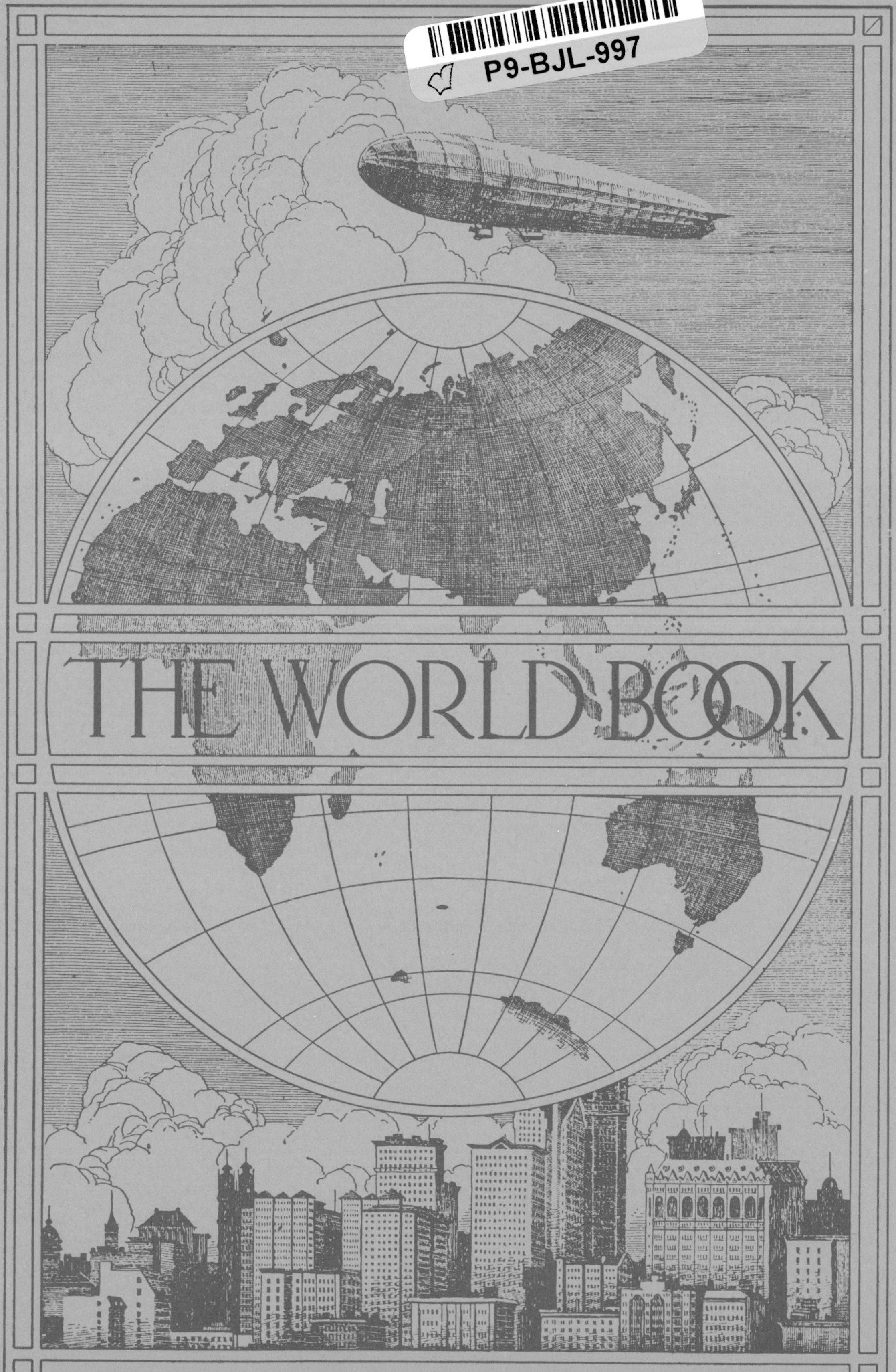

THE WORLD BOOK

M Volume 13

The World Book Encyclopedia

World Book, Inc.
a Scott Fetzer company

Chicago London Sydney Toronto

The World Book Encyclopedia

M is the 13th letter of our alphabet. It was also the 13th letter in the alphabet used by the Semites, who once lived in Syria and Palestine. They named it *mem,* their word for *water,* and adapted an Egyptian *hieroglyphic* (picture symbol) for water. The Greeks called it *mu.* See **Alphabet.**

Uses. *M* or *m* ranks as the 14th most frequently used letter in books, newspapers, and other printed material in English. It stands for *mile* or *meter* in measurements of distance. In chemistry, *m* is the short form for *metal.* *M* in the Roman numeral system stands for 1,000, while M̄ stands for 1,000,000. *M* is also the abbreviation for *Master* in college degrees, and *m* stands for *milli,* as in *millimeter.* In Germany, people use *M* to stand for the mark, the basic unit of their money. In French, *M* stands for *monsieur,* equal to our *mister.* It is the seventh letter of the Hawaiian alphabet.

Pronunciation. In English, a person pronounces *m* by closing both lips and making the sound through the nose. Double *m* usually has the same sound, as in *stammer.* But there are some words, like *immobile,* in which each *m* is often pronounced. These words come from a Latin prefix ending in *m* and a Latin stem beginning with *m.* The letter has almost exactly the same sound in French, German, Italian, and Spanish as it has in English. The Romans also gave it the same sound. The Portuguese nasalize the sound when it follows a vowel. See **Pronunciation.**   Marianne Cooley

Development of the letter m

The ancient Egyptians, about 3000 B.C., drew this symbol of waves of water.

The Semites adapted the Egyptian symbol about 1500 B.C. They named the letter *mem,* which was their word for *water.*

The Phoenicians changed the Semitic letter about 1000 B.C.

The Greeks added the letter *mu* to their alphabet about 600 B.C.

The Romans, about A.D. 114, gave the M its capital shape.

The small letter m appeared during the A.D. 300's as a rounded letter. By about 1500, it had developed its present shape.

A.D. 300   1500   Today

Special ways of expressing the letter m

International Morse Code

Braille

International Flag Code

Semaphore Code

Sign Language Alphabet

Common forms of the letter m

Mm *Mm* Mm *Mm* Mm *Mm*

Handwritten letters vary from person to person. *Manuscript* (printed) letters, *left,* have simple curves and straight lines. Cursive letters, *right,* have flowing lines.

Roman letters have small finishing strokes called *serifs* that extend from the main strokes. The type face shown above is Baskerville. The italic form appears at the right.

Sans-serif letters are also called *gothic letters.* They have no serifs. The type face shown above is called Futura. The italic form of Futura appears at the right.

Computer letters have special shapes. Computers can "read" these letters either optically or by means of the magnetic ink with which the letters may be printed.

Ma Yuan, *MAH yoo ehn,* was the most famous member of an honored family of painters. With his fellow painter Xia Gui (also spelled Hsia Kuei), Ma Yuan produced some of the greatest landscape paintings in ink during the early 1200's in the Southern Song (Sung) period in China. Ma Yuan's typical compositions are severely simple, with a framework of strong diagonal lines usually developed in one corner. His foregrounds may contain a few boldly silhouetted forms—rocks, a mountain path, a dramatically angular pine tree. The rest of the scene is largely mist, through which river banks or silhouetted faraway peaks can be seen.

Ma Yuan was born in Hezhong in Shanxi province. His birth and death dates are unknown.   Robert A. Rorex

Maas River. See Meuse River.

Maasai. See Kenya (Way of life).

Maazel, *muh ZEHL,* **Lorin,** *LAWR ihn* (1930-   ), has conducted several major orchestras throughout the world. He has served as music director of the Pittsburgh Symphony Orchestra since 1986.

Maazel was born to American parents in Neuilly, France, near Paris. He was a child prodigy, conducting several major American orchestras by the age of 15. He joined the Pittsburgh Symphony Orchestra as a violinist in 1948. In 1960, Maazel became the first American to conduct at the famous Bayreuth Festival in Germany. He was director of the Berlin Radio Symphony Orchestra from 1965 to 1975 and the German Opera in Berlin from 1965 to 1971. From 1971 to 1982, Maazel was music director of the Cleveland Orchestra. In 1982, Maazel became the first American to serve as director of the Vienna State Opera. He held that position until 1984.

John H. Baron

Mac, Mc. Biographies of persons whose names begin with *Mac,* such as *MacDonald,* are listed alphabetically under *Mac.* Names that begin with *Mc,* such as *McKinley,* are listed alphabetically under *Mc,* following all names beginning with *Ma* and *Mb.*

Macadamia nut, *MAK uh DAY mee uh,* is a large, round edible seed that grows on two species of trees. Macadamia trees are evergreens native to tropical Australia. The "smooth-shell" macadamia tree, the only commercially important species, grows more than 40 feet (12 meters) tall and bears creamy-white flowers. It was brought to Hawaii in the 1800's. Today, the nuts are an important crop there.

Macadamia nuts have a hard, smooth shell. The nuts are cracked, and the white kernels are then dried, roasted in oil, and salted. The roasted nuts are often used in cakes, candy, and ice cream. The nuts are also called *Australian nuts, bopple nuts, bush nuts,* and *Queensland nuts.*

WORLD BOOK illustration by James Teason

The macadamia nut

Scientific classification. Macadamia trees belong to the protea family, Proteaceae. The scientific name for the smooth-shell macadamia tree is *Macadamia integrifolia.*   Michael J. Tanabe

Macao, *muh KOW,* also spelled *Macau,* is a Portuguese territory on the southeast coast of China. It consists of the city of Macao, which occupies a peninsula, and three small islands. The territory has a population of about 436,000 and covers about $6\frac{1}{2}$ square miles (17 square kilometers). It lies at the mouth of the Zhu Jiang (Pearl River), about 40 miles (64 kilometers) west of Hong Kong. For location, see **Asia** (political map).

Some areas of Macao have old, pastel-colored houses that line cobblestone streets. Other sections include modern high-rise hotels and apartment buildings. More than 90 per cent of the people are Chinese, and most of the rest are Portuguese. Macao's economy is based on tourism and light industry, chiefly the manufacture of fireworks and textiles. Gambling casinos in Macao attract many tourists, mainly from Hong Kong.

A governor appointed by the president of Portugal heads Macao's government. A legislative assembly of appointed and elected members makes laws for the territory. But in practice, China dominates Macao's political life. The Chinese government may veto any government policies or laws concerning the territory.

The Portuguese established a permanent settlement in Macao in 1557. China has allowed them to remain because Macao contributes to China's economy. Macao buys almost all its food and drinking water from China. These purchases provide China with foreign currency, which it uses in international trade. However, in 1987, China and Portugal signed an agreement under which control of Macao will be transferred from Portugal to China in December 1999.   Donald W. Klein

Macaque, *muh KAHK,* is the name of a group of large, powerful monkeys. Some macaques weigh more than

© Warren Garst, Tom Stack & Assoc.

The Japanese macaque has brown fur and a short tail. Its reddish face and rump are features common to all macaques. Both male and female macaques protect and care for their young.

30 pounds (14 kilograms). Macaques have a wider geographical range than any other monkey or ape. Most species live in warm areas of southern Asia. One species, the *Barbary ape*, lives in northern Africa (see **Barbary ape**). Another, the *Japanese macaque*, lives as far north as Honshu Island, where snow falls in winter.

Most macaques have gray or brown fur, with pink or red skin on the face and rump. Some have long tails, and others have short tails or no tails at all. Males have long, sharp teeth that they use in fighting. Strong males rule most groups of macaques.

Many macaques live both in trees and on the ground. Most species eat fruits, grains, insects, and vegetables, but the *crab-eating macaque* eats crabs and clams.

The *rhesus monkey*, a macaque of India, was once widely used in medical research. India banned the export of rhesus monkeys in 1978 and since then their use in research has declined (see **Rhesus monkey**). People of Malaysia train the *pigtailed macaque* to pick coconuts from trees. Several species of macaques are threatened with extinction.

Scientific classification. Macaques make up the genus *Macaca* in the family Cercopithecidae.   Randall L. Susman

MacArthur, Douglas

MacArthur, Douglas (1880-1964), was a leading American general of World War II and the Korean War. He also won distinction as Allied supreme commander of the occupation of Japan after World War II.

Early career. MacArthur was born in Little Rock, Ark., on Jan. 26, 1880. His father, Arthur MacArthur, had been a hero as an officer in the Civil War (1861-1865). The elder MacArthur became a prominent general during the Spanish-American War (1898) and a revolt against U.S. control of the Philippines from 1899 to 1901.

MacArthur graduated from the United States Military Academy at West Point, N.Y., in 1903. He achieved one of the highest academic records in the school's history. During the next 10 years, he served as an aide and junior engineering officer in the Philippines, Panama, and the United States. MacArthur was on the general staff of the War Department for four years. In 1914, he served with the American forces that seized the Mexican city of Veracruz (see **Wilson, Woodrow** [Crisis in Mexico]).

World War I. MacArthur held the rank of major when the United States entered World War I in April 1917. He became chief of staff of the 42nd Division, nicknamed the Rainbow Division, and served in France. MacArthur became known as an outstanding combat leader, especially in the St.-Mihiel and Meuse-Argonne offensives. He was wounded twice and received many decorations for bravery. By June 1918, MacArthur had risen to the rank of brigadier general.

Between world wars. After occupation duty in Germany, MacArthur served as superintendent of the U.S. Military Academy from 1919 to 1922. Later in the 1920's, he served in the Philippines and again in the United States.

In 1930, at the age of 50, MacArthur became chief of staff of the U.S. Army. The Great Depression, a worldwide economic slump, hampered his efforts to modernize and expand the Army during his five years in this office. From 1935 to 1941, MacArthur served as military adviser to the Commonwealth of the Philippines. The Philippines, which had been a U.S. possession since 1898, were being prepared for independence.

National Archives

General Douglas MacArthur, *second from left,* returned to the Philippines when he waded ashore at Leyte on Oct. 20, 1944.

World War II. In July 1941, President Franklin D. Roosevelt made MacArthur commander of the Army forces in the Far East. On Dec. 7, 1941, Japanese planes bombed the U.S. naval base at Pearl Harbor in Hawaii and attacked American air bases in the Philippines. The United States entered World War II when it declared war on Japan on December 8. A major Japanese invasion of the Philippines began two weeks later.

MacArthur led the defense of the Philippines. He concentrated his Filipino and American troops on Bataan Peninsula and Corregidor Island in Manila Bay. In March 1942, under orders from Roosevelt, MacArthur and his family left Corregidor. Soon afterward, MacArthur flew to Australia. Upon reaching Australia, he made a pledge that became famous: "I shall return." See **Bataan Peninsula**.

MacArthur received the Medal of Honor for his defense of the Philippines. His father had won this medal, the nation's highest military award, for his heroism in the Civil War. The MacArthurs are the only father and son who have both received it.

Roosevelt appointed MacArthur commander of the Allied forces in the Southwest Pacific, and the general began an offensive against Japan. Early in 1943, MacArthur's forces drove the Japanese from southeast New Guinea. His troops then seized northeast New Guinea, western New Britain, and the Admiralty Islands. These victories isolated the Japanese base at Rabaul, the chief port of New Britain. By September 1944, MacArthur had also recaptured western New Guinea and Morotai.

On Oct. 20, 1944, MacArthur and his forces landed on the Philippine island of Leyte, thus carrying out his pledge to return. His troops landed on Mindoro in the central Philippines in December. MacArthur became a five-star general that same month. His troops invaded Luzon in January 1945 and recaptured most of that island by the time the war ended in August. He also retook the southern Philippines and Borneo.

Japan surrendered in August 1945, and MacArthur was appointed Allied supreme commander. He presided over the surrender ceremony aboard the U.S.S.

Missouri on September 2 and then took over as commander of the Allied occupation forces in Japan.

The occupation of Japan. From 1945 to 1951, MacArthur headed the Allied occupation of Japan. The occupation had the basic goals of demilitarizing Japan and making it a democratic nation. MacArthur administered the occupation with great independence, and he introduced major reforms in Japan's political, economic, and social institutions. The Japanese respected MacArthur's capable, firm leadership. He used the Japanese emperor and government to help carry out the reforms.

The occupation programs removed from power supporters of military conquest and reduced the control that a small group of Japanese families had over the nation's industry. A land reform program enabled farmers to own their own land. Labor unions were recognized, the government improved public health and education, and women received the right to vote. A new Japanese constitution went into effect in 1947. MacArthur also headed the U.S. Far East Command from 1947 to 1951.

The Korean War began on June 25, 1950, when North Korean troops crossed the 38th parallel, the border between North and South Korea. President Harry S. Truman appointed MacArthur head of the military force that the United Nations (UN) sent to defend South Korea. MacArthur led a surprise landing behind enemy lines at the South Korean port of Inchon. This move changed the course of the war, enabling the UN forces to capture Seoul and causing an almost total collapse of the North Korean army. MacArthur then invaded North Korea.

Before MacArthur could win a total victory over North Korea, however, Communist Chinese forces entered the war on the side of the North Koreans. The Chinese drove the UN forces south of the 38th parallel. As a result, MacArthur wanted to extend the war into China. However, some members of the UN feared that attacking China would start a third world war. MacArthur strenuously disagreed with Truman and the Joint Chiefs of Staff about limiting the war to Korea.

By March 1951, MacArthur's forces held positions close to the 38th parallel. In the meantime, MacArthur issued statements setting out his criticisms of the government's policy and strategy on the war. He was defying Truman's orders not to release policy statements on his own initiative. MacArthur also sent an unauthorized message demanding the surrender of the Chinese. On April 5, Joseph W. Martin, Jr., a Republican congressman, made public a letter from MacArthur that criticized official policy. Because of these disagreements, on April 11 President Truman relieved MacArthur as head of the UN Command, U.S. Far East Command, and occupation of Japan.

The American public welcomed MacArthur as a hero on his return to the United States. It was his first time back in the country since 1937. After a Senate investigation of his dismissal, popular support for his position declined sharply.

Last years. Some conservative Republicans tried in vain to get their party to nominate MacArthur for the presidency in 1944, 1948, and 1952. In 1952, MacArthur became chairman of the board of Remington Rand, Incorporated (now part of Unisys Corporation). Except for board duties and a few speeches, he lived in seclusion in New York City. His memoirs, *Reminiscences,* were published shortly before he died on April 5, 1964. After a state funeral, he was buried in a crypt of the MacArthur Memorial in Norfolk, Va.   D. Clayton James

See also **Korean War** (The land war); **World War II** (The war in Asia and the Pacific).

Additional resources

Finkelstein, Norman H. *The Emperor General: A Biography of Douglas MacArthur.* Dillon Pr., 1989. For younger readers.
James, D. Clayton. *The Years of MacArthur.* 3 vols. Houghton, 1970-1985.
Long, Gavin. *MacArthur as Military Commander.* Van Nostrand, 1969.
Manchester, William. *American Caesar: Douglas MacArthur, 1880-1964.* Little, Brown, 1978.

MacArthur Foundation is a private, independent organization that funds a variety of charitable and public service projects. It ranks as one of the 10 largest foundations in the world. Its official name is the John D. and Catherine T. MacArthur Foundation.

The MacArthur Foundation supports eight main programs. The MacArthur Fellows Program sponsors talented individuals of all skills and ages. The winners receive up to $375,000 to pursue their interests in whatever way they choose. The General Program develops special initiatives, which include projects not covered under the foundation's other programs. It also promotes diversity on television and radio.

Six separate programs finance specific research or development. The Community Initiatives Program supports cultural and community development in Palm Beach, Fla., and in Chicago, where the MacArthurs had homes. The Education Program encourages literacy, mathematics skills, and critical and creative thinking. The Health Program sponsors research on mental health and on diseases caused by parasites. The Program on Peace and International Cooperation aids the study and public understanding of international security. The Population Program seeks solutions to the problems caused by the rapid growth of the world's population. The World Environment and Resources Program promotes conservation as well as public education and studies about environmental issues.

John D. MacArthur created the foundation in 1970 with his fortune from insurance and real estate. The foundation announced its first grant winners in 1978. Its headquarters are at 140 S. Dearborn Street, Chicago, IL 60603.   Critically reviewed by the MacArthur Foundation

See also **Foundations.**

Macau. See Macao.

Macaulay, Thomas Babington (1800-1859), was the most widely read English historian of the 1800's. He also achieved fame for his essays and for his poems based on legends. But his writings—especially his poetry—have declined in popularity during the 1900's.

Macaulay was born in Leicestershire. His father, Zachary Macaulay, was a leading religious reformer. In 1825, Macaulay published his first article, an essay on the English poet John Milton, in the famous literary magazine *The Edinburgh Review.* The *Review* continued to publish many of Macaulay's scholarly but popular essays on historical and literary topics.

While Macaulay was gaining a reputation as an author, he was also pursuing a political career. He was elected to Parliament in 1830 and helped lead a movement to reform Great Britain's voting laws. His speeches in Parliament were so brilliant that he became a famous public figure. In 1833, the English East India Company appointed Macaulay to the Supreme Council, which governed the British colony of India. He served on the council until 1838. During this period, he lived in India and helped lay the foundations for English—in place of Oriental—systems of criminal law and education in the colony.

After Macaulay returned to England, he began his greatest work—*The History of England from the Accession of James II.* Macaulay published two volumes in 1848 and two more in 1855. After his death, his sister, Lady Trevelyan, edited the final volume, which was published in 1861. The *History* became a best seller in England and the United States because of its vivid descriptions and powerful prose style. The work contains some factual errors, and scholars have challenged Macaulay's slanted political views. But the *History* remains a highly readable introduction to a period of English history.

While working on his *History,* Macaulay remained a leading orator in Parliament and held several government positions. At the same time, he also wrote *Lays of Ancient Rome* (1842). This collection of poems about ancient Roman heroes became very popular and is still read by young people. The best-known poem in the collection is "Horatius."   Avrom Fleishman

See also **Horatius; Fourth estate.**

Macaw, *muh KAW,* is the name of about 18 *species* (kinds) of large, long-tailed parrots that live in forested areas of South America, Central America, and Mexico. Macaws are the largest parrots. They measure from 12 to 39 inches (30 to 100 centimeters) long. These birds have long pointed wings and a heavy, powerful bill. Beautifully colored feathers of blue, red, yellow, and green cover the body.

Macaws nest in holes in tall trees. They eat nuts, seeds, and fruit. They often can be seen flying swiftly in pairs over a tropical rain forest. Macaws can be easily tamed, but do not readily learn to talk. They are not common as household pets because they scream loudly and may bite.

Scientific classification. Typical macaws are members of the family, Psittacidae. They make up the genus *Ara.*

John W. Fitzpatrick

See also **Parrot** (picture: Scarlet macaw); **Animal** (picture: Animals of the tropical forests).

Macbeth, *muhk BEHTH* (? -1057), seized the throne of Scotland in 1040 after defeating and killing Duncan I. He based his claim to the crown on his wife's royal descent. Malcolm III, son of Duncan I, and Earl Siward of Northumberland defeated Macbeth at Dunsinane in 1054, but they did not dethrone him. Three years later, Malcolm III killed Macbeth at Lumphanan. Macbeth's stepson Lulach reigned for a few months, and then Malcolm III succeeded Lulach as king.

William Shakespeare based his play, *Macbeth,* upon a distorted version of these events which he found in Raphael Holinshed's *Chronicles of England, Scotland, and Ireland.* The only kernel of historical truth in the play is Duncan's death at the hand of Macbeth. From this fact, Shakespeare drew his portrait of ambition leading to a violent and tragic end.   Robert S. Hoyt

See also **Shakespeare, William** (*Macbeth*).

Maccabee, Judah. See Judah Maccabee.
MacCool, Finn. See Finn MacCool.
MacDonald, J. E. H. (1873-1932), was a member of the Group of Seven, a famous Canadian school of landscape painters. MacDonald is best known for his large, boldly designed and brightly colored paintings of the Algoma wilderness region of Ontario. Scandinavian landscape art of the early 1900's strongly influenced his work. Many of his decorative landscapes also reflect the influence of the *art nouveau* style of design (see **Art nouveau**).

James Edward Hervey MacDonald was born in Durham, England, and he settled in Canada in 1887. He worked as a graphics designer in Toronto before he devoted himself exclusively to landscape painting after 1911. MacDonald was the principal of the Ontario College of Art from 1929 to 1932. He wrote a number of poems that were collected in *West by East,* published in 1933, after his death.   Jeremy Adamson

See also **Group of Seven** (picture: *The Elements*).

MacDonald, James Ramsay (1866-1937), led Great Britain's first Labour Party government. He served as the first Labour Party prime minister of Britain in 1924. He was also prime minister from 1929 to 1935. MacDonald was secretary of Britain's Labour Party from the party's origin in 1900 until 1912.

MacDonald entered Parliament in 1906. As Labour Party leader in 1914, he opposed England's entry into World War I. His stand met considerable opposition within his own party. His pacifism resulted in his defeat for reelection to Parliament in 1918. But he was elected in 1922 and became prime minister in January 1924. MacDonald remained in office for only 10 months. He was defeated, in part, because his government was considered too friendly toward the Soviet Union. MacDonald accepted, but did not wholeheartedly support, the 1926 general strike on behalf of coal miners faced with reduced wages and longer working hours.

The Labour Party won the general election of 1929, and MacDonald formed his second government as prime minister. It achieved considerable success in international affairs. Diplomatic relations with the Soviet Union were resumed. MacDonald visited the United States to discuss with President Herbert Hoover proposals for naval reduction. He became chairman of the London arms conference in 1930. But MacDonald was unable to deal effectively with rapidly rising unemployment, and his government resigned in August 1931. MacDonald continued as prime minister, heading a national coalition government of Labour, Conservative, and Liberal Party members. A large majority of the Labour members of Parliament disapproved of his move. The Conservatives held an overwhelming majority in the government. They overshadowed MacDonald. Stanley Baldwin replaced him as prime minister in 1935.

MacDonald was born of farmer parents in the Scottish seaside village of Lossiemouth. He left school at the age of 13 to help support the family. Six years later, he went to London and worked as a clerk, accountant, and newspaper writer. He read widely in the fields of science, history, and economics. He became interested in socialism, joined the Fabian Society, and became one of its speakers.   Chris Cook

See also **Fabian Society.**

Sir John A. Macdonald

Prime Minister of Canada
1867-1873
1878-1891

Macdonald
1867-1873

Mackenzie
1873-1878

Macdonald
1878-1891

Abbott
1891-1892

Detail of a portrait by Frederick Arthur Verner; National Gallery of Canada, Ottawa (John Evans)

Macdonald, Sir John Alexander (1815-1891), was the first prime minister of the Dominion of Canada. He is often called the father of present-day Canada because he played the leading role in establishing the dominion in 1867. Macdonald served as prime minister from 1867 until 1873, and from 1878 until his death in 1891. He held the office for nearly 19 years, longer than any other Canadian prime minister except W. L. Mackenzie King, who served for 21 years.

Macdonald, a Conservative, entered politics when he was only 28 years old. During his long public career, Canada grew from a group of colonies into a self-governing, united dominion extending across North America. Macdonald stood out as the greatest political figure of Canada's early years. He helped strengthen the new nation by promoting western expansion, railway construction, and economic development.

A man of great personal charm, Macdonald knew how to make people like him. He was naturally sociable, with a quick wit and a remarkable ability to remember faces. Macdonald was not a flowery-speaking orator as were most politicians of his day. He kept his speeches short and filled with funny stories. People preferred his talks to the long, dull speeches of others.

Early life

Boyhood and education. John Alexander Macdonald was born on Jan. 11, 1815, in Glasgow, Scotland. He was the son of Helen Shaw Macdonald and Hugh Macdonald, an easygoing and usually unsuccessful busi-nessman. John had an older sister, Margaret, and a younger sister, Louisa. He was 5 years old when the family moved to Canada in 1820.

The Macdonalds settled in Kingston, Upper Canada (in present-day Ontario). Hugh opened a small shop, and the family lived above it. The business did not prosper. In 1824, the family moved westward to Hay Bay. They moved to Glenora in Prince Edward County in 1825, then back to Kingston. Hugh tried one business after another, but none brought him success.

As a boy, John developed an interest in books and was a bright student. He finished his formal schooling in 1829 when he was 14. The next year, John began to study law with George Mackenzie, a prominent Kingston lawyer.

Macdonald lived with the Mackenzie family and worked in the law office. In 1832, Mackenzie opened a branch office in nearby Napanee, and 17-year-old John became its manager. In 1833, John learned that a relative, a lawyer in Hallowell, Prince Edward County, was seriously ill. John agreed to take over his practice.

Lawyer. Macdonald returned to Kingston in 1835. He was admitted to the bar of Upper Canada in 1836. That same year, he took on his first apprentice-lawyer, Oliver Mowat, who became prime minister of Ontario.

During the Rebellion of 1837-1838, Macdonald served in the Frontenac County militia during the rebellion that broke out in Upper Canada in December 1837. In 1838, some of William Lyon Mackenzie's American supporters staged a raid into Canada. About 150 raiders were captured, and Macdonald defended some of them in court. Several Americans were hanged, but the case helped establish Macdonald's legal reputation. See **Rebellions of 1837; Mackenzie, William Lyon.**

In 1841, Upper Canada (part of present-day Ontario) and Lower Canada (part of present-day Quebec) united to form the Province of Canada. The Province of Canada, sometimes called United Canada, had one legislative assembly, with an equal number of members from Upper and Lower Canada.

Kingston, in Upper Canada, became the capital of the Province of Canada. Both the city and Macdonald's law practice grew prosperous. In 1843, Macdonald began a law partnership with Alexander Campbell, who had been his second apprentice-lawyer.

Marriages. On the same day that he set up his law partnership, Macdonald married his cousin, Isabella Clark. The Macdonalds had two sons, John Jr., who died at the age of 1, and Hugh John, who became premier of Manitoba. In 1845, Isabella was stricken by tuberculosis. Macdonald tried everything to cure her. He and his wife were separated for long periods while Isabella tried to restore her health in the United States. But she died in 1857. The years of his wife's illness were a strain on John Macdonald, both physically and financially. He remained at Isabella's bedside as much as possible. But he was also building a law practice and a political career. He often felt he was not giving enough attention to his wife, to his practice, or to politics.

In 1867, Macdonald married Susan Agnes Bernard, a widow. The couple had a daughter, Mary.

Early public career

In 1843, at the age of 28, Macdonald was elected an alderman in Kingston. In 1844, he accepted the Conservative nomination in Kingston for the Legislative Assembly of the Province of Canada. He easily won election.

Macdonald took his seat in the Assembly on Nov. 28, 1844. His associates soon recognized his abilities. In 1847, he was appointed receiver-general in the Conservative administration of William Henry Draper. But Draper's government was defeated later that year.

For the next few years, Macdonald helped rebuild the Conservative party. He wanted the party to include men of liberal and conservative views, French-Canadians and English-Canadians, Roman Catholics and Protestants, and rich and poor. A Liberal-Conservative coalition party was formed. It came to power in 1854 under Conservative leader Sir Allan McNab. Macdonald served as attorney general in this administration.

Associate provincial prime minister. In 1856, Macdonald and Étienne P. Taché became associate prime ministers of the Province of Canada. Taché was the senior prime minister in what was called the Taché-Macdonald government. The next year, Taché retired. Macdonald became senior prime minister with George É. Cartier as his associate prime minister. The Conservatives adopted a policy favoring confederation of all the British provinces in North America.

In 1858, the Macdonald-Cartier government was defeated. But Macdonald returned to power a week later when the governor-general asked Cartier to become senior prime minister and form a government. Cartier needed Macdonald's help in the task, and the new government became the Cartier-Macdonald government.

The formation of the Cartier-Macdonald government became known as the "double shuffle." The action was legal, but the opposition charged it was dishonest. Macdonald and Cartier simply took advantage of a provision in the law. This provision permitted a cabinet minister to resign and accept another cabinet position within a month without running for reelection. All the government ministers resigned and a few days later returned to office with new titles. Then they quickly dropped the new titles and resumed their former offices.

The Conservative government was defeated in 1862, although Macdonald won reelection to the assembly from Kingston. Macdonald served as leader of the opposition party until 1864. The Conservatives won the election that year. Taché came out of retirement, and the second Taché-Macdonald government was formed.

Forming the Dominion. In the early 1860's, the northern half of North America was called British North America. It consisted of only a few provinces. Most of the people lived in the east. The Maritime Provinces—New Brunswick, Newfoundland, Nova Scotia, and Prince Edward Island—lay along the Atlantic coast. The Province of Canada was next to them on the west. Of these five provinces, Nova Scotia and the Province of Canada were older and more developed. The other three had only begun to govern themselves in the 1840's and 1850's. Farther west was an expanse of mainly unsettled territory owned by the Hudson's Bay Company (see **Hudson's Bay Company**). On the west coast lay British Columbia, then a British colony.

For several years, the British provinces in North America had considered the idea of confederation. Several factors gave force to this idea. They included the frequent changes of provincial governments, the desire to expand to the west, and fear of U.S. expansion.

Nova Scotia and the Province of Canada took the lead in the confederation movement. In the Province of Canada, Macdonald joined forces with his opponent, Reform leader George Brown, to achieve confederation.

From 1864 to 1867, Macdonald led in planning confederation. In September 1864, he attended a conference in Charlottetown, P.E.I., to present the confederation plan to the Maritime Provinces. In October, delegates from all the provinces gathered at a second conference in Quebec. At this meeting, Macdonald was largely responsible for drawing up the Quebec Resolutions, the plan for confederation.

New Brunswick, Nova Scotia, and the Province of Canada approved the idea, but Newfoundland and Prince Edward Island rejected it. Final details were agreed upon at a conference in London, England, in 1866. In 1867, the British parliament passed the British North America Act, which brought the Dominion of Canada into being (see **British North America Act**). The new nation had four provinces: Ontario (previously Upper Canada), Quebec (previously Lower Canada), New Brunswick, and Nova Scotia. Governor General Charles S. Monck asked Macdonald to lead the first Dominion government as prime minister.

Confederation was largely Macdonald's achievement and Queen Victoria knighted him for it. The announcement of his knighthood came on July 1, 1867, the first day of the Dominion's existence. A general election was held in August, and the new Parliament assembled on Nov. 6, 1867.

First term as prime minister (1867-1873)

Completing the Dominion. Sir John A. Macdonald took office as prime minister of the Dominion of Canada on July 1, 1867. His goal was to enlarge the Dominion into a unified nation extending across the continent.

In 1869, the Canadian and British governments agreed with the Hudson's Bay Company to purchase the company's lands. The company was paid 300,000 pounds (about 1\frac{1}{2}$ million) and 5 per cent of the land south of the North Saskatchewan River. But the *métis* (persons of mixed white and Indian descent) in the territory rebelled. They were led by Louis Riel. They feared that an onrush of settlers would deprive them of their lands. Many Canadians also thought the United States might annex this land. Parliament passed the Manitoba Act in 1870, and in July 1870, the lands became the fifth Canadian province (see **Red River Rebellion**). British Columbia became the sixth province in 1871, and Prince Edward Island the seventh in 1873.

In 1871, delegates from Great Britain and the United States held a conference in Washington, D.C. Macdonald attended the meeting as the Canadian member

Important dates in Macdonald's life

1815 (Jan. 11) Born in Glasgow, Scotland.
1820 Macdonald family moved to Kingston, Upper Canada.
1836 Admitted to the bar of Upper Canada.
1843 (Sept. 1) Married Isabella Clark.
1844 (Oct. 14) Elected to Legislative Assembly of the Province of Canada.
1856 Became associate prime minister of Province of Canada.
1857 (Dec. 28) Mrs. Isabella Macdonald died.
1867 British Parliament passed the British North America Act. (Feb. 16) Married Susan Agnes Bernard. (July 1) Macdonald became the first prime minister of the Dominion of Canada and was knighted.
1869-1870 Louis Riel led the Red River Rebellion.
1870 Manitoba became the fifth Canadian province.
1871 British Columbia became the sixth province.
1873 Prince Edward Island became the seventh province.
1878 (Oct. 17) Became prime minister for second time.
1885 Riel led the North West Rebellion. The Canadian Pacific Railway (now CP Rail) was completed.
1891 Macdonald and the Conservatives won reelection. (June 6) Died in Ottawa, Ont.

Important events during Macdonald's Administrations

Fathers of the Confederation (1864), an oil painting on canvas by J. D. Kelly; Confederation Life Collection, Toronto, Canada

The Quebec Conference of 1864 drew up the plan that united the provinces of Canada into the Dominion of Canada. Macdonald, *standing at center,* became the new nation's first prime minister.

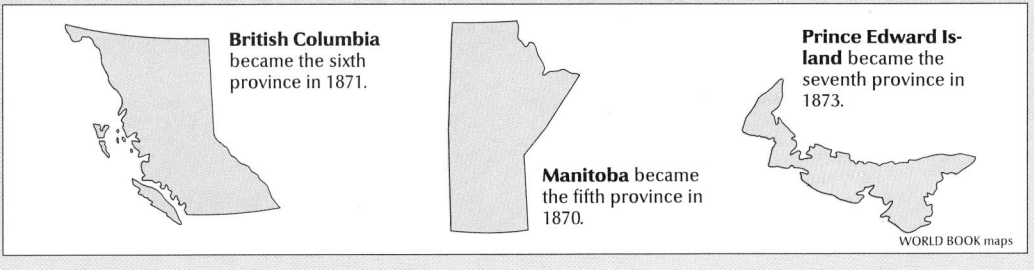

British Columbia became the sixth province in 1871.

Manitoba became the fifth province in 1870.

Prince Edward Island became the seventh province in 1873.

WORLD BOOK maps

of the British delegation. He tried to obtain a trade agreement with the United States, but failed. Nevertheless, Macdonald signed the Treaty of Washington. Among other points, this treaty granted the United States extensive fishing rights in Canadian waters. Macdonald felt that refusal to sign the treaty might encourage the United States to use force to win its demands. He was always careful to do nothing that might endanger the young Canadian nation. See **Washington, Treaty of.**

The Pacific Scandal. Next, Macdonald turned to the goal of building a transcontinental railroad to unify Canada. The completion of such a railroad had been one of the terms of British Columbia's entry into the Confederation.

Two financial groups competed with each other to build the line. Then, in 1873, it was learned that Sir Hugh Allan, head of one of the groups, had contributed a large sum of money to help reelect Macdonald's government in the 1872 election. Some Liberal members of parliament charged there had been an "understanding" between Allan and the government. They accused the government of giving Allan a charter to build the rail-

road because he had contributed to the Conservatives' election fund.

The incident became known as the Pacific Scandal. Macdonald claimed that he was innocent, but evidence showed that he and some of his associates had received money from Allan. Macdonald resigned as Prime Minister. He offered to resign as head of the Conservative Party, but his supporters persuaded him to remain in that post. The Conservatives lost the 1874 election, although Macdonald won reelection to parliament from Kingston. Alexander Mackenzie, the leader of the Liberal Party, succeeded Macdonald as Prime Minister.

The national policy. For the next four years, Macdonald led the opposition party in the house of commons. During this period, he worked to rebuild the Conservative Party. Macdonald formed a program of economic nationalism that he called the National Policy. This program called for developing Canada by protecting its industries against competing industries of other countries.

The idea appealed to Canadians, especially because a depression had begun in 1873. On the strength of the National Policy, the Conservatives defeated the Liberals

CP Rail

The Canadian Pacific Railway was completed in British Columbia with the driving in of the last spike in 1885.

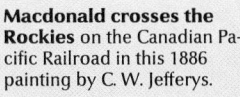

Louis Riel led revolts against the Canadian government in 1869-1870 and in 1885. English-Canadians called him a traitor. But French-Canadians hailed Riel as a hero.

Public Archives of Canada

Macdonald crosses the Rockies on the Canadian Pacific Railroad in this 1886 painting by C. W. Jefferys.

in the 1878 election. They returned to power with an election victory in almost every province.

Second term as prime minister (1878-1891)

National prosperity. Macdonald began his second term as prime minister on Oct. 17, 1878. In 1879, the government put tariffs on a variety of goods to protect the manufacturing and mining industries. Macdonald again began to push for construction of a transcontinental railroad. With government support, a new company was formed. By November, 1885, the Canadian Pacific Railway (now CP Rail) had been completed to the Pacific Ocean. Macdonald had achieved his program of western expansion, railway construction, and economic nationalism. Canada was riding a wave of prosperity.

Threats to Canadian unity. Macdonald had worked long and hard to build a unified Canadian nation. But beginning in 1885, a number of political developments seriously threatened this unity.

In 1885, the métis of northwest Canada rebelled for the second time. They were again led by Louis Riel. When Riel finally surrendered, the government found him guilty of treason and sentenced him to hang. The sentence caused severe bad feeling between French-Canadians and English-Canadians. For a time, the issue threatened to split the confederation. But Macdonald refused to give in to Riel's supporters. "He shall die though every dog in Quebec bark in his favour," Macdonald declared. Riel was hanged in November, 1885. See **North West Rebellion**.

Macdonald next faced an attack by the provincial prime ministers against his program for a strong central government. In 1888, the prime ministers met at a conference in Quebec. They proposed changes in the British North America Act that would decentralize the Canadian government. Great Britain rejected the prime ministers' demands. However, the conference showed the growing strength of provincial opinion against federal centralization.

Still another blow to Macdonald was the depression of 1883. The National Policy had not produced all the expected results. In 1886 and 1887, a demand arose for a change in Canada's financial policy. Some persons favored political federation with Great Britain. Others spoke of a commercial union with the United States. Macdonald opposed both proposals.

In the 1891 election, the Liberals adopted a party platform calling for unrestricted reciprocal trade with the United States (see **Reciprocal trade agreement**). The 75-year-old Macdonald fought this proposal with all the strength he could muster.

"Shall we endanger our possession of the great heritage bequeathed to us by our fathers," he asked the Canadian people, "and submit ourselves to direct taxation for the privilege of having our tariffs fixed at Washington, with the prospect of ultimately becoming a portion of the American Union? . . . As for myself, my course is clear. A British subject I was born, a British subject I will die." With this appeal, Macdonald won his last election.

Death. The strain of campaigning proved severe for Macdonald. He caught cold after a long day of speaking, and suffered a stroke on May 29, 1891. He died on June 6 in Ottawa. Macdonald was buried near his mother in Kingston, Ont.   G. F. G. Stanley

Related articles in *World Book* include:

Brown, George
Canada, Government of
Canada, History of
Cartier, Sir George É.
Mackenzie, Alexander
Monck, Viscount

Political party (Political parties in Canada)
Prime minister of Canada
Riel, Louis
Rose, Sir John
Taché, Sir Étienne-Paschal

Additional resources

Creighton, Donald G. *John A. Macdonald.* 2 vols. Macmillan (Toronto), 1965. First published in 1952 and 1955, respectively.
Sir John A.: An Anecdotal Life of John A. Macdonald. Ed. by Cynthia M. Smith and Jack McLeod. Oxford (Don Mills, Ont.), 1989.
Swainson, Donald. *John A. Macdonald: The Man and the Politician.* Oxford (Don Mills, Ont.), 1971.

MacDonald, John D. (1916-1986), was an American mystery writer best known for his 21 novels featuring Travis McGee, an amateur detective. He wrote more than 65 novels and over 500 short stories.

The first McGee novel was *The Deep Blue Good-By* (1964). McGee lives off the coast of Florida on a houseboat called *The Busted Flush.* He calls himself a "salvage consultant," but his real business is rescuing people from various kinds of trouble and recovering lost or stolen money. McGee is tough and cynical, but also sensitive and moral, and has a strong sense of honor. MacDonald used the character of McGee to expose the corruption that the author saw in modern American life. Typical McGee novels include *The Dreadful Lemon Sky* (1975) and *Free Fall in Crimson* (1981).

MacDonald's other works also show his skill as a mystery writer. Among his suspenseful thrillers are *The Executioners* (1958), *The Last One Left* (1967), and *Condominium* (1977). John Dann MacDonald was born in Sharon, Pa.   David Geherin

Macdonald, John Sandfield (1812-1872), served as joint prime minister of the Province of Canada from 1862 to 1864. The province was in what are now southern Ontario and southern Quebec. Macdonald was joint prime minister with Louis-Victor Sicotte from 1862 to 1863 and with Antoine-Aimé Dorion from 1863 to 1864. He also served as the first premier of Ontario from 1867 to 1871.

Macdonald belonged to the Reform Party, which eventually became the Liberal Party. In the early 1850's, he became a leader of the radical wing of the Reform Party in Upper Canada, the western part of the Province of Canada. But in 1856, control of the wing shifted to his political rival George Brown (see **Brown, George**).

Macdonald differed with Brown on several key issues. For example, Macdonald opposed the principle of *representation by population*—that is, basing the number of an area's elected representatives on the area's population. He felt this practice would weaken the rights of the French-speaking population in Lower Canada, the eastern part of the Province of Canada. Most of the province's people lived in Upper Canada and spoke English. Macdonald supported a *double majority system,* under which gov-

John S. Macdonald, portrait by Samuel B. Waugh, Public Archives of Canada, Toronto

John S. Macdonald

ernment proposals could be vetoed either by the representatives of Upper Canada or by those of Lower Canada. He also opposed Brown's goal of uniting the Canadian colonies under a central government. Macdonald was born in what is now St. Raphaels, Ont., near Alexandria.   J. M. Bumsted

Macdonald, Ross (1915-1983), was the pen name of Kenneth Millar, an American writer of detective novels. Macdonald's best-known books feature Lew Archer, a private detective. The Archer novels are "hard-boiled" detective fiction, which emphasizes realism and violence. But Macdonald also explored the psychological and social forces that lead to crime. His works are also noted for their highly literate prose style.

Much of Macdonald's work features the theme of a family broken by the loss of the father. Many of his characters seek close personal relationships and the meaning of life in a world that seems impersonal. The action takes place amid southern California's landscapes and changing life styles, which he portrayed vividly. Macdonald introduced Archer in *The Moving Target* (1949). Archer appeared in 17 other novels, including *The Chill* (1964), *The Far Side of the Dollar* (1965), *The Goodbye Look* (1969), *The Underground Man* (1971), and *The Blue Hammer* (1976). Macdonald's short stories were collected in *Lew Archer, Private Investigator* (1977).

Macdonald was born in Los Gatos, Calif., and grew up in Canada. His Canadian-born wife, Margaret Millar, also writes detective novels.   David Geherin

Macdonough, *muhk DAHN uh,* **Thomas** (1783-1825), an American naval officer, became a hero of the War of 1812. In 1814, he defeated the British on Lake Champlain at Plattsburgh, N.Y., in one of the most decisive battles ever fought by the U.S. Navy. When Macdonough took command of the Lake Champlain naval squadron in 1812, he found small, poorly armed vessels that lacked supplies and had untrained crews. After two years of preparations, he entered the harbor at Plattsburgh, carefully stationed his ships, and awaited the British. By fighting at anchor from an advantageous position rather than in open water, he captured the entire British fleet. His victory halted the British invasion of New York state and forced the British Army to retreat into Canada.

Macdonough was born in New Castle County, Delaware. He became a midshipman at 16. Macdonough became commander of the Mediterranean Squadron in 1824.   Michael J. Crawford

See also **War of 1812** (Lake Champlain).

MacDowell, Edward Alexander (1861-1908), was an American composer and pianist. During his lifetime, many people considered him the greatest composer in the history of American music. Today, he is primarily known for such short piano pieces as "To a Wild Rose" and "To a Water Lily." Both were part of a collection called *Woodland Sketches* (1896).

MacDowell studied in France and Germany from 1876 to 1888. His works reflect the rich harmonies of the European romantic composers, notably Edvard Grieg of Norway. MacDowell dedicated his *Norse Sonatas* (1900) and *Keltic Sonatas* (1901) to Grieg. MacDowell also composed many songs and a few orchestral works.

MacDowell was born in New York City. He headed the newly formed music department at Columbia University from 1896 to 1904.   Leonard W. Van Camp

Mace is a liquid tear gas that can be sprayed from a pressurized container. It causes a burning sensation and makes the eyes fill with tears. Mace causes temporary disability but no lasting effects. The terms *Mace* and *Chemical Mace* are trademarks of the Smith & Wesson Chemical Company, Inc., but other companies make similar hand-controlled liquid chemical irritants.

Many police departments in the United States use Mace and other irritant sprays to help control riots and violent demonstrations. Such sprays can be used on individual targets without affecting people nearby.

The U.S. Public Health Service reported in 1968 that its tests of Mace indicated no permanent effects on the eyes or nervous system. But all such substances should be used only by trained officers under careful control and regulation.   Frances M. Lussier

Mace is a club-shaped staff used as a symbol of authority. It is most often seen in legislatures where it is used chiefly to restore order. The mace originally was a weapon of the Middle Ages. It was a long-handled club, heavily weighted at one end. As the science of war developed, the weighted end became an iron ball. Archers and other unmounted warriors used the mace as a hand arm. Sergeants at arms, who guarded kings and other officials, and some church officials carried maces. Gradually the mace gained a ceremonial character. The mace used in the U.S. House of Representatives is about 3 feet (91 centimeters) long. It consists of ebony rods bound with a silver band. A longer ebony rod in the center of the bundle has a silver globe mounted on it with a silver eagle on top.   Whitney Smith

Mace is a highly flavored spice. It is the dried form of the red, netlike *aril,* or membrane, covering the nutmeg seed kernel (see **Nutmeg**). When fresh, this membrane is fleshy and smells and tastes like nutmeg. It is removed from the kernel and dried in the sun for its use as a spice. As it dries, the membrane turns orange-yellow and acquires a strong aroma. Mace is sold in whole or ground form.   James E. Simon

Macedonia is a historic region on the Balkan Peninsula of southeastern Europe. It covers all of a country that is also called Macedonia, plus parts of northern Greece and southwestern Bulgaria. The country of Macedonia has an area of 9,928 square miles (25,713 square kilometers). Greek Macedonia covers 13,206 square miles (34,203 square kilometers), and Bulgarian Macedonia 2,502 square miles (6,480 square kilometers). The region of Macedonia became powerful in ancient times, when Macedonian leader Alexander the Great conquered much of Asia and spread Macedonian and Greek culture throughout his empire.

The earliest known settlements in what is now Macedonia were villages established about 6200 B.C. A number of different peoples settled in the region over the next several thousand years. The people living there eventually came to be known as *Macedones,* and the region as

WORLD BOOK map

Macedonia

Macedonia. The name *Macedones* comes from the Greek word *makednon,* meaning *high*—a reference to the group's mountainous homeland.

The first known rulers of the Macedonians were members of the Argead *dynasty* (family of rulers), founded by King Perdiccas I about 650 B.C. During the 500's and 400's B.C., the Argeads expanded Macedonian rule into nearby regions.

King Philip II, an Argead, continued this expansion and eventually invaded central Greece. By 338 B.C., Philip controlled all of Greece. With these acquisitions, Macedonia gained valuable natural resources.

Philip was assassinated in 336. His son, Alexander, became king. Crowned King Alexander III, Philip's son became known as Alexander the Great. Alexander conquered the Persian Empire, which stretched from the Mediterranean Sea to India. The arts flourished under his rule. Macedonia also became very wealthy after acquiring the riches of the defeated Persian Empire.

Alexander died in 323 B.C., without leaving a strong successor. Political unity soon collapsed, as Macedonia's army generals divided up the empire.

Macedonia became a Roman province in the 140's B.C. The region became part of the Byzantine Empire in A.D. 395. In the A.D. 500's, Slavs from eastern Europe raided, and settled in, Macedonian towns. Bulgars from central Asia conquered Macedonia in the late 800's. In 1018, the Byzantine Empire regained control. The region came under Serbian rule in the early 1300's. But in 1371, Ottoman Turks conquered the region. Macedonia remained part of the Ottoman Empire for more than 500 years.

By the late 1800's, the Ottoman Empire had begun to collapse. In 1878, Bulgaria controlled Macedonia briefly. But most of Macedonia was returned to Ottoman rule that same year. At the end of the Second Balkan War (1913), Macedonia was divided among Serbia, Greece, and Bulgaria. Serbian Macedonia became the Yugoslav republic of Macedonia in 1946. The republic became an independent country in 1991.   Sabrina P. Ramet

Related articles in *World Book* include:

Alexander the Great	Macedonia (country)
Antigonid dynasty	Philip II
Balkans	Philippi
Greece (The land)	Thessaloniki

Macedonia is a disputed country in southeastern Europe. From 1946 to 1991, it was the southernmost of the six republics that made up the federal state of Yugoslavia. In 1991, after the republics of Croatia and Slovenia broke away from Yugoslavia, Macedonia also declared its independence. However, most nations have not recognized Macedonia.

Macedonia covers 9,928 square miles (25,713 square kilometers) and has a population of more than 2 million. The Macedonian ethnic group makes up the largest part of the population. Other groups include Albanians and Turks. Skopje is the country's capital.

From 1945 to 1990, Communists controlled all Yugoslavia, including Macedonia. In 1990, non-Communists gained control of Macedonia's government.

Government. A president is the highest official in Macedonia and is elected by the people to a four-year term. The Assembly of the Republic of Macedonia, the nation's lawmaking body, consists of 120 members who

Facts in brief

Capital: Skopje.
Official language: Macedonian.
Official name: Republika Makedonija (Republic of Macedonia).
Area: 9,928 sq. mi. (25,713 km²). *Greatest distances*—north-south, 105 mi. (170 km); east-west, 135 mi. (215 km).
Elevation: *Highest*—Mount Korabit, 9,026 ft. (2,751 m) above sea level. *Lowest*—Vardar River at southern border, 230 ft. (70 m) above sea level.
Population: *Estimated 1994 population*—2,096,000; density, 211 persons per sq. mi. (82 per km²); distribution, 54 percent urban, 46 percent rural. *1991 census*—2,033,964. *Estimated 1999 population*—2,182,000.
Chief products: *Agriculture*—apples, cattle, corn, cotton, grapes, hogs, peaches, plums, poultry, sheep, tobacco, wheat. *Manufacturing*—cement, iron and steel, refrigerators, sulfuric acid, textiles, tobacco products. *Mining*—chromium, copper, iron ore, lead, manganese, uranium, zinc.
National anthem: "Denes nad Makedonija se ragja" ("A new sun rises over Macedonia today").
Flag: The flag is red and has a yellow disk with 16 yellow rays in the center. It was adopted in 1992. See **Flag** (picture: Flags of Europe).
Money: *Basic unit*—denar.

are elected by the people to four-year terms. The president plays a leading role in establishing foreign policy. The president appoints a prime minister to handle day-to-day operations of the government. The Assembly must approve the appointment. Leading political parties include the Internal Macedonian Revolutionary Organization—Democratic Party for Macedonian National Unity, the Social Democratic Union of Macedonia (a group of former Communists), and the Albanian-supported Party of Democratic Prosperity. The country is divided into districts called *opštini* for purposes of local government. Local assemblies govern opštini.

Macedonia's highest court is the Supreme Court. The Assembly appoints justices of this court. About 9,000 men and women serve in Macedonia's armed forces.

People. About two-thirds of the people are Macedonian Slavs. About a fifth are Albanians, most of whom live in western Macedonia. The country has smaller numbers of Turks, Gypsies, and Serbs. Most ethnic Macedonians and Serbs are Eastern Orthodox Christians. Most Turks and Albanians are Muslims. The country's official language is Macedonian, a South Slavic language closely related to Serbo-Croatian and Bulgarian.

Almost 55 percent of Macedonia's people live in urban areas, and about 45 percent live in rural areas. Skopje, the capital and largest city, has about 500,000 people. Many city dwellers live in apartments in high-rise buildings. In rural villages, people have homes built of stone, red brick, or concrete brick.

Favorite Macedonian dishes include cold cucumber soup, garlic soup, *sarma* (stuffed grape leaves), and *sataraš*—a pork and veal dish spiced with onions and red peppers. The national drink of Macedonia is *šljivovica,* a plum brandy.

About 90 percent of the people can read and write. Children are required to attend school from the ages of 7 to 15. Macedonia has a university at Skopje and several other institutions of higher education.

Traditional Macedonian music shows many Turkish features introduced during Ottoman rule from the mid-1300's to the early 1900's. Popular folk dances include

Macedonia

▬▬▬	International boundary
────	Road
────	Railroad
⊛	National capital
•	Other city or town
+	Elevation above sea level

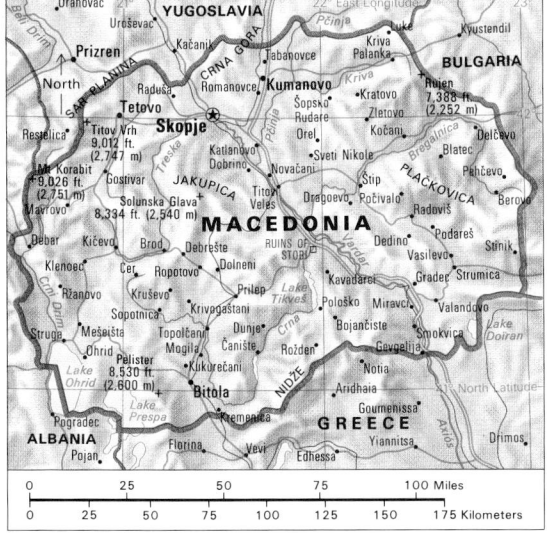

WORLD BOOK maps

the *oro,* a type of circle dance. Soccer is the country's most popular sport.

Land and climate. Macedonia is a rugged country, consisting largely of mountains and hills. Much of it occupies a plateau that lies between 2,000 and 3,000 feet (600 to 900 meters) above sea level. Some of Macedonia's mountains reach heights of more than 8,000 feet (2,500 meters). Mount Korabit, the highest peak, rises 9,026 feet (2,751 meters) along the western border. Forests of beech, oak, and pine grow in many areas of the country, particularly in the west. The Vardar is Macedonia's longest river. It rises in the northwest and flows through central and southern Macedonia.

Macedonia has cold, snowy winters. Summers are hot in the mountain valleys but cooler at higher elevations. Temperatures in Skopje average 34 °F (1 °C) in January and 75 °F (24 °C) in July. The city has an average annual rainfall of 21 inches (55 centimeters).

Economy. The government owns most factories and other businesses in Macedonia. About 40 percent of Macedonians work in industry and less than 10 percent in agriculture. Such service industries as government, health care, and trade employ most other Macedonians.

Macedonian factories produce cement, iron and steel, refrigerators, sulfuric acid, textiles, and tobacco products. The country's mines yield chromium, copper, iron ore, lead, manganese, uranium, and zinc.

Farms cover about a fourth of Macedonia. Chief crops include corn, cotton, tobacco, and wheat. Farmers also

grow apples, grapes, peaches, and plums. Some farmers raise cattle, hogs, poultry, and sheep. Logging is also an important economic activity in rural areas.

Paved roads connect most cities and large towns in Macedonia. A railroad system links Macedonia with Yugoslavia and Greece. The country has airports at Skopje and Ohrid. Leading daily newspapers in Macedonia include *Večer* and *Nova Makedonija*—both of Skopje. Most families own a television and one or more radios.

History. Until the early 1900's, the history of what is now the country of Macedonia was tied to that of the larger, historic area, also called Macedonia. The historic region of Macedonia includes the country of Macedonia and parts of northern Greece and southwestern Bulgaria. For information on historic Macedonia, see **Macedonia** (historic region).

By the late 1800's, historic Macedonia had been part of the Turkish-ruled Ottoman Empire for more than 500 years. But the Ottoman Empire had begun to fall apart, and Bulgaria and Serbia competed for possession of Macedonia. Bulgaria claimed that Macedonians were Bulgarians, while Serbia insisted they were "south Serbs." Bulgaria, Greece, and Serbia took Macedonia from the Ottoman Empire in the First Balkan War (1912-1913). In 1913, in the Second Balkan War, Bulgaria fought Greece, Montenegro, Romania, Serbia, and the

© Jerry Cooke, Photo Researchers

Skopje, Macedonia's capital, features many small shops along cobblestoned streets in its old town district, *above.* A domed mosque with a tower called a *minaret* rises in the background.

Ottoman Empire for control of the region. The war left Serbia with north and central Macedonia. Eastern Macedonia came under Bulgarian rule, and Greece gained southern Macedonia.

In 1918, Serbian Macedonia became part of the Kingdom of the Serbs, Croats, and Slovenes, which was renamed Yugoslavia in 1929. After World War II ended in 1945, a Communist government led by Josip Broz Tito took control of Yugoslavia. In 1946, the part of the Macedonia the Serbs had controlled became one of the six republics of the federal state of Yugoslavia.

Communists completely controlled the governments of Yugoslavia's republics and that of the central government. In the late 1980's, Communist power began to decline. In 1990, the Communists gave up their monopoly on power and allowed other parties to form. Later that year, Macedonia held its first multiparty elections, and the Communists lost control of the government. Macedonia and the republics of Croatia and Slovenia declared their independence from Yugoslavia in 1991.

Most European nations and the United States soon recognized Croatia and Slovenia as independent countries. However, Greek protests prevented recognition of Macedonia by most nations. Greece feared that Macedonia would use its name to claim territory in the region of Macedonia in northern Greece. Greece claimed that "Macedonia" was a Greek name and that the country of Macedonia had no right to use it. The lack of recognition prevented Macedonia from joining international organizations and interfered with its ability to receive economic aid. In 1993, Macedonia and Greece agreed to a compromise solution by which Macedonia was admitted to the United Nations under the temporary name of the Former Yugoslav Republic of Macedonia. The two countries agreed to negotiate a permanent settlement over Macedonia's name. Several European countries then recognized Macedonia's independence.

Sabrina P. Ramet

See also **Balkans; Berlin, Congress of; Macedonia** (historic region); **Skopje; Yugoslavia.**

MacGregor, Robert. See Rob Roy.

Mach, *makh,* **Ernst** (1838-1916), was an Austrian physicist and psychologist. He studied the action of bodies moving at high speeds through gases, and developed an accurate method for measuring their speeds in terms of the speed of sound. This method is important in problems of supersonic flight.

Mach's work remained obscure until the speed of aircraft began to approach the speed of sound. Then the term *Mach number* came to be used as a measure of speed. *Mach 0.5* is half the speed of sound, or *subsonic. Mach 1* is the speed of sound, or *transonic. Mach 2* is twice the speed of sound, or *supersonic,* and so on (see **Aerodynamics** [Shock waves and sonic booms]).

Mach was deeply interested in the historical development of the ideas on which the science of mechanics is based. He claimed that all knowledge of the physical world comes to us by the five senses—sight, hearing, smell, taste, and feeling. He also taught that a scientific law was only a correlation between observed data.

Mach was born at Turas, Moravia. He graduated from the University of Vienna. Arthur I. Miller

Mach number. See Aerodynamics (Shock waves and sonic booms); **Mach, Ernst.**

Machado de Assis, *mah SHAH du dih ah SEES,* **Joaquim Maria** (1839-1908), was a Brazilian author. His many novels and short stories combine a realistic style with sensitive psychological analyses of the characters. In his works, he experimented with the use of humor, irony, and different points of view.

Machado wrote chiefly about the lives of urban, middle-class Brazilians of the 1800's. In his stories, he explored the universal aspects of human nature, analyzed the reasons for the ways people think and act, and raised questions about the meaning of life.

Machado's first major novel was *Memórias Póstumas de Bras Cubas* (1881), which was translated as *Epitaph of a Small Winner.* His other novels include *Philosopher or Dog?* (1891), *Dom Casmurro* (1900), *Esau and Jacob* (1904), and *Memorial of Ayres* (1908). Some shorter fiction was translated into English and published after his death in *The Psychiatrist and Other Stories* (1963). Machado was born in Rio de Janeiro. Earl E. Fitz

Machaut, *ma SHOH,* **Guillaume de,** *gee YOHM duh* (1300?-1377), was a medieval French composer and poet. His best-known composition is his Mass, the earliest complete Mass for four voices by a single composer. He also wrote many French and Latin songs for one to four voices. The songs have elegant and expressive melodies, and often use offbeat rhythmic effects known as *syncopation.* Machaut's songs follow strict poetic forms. A typical song has its chief melody sung by the highest voice, accompanied by one or two voices or instruments in the tenor range. Machaut also wrote many songs for only one voice, like the songs of the poet-musicians called *troubadours* (see **Troubadour**).

Machaut was born in the region of Reims. During his early life, he traveled frequently with royal courts and with armies. He was a *canon* (priest attached to a cathedral) at Reims, and he also served the kings of Bohemia and France. Joscelyn Godwin

Machiavelli, MAK *ee uh VEHL ee* or MAH *kyah VEHL lee,* **Niccolò** (1469-1527), was an Italian statesman and writer whom many people consider the father of modern political science. He ranks as one of the most important political thinkers of the *Renaissance,* a period of great intellectual activity between the 1300's and the 1600's. The experience he acquired as a government official and his study of history led him to view politics in a new way. The political writers of the Middle Ages treated politics idealistically, within the framework of religion. But Machiavelli sought to explain politics realistically, based on his view of human nature within the framework of history.

Machiavelli viewed the state as an organism with its ruler as the head and its people as the body. He maintained that a healthy state is unified, orderly, and in balance, and that its people have happiness, honor, strength, and security. But an unhealthy state is disorderly and unbal-

Detail of *Niccolò Machiavelli* (about 1570), an oil painting on canvas by Santi di Tito; Palazzo Vecchio, Florence, Italy (Alinari/EPA)

Niccolò Machiavelli

anced, and may require strong measures to restore it to normal. Machiavelli called for a leader to use any means necessary to preserve the state, resorting to cruelty, deception, and force if nothing else worked. As a result, many people thought he supported the use of cruelty and deceit in politics. The word *Machiavellian* came to mean *cunning* and *unscrupulous.*

Machiavelli explained most of his ideas in *The Prince,* his best-known book, which was written in 1513 and published in 1532. This book describes the methods by which a strong ruler might gain and keep power. Machiavelli's other works include *Discourses upon the First Ten Books of Livy* (1517 or 1518) and *The Art of War* (1520 or 1521). He also wrote plays and poems.

Machiavelli was born in Florence, Italy. In 1498, he was appointed secretary of the second highest governing body in the Florentine republic. His duties consisted mainly of conducting diplomatic missions. He also organized a militia for the republic. In 1512, the republic collapsed. The Medici family, which had ruled Florence earlier, was then restored to power. Machiavelli was arrested, tortured, and imprisoned on suspicion of plotting against Medici rule, but he was released after less than a year.   John H. Geerken

See also **Italian literature** (Humanism and the Renaissance).

Additional resources

Anglo, Sydney. *Machiavelli: A Dissection.* Harcourt, 1970.
Gilbert, Felix. *Machiavelli and Guicciardini: Politics and History in Sixteenth-Century Florence.* Norton, 1984. First published in 1965.
Machiavelli, Niccolò. *The Portable Machiavelli.* Viking, 1979.
Muir, Dorothy E. *Machiavelli and His Times.* Greenwood, 1976. First published in 1936.

Machine is a device that does work. Machines are designed to make life easier for us. Some machines perform tasks that would be impossible to do without them.

We use machines all the time. Industries use giant drill presses, lathes, and presses to make the products we use. Businesses depend on typewriters, computers, and other office machines. Automobiles, buses, and airplanes transport people swiftly over great distances. Trucks, railroads, and ships haul goods to and from markets. Without machines, the residents of our cities would find it more difficult to live, and farmers could not raise enough food to feed us.

People have constructed a wide variety of machines to satisfy their needs. Early people made stone axes that served as weapons and tools. The machines that were gradually developed gave people great control over their *environment* (physical surroundings). To operate these improved machines, people harnessed the energy of falling water and of such fuels as coal, oil, and the atom. Today, we use so many machines that the age we live in is often called the *machine age.*

Principles of machines

A machine produces force and controls the direction and the motion of force. But it cannot create energy. A machine can never do more work than the energy put into it. It only transforms one kind of energy, such as electrical energy, and passes it along as mechanical energy. Some machines, such as diesel engines or steam turbines, change energy directly into mechanical motion. For example, the energy of steam rushing through the wheels of a turbine produces rotary motion. The mechanical energy of the turbine can be used to drive a generator that produces electricity. Other machines simply transmit mechanical work from one part of a device to another part. They include the six simple machines that are described below.

A machine's ability to do work is measured by two factors. They are (1) efficiency and (2) mechanical advantage.

How machines change the direction of motion

WORLD BOOK illustrations by Oxford Illustrators Limited

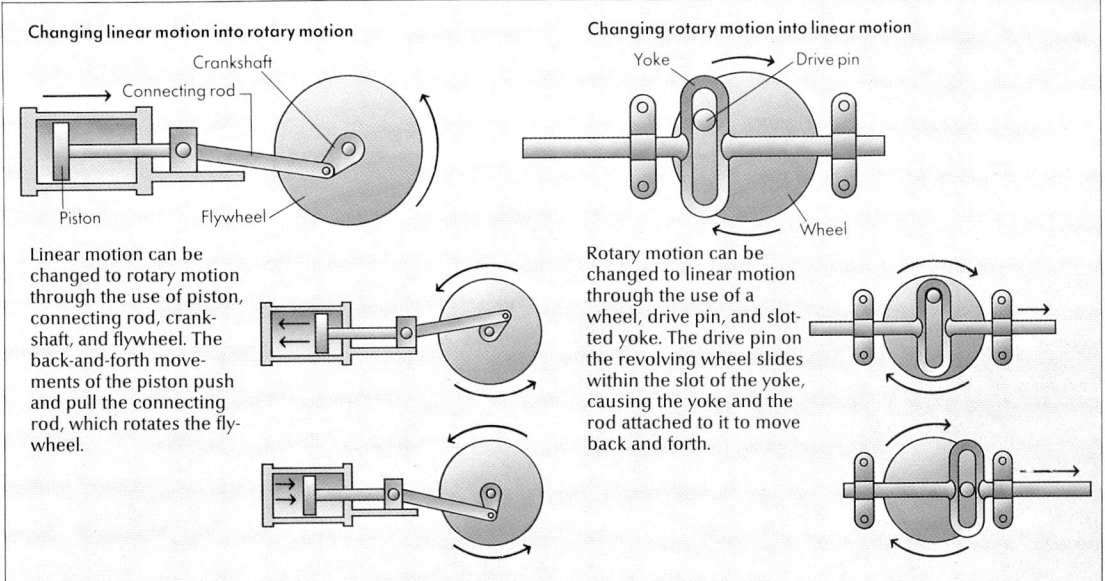

Changing linear motion into rotary motion

Crankshaft
Connecting rod
Piston   Flywheel

Linear motion can be changed to rotary motion through the use of piston, connecting rod, crankshaft, and flywheel. The back-and-forth movements of the piston push and pull the connecting rod, which rotates the flywheel.

Changing rotary motion into linear motion

Yoke   Drive pin
Wheel

Rotary motion can be changed to linear motion through the use of a wheel, drive pin, and slotted yoke. The drive pin on the revolving wheel slides within the slot of the yoke, causing the yoke and the rod attached to it to move back and forth.

Efficiency. The efficiency of a machine is the ratio between the energy it supplies and the energy put into it. No machine can operate with 100 per cent efficiency because the friction of its parts always uses up some of the energy that is being supplied to the machine. Although friction can be decreased by oiling any sliding or rotating parts, all machines produce some friction. For this reason, a perpetual-motion machine is impossible (see **Perpetual motion machine**).

A simple lever is a good example of a machine that has a high efficiency (see **Lever**). The work it puts out is almost equal to the energy it receives, because the energy used up by friction is quite small. On the other hand, an automobile engine has an efficiency of only about 25 per cent, because much of the energy supplied by the fuel is lost in the form of heat that escapes into the surrounding air. See **Efficiency.**

Mechanical advantage. In machines that transmit only mechanical energy, the ratio of the force exerted by the machine to the force applied to the machine is known as *mechanical advantage.* Mechanical advantage can be demonstrated with a crowbar, which is a type of lever. When one end of the crowbar is directly under the weight, a part of the crowbar must rest on a *fulcrum* (support). The closer the fulcrum is to the load, the less the effort required to raise the load by pushing down on the handle of the crowbar, and the greater the mechanical advantage of the crowbar. For example, if the load is 200 kilograms, and the distance from the load to the fulcrum is one fourth of the distance from the handle to the fulcrum, it will take 50 kilograms of effort to raise the load. Therefore, the mechanical advantage will be four to one. But the distance the load will be moved will be only one-fourth of the distance through which the effort is applied.

Six simple machines

Most machines consist of a number of elements, such as gears and ball bearings, that work together in a complex way. But no matter how complex they are, all machines are based in some way on six types of simple machines. These six types of machines are the lever, the wheel and axle, the pulley, the inclined plane, the wedge, and the screw.

Lever. There are three basic types of levers, depending on where the effort is applied, on the position of the load, and on the position of the fulcrum. In a first-class lever, such as a crowbar, the fulcrum is between the load and the applied force. In a second-class lever, such as a wheelbarrow, the load lies between the fulcrum and the applied force. In a third-class lever, the effort is applied between the load and the fulcrum. For example, when a person lifts a ball in the palm of the hand, the load is at the hand and the fulcrum is at the elbow. The forearm supplies the upward force that lifts the ball. See **Lever.**

Wheel and axle. The wheel and axle is essentially a modified lever, but it can move a load farther than a lever can. In a windlass used to raise water from a well, the rope that carries the load is wrapped around the axle of the wheel. The effort is applied to a crank handle on the side of the wheel. The center of the axle serves as a fulcrum. The mechanical advantage of the windlass depends upon the ratio between the radius of the axle and

Six simple machines

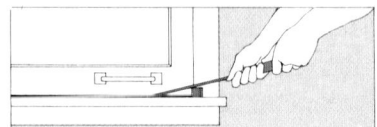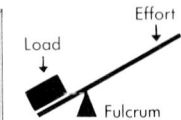

The lever is one of the earliest and simplest machines. Its advantage lies in the short distance between the fulcrum (pivotal point) and load, and in the long distance between the fulcrum and the point where effort is applied.

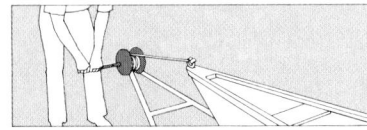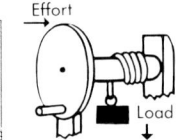

The wheel and axle has a rope attached to the axle to lift the load. The crank handle is the point where effort is applied. The effort is smaller than the load because it is at a greater distance from the axle which is the fulcrum.

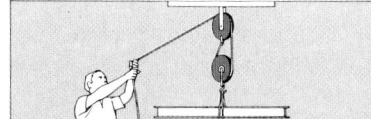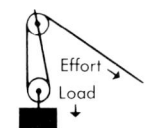

The pulley consists of a wheel with a grooved rim over which a rope is passed. It is used to change the direction of the effort applied to the rope. A block and tackle uses two or more pulleys to reduce the amount of effort needed to lift a load.

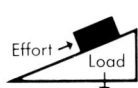

The inclined plane makes it easier to slide or skid a load upward than to lift it directly. The longer the slope, the smaller the effort required. The amount of work, however, is no less than if the load were lifted directly upward.

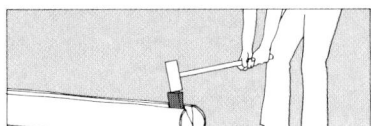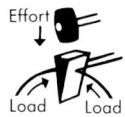

The wedge, when struck with a mallet or sledge, exerts a large force on its sides. A gently tapering, or thin, wedge is more effective than a thick one. The mechanical advantage of the wedge is of great importance.

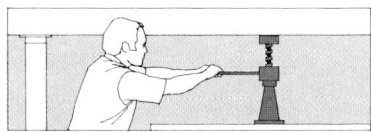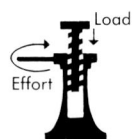

The screw is a spiral inclined plane. The jackscrew is a combination of the lever and the screw. It can lift a heavy load with relatively small effort. Therefore, it has a very high mechanical advantage for practical purposes.

the distance from the center of the axle to the crank handle. The wheel-and-axle machine has important applications when it is used to transport heavy goods by rolling rather than by sliding. The wheel itself is regarded as one of the most important inventions of all time. It is widely used in all types of machinery and motor vehicles. See **Wheel and axle.**

Pulley. A pulley is a wheel over which a rope or belt is passed. It is a form of the wheel and axle. The mechanical advantage of a single pulley is one, because the downward force exerted on the rope equals the weight lifted by the other end of the rope that passes over the pulley. The main advantage of the single pulley is that it changes the direction of the force. For example, to lift a load, a person can conveniently pull down on a rope, using the weight of the body. When one pulley is attached to a support and another is attached to the load and allowed to move freely, a definite mechanical advantage is obtained. See **Pulley.**

Inclined plane. The inclined plane is such a simple device that it scarcely looks like a machine at all. The average person cannot raise a 200-pound box up 2 feet into the rear of a truck. But by placing a 10-foot plank from the truck to the ground, a person could raise the load easily. If there were no friction, the force required to move the box would be exactly 40 pounds. The mechanical advantage of an inclined plane is the length of the incline divided by the vertical rise. The mechanical advantage increases as the slope of the incline decreases. But the load will then have to be moved a greater distance. By adding rollers, it is possible to make a roller conveyor that will reduce friction and have great efficiency. See **Inclined plane.**

Wedge. The wedge is an adaptation of the inclined plane. It can be used to raise a heavy load over a short distance or to split a log. The wedge is driven by blows from a mallet or sledge hammer. The effectiveness of the wedge depends on the angle of the thin end. The smaller the angle, the less the force required to raise a given load. See **Wedge.**

Screw. The screw is actually an inclined plane wrapped in a spiral around a shaft. The mechanical advantage of a screw is approximately the ratio of the circumference of the screw to the distance the screw advances during each revolution.

A *jackscrew,* such as those used to raise homes and other structures, combines the usefulness of the screw and the lever. The lever is used to turn the screw. The mechanical advantage of a jackscrew is quite high, and only a small effort will raise a heavy load. See **Screw.**

Designing machines

By combining the principles of simple machines, engineers develop new and specialized machines. They choose materials for the various parts of the machine that resist stress, friction, and *corrosion* (wear from chemicals). Engineers also design machines to be safe and efficient.   Richard M. H. Cheng

Related articles in *World Book* include:

Some kinds of machines

Archimedean screw	Catapult
Battering ram	Crane
Block and tackle	Die and diemaking

Electric generator	Treadmill
Engine	Turbine
Inclined plane	Water wheel
Lever	Wedge
Machine tool	Wheel and axle
Pulley	Windlass
Pump	Windmill
Screw	

Machine parts

Bearing	Governor	Safety valve
Gauge	Ratchet	Valve
Gear		

Uses of machines

See these articles and their lists of *Related articles:*

Airplane	Nuclear energy
Automation	Printing
Automobile	Rocket
Farm and farming	Tool

Other related articles

Cybernetics	Invention
Efficiency	Mechanical drawing
Energy (The conservation of energy)	Mechanics
	Perpetual motion machine
Industrial Revolution	Work

Machine age. See Machine; Industrial Revolution.

Machine gun is an automatic weapon that can fire from 400 to 1,600 rounds of ammunition each minute. Machine gun barrels range in size from .22 caliber to 20 millimeters. Ammunition is fed into the gun from a cloth or metal belt, or from a cartridge holder called a *magazine.* Because machine guns fire so rapidly, they must be cooled by water or air. Machine guns are heavy weapons and are usually mounted on a support.

Operation. In all machine guns, extremely high gas pressure provides the operating energy for the firing cycle. The cycle begins when the propellant charge in the cartridge case burns. This combustion creates the gas pressure that is used in the *blowback, gas,* and *recoil* operating systems. All three systems fire the projectile through the *bore* of the barrel, eject the cartridge case, place a new cartridge in the firing chamber, and ready the mechanism to repeat the cycle.

In the *blowback system,* the operating energy comes

William Allen, Photri
The M60 machine gun, a major infantry weapon, may be fired from the hip or shoulder, *above,* or on a support.

Machine guns of World Wars I and II. The heavy machine gun, *far left,* was the most destructive weapon of World War I. Machine guns used during World War II included light machine guns, *right,* and the submachine gun M3, carried by the standing soldier.

U.S. Army

from the cartridge case as the case is forced to the rear by the gas pressure. The case moves against the bolt, driving the bolt backward against a spring. The case is ejected, and the compressed spring drives the bolt forward. As the bolt moves forward, it cocks the firing mechanism, picks up a new cartridge, carries it into the chamber, and the cycle begins again.

In the *gas system,* the gas pressure drives a piston against the bolt. The bolt is driven to the rear, providing energy for a cycle like that of the blowback system.

In the *recoil system,* the bolt locks to the barrel when the gun is fired. These parts remain locked together as they are forced to the rear by the gas pressure. This movement provides energy to operate the gun.

Ground weapons. The 7.62-millimeter M60 machine gun is a major infantry weapon. It is air-cooled and gas-operated, and fires about 600 rounds a minute. The M60 replaced the Browning machine gun, an important weapon in World Wars I and II, and the Korean War.

Aircraft weapons. By the close of World War I, several types of machine guns were mounted on airplanes. These types included the Vickers, Maxim, Hotchkiss, Colt-Martin, and Lewis. Some machine guns were synchronized to fire in between the blades of propellers.

During World War II, fighters and bombers carried machine guns as armament. They also carried automatic cannon up to 20 millimeters in size. During the Vietnam War, helicopters called *gunships* carried machine guns or cannon. Today, most fighter planes and gunships carry rockets for air-to-air and air-to-ground use. Bombers use machine guns mounted in groups of two or four in power-driven turrets. The Vulcan 20-millimeter aircraft cannon has six rotating barrels. It can fire more than a ton of metal and explosives each minute.

Antiaircraft weapons. The .50-caliber Browning machine gun was used as an antiaircraft weapon during World War II. It was used alone, or in groups of two or four. Large-caliber automatic cannon that fired explosive shells were also developed as antiaircraft weapons. The 20-millimeter, Swiss-made Oerlikon gun was used on U.S. Navy ships. It was a self-fed, self-firing cannon that could fire 600 rounds a minute.

Early machine guns

Gatling gun

WORLD BOOK illustrations by Robert Addison

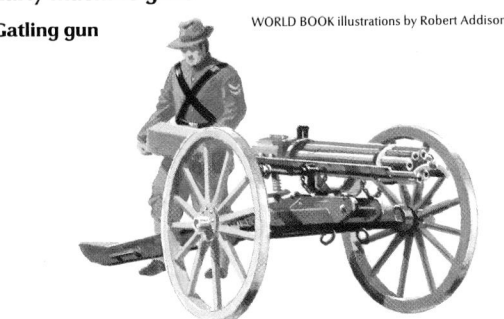

Richard Gatling built a hand-cranked machine gun in 1862.

Montigny mitrailleuse

The Montigny mitrailleuse was a 37-barrel machine gun.

Maxim gun

Hiram Maxim made the first fully automatic machine gun.

History. A type of machine gun appeared as early as the 1500's. It consisted of several guns bound together in a bundle or spread out in a row. A device that was fitted to the gun barrels caused them to fire simultaneously or in series. But little success was achieved until the Civil War, when many quick-fire guns appeared. Practical, rapid-fire, mechanical guns were used in the Franco-Prussian War, when soldiers operated them with a crank or lever. The French *Montigny mitrailleuse* and the American *Gatling* were among the more successful of these guns.

In 1883, Hiram Maxim, an American-born inventor, developed the first entirely automatic machine gun to gain wide acceptance. By the time of World War I, many different types of machine guns had come into use.

Joel D. Meyerson

See also **Gatling, Richard J.; Maxim, Sir Hiram Stevens.**

Machine tool is a power-driven machine used to shape metal. Basic machine tools use mechanical power to bend, cut, drill, grind, hammer, plane, and squeeze metal into desired shapes. More advanced machine tools use such power sources as electrical or chemical energy, heat, magnetism, and ultrasound. People who operate machine tools are called *machinists.*

Machine tools play an important part in the manufacture of almost all metal products. Machinists use them in making parts for such products as automobiles, radios, refrigerators, and television sets. Many other products are made by machines that were manufactured by machine tools. These include such products as books, furniture, and textiles.

There are about 500 kinds of machine tools. Some perform a single operation, such as grinding or drilling. Others, called *machining centers,* carry out several kinds of tasks. Machining centers have automatic tool changers and may use more than 100 tools.

Machine tools can be linked together to form a *flexible manufacturing system* (FMS). Each of the tools in an FMS performs a different metalworking operation. The metal being machined, called a *workpiece,* is moved from one tool to the next by conveyors, robots, and other automatic equipment. A single FMS can manufacture a variety of parts.

Machine tools come in a wide range of sizes. A machinist's choice of size is based on the size of the largest workpiece to be machined.

Basic machine tool operations

There are two chief kinds of machine tool operations: (1) metal removal and (2) metal forming. Basic metal removal operations involve either the cutting away or the *abrasion* (wearing away) of part of the workpiece. In metal forming, the workpiece is shaped without the removal of any material from it.

Metal removal. There are six basic types of metal removal processes. They are (1) turning; (2) hole machining; (3) milling; (4) sawing; (5) planing, shaping, and broaching; and (6) abrasive processes.

Turning is used chiefly to cut metal into round shapes. Turning machines are the most common machine tools in the United States. They manufacture gear blanks, shafts, wheels, and many other metal parts.

The *lathe* is the basic turning machine. On a lathe, the workpiece is fastened to a rotating spindle, and the cutting tool is mounted at the side of the workpiece. The tool moves against the rotating workpiece, peeling metal until the workpiece has the desired shape. A *turret lathe* has several kinds of cutting tools mounted on a revolving toolholder called a *turret.* This lathe can perform various cutting operations, one after the other.

Some turning machines have several spindles and cutting tools that operate at the same time. Such *multispindle machines* perform various operations at once on several workpieces. The machine moves each workpiece from one cutting tool to the next until all the operations have been performed.

Hole machining includes drilling, boring, reaming, and tapping. In *drilling,* round holes up to 3 inches (7.5 centimeters) in diameter are cut in a piece of metal. These holes, cut by a rotating *twist drill,* may be as small as a few thousandths of an inch in diameter.

In most machine shops, twist drills are mounted on large machines called *drill presses.* The machinist places the workpiece on a table beneath the drill and lowers the drill into the metal. The bit of the drill has several sharp cutting edges. Two or more spiral grooves along the bit help remove metal shavings from the hole.

In *boring,* round holes greater than 3 inches (7.6 centimeters) in diameter are cut. Boring is also used to en-

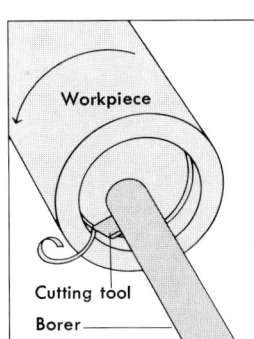

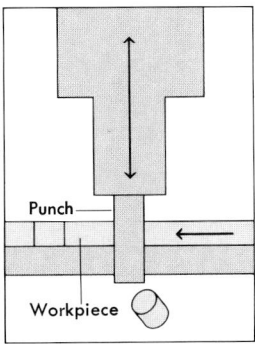

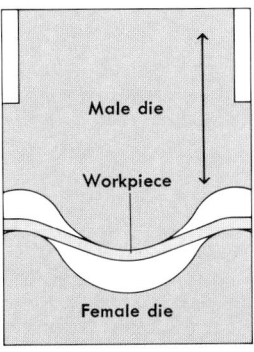

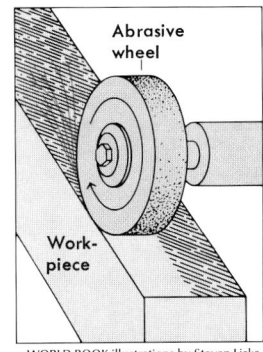

WORLD BOOK illustrations by Steven Liska

A borer cuts and smooths round holes. Its cutting tool has a single sharp edge.

A punch press is a forming machine that stamps holes into sheet metal.

Press brakes form metal into a desired shape by pressing it between two dies.

A grinding wheel rubs against the surface of a workpiece to make it smooth.

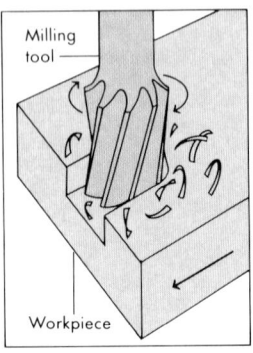
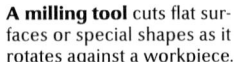

A milling tool cuts flat surfaces or special shapes as it rotates against a workpiece.

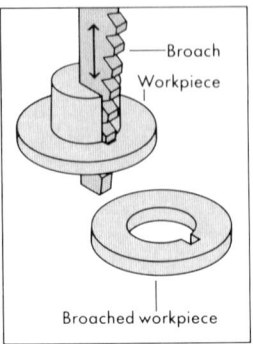

A broach changes the shape of a hole. It is pushed or pulled through a workpiece.

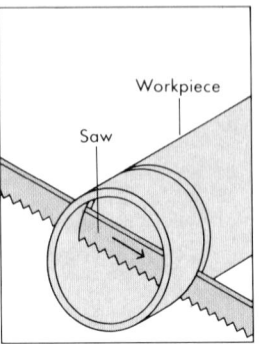

A saw cuts a piece of metal to a certain length or into a desired shape.

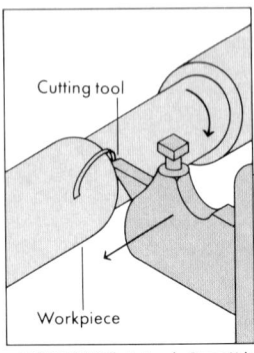

WORLD BOOK illustrations by Steven Liska

A turning machine has a cutting tool that peels metal from a rotating workpiece.

large and *finish* (smooth) holes already drilled.

Boring machines have a cutting tool with only one sharp edge. On small boring machines, the tool revolves and the workpiece remains stationary. On large machines, the tool is stationary and the workpiece revolves.

The process of *reaming* consists of smoothing the inside of a hole. *Tapping* involves the cutting of a screw thread inside a hole (see **Screw**).

To cut deep holes, machinists use special processes in which a single- or multiple-edged tool mounted at the end of a bar is driven into the workpiece. These processes involve the rotation of the tool, the workpiece, or both. During the operation, a fluid is forced into the hole to flush out shavings cut from the workpiece.

Milling. In this operation, a round tool with several cutting edges rotates against a workpiece. The cutting tool of most milling machines looks like a wheel with teeth projecting out of it. This tool makes flat surfaces on metal. Machinists use special milling tools to cut such shapes as those of bevels, gear teeth, and slots.

Some milling machines manufacture metal parts small enough to fit in a person's hand. Others, such as *special contour milling machines,* produce airplane wing sections as long as 80 feet (24 meters).

Sawing consists of machining a piece of metal with a cutting tool that has sharp teeth along one edge. There

are two types of machine-tool sawing, *cutoff sawing* and *contour sawing.* Machinists use cutoff sawing to cut metal bars to a certain length. Contour sawing cuts flat pieces of metal into the desired shape.

Planing, shaping, and broaching. Planing smooths flat surfaces of large pieces of metal. It resembles smoothing wood with a hand plane. But the cutting tool is stationary as the metal moves back and forth beneath it. Shaping flattens uneven surfaces and cuts slots. The cutting tool moves back and forth over a stationary workpiece. Broaching shapes holes in a piece of metal. For example, it can change round holes to square ones. A broach is a long metal bar with rows of teeth on it. Each tooth cuts a little deeper than the one before. A broach is pulled or pushed through a hole, and the teeth cut the metal to the desired shape.

Milling has replaced planing and shaping almost entirely. The cutting tools of milling machines can smooth metal surfaces faster than those of planers or shapers.

Abrasive processes include grinding, lapping, and honing. In *grinding,* metal is removed from the surface of a workpiece to make it smooth. A grinding machine has a *grinding wheel* that spins at high speed against the workpiece. This wheel is made of an abrasive material similar to that on sandpaper.

Two of the main types of grinding operations are *cy-*

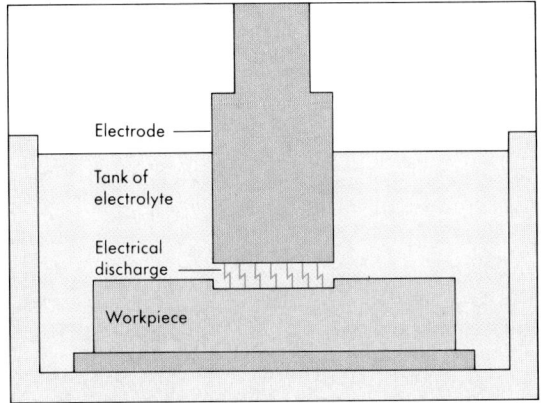

Electrical discharge machining (EDM) produces smooth, accurate holes in metal by means of an electric current.

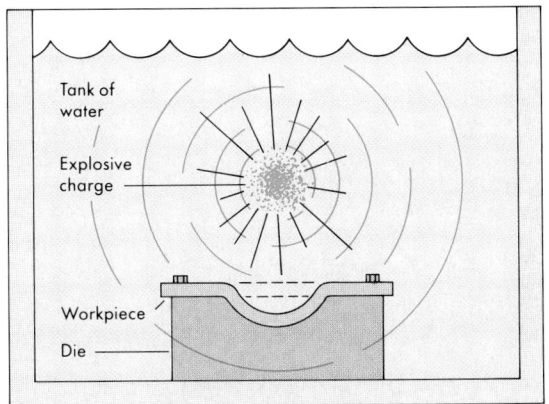

WORLD BOOK illustrations by Steven Liska

High-energy rate forming (HERF) uses an explosive charge to force sheet metal into the contours of a die.

lindrical and *surface.* In cylindrical grinding, a round workpiece rotates against the grinding wheel. A type of cylindrical grinding called *centerless grinding* is widely used in mass production. It involves two rotating wheels. One wheel rubs against the workpiece and turns it while the other grinds the workpiece. In surface grinding, a flat workpiece moves back and forth against a rotating wheel. In both cylindrical grinding and surface grinding, sharp edges of abrasive particles on the grinding wheel cut tiny chips from the workpiece, producing a smooth surface texture.

In *lapping,* an abrasive paste or other substance is used to remove metal. Lapping provides an extremely smooth surface when only a small amount of metal must be removed. A lapping machine has a metal plate covered with an abrasive. *Honing* assures maximum accuracy in finishing holes to precise dimensions. In this process, an abrasive paste is applied to cylindrical parts called *heads,* which are inserted into the hole. The heads rotate while moving up and down.

Metal forming operations include forging, pressing, bending, and shearing. There are four main types of forming machines: (1) forging machines, (2) presses, (3) press brakes, and (4) shears.

Forging machines form metal by hammering and squeezing it. Some of these machines hammer hot metal into any shape. Others squeeze hot metal in a *die* (mold) under great pressure. The metal flows to every part of the die and takes the desired shape. Forging machines produce extremely tough and durable metal parts.

Presses stamp a metal sheet into a certain shape. Then they use a die to squeeze this piece of metal, called a *blank,* into the final shape. *Punch presses* punch holes in metal sheets.

Press brakes bend sheets of metal to make products. These products include hoods and roofs for automobiles and the sides of cabinets and refrigerators.

Shears cut large sheets of metal much as scissors cut sheets of paper. Machinists then work the metal into finished parts of the desired shape and size.

Advanced machine tool operations

Advanced machine tools cut extremely hard metals into complex shapes by means of electrical or chemical energy, heat, magnetism, or other forces. Advanced machine tool operations are used chiefly to make large steel dies for the manufacture of automobile parts and other parts. These methods include (1) electrical discharge machining, (2) electrochemical machining, (3) chemical machining, and (4) high-energy rate forming.

Electrical discharge machining (EDM) cuts holes in extremely hard metals, including steel alloys that cannot be cut by traditional methods. EDM produces smooth, accurate holes, some of which have extremely complex shapes. It is the most widely used advanced machining process.

The energy for cutting comes from an electric current that flows through a part called an *electrode.* Most electrodes used in EDM are made of graphite, which has a high melting point. The electrode has the shape of the hole to be made in the workpiece. The electrode and the workpiece are submerged in an *electrolyte,* a liquid that conducts current. A current is then directed between the electrode and the workpiece, producing a

discharge of sparks. This discharge has the shape of the electrode. The sparks therefore erode a hole of the same shape in the workpiece.

Electrochemical machining (ECM) uses electric current to create a chemical reaction that erodes metal from a workpiece. In this method, current flows from a positively charged workpiece to a negatively charged cutting tool. An electrolyte pumped between the workpiece and the cutting tool conducts the current between them. The workpiece takes the shape of the face of the cutting tool.

Chemical machining. In this operation, the workpiece is covered by a chemically resistant mask. The mask has holes cut in it of the shape of those to be cut in the workpiece. The workpiece is dipped into a strong chemical solution, which dissolves the metal from the workpiece sections not covered by the mask.

High-energy rate forming (HERF) involves transmitting pressure through a liquid, usually water, to force sheet metal into the contours of a die. In most cases, the pressure is created by setting off an explosive in the liquid or by discharging an electric spark in it. HERF is used chiefly to make large metal parts that have an unusual shape, such as a dish-shaped radar antenna.

Other advanced machining operations. In *laser cutting,* machinists aim a thin beam of concentrated light at the workpiece. This light is created by a device called a *laser.* When a laser beam is aimed at an extremely small area, it may produce temperatures higher than 10,000 °F (5538 °C). Machinists use laser beams to make small, precise cuts or holes by melting through metal or other materials. See **Laser.**

In an operation called *magnetic forming,* an electromagnet is created when an electric current is directed through a coil. If the coil surrounds the workpiece, the electromagnetic force shapes the workpiece by pushing the metal in. If the coil is placed within the workpiece, the force pushes the metal out.

A process called *water-jet cutting* uses an extremely thin jet of water under very high pressure to cut soft metals. Minute abrasive particles are sometimes mixed with the water to increase the cutting rate.

In *plasma spraying and cutting,* machinists use a heated stream of ionized gas, called *plasma,* to melt holes in extremely hard metals. The plasma is sprayed at a high speed from an instrument called a *plasma torch* onto the workpiece. A similar process called *electron-beam machining* cuts holes in a workpiece by means of a stream of electrons traveling at high speed.

Another operation, called *ultrasonic machining,* cuts holes in extremely hard metal. The cutting tool of an ultrasonic cutter vibrates into the workpiece about 20,000 times a second. The workpiece is immersed in an abrasive fluid. Friction created by the tool vibrating against the abrasive grinds the metal into shape.

Numerical control of machine tools

Numerical control is a system of automating machine tools. In some systems, instructions are given by means of a *control tape.* This tape, which is made of paper or plastic, contains the instructions in the form of a number code. The numbers are represented on the tape by holes or by magnetized spots. The tape is fed into the machine, which has a control unit that reads the code.

This process creates electric signals that correspond to the code. The signals control the direction and speed of the machine as it moves across the workpiece.

In some other machining systems, computers have replaced control tapes. A system known as *computer numerical control* has a number of machine tools, each of which is directed by its own computer. In a system called *direct numerical control,* a single computer controls more than 100 machine tools.

A more highly automated machining system, called *adaptive control,* involves the use of a *microprocessor.* A microprocessor is a tiny electronic device that performs the work of a computer. The microprocessor regulates certain variables in the machining process such as the speed of a spindle, to make the process as efficient as possible. It also receives information from sensors that measure force, temperature, and other variables. It uses this information to operate the system at a level that is safe for the machine tool and the workpiece.

Another automated system, called *programmable machine control (PMC),* uses common computer programming languages to control machine tools. Under PMC, machine tools can operate for long periods of time without manual control.

History

The basic machine tool operations developed from processes originally used with hand tools that cut and shaped wood. The first modern machine tool was invented in 1775 by John Wilkinson, an English ironmaker. Wilkinson's invention, a boring machine, enabled workers to drill precise holes in metal. A number of other machine tools, including the planer, the shaper, and the first successful screw-cutting lathe, were also invented in England during the 1800's.

In the United States, the machine tool industry began about 1800. Machine tools were used chiefly to make guns and cannons for the armed forces. In 1873, C. M. Spencer of the United States developed a completely automatic lathe. In the 1920's, machine tools began to be linked together in series for use in mass production. The number of machine tools in the United States more than doubled during World War II (1939-1945).

Since the 1950's, the development of spacecraft and other aircraft has resulted in advanced machining operations. The use of numerical control, machining centers, computers, and microprocessors brought new speed and efficiency to the industry.   M. O. M. Osman

Related articles in *World Book* include:

Alloy (Alloys of iron)	Grinding and polishing	Nasmyth, James
Drill	Industrial Revolution	Steam hammer
Forging	(The steam engine)	

Machinists and Aerospace Workers, International Association of,

is a labor union affiliated with the American Federation of Labor and Congress of Industrial Organizations. It has local unions in the United States and its territories and in Canada. Membership in the union is open to men and women who work in the metalworking industries, on production lines, in machine shops, garages, toolrooms, and everywhere that machinery and equipment are manufactured, installed, repaired, or operated.

The union was founded in Atlanta, Ga., in 1888 as the National Association of Machinists. It became the International Association of Machinists in 1891, when it expanded its membership to include Canadian metalworkers. The union took its present name in 1965. It is one of the largest unions in the aerospace industry, as well as one of the largest among the railroad, automobile mechanics, airlines, machine tool, and business machine industry unions. Services include a research and statistical department, a department of safety and health, and a department of community services. The union publishes a monthly newspaper, *The Machinist.* Headquarters are at 1300 Connecticut Ave. NW, Washington, DC 20036. For membership, see **Labor movement** (table).

Critically reviewed by the
International Association of Machinists and Aerospace Workers

Machu Picchu, *MAH choo PEEK choo,* is the site of an ancient Inca city. It is located in south-central Peru, about 50 miles (80 kilometers) northwest of Cusco. The stone ruins of Machu Picchu stand on a mountain about 8,000 feet (2,400 meters) high. American explorer Hiram Bingham discovered the ruins in 1911.   David J. Robinson

See also **Peru** (picture; map); **Architecture** (Pre-Columbian architecture).

Macintosh, *MAK ihn tahsh,* **Charles** (1766-1843), a Scottish chemist and inventor, is best known as the inventor of waterproof fabrics. The *mackintosh,* a rubberized, waterproof outer garment, is named after him. Macintosh made many significant contributions to chemical technology. Macintosh opened a factory to manufacture alum and sal ammoniac before he was 20 years old. He also introduced into Great Britain the manufacture of lead and aluminum acetates and contributed to the technology of dyeing. Macintosh was born in Glasgow.   John A. Heitmann

See also **Rubber** (The rubber industry begins).

Mack, Connie (1862-1956), became one of the greatest managers in baseball history. He helped organize the American League, and served as owner-manager of the Philadelphia Athletics from 1901 to 1950. Mack spent more than 60 years in baseball. He led the Athletics to nine American League pennants and five World Series championships. His sons later sold the team and it was moved to Kansas City, Mo., in 1955. Mack was born in East Brookfield, Mass. His real name was Cornelius Alexander McGillicuddy. Mack was elected to the National Baseball Hall of Fame in 1937.   Jack Lang

Mackay, *MAK ee,* **John William** (1831-1902), was an American miner and financier. Along with another financier, James Gordon Bennett, Jr., Mackay organized the Commercial Cable Company and the Postal Telegraph Company in 1883. They laid two cables under the Atlantic Ocean and were beginning to lay one under the Pacific Ocean when Mackay died.

Mackay was born in Ireland, but came to New York City with his parents as a boy. In 1851, he went to California to seek gold. Mackay made his fortune as one of the owners of the "Big Bonanza" gold and silver mine. This mine, discovered in 1873 at Virginia City, Nev., was the richest deposit of gold and silver ore ever found. The value of a share in the mine shot up from 15 cents to $1,850. Mackay became a millionaire almost overnight. At their height, his earnings from the "Big Bonanza" were said to have reached $800,000 a month.

George H. Daniels

Alexander Mackenzie

**Prime Minister of Canada
1873-1878**

Macdonald
1867-1873

Mackenzie
1873-1878

Macdonald
1878-1891

Detail of a portrait by J. W. L. Forster;
Parliament Buildings, Ottawa (John Evans)

Mackenzie, Alexander (1822-1892), served as prime minister of Canada from 1873 to 1878. He was the second person, and the first Liberal, to hold that office.

Mackenzie faced many national economic problems as prime minister, chiefly because he served during a worldwide depression. But he strengthened the new nation by promoting honest, democratic government and greater independence from Great Britain. He won respect for his determination, hard work, and honesty.

Mackenzie, a Scottish immigrant, had little formal education. He worked as a stonemason before entering politics, and his appearance reflected his humble background. He had the muscular body and strong hands of a laborer. A reddish beard emphasized his strong chin. Mackenzie spoke with a Scottish accent.

Early life

Childhood and education. Alexander Mackenzie was born on Jan. 28, 1822, in the village of Logierait,

Important dates in Mackenzie's life

1822 (Jan. 28) Born in Logierait, Scotland.
1842 (May) Settled in Kingston, Upper Canada.
1845 (March 28) Married Helen Neil.
1852 (Jan. 4) Helen Neil Mackenzie died.
1853 (June 17) Married Jane Sym.
1861 Elected to the Legislative Assembly of the Province of Canada.
1873 (Nov. 7) Became prime minister of Canada.
1878 (Oct. 17) Resigned as prime minister.
1892 (April 17) Died in Toronto.

Scotland, about 50 miles (80 kilometers) north of Edinburgh. He was the third of the 10 children—all sons—of Alexander Mackenzie, a carpenter, and Mary Fleming Mackenzie. When Alexander was 10, he began to herd sheep to help support the family. His father, whose health had been poor, died three years later. Alexander then left school to train as a stonemason.

Alexander continued to read on his own and, in time, gave himself a good education. He finished his training as a stonemason when he was about 20 and got a job on a railroad construction project near Irvine, Scotland.

Emigration to Canada. In Irvine, Mackenzie fell in love with Helen Neil, the daughter of a stonemason. Her family emigrated to Canada in 1842, and Mackenzie went along. They settled in Kingston, the capital of the Province of Canada. The province consisted of Upper Canada (present-day Ontario) and Lower Canada (present-day Quebec). Mackenzie became a builder and contractor, and he and Helen were married in 1845.

In 1847, the young couple moved to what was then the Far West of Canada. They settled in Sarnia, Upper Canada. Helen and Alexander had three children, but only one, their daughter Mary, survived. Helen died in 1852. The next year, Mackenzie married Jane Sym, whose father was a Sarnia farmer.

Entry into political life

Member of the Reformers. Soon after settling in Canada, Mackenzie joined the Reform Party, a liberal political party. He became a follower of George Brown, a Reform leader and the publisher of the *Globe* in Toronto. In 1851, Mackenzie helped Brown win election to the Legislative Assembly of the Province of Canada.

Brown in time became the leader of the Reform Party. From 1852 to 1854, Mackenzie edited the *Lambton Shield,* a newspaper that supported the Reformers. In 1861, he won election to the Legislative Assembly from Lambton County, Upper Canada.

In 1867, several British colonies in North America united and formed the Dominion of Canada. Sir John A. Macdonald, the leader of the Conservative Party, became the first prime minister after Confederation. The Dominion's first elections took place in 1867. Mackenzie won election to the House of Commons, but Brown was defeated. Mackenzie then replaced Brown as head of the Reform Party. He united Reformers and liberals throughout Canada into a new Liberal Party.

Leader of the Opposition. The Conservatives won a majority in Parliament in the 1872 elections, and Macdonald remained prime minister. Mackenzie had unofficially led the Liberal Party since Confederation. In 1873, the party appointed him to the official position of *leader of the Opposition.* This office is held by the head of the second largest party in the House.

Later in 1873, a scandal disgraced the Macdonald administration. Two financial groups had competed for a government contract to build the Canadian Pacific Railway (now CP Rail) between eastern Canada and the Pacific Coast. The government gave the contract to the group headed by Sir Hugh Allan, the owner of a shipping line. But then it was learned that Allan had contributed $300,000 to the Conservative election campaign of 1872. Mackenzie and other Liberals attacked the Macdonald government about the so-called Pacific Scandal, and Macdonald resigned. On Nov. 7, 1873, Mackenzie became Canada's second prime minister.

Prime minister

Reforms. Mackenzie called for new elections to be held in January 1874. The Liberal Party won a large majority in the House. Under Mackenzie's leadership, Parliament took many steps to promote honest, democratic government. For example, it passed laws to prevent dishonest election practices and allow more citizens to vote. It also introduced the secret ballot, which was first used in 1878.

To guarantee honesty in his administration, Mackenzie himself took charge of the Department of Public Works. This department controlled the construction of such projects as railroads and public buildings. It spent more than any other government department—and thus offered the greatest possibilities for dishonesty.

Strengthening the new nation. Mackenzie's administration strengthened Canadian independence by dealing directly with the United States. Previously, British diplomats had met with representatives of other nations in Canada's behalf. Mackenzie also established the Royal Military College in 1874 and the Supreme Court of Canada in 1875. These institutions enabled Canada to handle more of its own military and legal affairs.

The Pacific Railway dispute occurred when the government ran short of time and money in building the Canadian Pacific Railway. In 1871, British Columbia had become part of Canada on the condition that the transcontinental railroad be started in 2 years and completed within 10 years. Mackenzie asked for more time, and the province threatened to secede from Canada.

The dispute between British Columbia and the Canadian government led to one of Mackenzie's most important achievements as prime minister. At that time, the British statesman Frederick T. Blackwood, Marquess of Dufferin and Ava, was governor general—the British monarch's representative in Canada. Lord Dufferin proposed that an official in London settle the dispute. However, Mackenzie protested against such an arrangement. He insisted that the governor general respect decisions that were made by Canadian officials. As a result, the British government revised the powers of the governor general and allowed Canada to handle its own internal affairs. The Canadian Pacific Railway was completed in 1885.

Economic difficulties and defeat. Mackenzie served as prime minister during a worldwide depression. With the Canadian economy in a slump, taxes did not provide enough income to pay expenses. Mackenzie, following the economic beliefs of his time, reduced government spending and increased taxes. But these steps failed to lift Canada out of the depression.

Hoping to win a vote of confidence, Mackenzie called for new elections to be held in September 1878. In the election campaign, the Conservatives attacked Mackenzie's leadership during the depression. Macdonald called for a "National Policy" that included tariff protection for Canadian industries. This idea appealed to many voters because of the nation's economic difficulties. The Conservatives won a large majority in Parliament, and Macdonald replaced Mackenzie as prime minister on Oct. 17, 1878.

Later years

Mackenzie was reelected to the House of Commons from Lambton County and again became leader of the Opposition. But the strain of office had damaged his health, and he resigned as Opposition leader in 1880. Mackenzie won reelection to the House three more times. He was still a member of Parliament when he died in Toronto on April 17, 1892.   Dale C. Thomson

See also **Brown, George; Canada, History of; Dufferin and Ava, Marquess of; Macdonald, Sir John A.; Prime minister of Canada.**

Additional resources

Buckingham, William, and Ross, G. W. *The Honourable Alexander Mackenzie: His Life and Times.* Haskell House, 1969. First published in 1892.
Thomson, Dale C. *Alexander Mackenzie: Clear Grit.* Macmillan (Toronto), 1960.

Mackenzie, Sir Alexander (1764-1820), was a Canadian explorer, trader, and businessman. He was the first white man to reach the Mackenzie River and to cross the northern part of North America to the Pacific Ocean.

In 1789, Mackenzie left Fort Chipewyan on Lake Athabasca with a small party of Canadians and Indian guides. He pushed his way north to Great Slave Lake and then followed the river that now bears his name. It took him to the Arctic Ocean. He had hoped the river would lead him to the Pacific Ocean.

Three years later, Mackenzie started on an expedition to the west coast. He followed the Peace River, crossed the Rocky Mountains, and reached the Pacific Ocean in 1793. This trip convinced him that a search for a Northwest Passage to the Orient would prove useless. However, he promoted the idea of carrying on trade across the Pacific Ocean.

He wrote *Voyages on the River Saint Lawrence and Through the Continent of North America to the Frozen and Pacific Oceans in the Years 1789 and 1793* (1801). This book contains much valuable information on Indian tribes and Canadian history.

Mackenzie was born in Stornoway, on the Scottish island of Lewis with Harris. In 1778, he went to Canada. He later became a partner in the North West Company, a leading Canadian fur-trading company. Mackenzie made a fortune as a fur trader. He spent his last years in Scotland.   Barry M. Gough

Mackenzie, Roderick (1760?-1844), was a Canadian frontiersman and fur trader. He accompanied his cousin, Sir Alexander Mackenzie, on a trip to western Canada in 1786. He commanded Fort Chipewyan in northeastern Alberta from 1789 to 1793. Mackenzie was a capable administrator rather than a trailblazer. He returned to eastern Canada in 1797, and became a partner in the North West Company in 1799. Later, he served in the Legislative Council of Lower Canada. Mackenzie was born in Scotland.   John Elgin Foster

Mackenzie, William Lyon (1795-1861), was a Canadian political leader and journalist. In the 1830's, he led a revolt against British rule in the North American colony of Upper Canada.

Mackenzie was born in Dundee, Scotland. He moved to Canada in 1820. In 1824, he founded the *Colonial Advocate,* a newspaper. In 1828, Mackenzie won election to the Legislative Assembly of Upper Canada as a member of the Reform Party. He argued for greater local self-government under British rule. In 1834, he became the first mayor of Toronto.

Mackenzie and the Reform Party were defeated in elections in 1836, and Mackenzie soon began to doubt the possibility of achieving peaceful reform. In 1837, he led a revolt to seek independence for Upper Canada from Britain. But local militia easily defeated the few hundred rebels. Mackenzie's revolt was one of the two unsuccessful Rebellions of 1837. In the other rebellion, Canadians in the colony of Lower Canada also fought against British rule.

Portrait by J. W. L. Forster
Public Archives of Canada, Ottawa
William L. Mackenzie

Mackenzie escaped to the United States. He established a temporary government on Navy Island in the Niagara River. U.S. authorities soon arrested him for breaking the neutrality laws. He was tried and imprisoned in 1839 but pardoned in 1840.

Mackenzie worked as a journalist in New York until 1849, when he was allowed to return to Canada. In 1851, he won election to the Legislative Assembly of the Province of Canada, a colony formed by a union of Upper and Lower Canada.   J. M. Bumsted

See also **Canada, History of** (The struggle for responsible government); **Rebellions of 1837; King, William Lyon Mackenzie.**

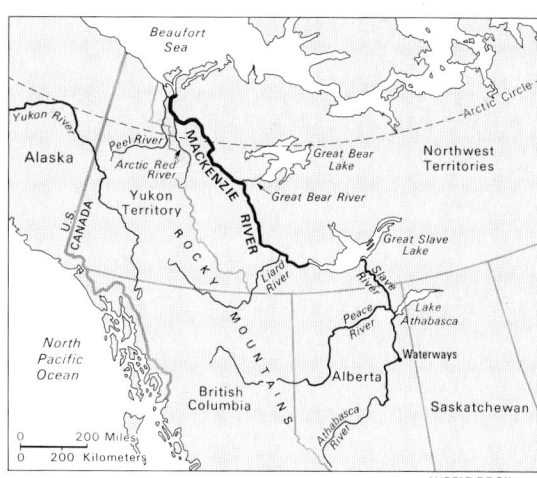

WORLD BOOK map
Location of the Mackenzie River

Mackenzie River, in the Northwest Territories, is the longest river in Canada. It flows north and west for about 1,071 miles (1,724 kilometers) from Great Slave Lake to the Beaufort Sea. Much of the river is more than 1 mile (1.6 kilometers) wide. Water flows into the Mackenzie from many tributaries, including the Liard, Great Bear, Arctic Red, and Peel rivers. Water also enters from Great Slave Lake. It reaches the lake through the Slave River, which collects water from the Peace and Athabasca rivers. The Mackenzie was named for the Canadian explorer Sir Alexander Mackenzie (see **Mackenzie, Sir Alexander**).

All the rivers mentioned above are part of the *Mackenzie River System,* Canada's largest river system. This vast system drains water from about 682,000 square miles (1,766,000 square kilometers). Its most distant water source is high in Alberta's Rocky Mountains, 2,635 miles (4,241 kilometers) from the Arctic mouth of the Mackenzie. In North America, only the Mississippi-Missouri system is longer than the Mackenzie system.

A 1,700-mile (2,740-kilometer) stretch of the Mackenzie system, from Waterways, Alberta, to the Beaufort Sea, is navigable. Only a 7-mile (11-kilometer) rapids on the Slave River interferes with shipping.

The Mackenzie River basin is rich in natural resources. The Peace River area of Alberta and British Columbia includes abundant farmland. The area also has petroleum and natural gas deposits and water for hydroelectric power. In the northern part of the basin, the delta at the mouth of the Mackenzie is a muskrat-trapping area. Hundreds of thousands of ducks, geese, swans, and cranes migrate to nesting grounds in the Mackenzie delta annually. The delta has little agriculture, but it has petroleum, radium, and uranium deposits.   G. Peter Kershaw

Mackerel, *MAK uhr uhl* or *MAK ruhl,* is the name of a number of valuable food fish that live in coastal areas of the Atlantic, Pacific, and Indian oceans. Mackerels have long, tapered bodies and forked tails. They swim in schools and are constantly on the move. Four common species are the *Atlantic, chub, king,* and *Spanish.*

The Atlantic mackerel, also called the *common mackerel,* lives in temperate parts of the North Atlantic

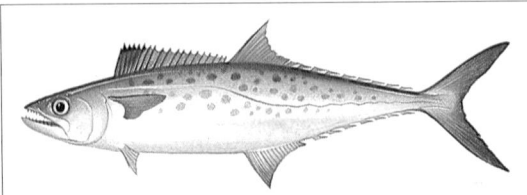

WORLD BOOK illustration by Colin Newman, Linden Artists Ltd.
The mackerel has blue-green skin and a forked tail.

Ocean. On the North American side of the Atlantic, this fish is found from North Carolina to Newfoundland. On the European side, it ranges from the Mediterranean Sea to Norway. Most Atlantic mackerel measure from 10 to 18 inches (25 to 46 centimeters) long. The fish *spawn* (reproduce) in the spring and summer near shore. Females can produce up to 200,000 eggs in a season.

The king and Spanish mackerels live mostly in tropical parts of the Atlantic. The king mackerel is found from Cape Cod to Rio de Janeiro, Brazil, and the Spanish mackerel ranges from Cape Cod to the Yucatán Peninsula in Mexico. Both species inhabit waters north of Florida only during the summer. They eat large quantities of small fish and smaller amounts of shrimp and squid. The largest king mackerels grow more than $5\frac{1}{2}$ feet (170 centimeters) long. Spanish mackerels can grow more than $2\frac{1}{2}$ feet (76 centimeters) long.

The chub mackerel, also called the *Pacific mackerel,* has a wide geographic distribution. Along the Pacific Coast of North America, chub mackerels range from southeastern Alaska to Baja California. Along the Atlantic Coast, they are found from Cape Cod to Cuba. Chub mackerels that live in the Atlantic have spots or wavy broken lines on their bellies. Chub mackerels grow to about 20 inches (51 centimeters) long.

Scientific classification. Mackerels belong to the family Scombridae. The scientific name for the Atlantic mackerel is *Scomber scombrus.* The chub mackerel is *S. japonicus.* The king mackerel is *Scomberomorous cavella,* and the Spanish mackerel is *Scomberomorous maculatus.*   Gary T. Sakagawa

See also **Bonito; Kingfish; Tuna.**

Mackinac, *MAK uh NAW* or *MACK uh NAK,* **Straits of,** is an important link in the water route between Lake Michigan and the Atlantic Ocean. The straits connect Lake Michigan and Lake Huron. They are at the northern end of the Lower Peninsula of Michigan (see **Michigan** [physical map]). Mackinac Island lies in the straits. The straits are about 40 miles (64 kilometers) long and about 5 miles (8 kilometers) wide at the narrowest point. The Mackinac Bridge across the straits is one of the world's longest suspension bridges. Its main span is 3,800 feet (1,160 meters) long. The bridge links Mackinaw City in the Lower Peninsula with the city of St. Ignace in the Upper Peninsula.   Richard A. Santer

Mackinac Island, *MAK uh NAW* or *MACK uh NAK,* is a north Michigan island summer resort in the Straits of Mackinac (see **Michigan** [political map]). It covers an area of about 4 square miles (10 square kilometers) and has a population of about 470. The Chippewa Indians called the island *Michilimackinac,* which is usually defined as *Great Spirits* or *Great Turtle.* No passenger cars are permitted on Mackinac. Ferries link the island with

the mainland. The world's longest freshwater yachting event is the Chicago-to-Mackinac Island race, which is held each July.

In 1671, Father Jacques Marquette established a mission at nearby Point St. Ignace. The French built forts at St. Ignace and Mackinac City, on the Michigan mainland. In 1761, the French surrendered the area to the British. The British built Fort Mackinac on the island in 1780. In 1796, the United States gained the island, but the British recaptured it in 1812. In 1815, the British returned it to the United States. The island became the headquarters of John Jacob Astor's American Fur Company. After the fort was abandoned in 1894, the federal government transferred much of the island to the state

Dwight Ellefsen, Shostal
Mackinac Island is an important summer resort in the Straits of Mackinac in northern Michigan. The island's fine harbor is a popular destination for owners of yachts and sailboats.

of Michigan. Most of this land became Mackinac Island State Park. Since the late 1950's, the island has experienced growth in tourism. The island and its surrounding area have also become a center of archaeological research and historical reconstruction.   Richard A. Santer

See also **Henry, Alexander.**

MacLeish, *mak LEESH* or *muh KLEESH,* **Archibald** (1892-1982), was an American poet, dramatist, and critic. He also served as librarian of Congress from 1939 to 1944 and assistant secretary of state in 1944 and 1945.

MacLeish's early work is lyrical and thoughtful, using free verse and other technical methods of such older poets as Ezra Pound and T. S. Eliot. *Conquistador* (1932) is a strong, individual achievement, describing in epic terms the Spanish exploration of the New World. The work gained MacLeish the first of his three Pulitzer Prizes. With social unrest in America and the rise of fascism abroad, MacLeish turned to more direct expression of the issues of his day. He particularly explored these issues in *Public Speech* (1936) and his two radio dramas, *The Fall of the City* (1937) and *Air Raid* (1938).

MacLeish's later work became less topical and more philosophic in tone. His verse drama *J.B.* raises the eternal problem of humanity's suffering, treating the Biblical story of Job in terms of modern American life. The play won the 1959 Pulitzer Prize for drama. His *Collected Poems, 1917-1952* won the 1953 Pulitzer Prize.

MacLeish's most mature reflections on the value of poetry as a means of knowledge are developed in *Po-*

etry and Experience (1961). He concludes, "To face the truth of the passing away of the world, and make song of it, make beauty of it, is not to solve the riddle of our mortal lives but perhaps to accomplish something more."

MacLeish was born in Glencoe, Ill. He received a law degree from Harvard, where he graduated first in his class. He practiced law from 1920 to 1923, when he decided to devote himself to literature. MacLeish lived in Europe from 1923 to 1928. He was professor of rhetoric and oratory at Harvard from 1949 to 1962.

Bonnie Costello

MacLennan, *mak LEHN an,* **Hugh** (1907-1990), was a Canadian author known for his novels about historic events and public issues in Canada. His strengths are his ability to convey the texture and tensions of society and his descriptions of places.

MacLennan based his first novel, *Barometer Rising* (1941), on an explosion that destroyed much of the city of Halifax, N.S., in 1917. *Two Solitudes* (1945) and *Return of the Sphinx* (1967) deal with conflicts between English Canadians and French Canadians. *Each Man's Son* (1951) is set in his native Cape Breton Island. *The Watch That Ends the Night* (1959) describes how a group of characters were affected by the Great Depression of the 1930's and by World War II (1939-1945).

MacLennan wrote many essays, including analyses of Canadian culture and sensitive descriptions of landscape. His collections of essays include *Cross Country* (1949), *Rivers of Canada* (1974), and *The Other Side of Hugh MacLennan* (1978). John Hugh MacLennan was born in Glace Bay, N.S.   Laurie R. Ricou

Macleod, *muh KLOWD,* **John James Rickard** (1876-1935), was a Scottish physiologist. He and Sir Frederick Banting won the 1923 Nobel Prize for physiology or medicine for their discovery of insulin in 1922 (see **Banting, Sir Frederick G.**). Macleod was born near Dunkeld, Scotland. He taught physiology in Cleveland, Toronto, and Aberdeen.   Dale C. Smith

MacMechan, *muhk MEHK uhn,* **Archibald McKellar** (1862-1933), was a Canadian essayist and educator. MacMechan described his personal responses to Nova Scotia's geography in *The Life of a Little College* (1914) and *The Book of Ultima Thule* (1927). In addition, he also wrote such historical works as *The Winning of Popular Government* (1916) and such literary history and criticism as *Headwaters of Canadian Literature* (1924). MacMechan's book of poems, *Late Harvest,* was published in 1934, after his death.

MacMechan was born in Berlin (now Kitchener), Ont. He was professor of English at Dalhousie University in Halifax, N.S., from 1889 to 1931.   Rosemary Sullivan

MacMillan, Donald Baxter (1874-1970), an American polar explorer, added much to our knowledge of Greenland and the Canadian Arctic. He advanced the belief that the glacier fields are pushing southward. MacMillan found coal deposits 9 degrees from the North Pole. These coal deposits contained remains of 36 kinds of trees, showing that the climate there had once been milder.

MacMillan's 1924 Arctic expedition used radio extensively. His 1925 expedition was one of the first to use airplanes in the Far North. His men made many special aerial photographs. MacMillan received the Special

United Press Int.

MacMillan's ship was often greeted by crowds as he returned from exploring Arctic waters. The explorer and a team of scientists studied the movements of glaciers and discovered coal deposits only 9 degrees from the North Pole.

Congressional Medal for surveying and charting Greenland and the Canadian Arctic for the U.S. Army during World War II (1939-1945). In 1957, at the age of 82, MacMillan went on his 31st trip to the Arctic. He wrote several books about his experiences, including *Four Years in the White North* (1918), *Etah and Beyond* (1927), and *How Peary Reached the Pole* (1932).

MacMillan was born in Provincetown, Mass. He studied at Bowdoin College and at Harvard University. MacMillan taught school until 1908, when he made his first polar expedition as assistant to Commander Robert Peary. MacMillan helped to train many younger explorers, including Richard Evelyn Byrd.   John Edwards Caswell

MacMillan, Sir Ernest Campbell (1893-1973), was a Canadian conductor, composer, organist, and educator. He brought professional standards to Canadian classical music. MacMillan conducted the Toronto Symphony Orchestra from 1931 to 1956. He served as principal of the Toronto Conservatory of Music from 1926 to 1942, and he was dean of the Faculty of Music at the University of Toronto from 1927 to 1952. MacMillan's performances of Johann Sebastian Bach's *Passion According to St. Matthew,* which he directed nearly every year from 1923 to 1957, were famous throughout Canada.

MacMillan composed the ballad opera *Prince Charming* (1933), orchestral music, choruses, songs, and a string quartet. He compiled *A Book of Songs* (1929), a popular school text. MacMillan was born in Mimico, Ont. He was knighted in 1935.   John H. Baron

Macmillan, Harold (1894-1986), served as prime minister of Great Britain from 1957 to 1963. Macmillan succeeded Anthony Eden in that office.

Macmillan was elected to the House of Commons in 1924 as a Conservative. In the 1930's, he became more progressive. He criticized British Prime Minister Neville

Chamberlain and the Munich settlement with Nazi Germany in 1938 (see **Munich Agreement**). He also urged action to combat Britain's economic depression.

From 1942 to 1945, Macmillan served in Prime Minister Winston Churchill's World War II government as British resident minister at Allied Headquarters in Northwest Africa. Macmillan served as

United Press Int.

Harold Macmillan

Churchill's minister of housing and local government from 1951 to 1954 and as minister of defense in 1954. He became foreign secretary under Eden in April 1955 and chancellor of the exchequer, Britain's chief financial officer, in December 1955.

Maurice Harold Macmillan was born in London. His grandfather founded the Macmillan publishing company. Harold Macmillan attended Eton College and Oxford University. He fought and was wounded in World War I (1914-1918). In 1984, he was granted the title Earl of Stockton.   Keith Robbins

Macon, *MAY kuhn* (pop. 106,612; met. area pop. 281,103), is a center of manufacturing and trade and one of the largest cities in Georgia. Macon lies on the Ocmulgee River in central Georgia and is called the *Heart of Georgia.* Its location helped Macon become a convention center for state and regional meetings. For location, see **Georgia** (political map).

Macon is the home of Wesleyan College, Macon College, and Mercer University. The Georgia Academy for the Blind is also in Macon. The Cherry Blossom Festival each March celebrates the city's more than 100,000 Japanese cherry trees. Macon's Hay House, a historic mansion, and Ocmulgee National Monument, the site of prehistoric Indian mounds, draw many visitors yearly. Visitors may also see the birthplace of poet Sidney Lanier.

Macon serves as the trading center for the famous peach region of Georgia and is a large poultry processor. One of the world's largest kaolin deposits lies near Macon. The city's most important industries are the manufacture of tobacco products, food products, and textiles. Other products made in Macon include aircraft parts, chemicals, furniture, paper products, and zippers. Two railroads provide freight service for Macon, and two interstate highways intersect there. Macon is a regional health center with six hospitals. The Macon area also has many companies in the aerospace industry.

Creek Indians first settled the Macon area. Thomas Jefferson established Fort Hawkins there in 1806. The city was chartered in 1823 and named for Nathaniel Macon, a North Carolina congressman. During the 1840's and 1850's, Macon became an important railroad center. Confederates repulsed a Union attack on Macon in 1864, during the Civil War.

Macon has six national historic districts. Major renewal took place in the downtown area in the early 1980's. Macon has a mayor-council form of government. It is the county seat of Bibb County.   Harriet F. Comer

Macon Act. See **War of 1812** (American reaction).

Macphail, *muhk FAYL,* **Agnes Campbell** (1890-1954), was the first woman ever elected to the Canadian House of Commons. She served in the federal Parliament from 1921 to 1940, and in the Ontario Legislature from 1943 to 1945 and from 1948 to 1951. She represented Canada in the Assembly of the League of Nations. Macphail was elected to Parliament as a United Farmers of Ontario candidate. She later supported the Co-operative Commonwealth Federation. She was born in Grey County, Ont., and taught in Canadian schools before entering politics.   David Jay Bercuson

Macramé, *MAK ruh may,* is the art of creating practical and decorative articles by knotting cord, rope, or string. It can be used to make clothing and such accessories as belts and purses, as well as sculptures, wallhangings, and other ornamental items.

Many individual cords are knotted together to make a macramé article. The two basic knots used are the clove hitch and the square knot (see **Knots, hitches, and splices** [illustrations: The clove hitch; The square knot]). These knots may be combined with each other or with different knots in an unlimited number of arrangements. Beads, bells, feathers, and other small objects can be tied into the work for variety.

Arabian weavers probably developed knotting during the 1200's. But the word *macramé* was not used until about the 1400's. The word comes from an Arabic or Turkish word for *towel,* or *napkin.* During the 1970's,

Macramé by Mary Walker Phillips; American Craft Council

A macramé wallhanging is made by knotting together different colored yarn and string into decorative patterns.

macramé enjoyed a revival as a modern handicraft. Fiber artists and craftworkers developed new patterns and modern uses for the finished fabrics. Macramé was often combined with basketmaking, embroidery, knitting, and other techniques.   Dona Z. Meilach

Macready, *muhk REE dee,* **William Charles** (1793-1873), was a famous English tragic actor. He encouraged the dramatic works of poets Lord Byron and Robert Browning and restored integrity and accuracy to the staging of William Shakespeare's plays. Macready had a violent temper, but his acting was restrained, dignified, and intellectual. A rivalry with American actor Edwin Forrest led to a riot in 1849 at the Astor Place Opera House in New York City, where Macready was performing in *Macbeth.* In the riot, 31 people were killed and about 150 were injured.

Macready was born in London. He made his stage debut in 1810 in Birmingham and his London debut in 1816. By 1819, he rivaled Edmund Kean, the leading English actor of the time, excelling in Shakespearean roles. Macready's diaries, covering his career to 1851, are an important source of theater history.　J. P. Wearing

Macrophage. See **Immunity** (Cells of the immune system); **Lymphatic system** (Lymph nodes; Fighting infection); **Disease** (Immune reactions; picture).

Madagascar is an African country made up of one large island and many tiny nearby islands. It lies in the Indian Ocean, about 240 miles (386 kilometers) southeast of the African mainland. The large island, also called Madagascar, is the fourth largest island in the world. Only Greenland, New Guinea, and Borneo are larger islands. Most of the country's people are farmers or herders of mixed black African and Indonesian descent. Antananarivo is Madagascar's capital and largest city.

Madagascar was a favorite base for sea pirates in the 1600's and 1700's, including the famous Captain William Kidd. Later, it became a haven for slave traders. In the early 1800's, most of Madagascar became part of the local Merina kingdom. The Merina kingdom fell to the French in 1896, and all of Madagascar became a French colony. Madagascar gained independence from France in 1960. The country was called the Malagasy Republic until 1975, when its name was changed to Madagascar (officially the *Democratic Republic of Madagascar*).

Government. The president of Madagascar is elected by the people. The president is the head of state. Madagascar's legislature is called the National Assembly. The 138 members of the National Assembly are elected by the people of the country. The National Assembly appoints a prime minister. A cabinet assists the prime minister in carrying out the functions of Madagascar's government.

People. The Malagasy people are made up of several ethnic groups of mixed Indonesian and black African descent. The ethnic groups of the central and south-central highlands tend to resemble Indonesians. Many raise rice in irrigated fields just as do farmers in Indone-

Madagascar

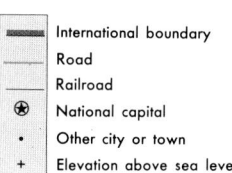

International boundary
Road
Railroad
⊛ National capital
· Other city or town
+ Elevation above sea level

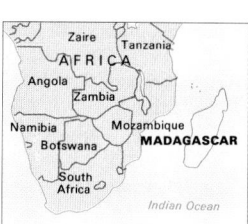

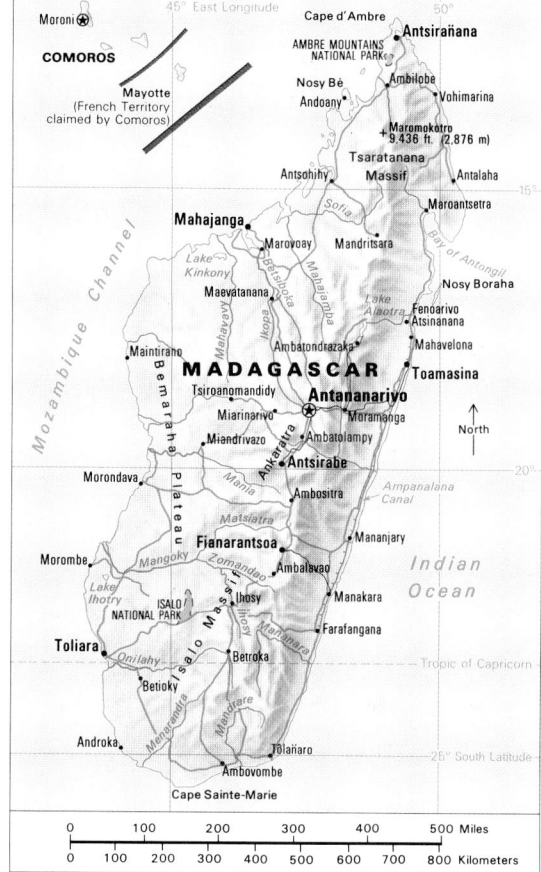

WORLD BOOK maps

Facts in brief

Capital: Antananarivo.
Official languages: Malagasy and French.
Area: 226,658 sq. mi. (587,041 km²). *Greatest distances*—north-south, 980 mi. (1,580 km); east-west, 360 mi. (579 km). *Coastline* —2,600 mi. (4,180 km).
Population: *Estimated 1994 population*—13,637,000; density, 60 persons per sq. mi. (23 persons per km²); distribution, 73 percent rural, 27 percent urban. *1975 census*—7,603,790. *Estimated 1999 population*—16,019,000.
Chief products: *Agriculture*—cassava, cloves, coffee, livestock, rice, sugar cane, vanilla. *Mining*—bauxite, chromite, coal, graphite. *Manufacturing*—food processing.
Flag: A white vertical stripe appears at the left, with a red horizontal stripe over a green one at the right. White is for purity, red for sovereignty, and green for hope. See **Flag** (picture: Flags of Africa).
National anthem: "Ry Tanindrazanay Malala O" ("Our Beloved Country").
Money: *Basic unit*—franc. See **Money** (table: Exchange rates).

sia. The coastal ethnic groups more closely resemble black Africans. Many herd cattle as do peoples of eastern Africa. Political rivalries exist between the coastal peoples and the highland peoples of the country. But coastal and highland people share control of Madagascar's government.

Malagasy is the language spoken throughout the country. It resembles Malay and Indonesian. French and Malagasy are the official languages. About half of the people are Christians, and about one-tenth are Muslims. The rest—especially those living along the coasts—practice local African religions. They worship ancestors and spirits and perform cattle sacrifices and other ceremonies at family tombs.

Many people of Madagascar wear European-style clothing. However, people of isolated southern tribes often wear little clothing. Most houses are built of brick,

Gerald Cubitt, Bruce Coleman Ltd.

The narrow streets of Antananarivo, the capital of Madagascar, are crowded on market day.

Gerald Cubitt, Bruce Coleman Ltd.

In southern Madagascar, people often use cattle like these zebus to transport goods and do heavy farm work.

and many are several stories high. They have tile or thatched roofs. The people eat rice, vegetables, fruit, and sometimes meat and fish.

About 55 per cent of the people can read and write. Almost all the children attend primary schools, but only about one out of every nine attends secondary school. The University of Madagascar's main campus is in Antananarivo.

Land. Northern Madagascar has fertile soil. Mountains separate it from the rest of the island. Western Madagascar has wide plains, some fertile river valleys, and a fairly sheltered coast. A narrow plain lies along the east coast, but reefs and storms make the east coast dangerous for ships. Some coastal shipping uses the Ampanalana Canal, which runs along the east coast between Mahavelona and Farafangana. The climate is warm and humid on the coast. The southern end of the island is mainly desert, and has a hot, dry climate.

Central Madagascar consists of highlands with altitudes of 2,000 to 4,000 feet (610 to 1,200 meters) and some higher mountains. The soil is *eroded* (worn away) and the region is *deforested* (cleared of trees), but it has the densest population. The highlands are cool, and temperatures at Antananarivo range between 55 °F (13 °C) and 67 °F (19 °C).

Most of Madagascar's animals and plants are not found anywhere else, except in the nearby Comoros islands. *Lemurs,* animals related to monkeys, are the best-known examples of such native animals (see **Lemur**).

Economy. Four-fifths of the people are farmers and herders. Rice is their chief food crop. Bananas, cassava, and sweet potatoes are also grown. Cattle are the country's most important livestock. Coffee is the chief export. Madagascar is the world's greatest producer of natural vanilla and cloves, which are also exported. Other exports include sugar and *sisal,* which is used to make binding twine. Bauxite, chromite, coal, and graphite are mined in Madagascar.

Most of the country's few industries process hides, meat, sisal, and sugar for export. Most of the foreign trade is with France. But the United States buys coffee, cloves, and vanilla from the country.

Roads, most of which are unpaved, link the chief cities and towns of Madagascar. But many roads have bad ruts and are impassable during the rainy season. Air Madagascar provides air service between the major cities and makes international flights from Antananarivo. Toamasina and Mahajanga are the leading seaports.

Seven daily newspapers, representing a variety of political opinions, are published in Madagascar. The government sometimes restricts what they may print.

History. Immigrants from Indonesia moved to the island in successive waves starting long before the time of Christ and lasting until the A.D. 1400's. They settled in the central highlands. Immigrants from Africa and the Arabian Peninsula settled on the coasts. A number of kingdoms developed, but in the early 1800's the Merina kingdom gained control of most of the island.

Radama I, who became king in 1810, outlawed the foreign slave trade in Madagascar. However, he kept many of the local people in domestic slavery. The king and his successors welcomed English and French traders and missionaries to the island. The missionaries opened churches and schools, but the Merina rulers allowed only the Merina people to attend the schools. In the 1840's, Queen Ranavalona I tried to end European influence and expelled Europeans from the island. Europeans returned after she died in 1861. The French expanded their political influence in Madagascar after 1869. Conflicts broke out between the French and the Merina. The French forces gained control, and France made all of Madagascar a French colony in 1896.

During World War I (1914-1918), Merina leaders began to demand independence. France gave the colony's people some control of financial matters and the right to elect an assembly in 1945. It also allowed them to elect representatives to the French Parliament. But this did not satisfy the people. An armed revolt that lasted almost two years broke out in 1947.

Madagascar became a self-governing state in the French Community in 1958. It gained independence from France in 1960. French influence remained strong in the country, which was called the Malagasy Republic. Philibert Tsiranana was elected the country's first president in 1959. Tsiranana was reelected president in 1965 and 1972.

In May 1972, demonstrations caused Tsiranana to resign. Army officers then took control of the government and set up a system of military rule. In June 1975, Didier Ratsiraka became the fourth in a series of military rulers to head the government. Under Ratsiraka and the earlier military leaders, the government took control of important parts of the country's economic activity, including many businesses owned by the French and other foreigners. In late 1975, the country changed its name from Malagasy Republic to Madagascar.

In 1977, a legislature was elected by the people of Madagascar. A presidential election was held in the country in 1982. The people elected Ratsiraka president. Since 1983, the government has lessened its role in Madagascar's economy. Ratsiraka was reelected in 1989. In 1991, a coalition of opposition parties organized protests and strikes and called for Ratsiraka's resignation. In February 1993, Albert Zafy, a leader of the opposition, was elected to replace Ratsiraka.   Bruce Fetter

See also **Antananarivo; Rosewood; Vanilla.**

Madder is a plant that was once commonly grown in Europe and Asia for use in making dyes. The madder has rough, prickly leaves and small greenish-yellow flowers. The fruit is black. The roots of the madder produce coloring extracts, such as alizarin and purpurin, that manufacturers can use to make dyes. These extracts are treated with a chemical solution to produce colors ranging from pink and red to yellow, purple, and brown. A madder that grows in the eastern Mediterranean region produces a dye called *Turkey-red.* People in ancient Egypt used Turkey-red dye for burial wrappings. Dyes made from madder have largely been replaced by synthetic dyes.

Scientific classification. Madder belongs to the family Rubiaceae. It is *Rubia tinctorum.*   Howard L. Needles

Madeira Islands, *muh DEER uh,* are a group of islands that belong to Portugal. The islands, of volcanic origin, lie in the Atlantic Ocean off the northwest coast of Africa. For location, see **Atlantic Ocean** (map).

The islands cover 307 square miles (794 square kilometers). Most of the about 271,000 residents live on Madeira, the larger of the two inhabited islands. The other inhabited island is Porto Santo. Noted for its sandy beaches, it lies about 26 miles (42 kilometers) northeast of Madeira. About 4,300 people live there. The Desertas and Selvagens are groups of tiny, uninhabited isles.

The island of Madeira, largest and most important of the group, is a great ocean mountain range rising to a height of 6,104 feet (1,860 meters) above sea level in the Pico Ruivo. Madeira is known as the *Rock Garden of the Atlantic* because its settlements and farms rise in terraces, covered with exotic flowers and trees. There are lush growths of orchids, bougainvillaea, bignonia, hibiscus, camellias, hydrangeas, wisteria, and jacaranda. Trees include the mimosa, eucalyptus, Brazilian araucaria, Indian fig, West Indies coral, and Japanese camphor, bamboo, laurel, and palm.

The richness of the vegetation is remarkable because rain falls only in the winter months. In order to grow crops, water has to be rationed and distributed by stone aqueducts, called *levadas.* Water retained from the rainy season flows down the levadas from the mountains to the farms and villages.

Chief crops include sugar cane, corn, vegetables, bananas, oranges, mangoes, pomegranates, and the grapes that have made Madeira famous for wine.

Wine production is the principal industry of Madeira. Next in importance are the making of willow wicker furniture and baskets, and embroidering. Most women embroider at home. Fishing also contributes to the economy. Britons handle much of Madeira's trade.

Funchal is the capital of the Madeira Islands. It is also the largest city, main seaport, and chief resort center of the group. Funchal has ship connections with Lisbon, Portugal, and English ports, and air links with European and North African cities. See **Funchal.**

Bernard Regent, Hutchison Library

The harbor of Funchal, Madeira, makes a picturesque sight with its old fortress. Ocean liners and freighters travel from Funchal to several European ports. The town is the main seaport and capital of the island group.

Madeira has several unusual kinds of local transportation. Oxen draw sleighs over the iceless steep streets and roads. Basket sleds for fast, downhill travel provide thrills. Visitors to remote places can also travel in hammocks carried on poles by two people.

History. The Romans called the Madeiras the *Purpuriarae*, or "Purple" islands. The Portuguese first sailed to the island of Madeira in 1419. They gave the island that name—which means *wood*—because it was heavily forested.

The Portuguese cleared some of the land by burning trees, the ashes from which gave the soil increased fertility. Funchal was founded in 1421. Porto Santo also was settled about that time. The Spaniards seized and held the islands from 1580 to 1640. The British occupied the Madeira Islands twice during the early 1800's.

Douglas L. Wheeler

Madeira River, *muh DEER uh,* is a large branch of the Amazon River and an important trade waterway of South America. *Madeira* in Portuguese means *wood* or *timber.* The river was named for the great amount of driftwood that floats on its waters.

The Madeira begins where several large streams meet on the boundary between Brazil and Bolivia. It flows northeast for about 2,000 miles (3,200 kilometers) before emptying into the Amazon River about 100 miles (160 kilometers) east of the city of Manaus. For the location of the Madeira River, see **Brazil** (terrain map).

The mouth of the Madeira River is nearly 2 miles (3 kilometers) wide. Ships can sail upstream about 700 miles (1,100 kilometers) until they reach a series of rapids. Twenty of these rapids extend for 230 miles (370 kilometers), with a drop of 475 feet (145 meters). The area surrounding the northern part of the river contains rich deposits of gold.

One branch of the Madeira is the Rio Teodoro, once called Rio Duvida. This stream is 1,000 miles (1,600 kilometers) long. Theodore Roosevelt explored the Rio Teodoro in 1914. Gregory Knapp

Madero, Francisco Indalecio. See **Mexico** (The revolution of 1910).

Madison, Ind. (pop. 12,006), is an Ohio River port and tobacco-auction center. It was once the largest city in Indiana. Madison is located in southeastern Indiana on the north bank of the Ohio River, 90 miles (145 kilometers) from Indianapolis. It is 46 miles (74 kilometers) from Louisville, Ky., and 88 miles (142 kilometers) from Cincinnati, Ohio. For the location of Madison, see **Indiana** (political map). Tobacco buyers from all parts of the United States attend tobacco auctions held in Madison.

Indiana's first railroad ran from Madison to Indianapolis, the state capital, in 1847. During the Civil War (1861-1865), Madison was a banking center. In 1862, James F. D. Lanier, a Madison banker, loaned about $1 million to the state administration of Governor Oliver P. Morton and kept Indiana from bankruptcy.

Madison's well-kept old mansions give the city an atmosphere of the middle 1800's. Among these old homes are the Shrewsbury House and the J.F.D. Lanier State Memorial. Francis Costigan, a famous architect of that period, built both houses. Clifty Falls State Park is situated on the bluff above Madison. Hanover College is located 7 miles (11 kilometers) outside the city.

Graham Taylor, Jr.

Madison, Wis. (pop. 191,262; met. area pop. 367,085), is the capital and second largest city of the state. Only Milwaukee has more people. Madison is the home of the largest campus of the University of Wisconsin System. It also is a center of medicine, dairy-based agribusiness, and recreation. The city serves as the trade center of a rich agricultural region. Madison lies in south-central Wisconsin. For location, see **Wisconsin** (political map).

Downtown Madison lies between Lakes Mendota and Monona, and Lake Wingra is in the western part of the city. These lakes help make Madison one of the nation's most beautiful state capitals.

Two land investors, James D. Doty and Stevens T. Mason, founded Madison in 1836. They named it for James Madison, the fourth President of the United States. Doty and Mason chose the site because its lakes provided scenic beauty.

Description. Madison covers about 62 square miles (100 square kilometers), including about 21 square miles (54 square kilometers) of inland water. It is the county seat of Dane County. The Madison metropolitan area includes the county—1,233 square miles (3,193 square kilometers).

The dome of the white granite state Capitol towers 286 feet (87 meters) above the heart of downtown Madison (see **Wisconsin** [picture: The State Capitol]). Federal, state, and municipal government buildings stand nearby. The University of Wisconsin campus lies about 1 mile (1.6 kilometers) west of the Capitol on the south shore of Lake Mendota.

Madison's public school system includes 29 elementary schools, 9 middle schools, and 4 high schools. The Madison Public Library consists of a main library and seven branch libraries. The University of Wisconsin-Madison is one of the nation's largest universities. The city is also the home of Edgewood College and the Madison Area Technical College. Madison serves as a medical center, with the University Medical School, three hospitals, and a number of clinics.

The city's cultural attractions include the State Historical Society of Wisconsin, Elvehjem Museum of Art, and the Madison Civic Center. The Civic Center includes two theaters and the Madison Art Center, an art gallery. The University of Wisconsin also operates the 1,200-acre (486-hectare) Arboretum in Madison. The zoo is in Henry Vilas Park. Lakes in and near Madison provide boating, fishing, water-skiing, and swimming.

Economy of Madison depends heavily on government operations and on trade. Federal, state, and municipal government agencies—plus the University of Wisconsin—employ about a third of Dane County's workers. Another third hold jobs in retail and wholesale trade and in such services as finance, insurance, and research. The city has more than 100 research and testing laboratories.

About a tenth of the county's workers are employed in the more than 400 manufacturing plants in the area. Farming and cattle raising in the area have helped make food processing the city's largest industry. Oscar Mayer Foods Corporation, one of the nation's biggest meat-packing firms, ranks as one of Madison's largest private employers. It has more than 2,800 workers in the city. The largest private employer is Wisconsin Physicians Service, an insurance company that employs more than

Edwin E. Proctor

Downtown Madison, Wis., lies on a narrow isthmus between Lakes Monona, *foreground,* and Mendota, *background.*

3,100 workers. Other major industries of Madison include the production of batteries, dairy equipment, and hospital supplies.

Railroad freight lines and bus and trucking companies serve Madison. Airlines use Dane County Regional Airport on Madison's east side.

Government and history. Madison has a mayor-council form of government. The voters elect the mayor and the 20 members of the Common Council to two-year terms.

Winnebago Indians lived in what is now the Madison area before white settlers came. In 1835, the site was bought by James D. Doty, a federal judge who later became governor of the Wisconsin Territory, and Stevens T. Mason, governor of the Michigan Territory. In 1836, the first legislature of the Wisconsin Territory made Madison the capital, even though the community did not yet exist. Madison's first white settlers, Eben and Rosaline Peck, arrived from nearby Blue Mounds in 1837. They erected a hotel for the workers who built the first Capitol.

Madison began functioning as the capital in 1838. It was incorporated as a village in 1846, with a population of 626. When Wisconsin gained statehood in 1848, Madison remained the capital. In 1856, Madison was incorporated as a city. By then, its population had reached about 9,500. By 1900, Madison had 19,164 people.

The Oscar Mayer company opened its meat-packing plant in the city in 1919 and helped make Madison a major food-processing center. During the 1920's, the city became the headquarters of the Progressive Party, led by the La Follette family of Madison. This party pioneered in social reform legislation.

During the 1960's, a rapid increase in employment by the federal, state, and municipal governments in Madison created a population boom in the city. Since the early 1970's, many buildings in downtown Madison have been rehabilitated. One major rehabilitation project was the creation of the Civic Center, a performing arts complex, which was completed in 1980. Part of the center was established in a 50-year-old theater and a former department store.   Terry Shelton

Madison, Dolley Payne (1768-1849), a famous Washington hostess, was the wife of President James Madison. She is best known for her flight from Washington in August 1814, when the British invaded the city during the War of 1812. She saved many state papers and a portrait of George Washington.

She and Madison were married in 1794 when he was a Congressman. While Madison served as secretary of state under President Thomas Jefferson, a widower, Mrs. Madison often helped Jefferson when he entertained guests. She also entertained frequently on her own. When Madison became President, official functions became more elaborate. Mrs. Madison was noted for her charm and tact. At her home, people of strongly differing views could meet at ease.

Mrs. Madison was born in Guilford County, North Carolina, the third child of Quaker parents. She did not spell her name "Dolly," as is done today. Tradition also says wrongly that her real name was "Dorothea." She spent her childhood in Scotchtown, Va. In 1783, the family moved to Philadelphia. Dolley and John Todd, Jr., a lawyer and a Quaker, were married in 1790. They had two sons. Todd and one of the sons died in 1793. When she married Madison in 1794, she was expelled from the Society of Friends because of her marriage to a non-Quaker. After Madison's two terms as President the couple retired to Montpelier, his Virginia plantation. In 1837, after his death, she returned to Washington to live.
          Robert J. Taylor

See also **Madison, James** (picture).

**4th President of
the United States 1809-1817**

Jefferson
3rd President
1801-1809
Democratic-
Republican

Madison
4th President
1809-1817
Democratic-
Republican

Monroe
5th President
1817-1825
Democratic-
Republican

George Clinton
Vice President
1809-1812

Elbridge Gerry
Vice President
1813-1814

Detail of an oil painting on wood (about 1810) by Gilbert Stuart; National Gallery of Art, Washington, D.C., Ailsa Mellon Bruce Fund.

Madison, James (1751-1836), the fourth President of the United States, is often called the Father of the Constitution. He played a leading role in the Constitutional Convention of 1787, where he helped design the checks and balances that operate among Congress, the President, and the Supreme Court. He also helped create the U.S. federal system, which divides power between the central government and the states.

Madison served his home state—Virginia—and the United States in many roles over his 40 years in public life. Before he became President, Madison had served as secretary of state under President Thomas Jefferson. Both as secretary of state and as President, Madison tried to keep the United States from being drawn into conflicts between European countries. In 1812, however, President Madison led the United States into a war against Great Britain after Britain had interfered with U.S. shipping. During the war, British troops captured Washington, D.C., where they burned the Capitol, the White House, and other government buildings. As President, Madison followed policies that generally resulted in U.S. economic growth and westward expansion.

Madison was a close friend of Thomas Jefferson, who also was a Virginian. The two men formed an important political partnership. During the Revolutionary War in America, they worked together for American independence.

After the United States won independence, Madison favored the formation of a strong federal government. In the 1790's, however, he and Jefferson resisted the efforts of Alexander Hamilton to establish a national bank and so make the central government even stronger. Hamilton was President George Washington's treasury secretary.

Madison and Jefferson also opposed Hamilton's attempts to promote the growth of manufacturing in the United States. They wanted the country to remain a farming republic. They organized people who opposed Hamilton's policies into the Democratic-Republican Party, the forerunner of today's Democratic Party.

Early life

James Madison was born in the home of his mother's parents on March 16, 1751 (March 5 by the calendar then in use). They lived at Port Conway, Va., about 12 miles (19 kilometers) from Fredericksburg. James was the eldest of 12 children. The families of his father, James Madison, and his mother, Nelly Conway Madison, had settled in Virginia during the 1600's. Many slaves worked on the Madison plantation, Montpelier, near what is now Orange, Va.

James was a frail and sickly child. He studied with private tutors and attended the Donald Robertson School in King and Queen County. At the age of 18, he entered the College of New Jersey (now Princeton University). He took an active interest in politics and was an early member of the American Whig Society. Madison studied very hard and completed the regular course at the college in two years. He graduated in 1771.

Madison spent the next six months studying Hebrew, philosophy, and other subjects that showed his deep interest in religious questions. A weak speaking voice prevented him from taking up a career as a minister. He soon turned his attention to politics.

Political and public career

Entry into politics. Madison entered politics in 1774, when he was elected to the Committee of Safety in Or-

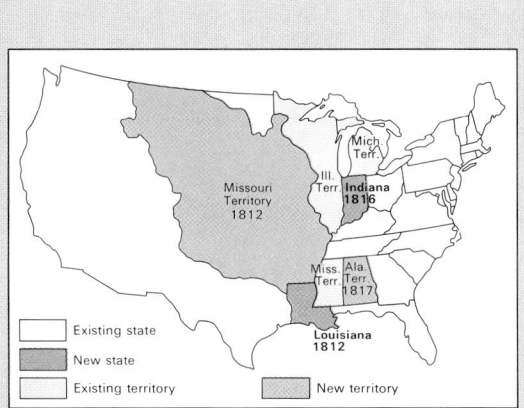

Existing state

New state

Existing territory

New territory

Two new states—Louisiana in 1812 and Indiana in 1816—joined the United States during Madison's presidency, making a total of 19 states in the Union. Congress established the Missouri Territory in 1812 and the Alabama Territory in 1817.

The world of President Madison

Construction of the National Road began in 1811. The road stretched from Maryland to Illinois and provided a major route to the West.

The steam-powered printing press, invented by the German printer Friedrich Koenig in 1811, enabled newspapers to print large numbers of copies cheaply.

The War of 1812 was fought by the United States and Great Britain from 1812 to 1815. British troops captured Washington, D.C., and burned the Capitol and other buildings. However, the war ended without a victory for either side.

Jane Austen's novels established her as one of the great writers in English literature. Her works included *Pride and Prejudice* (1813), *Mansfield Park* (1814), and *Emma* (1816).

"The Star-Spangled Banner," which became the national anthem of the United States, was written by Francis Scott Key in 1814. Key, an American lawyer, wrote the song after watching a British attack on Baltimore during the War of 1812.

The Hartford Convention, a meeting of New England leaders, took place in Hartford, Conn., in 1814 and 1815. The participants met to discuss their opposition to the War of 1812.

The Battle of Waterloo in 1815 brought defeat to the French Emperor Napoleon I and ended his plans to rule Europe.

The stethoscope, used to listen to the heart and other organs, was invented by French doctor René Laënnec in 1816.

The first savings banks in the United States were founded in Philadelphia and Boston in 1816. Such banks, which are nonprofit organizations created to promote saving, became the most common type of thrift institution in the Northeast.

WORLD BOOK map

ange County, Virginia. Committees of this kind provided local government in the days when the British colonial government was crumbling. In 1776, Madison helped draft a new Virginia constitution and the Virginia Declaration of Rights. Other colonies later drew upon these documents in writing their own constitutions.

Madison served in Virginia's revolutionary assembly in 1776, when he met Thomas Jefferson. The two men soon began a lifetime friendship.

Madison was defeated for reelection in 1777. But in 1778, the Virginia Assembly elected Madison to the Governor's Council, an advisory group. He held this post until December 1779, when he was elected to the Continental Congress.

Madison took his seat in Congress in March 1780. In those days, Congress had no power to raise taxes and found it difficult to pay national debts. Madison strongly favored increasing the powers of Congress in financial matters. He also advocated many other measures to stabilize and dignify the government.

Virginia assemblyman. Madison returned to Virginia in 1783. By that time, Americans generally recog-

Important dates in Madison's life

1751 (March 16) Born at Port Conway, Va.
1779 Elected to the Continental Congress.
1787 Served at the Constitutional Convention.
1789 Elected to the U.S. House of Representatives.
1794 (Sept. 15) Married Dolley Payne Todd.
1801 Appointed secretary of state.
1808 Elected President of the United States.
1812 Recommended war with Britain. Reelected President.
1829 Served at the Virginia Constitutional Convention.
1836 (June 28) Died at Montpelier, his family estate.

nized him as the ablest member of Congress. He planned to study law, history, and the sciences. Madison's studies were partially interrupted when the people of Orange County elected him to the state assembly for three successive one-year terms.

In the assembly, Madison continued the struggle Jefferson had begun for separation of church and state in Virginia. Madison's chief opponent was Patrick Henry, who favored state support for teachers of the Christian religion. In 1786, the assembly passed Virginia's Statute of Religious Freedom. Madison wrote to Jefferson that thus in Virginia "was extinguished forever the ambitious hope of making laws for the human mind."

Constitutional Convention. Madison represented Virginia at the Constitutional Convention of 1787. Although only 36 years old, he took a leading part. Madison fought for a stronger central government and drafted the Virginia Plan for the union. This plan, also called the Randolph Plan, foreshadowed the constitution that the convention finally adopted (see **Constitution of the United States** [The compromises]).

Madison proved valuable to the convention in many ways. He had read deeply in political history and knew firsthand the weaknesses of the Articles of Confederation, the basic law that the Constitution later replaced. Madison also kept a more complete record of the debates that took place at the convention than did anyone else who attended them.

Madison next served as a member of the convention that was called in Virginia to consider whether the state should ratify the new Constitution. He also joined Alexander Hamilton and John Jay of New York in writing *The Federalist,* a series of proratification letters to newspapers. Scholars still consider these letters the most authoritative explanation of the American constitutional system. See **Federalist, The.**

Congressman. Madison's efforts on behalf of the Constitution cost him the support of Virginians who opposed a stronger union. They united in the Virginia legislature to defeat him in 1788 for a seat in the first United States Senate. Early the next year, Madison defeated James Monroe in an election for the U.S. House of Representatives.

Madison, one of the ablest members of the House, proposed resolutions for organizing the Departments of State, Treasury, and War. He also drafted much of the first tariff act. Most important, he was largely responsible for drafting the first 10 amendments to the Constitution, the Bill of Rights (see **Bill of rights**).

At first, Madison supported many policies of President George Washington's first Administration. But he gradually came to oppose the financial plans of Washington's treasury secretary, Alexander Hamilton. Madison believed that Hamilton's plans favored wealthy Easterners at the expense of ordinary citizens, particularly small farmers in what were then the Southern and Western United States. As a result, Madison turned against the Washington Administration and Hamilton's Federalist Party. In 1791 and 1792, Madison and Jefferson formed the Democratic-Republican Party to oppose the Federalists.

In Philadelphia in 1794, Madison met and married Dolley Payne Todd, a young widow. By 1797, he had become weary of politics and retired to his estate. In 1798, Congress passed the Alien and Sedition Acts (see **Alien and Sedition Acts**). Madison was outraged. He drafted

Oil portrait on canvas (1817) by Bass Otis; New-York Historical Society, New York City

Dolley Madison, the President's wife, was famous for her hospitality. She served as White House hostess during the Administrations of both Madison and Thomas Jefferson, a widower.

the Virginia Resolutions of 1798, proposing joint action by the states in declaring these laws unconstitutional. He was elected to the Virginia legislature in 1799 and 1800 and led the fight against what he considered Federalist efforts to undermine basic human rights.

Secretary of state. Thomas Jefferson became President in 1801 and appointed Madison secretary of state. The purchase of Louisiana was the most important success in foreign relations during Jefferson's presidency (see **Louisiana Purchase**). War with the Barbary pirates between 1801 and 1805 caused excitement throughout the country. The peace treaty signed with Tripoli brought only brief satisfaction. The pirates soon began preying on U.S. shipping again (see **Barbary States**).

Madison and Jefferson failed to force Great Britain and France to respect the rights of Americans on the high seas. The British and French were fighting each other in the Napoleonic wars, and each had blockaded the other's coast. American ships that tried to trade with either country were stopped by warships of the other. Many American seamen were seized and forced to serve on British or French warships. The Embargo Act of 1807 attempted to protect American ships by prohibiting them from sailing into foreign ports. It also barred exports from the United States. But the loss of trade brought widespread economic distress to the United States, and many Northern merchants evaded the embargo. In the end, the embargo hurt Americans more than it did the British or French.

The Embargo Act was repealed in 1809. In its place, Congress passed the Non-Intercourse Act, which opened trade with all countries except Great Britain and France. Congress hoped this law would force the British and French to recognize American commercial rights.

Jefferson favored Madison to succeed him as President. Madison received 122 electoral votes to 47 for the Federalist candidate, former minister to France C. C. Pinckney. For votes by states, see **Electoral College** (table). Madison's running mate was George Clinton of New York.

Madison's first Administration (1809-1813)

Events leading to war. Trade with Britain and France was still the government's greatest problem when Madison became President. In spite of the Non-Intercourse Act, American merchants continued to trade with those two countries, and British and French warships continued to interfere with American shipping. In 1810, Congress passed a bill that reopened trade with Britain and France. This act stated that if either Britain or France ended its attacks on American ships, the United States would stop trading with the other country. But the plan backfired. The French Emperor Napoleon I announced that he would revoke the French blockade against neutral trade with Great Britain. But at the same time, he issued secret orders that maintained the French blockade against American shipping. Madison halted all trade with Great Britain, but the French continued to stop American ships.

Americans were angered by France. Reports that the British were stirring up Indians in the West also aroused feelings against the British. These reports seemed to be confirmed when Tecumseh, chief of the Shawnee tribe, tried to organize an Indian alliance to fight the Ameri-

Vice Presidents and Cabinet

Vice President	* George Clinton
	* Elbridge Gerry (1813)
Secretary of state	Robert Smith
	* James Monroe (1811)
Secretary of the treasury	* Albert Gallatin
	George W. Campbell (1814)
	Alexander J. Dallas (1814)
	* William H. Crawford (1816)
Secretary of war	William Eustis
	John Armstrong (1813)
	* James Monroe (1814)
	* William H. Crawford (1815)
Attorney general	Caesar A. Rodney
	William Pinkney (1811)
	Richard Rush (1814)
Secretary of the Navy	Paul Hamilton
	William Jones (1813)
	B. W. Crowninshield (1814)

*Has a separate biography in WORLD BOOK.

cans. The alliance dissolved after Governor William Henry Harrison of the Indiana Territory defeated the Indian forces in the Battle of Tippecanoe on Nov. 7, 1811 (see **Harrison, William Henry** [Entry into politics]). But people throughout the West believed the British as well as the Indians were their enemy.

Adding to the war feeling was a strongly nationalistic generation that had arisen in politics. It included many people who felt a war would result in the annexation of Canada and Spanish Florida. Henry Clay of Kentucky, Felix Grundy of Tennessee, and John Calhoun of South Carolina acted as its spokesmen in the House.

"Mr. Madison's War." Madison knew the United States was unprepared for war, and that New England merchants feared war would destroy trade. But he also knew people outside New England wanted it, and that the nation could tolerate no more insults from Britain. He finally recommended war, and Congress approved it

on June 18, 1812. The Federalists opposed the conflict and called it "Mr. Madison's War." A few months later, Madison was reelected President by 128 electoral votes to 89 for Mayor DeWitt Clinton of New York City (see **Electoral College** [table]). Madison's running mate was Governor Elbridge Gerry of Massachusetts.

Madison's second Administration (1813-1817)

Progress of the war. At the start of the war, the British Navy clamped on a blockade that the pitifully small U.S. Navy could not break. American land forces attacked Canada in 1812 but were defeated. The fight for Canada continued for two years, with no decisive victories on either side. In 1814, Napoleon was defeated in Europe. Britain then sent experienced troops to Canada, ending American hopes for conquest.

In the summer of 1814, General Winfield Scott fought the British to a standstill at Chippewa and Lundy's Lane in southern Ontario. British troops invaded Maryland and, on August 24, burned the Capitol and other public buildings in Washington. Only heroic resistance at Fort McHenry kept the British from capturing Baltimore.

In September 1814, American forces stopped an invasion of British troops that were moving south down the western shore of Lake Champlain. Early in 1815, Andrew Jackson won a stunning victory at New Orleans. The war ended with the Treaty of Ghent, which went into effect in February 1815. It settled none of the problems that had caused the war. But it did preserve American territorial integrity (see **Ghent, Treaty of; War of 1812**).

In 1814 and early 1815, before the end of the war, New England Federalists had held a closed meeting known as the Hartford Convention. The convention passed resolutions against the war and proposed making New England more independent of the federal government. Many people believed that the convention was planning secession of the New England states. As a re-

Library of Congress

The British captured Washington, D.C., in 1814, during the War of 1812. British troops burned the Capitol, the White House, and other government buildings. Madison fled to avoid capture.

sult, the Federalist Party was branded as unpatriotic, and it fell apart as a national organization shortly after James Monroe was elected President in 1816. See **Hartford Convention.**

The growth of nationalism. Albert Gallatin, Madison's first secretary of the treasury, believed that the War of 1812 had "renewed and reinstated the national feeling of character which the Revolution had given and which was daily lessening. The people . . . are more American; they feel and act more as a nation." The end of the war ushered in "the era of good feeling." With the end of the Federalist Party, political conflicts were submerged within the Democratic-Republican Party.

During the two years after the war, trade expanded, and the country experienced great economic growth. In 1816, Madison signed a bill that created the country's second national bank. The first such bank had operated from 1791 to 1811. Changes in federal policy also made it easier for settlers to buy frontier land, and the rate of westward migration increased. In addition, Madison approved the tariff of 1816, which introduced the principle of protecting American industries.

Life in the White House. Mrs. Madison began an extravagant round of parties as soon as her husband took office. She served elaborate dinners and delighted in surprising her guests with delicacies.

The British invasion of the capital and the burning of the White House ended social gaiety. The Madisons fled Washington. When they returned, they established a new residence in the Octagon House, a private home just west of the White House. In 1815, they moved to a house on the corner of Pennsylvania Avenue and 19th Street. Dolley Madison resumed her busy social life but longed to reoccupy the White House. However, reconstruction work proceeded slowly, and the Executive Mansion was not ready for occupancy until nine months after Madison left office in 1817.

Later years

In retirement at Montpelier, Madison busied himself with the affairs of his estate. After Jefferson's death in 1826, he became *rector* (president) of the University of Virginia. Madison died at Montpelier on June 28, 1836. His widow returned to Washington, where she lived until her death in 1849. The Madisons are buried in a family plot near Montpelier. They had no children, but they reared the son of Mrs. Madison by her first husband.   Robert J. Brugger

Related articles in *World Book* include:

Biographies

Clay, Henry	Henry, Patrick	Monroe, James
Clinton, George	Jefferson, Thomas	Washington,
Gallatin, Albert	Key, Francis Scott	George
Gerry, Elbridge	Madison, Dolley	
Hamilton, Alexander	Payne	

Other related articles

Alien and Sedition Acts	Federalist Party
Anti-Federalists	Kentucky and Virginia Resolu-
Bill of rights	tions
Constitution of the U.S.	Marbury v. Madison
Continental Congress	President of the United States
Democratic-Republican Party	States' rights
Embargo Act	United States, History of the
Federalist, The	

Quotations from Madison

The following quotations come from some of James Madison's speeches and writings.

Those who hold and those who are without property have ever formed distinct interests in society.
The Federalist, Number 10, November 1787

If men were angels, no government would be necessary.
The Federalist, Number 47, January 1788

The accumulation of all powers, legislative, executive, and judiciary, in the same hands, whether of one, a few, or many, and whether hereditary, self-appointed, or elective, may justly be pronounced the very definition of tyranny.
The Federalist, Number 47, January 1788

I believe there are more instances of the abridgment of the freedom of the people by gradual and silent encroachments of those in power than by violent and sudden usurpations.
Speech at the Virginia Ratifying Convention, June 16, 1788

Peace, at all times a blessing, is peculiarly welcome . . . at a period when the causes for the war have ceased to operate, when the government has demonstrated the efficiency of its powers of defense, and when the nation can review its conduct without regret and without reproach.
Message to Congress announcing the end of the War of 1812, Feb. 18,1815

The advice nearest to my heart and deepest in my convictions is that the Union of the states be cherished and perpetuated.
"Advice to my Country," 1834

Outline

I. Early life
II. Political and public career

A. Entry into politics	D. Congressman
B. Virginia assemblyman	E. Secretary of state
C. Constitutional Conven- tion	

III. Madison's first Administration (1809-1813)
    A. Events leading to war
    B. "Mr. Madison's War"
IV. Madison's second Administration (1813-1817)
    A. Progress of the war
    B. The growth of nationalism
    C. Life in the White House
V. Later years

Questions

Why is Madison called "the Father of the Constitution"?
What were some important principles that Madison supported in the Continental Congress?
What effect did Madison have on the relationship of church and state in Virginia?
How did Madison prove valuable in the first U.S. Congress?
How did the War of 1812 affect American nationalism?
Why did Madison draft the Virginia Resolutions of 1798?
What was Madison's relationship to *The Federalist?*
Why did Madison oppose the growth of U.S. manufacturing?
How did Dolley Madison shine as first lady?

Reading and Study Guide

See *Madison, James,* in the Research Guide/Index, Volume 22, for a *Reading and Study Guide.*

Additional resources

Brant, Irving. *James Madison.* 6 vols. Bobbs, 1941-1961.
Fritz, Jean. *The Great Little Madison.* Putnam, 1989. For younger readers.
Ketcham, Ralph L. *James Madison: A Biography.* Univ. Pr. of Virginia, 1990. First published in 1971.
Rutland, Robert A. *James Madison: The Founding Father.* Macmillan, 1987. *The Presidency of James Madison.* Univ. Pr. of Kansas, 1990.

Madonna and Child are the Virgin Mary and the infant Jesus in works of art. The Madonna and Child rank among the most important art subjects that the Christian religion has inspired.

Madonna means *my lady* in Italian. But the term has come to mean *the Virgin Mary.* Painters and sculptors produced some of their greatest works on the Madonna during the Renaissance (see **Renaissance**). Michelangelo's *Medici Madonna* is one of the finest sculptures of the Madonna. Terra-cotta figures of the Madonna by the sculptor Luca della Robbia are well known (see **Della Robbia, Luca** [picture: Luca della Robbia created *Madonna and Child Jesus*]). For other pictures of sculptures of the Madonna, see **Sculpture** (Medieval sculpture; picture); **Stoss, Veit.**

Painters of the Madonna. Saint Luke painted the first Madonna picture, according to legend. But the Virgin Mary and Child became symbols of the accepted Christian faith only after the Council of Ephesus, in present-day Turkey, in A.D. 431. Then the number of Madonna pictures began to increase. The oldest Madonna pictures are those found in the catacombs of the early Christians. Stiff images set against a gold background from the Byzantine period served as models for other artists until the 1200's. Then the painters of the early Renaissance introduced a style that featured more background scenery. Giovanni Cimabue, the first of these painters, tried to put natural life into his paintings instead of copying the Byzantine types of figures.

The Madonna and Child was one of the most popular

Madonna Enthroned with Saints by the Italian painter Giotto shows the Virgin Mary seated on a throne holding the Christ child. Saints and kneeling angels gaze at Mary and Jesus.

Tempera on wood panel, also called the *Ognissanti Madonna* (about 1300); Uffizi Gallery, Florence, Italy (SCALA) subjects for painters in the later Renaissance period. Raphael produced some of the greatest paintings of the Madonna. His painting *Sistine Madonna,* completed in 1515, hangs in Dresden, Germany. It shows the Virgin Mary carrying the infant Jesus in her arms. On one side, Pope Sixtus II kneels in prayer. Saint Barbara kneels on the other side. Below, two cherubs lean forward. Raphael originally painted this work as an altarpiece for the Church of San Sisto in Piacenza.

Other great painters who portrayed the Madonna included Giovanni Bellini, Leonardo da Vinci, Giorgione, Fra Filippo Lippi, Andrea del Sarto, and Titian.

Types of Madonna paintings. Paintings of the Madonna are usually divided into five classes, according to the general styles of treatment:

(1) *Portrait of the Madonna.* In this class, the Madonna usually appears as a half-length figure against a background of solid gold leaf, or with cherubs. She wears a blue robe, starred or marked with gold, often draped over her head. The first paintings of the Madonna, in the Greek or Byzantine period, belong to this group. This type evolved into the *Madonna of Humility,* in which the Madonna sits humbly on the ground while holding the Child (see **Angelico, Fra** [picture: *Madonna of Humility*]). Baldovinetti's *Madonna,* exhibited in the Louvre, Paris, is an example of this class of painting from the late Renaissance.

(2) *The Madonna enthroned.* The Madonna sits on a throne or platform in this largest class of paintings. The treatment varies widely. Two examples of this style are shown in color in the **Painting** article: *Enthroned Madonna and Child* by an unknown Byzantine artist and *Madonna of the Long Neck* by the Italian artist Parmigianino. For another example of this painting style, see **Lippi, Filippo** (picture: *Madonna and Child*).

(3) *The Madonna in glory.* The Madonna and her attendants hover in the sky in paintings of this group. Heaven is suggested by a *halo* (circle of light), clouds, or cherubs, or by posing the figures in air just above the earth. The halo originally surrounded the entire figure, instead of only the head. It was generally oval in shape. Examples of this type of painting include *The Sistine Madonna* by Raphael; and *Madonna of the Stars* by Fra Angelico, in the monastery of San Marco in Florence. El Greco's *The Virgin with Saint Inés and Saint Tecla* is another example of this type of painting.

(4) *The Madonna in pastoral scenes.* Paintings in this class have a landscape background. Two well-known examples are reproduced in the **Painting** article: *Madonna of the Goldfinch* by Raphael and *Madonna of the Rocks* by Leonardo da Vinci.

(5) *The Madonna in a home environment.* This type of composition shows the Madonna and Child receiving homage in a realistic setting. It was especially popular in northern European art. *Madonna* by Quentin Massys pictures a Flemish bedroom of the 1400's. In *The Madonna and Child with Chancellor Rolin,* Jan van Eyck pictured the Madonna in Flemish scenery of the 1430's (see **Renaissance** [picture: A northern Renaissance painting]). In the 1600's, Rembrandt followed this tradition by showing the Holy Family in Joseph's carpenter shop.

Eric M. Zafran

See also **Bearden, Romare** (picture); **Engraving** (picture: A Renaissance engraving).

Madonna lily. See Lily.

Madras, *muh DRAS* (pop. 3,276,622; met. area pop. 4,289,347), is India's fourth largest city. Only Bombay, Delhi, and Calcutta have more people. Madras lies on India's southeast coast. For location, see **India** (political map). Madras serves as the capital of the state of Tamil Nadu. Madras is also the state's chief port and commercial city.

A shipping center, Madras has one of India's busiest harbors. Its industrial plants include a railway coach factory; automobile assembly plants; cotton mills; tanneries; and cement, glass, and iron works. The city's landmarks include old Hindu temples and Christian churches, the University of Madras, and Fort St. George—formerly a British fort. An international airport serves Madras, and highways and railroads connect it with inland areas.

In 1640, the British—who later became the colonial rulers of India—built Fort St. George near the coast of what is now Madras. At that time, Madras was a small village called Madraspatam. Through the years, settlements grew up around the fort, and nearby towns were made part of Madras. Large industrial, commercial, and residential areas were established, and Madras grew into a huge urban area.   P. P. Karan

Madrasah. See Islam (The mosque); Islamic art (Madrasahs; picture).

Madrid, *muh DRIHD* (pop. 3,123,713), is the capital and largest city of Spain. It stands on a plateau about 2,150 feet (655 meters) above sea level and is one of the highest capitals in Europe. Madrid became the capital largely because of its location near the exact geographic center of Spain. For the location of Madrid, see **Spain** (political map).

Spain had reached its height as a colonial power when King Philip II made Madrid the capital in the mid-1500's. The Spanish colonial empire began to decline during the 1600's, but Madrid remained an important center of government and culture. Since the mid-1900's, Madrid has also become one of Spain's leading industrial cities.

The city covers about 234 square miles (606 square kilometers). Madrid suffered severe damage during the Spanish Civil War (1936-1939), and much of the city has been reconstructed or restored from the wartime ruins.

A large, crescent-shaped plaza called the Puerta del Sol (Gate of the Sun) marks the center of downtown Madrid. One of the city's main streets, the Calle de Alcalá, extends eastward from the Puerta del Sol. The old section of Madrid lies southwest of the Puerta del Sol. A number of the buildings that line the narrow, winding streets of this area were built during the 1500's and 1600's.

Madrid's modern business district is north of the Calle de Alcalá. Banks, hotels, restaurants, stores, and theaters line the Gran Vía, the main street of the business section. The Salamanca district, a residential area built chiefly in the late 1800's and the 1900's, occupies the near northeast part of the city. A huge park called the Retiro covers more than 350 acres (142 hectares) just southeast of the center of Madrid.

Nearly all of Madrid's famous buildings and monuments are in or near the old section and the central business district. The Royal Palace, built in the 1700's,

Madrid's Gran Vía is the main street of the city's modern business district. Banks, hotels, restaurants, stores, and theaters line both sides of this busy avenue.

stands at the western edge of the old section. The Spanish royal family lived in the palace until 1931, when King Alfonso XIII was forced to leave the country. Elaborate gardens border the palace, which is now a museum. Madrid also has a number of lovely old churches and impressive public squares with fountains and statues of famous Spaniards.

Since 1950, a rapid population growth has caused Madrid to expand in all directions. Today, residential areas and industrial suburbs surround the central city. Like other rapidly growing cities, Madrid has such problems as air pollution and crowded living conditions. Many of the city's trees have been cut down to widen streets and to provide parking space for the increasing number of automobiles.

The people of Madrid are called *Madrileños* (pronounced *MAH druh LAYN yohs*). They speak Castilian Spanish, the official language of Spain. Most people live in apartments because they cannot afford to buy a house.

Most stores and offices in Madrid open at 9 a.m. and close at about 1 p.m., when Madrileños leave work to eat a leisurely lunch. The business places are open again from 4 p.m. to about 7 p.m. Like other Spaniards, most Madrileños have dinner between 10 p.m. and midnight. They like to dine at Madrid's many fine restaurants, which feature beef, lamb, and seafood dishes. Sidewalk cafes throughout the city are favorite meeting places, where Madrileños chat with friends.

Large crowds attend the bullfights held at the Plaza de Toros. But soccer ranks as Madrid's most popular sport. The city's soccer stadium, one of the largest in the world, seats more than 100,000 spectators.

Education and cultural life. Madrid's educational institutions, museums, and libraries make the city the cultural center of Spain. The University of Madrid, the nation's largest university, occupies a section of Madrid called University City. The city also has a number of technical institutes.

Madrid is the home of one of the world's outstanding art museums, the Prado, also called the National Museum of Painting and Sculpture. The Prado houses a collection of more than 2,000 paintings by Spanish and foreign masters. The Prado's exhibits of Spanish paintings include more than 30 works by El Greco and more than 100 works by Francisco Goya. The museum also displays 50 paintings by Diego Velázquez, including *The Maids of Honor,* which appears in the **Painting** article in *World Book.*

Madrid has a number of other art museums, as well as many museums that feature exhibits on natural history and science. The city is also the home of Spain's National Library and the National Historical Archives.

Climate. Madrid has a dry climate, with hot summers and cool winters. It receives an average of less than 17 inches (43 centimeters) of rain a year. Temperatures average about 40 °F (4 °C) in January and about 74 °F (23 °C) in July. During August, which is usually the hottest

Mort Rabinow, Stock, Boston

Modern apartment buildings in and near Madrid house many families. Rapid population growth since 1950 has caused Madrid and its suburbs to expand in all directions.

month in Madrid, San Sebastián serves as the official seat of the Spanish government. San Sebastián lies on the country's cooler north coast.

Economy. From the mid-1500's to the mid-1900's, the economy of Madrid depended on the city's role as a government center. Most of the workers in Madrid had jobs related to politics or government administration. The city had almost no industry.

Since the mid-1900's, the Spanish government has encouraged large-scale industrial development in Madrid and its suburbs. Today, the city ranks second to Barcelona as a Spanish industrial center. Factories in the Madrid area manufacture automobiles, chemicals, clothing, leather goods, trucks, and other products.

Highways and railroads link Madrid to other Spanish cities. Barajas International Airport lies about 7 miles (11 kilometers) northeast of downtown Madrid.

History. In the A.D. 900's, the Moors, a Moslem people, built a fortress called Magerit on the site of what is now Madrid (see **Moors**). Spanish Christians, under King Alfonso VI of León and Castile, gained control of the area in 1083.

Madrid remained a small, unimportant town until 1561, when Philip II made it the capital of Spain. Philip, who ruled a huge colonial empire, chose Madrid primarily because of its central location. During the late 1500's and early 1600's, Madrid grew rapidly and became one of the great cities of western Europe. Wealthy aristocrats and royal officials built homes there. But the rapid population growth created problems. Most Madrileños

were poor and lived in shabby, crowded neighborhoods. Epidemics and a high crime rate made the city unsafe. During the 1700's, the government took steps that made Madrid a cleaner and safer city.

French forces under Napoleon I occupied Madrid from 1808 to 1813. On May 2, 1808, a group of Madrileños staged an unsuccessful revolt against the French. This uprising started a Spanish resistance movement that in time helped drive the French out of Spain.

Madrid, unlike many cities in a number of countries, failed to develop large industries during the 1800's. As a result, it did not attract large numbers of workers, and its rate of population growth dropped.

Madrid attracted worldwide attention during the Spanish Civil War, which began in 1936. The city was the scene of fierce fighting between the Loyalists, who supported the government, and the rebel forces of General Francisco Franco. The Loyalists moved the capital to Valencia in 1936 and to Barcelona in 1937. After the defeat of the Loyalists in 1939, Franco reestablished Madrid as the capital.

Since the mid-1900's, Madrid has again experienced rapid population growth. Government programs to develop industry and to build modern housing and office buildings in the city have helped contribute to Madrid's growth.   Stanley G. Payne

See also **Spain** (pictures).

Madrid Hurtado, Miguel de la. See De la Madrid Hurtado, Miguel.

Madrigal, *MAD ruh guhl,* is a pastoral song in which two or more voices sing separate melodies to a literary text. Most madrigals are contemplative songs that have no instrumental accompaniment. Madrigals are classified as vocal chamber music, with one voice to a part.

Italian composers began writing madrigals in the late 1300's. The form reached its high point in the 1500's and early 1600's in the works of Cipriano de Rore, Philippe de Monte, Luca Marenzio, Carlo Gesualdo, and Claudio Monteverdi. Outside of Italy, it developed chiefly in England. The madrigal had a number of names, including *song, canzonet,* and *ayre.* English madrigal composers of the late 1500's and early 1600's included William Byrd, Thomas Morley, Thomas Weelkes, and John Wilbye. A famous collection of English madrigals is *The Triumphes of Oriana* (1601), in which 21 composers wrote in praise of Queen Elizabeth I of England. Most madrigals were *secular* (nonreligious) songs, but such composers as Orlando di Lasso and Giovanni Palestrina wrote sacred madrigals.   Mary Vinquist

See also **Classical music** (The Renaissance period).

Madroña, *muh DROHN yuh,* also called *madrone,* is a small tree with white, urn-shaped flowers and leathery evergreen leaves. The rough, berrylike fruit has mealy flesh and hard seeds. It grows along the Pacific coast of North America, from southern California to British Columbia. See also **Heath.**

Scientific classification. Madroña belongs to the heath family, Ericaceae. Its scientific name is *Arbutus menziesii.*

James L. Luteyn

Maelstrom, *MAYL struhm,* is a swift and dangerous current in the Arctic Ocean. This current sweeps back and forth between two islands of the Lofoten group off the northwestern coast of Norway. It has been a menace to sailors for hundreds of years. The Maelstrom becomes more dangerous when the wind blows against it between high and low tide. The waters then form immense whirlpools that destroy small ships.

Writers, including the Norwegian poet Peter Dass and the American author Edgar Allan Poe, have greatly exaggerated the Maelstrom's power. As a result, the meaning of the word *maelstrom* has come to include any kind of whirlpool or any turmoil of widespread influence.   Mark A. Cane

See also **Whirlpool**.

Maeterlinck, *MAY tuhr lihngk,* **Maurice,** *moh REES* (1862-1949), was a Belgian dramatist, poet, naturalist, and philosopher. He won the 1911 Nobel Prize for literature. His literary works are symbolic and philosophical. Their stories suggest the soul's search for perfection and understanding. In his most famous play, the fairy talelike *The Blue Bird* (1908), a child searches the world for happiness, only to find it in his own home. The more realistic short plays *The Blind* and *The Intruder* (both 1891) are stories of unhappiness that also stress the need to find love and happiness in everyday life. *Pelléas and Mélisande* (1893) is a symbolic drama about ideal lovers destroyed by their search for perfection.

Maeterlinck also wrote two novels and four volumes of poetry. He turned from symbolic writing to direct expression of his philosophy in essays, such as the collection *The Treasure of the Humble* (1896). He often drew on his close study of nature in these essays. In *The Life of the Bees* (1901) and *Life and Flowers* (1907), he used his appreciation and understanding of nature as the basis for analysis of human behavior.

Maeterlinck was born in Ghent. He lived much of his life in France, and he wrote in French.

Gerald M. Berkowitz

See also **Drama** (Symbolism); **French literature** (Symbolism).

Maffei galaxies, *mah FAY ee,* often called *Maffei 1* and *Maffei 2,* are two large star systems. They probably belong to the group of galaxies that includes the earth's galaxy, the Milky Way. The Maffei galaxies are less than 12 million light-years from the earth. A light-year is the distance that light travels in a year. It equals about 5.88 trillion miles (9.46 trillion kilometers).

Each of the Maffei galaxies measures from 50,000 to 100,000 light-years in diameter. Maffei 1, the brighter of the two systems, may consist of as many as 100 billion stars. Maffei 2 has only about 10 billion stars. Astronomers classify Maffei 1 as an *elliptical galaxy* because of its oval shape. Maffei 2 resembles a flattened coil and is classified as a *spiral galaxy.*

The Maffei galaxies remained unknown until 1968 because they are hidden by dense clouds of cosmic dust and gas in the earth's galaxy. They were discovered that year by the Italian astronomer Paolo Maffei, for whom they were named. Maffei photographed the galaxies through a telescope by using film sensitive to *infrared rays,* the invisible heat rays given off by the galaxies. Infrared rays, unlike light rays, can penetrate dust clouds. In 1971, astronomers at several California observatories determined the approximate size and shape of the Maffei galaxies.   Frank D. Drake

Mafia, *MAH fee ah,* is a secret criminal society in Sicily. Crime groups stemming from the original Sicilian Mafia operate in the United States and other countries. *Mafia* is also used as a general term for any underworld criminal organization.

The Mafia is made up of extended kinship groups called *mafiosi.* A Mafia member is called a *mafioso.* These groups originally maintained an ideal of manliness developed during the 1600's, when Sicily was ruled by Spain. The ideal called for refusal to cooperate with authorities and self-control in the face of hardships. In personal quarrels, a mafioso took the law into his own hands and gained respect by using violence. Any offense might trigger a campaign of vengeance called a *vendetta* (see **Vendetta**). Mafiosi unofficially ruled part of western Sicily in the 1800's and early 1900's. Similar crime groups, such as the Camorra in Naples and the *Onorata Società* (Honored Society) in Calabria, developed in other parts of Italy.

In the late 1800's, southern Italians attempted to reproduce the Mafia in the United States. These groups did not have much power until Prohibition in the 1920's. Then, they greatly profited from *bootlegging*—the illegal making, selling, or transporting of alcoholic beverages. Also during this time, Italian dictator Benito Mussolini opposed mafiosi in western Sicily. Many fled to the United States and eventually became leaders of American organized crime.

After the end of Prohibition in 1933, these Italian-American groups, also called *crime families,* became active in other illegal practices. Their activities included gambling, *loan sharking* (lending money at unlawful rates of interest), and drug dealing. Authorities estimate that thousands of Mafia members and associates operate in the United States, particularly in New York City and Chicago.

Since the end of World War II (1939-1945), the Mafia in Italy has undergone major changes. Its rural base has moved into urban areas. It also has faced increased government opposition and feuds between Mafia groups.

Howard Abadinsky

See also **Sicily** (The people).

Additional resources

Abadinsky, Howard. *Organized Crime.* 3rd ed. Nelson-Hall, 1990.
Arlacchi, Pino. *Mafia Business: The Mafia Ethic and the Spirit of Capitalism.* Verso, 1987. First published in 1986.
Fox, Stephen R. *Blood and Power: Organized Crime in Twentieth Century America.* Morrow, 1989.
Harris, Jonathan. *Super Mafia: Organized Crime Threatens America.* Messner, 1984. Also suitable for younger readers.

Magarac, *MAG uh rak,* **Joe,** is a legendary hero of steelworkers. Folk tales about Magarac originated among Hungarian and other eastern European immigrants who settled in the steelmaking region of western Pennsylvania.

There has been a rich exchange of story elements between popular published versions of these legends and the oral traditions. Most of the legends about Magarac involve his great strength and physical endurance. Stories tell how he worked day and night at an open-hearth furnace. Magarac could squeeze hot steel through his fingers to make railroad rails and could forge horseshoes and cannonballs with his bare hands. According to one story, Magarac's life ended when he melted himself down to make the finest steel in the world. *Magarac* is a Slavic word that means *jackass,* but steelworkers used it as a term of admiration.   Ellen J. Stekert

Magazines reach millions of people. Most readers buy them at newsstands or have them delivered at home. A large readership helps a magazine attract advertising, a major source of income.

Magazine is a collection of articles or stories—or both—published at regular intervals. Most magazines also include illustrations.

Magazines provide a wide variety of information, opinion, and entertainment. For example, they may cover current events and fashions, discuss foreign affairs, or describe how to repair appliances or prepare food. Subjects addressed in magazines include business, culture, hobbies, medicine, religion, science, and sports. Some magazines seek simply to entertain their readers with fiction, poetry, photography, cartoons, or articles about television shows or motion-picture stars. The United States has about 12,300 magazines that are regularly listed as commercial periodicals. However, when smaller publications and more informal newsletters are included, the total number rises to at least 25,000. Canada, which also receives many U.S. magazines, publishes about 2,000 commercial magazines.

Magazines, like newspapers, represent the work of many writers. But magazines differ from newspapers in form and content. Magazines are designed to be kept much longer than newspapers. For this reason, most magazines are smaller and are printed on better paper. Many have covers and a binding of staples or stitching. In content, magazines have less concern with daily, rapidly changing events than do newspapers.

Some periodicals that appear in newspaper form are really magazines. On the other hand, some weekly newspapers feature long, detailed articles like those found in many magazines.

Writing of different types—ranging from factual or practical reporting to a more personal or emotional style—regularly appears in magazines. Some of the best writers and thinkers in the nation write either occasionally or regularly for magazines. Many well-known writers published their early works in magazines.

Kinds of magazines

Magazines are usually divided into two large categories. *Specialized magazines,* also called *trade magazines,* appeal to the special interests of business, industrial, and professional groups. They are usually mailed to their readers. *Consumer magazines* appeal to the broader interests of the general public and are the ones usually seen on the newsstands in stores. Consumer magazines are further classified by the various audiences they serve. These classifications include (1) children's magazines, (2) hobby magazines, (3) intellectual magazines, (4) men's magazines, (5) women's magazines, and (6) service magazines.

Children's magazines are published for young people of various ages. Most feature stories, jokes, and articles on subjects especially interesting to children, and instructions for making games or useful items.

Hobby magazines appeal to hobbyists in all fields. Their audiences include collectors of coins, stamps, and other items; people interested in certain sports or games; home decorators; and photography enthusiasts.

Intellectual magazines provide a thoughtful analysis of current cultural and political events. These publications include *opinion magazines,* which discuss current events from a particular economic or political viewpoint. Many intellectual magazines publish fiction and poetry as well as factual articles.

Men's magazines carry articles or stories on such subjects as adventure, entertainment, men's fashions, and sports. Some also have features and interviews about the arts and current affairs.

Women's magazines include many of the monthlies with the largest number of readers. These publications may offer ideas on skills such as cooking and home-decorating. Some women's periodicals deal with child-raising, fashion trends, or romance. Others discuss the role of women in society and provide career information.

Service magazines include a variety of advice, how-to, medical, self-help, and religious publications. This category includes magazines for the elderly. The number of elderly readers is growing, and magazines for the elderly may eventually become a separate classification.

Other magazines are more difficult to categorize. *News magazines* look like magazines, but because they summarize the week's news, their content is similar to that of newspapers. *Digests* reprint material, in a shorter form, that has appeared in other magazines or in books. The audiences of some large magazines are members of service or veterans' organizations and have a wide range of interests. Some business magazines have large circulations, even though their content is very specialized.

A growing number of magazines publish material of interest to various ethnic or racial groups. Some magazines for blacks, for example, feature news articles about blacks or offer specialized information for black business people.

How magazines are produced

Magazines must meet regular publishing deadlines. A newspaper may have one or more deadlines a day, but a magazine's deadlines are days or weeks apart.

Planning a magazine. Every issue of a magazine must be planned thoroughly before publication. Most monthlies, for example, are planned several months in advance. The editors and staff members first decide what major articles, stories, and other items will appear in the issue. They plan the illustrations, if any, at the same time. Regular columns and editorials must also be planned.

Making assignments. The editors assign articles to staff members or free-lance writers. Each article has a deadline and a specified length. Photographs may be taken by staff or free-lance photographers or purchased from picture agencies. Special drawings may be used to illustrate certain kinds of articles. Magazines sometimes publish unassigned articles and photographs by free-lance journalists who offer material for sale.

Scheduling the advertising. Ads are planned for an issue of a magazine while the writers work on their assignments. The editors and staff artists create a *layout,* which shows how the advertising and editorial material will be arranged on each page.

Editing and assembling an issue. After the articles have been written, one or more editors go over them to check their accuracy and readability. Members of the staff may write additional short articles or other items and choose letters from readers to be published. All the written material, called *copy,* is then set in type.

Photographs and other illustrations must be reduced or expanded in size if necessary. Then they have to be reproduced in some form—as engravings, for example—that can be used in making printing plates.

Proofreaders check proofs of the printed copy for errors. The editors examine proofs of the illustrations to be sure the color and size are accurate. Then they paste the text and illustration proofs on blank pages. This group of pages, called a *dummy,* shows how the printed magazine will look.

The magazine is printed according to the dummy. It may be printed by the *letterpress* process, which involves pressing inked lead type against paper. A more common method of magazine printing is *offset lithography,* which uses photographic printing plates of the pages to produce high-quality copies.

How magazines earn income

Most magazines receive income from two sources: (1) advertising and (2) sales of the publication by subscriptions or by newsstand purchases.

Advertising ranks as by far the most important source of income for almost all magazines. Advertisers put their messages in magazines because these publications are read by certain groups. For example, a photography magazine attracts camera fans who may find its ads helpful in choosing certain photographic equipment. Advertisers of such equipment can reach many potential customers by putting ads in such a magazine. Advertisers must spend many thousands of dollars for a single page of advertising space in a magazine that has a large circulation.

Many publishers conduct surveys to find out what groups of people read their magazines. These surveys can identify reader groups by age, income, occupation, race, sex, and other characteristics. Advertisers study such surveys to decide which magazines are read by the people most likely to buy their products.

Sales. Readers get almost all magazines by subscription through the mail or buy them at newsstands. Magazines to be sold on newsstands are shipped by airplane, train, and truck to local communities. Distribution companies then deliver them to newsstands.

Subscription and newsstand sales cannot cover the production costs of most magazine publishers. The actual selling of a magazine is also expensive. Attracting subscribers, for example, may involve an expensive promotional campaign that attracts only a small number of new subscriptions. In newsstand sales, the publisher gets paid only for the magazines actually sold.

History

The earliest magazines probably developed from newspapers or from bookseller catalogs. Such catalogs, which reviewed books on sale, first appeared during the 1600's in France and then in other countries. Pamphlets published at regular intervals appeared in England and America in the 1700's, primarily as literary publications. They included *The Tatler* and *The Spectator,* both published in England.

One of the first British magazines, *The Gentleman's Magazine,* was published from 1731 to 1914. Edward Cave, an English printer, started it as a collection of articles from various books and pamphlets. Later, the magazine published original material. Samuel Johnson, the famous English writer and critic, contributed to this magazine.

The first magazine published in America, the *American Magazine, or A Monthly View,* was published in

Producing a magazine

WORLD BOOK photo by Dan Miller

Each issue of a magazine is planned weeks or even months in advance by a group of editors, *above*. The editors choose topics to be covered in the magazine. They then make assignments and set deadlines for the writers, photographers, and illustrators assigned to the articles.

WORLD BOOK photo by Dan Miller

The writer may interview people to create an accurate, timely article.

WORLD BOOK photo by Tor Eigeland

The photographer takes dramatic pictures to illustrate the article.

WORLD BOOK photo by Dan Miller

A layout artist arranges the text and pictures in an attractive way.

WORLD BOOK photo by Dan Miller

After being printed, the magazine pages are assembled and stapled together. The finished copies are then trimmed, addressed, and mailed.

Leading magazines*

United States

Name	Publication period	Circulation
Reader's Digest	Monthly	16,306,000
TV Guide	Weekly	15,354,000
National Geographic	Monthly	9,921,000
Better Homes and Gardens	Monthly	8,003,000
Family Circle	17 times a year	5,152,000
Good Housekeeping	Monthly	5,028,000
McCall's	Monthly	5,009,000
Ladies' Home Journal	Monthly	5,003,000
Woman's Day	15 times a year	4,752,000
Time	Weekly	4,249,000
Redbook	Monthly	3,842,000
National Enquirer	Weekly	3,706,000
Playboy	Monthly	3,499,000
Sports Illustrated	Weekly	3,444,000
Newsweek	Weekly	3,420,000
People Weekly	Weekly	3,235,000
Star	Weekly	3,208,000
Prevention	Monthly	3,110,000
Cosmopolitan	Monthly	2,679,000
First for Women	Weekly	2,394,000
Southern Living	Monthly	2,385,000
U.S. News & World Report	Weekly	2,352,000
Smithsonian	Monthly	2,204,000
Glamour	Monthly	2,012,000
Field & Stream	Monthly	2,003,000

Canada

Name	Publication period	Circulation
Reader's Digest	Monthly	1,556,000
Chatelaine	Monthly	1,087,000
TV Guide	Weekly	810,000
National Geographic	Monthly	781,000
Maclean's	Weekly	597,000

*Not including newspaper supplements or magazines intended exclusively for members of an organization.
Source: Audit Bureau of Circulations, June 1991.

1741 in Philadelphia and lasted only three months. Mathew Carey, a Philadelphia printer and bookseller, started two early American magazines, *The Columbian* in 1786 and *The American Museum* in 1787.

In 1830, Louis A. Godey founded *Godey's Lady's Book,* the first American magazine for women. Sarah Josepha Hale edited the magazine, which helped shape the tastes of thousands of women. Among the first influential intellectual magazines was *The Dial,* published in the early 1840's by New England transcendentalists and edited by Margaret Fuller (see **Transcendentalism**). Around the mid-1800's, a number of important magazines were started. Frank Leslie began *Leslie's Weekly,* which was one of the first magazines to feature many illustrations. *Atlantic Monthly,* launched in 1857, was first edited by the famous poet James Russell Lowell. During the Civil War (1861-1865), many readers turned to a magazine called *Harper's Weekly* for its drawings of the battlefront.

In the late 1800's and early 1900's, reformers who exposed conditions in business, industry, and politics wrote for *Everybody's Magazine* and *McClure's Magazine.* These writers, called *muckrakers,* included Ray Stannard Baker, Lincoln Steffens, and Ida M. Tarbell. *McClure's Magazine,* founded by S. S. McClure, became one of the first successful inexpensive magazines. Before this time, magazines had been published mainly for wealthy people. *The Nation,* founded in 1865 as a liberal weekly newspaper, later became a magazine. The *La-*

dies' Home Journal, founded in 1883, worked for social causes under the editorship of Edward W. Bok after 1889. Important literary publications started during the early 1900's included *Vanity Fair* in 1914 and *The New Yorker* in 1925.

Henry R. Luce, who founded *Life, Time, Sports Illustrated,* and other magazines, was one of the leading magazine publishers of the 1900's. Another leading publisher, John H. Johnson, began publishing *Negro Digest* in 1942. Johnson later founded several other magazines written chiefly for black readers.

During the 1920's and 1930's, such *general magazines* as the *Saturday Evening Post* ranked as the major means of nationwide communication. These publications featured text and photographs on a wide range of subjects. But after the widespread growth of television in the 1950's, advertisers began to promote their products on TV rather than in general magazines. Television enabled the advertisers to reach larger audiences and to emphasize their message with motion. Since that time, the lack of advertising and an increase in overall costs have caused many general magazines to stop publishing or to publish less frequently.

Every year, many magazines are started and others die out. To last, a magazine must have an editorial content that remains useful to an audience. It also needs advertisers who want to reach that audience and believe they can do so most effectively by advertising in the magazine.

A magazine publisher once needed relatively little money to launch a publication. For example, two prominent American magazines, *The New Yorker* and *Time,* were started in the 1920's with little funds. But today, high costs—particularly those involving production and mailing—require a great deal of money to start and maintain a magazine.

To cut expenses, many magazines reduced the number and size of their pages during the 1960's and early 1970's. Many magazines that were launched during those years aimed for a small, specialized audience rather than a large readership. For example, such periodicals as *New York* were started mainly for residents of a particular geographical area. Such specialization enables publishers to cut the cost of production and postage and to attract advertisers who want to reach certain groups. Many publishers use statistical studies of the population to find possible subscribers.

Richard A. Schwarzlose

Related articles in *World Book* include:

Biographies

Adams, Samuel H.	Lowell, James R.
Buckley, William F., Jr.	Luce, Henry R.
Curtis, Cyrus H. K.	Monroe, Harriet
Fuller, Margaret	Munsey, Frank A.
Godey, Louis A.	Ross, Harold W.
Grosvenor, Gilbert H.	Sherwood, Robert E.
Hale, Sarah J.	Steffens, Lincoln
Howells, William D.	Steinem, Gloria
Johnson, John H.	Tarbell, Ida M.

Other related articles

Advertising	Literature for children
Commercial art	(Children's magazines)
Editorial	Trade publication
Journalism	Writing

Magazine is a military and naval term for a protected building or storage room for ammunition. The term comes from an Arabic word meaning *storehouse*. The ammunition supply chamber of a repeating rifle or machine gun is also called a magazine.

Shore magazines are usually concrete buildings shaped like beehives. They are half buried in the ground and are covered with earth. Some powder magazines are built in many compartments, each of which is covered with a light roof. If an explosion occurs, the damage will be confined to a small space and the force will move upward when the roof gives way.

On ships, magazines are placed as far as possible from the engines and firerooms and far below the water line. They are made up of many watertight rooms with steel walls. In the tropics, magazines are cooled by ventilators that pipe cool air from a refrigerator. Other pipes take away hot air.   Ann Alexander Warren

Magdalene. See Mary Magdalene.

Magellan, *muh JEHL uhn,* **Ferdinand** (1480?-1521), was a Portuguese sea captain who commanded the first expedition that sailed around the world. His voyage provided the first positive proof that the earth is round. Magellan did not live to complete the voyage, but his imaginative planning and courageous leadership made the entire expedition possible. Many scholars consider it the greatest navigational feat in history.

Early life

Magellan was born about 1480 in northern Portugal. His name in Portuguese was Fernão de Magalhães. His parents, who were members of the nobility, died when he was about 10 years old. At the age of 12, Magellan became a page to Queen Leonor at the royal court. Such a position commonly served as a means of education for sons of the Portuguese nobility.

At the court, Magellan learned about the voyages of such explorers as Christopher Columbus of Italy and Vasco da Gama of Portugal. He also learned the fundamentals of navigation. In 1496, Magellan was promoted to the rank of squire and became a clerk in the marine department. There, he helped outfit ships for trade along the west coast of Africa.

Magellan first went to sea in 1505, when he sailed to India with the fleet of Francisco de Almeida, Portugal's first viceroy to that country. In 1506, Magellan went on an expedition sent by Almeida to the east coast of Africa to strengthen Portuguese bases there. The next year, he returned to India, where he participated in trade and in several naval battles against Turkish fleets.

In 1509, Magellan sailed with a Portuguese fleet to Melaka, a commercial center in what is now Malaysia. The Malays attacked the Portuguese who went ashore, and Magellan helped rescue his comrades. In 1511, he took part in an expedition that conquered Melaka. After this victory, a Portuguese fleet sailed farther east to the Spice Islands (also called the Molucca Islands). Portugal claimed the islands at this time. Magellan's close personal friend Francisco Serrão went along on the voyage to the Spice Islands and wrote to Magellan, describing the route and the island of Ternate. Serrão's letters helped establish in Magellan's mind the location of the Spice Islands, which later became the destination of his great voyage.

Magellan returned to Portugal in 1513. He then joined a military expedition to Morocco. On this expedition, Magellan suffered a wound that made him limp for the rest of his life.

Voyage around the world

Planning the expedition. After returning to Portugal from Morocco, Magellan sought the support of King Manuel I for a voyage to the Spice Islands. The best maps available had convinced Magellan that he could reach the Spice Islands by sailing south of South America. Magellan believed such a route would be shorter than the eastward voyage around the southern tip of Africa and across the Indian Ocean. However, Manuel disliked Magellan and refused to support the proposed voyage.

Magellan then studied astronomy and navigation for about two years in Porto in northern Portugal. In Porto, he met Ruy Faleiro, an astronomer and geographer who strongly influenced his ideas. Magellan and Faleiro concluded from their studies that the Spice Islands lay in territory that had been awarded to Spain in 1494 (see **Line of Demarcation**). Therefore, Magellan decided to seek support for his plans from the king of Spain.

In 1517, Magellan went to Spain. There, he presented his proposal for visiting the Spice Islands as part of a westward circumnavigation of the earth. The next year, Magellan convinced Charles I of Spain to support such a voyage. The king promised Magellan a fifth of the profits from the voyage to the Spice Islands, plus a salary.

Preparations for the expedition took more than a year. The Spaniards became suspicious of Magellan, partly because he recruited many Portuguese sailors. As a result, the king forced Magellan to replace most of the Portuguese with Spanish crewmen.

The voyage begins. On Sept. 20, 1519, Magellan set sail from Sanlúcar de Barrameda in southern Spain. Magellan commanded a total of 241 men and a fleet of five ships, the *Concepción, San Antonio, Santiago, Trinidad,* and *Victoria.* Dissatisfaction among the crewmen plagued the voyage from the beginning, and hostility among the Spaniards toward Magellan grew rapidly. About a month after the voyage began, the Spanish captain of the *San Antonio* challenged Magellan's authority, and Magellan had the captain arrested.

The fleet sailed across the Atlantic Ocean to the coast of Brazil. The ships then followed the South American coast to the bay where Rio de Janeiro now stands. They remained there for two weeks and then sailed south in search of a passage to the Pacific Ocean. However, the ships could not find a passage before the end of summer in the Southern Hemisphere. In late March 1520, Magellan's fleet anchored for the winter at Puerto San Julián in what is now southern Argentina.

Real Academia de Bellas Artes de San Fernando, Madrid, Spain

Ferdinand Magellan

During the winter, a storm destroyed the *Santiago.* In addition, a mutiny broke out shortly after the men set up their winter quarters. Magellan and loyal crew members put down the mutiny and executed the leader. They also marooned two other mutineers when the fleet sailed again.

Magellan and his crew resumed their voyage on Oct. 18, 1520. Three days later, they discovered the passage to the Pacific—a passage known ever since as the Strait of Magellan. As the fleet sailed through the strait, the crew of the *San Antonio* mutinied and returned to Spain. On November 28, the three remaining ships sailed out of the strait and into the ocean. Magellan named the ocean the Pacific, which means *peaceful,* because it appeared calm compared with the stormy Atlantic.

Sailing across the Pacific involved great hardship for Magellan and his crew. They were the first Europeans ever to sail across the Pacific, and it was far larger than anyone had imagined. They sailed for 98 days without seeing any land except two uninhabited islands. Their food gave out and their water supply became contaminated. They ate rats, ox hides, and sawdust to avoid starvation. Most of the crew suffered from scurvy, a disease caused by the lack of fresh fruits and vegetables. Nineteen men died before the fleet reached Guam on March 6, 1521.

Conflicts with the people of Guam and the nearby island of Rota prevented Magellan from fully resupplying his ships. But the crew seized enough food and water to continue on to the Philippines.

Magellan and his crew remained in the Philippines for several weeks, and close relations developed between them and the islanders. Magellan took special pride in converting many of the people to Christianity. Unfortunately, however, he involved himself in rivalries among the people. On April 27, 1521, Magellan was killed when he took part in a battle between rival Filipino groups on the island of Mactan.

The end of the voyage. After the battle on Mactan, only about 110 of the original crew members remained —too few to man three ships. Therefore, the men abandoned the *Concepción,* and the two remaining vessels sailed southward to the Spice Islands. There, the ships were loaded with spices. The leaders of the fleet then decided that the two ships should make separate return voyages.

The *Trinidad,* under the command of Gonzalo Gómez de Espinosa, tried to sail eastward across the Pacific to the Isthmus of Panama. Bad weather and disease disrupted the voyage, and more than half of the crew of the *Trinidad* died. The surviving members of the crew were forced to return to the Spice Islands, where the Portuguese imprisoned them.

The *Victoria,* commanded by Juan Sebastián del Cano, continued its westward voyage back to Spain. Like the *Trinidad,* the *Victoria* experienced great hardship, and many of the crew died of malnutrition and starvation. The *Victoria* finally reached Sanlúcar de Barrameda on Sept. 6, 1522, nearly three years after the voyage had begun. Only Del Cano and 17 other survivors returned with the ship.

Results of the voyage. One of the crew members who returned with Del Cano was an Italian named Antonio Pigafetta. He had faithfully written down the events of the voyage, and his journal is the chief source of information about the expedition. According to Pigafetta, the voyage covered 14,460 leagues (50,610 miles or 81,449 kilometers). Pigafetta praised Magellan for his courage and navigational skill. However, nearly everyone else at the time gave Del Cano the credit for the voyage. The Portuguese considered Magellan a traitor, and the Spanish condemned Magellan after they received reports of his harshness and of his errors in navigation.

Magellan failed to find a short route to the Spice Islands, but his voyage contributed greatly to knowledge about the earth. In addition, the discovery of the Strait

The voyage of Magellan 1519 to 1522

This map traces Magellan's search for a western passage to the Spice Islands. He became the first European to sail across the Pacific Ocean. Magellan was killed on the island of Mactan in 1521. One of his ships, commanded by Juan Sebastián del Cano, completed the voyage.

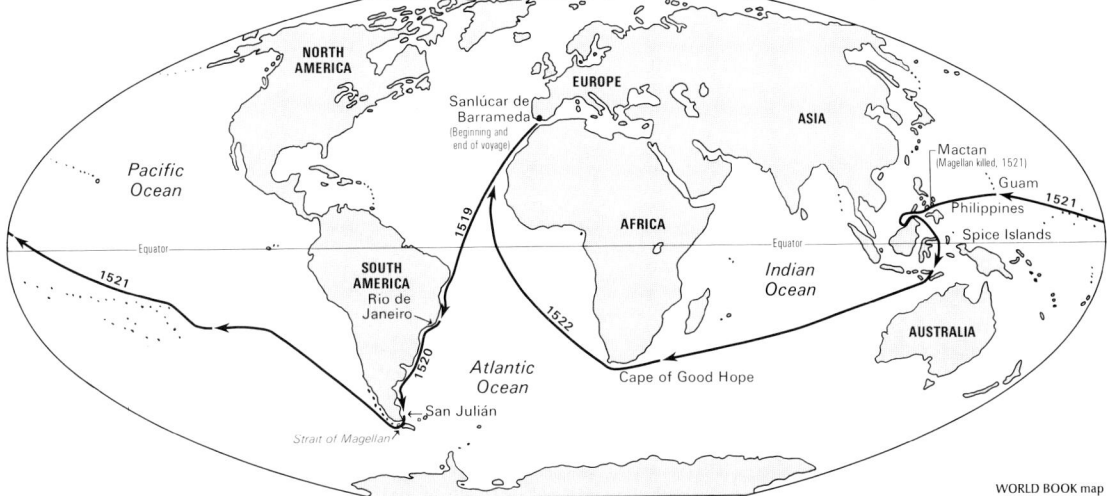

WORLD BOOK map

Detail of an engraving (1800's); Granger Collection

Magellan died in battle on the island of Mactan in the Philippines. Although he is remembered for leading the first naval expedition around the world, he did not complete the voyage.

of Magellan led to future European voyages to explore the vast Pacific. John Parker

See also **Exploration** (Magellan's globe-circling expedition).

Additional resources

Hargrove, Jim. *Ferdinand Magellan.* Childrens Pr., 1990. For younger readers.
Joyner, Tim. *Magellan.* International Marine, 1992.
Stefoff, Rebecca. *Ferdinand Magellan and the Discovery of the World Ocean.* Chelsea Hse., 1990. Also suitable for younger readers.

Magellan, *muh JEHL uhn,* **Strait of,** is a narrow, rough waterway that separates the islands of Tierra del Fuego from the mainland of South America. The Strait of Magellan is almost at the southern end of the continent.

The Strait of Magellan is located at the southern tip of South America. The strait experiences high winds and heavy rains throughout the year.

WORLD BOOK maps

In 1520, Ferdinand Magellan, the Portuguese explorer, led the first European expedition through the strait during the first voyage around the world.

The Strait of Magellan is 350 miles (563 kilometers) long and varies from 2 to 20 miles (3 to 32 kilometers) in width. Before the Panama Canal opened, the strait and Cape Horn were the shortest water routes from the Atlantic Ocean to the Pacific Ocean. Jerry R. Williams

See also **Cape Horn; Magellan, Ferdinand.**

Magellanic Clouds, *MAJ uh LAN ihk,* are two galaxies visible in the Southern Hemisphere as small, hazy patches of light. They are the galaxies closest to the Milky Way, the galaxy that contains the sun, the earth, and the rest of our solar system. The Large Magellanic Cloud is about 160,000 light-years away from the earth, and the Small Magellanic Cloud is about 180,000 light-years away. A light-year is the distance that light travels in one year—about 5.88 trillion miles (9.46 trillion kilometers).

Astronomers classify the Magellanic Clouds as *irregular galaxies* because the distribution of the stars within them does not follow a particular pattern. The Magellanic Clouds contain billions of stars, but individual stars can be distinguished only with the most powerful telescopes. As a result, the galaxies appear cloudy to the naked eye. The Magellanic Clouds also contain a huge quantity of gas. New stars are constantly forming from this gas, which is composed mainly of hydrogen. In addition, much of the light from the Magellanic Clouds comes from young, extremely luminous, hot blue stars that are surrounded by glowing clouds of this gas.

Because they are visible only in the Southern Hemisphere, the Magellanic Clouds were long unknown to astronomers in the Northern Hemisphere. They were first recorded in the early 1500's during the circumglobal voyage of the Portuguese explorer Ferdinand Magellan, after whom they were named. However, it was not until the early 1900's that the clouds were recognized as galaxies outside the Milky Way. Mark Morris

Maggiore, Lake. See **Lake Maggiore.**

Maggot, *MAG uht,* is the larva, or young, of many kinds of flies. The maggot has a soft body that usually tapers toward the front. It looks somewhat like a worm or caterpillar. It has no legs and no distinct head. Maggots move by wriggling or flipping their bodies. They are usually white but may be colored. Most maggots live buried in their food. Some are scavengers and live in dead or decaying matter. Others are parasites in animal and plant tissue. Still others prey on insects.

Sandra J. Glover

See also **Fly** (The life of a fly); **Larva.**

Magi, *MAY jy* or *MAJ eye,* were the hereditary members of a priestly class from Media, an ancient kingdom located in what is now northern Iran. A single member of the class was called *Magus.* The Magi were known for practicing magic, interpreting omens and dreams, and offering astrological sacrifices.

The Magi's vast knowledge of rituals gained them the reputation as the only true priests of Zoroastrianism, an ancient Persian religion founded by a prophet named Zoroaster. It is not known whether the Magi influenced Zoroaster, or if they became his followers. The Magi were said to keep watch upon a "Mount of the Lord" from generation to generation until a great star appeared that would signal the coming of a savior. From this tradition comes the narrative from the New Testament of the wise men, who followed that star to Bethlehem and presented gifts of gold, frankincense, and myrrh to the baby Jesus. According to one tradition, there were three wise men—Melchior, Balthasar, and Gaspar. The Magi are frequently connected with Persian religious tales and are often shown in early Christian art wearing Persian clothes.   Robert William Smith

Magic is the supposed use of unnatural or superhuman power by a person to try to control human actions or natural events. Magic often seems to achieve results, but the results actually have other causes. For example, a person might cast a magic spell to make an enemy sick. The enemy may learn about the spell, become frightened, and actually feel ill.

People throughout the world have practiced magic from the dawn of history. But beginning in the 1600's, science has provided an increasingly greater understanding of the true causes of natural events. This increased scientific knowledge has reduced people's dependence on magic. But many people in nonindustrial societies still believe in magic. Even in industrial societies, many people still trust in such forms of magic as astrology and fortunetelling.

The word *magic* also refers to entertainment in which the performer does tricks of so-called magic. In such entertainment, neither the magician nor the audience believes that the performer has supernatural powers. For information on magical performances, see **Magician.**

Elements of magic

The practice of magic includes the use of special words, actions, and objects. Most magic also involves a person called a magician, who claims to have supernatural powers.

Magic words. To work most magic, the magician sings or speaks special words in a certain order. These words are called *incantations* or *spells.* Some spells form prayers to demons, spirits, or other supernatural forces. Many societies believe the magic will not work unless the magician recites the spells perfectly. Other magic words have no meaning, though they supposedly possess power when spoken by a magician.

Magic actions accompany the words spoken in performing much magic. Many of these movements act out the desired effect of the magic. For example, a magician trying to make rain fall may sprinkle water on the ground. The magician's combined words and actions form a ceremony called a *rite* or *ritual.*

Magic objects include certain plants, stones, and other things with supposed supernatural powers. Any such object may be called a *fetish* (see **Fetish**). But this term often refers to an object—for example, a carving or a dried snake—honored by a tribe for its magic powers. Many tribes believe fetishes have magic power because spirits live in these objects.

Many people carry magic objects called *amulets, charms,* or *talismans* to protect themselves from harm (see **Amulet**). Many amulets and talismans are stones or rings engraved with magic symbols.

The magician. In some societies, nearly everyone knows how to work some magic. In other societies, only experts practice magic. Magicians may be called *medi-*cine *men, shamans, sorcerers,* or *witch doctors* (see **Shaman**). In many societies, magicians must inherit their powers. In others, any person may become a magician by studying the magical arts.

Many societies believe magicians must observe certain rules and *taboos* (forbidden actions) for their spells to work. For example, they may be required not to eat various foods or to avoid sexual activity for a certain period before the ceremony.

Kinds of magic

Many anthropologists classify magic as *homeopathic* or *contagious,* according to its basic principle. The Scottish anthropologist Sir James G. Frazer first described these two types of magic in his famous book *The Golden Bough* (1890).

Some people divide magic into *black magic* and *white magic.* Black magic harms people, but white magic helps them. Witches usually practice black magic. But a saint may cure a sick person using white magic.

Homeopathic magic is based on the belief that like produces like. In this type of magic, also called *imitative magic,* magicians act out or imitate what they want to happen. They often use a model or miniature of whatever they want to influence. For example, a fisherman may make a model of a fish and pretend he is netting it. He believes this ritual will assure him a good catch. In some European folk dances, the dancers leap high into the air to make their crops grow tall. People once believed that yellow flowers would cure *jaundice,* a yellowish discoloration of the body.

Many taboos come from homeopathic magic. People avoid certain harmless things because they resemble various harmful things. For example, Eskimo parents might warn their sons against playing a string game, such as *cat's cradle,* in which children loop string around their fingers. Playing such games might cause the children's fingers to become tangled in the harpoon lines they will use as adults.

Ray Manley, Shostal

A witch doctor is an important member of many African communities. Witch doctors perform magical ceremonies to heal the sick and protect people from harm.

Contagious magic comes from the belief that after a person has had contact with certain things, they will continue to influence that person. The most common examples of contagious magic involve parts of the body that have been removed, such as fingernails, hair, and teeth. A person's nails and hair supposedly can affect the rest of that person's body long after they have been cut off. A person can injure an enemy by damaging a lock of hair or a piece of clothing from the victim. A magician can even cripple an enemy by placing a sharp object in that person's footprint.

People who believe in contagious magic fear that an enemy can gain power over them by obtaining parts of their body. Therefore, they carefully dispose of their nails, hair, teeth, and even their body wastes.

Witches and voodoo magicians often practice a type of homeopathic magic called *envoûtement.* The magician makes a doll or some other likeness of an enemy. The magician harms the enemy by sticking pins into the doll or injuring it in some other way. In some societies, the doll includes a lock of hair or a piece of clothing from the enemy. This type of envoûtement is a combination of homeopathic and contagious magic.

Why people believe in magic

People turn to magic chiefly as a form of insurance—that is, they use it along with actions that actually bring results. For example, hunters may use a hunting charm. But they also use their hunting skills and knowledge of animals. The charm may give hunters the extra confidence they need to hunt even more successfully than they would without it. If they shoot a lot of game, they credit the charm for their success. Many events occur naturally without magic. Crops grow without it, and sick people get well without it. But if people use magic to bring a good harvest or to cure a patient, they may believe the magic was responsible.

People also tend to forget magic's failures and to be impressed by its apparent successes. They may consider magic successful if it appears to work only 10 per cent of the time. Even when magic fails, people often explain the failure without doubting the power of the magic. They may say that the magician made a mistake in reciting the spell or that another magician cast a more powerful spell against the magician.

Many anthropologists believe that people have faith in magic because they feel a need to believe in it. People may turn to magic to reduce their fear and uncertainty if they feel they have no control over the outcome of a situation. For example, farmers use knowledge and skill when they plant their fields. But they know that weather, insects, or diseases might ruin the crops. So farmers in some societies may also plant a charm or perform a magic rite to ensure a good harvest.

History

Ancient times. The use of magic goes back at least as far as 50,000 B.C. About that time, prehistoric people buried cave bears, probably as a magic rite. Scientists believe that much prehistoric art had magical purposes. Hunters, for example, probably used cave paintings of animals in rites intended to help them hunt the animals.

Magic was important to the ancient Egyptians, who used amulets, magic figures, and rites. The ancient

Greeks and Romans tried to tell the future from dreams. They also consulted priests called *oracles,* who interpreted advice from the gods (see **Oracle**).

According to one legend, the Three Wise Men who visited the baby Jesus were astrologers who located Him by magic use of the stars (see **Magi**). The Bible has many references to magic, sorcery, and witchcraft.

During the Middle Ages, nearly all Europeans believed in magic. The clergy considered magic sinful but believed in its power. The so-called science of *alchemy* included much magic (see **Alchemy**). Alchemists hoped to discover the *philosopher's stone,* a magic substance that could change iron, lead, and other metals into gold. They also sought the *elixir of life,* a miraculous substance that could cure disease and lengthen life.

Many men joined a secret brotherhood called the *Rosicrucians,* an early version of the present-day Rosicrucian Order. The Rosicrucians studied magic lore and devoted themselves to curing the sick and helping people in other ways. The Masons, another secret group, also had elements of magic in their rituals.

From the 1500's to the 1700's, belief in magic continued widespread. Even highly educated people believed in its power. The Swiss physician Philippus Paracelsus, for example, experimented with alchemy and believed in the power of talismans. Sir Isaac Newton,

Bettmann Archive

Tarot cards are used in fortunetelling. The cards above are from a French deck of the Middle Ages. The lovers card, *left,* usually indicates harmony. The strength card, showing a woman taming a lion, often stands for the power of gentleness.

the famous English astronomer and mathematician, studied alchemy. Thousands of persons were tried and executed as witches during this period.

Many forms of magic tried to predict the future. People believed a person's character could be described or the future foretold in various ways. These methods included studying the palm of a person's hand, facial features, or even the moles on a person's skin. Some people used *tarot cards,* a set of playing cards with special pictures, for fortunetelling.

After about 1600, advances in science gradually weakened people's belief in magic. But as late as the 1700's, the Italian magician Count Allesandro di Cagliostro won fame for his powers. Cagliostro traveled through Europe selling love potions and elixirs of life.

Magic today still plays an important role in the life of many ethnic groups. Even among modern peoples, magic has many followers with an interest in such subjects as astrology, fortunetelling, and witchcraft. For example, many people who have faith in astrology read their daily horoscope in a newspaper.

Countless people believe in superstitions that involve forms of magic. Some persons carry a fetish, such as a rabbit's foot or a lucky penny. They believe these articles have magic power to bring good luck. Homeopathic magic appears in the superstition that a newborn baby must be carried upstairs before it is carried down. This act supposedly guarantees that the child will rise in the world and have a successful life.

Magic also survives in much of today's advertising. The manufacturers of such products as gasolines and headache remedies boast of new, secret ingredients. Advertisements may indirectly suggest that a mouthwash or a toothpaste will magically transform an unpopular person into a popular one. Many people buy these and other products for the magic qualities suggested by such advertising.   Alan Dundes

Related articles in *World Book* include:

Astrology	Necromancy
Augur	Occultism
Clairvoyance	Omen
Divination	Palmistry
Evil eye	Psychical research
Exorcism	Superstition
Fortunetelling	Taboo
Genie	Voodoo
Kabbalah	Witchcraft
Mind reading	

Magician is an entertainer who performs tricks that seem impossible. Magicians make audiences believe they can pluck dollar bills out of the air and change one orange into three. They appear to read people's thoughts and produce bowls of goldfish from a scarf. Magicians even seem to make people disappear.

Many people think a magician's hands move so quickly that the audience cannot follow the actions and see how tricks are performed. But the hand is not quicker than the eye. Most magicians avoid rapid hand movements because they know such motions confuse people and weaken the effect of the trick.

Magicians base their tricks upon a variety of techniques from science and the arts that they cleverly use to deceive the mind and eye. The magician creates a drama designed to create the illusion that impossible things are happening. Creating this illusion involves acting ability, skillful physical movements, and the basic principles of such fields as chemistry, optics, psychology, and physics. Magicians use carefully planned actions and words to distract the audience by centering its attention on the wrong place at the right time. In addition, the spectators do not know that a magician uses various secret devices.

Professional magicians perform on television, in theaters, comedy clubs, night clubs, and restaurants. They frequently appear at trade shows, banquets, business sales meetings, and conventions. Many young people find magic a fascinating hobby, and some earn money by doing tricks at birthday parties and other gatherings. Young magicians can gain poise and self-confidence by performing before an audience. They also may develop mental alertness and skill in using their hands.

Kinds of magic

Magic includes a number of types of tricks. The most common kinds of magic are (1) sleight of hand, (2) close-up magic, (3) illusions, (4) escape magic, and (5) mentalist magic.

Sleight of hand, also called *conjuring, legerdemain,* and *prestidigitation,* requires especially skillful hand movements. The oldest known sleight-of-hand routine, which was performed in ancient Egypt and remains popular today, involves several small balls. The magician makes the balls appear, disappear, or change size while they are hidden under inverted cups or dishes. Gali Gali, a modern Egyptian magician, ended the trick by changing the balls into baby chicks. Paul Rosini, an American magician, turned the cups right side up and then poured out wine.

More varieties of sleight-of-hand tricks can be performed with a deck of cards than with any other objects. Cardini, a British magician, produced fans of cards at his fingertips. Then he made lighted cigarettes appear, followed by cigars and a pipe. Other magicians have used doves, handkerchiefs, clocks and watches, jewels, and lighted electric bulbs.

Close-up magic is performed with spectators close to the performer, sometimes surrounding the magician or at a table only a short distance away. In close-up magic, magicians work with cards, coins, sponges, and other small objects. For example, every time the magician Albert Goshman lifted a saltshaker, a silver coin appeared beneath it. Johnny Paul, another magician, borrowed a piece of paper currency from a spectator and put it at one end of the table. Then he made the money move across the table into his hand.

Illusions. Magicians called *illusionists* perform large-scale tricks with the aid of human assistants, animals, and elaborate equipment. One of the most famous illu-

Milbourne Christopher Collection

The "fantastic suitcase" was an amazing illusion developed by Robert-Houdin, a famous French magician of the 1800's. Robert-Houdin pulled birds, cages, hats, and pans from a thin suitcase. He ended the trick by lifting out his young son.

 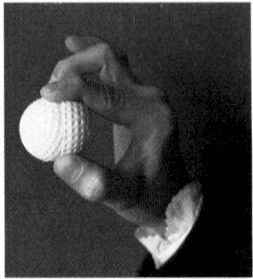 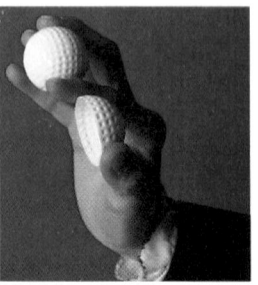 

Ken Baker's Magicland (WORLD BOOK photos by Steinkamp/Ballogg)

One ball changes into two in this sleight-of-hand trick. The magician uses a rubber ball and a metal shell that fits over it, as shown in the first photo above. The spectators believe they see one actual ball. The next two photos show the magician secretly separating the shell from the ball. The magician then displays the shell and the ball as if they were really two balls.

sions is sawing a woman in half. In 1921, magician Horace Goldin placed his assistant in a wooden box with her head, hands, and feet extending out through holes. He then sawed through the box without harming the body. Harry Blackstone, Jr., a modern illusionist, performs the same illusion by placing a young lady on a thin table without any covering. He then saws through her with a huge electric buzz saw. Although a board placed beneath her is cleanly cut in half, the lady is unharmed.

The first great modern illusionist was Robert-Houdin, a French magician who performed in the mid-1800's. Robert-Houdin became known as the father of modern magic because he contributed so many new tricks. For example, he suspended his young son in the air horizontally, with the boy's arm resting on the top of an upright

pole. Later, Adelaide Herrmann, a British illusionist, also performed this trick.

The three best-known illusionists in the United States during the 1900's were probably Harry Blackstone, Harry Kellar, and Howard Thurston. Blackstone made a camel disappear. Kellar featured an illusion in which he made a cage containing a live canary disappear in full view of the audience. Thurston fired a pistol, and an automobile on the stage immediately vanished.

Escape magic. Some magicians specialize in making apparently impossible escapes from various predicaments. The most famous escape performer was Harry Houdini, an American, who freed himself from police handcuffs, leg irons, and locked jail cells. He also let himself be handcuffed and placed in a crate that was nailed shut and lowered into a river. Houdini escaped in a few seconds. See **Houdini, Harry.**

Mentalist magic. Some magicians, called *mentalists,* perform mind-reading tricks and predict future events. Mentalists call out the names of strangers in an audience and duplicate designs drawn on a piece of paper by spectators and then sealed in envelopes. They also write the correct total of numbers selected later by volunteers. During a television broadcast, Dunninger, a famous American mentalist, seemingly read the mind of a stranger in a submerged submarine.

Becoming a magician

People enjoy magic because of its mystery. If they know how a trick is done, it loses its appeal—and so magicians seldom reveal the secrets of their tricks. But basic methods can be learned from books on magic. Some of these books can be obtained from general bookstores or from public libraries. Other such books are sold by stores that specialize in equipment for magicians.

Two organizations—the Society of American Magicians (S.A.M.) and the International Brotherhood of Magicians (I.B.M.)—have clubs in many cities of the United States and Canada. The S.A.M. mailing address is P.O. Drawer 1547, Mango, FL 33550-1547. The headquarters of the I.B.M. are at 103 Main St., Bluffton, OH 45817. Each group publishes a monthly magazine and holds an annual convention. At the annual convention, magicians give lectures and demonstrate new tricks, and dealers in magicians' supplies display new equipment.

Philip R. Willmarth

Houdini Museum, Niagara Falls, Ont.

Harry Houdini, an American magician, specialized in escaping from apparently impossible predicaments. In the water torture trick, *above,* Houdini freed himself from a box filled with water.

Additional resources

Blackstone, Harry, Jr., and others. *The Blackstone Book of Magic & Illusion.* Newmarket, 1985. Also suitable for older readers.
Eldin, Peter. *The Magic Handbook.* Messner, 1986.

Maginot Line, *MAZH uh noh,* is a fortified line of defense along the eastern border of France. It was constructed after World War I (1914-1918). Forts stand aboveground, flanked by pillboxes and barbed-wire entanglements. Underground chambers provide space for communications systems, hospitals, storerooms, garages, and living quarters for officers and men. In May 1940, the Germans invaded France through Belgium, passing north of the Maginot Line. In three weeks, they swept past and then behind the line, and captured it from the rear. The Maginot Line was overhauled in the 1950's for possible use in case of atomic war. See also **Siegfried Line.**   Theodore Ropp

Magma. See **Igneous rock; Rock** (Igneous rock); **Volcano** (How a volcano is formed; illustration).

Magna Carta, *MAG nuh KAHR tuh,* is a document that marked a decisive step forward in the development of constitutional government and legal ideas in England. In later centuries, much of the rest of the world also benefited from it because many countries followed English models in creating their own governments. These countries include the United States and Canada. The Latin words *Magna Carta* mean *Great Charter.*

English barons forced King John to approve the charter in June 1215 at Runnymede, southwest of London. In the charter, the king granted many rights to the English aristocracy. But the ordinary English people gained little. In later centuries, however, Magna Carta became a model for those who demanded democratic government and individual rights for all. In its own time, the greatest value of Magna Carta was that it limited royal power and made it clear that even the king had to obey the law.

Reasons for the charter. From the Norman invasion of England in 1066 through the 1100's, most of the kings who ruled England were able and strong. They usually tried to govern justly and respected feudal law. Under feudal law, nobles called *barons* received land in return for military and other services to the king. Law and custom established the barons' duties and what was expected of the king. But there was no actual control over the king's power. When John became king in 1199, he exercised his power even more forcefully than earlier kings. He demanded more military service than they did. He sold royal positions to the highest bidders. He demanded larger amounts of money without consulting the barons, which was contrary to feudal custom. He decided cases according to his wishes, and people who lost cases in his court had to pay crushing penalties.

English barons and church leaders began to express dissatisfaction with John's rule early in his reign. Their unhappiness grew when he lost most of the English possessions in France in warfare lasting from 1202 to 1206. In 1213, a group met at St. Albans, near London, and drew up a list of demands based in part on the coronation charter of Henry I, who had been king from 1100 to 1135. After John lost an important battle against France at Bouvines (in what is now western Belgium) in 1214, civil war broke out in England. John saw that he could not defeat his opponents' army, and so he agreed

to a set of articles on June 15, 1215. Four days later, the articles were *engrossed* (written out in legal form) as a royal charter. Copies of the charter were distributed throughout the kingdom.

Promises in the charter. Magna Carta contained 63 articles, most of which pledged the king to uphold feudal customs. These articles chiefly benefited the barons and other landholders. One article granted the church freedom from royal interference. A few articles guaranteed rights to residents of towns. Ordinary free people and peasants were hardly mentioned in the charter, even though they made up by far the largest part of England's population.

Some articles that in 1215 applied only to feudal landholders later became important to all the people. For example, the charter stated that the king could make no special demands for money without the consent of the barons. Later, this provision was used to support the argument that no tax should be raised without the consent of Parliament.

Still other articles became foundations for modern justice. One article says that the king will not sell, deny, or delay justice. Another says that no freeman shall be imprisoned, deprived of property, exiled, or destroyed, except by the lawful judgment of his *peers* (equals) or by the law of the land. The idea of due process of law, including trial by jury, developed from these articles. In John's time, however, there was no such thing as trial by jury in criminal cases.

The charter tried to make the king keep his promises by establishing a council of barons. If the king violated the charter and ignored warnings of the council, it could raise an army to force the king to live by the charter's provisions. But these measures were unsuccessful.

The charter after 1215. Magna Carta did not end the struggle between John and the barons. Neither side intended to abide by the charter completely. Pope Innocent III canceled the charter at the king's request, and war broke out immediately. After John's death in 1216, however, his son Henry III and later English kings promised to abide by the charter. The most famous of these promises was that of Edward I in 1297. Through these promises, the charter came to be recognized as part of the fundamental law of England.

In the 1600's, members of parliament used Magna Carta to rally support in their struggle against the strong rule of the Stuart kings. These lawmakers came to view the charter as a constitutional check on royal power. They cited it as a legal support for the argument that there could be no laws or taxation without the consent of Parliament. These members of Parliament used the charter to demand guarantees of trial by jury, safeguards against unfair imprisonment, and other rights.

In the 1700's, Sir William Blackstone, a famous lawyer, set down these ideals as legal rights of the people in his famous *Commentaries on the Laws of England* (see **Blackstone, Sir William**). Also in the 1700's, colonists carried these English ideals on legal and political rights to America. The ideals eventually became part of the framework of the Constitution of the United States.

Four originals of the 1215 charter remain. Two are in the British Library in London, one in Salisbury Cathedral, and one in Lincoln Cathedral. For many years, the document was commonly known as *Magna Charta.* But in

1946, the British government officially adopted the Latin spelling, *Magna Carta.*   Emily Zack Tabuteau

See also **Feudalism; John** (king of England), **Runnymede.**

Additional resources

Magna Carta and the Idea of Liberty. Ed. by James C. Holt. Krieger, 1982. First published in 1972.
Swindler, William F. *Magna Carta: Legend and Legacy.* Bobbs, 1965.

Magnesia, *mag NEE shuh* or *mag NEE zhuh,* is a white, tasteless substance. It is a chemical compound made up of magnesium and oxygen and is also called *magnesium oxide.* A form of magnesia is used in medicines to aid digestion. Manufacturers also use magnesia in refining metals from their ores and in making crucibles, insulating material, and special cements.

After magnesia is swallowed, it is converted by water in the digestive system to *magnesium hydroxide.* Magnesium hydroxide is a good antacid because it neutralizes excess stomach acid without releasing carbon dioxide. This property also makes it a good antidote against poisoning by acids. In acid poisoning, a build-up of gas in the stomach may cause a rupture. Doctors may also recommend *milk of magnesia,* a mixture of water and magnesium hydroxide, as a laxative.   Barbara M. Bayer

Magnesium, *mag NEE shee uhm* or *mag NEE zhee uhm,* a silver-white metal, is the lightest metal that is strong enough to use in construction. It weighs only about two-thirds as much as aluminum, another widely used light metal. Magnesium was discovered in 1808 by the English chemist Sir Humphry Davy.

Magnesium is a fairly abundant metallic element. However, pure magnesium does not occur in nature. Various minerals contain magnesium compounds. A few of these compounds, primarily magnesium chloride and magnesium sulfate, occur in dissolved form in seawater and in some pools of underground water. Seawater contains 0.13 per cent magnesium and provides a practically unlimited source of the metal. Magnesium occurs in the minerals magnesite, brucite, and dolomite, as well as in amphibole asbestos, olivine, serpentine, talc, and in certain of the other silicate minerals (see **Silicate**).

Magnesium plays a vital role in the life processes of plants and animals. Chlorophyll, which green plants use in photosynthesis, contains magnesium. Plants produce carbohydrates, a class of foods essential to living things, by means of photosynthesis. Magnesium also takes part in the duplication of substances called DNA and RNA, which have a key part in determining the heredity of all organisms (see **Heredity** [The chemical basis of heredity]). Magnesium also activates many of the enzymes that speed up chemical reactions in the human body.

Uses. Magnesium and its alloys are used in manufacturing many products. Their light weight makes them suitable for aircraft and automobile parts and for tools and equipment. Most magnesium alloys contain aluminum and zinc. These materials make magnesium alloys stronger and easier to shape. Some alloys may also contain small amounts of such elements as manganese, thorium, and zirconium that provide other properties.

Magnesium is used for a variety of nonstructural purposes because it is extremely active chemically. For example, pieces of magnesium are placed next to buried steel pipelines and water tanks. If magnesium were not present, oxygen and other chemicals in the earth would corrode the steel. Instead, the magnesium reacts with the chemicals. The pieces of magnesium can easily be replaced periodically at a cost much lower than that of replacing or repairing the steel. Protective strips of magnesium are also attached to the hulls of ships.

Steel manufacturers add magnesium to steel to remove sulfur and other impurities. In addition, magnesium is used in fireworks and flares because it burns with a brilliant white light. It also produces intense heat when it burns, making it useful for incendiary bombs.

Magnesium combines with other elements to form many useful compounds. These compounds include two commonly used medicines—milk of magnesia and Epsom salt (see **Magnesia**). Magnesium oxide resists heat and is used to line special types of furnaces. Also, magnesium oxide forms on the surface of magnesium metal and prevents it from corroding readily at low temperatures. If it were not for this protective layer, magnesium would not be a suitable structural material. Magnesium chloride is an important *catalyst* (substance that speeds up a chemical reaction) in the preparation of organic compounds. Other magnesium compounds are used in tanning leather; in dyeing textiles; and in making cement, fertilizer, and insulating materials.

Properties. Magnesium's chemical symbol is Mg. The metal belongs to the group of elements called *alkaline earth metals* (see **Element, Chemical** [Periodic table of the elements]). It has a density of 1.738 grams per cubic centimeter at 20 °C. Its atomic weight is 24.305, and its atomic number is 12. Magnesium melts at 650 °C and boils at 1090 °C.

Magnesium never occurs in nature as a pure metal because it is so active chemically. It readily combines with most acids and with many nonmetals, including nitrogen. When heated with the salts or oxides of many metals, magnesium replaces the other metal. In this process, called *reduction,* the magnesium purifies the other metal, preparing it for various uses.

How magnesium is obtained. Much of the magnesium used in the United States is recovered from seawater by the *Dow process.* In this process, lime obtained from the rock dolomite is mixed with seawater, which contains magnesium chloride. The lime and the magnesium chloride react to form magnesium hydroxide and calcium chloride. The magnesium hydroxide separates from the rest of the mixture. It is filtered out and mixed with hydrochloric acid, forming magnesium chloride and water. The water evaporates, leaving highly concentrated magnesium chloride, which is melted by being heated to a temperature above 708 °C. Then an electric current is passed through the melted compound. This kind of process is called *electrolysis* (see **Electrolysis**). The current changes the magnesium chloride into magnesium and chlorine gas. The molten magnesium is poured off and cast into forms called *ingots.*

A less widely used method of refining magnesium is known as the *ferrosilicon process* or *Pidgeon process.* This method, used primarily in Canada, involves heating dolomite in a vacuum with an alloy consisting of silicon and iron. The magnesium in the dolomite vaporizes, and then it condenses as crystals. The magnesium crystals are melted and cast into ingots.   Emily Jane Rose

Magnetic amplifier, also called a *saturable reactor,* is a device used to control large amounts of electric power. It is used where currents are too large, or other conditions are too severe, for transistor or vacuum tube amplifiers. For example, magnetic amplifiers are often used to control the speed of large motors or the brightness of airport runway lights.

A magnetic amplifier consists of two coils of wire—a *main coil* and a *control coil*—wound around an iron core. An alternating current flows through the main coil and creates a changing magnetic field around the core. This changing field limits the amount of current that can flow. But if direct current is passed through the control coil, the core becomes *saturated* (completely magnetized). The saturation cancels the limiting effect of the changing field, and enables much more current to flow through the main coil.   Glenn A. Burdick

Magnetic equator is an imaginary band that circles the earth near the geographic equator. The earth acts like a huge bar magnet whose poles lie close to the north and south geographic poles. The straight line between the poles of this imaginary magnet is called the *geomagnetic axis.* The magnetic equator lies on a plane that is at right angles to the geomagnetic axis.

An instrument called a *dipping needle* indicates the direction of the earth's magnetic field. A dipping needle is a magnetized needle mounted on a horizontal pivot so that it can swing up and down freely. At any point on the magnetic equator, the needle is horizontal. North of the magnetic equator, the north tip of the needle points downward. South of the magnetic equator, this tip points upward.   William C. Mahaney

Magnetic field. See Magnetism.

Magnetic levitation train, also called *maglev train,* is a vehicle that uses magnetic forces to travel at high speeds. Maglev trains float above a fixed track called a *guideway,* but do not touch it. The train's speed is not limited by the friction or vibration that contact with a track would cause. Maglev trains are expected to travel more than 300 miles (480 kilometers) per hour. But only low-speed maglev trains are in commercial use today.

Maglev trains have several advantages over other high-speed trains. For example, they can reach higher speeds and operate more quietly. Their guideways need little maintenance. In addition, maglev trains use elec-tricity for power and therefore produce little pollution themselves.

There are two kinds of maglev technology—*electrodynamic* and *electromagnetic.* Electrodynamic maglev uses magnetic *repulsion* (pushing away) to make the train float. Electromagnetic maglev uses magnetic attraction.

Electrodynamic maglev was invented in the early 1960's by nuclear engineer James R. Powell and physicist Gordon T. Danby of the United States. Since then, Japanese researchers have developed full-sized test models that can reach speeds over 300 miles (480 kilometers) per hour. Electrodynamic maglev trains use superconducting magnets—that is, magnets that are cooled to extremely cold temperatures and so conduct electricity without resistance. The magnets are placed on the bottom of the train. As the train moves, the magnets *induce* (create) currents in wire coils or metal sheets that are set in the guideway. The opposing magnetic force between the magnets and the induced currents lifts the vehicle. The train runs on wheels until it gains enough speed to lift off the guideway. It travels about 4 inches (10 centimeters) above the guideway.

Separate electric currents pass through other coils in the guideway. The currents produce a magnetic field that travels along the guideway, and pushes the train forward, much as an ocean wave pushes a surfer. The speed of the train remains constant as the magnetic force adjusts, even during travel uphill or downhill.

Electromagnetic maglev was developed by a group of West German companies, beginning in the early 1970's. The Germans have tested full-sized trains that run as fast as 250 miles (400 kilometers) per hour.

The underside of an electromagnetic maglev train carries electromagnets that ride beneath a T-shaped guideway. When current flows through the magnets, they are attracted upward to steel rails on the guideway. Currents flowing in wires in the steel rails create a shifting magnetic field that pushes the train forward.

An electromagnetic maglev train that uses conventional magnets travels only about $\frac{3}{8}$ inch (1 centimeter) above the track. To prevent the magnets from hitting the guideway, the lifting current must continually be adjusted by a fast-acting control system. Scientists have designed an electromagnetic maglev train that would use

WORLD BOOK diagram by J. Harlan Hunt, Koralik Associates

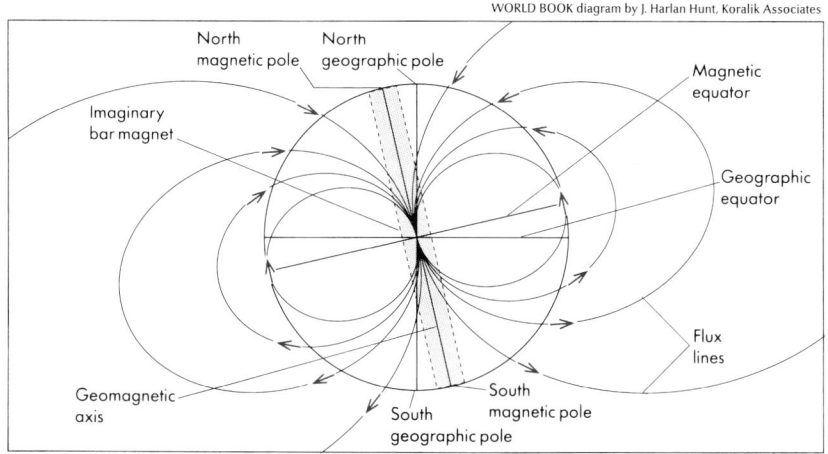

The magnetic equator is at right angles to the earth's *geomagnetic axis,* the straight line between the north and south magnetic poles. The earth's magnetic field, shown by imaginary *flux lines,* is shaped as if the earth were a bar magnet. The arrows show how a compass needle that can swing up and down aligns itself with this field.

A **maglev train** floats above a fixed track but does not touch it. Maglev trains like this one are lifted into the air when magnets that ride beneath the track are attracted upward to iron rails in the underside of the track.

© DPA from Photoreporters

superconducting magnets to lift the train about 2 inches (5 centimeters) above the track.

Low-speed maglev trains now operate in Birmingham, England, and Berlin, Germany. Researchers are developing electromagnetic and electrodynamic trains for high-speed intercity travel in Germany, Japan, the United States, and other countries.   Richard J. Gran

See also **Linear electric motor**.

Magnetic pole. See Earth (The earth's magnetism); North Pole; South Pole.

Magnetic resonance imaging (MRI) is a technique used in medicine for producing images of tissues inside the body. Physicians use these images to diagnose certain diseases, disorders, and injuries.

MRI is an important diagnostic tool because it enables physicians to identify abnormal tissue without opening the body through surgery. MRI does not expose the patient to radiation, unlike tests that use X rays. Also, MRI lets physicians see through bones and organs. MRI is safe for most people. But MRI uses a pow-

Siemens Medical Systems

Magnetic resonance imaging is used in medicine. The patient is placed inside a machine that has a huge magnet. The magnetic field causes the nuclei of certain atoms inside the body to line up. The machine then sends out a radio signal, which causes the nuclei to change direction. The changes create signals that a computer translates to produce detailed cross-sectional images on a video screen.

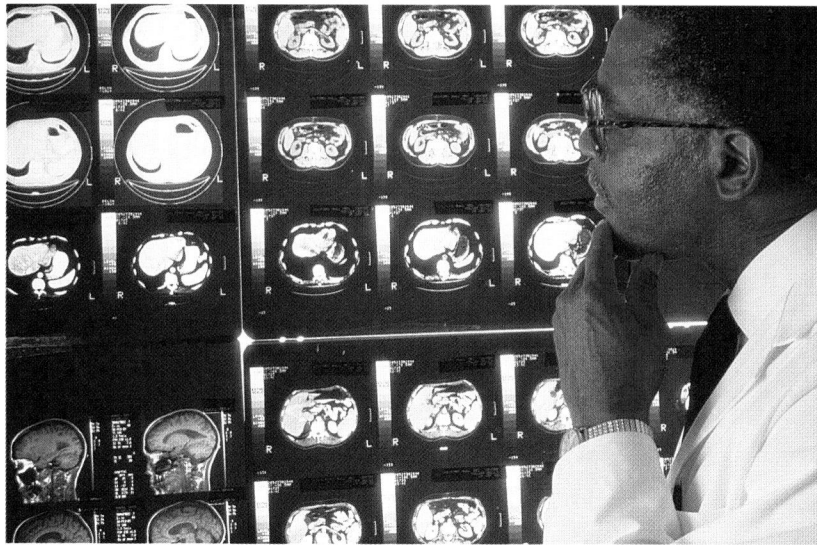

A doctor studies images produced by MRI. Physicians use MRI to identify abnormal tissue inside the body without performing surgery. It is most often used to study the head or spine.

Superstock

erful magnet and so cannot be used on people with metal implants, such as pacemakers or artificial joints.

An MRI unit consists mainly of a large cylindrical magnet, devices for transmitting and receiving radio waves, and a computer. During the examination, the patient lies inside the magnet, and a magnetic field is applied to the patient's body. The magnetic field causes nuclei in certain atoms inside the body to line up. Radio waves are then directed at the nuclei. If the frequency of the radio waves equals that of the atom, a *resonance condition* is produced. This condition enables the nuclei to absorb the energy of the radio waves. When the radio-wave stimulation stops, the nuclei return to their original state and emit energy in the form of weak radio signals. The strength and length of these signals—and therefore the kind of image produced—depend on various properties of the tissue. A computer translates the signals into highly detailed cross-sectional images.

An MRI examination is supervised by a *radiologist*—a physician trained in using images for medical diagnosis. The technique is most often used to study the head or spine. MRI is also used to examine the chest, abdomen, and joints. MRI has a high rate of success in detecting tumors, diseases of the circulatory system, abnormalities present since birth, and some types of injuries.

MRI devices are extremely costly and must be housed in special facilities. As a result, they are found chiefly in large medical centers. In some parts of the United States, several small hospitals share a mobile MRI unit.

MRI technology developed from a related technique called *nuclear magnetic resonance (NMR) spectroscopy.* Scientists use NMR spectroscopy to obtain detailed information about molecular structure.   Glenn S. Forbes

Magnetic storm is a strong fluctuation in the earth's magnetic field. A magnetic storm is caused by high-energy particles and intense radiation given off by the sun as a result of solar activity. The overall level of magnetic storm activity varies with the recurring 11-year *sunspot cycle* (see **Sun** [The sun's stormy activity]). It also varies with the 27-day period of the sun's rotation, as different active regions of the sun face the earth.

Many magnetic storms are associated with *coronal holes,* which are regions of low density in the sun's corona. A continuous flow of electrically charged particles from the sun called the *solar wind* emerges chiefly from the coronal holes. High-speed streams of the solar wind appear as the sun's activity increases. When the rapidly moving particles of these streams strike the earth's magnetic field, some of the particles are trapped by the field. The interaction of these particles with the earth's magnetic field produces a magnetic storm.

The solar wind is separated into large regions of either positive or negative magnetic polarity. A magnetic storm occurs when a boundary between such regions of opposite polarity is swept past the earth by the sun's rotation. The passage of these boundaries is the solar phenomenon most closely linked to magnetic storms.

Scientists believe many *solar flares,* which are eruptions on the sun's surface, also cause magnetic storms. Such storms start abruptly, unlike those associated with the solar wind, which begin gradually. Solar flares emit high-energy electrons and protons as well as radiation in the form of gamma rays and X rays. The electrons and protons are trapped by the earth's magnetic field. The gamma rays and X rays affect the field by causing changes in the ionosphere and in the *Van Allen belts,* which are doughnut-shaped regions of charged particles that surround the earth.

Magnetic storms demonstrate how solar activity directly affects the earth. They cause disturbances in the ionosphere, which interfere with short-wave radio reception. Scientists detect magnetic storms by means of such interference. In addition, abrupt changes in the earth's magnetic field resulting from magnetic storms can cause surges in power transmission lines. Magnetic storms are also accompanied by auroras.

The sun's increased magnetic field not only causes magnetic storms but also shields the earth from high-energy cosmic rays that originate in outer space. The resulting decrease in cosmic rays bombarding the earth is called the *Forbush effect.*   Jay M. Pasachoff

See also **Aurora; Solar wind; Sunspot.**

© Richard Hutchings

© Peter Pearson, Tony Stone Images

Fermi National Accelerator Laboratory

Magnetism causes a horseshoe magnet to attract paper clips, *top left,* and enables industrial magnets to lift heavy loads of scrap metal, *top right.* Magnets are also used in scientific devices. Physicists use magnets to boost atomic particles to high speeds in a particle accelerator, *above.*

Magnetism

Magnetism is the force that electric currents exert on other electric currents. Magnetism may be created by the motion of electrons in the atoms of certain materials, which are called magnets. Magnetic force may also be produced by ordinary electric current flowing through a coil of wire, called an *electromagnet.* The magnetic force may cause *attraction* or *repulsion*—that is, it may pull magnets together or push them apart.

The contributors of this article are Richard B. Frankel, Professor of Physics at California Polytechnic State University; and Brian B. Schwartz, Professor of Physics at Brooklyn College and Associate Executive Secretary and Education Officer of the American Physical Society.

Magnets have many different shapes. The most common are bars and thick disks, squares, or rectangles. A horseshoe magnet is a bar magnet bent into a U shape.

Magnets have a wide variety of uses. Magnets stick to certain metals, which makes them useful as fasteners and latches. Electric tools, appliances, and trains require magnets to run because all electric motors basically consist of a rotating electrical conductor situated between the poles of a stationary magnet. Huge magnets move iron and steel scrap. Tiny magnets on audiotape and videotape store sound and images. Magnets in telephones, radios, and TV sets help change electrical impulses into sounds. Scientists use powerful magnets to hold extremely hot gases in nuclear energy research.

Some rocks, minerals, and meteorites are natural magnets. The earth itself is a giant magnet, and so are the sun and other stars and most of the planets. Some insects, birds, and fish have extremely small magnets in their bodies. Biologists think these magnets may help animals find their way when migrating.

People in ancient Greece and China independently discovered magnetism when they found that the mineral magnetite attracted iron. Scientists could not explain what caused magnetism, however, until the mid-1800's.

What magnets do

Magnetic poles. A magnet with two poles, such as a bar magnet, is called a *magnetic dipole.* (The prefix *di-* means *two.*) If a bar magnet is hung by a string tied around its middle, it rotates until one end points north and the other end points south. The end that points north is called the *north pole,* and the south-pointing end is the *south pole.* In a disk or other flat magnet, the flat surfaces are the poles. If a magnet is broken or cut in half, each piece has a north and south magnetic pole.

Attraction and repulsion. Magnetism causes unlike magnetic poles to attract each other but like poles to *repel* (push away from) each other. If the north pole of a magnet is brought near the south pole of another magnet, the magnetic force pulls the magnets together. But two north poles or two south poles repel each other. If a bar magnet is suspended between the ends of a horseshoe magnet, it will move so that its north pole faces away from the horseshoe magnet's north pole.

Magnetic fields. The region around a magnet where the force of magnetism can be felt is said to contain a *magnetic field.* A magnetic field is invisible. You can picture the magnetic field of a bar magnet, however, if you place a piece of paper over the magnet and sprinkle iron filings on the paper. The filings bunch together near the poles and form a pattern around the magnet that corresponds to its magnetic field. A magnetic field can also be thought of as a set of imaginary lines called *field lines, flux lines,* or *lines of force.* We think of these lines going out from the north pole of a magnet, looping around, and returning to the magnet at its south pole. The lines lie closest to each other near the poles, where the magnetic field is strongest.

A magnetic field exerts a force on nearby magnets to make them align along its field lines. The needle of a magnetic compass, for example, is actually a slender bar magnet. It normally points north along one of the earth's magnetic field lines. But a strong bar magnet placed next to the compass will cause the needle to point along one of the bar magnet's field lines.

The strength of a magnetic field is measured in units called *gauss* or *tesla.* One tesla equals 10,000 gauss. The earth's magnetic field at its surface is about $\frac{1}{2}$ gauss. The field near the poles of a small horseshoe magnet may be several hundred gauss. Fields of magnets used in industry may measure more than 20,000 gauss (2 tesla).

Magnetization. A magnet attracts iron, steel, nickel, and certain other materials. The attracted materials then become magnets themselves in a process called *magnetization.* A steel nail placed near a magnet, for example, becomes magnetized and can attract a second nail. Magnetization occurs because the magnet causes spinning particles called *electrons* in the atoms of the nail to align along the magnet's field lines. The atoms with aligned electrons then act like tiny bar magnets.

Kinds of magnets

Most objects made of aluminum, concrete, copper, cotton, glass, gold, paper, plastic, rubber, silver, and wood are *nonmagnetic materials.* Magnets neither repel nor attract these substances, and magnetic fields pass through them without weakening. But other materials, called *magnetic materials,* become magnetized when exposed to a magnetic field. Magnetic materials are used in making temporary and permanent magnets. An electromagnet is produced by an electric current.

Temporary magnets are made of such materials as iron and nickel. These materials are known as *soft magnetic materials* because they usually do not retain their magnetism outside a strong magnetic field. A magnetized iron nail, for example, loses its magnetism if it is removed from a magnetic field.

Permanent magnets keep their magnetism after they have been magnetized. For this reason, they are

WORLD BOOK diagram by J. Harlan Hunt

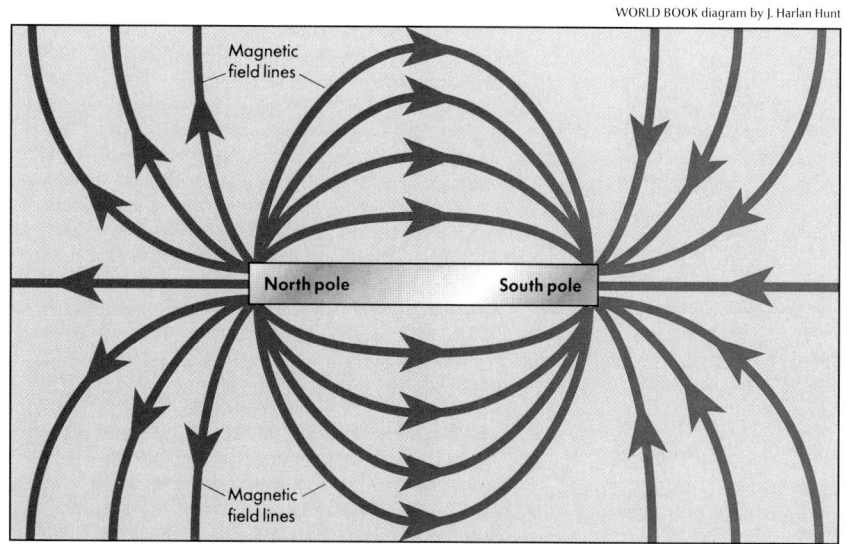

A magnetic field can be shown as imaginary lines that flow out of the north pole and into the south pole of a magnet. The magnetic field of a bar magnet, *left,* is strongest near the magnet's poles, where the lines lie closest to each other.

known as *hard magnetic materials.* Many strong permanent magnets are *alloys* (mixtures) of iron, nickel, or cobalt with other elements. These magnetic alloys include Alnico, a group of alloys usually containing a mixture of aluminum, nickel, cobalt, iron, and copper; and an alloy of cobalt and chromium called cobalt-chromium. Alloys containing metallic elements called *rare-earth elements* have produced some of the strongest permanent magnets. These alloys include samarium-cobalt, a mixture of cobalt and the rare-earth element samarium; and a combination of boron, iron, and the rare-earth element neodymium. Another important group of magnetic alloys, called *ferrites,* consist of iron, oxygen, and other elements. The best-known natural permanent magnet is a ferrite known as *magnetite* or *lodestone* (also spelled *loadstone*).

Some soft magnetic materials can be made into weak permanent magnets. An iron needle for a compass, for example, can be permanently magnetized by stroking it in one direction with a magnet.

Electromagnets are temporary magnets produced by electric currents. The simplest electromagnets consist of electric current flowing through a cylindrical coil of wire called a *solenoid.* One end of the solenoid becomes the north pole of the electromagnet, while the other end becomes the south pole. The poles switch position if the direction of the current is reversed. If the current is shut off, the solenoid loses its magnetism.

Many electromagnets have a cylinder of soft magnetic material, such as iron, within a coil of wire to strengthen the magnetic field the electromagnet produces. When current passes through the coil, the cylinder becomes strongly magnetized. The cylinder loses its magnetism, however, when the current is shut off. This characteristic of electromagnets makes them useful as switches in electric doorbells and telegraphs.

The strength of an electromagnet depends on the number of windings in the coil and the strength of the electric current. More windings and stronger current

Francis Bitter National Magnet Laboratory, M.I.T.

Technicians assemble a hybrid magnet by lowering an electromagnet into a superconducting magnet. Hybrid magnets can produce extremely strong fields of about 350,000 gauss.

produce more intense magnetic fields. Fields of about 250,000 gauss (25 tesla) have been produced by passing extremely strong electric current through a coil made of copper plates. These magnets require cooling systems that pump water past the coils, however, to prevent the heat produced by the current from melting the copper plates. Some electromagnets, called *superconducting magnets,* use coils that conduct current with no loss of energy and, thus, do not heat up. The strongest electromagnets, called *hybrid magnets,* consist of a water-cooled electromagnet within a superconducting magnet. These devices can produce magnetic fields of about 350,000 gauss (35 tesla).

Uses of magnets and magnetism

In homes, the attractive force between magnets makes them useful as latches on cabinet doors, as knife racks, and as fasteners for holding papers on refrigerators. The most important use of magnets in the home, however, is in electric motors. All electric motors use

Artstreet

Magnetite, also called *lodestone,* is a natural magnet that attracts iron nails and certain other metals. It belongs to an important group of magnetic materials called *ferrites.*

electromagnets or a combination of electromagnets and permanent magnets. These motors run refrigerators, vacuum cleaners, washing machines, compact disc players, blenders, hedge trimmers, drills, sanders, and such toys as electric trains, race cars, and robots.

Audiotape and videotape players have electromagnets called *heads* that record and read information on tapes covered with many tiny magnetic particles. The magnetic field of a recording head makes the magnetic particles on the tape form patterns that another type of head can read. The second head transforms the magnetic patterns into an electric signal. Magnets in speakers transform the signal into sound by making the speakers vibrate. An electromagnet called a *deflection yoke* in TV picture tubes helps form images on a screen.

In industry and business, magnets in electric motors help run almost any machine that makes something move or rotate. These devices include cranes, cutters, electric typewriters, fax machines, machine tools, photocopiers, and printing presses. Magnets in computers store information on magnetic tapes and disks. Powerful electromagnets attached to cranes move scrap iron and steel and separate metals for recycling.

One of the most important uses of magnets is electric power production. Generators in power plants rely on magnets similar to those in electric motors to produce electricity. Devices called *transformers* use electromagnets to change the high-voltage electricity carried by power lines to the lower voltage needed in homes and businesses.

In transportation. All electrified transportation systems depend on magnets in electric motors. These systems include trains, subways, trolleys, monorails, cable cars, escalators, elevators, and moving sidewalks. Electric motors operate windshield wipers, electric windows and doors, door locks, and other devices in automobiles, buses, and airplanes. Electromagnets also produce radio waves in radar systems, an important navigation aid for ships and airplanes.

Scientists and engineers have developed trains that use electromagnets to *levitate* (float) above a track without touching it. These trains, called *magnetic levitation* or *maglev* trains, eliminate the friction of wheels on the track and thus can move at much higher speeds than ordinary trains do.

In science and medicine. Magnets and magnetic fields are widely used in scientific research. Electromagnets in electron microscopes focus a beam of electrons on a sample to be studied. Powerful magnets called *bending magnets* help control beams of atomic particles that have been boosted to high speed in devices called *particle accelerators.* In nuclear energy research, physicists make the nuclei of atoms *fuse* (unite) in extremely hot gases called *plasmas.* The plasmas are so hot they would melt the walls of any container made of ordinary materials. Therefore, physicists hold the plasmas away from the container's walls in a strong magnetic field that functions as a "magnetic bottle."

In medicine, many devices for diagnosing diseases use magnets. In a technique known as *magnetic resonance imaging* (MRI), the patient lies inside a large cylindrical magnet. MRI uses magnetic fields and radio waves to produce images of the head, spine, internal organs, and other body parts. Other diagnostic devices enable physicians to observe magnetic fields generated by the brain, heart, and other internal organs.

How magnetism works

Magnetism and electricity are closely related. Together, they make a force called *electromagnetism,* one of the basic forces in the universe. A moving magnet near a coil of copper wire, for example, can *induce* (produce) an electric current in the coil. Similarly, an electric current flowing through a wire creates a magnetic field around the wire.

The direction of the magnetic field around a straight wire can be determined according to the *right-hand rule.* If the thumb of the right hand points along the flow

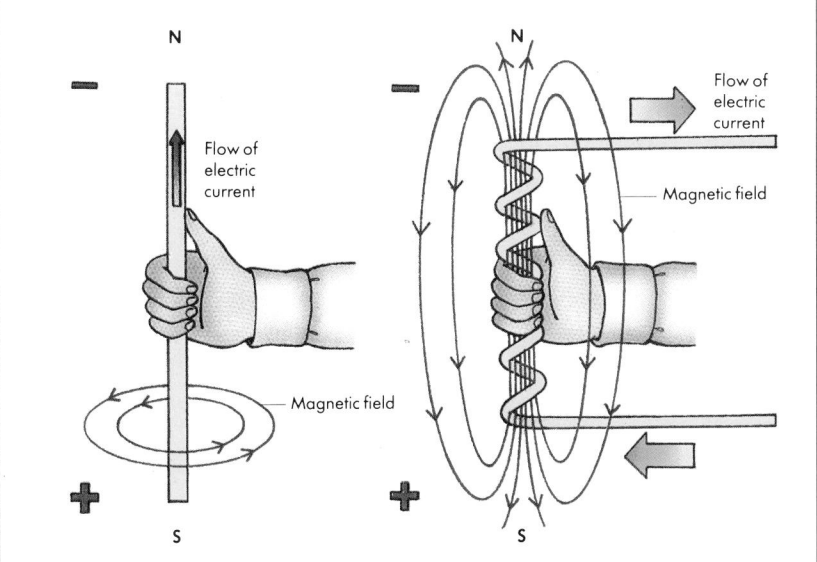

The right-hand rule shows the direction of the magnetic field around a wire that carries an electric current. If the thumb of the right hand points along the flow of current in a straight wire, *far left,* the fingers curl around the wire in the direction of the field. If a wire carrying current is wound into a coil, the magnetic field is strengthened. Such a coil is called a *solenoid.* The direction of the magnetic field surrounding a solenoid, *left,* can be found by wrapping the fingers around the coil in the direction of the current. The thumb then points to the solenoid's north pole and shows the direction of the field.

of current, the fingers curl around the wire in the direction of the magnetic field.

The right-hand rule also applies to the magnetic field produced by a coil or solenoid. Magnetic field lines flow through the length of a coil. If the fingers of the right hand curl around the coil in the direction of the current, the right thumb points to the coil's north pole and shows the direction of the magnetic field lines.

The right-hand rule is used when the current is thought of as a flow of positive electric charges. In a simple electric circuit connected to a battery, for example, the current is defined as flowing from the battery's positive terminal to its negative terminal.

Magnetism in atoms. Atoms have a small, dense center called a *nucleus* surrounded by one or more lighter, negatively charged electrons. Nuclei consist of *protons,* which have positive charges, and *neutrons,* which have no charge. Under most conditions, the atoms of each element contain an equal number of protons and electrons, and so the atoms are electrically neutral.

The relationship between magnetism and electricity also operates in the atom. The motion of negatively charged electrons around a nucleus makes an electric current, which produces a magnetic field. However, the effect of the electrons moving in one direction equals the effect of the electrons moving in the opposite direction. As a result, the magnetic fields of the moving electrons cancel each other out, and the atom has no magnetic field.

In addition to circling the nucleus, an electron spins on its axis like a top. This motion also produces an electric current and a magnetic field. But in most atoms, one electron spins in one direction for each electron that spins in the opposite direction. The magnetic fields caused by the spinning motion of the paired electrons cancel each other out.

The orbiting motions of paired electrons change slightly when an atom is placed in a magnetic field. The magnetic fields of the electrons then no longer cancel each other out, and their motions produce a weak magnetic field opposite to the external field. This effect is known as *diamagnetism* (opposite magnetism). The atoms making up most chemical compounds are held together by chemical links called *bonds* that consist of paired electrons. As a result, most compounds—including water, salt, and sugar—are diamagnetic. Diamagnetic materials are weakly repelled by magnets.

In some atoms, including those of cobalt, iron, nickel, oxygen, and the rare-earth element gadolinium, the spins of some electrons are not paired. As a result, each atom has a magnetic field and acts like a tiny magnet. Such an atom is called an *atomic dipole*. These atoms, like other magnets, tend to align themselves parallel to the lines of an external magnetic field. This alignment is called *paramagnetism* (same magnetism) and causes the individual atoms to be weakly attracted to magnets.

Magnetism of materials. In some paramagnetic materials, the atomic dipoles arrange themselves in certain patterns in relation to each other. These arrangements include *ferromagnetic, antiferromagnetic,* and *ferrimagnetic* ordering. In ferromagnetic materials, such as iron, an atomic dipole points in the same direction as neighboring dipoles. The ferromagnetic arrangement produces the most strongly magnetic substances. An atomic dipole in an antiferromagnetic material, how-

The magnetism of materials   Certain materials have magnetic properties because of the arrangement of their *atomic dipoles,* atoms that act like tiny magnets because they have unpaired electron spins. These arrangements include ferromagnetic, antiferromagnetic, and ferrimagnetic ordering.

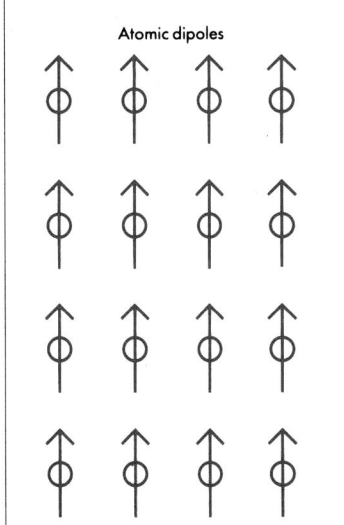

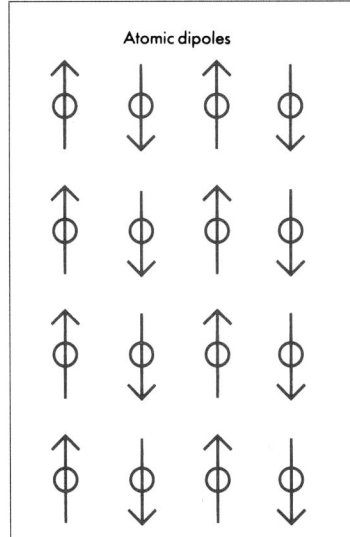

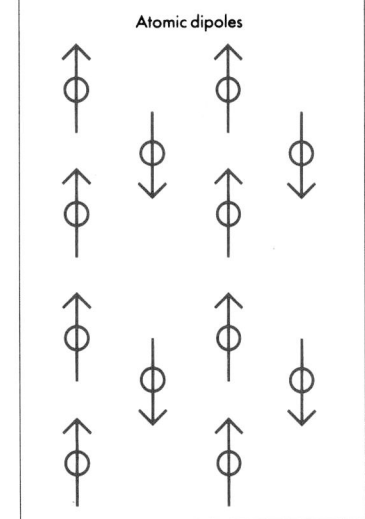

WORLD BOOK illustrations by Linda Kinnaman

Ferromagnetic materials have atomic dipoles that align in the same direction as neighboring dipoles. Such materials are strongly magnetic.

Antiferromagnetic materials, which are weakly magnetic, have atomic dipoles that align opposite to neighboring dipoles.

Ferrimagnetic materials have more atomic dipoles pointing in one direction than in the other and are strongly magnetic.

ever, points opposite to its neighbors. Antiferromagnetic materials are weakly magnetic. Ferrimagnetic ordering occurs in materials with several kinds of atoms, including magnetite and ferrite alloys. These materials have more dipoles pointing in one direction than in the other and are strongly magnetic.

Atomic dipoles of ferromagnetic and ferrimagnetic materials settle into an ordered arrangement when the material's temperature falls below its *magnetic ordering temperature* or *Curie point.* For antiferromagnetic materials, this temperature is called the *Néel temperature.* Iron, for example, has a magnetic ordering temperature of 1418 °F (770 °C); nickel, 676 °F (358 °C); and cobalt, 2050 °F (1121 °C). Above this temperature, stronger atomic vibrations prevent the atomic dipoles from arranging themselves in relation to each other. As a result, the materials then show only the weak magnetic attraction of paramagnetism.

In ferromagnetic and ferrimagnetic materials, the atomic dipoles usually align to form larger dipoles called *magnetic domains.* Domains combine the strength of the individual atomic dipoles. A piece of magnetic material may contain many magnetic domains. The domains often point in different directions, however, and tend to cancel each other out.

Ferromagnetic or ferrimagnetic materials become magnetized when exposed to a strong magnetic field. The domains parallel to the field grow as more atomic dipoles line up with it. If the magnetic field is extremely strong, all the atomic dipoles may align and the entire piece of material may become a single magnetic domain. The domains of a hard magnetic material remain aligned when removed from a magnetic field. Thus, the material becomes a permanent magnet. Soft magnetic materials, however, become *demagnetized* when removed from the field—that is, their original magnetic domains re-form and cancel each other out.

The magnetism of astronomical bodies

The magnetism of the earth. The earth is a giant magnet with poles called the *north magnetic pole* and the *south magnetic pole.* These poles are near the geographic North and South poles, respectively. The north magnetic pole attracts the north pole of a compass needle, so it is actually the south pole of the earth magnet. Similarly, the south magnetic pole is the north pole of the earth magnet because it repels the north pole of a compass needle.

The magnetic field at the surface of the earth, known as the *geomagnetic field,* has a strength of about $\frac{1}{2}$ gauss. The earth's inner structure creates the geomagnetic field. The earth's *crust* is the outermost portion on which we live. A rocky *mantle* lies beneath the crust. Under the mantle is a dense *core,* which has a solid inner part and a liquid outer part. Scientists believe the motion of electric charges in the liquid outer core produces the geomagnetic field.

Scientists who study the lava of ancient volcanoes have found that the geomagnetic field periodically reverses direction—that is, the earth's north and south magnetic poles switch places. Lava contains small particles of hard magnetic material. When the lava was hot, these magnetic particles were paramagnetic and, thus, were only weakly influenced by the earth's magnetic field. But once the lava cooled below the magnetic ordering temperature, the particles aligned themselves with the geomagnetic field like tiny compass needles. Thus, lava leaves a record of the geomagnetic field at the time when the lava cooled.

The earth's magnetic field also extends into space beyond the atmosphere. There, it is called the *magnetosphere.* The magnetosphere interacts with a flow of charged particles from the sun called the *solar wind.* This interaction produces displays of light called *auroras* and a zone of charged particles around the earth known as the *Van Allen belts.*

The magnetism of the sun. The sun has an overall magnetic field of about 1 to 2 gauss. But it also has stronger magnetic fields concentrated in relatively cooler areas of its surface called *sunspots.* These regions have magnetic fields of 250 to 5,000 gauss. Other solar features associated with strong magnetic fields include bright bursts of light called *flares* and huge arches of gas known as *prominences.*

The magnetism of other astronomical bodies. The moon has virtually no magnetic field because it does not have a liquid core. But moon rocks brought to the earth by astronauts show that the moon at one time had a stronger magnetic field. This evidence suggests that it once probably had a liquid core. Mercury, Venus, and Mars all have weaker fields than the earth's. But Saturn, Jupiter, Neptune, and Uranus have relatively strong magnetic fields and magnetospheres.

Some types of stars have magnetic fields much stronger than the sun's. These stars include *white dwarfs,* which can have magnetic fields of more than 1 million gauss. A type of collapsed star called a *neutron star* can have a field as strong as 10 trillion gauss.

Magnets in living things

Scientists have discovered that many animals—including pigeons, honey bees, salmon, tuna, dolphins, and turtles—are able to detect the earth's magnetic field and may use it to help find their way. Scientists have found particles of magnetite in the body tissues of some of these animals. They suspect that the particles form part of a system that senses the geomagnetic field.

Scientists have also found that some bacteria in water use the geomagnetic field to find their preferred habitat. Each of the bacteria, called *magnetotactic bacteria,* contains one or more chains of magnetite particles. The

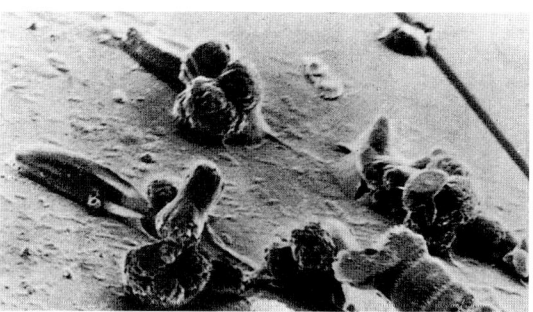

AP/Wide World

Magnetic bacteria contain extremely small chains of magnetite particles. These particles cause the bacteria, shown greatly magnified above, to align with the field lines of a bar magnet.

A *World Book* science project

Experimenting with magnetism

The purpose of this project is to demonstrate magnetic fields from permanent magnets and the magnetic effects of an electric current. The materials needed for this project are shown below. They can be purchased at most hardware or hobby stores.

Materials needed

WORLD BOOK illustrations by Oxford Illustrators Limited

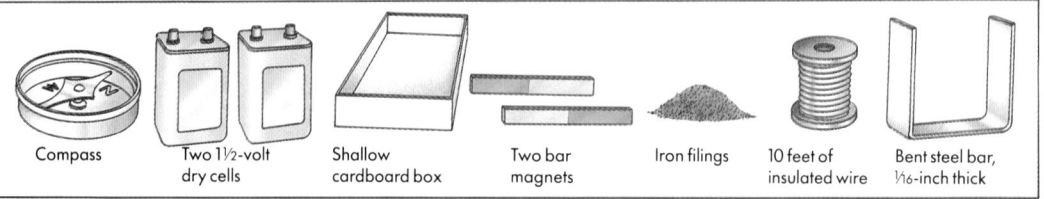

Compass   Two 1½-volt dry cells   Shallow cardboard box   Two bar magnets   Iron filings   10 feet of insulated wire   Bent steel bar, ⅛-inch thick

Mapping magnetic fields

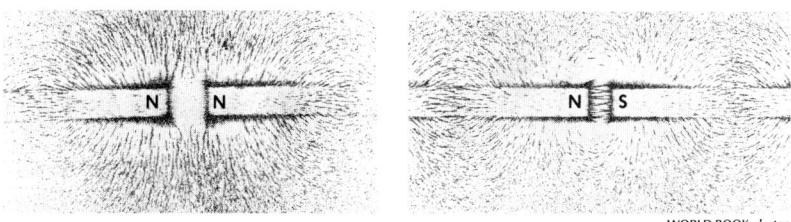

WORLD BOOK photos

Other experiments include mapping the field when one of the magnets is turned to a different position or when several magnets are placed under the paper. You can also study the effect of placing a steel coat hanger, coins, or other metal objects in contact with one or more magnets.

To map the field of a bar magnet, place the magnet under a sheet of white paper. Sprinkle iron filings on the paper and tap the paper gently. The filings will line up as shown. The field between two magnetic poles curves outward from the gap between the poles if they are alike, *left.* If opposite poles are used, the field extends across the gap from one pole to the other, *right.*

Magnetism and electricity

To see the magnetic effects of electricity, wrap about 10 turns of wire around a small box. Place a compass inside the box and turn the box so that the compass needle lines up with the wire. Strip the insulation from the ends of the wire, and connect the wire to the terminals of a dry cell. Then observe how the compass needle moves.

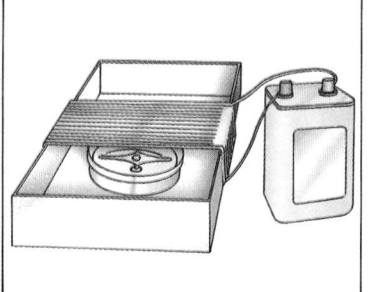

To experiment further, try switching the wires from one terminal to the other to see how the needle changes direction. By switching the wires at the proper rate, you may be able to make the needle spin completely around. Try changing the number of turns of wire to see the effect this has on the compass.

Experimenting with an electromagnet

To make an electromagnet, wind two layers of wire around a flat iron bar that is bent into the shape shown here. Strip the insulation from the ends of the wire and connect the wire to two dry cells. When you hold the compass between the poles of the electromagnet, the needle will pick up iron objects when the current is on.

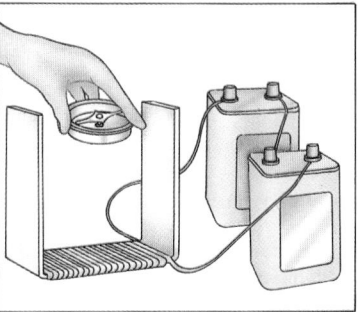

Electromagnet experiments. Try mapping the field of your magnet. You can also change the number of turns of wire and the number of dry cells to increase the lifting power of the magnet. The more turns of wire you add or the more dry cells you connect, the stronger your magnet will be.

bacteria use the particles as tiny compass needles to guide them along geomagnetic field lines.

The study of magnetism

Early discoveries. People in ancient Greece and China independently discovered that natural lodestone magnets attracted iron. The Chinese also found that a piece of lodestone would point in a north-south direction if it was allowed to rotate freely. They used this characteristic of lodestone to tell fortunes and as a guide for building. By A.D. 1200, Chinese and European sailors used magnetic compasses to steer their ships.

In 1269, a French soldier named Pierre de Maricourt (also known as Petrus Peregrinus) mapped the magnetic field around a lodestone sphere with a compass. He discovered that the sphere had two magnetic poles. William Gilbert, a physician of Queen Elizabeth I of England, concluded in 1600 that the earth itself is a giant magnet with north and south poles.

Electricity and magnetism. In 1820, Hans Christian Oersted, a Danish physicist and chemist, observed that an electric current flowing in a wire caused the needle of a magnetic compass to rotate. His discovery proved that electricity and magnetism were related. The French physicist André Marie Ampère worked out the mathematical relationship between current and the strength of the magnetic field during the 1820's. He also proposed that electric current in atoms caused magnetism. In the early 1830's, the English scientist Michael Faraday and the American physicist Joseph Henry independently discovered that a changing magnetic field induced a current in a coil of wire. In 1864, James Clerk Maxwell, a Scottish scientist, developed the mathematical theory that described the laws of electricity and magnetism.

The magnetic properties of materials became a focus of research in the late 1800's. The French physicist Pierre Curie found that ferromagnetic materials lose their ferromagnetism above a certain temperature, which became known as the Curie point.

In the early 1900's, a number of physicists developed the theory of quantum mechanics, which describes the behavior of electrons and other particles. The pioneers of quantum theory included Niels Bohr of Denmark, Wolfgang Pauli of Austria, and the German physicists Albert Einstein, Werner Heisenberg, Max Planck, and Erwin Schrödinger. Richard P. Feynman and Julian S. Schwinger of the United States and Sin-itiro Tomonaga of Japan later developed an improved theory of quantum electrodynamics. Their work led to a better understanding of the interaction between charged particles and an electromagnetic field. John H. Van Vleck of the United States and Louis E. F. Néel of France applied quantum mechanics to understand the magnetic properties of atoms and molecules.

Modern research in magnetism. In the 1940's, the American physicists Edward M. Purcell and Felix Bloch independently developed a way to measure the magnetic field of nuclei. They placed a substance in a strong magnetic field and exposed it to radio waves. They discovered that the waves interacted with the nuclei of the substance's atoms. This discovery, known as *nuclear magnetic resonance,* led to magnetic resonance imaging and other methods for studying the structure of living tissues.

The American physicist Francis Bitter pioneered in developing stronger magnets for research. In the 1930's, he developed electromagnets made of water-cooled copper plates that generated powerful magnetic fields. In the 1960's and 1970's, scientists developed superconducting materials. When cooled to near *absolute zero* (-459.67 °F or -273.15 °C), these materials could be used in magnets to generate fields as high as 200,000 gauss. Superconducting magnets are used in maglev trains and in nuclear research. In the 1980's and 1990's, researchers discovered materials that become superconducting at higher, though still extremely cold, temperatures—about -280 °F (-173 °C). These new superconductors will enable scientists to generate even stronger fields.   Richard B. Frankel and Brian B. Schwartz

Related articles in *World Book* include:

Compass	Magnetic amplifier
Cosmic rays	Magnetic equator
Earth (The earth's magnetism)	Magnetic levitation train
Electric generator	Magnetic resonance imaging
Electric motor	Magnetic storm
Electricity (Magnetism)	Magneto
Electromagnet	Magnetohydrodynamics
Electromagnetism	Magnetometer
Gauss	Permalloy
Hall effect	Quantum electrodynamics
Lenz's law	Quantum mechanics
Linear electric motor	Sun (Solar magnetism)
Loadstone	Superconductivity

Outline

I. **What magnets do**
 A. Magnetic poles
 B. Attraction and repulsion
 C. Magnetic fields
 D. Magnetization
II. **Kinds of magnets**
 A. Temporary magnets
 B. Permanent magnets
 C. Electromagnets
III. **Uses of magnetism**
 A. In homes
 B. In industry and business
 C. In transportation
 D. In science and medicine
IV. **How magnetism works**
 A. Magnetism and electricity
 B. Magnetism in atoms
 C. Magnetism of materials
V. **The magnetism of astronomical bodies**
 A. The magnetism of the earth
 B. The magnetism of the sun
 C. The magnetism of other astronomical bodies
VI. **Magnets in living things**
VII. **The study of magnetism**
 A. Early discoveries
 B. Electricity and magnetism
 C. The magnetic properties of materials
 D. Modern research in magnetism

Questions

How do hard magnetic materials and soft magnetic materials differ?

What do scientists think causes the earth's magnetic field?

What is a magnetic dipole?

How are atomic dipoles arranged in ferromagnetic materials?

Who developed the mathematical theory that describes the relationship between magnetism and electricity?

What is the right-hand rule?

Why are ferromagnetic and ferrimagnetic materials useful in making permanent magnets?

Who discovered magnetism?
What is the magnetic ordering temperature or Curie point?
How is a "magnetic bottle" used in nuclear energy research?

Additional resources

Catherall, Ed. *Exploring Magnets.* Steck-Vaughn, 1990. For younger readers.
Dobbs, E. Roland. *Electricity and Magnetism.* Routledge, 1984.
Lafferty, Peter. *Magnets to Generators.* Gloucester Pr., 1989. For younger readers.
Vogt, Gregory. *Electricity and Magnetism.* Watts, 1985. For younger readers.

Magnetite. See Loadstone.

Magneto, *mag NEE toh,* is an electric generator that provides spark ignition in some internal-combustion engines. Magneto ignitions are used in lawn mowers and in some aircraft and motorcycles. A magneto operates on two basic principles: (1) The movement of a conductor in a magnetic field produces an electric current in the conductor, and (2) A sudden interruption of the flow of the current in the conductor can *induce* (generate) large voltages.

A magneto consists of a magnet and a conductor made up of one or more coils of wire. The coils may rotate around the magnet, or the magnet may rotate inside the coils. The rotation induces an electric current in the coils. *Contacts* (connections) touching the coils are then opened, interrupting the flow of current and creating a high voltage in the coils. This voltage produces a spark that ignites fuel in the engine.   Glenn A. Burdick

See also **Electric generator; Ignition.**

Magnetohydrodynamics, *mag NEE toh HY droh dy NAM ihks,* often abbreviated MHD, is the study of the ways in which electric and magnetic fields interact with fluids that conduct electricity. These fluids include liquid metals and highly ionized gases called *plasmas.* MHD has played a role in developing generators and propulsion systems that use conducting fluids. MHD also helps scientists understand electric and magnetic effects around the earth and on the sun. These effects include sunspots, magnetic storms in the earth's magnetic field, and *auroras* (northern and southern lights).

The principles of MHD have many applications. They are used in MHD generators, which produce electricity from a high-speed stream of plasma. The plasma shoots through a duct in a magnetic field, where it generates current that is drawn off by electrodes. MHD generators provide a highly efficient power source, but they are still in the experimental stage. MHD propulsion systems use electricity from a plasma or another conducting fluid to produce thrust. Such propulsion systems may someday be used to power submarines and space vehicles.

The principles of MHD are also important in designing experimental *fusion reactors.* The fuel used in fusion reactors consists of plasma that has been heated many millions of degrees. But such extremely hot plasma would expand very quickly and would hit the walls of a container. The plasma would then be cooled and would lose energy too quickly for a fusion reaction to take place. Many physicists are trying to produce controlled fusion in superhot plasma with confinement achieved by externally imposed magnetic fields. See **Nuclear energy** (Nuclear fusion).   George Vahala

See also **Alfvén, Hannes O. G.; Aurora; Magnetic storm; Plasma** (physics); **Sunspot.**

Magnetometer, *MAG nuh TAHM uh tuhr,* is a device that measures the strength of a magnetic field. The simplest magnetometers can measure the magnetic field near an electric motor or the poles of a magnet. They have a tiny coil of wire. When the coil is moved through the magnetic field, an electric voltage is produced in the coil. This voltage indicates the strength of the field.

Such magnetometers as *optically pumped magnetometers* and *superconducting gradiometers* can measure weaker magnetic fields. Airplanes tow optically pumped magnetometers through the air in order to measure the slight irregularities in the earth's magnetic field. These measurements help prospectors locate deposits of iron ore, petroleum, and other natural resources. Superconducting gradiometers are becoming common in biomedical research. For example, they are used to measure magnetic fields from parts of the human body, such as the brain and heart.   Lynn W. Hart

See also **Petroleum** (Geophysical studies); **Plate tectonics.**

Magnifying glass is a lens which makes close objects appear larger. Both sides of the lens are usually curved to form a double convex lens. The magnifying glass can give two kinds of images. A glass held close to a page in a book forms a *virtual image.* The light rays which produce this image *diverge* (spread out) as they pass through the lens and appear to originate on the same side of the lens as the page. The virtual image appears upright and larger than the object.

A *real image* is formed when light rays from an object pass through the lens and are focused on the other side. The real image appears inverted, or upside down. Its size depends on the distance of the object from the lens. The distance from the center of the lens to the point where parallel light rays are focused is called the *focal length.* If the object is more than twice the focal length away from the lens, the image will be smaller. If the object is less than twice the focal length away, the image will be larger.

The magnifying power of a lens depends on its focal length. The greater the curve of a lens, the shorter its focal length and the greater its power. It bends the rays more, and they meet at a smaller distance from the lens. A lens with a focal length of 5 inches (13 centimeters) magnifies an image about two times.

A magnifying glass held between a piece of paper and the sun can be used to start a fire. Heat from the many rays focusing at a common point (focus) on the paper will make the paper burn.   Joseph A. Muscari

See also **Lens; Microscope.**

Magnitogorsk, *mag NEET uh gawrsk* (pop. 421,000), is the principal steel center of Russia. The city also makes mining machinery. Magnitogorsk is located in the Ural Mountains in southwestern Russia. For location, see **Russia** (political map). The city received its name from its rich deposits of magnetite, which is a type of iron ore. Magnitogorsk was founded in 1931.
    Roman Szporluk

Magnitude is the scale used by astronomers to measure the brightness of objects in space. The brighter a star or planet, the lower its magnitude number. The magnitude system is based on the work of the ancient Greek astronomer Hipparchus. About 125 B.C., Hipparchus classified the stars according to brightness. He called the brightest stars first magnitude; the next brightest, second magnitude; and so on down to the faintest stars visible with the unaided eye. He called such stars sixth magnitude.

Later astronomers found that first magnitude stars were about 100 times as bright as sixth magnitude stars. They adopted a system that made a star of any magnitude about $2\frac{1}{2}$ times as bright as a star of the next brightest magnitude. This scale has been extended to zero and negative magnitudes because some stars and planets are brighter than first magnitude ones. For example, the sun has a magnitude of -27.

The word *magnitude* generally refers to *apparent magnitude,* or the brightness of a star as seen from the earth. To compare actual brightness, astronomers use *absolute magnitude,* which shows how bright stars would appear if they all were the same distance—32.6 light-years—from the earth. At that distance, the sun would be a fifth magnitude star.   Thomas J. Balonek

See also **Sirius; Star** (Measuring brightness).

Magnolia is the name of a group of trees and shrubs that grow in the Americas and in Asia. Eight of the 80 kinds grow wild in the Eastern United States. These eight and others are commonly cultivated. Magnolias have large flowers, conelike fruits, and large leaves.

The *southern magnolia* is popular because of its large whitish flowers. This evergreen is native from North Carolina to Florida and west to Texas. It is the state tree and flower of Mississippi and the state flower of Louisiana. *Sweetbay,* also called *swamp magnolia,* has smaller flowers and leaves. Its leaves are green on top and whitish underneath.

The leaves of the *umbrella tree* and the *big-leaf magnolia* tend to stretch out from the ends of the branches like the ribs of an open umbrella. The big-leaf magnolia has the largest flowers of any tree native to the United States. They measure about 10 inches (25 centimeters) across and are creamy-white. The big-leaf magnolia also has the biggest undivided leaves, which are 15 to 32 inches (38 to 81 centimeters) long and up to 10 inches (25 centimeters) wide.

The *saucer magnolia* is an ornamental tree that has been widely planted in the United States. It is a hybrid of two Asian magnolias and has many light to dark pink flowers. Magnolia lumber is used mainly for furniture. The *cucumber tree,* a magnolia that gets its name from the shape of its fruits, has wood similar to that of the yellow-poplar (see **Yellow-poplar**).

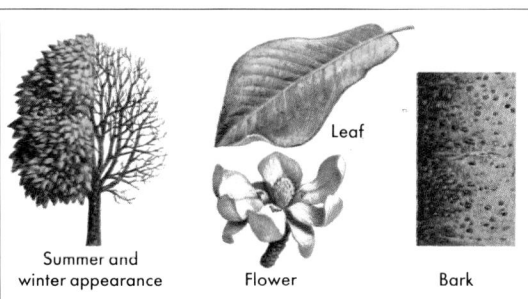

WORLD BOOK illustration by John D. Dawson

The big-leaf magnolia has large flowers and leaves.

Scientific classification. Magnolias belong to the magnolia family, Magnoliaceae. The southern magnolia is *Magnolia grandiflora.* The sweetbay is *M. virginiana;* the umbrella tree is *M. tripetala;* the big-leaf is *M. macrophylla;* the saucer is *M. Soulangiana;* and the cucumber tree is *M. acuminata.*

Kenneth R. Robertson

Magpie is a bird that belongs to the same family as crows, ravens, and jays. The *black-billed magpie* lives throughout Europe, central Asia, parts of Siberia, and western North America from Alaska to New Mexico. The *yellow-billed magpie* lives in California.

Both yellow- and black-billed magpies are black with white underparts and wing tops. The black feathers of the wings and tail are tinged with a shiny bronze-green. The long tail of the bird narrows at the tip, and the bird's bill is heavy.

Magpies eat chiefly insects, including grasshoppers and beetles. The bulky nest of the magpie is usually in a bush or tree and is covered with a loose canopy of thorny sticks. The female lays five to seven bluish-green eggs spotted with brown and tan. The female incubates

WORLD BOOK illustration by John Rignall, Linden Artists Ltd.

The magpie is related to the crow. Magpies can mimic various bird calls and often steal food from the nests of other birds.

the eggs by sitting on them, and the male feeds her. Both the male and the female feed the young. Magpies live up to 12 years.

Magpies travel in pairs or small groups. However, these birds may gather in large numbers at roosts or sources of food. They have a large number of calls, such as their well-known rattling chatter and the soft, warbling sounds that are used between mates at the nest. Tame magpies may imitate the human voice or the calls of other birds.

Scientific classification. Magpies are in the crow family, Corvidae. The black-billed magpie is *Pica pica.* The yellow-billed is *P. nuttalli.*   Edward H. Burtt, Jr.

Magritte, *ma GREET,* **René,** *ruh NAY* (1898-1967), was a Belgian surrealist painter. Magritte painted in a precise, realistic style that is often referred to as *Magic Realism.* His pictures present ordinary scenes but usually contain a combination of elements that normally do not belong together. This odd mixture gives his paintings an eerie, dreamlike quality. Many of Magritte's paintings include mysterious men wearing bowler hats. His painting *Golconda* shows a pattern of these men suspended in air.

Magritte was born in Lessines, near Ath. He studied art in Brussels. The artist's early paintings show the influence of cubism. Magritte's surrealist period began in 1922 after he saw a reproduction of a painting by the modern Italian artist Giorgio de Chirico.

Rebecca Jeffrey Easby

See also **Surrealism**.

Maguey, *MAG way* or *mah GAY,* is the name given to several kinds of agave plants that grow in Mexico. The name is usually used for the *pulque agave.* Mexicans often drink the juice of this plant. They use it to make *pulque* (a fermented drink) and *tequila* (a distilled liquor). The plant's leaves are green with gray spines, and may grow 9 feet (3 meters) long and 1 foot (30 centimeters) wide. The greenish flowers grow on stalks 20 feet (6 meters) high. People often eat parts of the stems and flowers. See also **Century plant.**

Scientific classification. The maguey is in the agave family, Agavaceae. The scientific name for the pulque agave is *Agave atrovirens.* Michael G. Barbour

Magyars, *MAG yahrz,* are a group of about 15 million people who are usually called Hungarians. They are traditionally considered to be descendants of the early Magyars, a people who founded Hungary in the late 800's. More than 10 million Magyars live in Hungary today, and they make up about 95 percent of the nation's population. About $3\frac{1}{2}$ million Magyars inhabit neighboring countries, and about $1\frac{1}{2}$ million live in the United States and other Western nations. The Magyar language belongs to the Finno-Ugric group of languages, which also includes Estonian and Finnish.

From about 3000 B.C. to A.D. 500, the Magyars lived between the Volga River and the Ural Mountains in what is now Russia. By the late 800's, they had moved southwest to settle in what became Hungary. From then until the mid-900's, they raided many neighboring peoples. During the 1000's, the Magyars adopted Christianity and founded a powerful kingdom.

In 1526, the Ottoman Empire, based in what is now Turkey, defeated the Magyars. Hungary was divided between the Ottoman Empire and the Austrian Habsburgs (or Hapsburgs). The Habsburgs expelled the Ottomans and gained complete control of Hungary in the early 1700's. Many Magyars became inhabitants of neighboring countries under the Treaty of Trianon, part of the peace settlement following World War I (1914-1918).

Steven Bela Vardy

See also **Hungary** (People; History).

Mah-jongg, *mah jawng,* also spelled *mah jongg* or *mah-jong,* is a Chinese game that developed in the 1800's. It is believed to be based on games played in China since about 500 B.C.

Mah-jongg is similar to the card game rummy. However, instead of cards, it is played with small, rectangular tiles engraved with Chinese drawings and symbols. There are 136 standard tiles, consisting of winds, dragons, and three kinds of suits—dots, craks, and bams. Suits are numbered from 1 to 9. There are four identical tiles of every kind. Most sets also have eight bonus tiles that represent flowers and seasons.

Two to six persons can play mah-jongg, but the game is best suited to four players. Rules vary. In general, players try to collect sets of three or four identical tiles or sequences within a suit by drawing from a pile of tiles, discarding tiles, and, in some versions of the game, exchanging tiles with other players. Players can also try to form special winning combinations that are worth different numbers of points. Usually, each player begins the game with chips equaling 1,000 points. Losers give chips to the winner equal to the value of the winning hand. R. Wayne Schmittberger

Mahabharata, *muh HAH BAH ruh tuh,* is an outstanding sacred writing of Hinduism and one of the two great epic poems of India. The other is the *Ramayana.*

According to Hindu tradition, the wise man Vyasa dictated the *Mahabharata* to Ganesh, the god of wisdom. Actually, the *Mahabharata* is a collection of writings by several authors who lived at various times. Parts of it may be more than 2,500 years old. The *Mahabharata* was written in Sanskrit, the principal literary language of ancient India.

The word *Mahabharata* means *Great King Bharata.* The epic tells the story of the descendants of King Bharata, two families who lived in northern India, per-

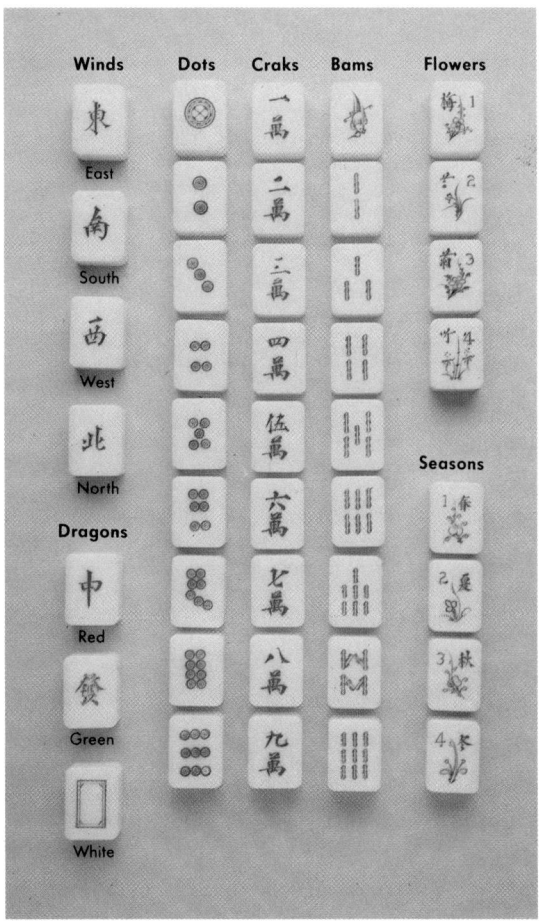

WORLD BOOK photo by Steinkamp/Ballogg

A mah-jongg set has four of each of the wind, dragon, dot, crak, and bam tiles. Most sets include flower and season tiles.

haps about 1200 B.C. The Pandava brothers lose their kingdom to their Kaurava cousins and engage in a mighty struggle to win it back. The story illustrates the futility of war. Some of the heroes are taken from history, and some represent human ideals and gods.

The main story of the *Mahabharata* is often interrupted by other stories and discussions of religion and other subjects. The part called the *Bhagavad-Gita* is an important writing of Hinduism.   Charles S. J. White

See also **Bhagavad-Gita; Ramayana; Hinduism.**

Mahan, *muh HAN,* **Alfred Thayer** (1840-1914), an American admiral, wrote many books on naval strategy and the influence of sea power on international affairs. His writings had an important effect on how nations viewed sea power in the 20 years before World War I (1914-1918). His great work, *The Influence of Sea Power upon History, 1660-1783* (1890), influenced President Theodore Roosevelt and others who supported colonial expansion overseas. Mahan argued in other writings for a strong navy, naval bases in Latin America and Asia, and an expanded merchant fleet. His ideas helped the United States develop as a world power and influenced naval experts in Great Britain and Germany.

Mahan thought that "Americans must now begin to look outward" to maintain the influence of the United States in world affairs. He believed a powerful navy was needed to achieve that end. Without overseas bases, he said, American ships in wartime "will be like land birds, unable to fly far from their own shores."

Mahan was born at West Point, N.Y. He studied at Columbia University and graduated from the U.S. Naval Academy in 1859. During the Civil War (1861-1865), he served on blockade duty in the South Atlantic Ocean and the Gulf of Mexico. His first book, *The Gulf and Inland Waters* (1883), was a naval history of the war.

Mahan lectured at the Naval War College in 1886. These speeches later became *The Influence of Sea Power upon History.* He headed the War College from 1886 to 1889 and again in 1892 and 1893. He retired in 1896 as as rear admiral. But in 1898, he was recalled to serve on the Naval War Board during the Spanish-American War. His books include *The Influence of Sea Power upon the French Revolution and Empire, 1793-1812* (1892); *Lessons of the War with Spain* (1399); and his autobiography, *From Sail to Steam* (1907).

Lewis L. Gould

Mahatma. See **Gandhi, Mohandas Karamchand.**

Mahican Indians, *muh HEE kuhn,* were important in the fur trade in North America during the 1600's. They struggled violently with the Mohawk Indians for control of the trade in the Hudson River Valley in New York. The Mahican Indians lived along the Hudson, and the name *Mahican* refers to the tides of the river near Albany. The Mahican are often confused with the Mohican, a fictional tribe created by American writer James Fenimore Cooper in his novel *The Last of the Mohicans.*

The Mahican lived in villages that were built on hills near rivers. A village consisted of from 3 to 16 large rectangular dwellings called *long houses.* Each long house sheltered several related families. A tall fence made of wooden stakes surrounded each village. The Mahican grew much of their food in gardens near their villages. They also fished, hunted, and gathered wild plants.

The struggle between the Mahican and the Mohawk

began about 1600. It lasted until the 1670's, when fur-bearing animals became so scarce in the valley that the fur trade no longer remained profitable. Increasing numbers of white farmers gradually forced the Mahican to move from their homelands. In 1736, many Mahican settled in Stockbridge, a community of Christian Indians in western Massachusetts. These Indians moved to central New York in the 1780's. In the 1820's, the federal government set up the Stockbridge Reservation in northeastern Wisconsin. Most of the remaining Mahican still live there.   T. Brasser

Mahler, Gustav (1860-1911), was a Bohemian-born composer of the romantic period. He completed nine symphonies and died before completing a 10th. He also composed numerous songs, many with orchestral accompaniment. Much of Mahler's music has a religious or philosophical basis. The early works often describe nature, and the later ones describe the struggles and triumphs of the soul. There is a note of sadness and resignation in many of his works. See **Classical music** (The romantic era).

Mahler's symphonies are large-scale works that try to include every human emotion. They employ a large orchestra, and four of them (Numbers 2, 3, 4, and 8) use voices. Although Mahler wrote for a large orchestra, he often used it very delicately. Mahler's songs are more intimate in style. They include *Kindertotenlieder* (*Songs on the Death of Children,* 1905) and *Das Lied von der Erde* (*The Song of the Earth,* 1911).

Bettmann Archive
Gustav Mahler

Mahler was born in Kaliště, Bohemia (now part of the Czech Republic). He studied at the Vienna Conservatory from 1875 to 1878. Mahler spent virtually his whole career as an opera and orchestra conductor. He worked his way up from small conducting jobs to the most prestigious positions in the music world. He directed the Vienna Court Opera from 1897 to 1907. After resigning this post, he visited the United States four times to conduct the New York Philharmonic Orchestra and at the Metropolitan Opera.   Joscelyn Godwin

Mahogany has long been considered one of the finest cabinet woods of the world, because it has most of the qualities desired for furniture making. It is strong and hard enough to stand ordinary use as furniture, yet soft enough to be easily sawed, planed, and carved. Mahogany does not shrink, swell, or warp as much as many other equally hard woods. The wood has an attractive color and grain, and a high luster.

Mahogany is a fairly heavy wood. Its color varies from light tan to dark reddish-brown. The wood darkens when exposed to daylight. It usually has an interlocking pattern or grain. Sometimes mahogany has curly, wavy, raindrop, or speckled figures. When mahogany is cut lengthwise through forks in the tree trunk, the wood shows a beautiful ostrich-plume effect. Workers often quartersaw or quarterslice mahogany into *veneer,* or thin sheets. They saw through the center of the log lengthwise so as to divide it into four sections. Then they cut planks alternately from each face of the quarter. Mahogany that has been quartersawed usually shows a ribbon or stripe figure.

The finest mahogany comes from the West Indies, where the tree *Swietenia mahogoni* grows to a height of more than 100 feet (30 meters). The long, clean tree trunk may reach a height of 60 to 80 feet (18 to 24 meters) before the first branch appears. Mahogany from this kind of tree is very scarce. Most mahogany used for fine woodworking today comes from southern Mexico, northern South America, and Africa. In Mexico and South America, the wood comes from the *Swietenia macrophylla* tree. In Africa, it is found in trees of the genus *Khaya.* Wood from trees of the genus *Cedrela* looks like mahogany, but is softer, lighter, and more brittle than true mahogany. *Philippine mahogany* comes from several trees in the genera *Shorea* and *Parashorea.* These trees are not true mahoganies.

The Cathedral of Santo Domingo in the Dominican Republic was the first building to use mahogany woodwork. The church was completed in 1540. People believe Sir Walter Raleigh used mahogany in 1595 to repair his ships in the West Indies. In the 1700's, Chippendale, Hepplewhite, and other furniture makers made mahogany furniture popular.   Jim L. Bowyer

See also **Wood** (picture: Some types of wood).

Mahomet. See Muhammad.

Mahony, Roger Michael Cardinal (1936-   ), was appointed a cardinal of the Roman Catholic Church by Pope John Paul II in 1991. The pope had named Mahony archbishop of Los Angeles in 1985.

Mahony was born in Hollywood, Calif. He was ordained a priest in 1962. In 1964, he received a master's degree in social work from the Catholic University of America. Also in 1964, Mahony became the administrator of St. Genevieve's Parish in Fresno, Calif., and was named pastor in 1967. Between 1968 and 1973, Mahony held several administrative positions in the diocese of Fresno. He served as rector of St. John's Cathedral in Fresno from 1973 to 1980. Mahony was chancellor of the diocese of Fresno from 1970 to 1977. He served as auxiliary bishop and vicar general of that diocese from 1975 to 1980, when he was appointed bishop of the diocese of Stockton, Calif.   Robert P. Imbelli

Maidenhair tree. See Ginkgo.

Maidu Indians, *MY doo,* are a group of tribes in north-central California who speak related languages. A Maidu tribe traditionally consisted of about three to five villages. The tribal center was the village with the largest *kum,* a structure that served as both a house and a place for religious worship. In summer, the Maidu traveled through their territory to fish in the rivers, hunt deer, and gather acorns and other foods. In winter, they returned to their villages and lived on the food gathered during summer. The Maidu depended heavily on their basket-weaving skills, which they used in making food containers, fish traps, clothing, sleeping mats, and many other items.

Between 1848 and 1910, the Maidu population dropped from about 9,000 to about 1,000. This dramatic decrease resulted from disease as well as from the Maidu's being driven off their lands by gold miners and ranchers and being moved by the United States government to distant reservations. Today, about 1,000 Maidu live in their traditional homeland. Most of them live on reservations. Maidu traditions are kept alive in religious ceremonies and in the work of modern Maidu artists.
      Lee Davis

Mail. See **Post office.**

Mail-order business is an industry involving the sale of products by mail. Mail-order companies, often called *mail-order houses,* have traditionally advertised by mailing leaflets, letters, or catalogs to customers. But today, many also advertise through magazines, newspapers, radio, and television. Many firms also encourage customers to place orders by telephone. Some firms invite customers to sales offices to select merchandise from catalogs or from samples on display. Because of the expanded scope of the traditional mail-order business, it is often referred to as the *direct-marketing business.* In the United States, total sales in direct marketing exceed $20 billion annually.

The first mail-order firms in the United States were retail merchants who took orders by mail for certain types of goods. In 1872, Montgomery Ward and Company of Chicago became the first mail-order business to sell general merchandise. Today, some mail-order firms sell only one product or a single related group of products. But others offer a wide variety of goods.

At first, the mail-order industry in the United States mainly served customers who lived on farms or in small towns. But after World War I (1914-1918), improved roads and the increased use of cars made it easier for rural people to shop in larger towns and cities. As a result, the mail-order industry began to decline. The larger mail-order firms, however, opened retail stores in urban areas.

After World War II ended in 1945, the mail-order business began to grow again despite a decreasing rural population. The industry recognized the importance of rapidly growing city and suburban markets, and it developed new methods of reaching customers there. These methods included telephone-order services, separate catalog-sales offices in towns and suburbs, and increased circulation of catalogs in city areas.

Today, the largest U.S. mail-order houses include the J. C. Penney Company and the Spiegel company. Sears Canada dominates the Canadian mail-order business.
      William H. Bolen

See also **Eaton, Timothy; Sears, Roebuck and Co.; Ward, Aaron Montgomery.**

Mailer, Norman (1923-   ), is an American author. Critics have sometimes attacked his work, but Mailer's readers usually find his essays and novels fascinating and disturbing. Mailer has analyzed the myths and unconscious impulses that underlie human behavior. He often stresses sex and violence. But Mailer uses these elements for artistic purposes, not merely to shock.

Mailer first achieved success with his war novel *The Naked and the Dead* (1948). In *Barbary Shore* (1951), he wrote about politics. *The Deer Park* (1955) describes the corruption of artistic and social values in Hollywood. *An American Dream* (1965) concerns events surrounding a man's murder of his wife. However, it is also a surrealistic journey through the power structures and obsessions of modern urban America. His novel *Why Are We in Vietnam?* (1967) extends such thematic concerns through an examination of the violence Mailer sees as basic to the American spirit. *The Executioner's Song* (1979) is based on the life of Gary Gilmore, a convicted murderer who was executed in 1977. The book won the 1980 Pulitzer Prize for fiction. *Tough Guys Don't Dance* (1984) is a violent detective story. *Harlot's Ghost* (1991) is a long, fictionalized history about the Central Intelligence Agency.

Dominique Nabokon, Gamma/Liaison
Norman Mailer

Many of Mailer's best essays about literature and culture were collected in *Advertisements for Myself* (1959) and *Existential Errands* (1972). *The Short Fiction of Norman Mailer* was published in 1967. *The Armies of the Night* (1968), which describes his experiences and observations during a peace demonstration, shared the 1969 Pulitzer Prize for general nonfiction. *Miami and the Siege of Chicago* (1968) represents Mailer's reactions to the 1968 national political conventions. He was born in Long Branch, N.J.   Victor A. Kramer

Maillol, *ma YAWL,* **Aristide,** *a rees TEED* (1861-1944), was a French sculptor. He devoted more than 40 years of his career to the theme of the female form. Maillol's figures are his visions of beautiful, robust women, usually graceful and sensual. They are most often portrayed in quiet, deeply thoughtful poses.

The style of Maillol's female figures changed very little during his career. Maillol was inspired by the late sculpture of French artist Pierre Auguste Renoir. He also tried to reproduce the calm, harmonious spirit of classical Greek sculpture. Much of Maillol's work is life-sized and cast in bronze.

Maillol was born in Banyuls-sur-Mer, near Perpignan. He worked as a painter and a tapestry designer before turning full-time to sculpture about the age of 40. He also made woodcuts to illustrate books.   Joseph F. Lamb

Maimonides, *my MAHN ih deez,* **Moses** (1135-1204), was the most important Jewish philosopher of the Middle Ages. Maimonides tried to demonstrate the compatibility of philosophy, as taught by the ancient Greek thinker Aristotle, with the Jewish tradition.

Maimonides' principal philosophical work, *The Guide for the Perplexed,* was written in Arabic and completed in 1190. It draws on Aristotle's works as transmitted by Greek and Muslim commentators. The *Guide* influenced Christian Aristotelian theologians, notably Saint Thomas Aquinas. In 1168, Maimonides completed a commentary to the *Mishnah,* the written version of traditional Jewish oral law. Maimonides completed the *Mishneh Torah* in about 1178. It became one of the most important Jewish law codes.

Maimonides was born in Córdoba, Spain. His Hebrew name was Solomon ben Maimon. Maimonides was a doctor by profession. However, he dedicated himself to the Jewish community in Cairo, Egypt, where he lived the last part of his life, and to furthering the study and practice of Judaism.   Gary G. Porton

Maine. The sinking of the United States battleship *Maine* helped cause the Spanish-American War. The *Maine* arrived in Havana, Cuba, on Jan. 25, 1898, to protect American lives and property in case of riots. On Feb. 15, 1898, it blew up, killing about 260 of the crew. A naval court of inquiry concluded that a submarine mine had caused the explosion. The United States accused Spain in this matter because Havana was then a Spanish port. But Spain claimed that an explosion inside the ship caused the disaster. The slogan "Remember the *Maine*" aroused widespread patriotic sentiment in favor of war against Spain.

In 1976, U.S. Navy researchers led by Admiral Hyman G. Rickover studied the incident. They concluded that heat from a fire in a coal bin exploded a nearby supply of ammunition.   H. Wayne Morgan

See also **Cuba** (picture); **Spanish-American War.**

National Archives, Washington

The sinking of the *Maine* in Havana Harbor on Feb. 15, 1898, angered the American people and helped spark the Spanish-American War. "Remember the *Maine*" became a popular patriotic slogan.

Tom Algire

The beautiful, rocky coast of Maine, with its thousands of bays and offshore islands, attracts vacationers to the state each year. The Portland Head Light, *above,* is one of the oldest and best-known American lighthouses. It was built in 1791.

Maine   *The Pine Tree State*

Maine forms the northeastern corner of the United States. West Quoddy Head, a small peninsula of Maine, is the country's easternmost piece of land. Nearby Eastport lies farther east than any other U.S. city. On a map, northern Maine looks like a giant wedge between the Canadian provinces of New Brunswick and Quebec. Augusta is the capital of Maine, and Portland is the largest city.

Maine, the largest of the New England States in area, is probably best known for its beautiful shore on the Atlantic Ocean. Along this famous "rock-bound" coast of the state are lighthouses, sandy beaches, quiet fishing villages, thousands of offshore islands, and Acadia National Park—the only national park in New England. Jagged rocks and cliffs, and thousands of bays and inlets, add to the rugged beauty of Maine's coast. Inland, the state has sparkling lakes, rushing rivers, green forests, and towering mountains.

Many cities and towns lie in the lowlands of southern Maine. But forests cover nearly 90 per cent of the state. Trees from Maine's forests provide raw materials for a giant wood-processing industry, and this industry forms the backbone of Maine's economy. Mills in Maine make

paper, pulp, toothpicks, and a variety of other products from trees. Maine leads the states in the production of toothpicks and ranks high in the manufacture of other wood products. Maine's nickname, the *Pine Tree State,* came from the tall pines that once made up much of the state's forests.

Service industries and fishing are also important in Maine. Thousands of people spend their summer vacations in Maine. They provide much income for lodging places, restaurants, and shops in the state. Maine leads all other states in lobster fishing.

Pioneering English colonists first settled in Maine in 1607, thirteen years before the Pilgrims landed at Plymouth Rock. Cold weather and lack of supplies forced the settlers back to England in 1608. English colonists made permanent settlements in Maine in the 1620's. Maine was a part of Massachusetts for the better part of 200 years. Then, on March 15, 1820, it became the 23rd state of the United States.

The name *Maine* probably means *mainland.* Early English explorers used the term *The Main* to distinguish the mainland from the offshore islands. New Englanders often refer to Maine as *Down East.* They call people who live in Maine *Down Easters* or *Down Easterners.* These terms probably come from the location of Maine east of, or downwind from, Boston. Ships from that port sailed down to Maine, and ships from Maine traveled up to Boston.

The contributors of this article are Richard H. Condon, Professor of History, and Paul B. Frederic, Professor of Geography, both at the University of Maine at Farmington.

Interesting facts about Maine

The first earmuffs were patented by Chester Greenwood of Farmington on March 13, 1877. Greenwood invented his first pair in 1873, when he was 15 years old. He later mass-produced earmuffs in his Farmington factory. Farmington, once known as the *Earmuff Capital of the World,* observes a Chester Greenwood Day each winter.

Earmuffs

The most easterly point of land in the continental United States is West Quoddy Head, a small peninsula near Lubec.

The first person to win a Pulitzer Prize for poetry, Edwin Arlington Robinson, was born in Head Tide and grew up in Gardiner. Robinson won his first Pulitzer Prize in 1922 for *Collected Poems.* He later won two more Pulitzer Prizes—for *The Man Who Died Twice* in 1925 and for *Tristram* in 1928.

Camp Fire Girls originated in Sebago Lake in 1910. Luther Halsey Gulick, a national leader in recreational programs for young people, and his wife, Charlotte Vetter Gulick, founded the organization. In 1975, the organization began admitting boys. Today, it is known as Camp Fire Boys and Girls.

More wooden toothpicks are produced in Maine than in any other state. Manufacturers use white birch to make toothpicks.

Toothpicks

Portland is the largest city in Maine and one of the chief ports on the Atlantic Coast. Portland is closer to Europe than any other U.S. transatlantic port.

A lobster fisherman removes a day's catch from his traps near Stonington. Maine has the largest lobster catch of any state.

Maine in brief

Symbols of Maine

The state flag, adopted in 1909, bears the state seal. On the seal, adopted in 1820, a farmer with a scythe represents agriculture. A seaman leaning on an anchor stands for commerce and fishing. These figures support a shield that displays a pine tree and a moose. The pine represents Maine's forests, and the moose symbolizes the state's undisturbed wildlife areas. At the top, the North Star represents Maine's northern location.

State flag

State seal

Maine (brown) ranks 39th in size among all the states and is the largest of the New England States (yellow).

General information

Statehood: March 15, 1820, the 23rd state.
State abbreviations: Me. (traditional); ME (postal).
State motto: *Dirigo* (I direct or I guide).
State song: "State of Maine Song." Words and music by Roger Vinton Snow.

The State Capitol is in Augusta, Maine's capital since 1832. Portland served as capital from 1820 to 1832.

Land and climate

Area: 33,128 sq. mi. (85,801 km²), including 2,263 sq. mi. (5,862 km²) of inland water but excluding 613 sq. mi. (1,587 km²) of coastal water.
Elevation: *Highest*—Mount Katahdin, 5,268 ft. (1,606 m) above sea level. *Lowest*—sea level along the coast.
Coastline: 228 mi. (367 km).
Record high temperature: 105 °F (41 °C) at North Bridgton on July 10, 1911.
Record low temperature: −48 °F (−44 °C) at Van Buren on Jan. 19, 1925.
Average July temperature: 67 °F (19 °C).
Average January temperature: 15 °F (−9 °C).
Average yearly precipitation: 41 in. (104 cm).

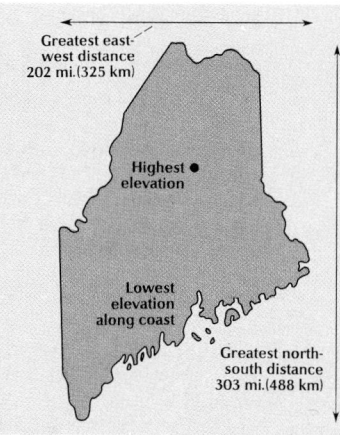

Greatest east-west distance 202 mi. (325 km)

Highest ● elevation

Lowest elevation along coast

Greatest north-south distance 303 mi. (488 km)

Important dates

English settlers established the Popham Colony near the mouth of the Kennebec River.

Maine became the 23rd state on March 15.

| 1000? | 1607 | 1775 | 1820 |

Vikings probably visited the Maine coast.

The first naval battle of the Revolutionary War took place off the Maine coast.

State bird
Chickadee

State flower
White pine cone and tassel

State tree
White pine

People

Population: 1,233,223 (1990 census)
Rank among the states: 38th
Density: 37 persons per sq. mi. (14 per km²), U.S. average 69 per sq. mi. (27 per km²)
Distribution: 55 per cent rural, 45 per cent urban
Largest cities in Maine

Portland	64,143
Lewiston	39,757
Bangor	33,181
Auburn	24,309
South Portland	23,163
Augusta	21,325

Source: U.S. Bureau of the Census.

Population trend

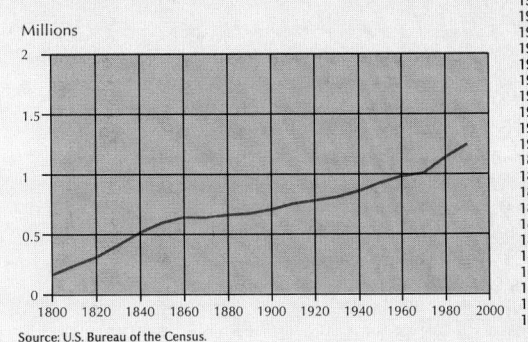

Millions

Source: U.S. Bureau of the Census.

Year	Population
1990	1,233,223
1980	1,125,030
1970	993,722
1960	969,265
1950	913,774
1940	847,226
1930	797,423
1920	768,014
1910	742,371
1900	694,466
1890	661,086
1880	648,936
1870	626,915
1860	628,279
1850	583,169
1840	501,793
1830	399,455
1820	298,335
1810	228,705
1800	151,719
1790	96,540

Economy

Chief products

Agriculture: milk, potatoes, eggs.
Fishing industry: lobsters.
Manufacturing: paper products, electrical equipment, transportation equipment, wood products, leather products, food products.
Mining: sand and gravel.

Gross state product

Value of goods and services produced in 1991: $24,469,000,000. *Services* include community, social, and personal services; finance; government; trade; and transportation, communication, and utilities. *Industry* includes construction, manufacturing, and mining. *Agriculture* includes agriculture, fishing, and forestry.

Source: U.S. Bureau of Economic Analysis.

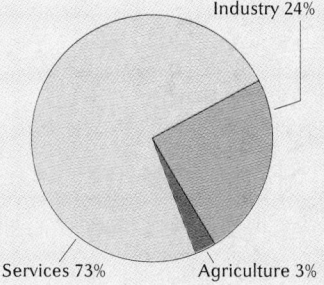

Industry 24%

Services 73%

Agriculture 3%

Government

State government

Governor: 4-year term
State senators: 35; 2-year terms
State representatives: 151; 2-year terms
Counties: 16

Federal government

United States senators: 2
United States representatives: 2
Electoral votes: 4

Sources of information

Tourism: Maine Publicity Bureau, P.O. Box 2300, Hallowell, ME 04347
Economy: Maine Department of Economic and Community Development, State House Station 59, Augusta, ME 04333
Government: Maine Department of Economic and Community Development, State House Station 59, Augusta, ME 04333
History: Maine Publicity Bureau, P.O. Box 2300, Hallowell, ME 04347

The Webster-Ashburton Treaty settled a long dispute over the Maine-Canada border.

Maine adopted personal and corporate income taxes.

| 1842 | 1851 | 1969 | 1980 |

Maine was the first state to outlaw alcoholic beverage sales.

The U.S. government agreed to pay $81½ million to Maine Indians for lands seized during the late 1700's and early 1800's.

Population. The 1990 United States census reported that Maine had 1,233,223 people. The population had increased $9\frac{1}{2}$ per cent over the 1980 figure, 1,125,030. According to the 1990 census, Maine ranks 38th in population among the 50 states.

About 45 per cent of Maine's people live in urban areas—that is, in or near municipalities with 2,500 or more people. The state's largest cities, in order of size, are Portland, Lewiston, Bangor, Auburn, South Portland, and Augusta. For more information, see the separate articles on Maine cities listed in the *Related articles* at the end of this article.

Three Metropolitan Statistical Areas are entirely within Maine (see **Metropolitan area**). They are Bangor, Lewiston-Auburn, and Portland. The Portsmouth-Rochester, N.H., Metropolitan Statistical Area extends into Maine. More than a third of the state's people live in these four areas. For the populations of these areas, see the *Index* to the political map of Maine.

About 96 of every 100 people in Maine were born in the United States. More than half of those born in other countries came from Canada. Maine's largest ancestry groups include people of English, French, Irish, French-Canadian, and German descent.

Schools. Colonial Maine offered little opportunity for formal education. Parents and local ministers often served as teachers. The first school in Maine may have been an Indian mission founded in 1696 by Sebastian Rasle, a Roman Catholic priest. Maine's first known school for white children opened in York in 1701. The first schoolhouse was constructed in Berwick in 1719. A school fund was provided by the state's Legislature in 1828. Schools in Maine began to receive tax support in 1868.

A commissioner of education and a nine-member board of education head Maine's public-school system. The governor of Maine appoints the members, subject to the approval of the Legislature, to five-year terms. The governor appoints the commissioner of education, subject to the approval of the Legislature. The commissioner serves a term of four years. Children between the ages of 7 and 17 are required to attend school. For the number of students and teachers in Maine, see **Education** (table).

Libraries. One of Maine's earliest libraries was formed in 1751. This collection of books alternated

Population density

Most of Maine's people live near the coast in the southwestern part of the state. Only a few tiny towns lie in the thinly populated, mountainous region of northwestern Maine.

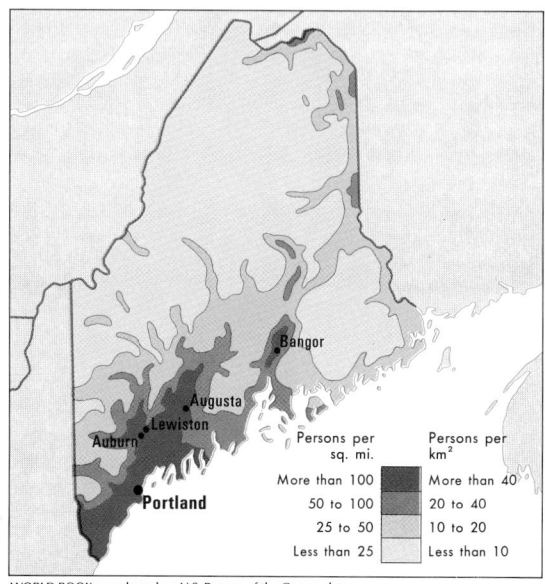

Persons per sq. mi.	Persons per km²
More than 100	More than 40
50 to 100	20 to 40
25 to 50	10 to 20
Less than 25	Less than 10

WORLD BOOK map; based on U.S. Bureau of the Census data.

Hanson Carroll, FPG

Fishing is a popular sport in Maine. The state's thousands of clear lakes, rivers, and streams offer a great opportunity for fishing enthusiasts. Hunting is also a popular form of recreation in Maine's vast woodlands.

between parish houses in Kittery and York. Maine now has about 250 public libraries.

The Maine State Library in Augusta and the Maine Historical Library in Portland own large collections of books about Maine and its history. The state's largest public libraries are the Bangor Public Library and the Portland Public Library.

Museums. The Maine State Museum in Augusta features exhibits on the state's history. The Bowdoin College Museum of Art has paintings and drawings by American, European, and Oriental artists. The Portland Museum of Art owns large collections of paintings and sculptures. The Robert Abbe Museum of Stone Age Antiquities features Indian items. Other museums in Maine include the Treat Gallery in Lewiston, the Brick Store Museum in Kennebunk, the William A. Farnsworth Library and Art Museum in Rockland, and the Maine Maritime Museum in Bath. See also the *Places to visit* section of this article.

Universities and colleges

Maine has 14 universities and colleges that grant bachelor's or advanced degrees and are accredited by the New England Association of Schools and Colleges. For enrollments and further information, see **Universities and colleges** (table).

Name	Mailing address
Atlantic, College of the	Bar Harbor
Bangor Theological Seminary	Bangor
Bates College	Lewiston
Bowdoin College	Brunswick
Colby College	Waterville
Husson College	Bangor
Maine, University of	*
Maine Maritime Academy	Castine
New England, University of	Biddeford
Portland School of Art	Portland
St. Joseph's College	Windham
Thomas College	Waterville
Unity College	Unity
Westbrook College	Portland

*For campuses and founding dates, see **Universities and colleges** (table).

Maine Historical Library

Maine Historical Society, in Portland, includes a large library of books and manuscripts dealing with the history of Maine and New England. The society was founded in 1822.

Steve Rosenthal

The Portland Museum of Art exhibits paintings and other works of art by American artists, especially artists from Maine.

University of Maine at Orono

The University of Maine has six four-year campus units. The campus at Orono, *above,* is the largest in the Maine system.

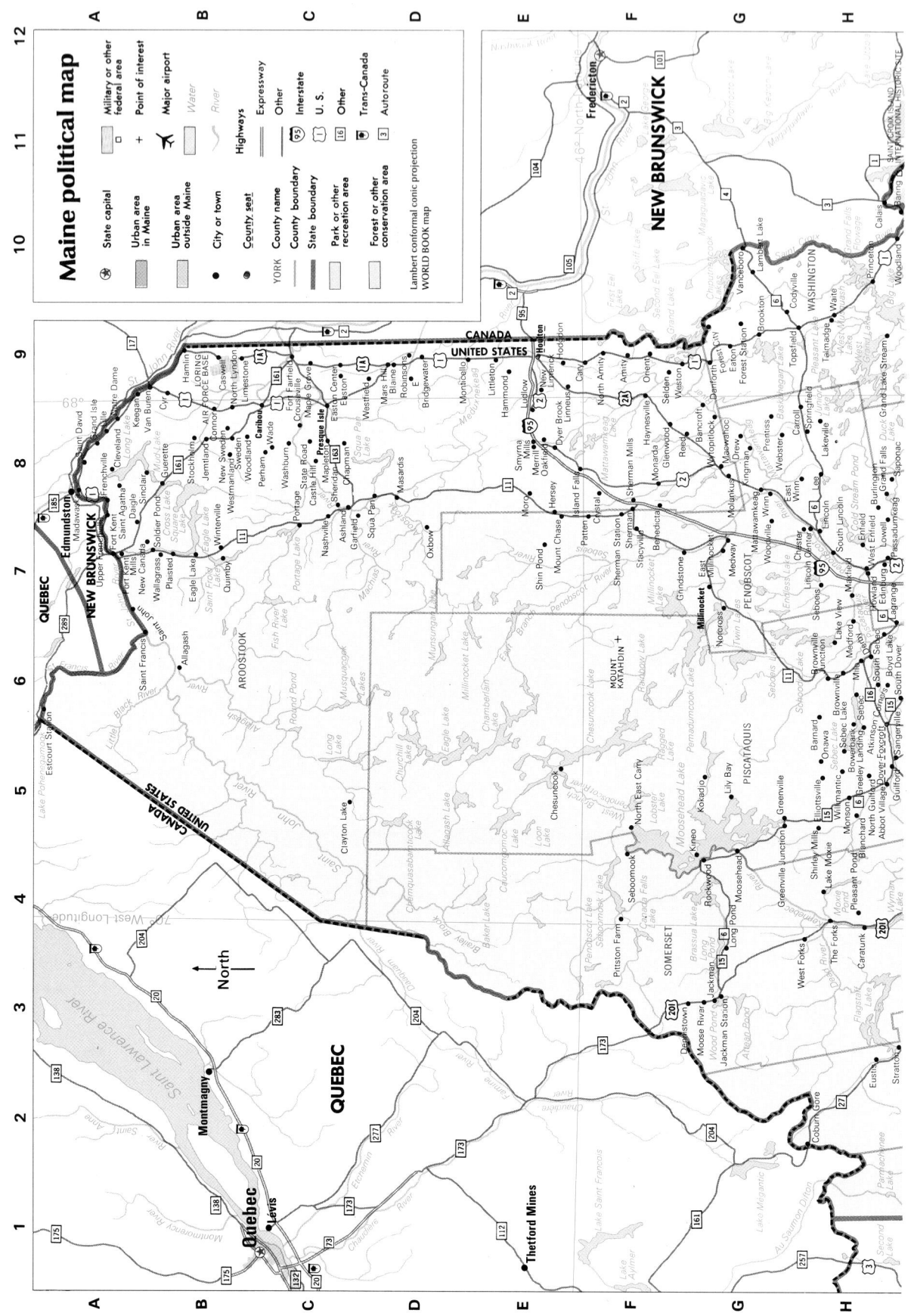

Maine political map

⊛	State capital
▨	Urban area in Maine
▨	Urban area outside Maine
●	City or town
○	County seat

YORK

County name

County boundary

State boundary

Park or other recreation area

Forest or other conservation area

☐	Military or other federal area
+	Point of interest
✈	Major airport
	Water
∼	River

Highways

Expressway

Other

Interstate

U. S.

Other

Trans-Canada

Autoroute

Lambert conformal conic projection
WORLD BOOK map

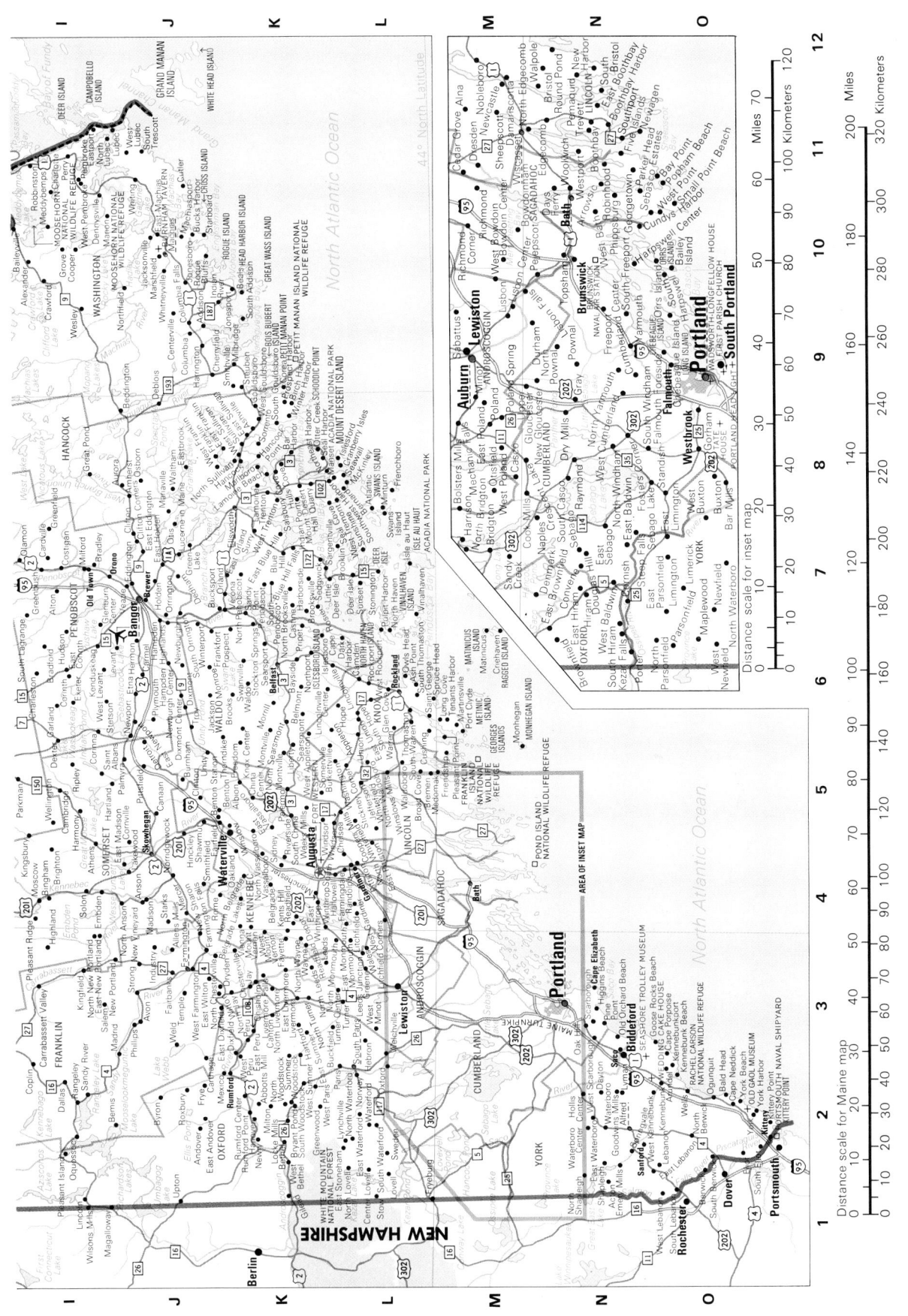

Maine map index

A traditional bagpipe band marches down a street in Bar Harbor during the town's annual Fourth of July parade.

Maine's beautiful coastal area attracts thousands of vacationers yearly. Visitors enjoy the rugged beauty of Atlantic waters pounding against rocky shores, and the many lighthouses along the coast. Hundreds of sandy beaches, bays, coves, and inlets provide areas for swimming, fishing, and sailing. Inland, hunters stalk bears, deer, and many other game animals in the vast wilderness of the north. People who enjoy fishing can try their luck in 2,500 lakes and ponds and 5,000 rivers and streams. Skiers and climbers enjoy Maine's mountains.

Maine's skiing season lasts from about mid-December to mid-April. In addition, the state has many historic sites, and picturesque landmarks such as small white churches.

Many of Maine's most popular annual events are sports contests. The summer months feature boat races and other water-sports contests. Among the state's outstanding annual events is the Maine Lobster Festival. This celebration is held in Rockland during the first weekend in August.

**Windjammer Days
at Boothbay Harbor**

Robert Mitchell

Places to visit

Black Mansion, in Ellsworth, is often called *Maine's Mount Vernon.* It resembles George Washington's Virginia home, Mount Vernon. Built about 1820, the Black Mansion has a low porch with a copper roof supported by decorative columns. Other features include fine china, silverware, furniture, and a winding staircase.

Burnham Tavern, in Machias, is the place where colonists met in 1775 to plot the capture of the British ship *Margaretta.* The *Margaretta* was captured during the first naval battle of the Revolutionary War. Burnham Tavern was built about 1770. The tavern still displays its original sign: "Drink for the thirsty, food for the hungry, lodging for the weary, and good keeping for horses."

First Parish Church is a Unitarian church in Portland. It was the site of Maine's only constitutional convention, which was held in 1819. Many of Portland's wealthiest families worshiped in the church during the 1700's and 1800's.

Fort Western, in Augusta, dates from 1754. It was at this fort that Benedict Arnold and his men met before marching up Maine to attack Quebec in 1775.

Old Gaol Museum, in York, is the oldest public building in Maine. It was built in 1653, and served as a *gaol* (jail) until 1860. Old Gaol Museum now houses local history relics.

Penobscot Marine Museum, in Searsport, displays valuable paintings, ship models, old sailing charts, navigation instruments, fishing and whaling equipment, ships' logs, books, and other historical items.

Portland Head Light, near Portland, towers 101 feet (31 meters) over the surf. Built in 1791, it ranks among the oldest and most famous American lighthouses.

Seashore Trolley Museum, near Kennebunkport, is the largest U.S. museum that exhibits only electric railroad equipment.

Shore Village Museum, in Rockland, contains the largest collection of lighthouse lenses and artifacts on display in the United States. Exhibits include buoys, life-saving gear, ship models, and *scrimshaw*—carvings or engravings made from whale teeth, whalebone, or sea shells.

Tate House is the oldest house in Portland. This three-story wooden structure was built in 1755. It includes quarters once used by slaves.

Wadsworth-Longfellow House, in Portland, ranks as Maine's most popular historic site. This building was the boyhood home of Henry Wadsworth Longfellow, the famous poet.

National parklands and forest. Acadia National Park, in southeastern Maine, is the only national park in New England. See **Acadia National Park.** Saint Croix Island International Historic Site, near Calais, marks the site of one of the first French settlements in North America. Part of White Mountain National Forest lies in southwestern Maine.

State parks and memorials. Maine has 30 state parks and 15 state memorials. It has no state forest system. For information on the parks and memorials, write to Director, Maine Bureau of Parks and Recreation, State House, Augusta, ME 04333.

Acadia National Park in southeast Maine

© Dean Abramson, Stock, Boston

© Brian Vanden Brink

Wadsworth-Longfellow House in Portland

Maine Office of Tourism

Black Mansion in Ellsworth

Annual events

January-June

Winter activities in Bethel, Carrabassett Valley, Greenville, Jackman, Kingfield, Rangeley, and other places (January and February).

July-December

Clam Festival in Yarmouth (July); Belfast Bay Festival in Belfast (July); Windjammer Days at Boothbay Harbor (July); Blueberry Festival in Union (August); Maine Festival of the Arts in Portland (August); Retired Skippers Race in Castine (August); Fairs in Bangor, Cumberland Center, Farmington, Fryeburg, Presque Isle, Skowhegan, Topsham, Union, and Windsor (various times during the summer and in early autumn).

Rockland Chamber of Commerce

Maine Lobster Festival in Rockland

Land and climate

Land regions. Maine has three natural land regions. They are, from southeast to northwest: (1) the Coastal Lowlands, (2) the Eastern New England Upland, and (3) the White Mountains Region.

The Coastal Lowlands cover southeastern Maine. They are part of a region of the same name that stretches along the entire New England coast. In Maine, the region extends from 10 to 40 miles (16 to 64 kilometers) inland from the Atlantic Ocean. Sandy beaches line the coast in the south. Old Orchard Beach, with 11 miles (18 kilometers) of hard-packed sand, is one of the longest and smoothest beaches on the Atlantic Coast. Salt marshes, crossed by tidal creeks, lie west of the beaches. In the northeast, the beaches shrink to small bays or strips of sand between high cliffs.

Most of the Coastal Lowlands lie near sea level. The land was once much higher than it is today. It was pushed down thousands of years ago, during the Ice Age, by the weight of ice and snow. The tops of sunken hills form more than 400 offshore islands from about 2 to 25 square miles (5 to 65 square kilometers) in area, and thousands of smaller islands. Mount Desert, the state's largest island, covers about 100 square miles (260 square kilometers).

The Eastern New England Upland lies northwest of the Coastal Lowlands. The entire upland extends from the Canadian border to Connecticut. In Maine, the region is from 20 to 50 miles (32 to 80 kilometers) wide. The land rises from elevations near sea level in the east to about 2,000 feet (610 meters) in the west. The Aroostook Plateau lies in the northeasternmost part of the region. The plateau's deep, fertile soil is good for agriculture. Farmers there grow one of the country's largest potato crops. Many lakes dot the Eastern New England Upland south of the Aroostook Plateau. Swift streams also flow through this area. Most of them are fed by springs and by melted snow. Mountains cut through the center of the region.

The White Mountains Region covers northwestern Maine and part of New Hampshire and Vermont. In Maine, the region is about 5 miles (8 kilometers) wide in the north and 30 miles (48 kilometers) wide in the south. The White Mountains Region includes hundreds of lakes and most of Maine's highest mountains. The mountains are an extension of New Hampshire's White Mountains.

Coastline of Maine has many deep harbors and thousands of bays, coves, and inlets. If the state's coastline is

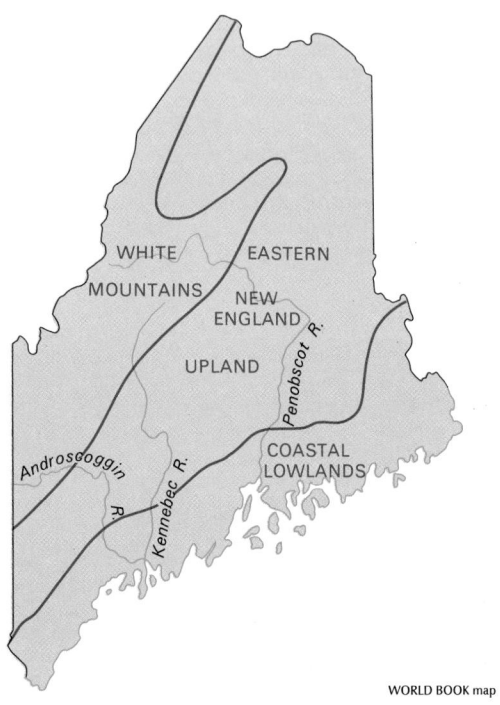

WORLD BOOK map

Land regions of Maine

Map index

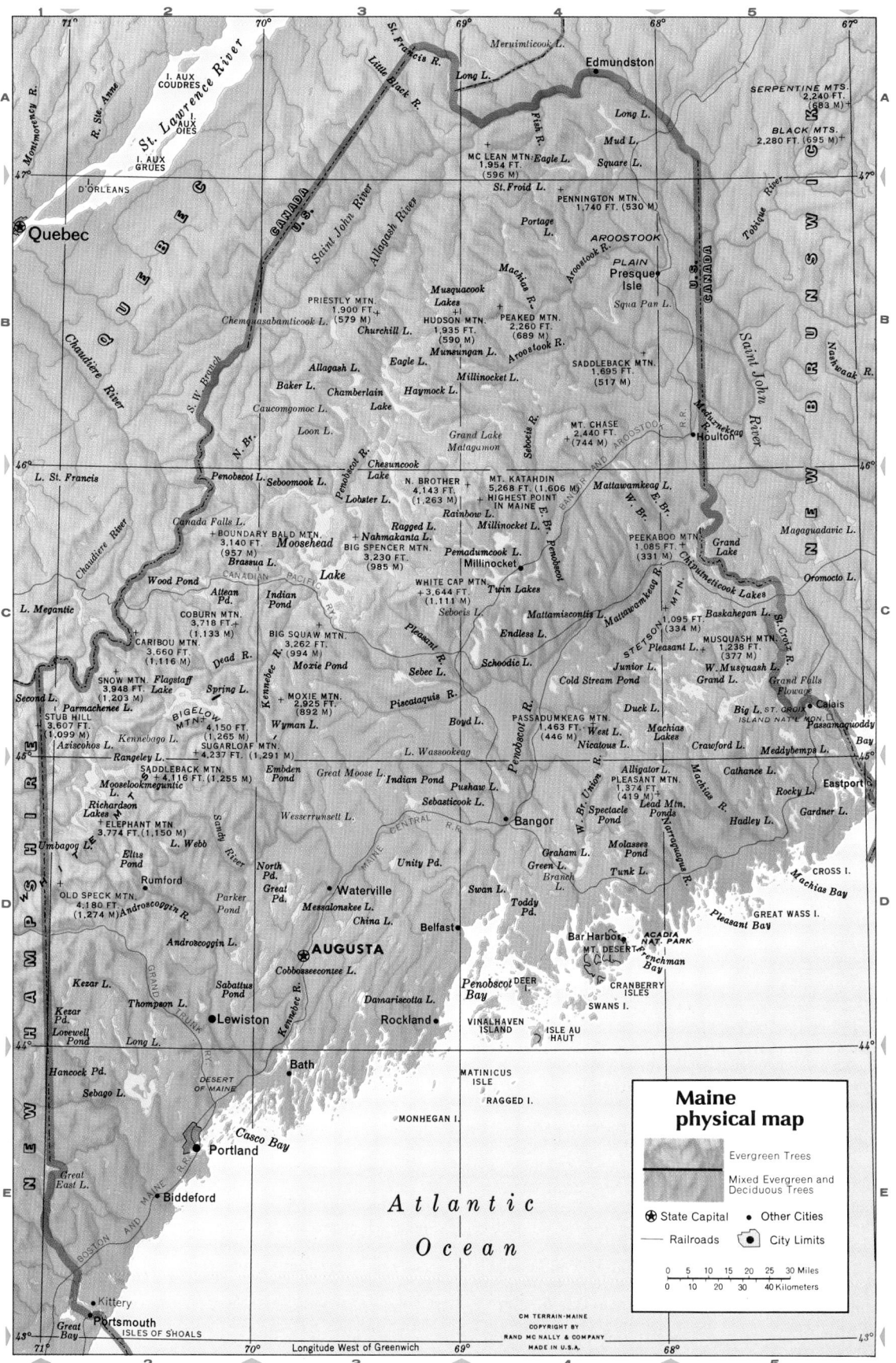

Maine
physical map

Evergreen Trees

Mixed Evergreen and
Deciduous Trees

⊛ State Capital   • Other Cities

— Railroads   City Limits

0 5 10 15 20 25 30 Miles
0 10 20 30 40 Kilometers

CM TERRAIN·MAINE
COPYRIGHT BY
RAND McNALLY & COMPANY
MADE IN U.S.A.

Longitude West of Greenwich

Specially created for *The World Book Encyclopedia* by Rand McNally and World Book editors

Tom Algire

Mount Katahdin, the highest peak in Maine, rises 5,268 feet (1,606 meters) in the central part of the state. Maine's mountains attract many skiers and climbers.

© Henry A. Harding

Allagash Falls rushes along the Allagash River through a pine forest in northwestern Maine. The winding river flows for about 80 miles (130 kilometers) through the state's wilderness.

measured in a straight line, it totals 228 miles (367 kilometers). However, if all of the area that is washed by water is measured, the coastline totals 3,478 miles (5,597 kilometers).

Mountains. Mount Katahdin, Maine's highest peak, rises 5,268 feet (1,606 meters) in the central part of the state. Nine other mountains are more than 4,000 feet (1,200 meters) high, and 97 others are over 3,000 feet (910 meters) high. Most of the mountains are forested and look green all year long. Cadillac Mountain towers 1,530 feet (466 meters) on Mount Desert Island. It is the highest point on the Atlantic coast between Labrador, Canada, and Rio de Janeiro, Brazil.

Rivers and lakes. Maine has more than 5,000 rivers and streams. Two of the chief rivers, the Androscoggin and the Saco, begin in New Hampshire. They flow across southern Maine and empty into the Atlantic Ocean. Two other important rivers, the Kennebec and the Penobscot, rise in lakes of north-central Maine. They wind down the center of the state, and empty into coastal bays. The St. Croix River forms the southern part of the border between Maine and New Brunswick. In northern Maine, the St. John River also is part of the border with New Brunswick. The St. John is the longest river in the northern part of the state.

Many of Maine's more than 2,500 lakes and ponds gleam like blue gems among dark forests. Moosehead, the largest lake, covers about 120 square miles (311 square kilometers) in the west-central part of the state.

Other large lakes in Maine include the Belgrades, the Grands, Rangeley, and Sebago.

Plant and animal life. Forests cover nearly 90 per cent of Maine. Valuable trees include the balsam fir, basswood, beech, hemlock, maple, oak, pine, spruce, and white and yellow birch. The speckled alder, a common shrub, thrives in Maine's swamps and pastures. Witch hazel borders much of the state's forestland. Chokeberries, shadbush, sumac, and thorn apples grow along country roads and farm fences. Blueberry bushes carpet the ground in much of Hancock and Washington counties and in a few other areas.

Maine's most common wild flowers are the anemone, aster, bittersweet, black-eyed Susan, buttercup, goldenrod, harebell, hepatica, Indian pipe, orange and red hawkweed, white oxeye daisy, and wild bergamot. Lady's-slippers and delicate mayflowers are found scattered through many of Maine's wooded areas. Jack-in-the-pulpit, knotgrass, lavender, and wild lily of the valley grow along the coast and many lakeshores.

Bobcats and black bears are found in several areas of Maine, particularly in the northern and western woods and mountains. Other fur-bearing animals of the forests include beavers, foxes, lynxes, martens, minks, raccoons, and skunks. Game animals found in Maine include rabbits, squirrels, white-tailed deer, black bears, and moose.

More than 320 kinds of birds live in Maine. The most common ones are buntings, chickadees, grackles, owls, sparrows, swallows, thrushes, and wrens. Ducks, gulls, loons, and other sea birds live on the coastal islands in the state.

The game fishes most commonly found in Maine's lakes and streams are brook trout, landlocked salmon, and smallmouth bass. Other fishes of the inland waters include bass, white and yellow perch, and pickerel. Every spring, thousands of alewives swim up Maine's coastal rivers to lay their eggs. Then they return to the ocean. Atlantic salmon are found in the Dennys, Machias, and other rivers. Fishes in the state's coastal waters include cod, flounder, hake, mackerel, pollock, striped bass, and tuna.

Climate. Maine has cooler weather than most of the rest of the United States. Arctic air and coastal winds from the *Labrador Current,* a cold ocean current that rises from the Arctic Ocean, keeps Maine from being warmed by Gulf Stream air. For this reason, Maine has few hot summer days.

Maine's temperature averages 15° F. (−9° C) in January and 67° F. (19° C) in July. The state's record low temperature, −48° F. (−44° C), was set in Van Buren on Jan. 19, 1925. Maine's record high temperature, 105° F. (41° C), was set in North Bridgton on July 10, 1911.

Maine's yearly *precipitation* (rain, melted snow, and other forms of moisture) averages about 41 inches (104 centimeters). The annual snowfall varies from about 70 inches (180 centimeters) near the coast to about 100 inches (250 centimeters) in the interior. The coastal area has much fog.

A moose drinks in a Maine pond. Moose, bobcats, and black bears live in the remote regions of northwest Maine.

Stan Osolinski, FPG

Average monthly weather

	Caribou Temperatures F° High Low		C° High Low		Days of rain or snow		Portland Temperatures F° High Low		C° High Low		Days of rain or snow
Jan.	18	−1	−8	−18	14	Jan.	31	11	−1	−12	12
Feb.	20	0	−7	−18	13	Feb.	32	11	0	−12	11
Mar.	31	13	−1	−11	12	Mar.	41	22	5	−6	11
Apr.	43	26	6	−3	13	Apr.	52	32	11	0	12
May	59	38	15	3	13	May	63	42	17	6	13
June	69	48	21	9	14	June	73	51	23	11	12
July	75	54	24	12	14	July	79	57	26	14	9
Aug.	72	51	22	11	12	Aug.	77	55	25	13	9
Sept.	63	43	17	6	11	Sept.	70	47	21	8	8
Oct.	51	33	11	1	11	Oct.	60	37	16	3	8
Nov.	36	22	2	−6	13	Nov.	47	28	8	−2	11
Dec.	22	7	−6	−14	14	Dec.	35	16	2	−9	11

Average January temperatures

Maine winters are warmer than winters of many inland places as far north. Temperatures are coldest in the far north.

Average July temperatures

Maine summers are mild. Temperatures are warmest along the Atlantic coast and get increasingly cooler northward.

Average yearly precipitation

The greatest area of precipitation lies along the coast. The interior of the state receives the highest yearly snowfall.

WORLD BOOK maps

Degrees Fahrenheit	Degrees Celsius
Above 18	Above -8
14 to 18	-10 to -8
10 to 14	-12 to -10
Below 10	Below -12

Degrees Fahrenheit	Degrees Celsius
Above 68	Above 20
66 to 68	19 to 20
65 to 66	18 to 19
Below 65	Below 18

Inches	Centimeters
More than 44	More than 112
40 to 44	102 to 112
38 to 40	97 to 102
Less than 38	Less than 97

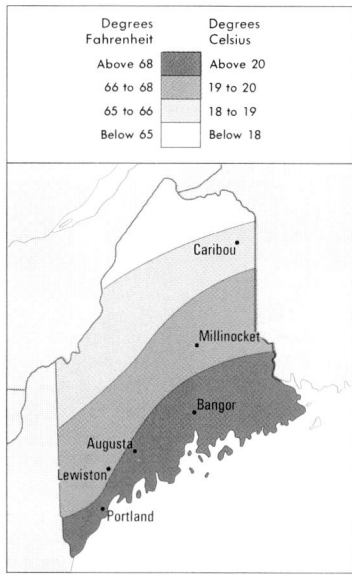

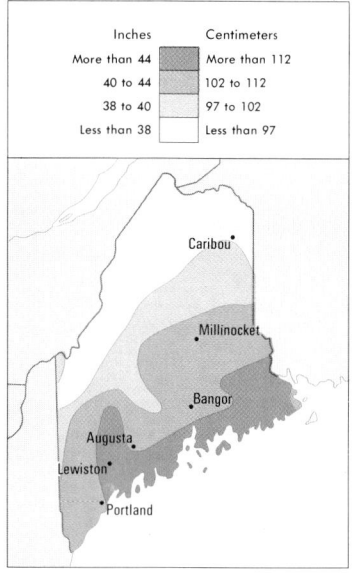

Service industries, taken together, account for nearly three-fourths of Maine's *gross state product*—that is, the total value of all goods and services produced in a state in a year. The state's leading industries are (1) community, social, and personal services and (2) manufacturing. Each supplies 18 percent of the gross state product. Farms are important in southern Maine and in Aroostook County. Millions of tourists visit Maine each year. Tourist activities contribute about $2 billion a year to the state's economy.

Natural resources of Maine include forests, fertile soils, and mineral deposits.

Soil in Maine ranges from sand in the western part of the state to heavy loams in the northern regions. Clay soils cover much of Maine's lowlands. Gravelly soils are common at Maine's higher elevations. These soils once supported many small family farms. Today, farms are larger, but most are still family-owned.

Minerals. Southern Maine has many granite and limestone deposits, but few of them are mined. Tourmaline, a gemstone that is Maine's state mineral, is found in southwestern Maine. Slate deposits lie near Brownville and Monson in the central part of the state. Aroostook County has one of the largest copper and zinc deposits in the United States. Other minerals include brick clay, feldspar, garnet, lead, peat, sand and gravel, silver, and stone. Most of the mines in Maine are on the coast.

Forests cover about 18 million acres (7.3 million hectares) in Maine, or nearly 90 percent of the total land area—the highest percentage of any state in the nation. The forests supply the raw material for many manufactured products of Maine. Private companies and individuals own nearly all of Maine's forestland. Until the late 1700's, the white pine tree was Maine's greatest resource. The white pine was used mainly to make masts for ships. By the mid-1800's, the pines had been cut down throughout the state. Today, most of the state's many pine trees are second-growth trees. Other valu-

Production and workers by economic activities

Economic activities	Percent of GSP* produced	Employed workers	
		Number of persons	Percent of total
Community, social, & personal services	18	125,800	23
Manufacturing	18	106,000	18
Finance, insurance, & real estate	17	25,000	4
Wholesale and retail trade	16	126,600	24
Government	13	96,000	18
Transportation, communication, & utilities	19	22,000	4
Construction	6	21,800	4
Agriculture & fishing	3	18,900	4
Mining	1	100	†
Total	**100**	**532,200**	**100**

*GSP = gross state product, the total value of goods and services produced in a year.
†Less than one-half of 1 per cent.
Figures are for 1991.
Sources: *World Book* estimates based on data from U.S. Bureau of Economic Analysis, U.S. Bureau of Labor Statistics, and U.S. Department of Agriculture.

able trees that grow in Maine include the balsam fir, basswood, beech, hemlock, maple, oak, spruce, and white and yellow birch.

Service industries account for 73 percent of the gross state product of Maine. Most of the state's service industries are concentrated in metropolitan areas.

Community, social, and personal services form Maine's leading service industry in terms of the gross state product. This industry consists of a variety of businesses, including doctors' offices and private hospitals, hotels, law firms, and repair shops.

Finance, insurance, and real estate rank second among the service industries. Real estate is the most important part of this industry. It includes the buying and selling of houses and the renting of apartments and office space. Portland is Maine's major center of banking and insurance.

Wholesale and retail trade rank third among the service industries. This industry employs more people than any of Maine's other industries. Portland, Bangor, and the Lewiston-Auburn metropolitan area are leading centers of Maine's wholesale and retail trade. Portland is one of the chief trading ports on the Atlantic coast. It plays a major role in the state's wholesale paper and pulp trade. Bangor is an important trade and distribution center on the Penobscot River. The Lewiston-Auburn area is a leading center of the textile trade. Important types of retail establishments include automobile dealerships, discount stores, grocery stores, and restaurants.

Government is the fourth-ranking service industry. Government services include public schools and hospitals, and military establishments. Government activities are based in Augusta.

Transportation, communication, and utilities are last in importance among Maine's service industries. Shipping and trucking firms are the major part of the state's transportation industry. Telephone companies provide most of the income in the communications sector. Utilities provide electric, gas, and water service. More infor-

© Eunice Harris, Photo Researchers

An outdoor cafe in Kennebunkport is a pleasant attraction for visitors. Tourism is important to Maine's economy.

Tom Tracy, FPG

Huge rolls of paper are manufactured in a Maine paper mill. The production of paper and paper products, such as cardboard boxes, paper bags, and pulp, is Maine's leading industry.

Farm, mineral, and forest products

This map shows where the state's leading farm, mineral, and forest products are produced. The major urban areas (shown on the map in red) are the state's important manufacturing centers.

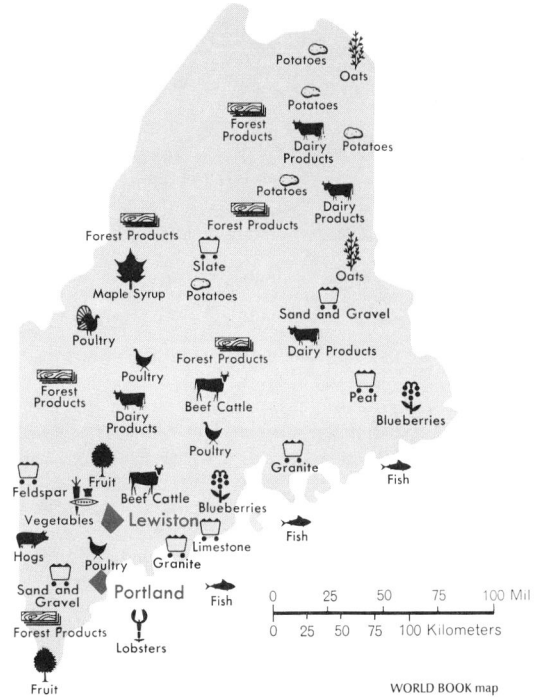

WORLD BOOK map

mation about transportation and communication appears later in this section.

Manufacturing in Maine accounts for 18 percent of the gross state product. Goods manufactured in the state have a *value added by manufacture* of about 5\frac{1}{2}$ billion a year. Value added by manufacture represents the increase in value of raw materials after they become finished products.

Paper products, which include cardboard boxes, paper bags, and pulp, as well as paper, are Maine's leading manufactured products. There are large paper and pulp mills in Bucksport, Jay, Lincoln, Madison, Old Town, Rumford, Skowhegan, Winslow, and Westbrook. Georgia-Pacific Corporation, with factories in Millinocket and East Millinocket, is one of the nation's largest producers of newsprint. Spruce and fir trees provide most of the wood used in Maine's paper and pulp industries.

Transportation equipment is the second most important manufactured product of Maine. Ship and boat-building and repair are important manufacturing activities in the state.

Wood products rank third among manufactured goods made in Maine. Lumber is the leading type of wood product. Sawmills and lumber camps operate in many parts of the state. They are especially important in northern Maine. Specialty wood products are also important in Maine. The state leads the nation in toothpick production. Other specialty wood products include clothespins, lobster traps, and matches.

Electrical equipment is the fourth-ranking manufac-

tured product. The value of the products manufactured by the electrical equipment industry in Maine has increased rapidly since the mid-1970's. The most valuable products made by this industry are electrical *components* (parts) used in making computers.

Other types of manufactured products made in Maine, in order of importance, include food products, leather products, printed materials, fabricated metal products, and plastic products. Canned and frozen foods are among the chief food products. Canned sardines and frozen French fries bring in much income. Maine food processing plants also pack lobsters, blueberries, and apples for shipping to other states. Bread, packaged chicken, and soft drinks are among the other processed foods produced in the state. Newspapers are the main type of printed material. Footwear is the most important type of leather product. The L. L. Bean Company of Freeport is famous for its boots and other outdoor wear.

Agriculture plays a small role in Maine's economy. Farmland covers only 5 percent of the state. Maine's approximately 7,100 farms average 200 acres (81 hectares) in size.

Livestock and livestock products account for most of the income of Maine farmers. Milk and eggs are the leading livestock products. Each earns about a fourth of the state's annual farm income. Most of Maine's dairy farms are located in Androscoggin, Kennebec, Penobscot, Somerset, and Waldo counties. Egg production is greatest in the southern part of the state. Beef cattle are Maine's third most valuable livestock product. Other

© Martin Rogers, FPG

Potatoes are Maine's most valuable farm crop. Maine is a leading potato-growing state.

livestock raised on Maine farms include chickens, hogs, sheep, and turkeys.

Potatoes, Maine's most valuable farm crop, earn about a fourth of the farm income. Maine is one of the leading potato-growing states. Most of Maine's 2-billion-pound (900 million-kilogram) annual potato crop comes from Aroostook County. Oats are an important field crop in Maine. Many farmers rotate oats and potatoes to keep soil fertile. Hay is raised chiefly as cattle feed. Many farmers also grow corn to feed cattle. Greenhouse and nursery products and dry beans, peas, and other vegetables are also grown in Maine.

Apples are Maine's most valuable fruit. They are grown chiefly in Androscoggin, Kennebec, Oxford, and York counties. The chief variety is McIntosh. Other varieties include Cortland, Delicious, and Golden Delicious. Other Maine fruits include blueberries, raspberries, and strawberries.

Fishing industry. Maine's annual fish catch is valued at about $135 million. Maine ranks high among the states in the value of fish and shellfish caught. Its yearly lobster catch of about 22 million pounds (10 million kilograms) is the largest of any state. Maine ranks second to Maryland in the quantity of soft-shell clams caught. The fish catch brings in valuable amounts of cod, flounder, ocean perch, pollock, and sea herring. Portland and Rockland are the chief fishing ports in Maine. Almost every community along the coast has at least a small fleet of fishing boats.

Mining provides less than one-half of 1 percent of the gross state product. The state's mineral industry is based on the production of sand and gravel and limestone. Southwestern Maine produces most of the state's sand and gravel. Sand and gravel are used mainly to make roadbeds and concrete. Limestone is crushed for use in cement. Knox and Aroostook counties have limestone quarries. Crushed sandstone, traprock, and marl are produced in Cumberland and Penobscot counties.

Maine's other mineral products include clays, garnet, gemstones, and peat. Garnet, used in grinding and polishing, is mined in Oxford County. Southwestern Maine also provides such gemstones as amethyst, topaz, and tourmaline. Brick manufacturers mine clays in Androscoggin and Cumberland counties. Washington County in eastern Maine has a large peat bog.

Northern Maine has large copper and zinc deposits.

Mining companies have been slow to develop these deposits, however, because they are difficult to mine.

Electric power. Nuclear plants account for about two-thirds of the electric power used in Maine. Hydroelectric plants provide about 20 percent of the state's power. The majority of the hydroelectric plants in Maine are located on the Androscoggin, Kennebec, Penobscot, and Saco rivers. Plants that burn petroleum provide most of the rest of Maine's electric power. The first United States power plant to produce electricity from peat began operation in Deblois in 1989. Maine purchases some electric power from Canada in order to help fulfill its needs.

Transportation. Maine began developing good roads during the early 1800's. Today, the state has about 22,000 miles (35,000 kilometers) of roads and highways, almost all of which are surfaced. The Maine Turnpike runs about 100 miles (160 kilometers) between York and Augusta. U.S. Interstate Highway 95 extends the turnpike from Augusta to Houlton, near the Canadian border. U.S. Highway 1 follows the coast of Maine.

Maine's first railroad was built in 1836 to carry lumber between Bangor and Old Town. Today, railroads provide freight service within the state. The largest of these are the Bangor & Aroostook, and Canadian Pacific. None of the freight railroads provide passenger service. VIA Rail Canada is the only passenger line that serves Maine. It links five Maine towns with Canadian cities in Quebec and New Brunswick.

Portland International Jetport is Maine's busiest airport. Bangor International Airport is the closest airport to Europe within the United States.

Large oceangoing vessels can dock at some Maine ports. Eastport, Portland, and Searsport have the state's busiest docks. Eastport is closer to Europe than any other U.S. transatlantic port. It is a major entry point for oil that is shipped by pipeline to Canada. At the Port of Portland, the Bath Iron Works in Bath runs one of the largest dry-dock facilities for ship repair on the east

Brian Smith, Stock, Boston

The Bath Iron Works in Bath is a leading U.S. shipbuilder. Many smaller Maine boatyards build fishing and sailing vessels.

coast. Ferries operate between both Portland and Bar Harbor, Me., and Yarmouth, N.S.

Communication. Maine has about 60 newspapers, 9 of which are dailies. The *Bangor Daily News* is the largest daily. The Gannett newspaper chain publishes the *Kennebec Journal* in Augusta, the *Central Maine Morning Sentinel* in Waterville, the *Portland Press Herald,*

and the *Maine Sunday Telegram,* also in Portland. The *Falmouth Gazette,* Maine's first paper, began in Falmouth (now Portland) in 1785. About 40 periodicals are published in the state.

Maine's first radio station, WABI, began operating in Bangor in 1924. The state's first television station, WABI-TV, started broadcasting in 1953 from Bangor.

Government

Constitution. Maine is governed under its original constitution. The Constitution was adopted in December 1819, about three months before Maine became a state. Amendments to the Constitution may be proposed by a two-thirds vote in both the Senate and the House of Representatives. To become law, these amendments need the approval of a majority of the state's voters in a regular election. Amendments also can be proposed by a constitutional convention. A two-thirds vote in both houses of the Legislature is needed to call a constitutional convention. Maine has never held such a convention.

Executive. The governor is the only Maine executive official elected by the people. The governor serves a four-year term. The governor may serve any number of terms but may not serve more than two of the terms in succession. Maine has no lieutenant governor. The Legislature elects the attorney general, secretary of state, and state treasurer to two-year terms. It elects the state auditor to a four-year term.

Legislature of Maine consists of a 35-member Senate and a 151-member House of Representatives. Each of the state's 35 senatorial districts elects one senator. Maine has 151 representative districts, each of which elects one representative. Senators and representatives are elected to two-year terms in even-numbered years. They hold two legislative sessions. The first one begins on the first Wednesday of December following the election. It may last until the third Wednesday in June. The second session begins on the Wednesday following the first Tuesday of January of the next even-numbered year. It may last until the third Wednesday in April. Either session may be extended for up to five days by a two-thirds vote of the Legislature.

In 1969, Maine voters approved a constitutional amendment requiring the Senate to be *reapportioned* (redivided) to give equal representation based on population. The Legislature drew up a reapportionment plan, but the governor vetoed it. In February 1972, the state Supreme Judicial Court ordered a plan which required a

The governors of Maine

	Party	Term		Party	Term
William King	Democratic	1820-1821	**Daniel F. Davis**	Republican	1880-1881
William D. Williamson	Democratic	1821	**Harris M. Plaisted**	Democratic	1881-1883
Benjamin Ames	Democratic	1821-1822	**Frederick Robie**	Republican	1883-1887
Albion K. Parris	Democratic	1822-1827	**Joseph R. Bodwell**	Republican	1887
Enoch Lincoln	Democratic	1827-1829	**S. S. Marble**	Republican	1887-1889
Nathan Cutler	Democratic	1829-1830	**Edwin C. Burleigh**	Republican	1889-1893
Joshua Hall	Democratic	1830	**Henry B. Cleaves**	Republican	1893-1897
Jonathan Hunton	National Republican	1830-1831	**Llewellyn Powers**	Republican	1897-1901
			John Fremont Hill	Republican	1901-1905
Samuel E. Smith	Democratic	1831-1834	**William T. Cobb**	Republican	1905-1909
Robert Dunlap	Democratic	1834-1838	**Bert M. Fernald**	Republican	1909-1911
Edward Kent	Whig	1838-1839	**Frederick W. Plaisted**	Democratic	1911-1913
John Fairfield	Democratic	1839-1841	**William T. Haines**	Republican	1913-1915
Edward Kent	Whig	1841-1842	**Oakley C. Curtis**	Democratic	1915-1917
John Fairfield	Democratic	1842-1843	**Carl E. Milliken**	Republican	1917-1921
Edward Kavanagh	Democratic	1843-1844	**Frederic H. Parkhurst**	Republican	1921
Hugh J. Anderson	Democratic	1844-1847	**Percival P. Baxter**	Republican	1921-1925
John W. Dana	Democratic	1847-1850	**Ralph Owen Brewster**	Republican	1925-1929
John Hubbard	Democratic	1850-1853	**William Tudor Gardiner**	Republican	1929-1933
William G. Crosby	Whig	1853-1855	**Louis J. Brann**	Democratic	1933-1937
Anson P. Morrill	Republican	1855-1856	**Lewis O. Barrows**	Republican	1937-1941
Samuel Wells	Democratic	1856-1857	**Sumner Sewall**	Republican	1941-1945
Hannibal Hamlin	Republican	1857	**Horace A. Hildreth**	Republican	1945-1949
Joseph H. Williams	Republican	1857-1858	**Frederick G. Payne**	Republican	1949-1952
Lot M. Morrill	Republican	1858-1861	**Burton M. Cross**	Republican	1952-1955
Israel Washburn, Jr.	Republican	1861-1863	**Edmund S. Muskie**	Democratic	1955-1959
Abner Coburn	Republican	1863-1864	**Robert Haskell**	Republican	1959
Samuel Cony	Republican	1864-1867	**Clinton Clauson**	Democratic	1959
Joshua L. Chamberlain	Republican	1867-1871	**John H. Reed**	Republican	1959-1967
Sidney Perham	Republican	1871-1874	**Kenneth M. Curtis**	Democratic	1967-1975
Nelson Dingley, Jr.	Republican	1874-1876	**James B. Longley**	Independent	1975-1979
Seldon Connor	Republican	1876-1879	**Joseph E. Brennan**	Democratic	1979-1987
Alonzo Garcelon	Democratic	1879-1880	**John R. McKernan, Jr.**	Republican	1987-

33-member Senate. The plan took effect in November 1972. In 1983, the state adopted a new plan, which required a 35-member Senate. It took effect in 1984.

Courts. The Supreme Judicial Court is Maine's highest court of appeals for all civil and criminal cases. The court has a chief justice and six associate justices. Each justice serves a seven-year term. Maine's superior court handles all cases requiring trial by jury, and all cases appealed from lower courts. The 14 superior court justices serve seven-year terms. Maine's 33 district courts, which are divided among the state's 13 districts, hear cases involving damages of less than $20,000. District court judges serve seven-year terms. The justices of the Supreme Judicial Court, the superior courts, and the district courts are appointed by the governor with the approval of two-thirds of the Senate. Each county in Maine has a probate court, whose judges are elected by the people to four-year terms.

Local government. Each of Maine's 22 cities has *home rule.* That is, each city may adopt or revise a charter without approval of the Legislature. Most cities have a mayor-council or city-manager form of government.

Maine has 467 towns and *plantations* (small incorporated areas). Most towns in Maine consist of several communities governed together as a unit. The town meeting is the most common form of government in Maine towns. It allows citizens to take a direct part in government. Each year, voters assemble to elect officials, approve budgets, and do other business. The chief town officials are called *selectmen.* Maine's plantations are each governed by a board of assessors. Maine also has 422 townships that have no organized government. In addition, the state has three self-governing Indian townships, each headed by a governor, a lieutenant governor, and a tribal council. Each of Maine's 16 counties has its own government.

Revenue. Taxation provides about 55 per cent of the state government's *general revenue* (income). Most of the rest comes from federal grants and other U.S. government programs. Sales taxes account for about half of the tax revenue, and income taxes account for about a third. Sales taxes, ranked in order of importance, include a general sales tax, and taxes on motor fuels, alcoholic beverages, tobacco products, utility bills, insurance, and horse races. Income taxes consist of personal and corporation income taxes. Other sources of tax revenue include license fees, a death and gift tax, and a state property tax. The property tax is the chief source of income for Maine's public school districts.

Politics. Maine was a Democratic state before the 1850's. But most Maine voters became Republicans in the period shortly before the Civil War. They favored the Republican Party's antislavery and pro-Northern policies. For about a hundred years, until the 1950's, Maine voters almost always elected Republicans in state, congressional, and presidential elections. The Republicans are still a strong party in Maine. But since the 1960's, the Democrats have received almost as much support, and at times even more. For example, the Democrats have controlled the state legislature since 1982.

Maine has voted for more Republican presidential candidates than any other state except Vermont. Since 1856, only four Democrats—Woodrow Wilson in 1912, Lyndon B. Johnson in 1964, Hubert H. Humphrey in 1968, and Bill Clinton in 1992—have won Maine's electoral votes. For years, Maine held its elections for Congress and governor in September. Its voters often chose candidates from the party that won November elections in other states. This led to the slogan, "As Maine goes, so goes the nation." In 1960, Maine began voting in November. For Maine's voting record in presidential elections, see **Electoral College** (table).

Maine's House of Representatives meets in the State Capitol in Augusta. Representatives serve two-year terms.

Indian days. Thousands of Indians lived in what is now Maine before white settlers came. The Indians belonged to the Abenaki and Etchemin tribes of the Algonquian Indian family. The Abenaki lived west of the Penobscot River, and the Etchemin lived east of the river. The Indians had villages, but often moved in search of food. Their enemy, the Iroquois, frequently raided their villages. Maine Indians lived in peace with the earliest white settlers.

Exploration and settlements. Vikings, led by Leif Ericson, probably visited Maine about A.D. 1000. Many historians believe that John Cabot, an Italian sea captain in the service of England, reached Maine in 1498. France sent many explorers to Maine. These explorers and the dates they reached Maine included Giovanni da Verrazzano (1524), Pierre du Gua (or du Guast), Sieur de Monts (1604), and Samuel de Champlain (1604). Champlain explored and named Mount Desert, the largest island along Maine's coast.

In 1605, Sir Ferdinando Gorges and Sir John Popham, two wealthy Englishmen, sent George Waymouth to explore the Maine coast. Waymouth's favorable reports about the area led Gorges and Popham to attempt a settlement in Maine. In 1607, they financed a group of colonists who established Popham Plantation, near the mouth of the Kennebec River. The death of Popham that winter and Indian troubles forced settlers to return to England in 1608. While in Maine, the settlers built a boat called the *Virginia.* It was the first boat built by English colonists in America. The English made many permanent settlements in Maine during the early 1620's. Perhaps the first one was the settlement made near present-day Saco in 1623.

Ownership disputes developed over Maine during the 1600's. In 1622, the Council for New England, an agency of the English government, gave Ferdinando Gorges and John Mason a large tract of land in present-day Maine and New Hampshire. The land was divided between the two men in 1629, and Gorges received the Maine section. Gorges established Maine's first government in 1636. In 1641, he made the community of Gorgeana (now York) a city. It was the first chartered English city in what is now the United States.

After Gorges died in 1647, the people of Kittery, Wells, and York united under a new government. Between 1652 and 1658, they and the people of Casco Bay, Kennebunk, Saco, and Scarborough agreed to make Maine a part of the Massachusetts Bay Colony. In 1660, the heirs of Gorges disputed Massachusetts' ownership of Maine, and claimed Maine for themselves. In 1664, an English board of commissioners ordered Maine restored to the Gorges family. Massachusetts finally gained clear title to Maine in 1677, when it bought the area from the Gorges family.

French and Indian wars were fought in Maine and the rest of New England off and on from 1689 to 1763. The French and their Indian allies battled to gain control of the area from the English colonists. William Pepperrell of Maine led the capture of the French fortress of Louisbourg, Nova Scotia, in 1745. The capture was one of the major events of the conflict. The French and Indian Wars ended with the Treaty of Paris in 1763. The treaty ended all French claims to Maine and most of the rest of North America.

The Revolutionary War. During the 1760's, Great Britain passed a series of laws that caused unrest in Maine and the rest of colonial America. Most of these laws either imposed severe taxes or restricted colonial trade. In 1774, a group of Maine patriots burned a supply of British tea stored at York. This event, called the *York Tea Party,* resembled the more famous Boston Tea Party of 1773.

The Revolutionary War (1775-1783) started at Lexington and Concord, Mass. Hundreds of Maine patriots joined the fight for independence. The war brought great hardships to Maine towns. In 1775, British troops burned Falmouth (now Portland) to punish the townspeople for opposing the king's policies.

The first naval battle of the Revolutionary War was fought off Machias in June 1775. In the battle, a group of Maine patriots captured the British ship *Margaretta.* Also in 1775, Benedict Arnold and his troops made a long march from Augusta to Quebec. They tried to capture Quebec from the British, but were pushed back. British troops occupied Castine in 1779. Colonial troops tried to recapture the town, but were badly defeated.

Maine's population increased greatly after the war. Massachusetts rewarded its soldiers with gifts of land in Maine, and sold Maine land to other persons.

In the early 1800's, Maine's economy depended on its pine forests. Wood from the forests was used to build ships and many other products. It was also traded for a variety of goods. The Embargo Act of 1807, which limited U.S. trade with other countries, hurt Maine's thriving shipping industry. But the slowdown in shipping forced Maine to seek new income by developing its manufacturing industries.

Statehood. In 1785, a movement began for the separation of Maine from Massachusetts and for Maine's admission to the Union. Many people in Maine protested heavy taxation, poor roads, the long distance to the capital city of Boston, and other conditions. But before the War of 1812, most voters wanted Maine to remain a part of Massachusetts. The separation movement grew much stronger after the war. Many of those who favored separation won election to the legislature. They swayed many voters to their side. The people voted for separation in 1819, and Maine entered the Union as the 23rd state on March 15, 1820. William King became the first state governor, and Portland was the first capital of Maine. Augusta became the capital in 1832.

Maine's admission to the Union became involved in the Missouri Compromise. The compromise called for Maine to enter the Union as a *free state* (a state without slaves) and Missouri to enter the Union as a slave state. This arrangement kept the number of slave and free states equal. See **Missouri Compromise**.

Ever since 1783, the boundary between Maine and New Brunswick had been disputed. The argument led to the so-called Aroostook War of 1839. The U.S. government sent General Winfield Scott to Maine, and he reached a temporary agreement with Canadian officials. No fighting took place. The boundary was finally set by the Webster-Ashburton Treaty of 1842. See **Webster-Ashburton Treaty**.

In 1846, Maine became the first state to pass a law prohibiting the manufacture and sale of alcoholic beverages. But the law did not provide for effective enforce-

Historic Maine

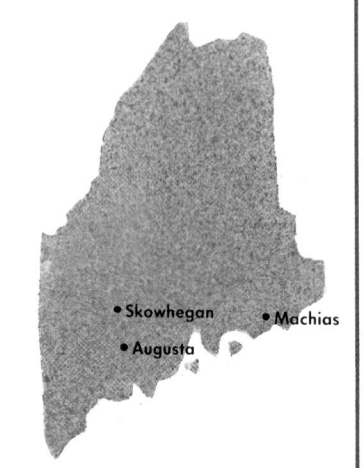

• Skowhegan   • Machias
• Augusta

Maine's northern boundary with Canada was fixed by treaty in 1842. Fort Kent was the center of an earlier dispute called the Aroostook War.

Maine entered the Union in 1820 as a free state (without slaves). Its admission was part of the Missouri Compromise.

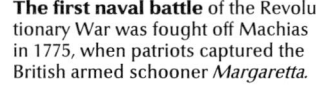

The first naval battle of the Revolutionary War was fought off Machias in 1775, when patriots captured the British armed schooner *Margaretta.*

In 1775, Benedict Arnold led an army through the Kennebec Valley into Canada to attack Quebec.

Margaret Chase Smith, a Maine Republican, became the first woman to be elected to both houses of the United States Congress. She was born in Skowhegan.

WORLD BOOK illustrations by Kevin Chadwick

Important dates in Maine

1000? Vikings probably visited the Maine coast.

1498 John Cabot probably explored the Maine coast.

1607 English settlers established the Popham Colony near the mouth of the Kennebec River.

1622 Maine lands were granted by royal charter to Sir Ferdinando Gorges and John Mason.

1641 Gorgeana (now York) became the first chartered English city in what is now the United States.

1677 Massachusetts bought Maine from the heirs of Ferdinando Gorges.

1763 The Treaty of Paris ended French efforts to gain control of Maine.

1775 The first naval battle of the Revolutionary War took place off the Maine coast.

1820 Maine became the 23rd state on March 15.

1842 The Webster-Ashburton Treaty settled a long dispute over the Maine-Canada border.

1851 Maine became the first state to outlaw the sale of alcoholic beverages.

1911 Maine adopted a direct-primary voting law.

1964 Maine voted for Lyndon B. Johnson, supporting a Democratic presidential candidate for the first time since 1912.

1969 Maine adopted personal and corporate income taxes.

1980 The U.S. government agreed to pay $81½ million to the Passamaquoddy and Penobscot Indians of Maine for lands seized during the late 1700's and early 1800's.

Ships built in Maine have been famous for more than 300 years. The *Roanoke, left,* was the largest wooden American full-rigged ship ever used in the merchant service. It was launched in 1892.

Maine Maritime Museum

ment. In 1851, the state passed a new law that banned the production and sale of alcoholic beverages. This law remained in force until 1934.

Antislavery feelings grew strong in Maine during the early 1830's. The state's Baptists and Congregationalists opposed slavery especially strongly. About 72,000 Maine men served with the Union forces during the Civil War (1861-1865). Hannibal Hamlin, a former U.S. senator and governor of Maine, served as Vice President of the United States during the war under President Abraham Lincoln.

Industrial development increased greatly after the Civil War. The textile and leather industries were among those that grew at record rates. Farming activity and rural populations decreased as industry grew. During the 1890's, Maine began developing hydroelectric power on its rivers. Businesses competed for the best power sites, and the state legislature acted to protect the state's power interests. In 1909, the legislature outlawed the sale of hydroelectric power outside the state in order to keep the power in Maine and attract new industries. The law remained in force until 1955.

The early 1900's. In 1907, Maine adopted an initiative and referendum law (see **Initiative and referendum**). The state adopted a direct primary voting law in 1911. This law gives Maine voters a voice in choosing candidates for state elections.

The number of small farms in Maine continued to decrease during the 1920's. Many large farms were started, especially in Aroostook County. These farms specialized in potato growing and in dairy and poultry products. Industrial growth also continued during the 1920's. However, some Maine textile mills moved to the South because of lower costs there. The state made up its loss with a greatly expanded paper and pulp industry. The Great Depression of the 1930's slowed Maine's econ-

omy. But conditions improved as the depression eased in the late 1930's.

The mid-1900's. Margaret Chase Smith, a Maine Republican, won fame during the 1940's. She became the first woman elected to both houses of the U.S. Congress. Smith served in the House of Representatives from 1940 to 1949 and in the Senate from 1949 to 1973.

During World War II (1939-1945), Maine mills and factories produced military shoes and uniforms. Shipyards in Bath and South Portland built cargo and combat vessels. After the war, the state legislature passed laws to encourage industry to come to Maine. These laws included reduced tax rates for new businesses. The highway system was expanded, and many motels were built

AT&T Bell Laboratories

A satellite earth station near Andover sends and receives signals and tracks satellites as they orbit the earth. An inflated dome, *background,* covers an antenna. The control building, *foreground,* houses computing and tracking equipment.

The Maine Indian Claims Settlement Act was signed by President Jimmy Carter on Oct. 10, 1980. During the late 1970's, the Passamaquoddy and Penobscot tribes of Maine sued to recover about 12 million acres (4.8 million hectares) of land taken by white settlers centuries ago. These tribes agreed to drop their lawsuit in exchange for an $81 $\frac{1}{2}$-million settlement from the federal government.

AP/Wide World

to accommodate Maine's growing tourist trade.

During the 1950's, Maine's economy was helped by the construction of Air Force bases. Small-scale farming all but ended in Maine, and some of the state's oldest textile mills closed. Many small electronics companies were established in the state during this period.

The state Department of Economic Development, established in 1955, and various community development groups helped bring new industries to Maine during the 1960's. Paper and pulp companies expanded, and Maine's food-processing industry also grew. Improved skiing facilities attracted thousands of winter tourists.

The Democratic Party gained strength during the 1950's and 1960's. In 1955, Edmund S. Muskie became Maine's first Democratic governor since 1937. In 1958, he became the first Democrat ever elected to the United States Senate by Maine voters. President Lyndon B. Johnson won Maine's electoral votes in 1964—the first time Maine voted for a Democratic presidential candidate in more than 50 years. Muskie was the Democratic vice presidential candidate in 1968. Maine supported him and presidential candidate Hubert H. Humphrey. In 1969, the Maine legislature approved state personal and corporate income taxes for the first time.

Recent developments. In 1980, the United States government agreed to pay $81 $\frac{1}{2}$ million to the Passamaquoddy and Penobscot Indians of Maine. The money was payment for Indian land seized through false and illegal treaties during the late 1700's and early 1800's.

Maine's economic development has been uneven since the early 1970's. The pulp and paper industry expanded rapidly at first, but increased automation has since eliminated many jobs. Maine's valuable fir and spruce forests have been overharvested and damaged by insects. A fishing boom in the late 1970's led to overfishing. The resulting lower fish catch and foreign competition damaged Maine's fishing industry in the 1980's. Also in the 1980's, Maine's potato farmers struggled with low prices and heavy debts, and many abandoned their farms. In addition, foreign competition has taken the jobs of many Maine shoeworkers.

Maine has benefited from efforts begun in the 1960's by environmentalists to clean up the state's rivers and harbors. Laws they sponsored have forced paper companies and municipalities to improve procedures to dispose of nuclear and other wastes. Waterways are cleaner, and attempts to set up oil refineries at various coastal sites have been defeated. Still, issues such as acid rain and heavy cutting of forests continue to challenge the state (see **Acid rain**).

Maine's economic problems occurred mainly in the northern and central areas of the state. Mainers in the southwestern area found jobs in shipbuilding and electronics and in new service industries. Coastal and ski areas profited from expanded tourism in the 1980's. These developments helped keep the state's unemployment rate below the national average. But at the end of the decade, Maine began to feel the effects of a slowing economic growth in New England.

Richard H. Condon and Paul B. Frederic

Study aids

Related articles in *World Book* include:

Biographies

Blaine, James G.	Longfellow, Henry W.
Coffin, Robert P. T.	Mitchell, George J.
Fessenden, William Pitt	Muskie, Edmund S.
Gilbreth, Frank and Lillian	Reed, Thomas B.
Hamlin, Hannibal	Sewall, Arthur
Jewett, Sarah Orne	Smith, Margaret Chase
King (William)	

Cities

Augusta	Bangor	Lewiston	Portland

History

Acadia	Missouri Compromise
Colonial life in America	Webster-Ashburton Treaty
French and Indian Wars	

Physical features

Kennebec River	Mount Desert Island

Passamaquoddy Bay   Saint John River
Penobscot River

Other related articles

Acadia National Park
Portsmouth Naval Shipyard
Saint Croix Island International Historic Site

Outline

I. People
  A. Population   C. Libraries
  B. Schools   D. Museums
II. Visitor's guide
  A. Places to visit
  B. Annual events
III. Land and climate
  A. Land regions   D. Rivers and lakes
  B. Coastline   E. Plant and animal life
  C. Mountains   F. Climate
IV. Economy
  A. Natural resources   F. Mining
  B. Service industries   G. Electric power
  C. Manufacturing   H. Transportation
  D. Agriculture   I. Communication
  E. Fishing industry
V. Government
  A. Constitution   E. Local government
  B. Executive   F. Revenue
  C. Legislature   G. Politics
  D. Courts
VI. History

Questions

What caused the Aroostook War?
What is Maine's most popular historic site?
What was Maine's first industry?
What is the legend of Wedding Cake House?
When did the English first try to settle in Maine?
What is Maine's most important economic activity?
What is Maine's largest island?
In what way was Maine involved in the Missouri Compromise?
To what state did Maine belong before it joined the Union in 1820?
What man from Maine served as Vice President of the United States?

Additional resources

Level I
Carpenter, Allan. *Maine.* Rev. ed. Childrens Pr., 1979.
Engfer, LeeAnne. *Maine.* Lerner, 1991.
Harrington, Ty. *Maine.* Childrens Pr., 1989.

Level II
Banks, Ronald F. *Maine Becomes a State: The Movement to Separate Maine from Massachusetts, 1785-1820.* Wesleyan, 1970.
Clark, Charles E. *Maine: A History.* Univ. Pr. of New England, 1990. First published as *Maine: A Bicentennial History* in 1977.
A History of Maine: A Collection of Readings on the History of Maine, 1600-1970. Ed. by Ronald F. Banks. Kendall-Hunt, 1969.
The Maine Atlas and Gazetteer. Ed. by David DeLorme. 15th ed. DeLorme Pub., 1991.
Maine in the Early Republic: From Revolution to Statehood. Ed. by Charles E. Clark and others. Univ. Pr. of New England, 1988.
Maine League of Historical Societies and Museums. *Maine, A Guide "Down East."* Ed. by Dorris A. Isaacson. 2nd ed. Courier-Gazette, Inc., 1970. A revised edition in the American Guide Series.
Rich, Louise D. *State O' Maine.* Down East, 1986. First published in 1964. *The Coast of Maine: An Informal History and Guide.* Rev. ed. Crowell, 1975.
Taylor, Alan. *Liberty Men and Great Proprietors: The Revolutionary Settlement on the Maine Frontier, 1760-1820.* Univ. of North Carolina Pr., 1990.

Maine, University of, is a coeducational, state-supported system of higher education. The official name of the system is the University of Maine System.

The system has campuses in Augusta, Farmington, Fort Kent, Machias, Orono, Portland, Gorham, and Presque Isle. The largest campus, at Orono, has colleges of business administration, sciences, education, forest resources, arts and humanities, social and behavioral sciences, engineering and technology, and applied sciences and agriculture. It offers bachelor's, master's, and doctor's degrees. The Augusta campus grants mostly associate's degrees. The Farmington, Fort Kent, Machias, and Presque Isle campuses offer bachelor's degrees. The Portland and Gorham campuses form the University of Southern Maine, which grants bachelor's, master's, and professional degrees. The Portland and Gorham campuses have a college of liberal arts, and schools of business and economics, education, law, and nursing.

The first campus was founded at Farmington in 1864. The University of Maine System was formed in 1968. For the enrollment of the University of Maine, see **Universities and colleges** (table).

Critically reviewed by the *University of Maine System*

See also **Maine** (picture).

Mainstreaming. See Special education.

Maintenon, *man tuh NAWN,* **Marquise de,** *mar KEEZ duh* (1635-1719), was the second wife of King Louis XIV of France. She had great influence in France during his reign.

The future marquise was born Françoise d'Aubigné in Niort, France. In 1652, she married the much older Paul Scarron, who died in 1660. In 1669, she became governess to Louis XIV's children by his mistress, the Marquise de Montespan. But Louis grew to prefer the governess, giving her land and the title Marquise de Maintenon. After Louis's wife, Queen Marie-Thérèse, died in 1683, he secretly married Maintenon. Scholars disagree on the year of the marriage.

For more than 30 years, Maintenon was the king's trusted adviser. She was deeply religious and tried to raise moral standards at court. Just before Louis's death, Maintenon helped him burn hundreds of documents that could have damaged his historical reputation. In 1686, she founded a school for girls at St. Cyr. She retired there after Louis died in 1715.   Maarten Ultee

See also **Louis XIV.**

Mainz, *mynts* (pop. 188,571), is a commercial and industrial city in southwestern Germany. It lies where the Rhine and Main rivers meet. For location, see **Germany** (political map). Mainz serves as the capital of the state of Rhineland-Palatinate.

Mainz has a beautiful, old inner town. Its numerous landmarks include a cathedral that was begun in 975 and Johannes Gutenberg University, which was founded in 1477. The city's old buildings include examples of Romanesque, Gothic, Renaissance, and Baroque architecture. Mainz produces wines from grapes grown nearby. Other industries include the production of cement, machinery, motor vehicles, and printed materials.

Roman soldiers established a military camp on the site of what is now Mainz in 38 B.C. During the Middle Ages, Mainz became a prosperous city and the seat of archbishops. St. Boniface became its first archbishop in A.D. 745.   Peter H. Merkl

Mair, Charles (1838-1927), was a Canadian poet and journalist. His best-known poetry vividly describes the beauty of the Canadian wilderness. Mair's poetry was collected in *Dreamland and Other Poems* (1868) and *Tecumseh: a Drama, and Canadian Poems* (1901). He also wrote *Through the Mackenzie Basin* (1908), a travel book describing the Mackenzie Basin in northwestern Canada. Mair's conservationist essay "The American Bison" (1890) led to the establishment of a sanctuary for one of the few remaining bison herds.

Mair was born in Lanark, Upper Canada (now in Ontario). During 1869 and 1870, he was a correspondent for the Toronto *Globe* and the Montreal *Gazette*. He helped found the "Canada First" movement, a group that promoted nationalist feeling after the formation of the Dominion of Canada in 1867.   Rosemary Sullivan

Maitland, *MAYT luhnd,* **Frederic William** (1850-1906), an English historian, pioneered in the study of early English legal history. His scholarship produced much of what is known today about the history of Anglo-Saxon law. Maitland was able to sift through masses of contradictory and confusing evidence and find the truth. His important works include *History of the English Law* (1895), which he wrote with Frederick Pollack, and *Domesday Book and Beyond* (1897).

Maitland was born in London, and attended Eton school and Cambridge University. He studied law at Lincoln's Inn, one of the four famous "Inns of Court" in London, where lawyers lived and studied. He practiced law for several years, then became a professor of English law at Cambridge in 1888.   Roland N. Stromberg

Maize. See Corn.

Majolica, *muh JAHL uh kuh* or *muh YAHL uh kuh,* is a type of pottery glazed with tin oxide to produce a soft white color. The name is sometimes spelled *maiolica.* Designs are painted on the white background with other metallic oxides. These oxides turn various colors on the background when the pottery is *fired* (baked).

Majolica is named for the Spanish island of Majorca, where pottery was exported to Italy. Spanish potters began exporting majolica to Italy in the mid-1400's. Centers for producing the pottery arose throughout Italy.

The word *majolica* should be used only to describe

The Bargello, Florence, Italy (Art Resource)

Majolica, a type of Italian pottery, is glazed with tin oxide to produce a soft white color and decorated with bright designs. The majolica medicine jars above were made during the 1600's.

Italian tin oxide-glazed pottery. But the term is also used to refer to the elaborately molded pottery that has been chiefly made in England since the mid-1800's. However, unlike true majolica, most of this pottery is coated with a lead glaze and is generally larger and more decorative than true majolica.   William C. Gates, Jr.

See also **Faïence**.

Major, John (1943-   ), became prime minister of the United Kingdom in November 1990. He took office after Conservative Party members of Parliament chose him as party leader. He succeeded Margaret Thatcher as both prime minister and party leader. Major, at 47, became the youngest British prime minister since 1894. Under his government, the United Kingdom played an important role in the Persian Gulf War of 1991. In 1992, Major's party won the parliamentary elections, and he remained prime minister.

Major was born in Merton, a borough of Greater London. He left school when he was 16. In 1965, Major took an entry-level job at a bank. He worked his way up to executive positions and also became active in London politics. In 1979, he won election to Parliament. Major served as an assistant government

© John Arthur, Impact

John Major

whip in 1983 and as senior whip in 1984. He became a minister for social security in 1985. He was named chief treasury secretary in 1987. Major served as foreign secretary from July to October 1989. He then became chancellor of the exchequer. Major held that post, which involves managing the economy, until he became prime minister.   Richard Rose

Majorca, *muh JAWR kuh,* also called Mallorca, *mah YAWR kuh* (pop. 534,511), is the largest island of the Balearic group. It lies about 100 miles (160 kilometers) off the eastern coast of Spain and is a Spanish possession. See **Spain** (political map). The island has an area of about 1,400 square miles (3,626 square kilometers). Palma is the only large city. Many tourists visit Majorca. Farming and tourism are the island's chief economic activities. Products include almonds, figs, olives, oranges, and wine. Majorca has limestone and marble quarries and some manufacturing. See also **Balearic Islands; Majolica; Spain** (picture: Palma).   Stanley G. Payne

Majority rule is a principle of democratic government that requires a decision to be approved by a majority of voters before it may take effect. A majority consists of at least one more than half the votes cast. Majority rule may be used to elect officials or decide a policy. It may be used by groups that range in size from a small private organization to a large nation. A majority differs from a *plurality.* A candidate with a plurality receives more votes than any other candidate, but not necessarily a majority. For example, in an election in which 10 people vote, a majority would require at least six votes. A plurality might be as few as two votes if one candidate got that number and no other candidate got more than one of the remaining eight votes.

In the United States, Congress and the state legislatures use majority rule to pass laws. A candidate for President also needs a majority of the 538 votes in the Electoral College to be elected. The plurality principle is followed in elections for Congress and for most state or local offices.   Alexander J. Groth

See also **Democracy** (Majority rule and minority rights).

Makalu, Mount. See Mount Makalu.

Makarios III, *muh KAR ee uhs* (1913-1977), a Greek Orthodox clergyman, became the first president of Cyprus in 1959. In July 1974, Cypriot troops led by Greek officers overthrew him, and he was forced to flee the country. He returned to Cyprus in December 1974 and served as president again until his death in 1977. While Makarios was out of office, Turkish troops took over a large part of northeastern Cyprus. See **Cyprus** (History).

Makarios was elected bishop of Kitium in 1948. In 1950, he was elected archbishop and *ethnarch* (national leader) of the Greek Cypriots. He led the Greek Cypriot movement for independence from Britain and for *enosis* (union with Greece). Britain exiled Makarios to Seychelles in 1956 but freed him in 1957. He was elected president after Britain agreed to independence for Cyprus.

Wide World
Archbishop Makarios

Archbishop Makarios was born in Pano Panayia, Cyprus. His real name was Michael Christodoulos Mouskos. He entered a monastery at age 13. He later studied at the National University of Athens in Greece. He also studied theology in the United States at Boston University.   H. Ibrahim Salih

Makeup. See Theater (Makeup techniques); **Cosmetics.**

Malabo, *mah LAH boh* (pop. 15,253), is the capital of Equatorial Guinea. The city lies on Bioko, an island in the Gulf of Guinea (see **Equatorial Guinea** [map]). Malabo is an important seaport. It handles such exports as bananas, cabinet woods, cacao, cinchona bark, coffee, kola nuts, and palm oil. Most of the city's people work for import-export companies. An airport lies near Malabo.

British businessmen and colonists founded the city in 1827. The British called it Clarencetown or Port Clarence. Spain took control of the city in 1844 and named it Santa Isabel. Malabo received its present name in 1973 after Equatorial Guinea had gained independence from Spain.   Immanuel Wallerstein

Malacca, *muh LAK uh,* **Strait of,** is a channel between the Malay Peninsula and the island of Sumatra. The strait connects the South China Sea and the Indian Ocean. It is about 500 miles (800 kilometers) long and from 25 to 100 miles (40 to 160 kilometers) wide. The city of Singapore lies on Singapore Island at the southeastern end of the strait. See **Indonesia** (map). The strait is an important shipping route.   David A. Ross

Malachi, *MAL uh ky,* **Book of,** is a book in the Hebrew Bible or Old Testament. It was written by an anon-

ymous prophet probably about 475 B.C. *Malachi* means *my messenger* and is probably not the writer's name, but a title taken from the book itself.

A central theme of the book is the corruption of the priesthood. This corruption, the book says, caused many people of Judah to question God's justice and to lose their faith. The prophet is also very concerned about intermarriage and predicts the coming of a "messenger" before God's final judgment. This messenger is identified with the prophet Elijah in the last verses. Later writers speculated that Elijah is to return from heaven to announce the Messiah and reunite Israel. This interpretation impressed both Jewish and Christian belief about the expected arrival of the Messiah.   Eric M. Meyers

See also **Elijah; Bible** (Books of the Old Testament).

Malachite, *MAL uh kyt,* is a beautiful green copper mineral. It consists of copper oxide, carbon dioxide, and water, and its chemical formula is $2CuO \cdot CO_2 \cdot H_2O$. Malachite is formed in layers that vary in color from apple green to dark gray-green (see **Mineral** [picture]). It is used chiefly as an ornamental stone. Fine pieces of malachite have been mined in the Ural Mountains of Russia and in Arizona. Other sources of the mineral include Africa, Australia, and Mexico.

In ancient times, people made bracelets of malachite because they thought it provided protection against disease, lightning, and witchcraft. Some scholars believe malachite is the stone the Israelites called *soham*. This stone was one of the sacred jewels in the high priest's breastplate.   Robert B. Cook

Malagasy Republic. See Madagascar.

Malamud, *MA luh mood,* **Bernard** (1914-1986), was an American author. Most of Malamud's fiction describes in a humorous but sympathetic way the misfortunes of city dwellers, particularly Jews.

Malamud's early stories, collected in *The Magic Barrel* (1958), are often comic and sometimes rely on supernatural elements for their humor. But many critics argue that he was at his best in realistic novels. These novels lead the reader to a deeper awareness of how even ordinary people can rise to noble stature, as in his first novel, *The Natural* (1952).

Malamud's novel *The Assistant* (1957) portrays the empty existence of Frank Alpine, a young man who robs a poor Jewish grocer. Alpine repents his crime and works for the grocer. In the process, he learns goodness and moral strength. After the grocer dies, Alpine converts to Judaism. Malamud won the 1967 Pulitzer Prize for fiction for *The Fixer* (1966). This novel examines how moral strength can be gained through oppression. The main character is a Russian Jew arrested for the murder of a Christian child. Although wrongly accused, he suffers quietly until a deepening sense of principle allows him to reach spiritual freedom.

Malamud's other novels are *A New Life* (1961), *The Tenants* (1971), *Dubin's Lives* (1979), and *God's Grace* (1982). His stories were collected in *The Stories of Bernard Malamud* (1983). Malamud was born in New York City.   Victor A. Kramer

Malamute. See Alaskan malamute.

Malaria is a dangerous parasitic disease common in tropical and subtropical areas. It is caused by protozoans called *Plasmodia* and is transmitted by the bite of the female *Anopheles* mosquito. Victims of malaria suffer attacks of chills and fever, and 1 to 2 million people die of the disease yearly.

There are four types of malaria, each of which is caused by a different species of *Plasmodium*. The four protozoans that cause malaria are *P. falciparum, P. vivax, P. ovale,* and *P. malariae.* (The *P.* stands for *Plasmodium.*)

Symptoms. Malaria causes periodic chills, with fevers that may reach 106 °F (41.1 °C). *P. falciparum, P. vivax,* and *P. ovale* cause attacks of chills and fever that recur about every 48 hours. In *P. malariae* infections, chills and fever recur about every 72 hours.

A malarial attack lasts two or more hours and is accompanied by headache, muscular pain, and nausea. After each attack, the patient perspires, causing the body temperature to drop to normal. Between attacks, the patient feels better but is weak and anemic.

The most serious type of the disease is caused by *P. falciparum.* Its victims become weaker with each attack of fever, and most die if untreated. In *P. vivax, P. ovale,* and *P. malariae* cases, the attacks get less severe and finally stop, even without treatment. But in *P. vivax* and *P. ovale* infections, the symptoms may reappear after a long period of apparent freedom from the disease.

Spread. The life cycle of the *Plasmodium* protozoan includes three basic stages. The first stage occurs in the mosquito's body, and the second and third stages take place in a person's body. The first stage begins when the mosquito bites someone who has malaria. *Plasmodia* enter the insect's body and reproduce in its stomach. The protozoan young find their way into the mosquito's saliva.

The second stage occurs after the mosquito bites another person. *Plasmodia* from the mosquito's saliva enter the person's blood. They travel to the liver, where they multiply and form clumps of parasites. After several days, these clumps burst and release new *Plasmodia.*

During the third stage, each *Plasmodium* invades a red blood cell, where it multiplies again. The infected blood cells eventually rupture and release large numbers of *Plasmodia,* which invade additional red blood cells. This invasion, multiplying, and cell rupture by the parasites continues, causing the periodic attacks of fever that are typical of malaria. An attack occurs each time the red blood cells rupture.

Some *Plasmodia* develop further in human blood and are able to reproduce in a mosquito's body. They enter the insect's body when the mosquito bites a person, and their life cycle begins again.

Treatment and prevention. Physicians diagnose malaria by identifying *Plasmodia* in a sample of the patient's blood. Most cases can be cured by using two drugs, chloroquine and primaquine. Some varieties of *P. falciparum* resist treatment by these drugs. In such cases, physicians prescribe quinine, mefloquine, or halofautrine.

Chloroquine can prevent malaria in addition to curing it. In most cases, people who plan to travel in areas where they could be exposed to malaria should take chloroquine before, during, and after their trip.

Prevention of malaria also involves controlling the *Anopheles* mosquito. To do so, workers spray people's homes with insecticides. They drain, spray, or fill in bodies of stagnant water where the insects breed. People also use mosquito netting and insect repellents and put screens on windows and doors.

During the 1950's and 1960's, the World Health Organization (WHO) tried to wipe out malaria. At first, the widespread use of insecticides, particularly DDT, eliminated malaria in some areas and greatly reduced the number of cases in others. However, the fight against malaria slackened, and the number of cases increased again. *Anopheles* mosquitoes became resistant to DDT and other insecticides, and some *Plasmodia* became resistant to drugs. Also, the cost of fighting malaria increased greatly. These problems prompted researchers to step up efforts to develop a vaccine that could help eliminate the disease.   Wasim A. Siddiqui

See also **Cinchona; Laveran, Charles L. A.; Mosquito** (pictures); **Quinine; Races, Human** (Susceptibility to genetic diseases); **Ross, Sir Ronald.**

WORLD BOOK illustrations by Patricia J. Wynne

The life cycle of the malaria parasite

Malaria is caused by protozoans called *Plasmodia.* These organisms spend part of their lives in the bodies of human beings and part in the bodies of *Anopheles* mosquitoes. The disease spreads from person to person through the bite of these mosquitoes.

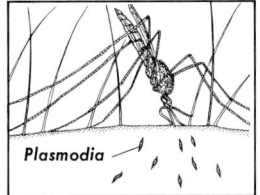

An infected mosquito injects *Plasmodia* with its bite.

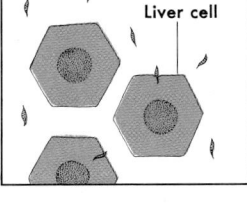

Each *Plasmodium* invades a liver cell and multiplies.

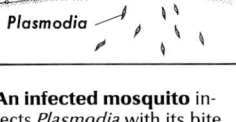

The cell bursts, releasing a new form of *Plasmodia.*

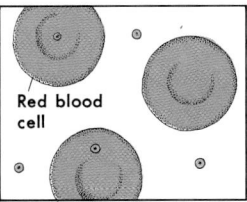

Each *Plasmodium* enters a red blood cell and multiplies.

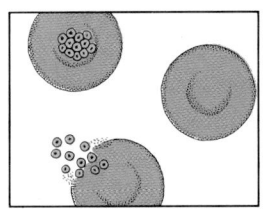

The cell ruptures, and *Plasmodia* invade more red cells.

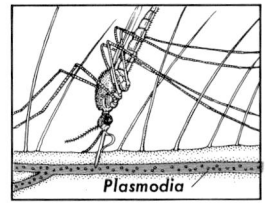

Some *Plasmodia* are able to infect mosquitoes.

Malawi

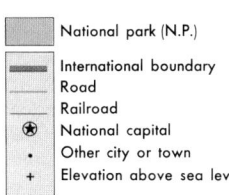

▨	National park (N.P.)
▬	International boundary
	Road
	Railroad
⊛	National capital
•	Other city or town
+	Elevation above sea level

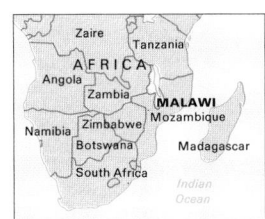

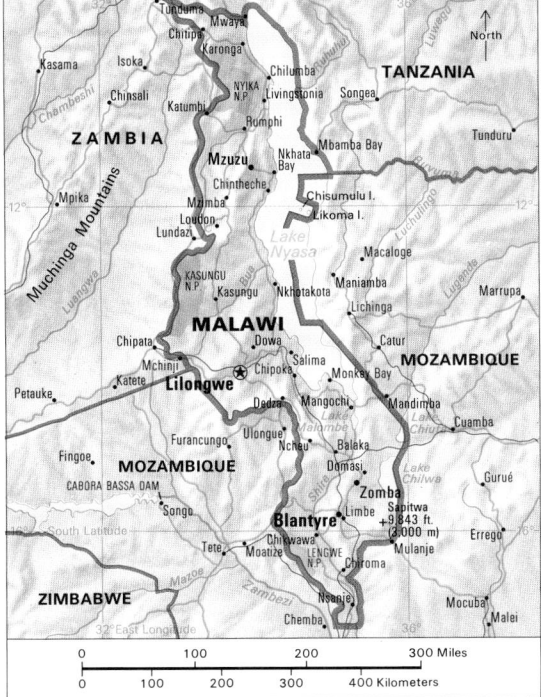

WORLD BOOK maps

Malawi, *mah LAH wee,* is a small scenic country in southeastern Africa. It is about 520 miles (837 kilometers) long and from 50 to 100 miles (80 to 160 kilometers) wide. Malawi lies on the western shore of Lake Nyasa, called Lake Malawi in that country.

Ancient volcanic activity left Malawi with rich soil. But only about one-third of the land is suitable for agriculture because mountains, forests, and rough pastures cover most of the country.

The country takes its name from the Malawi kingdom, which was established by local people during the 1500's. Once the British protectorate of Nyasaland, Malawi became an independent country in 1964. Lilongwe is the capital of Malawi, and Blantyre is the largest city.

Government. Malawi is a republic, with a president as its head of state and chief executive. The president appoints a Cabinet to help govern the country. Under the constitution, the people elect the president to a five-year term. However, in 1970, a constitutional amendment made Hastings Kamuzu Banda president for life. The people elect 101 members to Malawi's parliament. In addition, the president may appoint any number of additional members. All members serve five-year terms.

People. Most of Malawi's about 10 million people are black Africans who live in small villages. In these rural areas, the people live in round or oblong houses with mud walls and thatched roofs. Most of the people belong to Bantu groups. The leading groups are the Chewa (Cewa), Lomwe, Nyanja, Yao, and Ngoni (Angoni). Also, about 9,000 Europeans and about 14,000 Asians and people of mixed origin live in Malawi.

In most Western cultures, the father is the head of the family and descent is determined through him. But most Malawi people determine descent through the mother. New families often establish households near their mother or relatives of their mother. Mothers have traditionally raised the family's food crops, while the fathers have provided the family's meat and fish. But today both men and women farm the land. Women grow food crops for their families, and men raise most of the crops for sale, such as sugar cane, tea, and tobacco.

Chichewa and English are Malawi's official languages. Nyanja and Yao are the most popular languages in central and southern Malawi. Most of the people in northern Malawi speak Tumbuka.

Many of Malawi's people practice traditional African religions. About 700,000 of the people are Christians, and about 500,000 are *Muslims* (followers of Islam).

About 800,000 children—about 70 percent of the boys and 50 percent of the girls—attend primary schools. But only about 4,500 children attend the country's 17 secondary schools. The University of Malawi is in Zomba. It has branch colleges or institutes in other cities.

Land. Malawi is a land of great scenic beauty. Grassland and *savanna* (areas of coarse grass and trees) cover much of the land. The Great Rift Valley runs the length of Malawi from north to south. Lake Nyasa fills most of the valley. It is 1,550 feet (472 meters) above sea level. The Shire River flows out of the southern end of the lake to the Zambezi River. West of the lake, the land rises steeply to a plateau about 4,000 feet (1,200 meters) above sea level. Malawi's highest mountain, Sapitwa (9,843 feet, or 3,000 meters), rises on a plateau southeast of the Shire River.

The lowlands in the Shire Valley and along the lake have a hot, humid, tropical climate. The temperature in this area averages from 74 to 78 °F (23 to 26 °C). The plateaus are much cooler. They average about 58 °F (14 °C) in higher areas and about 65 °F (18 °C) in lower areas. The northern parts of the country average about 70 inches (180 centimeters) of rainfall a year. The southwestern parts get an average of only 30 inches (76 centimeters) a year.

Facts in brief

Capital: Lilongwe.
Official languages: Chichewa and English.
Area: 45,747 sq. mi. (118,484 km²).
Population: *Estimated 1994 population*—10,096,000; density, 221 persons per sq. mi. (85 persons per km²); distribution, 86 per cent rural, 14 per cent urban. *1987 census*—7,982,607. *Estimated 1999 population*—11,959,000.
Chief products: *Agriculture*—corn, cotton, hides and skins, peanuts, sorghum, sugar cane, tea, tobacco. *Manufacturing and processing*—bricks, cement, cotton goods, food processing.
Flag: The flag has black, red, and green horizontal stripes, with a red rising sun on the black stripe. See **Flag** (picture: Flags of Africa).
Money: *Basic unit*—kwacha.

Economy. Malawi is a poor country. It has no important mineral deposits. Its economy is based on agriculture, but only about a third of the land is suitable for farming. The most important export crop is tea, which is grown on estates in the highlands that are owned by Europeans. Important crops grown by Africans include sorghum, sugar cane, tobacco, cotton, corn, and peanuts. Many farmers raise livestock. Fishing in Lake Nyasa has also become an important industry. Malawi's few manufacturing industries produce such goods as bricks, cement, cotton goods, and processed foods. Valuable hardwood forests cover the northwest part of the country, but they are too difficult for trucks to reach.

Malawi has more than 7,000 miles (11,000 kilometers) of roads, but only about 500 miles (800 kilometers) are paved. A main road runs the length of the country, and Malawi has roads linking it with Tanzania, Zambia, and Zimbabwe. A railroad in the Shire Valley connects Malawi with the Mozambique port of Beira on the Indian Ocean. An international airport near Blantyre provides air service to eastern and southern Africa.

History. Bantu-speaking people began living in Malawi about 2,000 years ago. They formed kingdoms as well as smaller political groups. In the 1830's, two other Bantu groups, the Ngoni and Yao, invaded the area. The Yao were slave traders who sold slaves to the Arabs along the eastern coast of Africa.

The British missionary David Livingstone reached the area in 1859. He found it torn by local wars, and saw the suffering the slave traders caused. Livingstone called for "commerce and Christianity" to bring peace to the area. In 1875, the Free Church of Scotland set up a mission that later became an important religious center. Scottish businessmen formed the African Lakes Corporation three years later to introduce lawful business instead of the slave trade. In 1889, the British made treaties with the local chiefs on the western shore of Lake Nyasa. Two years later, Britain proclaimed the territory as the Protectorate of Nyasaland.

In 1953, the British made the protectorate part of a federation with Northern and Southern Rhodesia, the Federation of Rhodesia and Nyasaland. The Africans living there opposed the creation of the federation, and protested strongly against it. In 1958, Hastings Kamuzu Banda, a physician educated in the United States, became the leader of an independence movement in the protectorate. In July 1964, the protectorate gained independence as the nation of Malawi, and it installed a one-party system of government. The Malawi Congress Party became the only political party. In 1966, Malawi adopted a new constitution and became a republic. A constitutional amendment passed in 1970 made Banda president for life. In 1993, Malawi's people voted to adopt a multiparty political system.

During colonial times, many Malawian men went to neighboring lands to find work. Since independence, the government of Malawi has encouraged increased economic production within the country. As a result, the number of laborers migrating to other countries has decreased greatly. The government has also encouraged foreign investment and assistance, including aid from the white-ruled black country of South Africa. Malawi has also maintained good relations with neighboring black-ruled nations.   Bruce Fetter

See also **Banda, Hastings K.; Lilongwe.**

Malaya, muh LAY uh, is a former name of Peninsular Malaysia—a region of the nation of Malaysia. For details on the region, see **Malaysia.**

Malays, MAY layz or muh LAYZ, are a group of Southeast Asian peoples. Most of the approximately 130 million Malays live in Indonesia and Malaysia. The Malays belong to the Asian geographical race, which also includes the Chinese and Japanese.

The Malay culture is extremely diverse. It consists of about 300 ethnic groups that speak various dialects of the Malay language. Most of the groups are Muslims and work as civil servants or rice farmers. Both men and women often dress in a traditional length of cloth worn as a skirt. In general, the Malays place a high value on social harmony, courtesy, and respect for authority.

Anthropologists believe the ancestors of the Malays migrated to Southeast Asia from southern China thousands of years ago. These ancestors practiced a religion based on *animism,* the belief that all things in nature—even lifeless objects—have spirits. Some Malays today combine animist beliefs with Islam or other religions.

In the first century A.D., traders from India brought Hinduism and Buddhism to the Malay region. For hundreds of years, rival Hindu and Buddhist Malay kingdoms struggled against each other. In the 1400's, Muslim merchants and teachers from the Near East and India introduced Islam to the Malays. The ruler of Melaka, an important Malay kingdom, converted to Islam and promoted its spread.

In the 1500's, the Portuguese captured Melaka and became the first Europeans to influence the Malays. For most of the period from the 1700's to the mid-1900's, the Dutch ruled Indonesia and the British governed Malaysia. Indonesia and Malaysia then gained independence, and the Malays played a major role in shaping the two nations.   James L. Peacock

See also **Indonesia** (People; History); **Malaysia** (People; History).

Malaysia, muh LAY zhuh, is a country in Southeast Asia. It consists of two regions about 400 miles (644 kilometers) apart, which are separated by the South China

Malawi fishermen set out in canoes to catch fish in Lake Nyasa. Malawi is a beautiful but poor country, and fishing has become an important industry as well as a source of food.

Peter Schmid, Shostal

Sea. The regions are Peninsular (formerly West) Malaysia, on the southern part of the Malay Peninsula; and Sarawak and Sabah (formerly East Malaysia), on the northern part of the island of Borneo.

Malaysia is a tropical land, much of which is covered by dense rain forests. It ranks as the world's largest producer of natural rubber and palm oil (vegetable oil from palm tree nuts). Malays and Chinese people make up most of the country's population. Kuala Lumpur is Malaysia's capital and largest city.

The nation of Malaysia was formed in 1963, when Malaya, Sarawak, Sabah, and Singapore united. Malaya was an independent nation that occupied what is now Peninsular Malaysia. Sarawak and Sabah were separate British colonies that covered what is now the Malaysian region of Sarawak and Sabah. Singapore was a British colony south of Malaya. Singapore withdrew from the nation in 1965.

Government

Malaysia is a constitutional monarchy. A Parliament makes the country's laws, and a prime minister and Cabinet carry out the operations of the government. The prime minister is the top government official. Local government is administered through 13 states and the federal territory of Kuala Lumpur. A king, called the *yang dipertuan agong,* serves as head of state, but his duties are largely ceremonial.

National government. Malaysia's Parliament is made up of a 154-member House of Representatives and a 68-member Senate. The people elect the House members to five-year terms. The head of the political party with the most seats in the House serves as prime minister. The prime minister selects the Cabinet members. Each state legislature elects two of the Senate members, and the king appoints the other senators on the advice of the prime minister. The senators serve six-year terms. Every five years, the rulers of nine of Malaysia's states elect a king from their number.

Local government. Hereditary rulers, most of whom are called *sultans,* head 9 of Malaysia's 13 state governments. Federally appointed governors head the four other states and the federal territory. Each state has a constitution and a legislature elected by the people. The states are divided into administrative districts, each of which is governed by a district officer.

Political parties. The National Front, a coalition of political parties, is Malaysia's most powerful political group. Other political groups include the Democratic Action Party and the Pan-Malayan Islamic Party.

Courts. The Supreme Court is Malaysia's highest court. It has 10 members, who are appointed by the king on the advice of the prime minister. The Supreme Court hears appeals from High Courts—Malaysia's second level of courts. Malaysia's lower courts include local, juvenile, and religious courts.

Armed forces of Malaysia include an army, an air force, and a navy. About 125,000 people serve in the armed forces. All service is voluntary.

People

Population and ethnic groups. Malaysia has a population of about 20 million. About half of the people live in rural areas. More than 80 percent of the people live in

Leon V. Kofod

Kuala Lumpur, Malaysia's capital, is a bustling, crowded city. The modern National Mosque, an Islamic house of worship, *above center,* stands near an expressway.

Peninsular Malaysia. Kuala Lumpur, Malaysia's largest city, has about 938,000 people.

Malaysia's largest population groups are, in order of size, the Malays, Chinese, and Asian Indians. Malays make up about 50 percent of the population, Chinese about 35 percent, and Indians about 10 percent. A number of other ethnic groups who live chiefly in Sarawak and Sabah make up the rest of the population. The largest groups in Sarawak and Sabah are the Dyaks and the Kadazans (see **Dyaks**).

Malaysia's ethnic groups speak separate languages or dialects, and, in many areas, have different ways of life. Malays make up the most powerful group in Malaysian politics, but the Chinese control much of the nation's economy. Social, economic, and political differences between the Chinese and Malays have led to friction and—sometimes—violence between the two groups.

Facts in brief

Capital: Kuala Lumpur.
Official language: Bahasa Malaysia.
Area: 127,317 sq. mi. (329,749 km²).
Elevation: *Highest*—Mount Kinabalu, 13,431 ft. (4,094 m) above sea level. *Lowest*—sea level, along the coast.
Population: *Estimated 1994 population*—19,564,000; density, 154 persons per sq. mi. (59 per km²); distribution, 53 percent rural, 47 percent urban. *1980 census*—13,183,005. *Estimated 1999 population*—21,528,000.
Chief products: *Agriculture*—cacao, coconuts, palm oil, pepper, pineapples, rice, rubber, timber. *Manufacturing*—air conditioners, cement, processed foods, rubber goods, semiconductors, textiles. *Mining*—bauxite, copper, gold, iron ore, natural gas, petroleum, tin.
National anthem: "Negara Ku" ("My Country").
Flag: A yellow crescent and star lie on a blue background in the upper left corner. The crescent represents Islam. The star's 14 points and the flag's 14 red and white stripes symbolize Malaysia's 14 original states. See **Flag** (picture: Flags of Asia and the Pacific).
Money: *Basic unit*—ringgit (sometimes called Malaysian dollar). See **Money** (table: Exchange rates).

David Moore, Black Star

People of various ethnic groups live in Peninsular Malaysia. Malays make up the largest group, followed by Chinese and Indians. Most of the people in the scene above are Malays.

Languages. Bahasa Malaysia, a form of the Malay language, is used by most of the Malay people and is the country's official language. Most Chinese use the Chinese language, and most Indians use Tamil. Many Malaysians also know English, which is widely used in business and everyday life.

Way of life. Peninsular Malaysia includes many crowded cities as well as large rural regions. Sarawak and Sabah is chiefly a rural area.

The majority of the country's Malays live in rural areas on the peninsula. Most of them work as farmers and live in settlements called *kampongs*. Many houses in rural areas are made of wood. Most have thatch roofs, but some have roofs made of tile. Some houses are raised above the ground on stilts. Most Malays who live in cities work in industry or in government jobs.

Most of Malaysia's Chinese people live in cities. Large numbers of them work in stores, banks, or business offices. Chinese people own a large proportion of Malaysia's businesses. Wealthy and middle-class Chinese live in high-rise apartments in downtown areas or in suburban homes. In the cities, some low-income Chinese—as well as Malays and Indians—live in crowded, run-down areas.

Large numbers of Malaysia's Indians work on rubber plantations. Many others hold city jobs.

Most people of Sarawak and Sabah live in small settlements in rural areas. Several families often live together in *long houses* along rivers. Many of these rural farm families must struggle to produce enough food for their own use.

Clothing. The clothing of most of Malaysia's Chinese and many members of its other ethnic groups is similar to that worn in Western nations. But many Malay men and women, especially in rural areas, wear a skirt called a *sarong* and a jacket.

Food. Rice is the main food of most Malaysians. The people may serve rice with meat, fish or a fish sauce, fruit, or vegetables. *Satay* is a popular Malaysian dish. It consists of small chunks of meat that are put on a skewer, grilled, and dipped in hot sauce.

Religion. Islam, the Muslim faith, is Malaysia's official religion. But the constitution grants freedom of religion.

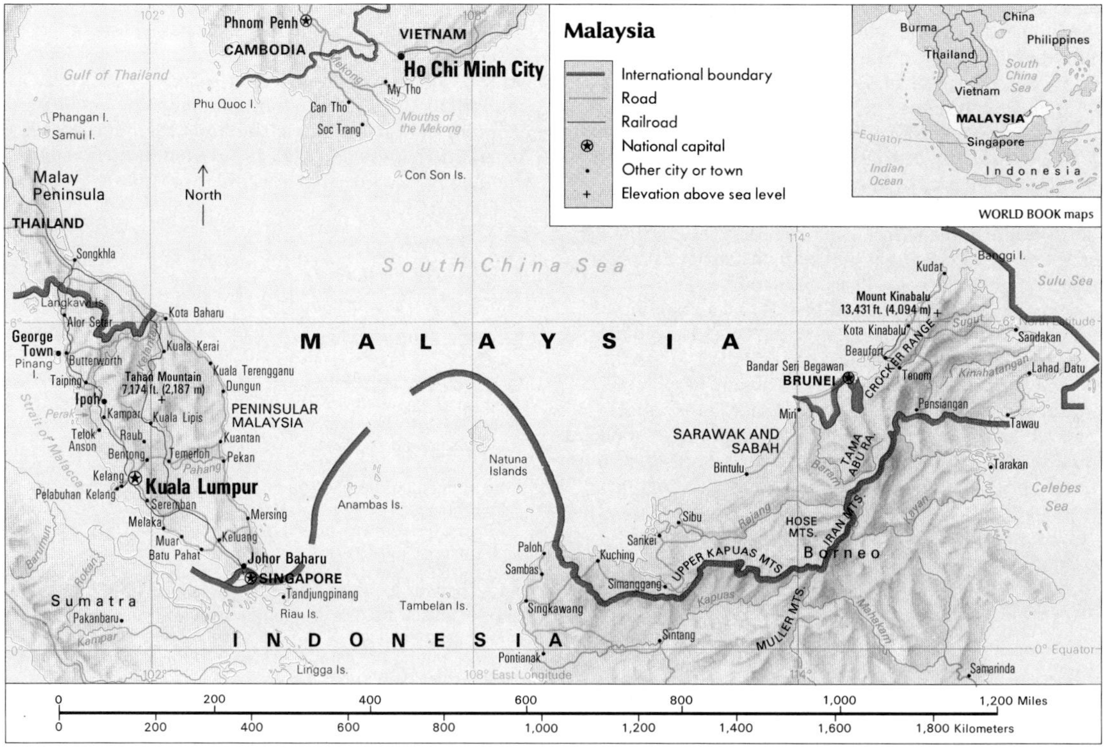

Malaysia

———	International boundary
	Road
	Railroad
✹	National capital
•	Other city or town
+	Elevation above sea level

WORLD BOOK maps

Nearly all Malays are Muslims. Most Chinese follow Buddhism, Confucianism, or Taoism, and most Indians practice Hinduism. Many ethnic groups in Sarawak and Sabah follow local traditional religions. Christianity is practiced by some members of each of Malaysia's ethnic groups.

Education. Most Malaysian children complete elementary school. But large numbers of them do not attend high school. They are from poor families and leave school to begin work. About 70 percent of Malaysia's people 10 years of age or older can read and write. Malaysia has 7 universities and 7 colleges.

The arts. Traditional arts of Malaysia include folk dances and puppet dramas. The folk dances may represent scenes of adventures, battles, or love. In the puppet dramas, the puppeteer sits behind a screen and moves leather or wood puppets to act out stories. The puppeteer tells the story and speaks the part of each puppet.

Land and climate

Malaysia covers 127,317 square miles (329,749 square kilometers). It is divided into two regions. The regions and their areas are Peninsular Malaysia, 50,806 square miles (131,588 square kilometers); and Sarawak and Sabah, 76,511 square miles (198,161 square kilometers).

Peninsular Malaysia covers the southern part of the Malay Peninsula. Mountains extend down the center of the peninsula in a north-south direction. Thick tropical rain forests cover much of this mountainous region. Low, swampy plains spread out over parts of the peninsula west and east of the mountains to the coasts. The west coast, which borders the Strait of Malacca, has most of Peninsular Malaysia's cities and major seaports. Much of the land east of the mountains is covered by tropical rain forests. The east coast borders the South China Sea. Major rivers in Peninsular Malaysia include the Kelantan, Perak, and Pahang.

Sarawak and Sabah covers most of the northern part of Borneo. Much of the coastal area, which borders the South China Sea, is low and swampy. Inland areas are mountainous and covered with tropical rain forests. Mount Kinabalu, the highest peak in Malaysia, rises 13,431 feet (4,094 meters) in the northeast part of Sarawak and Sabah. Major rivers include the Kinabatangan and the Rajang.

Animal life and vegetation. Many kinds of wild animals live in Malaysia. They include civets, deer, elephants, monkeys, tapirs, tigers, and wild oxen. Other animals include such reptiles as cobras, crocodiles, lizards, and pythons; more than 500 kinds of birds; and an enormous variety of butterflies.

Mangrove and palm trees cover much of Malaysia's swampy coastal areas. Other vegetation in the country includes camphor, ebony, fig, mahogany, rubber, and sandalwood trees.

Climate. Both Peninsular Malaysia and Sarawak and Sabah have tropical climates. Coastal temperatures usually stay between 70 and 90 °F (21 and 32 °C). Mountain temperatures range from 55 to 80 °F (13 to 27 °C). About 100 inches (250 centimeters) of rain falls annually in Peninsular Malaysia, and Sarawak and Sabah receives about 150 inches (381 centimeters).

Economy

Malaysia has one of the strongest economies in Southeast Asia. Its economy depends heavily on the production of petroleum, rubber, timber, and tin. But the country also produces a variety of farm crops and manufactured goods.

Agriculture. Malaysia is the world's leading producer of natural rubber and of palm oil. Nearly all of the country's rubber and palm oil is raised on large plantations for export. Farmers grow rice, Malaysia's chief food crop, on small farms throughout the country. The small farms also produce coconuts, pepper, pineapples, vegetables, and *cacao* (seeds used in making chocolate). Some farmers raise cattle or pigs for meat. About four-fifths of Malaysia's farms cover less than 5 acres (2 hectares) each.

The country's tropical rain forests yield large amounts

Milt and Joan Mann

J. Allan Cash Ltd.

Urban and rural areas in Malaysia contrast sharply. A heavily populated Chinese section of Kuala Lumpur, *left,* has narrow streets crowded with motor vehicles. A quiet rural area scene, *above,* shows a house that is raised on stilts.

of timber. In addition, Malaysians catch shrimp and such fishes as anchovies and mackerel in coastal waters.

Mining. Since the 1970's, Malaysia's production of petroleum and natural gas has increased, and petroleum is now the country's chief export. The country's other minerals include *bauxite* (aluminum ore); copper; gold; iron ore; *ilmenite,* an ore that contains a valuable metal called titanium; and tin.

Manufacturing. The chief manufactured products of Malaysia include air conditioners, cement, rubber goods, semiconductors for computers, and textiles. Food processing is another major industrial activity in the country.

Foreign trade. Malaysia's chief exports include electronic equipment, machinery, petroleum, palm oil, rubber, timber, and tin. Imports include chemicals and machinery. Malaysia's chief trading partners are Japan, Singapore, and the United States.

Transportation and communication. Malaysia has a good road system. The country has an average of about 1 automobile for every 15 people. Most Malaysians travel by bus or shared taxi. Railroads link Kuala Lumpur with Singapore and with Bangkok, Thailand. Kuala Lumpur, Kota Kinabalu, Kuching, and Pinang Island have international airports. Malaysian Air System (MAS) provides domestic and international air service.

Radio Television Malaysia, a government-owned network, broadcasts radio and television programs in Bahasa Malaysia, Chinese, English, Tamil, and various other languages. The country has about 40 daily newspapers.

History

Early days. Archaeological evidence indicates that there were human settlements in what is now Peninsular Malaysia in prehistoric times. About 4,000 years ago, ancestors of the Malays moved into the area from southern China. The peninsula became a crossroads for trade between China and India. Chinese and Indian people settled there through the years.

By the A.D. 800's, several small city-states had grown up along the east and west coasts of the peninsula. Indian traders brought Indian culture, including Buddhism and Hinduism, to the area. In the 1400's, Melaka, on the west coast, became a major trading center. Indians and Arabs introduced Islam there, and many Malays on the peninsula soon became Muslims.

European conquest. Portuguese forces captured Melaka in 1511 and lost it to the Dutch in 1641. During the 1700's, many people from the Dutch-controlled islands of Sulawesi (Celebes) and Sumatra settled on the peninsula. In the late 1700's, immigrants from Sulawesi and Sumatra formed Malay states on the peninsula.

Also in the late 1700's, people from Britain began setting up trading posts on the peninsula and nearby islands and British forces captured Melaka from the Dutch. In 1826, the British formed a colony that included Melaka, the island of Pinang, and the island of Singapore. It was called the Colony of the Straits Settlements. During the 1800's and early 1900's, the British gained control of the Malay states on the peninsula and of what is now Sarawak and Sabah.

Under British rule, the peninsula's economy prospered. The rapid growth of the rubber industry and tin mining attracted thousands of workers from India and China. The British delegated much of their authority in the area to local rulers called *sultans.*

Independence. In the early 1940's, during World War II, Japan conquered what is now Malaysia. The area returned to British rule following Japan's defeat in 1945. In 1948, the states on the Malay Peninsula, plus Pinang, united to form the Federation of Malaya, a partially independent territory under British protection. During the late 1940's and the 1950's, Chinese Communists and other rebels on the peninsula fought against the British. The conflict ended after the Federation of Malaya

Cameramann International, Ltd. from Marilyn Gartman

Farmers grow rice, Malaysia's chief food crop, on small farms like the one above near Kuala Lumpur. Malaysian farms also produce cacao seeds, coconuts, pepper, pineapples, and livestock.

Jean-Claude Lejeune, Black Star

Tropical rain forests cover most mountain areas in Malaysia. This village is in the Sarawak and Sabah region. Mount Kinabalu, the country's highest peak, rises in the background.

Leon V. Kofod

Rubber processing is one of Malaysia's chief industries. Factory workers make sheets of rubber from a milky fluid called latex, *above*. The fluid comes from rubber trees.

gained complete independence from Britain in 1957.

In 1963, Malaya, Singapore, and what is now Sarawak and Sabah united and formed the new independent nation of Malaysia. Disagreements soon arose between Singapore and the rest of the nation, and Singapore left the nation in 1965. Tengku Abdul Rahman became Malaysia's first prime minister.

Malaysia today has one of the strongest economies in Southeast Asia. Continued prosperity depends on the country's ability to strengthen export markets. Malaysia has greatly increased its manufacturing to lessen its economic reliance on agriculture and mining.

Malays account for a high percentage of Malaysia's poor people, and Chinese make up a high percentage of its wealthy class. But Malays control the country's political system. This situation has helped cause friction between Malay and Chinese people. The friction is one of Malaysia's chief problems.

Abdul Razak became prime minister in 1970. He died in 1976, and Hussein Onn became prime minister. Mahathir bin Mohamad succeeded Hussein Onn in 1981.   David P. Chandler

Related articles in *World Book* include:

Association of Southeast Asian Nations	George Town
Borneo	Kuala Lumpur
Clothing (picture: Traditional costumes)	Kuching
	Melaka
	Singapore (History)

Malcolm X (1925-1965) was one of the most influential black-American leaders of the 1950's and 1960's. He transformed himself from a petty criminal into an important defender of the rights of blacks.

Malcolm X was born Malcolm Little in Omaha, Nebr. His father was a follower of Marcus Garvey, a black leader who worked to establish close political and economic ties to Africa. In 1931, Malcolm's father was found dead after being run over by a streetcar. Malcolm believed white racists were responsible for his father's death. When Malcolm was 12 years old, his mother was committed to a mental hospital. Malcolm spent the rest of his childhood in foster homes. He also became discouraged by racial prejudice around him.

In 1941, Malcolm moved to Boston. The youth became involved in criminal activities. In 1946, he was arrested for burglary and sent to prison. In prison, he joined the Nation of Islam, commonly called the Black Muslims. The Nation of Islam taught that white people were devils. After Malcolm was released from prison in 1952, he adopted "X" as his last name. The letter stood for the unknown African name of Malcolm's slave ancestors.

Malcolm X quickly became the Nation of Islam's most effective minister. He was a fiery orator, urging blacks to live separately from whites and to win their freedom "by any means necessary." But he became dissatisfied with the Nation of Islam, in part because the group avoided political activity.

In 1964, Malcolm X broke with the Nation of Islam. Soon afterward, he traveled to the Muslim holy city of Mecca in Saudi Arabia. He met Muslims of many ethnic backgrounds and rejected the view that all white people are devils. Malcolm X adopted the Muslim name El-Hajj Malik El-Shabbazz. After returning to the United States, he formed his own group, the Organization of Afro-American Unity.

Frank Castoral, Photo Researchers

Malcolm X

Malcolm X rejected nonviolence as a principle, but he sought cooperation with Martin Luther King, Jr., and other civil rights activists who favored *militant* (aggressive) nonviolent protests. But by this time, some Black Muslims had condemned Malcolm X as a hypocrite and traitor because of his criticisms of the group's leader, Elijah Muhammad. On Feb. 21, 1965, Malcolm X was fatally shot while giving a speech in New York City. Three members of the Nation of Islam were convicted of the crime. Malcolm's views reached many people after his death through his *Autobiography of Malcolm X* (1965).

Clayborne Carson

See also **Black Muslims.**

Additional resources

The Autobiography of Malcolm X. Ed. by Alex Haley. Ballantine, 1987. First published in 1965.
Goldman, Peter L. *The Death and Life of Malcolm X.* 2nd ed. Univ. of Illinois Pr., 1979.

Maldives, *MAWL deevz* or *MAL dyvz,* is the smallest independent country in Asia and one of the smallest in the world. It consists of about 1,200 small coral islands that form a chain 475 miles (764 kilometers) long and 80 miles (129 kilometers) wide in the Indian Ocean. The northern tip of the Maldives is about 370 miles (595 kilometers) south of India. These tropical islands cover a total of only 115 square miles (298 square kilometers). Fishing and tourism are the main economic activities.

Maldives

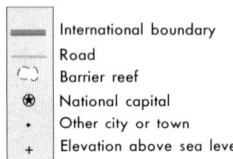

International boundary
Road
Barrier reef
National capital
Other city or town
Elevation above sea level

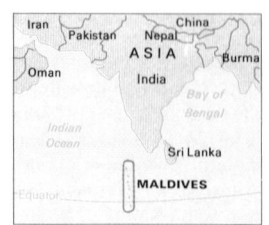

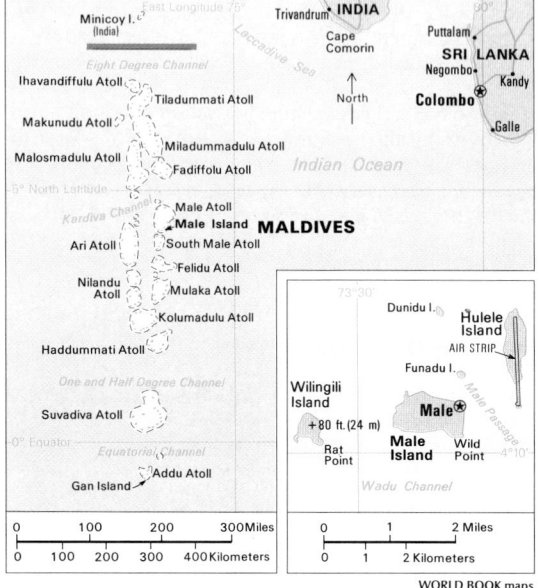

WORLD BOOK maps

Britain governed the Maldives as a protectorate for 78 years. The islands became independent in 1965. The country's official name in Divehi, the official language, is Divehi Raajje (Republic of Maldives). Male, the capital, has about 56,000 people.

Government. The Maldives is a republic. The president, who is head of the government, is elected to a five-year term by the *Majlis* (legislature). A nine-member Cabinet assists the president. The 48 members of the Majlis serve five-year terms. The people elect 40 members, and the president appoints 8. An elected committee handles local government on each *atoll* (cluster of islands). The government appoints a *kateeb* (headman) for each island. A chief justice appointed by the president administers the laws. Law in the Maldives is based on the Sunni Muslims' code of law.

People. Most Maldivians are descendants of Sinhalese people who came from Sri Lanka. Some Maldivians are descendants of people from southern India and Arab traders and sailors. Almost all Maldivians belong to the Sunni Muslim sect. Maldivians live on only about 210 of the country's islands. Many Maldivian men go to sea every day in thousands of boats to catch fish. Most build their boats of coconut or other timber that grows on the islands. Most of the boats are 36 feet (11 meters) long and 8 or 9 feet (2.4 or 2.7 meters) wide at the widest point. Each boat can hold about a dozen fishermen. The fishermen sail 15 or 20 miles (24 or 32 kilometers) out from the islands, and use rods and reels to haul in bonito, tuna, and other fish.

When the boats return home, the women prepare the fish. They cook and smoke them over a fire. Most of the fish are exported to Japan and Sri Lanka. The people eat some of the fish. Their diet also includes coconuts, papayas, pineapples, pomegranates, and sweet potatoes.

Land. The 1,200 small islands are grouped together in about 12 clusters called *atolls.* Barrier reefs around the atolls help to protect the islands from the sea.

None of the islands covers more than 5 square miles (13 square kilometers), and most are smaller than that. Most are like little platforms about 6 feet (1.8 meters) above sea level. An 80-foot (24-meter) elevation on Wilingili Island is the highest point. The islands have clear lagoons and white sand beaches. The land is covered with grass and low-growing tropical plants. Coconut palms and fruit trees grow on the islands.

The climate is hot and humid. Daytime temperatures average about 80 °F (27 °C). The northern islands receive at least 100 inches (250 centimeters) of rain a year, and those in the south receive almost 150 inches (381 centimeters). Two *monsoons* (seasonal winds) blow over the islands each year and bring most of the rain.

Economy of the Maldives is heavily based on the government-controlled fishing industry. The sale of dried fish in Sri Lanka is one of the chief sources of government income. Tourism is also important. About one-fifth of the national income comes from tourism.

The people raise breadfruit, chili peppers, coconuts, millet, and sweet potatoes. Women use the coconut husk fibers, called *coir,* to make yarn and ropes. The women also collect cowrie shells from the shores and weave reed mats. Gan Island has two large clothing factories that produce shirts and sweaters. Fish is the Maldives' chief export. Other exports include coir yarn, *copra* (dried coconut meat), cowrie shells, and fish meal. Rice, sugar, wheat flour, and manufactured goods are the major imports. India, Japan, Singapore, and Sri Lanka are the country's chief trading partners.

Sailboats are the most common form of transportation in the Maldives. Steamships sail regularly between Male and Sri Lanka.

History. Little is known about the Maldives before they came under Portuguese rule during the 1500's. From 1656 to 1796, the Dutch ruled the islands from Sri Lanka. In 1887, the Maldives officially became a British

Facts in brief

Capital: Male.
Official language: Divehi.
Total land area: 115 sq. mi. (298 km²). *Greatest distances—* north-south, 550 mi. (885 km); east-west, 100 mi. (161 km).
Elevation: *Highest—*80 ft. (24 m) above sea level, on Wilingili Island. *Lowest—*sea level.
Population: *Estimated 1994 population—*239,000; density, 2,078 persons per sq. mi. (802 per km²); distribution, 74 per cent rural, 26 per cent urban. *1990 census—*213,215. *Estimated 1999 population—*273,000.
Chief products: *Agriculture—*chili peppers, coconuts, millet, sweet potatoes. *Fishing—*bonito, tuna. *Handicrafts—*coir yarn, cowrie shells, shirts and sweaters, woven mats.
Flag: The flag has a white crescent on a dark green rectangle with a red border. The colors and the crescent on the flag stand for Islam. It was adopted in 1965. See **Flag** (picture: Flags of Asia and the Pacific).
Money: *Basic unit—*rufiyaa.

Bernard Regent, Hutchison Library

Fishermen in the Maldives catch mainly tuna and bonito. Fish, one of the nation's leading foods, is also the chief export.

protectorate. As a protectorate, the Maldives had internal self-government, and Britain handled foreign affairs. In the 1950's, a dispute between the Maldivians and the British over an air base on Gan Island led to the *secession* (withdrawal) of three southern atolls. The Maldivian government accused Britain of backing the rebellion. It crushed the rebellion in 1960.

In 1960, Britain and the Maldives signed an agreement that gave Britain free use of the Gan Island base. The Maldivians received the right to conduct most of their foreign affairs. Britain promised the islands about $2 million for economic development.

On July 26, 1965, Britain and the Maldives signed a new agreement that gave the islands complete independence. The Maldives became a republic in November 1968. In 1976, Britain withdrew from the Gan Island air base. The Maldives joined the Commonwealth of Nations in 1982. In 1985, the Maldives and six other countries established the South Asian Association for Regional Cooperation (SAARC), a regional association that deals with social and economic issues. The other countries are Bangladesh, Bhutan, India, Nepal, Pakistan, and Sri Lanka.   Myron Weiner

See also **Colombo Plan; Male.**

Male. See Reproduction; Sex.

Male, *MAH lay* (pop. 46,334), is the capital and chief port of the Maldives. It lies on Male Island, in the Indian Ocean. For location, see **Maldives** (map).

Housing in Male ranges from palm thatched structures with tin roofs to buildings made of crushed coral with tile roofs. Male has many *mosques* (Islamic houses of worship). Its landmarks include the Islamic Center, a

gold-painted mosque and meeting place; and the national museum, which is on the grounds of the demolished sultan's palace. The museum displays items from Arab, Dravidian, and Sri Lankan cultures. Male attracts many tourists. Tourist and government activities employ many of the city's people.

The origin of Male is unknown. But it may have been founded as the capital when the first people reached the Maldives in the 300's B.C.   Robert LaPorte, Jr.

Malemute. See Alaskan malamute.

Malenkov, *MAH luhn KAWF* or *mah lehn KAWF,* **Georgi Maximilianovich,** *gay AWR gih MAH ksih mih LYAH nah vihch* (1902-1988), became premier of the Soviet Union after the death of Joseph Stalin in March 1953. Nikita S. Khrushchev forced him to resign as premier in February 1955, and Malenkov became deputy premier under Premier Nikolai Bulganin. In June 1957, Malenkov tried to unseat Khrushchev as first secretary of the Soviet Communist Party. He failed, and was sent to Kazakhstan to manage a power plant. He was expelled from the party in 1964.

Malenkov was born in Orenburg. He became Stalin's private secretary in 1925. He became a member of the Politburo in 1946, and second secretary of the Presidium in 1952.   Albert Parry

Malherbe, *mal EHRB,* **François de,** *frahn SWAH duh* (1555-1628), was a French poet who became a haughty critic of French poetic language and style. He ridiculed the French poets of the 1500's, mercilessly attacking their flowery vocabularies and elaborate sentences. Some scholars believe that Malherbe smothered French lyric poetry by setting rigid rules that dominated poets until the romantic period of the early 1800's. But he also gave the language simplicity, clarity, force, and dignity.

Malherbe insisted that poetry be understandable, even to the poorest people of Paris. But he sternly avoided expressing personal feelings. Instead, Malherbe wrote about love and death, the great moral truths, and patriotic subjects of his day. His poetry consists of *Odes* and *Stanzas* (1600-1628). Malherbe was born in Caen.   Robert B. Griffin

Mali, *MAH lee,* is a large country in western Africa. The Sahara, Africa's great desert, covers the northern half of the country. Rolling grassland spreads across most of the rest of Mali. Mali covers about 479,000 square miles (1,240,000 square kilometers). Thinly populated, it has only about 10 million people.

Mali is a poor, agricultural country. At times, droughts have led to large numbers of deaths of people and animals there. Most of Mali's people are black Africans who live in small rural villages and farm for a living. Many farmers produce only enough food for their own families. Many others raise livestock in the desert. Mali has a variety of mineral and water resources, but they are largely undeveloped. Manufacturing and mining contribute relatively little to the economy.

From about the A.D. 300's to the late 1500's, one or more of three powerful black empires—Ghana, Mali, and Songhai—thrived in what is now Mali. France ruled Mali from 1895 to 1959. Mali became an independent nation in 1960. Its name in French, the official language, is République du Mali (Republic of Mali). Bamako is Mali's capital and largest city.

Government. The president, Mali's top government official, is elected by the people to a five-year term. The president may serve a maximum of two terms. The president appoints a prime minister and other government ministers, who carry out the day-to-day operations of the government. Mali has a 129-member legislature called the *National Assembly*. The members are elected by the people.

Mali's court system includes a Supreme Court, a Constitutional Court, and lower courts. For purposes of local government, Mali is divided into eight regions and the District of Bamako.

Facts in brief

Capital: Bamako.
Official language: French.
Area: 478,841 sq. mi. (1,240,192 km²). *Greatest distances*—east-west, 1,150 mi. (1,851 km); north-south, 1,000 mi. (1,609 km). *Coastline*—none.
Elevation: *Highest*—Hombori Tondo, 3,789 ft. (1,155 m) above sea level; *Lowest*—75 ft. (23 m) above sea level, at the western border.
Population: *Estimated 1994 population*—10,443,000; density, 22 persons per sq. mi. (8 per km²); distribution, 79 per cent rural, 21 per cent urban. *1987 census*—7,696,348. *Estimated 1999 population*—12,231,000.
Chief products: *Agriculture*—cassava, corn, cotton, livestock, millet, peanuts, rice, sorghum, sugar cane, yams. *Fishing*—carp, catfish, perch. *Manufacturing*—food products, leather products, textiles. *Mining*—salt, gold.
Flag: The flag has vertical stripes of green, gold, and red. The stripes symbolize devotion to a republican form of government and the Declaration of the Rights of Man. See **Flag** (picture: Flags of Africa).
National anthem: "A Ton Appel Mali" ("At Your Call Mali").
Money: *Basic unit*—franc.

People. The vast majority of Mali's people are black Africans. The Fulani and a related people called the Toucouleur make up the largest group of Mali's people. The Fulani are descended from both blacks and whites. The Mandingos form the next largest Malian group. There are three main Mandingo subgroups—the Bambara, Malinke, and Soninke. Other large black groups in Mali include the Dogon, Songhai, and Voltaic peoples. Whites account for about 5 per cent of Mali's population. The whites include Arabs, Europeans—chiefly French—Moors, and Tuareg.

The Fulani and Toucouleur speak Fulani. Most of Mali's other people speak Bambara or other local languages. The Arabs and Moors speak Arabic, and the Tuareg use an ancient Berber language. French is spoken mainly by the Europeans, and by people in government offices and schools.

Islam is the chief religion in Mali. About 65 per cent of the people are *Muslims* (followers of Islam). The Bambara, Malinke, and Voltaic peoples practice traditional African religions. About 5 per cent of the people are Christians.

About four-fifths of Mali's people live in rural areas, and about a fifth live in urban areas. Most of the blacks reside in small rural villages in southern Mali and grow crops for a living. They generally work on village-owned plots. Many can raise only enough food for their own use. Their foods include cassava, corn, millet, rice, sorghum, and yams. Most Malian farmers cannot afford agricultural machinery, and so they use hand tools for almost all their work. Most village families live in small houses made of mud or branches.

A majority of Mali's Fulani farm for a living. They live in dome-shaped huts thatched with straw and lined with mats. But others raise cattle in the Sahel, a semidesert

Mali

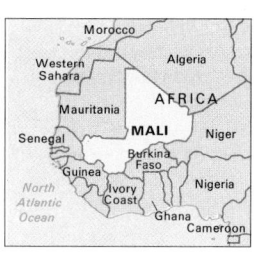

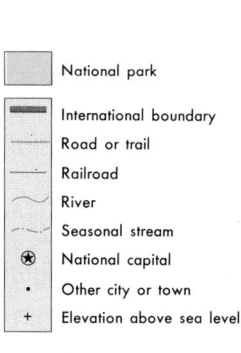

National park
International boundary
Road or trail
Railroad
River
Seasonal stream
National capital
Other city or town
Elevation above sea level

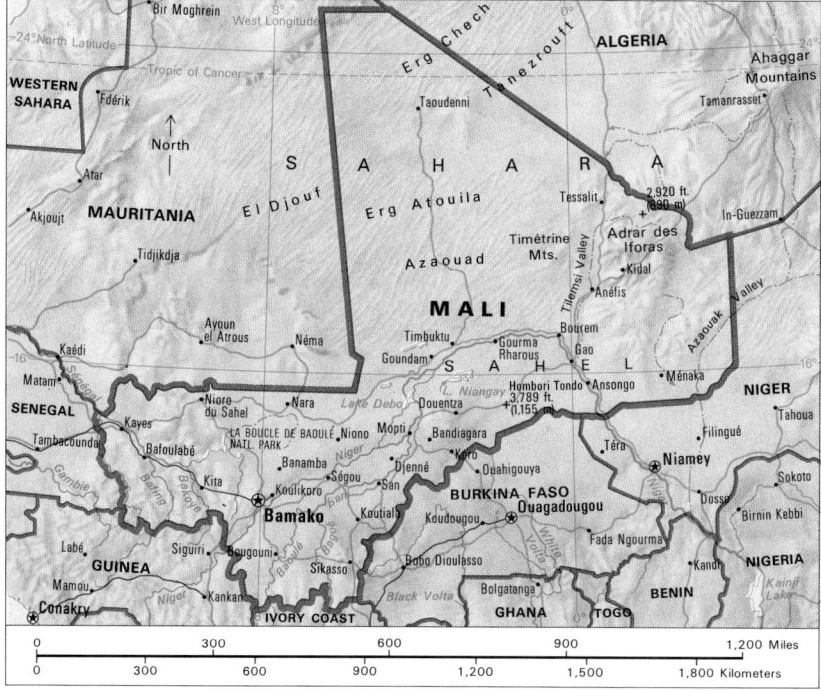

Georg Gerster, Photo Researchers

Farmers in Mali bundle and stack stalks of millet to dry in the sun after the harvest. Millet is one of the chief food crops of this large, west African country.

region, and in the southern grasslands. These herders live in low huts made of straw mats or branches.

Many of Mali's Arabs and Moors and almost all the Tuareg are nomads. The nomads herd cattle, goats, sheep, and donkeys back and forth across the Sahel and Sahara in search of water and pasture for grazing. They live in portable tents made of camel hair. Their basic foods include dates and millet. The nomads travel in groups led by *marabouts* (holy men) and are fiercely independent. They are more loyal to their marabouts than to Mali's government.

Many of Mali's Europeans are descendants of French colonists. Most live in modern houses in Bamako and other urban areas. Bamako, with a population of about 400,000, is Mali's largest city (see **Bamako**). Many Europeans own businesses or have government or professional jobs. Others work in banks, stores, and offices.

Women play a key role in farming in Mali. They help plant and harvest crops and raise livestock. The government has set up modern job training programs for women. But relatively few have enrolled because of their heavy workloads and family responsibilities.

Mali, like other developing nations, faces major social problems. Many of its people suffer from a lack of education. About 90 per cent of Mali's adults cannot read and write, and only about 27 per cent of its school-age children attend school. Mali has several schools of higher education. But many Malian students prefer to get higher degrees and professional training in other nations, mainly France and Senegal.

Mali is also challenged by poor health conditions. The average life expectancy for infants in Mali is less than 50 years. About a fifth of the babies born in rural areas die as infants. Malaria is widespread and is a chief cause of death among children. Mali has only a few hundred doctors to serve its entire population. Most of them work in urban areas.

Land and climate. Mali has three main land regions: the harsh Sahara in the north, the semidesert Sahel in central Mali, and rolling grasslands in the south. Mali has few mountains. Its highest point, Hombori Tondo, a mountain in the south, rises 3,789 feet (1,155 meters) above sea level.

The Sénégal and Niger are Mali's chief rivers. Most of the country's people live in villages and urban areas along or near these rivers and their branches. The Sénégal flows through southwestern Mali. The Niger enters Mali near Bamako and flows northeastward into the interior delta, Mali's most fertile area. It then makes a great turn called the Niger Bend and flows southeastward into the country of Niger. It spreads out into a network of branches and lakes in Mali.

Mali has three seasons. Its weather is hot and dry

Wendy Watriss, Woodfin Camp, Inc.

A street market stretches along a sidewalk in Bamako, Mali's capital and largest city. Such markets serve as social centers as well as places to buy or trade food and other goods.

Carl Purcell, Click/Chicago

Nomads camp in a desert area of Mali. They travel with their herds in search of grazing land and water. The dry Sahara covers much of the northern part of the country.

Wendy Watriss, Woodfin Camp, Inc.

Vast grasslands stretch across much of southern Mali. This area receives abundant rainfall and supports many kinds of wild animals, including elephants, giraffes, and lions.

from March to May, warm and rainy from June to October, and relatively cool and dry from November to February. Average annual temperatures are between 80 and 85 °F (27 and 29 °C) in much of the country. From March to May, temperatures often exceed 100 °F (38 °C). In the scorching Sahara, they may rise to more than 110 °F (43 °C) during the day. But at night, Sahara temperatures may be as low as about 40 °F (4 °C). The Sahara receives an average of about 10 inches (25 centimeters) of rain a year, and southern Mali averages about 35 inches (89 centimeters).

Animal and plant life. Many wild animals roam across southern Mali. They include elephants, gazelles and other antelope, giraffes, hyenas, leopards, and lions. Crocodiles and hippopotamuses live in the river areas.

Mali has a variety of plant life. Trees scattered throughout the southern grasslands include cailcedra, kapioka, karite, and nere. The Sahel has baobab, down palm, and palmyra trees. It also features acacia, cram-cram, mimosa, and other short, thorny plants.

Economy. Mali is a poor country with a developing economy. More than three-fourths of its workers farm or herd livestock for a living. Millet, rice, and sorghum are the main food crops. Other food crops include cassava, corn, and yams. Cotton, peanuts, and sugar cane are important cash crops. Nomads raise large herds of cattle, goats, and sheep. Fishing is also an important economic activity. The largest catches are carp, catfish, and perch. The fish come mainly from the Bani and Niger rivers and Lake Debo.

Service industries, such as government, tourism, and wholesale and retail trade, employ about 15 per cent of Mali's labor force. Most of these people work in Bamako and other urban areas.

Manufacturing provides jobs for about 10 per cent of the workers. The production of textiles is the leading manufacturing activity. The production of food and leather products is also important. The government owns almost all of the largest factories, but it encourages increased private enterprise. Most of the country's largest industrial plants were built with foreign aid. They include a cement factory, sugar mill, tannery, and textile plant.

Mali has deposits of bauxite, copper, gold, iron ore, manganese, phosphates, salt, and uranium. However, the production of salt is the only major mining activity. Some gold is produced.

Cotton is Mali's chief export. It earns about half the country's export income. Mali also exports fish, leather products, livestock, meat, and peanuts. Its leading imports include chemicals, food, machinery, petroleum, and textiles. Mali trades chiefly with other countries of western Africa, and with France and other Western European nations.

Mali has about 11,200 miles (18,000 kilometers) of roads, but only about 10 per cent are paved. The Niger River is navigable throughout its course in Mali. A railroad links Bamako and Dakar, Senegal. Air Mali, the national airline, operates in Mali and has flights to other African countries and to Europe.

The government controls communications in Mali. It publishes two daily newspapers and operates a national radio station.

Mali faces several economic problems. It depends heavily on agriculture, but only about a fifth of its land is fertile. The government has sometimes discouraged farming by keeping food prices low. Crop production has also often suffered from below normal rainfall. In addition, pasture for grazing has become increasingly scarce. In the 1970's and early 1980's, severe droughts destroyed much of the plant life in the Sahel and caused the death of millions of cattle, goats, and sheep. Mali's economy also has been troubled by sharp drops in world cotton prices and large increases in the cost of imported petroleum and other fuels.

History. Mali has a rich cultural heritage. From about the A.D. 300's to the late 1500's, areas in what is now Mali formed part of one or more of three great black empires. These empires—Ghana, Mali, and Songhai—grew prosperous because they controlled important trade routes.

The Ghana Empire began during the 300's and lasted until the mid-1000's. It became known as "the land of gold" because traders brought gold there from fields farther south and exchanged it for salt and other goods from North Africa. See **Ghana Empire.**

Ronald Trigg

Timbuktu is now a small trading town in central Mali. But as late as the 1500's, it was a great center of learning and one of the richest commercial cities in Africa.

The Mali Empire flourished from about 1240 to 1500. In the 1300's, it ranked as the wealthiest and most powerful state in western Africa. Mansa Musa, its king from 1312 to 1337, brought Muslim scholars to the empire, and the city of Timbuktu started to become a center of Muslim learning. See **Mali Empire; Timbuktu.**

The Songhai Empire began in the 700's. The Malian city of Gao served as capital of the empire. Under Askia Muhammad, who ruled the empire from 1493 to 1528, Timbuktu reached its peak as a center of wealth and Muslim learning. Invaders from Morocco overran Songhai in 1591. Many small kingdoms later ruled the area. See **Songhai Empire; Askia Muhammad.**

During the mid-1800's, France tried to set up a colony in what is now Mali. But French troops met fierce resistance from black Africans and did not gain control of the area until 1895. In 1904, the colony, then called French Sudan, became part of French West Africa. In 1946, France gave French Sudan the status of a territory in the French Union. See **French West Africa.**

In 1958, French Sudan became a self-governing republic within the French Community. The next year, French Sudan and Senegal united to form the Federation of Mali. Modibo Keita, a Malian leader, became head of the federation. The federation broke up in August 1960. On Sept. 22, 1960, French Sudan gained complete independence as the Republic of Mali.

Keita became Mali's first president. He tried to develop the economy, partly by establishing close ties with the Soviet Union and other Communist nations. Several Communist countries built factories in Mali. But worldwide inflation and an unsuccessful attempt to set up a new money system led Mali into debt.

In 1968, a group of Malian military leaders overthrew Keita. Moussa Traoré, one of the leaders, took control of Mali's government as head of a military committee.

In 1974, Malians approved a Constitution that called for the gradual establishment of an elected president and legislature. Legislative and presidential elections— the first elections under the Constitution—were held in 1979. All the candidates belonged to the Mali People's Democratic Union. Traoré, who headed the party, was elected president.

During the 1970's and early 1980's, severe droughts struck the Sahel and brought widespread famine to Mali. Millions of cattle, goats, and sheep died. Thousands of Fulani and Tuareg herders, who depended on their livestock for meat and milk, died from malnutrition. Thousands of other nomads poured into Mali's urban areas seeking food. The United Nations and a number of countries gave Mali food to prevent mass starvation.

Today, Mali's lack of industry and heavy reliance on agriculture limit economic progress. Malians are working to establish a more balanced economy to lessen the economic disasters caused by droughts and other agricultural problems.

In 1991, Malian government forces killed many people in a crackdown against antigovernment protests. Later that year, military leaders overthrew Traoré's government. They formed a temporary government composed of military and civilian members. In 1992, a new constitution was adopted. It provided for a multiparty system and an elected government. A new civilian president, Alpha Oumar Konare, was elected. A new National Assembly was also elected. Former president Traoré was tried for his government's actions against the antigovernment protests of 1991. In 1993, he was convicted and sentenced to death.   Clement Henry Moore

See also **Africa** (pictures); **Senegal.**

Mali Empire, *MAH lee,* was a black empire that flourished in west Africa from about 1240 to 1500. At its height, the Mali Empire controlled most of what are now Gambia, Guinea, Mali, and Senegal, and parts of present-day Burkina Faso, Mauritania, and Niger.

Between 1235 and 1240, Sundiata, the king of Kanga-

The Mali Empire in 1337

This map shows the Mali Empire, in dark gray, at the height of its power in 1337. Mali controlled an area in west Africa including most of what are now Gambia, Guinea, Senegal, and Mali. The present boundaries are shown as white lines.

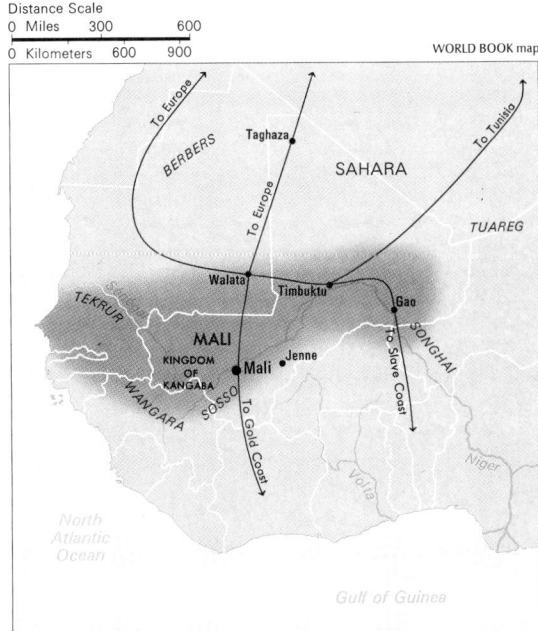

Distance Scale

WORLD BOOK map

ba, conquered the nearby lands of the Sosso. He built a new city, Mali, to be the capital of his empire (see **Sundiata Keita**). Later, under Mansa Musa, who ruled from 1312 to about 1337, the empire spread eastward to Gao. Mansa Musa brought the empire to the peak of its political power and cultural achievement. Timbuktu became a famous center of learning, especially in law and the study of Islam, the Muslim religion.

The cities of the Mali Empire were centers for the caravan trade from beyond the Sahara. The people were successful farmers and herders. Members of the governing classes were Muslims, but most of the people continued to worship traditional local African gods.

Control of the vast empire required skill and power that Mansa Musa's successors lacked. After about 1400, Songhai and other states conquered Mali's outlying areas. By 1500, the Songhai Empire controlled most of the Mali Empire.   Leo Spitzer

See also **Timbuktu; Jenne; Walata; Mansa Musa.**

Malibran, *mah lee BRAHN,* **Maria Felicita** (1808-1836), was a famous Spanish opera singer. She was known for the power and flexibility of her voice and for her broad vocal range. She was a contralto but could also sing in the higher soprano range. She had a fiery temperament that added excitement to many performances and contributed to her international fame.

Malibran was born Maria García in Paris and studied with her father, Manuel García, a famous tenor and composer. In 1825, she made her professional debut in London, singing the role of Rosina in *The Barber of Seville.* She spent two years in New York City singing with her father's opera company. There she married François Eugène Malibran. She returned to Europe in 1827 and performed in most major opera houses. Malibran was thrown from a horse while riding in April 1836. Her injuries led to her death several months later.   Ellen Pfeifer

Malignancy, *muh LIHG nuhn see,* is the tendency of a disease to be severe and possibly cause death. It most frequently refers to a *malignant tumor,* or cancer, in contrast to a *benign* (mild) tumor (see **Cancer; Tumor**). Benign tumors remain in one part of the body and grow slowly. Malignant tumors can invade surrounding normal tissue, or spread to distant organs of the body through the blood, a process called *metastasis.* Malignant cells often resemble the normal cells that they originate from, but they have unique characteristics that make them malignant. Many people say *malignancy* when they mean *cancer.*   Joseph V. Simone

Malinke. See **Mandingo.**

Malinowski, *MAH lih NAWF skee,* **Bronislaw,** *braw NEE slahf* (1884-1942), was a British anthropologist. He became known for his study of the culture of the peoples of the Trobriand Islands in the southwest Pacific, and for his contributions to theories on human culture.

Malinowski was born in Poland. He taught at the University of London and at Yale University. He wrote *Argonauts of the Western Pacific, Sexual Life of Savages in North West Melanesia,* and *Coral Gardens and Their Magic.*   David B. Stout

See also **Anthropology** (Development of field research); **Mythology** (How myths began).

Mall. See **Shopping center.**

Mallard is one of the most common wild ducks. It is found throughout much of North America, Europe, and

WORLD BOOK illustration by Trevor Boyer, Linden Artists Ltd.
Mallards are wild ducks found in much of the Northern Hemisphere. The female, *top,* has brownish feathers. In the breeding season, the male, *bottom,* has brightly colored plumage.

Asia. Mallards range from 20 to 28 inches (51 to 71 centimeters) in length. During the breeding season, the male is strikingly colored, having a glossy green head, a white neck ring, and a purplish-chestnut breast. Gray feathers cover the back, and the center of the tail has black feathers that curl up at the end. The female has duller, brownish feathers. The male loses its bright-colored feathers after breeding and becomes similar in appearance to the female.

During warmer months, mallards nest chiefly near northern prairie marshes and ponds. They migrate to southern wetlands for the winter. Most mallards nest on the ground. The females usually lay 8 to 10 dull yellow or greenish eggs. The males flock together after the eggs are laid, and the young are cared for by the females alone. Mallards feed chiefly on water insects, snails, and crustaceans during early summer. They eat mainly seeds and plants the rest of the year.

Scientific classification. The mallard belongs to the family Anatidae. It is *Anas platyrhynchos.*   Milton W. Weller

See also **Duck.**

Mallarmé, *mah lahr MAY,* **Stéphane,** *stay FAHN* (1842-1898), was a French poet and critic born in Paris. He is best known for his dream poem *L'Après-midi d'un faune* (*The Afternoon of a Faun,* 1876). Except for weekly meetings with a group of European poets and artists in Paris, Mallarmé lived detached from society. Mallarmé considered society hostile to the values of the poet.

Recognized by the younger generation as a master of poetic theory, Mallarmé became the mentor of a literary movement known as *symbolism* (see **Symbolism**). According to him, the poet must suggest, not describe, the natural object. Poets must deliberately make their poetic image ambiguous, so that reality is presented in an atmosphere of mystery. Mallarmé's other works include esoteric sonnets; a metaphysical prose poem, *Igitur;* and *L'Hérodiade,* a long poem about Salome. His last poem, "Un Coup de dés jamais n'abolira le hasard" (1897), expresses the confrontation between the chaos of the universe (*le hasard*) and the desire of people to shape their own destiny (*le coup de dés*).   Anna Balakian

See also **French literature** (Symbolism).

Malleability, MAL *ee uh BIHL uh tee,* is the ability of many metals to be pressed or hammered into thin sheets. A malleable metal can be squeezed into a thin sheet by pushing on it in opposite directions. The most malleable metals include copper, gold, and silver. For example, gold can be shaped into foils 10 times as thin as a sheet of paper. Some gold foils measure only 0.0001 inch (0.00254 millimeter) thick. Certain metals are not malleable at room temperature, but they gain malleability when heated and kept at a high temperature. Malleable metals also exhibit *ductility*—that is, they can be permanently stretched to a considerable degree without breaking.   Johannes Weertman

See also **Ductility; Elasticity.**

Mallon, Mary. See Typhoid Mary.

Mallorca. See Majorca.

Mallory, MAL *uh ree,* **Stephen Russell** (1813?-1873), was secretary of the Confederate Navy during the Civil War (1861-1865). He was born on the Caribbean island of Trinidad but grew up in Key West, Fla., where his family settled in 1820.

Mallory was appointed inspector of *customs* (import taxes) in Key West in 1833, and he studied law while holding that position. In 1845, United States President James K. Polk appointed him collector of customs in Key West. In 1850, Mallory was elected to the U.S. Senate from Florida.

Florida *seceded* (withdrew) from the Union in 1861, and Mallory resigned from the Senate. Confederate President Jefferson Davis appointed him secretary of the Navy, which was then almost nonexistent. Mallory had to organize the Navy and direct it. He also had to build and equip ships from what little material he found available.

Mallory attacked his task with great ability. He succeeded in building a small but efficient Navy and showed much foresight in ordering ironclads built instead of the older type of wooden warships. His naval experts developed deadly torpedoes and underwater devices which kept the Union Navy out of the great rivers of Virginia until late in the war.

After the fall of Richmond, Va., in 1865, Mallory fled south with President Davis and was captured in Georgia. He was held prisoner for nearly a year but was pardoned by U.S. President Andrew Johnson in 1867. He then practiced law in Pensacola, Fla., until his death.

Michael Perman

Mallow, MAL *oh,* is the popular name of a large family of plants. The mallow family includes about 1,000 kinds of herbs, shrubs, and trees that grow in tropical and temperate regions of the world. The plants of this family have fibrous stems and sticky sap. They bear flowers with many *stamens* (male reproductive parts) that are fused together into a tubelike structure. The hibiscus, hollyhock, and marsh mallow all belong to the mallow family. The cotton plant and okra also are members.

Scientific classification. Mallows make up the mallow family, Malvaceae.   Walter S. Judd

Related articles in *World Book* include:

Cotton	Flowering maple	Hibiscus
Hollyhock	Okra	Velvetleaf
Marsh mallow	Rose of Sharon	

Malmö, MAL *moh* (pop. 229,107; met. area pop. 455,017), is the third largest city in Sweden. Only Stockholm and Göteborg have more people. Malmö lies at the southern tip of Sweden, 16 miles (26 kilometers) from Copenhagen, Denmark. For location, see **Sweden** (political map). The city exports food and other products to European ports. Eight railroad lines connect it with other cities of Sweden. Malmö has a modern airport. Its beautiful town hall dates from 1546.   M. Donald Hancock

Malnutrition, MAL *noo TRIHSH uhn,* is an unhealthy condition caused by a poor or inappropriate diet or by the body's inability to absorb or use nutrients. *Primary malnutrition* results when the body gets too much food, not enough food, or the wrong kinds of food. *Secondary malnutrition* occurs when, because of disease, the body cannot use nutrients even though they are present in the food.

There are a number of types of malnutrition. Obesity and starvation are extreme forms of malnutrition. Obesity occurs when people eat much more food than they need. Undernutrition or starvation occurs when a person does not get enough food or does not consume enough of a particular nutrient or nutrients. Symptoms of undernutrition and starvation include cramps, diarrhea, weakness, and weight loss. *Protein-energy malnutrition,* also called *protein-calorie malnutritution,* occurs when the diet is low in both proteins and calories. This condition is called *marasmus* if the diet is particularly low in calories. It is called *kwashiorkor* if the diet is especially low in proteins.

Malnutrition caused by a low intake of vitamins may lead to *vitamin deficiencies.* Various diseases result from deficiencies of different vitamins. Malnutrition may also be due to *mineral deficiencies.* For example, lack of iron or copper can cause an abnormal condition of the blood called *anemia.* Social and economic conditions as well as natural disasters such as flooding and drought may produce malnutrition. Poverty, war, disease, and ignorance regarding a balanced diet also cause countless cases of malnutrition.   Mary Frances Picciano

Related articles in *World Book* include:

Anemia	Food	Nutrition	Scurvy
Beriberi	Goiter	Pellagra	Vitamin
Diet	Kwashiorkor	Rickets	

Malory, MAL *uh ree,* **Sir Thomas** (? -1471?), was the author of the book *Le Morte Darthur.* This title is French for *The Death of Arthur.* In *Le Morte Darthur,* Malory told the whole story of King Arthur of Britain and the careers of such knights of the Round Table as Lancelot, Gareth, and Tristan. The book provides the fullest version of the legends about Arthur and his court ever written in English.

Scholars disagree on the identity of the author of *Le Morte Darthur.* Records from the 1400's show that several Englishmen named Thomas Malory lived at this time. A knight of Warwickshire, who was imprisoned for a series of crimes, is usually identified as the author.

Malory translated and adapted much of his work from earlier French and English writings about Arthur. He completed his work about 1470. William Caxton, the first English printer, published the first edition of the book in 1485. He made the title of Malory's last section, *Le Morte*

Darthur, stand for the entire book. A manuscript copy of Malory's work was found at Winchester College in England in 1934. The most accurate and complete modern editions of *Le Morte Darthur* are based on the Winchester manuscript.

Malory's book has influenced the work of many artists and writers. Such writers include the English poets Edmund Spenser and Lord Tennyson.   Edmund Reiss

See also **Arthur, King; Round Table.**

Additional resources

Hicks, Edward. *Sir Thomas Malory, His Turbulent Career: A Biography.* Octagon, 1970. First published in 1928. A standard biography.

McCarthy, Terence. *Reading the Morte Darthur.* D. S. Brewer, 1988.

Malpighi, *mahl PEE gee,* **Marcello,** *mahr CHEHL loh* (1628-1694), an Italian anatomist, physician, and botanist, became famous for his research on animal tissues and his mastery of the use of the microscope in his work. Malpighi made fundamental discoveries about human anatomy.

In 1659, Malpighi began to dissect the lungs of dogs and frogs. He examined the tissues under a microscope and discovered that lungs are made up of tiny air sacs, called *alveoli.* He also discovered that the veins connect to the arteries by microscopic blood vessels, called *capillaries.*

Malpighi was the first person to observe and describe red blood cells, though he did not understand their significance. He described the tiny structures of the liver, spleen, and kidneys, as well as some of their functions. Later, he provided the first full accounts of the body structures of insects and of developing chick embryos. Other research by Malpighi advanced understanding of the structure of plants.

Malpighi was born in Crevalcore, near Bologna. He studied medicine and philosophy at the University of Bologna. Malpighi became a professor of medicine at the universities of Pisa, Bologna, and Messina. He later served as physician to Pope Innocent XII.

John Scarborough

Malpractice suit is a lawsuit in which a professional person is accused of injuring a patient or client through negligence or error. Most malpractice suits involve physicians. A smaller number involve lawyers.

The number of malpractice suits against doctors increased greatly in the United States beginning in the early 1970's. Most of these suits are filed against surgeons and other specialists who perform medical procedures that involve great risks to patients or that can have lifelong consequences. The amount of money awarded in successful malpractice suits also increased. Many such awards have greatly exceeded $1 million.

With the increased number of suits and the large amounts of money awarded, the cost of malpractice insurance for physicians soared in the 1970's and 1980's. But some insurance companies dropped all malpractice coverage. The higher cost of malpractice insurance, like the rise in number of suits and in amounts awarded, contributed to sharp rises in the cost of medical care. Physicians passed the higher insurance cost on to patients by increasing their fees. Some physicians also began to order expensive laboratory tests and X rays to protect themselves in case they were later sued. Some

surgeons became hesitant to perform risky operations, and some older doctors retired.

Physicians and many state legislatures proposed various solutions to the problem. One proposal involved the creation of panels of doctors, lawyers, and other people to review malpractice cases before the suits go to court. Other approaches included laws that set limits on the amount of money awarded and on the fee of the trial lawyers. Some courts have ruled that such statutes are unconstitutional, and others have upheld them.

Malpractice suits against other professionals have also increased since the early 1970's. Many clients sued attorneys who lost a case. Most of these suits resulted from a technical mistake, such as failing to file a suit on time. Others involved lawyers who failed to complete the legal work on a case. Malpractice suits have also been brought against accountants and clergy.

Troyen Brennan

Malraux, *mal ROH,* **André,** *ahn DRAY* (1901-1976), was a French author who combined intellectual achievement with political activity. Malraux was born in Paris. From 1923 to 1927, he traveled in the Far East as a student of archaeology, Oriental languages, and art. While there, Malraux became involved in local revolutionary struggles for freedom. In the 1930's, he participated in the struggles against Nazism in Germany, and Fascism in Spain. In World War II, he fought with the French resistance forces against the Germans. Malraux served as France's first secretary of cultural affairs, from 1959 to 1969.

Malraux's novels reflect his involvement in battles for freedom. However, his books are not autobiographical. Malraux's fiction explores humanity's devotion to ideals. He wanted art "to give men a consciousness of their own hidden greatness." His style is simple, concise, and fact-filled. But it may burst into poetic imagery and suggests our solitude and everpresent sense of death. His best novels include *The Royal Way* (1930), *Man's Fate* (1933), *Days of Wrath* (1935), and *Man's Hope* (1937). Malraux also wrote *The Voices of Silence* (1951) and other important works on art that compare works of different periods and civilizations.   Elaine D. Cancalon

Malt is a food product that results when barley and certain other grains are specially treated. In the United States and Canada, beer makers use 95 percent of the malt that is produced. It is also used in distilling, and as a source of flavor or aroma in a variety of baked goods, candies, cereals, and infant formulas.

In the malting process, manufacturers steep grain in cool water for 20 to 50 hours. They then spread the grain on large, ventilated floors and allow it to sprout and grow for 4 to 6 days. Temperature and moisture are carefully controlled. Next, large *kilns* (ovens) dry the grain for 2 or 3 days. After drying, the malt is cooled and the rootlets, which are used in animal feed, are removed from the sprouts. Finally, after cleaning, the malt is aged for 4 to 8 weeks before manufacturers use it.

During the malting process, certain chemical changes take place in the grain. Malting releases enzymes called *amylases.* These enzymes bring about the conversion of starch in the grain to sugars. Malting also produces enzymes called *hydrolases,* which are involved in breaking down proteins and nucleic acids.   Robert D. Wych

See also **Barley; Brewing; Maltose.**

Malta is an island country in the Mediterranean Sea, about 60 miles (97 kilometers) south of Sicily. It consists of the inhabited islands of Malta, Gozo, and Comino, and the tiny, uninhabited islands of Cominotto and Filfla. It is one of the most densely populated countries in the world, with 2,943 persons per square mile (1,136 persons per square kilometer).

Terrace farming over much of Malta makes the countryside look much like giant steps. The balmy climate attracts many visitors. Tourists also come to Malta to view some of the world's finest examples of Baroque and Renaissance art and architecture.

Malta was once a British crown colony. In 1964, Malta became an independent country. Valletta, on the island of Malta, is the capital and chief port. See **Valletta**.

Government. Malta is a republic. The president is head of state and is appointed by parliament to a five-year term. The prime minister is usually the leader of the majority party in parliament. The prime minister is the country's most powerful official. A Cabinet assists the prime minister in carrying out government operations. The 65 members of the House of Representatives are elected by the people to five-year terms.

People. Malta has a population of about 359,000. The Maltese have the medium height, black hair, and dark eyes of most Mediterranean peoples. Most of them speak Maltese, a West Arabic dialect with some Italian words. Both English and Maltese are official languages. Maltese is used in the courts. The country has both Maltese and English newspapers. Roman Catholicism is the state religion of Malta.

Land. Malta covers a total area of 122 square miles (316 square kilometers). Malta island covers 95 square miles (246 square kilometers). Gozo covers 26 square miles (67 square kilometers). Comino covers about 1 square mile (3 square kilometers).

Malta has a mild climate. Winters are moist and mild, and frost is unusual. Summers are hot and dry, but the heat is moderated by sea breezes. Malta gets about 21 inches (53 centimeters) of rainfall a year. Northwest winds sometimes reach hurricane force in autumn and winter.

Economy. Many of the people work at the dockyards and in the building industry. The one-time British naval dockyards are now used for commercial shipbuilding and repair. A few light industries have been set up. Malta is becoming more dependent upon tourists.

Maltese farmers raise cauliflowers, flowers for export,

Facts in brief

Capital: Valletta.
Official languages: Maltese and English.
Area: 122 sq. mi. (316 km²).
Population: *Estimated 1994 population*—359,000; density, 2,943 persons per sq. mi. (1,136 per km²); distribution, 89 per cent urban, 11 per cent rural. *1985 census*—345,418. *Estimated 1999 population*—365,000.
Chief products: *Agriculture*—grapes, milk, onions, potatoes, tomatoes. *Manufacturing and processing*—beverages, processed food, shipbuilding and repair.
National anthem: "Innu Malti" ("Maltese Anthem").
Flag: A replica of the George Cross, a British medal awarded to Malta for bravery in World War II, appears on a white and red field. See **Flag** (picture: Flags of Europe).
Money: *Basic unit*—lira. See **Money** (table: Exchange rates).

Malta

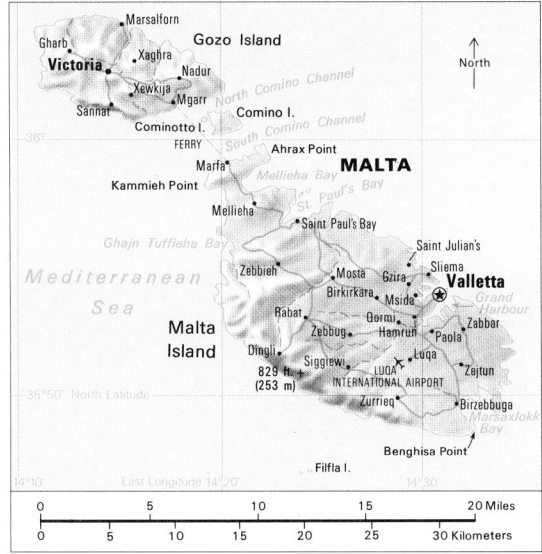

Road
Seasonal stream
National capital
Other city or town
Elevation above sea level

WORLD BOOK maps

grapes, onions, potatoes, tomatoes, and wheat. However, crops are small because of the rocky soil. Maltese farms also produce milk, pork, and poultry. But Malta must import most of its food. It has no minerals or natural resources, except salt and limestone.

Malta imports more goods than it exports. It carries on more than half of its trade with Britain, Germany, and Italy.

The country has a good road network and extensive local bus service. Ferry service links Malta with Gozo. Luqa has an international airport.

Malta has compulsory elementary education for all children from 6 to 16 years old. The country has both public schools and Roman Catholic schools. By law, the teachings of the Roman Catholic Church that are taught in Catholic schools must also be included in public school courses. Instruction is in both English and Maltese. The University of Malta is in Msida, near Valletta.

History. Malta is a region of great historical interest. Through the years, it has had much military importance because of its strategic location and natural harbors.

Remains of late Stone Age and Bronze Age people have been found in limestone caverns on the islands. Rough stone buildings from early ages have also been discovered in Malta. The Phoenicians colonized Malta in about 1000 B.C. Temples, tombs, and other relics of the Phoenicians still stand. Greek, Carthaginian, Roman, and Arab conquerors followed the Phoenicians into Malta. According to tradition, Saint Paul the Apostle was shipwrecked near Malta about A.D. 60 and converted the inhabitants to Christianity.

Malta passed to the Norman kings of Sicily around 1090. About 1520, the Holy Roman Emperor Charles V inherited the area when he received the crown of Spain. In 1530, Charles V gave Malta to the Knights Hospitallers. For this reason, the Knights are sometimes called the Knights of Malta. The Knights Hospitallers wore the Maltese cross as their badge (see **Cross** [picture]). They had fought against the Muslims since the time of the First Crusade in the 1090's. In 1565, the Turks laid siege to Malta with naval and military forces. Though heavily outnumbered, the Knights held out against the Turks for months, and finally defeated them. The town of Valletta was named after Jean de la Vallette, the Grand Master who led the Knights against the Turks.

The French under Napoleon Bonaparte took Malta from the Knights Hospitallers in 1798. British forces drove out the French in 1800. The people of Malta offered control of the colony to Great Britain. Britain's control was not completely recognized, however, until peace was made with France in 1815, after the Napoleonic Wars. Great Britain developed its Mediterranean military headquarters on Malta.

During World War I (1914-1918), Malta served as a strategic naval base for Allied forces. Great Britain granted Malta a measure of self-government in 1921. However, political crises in Malta caused Britain to revoke the Maltese political power. Malta's constitution was suspended in 1930 because of a dispute between the state and Roman Catholic authorities. They disagreed about the role of the church in state affairs. The constitution was reestablished in 1932, then withdrawn a year later. This time the pro-Italian sympathies of the Maltese government led Britain to suspend the constitution. Full authority was returned to the governor in 1936.

During World War II (1939-1945), Malta controlled the vital sea lanes between Italy and Africa. The natural rocks and deep inlets of the colony concealed anchorages and submarine bases. Many underground passages provided bomb shelters. Fighter planes based on Malta defended convoys of ships. The colony suffered heavy bomb damage. In 1942, King George VI of England awarded the George Cross to Malta in recognition of the courage and endurance of the Maltese people during the war. In 1953, the North Atlantic Treaty Organization (NATO) established its Mediterranean military headquarters on Malta.

The constitution of 1947 gave the colony increased partial self-government. The Maltese Labour Party gained control of the assembly and proposed political integration with Great Britain. In a 1956 referendum, the people voted for integration. A bill was prepared in the British Parliament, providing for local government in Malta and giving it three members in Britain's House of Commons. No further progress was made because the Maltese wanted guaranteed work in the dockyards.

An independence movement began to grow in Malta in 1958. A constitution approved in 1962 provided that the colony become a state with internal self-government. The new legislative assembly favored full independence. Britain agreed to grant full independence in May 1964. But disagreement among Malta's political factions delayed the action until September 1964.

Malta's political parties could not agree on whether to become a republic or a constitutional monarchy after independence. Some factions did not even want independence from Great Britain. But the Nationalist Party defeated the Labour Party on these measures and Malta became an independent constitutional monarchy on Sept. 21, 1964. Dr. Borg Oliver, leader of the Nationalists, became prime minister. In 1971, the Labour Party won a majority in parliament. Party leader Dom Mintoff became prime minister.

In 1974, Malta's parliament amended the constitution to change the form of government to a republic. Mintoff remained as prime minister. The Labour Party kept its majority in parliament in the 1976 and 1981 elections, and Mintoff continued to serve as prime minister until he resigned in 1984. He was succeeded by Karmenu Mifsud Bonnici, also of the Labour Party.

In 1979, an agreement between Great Britain and Malta that permitted Britain's use of military facilities on Malta expired. Britain and NATO then withdrew their military forces from Malta.

In 1987, the Nationalist Party won a majority in Parliament. Nationalist Party leader Eddie Fenech Adami became prime minister.   Dale D. Doreen

See also **Knights Hospitallers.**

Malta fever. See **Brucellosis.**

Valletta, Malta, borders the Mediterranean Sea. The city has been Malta's capital since 1571. It is also the country's chief port.

Maltese was probably the world's first lap dog. It developed on the Mediterranean island of Malta more than 2,000 years ago. Ladies in Greek and Roman noble families were fond of these dogs. They carried them in the sleeves of their robes and waited on the dogs as though they were babies. The Maltese grew to be one of the gentlest of all toy dogs. It usually weighs from 4 to 6 pounds (1.8 to 2.7 kilograms). Its black eyes have dark rims that make the eyes look large. Its white coat falls from a part down its back, and may grow so long it trails on the ground. See also **Dog** (picture: Toy dogs).

Critically reviewed by the American Kennel Club

Malthus, *MAL thuhs,* **Thomas Robert** (1766-1834), was an English economist. He is best known for his *Essay on the Principle of Population* (1798). His main idea in this book is that population tends to increase more rapidly than food supplies. He believed that wars and disease would have to kill off the extra population, unless people limited the number of their children.

Malthus' *Essay* suggested to Charles Darwin the relationship between progress and natural selection. This was a basic idea in Darwin's theory of evolution (see **Darwin, Charles R.**). Malthus' prediction failed to come true in the 1800's. Improved methods of agriculture provided enough food for most people. But rapid population growth in the 1900's, especially in underdeveloped countries, led to renewed interest in Malthus' theories. Many conservationists warned that food production could not keep pace with population indefinitely. The *neo-Malthusians* urged the use of birth control, though Malthus had rejected that solution.

Malthus was born on Feb. 17, 1766, in Surrey. He decided to be a clergyman, and was graduated from Cambridge University. About 1796, he took a parish in Surrey. He became a professor of history and political economy in the college of the East India Company in 1805, and held this post until his death.   H. W. Spiegel

See also **Population** (Effects).

Additional resources

Malthus, Thomas R. *An Essay on the Principle of Population.* Norton, 1976. First published in 1798.
Malthus Past and Present. Ed. by Jacques Dupaquier and others. Academic Pr., 1983.

Maltose, *MAWL tohs,* is the chemical term for malt sugar. The formation of maltose in the body is the first step in the digestion of starchy foods. The enzyme *ptyalin* in saliva changes starch into maltose. Other enzymes in the body split the maltose into glucose (see **Glucose**). Commercially, the enzyme *diastase* in malt changes starch into maltose. Fermentation changes maltose into alcohol. This is recovered by distillation. Maltose is used for sweetening some foods. See also **Brewing; Digestive system; Malt.**   Kay Franzen Jamieson

Mamba, *MAHM buh* or *MAM buh,* is the name of three deadly snakes of central and southern Africa. Mambas are closely related to the cobras, but, unlike cobras, they do not have a hood (see **Cobra**).

The mambas are slender and look somewhat like whips. They are usually about 6 to 8 feet (1.8 to 2.4 meters) long, but may be as long as 14 feet (4.3 meters). Mambas glide very rapidly in trees as well as on the ground. They produce a deadly poison. The black mamba is green when young and dark brown when

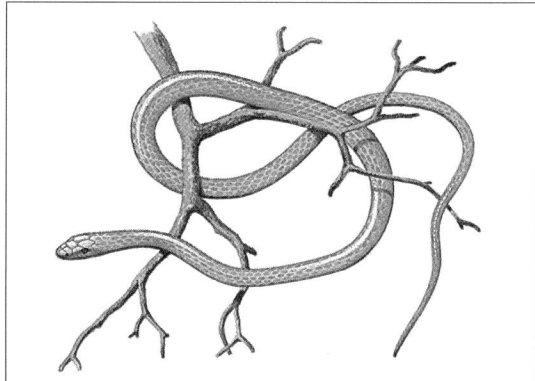

WORLD BOOK illustration by Richard Lewington, The Garden Studio
The mamba, a close relative of the cobra, is a poisonous snake that lives in central and southern Africa.

adult. The green mamba is green throughout its life.

Scientific classification. The mambas belong to the family Elapidae. The black mamba is *Dendroaspis polylepis.* The green mamba is *D. angusticeps.*   Albert F. Bennett

Mamelukes, *MAM uh looks,* were a military group that ruled Egypt from about A.D. 1250 to 1517. They were originally Turkish, Mongol, and Circassian slaves first brought to Egypt in the late 1100's. *Mameluke* is an Arabic term meaning *owned* or *slave.* The Mamelukes were trained as soldiers and rose to high army and government posts before they revolted and seized control of Egypt. See **Egypt** (History; picture). In time, the Mamelukes extended their rule to Palestine, Syria, and southern Asia Minor (now Turkey).

The Ottoman Turks defeated the Mamelukes and conquered Egypt in 1517. But the Mamelukes quickly regained influence under the Ottomans. In 1811, Muhammad Ali, the Ottoman governor of Egypt, ordered the massacre of the Mamelukes. A few escaped to Nubia to reorganize. But they could not defeat Ali's modern army and soon disappeared.   Andrew C. Hess

Mamet, *MAM eht,* **David** (1947-   ), is a leading American playwright. In his major plays, Mamet uses forceful, realistic dialogue to create a world he sees as corrupt and morally decayed and ready for radical change. Mamet often focuses on how following an amoral business ethic reduces people to commodities and creates an emotional and spiritual wasteland.

Mamet first gained attention for two short plays, *Duck Variations* (1972) and *Sexual Perversity in Chicago* (1974). His first major full-length drama was *American Buffalo* (1977), a naturalistic study of three petty criminals. *Glengarry Glen Ross* (1984) is an exposé of greed and cynicism among real estate salesmen. The play won the 1984 Pulitzer Prize for drama. *Speed-the-Plow* (1988) is a satiric behind-the-scenes portrait of the movie industry in Hollywood. *Oleanna* (1992) examines charges of sexual harassment between a male college professor and a female graduate student.

Mamet has written several successful screenplays, including *The Postman Always Rings Twice* (1981), *The Verdict* (1982), and *The Untouchables* (1987). Selections of his nonfiction pieces were published as *Writing in Restaurants* (1986) and *Some Freaks* (1990). Mamet was born in Chicago.   Thomas P. Adler

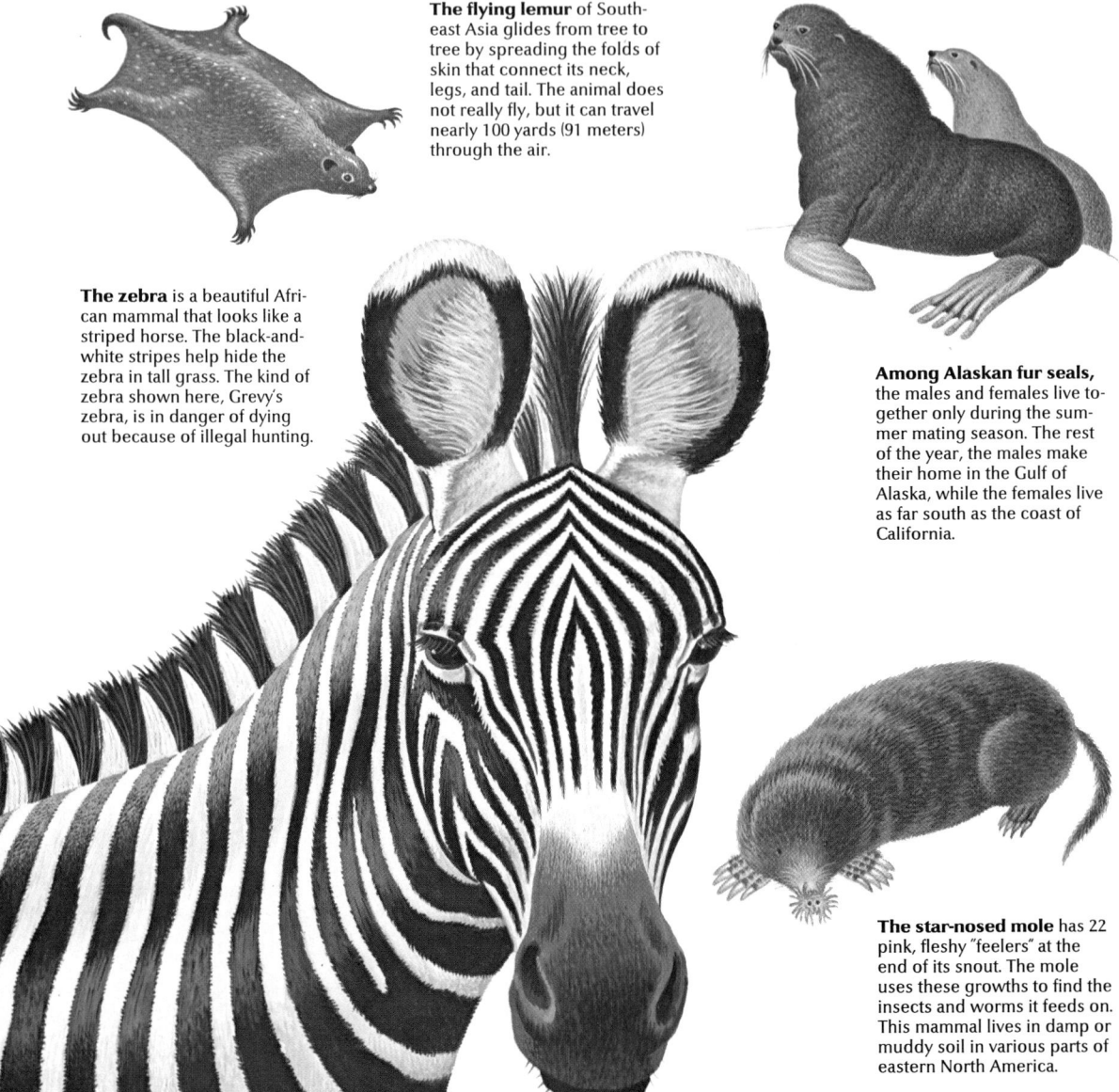

The flying lemur of Southeast Asia glides from tree to tree by spreading the folds of skin that connect its neck, legs, and tail. The animal does not really fly, but it can travel nearly 100 yards (91 meters) through the air.

The zebra is a beautiful African mammal that looks like a striped horse. The black-and-white stripes help hide the zebra in tall grass. The kind of zebra shown here, Grevy's zebra, is in danger of dying out because of illegal hunting.

Among Alaskan fur seals, the males and females live together only during the summer mating season. The rest of the year, the males make their home in the Gulf of Alaska, while the females live as far south as the coast of California.

The star-nosed mole has 22 pink, fleshy "feelers" at the end of its snout. The mole uses these growths to find the insects and worms it feeds on. This mammal lives in damp or muddy soil in various parts of eastern North America.

Mammal

Mammal is a *vertebrate* (backboned animal) that feeds its young on the mother's milk. There are about 4,500 kinds of mammals, and many of them are among the most familiar of all animals. Cats and dogs are mammals. So are such farm animals as cattle, goats, hogs, and horses. Mammals also include such fascinating animals as anteaters, apes, giraffes, hippopotamuses, and kangaroos. And people, too, are mammals.

Richard G. Van Gelder, the contributor of this article, is Curator Emeritus of Mammals at the American Museum of Natural History and the author of Biology of Mammals.

Mammals live almost everywhere. Such mammals as monkeys and elephants dwell in tropical regions. Arctic foxes, polar bears, and many other mammals make their home near the North Pole. Such mammals as camels and kangaroo rats live in deserts. Certain others, including seals and whales, dwell in the oceans. One group of mammals, the bats, can fly.

The largest animal that has ever lived, the blue whale, is a mammal. It can measure more than 100 feet (30 meters) long and can weigh more than 150 short tons (135 metric tons). The smallest mammal is the Kitti's hog-nosed bat of Thailand. It is about the size of a bumble bee and weighs only about $\frac{1}{14}$ ounce (2 grams).

Some mammals live a long time. Elephants, for example, live about 60 years, and some human beings reach

The sloth spends most of its life in the treetops. This South American mammal moves very slowly along the underside of branches, hanging upside down by its long claws.

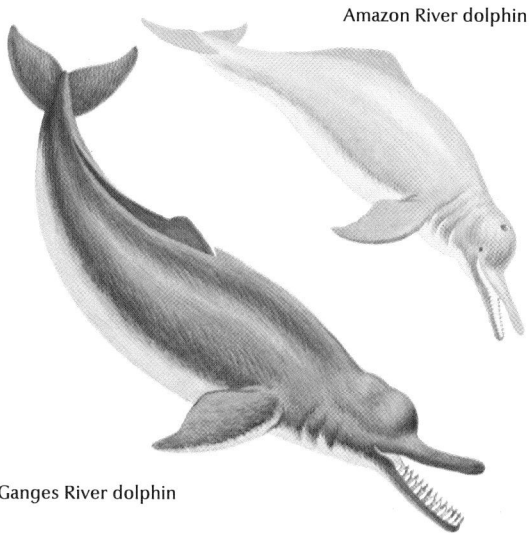

Amazon River dolphin

Ganges River dolphin

Dolphins are mammals that live in water. Most kinds of dolphins live in the ocean. However, the Amazon River dolphin and the Ganges River dolphin dwell in fresh water.

Interesting facts about mammals

The largest mammal—and the largest animal that has ever lived—is the blue whale. It measures up to 100 feet (30 meters) long when fully grown.

The Kitti's hog-nosed bat of Thailand is the smallest mammal. It is about the size of a bumblebee and weighs no more than a penny.

WORLD BOOK illustration by John Dawson

Kitti's hog-nosed bat

The potto, a small African tree dweller, has one of the strongest grips of all mammals. A potto can grasp a branch so tightly with its hands and feet that the animal may remain clinging to the branch even after it has died.

Potto

The rhinoceros has horns that look like closely packed hairs. Actually, they consist of many fibers of *keratin,* the horny substance that makes up the nails of people. African rhinos have two horns. Indian rhinos have one.

African rhinoceros

A young marmoset rides on its father's back. Most male mammals have little to do with raising their offspring. But among these South American monkeys, the father and mother share the job of carrying and protecting their babies.

Marmosets

The hyrax is a small mammal that looks much like a guinea pig. But scientists believe that its nearest relatives are actually elephants. Hyraxes, which are also known as conies, live in Africa and the Middle East.

Hyrax

WORLD BOOK illustrations by James Teason unless otherwise credited

the age of 100 years or more. On the other hand, many mice and shrews live less than a year.

Mammals differ from all or most other animals in five major ways. (1) Mammals nurse their babies—that is, they feed them on the mother's milk. No other animals do this. (2) Most mammals give their young more protection and training than do other animals. (3) Only mammals have hair. All mammals have hair at some time in their life, though in certain whales it is present only before birth. (4) Mammals are *warm-blooded*—that is, their body temperature remains about the same all the time, even though the temperature of their surroundings may change. Birds are also warm-blooded, but nearly all other animals are not. (5) Mammals have a larger, more well-developed brain than do other ani-

mals. Some mammals, such as chimpanzees, dolphins, and especially human beings, are highly intelligent.

This article provides general information about mammals. Several hundred separate *World Book* articles give details on specific kinds of mammals. Readers can find these articles by consulting the general articles listed in the *Related articles* at the end of this article. In addition, the article **Animal** has much information on mammals, such as the tables *Names of animals and their young* and *Length of life of animals.*

The importance of mammals

How people use mammals. Since the earliest times, human beings have hunted other mammals. Prehistoric people ate the flesh of wild mammals, used their skins for clothing, and made tools and ornaments from their bones, teeth, horns, and hoofs.

About 10,000 years ago, people learned they could *domesticate* (tame and raise) certain useful mammals. Hunters bred dogs, one of the first domestic animals, to track and bring down game animals. People later domesticated the wild ancestors of today's cattle, goats, hogs, and sheep. Since then, these mammals have provided meat and other products. Horses and oxen have long been used to carry people or their goods. Camels, elephants, goats, llamas, reindeer, and even dogs have also been used in this way.

Some mammals, especially cats, dogs, hamsters, and rabbits, are popular pets. Certain mammals are used in scientific research. For example, new drugs are tested on domestic mice and rats and on dogs, guinea pigs, and monkeys.

Although domestic mammals provide many products, people still hunt wild mammals. They hunt such mammals as antelopes, deer, rabbits, and squirrels for their flesh or hides. Whales are killed for their meat and oil, and seals for their skins. Beavers, muskrats, otters, and other wild mammals that have thick coats are trapped for their fur. Elephants, hippopotamuses, and walruses are killed for their tusks, which consist of ivory.

Wild mammals are also a source of enjoyment. Many people travel to national parks to delight in viewing bears, deer, moose, and other mammals in their natural homes. Other people visit zoos, where they can see interesting mammals from many countries. Even in the largest cities, people can still find some wild mammals to enjoy, such as the friendly gray squirrel.

Mammals in the balance of nature. Mammals are important not only to people but also to the whole system of life on the earth. Many mammals help plants grow. For example, animals that eat plants leave seeds in their *droppings* (body wastes). Many of these seeds sprout into plants. Similarly, many of the nuts that squirrels bury for a food supply grow into trees. Gophers, moles, prairie dogs, and other burrowing mammals dig up the soil. This activity enables air, moisture, and sunlight to break down the soil, which can then be used by growing plants.

Flesh-eating mammals also help maintain the balance of nature by feeding on plant-eating animals. If such flesh-eaters as coyotes, mongooses, and weasels did not control the number of plant-eaters, certain species of plants in an area could be drastically reduced or even wiped out. Other mammals help keep the insect population under control. For example, aardvarks, giant anteaters, and pangolins eat millions of ants and termites at each meal. Every night, bats eat great numbers of insects. *Scavenger* mammals, such as hyenas and jackals, clean up the remains of large animals that have been killed or that died naturally.

Even the wastes and dead bodies of mammals are important to the balance of nature. Mammal droppings are a valuable fertilizer. The bones of dead mammals break down into chemicals that are needed by animals and plants. For more information, see **Balance of nature.**

The bodies of mammals

Mammals have many ways of life, and each species has a body adapted to its particular way of life. However, all mammals share some basic body characteristics. These characteristics include certain features of their (1) skin and hair, (2) skeleton, and (3) internal organ systems.

Skin and hair cover the body of mammals. Skin consists of an inner layer, the *dermis,* and an outer layer, the *epidermis.* The dermis contains the arteries and veins that supply the skin with blood. The epidermis, which has no blood vessels, protects the dermis. It also produces special skin structures, including hair, horns, claws, nails, and hoofs.

The skin of mammals has a rich supply of glands. *Mammary glands* produce the milk that female mammals use to nurse their young. *Sebaceous glands* give off oil that lubricates the hair and skin. *Sweat glands* eliminate small amounts of liquid wastes, but their main purpose is to help mammals cool off. As sweat evaporates from the skin, it cools the surface. Many mammals, such as dogs and skunks, also have *scent glands.* Dogs use their scent glands for communication and identification. Skunks spray a bad-smelling odor from their scent glands as a means of self-defense.

Many mammals have two coats of hair. The *underhair* consists of soft, fine hairs that provide a thick, warm coat. The outer *guard hair* consists of longer, slightly stiffened hairs that give shape to a mammal's coat and protect the underhair. Many mammals have long, stiff hairs about the mouth or other parts of the head. These hairs, called *vibrissae* or *tactile hairs,* serve as highly sensitive touch organs. The whiskers of cats and mice are examples of such hairs.

Hair serves many purposes. The hair color of many mammals blends with the animals' surroundings and so helps them hide from their enemies or prey. Some mammals have specialized guard hairs, such as the quills on a porcupine, that provide protection from enemies. But the main purpose of hair is to keep the animal warm. Dolphins and whales, which lack body hair, have a thick layer of fat that provides warmth. Other mammals with little hair, such as elephants and rhinoceroses, live in warm climates. See **Skin; Hair.**

Skeleton of mammals provides a framework for the body and protects vital organs. In addition, the muscles that enable a mammal to move about are attached to the skeleton. The skeleton of all adult mammals— whether blue whales or shrews—consists of more than 200 bones. Some of these bones are *fused* (united) and so form a single structure. The skeleton has two main parts. They are (1) the axial skeleton and (2) the appendicular skeleton.

The axial skeleton consists of three regions. These regions are the skull, the vertebral column, and the thoracic basket.

The skull houses the brain in a bony box called the *cranium.* The skull also includes the jaws and teeth and areas for the organs of hearing, sight, and smell. Some mammals have bony growths from the skull, such as the antlers on deer.

The vertebral column, or spine, consists of five kinds of *vertebrae* (spinal bones): *cervical,* in the neck; *thoracic,* in the chest; *lumbar,* in the lower back; *sacral,* in the hip; and *caudal,* in the tail. All mammals, except manatees and sloths, have seven cervical vertebrae. The number of each of the other kinds of vertebrae varies with the species of mammal.

The thoracic basket is made up of the ribs, which are attached to the thoracic vertebrae. Most of the ribs also are joined to the breastbone. The thoracic basket forms a bony cage that protects the heart, lungs, and other vital organs.

The appendicular skeleton is made up of the limbs and their supports. The forelimbs are attached to the axial skeleton by the shoulder girdle, which consists of a broad shoulder blade and, in most species, a narrow collarbone. The hindlimbs are attached to the sacral vertebrae by a hip girdle consisting of three bones. In many mammals, the three bones of the hip girdle are fused to one another and to the sacral vertebrae.

A single bone forms the upper portion of each limb. In most mammals, the lower part of each limb has two bones. These bones are fused in some mammals. The wrist, palm, ankle, and sole consist of several small bones. The number of these depends on how many fingers or toes the mammal has. See **Skeleton.**

Internal organ systems are groups of organs that serve a particular function. The major systems of mammals include (1) the circulatory system, (2) the digestive system, (3) the nervous system, and (4) the respiratory system.

The circulatory system consists of the heart and blood vessels. Mammals have an extremely efficient four-chambered heart, which pumps blood to all parts of the body. The blood, in turn, carries food and oxygen to the body tissues, where they are burned to release energy. The red blood cells of mammals can carry more oxygen than can the cells of all other animals except birds. The high efficiency of the circulatory system is associated with warm-bloodedness. Mammals must burn large amounts of food to maintain a high body temperature. See **Heart; Blood.**

The digestive system absorbs nourishing substances from food. It consists basically of a long tube that is formed by the mouth, the esophagus, the stomach, and the intestines. The digestive system of mammals varies according to the kind of food an animal eats. Mammals that eat flesh, which is easy to digest, have a fairly simple stomach and short intestines. Most mammals that eat plants, however, have a complicated stomach and long intestines. For example, such mammals as cows and sheep have a four-chambered stomach. Each chamber helps break down the coarse grasses that the animals eat. See **Digestive system; Ruminant.**

The nervous system regulates most body activities. It consists mainly of the brain and spinal cord and their associated nerves. Most kinds of mammals have a larger brain than do other animals of similar size. In addition, mammalian brains have an extremely well-developed

Some major characteristics of mammals

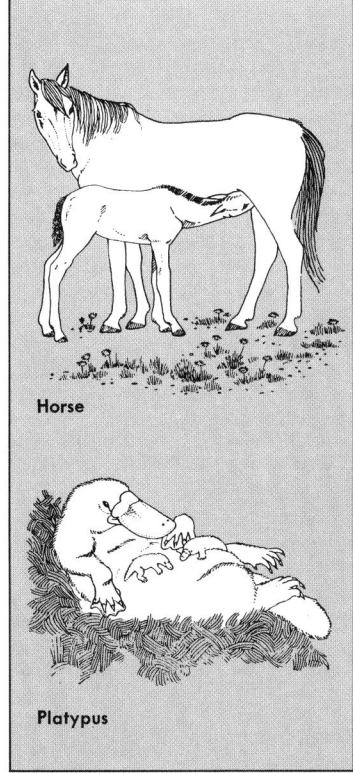

Horse

Platypus

Alpaca

Porcupine

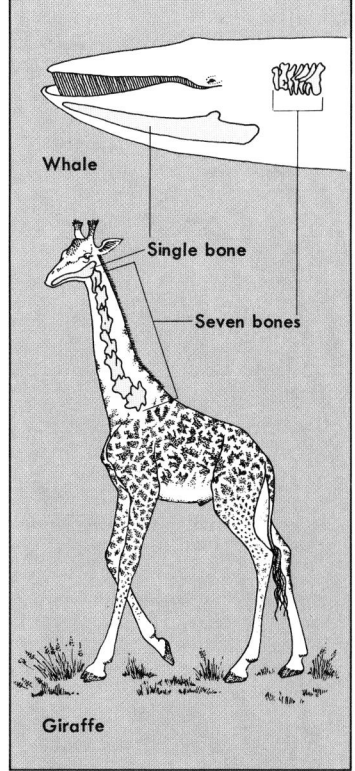

Whale

Single bone

Seven bones

Giraffe

WORLD BOOK illustrations by Jean Helmer

Mammals nurse their young. A colt, like most baby mammals, sucks milk from his mother's nipples. Baby platypuses lap milk from their mother's abdomen.

Mammals have hair. In the alpaca and most other mammals, a thick coat of hair provides warmth. The porcupine's quills are special hairs used for self-defense.

Mammals have similar skeletons. Only one bone forms each side of the lower jaw in mammals. Almost all mammals have seven bones in the neck.

The anatomy of a mammal

Although mammals differ greatly in size and shape, they all share a number of physical characteristics. These characteristics include the same basic skeletal and internal organ systems. The diagrams below show the skeleton and internal organs of a male dog.

WORLD BOOK diagrams by Jean Helmer

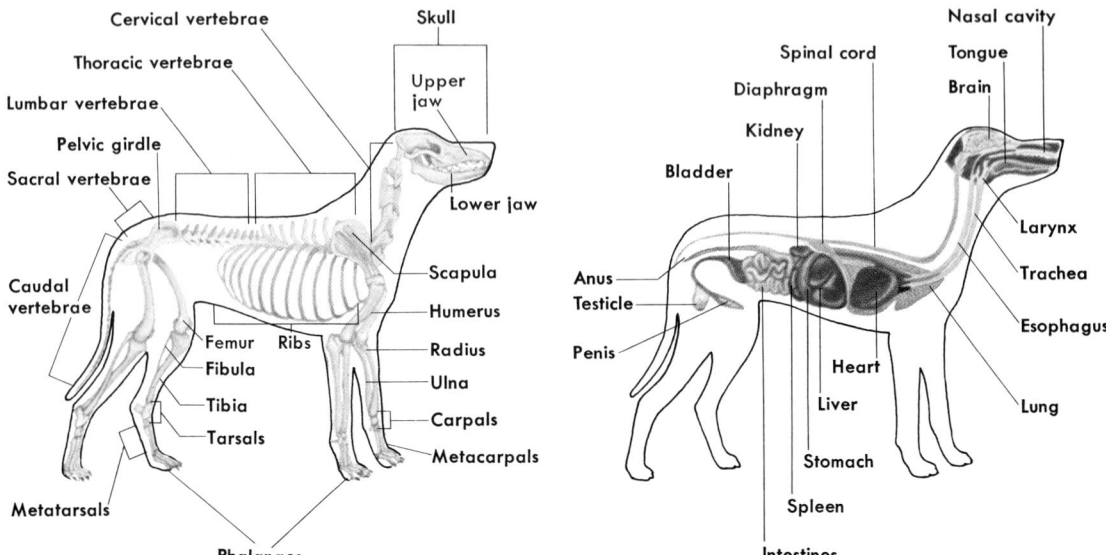

cerebral cortex. This part of the brain serves as the center for learning and gives mammals superior intelligence. See **Brain; Nervous system.**

The respiratory system enables mammals to breathe. It is made up of two lungs and various tubes that lead to the nostrils. A muscular sheet called the *diaphragm* divides the chest cavity from the abdominal cavity and aids in breathing. Only mammals have a muscular diaphragm. In most mammals, the nostrils are at the end of the snout or nose. Dolphins and whales have their nostrils, called *blowholes,* at the top of the head. Dolphins and some whales have one nostril. Other whales have two. See **Lung; Respiration.**

Other organ systems of mammals include the endocrine, excretory, and reproductive systems. The endocrine system consists of glands that produce *hormones,* substances which help regulate body functions. The excretory system eliminates wastes from the body by means of the kidneys. For information on these two systems, see the articles **Hormone** and **Kidney.** For a discussion of the mammalian reproductive system, see the section of this article titled *How mammals reproduce.*

The senses and intelligence of mammals

Senses. Mammals rely on various senses to inform them of happenings in their environment. The major senses of mammals are (1) smell, (2) taste, (3) hearing, (4) sight, and (5) touch. However, the senses are not equally developed in each species of mammal. In fact, some species do not have all the senses.

Smell is the most important sense among the majority of mammals. Most species have large nasal cavities lined with nerves that are sensitive to odors. These animals rely heavily on smell to find food and to detect the presence of enemies. In many species, the members communicate with one another through the odors produced by various skin glands and body wastes. For ex-

ample, a dog urinates on trees and other objects to tell other dogs it has been there. A few species of mammals, especially human beings, apes, and monkeys, have a poorly developed sense of smell. Dolphins and whales seem to lack the sense entirely. See **Smell.**

Taste helps mammals identify foods and so decide what foods to eat. This sense is located mainly in *taste buds* on the tongue. However, much of the sense of taste is strongly affected by the odor of food. See **Taste.**

Hearing is well developed in most mammals. The majority of species have an outer ear, which collects sound waves and channels them into the middle and inner ear. Only mammals have an outer ear. See the article **Ear** for a description of the human ear, which is typical of the ears of most mammals.

Some mammals use their sense of hearing to find food and avoid obstacles in the dark. Bats, for example, produce short, high-pitched sounds that bounce off surrounding objects. Bats can use these sounds and their echoes to detect insects and even thin wires. Dolphins and whales also use this system, called *echolocation,* to find food and avoid objects underwater. However, most of the sounds they make are pitched much lower than are the sounds made by bats. Other echolocating mammals include sea lions, seals, and shrews.

Sight is the most important sense among the *higher primates* (apes, monkeys, and people). The structure and function of the eye is similar in all mammals (see **Eye**). However, the eyes of the higher primates have more *cones* than do those of most other mammals. These structures give apes, monkeys, and people sharp daytime vision and the ability to tell colors apart. A few other mammals that are active during the day have some color vision, but most mammals are color blind. Many species of mammals that are active at night have large eyes with a reflector at the rear. This reflector, called the *tapetum lucidum,* helps the animal see in the dark. It produces the *eyeshine* a person sees when light strikes the eyes of a cat or a deer at night.

Touch. Most mammals have a good sense of touch. *Tactile nerves*—that is, nerves which respond to touch—are found all over a mammal's body. But some areas have an especially large number of these nerves and are very sensitive to touch. The whiskers of such mammals as cats, dogs, and mice have many tactile nerves at their base. These whiskers help the animals feel their way in the dark. Moles and pocket gophers have a highly sensitive tail, which aids them when backing up in their dark, narrow tunnels. Primates' fingers also have many tactile nerves as do the paws of raccoons.

Intelligence is related to the ability to learn. Through learning, an animal stores information in its memory and then later uses this information to act in appropriate ways. Mammals, with their highly developed cerebral cortex, can learn more than other kinds of animals.

Intelligence is hard to measure, even in human beings. But chimpanzees, dogs, and dolphins can learn much when trained by people. These species are among the most intelligent mammals. The amount of the surface area of the brain, especially of the cerebral cortex, generally indicates an animal's learning ability. In the more intelligent mammals, the cerebral cortex is fairly large and has many folds, which further increase its surface area. Human beings have the most highly developed cerebral cortex.

What mammals eat

Most mammals are *herbivorous*—that is, they eat plants. Plant food is generally tough and so tends to wear teeth down. Herbivorous mammals have special teeth that help counteract such wear. Many plant-eating mammals, including cattle, elephants, and horses, have high-crowned teeth that wear down slowly. The front teeth of beavers, rats, and other rodents grow continuously and thus never wear down.

Some mammals are *carnivorous.* They eat animal flesh. Many of them are speedy animals that catch, hold, and stab their prey with long, pointed *canine teeth.*

Such mammals, which include leopards, lions, and wolves, do not thoroughly chew their food. They swallow chunks of it whole. Dolphins, seals, and other fish-eating mammals also use their teeth to grasp prey, which they swallow whole. Some carnivorous mammals commonly feed on the remains of dead animals, instead of hunting and killing fresh prey. Hyenas are especially adapted to such a diet and have extremely powerful jaws that can crush even large bones.

Various mammals eat insects. Many of these *insectivorous* mammals, such as bats and shrews, have teeth that can crush and slice off the hard outer parts of insects. This action exposes the softer flesh and juices, which the mammals feed on. Other insect-eaters, such as aardvarks, anteaters, echidnas, numbats, and pangolins, have weak teeth or none at all. These mammals eat ants and termites, which they lick up with their long, sticky tongues and swallow without chewing.

Some mammals eat both plants and animals. These *omnivorous* mammals have teeth that can grind up plants and tear off flesh. They include bears, hogs, opossums, and human beings. Some omnivorous mammals change their diet with the seasons. For example, spotted skunks feed mostly on fruits, seeds, and insects in summer. In winter, they eat mainly mice and rats.

How mammals move

On land. Most mammals live on the ground. The majority of these *terrestrial* animals move about on four legs. They walk by lifting one foot at a time—first one forefoot, then the opposite hindfoot, next the other forefoot, and then the opposite hindfoot. At faster speeds, most four-legged mammals *trot,* lifting one forefoot and the opposite hindfoot at the same time. A few species, such as camels, elephants, and giraffes, pace rather than trot. *Pacing* involves lifting both feet on one side of the body at the same time. At their fastest speed, most terrestrial mammals *gallop.* While galloping, the animal usually has only one foot on the ground at a time. At some point during the gallop, all four feet are in the air.

Jerboas, kangaroos, and kangaroo rats are terrestrial

The teeth of mammals   Mammals have three basic types of teeth: (1) *incisors* (front teeth), (2) *canines* (side teeth), and (3) *premolars* and *molars* (cheek teeth). The number and shape of these teeth vary according to diet.

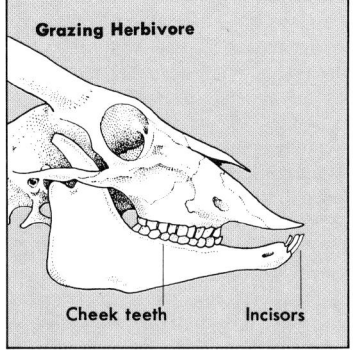

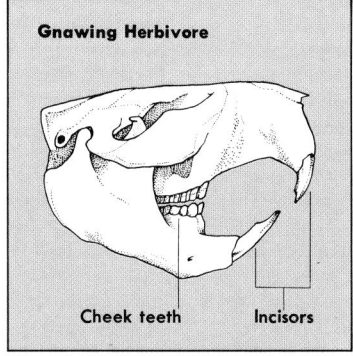

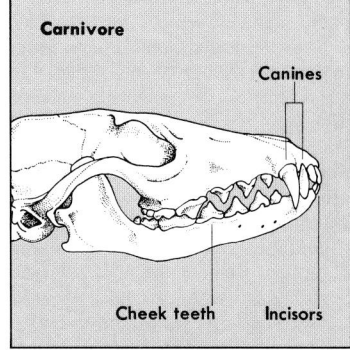

WORLD BOOK illustrations by Jean Helmer

Sheep teeth. A sheep snips off grass by pressing its lower incisors against a pad on its upper jaw. It uses the cheek teeth for grinding and has no canine teeth.

Beaver teeth. A beaver uses its huge incisors to gnaw the bark off plants. Like sheep, beavers use the cheek teeth for grinding and have no canine teeth.

Red fox teeth. A red fox has small incisors but large, pointed canine teeth, which it uses to stab and hold prey. The cheek teeth are for cutting and crushing.

How the skeleton is adapted for movement   Although all mammals have a basic skeleton in common, it is adapted in each species to suit the particular way the animals move. These illustrations show various adaptations of the forelimb.

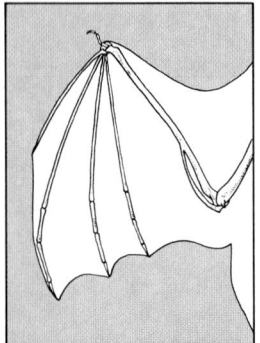
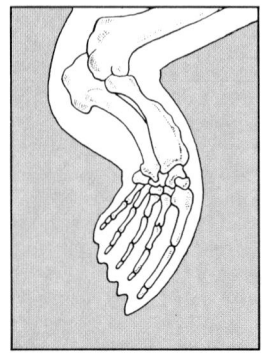
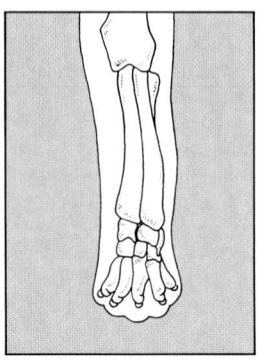
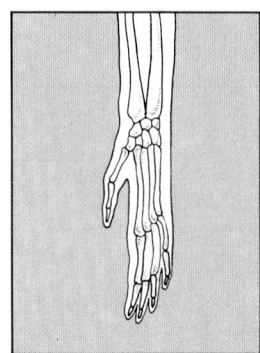

WORLD BOOK illustrations by Jean Helmer

A bat's forelimb is adapted for flying. The bones of the hand and forearm provide the framework of the bat's wing.

A walrus' forelimb forms a paddle-shaped flipper, which the animal uses to pull itself through the water.

An elephant's forelimb provides a sturdy, pillarlike support to carry the enormous body over the ground.

A gibbon's forelimb is adapted for swinging through trees. The animal has powerful arms and flexible fingers.

mammals that move by hopping. These animals have powerful hind legs. They also have a long tail that is used for balance.

In trees. Many mammals that live in forested areas spend most of their time in the trees. These *arboreal* animals have a number of special body features that help them move through the trees. Monkeys, for example, can use their hands and feet to grasp tree branches. Many monkeys of Central and South America also have a *prehensile* (grasping) tail, which they can wrap around branches for support. Other arboreal mammals with a prehensile tail include kinkajous, opossums, and phalangers. Some species of anteaters, pangolins, and South American porcupines also have such a tail. Squirrels and tree shrews have sharp, curved claws that aid them in climbing trees. The claws of tree sloths are so long and curved that the animals cannot walk erect on the ground. These mammals spend most of their life hanging upside down from branches.

In water. Dolphins, porpoises, manatees, and whales are mammals that live their entire life in water. They have a streamlined body and a powerful tail, which they move up and down to propel themselves through the water. Their forelimbs are paddlelike flippers, used for balance and steering. They have no hindlimbs.

Many other mammals spend much, but not all, of their time in water. Some of these animals, such as capybaras, hippopotamuses, and walruses, swim by moving their forelimbs and their hindlimbs. Other species use mainly their forelimbs. Such swimmers include platypuses, polar bears, and fur seals and sea lions. Still other mammals use only their hindlimbs to swim. These animals include beavers and hair seals.

In the air. Bats are the only mammals that can fly. Their wings consist of thin skin stretched over the bones of the forelimbs. Bats fly by beating their wings forward and downward, then upward and backward.

The so-called flying lemurs, flying phalangers, and flying squirrels cannot actually fly. These mammals have a fold of skin between the forelimb and hindlimb on each side of the body. By stretching out these "wings," the animals can glide from tree to tree.

Underground. Pocket gophers, moles, and certain other mammals spend almost all their life underground. Most of these *fossorial* mammals have strong claws and powerful forelimbs. Many of them have poor vision, and some are blind. The forelimbs of moles are turned so that the broad palms face backward and the elbows point upward. Strong chest muscles attached to the forelimbs enable moles to "swim" through the soil, much as a person swims when doing the breaststroke.

How mammals reproduce

All mammals reproduce sexually. In sexual reproduction, a *sperm* (male sex cell) unites with an *egg* (female sex cell) in a process called *fertilization.* The fertilized egg develops into a new individual. In all species of mammals, the eggs are fertilized inside the female's body. Male mammals have a special organ, the penis, which releases sperm into the female during *copulation* (sexual intercourse).

Mating occurs among most mammals only during the period when the female is in *estrus,* or *heat.* At this time, the female is sexually receptive and will permit copulation. See **Estrous cycle.**

The time of the estrous period varies with different species. Among many mammals, especially those that live where the climate is constant the year around, the females may come into heat at any time. Such *polyestrous* (many-estrous) mammals include elephants and giraffes. Among species that live in regions with distinct seasons, all the females may come into heat at a particular time of year. This *breeding,* or *rutting,* season is so timed that the offspring will be born when environmental conditions are best for their survival. Some seasonal breeders have one heat period a year. Such *monestrous* (one-estrous) species include certain bats, bears, and deer. Other species, such as cottontail rabbits, have several heat periods during their breeding season. These mammals are *seasonally polyestrous.*

Most smaller mammals are *promiscuous* in their mating behavior. No lasting bond forms between the mates. They remain together only long enough to copulate. Some other species are *polygamous.* The males of such species, which include American elks and fur seals, gather a *harem* (group of females) just before and during the mating season. The male tries to mate with each member of his harem. The association between the male and the harem ends after the breeding season. Among many kinds of mammals, the males and females remain together for some time after mating. However, only a few mammals seem to take one mate for life. Zoologists believe that such *monogamous* species include beavers, wolves, and a tiny antelope called a dik-dik.

Reproduction. Mammals can be divided into three groups according to the way in which new individuals develop from the fertilized eggs. These groups are (1) placentals, (2) marsupials, and (3) monotremes.

Placentals give birth to fairly well-developed offspring. The vast majority of mammals are placentals. After fertilization occurs, a placental mammal begins to develop in the *uterus,* a hollow organ in the mother's abdomen. Another organ, called the *placenta,* attaches the developing mammal to the uterus wall. The developing mammal receives nourishment from the mother through the placenta.

The time during which the unborn young develops in the uterus is called the *gestation period.* Among placen-

How mammals reproduce	All mammals reproduce sexually. A new individual begins to form after a *sperm* (male sex cell) unites with an *egg* (female sex cell). This union is called *fertilization.* Mammals can be divided into three groups according to the way in which the fertilized egg develops into a new individual. These groups are (1) placentals, (2) marsupials, and (3) monotremes.

Norman Myers, Bruce Coleman Inc.

Placentals give birth to fairly well-developed offspring, such as the newborn zebra shown above. A young placental mammal develops inside its mother, receiving nourishment from her through an organ called the *placenta.* Placentals make up the vast majority of mammals.

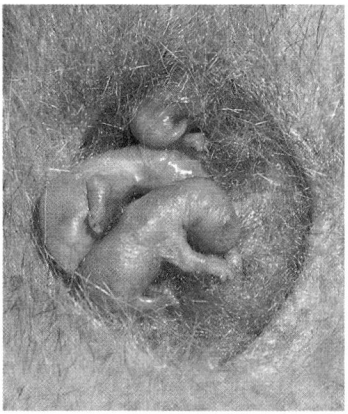

Leonard Lee Rue III, Bruce Coleman Inc.

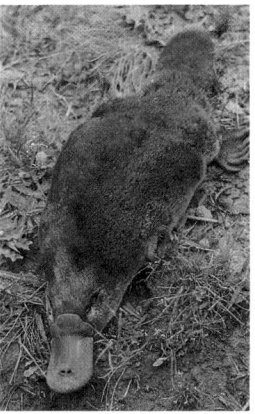

Warren Garst, Tom Stack & Assoc.

WORLD BOOK diagram by Jean Helmer

Marsupials give birth to poorly developed young, such as these baby opossums. The young complete their development attached to the mother's nipples.

Monotremes, such as the platypus, *left,* lay eggs rather than bear their young alive. The female platypus digs a long tunnel in the bank of a stream, *right.* There she lays one to three eggs that have a leathery shell. The only other monotremes are the echidnas, or spiny anteaters. Platypuses and echidnas live in Australia and on nearby islands.

A lion cub sucks nourishing milk from its mother's nipple. All baby mammals feed on mother's milk. Among many species, the young continue to nurse long after they can eat solid foods.

A mother brown bear shows her cubs how to catch fish. Many young mammals learn how to obtain food by watching and imitating the behavior of their parents and other adults.

Young wild dogs romp together in a make-believe fight. This kind of play serves as an important learning experience. It helps the puppies develop the skills they will need for hunting.

tal mammals, the gestation period ranges from about 16 days in golden hamsters to about 650 days in elephants. Most species with a short gestation period give birth to young that are generally helpless and may be blind and hairless. Most species with a long gestation period bear young that are alert soon after birth. The newborns may also be fully haired, and some can even walk or run almost immediately.

Marsupials give birth to very tiny, poorly developed offspring. Directly after birth, the young attach themselves to the mother's nipples. The babies remain attached until they develop more completely. The nipples of most female marsupials are in a pouch, called the *marsupium,* on the stomach. Marsupials are often known as *pouched mammals.* However, not all female marsupials have a pouch. Certain South American species, for example, lack this feature.

There are about 260 species of marsupials. About two-thirds of them live in Australia and nearby islands. Australian marsupials include kangaroos, koala bears, and wombats. About 80 kinds of opossums, which are marsupials, live in Central and South America. One species lives in the United States and Canada.

Monotremes, unlike all other kinds of mammals, do not give birth to live young. Instead, they lay eggs that have a leathery shell. After an incubation period, the eggs hatch. The only monotremes are the echidnas and the platypus. They live in Australia, New Guinea, and Tasmania.

Care of the young. All baby mammals feed on milk from their mother's mammary glands. Baby placentals and marsupials suck the milk from the mother's nipples. Female monotremes do not have nipples. The milk is released through pores on the mother's abdomen, and the young lap it up. The nursing period lasts only a few weeks in mice, hares, and many other species. But among some mammals, such as elephants and rhinoceroses, the young may nurse several years before they are *weaned*—that is, taken off the mother's milk. In most species, the young can eat solid food long before they are weaned.

Young mammals must learn many of the skills they need to survive. Much of this learning occurs during the nursing period, when the young are taught how to obtain food and how to avoid dangers. Among most kinds of mammals, the mother alone raises the young. However, the males of some species help care for their offspring. For example, male mice of certain species aid in nest building. Male coyotes and African wild dogs bring back food for the mother and puppies. Male lions help protect the mother and cubs from attacks by hyenas and other lions.

Among many smaller mammals, such as mice and shrews, the young leave the parental nest or den as soon as they are weaned. But among cheetahs, elephants, wolves, and many other species, the young stay with their parents long after the nursing period ends.

Ways of life

Group life. Many mammals live in *social groups* of several individuals. The simplest social group consists of an adult male and female and their offspring. Beavers and certain species of monkeys form such family groups. A larger social group, such as a wolf pack, may have a number of adult and young animals of both sexes. Zebra herds, which consist of an adult male and several females and their young, make up another kind of social group.

Among many social species, the group members are ranked according to a *dominance hierarchy.* The *dominant* (controlling) members of the group get first choice of food and mates. They may establish their dominance at first by winning fights. Thereafter, they keep their position mostly by threats. See **Dominance.**

Group life offers several advantages. Coyotes, lions, wolves, and other *predators* (hunters) that live in groups cooperate in surrounding and bringing down prey. However, prey species can also profit from group life. If one deer senses danger, for example, it can warn the entire herd by flashing the white underside of its tail. Among some prey species, such as baboons and musk oxen, the group assembles into a defensive formation for protection against predators.

Some mammals spend most of their life alone. Such *solitary* mammals include leopards, tigers, and most other cats except lions. However, even solitary mammals spend some time with members of their species. For example, adult males and females get together to mate,

and a mother remains with her young at least until they are weaned.

Solitary mammals have several advantages over social species. They do not have to share available food and shelter. In addition, a solitary predator can hunt its prey more silently than can a group. Among prey species, a solitary animal attracts less attention than a group does, and it can hide more easily.

Territoriality is a form of behavior in which an animal or group of animals claims and defends a particular area. Other members of the species are kept out of the territory. Many species of mammals establish territories only during the breeding season. For example, a male fur seal claims a territory before mating. He drives all other males from his territory, while he tries to herd as many females as possible into the area. Other mammals, such as gibbons and howler monkeys, claim a territory to help ensure the group of an adequate food supply.

Mammals mark the boundaries of their territories in various ways. For example, hyenas leave solid body wastes and scents produced by special glands to indicate their territorial borders. Wolf packs mark their territories with urine. Such markers serve as No Trespassing signs to other members of the species.

Rod Allin, Bruce Coleman Inc.

Barren ground caribou are *social mammals*—that is, they live in groups. Caribou herds may include hundreds of members. The herds spend the summer in the Arctic tundra. As autumn approaches, they migrate south to evergreen forests, where they can get food during the winter.

R. T. W. from Carl E. Östman

Vervets, like all other species of monkeys, are social mammals. Vervets generally form bands of no more than 20 members. These monkeys are common throughout much of Africa.

K. W. Fink, Bruce Coleman Inc.

A male sea lion, *center,* claims a territory during the mating season. He keeps all other males out of his territory but tries to gather as many females as possible into the area.

Mammals usually defend their territories by threats rather than by actually fighting. A group of howler monkeys, for instance, keeps other howlers out of its territory by shouting at them.

Many mammals are not territorial. But most species, including those that do not claim a territory, have a *home range.* A mammal wanders over its home range during the daily activities of feeding, drinking, and seeking shelter. Unlike a territory, a home range is not defended against members of the same species. See **Territoriality.**

Migration. Many kinds of mammals make seasonal migrations to obtain a better food supply, to avoid harsh weather, or to do both. For example, various species of North American bats migrate southward each autumn because the insects that they feed on become scarce during the cold northern winter. Wildebeests and zebras in central Africa migrate in search of green grass during the yearly dry season. American elks of Canada and the Western United States spend the summer on high mountain slopes. In winter, they live in the valleys below, where the snow is not as deep.

Some mammals migrate to an area to give birth or to mate. Every fall, for example, gray whales swim from

their Arctic feeding grounds to the warmer waters off the northwest coast of Mexico. These waters provide little or no food for the whales. The animals make the journey to give birth because newborn whales could not survive in the cold Arctic waters. See **Migration.**

Hibernation. Some kinds of mammals hibernate to avoid winter food shortages. During hibernation, an animal goes into *torpor,* a type of sleep from which it cannot be awakened quickly. The body temperature of a hibernating mammal is lower than normal. In fact, the temperature of most hibernators drops to nearly that of the surrounding air. The heartbeat and breathing slow down greatly. A hibernating mammal does not eat. It lives off the fat in its body. Some hibernating mammals pass in and out of torpor all during the winter.

Mammals that hibernate include certain kinds of bats; echidnas; and chipmunks, woodchucks, and some other rodents. Most of these animals become extremely fat before they go into hibernation. They usually spend the winter in a den or some other protected place where the temperature is not likely to fall below freezing.

Some bears also enter into a sleeplike state during much of the winter. Many scientists believe that a bear's winter sleep can be classified as hibernation. However, many other scientists do not consider bears to be true hibernators because their body temperature falls only slightly during winter sleep.

A few kinds of mammals, mostly rodents, become torpid during the hottest, driest part of the summer. This summer torpor is called *estivation.* See **Estivation; Hibernation.**

Methods of attack and defense. Mammals that hunt rely mainly on their sharp teeth to catch and kill prey. Most of these predators also have sharp claws, which they use to grab and hold their victims. Solitary predators generally stalk their prey by slinking and hiding, and many of these hunters have coats that blend with their surroundings. After a predator has sneaked up on its prey, it makes a final dash at high speed to catch the animal before it can escape. Group hunters, such as African hunting dogs and wolves, usually take turns in the chase until they have worn the prey out.

Most mammals try to escape predators by fleeing. Many hoofed mammals, such as deer and impalas, can run swiftly for long distances. Gophers, prairie dogs, and many other small mammals rush into a burrow or other hiding place. On the other hand, fawns and rabbits sometimes escape hunters by remaining absolutely still. This defense works because many predators are "sight hunters" and are attracted mainly by movement. The American opossum takes this defense one step further. It "plays dead" by going completely limp. Many predators lose interest in the apparently dead animal.

Some mammals have special features that help protect them from enemies. The bony shell of armadillos and the scales of pangolins serve as protection against sharp-clawed predators. The thick skin of elephants and rhinoceroses serves the same purpose. Echidnas, hedgehogs, and porcupines have sharp, stiff quills that stop most attackers. Skunks and their relatives spray a foul-smelling liquid when threatened. An animal that has been sprayed by a skunk will probably not want to threaten it again. The skunk's bold black-and-white markings make it easy for predators to remember to

Methods of attack and defense   Mammals have various means of capturing prey and of defending themselves against enemies. The most important means include speed, concealment, and special protective body structures.

Jack Couffer, Bruce Coleman Inc.

A lion chases a waterbuck. In this contest, both mammals rely on speed—the lion to attack, and the waterbuck to escape. In most instances, a healthy adult waterbuck will escape.

George Schaller, Bruce Coleman Inc.

A tiger's striped coat provides almost total concealment in tall grass, enabling the animal to sneak up on its prey.

Leonard Lee Rue III, FPG

An armadillo's bony shell protects the animal like a suit of armor. When attacked, the armadillo curls up into a tight ball.

avoid the animal. Most prey species, however, have protective coloration that blends with their surroundings. The coat of some species changes seasonally to match the color of the terrain. For example, the coat of Arctic hares is brownish in summer. In winter, the coat turns white and so helps hide the animals against the snow.

The evolution of mammals

The ancestors of mammals. Mammals *evolved* (developed gradually) from a group of reptiles called the *synapsids.* These reptiles arose during the Pennsylvanian Period (330 million to 290 million years ago). By the middle of the Permian Period (290 million to 240 million years ago), a branch of the synapsids called the *therapsids* had appeared. Over tens of millions of years, the therapsids developed many features that would later be associated with mammals. The therapsids are often referred to as the *mammallike reptiles.* One group of therapsids, the *cynodonts,* developed especially mammallike teeth, skulls, and limbs. Most scientists believe that the first mammals evolved from the cynodonts.

The first mammals probably split off from the cynodonts late in the Triassic Period (240 million to 205 million years ago). Numerous fossils from this period might be either early mammals or cynodonts. Scientists cannot be sure because many characteristics of mammals— such as hair, mammary glands, and warm-bloodedness—are not preserved in the fossil record.

By the start of the Jurassic Period (205 million to 138 million years ago), mammals had definitely evolved. They were tiny, shrewlike animals that probably ate insects and worms. Mammals remained fairly small throughout the Jurassic Period and the Cretaceous Period (138 million to 63 million years ago). Dinosaurs ruled the land during these periods. But many primitive groups of mammals developed in Jurassic times. Most scientists believe that one of these early groups led directly to modern monotremes, though the fossil record of egg-laying mammals is extremely incomplete. Many other early groups died out in the Cretaceous Period. But one group, the *pantotheres,* probably gave rise to marsupials and placentals by the middle of the period.

A classification of mammals

Mammals make up the class Mammalia, one of the eight classes of vertebrates. Zoologists divide the class into various orders of related species. The classification used here recognizes 18 orders of living mammals. The orders are listed according to their probable evolutionary development.

WORLD BOOK illustrations by Jean Helmer

Order Monotremata—monotremes. Primitive mammals that lay eggs. Mammary glands lack nipples. Teeth present only in young; adults have horny beak. Order consists of two species of echidnas and one species of platypus.

Echidna

Order Marsupialia—marsupials. Varied group of mammals whose young are poorly developed at birth. They complete development attached to the mother's nipples, which are in a pouch in most species. Order consists of about 260 species, including kangaroos, koalas, and wombats.

Kangaroo

Order Insectivora—moles, shrews. Small mammals with teeth adapted for crushing insects. Most have pointed snout and five-toed feet. Order consists of about 380 species, including elephant shrews, hedgehogs, moles, and shrews.

Hedgehog

Order Dermoptera—flying lemurs. Tree-dwelling Asian mammals with flaps of skin adapted for gliding. Order consists of two species of flying lemurs, or colugos.

Flying Lemur

Order Chiroptera—bats. Only mammals that are capable of true flight, having forelimbs adapted as wings. Order consists of about 900 species of bats.

Bat

Order Primates—primates. Most species are tree dwellers. Hands have five fingers, and feet five toes. Many species have thumbs and big toes capable of grasping. Order consists of about 180 species, including apes, human beings, lemurs, and monkeys.

Baboon

Order Edentata—edentates. Mammals that lack teeth or have only molars. Forelimbs adapted for digging or for clinging to branches. Order consists of about 30 species of anteaters, armadillos, and sloths.

Armadillo

Order Pholidota—pangolins. Toothless mammals covered with horny scales. A few hairs grow between scales. Order consists of seven species of pangolins.

Pangolin

Order Lagomorpha—lagomorphs. Small mammals with two pairs of upper incisors, no canine teeth, and molars without roots. Tail short or absent. Order consists of about 65 species of hares, pikas, and rabbits.

Hare

Order Rodentia—rodents. Small, gnawing mammals with one pair of chisellike upper incisors; no canines. Order consists of about 1,750 species, including beavers, gophers, mice, porcupines, rats, and squirrels.

Squirrel

Order Cetacea—cetaceans. Aquatic mammals with streamlined bodies, paddlelike forelimbs, no hindlimbs, horizontally flattened tail, and nostrils on top of head. Order consists of about 80 species of dolphins, porpoises, and whales.

Dolphin

Order Carnivora—carnivores. Most are meat-eaters and have claws and large canine teeth. Order consists of about 270 species, including bears, cats, raccoons, seals, walruses, weasels, and wolves. Seals and walruses sometimes put in separate order.

Wolf

Order Tubulidentata—aardvark. Burrowing, insect-eating mammal with long, piglike snout and long, sticky tongue. Order consists of only one species.

Aardvark

Order Proboscidea—elephants. Large, thick-skinned mammals. Nose and upper lip form trunk; upper incisors enlarged as tusks. Order consists of two species, African elephant and Indian elephant.

Elephant

Order Hyracoidea—hyraxes. Small mammals with hooflike claws and short tail. Order consists of seven species of hyraxes.

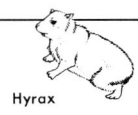
Hyrax

Order Sirenia—sea cows. Aquatic mammals with paddlelike forelimbs, no hindlimbs, and flattened muzzle. Order consists of four species of dugongs and manatees.

Manatee

Order Perissodactyla—odd-toed ungulates. Hoofed mammals with one or three toes on each foot. Axis of limb passes through middle toe. Order has about 17 species, including horses, rhinoceroses, and tapirs.

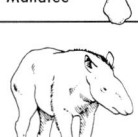
Tapir

Order Artiodactyla—even-toed ungulates. Hoofed mammals with two or four toes on each foot. Axis of limb passes between middle of toes. Order consists of about 185 species, including antelopes, bison, camels, deer, giraffes, goats, hippopotamuses, hogs, pronghorns, and sheep.

Deer

The Age of Mammals began with the extinction of the dinosaurs at the end of Cretaceous times. During the Cenozoic Era (63 million years ago to the present), mammals became the dominant land vertebrates. By the end of the Eocene Epoch (55 million to 38 million years ago), all the modern *orders* (main groups) of mammals had developed. The modern families of mammals appeared during the Oligocene Epoch (38 million to 24 million years ago).

Mammals reached their greatest variety during the Miocene Epoch (24 million to 5 million years ago). The number of mammalian species began to decline during the Pliocene Epoch (5 million to 2 million years ago). The Pleistocene Epoch, which began about 2 million years ago, brought enormous changes in climate. Several waves of glaciers advanced over much of North America, Europe, and Asia. Many mammals—including ground sloths, mammoths, saber-toothed cats, and woolly rhinoceroses—died out. Most of these extinctions were probably due to the changes in climate. But some might have been caused by a group of new, terribly skillful predators—human beings.

The future of mammals. Although extinctions are a normal part of evolution, human beings have caused an increasingly rapid decline in the number of wild mammals. Human hunters have exterminated such mammals as the blaubok, or bluebuck, of Africa; the zebralike quagga; and Steller's sea cow. Human beings have also reduced the population of orangutans, rhinoceroses, tigers, and many other mammals to a size so low that these species might not survive.

Most large wild mammals are now few in number and confined to parks, some of which provide little protection or insufficient living space. Other large mammals are still hunted. Every year, people turn more and more wild lands into farms and so increasingly deprive mammals of living space. The survival of most wild mammals will depend on the establishment and careful management of large nature preserves and parks.

Richard G. Van Gelder

Related articles in *World Book* include:

Mammals

See the following general articles and their lists of *Related articles:*

Antelope	Dog	Ox
Ape	Edentate	Rabbit
Bat	Goat	Raccoon
Bear	Hog	Rodent
Camel	Horse	Sheep
Carnivore	Human being	Sirenia
Cat	Insectivore	Ungulate
Cattle	Marsupial	Weasel
Cetacean	Monkey	Whale
Deer		

Other related articles

Lactation	Prehistoric animal (The Age of
Mammary glands	Mammals)
	Warm-blooded animal

Outline

I. The importance of mammals
   A. How people use mammals
   B. Mammals in the balance of nature
II. The bodies of mammals
   A. Skin and hair   C. Internal organ systems
   B. Skeleton

III. The senses and intelligence of mammals
   A. Senses
   B. Intelligence
IV. What mammals eat
V. How mammals move
   A. On land   D. In the air
   B. In trees   E. Underground
   C. In water
VI. How mammals reproduce
   A. Mating   C. Care of the young
   B. Reproduction
VII. Ways of life
   A. Group life   D. Hibernation
   B. Territoriality   E. Methods of attack
   C. Migration   and defense
VIII. The evolution of mammals
   A. The ancestors of   C. The Age of Mammals
      mammals   D. The future
   B. The first mammals   of mammals

Questions

How do monotremes differ from all other mammals?
What are some of the purposes of hair?
Which is the most important sense among most mammals?
How does the diet differ among herbivorous, carnivorous, and omnivorous mammals?
What are *domestic* mammals?
When did the first mammals probably appear? From which group of animals did they evolve?
What are some of the advantages of group life?
What is the *cerebral cortex*? Why is it important to mammals?
How does a *territory* differ from a *home range*?
What are some of the special body features of *arboreal* mammals?

Additional resources

Level I
Minelli, Giuseppe. *Mammals.* Facts on File, 1988.
National Geographic Soc. *Wild Animals of North America.* Rev. ed. The Society, 1987.
Parker, Steve. *Mammal.* Knopf, 1989.

Level II
The Encyclopedia of Mammals. Ed. by David W. Macdonald. Facts on File, 1984.
Savage, Robert J. G. *Mammal Evolution: An Illustrated Guide.* Facts on File, 1986.
Van Gelder, Richard G. *Biology of Mammals.* Scribner, 1969.
Walker, Ernest P., and others. *Walker's Mammals of the World.* 2 vols. 4th ed. Johns Hopkins, 1983.

Mammals, Age of. See Mammal (The Age of Mammals); **Earth** (The Cenozoic Era; table); **Prehistoric animal** (The Age of Mammals).

Mammary glands are special glands found in all mammals. In female mammals, the mammary glands produce milk. They are one of the major features that distinguish mammals from other kinds of animals (see **Mammal**).

In males, the mammary glands remain undeveloped. In female human beings, they enlarge and develop at the beginning of adolescence. The gland itself consists of several *lobes* (compartments) surrounded by cells of fat. The amount of fat determines the size of the mammary glands. The lobes are made up of smaller *lobules,* also called *acini,* which are lined by cells that secrete milk. Many *ducts* (tubes) are connected to these lobules. The ducts combine and form several main ducts that empty milk from the mammary glands at the nipple. Mammary gland development and milk production are controlled by certain chemicals called *hormones.*

Lawrence C. Wit

See also **Breast; Lactation.**

Field Museum of Natural History (Painting by Charles R. Knight)

The woolly mammoth is an extinct relative of the modern elephant. Mammoths lived in frozen regions of North America, Europe, and Asia. The animal's coat protected it from the cold.

Mammoth, *MAM uhth,* was a prehistoric animal closely related to present-day elephants. Mammoths were huge, lumbering beasts. Some measured more than 14 feet (4.3 meters) high at the shoulders. Mammoths had trunks and tusks. Many had tusks 13 feet (4 meters) long. The tusks curved down from the animal's upper jaw, then curved up and crossed in front of the trunk. Certain mammoths, called *woolly* or *hairy* mammoths, had long hair on their bodies, which helped protect them from the severe cold of the Ice Age.

Mammoths rank among the most common fossils. The bodies of mammoths have been found perfectly preserved in ice in Siberia. Fossils of mammoths also have been found in Europe and in almost every state of the United States. Alaskan miners often find petrified mammoth bones and teeth when they pan for gold.

The oldest known mammoth bones date from 4 million years ago in Africa. Mammoths spread to other continents and reached North America about $1\frac{1}{2}$ million years ago, during the Ice Age. Prehistoric people hunted them for food. Pictures of mammoths drawn by cave dwellers can be seen on cave walls in southern France. Mammoths died out about 10,000 years ago.

Scientific classification. Mammoths belong to the elephant family, Elephantidae. They make up the genus *Mammuthus.*

Michael R. Voorhies

See also **Fossil** (How fossils form); **Mastodon; Prehistoric animal** (picture).

Mammoth Cave National Park, *MAM uhth,* surrounds Mammoth Cave, part of the world's longest known cave system. The park lies in central Kentucky, about 90 miles (140 kilometers) south of Louisville. The Green and Nolin rivers flow through the park. Mammoth Cave National Park was established in 1941. It attracts about $1\frac{3}{4}$ million visitors annually. For area, see **National Park System** (table: National parks).

Mammoth Cave is often called one of the wonders of the Western Hemisphere. The cave is located in a ridge that consists mainly of limestone. Through millions of years, mildly acidic water trickled through cracks in the limestone and wore it away, forming the cave. Visitors can be guided through 12 miles (19 kilometers) of corridors on five levels in the cave. The lowest level lies 360 feet (110 meters) below the surface of the earth. Many rocks in the cave have interesting colors and shapes. These rocks resemble flowers, trees, and waterfalls.

The cave contains several lakes, rivers, and waterfalls. The largest river, Echo River, varies in width from 20 to 60 feet (6 to 18 meters) and in depth from 5 to 25 feet (1.5 to 8 meters). Strange eyeless fish live in Echo River (see **Cavefish**). These colorless creatures are about 3 inches (8 centimeters) long. Other blind creatures living in Mammoth Cave include beetles and crayfish. Several species of bats live in parts of the cave that are not visited frequently by people.

Historians believe that the first white people to see Mammoth Cave were local settlers who came to the area during the late 1700's. A deed filed in 1798 describes a large cave that probably was Mammoth Cave. But moccasins, simple tools, torches, and the remains of mummies found in the cave indicate that it was known to prehistoric Indians. Saltpeter, used to make gunpowder, was mined in the cave during the War of 1812. Mammoth Cave contained the only large supply of saltpeter that was known in the United States at that time. After the war ended, miners stopped working in the cave. It became a public showplace in 1816.

Another famous cave, Floyd Collins Crystal Cave, lies within the national park. Collins, a cave explorer, discovered Crystal Cave in 1917. Crystal Cave forms part of the Flint Ridge cave system, one of three cave systems in the park. The other two are the Joppa Ridge and the Mammoth Cave systems. In 1972, explorers discovered a connection between Mammoth Cave and the Flint Ridge cave system. The combined Mammoth-Flint Ridge cave system is the longest known cave system in the world. It has about 200 miles (320 kilometers) of explored passages.   Critically reviewed by the National Park Service

See also **Kentucky** (Places to visit; picture).

Man. See **Human being.**

Man, Isle of, is an island in the Irish Sea. It is a dependency of the British Crown and lies about halfway between England and Ireland and about 20 miles (32 kilometers) south of Scotland. The island has an area of 227 square miles (588 square kilometers) and a population of about 65,000. Most of the people have Celtic ancestry, and a few speak a Celtic language called *Manx* in addition to English. A breed of cats called *Manx,* most of

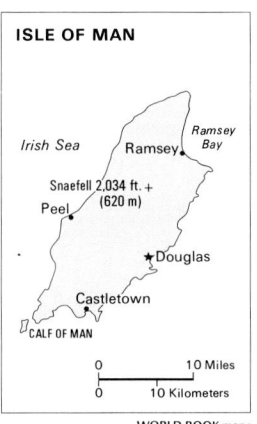

ISLE OF MAN

Irish Sea

Ramsey
Ramsey Bay

Snaefell 2,034 ft. +
(620 m)

Peel

★Douglas

Castletown

CALF OF MAN

| 0 | | 10 Miles |
| 0 | | 10 Kilometers |

WORLD BOOK maps

The Isle of Man, which lies in the Irish Sea, belongs to Great Britain.

which have no tail, originated on the island (see **Cat** [picture]).

There are several theories about the origin of the island's name. One of the most widely held theories is that the name *Man* comes from the Celtic word *monadh,* meaning *mountain.* Most of the Isle of Man is covered by farmland and *moors* (wastelands of coarse grasses and evergreen shrubs called *heather*). A low mountain chain runs the length of the island. The highest peak, Snaefell, rises 2,034 feet (620 meters) above sea level. Douglas, the island's capital, lies on the east coast.

The Isle of Man is a popular summer resort for the people of the British Isles. An international motorcycle race, held each June, is a major attraction of the island. In addition to tourism, important industries include agriculture and fishing. In 1961, the Isle of Man greatly lowered its taxes on individuals and companies. The low taxes have helped attract new residents and industries.

The Isle of Man was ruled at various times by Ireland, Wales, Norway, Scotland, and England. Great Britain bought the Isle of Man from local rulers in 1765 and has controlled it ever since. However, British laws do not apply to the Isle of Man unless they specifically name the island. A British lieutenant governor represents Great Britain on the island. A 1,000-year-old parliament called Tynwald Court regulates the internal affairs of the Isle of Man.   H. R. Jones

Man-of-war bird. See Frigatebird.

Management. See Industry (Management); Personnel management.

Management and Budget, Office of (OMB), is a United States government agency that assists the President in preparing the federal budget and evaluating government programs and organization. The OMB determines the performance and objectives of each government program and recommends to the President how much money the government should spend. The OMB also reviews and approves all regulations issued by agencies of the executive branch. Other functions of the OMB include improving the financial management of government agencies, improving government organization and administrative management, and establishing government policies for obtaining goods and services. The OMB issues *The Budget of the United States Government* and other publications.

Before 1970, the OMB was known as the Bureau of the Budget. The bureau was created in 1921 as part of the Treasury Department. It became a part of the Executive Office of the President in 1939.

Critically reviewed by the Office of Management and Budget

See also **Congressional Budget Office.**

Management information systems are computer systems designed to aid the executives who run businesses, government agencies, and other organizations. Businesses have long relied on computers to handle basic bookkeeping jobs, such as payroll and billing. But management information systems actually help managers make complex business decisions.

The establishment of a management information system involves the preparation of specific *programs* (sets of instructions) for the computer. For example, one program might call for the computer to issue *exception reports.* These reports list any unusual developments, such as products with very low or very high sales. In most cases, computer specialists develop programs from information provided by managers.

Management information systems may be used to handle *programmable* or *nonprogrammable* decisions. Programmable decisions are simple decisions that a computer can make by itself, using the data it receives. For example, a management information system can determine how often to order supplies by processing information about rates of use and storage costs.

Nonprogrammable decisions are more complex decisions that require an *interface* (exchange of information) between human managers and the computer system. For example, a manager's decision to raise prices may hinge on the computer's analysis of how rising costs will affect sales.   Donald W. Kroeber

Managua, *mah NAH gwah* (pop. 701,466), is the capital, largest city, and chief commercial center of Nicaragua. It lies on the southern shore of Lake Managua in western Nicaragua (see **Nicaragua** [map]).

Managua was severely damaged in 1972 by an earthquake that killed about 5,000 people and destroyed almost the entire downtown area. Today, the city has no central business district. The former downtown section consists of empty fields, except for those now used as sports fields or as sites for monuments honoring national heroes. A few concrete buildings survived the earthquake. These include the Palace of the Heroes of the Revolution, the Presidential Palace, and the badly damaged Metropolitan Cathedral.

Since the earthquake, residential and business areas have been built on the outskirts of Managua. Large villages of housing units were built for thousands of families left homeless by the earthquake. Other new construction included schools, hospitals, and shopping centers. These buildings were specially constructed to withstand severe earthquakes.

Managua's economy is based mainly on trade. The city is Nicaragua's chief trading center for coffee, cotton, and other crops. Managua lies on the Pan American Highway, the country's major north-south route. It is also an important industrial center. Its chief products include beer, coffee, matches, textiles, and shoes.

Managua was built in the 1850's on the site of an Indian community. It was established as the capital to settle disputes between two feuding political parties. Previously, the capital had alternated between Leon, controlled by the Liberal Party; and Granada, headquarters of the Conservative Party. Managua's location between the rival cities and its position on the lake made it an attractive site for the capital.

Managua occupies an area on a *fault* (break in the earth's crust) and suffered a major earthquake in 1931 as well as in 1972. *Seismologists* (scientists who study earthquakes) predict that Managua will continue to experience a severe earthquake every 50 years or less.

Nathan A. Haverstock

See also **Nicaragua** (picture).

Manakin, *MAN uh kihn,* is a type of small, tropical bird. There are more than 50 species of manakins. They live in woodlands and forests from Mexico to Argentina. These birds are very active and show little fear of people. Most manakins measure less than 5 inches (13 centimeters) long.

Manakins have a chunky body with a short, broad bill

© John S. Dunning, Photo Researchers

The manakin is a small bird found in the tropical forests of Central and South America. The male, *above,* has brilliantly colored feathers. The female's feathers are generally olive-green.

and short wings. Most species have a short tail, but a few have longer tail feathers. The males of most species have a bold color pattern. They are partly black or olive-brown and partly brightly colored in red, yellow, or blue feathers. Females are olive-green in color.

Male manakins perform elaborate courtship rituals to attract females. They often produce unusual sounds with their wings as part of these rituals. In some species, the male does a solitary hopping or flying dance. Other species are known for displays in which many males gather on a specially selected dancing ground called a *lek.* There they perform courtship displays in competition with each other. The female manakin visits the lek and selects a mate as the males perform. Once mating occurs, the female builds a nest and raises the family alone, while the male continues to court other females.

Manakins feed mainly on insects and small fruit. Recent studies indicate that some manakins may live more than 20 years. Most other birds of similar size have a much shorter life span.   Donald F. Bruning

Scientific classification. Manakins make up the family Pipridae.

Manama, *muh NAM uh* (pop. 121,986), is the capital, largest city, and chief port of Bahrain, an island nation in the Persian Gulf (see **Bahrain**). Manama lies on the northern tip of the country's main island, which is also called Bahrain.

Manama was probably founded in the 1300's. It became an important port, largely because it lies along major trade routes. Today, the city is a major center of trade, finance, and shipping for the Persian Gulf region. It has numerous warehouses, banks, and stores, as well as modern hotels and government offices. About 40 per cent of Bahrain's people live in Manama.

In 1962, the government of Bahrain opened a new harbor for Manama. This harbor is suitable for modern ocean vessels. Manama has been developing its industries since the mid-1900's. These industries include the construction and repair of ships.   Robert Geran Landen

Manassas, Battles of. See Civil War (First Battle of Bull Run; Second Battle of Bull Run; table: Major battles).

Manatee, *MAN uh TEE,* sometimes called *sea cow,* is a large water mammal. It belongs to the same group of mammals—the order *Sirenia*—as the dugong. There are three species of manatees. The *Caribbean manatee* lives in the Caribbean Sea and along the northeastern coast of South America. It is also found in the coastal waters of the Southeastern United States, particularly in the bays and rivers of Florida. The *Amazon manatee* is only found in fresh water. It dwells in the Amazon and Orinoco river systems. The *African manatee* lives in the rivers and coastal waters of western Africa. All three species have been hunted for their flesh, hide, and oil, and are endangered or threatened.

The manatee feeds on water plants. Its upper lip is divided into halves, which close like pliers on the plants. A manatee can consume more than 100 pounds (45 kilograms) of plants in a day. In Guyana, manatees have been used to keep waterways free of weeds.

A manatee has light to dark gray skin, with bristly hairs scattered over its body. Its front legs are paddle shaped, and its tail is rounded. It has no hind legs. The Caribbean manatee may grow to 13 feet (4 meters) long

© M. Timothy O'Keefe, Tom Stack & Assoc.

Manatees feed on water plants. These huge mammals can eat more than 100 pounds (45 kilograms) of plants in a day.

and weigh up to 3,500 pounds (1,600 kilograms).

Scientific classification. Manatees make up the genus *Trichechus* in the family Trichechidae. The Caribbean manatee is *T. manatus;* the Amazon manatee, *T. inunguis;* the African manatee, *T. senegalensis.*   Daniel K. Odell

See also **Dugong; Sea cow; Sirenia.**

Manchester (pop. 397,400; met. area pop. 2,445,200) is one of the largest cities in England, one of the political divisions of the United Kingdom. Manchester is the center of England's third largest metropolitan area. Only the metropolitan areas of London and Birmingham have more people. Manchester is the main city of Greater

Manchester County, one of the United Kingdom's chief economic centers. The city is on the Irwell River about 35 miles (56 kilometers) east of the Irish Sea, an arm of the Atlantic Ocean (see **England** [political map]). The Manchester Ship Canal connects the city to the mouth of the Mersey River, which flows into the Irish Sea. The canal makes Manchester an inland port.

The city. The downtown area of Manchester has many buildings that date from the 1800's, when the city became a major industrial and trade center. A number of the buildings were constructed to serve the needs of industry and trade but are now used for other purposes. For example, the Royal Exchange, formerly a trading center for the British cotton industry, is now a theater. The Free Trade Hall was once a center for free-trade and radical political movements. Today, the world-famous Hallé Orchestra performs there. Manchester's magnificent Town Hall also dates from the 1800's. All these buildings are architectural landmarks and reminders of Manchester's former great wealth. Manchester Cathedral, built in the 1400's, is another famous landmark.

During the 1970's, a huge educational district was developed south of the downtown area. The district is more than 2 miles (3.2 kilometers) long and includes two universities, a technical school, a college of music, and a college of education.

Economy. Manchester is one of the United Kingdom's chief centers of trade and finance. Its port handles about 14 million short tons (13 million metric tons) of cargo annually. The city has many banks and insurance companies and a stock exchange. The Manchester area is also a leader in manufacturing in the United Kingdom. Products include chemicals, clothing and textiles, computers, electronic equipment, industrial machinery and machine tools, paper, precision instruments, and processed foods.

Manchester has an international airport. The city is a center of railroad transportation and of radio and television broadcasting.

History. About A.D. 80, Roman soldiers built a fort on the site of what is now Manchester. Anglo-Saxons from northeastern England established a village there about 700. By the 1500's, Manchester had become an important center for the wool trade.

During the 1800's, Manchester developed into one of the world's chief centers for the production of cotton textiles. The city and its surrounding communities grew into a major industrial area. Large numbers of people moved there to find jobs. The Manchester Ship Canal opened in 1894 and made the city an inland port. The production of cotton textiles declined steadily during the first half of the 1900's. However, the development of other businesses in the city and surrounding communities helped the Manchester area retain its economic importance.   Anthony Sutcliffe

Manchester, N.H. (pop. 99,567; met. area pop. 173,783), is the largest city and chief manufacturing and financial center of the state. Manchester lies in south-central New Hampshire, about 17 miles (27 kilometers) south of Concord, the capital (see **New Hampshire** [political map]). The city covers about 34 square miles (88 square kilometers) along both banks of the Merrimack River. The Uncanoonuc Mountains curve around the western part of the city.

Nearly 10 per cent of the people of Manchester are foreign-born. About a fourth of the population are of French-Canadian ancestry.

The city is the home of the Manchester Institute of Arts and Sciences, the Currier Gallery of Art, the Association Canado-Américaine, and the Carpenter Memorial Library. New Hampshire, Notre Dame, and St. Anselm colleges and a campus of the University of New Hampshire are also in the city. The home of General John Stark, a figure of the Revolutionary War, is in the city.

Manchester was once known as the home of the largest cotton mills in the world. The mills failed in the 1930's. Today, the city's chief products include boots and shoes and cotton and woolen goods. It is an insurance center and distributing point. The city is served by Manchester Airport, several bus lines, and a freight railroad. No railroad passenger trains stop in Manchester.

Manchester's first white settlement was started in 1722. Manchester was first called Harrytown, and then Derryfield. It received its present name in 1810. Manchester became a city in 1846. It has a mayor-alderman form of government.   Donald C. Anderson

Manchester terrier is a breed of dog that originated in Manchester, England, in the 1800's. Dog breeders

Sefton Photo Library

The Town Hall of Manchester, England, *above,* was completed in 1877. Manchester is one of England's largest cities and a major center of trade and finance.

produced the terrier to compete in rat-killing matches. In these matches, people bet on how many rats a dog could kill in a given period of time. By mating the black-and-tan terrier, an excellent ratcatcher, with the swift whippet, the breeders hoped to produce a superior ratter. Today, Manchesters are popular house pets. They are loyal to their owners and make excellent watchdogs.

Manchesters have a smooth, black coat; and a tan mark over each eye, on each cheek, and on the chest. The front of the forelegs and the inside of the hind legs are tan with black markings. The ears are set high on the long, narrow head. The dog has a whiplike tail.

The Manchester terrier has two varieties—the standard and the toy. The standard Manchester weighs 12 to 22 pounds (5.4 to 10 kilograms). Its ears may naturally stand erect or may fold over, with the tips falling to the front. Some owners have the ears *cropped* (cut) to make them stand straight up. The toy Manchester weighs 5 to 12 pounds (2.3 to 5.4 kilograms). Its ears are naturally erect. The toy was bred from the standard.

Critically reviewed by the American Manchester Terrier Club

See also **Dog** (picture: Terriers).

Manchuria, *man CHOOR ee uh,* is a region in northeastern China known for its rich natural resources, especially coal and iron. Much of China's heavy industry centers around the Manchurian cities of Changchun, Harbin, and Shenyang. The region also has fertile soil and produces much of China's food. In China today, Manchuria is called *the Northeast.* Manchuria consists of the Chinese provinces of Heilongjiang, Jilin, and Liaoning; and the northeastern part of Inner Mongolia, a self-governing region of China. Manchuria covers 474,906 square miles (1,230,000 square kilometers).

People. Manchuria has a population of about 91 million. About 90 per cent of the people are descendants of Chinese who migrated to Manchuria around 1900. Manchus, the original people of Manchuria, make up about 5 per cent of the region's population. Smaller population groups include Koreans and Mongols. Large numbers of these minority peoples have been absorbed into Chinese society through intermarriage and public education. Today, almost all the people of Manchuria speak Northern Chinese (Mandarin), the official language of China. They follow Chinese customs and live as do the people of any other part of China.

Land and climate. A broad central plain makes up most of Manchuria. Forested mountains border the plain on the east, north, and west. In the south, the Liaodong Peninsula extends into the Yellow Sea. The Amur and Ussuri rivers separate Manchuria from Russia on the northeast. Korea lies across the Yalu River to the southeast. Manchuria has long, cold winters and short, hot summers.

Economy. Manchuria has rich deposits of coal and iron, both used in making steel. Its factories make such steel products as machinery, railroad equipment, tools, and trucks. They also produce cement, chemicals, electrical equipment, and paper. Grains, especially sorghums and soybeans, make up much of Manchuria's agricultural production. The region's farmers also grow cotton, sugar beets, and tobacco. Manchuria has reclaimed large areas of wasteland for farming by using irrigation and other methods. Lüda, one of China's busiest ports, lies in the southern part of Manchuria.

History. In early times, Manchu warriors on horseback frequently invaded and conquered parts of China. The Manchus conquered northern China in 1644, and gradually extended their control to the whole country. The Manchus ruled until 1912. Chinese rulers since 1912 have looked upon Manchuria as part of China.

Russia expanded across Asia during the 1800's and seized land from China. In 1860, Russia and China signed an agreement giving Russia all the territory north of the Amur River and east of the Ussuri River. In 1896, China agreed to permit Russia to build the Chinese Eastern Railway across Manchuria to the Russian port of Vladivostok. Two years later, Russia leased land on the Liaodong Peninsula and built a naval base at Lüshun (Port Arthur) and a port at Lüda.

In the Russo-Japanese War (1904-1905), Japan defeated Russia and took control of the Liaodong Peninsula. In 1931, the Japanese conquered the rest of Manchuria. They made the region a puppet state called *Manchukuo.* During World War II (1939-1945), Manchuria was an important industrial base for Japan.

During the last days of World War II, the Soviet Union—which had been formed in 1922 under Russia's leadership—declared war on Japan and occupied Man-

Manchuria

This map shows the northeastern part of China, called Manchuria. Manchuria is important for its heavy industry.

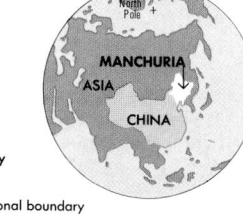

⊛ National capital   • Other city or town

★ Provincial capital

International boundary

Provincial boundary

WORLD BOOK map

churia. Before returning Manchuria to China in 1946, the Soviet Union helped the Chinese Communists seize power. The Communists conquered all of China in 1949.

During the 1960's, China claimed some Soviet territory beyond Manchuria. In 1969, China and the Soviet Union clashed over control of an island in the Ussuri River. The fighting stopped after the two nations agreed to discuss their differences. But when the Soviet Union broke up in 1991, the border claims had not yet been settled. Russia and China planned to negotiate to settle the claims.　　Norma Diamond

Related articles in *World Book* include:

China	Lüshun	Shenyang
Harbin	Russo-Japanese	Yalu River
Japan (Imperialism)	War	

Manchus, *MAN chooz,* were a people who conquered China in the 1600's. They invaded from Manchuria, in what is now northeast China, in 1644. They established the *Qing* (*Pure*) dynasty that same year and gradually took control of China. The Qing dynasty prospered in the 1700's but declined in the 1800's. It ended in 1912, when the Chinese overthrew the Manchus.

Manchu rulers forbade marriage between Manchus and the Chinese until the early 1900's. Since then, many Manchus and Chinese have intermarried. Most Manchus now have taken Chinese names.

The Manchus are descended from a people called the Jurchen (also spelled Juchen). The Jurchen, who also came from Manchuria, had occupied all of northern China by 1127 and ruled the area until 1234.

　　Richard L. Davis

See also **Manchuria** (History); **China** (History).

Mandalay, *MAN duh LAY* (pop. 472,512), is Burma's second largest city and chief inland river port. Only Rangoon has more people. Mandalay lies in central Burma on the Irrawaddy River (see **Burma** [map]). It is known for its old pagodas, temples, and monasteries. It is the home of the Mandalay Arts and Science University.

The Burmese founded Mandalay in 1857. It was the capital of Burma from 1860 to 1885, when the British captured the city. The British moved the capital to Rangoon. Mandalay suffered much damage during World War II (1939-1945).　　James F. Guyot

Mandamus, *man DAY muhs,* is a court order that requires a person, lower court, government official, or an officer of a corporation to do a legal duty. On many occasions, a public official may be required to perform an act, such as to make a commission or sign a paper. If the official refuses to do the act, a *writ of mandamus* may be sought, and a court may order the official to do the act.

Mandamus can be obtained only where the law says the official must do the act, but not where the law says the official may decide whether to do it or not. In such a case, a court will not compel the official to decide in favor of the person seeking the writ of mandamus. But the court may compel the official to decide one way or the other.　　Paul C. Giannelli

See also **Injunction; Writ.**

Mandan Indians are a tribe that has lived in western North Dakota, along the Missouri River, for more than 500 years. The Mandan were originally village dwellers and lived in large, earth-covered lodges. They hunted and also cultivated fields of beans, corn, squash, sunflowers, and tobacco. The early Mandan exchanged

their crops for goods that other tribes brought to their villages. During the 1700's, the Mandan began to trade with European explorers and traders.

In 1837, a smallpox epidemic nearly wiped out the Mandan. The survivors found refuge in the nearby villages of the Arikara and the Hidatsa tribes. From the 1840's to the 1860's, the three tribes settled on what is now the Fort Berthold Reservation in North Dakota.

In the late 1800's, the U.S. government began to divide the reservation into small parcels of land, which were assigned to each eligible Arikara, Hidatsa, and Mandan. The three tribes then left their villages and moved to

Oil painting on canvas (1832) by George Catlin; National Museum of American Art, Smithsonian Institution, Gift of Mrs. Sarah Harrison

A Mandan medicine man, wearing moccasins with attached foxtails, holds ceremonial pipes decorated with feathers.

their assigned lands. In the late 1940's, the government took about a fourth of the reservation to build Garrison Dam, a huge hydroelectric project. Indian families who lived on this land had to settle elsewhere on the reservation. Today, about 400 Mandan live there. Most are farmers or ranchers.　　Beatrice Medicine

See also **Indian, American** (pictures: A Mandan chief).

Mandarin, *MAN duhr ihn.* English-speaking people used the name *mandarin* for any high military or civil official of the Chinese Empire. The Chinese term is *guan,* which means *a public official.* The dialect of North China, the language these officials spoke, is called *Northern Chinese* or *Mandarin.* The Chinese call the dialect *putonghua,* meaning *common language.* Today it is China's official language. See **Chinese language.**

A Chinese became a mandarin by taking promotional examinations. He showed his rank by the color of the buttons on his cap. Governors and generals had red coral buttons. Lieutenant governors and judges wore blue ones. Lower officers had other colors.

Each mandarin had an official robe. The military man's robe had beasts embroidered on it. The civil official had decorative birds on his robe. Judges wore plainer robes.

A mandarin could not marry or acquire property in the province to which he was sent. He could not serve over three years in one province.   Richard L. Davis

Mandarin, *MAN duhr ihn,* is a citrus fruit that has a sweet, juicy pulp. Most varieties have an orange-colored rind that separates easily from the edible interior. In the United States, mandarins are commonly called *tangerines.* Mandarins and mandarin hybrids form a large group of citrus fruits. Hybrids include the *tangelo,* a cross with a grapefruit, and the *tangor,* a cross with an orange.

Mandarins originated in Southeast Asia. They are now grown in Brazil, China, Italy, Japan, Spain, and other countries. In the United States, Arizona, California, and Florida are the leading mandarin-producing states.

Scientific classification. Mandarins belong to the rue family, Rutaceae. They are *Citrus reticulata.*   Wilfred F. Wardowski

See also **Tangelo; Tangerine; Tangor.**

Mandated territory. After World War I, certain colonies and territories were taken from the defeated nations and placed under the administration of one or more of the victorious nations. These areas were called *mandated territories.* The League of Nations supervised the governing countries in the administration of the territories. The League expected the governing countries to improve living conditions in the territories, and to prepare the people for self-government.

The mandated territories included areas that once were controlled by Germany and the Ottoman Empire. Britain received mandates for Mesopotamia (later renamed Iraq); Tanganyika (now part of Tanzania); and Palestine. Palestine was later divided into Palestine and Transjordan (later renamed Jordan). France received Syria, which was later divided into Syria and Lebanon. Both Britain and France were given parts of the Cameroons and Togoland. Belgium received Ruanda-Urundi. Japan was given German islands in the North Pacific Ocean. Australia received German islands in the South Pacific, including the northeastern section of New Guinea and Nauru. New Zealand received Western Samoa, and the Union of South Africa (now South Africa) got German Southwest Africa (now called Namibia).

The mandate system ended in 1947. By that time, several mandated territories, including Iraq, Syria, Lebanon, and Jordan, had become independent countries. The remaining territories, except Namibia, were placed under the stronger United Nations trusteeship system. The same countries continued to administer the territories, but they were under the control of the UN Trusteeship Council and General Assembly (see **Trust territory**). South Africa resisted UN attempts to bring Namibia into the trusteeship system. Namibia became independent in March 1990.   Anthony D'Amato

Mandela, *man DEHL uh,* **Nelson** (1918-   ), is a leader of black protest against policies of the white-minority government of South Africa. These policies have included denying blacks the right to vote in national and provincial elections and enforcing a form of racial segregation called *apartheid* (see **Apartheid**). In July 1991, Mandela was elected president of the African National Congress (ANC), a group opposed to South Af-

rican government policies that discriminate against blacks (see **African National Congress**).

Birth and career. Nelson Rolihlahla Mandela was born in Umtata, in the Transkei territory of South Africa. His father was a tribal chief. Mandela became a lawyer and, in 1944, joined the ANC. He first won national prominence as a black leader through protests in the 1950's.

In 1956, Mandela was charged with treason and other serious crimes but was found not guilty in 1961. He then renewed the protests and went into hiding. He was arrested in 1962 and later convicted of sabotage and conspiracy and sentenced to life imprisonment.

While imprisoned from 1962 to 1990, Mandela became a symbol of the black struggle for racial justice. Many South African groups made his release the precondition for any serious negotiations on the country's future. The government released Mandela in February 1990 after he expressed his willingness to "contribute to the creation of a climate which would promote peace in South Africa." Shortly before his release, the government recognized the ANC as a legal political organization. The government had outlawed the ANC in 1960.

Beginning in May 1990, Mandela led a team of negotiators in formal talks with South African president F. W. de Klerk and other South African officials. The series of talks were aimed at clearing the way for negotiations on a new South African constitution that would grant more political power to the country's black majority. In August 1990, Mandela suspended the armed struggle that the ANC had been waging against the South African government since 1960.

In 1991, the government repealed the last of the laws that formed the legal basis of apartheid. But Mandela continued to fight remaining forms of racial injustice in South Africa, including the laws that denied blacks the right to vote in national and provincial elections. In 1993, partly as a result of Mandela's efforts, elections for a transitional government were scheduled. The elections, planned for early 1994, were to be the first in which black South Africans would be allowed to vote. The transitional government was expected to write a new constitution.

Marriage to Winnie Mandela. In 1958, Mandela married Winifred Nomzamo Madikizela. Winifred, commonly known as Winnie, became increasingly involved in the movement against apartheid after Nelson's imprisonment. Her defiance of South Africa's white authorities won her worldwide admiration.

But Winnie's popularity dropped during the late 1980's, largely because of her links to a group called the Mandela United Football Club. The leader of the club was convicted of kidnapping, murder, and other crimes in 1990. In 1991, Winnie was convicted of kidnapping and being an accessory to assault in connection with the football club's crimes. She was sentenced to six

© De Keerle, UK Press from Gamma/Liaison

Nelson Mandela

years in prison but remained free while waiting for her case to be reviewed. In 1993, a higher court upheld her kidnapping conviction but overturned her conviction on being an accessory to assault and in effect reduced her sentence to fines. In 1992, Nelson announced that he and Winnie agreed to separate.   Sanford J. Ungar

Mandible, *MAN duh buhl,* or lower jawbone, is shaped like a horseshoe. A person can feel the entire bone from chin to temple. The *corpus* (body) of the mandible runs backwards from the chin to the *angle,* at which point it turns upward to form the *ramus.* The ramus makes a joint at the temple. This joint allows the mouth to open and close. In adults, the corpus has eight teeth on each side. The chewing muscles attach to the ramus and the back part of the corpus. Most of the tongue muscles attach to the corpus. See also **Head** (picture).   Charles W. Cummings

Mandingo, *man DIHNG goh,* is the name of a group of west African people. The Mandingo are descendants of the founders of the powerful Mali Empire. Most of the 1$\frac{1}{2}$ million Mandingo live in Mali, but many live in Gambia, Guinea-Bissau, the Ivory Coast, and Senegal. The Malinke are the most important Mandingo group.

The Mandingo speak a language that belongs to the *Mande* language group. This group has many *dialects* (local forms of speech). Mandingo who speak different dialects may not be able to understand one another.

During the 1200's, Mande-speaking people lived in independent states in Africa. The largest and most famous Mandingo state, the Mali Empire, flourished from about 1240 to 1500. Its leaders converted to Islam, the religion of the Muslims, but few of the Mandingo people became Muslims. Today, many Mandingo still practice traditional African religions. Most of the rural people are farmers or cattle herders, though many city dwellers are traders or artists.   Leo Spitzer

Mandolin, *MAN duh lihn,* is a stringed musical instrument. It has a narrow, *fretted* (ridged) neck attached to a pear-shaped body that resembles the body of a lute. Most mandolins have four pairs of strings. Others have five pairs. The strings run from the top of the neck to a low bridge near the bottom of the body. The player strums the strings with a *plectrum* (pick) held between the thumb and index finger of the right hand. With the fingers of the left hand, the player presses down the strings along the neck to vary the pitch. In the 1700's, the mandolin gained some use in classical music. Today, it is chiefly played in popular music.   Abram Loft

Mandrake is the name of two similar plants that belong to the nightshade family. Mandrakes grow wild in southern Europe and Asia. The stem of a mandrake cannot be seen, and the leaves seem to grow from the roots. Most mandrakes have one large, thick root that ta-

WORLD BOOK illustration by James Teason
A mandrake has a large, thick root. Some people believe these roots have magical and medicinal properties.

pers to a point. The white, bluish, or purple flowers of a mandrake grow on slender stalks among the leaves.

People have had superstitious beliefs about the mandrake since early times. The plant contains *scopolamine* and *hyoscyamine,* two chemical compounds that may be used as medicines or poisons. Ancient peoples of the Near East and Europe used the root of the plant as a narcotic and anesthetic. Some people thought mandrakes were magical plants and used them in so-called *love potions.* Mandrakes are mentioned in the Bible and in the Ebers Papyrus, an Egyptian medical text which dates from about 1550 B.C. or earlier. The Egyptians probably used the plant to prepare sedatives and pain-relieving drugs. Today, some peasants in Europe may still use the plant's root in drinks believed to have magical effects.

Scientific classification. Mandrakes are in the nightshade family, Solanaceae. The two species of mandrakes are *Mandragora autumnalis* and *M. officinarum.*   John E. Averett

Mandrill, *MAN druhl,* is a colorful monkey that lives in the forests of Cameroon and other parts of western Africa. Male mandrills are among the largest monkeys, weighing as much as 90 pounds (40 kilograms). Female mandrills weigh half as much. Mandrills resemble baboons, having long arms, small, piglike eyes, large canine teeth, and a muzzle similar to that of a dog. The

David R. Frazier
The mandolin has been popular for hundreds of years, particularly among southern Europeans and Latin Americans.

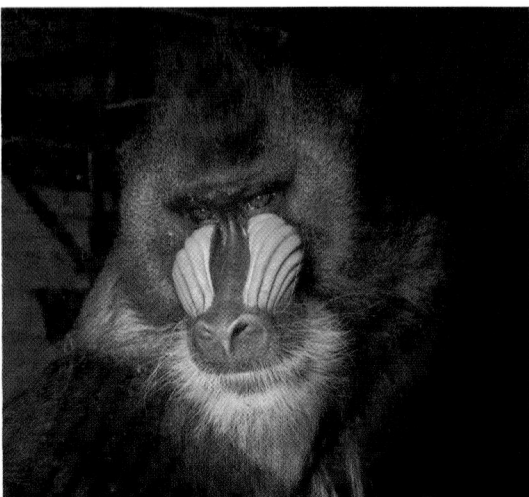

George H. Harrison from Grant Heilman

The male mandrill has vivid coloring that helps make it one of the most unusual looking monkeys. The colors become even more brilliant when this west African monkey is excited.

male mandrill is especially colorful. Its cheeks are blue; its long, flat nose is red; and its rump is red and blue.

Like most other monkeys, mandrills live in groups. Mandrill groups range from 15 to 95 individuals, though as many as 150 mandrills may band together for short periods of time. Males protect the group against leopards and other enemies. Mandrills move about on the ground and in trees. They feed on vegetation—especially fruits—and many kinds of insects. In captivity, mandrills have lived for more than 40 years.

Scientific classification. The mandrill belongs to the Old World monkey family, Cercopithecidae. It is *Mandrillus sphinx.*

Randall L. Susman

Maned wolf. See Fox (South American "foxes").
Manet, *ma NAY,* **Edouard,** *ay DWAR* (1832-1883), a French painter, helped break tradition by using his subject matter in unexpected ways. His subjects often combine elements of traditional art with themes from the life of his time. Manet also painted in a bold, simplified manner, stressing the general visual effect. Since Manet's time, painting has been dominated by this concern with the importance of the picture itself, rather than with the picture's storytelling function.

Manet is often identified with the impressionist style of painting, and he and the impressionist artists influenced each other. However, Manet refused to exhibit his works in impressionist shows. The public considered impressionism revolutionary and treated it hostilely. Manet preferred to seek popular success by exhibiting in conservative shows sponsored by the government.

Manet was born in Paris. From 1850 to 1856, he studied with the skillful but traditional artist Thomas Couture. From Couture, Manet learned how to use outline expressively, how to obtain a lively effect with broken brushstrokes, and how to achieve strong lighting with a minimum of tones. Manet wanted to use this technical knowledge to portray modern life in a spontaneous way.

In 1863, Manet shocked the people of Paris with his painting *Luncheon on the Grass.* This picture shows a female nude at a picnic with two men who are wearing modern clothing. Many people felt that the painting was indecent. *Luncheon on the Grass* is reproduced in the *World Book* article on **Painting.** In 1865, Manet's *Olympia,* a painting of a female nude, created an even greater scandal. The public objected to the nude's bold pose, to her direct and outward gaze, and to the picture's severe lighting contrasts and flat silhouetted forms.

During the 1860's, Manet also painted scenes from modern history, though Biblical and ancient historical scenes were popular at the time. One painting shows

Courtauld Institute Gallery, London

Art Institute of Chicago

Edouard Manet completed *Bar at the Folies Bergère, left,* in 1882. The painting shows the firm modeling and bright, vivid colors that are typical of much of his work. The portrait of Manet, *above,* was painted by his friend Henri Fantin-Latour in 1867.

the execution of Emperor Maximilian of Mexico in 1867. Another of Manet's modern historical scenes, *Combat of the Kearsarge and the Alabama* (about 1865), shows a naval battle of the American Civil War. It is reproduced in the **Alabama** (ship) article.

Manet's last great painting was *Bar at the Folies Bergère* (1882). This work is remarkable for its dazzling color and rich textures, as well as its detailed portrayal of Parisian society.   Richard Shiff

See also **Impressionism**.

Manganese is a brittle, silver-gray, metallic element. It has many industrial uses and is especially important in the production of steel. Manganese has an atomic weight of 54.938, and its atomic number is 25. Its chemical symbol is *Mn*. See **Element, Chemical** (Periodic table of the elements).

Manganese is a plentiful element that is found throughout much of the earth's crust. However, the metal occurs only in combination with other chemical elements. Minerals that contain large amounts of manganese include braunite, hausmannite, manganite, psilomelane, and pyrolusite. Manganese was first isolated as a pure metal in 1774 by Johan Gottlieb Gahn, a Swedish chemist.

All plants and animals require small amounts of manganese. In plants, a lack of manganese affects the production of chlorophyll and causes leaves to turn yellow. In human beings and other animals, a manganese deficiency disrupts growth and results in various disorders of the bones and the central nervous system. A diet that includes beets, blueberries, whole wheat, or wheat bran provides adequate amounts of manganese.

Uses. Most manganese is used in the form of alloys and compounds. *Ferromanganese,* an iron alloy that contains about 80 per cent manganese, is used in producing steel. Manganese removes oxygen and sulfur from steel and so strengthens the metal. Bubbles of oxygen weaken steel, and sulfur causes steel to break during the *forging process,* in which the metal is heated and shaped. Other iron alloys that have a high manganese content and are important in manufacturing steel include *silicomanganese* and *spiegeleisen.*

A steel alloy called *manganese steel* contains up to 14 per cent manganese. It is extremely durable and is used in making heavy-duty machinery and safes. In addition, the electronics industry uses manganese steel in certain electromagnets. These devices are utilized in radar transmitters, radios, and computer storage units called *magnetic core memories.*

Manganese is also used in *stainless steel* and in various alloys of aluminum, copper, and magnesium. Manganese makes these alloys harder and more resistant to rust.

The most widely used compound of manganese is *manganese dioxide,* which is important in manufacturing dry cell batteries and many dyes. Manufacturers of paints and varnish driers use large quantities of *manganese sulfate* in their production process. Manganese sulfate also is a key ingredient in certain fertilizers.

Another manganese compound, *potassium permanganate,* is a disinfectant and deodorizer. It is frequently used in water purification. Such compounds as *manganous nitrate* and *manganous oxide* serve as *catalysts* in the production of various petrochemicals, plastics, and

Leading manganese-mining countries

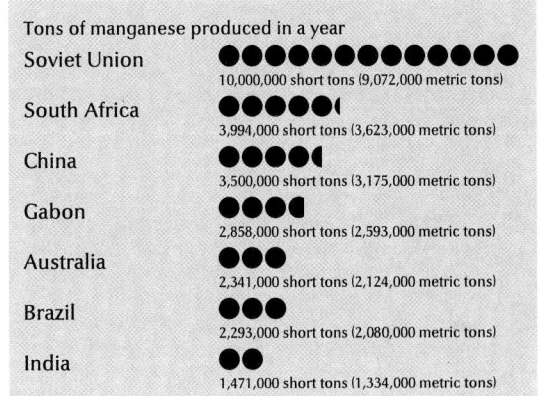

Tons of manganese produced in a year

Soviet Union — 10,000,000 short tons (9,072,000 metric tons)
South Africa — 3,994,000 short tons (3,623,000 metric tons)
China — 3,500,000 short tons (3,175,000 metric tons)
Gabon — 2,858,000 short tons (2,593,000 metric tons)
Australia — 2,341,000 short tons (2,124,000 metric tons)
Brazil — 2,293,000 short tons (2,080,000 metric tons)
India — 1,471,000 short tons (1,334,000 metric tons)

Figures are for 1989, prior to the breakup of the Soviet Union.
Source: U.S. Bureau of Mines.

synthetic fibers. Catalysts are substances that accelerate chemical reactions.

Properties. Manganese is hard enough to scratch glass and so brittle that it cannot be used alone as a building material. It combines with many other elements, including boron, carbon, phosphorus, silicon, and sulfur. Manganese melts at 1244 $\pm$ 3 °C and boils at 1962 °C.

Manganese can exist in four different forms. These forms, called *allotropes,* have different chemical and physical properties. For example, the allotrope *alpha manganese* is brittle and has a density of 7.44 grams per cubic centimeter at 20 °C. Another allotrope, *gamma manganese,* is flexible and has a density of 7.18 grams per cubic centimeter at 20 °C.

Manganese reacts slowly in cold water and rapidly in hot water. The metal tarnishes when exposed to air, and it rusts in moist air. When placed in dilute inorganic acids, manganese dissolves and forms manganese salts and hydrogen gas. At high temperatures, manganese burns when placed in nitrogen, and it reacts with both carbon monoxide and carbon dioxide.

Sources. Most manganese occurs in iron ores. A high manganese content makes an ore more valuable. Ores that contain from 5 to 10 per cent manganese are called *manganiferous ores.* Those that have from 10 to 35 per cent manganese are called *ferruginous manganese ores,* and those with 35 per cent or more manganese are called *manganese ores.*

Before its breakup, the Soviet Union was the world's leading producer of manganese ore, followed by South Africa, China, and Gabon. The United States has few deposits of high-grade manganese ore, and so it must import more than 90 per cent of the manganese that it uses.

The ocean floor has large deposits of manganese in the form of round masses called *nodules.* However, the high cost of mining these deposits has prevented their commercial development.

Manganese ores are purified by several methods. In one method, manganese ore is placed in an electric furnace with aluminum and silicon and undergoes *reduction* (see **Reduction**). Another method involves the electrolysis of sulfate solutions of manganese. This method is the most economical and produces the purest manganese. Manganese ores are converted to manganese oxides by heating. The oxides are mixed with sulfuric acid to form manganous sulfate. This solution is purified and subjected to electrolysis.   Theophilus Sorrell

See also **Trace elements.**

Mange, *maynj,* is a contagious skin disease that certain types of mites cause in dogs, cats, sheep, horses, goats, and swine. The mites usually cause mange in animals that are ill, dirty, or neglected, or that live in crowded conditions.

Mange occurs when the mites burrow into the skin of animals, causing an irritation. Animals with mange experience severe itching and have areas of redness and swelling. As the disease progresses, the condition of the sores and areas of swelling worsens and patches of hair or wool fall out. Continuous scratching may cause open sores.

Veterinarians treat mange chiefly by using antimite sprays or by carefully washing afflicted animals with sulfur or lime-sulfur shampoos. The disease can be prevented by keeping animals' coats clean and well-groomed and by providing the animals with a proper diet; a clean, dry place; and adequate space.

Lawrence D. McGill

See also **Mite.**

Mango is a fruit that grows in tropical regions throughout the world. It serves as the main food of many people in tropical countries and is often called the *king of tropical fruits.* Mangoes are eaten fresh or are used in making desserts, preserves, and some other foods. The fruit is an excellent source of vitamins A and C.

Most mangoes are kidney-shaped, oval, or round. They vary from about 2 to 10 inches (5 to 25 centimeters) in length and from 2 ounces to 5 pounds (57 grams to 2.3 kilograms) in weight. Mangoes have a smooth, leathery skin that surrounds a juicy, yellow or orange pulp and a hard inner pit. The skin may be green, purple, or various shades of orange, red, or yellow. Many mangoes have tough fibers in their pulp, and some of the fruits have an unpleasant turpentinelike odor. However, mangoes grown commercially have a soft, fiberless pulp and a sweet, spicy taste and odor.

The mango tree is an evergreen that grows about 70 feet (21 meters) tall. It has long, slender leaves and small, pinkish-white flowers. The fruit develops from the ovaries of the blossoms and ripens about five months after the flowers bloom.

Mangoes were first cultivated about 4,000 years ago in India and the Malay Archipelago. In the 1700's and 1800's, European explorers brought mangoes from India to other tropical countries. Today, farmers grow mangoes in Brazil, India, Mexico, and the Philippines. In the United States, mangoes grow in Florida and in Hawaii.

Scientific classification. The mango belongs to the cashew family, Anacardiaceae. It is *Mangifera indica.*   Philip J. Ito

Mangosteen, *MANG guh steen,* is a tree that grows in Southeast Asia. It is about 30 feet (9 meters) tall. The large, shiny green leaves are thick and leathery. The white to pinkish flowers measure almost 2 inches (5 centimeters) across. The edible fruit is shaped like a tangerine. It is yellowish to reddish-purple and has juicy, white flesh. The fruits are about $2\frac{1}{2}$ inches (6 centimeters) across. Cold weather kills the mangosteen. A few of these plants grow in gardens in the southernmost parts of the United States.

Leaves

Up to
30 ft. (9 m)

Fruit

Bark

WORLD BOOK illustration by John D. Dawson

The mangosteen is a tree from Southeast Asia that produces edible, juicy fruit with a yellowish to reddish-purple rind.

Scientific classification. Mangosteens belong to the garcinia family, Guttiferae. They are classified as *Garcinia mangostana.*   Alwyn H. Gentry

Mangrove, *MANG grohv,* is a tree that grows along tropical coasts in salty ocean water. The best-known species is the *red mangrove.* As this type of mangrove develops, it sends down roots from its branches. Eventually, a network of many stiltlike roots supports its leafy crown above the water.

Mangroves form the chief plant growth along long stretches of tropical coasts. They usually grow in places by quiet ocean water. Large mangrove thickets, or forests on stilts, often grow in shallow waters along bays, lagoons, and river mouths. The thousands of stiltlike roots catch silt, which piles up in the water. At the mouths of streams, the roots slow down the current and help settle the silt. Thus, mangroves may aid in building

WORLD BOOK illustration by Kate Lloyd-Jones, Linden Artists Ltd.

Mangoes are delicious tropical fruit. They grow from clusters of tiny pink flowers on the evergreen mango tree.

© P. Laboute, Jacana

Mangroves have long, spreading roots that anchor the trees in tropical coastal waters. The roots catch and hold particles of dirt and sand, which helps build up shorelines.

up dry land. The roots also form a breeding place for many fish and other marine life.

Mangrove seeds often germinate while the fruit is on the tree. A seed sends down a root up to 1 foot (30 centimeters) long. When the fruit falls, the heavy root holds it upright as it floats on the water. The root tip eventually strikes mud and a new tree begins to grow.

The red mangrove is found along coasts from Florida to northern South America and in West Africa. The tree most commonly grows only to the height of a shrub or small tree. Related species can grow up to 82 feet (25 meters) tall. People use the wood of the red mangrove for wharf piles and fuel. The bark is rich in tannic acid, which is used for tanning hides and making dyes.

Scientific classification. The mangrove belongs to the mangrove family, Rhizophoraceae. The scientific name for the red mangrove is *Rhizophora mangle.* Alwyn H. Gentry

Manhattan Island is one of the commercial, financial, publishing, and cultural centers of the world. Millions of people commute there every day to work in offices, factories, shops, and theaters. Manhattan has a population of 1,487,536 and an area of 34 square miles (88 square kilometers), including 12 square miles (31 square kilometers) of inland water. The island forms the smallest, in size, of the five *boroughs* (districts) of New York City. The East River is its eastern border, with Upper New York Bay on the south, the Hudson River on the west, and the Harlem River and Spuyten Duyvil Creek on the north. Bridges, tunnels, and ferries connect the island with the other boroughs and with New Jersey (see **New York City** [map]).

Manhattan Island has many famous landmarks and tourist attractions. They include Broadway, Central Park, Chinatown, the Empire State Building, Greenwich Village, Rockefeller Center, Times Square, the United Nations headquarters, Wall Street, the World Trade Center, and many churches, colleges, museums, skyscrapers, and theaters. Most of New York City's municipal buildings stand on Manhattan Island.

Peter Minuit, governor (or director-general) of the colony of New Netherland, bought the island in 1626 from Indians who may have been passing through the area. Minuit paid for the island with beads, cloth, and trinkets worth $24. Michael K. Heiman

See also **Minuit, Peter; New York City** (Manhattan).

Manhattan Project was created by the United States government in 1942 to produce the first atomic bomb. The official agency that produced the bomb was the Corps of Engineers' Manhattan Engineer District, commanded by Major (later Lieutenant) General Leslie R. Groves. Physicist J. Robert Oppenheimer directed the design and building of the bomb. Industrial and research activities took place at such sites as Los Alamos, N. Mex.; Oak Ridge, Tenn.; and Hanford, Wash.

The idea for the project began in 1939, shortly before World War II began. United States scientists feared Germany might be the first country to develop an atomic bomb. They alerted President Franklin D. Roosevelt to this possibility. Manhattan Project scientists successfully exploded the first atomic bomb on July 16, 1945, near Alamogordo, N. Mex. Lucille B. Garmon

See also **Nuclear weapon**.

Additional resources

Larsen, Rebecca. *Oppenheimer and the Atomic Bomb.* Watts, 1988. Suitable for younger readers.
Rhodes, Richard. *The Making of the Atomic Bomb.* Simon & Schuster, 1987. Pulitzer Prize winner.

Manic-depressive disorder. See Mental illness (Mood disorders).

Manichaeism, *MAN uh KEE ihz uhm,* is a philosophical and religious system based on the teachings of a Babylonian prophet named Mani, who lived during the A.D. 200's. According to Manichaeism, two opposing forces govern the universe—the kingdom of light (good) and the kingdom of darkness (evil). The soul, which is a part of the kingdom of light, is trapped inside the body, a part of the kingdom of darkness. The soul yearns to escape the body. This escape can only occur in death, when the soul returns to God.

Manichaeans believed that while living on earth in a mortal body, people must lead lives of self-denial and avoid lusts of the flesh. Only through wisdom can a person hope to avoid the evils of material and sensual things. Wisdom and knowledge will come from a savior who will reveal a plan for salvation and redemption. This savior appears as the prophets Zoroaster, Buddha, and Jesus, and finally as Mani. Manichaeism taught several sacraments necessary for self-denial, such as vegetarianism, simplicity in daily activity, and refraining from sexual intercourse. Robert William Smith

Manifest destiny was a term used to describe the belief in the 1840's in the inevitable territorial expansion of the United States. People who believed in manifest destiny maintained that the United States should rule all North America because of U.S. economic and political superiority, because the U.S. population was growing rapidly, and because it was God's will that the United States should do so. The phrase was first used in 1845 by John L. O'Sullivan in an article on the annexation of Texas. The spirit of manifest destiny was revived at the end of the 1800's, during and after the Spanish-American War (see **Spanish-American War**). See also **United States, History of the** (Expansion). Jerome O. Steffen

Manila (pop. 1,876,195; met. area pop. 6,720,050) is the capital and largest city of the Philippines. It is also the country's leading port and chief cultural, social, educational, and commercial city. Spanish invaders of the Philippines founded the city more than 400 years ago. Manila is a place of sharp contrasts, with some people possessing exceptional wealth and others suffering from severe poverty. The city's beautiful setting and architectural landmarks earned it the name *Pearl of the Orient.* But Manila also has many slums.

Location and size. Manila stretches along the east shore of Manila Bay on the island of Luzon. A crescent of mountains surrounds the city on the north, east, and south. The Pasig River divides the city into two sections. Manila covers a total area of about 15 square miles (38 square kilometers). It is the center of a large metropolitan area that covers 246 square miles (636 square kilometers). For the location of Manila, see **Philippines** (map).

Description. Intramuros, or the Walled City, stands on the south bank of the Pasig River. Spaniards began construction of Intramuros in 1571, and completed it in 1739. They built high city walls and a wide moat to protect themselves from attacks by unfriendly Filipinos. The walls and some of the churches, convents, monasteries, and public buildings still stand, despite heavy bombing in the early 1940's during World War II. Outstanding among the old buildings is San Agustin Church, completed in 1601.

Rizal Park, which is one of Manila's favorite parks, looks across Manila Bay from just outside Intramuros. A statue of José Rizal stands on the spot in the park where this national hero was executed by the Spanish on Dec. 30, 1896. Roxas Boulevard runs south along Manila Bay from Rizal Park. This picturesque drive passes the mansions of wealthy Manilans and lovely hotels. It also runs

Hutchison Library

Downtown Manila lies on both banks of the muddy Pasig River. The river cuts through the heart of the city and forms an essential part of the harbor on Manila Bay. Several bridges span the river and connect the two parts of the city.

through poor areas of the city.

The original business district of Manila lies on the north bank of the Pasig River. Six bridges connect it with the south bank. A large Chinatown lies on the north bank of the Pasig River. Many tourists travel to Quiapo, just north of the river, to visit its colorful market and lively restaurants, shopping centers, and movie houses. Thousands of people go to the Quiapo Church every Friday to worship before the shrine of the miraculous image of the Black Nazarene. Tondo, in the northwestern corner of the city, is a large poor section. The most modern center in the Manila area lies in suburban Makati.

Important buildings in Manila include Malacañang—home to many Philippine presidents—and the José Rizal Memorial Stadium. Outstanding government buildings include the Legislative Building, the City Hall, and the Post Office. Japanese bombings during World War II destroyed the Manila Cathedral, originally built in 1654, but it was rebuilt in 1958.

Economy. Manila is the banking, financial, and commercial center of the Philippines. The Asian Development Bank, which lends money to promote economic growth in Asia, has its headquarters in Manila. Industries in Manila turn out a variety of textiles and clothing, and accessory manufacturers produce costume jewelry, hats, leather goods, pearl buttons, and shoes. Handmade items include embroidered goods and furniture. Processing plants in Manila produce beer, coconut oil, processed foods, soap, and tobacco products. Other products include building materials, cosmetics, drugs, electronic products, glass, ink, machinery, matches, nails, paints, pencils, radio equipment, and rope and twine.

Manila is one of the leading trade centers of the Pacific area. The city's major exports are electronic products, clothing and textiles, and processed foods. Other exports include mineral ores, timber products, and abacá, from which rope is made. Large corporations in the United States, Europe, and Japan and other Asian nations have invested in large manufacturing operations in Manila, including facilities for electronics, drugs, and food processing.

Transportation and communication. Manila's superb harbor and location make it an important port on Pacific and Far East trade routes. Piers in the harbor can handle up to 12 large ships at one time. Manila also has an international airport. The Philippine National Railways links Manila with other cities on Luzon. The Manila area also has an elevated rail rapid transit system.

Manila has many radio and television stations. Publishers in Manila print a number of newspapers and magazines.

Education and cultural life. Manila has 17 universities. The University of Santo Tomás, the oldest, was founded in 1611. The University of the Philippines stands in Quezon City. Many colleges also operate in Manila. The National Museum and Santo Tomás Museum have interesting collections. The city also has a number of public libraries. The Manila Symphony Orchestra plays concert music. Ballet and opera groups are also active in the city.

Government. The entire Manila metropolitan area is part of *Metro-Manila.* A five-member commission heads

M. Harvey, Hutchison Library

Rizal Park is one of several spacious parks that add to the beauty of Manila. The park overlooks Manila Bay, *background.* A scenic boulevard runs nearby.

this areawide governmental unit. There are 4 cities and 13 towns within Metro-Manila. Each of the cities and towns has an elected mayor. Manila and Quezon City are the largest of the cities.

History. Before the coming of Europeans, the Manila area was a small sultanate that was ruled by Rajah Soliman and Rajah Lakandula. The Spanish conquered these rulers, and Miguel López de Legazpi, a conquistador, founded a Spanish city at the site of Manila in 1571. The Ayuntamiento in Intramuros was built in 1735 to house the city council and the mayor's office. This building became the seat of the national government of the Philippines when the United States took possession of the country. An earthquake destroyed a large part of Manila in 1863.

Spain surrendered Manila to the United States in 1898, during the Spanish-American War. The American administration of the city installed a modern water supply system and electric lighting, and made several other improvements.

Japanese forces seized Manila on Jan. 2, 1942, just four weeks after the beginning of World War II in the Pacific. United States forces began the liberation of the city on Feb. 3, 1945, and a bitter four-week battle followed. Among the first places liberated were the Santo Tomás internment camp and the Bilibid Prison, where the Japanese had kept United States prisoners. Few buildings in Manila remained standing when the Japanese finally surrendered the city on March 4. However, the Filipinos began rebuilding almost immediately afterward.

Manila became the national capital of the Philippines when independence was proclaimed on July 4, 1946. In 1948, the Philippine government made Quezon City the official capital of the country. But Manila continued to serve as the seat of the government, pending the completion of new government buildings in Quezon City. In 1976, the government made Manila the country's official capital again. David J. Steinberg

See also **Philippines** (pictures); **World War II** (The war in Asia and the Pacific).

Manila Bay is the entrance to the city of Manila on Luzon, a northern island in the Philippines. The bay is an extension of the South China Sea. For location, see **Philippines** (map). Manila Bay is about 40 miles (64 kilometers) long and 35 miles (56 kilometers) wide. Its waters are deep enough for large ships. There are two excellent harbors at Cavite and Manila.

The rocky, fortified island of Corregidor is at the mouth of Manila Bay. Some of the most bitter fighting of World War II (1939-1945) took place on Corregidor. The island was attacked by the Japanese during the first days of the war. During the Spanish-American War, in 1898, an American fleet under the command of Commodore George Dewey destroyed a Spanish fleet in a battle at Manila Bay. David A. Ross

See also **Bataan Peninsula; Corregidor; Spanish-American War.**

Manila Bay, Battle of. See Spanish-American War (Chief events).

Manila hemp. See Abacá.

Manioc. See Cassava.

George Hunter, Photri

A vast field of Manitoba wheat that spreads out beyond the village of Wellwood

Manitoba

Manitoba, *MAN uh TOH buh,* is one of Canada's three Prairie Provinces. The other two are Alberta and Saskatchewan. Manitoba lies midway between the Atlantic and Pacific oceans. Winnipeg, Manitoba's capital and largest city, is the main transportation center linking eastern and western Canada.

More than half the people of Manitoba live in the Winnipeg metropolitan area. Winnipeg is the province's major industrial center. Busy food-processing plants and other factories are located in Winnipeg. In addition, the Winnipeg metropolitan area also has clothing factories and plants that make transportation equipment and electrical products.

Winnipeg lies in rolling plains that cover the southern section of Manitoba. This fertile region has the richest farmlands in the province. In summer, vast fields of wheat and other grains wave in the sun. Large numbers of beef cattle graze in fenced pastures. Other important farm products of this southern region include barley, canola, hogs, and milk.

A vast, rocky region lies across the northern two-

The contributors of this article are John S. Brierley, Professor of Geography at the University of Manitoba; and J. M. Bumsted, Professor of History at St. John's College, University of Manitoba.

thirds of Manitoba. This thinly populated region has great deposits of copper, gold, nickel, and zinc. Thompson has one of the few facilities in the Western world for all stages of nickel production, from mining to processing. This thriving town was carved out of the wilderness after prospectors discovered vast deposits of nickel in the area. Manitoba supplies 30 per cent of the nickel produced in Canada. The province ranks among the leading North American producers of nickel and zinc.

Thick forests stretch across the southern half of the region. Balsam fir, spruce, and other trees that grow in this area provide wood for Manitoba's furniture factories and paper mills.

Manitoba's many rivers and lakes cover almost a sixth of the province and help make it a popular vacationland. Tourists enjoy boating and swimming in the clear, sparkling waters. Fishing enthusiasts come from many parts of North America to cast for bass, pike, and trout. In the rugged forests of Manitoba, hunters track caribou, elk, moose, and smaller game. In the province's marshes and prairies, hunters shoot ducks, geese, partridges, and ruffed grouse.

Beavers and other fur-bearing animals made the Manitoba region important during the late 1600's. English fur traders entered the rich fur country from Hudson Bay in

Downtown Winnipeg

George Hunter, Masterfile

Interesting facts about Manitoba

WORLD BOOK illustrations by Kevin Chadwick

Two of the world's best collections of Inuit Eskimo art are located in Manitoba. One is at the Eskimo Museum in Churchill, which is devoted entirely to Inuit art. The other, housed at the Winnipeg Art Gallery, contains about 6,000 examples.

Manitoba's seaport, at Churchill, is the only seaport in the Prairie Provinces.

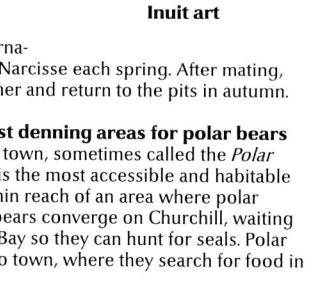

Inuit art

Thousands of garter snakes emerge from hibernation in limestone pits near Narcisse each spring. After mating, they disperse for the summer and return to the pits in autumn.

One of the world's largest denning areas for polar bears lies south of Churchill. The town, sometimes called the *Polar Bear Capital of the World,* is the most accessible and habitable area in the world lying within reach of an area where polar bears live. Each fall, polar bears converge on Churchill, waiting for ice to form on Hudson Bay so they can hunt for seals. Polar bears often wander close to town, where they search for food in garbage dumps.

Polar bears

the northeast. French-Canadian traders came westward from Quebec during the early 1700's. The adventurous fur traders paddled their birchbark canoes up Manitoba's rivers and traveled through unexplored forests and plains. They traded with the Indians of the region and built forts and trading posts in the wilderness. Irish and Scottish farmers began breaking up the plains of Manitoba in the early 1800's. Vast wheat fields were created in the fertile Red River Valley. Manitoba began exporting wheat, and the grain became famous for its high quality.

The word *Manitoba* probably came from the Algonquian language of the Indians. The tribes thought the *manito* (great spirit) made the echoing sounds that came from a strait of Lake Manitoba. These sounds were actually made by waves dashing against limestone ledges on the shore. The Indians called this part of the lake *Manito waba* (great spirit's strait).

Manitoba's nickname is the *Keystone Province.* It earned this nickname because of its location in the central, or keystone, position of the "arch" formed by the 10 Canadian provinces.

For the relationship of Manitoba to the other Canadian provinces, see the *World Book* articles on **Canada; Canada, Government of; Canada, History of; Prairie Provinces.**

George Hunter, Masterfile

Copper and zinc mining near Lynn Lake

Manitoba in brief

Symbols of Manitoba

The provincial flag, adopted in 1966, bears Manitoba's coat of arms and the British Union Flag. On the coat of arms, adopted in 1905, the buffalo symbolizes the importance of the animal in Manitoba's early history. Above the buffalo is the red cross of St. George, which represents Manitoba's bond with Great Britain.

Provincial flag

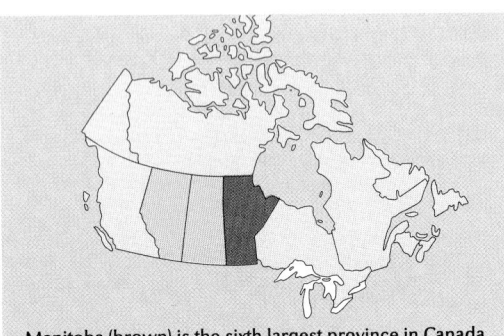

Manitoba (brown) is the sixth largest province in Canada and the smallest of the Prairie Provinces (yellow).

General information

Entered the Dominion: July 15, 1870, the fifth province.
Provincial abbreviation: MB (postal).
Provincial motto: none.

The Manitoba Legislative Building is in Winnipeg, the province's capital since it entered the Dominion in 1870.

Land and climate

Area: 250,947 sq. mi. (649,950 km²), including 39,224 sq. mi. (101,590 km²) of inland water.
Elevation: *Highest*—Baldy Mountain, 2,729 ft. (832 m) above sea level. *Lowest*—sea level, along Hudson Bay.
Coastline: 570 mi. (917 km).
Record high temperature: 112° F. (44° C) at Treesbank, near Wawanesa, on July 11, 1936, and at Emerson on July 12, 1936.
Record low temperature: −63° F. (−53° C) at Norway House on Jan. 9, 1899.
Average July temperature: 66° F. (19° C).
Average January temperature: −4° F. (−20° C).
Average yearly precipitation: 20 in. (50 cm).

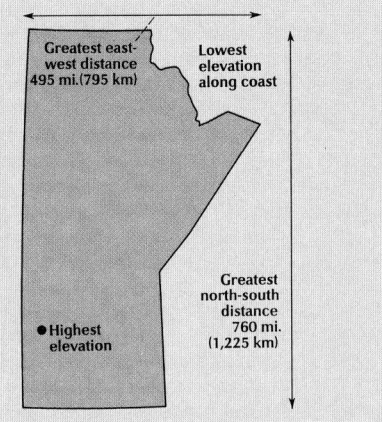

Greatest east-west distance 495 mi.(795 km)

Lowest elevation along coast

●Highest elevation

Greatest north-south distance 760 mi. (1,225 km)

Important dates

Pierre Gaultier de Varennes, Sieur de la Vérendrye, built Fort Rouge at the site of present-day Winnipeg.

Louis Riel led métis in the Red River Rebellion.

| 1612 | 1738 | 1812 | 1869-1870 |

Sir Thomas Button of England explored the west coast of Hudson Bay.

Settlers sent by the Earl of Selkirk established the Red River Colony.

Provincial
coat
of arms

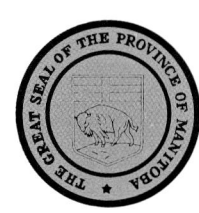

Provincial
seal

Floral emblem
Pasqueflower

People

Population: 1,091,942 (1991 census)
Rank among the provinces: 5th
Density: 4 persons per sq. mi. (2 per km²), provinces average 13 per sq. mi. (4 per km²)
Distribution: 72 per cent urban, 28 per cent rural
Largest cities and towns

Winnipeg	616,790
Brandon	38,567
Thompson	14,977
Portage la Prairie	13,186
Selkirk	9,815
Dauphin	8,453

Source: Statistics Canada.

Population trend

Source: Statistics Canada

Year	Population
1991	1,091,942
1986	1,071,232
1981	1,026,241
1976	1,021,506
1971	988,247
1966	963,066
1961	921,686
1951	776,541
1941	729,744
1931	700,139
1921	610,118
1911	461,394
1901	255,211
1891	152,506
1881	62,260
1871	25,228

Economy

Chief products

Agriculture: wheat, beef cattle, hogs, barley, canola, milk.
Manufacturing: food products, transportation equipment, printed materials, electrical equipment.
Mining: nickel.

Gross domestic product

Value of goods and services produced in 1991, $21,329,000,000.* *Services* include community, business, and personal services; finance; government; trade; transportation and communication; and utilities. *Industry* includes construction, manufacturing, and mining. *Agriculture* includes agriculture, fishing, and forestry.

*Canadian dollars.
Source: The Conference Board of Canada.

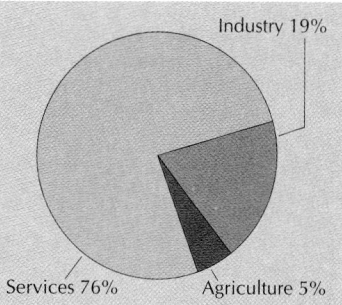

Industry 19%

Services 76%

Agriculture 5%

Government

Provincial government

Premier: term of up to 5 years
Legislative Assembly: 57 members, terms of up to 5 years.

Federal government

Members of the House of Commons: 14
Senators: 6

Sources of information

Tourism: Travel Manitoba, 7-155 Carlton Street, Winnipeg, MB R3C 3H8
Economy: Citizens Inquiry, Room 511, 401 York Avenue, Winnipeg, MB R3C OP8
Government: Information Services, Room 29, Legislative Building, Winnipeg, MB R3C OV8
History: Culture, Heritage & Citizenship Department, 3rd floor, 177 Lombard Avenue, Winnipeg, MB R3B OW5

The Canadian government extended Manitoba's northern boundary to Hudson Bay.

Winnipeg and its suburbs merged into one city, making Winnipeg one of Canada's largest cities.

1870   **1912**   **1960**   **1972**

Manitoba became Canada's fifth province on July 15.

Nickel mining operations began in Thompson.

Bill Brooks, Masterfile

Winnipeg's Old Market Square lies in a restored historic area of the city. Many people visit the square during the summer to enjoy its outdoor flea market, *above,* and live entertainment.

Population. The 1991 Canadian census reported that Manitoba had 1,091,942 people. The population of the province had increased about 2 per cent over the 1986 figure of 1,071,232.

About three-fourths of the people of Manitoba live in cities and towns. About 58 per cent—625,304 people— live in the metropolitan area of Winnipeg. Winnipeg is Manitoba's largest city and chief industrial center. It has the province's only Census Metropolitan Area as defined by Statistics Canada.

Besides Winnipeg, Manitoba has three cities that have populations of more than 12,000. These cities are, in order of size, Brandon, Thompson, and Portage la Prairie. See the separate articles on the cities and towns of Manitoba listed in the *Related articles* at the end of this article.

About 85 out of 100 Manitobans were born in Canada. Of the people born outside of Canada, most come from European countries. About a third of the people in Manitoba have some English ancestry. Other large ethnic groups in the province, in order of size, include Scots, Germans, Ukrainians, Irish, and French. The St. Boniface district of Winnipeg is the center of French-Canadian culture in the province.

Manitoba has about 33,000 *métis* (persons of mixed white and Indian ancestry). About 56,000 Indians and about 700 Eskimos live in the province. Southwestern Manitoba has more than a hundred Indian reservations. Most of the Eskimos live near Churchill.

Schools. The first school in the Manitoba region was established by the first settlers to the Red River Colony, in 1812. In 1818, Roman Catholic missionaries, led by Joseph Provencher, began setting up schools along with churches. John West, an Anglican missionary, opened the region's first Protestant school in 1820.

In 1871, a church-supported educational system, which had developed, was ended. The province created a board of education to direct the schools and provide

Population density

More than half of Manitoba's people live in and around Winnipeg, the province's largest city. The northern areas are thinly populated, partly because they have a severe climate.

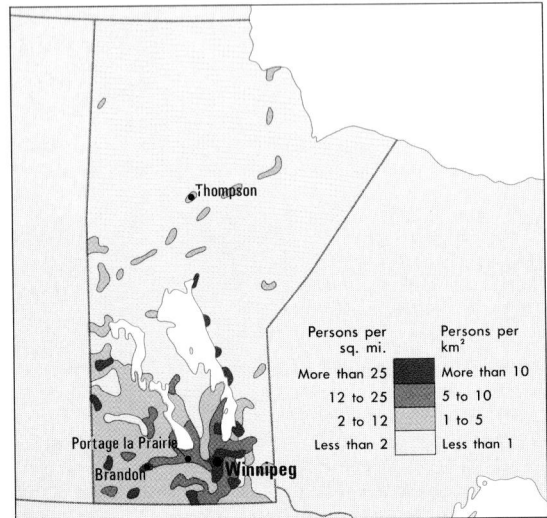

Persons per sq. mi.	Persons per km²
More than 25	More than 10
12 to 25	5 to 10
2 to 12	1 to 5
Less than 2	Less than 1

WORLD BOOK map; based on the *National Atlas of Canada*

them with public funds. Roman Catholic board members managed the Roman Catholic schools, and Protestant members supervised the Protestant schools. In 1890, the province abolished the board of education and its double school system. The provincial Department of Education was created to head a single education system. In 1908, the cabinet office of minister of education was established in Manitoba.

Manitoba law requires all children between the ages of 7 and 16 to attend school. The province has about 700 public schools and about 100 government-funded private schools. For information on the number of students and teachers in Manitoba, see **Education** (table).

Libraries and museums. The most important libraries in the province include the University of Manitoba Library, the University of Winnipeg Library, the Legislative Library, and the Centennial Library. All of these libraries are in Winnipeg.

Students of early Manitoban history use a special library of the Hudson's Bay Company that is operated by the Provincial Archives. The Museum of Man and Nature and the St. Boniface Historical Museum, both in Winnipeg, attract thousands of visitors yearly.

Universities and colleges

Manitoba has six degree-granting universities and colleges that are members of the Association of Universities and Colleges of Canada, listed below. For enrollments, see **Canada** (table: Universities and colleges).

Name	Mailing address
Brandon University	Brandon
Manitoba, University of	Winnipeg
St. Boniface, University College of	Winnipeg
St. John's College	Winnipeg
St. Paul's College	Winnipeg
Winnipeg, University of	Winnipeg

Manitoba map index

Metropolitan area

Cities, towns, and villages

*Does not appear on map; key shows general location.
†Unincorporated place.
‡City on Manitoba-Saskatchewan border; total population 7,449.
Sources: 1991 census for incorporated places; 1986 census for unincorporated places.

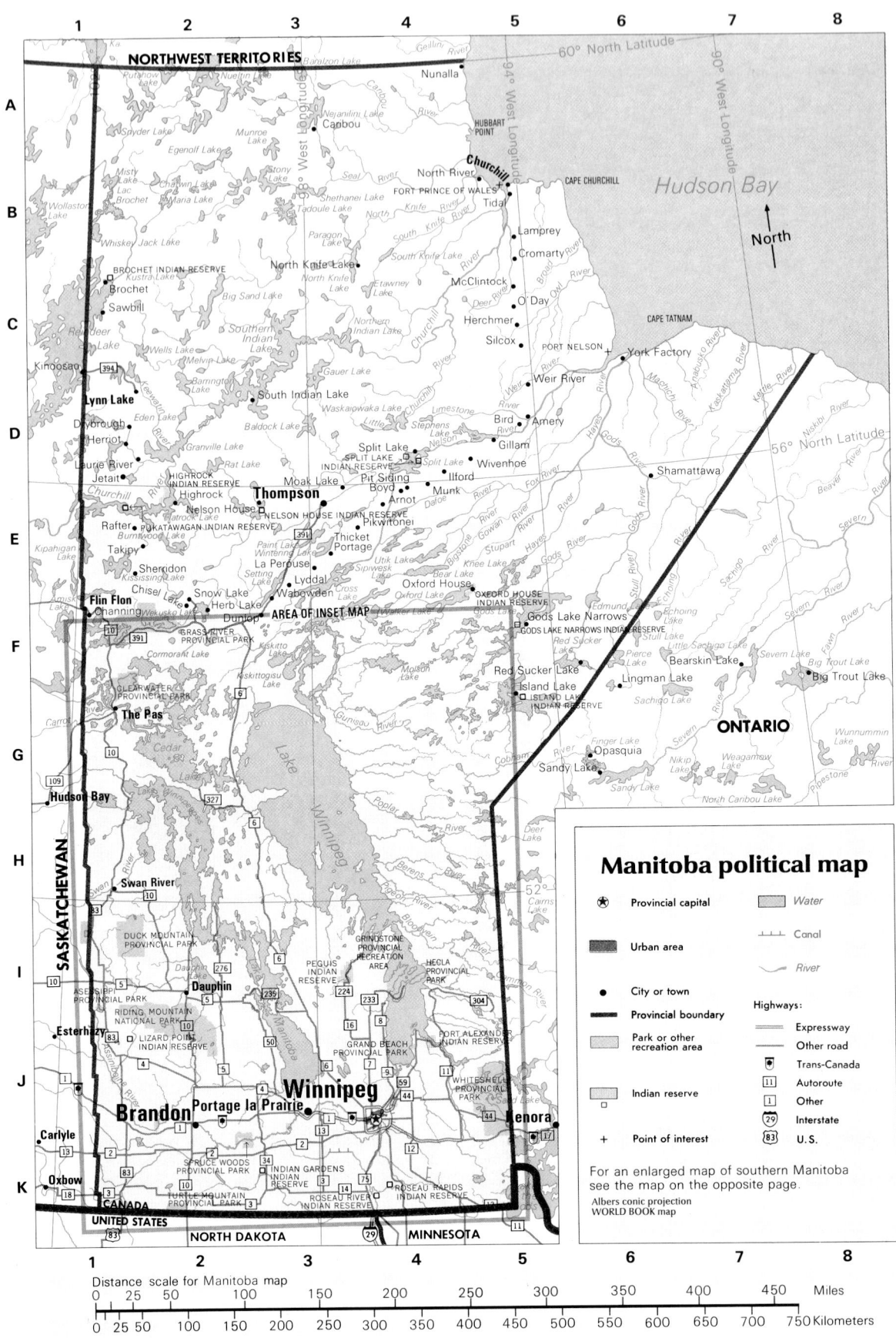

Manitoba political map

⊛ Provincial capital	▨ Water
▬ Urban area	⊥⊥⊥ Canal
● City or town	River
▬ Provincial boundary	**Highways:**
Park or other recreation area	═ Expressway
	— Other road
▫ Indian reserve	Trans-Canada
+ Point of interest	11 Autoroute
	1 Other
	29 Interstate
	83 U.S.

For an enlarged map of southern Manitoba
see the map on the opposite page.
Albers conic projection
WORLD BOOK map

Distance scale for Manitoba map

0   25   50   100   150   200   250   300   350   400   450   Miles

0 25 50   100   150   200   250   300   350   400   450   500   550   600   650   700   750 Kilometers

NORTHWEST TERRITORIES

60° North Latitude

Hudson Bay

North

SASKATCHEWAN

ONTARIO

CANADA
UNITED STATES
NORTH DAKOTA   MINNESOTA

56° North Latitude

Winnipeg
Brandon
Portage la Prairie
Dauphin
The Pas
Flin Flon
Thompson
Churchill
Kenora

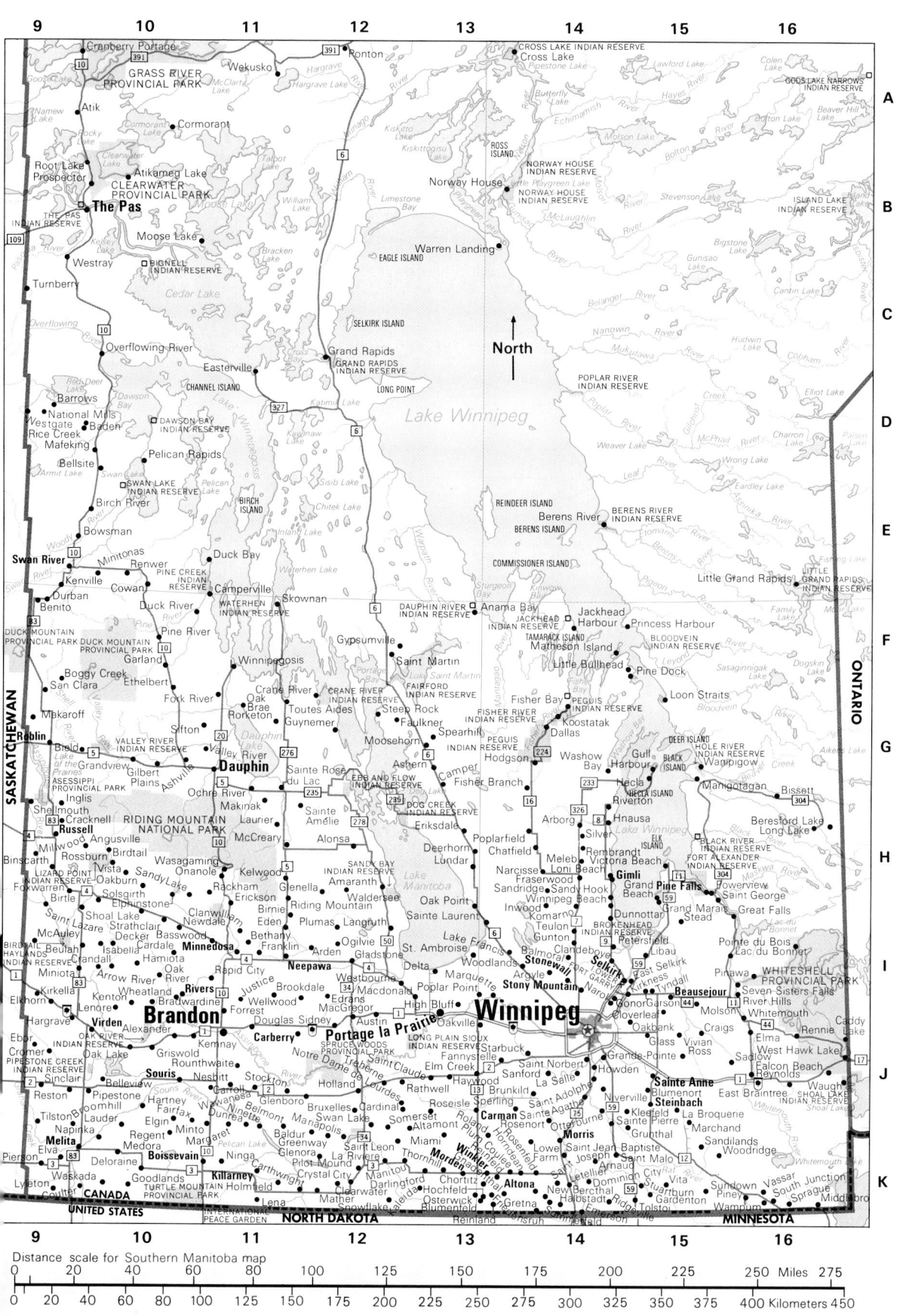

Distance scale for Southern Manitoba map

Visitors to Manitoba can see many reminders of the province's colorful history. Forts and trading posts of the early fur-trading days are popular attractions. The Basilica of St. Boniface, in Winnipeg, stands on the site of the first Roman Catholic church in western Canada. It is perhaps the most beautiful cathedral in the region. Many people who helped make Manitoba history are buried in the churchyard. They include Louis Riel, who led two uprisings of the métis.

Lake Winnipeg and many other beautiful lakes of Manitoba have popular summer resorts that offer boating and swimming. The province also has fine golf courses. People come from many parts of North America to fish for pike, smallmouth bass, trout, and walleye in the province's lakes and rivers. Hunters seek black bears, ducks, geese, and moose in the forests and marshes of Manitoba. Many visitors attend performances by the Royal Winnipeg Ballet, the Winnipeg Symphony Orchestra, and other cultural groups.

Manitoba's annual events include many colorful festivals. The Folk Festival, featuring folk musicians and singers, is held in Birds Hill Park each July. The National Ukrainian Festival is held every July in Dauphin. Folklorama features Winnipeg's ethnic groups each August.

Places to visit

Following are brief descriptions of some of Manitoba's many interesting places to visit:

Centennial Centre, in Winnipeg, includes the popular Museum of Man and Nature and the Manitoba Theatre Center. It also has a concert hall and a planetarium.

Fort Prince of Wales, near Churchill, overlooks Hudson Bay. It is the massive remains of the northernmost fortress in North America. The stone structure was built by the Hudson's Bay Company between 1732 and 1772. It became a national historic park in 1940.

International Peace Garden lies partly in Manitoba and partly in North Dakota. It honors the long friendship between Canada and the United States. A *cairn* (memorial made of stones) consisting of rocks from both countries marks the international boundary.

Lower Fort Garry, 20 miles (32 kilometers) north of Winnipeg, is the only stone fur-trading fort in Canada still standing complete. It was built during the 1830's by the Hudson's Bay Company on the Red River. The area became a national historic park in 1951.

Manitoba Agricultural Museum and Homesteaders Village, in Austin, features Canada's largest collection of operating steam engines, gasoline tractors, and other antique farm equipment. It also includes a pioneer village in a beautiful wooded setting.

Mennonite Heritage Village, in Steinbach, is a reproduction of an authentic Mennonite village. It includes a blacksmith shop, a general store, farmhouses, a livery barn, and a sod house. A huge windmill towers over the site.

Spirit Sands, in Spruce Woods Provincial Park, features high sand dunes and plants and animals that are rare to Manitoba.

National and provincial parks. Riding Mountain National Park lies west of Lake Manitoba. For its area and chief features, see **Canada** (National parks). Manitoba has 12 provincial parks. For information, write to Department of Natural Resources, Room 402, 258 Portage Avenue, Winnipeg, MB R3C 0B6.

Travel Manitoba

Dog derby during the Trappers' Festival in The Pas

Bill Brooks, Masterfile

Windmill at the Mennonite Heritage Village in Steinbach

Annual events

February-April
Festival du Voyageur in Winnipeg (February); Trappers' Festival in The Pas (February); Royal Manitoba Winter Fair in Brandon (March).

June-October
Provincial Exhibition in Brandon (June); Winnipeg International Children's Festival (June); Flin Flon Trout Festival (July); Manitoba Stampede and Exhibition in Morris (July); Selkirk Highland Gathering (July); Threshermen's Reunion in Austin (July); Folklorama in Winnipeg (August); Icelandic Festival in Gimli (August); Oktoberfest in Winnipeg (September); All Canada Goose Shoot in Lundar (October).

Canadian Government Office of Tourism

Travel Manitoba

National Ukrainian Festival in Dauphin

Dancers of the Royal Winnipeg Ballet

Canadian Government Office of Tourism

Threshermen's Reunion and Stampede in Austin

Land and climate

Land regions. Manitoba has four main land regions. They are, from northeast to southwest: (1) the Hudson Bay Lowland, (2) the Canadian Shield, (3) the Manitoba Lowland, and (4) the Saskatchewan Plain.

The Hudson Bay Lowland is a wet plain bordering the southern part of Hudson Bay. In Manitoba, this almost treeless flatland extends about 100 miles (160 kilometers) into the interior. Few persons live there.

The Canadian Shield is a vast, horseshoe-shaped region that covers almost half of Canada and part of the United States. The rough shield, made up mostly of granites and other kinds of rocks, covers nearly two-thirds of Manitoba. It has many lakes, streams, and forests, and deposits of copper, nickel, and other minerals. See **Canadian Shield.**

The Manitoba Lowland forms part of the Western Interior Plains, the Canadian section of the North American Great Plains. It is a flat area of forests, lakes, limestone rock, and swamps. The forests have great stands of timber, and the lakes are rich in fish.

The Saskatchewan Plain also forms part of the Western Interior Plains. This region is a rolling plain broken by low hills. Its rich, well-drained soils make it the main farming region of Manitoba.

Coastline. Manitoba has 570 miles (917 kilometers) of coastline along Hudson Bay in the northeastern part of the province. Few inlets or islands lie along the coast.

T. Klassen, Hot Shots

A polar bear roams in the Hudson Bay Lowland, a flat, treeless region that extends about 100 miles (160 kilometers) inland from Hudson Bay. Few people live in this region.

Hudson Bay waters are frozen much of the year, and so commercial shipping activities are limited in the coastal region.

Mountains. The Duck, Porcupine, and Riding mountain ranges form the Manitoba Escarpment. It rises between the two plains regions. The highest point in Manitoba is 2,729-foot (832-meter) Baldy Mountain, in the Duck Mountain range near the Saskatchewan border. The Turtle and Pembina hills of North Dakota extend into the southern part of Manitoba.

Rivers and lakes cover almost a sixth of Manitoba, or 39,225 square miles (101,592 square kilometers). The rivers form a great waterway system that drains western Canada from as far west as the Rocky Mountains. The Red, Saskatchewan, and Winnipeg rivers flow into Lake Winnipeg. Important branches of the Red River are the Assiniboine and Pembina rivers. The Nelson River flows out of Lake Winnipeg across the Canadian Shield, and empties into Hudson Bay. The Churchill and Hayes rivers also drain northern Manitoba.

Manitoba has about 100,000 lakes. Three lakes are so large that they are often called the *Great Lakes of Manitoba.* Lake Winnipeg, which covers 9,398 square miles (24,341 square kilometers), is the largest body of water entirely within any province or state. Lake Winnipegosis covers 2,103 square miles (5,447 square kilometers), and Lake Manitoba spreads over 1,817 square miles (4,706 square kilometers). Other lakes include Dauphin, Gods, Island, Reindeer, Southern Indian, and Tadoule.

Plant and animal life. Manitoba has about 99,230 square miles (257,000 square kilometers) of forests. The

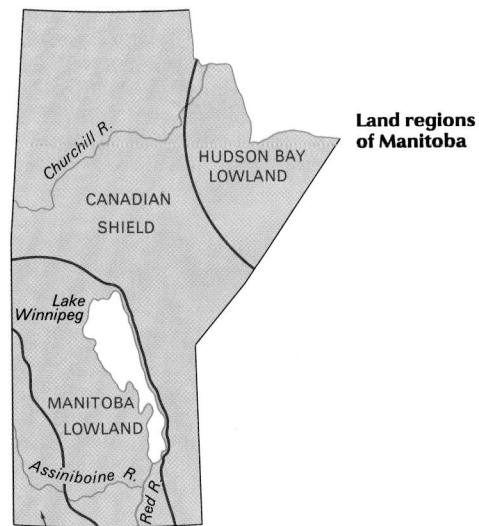

Land regions of Manitoba

HUDSON BAY LOWLAND

CANADIAN SHIELD

Churchill R.

Lake Winnipeg

MANITOBA LOWLAND

Assiniboine R.

Red R.

SASKATCHEWAN PLAIN

WORLD BOOK map

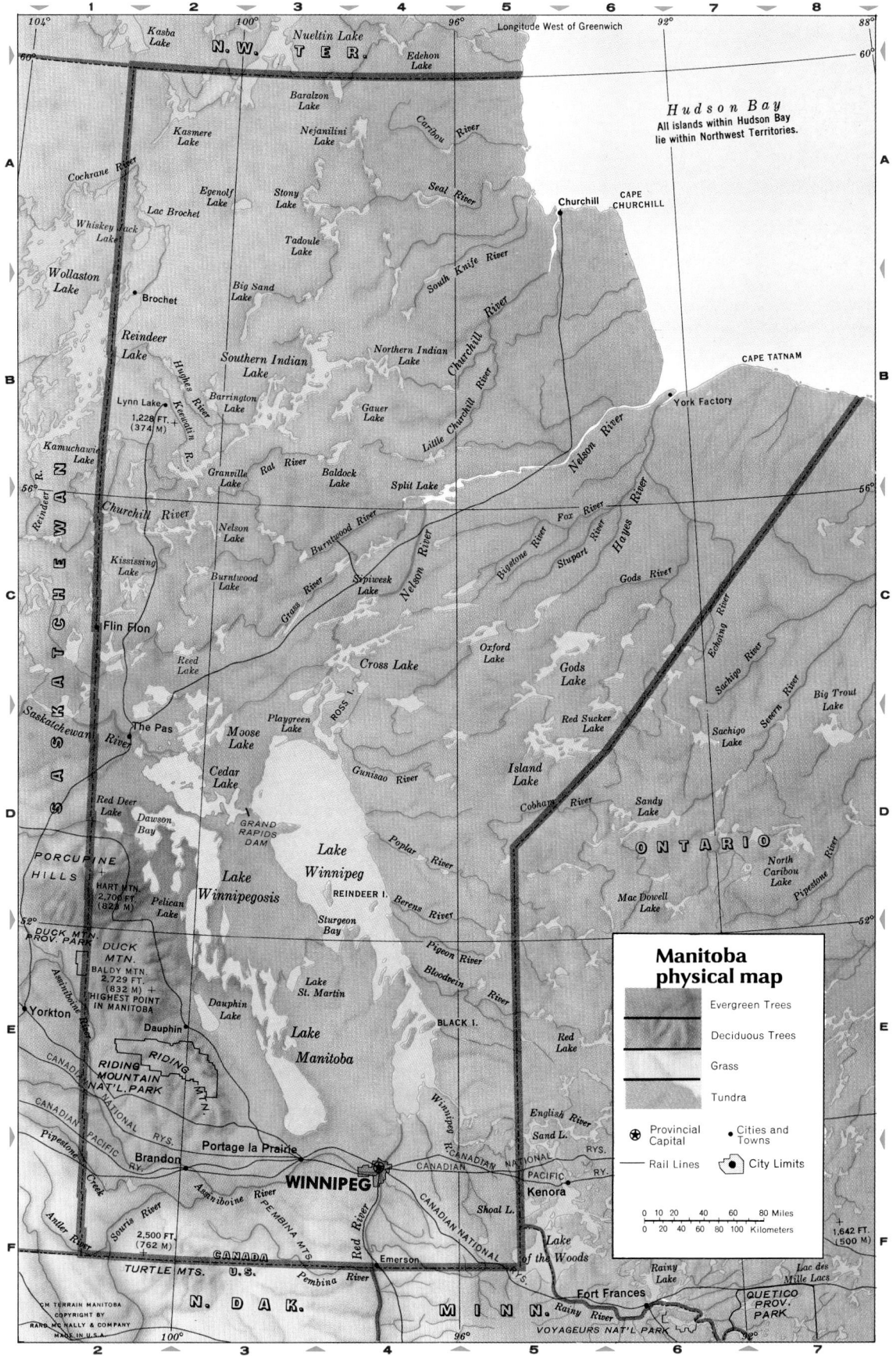

Manitoba
physical map

Evergreen Trees
Deciduous Trees
Grass
Tundra

⊛ Provincial Capital
━ Rail Lines
• Cities and Towns
City Limits

0 10 20   40   60   80 Miles
0 20 40 60 80 100 Kilometers

Manitoba Department of Economic Development and Tourism

Forests and lakes are abundant in the rocky region called the Canadian Shield, which covers almost two-thirds of Manitoba.

most common trees are the aspen, black spruce, jack pine, and white spruce. Others include ash, birch, maple, oak, and tamarack. Columbines, fireweeds, and other wild flowers grow in many parts of the province.

Caribou, elk, and moose live in the northern forests. Deer thrive there and in most parts of southern Manitoba. Fur-bearing animals of the forests include the beaver, fox, lynx, mink, and muskrat. Other animals include the bear, coyote, ermine, otter, and raccoon. Ducks and geese fly north in spring to breed in Manitoba's lakes and ponds. Grouse, partridges, prairie chickens, ptarmigan, and other game birds live in Manitoba. Fish there

include bass, goldeye, perch, pickerel, pike, sauger, sturgeon, trout, tullibee, and whitefish.

Climate. Manitoba has long, bitterly cold winters and warm summers. In general, the temperature decreases from the southwestern part of the province to the northeastern section. The average January temperature is 0° F. (−18° C) in the south and −17° F. (−27° C) in the north. The lowest recorded temperature, −63° F. (−53° C), occurred in Norway House on Jan. 9, 1899. Average July temperatures range from 68° F. (20° C) in the south to 55° F. (13° C) in the north. The highest temperature was 112° F. (44° C), recorded in Treesbank, near Wawanesa, on July 11, 1936, and in Emerson on July 12, 1936. Manitoba's *precipitation* (rain, melted snow, and other forms of moisture) averages 20 inches (50 centimeters) a year. About 50 inches (130 centimeters) of snow falls a year.

Average monthly weather

	The Pas						Winnipeg				
	Temperatures				**Days of rain or snow**		**Temperatures**				**Days of rain or snow**
	F°		**C°**				**F°**		**C°**		
	High	**Low**	**High**	**Low**			**High**	**Low**	**High**	**Low**	
Jan.	3	−16	−16	−27	7	Jan.	9	−8	−13	−22	12
Feb.	10	−12	−12	−24	7	Feb.	14	−5	−10	−21	10
Mar.	25	1	−4	−17	7	Mar.	28	9	−2	−13	9
Apr.	44	21	7	−6	7	Apr.	48	28	9	−2	9
May	60	36	16	2	7	May	64	41	18	5	10
June	69	46	21	8	11	June	73	51	23	11	12
July	76	53	24	12	11	July	80	57	27	14	10
Aug.	73	50	23	10	10	Aug.	78	54	26	12	9
Sept.	61	40	16	4	10	Sept.	66	45	19	7	9
Oct.	47	29	8	−2	9	Oct.	52	34	11	1	8
Nov.	25	9	−4	−13	9	Nov.	30	16	−1	−9	11
Dec.	9	−8	−13	−22	8	Dec.	15	1	−9	−17	11

Average January temperatures

Manitoba has long, cold winters. The province's temperatures decrease steadily from the far south to the north.

Average July temperatures

The province has mild summers. The southern section of Manitoba has the warmest summertime temperatures.

Average yearly precipitation

The southeastern portion of Manitoba has the greatest amount of precipitation. The far north is the driest area.

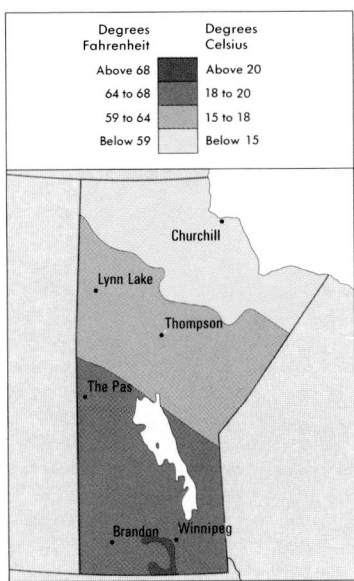

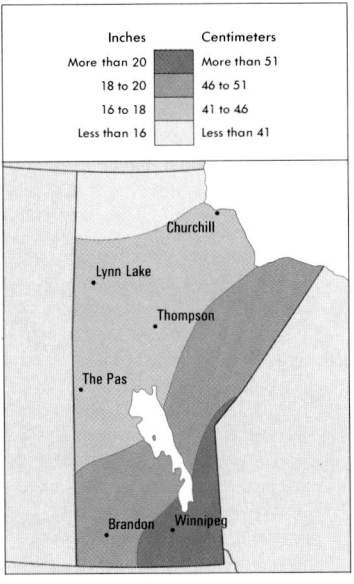

WORLD BOOK maps; based on the *National Atlas of Canada.*

For many years, the economy of Manitoba was based chiefly on agriculture. Many new industries developed in the 1940's, and manufacturing increased rapidly. Today, service industries, taken together, make up the largest part of Manitoba's *gross domestic product* (GDP) —the total value of all goods and services produced. Manufacturing ranks second. All values given here are in Canadian dollars. For the value of the Canadian dollar in U.S. money, see **Money** (table).

Natural resources. The forests and wildlife of Manitoba are important to the province's economy. Manitoba's chief natural resources also include fertile soils and rich mineral deposits.

Soil. The deep, fertile soils of the southern plains are perhaps the province's chief natural resource. Some of these soils were deposited by glaciers or by ancient glacial lakes. The soils of southern Manitoba vary from clays to bog and peat. The soils of the Hudson Bay Lowland contain clay.

Minerals. The Canadian Shield region of Manitoba has large deposits of cobalt, copper, nickel, zinc, and other minerals. Deposits of gypsum lie just north of Lake Manitoba. Southwestern Manitoba's minerals include bentonite, limestone, petroleum, and potash.

Service industries provide 76 per cent of Manitoba's gross domestic product. Service industries are concentrated in Winnipeg.

Community, business, and personal services form the leading service industry in Manitoba. This industry includes such activities as education, health care, legal services, and the operation of hotels and repair shops. Community, social, and personal services employ about a third of the province's workers.

Finance, insurance, and real estate rank next among Manitoba service industries in terms of the gross domestic product. Real estate is the most important part of this industry because of the large sums of money involved in the selling and leasing of homes, office space, and other property. Many of Canada's largest financial companies have major branch offices in Winnipeg.

Wholesale and retail trade make up the third most important type of service industry in Manitoba. Wholesale companies buy goods from producers and sell the goods mainly to other businesses. The wholesale trade of cattle, groceries, and wheat is a major part of the province's economy. Retail businesses sell goods directly to the public. Common types of retail establishments are automobile dealerships, food stores, and department stores.

Other service industries are transportation and communication, government, and utilities. Railroads and trucking firms are the major part of the transportation industry. Telephone companies are the leading type of communication business. Utility companies provide electric, gas, and water service.

Manufacturing accounts for 11 per cent of Manitoba's GDP. Goods manufactured in the province have a *value added by manufacture* of about $3 billion yearly. This figure represents the increase in value of raw materials after they become finished products.

Food and beverage processing is the major manufacturing activity. It accounts for about a fourth of all manufacturing in Manitoba. Meat packing is the most important type of food-processing activity. It is concentrated in the St. Boniface area of Winnipeg. Other leading food-processing establishments in Manitoba produce canned and frozen vegetables, dairy products, livestock feed, soft drinks, and vegetable oil.

The production of transportation equipment and printed materials rank next in importance among manufacturing activities in Manitoba. Winnipeg is a leading Canadian producer of aerospace equipment and buses. Newspaper companies and print shops turn out most of the province's printed materials.

Other manufactured products made in Manitoba, in order of value, include electrical equipment, clothing, fabricated metal products, primary metals, and machinery. Most of these items are produced mainly in Winnipeg. Computer parts and telecommunications equipment are the major electrical products. Women's sportswear is the leading type of clothing made in Manitoba. Machine tools and structural metal are among the province's fabricated metal products. A nickel smelter in Thompson and a copper and zinc smelter in Flin Flon produce primary metals. Agricultural equipment is the leading type of machinery produced in the province.

Agriculture accounts for 5 per cent of the province's gross domestic product. It provides the economic base for most rural communities in southern Manitoba. There, about 27,000 farms occupy about 19 million acres (7.7 million hectares). The farms average about 690 acres (280 hectares). Wheat, the most valuable farm product, accounts for 30 per cent of the income. Wheat farmers primarily raise varieties of hard red spring wheat. Barley and canola rank next in value. Wheat and barley production is heaviest in the region southwest of Winnipeg. Canola, flaxseed, mustard seed, and sunflowers are grown for their oil. Other important field crops in Manitoba include oats, potatoes, and rye. Most of the province's vegetable farms lie near Portage la Prairie and Winkler.

Livestock farms are more common in western Manitoba than eastern Manitoba. The raising of beef cattle

Production and workers by economic activities

Economic activities	Per cent of GDP* produced	Employed workers	
		Number of persons	Per cent of total
Community, business, & personal services	25	178,000	36
Finance, insurance, & real estate	15	25,000	5
Transportation & communication	12	38,000	8
Wholesale & retail trade	12	84,000	17
Manufacturing	11	55,000	11
Government	8	38,000	8
Construction	6	20,000	4
Agriculture	5	43,000	9
Utilities	4	6,000	1
Mining	2	6,000	1
Total	100	493,000	100

*GDP = gross domestic product, the total value of goods and services produced in a year.
Figures are for 1991.
Sources: *World Book* estimates based on data from The Conference board of Canada and Statistics Canada.

provides about 15 per cent of the value of the province's farm output. Dairy farming is most important in south-central Manitoba. Chickens, eggs, and hogs are also produced.

Mining provides 2 per cent of Manitoba's gross domestic product. Nickel production accounts for more than half of the province's mining income. Ontario is the only region in North or South America that produces more nickel than Manitoba. Thompson is the chief center of nickel production in Manitoba. Nickel also comes from a mine just northwest of The Pas.

Other minerals produced in Manitoba, in order of value, include copper, zinc, petroleum, and sand and gravel. Copper is obtained as a by-product of nickel mining. It also occurs along with zinc. Large copper-zinc mines operate near Flin Flon, Leaf Rapids, Lynn Lake, and Snow Lake.

All of the petroleum produced in Manitoba comes from the southwestern part of the province. Oil production is heaviest in the Virden, Pierson, and Waskada areas. The province's other mineral products include cobalt, limestone, lithium, platinum, silver, and tantalum.

Electric power. Hydroelectric power plants generate most of the province's electricity. Plants on the Laurie, Nelson, Saskatchewan, and Winnipeg rivers supply power to Manitoba, nearby provinces, and parts of the United States. The major source of electric power is the lower Nelson River. Manitoba's largest station, at Limestone Rapids, began full operation in 1992.

Transportation. Major airlines offer flights from Winnipeg to large cities in other provinces. Smaller airlines connect Winnipeg to Brandon, The Pas, Thompson, Churchill, and other communities in Manitoba.

Manitoba's main rail lines branch out from Winnipeg to the east and to the west. Brandon and Portage la Prairie are also important rail centers. The main rail line in northern Manitoba connects The Pas, Thompson, and Churchill.

Most of Manitoba's roads are in the southern part of the province. The most important one is the cross-

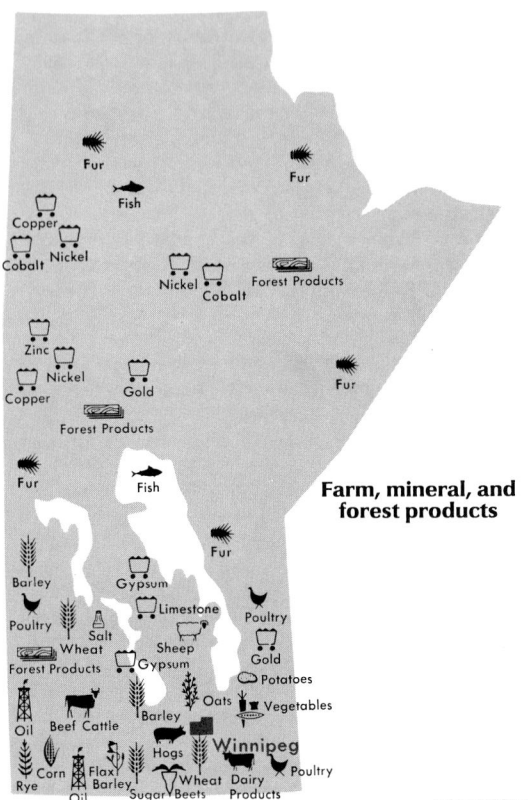

Farm, mineral, and forest products

WORLD BOOK map

This map shows where the province's leading farm, mineral, and forest products are produced. The major urban area (shown in red) is the province's most important manufacturing center.

country Trans-Canada Highway, which crosses Manitoba through Winnipeg and Brandon. Other major roads link Flin Flon and Winnipeg with North Dakota, and Winnipeg with Thompson. In winter, bulldozers pack the snow to make roads in northern Manitoba.

Churchill, on Hudson Bay, is Manitoba's only seaport. It is blocked by ice during winter and spring. Shipping from the port occurs only during the months of August, September, and October. Trains carry wheat to Churchill for export to Britain and other European countries. Manitoba's most important inland waterways are Lake Winnipeg and the Red River.

Communication. The first newspaper published in Manitoba, *The Nor' Wester,* was issued in 1859 in Fort Garry (now Winnipeg). Today, the province has five daily newspapers, the largest of which is the *Free Press* of Winnipeg. About 70 weekly newspapers are also published in the province. *The South Lance,* printed in Winnipeg, has the largest circulation of these weekly papers. A French-language weekly, *La Liberté,* is published in the St. Boniface district of Winnipeg.

The first radio station in Manitoba, CKY, began broadcasting from Winnipeg in 1922. The first television station, CBWT, began operating in Winnipeg in 1954. Two French-language radio stations broadcast from the St. Boniface area. Manitoba has 28 radio stations and 7 TV stations.

Freeman Patterson, Masterfile

Cattle graze on a pasture in southern Manitoba. Raising beef cattle is one of the province's most valuable agricultural activities. Farmers in Manitoba also raise dairy cattle and hogs.

Travel Manitoba

Manitoba's Legislative Assembly is a one-house legislature. Its 57 members serve terms of up to five years.

Lieutenant governor of Manitoba represents the British monarch, Queen Elizabeth II, in her role as the queen of Canada. The lieutenant governor is appointed by the governor general in council of Canada. The position of lieutenant governor is largely honorary.

Premier of Manitoba is the actual head of the provincial government. The province, like the other provinces and Canada itself, has a *parliamentary* form of government. The premier is an elected member of the Legislative Assembly. The person who serves as premier is usually the leader of the majority party in the Legislative Assembly.

The premier presides over the executive council, or cabinet. The cabinet also includes ministers chosen by the premier from among party members in the Legislative Assembly. Each minister directs one or more departments of the provincial government. The cabinet, like the premier, resigns if it loses the support of a majority of the assembly.

Legislative Assembly is a one-house legislature that makes the provincial laws. It has 57 members elected from 57 electoral districts. Members of the Legislative Assembly serve terms that may last up to five years. However, the lieutenant governor, on the advice of the premier, normally calls an election before the end of the five-year period.

Courts. The highest court in Manitoba is the court of appeal. It is made up of the chief justice of Manitoba and six judges of appeal. The court of queen's bench hears all major civil and criminal cases. It consists of a chief justice and 33 associate justices. Nine of the associate justices make up a special family division. This division is headed by an associate chief justice.

The governor general in council appoints all of Manitoba's higher-court judges. They serve until the age of 75. Minor court officials, such as provincial judges, are appointed by provincial authorities.

Local government. Manitoba has about 185 incorporated cities, towns, villages, and rural municipalities. Each is governed by a council headed by a mayor or a reeve. All these officials are elected to three-year terms. The number of council members ranges from 4 to 15, depending on the area's population. The province also has 17 local government districts in remote or thinly settled areas. These districts are governed by resident ad-

ministrators, appointed by the provincial government.

The five cities of Manitoba received their charters under special acts of the Legislative Assembly. The towns, villages, and rural municipalities of Manitoba were incorporated under the province's municipal act. They are supervised by the department of rural development.

In 1971, the Manitoba legislature passed a law that combined Winnipeg and 12 of its suburbs into one municipality, the city of Winnipeg. The suburbs included St. Boniface and St. James-Assiniboia. The legislature also eliminated the Metropolitan Corporation of Greater Winnipeg, a regional authority that had administered services for Winnipeg and its suburbs.

Revenue. The provincial government of Manitoba gets about 52 per cent of its *general revenue* (income) from taxation. Most of this money comes from taxes on personal income and retail sales. Other taxes include those levied on corporate incomes and sales of gasoline and tobacco. Such financial agreements as national and provincial tax-sharing arrangements account for about 35 per cent of Manitoba's revenue. Additional revenue is received from license fees and from the sale of liquor, which is controlled by the provincial government of Manitoba.

Politics. The major political parties of Manitoba are the Progressive Conservative Party, the New Democratic Party, and the Liberal Party.

The Progressive Conservative Party was formerly named the Conservative Party, and today members are usually simply called Conservatives. The New Democratic Party is a democratic socialist party. It was formerly called the Co-operative Commonwealth Federation. In 1932, the Liberals joined the provincial government headed by a farmers' organization called the Progressives. They were called the Liberal Progressives until 1961. A Manitoba citizen must be at least 18 years old to vote in an election.

The premiers of Manitoba

	Party	Term
Alfred Boyd	None	1870-1871
Marc A. Girard	Conservative	1871-1872
Henry J. H. Clarke	None	1872-1874
Marc A. Girard	Conservative	1874
Robert A. Davis	None	1874-1878
John Norquay	Conservative	1878-1887
David H. Harrison	Conservative	1887-1888
Thomas Greenway	Liberal	1888-1900
Hugh J. MacDonald	Conservative	1900
Rodmond P. Roblin	Conservative	1900-1915
Tobias C. Norris	Liberal	1915-1922
John Bracken	Liberal Progressive	1922-1943
Stuart S. Garson	Liberal Progressive	1943-1948
Douglas L. Campbell	Liberal Progressive	1948-1958
Duff Roblin	Progressive Conservative	1958-1967
Walter Weir	Progressive Conservative	1967-1969
Edward R. Schreyer	New Democratic	1969-1977
Sterling R. Lyon	Progressive Conservative	1977-1981
Howard R. Pawley	New Democratic	1981-1988
Gary Filmon	Progressive Conservative	1988-

Indian days. Five Indian tribes lived in the Manitoba region when the first explorers and fur traders arrived. The Chipewyan Indians hunted caribou across the northern section. The Woods Cree, who hunted beavers and moose, lived in the central forests. The Plains Cree fished and trapped animals in the prairies and wooded lowlands. The Assiniboine lived on the southwestern plains. These allies of the Cree were buffalo hunters. The Chippewa, who also hunted buffalo, lived in the south-eastern section of the plains.

Exploration. The English explorer Sir Thomas Button and his crew were the first white people in the Manitoba region. They sailed down the west coast of Hudson Bay in 1612. Button and his crew spent the winter at the mouth of the Nelson River, and claimed the land for England. Two English seamen, Luke Foxe and Thomas James, explored Hudson Bay and its west coast in 1631.

In 1670, King Charles II of England granted trading rights in the region to the Hudson's Bay Company of London. The region was called Rupert's Land. By 1690, English fur traders had fought many battles with their French-Canadian rivals, who were pushing westward into the Hudson Bay region. The company sent Henry Kelsey on an expedition to find new sources of fur. Kelsey left the company's outpost in York Factory and traveled among the Indians of central and southern Manitoba from 1690 to 1692. He persuaded many of them to bring furs north to the company trading posts. See **Hudson's Bay Company.**

In 1731, Pierre Gaultier de Varennes, Sieur de La Vérendrye, left Montreal in search of an overland route to the Pacific Ocean. He and his men were French-Canadian fur traders. They built a series of forts between the Lake Superior area and the lower Saskatchewan River. These outposts included Fort Rouge, which La Vérendrye built on the site of present-day Winnipeg in 1738. The fur trade that he established cut heavily into that of the Hudson's Bay Company.

In 1763, the British defeated the French in the French and Indian War. France gave up its Canadian lands to Great Britain, and French exploration and trade in the Manitoba region stopped. In the 1770's, the North West Company was first established in Montreal to compete with the Hudson's Bay Company. The new firm soon disbanded. A new agreement drafted in 1784 reestablished the firm and officially adopted the name North West Company. See **North West Company.**

The Red River Colony. While the two fur companies competed for trade, plans were made for the Manitoba region's first agricultural settlement. In 1811, Thomas Douglas, fifth Earl of Selkirk, obtained a land grant from the Hudson's Bay Company. It consisted of more than 100,000 square miles (260,000 square kilometers) and covered much of the present areas of Manitoba, North Dakota, and Minnesota. Between 1812 and 1816, Selkirk sent several parties of Scottish Highlanders and Irish to the Red River region around present-day Winnipeg. The immigrants founded the Red River Colony. See **Selkirk, Earl of.**

The early colonists suffered great hardships. Frosts, floods, and grasshoppers ruined many crops. At first, the settlers depended heavily on buffalo and other animals for meat. However, the colony lay in the heart of the North West Company's area of operations. As the colony expanded, there was much competition for food, especially buffalo meat. The North West Company became increasingly hostile. It turned local residents, including the *métis* (people of mixed European and Indian ancestry), against the colonists. The métis attacked the colony in 1815. In 1816, they massacred Robert Semple, the colonial governor, and 20 others in the Battle of Seven Oaks. Peace came when the North West Company and the Hudson's Bay Company merged in 1821.

The Red River Rebellion. The Dominion of Canada, a reunion of four provinces, was created in 1867. In 1868, it arranged the transfer of almost all of Rupert's Land from the Hudson's Bay Company to itself in return for 1\frac{1}{2}$ million and land concessions. This area included the Manitoba region and the Red River Colony. The métis feared they would lose their land to settlers who would rush in after the area became part of the Dominion of Canada. The métis and other local inhabitants opposed the transfer. Louis Riel, the leader of the métis, directed a rebellion in 1869. See **Red River Rebellion.**

In 1870, the Canadian government granted the métis a bill of rights in the Manitoba Act. This act made Manitoba Canada's fifth province on July 15, 1870. The new province covered only the old Red River settlement boundaries, the southeastern corner of present-day Manitoba. Winnipeg became the capital, and Alfred Boyd was the first premier.

Growth as a province. The expected rush of settlers into Manitoba began after 1870. Between 1871 and 1881, the population more than doubled, rising from 25,228 to 62,260. Most of the new arrivals came from Ontario.

In 1876, Manitoba began to export wheat. Farmers in the Red River Valley shipped wheat south along the Red River to Minnesota and to Toronto, Ont. Wheat soon replaced fur as Manitoba's most valuable product. In 1878, the first railroad in the province connected Winnipeg and St. Paul, Minn. In 1881, other lines linked Winnipeg with cities in eastern Canada and the wheat-producing regions with Lake Superior. Manitoba grain could then

Illustration (1888) by Frederic Remington; Glenbow Archives

Fur-trappers of the North West Company competed for land with farmers of the Red River Colony during the early 1800's. Several skirmishes took place, but peace was restored by 1821.

Historic Manitoba

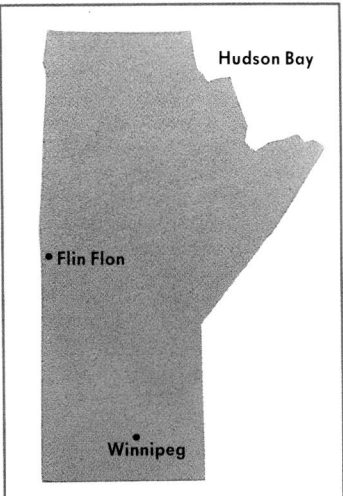

Sir Thomas Button and his crew reached the west coast of Hudson Bay in 1612. They were the first white people in the Manitoba region.

The first permanent settlement in Manitoba, the Red River Colony, was established in 1812 by Scottish and Irish settlers.

Flin Flon became a mining center in 1930 with the start of operations there by the Hudson Bay Mining and Smelting Company. Flin Flon has deposits of copper, gold, silver, and zinc.

Louis Riel led people of mixed white and Indian descent called *métis* in the Red River Rebellion in 1869.

Canada's first transcontinental train arrived in Winnipeg in 1886.

Important dates in Manitoba

WORLD BOOK illustrations by Kevin Chadwick

1612 Sir Thomas Button, leader of the first white people in Manitoba, explored the west coast of Hudson Bay.

1690-1692 Henry Kelsey of the Hudson's Bay Company explored inland from Hudson Bay to what is now southern Manitoba.

1738 Pierre Gaultier de Varennes, Sieur de La Vérendrye, a French-Canadian fur trader, arrived at the site of present-day Winnipeg.

1812 Settlers sent by the Earl of Selkirk established the Red River Colony.

1869-1870 The métis revolted against the Canadian government in the Red River Rebellion.

1870 Manitoba became Canada's fifth province.

1876 Manitoba farmers began exporting wheat.

1878 The first railroad in Manitoba connected Winnipeg and St. Paul, Minn.

1912 The Canadian government extended Manitoba's northern boundary to Hudson Bay.

1960 Nickel mining operations began in Thompson.

1969 The voters of Manitoba elected the first Socialist government in Canada outside Saskatchewan.

1972 Winnipeg and its suburbs merged into one city, making Winnipeg one of Canada's largest cities.

1985 The Supreme Court of Canada ruled that all of Manitoba's laws, written only in English, must be translated to French.

be shipped to Canadian and European markets through ports on the Great Lakes.

Beginning in the 1890's, Manitoba experienced a major wave of new settlers. Many settlers came from eastern Canada and many others from Britain and other areas of Europe. The production of grain expanded rapidly, especially from 1900 to 1913. During these prosperous years, Winnipeg became the rail center for the entire prairie region of Canada.

By 1901, Manitoba's population had increased to more than 10 times that of 1871. The Canadian government extended the provincial boundary west to what is now Saskatchewan in 1881, and east to Ontario in 1884. In 1912, the northern boundary was extended to Hudson Bay, giving Manitoba its present size and shape.

Economic developments. Manitoba's boundary extension to Hudson Bay opened up lands for mineral development, and military needs of World War I encouraged exploration. In 1915, prospectors discovered huge deposits of copper and zinc on the site of Flin Flon. Mining operations became fully developed in 1930, and the town soon began to develop rapidly. Extensive mining of gold, nickel, and silver also began during the 1930's, particularly in areas around northern Lake Winnipeg.

Cheap power, plentiful water, and availability of labor encouraged the growth of many industries during the 1920's and 1930's. A pulp and paper plant opened in Pine Falls in 1927. Fur processing and clothing trades developed rapidly in Winnipeg during the 1930's.

Political developments. Between 1878 and 1922, Manitoba was governed alternately by the Conservative and Liberal parties. The Liberal Administration of Thomas Greenway (1888-1900) presided over the expansion of railroads and settlement.

The Conservative Party, led by Sir Rodmond P. Roblin, a Winnipeg grain dealer, controlled the government from 1900 to 1915. It concentrated on economic development and boundary expansion. The Liberal government of Tobias C. Norris ran the province from 1915 to 1922 and passed much reform legislation. Some of these reforms provided for female suffrage, workmen's compensation, compulsory education to age 14, and rural farm credit. In spite of the reforms, however, Winnipeg remained a hotbed of labor unrest during World War I (1914-1918). The city's labor problems erupted into the Winnipeg General Strike of 1919, in which 52 unions struck at once. The federal government and citizens groups worked to keep the province's services running, and the strike failed.

In 1922, a group of organized farmers formed the Progressive Party. The Progressives defeated the Liberal government. They formed a new government under John Bracken, the principal of the Manitoba Agricultural College. Bracken urged a union of parties. This union occurred in 1932, when the Liberal and Progressive parties merged to form the Liberal Progressive Party.

The Great Depression of the 1930's created much hardship in Manitoba. Farm prices, especially for grain, were extremely low. The province, still dependent on agriculture, suffered widespread unemployment.

During the 1930's, two new political parties appeared in Manitoba. The Co-operative Commonwealth Federation, later called the New Democratic Party, was made up of farmers and factory workers. The other was the

Provincial Archives of Manitoba

Large oil fields near Virden were developed during the early 1950's. Geologists also discovered important deposits of copper, nickel, and zinc in Manitoba during the 1940's and 1950's.

Social Credit Party. Its members believed that governments should pay all citizens a dividend based on economic production.

The mid-1900's. World War II (1939-1945) created a great demand for Manitoba cattle, metals, wheat, and wood. Many industries built new plants in the province during the war, and manufacturing continued to grow rapidly in the late 1940's. By 1950, for the first time in Manitoba's history, manufacturing outranked agriculture as the province's main source of income.

After World War II, Manitoba began to need fewer farmworkers because of the increased use of machines and new farming methods. Thousands moved from rural areas to cities and found jobs in factories and service industries.

Geologists discovered important mineral deposits in Manitoba during the 1940's and 1950's. Copper, nickel, and zinc ores were found in a northwestern area in 1945. Oil companies developed rich oil fields near Virden in the early 1950's. In 1956, prospectors found huge nickel deposits in the Moak Lake-Mystery Lake area. The International Nickel Company of Canada, Limited (now Inco Limited), built a complex at Thompson, and nickel mining began there in 1960. Thompson became one of the world's largest nickel-producing centers.

The province continued to develop its rich sources of electric power in the 1950's and 1960's. By 1954, all rural areas had electricity. In 1963, the first laboratories began operating at the Whiteshell Nuclear Research Establishment at Pinawa, near Winnipeg. A nuclear reactor went into operation there in 1965.

The biggest growth, however, was in the service and

public sectors. By 1970, the federal, provincial, and local governments were the largest employers in Manitoba.

The Liberal Progressive Party governed Manitoba during the 1940's and most of the 1950's. The Progressive Conservative Party won power in 1958 and held it until 1969. That year, voters elected the first socialist government ever to hold office in Canada outside Saskatchewan. The government was headed by Edward R. Schreyer of the New Democratic Party. The Progressive Conservatives regained control of the government in 1977. Sterling R. Lyon became premier.

Recent developments. In the late 1970's and early 1980's, problems arose concerning French language rights. French had been removed as an official language of Manitoba in 1890. In 1979, however, this removal was ruled unconstitutional by the Supreme Court of Canada. In 1980, the constitutionality of speeding tickets issued only in English was challenged in court.

The New Democratic Party returned to power in 1981, with Howard R. Pawley as premier. The government offered the French-speaking community translation of key legislation and extension of some French-language services throughout the province in return for an end to constitutional challenges. But it was unable to enact the compromise package. In 1985, the Supreme Court of Canada ruled that all of Manitoba's 4,500 laws, which were enacted in English only, must be translated into French. In 1988, the Progressive Conservatives returned to power, with Gary Filmon as premier.

The debate over providing widespread services in French continues. The province faces other major issues as well. Much of central Winnipeg has become run down. In addition, the provincial debt has risen rapidly as the government has increased public services without a major raise in taxes. Still, because the province's economy is based on a variety of goods and services, Manitoba has remained relatively stable. The cost of living, especially in Winnipeg, is among the lowest in Canada. Provincial unemployment has remained at well under 10 per cent of the labor force. Furthermore, the province's population has grown steadily since the early 1980's.   John S. Brierley and J. M. Bumsted

Study aids

Related articles in *World Book* include:

Biographies

Bowell, Sir Mackenzie
Riel, Louis
Roy, Gabrielle
Schreyer, Edward R.
Selkirk, Earl of
Strathcona and Mount Royal, Baron of
Woodsworth, James S.

Cities and towns

Brandon
Flin Flon
Thompson
Winnipeg

Physical features

Canadian Shield
Churchill River
Hudson Bay
Lake Manitoba
Lake Winnipeg
Nelson River
Red River of the North
Saskatchewan River
Winnipeg River

Other related articles

Hudson's Bay Company
Prairie Provinces
Red River Rebellion

Outline

I. People
  A. Population
  B. Schools
  C. Libraries and museums
II. Visitor's guide
  A. Places to visit
  B. Annual events
III. Land and climate
  A. Land regions
  B. Coastline
  C. Mountains
  D. Rivers and lakes
  E. Plant and animal life
  F. Climate
IV. Economy
  A. Natural resources
  B. Service industries
  C. Manufacturing
  D. Agriculture
  E. Mining
  F. Electric power
  G. Transportation
  H. Communication
V. Government
  A. Lieutenant governor
  B. Premier
  C. Legislative Assembly
  D. Courts
  E. Local government
  F. Revenue
  G. Politics
VI. History

Questions

What is Manitoba's largest city?
Why is Manitoba called the *Keystone Province*?
How much of Manitoba do rivers and lakes cover?
Who were the *métis*? Why did they rebel in 1869?
What is the province's most important crop?
Why did the English and French Canadians fight each other during the region's early days?
Where do Manitoba's Indians and Eskimos live?
Where is Manitoba's nickel-producing center?
Which land region covers two-thirds of the province?

Additional resources

Level I
Animals of Manitoba. Ed. by Robert E. Wrigley. Manitoba Museum of Man and Nature, 1974.
Campbell, Maria. *Riel's People: How the Métis Lived.* Douglas & McIntyre (North Vancouver), 1978.
Chafe, James W. *Extraordinary Tales from Manitoba's History.* McClelland (Toronto), 1973.
Grisdale, Alex. *Wild Drums: Indian Legends of Manitoba.* Peguis (Winnipeg), 1972.
Kurelek, William. *A Prairie Boy's Winter.* Tundra (Montreal); Houghton (Boston), 1973. *A Prairie Boy's Summer.* 1984. First published in 1975.
Manitoba: Past and Present. Ed. by Denise Dawes and Thora Cooke. Peguis (Winnipeg), 1971.

Level II
Coates, Ken, and McGuinness, Fred. *Manitoba: The Province and the People.* Hurtig (Edmonton), 1987.
Jackson, James A. *The Centennial History of Manitoba.* Manitoba Historical Society (Winnipeg), 1970.
Johnson, Earl R. *Manitoba Montage.* Panther (Winnipeg), 1985.
Morton, William L. *Manitoba: A History.* 2nd ed. Univ. of Toronto Press, 1967.
Taylor, Robert R. *Manitoba.* Oxford (Don Mills, Ont.), 1981. A book of photographs.

Manitoba, Lake. See Lake Manitoba.

Manitoba, University of, is western Canada's oldest university and the largest school in Manitoba. It is a coeducational, government-supported school and has its main campus in Fort Garry, a suburb of Winnipeg. The university was founded in Winnipeg in 1877. The university offers undergraduate degrees in agriculture, architecture, arts, dentistry, education, engineering, fine arts, human ecology, law, management, medicine, medical rehabilitation, music, nursing, pharmacy, physical education and recreation studies, science, and social work. The Faculty of Graduate Studies offers graduate degrees in most of these areas. Four colleges are affiliated with the university. They are St. John's, St. Paul's, St. Andrew's, and St. Boniface colleges. St. Boniface College offers its classes in French. The University of Manitoba also has a smaller campus in Winnipeg for the health sciences. For enrollment, see **Canada** (table: Universities and colleges).   Critically reviewed by the University of Manitoba

Manitoulin Island, *MAN ih TOO lihn* (pop. 9,823), in Lake Huron, is famed for its resorts. The island is part of Ontario. It lies northwest of Georgian Bay and is separated from the north shore of Lake Huron by the North Channel. Manitoulin is formed by the northern section of the Niagara Escarpment. It is the world's largest inland island, covering an area of 1,067 square miles (2,764 square kilometers). Chippewa Indians named the island for their great god Manitou, whose home they believed it to be. Many Indians live on Manitoulin. The island has several Indian reservations. A *causeway* (raised road) from Little Current in the northeastern part of the island connects Manitoulin to mainland Ontario. Ferry service is provided between the island and the mainland.

George B. Priddle

Mann, Horace (1796-1859), played a leading part in establishing the elementary school system of the United States. He aroused public interest in educational problems. He summed up his great desire to serve humanity in his last public statement: "Be ashamed to die until you have won some victory for humanity."

Mann gave up his law practice in 1837 to become the secretary of the newly established Massachusetts State Board of Education. He fought so well for educational reforms that nearly every one of the states profited. He has been called the *Father of the Common Schools.*

Mann strengthened education in his own state through a series of laws that improved the financial support and public control of schools. He founded the first state normal school in the United States in 1839 in Lexington, Mass. This improved the quality of public school teachers. His study of European educational methods in 1843 was the subject of one of his 12 annual reports. These influential reports covered almost every phase of the problems facing the U.S. educational system.

Mann resigned from the State Board of Education in 1848 to take a seat in the U.S. House of Representatives as an antislavery Whig. Mann was defeated as a Free Soil Party candidate for governor of Massachusetts. He was president of Antioch College (now Antioch University) in Yellow Springs, Ohio, from 1853 until his death.

Mann was born on May 4, 1796, in Franklin, Mass., and graduated from Brown University. He began his public career as a member of the Massachusetts state legislature in 1827. He was elected to New York University's Hall of Fame when it was established in 1900 to honor great Americans.   Claude A. Eggertsen

Additional resources

Downs, Robert B. *Horace Mann: Champion of Public Schools.* Twayne, 1974.
Messerli, Jonathan. *Horace Mann: A Biography.* Knopf, 1972.
Tharp, Louise H. *Until Victory: Horace Mann and Mary Peabody.* Greenwood, 1977. First published in 1953.

Mann, *mahn,* **Thomas** (1875-1955), a German novelist, won the 1929 Nobel Prize for literature. His writings combine wisdom, humor, and philosophical thought. His intellectual scope, keen psychological insight, and

critical awareness of cultural and political conditions made him one of the foremost humanistic writers of his time. His writing has a tone of gentle irony, which creates an atmosphere of artistic detachment and tolerance. He often wrote in a highly stylized, stilted manner as a parody of earlier writers, especially Goethe.

A superb literary craftsman, Mann maintained a balance in his writings between the traditional realism of the 1800's and experimentation with style and structure. He was a critical, yet sympathetic, analyst of European middle class values and attitudes. The central theme in his writings is a dualism between spirit and life. Mann expressed *spirit* as intellectual refinement and creativity, and *life* as naive and unquestioning vitality. He often presented this dualism through the conflict between the attitudes of the artist and the middle class.

Mann's first novel, *Buddenbrooks* (1901), made him famous. It describes the physical decline and accompanying intellectual refinement of a merchant family similar to Mann's. Variations on this theme appear in two shorter works, *Tristan* (1903) and *Tonio Kröger* (1903). The short novel *Death in Venice* (1912) portrays a writer's moral collapse through an uncontrollable and humiliating passion for a young boy.

Mann published the novel *The Magic Mountain* in 1924, after working on it for 12 years. In the book, patients of a tuberculosis sanitarium represent the conflicting attitudes and political beliefs of European society before World War I. Mann's longest work is *Joseph and His Brothers* (1933-1943). In this series of four novels, Mann expands on the Biblical story of Joseph by analyzing it from the standpoint of psychology and mythology.

Doctor Faustus (1947) is Mann's most despairing novel. In it, a German composer rejects love and moral responsibility in favor of artistic creativity. His story symbolically parallels the rise of Nazism. *Confessions of Felix Krull, Confidence Man* (1954) is a delightful novel about a rogue's adventures in middle-class society.

Mann's essays deal with politics, literature, music, and philosophy. Collections include *Order of the Day* (1942) and *Essays of Three Decades* (1947). *Last Essays* was published in 1959, after his death. Many volumes of his letters and diaries have also been published.

Mann was born into a wealthy merchant family in Lübeck. He left Germany when the Nazis took power and lived in Switzerland from 1933 to 1938, when he moved to the United States. He became a U.S. citizen in 1944. He returned to Switzerland in 1952 and died there. His brother, Heinrich Mann, and his son, Klaus Mann, were also writers.   Werner Hoffmeister

Additional resources

Bürgin, Hans, and Mayer, Hans-Otto. *Thomas Mann: A Chronicle of His Life.* Univ. of Alabama Pr., 1969.
Feuerlicht, Ignace. *Thomas Mann.* Twayne, 1968.
Leser, Esther H. *Thomas Mann's Short Fiction: An Intellectual Biography.* Fairleigh Dickinson, 1989.
Winston, Richard. *Thomas Mann: The Making of an Artist, 1875-1911.* Knopf, 1981.

Manna, *MAN uh,* in the Old Testament, was the food given by God to the Israelites during their 40 years of wandering in the wilderness (Exod. 16 and Num. 11). It consisted of small, round, yellowish-white flakes and tasted like wafers made with honey. Manna appeared with the dew each morning. It was gathered early because it melted in the sun. The daily portion of each person was an *omer*. Estimates of the size of an omer range from about 2 quarts (1.9 liters) to about 4 quarts (3.8 liters). The people gathered up just enough food for each day. The manna spoiled and was unfit to eat if more was gathered. But twice the usual amount was said to fall on the sixth day. Each person then took two omers, because the Sabbath was a day of worship and rest. This manna stayed fresh two days. The fall stopped when the Israelites crossed into Canaan, the Promised Land. Some historians say manna was a gluey sugar from the tamarisk shrub.   H. Darrell Lance

Manned Spacecraft Center. See Johnson Space Center.

Mannerheim, Carl Gustaf Emil von (1867-1951), a Finnish military and political leader, helped found the Republic of Finland in 1919. He had a fortified line built across the Karelian Isthmus called the *Mannerheim Line*. He directed the Finnish defense against Russian invaders in the famous "Winter War" of 1939-1940, and in fighting that lasted from 1941 to 1944. He was president of Finland from 1944 to 1946.

Mannerheim was born in Villnäs, near Turku, Finland, which was then under Russian control. He served in the Russian Army in the Russo-Japanese War (1904-1905) and in World War I. An anti-Communist, Mannerheim left Russia after the Communist revolution of 1917.

Mannerheim took command of the Finnish Army in January 1918, after Finland declared its independence from Russia. In December 1918, he became *regent* (temporary ruler) of Finland, and toured Europe seeking recognition for his country and food for his people. In 1919, Mannerheim ran unsuccessfully for president of Finland. He then retired from public life until the 1930's, when he took over command of Finnish defenses.

Alfred Erich Senn

Mannerism was a style of European art that flourished from about 1520 to 1600. The style appears most fully and typically in central Italian art. However, some mannerist traits can be found in all European art of the time, including architecture and the late works of the great Renaissance artists Raphael and Michelangelo.

Mannerist artists tended to value artistic invention and imagination more than faithful reproduction of nature. Space in many mannerist paintings appears illogical or unmeasurable, with abrupt and disturbing contrasts between figures close to the viewer and those far away. Most of the paintings stress surface patterns. Strongly three-dimensional forms compressed within these patterns create an effect of confinement or of a struggle between a figure and its setting. Many figures in mannerist paintings are distorted in proportion and have contorted poses.

Mannerism was an elegant, courtly style. It flourished in Florence, Italy, where its leading representatives were Giorgio Vasari and Bronzino. The style was introduced to the French court by Rosso Fiorentino and by Francesco Primaticcio. The Venetian painter Tintoretto was influenced by the style. El Greco brought mannerism from Venice to Spain, where he developed it in his own distinctive way.

The mannerist approach to painting also influenced other arts. In architecture, the work of Italian architect Giulio Romano is a notable example. The Italians Ben-

venuto Cellini and Giovanni Bologna were the style's chief representatives in sculpture.   Eric M. Zafran

See also **Painting** (Mannerism [with picture]); **Sculpture** (Michelangelo); **Cellini, Benvenuto; Greco, El; Tintoretto.**

Manners and customs. See Custom; Etiquette.

Mannheim, *MAN hym* (pop. 294,984), is a city in southern Germany. It lies near the point where the Neckar and Rhine rivers meet (see **Germany** [political map]). Mannheim is the center of a major industrial area. Its chief products include chemicals, machinery, and precision instruments. Together with the nearby city of Ludwigshafen, it forms an important river port.

A fishing village existed on the site of Mannheim as early as the 700's. German officials began building the city there in the 1600's. They laid out the city in an orderly pattern of rectangular city blocks and constructed many buildings in the baroque style. Mannheim's chief baroque building is the Residence of the Elector. Built as a palace in the early 1700's, it now houses Mannheim University and many art treasures. Much of Mannheim was damaged in World War II (1939-1945). The damaged areas were rebuilt, giving much of Mannheim a modern appearance.   Peter H. Merkl

Manometer, *muh NAHM uh tuhr,* is an instrument used to measure the pressure of a gas or vapor. There are several types of manometers. The simplest kind consists of a U-shaped tube with both ends open. The tube contains a liquid, often mercury, which fills the bot-

Supper at Emmaus (1525), an oil painting on canvas by Jacopo Pontormo; Uffizi Gallery, Florence (SCALA/Art Resource)

A mannerist painting shows the exaggeration, distorted space, and elongated figures that give the style its strong dramatic quality. Mannerism flourished in Italy in the 1500's.

tom of the U and rises in each of the arms. The person using this type connects one of the arms to the gas whose pressure is to be measured. The other arm remains open to the atmosphere. In this way, the liquid is exposed to the pressure of the gas in one arm and atmospheric pressure in the other.

If the pressure of the gas is greater than that of the atmosphere, the liquid rises in the arm of the tube exposed to the air. The user measures the difference between the heights of the liquid in the two arms to determine the pressure of the liquid. The liquid pressure is equal to the product of the measured height difference and the *specific weight* (weight per unit volume) of the liquid. The sum of the liquid pressure and the atmospheric pressure is the gas pressure.

In some manometers, the air is removed from one arm of the tube and that end is sealed. This eliminates the need for corrections due to changes in atmospheric pressure. The difference between the levels of the liquid in the arms shows the pressure of the gas. Gas pressure is often measured in units of the height of the liquid. For example, manometers called *barometers* commonly measure atmospheric pressure in centimeters of mercury (see **Barometer**). Some manometers work on the principle of a spring attached to an indicator. The indicator moves in front of a graduated scale that gives direct pressure readings. Physicians use a type of manometer called a *sphygmomanometer* to measure blood pressure.   Richard A. Martin

Manor. See Manorialism.

Manorialism was the economic system of Europe from the end of the Roman Empire to the 1200's. The name comes from *manerium,* the Latin word for *manor,* meaning a large estate controlled by a lord and worked by *peasants.* Manors covered most of Europe. They supplied food, clothing, shelter, and nearly everything else needed by the lords and peasants.

Most manors were made up of the lord's land and small plots of land held by the peasants. The lord lived in a manor house, which was usually surrounded by a garden, an orchard, and farm buildings. The peasants' huts were clustered nearby. Most manors also included a church, a mill for grinding grain into flour, and a press for making wine.

The peasants depended on the lord for protection from enemies, for justice, and for what little government there was. The peasants farmed both the lord's land and their own. They were *bound to the soil.* This means that they were part of the property, and they remained on the land if a new lord acquired it. Unlike slaves, they could not be sold apart from the land. Peasants rarely traveled far from the manor.

The manorial system began to decline when trade and industry revived. This revival brought back an economic system based on payment with money for goods and services. Manorialism ended first in western Europe. It remained as late as the 1800's in some parts of central and eastern Europe. Large family estates in Great Britain and other parts of Europe still exist as reminders of manorialism.   Bryce Lyon

See also **Feudalism; Middle Ages; Serf; Villein.**

Manpower. See Labor force.

Mansa Musa, *MAHN sah MOO sah* (?   -1337?), was the ruler of the Mali Empire in Africa from 1312 to about 1337. He was a grandson of Sundiata Keita, an earlier Mali ruler. Mansa Musa greatly expanded the empire and made it the political and cultural leader of West Africa. He brought the trading cities of Gao and Timbuktu under his rule and made Timbuktu a center of learning.

Mansa Musa spread Islam, the Muslim religion, throughout the empire. In 1324, he traveled to Mecca, the holy city of the Muslims. Mansa Musa's party supposedly included thousands of his people and hundreds of camels bearing gold and gifts. He brought back many learned people, including an architect who designed *mosques* (Muslim houses of worship) for Gao and Timbuktu. After Mansa Musa died, his son, Mansa Maghan I, became ruler of the empire.   Leo Spitzer

Mansfield, Arabella Babb (1846-1911), was the first woman admitted to the practice of law in the United States. She did not work as a lawyer but instead pursued a college teaching career.

Mansfield was born on a farm near Burlington, Iowa, and graduated from Iowa Wesleyan College. Her original name was Belle Aurelia Babb, but she came to be called Arabella. In 1868, she married John Melvin Mansfield, a professor of natural history. The couple joined the faculty of Iowa Wesleyan, where Arabella taught English and history. She studied law and was admitted to the legal profession in 1869. In 1870, she helped found the Iowa Woman Suffrage Association, which worked to gain voting rights for women.

In 1879, the Mansfields moved to Indiana Asbury University, now DePauw University. There, Arabella became dean of the school of art in 1893 and dean of the school of music in 1894. She held both positions until her death.   June Sochen

Mansfield, Katherine (1888-1923), a British author, wrote symbolic short stories about everyday human experiences and inner feelings. She has often been compared to the Russian author Anton Chekhov in her mastery of the forms of short fiction. Many of her stories are studies of childhood, based on her early years in Wellington, New Zealand.

Mansfield often used herself and her brother as models for the main characters. Her stories were published in *In a German Pension* (1911), *Prelude* (1918), *Bliss* (1920), and *The Garden Party* (1927). Her *Journal* (1927) gives a fascinating picture of her mind and the development of her writing.

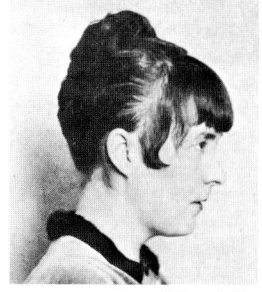
Bettmann Archive
Katherine Mansfield

Katherine Mansfield was born Kathleen Mansfield Beauchamp in Wellington. She began her literary career after moving to England in 1908. She suffered from tuberculosis, and spent much of her life in hospitals and sanitariums.   Jane Marcus

Mansfield, Mike (1903-   ), a Montana Democrat, served as majority leader of the United States Senate from 1961 to 1977, longer than any other person. He served as a member of the U.S. House of Representatives for 10 years before he was elected to the Senate in 1952. From 1977 to 1988, he was U.S. ambassador to

Japan under Presidents Jimmy Carter and Ronald Reagan. Mansfield also carried out foreign assignments for Presidents Dwight D. Eisenhower, John F. Kennedy, and Lyndon B. Johnson.

Michael Joseph Mansfield was born in New York City and was raised in Montana. At the age of 14, he dropped out of eighth grade and joined the U.S. Navy. He served as a seaman during World War I, spent the next year as a private in the U.S. Army, and was in the U.S. Marine Corps from 1920 to 1922. Mansfield worked as a miner and mining engineer from 1922 to 1930. Although he never went to high school, he graduated from Montana State University in 1933 and earned a master's degree there in 1934. Mansfield taught Latin-American and Far Eastern history at Montana State until he entered Congress in 1943. Mansfield served in the U.S. Senate from 1953 to 1977.   William J. Eaton

Mansfield, Richard (1854-1907), was the leading actor in the American theater from the 1880's to the early 1900's. Mansfield won acclaim for his performances in such classics as *Richard III* and *Henry V* by William Shakespeare. He also starred in works by modern playwrights, notably George Bernard Shaw and Henrik Ibsen. Mansfield became especially popular for his skillful physical impersonation of characters. His most famous performance was in the dual role of Dr. Jekyll and Mr. Hyde, in a dramatic adaptation of a famous horror story by Robert Louis Stevenson.

Mansfield was born in Berlin, Germany, to an English father and a Dutch mother. He lived in England and elsewhere in Europe before coming to the United States at the age of 18. Mansfield moved back to England in 1877. He made his American professional acting debut in 1882.   Stanley L. Glenn

Manslaughter is the legal term for the wrongful unplanned killing of another person. It is different from *murder* in that it is not done with malice.

The law recognizes two kinds of manslaughter, *voluntary* and *involuntary.* Voluntary manslaughter, also called *nonnegligent manslaughter,* is a killing done in a heated moment, without previous plan, and in reaction to provocation by the victim. This provocation is such that it would enrage a person for a period in which an ordinary person would not have calmed down. A person who kills someone in a violent quarrel without first planning to do so is guilty of voluntary manslaughter. Involuntary manslaughter, also called *manslaughter by negligence,* is done while the offender is engaged in some wrongful act. If a reckless driver kills someone, the driver is guilty of involuntary manslaughter.

Punishment for manslaughter varies by state and country. The usual penalty in the United States is imprisonment for 1 to 14 years.   Charles F. Wellford

See also **Homicide; Murder.**

Manson, Sir Patrick (1844-1922), a Scottish physician, was called the *father of tropical medicine.* He demonstrated in 1877 that the parasite *Filaria* caused the disease elephantiasis. He later showed that mosquitoes carried the parasite (see **Filaria**). In 1894, Manson suggested that mosquitoes also transmitted malaria to human beings, a theory later proven by the British physician Sir Ronald Ross (see **Ross, Sir Ronald**). In 1900, Manson confirmed Ross's findings.

Manson was born in Aberdeenshire (now Grampian Region), Scotland. Soon after graduating from the Aberdeen Medical School in 1866, he traveled to China, where he worked for 24 years. He helped establish the London School of Tropical Medicine in 1899.   Kenneth R. Manning

Manta ray. See **Ray; Fish** (picture: Fish of coastal waters and the open ocean).

Mantegna, *mahn TEH nyah,* **Andrea,** *ahn DREH ah* (1431-1506), was a leading painter of the Italian Renaissance. He painted sculpturelike figures that are sharply outlined and precisely detailed. The surfaces of his figures seem like marble. Mantegna used perspective for dramatic effects, with many figures appearing as if seen from below. He was also a famous engraver. Mantegna's engravings influenced many other painters, including the famous German artist Albrecht Dürer.

Mantegna was born in Isola di Carturo, Italy, near Padua. He received his early art training in Padua and soon earned a reputation as a painter. In 1459 or 1460,

The Risen Christ Between Saint Andrew and Saint Longinus (about 1500); Rijksprentenkabinet, Rijksmuseum, Amsterdam, the Netherlands

An engraving by Mantegna shows the sculpturelike figures and precise details that are typical of the artist's style.

he entered the service of the ruling Gonzaga family in Mantua. Mantegna spent the rest of his life there and painted the Gonzagas in superb frescoes. One of these frescoes, *Family and Court of Ludovico Gonzaga II,* is shown in the **Painting** article. Mantegna also painted several portraits and altarpieces.   David Summers

See also **Engraving** (picture: A Renaissance engraving); **Fresco** (picture); **Jesus Christ** (picture: Jesus was arrested); **Renaissance** (picture: The ruling families).

Mantid is an insect that is sometimes called *praying mantis* because it usually holds its front legs as if it were praying. Most mantids live in tropical or warm climates. But the *European mantid* is native to cool parts of Europe. It was introduced to the Rochester, N. Y., area about 1899 and has since spread through the Eastern United States.

Mantids prey on other insects, including other man-

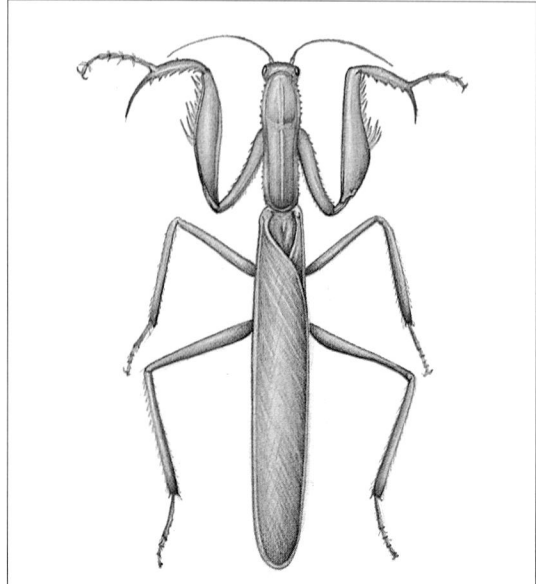

WORLD BOOK illustration by Shirley Hooper, Oxford Illustrators Limited

The mantid has armlike forelegs with sharp hooks used to hold its food. The insect's slender body and green color allow it to escape attention on the plants on which it lives.

tids. They even seize and eat small tree frogs. A female mantid will sometimes devour her own mate, but the male is able to continue mating with the female even after his head and brain have been eaten.

A full-grown mantid measures from 2 to 5 inches (5 to 13 centimeters) in length, depending on the species. Mantids resemble the color, and sometimes the form, of the plants on which they stay. As a result, predators often fail to see them. A mantid uses its armlike forelegs to grasp and capture its prey. The forelegs have sharp spines and hooks that hold captives.

Female mantids lay their eggs in masses. The eggs can be found attached to trees and shrubs during the winter when leaves no longer hide them. The eggs are light brown and ribbed.

Scientific classification. Mantids are usually classified in the order Orthoptera. They make up the mantid family, Mantidae. Some scientists classify mantids in the order Mantodea.

James E. Lloyd

See also **Life** (picture).

Mantissa. See **Logarithms** (Common logarithms).
Mantle is a membrane or a tissue. See **Shell** (How shells are formed); **Oyster** (Shell; diagram).
Mantle. See **Earth** (Inside the earth); **Plate tectonics.**
Mantle, Mickey (1931-   ), ranks among the leading home run hitters in baseball history. Mantle hit 536 home runs in regular season play. He spent his entire major league career with the New York Yankees —from 1951 through 1968. He mainly played center field and was a switch hitter.

Mantle led the American League in home runs four times. He was named the most valuable player in the American League three times. Mantle hit 18 World Series home runs, a record. Unlike most sluggers, he had great speed. However, various leg injuries reduced

Mantle's base running effectiveness during the 1960's.

Mickey Charles Mantle was born in Spavinaw, Okla. He was elected to the National Baseball Hall of Fame in 1974. Mantle's autobiography, *The Mick,* was published in 1985.   Dave Nightingale

Mantra. See **Buddhism** (The Mantrayana); **Transcendental meditation.**
Manu, *MAN oo,* in Hindu mythology, was the man who systematized the religious and social laws of Hinduism. These ancient laws are called the *Manu Smriti* (*Code of Manu*). They still influence the religious and social life of India, where Hinduism is the chief religion. The *Manu Smriti* has three main parts: (1) *varna,* (2) *ashrama,* and (3) *dharma.*

Varna sets forth the basis of *caste,* the strict Hindu class system. Hinduism has four major *varnas* (groups of castes). See **Hinduism** (Caste).

Ashrama describes the four ideal stages of a Hindu man's life. First, he studies Hindu scriptures called the *Vedas,* and the duties of his caste. Second, he marries. Third, after he fulfills his family obligations, he retires with his wife to a forest to meditate. Finally, in old age, the husband and wife separate and wander as beggars called *sannyasis,* preparing for death.

Dharma describes the four goals of life. They are (1) *dharma*—fulfilling one's religious obligation in society, (2) *kama*—enjoying sex and other physical pleasures, (3) *artha*—achieving worldly success through one's occupation, and (4) *moksha*—gaining spiritual release from worldly existence.   Charles S. J. White

Manual training. See **Industrial arts.**
Manuel II. See **Portugal** (The first Portuguese republic).
Manuelito, *mahn yoo ayl EE toh* (1818?-1893), was a leader of the Navajo Indians. He played an important part in the Navajos' fight to prevent white settlers from taking over their land.

In 1860, following conflicts between the Navajos and the settlers, Manuelito helped lead an attack on Fort Defiance in what is now Arizona. The next year, he and other Navajo leaders signed a peace treaty with the United States. But fighting soon broke out again. In 1863 and 1864, U.S. Army troops led by the frontiersman Kit Carson forced thousands of Navajos to surrender. The Army did not capture Manuelito, but he surrendered in 1866.

In 1868, the United States government established a reservation for the Navajos in what became parts of Arizona, New Mexico, and Utah. Manuelito headed the first Navajo police force, which was founded in 1872 to protect the reservation. He was probably born in Bear's Ears, near what is now Moab, Utah.

Smithsonian Institution, National Anthropological Archives, Washington, D.C.
Manuelito

Ruth W. Roessel

Manufactured home. See **Mobile home.**
Manufacturers, National Association of. See **National Association of Manufacturers.**

Manufacturing is the industry that makes automobiles, books, clothing, furniture, paper, pencils, and thousands of other products. The word *manufacture* comes from the Latin words *manus* (hand) and *facere* (to make). Today, manufacturing means the making of articles by machinery as well as by hand.

Manufacturing plants have great importance to the welfare of their communities. When a factory hires 100 workers, for example, it also creates about 175 jobs outside the factory. These include jobs for people in restaurants, stores, and other businesses that provide the factory employees with goods and services.

Until the early 1900's, the world's greatest manufacturing centers were in western Europe. The United States became the leading manufacturing nation during World War I. Since then, the United States has ranked as the world's greatest producer of manufactured goods.

Manufacturing is an important industry in the United States and Canada. It earns about one-fifth of the *gross domestic product* (GDP) of each nation. GDP is the value of all the goods and services produced in a country within a given period. Manufacturing employs about one-fifth of the two nations' workers.

Kinds of manufacturing

Manufactured items may be divided into heavy or light, and durable or nondurable goods. A *durable* product lasts for a long time. A *nondurable* product is used up quickly. A locomotive is a heavy durable product. A loaf of bread is a light nondurable item.

All manufactured products are either consumer goods or producer goods. Retail stores, such as groceries or drugstores, sell *consumer goods* to millions of buyers. These products include radios, rugs, food, and thousands of other items. *Producer goods* are products used to make other products. They include springs, bearings, printing presses, and many other items.

Manufacturing around the world

Manufacturing industries are usually located in regions that have abundant natural resources, good transportation, mild climates, and large populations. North America, Europe, and Asia rank as leaders in all these categories. Together they produce more than 90 per cent of the world's manufactured goods.

In the United States, manufacturing companies operate more than 360,000 factories. These companies include individually owned firms, partnerships, and corporations. Much of the money invested in manufacturing is for the plant and equipment. The rest is represented by the inventory of materials waiting to be worked on or sold. Manufacturing firms employ about 18 million people and account for about $19 of every $100 earned in the nation.

Most big U.S. manufacturers are near large cities. The 15 major manufacturing regions, in order of importance, are Los Angeles-Long Beach, Chicago, New York City, Philadelphia, Detroit, Houston, Dallas-Fort Worth, Boston, St. Louis, Rochester, Newark, San Francisco-Oakland, Cleveland, Milwaukee, and Baltimore. See **United States** (Manufacturing).

In Canada. Canada ranks among the leading manufacturing countries. Its major manufacturing industry produces transportation equipment. Other important in-

Leading manufactured products in the United States

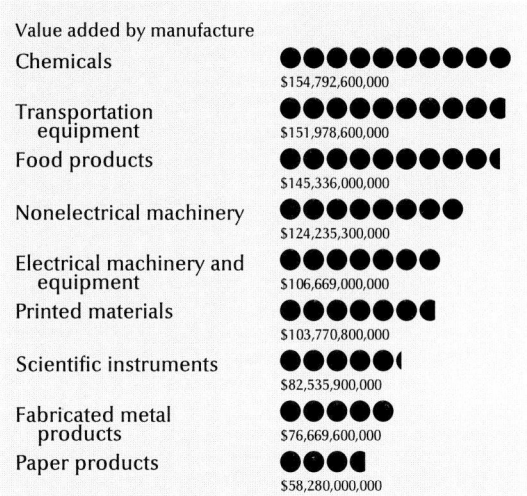

Value added by manufacture

Chemicals	$154,792,600,000
Transportation equipment	$151,978,600,000
Food products	$145,336,000,000
Nonelectrical machinery	$124,235,300,000
Electrical machinery and equipment	$106,669,000,000
Printed materials	$103,770,800,000
Scientific instruments	$82,535,900,000
Fabricated metal products	$76,669,600,000
Paper products	$58,280,000,000

Figures are for 1991. Source: U.S. Bureau of the Census.

dustries make food products, paper products, chemicals, electrical machinery and equipment, and primary metals. Ontario produces about half of Canada's manufactured goods. Quebec produces about a fourth. The nation has about 39,000 factories that employ about 2 million people. They produce goods with a *value added by manufacture* of about $110 billion a year in United States dollars. This figure represents the value created in products by industries, not counting such costs as materials, supplies, and fuel. See **Canada** (Manufacturing).

In Europe. Europe ranks after the United States as the world's main manufacturing region. The major

Leading manufacturing states and provinces

Value added by manufacture

California	$144,907,800,000
New York	$85,480,200,000
Texas	$79,394,700,000
Ohio	$79,244,400,000
Illinois	$70,015,700,000
Michigan	$66,131,000,000
Pennsylvania	$62,713,500,000
North Carolina	$56,417,600,000
Ontario	$55,176,100,000
New Jersey	$45,064,700,000

Figures are for 1989. Sources: U.S. Bureau of the Census; Statistics Canada.

50 leading U.S. manufacturers

Manufacturer	Sales*	Assets*	Employees
1. General Motors	132,775	191,013	750,000
2. Exxon	103,547	85,030	95,000
3. Ford Motor	100,786	180,545	325,333
4. International Business Machines	65,096	86,705	308,010
5. General Electric	62,202	192,876	268,000
6. Mobil	57,389	40,561	63,700
7. Philip Morris	50,157	50,014	161,000
8. E. I. du Pont de Nemours	37,643	38,870	125,000
9. Chevron	37,464	33,970	49,245
10. Texaco	37,130	25,992	37,582
11. Chrysler	36,897	40,653	128,000
12. Boeing	30,184	18,147	158,600
13. Procter & Gamble	29,890	24,025	106,200
14. Amoco	25,543	28,453	47,400
15. PepsiCo	22,084	20,951	372,000
16. United Technologies	22,032	15,928	178,000
17. Shell Oil	21,702	26,970	25,308
18. ConAgra	21,219	9,759	80,787
19. Eastman Kodak	20,577	23,138	132,600
20. Dow Chemical	19,177	25,360	61,353
21. Xerox	18,261	34,051	99,300
22. Atlantic Richfield	18,061	24,256	26,800
23. McDonnell Douglas	17,513	13,781	87,377
24. Hewlett-Packard	16,427	13,700	92,600
25. USX	16,186	17,252	45,582
26. RJR Nabisco Holdings	15,734	32,041	64,000
27. Digital Equipment	14,027	11,284	113,800
28. Minnesota Mining & Mfg. ...	13,883	11,955	87,015
29. Johnson & Johnson	13,846	11,884	84,900
30. Tenneco	13,606	16,584	79,000
31. International Paper	13,600	16,459	73,000
32. Motorola	13,341	10,629	107,000
33. Sara Lee	13,321	9,989	128,000
34. Coca-Cola	13,238	11,052	31,000
35. Westinghouse Electric	12,100	10,398	109,050
36. Allied-Signal	12,089	10,756	89,300
37. Phillips Petroleum	11,933	11,468	21,400
38. Goodyear Tire and Rubber .	11,924	8,564	95,712
39. Georgia-Pacific	11,847	10,890	52,000
40. Bristol-Myers Squibb	11,805	10,804	52,600
41. Anheuser-Busch	11,401	10,538	41,000
42. IBP	11,130	1,499	27,500
43. Rockwell International	10,995	9,731	78,685
44. Caterpillar	10,194	13,935	50,749
45. Lockheed	10,138	6,754	71,700
46. Coastal	10,063	10,580	16,570
47. Merck	9,801	11,086	38,400
48. Ashland Oil	9,596	5,668	33,700
49. Aluminum Co. of America ...	9,588	11,023	63,600
50. Archer Daniels Midland	9,344	7,525	13,524

*In millions of dollars. Figures may include income from nonmanufacturing activities.
Source: "The Fortune 500," *Fortune,* April 19, 1993, © 1993 Time Inc. All rights reserved.

manufacturing nations of Western Europe are France, Germany, Italy, the Netherlands, Spain, Sweden, and the United Kingdom. Major manufacturing nations of Eastern Europe include Poland, Russia, and Ukraine. See **Europe** (Manufacturing); **European Community.**

In Asia, large-scale manufacturing is mostly centered in China, India, Japan, Russia, South Korea, and Taiwan. Most countries produce only a few goods which workers make by hand. But Asia leads the world in silk production. Japan is a major manufacturer of such products as automobiles, machine tools, radios, and steel. Today, Japan manufactures more products than any Western European country. See **Asia** (Industry).

In Africa, there is almost no manufacturing. The continent has poor transportation and includes vast areas with sparse populations. Africa has about a third of the world's potential water power. But most of the sites for power plants are in regions where it would be difficult to develop industries. Less than 1 per cent of Africa's available water power is used. See **Africa** (Manufacturing).

In Latin America, manufacturing has gradually increased in importance. The region's leading manufacturing countries include Brazil and Mexico, which make such products as automobiles, chemicals, and steel. Many nations produce cement, processed foods, and textiles. A number of countries, including Mexico and Venezuela, manufacture petroleum products.

The main steps in manufacturing

Design and engineering. Manufacturers must design products that will be easy and safe to use, without being too expensive to make and ship. Makers of consumer goods often change the styles of their products. The new designs attract the public's interest and frequently include improvements on the old styles.

After the basic product design has been determined, engineers with different skills work to produce instructions for making the product. They often build and test a *prototype* (sample of the product) before selling the item.

Purchasing. The raw materials and purchased parts used in making the finished product must be bought and delivered to the plant. Raw materials come from farms, forests, fisheries, mines, and quarries. Some manufacturers, such as those that make food products, buy most of their raw materials from nearby areas. Others may require raw materials that must be shipped from the other side of the world. For example, Ohio manufacturers make the most tires in the world. But the rubber for these factories comes from Asia. Some manufacturers purchase parts that are already made. For example, automobile manufacturers buy finished tires and use them to build their own finished product—automobiles.

Making products involves one or more of three processes. These processes are (1) synthetic, (2) analytic, and (3) conditioning.

Manufacturers who use the *synthetic* process mix ingredients or assemble ready-made parts. A paint manufacturer mixes chemicals to produce paint, and an automobile company assembles parts to make a car.

In the *analytic* process, the manufacturer breaks down a raw material. Oil refineries break crude oil down into gasoline, oil, and other parts. A hog goes through an analytic process at a packing house and comes out as ham, bacon, and other pork products.

The *conditioning* process changes the form of raw materials. Ore from mines becomes ingots (bricks) or sheets of metal, which then may be formed into usable parts. Rocks from quarries are made into gravel.

Besides making the product, a manufacturer must have a system of *quality control.* Specially trained workers check the raw materials and examine the finished products. They make sure that the products meet company standards. Careful *production control* is also essential. Experts make sure that the right materials in the right amounts go to the proper place at the proper time.

Distribution and sales account for a large part of the prices we pay for products. For example, 1 gallon

25 leading manufacturers outside the United States

Manufacturer	Sales*	Employees	Manufacturer	Sales*	Employees
1. Royal Dutch/Shell Group			**14. Siemens** (Germany)	39,228	373,000
(Netherlands/Great Britain)	107,204	761,400	**15. Nestle** (Switzerland)	33,359	199,021
2. Toyota Motor (Japan)	64,516	96,849	**16. Elf Aquitaine** (France)	32,939	90,000
3. IRI (Italy)	61,443	419,500	**17. Philips' Gloeilampenfabrieken**		
4. British Petroleum (Great Britain)	59,541	116,750	(Netherlands)	30,866	272,800
5. Daimler-Benz (Germany)	54,259	376,785	**18. Toshiba** (Japan)	30,182	142,000
6. Hitachi (Japan)	50,686	290,891	**19. Renault** (France)	30,050	157,378
7. Fiat (Italy)	47,752	303,238	**20. Peugeot** (France)	29,380	191,100
8. Samsung (South Korea)	45,052	†	**21. BASF** (Germany)	29,184	134,647
9. Volkswagen (Germany)	43,710	268,744	**22. Hoechst** (Germany)	27,750	172,890
10. Matsushita Electric			**23. Asea Brown Boveri**		
Industrial (Japan)	43,516	198,299	(Switzerland)	27,705	215,154
11. ENI (Italy)	41,762	130,745	**24. Honda Motor** (Japan)	27,070	79,200
12. Nissan Motor (Japan)	40,217	129,546	**25. Alcatel Alsthom** (France)	26,456	205,500
13. Unilever (Great Britain/Netherlands)	39,971	304,000			

*In millions of dollars. Figures may include income from nonmanufacturing activities.
†Not available

Source: "The Fortune Directory," *Fortune*, July 29, 1991, © 1991 Time, Inc.

(3.8 liters) of paint costs much more than the chemicals and labor needed to manufacture it. The final price of a product includes the costs of advertising, packaging, shipping, storage, commissions to salespeople, office work, and taxes. In addition to these costs, the price must give a fair profit to the manufacturer, the wholesalers, and the retailers.

How science helps manufacturing

Engineers and scientists continually experiment and search for new materials that will improve manufactured items. As a result of research since the early 1800's, manufacturers use hundreds of kinds of plastics. Plastics products have replaced less sturdy, less attractive, and more expensive materials. See **Plastics**.

Research not only develops new products, but also finds new uses for old ones. In addition, it leads to lower prices as manufacturers discover more efficient ways to make products. For example, until automobile companies developed the assembly-line method of manufacturing in the early 1900's, only the wealthiest families could afford automobiles (see **Assembly line**).

Steps in manufacturing

The steps in manufacturing are the same for nearly all types of products, including the automobile tires shown in the photographs at the right. First, the manufacturer designs the product. For example, tire treads may be designed using a computer. Next, the producer buys the raw materials, such as bales of rubber from Indonesia. Then, the manufacturer produces and inspects the product. Finally, the products are distributed to stores where customers may examine and purchase them. New methods and materials for conducting electricity have led to the development of many new products, including computers, industrial robots, and video games.

Designing the product

Obtaining the raw materials

Making the product

Goodyear Tire and Rubber Company

Selling the product

Widespread industrial research began after World War I, when research became more and more important as a part of manufacturing. Today, companies in the United States spend about $50 billion a year for industrial research. About 500,000 scientists and engineers take part in research work performed by about 15,000 companies.

How governments help manufacturing

Thousands of government laws and regulations protect a manufacturer's property. The government also provides legal ways to buy and sell property and to establish companies. Government helps keep money stable so that its value does not change greatly from day to day and from one area to another. The government permits manufacturers to patent new products or methods that they have developed (see **Patent**).

Governments furnish businesses with statistics that help them plan their sales and purchases. They give manufacturers loans at low rates of interest, and sometimes give them *subsidies,* or outright grants (see **Subsidy**). Governments protect home industries by levying tariffs on goods imported from other countries (see **Tariff**). Many nations encourage manufacturers to build factories by not levying taxes on their profits for a certain number of years. The U.S. government also provides funding to colleges and universities for manufacturing-related research. Ronald G. Askin

Related articles. See the section on *Manufacturing* in each state, province, and country article. See also articles on specific products such as **Automobile.** Other related articles include:

Aviation	Forest products	Printing
Careers (Manufac-	Industrial Revolution	Publishing
turing)	Industry	Technology
Ceramics	Machine	Textile
Clothing	Mass production	Transportation
Factory	Metal	Value added by
Food	Plastics	manufacture

Manure is any substance produced by animals or plants that is used as fertilizer. Most manure consists of animal waste mixed with straw or hay from barnyards, though it may be pure animal waste. This waste is collected and spread onto fields. When it decays, it releases important nutrients that enrich the soil and aid plant growth. Manure also loosens the soil and improves its ability to absorb water. A special kind of manure called *green manure* is obtained from plants that are plowed into the soil and allowed to decay.

The content of animal manure varies widely, depending on the kind of manure and whether it is fresh, dried, or partly decayed. Most animal manure in the United States is from the wastes of cattle and chickens. Horses, hogs, and sheep also provide manure. Animal manure is an excellent source of *organic matter* (substances containing carbon) for the soil. But it is low in such important nutrients as nitrogen, phosphorus, and potassium. In general, it takes about 2,000 pounds (907 kilograms) of manure to supply as much of these three substances as 100 pounds (45 kilograms) of a commercial fertilizer.

The most common green manure plants are grasses and *legumes.* Legumes are plants that belong to the pea family. They include alfalfa, beans, clover, and peas. Grasses and legumes provide the soil with organic matter and large amounts of nitrogen. Taylor J. Johnston

See also **Fertilizer.**

Manuscript is a term for any document written by hand or by a machine such as a typewriter or a personal computer. The word is often used to distinguish an author's original version of a work from the printed copy. In addition, manuscript refers to any handwritten document from ancient times until the introduction of printing in the 1400's. This article discusses such historical manuscripts.

Most manuscripts can be identified with certain times or areas by the material on which they were written. In ancient times, for example, people living around the Mediterranean Sea wrote manuscripts on papyrus, leather, and wax tablets. During the Middle Ages, manuscripts were written on parchment and on a refined form of parchment called *vellum.* By the 1400's, paper was replacing parchment for manuscripts. Paper made practical the printed books that became the principal means of transmitting the written word.

Ancient and medieval manuscripts tell about the lives and activities of people who lived hundreds and even thousands of years ago. Scholars learn from manuscripts about business transactions, customs and laws, family affairs, literature, government, and religious beliefs. Many of these manuscripts are also considered works of art because they are beautifully decorated or painted.

Manuscripts of the ancient Near East

Papyrus manuscripts. Papyrus was the principal writing material of the ancient Egyptians, Greeks, and Romans who lived in the lands surrounding the Mediterranean Sea. Papyrus manuscripts appeared as early as 2700 B.C. and continued in use even after parchment books became common in the A.D. 300's.

Papyrus was made from a tall, reedlike plant that grew in the swamps of the Nile River in Egypt. Papyrus was manufactured from the stem of the plant by removing the hard rind and cutting the fibrous core into long strips that were pressed together into sheets. The sheets, in turn, were pasted together to form scrolls or rolls. The scrolls varied in size but they averaged about 1 foot (0.3 meter) wide and 20 feet (6 meters) long.

The papyrus scroll was the manuscript book of the ancient world, but it had drawbacks. First, papyrus was a vegetable substance that decayed rapidly in damp climates. While it was satisfactory in the dry climate of Egypt, it was not durable enough for the damper European weather. Second, the scroll was awkward to read and difficult to use if the reader only wanted to locate one portion of the manuscript. Finally, it was possible to write on only one side of the papyrus.

Wax tablets. People of the Greek and Roman worlds also wrote on wax tablets with a sharp, pointed instrument called a *stylus.* On the end opposite the point, the stylus had a flat or rounded surface, which was used to erase the writing by smoothing the wax. Sometimes, several wax tablets were laced together on one side to form a *codex,* which became the ancestor of the book.

Parchment manuscripts. Parchment was made from cleaned and scraped skins, chiefly sheep, goat, or calf skins. It was an improved version of the animal skins used for ancient Persian and Hebrew religious writings. Sheets of parchment were trimmed into rectangles. About four sheets were stacked together, folded, and

Trinity College, Dublin, Ireland, The Green Studio Ltd.

The Book of Kells is an illuminated manuscript of the Gospels created in Ireland between the mid-700's and early 800's.

sewed at the fold to form a gathering. The entire manuscript could be bound between boards into a codex.

The parchment codex was more durable than the older papyrus scroll that it largely replaced. It could be read more easily, and could be conveniently stored on a shelf. Papyrus scrolls were often kept in bins or boxes. Both sides of parchment could also be used for writing.

Other manuscripts. Other materials were used for ancient manuscripts. From about 3500 B.C., the peoples of Mesopotamia wrote on small clay tablets that were baked like bricks to preserve them. Some manuscripts were written on the bark of various trees, on wood, or on thin sheets of copper that were rolled up.

Manuscripts of the ancient Far East

Paper manuscripts. The Chinese had invented paper by A.D. 1. Their first books written on paper took the form of scrolls. Later, they made books by folding long strips of paper into accordionlike pleats.

Before the Chinese invented paper, they wrote on bones and silk. They also wrote on bamboo strips that measured about $\frac{1}{4}$ inch (0.6 centimeter) wide and 6 to 9 inches (15 to 23 centimeters) long. They wrote on the strips in column form from top to bottom. Then they tied the strips together with string in much the same way that bamboo screens and window shades are made.

Palm leaf manuscripts. In ancient India and some surrounding lands, the people also made books of strips, only cut from palm leaves. They used strips about $1\frac{1}{2}$ to 3 inches (4 to 8 centimeters) wide and 24 inches (61

centimeters) or more long. They made holes in the strips and then strung them together, forming the books.

European manuscripts of the Middle Ages

Parchment and vellum were the chief writing materials in Europe during the Middle Ages. They were generally replaced by the 1400's by the adoption of paper and the invention of printing.

Monks produced most manuscripts in special workshops called *scriptoria* in their monasteries. The monks were often assisted by outside craftsmen. The manuscript writers were called *scribes.* Their work was highly specialized. One group of monks produced the parchment and another group did the writing. A third group decorated the manuscripts with designs or paintings, and a fourth group bound the finished pages into books. Monasteries traded manuscripts for books made in other monasteries, and some were sold.

Medieval scribes made important contributions to the development of modern books. For example, scribes separated words with spaces, while the Greeks and Romans had run words together without spacing. The scribes used capital and small letters and established a system of punctuation to make reading easier. Most of these developments occurred in the Carolingian period, during the late 700's and 800's in the scriptoria of what are now France and western Germany.

Many manuscripts of the Middle Ages were beautifully decorated in various colors. Often, gold or silver leaf was used on the initial letters and the decoration. Such manuscripts were called *illuminated,* because they looked as if they had been lit from inside. Today, we use the term *illuminated* to refer to any decorated manuscript, whether or not it has gold or silver.

Distinctive styles of illumination developed in differ-

Newberry Library, Ayer Collection

Aztec manuscript of the mid-1500's shows property records of a Mexican village. It is made of fiber from the maguey plant.

ent parts of Europe. There were, for example, Byzantine, English, French, Irish, and Italian styles of illumination. All these styles used six basic forms of decoration: (1) animals and human figures, (2) branches with leaves or berries, (3) geometric designs, (4) ornamental letters, (5) *plaits* (braids), and (6) scrollwork.

Many books produced during the Middle Ages were Bibles, parts of the Bible, or other religious books. There were also many nonreligious books produced, including *bestiaries* (books about animals), romances, histories, legends, and writings by ancient Greeks and Romans.

Illustrated manuscripts

Some of the oldest illustrated manuscripts in existence are copies of the Egyptian *Book of the Dead*. These scrolls date from the 18th Dynasty (1554-1304 B.C.). The Egyptians placed copies of the book, which contained prayers and hymns, in their tombs. Illustrated papyrus rolls were also common in ancient Greece and Rome.

After the codex form came into use, illustrations took on greater importance as they occupied more space on a page and were framed in decorative borders. Full-page illustrations appeared during the early Middle Ages. Portraits, which were derived from Greek, Roman, or Byzantine models, began to appear in the late 700's.

By the 1000's, the custom had developed of beginning some sections of a manuscript with a small picture called a *miniature*. Some miniatures were painted within the large initial letter, called a *historiated* initial, that began a manuscript section.   Paul H. Mosher

Related articles in *World Book* include:

Bible (pictures)	Gothic art (picture)	Paper
Book (History)	Hieroglyphics	Papyrus
Calligraphy	Library (History)	Parchment
Carolingian art	Limbourg, Pol de	Scribe
City (pictures)	Middle Ages (pictures)	Scroll
England (picture: The Battle of Crécy)	Painting (Medieval)	World, History of the (picture: Medieval monks)
Europe (pictures)	Paleography	Writing

Manx. See Cat (Breeds of cats); **Man, Isle of.**
Manzanita, *MAN zuh NEE tuh,* is the name of a group of evergreen shrubs that grow chiefly from British Columbia to California. The shrubs measure about 3 to 13

WORLD BOOK illustration by Stuart Lafford, Linden Artists Ltd.

A manzanita plant has bright red berries and attractive, oval leaves. Manzanitas are popular ornamental shrubs.

feet (0.9 to 4 meters) in height. Their leaves have smooth edges. White hairs cover the undersurface of the leaves. The small, bell-shaped flowers of manzanitas are pink or white. The fruit of manzanitas is red and fleshy. See also **Heath; Madroña.**

Scientific classification. Manzanitas belong to the genus *Arctostaphylos* in the heath family, Ericaceae.   James L. Luteyn

Manzoni, *mahnd ZAW nee,* **Alessandro,** *ah lehs SAHN draw* (1785-1873), ranks as one of Italy's greatest novelists on the basis of his only novel, *The Betrothed.* This work, published in 1827 and again with revisions from 1840 to 1842, set the standard for modern Italian prose. *The Betrothed* is a long historical story set in Lombardy during the 1600's, when the province was ruled by Spain. It describes the adventures of two simple young silk weavers, Renzo and Lucia, whose marriage is prevented by a local tyrant, Don Rodrigo. The story is set against the background of larger historical events, including a war, a plague, and a famine.

Manzoni was born in Milan. At the age of 16, he began writing poetry, classical in style and patriotic in inspiration and content. Manzoni was baptized a Roman Catholic, but paid little attention to his faith until 1810. He then underwent a crisis that led him back to Catholicism. That crisis deeply influenced all his works. Manzoni wrote five religious *Sacred Hymns* (1812-1822) and an ode to Napoleon. In addition, Manzoni wrote two historical plays.   Richard H. Lansing

See also **Italian literature** (Romanticism).
Mao Tse-tung. See Mao Zedong.
Mao Zedong, *mow zeh dawng* (1893-1976), also spelled *Mao Tse-tung,* led the long struggle that made China a Communist nation in 1949. He then became the ruler of China and one of the world's most powerful people. Mao controlled China's artistic, intellectual, military, industrial, and agricultural planning and policies.

After the Communist victory, Mao's face became familiar throughout the world. Pictures of him appeared everywhere in China. Young and old learned his slogans and studied his writings. His writings, particularly on guerrilla warfare and the role of peasants in Communist revolutions, were influential outside China. Mao also wrote poetry.

Eastfoto

Mao Zedong

His life. Mao was born to a peasant family in Shaoshan, a village in Hunan Province. He was still a student when the revolution of 1911-1912 overthrew the Manchu government and made China a republic. While he was employed as a library worker at the National University in Beijing (Peking) in 1918, Mao became attracted to the ideas of Communism. In 1921, Mao and 11 other people founded the Chinese Communist Party in Shanghai.

The Communists joined forces with Sun Yat-sen's *Kuomintang* (Nationalist Party) in the effort to unite China. But distrust between the Communists and Chiang Kai-shek, who became Nationalist leader after Sun's death in 1925, soon led to warfare between the two groups. Mao and other Communist leaders led small bands to Jiangxi province in 1928. By 1931, that province had become Chiang's chief target. He began a series of "extermination campaigns" that nearly wiped the Communists out. In 1934, Mao led the Communists to Shaanxi (Shensi) province, in what is called *The Long March*. The 6,000-mile (9,700-kilometer) march lasted over a year and welded the survivors into a tightly-knit group under Mao's leadership.

Japan had invaded Manchuria in 1931, and launched full-scale war against China in 1937. The Communists and Nationalists joined in an uneasy alliance until World War II ended in 1945. As the Nationalist armies were driven inland during the war, Mao organized guerrilla warfare to spread Communism. By 1945, the Communists controlled areas populated by nearly 100 million Chinese. In 1946, fighting between Communists and Nationalists began in Manchuria. The Communists gained control of China by October 1949, and the Nationalists withdrew to Taiwan.

His leadership. Mao formed the Chinese into a tightly controlled society more quickly than most observers thought possible. After taking power, he made an alliance with the Soviets, who helped strengthen the Chinese army when Chinese forces aided North Korea during the Korean War (1950-1953).

After the Korean War, Mao began programs to expand agricultural and industrial production. In 1958, a crash program called the *Great Leap Forward* failed. In the 1960's, a split developed between China and the Soviet Union. Mao ordered nuclear research that led to Chinese nuclear explosions in the 1960's.

In 1959, Mao gave up his title of chairman of the People's Republic. But he kept control of the country and of the Communist Party. By the 1960's, disputes between China and the Soviet Union had expanded into a struggle for leadership of the Communist world. Mao considered himself the true interpreter of Marx, Lenin, and Stalin. Mao believed that poor nations would inevitably revolt against richer nations. He also accused Soviet Communists of being soft toward the United States.

In the mid-1960's, China suffered a series of diplomatic defeats, and Mao launched a campaign against so-called *revisionists* (those favoring changes), to maintain revolutionary enthusiasm. Young *Red Guards* publicly disgraced many officials. In the early 1970's, China improved its relations with the United States and other Western nations. Mao died in September 1976, after a long illness. After Mao's death, Chinese leaders reversed many of his policies and ended the emphasis on his personality. They looked to Japan, the United States, and European countries for help in modernizing China's industry, agriculture, science, and armed forces. These goals were called the *Four Modernizations*.

Marius B. Jansen

See also **China** (History); **Jiang Qing**.

Additional resources

Lawson, Don. *The Long March: Red China Under Chairman Mao.* Harper, 1983. Suitable for younger readers.
Terrill, Ross. *Mao: A Biography.* Harper, 1980.

Maoris, *MAH oh reez* or *MOW reez,* were among the first inhabitants of New Zealand. They are a Polynesian people. About 300,000 Maoris live in New Zealand. They make up about 9 per cent of its population.

Most Maoris are tall and have broad faces; brown eyes; and black, wavy hair. Through the years, many Maoris have intermarried with people of European ancestry. As a result, large numbers of New Zealanders of mixed parentage resemble Maoris. These New Zealanders are also called Maoris.

The original Maoris lived in isolated villages. They fished and hunted. Later, they also became farmers. The Maoris were skilled woodcarvers, and they decorated war canoes and communal houses with complicated designs. Their religion was based on *taboos* (prohibitions on certain objects, persons, and places).

During World War II (1939-1945), educational and job opportunities drew many Maoris into various cities. Today, Maoris hold positions in government, industry, and professional fields. They live in much the same way as New Zealanders of European ancestry.

The Maoris have pride in their cultural heritage, and many old customs remain part of their way of life. For example, they greet each other by pressing their noses together. They enjoy eating fermented crayfish and performing dances called *action songs*. The Maoris hold large gatherings known as *hui*. These gatherings, which are held at social centers called *marae,* celebrate such ceremonial events as funerals, weddings, and the opening of new buildings. Although most Maoris speak English, they generally use only their own language, called Maori, at these gatherings. About 20 per cent of the people speak the Maori language in their homes.

Alan Howard

See also **New Zealand; Mythology** (Mythology of the Pacific Islands).

Rubin Smith, Shostal

A Maori woman in traditional dress wears a feather cloak. She stands outside a village hut built of branches. On a pole behind the hut is an example of Maori woodcarving.

David Austen, Stock, Boston

© Journalism Services

© Bob Daemmrich, The Image Works

Maps have many uses. For example, geologists, *top,* study maps of the earth's surface to find likely deposits of oil. A student may use a world map to learn where different countries are, *above left.* A navigator on an ocean freighter, *above right,* plots a course on a map called a *nautical chart.*

Map

Map is a drawn or printed representation of the earth or any other heavenly body. Most maps show part or all of the earth's surface. But maps also may show other planets, the moon, or the positions of stars in space. Most maps are flat, though some have raised surfaces. A globe is a map in the shape of a ball.

Maps express information through lines, colors, shapes, and other symbols. These symbols stand for such features as rivers, roads, and cities. The features represented on a map are greatly reduced in size. An inch (2.5 centimeters) on a map, for example, might represent a distance of 100 miles (160 kilometers).

We use maps to locate places, measure distances, plan trips, and find our way. Pilots of ships and airplanes use maps to navigate. Maps may also give us information about a place, such as its climate, population, and transportation routes. They can also show such patterns as where people live and how they use the land. We also use maps to make comparisons and draw conclusions. Geologists, for example, study maps of the earth's structure to help locate natural resources.

People probably made crude maps even before the development of written language some 5,500 years ago. Through the years, people have explored more of the world, adding new information to maps. Scientific discoveries have made maps more accurate. Today, most maps are based on photographs taken from the air. *Cartography* is the making and study of maps. Someone who makes or studies maps is a *cartographer.*

Types of maps

There are many kinds of maps. The most familiar types are (1) *general reference maps,* (2) *mobility maps,* (3) *thematic maps,* and (4) *inventory maps.*

General reference maps identify and locate a variety of geographic features. Such maps may include land features, bodies of water, political boundaries, cities and towns, roads, and many other elements. People use general reference maps to locate specific places and to observe their location in relation to other places. The maps of states, countries, and continents in atlases are examples of general reference maps. Maps that emphasize the boundaries of counties, states, countries, or other political units are called *political maps.* Maps that emphasize the location of such features of the earth's surface as mountains, rivers, and lakes are called *physical maps* or *terrain maps.*

Mobility maps are designed to help people find their way from one place to another. There are mobility maps for travel on land, on water, or in the air. A map used to navigate a ship or an airplane is called a *chart.*

Road maps are the most familiar kind of mobility map. Road maps represent different categories of roads, such as divided highways, four-lane roads, and scenic routes. They also show the cities, towns, state parks, and other places connected by those roads. Travelers use road maps to plan trips and follow lengthy routes.

Street maps are similar to road maps. But street maps show a much smaller area in much greater detail. People use street maps to find specific addresses and to plan and follow short routes.

Transit maps show the routes of buses, subways, and other systems of *mass transit* (public transportation in cities). Transit maps help people reach their destination by means of public transportation.

Aeronautical charts are maps used to navigate airplanes. Many pilots of small, low-flying aircraft plan and follow a course by using VFR (visual flight rules) charts. VFR charts show such landmarks as bridges, highways, railroad tracks, rivers, and towns. They also show the location of airports and the heights of mountains and

Map   177

other obstructions. Other pilots of low-flying planes—and all crews of high-flying aircraft—use IFR (*i*nstrument *f*light *r*ules) charts, which are designed for radio navigation. IFR charts locate transmitters that beam very high frequency radio signals, which help airplane crews determine their position and course.

Nautical charts are maps used to navigate ships and boats. Nautical charts show water depths, lighthouses, buoys, islands, and such dangers as coral reefs and underwater mountains that come near the surface. They also locate the source of radio signals that navigators use to determine their course and position.

Thematic maps show the distribution of a particular feature such as population, rainfall, or a natural resource. They are used to study overall patterns. A thematic map might show, for example, where petroleum is produced in North America or how the average yearly rainfall varies from one part of Canada to another.

Many thematic maps express quantities by means of symbols or colors. For example, the *Population density* map in the **Maryland** article in *World Book* uses color to show how heavily settled that area is. In this map, shades of orange indicate four levels of population density.

Some thematic maps express quantities by using lines that pass through points of equal value. General terms for such lines include *isograms, isolines,* and *isarithms.* Specific types of isograms have special names. On a

weather map, for example, lines called *isobars* connect places that have the same air pressure (see **Isobar**). Isograms may also indicate temperatures, precipitation, and other measurements. On *topographic maps,* which show surface features of the land, isograms called *contour lines* are used to depict areas of equal elevation.

Some thematic maps use variations in size and shape to express quantities. A map of the international petroleum trade might indicate a large flow of oil with thick arrows and a small flow of oil with thin arrows.

Inventory maps, like thematic maps, concentrate on a specific feature. But unlike thematic maps, which show distributional patterns, inventory maps show the precise location of the specific feature. A map showing every building in a community is an example.

Reading a map

Using a map requires certain skills. To read a map, it is necessary to understand *map legends, scale, geographic grids,* and *map indexes.*

Map legends list and explain the symbols and colors on a map. Some map symbols resemble or suggest the features they represent. For example, a tree-shaped symbol may stand for a forest or an orchard. But many symbols have no resemblance to what they represent, as when a circle stands for a city. In addition, the same symbol may represent different features on different maps. A circle, for instance, may represent 20 mobile

---

Types of maps

Of the many types of maps, the most familiar are (1) general reference, (2) mobility, (3) thematic, and (4) inventory maps.

General reference maps, such as the one at the top left, show various geographic features. This example includes both land and political features.

Mobility maps, like the road map at the top right, help us find our way from one place to another.

Thematic maps, such as the population density map at the bottom left, show distribution patterns for a specific feature. In this map, darker colors indicate more populated areas.

Inventory maps, like the land use map at the bottom right, show the location of specific features. This map shows the location of forestlands in dark green, of croplands in light green, and of urban lands in tan.

WORLD BOOK maps

General reference map

Road map

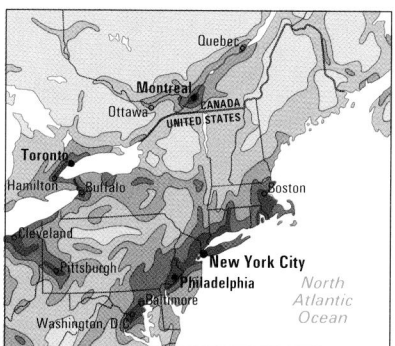

Population density map

Land use map

How to read a map

The illustrations on this page and the next demonstrate skills that are needed to read a map. They show how to use map legends and indexes, and they explain geographic grids and map scales.

Map legends   A map legend explains what the symbols and colors on a map represent. The illustration below shows the complete legend and part of the political map from the **Washington** article. The white ovals have been added to the map to point out some of the features explained in the legend.

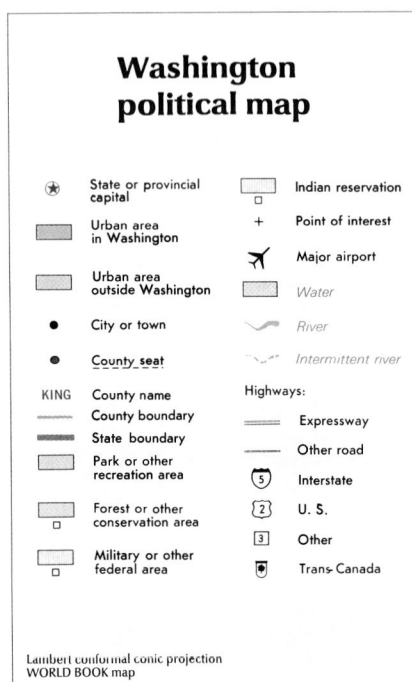

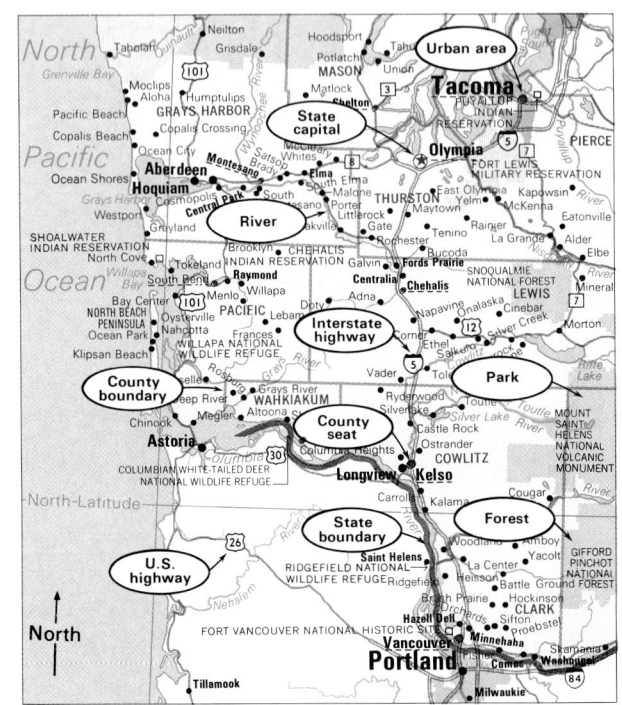

Map indexes   A map index helps us locate places. The example below, again taken from the **Washington** article, shows how to locate Walla Walla, Wash. The Walla Walla index entry is followed by the letter I and the number 14. This tells us that Walla Walla is found where row I and column 14 cross.

Washington map index (partial)

University
  Place* ....20,381..F   8
Urban C   7
Usk ....D 16
Utsalady ....P   2
Vader ....406..H   7
Valley ....D 15
Valley
  Ridge* ....17,961..E   8
Valleyford ....F 16
Vancouver .... 42,834°..J   7
Vantage ....G 11
Van Zandt C   8
Vashon I   2
Vashon Heights I   2
Vaughn ....J   1
Veradale ....7,256..E 16
Verlot ....D   9
Wahkiacus ....J 10
Waitsburg ....1,035..I 14
Waldron C   7
Walla Walla ......25,618..I 14
Walla Walla
  East* ....3,285..I 14
Wallula ....I 13
Wapato ....3,307..H 11
Warden ....1,479..G 13
Washougal ....3,834..J   8
Washtucna ....266..G 14
Waterville ....908°..E 11
Wauconda ....C 13
Waukon ....F 15

Wenatchee .... 17,237°..F 11
West Clarkston-
  |Highland]* .....3,683..H 16
West Federal
  Way* ....16,872..E   8
West Pasco* ......5,729..I 13
West Richland ....2,938..I 13
West
  Wenatchee* ....2,187..F 11
Westport ....1,954..G   5
Wheeler ....G 13
White Center
  |-Shorewood]* .19,362..E   8
White Salmon ......1,853..J   9
White Swan ....H 10
Whites ....G   6
Wickersham C   8
Wilbur ....1,122..E 14
Wilkeson ....321..K   3
Willapa ....H   6
Wilson Creek ....222..F 13
Winchester ....F 12
Winlock ....1,052..H   7
Winona ....G 15
Winslow ....2,196..H   2
Winthrop ....413..C 11
Winton ....E 10
Wishram ....E 10
Withrow ....E 12
Woodinville ....H   3
Woodland ....2,341..I   7
Woodway* ....832..E   8
Yacolt ....544..J   8
Yakima ....49,826°..H 11
Yarrow Point .....1,064..H   3
Yelm ....1,294..G   7
Zenith
  |-Saltwater]* .....8,982..E   8
Zillah ....1,599..H 11

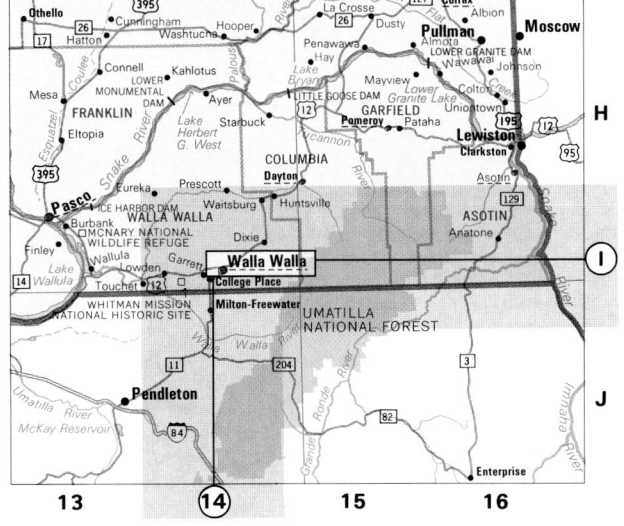

Map 179

Geographic grids Geographic grids are networks of lines on a map that enable us to find and describe locations. The most common geographic grid uses east-west lines called *parallels,* or *lines of latitude,* and north-south lines called *meridians,* or *lines of longitude.* This network is known as the *graticule.*

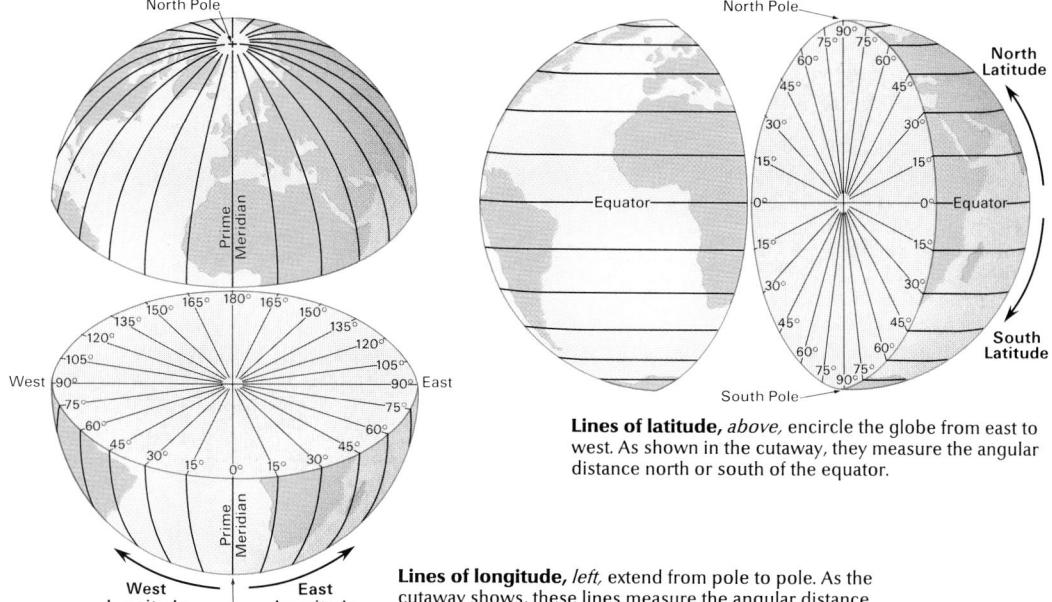

Lines of latitude, *above,* encircle the globe from east to west. As shown in the cutaway, they measure the angular distance north or south of the equator.

Lines of longitude, *left,* extend from pole to pole. As the cutaway shows, these lines measure the angular distance east or west of the prime meridian.

WORLD BOOK maps

Map scales A map's scale shows the relationship between the distances on the map and on the earth's surface. The photos below show how to use a scale that marks off distances along a line.

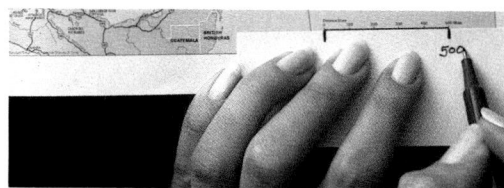

Next place the paper along the map's scale, with the left mark at 0. If, as in this case, the scale is shorter than the distance, mark on the paper the end point of the scale and distance it represents—500 miles in this example.

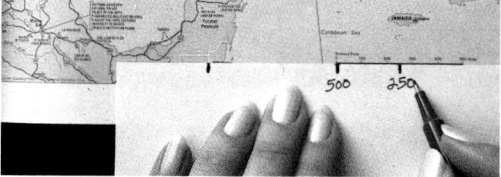

WORLD BOOK photos by Steinkamp/Ballogg

To find the distance between two points, such as Chicago and Montreal, first mark a piece of paper to show the distance between the two points on the map.

Then place the 500-mile mark at 0. The mark that represents Montreal is at about 250 on the scale. Thus, Chicago and Montreal lie about 500 plus 250, or 750, miles apart.

homes on one map and a petroleum deposit on another. It is important to read the map legend to find out exactly what the symbols mean.

Most maps are printed to show north at the top. Many map legends include an arrow that indicates which direction is north.

Scale. A map's scale shows the relationship between distances on the map and the corresponding distances on the earth's surface. Many maps show scale by marking off distances on a straight line. Each mark represents a certain number of miles or kilometers.

Other maps indicate scale in words and figures. For example, the scale might appear as "1 inch:15 statute miles." In other words, a distance of 1 inch on the map represents a distance of 15 miles on the earth's surface.

Another common method of expressing scale is by a *representative fraction,* such as "1:100,000" or "$\frac{1}{100,000}$." This means that a single unit of length on the map represents 100,000 of those units on the earth's surface. A centimeter on the map, for example, would represent 100,000 centimeters—1 kilometer—on the surface of the earth.

The amount of detail that a map can show depends on the scale chosen. A *large-scale* map would be chosen to show an area in great detail. Such a map has a large size relative to the area represented. It might have a scale in which 1 inch represents $\frac{1}{10}$ mile. A *small-scale* map, on the other hand, has a small size relative to the area represented and must leave out much detail. On such a map, 1 inch might represent 100 miles.

Geographic grids are networks of lines on maps that help us find and describe locations. The most common geographic grid uses east-west lines called *parallels* and north-south lines called *meridians.* The network of parallels and meridians is known as the *graticule.*

Parallels are lines that encircle the globe from east to west. The equator is the parallel that lies exactly halfway between the North Pole and the South Pole. Parallels are used to measure latitude—that is, the angular distance from the equator toward either pole. Latitude is measured in degrees of a circle. Any point on the equator has a latitude of zero degrees, written 0°. The North Pole has a latitude of 90° north and the South Pole a latitude of 90° south. Every other point on the earth has a latitude somewhere between 0° and 90°. Parallels are sometimes called *lines of latitude.* See **Equator; Latitude.**

Meridians are lines that extend halfway around the globe from the North Pole to the South Pole. By international agreement, mapmakers begin counting meridians from the line that passes through Greenwich, England, a borough of London. The Greenwich meridian is also known as the *prime meridian.* Meridians are used to measure longitude—that is, the angular distance east or west of the prime meridian. Like latitude, longitude is measured in degrees of a circle. Meridians, which are sometimes called *lines of longitude,* run from 0° at Greenwich to 180°. The 180° meridian lies halfway around the world from the prime meridian. Between the prime meridian and the 180° meridian are lines of west longitude (west of the prime meridian) and lines of east longitude (east of the prime meridian). See **Greenwich meridian; Longitude.**

Longitude and latitude can be used to pinpoint any place on earth. For example, only one place can lie at 30°

north latitude and 90° west longitude. An examination of a map of the United States reveals that this place is New Orleans, La.

Map indexes help us locate places on a map. A map index lists the features shown on a map in alphabetical order. In many atlases, each entry in the index is listed with its longitude and latitude. We can then use the longitude and latitude to find that feature on a map.

Many maps are divided into horizontal rows and vertical columns by an index grid. In most cases, letters along the sides of the map label the horizontal rows. Numbers across the top and bottom of the map label the vertical columns. Each entry in the map index is followed by a letter and a number corresponding to a row and a column on the map. The feature will be found where that row and column cross.

Map projections

Any system for transferring parallels and meridians from a globe onto a flat map is called a *projection.* Map-

Map projections

A map projection is a system for transferring the surface of the globe to a flat map. The maps at the bottom of the following panels show three common types of projections: cylindrical, conic, and azimuthal. The diagrams at the top of the panels show the relationship between the surface of the globe and that of the map.

WORLD BOOK maps

Cylindrical projection

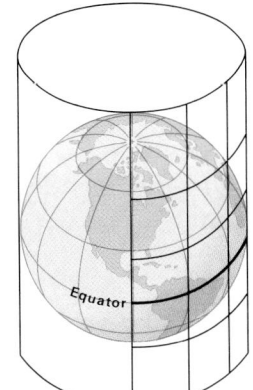

Cylindrical projections can be visualized by imagining a paper cylinder wrapped around an illuminated globe. The lines of the graticule would be projected onto the cylinder. The resulting map is free from distortion along the one or two lines where the cylinder touches the globe. But because the meridians do not meet at the poles, cylindrical projections seriously stretch regions near the poles.

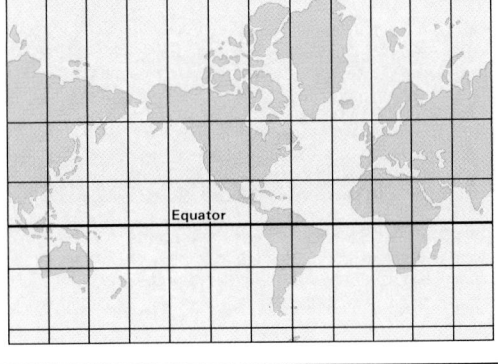

Equator

Map 181

makers create projections according to mathematical formulas, often with the aid of computers.

It is impossible to project a sphere, such as the earth's surface, onto a flat surface with complete accuracy. Every flat map has inaccuracies in scale that result from shrinking the globe in some places and stretching it in others to flatten it.

Some maps *distort* (show inaccurately) distances. On such maps, equal land areas may not appear of equal size. Many maps distort angles, resulting in misshapen seas and continents. Nearly all maps have one or two points or lines where there is no distortion. These are called *standard points* or *standard lines.* As we move away from them, the distortion of scale increases in a predictable way.

A map projection may be classified according to which properties of the globe it distorts least. *Equal-area projections* represent the sizes of regions in correct relation to one another but distort shapes. *Conformal projections* show angles and directions at any point accurately but distort size relationships. A map cannot be both equal-area and conformal, but many maps are neither. There is no name for this third category of projections classified by distortion.

A second way of classifying projections is according to the geometrical shape of the surface onto which the projection is drawn. Many maps are—in theory—projections onto a cylinder, a cone, or a plane.

Cylindrical projections are projections of the globe onto a cylinder. Although constructed by mathematical formulas, such projections can be visualized by imagining a paper cylinder wrapped around an illuminated globe. Lines from the globe would be projected onto the cylinder, which would then be slit and unrolled. The resulting map has one or two lines that are free from distortion. They occur where the cylinder touches the globe. On a cylindrical projection, all meridians will appear parallel on the map. The meridians thus fail to meet at the poles. As a result, such a map seriously stretches regions near the poles. Greenland, for example, will appear wider than South America, though it is actually much narrower.

The most famous cylindrical projection is the *Mercator projection.* This conformal projection is useful to navigators because a straight line drawn between any two points on the map provides a route that can be followed without changing compass direction.

Conic projections are projections of a globe onto a cone. To visualize a conic projection, imagine a paper cone with its open end resting over part of an illuminated globe. Lines from the globe would be projected onto the cone, which would then be slit and unrolled. If the point of the cone lies directly above one of the poles, the meridians are projected as straight lines radiating from the pole. The parallels appear as portions of a circle.

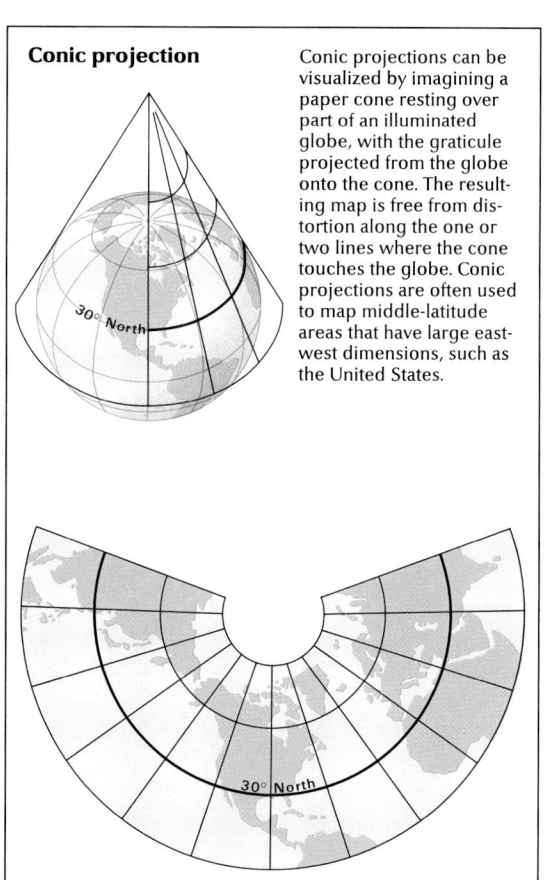

Conic projection

Conic projections can be visualized by imagining a paper cone resting over part of an illuminated globe, with the graticule projected from the globe onto the cone. The resulting map is free from distortion along the one or two lines where the cone touches the globe. Conic projections are often used to map middle-latitude areas that have large east-west dimensions, such as the United States.

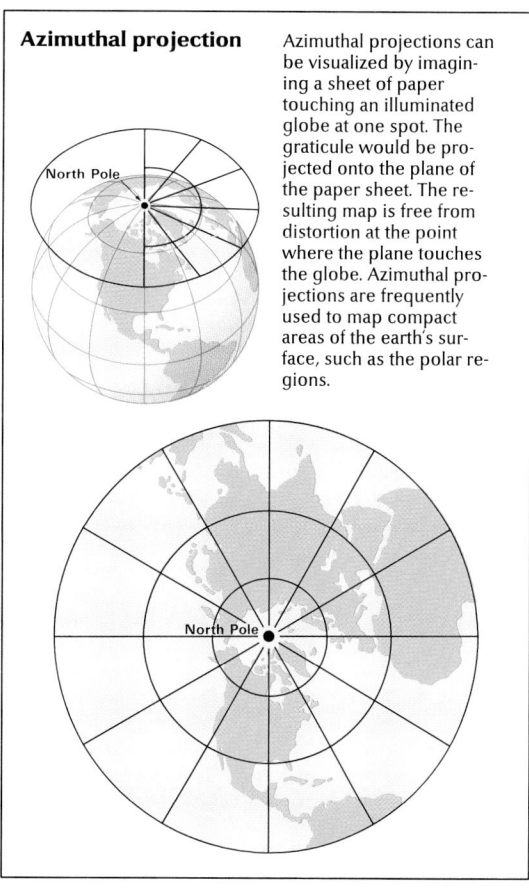

Azimuthal projection

Azimuthal projections can be visualized by imagining a sheet of paper touching an illuminated globe at one spot. The graticule would be projected onto the plane of the paper sheet. The resulting map is free from distortion at the point where the plane touches the globe. Azimuthal projections are frequently used to map compact areas of the earth's surface, such as the polar regions.

One or two lines free from distortion occur where the cone touches the surface of the globe. With its point over a pole, the cone touches the globe at the middle latitudes. Therefore, such conic projections are commonly used to map middle-latitude areas with large east-west dimensions, such as the United States and Russia. Some conic projections combine slices from several cones to increase accuracy.

Azimuthal projections are projections of a globe onto a plane. To visualize an azimuthal projection, imagine a sheet of paper touching an illuminated globe at one spot. The lines of the globe would be projected onto the sheet. The point on the map projection where the plane touches the globe is free from distortion. Cartographers can also draw azimuthal projections in which the plane theoretically slices through the globe. On these projections, the circular line where the plane intersects the globe is free from distortion.

Azimuthal projections are used most commonly to map compact areas of the earth's surface, such as the polar regions. One type of azimuthal projection, called a *gnomonic projection,* shows the shortest distance between any two points on the earth as a straight line. This distance is known as a *great-circle route* (see **Great-circle route**). Gnomonic projections are especially useful for planning intercontinental flights.

Other projections. Several useful projections are not based on the cylinder, cone, or plane. For example, projections that are oval in shape fall into a different category. Equal-area oval projections have little distortion along the equator and along the meridian that runs through their center. Mapmakers can achieve even less distortion by splitting the oval into several arching shapes.

How maps are made

Experts from many fields gather the information that cartographers need. The cartographer then transforms this information into a meaningful visual representation. In general, mapmaking follows these steps: (1) observation and measurement, (2) planning and design, (3) drawing and reproduction, and (4) revision.

Observation and measurement. A variety of experts obtain the information shown on maps. The *geodesist* provides precise measurements of the earth's size and shape. The *surveyor* works out the location and boundaries of places by measuring distances, angles, and elevations. The *photogrammetrist* obtains measurements from aerial photographs. Some of the other specialists who contribute information include census takers, geographers, geologists, and meteorologists.

The production of new maps based on aerial photographs and other original surveys is called *base mapping.* Most maps made by base mapping are topographic maps that are large in scale and include much detail. They become the basis for many other maps made by the process of *compilation mapping.* Compilation mapping involves selecting information from large-scale maps and displaying it on a map at a smaller scale. Cartographers may also *compile* (collect) information from censuses and other sources for presentation on the finished map.

Planning and design. In planning a map, the cartographer considers the map's purpose and its likely users.

This information helps the cartographer decide which map projection and scale to use and which information to highlight or eliminate. The map's design helps communicate information effectively. In designing a map, the cartographer selects suitable symbols, writes titles and labels, and chooses lettering. In many cases, a graphic artist helps the cartographer design a map.

Drawing and reproduction. Maps may be drawn in several ways. Cartographers sometimes draw a map directly on paper or plastic drafting film. More commonly, however, they use a technique called *scribing.* In scribing, the mapmaker uses special tools to cut away the colored surface coating on a sheet of clear plastic. Lines and areas of the clear plastic are thereby exposed. These lines and areas correspond to lines and areas to be printed in ink on the map. Scribing produces maps with sharp, fine lines that would be difficult to achieve by the direct drawing method.

Cartographers today increasingly use computers to draw maps. A device called a *plotter,* which attaches to a computer, produces maps by scribing or by drawing with pen and ink. Computers can also use a beam of light from a laser to plot maps by exposing areas of photographic film. In addition, computers can scan base maps, aerial photographs, or actual physical surfaces and then use the data to print a map.

Cartographers often supervise the reproduction of maps so that the correct colors and symbols appear in the proper place on the final map. Most paper maps are printed from printing plates.

Additional steps are needed to produce maps that have a raised surface. These maps include *raised relief maps,* which have elevated surfaces to represent hills

Chicago Aerial Survey, Inc.

A cartographer scribes a map by cutting away the colored surface coating from a sheet of plastic. The scribed sheet is then used to make a printing plate. The clear areas on the sheet correspond to the areas that will print in ink on the finished map.

Map 183

NASA

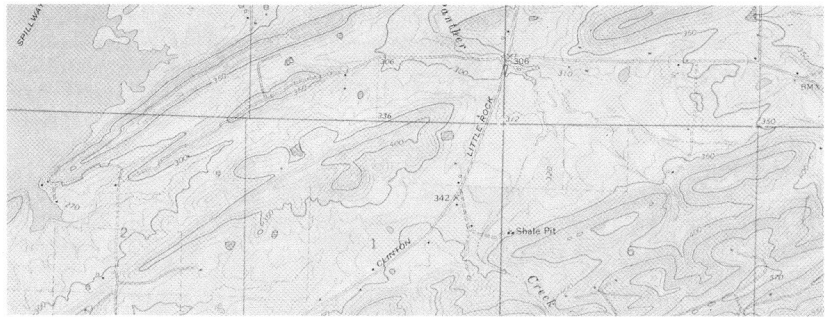

U.S. Geological Survey

Contour mapping begins with aerial photography. This photograph, *top,* shows the landscape around Hamlet, Ark., including hills and part of a lake, *upper left.* A machine called a *stereoplanigraph* traces the contours of the landscape from the photo onto a sheet of paper. The resulting contour map, *bottom,* shows elevations at regular intervals.

and mountains, and *tactual maps,* which have raised symbols that blind people can read by touch. To make such maps, cartographers first build a three-dimensional model of the map's raised surface, using plaster or a similar material. Next, the map's symbols and letter-

Chicago Aerial Survey, Inc.

A pen-and-ink plotter, *above,* uses information stored in a computer to draw contour lines on a topographic map. Other plotters can scribe maps according to computer data. Computer-linked plotters have become increasingly common.

ing are printed on a flat plastic sheet. The plastic sheet is then softened by heating, molded to the shape of the three-dimensional model, and hardened.

Revision. Cartographers must revise maps to keep them up to date. For example, changes in the population of cities, the shape of waterways, or the area of forests may require revisions on maps. Aerial photographs are commonly used to survey changes that have occurred since the map was last revised.

History

Ancient maps. The oldest existing map appears on a clay tablet made in Babylonia (now part of Iraq) around 2500 B.C. This map seems to show a settlement in a mountain-lined river valley. The Babylonians had a lasting influence on mapmaking. They developed the system of dividing a circle into 360 equal parts called degrees. We use this system to measure latitude and longitude.

The Egyptians made maps as early as 1300 B.C. They developed techniques of surveying, probably to remap property boundaries each year after the Nile River flooded its banks.

The Greeks made great advances in geometry and surveying, and they developed systems of map projection. The Greeks also speculated about the size and shape of the earth. Many of them believed it was a sphere. The Greek mathematician Eratosthenes calculated the circumference of the earth with remarkable accuracy around 250 B.C.

The most influential mapmaker of ancient times was probably Claudius Ptolemy, a Greek astronomer and geographer who worked in Alexandria, Egypt, around A.D. 150. Ptolemy brought together what was known about the world in his eight-volume *Geography.* It included maps and a list of about 8,000 places along with their latitude and longitude. Ptolemy also provided instructions for various systems of map projection.

Maps in the Middle Ages. Little scientific progress occurred in European mapmaking during most of the Middle Ages, the period that lasted from about 400 to the late 1400's. During the 1300's, however, European mapmakers began producing *portolan charts,* a group of maps notable for their accuracy. These navigation aids showed the coastline of the Mediterranean Sea and nearby regions in great detail. Lines across the map helped sailors determine compass directions.

During the Middle Ages, progress in mapmaking occurred mainly in the Arab world and China. Arab scholars developed methods of determining latitude and longitude after Ptolemy's *Geography* was translated into Arabic in the 800's. The earliest known printed map appeared in a Chinese encyclopedia around 1155, more than 300 years before printed maps were produced in Europe.

Advances in European cartography followed several developments of the 1400's. First, the translation of Ptolemy's works into Latin led to the rediscovery of his methods of map projection and of locating places systematically. Second, the invention of the printing press in the mid-1400's made maps more widely available. Many identical copies could be produced by printing maps instead of copying them by hand. Third, an age of exploration opened in the late 1400's, which increased knowledge of the world and interest in mapmaking.

By the late 1400's, educated Europeans had accepted the idea that the world is round. In 1492, the year that Christopher Columbus discovered the New World, a German merchant and navigator named Martin Behaim produced a globe that recorded the world as Europeans knew it before Columbus' voyage. Behaim's globe lacked the Americas, of course, and it depicted the Atlantic Ocean as much smaller than it actually is. By the early 1500's, mapmakers had begun including the New World on their maps. The name *America* first appeared

Harvard Semitic Museum

The oldest map known is a clay tablet found in Iraq. Made about 2500 B.C., it probably shows a settlement in a valley.

on a map produced in 1507 by a German cartographer, Martin Waldseemüller.

In 1569, Flemish geographer Gerardus Mercator published the first map based on his Mercator projection, which was of great value to sailors. The first collection of maps made specifically to be combined into an atlas was produced by the Flemish mapmaker Abraham Ortelius in 1570.

Scientific activity during the 1500's, 1600's, and 1700's produced new instruments and techniques that made measurements of location and elevation more accurate. Jean-Domenique Cassini, an astronomer at the Paris Observatory, began the detailed and accurate mapping of France's *topography* (surface features) in the late 1600's. That work continued for more than 100 years. In England, the astronomer Edmond Halley published a map of

From Ptolemy's *Geography*, published in Ulm by Leinhart Holle, 1482, Library of Congress

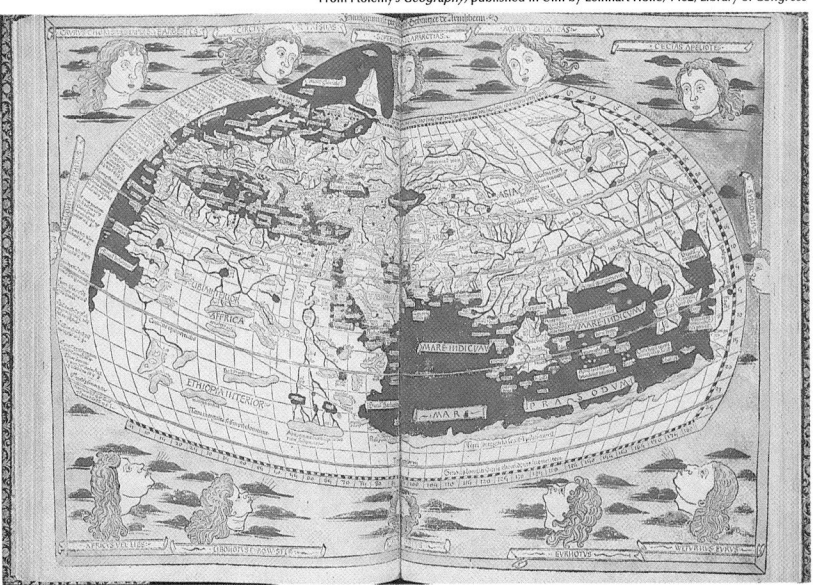

A map of the world formed part of Ptolemy's eight-book *Geography.* Ptolemy was a Greek geographer and astronomer who lived about A.D. 150. Few people knew about his maps until they were printed in an atlas in the late 1400's. The map at the left is from an edition of *Geography* published in 1482.

Map 185

the trade winds in 1686, which is considered the first *meteorological* (weather) map. Halley's map of the earth's magnetic fields in 1700 was the first published map that used isograms to connect points of equal value.

Mapping the New World. During the 1600's and 1700's, the colonization of the New World created a need for many new maps. The Spanish surveyed and mapped land under their control. In 1612, the English adventurer Captain John Smith published a map of Virginia's coastline. Smith also made the first English map of New England. During the early 1600's, the French explorer Samuel de Champlain mapped the region from Maryland to the St. Lawrence River in Canada.

Surveying was an important activity in the American Colonies. Surveyors Joshua Fry and Peter Jefferson published a map of the region from Virginia to the Great Lakes in 1751. In 1755, John Mitchell, a Virginia colonist, published his *Map of the British and French Dominions in America.* A copy of this map was used to mark the boundaries of the United States of America after the Revolutionary War ended in 1783.

As the pioneers moved westward during the 1800's, explorers and army engineers mapped trails and surveyed government lands. The United States government eventually established two agencies with responsibility for detailed, large-scale mapping. The Survey of the Coast—now the National Ocean Survey—was founded in 1807. The U.S. Geological Survey was officially created in 1879.

The development of thematic mapping. By the 1800's, the systematic collection of data through censuses had become common. Cartographers then created thematic maps to display and study this wealth of new information. The British cartographer Henry D. Harness advanced thematic mapping with several maps of Ireland published in 1837. Those maps used tones to indicate population density, black circles of different sizes to show the populations of cities, and lines of different thickness to represent traffic flow.

In 1855, John Snow, an English physician, dramatically demonstrated the value of thematic mapping for scientific research. On a map of London neighborhoods, Snow used a dot to represent each person who had died of cholera during an epidemic that year. A large number of dots clustered around a water pump on Broad Street helped locate the source of the infection.

Mapmaking and modern technology. During the 1900's, improvements in printing and photography have made it cheaper and easier to produce maps. Maps became more widespread as a result. The development of the airplane during the early 1900's made aeronautical charts necessary. Airplanes also made it possible to photograph large areas from the air.

Since the mid-1900's, the use of computers in mapmaking has increased greatly. Computers store, sort, and arrange data for mapping. They create map projections and control plotters that draw or scribe maps. The computer may even draw the map directly on its display monitor.

Space exploration also has contributed many devices to mapmaking and has furthered the mapping of moons, other planets, and the vast reaches of space. Artificial satellites carry *remote sensing devices* that send a variety of signals back to earth. These signals can be used in mapping landforms, mineral deposits, patterns of vegetation growth, environmental pollution, and other subjects.
                                   Judy M. Olson

Related articles in *World Book.* See the maps with the state, province, country, and continent articles. See also the following articles:

Airplane (Flight navigation)	Longitude
Atlas	Mercator, Gerardus
Azimuth	Navigation
Colonial life in America	Photogrammetry
(map: "The Duke's Plan	Plane table
of 1661")	Radar (Pulse radar;
Equator	picture: Radar mapping)
Geodesy	Satellite, Artificial
Geography	Surveying
Globe	Topography
Greenwich meridian	Weather (Making a
International date line	weather map; map)
Isobar	World, History of the
Isotherm	(picture: An atlas
Latitude	printed in 1547)

Outline

Questions

How do general reference maps differ from thematic maps?
What does a map's scale show?
What three developments of the 1400's advanced European mapmaking?
Why do all flat maps have inaccuracies in scale?
Which parallel lies exactly halfway between the North Pole and the South Pole?
What information do geodesists, surveyors, and photogrammetrists obtain for mapmakers?
What is a *map projection?*
How are computers used in mapmaking?
What does a *gnomonic projection* show?
How did air travel affect mapmaking during the early 1900's?

Additional resources

Level I

Baynes, John. *How Maps Are Made.* Facts on File, 1987.
Carey, Helen H. *How to Use Maps and Globes.* Watts, 1983.
Ryan, Peter. *Explorers & Mapmakers.* Lodestar, 1989.

Level II

Blandford, Percy W. *Maps & Compasses: A User's Handbook.* TAB, 1984.
Greenhood, David. *Mapping.* Rev. ed. Univ. of Chicago Pr., 1964.
Robinson, Arthur H., and others. *Elements of Cartography.* 5th ed. Wiley, 1984.
Wilford, John N. *The Mapmakers.* Knopf, 1981. A history of maps from the earliest to the present day.

Grant Heilman

E. R. Degginger

The sugar maple ranks as one of the most valuable trees of North America. Its sweet sap is used in making maple syrup, and its hard wood makes excellent lumber.

The silver maple is named for the silvery-white underside of its leaves.

Maple is any of about 120 species of broadleaf trees and shrubs common in forests of the Northern Hemisphere. Most maples grow in regions with climates that are neither very cold nor very warm. About two-thirds of all maple species are native to China. Other species are native to other parts of Asia, Europe, North America, and northern Africa.

Maples are easy to recognize because their leaves

E. R. Degginger

Jerome Wexler, APF

The Norway maple, *above,* is an important timber tree in northern Europe. It was introduced into North America, where it has become popular as a street tree. In spring, the tree has bright-yellow blossoms, *left.*

grow in pairs on opposite sides of the branch, and each leaf has several lobes. No other North American tree has opposite, lobed leaves. Nearly all maples lose their leaves in the autumn. In numerous species of maples, the leaves turn bright orange, red, or yellow before they drop off.

Maples flower in the spring, either before or at the same time the leaves appear. Most maples bear male and female flowers on the same tree. Maple seeds, sometimes called *keys,* grow in pairs and have flat, thin wings that make them whirl and float in the wind as they fall. Breezes can carry the seeds far from the parent tree, thus helping maples spread to new areas.

Maples are an important source of lumber. Some species have very hard, strong wood. Manufacturers use it to make furniture and musical instruments. The sap of certain maple species is used to make maple syrup. People also plant maples as shade trees.

North American maples

Fourteen species are native to North America. They grow mostly in the eastern half of the continent.

Sugar maple is one of the most common trees in the broadleaf forests of southeastern Canada and the northeastern quarter of the United States. This tree typically grows 75 to 100 feet (23 to 30 meters) tall and measures 2 to 3 feet (60 to 90 centimeters) in diameter at its base. However, it may reach a height of 135 feet (41 meters) tall and a diameter of 5 to 6 feet (1.5 to 1.8 meters). The sugar maple is most common in areas that are neither swampy nor very dry.

Sugar maple wood is the hardest and strongest maple wood. It polishes well and is widely used for furniture, cabinets, and violins and other musical instruments. It is also used for making bowling alleys. Some sugar maple wood has an unusual grain pattern that makes it particularly beautiful and valuable. This wood, called *curly maple* or *bird's eye maple,* is used in fine furniture and stringed musical instruments.

People also value the sugar maple for its sweet, flavorful sap. The sap rises in the trunks in the spring. Syrup producers collect the sap from pipes driven into the tree trunks. They then boil the sap down to make maple syrup and maple sugar. Maple syrup production is a multimillion dollar industry in New England and southern Canada. See **Maple syrup.**

Red maple is common in eastern and midwestern forests of the United States and in southeastern Canada. This tree thrives in rich, moist woods; on rocky ridges with thin, dry soil; and in swampy areas that are flooded for part of the year. Most red maples grow 70 to 90 feet (21 to 27 meters) tall.

The red maple has red twigs. In the fall, its leaves usually turn red. People sometimes plant the red maple as a shade tree in yards and along streets because it is colorful in both spring and fall and grows well in most soils. Furniture makers sometimes use the wood of the red maple.

Silver maple is common along rivers and streams in much of the eastern and midwestern parts of the United States and in southeastern Canada. Unlike most trees, the silver maple produces seeds in the spring instead of in the fall. Botanists believe this characteristic developed as an adaptation to growing near rivers that flood in the spring. Such flooding washes away plants and soil, leaving bare areas of ground. Many silver maple seeds fall on these bare areas and begin growing without competition from other plants.

The silver maple was once popular as an ornamental tree because it grows fast. But people seldom plant it today because its branches break off easily in storms and the leaves are not colorful in the fall. The silver maple produces brittle wood with limited economic value.

Boxelder, sometimes called *ashleaf maple,* is the most widespread maple in North America. It often grows along streams and swamps throughout much of the United States and Canada. It is also found in parts of Mexico and Central America. The boxelder has *compound leaves*—that is, each leaf consists of several leaflets. The male and female flowers of the species grow on different trees. Female trees grow in wetter sites, and male trees grow in drier places.

In the past, landscapers often used the boxelder as a street tree because it grows fast when young. However, they rarely plant it today because its branches split off easily. Boxelders produce soft, weak wood that has little

Charles E. Mohr, NAS   Jerome Wexler, NAS

The fruit of maple trees consists of a pair of winged seeds, *left.* The wind carries the seeds away from the tree, and the seeds take root and start to grow, *right.*

economic value. See **Boxelder.**

Bigleaf maple is the only tree-sized maple found in the Pacific Northwest. It often grows in open areas and near lowland streams. It is also found growing under the giant evergreen trees of the Pacific Coast rain forest. Bigleaf maple leaves may measure 6 to 12 inches (15 to 30 centimeters) across. The wood is sometimes used for furniture and musical instruments.

Other maples

Several species of maples native to Europe have been planted widely in North America. The *Norway maple* averages about the same size as the red maple. It is an important timber tree in northern Europe. Landscapers use the Norway maple as a street tree in North America because it tolerates pollution well. The *sycamore maple* ranks as an important timber tree in central and southern Europe. It, too, is sometimes planted as a street tree in North America.

Certain species of maples native to Asia are widely planted as ornamental shrubs. They include the *Japanese maple* and the *fullmoon maple.* Some cultivated kinds of these trees have red or bronze-colored leaves.

Scientific classification. Maples make up the genus *Acer* in the maple family, Aceraceae. The scientific name for the sugar maple is *Acer saccharum.* The red maple is *A. rubrum;* the silver maple, *A. saccharinum;* the boxelder, *A. negundo;* the bigleaf maple, *A. macrophyllum.* The Norway maple is *A. platanoides;* the sycamore maple, *A. pseudoplatanus;* the Japanese maple, *A. palmatum;* and the fullmoon maple, *A. japonicum.*

Douglas G. Sprugel

See also **Tree** (Familiar broadleaf and needleleaf trees of North America [picture]).

Some kinds of maple leaves

Maple leaves grow in pairs and typically have several lobes. Most maples lose their leaves in autumn. The leaves may turn a brilliant orange, red, or yellow before they drop off.

Werner Schulz   Walter Chandoha   E. R. Degginger   C. G. Maxwell, NAS

Norway maple   **Sugar maple**   **Silver maple**   **Japanese maple**

Maple, Flowering. See Flowering maple.

Maple syrup is a sweet, thick liquid obtained from the sap of certain maple trees. The *sugar maple* tree ranks as the chief source of this delicious food product. Vermont and New York lead the states of the United States in maple syrup production. But the Canadian province of Quebec produces more maple syrup than all the states together.

Some people pour pure maple syrup on pancakes, waffles, and other foods. But the "maple" syrups that most people use contain only a small amount of actual maple syrup. Most of these products are a combination of maple syrup, cane sugar syrup, and corn syrup. Maple syrup producers use some syrup to make maple sugar, maple butter and cream, and soft maple candy.

Maple sap is a colorless, watery solution that contains sugar and various acids and salts. Standards set by the U.S. government require that maple syrup consist of at least $65\frac{1}{2}$ per cent of these solids. It usually takes from 35 to 45 gallons (132 to 170 liters) of sap to make 1 gallon (3.8 liters) of maple syrup.

The typical maple flavors and *amber* (golden brown) colors develop during processing. Syrup is often classified by color, ranging from the palest amber, called *light amber* or *Fancy,* to the darkest amber, called *Commercial.* All maple syrups have the same food value, but they differ in flavor. In general, the lighter the syrup, the more delicate the taste.

Production. Syrup producers begin to collect sap from maple trees in late winter or early spring. The nights are cold during the *sapping* season, which lasts only a few weeks, but the days are warmer. This daily rise and fall in temperature starts the sap flowing.

Syrup producers use one of two methods to collect the sap from the trees. In the older method, a producer drills one or more holes into a tree and drives a metal spout into each hole. The sap runs through the spout into a bucket that hangs from the spout. After all the buckets are filled, the producer empties their contents into a large bucket, which is taken by sled or wagon to a building called a *sugarhouse.*

In the more modern method, a producer inserts plastic spouts into holes drilled in the trees. The sap runs

Leading maple syrup producing states and provinces

Amount of maple syrup produced in a year

Quebec	●●●●●●●●●●●●●●●●●●●●●●● 2,024,000 gallons (7,662,000 liters)
Vermont	●●●●●◐ 525,000 gallons (1,987,000 liters)
New York	●●● 315,000 gallons (1,192,000 liters)
Ontario	●●◐ 221,000 gallons (837,000 liters)
Wisconsin	● 110,000 gallons (416,000 liters)
New Hampshire	● 92,000 gallons (348,000 liters)

Includes maple syrup later made into maple sugar and maple taffy; figures are for 1985.
Sources: Economic Research Service, U.S. Department of Agriculture; Statistics Canada.

through tubes connected to the spouts and into a pipeline system that carries sap to the sugarhouse. A properly managed pipeline system yields more sap than the bucket method. It also requires less time and labor.

After the sap reaches the sugarhouse, it is boiled in a long, shallow pan called an *evaporator.* The maple color and flavor develop during this process, and most of the water in the sap evaporates. Pure maple syrup remains. Some producers let part of the sap boil beyond the syrup stage until it becomes maple sugar. These producers then hold *sugaring off* gatherings at which people sample both products.

History. Indians who lived near the Great Lakes and the St. Lawrence River produced maple sugar and syrup long before white explorers came to North America. Early French and English explorers wrote of the "sweet water" that the Indians drew from trees and heated to make the maple products.

During the 1700's and 1800's, maple sugar ranked as an important food item. People in maple sugar producing areas traded it for various foods and services. Gradually, white cane sugar became less expensive than maple sugar. By the late 1800's, cane sugar had replaced

Maple syrup comes from the sap of certain maple trees, chiefly the sugar maple. Syrup producers collect the sap in buckets, *left,* or use a system of plastic pipelines, *above.* The pipelines run into a *sugarhouse,* where the syrup is made.

Constantine Manos, Magnum

In the sugarhouse, the maple sap is boiled. This process turns the sap into thick syrup, which is collected in buckets, *above*.

maple sugar for most purposes. At about that time, food manufacturers developed the blend of maple syrup and other syrups that became "maple" syrup.

Today, some food companies use artificial maple flavorings in certain foods. But these flavorings taste somewhat different from real maple syrup.   Manon Côté

See also **Maple** (The sugar maple).

Maputo, *muh POOT oh* (pop. 1,006,765; met. area pop. 1,551,457), is the capital and largest city of Mozambique. It has an excellent harbor and is the chief port of Mozambique and several nearby countries. It is located in southern Mozambique on Delagoa Bay, an inlet of the Indian Ocean. For the location of Maputo, see **Mozambique** (map).

The Portuguese founded the city about 1780 and named it Lourenço Marques. The city became the major

white settlement in Mozambique, but most of the whites left in 1975 after Mozambique gained independence from Portugal. In 1976, the city's name was changed to Maputo.

The main sections of Maputo have wide, tree-lined streets and large beaches. The fortress of Nossa Senhora da Conceição, built in 1871, is a famous landmark. Food processing is the city's most important industry.   John D. Metzler

Maquis, *mah KEE,* were French patriots who formed a secret army to fight German occupation forces in France during World War II (1939-1945). *Maquis* is a French word for the tough, scrubby vegetation of the Mediterranean Coast. People from all classes joined the Maquis to support the Free French, and to escape from being forced into German labor camps.

The Maquis conducted intelligence and small-scale operations, blowing up trains, and sabotaging military production. Members lived in hiding in the mountains of southern and eastern France. The Allies parachuted supplies to them. When the war ended, the French government publicly thanked the Maquis for their services.
          Stefan T. Possony

Mar del Plata, *MAHR dehl PLAHT uh* (pop. 407,024), is one of the most popular resort cities in Argentina. Its pleasant climate and beautiful beaches draw more than 2 million vacationers each year. The city lies in eastern Argentina and borders the Atlantic Ocean. For location, see **Argentina** (political map).

Modern, high-rise apartment buildings and hotels line Mar del Plata's beaches. The city has a huge casino, fashionable shops, and plazas filled with trees and flowers. Tourism is Mar del Plata's principal industry. Other important industries in the city include fishing and fish processing.

Mar del Plata was founded in 1874. It became a favor-

Geoslides

Maputo is the capital and largest city of Mozambique. Modern buildings rise along the city's tree-lined streets, *above*. Maputo lies on an inlet of the Indian Ocean and is a major port.

Loren McIntyre

Mar del Plata is a popular resort city in eastern Argentina. The city's beaches are lined with modern, high-rise apartment buildings and hotels.

ite resort of wealthy Argentines during the late 1800's. Middle- and lower-income people began vacationing there during the mid-1900's. During the 1970's, the city's permanent population grew sharply, rising by more than 100,000.   Richard W. Wilkie

Marabou, *MAIR uh boo,* is one of the largest birds in the stork family. The marabou lives throughout Africa. Two closely related species, the *greater adjutant* and the *lesser adjutant,* are found in India and Southeast Asia. See **Adjutant.**

The marabou has long legs and stands up to 5 feet (1.5 meters) tall. The wings and upper body are slate-gray or black, and the underparts are white. The bird has beautiful, soft, white tail feathers, which are also called *marabou.* Manufacturers once used these feathers to make scarves and to trim hats and gowns. The head and neck of the marabou are almost featherless. A

C. Haagner, Bruce Coleman Inc.

Marabous have a long, pointed bill and a nearly bald head and neck. These large storks are found in Africa. They measure up to 5 feet (1.5 meters) tall.

long pouch of reddish skin hangs down from the neck. The marabou can inflate this pouch with air, but its exact function is not known.

Marabous feed largely on the remains of dead animals. They also eat live prey, including frogs, fish, reptiles, and locusts. Marabous nest in colonies. They build platformlike nests high in trees or on rocks and lay two or three white eggs.

Scientific classification. The marabou belongs to the stork family, Ciconiidae. Its scientific name is *Leptoptilos crumeniferus.*   James J. Dinsmore

See also **Stork.**

Maracaibo, *MAR uh KY boh* (pop. 1,151,933), is Venezuela's chief coffee-exporting port and second largest city. Only Caracas has more people.

The discovery of petroleum in 1912 made Maracaibo one of the world's great oil cities, and a thriving metropolis. Maracaibo lies on the west shore of the narrows that connect the Gulf of Venezuela with Lake Maracaibo

Shostal

Maracaibo has wide boulevards and modern high-rise office buildings in the downtown area, *above.* Maracaibo is Venezuela's second largest city. Only Caracas has more people.

(see **Venezuela** [political map]). The city has a good harbor. A bridge $5\frac{1}{2}$ miles (8.9 kilometers) long across Lake Maracaibo connects Maracaibo with the east shore of the narrows. Maracaibo was founded in 1529.

Jerry R. Williams

Maracaibo, Lake. See Lake Maracaibo.

Maracas. See Venezuela (Recreation).

Marajó, *MAH rah ZHAW,* is a large island that belongs to Brazil. It covers 15,444 square miles (40,000 square kilometers) between the *estuaries* (river mouths) of the Amazon and Pará rivers in northeastern South America. For location, see **Brazil** (terrain map). About 270,000 people live on the island.

Marajó is a plain just above sea level. Much of the plain is flooded during the six-month rainy season. The vast grasslands that cover most of the island make good pasture for water buffalo. Forests fringe the shores and banks of waterways. Rubber trees are scattered through these forests.   J. H. Galloway

Maraschino cherry, *MAR uh SKEE noh* or *MAR uh SHEE noh,* is a preserved cherry. Maraschino cherries are used to decorate and add flavor to desserts and beverages. The cherries received their name because they were originally preserved in *maraschino,* a liqueur distilled from the fermented juice of the marasca cherry. Today, the cherries are artificially colored, flavored, and preserved. Several varieties of cherries are used. They are picked before they have fully ripened, and are pitted by a machine.   Margaret McWilliams

Marat, *mah RAH,* **Jean Paul,** *zhahn pawl* (1743-1793), was one of the most radical leaders of the French Revolution (1789-1799). He helped increase the violence of the period by demanding death for all opponents of the revolution.

Marat was born in Boudry, Switzerland, near Neuchâtel. He became a physician and a writer. During the 1770's and 1780's, Marat wrote books on electricity, heat, light, and physiology, as well as on law and political theory. The French Academy of Sciences rejected Marat's chief ideas, and Marat believed that officials of the academy had cooperated to keep him from winning the recognition he deserved.

Marat strongly supported the French Revolution, which began in 1789. He believed it would improve conditions, especially for the poor. Marat founded a newspaper, *L'Ami du Peuple* (The Friend of the People). The paper violently criticized those who opposed the revolution.

Portrait by Joseph Boze, Musee Carnavalet, Paris (Bulloz)
Jean Paul Marat

In August 1792, the people of Paris put King Louis XVI and his family in prison. Marat called for death for those who continued to support the king. Indirectly, he contributed to the violent mood of the public that led to the massacres in Paris in September. That month, bands of revolutionaries broke into the city's prisons and killed over 1,000 prisoners, including priests and aristocratic supporters of the king.

Later in September, Marat was elected to the National Convention, a body that was writing a new constitution for France. He joined a group called the *Jacobins,* who demanded the king's execution. Marat soon became the main target of moderate members of the convention, known as *Girondists.* They accused Marat of plotting against them and brought him to trial. He was acquitted and, in turn, called for the expulsion of Girondist leaders from the convention. They were expelled and then arrested in June 1793. In July, Marat was stabbed to death by Charlotte Corday, an aristocrat who supported the Girondists.   Isser Woloch

See also **French Revolution; Corday, Charlotte.**

Additional resources

Gottschalk, Louis R. *Jean Paul Marat: A Study in Radicalism.* Ayer, 1972. First published in 1927.
Hibbert, Christopher. *The Days of the French Revolution.* Morrow, 1980.

Marathon, *MAIR uh thahn,* a coastal plain in Greece, was the site of one of the most important battles in the history of Western civilization. There, in 490 B.C., a Greek army defeated an invading army of Persians and saved Greece from becoming part of the Persian Empire. Marathon lies about 25 miles (40 kilometers) northeast of Athens.

Causes of the battle. In 507 B.C., the Athenians asked King Darius I of Persia to become their ally against Sparta, a powerful city-state in southern Greece. To form the alliance, representatives of Athens promised Athenian obedience to Darius. The Athenian government later rejected the agreement, but Darius continued to consider himself the rightful ruler of Athens.

Beginning in 499 B.C., Greeks living under Persian rule in Asia Minor (now Turkey) rebelled against Darius. The Athenians sent soldiers and 20 ships to aid the rebels. Then the Greek forces attacked and burned Sardis, a city that served as Darius' capital in Asia Minor. Darius vowed that he would take revenge on the Athenians by conquering and burning Athens.

The battle. In 490 B.C., Darius sent his nephew Artaphernes and Datis, one of his generals, with an army and a fleet of about 200 ships to conquer Athens. The Persians first destroyed Eretria, a city on the Greek island of Euboea, and then sailed for Marathon. The Athenian general Militiades positioned the Athenian troops on the inland edge of the plain. The Persians occupied the seaward edge. Both armies waited several days. The Persians awaited a signal that Athenians allied to them had weakened Athens by starting a civil war in the city. Meanwhile, the Athenian army waited for expected help from Sparta. But only about 600 soldiers from Plataea, a city near Athens, joined the Athenians at Marathon.

A few days later, the Persian leaders, hoping that civil war had broken out in Athens, loaded part of their forces on ships. The Persians on the ships prepared to sail to Athens and attack the city. Seeing their chance for a victory, the Athenians charged the army of Persians that remained on the plain. The Greeks surrounded and thoroughly defeated the Persians at Marathon.

The Persians, not worried about the defeat at Marathon, sailed for Athens. They reached Phaleron—Athens' harbor—a few days later. There, they found that civil war had not broken out and that the Athenian army at Marathon had reached Athens before the Persian ships did. As a result, the Persians returned to Persia.

According to tradition, Miltiades sent the runner Pheidippides from Marathon to Athens with news of the Athenian victory. Pheidippides raced the 25 miles (40 kilometers) to Athens at top speed, delivered his message, and fell to the ground, dead. Today, the word *marathon* refers to a foot race of 26 miles 385 yards (42.2 kilometers) or of similar length.   Jack Martin Balcer

Maravich, Pete (1947-1988), was one of the greatest scorers in basketball history. His sensational shooting earned him the nickname "Pistol Pete." Maravich's brilliant passing and behind-the-back dribbling also made him one of the game's most exciting players.

Maravich, a guard, played at Louisiana State University from 1967 to 1970. He led all college players in scoring during each of his three varsity seasons. His total of 3,667 points and average of 44.2 points a game are National Collegiate Athletic Association (NCAA) career records. Maravich played for 10 seasons in the National Basketball Association (NBA) with four teams, beginning with the 1970-71 season. He averaged 24.2 points a game in the NBA and led the league in scoring during the 1976-1977 season. Peter Press Maravich was born in Aliquippa, Pa. He died at the age of 40 from heart failure caused by a natural heart defect.   Bob Logan

Marble is a rock widely used in buildings, monuments, and sculptures. It consists chiefly of calcite or dolomite, or a combination of these carbonate minerals. Marble is a type of *metamorphic rock* formed from limestone (see **Metamorphic rock**).

Most marble of commercial value was formed in the *Paleozoic Era* or earlier in *Precambrian Time* (see **Earth** [Outline of the earth's history]). Marble is found in many countries, including Belgium, France, Great Britain, Greece, India, Italy, and Spain. South American nations also have large marble deposits. In the United States, Georgia produces the most marble. Other chief marble-producing states include Alabama, Colorado, Montana, Tennessee, Texas, and Vermont.

Field Museum of Natural History, Chicago (WORLD BOOK photo)

Marble occurs in many colors. It consists chiefly of calcite or dolomite, or a combination of these minerals. Impurities in the minerals produce the variations in color.

WORLD BOOK photo

The beauty of marble makes it an attractive building stone. The desk and walls shown above are made of marble.

Georgia Marble Company

Marble is mined in quarries such as this one in Georgia. Special mining equipment is used to cut the marble into blocks and remove it from the quarry.

Properties. Marble is formed from limestone by heat and pressure in the earth's crust. These forces cause the limestone to change in texture and makeup. This process is called *recrystallization.* Fossilized materials in the limestone, along with its original carbonate minerals, recrystallize and form large, coarse grains of calcite.

Impurities present in the limestone during recrystallization affect the mineral composition of the marble that forms. At relatively low temperatures, silica impurities in the carbonate minerals form masses of chert or crystals of quartz. At higher temperatures, the silica reacts with the carbonates to produce diopside and forsterite. At extremely high temperatures, rarer calcium minerals, such as larnite, monticellite, and rankinite, form in the marble. If water is present, serpentine, talc, and certain other hydrous minerals may be produced. The presence of iron, alumina, and silica may result in the formation of hematite and magnetite. In some cases, all these impurities may react to form garnets, hornblendes, and pyroxenes.

The minerals that result from impurities give marble a wide variety of colors. The purest calcite marble is white. Marble containing hematite has a reddish color. Marble that has limonite is yellow, and marble with serpentine is green.

Marble does not split easily into sheets of equal size and must be mined carefully. The rock may shatter if explosives are used. Blocks of marble are mined with *channeling machines,* which cut grooves and holes in the rock. Miners outline a block of marble with rows of grooves and holes. They then drive wedges into the openings and separate the block from the surrounding rock. The blocks are cut with saws to the desired shape and size.

Uses. Marble has long been highly valued for its beauty, strength, and resistance to fire and erosion. The ancient Greeks used marble in many buildings and statues. The Italian artist Michelangelo used marble from Carrara, Italy, in a number of sculptures. Marble from Tennessee was used in parts of the National Gallery of Art in Washington, D.C. The Lincoln Memorial, also in Washington, was built of marble from Alabama, Colorado, and Georgia.

Extremely pure calcite marble is used for most statues. This kind of marble is *translucent*—that is, light penetrates a short distance below the surface of the marble before it is reflected. Large blocks of colored marble are used for columns, floors, and other parts of buildings. Smaller pieces of such marble are crushed or finely ground and used as abrasives in soaps and other products. Crushed or ground marble is also used in paving roads and in manufacturing roofing materials and soil treatment products.   Robert W. Charles

Related articles in *World Book* include:

Building stone (Marble)	Limestone	Rock (pictures)
Carbonate	Metamorphism	Sculpture (pictures)
Dolomite	Onyx	

Marble, Alice. See Tennis (tables).
Marble bones. See Osteosclerosis.
Marbles is a children's game played with small balls, usually made of glass. Each ball is called a marble. There are many types of marbles games. Most games are played outdoors on a level surface. Marbles can be an

National Marbles Tournament

Marbles is a game generally played with small glass balls. Players shoot marbles by flicking a large marble toward smaller ones. Skilled players may compete in tournaments, *above*.

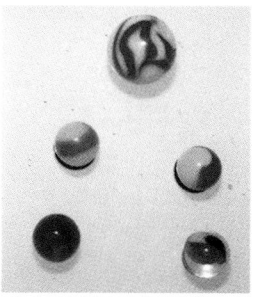

Jerry Brule, Marble Collectors Unlimited

Kinds of marbles include antique handmade marbles, *left*, and modern marbles made by machine, *right*.

organized sport, but it is most popular as a form of recreation.

Players shoot marbles by balancing a large marble called a *shooter* between the thumb and index finger. With the thumb, the player flicks the shooter toward one or more smaller marbles, called *object marbles*. Usually, players must *knuckle down* when shooting—that is, they must keep at least one knuckle on the ground as they shoot.

Marbles of various materials and colors have their own slang names. For example, glass marbles with colored swirls are known as *glassies*. Steel ball bearings used as marbles are called *steelies*.

In the United States, a game called *ringer* is played in tournaments. In ringer, players try to knock object marbles out of a circle 10 feet (3 meters) in diameter. Before play begins, a referee arranges 13 object marbles into the shape of a cross in the center of the circle. Players start their turns by knuckling down outside the circle. From there, a player must knock at least one object marble from the circle, and the player's shooter must remain in the circle. If successful, a player continues to shoot from wherever the shooter comes to rest. The turn ends when a player fails to knock out a marble or the shooter leaves the circle. The next player then takes a turn. The first player to knock seven object marbles out of the circle wins the game.

Marbles made of baked clay have been found in pre-

historic caves. The ancient Romans played games of marbles 2,000 years ago.   Rachel Gallagher

Marbury v. Madison marked the first time the United States Supreme Court declared a federal law unconstitutional. This 1803 case is one of the most important decisions in history. It established the supremacy of the Constitution over laws passed by Congress and the right of the court to review the constitutionality of legislation.

In 1801, President John Adams appointed William Marbury justice of the peace in the District of Columbia. But Adams' term ended before Marbury took office, and James Madison, the new secretary of state, withheld the appointment. Marbury asked the Supreme Court, under Section 13 of the Judiciary Act of 1789, to force Madison to grant the appointment. But the court refused to rule on the appointment because Section 13 gave the Supreme Court powers not provided by the Constitution and, therefore, the court declared Section 13 unconstitutional.   Stanley I. Kutler

See also **Jefferson, Thomas** (The courts); **Marshall, John** (Chief justice).

Marcel, Gabriel (1889-1973), was a French philosopher. He was an unsystematic thinker who presented his philosophy for the most part in three philosophical diaries: *Metaphysical Journals* (1927), *Being and Having* (1935), and *Presence and Immortality* (1959). His philosophy consists of reflections on concrete human experiences such as love and fidelity. He believed human experience can be understood only by directly participating in it. Therefore, he tried not merely to observe but to relive these experiences in the course of his reflections. His other works include *Homo Viator* (1944), an analysis of hope; and *Man Against Society* (1951), an examination of the effects of a technological society on the human personality.

Marcel was born in Paris. He became a Roman Catholic at 39. He is often classified as a Christian existentialist (see **Existentialism**).   Ivan Soll

March is a highly rhythmic musical composition that is performed mainly to accompany marching. Marches are intended to raise the morale of military troops, provide color and pageantry at sports events, and lend dignity to official ceremonies. In addition, some ballets, operas, and classical instrumental works include marches.

Most marches consist of a main melody called a *march* and a contrasting section called a *trio*. The trio generally is quieter and more melodious than the march and is played in a different key.

There are various kinds of marches. Two of the most common kinds are the *military march* and the *ceremonial march*. Military marches have a quick tempo and are used to help large groups march in an orderly manner. The American bandmaster John Philip Sousa wrote many popular military marches. Ceremonial marches are slower than military marches and are played at serious events, such as coronations and school graduations. The English composer Sir Edward Elgar wrote five famous ceremonial marches that are called *Pomp and Circumstance*. Other types include *circus marches*, which have fast tempos, and *funeral marches*, which have the slowest tempos of all marches.   R. M. Longyear

See also **Elgar, Sir Edward; Sousa, John Philip; King, Karl.**

March is the third month of the year according to the Gregorian calendar, which is used in almost all the world today. It was the first month on the early Roman calendar and was called *Martius*. Later, the ancient Romans made January 1 the beginning of the year, and March became the third month. March has always had 31 days. Its name honors Mars, the Roman god of war.

March brings in spring and ends the winter. Spring in the northern half of the world begins with the *vernal equinox*, which occurs on March 20 or 21. On this day, the center of the sun is directly over the equator. March can be both wintry and springlike. Blustery, windy days occur as frequently as mild, sunny days.

In the Northern Hemisphere, many animals end their hibernation, and many plants come to life again, during March. Sap flows in the trees, and green buds begin to appear. The first pussy willows and wild flowers can be found in the woods. Most frogs lay their eggs. Hibernating animals, such as bears, chipmunks, and wood-chucks, leave their winter sleeping places. Wild geese and ducks begin their northward flights. In March, people begin to look for the first robin as a sign that spring has really come.

Special days. March has no national holidays, but there are several important state and religious holidays. Nebraskans celebrate the admission of their state to the Union on March 1. Texas celebrates March 2 as the anniversary of its independence from Mexico. On March 4, the people of Pennsylvania commemorate the granting of the state's charter to William Penn in 1681. The Irish celebrate March 17 as the feast day of St. Patrick. In Maryland, March 25 is set apart for a celebration of the arrival of the first Maryland colonists in 1634. The Jewish festival of Purim usually occurs in March. It is held on the day corresponding to the 14th day of Adar on the Hebrew calendar.

Popular beliefs. There are many superstitions about March. We often hear that "March comes in like a lion

Important March events

1 Ohio became the 17th state, 1803.
— Augustus Saint-Gaudens, American sculptor, born 1848.
— Nebraska became the 37th state, 1867.
2 Sam Houston, American political leader, born 1793.
— Bedřich Smetana, Czech composer, born 1824.
— Carl Schurz, American political leader, born 1829.
— Texas declared its independence from Mexico, 1836.
— Pope Pius XII born 1876.
— Kurt Weill, German composer, born 1900.
3 Missouri Compromise passed, 1820.
— George Pullman, American inventor and businessman, born 1831.
— Florida became the 27th state, 1845.
— Inventor Alexander Graham Bell born 1847.
— Russia signed the Treaty of Brest-Litovsk, 1918.
4 William Penn received grant of Pennsylvania, 1681.
— The first Congress under the U.S. Constitution met, 1789. This date was used as Inauguration Day until 1937.
— Vermont became the 14th state, 1791.
— Knute Rockne, American football coach, born 1888.
5 Gerardus Mercator, Flemish geographer, born 1512.
— British soldiers fired on a mob in the Boston Massacre, 1770.
— Heitor Villa-Lobos, Brazilian composer, born 1887.
— Joseph Stalin, Soviet dictator, died 1953.
6 Italian artist Michelangelo, born 1475.
— Elizabeth Barrett Browning, English poet, born 1806.
— Santa Anna captured the Alamo, 1836.
— Ring Lardner, American humorist, born 1885.
7 Luther Burbank, American horticulturist, born 1849.
— Tomáš Masaryk, cofounder of Czechoslovakia, born 1850.
— Maurice Ravel, French composer, born 1875.
— Alexander Graham Bell patented the telephone, 1876.
8 Jurist Oliver Wendell Holmes, Jr., born 1841.

9 Amerigo Vespucci, Italian explorer, born 1454.
— The *Merrimack* (then called the *Virginia*) fought the *Monitor,* 1862.
— Samuel Barber, American composer, born 1910.
10 Arthur Honegger, French composer, born 1892.
11 Torquato Tasso, Italian poet, born 1544.
12 Canadian politician William Mackenzie born 1795.
— Sir John J. C. Abbott, prime minister of Canada, born 1821.
— Clement Studebaker, American manufacturer, born 1831.
— Gabriele d'Annunzio, Italian poet, born 1863.
— Juliette Low founded the Girl Scout movement in America, 1912.
— First transatlantic radio broadcast, 1925.
— President Harry S. Truman announced the Truman Doctrine, 1947.
13 Joseph Priestley, English chemist, born 1733.
— Johann Wyss, Swiss author, born 1781.
14 Eli Whitney patented the cotton gin, 1794.
— Johann Strauss, Austrian composer, born 1804.
— Albert Einstein, German-born American physicist, born 1879.
15 Julius Caesar assassinated, 44 B.C.
— Andrew Jackson, seventh President of the United States, born in Waxhaw settlement, either North Carolina or South Carolina, 1767.
— Maine became the 23rd state, 1820.
— American Legion founded, 1919.
16 James Madison, fourth President of the United States, born at Port Conway, King George County, Va., 1751.
— Georg S. Ohm, German physicist, born 1787.
— United States Military Academy founded at West Point, N.Y., 1802.

March birthstone—
bloodstone

March flower—
violet

March 5—
Boston Massacre

March 6—
Michelangelo born

and goes out like a lamb." This means that the first day of March is often stormy, and the last day is mild and warm. Another saying is, "April borrowed from March three days, and they were ill." This refers to the first three days of April, which are generally rough and blustery like March. A third saying calls the first three days of March "blind days" because they are "unlucky." If rain falls on these days, farmers supposedly will have poor harvests.

March symbols. The flower for March is the violet. The birthstones are the bloodstone (a variety of chalcedony) and the aquamarine. Sharron G. Uhler

Quotations

The stormy March has come at last,
With wind, and cloud, and changing skies;
I hear the rushing of the blast
That through the snowy valley flies.
William Cullen Bryant

I wonder if the sap is stirring yet,
If wintry birds are dreaming of a mate,
If frozen snowdrops feel as yet the sun,
And crocus fires are kindling one by one.
Christina Rossetti

And the Spring arose on the garden fair,
Like the Spirit of Love felt everywhere;
And each flower and herb on Earth's dark breast
Rose from the dreams of its wintry rest.
Percy Bysshe Shelley

The year's at the spring
And day's at the morn; . . .
God's in His heaven—
All's right with the world!
Robert Browning

Related articles in *World Book* include:

Aquamarine	Equinox	St. Patrick's Day
Calendar	Mars	Spring
Chalcedony	Purim	Violet

Important March events

17 St. Patrick's Day.
— British evacuated Boston, 1776.
18 John C. Calhoun, American statesman, born 1782.
— Grover Cleveland, 22nd and 24th President of the United States, born in Caldwell, N.J., 1837.
— Nikolai Rimsky-Korsakov, Russian composer, born 1844.
— Rudolf Diesel, German inventor, born 1858.
19 Missionary and explorer David Livingstone born 1813.
— Political leader William Jennings Bryan born 1860.
— Ballet producer Sergei Diaghilev born 1872.
20 Henrik Ibsen, Norwegian poet and dramatist, born 1828.
— Lauritz Melchior, Danish tenor, born 1890.
21 Johann Sebastian Bach, German composer, born 1685.
— Benito Juárez, Mexican political leader, born 1806.
— Modest Mussorgsky, Russian composer, born 1839.
22 Sir Anthony Van Dyck, Flemish painter, born 1599.
— Randolph Caldecott, English illustrator, born 1846.
— Robert Millikan, American physicist, born 1868.
23 Patrick Henry, according to tradition, declared "Give me liberty, or give me death!" 1775.
— Roger Martin du Gard, French novelist and Nobel Prize-winner for literature, born 1881.
24 William Morris, English poet and artist, born 1834.
— Andrew Mellon, American financier, born 1855.
25 Lord Baltimore's colonists landed in Maryland, 1634.
— British Parliament abolished slave trade, 1807.
— Arturo Toscanini, Italian conductor, born 1867.
— Béla Bartók, Hungarian composer, born 1881.
26 A. E. Housman, English poet, born 1859.
— Robert Frost, American poet, born 1874.
— James Conant, American chemist and educator, born 1893.
— Tennessee Williams, American playwright, born 1911.

26 Sandra Day O'Connor, first woman justice of Supreme Court of the United States, born 1930.
27 Louis XVII of France born 1785.
— Lithographer Nathaniel Currier born 1813.
— Wilhelm Roentgen, German physicist who discovered X rays, born 1845.
— Ludwig Mies van der Rohe, German-born architect, born 1886.
28 Pierre Laplace, French astronomer and mathematician, born 1749.
— Aristide Briand, French statesman, born 1862.
29 John Tyler, 10th President of the United States, born at Greenway Estate, Charles City County, Va., 1790.
— Parliament passed the British North America Act, 1867.
— Cy Young, American baseball player, born 1867.
30 Francisco Goya, Spanish painter, born 1746.
— Treaty of Paris ended the Crimean War, 1856.
— United States purchased Alaska from Russia, 1867.
— Amendment 15 to the U.S. Constitution, stating that a person cannot be denied the ballot because of race or color, proclaimed, 1870.
— Albert Einstein announced revised Unified Field Theory, 1953.
31 René Descartes, French philosopher-scientist, born 1596.
— Joseph Haydn, Austrian composer, born 1732.
— Commodore Matthew C. Perry made the first treaty between the United States and Japan, 1854.
— United States took possession of the Virgin Islands by purchase from Denmark, 1917.
— Daylight Saving Time went into effect in the United States, 1918.
— Newfoundland became the 10th province of Canada, 1949.

WORLD BOOK illustrations by Mike Hagel

March 12—
Girl Scout movement founded

March 14—
Albert Einstein born

March 17—St.
Patrick's Day

March 23—famous
Patrick Henry speech

March, Peyton Conway, *PAY tuhn* (1864-1955), was chief of staff of the United States Army during World War I. He directed the operations that landed about 2 million American troops in France. March has been called the father of the modern U.S. Army. He combined the Regular Army, the National Guard, and the National Army divisions into a single force. He also reorganized the War Department, and built a small, well-organized army around a core of professional soldiers. March believed a small corps of trained officers could build a large, powerful army in time of emergency.

March was born in Easton, Pa. He graduated from the U.S. Military Academy (West Point) in 1888, and fought in the Spanish-American War. He retired from active service in 1921. He described his World War I experiences in *The Nation at War* (1932).   Maurice Matloff

March of Dimes Birth Defects Foundation is a health agency that supports research, education, and medical and social services for children and pregnant women. It is a leading authority on such issues as birth defects, low birth weight, infant mortality, and maternal drug and alcohol abuse.

The agency was established in 1938 by President Franklin D. Roosevelt to combat epidemic poliomyelitis, or polio. It was then called the National Foundation for Infantile Paralysis. It funded the development of the Salk and Sabin vaccines that help prevent polio. In 1958, the agency began working to prevent birth defects and also changed its name to National Foundation—March of Dimes. March of Dimes referred to the dimes sent to the White House during Roosevelt's presidency for the agency's annual fund-raising drive. The agency adopted its present name in 1979.

The March of Dimes is supported by donations and assisted by volunteers. Headquarters are at 1275 Mamaroneck Avenue, White Plains, NY 10605.
Critically reviewed by the March of Dimes Birth Defects Foundation

Marciano, *MAHR see AH noh,* **Rocky** (1923-1969), was the world heavyweight boxing champion from 1952 to 1956. He retired in 1956 after winning all of his 49 professional fights. Marciano won the title on Sept. 23, 1952, by knocking out Jersey Joe Walcott in the 13th round in Philadelphia. Eight months later, in his first title defense, Marciano knocked out Walcott in the first round. Marciano then successfully defended his title five more times. Marciano is considered one of the hardest punchers in boxing history. His victories include 43 knockouts, with 11 in the first round. In 1951, he ended the comeback of former world champion Joe Louis by knocking him out in the 8th round.

Marciano was born Rocco Marchegiano in Brockton, Mass. He turned professional in 1947. Marciano died in the crash of a private airplane.   Bert Randolph Sugar

Marco Polo. See Polo, Marco.

Marconi, *mahr KOH nee,* **Guglielmo,** *goo LYEHL moh* (1874-1937), was an Italian inventor and electrical engineer who gained international fame for his role in developing *wireless telegraphy,* or radio (see **Radio**). In 1895, he sent the first telegraph signals through the air. Telegraph signals previously had been transmitted through electric wires, and so Marconi's system became known as wireless telegraphy. In 1901, Marconi transmitted the first transatlantic wireless communication. He shared the 1909 Nobel Prize in physics with Karl Ferdi-

nand Braun of Germany, who had invented a tube that improved wireless transmission. Their work helped lead to the development of radio broadcasting. Marconi also pioneered tests with short waves and microwaves.

Early life. Marconi was born in Bologna, Italy. His father was a wealthy landowner. As a child, Guglielmo was educated primarily by tutors and took a strong interest in science. He later failed the University of Bologna entrance exam and decided to pursue his scientific studies on his own.

Marconi read about the German physicist Heinrich Hertz's work with electromagnetic waves, and began experimenting with wireless telegraphy in 1894. He set up equipment in the attic of his father's estate and transmitted signals across the room. Marconi later began to experiment outdoors. Marconi found when his transmitter and receiver were *grounded* (connected to earth), he could greatly extend the signal's range by increasing the antenna's height. After this discovery, he transmitted signals farther than had ever been done before.

The Italian government showed no interest in the young, unschooled inventor's work, so Marconi went to Great Britain. There, in 1896, he received the first patent on wireless telegraphy. Marconi also gained financial support and formed the Wireless Telegraph and Signal Company, Ltd., in 1897 in London. In 1899, three British warships were equipped with Marconi's wireless equipment. That same year, he sent a wireless message across the English Channel to France. Private ships also began to use Marconi's system.

First transatlantic signal. On Dec. 12, 1901, Marconi and his staff sent the first wireless transatlantic communication in history. They transmitted the Morse code letter *s* from Poldhu, Cornwall, England, to St. John's, Canada. Soon afterward, ships used Marconi's equipment to communicate with each other and with the shore over distances up to 2,000 miles (3,200 kilometers).

Marconi's fame grew when his wireless equipment helped bring rescue ships for the sinking ocean liners *Republic* in 1909 and *Titanic* in 1912, saving many lives.

Brown Bros.

Guglielmo Marconi centered his life around wireless telegraphy. In his yacht, *above,* Marconi experimented sending and receiving messages while crossing the Atlantic.

These accidents led to laws requiring that all large passenger ships have wireless equipment.

Short-wave experiments. During the 1920's, Marconi turned his attention to short waves and microwaves. Marconi and other inventors had developed commercial wireless equipment using long airwaves, which required large, powerful transmission systems. But short-wave stations did not require such transmitters, and they cost less to build and operate. Short waves, unlike long waves, could be used as effectively during the day as at night. Marconi and his staff perfected the *beam system,* which used directional aerials and reflectors. This system made short-wave radio an efficient and reliable method of communication. Marconi's team also built the first microwave telephone system in 1932 and helped open the way for a revolution in microwave electronic communication.

Besides the Nobel Prize, Marconi received many other honors and awards. King George V of Great Britain gave him the honorary title of Knight Grand Cross of the Royal Victoria Order in 1914. Marconi also received the John Fritz Medal, the most prestigious award in American engineering.   David A. Hounshell

Additional resources

Gunston, David. *Marconi: Father of Radio.* Crowell Collier, 1965. First published in 1962. For younger readers.
Jacot de Boinod, B. L., and Collier, D. M. B. *Marconi: Master of Space.* Hutchinson (London), 1935. A classic biography.

Marcos, Ferdinand Edralin (1917-1989), served as president of the Philippines from 1965 to 1986. In 1973, the Philippines adopted a constitution that gave him broad powers as both president and prime minister. In 1978, Marcos took the title of prime minister while remaining as president. In 1981, he was replaced as prime minister, but he kept his broad powers. Marcos' political party was accused of widespread election fraud in a presidential election held in February 1986. He was forced to leave the country after widespread protests against him broke out. Corazon Aquino, his main election opponent, was officially declared winner and was sworn in as president. Marcos settled in Honolulu, Hawaii. See **Philippines** (The Philippines today).

In 1988, Marcos and his wife, Imelda, were indicted by the United States government. The indictment included charges that they had embezzled money from the Philippines and used it to buy buildings in the United States. But Marcos became seriously ill and, as a result, the charges against him were dropped. He died in exile in September 1989. In 1990, a jury found Imelda not guilty. In 1991, Imelda returned to the Philippines to face civil and criminal charges there. The Philippine government is attempting to recover much of the money the Marcoses had supposedly embezzled. In 1992, Imelda ran for president of the Philippines but lost.

Marcos was born in Sarrat. While a law student at the University of the Philippines, he was accused, tried, and convicted of murdering a man who had defeated his father in an election for the National Assembly. But the Supreme Court acquitted him. Marcos served in the Philippine House of Representatives from 1949 to 1959. He was elected to the Senate in 1959.   Jean Grossholtz

Marcus Aurelius, *aw REE lee uhs* (A.D. 121-180), was a Roman emperor and philosopher. He became a fol-

lower of Stoicism, a school of philosophy that originated in Greece about 300 B.C. Marcus wrote a series of thoughts that were collected and published as *Meditations.* This work is an intimate self-portrait and a classic of Stoic philosophy. See **Stoic philosophy.**

Marcus was born in Rome to a noble family. Before Antoninus Pius became emperor in A.D. 138, he adopted Marcus and Lucius Verus. Marcus became emperor in 161 and named Lucius co-emperor. Marcus and Lucius ruled jointly until Lucius' death in 169. During much of Marcus' reign, the Roman Empire suffered from epidemics, revolts, and frequent wars along its frontiers. Marcus turned to Stoic philosophy for personal comfort.

Marcus accepted the Stoic belief that the world is ruled by a benevolent universal force. He was inspired by the Stoic belief in the harmony of natural and moral law that represented the divine spirit present in all things. Marcus believed that the soul did not survive after death, but instead was reabsorbed into the universe. He saw this reabsorption as a reason to accept death calmly. Marcus hated selfishness and taught himself to ignore or forgive offenses. Perhaps his noblest quality was his sense of responsibility to humanity and his belief that all people are citizens of the universe and should live for each other.   Elaine Fantham

Mardi Gras, *MAHR dee GRAH,* is a lively, colorful celebration held on Shrove Tuesday, the day before Lent begins. The date of Mardi Gras depends on the date of Easter. Mardi Gras takes place at the end of a long carnival season that begins on January 6, or Twelfth Night. It is celebrated in many Roman Catholic countries and other communities. *Mardi Gras* means *fat Tuesday* in French. The term may have arisen in part from the custom of parading a fat ox through French towns and villages on Shrove Tuesday.

French colonists introduced Mardi Gras into America in the early 1700's. The custom became popular in New Orleans, La., and spread through several Southern States. Mardi Gras is a legal holiday in Alabama and Florida and in eight *parishes* (counties) of Louisiana. The New Orleans celebration is the most famous. But Biloxi, Miss., and Mobile, Ala., also celebrate Mardi Gras.

Mardi Gras in New Orleans attracts tourists from around the world. Parades begin the week before Mardi Gras Day. Societies called *krewes* organize and pay for the parades and other festivities. During the carnival season, the krewes give balls and parties. They parade in masks and fancy dress. A parade of beautiful floats and marching bands climaxes the carnival on Mardi Gras Day. Riders on the floats throw necklaces, toys, and coins called *doubloons* to the onlookers. Each year, the festivities have a theme.

Mardi Gras goes back to an ancient Roman custom of merrymaking before a period of fast. In Germany Mardi Gras is called *Fastnacht.* In England it is called *Pancake Day* or *Pancake Tuesday.*   Robert J. Myers

See also **Louisiana** (picture); **Mask** (picture: Colorful masks); **Shrove Tuesday.**

Marduk, *MAHR duk,* was the chief god of the ancient Babylonians. He was originally a god of only the city of Babylon. But as Babylon emerged as the most important and powerful city of Mesopotamia, Marduk became the most important god of the area. He was called the "great lord, the lord of heaven and earth." His power was said to lie in his wisdom, which he used to help good people and to punish the wicked.   C. Scott Littleton

Mare. See **Horse** (Life history).

Marfan syndrome is a disorder characterized by abnormalities of the skeleton, eye, and heart. It is caused by a genetic defect that is thought to affect the development of some of the body's connective tissues. People who have Marfan syndrome typically die before the age of 50, usually from heart complications.

People with Marfan syndrome tend to be unusually tall, often with long, thin arms and legs and an arm span that exceeds the height of the body. The hands, fingers, feet, and toes also may be unusually long. Other, less common skeletal abnormalities include a long, narrow face, funnel-shaped deformities of the chest; and curvature of the spine. An abnormality in the position of the lens of the eye causes vision problems in many Marfan patients. Heart problems associated with the syndrome primarily involve the connections of the large blood vessels to the heart. These vessel walls may gradually weaken and balloon out, eventually rupturing or splitting, which results in death.

Researchers estimate that 5 of every 100,000 people have Marfan syndrome. A child of an affected parent has a 50 per cent chance of inheriting the syndrome. Doctors know of no cure for it.   Thomas J. Schnitzer

Margarine, also called *oleomargarine,* is a butterlike food made from vegetable oils or animal fats, or both. Many people cook with margarine and use it on bread and other foods. Many bakeries and other food manufacturers also use it.

In the United States, people use more than twice as much margarine as butter. Margarine usually costs less than butter, and it can be processed so that it has the same food value. It also contains a greater proportion of *polyunsaturated fatty acids* and much less of a fatty substance called *cholesterol.* Many doctors warn that too much cholesterol in the blood can lead to a heart attack. See **Fat** (Fats and disease).

How margarine is made. The U.S. government requires that margarine contain at least 80 per cent fat. The fat must be *emulsified* (evenly distributed) in milk, water, or a type of milk made from soybeans. Margarine also must be fortified with vitamin A at a level equal to that in butter. Most margarine also contains butterlike flavoring, salt, vitamin D, and yellow coloring. Preservatives are added to prevent decay. One or more vegetable oils provide the fat content of most margarine. Soybean oil is the most commonly used oil. But processors also may use corn, cottonseed, palm, peanut, and safflower oils. Some margarine is made with animal fats.

To make margarine, manufacturers emulsify melted oils with milk or water and chill the resulting substance until it hardens. Most household margarine is made in sticks or is packaged in small tubs. Manufacturers also make large blocks of hard margarine for commercial bakeries, and fluid household margarine in plastic squeeze bottles.

History. Hippolyte Mege-Mouries, a French chemist, developed margarine in the late 1860's as a substitute for butter. He called it *oleomargarine* because its chief ingredients were beef fat, called *oleo,* and *margaric acid.* The product was introduced into the United States in the early 1870's. Almost immediately, U.S. dairy farmers protested that it would ruin the butter market. As a result, Congress put a tax on margarine in 1886 to discourage its sale. By the 1930's, many states had banned the sale of yellow-colored margarine. Such margarine was more popular than the natural white variety.

People bought margarine despite the restrictions, and criticism of the federal tax increased. Congress ended the tax in 1950. By 1967, all state bans on colored margarine had also ended. Margarine sales more than doubled from 1950 to 1970.   Kay Franzen Jamieson

Margay, *MAHR gay,* is a wildcat that lives in Central and South America from northern Mexico to Bolivia and

Jeff Foott, Bruce Coleman Ltd.

The margay is a wildcat that lives in Central and South America. Its markings are similar to those of the ocelot. The margay has a small head and a very long tail.

Brazil. Its reddish or grayish fur is thickly marked with black spots and streaks. Its tail is longer than the head and body. The margay is $2\frac{1}{2}$ to 4 feet (76 to 122 centimeters) long and weighs 10 to 20 pounds (4.5 to 9 kilograms). It resembles the *ocelot* (tiger cat) but is smaller, more slender, and has a longer tail (see **Ocelot**). The margay's name may have come from an Indian term for "little ocelot." Zoologists know little about its habits.

Scientific classification. The margay belongs to the cat family, Felidae. It is *Felis wiedii.*   Elizabeth S. Frank

Margin in a stock exchange refers to funds that speculators deposit with their brokers to protect the brokers against loss. The deposit safeguards the brokers, in case speculators lose money after they have bought stocks. It must cover the difference between the selling price of the stocks and the amount the brokers can borrow from a bank, plus an amount to cover possible losses that might result from stocks quickly changing prices. In the United States, the Federal Reserve System sets the amount of margin required.   Robert Sobel

Margrethe II, *mahr GRAY tuh* (1940-   ), is queen of Denmark. She succeeded her father, Frederik IX, upon his death in 1972.

Margrethe was born in Copenhagen. Her full name is Margrethe Alexandrine Torhildur Ingrid. She became next in line for the throne in 1953, when changes in the Danish Constitution enabled women to rule for the first time. A lack of male heirs to the throne forced the change. In preparation for her reign, Margrethe attended universities in Denmark, England, and France. She presided over the Danish Cabinet at formal functions when her father was ill.

During the 1960's, Margrethe traveled to Africa, the Far East, and the Middle East in connection with her interest in archaeology. In 1967, she married Henri de

Laborde de Monpezat, a French count, who became Prince Henrik of Denmark. They have two sons, Frederik, the crown prince, and Joachim. In addition to performing her royal functions, Margarethe is an artist and book illustrator. Her works have been exhibited publicly.   Ulla Skovgaard Jensen

Maria Theresa (1717-1780) was Holy Roman empress, queen of Hungary and Bohemia, and archduchess of Austria. She was a powerful force in European affairs and one of the wisest and most able rulers in Austrian history. With the aid of her brilliant chancellor and foreign minister, Prince Kaunitz, she managed foreign affairs skillfully. Her economic reforms promoted the prosperity of her empire. She had 16 children. One daughter, Marie Antoinette, was queen of France (see **Marie Antoinette**).

Maria Theresa was born in Vienna. Her father, Emperor Charles VI, was the last male Habsburg (or Hapsburg) heir. In 1724, he announced publicly a decree, called a Pragmatic sanction, that had been issued privately in 1713. This decree allowed Maria Theresa to inherit his territories. The rulers of the principal states of Europe accepted the decree and promised not to attack Maria Theresa's lands (see **Pragmatic sanction**).

Charles VI died in 1740. Prussia was the first to attack in the War of the Austrian Succession and was soon joined by Bavaria, France, and Spain. They all claimed parts of Maria Theresa's territories in spite of their promises. At first, Sardinia and Saxony also opposed Maria Theresa. But they later joined the Netherlands and Britain in aiding Maria Theresa's forces in the war. In 1745, Maria Theresa's husband, Francis Stephen, former Duke of Lorraine, became Holy Roman emperor as Francis I. But she kept control over most state affairs.

Maria Theresa of Austria, portrait by Martin Van Mytens, Brooks Memorial Art Gallery, Memphis, Tenn.

Maria Theresa of Austria

The War of the Austrian Succession ended in 1748 with the Treaty of Aix-la-Chapelle. By this treaty, Maria Theresa lost almost all of the rich province of Silesia to Frederick II of Prussia (see **Frederick II** [of Prussia]). The powers of Europe recognized her rights to her other possessions. See **Succession wars**.

During the early 1750's, Maria Theresa strengthened her power at home and built a large army. In 1756, while she was planning to seek revenge for the loss of Silesia, Frederick II suddenly attacked again. The Seven Years' War followed, and Maria Theresa was forced to give up all claims to Silesia (see **Seven Years' War**). Her husband died in 1765, and her oldest son became Holy Roman emperor as Joseph II. In 1772, Maria Theresa joined with Russia and Prussia in a division of Poland and gained most of the region of Galicia. In 1775, she took the region of Bukovina from Turkey. Maria Theresa died in Vienna.   Charles W. Ingrao

Mariana Islands, *MAIR ee AN uh,* are formed by the summits of 15 volcanic mountains in the Pacific. They are the southern part of a submerged mountain range

that extends 1,565 miles (2,519 kilometers) from Guam almost to Japan (see **Pacific Islands** [map]). The Marianas are the northernmost islands of a larger island group called *Micronesia,* which means *small islands.* The Marianas have a total land area of 396 square miles (1,026 square kilometers) and a population of about 176,500. About 133,000 people live on Guam, and about 39,000 live on Saipan. The rest of the people live on other islands.

The Mariana Islands, except Guam, are a commonwealth of the United States. Island residents are U.S. citizens. Saipan is the capital of the commonwealth.

The 10 northern Marianas are rugged islands. Some of them have volcanoes that erupt periodically. Pagan, Agrihan, and Anatahan are the largest islands in this group. The limestone or reef rock terraces on volcanic slopes in the five southern Marianas show that they are older than the northern group. Guam is the largest of the southern islands. Other important islands are Rota, Saipan, and Tinian. Tourism is the major industry of Guam and Saipan. In addition, the U.S. military service employs many people on Guam.

The native islanders are called *Chamorros.* Their ancestors, who were among the earliest settlers of Micronesia, arrived from Asia thousands of years ago. The Chamorros have intermarried with Europeans, Filipinos, and other peoples. Today, they practice many Western customs.

The Portuguese explorer Ferdinand Magellan led the first European expedition to Guam and Rota. His party arrived in 1521. His sailors called the islands *Islas de los Ladrones,* or *Islands of Thieves,* because the islanders helped themselves to articles on the ships after furnishing supplies of food and water. The islands received their present name from Spanish Jesuits who arrived in 1668. Spain governed the islands from 1668 to 1898.

After the Spanish-American War (1898), the United States kept Guam as a naval base. Spain sold the rest of the islands to Germany. Japan occupied Guam in 1941, but American armed forces recaptured the island in July and August 1944 and built naval air bases on several of the islands. The Marianas, except for Guam, were governed by the United States as part of the United Nations Trust Territory of the Pacific Islands. In 1976, the United States agreed to form the Commonwealth of the Northern Mariana Islands, which would include all of the Marianas except Guam. This agreement went into effect in November 1986, making the people U.S. citizens. The government of the commonwealth controls its internal affairs, but the United States remains responsible for foreign affairs and defense.   Robert C. Kiste

See also **Guam; Pacific Islands, Trust Territory of the; Saipan.**

Mariana Trench. See Ocean (Depth).

Marie Antoinette, *AN twuh NEHT* (1755-1793), was the beautiful queen of France who died on the guillotine during the French Revolution. Her frivolity and plotting helped undermine the monarchy.

The young queen was lively and extravagant. The stiff formalities of court life bored her, so she amused herself with such pleasures as fancy balls, theatricals, and gambling. Marie lacked a good education and cared very little for serious affairs. She did not hesitate to urge the dismissal of the able ministers of France whose efforts to reduce royal spending threatened her pleasures. Louis XVI gave her the château called the Petit Trianon, where the queen and her friends amused themselves (see **Versailles, Palace of**).

Marie became very unpopular and was blamed for the corruption of the French court. She lavished money on court favorites and paid no attention to France's financial crisis. Vicious stories were told about her. One of these stories illustrates the haughty attitude people associated with her name. According to the story, Marie once asked an official why the Parisians were angry. "Because they have no bread," was the reply. "Then let them eat cake," said the queen. The suffering people of Paris readily believed this false story.

Her early life. Marie was born in Vienna. She was the youngest and favorite daughter of Emperor Francis I and Maria Theresa, rulers of the Holy Roman Empire. Marie was brought up in the hope that she might one day be queen of France. She married the French *dauphin* (crown prince) in 1770. Four years later, he became King Louis XVI, and Marie became queen.

The revolution. Tragedy struck Marie twice in 1789. Her eldest son died, and the French Revolution started. Her weak-willed husband lost control of the nation. Marie tried to stiffen King Louis' will, but only made people angrier by her stubborn opposition to the revolutionary changes.

The king, partly on Marie's advice, assembled troops around Versailles twice in 1789. Both times violence followed, and royal authority became weaker. The second time, early in October 1789, a hungry and desperate Parisian crowd marched to Versailles and forced the royal family to move to the Tuileries palace in Paris. From then on, Louis and Marie were virtual prisoners.

The rulers might have been able to rally the nation in support of a constitutional monarchy like that of England, had they followed the advice of moderate statesmen like the Comte de Mirabeau (see **Mirabeau, Comte de**). Instead, Marie Antoinette plotted for military aid from the rulers of Europe—especially from her brother, Leopold II of Austria. She refused to make any concessions at all to the revolutionists.

Downfall of the monarchy. Finally, Marie influenced Louis to flee from Paris on the night of June 20, 1791. The royal family set out in disguise by carriage for the eastern frontier of France. But an alert patriot recognized the king from his picture on French paper money. The king and queen were halted at Varennes, and returned under guard to Paris. The flight of Louis and Marie made the people distrust their rulers even more. But Louis promised to accept a new constitution that limited his powers.

Marie now worked to get aid from abroad, and, when war with Austria and Prussia came in 1792, she passed military secrets on to the enemy. The people suspected such treason. On Aug. 10, 1792, they threw the royal family into prison, ending the monarchy. Louis XVI died on the guillotine on Jan. 21, 1793. After bravely enduring imprisonment, Marie Antoinette, called Widow Capet by the revolutionists, was tried for treason. She died on the guillotine on Oct. 16, 1793.   Isser Woloch

See also **French Revolution; Louis XVI; Maria Theresa; Swiss Guard**.

Additional resources

Erickson, Carolly. *To the Scaffold: The Life of Marie Antoinette*. Morrow, 1991.
Haslip, Joan. *Marie Antoinette*. Weidenfeld & Nicolson, 1987.
Seward, Desmond. *Marie Antoinette*. St. Martin's, 1981.
Zweig, Stefan. *Marie Antoinette: The Portrait of an Average Woman*. Century Bookbindery, 1983. First published in 1933. A standard source.

Marie Louise (1791-1847) was the second wife of Napoleon Bonaparte and the daughter of Emperor Francis I of Austria. She married Napoleon in 1810 after his divorce from Josephine. Napoleon and Marie Louise had a son in 1811 who became known as Napoleon II.

Marie Louise was not permitted to go with Napoleon when he was exiled. She and her son lived at Schönbrunn, near Vienna. She received the Italian duchies of Parma, Piacenza, and Guastalla in 1816, and governed them until her death. Marie Louise was married twice after the death of Napoleon. She was born in Vienna, Austria.   Donald Sutherland

See also **Josephine; Napoleon I; Napoleon II**.

Marietta (pop. 15,026), the oldest town in Ohio, is a major manufacturing and trading center. The city lies on the north bank of the Ohio River at the mouth of the Muskingum River. Marietta and Parkersburg, W. Va., form a metropolitan area with a population of 149,169. For location, see **Ohio** (political map).

Marietta serves as a market for farm products of the Muskingum Valley. The chief manufactures include medical equipment, paints, gasoline, lubricating oils, concrete products, alloys, phenol, and polystyrene. The city is the home of Marietta College.

Pioneers led by General Rufus Putnam founded Mari-

Marie Antoinette and Her Children in the Petit Trianon Park (detail) by Ulrich Wertmüller. Nationalmuseum, Stockholm

Marie Antoinette was a teen-ager when she became queen of France in 1774. She was executed less than 20 years later.

etta in 1788. The city was named for Queen Marie Antoinette of France. It has a mayor-council government and is the seat of Washington County.   Thomas W. Schmidlin

See also **Putnam, Rufus.**

Marigold is a hardy flowering plant commonly grown in gardens. Marigolds range from 6 inches to 3 feet (15 to 90 centimeters) in height. They generally have feathery, fernlike leaves and yellow, orange, or reddish-brown blossoms. Most marigolds have a strong odor. All cultivated marigolds are *annuals*—that is, they live for only one year.

WORLD BOOK illustration by John F. Eggert

The African marigold, *above,* is cultivated in many gardens. Marigolds are popular garden flowers because they are easy to grow and survive periods of dry weather well.

There are about 50 species of marigolds. Six of these species are commonly cultivated: (1) African, also called Aztec or big, (2) French, (3) sweet-scented, (4) signet, (5) Irish lace and (6) Muster-John-Henry. All marigolds are native to an area that extends from the Southwestern United States to Argentina. Spanish explorers brought marigolds to Europe in the early 1500's.

Marigolds are easy to grow. They can survive periods of dry weather better than most other garden flowers can. Many gardeners plant marigold seeds indoors in late winter or early spring. The seedlings are transplanted outdoors in a warm, sunny place in late spring. Some marigolds produce an oil that repels *nematodes,* small worms that live as parasites on plant roots. Gardeners sometimes grow such marigolds with other plants to protect those plants from nematodes.

Scientific classification. Marigolds belong to the composite family, Compositae.   Margaret R. Bolick

See also **Flower** (picture: Garden annuals).

Marijuana, also spelled *marihuana,* is a drug made from the dried leaves and flowering tops of the hemp plant. Marijuana has many psychological and physical effects. People usually smoke marijuana in cigarettes or pipes, but it also can be mixed with food and beverages. Almost all nations, including the United States and Canada, have laws that prohibit the cultivation, distribution, possession, and use of marijuana.

Marijuana has many nicknames, including *grass, pot,*

and *weed.* It is also called *cannabis,* a word that comes from *Cannabis sativa,* the scientific name for hemp.

Effects. Marijuana contains more than 400 chemicals. When smoked, it produces over 2,000 chemicals that enter the body through the lungs. These chemicals have a variety of immediate, short-term effects. In addition, the repeated use of marijuana has been linked to a number of long-term effects.

Short-term effects of marijuana include both psychological and physical reactions. These reactions usually last for three to five hours after a person has smoked marijuana. The psychological reaction, known as a *high,* consists of changes in the user's feelings and thoughts. Such changes are caused mainly by *THC,* a chemical in marijuana that impairs brain function.

The effects of a marijuana high vary from person to person and from one time to another in the same individual. In most cases, the high consists of a dreamy, relaxed state in which users seem more aware of their senses and feel that time is moving slowly. Sometimes, however, marijuana produces a feeling of panic and dread. The different reactions result partly from the concentration of THC in the marijuana. Other factors, such as the setting in which marijuana is used and the user's expectations, personality, and mood, also affect a person's reaction to the drug.

The short-term physical effects of marijuana include redness in the eyes and a rapid heartbeat. The drug also interferes with a person's judgment and coordination. Therefore, driving a motor vehicle while under the influence of marijuana is particularly dangerous.

Long-term effects of marijuana are not completely known. But studies have shown that some people who have used marijuana regularly for several months or longer develop serious long-term problems. Use of marijuana harms memory and motivation. Some chronic users suffer bronchitis, coughing, and chest pains. Marijuana smoke also contains cancer-causing substances. Among males, marijuana use can reduce the production of sperm and of the male sex hormone *testosterone.* Among females, it can cause menstrual irregularity and reduced fertility. Extended use of marijuana also has a long-term psychological effect on many people. These individuals lose interest in school, their job, and social activities.

Why people use marijuana. Most people who use marijuana begin to do so between the ages of 12 and 18. They try the drug because of curiosity. Some people believe marijuana improves their talents and capabilities. But scientists have found that marijuana impairs all abilities. Marijuana may increase a person's willingness to accept new ideas without determining whether they are true or false. As a result, some users think marijuana gives them new understanding about life.

Many people who try marijuana use it only a few times or infrequently. However, others become regular users. Some regular users become dependent on the drug and have great difficulty in stopping its use.

History. Marijuana has been used as a medicine and an intoxicant for thousands of years in many parts of the world. In the United States, marijuana use has been prohibited by state and local laws since the early 1900's, and by federal law since 1937. In spite of these laws, use of the drug became widespread during the 1960's and

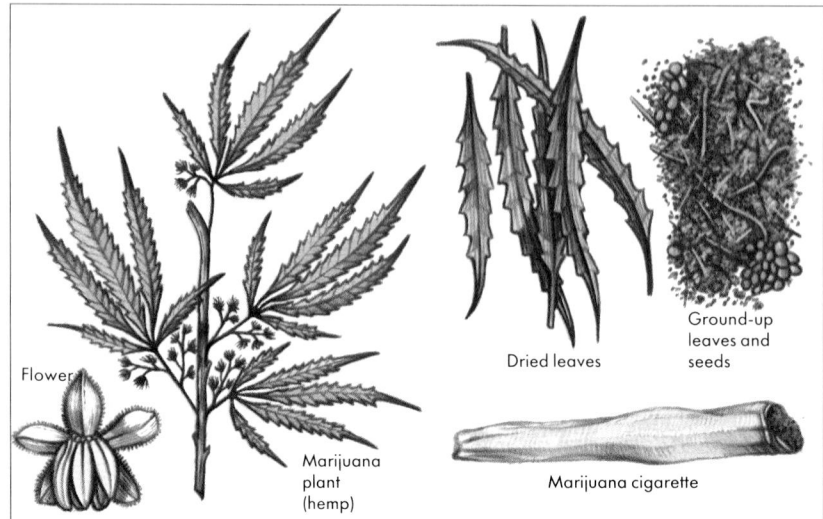

Marijuana is an illegal drug that produces psychological and physical effects. It is made from the dried leaves and flowering tops of the hemp plant. Users commonly smoke marijuana in cigarettes or pipes.

Flower

Dried leaves

Ground-up leaves and seeds

Marijuana plant (hemp)

Marijuana cigarette

WORLD BOOK illustration by Carol A. Brozman

1970's, especially among young people. Between 1969 and 1978, the federal and many state governments reduced the criminal charge for possession of small amounts of marijuana from a felony to a misdemeanor. Some states even substituted fines for jail sentences. Surveys indicated a decline in marijuana use among high school students during the 1980's as more young people became aware of the drug's harmful effects.

Many people have urged investigation of the possible medical uses of marijuana and the chemicals in it. Others have opposed such investigations, fearing they would lead to increased availability and recreational use of the drug. In 1980, the U.S. Food and Drug Administration (FDA) approved the limited use of THC pills to control nausea brought on by anticancer medicines. Under a tightly regulated investigational program, the FDA has provided marijuana cigarettes to a few cancer and glaucoma patients. In 1985, the FDA approved *Marinol,* a drug containing THC, for use under a physician's supervision.   Robert L. DuPont

See also **Drug abuse; Hashish; Hemp.**

Additional resources

Godfrey, Martin. *Marijuana.* Watts, 1987. Also suitable for younger readers.
Jones, Helen C., and Lovinger, P. W. *The Marijuana Question: And Science's Search for an Answer.* Dodd, 1985.

Marimba, *muh RIHM buh,* is a percussion instrument that consists of a number of bars arranged on a frame like the keys of a piano. Most marimbas have bars of rosewood, but some have plastic bars. A musician strikes the bars with mallets that have heads of soft or hard rubber or of yarn. The sounds are amplified by metal tubes called *resonators,* one of which lies beneath each bar. Most marimbas have 49 to 52 bars with a range of from 4 to $4\frac{1}{2}$ octaves. The instrument produces a rich, mellow sound. Marimbalike instruments date from prehistoric times. Marimbas have become especially popular in Africa, and in Latin America. Some Latin-American marimbas are so long that four or five musicians can play at one time.   John H. Beck

Marin, *MAIR uhn,* **John** (1870-1953), was one of the first American artists to paint in a modern style. He combined realistic images with elements of an abstract style called *cubism* (see **Cubism**). Marin's paintings include bold, angular lines; vivid colors; patches of bare paper or canvas; and overlapping planes. Some of these planes cluster at the edge of the work to reinforce the frame. Many of Marin's water color and oil paintings are seascapes and landscapes that express in abstract ways the powerful forces of change in nature. The active forms he used in his representation of objects give his work a sense of movement and energy.

Marin was born in Rutherford, N.J. He lived in Europe from 1905 to 1911. During this period, his work showed

Karl Kummels, Shostal

The marimba is similar to a xylophone. Some Latin-American marimbas, such as the one shown above, are so long that several musicians can play the instrument at one time.

Peter A. Juley & Son

John Marin became famous for his vivid water color paintings. Many of his works show dramatic scenes from nature. Marin's *Maine Islands, left,* reflects the blend of abstract and realistic elements that are typical of his style.

Water color (1922); the Phillips Collection, Washington, D.C.

the influence of James A. M. Whistler, an American painter of the late 1800's. Marin first exhibited his paintings in Paris in 1908. His work was shown in the United States for the first time in 1909, at the gallery of Alfred Stieglitz in New York City. Stieglitz, a photographer and art promoter, was the chief spokesman for modern art in the United States. He became Marin's most active supporter.

Marin returned to the United States in 1911 and began to develop a distinctive personal style in response to both the urban scene and nature. Most of Marin's paintings portray his immediate surroundings, such as New York City and the seacoast of Maine. A Maine seascape, the water color *Off Stonington* (1921), appears in the **Painting** article. He painted his impression of New York City in *Lower Manhattan* (1922). Marin traveled to other parts of the country to find new subjects for his paintings. *Storm Over Taos* (1930) reflects some of the beauty he saw in New Mexico.

Alison McNeil Kettering

Marine is a soldier who serves at sea and in special missions on land and in the air. Marines also serve in *amphibious operations*—seaborne operations that involve naval, air, and land forces. Marines receive specialized training for the tasks they are expected to perform. Nearly all of the major maritime nations maintain marine forces or some type of naval infantry.

In amphibious operations, marines attack from the sea to capture important enemy-held islands, beaches, or other locations on shore. By going ashore first, marines prepare the way for other soldiers to land and build bases or fight the enemy.

Some marine forces perform special or difficult missions, such as nighttime raids and actions against terrorists. Marines may also guard navy ships, navy yards, and

government embassies. United States marines serve as guards at American embassies throughout the world. For more information on U.S. marines, see **Marine Corps, United States**.

Marines of other lands. The United States has the largest corps of marines in the world, with about 195,000 soldiers. Other nations that maintain large marine forces include Argentina, France, the Netherlands, the Philippines, Russia, South Korea, and the United Kingdom.

After the breakup of the Soviet Union, Russia main-

Globe Photos

British Royal Marines prepare to attack Argentine forces in a 1982 battle over the ownership of the Falkland Islands.

tained 12,000 troops in its *Morskaia Pekoota,* or "sea infantry." In the 1980's, these soldiers helped Afghanistan's government fight antigovernment rebels.

The British Royal Marines are part of the Royal Navy. The 8,000-member force operates landing craft and helicopters, and stages amphibious raids. The Royal Marines fought in the British-held Falkland Islands in 1982, after Argentine troops invaded and occupied the islands. Both the British and the Dutch marines have specially trained antiterrorist units.

History. The first marines were the *epibatae,* or "heavily armed sea-soldiers," of the Greek navies in the 500's B.C. Later, Roman warships carried *milites classiarii,* or "soldiers of the fleet." Both the Greeks and the Romans used their marines to fight at sea while sailors maneuvered the ships.

During the Middle Ages, European states did not maintain organized armies, navies, and marine forces. But it was common practice to put soldiers aboard ship whenever sea combat was expected. In the 1600's, nations began once again to organize permanent armed forces. Both England and the Netherlands recognized the need for regular troops aboard their warships. The British formed a corps of marines in 1664, and the Dutch did so in 1665. When the American Colonies revolted in 1775, the Continental Congress organized a force of marines modeled after the British Royal Marines.

In the 1900's, marine forces began to develop ways of getting soldiers ashore more quickly. Marines of several nations fought in World War I (1914-1918), World War II (1939-1945), the Korean War (1950-1953), and the Vietnam War (1957-1975). U.S. Marine units served in Lebanon from 1982 until 1984 as part of an international peacekeeping force there.   John W. Gordon

See also Navy.

Marine animal. See Marine biology with its list of *Related articles.*

Marine Band, United States. See Marine Corps, United States (introduction).

Marine biology is the study of organisms that live in the sea. It deals with all forms of marine life, from huge whales to creatures so tiny they can be seen only under a microscope. Marine organisms dwell in all parts of the ocean, from shallow shore areas to the deepest points on the ocean floor. Marine biologists try to discover how these organisms develop and grow, how they get food, how their bodies function, and how they live in relation to other marine organisms. Marine biologists also try to classify marine organisms. Marine biology has become increasingly important in recent years as people have increased their use of ocean resources.

Some marine biologists study marine organisms in their natural surroundings. Other marine biologists may do most of their work in specially equipped laboratories. Marine biologists who study marine life from specially equipped research vessels are often called *biological oceanographers.*

Marine biologists use marine organisms in laboratory experiments that are designed to increase our knowledge of human life processes. For example, much of our knowledge of human reproduction and development has been developed through experiments with marine animals. Chemical substances that influence different animal *embryos* (developing young) were first discovered in marine organisms. The sea urchin is one of the animals most often used by biologists in these experiments. It produces many large eggs that make experiments and observations easier (see **Sea urchin**).

Marine biologists have used the squid's giant nerve fibers to do valuable research in discovering how nerves work. The squid's nerve fibers are larger and easier to handle and observe than those of most animals. The fibers are so large that scientists can place instruments inside different parts of the nerve. The instruments are then used to record the nerves' mechanical, chemical, and electrical responses. These experiments may lead to greater understanding of how messages are sent from the brain to various points of action in the human body.

Joe Viesti

Marine biologists study marine life in its environment. These scientists may travel long distances to an isolated area to study a particular marine animal. They collect data on the animal and on characteristics of its environment, such as water temperature and salt content.

Marine biologists also use organisms from the sea to produce substances that are valuable to human beings. Marine scientists have found substances in sponges, sea cucumbers, corals, and seaweed that can be used in treating such things as viral and bacterial infections, and cancer. Substances from certain subtropical sponges can be used to treat skin infections, food and blood poisoning, and pneumonia caused by *staphylococcal* bacteria (see **Staphylococcus**).

Some marine biologists have found that the poisons from certain kinds of shellfish and puffers are 200,000 times more powerful as anesthetics than drugs that are now being used for this purpose. They have found that the saliva of the octopus contains a substance that can be used as a powerful heart stimulant. The octopus also uses its saliva to paralyze crabs and then eat them. Scientists specializing in the study of marine life believe that many of these substances will eventually be refined for use as commercial drugs.

Most of the experiments with marine organisms are carried out at marine laboratories. Among the oldest and most famous of these are the Stazione Zoologica in Naples, Italy; the Laboratory of the Marine Biological Association of the United Kingdom in Plymouth, England; and the Marine Biological Laboratory at Woods Hole, Mass.

Biological oceanographers try to find out how marine organisms live in relationship to one another and to their environment. They study how organisms live in the sea, and try to trace how they *evolved* (gradually developed), adapted, and spread. They try to find out how the body organs of marine creatures can work deep in the sea at pressures as high as 15,000 pounds per square inch (1,060 kilograms per square centimeter). They want to learn how organisms living on the sea floor can locate their mates and find their food, despite the fact that they live in constant darkness, where food is scarce.

Some marine oceanographers go down into the sea to observe and conduct experiments in the natural environment of marine organisms. Oceangoing vessels with deep-sea nets and dredges are used to capture organisms for study. Scientists often record environmental conditions, such as water temperature and the salt and oxygen content in given ocean areas, by using specialized instruments that are lowered from research vessels. Deep-sea cameras are used to map the sea floor and to locate certain organisms. Scientists also now use special underwater cameras to make detailed photographic records of marine life at great depths. Special sound devices are used to record the vertical motion of fish.

Among the leading U.S. organizations equipped for such studies are the Woods Hole (Mass.) Oceanographic Institution, the Scripps Institution of Oceanography in La Jolla, Calif., the Lamont Geological Observatory in New York City, and the Institute of Marine Science in Miami, Fla.

Many marine scientists use scuba diving equipment to make underwater studies, especially in clear tropical waters along coral reefs. The French undersea explorer Jacques-Yves Cousteau pioneered the use of undersea stations where divers can live for relatively long periods to study marine life (see **Cousteau, Jacques-Yves**). The U.S. Navy, in its Man-in-the-Sea program conducted off the California coast, and scientists at the Oceanic Insti-

tute in Hawaii have also used this method. But these studies are limited to shallow ocean regions.

To observe deep-sea life, biological oceanographers must use special equipment, such as research submarines. Some research vessels, such as bathyscaphs, can withstand the great pressures found at the deepest parts of the ocean. The bathyscaph *Trieste,* built by Swiss scientists Auguste and Jacques Piccard, made a record dive of 35,800 feet (10,910 meters) in the Mariana Trench of the Pacific Ocean off Guam, in 1960 (see **Bathyscaph**). More recently, a deep-submersible called *Alvin* has been used in numerous studies of deep-sea life. In 1979, scientists used *Alvin* to explore the sea bottom on the East Pacific Rise near the Galapagos Islands. They discovered rich populations of bottom-dwelling marine life surrounding deep-sea hot springs. Scientists believe these communities thrive by using chemical energy produced in the hot springs.   David L. Garrison

Related articles. See **Ocean**. See also the following articles:

Marine life

Algae	Kelp
Animal (Animals of the oceans)	Mollusk
	Plankton
Cnidarian	Puffer
Crustacean	Sea cow
Diatom	Seal
Dolphin	Seaweed
Dugong	Sponge
Echinoderm	Turtle
Fish	Walrus
Irish moss	Whale

Other related articles

Careers (Marine science; picture: Marine biology)	Scripps Institution of Oceanography
Diving, Underwater	Woods Hole Oceanographic Institution

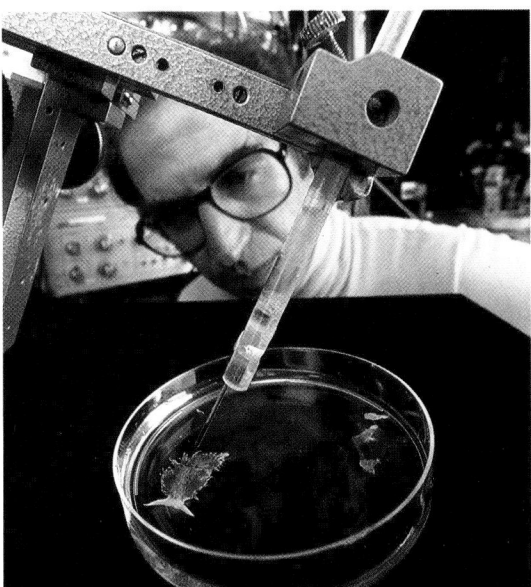

Dan McCoy, Rainbow

Marine biologists use laboratories to study marine life in order to better understand human life processes. The scientist above is doing research on the memory of snails.

The Marine Corps War Memorial in Arlington, Va., *above,* honors all marines who have died in action since 1775, the year the corps was founded. The memorial portrays the raising of the U.S. flag on Iwo Jima during World War II. The Marine Corps emblem is shown at the right.

Marine Corps, United States, is the branch of the armed services that is especially trained and organized for amphibious assault operations. Marine assault troops, supported by air units, attack and seize enemy beachheads and bases. As the nation's amphibious force, marines in many strategic parts of the world stand alert to speed to any trouble spot. A well-known military saying is "The marines have landed, and the situation is well in hand." Marines have been the first to fight in almost every major war of the United States. Since 1775, these "soldiers of the sea" have grown from two battalions of sharpshooters into a combat organization of highly mobile ground divisions and air wings. Marines have made more than 300 landings on foreign shores, and have served in areas ranging from the polar regions to the tropics.

During the late-1980's, the Marine Corps had a strength of about 185,000 men and 10,000 women. The corps is a separate branch of the armed forces within the Department of the Navy in the Department of Defense. Marines are often called *leathernecks,* because in the early days they wore high leather collars around their necks. The *WM's,* or women marines, have the same ranks as male marines.

The motto of the corps, adopted in 1880, is *Semper Fidelis* (Always Faithful). The Marine emblem was adopted in 1868. "The Marines' Hymn," written in the 1800's, begins with the stirring words "From the halls of Montezuma to the shores of Tripoli." John Philip Sousa wrote the corps' march, "Semper Fidelis," while serving as leader of the Marine band. The band is called "The President's Own," because it plays for state affairs in the White House. The official colors of the corps are scarlet and gold.

Why we have a marine corps

Every great maritime nation such as the United States must be able to defend its interests on land and sea, and protect the lives and property of its citizens in other regions. During war and other emergencies, the United States must be ready to send well-trained, disciplined forces to accomplish these goals.

The Marine Corps maintains fleet marine forces of combined air and ground units to seize and defend advance bases, and for land operations that are carried out as part of a naval campaign. It develops the tactics, techniques, and equipment for the amphibious landing operations. The corps provides detachments for service aboard warships and for the protection of naval bases and stations. It guards U.S. embassies, legations, and

Development of the Marine Corps uniform

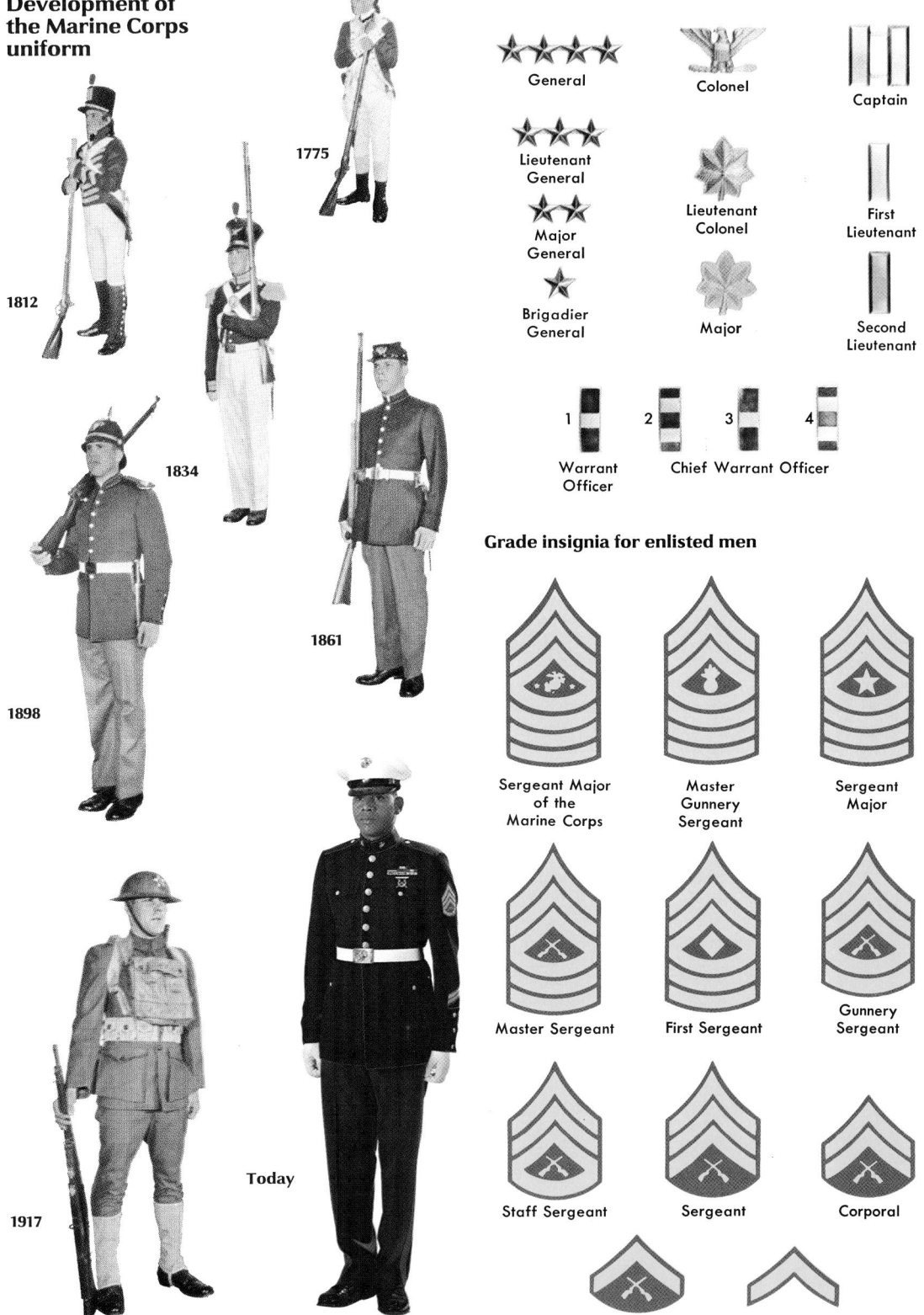

1775

1812

1834

1861

1898

1917

Today

Grade insignia for officers

General

Colonel

Captain

Lieutenant General

Lieutenant Colonel

First Lieutenant

Major General

Brigadier General

Major

Second Lieutenant

1 Warrant Officer

2   3   4 Chief Warrant Officer

Grade insignia for enlisted men

Sergeant Major of the Marine Corps

Master Gunnery Sergeant

Sergeant Major

Master Sergeant

First Sergeant

Gunnery Sergeant

Staff Sergeant

Sergeant

Corporal

Lance Corporal

Private First Class

consulates in other countries, and performs such other duties as the President may direct.

Life in the Marine Corps

Training a marine. Marine recruits receive basic training in *boot camp*. Recruits are called *boots* because in early days they wore leather leggings that looked like boots.

Male recruits receive about 10 weeks of basic training at one of two recruit depots—in Parris Island, S.C., or in San Diego, Calif. They undergo physical conditioning and learn how to shoot, drill, obey orders, and follow the traditions of the corps. Women receive 10 weeks of basic training in Parris Island, S.C. They are trained in most of the same disciplines as men. But their fitness program differs from that of male recruits, and they learn defensive rather than offensive tactics.

Training an officer. Marine Corps officers come from four main sources: (1) the U.S. Naval Academy, (2) the Naval Reserve Officers Training Corps, (3) civilian universities, and (4) the enlisted ranks of the corps. Each officer receives five or more months of initial training at the Marine Corps Basic School in Quantico, Va. Much of this training is in field tactics, leadership, marksmanship, infantry weapons and supporting arms, drill, military law, and physical fitness.

A typical day. Because of the wide variety of marine duties, there is no completely typical day. Nevertheless, the following routine would be familiar to any marine in peacetime. At 6 a.m., reveille is sounded. The marine rises, washes, makes the bunk, and has light physical training. Breakfast is followed by police call, when quarters and outside areas are *policed* (cleaned). At 8 a.m. comes morning colors, when the flag is hoisted while the band plays the National Anthem. After colors, troop inspection and guard mount take place. All marines are inspected and drilled, and the guard is relieved. Drills and instructions go on until recall at about 11 a.m. Dinner is served at 11:30 a.m. At 1 p.m., drill call sounds again, and afternoon training lasts until the day's work is finished. Liberty call then announces that eligible marines may "go ashore," or leave the post. Supper is served at 5 p.m. In the evening, marines are free unless night training is planned. Taps sounds at 10 p.m.

Careers in the Marine Corps. Young men between the ages of 17 and 28 may enlist in the corps for three, four, or six years. Women between the ages of 18 and 28 may enlist. Men may serve in a wide variety of job fields. Women can serve in all military job fields except the air, armor, artillery, and infantry crews.

Marines who reenlist may, if qualified, rise to jobs as senior noncommissioned officers. The most capable marines can win appointments to the U.S. Naval Academy, receive direct commissions as officers, or be chosen as warrant officers. Marines may retire with pay after 20 years' service.

Weapons and equipment

Marine ground weapons. The M16A2 rifle is the basic infantry weapon of the corps. Marines also use grenades, pistols, and machine guns.

Artillery provides support for Marine infantry. Marine artillery includes mortars, guns, and howitzers. Armored units have tanks with heavy guns. Antiaircraft weapons include Hawk guided missiles and shoulder-fired Redeye and Stinger missiles. Special marine teams ashore use radio to direct gunfire from warships.

Marine aviation provides close air support for fleet marine and other troops. It reinforces naval aviation. Marine aviation attacks enemy forces so close to marine land operations that detailed coordination between air and ground units is required. The Marines have aviators with ground units at the front lines to control and direct air support. They fly the same kinds of aircraft as the Navy (see **Navy, United States** [Naval aviation]). The Marines also fly the Harrier, a type of V/STOL (Vertical/Short Take-Off and Landing) aircraft. In addition, the Marines operate assault helicopters to land men from naval helicopter carriers.

Organization of the Marine Corps

Headquarters of the Marine Corps is in Washington, D.C. The corps is one of the two naval services. It is a partner, but not a part, of the Navy. A commandant, appointed by the President, heads the corps. The commandant usually serves four years and has the rank of general. The commandant serves as a member of the Joint Chiefs of Staff and is responsible directly to the secretary of the Navy. The principal assistants of the commandant include the assistant commandant and chief of staff, the deputy and assistant chiefs of staff, and the directors of headquarters departments and divisions.

Operating forces account for almost two-thirds of the entire Marine Corps. They consist of (1) the fleet marine forces, (2) marines aboard ships, and (3) security forces. The fleet marine forces make up the corps' combat strength and form parts of the Atlantic and Pacific fleets. They consist of three Marine divisions, three Marine aircraft wings, and various support units. The combat units operate as air-ground teams. One division and wing team is based on the East Coast of the United States, another is on the West Coast, and the third is in the Far East and Hawaii. The teams are kept combat ready at all times. A fourth division and wing team, composed of elements of the Marine Corps Reserve, is prepared to reinforce the active forces when needed.

Marines serve on many warships. They provide internal security aboard the vessels. They also take part in amphibious warfare and land operations in connection with naval campaigns. Marine airplane and helicopter squadrons may fly from carriers.

Security forces include marines who guard American embassies and other important government installations and naval bases around the world.

The supporting establishment provides administrative, supply, training, and recruiting support for the operating forces. The Marine schools combine the corps' education and military development activities. The corps' two recruit depots handle basic training. The Marine *logistics* (supply) bases provide support.

Reserves. The Marine Corps Reserve consists of (1) the Ready Reserve, (2) the Standby Reserve, and (3) the Retired Reserve. Many members of the Ready Reserve enlist for six years to serve in selected reserve units. They train one weekend a month and serve two weeks of active duty each year. Other members of the Ready Reserve may volunteer to train with these reserve units, or they may take other types of training.

The Standby Reserve is for Marines who complete their military obligation and remain in the reserves. They do not undergo the scheduled training required of the Ready Reserve. The Retired Reserve is made up of reserve marines who have been active in training for 20 years or more. There are about 110,000 marines in the reserves, and all of them may be called to active duty, depending on the situation.

History

The Revolutionary War. The Continental Congress established a marine corps on Nov. 10, 1775, to fight in

the war, no marine corps as such existed. The U.S. Congress re-created the Marine Corps as a military service in 1798.

The shores of Tripoli. Marines took part in the hard-fought naval battles that U.S. ships fought against France in 1797. In 1805, marines led the storming of the Barbary pirates' stronghold at Derna, Tripoli, helping end the pirate menace in the Mediterranean Sea.

The War of 1812 saw marines in all major American naval victories. Captain John Gamble showed such ability that he was given command of a captured British warship. He became the only Marine officer ever to

Combat uniform

Aviator uniform

Women's service uniform   **Blue dress uniform**

© Captain Donna J. Neary, U.S. Marine Corps Reserve

the Revolutionary War in America (1775-1783). Marines also served with the Continental Army in the battles of Trenton, Assunpink, Morristown, and Brandywine. After

Important dates in Marine Corps history

1775 The Continental Congress authorized the formation of two battalions of marines.
1776 Marines made their first landing, on the Bahama Islands during the Revolutionary War.
1798 Congress re-created the Marine Corps as a separate military service.
1805 Marines stormed the Barbary pirates' stronghold at Derna on the shores of Tripoli.
1834 Congress placed the Marine Corps directly under the secretary of the Navy.
1847 Marines occupied "the halls of Montezuma" in Mexico City during the Mexican War.
1913 The Marine Corps established its aviation section.
1918 Marines fought one of their greatest battles at Belleau Wood in France during World War I.
1942 Marines invaded Guadalcanal Island in the first United States offensive of World War II.
1945 Marines seized Iwo Jima Island in the western Pacific in the largest all-marine battle.
1950 Marines stormed ashore at Inchon, Korea, in the first major landing of the Korean War.
1952 The marine commandant became a member of the Joint Chiefs of Staff.
1965-1971 The Third Amphibious Force, the largest field command in Marine Corps history, served in Vietnam.

command a naval ship. Marines helped Andrew Jackson's army administer the worst defeat of the war to the British in the defense of New Orleans in 1815.

The Creek and Seminole wars. In 1836, the Army was assigned to move the Creek and Seminole Indians of Georgia and Florida to new reservations. When the tribes refused to move, Marine Commandant Archibald Henderson personally led marines to reinforce the army. He was promoted to brigadier general for gallantry at the Battle of Hatchee-Lustee in Florida in 1837. Henderson became the corps' first general officer.

The halls of Montezuma. During the Mexican War, from 1846 to 1848, marines made many landings on both coasts of Mexico. Marines entered the city gates of Mexico City. They raised the American flag over the National Palace, which later became known as "the halls of Montezuma."

The Civil War. When John Brown and his followers captured the army arsenal at Harpers Ferry, Va., in 1859, marines from Washington were the only troops available. They helped capture Brown and occupied the arsenal. In the Civil War (1861-1865) itself, marines fought in many land and naval battles.

In the Far East. During the late 1800's and early 1900's, marines landed 17 times in China to protect American interests. They defended the besieged legations in Beijing during the Boxer Rebellion in 1900, and also fought at Tianjin in the Beijing relief force.

The Spanish-American War. Marines were the first American troops to land in Cuba. A battalion seized Guantánamo Bay in 1898. Marines were also the first American forces to land in the Philippines. They occupied Guam and took part in the seizure of Puerto Rico. A Marine brigade served with the Army during the Philippine insurrection from 1899 to 1903.

In Central America. Marines landed in Panama six times between 1885 and 1903 to protect American lives and property and to keep the Isthmus of Panama open. They also fought in two campaigns to stabilize Nicaragua, in 1912 and again from 1926 to 1933. Marine brigades exercised American protectorates over Haiti and Santo Domingo in the early 1900's.

World War I. Marines arrived in France in June 1917 with the first troops of the American Expeditionary Forces. They dismayed the Germans with long-range rifle fire and fierce assaults at Soissons, St.-Mihiel, Blanc Mont Ridge, and the Meuse-Argonne.

World War II. In August 1942, the Marines invaded Guadalcanal in the Solomon Islands and launched the first American offensive of the war. Marines under Lieutenant General Holland M. Smith led the amphibious landings of the island-hopping drive westward through the Central Pacific. The conquest of Iwo Jima during February and March of 1945 was the largest all-marine battle in history (see **Iwo Jima; Washington, D.C.** [picture]). Strength of the corps reached nearly 500,000 during World War II.

The Korean War. In August 1950, marines arrived in Korea to help rescue the crumbling Pusan perimeter. They later made the amphibious landing at Inchon. After Chinese Communist troops entered the Korean War, marines smashed seven enemy divisions in their winter march south from the Chosin Reservoir.

Recent developments. The Marines have taken part in several operations since the Korean War. During the Suez crisis in 1956, a Marine battalion aided the evacuation of American citizens from the trouble zone. In 1958, a Marine regiment helped prevent the overthrow of the Lebanese government. Marine units ended fighting in the Dominican Republic in 1965. From 1965 to 1973, about 450,000 marines served in the Vietnam War.

From 1982 to 1984, several Marine units formed part of an international force attempting to preserve order in Lebanon (see **Lebanon** [War and terrorism]). In 1983, marines participated in a successful military operation against rebel forces that had seized the government of Grenada.

About 94,000 marines served in the Persian Gulf War (1991). Marine aircraft bombed Iraq and Iraqi-occupied Kuwait. Marine and allied Arab ground forces attacked through southern Kuwait, breaking through Iraqi defenses along the border of Saudi Arabia and Kuwait.

Critically reviewed by the United States Marine Corps

Related articles in *World Book*. See Navy, **Department of the; Navy, U.S.** Additional related articles include:

Marine Corps installations

Camp H. M. Smith
Camp Lejeune
Camp Pendleton
Cherry Point Marine Corps
  Air Station
El Toro Marine Corps
  Air Station

Parris Island Marine Corps
  Recruit Depot
Quantico Marine Corps
  Combat Development
  Command
San Diego Marine Corps
  Recruit Depot

History

Civil War   Korean War   Mexican War

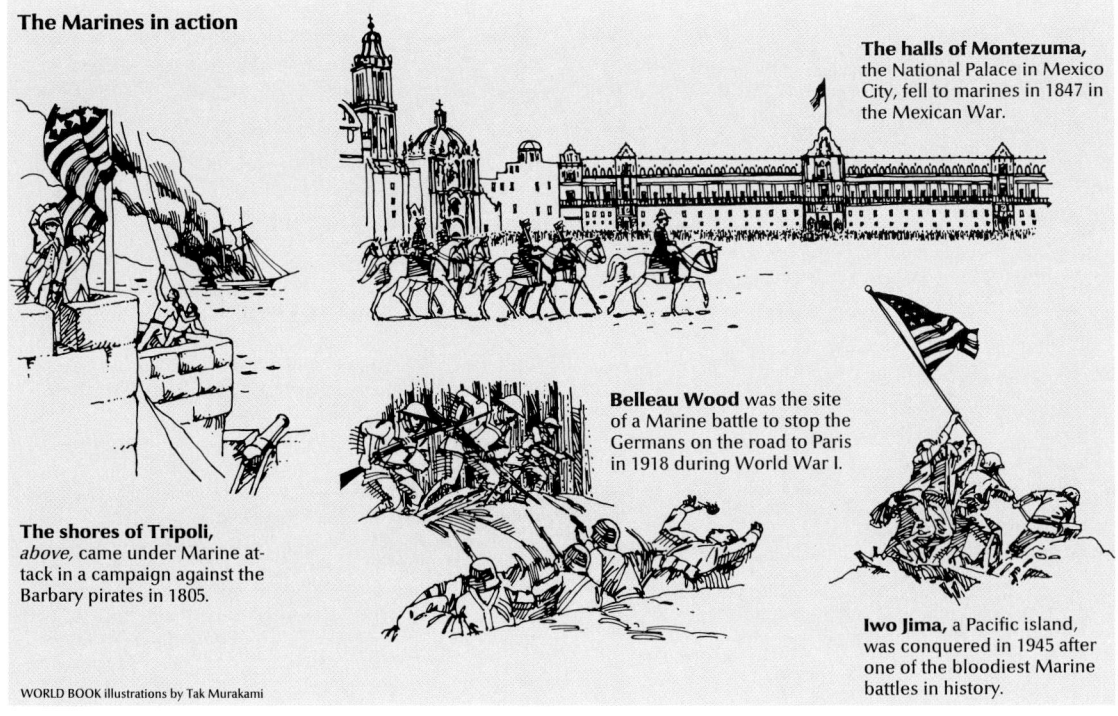

The Marines in action

The halls of Montezuma, the National Palace in Mexico City, fell to marines in 1847 in the Mexican War.

Belleau Wood was the site of a Marine battle to stop the Germans on the road to Paris in 1918 during World War I.

The shores of Tripoli, *above,* came under Marine attack in a campaign against the Barbary pirates in 1805.

Iwo Jima, a Pacific island, was conquered in 1945 after one of the bloodiest Marine battles in history.

WORLD BOOK illustrations by Tak Murakami

Outline

I. Why we have a Marine Corps
II. Life in the Marine Corps
   A. Training a marine
   B. Training an officer
   C. A typical day
   D. Careers in the Marine Corps
III. Weapons of the Marine Corps
   A. Marine ground weapons
   B. Marine aviation
IV. Organization of the Marine Corps
   A. Headquarters
   B. Operating forces
   C. The supporting establishment
   D. Reserves
V. History

Questions

What is the Marine Corps motto? What does it mean?
Why are marines often called *leathernecks*?
What are Marine operating forces? Support forces?
What are the duties of marines aboard warships?
What are some Marine ground weapons?
What is the chief purpose of the Marine Corps?
What is "boot camp"?
What is the fleet marine force?

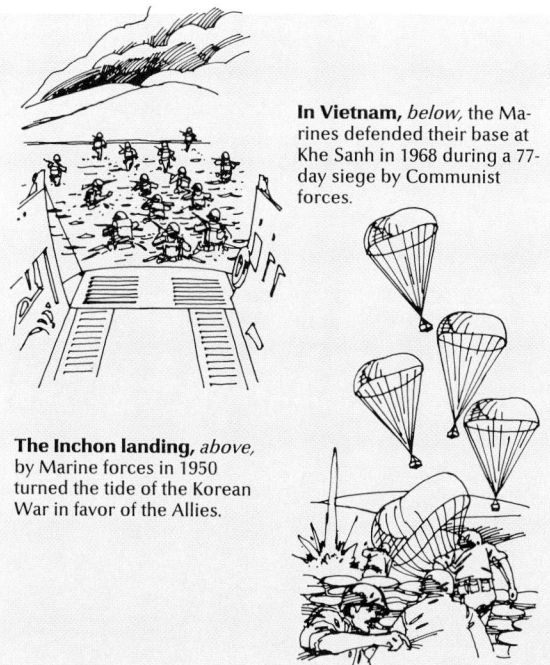

In Vietnam, *below,* the Marines defended their base at Khe Sanh in 1968 during a 77-day siege by Communist forces.

The Inchon landing, *above,* by Marine forces in 1950 turned the tide of the Korean War in favor of the Allies.

WORLD BOOK illustrations by Tak Murakami

Why is Marine aviation important to Marine ground units?
When did the corps establish its aviation section?
Where did marines make their first landing?

Additional resources

Da Cruz, Daniel. *Boot: The Inside Story of How a Few Good Men Became Today's Marines.* St. Martin's, 1987.
Lawliss, Chuck. *The Marine Book: A Portrait of America's Military Elite.* Thames & Hudson, 1988.
Millett, Allan R. *Semper Fidelis: The History of the United States Marine Corps.* Macmillan, 1980.
Moskin, John R. *The U.S. Marine Corps Story.* Rev. ed. McGraw, 1987.
Parry, Francis F. *Three-War Marine: The Pacific, Korea, Vietnam.* Pacifica Pr., 1987.
Rummel, Jack. *The U.S. Marine Corps.* Chelsea Hse., 1990. Also suitable for younger readers.

Marine plant. See **Marine biology** and its list of *Related articles.*

Mariner space probe. See **Venus** (planet); **Mars.**

Marino, Eugene Antonio (1934-   ), became the first black American to be named an archbishop of the Roman Catholic Church. Appointed by Pope John Paul II, Marino was archbishop of Atlanta from 1988 to 1990.

Marino was born in Biloxi, Miss. He was ordained a priest in 1962. In 1971, Marino became the first black vicar general of a major Roman Catholic religious order, St. Joseph's Society of the Sacred Heart, also called the Josephites. He held this position until 1974, when he was appointed auxiliary bishop of Washington, D.C. Marino was auxiliary bishop until his appointment as archbishop of Atlanta. He was also the first black secretary of the National Conference of Catholic Bishops.

Kenneth Guentert

Marion, Francis (1732?-1795), was an American military leader from South Carolina whose shrewd, daring raids in the Revolutionary War in America won him the nickname of The Swamp Fox. He and his soldiers repeatedly darted out of the marshes to attack the British and Americans who supported them and then vanished before their victims could strike back.

Marion was born in Berkeley County, South Carolina. He spent his youth on his parents' farm near Georgetown, S.C. He had his first experience in war as a lieutenant of colonial militia in 1761, when he led a successful attack against the Cherokee Indians.

In 1775, at the start of the Revolutionary War, Marion became captain of a militia company. He helped defend Charleston, S.C., against a British attack in 1776. The British captured Charleston in May 1780. But Marion had left the city before it surrendered.

Few American troops remained in South Carolina after the British won the Battle of Camden in August 1780. Marion could form only a band of fighters, which was too small to fight the British in open battle. So Marion used the group as guerrillas, favoring ambushes and sudden raids. Ammunition was so scarce in many battles that each soldier often carried no more than three rounds.

Marion's band hid on Snow Island in the Pee Dee River, in northeastern South Carolina. From there, he and his soldiers made lightning-quick raids on British communications and supply depots and rescued captured Americans. British Lieutenant Colonel Banastre Tarleton spent much time chasing Marion through the swamps but could not catch him. For this reason, Tarleton gave Marion his nickname. After the war, Marion served several terms in the South Carolina Senate. He died on his plantation at Pond Bluff.   James Kirby Martin

Marionette. See Puppet (Marionettes).

Mariposa lily, *MAIR uh POH suh* or *MAIR uh POH zuh,* is a group of about 60 species of spring-blooming flowers of the lily family. The beautiful flowers are sometimes called *fairy lantern, globe tulip, sego lily,* or *butterfly lily.* The petals of the blossoms resemble a butterfly's wings. *Mariposa* is the Spanish word for *butterfly.*

WORLD BOOK illustration by Robert Hynes

Mariposa lilies have lovely, tulip-shaped flowers that vary in color. These hardy plants thrive in moist, sandy soil.

Native to the Western United States, mariposa lilies have narrow leaves shaped like blades of grass. The cup-shaped flowers grow singly or in small clusters and look like tulips. Colors range from white to purple to deep yellow or orange. The lilies grow well in sandy, porous soil, but need a lot of water. They grow from underground bulbs. Bulbs should be dried out in summer for fall planting. In their native regions, the lilies make excellent flowers for woodland or rock gardens.

Scientific classification. Mariposa lilies make up the genus *Calochortus* in the family Liliaceae.   Anton A. Reznicek

See also **Sego lily.**

Maris, *MAIR ihs,* **Roger** (1934-1985), hit more home runs in one season than any other major league baseball player. He set a record in 1961 when he hit his 61st homer on the last day of the season. His team, the New York Yankees, played a 162-game schedule that year. In 1927, Babe Ruth, also a Yankee, hit 60 homers in a 154-game schedule. Both totals were considered records until 1991, when Maris' 61 homers were recognized as the sole record. See **Baseball** (Recent developments).

Maris, an outfielder, batted left handed and threw right handed. He started his major league career with the Cleveland Indians in 1957 and was traded to

UPI

Roger Maris

the Kansas City Athletics in 1958. In 1960, his first year with the Yankees, he hit 39 home runs. Maris was voted the American League's most valuable player in 1960 and 1961. After the 1966 season, he was traded to the St. Louis Cardinals. He retired from baseball following the 1968 season. Roger Eugene Maras was born in Hibbing, Minn., and grew up in Fargo, N. Dak. He changed his last name to Maris in 1955.   Dave Nightingale

Marisol, *MAIR uh SAHL* (1930-   ), is an American sculptor known for her witty, life-sized wooden figures. She constructs her figures with crudely carved wooden blocks, on which she draws or paints realistic facial features and other details, such as clothing. Marisol often attaches everyday objects as well as plaster casts of her own face, hands, or feet to her sculptures.

Although she occasionally makes sculptures of recognizable personalities, most of Marisol's works portray fictional, ordinary people. Many of Marisol's sculptures consist of groupings of several physically independent figures. An example is *The Family,* which appears in the **Sculpture** article. Marisol's work has often been associated with the pop art movement. But unlike pop artists, she rarely depicts commercial objects or designs.

Marisol Escobar was born in Paris of Venezuelan parents. She emigrated to the United States in 1950.

Deborah Leveton

Maritain, *ma ree TAN,* **Jacques,** *zhahk* (1882-1973), was a French philosopher and one of the most influential Roman Catholic scholars of the 1900's. He was a leader of *neo-Thomism,* a revival of the philosophical system developed by the medieval theologian Saint Thomas Aquinas. The system attempted to reconcile faith and reason.

Much of Maritain's work dealt with the theory of knowledge. In *The Degree of Knowledge* (1932), he analyzed the structure of thought, identifying three types of knowledge. They were, in ascending order, (1) scientific knowledge of empirical reality, (2) metaphysical knowledge of the principles of "being as such," and (3) suprarational knowledge of God through divine revelation. By suprarational knowledge, Maritain meant knowledge beyond the comprehension of human reason.

Maritain was born in Paris. He converted from Protestantism to Roman Catholicism in 1906. He taught at the Catholic Institute from 1914 to 1939 and was the French ambassador to the Vatican from 1945 to 1948. Maritain's other major books include *Art and Poetry* (1935), *Integral Humanism* (1936), *The Range of Reason* (1948), and *Man and the State* (1951).   David E. Klemm

Maritime Administration, *MAIR ih tym,* is an agency of the United States Department of Transportation. The agency promotes a strong and efficient U.S. merchant marine. It works to meet the nation's waterborne shipping demands in times of peace and to support the armed forces during a national emergency. It also conducts promotional and marketing programs to increase domestic shipping, port development, and the use of U.S. vessels in foreign trade.

The agency trains young men and women to become deck and engineering officers at the U.S. Merchant Marine Academy at Kings Point, N.Y. (see **Merchant marine**). In addition, the agency provides support to six state-operated maritime academies.

The Maritime Administration negotiates maritime

agreements with other nations and participates in international maritime forums. It also maintains a National Defense Reserve Fleet for use in national emergencies. The Maritime Administration was established in 1950.

Critically reviewed by the Maritime Administration

Maritime Commission, Federal. See Federal Maritime Commission.

Maritime law regulates commerce and navigation on the high seas or other navigable waters, including inland lakes and rivers. It involves all vessels, from huge passenger liners to small pleasure boats, and covers such matters as contracts, insurance, property damage, and personal injuries. Maritime law is sometimes referred to as *admiralty law,* because at one time it was administered under the jurisdiction of admirals.

Although a general maritime law has developed internationally, it operates in any nation according to the laws and usages of that country. Each nation bases its own maritime law on the general law. There is no international court to enforce maritime decisions. But all nations that have vessels on the sea set up national courts. These courts consider maritime cases in much the same way that civil courts hear other kinds of complaints. Federal district courts administer maritime law in the United States. Admiralty courts handle maritime cases in Great Britain.   George P. Smith II

See also **Flotsam, jetsam, and lagan; Salvage; International Maritime Organization.**

Maritime Provinces. See Atlantic Provinces.

Marius, *MAIR ee uhs,* **Gaius,** *GAY uhs* (157-86 B.C.), was a Roman general and statesman. He was not of noble ancestry, but he worked his way into political leadership. He served seven times as one of the two *consuls* (chief government officials) of Rome, between 107 and 86 B.C. He opposed Rome's aristocratic *oligarchy* (rule by a few).

As a general, Marius reorganized Rome's infantry legions, improved training methods, and opened military service to men of the lowest social classes. A strong professional army developed. The troops, if treated well, often became more loyal to their generals than to the state, so successful military command became a means to political power. Marius was born near Arpinum, in central Italy. He won his greatest military victories against the Numidians in North Africa, and the Cimbri and Teutone tribes in northern Italy.   Arther Ferrill

Marivaux, *ma ree VOH,* **Pierre** (1688-1763), was a French playwright and novelist. His novels and some of his plays deal with the rising middle class, which was slowly replacing the nobility as the ruling social force in France. Many of his plays offer subtle analysis of the psychology of love.

Marivaux is best known for his comedies. His originality lies in his basing them on the birth of love and its struggle against the individual's pride. His heroines are elegant, intellectual, and cunning, and their speech is delicate and refined. His comedies include *The Double Inconstancy* (1723), *The Game of Love and Chance* (1730), and *The False Confessions* (1737). His two unfinished novels, *The Life of Marianne* (1731-1741) and *The Successful Peasant* (1735-1736), were among the first French novels to give a realistic picture of the middle class. Marivaux was born Pierre Carlet de Chamblain de Marivaux in Paris.   Carol L. Sherman

Marjoram, *MAHR juh ruhm,* is the name of a group of fragrant plants that belong to the mint family. Marjoram is a source of *oregano,* a seasoning used for many Italian foods. Most oregano sold in the United States is made from the dried leaves of wild marjoram. Wild marjoram is native to dry areas from western Europe to central Asia. In eastern North America, it has escaped from cultivation and grows as a weed. This plant grows from 2 to 4 feet (61 to 121 centimeters) tall. It has purplish stems and leaves with white or purplish clusters of flowers.

© Giuseppe Mazza

Marjoram

Another type of marjoram, called sweet marjoram, is native to northern Africa and southwestern Asia. It grows to about 2 feet tall and has white, purplish, or pink flower clusters. Sweet marjoram is a popular cooking herb, especially for French foods. It also serves as a scent for soap, perfume, and other toiletries.

Scientific classification. Marjoram is in the mint family, Lamiaceae or Labiatae. The scientific name for wild marjoram is *Origanum vulgare.* Sweet marjoram is *O. majorana.*

Donna M. Eggers Ware

Mark is the monetary unit of Germany. In 1924, it became known as the *reichsmark.* It is now called the *Deutsche mark.* See also **Money** (table: Exchange rates).

Mark, Saint, sometimes called John Mark, was an early Christian who accompanied Saint Paul on his first missionary journey. The Acts of the Apostles reports that Mark caused a dispute between Paul and Barnabas, another of Paul's companions. Mark left them to return to Jerusalem, his home. Mark and Barnabas traveled together as missionaries to Crete after the disagreement. Mark may have been related to Barnabas. According to tradition, Mark was the author of the second Gospel. Mark is also said to have been Saint Peter's "interpreter" in Rome and to have founded the church in Alexandria, Egypt. He is also said to have died a martyr's death. His feast day is April 25.   Richard A. Edwards

Mark Antony. See Antony, Mark.

Market economy. See Capitalism.

Market research is the process of gathering and analyzing information to help business firms and other organizations make marketing decisions. Business executives use market research to help them identify *markets* (potential customers) for their products and decide what marketing methods to use. Government officials use such research to develop regulations regarding advertising, other sales practices, and product safety.

Market research services are provided by several kinds of companies, including advertising agencies, management consultants, and specialized market research organizations. In addition, many large business companies have their own market research department.

Market researchers handle a wide range of tasks. They estimate the demand for new products and services, describe the characteristics of probable customers, and measure potential sales. They determine how prices influence demand, and they test the effectiveness of current and proposed advertising. Market researchers also assess a company's sales personnel and analyze the public "image" of a company and its products.

A market research study begins with a statement of the problem that the client wants to solve. This statement leads to a detailed definition of the information to be gathered. There are two types of market research information, *secondary data* and *primary data.*

Secondary data are statistics and other information that are already available from such sources as government agencies and universities. To save time and money, market researchers use secondary sources as much as they can. Primary data are data that must be obtained through research. The chief techniques for gathering such data include mail questionnaires, interviews, retail store shelf audits, use of electronic scanners at retail checkout counters, and direct observation in stores. The researchers design and test research materials, such as questionnaires or guides for interviewers. Finally, they collect the data, analyze the information, and report the results of their study. The computer is an important tool in analyzing market research data.

Market research can reduce the risk involved in many business decisions, but some risk always remains. Expenditures for market research must be carefully controlled so that the costs do not exceed the probable benefits from reduced risk.   Frederick E. Webster, Jr.

See also **Advertising** (Research); **Automobile** (Market research); **Marketing; Public opinion poll.**

Additional resources

Breen, George, and Blankenship, A. B. *Do-It-Yourself Marketing Research.* 3rd ed. McGraw, 1989.
Pinson, Linda, and Jinnett, J. A. *Marketing: Researching and Reaching Your Target Market.* Out of Your Mind and into the Marketplace, 1988.

Marketing is the process by which sellers find buyers and by which goods and services move from producers to consumers. Everyday life involves many marketing activities. For example, advertising and selling are part of the marketing process. Other marketing activities include financing by banks and deliveries to stores and homes. Marketing is so important to industry that about half the cost of goods and services results from the marketing process. More people work in marketing than in production.

Consumers in the United States, Canada, and most other non-Communist countries can choose from a huge variety of products and services. Therefore, a company must have an effective marketing program to make its products and services attractive to customers. In a large firm, executives called *marketing managers* direct marketing. But every business, regardless of size, engages in five major marketing activities: (1) market research, (2) product development, (3) distribution, (4) pricing, and (5) promotion.

Market research is the study of the probable users of a product or service. Such potential customers are called a *market.* There are many sources of market information. For example, government statistics about population and income indicate the size of a market and its purchasing power.

Product development includes determining the various goods to be offered, as well as developing the

products themselves. Manufacturers continually meet the demands of the public by adding new products, changing existing ones, and dropping others.

Distribution is the movement of goods and services from producer to consumer. A manufacturer must establish a system that keeps products moving steadily from the factory to the customer. Such a system is called a *marketing channel* or a *channel of distribution.*

Many types of companies take part in distribution. They include *wholesalers,* who sell large quantities of goods to *retailers.* The retailers, in turn, sell small numbers of products to consumers. Independent dealers called *jobbers* buy goods from manufacturers in large quantities and sell them to retail dealers in small quantities. Other firms provide such services as financing, transportation, and storage.

Pricing. When setting the price of a product, most manufacturers start with their *unit production cost,* the expense of making one unit of the item. They add a percentage of this cost to provide a profit for themselves. Every company in the marketing channel then sells the product for more than it cost. Each firm adds an amount that covers its expenses and enables it to make a profit. The amount added at each stage is called a *markup.* The final selling price of an item equals its production cost plus the total of the markups. See **Price; Profit.**

Some people believe a large part of the money spent on marketing is wasted. But most economists believe the marketing process actually benefits consumers. For example, market research helps industry offer what customers need and want. Marketing also provides consumers with shopping information and makes products available in convenient quantities at nearby locations.

Promotion includes advertising, catalogs, coupons, direct-mail, in-store displays, and personal selling. Companies engage in a variety of promotional activities to inform customers about products and services and to persuade them to buy. See the articles on **Advertising** and **Salesmanship** for more information about this phase of marketing.   Frederick E. Webster, Jr.

Related articles in *World Book* include:

Careers (Marketing and distribution)	Food (Marketing)
Consumption	Livestock (Marketing livestock)
Cooperative (Marketing cooperatives)	Market research
Farm and farming (Marketing farm products)	Packaging
	Retailing
	Trade

Additional resources

Lant, Jeffrey. *Money Making Marketing.* JLA Pubns., 1987.
Tedlow, Richard S. *New and Improved: The Story of Mass Marketing in America.* Basic Bks., 1990.

Markham, *MAHR kuhm,* **Edwin** (1852-1940), was an American poet. He wrote many volumes of poetry, but he is best remembered for two individual poems. They are "The Man with the Hoe" (1899) and "Lincoln, the Man of the People" (1901).

"The Man with the Hoe" is a powerful work of social protest based on a painting by Jean François Millet of France. The poem sympathetically portrays a poor farmer who has become brutalized by years of overwork. It refers to the farmer as ". . . a brother to the ox" and attacks those who have taken advantage of his labor. In "Lincoln, the Man of the People," Markham commemorated the American President Abraham Lincoln.

Markham was born in Oregon City, Ore. His real name was Charles Edward Anson Markham. He worked as a schoolteacher and school principal before the popularity of "The Man with the Hoe" enabled him to devote himself to writing. William Harmon

Markova, *mahr KOH vuh,* **Dame Alicia** (1910-   ), is considered the first great English ballerina. At 14, she joined Sergei Diaghilev's Ballets Russes and became a soloist. After the company disbanded in 1929, she danced with Ballet Rambert and with the Sadler's Wells Ballet (now the Royal Ballet). With these companies, she performed all the principal ballerina roles in the first English productions of the classics. In 1935, she formed the Markova-Dolin Ballet with English dancer Sir Anton Dolin. Her greatest role was the title character in *Giselle.* Markova described her experiences in the role in *Giselle and I* (1960). She also wrote a memoir, *Markova Remembers* (1986).

Markova was born in London. Her real name is Lillian Alicia Marks. She retired as a dancer in 1963 and then served as director of the Metropolitan Opera Ballet in New York City until 1969. She has remained active as a coach, teacher, and lecturer. Markova was made Dame Commander of the Order of the British Empire in 1963.

Dorothy Lourdou

See also **Dolin, Sir Anton.**

Marl, *mahrl,* is the common name for *calcareous mudstone,* a type of rock that consists of almost equal amounts of clay and calcite or dolomite. It is a *sedimentary rock,* a layered rock formed by the accumulation of other rocks and mineral fragments. Many marls form at the edges of freshwater lakes and contain fossils.

People use marl in various ways, depending on the impurities present. *Greensand marl* has much phosphorus and potash, and farmers use it as a fertilizer. *Shell marl* contains many fossil shells and is used as a decorative stone. Ray E. Ferrell, Jr.

Marlborough, *MAWL buh ruh,* **Duke of** (1650-1722), was one of England's greatest generals. He won a series of brilliant victories at Blenheim, Ramillies, Oudenaarde, and Malplaquet in his campaigns in the War of the Spanish Succession (see **Blenheim, Battle of; Succession wars** [The War of the Spanish Succession]).

His character and motives have been criticized, but his military genius has never been questioned. He was also a successful diplomat.

Marlborough deserted King James II to support William of Orange when English leaders invited William to invade England in 1688 (see **James** [II]; **William III**). William made him earl of Marlborough, and gave him commands in the army. Marlborough's position became stronger when William died and Princess Anne came to the throne as Queen Anne (see **Anne**). Marlborough's wife, Sarah Jennings (1660-1744), was the queen's closest friend. Anne made Marlborough commander of all the armed forces at home and in Europe. In the War of the Spanish Succession, Marlborough, then a duke, won a series of victories.

At the peak of his success, Marlborough lost his influence at home. His political enemies had turned the queen against him and his wife. He was removed from his command, and retired from public life. His final downfall was not due to lack of ability. It was the fault of

his wife, who was domineering and ill tempered. England generously rewarded him for his services. He received an estate in Oxfordshire, and Blenheim Palace was built for him there in 1705.

Marlborough was born in Devonshire. His given name was John Churchill. He was an ancestor of Sir Winston Churchill, who wrote a biography of him. Marlborough served in the war against the Netherlands, under the French Marshal Turenne, the greatest military leader of that day. Philip Dwight Jones

Marlin, *MAHR luhn,* is the name of a group of large game fishes that live in the ocean. They are related to the spearfishes and sailfishes. Most marlins weigh from 50 to 400 pounds (23 to 180 kilograms), but some weigh much more. The largest ever caught, a *black marlin,* weighed 1,560 pounds (708 kilograms). The marlin has a pointed spear that may measure 2 feet (61 centimeters) long. The marlin's *dorsal* (back) fin looks like a sickle, and its tail is crescent shaped. *White marlins* live in the

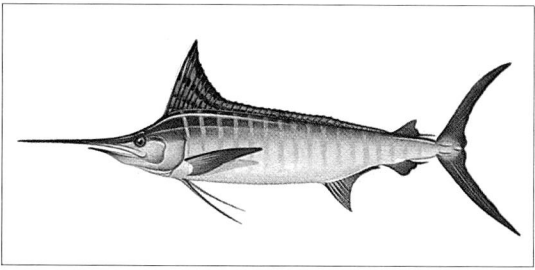

WORLD BOOK illustration by Colin Newman, Linden Artists Ltd.

A marlin is a large game fish related to the swordfish and the sailfish. The marlin has a pointed spear and a crescent-shaped tail. The fish's *dorsal* (back) fin looks like a sickle.

Atlantic Ocean and *striped marlins* live in the Pacific. Black marlins and *blue marlins* live in both the Atlantic and Pacific. Marlins often leap high in the air. See also **Fish** (pictures: Fish of coastal waters and the open ocean); **Sailfish; Swordfish.**

Scientific classification. Marlins belong to the family Istiophoridae. The blue marlin is *Makaira nigricans;* the black marlin, *M. indica;* the white marlin, *Tetrapturus albidus;* and the striped marlin, *T. audax.* William J. Richards

Marlowe, Christopher (1564-1593), was the first great Elizabethan writer of tragedy. His most famous work, *The Tragical History of Doctor Faustus* (about 1588), is an imaginative view of a legendary scholar's fall to damnation through lust for forbidden knowledge, power, and sensual pleasure. Never before in English literature had a writer so powerfully shown the soul's conflict with the laws defining the place of human beings in a universal order. See **Faust.**

Marlowe was born in Canterbury and studied at Cambridge. Evidently at some time during his university years, he did secret service work for the government. The few years before his death in a tavern fight have left evidence of his duels and reports of his unconventional, skeptical political and religious thought.

Marlowe established his theatrical reputation with *Tamburlaine the Great* (about 1587). In "high astounding" poetry and spectacle, Marlowe wrote about an awe-inspiring conqueror, Tamburlaine. These plays reflect the widespread fascination in Marlowe's time with the reach and limits of the human will's desire for dominion. In *Tamburlaine*, Marlowe influenced later drama with his concentration on a heroic figure and his development of *blank verse* (unrhymed poetry) into a flexible poetic form for tragedy. His later plays focus on what were considered the dangerous and subversive elements in Renaissance culture, such as atheism, witchcraft, and homosexuality. These plays are *The Jew of Malta* (c. 1589), *Edward II* (c. 1592), and *Doctor Faustus*. Marlowe's nondramatic poetry includes the unfinished *Hero and Leander*, which became an immediate classic; translations from the Roman poets Ovid and Lucan; and the pastoral lyric "The Passionate Shepherd to His Love."

Stephen Orgel

Marmara, *MAHR muhr uh,* **Sea of,** is part of the trade waterway that links the Black Sea with the Mediterranean Sea. The Sea of Marmara was once called *Propontis.* The Bosporus, a strait, connects it with the Black Sea on the east. Another strait, the Dardanelles, links it with the Aegean Sea on the west. The Sea of Marmara is about 170 miles (275 kilometers) long and 50 miles (80 kilometers) across at its widest point. It covers about 4,300 square miles (11,100 square kilometers). See also **Bosporus; Dardanelles.**   John J. Baxevanis

Location of the Sea of Marmara

Marmoset, *MAHR muh zeht,* is one of the world's smallest kinds of monkey. Most marmosets are less than 1 foot (30 centimeters) long, not including the tail, and weigh from 10 to 12 ounces (300 to 350 grams). The thick, soft coats of marmosets range in color from silvery-white to dark gray or brown. Patches of hair stick out from the head and ears of some marmosets. Unlike most other monkeys, marmosets have claws instead of nails. They live in trees and walk on all four legs, much like squirrels. Marmosets feed mainly on insects and fruit. They also chew holes in certain trees to eat the gum or sap. Most marmosets live in groups of three to eight in the tropical forests and woodland plains of Central and South America.

There are 10 types of marmosets. The *pygmy marmoset* is $5\frac{1}{2}$ to $6\frac{1}{4}$ inches (14 to 16 centimeters) long and weighs between 5 and 7 ounces (150 and 200 grams). Pygmy marmosets are found from southern Colombia to southeastern Peru, and in parts of Ecuador and Brazil. Other marmosets live in Brazil and Bolivia.

Marmosets are kept as pets and are used in medical

Rod Williams, Bruce Coleman Inc.

A pygmy marmoset, *above,* feasts on a grape. Marmosets eat insects, fruit, and the gum or sap of trees.

research. They are threatened by the increasing destruction of their tropical forest habitat.

Scientific classification. Marmosets are members of the marmoset and tamarin family, Callitrichidae. The scientific name for the pygmy marmoset is *Cebuella pygmaea.* Other marmosets are in the genus *Callithrix.*   Roderic B. Mast

See also **Tamarin.**

Marmot, *MAHR muht,* is the largest member of the squirrel family. Marmots live in burrows, and are found in much of the Northern Hemisphere. They are rodents. The woodchuck is a kind of marmot that lives in open areas (see **Woodchuck**). North American marmots are from 1 to 2 feet (30 to 61 centimeters) long. They have short legs, small ears, and furry tails up to 9 inches (23 centimeters) long. Most marmots have gray fur on their backs and yellowish-orange fur on their bellies. Marmots eat plants. They grow fat in autumn and sleep through winter. Female marmots give birth to four or five young in May. Marmots live in *colonies* (groups) on mountain slopes.

Scientific classification. Marmots belong to the squirrel family, Sciuridae. The scientific name for the common marmot is *Marmota flaviventris.*   Clyde Jones

Marne, Battles of the. See World War I (The Western Front; The last campaigns).

Marne River, *mahrn,* is the largest branch of the Seine River in France. It rises in eastern France on the Langres Plateau and flows north and west for 310 miles (500 kilometers) through rich grain land. It empties into the Seine River southeast of Paris (see **France** [physical map]). Large barges can navigate the river. The Marne is linked to the east by a canal that runs through Nancy to Strasbourg on the Rhine River.   Hugh D. Clout

Marot, *ma ROH,* **Clement,** *klay MAHN* (1496-1544), was a French poet who served in the households of King Francis I and Marguerite de Navarre. Marot composed light, elegant, witty verse that pleased the wealthy members of court society. But his poetry also reveals, with great artistry and devotion to truth, the social and intellectual realities of the time and an interest in the religious controversies of the Reformation.

Shortly before his death, he published a significant translation of the Psalms. Some critics consider him an unimportant court poet. Others, especially modern critics, call him a genuine moralist who wrote with delicacy and discretion. Marot was born in Cahors. He died in Italy, exiled from Roman Catholic France because of his Protestant beliefs.   Robert B. Griffin

Marquand, *mahr KWAHND,* **John Phillips** (1893-1960), an American novelist, pictured the decayed aristocratic society in Boston with gentle but effective satire. He won the 1938 Pulitzer Prize for fiction for *The Late George Apley* (1937). This, and *Wickford Point* (1939), *H. M. Pulham, Esq.* (1941), and *Point of No Return* (1949) are usually considered his best works. They show how the inheritors of wealth conform to old customs without understanding the duties of a new age.

Marquand was born in Wilmington, Del. After graduating from Harvard University, he became a reporter for the Boston *Transcript.* Marquand won his first success as an author with romantic novels and with serialized detective stories about Mr. Moto, a secret agent. *Thirty Years* (1954) contains essays and reports on Marquand's own observations.   Bert Hitchcock

Marquesas Islands, *mahr KAY suhz,* are a group of about 10 volcanic islands in the South Pacific Ocean. The islands lie about 900 miles (1,400 kilometers) northeast of Tahiti and have a total area of 492 square miles (1,274 square kilometers). France governs the islands as part of the territory of French Polynesia. For location, see **Pacific Islands** (map).

The main islands in the Marquesas group are Hiva Oa, the largest island; Nuku Hiva; Ua Huka; and Ua Pou. The village of Tai o Hae, on Nuku Hiva, serves as the main port and administrative center. Most of the islands have steep mountains that drop sharply to the sea and fertile valleys with many streams and waterfalls. The Marquesas have a warm, humid climate, with an average temperature of about 78 °F (25 °C) throughout the year. Annual rainfall varies from about 50 inches (125 centimeters) to more than 100 inches (250 centimeters).

About 7,000 people, mainly Polynesians, live on the Marquesas Islands. Most of them farm or fish to provide their own food. The chief crops are bananas, breadfruit, coconut, sweet potatoes, and taro. *Copra* (dried coconut meat) is the main export.

The first settlers on the Marquesas Islands arrived about 2,000 years ago. Historians are not sure whether these settlers came from Polynesia or South America. Remains of stone platform foundations for houses and large courtyards for religious ceremonies built by early settlers still exist. A Spanish explorer, Álvaro de Mendaña, reached the southernmost islands in 1595. He named them after the Marques de Mendoza, the Spanish viceroy of Peru. In 1791, Joseph Ingraham, an American sea captain, sailed among the northern islands.

Many American whalers visited the islands from old the 1820's to the 1860's. Thousands of Marquesans died of diseases brought by the whalers. In 1842, France annexed the Marquesas Islands and stationed troops on Nuku Hiva. In 1870, France took control of all the Marquesas Islands. American author Herman Melville described the islands in his novel *Typee* (1846). Paul Gauguin, a French painter who died in 1903, spent the last two years of his life on Hiva Oa and is buried there.
          Robert Langdon

Marquess, *MAHR kwihs,* is a degree of nobility in the British peerage. A marquess, also spelled *marquis,* ranks higher than an earl or a baron, and second only to a duke. The name *marquess* once meant the ruler of an outlying province. A marquess's wife is a marchioness.

Marquetry. See Inlay.

Marquette, *mahr KEHT,* **Jacques,** *zhahk* (1637-1675), was a French explorer and Roman Catholic missionary in North America. He joined the French-Canadian explorer Louis Jolliet on a trip down the Mississippi River. They were probably the first whites to explore the upper Mississippi and parts of Illinois and Wisconsin.

Early life. Marquette was born in Laon, France, and attended schools run by Jesuit priests. He joined the Jesuit order in 1656 and spent the next 10 years studying and teaching in France. In 1666, he was sent as a missionary to the French province, New France.

Victor Englebert

The island of Ua Pou is one of the largest of the Marquesas Islands. These volcanic islands are noted for their healthful climate and lush vegetation. Breadfruit and coconuts are among the crops that grow well in the islands' fertile soil.

In New France, Marquette spent two years learning Indian languages. In 1668, he established a mission among the Ottawa Indians at Sault Sainte Marie in what is now Ontario. He went to the St. Esprit mission on Lake Superior in 1669 and worked among the Huron and Ottawa Indians. In 1671, he moved with them to the St. Ignace mission on northern Lake Michigan.

The Indians often talked about a great river called the Mississippi, a word that meant *big river* in their language. At that time, little was known about the geography of North America. Marquette and others thought the river might flow into the Pacific Ocean.

Exploration and discovery. Governor General Comte de Frontenac of New France believed the Mississippi might provide an easy route to the Far East for traders. In 1673, he sent Louis Jolliet to find the river and trace its course. Marquette knew some Indian languages, and so he was chosen to go with Jolliet.

In May 1673, Marquette, Jolliet, and five other men set out in two canoes from St. Ignace. They paddled south on Lake Michigan, into the Fox River, and up through what is now Wisconsin. They traveled overland from the Fox to the Wisconsin River. At the mouth of the Wisconsin, they saw the Mississippi.

The explorers paddled down the Mississippi and realized that it flowed south. They decided that the river probably flowed into the Gulf of Mexico, rather than into the Pacific Ocean. Along the way, they met many friendly Indians. But when the men reached the mouth of the Arkansas River, they encountered hostile Indians. A friendly Indian told Marquette that whites lived farther south on the river. The explorers realized these people must be Spaniards who had settled along the Gulf of Mexico. Marquette and Jolliet feared that the Indians and Spaniards would attack them. Having learned the course of the river, they turned back.

The expedition traveled up the Mississippi to the Illinois River and from there to the Kankakee River. They journeyed overland from the Kankakee to the Chicago

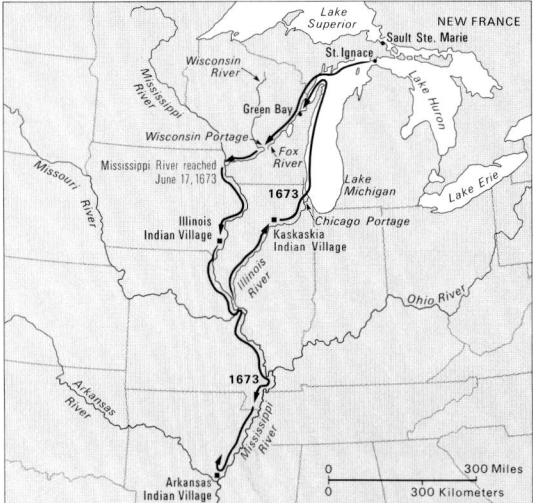

Jacques Marquette was one of the first whites to explore the upper Mississippi River and nearby areas. In 1673, he made a historic trip down the river with the explorer Louis Jolliet.

River and on to Lake Michigan. Their journey had taken about five months.

Final journey. In 1674, Marquette set out from near present-day Green Bay, Wis., to establish a mission among the Kaskaskia Indians in the area of Ottawa, Ill. However, he became ill and spent the winter in a hut on the Chicago River. He reached his destination in the spring of 1675, but his health became worse. He started out to St. Ignace for medical aid but died on the way.

David P. Hardcastle

See also **Illinois** (French and English control); **Jolliet, Louis.**

Additional resources

Donnelly, Joseph P. *Jacques Marquette, S. J., 1637-1675.* Loyola Univ. Press, 1968.
Stein, R. Conrad. *The Story of Marquette and Jolliet.* Childrens Pr., 1981. For younger readers.

Marquette University is an independent coeducational school in Milwaukee, Wis. It is sponsored by the Society of Jesus (Jesuits) and governed by a board of trustees composed of Jesuits and lay people. The courses offered lead to degrees in arts and sciences, business administration, journalism, education, engineering, nursing, speech, dentistry, law, and allied health fields. The university has a graduate school and an evening division, and also offers summer sessions.

Marquette was chartered in 1864 and opened in 1881. It became a university in 1907. For enrollment, see **Universities and colleges** (table).

Critically reviewed by Marquette University

Marquis. See Marquess.

Marquis, *MAHR kwihs,* **Don** (1878-1937), was an American humorist and journalist. He became best known for his fictional creations archy the cockroach and his companion, mehitabel the alley cat. They first appeared in Marquis' daily newspaper column in 1916. archy typed accounts of his adventures with mehitabel on Marquis' typewriter at night. Because archy could not depress the shift key, he typed only in small letters, giving Marquis' columns a distinctive appearance. The cockroach mocked many subjects that irritated Marquis, including free verse, missionaries, organized labor, technology, and popular science writers. The cat ridiculed sober morality and pretentious social attitudes.

Marquis was born in Walnut, Ill. His full name was Donald Robert Perry Marquis. He was a journalist in Atlanta, Ga., from 1902 to 1909 and in New York City from 1909 to 1925. Marquis also wrote humorous verse, short stories, novels, and plays.   Sarah Blacher Cohen

Marrakech, *muh RAH kehsh* or *MAR uh KEHSH* (pop. 332,741), is one of the largest cities in Morocco. It is also one of the country's traditional capitals. Marrakech lies in west-central Morocco. For location, see **Morocco** (map). The city is noted for its *mosques* (Muslim houses of worship), parks, gardens, and pink clay buildings. Its chief industries include food processing, flour milling, and leather and textile manufacturing.

Marrakech was once the capital of a vast Berber empire. The city was founded by the Berber ruler Yusuf ibn Tashfin in 1062 and reached the height of its prosperity in the 1400's. Its importance declined when a succession of Arab rulers replaced the Berbers in Morocco.

Kenneth J. Perkins

© Brian Seed, TSW/Chicago Ltd.

A bride and groom exchange marriage vows at a wedding ceremony. Couples traditionally include a *best man* and a *maid of honor* in the ceremony to serve as official witnesses.

Marriage is the relationship between a man and a woman who have made a legal agreement to live together. When a man and woman marry, they become husband and wife. Marriage is also an important religious ceremony in many of the world's religions.

Most couples decide to marry because they love each other and want to spend the rest of their lives together. A man and woman who marry usually hope to share a special sexual relationship and a permanent romantic attraction. But each hopes the other will always be a close friend as well. Each also expects the other to help with many problems and to share certain responsibilities. These responsibilities include earning a living, budgeting money, paying bills, preparing meals, and taking care of a home.

Most couples who marry plan to have children and to raise them together. A husband and wife are required by law to protect and care for their children. Marriage thus serves as the basis of family life (see **Family**).

In the United States, about $2\frac{1}{2}$ million couples marry each year. However, many people choose never to marry. Some people who remain single may not find a mate with whom they want to share their life. Others may not want the many responsibilities required of a successful marriage. Still others prefer to stay unmarried because they enjoy their independence.

Many married couples find they are not happy as husband and wife. Some marriages fail because the man and woman married when they were young and inexpe-

rienced in many ways. People who marry before they are 18 years old are much more likely to have unsuccessful marriages than if they had waited until they were older. A man and woman also have less of a chance of achieving a happy marriage if they marry primarily because the woman is pregnant. In addition, if a man and woman are of a different age, nationality, religion, or background, their chances of a successful marriage drop significantly.

In the United States, the rate of divorce among young couples has increased sharply since the mid-1960's. Statistics indicate that about half the marriages that took place during the 1970's will likely end in divorce. Most divorced people remarry, and many have a successful marriage with another partner. See **Divorce**.

Dating and courtship. In India and many other countries, most marriages are arranged by parents' deciding whom their children will marry. But in Western countries, including the United States and Canada, nearly everyone makes his or her own decision about whom and when to marry.

Before people marry, they date members of the opposite sex. A man and woman who date each other spend a lot of time together learning to know the other person. After they have dated over a period of time, they may find that they love each other and decide to become engaged.

In many cases, the man gives the woman an engagement ring as a token of their agreement to marry. The use of a ring as an engagement token comes from the ancient custom of using a ring to seal an important agreement.

The age at which people start to date varies widely. But generally, the younger that a man and a woman are

WORLD BOOK photo

Raising a family is one of the many rewards of marriage, but it is also a serious responsibility for the parents. The family shown above is enjoying a meal together at home.

The contributor of this article is Carlfred B. Broderick, Professor of Sociology at the University of Southern California.

© John Coletti, Stock, Boston

A husband and wife prepare a meal as a team. Many married couples today share household tasks that were traditionally handled by either the wife or the husband.

when they begin to date, the younger they are when they marry.

Most men and women date and marry people they live near, or with whom they work or go to school. Most people also date and marry those whom they consider attractive and who, in turn, regard them as attractive. In addition, people tend to date and marry individuals who are like themselves in certain ways. For example, people of the same nationality, ethnic group, and religion tend to marry each other. A man and woman are more likely to marry if they have similar social and educational backgrounds. They are also more likely to marry if they are about the same age.

Laws concerning marriage. A man and woman must follow certain laws when they marry. The United States and Canada have basically the same marriage laws. Neither nation has federal marriage laws, but each state and province has its own regulations.

In all except four states, both the man and woman must be at least 18 years old to marry without parental consent. Nebraska and Wyoming require a couple to be at least 19. Mississippi and Rhode Island have a minimum age of 21. Most states allow people to marry as young as 16 with parental consent. In some states, a person under age 16 needs a judge's permission to marry.

According to law, both the man and woman must freely consent to marry. If a person is forced or tricked into marrying against his or her will, a judge will *annul* (cancel) the marriage.

State laws prohibit close relatives from marrying each other. Laws also forbid a person to marry if he or she is married to someone else. A person who marries a second time while a first marriage is still in effect commits the crime of *bigamy.*

Some states permit a couple to marry even if the bride or groom cannot be present at the wedding ceremony. However, another person must serve as a *proxy* (substitute) for the absent bride or groom. This type of marriage is called *marriage by proxy.*

In nearly all states, a couple must have a marriage license to marry. Some states require both the man and woman to have a blood test before they can obtain a marriage license. This test shows whether or not a person has syphilis, a sexually transmitted disease (see **Syphilis**). Some states also require that the blood be tested for immunity to rubella. In some states, both the man and woman must also have a medical examination before they can get a marriage license.

Most states require a waiting period between the day a couple apply for a license and the day they marry. This period, which averages from three to five days, gives both people time to make sure they want to marry. The waiting period developed from a Roman Catholic custom that required a couple to announce their engagement publicly on each of the three Sundays before the wedding day. During the time between the first announcement and the wedding, anyone who believed that the couple should not marry was expected to say so. Today, some couples announce their engagement at church services or through church bulletins. Such announcements are called *banns.*

Marital status of the United States population
Percent of persons 18 years old and over

Year	Married	Single	Widowed	Divorced
1910	62.7	28.6	8.1	0.6
1920	64.8	25.7	8.5	1.0
1930	65.6	24.5	8.5	1.4
1940	65.8	24.1	8.6	1.5
1950	72.2	16.8	9.0	2.0
1960	73.9	14.7	8.9	2.5
1970	71.7	16.2	8.9	3.2
1975	69.6	17.5	8.3	4.6
1980	65.5	20.3	8.0	6.2
1985	63.0	21.5	7.9	7.6
1990	61.9	22.2	7.6	8.3
1992	61.1	22.6	7.5	8.8

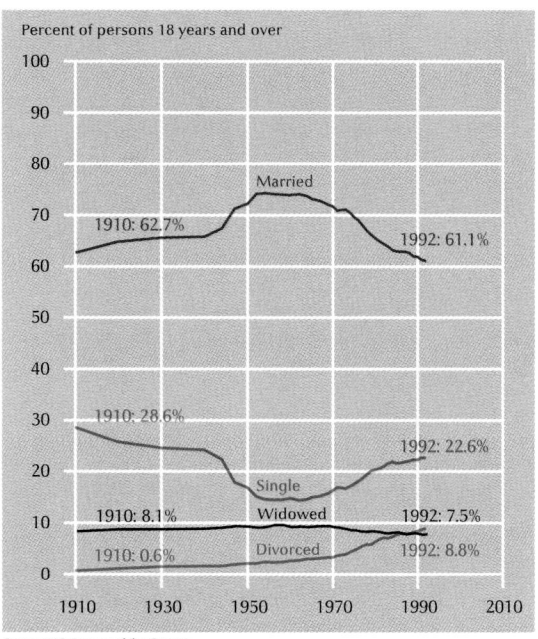

Source: U.S. Bureau of the Census.

If an unmarried couple live together as husband and wife, a court may declare them married after a certain period of time. The time period varies among the states that permit such *common-law marriages.* It is usually several years. A couple do not have to have a license or wedding ceremony for a common-law marriage.

Most states have laws forbidding people of the same sex to marry. However, many homosexual couples establish long-term relationships that are similar to marriage and consider themselves married.

Wedding ceremonies and customs. Most wedding ceremonies involve two requirements. First, the man and woman must say that they want to become husband and wife. Second, the ceremony must have witnesses, including the official who marries the couple. If the couple have a religious ceremony, it is conducted by a member of the clergy, such as a minister, priest, or rabbi. If a couple are married in a *civil* (nonreligious) ceremony, a judge or some other authorized official performs it. During the days of long sea voyages, the captain of a ship was authorized to conduct a marriage ceremony while the ship was at sea.

Many couples prefer a traditional religious ceremony, though some people depart from custom. Some even write their own wedding service. A traditional marriage ceremony begins with the bridesmaids and ushers walking slowly down a center aisle to the altar. They stand on each side of the altar throughout the ceremony. The groom enters and waits for the bride at the altar. The bride then walks down the aisle with her father, another male relative, or a family friend. She wears a white dress and veil and carries a bouquet. At the altar, the bride and groom exchange marriage vows and accept each other as husband and wife. The groom puts a wedding ring on the ring finger of the bride's left hand, and the bride may also give the groom a ring. After the ceremony, the bride and groom kiss and then leave down the main aisle.

People of many backgrounds follow the traditional wedding ceremony, but certain religious groups add their own features to it. For example, different Protestant groups have their own versions of the ceremony. Many Roman Catholic weddings take place during a Mass, and the bride and groom receive Holy Communion. Marriage is a *sacrament* (important religious ceremony) in the Roman Catholic and Eastern Orthodox churches (see **Sacrament**).

Most Jewish weddings are held under a special canopy that represents the couple's future home. At the end of the ceremony, an empty glass or other breakable object is placed on the floor and the groom breaks it with his foot. This act symbolizes the destruction of the ancient Jewish Temple in Jerusalem and reminds the couple that a marriage can also break if it is not protected.

Mormon weddings are held privately in Mormon temples. Only church members in good standing can attend these ceremonies. Mormons believe that marriage and family life continue after death.

A Quaker man and woman marry at a public gathering where they declare their commitment to each other. Quakers believe that God makes a couple husband and wife, and so a minister or other official is not required.

Many wedding customs have been popular since ancient times. For example, Roman brides probably wore

J. M. Bertrand, Shostal

Some societies permit *polygamy,* the practice of having more than one wife or husband. This photograph shows an African prince with five of his wives.

veils more than 2,000 years ago. Bridal veils became popular in Great Britain and the New World during the late 1700's. The custom of giving a wedding ring probably dates back to the ancient Egyptians. The roundness of the ring probably represents eternity, and the presentation of wedding rings symbolizes that the man and woman are united forever. Wearing the wedding ring on the ring finger of the left hand is another old custom. People once thought that a vein or nerve ran directly from this finger to the heart. An old superstition says that a bride can ensure good luck by wearing "something old, something new, something borrowed, and something blue." Another superstition is that it is bad luck for a bride and groom to see each other before the ceremony on their wedding day.

After many weddings, the guests throw rice at the bride and groom as a wish for children and good fortune. Rice was once a symbol of fertility, happiness, and long life. The bride may toss her bouquet to the unmarried female guests. The woman who catches the flowers will supposedly be the next to marry. This custom probably started in France in the 1300's. The bride may also throw her garter to the unmarried men. The man who catches it will supposedly be the next male to marry.

Marriage problems. A man and woman expect certain things of each other even before they marry. After marriage, some husbands and wives cannot satisfy their partner's expectations. They may become disappointed and unhappy with each other and have problems with their marriage.

A couple may argue about almost anything, such as how to spend their money or how to treat their children. If they do not work out their differences, they may find it difficult to be friends, romantic partners, or good parents.

Couples with marriage problems should seek help from a trained marriage counselor. Only a few states require marriage counselors to be licensed. A couple can obtain the names of qualified counselors in their area from the American Association for Marriage and Family

Therapy, 1100 17th Street NW, 10th Floor, Washington, DC 20036.

Changing attitudes about marriage. Almost every society has certain traditional ideas about marriage. For example, most societies expect men and women to marry. Most cultures also have traditions about the role and duties of a husband and wife. Traditionally, the husband is expected to earn a living, and the wife is expected to keep house and raise children.

Many Americans disregard traditional marriage patterns. For example, a large number of married couples share responsibilities that have been traditionally handled by either the husband or the wife. An increasing number of married women have paying jobs and help support their families financially. In 1940, about 15 per cent of all married women earned money. Today, about 50 per cent hold a full- or part-time job. More and more husbands share responsibilities traditionally handled by women. Such responsibilities include cooking, doing housework, and caring for the children.

On the average, men and women stay single longer than they once did. In 1950, men married at an average age of 23, and women married at an average age of 20. By the late 1980's, the average marriage age was about 26 for men and about 24 for women.

An increasing number of people choose not to marry. If a man and woman wish to avoid marriage, they may decide to live together with no formal obligations to each other. This arrangement is more common among young adults, but some couples of all ages live together without marrying.

Marriage in other cultures. In most countries, one man marries one woman, and they stay married unless one of them dies or they are divorced. This system of marriage is called *monogamy.* Some societies permit *polygamy,* in which a man has more than one wife, or a woman has more than one husband. The marriage of a man to more than one woman is called *polygyny* and is practiced by many African and Middle Eastern peoples. Islamic law permits a man to have as many as four wives. Some societies practice *polyandry,* the marriage of a woman to more than one man.

In certain cultures, marriage involves a gift from the family of the bride or groom to the other's family. In many societies, for example, the bride's family gives money or property to the groom or his family. Such a gift is called a *dowry.* In some cases, the dowry is given to the bride so that she and her husband may benefit from it. In other cultures, the groom and his family present gifts to the family of the bride. This offering is called a *bride price.*

Some societies require a person to marry someone who belongs to his or her own tribe or group. This custom is called *endogamy.* In other places, an individual must follow the rules of *exogamy* and marry a person from another tribe or village. The most common rule of exogamy requires a man or woman to marry someone outside his or her own family.

Each culture has its own rules about which family members a person is forbidden to marry. However, most societies forbid *incest,* which is marriage or sexual relations between certain close relatives. In nearly all cultures, such relatives include a parent and child or a brother and sister. Carlfred B. Broderick

Related articles in *World Book* include:

Africa (Marriage and the family; picture)	Family
Annulment	Gretna Green
Bigamy	Indian, American (Marriage)
Breach of promise	Poland (picture: Weddings)
Culture (pictures)	Polygamy
Divorce	Proxy
Dower	Sex
Eugenics	Wedding anniversary

See also *Marriage and divorce* in the Research Guide/Index, Volume 22, for a *Reading and Study Guide.*

Additional resources

Handbook of Marriage and the Family. Ed. by Marvin B. Sussman and S. K. Steinmetz. Plenum, 1987.
Lauer, Jeanette C. and R. H. *Til Death Do Us Part: How Couples Stay Together.* Haworth Pr., 1986.
Lindsay, Jeanne W. *Teenage Marriage: Coping with Reality.* Rev. ed. Morning Glory, 1988. *Teens Look at Marriage: Rainbows, Roles and Realities.* 1985.
Marks, Stephen R. *Three Corners: Exploring Marriage and the Self.* Lexington Bks., 1986.

Marric, J. J. See Creasey, John.

Marrow. See Bone (Structure of the bones).

Marryat, Frederick (1792-1848), was an English author whose novels about life at sea were widely read during the 1800's. Marryat's novels have declined in popularity, but they remain fine examples of adventure stories.

Marryat was born in London. As a boy, he tried to run away to sea several times. When Marryat was 14 years old, his father allowed him to join the navy. Marryat's 23 years of sea adventures in the British navy provided material for his writing. *The Naval Officer, or Scenes and Adventures in the Life of Frank Mildmay* (1829), for example, is largely an autobiographical novel. Marryat's other sea novels include *The King's Own* (1830), *The Pirate and the Three Cutters* (1836), and *Mr. Midshipman Easy* (1836). His children's stories include *Masterman Ready* (1841-1842). K. K. Collins

Mars was the god of war in Roman mythology. The ancient Romans gave Mars special importance because they considered him the father of Romulus and Remus, the legendary founders of Rome.

Originally, Mars was a god of farmland and fertility. The month of March, the beginning of the Roman growing season, was named for him. Since ancient times, the area enclosed by a bend in the Tiber River in Rome has been called the Field of Mars. The early Romans dedicated this section of land to Mars because of its fertility.

Mars became the god of war after the Romans came into contact with Greek culture. They gave him many characteristics of the Greek god of war, Ares. In time, the Romans associated Mars principally with war. Before going into battle, Roman troops offered sacrifices to him. After winning a battle, they gave Mars a share of their spoils. The word *martial,* which means *warlike,* is based on the god's name. The planet Mars is named for him.

Artists show Mars in armor and wearing a crested helmet. Editorial cartoonists still use this image of Mars as a symbol for war. The wolf and the woodpecker were associated with Mars. His love affair with Venus, the Roman goddess of love, became a popular subject for poets and painters. E. N. Genovese

See also **Ares; Mythology** (Roman mythology).

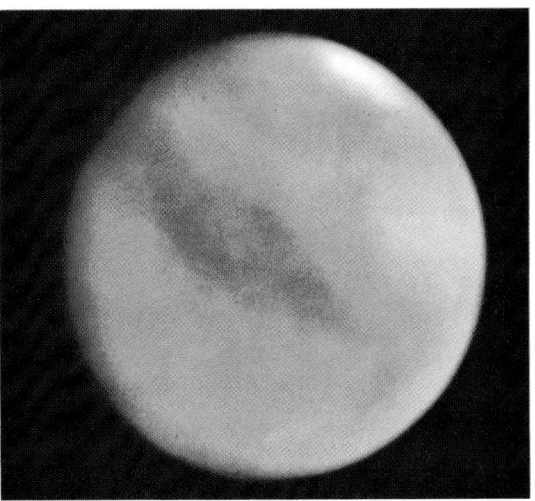
Hale Observatories

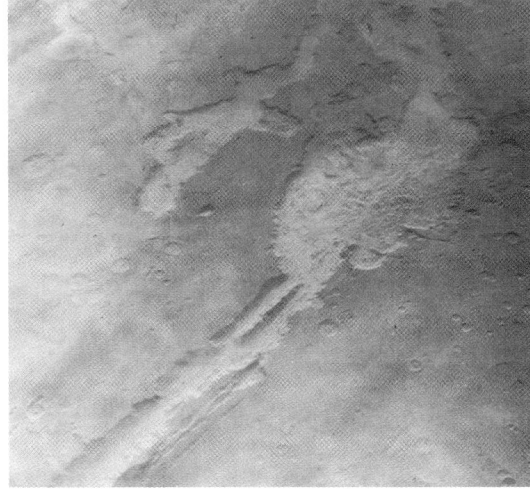
NASA

Mars's surface features, including light areas, dark areas, and polar cap, are visible in this photograph taken from the earth, *left.* The earth's atmosphere makes the picture blurry. A series of canyons called the Valles Marineris (Mariner Valleys) make up the diagonal landform in the photo at the right, taken by the *Viking 1.* This landform is more than 2,500 miles (4,000 kilometers) long.

Mars is the only planet whose surface can be seen in detail from the earth. It is reddish in color, and was named Mars after the bloody-red god of war of the ancient Romans.

Mars is the fourth closest planet to the sun, and the next planet beyond the earth. Its mean distance from the sun is 141,600,000 miles (227,900,000 kilometers), compared with about 93,000,000 miles (150,000,000 kilometers) for the earth. At its closest approach to the earth, Mars is 34,600,000 miles (55,700,000 kilometers) away. Venus is the only planet that comes closer to the earth.

The diameter of Mars is 4,223 miles (6,796 kilometers), a little over half that of the earth. Pluto and Mercury are the only planets smaller than Mars.

Orbit. Mars travels around the sun in an *elliptical* (oval-shaped) orbit. Its distance from the sun varies from about 154,800,000 miles (249,200,000 kilometers) at its farthest point, to about 128,400,000 miles (206,600,000 kilometers) at its closest point. Mars takes about 687 earth-days to go around the sun, compared with about 365 days, or 1 year, for the earth.

Rotation. As Mars orbits the sun, it spins on its *axis,* an imaginary line through its center. Mars's axis is not *perpendicular* (at an angle of 90°) to its path around the sun. The axis tilts at an angle of about 24° from the perpendicular position. For an illustration of the tilt of an axis, see **Planet** (The axes of the planets). Mars rotates once every 24 hours and 37 minutes. The earth rotates once every 23 hours and 56 minutes.

Surface. The surface conditions on Mars are more like the earth's than are those of any other planet. But the present plants and animals of the earth could not live on Mars. The surface temperature on Mars is much lower than that on earth, rarely rising above the freezing

The contributor of this article is Hyron Spinrad, Professor of Astronomy at the University of California, Berkeley.

Mars, shown in blue in the diagram, is the next planet beyond the earth. The ancient symbol for Mars, *right,* is still used today.

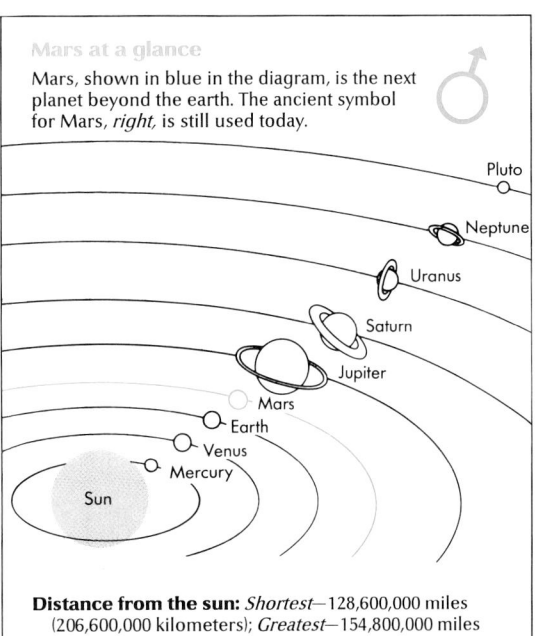

Distance from the sun: *Shortest*—128,600,000 miles (206,600,000 kilometers); *Greatest*—154,800,000 miles (249,200,000 kilometers); *Mean*—141,600,000 miles (227,900,000 kilometers).

Distance from the earth: *Shortest*—34,600,000 miles (55,700,000 kilometers); *Greatest*—248,000,000 miles (399,000,000 kilometers).

Diameter: 4,223 miles (6,796 kilometers).

Length of year: About 1 earth-year and $10\frac{1}{2}$ months.

Rotation period: 24 hours and 37 minutes.

Temperature: $-225°$ to 63° F. ($-143°$ to 17° C).

Atmosphere: Carbon dioxide, nitrogen, argon, oxygen, carbon monoxide, neon, krypton, xenon, and water vapor.

Number of satellites: 2.

NASA

The windblown plains of Mars are covered by red sand dunes and jagged rocks. They resemble the deserts of southwestern North America. This photo of Mars's surface was taken in 1976 by the U.S. *Viking 1* space probe. A part of the probe's equipment appears in the center.

point of water, which is 32° F. (0° C). The planet seems to have had large amounts of surface water millions of years ago, but almost none exists today. However, scientists think that water may be frozen in the planet's large polar caps or beneath its surface. The atmosphere surrounding Mars contains only a trace of oxygen. In spite of the scarcity of liquid water and oxygen, many scientists believe some form of life may exist on Mars. But none has been found yet.

As seen from the earth through a telescope, the surface of Mars has three outstanding features—bright areas, dark areas, and polar caps. There are no oceans on Mars, but there are numerous craters caused by meteors crashing into its surface. Photographs sent back by unmanned space probes show that Mars also has canyons, deep gorges, and surface features that resemble dry riverbeds. Such features seem to support the view of some scientists that large quantities of water once flowed on the planet's surface. A region near Mars's equator is dominated by giant volcanoes. The largest of these volcanoes are bigger and higher than those of the Hawaiian islands on the earth. In fact, the highest volcano on Mars stands twice as high as Mount Everest. A huge canyon near this volcano may be a *fault line* (a break in the planet's crust).

Bright areas of Mars are reddish rust-brown in color and cover about two-thirds of the planet's surface. They are dry, desertlike regions that are covered by dust, sand, and rocks. Much of the surface material seems to contain a brick-colored mineral called *limonite,* which is found in various deserts on the earth.

Dark areas of Mars cover about one-third of the planet's surface. They form irregular patterns, and generally appear greenish-gray or bluish-gray. These dark regions have historically been called *maria* (seas), even though they do not contain measurable amounts of water.

The color and size of Mars's dark areas vary throughout the planet's year. Parts of the maria become lighter in color or disappear during the Martian fall and winter. They become darker and larger during the Martian spring and summer. Many astronomers think the variation is caused by blowing sand and dust that covers and uncovers parts of Mars's surface.

A series of lines running between Mars's dark areas was discovered in 1877 by Giovanni V. Schiaparelli, an Italian astronomer. Schiaparelli called these lines "channels," but when the word was translated from Italian into English, it became "canals." As a result of this error, some scientists thought the lines might be waterways constructed by living beings. Astronomers now know that the canals never existed. They were an illusion.

Polar caps of Mars cover small areas located at the planet's north and south poles. The polar caps appear white from the earth, and they may contain large amounts of frozen water. Like the maria on the planet, each polar cap grows and shrinks with the Martian seasons. A cap appears to evaporate and become smaller when it is tilted toward the sun, and then freeze and get larger when it is tilted away from the sun. The evaporating polar caps may provide some of the water vapor that is present in the atmosphere of the planet.

Atmosphere of Mars is much thinner than that surrounding the earth. It consists chiefly of carbon dioxide,

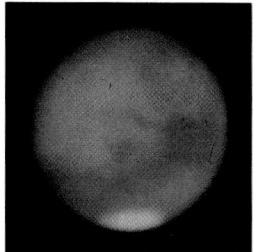

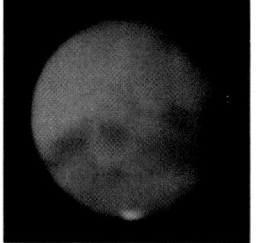

Lowell Observatory

Seasons on Mars cause changes in the planet's surface features. During a Martian winter, the polar cap is large and the dark areas are small, *left*. During a Martian summer, the polar cap shrinks and the dark areas become larger, *right*.

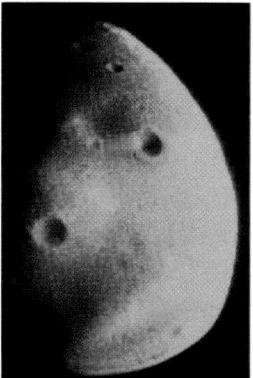

NASA   Lowell Observatory

Mars has two satellites, Deimos and Phobos. Deimos, *left,* was photographed by the *Viking Orbiter 1* space probe. Viewed through a telescope, *right*, Phobos appears as a bright spot to the left of Mars. Deimos is farther away, to the right.

with small amounts of nitrogen, argon, oxygen, carbon monoxide, neon, krypton, and xenon. Mars's atmosphere also contains tiny traces of water vapor. The *atmospheric pressure* (force exerted by the weight of the gases) on Mars is about 0.1 pound per square inch (0.007 kilogram per square centimeter)—less than one-hundredth the atmospheric pressure on the earth.

Three general types of clouds can be seen in the Martian atmosphere. Pink clouds of dust often cover large areas of Mars. Thin blue clouds appear to be made up of ice crystals. Thicker white clouds, which are thought to consist of water vapor, occasionally move across the planet.

Temperature. The tilt of Mars's axis causes the sun to heat the planet's northern and southern halves unequally, resulting in seasons and temperature changes. The seasons on Mars last about twice as long as those on the earth because Mars takes almost twice as long to make one revolution around the sun as the earth does.

Temperatures on Mars are lower than those on the earth because Mars is farther from the sun than the earth is. The lowest nighttime temperature recorded on Mars in winter was −191° F. (−124° C) at about 50° north latitude. The highest recorded daytime temperature in summer was −24° F. (−31° C) closer to the planet's

equator. Scientists calculate, however, that temperatures on Mars may occasionally rise as high as 63° F. (17° C) at the equator and drop as low as −225° F. (−143° C) at night near the poles.

Density and mass. Mars is about four-fifths as *dense* as the earth (see **Density**). The *mass* of Mars is only about a tenth that of the earth (see **Mass**). Because of the planet's smaller mass, its force of gravity is about three-eighths as strong as the earth's. A 100-pound object on the earth would weigh about 38 pounds on Mars.

Satellites. Two small *satellites* (moons) travel around Mars. The closer and larger one, named Phobos, is about 5,800 miles (9,330 kilometers) from the center of Mars. Its diameter is about 14 miles (23 kilometers) at its equator and 11 miles (18 kilometers) from pole to pole. It travels around Mars once about every 7½ hours. Deimos, the smaller satellite, is about 14,600 miles (23,500 kilometers) from Mars's center, and circles the planet once about every 30 hours. Deimos has a diameter of about 6 miles (10 kilometers). An American astronomer, Asaph Hall, discovered both satellites in 1877.

Flights to Mars. The unmanned U.S. spacecraft *Mariner 4* flew as close as 6,118 miles (9,846 kilometers) to Mars in 1965. *Mariner 6* and *Mariner 7* flew within about 2,000 miles (3,200 kilometers) of Mars in 1969.

Mars   The first detailed map of Mars, *below,* was prepared from photographs taken by the *Mariner 9* spacecraft. This map shows volcanic craters and peaks, windblown plains, and the Valles Marineris, a series of canyons extending over 2,500 miles (4,000 kilometers) across the planet.

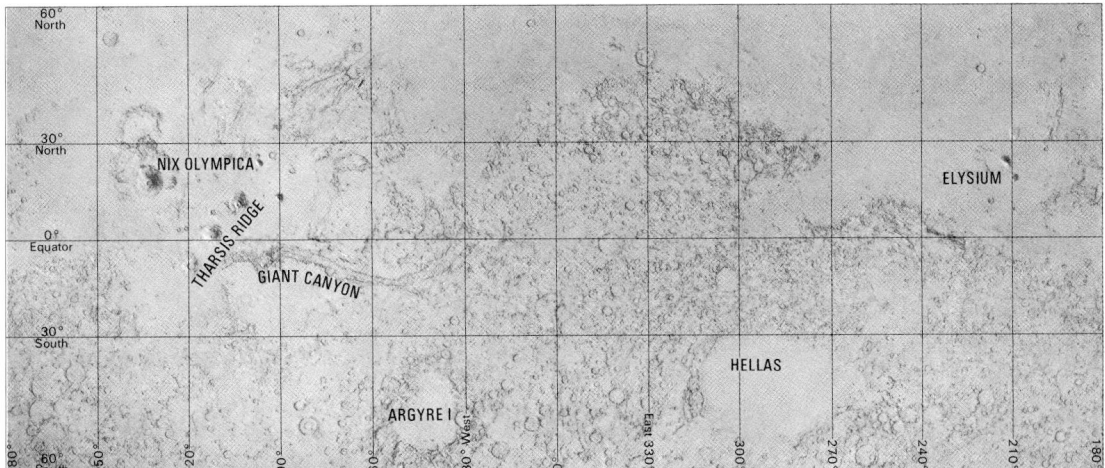

North and south polar regions

Polar caps, which appear white from the earth, cover small areas at the north and south poles of Mars, *right.* The polar caps remain frozen the year around, though their size varies with the seasons on Mars.

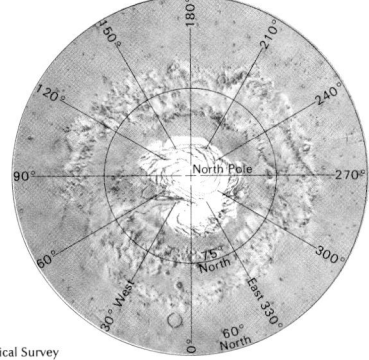
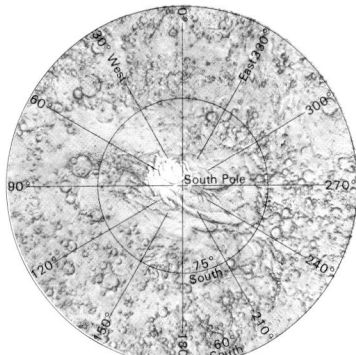

WORLD BOOK maps
Base maps provided by Center of Astrogeology, U.S. Geological Survey

In 1971 and 1972, *Mariner 9* orbited Mars at a distance of about 1,000 miles (1,600 kilometers). It photographed both Martian satellites, a dust storm on the planet, and many surface details. A Soviet probe, *Mars 3,* also orbited the planet in 1971. It released a capsule that made the first soft landing on Mars. But the capsule transmitted information for only 20 seconds before it unexpectedly fell silent.

Photographs sent to the earth from *Mariner 4* and *Mariner 9* revealed meteor craters on Mars's surface. Astronomers had never seen craters in observations from the earth. *Mariner 4* instruments showed that Mars has no measurable magnetic field.

On July 20, 1976, the U.S. *Viking 1* space probe landed on Mars in a desertlike region near the planet's equator. A second unmanned U.S. craft, *Viking 2,* landed farther north on September 3 of the same year. Both probes transmitted high-quality, close-up photographs of the planet's surface features. In addition, their instruments analyzed Mars's atmosphere and soil to seek signs of life. In spite of these experiments, however, scientists still have not been able to determine whether life exists on the planet.

The Soviet Union launched two unmanned spacecraft to Mars in 1988. One craft became lost in space. Communications with the other spacecraft broke down shortly before its scheduled landing in 1989.

Hyron Spinrad

See also **Planet; Solar system; Space exploration.**

Additional resources

Ezell, Edward C. and L. N. *On Mars: Exploration of the Red Planet 1958-1978.* NASA, 1984.
Fisher, David E. *The Third Experiment: Is There Life on Mars?* Atheneum, 1985. Suitable for younger readers.
Fradin, Dennis B. *Mars.* Childrens Pr., 1989. For younger readers.
Moore, Patrick A. *Guide to Mars.* Norton, 1978.

Marseillaise, *MAHR suh LAYZ,* is the national hymn of France. Claude Joseph Rouget de Lisle, a French army engineer, composed the words and the music in Strasbourg on the night of April 25-26, 1792. He wrote the hymn as a marching song after France declared war on Austria and Prussia. Rouget de Lisle called his hymn "Song of the Rhine Army," in honor of the garrison to which he belonged. The hymn begins:

Allons enfants de la patrie,
Le jour de gloire est arrivé!
Contre nous, de la tyrannie,
L'étendard sanglant est levé.
L'étendard sanglant est levé.

(Arise you children of our motherland,
O now is here our glorious day!
Over us the bloodstained banner
Of tyranny holds sway!
Of tyranny holds sway!)

The fighting against Austria and Prussia occurred during the French Revolution (1789-1799). Rouget de Lisle supported the monarchy. His song, however, became a rallying cry of the revolutionary leaders and the common people. It became associated with the revolution when soldiers from Marseille sang it in August 1792 as they marched to storm the Tuileries, a palace in Paris where King Louis XVI lived. From this time on, the song was called "The Marseillaise." It has been used as a national hymn of France since 1795. It was officially adopted as the national hymn in 1879.

Valerie Woodring Goertzen

Marseille, *mahr SAY* (pop. 874,436; met. area pop. 1,115,697), is the second largest city in France and the country's main seaport. Paris is the only larger French city. Marseille, the nation's oldest city, lies in southeast France on the Mediterranean Sea. For location, see **France** (political map).

The city has the shape of a half-circle. It extends inland from an old port that is too small for modern ships. This port, called Old Harbor, is filled with pleasure boats and surrounded by restaurants and cafes. It is the city's major tourist attraction. The Canèbiere, a main street lined with modern shops, extends inland from Old Harbor. It also attracts tourists.

A huge, modern port—which is one of the world's busiest—extends about 5 miles (8 kilometers) west of Old Harbor. Trading ships from many parts of the world dock at the port. Crew members of the ships visit the city and give it a busy, international flavor. Marseille also has attracted many workers from other countries, especially the countries of northern Africa.

Marseille has many beautiful churches. Notre-Dame-de-la-Garde, one of the churches, has a large image of

© Francis de Richemond, The Image Works

Marseille is the oldest city in France. It lies in the southeast part of the country, on the Mediterranean Sea. The Old Harbor, *left,* is the city's main tourist attraction. The harbor area has many restaurants and cafes.

the Virgin Mary on its tall steeple. The image can be seen far out at sea.

Economy of Marseille is based on trade and manufacturing. The city's port handles about a third of the traffic of all French seaports. About 4,500 ships use the port annually. Industries in the Marseille area process chemicals, food, and petroleum from many parts of the world. The city's chief manufactured products include bricks, candles, engines, medicines, soap, and tiles. Marseille has an airport, and highways and trains connect the city with other major European cities, particularly Paris.

History. Marseille was founded about 600 B.C. by Greek adventurers from Asia Minor, who called it *Massalia.* Marseille was an independent city until the first century before the birth of Christ. It then came under Roman domination and fell into decline. In the Middle Ages, the city regained its importance during the Crusades, a series of Christian military expeditions to recapture the Holy Land from the Muslims. Many soldiers and supplies were sent through the port to the Holy Land.

Provence, the region where Marseille is located, became part of France in 1481. Bloody struggles took place in Marseille in the late 1700's during the French Revolution. The opening of the Suez Canal in 1869 provided a water route between the Mediterranean Sea and Indian Ocean. The canal greatly increased the city's importance as a shipping center.   William M. Reddy

For the monthly weather in Marseille, see **France** (Climate). See also **Marseillaise.**

Marsh is a type of wetland where nonwoody plants such as cattails grow. Trees and shrubs are not commonly found in marshes. Many kinds of animals make their homes in marshes. Typical marsh animals include muskrats, turtles, frogs, red-winged blackbirds, and dragonflies.

There are two kinds of marshes—*freshwater marshes* and *salt marshes.* Freshwater marshes develop where the water level is above the surface of the ground for most, if not all, of the year. They generally occur along the shores of lakes, ponds, rivers, and streams where the water is shallow. Plants commonly found in freshwater marshes include bulrushes, horsetails, and reeds.

Salt marshes lie along coasts where fresh water flows into the sea—for example, at river mouths. They are thus exposed to both fresh and salt water and experience daily changes in water level due to tidal activity. Grasses, especially cordgrass and salt-meadow grass, are often the most abundant plants in salt marshes.

Many marshes have been destroyed to make way for buildings and roads or have been damaged by water pollution. Public awareness of the ecological importance of marshes has led to the protection and preservation of many of them. Despite this awareness, a significant number of marshes continue to be eliminated each year.   Eric F. Karlin

See also **Swamp; Wetland.**

Marsh, Reginald (1898-1954), was an American artist famous for his realistic pictures of New York City life. He excelled at portraying crowds on skid row or Coney Island, on subways or in burlesque houses. Some of his scenes have a grim feeling of the Great Depression of the 1930's. But most are full of vitality. Marsh worked in various painting media, often experimenting with the

techniques and materials used by the great painters before 1700. He was also an accomplished draftsman.

Marsh was born in Paris of American parents and grew up in New Jersey. After graduating from Yale University, he was an illustrator for the New York *Daily News.* He taught at the Art Students League in New York from the early 1930's until his death.   Charles C. Eldredge

See also **Realism** (picture).

Marsh gas. See Methane.

Marsh hawk. See Northern harrier.

Marsh hen. See Coot.

Marsh mallow is a plant that grows in meadows and marshes of eastern Europe. It is now grown in the United States. The marsh mallow has woody stalks, which grow 2 to 4 feet (61 to 120 centimeters) high, and large leaves. Downy hair covers both stalks and leaves.

WORLD BOOK illustration by Christabel King

The marsh mallow grows in meadows and marshy areas. It has woody stalks and bluish to pink flowers.

The plant has bluish to pink flowers. Its root is white and shaped like a carrot. People have eaten the roots and leaves of the plant during famines. These parts also are sometimes used for medicinal purposes.

Scientific classification. The marsh mallow belongs to the mallow family, Malvaceae. Its scientific name is *Althaea officinalis.*   Walter S. Judd

Marshal is the highest title in the armies of many countries. *Marshal* is also the title of a police officer having the same powers and duties as a sheriff in many small towns or villages.

In England, the word *marshal* was used to mean *commander of the army* as early as the 1100's. Under the early Frankish kings, the marshal was first a master of horse and later a commander of cavalry. The title grew in dignity and honor until *Maréchal de France* (Marshal of France) became one of the highest honors that could be conferred upon a person. The countries of Europe have given the title *marshal* to top-ranking military commanders. Joseph Stalin, former dictator of the Soviet Union, used the title *Marshal* during World War II. The British Army uses the title *field marshal,* and the head of the British air forces is called an *air marshal.* The *provost marshal* is the highest military police officer.

In the United States, officers of the federal court are called *United States marshals.* They open and close sessions of district courts and courts of appeals, and may serve writs, orders, and other processes of the courts in their districts. *Deputy United States marshals* can make arrests for violation of federal laws. A United States marshal is assigned to each federal court district.

Temporary police are sometimes called marshals, and in some towns the head of the fire department is called the *fire marshal.*   Jack M. Kress

Marshall, Alfred (1842-1924), was a British educator and the most influential economist of his day. He combined two different theories about what determines the value or price of a good. "Classical" theorists had said price was determined mainly by the cost of producing the good, and theorists of the late 1800's had stressed the *utility* (usefulness) of the good and the consumer demand for it. In *Principles of Economics* (1890), Marshall said that all of these factors helped determine price.

Marshall also believed that a self-regulating economy, free of major government interference and based on free competition and private enterprise, would lead to better social conditions, a fair distribution of income, and full employment. Marshall's emphasis on consumer welfare led to the development of *welfare economics.* This branch of economics judges economic systems according to how well they contribute to consumer satisfaction and human well-being.

Marshall was born in London. In 1883, he began teaching economics at Oxford University. He taught at Cambridge University from 1885 to 1908. At Cambridge, Marshall helped train a generation of economists who made the "Cambridge school" the most important of its time.   Daniel R. Fusfeld

Marshall, George Catlett (1880-1959), an American soldier and statesman, served as chief of staff of the United States Army during World War II (1939-1945). He also served as secretary of state from 1947 to 1949 and as secretary of defense from 1950 to 1951. Marshall was the first professional soldier to become secretary of state. In 1947, while serving in that post, he proposed the European Recovery Program, also called the Marshall Plan. Under this plan, the United States spent billions of dollars to rebuild war-torn western Europe. The Marshall Plan is credited with helping check the spread of Communism in Europe. Marshall's role in European reconstruction earned him the 1953 Nobel Peace Prize.

His early life. Marshall was born on Dec. 31, 1880, in Uniontown, Pa. He was the youngest of four children. His father owned coal and coke properties. The senior Marshall was extremely proud of his distant cousin John Marshall, former chief justice of the Supreme Court (see **Marshall, John**).

Marshall graduated from the Virginia Military Institute in Lexington, Va., in 1901. He was not an out-

U.S. Army
George C. Marshall

standing student, but he ranked in the upper half of his class. He received an army commission as a second lieutenant of infantry in 1902. Marshall married Elizabeth Carter Coles in 1902. She died in 1927, and Marshall married Katherine Tupper Brown in 1930.

His early career. Marshall began his Army career in the Philippines in 1902. He returned home in 1903, and attended the Army School of the Line and the Army Staff College at Fort Leavenworth, Kansas. He graduated first in his class from the School of the Line. He said later of this achievement, "Ambition had set in." He also served at various military posts in the United States.

Assigned to the Philippines again in 1913, he showed great ability for planning and tactics in mock battles. In 1916, he returned to the United States and was promoted to captain. When the United States entered World War I in 1917, Marshall sailed for France with the first field units to go overseas. He served for a year as training officer and then as chief of operations of the First Division. He was transferred to the First Army in 1918 and served as chief of operations in the closing months of the war.

Marshall helped plan the First Army's attack on St.-Mihiel. He directed the movement of more than 400,000 men and 2,700 guns from St.-Mihiel to the Meuse-Argonne front for the final American battle of the war. This transfer, made at night in less than two weeks, completely surprised the Germans. General John J. Pershing, commander of the U.S. forces, hailed it as one of the great accomplishments of the war.

Marshall served as senior aide to Pershing from 1919 to 1924. From 1924 to 1927, he served in China as executive officer of the 15th Infantry Regiment.

From 1927 until 1932, Marshall was assistant commandant in charge of training at the Infantry School, Fort Benning, Georgia. He did much to raise the level of instruction there. He later helped organize and administer Civilian Conservation Corps (CCC) camps.

World War II. Marshall was made a brigadier general in 1936. In 1938, he became chief of the war plans division of the War Department and then deputy chief of staff of the Army. On Sept. 1, 1939, the day World War II began in Europe, Marshall became chief of staff of the United States Army, which then had less than 200,000 men, including the Army Air Corps. He also became a four-star general.

Marshall introduced mass maneuvers in which soldiers gained experience under simulated combat conditions. He organized the army into units trained to take part in desert, mountain, and jungle warfare.

Marshall helped make the U.S. Army the greatest fighting force in history by 1945. He remained in Washington, D.C., throughout the war. His work there was so important that he could not be spared to serve as a battle leader. He was responsible for building, arming, and supplying a force of 8,250,000 soldiers and airmen. He was a leader in planning the overall war strategy, and the directing force behind the movements of U.S. armies. Under his command, General Dwight D. Eisenhower and General Douglas MacArthur led American forces to victory in Europe and the Pacific.

On Dec. 16, 1944, Marshall became a General of the Army. In November 1945, a few months after the war ended, he retired as chief of staff. After he retired, President Harry S. Truman appointed him special representative to China. He spent much of the next year in China trying to end the civil war between the Chinese Nationalists and the Communists.

Statesman. Marshall returned to the United States in January 1947, to assume the post of secretary of state in President Truman's Cabinet. As secretary, he urged Congress to pass the European Recovery Program. Under the plan, the United States sent about $13 billion in aid to European countries. Marshall also worked to secure aid for Greece and Turkey and to supply food to West Berlin when the Communists blockaded that city. These programs and the Marshall Plan did much to check Communist influence in Europe (see **Marshall Plan**). Marshall also began negotiations that led to the North Atlantic Treaty Organization (NATO). In 1949, he resigned his Cabinet post because of poor health.

Marshall served as president of the American Red Cross in 1949 and 1950. When the Korean War began in 1950, Truman asked Marshall to head the Department of Defense. An act of Congress set aside the rule that the secretary of defense must be a civilian. Marshall helped strengthen NATO and build up the United Nations fighting forces in Korea. He resigned as secretary of defense in September 1951.

Marshall died on Oct. 16, 1959, and was buried at Arlington National Cemetery. In 1964, the George C. Marshall Research Library, containing his papers and souvenirs, opened in Lexington, Va.   Theodore A. Wilson

Additional resources

Cray, Ed. *General of the Army: George C. Marshall, Soldier and Statesman.* Norton, 1990.
Pogue, Forrest C. *George C. Marshall.* 3 vols. Viking, 1963-1987.

Marshall, James Wilson (1810-1885), discovered gold in California on Jan. 24, 1848. He found pieces of gold while building a sawmill for John Sutter 48 miles (77 kilometers) north of Sutter's Fort. News of the discovery started the gold rush of 1849. In spite of his discovery, Marshall died a poor and bitter man. The first people who came to the gold site paid a small fee, but later arrivals refused to pay. The claims of Marshall and Sutter were swept aside. Marshall was born in Hunterdon County, New Jersey.   Dan L. Flores

Marshall, John (1755-1835), the fourth chief justice of the United States, established the Supreme Court as an important branch of the federal government. He served from 1801 until his death 34 years later, longer than any other chief justice. Marshall is known as the "Great Chief Justice" because of his tremendous impact on the U.S. judicial system.

When Marshall became chief justice, the Supreme Court commanded little respect. Marshall raised the court to a level equal to the executive and legislative branches of the government. He used the court's authority to restructure and clearly define the boundaries of power between the states and the federal government. Marshall established broad judicial principles. Some of these principles laid the foundation for modern decisions that made possible the court's ruling in such areas as civil rights and criminal justice.

During Marshall's years as chief justice, the United States was governed by Democratic-Republicans and Democrats. Most of these leaders—President Thomas

Detail of an oil painting on canvas (about 1832) by William James Hubbard; National Portrait Gallery, Smithsonian Institution, Washington, D.C.

John Marshall, the fourth chief justice of the United States, established the court's power to review legislative acts.

Jefferson, in particular—believed in states' rights. Marshall, however, was a Federalist. He believed that the United States, still a young nation in the early 1800's, greatly needed a strong central government. Marshall felt that such a government—rather than strong state governments—could best help the United States grow strong and safe. Through the force of his arguments, Marshall gave the court the power to overrule the states when national and state interests collided.

Early life. Marshall was born on Sept. 24, 1755, in a log cabin near Germantown, Va. His mother was related to Thomas Jefferson. John's father served in the Virginia House of Burgesses and as a county sheriff. John spent much of his first 20 years helping to raise his 14 younger brothers and sisters on the family farm. He had little formal schooling.

Marshall joined the Continental Army in 1776, during the Revolutionary War in America. He spent the winter of 1777-1778 with General George Washington's forces at Valley Forge, and he was promoted to captain in 1778. In 1780, Marshall studied law briefly at the College of William and Mary and was admitted to the Virginia bar.

Political career. In 1782, Marshall was elected to his first term in the Virginia legislature and moved to Richmond. That same year, he became a member of the Council of State, the executive branch of government in Virginia. In 1783, Marshall married Mary Willis Ambler of Richmond. He resigned from the Council of State in 1784, when it was decided he could not practice law at the same time. However, Marshall quickly regained his seat in the state legislature and continued his distinguished legal career. In 1788, Marshall was elected to the state convention called to decide whether to *ratify* (approve) the proposed Constitution of the United States. He helped win ratification by Virginia.

Marshall served several more terms in the Virginia legislature until 1797, when he became a U.S. minister to France under President John Adams. Adams sent Marshall and two other ambassadors to Paris to negotiate with the French government over French interference with American trade. When Marshall returned in 1798, he was hailed as a hero for refusing to give in to unreasonable and somewhat dishonorable French demands in what became known as the XYZ Affair (see **XYZ Affair**). Marshall was elected to the U.S. House of Representatives in 1799. He quickly became the leader of the moderate Federalists and championed the policies of President Adams. This position made him a rival of his distant cousin and fellow Virginian, Thomas Jefferson, and the two men never agreed on many things again. In 1800, Adams appointed Marshall secretary of state.

Chief justice. In January 1801, as Adams' term neared a close, he appointed Marshall chief justice of the United States. The U.S. Senate quickly confirmed the nomination, and Marshall took the position on Feb. 4, 1801. Marshall believed that the Constitution, upon which the national government was based, must be accepted as the supreme law of the land.

In 1803, Marshall wrote the opinion in the landmark case of *Marbury v. Madison.* In this case, the Supreme Court struck down an act of Congress that was in conflict with the Constitution. The decision firmly established the court's power to declare laws unconstitutional, a power known as *judicial review.* Afterward, Marshall used the power of his position to persuade his fellow justices to accept his view of the Constitution and the need for a strong judiciary and a strong central government, especially in the area of commerce. President Thomas Jefferson and his fellow Democratic-Republicans feared that the Supreme Court would use its power to help the Federalists weaken the states. However, judicial review strengthened the Constitution and remained one of the Supreme Court's greatest powers.

The *Marbury v. Madison* ruling opened the way for a series of landmark Supreme Court decisions. One of the most important cases in the court's history was *McCulloch v. Maryland* (1819). The court ruled that Congress possessed *implied powers*—that is, powers not specifically stated in the Constitution. In this case, Marshall upheld the power of Congress to create the United States Bank and ruled that the state of Maryland's attempt to tax the bank was unconstitutional. This decision was crucial to the growth of the United States because it allowed for changes in the needs of the nation over time. It also firmly established the superiority of federal power over state power in case of conflict.

In the case of *Fletcher v. Peck* (1810), Marshall established that the Constitution protects contracts against interference from the states. In this case, the court declared a state law unconstitutional for the first time.

In *Gibbons v. Ogden* (1824), the court rejected the authority of a New York law that hindered out-of-state commercial steamboats from doing business in its waters. Marshall's opinion defined national power over interstate commerce, opening the way for easy trade between the states and national economic growth. By the time Marshall died, the judicial branch of the federal government had become equal in authority with the executive and legislative branches.　Charles T. Cullen

See also **Supreme Court of the U.S.; Liberty Bell**.

Additional resources

Beveridge, Albert J. *The Life of John Marshall.* Cherokee Pub. Co., 1990. First published in 1916 and 1919. The standard work.
Stites, Francis N. *John Marshall: Defender of the Constitution.* Little, Brown, 1981.

Marshall, Thomas Riley (1854-1925), served as Vice President of the United States from 1913 to 1921, under President Woodrow Wilson. He made the famous remark: "What this country needs is a good 5-cent cigar." Marshall served two terms as Vice President, but he had little influence in the Wilson Administration. He was the first Vice President to preside at a Cabinet meeting in the absence of the President. In 1919, after Wilson became seriously ill, Marshall refused to listen to those who urged him to declare himself President.

Marshall was born in North Manchester, Ind., and graduated from Wabash College. He practiced law and served as governor of Indiana from 1909 to 1913. Marshall sought the Democratic presidential nomination in 1912. However, he was nominated for the vice presidency instead.　Kendrick A. Clements

See also **Vice President of the U.S.** (picture).

Marshall, Thurgood (1908-1993), was the first black justice of the Supreme Court of the United States. He served as an associate justice from 1967 until his retirement in 1991. Marshall was appointed by President Lyndon B. Johnson. As a justice, Marshall took liberal positions on a wide variety of issues, including capital punishment, free speech, school desegregation, the rights of welfare recipients, and affirmative action (see **Affirmative action**).

Marshall was born in Baltimore. He graduated from Lincoln University and studied law at Howard University. He began practicing law in 1933. From 1938 to 1950, Marshall served as chief counsel for the National Association for the Advancement of Colored People (NAACP). From 1940 to 1961, he was director and chief counsel for the NAACP Legal Defense and Educational Fund. Marshall presented the legal argument that resulted in the 1954 Supreme Court decision that racial segregation in public schools is unconstitutional. In 1961, Marshall was appointed to the U.S. Court of Appeals. In 1965, he was appointed solicitor general of the United States. Marshall won the Spingarn Medal in 1946.　Owen M. Fiss

© National Geographic Society from Supreme Court Historical Society

Thurgood Marshall

Marshall Islands are a group of 34 low-lying coral atolls and islands in the central Pacific Ocean. The group is located in the part of the Pacific called Micronesia, meaning *small islands.* The Marshall Islands are a self-governing political unit in free association with the United States.

The Marshall Islands have a total land area of about

70 square miles (181 square kilometers). They lie in two parallel chains about 130 miles (209 kilometers) apart. Each chain extends about 650 miles (1,050 kilometers) in a curve from northwest to southeast. The eastern group is the *Ratak* or *Sunrise Chain*, and the western group is the *Ralik* or *Sunset Chain*. About 1,150 islets lie along the reefs that form the atolls.

The climate is tropical, but ocean breezes cool the air. Rainfall is light on the northern islands but heavier on those to the south. Only a few kinds of plants can grow in the coral sand that covers the land. They include coconut palms, banana and papaya plants, and pandanus and breadfruit trees. *Copra* (dried coconut meat) is the chief product. Fish are plentiful among the reefs.

The people are called Micronesians. They are noted for their handicraft. Many Micronesians died of diseases brought to the islands by Europeans in the 1800's. The islands' population is about 42,000.

The first white person to visit the Marshall Islands was probably Alvaro de Saavedra, a Spanish navigator who sailed the Pacific in 1529. The islands were named for John Marshall, a British sea captain who explored them in 1788. Germany gained possession of the islands in 1885 and bought them from Spain along with the Mariana and Caroline islands in 1899. Japanese forces occupied the Marshalls during World War I (1914-1918). After the war, Japan was allowed to rule the islands under a mandate of the League of Nations. But in 1933, Japan left the League. The Japanese declared themselves the owners of the Marshalls. They closed the islands to Europeans and built war bases on them.

Early in 1944, during World War II, U.S. forces invaded Kwajalein and Enewetak, in the Marshalls, and, later, took possession of all the islands (see **Enewetak**). In 1947, after the war, the Marshall Islands became part of the United Nations Trust Territory of the Pacific Islands, which was administered by the United States. In 1986, the United States granted the Marshalls a form of self-government called *free association*. Under this system, the people of the Marshalls control their internal and foreign affairs. But the United States is obligated to defend the islands in emergencies.   Robert C. Kiste

Marshall Plan encouraged European nations to work together for economic recovery after World War II (1939-1945). In June 1947, the United States agreed to administer aid to Europe if the countries would meet to decide what they needed. The official name of the plan was the European Recovery Program. It is called the Marshall Plan because Secretary of State George C. Marshall first suggested it.

The Marshall Plan began in April 1948, when Congress established the Economic Cooperation Administration (ECA) to administer foreign aid. Seventeen nations formed the Organization for European Economic Cooperation (OEEC) to assist the ECA and develop cooperation among its members. The United States sent about $13 billion in food, machinery, and other products to Europe. Aid ended in 1952.

In 1961, the Organization for Economic Cooperation and Development (OECD) succeeded the OEEC. Twenty nations, including the United States and Canada, formed the OECD to promote the economic growth of member nations and aid developing areas.   Theodore A. Wilson

See also **Europe** (History); **Foreign aid; Marshall,**

George C.; Organization for Economic Cooperation and Development; Truman, Harry S. (The Marshall Plan).

Additional resources

Hogan, Michael J. *The Marshall Plan: America, Britain, and the Reconstruction of Western Europe, 1947-1952.* Cambridge, 1987.
Mee, Charles L., Jr. *The Marshall Plan: The Launching of the Pax Americana.* Simon & Schuster, 1984.

Marston, John (1576-1634), was an English playwright. Two of his plays reflect the pessimism of their time, when the glories of the Elizabethan Age were becoming clouded by the uncertainties of life in the 1600's. *Antonio's Revenge* (1600) is a sensational drama of revenge about the murder of a tyrant. With *Hamlet,* it is among the first examples of tragedy in English drama. *The Malcontent* (1604) is a somber comedy of intrigue, bitter in its satire but intended to correct, not to condemn.

Marston was probably born in Coventry. His talent for satire led to a quarrel with Ben Jonson. He was briefly imprisoned in 1608 for critical comments about King James I. Later, Marston studied theology and in 1616 became rector of a country parish.   Albert Wertheim

Marsupial is a mammal whose young are born in an extremely immature state. The newborn undergoes most of its development attached to one of its mother's nipples and nourished by her milk. In most species, the nipples are located in a pouch called the *marsupium*.

There are about 260 species of marsupials, all of which live in either the Americas or Australasia. They include kangaroos, koalas, and opossums. Marsupials inhabit many environments, including forests, plains, and deserts. Kangaroos are the biggest marsupials. Most male red kangaroos stand about 6 feet (1.8 meters) tall. The smallest marsupials are the marsupial mice, some of which measure less than $3\frac{3}{4}$ inches (9.5 centimeters) long, including their tail.

Characteristics of marsupials. Marsupials differ from other mammals by giving birth to extremely undeveloped young. Most mammals give birth to relatively well-developed offspring. Such mammals are called *placentals*. At the other extreme are *monotremes,* which lay eggs. See **Mammal** (Reproduction).

At birth, a marsupial is expelled from the birth canal onto the base of its mother's tail. It wiggles along the mother's fur until it reaches the nipples. The young attaches itself to a nipple and begins to nurse. The nipple expands in the youngster's mouth, so there is little danger of separation. A young marsupial stays attached to its mother's nipples for several months. Then it separates itself from its mother but continues to stay close to her. If it is frightened, it returns to her, hopping into her pouch, or clinging to her teats.

Marsupials also differ from most other mammals in the details of their skeleton. Marsupials have two bones, called the *marsupial bones* or *epipubic bones,* that extend forward from the pelvis. The only other mammals that share this skeletal feature are the monotremes.

Kinds of marsupials. There are six major groups of marsupials. Two are found only in the Americas. One American group, the *didelphids,* contains the opossums. The common opossum is the only marsupial found north of Mexico. Other opossum species live in Central and South America. Most didelphids eat almost

© Ray Williams

© Tom McHugh, Photo Researchers

Marsupials are born at an extremely immature stage of development. The photograph on the left shows a newborn wallaby attached to a nipple in its mother's pouch. An adult female wallaby with a much older offspring in her pouch is shown in the photograph on the right.

any plant and animal food. The rat opossums make up the other American group, the *caenolestids*. Rat opossums live in western South America. They eat insects and other invertebrates.

The remaining four major groups of marsupials are found only in Australia, New Guinea, and neighboring islands. The *macropods* include kangaroos and wallabies. Macropods have hind legs that are larger than their front legs. They eat mainly grasses.

The *phalangers* often nest in hollow places in trees. They eat mainly fruits, flowers, and nectar. Many Phalanger species are commonly called *possums,* but should not be confused with the opossums of the Americas.

The *dasyurids* include meat-eaters. Most are small insect-eating animals, often called *marsupial mice.* The group also includes the native cat and Tasmanian devil.

Bandicoots make up the *peramelids.* Most bandicoots are about the size of a large rat and have long pointed noses, which they use to root in the soil for insects.

Koalas and wombats do not fit easily into any of these six major groups. Koalas eat eucalyptus leaves. Wombats are burrowers that eat mainly grasses.

History of marsupials. Scientists think marsupials originated on a large continent that later split to become present-day South America, Antarctica, and Australia. Many of the American marsupials eventually became extinct as a result of competition with placental mammals. But the Australian marsupials were isolated from most placentals. They flourished and developed into the unique animals found in Australia today.

Many Australian marsupials face extinction. They are threatened chiefly by placental mammals, such as foxes, rabbits, and *dingoes* (wild dogs), which have been introduced to Australia by human beings.

Scientific classification. Marsupials make up the order Marsupialia.   Michael L. Augee

Related articles in *World Book* include:
Australia (Native animals; map)   Bandicoot

Cuscus	Native cat	Tasmanian devil
Kangaroo	Opossum	Tasmanian tiger
Koala	Possum	Wombat

Additional resources

Lavine, Sigmund A. *Wonders of Marsupials.* Dodd, 1979. For younger readers.
Morcombe, Michael K. *Michael Morcombe's Australian Marsupials and Other Native Mammals.* Scribner, 1972.

Martel, Charles. See Charles Martel.

Marten is a slim, fur-covered mammal that looks like an oversized weasel. It lives in mountainous and forested areas of Asia, Europe, and North America.

The best-known North American species is the *American marten.* It is fairly common in the Rocky Mountains and the Far North from Newfoundland and Quebec to Alaska. This marten has thick, golden-brown fur with darker feet and a paler face. It usually has an orange patch on the throat and chest. It grows to 26 inches (66 centimeters) long, including its tail. Martens weigh 2 to

Joe Van Wormer, Bruce Coleman Inc.

The marten, a member of the weasel family, usually builds its den in a hollow tree. From there, the marten can gracefully leap from branch to branch in pursuit of small animals for food.

3 pounds (0.9 to 1.4 kilograms). The males are slightly larger than the females. The American marten eats mice, rabbits, squirrels, and birds. It lives in hollow trees and rock crevices. About nine months after mating, the female gives birth, usually to two or three young.

From November to March, when the American marten's coat is thick and soft, trappers in Canada and the United States kill about 50,000 to 130,000 animals. The fur is used in coats, hats, and muffs.

The *fisher* is related to the American marten. A male fisher weighs up to 20 pounds (9 kilograms). It has dark brown or grayish-brown fur. Now rare, the fisher is found in nearly the same areas as the American marten. It lives on the ground or in trees. It eats mostly small rodents. It also feeds on porcupines and snowshoe hares. Well-known European martens include the *beech marten,* which has white fur on its throat and chest, and the *pine marten,* with yellowish fur on these parts.

Scientific classification. Martens are in the weasel family, Mustelidae. The American marten is *Martes americana.* The fisher is *M. pennanti;* the beech, *M. foina;* and the pine, *M. martes.* Charles A. Long

See also **Sable.**

Martha's Vineyard, an island 4 miles (6 kilometers) off the southeastern coast of Massachusetts, is a popular summer resort. Vineyard Sound separates it from the mainland. The island covers about 100 square miles (260 square kilometers). For location, see **Massachusetts** (physical map). Its attractions include a mild climate, beaches, fishing, shopping, and yachting. About 12,000 people live on the island. However, tens of thousands of tourists visit the island in the summer. Many take a ferry to the island from either Woods Hole or Falmouth on the coast of Massachusetts. Explorer Bartholomew Gosnold named the island for his daughter and for the grapevines he found there in 1602. Laurence A. Lewis

Martí, *mahr TEE,* **José Julián** (1853-1895), was a Cuban political activist, journalist, and author. He was devoted to achieving Cuba's independence from Spain. Martí was killed during a battle with the Spaniards.

Martí was a leader in the Modernist movement in Spanish literature, (see **Latin-American literature** [Modernism]). All of Martí's writing is characterized by rhythmic flow and an original choice of words. His poetry and especially his prose represent an effort by the Modernist movement to give literary Spanish a new beauty. His poetry collections *Ismaelillo* (1882) and *Simple Verses* (1891) attempt to move beyond the romanticism of the time. His eloquent political writings were influential in Spanish America.

Martí was born in Havana. He lived in exile in the United States from 1881 to 1895. Naomi Lindstrom

Martial, *MAHR shuhl* (A.D. 40?-104?), was an ancient Roman writer. He became famous for developing the *epigram* into its modern form—a sharp, stinging poem or saying (see **Epigram**). Martial wrote more than 1,500 short verses and epigrams. They contain witty and sometimes obscene comments about the vices of ancient Roman society. He also wrote several serious pieces, including one on the death of a slave girl named Erotion, whom he loved.

Martial's full name was Marcus Valerius Martialis. He was born in Bilbilis, Spain. He came to Rome in A.D. 64 and became known for his witty verse. Elaine Fantham

Martial arts, *MAHR shuhl,* is a general term for various types of fighting arts that originated in the Orient. Most martial arts practiced today came from China, Japan, and Korea. There are hundreds of martial arts, each divided into specific *styles* or *systems.*

Technically, the martial arts fall into two categories, *percussive* and *nonpercussive.* In percussive martial arts, such as *karate-do* (pronounced *kuh RAH tee doh*) and *tae kwon do* (*TY kwahn DOH*), people kick and strike with their hands, feet, elbows, knees, and head. Nonpercussive martial arts involve throwing, locking, and neutralizing the opponent without striking him or her. *Judo* and *aikido* (*eye KEE doh*) are the most popular martial arts in this category. See **Judo; Karate.**

Weapons are often used in advanced training in martial arts to preserve ancient tradition. But in some martial arts, weapons are part of the basic training.

Today, people practice the martial arts for exercise, as a means of self-defense, and as a sport. Martial sports have many variations, from judo and traditional karate, in which the blows are pulled short of contact, to kickboxing or full-contact karate, in which the objective is to win by knockout, as in professional boxing.

Chinese martial arts are called *kung fu (kung foo)* in the West. In China they are known as *wushu (woo shoo).* Kung fu, a general term for hundreds of Chinese martial arts, means "skill" or "ability." Kung fu represents systems created for combat, health and exercise, or dance. The most popular styles are *Shaolin* (*shah oh LIHN*) and *t'ai chi chuan* (*ty jee chwahn*), also spelled *taijiquan.* Shaolin developed in northern China and involves straight-line attacks and retreats, emphasizing strength and speed. T'ai chi chuan, the southern style, consists of circular motions and intricate foot patterns and emphasizes gentle force and inner harmony.

The origins of kung fu are unknown. Some historians believe it started as early as the 1500's B.C. Kung fu reached the West in the mid-1800's, with the first migration of Chinese laborers to the United States. Many were skilled in kung fu and restricted its teachings to those of immediate Chinese ancestry. This custom ended in 1964, when a kung fu instructor in Los Angeles opened his school to non-Chinese.

Japanese martial arts. Two major martial arts evolved in Japan, the *bujutsu* (*boo JUHT soo*), or "ancient martial arts," and the *budo,* or "new martial ways." Although their philosophies differ, both schools are based on spiritual concepts found in Zen Buddhism and Shinto. Bujutsu emphasizes combat and willingness to face death as a matter of honor. It contains the philosophy and techniques of the Japanese samurai warriors and includes such arts as *jujutsu* (*joo JUHT soo*) and *karate-jutsu* (*kuh RAH tee JUHT soo*). Budo, which started during the late 1800's, focuses on moral and aesthetic development. People who practice budo seek to avoid conflict and use martial arts only as a last resort. Karate-do, judo, and aikido are forms of budo.

Another martial art that developed in Japan is *ninjutsu* (*nihn JUHT soo*), which means "the art of stealing in," or espionage. People who practice ninjutsu are called *ninja.* Mountain mystics developed ninjutsu in the late 1200's. At that time, ninja were masters at all forms of armed and unarmed combat, including the use of disguises, bombs, and poisons. Although the rulers of

Japan banned ninjutsu in the 1600's, the ninja practiced it secretly and preserved its techniques. Ninjutsu gained international interest in the mid-1980's. Today, ninja practice their art not as espionage, but as a traditional martial art with a nonviolent philosophy.

Korean martial arts. The most popular martial art in Korea is *tae kwon do,* "the art of kicking and punching." Tae kwon do combines the abrupt movements of karate and the circular patterns of kung fu with its own spectacular jumping and spinning kicks. It also employs punching, dodging, and blocking techniques.

The Korean martial arts probably originated during the Great Silla dynasty (A.D. 668-935). In the mid-1900's, several Korean martial arts styles called *kwans* merged to form tae kwon do. In the 1960's, tae kwon do began to spread internationally and now ranks as one of the world's most popular martial arts.

American martial arts. Since 1902, when judo was introduced, the United States has become a melting pot of Oriental martial arts and styles. Karate was introduced in 1946 and today has more U.S. practitioners than anywhere else in the world. Beginning in the late 1960's, U.S. instructors started breaking their ties with Oriental traditions and philosophies to form what is known as *American karate.*

Martial arts in other countries. During the 1970's, the art of *escrima (eskreema)* spread from the Philippines throughout the Western world. It is an art in which bare hand techniques and knife/stick techniques are interchangeable. During the same period, the arts of *Pentjak Silat* developed in Indonesia and Malaysia. They contain many empty hand and weapons styles.

Paul Crompton

Additional resources

Barrett, Norman S. *Martial Arts.* Watts, 1988. For younger readers.
Corcoran, John, and Farkas, Emil. *Martial Arts: Traditions, History, People.* W. H. Smith, 1983.
Crompton, Paul H. *The Complete Martial Arts.* McGraw, 1989.

Martial law, *MAHR shuhl,* is a temporary, emergency form of government under military rule. It may be organized in an emergency, such as a natural disaster, a political or economic crisis, or a riot. For example, martial law was declared in the Philippines in 1972 to control groups that opposed the civil government's policies. The new military government then restricted the activities of these groups, which included political parties, labor unions, and other organizations. In wartime, a country may declare martial law in its own territory or in enemy territory then in its possession.

Under martial law, military laws and the decisions of military institutions are substituted for all civil laws and civil courts. Martial law does not exist if the civil government remains in power but uses military forces to maintain order.

The Constitution of the United States does not specifically provide for martial law. It implies the power, however, by giving the federal government the right and responsibility to protect a state from invasion or internal violence. During the Civil War (1861-1865), President Abraham Lincoln put U.S. troops in control of parts of the Northern United States. But strictly speaking, martial law has never been declared in the United States.

Robert C. Mueller

Martin is the name for several birds in the swallow family. The *purple martin* is the best-known martin in North America. It is about 8 inches (20 centimeters) long. The male is a dark purplish-blue color. The birds migrate to Central and South America in the winter. They have been seen in summer as far north as the Saskatchewan Valley in Canada. Purple martins nest in *colonies* (large groups). They originally built their nests in holes in dead trees, but they now nest primarily in large, multiroomed birdhouses built especially for them. Martins will return to the same birdhouse year after year. The female lays from three to eight white eggs.

Martins help people by eating ants, flies, beetles, mosquitoes, and other winged insect pests. In New England, house sparrows and starlings have driven most of the martins from their homes.

Scientific classification. Martins belong to the swallow family, Hirundinidae. The scientific name for the purple martin is *Progne subis.*   Donald F. Bruning

See also **Bird** (picture: Birds' eggs).

WORLD BOOK illustration by John Rignall, Linden Artists Ltd.

The martin is a swallow. The male purple martin, *bottom,* is purplish in color. The female purple martin, *top,* is dull gray.

© Leonard Lee Rue III, Animals Animals

A purple martin birdhouse is divided into separate "apartments," allowing the birds to nest in groups called *colonies.*

Martin V (1368-1431) was elected pope in 1417. His election at the Council of Constance ended the Great Schism that had divided the papacy since 1378 (see **Roman Catholic Church** [The Great Schism]).

Martin labored to restore order to the church. Although he placed many of his relatives in positions of authority, he did attempt to reform some of the worst abuses within the church. Martin also arranged *concordats* (agreements) with Germany, France, Italy, Spain, and England. According to a decree of the Council of Constance, Martin had to call councils regularly. He convened a council at Pavia, Italy, in 1423 and another at Basel, Switzerland, in 1431. Radical reformers eventually took over the Basel council, but Martin died shortly before it met for the first time.

Martin's given and family name was Oddone Colonna. He was born into a famous and powerful family in Rome.   Kenneth Pennington

Martin du Gard, *mahr TAN dyoo GAHR,* **Roger,** *raw ZHAY* (1881-1958), a French novelist, received the 1937 Nobel Prize for literature. His novel *Jean Barois* (1913) explores the intellectual agonies experienced by many French people over the unjust treatment of the French army officer Alfred Dreyfus (see **Dreyfus, Alfred**). *Jean Barois* also deals with a theme found in the author's other works—the conflict between religious beliefs and a scientific approach to life.

Martin du Gard published an eight-part saga called *The World of the Thibaults* (1922-1940). It follows the lives of two French families, one Protestant and the other Roman Catholic, from the early 1900's to the outbreak of World War I in 1914.

Martin du Gard was trained in the study of old documents and was noted for his attention to detail and historical accuracy in his writing. He was born in Neuilly-sur-Seine.   Dora E. Polachek

Martin Luther King, Jr., Day is a United States national holiday honoring the birthday of civil rights leader Martin Luther King, Jr. The holiday is observed each year on the third Monday in January. King's actual birthday was Jan. 15, 1929.

On Martin Luther King, Jr., Day, people take part in religious services, candlelight vigils, parades, and other programs honoring the civil rights leader. Most government offices and schools close for the day, but many private businesses remain open.

A campaign to establish a holiday honoring King began soon after he was assassinated in 1968. In 1983, Congress made his birthday a federal holiday, first celebrated on Jan. 20, 1986. Today, the holiday is observed by the federal government and by nearly every state.
        Alton Hornsby, Jr.

Martin of Tours, Saint (316?-397), is the patron saint of France. During his lifetime, he became famous for healing the sick, performing miracles, and founding churches and monasteries.

Martin was born into a pagan family in what is now Szombathely, Hungary, and grew up in Pavia, Italy. At the age of 15, he joined the Roman Army. Three years later, he was baptized a Christian. Martin was discharged from the army about 356 and became a follower of Hilary, the bishop of Poitiers, France. About 360, Hilary helped Martin found the first French monastery, located at Ligugê, near Poitiers. About 371, Martin became bishop of Tours, France. He was responsible for destroying many pagan shrines and temples but always tried to build a church or monastery in their place.

Martin's friend Sulpicius Severus wrote a biography of the saint that helped to promote monasticism and the reputation of Martin in the West. The biography includes the most famous legend about Martin. It tells that, while a soldier, Martin divided his cloak with a freezing beggar. Later, in a dream, the beggar was revealed to Martin as Jesus Christ. Martin's feast day is November 11.   Richard R. Ring

Martineau, *MAHR tih NOH,* **Harriet** (1802-1876), was a British writer and social reformer who wrote widely on economic, philosophic, and social issues. She became famous for a series of stories called *Illustrations of Political Economy.* These stories, published between 1832 and 1834, explained economics for the ordinary reader. Martineau also wrote biographies, essays, fiction, history, poetry, religious works, and children's stories.

In her writings, Martineau opposed cruel treatment of children in factories and supported voting rights for women. She also called for better education and health care for the poor and the mentally ill. From 1834 to 1836, she traveled in the United States. She met leading abolitionists and became a strong opponent of slavery. She attacked slavery in her book *Society in America* (1837).

Martineau was born in Norwich, England. She was educated at home because of poor health. Her father died in 1826, and she began writing to support herself. She wrote more than 30 books and thousands of articles in spite of nearly constant illness.   Cynthia F. Behrman

Martini, Simone. See Simone Martini.

Martinique, *MAHR tuh NEEK,* is a French island in the West Indies. The oval-shaped island covers 425 square miles (1,100 square kilometers). Martinique's capital is Fort-de-France. For location, see **West Indies** (map).

Martinique has many volcanic mountains. The highest and most famous of these is Mont Pelée, which rises 4,583 feet (1,397 meters). This volcano suddenly erupted in 1902 and destroyed the city of St.-Pierre. About 38,000 people died. Only one person survived.

Martinique has about 360,000 people. Ninety per cent of the people are blacks. Others are of European ancestry, mainly French. Martinique's sunny climate and beautiful scenery help make tourism its most important industry. Its chief crop is sugar cane. Bananas, cotton, pineapples, and tobacco also grow there. Other industries include petroleum refining and rum distilling.

Christopher Columbus reached Martinique in 1502, on his fourth voyage. The French began to colonize the island in 1635. They made Fort-de-France (originally Fort Royal) the capital in 1692. The Empress Josephine, first wife of Napoleon I, was born at Trois-Ilets in Martinique. The French made Martinique an overseas *department* (administrative district) in 1946. In 1958, Martinique chose to remain a department. It is governed by a general council elected by the people. In 1974, the island also became a region of France. As a region, it has a regional council responsible for social and economic planning. The island sends representatives to the French Parliament.   Gerald R. Showalter

See also **Fort-de-France; Mont Pelée.**

Martins, Peter (1946-   ), is a Danish-born dancer and *choreographer* (dance creator). As a featured performer with the New York City Ballet, he gained fame for his fine classical technique. He was co-ballet master in chief of the New York City Ballet with Jerome Robbins from 1983 until Robbins resigned in 1990. Martins then assumed sole artistic leadership as Ballet Master in Chief.

New York City Ballet

Peter Martins

Martins was born in Copenhagen and received traditional dance training at the Royal Danish Ballet beginning at the age of 8. He joined that company in 1964 and became a solo dancer in 1967. From 1970 to 1983, Martins was a principal dancer for the New York City Ballet. He created many roles in ballets by George Balanchine and Jerome Robbins, notably through his partnerships with Suzanne Farrell and other leading ballerinas. Martins has choreographed many works for the company, beginning with *Calcium Light Night* (1977).   Selma Landen Odom

Martyr, *MAHR tuhr,* is a person who defends a principle, even though it means sacrificing many things, perhaps even his or her life. Almost every religious movement has had such persons. Many social and political movements have created martyrs. *Martyr* comes from the Greek, and means *witness.* See also **Roman Catholic Church** (The first 300 years).   Jonathan Z. Smith

Marvel-of-Peru. See Four-o'clock.

Marvell, *MAHR vuhl,* **Andrew** (1621-1678), was perhaps the finest of the English metaphysical poets of the mid-1600's. In addition to the influence of John Donne, Marvell also showed the influence of the English classical poet Ben Jonson. Marvell's verse blends argumentative vigor with classical smoothness and control, a blend that critic and poet T. S. Eliot described as "a tough reasonableness beneath the slight lyric grace." Marvell's best poems are a series of lyrics written about 1650. They include "The Garden" and "To His Coy Mistress." The latter poem includes the famous lines:

> Had we but world enough and time,
> This coyness, lady, were no crime.

and

> But at my back I always hear
> Time's winged chariot hurrying near. . . .

Marvell was born near Hall in Yorkshire. During the Puritan revolution, he supported Oliver Cromwell and assisted John Milton when Milton was a high government official. Marvell served in Parliament from 1659 to his death. During his later years, he wrote political satire against the king and court.   Gary A. Stringer

See also **Metaphysical poets.**

Marx, Karl (1818-1883), was a German philosopher, social scientist, and professional revolutionary. Few writers have had such a great and lasting influence on the world. Marx was the chief founder of two of the most powerful mass movements in history—democratic socialism and revolutionary communism. See **Communism; Socialism.**

Marx was sometimes ignored or misunderstood, even by his followers. Yet many of the social sciences—especially sociology—have been influenced by his theories. Many important social scientists of the late 1800's and the 1900's can be fully understood only by realizing how much they were reacting to Marx's beliefs.

The life of Marx

Karl Heinrich Marx was born and raised in Trier, in what was then Prussia. His father was a lawyer. Marx showed intellectual promise in school and went to the University of Bonn in 1835 to study law. The next year, he transferred to the University of Berlin. There he became much more interested in philosophy, a highly political subject in Prussia, where citizens were not permitted to participate directly in public affairs. Marx joined a group of radical leftist students and professors whose philosophic views implied strong criticism of the severe way in which Prussia was governed.

In 1841, Marx obtained his doctorate in philosophy from the university in Jena. He tried to get a teaching position but failed because of his opposition to the Prussian government. He became a free-lance journalist and helped create and manage several radical journals. After his marriage in 1843, he and his wife moved to Paris. There they met Friedrich Engels, a young German radical, who became Marx's best friend and worked with him on several articles and books. Marx lived in Brussels, Belgium, from 1845 to 1848, when he returned to Germany. He edited the *Neue Rheinische Zeitung,* which was published in Cologne during the German revolution of 1848. This journal made Marx known throughout Germany as a spokesman for radical democratic reform. After the collapse of the 1848 revolution, Marx fled from Prussia. He spent the rest of his life as a political exile in London.

Marx led a hand-to-mouth existence because he was too proud—or too much a professional revolutionary—to work for a living. He did write some articles for newspapers. His most regular job of this kind was that of political reporter for the *New York Tribune.* But generally, Marx, his wife, and their six children survived only because Engels sent them money. In 1864, Marx founded *The International Workingmen's Association,* an organization dedicated to improving the life of the working classes and preparing for a socialist revolution.

Marx suffered from frequent illnesses, many of which may have been psychological. Even when physically healthy, he suffered from long periods of apathy and depression and could not work. Marx was learned and sophisticated, but he was often opinionated and arrogant. He had many admirers but few friends. Except for Engels, he lost most of his friends—and many of them became his enemies.

Marx's writings

Most of Marx's writings have been preserved. They include not only his books,

Brown Bros.

Karl Marx

but also most of his correspondence and the notes of his speeches.

Philosophic essays. Some of Marx's philosophic essays were published during his lifetime, but others were not discovered until the 1900's. Marx wrote some of them alone and some with Engels. The essays range from one of about 15 sentences to a 700-page book, *The German Ideology* (1845-1846), written with Engels.

Marx wrote his essays between 1842 and 1847. They spell out the philosophic foundations of his radicalism. The chief themes in the essays include Marx's bitter view that economic forces were increasingly oppressing human beings and his belief that political action is a necessary part of philosophy. The essays also show the influence of the philosophy of history developed by the German philosopher Georg Wilhelm Friedrich Hegel (see **Hegel, G. W. F.**).

The *Communist Manifesto* was a pamphlet written jointly with Engels on the eve of the German revolution of 1848. Its full title is the *Manifesto of the Communist Party.* The manifesto is a brief but forceful presentation of the authors' political and historical theories. It is the only work they produced that can be considered a systematic statement of the theories that became known as *Marxism.* The *Communist Manifesto* considers history to be a series of conflicts between classes. It predicts that the ruling middle class will be overthrown by the working class. The result of this revolution, according to Marx and Engels, will be a classless society in which the chief means of production are publicly owned.

Das Kapital (*Capital*) was Marx's major work. He spent about 30 years writing it. The first volume appeared in 1867. Engels edited the second and third volumes from Marx's manuscripts. Both of these volumes were published after Marx's death. The fourth volume exists only as a mass of scattered notes.

In *Das Kapital,* Marx described the free enterprise system as he saw it. He considered it the most efficient, dynamic economic system ever devised. But he also regarded it as afflicted with flaws that would destroy it through increasingly severe periods of inflation and depression. The most serious flaw in the free enterprise system, according to Marx, is that it accumulates more and more wealth but becomes less and less capable of using this wealth wisely. As a result, Marx saw the accumulation of riches being accompanied by the rapid spread of human misery. See **Capitalism.**

Other writings. Marx and Engels also wrote what today might be called political columns. They discussed all sorts of events in and influences on national and international affairs—personalities, overthrowing of governments, cabinet changes, parliamentary debates, wars, and workers' uprisings.

Marx also wrote about the practical problems of leading an international revolutionary movement. The major source of these comments is his correspondence with Engels and other friends.

Marx's theories

Marx's doctrine is sometimes called *dialectical materialism,* and part of it is referred to as *historical materialism.* These terms were taken from Hegel's philosophy of history. Marx never used them, but Engels did and so have most later Marxists. The concepts of dialectical and

historical materialism are difficult and obscure and may be unnecessary for an understanding of Marx's theories. See **Materialism.**

Marx's writings cover more than 40 years. His interests shifted and he often changed his mind. But his philosophy remained surprisingly consistent—and very complex. Aside from the brief *Communist Manifesto,* he never presented his ideas systematically.

Production and society. The basis of Marxism is the conviction that socialism is inevitable. Marx believed that the free enterprise system, or capitalism, was doomed and that socialism was the only alternative.

Marx discussed capitalism within a broad historical perspective that covered the history of the human race. He believed that the individual, not God, is the highest being. People have made themselves what they are by their own labor. They use their intelligence and creative talent to dominate the world by a process called *production.* Through production, people make the goods they need to live. The means of production include natural resources, factories, machinery, and labor.

The process of production, according to Marx, is a collective effort, not an individual one. Organized societies are the principal creative agents in human history, and historical progress requires increasingly developed societies for production. Such developed societies are achieved by continual refinement of production methods and of the *division of labor.* By the division of labor, Marx meant that each person specializes in one job, resulting in the development of two classes of people—the rulers and the workers. The ruling class owns the means of production. The working class consists of the nonowners, who are *exploited* (treated unfairly) by the owners.

The class struggle. Marx believed there was a strain in all societies because the social organization never kept pace with the development of the means of production. An even greater strain developed from the division of people into two classes.

According to Marx, all history is a struggle between the ruling and working classes, and all societies have been torn by this conflict. Past societies tried to keep the exploited class under control by using elaborate political organizations, laws, customs, traditions, ideologies, religions, and rituals. Marx argued that personality, beliefs, and activities are shaped by these institutions. By recognizing these forces, he reasoned, people will be able to overcome them through revolutionary action.

Marx believed that private ownership of the chief means of production was the heart of the class system. For people to be truly free, he declared, the means of production must be publicly owned—by the community as a whole. With the resulting general economic and social equality, all people would have an opportunity to follow their own desires and to use their leisure time creatively. Unfair institutions and customs would disappear. All these events, said Marx, will take place when the *proletariat* (working class) revolts against the *bourgeoisie* (owners of the means of production).

Political strategy. It is not clear what strategy Marx might have proposed to achieve the revolution he favored. An idea of this strategy can come only from his speeches, articles, letters, and political activities. As a guideline for practical politics, Marxism is vague. Marx's followers have quarreled bitterly among themselves over different interpretations and policies.

Marx today

Today, Marx is studied as both a revolutionary and an economist. His importance as a pioneer in the social sciences is being recognized increasingly. Marx has often been attacked because he rebelled against all established societies, because he was an arrogant writer who scorned his critics, and because of his radical views.

As the founder of the Communist movement, Marx is regarded by Communists as one of the greatest thinkers of all time. Many Communists believe his writings are the source of all important truths in social science and philosophy. They believe a person cannot be an intelligent student of society, history, economics, philosophy, and many other fields without studying Marx or his principal disciples.

Scholars in the Western world were slow to recognize the importance of Marx. For many years, few Americans bothered to study his writings. But today, in a variety of fields, it has become essential to have some knowledge of Marx. One of these fields is economics. Although his methods of analyzing capitalism are considered old-fashioned, many scholars recognize the brilliance of this analysis. Many people consider his criticism of capitalism and his view of what humanity has made of the world as timely today as they were 100 years ago. Even the analysis that Marx made of the business cycle is studied as one of the many explanations of inflation and depression.

In sociology, Marx's work is also regarded with increasing respect. Without his contributions, sociology would not have developed into what it is today. Marx did pioneering work in many areas with which sociology deals. He wrote on social classes, on the relationship between the economy and the state, and on the principles that underlie a political or economic system.

Many people still turn to Marx for an explanation of current social, economic, and political evils. But most are unlikely to agree with his view of the ease with which workers will overthrow the class system and establish a Communist society.   Alfred G. Meyer

See also **Economic determinism; Engels, Friedrich; Lenin, V. I.** For a *Reading and Study Guide,* see *Marx, Karl,* in the Research Guide/Index, Volume 22.

Additional resources

Appelbaum, Richard P. *Karl Marx.* Sage, 1988.
Feinberg, Barbara S. *Marx and Marxism.* Watts, 1985. Suitable for younger readers.
Suchting, Wallis A. *Marx: An Introduction.* New York Univ. Pr., 1983.

Marx brothers were three American brothers who became famous for their zany antics in motion pictures. The brothers were Groucho (Julius, 1890-1977), Chico (Leonard, 1886-1961), and Harpo (Adolph, later changed to Arthur, 1888-1964). Groucho became known for his insults, long cigar, and bushy mustache and eyebrows. Chico spoke in an Italian accent and played the piano. Harpo, who never spoke in the films, played the harp.

The Marx brothers as a team made 13 movies, many of which ridiculed parts of society. The brothers' first two films, *The Cocoanuts* (1929) and *Animal Crackers* (1930), were based on Broadway shows in which they

United Press Int.

The Marx brothers starred in *Horse Feathers,* a zany 1932 motion-picture comedy. They were Chico, *left,* holding an apple; Groucho, smoking the cigar; and Harpo, *far right.*

had starred. Their other movies include *Monkey Business* (1931), *Horse Feathers* (1932), *Duck Soup* (1933), *A Night at the Opera* (1935), and *A Day at the Races* (1937).

The Marx brothers were born in New York City and began their career when they were children. With two other brothers, they starred in vaudeville and several Broadway shows before making movies. Zeppo (Herbert) played romantic roles in their films until he left the team in the mid-1930's. Gummo (Milton) appeared on the stage but made no movies.   Roger Ebert

Marxism. See Marx, Karl.

Mary was the mother of Jesus. She is also known as the Virgin Mary, the Blessed Virgin Mary, or the Blessed Virgin. According to the Gospels of Luke and Matthew, Mary gave birth to Jesus in Bethlehem. According to Luke, her family lived in Nazareth, and she had gone to Bethlehem with Joseph to have their names recorded as members of the House of David.

The sufferings of Jesus brought great sorrow into Mary's life. At the Crucifixion, according to John 19, Jesus asked His beloved disciple, perhaps John, to take care of her. Little is known about her later life. It is believed that she died in Jerusalem about A.D. 63. Mary is venerated by the Roman Catholic, Anglican, and Eastern Orthodox churches as the "Mother of God."

The story of Mary has always been a favorite subject of artists and musicians. Many great paintings and songs have been based on the incidents and traditions of her life.   J. H. Charlesworth

Related articles in *World Book* include:

Anne, Saint	Fátima, Our	Jesus Christ
Annunciation	Lady of	Joseph
Assumption	Immaculate Con-	Lourdes
Christmas	ception	Madonna and
		Child

Mary I (1516-1558) was queen of England from 1553 until her death in 1558. She was the daughter of King

Henry VIII and Catherine of Aragon. Mary became queen after her half brother, King Edward VI, died. An attempt to set her aside in favor of her cousin Lady Jane Grey, "the nine day queen," failed. The English people preferred Mary because they considered her the rightful heir. See **Grey, Lady Jane; Tudor, House of.**

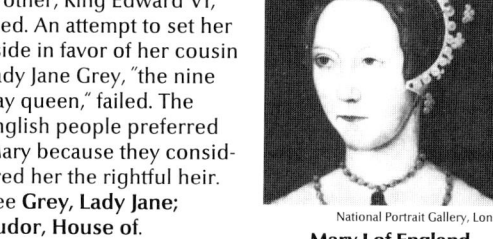

National Portrait Gallery, London
Mary I of England

Mary was a devout Roman Catholic and tried to bring England back to the Roman Catholic Church. She repealed a law that had made Protestantism the state religion. Mary also reestablished certain severe laws against heresy or disbelief in Roman Catholic doctrine.

Mary became known as "Bloody Mary" because of the persecutions she caused. More than 300 people were burned at the stake during her reign. Among them were Thomas Cranmer, Nicholas Ridley, and Hugh Latimer, all high-ranking Protestant clergymen (see **Cranmer, Thomas; Latimer, Hugh; Ridley, Nicholas**). Mary also drove many Protestant clergymen into exile.

Mary married King Philip II of Spain. Their marriage was unpopular because many English people viewed Spain as England's greatest enemy. Philip persuaded Mary to join Spain in a war against France. But France won the war, which officially ended in 1559, after Mary's death. Mary died childless and was succeeded by her Protestant half sister, Elizabeth (see **Elizabeth I**).

Roger Howell, Jr.

See also **Ireland** (The conquest of Ireland).

Mary II (1662-1694) was the queen of England from 1689 to 1694. She ruled jointly with her husband, King William III. Mary devoted much of her time to religious and charitable projects. She helped found the College of William and Mary in Virginia in 1693. Mary was born in London. She was the daughter of King James II. Although her father was a Roman Catholic, Mary was raised a Protestant. In 1677, she married William of Orange, the Protestant ruler of the Netherlands. In the Glorious Revolution of 1688, William's forces invaded England and forced James to flee the country. William and Mary became the rulers of England in 1689.

Roger Howell, Jr.

See also **William III.**

Mary, Queen of Scots (1542-1587), was the only surviving child of King James V of Scotland. The princess, whose mother was Mary of Guise, was only a week old when James V died. However, she was immediately proclaimed queen of Scotland.

Mary was sent to France at the age of 5 to be educated. She married the French *dauphin* (crown prince) at the age of 15. The dauphin became king of France soon after their marriage, but he died in 1560.

Her reign. Mary returned to Scotland in 1561, soon after it had officially become a Protestant country. Before the 1560's, the Roman Catholic Church had been Scotland's official church. Although Mary was a Catholic, she did not oppose the spread of the Protestant faith at first.

But in 1565, she married her cousin Henry Stuart, who was also known as Lord Darnley. This young Catholic nobleman's rise to power caused leading Protestant lords to revolt. The rebellion was quickly put down. But the queen soon discovered that she had married an ineffective and overly ambitious husband, and she came to hate him.

A rumor began to develop that Mary was having an affair with her private secretary, an Italian musician named David Riccio (also spelled Rizzio). A band of Protestant nobles dragged Riccio from Mary's presence and stabbed him to death in March 1566. Darnley, Mary's husband, was one of the leaders in the murder, but Mary fled with him to Dunbar and thus preserved her power. Mary gave birth to a son three months later. This son eventually became King James I of England (see **James [I]**).

Mary still hated her husband. Before long she began to show marked attention to James Hepburn, Earl of Bothwell (see **Bothwell, Earl of**). Early in 1567, Bothwell murdered Darnley. Mary married Bothwell three months later.

Her death. This marriage was Mary's fatal mistake. She was forced to abdicate in favor of her son in June 1567 and was imprisoned. She escaped in 1568 and raised a small army, but most people in Scotland opposed her. Her forces were defeated, and she fled to England.

Mary was next in line for the English throne after her second cousin Queen Elizabeth I. However, Mary refused to recognize Elizabeth as queen. Beginning in 1569, Mary supported a series of plots to overthrow her (see **Elizabeth I**).

Detail of a pen drawing (1560) by an unknown artist; Musée Condé, Chantilly, France (Giraudon/Art Resource)
Mary, Queen of Scots

Elizabeth kept Mary confined and for years refused demands for her execution. Eventually, however, Elizabeth had her tried for high treason. Mary was found guilty, and Elizabeth reluctantly signed Mary's death warrant. Mary was beheaded on Feb. 8, 1587.

Richard L. Greaves

Additional resources

Fraser, Antonia. *Mary, Queen of Scots.* Dell, 1984. First published in 1969.
Stepanek, Sally. *Mary, Queen of Scots.* Chelsea Hse., 1987. Suitable for younger readers.

Mary, Virgin. See Mary.

Mary Magdalene, *MAG duh leen,* a follower of Jesus, was called Magdalene because she was reputed to be from the village of Magdala. Luke gives her name at the head of a list of women of Galilee (Luke 8:2). She was known as one out of whom Jesus had cast "seven demons." She followed Jesus the rest of His life, and may have stood at the cross when He was crucified (John 19:25). She was remembered as the first person to see Him after He arose from the tomb (John 20). See also **Jesus Christ** (The Resurrection). J. H. Charlesworth

Tom Algire, FPG

Tilghman Island in Chesapeake Bay provides a natural harbor for pleasure boats. The bay divides Maryland into two parts, called the Eastern Shore and the Western Shore. The state's long Chesapeake Bay shoreline offers opportunities for recreational boating, fishing, and swimming.

Maryland   *The Old Line State*

Maryland is an important industrial and shipping state of the United States. It lies in the northeastern corner of the Southern States. Chesapeake Bay, which cuts deep into Maryland, provides the state with several excellent harbors. Historic Baltimore, the state's largest city, is one of the world's greatest port cities. Annapolis, the home of the United States Naval Academy, is the capital of Maryland.

Chesapeake Bay divides Maryland into two parts. The part of Maryland east of the bay is called the Eastern Shore. The part west of the bay is the Western Shore. The two parts join north of the bay in the northeastern corner of the state. The Eastern Shore shares the Delmarva Peninsula with parts of Delaware and Virginia. The Eastern Shore and part of the Western Shore are low and relatively flat. But western Maryland has rolling plains, hills and valleys, mountains, and plateaus. Most parts of Maryland have good farmland. Forests cover about 40 per cent of the state.

Service industries, such as government and trade, play a leading role in Maryland's economy. The state's chief manufactured products are electrical equipment, electrical devices, and processed foods. Manufacturing in Maryland is centered in the Baltimore area and in the Maryland suburbs of Washington, D.C.

The contributors of this article are Robert D. Mitchell, Associate Professor of Geography at the University of Maryland, and Edward C. Papenfuse, Archivist for the Maryland State Archives.

Many farms on the Eastern Shore raise chickens. Many dairy farms lie in the river valleys of the Western Shore. Greenhouse and nursery products are important in the larger cities. Maryland is an important producer of clams, soft-shell crabs, and oysters.

Maryland was named for Queen Henrietta Maria, the wife of King Charles I of England. In 1632, Charles granted the Maryland region to Cecilius Calvert, the second Lord Baltimore. Calvert, a Roman Catholic, believed in religious freedom, and welcomed settlers of all faiths to Maryland. Calvert and his descendants—the Lords Baltimore—ruled Maryland during most of the period when it was an English colony. During the Revolutionary War in America (1775-1783), the Second Continental Congress met for about three months in Baltimore. After the war, the Congress of the Confederation met for several months in the Maryland State House in Annapolis. In 1791, Maryland gave part of its land to the federal government for the District of Columbia.

Francis Scott Key wrote "The Star-Spangled Banner" while watching the British bombard Baltimore's Fort McHenry during the War of 1812. Maryland, although a southern state, remained loyal to the Union during the Civil War. Several Civil War battles were fought in Maryland, including the Battle of Antietam—one of the bloodiest of the war.

Maryland is nicknamed the *Old Line State* after its heroic "troops of the line." These troops won praise from George Washington, who was commander in chief of the Continental Army during the Revolutionary War.

Interesting facts about Maryland

WORLD BOOK illustrations by Kevin Chadwick

The largest white oak tree in the United States is the Wye Oak in Wye Mills. This tree is 107 feet (33 meters) tall, and has a circumference of $34\frac{1}{2}$ feet (10.5 meters) at the base of the trunk. It is more than 400 years old.

The first umbrella factory in the United States was established in Baltimore in 1828. The slogan "Born in Baltimore—raised everywhere" came to describe the umbrellas made there.

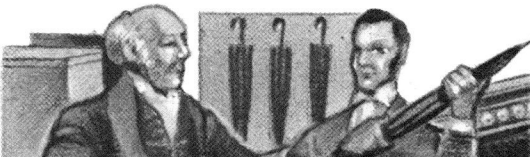

First umbrella factory

The first elevated electric railway in the United States was built in Baltimore in 1893.

Jousting is the official state sport of Maryland. *Jousting*, which is fighting with lances on horseback, was a popular sport during the Middle Ages. Maryland holds a state championship jousting tournament each October.

The Baltimore Department of Health is the oldest continuously operating municipal health department in the United States. It was organized in 1793 to help prevent the spreading of diseases.

Jousting

Eric Carle, Shostal

Martin's Head, a peak near Cumberland, offers a scenic view of the Allegheny Mountains in the Appalachian Plateau region of western Maryland. Eastern Maryland is low and flat, but the western part of the state has mountains, valleys, and plateaus.

Eric Carle, Shostal

Johns Hopkins University in Baltimore has gained international recognition for its scholarship and research.

Robert Rathe, FPG

Office workers gather at lunchtime in a Baltimore plaza. Baltimore is Maryland's largest city and commercial center.

Maryland in brief

Symbols of Maryland

The state flag, adopted in 1904, bears the coats of arms of two families related to Lord Baltimore—the Calverts and the Crosslands. The black-and-gold quarters are the Calverts' arms. The red-and-white quarters represent the Crosslands. The state seal was adopted in 1876. The front shows Lord Baltimore as a knight. On the back, the farmer symbolizes Maryland. The fisherman represents Lord Baltimore's Newfoundland colony.

State flag

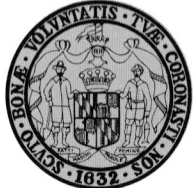

State seal

Maryland (brown) ranks 42nd in size among all the states, and 13th in size among the Southern States (yellow).

General information

Statehood: April 28, 1788, the seventh state.
State abbreviations: Md. (traditional); MD (postal).
State motto: *Fatti Maschii Parole Femine* (Manly Deeds, Womanly Words), Italian motto of the Calvert family.
State song: "Maryland, My Maryland," sung to the music of "O, Tannenbaum." Words by James Ryder Randall.

The State Capitol is in Annapolis, Maryland's capital since 1694. St. Marys City was the capital from 1634 to 1694.

Land and climate

Area: 10,455 sq. mi. (27,077 km²), including 680 sq. mi. (1,761 km²) of inland water but excluding 1,842 sq. mi. (4,771 km²) of coastal water.
Elevation: *Highest*—Backbone Mountain, 3,360 ft. (1,024 m) above sea level. *Lowest*—sea level along the coast.
Coastline: 31 mi. (49 km); including Chesapeake Bay, Potomac River, and other rivers, 3,190 mi. (5,134 km).
Record high temperature: 109 °F (43 °C) in Allegany County on July 3, 1898, and at Cumberland and Frederick on July 10, 1936.
Record low temperature: −40 °F (−40 °C) at Oakland on Jan. 13, 1912.
Average July temperature: 75 °F (24 °C).
Average January temperature: 33 °F (1 °C).
Average yearly precipitation: 43 in. (109 cm).

Greatest east-west distance 238 mi. (383 km)

Highest elevation

Greatest north-south distance 124 mi. (199 km)

Lowest elevation along coast

Important dates

King Charles I of England granted the Maryland charter to Cecilius Calvert, second Lord Baltimore.

Maryland became the seventh state on April 28.

| 1608 | 1632 | 1774 | 1788 |

Captain John Smith explored Chesapeake Bay.

Marylanders burned the *Peggy Stewart* in protest of the Boston Port Act.

State bird
Baltimore oriole

State flower
Black-eyed Susan

State tree
White oak

People

Population: 4,798,622 (1990 census)
Rank among the states: 19th
Density: 459 persons per sq. mi. (177 per km²), U.S. average 69 per sq. mi. (27 per km²)
Distribution: 81 percent urban, 19 percent rural

Largest cities in Maryland

Baltimore	736,014
Silver Spring	76,046
Columbia*	75,883
Dundalk*	65,800
Bethesda*	62,936

*Unincorporated place.
Source: U.S. Bureau of the Census.

Population trend

Millions

Source: U.S. Bureau of the Census.

Year	Population
1990	4,798,622
1980	4,216,941
1970	3,923,897
1960	3,100,689
1950	2,343,001
1940	1,821,244
1930	1,631,526
1920	1,449,661
1910	1,295,346
1900	1,188,044
1890	1,042,390
1880	934,943
1870	780,894
1860	687,049
1850	583,034
1840	470,019
1830	447,040
1820	407,350
1810	380,546
1800	341,548
1790	319,728

Economy

Chief products

Agriculture: chickens, milk, greenhouse and nursery products.
Manufacturing: electrical equipment, food products, chemicals, printed materials.
Mining: crushed stone, coal, sand and gravel.

Gross state product

Value of goods and services produced in 1991: $106,519,000,000. *Services* include community, social, and personal services; finance; government; trade; and transportation, communication, and utilities. *Industry* includes construction, manufacturing, and mining. *Agriculture* includes agriculture, fishing, and forestry.

Source: U.S. Bureau of Economic Analysis.

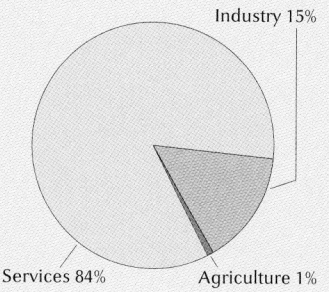

Industry 15%
Services 84%
Agriculture 1%

Government

State government

Governor: 4-year term
State senators: 47; 4-year terms
State delegates: 141; 4-year terms
Counties: 23

Federal government

United States senators: 2
United States representatives: 8
Electoral votes: 10

Sources of information

Tourism: Department of Economic and Employment Development, Office of Tourism Development, 217 East Redwood Street, 9th Floor, Baltimore, MD 21202
Economy: Department of Economic and Employment Development, Division of Business Development, 217 East Redwood Street, 10th Floor, Baltimore, MD 21202
Government: Office of the Governor, State House, Annapolis, MD 21401
History: State Archives, Hall of Records, 350 Rowe Boulevard, Annapolis, MD 21401

Maryland gave land for the District of Columbia.

Maryland adopted a constitution abolishing slavery.

Maryland voters approved a lottery to raise money for the state government.

1791 **1828** **1864** **1919-1933** **1972**

Construction of the Baltimore & Ohio Railroad began.

Maryland resisted the nation's prohibition laws and became known as the Free State.

Population. The 1990 United States census reported that Maryland had 4,798,622 people. The population had increased 14 percent over the 1980 figure, 4,216,941. According to the 1990 census, Maryland ranks 19th in population among the 50 states.

About four-fifths of the people of Maryland live in urban areas of the state. That is, they live in or near cities and towns that have a population of 2,500 or more. About one-fifth of the people of Maryland live in rural communities.

About 93 percent of the people in Maryland live in one of the state's five metropolitan areas (see **Metropolitan area**). These include the Baltimore, Cumberland, and Hagerstown metropolitan areas, and the Maryland portions of the Washington, D.C., and Wilmington, Del., metropolitan areas. For the populations of these metropolitan areas, see the *Index* to the political map of Maryland.

Baltimore is the state's largest city. Other large population centers, in order of population, are Silver Spring, Columbia, Dundalk, and Bethesda.

About a fourth of Maryland's people are blacks. Other large population groups in Maryland include people of German, Irish, English, Italian, Polish, and American Indian descent.

Schools. Church leaders and private tutors taught children in colonial Maryland. Only the children of wealthy families received schooling. The colony first provided funds for public education in 1694. King William's School in Annapolis was the colony's first free school. It was founded in 1696 and became St. John's College in 1784. In 1826, Maryland provided for the establishment of public schools throughout the state. The office of superintendent of public instruction was created in 1865. The state board of education was established in 1870.

Today, the state board of education administers the public school system. The governor appoints 11 board members to four-year terms and 1 nonvoting student member to a one-year term. The board appoints the state superintendent of schools to carry out its policies. A state law requires children to attend school from ages 5 through 15. For the number of students and teachers in Maryland, see **Education** (table).

Libraries. In 1699, Thomas Bray, an Episcopal minister, set up 30 *parish* (church district) libraries in the colony, with a central library in Annapolis. These were Maryland's first libraries and probably the first in the colonies to loan books. In 1886, Enoch Pratt, a Baltimore iron merchant, established the Enoch Pratt Free Library of Baltimore, one of the oldest public library systems in the United States.

The Johns Hopkins University library in Baltimore has a large collection of medical history materials. The Maryland Historical Society, founded in 1844, has an outstanding collection of books and manuscripts dealing with the history of Maryland. The Maryland State Law Library, in Annapolis, has many rare books, maps, and newspapers.

Museums. The Peale Museum, also called the Municipal Museum of the City of Baltimore, is one of the oldest museums in the United States. It opened in 1814 as the Baltimore Museum and Gallery of the Fine Arts. Rembrandt Peale, the founder of the museum, was the

Population density

Most of the people of Maryland live in the Baltimore or Washington, D.C., metropolitan areas. Relatively few people live in the southeastern part of the state.

Persons per sq. mi.	Persons per km²
More than 1,000	More than 400
250 to 1,000	100 to 400
100 to 250	40 to 100
Less than 100	Less than 40

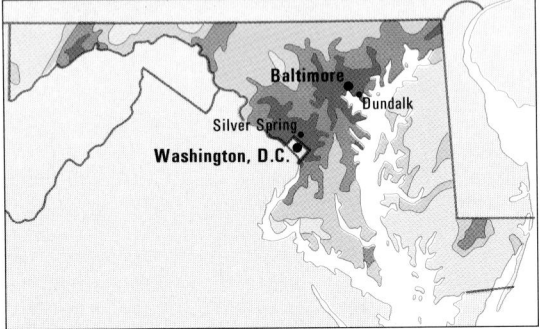

WORLD BOOK map; based on U.S. Bureau of the Census data.

son of the famous painter, Charles Willson Peale. The museum displays many works, including those of both Peales.

The Baltimore Museum of Art has exhibits of paintings, prints, and sculpture. Its collection of paintings by the French artist Henri Matisse is the largest in any public gallery.

The Maryland Historical Society in Baltimore owns the original manuscript of "The Star-Spangled Banner." The society's Noel Wyatt and Elizabeth Patterson Bonaparte collections include Empire furniture, miniatures, glass, jewelry, and lace. Other important museums include the Walters Art Gallery in Baltimore and the U.S. Naval Academy Museum in Annapolis.

Universities and colleges

Maryland has 27 universities and colleges that grant bachelor's or advanced degrees and are accredited by the Middle States Association of Colleges and Schools. For enrollments and further information, see **Universities and colleges** (table).

Name	Mailing address
Baltimore, University of	Baltimore
Baltimore Hebrew University	Baltimore
Bowie State University	Bowie
Capitol College	Laurel
Columbia Union College	Takoma Park
Coppin State College	Baltimore
Frostburg State University	Frostburg
Goucher College	Towson
Hood College	Frederick
Johns Hopkins University	*
Loyola College in Maryland	Baltimore
Maryland, University of	*
Maryland Institute College of Art	Baltimore
Morgan State University	Baltimore
Mount St. Mary's College	Emmitsburg
Notre Dame of Maryland, College of	Baltimore
St. John's College	Annapolis
St. Mary's College of Maryland	St. Marys City
St. Mary's Seminary and University	Baltimore
Salisbury State University	Salisbury
Sojourner-Douglass College	Baltimore
Towson State University	Baltimore
United States Naval Academy	Annapolis
Villa Julie College	Stevenson
Washington College	Chestertown
Washington Theological Union	Silver Spring
Western Maryland College	Westminster

*For campuses and founding dates, see **Universities and colleges** (table).

Maryland map index

Metropolitan areas

Baltimore 2,382,172
Cumberland 101,643
  (74,946 in Md.;
  26,697 in W. Va.)
Hagerstown 121,393
Washington,
  D.C., ... 4,223,485
  (1,789,029 in Md.;
  1,732,377 in Va.;
  606,900 in D.C.;
  95,179 in W. Va.)
Wilmington-
  Newark (Del.) 513,293
  (441,946 in Del.;
  71,347 in Md.)

Counties

Cities, towns, and villages

---

*Does not appear on map; key shows general location.
†Census designated place—unincorporated, but recognized as a significant settled community by the U.S. Bureau of the Census.

‡Independent city.
°County seat.

Source: 1990 census. Places without population figures are unincorporated areas.

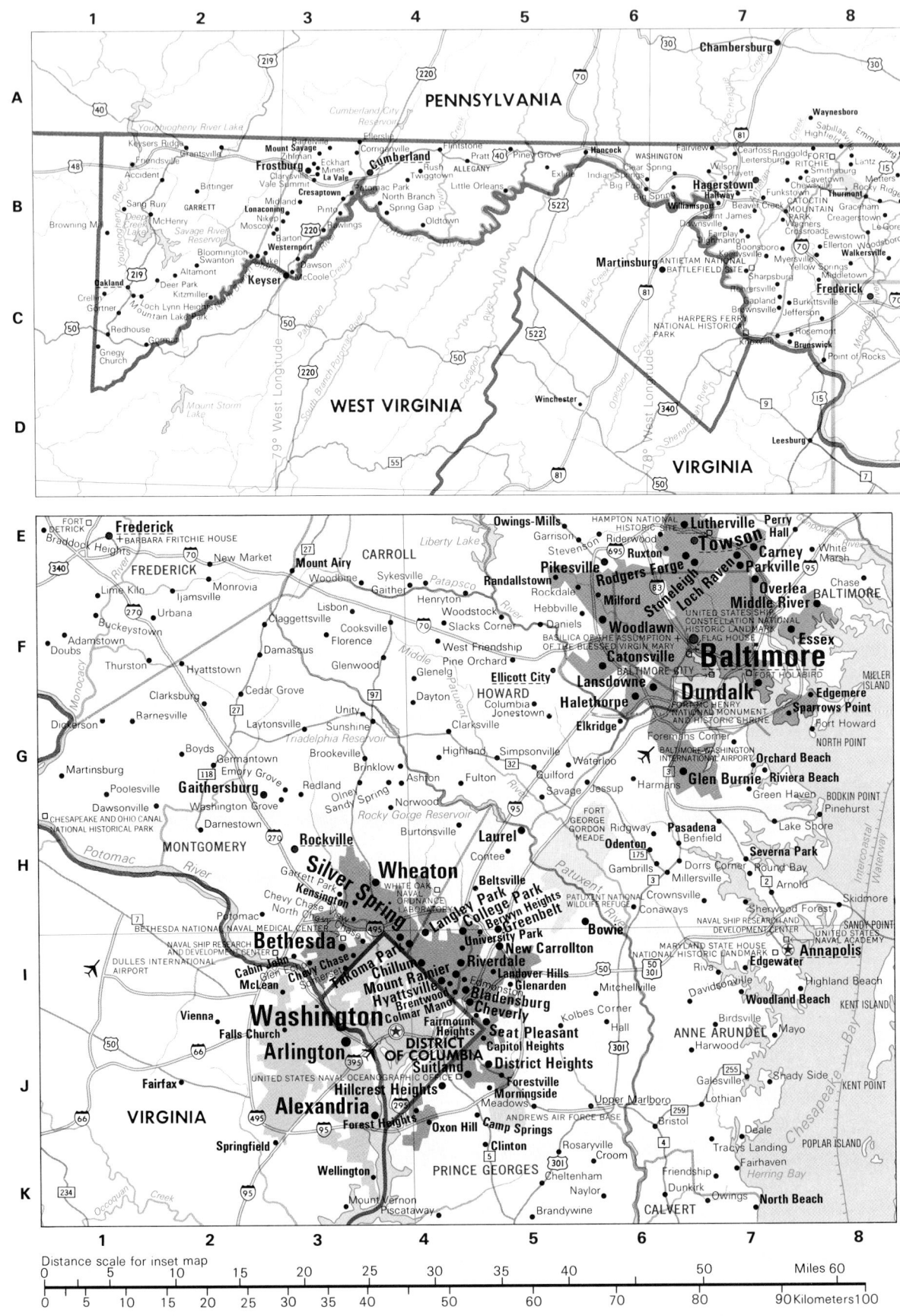

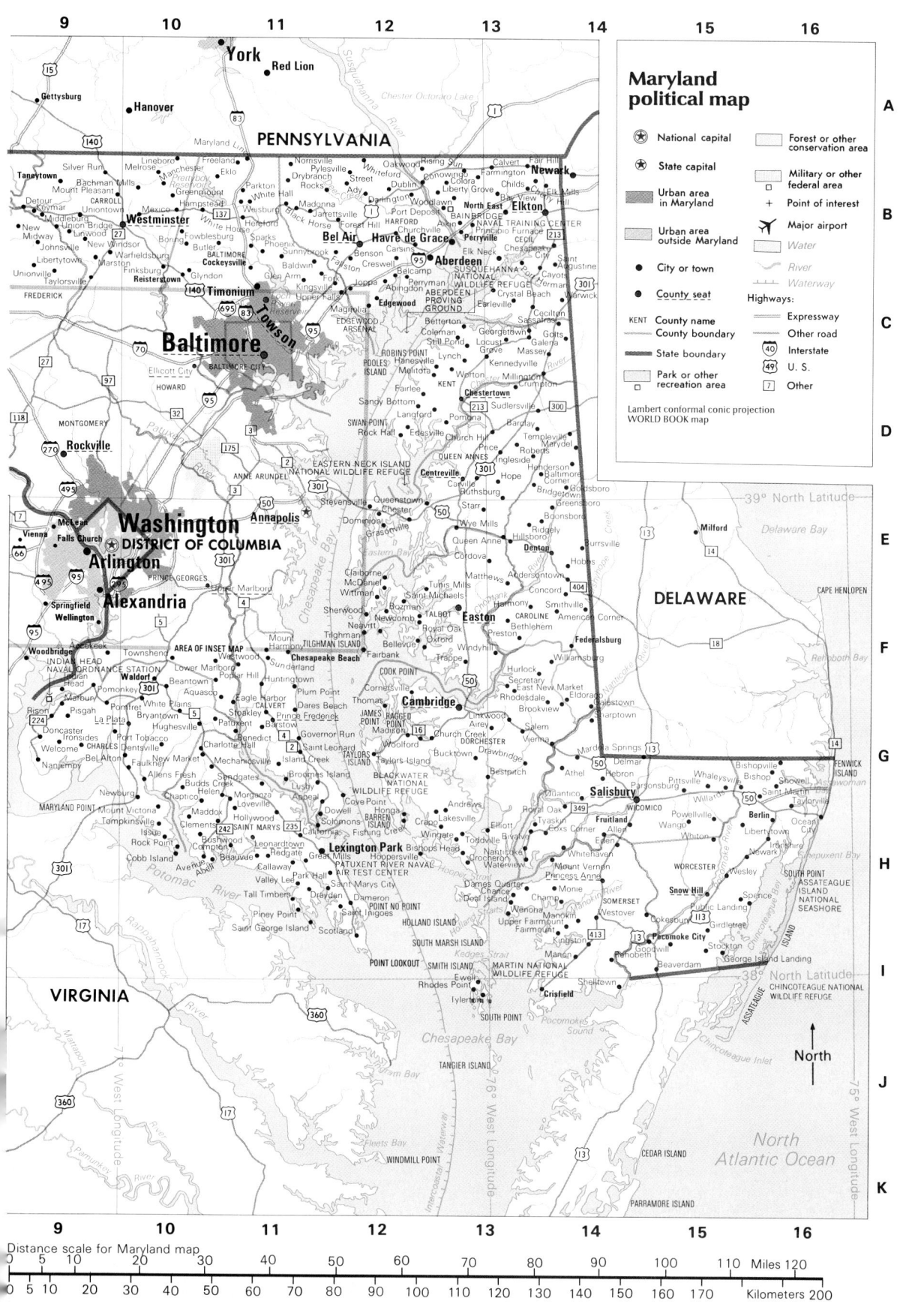

Maryland
political map

★ National capital
☆ State capital

Urban area in Maryland

Urban area outside Maryland

● City or town
● County seat

KENT County name
County boundary
State boundary

Park or other recreation area

Forest or other conservation area

Military or other federal area

+ Point of interest
✈ Major airport
Water
River
Waterway

Highways:
Expressway
Other road
40 Interstate
49 U.S.
7 Other

Lambert conformal conic projection
WORLD BOOK map

Distance scale for Maryland map

Maryland's long Chesapeake Bay shoreline offers opportunities for boating, fishing, and swimming. Visitors can hunt game birds and animals in the fields and forests, and along rivers. Old mansions and historic sites throughout the state appeal to sightseers. Visitors can still watch a form of old English jousting, in which galloping riders try to catch small rings on a spear.

One of Maryland's most famous annual events is the Preakness Stakes, a horse race run each May at the Pimlico race track in Baltimore. The Preakness, the Kentucky Derby, and the Belmont Stakes make up the famous Triple Crown of horse racing.

Maryland Department of Economic and Community Development

Barbara Fritchie House and Museum in Frederick

Colonial reconstruction in St. Marys City, near Lexington Park.

Everett C. Johnson from Marilyn Gartman

Places to visit

Barbara Fritchie House and Museum, in Frederick, has a reproduction of the house where Barbara Fritchie (also spelled Frietchie) supposedly defied Confederate forces. The museum has an audio-visual presentation of Barbara Fritchie's story.

Chesapeake Bay Maritime Museum, in St. Michael's, features a lighthouse, a saltwater aquarium, and a waterfowling exhibit. The museum also has a floating collection of Chesapeake Bay ships and boats.

Inner harbor area of Baltimore includes a number of attractions. *Harborplace* is an enclosed complex of shops and restaurants. *Maryland Science Center* features a science museum, a planetarium, and a theater. *National Aquarium in Baltimore* has thousands of fish, reptiles, and birds. *U.S.S. Constellation,* an early United States warship docked in the harbor, is a national landmark.

St. Marys City, a village near Leonardtown, became Maryland's first colonial settlement in 1634. A copy of the first Maryland state house stands in the historic village. Other attractions in St. Marys City include a replica of the *Dove,* Lord Baltimore's ship; a reconstruction of a tobacco plantation; a natural history museum; and a reconstructed inn of the 1600's.

Star-Spangled Banner Flag House, in Baltimore, was built in 1793. In this brick building, Mary Pickersgill made the huge flag that inspired Francis Scott Key to write "The Star-Spangled Banner."

National monuments and historic sites. Antietam National Battlefield, near Sharpsburg, was the site of one of the bloodiest Civil War battles. On Sept. 17, 1862, Union forces at Antietam turned back the first Confederate invasion of the North. Fort McHenry National Monument and Historic Shrine in Baltimore honors the defense of Baltimore against the British during the War of 1812. During that defense, on Sept. 13 and 14, 1814, Francis Scott Key was inspired to write "The Star-Spangled Banner."

Other historic sites in Maryland include the Maryland State House and the United States Naval Academy, both in Annapolis. Chesapeake and Ohio Canal National Historic Park extends from Cumberland to Washington, D.C.

State parks and forests. Maryland has 35 state parks and 9 state forests. For information on the state parks of Maryland, write to Director, State Forest and Park Service, Tawes Building, 580 Taylor Avenue, Annapolis, MD 21401.

Annual events

January-March
Governor's Open House in Annapolis (January 1); Winterfest in McHenry (March); Maryland Day in St. Marys City (Sunday nearest March 25).

April-June
Fish & Fowl Day in Snow Hill (April); Preakness Celebration in Baltimore (May); Commissioning Week at the U.S. Naval Academy in Annapolis (May); Flag Day Ceremonies at Fort McHenry in Baltimore (June); Heritage Days Festival in Cumberland (June).

July-September
American Indian Inter-Tribal Cultural Powwow in McHenry (July); Artscape in Baltimore (July); State Jousting Championships in different locations (August-October); National Hard Crab Derby in Crisfield (Labor Day weekend); Deal Island Skipjack Races (Labor Day weekend); Heritage Weekend in Annapolis (September); Pemberton Hall Colonial Fair in Salisbury (September).

October-December
Autumn Glory Festival in Garrett County (October); Seaport Days in Cambridge (October); Chesapeake Appreciation Day Festival near Annapolis (late October); Waterfowl Festival in Easton (November).

© Stuart L. Craig, Bruce Coleman Inc.

Inner Harbor area of Baltimore

© Jerry Wachter, Focus on Sports

Preakness Stakes at Baltimore's Pimlico race track

J. Blank, FPG

Fort McHenry National Monument in Baltimore

Eric Carle, Shostal

Dress parade at U.S. Naval Academy in Annapolis

Land regions. Chesapeake Bay divides most of Maryland into two sections. The area east of Chesapeake Bay is called the Eastern Shore. The area west of the bay is called the Western Shore. Maryland has five main land regions. They are, from east to west: (1) the Atlantic Coastal Plain, (2) the Piedmont, (3) the Blue Ridge, (4) the Appalachian Ridge and Valley, and (5) the Appalachian Plateau.

The Atlantic Coastal Plain stretches along the east coast of the United States from New Jersey to southern Florida. In Maryland, the coastal plain covers the entire Eastern Shore and part of the Western Shore. The plain touches a narrow tip of northeastern Maryland. It extends across southern Maryland from the southeastern corner of the state almost to Washington, D.C. The Atlantic Coastal Plain has little elevation on the Eastern Shore, but it rises to about 400 feet (120 meters) on the Western Shore.

The Eastern Shore has some marshy areas. The Pocomoke Swamp, which is 2 miles (3 kilometers) wide, extends from Pocomoke Sound to the Delaware border. The part of the Western Shore south of Baltimore is called Southern Maryland. Tobacco has been raised in Southern Maryland since colonial times.

The Piedmont extends from New Jersey to Alabama. In Maryland, the Piedmont is about 50 miles (80 kilometers) wide. It stretches from the northeastern to the central part of the state. Low, rolling hills and fertile valleys cover the region. The Piedmont rises to about 880 feet (268 meters) at Parrs Ridge, and to about 1,200 feet (366 meters) at Dug Hill Ridge on the Pennsylvania border. Both of these ridges run in a southwesterly direction. They form the divide between streams flowing west-

ward into the Potomac River and those flowing eastward into Chesapeake Bay. Frederick Valley, which lies along the Monocacy River, is a rich dairy-farming area.

The Blue Ridge region extends from southern Pennsylvania to northern Georgia. In Maryland, the region is a narrow, mountainous strip of land between the Piedmont and the Appalachian Ridge and Valley region. South Mountain and Catoctin Mountain form most of the Blue Ridge. Nearly all the region is over 1,000 feet (300 meters) above sea level. It rises to a height of over 2,000 feet (610 meters) near the Pennsylvania border. The Blue Ridge region was named for the blue haze that sometimes hangs over its forest-covered ridges.

The Appalachian Ridge and Valley is a land region that stretches southwestward from New Jersey to Alabama. The Maryland portion is a strip of land that separates Pennsylvania from West Virginia. At Hancock, Maryland measures less than 2 miles (3 kilometers) from its northern to its southern borders.

The Great Valley, known in Maryland as Hagerstown Valley, covers the eastern portion of the state's ridge and valley region. Much of this fertile valley is filled with orchards and farms. West of the valley, a series of ridges crosses the state from northeast to southwest. Some of the ridges rise to almost 2,000 feet (610 meters). Forests cover about two-thirds of the region.

The Appalachian Plateau extends from New York to Georgia. It covers a triangle-shaped area in the extreme western part of Maryland. The Allegheny Mountains cover most of the region. They make up part of the huge Appalachian Range. Backbone Mountain, in the northwest, is Maryland's highest point. It rises 3,360 feet (1,024 meters). Streams have cut deep valleys into the

Maryland Department of Economic and Community Development

The Pocomoke River, in the southern part of Maryland's Eastern Shore, flows through the Atlantic Coastal Plain.

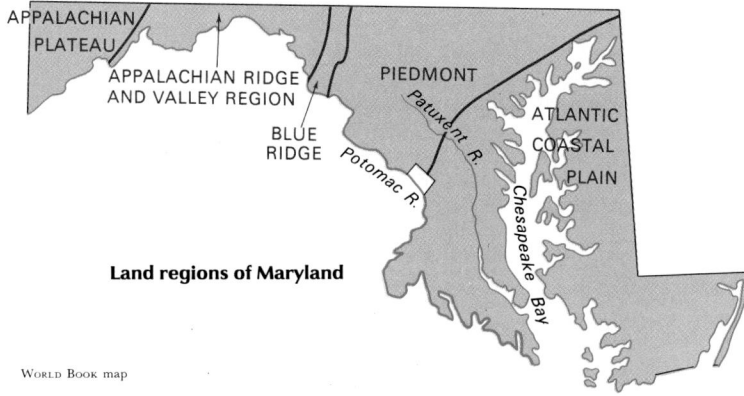

Land regions of Maryland

WORLD BOOK map

Map index

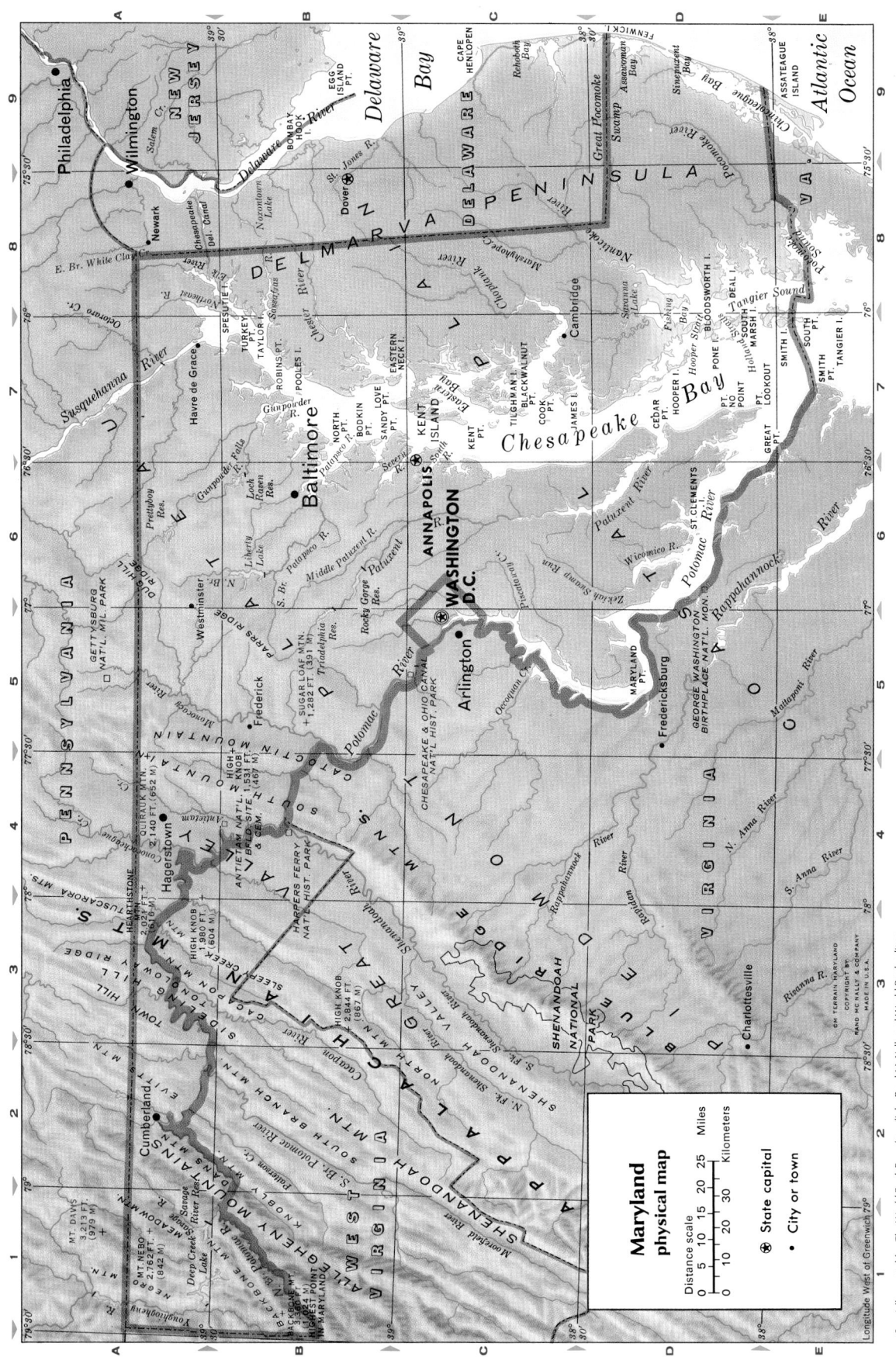

Maryland
physical map

Distance scale

Miles

Kilometers

⊛ State capital

• City or town

Specially created for *The World Book Encyclopedia* by Rand McNally and World Book editors

Longitude West of Greenwich 79°

Appalachian Plateau. The valleys served as early trails to the West. Forests cover nearly three-fourths of the plateau region.

Coastline of Maryland measures only 31 miles (49 kilometers) along the Atlantic Ocean. But the many arms and inlets of Chesapeake Bay give Maryland a total coastline of 3,190 miles (5,134 kilometers). These arms and inlets provide excellent harbors. Islands in Chesapeake Bay include Bloodsworth, Deal, Hooper, Kent, Smith, South Marsh, Taylors, and Tilghman.

Rivers and lakes. Most of Maryland is drained by rivers that flow into Chesapeake Bay. Seven large rivers cross the Eastern Shore area. They are the Chester, Choptank, Elk, Nanticoke, Pocomoke, Sassafras, and Wicomico. The Susquehanna River flows into the state from Pennsylvania and empties into Chesapeake Bay. The Gunpowder, Patapsco, and Patuxent rivers all drain the Western Shore and flow into the bay.

The Potomac River forms Maryland's southern and southwestern boundary. South of Washington, D.C., it widens into an arm of Chesapeake Bay. Tributaries of the Potomac drain much of western Maryland.

All Maryland lakes are artificially created. The largest, Deep Creek Lake in the Allegheny Mountains, covers about 4,000 acres (1,600 hectares). It was formed by a dam built across a small tributary of the Youghiogheny River. The dam provides hydroelectric power.

Plant and animal life. Forests cover about 40 per cent of Maryland's land area. The state has over 150 kinds of trees. Oaks are the most common. Others include the ash, beech, black locust, hickory, maple, and tupelo.

The black-eyed Susan, Maryland's state flower, grows on the Western Shore. The Western Shore also has many kinds of berries, including blackberries, dewberries, raspberries, and wild strawberries. Grasses and grasslike plants called *sedges* grow on the Eastern Shore. Azaleas, laurel, and rhododendrons grow along the edges of the woods.

Maryland's animal life includes eastern cottontail rabbits, minks, opossums, raccoons, red and gray foxes, and white-tailed deer. The north-central part of the state has chipmunks, otters, squirrels, and woodchucks. Hunters find grouse, partridge, wild turkeys, and woodcocks in western Maryland, and wild ducks and geese along the coastal plain. Songbirds are plentiful.

Average monthly weather

	Baltimore						Washington, D.C.				
	Temperatures				Days of rain or snow		Temperatures				Days of rain or snow
	F°		C°				F°		C°		
	High	Low	High	Low			High	Low	High	Low	
Jan.	43	26	6	−3	12	Jan.	44	29	7	−2	11
Feb.	44	26	7	−3	8	Feb.	46	29	8	−2	10
Mar.	53	33	12	1	13	Mar.	55	36	13	2	12
Apr.	63	42	17	6	11	Apr.	65	45	18	7	11
May	73	53	23	12	11	May	76	55	24	13	12
June	83	62	28	17	10	June	84	64	29	18	11
July	87	66	31	19	6	July	87	68	31	20	11
Aug.	85	64	29	18	10	Aug.	85	67	29	19	11
Sept.	78	58	26	14	9	Sept.	79	61	26	16	8
Oct.	67	46	19	8	7	Oct.	68	49	20	9	8
Nov.	55	36	13	2	9	Nov.	57	39	14	4	9
Dec.	44	27	7	−3	9	Dec.	46	31	8	−1	10

Maryland's coastal waters have great quantities of bluefish, crabs, diamondback terrapins, menhaden, oysters, sea trout, shrimps, and striped bass (called *rockfish* or *rock* in Maryland). Each spring croakers, alewives, and other fishes swim up Chesapeake Bay to lay their eggs in the larger rivers. Trout live in the cold rivers and streams of northern and western Maryland. Carp, catfish, and suckers are found in the waters of the Piedmont and the coastal plain.

Average yearly precipitation

Maryland has a humid climate. Rain falls fairly evenly throughout the state. Snowfall ranges from light amounts in the southeast to heavy accumulations in the northwest.

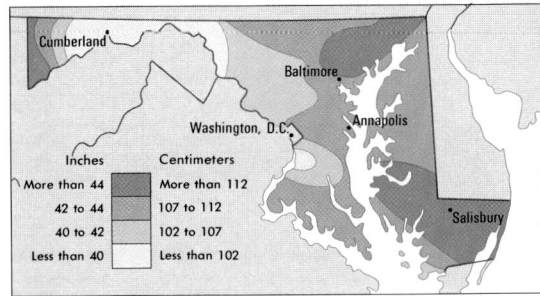

Average January temperatures

Maryland has mild winters. Temperatures in the mountainous regions of the northwest are lower than those along the Atlantic coast and in the Chesapeake Bay sections.

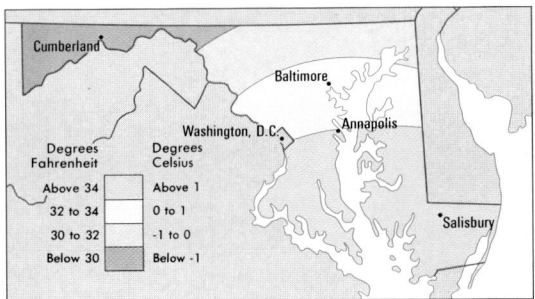

Average July temperatures

Maryland's summers are generally very warm. There is little variation in temperature throughout much of the state. The area around the Chesapeake Bay has the highest temperatures.

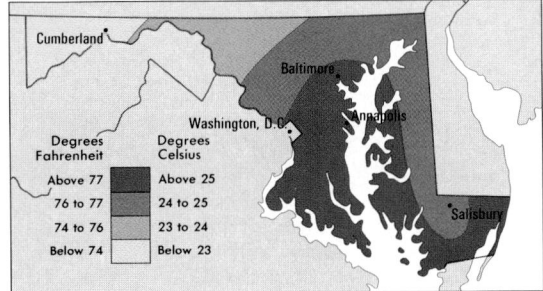

WORLD BOOK maps

Climate. Maryland has a humid climate, with hot summers and generally mild winters. Temperatures in the mountainous northwest are lower than those along the Atlantic coast and in the Chesapeake Bay region. January temperatures average 29 °F (−2 °C) in the northwest, and 39 °F (4 °C) along the Atlantic coast. Average July temperatures range from 68 °F (20 °C) in the northwest to about 75 °F (24 °C) in the Chesapeake Bay region. The record high temperature, 109 °F (43 °C), occurred in

Allegany County on July 3, 1898, and at Cumberland and Frederick on July 10, 1936. Oakland had the lowest temperature, −40 °F (−40 °C), on Jan. 13, 1912.

Maryland's *precipitation* (rain, melted snow, and other forms of moisture) averages about 43 inches (109 centimeters) a year. Rain falls fairly evenly throughout the state. Snow ranges from about 9 inches (23 centimeters) a year in the southeast to about 78 inches (198 centimeters) in the Appalachian Plateau.

Economy

Maryland's economy is based largely on service industries. These industries taken together account for more than four-fifths of Maryland's *gross state product—* the total value of all goods and services produced in a state in a year. Because Maryland lies next to the District of Columbia, the federal government plays a major role in the state's economy. Many federal offices are in the section of the Washington, D.C., metropolitan area that lies within Maryland. In addition, many businesses in this region provide support services to federal agencies. The Baltimore area is Maryland's other major economic center. It is one of the East Coast's leading areas for finance, manufacturing, and trade.

Natural resources of Maryland include fertile soils and many minerals. Light, sandy loams and stiff, clay soils cover much of the Eastern Shore. The Western Shore south of Baltimore also has loam and clay soils. North-central Maryland has fertile, limestone soils. The valleys of western Maryland have a thin covering of soil. Sand and gravel deposits are found in many counties on the Western Shore. Other minerals include clays, coal, granite, limestone, natural gas, and talc.

Service industries account for 84 per cent of the gross state product of Maryland. The state's leading category of service industries consists of community, social, and personal services. The most important activities in this industry in Maryland are private health care and support services for business and government. Private health care consists chiefly of doctors' offices and private hospitals. Support services include computer programming, consulting, data processing, janitorial help, and security.

Government services form the second most important service industry in Maryland. This industry includes public schools and hospitals, and military activities. Agencies of the federal government in Maryland include the National Institutes of Health and the Bureau of the Census. Military facilities include several bases, the Bethesda Naval Medical Center, Goddard Space Flight Center, and the U.S. Naval Academy. Most state government offices are in Annapolis and Baltimore.

Next, and equal, among service industries in terms of Maryland's gross state product are (1) wholesale and retail trade and (2) finance, insurance, and real estate. The Port of Baltimore is a center of wholesale trade. It handles large numbers of imported motor vehicles and large amounts of exported chemicals. Much exported and imported machinery also travels through the port. The leading types of retail trade establishments are automobile dealerships, food stores, and restaurants. Baltimore ranks among the leading financial centers in the

Eastern United States. Several major commercial banking companies and holding companies are headquartered in or near the city.

Transportation, communication, and utilities rank fifth in importance among Maryland service industries. Many shipping and trucking firms operate in the Baltimore area. Telephone companies are the most important part of the communications industry. Baltimore Gas & Electric is the state's largest utility company. More information about transportation and communication appears later in this section.

Manufacturing in Maryland accounts for 10 per cent of the gross state product. Manufactured goods have a *value added by manufacture* of about $14 billion a year. Value added by manufacture represents the increase in value of raw materials after they become finished products. Most of Maryland's manufacturing activity takes place within the Baltimore area and the urban areas near Washington, D.C.

Electrical equipment and devices are the leading type of manufactured product in Maryland. Communication equipment is the most important type of electrical equipment manufactured in the state. The production of military communication systems and television broadcasting equipment is especially important.

Food products rank second in importance in terms of value added by manufacture. Maryland's major types of

Production and workers by economic activities

Economic activities	Per cent of GSP* produced	Employed workers	
		Number of persons	Per cent of total
Community, social, & personal services	23	619,100	29
Government	18	414,600	19
Wholesale and retail trade	17	507,400	24
Finance, insurance, & real estate	17	130,600	6
Manufacturing	10	192,800	9
Transportation, communication, & utilities	9	100,400	5
Construction	5	130,100	6
Agriculture	1	38,000	2
Mining	†	1,600	†
Total	**100**	**2,134,600**	**100**

*GSP = gross state product, the total value of goods and services produced in a year.
†Less than one-half of 1 per cent.
Figures are for 1991.
Sources: *World Book* estimates based on data from U.S. Bureau of Economic Analysis, U.S. Bureau of Labor Statistics, and U.S. Department of Agriculture.

processed foods are soft drinks, alcoholic beverages, spices, and bread. One of the nation's largest spice makers is based near Cockeysville.

Other leading manufactured products in Maryland are chemicals and printed materials. Soaps and bathroom cleaners are the most important chemical products made in the state. Large numbers of newspapers are printed in the Baltimore area. Plants in southern Maryland print documents for the federal government. The state's other manufactures include, in order of value, transportation equipment, primary metals, and machinery.

Agriculture accounts for 1 per cent of Maryland's gross state product. Farmland covers about 35 per cent of the state. Maryland's 15,400 farms average about 146 acres (59 hectares) in size.

Livestock and livestock products provide about 60 per cent of Maryland's farm income. *Broilers* (chickens from 5 to 12 weeks old) are Maryland's leading farm product. They account for nearly half of the livestock income. Most of the state's broilers are raised in the central and southern parts of the Eastern Shore. Milk is Maryland's second most important farm product. Frederick County leads the state in milk production. Other livestock products include beef cattle, eggs, hogs, and sheep.

Crops in Maryland account for about 40 per cent of the farm income. Greenhouse and nursery products—including flowers, ornamental shrubs, and young fruit trees—make up the leading category of crops in Maryland. The state's leading field crops are soybeans, corn, and wheat. Maryland farmers also grow barley, hay, and tobacco. Tomatoes are the state's most important vegetable. Apples are the leading fruit.

Mining in Maryland accounts for less than half of 1 per cent of the gross state product. Crushed stone ranks as the most valuable mineral product. It is used mainly in the construction industry. The Piedmont region has the state's largest stone quarries. Coal is the second most valuable mineral in Maryland. Allegany and Garrett counties, in western Maryland, mine all of the state's coal. Large quantities of sand and gravel come from pits on the Western Shore. Clay is mined in the Piedmont. Frederick County produces all of the state's limestone. Natural gas comes from Garrett County. Other minerals mined in Maryland include gemstones and peat.

Fishing industry. The annual fish catch in Maryland is valued at about $50 million. Maryland ranks among the leading states in the production of clams, crabs, and oysters. Valuable catches in the waters of Chesapeake Bay include bluefish, catfish, clams, crabs, menhaden, oysters, striped bass, turtles, and white perch. Fish caught in Atlantic coastal waters include bluefish, croakers, flounder, fluke, mackerel, marlin, shark, striped bass, swordfish, and whiting.

Electric power. Plants that burn coal generate about 60 per cent of the electric power used in Maryland about 25 per cent comes from nuclear plants. Hydroelectric plants and plants that burn petroleum or natural gas supply the rest of Maryland's electricity.

Transportation. Early transportation in the Maryland region was provided by steamboats traveling over Chesapeake Bay and its tributaries. In 1828, construction began on the Baltimore and Ohio Railroad. This railroad was the first in the Western Hemisphere to carry both passengers and freight. The Chesapeake and Delaware Canal was completed in 1829, connecting Chesapeake

© Martin Rogers, Woodfin Camp, Inc.

Ships dock in Baltimore harbor, one of the largest natural harbors in the world. Baltimore is Maryland's chief industrial and trade center and one of the Atlantic Coast's leading ports.

Farm and mineral products

This map shows where the leading farm and mineral products are produced. The major urban areas (shown in red) are the important manufacturing centers.

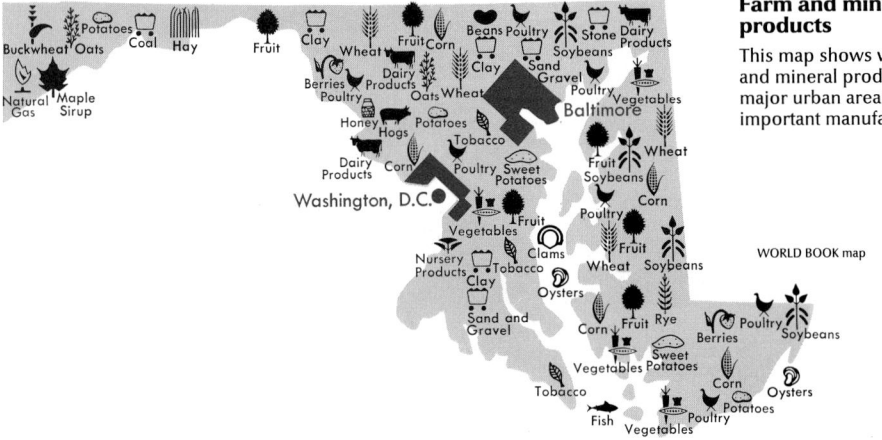

WORLD BOOK map

Bay with the Delaware River. In the 1920's, motor trucks and buses replaced steamboat transportation in the Chesapeake Bay country.

Nearly all Maryland's 29,000 miles (46,000 kilometers) of roads and highways are surfaced. In 1963, the John F. Kennedy Expressway became the state's first modern tollway. It is part of Interstate 95, which extends from Florida to Maine. Baltimore-Washington International Airport, near Baltimore, is Maryland's chief airport. Some people who travel to or from the Washington, D.C., area use it. Passenger trains serve Baltimore and Washington, D.C. Baltimore is a leading Atlantic Coast seaport.

Communication. The *Maryland Gazette,* published in Annapolis from 1727 to 1734, was the first colonial newspaper south of Philadelphia, and one of the first in the colonies. In 1844, the first telegraph line in the United States opened between Baltimore and Washington, D.C. Maryland's oldest radio stations, WCAO and WFBR of Baltimore, began broadcasting in 1922. The state's first television station, WMAR-TV, was established in Baltimore in 1947.

Today, Maryland has about 130 newspapers, about 15 of which are dailies, and about 370 periodicals. *The Sun* in Baltimore is the largest daily. The state has about 100 radio stations and about 15 television stations.

Government

Constitution. The current Maryland Constitution was adopted in 1867, shortly after the Civil War. Earlier constitutions were adopted in 1776, 1851, and 1864.

An *amendment* (change) in the Constitution may be proposed by the state legislature or by a constitutional convention. Legislative amendments must be approved by three-fifths of the members of both houses of the legislature. All amendments must be approved by a majority of the people who vote on the amendment.

Executive. Maryland's governor serves a four-year term. The governor may be elected to an unlimited number of terms but may not serve more than two terms in a row.

The people elect the lieutenant governor, the attorney general, and the comptroller to four-year terms. The governor appoints the secretary of state, the adjutant general, and most members of state boards. The legislature elects the state treasurer to a four-year term.

Legislature, called the *General Assembly,* consists of a 47-member Senate and a 141-member House of Delegates. Each of the state's 47 legislative districts elects one senator and three delegates. All Maryland legislators serve four-year terms. Legislative sessions begin on the second Wednesday in January and are limited to 90 days. However, regular sessions may be extended 30 days by a three-fifths vote of the members of each

The state governors of Maryland

	Party	Term		Party	Term
Thomas Johnson	None	1777-1779	Philip Francis Thomas	Democratic	1848-1851
Thomas Sim Lee	None	1779-1782	Enoch Louis Lowe	Democratic	1851-1854
William Paca	None	1782-1785	Thomas Watkins Ligon	Democratic	1854-1858
William Smallwood	Unknown	1785-1788	Thomas Holliday Hicks	Know-Nothing	1858-1862
John Eager Howard	Federalist	1788-1791	Augustus W. Bradford	Union	1862-1866
George Plater	Federalist	1791-1792	Thomas Swann	Democratic	1866-1869
James Brice	Unknown	1792	Oden Bowie	Democratic	1869-1872
Thomas Sim Lee	Federalist	1792-1794	William Pinkney Whyte	Democratic	1872-1874
John H. Stone	Federalist	1794-1797	James Black Groome	Democratic	1874-1876
John Henry	Federalist	1797-1798	John Lee Carroll	Democratic	1876-1880
Benjamin Ogle	Federalist	1798-1801	William T. Hamilton	Democratic	1880-1884
John Francis Mercer	Dem.-Rep.*	1801-1803	Robert M. McLane	Democratic	1884-1885
Robert Bowie	Dem.-Rep.	1803-1806	Henry Lloyd	Democratic	1885-1888
Robert Wright	Dem.-Rep.	1806-1809	Elihu E. Jackson	Democratic	1888-1892
James Butcher	Unknown	1809	Frank Brown	Democratic	1892-1896
Edward Lloyd	Dem.-Rep.	1809-1811	Lloyd Lowndes	Republican	1896-1900
Robert Bowie	Dem.-Rep.	1811-1812	John Walter Smith	Democratic	1900-1904
Levin Winder	Federalist	1812-1816	Edwin Warfield	Democratic	1904-1908
Charles Ridgely	Federalist	1816-1819	Austin L. Crothers	Democratic	1908-1912
Charles Goldsborough	Federalist	1819	Phillips Lee Goldsborough	Republican	1912-1916
Samuel Sprigg	Dem.-Rep.	1819-1822	Emerson C. Harrington	Democratic	1916-1920
Samuel Stevens, Jr.	Dem.-Rep.	1822-1826	Albert C. Ritchie	Democratic	1920-1935
Joseph Kent	Democratic	1826-1829	Harry W. Nice	Republican	1935-1939
Daniel Martin	Democratic	1829-1830	Herbert R. O'Conor	Democratic	1939-1947
Thomas King Carroll	Democratic	1830-1831	Wm. Preston Lane, Jr.	Democratic	1947-1951
Daniel Martin	Democratic	1831	Theodore R. McKeldin	Republican	1951-1959
George Howard	Democratic	1831-1833	J. Millard Tawes	Democratic	1959-1967
James Thomas	Whig	1833-1836	Spiro T. Agnew	Republican	1967-1969
Thomas W. Veazey	Whig	1836-1839	Marvin Mandel	Democratic	1969-1979†
William Grason	Democratic	1839-1842	Harry R. Hughes	Democratic	1979-1987
Francis Thomas	Democratic	1842-1845	William D. Schaefer	Democratic	1987-
Thomas G. Pratt	Democratic	1845-1848			

*Democratic-Republican
†Lieutenant Governor Blair Lee III served as acting governor from June 4, 1977, to Jan. 15, 1979.

house. The governor also may call to have a regular session extended. Special sessions may be called by the governor, or by the legislature if a majority of its members sign a petition requesting such a session.

Courts. Maryland's chief courts include the Court of Appeals, the Court of Special Appeals, and 24 circuit courts divided among eight judicial circuits. The Court of Appeals, the highest state court, hears appeals of civil cases and of criminal cases involving the death sentence. It has seven judges. The Court of Special Appeals hears appeals of criminal cases and of certain civil cases, such as automobile accidents. This court consists of 13 judges. The circuit courts hear general cases. The number of judges in each circuit varies from 6 to 25. The governor appoints all appeals court and circuit court judges to serve for at least one year. At the next general election, appeals court judges may run for 10-year terms, and circuit court judges may run for 15-year terms. The governor also designates the chief judges who head each of the appeals courts.

Maryland also has a district court system. It consists of 12 courts that hear minor civil and criminal cases and traffic cases. A chief judge heads the system. The number of associate judges in each district varies from 3 to 23. The governor appoints all district court judges to 10-year terms, subject to confirmation by the Maryland Senate. The chief judge of the Court of Appeals appoints the chief judge of the District Court, who serves a 10-year term and administers the state court system.

Local government in Maryland is centered in the state's 23 counties and in the city of Baltimore. Incorporated cities function as independent units of government. But all other areas in a county come under the jurisdiction of county government.

More than half of Maryland's counties are governed by elected boards of commissioners. These boards serve executive and legislative functions. Board members are elected to four-year terms. The other counties are governed by county councils or county executives, or a combination of both. Council members are elected to four-year terms. Voters also choose such county officers as circuit court clerk, state's attorney, sheriff, and treasurer or financial director.

Baltimore, which is not part of any county, is governed by a mayor, an 18-member city council, and a council president. Most other cities use the mayor-council or commissioner form of government.

Counties in Maryland may adopt either of two forms of *home rule,* both of which allow them to govern many of their own affairs without control by the state legislature. Thirteen Maryland counties have adopted home rule. Incorporated cities in Maryland also have it.

Revenue. Sales taxes account for about 14 per cent of the state government's *general revenue* (income). Individual state income taxes account for about 26 per cent. Other sources of income include a corporate income tax, franchise and gross receipts taxes, transportation taxes, property taxes, and a state lottery. About 20 per cent of the state revenue comes from federal grants and programs.

Politics. In most elections, Maryland is strongly Democratic, with the greatest Democratic strength in the city of Baltimore. The Republican Party's strength is limited to a few counties in central and western Maryland. Only five Republicans have ever served as governor of Maryland. But in presidential elections since 1920, about an equal number of Democratic and Republican candidates have won the state's electoral votes. For Maryland's electoral votes and its voting record in presidential elections, see **Electoral College** (table).

History

Indian days. Indians probably lived in the Maryland region hundreds of years before white people came. Early European explorers found Algonquian Indians and a few Susquehannock in the region. The Algonquian tribes included the Choptank, Nanticoke, Patuxent, Portobago, and Wicomico. Most of the Indians left the region during the early years of colonial settlement. But they gave their names to many of Maryland's rivers, towns, and counties.

Exploration and settlement. The Spaniards became the first Europeans to visit the Maryland region when they explored Chesapeake Bay in the 1500's. In 1608, Captain John Smith of Virginia sailed northward up Chesapeake Bay into the Maryland region. Smith wrote a description of what he saw. In 1631, William Claiborne, also of Virginia, opened a trading post on Kent Island in the bay. Claiborne's was the first colonial settlement in the Maryland region.

In 1632, King Charles I of England granted the Maryland region to George Calvert, the first Lord Baltimore. But Calvert died before the king signed the charter. King Charles then chartered the region to Calvert's son, Cecilius, the second Lord Baltimore. The region was named *Maryland* in honor of Queen Henrietta Maria, the wife of Charles. Cecilius Calvert sent colonists to Maryland on two ships, the *Ark* and the *Dove.* In 1634, the two ships anchored off St. Clements Island in the Potomac River. The colonists established St. Marys City near the southern tip of the Western Shore.

Colonial days. Cecilius Calvert appointed his brother, Leonard, as governor of the Maryland Colony. Cecilius encouraged the colonists to suggest laws and to assist his brother in the colony's administration. Cecilius was a Roman Catholic, but he had to support the Church of England. However, he wanted freedom of worship for those of his faith, and he also wanted people of other faiths to settle in Maryland. He believed that religious restrictions would interfere with the colony's growth and development. In 1649, the colonial assembly approved Cecilius Calvert's draft of a religious toleration law, granting religious freedom to all Christians. After the law was passed, a band of Puritans fled from Virginia and came to Maryland. Maryland became famous for its religious freedom.

William Claiborne's trading settlement on Kent Island was part of the Maryland Colony. But Claiborne refused to recognize Cecilius Calvert's authority. In 1654, Claiborne led a group of Protestant settlers who overthrew Calvert's government. Claiborne controlled Maryland for four years.

Historic Maryland

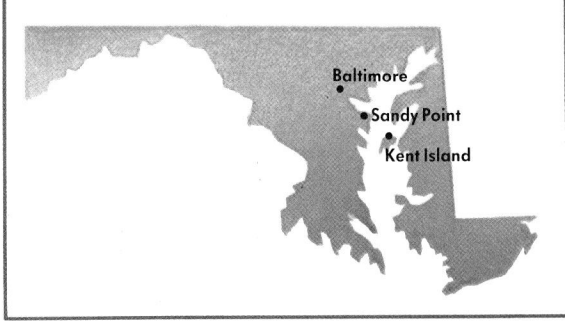

Francis Scott Key wrote the "Star-Spangled Banner" after watching the British bombard Baltimore's Fort McHenry in 1814.

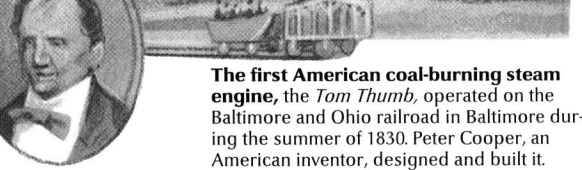

The first American coal-burning steam engine, the *Tom Thumb,* operated on the Baltimore and Ohio railroad in Baltimore during the summer of 1830. Peter Cooper, an American inventor, designed and built it.

The first telegraph line in America was opened in 1844. The words "What hath God wrought" were sent by inventor Samuel F. B. Morse from Washington, D.C., to Baltimore.

The William P. Lane, Jr., Memorial Bridge connects Maryland's two shores. The 4⅓-mile (7-kilometer) bridge opened in 1952. It was first called the Chesapeake Bay Bridge.

Important dates in Maryland

WORLD BOOK illustrations by Kevin Chadwick

1608 Captain John Smith explored Chesapeake Bay.

1631 William Claiborne established a trading post on Kent Island.

1632 King Charles I of England granted the Maryland charter to Cecilius Calvert, second Lord Baltimore.

1634 The first settlers arrived in Maryland.

1649 Maryland passed a religious toleration act.

1654 William Claiborne seized control of the colony.

1658 Cecilius Calvert regained control.

1691 England assumed direct rule of the colony.

1715 The Calvert family regained proprietorship of the colony.

1767 Mason and Dixon completed their survey of the Maryland-Pennsylvania boundary, begun in 1763.

1774 Marylanders burned the *Peggy Stewart* and its cargo of tea in protest against the Boston Port Act.

1776 Maryland declared its independence.

1776-1777 The Second Continental Congress met in Baltimore.

1783 George Washington resigned his commission as commander in chief at Annapolis.

1786 The Annapolis Convention met.

1788 Maryland became the seventh state on April 28.

1791 Maryland gave land for the District of Columbia.

1814 Francis Scott Key wrote "The Star-Spangled Banner" during the British bombardment of Fort McHenry.

1828 Construction of the Baltimore & Ohio Railroad began.

1850 The National (Cumberland) Road, west from Cumberland, was completed.

1862 Federal forces drove back the Confederates from Antietam Creek near Sharpsburg.

1864 A constitution abolishing slavery was adopted.

1919-1933 Maryland resisted the nation's prohibition laws and became known as the *Free State.*

1950 Baltimore's Friendship International Airport (now Baltimore-Washington International Airport) opened.

1952 The Chesapeake Bay Bridge (now the William Preston Lane, Jr., Memorial Bridge) was opened to traffic.

1972 Maryland voters approved a state lottery to raise money for the state government.

1980 The completion of Harborplace, a modern complex of shops and restaurants, marked a major development in the renewal of Baltimore's Inner Harbor.

On orders from the English government, Claiborne returned Maryland to Calvert in 1658. Calvert promised to uphold the religious freedoms established in 1649. But many Protestants in Maryland resented a Roman Catholic as owner of the colony. In 1689, the Protestant Association, a group led by John Coode, seized control of the colony. Coode demanded that England take over the government of Maryland. As a result, royal governors appointed by the English crown began to rule the colony in 1691.

The Calvert family regained control of Maryland in 1715 under Benedict Leonard Calvert, the fourth Lord Baltimore, who was a Protestant. In 1718, Roman Catholics in Maryland lost the right to vote. They did not regain this right until 1776. Maryland remained in the hands of the Calverts until the Revolutionary War. Maryland prospered during the years before the war. Tobacco farming in the colony became profitable. Many colonists grew wealthy and built beautiful mansions. Maryland's population grew rapidly. In the 1700's, Maryland and Pennsylvania quarreled over the boundary line between them. In 1763, both colonies agreed to have Charles Mason and Jeremiah Dixon of England survey the land. The survey was completed in 1767, and the boundary became known as Mason and Dixon's Line.

The Revolutionary War. In the mid-1700's, Great Britain found itself deeply in debt. To help raise money, Britain placed severe taxes and trade restrictions on the American Colonies. The people of Maryland, like those of the other colonies, opposed these measures. Marylanders resisted the Stamp Act of 1765 (see **Stamp Act**). In 1774, colonists in Maryland protested the Boston Port Act. This act was a British attempt to punish the people of Boston for the Boston Tea Party (see **Boston Port Act**). Marylanders burned the British ship *Peggy Stewart* and its cargo of tea in Annapolis.

In 1774, delegates from Maryland attended the First Continental Congress in Philadelphia. They supported a policy forbidding the colonists to trade with Great Britain. The Revolutionary War in America began in Massachusetts in April 1775. That May, the Second Continental Congress met in Philadelphia, and on July 2, 1776, Maryland delegates voted for independence. Maryland adopted its first constitution on Nov. 8, 1776. In December 1776, the Continental Congress moved to Baltimore because the British threatened Philadelphia. The congress remained there until the following March. Thomas Johnson, Maryland's first governor under its constitution, took office on March 21, 1777.

Maryland troops fought throughout the Revolutionary War. Baltimore industries built ships and cannons for the colonial forces. But little fighting took place on Maryland soil. British Vice Admiral Richard Howe sailed up Chesapeake Bay in 1777 and landed troops at the mouth of the Elk River. The troops moved into Pennsylvania that same year, and they defeated General George Washington in the Battle of Brandywine.

Statehood. During the war, the Continental Congress formed a government of the United States under the Articles of Confederation. Some of the states claimed western land that extended beyond their colonial boundaries. Maryland refused to sign the Articles of Confederation until the states promised to turn these western lands over to the United States government.

Maryland signed the Articles of Confederation on March 1, 1781.

After the war, the Congress of the Confederation accepted Maryland's invitation and met at the Maryland State House in Annapolis from November 1783, to June 1784. George Washington resigned his commission as commander in chief of the Continental Army in the State House. Congress also ratified the Treaty of Paris, ending the Revolutionary War, in the State House.

During the early 1780's, Maryland and Virginia disagreed over navigational rights in Chesapeake Bay and on the Potomac River. In 1785, commissioners from the two states approved the Mount Vernon Compact, which allowed both states to benefit from use of the waterways. Another interstate conference, the Annapolis Convention, met in Annapolis on Sept. 11, 1786, to discuss trade and commerce problems. When the meeting attracted representatives from only five states, the delegates called for a meeting of all the states in Philadelphia in 1787. The delegates who met in Philadelphia wrote the Constitution of the United States. Maryland *ratified* (approved) the Constitution on April 28, 1788, and became the seventh state of the Union. In 1781, Maryland gave land to Congress for the District of Columbia, the new national capital.

The War of 1812 and industrial development. Several battles of the War of 1812 were fought in Maryland. In 1813, the British raided a number of Maryland towns and farmhouses along Chesapeake Bay. During the summer of 1814, a large British force under General Robert Ross sailed up the Patuxent River. Ross's troops defeated American forces in the Battle of Bladensburg on Aug. 24, 1814. The British moved on to Washington, D.C., that same day. They burned the Capitol and other government buildings.

On Sept. 12, the British attacked Baltimore. British troops landed at North Point, southeast of Baltimore at the mouth of the Patapsco River. British ships sailed up the river and fired on Fort McHenry. But American forces defended the city and drove the British out of Maryland. The Battle of Baltimore inspired Francis Scott Key to write "The Star-Spangled Banner," which later became the national anthem of the United States. See **Star-Spangled Banner.**

During the early and middle 1800's, Baltimore grew into an important industrial city. It became a leading seaport, and one of the nation's shipbuilding centers. Goods were shipped between Baltimore and the West on the Baltimore and Ohio Railroad and on the Chesapeake and Ohio Canal. Goods were shipped eastward on the Chesapeake and Delaware Canal. In 1830, Peter Cooper built the *Tom Thumb,* the first coal-burning American steam locomotive. The Baltimore and Ohio Railroad used the *Tom Thumb* between Baltimore and Ellicott's Mills (now Ellicott City). The *De Rosset,* the first oceangoing iron steamship built in the United States, was completed in Baltimore in 1839. Maryland adopted a new constitution in 1851, its first since 1776.

The Civil War. Maryland was a slave state, but it also was one of the original 13 states of the Union. When the Civil War began in 1861, Marylanders were divided in their loyalties between the Union and the Confederacy. After Virginia joined the Confederacy, the fate of Washington, D.C., depended on whether Maryland remained

Lithograph (1887); Maryland Historical Society

The Battle of Antietam halted General Robert E. Lee's first invasion of the North during the Civil War. The bloody battle was fought near Sharpsburg on Sept. 17, 1862.

in the Union. If Maryland joined the Confederacy, Washington, D.C., would be surrounded by Confederate territory. Union forces rushed across Maryland to defend the nation's capital. Maryland finally decided to stay in the Union, but many Marylanders joined the Confederate armies.

Several Civil War battles were fought on Maryland soil. In 1862, General Robert E. Lee's Confederate troops invaded Maryland. Union forces fought them in the Battle of Antietam, near Sharpsburg, on September 17. That day, more than 12,000 Union soldiers and 10,000 Confederates were killed or wounded. Lee withdrew to Virginia the next day. In June 1863, Lee led his troops across Maryland into Pennsylvania, where he was defeated in the Battle of Gettysburg. In 1864, Confederate General Jubal A. Early crossed the Potomac River into Maryland. He defeated a Union division in the Battle of Monocacy, near Frederick, on July 9. Early's forces advanced to within sight of Washington, D.C., before Union forces drove them back.

In 1864, Maryland adopted a constitution that abolished slavery. The new constitution also placed harsh penalties on Marylanders who had supported the Confederate cause. A less severe constitution was adopted in 1867, and is still in effect.

Maryland maintained its industrial and commercial development after the Civil War. Baltimore, already a great industrial city, became a well-known cultural center in the middle and late 1800's.

The early 1900's. Maryland's industrial expansion continued into the 1900's. The state's factories and shipyards expanded greatly after the United States entered World War I in 1917. The U.S. Army established the Aberdeen Proving Ground, its first testing center, along the northwest shore of Chesapeake Bay in 1917.

In 1919, the U.S. Congress passed a law making it illegal to manufacture, sell, and transport alcoholic beverages. Marylanders were among the leading opponents of prohibition law, because they considered it a violation of their state's rights. As a result, Maryland became

known as the Free State. This nickname is still sometimes used to honor Maryland's traditions of political and religious freedoms.

The Great Depression of the 1930's struck the industrial city of Baltimore particularly hard. Maryland passed social and welfare laws in cooperation with the federal government to ease hardships. In 1938, the state legislature approved the first state income tax law and a $15-million federal housing project.

The mid-1900's. During World War II (1939-1945), manufacturing activity increased greatly in Maryland. Thousands of workers came to the state from the Appalachian mountain region and other parts of the South.

After the war, Maryland's industry and population continued to grow, and the state improved its transportation systems. Baltimore's Friendship International Airport (now Baltimore-Washington International Airport) opened in 1950. Between 1952 and 1963, the state completed the Baltimore Harbor Tunnel, the Chesapeake Bay Bridge (now the William P. Lane, Jr., Memorial Bridge), the John F. Kennedy Expressway, and an expressway connecting Baltimore and Washington.

The growth of Maryland's urban population created political problems. Until the 1960's, voters in thinly populated rural areas were electing most of the state's legislators. Between 1962 and 1966, Maryland *reapportioned* (redivided) its state legislative and United States congressional districts for more equal representation.

Maryland expanded its school system during the 1960's and 1970's. The University of Maryland, which has its main campus in College Park, opened branches in Baltimore, Catonsville, and Princess Anne. Several state teachers' colleges became general state colleges, and many two-year community colleges opened.

In 1967, Spiro T. Agnew became the fifth Republican governor in Maryland's history. In 1969, Agnew took office as Vice President of the United States under President Richard M. Nixon. Nixon and Agnew won reelection in 1972. But Agnew resigned as Vice President in 1973. He left the office when a federal grand jury investigated charges that he had participated in widespread graft as an officeholder in Maryland and as Vice President (see **Agnew, Spiro T.**).

Recent developments. Maryland's industrial growth and its location on Chesapeake Bay have tied the state economically to the northeastern industrial states. Many new cities, suburbs, and industrial communities grew up between Baltimore and Washington. The state faced the challenge of providing these expanding areas with schools, water and power supplies, and other services. In 1972, Maryland voters approved a state lottery to raise money for the state government. State officials also emphasized the need to solve the problems of air and water pollution.

The population increase during and after World War II brought changes in housing and education that are still going on in Maryland. Thousands of the people who moved to Maryland from the South were blacks. As more and more blacks settled in Baltimore, increasing numbers of white families moved to the city's suburbs. At this time, black children in Maryland attended segregated schools, as required by state law. But in 1954, the Supreme Court of the United States ruled that compulsory segregation of public schools was unconstitutional. Baltimore desegregated its public schools almost immediately. School desegregation in the rest of the state proceeded slowly but steadily, and all of Maryland's school systems are now racially integrated.

Baltimore, like many cities, had racial violence after the assassination of civil rights leader Martin Luther King, Jr., in 1968. Since then, federal, state, and local agencies have increased their efforts to end racial discrimination in education, employment, and housing.

In 1982, Maryland's government began planning a major effort to clean up Chesapeake Bay. The cleanup began in 1985 and will continue throughout the 1990's. The project involves close cooperation with Virginia, Pennsylvania, Delaware, and Washington D.C.

Today, Maryland is a national center for space research, development, and production. Basic planning for space projects is carried out at the National Aeronautics and Space Administration's Goddard Space Flight Center in Greenbelt.

Robert D. Mitchell and Edward C. Papenfuse

Study aids

Related articles in *World Book* include:

Biographies

Agnew, Spiro T.	Jenifer, Daniel of St. Thomas
Banneker, Benjamin	Key, Francis Scott
Calvert, Cecilius	McHenry, James
Calvert, Charles	Mencken, H. L.
Calvert, George	Paca, William
Carroll (family)	Ruth, Babe
Chase, Samuel	Shehan, Lawrence J. Cardinal
Davis, David	Shriver, Sargent
Decatur, Stephen	Stoddert, Benjamin
Few, William	Stone, Thomas
Hanson, John	Taney, Roger B.
Hopkins, Johns	

Cities

Annapolis	Baltimore

History

Annapolis Convention	Mason and Dixon's Line
Civil War	Revolutionary War in America
Claiborne's Rebellion	Star-Spangled Banner
Colonial life in America	War of 1812

Physical features

Allegheny Mountains
Appalachian Mountains
Chesapeake Bay
Potomac River
Susquehanna River

Other related articles

Aberdeen Proving Ground	Fort McHenry National Monument and Historic Shrine
Andrews Air Force Base	
Camp David	Maryland Day
Fort George G. Meade	National Naval Medical Center

Outline

I. People
  A. Population
  B. Schools
  C. Libraries
  D. Museums
II. Visitor's guide
  A. Places to visit
  B. Annual events
III. Land and climate
  A. Land regions
  B. Coastline
  C. Rivers and lakes
  D. Plant and animal life
  E. Climate
IV. Economy
  A. Natural resources
  B. Service industries
  C. Manufacturing
  D. Agriculture

  E. Mining
  F. Fishing industry
  G. Electric power
  H. Transportation
  I. Communication
V. Government
  A. Constitution   E. Local government
  B. Executive   F. Revenue
  C. Legislature   G. Politics
  D. Courts
VI. History

Questions

For whom was Maryland named?

Why did Maryland delay signing the Articles of Confederation?

What important developments in transportation occurred in Maryland during the 1800's?

Why does the federal government play an important role in Maryland's economy?

Why did the fate of Washington, D.C., depend on whether Maryland remained in the Union during the Civil War?

What are Maryland's two leading manufacturing industries?

What famous Marylander wrote "The Star-Spangled Banner"? Under what circumstances?

When and why did Maryland give land to the U.S. government?

By what name has the Maryland-Pennsylvania boundary become known? Why?

Why is Maryland called the *Old Line State? The Free State?*

Additional resources

Level I

Boyce-Ballweber, Hettie. *The First People of Maryland.* Maryland Hist. Pr., 1987.

Carpenter, Allan. *Maryland.* Rev. ed. Childrens Pr., 1979.

Finlayson, Ann. *Colonial Maryland.* Thomas Nelson, 1974.

Fradin, Dennis B. *The Maryland Colony.* Childrens Pr., 1990.

Kent, Deborah. *Maryland.* Childrens Pr., 1990.

Wilson, Richard, and Bridner, E. L., Jr. *Maryland: Its Past and Present.* Rev. ed. Maryland Hist. Pr., 1987. First published in 1983.

Level II

Bode, Carl. *Maryland: A Bicentennial History.* Norton, 1978.

Brugger, Robert J. *Maryland: A Middle Temperament, 1634-1980.* Johns Hopkins, 1988.

Callcott, George H. *Maryland and America: 1940 to 1980.* Johns Hopkins, 1985.

Carey, George G. *Maryland Folklore.* Rev. ed. Tidewater, 1989.

DiLisio, James E. *Maryland: A Geography.* Westview, 1983.

Evitts, William J. *A Matter of Allegiances: Maryland from 1850 to 1861.* Johns Hopkins, 1974.

Iams, James D. *Bayside Impressions: Maryland's Eastern Shore and the Chesapeake Bay.* Tidewater, 1984.

Maryland: A History, 1632-1974. Ed. by Richard Walsh and W. L. Fox. Maryland Hist. Soc., 1974.

Maryland: A New Guide to the Old Line State. Ed. by Edward C. Papenfuse and others. Johns Hopkins, 1976.

Rollo, Vera A. F. *The Black Experience in Maryland: An Illustrated History.* 2nd ed. Maryland Hist. Pr., 1984.

Maryland Day is a holiday observed on March 25 in the state of Maryland. It commemorates the first Roman Catholic Mass colonists celebrated when they landed in 1634. The first action of the colonists after landing on the shores of St. Clements Island in the Potomac River was to celebrate the Feast of the Annunciation.

Maryland System, University of, is a coeducational, state-assisted system of higher education. It includes 11 degree-granting institutions and 3 major research and service centers.

Five of the University of Maryland System's degree-granting institutions are located in the Baltimore region. They are the University of Baltimore, the University of Maryland at Baltimore, Coppin State College, and Tow-

University of Maryland

The University of Maryland campus in College Park, Md., lies in a wooded area near Washington, D.C.

son State University, all in Baltimore; and the University of Maryland Baltimore County, in Catonsville. The system's other degree-granting institutions are Bowie State University, in Bowie; Frostburg State University, in Frostburg; Salisbury State University, in Salisbury; the University of Maryland College Park, in College Park; the University of Maryland Eastern Shore, in Princess Anne; and the University of Maryland University College, headquartered in College Park.

The various campuses of the University of Maryland System offer instruction in many fields, including arts and humanities, journalism, business, education, social work, engineering, science, health science, and law. Each campus grants bachelor's and master's degrees. Four campuses also grant doctor's degrees in certain fields.

The University of Maryland College Park is the largest school in the system. The College Park campus offers 125 undergraduate majors and more than 80 graduate programs. The University of Maryland at Baltimore, founded in 1807, is one of the nation's oldest and largest centers of graduate and professional education. The University of Maryland University College offers part-time programs at about 20 locations in Maryland, Virginia, and Washington, D.C. Its European and Asian divisions offer degree programs to United States military families in more than 20 countries.

The University of Maryland System's major research and service centers are the Center for Environmental and Estuarine Studies, the Maryland Biotechnology Institute, and the Maryland Institute for Agriculture and

Natural Resources. The Maryland legislature established the University of Maryland System in 1988. For the enrollment at various campuses, see **Universities and colleges** (table).

Critically reviewed by the University of Maryland System

Masaccio, *muh SAH chee OH* (1401-1428), an Italian painter, was one of the first great masters of the Italian Renaissance. He brought a new naturalness to painting through the use of strong modeling and lifelike poses. His *The Holy Trinity* is the first monumental painting to use the newly invented device of perspective. The effects of light and atmosphere also gave a new realism to his work. Masaccio's art was admired by many famous Italian painters, including Michelangelo and Raphael.

The Holy Trinity with the Virgin and Saint John (1425), a fresco in the church of Santa Maria Novella, Florence, Italy; SCALA

A painting by Masaccio shows his ability to create solid-looking forms through the use of perspective and light and shade.

Masaccio was born in San Giovanni di Valdarno, Italy, near Florence. His real name was Tommaso Cassai, but he was nicknamed Masaccio—which means *simple Tom* —because of his absent-mindedness. He studied art in Florence and gained recognition as a master painter by the time he was 21.

Masaccio's most important work is a series of frescoes in the church of Santa Maria del Carmine in Florence. One of the paintings in this series, *The Tribute Money,* shows his advanced use of form and perspective. It is reproduced in color in the **Painting** article.

David Summers

See also **Painting** (The Renaissance); **Renaissance** (The fine arts).

Masada, *muh SAHD uh* or *muh SAYD uh,* was a historic Jewish fortress that stood on a huge rock in Judea (now southern Israel). The rock is also called *Masada,* the Hebrew word for *mountain fortress.* In A.D. 73, 960 Jewish patriots killed themselves at Masada rather than surrender to Roman troops. For many Israelis, this devotion to liberty is a national symbol called the "spirit of Masada."

The rock is about 20 miles (32 kilometers) southeast of Hebron. For location, see **Dead Sea** (map). Masada has cliffs that rise 1,400 feet (427 meters). The top of the rock is flat and measures about 1,900 feet (579 meters) long and 650 feet (198 meters) wide.

The Jewish leader Jonathan established the fortress during the Hasmonean Revolt (167-142 B.C.). During that period, the Jews successfully fought for their independence from the Syrians. In 63 B.C., the Romans gained control of Judea. Herod the Great, who was appointed king of Judea by the Romans in 40 B.C., reinforced the fortress and also built two palaces on the rock.

Jewish patriots called *Zealots* captured Masada in A.D. 66, when the Roman governor Gessius Florus ruled Judea. In A.D. 73, just before the Romans recaptured the fortress, Eleazer Ben Jair, the leader of the Zealots, persuaded the Jews to burn the camp and commit suicide. Only two women and five children survived. Byzantine monks settled briefly on Masada during the 400's and 500's.

From 1963 to 1965, an archaeological expedition headed by Yigael Yadin of Israel discovered various ruins of ancient Masada, including Herod's palaces. The expedition also found armor, Biblical and other scrolls, coins, ritual baths, and a synagogue. Today, many tourists and Israeli citizens visit Masada.   Jane S. Gerber

See also **Jews** (Roman rule).

Masai. See **Kenya** (Way of life; picture).

Masaryk, *MAS uh rihk,* was the family name of two Czech statesmen, father and son.

Tomáš Garrigue Masaryk, *TAW mahsh guh REEG* (1850-1937), was a scholar and a statesman who, with his student Eduard Beneš, founded Czechoslovakia in 1918 (see **Beneš, Eduard**). Masaryk became the country's first president in 1918, and served until 1935.

Czech Embassy

Tomáš Masaryk

He began his career in 1891 in the Austro-Hungarian parliament, where he fought for the rights of Slavic minority groups. When World War I broke out, he fled to Switzerland and then to England. In his absence, the Austro-Hungarian government in 1916 sentenced him to death for high treason.

Masaryk came to the United States in 1917 to seek support for his dream of an independent Czechoslovakia. He met with President Woodrow Wilson, and with Czechs, Slovaks, and Ruthenes who lived in America. Masaryk gained his objective when the Allied armies defeated Austria-Hungary in 1918. The Republic of Czechoslovakia was created from a part of Austria-Hungary.

Masaryk's 17-year term as president of the Czechoslovak republic was generally a time of peace and prosperity. But the Slovaks gradually became restless, because they thought he had not fulfilled a promise to grant them the right of self-government. Also, the German minority group turned increasingly to Nazi Germany for sympathy and help. Masaryk resigned in 1935 because of poor health. Beneš succeeded him.

Masaryk was born on an estate in Moravia, where his father served as a coachman to the Austrian emperor, Francis Joseph. He was educated at the universities of Vienna and Leipzig. He taught philosophy and sociology at Charles University in Prague.

Jan Garrigue Masaryk, *yahn guh REEG* (1886-1948), the son of Tomáš, entered the Czechoslovak foreign service in 1919, and served as minister to London from 1925 to 1938. In 1940, he became foreign minister of the Czechoslovak government-in-exile. When the government returned to Czechoslovakia after World War II (1939-1945), Masaryk kept the post of foreign minister. He fought a losing battle from 1945 to 1948 against the increasing level of Communist domination of Czechoslovakia.

© Manley Features from Shostal

Masada was a Jewish fortress in what is now southern Israel. In A.D. 73, more than 900 Jewish patriots committed suicide there rather than surrender to Roman troops.

Masaryk died mysteriously in 1948. His body was found in a courtyard, three stories under his apartment window in Prague. It has never been determined whether he was murdered or killed himself in protest against the Communist seizure of the government in February 1948. He was born in Prague.   R. V. Burks

See also **Czechoslovakia** (History).

Masbate. See Philippines (The main islands).

Mascagni, *mahs KAH nyee,* **Pietro,** *PYEH traw* (1863-1945), was an Italian opera composer. He studied music in Livorno, his birthplace. In 1888, Mascagni entered a one-act opera in a competition and won first prize. The opera, *Cavalleria Rusticana,* was a drama of raw passion in a Sicilian village. It was presented in Rome in 1890 and made Mascagni world famous as the leader of a realistic, boisterous operatic style called *verismo* (see **Opera** [*Cavalleria Rusticana*]). Mascagni never came close to repeating his first success. He composed 15 operas, but the only other one still performed is *L'Amico Fritz* (1891).

Mascagni died a disappointed and almost discredited composer. He seemed to lack the creative imagination to overcome public expectations after the worldwide success of *Cavalleria.* The opera remains popular because of its emotional melodies and the theatrical force of its *libretto* (words).   Charles H. Webb

Mascons. See Moon (Gravity).

Masculine gender. See Gender.

Masefield, John (1878-1967), was an English poet, novelist, critic, and playwright. He was appointed poet laureate of England in 1930 (see **Poet laureate**). His 37-year term as poet laureate is among the longest and most distinguished in English literature.

Masefield was born at Ledbury in what is now the county of Hereford and Worcester. He was apprenticed as a seaman when he was 13 and spent four years at sea. His experiences influenced his poetry and his fiction. Masefield is most celebrated as a sea poet and as one who sings of "the dust and scum of the earth" and of "the maimed, of the halt and the blind in the rain and the cold." Many of his works tell tales of love and tragedy among the people of Shropshire and among vagabonds and men of the sea.

British Combine
John Masefield

Masefield wrote more than 100 books. He first won recognition for his collection of poetry *Salt-Water Ballads* (1902). His best-known works are the long narrative poems *The Everlasting Mercy* (1911), *The Widow in the Bye Street* (1912), *Dauber* (1913), and *Reynard the Fox* (1919). His individual poems include "A Consecration," "On Growing Old," and "Sea Fever." His popular novels include the adventure tales *Sard Harker* (1924) and *The Bird of Dawning* (1933). Masefield also wrote an autobiography, *So Long to Learn* (1952).   William Harmon

Maser, *MAY zuhr,* is a device that generates or amplifies microwaves. The word *maser* stands for *Microwave Amplification by Stimulated Emission of Radiation.*

The essential part of a maser is a substance that has been put into an *excited* (higher energy) state. In this state, the atoms of the substance are able to radiate energy of a particular frequency when *stimulated* (triggered) by a microwave of the same frequency. The energy released by the atoms is added to the stimulating wave, amplifying it.

In the *ammonia maser,* heat is used to excite ammonia gas. The first ammonia maser was built in the United States in 1954. Masers are used for the amplification of weak microwave signals from distant stars and for communications.   William B. Case

See also **Laser.**

Maseru, *MAZ uh ROO* (pop. 109,382), is the capital of Lesotho. It lies near the northwest border. For location, see **Lesotho** (map). A railroad links Maseru with cities in South Africa, which surrounds Lesotho. The city is the seat of government for the country, and has a hospital and technical training school where manual and local arts are taught. Most of the people who live in Maseru are black Africans called *Sotho.* Maseru's other people include Europeans and black refugees from South Africa.   Bruce Fetter

Mash. See Whiskey; Brewing.

Mask is a covering that disguises or protects the face. Most masks worn as a disguise have the features of a human being or an animal. In the United States, such masks are generally worn for fun at masquerades and on Halloween and other special occasions. Various kinds of protective masks serve different purposes. For example, a welder wears a steel mask with a special lens that protects his eyes from the intense light produced by welding.

Throughout history, people in almost every society have used masks as a disguise. By hiding the features of the face, masks prevent other people from making judgments about the wearer's personality and character. Most of these masks not only hide the identity of the wearer but supposedly also give him magic powers. Such masks represent gods or spirits. The custom of wearing masks probably began with animal heads worn by people. Such masks may have been used in hunting. They probably served as disguises and as magic symbols to make the hunt successful. However, masks may have developed from the practice of marking the face with colorful designs that had magic powers.

Some masks are made of paper or are carved from wood or stone. Others are made of cloth, grass, hide, leather, metal, or shell. Some masks have realistic human or animal features, but others give the wearer a grotesque appearance. Many masks represent the art forms of a society. The masks may involve highly developed craft skills and may be painted with symbolic designs and colors.

This article discusses masks worn for other purposes than to protect the face. Such masks may be divided into four groups according to their major use: (1) ceremonial masks, (2) theatrical masks, (3) burial masks and death masks, and (4) festival masks. These categories overlap, however. Many burial masks, for example, serve ceremonial purposes.

Ceremonial masks developed from the belief of many primitive societies that gods controlled the forces of nature. Dancers at various ceremonies wore masks

Marvin Newman, Woodfin Camp, Inc.

Colorful masks are worn in many countries during *carnival,* a period of merrymaking just before Lent. Carnival celebrations include such festivities as masked balls, parades, and dancing in the streets. The drummers shown above are marching in a carnival procession in Basel, Switzerland.

Field Museum of Natural History (WORLD BOOK photo)

Some masks have skirts that cover much of the wearer's body. The mask on the left was made by the Cubeo Indians of Colombia; the one on the right, by the Senesi people of Papua New Guinea.

Field Museum of Natural History (WORLD BOOK photo)

Many masks have grotesque features. A demon mask from Sri Lanka, *left,* has fangs and bulging eyes. A Chinese theatrical mask, *right,* represents an official of hell in a religious play.

that represented these gods. A mask made its wearer unrecognizable, and so he seemed to almost lose his identity and become the spirit itself. When these ceremonial dancers wore such masks, the people believed that the gods were actually present. If people wore a mask that represented a certain spirit, the powers of that spirit supposedly remained for many generations. After the wearer of the mask died, another man took his place in wearing it.

Many Indian tribes of North America used masks in their ceremonies. Male members of the False Face Society of the Iroquois Indians wore wooden masks at ceremonies held to heal the sick. The False Face performers visited villages and were often escorted by male clowns called Shuck Faces, who wore masks made of braided corn husks. Adults welcomed the masked visitors, but most of the children became terrified.

The Indians of the northwest Pacific Coast used masks with a movable mouth and eyelids. They wore these masks in ceremonies honoring certain animals. Many of these masks actually consisted of two or three masks. The outer mask of a double mask—or the two outer masks of a triple mask—represented a bird or some other animal. The outer mask could be folded back, revealing a mask of a human face. Such masks are related to the belief that some human beings had the power to change into animals and back again. This belief was common among many societies.

Some peoples in New Guinea, West Africa, the Amazon region of South America, and the southwestern United States still use masks in spiritual ceremonies. For example, the Hopi Indians of Arizona have special ceremonies in which male dancers wear masks that represent their ancestors or certain gods. The people believe the ceremonies bring visits from these beings, who appear in the form of spirits called *Kachinas.* Kachinas produce rain, make corn grow, and sometimes whip young boys and girls who are about to be formally initiated into adulthood. The masks are also called Kachinas.

Some primitive peoples wore grotesque masks when they went to war. They believed that the appearance of these masks, which represented their gods, would frighten the enemy.

Theatrical masks. The ancient Greeks used masks in their classical drama, which developed from religious ceremonies of earlier times. Masked singers and dancers represented gods and mythological heroes. The masks also expressed anger, joy, love, and other emotions. These masks were needed to let the audience follow the action of the play. The theaters were so large that many people could not see the facial expressions of the actors. Also, simple amplifiers built into the masks helped carry an actor's voice a great distance.

Since ancient times, Chinese drama has used masks to help portray types of characters. The color of the mask plays an important part in the drama. For example, red represents a loyal person, and white represents a cruel one. A type of dramatic entertainment called a *masque* developed from the use of masks as disguises in musical pageants during the Renaissance (see **Masque**). A type of Japanese play called *no* uses many masks, each representing a different emotion.

Burial masks and death masks have had an important role in many societies. The ancient Egyptians put a personalized mask over the face of every mummy, or they made the mask part of the mummy case. The mask supposedly identified the dead person so that the wandering soul could always find its body.

Some peoples still use masks in ceremonies relating to death. In an annual mourning ceremony held on New Ireland, an island near Australia, dancers wear masks that represent certain dead persons. The spirits of the dead supposedly return during the ceremony.

The Aleuts, who live on the Aleutian Islands of Alaska, put a mask on people after they die. They believe the mask protects the dead from the dangerous glances of spirits. Some Indian tribes of the Andes Mountains of South America also follow this custom.

In Western countries, death masks are sometimes used to preserve the features of the dead. A plaster cast is made of the face, and plaster likenesses are made from this mold. Famous death masks include those of Ludwig van Beethoven and Napoleon Bonaparte.

Granger Collection

Museum of the American Indian, New York City

Burial masks are important in many societies. The Egyptian king Tutankhamen's golden burial mask was made from a cast of his face taken after he died. The Aleuts—a people native to Alaska—cover the faces of their dead with a wooden mask.

Festival masks developed from masks used in religious ceremonies. Some North American Indian tribes continue to use such masks in harvest festivals. Processions and festivals in China, India, and other countries also include masked people. In the United States, people wear masks at Mardi Gras. Alan Dundes

For pictures of masks, see **Africa; Drama** (Greek drama); **Indian, American.**

Maslow, *MAS loh,* **Abraham Harold** (1908-1970), was an American psychologist whom many people consider the founder of a movement called *humanistic psychology.* The movement developed as a revolt against behaviorism and psychoanalysis, the two most popular psychological views of the mid-1900's. Humanistic psychologists believe individuals are controlled by their own values and choices and not by the environment, as behaviorists think, or by unconscious drives, as psychoanalysts believe. Maslow stressed the importance of studying well-adjusted people in society instead of only disturbed ones.

Maslow identified several levels of human needs, the most basic of which must be satisfied before the next levels can be fulfilled. The most basic needs are bodily drives, such as hunger and thirst. Succeeding levels include the needs for safety and love. The highest need is for the fulfillment of one's unique potential, which Maslow called *self-actualization.*

Maslow was born in New York City. He wrote several books, including *Motivation and Personality* (1954) and *Toward a Psychology of Being* (1962). Ricardo B. Morant

Mason (bricklayer). See **Building trade.**

Mason (Freemason). See **Masonry.**

Mason, Charles. See **Mason and Dixon's Line.**

Mason, George (1725-1792), was a Virginia statesman who wrote the first American bill of rights, the Virginia Declaration of Rights of 1776. In 1787, Mason played an important role in the Constitutional Convention, though he refused to sign the final draft of the United States Constitution. Mason held few public offices, but his writings and leadership had great influence.

Perhaps Mason's most important work was his writing of the Virginia Declaration of Rights. Thomas Jefferson drew on this document when he wrote the Declaration of Independence. James Madison also used Mason's ideas in 1789

Virginia Museum of Fine Arts, Gift of K. E. Bruce

George Mason

when he drafted the 10 constitutional amendments that became the Bill of Rights.

His constitutional views. Mason played an active role in creating the Constitution but disagreed with parts of it. For example, he favored a system of *proportional representation,* in which a state's population determines the number of its members in Congress. But he eventually supported the compromise that gave each state an equal vote in the Senate and a proportional vote in the House of Representatives.

Mason objected strongly to the compromise that allowed the importation of slaves to go on until 1808. He was one of the few Southerners who opposed slavery. He felt slaves should be educated and gradually freed.

Mason also had other concerns. He opposed concentrating executive power in one person—the President— without an advisory council appointed by the House of Representatives. He feared that the Senate might develop into an aristocratic institution that would dominate the government. He was concerned that the economic interests of the South might be damaged if laws regulating commerce could be passed by a simple majority in each house of Congress. Mason also wanted a bill of rights to protect personal liberties against possible interference by the federal government.

Mason was dissatisfied because his fellow delegates did not meet these concerns, and he refused to sign the Constitution. When the Constitution was submitted to the states for ratification, he opposed it, and made the absence of a bill of rights his main objection. The Bill of Rights was finally added in 1791.

Early life. Mason was born in Fairfax County, Virginia, where his family had extensive landholdings. He studied law, managed his plantation, and was active in community affairs. His paper *Extracts from the Virginia Charters* (1773) formed a basis for U.S. claims to land south of the Great Lakes.

Mason preferred private life and refused many public offices. Finally, he became a member of the second Virginia Convention in Richmond in 1775. He also attended the third Virginia Convention in Williamsburg in 1776, where he wrote the Declaration of Rights and a large part of the state Constitution.   Jack N. Rakove

Mason, James Murray (1798-1871), served as Confederate commissioner to Britain during the American Civil War (1861-1865). As commissioner, he became a key figure in a naval incident called the Trent Affair.

In 1861, Commissioner Mason sailed for Europe aboard a British ship, the *Trent.* His primary mission was to gain British aid for the South. While at sea, a Union warship stopped the *Trent* and seized Mason and John Slidell, the Confederate commissioner to France. This action resulted in a diplomatic crisis that nearly caused Britain to declare war on the Union. The crisis passed after Mason and Slidell were released in 1862. Mason went on to London but failed to win aid for the South.

Mason was born in what is now Washington, D.C. He represented Virginia in the U.S. House of Representatives from 1837 to 1839 and in the Senate from 1847 to 1861. Mason's grandfather George Mason wrote the Virginia Declaration of Rights of 1776, which formed the basis for the U.S. Bill of Rights.   Michael Perman

See also **Mason, George; Slidell, John; Trent Affair.**

Mason, Lowell (1792-1872), was an influential American music educator and composer of hymn tunes. He wrote over 1,650 religious compositions and published many popular works, including hymn collections and books on music and music education. His best-known compositions include "Nearer My God to Thee" and "From Greenland's Icy Mountains." Mason was the first music teacher in American public schools, and became superintendent of music for Boston public schools in 1838. He founded the Boston Academy of Music with George J. Webb in 1833. Mason was born in Medfield, Mass. See also **America** (hymn).   Leonard W. Van Camp

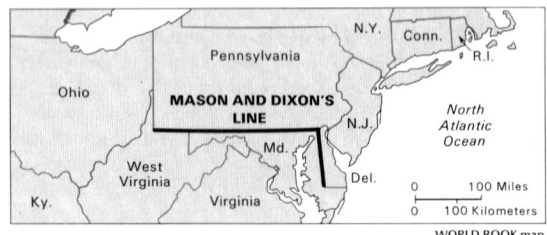

Location of Mason and Dixon's Line

Mason and Dixon's Line is usually thought of as the line that divides the North and the South. Actually it is the east-west boundary line that separates Pennsylvania from Maryland and part of West Virginia, and the north-south boundary between Maryland and Delaware. Before the Civil War, the southern boundary of Pennsylvania was considered the dividing line between the slave and nonslave states.

In the 1700's, a boundary quarrel arose between Pennsylvania and Maryland. The two agreed to settle the dispute by having the land surveyed. In 1763, they called in two English astronomers, Charles Mason and Jeremiah Dixon. They completed their survey in 1767. The line was named after them.

The surveyors set up milestones to mark the boundary. Through the years, souvenir hunters removed many stones and used them as doorsteps and curbstones. However, authorities recovered many of these stones and replaced nearly all the stolen markers. Occasionally a dispute arose as to the exact location of the line. But surveys made in 1849 and 1900 showed there was no important error in the line Mason and Dixon decided upon. A survey during the 1960's resulted in a slight shift of the line, which is now at 39°43'19.521" north latitude.   Ray Allen Billington

Mason and Slidell. See Mason, James Murray; Slidell, John.

Masonry, also called Freemasonry, is the name of one of the oldest and largest fraternal organizations in the world. The organization's official name is Free and Accepted Masons. Masonry is dedicated to the ideals of charity, equality, morality, and service to God. Masons donate millions of dollars each year to charitable projects, including hospitals; homes for widows, orphans, and the aged; relief for people in distress; and scholarships. The organization has millions of members worldwide, including more than $2\frac{1}{2}$ million in the United States.

Symbols and rituals are an important part of Masonry. At times, some Masons dress in elaborate, colorful costumes and take part in dramatic ceremonies, many of which are kept secret from all except members. Most masonic symbols and rituals are based on the tools and practices of the building professions. Masons call God the "Great Architect of the Universe."

Masons try to promote "morality in which all men agree, that is, to be good men and true." Throughout its history, Masonry has sought to bring together men of different religious beliefs and political opinions. Men of any religion who profess belief in one God may join. Historically, however, most Masons have been Protestants. During much of its history, Masonry normally did

33rd degree Mason

F. N. Kistner Co. (WORLD BOOK photos)
Knight Templar

Oil painting on canvas by Stanley Massey Arthurs; Acacia Mutual Life Insurance Co., Washington, D.C.

George Washington, wearing his regalia as a member of the Masons, laid the cornerstone of the United States Capitol in Washington, D.C., in 1793. The historic ceremony took place under the sponsorship of the Grand Lodge of Maryland.

not admit Roman Catholics as members, in part because the Catholic Church prohibited Catholics from becoming Masons.

The lodges and degrees of Masonry. Men who .wish to become Masons must apply for membership. They are not invited to join. Most of these individuals apply through a friend who is already a member. After a man has been accepted by the Masons, he joins a *Blue Lodge,* the basic organization of Masonry. Members of Blue Lodges may hold three degrees. When they join, they automatically receive the *Entered Apprentice* degree. Later, they may earn the second degree, called *Fellowcraft,* and the third degree, called *Master Mason.* To earn each degree, a Mason must learn certain lessons and participate in a ceremony that illustrates them. After a Mason acquires the third degree in a Blue Lodge, he may be invited to join either or both of the two branches of advanced Masonry—the *Scottish Rite* and the *York Rite.* He may receive further degrees as a member of these branches.

If a Mason enters the Scottish Rite, he may advance through 29 degrees that are designated both by names and numbers. The first degree in the Scottish Rite is the fourth degree in Masonry. The highest degree in the Scottish Rite is the 33rd, an honorary degree that members receive in recognition of outstanding service to Masonry, the community, or the nation. This degree is commonly called *Sovereign Grand Inspector General.*

If a Mason chooses to advance in the York Rite, the first four degrees he receives are called *Degrees of the Chapter.* The next three degrees make up the *Degrees of the Council.* In some U.S. states, members of the York Rite do not have to receive the Degrees of the Council in order to go on to higher degrees in the rite. The three highest degrees make up the *Orders of the Commandery.* The highest degree in the York Rite is that of *Knight Templar.*

The names *Scottish Rite* and *York Rite* are symbols of early times in Masonry. The earliest traditions are associated with Scotland and the city of York, England.

Organization. In most countries, all the Blue Lodges are governed by a National Grand Lodge headed by a Grand Master. But neither the United States nor Canada has a National Grand Lodge. Instead, each state or province has its own Grand Lodge and Grand Master.

More than a hundred fraternal organizations have a relationship with Masonry, but they do not form part of its basic structure. One of the best known is the *Order of the Eastern Star,* an organization for women relatives of Masons who have achieved at least the degree of

Master Mason. The Masons and the Order of the Eastern Star also sponsor organizations for boys and girls. Boys may join the *Order of DeMolay.* Girls may become members of *Job's Daughters* in some U.S. states and *Rainbow for Girls* in others.

The *Ancient Arabic Order of Nobles of the Mystic Shrine* admits members who are at least 32nd degree Masons in the Scottish Rite or Knights Templar in the York Rite. There are three Shrine-associated organizations for wives and some female relatives of Shrine members. They are the *Ladies Oriental Shrine of North America, Daughters of the Nile,* and *Imperial Council Shrine Guilds of America, Inc.*

Prince Hall Freemasonry is a separate masonic organization for men. Almost all of its 275,000 members are black Americans. Nearly all other Masons are white. Prince Hall Masons are devoted to the same ideals as other Masons. In addition, the structure of the organization of Prince Hall Freemasonry resembles that of the principal Masonry group. For example, in each state with Prince Hall lodges, one Grand Master heads all lodges in the state. Prince Hall members also earn degrees that are similar to those earned by other Masons. However, many white Masons claim that Prince Hall Freemasonry is not a true Masonic organization.

History. Many of the ideas and rituals of Masonry originated in the period of cathedral building from the 900's to the 1600's. At that time, stonemasons formed associations called *guilds* in various European cities and towns. With the decline of cathedral building in the 1600's, many masons' organizations became social societies. They began accepting members who had never been stoneworkers and called these men *speculative masons.*

In the early 1700's, speculative masons created the complicated masonic system of rituals and symbols that is still in use today. The system is based on stonemason traditions and on ideas developed during the Age of Reason (see **Age of Reason**).

In 1717, four fraternal lodges, which originally may have been masons' organizations, united under the Grand Lodge of England. The Masons of today consider the formation of the Grand Lodge of England to be the beginning of their organized society. The order spread quickly to other lands and included such famous men as the American statesman Benjamin Franklin, King Frederick II of Prussia, the Austrian composer Wolfgang Amadeus Mozart, U.S. President George Washington, and the French philosopher Voltaire.

British colonists brought Masonry to North America, where it developed into two separate organizations, one for whites and one for blacks. White Masonry was popular in the early 1800's. But its involvement in politics and its secrecy contributed to an antimasonic movement in the late 1820's and early 1830's. This movement almost destroyed the organization. White Masonry regained its popularity by the mid-1860's. By the 1880's, it had become a highly respected organization whose members included prominent businessmen, ministers, and politicians. During the 1900's, white Masonry became one of the world's largest fraternal organizations.

The organization for blacks, Prince Hall Freemasonry, was founded by Prince Hall, a free black Methodist minister who settled in the Boston area in 1765. White American Masons had refused to admit blacks into their lodges. But in 1775, a British Army lodge admitted Hall and 14 other free blacks. Soon these 15 men formed African Lodge 1, but white American Masons refused to grant the lodge a charter. It received its charter, as African Lodge 459, in 1787 from the Grand Lodge of England. In 1791, the American Prince Hall Grand Lodge was established. Before the Civil War (1861-1865), this lodge spread mainly throughout the U.S. states in which slavery was illegal. After the war, the lodge expanded into the South.

Prince Hall and other early black Masons protested slavery and sought to improve the status of free blacks. More recently, many Prince Hall lodges have taken part in the U.S. civil rights movement. Prince Hall members have included the historian and sociologist W. E. B. Du-Bois and Thurgood Marshall, the first black justice of the U.S. Supreme Court.   Lynn Dumenil

Related articles in *World Book* include:
De Molay, Order of   Rainbow for Girls
Eastern Star   Shrine, The
Job's Daughters

Masqat. See Muscat.

Masque, *mask* or *mahsk,* was an elaborate form of entertainment presented at European courts. The masque reached its height in England during the early 1600's. English masques combined dancing, drama, music, and poetry with lavish sets and costumes, often to convey a moral message. Masques were presented as part of banquets to honor visiting royalty or to celebrate such events as a coronation, holiday, or wedding.

The English architect Inigo Jones was the most gifted designer of English masques. Beginning in 1605, he collaborated in the production of masques with the English poet and playwright Ben Jonson. Many of their works opened with an *antimasque*—that is, an *allegory* (symbolic story) in song, dance, and poetry involving gro-

tesque and comic characters. The masque followed, portraying in allegory the triumph of the forces of good and virtue—roles often acted and danced by the royal hosts and their courtiers. At the close, actors danced with partners from the audience.   Albert Wertheim

See also **Drama** (picture: Masques).

Mass is often defined as the amount of matter in an object. However, scientists usually define mass as a measure of *inertia,* which is a property of all matter. Inertia is the tendency of a motionless object to remain motionless and of a moving object to continue moving at a constant speed and in the same direction. See **Inertia.**

The greater an object's mass, the more difficult it is to change its velocity. For example, a locomotive has a greater mass than an automobile. For this reason, it takes more force to stop a locomotive than to stop an automobile if both are moving at the same speed.

Force, mass, and acceleration are related by Newton's *second law of motion* (see **Motion** [Newton's laws of motion]). This law is represented by the equation $F=ma,$ where F is force, m is mass, and a is acceleration.

The unit of mass depends on the system of *mechanical units* used. Scientists prefer to use the Meter-Kilogram-Second (MKS) absolute system, in which the unit of mass is the kilogram (1,000 grams). Engineers prefer the Foot-Pound-Second (FPS) gravitational system, in which the unit of mass is the *slug.* One slug equals 14.594 kilograms.

Mass and weight are not the same thing. Weight is the force on an object due to the gravitational pull of a planet or other heavenly body. An object within a planet's pull of gravity weighs less the farther it is from the planet's surface. However, the object's mass remains constant, no matter where it is.

Conservation of mass. The law of the conservation of mass states that mass cannot be created or destroyed. This law has also been called the law of conservation of matter because scientists once thought that an object lost mass only by giving up some of its matter. However, we now know that an object also loses mass when it loses energy and gains mass when it gains energy.

In chemical reactions, the mass changes are very small. For example, when coal burns, it produces heat energy along with carbon dioxide, water vapor, and ash. This reaction results in a loss of only 0.0003 gram for every million grams of coal burned. But nuclear reactions, such as those that occur in a nuclear reactor, result in a huge release of energy accompanied by a significant loss of mass. A million grams of uranium undergoing nuclear fission loses about 750 grams.

Most of the energy lost by burning coal or fissioning uranium is reabsorbed by other atoms and becomes mass again, according to Albert Einstein's famous equation $E=mc^2.$ In this formula, E represents energy, m represents mass, and c is the speed of light. See also **E=mc².**   Lucille B. Garmon

Related articles in *World Book* include:
Density   Lavoisier, Antoine L.
Energy   Matter
Force   Weight
Gravitation

Mass is the name used by several Christian churches for the celebration of the sacrament of the Eucharist, or Lord's Supper. In this important ritual, the worshiping community gathers to give thanks and praise to God and to participate in the ongoing mystery of the death and Resurrection of Jesus Christ. This celebration is called the Mass by Roman Catholics, and by some Episcopal and Lutheran churches. The Eastern Orthodox service known as the *Divine Liturgy* is similar to the Mass. Other Christians celebrate it in similar rituals.

The Mass has two major parts. The first part is a service that includes readings from Scripture and a sermon. The second part is a Eucharistic rite of prayer focusing on a remembrance of the Last Supper, the basis of the sacrament of Holy Communion (see **Communion**). Worshipers sing hymns and say prayers during the Mass.

The Eucharist was instituted by Jesus, who shared bread and wine with His disciples at the Last Supper. Most Christians believe that Jesus intended His words and actions during the Last Supper to be continued in a sacramental ritual. They base their belief upon accounts of the Last Supper in the Gospels and 1 Corinthians in the New Testament.

The word *Mass* comes from the Latin word *mittere,* meaning "to send." People who had gathered to celebrate the Lord's Supper or the "breaking of the bread" were then sent forth to practice what they had celebrated.   Richard L. Schebera

See also **Liturgy; Religion** (picture: The Mass); **Roman Catholic Church** (The Eucharist).

Mass media. See **Advertising** (Social effects); **Communication.**

Mass number. See **Atom** (The mass number).

Mass production is the production of machinery and other articles in standard sizes in large numbers. Mass production makes it possible to manufacture things faster, and often at less cost. It also means that a replacement can be obtained for any part of a manufacturing machine or other product that breaks down.

Mass production began in 1800, when the United States was building up its army. Until that time, gunsmiths started a second gun only after they had completed the first one. Thus, each gun was a little different.

In 1798, the government hired the inventor Eli Whitney to make 10,000 muskets in two years. By 1800, Whitney had delivered only 500. He was called to Washington to explain the delay.

In front of a board of experts, Whitney placed 10 musket barrels, 10 stocks, 10 triggers, and so on, in separate piles. Then he assembled 10 muskets from the pieces, showing that anyone could do this if the parts were identical. In this way, Whitney demonstrated the basis of mass production—the interchangeability of parts. He had spent about two years developing *machine tools* that made identical parts.

In 1918, five engineering societies established what is now the American National Standards Institute, Inc. The institute studies and sets up standards of quality and methods of interchangeability for mass-produced parts in most U.S. industries.

In the early 1900's, Henry Ford originated the moving assembly line for manufacturing automobiles. After the automobile parts are made, the automobile frame is attached to a conveyor belt. This belt consists of a chain that moves along the floor of the factory. Workers are stationed along the chain in an assembly line. As the car moves slowly along the line, each worker does a special

task. The task must be done in a certain length of time, and with exactness, because the work of the entire line is stopped if it is necessary to halt the moving chain. Mass production led to the *division-of-labor* system, in which each worker is skilled in a single operation. See **Assembly line; Conveyor belt.**   Marvin F. DeVries

See also **Airplane** (Building an airplane); **Automobile** (The birth of the automobile industry); **Industrial Revolution** (diagram); **Machine tool; Whitney, Eli.**

Mass spectroscopy, *spehk TRAHS kuh pee,* also called *mass spectrometry,* is a method of separating ionized atoms or molecules according to their mass (m) and electric charge (z). It involves the use of an instrument called a *mass spectrometer.* Mass spectroscopy provides an effective means of identifying elements, isotopes, and molecules. It can also be used to determine the chemical composition and structure of more complex substances.

In a basic mass spectrometer, a sample of a substance is placed in a vacuum. Electrons bombard the sample, forming ions. An electric field forces a stream of ions away from the sample and separates them according to the strength of their charges. Each group of ions then passes through a magnetic field. This field deflects lighter ions more than heavier ions, producing a pattern called a *mass spectrum.* This pattern has peaks that correspond to the *m/z values* of each type of ion in the sample. An m/z value is the ratio of the mass of an ion to the ion's charge. The mass spectrum is scanned by varying the intensity of the magnetic field. Each m/z value is recorded by an electrical detector.

Most mass spectrometers are combined with a computer, which stores, manipulates, and interprets the data. A mass spectrometer also can be combined with such separating devices as *gas chromatographs* and *liquid chromatographs* to analyze mixtures made up of hundreds of components (see **Chromatography**).

Mass spectroscopy has many important uses in science and industry. Common uses include distinguishing one isotope from another, measuring atomic and molecular masses, and detecting impurities in silicon, which is used in transistors and other electronic devices. Government regulatory agencies sometimes use mass spectroscopy to detect—and measure the amounts of—pollutants in water, soil, and other substances.

Margaret E. Wickham St. Germain

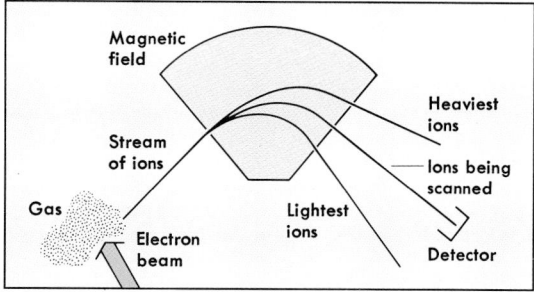

WORLD BOOK diagram

In a basic mass spectrometer, electrons bombard a gas sample to form ions. A magnetic field deflects the lighter ions more than the heavier ones. By varying the field's intensity, each of the deflected ions is exposed in rapid succession to a detector that measures the ion's mass and charge.

©Steve Dunwell

Autumn colors frame a colonial church in Brimfield, located in south-central Massachusetts. The state's natural beauty and its many historic landmarks make it one of the main tourist attractions in the United States. About 23 million people visit Massachusetts each year.

Massachusetts *The Bay State*

Massachusetts is the sixth smallest state of the United States, but it stands among the leaders in many fields. Only New Jersey, Hawaii, Connecticut, Delaware, and Rhode Island have smaller areas. Massachusetts ranks third among the most densely populated states, behind New Jersey and Rhode Island. Boston, the state's capital and largest city, is a major U.S. seaport and air terminal. It is New England's major center of finance and trade. Universities in and around Boston help make the area one of the world's great cultural, educational, medical, and research centers. Historic landmarks make Massachusetts one of America's main tourist spots.

The land in Massachusetts is a series of hills and valleys. From sea level near the Atlantic Ocean, the state

---

The contributors for this article are Winfred E. A. Bernhard, Professor of Early American History at the University of Massachusetts at Amherst; Michael G. Mensoian, Professor of Geography and Director of Armenian Studies at the University of Massachusetts at Boston; and Robert L. Turner, Political Columnist of The Boston Globe.

---

reaches a height of about 3,500 feet (1,100 meters) near its western border. The best farmland lies in the river valleys and near the coastline. Massachusetts produces more cranberries than any other state. Boston, Gloucester, and New Bedford are important fishing ports and centers for the canning and processing of fish.

The Norse explorer Leif Ericson may have visited the Massachusetts region about the year 1000. He was one of the first Europeans to sail to North America. In 1620, the Pilgrims settled at what is now Plymouth. The Puritans came in 1630. Both these groups left England in search of better economic opportunities and freedom to pursue their religious beliefs. The first newspaper, printing press, and library in the British colonies were established in Massachusetts. The first college, Harvard, was founded at Cambridge in 1636. Boston Latin School, the first secondary school in the colonies, opened in 1635. The first public high school in the United States, Boston English High School, opened in 1821.

Many of the events that led up to the Revolutionary War took place in Massachusetts. These included the Boston Massacre in 1770 and the Boston Tea Party in

Interesting facts about Massachusetts

Volleyball was developed by William Morgan in 1895. Morgan was a director of the YMCA in Holyoke.

The National Woman's Rights Convention was held in Worcester on Oct. 23 and 24, 1850. It was the first national convention of women in favor of woman's suffrage.

National Woman's Rights Convention

The oldest voluntary military organization in the world, the Ancient and Honorable Artillery Company, was established in Boston in 1838. Its purpose was to help men improve their military skills.

The first post office in the American Colonies was established at the tavern of Richard Fairbanks in Boston in 1639. The Massachusetts Bay Colony gave Fairbanks the right to process mail sent to or delivered from England.

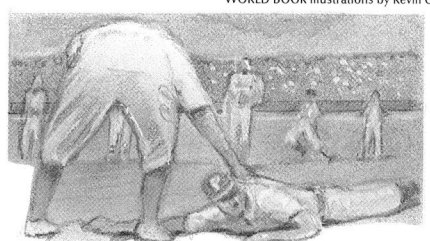

WORLD BOOK illustrations by Kevin Chadwick

First World Series

The first World Series in baseball history was played in Boston from Oct. 1 to Oct. 13, 1903. The Boston Pilgrims beat the Pittsburgh Pirates in the series, five games to three.

Basketball was invented in Springfield in 1891 by James A. Naismith, a physical-education instructor at the School for Christian Workers (now Springfield College). He invented the game to create a team sport that could be played indoors in winter.

Jeff Gnass, West Stock

Fishing boats dock at Provincetown Harbor on Cape Cod. Many fine harbors line the coast of Massachusetts, helping to make it one of the leading commercial fishing states.

1773. On the night of April 18, 1775, Paul Revere made his famous ride to warn his fellow patriots that British troops were coming. On April 19, 1775, minutemen at Lexington and then at Concord fought the first battles of the Revolutionary War. On Feb. 6, 1788, Massachusetts ratified the U.S. Constitution, becoming the sixth state to join the Union.

Four U.S. Presidents were born in Massachusetts. John Adams, the second President, and his son, John Quincy Adams, the sixth President, were both born in Braintree (now Quincy). John F. Kennedy, the 35th President, was born in Brookline. George Bush, the 41st President, was born in Milton.

Massachusetts gets its name from the Massachuset Indian tribe, which lived in the region when the Pilgrims arrived. The name probably means *near the great hill,* or *the place of the great hill.* Historians believe it refers to the Great Blue Hill south of Boston. Massachusetts is often called the *Bay State* because the Puritans founded their colony on Massachusetts Bay. Massachusetts is one of four states officially called *commonwealths.* The others are Kentucky, Pennsylvania, and Virginia.

Cy Furlan

The Faneuil Hall Marketplace in downtown Boston attracts thousands of people each day. The marketplace, developed in 1976, has more than 150 shops, food stalls, restaurants, and bars.

Massachusetts in brief

Symbols of Massachusetts

The state flag, adopted in 1971, bears a shield with the figure of an Indian. The Indian has been a symbol of Massachusetts since 1629. The star represents Massachusetts as one of the original 13 Colonies. A crest above the shield, an arm wielding a sword, coincides with the motto. The state seal, adopted in 1885, bears the same symbols as the flag.

State flag

State seal

Massachusetts (brown) ranks 45th in size of all the states and 4th in size among the New England States (yellow).

General information

Statehood: Feb. 6, 1788, the sixth state.
State abbreviations: Mass. (traditional); MA (postal).
State motto: *Ense petit placidam sub libertate quietem* (By the sword we seek peace, but peace only under liberty).
State song: "All Hail to Massachusetts" by Arthur J. Marsh.

The State House is in Boston, the capital of Massachusetts since 1630.

Land and climate

Area: 8,262 sq. mi. (21,398 km²), including 424 sq. mi. (1,098 km²) of inland water but excluding 979 sq. mi. (2,536 km²) of Atlantic coastal water.
Elevation: *Highest*—Mount Greylock, 3,491 ft. (1,064 m) above sea level. *Lowest*—sea level along the Atlantic Ocean.
Coastline: 192 mi. (309 km).
Record high temperature: 107 °F (42 °C) at New Bedford and Chester on Aug. 2, 1975.
Record low temperature: −34 °F (−37 °C) at Birch Hill Dam on Jan. 18, 1957.
Average July temperature: 71 °F (22 °C).
Average January temperature: 25 °F (−4 °C).
Average yearly precipitation: 45 in. (114 cm).

Greatest east-west distance 183 mi. (295 km)

● Highest elevation

Greatest north-south distance 113 mi. (182 km)

Lowest elevation along coast

Important dates

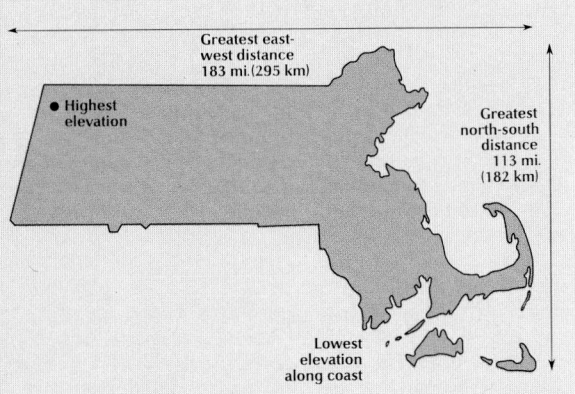

The Puritans founded Boston.

Patriots dumped British tea into Boston Harbor during the Boston Tea Party.

| 1620 | 1630 | 1636 | 1773 | 1775 |

The Pilgrims landed at Plymouth.

Harvard became the first college in the colonies.

The American Revolutionary War began at Lexington and Concord.

| **State bird** | **State flower** | **State tree** |
| Chickadee | Mayflower | American elm |

People

Population: 6,029,051 (1990 census)
Rank among the states: 13th
Density: 730 persons per sq. mi. (282 per km²), U.S. average 69 per sq. mi. (27 per km²)
Distribution: 84 percent urban, 16 percent rural
Largest cities in Massachusetts

Boston	574,283
Worcester	169,759
Springfield	156,983
Lowell*	103,439
New Bedford	99,922
Cambridge	95,802

*Unincorporated place.
Source: U.S. Bureau of the Census.

Population trend

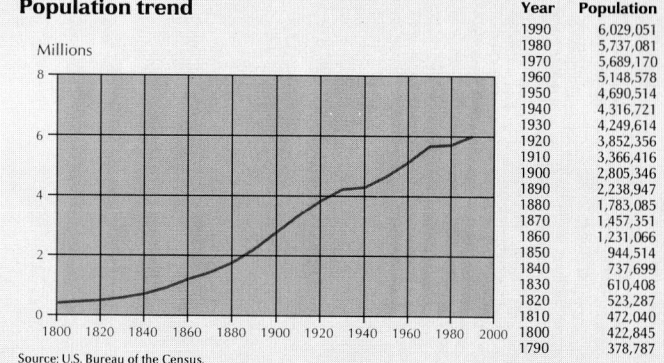

Millions

Source: U.S. Bureau of the Census.

Year	Population
1990	6,029,051
1980	5,737,081
1970	5,689,170
1960	5,148,578
1950	4,690,514
1940	4,316,721
1930	4,249,614
1920	3,852,356
1910	3,366,416
1900	2,805,346
1890	2,238,947
1880	1,783,085
1870	1,457,351
1860	1,231,066
1850	944,514
1840	737,699
1830	610,408
1820	523,287
1810	472,040
1800	422,845
1790	378,787

Economy

Chief products

Agriculture: greenhouse and nursery products, cranberries, milk.
Fishing industry: flounder, scallops.
Manufacturing: scientific instruments, electrical equipment, machinery, printed materials, fabricated metal products, transportation equipment.
Mining: sand and gravel, crushed stone.

Gross state product

Value of goods and services produced in 1991: $147,627,000,000. *Services* include community, social, and personal services; finance; government; trade; and transportation, communication, and utilities. *Industry* includes construction, manufacturing, and mining. *Agriculture* includes agriculture, fishing, and forestry.

Source: U.S. Bureau of Economic Analysis.

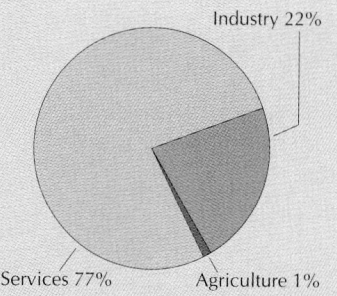

Industry 22%

Services 77%   Agriculture 1%

Government

State government

Governor: 4-year term
State senators: 40; 2-year terms
State representatives: 160; 2-year terms
Counties: 14

Federal government

United States senators: 2
United States representatives: 10
Electoral votes: 12

Sources of information

Tourism: Office of Travel and Tourism, 100 Cambridge Street, 13th floor, Boston, MA 02202
Economy: Office of Business Development, 1 Ashburton Place, 21st floor, Boston, MA 02108
Government: Office of the Secretary of State, Citizen Information Service, 1 Ashburton Place, Room 1611, Boston, MA 02108
History: Office of the Secretary of State, Citizen Information Service, 1 Ashburton Place, Room 1611, Boston, MA 02108

Massachusetts became the sixth state on February 6.

William Lloyd Garrison began publishing his antislavery newspaper *The Liberator* in Boston.

| 1788 | 1807 | 1831 | 1971 |

The Embargo Act ruined Massachusetts shipping and led to the rise of manufacturing.

Massachusetts began a major reorganization of its state government.

Population. The 1990 United States census reported that Massachusetts had 6,029,051 people. The population had increased 5 percent over the 1980 figure, 5,737,081. According to the 1990 census, Massachusetts ranks 13th in population among the 50 states.

About 84 percent of the people of Massachusetts live in urban areas. That is, they live in or near municipalities of 2,500 or more people. About 16 percent of the people live in rural areas. About 95 percent of the people in Massachusetts live in one of the metropolitan statistical areas that are either entirely or partly in the state (see **Metropolitan area**). These areas are Barnstable-Yarmouth, Boston, Brockton, Fitchburg-Leominster, Lawrence, Lowell, New Bedford, Pittsfield, Providence-Fall River (R.I.)-Warwick, Springfield, and Worcester. For the populations of these areas, see the *Index* to the po-

Massachusetts has some of the nation's most highly regarded *prep schools* (private schools that prepare students for college). The state's universities and colleges are highly acclaimed.

Libraries. The first library in the American Colonies was established in Massachusetts in 1638, when John Harvard gave his collection of books to Harvard College. Harvard's library is now the largest university library in the world. It has more than 11 million volumes. Today, Massachusetts has 374 public libraries.

Several Boston libraries own outstanding collections. These libraries include the Athenaeum, which has George Washington's collection of books; the John F. Kennedy Library; the Massachusetts Historical Society; the State Library, in the State House; and the Boston Public Library.

Population density

About half the people of Massachusetts live in the Boston metropolitan area. Mountainous regions in the west are among the most thinly populated parts of the state.

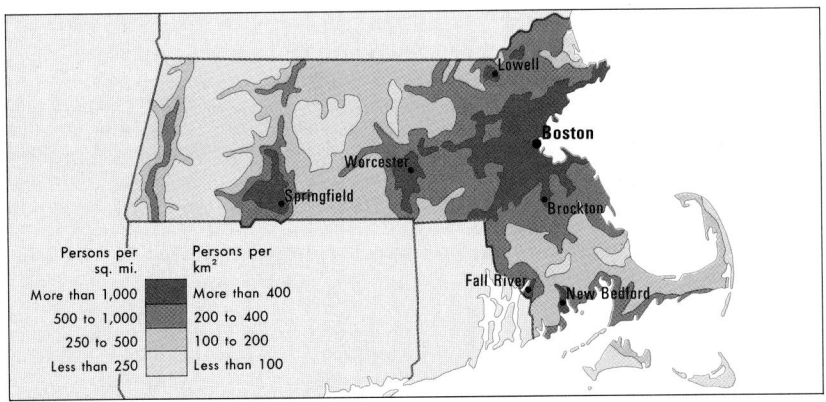

Persons per sq. mi.	Persons per km²
More than 1,000	More than 400
500 to 1,000	200 to 400
250 to 500	100 to 200
Less than 250	Less than 100

litical map of Massachusetts.

Boston is the state's largest city and the capital of Massachusetts. Other large cities in Massachusetts, in order of population, are Worcester, Springfield, Lowell, New Bedford, and Cambridge.

About 88 percent of the people living in Massachusetts were born in the United States. The largest groups of people born in other countries came from Canada, Italy, and the United Kingdom. The state's largest population groups include people of Irish, English, Italian, and French descent.

Schools. The Puritans of Boston built the first school in Massachusetts in 1635. This school, the Boston Latin School, was the first secondary school in the American Colonies. In 1647, the Massachusetts Bay Colony ordered that elementary schools be established in all towns where there were 50 or more families. This action marked the first time that any government in the world provided free public education at public expense. In 1852, Massachusetts became the first state to require its children to attend school.

The state department of education supervises public education from kindergarten through secondary school. The department has a commissioner, a deputy commissioner, and a 15-member board of education. Children from ages 6 through 15 must attend school. For the number of students and teachers in Massachusetts, see **Education** (table).

Other Massachusetts libraries with important collections include the Essex Institute in Salem and the American Antiquarian Society in Worcester. The Harvard library owns collections of rare books and old Indian manuscripts.

The Worcester Art Museum has 42 galleries with works ranging from ancient Egyptian sculptures to modern European and American painting. It also has Oriental and Indian art.

© Steve Hanson

The Boston Athenaeum is a small but well-known private library. The Athenaeum has many rare volumes, including a collection of books originally owned by George Washington.

© Steve Dunwell

Harvard University, in Cambridge, is the oldest institution of higher learning in the United States. The university was founded in 1636. The Charles River flows near the campus.

Museums. The Museum of Fine Arts in Boston is one of the world's great museums. It has the finest collection of Oriental art in the world. The Isabella Stewart Gardner Museum in Boston has many outstanding Renaissance paintings. Boston's children's museum is one of the oldest and largest in the nation. The George Walter Vincent Smith Art Museum in Springfield, the Worcester Art Museum, and the Sterling and Francine Clark Art Institute in Williamstown are among the nation's best-known smaller museums. The Addison Gallery of American Art of Phillips Academy in Andover owns a valuable collection of American paintings. Other museums include the Museum of Science in Boston, the Whaling Museum in New Bedford, the Peabody Museum of Salem, the Norman Rockwell Museum in Stockbridge, and the John Woodman Higgins Armory in Worcester.

Universities and colleges

Massachusetts has 75 universities and colleges that grant bachelor's or advanced degrees and are accredited by the New England Association of Schools and Colleges. For enrollments and further information, see **Universities and colleges** (table).

Name	Mailing address	Name	Mailing address
American International College	Springfield	Lasell College	Newton
Amherst College	Amherst	Lesley College	Cambridge
Andover Newton		Massachusetts, University of	*
Theological School	Newton Centre	Massachusetts College of Art	Boston
Anna Maria College	Paxton	Massachusetts College	
Arthur D. Little Management		of Pharmacy and	
Education Institute	Cambridge	Allied Health Sciences	Boston
Assumption College	Worcester	Massachusetts Institute of Technology	Cambridge
Atlantic Union College	South Lancaster	Massachusetts Maritime Academy	Buzzards Bay
Babson College	Babson Park	Massachusetts School of	
Bay Path College	Longmeadow	Professional Psychology	Dedham
Bentley College	Waltham	Merrimack College	North Andover
Berklee College of Music	Boston	MGH Institute of Health Professions	Boston
Boston Architectural Center	Boston	Mount Holyoke College	South Hadley
Boston College	Chestnut Hill	Mount Ida College	Newton Centre
Boston Conservatory	Boston	New England College of Optometry	Boston
Boston University	Boston	New England Conservatory of Music	Boston
Bradford College	Bradford	Nichols College	Dudley
Brandeis University	Waltham	North Adams State College	North Adams
Bridgewater State College	Bridgewater	Northeastern University	Boston
Cambridge College	Cambridge	Our Lady of the Elms, College of	Chicopee
Clark University	Worcester	Pine Manor College	Chestnut Hill
Conway School of Landscape Design	Conway	Regis College	Weston
Curry College	Milton	St. Hyacinth College and Seminary	Granby
Eastern Nazarene College	Wollaston	St. John's Seminary	Brighton
Emerson College	Boston	Salem State College	Salem
Emmanuel College	Boston	Simmons College	Boston
Endicott College	Beverly	Simon's Rock College of Bard	Great Barrington
Fitchburg State College	Fitchburg	Smith College	Northampton
Framingham State College	Framingham	Springfield College	Springfield
Gordon College	Wenham	Stonehill College	North Easton
Gordon-Conwell		Suffolk University	Boston
Theological Seminary	South Hamilton	Tufts University	Medford
Gordon Institute	Wakefield	Wellesley College	Wellesley
Hampshire College	Amherst	Wentworth Institute of Technology	Boston
Harvard University	*	Western New England College	Springfield
Hebrew College	Brookline	Westfield State College	Westfield
Hellenic College-Holy Cross		Wheaton College	Norton
Greek Orthodox		Wheelock College	Boston
School of Theology	Brookline	Williams College	Williamstown
Holy Cross,		Worcester Polytechnic Institute	Worcester
College of the	Worcester	Worcester State College	Worcester

*For campuses, see **Universities and colleges** (table).

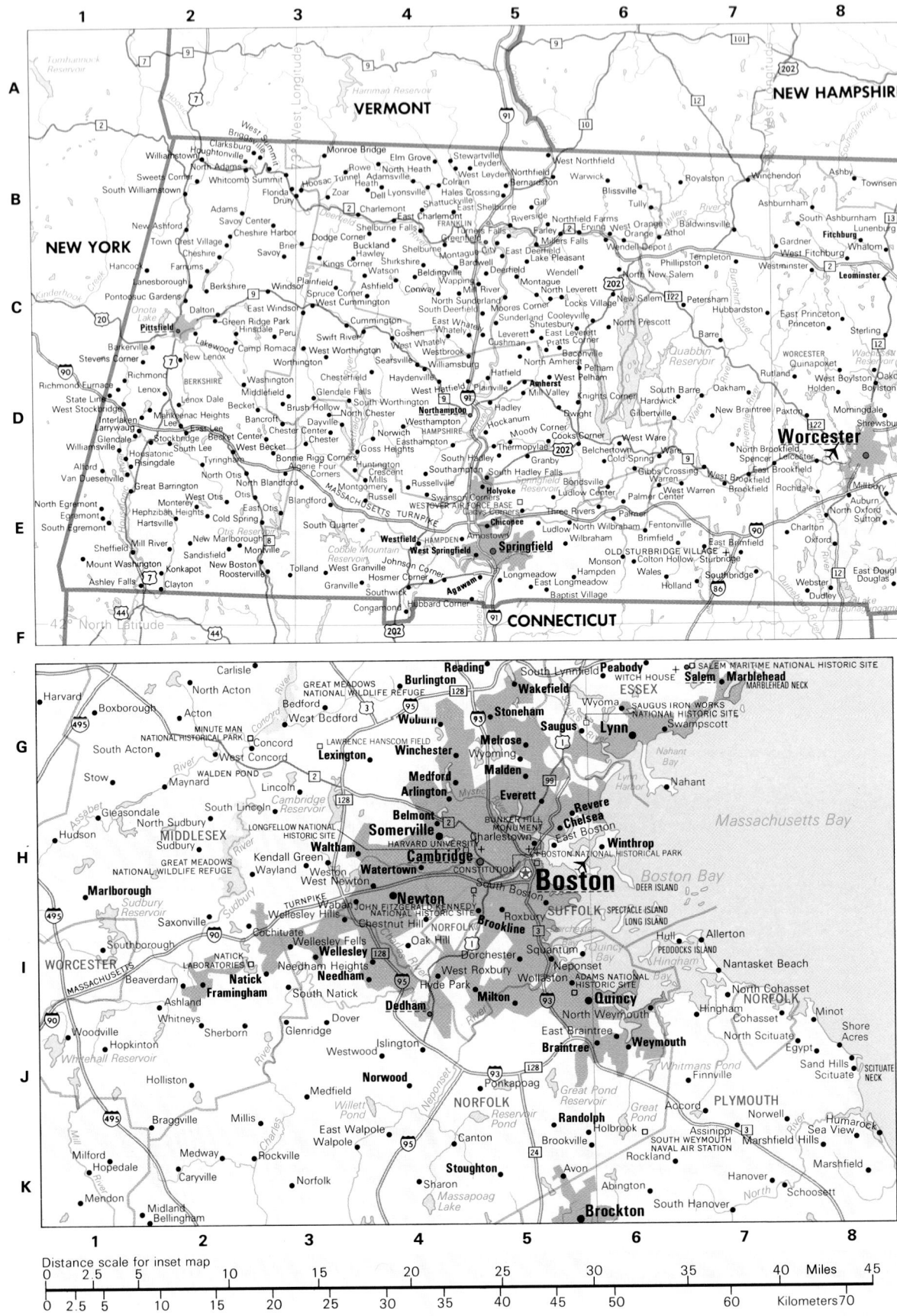

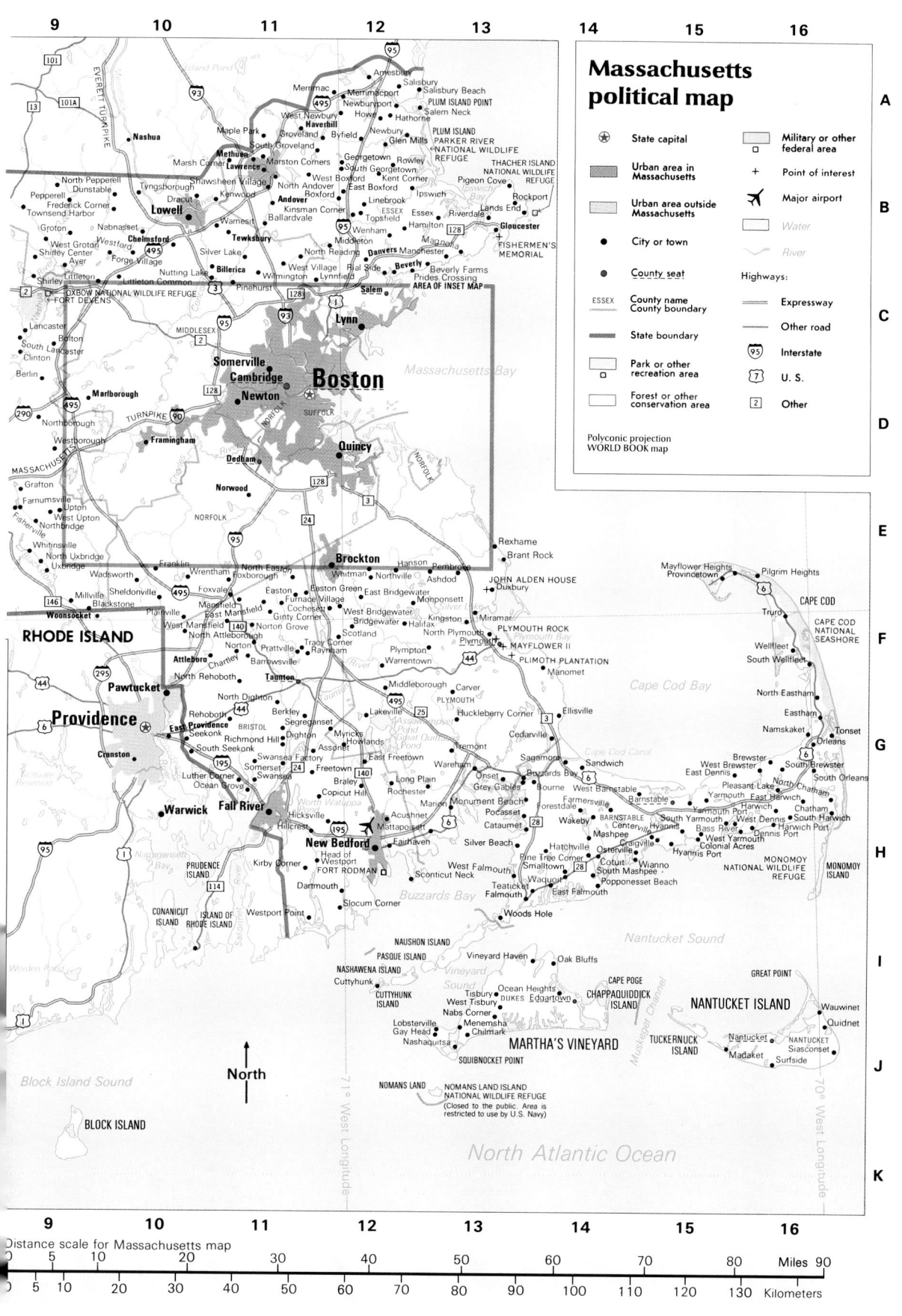

Massachusetts political map

Legend:

- State capital
- Urban area in Massachusetts
- Urban area outside Massachusetts
- City or town
- County seat
- ESSEX — County name / County boundary
- State boundary
- Park or other recreation area
- Forest or other conservation area
- Military or other federal area
- Point of interest
- Major airport
- Water
- River

Highways:
- Expressway
- Other road
- 95 Interstate
- 7 U.S.
- 2 Other

Polyconic projection
WORLD BOOK map

Distance scale for Massachusetts map

Miles 90

Kilometers

Massachusetts map index

*Does not appear on map, key shows general location.
†Census designated place—unincorporated, but recognized as a significant settled community by the U.S. Bureau of the Census.
▲Entire town (township), including rural area.
°County seat.
Source: 1990 census. Places without population figures are unincorporated areas.

© Steve Dunwell

Court Square is a popular park in downtown Springfield. The Soldiers Monument, *center,* stands in the square, honoring men from Massachusetts who fought in the Civil War.

Skiing brings many visitors to the Berkshire Hills and to other parts of Massachusetts. The Atlantic Ocean and many lakes and rivers attract swimmers, fishing enthusiasts, and boaters. But Massachusetts offers perhaps its greatest rewards to the student of American history. Historic sites date back to the Pilgrims, to colonial witchcraft trials, and to the Revolutionary War.

One of the outstanding yearly events in Massachusetts is the Tanglewood Music Festival, held in the Tanglewood Music Shed near Lenox. This 210-acre (85-hectare) estate in the Berkshires is also the summer home of the Boston Symphony Orchestra.

T. Blank, Freelance Photographers Guild

Plimoth Plantation in Plymouth

Susan Lapides, Wheeler Pictures

Summer resort on Cape Cod

Places to visit

Following are brief descriptions of some of Massachusetts' many interesting places to visit:

Basketball Hall of Fame, in Springfield, honors outstanding basketball players and features exhibits on the history of the game.

Bearskin Neck, in Rockport, is a long stretch of restored cottages in a former fishing village. The cottages now house craft shops, restaurants, and galleries. A restored fishing shanty near the end of Bearskin Neck is a popular subject for painters and photographers.

Black Heritage Trail winds along Beacon Hill's north slope, a neighborhood where black Bostonians of the 1800's lived. The trail has nine sites, including a *station* (hiding place) on the *underground railroad,* which aided slaves fleeing to the free states or to Canada.

Boston is a major cultural center and one of the nation's great historic cities. The city became known as the *Cradle of Liberty* when it led the American colonies in their struggle for independence. Visitors may follow the Freedom Trail, a three-mile-long red line along the city's sidewalks that connects 16 historic sites. See **Boston** (Downtown Boston; illustration: Boston's Freedom Trail).

Cape Cod, a peninsula in southeastern Massachusetts, is a famous summer resort and vacation area. The peninsula faces Cape Cod Bay on the north, Nantucket Sound on the south, and the Atlantic Ocean on the east. Long sandy beaches stretch along the cape.

Constitution, also called *Old Ironsides,* is docked at the Charlestown Navy Yard in Boston. This early U.S. Navy frigate became famous during the War of 1812. Oliver Wendell Holmes honored the ship with his famous poem "Old Ironsides."

Harvard University, in Cambridge, is one of the world's most famous universities. Harvard was founded in 1636. It is the oldest institution of higher learning in the United States. Harvard Yard, the center of the original college, still retains much

of its early charm. Notable libraries and museums on the campus include Widener Library and the Fogg Art Museum.

Martha's Vineyard, an island 4 miles (6 kilometers) off the southeastern coast of Massachusetts, is a popular resort area. The island features long stretches of unspoiled beaches and forests.

Nantucket Island is a former whaling port that is now an important resort center. Beaches and moors cover much of the island.

Old Sturbridge Village, in Sturbridge, is a re-creation of a typical New England town of the 1830's.

Plimoth Plantation, in Plymouth, is a re-creation of a 1627 Pilgrim village. *Mayflower II,* built the way the original *Mayflower* is thought to have looked, is maintained by the plantation.

Salem has attractions that include the birthplace of American author Nathaniel Hawthorne and Witch House, the home of a judge of the witchcraft trials of 1692.

Walden Pond, near Concord, has become a symbol of nature. The American writer Henry David Thoreau built a simple cabin on its shore and lived there for two years. His book *Walden* describes his experiences at the pond and his views on nature and life.

National historical parks, seashores, and historic sites. Minute Man National Historical Park is located between Lexington and Concord. Cape Cod National Seashore includes beaches, marshes, and woodland areas on outer Cape Cod. Saugus Iron Works National Historic Site in Saugus is a reconstruction of the first successful ironworks in North America. Massachusetts has several other national historic sites. For information on these areas, see the map and tables in the article on **National Park System.**

State parks and forests. Massachusetts has 107 state parks, forests, and recreational areas. For information, write to Director, Division of Forests and Parks, 100 Cambridge Street, Boston, MA 02202.

Annual events

January-March
The Boston Festival (mid-February); Bay State Games in Williamstown and North Adams (last week in February); Spring Garden and Flower Show in Worcester (March); St. Patrick's Day Parade in Holyoke (March 17).

April-June
Daffodil Festival on Nantucket Island (April); Whale Watch Cruises from Cape Ann to Cape Cod (April-October); Hanging of Lanterns in the steeple of the Old North Church in Boston (third Sunday in April); Boston Marathon (third Monday in April); Cambridge River Festival (May); Antique Automobile Show in Stockbridge (Sunday of Memorial Day weekend); ACC Craftfair in West Springfield (June); Cape Cod Chowder Festival in Hyannis (June); Williamstown Theatre Festival (June-August); Bunker Hill Day in Charlestown (June 17); Tanglewood Music Festival in Lenox (mid-June-August); Blessing of Fishing Fleets in Gloucester and Provincetown (late June).

July-September
Esplanade Concerts in Boston (July); Harborfest in Boston (July); Jacob's Pillow Dance Festival in Becket (July-August); Pilgrim Progress Processional in Plymouth (Fridays, July-August); Sandcastle Contest in Nantucket (August); Teddy Bear Rally in Amherst (August); Fishermen's Memorial Service in Gloucester (August); The "Big E" State Fair in West Springfield (September); World Kielbasa Festival in Chicopee (weekend after Labor Day); Cranberry Harvest Festival in Harwich (weekend after Labor Day); Apple/Peach Festival in Acushnet (second weekend in September).

October-December
Scallop Festival in Buzzards Bay (October); Rowing Regatta on the Charles River in Boston and Cambridge (October); Haunted Happenings in Salem (October); Pilgrim Progress Processional and Pilgrim Thanksgiving Day in Plymouth (Thanksgiving Day); A and D Toy-Train Village Christmas Festival in Middleboro (November-December).

Michael Philip Manheim, West Stock

Rowing regatta on the Charles River in Cambridge

Jerry Howard, Stock, Boston

Tanglewood Music Shed near Lenox

Lois Greenfield

Jacob's Pillow Dance Festival

Land and climate

Land regions. Massachusetts has six main land regions. They are, from east to west: (1) the Coastal Lowlands, (2) the Eastern New England Upland, (3) the Connecticut Valley Lowland, (4) the Western New England Upland, (5) the Berkshire Valley, and (6) the Taconic Mountains.

The Coastal Lowlands are part of a large land region that extends over the entire New England coastline. The lowlands make up the eastern third of Massachusetts. They also include Nantucket Island, Martha's Vineyard, the Elizabeth Islands, and other smaller offshore islands. The region has many rounded hills, swamps, small lakes and ponds, and short shallow rivers. The lowlands are dotted with glacial deposits. These were left by glaciers thousands of years ago during the Ice Age. The Great Blue Hill, south of Boston, rises to a height of about 635 feet (194 meters). Several excellent harbors lie along the coast. They include Boston, Gloucester, and New Bedford.

The Eastern New England Upland makes up part of a land region that stretches from Maine to New Jersey. The upland is an extension of the White Mountains of New Hampshire. In Massachusetts the upland extends westward from the Coastal Lowlands for 40 to 60 miles (64 to 97 kilometers). The upland region rises to a height of about 1,000 feet (300 meters) and then gradually slopes downward toward the Connecticut Valley Lowland. Many streams cut through the Eastern New England Upland.

The Connecticut Valley Lowland is a long, sausage-shaped region. It extends from northern Massachusetts to southern Connecticut. In Massachusetts, the valley, which is 20 miles (32 kilometers) wide, is hemmed in by hills to the north, east, and west. The Connecticut River flows through the valley region. Rich soil and a mild climate provide good farming.

The Western New England Upland extends through Vermont, Massachusetts, and Connecticut. In Massachusetts, the region stretches 20 to 30 miles (32 to 48 kilometers) westward from the Connecticut Valley Lowland to the Berkshire Valley. The Berkshire Hills, a range that covers this region, is an extension of the Green Mountains of Vermont. In Massachusetts, the Western New England Upland region itself is often called the Berkshire Hills. The land rises from the Connecticut Valley to rugged, beautiful heights of more than 2,000 feet (610 meters). In this region is Majestic Mount Greylock, which rises 3,491 feet (1,064 meters) and is the highest

point in Massachusetts. Farms and towns lie on the region's slopes.

The Berkshire Valley is a narrow path of lower land that extends into northern Connecticut. In Massachusetts, it winds between the Berkshire Hills and the Taconic Mountains. This valley region is less than 10 miles (16 kilometers) wide. Its many green meadows are good for dairy farming.

The Taconic Mountains extend into Vermont. This region skirts the extreme western edge of Massachusetts. At its widest point, the region measures no more than 6 miles (10 kilometers) across. The Taconic Range slopes from northwestern Massachusetts to the southwestern corner of the state, where Mount Everett rises 2,602 feet (793 meters).

Coastline of Massachusetts measures 192 miles (309 kilometers). If the coastline of each bay and inlet were added to the total, the state's coastline would measure more than 1,500 miles (2,410 kilometers). Boston is the state's most important harbor. Other important harbors include Gloucester in the north, Quincy and Weymouth in Boston Bay, and New Bedford and Fall River in the south.

Islands. The Elizabeth Islands, Martha's Vineyard, and Nantucket Island are the state's largest and most important islands. Together with Cape Cod, these islands form the boundaries of Nantucket Sound. Martha's Vineyard and Nantucket Island are important resort centers. A number of smaller islands also lie along the coast of Massachusetts.

Land regions of Massachusetts

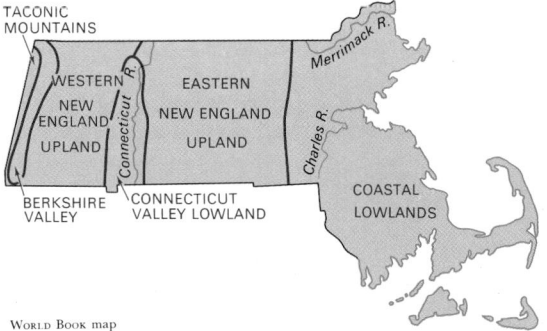

WORLD BOOK map

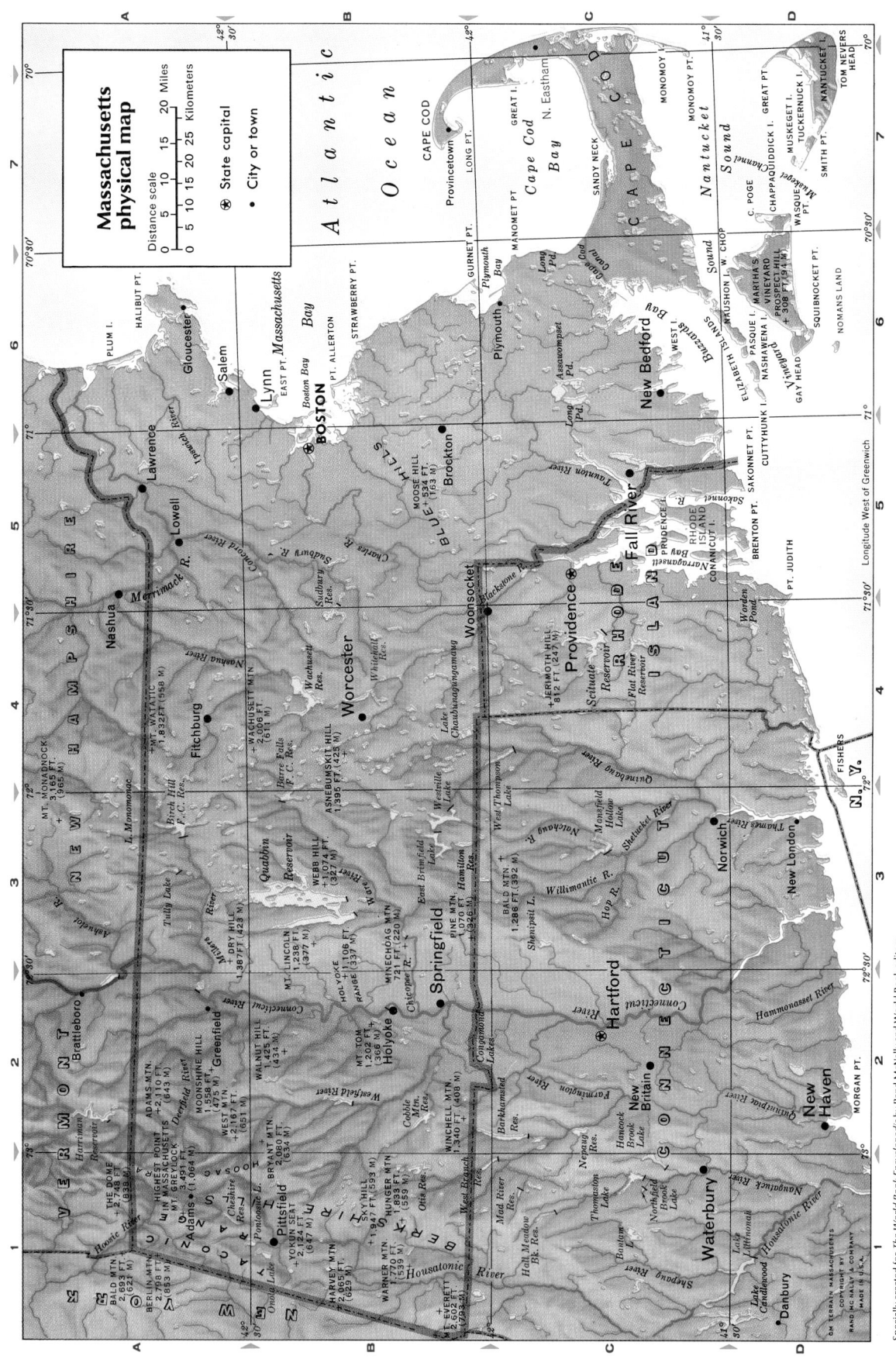

Massachusetts physical map

Distance scale

⊛ State capital

• City or town

0 5 10 15 20 25 Kilometers

0 5 10 15 20 Miles

Specially created for *The World Book Encyclopedia* by Rand McNally and World Book editors

Rivers and lakes. Massachusetts has 4,230 miles (6,808 kilometers) of rivers. The Connecticut River is the state's most important waterway. It flows southward and provides water for the most fertile Massachusetts farmlands. The Connecticut's chief tributaries include the Deerfield and Westfield rivers to the west, and the Chicopee and Millers rivers to the east.

The far western part of Massachusetts has two important rivers—the Hoosic River and the Housatonic River. The Hoosic River flows northward and westward into Vermont, and finally drains into the Hudson River. The scenic Housatonic River flows southward into Connecticut. The Blackstone River drains Massachusetts' eastern upland region. It then flows southeastward into Rhode Island.

The Merrimack River is the most important river in the Coastal Lowlands. It enters the state from New Hampshire. Then the Merrimack turns abruptly northeastward and flows almost parallel to the Massachusetts border until it empties into the Atlantic Ocean at Newburyport. The Nashua and Concord rivers are the Merrimack's main tributaries. The Charles, Mystic, and Neponset rivers all empty into Boston Harbor. The Taunton River flows southward into Rhode Island's Mount Hope Bay.

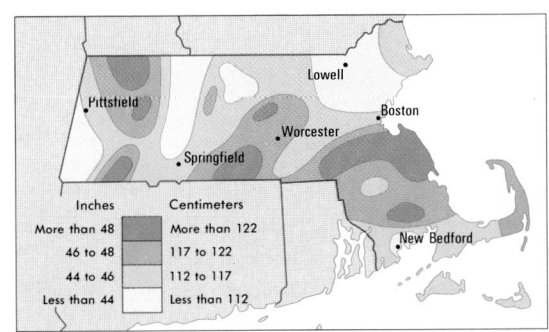

Shostal

Mount Greylock, the highest point in Massachusetts, rises 3,491 feet (1,064 meters) in the state's Western New England Upland region. This area is often called the Berkshire Hills.

Average monthly weather

	Boston						Pittsfield				
	Temperatures				Days of rain or snow		Temperatures				Days of rain or snow
	F°		C°				F°		C°		
	High	Low	High	Low			High	Low	High	Low	
Jan.	37	22	3	−6	12	Jan.	30	13	−1	−11	14
Feb.	37	22	3	−6	10	Feb.	31	13	−1	−11	13
Mar.	45	30	7	−1	12	Mar.	40	22	4	−6	14
Apr.	55	39	13	4	11	Apr.	53	31	12	−1	14
May	66	49	19	9	11	May	66	43	19	6	14
June	76	58	24	14	10	June	74	52	23	11	11
July	80	64	27	18	10	July	79	56	26	13	12
Aug.	79	64	26	18	10	Aug.	78	54	26	12	9
Sept.	73	56	23	13	9	Sept.	70	47	21	8	10
Oct.	63	47	17	8	9	Oct.	59	36	15	2	8
Nov.	52	37	11	3	10	Nov.	46	28	8	−2	12
Dec.	40	26	4	−3	11	Dec.	33	16	1	−9	13

Average yearly precipitation

Amounts of precipitation are uneven throughout Massachusetts. In general, the east gets more precipitation than the west.

Inches	Centimeters
More than 48	More than 122
46 to 48	117 to 122
44 to 46	112 to 117
Less than 44	Less than 112

Average January temperatures

The eastern part of the state has the mildest wintertime temperatures. The winters are increasingly cold to the west.

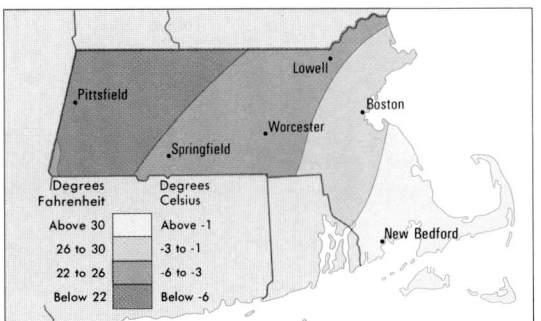

Degrees Fahrenheit	Degrees Celsius
Above 30	Above −1
26 to 30	−3 to −1
22 to 26	−6 to −3
Below 22	Below −6

Average July temperatures

Massachusetts has even summer temperatures. Only the area around Worcester averages below 70° F. (20° C.).

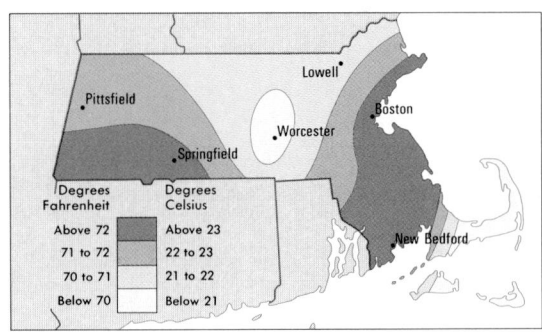

Degrees Fahrenheit	Degrees Celsius
Above 72	Above 23
71 to 72	22 to 23
70 to 71	21 to 22
Below 70	Below 21

WORLD BOOK maps

Massachusetts has more than 1,300 lakes and ponds. More than a fourth of these lakes supply drinking water to nearby cities and towns. The state's two largest lakes—Quabbin and Wachusett—are artificially created reservoirs. Quabbin Reservoir, near Ware in the center of the state, is one of the nation's largest reservoirs of drinking water. It covers more than 39 square miles (101 square kilometers). Wachusett Reservoir, north of Worcester, covers $6\frac{1}{2}$ square miles (17 square kilometers). These reservoirs supply water to the Boston metropolitan area.

Many of the state's lakes have Indian names. For example, Lake Chaubunagungamaug, also called Lake Webster, received its name from the Nipmuc Indians. The long form for this name is Chargoggagogg-manchauggagoggchaubunagungamaug. The name means "You fish your side of the lake. I fish my side. Nobody fishes the middle."

Plant and animal life. Forests cover about three-fifths of the land area of Massachusetts. The most common softwood trees include the eastern white and red pines, the eastern hemlock, and the pitch pine. Common hardwoods include ash, beech, birch, maple, and oak trees.

Every spring, blue and white violets blossom along the river valleys and in the lower portions of the upland regions. Marsh marigolds, skunk cabbages, and white helebores also cover these regions in the springtime. Common shrubs and plants in the western hilly regions include azaleas, dogwoods, ferns, mountain laurels, rhododendrons, and viburnums. Mayflowers, Solomon's-seals, and trilliums are also common in the western regions. Rushes and sedges thrive along the seacoast and in the Coastal Lowlands.

Massachusetts' forests and woodlands are filled with foxes, muskrats, porcupines, rabbits, raccoons, and skunks. The tiny meadow mouse is the state's most common animal. Deer live throughout the state. Great numbers of beavers live in the streams of the Berkshire Hills. Partridge, pheasant, and other game birds are found in the fields and forests. Many kinds of water, marsh, and shore birds, especially gulls and terns, nest along the seacoast.

Bass, pickerel, sunfish, trout, and white and yellow perch swim in the state's lakes and ponds. Clams, fishes, lobsters, and oysters are found in the coastal waters. Massachusetts has many kinds of snakes. Poisonous copperheads and timber rattlesnakes live in the Berkshire and Blue hills.

Climate. Western Massachusetts is colder than the eastern part of the state. Boston, on the eastern edge of the state, has an average July temperature of 72 °F (22 °C) and an average January temperature of 29 °F (−2 °C). In the west, Pittsfield averages 68 °F (20 °C) in July and 21 °F (−6 °C) in January. Worcester, in the central portion of the state, has a July average of 70 °F (21 °C) and a January average of 24 °F (−4 °C). The highest temperature ever recorded in the state was 107 °F (42 °C) at New Bedford and Chester on Aug. 2, 1975. The lowest recorded temperature, −34 °F (−37 °C), occurred at Birch Hill Dam on Jan. 18, 1957.

The state's *precipitation* (rain, melted snow, and other forms of moisture) ranges from about 47 inches (119 centimeters) a year in the west to about 43 inches (109 centimeters) near the coast. From 55 to 75 inches (140 to 191 centimeters) of snow falls in the western mountains of Massachusetts each year. The central part of the state averages about 49 inches (124 centimeters) a year and the coastal area about 42 inches (107 centimeters). Hurricanes occasionally lash the Massachusetts coastline. Especially destructive hurricanes hit the state in 1938, 1944, and 1985.

Economy

Service industries, taken together, account for more than three-fourths of Massachusetts' *gross state product* —the total value of all goods and services produced in a state in a year. Service industries include such activities as banking, health care, real estate, and trade. The manufacture of computers and electronic products is also a major part of the Massachusetts economy.

Each year, about 23 million tourists visit Massachusetts, contributing about $6 billion to the state's economy. Tourism thrives around the Boston area, on Cape Cod and neighboring islands, and in the Berkshires.

Natural resources include fertile river valley soils and deposits of sand and gravel and other minerals.

Soil. Most of the river valleys have deep soils that are rich in peat. The Connecticut River Valley has the most fertile soil in the state. The marshy soils of the Coastal Lowlands, with underground peat deposits, are also quite rich. But much of the state's soil contains sand and gravel. Stones and boulders, deposited long ago by melting glaciers, are also common. These gravel and sandy acid soils are not very fertile. Farmers must treat them with large amounts of fertilizer.

Minerals. Most of the minerals found in Massachusetts are valuable building materials. Sand and gravel deposits lie mostly in east-central Massachusetts. The richest granite deposits are near West Chelmsford. Deposits of dolomitic marbles are found in Ashley Falls, Lee, and West Stockbridge.

Service industries account for 77 percent of the gross state product of Massachusetts. Service industries operate chiefly within the state's 12 metropolitan areas, especially the Boston metropolitan area.

Community, social, and personal services form the most valuable service industry in Massachusetts in terms of the gross state product. This industry also employs more people than any other economic activity in the state. Community, social, and personal services consist of a variety of establishments. These include doctors' offices and private hospitals, private schools, law firms, computer programming services, and engineering companies. The Massachusetts General Hospital in Boston is one of the world's leading centers of medical research. Cambridge is the home of two highly respected private universities, Harvard University and the Massachusetts Institute of Technology.

Next in importance among service industries in Massachusetts, in terms of the gross state product, are finance, insurance, and real estate. Boston ranks among the nation's major financial centers. Two of the largest U.S. banking companies, the Bank of New England and the Bank of Boston, are headquartered in the city. Boston is also the home of a stock exchange and many large insurance firms and holding companies. Large financial companies are also based in Springfield and Worcester. Real estate is a major part of the economy because of the large sums of money involved in the buying and selling of property.

Wholesale and retail trade rank third among the state's service industries. Massachusetts wholesalers purchase such goods as automobiles, groceries, and petroleum from producers and sell them to retailers. Such retail establishments as automobile dealerships, food stores, and gas stations sell goods to consumers.

Government ranks fourth among service industries in Massachusetts. Government services include public schools and hospitals, and military bases. State government activities are based in Boston. Public education is one of the state's major employers.

Transportation, communication, and utilities rank last among service industries in Massachusetts. Telephone companies are the major part of the communications industry. Northeast Utilities, headquartered in West Springfield, is the largest utility company in Massachusetts. More information about transportation and communication appears later in this section.

Manufacturing accounts for 18 percent of the gross state product of Massachusetts. The state's manufactured goods have a *value added by manufacture* of about $34 billion a year. Value added by manufacture represents the increase in value of raw materials after they become finished products.

Scientific instruments are the state's leading manufactured product in terms of value added by manufacture. Factories in the Boston area produce automation control devices, oscilloscopes, and other instruments.

Electrical equipment ranks second among manufactured products in Massachusetts. Electronic components and communications equipment are the leading goods made by this industry. Communications equipment includes broadcasting devices, military communications systems, and telephone equipment. Essex and Middlesex counties in northeastern Massachusetts produce most of the state's electrical equipment.

Machinery ranks third among the manufactured products. Computers are the major type of machinery produced in the state. Digital Equipment, one of the nation's largest computer companies, is headquartered in Massachusetts. The Greater Boston area has many factories that make computers. Other types of machinery manufactured in Massachusetts include metalworking machinery and printing equipment.

Printed materials are fourth among the manufactured products. Most printed materials are manufactured in Boston. Books and newspapers are the major kinds of printed materials made in Massachusetts.

Other types of products manufactured in Massachusetts, in order of value, include fabricated metal products, transportation equipment, food products, chemicals, plastics products, and paper products. Such fabricated metal products as hand tools, knives, stampings, and valves are made in Massachusetts. Automobiles, which are assembled in Framingham, are the major kind of transportation equipment. Most of the state's food processing takes place in the Boston area. Bread, candy, dairy products, fish products, and soft drinks are the main food products made in the state.

Agriculture. Farmland covers 14 percent of Massachusetts. The state's approximately 6,900 farms average about 99 acres (40 hectares) in size.

Greenhouse and nursery products, such as flowers and ornamental shrubs, are the leading source of farm income in Massachusetts. These products supply about a fourth of the farm income.

Cranberries rank second in value among farm products in Massachusetts. The state provides about half of the cranberries grown in the United States. Most of the state's cranberries are grown in bogs in marshy areas of the coastal lowlands.

Production and workers by economic activities

Economic activities	Percent of GSP* produced	Employed workers	
		Number of persons	Percent of total
Community, social, & personal services	27	889,900	31
Manufacturing	18	484,500	17
Finance, insurance, & real estate	17	203,900	7
Wholesale & retail trade	16	649,500	23
Government	10	384,500	14
Transportation, communication, & utilities	7	124,200	4
Construction	4	79,300	3
Agriculture & fishing	1	35,200	1
Mining	†	1,200	†
Total	**100**	**2,852,200**	**100**

*GSP = gross state product, the total value of goods and services produced in a year.
†Less than one-half of 1 percent.
Figures are for 1991.
Sources: *World Book* estimates based on data from U.S. Bureau of Economic Analysis, U.S. Bureau of Labor Statistics, and U.S. Department of Agriculture.

Bill Gallery, Stock, Boston

High technology industries began to flourish in the Boston area during the 1970's. The worker shown above is assembling a computer board in a factory in Marlborough.

Farm and mineral products

This map shows where the state's leading farm and mineral products are produced. The major urban areas (shown on the map in red) are the state's important manufacturing centers.

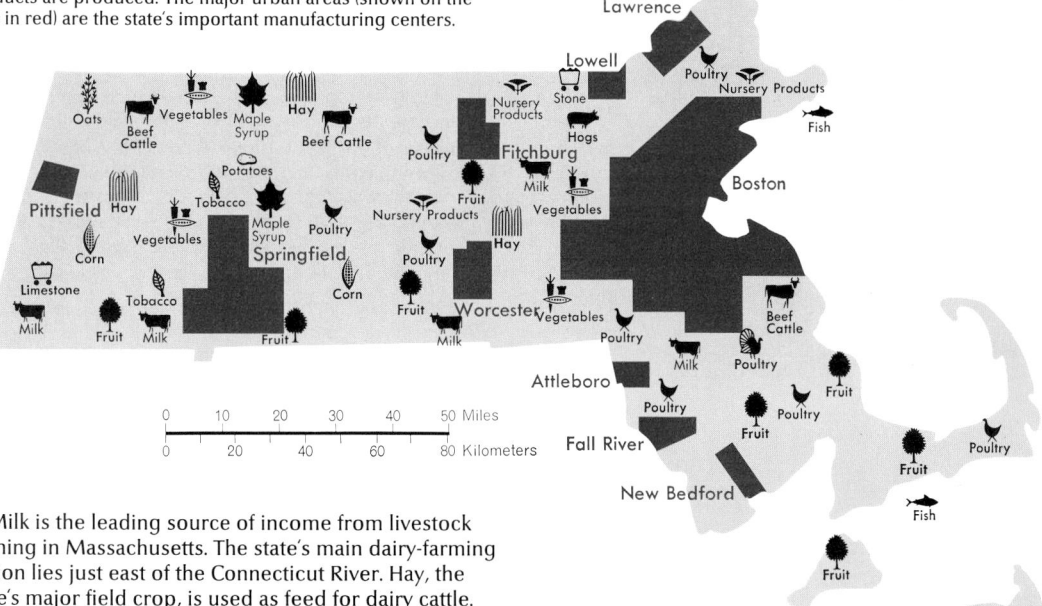

WORLD BOOK map

Milk is the leading source of income from livestock farming in Massachusetts. The state's main dairy-farming region lies just east of the Connecticut River. Hay, the state's major field crop, is used as feed for dairy cattle. Massachusetts farmers also produce apples, beef cattle, eggs, and sweet corn.

Mining in Massachusetts accounts for less than half of 1 percent of the gross state product. The production of sand and gravel and crushed stone provides most of the state's mining income. Central Massachusetts leads in sand and gravel production. Sand and gravel are used to make concrete and roadbeds. Traprock quarries in eastern Massachusetts are the main source of crushed stone. Crushed traprock is used to make asphalt pavement and other road surfaces. Clays, granite, and peat are also mined in Massachusetts.

Fishing industry. Massachusetts ranks among the leading commercial fishing states. The state's annual fish catch is valued at about $260 million. New Bedford's catch is more valuable than that of any other port in the United States. New Bedford accounts for about half the scallops produced in the United States. Gloucester's fish catch is the second most valuable in Massachusetts. Gloucester's chief products include cod, flounder, haddock, ocean perch, and whiting. The fishing industry in Boston specializes in cod and haddock. Other valuable products of the Massachusetts fishing industry include clams, crabs, hake, herring, lobster, pollock, squid, swordfish, and tuna.

Electric power. Plants that burn petroleum supply about 45 percent of the electric power used in Massachusetts. Plants that burn coal supply about 35 percent. Nuclear power plants and plants that burn natural gas each contribute about 10 percent of the state's electric power. Hydroelectric plants produce less than 1 percent of the power.

Transportation. Logan International Airport in Boston is the busiest airport in Massachusetts and one of the busiest airports in the world. Eleven railroads provide freight service in the state, and passenger trains serve several cities.

Massachusetts has about 34,000 miles (55,000 kilometers) of roads and highways, nearly all of which are paved. The Massachusetts Turnpike, a toll road, stretches westward from Boston to the New York state line. Two major highways swing in an arc around Boston—Route 128 and, farther west, Route 495.

Boston is the main seaport for Massachusetts and for much of New England. Fall River, the second most important port in Massachusetts, handles mostly petroleum products.

Communication. In 1639, Stephen Daye established the first printing press in the English colonies in Cambridge. This was only 19 years after the Pilgrims landed in Massachusetts. In 1640, Daye printed the *Bay Psalm Book,* the first English-language book published in America.

The first two newspapers in the colonies were published in Boston. *Publick Occurrences Both Forreign and Domestick* was established in 1690. *The Boston News-Letter,* which was established in 1704, was the first successful newspaper in America.

Today, Massachusetts publishers issue about 240 newspapers. About 50 of the newspapers are dailies. The chief newspapers include *The Boston Globe,* the *Boston Herald, The Christian Science Monitor* in Boston, *The Patriot Ledger* in Quincy, the *Springfield Union-News, The Standard Times* in New Bedford, and the *Telegram & Gazette* in Worcester. About 400 periodicals also are issued by publishers in Massachusetts.

The state's first radio station, WGI, began broadcasting in Medford in 1920. The first television stations in Massachusetts, WBZ-TV and WNAC-TV, started in Boston in 1948. Today, Massachusetts has about 170 radio stations and 13 television stations.

Constitution. Massachusetts adopted its Constitution in 1780, during the Revolutionary War. Its Constitution is the oldest state constitution still in use, though it has been *amended* (changed) more than 100 times.

The Constitution provides for two kinds of amendments. *Legislative amendments,* the more common type, are introduced by members of the legislature. *Initiative amendments* are introduced to the legislature on petitions signed by a specified number of qualified voters. Both types of amendments must be approved during joint sessions of the legislature. Legislative amendments require approval by a majority of the legislature. Initiative amendments must be approved by one-fourth of the legislators. All amendments must then be approved in a similar manner by the next legislative body. Finally, an amendment must be approved by a majority of the people voting on it in a general election. An initiative amendment must also receive approving votes equal to 30 per cent of the total number of ballots cast in the election.

A third procedure for a constitutional amendment, set by precedent in 1779, allows for the calling and holding of a constitutional convention. Before a constitutional convention can meet, it must be approved by a majority of the legislators and two-thirds of the state's voters.

Executive. The governor and lieutenant governor of Massachusetts are elected to four-year terms. The voters also elect the secretary of the commonwealth, the treasurer and receiver general, the attorney general, and the state auditor to four-year terms.

The governor is assisted by an 11-member cabinet, made up of the appointed heads of the state's 11 executive departments. The governor appoints the heads of state departments and the members of state agencies and nominates judges. The governor's judicial nominations are subject to approval by the Executive Council. The council consists of the lieutenant governor and one member elected from each of eight state districts. Massachusetts has no official residence for its governor.

Legislature, called the *Great and General Court,* consists of a 40-member senate and a 160-member house of representatives. Each of the 40 senatorial districts in Massachusetts elects one senator, and each of the state's representative districts elects one representative. All members of the legislature serve two-year terms. Both houses meet every year beginning on the first Wednesday in January. The session is scheduled to end on the Tuesday that precedes the first Wednesday in the following January. But it may end earlier if the legislature and the governor agree that all business is completed. Any Massachusetts citizen has the right to file a bill with the legislature.

Courts. All judges in Massachusetts are appointed by the governor and may serve until the age of 70. The su-

The state governors of Massachusetts

	Party	Term		Party	Term
John Hancock	None	1780-1785	Benjamin F. Butler	Democratic	1883-1884
James Bowdoin	None	1785-1787	George D. Robinson	Republican	1884-1887
John Hancock	None	1787-1793	Oliver Ames	Republican	1887-1890
Samuel Adams	None	1794-1797	John Q. A. Brackett	Republican	1890-1891
Increase Sumner	Federalist	1797-1799	William E. Russell	Democratic	1891-1894
Caleb Strong	Federalist	1800-1807	Frederic T. Greenhalge	Republican	1894-1896
James Sullivan	*Dem.-Rep.	1807-1808	Roger Wolcott	Republican	1896-1900
Levi Lincoln	Dem.-Rep.	1808-1809	Winthrop M. Crane	Republican	1900-1903
Christopher Gore	Federalist	1809-1810	John L. Bates	Republican	1903-1905
Elbridge Gerry	Dem.-Rep.	1810-1812	William L. Douglas	Democratic	1905-1906
Caleb Strong	Federalist	1812-1816	Curtis Guild, Jr.	Republican	1906-1909
John Brooks	Federalist	1816-1823	Eben S. Draper	Republican	1909-1911
William Eustis	Dem.-Rep.	1823-1825	Eugene N. Foss	Democratic	1911-1914
Marcus Morton	Dem.-Rep.	1825	David I. Walsh	Democratic	1914-1916
Levi Lincoln	Dem.-Rep.	1825-1834	Samuel W. McCall	Republican	1916-1919
John Davis	Whig	1834-1835	Calvin Coolidge	Republican	1919-1921
Samuel Armstrong	Whig	1835-1836	Channing H. Cox	Republican	1921-1925
Edward Everett	Whig	1836-1840	Alvin T. Fuller	Republican	1925-1929
Marcus Morton	Democratic	1840-1841	Frank G. Allen	Republican	1929-1931
John Davis	Whig	1841-1843	Joseph B. Ely	Democratic	1931-1935
Marcus Morton	Democratic	1843-1844	James M. Curley	Democratic	1935-1937
George N. Briggs	Whig	1844-1851	Charles F. Hurley	Democratic	1937-1939
George S. Boutwell	Democratic	1851-1853	Leverett Saltonstall	Republican	1939-1945
John H. Clifford	Whig	1853-1854	Maurice J. Tobin	Democratic	1945-1947
Emory Washburn	Whig	1854-1855	Robert F. Bradford	Republican	1947-1949
Henry J. Gardner	†American	1855-1858	Paul A. Dever	Democratic	1949-1953
Nathaniel P. Banks	Republican	1858-1861	Christian A. Herter	Republican	1953-1957
John A. Andrew	Republican	1861-1866	Foster Furcolo	Democratic	1957-1961
Alexander H. Bullock	Republican	1866-1869	John A. Volpe	Republican	1961-1963
William Claflin	Republican	1869-1872	Endicott Peabody	Democratic	1963-1965
William B. Washburn	Republican	1872-1874	John A. Volpe	Republican	1965-1969
Thomas Talbot	Republican	1874-1875	Francis W. Sargent	Republican	1969-1975
William Gaston	Democratic	1875-1876	Michael S. Dukakis	Democratic	1975-1979
Alexander H. Rice	Republican	1876-1879	Edward J. King	Democratic	1979-1983
Thomas Talbot	Republican	1879-1880	Michael S. Dukakis	Democratic	1983-1991
John D. Long	Republican	1880-1883	William F. Weld	Republican	1991-

*Democratic-Republican   †Know-Nothing

preme judicial court is the state's highest court. It has a chief justice and six associate justices. The appeals court handles appeals of civil and criminal cases. It consists of a chief justice and 13 associate justices. The superior court is the main trial court in the state. This court has a chief justice and 71 associate justices. Other state courts include district, housing, juvenile, land, Boston Municipal, and probate and family courts. The district, Boston Municipal, and juvenile courts are the lowest courts in Massachusetts.

Local government in Massachusetts is centered in 39 chartered cities and in 312 incorporated towns. Most of the cities have a mayor-council government. Some use a council-manager system. A *town* in Massachusetts is similar to a *township* in other states. Like a township, a town may consist of several villages and rural areas. The entire town is governed as a single unit.

Towns in Massachusetts are governed by annual town meetings. Many small towns hold open meetings at which any voter in the town can participate. Most large towns hold representative meetings at which only elected members are allowed to vote. Voters express their opinions about town issues and make plans for the coming year. They also choose officials called *selectmen* to carry out the town's business until the next meeting.

Massachusetts cities and towns have *home rule* (self-government). Under the state's home rule, communities may pass some laws dealing with local matters without interference from the state government.

Counties serve mainly as judicial boundaries. The state's 14 counties are divided into districts. Each county has one or more district courts. Each county elects a register of deeds, a register of probate and insolvency, a district attorney, a sheriff, and clerks of court. All the counties except Nantucket and Suffolk elect commissioners and treasurers.

Revenue. Taxation provides about three-fourths of Massachusetts' *general revenue* (income). Most of the rest comes from federal grants and programs. Income taxes are the largest source of tax revenue. Other key sources of tax revenue in the state include a corporate excise tax, a motor fuel tax, and sales taxes.

Politics. Massachusetts has elected about an equal number of Democrats and Republicans to the United States Senate. More Republicans than Democrats have served as governor. In presidential elections that have occurred since 1900, more Democrats than Republicans have won the state's electoral votes. For Massachusetts' electoral votes and voting record in presidential elections, see **Electoral College** (table).

History

Indian days. Indians probably lived in the Massachusetts region more than 3,000 years ago. Early white explorers saw Algonquian Indians in the region about 1500. The Algonquian tribes included the Massachuset, Nauset, Nipmuc, Pennacook, Pocomtuc, and Wampanoag. Disease killed many of these Indians in 1616 and 1617. By the time the Pilgrims arrived in 1620, the Indian population had dropped from about 30,000 to about 7,000.

Early exploration. The first Europeans to reach Massachusetts were probably Vikings led by Leif Ericson in about the year 1000. Some French and Spanish fishermen may have visited the region during the 1400's. Historians believe that John Cabot sighted the Massachusetts coast in 1498.

In 1602, Bartholomew Gosnold of England landed on Cuttyhunk Island in the Elizabeth Islands. He gave Cape Cod its name. In 1605 and 1606, Samuel de Champlain of France drew maps of the New England shoreline. John Smith, an English sea captain, sailed along the coast of Massachusetts in 1614. Smith's book, *A Description of New England,* guided the Pilgrims to Massachusetts.

The Pilgrims. In the early 1600's, a group of English Protestants separated from the Church of England. These people, called *Separatists,* wanted to worship God in their own way, but were not permitted to do so. On Sept. 16, 1620, 41 Separatists and 61 other people from England became the first group of Pilgrims to journey to America. These Pilgrims sailed from Plymouth, England, in the *Mayflower.* That November, the *Mayflower* anchored in what is now Provincetown harbor. Before leaving the ship, the Pilgrims drew up a plan of self-government, which they called the Mayflower Compact. In December, the Pilgrims sailed across Cape Cod Bay and settled in Plymouth.

The Pilgrims suffered great hardships during their first winter in America. They had little food other than the game they could hunt. Their houses were crude bark shelters. About half the settlers died during the winter of 1620-1621.

Early in 1621, the Pilgrims became friendly with some Indians. The Indians taught them how to plant corn and beans. By the time cold weather came again, the settlers were living more comfortably. They had enough food to last through the winter. The Pilgrims celebrated the first New England Thanksgiving in 1621. They gave thanks to God for delivering them from hunger and hardship (see **Thanksgiving Day**).

More settlers came to the Plymouth Colony during the years that followed. Within 20 years after the Pilgrims landed, Plymouth Colony had eight towns and about 2,500 people.

The Puritans. In 1629, King Charles I of England granted a charter to a group called the Puritans. The charter gave the Puritans the right to settle and govern an English colony in the Massachusetts Bay area. John Winthrop, an English lawyer and country gentleman, led about 1,000 Puritans to Massachusetts in 1630. They joined a settlement that had been established in Salem about three years earlier. In 1630, they left Salem and founded a settlement in the area of present-day Boston. The colony prospered and grew. By 1640, the Massachusetts Bay Colony had about 10,000 settlers.

Colonial days. The Massachusetts Bay Colony established political freedom and a representative form of government. In 1641, the first code of laws of the colony was set down in a document known as the Body of Liberties. But the Puritans permitted no religion except their own in the colony. Some religious groups were put out of the colony, and others left on their own.

Historic Massachusetts

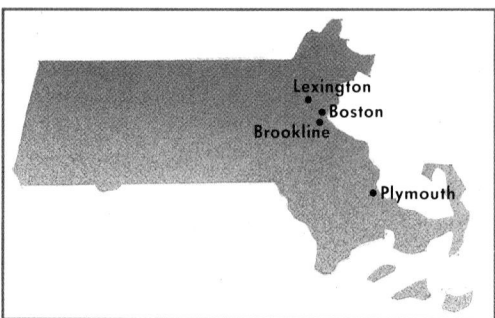

The Pilgrims landed at Plymouth in December 1620, after a voyage of more than three months from England.

The Boston Tea Party of Dec. 16, 1773, was a protest by colonists. Dressed as Indians, they threw cargoes of tea from British ships into Boston Harbor.

The Revolutionary War began when the patriots fought the British at Lexington and Concord on April 19, 1775.

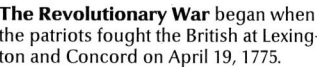

The telephone was invented by Alexander Graham Bell in Boston. It was patented on March 7, 1876.

John F. Kennedy, born in Brookline, became the 35th President of the United States on Jan. 20, 1961.

WORLD BOOK illustrations by Kevin Chadwick

Important dates in Massachusetts

1602 Bartholomew Gosnold, an English explorer, visited the Massachusetts region.

1620 The Pilgrims landed at Plymouth.

1630 The Puritans founded Boston.

1636 Harvard became the first college in the colonies.

1641 Massachusetts adopted its first code of law, the Body of Liberties.

1675-1676 Massachusetts colonists won King Philip's War against the Indians.

1689-1763 Massachusetts colonists helped the British win the French and Indian Wars.

1691 Plymouth and the Massachusetts Bay colonies were combined into one colony.

1764 The colonists began to resist enforcement of British tax laws.

1770 British soldiers killed several colonists in the Boston Massacre.

1773 Patriots dumped British tea into Boston Harbor during the Boston Tea Party.

1775 The American Revolutionary War began at Lexington and Concord.

1780 Massachusetts adopted its constitution.

1788 Massachusetts became the sixth state in the union on February 6.

1797 John Adams of Massachusetts became President of the United States.

1807 The Embargo Act ruined Massachusetts shipping, and led to the rise of manufacturing.

1825 John Quincy Adams of Massachusetts became President of the United States.

1912 A strike of textile workers at Lawrence led to improved conditions in the textile industry.

1919 Settlement of the Boston police strike brought national prominence to Governor Calvin Coolidge.

1959 The U.S. Navy launched its first nuclear-powered surface ship, the cruiser *Long Beach,* at Quincy.

1961 John F. Kennedy of Massachusetts became President of the United States.

1971 Massachusetts began a major reorganization of its state government, including the consolidation of more than 150 smaller agencies into about 10 new departments.

Illustration (1907) by Howard Pyle (Granger Collection)

The Salem Witchcraft Trials, held in 1692, resulted in the execution of 19 people, both men and women, who were convicted as witches. These were the last witchcraft executions in America.

These Massachusetts settlers helped colonize other parts of New England in their search for religious freedom. They established settlements in Connecticut in 1635, Rhode Island in 1636, New Hampshire in 1638, and Maine in 1652. Connecticut and Rhode Island soon became independent colonies. New Hampshire did not separate from Massachusetts until 1680. Maine remained a part of Massachusetts until 1820.

King Philip's War. Massasoit, chief of the Wampanoag tribe, had been a close friend of the Plymouth colonists. But his son, King Philip, who became chief in 1662, feared the white settlers. He believed that they would wipe out the Indians and seize their lands.

In 1675, King Philip rose up against the colonists in an attempt to protect his people and their homelands. He planned to massacre all white settlers in New England. The struggle became known as King Philip's War. White and Indian settlements were burned and hundreds of men, women, and children died on both sides. An Indian serving with colonial troops killed King Philip in 1676, ending the war in southern New England. Fighting continued in northern New England until 1678. The Indian danger in eastern, central, and southern Massachusetts ended. But a tenth of Massachusetts' white male population had been wiped out.

Troubles with England. Although Massachusetts belonged to England, the colonists often resisted controls from across the sea. England believed that its colo-

nists should trade only with the mother country. But many Massachusetts colonists disagreed, and traded with other countries. Attempts at stricter control had little effect on some of the colonists. In 1684, King Charles II canceled the Massachusetts charter. James II became king of England in 1685.

In 1686, King James established a government in Massachusetts and other northern colonies called the Dominion of New England. The king made Sir Edmund Andros governor of the dominion. King James was overthrown in 1688. His daughter, Mary, and her husband, Prince William of Orange, became joint rulers of England. When the Massachusetts colonists received the news, they put Andros out of office and set up a temporary government of their own. William and Mary granted a new charter to Massachusetts in 1691. This charter combined the Plymouth Colony with the Massachusetts Bay Colony and added the island of Martha's Vineyard.

In 1692, Sir William Phips became Massachusetts' first royal governor. One of his most important acts was to end the persecution of persons believed to be witches (see **Witchcraft**).

The French and Indian wars. In 1689, the first of the four French and Indian wars broke out. The English colonists fought the French colonists and France's Indian allies. Between 1689 and 1713, settlers along Massachusetts' northern and western borders fought off continuous French and Indian attacks. In 1713, Great Britain, France, and other European nations signed a peace treaty at Utrecht, the Netherlands. An era of prosperity began in Massachusetts. Dozens of towns sprang up in the central and western areas of the colony. But the wars broke out again in the 1740's. They finally ended in 1763 with victory for the British.

Pre-Revolutionary days. The colonial wars left Britain in debt. To help pay for defense of the colonies, the British placed severe taxes on the American colonies. The Massachusetts colonists ignored most of these taxes. But the Stamp Act of 1765 led to bitter protests (see **Stamp Act**). The cry of "no taxation without representation" spread through the colony. An angry mob destroyed the lieutenant governor's home. The presence of British soldiers in Boston added to the bitterness between the colonists and the Crown. In 1770, British soldiers killed several colonists while fighting a Boston mob. This incident became known as the Boston Massacre. In 1773, angry colonists staged the Boston Tea Party to protest a British tea tax. The colonists dumped 342 chests of British tea into Boston Harbor.

The British passed a series of measures to punish the colonists. But these measures merely angered the colonists more and helped bring all the American colonies together. On April 18, 1775, British troops marched from Boston to seize or destroy supplies of gunpowder hidden by the colonists at Concord. Paul Revere and others rode across the Massachusetts countryside to warn their fellow patriots that the British were coming. The next morning, American minutemen at Lexington fought the opening battle of the Revolutionary War (see **Minutemen**).

The Revolutionary War began in Massachusetts. Much of the early fighting took place on Massachusetts soil. Massachusetts soldiers fought bravely at Lexington,

Boston Harbor in 1768 is shown in an engraving by Paul Revere. British warships are anchored in the harbor.

Massachusetts Historical Society

Concord, and at Bunker Hill. On July 3, 1775, General George Washington took command of the Continental Army in Cambridge. In the spring of 1776, Washington drove the British out of Boston in the first major American victory of the war. Much of the fighting moved out of Massachusetts and into New York, New Jersey, and Pennsylvania in 1776. But Massachusetts continued to send soldiers and supplies to the American forces. At sea, Massachusetts ships inflicted heavy damage on British merchant ships.

The effects of the Revolutionary War in Massachusetts were felt most by the farmers. Prices of farm products dropped after the war ended in 1783. Money became so scarce that many farmers could not pay their taxes or debts. The farmers, facing the danger of losing their farms and going to prison, grew restless. In September 1786, Daniel Shays led a group of angry farmers to protest in front of the courthouse in Springfield. Fighting broke out between the farmers and government troops. The fighting, which became known as Shays' Rebellion, ended when the farmers surrendered in February 1787.

Massachusetts farmers also opposed *ratification* (approval) of the United States Constitution. They felt that the Constitution was more favorable to trade and finance than to agriculture. On Feb. 6, 1788, Massachusetts ratified the Constitution and became the sixth state in the Union. Massachusetts ratified the Constitution only on the condition that certain amendments concerning individual rights be added. The Bill of Rights to the U.S. Constitution went into effect on Dec. 15, 1791.

Progress as a state. Massachusetts prospered during its early years as a state. In the early 1800's, France and Britain were at war. American shipowners who were willing to send their vessels into European waters could make huge profits. But both the British and the French tried to attack ships bound for their enemy's ports. President Thomas Jefferson feared that such an attack on an American ship might force the United States into the war. In 1807, he persuaded Congress to pass the Embargo Act, which stopped American exports to other countries and prohibited U.S. ships from sailing into foreign ports.

Hardships resulting from the embargo and the War of

1812 forced a new way of life upon the people of Massachusetts. Goods had to be manufactured at home rather than imported. In 1814, Francis Cabot Lowell built a textile factory in Waltham. It was one of the first factories in the United States. A number of other textile mills were soon operating in eastern Massachusetts. With the opening of New York's Erie Canal in 1825, crops could be brought to New England from the west. Farming in Massachusetts suffered. Many farmers left the state or went to work in factories.

The whaling industry flourished in New Bedford, Nantucket, and Boston until the early 1860's. It declined after kerosene replaced whale oil.

The *abolitionist* (antislavery) movement received wide support in Massachusetts. In 1831, William Lloyd Garrison of Boston began publishing his antislavery newspaper *The Liberator.* In 1832, abolitionists formed the New England Anti-Slavery Society in Boston. The society helped slaves escape to Canada. Some people in Massachusetts opposed the abolitionists. They objected to what they considered extremist tactics. They also feared that the Southern planters might cut off the cotton supply for the Massachusetts textile industry.

In 1850, Congress passed a series of acts which it hoped would settle the conflict between slave-owners and those who opposed slavery. These acts were called the Compromise of 1850 (see **Compromise of 1850**). Senator Daniel Webster of Massachusetts defended the compromise as necessary to preserve the Union. But many persons in Massachusetts disagreed. Abraham Lincoln and the Republican Party carried the state in the 1860 presidential election.

Massachusetts gave strong support to the Union during the Civil War (1861-1865). The state furnished more than 125,000 men to the Union Army and about 20,000 men to the Navy. Massachusetts shipbuilders built and equipped many Union ships.

Industry in the state expanded after the war. The textile industry prospered, and the leather and metal products industries also grew rapidly. Thousands of immigrants poured into the state to meet the great demand for industrial labor.

In 1876, the American inventor Alexander Graham Bell developed the telephone in Boston. A telephone line between Boston and Providence, R.I., was installed in 1881.

The early 1900's. Massachusetts' population swelled to about $2\frac{1}{2}$ million by 1900. About 30 per cent of these people came to the United States from other countries. This huge number of people, with their variety of backgrounds, brought new problems to the state. Communities had to provide such services as water supply, sewerage, housing, and police protection. Industrial workers became unhappy with wages and working conditions. A textile strike in Lawrence in 1912 brought nationwide attention to poor working conditions in the textile industry. Improvements followed the strike.

The United States entered World War I in 1917. The Yankee (26th) Division of Massachusetts was the first National Guard division to reach the battlefields of France. Prices climbed in Massachusetts during the war, and workers demanded higher wages to meet the increased cost of living. But often such demands were not met. In 1919, the mayor of Boston refused to let the city's police form a union. About three-fourths of the Boston police force went on strike. Governor Calvin Coolidge helped end the strike by sending the National Guard into Boston. Coolidge gained nationwide fame because of his action and was elected Vice President of the United States in 1920. Three years later, Coolidge became President after President Warren G. Harding died.

Massachusetts' economy suffered during the 1920's because of competition from the textile and shoe industries in Southern and Western states. But other industries continued to prosper. In 1929, the Great Depression hit the United States. Massachusetts carried on its own unemployment-relief program until the federal government organized nationwide programs. In 1938, a hurricane killed hundreds of persons in Massachusetts and caused great property damage.

The mid-1900's. The state's economy soared during World War II (1939-1945). Massachusetts factories and shipyards produced huge quantities of war materials.

Many traditional Massachusetts industries, including the manufacture of shoes and textiles, declined greatly during the 1950's and 1960's. Many industries in the state began to switch to space and rocket research or the production of electronics equipment. Hundreds of research laboratories developed in and around Boston, using the facilities and personnel of the many colleges and universities in the area. The United States Navy launched its first nuclear surface ship, the cruiser *Long Beach,* at Quincy in 1959.

Like many other states, Massachusetts faced serious racial problems during the mid-1900's. In 1957, the state legislature prohibited segregation in public housing. New legislation in 1963 made segregation illegal in most private dwellings as well. During the mid-1970's, Boston's public schools were desegregated by order of a federal court.

During the 1950's and 1960's, the Kennedy family of Brookline became powerful in state and national politics. John F. Kennedy served as President of the United States from 1961 until his assassination in 1963. When elected President, he was representing Massachusetts in the U.S. Senate. His brother, Robert F. Kennedy, served as U.S. attorney general from 1961 to 1964. Robert Kennedy was elected to the U.S. Senate from New York in 1964. He was assassinated in 1968 while campaigning for the Democratic presidential nomination. The youngest Kennedy brother, Edward M. Kennedy, has served as a U.S. senator from Massachusetts since 1962.

Recent developments. Since the mid-1900's, large numbers of people and industries have moved from the cities to suburbs. However, this trend began to reverse in the late 1970's, largely because of rising transportation costs for commuters and a state government policy favoring growth in the cities.

Massachusetts has remained a center for military research and development, and it is a leader in banking, education, insurance, and medical care. The state's economy improved steadily from the mid-1970's through the mid-1980's. However, Massachusetts' economic growth slowed in the late 1980's and early 1990's as the northeastern region of the country faced economic problems.

In the late 1980's, lower tax revenues and increased government spending combined to create a large deficit in the state government's budget. The decreased tax revenues were caused partly by cuts in property taxes and state taxes that occurred earlier in the 1980's. Massachusetts' sluggish economy contributed to the decrease. In response to the deficit, Massachusetts cut state spending and raised income taxes. These measures helped Massachusetts eliminate its budget deficit in the early 1990's.

Today, Massachusetts officials are also working to ease several other problems common to many states. These problems include air and water pollution, a housing shortage in cities, and racial tension.

Winfred E. A. Bernhard, Michael G. Mensoian, and Robert L. Turner

Study aids

Related articles in *World Book* include:

Biographies

Adams, Charles F.	Bradford, William	Coolidge, Calvin	Gage, Thomas
Adams, John	(Plymouth governor)	Cotton, John	Gerry, Elbridge
Adams, John Q.	Bradstreet, Anne D.	Curley, James M.	Goddard, Robert H.
Adams, Samuel	Brandeis, Louis D.	Daye, Stephen	Gorham, Nathaniel
Alden, John and Priscilla	Brewster, William	Dickinson, Emily	Hancock, John
Attucks, Crispus	Brooke, Edward W.	Dudley, Thomas	Harvard, John
Bartlett, John	Bulfinch, Charles	Dukakis, Michael S.	Hawthorne, Nathaniel
Barton, Clara	Bulfinch, Thomas	Eliot, John	Holmes, Oliver Wendell
Bowditch, Nathaniel	Carver, John	Emerson, Ralph Waldo	Holmes, Oliver W., Jr.
		Endecott, John	Hutchinson, Anne M.
		Everett, Edward	Hutchinson, Thomas
		Franklin, Benjamin	Kennedy (family)

Kennedy, Edward M.
Kennedy, John F.
Kennedy, Robert F.
Knox, Henry
Lodge, Henry Cabot
Lodge, Henry Cabot, Jr.
Lowell, Amy
Lowell, James Russell
Mann, Horace
Massasoit
Mather (family)
McCormack, John W.
O'Neill, Thomas P.
Otis, James
Paine, Robert T.
Parker, Theodore
Phillips, Wendell
Pickering, Timothy
Randolph, Edward

Revere, Paul
Richardson, Elliot L.
Samoset
Sampson, Deborah
Sewall, Samuel
Shirley, William
Squanto
Standish, Miles
Sumner, Charles
Thoreau, Henry David
Warren, Joseph
Wheatley, Phillis
White, Peregrine
Whittier, John G.
Williams, Roger
Wilson, Henry
Winslow, Edward
Winthrop, John

Cities and towns

Boston
Cambridge
Concord
Fall River
Gloucester
Lowell
Nantucket

New Bedford
Plymouth
Quincy
Salem
Springfield
Worcester

History

Architecture (pictures: Early American architecture)
Boston Massacre
Boston Tea Party
Brook Farm
Civil War
Colonial life in America
Massachusetts Bay Colony
Mayflower
Mayflower Compact

Money (History of United States currency: picture)
Pilgrims
Pine-tree shilling
Plymouth Colony
Plymouth Rock
Puritans
Revolutionary War in America
Shays' Rebellion
Witchcraft

Physical features

Cape Cod
Connecticut River
Housatonic River

Martha's Vineyard
Merrimack River

Outline

I. People
  A. Population
  B. Schools
  C. Libraries
  D. Museums
II. Visitor's guide
  A. Places to visit
  B. Annual events
III. Land and climate
  A. Land regions
  B. Coastline
  C. Islands
  D. Rivers and lakes
  E. Plant and animal life
  F. Climate
IV. Economy
  A. Natural resources
  B. Service industries
  C. Manufacturing
  D. Agriculture
  E. Mining
  F. Fishing industry
  G. Electric power
  H. Transportation
  I. Communication
V. Government
  A. Constitution
  B. Executive
  C. Legislature
  D. Courts
  E. Local government
  F. Revenue
  G. Politics
VI. History

Questions

What nationwide holiday was first observed in Massachusetts? What was the occasion?
What distinction does the Massachusetts constitution have among all state constitutions?

What section of Massachusetts has the most fertile soil?
When and where was the first printing press in the British colonies set up?
What was Shays' Rebellion?
What great stride in education took place in the Massachusetts Bay Colony in 1647?
What mountain ranges extend into Massachusetts? What is the state's most important waterway?
Why did Britain tax the American colonies after the French and Indian wars? How did these taxes start a chain of events that led to the Revolutionary War?
Which three U.S. Presidents were born in Massachusetts?
How does local government operate in Massachusetts towns?

Additional resources

Level I
Anderson, Joan. *The First Thanksgiving Feast.* Clarion, 1984.
Carpenter, Allan. *Massachusetts.* Rev. ed. Childrens Pr., 1978.
Fradin, Dennis B. *Massachusetts in Words and Pictures.* Childrens Pr., 1981.
Kent, Deborah. *Massachusetts.* Childrens Pr., 1987.
Monke, Ingrid. *Boston.* Dillon Pr., 1988.
Morison, Samuel Eliot. *Story of the Old Colony of New Plymouth (1620-1692).* Knopf, 1956.
Sewall, Marcia. *The Pilgrims of Plimoth.* Atheneum, 1986.

Level II
Brown, Richard D. *Massachusetts: A Bicentennial History.* Norton, 1978.
Fleming, Thomas J. *One Small Candle: The Pilgrims' First Year in America.* Norton, 1964.
Forbes, Esther. *Paul Revere and the World He Lived In.* Houghton, 1972. First published in 1942.
Formisano, Ronald P. *The Transformation of Political Culture: Massachusetts Parties, 1790s-1840s.* Oxford, 1983.
A Guide to the History of Massachusetts. Ed. by Martin Kaufman and others. Greenwood, 1988.
Labaree, Benjamin W. *Colonial Massachusetts: A History.* Kraus-Thomson, 1979.
The Massachusetts Miracle: High Technology and Economic Revitalization. Ed. by David Lampe. MIT Press, 1988.
Morison, Samuel Eliot. *The Maritime History of Massachusetts, 1783-1860.* Northeastern Univ. Pr., 1979. First published in 1921. *Builders of the Bay Colony.* 1982. Reprint of 1964 revised edition.
Whitehill, Walter M., and Kotker, Norman. *Massachusetts: A Pictorial History.* Scribner, 1981. First published in 1976.
Williams, Selma R. *Kings, Commoners, and Colonists: Puritan Politics in Old New England, 1603-1660.* Atheneum, 1974.

Massachusetts, University of, is a state-supported coeducational university. It has campuses in Amherst, Boston, and North Dartmouth, and a medical center in Worcester, Mass.

The Amherst campus has colleges of arts and sciences and of food and natural resources, and schools of education, engineering, health science, management, and physical education. It grants associate, bachelor's, master's, and doctor's degrees. The Boston campus has colleges of arts and sciences, management, and public and community service; a school of nursing; and a college of education. It offers bachelor's, master's, and doctor's degrees. The North Dartmouth campus has colleges of arts and sciences, business and industry, nursing, and visual and performing arts. It grants bachelor's and master's degrees. The university's medical school and graduate schools of nursing and biomedical science are part of the medical center located in Worcester.

The University of Massachusetts and Amherst, Hampshire, Mount Holyoke, and Smith colleges have set up cooperative programs. One program allows a student to take courses at any of the other schools if they are not offered at his or her own school. The schools also offer doctor's degrees jointly in several fields.

The university was chartered in 1863 as Massachusetts Agricultural College. It took its present name in 1947. For enrollment, see **Universities and colleges** (table).

Critically reviewed by the University of Massachusetts

Massachusetts Bay Colony was the largest and most successful early New England settlement. It was established in 1628 by the New England Company, a joint-stock company composed of English Puritans. That year, John Endecott led the first group of colonists to Naumkeag, an English settlement that he renamed Salem. In 1629, King Charles I granted a new charter that changed the name of the company to the Massachusetts Bay Company. In 1630, the company's new governor, John Winthrop, brought the charter and about 1,000 more people to settle the Massachusetts Bay region, including the area that is now Boston.

The Puritans observed a simple form of worship without the ceremonies of the Church of England. Each community established self-governing congregations. The Puritans wanted to make their church and society an example for people in other parts of the world to follow. Newcomers were expected to follow the Puritans' religious beliefs and practices. People who refused were sent back to England or expelled to such other settlements as Rhode Island and New Hampshire.

England rarely interfered with the colony's government and trade. Beginning in 1660, Puritans refused to obey new English trade laws. In 1684, the colony lost its charter. In 1691, King William III granted a new charter that included Plymouth Colony as part of the Massachusetts Bay Colony. This charter lasted until the Revolutionary War in America began in 1775.

The colonists of the Massachusetts Bay Colony made many contributions to American life. Among the most important of these were a practical, local self-government and a love of learning.   T. H. Breen

See also **Endecott, John; Massachusetts** (History); **Puritans; Williams, Roger; Winthrop, John; Winthrop, John, Jr.**

Additional resources

Labaree, Benjamin W. *Colonial Massachusetts: A History.* Kraus, 1979.
Morison, Samuel E. *Builders of the Bay Colony.* Rev. ed. Houghton, 1964.
Smith, Robert. *The Massachusetts Colony.* Crowell Collier, 1969. For younger readers.
Wall, Robert E. *Massachusetts Bay: The Crucial Decade, 1640-1650.* Yale, 1972.

Massachusetts Institute of Technology

(M.I.T.) is a private coeducational university in Cambridge, Mass. It is famous for its scientific research activities and for combining education and research in all programs. The institute includes schools of architecture and planning, engineering, humanities and social science, management, and science. All these schools offer graduate programs. M.I.T. grants bachelor's, master's, and doctor's degrees.

M.I.T. has research centers in several broad fields, including cancer, communications sciences, earth and life sciences, energy, international and urban studies, and nuclear and space science. More than 70 laboratories at the institute conduct research in all fields represented at M.I.T. The institution has a wide sports program and sponsors activities in drama, music, publications, and other cultural areas.

M.I.T. was founded in Boston in 1861 and moved to Cambridge in 1916. The campus extends for more than a mile (1.6 kilometers) along the Charles River. For enrollment, see **Universities and colleges** (table).

Critically reviewed by Massachusetts Institute of Technology

Massage, *muh SAHZH,* is a method of manipulating the skin to produce healthful effects on the skin and underlying tissues. "Western massage" consists of stroking, rubbing, kneading, and striking the skin, usually with the hands or fingers. "Eastern massage" includes these same methods, but it also focuses on applying pressure at specific points of the body according to acupuncture techniques (see **Acupuncture**).

Massage can improve blood circulation, relax muscles, stimulate nerve endings in the skin, and promote a feeling of general well-being. Depending on how the massage is given, its effects can be relaxing or invigorating. It is often used to promote healing of an injury or muscle soreness, or to relieve tension. People who give massages should be well trained, and they should be knowledgeable about physiology.   Mary T. Moffroid

Massasoit, *MAS uh soyt* (1580?-1661), was a chief of the Wampanoag tribe of Indians who lived in what is now southern Massachusetts and Rhode Island. He made a treaty with Governor John Carver of Plymouth Colony in the spring of 1621, shortly after the Pilgrims landed in America.

Massasoit agreed that his people would not harm the Pilgrims as long as he lived. In turn, the Pilgrims guaranteed to protect the Indians and their rights. Massasoit kept the peace all his life.

In the autumn of 1621, the Pilgrims harvested their

Bronze statue (1921); Artstreet

A statue of Massasoit by the American sculptor Cyrus Dallin stands on a Pilgrim burial ground in Plymouth, Mass.

first crop of Indian corn and invited Massasoit and about 90 of his people to share the first Thanksgiving feast. The Indians brought five deer to add to the feast, which lasted three days.

When Massasoit died, he was succeeded by his elder son, Wamsutta, whom the colonists called Alexander. Massasoit's younger son, Metacomet, called King Philip by the colonists, succeeded Alexander.   James Axtell

See also **Philip, King; Plymouth Colony** (The first year).

Massenet, *MAS uh NAY,* **Jules,** *zhool* (1842-1912), was a French composer best known for his operas. Massenet's operas are noted for their dramatic sense and graceful melodies. Perhaps the best known of his 25 operas is *Manon* (1884). The leading roles of Manon and her lover, Des Grieux, are still popular with singers. Massenet's other operas include *Werther* (1892), *Thaïs* (1894), and *Don Quichotte* (1910). He also wrote orchestral works, works for orchestra and voice, and more than 200 songs that rank among his best compositions.

Jules Émile Frédéric Massenet was born in Montaud, near St.-Étienne. His early piano lessons with his mother helped him gain admission to the Paris Conservatory at the age of 11. From 1878 to 1896, he was a professor of composition at the conservatory.   Steven E. Gilbert

Massey, Vincent (1887-1967), was the first Canadian-born governor general of Canada. He served in this position from 1952 to 1959. All previous governors general had come from Britain. Massey traveled extensively in Canada, promoting a feeling of national identity among Canada's French- and English-speaking citizens.

Charles Vincent Massey was born in Toronto, Ont. He received a bachelor's degree from the University of Toronto and a master's degree from Balliol College of Oxford University. Massey was a history lecturer at the university from 1913 to 1915. From 1921 to 1925, he was president of the family's Massey-Harris Company, which manufactured farm machinery.

In 1926, Massey joined the Canadian delegation at the Imperial Conference in London. Canada's independent status in the British Commonwealth of Nations, as the British Empire then became known, was recognized at this conference. Massey served as Canada's first minister to the United States from 1926 to 1930. From 1935 to 1946, he was High Commissioner for Canada in Britain.

In 1949, the Canadian government made Massey chairman of the Royal Commission on National Development in the Arts, Letters and Sciences. The commission's work led to increased government financial aid to help promote the arts and sciences. Massey served as chancellor of the University of Toronto from 1947 to 1953. In 1961, he founded Massey College, a graduate college of the university. Massey published several volumes of his speeches. He also wrote an autobiography, *What's Past Is Prologue* (1963).   Jacques Monet

Massine, *mah SEEN,* **Leonide,** *lay aw NEED* (1896-1979), was a great Russian dancer and *choreographer* (dance creator). Massine invented a dance form called *symphonic ballet,* in which *abstract* (storyless) ballets were choreographed to well-known symphonies. His *Les Présages* (1933) to Tchaikovsky's Symphony No. 5 was the first of these ballets. He also choreographed and danced in many other kinds of ballets, such as *The Three-Cornered Hat* (1919), *Le Beau Danube* (1933), and

Gaîté Parisienne (1938). As a dancer, he had a strong personality, especially in comic or character roles.

Massine was born in Moscow. He joined Sergei Diaghilev's Ballets Russes as a dancer in 1913. By 1917 he had created several ballets, including the first cubist ballet, *Parade.* Massine was director, dancer, and choreographer of the Ballets Russes from 1932 to 1938 and of the Ballet Russe de Monte Carlo from 1938 to 1941. He also appeared in films, including *The Red Shoes* (1948) and *Tales of Hoffmann* (1951).   Dorothy Lourdou

Massinger, *MAS uhn juhr,* **Philip** (1583-1640), an English playwright, is best known for his comedy *A New Way to Pay Old Debts* (1621 or 1622). The play's chief character, the monstrous villain Sir Giles Overreach, so appealed to actors and audiences that the play was performed longer than any other non-Shakespearean play of the 1600's. The character of Sir Giles Overreach is based on the scandalous activities of a real nobleman, and the action is taken from Thomas Middleton's play *A Trick to Catch the Old One* (1608).

Massinger was born in Salisbury of a prominent family. He wrote nearly 40 plays, some of them in collaboration with other playwrights. About 20 of his plays survive. From 1625 to his death, Massinger wrote one or two plays a year for The King's Men, the leading acting company of the day.   Albert Wertheim

Masson, André. See **Painting** (Surrealism; picture); **Surrealism.**

Mastaba. See **Pyramids** (Egyptian pyramids).

Mastectomy, *mas TEHK tuh mee,* is the surgical removal of a breast. Surgeons generally perform a mastectomy to treat women for breast cancer. The operation removes cancer cells in the breast and prevents them from spreading to other body organs.

There are four main types of mastectomies. The type of mastectomy performed depends on the size and location of the tumor, the extent of the cancer, and the age and health of the patient. The *conventional radical mastectomy* removes the breast, the lymph nodes in the underarm, and the chest wall muscles. The *modified radical mastectomy* removes the breast and the underarm lymph nodes. A *simple mastectomy,* also called *total mastectomy,* removes only the breast. A *subcutaneous mastectomy* removes breast tissue but spares the overlying skin and nipple.

Until the 1970's, the conventional radical mastectomy was the most common type of breast removal for cancer. It was developed in 1894 by William S. Halsted, an American surgeon. It leaves the patient with a long, unsightly scar, a depression beneath the collarbone, and often some difficulty in using the arm. In the 1950's, some surgeons began using the modified radical mastectomy, which resulted in less disfigurement for the woman. By the late 1970's, studies indicated that the modified radical was probably as effective as the conventional radical. Today, the modified radical mastectomy is the most commonly used surgical procedure for breast cancer. It offers the woman good options for breast reconstruction and normal use of her arm.

Most women who have had mastectomies wear an artificial breast called a *breast prosthesis.* Some women have their breast reconstructed through surgery. The breast is reconstructed by placing an implant filled with either saltwater or a material called *silicone gel* under the muscle or skin or by using skin and tissue from another part of the patient's body.

In the 1980's, many surgeons began recommending a procedure called *lumpectomy,* followed by radiation therapy, as an alternative to mastectomy in treating small tumors. A lumpectomy removes just the cancerous growth and the underarm lymph nodes. The breast is then treated with radiation to prevent any remaining cancer cells from spreading. Research suggests that a lumpectomy followed by radiation treatment may be just as effective as the modified radical mastectomy in treating small tumors.   Melvin J. Silverstein

See also **Breast; Cancer.**

Masters, Edgar Lee (1868-1950), was an American author. He wrote novels, poetry, plays, biography, and history, but he became famous chiefly for one volume of poems, *Spoon River Anthology* (1915).

Masters modeled the *Anthology* on a collection of ancient Greek short poems and sayings called *The Greek Anthology.* Spoon River is an imaginary Midwestern village. Masters' work consists of more than 200 short poems in free verse. Each poem is spoken by a former resident of the village, now dead and buried in the Spoon River cemetery. Each of the dead persons seeks to interpret, from the grave, the meaning of life on earth.

Through the poems, Spoon River comes to life again. Sometimes the histories of whole families are told. Spoon River is seen as a place where life was hard but could be good and satisfying. One of the best-known poems is spoken by Petit, the village poet. Another poem is spoken by Ann Rutledge, a real-life girl whom young Abraham Lincoln supposedly loved.

Masters was born in Garnett, Kans., and grew up in Lewistown, Ill. His father's financial situation prevented Edgar from completing college. But he studied law under his father and was an attorney in Chicago from 1895 to 1920. From 1903 to 1911, he was a partner in the law firm of the famous defense attorney Clarence Darrow. In 1923, Masters settled in New York City. His autobiography, *Across Spoon River,* appeared in 1936.
Bonnie Costello

Masters and Johnson, two American researchers, have made important contributions to the understanding of human sexual behavior. William Howell Masters (1915-   ), a physician, and his research associate, Virginia Eshelman Johnson (1925-   ), pioneered in the scientific study of sexual arousal and the treatment of sexual problems.

Masters began the sex research program at Washington University in St. Louis in 1954, and Johnson joined him in 1957. At that time, scientists knew little about the human body's physiological responses to sexual stimulation. Masters and Johnson used motion pictures and various special instruments to record such responses in men and women who volunteered to engage in sexual activity.

Masters and Johnson wrote a summary of their findings called *Human Sexual Response* (1966). This book was written in technical language for physicians and other health scientists, but it became a best seller. The research of Masters and Johnson created great controversy. Their critics called them immoral and accused them of dehumanizing sex.

In 1964, Masters and Johnson established the Repro-

ductive Biology Research Foundation (now called the Masters and Johnson Institute) in St. Louis. This clinic treats couples with sexual problems, trains other therapists, and conducts further research.

Masters and Johnson also wrote *Human Sexual Inadequacy* (1970), *The Pleasure Bond* (1975), and *Homosexuality in Perspective* (1979). Masters received his M.D. from the University of Rochester School of Medicine and Dentistry. Johnson began as a research assistant in the sex research project. Masters and Johnson were married in 1971. They divorced in 1993.   Martin Weisberg

Master's degree. See Degree, College.

Mastersinger was one of a group of German poet-musicians who treated literary art as a sort of craft or trade. The name *mastersinger* comes from the German word *meistersinger.*

The tradition of the mastersingers began in the late Middle Ages when middle-class poets tried to revive the declining art of the *minnesingers.* The minnesingers were wandering poet-musicians, originally chiefly aristocrats (see **Minnesinger**). Sometime between the late 1200's and the late 1400's, the mastersingers developed rules for song composition and organized song schools modeled after medieval guilds. Members passed examinations for admission and promotion. Singing competitions were held and prizes were awarded.

Most mastersingers were businessmen and craftsmen. The most famous mastersinger was Hans Sachs, a Nuremberg shoemaker. The mastersingers reached their peak in the early 1500's, though the tradition continued into the 1800's.

In the early period, the *Tabulatur* (rulebook) permitted composition only to prescribed melodies. But by the 1500's, original compositions were required to gain the title of *master.* Poetic themes were usually instructive stories. Mastersingers did not produce great literature, but achieved lasting fame through Richard Wagner's opera *Die Meistersinger.*   James F. Poag

Masterson, Bat (1853-1921), was a famous frontiersman and peace officer in the American West. As a young man, he became known as a courageous buffalo hunter and Indian fighter. As a peace officer, he was viewed as a cold-blooded gunfighter, but that reputation was untrue.

Masterson began his career as a peace officer in 1876, when he became a deputy marshal in Dodge City, Kans., county seat of Ford County. From 1878 to 1880, he was sheriff of Ford County. In 1881, he helped his friend Wyatt Earp, a deputy United States marshal in Tombstone, Ariz., enforce the law there. Masterson served as city marshal of Trinidad, Colo., in 1882. At times, he earned his living as a gambler. Masterson managed a gambling house in Creede, Colo., in 1892.

Bartholomew Masterson was born in Henryville, Que. He later called himself William Barclay Masterson. In 1902, he moved to New York City, where he became a sportswriter for the *New York Morning Telegraph* and an authority on boxing.   Odie B. Faulk

Mastic is a resin drawn from *Pistacia lentiscus,* a tree or small shrub native to the Mediterranean region. Mastic was once widely used as a protective dressing for wounds. Today, it is used to make high-grade varnishes for artwork.

The term *mastic* also refers to a group of adhesive

compounds used to fasten floor, ceiling, and wall tiles. Such mastics are usually applied in thick layers with a knife or with such tools as *trowels* or *spatulas,* which have a broad, flat blade.   Lewis T. Hendricks

Mastication, *MAS tuh KAY shuhn,* is the first process in the digestion of food. It involves chewing or breaking the food into small pieces by grinding with the teeth. Mastication mixes the food with saliva, which reacts chemically with the food and also gives it a pasty texture. Saliva contains enzymes, including *ptyalin,* or *amylase,* which digests cooked starches into sugars; and *lipase,* which digests fats. It also contains a slimy *mucus* that lubricates the food so it can be swallowed. In addition, saliva contains *bicarbonate of soda* and other salts that buffer the acids or alkalis found in some foods and drinks. Poor mastication causes overworking of digestive organs and indigestion. See also **Digestive system; Indigestion.**   André Dubois

Mastiff, *MAS tihf,* also called Old English Mastiff, is a breed of dog that was developed in the Middle East in ancient times. Mastiffs have been bred in England for centuries, perhaps since 55 B.C. Their short coat is usually apricot or brownish. Most mastiffs have a dark brown or black mouth, nose, and ears. The dogs stand about 30 inches (76 centimeters) high at the shoulder, and most weigh about 165 to 185 pounds (75 to 84 kilograms). See also **Dog** (picture: Working dogs); **Great Dane; Bullmastiff.**   Olga Dakan

Mastodon, *MAS tuh dahn,* was an animal much like the elephant. It is now extinct. Mastodons first lived in North Africa about 40 million years ago. They spread to Asia, Europe, and the rest of Africa. Mastodons reached America about 14 million years ago and lived there until about 10,000 years ago.

Mastodons were related to another group of prehistoric elephantlike animals called *four-tuskers.* Mastodons and four-tuskers were stockier than and not as tall as elephants or mammoths. Early species had tusks in both jaws. Some of the later species lost the lower tusks.

Painting by Charles R. Knight, © American Museum of Natural History

The mastodon is a prehistoric relative of the modern elephant. Mastodons lived in Africa, Asia, Europe, and North America.

Others developed great, flat, lower tusks. These species are called *shovel-tuskers.* The mastodon's teeth were up to 3 inches (7.5 centimeters) wide and 6 inches (15 centimeters) long. Each tooth had four to six cross-rows of heavy enamel cones which the mastodon used to grind plants it ate.

Scientific classification. Mastodons belong to the mastodon family, Mammutidae. The American mastodon is *Mammut americanum.*   Michael R. Voorhies

See also **Mammoth; Prehistoric animal** (The age of mammals).

Mastoid, *MAS toyd,* is one of the five parts of the temporal bone of the skull. It is located at the side of the skull, just behind the ear. The name *mastoid* means *nipple-shaped.* This describes the bottom of the mastoid, which extends downward, forming the *mastoid process.* The mastoid process may be felt as the hard area just behind and below the ear.

The mastoid process is porous, like a sponge. The *pores,* or hollow spaces, are called the *mastoid cells.* They vary greatly in size and number in different individuals. They connect with a larger, irregularly shaped cavity called the *tympanic antrum,* or *cavity.* This cavity opens into the middle ear. The mucous membrane of the middle ear extends into the tympanic antrum and the mastoid cells. Infections of the middle ear spread through these connections and may infect the mastoid cells. Doctors call this infection *mastoiditis.*

Mastoiditis may be serious because the mastoid cells are close to the organs of hearing, to important nerves, to the covering of the brain, and to the jugular vein. A mastoid infection may spread to any of these.

Mastoiditis may result from blowing the nose the wrong way. If both nostrils are held closed when a person blows his or her nose, germs may be forced from the throat into the *Eustachian tubes.* These tubes link the back of the nose with the middle ear. Antibiotics have cured mastoiditis, but severe cases may require surgery (see **Antibiotic**).   Charles W. Cummings

Masur, *Mah ZOOR,* **Kurt** (1927-   ), is a German conductor who specializes in music of the classical and romantic periods. In 1991, Masur became musical director of the New York Philharmonic Orchestra.

Masur began his career conducting operas. He was musical director of the Komische Oper in East Berlin, from 1960 to 1964. He was chief conductor of the Dresden Philharmonic from 1967 to 1972, and has been director of the Leipzig Gewandhaus Orchestra since 1970. He has toured widely with the Leipzig orchestra. Masur has appeared as guest conductor in orchestras throughout the world. He made his American debut with the Cleveland Symphony Orchestra in 1974 and first conducted the New York Philharmonic in 1981.

Masur was born in Brieg, Germany (now Brzeg, Poland). He studied piano and cello at the National Music School in Breslau, Germany (now Wrocław, Poland), from 1942 to 1944. From 1946 to 1948, he studied piano, composition, and conducting at the Leipzig Conservatory.   John H. Baron

Mata Hari, *MAH tuh HAH ree* (1876-1917), a Dutch dancer, was executed by the French on charges of being a German spy during World War I. She began her stage career after an unhappy marriage. She soon became popular throughout Europe, pretending to be a Java-

Mata Hari was an exotic dancer who lived in France and spied for the Germans during World War I. In 1917, the French executed her on charges of being a German spy. UPI/Bettmann

nese dancer. She apparently became associated with the German spy network when her strange dances lost popularity. She was born Margaretha Geertruida Zelle at Leeuwarden, in the Netherlands.   James L. Stokesbury

Matador. See Bullfighting.

Matanuska Valley, *mat uh NOOS kuh,* lies in south-central Alaska, near Anchorage. High mountains to the north and warm ocean currents from Cook Inlet to the south help prevent extreme temperatures in the valley.

The Matanuska Valley was the site of a large-scale farming experiment begun by the federal government during the Great Depression. In 1935, the government established 202 economically depressed families from Michigan, Minnesota, and Wisconsin on farms in the Matanuska Valley. Dairy farming, poultry raising, and vegetable growing became important activities there. The valley became the chief center of Alaska's relatively small agricultural activity. The farm operations began to decline in the 1960's, when reliable air freight service from farming areas outside Alaska was established. Today, the Matanuska Valley remains Alaska's chief farming center. However, many of the valley's residents are now employed in jobs in Anchorage.

Claus-M. Naske

See also **Alaska** (picture: The Matanuska Valley).

Match is a slender piece of cardboard or wood with a tip made of a chemical mixture that burns easily. Matches are used to produce fire. When the tip is rubbed against a rough or specially prepared surface, the chemicals burst into flame and ignite the match.

India is the world's leading producer of matches. Brazil, South Africa, and the United States also have large match industries. Matches, which were invented in the early 1800's, provided the first cheap, convenient method of producing fire.

Kinds of matches

The matches we use today are of two chief types, the strike-anywhere match and the safety match.

Strike-anywhere matches will light when drawn across any rough surface. They are wooden matches with heads of two colors, usually red and white. The white tip, called the *eye,* contains the firing substance. It is made chiefly of the chemical preparation, sesquisulfide of phosphorus. The rest of the bulblike head will not fire if struck, but will burn after the flaming eye sets it afire. It is larger around than the eye. This protects the matches from setting fire to each other by friction when they are packed into a box. When the match is lighted, the paraffin in which the matchstick had been dipped carries the flame from the head to the wood part.

Safety matches can be lighted only by striking them across a special surface, usually on the side of the box in which they are contained. The match head is made of a substance containing chlorate of potash. The striking surface is made of a compound of red phosphorus and sand. *Book* matches are a type of safety match made of paper and bound into a folding paper cover. The striking surface is on the outside back of the cover.

Matches can be dangerous

Many disastrous fires and hundreds of deaths have been caused by the careless use of matches. All kinds of matches should be stored where children cannot reach them. Strike-anywhere matches should be placed out of the reach of mice. Rats or mice can set off matches by gnawing at the striking heads. A match should not be thrown away until the flame is out. Even then, it should be placed in a metal or other fire-resistant container.

How matches are made

Wooden matches are made by complex automatic machines that can manufacture and package more than a million matches an hour. First, a machine cuts *splints* (matchsticks) from thin strips of poplar wood. The splints are processed through an *anti-afterglow* solution, which prevents embers from forming after a match is blown out. Then the splints are dried and put into a matchmaking machine.

The matchmaking machine puts the splints into small holes in a belt of metal plates. As the belt fills up with splints, it dips them into a series of chemicals. The splints are first dipped into paraffin, which provides a base that carries the flame from the match head to the wood. The belt also passes the splints through a chemical mixture that forms the bulbs and eyes of the

Combs of matches are loaded into a booking machine, which cuts the combs to the proper size and staples them into matchbook covers. Workers then pack the matchbooks into boxes. Universal Match Corporation

A matchbook collection may include covers designed for a variety of purposes, including advertising and the observance of an important public event.

matches. The heads may also receive a final chemical coating that protects them from moisture in the air. The finished matches are then punched from their plates, counted, and boxed in one automatic operation.

Book matches are made by two machines from rolls of heavy paper called *paperboard* that has been treated with an anti-afterglow solution. The first machine, called a *match machine,* cuts the paperboard into *combs* (strips). Each comb is divided into from 60 to 120 smaller strips. These smaller strips eventually become matches. The machine dips the combs into paraffin and then dips the tips of the combs into the match-head solution.

Next, the combs are loaded into a *booking,* or *stitching,* machine. This machine cuts the combs into the size of an individual matchbook. It also fits them into printed covers. Finally, the machine staples the combs and the covers together to form the finished matchbooks, and workers pack the matchbooks into boxes.

Collecting matchbook covers

Collecting matchbook covers is an interesting and enjoyable hobby shared by thousands of persons. Match hobbyists collect covers from places they visit, trade covers with other collectors, and even buy rare or unusual covers from hobby shops or through advertisements in hobby magazines. Some match covers have become valuable because of their rarity.

Matchbook collectors are called *phillumenists,* which means *lovers of light.* They often form clubs to help them trade covers and meet fellow hobbyists. The clubs hold meetings and conduct contests that award prizes to the best collections. Several clubs are organized on a nationwide basis.

Because of the great variety of matchbook covers, collectors classify them in order to store or display them more easily. Collectors often specialize in certain kinds, such as covers from hotels, railroads, and government organizations. Covers can also be classified by size. Most collectors prefer covers that have not been used. However, collectors will often keep a used cover until they can find an unused one to replace it in their collections.

Collectors usually store covers in albums which they buy from hobby shops or make themselves. A matchbook album should have slots to hold the covers. A cover that is pasted in an album loses its value.

History

Early fire-making devices were developed as scientists learned of chemical reactions that produced fire. In 1780, a group of French chemists invented the *phosphoric candle,* or *ethereal match,* a sealed glass tube containing a twist of paper. The paper was tipped with a form of phosphorus that burned upon exposure to oxygen. When a person broke the tube, air ignited the phosphorus. This and other early fire-producing devices were dangerous because of the poisonous fumes and extreme flammability of phosphorus.

The first matches resembling those of today appeared in 1827, when John Walker, an English pharmacist, began to make and sell *congreves.* A congreve was a splint 3 inches (8 centimeters) long, tipped with antimony sulfide, chlorate of potash, gum arabic, and starch. A person lit one by drawing it through a fold of sandpaper. The match burst into flame with a series of small explosions that showered the user with sparks.

Charles Sauria, a French chemistry student, produced the first strike-anywhere match in the early 1830's. The match tip included phosphorus. Alonzo D. Phillips of Springfield, Mass., patented the first phosphorus matches in the United States in 1836. He made the matches by hand and sold them from door to door.

Neither Sauria nor Phillips knew that fumes from their phosphorus matches could cause a deadly disease called necrosis of the jaw, or *phossy jaw.* But after match factories began to operate during the mid-1800's, a number of workers who were exposed to phosphorus fumes died from the disease. As the match industry grew, the threat of widespread necrosis became alarming. In 1900, the Diamond Match Company purchased a French patent for matches with a striking head of sesquisulfide of phosphorus, a nonpoisonous compound. But the French formula would not work in the United States because of the difference in climate.

In 1910, as a result of the spread of necrosis, the United States placed such a high tax on phosphorus matches that the match industry faced extinction. In 1911, William A. Fairburn, a young engineer, solved the problem by adapting the French formula for sesquisulfide of phosphorus to the climate of the United States. The threat of necrosis ended.

The first safety matches were invented by Gustave E. Pasch, a Swedish chemist, in 1844. John Lundstrom, a Swedish manufacturer, began to produce them in large quantities in 1852.

The match industry centered in Sweden for many years. In the early 1900's, Ivar Kreuger, a Swedish promoter, formed the Swedish Match Company, a giant international match empire that owned factories, forests, and mines. The company operated match factories in about 40 countries and made most of the world's matches. The stock market crash of 1929 weakened Kreuger's influence, and he committed suicide in 1932. But the Swedish Match Company survived the crash and operated successfully under new management.

The invention of book matches. Joshua Pusey, a Philadelphia attorney, patented the first book matches in 1892. He called them *flexible matches.* Pusey made his matches in packages of 50. The striking surface was on the inside cover, dangerously near the heads of the matches. Because of this, book matches did not become popular until World War I (1914-1918). By that time, the Diamond Match Company had purchased Pusey's patent and made book matches safe and usable.

During World War II (1939-1945), when the United States Army had to fight the Japanese in areas where long rainy seasons prevailed, the match industry was called upon to produce a waterproof match. In 1943, Raymond D. Cady, a chemist with the Diamond Match Company, produced a formula which protected wooden matches so well that they would light after eight hours under water. This waterproof match is coated with a water- and heat-resistant substance. The substance does not interfere with the creation of enough friction to light the match.   Mark C. Bean

See also **Fire** (Methods of starting fires).

Mate is the title of a merchant marine officer or naval petty officer. The term *mate* comes from an Old English word meaning *comrade* or *companion.* On merchant ships, the first mate is second in command. In the U.S. Navy, mates serve under warrant officers.

Maté, *MAH tay,* also called *Paraguay tea,* is a drink made from the dried leaves and shoots of a plant that grows in South America. People make the tea by pouring boiling water over the leaves and stems. Maté has a large amount of caffeine and produces a stimulating effect. The maté plant has dark green leaves 3 to 6 inches (8 to 15 centimeters) long, small greenish-white flowers,

WORLD BOOK illustration by John D. Dawson

The maté plant is the source of a South American tea. The tea is made by pouring boiling water over the leaves and stems.

and small, dark red fruits. Maté growing is a large industry in Paraguay, Argentina, and southern Brazil, where drinking maté is an important part of the culture. Exporters also ship maté to other countries in South America. Maté is sometimes called *yerba maté.*

Scientific classification. The maté plant is in the family Aquifoliaceae. Its scientific name is *Ilex paraguariensis.*
Alwyn H. Gentry

Materialism is a philosophical position that states that everything is material, or a state of matter. The word comes from the Latin *materia,* meaning *matter.* Materialists particularly deny that the human self is a spiritual—or in any way nonmaterial—entity. They interpret beliefs, thoughts, desires, sensations, and other mental states as properties of material systems. Materialism is often considered a "scientific" philosophy because it is closely associated with the view that everything that occurs can be explained by scientific laws—perhaps even by the laws of physics alone.

The Greek philosophers Leucippus and Democritus developed an early form of materialism called *atomism* in the 400's B.C. They believed that invisible, indivisible material particles, called *atoms,* of various sizes and shapes make up everything that exists. According to atomism, the mind itself is made up of small, round, material atoms. Later atomists included the Greek philosopher Epicurus and the Roman poet Lucretius.

The growth of Christianity, with its emphasis on spiritual concerns, led to a decline in materialism for many centuries. Materialism reemerged as a significant intellectual force during the rise of modern science in the 1600's. In France, Pierre Gassendi, a philosopher and scientist, revived some of the doctrines of ancient atomism. The English philosopher Thomas Hobbes developed an uncompromisingly materialist philosophy. The French philosophers Denis Diderot and Julien de la Mettrie also were among the best-known materialists of the 1700's.

A version of materialism known as *dialectical materialism* emerged in the late 1800's with the works of the German philosopher Karl Marx and the German social scientist Friedrich Engels. The German philosopher G. W. F. Hegel had used the term *dialectic* to indicate a necessary transition from one phase of the world or society or thought to another phase. This transition occurs as a result of inadequacies or "contradictions" in the earlier phase. Hegel identified dialectical processes with the development of reason or spirit, but Marx and Engels combined the notion of dialectic with the view that the forces underlying historical development are always material. Marx and Engels particularly believed that economic factors determine social structure and change. Dialectical materialism provides the philosophical basis for Communism, a political and economic movement.

Since the 1950's, many scientifically oriented philosophers have defended materialist positions in *metaphysics,* a branch of philosophy that is concerned with the basic nature of reality (see **Metaphysics**). These philosophers uphold materialist positions independent of any political ideology or theory of social development.

Margaret D. Wilson

See also **Atomism; Democritus; Marx, Karl.**

Materials are solid substances of which manufactured products are made. Materials belong to two groups: (1) *natural materials* and (2) *extracted materials.* Natural materials, which include stone, wood, and wool, are used much as they occur in nature. Extracted materials, such as plastics, *alloys* (metal mixtures), and ceramics, are created through the processing of various natural substances.

Manufacturers determine which material to use for a given product by evaluating *properties* (qualities) of materials. For example, wood is used for boats because of its low *density* (weight per unit of volume). Stainless steel, an alloy, serves as a material for pots and pans largely because of its resistance to heat and *corrosion* (chemical attack by the environment).

Some properties can be linked with a material's *macrostructure* (structure visible to the unaided eye). For example, the long, parallel fibers of wood give this material relatively strong resistance to a force applied along the *grain* (the direction of the fibers), but relatively weak resistance to a force applied at a right angle to the grain. Other properties are explained by a material's *microstructure* (structure that can be seen only through a microscope). The low density of wood is due to the open structure of its cells, which are visible only when viewed through a microscope. At the most basic level, properties of materials are determined by *chemical bonds,* forces that attract atoms to one another and hold them together.

Materials scientists study how the structure of materi-

als relates to their properties. A large part of their work involves experimentation. For example, they alter the microstructure of a material, then determine how the changes affect the properties. *Materials engineers,* who work in much the same way, develop new materials for use in commercial products.

Materials scientists and engineers have developed a wide variety of engineered materials in recent years. These include strong but lightweight alloys of titanium used for aircraft parts. An important new class of substances called *composite materials* are produced by combining other substances. For example, some tennis rackets are made of a composite of carbon fibers and plastic.

Properties of materials

Scientists group the properties of materials according to various functions that must be performed by objects made of the materials. For example, *mechanical properties* are critical in a material for a part such as a beam of a bridge that must resist strong mechanical forces.

Most properties of materials fall into six groups: (1) mechanical, (2) chemical, (3) electrical, (4) magnetic, (5) thermal, and (6) optical.

Mechanical properties are critical in a wide variety of structures and objects—from bridges, houses, and space vehicles to chairs and even food trays. Some of the most important mechanical properties are (1) stiffness, (2) yield stress, (3) toughness, (4) strength, (5) creep, and (6) fatigue resistance.

Stiffness measures how much a material bends when first subjected to a mechanical force. For example, the degree to which a shelf first bends when a book is put on it depends on the shelf's stiffness.

Yield stress measures how much force per unit area must be exerted on a material for that material to permanently *deform* (change its shape). Materials that deform easily—that is, those that have a low yield stress—are generally not desirable.

Toughness measures a material's resistance to cracking. The tougher a material, the greater the stress necessary to break that material near a crack.

Strength measures the greatest force a material can withstand without breaking. A material's strength depends on many factors, including its toughness and its shape.

Creep is a measure of a material's resistance to gradual deformation under a constant force. At room temperature, creep is almost nonexistent in many metals, including aluminum and steel. However, manufacturers of metal parts such as jet engine turbine blades that operate at high temperatures must consider creep.

Fatigue resistance measures the resistance of a material to repeated applications and withdrawals of force. Metal that is used for gears must have a high resistance to fatigue because, as a gear rotates, force is repeatedly applied to, and withdrawn from, the individual gear teeth.

Chemical properties include *catalytic properties* and *resistance to corrosion.* Catalytic properties measure the ability of a material to function as a *catalyst*—that is, its ability to provide a favorable site for a certain chemical reaction to occur. Automobile pollution-controlling devices called *catalytic converters* are made

Uses of materials   **A variety of materials** are used in different products. Basic types of materials range from wood, which has been used for thousands of years, to composite materials, which are still under development. The photos below show products made of several materials.

Superstock
Iron beams

Broyhill Furniture, Inc.
Wooden desk

Corning Incorporated
Ceramic cookware

Goodyear
Rubber tire

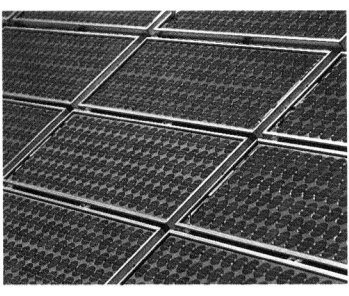
Comstock
Semiconducting solar cells

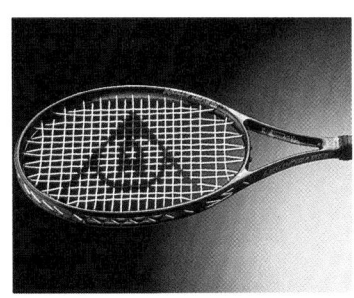
Dunlop Slazenger Corporation
Composite tennis racket body

partly of metals such as platinum that reduce pollution by causing certain chemical reactions.

Resistance to corrosion measures how well a material holds up to chemical attack by the environment. For example, iron has low resistance to corrosion by oxygen. It reacts with oxygen in the air to form rust.

Electrical properties are important in products designed either to *conduct* (carry) or block the flow of electric current. *Electrical resistance* is a measure of the energy lost when a current passes through a given material. The lower the resistance, the lower the loss of energy. Copper and other materials that have low resistance are good conductors.

Dielectric strength describes a material's response to an electric field. It is used to evaluate how well a material can act as an *insulator* (an object that blocks current). A material's dielectric strength is the highest voltage difference a given thickness of the material can withstand before a current passes through it.

Magnetic properties indicate a material's response to a *magnetic field*—the region around a magnet or a conductor where the force of magnetism can be felt. *Magnetic susceptibility* is a measure of how well a material can be magnetized by an external magnetic field. A material is *ferromagnetic* if a magnetic field remains inside the material after the external magnetic field has been removed. The object composed of this material then becomes a permanent magnet.

Thermal properties reflect a material's response to heat. *Thermal conductivity* is a measure of how well a material conducts heat. Pots and pans are best made of materials that have a high thermal conductivity so they

can efficiently and evenly transfer heat to food. *Heat capacity* measures a material's ability to contain heat. This property can be important in insulation materials.

Coefficient of thermal expansion indicates the increase in length of materials as they heat up. This is an important property to consider, for example, when building a telescope to orbit the earth. There is no air in outer space to equalize temperatures. Therefore, a spot on a telescope that is exposed to direct sunlight becomes much hotter than one not so exposed. If the telescope were made of material with a high coefficient of thermal expansion, its hot parts would expand much more than its cold parts, causing the telescope to warp.

Optical properties indicate how a material responds to light. The *refraction index* of a material indicates the degree to which the material changes the direction of a beam of light going through it. Manufacturers of eyeglasses use materials with a high refraction index because the higher the index is, the thinner the lenses can be made. These manufacturers must also consider *optical absorption,* a measure of how much light a material absorbs. The lower the optical absorption, the more transparent the material.

Natural materials

Natural materials generally are used as they are found, except for being cleaned, cut, or processed in a simple way that does not use much energy. Natural materials include stone and biological materials.

Stone. Certain types of rock are extremely strong and hard, and are therefore used as building stone. There are two types of building stone—*crushed stone* and *dimension stone.* Crushed stone is mixed with tarlike substances such as asphalt to make paving material. It is also mixed with portland cement and sand to make concrete. Common crushed stone includes limestone and granite. Dimension stone is used for finishing and decorating buildings. Common building stones include granite, limestone, marble, sandstone, and slate.

Biological materials are substances that develop as part of a plant or animal. Common plant materials include wood and various fibers such as cotton. Animal materials include leather and fibers such as wool.

Wood is a valuable biological material because of its strength, toughness, and low density. These properties make wood an excellent material for thousands of products, including houses, sailboats, furniture, baseball bats, and railroad ties. In addition, wood serves as a raw material for a wide variety of products, including paper, rayon, and charcoal.

Plant fibers used in their natural state include cotton, flax, and jute. Many plant fibers are flexible and can be spun into yarn. Cotton cloth is soft, absorbs moisture well, and is comfortable to wear. Flax is a strong fiber made from the stems of flax plants. It is made into linen fabric and other products, including thread and rope. Jute is a long, soft fiber that can be spun into coarse, strong threads. Jute products include cloth for wrapping bales of raw cotton.

Leather is a tough, flexible material made from the skin of animals. It is strong and durable. Leather can be made as flexible as cloth or as stiff as wood. Leather products range from shoes, belts, and gloves to baseballs, basketballs, and footballs. A soft leather known as *suede* serves as a clothing material.

Animal fibers include fur, wool, and silk. Fur and wool consist of animal hair. Because these materials can trap air, they are excellent insulators and are therefore used for clothing. Silk is the strongest natural fiber. Manufacturers unwind strands of silk from silkworm cocoons and make yarn for clothing and decorative fabrics.

Extracted materials

An extracted material is created through processes that expend a great deal of energy or alter the microstructure of the substances used to make the material. Extracted materials include ceramics, metals and their alloys, plastics, rubber, composite materials, and semiconductors.

Ceramics include such everyday materials as brick, cement, glass, and porcelain. These materials are made from mineral compounds called *silicates,* including clay, feldspar, silica, and talc.

The properties of ceramics make them useful in a number of ways. Exposure to acids, gases, salts, and water generally does not corrode ceramics. Their freedom from corrosion makes ceramics an excellent material for dinnerware and for bathroom fixtures. Such ceramics as bricks and concrete are used in construction because of their low price and their resistance to crushing. The high dielectric strength of ceramics suits them for use as insulators for electric power lines. Their high melting points make them useful as materials for cookware. The transparency and strength of glass make it an obvious choice for applications ranging from windows

to precision lenses for microscopes.

Certain advanced ceramics have an unusual property known as *superconductivity.* At extremely low temperatures, these materials conduct electric current with no resistance. Like other ceramics, however, these materials are brittle. Materials engineers are working to make them into commercially useful products.

Metals and alloys. People have used such metals as copper, gold, iron, and silver for thousands of years to make various practical and decorative objects. Today, metals are important in all aspects of construction and manufacturing. Metals are strong and are good conductors of heat and electric current. They are also easy to hammer into thin sheets and can be drawn out into wires.

Most metals are not used in their pure form because they are soft. Instead, they are used as ingredients in alloys.

One exception is copper, which is used in its pure form in electric wiring. Copper is an excellent conductor of electricity. The only better conductor is silver, but silver is too expensive for common use.

Iron and steel are the chief metals used in construction. Steel is an alloy of iron and carbon, as are the materials called *cast iron* and *wrought iron.*

The addition of other elements gives various kinds of steel different properties. For example, stainless steel, which contains at least 12 percent chromium, resists corrosion better than any other kind of steel. Nickel increases the hardness of steel. Tungsten makes steel more resistant to heat.

Plastics are synthetic materials made up primarily of long chains of molecules called *polymers.* There are two basic types of plastics: (1) *thermosetting plastics* (usually called *thermosets*) and (2) *thermoplastics.*

Thermosets can be heated and set only once; they cannot be remelted or reshaped. Because they are highly resistant to heat, thermosets are used for electrical parts, insulation foam, oven gaskets, and appliance handles. Other objects made of thermosets include luggage and parts for automobile bodies.

Thermoplastics can be melted and reshaped. Thermoplastics are used much more widely than thermosets because they are easier to process and require less time to set. Common thermoplastic products include telephone bodies, packaging, and bottles.

Rubber is made up of *elastomers,* polymers that stretch easily to several times their length and then return to their original shape. This property is known as *elasticity.* Rubber's elasticity, its ability to hold air and keep out water, and its toughness make it an important material.

About three-fifths of the rubber used in the United States goes into tires and tubes. Other uses include mechanical products such as gaskets, and waterproof clothing such as boots and raincoats. *Natural rubber* comes from the juice of a tree. *Synthetic rubber* is made from petroleum.

Composite materials. Engineers may artificially combine various materials to create a new *composite material.* Many composite materials contain a large amount of one substance to which fibers, flakes, or layers of another substance are added. Fiberglass, for example, consists of glass fibers and a polymer such as epoxy. This composite, in turn, can be used as an ingredient in another composite called a *fiberglass-reinforced plastic.* This is made up of cloth, mats, or individual strands of fiberglass added to a plastic. Fiberglass-reinforced plastics are used for such products as automobile bodies, fishing rods, and aircraft parts. Other common composites include carbon-reinforced plastics, which are used for such products as tennis rackets and golf clubs.

Composite materials usually have the favorable qualities of their ingredient materials. For example, fiberglass-reinforced plastics have the stiffness of glass but, like plastic, weigh less than glass.

Semiconductors are materials that conduct electricity better than insulators, but not as well as conductors, at room temperature. Extremely pure crystals of semiconductor material *doped* (combined) with small, precisely controlled amounts of other substances can perform many electronic functions. Such crystals, usually of silicon, are the building blocks of computer chips. In addition, *photovoltaic cells,* also called *solar cells,* consist of thin slices of doped semiconductor materials. When the sun shines on a photovoltaic cell, electric current flows from one side of the cell to the other. Photovoltaic cells power most artificial satellites.

The role of bonds

Wide differences in the properties of certain kinds of materials are a result of differences in *bonds*—forces that attract atoms and molecules to one another and hold them together. *Chemical bonds* hold atoms together through the transfer or sharing of *electrons,* the negatively charged particles that whirl about the positively charged nucleus of an atom (see **Atom**). Weaker forces called *physical bonds* hold molecules together in a group.

Chemical bonds are *ionic, covalent,* or *metallic.* Ionic bonds are created by the transfer of electrons from one atom to one or more other atoms. In covalent bonding, two or more atoms share pairs of electrons. A shared pair consists of one electron from each of two atoms. In metallic bonding, all the atoms in a metal crystal share electrons. The shared electrons are free to move throughout the crystal. This movement creates a "sea" of negative electrons that surrounds and holds together the metal nuclei.

Physical bonds, also called *van der Waals forces,* hold molecules together in a group. Van der Waals forces are electrical forces caused by an interaction between charges of neighboring molecules. They are much weaker than chemical bonds because no transfer or sharing of electrons occurs.

One example of how bonding determines properties occurs in the area of electrical resistance. Ordinary ceramics are held together chiefly by covalent and ionic bonds. In these bonds, electrons are positioned near individual atoms. Much energy is therefore needed to make these electrons flow as electric current. Ceramics thus have a high resistance. By contrast, metals are held together by metallic bonds. Because many atoms share electrons, the electrons can circulate easily within the material. Metals therefore conduct current and have a low electrical resistance.

Bonding also determines important properties of

polymers. These materials are made of long molecules featuring chainlike structures of carbon atoms linked by covalent bonds. In some polymers, covalent bonds also join chains to one another. These polymers are said to be *cross-linked.*

When a thermoset is heated for the first time, its chains cross-link. When the material is heated again, the cross-links do not break, so the material does not melt. A thermoplastic, however, does not form crosslinks. When it is heated, its physical bonds become so weak that the chains can slide past one another. The material therefore melts.   Andreas Mortensen

Related articles in *World Book* include:

Materials

World Book has hundreds of separate articles on materials. See **Ceramics; Composite materials; Metal; Plastics; Rock; Semiconductor; Textile; Wood;** and their lists of related articles.

Properties of materials

Absorption and adsorption	Dynamics	Light (How light behaves)
Acoustics	Elasticity	Magnetism
Aerodynamics	Electricity (Conduction of electric current)	(Magnetism of materials)
Catalysis		Melting point
Corrosion	Heat (How heat travels)	Refraction
Density	Hydraulics	Reflection
Ductility		Thermodynamics
		Viscosity

Other related articles

Atom	Cell	Molecule
Bond	Crystal	

Materials engineering. See Engineering (Materials engineering).

Materials science is the study of the structure, properties, and uses of materials. By combining atoms and molecules in new ways, materials scientists can create unusual materials with specific properties.

The materials that the scientists study can be grouped into five major categories. Each category has special properties. *Metals and alloys* are typically strong and conduct electricity and heat well. *Ceramics* are normally brittle and conduct electricity and heat poorly, which makes them good *insulators.* Materials called *Polymers,* such as plastics, are typically good electrical insulators but less heat-resistant than metals or ceramics. *Semiconductors* have unique electronic behavior that makes transistors, microprocessors, and solar cells possible. *Composites* combine different materials to achieve unusual properties. For example, ceramic fibers might be added to metal to make the metal stronger at high temperatures.

Materials science has contributed to many advances in technology. For example, specially designed glass fibers used in fiber-optic cables have revolutionized the transfer of information by telephone (see **Fiber optics**). Certain ceramic compounds act as *superconductors,* which conduct electricity with no resistance (see **Superconductivity**). The B-2 Stealth bomber is designed to evade radar detection by means of composite materials that absorb radar signals, rather than reflect them.

Donald R. Askeland

Mathematical symbol. See Algebra (Symbols in algebra); **Set theory.**

© Alvis Upitis, The Image Bank **A mathematician teaching problem solving** © Steve Dunwell, The Image Bank **Engineers designing machinery** © Alvis Upitis, The Image Bank **A bank teller directing funds**

The uses of mathematics are wide-ranging. For example, mathematics may be used to solve scientific problems, design industrial projects, and carry out business transactions.

Mathematics

Mathematics is one of the most useful and fascinating divisions of human knowledge. It includes many topics of study. For this reason, the term *mathematics* is difficult to define. It comes from a Greek word meaning "inclined to learn."

Most of the basic mathematics taught in school involves the study of number, quantity, form, and relations. *Arithmetic,* for example, concerns problems with numbers. *Algebra* involves solving *equations* (mathematical statements of equality) in which letters represent unknown quantities. *Geometry* concerns the properties and relationships of figures in space.

The most important skills in mathematics are careful analysis and clear reasoning. These skills can help us solve some of the deepest puzzles we must face. Mathematics is based upon logic. Starting from widely accepted statements, mathematicians use logic to draw conclusions and develop mathematical systems.

The importance of mathematics

The work of mathematicians may be divided into *pure mathematics* and *applied mathematics.* Pure mathematics seeks to advance mathematical knowledge for its own sake rather than for any immediate practical use. For example, a mathematician may create a system of geometry for an imaginary world where objects have more dimensions than just length, width, and depth. Applied mathematics seeks to develop mathematical techniques for use in science and other fields.

Joseph W. Dauben, the contributor of this article, is Professor of History and History of Science at Herbert H. Lehman College and the Graduate Center of the City University of New York. He is the editor of The History of Mathematics from Antiquity to the Present. *The drawings in this article were prepared for* World Book *by Zorica Dabich.*

The boundary between pure and applied mathematics is not always clear. Ideas developed in pure mathematics often have practical applications, and work in applied mathematics frequently leads to research in pure mathematics.

Nearly every part of our lives involves mathematics. It has played an essential role in the development of modern *technology*—the tools, materials, techniques, and sources of power that make our lives and work easier.

In everyday life, we use mathematics for such simple tasks as telling time from a clock or counting our change after making a purchase. We also use mathematics for such complex tasks as making up a household budget or figuring our income tax. Cooking, driving, gardening, sewing, and many other common activities involve mathematical calculations. Mathematics is also part of many games, hobbies, and sports.

In science. Mathematics is an essential part of nearly all scientific study. It helps scientists design experiments and analyze data. Scientists use mathematical formulas to express their findings precisely and to make predictions based on these findings.

The physical sciences, such as astronomy, chemistry, and physics, rely heavily on mathematics. Such social sciences as economics, psychology, and sociology also depend greatly on statistics and other kinds of mathematics. For example, some economists create mathematical models of economic systems. These models are sets of formulas used to predict how a change in one part of the economy might affect other parts.

In industry. Mathematics helps industries design, develop, and test products and manufacturing processes. Mathematics is necessary in designing bridges, buildings, dams, highways, tunnels, and other architectural and engineering projects.

In business, mathematics is used in transactions that involve buying and selling. Businesses need mathematics to keep records of such things as inventory and employees' hours and wages. Bankers use mathematics to handle and invest funds. Mathematics helps insurance companies calculate risks and compute the rates charged for insurance coverage.

Branches of mathematics

Mathematics has many branches. They may differ in the types of problems involved and in the practical application of their results. However, mathematicians working in different branches often use many of the same basic concepts and operations. This section discusses several of the main kinds of mathematics.

Arithmetic includes the study of whole numbers, fractions and decimals, and the operations of addition, subtraction, multiplication, and division. It forms the foundation for other kinds of mathematics by providing such basic skills as counting and grouping objects, and measuring and comparing quantities. See **Addition; Arithmetic; Division; Multiplication; Subtraction.**

Algebra, unlike arithmetic, is not limited to work with specific numbers. Algebra involves solving problems with equations in which letters, such as x and y, stand for unknown quantities. Algebraic operations also use negative numbers and *imaginary numbers* (the square roots of negative numbers). See **Algebra; Square root** (Square roots of negative numbers).

Geometry is concerned with the properties and relationships of figures in space. *Plane geometry* deals with squares, circles, and other figures that lie on a plane. *Solid geometry* involves such figures as cubes and spheres, which have three dimensions.

About 300 B.C., Euclid, a Greek mathematician, stated the definitions and assumptions of the system of geometry that describes the world as we usually experience it. But later mathematicians developed alternative systems of geometry that rejected Euclid's assumption about the nature of parallel lines. Such *non-Euclidean geometries* have proven useful, for example, in the theory of relativity—one of the outstanding achievements of scientific thought. See **Geometry.**

Analytic geometry and trigonometry. Analytic geometry relates algebra and geometry. It provides a way to represent an algebraic equation as a line or curve on a graph. It also makes it possible to write equations that exactly describe many curves. For example, the equation $x = y^2$ describes a curve called a *parabola.*

Trigonometry is used widely by astronomers, navigators, and surveyors to calculate angles and distances when direct measurement is impossible. It deals with the relations between the sides and angles of triangles, especially *right triangles* (triangles that have a 90° angle). Certain relations between the lengths of two sides of a right triangle are called *trigonometric ratios.* Using trigonometric ratios, a person can calculate the unknown angles and lengths in a triangle from the known angles and lengths. Formulas involving trigonometric ratios describe curves that physicists and engineers use to analyze the behavior of heat, light, sound, and other natural phenomena. See **Trigonometry.**

Calculus and analysis have many practical uses in engineering, physics, and other sciences. Calculus provides a way of solving many problems that involve motion or changing quantities. *Differential calculus* seeks to determine the rate at which a varying quantity changes. It is used to calculate the slope of a curve and the changing speed of a bullet. *Integral calculus* tries to

find a quantity when the rate at which it is changing is known. It is used to calculate the area of a curved figure or the amount of work done by a varying force. Unlike algebra, calculus includes operations with *infinitesimals* (quantities that are not zero but are smaller than any assignable quantity). See **Calculus.**

Analysis involves various mathematical operations with infinite quantities and infinitesimals. It includes the study of *infinite series,* sequences of numbers or algebraic expressions that go on indefinitely. The concept of infinite series has important applications in such areas as the study of heat and of vibrating strings. See **Series** (Working with infinite series).

Probability and statistics. Probability is the mathematical study of the likelihood of events. It is used to determine the chances that an uncertain event may occur. For example, using probability, a person can calculate the chances that three tossed coins will all turn up heads. See **Probability.**

Statistics is the branch of mathematics concerned with the collection and analysis of large bodies of data to identify trends and overall patterns. Statistics relies heavily on probability. Statistical methods provide information to government, business, and science. For example, physicists use statistics to study the behavior of the many molecules in a sample of gas. See **Statistics.**

Set theory and logic. Set theory deals with the nature and relations of *sets.* A set is a collection of items, which may be numbers, ideas, or objects. The study of sets is important in investigating most basic mathematical concepts. See **Set theory.**

In the field of logic—the branch of philosophy that deals with the rules of correct reasoning—mathematicians have developed *symbolic logic.* Symbolic logic is a formal system of reasoning that uses mathematical symbols and methods. Mathematicians have devised various systems of symbolic logic that have been important in the development of computers.

History

Early civilization. Prehistoric people probably first counted with their fingers. They also had various methods for recording such quantities as the number of animals in a herd or the days since the full moon. To represent such amounts, they used a corresponding number of pebbles, knots in a cord, or marks on wood, bone, or stone. They also learned to use regular shapes when they molded pottery or carved arrowheads.

By about 3000 B.C., mathematicians of ancient Egypt used a *decimal system* (a system of counting in groups of 10) without place values. The Egyptians pioneered in geometry, developing formulas for finding the area and volume of simple figures. Egyptian mathematics had many practical applications, ranging from surveying fields after the annual floods to making the intricate calculations necessary to build the pyramids.

By 2100 B.C., the people of ancient Babylonia had developed a *sexagesimal system*—a system based on groups of 60. Today, we use such a system to measure time in hours, minutes, and seconds. Historians do not know exactly how the Babylonian system developed. They think it may have arisen from the use of weights and measures based on groups of 60. The system had

(Text continued on page 306)

The following problems all require the use of important mathematical skills, including careful analysis of situations and reasoning to reach solutions. Try to solve the problems and then compare your work with the solutions provided.

1. *Which salary would you choose?* Your boss offers you one of two salary arrangements. "Which would you prefer," she asks, "a salary starting at $16,000 a year with an $800 increase each year, or one starting at $8,000 for a half year with a $200 increase each half year?" Which choice offers the higher salary?

Make a chart to show the two choices of salary over a number of years.

Year	Choice 1	Choice 2
First year	$16,000	$8,000 + $8,200 = $16,200
Second year	$16,800	$8,400 + $8,600 = $17,000
Third year	$17,600	$8,800 + $9,000 = $17,800
Fourth year	$18,400	$9,200 + $9,400 = $18,600

Choice 2 gives you $200 more each year than choice 1 does.

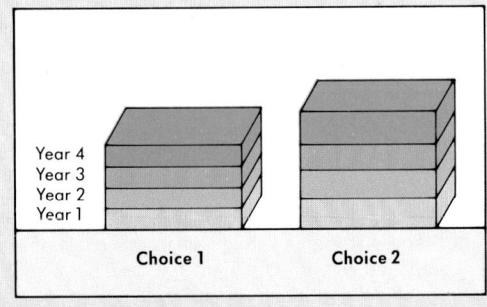

Year 4
Year 3
Year 2
Year 1

Choice 1   Choice 2

3. *A little pile of paper.* Imagine that you have a huge sheet of paper only $\frac{1}{1,000}$ inch (0.025 millimeter) thick. You cut the sheet in half and put one piece of paper on top of the other.

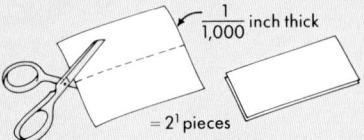

$\frac{1}{1,000}$ inch thick

= 2^1 pieces

You cut these two pieces in half and put the resulting four pieces together in a pile. Then you cut the pile of four pieces in half and put the resulting eight pieces in a pile. Suppose that you continue in this manner until you have cut the pile in half 50 times, each time piling up the resulting pieces. How high do you think the final pile would be?

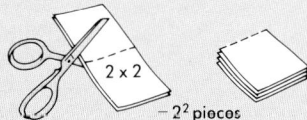

2 x 2

= 2^2 pieces

After the first cut, you have 2 pieces. After the second cut, you have 2 × 2, or 2^2 pieces. Following the third cut, you have 2 × 2 × 2, or 2^3 pieces. Therefore, after the 50th cut, you should have 2^{50} pieces. Two multiplied by itself 50 times is about 1,126,000,000,000,000. Because there are 1,000 pieces of paper to the inch, divide by 1,000 to find the number of inches in the pile. Next, divide the number of inches by 12 to find the number of feet in the pile. Then divide the number of feet by 5,280 to find the number of miles. You may be surprised to find that the pile of paper is about 17,770,000 miles (28,600,000 kilometers) high!

2. *Find the counterfeit.* You have nine rare and valuable coins. Although they appear to be identical, you know that one is counterfeit and weighs less than the others. Using a balance scale only twice, how can you find the fake coin?

First, divide the coins into three groups of three coins.

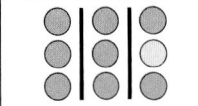

Next, take the group of three coins that contains the fake.

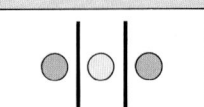

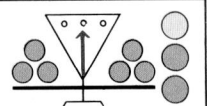

Weigh one group against another. If they balance, then the fake, or light, coin is in the group you have not weighed.

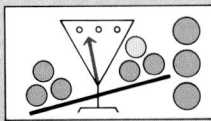

If the two groups of coins do not balance, then the fake coin is in the lighter group on the scale.

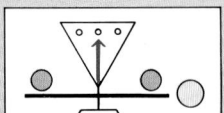

Weigh two coins from this group against each other. If they balance, then the coin you have not weighed is the fake.

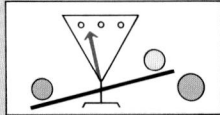

If the two coins do not balance, then the lighter coin on the scale is the counterfeit.

4. *Where to start?* From what point or points on the earth's surface could you walk 12 miles (19 kilometers) due south, then walk 12 miles due east, then walk 12 miles due north, and find yourself back at your starting point?

The usual answer to this old riddle is the North Pole. But the earth actually has an infinite number of points from which you could begin such a walk.

In theory, the equator forms a circle of latitude around the middle of the earth. As one goes north or south from the equator, the circumference of the circles of latitude gets progressively smaller until you reach the poles. Near the South Pole, there is a circle of latitude exactly 12 miles in circumference. Twelve miles north of this first circle is a second circle of latitude. You can start your walk at any point on this outer circle. You walk 12 miles south and find yourself on the inner circle. Then you walk 12 miles east around this circle—that is, you walk once around the earth, which is only 12 miles in circumference at this latitude. You then walk 12 miles north and arrive back at your starting point.

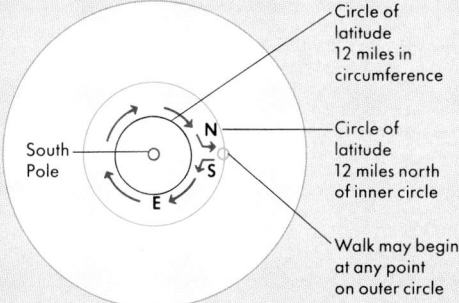

Circle of latitude 12 miles in circumference

Circle of latitude 12 miles north of inner circle

South Pole

Walk may begin at any point on outer circle

An infinite number of other points also can serve as your starting place. There are circles of latitude closer to the South Pole that have a circumference of 6 miles, 3 miles, 2 miles, and so forth. By starting at any point 12 miles north of any of these circles, you could take the walk described. Suppose, for example, you start 12 miles north of the circle of latitude that has a circumference of 1 mile. First you walk 12 miles south. Then you walk 12 miles east—that is, you go around the inner circle 12 times. Then, after walking north for 12 miles, you will arrive at your starting point on the outer circle.

5. *Whose turn to win?* Your friend Rachel challenges you to a game. There are six marbles in a bowl. At a turn, a player may take either one or two marbles. The player who takes the last marble wins the game. Rachel offers to let you take the first turn. If you accept, who wins?

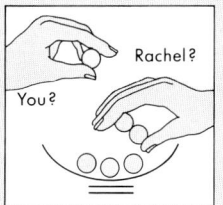

Rachel?

You?

Assume that each player will always make the best move. The winner will take the winning turn when either one or two marbles are left. Therefore, the winner will be the player who leaves the opponent three marbles. If you make the first move and take one marble, Rachel can take two—leaving three for you and winning on her next turn. If, on the first move, you take two marbles, then Rachel can take one—again leaving three for you and winning on her next move. If you accept her kind offer to take the first turn, Rachel will win the game!

6. *The well-dressed doctors.* Doctors Black, Brown, Gray, Green, and White are seated around a circular table, discussing golf. Each doctor wears a suit of a color that corresponds to the name of one of the other doctors. Each suit is of a different color. Based on the following clues, what is the name of the doctor wearing the black suit? (1) The doctor in the black suit sits two places to the left of Dr. Gray. (2) The doctor in the green suit is two places to Dr. Green's right. (3) The doctor in the brown suit sits on Dr. Brown's left. (4) Dr. Black sits to the right of the doctor wearing the white suit.

Draw a circle and label the seating positions A, B, C, D, and E, moving clockwise around the circle. Assign Dr. Gray to position A. It will also help to set up a chart to show the information in the clues. The information provided by clue 1 is shown in the chart below.

Position	Name	Suit color
A	Gray.	Not gray. Not black.
B	Not Gray.	Not black.
C	Not Gray. Not Black.	Black.
D	Not Gray.	Not black.
E	Not Gray.	Not black.

Based on clue 2, you can conclude that the doctor in green does not sit two places to Dr. Gray's right, at position D. In addition, Dr. Green does not occupy position E, because the doctor in black, not green, sits two seats to the right, at position C. Reasoning in this manner, fill in the chart with the information provided by clues 2, 3, and 4.

The completed chart should indicate that the doctor at B cannot be Drs. Gray, Black, or Brown. If you assume that Dr. Green is at B, he or she must wear gray. Then, according to clue 2, the doctor at E wears green and

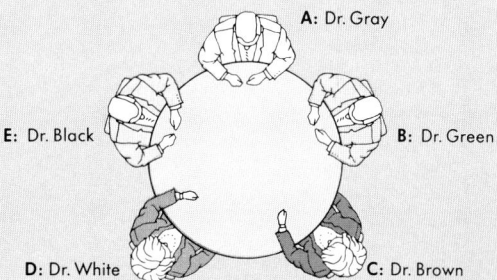

A: Dr. Gray

E: Dr. Black

B: Dr. Green

D: Dr. White

C: Dr. Brown

could be Dr. White or Dr. Black. If Dr. Black is at E, then, according to clue 4, Dr. Gray wears white. This leaves the brown suit for the doctor at D. Then, according to clue 3, Dr. Brown occupies C. This leaves only Dr. White, who must occupy D. Therefore, the doctor in the black suit is Dr. Brown.

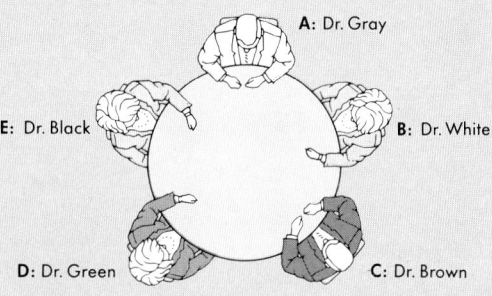

A: Dr. Gray

E: Dr. Black

B: Dr. White

D: Dr. Green

C: Dr. Brown

important uses in astronomy, and also in commerce, because 60 can be divided easily. The Babylonians went well beyond the Egyptians in algebra and geometry.

The Greeks and Romans. Ancient Greek scholars became the first people to explore pure mathematics, apart from practical problems. They made important advances by introducing the concepts of logical deduction and proof in order to create a systematic theory of mathematics. According to tradition, one of the first to provide mathematical proofs based on deduction was the philosopher Thales, who did his work in geometry about 600 B.C.

The Greek philosopher Pythagoras, who lived about 550 B.C., explored the nature of numbers, believing that everything could be understood in terms of whole numbers or their ratios. However, about 400 B.C., the Greeks discovered *irrational numbers* (numbers that cannot be expressed as a ratio of two whole numbers), and they recognized that Pythagorean ideas were incomplete. About 370 B.C., Eudoxus of Cnidus, a Greek astronomer, formulated a theory of proportions to resolve problems associated with irrational numbers. He also developed the *method of exhaustion,* a way of determining areas of curved figures, which foreshadowed integral calculus.

Euclid, one of the foremost Greek mathematicians, wrote the *Elements* about 300 B.C. In this book, Euclid constructs an entire system of geometry by means of abstract definitions and logical deductions. During the 200's B.C., the Greek mathematician Archimedes extended the method of exhaustion. Using a 96-sided figure to approximate a circle, he calculated a highly accurate value for *pi* (the ratio of a circle's circumference to its diameter). About A.D. 150, the Greek astronomer Ptolemy applied geometry and trigonometry to astronomy in a 13-part work on the motions of the planets. It became known as the *Almagest,* meaning *the greatest.*

The Romans showed little interest in pure mathematics. However, they applied mathematical principles in such fields as commerce, engineering, and warfare.

Arab mathematics. Scholars in the Arab world translated and preserved the works of ancient Greek mathematicians and made their own original contributions as well. A book written about 825 by the Arab mathematician al-Khowarizmi described a numeration system developed in India. This decimal system, which used place values and zero, became known as the Hindu-Arabic numeral system. Al-Khowarizmi also wrote an influential book about algebra. The word *algebra* comes from the Arabic title of this book.

In the mid-1100's, a Latin translation of al-Khowarizmi's book on arithmetic introduced the Hindu-Arabic numeral system to Europe. In 1202, Leonardo Fibonacci, an Italian mathematician, published a book on algebra that helped promote this system. Hindu-Arabic numerals gradually replaced Roman numerals in Europe.

Arab astronomers of the 900's made major contributions to trigonometry. During the 1000's, an Arab physicist known as Alhazen applied geometry to optics. The Persian poet and astronomer Omar Khayyam wrote an important book on algebra about 1100. In the 1200's, Nasir Eddin al-Tusi, a Persian mathematician, created ingenious mathematical models for use in astronomy.

The Renaissance. During the 1400's and 1500's, European explorers sought new overseas trade routes,

Important dates in mathematics

c. 3000 B.C. The Egyptians used a system based on groups of 10 and developed basic geometry and surveying techniques.

c. 370 B.C. Eudoxus of Cnidus developed the method of exhaustion, foreshadowing integral calculus.

c. 300 B.C. Euclid constructed a system of geometry by means of logical deduction.

Mid-1100's A translation of al-Khowarizmi's book on arithmetic introduced the Hindu-Arabic numeral system to Europe.

1614 John Napier published his discovery of logarithms, an aid in simplifying calculations.

1637 René Descartes published his discovery of analytic geometry, proposing mathematics as the perfect model for reasoning.

Mid-1680's Sir Isaac Newton and Gottfried Wilhelm Leibniz published their independent discoveries of calculus.

Early 1800's Karl F. Gauss, Janos Bolyai, and Nikolai Lobachevsky separately developed non-Euclidean geometries.

Early 1820's Charles Babbage began to develop mechanical computing machines.

1854 George Boole published his system of symbolic logic.

Late 1800's Georg Cantor developed set theory and a mathematical theory of the infinite.

1910-1913 Alfred North Whitehead and Bertrand Russell published *Principia Mathematica,* which argues that all mathematical propositions can be derived from a few axioms.

Early 1930's Kurt Gödel showed that in any system of axioms, there are statements that cannot be proven.

Late 1950's and 1960's New mathematics was introduced in classrooms in the United States.

1970's and 1980's Computer-based mathematical models came into wide use in studies in business, industry, and science.

stimulating the application of mathematics to navigation and commerce. Mathematics also played a part in artistic creativity. Renaissance artists applied principles of geometry and created a system of linear perspective that gave their paintings an illusion of depth and distance. The invention of printing with movable type in the mid-1400's resulted in speedy and widespread communication of mathematical knowledge.

The Renaissance also brought major advances in pure mathematics. In a book published in 1533, a German mathematician known as Regiomontanus established trigonometry as a field separate from astronomy. French mathematician François Viète made advances in algebra in a book published in 1591.

Mathematics and the scientific revolution. By 1600, the increased use of mathematics and the growth of the experimental method were contributing to revolutionary advances in knowledge. In 1543, Nicolaus Copernicus, a Polish astronomer, published an influential book in which he argued that the sun, not the earth, is the center of the universe. His book sparked intense interest in mathematics and its applications, especially to the study of the motions of the earth and other heavenly bodies. In 1614, John Napier, a Scottish mathematician, published his discovery of *logarithms,* numbers that can be used to simplify such complicated calculations as those used in astronomy. Galileo, an Italian astronomer of the late 1500's and early 1600's, found that many types of motion can be analyzed mathematically.

In a book published in 1637, French philosopher René Descartes proposed mathematics as the perfect model for reasoning. His invention of analytic geometry illustrated the exactness and certainty that mathematics can provide. Another French mathematician of the 1600's, Pierre de Fermat, founded modern number theory. He and French philosopher Blaise Pascal explored probability theory. Fermat's work with infinitesimals helped lay a foundation for calculus.

The English scientist Sir Isaac Newton invented calculus in the mid-1660's. He first mentioned his discovery in a book published in 1687. Working independently, the German philosopher and mathematician Gottfried Wilhelm Leibniz also invented calculus in the mid-1670's. He published his findings in 1684 and 1686.

Developments in the 1700's. A remarkable family of Swiss mathematicians, the Bernoullis, made many contributions to mathematics during the late 1600's and the 1700's. Jakob Bernoulli did pioneering work in analytic geometry and wrote about probability theory. Jakob's brother Johann also worked in analytic geometry and in mathematical astronomy and physics. Johann's son Nicolaus helped advance probability theory. Johann's son Daniel used mathematics to study the motion of fluids and the properties of vibrating strings.

During the mid-1700's, Swiss mathematician Leonhard Euler advanced calculus by showing that the operations of differentiation and integration were opposites. Beginning in the late 1700's, French mathematician Joseph L. Lagrange worked to develop a firmer foundation for calculus. He was suspicious of relying on assumptions from geometry and, instead, developed calculus entirely in terms of algebra.

In the 1800's, public education expanded rapidly, and mathematics became a standard part of university education. Many of the great works in mathematics of the 1800's were written as textbooks. In the 1790's and early 1800's, French mathematician Adrien Marie Legendre wrote particularly influential textbooks and did work in calculus, geometry, and number theory. Important calculus textbooks by French mathematician Augustin Louis Cauchy were published in the 1820's. Cauchy and Jean Baptiste Fourier, another French mathematician, made significant advances in mathematical physics.

Carl Friedrich Gauss, a German mathematician, proved the fundamental theorem of algebra, which states that every equation has at least one root. His work with imaginary numbers led to their increased acceptance. In the 1810's, Gauss developed a non-Euclidean geometry but did not publish his discovery. Working separately, Janos Bolyai of Hungary and Nikolai Lobachevsky of Russia also developed non-Euclidean geometries. They published their discoveries about 1830. In the mid-1800's, Georg Friedrich Bernhard Riemann of Germany developed another non-Euclidean geometry.

During the early 1800's, the works of German mathematician August Ferdinand Möbius helped develop a study in geometry that became known as *topology.* Topology explores the properties of a geometrical figure that do not change when the figure is bent or stretched. See **Topology.**

In the late 1800's, German mathematician Karl Theodor Weierstrass worked to establish a more solid theoretical foundation for calculus. In the 1870's and 1880's, his student Georg Cantor developed set theory and a mathematical theory of the infinite.

Much exciting work in applied mathematics was performed in the 1800's. In Great Britain, Charles Babbage developed early mechanical computing machines, and George Boole created a system of symbolic logic. During the late 1800's, French mathematician Jules Henri Poincaré contributed to probability theory, celestial mechanics, and the study of electromagnetic waves.

Philosophies of mathematics in the 1900's. Many mathematicians of the 1900's have shown concern for the philosophical foundations of mathematics. In order to eliminate contradictions, some mathematicians have used logic to develop mathematics from a set of *axioms* (basic statements considered to be true). Two British philosophers and mathematicians, Alfred North Whitehead and Bertrand Russell, promoted a philosophy of mathematics called *logicism.* In their three-volume work, *Principia Mathematica* (1910-1913), they argued that all *propositions* (statements) in mathematics can be derived logically from just a few axioms.

David Hilbert, a German mathematician of the early 1900's, was a *formalist.* Formalists consider mathematics to be a purely formal system of rules. Hilbert's work led to the study of imaginary spaces with an infinite number of dimensions.

Beginning in the early 1900's, Dutch mathematician Luitzen Brouwer championed *intuitionism.* He believed people understand the laws of mathematics by *intuition* (knowledge not gained by reasoning or experience).

In the early 1930's, Austrian mathematician Kurt Gödel demonstrated that for any logical system, there are always theorems that cannot be proven either true or false by the axioms within that system. He found this to be true even of basic arithmetic.

Mathematicians have made major advances in the study of abstract mathematical structures during the 1900's. One such structure is the *group.* A group is a collection of items, which may be numbers, and rules for some operation with these items, such as addition or multiplication. Group theory is useful in many areas of mathematics and such fields as subatomic physics.

Since 1939, a group of mathematicians, most of whom are French, have published an influential series of books under the pen name Nicolas Bourbaki. This series takes an abstract approach to mathematics, using axiom systems and set theory.

New areas of mathematical specialization have arisen during the 1900's, including systems analysis and computer science. Advances in mathematical logic have been essential to the development of electronic computers. Computers, in turn, enable mathematicians to complete long and complicated calculations quickly. Since the 1970's, computer-based mathematical models have become widely used to study weather patterns, economic relationships, and many other systems.

Trends in teaching mathematics. Before the 1950's, most mathematics courses in elementary, junior high, and high schools in the United States stressed the development of basic computational skills. During the late 1950's and the 1960's, *new mathematics* was introduced. New mathematics is a way of teaching mathematics that stresses understanding concepts rather than memorizing rules and performing repetitious drills. In the 1970's and 1980's, educators continued to use new mathematics, but they gave added emphasis to problem solving and computational skills.

At the college level, educators have moved away from teaching mathematics in the same way to all students. Instead, colleges and universities offer more courses in specialized applications of mathematics in such fields as economics, engineering, and physics.

Careers

A strong background in mathematics is excellent preparation for a wide variety of careers in business, education, government, and industry. Students who wish to study mathematics in college should take high school courses in algebra, geometry, trigonometry, and calculus, if available. These courses also are useful preparation for study in architecture, engineering, and physics.

In college, the basic courses for a major in mathematics include advanced calculus, differential equations, abstract algebra, numerical analysis, number theory, theories of real and complex variables, probability, and statistics. Courses in logic and computer programming also are useful in preparing for many careers.

Mathematicians teach at all levels. High school mathematics teachers must have at least a bachelor's degree in mathematics. Many mathematicians with a doctor's degree teach at colleges and universities.

Large numbers of mathematicians work in business or industry. Those with a bachelor's degree may find work as accountants, computer operators, and statisticians. Many people who have earned a master's or doctor's degree in mathematics conduct research for the communications, energy, manufacturing, or transportation industries. Some mathematicians serve as consultants who apply their training to industrial problems. Mathematicians also work in the computer industry as programmers or as systems analysts who determine the most efficient use of a computer in any given situation. Insurance companies employ mathematicians as actuaries to calculate risks and help design policies.

Mathematicians also work for government agencies. They analyze census data, gather information about the economy, plan space flights, analyze military needs, and perform other services.   Joseph W. Dauben

Related articles in *World Book* include:

American mathematicians

Banneker, Benjamin	Rittenhouse, David
Bowditch, Nathaniel	Steinmetz, Charles P.
Gibbs, Josiah W.	Von Neumann, John
Peirce, Charles S.	Wiener, Norbert

British mathematicians

Babbage, Charles	Russell, Bertrand
Napier, John	Turing, Alan M.
Newton, Sir Isaac	Whitehead, Alfred North

French mathematicians

Châtelet, Marquise du	Lagrange, Joseph-Louis
Descartes, René	Laplace, Marquis de
Fermat, Pierre de	Pascal, Blaise

German mathematicians

Bessel, Friedrich	Kepler, Johannes
Clausius, Rudolf J. E.	Leibniz, Gottfried W.
Gauss, Carl F.	

Other mathematicians

Archimedes	Omar Khayyam
Eratosthenes	Ptolemy
Euclid	Pythagoras
Euler, Leonhard	Thales
Fibonacci, Leonardo	Torricelli, Evangelista
Huygens, Christiaan	

Applied mathematics

Accounting	Insurance	Navigation
Bookkeeping	Interest	Surveying
Budget	Map	Systems analysis
Discount	Mechanical draw-	Weights and
Econometrics	ing	measures
Engineering		

Branches of mathematics

Algebra	Geometry	Topology
Arithmetic	Probability	Trigonometry
Calculus	Statistics	

Mathematical machines and devices

Abacus	Computer
Adding machine	Vernier
Calculator	

Other related articles

Algorithm	Maya (Communica-	Numeration sys-
Chaos	tion and learning)	tems
Decimal system	Möbius strip	Progression
Determinant	New mathematics	Series
Fractal	Number and nu-	Set theory
Game theory	meral	Sieve of
Infinity	Number theory	Eratosthenes
Integer		Square root

Outline

I. The importance of mathematics
 A. In everyday life   C. In industry
 B. In science   D. In business
II. Branches of mathematics
 A. Arithmetic   E. Calculus and analysis
 B. Algebra   F. Probability and statistics
 C. Geometry   G. Set theory and logic
 D. Analytic geometry and
    trigonometry
III. History
IV. Careers

Questions

What type of system do we use when measuring time in hours, minutes, and seconds?
Which two men independently invented calculus?
What did Euclid accomplish in his book the *Elements*?
How does analytic geometry relate algebra to geometry?
Which branch of mathematics got its name from the title of a book by al-Khowarizmi?
How does *pure mathematics* differ from *applied mathematics*?
What do mathematicians do as consultants to companies?
How were Hindu-Arabic numerals introduced to Europe?
How does trigonometry help astronomers, navigators, and surveyors?
Which branch of mathematics would you use to calculate the chances that three tossed coins will all turn up heads?

Additional resources

Level I
Adler, Irving. *Mathematics.* Doubleday, 1990.
Burns, Marilyn. *Math for Smarty Pants.* Little, Brown, 1982. Includes trivia, puzzles, and problems for both math haters and math lovers.
Kaplan, Andrew. *Careers for Number Lovers.* Millbrook, 1991.

Level II
Kline, Morris. *Mathematics and the Search for Knowledge.* Oxford, 1985.
Paulos, John A. *Beyond Numeracy.* Knopf, 1991. Essays on a number of mathematical topics.
Peterson, Ivars. *The Mathematical Tourist: Snapshots of Modern Mathematics.* W. H. Freeman, 1988.

Mather was the name of a family of intellectual and religious leaders—father, son, and grandson—in colonial America.

Richard Mather (1596-1669) was born in Lancashire, England. He was ordained a minister of the Church of England in 1620. But his Puritan beliefs antagonized church authorities, who suspended him from his ministry in 1633. In 1635, he came to the Massachusetts Bay Colony, where he helped establish the Congregational Church in America. From 1636 until his death, he was pastor of the parish in Dorchester, near Boston.

Mather helped compile the *Bay Psalm Book* (1640), the first book printed in the American Colonies (see **Bay Psalm Book**). He also helped write the *Cambridge Platform,* which set forth the principles of Congregational Church discipline and government. The Cambridge Platform was adopted in 1648. About 1655, after his first wife died, Mather married the widow of John Cotton, who was the most prominent theologian of early colonial America.

Increase Mather (1639-1723), the son of Richard, was born in Dorchester. He graduated from Harvard College in 1656 and received his M.A. degree from Trinity College in Dublin, Ireland, in 1658. He returned to America in 1661 and married the daughter of John Cotton in 1662. In 1664, Mather joined the Second Church of Boston in the important post of teacher. He became president of Harvard in 1686.

During the late 1600's, many people opposed the strong governing powers of the Congregational Church. Some of these people, especially those in the Boston area, tried to liberalize the requirements for church membership. Mather was conservative in religious matters and strongly opposed the liberals. This opposition led to his removal as president of Harvard in 1701. For the rest of his life, Mather wrote pamphlets attacking people who he thought threatened established church practices.

Cotton Mather (1663-1728), the son of Increase, was born in Boston. He entered Harvard at the age of 12 and received his B.A. degree in 1678 and his M.A. in 1681. About 1680, he joined his father at the Second Church of Boston as an assistant. He remained there until his death.

Portrait c. 1727 by Peter Pelham, American Antiquarian Society, Worcester, Mass.

Cotton Mather

Mather published more than 400 books and pamphlets, many of which dealt with scientific subjects. In recognition of his scientific writings, he became the first American elected to the Royal Society, the famous British scientific academy. Both he and his father supported smallpox inoculation, though most colonists regarded it with suspicion.

Mather's best-known book is *Magnalia Christi Americana* (1702). This book contains much information about the people and issues that were important in the early history of New England.

Many historians believe that Increase and Cotton Mather helped stir up the Salem witchcraft trials of the 1690's with their writings and sermons. The trials resulted in the execution of 19 people as witches and the pressing to death of a man who refused to plead to the witchcraft charge. Other historians believe that the Mathers' reputation for persecution during the trials has been greatly exaggerated.   Robert L. Ferm

Additional resources

Levin, David. *Cotton Mather: The Young Life of the Lord's Remembrancer, 1663-1703.* Harvard, 1978.
Middlekauff, Robert. *The Mathers: Three Generations of Puritan Intellectuals, 1596-1728.* Oxford, 1971.
Silverman, Kenneth. *The Life and Times of Cotton Mather.* Harper, 1984.

Mathewson, Christy (1880-1925), was one of baseball's greatest right-handed pitchers. He won 373 games, 372 of them while pitching for the New York Giants from 1900 to 1916. He won one game for the Cincinnati Reds in 1916 before retiring. Mathewson became the first pitcher in the 1900's to win 30 games a season three years in a row. He also pitched 20 or more victories for 12 consecutive seasons.

Christopher Mathewson was born in Factoryville, Pa. He became famous for developing a reverse curve pitch which was called a *fadeaway* by hitters of his time. Today the pitch is known as a *screwball.* Mathewson pitched three shutouts in the 1905 World Series. In 1908, he won 37 games. Mathewson led the league in strikeouts for five seasons—1903, 1904, 1905, 1907, and 1908. He became one of the first five players elected to the National Baseball Hall of Fame in 1936.   Jack Lang

See also **Baseball** (picture).

Matisse, *mah TEES,* **Henri,** *ahn REE* (1869-1954), a French painter, was one of the most influential artists of the 1900's. He was the leader of the Fauves, a group of painters who started the first important art movement of the era. Matisse was also a noted sculptor and graphic artist.

Matisse's favorite subjects included human figures, still lifes, and scenes of interiors. He believed that the arrangement of colors and forms was as important as the subject matter to communicate the meaning of a painting. Although he made few entirely abstract images, he avoided detailed illusion. Instead, he used intense colors and strong lines to produce patterns and a sense of movement. These features often produce a tension with the figurative subjects of his paintings. Matisse's works, especially those of the 1920's, have a decorative quality similar to the art of the Near and Middle East. He was one of the first European artists to be influenced by Afri-

Collection of S. Max Becker, Jr., Glencoe, Ill.   © Gisele Freund, Photo Researchers

Henri Matisse was a famous French artist. The self-portrait on the left and the photograph on the right both date from 1949.

The Royal Museum of Fine Arts, Rump Collection, Copenhagen

Portrait of Madame Matisse, painted in 1905, shows Matisse's emphasis on color, which is typical of the Fauve movement.

can masks and sculpture.

Matisse was born in Le Cateau, near Cambrai. He entered law school in 1887 but began to paint in 1890 as a pastime while recovering from an operation. In 1891, Matisse moved to Paris to study art. In the early 1890's, he painted with dark colors. But he showed the influence of the bright colors of the impressionists in his painting *The Dinner Table* (1897).

In 1905, works by Matisse and other Fauve painters were exhibited together. The brilliant colors and bold patterns of these paintings shocked the Paris art world. One of Matisse's Fauve paintings, *Landscape at Collioure,* appears in the **Painting** article. See also **Fauves**.

From 1907 to about 1920, Matisse painted increasingly simplified designs that reflected the influence of the French artist Paul Cézanne and of the cubists. Matisse also did his most important work as a sculptor during this period. In his last years, Matisse created large, decorative compositions made of cut paper. From 1948 to 1951, he designed and decorated the Chapel of the Rosary in Vence, France. Nancy J. Troy

Additional resources

Flam, Jack D. *Matisse: The Man and His Art, 1869-1918.* Cornell Univ. Pr., 1986.
Schneider, Pierre. *Matisse.* Thames & Hudson, 1989. First published in 1984.

Matriarchal family. See Family (Traditional families in other cultures).

Matter is the substance of which all things are made. All objects consist of matter. The objects may differ widely from one another. But they have one thing in common—they all occupy space. Therefore, scientists usually define matter as anything that occupies space. All matter has *inertia.* This means that it resists any change in its condition of rest or of motion. The quantity of matter in an object is called its *mass,* but scientists usually prefer to define mass as a measure of inertia. The earth's gravitational attraction for a given mass gives matter its *weight.* Gravity's pull on an object decreases as it moves away from the earth. For this reason, objects that move from the earth into outer space "lose weight" even though their masses remain the same.

When we see people, animals, or machines working, feel heat from a fire, or see light from an electric bulb, we become aware of energy. Heat is the variety of energy most familiar to us. All other kinds of energy may be changed into heat. See **Energy.**

Matter can be changed into energy and energy into matter. For example, matter changes into energy when radium and other radioactive elements disintegrate and when atomic bombs explode. Energy changes into matter when subatomic particles collide at high speeds and create new, heavier particles.

The properties of matter

All of us easily recognize many varieties of matter. Each variety possesses certain characteristics common to all samples of its kind. We base our recognition of each variety of matter on knowledge of its special characteristics, or *properties.* These properties distinguish one kind of matter from others. Matter has two main types of properties—physical and chemical.

Physical properties. People recognize certain kinds of matter by sight, smell, touch, taste, or hearing. We can recognize gold by color, sugar by taste, and gasoline by odor. These are examples of physical properties of matter. Another such property is *density,* the amount of mass for each unit of volume. Because of the difference in density, a block of cork weighs less than a block of all common woods the same size. *Solubility* (the ability of one kind of matter to dissolve in another) and *conductivity* (the ability of matter to conduct heat or electricity) are also physical properties.

Chemical properties of matter describe how a substance acts when it undergoes chemical change. For example, a chemical property of iron is its ability to combine with oxygen in moist air to form iron oxide, or rust. Scientists call such changes in the composition of matter *chemical changes.* Some changes alter the value of physical properties, such as weight or density, but produce no change in the composition of the matter. Scientists call these *physical changes.* When water changes to steam it undergoes physical, but not chemical, change (see **Physical change**).

Compounds and elements. By using chemical processes, scientists may be able to separate a substance into two or more simpler kinds of matter with new properties. If so, they call the substance a *compound substance,* or a *chemical compound.* Substances that do not break down into simpler varieties of matter by chemical means are called *elementary substances,* or *chemical elements* (see **Element, Chemical**).

Structure of matter

All ordinary matter is made up of *atoms.* An atom is the smallest quantity of an element that can enter into chemical reaction to form a compound. Atoms are composed of particles called *protons, neutrons,* and *electrons.* Protons and neutrons, in turn, are made up of particles called *quarks.* Quarks are held together by particles called *gluons.*

All the atoms of an elementary substance have identical chemical properties. When two or more elements combine to form a compound, the atoms of one substance combine with the atoms of the other substances. The atoms form larger particles called *molecules.* Water consists of molecules, each of which contains two atoms of hydrogen and one of oxygen. Atoms and molecules are extremely small. If the molecules in one drop of water were counted at the rate of 10 million each second, a person would need about 5 million years to count them all.

Compounds may be *organic* or *inorganic.* Organic compounds contain the element carbon. They are called organic because most of the compounds found in living organisms contain carbon. All other compounds are classed as inorganic. These classifications are not completely rigid. Organic molecules are among the largest molecules. Organic molecules may contain thousands of atoms.

Molecules are bound together by electrical force. This force comes from the electrons in the atoms. Electrons in a molecule may be exchanged between atoms in what chemists call *ionic bonding.* In addition, electrons may be shared between atoms in what chemists call *covalent bonding* (see **Chemistry** [Fundamental ideas of chemistry]).

Conservation of matter

Before the famous German-born scientist Albert Einstein developed his theory of relativity, scientists believed that matter was never created or destroyed (see **Relativity**). This idea was called the *conservation of matter.* But Einstein proved that mass and energy are interchangeable. For example, if a chemical change gives off energy as heat and light, then the substances that changed must have lost some mass. In all ordinary chemical reactions that take place in factories, homes,

and laboratories, the amount of mass lost is far too small to be measured. Measurable quantities of mass are changed into energy only in nuclear reactions such as those that occur in nuclear reactors, atomic bombs, or particle accelerators. Because of Einstein's work, scientists now state the conservation law this way: Mass-energy may not be created or destroyed, but each may be converted into the other.

States of matter

Matter can ordinarily exist in three physical states—solid, liquid, and gas. For example, ice is solid water. When heated, it melts at a definite temperature to form liquid water. When heat causes the temperature of the water to rise to a certain point, the water boils, producing steam, a gas. Removal of heat reverses these processes. In spite of these changes, the chemical composition of water remains the same. A fourth state of matter, called plasma, exists under special conditions.

Solids. All solids have *form.* They also have *hardness* and *rigidity,* or the ability to oppose a change of shape. For example, stone does not change shape easily. Some solids, like salt or sulfur, are *brittle* and will shatter when struck. Others have great *tensile strength* and resist being pulled apart. Still others, particularly metals, have *malleability* (the ability to be beaten into thin sheets) and *ductility* (the ability to be drawn into wires). These properties depend on the particles that make up the substance and the forces acting among them. The atoms in almost all solids are arranged in regular patterns, called crystals. See **Solid.**

Liquids have no shape of their own. But they have the ability to flow. They take the shape of any container in which they are placed. They fill it only when their volume equals that of the container. Iron and steel are rigid in their solid state. But manufacturers often melt them and pour them into molds. See **Liquid.**

Gases. All gases, regardless of the composition of their molecules, have almost identical physical behavior. Compared with liquids or solids, they have low densities. They exert pressure equally in all directions. All are compressible. When heated, gases expand or exert a greater pressure when confined in a vessel of fixed volume. See **Gas.**

Plasmas form in the interior of stars, in outer space, in neon lamps and fluorescent lamps, and in some laboratory experiments. Plasmas result when the atoms in a gas become *ionized* (electrically charged). Electrical forces between the gas atoms give the gas new physical properties.

Dark matter

The visible universe is made up chiefly of the two lightest elements. It consists of about 75 per cent hydrogen and 24 per cent helium, with the heavier elements making up the remainder. However, there is convincing evidence that most of the matter in the universe is not visible. This invisible matter is called *dark matter.* Many scientists believe that dark matter may not be composed of atoms, or even of electrons, protons, neutrons, or quarks. Instead, it may be composed of yet undiscovered types of particles. The nature of dark matter is one of the most important questions in science today. See **Dark matter.**   Joel R. Primack

WORLD BOOK illustration

Matter exists in three forms—solids, such as rocks; liquids, such as water; and gases, such as air.

Related articles in *World Book* include:

Adhesion	Energy	Malleability
Antimatter	Expansion	Materialism
Atom	Gas	Molecule
Cohesion	Gravitation	Plasma (physics)
Dark matter	Inertia	Shadow matter
Density	Lavoisier, Antoine L.	Solid
Elasticity	Liquid	Viscosity

Matterhorn, *MAT uhr HAWRN,* is a famous mountain peak in the Pennine Alps. It rises 14,692 feet (4,478 meters) on the boundary between the *canton* (state) of Valais in southern, Switzerland and the Piedmont region of Italy. For location, see **Switzerland** (political map).

The peak of the Matterhorn rises like a pyramid from the surrounding mountain base. Snow always covers the upper slopes of this peak. Many climbers have scaled its steep sides. The first person to make the challenging climb to the top of the Matterhorn was Edward Whymper in 1865.   Howell C. Lloyd

Chris Bonington, Bruce Coleman Ltd.

The Matterhorn has one of the highest peaks in the Pennine Alps, which lie in Italy and Switzerland. The spectacular peak towers above snow-packed glaciers and quiet mountain lakes.

See also **Alps; Mountain** (diagram: Major mountains); **Switzerland** (picture).

Matthew, Saint, was one of the 12 apostles of Jesus Christ. The Gospel of Matthew states that Matthew was working as a tax collector when he was called to follow Jesus. However, the Gospels of Mark and Luke state that the tax collector's name was *Levi.* Some scholars have suggested that Levi was Matthew's second name and that all of the Gospels refer to the same person.

Matthew has traditionally been regarded as the author of the first Gospel, perhaps written in Hebrew or Aramaic. Many modern scholars, however, believe that Matthew was not the author and that this Gospel was originally written in Greek. According to tradition, Matthew preached in Africa and Persia, where he was martyred.

Matthew's feast day is celebrated on September 21 in the Roman Catholic Church. The Eastern Orthodox Churches celebrate his feast day on November 16.
    Richard A. Edwards

See also **Apostles; Gospels.**

Matthias, *muh THY uhs,* **Saint,** was an early Christian. He is mentioned once in the New Testament as a follower of Jesus who was chosen by the remaining 11 apostles to replace Judas Iscariot (Acts 1:15-26). According to later tradition, Matthias traveled in Judea, Turkey, and Ethiopia as a missionary. His feast day is May 14 in the West and August 9 in the Eastern Orthodox Churches.   Richard A. Edwards

Matthias Corvinus. See **Hungary** (The Kingdom of Hungary).

Mattress. See **Bed.**

Matzah. See **Passover.**

Matzeliger, Jan Ernst (1852-1889), invented a machine that revolutionized the shoe industry. He made the first shoe-lasting machine, which shaped and fastened the leather over the sole of a shoe. This process, previously done by hand, led to the mass production of shoes and greatly reduced their price.

Matzeliger, a black, was born in Paramaribo, Dutch Guiana (now Suriname). As a boy, he worked in a government machine shop there. In 1873, Matzeliger settled in Philadelphia and worked as a cobbler. In 1877, he took a job in a shoe factory in Lynn, Mass.

Matzeliger completed his shoe-lasting machine in 1882 and patented it in 1883. He did not have enough money to produce and sell the machine himself, and so in 1885 he sold the patent to a company in Lynn. This company later became the United Shoe Machinery Company.

Matzeliger died of tuberculosis at the age of 37. He shared only partly in the great profits that resulted from his invention.   Raymond W. Smock

Mau Mau, *MOW mow,* was a secret movement that included Africans who wanted to end European colonial rule in Kenya. Most who took the oath of unity were Kikuyu people who lived in overcrowded areas. The movement began in the late 1940's. British forces started a drive to wipe out the movement after a series of murders and other terrorist attacks by the Mau Mau started in 1952. Jomo Kenyatta, who later became president of Kenya, was convicted of leading the movement and was held in a remote area until 1961. When the fighting ended in 1956, about 11,500 Kikuyu had been killed. About 2,000 other Africans, 95 Europeans, and 29 Asians lost their lives supporting the colonial government.
    Carl G. Rosberg

See also **Kenya** (Opposition to the British).

Maugham, *mawm,* **W. Somerset** (1874-1965), was a fiction and drama writer who became one of the most popular British authors of the 1900's. However, Maugham's reputation stood far higher with the public than with critics.

Maugham usually wrote in a detached, ironic style, yet he often showed sympathy for his characters. His semiautobiographical novel *Of Human Bondage* (1915) established his position as a serious writer. Considered his finest work, it is a realistic story of a medical student's bondage to his lameness and his love for an unappreciative woman. *Cakes and Ale* (1930) is generally ranked next among Maugham's novels. It is a comic satire about an English author.

Maugham based his novel *The Moon and Sixpence* (1919) on the life of the painter Paul Gauguin. Maugham's experiences in the British secret service during World War I provided the background for a group of related stories published as *Ashenden* (1928).

Balkin, Pix

W. Somerset Maugham

Maugham's *Collected Short Stories* was published in four volumes in 1977 and 1978. *The Summing Up* (1938) and *A Writer's Notebook* (1949) are the direct, personal observations of a professional writer.

Maugham wrote many sophisticated plays, beginning with *Lady Frederick* (1907). His most popular comedies include *The Circle* (1921) and *The Constant Wife* (1927).

William Somerset Maugham was born in Paris, the son of a British embassy official. He studied medicine at the request of his family, but he never practiced after completing his internship.   Sharon Bassett

Maui. See Hawaii (The islands).

Mauldin, *MAWL dihn,* **Bill** (1921-   ), is an American editorial cartoonist. He became famous during World War II (1939-1945) for his drawings of U.S. Army life in *Stars and Stripes,* the armed forces newspaper. The main characters in these cartoons, two American GI's named Willie and Joe, often showed the resentment of enlisted soldiers toward officers. Mauldin won the Pulitzer Prize for cartooning in 1945 and 1959.

William Henry Mauldin was born in Mountain Park, N. Mex. He served in the Army from 1940 to 1945. After his release from the Army, he worked for several years as a cartoonist for United Features Syndicate. In 1958, Mauldin became editorial cartoonist for the *St. Louis Post-Dispatch,* where he became known for his satirical wit and liberal views. In 1962, he joined the *Chicago Sun-Times.* His cartoons are syndicated to about 200 newspapers. Collections of his cartoons include *Up Front* (1945), *Back Home* (1947), *The Brass Ring* (1971), and *Mud and Guts* (1978).   Michael Emery

See also **Kennedy, John F.** (picture: The nation's sorrow).

Mauna Kea, *MOW nuh KAY uh,* is a volcano on the island of Hawaii. Its peak rises 13,796 feet (4,205 meters) above sea level and 33,476 feet (10,203 meters) above the base of the mountain on the floor of the Pacific Ocean. Its rise from base to peak is the greatest in the world. This distance is 4,448 feet (1,356 meters) longer than the rise from sea level to the peak of Mount Everest. The name Mauna Kea means *white mountain.* See also **Mountain** (diagram: Major mountains).

Mauna Loa, *MOW nuh LOH uh,* a volcanic mountain on the island of Hawaii, rises 13,677 feet (4,169 meters) above sea level in Hawaii Volcanoes National Park (see **Hawaii** [physical map]). It is the world's largest volcano. At the top is Mokuaweoweo, a crater. Kilauea volcano lies on the southeastern slope.

Mauna Loa's longest eruption lasted 18 months in 1855-1856. Most of the lava produced by eruptions comes from the sides of the mountain, not from the peak crater. In 1926, lava destroyed a fishing village. Parts of other villages were buried in 1950. A 1984 eruption sent lava flowing to within 4 miles (6.4 kilometers) of the city of Hilo.   Lyndon Wester

See also **Kilauea; Mountain** (diagram: Major mountains); **Volcano** (Shield volcanoes; table; picture).

Maundy Thursday, *MAWN dee,* also called Holy Thursday, is observed on the Thursday during Holy Week in the Christian calendar. It comes three days before Easter. Maundy Thursday celebrates two events of Jesus Christ's last week on earth—washing the feet of His disciples and sharing the Last Supper with them.

The name *Maundy* probably comes from a Latin word that means *mandate* or *commandment.* It refers to Jesus' commandment that His disciples wash one another's feet as He had washed theirs. The commandment is linked with His words to the disciples (John 13: 34): "A new commandment I give unto you, That ye love one another."

Special services on Maundy Thursday may include a reenactment of the washing of feet and the administer-

Courtesy of Mr. and Mrs. Sidney Simon, New York, New York

"Beautiful view! Is there one for the enlisted men?"

Cartoonist Bill Mauldin accurately pictured the favorite gripes and the plight of the common soldier in World War II. This drawing lampooning officers became one of his most famous.

ing of Communion. Both acts help to visibly remind Christians of their share in Christ's love.

David G. Truemper

See also **Holy Week.**

Maupassant, Guy de. See De Maupassant, Guy.

Maurer, *MOW rur,* **Ion Gheorghe,** *yahn gay AWR gay* (1902-   ), served as prime minister of Romania from 1961 until he resigned in 1974. He was a member of the Presidium, the Romanian Communist Party's chief executive body, from 1965 to 1974.

Maurer was born in Bucharest and earned a law degree at Bucharest University. During the 1930's, he served as defense attorney for Communists in various trials. Maurer joined the party in 1936. In 1945, he was named undersecretary for communications. From 1948 to 1955, Maurer was director of the Institute for Juridical Research of the Academy of Sciences. He became vice president of the National Assembly in 1957 and minister for foreign affairs in 1958.   Stuart D. Goldman

Mauretania. See **Moors; Rome, Ancient** (map: The Roman world).

Mauriac, *maw RYAK,* **François,** *frahn SWAH* (1885-1970), a French author, won the 1952 Nobel Prize for literature. His novels are set among middle-class people in his native Bordeaux. The attitudes toward sin and love expressed in his fiction reflect his Roman Catholic faith. Mauriac's novels explore the mysteries of human existence, the nature of destiny, and human guilt before a judging though forgiving God. His stories are noted for their psychology and beautiful language. Mauriac's major novels include *The Kiss to the Leper* (1922), *Thérèse Desqueyroux* (1927), *Vipers Tangle* (1932), and *The Frontenac Mystery* (1933).

In 1934, Mauriac began to write essays on his view of life and literature for the newspaper *Le Figaro.* These essays have been republished periodically in collections called *Journals.* Mauriac also wrote several plays, including *Asmodée* (1938) and *Le Feu sur la terre* (1951). His poetry was collected in *Le Sang d'Atys* (1940). His biographies include two studies of Christ, *Life of Jesus* (1936) and *The Son of Man* (1958).

Mauriac was elected to the French Academy in 1933. Claude Mauriac, his son, is also a well-known novelist.

Elaine D. Cancalon

Mauritania, *MAWR ih TAY nee uh,* is a country in western Africa. It stretches eastward from the Atlantic coast into the Sahara. Arabic-speaking people called Moors make up most of the population. Black Africans form a large minority group.

Mauritania was once a colony in French West Africa. It became independent in 1960. Its name in French is République Islamique de Mauritanie (Islamic Republic of Mauritania). The name comes from the fact that almost all the people are Muslims. Nouakchott, a town of about 350,000 people, is the capital and largest city.

Government. A president serves as head of state of Mauritania, and a prime minister as head of government. The president manages the nation's foreign affairs. The prime minister, with the help of the *Council of Ministers* (cabinet), directs the day-to-day operations of the government. A legislature passes the laws. The legislature consists of a Senate with 53 members and a National Assembly with 79 members. The people elect the president and the members of the legislature. The presi-

dent appoints the prime minister, who then appoints members to the Council of Ministers.

Mauritania is divided into 12 regions and 1 district for purposes of local government. The capital makes up the district. The Republican Democratic and Social Party (PRDS) is the largest political party in Mauritania.

People. About 99 per cent of the people are Muslims. The way of life differs among the various groups.

The majority of people are Moors, descendants of Arabs and Berbers. Most Moors speak Arabic. Some lead a nomadic life, living in tents and moving over the desert with their cattle in search of waterholes and pastureland. Others live in cities or villages, or in rural areas where they farm.

The Moors are divided into two main groups, *white Moors* and *black Moors.* The terms *white* and *black* refer to social status and family lineage rather than to skin color. The white Moors, who have the higher status, are in turn divided into two groups, the warriors and the *marabout* (saintly) tribes. Before French rule, the warriors were a nobility who kept black slaves. Other tribes served the warriors, whose chief occupation was fighting. The marabout have always raised cattle, sheep, and other livestock. Traditionally, leading marabout families were a learned class who studied religion and law and advised the warriors.

About a third of Mauritania's people are black Africans belonging to any of several ethnic groups. Many are farmers who live in villages along the Senegal River. Their circular huts, with walls made of sun-dried mudbrick, stand along narrow, twisting village pathways. The largest black ethnic group is the *Toucouleur.* Other groups include the *Fulbe* (also called *Fulani*), the *Soninké,* the *Wolof,* and the *Banbara.* The blacks were the first to gain a modern education, and many hold jobs in government and as teachers.

Mauritania has two main languages, Arabic and French. Both have been used extensively in government

Wolfgang Kaehler

Mauritanians gather in Nouadhibou, the nation's chief port. Arabic-speaking people called Moors make up most of the country's population. Black Africans form a large minority group.

Facts in brief

Capital: Nouakchott.
Official language: Arabic. *National languages*—Arabic, Poular, Soninké, Wolof.
Area: 397,956 sq. mi. (1,030,700 km²). *Greatest distances*—north-south, 800 mi. (1,287 km); east-west, 780 mi. (1,255 km). *Coastline*—414 mi. (666 km).
Elevation: *Highest*—Kediet Ijill, 3,002 ft. (915 m) above sea level. *Lowest*—sea level along the coast.
Population: *Estimated 1994 population*—2,266,000; density, 6 persons per sq. mi. (2 per km²); distribution, 54 per cent urban, 46 per cent rural. *1988 census*—1,864,236. *Estimated 1999 population*—2,614,000.
Chief products: *Agriculture*—dates, gum arabic, livestock (cattle, sheep, goats), millet. *Mining*—iron ore. *Fishing*—ocean and freshwater fish.
Flag: The flag is green and has a yellow star and crescent in the center. The green color and the star and crescent stand for Mauritania's ties to Islam and the rest of northern Africa. The yellow stands for the country's ties to nations south of the Sahara. See **Flag** (picture: Flags of Africa).
Money: *Basic unit*—ouguiya.

and education. But black ethnic groups also speak their own languages. Serious disputes over language use have broken out over the years. In 1991, Arabic became the country's official language. At the same time, Arabic and three black languages—Poular, Soninké, and Wolof—were recognized as national languages. Both Moors and blacks seek to promote their own interests in language and other matters.

Only 10 per cent of Mauritania's children attend primary school, and an even smaller percentage attend high school. The country's first university, the University of Nouakchott, opened in 1983.

Land. An imaginary line drawn between Nouakchott on the coast and Néma in the southeast divides Mauritania into two major land regions. The Sahara covers most of the area north of the Nouakchott-Néma line. It is broken only by rocky plateaus and a few oases.

The small part of the country south of the line receives enough rainfall to support farming and livestock-raising. It contains two fertile areas—a narrow plain along the Sénégal River and a *savanna* (grassland with scattered trees) in the southeast. Farmers raise millet, rice, and other crops on the plain. Herders raise livestock in the savanna area. Eighty per cent of the people live in the south.

Mauritania's climate is hot, but temperatures vary greatly. Desert temperatures may fall from over 100 °F (38 °C) during the day to 45 °F (7 °C) at night. The average monthly temperatures at Nouadhibou (formerly Port-Étienne) vary from a 91 °F (33 °C) high in September to a 54 °F (12 °C) low in January. There is little rain in the north. Southern Mauritania receives more than 20 inches (51 centimeters) of rain a year.

Economy. Mauritania's economy is based on agriculture and about 65 per cent of the people are farmers and livestock herders. Chief food crops include millet, dates, corn, red beans, and rice. Gum arabic, used to make mucilage, and livestock on the hoof are important exports. A rich fishing ground lies off the coast.

Large high-grade iron ore deposits near Fdérik are Mauritania's most important mineral resource. The ore is exported chiefly to Britain, Germany, and Italy. It provides a large part of the government's revenue.

Incomes in Mauritania are low, and most workers make only enough to provide for their families. The government depends on aid from other countries—chiefly France—to balance its budget. The government has expanded the fishing industry, which is now an important part of the economy. Poor communications and transportation hinder economic development.

Mauritania's railroad is about 420 miles (670 kilometers) long. It links Zouirât and Akjoujt with Nouadhibou, the chief port. Less than a fifth of the nation's 5,500 miles (8,900 kilometers) of roads are paved.

History. From the A.D. 300's to the 1500's, areas of what is now Mauritania were part of three great West African empires—Ghana, Mali, and Songhai. In the early 1900's, archaeologists identified ruins in southeastern Mauritania as part of Kumbi Saleh, the capital of the Ghana Empire. See **Ghana Empire; Mali Empire; Songhai Empire.**

The Portuguese landed in Mauritania in the 1400's, but continuous European contact did not begin until the 1600's. Between the 1600's and the 1800's, Britain, France, and the Netherlands competed for the Mauritanian gum arabic trade.

Mauritania

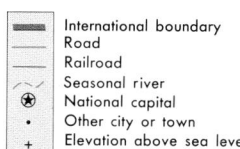

International boundary
Road
Railroad
Seasonal river
National capital
Other city or town
Elevation above sea level

WORLD BOOK maps

France began to occupy Mauritania in 1902 and set up a protectorate there in 1903. Xavier Coppolani became the first governor. Modern Mauritania is largely the result of Coppolani's work in promoting Mauritanian identity separate from neighboring states and of his successors' ability to extend French rule over the country. Mauritania became a French colony in 1920.

After World War II (1939-1945), Mauritanian political leaders began to gain power. In 1946, Mauritania became a territory in the French Union. It became a self-governing republic in the French Community in 1958. Mokhtar Ould Daddah was elected prime minister in 1959. Supported by many Moorish leaders and the small group of educated black leaders, he favored independence and close ties with west African countries. On Nov. 28, 1960, Mauritania became fully independent. Morocco claimed that Mauritania was historically Moroccan territory and did not recognize its independence. Some of Ould Daddah's opponents fled to Morocco and worked to unite the two countries. But Morocco recognized Mauritania's independence in 1970.

In 1961, Mauritania adopted a constitution that set up a presidential system of government. Ould Daddah, elected the first president, merged Mauritania's four political parties into a single party, the Mauritanian People's Party. A 1965 constitutional amendment officially made Mauritania a one-party state.

In 1976, Spain gave up control of its overseas province of Spanish Sahara, and Mauritania and Morocco took over its administration. This area—which borders Mauritania, Morocco, and Algeria—is now called Western Sahara. Mauritania claimed the southern part of the area, and Morocco claimed the northern part. But Algeria and an organization of people of Western Sahara called the Polisario Front opposed the claims. Fighting broke out between Polisario Front troops and troops from Mauritania and Morocco. In 1979, Mauritania gave up its claim to Western Sahara and ended its role in the fighting.

In the early 1980's, a severe drought caused widespread food shortages and losses of livestock in Mauritania. The drought became more severe in the mid-1980's, causing many people to move from rural areas to cities. The cities became overpopulated. Farm production fell sharply, and Mauritania's dependence on foreign aid increased.

In 1978, military leaders overthrew Ould Daddah and took control of the government. Military leaders then ruled the country until 1992, when Mauritania established a multiparty democracy. In 1992, Maawiya Ould Sid Ahmed Taya, an army colonel who had served as president of the military government, was elected president. Parliamentary elections were also held that year.

Kenneth J. Perkins

See also **French West Africa; Nouakchott.**

Mauritius, *maw RIHSH uhs,* is an island nation in the Indian Ocean. Its chief island, also called Mauritius, lies about 500 miles (800 kilometers) east of Madagascar and about 2,450 miles (3,943 kilometers) southwest of India. Overpopulation is one of the country's problems.

Sugar cane fields cover about half of the island. Bare, black volcanic peaks tower over the sugar cane fields. Sugar is the island's chief product.

The Dutch claimed Mauritius in 1598. Later, France

Mauritius

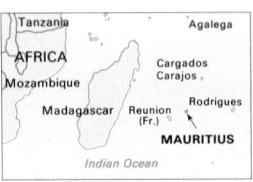
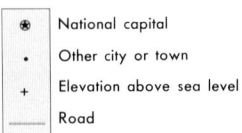
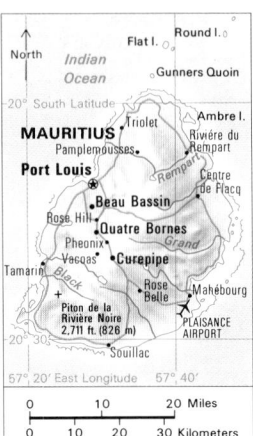

WORLD BOOK maps

and then Britain ruled the island. Mauritius gained its independence from Britain in 1968. It remained a member of the Commonwealth of Nations. Port Louis, a city of about 138,000 people, is the nation's capital and leading port.

Government. Mauritius is a constitutional monarchy. A governor general, who is appointed by Britain, represents the British Crown. But a prime minister, who is chosen by the majority party in the assembly, runs the government.

The 70-member Legislative Assembly passes laws for the country. Elections for the assembly are held at least once every five years. Adults cast three votes, and elect three assembly members from each of the island's 20 districts. To guarantee fair representation for minority groups, an electoral supervisory commission chooses eight more members from among unsuccessful candidates. They choose four members from minorities that do not have enough representatives in the assembly in proportion to their numbers in the population. They choose the other four on the basis of minority groups and political party.

Throughout Mauritius, councils govern villages and towns. The members of these councils are elected by adult voters.

People. The people of Mauritius are descendants of European settlers, African slaves, Chinese traders, and

Facts in brief

Capital: Port Louis.
Official language: English.
Area: 788 sq. mi. (2,040 km²). *Greatest length*—38 mi. (61 km). *Greatest width*—29 mi. (47 km). *Coastline*—100 mi. (161 km).
Elevation: *Highest*—2,711 ft. (826 m). *Lowest*—sea level.
Population: *Estimated 1994 population*—1,103,000; density, 1,400 persons per sq. mi. (541 per km²); distribution, 59 per cent rural, 41 per cent urban. *1990 census*—1,056,660. *Estimated 1999 population*—1,161,000.
Chief product: *Agriculture*—sugar.
National anthem: "Motherland."
Flag: The flag's four horizontal stripes are red, blue, yellow, and green (top to bottom). Red stands for the struggle for freedom, blue for the Indian Ocean, yellow for the light of independence shining over the island, and green for agriculture. Adopted 1968. See **Flag** (picture: Flags of Africa).
Money: *Basic unit*—rupee.

Indian laborers and traders. Almost 70 per cent of the people are Indians, and almost 30 per cent are people of European and African or European and Indian ancestry called *Creoles.* The rest are Chinese or Europeans. Most Europeans are of French descent.

About half of the people live in villages and other rural areas. Most Europeans live in towns. Most villagers live in houses with concrete or wood walls and corrugated iron roofs. Most men wear Western-style clothes. Indian women wear the *sari* (a straight piece of cloth draped around the body).

English is the official language, but French may also be used in the Legislative Assembly. Most of the people speak *Creole,* a French dialect. Some Indians speak one or more of six Indian dialects, and the Chinese speak two Chinese dialects. Most Europeans speak French.

More than 50 per cent of the people are Hindus. About 30 per cent are Christians, and over 17 per cent are Muslims. Hindu temples, Muslim mosques, Buddhist pagodas, and Christian churches dot the land.

Primary and secondary education are free, but not compulsory. About 60 per cent of the people can read and write. Mauritius has an agricultural college, a teachers' training college, and a university college.

Land. Mauritius covers a total of 788 square miles (2,040 square kilometers). The country consists of the island of Mauritius, which has an area of 720 square miles (1,865 square kilometers), and several other islands. The other islands include Rodrigues, about 350 miles (563 kilometers) east of Mauritius; Agalega, two small islands about 580 miles (933 kilometers) north of Mauritius; and the Cargados Carajos Shoals, about 250 miles (402 kilometers) north. Mauritius also claims the Chagos Archipelago, an island group about 1,300 miles (2,100 kilometers) northeast of the island of Mauritius. The archipelago makes up the British Indian Ocean Territory and is controlled by Great Britain. The archipelago includes the island of Diego Garcia, the site of a U.S. naval base.

The island of Mauritius was formed by volcanoes that left the land covered with rocks and a thick layer of lava. A misty plateau in the center of the island rises 2,200 feet (671 meters) above sea level. This area may receive up to 200 inches (510 centimeters) of rain a year. In the north, the plateau slopes to the sea. But it drops sharply to the southern and western coasts. Dry regions that receive only about 35 inches (89 centimeters) of rain a year lie in the southwest. Coral reefs surround all but the southern part of the island.

Summer lasts from November to April, and the temperatures then average about 79 °F (26 °C). Southeast winds bring rains to the plateau. Sometimes cyclones strike the island. Winter lasts from June to October. Temperatures then average about 72 °F (22 °C).

Economy. More than a third of the nation's income comes from the sugar industry, and almost all its exports are sugar or sugar products. About one-third of all workers grow, harvest, or process sugar cane. About 90 per cent of the farmland is planted with sugar cane. About 20 large sugar estates produce over half of the cane. The rest is produced by more than 27,500 small planters. Sugar is processed in factories on the island.

Farmers also raise tea in the wet uplands. About two-thirds of the tea crop is exported. Some tobacco is raised and made into cigarettes. People grow vegetables in small gardens or between the rows of sugar cane. A few keep cattle, goats, or chickens. But almost all of the country's food, including rice, cattle, grain, meat, and wheat flour, must be imported. The country has some small industries. Tourism also contributes to the economy. Mauritius has about 550 miles (885 kilometers) of paved roads.

History. In the 1500's, Portuguese sailors became the first Europeans to visit Mauritius island. Mauritius was uninhabited until the Dutch claimed it in 1598, and named it after Prince Maurice of Nassau. The Dutch brought slaves from Madagascar to cut down the ebony forests, but they abandoned Mauritius in 1710.

In 1715, France took possession of the island, and renamed it Île de France. French colonists from the neighboring island of Bourbon (now Reunion) moved to Mauritius in 1722. They imported slaves, built a port, and planted coffee, fruit, spices, sugar, and vegetables.

During the Anglo-French wars of the 1700's, the French launched attacks from the island against British shipping in the Indian Ocean and against British settlements in India. The British captured the island in 1810, made it a colony, and renamed it Mauritius.

In 1833, Britain ordered the abolition of slavery in its empire. More than 75,000 slaves were freed in Mauritius. Most of them refused to continue working on the sugar plantations. Planters then brought in nearly 450,000 Indian laborers between 1835 and 1907.

Mauritius began to achieve self-government in the 1950's and became independent in March 1968. From 1968 to 1982, the Labor Party led by Prime Minister Sir Seewoosagur Ramgoolam controlled the government. In 1982, the leftist Mauritian Militant Movement (MMM) gained control through elections. Aneerood Jugnauth became prime minister. In 1983, he broke from the MMM and formed the Militant Socialist Movement (MSM). The party formed an alliance with two other political parties and won elections held in August 1983. Jugnauth remained as prime minister.   Burton Benedict

See also **Port Louis; Dodo; Diego Garcia**.

Maurois, *maw RWAH,* **André,** *ahn DRAY* (1885-1967), was the pen name of Émile Herzog, a French novelist and biographer. Maurois tried to attain in his life and writings the spirit of the French writer Michel de Montaigne—a skeptical detachment from life, mixed with humor. These qualities appear in his best works.

Maurois' place in literature probably rests with his biographies of English and French authors. His most notable works include the lives of Percy Shelley (*Ariel,* 1923), Benjamin Disraeli (*Disraeli: A Picture of the Victorian Age,* 1927), Lord Byron (*Don Juan,* 1930), George Sand (*Lélia,* 1952), Victor Hugo (*Olympio,* 1954), and three generations of Alexandre Dumas's family (*The Titans,* 1957).

Maurois was born in Elbeuf. During World War I, he served as a French liaison officer with the British Army. His first works were two humorous novels based on his war experiences, *The Silence of Colonel Bramble* (1919) and *Les Discours du Docteur O'Grady* (*The Return of Dr. O'Grady,* 1922). *Climats* (*Whatever Gods May Be,* 1928) established Maurois as a skillful novelist with an elegant style. He also wrote popular histories of France, England, and the United States. Maurois was elected to the French Academy in 1938. Maurois' *Memoirs: 1885-1967* was published in 1970.   Elaine D. Cancalon

Maury, *MAWR ee,* **Matthew Fontaine** (1806-1873), was a United States naval officer and scientist who did much to improve ocean travel. He has been called the *Pathfinder of the Seas.* Maury spent years collecting information on winds and currents. His *Wind and Current Charts* formed the basis for all pilot charts issued by the U.S. government. His *Explanations and Sailing Directions,* which accompanied the charts, enabled ships to save time and money on voyages. Maury's *Physical Geography of the Sea and Its Meteorology* was the first textbook of modern oceanography. In the 1850's, Maury aided in laying a transatlantic telegraph cable.

Maury entered the Navy as a midshipman in 1825. He took charge of the Navy Department's Depot of Charts and Instruments in 1842. In this position, he helped develop the Naval Observatory and the Hydrographic Office. He became a commander, effective in 1855.

During the Civil War, Maury joined the Confederate forces. He was in charge of all coast, harbor, and river defenses. The Confederacy sent him to England as a special envoy. While there, he perfected an electric mine for harbor defense. After the war, he tried unsuccessfully to set up a colony of Virginians in Mexico. Later, he went to England, where he wrote textbooks and received honors and financial aid. When President Andrew Johnson pardoned Confederate leaders in 1868, Maury returned home. He became a professor of meteorology at the Virginia Military Institute.

Maury was born near Fredericksburg, Va. In 1930, he was elected to the Hall of Fame. *James C. Bradford*

Maurya Empire, *MOW ree uh,* was the first empire of India to provide a uniform government for almost the entire country. The Maurya emperors ruled from about 321 to 185 B.C. During its early period, the empire provided efficient, stern government, resulting in prosperity but little freedom.

Chandragupta Maurya, who ruled from about 321 to 298 B.C., conquered much of North India and West Pakistan and part of Afghanistan. His son Bindusara held the throne from about 298 to 272 B.C., and Bindusara's son Asoka governed from about 272 to 232 B.C. Both expanded the empire far into South India. Asoka eventually gave up further conquest. The empire broke up into smaller units after Asoka's death.

During the Maurya Empire, public irrigation works helped farms produce good harvests. Craftworkers made cloth, gold, jewelry, and wood products. Many people worked in farms, forests, mines, and workshops owned by the state. Many peasants and war prisoners worked as slaves to develop new agricultural lands. A system of royal inspectors, spies, and informers made sure that officials and citizens alike obeyed the emperor's will. The Maurya Empire traded with Ceylon, Greece, Malaya, Mesopotamia, and Persia. Broach, near the mouth of the Narbada River, was a seaport for commerce with the Persian Gulf states.

Pataliputra, the Maurya capital, stood at what is now Patna. It was surrounded by a wall with 570 watchtowers and 64 gates. The wooden palace of Chandragupta was in a park filled with flowering trees, fountains, and fish ponds. Asoka built a new palace of stone and also erected many stone monuments. *J. F. Richards*

See also **Asoka; Chandragupta Maurya.**
Mausoleum. See Tomb.

Mauve, *mohv,* is a delicate pale purple or violet dye. In 1856, W. H. Perkin, an English chemist, discovered that the oxidation of *aniline* and *potassium dichromate* produces mauve dye (see **Oxidation**). Mauve is a mixture of derivatives of phenazine. It was the first synthetic coloring to be obtained from coal tar chemicals.
Howard L. Needles

See also **Dye.**
Mave, Queen. See Mythology (The Irish cycles).
Maverick, *MAV ur ihk,* **Samuel Augustus** (1803-1870), was a prominent Texas pioneer and statesman. He helped establish the Republic of Texas. His name has become part of the American language. In 1845, Maverick took a herd of 400 cattle in payment of a debt. He did not brand his cattle. They strayed, and neighboring ranchers called them *mavericks.* This came to be the name given to all unmarked cattle.

Maverick was born in South Carolina. He graduated from Yale University and practiced law in Virginia and Alabama before going to Texas. *Clifford L. Egan*

Max Planck Society for the Advancement of Science is the principal organization for scientific research in Germany. The society distributes government funds for research in the natural and social sciences. It supports about 65 research institutes in a wide variety of fields and employs more than 5,000 scientists. The society also maintains libraries and training institutions. More than 20 winners of Nobel Prizes have been members of the society.

The Max Planck Society, formerly called the Kaiser Wilhelm Society, was founded in 1911 by the German philosopher Adolph von Harnack. In 1948, the society changed its name to honor Max Planck, a German physicist who helped formulate the quantum theory. The society publishes a journal, *Die Naturwissenschaften* (*The Natural Sciences*). *Robert H. March*

Maxim, *MAK sihm,* **Sir Hiram Stevens** (1840-1916), was an inventor who developed an automatic weapon called the Maxim gun. This gun uses the force of recoil caused by the explosion of a cartridge to throw out the empty shell and ram home a new one. Its invention changed many warfare methods.

Maxim was born near Sangerville, Me. He worked for a time in a machine shop and in a shipbuilding yard. He did early inventive work on gas-generating plants and electric lighting. He lost his rights to an important patent in a lawsuit with Thomas Edison. Maxim then moved to England, where he set up the Maxim Gun Company. The company later merged with the Vickers munitions company. Maxim experimented with internal-combustion engines for automobiles and airplanes. In 1894, he tested a steam-powered airplane that actually lifted itself off the ground. Maxim became a British citizen in 1900, and was knighted in 1901. See **Airplane** (Powered flight); **Machine gun.** *Merritt Roe Smith*

Maxim, Hudson (1853-1927), was an American inventor and explosives expert. He invented *maximite,* an explosive one and a half times as powerful as dynamite. Maxim also developed a smokeless powder and other types of explosives; a self-propelled torpedo; and a torpedo ram.

Maxim was born in Orneville, Me., and worked first as a book publisher. He later became interested in explosives and worked briefly in the gun factory of his brother Sir Hiram Maxim. In 1893, Hudson Maxim established the Maxim Powder Company to manufacture explosives. Four years later, he sold the plant and his patents to E. I. du Pont de Nemours & Company. Maxim served as an adviser to the Du Pont Company from 1897 until his death.   Merritt Roe Smith

Maximilian, *MAK suh MIHL yuhn* (1832-1867), ruled as emperor of Mexico from 1864 to 1867. His reign was part of French Emperor Napoleon III's attempt to gain possessions and influence in North America.

The French had landed in Mexico in 1862 to collect debts. They advanced inland and captured Mexico City. Napoleon III wanted to control Mexico, and so he offered the crown to Maximilian, who was then Archduke of Austria. Maximilian accepted on the basis of "proof" given by Napoleon and by Mexican exiles in France that the Mexican people wanted him. He became emperor of Mexico in 1864. Maximilian's government adopted policies and laws that increased investments, European immigration, and the protection of private property. These measures helped lead to the modernization of Mexico.

Benito Juárez, president of Mexico, resisted the French (see **Juárez, Benito Pablo**). In 1865, Maximilian ordered that Juárez' supporters be shot on sight. His advisers assured him that resistance had ended, and that this order would prevent further trouble.

Maximilian's empire was doomed when the American Civil War ended in 1865. The United States could now enforce the Monroe Doctrine, which forbade European intervention in the Americas. Napoleon III was forced to withdraw his troops from Mexico in 1866 and 1867, leaving Maximilian without support. Maximilian's wife Carlota went to Europe to seek aid from Napoleon III and from Pope Pius IX, but failed.

Maximilian left Mexico City in 1867 to fight Juárez. He and his soldiers marched to Querétaro, where General Gómez, a trusted aide, betrayed him. He was captured by troops of the Mexican Republic, and was executed by a firing squad on June 19, 1867.

Maximilian was born in Vienna. His full name was Ferdinand Maximilian Joseph. He was a brother of Austrian Emperor Francis Joseph. He trained with the Austrian navy and served briefly as its commander in chief. He married Carlota, daughter of King Leopold I of Belgium, in 1857.   W. Dirk Raat

See also **Mexico** (The French invasion).

Maximilian I, *MAK suh MIHL yuhn* (1459-1519), reigned as Holy Roman Emperor from 1493 to 1519. He extended the power of the House of Habsburg through wars and marriages (see **Habsburg, House of**).

Maximilian, son of Emperor Frederick III, married Mary, daughter of Charles the Bold of Burgundy, in 1477. He fought Mary's war with Louis XI of France for possession of Burgundy and the Netherlands. He won the war, but the Netherland states, hostile to him, signed a treaty with Louis XI in 1482. The treaty forced Maximilian to give Burgundy back to Louis XI. Mary died the same year.

Maximilian became emperor in 1493. He married Bianca, daughter of the *regent* (temporary ruler) of Milan, in 1494. He fought another long war with France for control of possessions in Italy, and lost. Maximilian was forced to grant Switzerland its independence after a war in 1499.

Maximilian arranged the marriage of his son, Philip, Archduke of Austria, to Juana of Castile, daughter of Ferdinand and Isabella of Spain, in 1496. The marriage gave Spain to the Habsburgs when Philip and Juana's son became king of Spain and, later, emperor as Charles V. Maximilian established claims on Hungary and Bohemia when his grandchildren married heirs of these countries. Maximilian was also an important patron of the arts. He was born in Wiener Neustadt, Austria.

Jonathan W. Zophy

Maximum security prison. See Prison (Types of correctional institutions).

Maxwell. See Weber.

Maxwell, James Clerk (1831-1879), a Scottish scientist, was one of the greatest mathematicians and physicists of the 1800's. He is best known for his research on electricity and magnetism and for his *kinetic theory of gases.* This theory explains the properties of a gas in terms of the behavior of its molecules. Maxwell also investigated color vision, elasticity, optics, Saturn's rings, and *thermodynamics,* a branch of physics that deals with heat and work.

Maxwell based his work on electricity and magnetism on the discoveries of the English physicist Michael Faraday. In 1864, Maxwell combined his ideas with those of Faraday and certain other scientists and formed a mathematical theory that describes the relationship between electric and magnetic fields. Both these fields exert forces on electrically charged objects. Maxwell showed that waves in combined electric and magnetic fields, called *electromagnetic waves,* travel at the speed of light. In fact, Maxwell argued that light itself consists of electromagnetic waves. In the late 1880's, the German physicist Heinrich R. Hertz conducted experiments that confirmed Maxwell's theory. See **Electromagnetic waves; Faraday, Michael; Hertz, Heinrich R**.

In his research on the kinetic theory of gases, Maxwell developed a statistical law that gives the distribution of velocities among molecules of a gas. He was the first scientist to use such a law to show how molecular behavior determines pressure, temperature, and other properties of a gas.

Maxwell was born in Edinburgh, Scotland, and studied at the University of Edinburgh. He graduated from Cambridge University in 1854 and taught there until 1856. He then became a professor of physics at Marischal College in Aberdeen, Scotland.

From 1860 to 1865, Maxwell taught physics at King's College in London. In 1865, he retired to his family estate and devoted his time to scientific writing. In 1871, Maxwell became the first professor of experimental physics at Cambridge and director of the newly established Cavendish Laboratory there.

Maxwell edited many research papers by the English physicist Henry Cavendish. These papers described Cavendish's discoveries about electricity. Maxwell's most famous work was *Treatise on Electricity and Magnetism* (1873). The key ideas of this work are often considered the basis of such developments in modern physics as the theory of relativity and the quantum theory.

Richard L. Hilt

See also **Light** (The electromagnetic theory); **Physics** (Developments in the 1800's); **Radar** (The development of radar).

May is one of the most beautiful months of the year in the North Temperate Zone. The snow and ice have melted, and summer's intense heat has not yet begun. The first garden crops begin to sprout in May. The trees and grass are green, and wild plants are in bloom. Wild flowers that blossom in different parts of the United States include the jack-in-the-pulpit, anemone, hepatica, forsythia, dogwood, and blue, yellow, and white violets. Many birds have built their nests, and mother birds are sitting on the eggs, which will soon hatch.

May was the third month according to the early Roman calendar, and March was the first. Later, the ancient Romans used January 1 for the beginning of their year, and May became the fifth month. May has always had 31 days.

There are several stories about how the month of May was named. The most widely accepted explanation is that it was named for Maia, the Roman goddess of spring and growth. Her name seems to be related to a Latin word that means *increase* or *growth*. The ancient Romans held ceremonies in Maia's honor on May 1 and again on May 15.

May customs. Even in ancient times, May 1 was a day for outdoor festivals. In Rome, May 1 fell at a time that was sacred to Flora, the goddess of flowers. The Romans celebrated the day with flower-decked parades. The English also observed many beautiful May Day customs. Maypoles were erected in village parks. On the morning of May 1, the village youths went to the woods and gathered "mayflowers," or hawthorn blossoms, to decorate the Maypole. The girls wore their prettiest dresses, each hoping that she would be elected May queen. The queen danced around the Maypole with her "subjects."

Special days. In most states of the United States, the last Monday in May is observed as Memorial Day, or Decoration Day. It is a legal holiday in memory of those who died while serving the United States in war. The graves of war heroes are decorated with flowers. Memorial Day was first observed in 1866.

Two special days in May have been designated by Presidential proclamations. Mother's Day, first observed in 1908, was recognized officially by Congress and the President in 1914. It is celebrated in honor of the

Important May events

1 The Act of Union joined England and Wales with Scotland to form Great Britain, 1707.
— Empire State Building opened, 1931.
2 Hudson's Bay Company chartered 1670.
— Catherine the Great of Russia born 1729.
3 Niccolò Machiavelli, author of *The Prince,* born 1469.
— First U.S. medical school opened in Philadelphia, 1765.
4 Thomas Huxley, English biologist, born 1825.
— Haymarket Riot took place in Chicago, 1886.
5 Karl Marx, author of *Das Kapital,* born 1818.
— Napoleon died on St. Helena, 1821.
— Mexicans defeated French at Puebla, 1862.
— Memorial Day first observed, 1866.
6 First postage stamp issued in England, 1840.
— Robert E. Peary, American Arctic explorer, born 1856.
— Sigmund Freud, founder of psychoanalysis, born 1856.
— Airship *Hindenburg* blew up and burned, 1937.
7 Robert Browning, English poet, born 1812.
— Composer Johannes Brahms born 1833.
— Peter Ilich Tchaikovsky, Russian composer, born 1840.
— A German submarine sank the passenger liner *Lusitania* in World War I, 1915.
8 Harry S. Truman, 33rd President of the United States, born in Lamar, Mo., 1884.
— Victory in Europe Day (V-E Day) first celebrated on the day after Germany surrendered, ending World War II in Europe, 1945.
9 John Brown, American abolitionist, born 1800.
— Sir James Barrie, Scottish author, born 1860.

— Mother's Day became a public holiday, 1914.
— Explorers Richard E. Byrd and Floyd Bennett credited with first flight over the North Pole, 1926.
10 Second Continental Congress met, 1775.
— First transcontinental railway completed in Promontory, Utah, 1869.
— Franco-Prussian War ended, 1871.
11 Minnesota admitted to the Union, 1858.
— Irving Berlin, American songwriter, born 1888.
12 King Gustavus I of Sweden born 1496.
— Edward Lear, English writer and artist, born 1812.
— Florence Nightingale, English nurse, born 1820.
— Roald Amundsen flew over the North Pole, 1926.
13 Austrian Empress Maria Theresa born 1717.
— Sir Arthur Sullivan, English composer, born 1842.
— United States declared war on Mexico, 1846.
14 Gabriel Fahrenheit, German physicist, born 1686.
— Robert Owen, social reformer, born 1771.
— Edward Jenner, a British physician, performed the first vaccination against smallpox in 1796.
— Lewis and Clark began trip up Missouri River, 1804.
— Israel became an independent country as the last British troops left Palestine, 1948.
15 Pierre Curie, codiscoverer of radium, born 1859.
— U.S. began first regular airmail service, 1918.
16 William Seward, American statesman who arranged the purchase of Alaska, born 1801.
17 King George VI became the first reigning British monarch to visit Canada, 1939.

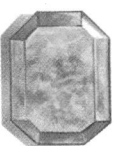

May birthstone—
emerald

May flower—
lily of the valley

May 6—airship
Hindenburg exploded

May 7—ocean liner
Lusitania sunk

nation's mothers on the second Sunday in May. The third Saturday of the month is Armed Forces Day, when the United States honors the men and women of the military services. In 1950, the Armed Forces Day celebration combined the Army, Navy, and Air Force tributes, which had been held at separate times.

The Kentucky Derby, the most famous horse race in the United States, takes place on the first Saturday in May at Churchill Downs, Louisville, Ky.

Many Mexican Americans celebrate May 5, which they call *Cinco de Mayo*. This day, a national holiday in Mexico, is the anniversary of the Mexican victory over the French at Puebla in 1862.

May symbols. The hawthorn and the lily of the valley are considered the flowers for May. The birthstone is the emerald.   Sharron G. Uhler

Quotations

Here's to the day when it is May
  And care as light as a feather,
When your little shoes and my big boots
  Go tramping over the heather.   *Bliss Carman*

'Twas as welcome to me as flowers in May.
          James Howell

The maple puts her corals on in May.
          James Russell Lowell

Then came fair May, the fairest maid on ground,
Deck'd all with dainties of the season's pride,
And throwing flowers out of her lap around.
          Edmund Spenser

Hail, bounteous May, that doth inspire
Mirth, and youth, and warm desire;
Woods and groves are of thy dressing,
Hill and dale doth boast thy blessing.
          John Milton

When May, with cowslip-braided locks,
Walks through the land in green attire.
          Bayard Taylor

Related articles in *World Book* include:

Armed Forces	Hawthorn	May Day
Day	Kentucky Derby	Memorial Day
Calendar	Lily of the valley	Mother's Day
Emerald		

Important May events

18 Czar Nicholas II of Russia born 1868.
— Bertrand Russell, British philosopher and mathematician, born 1872.
— Dame Margot Fonteyn, British ballerina, born 1919.
19 Johns Hopkins, American philanthropist, born 1795.
20 Honoré de Balzac, French novelist, born 1799.
— John Stuart Mill, English philosopher and writer, born 1806.
— Homestead Act signed by President Abraham Lincoln, 1862.
— Amelia Earhart began the first solo flight by a woman across the Atlantic Ocean, 1932.
21 Albrecht Dürer, German engraver, born 1471.
— Alexander Pope, English poet, born 1688.
— First Democratic National Convention held, 1832.
— Clara Barton founded what became the American Red Cross, 1881.
— Charles Lindbergh finished first transatlantic solo flight, 1927.
22 Richard Wagner, German composer, born 1813.
— Sir Arthur Conan Doyle, British author and creator of Sherlock Holmes, born 1859.
— Laurence Olivier, British actor, born 1907.
23 Carolus Linnaeus, Swedish botanist, born 1707.
— South Carolina became the eighth state, 1788.
24 First permanent English settlement in America established in Jamestown, Va., 1607.
— Queen Victoria of Great Britain, born 1819.
— Brooklyn Bridge opened to traffic, 1883.

25 Constitutional Convention opened in Philadelphia with George Washington as president, 1787.
— Ralph Waldo Emerson, American essayist and poet, born 1803.
26 Lord Beaverbrook, British publisher, born 1879.
27 Julia Ward Howe, American poet who wrote "The Battle Hymn of the Republic," born 1819.
— Jay Gould, American financier, born 1836.
— Isadora Duncan, American dancer, born 1878.
— Golden Gate Bridge opened at San Francisco, 1937.
28 William Pitt, English statesman and prime minister, born 1759.
29 The Turks captured Constantinople, 1453.
— King Charles II of England born 1630.
— Monarchy restored to England, 1660.
— Patrick Henry, American statesman and orator, born 1736.
— Rhode Island ratified the Constitution, becoming the 13th state, 1790.
— Wisconsin became the 30th state, 1848.
— G. K. Chesterton, English author, born 1874.
— John F. Kennedy, 35th President of the United States, born in Brookline, Mass., 1917.
30 Joan of Arc burned at the stake, 1431.
— Christopher Columbus began his third voyage, 1498.
31 U.S. copyright law enacted, 1790.
— Walt Whitman, American poet, born 1819.
— Amendment 17 to the Constitution, providing direct election of senators, proclaimed, 1913.

WORLD BOOK illustrations by Mike Hagel

May 10—first transcontinental railway completed

May 14—Edward Jenner performed first smallpox vaccination

May 21—Charles Lindbergh flew across the Atlantic

May 27—Golden Gate Bridge opened

May apple. See Mayapple.

May beetle. See Junebug.

May Day (May 1) is celebrated as a spring festival in many countries. It marks the revival of life in early spring after winter. May Day celebrations may go back to the spring festivals of ancient Egypt and India.

The English and other peoples whom the Romans conquered developed their May Day festivals from the Roman festival called Floralia. In the April festival of Floralia, the Romans gathered flowers to honor the goddess of springtime, Flora. Eventually, Floralia was combined with a Celtic celebration called Beltane, which was held on May 1. The Celts believed that on Beltane, the fairies were especially active.

In medieval times, May Day became the favorite holiday of many English villages. People gathered flowers to decorate their homes and churches. They sang spring carols and received gifts in return. They chose a king and queen of May. Villagers danced around a Maypole, holding the ends of ribbons that streamed from its top. They wove the ribbons around the pole until it was covered with bright colors. Dew collected on May Day morning was said to restore youth.

Other European countries had their own May Day customs. In some, the day became a time for courting. In Italy, for example, boys serenaded their sweethearts. In Switzerland, a May pine tree was placed under a girl's window. In France, May Day had religious importance. The French considered the month of May sacred to the Virgin Mary. They enshrined young girls as May queens in their churches. The May queens led processions in honor of the Virgin Mary.

The Puritans disapproved of May Day, and the day has never been celebrated with the same enthusiasm in the United States as in Britain. But in many American towns and cities, children celebrate the day with dancing and singing. They often gather flowers in handmade paper baskets and hang them on the doorknobs of the homes of friends and neighbors on May Day morning. At May Day parties, children select May queens, dance around the Maypole, and sing May Day songs. May is also celebrated in the Roman Catholic Church by electing May queens who wear flowers and lead parades called *May processions.* Such customs are probably pre-Christian in origin.

In 1889, a congress of world Socialist parties held in Paris voted to support the United States labor movement's demands for an eight-hour day. It chose May 1, 1890, as a day of demonstrations in favor of the eight-hour day. Afterward, May 1 became a holiday called Labor Day in many nations. It resembles the September holiday in the United States (see **Labor Day**). Government and labor organizations sponsor parades, speeches, and other celebrations to honor working people. The holiday has had special importance in socialist and Communist countries.   Jack Santino

See also **May** (May customs); **Walpurgis Night.**

May fly. See Mayfly.

Maya, *MAH yuh,* were an American Indian people who developed a magnificent civilization in Central America and south Mexico. The Maya civilization reached its period of greatest development about A.D. 250 and continued to flourish for hundreds of years. The Maya produced remarkable architecture, painting, pottery, and sculpture. They made great advancements in astronomy and mathematics and developed an accurate yearly calendar. They were one of the first peoples in the Western Hemisphere to develop an advanced form of writing.

The Maya lived in an area of about 120,000 square miles (311,000 square kilometers). Today, their territory is divided among Mexico and several Central American countries. It consists of the Mexican states of Campeche, Yucatán, and Quintana Roo and part of the states of Tabasco and Chiapas. It also includes Belize, most of Guatemala, and parts of El Salvador and of Honduras.

The Maya civilization was at its peak from about A.D. 250 to 900. During that time, known as the Classic Period, it was centered in the tropical rain forest of the lowlands of what is now northern Guatemala. Many of the major Maya cities, such as Piedras Negras, Tikal, and Uaxactún, developed in this area. By about 900, most of the Maya abandoned the Guatemalan lowlands and moved to areas to the north and south, including Yucatán and the highlands of southern Guatemala. In those areas, they continued to prosper until Spain conquered almost all of the Maya in the mid-1500's.

Today, descendants of the Maya live in Mexico and Central America. They speak Maya languages and carry on some religious customs of their ancestors.

Way of life

Religion. The Maya worshiped many gods and goddesses. One Maya manuscript mentions more than 160 of them. For example, the Maya worshiped a corn god, a rain god known as *Chac,* a sun god called *Kinich Ahau,* and a moon goddess called *Ix Chel.* Each god or goddess influenced some part of Maya life. Ix Chel, for instance, was the goddess of medicine and weaving.

Religion played a central part in the daily life of the Maya. Each day had special religious importance, and

The land of the Maya included parts of present-day Mexico, Guatemala, Honduras, and El Salvador, and all of Belize. This map shows the area inhabited by three chief Maya groups and the location of major Maya cities.

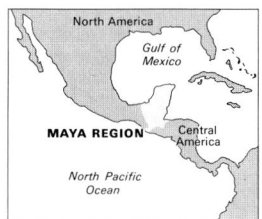

WORLD BOOK maps

A **Maya city called Tikal** lies in what is now Guatemala. This illustration is an artist's idea of how the city may have looked about A.D. 750. In the foreground, a priest prepares for a ceremony. In the background, other priests climb the stairway to the temple, 150 feet (45 meters) high.

WORLD BOOK illustration by Alton S. Tobey

religious festivals in honor of particular gods took place throughout the year. The Maya regarded their gods as both helpful and harmful. To obtain the help of the gods, the Maya fasted, prayed, offered sacrifices, and held many religious ceremonies. Deer, dogs, and turkeys were sacrificed to feed the gods. The Maya frequently offered their own blood, which they spattered on pieces of bark paper. They practiced some human sacrifice, such as throwing victims into deep wells or killing them at the funerals of great leaders.

In their cities, the Maya built tall pyramids of limestone with small temples on top. Priests climbed the stairs of the pyramids and performed ceremonies in the temples. Major religious festivals, such as those for the Maya New Year and for each of the Maya months, took place in the cities.

The Maya observed special ceremonies when burying their dead. Corpses were painted red and then were wrapped in straw mats with a few of their personal belongings. They were buried under the floor of the houses where they had lived. Maya rulers and other important persons were buried in their finest garments within the pyramids, under the temples. Servants were killed and buried with them, along with jewelry and utensils, for use in the next world.

Family and social life. Entire Maya families, including parents, children, and grandparents, lived together. Everyone in a household helped with the work. The men and the older boys did most of the farmwork, such as clearing and weeding the fields and planting the crops. They also did most of the hunting and fishing. The women and the older girls made the family's clothes, prepared meals, raised the younger children, and supplied the house with firewood and water. The Maya had no schools. The children learned various skills by observing adults and helping them.

Religious festivals provided one of the favorite forms of recreation for the Maya. These festivals were held on special days throughout the year. Dancing and feasts

took place at the festivals. In addition, the Maya had a sacred game that was played on special courts. The players tried to hit a rubber ball through a stone ring with their hips.

Food, clothing, and shelter. Maya farmers raised chiefly beans, corn, and squash. Corn was the principal food of the Maya, and the women prepared it in a variety of ways. They made flat corn cakes, which today are called *tortillas,* as a type of bread. The Maya also used corn to make an alcoholic drink called *balche,* which they sweetened with honey and spiced with bark. The Maya also raised avocados, chili peppers, and sweet potatoes.

Farmers became skilled at making the best use of natural resources. They dug canals in swampy lowlands to drain the soil and used the unearthed soil to build raised fields in which they grew crops. On sloping land, farmers built terraces to hold the soil in place and walls to control water flow. With such methods, the Maya grew enough food to feed a large population.

Dogs were the only tame animals of the Maya, but the people raised turkeys and honey bees on their farms. The Maya hunted deer, rabbits, piglike animals called *peccaries,* and other wild animals. They fished and collected shellfish from the rivers and sea. They also gathered fruits and vegetables from the countryside.

The clothing of the Maya kept them comfortable in the hot, tropical climate. Men wore a *loincloth,* a strip of cloth tied around their hips and passed between their legs. Women wore loose dresses that reached their ankles. The people wove these garments from cotton or other fibers. The people of the upper classes wore finer clothes decorated with embroidery and ornaments. They had splendid headdresses made of the brightly colored feathers of tropical birds. The wealthy also wore large amounts of jewelry, much of which was carved out of green jade and colorful shells.

Maya farmers lived in rural homesteads or small villages near their fields. They built their houses from poles lashed together and used palm leaves or grass to thatch the roofs. Many Maya cities were home to tens of thousands of people. The largest known city of the Classic Period, Tikal may have had a population of about 100,000 at its peak. People from the countryside gathered in the cities for markets, religious festivals, and other important events.

Trade and transportation. The Maya took part in a trade network that linked a number of groups in Central America. The people of the Maya lowlands exported many items, including handicrafts, forest and sea products, and jaguar pelts. They imported jade, volcanic glass, and the feathers of a bird called the *quetzal* from the highlands of Guatemala, where other Maya-speaking peoples lived.

The Maya of Yucatán sent salt and finely decorated cottons to Honduras. In return, they received cacao beans, which they used in making chocolate. The Maya also transported goods as far as the Valley of Oaxaca in Mexico and the city of Teotihuacán, near what is now Mexico City. They carried most goods on their backs or on rivers in dugout canoes. They did not use the wheel or any beasts of burden, such as horses or oxen.

Government. Each Maya city governed its surrounding area, and some large cities each controlled one or more smaller cities. A city ruler would usually be succeeded by his younger brother or by his son. In some cases, generations of a single family ruled for hundreds of years. For example, a series of at least 29 kings from one family ruled Tikal from before A.D. 300 until sometime after 869. The Maya never united to form a central governmental unit. But in late Maya times, the governments of such cities as Chichén Itzá and Mayapán controlled large parts of the Maya population.

Communication and learning. The Maya developed an advanced form of writing that consisted of many symbols. These symbols represented combinations of sounds or entire ideas and formed a kind of *hieroglyphic* writing (see **Hieroglyphics**).

The Maya kept records on large stone monuments called *stelae,* as well as on some buildings and household utensils. They used the stelae to record important dates and to take note of great events in the lives of their rulers and the rulers' families. The Maya also made books of paper made from fig tree bark. Several books from the 1100's to the early 1500's have survived. They contain astronomical tables, information about religious ceremonies, and calendars that show lucky days for such activities as farming and hunting.

Other cultural advances by the Maya included the development of mathematics and astronomy. The Maya used a mathematical system based on the number 20, instead of 10 as in the decimal system. A dot represented the number one, a bar represented five, and a special symbol represented zero. The Maya are believed to have been the first people to use the idea of zero. Maya priests observed the positions of the sun, moon, and stars. They made tables predicting eclipses and the orbit of the planet Venus.

The priests also used mathematics and astronomy to develop two kinds of calendars. One was a sacred almanac of 260 days. Each day was named with one of 20 day names and a number from 1 to 13. Each of the 20 day names had a god or goddess associated with it. The priests predicted good or bad luck by studying the combinations of gods or goddesses and numbers. The Maya also had a calendar of 365 days, based on the orbit of the earth around the sun. These days were divided into 18 months of 20 days each, plus 5 days at the end of the year. The Maya considered these last 5 days of the year to be extremely unlucky. During that period they fasted, made many sacrifices, and avoided unnecessary work.

Clay sculpture (A.D. 700 to 900), 5 in. (12.5 cm) high; Museo Nacional de Antropologia e Historia, Mexico City (Bradley Smith)

A Maya ballplayer wore thigh guards and a thick protective belt to compete in a sacred ball game. The players hit a rubber ball through a stone ring with their hips.

Clay sculpture, 16 in. (40 cm) high; Museo Nacional de Antropologia e Historia, Mexico City (Lee Boltin)

A sculpture of the Maya corn god has ears of corn in its headdress. Corn was the chief food of the Maya. They prayed to this god for plentiful harvests and offered sacrifices to him.

The Maya used herbs and magic to treat illness. Scholars know little else about Maya medicine.

Arts and crafts. The Maya produced exceptional architecture, painting, pottery, and sculpture. Highly skilled architects built tall pyramids of limestone, with small temples on top. The Maya also built large, low buildings where rulers and other nobles lived. Many buildings had flat ornaments called *roof combs,* which extended from the high point of the roof. The combs gave buildings the appearance of great height.

Maya artists decorated walls with brightly colored murals that featured lifelike figures taking part in battles and festivals. The artists outlined the figures and then filled in the color. They rarely shaded the colors. A similar type of painting appears on Maya pottery.

The Maya made small sculptures of clay and carved huge ones from stone. Most of the small sculptures were figures of men and women. The large sculptures, some standing over 30 feet (9 meters) high, were carved with portraits of rulers.

History

The Preclassic Period. The heart of the Maya civilization centered around what is now the *department* (state) of El Petén in the lowlands of northern Guatemala. The first farmers may have settled there as early as 1000 B.C. They came from areas surrounding El Petén—mostly from highlands to the west and south—in search of fertile land. The new settlers lived in small villages. They gathered food from the surrounding forest and raised crops.

By 800 B.C., the Maya lowlands were completely settled. At that time, the Olmec lived west of the Maya. The Olmec were probably the Central American inventors of numbers and writing. They also had well-developed art. The Olmec civilization influenced Maya culture. The

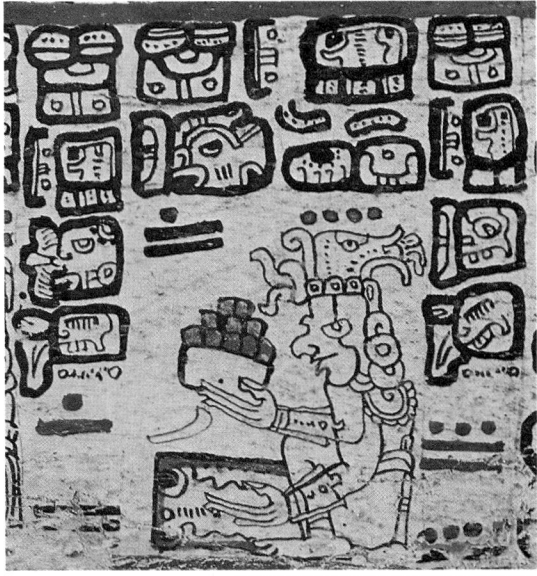

Codex Tro-Cortesianus (late 1400's); Museo de America, Madrid, Spain (Ampliaciones y Reproducciones MAS)

Maya writing used symbols that represented entire ideas or combinations of sounds. This section of a Maya manuscript came from an astrology book used by priests.

Stone sculpture (A.D. 784) by an unknown Maya artist; Lee Boltin

A Maya monument called a *stele* stands in Copán, a city in what is now Honduras. The Maya used such sculptures to record important dates and to note events in their rulers' lives.

Maya, like the Olmec, began to build pyramids and carve stone monuments. See **Olmec Indians.**

The Maya built their first large pyramids between 600 and 400 B.C., during the middle of the Preclassic Period. By late in the Preclassic Period, between 400 B.C. and A.D. 250, there were several large Maya settlements in the lowlands. Some of the largest Maya pyramids stood in one of these settlements, at a site now called El Mirador, in northern Guatemala.

The Classic Period of the Maya civilization lasted from about A.D. 250 to 900. During those years, the Maya founded their greatest cities and made their remarkable achievements in the arts and sciences. They also perfected the practice of erecting stelae to honor the most important events in the lives of their leaders.

During the first 300 years of the Classic Period, the city of Teotihuacán, near present-day Mexico City, had a strong influence on Maya art and architecture. Throughout the Classic Period, populations grew, and new cities were founded. Toward the end of the period, as competition for land and other resources increased, rival cities began to fight each other. Sometimes a growing city would break away from a larger city's control. In other cases, one city conquered another and captured its ruler. Defeated rulers and other important prisoners of war were sacrificed in religious ceremonies, and the conquered city probably paid something to the victor. By about 700, the Maya of the Classic Period reached their peak in population and prosperity.

Then, beginning in the 800's, the Maya stopped erecting stelae in city after city. They abandoned their major centers in the Guatemala lowlands one by one and finally left most of this lowland region. Scholars are still trying to discover the reasons for the collapse of Classic Maya society. Some experts point to a combination of such factors as overpopulation, disease, exhaustion of natural resources, crop failures, and the movement of other groups into the Maya area.

The Postclassic Period began about 900, when the Maya abandoned their cities in the Guatemalan lowlands. Some Maya moved north to build new cities in the lowlands of Yucatán. Others moved to southern Guatemala's highlands and built cities there.

Important changes took place in Maya political and economic systems during the Postclassic Period. For example, sea trade became much more common, resulting in prosperity for Maya cities near the sea coasts. Between 900 and 1200, Chichén Itzá, in Yucatán, grew to be the largest and most powerful Maya city. It was governed by a council of nobles—unlike Maya cities of the Classic Period, which each had a single ruler. Chichén Itzá dominated Yucatán by a combination of military strength and control over important trade routes. Chichén Itzá traded with, and formed other ties to, regions beyond the Maya area. These areas included Tula, the capital of the Toltec Indians' empire in the highlands of what is now central Mexico. See **Toltec Indians.**

Chichén Itzá declined around 1200, and Mayapán replaced it as the chief Maya city. Although Mayapán never became as powerful as Chichén Itzá had been, it controlled much of Yucatán for another 200 years.

About 1440, the leaders of some Maya cities revolted against the Mayapán rulers and defeated them. Yucatán was then divided into separate warring states. About the same time, several Maya states in the highlands of southern Guatemala used military force to dominate other Maya in that region. Then, in the early 1500's,

WORLD BOOK photo by Joya Hairs

The ruins of Tikal in Guatemala are all that remain of the great Maya city. The restored Temple of the Giant Jaguar, *left,* rises 150 feet (45 meters) above the site.

Spanish conquerors invaded the Maya territories. By the mid-1500's, they had overcome almost all the Maya.

The Maya heritage. Today, many people of Mexico and Central America speak one of more than 20 languages and dialects that developed from the ancient Maya language. Some of these people live in the highlands of Mexico and Guatemala. Others inhabit the northern part of the Yucatán Peninsula in Mexico. Many descendants of the Maya farm as did their ancestors and carry on some of the traditional religious customs.

The ruins of the Maya cities are tourist attractions. Sites in Mexico include the ruins of Bonampak and Palenque in Chiapas, and Chichén Itzá in northern Yucatán. Tourists also visit the ruins of Tikal in Guatemala and of Copán in Honduras.   Robert J. Sharer

See also **Guatemala; Honduras** (picture: A Maya ball court); **Indian, American; Mexico** (picture: Ruins of an ancient Maya temple); **Stephens, John Lloyd.** For a *Reading and Study Guide,* see *Maya* in the Research Guide/Index, Volume 22.

Additional resources

Level I
Beck, Barbara L., and Greenberg, Lorna. *The Ancient Maya.* Rev. ed. Watts, 1983.
Odijk, Pamela. *The Mayas.* Silver Burdett, 1989.

Level II
Farriss, Nancy M. *Maya Society Under Colonial Rule: The Collective Enterprise of Survival.* Princeton, 1984.
Hammond, Norman. *Ancient Maya Civilization.* Rutgers, 1982.
Meyer, Carolyn, and Gallenkamp, Charles. *The Mystery of the Ancient Maya.* Atheneum. 1985.
Schele, Linda, and Miller, M. E. *The Blood of Kings: Dynasty and Ritual in Maya Art.* Kimbell Art Museum, 1986.

Mayapple is a plant that grows wild in wooded areas of the eastern half of the United States, as far west as Texas. It is also called *mandrake, wild lemon,* and *wild jalap.* The mayapple grows in large groups or colonies. Its large leaves have 5 to 7 lobes. The leaves look somewhat like small umbrellas. They usually grow in pairs, on a stem about 1 foot (30 centimeters) high. A white flower grows on a short stalk in a fork of the stem. The flower is about 2 inches (5 centimeters) wide.

The mayapple produces a small, round fruit about the size of a golf ball. Before it ripens, the fruit is green and bitter. If eaten, it can cause severe stomach pain. The ripe fruit is yellow and can be eaten. Podophyllum resin, a drug used to remove warts, comes from the *rhizomes* (underground stems) of the mayapple.

Scientific classification. The mayapple belongs to the barberry family, Berberidaceae. Its scientific name is *Podophyllum peltatum.*   Fred T. Davies, Jr.

See also **Flower** (picture: Flowers of woodlands and forests).

Maybach, *MY bahk,* **Wilhelm,** *VIHL hehlm* (1846-1929), was a German inventor, engineer, and designer. In the early 1870's, he began working for German automotive pioneer Gottlieb Daimler (see **Daimler, Gottlieb**). In 1883, the two men developed an improved gasoline engine. They modified this engine, and in 1885 installed it on a bicycle, thus creating the first motorcycle. In 1886, they used a slightly more powerful engine to power a carriage. Daimler founded the Daimler Motor Company in 1890. In 1895, Maybach became the company's technical director and played a key role in the design of the company's first Mercedes car in 1901. In 1907, he left the company to build engines for airships manufactured by German aircraft pioneer Ferdinand von Zeppelin. Maybach was born in Heilbronn.

Joel W. Eastman

Mayer, *MY uhr,* **Julius Robert von** (1814-1878), was a German physician and physicist. He and James Joule shared credit for discovering the universal law of conservation of energy (see **Joule, James**). This principle, known as the first law of thermodynamics, states that the total energy of the universe remains the same, and cannot be increased or lessened.

Mayer published his article on heat and energy in 1842. Joule, an English physicist, reached the same conclusions while working independently. It has never been determined which scientist made the first discovery. Mayer was born at Heilbronn.   Richard G. Olson

See also **Heat** (Heat and energy).

Mayer, *MY uhr,* **Maria Goeppert,** *GOH puhrt* (1906-1972), a German-born physicist, shared the 1963 Nobel Prize in physics with J. Hans Jensen of Germany and Eugene Paul Wigner of the United States. Mayer and Jensen, working independently, prepared almost identical papers on the shell structure of atomic nuclei. They discovered that atomic nuclei possess shells similar to the electron shells of atoms. These shells contain varying numbers of protons and neutrons, which permits systematic arrangement of nuclei according to their properties. Maria Goeppert was born in Kattowitz, Germany (now Katowice, Poland). She married Joseph E. Mayer, an American chemist, in 1930, and moved to the United States. In 1960, they both joined the faculty of the University of California, San Diego.   Richard L. Hilt

Mayflower. See Arbutus.

Mayflower was the ship that carried the first Pilgrims to America, in 1620. It was built around 1610 and probably had three masts and two decks. It probably meas-

Wide World

The *Mayflower II,* built as the original *Mayflower* is thought to have looked, made a 54-day voyage across the Atlantic Ocean in 1957. This was 11 days fewer than the Pilgrims' trip in 1620.

ured about 90 feet (27 meters) long and weighed about 180 short tons (163 metric tons). Its master, Christopher Jones, was a quarter-owner.

The *Mayflower* left England on Aug. 15, 1620 (August 5 according to the calendar then in use) with another ship, the *Speedwell.* After turning back twice because of leaks on the *Speedwell,* the *Mayflower* sailed alone from Plymouth on September 16 (September 6), with 102 passengers. The ship reached Cape Cod on November 21 (November 11), off what is now Provincetown Harbor. It reached the present site of Plymouth, Mass., on December 26 (December 16), five days after a small party explored the site.

The *Mayflower* left America on April 15, 1621 (April 5, 1621). Historians are not certain what happened to the ship after it returned to England. Some believe it was dismantled after Jones died in 1622, although a ship called the *Mayflower* made trips to America after that. Others believe that William Russell bought the *Mayflower* for salvage, and used its hull as a barn roof. The barn stands in Jordans, a village outside London.

The *Mayflower II,* built the way the original *Mayflower* is thought to have looked, is kept in Plymouth, Mass. In 1957, it crossed the Atlantic in 54 days. The Britons who built the replica gave it to the American people as a symbol of friendship.   Joan R. Gundersen

See **Plymouth Rock; Plymouth Colony; Pilgrims.**

Mayflower Compact was the first agreement for self-government ever put in force in America. On Nov. 21 (then Nov. 11), 1620, the ship *Mayflower* anchored off Cape Cod, Mass. The Pilgrim leaders persuaded 41 male adults aboard to sign the *Mayflower Compact,* and set up a government in Plymouth Colony. The original compact has since disappeared. The version below follows the spelling and punctuation given in the history *Of Plimoth Plantation,* written by William Bradford, second governor of Plymouth colony.

"In ye name of God Amen. We whose names are underwritten, the loyall subjects of our dread soveraigne Lord King James, by ye grace of God, of Great Britaine, Franc, & Ireland king, defender of ye faith, &c. Haveing undertaken, for ye glorie of God, and advancemente of ye Christian faith and honour of our king & countrie, a voyage to plant ye first colonie in ye Northerne parts of Virginia, doe by these presents solemnly & mutualy in ye presence of God, and one of another, covenant, & combine ourselves together into a Civill body politick; for our better ordering, & preservation & furtherance of ye ends aforesaid; and by vertue hereof to enacte, constitute, and frame such just & equall Lawes, ordinances, Acts, constitutions, & offices, from time to time, as shall be thought most meete & convenient for ye generall good of ye colonie: unto which we promise all due submission and obedience. In witnes whereof we have hereunder subscribed our names at Cap-Codd ye -11- of November, in ye year of ye raigne of our soveraigne Lord King James of England, France, & Ireland ye eighteenth, and of Scotland ye fiftie fourth. Ano Dom. 1620."

Joan R. Gundersen

See also **Plymouth Colony** (The founding of Plymouth Colony).

Mayfly is a dainty insect with lacy wings and a slender, forked tail that trails behind it in flight. Mayflies are commonly called *dayflies* because of their short lives. Adult mayflies live only a few hours or a few days. They do not eat and usually have undeveloped mouthparts. Mayflies actually are not true flies. A true fly has two wings. Mayflies have four wings. Mayflies are also known as *shad flies* or *duns.* Imitation mayflies are used as fishing lures.

Young mayflies are called *nymphs* or *naiads.* They hatch from eggs laid in streams and ponds. A nymph breathes through gills and feeds on water plants. It lives for a few months to two years in the water. It then leaves the water, sheds its skin, and becomes a winged *subimago,* or subadult. Mayflies are the only insects

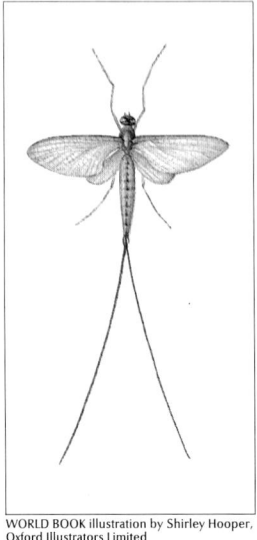

WORLD BOOK illustration by Shirley Hooper, Oxford Illustrators Limited
Mayfly

that go through this stage. After a few hours, the subimago sheds its skin and becomes a full-grown adult. Mayflies are most common in early spring, but may occur until late fall. The nymphs serve as food for fish.

Scientific classification. Mayflies make up the order Ephemeroptera. Sandra J. Glover

Mayhem, *MAY hehm,* in law, is the offense of making a person less capable of self-defense by maiming the body or by destroying or injuring one of its members. Such injuries call for legal distinctions, because not all injuries which result from assault are mayhem. Biting off a person's ear or nose was not mayhem under the old common law. But cutting off a finger or destroying an eye came under that law, because such an injury would make a person less capable of self-defense.

Modern statutes now regard as mayhem any crime of violence which causes a permanent bodily injury. The person who inflicts the injury is subject to a civil suit as well as to criminal prosecution. The word is an old form of the word *maim.* George T. Felkenes

Maynor, Dorothy (1910-), a black American singer, gained fame for her pure, sweet soprano voice. She was especially effective performing the music of Wolfgang Amadeus Mozart and George Frideric Handel. She also excelled in singing spirituals and German *lieder* (songs). Maynor's career was limited to concerts and recordings because major opera houses would not hire black artists while she was active.

Maynor was born in Norfolk, Va. Her father was a clergyman, and she first sang in his church's choir. Conductor Serge Koussevitzky heard her at the Tanglewood Festival in 1939 and hired her as a soloist with the Boston Symphony Orchestra. Martin Bernheimer

Mayo, Charles Horace (1865-1939), was a prominent American surgeon. He helped his father and his older brother, William, found the Mayo Clinic in Rochester, Minn. (see **Mayo Clinic**). Mayo and his brother pioneered the use of medical group practice at the clinic. They also started the Mayo Foundation and the Mayo Graduate School of Medicine.

Mayo was born in Rochester. He graduated from Chicago Medical College (now Northwestern University Medical School) in 1888. Mayo was best known for his skill in thyroid surgery. He was professor of surgery at the University of Minnesota Medical School from 1915 to 1936. He was president of the American Medical Association in 1917 and the American College of Surgeons in 1925. Mayo also served in the armed forces during World War I (1914-1918) and became a brigadier general in the medical reserve in 1921. Dale C. Smith

Mayo, William James (1861-1939), an American physician, helped found the Mayo Clinic in Rochester, Minn., along with his father and his younger brother, Charles (see **Mayo Clinic**). William and his brother pioneered the development of medical group practice at the clinic. The brothers donated $1½ million in 1915 to establish the Mayo Foundation and the Mayo Graduate School of Medicine. The school became one of the world's most important graduate medical centers.

Mayo graduated from the University of Michigan in 1883. He was president of the American Medical Association in 1906 and the American Surgical Association in 1914. He served in the Army Medical Reserve Officers Corps during World War I (1914-1918) and became a brigadier general in the medical reserve in 1921. Mayo was born in Le Sueur, Minn. Dale C. Smith

Mayo, William Worrall (1819-1911), a surgeon, made important contributions to American medicine. With his sons William and Charles, he founded the internationally famous Mayo Clinic in Rochester, Minn.

Mayo was born in Manchester, England, and studied at Owens College there. He came to the United States in 1845. He graduated from the University of Missouri in 1854. Mayo began practicing medicine in Minnesota in 1855 and soon became the leading physician and surgeon in the area. He was one of the first doctors in the West to use a microscope in diagnosis.

Mayo also took an active part in organizing the Minnesota Territory. In 1862, he served as a volunteer surgeon during an outbreak of fighting with Sioux Indians. He became provost surgeon for southern Minnesota in 1863. In 1883, after a cyclone struck Rochester, Mayo was placed in charge of an emergency hospital. Sisters of the Order of St. Francis assisted him and then built a permanent hospital in Rochester. This hospital, called St. Marys Hospital, opened in 1889, and Mayo served as its chief of staff until he was succeeded by his sons. Together, the three Mayos built up the practice that eventually became known as the Mayo Clinic. Dale C. Smith

See also **Mayo Clinic**.

Additional resources

Clapesattle, Helen. *The Doctors Mayo.* 3rd ed. Mayo Found., 1989.
Crofford, Emily. *Frontier Surgeons: A Story About the Mayo Brothers.* Carolrhoda, 1989. For younger readers.

Mayo Clinic, *MAY oh,* in Rochester, Minn., is one of the world's largest medical centers. Staff physicians care for clinic patients through an integrated group practice of medicine. A 12-member board of governors, which functions through several committees, administers the clinic. The clinic has nearly 900 physicians and medical scientists on its staff. About 800 younger doctors assist the staff of the Mayo Clinic as part of their residency training in medical and surgical specialties.

William Worrall Mayo and his sons, William James and Charles Horace Mayo, began their team practice in 1889 as staff physicians for St. Marys Hospital. Their successes in surgery became widely recognized, and the number of physicians on their staff gradually increased. In 1914, the brothers built their own medical center. The Mayo Clinic now registers about 280,000 patients a year. The clinic has cared for about 4 million patients since 1907. In 1986, the Mayo Clinic merged with St. Marys Hospital and Rochester Methodist Hospital, both in Rochester.   Critically reviewed by the Mayo Clinic

Mayor is the head of a city government in the United States and many other countries. The people of England have used the title for hundreds of years. Colonists in America brought the name and office with them from England. In the United States, two kinds of mayors, called strong and weak, developed.

In cities that have a *strong-mayor* government, the mayor takes a leading part in city administration. Such mayors enforce laws passed by the city council and can veto council rulings. They appoint lesser officials and may name a managing director or chief administrative officer to supervise government operations. In most strong-mayor governments, the mayor is chosen by the voters in a direct election.

In cities that have a *weak-mayor* government, the mayor has little executive authority. The mayor is the head of the government of the city. But the city council has the final authority in directing the city's administration. In most weak-mayor governments, the council elects one of its members as mayor.

In Austria, Belgium, Germany, and the Netherlands, the mayor is often called the *burgomaster.* The duties of a burgomaster are substantially those of a mayor in the United States. The position of mayor in the United Kingdom is largely honorary. In Canada, the mayor enforces ordinances, supervises lower officials, and presents proposals to the city council.   Susan H. Ambler

See also **City government.**

Maypole. See May Day; May (May customs).

Mays, Benjamin Elijah (1894-1984), was an American Baptist minister, educator, and public speaker. He was president of Morehouse College in Atlanta, Ga., from 1940 to 1967. Mays was president of Morehouse when civil rights leader Martin Luther King, Jr., attended the college. King's admiration for Mays influenced his decision to become a minister. Mays delivered a nationally televised speech at a memorial service for King, who was shot to death in 1968.

Mays was born in Epworth, near Greenwood, S.C. He earned a B.A. degree at Bates College in Maine and a Ph.D. degree at the University of Chicago. He became a minister in 1922. Mays was dean of the School of Religion at Howard University from 1934 to 1940. He wrote *The Negro's God as Reflected in His Literature* (1938), and was coauthor of *The Negro's Church* (1933). Mays also wrote an autobiography, *Born to Rebel,* which was published in 1971. In 1982, Mays received the Spingarn Medal for his work in education and theology.
Edgar Allan Toppin

Mays, Willie (1931-   ), became one of the most exciting players in baseball history. He electrified crowds with his sensational fielding, explosive hitting, and daring base running. In his major league career, he hit 660 home runs. Only Henry Aaron and Babe Ruth hit more.

Mays played center field for the New York (later San Francisco) Giants during most of his major league career. He was named the National League's Most Valuable Player in 1954 and 1965. He led the league in home runs four times and in stolen bases four times.

UPI/Bettmann
Newsphotos

Willie Mays

Mays won the league batting championship in 1954 and had a career batting average of .302. During the 1954 World Series, Mays had a spectacular running, over-the-shoulder catch of a long fly hit by Vic Wertz of the Cleveland Indians. The catch ranks among the most memorable plays in series history.

Willie Howard Mays was born in Westfield, Ala., a town near Fairfield. He joined the Giants in 1951. In 1972, he was traded to the New York Mets. He retired as a baseball player in 1973. Mays was elected to the National Baseball Hall of Fame in 1979.   Dave Nightingale

Mazarin, *MAZ uh rihn* or *ma za RAN,* **Jules Cardinal** (1602-1661), was a French statesman and a cardinal of the Roman Catholic Church. When Cardinal Richelieu, King Louis XIII's chief minister, died in 1642, Mazarin became chief minister of France. Anne of Austria, mother of the 4-year-old king, Louis XIV, ruled as her son's regent after Louis XIII died in 1643. She relied heavily on Mazarin's advice.

Mazarin sought to strengthen the French rulers at the expense of the aristocracy. Abroad, he employed diplomacy and the army to break out of the encirclement imposed upon France by the Spanish and Austrian Habsburgs. This program helped the French rulers, but placed a tax burden upon the common people.

In serving his king, Mazarin never lost an opportunity to enrich himself. When he died a wealthy man, Mazarin was mourned by both the monarchy and the aristocrats. However, the common people of France disliked Mazarin because he taxed them heavily and thought little about their needs.

Mazarin was born in the south-central Italian district of Abruzzi. He was a captain of infantry in the pope's army in the early campaigns of the Thirty Years' War. His skill in diplomacy led to a mission to France, where he attracted the notice of Cardinal Richelieu. Mazarin entered the service of France and became a French citizen. In 1641, he became a cardinal.   Richard M. Brace

See also **Anne of Austria; Louis XIV; Library** (Libraries of the 1600's and 1700's).

Maze. See Labyrinth.

Mazowiecki, *mah zoh VYEHT skee,* **Tadeusz,** *tah DAY oosh* (1927-   ), served as prime minister of Poland from August 1989 until November 1990. He was the first non-Communist to head the country's government since 1945.

Mazowiecki was born in Plock. After World War II (1939-1945), he studied law at the University of Warsaw. In the 1950's, Mazowiecki became a leader in Roman

Catholic organizations that sought to win greater religious freedom from Poland's Communist government.

In 1980, Mazowiecki helped Polish labor leader Lech Walesa negotiate a major agreement with the government. The agreement made Solidarity the first independent labor union in a Communist country. From then on, Mazowiecki was one of Walesa's closest advisers. In 1981, the government suspended Solidarity's activities and imprisoned Mazowiecki and most other Solidarity leaders. Mazowiecki was released from prison in 1982. In 1989, he played an important role in talks that led to an agreement to legalize Solidarity and to hold free parliamentary elections that June. Non-Communists received great support in the elections, and the lower house of parliament elected Mazowiecki prime minister in August.

Disagreements soon arose between Mazowiecki and Walesa. In November 1990, both men and another candidate ran for president of Poland. Mazowiecki finished last in the election and then resigned from his office of prime minister.   Stuart D. Goldman

Mazzei, *maht TSA ee,* **Philip** (1730-1816), was an Italian physician and merchant who supported the American Colonies during the Revolutionary War (1775-1783). He was a friend of Thomas Jefferson, who became the third President of the United States.

Mazzei was born in Poggio-a-Caiano, Italy, near Florence. He was trained as a surgeon and practiced medicine in Turkey until 1755, when he moved to London and became a wine merchant. In 1773, Mazzei went to America. He conducted agricultural experiments and established a wine, olive oil, and silk company in Virginia. Jefferson was a partner in the firm, and Mazzei lived near Monticello, Jefferson's estate.

Mazzei wrote many articles that demanded independence for the American Colonies. Jefferson translated these articles from Italian into English. In 1779, Mazzei went to Italy, where he collected political and military information for Virginia's leaders. He returned to Virginia after the war but moved to France in 1785. In 1791, Mazzei went to Poland, where he served as an adviser to the king. He returned to Italy in 1792 and spent the rest of his life there.   William Morgan Fowler, Jr.

Mazzini, *maht TSEE nee,* **Giuseppe,** *joo ZEHP peh* (1805-1872), was an Italian patriot and republican leader who played an important part in uniting Italy in 1861. He spent many years in exile because he wanted to free Italy from Austrian rule and unite it as a republic.

Mazzini began his political career in 1830 by joining the *Carbonari,* a group that wanted to unify Italy. A bold and active leader, he was exiled from Italy in 1830. Mazzini lived in exile for 18 years—first in Marseille, France, and later in Switzerland—and kept in contact with the liberal republicans in Italy. In 1832, he organized a society, called *Young Italy,* to work for Italian unity. One of his followers was Giuseppe Garibaldi, who later played an important role in the unification of Italy.

Mazzini returned to Italy in 1848, when revolutions broke out in many European countries. He helped organize a republic at Rome, and became one of its leaders. But French troops attacked the new government and captured Rome. Mazzini again fled to Switzerland, and later to London.

Italy finally was united in 1861 under King Victor Em-

manuel II of Sardinia, but only half of Mazzini's dream was realized. He wanted a republic, not a monarchy. He tried to organize a republican revolt in Palermo, Sicily, in 1870, but it failed. Mazzini was born in Genoa.
                                                R. John Rath

See also **Garibaldi, Giuseppe; Italy** (The French Revolution and Napoleon).

Mbabane, *EHM buh BAHN* (pop. 38,636), is the administrative capital of Swaziland, a country in southern Africa. Mbabane lies in a mountainous region of Swaziland 200 miles (320 kilometers) east of Johannesburg, South Africa (see **Swaziland** [map]). Mbabane was founded as a mining camp. Tin mining and farming are major occupations. Most people living there are Swazi. The Swazi are Bantu-speaking people who have much in common with the Zulus of South Africa.   Bruce Fetter

Mc. See Mac.

McAdam, John Loudon (1756-1836), a Scottish engineer, originated the *macadam* type of road surface. He was the first person to recognize that normal soil, if well-prepared, drained, and protected, can support the weight of traffic without an expensive foundation made of rock. His macadam pavements consisted of small stones packed into layers over dry, prepared soil. The stones provided a smooth surface and kept the soil dry. McAdam was born in Ayr, Scotland.   Terry S. Reynolds

See also **Industrial Revolution** (Roads); **Road** (Paving).

McAfee, Mildred Helen (1900-   ), an American educator, commanded the WAVES during World War II. She received the Distinguished Service Medal in 1945 for her work as the first director of the WAVES, the women's reserve of the U.S. Navy. She was president of Wellesley College from 1936 to 1949.

McAfee was born in Parkville, Mo. She graduated from Vassar College and received a master's degree from the University of Chicago. In 1945, she married Douglas Horton, a clergyman. She was the first woman chosen to the board of directors of Radio Corporation of America (RCA).   Miriam Schneir

McAuliffe, *muh KAW lihf,* **Christa** (1948-1986), was chosen to become the first schoolteacher to travel in space. McAuliffe was selected by the National Aeronautics and Space Administration (NASA) from more than 11,000 teachers who had applied for the post. She planned to document her flight in three parts—a diary beginning at the time of her selection, a journal of the actual flight, and her thoughts following the flight. On Jan. 28, 1986, the space shuttle *Challenger,* which carried McAuliffe, exploded shortly after take-off. The explosion killed McAuliffe and the six other crew members.

Sharon Christa Corrigan was born in Boston. She married Steven McAuliffe in 1970. They had two children. McAuliffe earned a bachelor's degree from Framingham State College in 1970. She received a master's degree in education from Bowie State College in 1978. From 1982 until her death, McAuliffe taught social studies at Concord High School in Concord, N.H.   Lillian D. Kozloski

McBain, Ed (1926-   ), is the pen name of Evan Hunter, a leading American writer of detective fiction. He is best known for his 87th Precinct series of novels set in a large American city. Each novel features members of the precinct police squad as the heroes. The series began with *Cop Hater* (1956) and is noted for its realism, sense of humor, and rich variety. Another series of mystery novels features a Florida lawyer named Matthew Hope. The series began with *Goldilocks* (1978).

McBain was born in New York City. His given and family name was Salvatore Lombino. In 1952, he legally changed his name to Evan Hunter. Among his best-known works under this name are the novels *The Blackboard Jungle* (1954) and *Last Summer* (1968). As Hunter, he also wrote the screenplay for the Alfred Hitchcock film *The Birds* (1963). His other pen names include Curt Cannon, Hunt Collins, and Richard Marsten.

David Geherin

McCarthy, Eugene Joseph (1916-   ), served as a United States senator from Minnesota from 1959 to 1971. He was a leading candidate for the 1968 Democratic presidential nomination. As a candidate, he consolidated the widespread opposition to the Vietnam War. He attracted much student support, and won primary elections in Wisconsin and Oregon. He was narrowly defeated by President Lyndon B. Johnson in the opening primary in New Hampshire.

McCarthy's success in the New Hampshire primary influenced Senator Robert F. Kennedy of New York to enter the Democratic race. It also helped persuade Johnson not to run for reelection. McCarthy lost in three states to Kennedy, and Vice President Hubert H. Humphrey won the Democratic nomination. McCarthy was also an unsuccessful candidate for the 1972 and 1992 Democratic presidential nominations. In 1976 and 1988, he ran for the presidency as an independent candidate but received less than 1 per cent of the popular vote in each election.

Eugene J. McCarthy

McCarthy was born in Watkins, Minn. He earned degrees from St. John's University and the University of Minnesota, and taught high school and college for 10 years. He was elected to the U.S. House of Representatives in 1948. He served in the House from 1949 to 1959.

Charles Bartlett

McCarthy, Joseph Raymond (1908-1957), a Republican United States senator from Wisconsin, was one of the most controversial figures in American politics. He gained worldwide attention in the early 1950's by charging that Communists had infiltrated the government. McCarthy conducted several public investigations of Communist influence on U.S. foreign policy. Some people praised him as a patriot, but others condemned him for publicly accusing people of disloyalty without sufficient evidence. He did not succeed in identifying any Communists employed by the government. His widely scattered charges gave rise to a new word, *McCarthyism*. See **McCarthyism**.

McCarthy was elected to the Senate in 1946. He attracted national attention in 1950 by accusing the Department of State of harboring Communists. President Harry S. Truman, a Democrat, and Secretary of State Dean Acheson denied McCarthy's charges. But most of McCarthy's fellow senators of both parties were aware

of his widespread support and were anxious to avoid challenging him. So was General Dwight D. Eisenhower, both as Republican presidential candidate and soon after becoming President in 1953. McCarthy also accused the Eisenhower Administration of treason.

A number of circumstances caused many Americans to believe McCarthy's charges. These

United Press Int.

Joseph R. McCarthy

included the frustrations of the Korean War, the Chinese Communist conquest of mainland China, and the conviction of several Americans as Soviet spies.

During nationally televised hearings in 1954, McCarthy accused the U.S. Army of "coddling Communists." The Army made countercharges of improper conduct by members of McCarthy's staff. As a result of the hearings, McCarthy lost the support of millions of people. The Senate condemned him in 1954 for "contemptuous" conduct toward a subcommittee that had investigated his finances in 1952, and for his abuse of a committee that recommended he be censured.

McCarthy was born in Grand Chute, Wis., and graduated from Marquette University. He wrote *America's Retreat from Victory: The Story of George Catlett Marshall* (1951) and *McCarthyism: The Fight for America* (1952).

Charles Bartlett

Additional resources

Fried, Richard M. *Nightmare in Red: The McCarthy Era in Perspective.* Oxford, 1990.
Oshinsky, David M. *A Conspiracy So Immense: The World of Joe McCarthy.* Free Pr., 1985. First published in 1983.
Reeves, Thomas C. *The Life and Times of Joe McCarthy: A Biography.* Stein & Day, 1982.

McCarthy, Mary (1912-1989), was an American author. She wrote novels, short stories, criticism, essays, travel books, and autobiography. Much of her work is satirical and deals with events and issues of the day.

Mary Therese McCarthy was born in Seattle. She described her childhood and early life in *Memories of a Catholic Girlhood* (1957) and *How I Grew* (1987). McCarthy graduated from Vassar College in 1933 and served as drama critic for the *Partisan Review* from 1937 to 1948. Her reviews and other criticism from 1937 to 1956 were collected in *Sights and Spectacles* (1956) and *Theatre Chronicles* (1963).

McCarthy's fiction draws heavily on her own life. Her best-known novel, *The Group* (1963), follows the lives of several women who attended Vassar in the 1930's. Her other novels include *The Company She Keeps* (1942), *The Oasis* (1949), *The Groves of Academe* (1952), *A Charmed Life* (1955), *Birds of America* (1971), and *Cannibals and Missionaries* (1979). Many of her short stories appear in *Cast a Cold Eye* (1950).

McCarthy wrote two travel books, *Venice Observed* (1956) and *The Stones of Florence* (1959). Her literary essays were collected in *On the Contrary* (1961), *The Writing on the Wall* (1970), and *Ideas and the Novel* (1980).

Barbara M. Perkins

McCarthyism is a term for the widespread accusations and investigations of suspected Communist activities in the United States during the 1950's. The word came from the name of Senator Joseph R. McCarthy. McCarthy, a Wisconsin Republican, made numerous charges—usually with little evidence—that certain public officials and other individuals were Communists or cooperated with Communists.

McCarthyism developed during the Cold War, a period of great hostility between the Communist and non-Communist nations. In the late 1940's and the 1950's, a number of events related to this struggle alarmed and frustrated many Americans. For example, Communists took over Czechoslovakia and China. The Soviet Union exploded its first atomic bomb and equipped the North Korean Communist forces that invaded South Korea. This invasion touched off the Korean War (1950-1953).

Meanwhile, charges that Americans had served as Soviet spies received wide attention. Alger Hiss, a former official of the U.S. Department of State, was accused of giving government secrets to a Soviet spy during the 1930's. Julius and Ethel Rosenberg, an American couple, were convicted of passing military secrets to Soviet agents in the 1940's. See **Hiss, Alger; Rosenberg, Julius and Ethel.**

As Communism appeared more and more threatening, the federal government began to search for secret Communists among its employees. In 1947, President Harry S. Truman established agencies called *loyalty boards* to investigate federal workers. Truman ordered the dismissal of any government employee whose loyalty appeared questionable. That same year, the U.S. attorney general established a list of organizations that the Department of Justice considered disloyal. Government agencies used the list as a guide to help determine the loyalty of employees and of people seeking jobs.

McCarthy first gained national attention in 1950, when he charged that Communists dominated the State Department. The Senate Foreign Relations Committee investigated the department but found no Communists or Communist sympathizers there. Nevertheless, McCarthy made numerous additional accusations and gained many followers. He and other conservatives blamed many of the nation's problems on the supposed secret presence of Communists in the government.

The accusations and investigations spread quickly and affected thousands of people. Librarians, college professors, entertainers, journalists, clergy, and others came under suspicion. Some firms *blacklisted* (refused to hire) people accused of Communist associations. Many employees, to keep their jobs, were required to take oaths of loyalty to the government. McCarthyism gradually declined after 1954. Among the factors that contributed to its decline were the end of the Korean War in 1953 and the condemnation of McCarthy by the Senate for conduct unbecoming a senator in 1954. In addition, from 1955 to 1958, the Supreme Court of the United States made a series of decisions that helped protect the rights of people accused of sympathizing with Communists. Today, the term *McCarthyism* is sometimes used to refer to reckless public accusations of disloyalty to the United States.   Thomas C. Reeves

See also **Cold War; McCarthy, Joseph R.; Un-American Activities Committee.**

McCartney, Paul (1942-   ), is a famous English singer, songwriter, and musician. He first became prominent as a member of the Beatles, the most popular group in the history of rock music (see **Beatles**).

James Paul McCartney was born in Liverpool. He played bass with the Beatles. McCartney and guitarist John Lennon wrote most of the Beatles' music. With the Beatles, McCartney sang and wrote many of their melodic ballads. These ballads included "Yesterday" (1965), "Hey Jude" (1968), and "Let It Be" (1970). He also contributed some harder rock numbers, such as "I'm Down" (1965) and "Helter Skelter" (1968).

The Beatles disbanded in 1970. McCartney has continued to perform as a soloist. He also became the leader of Wings, a rock band that included his wife, Linda Eastman McCartney. His most popular albums since 1970 include *Band on the Run* (1973) and *Tug of War* (1982). In 1989, McCartney released "Flowers in the Dirt," an album that many critics considered one of his best since his recordings with the Beatles. In addition, he composed a classical work, *Liverpool Oratorio* (1991), with the American composer Carl Davis.   Don McLeese

McCarty, Henry. See Billy the Kid.

McClellan, George Brinton (1826-1885), served for a time as the general in chief of the Union Army during the American Civil War (1861-1865). He was a brilliant organizer and trainer of troops and a scholar of military strategy. McClellan was called "Young Napoleon" after the famous French military genius Napoleon I. Some authorities rank McClellan as a great general, but most believe he was too cautious on the battlefield. In 1864, McClellan was the Democratic candidate for President. He lost to his Republican opponent, Abraham Lincoln.

Military career. At the outbreak of the Civil War, McClellan became a major general in command of Ohio volunteers. After becoming a major general in the regular army, he cleared western Virginia of Confederate forces. In the summer of 1861, he took command of the Union Army in the East, which became known as the Army of the Potomac. In November 1861, he became general in chief of all armies. President Lincoln grew impatient because McClellan did not move against the Confederates. He relieved him as supreme general in March 1862. McClellan remained an Army commander.

McClellan finally advanced in the spring of 1862, moving against Richmond from the east in the Peninsular Campaign. After fighting at Williamsburg and Fair Oaks, he drew close to Richmond. The Confederates, under General Robert E. Lee, then attacked him in the Battles of the Seven Days and drove him back to Harrison's Landing on the James River. Washington authorities then transferred McClellan's army to northern Virginia, uniting most of his troops temporarily with a force under General John Pope's command. After Pope's defeat at the Second Battle of Bull Run, or Manassas, McClellan became head of all troops in the Washington area.

Brown Bros.

George B. McClellan

McClellan led his army into Maryland to meet a Confederate invasion. The two armies clashed in the Battle of Antietam on Sept. 17, 1862, the bloodiest day of the war. About 12,500 Northerners and almost 11,000 Southerners were killed or wounded in the battle. McClellan forced the Confederates to retreat, but he did not immediately pursue them. His delay angered Lincoln. Lincoln replaced McClellan with General Ambrose Burnside in November 1862, and McClellan's military career was ended.

Other activities. McClellan was born in Philadelphia. He graduated from the U.S. Military Academy in 1846, second in his class. He served in the Mexican War (1846-1848) and went to Europe in 1855 to study European military systems. In 1857, McClellan became chief engineer of the Illinois Central (now Illinois Central Gulf) Railroad. He became vice president of that railroad, and later served as president of a division of the Ohio and Mississippi Railroad. McClellan was governor of New Jersey from 1878 to 1881.   Gabor S. Boritt

See also **Civil War** (The war in the East); **President of the United States** (picture: Abraham Lincoln).

Additional resources

Sears, Stephen W. *George B. McClellan: The Young Napoleon.* Ticknor & Fields, 1988.
Wheeler, Richard. *Sword over Richmond: An Eyewitness History of McClellan's Peninsula Campaign.* Fairfax Pr., 1989. First published in 1986.

McClintock, Barbara (1902-1992), an American geneticist, won the 1983 Nobel Prize for physiology or medicine. She received the award for her discovery that certain genes can change their position on the chromosomes of cells. These genes, called *mobile genetic elements,* occur in all organisms.

McClintock studied the way corn inherits its traits. In 1931, she showed that chromosomes can break and join together differently during the formation of eggs or sperm. This process is important because it allows each egg and sperm to contain a different combination of genes. In 1951, McClintock announced her discovery of mobile genetic elements. In some corn plants, the mobile gene might be in one place on a chromosome, but in others it would be somewhere else. McClintock could tell where the mobile gene was because of its effects on nearby genes.

McClintock was born in Hartford, Conn. She received a Ph.D. degree from Cornell University in 1927. She became a member of the Carnegie Institution of Washington, D.C., in 1941.   Daniel L. Hartl

McCloskey, John Cardinal (1810-1885), was the first American to be named a cardinal of the Roman Catholic Church. He served as the second archbishop of the Roman Catholic archdiocese from 1864 until his death. Pope Pius IX named him a cardinal in 1875 despite McCloskey's opposition to the definition of papal infallibility at Vatican Council I.

McCloskey was born in New York City. He was ordained a priest in 1834 and a bishop in 1844. From 1847 to 1864, he served as the first bishop of Albany, N.Y. There he won the respect of politicians, helped reduce widespread anti-Catholic sentiment, and oversaw a large building program of new schools and churches. While serving as archbishop, he saw to the needs of thousands of immigrants. McCloskey also supervised the completion of St. Patrick's Cathedral in New York City.   David G. Schultenover

McClung, Nellie (1873-1951), was a leading Canadian feminist and an author. She fought successfully for political and legal rights for Canadian women. In 1912, she helped found the Winnipeg (Man.) Political Equality League, which campaigned for female *suffrage* (voting rights) in Canada. Manitoba was one of several provinces that in 1916 gave women the right to vote. Female suffrage became nationwide in 1918.

From 1921 to 1926, McClung served in the Alberta legislature. She was one of five women who began a court battle in 1927 to determine whether women were "persons" under the British North America Act, which serves as Canada's constitution. The Privy Council in England, the highest judicial authority in the British Empire, ruled in their favor in 1929. This ruling enabled women to serve in the Canadian Senate.

Nellie McClung

McClung wrote several books about Canadian life and the women's movement. They included *In Times Like These* (1915) and *Purple Springs* (1921). Nellie Letitia McClung was born in Chatsworth, Ont.   Patricia Monk

McClure, Sir Robert John Le Mesurier (1807-1873), also spelled *M'Clure,* was a British explorer who led the first expedition to cross the Northwest Passage. He discovered the route through the Arctic region during an expedition from 1850 to 1854. McClure found the passage during an unsuccessful search for Sir John Franklin, a British explorer who had not returned from an Arctic voyage begun in 1845. McClure sailed across the Beaufort Sea and around Banks Island, where his ship became stuck in ice. McClure and his crew almost starved to death, but a search party rescued them in 1853. McClure then covered the rest of the passage, traveling by ship and sled to Baffin Bay. After returning to England in 1854, McClure was knighted and promoted to captain in the British navy. McClure was born in Wexford, Ireland. He joined the British navy in 1824. See also **Northwest Passage.**   Barry M. Gough

McClure, Samuel Sidney (1857-1949), was an American editor and publisher. He founded the McClure Syndicate in New York City in 1884. This was one of the first newspaper syndicates. In 1893, he founded *McClure's Magazine,* one of the first successful inexpensive magazines. He was briefly connected with the S. S. McClure Newspaper Corporation, which was formed in 1915 when he bought the *New York Mail.*

McClure was born in Forcess, Ireland. His works include *My Autobiography, Obstacles to Peace,* and *The Achievements of Liberty.*   John Eldridge Drewry

McCollum, Elmer Verner (1879-1967), was an American biochemist known for his work on the influence of diet on health. He pioneered in the study of vitamins and minerals by experimenting with the diets of small animals. McCollum discovered or helped discover a number of vitamins and originated the letter system of naming vitamins. He showed that vitamin D—a previously unknown vitamin—prevents *rickets,* a bone disease. McCollum's book *The Newer Knowledge of Nutrition* (1918) influenced a generation of dietitians.

McCollum was born near Fort Scott, Kans., and studied at Yale University. He was a professor of agricultural chemistry at the University of Wisconsin and a professor of biochemistry at Johns Hopkins University.

Martin D. Saltzman

McConnell Family Foundation, J. W., is the largest private foundation in Canada. It seeks to advance the quality of life in Canada through grants and awards to not-for-profit organizations that help solve cultural, educational, environmental, health, or social problems.

Programs funded by the foundation include those that (1) promote the artistic development of people seeking to become professional artists; (2) provide alternatives to institutional living for elderly or disabled people; (3) increase public awareness of environmental issues; (4) aid rural communities, homeless people, or disadvantaged youth; or (5) help not-for-profit companies improve their management and fund-raising skills. The foundation makes grants only to nonprofit organizations and only for clearly charitable purposes. It does not make grants to individuals.

In 1937, John Wilson McConnell, a Canadian financier, set up the J. W. McConnell Foundation. In 1966, that organization established the Griffith Foundation. In 1987, the two foundations were combined to form the J. W. McConnell Family Foundation, with headquarters in Montreal. For assets, see **Foundations** (table).

Critically reviewed by the J. W. McConnell Family Foundation

McCord, David (1897-   ), an American writer, is best known for his poetry for young children. He writes humorous poems filled with imaginative wordplay that emphasizes the sounds and rhythms of language. Many of his poems are about small animals and children.

McCord has written several books of poetry for children. Five of the books were collected in *One at a Time* (1977). His other books of poetry include *Every Time I Climb a Tree* (1967), *The Star in the Pail* (1975), and *Speak Up: More Rhymes of the Never Was and Always Is* (1980).

David Thompson Watson McCord was born in New York City. McCord is also a painter and has taught creative writing. Nancy Lyman Huse

McCormack, John (1884-1945), was perhaps the most famous of Irish tenors. His popularity as a concert artist was almost unrivaled. It enabled him to amass a fortune estimated at over $1 million. McCormack commanded a light, clear voice and sang with perfect diction and great vocal finesse. He sang airs of the 1700's and Irish ballads with equal eloquence.

McCormack began his career at the age of 18 by winning a gold medal at the National Irish Festival in Dublin. After study in Italy, he won immediate success in Naples, London, New York, Boston, and Chicago. McCormack abandoned opera after 1913 in favor of concerts. He was born in Athlone, Ireland, but became a U.S. citizen in 1917. Martin Bernheimer

McCormack, John William (1891-1980), a Democrat from Massachusetts, served as Speaker of the United States House of Representatives from 1962 to 1971. Be-

fore his election as Speaker, McCormack had been deputy to Sam Rayburn, the top House Democrat from 1940 until his death in 1961.

McCormack was born in Boston and attended public schools there. He served in the Massachusetts legislature from 1920 to 1926, and represented his South Boston district in the U.S. House of Representatives from 1928 to 1971. McCormack gained a reputation in Congress as a strong supporter of his party's legislative programs. In 1969, a group of liberal House Democrats tried to replace McCormack as Speaker, but he was re-elected by a wide margin. McCormack retired from the House in January 1971, after more than 42 consecutive years of service. Charles Bartlett

McCormick, Cyrus Hall (1809-1884), invented a reaping machine that revolutionized grain harvesting in the United States. His horse-drawn reaper enabled farmers to harvest more than 10 acres (4 hectares) of grain per day. Before his invention, farmers harvested with cradle scythes and a skilled worker could harvest at most 2 or 3 acres (0.8 to 1.2 hectares) per day.

McCormick was born on a farm in Rockbridge County, Virginia. As a youth, he experimented with various tools in the hope of designing equipment that would simplify farmers' work. He also observed his father's unsuccessful efforts to construct a mechanical reaper. In 1831, Cyrus built his first reaper. He tested the device on wheat and oats and continued to make adjustments before patenting it in 1834. McCormick finally offered his reaper for sale in Virginia in 1840.

The reaper sold well, and McCormick expanded sales to other parts of the country in 1844. Sales boomed because the machine's efficiency enabled farmers to raise more grain and greatly increase their income.

In 1847, McCormick moved his manufacturing operation to Chicago to increase sales. Centrally located in the Midwest, he used the Great Lakes to transport reapers to the Eastern States, and the Mississippi River to ship reapers into the South. McCormick gained worldwide fame in 1851, when he demonstrated his machine at an exhibition in London. By late 1851, Chicago newspapers boasted that the McCormick Harvesting Machine Company was the largest implement factory in the world. McCormick's sales and distribution grew further in the 1850's, when Chicago became a major railroad center.

McCormick remained president of the McCormick Harvesting Machine Company until his death. In 1902, the company merged with four other implement companies to form the International Harvester Company (now Navistar International Corporation). R. Douglas Hurt

See also **Reaper.**

McCormick, Robert Rutherford (1880-1955), an American editor and publisher, made the *Chicago Tribune* one of the nation's most important newspapers. His grandfather, Joseph Medill, gave the *Tribune* its first fame (see **Medill, Joseph**). With his cousin, Joseph Medill Patterson, McCormick built an enterprise that included the *Tribune,* the New York *Daily News,* and the *Washington* (D.C.) *Times-Herald.* He took over sole control of the *Tribune* in 1925. A conservative Republican, McCormick fought the New Deal (see **New Deal**). He was born in Chicago. Kenneth N. Stewart

McCoy, Elijah, *ih LY juh* (1843-1929), was a black American engineer and inventor who developed the automatic lubricator. His invention, the *lubricator cup,* continuously supplies lubricants to moving parts of various types of machines.

Before McCoy's invention in the early 1870's, workers had to lubricate the parts of machines regularly. The lubricator cup automatically oils machine parts as they operate, and has eliminated the need for such workers. Throughout his life, McCoy worked to improve lubricating systems for locomotives and other machines. The expression *the real McCoy,* meaning *the real thing,* may have originated with machinery buyers who insisted that their new equipment have only McCoy lubricators.

McCoy was born in Colchester, Ont. His parents had been slaves who fled to Canada from Kentucky. McCoy was apprenticed to a mechanical engineer in Scotland and later worked as a fireman-oilman for several railroads in Michigan. W. Bernard Carlson

McCrae, *muh KRAY,* **John** (1872-1918), was a Canadian physician, soldier, and poet. He contributed verses to Canadian periodicals before World War I. But he did not become famous until 1915 when he published "In Flanders Fields" in *Punch,* an English magazine. His poems were published after his death under the title *In Flanders Fields, and Other Poems* (1919). The second stanza of his famous poem is:

> We are the Dead. Short days ago
> We lived, felt dawn, saw sunset glow,
> Loved and were loved, and now we lie
> In Flanders fields. *Reprinted by permission of Punch*

McCrae was born in Guelph, Ont., and graduated from the University of Toronto. After serving in the Canadian Army in South Africa in 1899 and 1900, he became a pathologist at McGill University and at Montreal General Hospital. As the chief medical officer at a hospital in Boulogne, France, in World War I, he witnessed the suffering and death he wrote about. He died of pneumonia before the war ended. Rosemary Sullivan

McCullers, Carson (1917-1967), was an American novelist known for her stories of small-town life in the South. Many of her characters are lonely, disappointed people. McCullers was particularly interested in adolescents who learn the meaning of loneliness while appearing to be part of a close family. *The Member of the Wedding* (1946), perhaps her most famous novel, portrays a 12-year-old girl experiencing the pains of growing up. Her other major themes include the search for individual identity, the nature of love, and the inevitability of death.

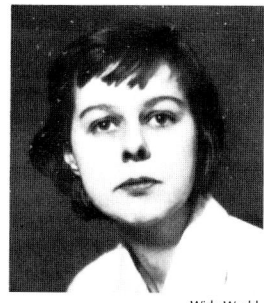
Wide World
Carson McCullers

Many characters in McCullers' books are lonely because they are deformed. For example, two characters in her short novel *The Ballad of the Sad Café* (1951) are a dwarf and an abnormally large woman. Her other novels—*The Heart Is a Lonely Hunter* (1940), *Reflections in a Golden Eye* (1941), and *Clock Without Hands* (1961)—show the violence and pain that may accompany loneliness and lack of love. McCullers wrote two plays—an adaptation of *The Member of the Wedding* (1950) and *The Square Root of Wonderful* (1957). *The Mortgaged Heart* (1971) contains essays, poems, and early fiction. Her *Collected Stories* was published in 1987, after her death. She was born in Columbus, Ga. Noel Polk

McCulloch v. Maryland resulted in one of the most important decisions in the history of the U.S. Supreme Court. The court ruled in 1819 that Congress has implied powers in addition to those specified in the Constitution. The decision was based on a section of the Constitution called the "necessary and proper" clause. This clause gives Congress power "to make all laws which shall be necessary and proper" to carry out its other powers. The court also ruled that when federal and state powers conflict, federal powers prevail.

James McCulloch, cashier of the Baltimore branch of the Bank of the United States, refused to pay a Maryland state tax on the bank. The court first upheld the implied power of Congress to create a bank, because Congress needed a bank to exercise its specified powers. It then declared the tax unconstitutional because it interfered with an instrument of the federal government. In a famous opinion, Chief Justice John Marshall said that the American people "did not design to make their government dependent on the states." Stanley I. Kutler

McDougall, William. See Red River Rebellion.

McEnroe, John (1959-   ), is one of the world's best tennis players. He won the U.S. Open singles title in 1979, 1980, 1981, and 1984 and the All-England (Wimbledon) singles championship in 1981, 1983, and 1984. With Peter Fleming, he won the Wimbledon doubles title in 1979, 1981, 1983, and 1984 and the U.S. doubles title in 1979, 1981, and 1983.

McEnroe, a left-hander, became noted for his powerful serve and for his speed and quickness. He plays well on all court surfaces. His aggressiveness and intensity have also contributed to his success. McEnroe has stirred much controversy for his frequent conflicts with officials during matches.

John Patrick McEnroe

© Sh. Steiner, Sygma
John McEnroe

was born in Wiesbaden, Germany, where his father was serving in the U.S. Air Force. McEnroe became a professional tennis player in 1978. Patrick McEnroe, John's younger brother, is also a leading professional tennis player. J. Norman Arey

See also **Tennis** (picture: Modern men tennis stars).

McGill, James (1744-1813), a wealthy Canadian merchant, founded McGill University in Montreal, Quebec. He willed money and property to the institution, which was chartered in 1821 and opened in 1829. Born in Glasgow, Scotland, McGill settled in Montreal in 1770, and became a fur trader. He served in the first parliament of Lower Canada. Galen Saylor

McGill University is a coeducational university in Montreal, Canada. It is supported chiefly by the province of Quebec. Courses are conducted in English, though Montreal is primarily a French-speaking city.

The university offers programs in architecture, arts, computer science, dentistry, education, engineering, law, library science and information studies, management, medicine, music, nursing, physical and occupational therapy, religious studies, science, social work, and urban planning. It grants bachelor's, master's, and doctor's degrees. The university has a division of agriculture and a school of dietetics and human nutrition in nearby Ste.-Anne-de-Bellevue. It operates a subarctic research laboratory in Schefferville, Que., an institute for research in the natural sciences in Mont-St.-Hilaire, Que., and a facility in Barbados for research on tropical animals, plants, geography, and geology.

James McGill, a Canadian merchant, willed money and land to set up the university. It was chartered in 1821 and opened in 1829. For enrollment, see **Canada** (table: Universities and colleges).

Critically reviewed by McGill University

McGillicuddy, Cornelius. See Mack, Connie.

McGillivray, Alexander (1759?-1793), was an influential Creek Indian leader around the time of the Revolutionary War in America (1775-1783). He helped protect Creek lands from American settlers.

McGillivray was born near what is now Montgomery, Ala. His father was a wealthy Scot, and his mother was half Creek and half French. McGillivray believed that an independent United States would threaten all Indian lands. He helped keep the Creeks loyal to the British during the Revolutionary War. McGillivray and his Creek warriors fought wars with Georgia and Tennessee from 1785 to 1787. In 1790, he signed a treaty with the United States that guaranteed the Creeks certain territory where settlement by U.S. citizens was prohibited.

McGillivray worked hard to unite the Creeks under a strong central government. He called for changes in the way the Creeks viewed politics, but died before the Creeks carried out his reforms. The Creeks adopted many of his ideas in the 1820's. Michael D. Green

McGillivray, William (1764?-1825), served as director of the North West Company, in what is now Canada, from 1804 to 1821. This company, a fur-trading organization, consisted of a group of Montreal fur-trading firms.

McGillivray was born in the county of Inverness-shire in Scotland. He settled in Montreal in 1784 and went to work as a clerk for the North West Company. In 1786, McGillivray took charge of a trading post for the firm. He became a partner in the firm in 1790.

McGillivray helped develop the fur trade by sending traders into wilderness regions of western Canada. In 1821, he realized that the North West Company could not compete with the Hudson's Bay Company, a British fur-trading firm. He helped unite the two firms under the name of the Hudson's Bay Company. P. B. Waite

McGinley, Phyllis (1905-1978), was a leading American author of light verse. Her collection *Times Three: Selected Verse from Three Decades* won the 1961 Pulitzer Prize for poetry.

McGinley praised the virtues of the ordinary life with affection and humor, and she celebrated but also satirized life's absurdities. She defended femininity, morality, and domestic and suburban living in *Times Three* and in two books of witty essays, *The Province of the Heart* (1959) and *Sixpence in Her Shoe* (1964). McGinley

summed up her point of view by quoting a man who said he had failed as a philosopher because "cheerfulness was always breaking in." She wrote many books for young people, including *The Horse Who Lived Upstairs* (1944) and *Sugar and Spice* (1960).

McGinley was born in Ontario, Ore. She lived in a suburb of New York City, which provided the setting for much of her writing. Bonnie Costello

McGovern, George Stanley (1922-), was the Democratic presidential nominee in 1972. He lost to his Republican opponent, President Richard M. Nixon.

When McGovern ran for President, he was serving his second term as a U.S. senator. In 1962, he had been elected South Dakota's first Democratic senator since the 1930's. During the 1950's, he twice won election to the U.S. House of Representatives.

Early life. McGovern was born on July 19, 1922, in Avon, S. Dak. He graduated from Dakota Wesleyan University and later taught history there. He earned a master's degree and a Ph.D. at Northwestern University. During World War II (1939-1945), McGovern served as a bomber pilot and won the Distinguished Flying Cross. In 1943, he married Eleanor Faye Stegeberg (1921-). They had five children—Ann (1945-), Susan (1946-), Teresa (1949-), Steven (1952-), and Mary (1955-).

George S. McGovern

Career in Congress. McGovern was elected to the U.S. House of Representatives in 1956. He was reelected in 1958 and ran unsuccessfully for the U.S. Senate two years later. McGovern won election to the Senate in 1962 and was reelected in 1968. In 1969, McGovern became chairman of a commission to recommend ways to reform the Democratic Party. In 1974, McGovern won reelection to a third term in the Senate, but he was defeated in his bid for a fourth term in 1980.

Presidential candidate. In 1972, the Democratic National Convention nominated McGovern for President and Senator Thomas F. Eagleton of Missouri for Vice President. Twelve days after Eagleton's nomination, he revealed that he had been hospitalized three times in the 1960's for treatment of emotional exhaustion and depression. Eagleton's qualifications for the vice presidency became the subject of a nationwide debate, and he resigned from the ticket at McGovern's request. He was replaced by Sargent Shriver, former director of the Peace Corps. McGovern and Shriver were defeated by Nixon and Vice President Spiro T. Agnew. For the electoral vote, see **Electoral College** (table).

McGovern also ran for the 1984 Democratic presidential nomination. He withdrew from the race after failing to win any early primary elections. David S. Broder

See also **Democratic Party; Eagleton, Thomas F.; Shriver, Sargent.**

McGuffey, William Holmes (1800-1873), was an American educator and clergyman. From 1836 to 1857, he published illustrated reading books. More than 120

14   NEW SECOND READER.

LESSON II.

flew	trees	catch	ver'y	lit'tle
once	birds	think	po'ny	tall'er
been	knew	found	ta'ble	a-way'
come	grass	would	wi'ser	sum'mer
much	shone	school	stud'y	morn'ing

THE SCHOOL-BOY.

1. I once knew a boy. He was not a big boy.

2. If he had been a big boy, he would have been wi-ser.

3. But he was a lit-tle boy. He was not much tall-er than the ta-ble.

Newberry Library, Chicago

William H. McGuffey's *Eclectic Reader* was used in schools throughout the United States during the 1800's. Millions of copies were sold. A page from the reader is shown above.

million copies of his *Eclectic Reader* were sold, and for many years nearly all American schoolchildren learned to read from it. The book played a major part in forming American moral ideas and literary tastes in the 1800's.

McGuffey was born in Washington County, Pennsylvania. He became a Presbyterian minister in 1829. McGuffey taught at Miami University in Ohio and at the University of Virginia. He was president of Ohio University from 1839 to 1845.   Glenn Smith

McHenry, *muhk HEHN rih,* **James** (1753-1816), a doctor and politician, was a Maryland signer of the Constitution of the United States. He was absent from many early sessions of the Constitutional Convention in 1787 but helped shape the final document. He helped win *ratification* (approval) of the Constitution by Maryland.

McHenry was born in Ballymena, Ireland. He moved to Philadelphia in 1771 and studied medicine. During the Revolutionary War in America (1775-1783), McHenry served as an army surgeon and as secretary to Generals George Washington and the Marquis de Lafayette. He served in the Maryland legislature from 1781 to 1786

and from 1791 to 1796, and he attended the Congress of the Confederation from 1783 to 1785. In 1796, President George Washington appointed him secretary of war. McHenry continued in this office under President John Adams until 1800.   Joan R. Gundersen

McKay, Alexander (1770?-1811), also spelled *MacKay,* was a Canadian fur trader and explorer. In 1793, he accompanied Alexander Mackenzie on the first overland crossing of northern North America by whites (see **Mackenzie, Sir Alexander**). In 1810, McKay became a partner in American businessman John Jacob Astor's Pacific Fur Company. McKay helped found Astoria, the first white settlement in Oregon, in 1811. That same year, he took part in a trading mission in the ship *Tonquin* along the Pacific coast north of Astoria. Against McKay's advice, the ship's crew abused the coast Indians. The Indians took revenge by killing McKay and all but one of the ship's crew. McKay was born in what is now the state of New York.   D. Peter MacLeod

McKay, Claude (1890-1948), was a black poet and novelist. His poetry is noted for its lyricism and its powerful statements of black militancy. The best known of McKay's three novels is *Home to Harlem* (1928), the story of a black American soldier's life after his return from France after World War I (1914-1918). This novel became controversial because some black critics protested that it emphasized exotic elements in black life but ignored the major problems of African-Americans. McKay's 10 other books include *Harlem Shadows* (1922), a collection of poems; *Banana Bottom* (1933), a novel; *A Long Way from Home* (1937), an autobiography; and *Selected Poems* (published in 1953, after his death).

McKay was born in Jamaica. His first two works were collections of dialect poetry published there. McKay moved to the United States in 1912 to attend college. He lived both in Europe and in the United States.
William L. Andrews

See also **American literature** (The Harlem Renaissance).

McKay, Donald (1810-1880), was a Canadian master craftsman who designed and built more than 90 clipper ships. Famed for grace and seaworthiness, they were the fastest sailing vessels ever built. The *Flying Cloud,* launched in 1851, sailed around Cape Horn from New York to San Francisco in 89 days. It covered 374 nautical miles (693 kilometers) in one day. Both the speed of the cruise and the length of the day's run set world records for sailing ships. McKay launched the *Great Republic,* the largest wooden sailing ship ever built, in 1853. The vessel measured 335 feet (102 meters) in length. McKay built most of his ships in Boston. He was born in Shelbourne County, Nova Scotia. See also **Ship** (Clipper ships).   James C. Bradford

McKean, *muh KEEN,* **Thomas** (1734-1817), an American statesman, was a Delaware signer of the Declaration of Independence. He was a Delaware delegate to the Continental Congress and the Congress of the Confederation almost continuously from 1774 to 1783. McKean also served as chief justice of Pennsylvania from 1777 to 1799. He was governor of that state from 1799 to 1808.

McKean was born in New London, Pa. He studied law and, in 1776, wrote most of the Delaware state Constitution.   James H. Hutson

McKinley, Mount. See **Mount McKinley.**

**25th President of
the United States 1897-1901**

Cleveland
24th President
1893-1897
Democrat

McKinley
25th President
1897-1901
Republican

T. Roosevelt
26th President
1901-1909
Republican

**Garret A.
Hobart**
Vice President
1897-1899

**Theodore
Roosevelt**
Vice President
1901

Oil painting on canvas (1900) by William T. Mathews; Corcoran Gallery of Art, Washington, D.C.

McKinley, William (1843-1901), helped shape the modern presidency and set the United States on a path toward world leadership. During his two Administrations, the nation emerged from a depression. American soldiers and sailors won the Spanish-American War (1898). The United States took possession of Guam, Hawaii, the Philippines, Puerto Rico, and part of American Samoa. Victory at war and control of new lands made the United States a world power, and thus also increased the power of the presidency.

McKinley led the Republican Party during the 1890's. He supported his party's belief in *protective tariffs,* taxes on imports to protect American industries from foreign competition. He and his party also promoted the growth of big business in the United States. McKinley succeeded President Grover Cleveland and twice defeated the well-known statesman William Jennings Bryan for the presidency. An assassin shot and killed McKinley about six months after the start of his second term, and Vice President Theodore Roosevelt became President. McKinley was the third President to be assassinated. The first two were Abraham Lincoln and James A. Garfield.

Following the hard times of the mid-1890's, McKinley's two Administrations were filled with national optimism and confidence. The motion picture, the automobile, and the telephone were becoming part of everyday life. Businesses were growing, but social problems remained. Blacks faced segregation, violence, and lynchings in the South. Industrial workers labored an average of 59 hours a week. And women had full voting rights in only four states—Colorado, Idaho, Utah, and Wyoming. There were already stirrings of a spirit of reform that would sweep through the United States after 1901.

History has not been kind to McKinley. Historians and political scientists have often underestimated his achievements as President. They have seen McKinley as a colorless, cautious President compared with more exciting leaders, such as Theodore Roosevelt and Woodrow Wilson. In fact, McKinley's presidency was a time of great change for the nation, and he did much to shape that change. He strengthened the powers of his office and expanded the nation's role in world affairs.

Early life

Childhood. William McKinley was born on Jan. 29, 1843, in Niles, Ohio, a rural town with a population of about 300. His parents, William, Sr., and Nancy McKinley, owned an iron foundry. His grandfather James McKinley had moved to Ohio in the early 1800's to manage an iron foundry in Columbiana County.

Education. William, the seventh of nine children, attended school in Niles. When William was 9 years old, the family moved to Poland, Ohio, near Youngstown, in search of better schools. The boy entered a private school, the Poland Seminary. McKinley's father stayed in Niles to run his iron foundry, spending much time away from the family. At the age of 10, McKinley joined the Methodist Episcopal Church. When he was 17, he entered Allegheny College in Meadville, Pa. But he soon became ill and dropped out.

Bravery under fire. When the Civil War began in 1861, McKinley was the first man in the town of Poland to volunteer to fight. He joined the 23rd Ohio Infantry commanded by future U.S. President Rutherford B. Hayes. At the Battle of Antietam in 1862, McKinley brought food to his regiment while it was under intense enemy assault. This bravery under fire helped earn him a promotion to second lieutenant. He ended the war

The explosion of the U.S. battleship *Maine* on Feb. 15, 1898, in Havana helped trigger the Spanish-American War.

The Klondike gold rush attracted thousands of fortune hunters to the Yukon Territory of Canada in the late 1890's.

The world of President McKinley

Press sensationalism arose during the late 1800's, as newspapers competed for readers. William Randolph Hearst's *New York Journal* and Joseph Pulitzer's *New York World* battled for public attention with sensational headlines and exaggerated reporting that became known as "yellow journalism."

Hawaii, Puerto Rico, and the Philippines became American possessions between 1898 and 1900.

Spanish-American War heroes came home to public acclaim. Admiral George Dewey was the hero of the Battle of Manila. Theodore Roosevelt captured national attention as a commander of the Rough Rider Regiment that helped defeat Spanish forces at the Battle of San Juan Hill in Cuba.

Walter Reed, a U.S. Army doctor, conducted experiments in Cuba during the Spanish-American War that led to important advances in the control of typhoid and yellow fever.

Marie and Pierre Curie of France discovered the elements radium and polonium in 1898 while studying the radioactive properties of uranium.

The Boer War broke out in South Africa in 1899. British and mainly Dutch forces fought for control of territory.

Temperance crusader Carry Nation began smashing saloons in Kansas in 1899. Her efforts helped bring about national prohibition 20 years later.

The Boxer Rebellion erupted in China in 1900. Chinese nationalists who opposed the spread of Western influence in China battled Europeans and Chinese Christians.

The first Texas oil strike occurred on Jan. 10, 1901, when oil was found at the Spindletop oil field near Beaumont.

Chicago Historical Society; Brown Bros.

with the rank of *brevet* (honorary) major. Later, during his political career, he was known as Major McKinley.

After the war ended in 1865, McKinley studied law. He worked for a county judge in Youngstown for about 18 months. In 1866, he entered law school in Albany, N.Y. In 1867, he began practicing law in Canton, Ohio.

Political and public activities

Entry into politics. McKinley was a gifted public speaker and a naturally popular figure in the community. He began his political career in 1869, when he was elected prosecuting attorney of Stark County, Ohio. McKinley narrowly lost reelection in 1871.

McKinley's family. On Jan. 25, 1871, McKinley married Ida Saxton (June 8, 1847-May 26, 1907), whose grandfather had founded the first newspaper in Canton. The McKinleys had two daughters. In 1873, the younger one died when she was 4 months old. That same year, Mrs. McKinley's mother died. Two years later, the McKinleys' other daughter, Katherine (1871-1875), died. The grief and shock caused by these deaths left Ida an invalid. Later, she developed epilepsy.

Congressman. McKinley won election to the U.S. House of Representatives in 1876. He served seven

Important dates in McKinley's life

1843	(Jan. 29) Born in Niles, Ohio.
1876	Elected to U.S. House of Representatives.
1891	Elected governor of Ohio.
1896	Elected President of the United States.
1900	Reelected President of the United States.
1901	(Sept. 6) Shot by assassin in Buffalo, N.Y.
1901	(Sept. 14) Died in Buffalo.

terms, from 1877 to 1891, except for about 9 months in 1884-1885. In 1884, the House ruled that McKinley's opponent, lawyer Jonathan H. Wallace, had actually received the most votes in the 1882 election. Wallace took McKinley's seat for the rest of the term, but McKinley returned to Congress in 1885 with a clear victory in the 1884 election.

In Congress during the late 1870's, McKinley voted for *free silver*. Free silver was a plan to increase the country's supply of money by allowing the treasury to mint silver coins in addition to gold coins. See **Free silver.**

McKinley also gained fame as a strong supporter in Congress of the protective tariff. The protective tariff is a policy, he said, that believes "in American work for

Foto/Find

William McKinley's birthplace was this frame building on South Main Street in Niles, Ohio. The building was later moved and then was destroyed by fire in 1937.

American workmen, that believes in American wages for American laborers, that believes in American homes for American citizens." The McKinley Tariff Act of 1890 raised taxes on imports to a record high and supported trade agreements with Latin-American countries.

Governor. In 1890, McKinley lost his bid for an eighth term in Congress. This loss came in part because the McKinley Tariff had greatly increased consumer prices and so became unpopular. In addition, the Democrats had *gerrymandered* (unfairly redrawn the boundaries of) his district. In 1891, however, voters elected McKinley governor of Ohio. McKinley improved the state's canals, roads, and public institutions. He also established a state board to settle labor disputes.

As McKinley's national reputation grew, people began to consider him for the presidency. In addition, McKinley had become friends with Cleveland businessman and millionaire Mark Hanna. Legend describes Hanna as leading McKinley to political power and success. But in fact, McKinley used Hanna to meet his own political goals. In 1892, Hanna opened an unofficial McKinley-for-President headquarters at the Republican National Convention in Minneapolis, Minn. McKinley received a flurry of support for the nomination. In balloting at the convention, he accumulated 182 votes but lost to President Benjamin Harrison, who got 535 votes.

Crisis and triumph. In 1893, McKinley faced a personal crisis that almost sidetracked his political career. He had co-signed bank notes totaling more than $100,000 to help a friend start a business manufacturing tin plate. But the business failed, and McKinley was expected to repay the bank loans. McKinley did not have the money. His friends, led by Hanna, raised enough funds to pay the obligation. The public sympathized with McKinley and reelected him governor in 1893.

As the 1896 presidential election approached, people

again supported McKinley for President. His popularity within the party and an absence of strong rivals led to his nomination at the Republican National Convention in St. Louis, Mo. The Republicans chose Garret A. Hobart of New Jersey to run as Vice President.

The Democrats nominated the great orator William Jennings Bryan of Nebraska as McKinley's opponent. Bryan chose Arthur Sewall, a wealthy Maine shipbuilder, as his running mate.

The front-porch campaign. McKinley stayed in Canton during the campaign and spoke to visiting delegations from his front porch. More than 750,000 people visited Canton to hear him speak. Newspapers nationwide reprinted his speeches. As McKinley's campaign manager, Hanna helped raise some 3½ million in campaign funds from banks and other businesses.

McKinley had wanted to stress the protective tariff as the campaign theme. But Bryan electrified the Democratic National Convention with his "cross of gold" speech in favor of free silver. Bryan's appeal for an unlimited number of silver coins made currency the main issue. McKinley no longer supported free silver as he did in Congress. Instead, he called for the United States to maintain the *gold standard,* a system in which the dollar was defined as worth a certain quantity of gold. He also proposed higher tariffs. McKinley told voters that free silver would increase consumer prices, but that high tariffs would promote national prosperity. In the November election, McKinley won with more than 7 million of the nearly 14 million votes.

McKinley's first Administration (1897-1901)

McKinley took office on March 4, 1897. His first priority was to increase the protective tariff. He called Congress into special session, and the Dingley Tariff of 1897 was passed. This act raised taxes on imports to record highs. Three years later, Congress passed the Gold Standard Act of 1900. This act made only gold—not silver—exchangeable for money in the United States.

McKinley developed new policies toward the press that laid the basis for modern techniques of informing the public about the President. McKinley's secretary, George B. Cortelyou, adopted new procedures for distributing press releases and conducting presidential travel. Also, McKinley made himself accessible to the press corps and provided space in the White House where reporters could work.

The Spanish-American War (1898). In 1895, Cubans began a rebellion against Spain, which had ruled Cuba for almost 400 years. After McKinley took office in 1897, he pressed Spain to negotiate with the rebels. The new President had wanted to remain neutral in the affair. However, McKinley said that the United States would go

The Western Reserve Historical Society

Ida McKinley was an invalid when she became first lady. But her illnesses, including epilepsy, did not keep her from attending many White House functions with her devoted husband.

McKinley's first election

Place of nominating convention	St. Louis
Ballot on which nominated	1st
Democratic opponent	William Jennings Bryan
Electoral vote*	271 (McKinley) to 176 (Bryan)
Popular vote	7,108,480 (McKinley) to 6,511,495 (Bryan)
Age at first inauguration	54

*For votes by states, see **Electoral College** (table).

to war if necessary to protect U.S. interests.

On Feb. 15, 1898, the battleship U.S.S. *Maine* exploded in Havana harbor in Cuba. Today, historians believe the explosion was an accident. But at the time, the public blamed Spain. Many politicians, newspaper publishers, and those in favor of expanding U.S. territorial control urged McKinley to help Cuba. McKinley hoped the Spaniards would peacefully leave the island. But no Spanish politician could accept the loss of Cuba and remain in power.

Greatly pressured by public opinion, McKinley asked Congress for authority to take action. On April 25, the United States declared war on Spain. U.S. Army and Navy troops overpowered Spanish forces. Key battles took place in the Philippines and off the coast of Cuba. In July, the Spanish forces in Cuba surrendered. In August, an armistice ended the fighting. On December 10, Spain and the United States signed the Treaty of Paris. Under this agreement, Spain surrendered Guam and Puerto Rico to the United States. It also gave the United States the Philippines for $20 million. See **Spanish-American War.**

America becomes a world power. The war with Spain lasted only 113 days, but it had far-reaching effects. As a result of the conflict, the United States took over most of Spain's overseas territories, leaving it with only a few outposts in northern Africa. Also in 1898, the United States took possession of what had been the Republic of Hawaii. In 1899, the United States signed a treaty with Germany and Britain, gaining what is now part of American Samoa. Because of its new possessions in the Pacific Ocean, the United States became more involved in Asian politics.

In February 1899, a Filipino patriot named Emilio Aguinaldo led a revolt against American control of the Philippines. The rebels waged *guerrilla warfare,* which involved small-scale hit-and-run attacks, for over three years. To defeat the guerrillas, U.S. soldiers used cruel tactics, including the killing of civilians. As a result, many Americans turned against U.S. *imperialism* (controlling territories for political or economic gain).

The United States also used military force in China. In 1899, McKinley's secretary of state, John M. Hay, issued what became known as the Open-Door Policy. This policy sought to give all nations equal access to the profitable trade in China. Since the 1890's, a secret Chinese society known as the *Boxers* had opposed Western and Japanese influence in China. In 1900, the Boxers began an uprising called the Boxer Rebellion to drive out the foreigners. McKinley sent 5,000 U.S. troops to help Germany, Japan, Russia, and other nations crush the rebellion and rescue Europeans and Americans held in Beijing. By thus using his authority as commander in chief, McKinley helped strengthen the presidency. See **Boxer Rebellion; Open-Door Policy.**

Life in the White House remained simple during McKinley's two Administrations. Because of her illness, Mrs. McKinley was not socially active. Her relatives and the President's nieces often served as official hostesses. The President reserved a room to greet his many visitors. Mrs. McKinley usually sat beside the President as he stood in a receiving line.

"President of the whole people." In 1900, the Republicans again nominated McKinley for President. They selected Theodore Roosevelt, a hero of the Spanish-American War and governor of New York, to run for Vice President. Bryan again became the Democratic candidate. His running mate, Adlai E. Stevenson, had been Vice President under Grover Cleveland from 1893 to 1897.

Culver

McKinley's reelection campaign promised continued prosperity, with "A Full Dinner Bucket." The campaign button above pictures McKinley and his running mate, Theodore Roosevelt.

During the presidential campaign, Bryan attacked McKinley on the issues of imperialism, free silver, and the growth of big business and illegal monopolies called *trusts.* But the major campaign issue became prosperity. McKinley said, "We have prosperity at home and prestige abroad." McKinley and Roosevelt won a sweeping victory. Afterward, McKinley said: "I can no longer be called the President of a party; I am now the President of the whole people."

McKinley's second Administration (1901)

During McKinley's short second term, the United States extended the policies that McKinley had already established. In March 1901, the country enacted the Platt Amendment, which later became part of Cuba's Constitution. This amendment gave the United States the right to intervene if Cuba's affairs became unsettled. In May, the U.S. Supreme Court of the United States decided the Insular Cases, which found that the United States could control territories without granting their people citizenship. In July, McKinley set up a civilian government in the Philippines.

Revised policies. By 1901, McKinley no longer fully supported the growth of big business. He told aides that government would have to address the problem of industrial consolidation, in which companies in the same industry combined to form a single company. Business owners in the United States had formed huge trusts and other monopolies that hurt competition and kept prices high for consumers.

Also by 1901, McKinley had modified his views on tariffs. He no longer supported protective tariffs to help businesses. Instead, he favored freer commerce through *reciprocal trade agreements,* arrangements with other countries to reduce tariffs on each other's exports. McKinley introduced this policy at the Pan American Exposition in Buffalo, N.Y., on Sept. 5, 1901. He said, "By sensible trade relations which will not interrupt our home

McKinley's second election

Place of nominating convention	Philadelphia
Ballot on which nominated	1st
Democratic opponent	William Jennings Bryan
Electoral vote*	292 (McKinley) to 155 (Bryan)
Popular vote	7,218,039 (McKinley) to 6,358,345 (Bryan)
Age at second inauguration	58

*For votes by states, see **Electoral College** (table).

McKinley was shot by an anarchist named Leon Czolgosz at the Pan American Exposition in Buffalo, N.Y., on Sept. 6, 1901. The President died eight days later.

Vice Presidents and Cabinet

Vice President	*Garret A. Hobart
	*Theodore Roosevelt (1901)
Secretary of state	*John Sherman
	William R. Day (1898)
	*John M. Hay (1898)
Secretary of the treasury	Lyman J. Gage
Secretary of war	Russell A. Alger
	*Elihu Root (1899)
Attorney general	Joseph McKenna
	John W. Griggs (1898)
	Philander C. Knox (1901)
Postmaster general	James A. Gary
	Charles E. Smith (1898)
Secretary of the navy	John D. Long
Secretary of the interior	Cornelius N. Bliss
	Ethan A. Hitchcock (1898)
Secretary of agriculture	James Wilson

*Has a separate biography in *World Book.*

production, we shall extend the outlets for our increasing surplus" of products. He concluded, "The period of exclusiveness is past."

Assassination. On September 6, the day after McKinley's trade speech, the President held a reception in the exhibition's Temple of Music. Among the crowd of people attending was Leon F. Czolgosz, an *anarchist* (person who opposes regulations and government). A handkerchief covered a revolver that Czolgosz carried in his right hand. When McKinley approached him to shake hands, Czolgosz fired two bullets at the President. One bullet ricocheted off McKinley's button, but the other pierced the President's stomach. McKinley was rushed to a hospital for surgery. He lived for eight days before gangrene and infection overwhelmed him. McKinley died the morning of Sept. 14, 1901, just over six months after beginning his second term as President. Czolgosz was later convicted of murder and electrocuted.

Roosevelt rushed from a vacation in the Adirondack Mountains when he learned McKinley was near death. But by the time Roosevelt reached Buffalo on Septem-

ber 14, McKinley had died. Roosevelt took the oath of office that same day and became President. Mrs. McKinley died in 1907 in Canton. She and her husband are buried there at the McKinley National Memorial.

Lewis L. Gould

Related articles in *World Book* include:

Bryan, William Jennings
Buffalo (Other interesting places to visit)
Cuba (History)
Hanna, Mark
Hobart, Garret A.
Philippines (History)

President of the United States
Puerto Rico (History)
Roosevelt, Theodore
Spanish-American War
Tariff
Territory

Questions

What was McKinley's relationship to: Mark Hanna? William Jennings Bryan? Theodore Roosevelt?
How did McKinley begin his political career in Ohio?
How did the United States change its position in world affairs during McKinley's Administrations?
What policy was McKinley famous for supporting when he was in Congress?
How did McKinley strengthen the presidency during his terms?
What was McKinley's policy toward Spain and Cuba in 1897?
What were two improvements McKinley made as governor of Ohio?
What stand did McKinley take on free silver during the 1896 campaign? Why?
Who shot McKinley? Where and when did it occur?
What two policies did McKinley no longer fully support in his second Administration?

Additional resources

Gould, Lewis L. *The Presidency of William McKinley.* Univ. Pr. of Kansas, 1980.
Kent, Zachary. *William McKinley: Twenty-Fifth President of the United States.* Childrens Pr., 1988. For younger readers.
Leech, Margaret K. *In the Days of McKinley.* Greenwood, 1975. First published in 1959. Pulitzer Prize winner.
Morgan, H. Wayne. *William McKinley and His America.* Syracuse Univ. Pr., 1963. *From Hayes to McKinley: National Party Politics, 1877-1896.* 1969.

McKissick, Floyd Bixler (1922-1991), was a black American civil rights leader. He became known for his efforts to help blacks gain political and economic control over their communities.

McKissick was born in Asheville, N.C. He received a law degree from North Carolina College (now North Carolina Central University) in 1951. Later, as a lawyer, he won lawsuits that allowed his children to enter previously all-white schools.

In 1960, McKissick became legal counsel for the Congress of Racial Equality (CORE), a civil rights organization. He was its national chairman from 1963 to 1966 and its national director from 1966 to 1968.

After leaving CORE, McKissick worked to help blacks

obtain positions of power in cities where they made up a large part of the population. He also formed a company to promote black business projects.

In 1974, McKissick's company began building Soul City, a new town near Henderson, N.C. This project was financed in part by the federal government. In 1979, however, the government announced plans to end its support of Soul City. McKissick withdrew from the project the next year and returned to practicing law. In 1990, he was appointed to serve as a judge in the Ninth Judicial District in North Carolina.   Alton Hornsby, Jr.

McKuen, *muh KYOON,* **Rod** (1933-   ), is a popular American poet and composer. Most of his poems and songs describe loneliness or love. McKuen often has performed his works in concerts and on recordings.

McKuen's most popular books of poetry include *Stanyan Street and Other Sorrows* (1966), *Lonesome Cities* (1968), and *In Someone's Shadow* (1969). He has written more than 1,000 songs, and many of the lyrics were published in *Listen to the Warm* (1967). He also has composed classical music and music for motion pictures. McKuen's book *Finding My Father* (1976) tells about his search for his father, who deserted the family shortly before McKuen's birth.

Rod Marvin McKuen was born in Oakland, Calif. He ran away from home when he was 11 years old. For several years, he wandered throughout the West doing odd jobs. His first book of poems, *And Autumn Came,* was published in 1954.   John S. Wilson

McLaughlin, *muhk LAHK lihn,* **Audrey Marlene** (1936-   ), was elected leader of Canada's New Democratic Party (NDP) in 1989. She thus became the first woman to head an important national political party in Canada. McLaughlin succeeded Edward Broadbent as the party's leader. She became known as a moderate social democrat and supported a mixture of public and private enterprise in the Canadian economy.

McLaughlin was born in Dutton, Ont. She earned a Bachelor of Arts degree from the University of Western Ontario in 1964. In 1970, she received a Master of Social Work degree from the University of Toronto and became a social worker. McLaughlin moved to the Yukon Territory in 1979. Since 1987, she has represented the Yukon in the Canadian House of Commons.   Kendal Windeyer

House of Commons, Ottawa
Audrey McLaughlin

McLoughlin, *muk LAWF lihn,* **John** (1784-1857), a Canadian-born trader, is sometimes called the *father of Oregon.* He played a leading part in settling Oregon Territory. He became a partner in the North West Company, a fur trading company, in 1814 and took charge of Fort William in 1815. After the North West and Hudson's Bay companies merged in 1821, he directed their business in the Oregon country from 1824 to 1846. He developed trading posts and friendly relations with the Indians, whose cultures he found interesting. He had to resign for helping new settlers at his company's expense.

McLoughlin was born at La Rivière du Loup, Que. Oregon placed his statue in the United States Capitol in 1953.   Dan L. Flores

McLuhan, *muhk LOO ihn,* **Marshall** (1911-1980), was a Canadian professor and writer whose theories on mass communication have caused widespread debate. According to McLuhan, electronic communication —especially television—dominates the life of all Western peoples. It affects their ways of thinking as well as their institutions. McLuhan analyzed the effects of communications media on people and society in *The Mechanical Bride* (1951), *The Gutenberg Galaxy* (1962), *Understanding Media* (1964), *The Medium Is the Massage* (1967), and *War and Peace in the Global Village* (1968).

McLuhan argued that each major period in history takes its character from the medium of communication used most widely at the time. For example, he called the period from 1700 to the mid-1900's the *age of print.* At that time, printing was the chief means by which people gained and shared knowledge. McLuhan claimed that printing encouraged individualism, nationalism, democracy, the desire for privacy, specialization in work, and the separation of work and leisure.

According to McLuhan, the electronic age has replaced the age of print. Electronics speeds communication so greatly that people in all parts of the world become deeply involved in the lives of everyone else. As a result, said McLuhan, electronics leads to the end of individualism and nationalism and to the growth of new international communities.

Interest in McLuhan's work resurfaced in the 1980's. He is among the first of the *post-modernist writers,* who believe that our society has become driven by computers and electronics. They argue that electronics have revolutionized work, politics, culture, and art.

McLuhan was born in Edmonton, Alta. His full name was Herbert Marshall McLuhan.   James W. Carey

M'Clure, Sir Robert John Le Mesurier. See McClure, Sir Robert John Le Mesurier.

McMurtry, Larry (1936-   ), is an American novelist whose fiction reflects his Southwestern heritage. McMurtry writes about dissatisfied, lonely characters living in dying Western towns. His novels move beyond traditional Western fiction through their use of black humor, their frank treatment of sex, and their theme of the rootless Texan lost in the big city. McMurtry contrasts dreams of grandeur with the harsh realities and limited options open on the contemporary frontier. There is a mournful tone to much of his fiction in response to the fading away of traditions of simplicity and freedom usually associated with the West.

Larry Jeff McMurtry was born in Wichita Falls, Tex. His early novels, such as *Horseman, Pass By* (1961) and *The Last Picture Show* (1966), reflect cheerless life on the ranches and in the small towns of west Texas. *Terms of Endearment* (1975) and McMurtry's other novels of the 1970's explore Texas characters who have been attracted to the urban environment. *Lonesome Dove* (1985) describes a cattle drive of the 1800's. The novel won the 1986 Pulitzer Prize for fiction. *Buffalo Girls* (1990) uses historical figures from Western history to portray the passing of the Wild West era.   Arthur M. Saltzman

McNamara, Robert Strange (1916-   ), was United States secretary of defense from 1961 to 1968. He served under Presidents John F. Kennedy and Lyndon B. Johnson. As secretary, McNamara became an important adviser to the Presidents in economic and foreign affairs as well as in military matters. He introduced systems of estimating military needs and costs 10 to 15 years into the future. From 1968 to 1981, McNamara served as president of the World Bank.

McNamara was born in San Francisco. He graduated from the University of California and the Harvard Business School, and taught at Harvard from 1940 to 1943. He was in the U.S. Army Air Forces in World War II, and then served as an executive at the Ford Motor Company from 1946 to 1961. He became president of Ford in 1960.

James I. Lengle

McNary, *muhk NAIR ih,* **Charles Linza,** *LIHN zuh* (1874-1944), served as a United States senator from Oregon from 1917 until his death. He was the Republican candidate for Vice President of the United States in 1940. He and presidential candidate Wendell L. Willkie lost to President Franklin D. Roosevelt and Henry A. Wallace. A liberal Republican, McNary supported federal aid to farmers during the 1920's and many New Deal programs in the 1930's (see **New Deal**). He served as Senate minority leader from 1932 until his death. Born near Salem, Ore., he attended Stanford University.

David E. Kyvig

McNaughton, *muhk NAW tuhn,* **Andrew George Latta,** *LAT uh* (1887-1966), was a noted Canadian soldier of World Wars I and II. He took command of the First Canadian Division at the outbreak of World War II in 1939. He commanded the Canadian Corps from 1940 to 1942 and the Canadian Army in 1942 and 1943. In 1944, McNaughton served as defense minister under Prime Minister Mackenzie King. He was chairman of the Canadian sections of the Canada-United States Permanent Joint Board on Defense from 1945 to 1962 and of the International Joint Commission from 1950 to 1962 (see **International Joint Commission**).

McNaughton served as a gunnery officer in World War I (1914-1918) and became a brigadier general in 1918. He was credited with developing techniques for locating enemy artillery so that it could be disabled.

McNaughton was the co-inventor of a cathode-ray direction finder used in airplanes (see **Cathode rays**). He served as chairman of the Canadian National Research Council from 1935 to 1939. McNaughton was born in Moosomin, Sask.

Desmond Morton

McPherson, *muhk FUR suhn,* **Aimee Semple** (1890-1944), a colorful American evangelist, founded the International Church of the Foursquare Gospel. She also founded the Lighthouse of International Foursquare Evangelism Bible College. McPherson stressed salvation, divine healing, baptism by the Holy Spirit, and the Second Coming of Christ. She worked as a revivalist in the Full Gospel Assembly from 1908 to 1910 and was a missionary in China in 1910 and 1911. She built Angelus Temple in Los Angeles in 1922. McPherson was born in Salford, Ont., Canada.

Henry Warner Bowden

Mead, Lake. See Lake Mead.

Mead, *meed,* **Margaret** (1901-1978), was an American anthropologist known for her studies of how culture influences the development of personality. She lived among peoples of the Pacific Islands to study their ways of life. Mead described how cultures differ in what behavior they consider appropriate. She also studied how children learn to become part of their culture.

Mead's best-known book, *Coming of Age in Samoa* (1928), compares the lives of adolescents in a Samoan village and in Western societies. The accuracy of her comparisons was later challenged, causing anthropologists to become even more aware that such field research may be interpreted in more ways than one. Her

WORLD BOOK photo by Kenneth Heyman
Margaret Mead

other books include *Growing Up in New Guinea* (1930), *Sex and Temperament in Three Primitive Societies* (1935), *Male and Female* (1949), and *Culture and Commitment* (1970).

Mead was born in Philadelphia. She graduated from Barnard College and received a Ph.D. degree in anthropology from Columbia University. From 1926 to 1969, she was a curator of ethnology at the American Museum of Natural History in New York City.

Judith Modell

See also **Anthropology** (picture: Margaret Mead).

Additional resources

Howard, Jane. *Margaret Mead: A Life.* Fawcett, 1990. First published in 1984.
Ziesk, Edra. *Margaret Mead.* Chelsea Hse., 1990. For younger readers.

Meade, *meed,* **George Gordon** (1815-1872), was a Union general in the Civil War (1861-1865). He commanded the victorious Union Army at the Battle of Gettysburg in July 1863. This battle, between about 90,000 Union troops and 75,000 Southerners, has been called the greatest engagement ever fought on U.S. soil.

When the Civil War began, Meade became a brigadier general of volunteers from Pennsylvania. Beginning in 1862, he fought in most of the important battles in the East, including the peninsular campaign, the Second Battle of Bull Run (also called Manassas), and the battles of Antietam (also called Sharpsburg), Fredericksburg, and Chancellorsville. He became a major general of volunteers after Antietam and a corps commander after Fredericksburg. In June 1863, he replaced General Joseph Hooker as commander of the Army of the Potomac. Three days later, Meade showed his skill and military judgment in defeating the Confederates at Gettysburg. Jealous subordinates and Republican politicians criticized Meade's battlefield leadership and blamed him for the Confederate Army's escape into Virginia. But he remained in his command for the rest of the war, and his major decisions and actions proved to be correct.

Meade was born in Cádiz, Spain, the son of an Ameri-

Photograph by Mathew B. Brady, The National Archives, Washington, D.C.
George Meade

can naval agent. He was educated in the United States and graduated from the U.S. Military Academy in 1835. He served in the Second Seminole War (1835-1842) and in the Mexican War (1846-1848). After the Civil War, Meade held various military commands.

James E. Sefton

Meadow saffron. See Colchicum.

Meadowlark is the common name of two similar species of North American birds that inhabit grassy fields, meadows, and prairies. The *eastern meadowlark* usually lives in moister habitats than does the *western meadowlark*. The eastern meadowlark is found from southern Ontario south to the Amazon River in South America, and it ranges westward to Arizona. The western meadowlark is found from southern British Columbia to central Mexico, and as far east as Ohio.

WORLD BOOK illustration by Trevor Boyer, Linden Artists Ltd.

Eastern meadowlark

Meadowlarks are not true larks. They belong to the same family as blackbirds and orioles. Meadowlarks are about the size of robins but have a heavier body, shorter tail, and longer bill. The back, wings, and tail of the meadowlark are brownish, streaked with black. The throat and underparts of the bird are bright yellow with a large, black, V-shaped band on the breast. White feathers on each side of the tail are flashed when the meadowlark is nervous or in flight.

The eastern meadowlark's song consists of two clear whistles, the second ending as a slurred, drawn-out note. It is one of the first bird songs of spring. The song of the western meadowlark consists of 7 to 10 flutelike, gurgling notes.

The meadowlark builds its nest on the ground, usually with a dome-shaped roof of grass hiding the eggs. Both species lay three to seven white eggs speckled with reddish-brown. Meadowlarks eat some waste grain and vast quantities of weed seeds and harmful insects.

Scientific classification. Meadowlarks belong to the subfamily Icterinae of the emberizid family, Emberizidae. The scientific name for the eastern meadowlark is *Sturnella magna*. The western meadowlark is *S. neglecta*.   Edward H. Burtt, Jr.

See also **Bird** (table: State and provincial birds; pictures: Birds of grasslands; Birds' eggs).

Mean, in statistics, is the sum of a series of numbers divided by the number of cases. Suppose five boys weigh 67, 62, 68, 69, and 64 pounds. The sum of their weights is 330 pounds. Divide this sum by 5, the number of boys, or cases: $330 \div 5 = 66$. The *mean* of this series of numbers is 66 and the *mean weight* of the boys is 66 pounds. This single weight of 66 pounds can be used to represent the differing weights of all five boys, even though none of them weighs exactly 66 pounds. The mean is often called the *arithmetic average* or *arithmetic mean*. See also **Average; Median; Mode; Statistics** (Probability).   Doris F. Hertsgaard

Meany, George (1894-1980), served as the first president of the American Federation of Labor and Congress of Industrial Organizations (AFL-CIO). He held the office from 1955, when the AFL and CIO merged, until he retired in 1979. Before the merger, Meany had served as president of the AFL since 1952.

Meany made it one of his chief tasks to eliminate corruption in labor unions. He was influential in expelling the big and powerful Teamsters Union from the AFL-CIO in 1957, after its leaders were accused of unethical practices.

Wide World

George Meany

Meany played a major role in the AFL-CIO's international activities. He tried to strengthen anti-Communist forces in labor, and he strongly supported United States policy on the Vietnam War (1957-1975). In 1963, Meany received the Presidential Medal of Freedom.

Meany was highly critical of President Richard M. Nixon's efforts to halt inflation. However, he agreed in 1971 to serve on a Pay Board that Nixon set up to control wage increases. Several months later, Meany resigned from the Pay Board, accusing the Nixon Administration of favoring business over labor.

Meany was born in New York City. He became an apprentice plumber when he was 16 years old. Meany served as president of the New York State Federation of Labor from 1934 to 1939 and as secretary-treasurer of the AFL from 1940 to 1952.   Gerald G. Somers

See also **Labor movement** (Reunification of the AFL and the CIO; picture).

Measles is a disease that causes a pink rash all over the body. It is extremely contagious. The disease occurs chiefly in children, but some young adults also catch it. Few people in the United States or Canada die of measles. But the disease kills many undernourished children in developing countries. The medical name for measles is *rubeola*. *German measles,* known medically as *rubella,* is a different disease with similar symptoms (see **Rubella**).

Before the 1960's, most children in the United States caught measles. In 1963—in a major medical advance—a team of virologists headed by the American researcher John F. Enders developed a measles vaccine. By the early 1980's, the use of this vaccine had practically eliminated measles from the United States. But widespread outbreaks of measles among children and young adults beginning in the late 1980's have caused U.S. health officials to intensify vaccination programs against the disease.

Cause and effects. A virus causes measles. People who have the disease spread the virus by coughing and sneezing. The first symptoms appear about 10 days after the virus enters a person's body. A fever, cough, and runny nose develop, and the eyes become red and watery and sensitive to light. The fever may reach 105 °F (41 °C). Small pink spots with gray-white centers develop inside the mouth, especially on the insides of the cheeks. They are called *Koplik's spots.* A person with symptoms of measles should call a physician.

Three to five days after the first symptoms appear,

faint pink spots break out on the face near the hairline. The rash spreads all over the body within two or three days. About the time it reaches the feet, the patient's fever drops and the runny nose and cough disappear. The patient's rash begins to fade at the same time. Some people who are weakened by measles suffer various complications, including infections of the lungs and the middle ear. The virus can harm the brain, but this is not common.

No drug exists to cure measles after it develops. Patients should be kept comfortable while the disease lasts. In most cases, a person has measles only once. The body produces *antibodies* (substances that fight infection) during the disease. These antibodies normally provide lifelong *immunity* (protection) from later attacks.

Prevention. In 1954, Enders separated the measles virus from other substances and grew it in living cells in test tubes. He later developed a vaccine from the virus. Since 1963, millions of young children have received a single injection of the vaccine to prevent measles. It usually is given when the child is about 15 months old. Most American physicians recommend a second injection for older children or adolescents.

Measles vaccine contains live measles virus that has been weakened by a long period of growth in animal cells in a test tube. When injected into a person's body, this virus produces a mild form of the condition and, in most people, no symptoms appear. But the body reacts to the weakened virus just as it would to an ordinary virus. That is, it produces antibodies that fight the virus and provide immunity to measles. Scientists do not know how long the immunity lasts. In most people, it continues for many years—perhaps for life. In the United States, measles occasionally occurs in adolescents and young adults who have never received the measles vaccine or who have received it only once.

The vaccine cannot stop measles from developing in someone who already has the virus. For a very few children who have been exposed to measles and who are at risk of developing other, more severe disease, doctors may try to prevent measles by using *gamma globulin treatment.* In this treatment, a doctor injects gamma globulin, a part of the blood. The gamma globulin that is used comes from people who have had measles, and so it contains antibodies.   Neil R. Blacklow

See also **Disease** (table); **Enders, John F.**

Measure. See **Music** (Rhythm; Musical notation).

Measurement. See **Weights and measures.**

Measuring worm is a moth caterpillar that moves by looping its body forward. Measuring worms are also called *inchworms, loopers,* or *spanworms.* A measuring

worm crawls by pulling the back part of its body toward the front part, forming a hump in the middle. It then reaches forward with its six front legs to "measure" the distance it can reach by straightening its body. It moves in this way because it has only two or three pairs of *prolegs* (leglike structures) on the back part of its body. Most other caterpillars have five pairs of prolegs. A measuring worm can stand upright and motionless on a twig. By doing this, it resembles a branch of the twig and can escape the notice of its enemies.

There are thousands of species of measuring worms. Some species, such as the *spring cankerworm* and the *fall cankerworm,* are serious pests of fruit and shade trees (see **Cankerworm**). Other species, including the *cabbage looper* and the *omnivorous looper,* damage crops. Measuring worms usually form loose cocoons to enter the pupa stage. The moths that later appear are medium-sized with broad wings that have delicate lined patterns.

Scientific classification. Most measuring worms belong to the family Geometridae. Others are in the family Noctuidae.

Charles V. Covell, Jr.

Meat is animal flesh that is eaten as food. Meat consists largely of muscles, but fat and other animal tissue are also considered meat. The most commonly eaten meats in the United States and Canada come from animals that are raised for food. These animals—and the meats that come from them—are cattle (beef and veal), hogs (pork), sheep (lamb and mutton), and poultry (chicken, duck, and turkey). *Game,* which is meat from wild animals, is also frequently eaten. In addition, fish is included among meat-producing animals. This article discusses meat from cattle, hogs, and sheep, all called *red meat.* For information on poultry and fish, see **Poultry; Fishing industry.**

About 30 billion pounds (14 billion kilograms) of red meat is eaten in the United States each year. That averages 120 pounds (54 kilograms) of red meat per year for each person. About 74 pounds (34 kilograms) is beef; 43 pounds (20 kilograms) is pork; 2 pounds (0.9 kilogram) is veal; and 1 pound (0.45 kilogram) is lamb and mutton. Canadians eat an average of 105 pounds (47 kilograms) of red meat per person each year. Only the people of Argentina, New Zealand, and Uruguay eat more red meat than North Americans.

Food value of meat. Most nutritionists consider meat an important part of a well-balanced diet. Meat provides protein, vitamins, minerals, and fat necessary for good health and growth. Meat protein contains essential *amino acids* (protein elements) needed to build and maintain body tissue. See **Amino acid.**

Red meat is an excellent source of the vitamin B complex group. Thiamine (B_1) is especially abundant in pork. Thiamine helps maintain the circulatory and nervous systems and aids the body in storing and releasing energy. Riboflavin (B_2) is needed for normal growth and healthy skin. Pyridoxine (B_6) helps prevent nervous disorders and skin diseases and vitamin B_{12} helps maintain red blood cells. Niacin is important in preventing a disease called pellagra (see **Pellagra**). Liver, an especially nutritious meat, also provides vitamins A and C. The body needs these vitamins for normal vision and healthy gums and tissue.

Meat is rich in iron, which is needed to build and

© Anthony Bannister, N. H. P. A.

The measuring worm crawls by arching its body.

maintain red blood cells and muscle growth. Meat is also a source of copper, phosphorus, and zinc. The fat in meat is an excellent source of energy and certain fatty acids the body cannot produce itself. About half of the fatty acids in meat fat are *saturated.* Saturated fats help form a fatty substance called *cholesterol.* Some doctors believe large amounts of cholesterol in the body may contribute to heart disease, and advise eating only moderate amounts of foods containing saturated fats. See Cholesterol; Fat.

Kinds of meat. There are several different types of red meat. The names for meat from cattle and sheep tell the age of the animal from which the meat was taken.

Veal is the flesh of calves less than 14 weeks old. It is light pink and contains little fat. Veal is more tender than beef and has a milder flavor. Meat from calves over 14 weeks old is called *calf.*

Beef is the flesh of full-grown cattle. Most beef sold at stores comes from animals 1 to 2 years old. Beef is bright red and has white fat. Flecks of fat called *marbling* help make beef tasty and juicy.

Lamb is the flesh of sheep less than 1 year old. It is red and has white fat. Lamb has a milder taste than mutton.

Mutton is the flesh of sheep over 1 year old. It has a deep red to purple color. Mutton has a stronger flavor and a coarser texture than lamb.

Pork is the flesh of hogs. Most pork comes from animals from 4 to 7 months old. Pork has a light pink color, with white fat. It has a mild taste. Many cured meats, such as ham and bacon, are made from pork.

Variety meat is the general name for various organs and glands of meat animals. Common variety meats include the brains, hearts, kidneys, livers, and tongues of animals. Some other variety meats are chitterlings (hog large intestines), sweetbreads (pancreas and thymus glands), and tripe (linings of first and second cattle stomachs). Most variety meats are good sources of vitamins and minerals.

Meat is available in fresh, frozen, canned, and cured

Average consumption of various meats

This graph shows the average amounts of various kinds of meat consumed per person in the United States in a year. The amounts are based on the weight of retail cuts of meat.

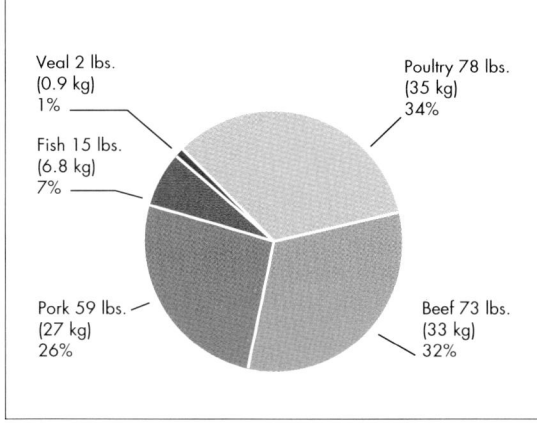

Veal 2 lbs. (0.9 kg) 1%

Fish 15 lbs. (6.8 kg) 7%

Poultry 78 lbs. (35 kg) 34%

Pork 59 lbs. (27 kg) 26%

Beef 73 lbs. (33 kg) 32%

Figures are for 1987. Source: U.S. Department of Agriculture.

forms. Fresh meat is raw meat. Fresh meat spoils quickly and must be refrigerated until it is cooked. People can keep fresh meat from spoiling by freezing it. Frozen meat is also sold in stores. It has the same food value as fresh meat and is often used by restaurants. Frozen meat should be cooked as soon as it thaws and should not be refrozen.

Canned meat has been sealed in a metal can and then heated. The heat cooks the meat and destroys bacteria. Meat is often canned with other ingredients, such as vegetables or gravy. Cured meat, such as ham, bacon, and sausage, has been treated with salt and sodium nitrite to control bacterial growth.

How to select meat. All meat sold in stores is inspected by the U.S. Department of Agriculture (USDA) or by a state inspection service. Meat sold in stores is often graded according to its quality. Meat may be graded on a system used by the USDA, or individual stores may do their own grading. Higher grades of meat are more tender, juicy, and flavorful than lower grades. The grade of a meat is stamped directly on the meat in purple vegetable dye or on the package label.

The USDA grades for beef are prime, choice, select, standard, commercial, utility, cutter, and canner. Prime, the highest and most expensive grade of beef, is mainly sold to restaurants but can sometimes be bought in stores. Choice and select meats are commonly sold in stores. The lower grades of beef are usually used to make processed meat products, such as bologna. Veal and lamb are graded on similar systems ranging from prime (the highest grade) to cull (the lowest grade). Pork is often not graded because it is uniform in quality.

Grading is based on such quality factors as age, marbling, fat, firmness and texture, and color of the meat. Because marbling makes meat more tasty and juicy, good meats will contain more marbling than poor meats. White to creamy-white firm fat is preferable to yellow fat, and a fine meat texture is better than a coarse one.

How meat is cooked. There are two main ways to cook meat: (1) with dry heat and (2) with moist heat. The method is determined by a meat's cut and degree of tenderness. The table *Cuts of meat and how to cook them* with this article lists the best methods for various types of meat.

Dry heat methods include broiling, panbroiling, roasting, panfrying, and deep-fat frying. These methods are best for tender cuts of meat. Broiled (grilled) meat is cooked directly above or below a source of heat. Meat may be broiled on a grill over hot coals or under the heating element of an open oven. In panbroiling, meat is cooked in a pan or griddle over low heat. In roasting (baking), meat is cooked in a shallow pan in an oven. It is best to raise the meat on a rack in the pan so the heat can circulate around the meat. In panfrying, or sautéing, meat is cooked in a small amount of fat over low heat. In deep-fat frying, meat is covered by hot fat.

Moist heat methods, such as braising and cooking in liquid, are best for less tender meats. Moist heat tenderizes meat by softening its connective tissues. In braising, meat is placed in a tightly covered pan at a low temperature. The meat cooks in its own juices or in other liquids that may be added. Simmering and stewing are two ways to cook meat in liquid. Meat is simmered just

How to carve meat

Carving will be easier if you remember a few helpful hints. Allow a large roast to stand for about 30 minutes after it has been taken out of the oven. This will make it easier to cut. Carve across the grain of the meat to prevent stringy slices. To carve neat slices, keep the knife at the same angle while cutting each slice. The directions given on this page and the following page are for right-handed carvers. Left-handed carvers should substitute *left* for *right* and *right* for *left* in the instructions.

Diagrams prepared through the cooperation of the National Live Stock and Meat Board

Pork loin roast
A pork loin roast is easier to carve if you have a butcher cut between the backbone and the ends of the ribs.

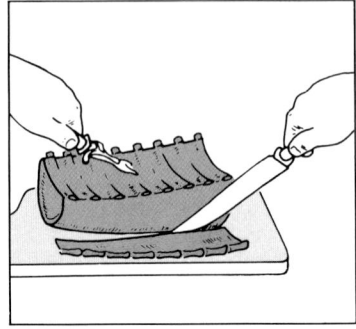 

Remove the backbone before slicing the meat. Use the ribs as a guide to cut off the backbone. If a butcher has already separated the backbone from the ribs, it will be loose and easy to remove.

Slice the meat with the fork inserted firmly in the top of the roast. Cut close to each rib. The size of the loin will determine how many boneless slices you can cut between the ribs.

Roast leg of lamb
The thick, meaty section of a roast leg of lamb is called the *cushion* of the leg. When carving begins, as shown in the first diagram below, the leg should be placed on the platter so that the cushion is turned away from the carver.

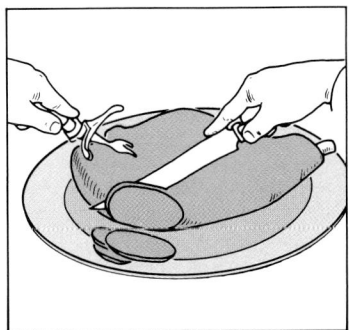 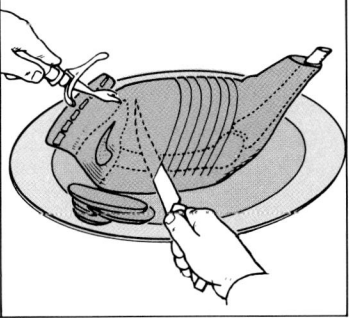 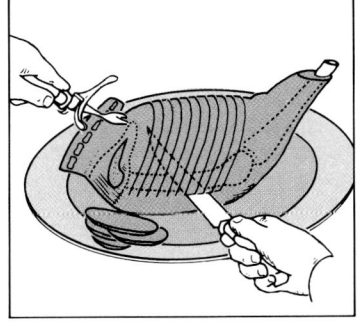

Place the shankbone to your right, keeping the cushion away from you. Insert the fork firmly and carve two or three slices from the thin side of the roast opposite the cushion.

Turn the roast up, so it rests on the surface just cut. Insert the fork at the left of the roast. Starting at the shank end, opposite your fork, make parallel slices down to the bone.

Release all the slices at the same time by running the knife along the leg bone at the bottom of the parallel cuts. The slices can then be lifted off the bone and placed on a platter for serving.

Roast turkey
A roast turkey has both dark meat and white meat. The dark meat comes from the turkey's legs (drumsticks) and thighs. The white meat comes from the turkey's wings and breast. Roast turkey is a popular main course of many holiday meals, and is often carved at the table.

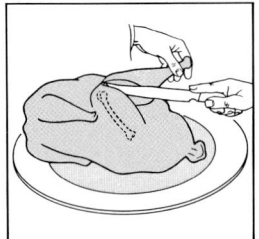 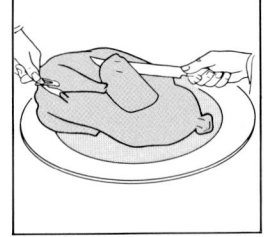 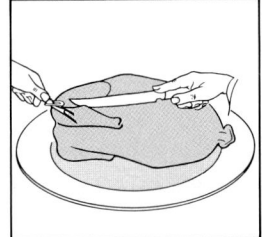 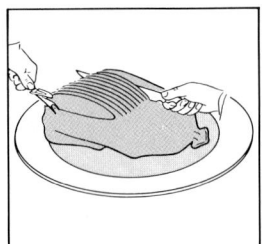

Remove the drumstick by turning the turkey on its side with its breastbone away from you. Pull the end of the drumstick away from you as you cut through the joint.

Carve the thigh next, cutting slices until the bone is exposed. Remove the thighbone by prying it loose with the tip of the knife. Then finish slicing the thigh meat.

For large slices, carve the breast with the grain. Slice until you reach the wing joint. Remove the wing and then slice all the white meat from one side of the breast.

For small slices, carve the breast across the grain. Remove the wing and then cut slices reaching down to the keel bone. Cut across the bone to release the slices.

Blade pot roast   A blade pot roast contains part of the bladebone and part of a rib. The tissue around the bones softens as the meat is cooked, making it easy to remove the bones when the pot roast is carved.

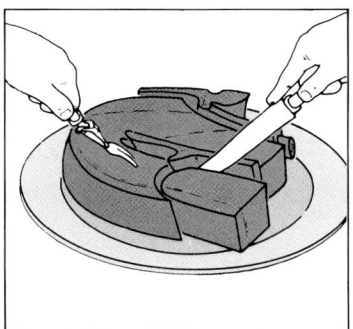
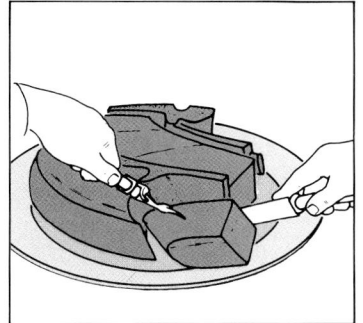
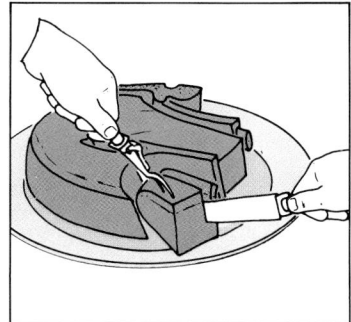

Hold the roast firmly in place with the fork inserted in the top of the meat. Separate a section of the roast by running the knife between two muscles and along the bone, as shown.

Turn the section just separated from the roast so that you can cut across the grain of the meat. Insert the fork firmly in the top of the section to hold the meat in place while it is sliced.

Carve the section by cutting thin slices across the grain. Cut and slice the other sections of the pot roast in the same manner. Remove the bones from the platter before serving.

Standing rib roast   A standing rib roast has at least two and sometimes three ribs. The meat may be cut into thick or thin slices. When carving this large cut of meat, it is helpful to have a second platter nearby to hold the slices of meat you cut from the roast.

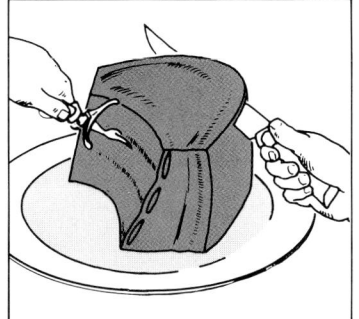

Place the roast on the platter so the small cut surface is up and the ribs are to your left. Insert the fork between the top two ribs. Starting from the outside edge, slice across the grain to the ribs.

Release each slice as it is cut by running the tip of the knife along the edge of the rib. After a slice has been released, remove it from the roast so the next slice can be cut.

Remove each slice by lifting it off the roast with the blade of the knife. Slide the knife under the slice and hold the meat in place with the fork. Then place the slice on a platter for serving.

Other cuts of meat   Many other cuts of meat are popular foods in the United States. Such cuts include beef tongue, half ham, center-cut ham slice, and beef brisket. These cuts are shown in the diagrams below, along with instructions for carving them.

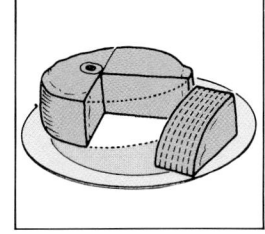

Beef tongue should be carved from the larger to the smaller end in thin, parallel slices. The larger end may have excess tissue that should be trimmed from the meat.

Half ham has a cushion section that can be easily removed and sliced. Separate the other section from the shank and remove the bone. Then slice the boned section.

Center-cut ham slice should be cut into three pieces before it is sliced. Slice each piece across the grain of the meat. Remove the bone before slicing the end piece.

Beef brisket often has excess fat that should be removed before carving. Position the rounded side of the brisket away from you and cut slices from it in rotation as shown.

below the boiling point. In stewing, the meat is slowly boiled in a covered pot or pan.   Larry L. Borchert

Related articles in *World Book* include:

Kinds of meat

Beef	Ham	Mutton	Poultry
Fish	Lamb	Pork	Veal

Other related articles

Cooking	Food	Meat packing

Meat extract is a paste with a highly concentrated meaty flavor. Cooks often flavor soups and sauces with meat extract. Food manufacturers use beef extract or chicken extract in making bouillon cubes. When dissolved in hot liquid, these cubes produce a fragrant broth.

Food manufacturers make meat extract by boiling fresh, lean meat in a vacuum kettle. They boil the meat until it loses nearly all its color and the water turns brown. Then they remove the meat and boil the juice again until most of the liquid has evaporated. As the remaining extract cools, it forms a paste. Meat extract has a yellowish-brown color, and a pleasant, meaty odor and flavor.

Meat extract has little food value, though it does contain some protein and minerals. The meat left after boiling, even though flavorless, usually contains more food value than the extract. To add to the extract's food value, sometimes the boiled meat is ground or powdered and put back in the broth.   Donald H. Beermann

Meat Inspection Act. See **Roosevelt, Theodore** (Domestic problems).

Meat packing is the business of slaughtering cattle, hogs, and sheep, and preparing the meat for transportation and sale. The term *meat packing* comes from the once-common practice of packing highly salted meat in wooden barrels. The American colonists used this technique to preserve meat for storage or for shipment overseas. Today, meat packers use refrigeration as well as smoking, curing, and canning to preserve meat.

Oscar Mayer Foods Corporation
Meat cutters use special knives to carve portions of livestock carcasses into smaller wholesale or retail cuts.

Meat packing is a major industry in many countries. China produces the most *red meat* (meat of cattle, hogs, and sheep). Other leading producers of red meat include Brazil, France, Germany, and the United States.

In the United States alone, the meat-packing industry produces more than 39 billion pounds (17.7 billion kilograms) of meat annually. About 140 million farm animals must be slaughtered yearly to produce this amount of meat. Raising and slaughtering these animals and processing the meat provide jobs for thousands of farmers, ranchers, butchers, and meat packers. About 5,000 meat-packing and processing plants in the United States employ about 225,000 workers.

Marketing of livestock

Kinds of markets. Each weekday, farmers and ranchers in the United States sell about 500,000 meat animals. More than two-thirds of the cattle, hogs, and sheep are sold directly to meat packers, a practice called *direct marketing.* Some livestock owners sell their animals through large trading centers called *terminal markets.* There are about 50 terminal markets in the United States. Stockyards at these markets provide pens, weight scales, and other facilities for handling and selling large numbers of livestock. Farmers and ranchers also sell animals through smaller markets called *auction markets* or *sale barns,* which operate throughout the farming areas of the United States. Animals are shipped to packers or to market by train or truck.

Many meat packers operate slaughterhouses in terminal-market cities. But not all animals shipped to terminal markets are sold and processed in those areas. Some are shipped on to other markets and then sold. Others are bought and shipped on to meat-packing plants in other cities. The nation's largest terminal markets include those in Omaha, Neb.; Sioux Falls, S. Dak.; and South St. Paul, Minn.

Selling livestock. In the direct-marketing process, livestock owners obtain bids from meat packers. The owners get bids by telephone or from a packing company buyer who visits their feedlot or farm. To make sure that the price is satisfactory, owners may listen to market reports on the radio or get price quotations from other meat packers. After a price has been agreed upon, the animals are shipped to the packer's slaughterhouse.

At terminal markets, livestock owners usually sell their animals through a *commission firm.* This firm acts as an agent for the owner. It sells the livestock to a meat packer or other buyer at the highest possible price. The commission firm receives a commission from the livestock owner for this service. The stockyard also charges the owner for the feed and facilities used by the animals.

Livestock buyers determine a price per 100 pounds (45 kilograms), on the basis of live weight. Factors such as age, sex, weight, grade of the animal, and degree of fatness help buyers determine the price they pay. Expert livestock buyers can accurately estimate the meat yield of a live animal. Their estimate seldom varies more than 1 per cent from the actual meat yield after slaughtering and *dressing* (preparing meat for sale).

Packing processes

Meat goes through more than 25 operations before it hangs dressed in packing-house coolers. Skilled workers perform these operations with great speed. Many packing plants slaughter and dress as many as 150 head of cattle or 600 to 1,200 hogs in an hour.

Slaughtering and dressing. Workers use mechanical stunners to make the cattle unconscious, after which the animals are killed and dressed. The carcasses are suspended from an overhead rail for the dressing operation, in which the hide and *viscera* (internal organs) are removed. Workers cut the dressed carcasses into halves, wash them, and move them along the rail to refrigerated rooms. There the carcasses chill to about 35 °F (2 °C) for 12 to 24 hours. Then workers may cut the halves into forequarters and hindquarters.

At wholesale or retail establishments, butchers divide the hindquarter cuts into flank, short loin, sirloin, and round. These cuts make up about half of a dressed beef carcass. The forequarter cuts, the other half, are divided into brisket, chuck, foreshank, rib, and short plate. A choice grade steer that weighs 1,000 pounds (450 kilograms) when alive will yield a carcass of about 600 pounds (270 kilograms).

Calves and lambs are made unconscious by an electric shock. Then workers slaughter and dress them in much the same way as cattle. Packers ship most calves and lambs to wholesalers and retailers as whole carcasses.

Hogs are made unconscious by electricity or gas before they are killed. The carcasses are then scalded and dehaired. The viscera are removed and the carcasses are washed before being cooled overnight in a hog-chill cooler at a temperature of about 35 °F (2 °C). The next day, butchers cut the carcasses into wholesale cuts—hams, shoulders, loins, bellies, spareribs, and other cuts. The cuts are then sent to the shipping room, where they are graded by weight, boxed, and marked for ship-

ment to markets or for further processing.

Lard makes up about 10 per cent of the weight of a dressed hog. Grinding and heating operations *render* (separate) the lard from the protein in the raw fat. The fat around the kidneys may be made into leaf lard, the best grade.

Curing and smoking processes were once used primarily to preserve meat. Today, meat is preserved mainly by refrigeration, though curing and smoking are still important for long-term preservation. Curing and smoking also produce the special flavor of bacon, ham, and other cuts.

Packers cure most meat by pumping a curing solution into the arteries of the meat, or by injecting the solution directly into the meat. The curing solution is made up largely of salt and water, but sugar may be included. Other ingredients, such as sodium nitrate and sodium ascorbate, are usually added to help develop the cherry-red color of cured meat and to preserve the flavor.

Smoking produces the distinctive smoked-meat flavor which consumers demand in certain meats. Modern smokehouses consist of air-conditioned, stainless-steel rooms. Controlled amounts of smoke from special hardwood sawdust are drawn into the rooms. The warm, fragrant smoke gives the meat a unique flavor and color.

Tenderizing. Consumers want tenderness, as well as flavor, in the meat they buy. Less-tender cuts of meat may be ground to tenderize them. For example, ground beef makes up about 30 per cent of all fresh beef consumed in the United States.

In recent years, chemical tenderizers that are enzymes taken from fruits such as pineapple, papaya, and figs have been used by both packers and consumers. When meat is cooked, the heat activates these tenderizers. Consumers buy tenderizers in liquid or powder form.

Sausage making. Packers make more than 200 varieties of sausage, but they use the same basic process to make most varieties. Meat is chopped or ground and mixed with seasonings and curing ingredients. Generally, this mixture is forced into *casings* (long tubes usually made from cellulose or from an animal protein called *collagen*). The casings are tied or twisted at regular intervals to form sausage links. Then the sausage may be smoked, cooked, or dried, depending on the type of sausage being made.

Some sausages are ready to eat. Others require cooking. The most popular is the frankfurter, also called the hot dog or wiener.

By-products

Modern production methods make it possible for meat packers to use much material that was once considered waste. In fact, packers are sometimes credited with using "every part of the pig but the squeal." Livestock producers would get less money for the animals they sell if meat packers depended only upon the sale of meat from the carcass to make a profit.

Manufacturers divide by-products into two classes: (1) edible by-products or variety meats and (2) by-products, such as animal hides, that are not eaten.

The variety meats of cattle include the heart, liver, kidney, tongue, brains, *sweetbreads* (thymus), and *tripe* (first and second stomachs). In addition to variety meats,

Oscar Mayer Foods Corporation

A frankfurter machine stuffs meat into long tubes and shapes the tubes into links at a rate of 36,000 links per hour.

hogs yield edible by-products such as ears, feet, *chitterlings* (small intestines), and lard.

More than a hundred different articles are made as by-products of meat packing. Some of these are listed in a table that appears in this article.

U.S. government inspection

The Wholesome Meat Act of 1967 requires each state to provide inspection equal to federal standards for packers who sell in and have plants in that state. The U.S. Department of Agriculture must impose federal inspection standards on all plants in a state if that state's inspection standards do not equal federal standards. The law also requires that all meat produced in one state and sold in another must be inspected by the U.S. Department of Agriculture.

The inspection process extends through each stage of preparation of meat for sale. Labels used on federally inspected meat products must be approved, and they must give complete and accurate information.

The Department of Agriculture inspects about 90 per cent of all meat produced in the United States. It administers federal laws that control the slaughtering and dressing of animals, and the preparation of meat for sale. It also inspects meat and meat products brought into the United States from abroad and inspects the wholesomeness of meat exported to other countries.

Government inspectors, many of them veterinarians, examine each animal to be certain it is produced under sanitary conditions. They make sure that meat products are wholesome and *unadulterated* (have no improper substances added). Inspectors check the construction, equipment, and sanitation in slaughtering and processing plants. They also inspect plants that make prepared meats such as luncheon meats; frozen meat pies and dinners; and canned and dehydrated soups.

History

Meat packing in the American Colonies began to develop as an industry during the 1640's. Packing houses packed pork in salt for shipment to plantations in the West Indies. The number of packing houses grew as communities developed that did not produce their own meat animals. In most cases, a packing house then served only one small community. When that community's farms failed to produce enough livestock, animals were herded in from other communities.

Before 1850, packing plants operated only during the winter. Many meat-packing plants were connected with icehouses. Workers cut ice from rivers and lakes in winter, and stored it in icehouses for use in warm weather. Meat packing became a year-round business after artificial refrigeration was developed.

However, until the industry developed refrigerated railway cars, packing plants had trouble keeping meat fresh during the time needed to ship it to big Eastern cities. By the 1880's, meat packers had perfected refrigerated railway cars. In the early 1900's, inventor Frederick McKinley Jones developed a refrigeration process that could be used in trucks.

Modern meat packing also began during this period when packers perfected assembly line production methods. In 1890, Congress passed a meat inspection law for meats to be exported. In 1906, a law was passed providing for federal inspection of meats shipped in interstate commerce.

Recent developments. Since 1945, several hundred meat-packing plants have been built in towns and cities close to the farms and ranches where livestock are raised. Companies have lowered their transportation costs by building packing plants where livestock are raised. Many plants which make prepared foods have been built in and near big cities. These plants supply the processed meats that are sold in neighborhood supermarkets, butcher shops, and grocery stores.

Since the 1950's, the increased use of machinery has helped speed up meat-packing operations. Mechanical developments include continuous-process, frankfurter-making machines; semiautomatic slicing and weighing systems for packaged bacon; and mechanical knives and

Animal by-products

Blood		Fats and oils	
Adhesives	Plaster retardants	Antifreeze	Leather dressing
Animal feed	Plastics	Candies	Medicinal capsules
Leather preparations	Textile sizing	Candles	Nitroglycerin
Pharmaceuticals		Cellophane	Ointments
		Chewing gum	Paints
Bones, horns, and hoofs		Cosmetics	Plastics
Bone china	Ornaments and novelties	Detergents	Shortenings
Bone meal	(such as combs, buttons,	Food preservatives	Soap
Gelatin	and umbrella handles)	Frozen desserts	Solvents
Glue		Illuminating and	Synthetic rubber
		industrial oils	Tar
Hair		Insecticides	Weedkillers
Air filters	Felt padding	Rug pads	Lard	
Brushes	Plastering materials	Upholstery		

Hide		
Athletic equipment	Furniture	Luggage
Belting	Gelatin	Shoes and soles
Chamois	Glue	Wallets and pocketbooks
Drumheads	Harnesses	Wearing apparel
Fertilizer	Jewelry	

Organs, glands, and viscera (for medical use)		
ACTH	Growth hormone	Progesterone
Bile salts	Heart valves	Rennet
Cortisone	Heparin	Surgical sutures
Epinephrine	Insulin	Thyroid extract
(adrenalin)	Liver extract	Vasopressin
Glucagon	Pepsin	

saws. Mechanically refrigerated trucks and railroad cars have eliminated the need for ice and salt to preserve meat that is shipped long distances. Most meat packers now use computers in their production operations.

Trends in new product development include more prepackaging of retail meat items containing recipes and detailed cooking instructions, and more precooked meat products. Many meat packers offer the consumer canned meats—hams, luncheon meats, sandwich spreads, and combination dishes that consumers can store easily and serve quickly. Nearly all meat is sold in prepackaged form. Much of the meat is boned, shaped, and ready for cooking. New methods of breeding and feeding have produced younger animals of the desired market weight and quality. As a result, meat is leaner and more tender.   Joseph G. Sebranek

Related articles in *World Book* include:

Armour, Philip D.	Lamb	Soybean (How
Bacon	Meat	soybeans are
Beef	Meat extract	used)
Cudahy, Michael	Mutton	Suet
Fat	Pork	Sweetbread
Food	Pure food	Swift, Gustavus F.
preservation	and drug laws	Tripe
Ham	Sausage	Veal

Mecca, *MEHK uh* (pop. 463,000), is the holiest city of Islam, the religion of the Muslims. It lies in western Saudi Arabia in a dry, barren valley that is surrounded by desolate hills and mountains. For the location of Mecca, see **Saudi Arabia** (political map). The city is the birthplace of Muhammad, the prophet of Islam. Mecca is also the site of the *Kaaba,* the shrine that Muslims face when they pray.

Only Muslims may enter Mecca, which Islam considers to be a sacred city. Islam requires every Muslim to make the *hajj* (a pilgrimage to Mecca) at least once if he or she is able to do so (see **Hajj**).

The city. The Great Mosque, the center of worship for all Muslims, stands in the heart of Mecca. The outside of the mosque consists of an *arcade,* a series of arches supported by pillars. The arcade encloses a courtyard that measures about 600 by 800 feet (180 by 240 meters). The Kaaba, a cube-shaped stone building, is located in this open area. The Kaaba contains the Black Stone, which Muslims believe was sent from heaven by Allah (God).

In the 1950's, the Saudi government began a program to modernize Mecca. This program included the construction of tall, modern hotels for pilgrims. The government also added lighting and other facilities, built better roads, and increased the health and security services of the community. Modern houses replaced a large number of traditional dwellings. New suburbs were also built, and many wealthy Meccans moved to those areas. Mecca is the home of the Saudi Arabian Institute for Higher Education and of one of Saudi Arabia's royal palaces.

People. In the past, many Muslims who came to Mecca on the hajj settled there later. The city's population became a mixture of various nationalities. But since the 1930's, the government has strongly discouraged immigration to Mecca because it wants to preserve jobs in the area for people of Saudi Arabia.

Economy of Mecca depends on money spent by pilgrims. A hajj must be made between the 8th and 13th

Keystone

The Great Mosque in Mecca is the center of worship for all Muslims. The Kaaba, Islam's most sacred shrine, stands in the mosque's courtyard. More than a million Muslims make a pilgrimage to the Great Mosque annually.

day of the last month of the Muslim year. About $1\frac{1}{4}$ million pilgrims crowd into Mecca within those few days. About half of them come from other countries. The city takes in more than $100 million during the annual great pilgrimage. The Saudi government spends almost $50 million yearly to provide health care, security, and other services for pilgrims.

Mecca has some minor industries. For example, a factory makes products from clay. But the city no longer plays a major part in Saudi Arabia's economy, which has been based on oil exports since the late 1940's.

History. Mecca became a trading center about A.D. 400. The people of Mecca worshiped many gods, whose idols stood at the Kaaba. Muhammad was born in the city about 570.

The Meccans rejected Muhammad's religious teachings, and he and his disciples fled from the city in 622. Eight years later, Muhammad and his followers captured Mecca and destroyed the idols. They spared the Kaaba, which has remained as the Muslim shrine.

Mecca became the heart of the first Arab-Islamic empire. The city's political importance declined during the mid-600's, when Muslim conquests spread through distant lands. But Mecca kept its importance as the religious center of Islam.

A series of *sharifs* (descendants of Muhammad) ruled Mecca from 960 until 1924. That year, Abd al-Aziz ibn Saud, an Arab leader, conquered the city. Mecca became part of his kingdom, which he named Saudi Arabia in 1932. Beginning in the 1950's, the Saudi Arabian government has worked to modernize Mecca and to ensure the comfort and safety of pilgrims to the city. During the 1970's and 1980's, Mecca experienced major population growth as many rural people moved there.

Malcolm C. Peck

See also **Kaaba; Muhammad; Saudi Arabia.**

Mechanical drawing, also called *technical drawing,* refers chiefly to a drawing produced with instruments. However, some mechanical drawings are made freehand. Drafters make mechanical drawings to show exactly how to construct or use machines, buildings, or other objects. No ship, airplane, automobile, bridge, dam, engine, or any of the tools of industry could be made without such drawings. The father of modern drawing was the Italian artist Leonardo da Vinci. He practiced and taught a method of drawing that recorded ideas about mechanical objects and systems.

Mechanical drawings do not show objects as they appear in photographs because photographs do not indicate true dimensions. Instead, a mechanical drawing shows as many views of an object as may be necessary to define its exact shape and size. The most common method is called *orthographic,* or right-angle, projection. This presents views of an object as seen from the

Mechanical drawing

Drafters prepare mechanical drawings to provide technical information. Unlike a photograph or a perspective drawing, a mechanical drawing presents various views of an object to define its dimensions. Common drafting methods include *orthographic projection* and *isometric drawing.*

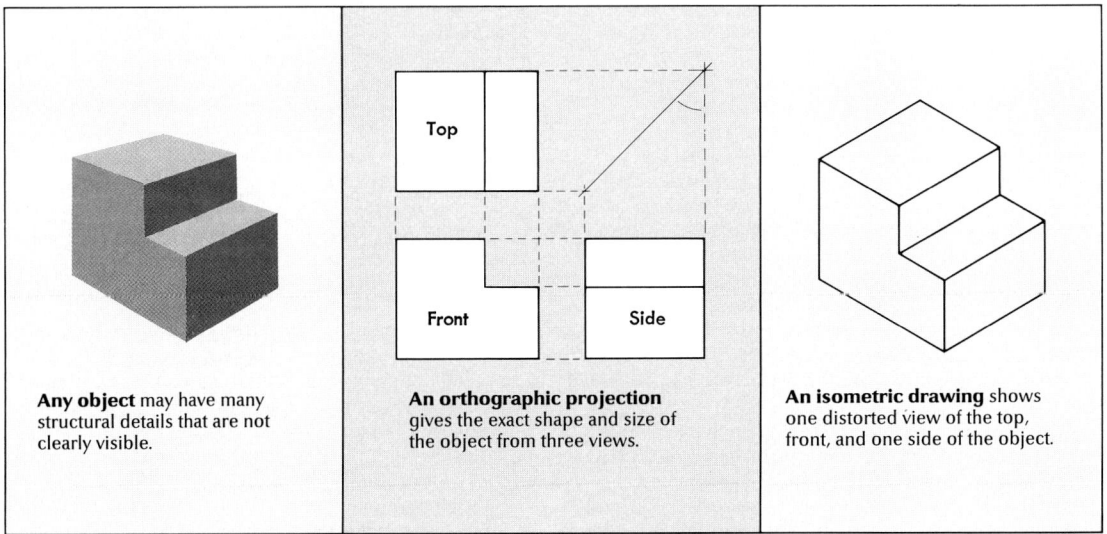

Any object may have many structural details that are not clearly visible.

An orthographic projection gives the exact shape and size of the object from three views.

Top

Front   Side

An isometric drawing shows one distorted view of the top, front, and one side of the object.

WORLD BOOK diagrams

Rich Franzon, Artstreet

Mechanical drawing requires skill and attention to detail. A drafter uses a variety of instruments to create a drawing that indicates the exact shape and size of an object.

WORLD BOOK photo by Steinkamp/Ballogg

A drafting machine, such as the one shown above, combines several drawing tools—a protractor, scale, T square, and triangle. The device helps a drafter work quickly and efficiently.

front, side, and above. Another method, called *isometric* drawing, gives a distorted view of the front, top, and one side of an object.

Materials needed. A simple set of instruments to make mechanical drawings consists of a drawing board, a scale, a T square, triangles, a compass, drafting tape, drawing pencils, an eraser, and drafting paper. Curves, inking pens, dividers, protractors, a ruler, and blueprinting or other copying machines may also be used. A device called a *drafting machine* is a combination of several drawing tools. Much of the mechanical drawing that is done today is accomplished by using computer-aided design and drafting.

Career opportunities. Mechanical drawing is exacting work, and expert drafters are in great demand. Courses are taught in high schools, technical institutes, and colleges. Engineers who wish to concentrate on design must have a good background in drafting and be familiar with mathematics, physics, chemistry, mechanics, thermodynamics, and projection. A knowledge of certain shop practices is also important. Todd I. Blue

See also **Blueprint; Pantograph; Protractor.**

Mechanical engineering. See Engineering (The branches of engineering).

Mechanics is a science that studies the effects of forces on solids, liquids, and gases at rest or in motion. Engineers use mechanics to determine stresses and deformations in machine parts, such as gear teeth, and in structural elements, such as support columns. The principles of mechanics are used by engineers to design products that range in size from tiny computer parts to huge dams; by astronomers to predict the motion of stars, planets, and other celestial bodies; and by physicists to study the motion of atomic particles.

Mechanics can be divided into two branches—statics and dynamics. *Statics* studies bodies at rest, or in motion at a constant speed and in a constant direction. *Dynamics* is the study of bodies that undergo a change of speed or direction, or both, because of forces acting upon them.

Solid mechanics is the study of the motions of rigid bodies and deformable solid bodies, and of the forces that cause such motions. *Continuum mechanics* deals with deformable bodies. Deformable bodies are gases, liquids, and deformable solids. Areas of specialization in continuum mechanics include *theory of elasticity,* the study of the reversible deformation of solids; *theory of plasticity,* the study of the permanent deformation of solids; *fluid dynamics,* the study of fluids in motion; *aerodynamics,* the study of gases in motion around a body; and *hydraulics,* the study of liquids at rest or in motion. James D. Chalupnik

See also **Aerodynamics; Dynamics; Hydraulics; Statics.**

Mechanic's lien. See Lien.

Mechanist philosophy, *MEHK uh nihst,* states that physical phenomena must be explained in terms of laws of cause and effect that describe the motion of matter. Mechanist philosophers believe that all of nature can be understood by describing the size, shape, arrangement, and motion of small particles of matter called *atoms* or *corpuscles.* Many mechanists characterize their philosophy as the claim that the world is like a gigantic machine. Just as the interaction of cogs, springs, and

wheels makes a machine work, so the interaction of tiny corpuscles or atoms ultimately causes all the different phenomena in nature.

Mechanism is opposed to the philosophical doctrine of *teleology.* Teleology comes from the Greek word *teleos,* meaning *goal* or *end.* A teleological theory seeks to understand physical phenomena in terms of purposes. For example, these two philosophies would give different answers to the question, "Why does fire travel upward?" A mechanist would explain that the atoms or corpuscles making up the fire collide, bouncing one another upward according to the laws of impact. The teleological answer would be that it is the nature of fire to blaze upward in search of its natural place above the earth.

During the 1600's, Thomas Hobbes and John Locke in England and René Descartes in France developed influential mechanistic philosophies as a reaction against teleology. During this time, mechanistic philosophy became an important part of the Scientific Revolution. But in the 1800's, physicists began to realize that mechanism was inadequate to explain such phenomena as electricity and magnetism. Thus, the original mechanistic goal of explaining all of nature in terms of matter and motion had to be abandoned. Douglas M. Jesseph

See also **Descartes, René; Hobbes, Thomas; Locke, John; Philosophy** (Metaphysics; Modern philosophy).

Mecoptera. See Insect (table).

Medals, decorations, and orders are honors that are awarded to people for bravery or merit. These honors are generally given by a monarch or head of state. People granted such honors receive a badge that may be worn or displayed. In most cases, the badges are suspended from a ribbon. The designs and colors of the ribbon usually symbolize the national colors of a country or such characteristics as virtue or bravery.

Medals are usually round and bear the likeness of a head of state or other symbol surrounded by an inscription. Most medals are made of gold, silver, or bronze. Medals generally hang from a ribbon. Medals are usually presented for participation in a campaign, long service, or good conduct. An example of a medal is the United States Navy Civil War campaign medal.

Decorations are usually in the shape of a cross or star, suspended from a ribbon. They are usually given in wartime for a single act of outstanding gallantry. In the military, decorations are generally more important than medals. The Victoria Cross of Great Britain is an example of a decoration.

Orders have a variety of shapes, but stars and crosses are used most frequently. The most common type of cross is the *Maltese cross.* Its four arms have V-shaped ends. Traditionally, orders have been exclusive societies with a limited membership determined by the head of state. In countries where orders exist, membership in an order is generally considered the highest possible degree of honor. The United States and Switzerland are among the few countries that do not have orders. The French Legion of Honor is an example of an order.

United States medals and decorations

Military awards. During the late 1700's and early 1800's, the idea of medals and decorations was unpopu-

Medals and decorations of the United States

WORLD BOOK photos unless otherwise credited

Medal of Honor
(Army)

Medal of Honor
(Air Force)

Medal of Honor
(Navy)

Distinguished Service Cross

Army   Navy Cross   Air Force Cross

Distinguished Service Medal

Air Force   Army   Navy   Defense

U.S. Army

Silver Star

Legion of Merit
(Chief Commander)

Distinguished
Flying Cross

Purple Heart

Young American
Medal for Bravery

Presidential
Medal
of Freedom

Congressional Space
Medal of Honor

NASA

lar in the United States because it was associated with customs of the European upper classes. As a result, no general system of military medals or decorations was organized until the Civil War. However, a few individual awards were granted during the Revolutionary War.

George Washington received the first American medal. In 1776, Congress gave him a gold medal for forcing the British to abandon Boston.

In 1782, Washington established the Purple Heart, formally called the Badge of Military Merit. This badge,

United States military medals and decorations

Name of medal	Year established	People eligible	Awarded for
Medal of Honor	1861 (Navy)	All ranks	Gallantry in action
	1862 (Army)	All ranks	Gallantry in action
	1963 (Air Force)	All ranks	Gallantry in action
Distinguished Service Cross (Army)	1918	All ranks	Exceptional heroism in combat
Navy Cross	1919	All ranks	Exceptional heroism in combat
Air Force Cross	1960	All ranks	Exceptional heroism in combat
Distinguished Service Medal	1918 (Army)	High-ranking officers	Exceptional meritorious service
	1919 (Navy)	High-ranking officers	Exceptional meritorious service
	1949 (Coast Guard)	High-ranking officers	Exceptional meritorious service
	1960 (Air Force)	High-ranking officers	Exceptional meritorious service
	1970 (Defense)	High-ranking officers assigned to the Department of Defense	Distinguished service
Silver Star (citation)	1918	All ranks of the armed forces	Gallantry in action
(medal)	1932	All ranks of the armed forces	Gallantry in action
Legion of Merit	1942	Normally to officers or high foreign officials	Exceptionally meritorious service in peace or war
Distinguished Flying Cross	1926	All ranks of the armed forces	Heroism or extraordinary achievement in flight
Soldier's Medal	1926	All ranks of the Army	Heroism not involving conflict with the enemy
Navy and Marine Corps Medal	1942	All ranks of the Navy or Marine Corps	Heroism not involving conflict with the enemy
Airman's Medal	1960	All ranks of the Air Force	Heroism not involving conflict with the enemy
Coast Guard Medal	1951	Any person serving with the Coast Guard	Heroism not involving conflict with the enemy
Bronze Star	1944	All ranks of the armed forces	Heroic or meritorious achievement during military operations
Air Medal	1942	All ranks of the armed forces	Meritorious achievement in flight
Commendation Medal	1944 (Navy)	All ranks	Meritorious service in war or peace
	1945 (Army)	All ranks	Meritorious service in war or peace
	1947 (Coast Guard)	All ranks	Meritorious service in war or peace
	1958 (Air Force)	All ranks	Meritorious service in war or peace
Purple Heart (original)	1782	All ranks of the armed forces	Wounds or death in combat
(modern)	1932 (Army)	All ranks of the armed forces	Wounds or death in combat
	1942 (Navy)	All ranks of the armed forces	Wounds or death in combat

United States civilian medals and decorations

Presidential Medal of Freedom	1963	U.S. citizens	Nation's highest civilian honor for exceptional merit toward national security, world peace, culture, or other public service
Presidential Citizens Medal	1969	U.S. citizens	Exemplary deeds of service
Gold and Silver Lifesaving Medals	1874	Any person	Lifesaving in maritime waters at personal risk of life
National Security Medal	1953	Any person	Distinguished contribution to the U.S. national intelligence effort
President's Award for Distinguished Federal Civilian Service	1957	Federal employees	Outstanding service
Young American Medal for Bravery	1950	U.S. citizens under 19	Exceptional courage in lifesaving
Young American Medal for Service	1950	U.S. citizens under 19	Outstanding service
Congressional Space Medal of Honor	1969	Astronauts	Exceptional meritorious contribution to national welfare
National Aeronautics and Space Administration Distinguished Service Medal	1959	Federal employees	Contributions to aeronautical or space exploration

which consisted of a heart made of purple cloth, was awarded to Revolutionary War soldiers for unusual bravery. The modern Purple Heart, established in 1932, is given to members of the armed forces who have been wounded or killed in action.

During the Civil War, Congress authorized the first permanent U.S. military medal or decoration—the Medal of Honor. Today this award, often called the Congressional Medal of Honor, is the highest military decoration that the United States grants to members of its armed forces. Congress approved the Navy Medal of Honor in 1861, and the Army Medal of Honor in 1862. Originally, the Army Medal of Honor was awarded only to noncommissioned officers and privates. Beginning in 1863, this honor was also given to officers. The Air Force Medal of Honor was approved by Congress in 1963. Before then, Air Force personnel received the Army Medal of Honor because the Air Force was originally a division of the Army.

Campaign medals, also known as war service medals, have been awarded to all ranks of the military for service in every war fought by the United States from the Civil War to the present. The first campaign medal approved by Congress was the Manila Bay Medal, also called the Dewey Medal. This medal was awarded in 1898 to members of the Navy and Marine Corps who took part in the battle of Manila Bay during the Spanish-American War. The U.S. War Department authorized the Army Civil War Campaign Medal in 1907—42 years after the conflict ended.

Civilian awards. Congress established the gold and silver Treasury Department Lifesaving Medals in 1874. They are awarded by the Coast Guard for extreme and heroic daring in rescue at sea.

In 1904, Andrew Carnegie established the Carnegie Hero Fund Commission. The commission provides awards in North America and Western Europe for saving or attempting to save lives. Carnegie Medals have been awarded in gold, silver, and bronze.

The Department of Justice awards the Young American Medal for Bravery and the Young American Medal for Service. Only two of each of these medals can be awarded each year. They are given to young people under the age of 19.

The National Aeronautics and Space Administration (NASA) awards the Distinguished Service Medal to astronauts or any other federal employees who have made a great contribution to aeronautical or space exploration. Astronauts are also eligible for the Congressional Space Medal of Honor.

The Presidential Citizens Medal is occasionally awarded to distinguished United States citizens. Recipi-

Medals and decorations of other countries

WORLD BOOK photos

Order of Canada
Canadian Government House

Order of Merit of the Italian Republic (Italy)

Grand Cordon of the Supreme Order of the Chrysanthemum (Japan)

Consulate General of Japan, New York

Legion of Honor (France)

Iron Cross (Germany)

Order of the Aztec Eagle (Mexico)

Order of the Seraphim (Sweden)
© Alexis Daflos, Kungl. Husgerådskammaren

Victoria Cross (Great Britain)

ents of the medal have included composer Irving Berlin and comedian Bob Hope. Congress awards the Medal for Merit to United States and foreign civilians who perform distinguished service in wartime. Another medal, the Presidential Medal of Freedom, is the nation's highest civilian honor. It is awarded by the President for outstanding service.

Other awards. Most of the states give members of their National Guard medals and decorations that resemble federal military awards. In addition, some cities, schools, associations, and foundations award decorations.

The Constitution forbids U.S. citizens who work for the federal government to accept foreign decorations without the consent of Congress. Congress has passed special laws authorizing specified people to accept decorations awarded by another country.

Foreign orders and decorations

Medals and decorations are awarded by nearly every country in the world. Most nations have national orders of merit. The highest awards for valor or service in some countries are the grand orders of knighthood. New systems of awards have developed as kingdoms have been replaced by other forms of government. Many former colonies that are now independent also have set up their own systems of awards.

The Americas. Mexico awards the Order of the Aztec Eagle to foreigners who have given distinguished service to Mexico. Bolivia's highest award is the National Order of the Condor of the Andes. It is given to foreigners and Bolivian citizens for exceptional civil or military merit. Peru awards the Order of the Sun of Peru to Peruvians and foreigners for distinguished service in civilian or military affairs. The Order of the Sun of Peru was established in 1821.

Europe. The Victoria Cross ranks as the highest honor in Great Britain. Queen Victoria instituted this award in 1856. It is usually given to members of the military for a single act of extreme heroism. Britain's Royal Humane Society is probably the world's best-known lifesaving society. Each year, this society grants more than

Medals, decorations, and orders of some other countries

Country	Name of award	Year established	People eligible	Awarded for
Belgium	**Order of Leopold**	1832	Belgians and citizens of other countries	General civilian and military merit
Brazil	**National Order of the Southern Cross**	1822	Citizens of other countries	Civil or military merit
British Commonwealth	**Victoria Cross**	1856	All ranks of the armed forces	Conspicuous bravery in action
	George Cross	1940	Civilians and military	Conspicuous bravery
Canada	**Order of Canada**	1967	Canadian citizens	Outstanding achievement in any field
Chad	**National Order of Chad**	1960	Chadians	Distinguished service to Chad
China	**Order of Socialist Labor**	1949	Chinese Communists	Distinguished service to China
Denmark	**Order of the Dannebrog**	1219; revived 1671	Danes and foreigners	General merit
France	**Legion of Honor**	1802	French citizens and citizens of other countries	General merit
Gabon	**Order of the Equatorial Star**	1959	All people over 29 years old	Contributions to the work of Gabon; acts of courage or devotion to duty
Germany	**Iron Cross**	1813	German and allied military	Exceptional bravery in combat and outstanding leadership of troops
Great Britain	**Order of the Garter**	1348	Sovereign and 26 knights	Service to the British monarch
Greece	**Order of the Redeemer**	1829	Greeks and citizens of other countries	General merit
Israel	**Hero of Israel**	1949	Military personnel	Gallantry in combat
Italy	**Order of Merit of the Italian Republic**	1951	Italian citizens and foreigners	Outstanding service to Italy
Japan	**Supreme Order of the Chrysanthemum**	1876 or 1877	Japanese male royalty and heads of state	Great service to the emperor
Mexico	**Order of the Aztec Eagle**	1933	Foreign heads of state, diplomats, and distinguished foreigners	Distinguished service to Mexico or to humanity
Nepal	**Order of Mahendra-Mala**	1961	Foreign monarchs	Service to Nepal
Pakistan	**Sign of Haider**	1958	Pakistani military	Acts of great heroism in action
Philippines	**Ancient Order of Sikatuna**	1951	Philippine and foreign diplomats and heads of state	Outstanding achievement
Somalia	**Order of the Somali Star**	1960	All people	Outstanding civil or military merit
Sweden	**Order of the Seraphim**	1748	Royalty and heads of state	Service to humanity
Syria	**Order of the Omayyad**	1924	All people	Outstanding civil or military merit
Turkey	**Independence Medal**	1924	Turkish citizens	Outstanding contribution to the formation of the Turkish Republic
The Vatican	**Order of Pius**	1847	Distinguished Roman Catholics	Personal service to the pope

50 medals for lifesaving. France's highest award is the Legion of Honor. This award was instituted by Emperor Napoleon I in 1802. It is given to foreigners and French citizens for gallantry or civil achievement. The Legion of Honor was the first order based solely on merit and was open to all citizens. One of the oldest European awards is Denmark's Order of the Dannebrog. It was established in 1219 and revived in 1671. It is given to Danes and foreigners for distinguished service in civilian and military affairs.

Middle East. Lebanon gives the National Order of the Cedar to foreigners and to Lebanese for exceptional service or for acts of extreme courage. Egypt's highest award is the Order of the Nile. This award is given to Egyptian citizens and foreigners for distinguished military or civilian service. Israel gives the Medal for Valour to members of the Israeli military who have performed acts of supreme heroism. Gabon awards the Order of the Equatorial Star for acts of courage or devotion to duty and for contributions to the work of the country.

Africa. Kenya awards the Order of the Golden Heart of Kenya to citizens of Kenya and foreigners who have performed exceptional service to the country. Morocco's highest award is the Order of Muhammad. The Order of Muhammad award is given to members of the royal family, foreign heads of state, and civil and military leaders for exceptional service to Morocco. Malawi gives the Order of the Lion of Malawi to foreigners and citizens of Malawi who have performed distinguished and outstanding service to Malawi. The Order of the Pioneers of Liberia is Liberia's award for exceptional service to Liberia in the arts, science, or government, as well as for heroism.

Australia and Asia. Australia's highest award is the Order of Australia. It is given to Australians and foreigners for outstanding civil or military merit. India awards the Bharat Ratna (Jewel of India) to Indian citizens who have done exceptional work in art, literature, science, or public service. Thailand's greatest honor is the Most Illustrious Order of the Royal House of Chakri. Membership is limited to 43 people who have performed outstanding service to Thailand. The Supreme Order of the Chrysanthemum is Japan's highest award. This award is given to Japanese royalty, nobility, and foreign heads of state (male only). The Supreme Order of the Chrysanthemum was established in 1876 or 1877.

History

Since the beginning of history, monarchs and heads of state have rewarded individuals for bravery and merit. The ancient Greeks rewarded military and athletic heroes with wreaths made of laurel leaves. The tradition of the laurel wreath has had a lasting influence. Today, many medals have an image of a laurel wreath surrounding an inscription or the *bust* (sculpted head) of a head of state.

The ancient Romans crowned their heroes with gold laurel wreaths. Gold collars, chains, medallions, and arm rings were also awarded for outstanding bravery. The most significant award was the *phalera,* a gold or silver disk formed into the head of a god, man, or animal. These awards were given for bravery in battle and represented an early stage in the development of breast stars and chest decorations.

Knights of the Middle Ages formed orders. Each order created a distinctive badge that displayed the symbol of the order. A knight wore the badge on a chain around his neck. Knights also received medals of gold, silver, or bronze. These round medals were meant to be displayed on a table, not worn.

The first ribboned medals, similar to today's medals, appeared in Austria and Russia during the 1600's. Most of these types of medals celebrated participation in famous battles, and they were generally awarded only to military officers.

By the mid-1800's, almost every country in Europe had at least one national order for merit. Orders were created to reward merit in many fields, including the arts, science, and agriculture, as well as for military and civil merit. During the last half of the 1800's, trade and the expansion of colonial empires led much of the rest of the world to adopt awards systems based on those of Western Europe.   J. Robert Elliott

See also **Knighthood, Orders of** (picture: Some symbols of leading orders of knighthood).

Additional resources

Borthick, David, and Britton, J. L. *Medals, Military and Civilian of the United States.* MCN Pr., 1984.
Gaylor, John. *Military Badge Collecting.* 3rd ed. Secker & Warburg, 1983.
Kerrigan, Evans E. *American Medals and Decorations.* Mallard Pr., 1990.
Werlich, Robert. *Orders and Decorations of All Nations: Ancient and Modern, Civil and Military.* 2nd ed. Quaker Pr., 1974.

Medan, *may DAHN* (pop. 1,715,670), is a city on the island of Sumatra, Indonesia. It is a commercial center for a forested and agricultural area. Its products include rubber, tobacco, palm oil, tea, and fibers.

Medea, *mih DEE uh,* was a woman in Greek mythology who had magical powers. She helped the hero Jason capture the Golden Fleece, the famous golden wool of a flying ram.

Medea was the daughter of Aites, the king of Colchis. The Golden Fleece hung in a grove of trees there, guarded by a dragon that never slept. Medea fell in love with Jason when he and his companions, the Argonauts, came to Colchis to capture the fleece. She put a spell on the dragon so Jason could take the fleece.

Medea and her brother, Apsyrtos, sailed from Colchis with Jason and the Argonauts. When Aites tried to overtake them, Medea killed Apsyrtos and cut him into little pieces, which she threw into the water. The king stopped to recover the pieces of his son's body, and Jason and Medea escaped.

The expedition traveled to Iolkos, the Greek city where Jason had been born. There, Medea plotted against King Pelias, who had seized the throne of Iolkos from Jason's father. She told the king's daughters that she had a magic charm to make the king young again. However, Medea withheld the correct ingredients. The daughters tried the magic on the king, and he died. The king's son forced Jason and Medea to flee, and they settled in the city of Corinth.

Jason and Medea had two children and lived happily in Corinth for 10 years. But then Jason fell in love with Glauke, also called Creusa, the daughter of the king of Corinth. He left Medea and prepared to marry Glauke. Medea gave her rival a magic robe that burned Glauke to death when she put it on. Medea then killed the two sons she had by Jason and fled to Athens.

Medea lived with Aegeus, the king of Athens, and they had a son named Medus. When the king's first son, Theseus, came to Athens, Medea feared he would replace Medus as the heir to the Athenian throne. She tried to poison Theseus, but Aegeus learned about the plot and banished Medea. Medea returned to Colchis, where she lived the rest of her life.

Medea is the central character in tragedies by the ancient Greek playwright Euripides and the Roman author Seneca. Her story is also told in *Médée* (1635) by Pierre Corneille of France and in *Medea* (1946) by the American poet Robinson Jeffers. C. Scott Littleton

See also **Argonauts; Golden fleece; Jason.**

Medeiros, *may DAY rohs,* **Humberto S. Cardinal** (1915-1983), was appointed a cardinal of the Roman Catholic Church by Pope Paul VI in 1973. Medeiros was born on São Miguel Island in the Azores. He emigrated to the United States in 1931 and became a U.S. citizen in 1940. Medeiros was ordained a priest in 1946. In 1966, he was ordained a bishop and became bishop of Brownsville, Tex. He became known for his support of Mexican-American farmworkers who were campaigning for higher wages. Medeiros was named archbishop of Boston in 1970. Kenneth Guentert

Medellín, *meh deh YEEN* (pop. 1,468,089), is the second largest city of Colombia. Only Bogotá has more people. Medellín is located in northwestern Colombia, nearly 5,000 feet (1,500 meters) above sea level in a lovely valley east of the Cauca River. For location, see **Colombia** (map). Medellín is a center of Colombia's industrial activity. Factories there produce most of the country's textiles, as well as large amounts of clothing, processed food, agricultural machinery, glass and chinaware, paints, and chemicals. Medellín has four universities. Residential neighborhoods and modern industrial parks surround the city.

Medellín was founded in 1675 near important gold fields. Later, the area became noted for its coffee production. Medellín is a chief center for illegal drug trade in Colombia. Beginning in the 1980's, fighting between drug dealers and police took place in the city. For more information, see **Colombia** (Colombia today).

William J. Smole

Media, *MEE dee uh,* was an ancient country in what is now Northern Iran. It became the center of a large empire in the 500's B.C. Media was the homeland of the Medes, a nomadic people. The Medes settled in Media in the 900's B.C. and then moved slowly southward.

Scholars have traced the recorded history of the Medes back to 836 B.C., when the Assyrians under King Shalmaneser III invaded Media. This was the first of

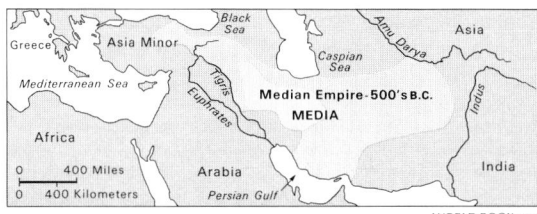

Location of Media

many Assyrian invasions of Media. The Medes reached the peak of their power under Cyaxares, who reigned from 625 to 585 B.C. Cyaxares defeated Assyria and built an empire that included parts of what are now Turkey, Iran, Afghanistan, and Pakistan. Astyages, the son of Cyaxares and the last Median king, was defeated by Cyrus the Great of Persia about 550 B.C. Cyrus incorporated Median lands into the Persian Empire and made Media a Persian province. Jacob J. Finkelstein

Media. See **Advertising** (Ways of advertising); **Magazine; Newspaper; Radio; Television.**

Median, *MEE dee uhn,* in statistics, is the middle value in a group of numbers arranged in numerical order. Suppose five students receive test scores of 62, 84, 99, 77, and 88. To find the median of these scores, arrange them in numerical order: 62, 77, 84, 88, and 99. The number in the middle is now 84. The *median* of this group is 84, and the *median score* is 84. The *arithmetic average* or *mean score* is 82. If the number of cases is even, there will be no number in the middle. In such instances, the median is the average of the two middle values. If the median mark on a test is 84, we know that just as many students received marks above 84 as marks below 84. Doris F. Hertsgaard

See also **Average; Mean; Mode; Statistics.**

Mediation. See **Labor movement** (Handling labor disputes); **National Mediation Board.**

Medic Alert is a metal emblem that identifies its wearer as someone who has a certain medical problem. Such a problem may be a drug allergy, diabetes, heart disease, or some other condition that a doctor should know about before giving medical treatment. For example, people with severe allergies may become seriously ill or die if they take certain drugs. Such people might someday require emergency care while unconscious. If they wear a Medic Alert emblem that identifies their problem, the doctor will not give them the drugs.

The emblems are provided in the form of necklaces or bracelets by the Medic Alert Foundation International, a nonprofit organization. The symbol of the medical profession and the words *Medic Alert* appear on the front of each emblem. On the reverse side are engraved the name of the individual's medical problem, his or her membership number in the foundation, and the foundation's telephone number. The doctor or other medical workers attending the patient in an emergency can call the foundation collect for further information about the patient.

Critically reviewed by the Medic Alert Foundation International

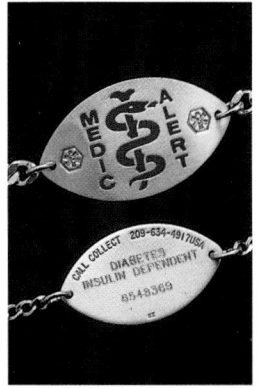

Medic Alert Foundation International

Medic Alert bracelet

Medicaid, *MEHD uh kayd,* is a federal-state program in the United States that provides medical care for many people who cannot pay for it. A state has considerable freedom to choose what medical services it provides. But to take part in the Medicaid program, a state must meet standards that are set by the federal government. One requirement is that a state's Medicaid plan provide medical care for all persons who are receiving public assistance. A plan may also include people called *medically indigent.* Such people are able to provide for their daily needs but cannot afford large medical expenses.

The federal government pays a state from 50 to about 80 percent of the state's Medicaid costs. The percentage the federal government pays depends on the average income of people in the state. All states have the program.

Congress established Medicaid in 1965 and has expanded the program several times. In 1990, about $25\frac{1}{4}$ million people received services under Medicaid. Since the 1980's, many physicians have refused to treat new Medicaid patients because of the low fees Medicaid pays for medical service.   Robert I. Lerman

See also **Blue Cross and Blue Shield.**

Medicare is a United States government health insurance program. It consists of hospital insurance and supplementary medical insurance. The program is for nearly all people age 65 or older, for people who have received social security disability benefits for at least two years, and for certain people with kidney disease. Eligible people can gain Medicare coverage by signing up at a social security office. Medicare beneficiaries normally must pay premiums and some of their own medical expenses. But for certain low-income people, a welfare program called Medicaid pays part or all of these premiums and expenses. The Medicare program is managed by the Health Care Financing Administration of the U.S. Department of Health and Human Services.

Hospital insurance helps pay the cost of hospital care, certain skilled nursing facility care after leaving the hospital, and home health services. The patient pays a set amount of the hospital bill in each *benefit period.* A benefit period begins when a person is admitted to a hospital and ends when the person has been out of the hospital for 60 consecutive days. In 1993, the set amount the patient paid during a benefit period was $676. Medicare pays the rest of the patient's covered hospital expenses for the first 60 days of the benefit period, and all but a fixed amount a day for 30 more days. In 1993, the daily amount not paid by Medicare was $169. Medicare also pays all covered expenses for the first 20 days of skilled nursing facility care and all but a certain amount a day for the next 80 days. The daily amount not paid by Medicare was $84.50 in 1993. Within each benefit period, a person may use all 90 days of hospital and 100 days of nursing facility benefits.

The patient is eligible again for these benefits anytime he or she has gone for 60 days in a row without receiving skilled care in a hospital or any other Medicare-certified facility. The patient also has a "lifetime reserve" of 60 hospital days. These days can be used at any time and cover all costs over a fixed amount a day. In 1993, the fixed amount was $338. Medicare also has an optional hospice benefit that is available for terminally ill patients (see **Hospice**). Hospital insurance is financed by a tax paid by workers and their employers and by self-employed people.

Medical insurance helps pay for physicians' services and certain other costs not covered by hospital insurance. The insured member pays a set amount of cov-

ered medical expenses in a calendar year. In 1993, this amount was $100. Medicare then generally pays 80 percent of an approved amount for covered services for the rest of the year. The program is financed by monthly payments from members and by federal payments. In 1993, most members paid $36.60 a month.

Critically reviewed by the Health Care Financing Administration

Additional resources

Fein, Rashi. *Medical Care, Medical Costs: The Search for a Health Insurance Policy.* Harvard, 1986. Includes information on the implementation of Medicare.
Sieforth, Jeannine M. *Medicare Savings and Sense: A Practical Complete Guide and Reference Manual.* 3rd ed. Duo, 1988.

Medici, *MEHD ih chee,* was the name of a ruling family of Florence, Italy. Members of the family played important parts in the history of Italy and France from the 1400's to the 1700's. Their great wealth and influence as bankers first gave them control of Florence.

Except for brief periods, the Medici ruled Florence until 1737. Their cultural interests led them to become patrons of the arts, and Florence became an art center under their rule. Michelangelo and Raphael were among the great artists the Medici helped.

The Medici influence extended to Rome when three members of the family became popes. Leo X reigned from 1513 to 1521 and Clement VII from 1523 to 1534 (see **Leo X; Clement VII**). Leo XI was pope for only 27 days in 1605. Two women of the Medici family became queens of France. They adopted the French spelling of the name, *de Médicis.* Catherine de Médicis, the wife of Henry II and mother of three French kings, was a powerful force in France from 1559 until her death in 1589 (see **Catherine de Médicis**). Marie de Médicis married Henry IV. After his death in 1610, Marie reigned until her son Louis XIII took over.

Giovanni de' Medici (1360-1429) made a fortune in banking and commerce. Giovanni de' Medici is considered the first of the great Medici.

Cosimo de' Medici (1389-1464), the son of Giovanni, became the first Medici to win wide fame. He gave large sums of money to promote the arts. Cosimo wielded great influence in the city of Florence and was called the *Father of his Country.*

Lorenzo the Magnificent (1449-1492), the grandson of Cosimo, became the most famous Medici. Lorenzo made Florence the most powerful state in Italy and worked to make it one of the world's beautiful cities. He built beautiful buildings and promoted the establishment of libraries.

While the people of Florence devoted themselves to luxury, Lorenzo took over the state government. The Medici family first lost power under Pietro de' Medici (1471-1503), the weak son of Lorenzo.   Franklin D. Scott

See also **Florence** (History); **Michelangelo; Renaissance** (Political background; picture).

Additional resources

Cleugh, James. *The Medici: A Tale of Fifteen Generations.* Doubleday, 1975.
Hibbert, Christopher. *The House of Medici: Its Rise and Fall.* Morrow, 1980. First published in 1974.
Hook, Judith. *Lorenzo de' Medici: An Historical Biography.* Hamish Hamilton, 1984.
Schevill, Ferdinand. *The Medici.* Arden Lib., 1981. First published in 1949.

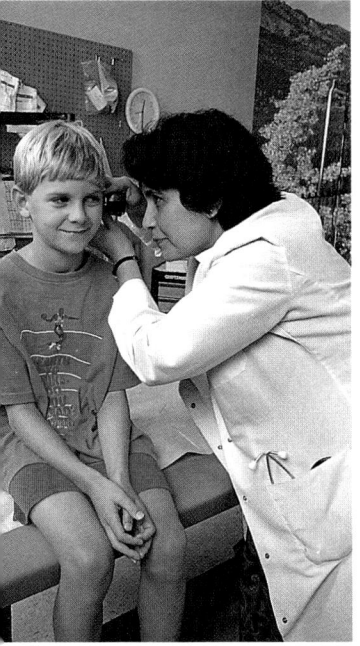
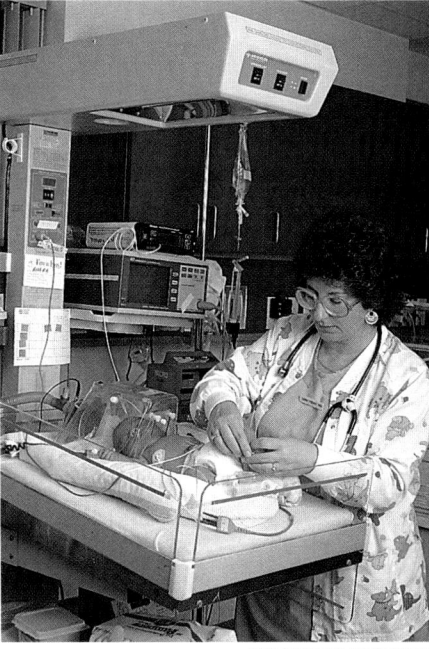

Robert Crandall, Medical Images   Nicholas Thomas, Medical Images   Paul Almasy, World Health Organization

Medical care is provided by a variety of trained people. Doctors take charge of treating the sick. Nurses work with doctors to provide care. Other trained workers also provide basic and specialized care. The worker at the right is vaccinating patients in Afghanistan.

Medicine

Medicine is the science and art of healing. Medicine is a science because it is based on knowledge gained through careful study and experimentation. It is an art because it depends on how skillfully doctors and other medical workers apply this knowledge when dealing with patients.

The goals of medicine are to save lives, to relieve suffering, and to maintain the dignity of ill individuals. For this reason, medicine has long been one of the most respected professions. Thousands of men and women who work in the medical profession spend their lives caring for the sick. When disaster strikes, hospital workers rush emergency aid to the injured. When epidemics threaten, doctors and nurses work to prevent the spread of disease. Researchers in the medical profession continually search for better ways of fighting disease.

Human beings have suffered from illnesses since they first appeared on the earth about $2\frac{1}{2}$ million years ago. Throughout most of this time, they knew little about how the human body works or what causes disease. Treatment was based largely on superstition and guesswork.

James Webster, the contributor of this article, is Professor of Medicine and Director of the Buehler Center on Aging at Northwestern University Medical School. Unless otherwise credited, the photographs in the article were taken for World Book *by Stephen Feldman through the courtesy of Rush-Presbyterian-St. Luke's Medical Center in Chicago.*

Medicine has made tremendous progress in the last several hundred years. Today, it is possible to cure, control, or prevent hundreds of diseases. People live longer than they did in the past as a result of new drugs, machines, and surgical operations. Medical progress in the control of infectious diseases, improvements in health care programs for mothers and children, and better nutrition, sanitation, and living conditions have given people a longer life expectancy. In 1900, most people in the United States did not live past the age of 50. Today, Americans have an average life span of about 75 years.

As medicine has become more scientific, it has also become more complicated. In the past, doctors cared for patients almost single-handedly. Patients received treatment at home for most kinds of illnesses. Today, doctors no longer work by themselves. Instead, they head *medical teams* made up of nurses, laboratory workers, and many other skilled professionals. The care provided by such teams cannot generally be started at home. As a result, clinics and hospitals have become the chief centers for medical care in most countries.

Medical care is often considered part of the larger field of *health care.* In addition to medical care, health care includes the services provided by dentists, clinical psychologists, social workers, physical and occupational therapists, and other professionals in various fields of physical and mental health. This article deals chiefly with the kind of health care provided by physicians, including doctors of medicine (M.D.'s) and doctors of osteopathy (D.O.'s), and by people who work with physicians. Information about other kinds of health care can be found in separate *World Book* articles, such as **Clinical psychology; Dentistry; Optometry;** and **Podiatry.**

Medical care has three main elements: (1) *diagnosis,* or identification, of disease or injury; (2) *treatment* of disease or injury; and (3) *prevention* of disease.

Diagnosis. Serious ailments require diagnosis by an expert, who, in most cases, is a doctor. Doctors use three main types of "clues" in making a diagnosis: (1) the patient's *case history;* (2) the doctor's *physical examination* of the patient; and (3) the results of *medical tests.*

Patients provide their own medical history by answering questions about their physical condition and past illnesses. Doctors use certain basic tools and techniques to perform a physical examination. For example, they use a stethoscope to listen to a patient's heart and lungs. By pressing and probing various areas of the body, they check internal organs for unusual hardness, softness, or changes in size or shape. A lighted instrument called an *endoscope* allows doctors to see the interior of hollow organs, such as the stomach or intestines. Doctors also insert medical instruments through endoscopes to obtain pieces of tissue for study.

Medical laboratories aid diagnosis by making chemical and microscopic tests on body fluids and tissues. A physician may also order tests that use radioactive trace elements, X rays, or sound or electric waves to detect disease by literally looking inside the body (see **Radioactivity** [In medicine]; **Ultrasound; X rays**).

To make a final diagnosis, the doctor fits together all the clues from the patient's case history, physical examination, and medical tests. If the diagnosis is complicated, the doctor may ask the opinion of other experts.

Treatment. People usually recover from minor illnesses and injuries without special treatment. In these cases, doctors may simply reassure their patients and allow the body to heal itself. But serious ailments generally require special treatment. In these cases, a doctor may prescribe drugs, surgery, or other treatment.

For thousands of years, drugs and surgery have provided two of the chief methods of treating disease. But modern science has helped make these methods much more effective than they used to be. Penicillin and other "wonder drugs" help cure many infectious diseases that were once extremely difficult to treat. With the help of machines, surgeons can repair or replace organs that have been seriously damaged, including the heart and kidneys. Science has also helped develop entirely new methods of treatment. *Radiotherapy,* for example, makes use of X rays and radioactive rays to treat cancer.

Prevention. Doctors help prevent disease in various ways. For example, they give vaccinations to guard against such diseases as polio, hepatitis, and measles. They may also order a special diet or drug to strengthen a patient's natural defenses against illness. People can also help themselves remain healthy by exercising, by not smoking, and by avoiding use of alcohol or illegal drugs. Doctors can prevent many diseases from becoming serious by diagnosing and treating them in their early stages. For this reason, most doctors recommend regular physical examinations. See **Disease** (Preventing disease).

Local governments help prevent disease by enforcing public health measures. For example, they make sure the community has pure drinking water and a system of garbage and sewage disposal. See **Public health**.

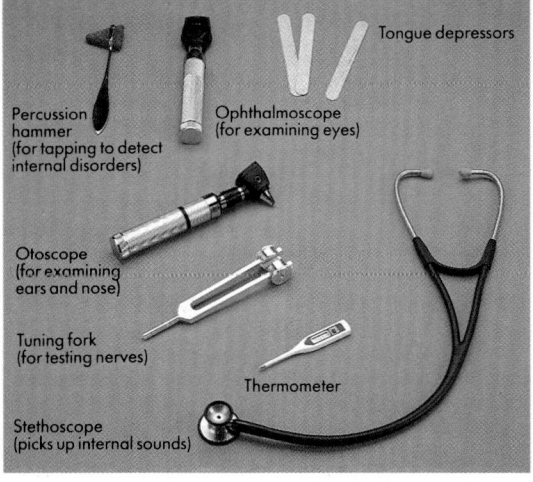

Percussion hammer
(for tapping to detect internal disorders)

Tongue depressors

Ophthalmoscope
(for examining eyes)

Otoscope
(for examining ears and nose)

Tuning fork
(for testing nerves)

Thermometer

Stethoscope
(picks up internal sounds)

WORLD BOOK photo by Ralph J. Brunke

Some basic tools of medicine. A doctor uses the equipment shown above in making physical examinations.

Beebe, Custom Medical

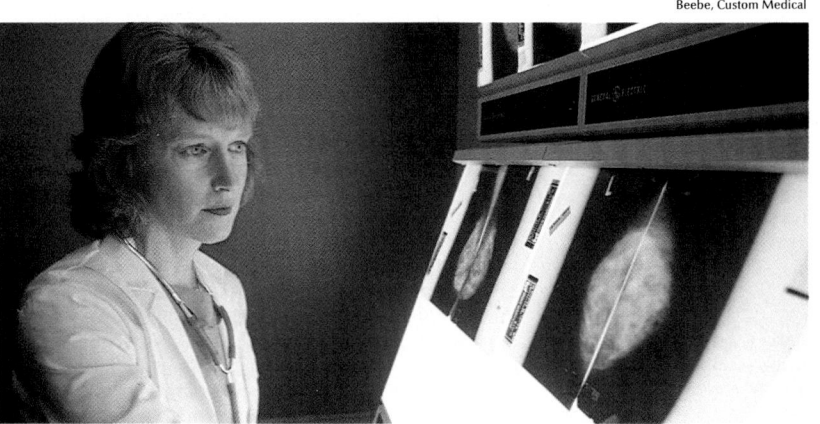

A doctor studies X rays to determine whether a patient has breast cancer, *left.* X-ray machines and other devices help doctors diagnose and treat illnesses and injuries.

In industrially developed countries, most people can get high-quality medical care when they need it. These countries include Canada, Japan, the United States, and most Western European nations. Certain developing countries of Africa, Asia, and Latin America lack the facilities for high-quality medical care. Some of these countries have only 1 doctor for every 20,000 to 60,000 persons. Some developed countries, on the other hand, have 1 doctor for every 450 persons.

This section discusses how and where medical care is provided in the United States and Canada. It also describes efforts to improve the quality of medical care in various parts of the world.

How medical care is provided

In case of illness or injury, people first of all need someone to diagnose their condition and prescribe or give the necessary treatment. This kind of basic medical care is called *primary care.* It is provided by such doctors as family practitioners and internists to whom people can go directly, without having to be referred by another doctor or medical worker. If a case is complicated or severe, the person who provides primary care refers the patient to a doctor or a hospital or other institution that provides *specialized care.*

The role of the doctor. Doctors have detailed knowledge of the human body and how it works, and they are specially trained in the diagnosis, treatment, and prevention of disease. For this reason, they make all major decisions regarding the care of patients.

In the early 1990's, the United States had about 525,000 doctors whose chief duty is to provide medical care. Canada had about 48,000 such doctors. Other doctors in both countries serve as medical researchers, teachers of medicine, or administrators of medical institutions. Doctors who provide medical care are (1) *family practitioners* or (2) *specialists.*

Family practitioners provide primary care only. But they treat a wide variety of ailments. In many small

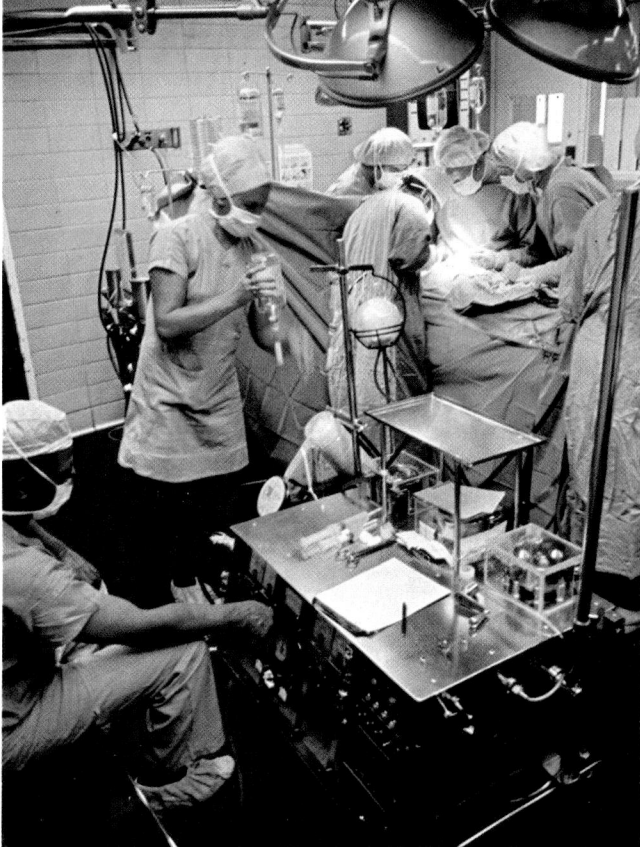

A surgical team, headed by a skilled surgeon, includes other doctors plus nurses and medical technicians. The team shown above is performing open-heart surgery. Most doctors depend on such teams to help them care for seriously ill patients.

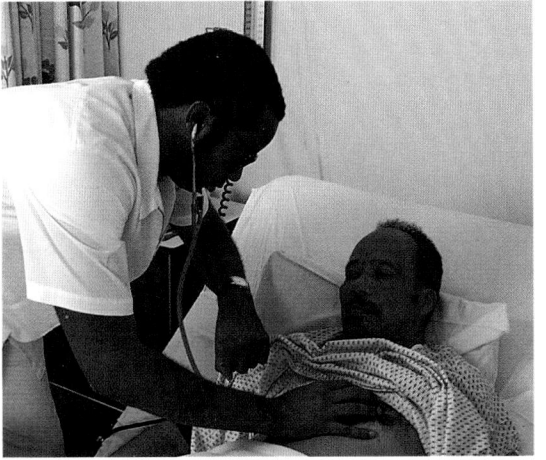

C. C. Duncan, Medical Images

Nurses with special training may relieve doctors of various routine duties, such as examining patients. In this photograph, a male nurse checks the heartbeat of a patient.

© Rick Brady, Medichrome

Home care workers provide certain medical services in the home, including periodic checkups of an elderly patient, *above.* Hospitals or clinics employ most of these workers.

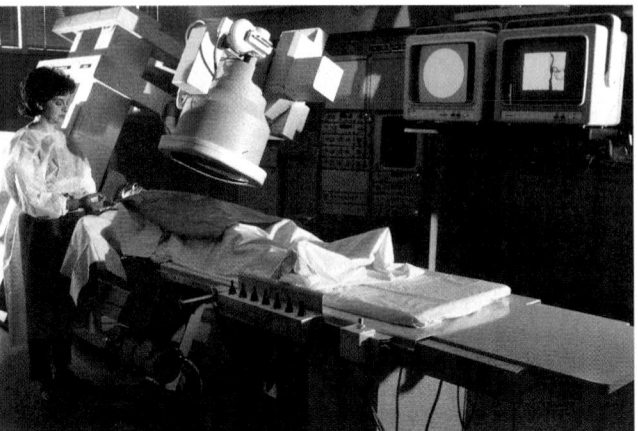
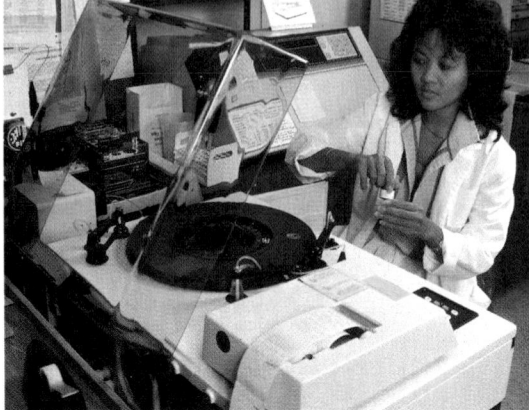

WORLD BOOK photo by Robert Frerck   © Larry Mulvehill, Science Source from Photo Researchers

Skilled technicians play a key role in modern medicine. Some operate complex hospital equipment, such as the computer equipment used to photograph blood vessels, *left*. Others perform laboratory tests that aid doctors in diagnosing disease, *right*.

towns, the only doctor is a family practitioner, who does everything from delivering babies to setting broken bones. Family practitioners provide care for every member of the family, regardless of age. During the mid-1980's, about 12 percent of all U.S. doctors and 50 percent of all Canadian doctors were family practitioners.

Specialists. In the past, almost all doctors were general practitioners. But medical knowledge has increased so rapidly during the 1900's that no doctor can possibly keep up with all the important advances. As a result, more than 80 percent of all U.S. doctors and about 50 percent of all Canadian doctors today specialize in a particular field of medicine. *Dermatologists,* for example, specialize in diseases of the skin. *Pediatricians* specialize in children's diseases. Some specialists also provide primary care. They include *internists* who specialize in the diagnosis and nonsurgical treatment of diseases of adults; and pediatricians, who often provide primary care for children.

The growth of the medical specialties has led to a great improvement in the quality of medical care. Seriously ill patients, especially, receive much more effective treatment than ever before. But as more and more doctors become specialists, fewer doctors may be available for primary care.

During the 1980's, the trend to specialization reversed somewhat as a growing number of family practitioners and general pediatricians and internists were trained. A table in the section *A career as a doctor* describes the major medical specialties.

The role of medical workers. Doctors could not do their job without the help of many other skilled professionals. *Registered nurses,* for example, work closely with doctors in clinics, hospitals, and doctors' offices. Nurses also provide many services to patients independent of doctors. *Pharmacists* fill prescriptions and give advice on the drugs prescribed. Various kinds of *therapists* give special treatment as ordered by the doctor. Other skilled workers serve in clinics, medical laboratories, X-ray departments, and operating rooms. The

section *Other careers in medicine* discusses the jobs of various kinds of medical workers.

Where medical care is provided

In the doctor's office. Most of the U.S. and Canadian doctors who provide primary or specialized care have an office-based practice. In their offices, they examine patients and, based on the findings, provide treatment. Patients either pay the doctor a fee for the services they receive or have prepaid medical insurance, such as that provided by a health maintenance organization (HMO). Most doctors in office-based practice are associated with a hospital where they send patients who need special care.

Office-based doctors practice alone or in a *group practice,* where three or more doctors share the same office area, equipment, and personnel. Group practice reduces each doctor's expenses, enabling doctors to offer more services under the same roof. Such services include X-ray and laboratory tests and specialized treatment. Many doctors in larger group practices work for HMO's, medical schools, or corporations.

In hospitals. The United States has about 7,000 hospitals, and Canada has about 1,200. More than 35 million patients are admitted to U.S. hospitals each year. Canadian hospitals admit over $3\frac{1}{2}$ million patients yearly. The hospitals range from small private institutions to huge community hospitals.

Hospitals offer services not available anywhere else. Patients receive round-the-clock care from a full-time staff of doctors, nurses, and other skilled workers. The largest, most modern hospitals have a variety of advanced equipment. Such equipment includes *heart-lung machines,* which may take over the work of a patient's heart and lungs during a complicated heart operation. Modern hospitals also have *intensive care units,* which use television and electronic devices to keep constant watch over seriously ill patients. The units are also equipped with highly technical lifesaving equipment. For more information about the various kinds of hospitals and the services they provide, see **Hospital**.

In clinics. Clinics provide primary care for *outpatients*—that is, for patients who are not hospitalized. Some clinics are part of a hospital or a corporation. The doctors and medical workers who staff such clinics may be employees of the hospital or corporation, or volunteers. Other clinics are run by doctors in group practice or by community organizations. These clinics often operate on a nonprofit basis and offer free or inexpensive care for poor people. The doctors and medical workers who staff the clinics charge the patients a small fee or none at all. Some community clinics, called *neighborhood health centers,* receive financial aid from the U.S. government or from the government of the city in which they are located.

Some clinics have both specialists and general practitioners on their staff. Others have specialists only. Many communities have certain types of specialized clinics, such as those that diagnose and treat alcohol and drug abuse, psychiatric disorders, or AIDS (Acquired Immunodeficiency Syndrome).

In nursing homes. Many nursing homes do not provide medical care on a regular basis. But others have professional nurses on the staff. Such homes are called *skilled nursing care facilities.* They accept patients who need round-the-clock care but do not need to be hospitalized. Doctors visit the patients on a regular basis. Most nursing homes are privately owned.

In the home. Some people need continuing medical attention but not the round-the-clock care given in hospitals and nursing care homes. Various public and private agencies and some hospitals sponsor home care programs for these people. The programs offer extensive therapy and nursing care.

Because of the highly technical nature of modern medical care, few doctors make house calls today. But in some large cities, emergency medical services employ doctors who make house calls on request. In addition, many patients avoid the high cost of hospital stays by receiving care at home from visiting nurses and therapists. They may even receive intravenous drugs and other treatments formerly available only to hospital patients.

Improving the quality of medical care

The role of medical organizations. A number of national and international organizations work to improve the quality of medical care. These organizations encourage medical education and research, help standardize medical practice, and enforce codes of professional conduct. The American Medical Association (AMA) is the largest medical organization in the United States. It is composed of doctors of medicine. The American Osteopathic Association (AOA) is the chief medical organization for doctors of osteopathy. The National Medical Association has a membership made up largely of black physicians. The Canadian Medical Association is Canada's main medical organization.

Many specialty medical organizations in the United States work to set and raise standards of care in a particular area of practice. These organizations include the American College of Physicians, the American College of Surgeons, and the Joint Commission on Accreditation of Health Care Organizations.

The World Health Organization (WHO) is the chief international medical organization. It promotes public health programs and the exchange of medical knowledge. WHO is especially dedicated to improving the quality of medical care in developing countries.

Jim Brown, The Stock Market

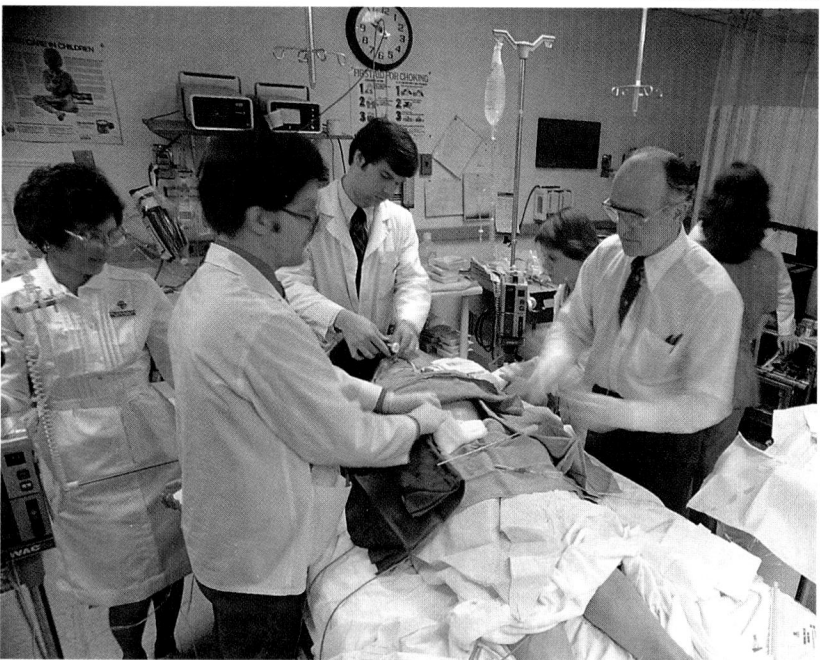

A modern hospital provides many services that are unavailable elsewhere. In an emergency room, *left,* doctors provide immediate care for accident victims and people who have suddenly become ill.

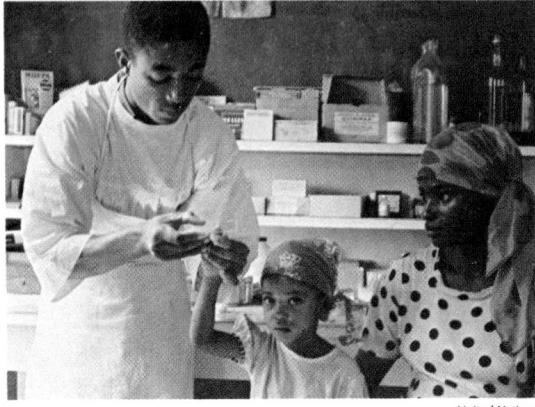

Brunei N. Borneo, DPI   United Nations

Providing medical care in developing countries requires overcoming great distances and a shortage of doctors. The medical team at the left reaches remote areas in Borneo by helicopter. A specially trained medical worker, *right,* tests for malaria in Cameroon.

Most developing countries have a shortage of doctors and hospitals. Many people rely on such practices as the use of plant medicines or even treatment by medicine men or witch doctors. Infectious diseases, such as malaria and tuberculosis, still take a heavy toll. To help remedy this situation, medically advanced members of WHO help train medical personnel for the less advanced members. They also provide the less advanced members with badly needed medical supplies and equipment.

The role of medical research. Progress in medicine depends largely on the work of medical research. Medical researchers strive to increase our knowledge of (1) how the healthy body works; (2) how it is disturbed by disease; and (3) how disease can be prevented or cured.

Some medical researchers are physicians, but others do purely research work. Much medical research is done in laboratories. But physicians also carry on research by observing groups of patients.

Most medical discoveries provide clues to only part of the solution of a difficult medical problem. As a result, the problem is solved only after years of work by many people. But researchers sometimes make dramatic discoveries. An outstanding example of a dramatic discovery in medicine was the development of an effective polio vaccine by the American research scientist Jonas E. Salk in the early 1950's. For more information on medical research, see the section of this article on *Current problems in U.S. medicine.* See also the article **Science** (The history of science).

Careers in medicine

A career as a doctor

Young men and women who choose a career as a doctor face a long, difficult, and expensive training period. This section discusses the training and licensing of doctors in the United States and Canada.

Premedical education begins in college. Most medical schools accept only four-year college graduates. But some schools admit students after two or three years of college. Some medical schools also offer a six- or seven-year program that awards both a medical degree and a liberal arts degree. The majority of premedical students take a liberal arts program, including courses in chemistry, higher mathematics, physics, and biology.

Medical schools are crowded and can admit only a certain number of new students each year. Most schools accept only applicants whose past school records, test scores, and personal interviews indicate high potential.

Medical education. Most medical schools are part of a university. In the United States during the early 1990's, the tuition at the medical schools of private universities averaged more than $20,000 a year. At state universities, it averaged about $6,000 for state residents. The annual tuition at all Canadian medical schools averaged about $2,000 (in Canadian currency).

Traditionally, a medical school offers a four-year course of study. The first two years consist largely of *preclinical training.* Students study such basic medical sciences as biochemistry, cell biology and physiology, microbiology, pathology, pharmacology, and organ physiology. The last two years consist largely of *clinical training*—that is, training by observing and caring for patients. Students ordinarily receive clinical training in a hospital associated with their medical school.

Students must pass all their courses to graduate from medical school. Upon graduation, they receive either a Doctor of Medicine (M.D.) degree or a Doctor of Osteopathy (D.O.) degree, depending on whether their school has been approved by the AMA or the AOA.

Internship and residency. After graduating from medical school, doctors serve at least a year as a hospital *intern.* Interns examine patients and prescribe treatment. But they are supervised by experienced doctors.

Most doctors specialize in a particular field of medi-

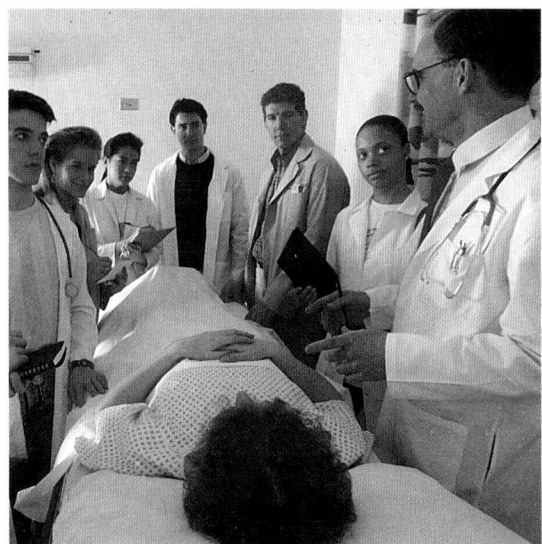

Hospital interns work under the supervision of experienced doctors for at least a year. After their internship, most doctors spend several years training to become specialists.

cine after their internship. To prepare for a specialty, they must train for at least three years as a hospital *resident.* During residency, doctors work with the kinds of patients they will treat as specialists. A surgical resident, for example, works with surgical patients. Like interns,

residents learn through experience. But they have more responsibility than do interns. Hospitals in the United States and Canada pay interns and residents an annual salary, which varies from hospital to hospital.

To become *certified* specialists, doctors must complete residency training and pass a rigorous examination given by their *specialty board.* A separate board governs each specialty field and certifies specialists. Some doctors undertake further very specialized training, called a *fellowship,* for two or three years. These doctors, known as *fellows,* must pass another difficult examination after completing their training.

Licensing. In the United States, every state requires doctors to obtain a license before they may practice medicine in the state. In each state, a state medical board sets licensing requirements and issues licenses. To obtain a license, a person must have an M.D. or a D.O. degree from an approved school and must pass an examination approved by the state medical board. Most states also require completion of a one-year internship. To practice in another state, a doctor must obtain a license from that state. Most states grant licenses by *endorsement,* or *reciprocity,* to doctors from states whose licensing requirements and examination are the same as its own. In such cases, doctors do not have to take the licensing examination again. Each Canadian province has its own licensing requirements, which are similar to those in the United States.

Rewards and responsibilities. Doctors rank among the highest paid professionals. In the late 1980's, the average income of U.S. doctors was about $120,000 a year. In Canada, the average annual income of doctors was

Major medical specialty fields

Allergy and immunology, *IHM* yuh NAHL uh jee, deals with disorders of the immune system, including allergies, autoimmune diseases, and immune deficiencies.

Anesthesiology, *AN* uhs THEE zee AHL uh jee, is the study of anesthesia and anesthetics. *Anesthesiologists* give anesthetics during operations or supervise the administration of these drugs.

Cardiology, *KAHR* dee AHL uh jee, is the diagnosis and treatment of disorders of the heart.

Colon and rectal surgery is the surgical treatment of disorders of the lower digestive tract.

Dermatology diagnoses and treats diseases of the skin, nails, and hair.

Emergency medicine deals with the immediate recognition and treatment of acute injuries, illnesses, and emotional crises.

Family practice is the supervision of the total health care of patients and their families, regardless of age.

General surgery treats diseases by operations, except for those diseases treated by other surgical specialties.

Internal medicine is the diagnosis and nonsurgical treatment of diseases of adults. Specialists are called *internists.* Some internists limit their practice to allergies; diseases of the heart and blood vessels; disorders of the digestive tract; diseases of the lungs; diseases of the joints; or disorders of the kidneys.

Neurological surgery, or *neurosurgery,* is the surgical treatment of disorders of the nervous system.

Nuclear medicine is the use of radioactive isotopes to diagnose and treat disease.

Obstetrics and gynecology, *ahb STEHT rihks,* *GY* nuh KAHL uh jee, provide the special medical care required by women. *Obstetricians* provide care for women during pregnancy and during and immediately after childbirth. *Gynecologists* diag-

nose and treat diseases of the female reproductive organs.

Oncology, *ahng KAHL uh jee,* is the study of tumors.

Ophthalmology, *AHF* thal MAHL uh jee, is the diagnosis, treatment, and prevention of eye diseases.

Orthopedics is the diagnosis and treatment of disorders of the skeletal and muscular systems.

Otolaryngology, *OH* tuh LAR ihng GAHL uh jee, diagnoses and treats ear, nose, and throat diseases.

Pathology, *puh THAHL uh jee,* is the study of changes in the body that cause disease or are caused by disease.

Pediatrics, *PEE* dee AT rihks, is the diagnosis, treatment, and prevention of children's diseases.

Physical medicine and rehabilitation, or *physiatrics,* treats diseases and disabilities by such physical means as light, heat, and water therapy.

Plastic surgery restores or rebuilds certain parts of the body that are imperfect or have been damaged.

Preventive medicine deals with the relation between environment and health. Specialists may limit their practice to such fields as *public health* or *aviation medicine.*

Psychiatry and neurology deal with the mind and nervous system. *Psychiatrists* diagnose and treat mental disorders. *Neurologists* provide nonsurgical treatment of diseases of the nervous system.

Radiology is the use of X rays and radium to diagnose and treat disease.

Thoracic surgery, *thaw RAS ihk,* is the surgical treatment of diseases of the heart, lungs, or large blood vessels in the chest.

Urology, *yu RAHL uh jee,* deals with diseases of organs that pass urine and of the male reproductive organs.

about $100,000 (in Canadian currency). In addition to the high earnings, doctors also have the satisfaction of helping patients regain their health.

Every state and province requires doctors to meet certain standards of professional conduct. Doctors who do not meet these standards are liable to lawsuits. Doctors also have their own *code of ethics.* It includes charging reasonable fees, providing the best quality of care, and respecting a patient's confidence, dignity, and privacy. Doctors must keep up with medical progress by reading medical journals and books, attending conferences, and consulting with other specialists.

Other careers in medicine

Medical careers outside those requiring an M.D. or a D.O. degree range from laboratory work to nursing or pharmacy. The articles **Nursing** and **Pharmacy** tell about a career as a nurse or pharmacist. This section deals mainly with other medical careers. Further information can be obtained from the American Medical Association, Division of Medical Education and Scientific Policy, 535 N. Dearborn Street, Chicago, IL 60610.

Working with patients. Some medical workers help care for patients by taking the place of physicians under certain conditions. Such workers are sometimes called *paramedical workers* or *paramedics.* Paramedics free doctors from routine medical duties and so enable them to spend more time on cases that only a doctor can handle. Two of the chief types of paramedics are *nurse practitioners* and *physician's assistants.*

Nurse practitioners are registered nurses who have had additional medical training. This training enables them to take a patient's medical history, perform physical examination, make a diagnosis, and prescribe treatment. The nurse practitioner calls a doctor if a patient needs more than routine medical care. Some nurse practitioners are trained to assist specialists.

Physician's assistants also provide certain types of routine medical care. But unlike a nurse practitioner, a physician's assistant does not have to be a registered nurse. Many physician's assistants are trained in special programs conducted by university medical schools. Some physician's assistants work in doctors' offices or in hospitals. Many physician's assistants formerly were in a medical branch of the armed forces.

Many other kinds of medical workers also work with patients. *Medical assistants* take case histories and do clerical and laboratory work in the doctor's office. *Occupational therapists* teach useful activities to people with disabilities to help them overcome or lessen their disability (see **Occupational therapy**). *Physical therapists* use such physical means as exercise, heat, or ultraviolet light to treat ailments (see **Physical therapy**). *Medical social workers* help patients prepare for their care after leaving the hospital. For example, they arrange for therapists and nurses to visit the patient's home. They also provide counseling to patients and their families.

Providing technical support. Many important medical careers require special technical skills. Laboratory workers, for example, perform chemical and microscopic tests that may be needed for accurate diagnosis. *Medical technologists* perform the most difficult and highly specialized laboratory tests. They also supervise *laboratory technicians* and *assistants,* who perform more routine laboratory tasks. *Radiologic technologists* prepare patients for X rays and other imaging techniques, such as ultrasound, computer axial tomography (CAT), and magnetic resonance imaging (MRI). These technologists also operate the imaging equipment under a doctor's supervision. *Nuclear medicine technologists* and *technicians* work with the nuclear equipment and materials used in diagnosis and treatment.

Financing medical care

In the United States

Medical costs have risen sharply in the United States since the early 1960's. The greatest increase has been in the cost of hospital care. Most hospitals have granted large pay raises to their employees. Many hospitals have also installed expensive new equipment. To meet these expenses, hospitals raised their service charges by about 600 percent between 1970 and 1987.

There are three main methods of financing medical care in the United States. They are (1) private insurance; (2) government insurance and other government aid; and (3) direct personal payments.

Private insurance. About 80 percent of all Americans have some kind of private health insurance. The insured person, his or her employer, or the government pays a specified sum for medical benefits. Private health insurance in the United States is offered mainly by (1) insurance companies; (2) medical service plans; (3) health maintenance organizations; and (4) employers.

Insurance companies generally pay benefits to the insured person rather than to the provider of medical service. Medical service plans pay *service benefits.* A service benefit is a direct payment to the hospital or physician that provided the medical care. Blue Cross and Blue Shield are the largest medical service plans in the United States.

Health maintenance organizations (HMO's) provide nearly complete health care services for a prepaid monthly or yearly fee. However, the patient usually has to choose from a limited number of doctors or hospitals. Employers may pay for the health care costs of their employees rather than buy insurance. Many larger companies have such arrangements. However, many insurance plans cover only a portion of health-care costs and patients may have to pay a portion by means of deductions or copayments.

Prior to the 1970's, most health policies offered benefits only for hospital care and associated doctors' fees. Today, many medical prepayment plans cover a wide variety of outpatient expenses, including drugs, eyeglasses, and home care. For more information about the various kinds of private health insurance, see **Health care plans** and **Insurance** (Private health insurance).

Government aid. The federal, state, and local governments pay about 40 percent of all health care costs in the United States. The federal government pays by far the largest share. It supports hospitals run by the Public Health Service as well as those run by the Department of Veterans Affairs. The National Institutes of Health, an agency of the U.S. Public Health Service, funds much of the medical research in the United States (see **National Institutes of Health**). Federal funds also help pay for hospital construction and help support medical schools.

The federal *Medicare* program is the largest public health care program in the United States. It helps elderly people pay for outpatient, hospital, and nursing home care. Social security contributions support the program. People covered by Medicare may obtain additional government medical insurance at low cost to help pay for medical expenses. The federal government has also developed cost-control measures to help ensure that Medicare patients receive efficient and appropriate care. For example, hospitals are paid a fixed rate for treating Medicare patients. The rate is determined by the average cost of treating a specific ailment. Ailments are classified into about 480 categories called *diagnosis-related groups (DRG's),* and a fixed rate is set for each DRG. If the cost of treatment exceeds the set payment for that DRG, the hospital loses money. If the cost is less, the hospital makes a profit. Doctors also are paid a fixed fee

for taking care of Medicare patients.

The U.S. government cooperates with state governments to finance *Medicaid,* a health care plan for people of any age who cannot afford private health insurance. Each state decides what health services to include under its Medicaid plan. See **Medicare; Medicaid**.

Direct personal payments. Most insurance policies do not cover the cost of drugs, eyeglasses, and medical appliances. In addition, they often cover only part of the cost of outpatient care. People ordinarily must pay these expenses themselves. About 25 percent of all U.S. health care costs are paid in this way. Charitable organizations pay about 3 percent of U.S. health care costs.

In Canada

Each Canadian province has its own program of public health insurance. Almost all Canadians are covered under the provincial programs. The programs pay all major health care expenses. Private insurance companies offer additional coverage for those who desire it.

The Canadian government shares the costs of public health insurance with the provinces. It pays about half the total costs, using general tax funds. The provinces finance their share of the costs in various ways. In most provinces, families or individuals covered by the plan must contribute a certain amount through regular payments or payroll deductions. The provinces contribute

Expenditures for health care in the United States The graphs at the left show how health care costs have risen since 1940. The graphs at the right show how health care money is spent and where it comes from.

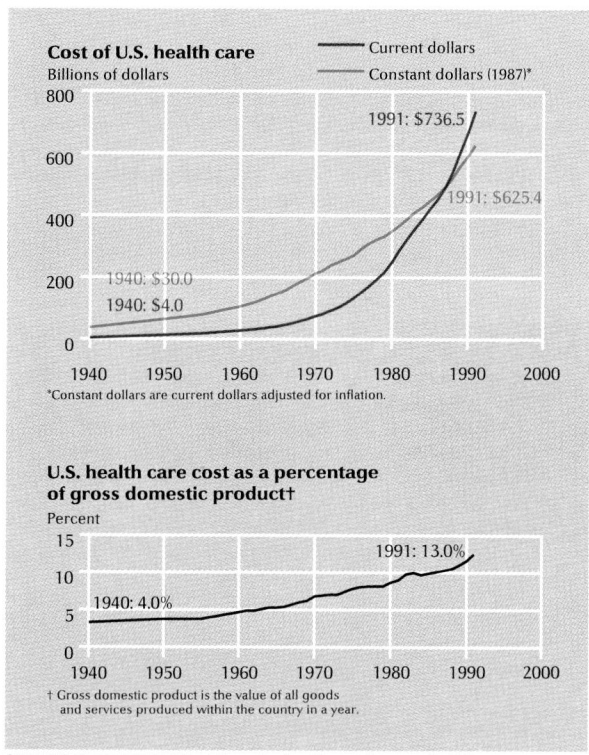

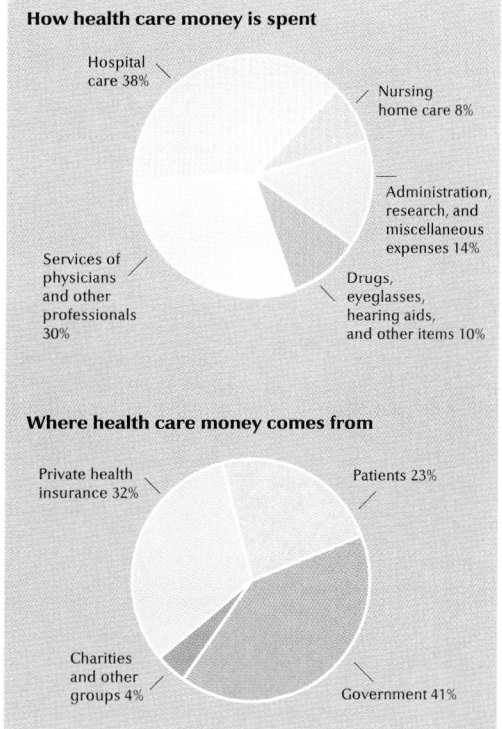

Source: U.S. Department of Health and Human Services. Pie graph figures are for 1990.

WORLD BOOK graphs

varying amounts from general tax funds, depending on how much is collected from individuals and families.

In other countries

In China and some other countries, medicine is completely *socialized*—that is, all medical facilities are publicly owned and all medical personnel are paid from public funds. Every citizen receives medical care free or at very low cost. In some countries, medicine is largely socialized. The United Kingdom is the best-known example. In the United Kingdom, the central government owns most medical facilities and pays most medical personnel. Therefore, the government can provide most

medical care free or at low cost.

In many other countries, including most Western European countries, medicine is partly socialized. The central government does not own most medical facilities, nor does it pay most doctors, who are self-employed. But these countries have a national health insurance plan that provides free medical care or refunds almost all the money a patient spends for medical care. The plan is financed through the social security system in almost all the countries and is compulsory for workers covered by social security. Doctors who take part in the national plan must charge a set fee. But patients generally may choose their doctor and hospital.

History

In prehistoric times, people believed that angry gods or evil spirits caused disease. To cure the sick, the gods had to be pacified or the evil spirits driven from the body. In time, this task became the job of the first "physicians"—the tribal priests who tried to pacify the gods or drive out the evil spirits.

The first-known surgical treatment was an operation called *trephining*. Trephining involved use of a stone instrument to cut a hole in a patient's skull. Scientists have found fossils of such skulls that date as far back as 10,000 years. Early people may have performed the operations to release spirits believed responsible for headaches, mental illness, or epilepsy. However, trephining could have brought relief in some cases. Surgeons still

practice trephining to relieve certain types of pressure on the brain.

Prehistoric people probably also discovered that many plants can be used as drugs. For example, the use of willow bark to relieve pain probably dates back thousands of years. Today, scientists know that willow bark contains *salicin*, a substance related to the *salicylates* used in making aspirin.

Ancient times

The Middle East. By about 3000 B.C., the Egyptians, who had developed one of the world's first great civilizations, began making important medical progress. The world's first physician known by name was the Egyptian

Highlights in medical history

Prehistoric people practiced *trephining*— the first-known surgical treatment.

Hippocrates showed that diseases have only natural, not supernatural, causes.

The first university medical schools developed in Europe.

| c. 8000 B.C. | c. 2500 B.C. | 400's B.C. | A.D. 100's | 1100's |

Egyptian physicians developed the first systematic methods of treating diseases.

Galen formulated the first medical theories based on scientific experimentations.

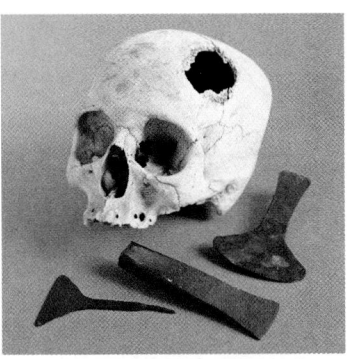

International College of Surgeons Museum, Chicago (WORLD BOOK photo)

Trephining involved cutting a hole in the skull, perhaps to release evil spirits. The ancient trephined skull and cutting tools shown above were found in Peru.

Relief sculpture (A.D. 100's) by an unknown Greek sculptor; British Museum, London (Michael Holford)

Ancient Greek physicians, such as the one shown above examining a young patient, raised medicine to the level of a science. Hippocrates led this development.

Detail of a manuscript (about 1300); International College of Surgeons Museum, Chicago (WORLD BOOK photo)

During the Middle Ages, doctors had little scientific knowledge. The doctor above is using all his strength to bandage a fractured jaw as tightly as possible.

Imhotep, who lived about 2650 B.C. The Egyptians later worshiped him as the god of healing (see **Imhotep**). About 2500 B.C., Egyptian surgeons produced a textbook that told how to treat dislocated or fractured bones and external abscesses, tumors, and wounds.

Other ancient Middle Eastern civilizations also contributed to medical progress. The ancient Israelites, for example, made progress in preventive medicine from about 1200 to 600 B.C. The Israelites required strict isolation of persons with gonorrhea, leprosy, and other contagious diseases. They also prohibited the contamination of public wells and the eating of pork and other foods that might carry disease.

China and India. The ancient Chinese developed medical practices that have been handed down almost unchanged to the present day. This traditional medicine is based on the belief that two life forces, *yin* and *yang,* flow through the human body. Disease results when the two forces become out of balance. To restore the balance, the Chinese developed the practice of *acupuncture*—inserting needles into parts of the body thought to control the flow of yin and yang. Chinese doctors still practice acupuncture. The technique has gained some popularity in Western countries, where it is occasionally used to treat certain pain disorders. But most experts question its value. See **Acupuncture.**

In ancient India, the practice of medicine became known as *ayurveda.* It stressed the prevention as well as the treatment of illness. By 600 to 500 B.C., practitioners of ayurveda had developed impressive knowledge of drugs to treat illness and of surgery. Indian surgeons successfully performed many kinds of operations, including amputations and plastic surgery.

Greece and Rome. The civilization of ancient Greece was at its peak during the 400's B.C. Throughout this period, sick people flocked to temples dedicated to the Greek god of healing, Asclepius, seeking magical cures. But at the same time, the great Greek physician Hippocrates began showing that disease has only natural causes. He thus became the first physician known to consider medicine a science and art separate from the practice of religion. The *Hippocratic oath,* an expression of early medical ethics, reflects Hippocrates' high ideals. But the oath was probably composed from a number of sources rather than by Hippocrates himself. For the text of the oath, see the article **Hippocrates.**

After 300 B.C., the city of Rome gradually conquered much of the civilized world, including Egypt and Greece. The Romans got most of their medical knowledge from Egypt and Greece. Their own medical achievements were largely in public health. The Romans built aqueducts that carried 300 million gallons (1.1 billion liters) of fresh water to Rome each day. They also built an excellent sewerage system in Rome.

The Greek physician Galen, who practiced medicine in Rome during the A.D. 100's, made the most important contributions to medicine in Roman times. Galen performed experiments on animals and used his findings to develop the first medical theories based on scientific experiments. For this reason, he is considered the founder of *experimental medicine.* But because his knowledge of anatomy was based largely on animal experiments, Galen developed many false notions about how the human body works. Galen wrote numerous books de-

---

Vesalius published the first scientific study of human anatomy.	Harvey started modern physiology with his book on blood circulation.	Jenner gave the first officially recognized vaccination, against smallpox.

| 1543 | Mid-1500's | 1628 | 1670's | 1796 |

Paré, the "father of modern surgery," introduced advanced surgical techniques.

Leeuwenhoek discovered bacteria, which helped lead to the germ theory of disease.

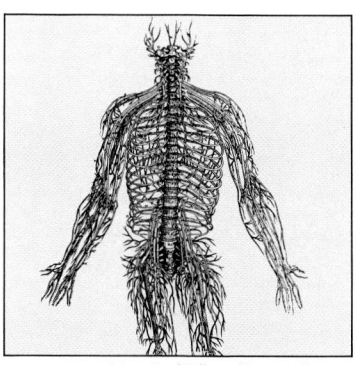

International College of Surgeons Museum, Chicago (WORLD BOOK photo)

The scientific study of anatomy began with Andreas Vesalius' book *On the Structure of the Human Body.* This drawing from the book shows spinal nerves.

Wood engraving (1594) by an unknown artist (Bettmann Archive)

Surgical advances by Ambroise Paré included sewing through pieces of cloth glued to the patient's skin instead of stitching through the skin itself.

Detail of an engraving after a painting (late 1800's?) by Georges Gaston Théodore Melingue (Granger Collection)

Edward Jenner vaccinates a child. Jenner's discovery of a smallpox vaccine led to the development of vaccines to prevent many other diseases as well.

scribing his medical theories. These theories, many of which were wrong, guided doctors for hundreds of years.

The Middle Ages

During the Middle Ages, which lasted from the A.D. 400's to the 1500's, the Islamic empire of Southwest and Central Asia contributed greatly to medicine. Rhazes, a Persian-born physician of the late 800's and early 900's, wrote the first accurate descriptions of measles and smallpox. Avicenna, an Arab physician of the late 900's and early 1000's, produced a vast medical encyclopedia called *Canon of Medicine.* It summed up the medical knowledge of the time and accurately described meningitis, tetanus, and many other diseases. The work became popular in Europe, where it influenced medical education for more than 600 years.

A series of epidemics swept across Europe during the Middle Ages. Outbreaks of leprosy began in the 500's and reached their peak in the 1200's. In the mid-1300's, a terrible outbreak of plague, now known as the *Black Death,* killed about a fourth of Europe's people. Throughout the medieval period, smallpox and other diseases attacked hundreds of thousands of people.

The chief medical advances in Europe during the Middle Ages were the founding of many hospitals and the first university medical schools. Christian religious groups established hundreds of charitable hospitals for victims of leprosy. In the 900's, a medical school was started in Salerno, Italy. It became the chief center of medical learning in Europe during the 1000's and 1100's. Other important medical schools developed in Europe

after 1000. During the 1100's and 1200's, many of these schools became part of newly developing universities, such as the University of Bologna in Italy and the University of Paris in France.

The Renaissance

A new scientific spirit developed during the Renaissance, the great cultural movement that swept across Western Europe from about 1300 to the 1600's. Before this time, most societies had strictly limited the practice of *dissecting* (cutting up) human corpses for scientific study. But laws against dissection were relaxed during the Renaissance. As a result, the first truly scientific studies of the human body began.

During the late 1400's and early 1500's, the Italian artist Leonardo da Vinci performed many dissections to learn more about human anatomy. He recorded his findings in a series of more than 750 drawings. Andreas Vesalius, a physician and professor of medicine at the University of Padua in Italy, also performed numerous dissections. Vesalius used his findings to write the first scientific textbook on human anatomy, a work called *On the Structure of the Human Body* (1543). This book gradually replaced the texts of Galen and Avicenna.

Other physicians also made outstanding contributions to medical science in the 1500's. A French army doctor named Ambroise Paré improved surgical techniques to such an extent that he is considered the father of modern surgery. For example, he opposed the common practice of *cauterizing* (burning) wounds with boiling oil to prevent infection. Instead, he developed the much more effective method of applying a mild oint-

Long and Morton introduced the use of ether, the first practical anesthetic.		Virchow pioneered in *pathology,* the scientific study of disease.		Lister introduced antiseptic methods to surgery.
◉ 1842-1846	◉ Mid-1800's	◉ 1850's	◉ Mid- to late 1800's	◉ 1865
	Nightingale founded the modern nursing profession.		Pasteur and Koch proved that certain bacteria cause certain diseases.	

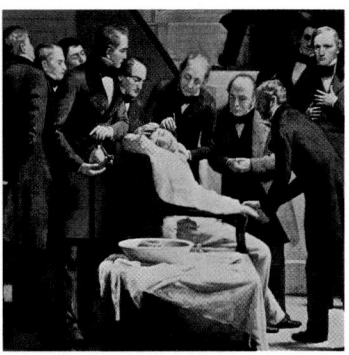

Detail of a mural (1893) by Robert Hinckley; Boston Medical Library

Ether anesthesia was first demonstrated publicly at Massachusetts General Hospital in 1846. William Morton, *left,* administered the drug.

Staffordshire pottery figures (mid-1800's); Wellcome Historical Medical Museum, London

Florence Nightingale introduced modern nursing methods during the Crimean War (1853-1856). These pottery figures show her with a wounded British soldier.

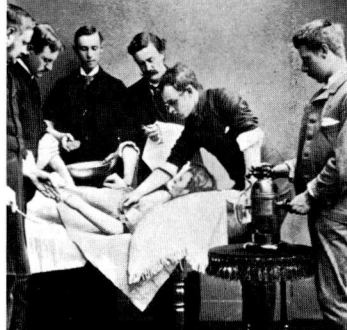

Detail of photograph taken about 1870 in Edinburgh, Scotland; Bettmann Archive

Antiseptic surgery involved spraying surgical wounds with carbolic acid to prevent infection. Joseph Lister invented this procedure in 1865.

ment and then allowing the wound to heal naturally. Philippus Paracelsus, a Swiss physician, stressed the importance of chemistry in the preparation of drugs. He pointed out that in many drugs consisting of several ingredients, one ingredient made another useless.

Modern times

The beginnings of modern research. The English physician William Harvey performed many experiments in the early 1600's to learn how blood circulates through the body. Before Harvey, scientists had studied only parts of the process and invented theories to fill in the gaps. Harvey studied the entire problem. He performed dissections on both human beings and animals and made careful studies of the human pulsebeat and heartbeat. Harvey concluded that the heart pumps blood through the arteries to all parts of the body and that the blood returns to the heart through the veins.

Harvey described his findings in *An Anatomical Study of the Motion of the Heart and of the Blood in Animals* (1628). His discovery of how blood circulates marked a turning point in medical history. After Harvey, scientists realized that knowledge of how the body works depends on knowledge of the body's structure.

In the mid-1600's, a Dutch amateur scientist named Anton van Leeuwenhoek began using a microscope to study organisms invisible to the naked eye. Today, such organisms are called *microorganisms, microbes,* or *germs.* In the mid-1670's, Leeuwenhoek discovered certain microbes that later became known as *bacteria.* Leeuwenhoek did not understand the role of microbes in nature. But his research paved the way for the even-

tual discovery that certain microbes cause disease.

The development of immunology. Smallpox was one of the most feared and highly contagious diseases of the 1700's. It killed many people every year and scarred others for life. Doctors had known for hundreds of years that a person who recovered from smallpox developed lifelong *immunity* (resistance) to it. To provide this immunity, doctors sometimes inoculated people with matter from a smallpox sore, hoping they would develop only a mild case of the disease. But such inoculations were dangerous. Some people developed a severe case of smallpox instead of a mild one. Other inoculated persons spread the disease.

In 1796, an English physician named Edward Jenner discovered a safe method of making people immune to smallpox. He inoculated a young boy with matter from a cowpox sore. The boy developed cowpox, a relatively harmless disease related to smallpox. But when Jenner later injected the boy with matter from a smallpox sore, the boy did not come down with the disease. His bout with cowpox had helped his body build up an immunity to smallpox. Jenner's classic experiment was the first officially recorded vaccination. The success of the experiment initiated the science of immunology—the prevention of disease by building up resistance to it.

Discovery of the first anesthetic. For thousands of years, physicians tried to dull pain during surgery by administering alcoholic drinks, opium, and various other drugs. But no drug had proved really effective in reducing the pain and shock of operations. Then in the 1840's, two Americans—Crawford Long and William T. G. Morton—discovered that ether gas could safely be used

Roentgen discovered X rays, used in diagnosing diseases and treating cancer.

Freud developed the psychoanalytic method of treating mental illness.

| 1895 | 1898 | c. 1900 | Early 1900's |

The Curies discovered radium, used in treating cancer.

Eijkman and Hopkins demonstrated the existence of vitamins.

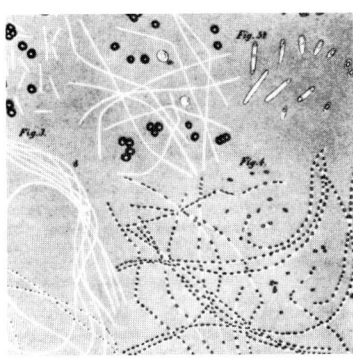

Detail of sketch by Robert Koch (1876); Aldus Archives

Anthrax germs were the first microorganisms identified as a cause of illness. Robert Koch made the discovery and sketched the anthrax germs, *above.*

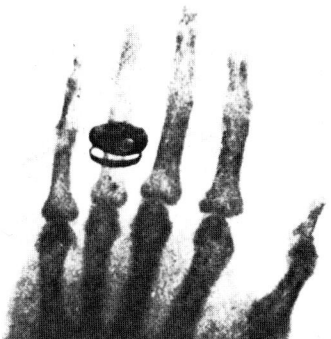

Wellcome Historical Medical Museum, London

An early X-ray photograph by Wilhelm Roentgen shows his wife's left hand and wedding ring. Roentgen took the photograph the year he discovered X rays.

Detail of an illustration (1904) from *Vanity Fair* magazine; Wellcome Historical Medical Museum, London

Marie and Pierre Curie, the discoverers of radium, are shown at work in their laboratory. Until the mid-1950's, radium was widely used for treating cancer.

to put patients to sleep during surgery. Long, a physician, and Morton, a dentist, made the discovery independently. With an effective anesthetic, doctors could perform operations never possible before.

The scientific study of disease, called *pathology,* developed during the 1800's. Rudolf Virchow, a German physician and scientist, led the development. Virchow believed that the only way to understand the nature of disease was by close examination of the affected body cells. He did important research in such diseases as leukemia and tuberculosis. The development of much improved microscopes in the early 1800's made his studies possible.

Scientists of the 1800's made dramatic progress in learning the causes of infectious disease. As early as the 1500's, scholars had suggested that tiny, invisible "seeds" caused some diseases. The bacteria discovered by Leeuwenhoek in the 1600's fitted this description. In the late 1800's, the research of Louis Pasteur and Robert Koch firmly established the *microbial,* or *germ, theory* of disease.

Pasteur, a brilliant French chemist, proved that microbes are living organisms and that certain kinds of microbes cause disease. He also proved that killing specific microbes stops the spread of specific diseases. Koch, a German physician, invented a method for determining which bacteria cause particular diseases. This method enabled him to identify the germ that causes *anthrax,* a severe disease of people and animals. The anthrax germ thus became the first germ definitely linked to a particular disease. Other research scientists followed the lead of these two pioneers. By the end of the

1800's, researchers had discovered the kinds of bacteria and other microbes responsible for such infectious diseases as plague, cholera, diphtheria, dysentery, gonorrhea, leprosy, malaria, pneumonia, tetanus, and tuberculosis.

Introduction of antiseptic surgery. Hospitals paid little attention to cleanliness before the mid-1800's. Operating rooms were often dirty, and surgeons operated in street clothes. Up to half of all surgical patients died of infections. In 1847, a Hungarian doctor, Ignaz Semmelweis, stressed the need for cleanliness in childbirth. But Semmelweis knew little about the germ theory of disease.

Pasteur's early work on bacteria convinced an English surgeon named Joseph Lister that germs caused many of the deaths of surgical patients. In 1865, Lister began using carbolic acid, a powerful disinfectant, to sterilize surgical wounds. But this method was later replaced by a more efficient technique known as *aseptic surgery.* This technique involved keeping germs away from surgical wounds in the first place instead of trying to kill germs already there. Surgeons began to wash thoroughly before an operation and to wear surgical gowns, gloves, and masks.

The beginnings of organized medicine. During the 1800's and early 1900's, groups were founded in the United States and Canada to organize and reform the medical profession in the two countries. In 1847, U.S. doctors founded the AMA to help raise the nation's medical standards. Partly as a result of the AMA's efforts, the first state licensing boards were set up in the late 1800's. The Canadian Medical Association was founded

Fleming discovered penicillin, the first antibiotic drug.

American surgeons transplanted a kidney—the first successful organ transplant.

American surgeons performed the first implantation of a permanent artificial heart.

| 1928 | Early 1950's | 1954 | Early 1970's | 1982 | 1990 |

Salk developed the first successful polio vaccine.

Scientists intensified investigation of viruses as a possible cause of cancer.

American surgeons first used gene therapy to treat a patient.

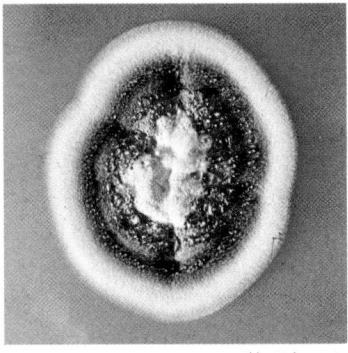

Abbott Laboratories

Penicillium **mold,** discovered by Alexander Fleming, is grown in laboratories to make penicillin. This photograph shows the mold after four days' growth.

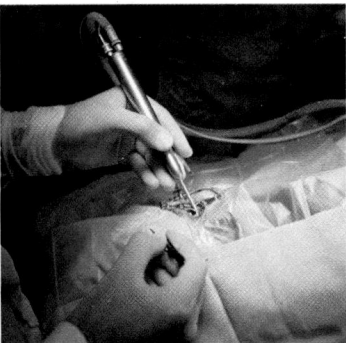

WORLD BOOK photo by Stephen Feldman, courtesy Rush-Presbyterian-St. Luke's Medical Center, Chicago

Cryosurgery, the use of extreme cold in surgery, was developed in the 1960's. The cold is applied by tools like the one above, shown "gluing" a detached retina.

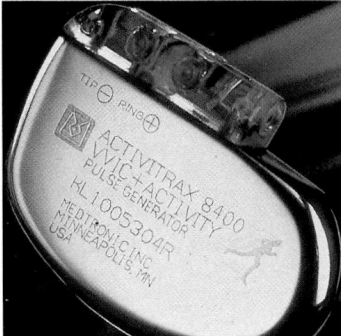

Medtronic, Inc.

A pacemaker can be implanted near the heart to make the organ beat steadily. An early, battery-powered pacemaker of the 1980's is shown in this photograph.

in 1867 for much the same purpose. The National Medical Association was started in 1895 by black doctors who felt discriminated against by the AMA. Osteopathic physicians founded the AOA in 1897.

In 1910, the Carnegie Foundation for the Advancement of Teaching issued a report called *Medical Education in the United States and Canada.* The U.S. educator Abraham Flexner prepared the report for the foundation. Flexner's report stated that only 1 of the 155 medical schools in the United States and Canada at that time provided an acceptable medical education. That school was the Johns Hopkins Medical School, founded in Baltimore in 1893. Flexner's report and the example of the Johns Hopkins school helped bring far-reaching reforms in U.S. and Canadian medical education.

The medical revolution. Advances in many fields of science and engineering have created a medical revolution in the 1900's. For example, the discovery of X rays by the German physicist Wilhelm Roentgen in 1895 enabled doctors to "see" inside the human body to diagnose illnesses and injuries. The discovery of radium by the French physicists Pierre and Marie Curie in 1898 provided a powerful weapon against cancer.

In the early 1900's, Christiaan Eijkman of the Netherlands, Frederick G. Hopkins of England, and a number of other physician-scientists showed the importance of vitamins. Their achievements helped conquer such nutritional diseases as beriberi, rickets, and scurvy. About 1910, the German physician and chemist Paul Ehrlich introduced a new method of attacking infectious disease. Ehrlich's method, called *chemotherapy,* involved searching for chemicals to destroy the microbes responsible for particular diseases.

Ehrlich's work greatly advanced drug research. In 1935, a German doctor, Gerhard Domagk, discovered the ability of sulfa drugs to cure infections in animals. His discovery led to the development of sulfa drugs to treat diseases in human beings. In 1928, the English bacteriologist Sir Alexander Fleming discovered the germ-killing power of a mold called *Penicillium.* In the early 1940's, a group of English scientists headed by Howard Florey isolated penicillin, a product of this mold. Penicillin thus became the first antibiotic.

Since the discoveries made by Domagk and Fleming, scientists have developed hundreds of antibiotics. These drugs have helped control the bacteria that cause most of the serious infectious diseases. Other drugs have been developed to fight such disorders as diabetes, high blood pressure, arthritis, heart attacks, and cancer.

The development of new vaccines has helped control the spread of such infectious diseases as polio, hepatitis, and measles. During the 1960's and 1970's, the World Health Organization conducted a vaccination program that eliminated smallpox from the world.

Since 1901, many people have received Nobel Prizes in physiology or medicine. For a list of the winners and their achievements, see the article **Nobel Prizes**.

Much progress in modern medicine has resulted from engineering advances. Engineers have developed a variety of instruments and machines to aid doctors in the diagnosis, treatment, and prevention of diseases and disorders (see **Biomedical engineering**). Microsurgery

Engineering advances led to the development of intensive care units in hospitals. Information about patients' body functions appears on screens in the unit's monitoring station.

done through small instruments eliminates the need for large incisions and enables many patients to avoid hospitalization (**Surgery** [Technique]). Some devices have helped surgeons develop new lifesaving techniques, especially in the fields of heart surgery and organ transplants (see **Heart** [History of heart research]; **Transplant**). Other advances have opened up whole new fields of medicine, such as *aviation medicine* and *occupational medicine.*

Current problems in U.S. medicine

Financial problems. Since the early 1960's, medical costs in the United States have risen rapidly. As a result, most people need some kind of health insurance. However, some Americans do not have any health insurance at all, and many other people are only partially covered.

Various plans have been suggested to guarantee more complete health coverage for all Americans. One such plan calls for employers to provide insurance that would protect all employees from large medical expenses. Under this plan, the government would provide increased health care benefits for the elderly, the poor, and the unemployed. Another plan calls for comprehensive national health insurance to cover all people. These health care plans would be financed largely through general tax revenues and increased premiums on the health insurance now provided by employers.

One factor driving up the price of medical care in the United States has been the sharp rise in the cost of hospital services. To deal with this problem, the United States Department of Health, Education, and Welfare started issuing health planning guidelines in 1978. These guidelines were designed to hold down hospital costs by preventing the expensive duplication of hospital facilities, equipment, and services, and by improving care. Numerous professional groups have developed similar but more extensive practice guidelines to deal with hundreds of medical problems. However, such measures cannot eliminate increases in hospital costs resulting from inflation, expensive new equipment, and the increased range and amount of services needed by the growing number of elderly people in the United States.

An increase in the number of malpractice suits during the 1970's also forced up the cost of medical care. As the price of malpractice insurance increased, doctors were forced to raise their fees. To protect themselves from malpractice charges, many physicians began to order more medical tests for their patients and to prescribe more cautious—and more expensive—treatment.

Poor distribution of doctors. Health experts believe the United States has enough physicians, but that the supply of physicians is badly distributed. Many rural areas and inner cities do not have enough doctors, while many suburban areas have more doctors than they need. To help remedy this situation, the federal government established the National Health Service Corps (NHSC) in 1970. Through NHSC, the government recruits physicians to work in areas that have a shortage of doctors. Another problem is an overabundance of specialists and a shortage of primary-care doctors.

Legal and ethical questions. Malpractice is the main legal dilemma confronting doctors today. Doctors may be accused of malpractice if a patient believes that he or she has been injured through the doctor's mistake or negligence. Some doctors believe that malpractice

suits have become more common because many patients now have unrealistic expectations about medical care. Patients expect their treatment to be successful, even though some modern medical techniques are highly complicated and potentially dangerous.

Medical progress has raised a large number of new, complex, and difficult problems in the day-to-day practice of medicine. For example, modern medicine's ability to prolong life raises the question of when death actually occurs. In the past, people were considered legally dead when their heart and lung action stopped. But today, machines can keep a patient's heart and lungs working for days or even months after they can no longer function by themselves. As a result, many experts believe that a person should be considered legally dead when the brain stops functioning.

Other ethical questions raised by modern medicine concern organ transplants, abortion, *euthanasia* (helping or allowing patients to die), gene therapy, and the use of human subjects in medical experiments. Some hospitals have established ethics committees which doctors can consult when faced with an ethical question.

Problems for research. Medical research has yet to find the underlying causes of diseases of the heart and blood vessels and of cancer—the chief causes of death in the United States. Knowledge of the molecular and cellular causes of these disorders will help scientists develop better ways of treating and preventing them. Women's health issues, especially breast cancer, hip fracture, and mother-and-child care, are also receiving attention from researchers. In addition, many researchers are studying how preventive strategies, such as exercising, eating a balanced diet, and avoiding alcohol and cigarettes, can be made part of daily routines. Such strategies can reduce death rates, especially among middle-aged and younger adults.   James Webster

Study aids

Laveran, Charles
Louis Alphonse

Paré, Ambroise
Pasteur, Louis

German

Baer, Karl E. von
Domagk, Gerhard
Ehrlich, Paul
Hahnemann, Samuel
Koch, Robert
Krebs, Sir Hans A.

Mayer, Julius R. von
Roentgen, Wilhelm C.
Schweitzer, Albert
Virchow, Rudolf
Wassermann, August von
Weismann, August

Italian

Galvani, Luigi
Golgi, Camillo
Malpighi, Marcello

Morgagni, Giovanni B.
Spallanzani, Lazzaro

Others

Avicenna
Barnard,
  Christiaan N.
Burnet,
  Sir Macfarlane
Einthoven, Willem
Finlay, Carlos J.

Freud, Sigmund
Galen
Hippocrates
Imhotep
Kocher, Emil T.
Mesmer,
  Franz Anton

Metchnikoff, Élie
Paracelsus,
  Philippus A.
Pavlov, Ivan P.
Semmelweis,
  Ignaz P.
Vesalius, Andreas

Diagnosis

Amniocentesis
Angiography
Arthroscopy
Biopsy
Blood count
Bronchoscope
Electrocardio-
  graph
Electroencepha-
  lograph

Endoscope
Fluoroscopy
Gastroscope
Laparoscopy
Liquid crystal
Magnetic
  resonance
  imaging
Manometer

Ophthalmoscope
Positron emission
  tomography
Spirometer
Stethoscope
Thermography
Ultrasound
X rays

Diseases

See **Disease** and **Mental illness** with their lists of *Related articles.*

Medical organizations

American Medical Association
Cancer Society, American
Emergency Medical Service
Health care plans
Heart Association, American
Medic Alert

Menninger Clinic
National Medical Association
Public Health Service
World Health Organization
World Medical Association

Preventive medicine

Antitoxin
Health
Holistic medicine

Immunity
Immunization

Inoculation
Sanitation

Medical sciences

Aerospace medicine
Anatomy
Anesthesiology
Bacteriology
Biochemistry
Cardiology
Dermatology
Embryology
Genetics

Geriatrics
Histology
Internal medicine
Microbiology
Neonatology
Neurology
Nutrition
Obstetrics and gyne-
  cology

Oncology
Ophthalmology
Orthopedics
Osteology
Pathology
Pediatrics
Pharmacology
Physiology
Psychiatry

Treatment

Angioplasty
Blood
  transfusion
Chelation therapy
Chemotherapy
Diathermy
Diet

Drug
First aid
Gamma rays
Gene therapy
Hydrotherapy
Hyperbaric
  oxygen therapy

Infrared rays
Iron lung
Irradiation
Massage
Occupational
  therapy
Oxygen tent

Physical
  therapy
Plasma
Plastic
  surgery
Prosthetics

Psychoanalysis
Psychosomatic
  medicine
Psychotherapy
Respirator
Serum

Sports medicine
Sun lamp
Surgery
Transplant
Ultraviolet rays

Other related articles

Abortion
Allopathy
Asclepius
Biofeedback
Biomedical engi-
  neering
Biotechnology
Bone bank
Chiropractic
Dentistry
Emergency Medical
  Services
Euthanasia

Eye bank
Health insurance,
  National
Homeopathy
Hope, Project
Hospital
Isotope (Uses of ra-
  dioisotopes)
Malpractice suit
Nobel Prizes
Nursing
Optometry

Osteopathic
  medicine
Paramedic
Pharmacy
Placebo
Podiatry
Poison Control
  Center
Pure food and
  drug laws
℞
Sanitarium
Trauma center

Outline

I. Elements of medical care
  A. Diagnosis   C. Prevention
  B. Treatment
II. Providing medical care
  A. How medical care is provided
  B. Where medical care is provided
  C. Improving the quality of medical care
III. Careers in medicine
  A. A career as a doctor
  B. Other careers in medicine
IV. Financing medical care
  A. In the United States   C. In other countries
  B. In Canada
V. History
VI. Current problems in U.S. medicine

Questions

What are the three main methods of paying for medical care in
  the United States?
Why is medicine both a science and an art?
What is primary care? Who provides it?
What are the three main elements of medical care?
Who proved that certain microbes cause disease?
What are *paramedical workers? Medical technologists*?
Who wrote the first scientific textbook on human anatomy?
What are the requirements for obtaining a license to practice
  medicine in each state of the United States?
What is the World Health Organization? What does it do?
Who was the first physician known to consider medicine a sci-
  ence and art separate from religion?

Reading and Study Guide

See *Medicine* in the Research Guide/Index, Volume 22, for a
Reading and Study Guide.

Additional resources

Altman, Lawrence K. *Who Goes First? The Story of Self-
  Experimentation in Medicine.* Random Hse., 1987.
Epstein, Rachael S. *Careers in Health Care.* Chelsea Hse., 1989.
  Also suitable for younger readers.
Fradin, Dennis B. *Medicine: Yesterday, Today, and Tomorrow.*
  Childrens Pr., 1989. Also suitable for younger readers.
Lambert, Mark. *Medicine in the Future.* Bookwright, 1986. For
  younger readers.
Nuland, Sherwin B. *Doctors: The Biography of Medicine.* Knopf,
  1988.
Shorter, Edward. *The Health Century.* Doubleday, 1987.
Weiss, Ann E. *Bioethics: Dilemmas in Modern Medicine.* Ens-
  low, 1985. Also suitable for younger readers.

Medicine Hat (pop. 43,625) is a city on the South Saskatchewan River in southeastern Alberta. For location, see **Alberta** (political map). Warm winds called *chinooks* usually keep Medicine Hat warmer than most other cities in the same latitude.

One of the largest known natural-gas fields in the world surrounds Medicine Hat and provides the basis for its industries. The city owns its own gas reserves, which are part of the field.

Medicine Hat serves as a trading center for a large farming and ranching area. Its factories use gas for power, and this keeps Medicine Hat free from smoke. The chief products include flour, glass, linseed oil, cement, petrochemicals, rubber products, brick and tile, pottery, and machinery. Workers process lignite coal and clay found nearby. The city has a fertilizer plant, a carbon black plant, a tire plant, and several greenhouses. One of these greenhouses, with 10 acres (4 hectares) under glass, is the second largest in Canada.

Medicine Hat was founded in 1883 and chartered as a city in 1906. The city's name is the translation of the Blackfoot Indian word *saamis* (the headdress of a medicine man). A Blackfoot legend says a Cree medicine man lost his saamis there while deserting a battle against the Blackfoot. Medicine Hat has a mayor-council form of government.   Peter R. Mossey

Médicis, Catherine de. See Catherine de Médicis.
Medieval period. See Middle Ages.
Medill, *muh DIHL,* **Joseph** (1823-1899), a crusading American editor and publisher, made the *Chicago Tribune* one of the world's most successful newspapers. He served as managing editor from 1855 to 1863, as editor in chief from 1863 to 1866, and as publisher from 1874 until his death. Many of his editorials concerned government reforms.

Medill worked hard to build the Republican Party. Some authorities believe he named the party. He helped sponsor Abraham Lincoln as a candidate for the presidency. Medill served at the Illinois Constitutional Convention of 1869, on the Civil Service Commission under President Ulysses S. Grant, and as mayor of Chicago from 1872 to 1874. He was born near Saint John, New Brunswick, Canada.   John Tebbel

Medina, *muh DEE nuh* (pop. 198,186), is a city in western Saudi Arabia. It lies on a fertile plain about 270 miles (434 kilometers) north of Mecca (see **Saudi Arabia** [political map]). Medina and Mecca are the holiest cities in Islam, the Muslim religion, and only Muslims may enter them. The Holy Mosque of the Islamic prophet Muhammad is located in Medina. This mosque holds Muhammad's tomb. Islam requires every Muslim to make at least one pilgrimage to Mecca if possible. Most pilgrims who visit Mecca also go to Medina.

Farmers grow fruits and vegetables in the area around Medina. Agriculture and money spent by pilgrims form the basis of Medina's economy. The city is the home of the Islamic University. Medina has kept much of its traditional appearance. As Medina has grown, however, the walls of the old city have disappeared. New suburbs have grown up, and wealthy residents live in these areas.

No one knows when Medina was founded. It was originally called *Yathrib,* and farmers settled there before 200 B.C. Medina received its present name, which means *town* or *city,* about A.D. 600. Muhammad and his disciples found safety in Medina after they were forced to flee from Mecca in 622. Medina became the center of the Muslim community, but its political importance fell as the Islamic empire grew.   Malcolm C. Peck

See also **Muhammad** (His teachings; The Hegira).
Medina, *muh DEE nuh,* **Harold Raymond** (1888-1990), an American judge, won international fame for his fair conduct of the trial of 11 American Communist Party leaders in 1949. These leaders were convicted of conspiring to teach and advocate the overthrow of the U.S. government by force. Medina urged the jury to be calm and cautioned that "justice does not flourish amidst emotional excitement and stress."

Judge Medina was born in Brooklyn, N.Y., and graduated from Princeton University. He received his law degree from Columbia University in 1912 and taught there from 1915 to 1947. He practiced law in New York City until he was appointed a federal judge in 1947. He retired from that post in 1958.   David M. O'Brien
Meditation. See Religion (Religious rituals); Transcendental Meditation.
Mediterranean fruit fly is an insect that destroys fruits, nuts, and vegetables. It attacks more than 200 kinds of plants, especially tropical species.

Scientists believe that the Mediterranean fruit fly, popularly called the *Medfly,* originated in tropical west Africa. Long ago it made its way to northern and southern Africa, southern Europe, and Asia. It had spread throughout the Mediterranean region by 1850. The fly was found in Australia in the late 1800's, and it appeared in Brazil and Hawaii in the early 1900's.

In 1929, the Medfly was discovered in Florida. A quarantine was quickly ordered in the infested area to prevent the fly from spreading. By mid-1930, all of these flies in the United States had apparently been destroyed. Several invasions of the fly in Florida and Texas between 1930 and 1979 were also stopped.

The Medfly first appeared in California in 1975. This infestation was eliminated by 1976. In June 1980, Medflies were found in northern and southern California. The infestations were attacked by stripping damaged fruit from the trees and by spraying with insecticide from machines on the ground. Large numbers of sterile flies, which mate with fertile flies and cause them to lay infertile eggs, were also released. These measures eliminated the southern infestation. In northern California, however, the infestation became so widespread that, in 1981, the area had to be aerially sprayed with insecticide-treated bait. The spraying apparently was successful, and the Medfly infestation was declared eradicated in 1982.

In 1984, 1985, 1987, and 1990, the Medfly appeared in Miami, Fla. The insect also was found in California every year from 1987 to 1992. Infestations were treated by aerially spraying malathion and releasing sterile flies.

WORLD BOOK illustration by
Oxford Illustrators Limited
Mediterranean fruit fly

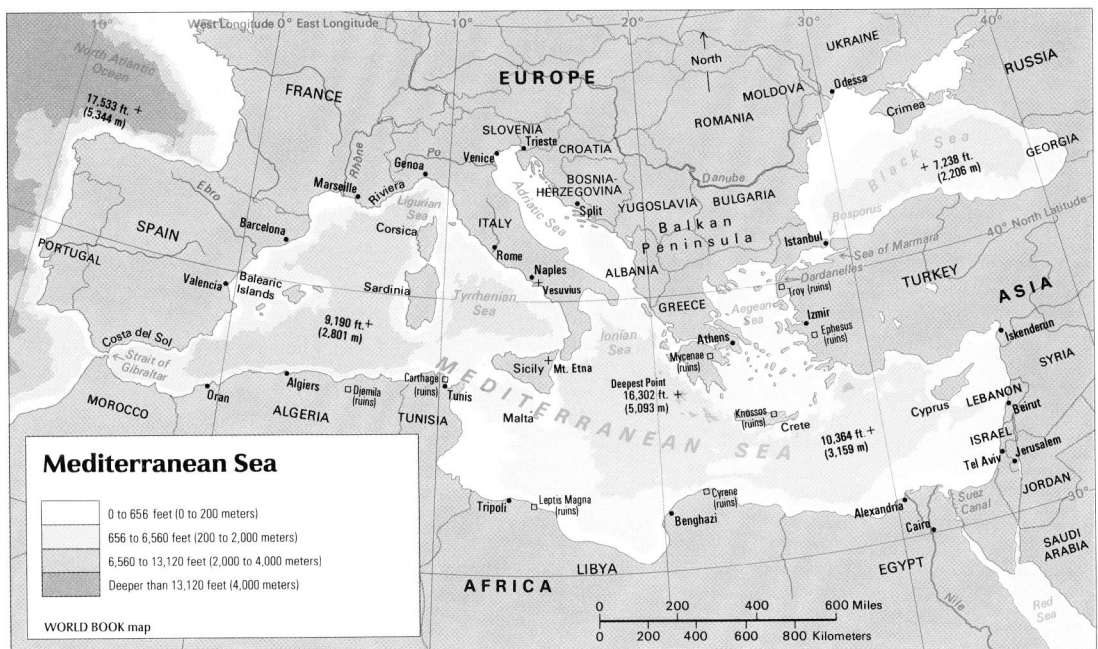

Mediterranean Sea

- 0 to 656 feet (0 to 200 meters)
- 656 to 6,560 feet (200 to 2,000 meters)
- 6,560 to 13,120 feet (2,000 to 4,000 meters)
- Deeper than 13,120 feet (4,000 meters)

WORLD BOOK map

The Medfly is slightly smaller than a common house fly. Its wings have yellowish-orange spots. The female fruit fly can lay as many as 1,000 eggs in her lifetime and up to 40 per day. She typically lays her eggs in a ripe fruit that is still on the tree. She drills tiny holes into the skin or rind of the fruit, and lays from two to six eggs in each hole. The eggs hatch into larvae, which eat their way through the fruit, causing it to drop to the ground. The larvae later burrow into the ground for the next stage of development, which is called the *pupal stage.* When the insects come out of the ground, they are adult Medflies.

The Mediterranean fruit fly thrives in a warm climate. Extremely hot or cold weather can kill it. There are also several insect parasites that destroy the larvae and pupae of the Medfly. These parasites can help control the fly, but they cannot eliminate it. A person who suspects that fruit is infested with larvae of the Medfly should have the fruit examined by an expert.   Donald L. Dahlsten

Mediterranean Sea, MEHD *uh tuh* RAY *nee uhn,* has been one of the world's chief trade routes since ancient times. Many early civilizations, including those of Egypt, Greece, Phoenicia, and Rome, developed along its shores. Today, the islands and coastal areas of the Mediterranean rank among the most popular tourist attractions in the world.

Location and size. The Latin word *mediterranean* means *in the middle of land,* and land almost surrounds the Mediterranean Sea. Europe lies to the north, Asia to the east, and Africa to the south.

On the west, the Strait of Gibraltar connects the Mediterranean with the Atlantic Ocean. Another strait, the Dardanelles, links the Mediterranean on the east with the Sea of Marmara, the Bosporus, and the Black Sea. On the southeast, the Isthmus of Suez separates the Mediterranean and Red seas. The Suez Canal, an artifi-

cial waterway, crosses this thin strip of land. Ships sail through the canal between the Mediterranean and the Red Sea and Indian Ocean.

The Mediterranean covers about 969,100 square miles (2,510,000 square kilometers). The Black Sea, which many people consider part of the Mediterranean, has an area of about 173,000 square miles (448,000 square kilometers). Several other arms of the Mediterranean are large enough to be called seas. They include the Adriatic, Aegean, Ionian, and Tyrrhenian seas.

Excluding the Black Sea, the Mediterranean is more than twice as long as it is wide. It has a maximum length of about 2,200 miles (3,540 kilometers), between the Strait of Gibraltar and Iskenderun, Turkey. The widest part of the sea lies between Libya and Croatia, a distance of about 1,000 miles (1,600 kilometers).

The seabed. An underwater ridge between Sicily and Tunisia divides the Mediterranean into two basins. The eastern basin is deeper than the western one. The sea has an average depth of 4,926 feet (1,501 meters). It reaches its greatest depth—16,302 feet (5,093 meters)—in a depression called the Hellenic Trough that lies between Greece and Italy.

Earthquakes occur frequently throughout the Mediterranean region, especially in Greece and western Turkey. Volcanic action formed many of the islands in the Mediterranean Sea. A few volcanoes still erupt in the area. They include Mount Etna, Stromboli, and Vesuvius.

Earth scientists explain the earthquakes and volcanic activity by the theory of *plate tectonics.* According to this theory, the earth's outer shell consists of about 30 rigid plates that are in slow, continuous motion. Movements of plates that carry the European and African continents and the Mediterranean seabed squeeze and stretch the earth's crust in the Mediterranean region, causing earthquakes and volcanoes.

Coastline and islands. Many bays and inlets indent the coastline of the Mediterranean. Several large peninsulas, including Italy and the Balkan Peninsula, jut out into the sea. Along most of the coast, rugged hills rise sharply from the water. Egypt and Libya have flatter coastal areas, with plains lying next to the sea.

Sicily, the largest island in the Mediterranean, covers 9,926 square miles (25,708 square kilometers). Other large islands include, in order of size, Sardinia, Cyprus, Corsica, and Crete.

Climate. The temperature at the surface of the Mediterranean averages about 61° F. (16° C). In summer, the surface temperature may reach 80° F. (27° C). Even in winter, it seldom drops below 40° F. (4° C). The water varies little in temperature in the middle depths and near the bottom. It stays between 55° and 59° F. (13° and 15° C) throughout the year.

The tremendous volume of warm water helps give the land surrounding it a warm, subtropical climate. Most Mediterranean countries have hot, dry summers and mild, rainy winters. These conditions provide what has become known as a "Mediterranean climate," even when they occur elsewhere. Two Mediterranean countries, Egypt and Libya, have tropical climates, hotter and dryer than the typical Mediterranean type.

A hot wind known as the *sirocco* blows across the Mediterranean from Africa toward southern Europe. A cold, dry wind called the *mistral* blows the other way, from France out over the sea. See **Sirocco.**

The water of the Mediterranean comes mostly from the Atlantic Ocean and the Black Sea. Several large rivers also empty into the Mediterranean. The largest include the Ebro of Spain, the Nile of Egypt, the Po of Italy, and the Rhône of France. The Nile has contributed less water since 1964, when the Aswan High Dam in Egypt began partly blocking its flow.

The warm, dry climate gives the sea a high rate of evaporation. As a result, the water of the Mediterranean is saltier than that of the Atlantic.

The Mediterranean has almost no tides. A strong current flows into the Mediterranean from the Black Sea. Another flows in from the Atlantic through the Strait of Gibraltar. In the days of sailing ships, this Atlantic current made it difficult for vessels to reach the ocean from the Mediterranean. Beneath the surface current, a deeper current of dense salty water flows from the Mediterranean to the Atlantic.

Economic importance. The warm climate, beautiful scenery, and historical importance of the Mediterranean region attract millions of tourists yearly. The region includes such popular resort areas as the Greek islands and the French and Italian rivieras.

The Mediterranean has little large-scale commercial fishing, but it is an important source of food for the people of the region. The chief seafoods from the Mediterranean Sea include anchovies, sardines, shrimp, and tuna. Other products harvested from the sea include coral and sponges.

The Mediterranean serves as an important waterway that links Europe, the Middle East, and Asia. Ships use the Suez Canal as a route between the Mediterranean and Red seas.

Formation of the Mediterranean Sea can be explained by the theory of plate tectonics. About 250 million years ago, the continents formed a single land mass called Pangaea. The Tethys Sea, a huge bay that developed into the Mediterranean, indented the east coast of Pangaea. Through the centuries, Pangaea broke up into continents that began to drift slowly toward their present location. As they drifted, Africa turned counterclockwise, and Eurasia turned clockwise. Their movement opened a waterway at the western end of the sea, linking it with the ocean. By about 65 million years ago, the rotation of these two continents had almost closed the eastern end of the Tethys Sea. The sea thus acquired its present shape.

Some earth scientists believe the Mediterranean dried up about a dozen times between $7\frac{1}{2}$ and $5\frac{1}{2}$ million years ago. During this period, the movement of the European and African continents repeatedly closed and reopened the Strait of Gibraltar. Each time it closed, the sea began to dry up. After about 1,000 years of evaporation, only a large desert remained. A few salty lakes, like Great Salt Lake in Utah, dotted this desert. When the strait reopened, water from the Atlantic rushed in, forming a huge waterfall. The waterfall carried about 1,000 times as much water as does Niagara Falls, and it refilled the Mediterranean in about 100 years.

In 1970, scientists found evidence that supported the desert theory. That year, geologists aboard a research vessel called the *Glomar Challenger* drilled cores of rock from the Mediterranean floor. The cores contained minerals, known as *evaporites,* that are formed by the evaporation of salty water.

History of the Mediterranean. Many historians believe Western civilization was born in the Mediterranean region. Ancient cultures grew up on the banks of the sea, where conditions favored their development. The mild climate encouraged human settlement. The sea's calm waters and steady winds most of the year made seafaring relatively easy. The sea also had natural harbors and many islands that sailors could use as ports.

Probably the first great civilization to develop in the Mediterranean region was that of ancient Egypt. The Egyptians had a unified national government by about 3100 B.C. and had begun using a writing system by 3000 B.C. The first important European civilization, the Minoan culture, arose on the island of Crete about 3000 B.C. Another culture, the Helladic civilization, grew up on the Greek mainland. One city, Mycenae, became so powerful that some historians call the later Helladic civilization *Mycenaean.* By about 1450 B.C., Mycenaean ships controlled the Mediterranean. They traded with cities as far away as what are now Lebanon and Syria.

After about 1200 B.C., the Phoenicians began to win control of the Mediterranean. From their homes on the eastern shore, they sailed to all parts of the sea. Phoenician sailors even traveled through the Strait of Gibraltar into the Atlantic. Carthage, a colony founded by the Phoenicians, became another great sea power after about 600 B.C. By the A.D. 100's, the Roman Empire ruled all the lands that bordered the sea. The Romans called the Mediterranean *Mare Nostrum* (Our Sea).

For centuries, the Mediterranean served as the greatest water route in the world. From the 1100's to the 1400's, such Mediterranean trading centers as Barcelona, Constantinople, Genoa, and Venice linked Europe and Asia. The ships of these cities brought goods from

India and China across the sea to Europe. The Portuguese explorer Vasco da Gama sailed around Africa in 1497, reaching India in 1498. Trading ships then began to use this easier, all-water route to the East. As a result, the importance of the Mediterranean as a trade route declined until the 1800's.

The opening of the Suez Canal in 1869 made the Mediterranean a part of the shortest water route between Europe and Asia. For nearly 100 years, the sea ranked as one of the world's busiest shipping lanes. The canal was closed during the Arab-Israeli War of 1967. It was reopened in 1975.

During the 1970's, water pollution became a serious problem in the Mediterranean. Garbage, industrial wastes, oil, pesticides, and sewage polluted the sea and threatened fishing and tourism in the region. In 1976, most of the nations with borders on the Mediterranean signed a treaty in which they agreed to work to reduce the pollution. Since that time, they have followed detailed plans of action that have helped reduce the pollution somewhat.   Warren E. Yasso

Related articles in *World Book* include:

Adriatic Sea	Crete	Ionian Sea
Aegean Sea	Cyprus	Sardinia
Black Sea	Dardanelles	Sicily
Bosporus	Gibraltar	Suez Canal
Corsica	Gibraltar, Strait of	Tyrrhenian Sea

Additional resources

Bradford, Ernle D. S. *Mediterranean: Portrait of a Sea.* Harcourt, 1971.
Carrington, Richard. *The Mediterranean: Cradle of Western Culture.* Viking, 1971.
The Mediterranean. Ed. by Pat Hargreaves. Silver Burdett, 1981. For younger readers.

Medulla oblongata. See **Brain** (The brain stem).

Medusa. See **Jellyfish**.

Medusa, *muh DOO suh,* was one of the three Gorgons, and the only mortal Gorgon (see **Gorgons**). Medusa and her two sisters had writhing snakes for hair, staring eyes, hideous grins, and protruding fangs. They were so ugly that anyone who saw them turned to stone.

Unlike her sisters, Medusa had been beautiful in her youth, and was still proud of her hair. She boasted of her beauty to Athena, who became jealous and changed her into a hideous person.

Perseus killed Medusa by looking into his mirrorlike shield as he cut off her head (see **Perseus**). At that time, Medusa had been made pregnant by the sea god Poseidon. The winged horse Pegasus sprang from her beheaded body, and poisonous snakes arose from the blood that dripped from her head. Athena saved blood from Medusa's body and gave it to Asclepius, the god of healing (see **Asclepius**). The blood from Medusa's left side was a fatal poison, but that from her right side had the power to revive the dead.   Justin M. Glenn

Meech Lake accord. See **Quebec** (Recent developments).

Meeker, Ezra (1830-1928), was an American pioneer and author. In 1852, he took a five-month journey by oxcart along the Oregon Trail from Iowa to Portland, Ore., with his wife and infant son. He returned to Iowa by the same route in 1906, painting inscriptions on landmarks along the way as part of a memorial observance. He made a similar trip by automobile in 1915. He spent much of his time after the age of 75 promoting the mem-

ory of the Oregon Trail. Meeker founded the Oregon Trail Association. His books include *Ox-Team Days on the Oregon Trail* (1922) and *Kate Mulhall* (1926). Meeker was born in Huntsville, Ohio.   Jesse L. Gilmore

Meerkat is a small burrowing animal of Africa. It lives from southwestern Angola to South Africa. The meerkat, also called *suricate,* is found in open, dry country where the ground is hard and stony.

Adult meerkats measure about 20 inches (51 centimeters) long, including a tail of about 8 inches (20 centimeters). They weigh about 2 pounds (900 grams). Meerkats have front feet with strong, curved claws for digging, and stocky hind legs. They have broad, rounded heads and sharply pointed noses. Most meerkats are silvery-brown, with dark bands across their backs.

Meerkats live in underground colonies of up to 30 in-

© Charles G. Summers, Jr., Tom Stack & Assoc.

Meerkats often stand upright to search for birds that may attack them. These burrowing animals live in southern Africa.

dividuals. Their burrows have many tunnels and entrances. Meerkats leave their burrows only during the day. They often stand upright, exposing their chests and bellies to the sun. They also stand upright to search for large birds that hunt them. Meerkats eat mostly spiders and insects, including beetles and grasshoppers.

Scientific classification. The meerkat belongs to the family Herpestidae. Its scientific name is *Suricata suricatta.*

Duane A. Schlitter

Meerschaum, *MIHR shuhm,* is a soft, whitish fibrous or flaky clay. Manufacturers use it to make tobacco pipes. Meerschaum is also called *sepiolite.* It is so light that it will float in water. In German, the word *meerschaum* means *sea foam.* The mineral gets its name because it floats and has the look of foam. Large quantities of meerschaum are found in Asia Minor. Lumps of meerschaum are found in masses of other types of clay. Meerschaum is a compound of magnesium, silicon, oxygen, and water. The mineral is a water-bearing magnesium silicate.

Many smokers prefer meerschaum tobacco pipes. The bowls of meerschaum pipes are white when new. With careful handling and use, the bowl slowly colors a rich brown. Meerschaum pipes break easily.

Ray E. Ferrell, Jr.

Megalithic monuments, *MEHG uh LIHTH ihk,* are structures built of large stones by prehistoric people for burial or religious purposes. The word *megalith* means

Ronald Sheridan

A megalithic monument near Carnac, France, consists of single upright stones called *menhirs* arranged in rows called *alignments*. Menhirs are common in megalithic monuments.

large stone. The stones may weigh from 25 to 100 short tons (23 to 91 metric tons) each. Megalithic monuments can be found in various parts of the world. The best-known ones are in western Europe and were built between 4000 and 1500 B.C. Many megalithic structures served as tombs. Some of these tombs had passages. Other tombs, called *dolmens,* consisted of a small, simple chamber. Such tombs have been discovered in many parts of western and southern Europe.

Single, erect stones are called *menhirs.* A monument composed of menhirs arranged in a circle and surrounded by a bank of earth and a ditch is called a *henge.* The most famous henge, Stonehenge, stands near Salisbury, England (see **Stonehenge**). Menhirs were also arranged in parallel rows called *alignments.* Elaborate alignments near Carnac in northwestern France extend over 2 miles (3 kilometers). Bruce Kraig

Megalopolis, *mehg uh LAHP uh lihs,* is a region made up of two or more metropolitan areas. A metropolitan area consists of a central city that has a population of at least 50,000 and the suburbs that surround the city. Metropolitan areas form a megalopolis if they attract

Megalopolis

The map below shows in light red the largest developing *megalopolis* (continuous metropolitan area) in the United States. Built-up areas are shown in dark red.

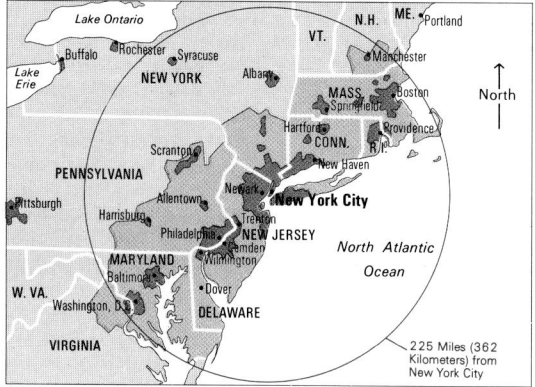

enough people and industry and then expand and begin to grow together.

The largest megalopolis in the United States includes the metropolitan areas of Boston, New York City, Philadelphia, Baltimore, and Washington, D.C. It extends about 600 miles (960 kilometers) from southern New Hampshire into northern Virginia. It covers over 50,000 square miles (130,000 square kilometers) and has about 42 million people. Other megalopolises developing in the nation include (1) the area from San Francisco, through Los Angeles, to San Diego; (2) the area from Milwaukee, through Chicago and Cleveland, to Pittsburgh; and (3) the area from Dallas and Fort Worth to Houston.

The French geographer Jean Gottmann introduced the term *megalopolis* in 1961 to describe the urban development in the Northeastern United States. The term comes from the Greek words *megalo* and *polis,* meaning *great city.* Megalopolises developing outside the United States include the Tokyo-Yokohama-Osaka area in Japan and the Ruhr Industrial Basin in Germany, the Netherlands, and Belgium. Louis H. Masotti

See also **Metropolitan area.**

Megaphone, *MEHG uh fohn,* is a hollow, cone-shaped device used to make a voice sound louder. A person speaks or shouts into the small opening at one end of the megaphone, and the sound of the voice comes out at the wide end. The megaphone makes the voice sound louder by pointing sound waves in one direction and reducing the spreading of the waves in other directions. Megaphones vary in size, and some are over 2 feet (61 centimeters) long. Cheerleaders often use megaphones. A portable, battery-powered megaphone that combines a microphone, an amplifier, and a loudspeaker is called a *bullhorn.* Carol E. Stokes

Megara. See Hercules.

Mehmed II. See Muhammad II

Mehta, *MAY tuh,* **Zubin,** *ZOO bihn* (1936-), is a symphony orchestra conductor. Mehta won fame for his conducting of such large-scale romantic compositions as the works of the French composer Hector Berlioz. His interpretations are forceful, though they have been criticized as lacking refinement and being too showy.

Mehta was born in Bombay, India. From 1954 to 1960, he studied conducting in Vienna, Austria, under conductor Hans Swarowsky. Mehta became music director of the Montreal Symphony Orchestra in 1960. In 1962, Mehta took the same position with the Los Angeles Symphony, becoming the youngest conductor of a major symphony orchestra in the United States. He served as director of both orchestras until 1967, when he resigned from the Montreal post.

In 1978, Mehta left the Los Angeles Symphony to become music director of the New York Philharmonic, a position he held until 1991. He has also served as music director of the Israel Philharmonic Orchestra since 1968. Charles H. Webb

Christine Steiner, New York Philharmonic

Zubin Mehta

Arthur Meighen

Prime Minister of Canada
1920-1921
1926

Detail of a portrait by Ernest Fosbery;
Parliament Buildings, Ottawa (John Evans)

Borden	Meighen	King	Meighen	King
1911-1920	1920-1921	1921-1926	1926	1926-1930

Meighen, *MEE uhn,* **Arthur** (1874-1960), served as prime minister of Canada two times during the 1920's. He first took office as prime minister in July 1920, succeeding Sir Robert L. Borden. Meighen served as prime minister until December 1921. He held the office again from June to September in 1926. Meighen led the Conservative Party from 1921 to 1926 and in 1941 and 1942.

Meighen accomplished little as prime minister. But he was noted for his bitter and unsuccessful power struggle with Liberal Party chief W. L. Mackenzie King. Meighen failed to lead his party to a parliamentary majority in the elections of 1921, 1925, and 1926. Each time, King became—or remained—prime minister.

Meighen, a lawyer, had a remarkable memory and a gift for eloquent expression. He especially liked to argue and became the most skilled debater in Parliament. A newspaper paid tribute to Meighen's sharpness with words by calling him "The First Swordsman of Parliament." Meighen became one of Borden's chief aides during World War I (1914-1918). During this period, Meighen either developed or defended almost all the government's most controversial policies.

Some Canadians viewed Meighen as a brilliant, honest, and courageous statesman. But many others regarded him as quarrelsome and unwilling to compromise, and still others disliked his critical comments about King. Meighen himself felt that the public often misunderstood him.

Early life

Arthur Meighen was born on June 16, 1874, on a farm near St. Mary's, Ont. He was the second of the six children of Joseph Meighen and Mary Bell Meighen. His parents placed a high value on education, and Arthur became a bright and eager student. He was a serious youth and made it clear to the family that he preferred to be called Arthur rather than Art. In 1896, he graduated from the University of Toronto with honors in mathematics.

Soon afterward, Meighen became a high-school teacher in Caledonia, Ont. But he did not like teaching and quit after a year. In 1898, Meighen moved to Winnipeg. He began to study law there as a clerk in a law firm. He was admitted to the bar in 1903 and established a law practice in Portage la Prairie, Man.

In June 1904, Meighen married Isabel Cox (1883-1985), a schoolteacher from Birtle, Man. They had two sons, Theodore and Maxwell, and a daughter, Lillian.

Entry into public life

Meighen began his political career in 1908, when he won election to the Canadian House of Commons as a Conservative from Portage la Prairie. He was reelected in 1911. In 1913, Meighen was appointed solicitor general after working out a method to cut off a bitter debate over a naval bill that Prime Minister Borden had introduced in the House of Commons. In 1917, Borden named Meighen secretary of state and minister of mines and, later that year, minister of the interior.

During World War I, Meighen played a key role in the development of several controversial measures. One such bill enabled the government to take possession of some important railroads that had gone into debt. Another established a military draft. These bills made

Meighen unpopular in Quebec, where Montreal business executives disliked the railroad take-over and French-speaking Canadians bitterly opposed the draft.

In October 1917, Borden formed a government almost entirely of English-speaking Conservative and Liberal supporters of the draft. This administration became known as the Union Government. Two months later, Borden led the Unionists to victory in a general election. In 1920, he retired because of poor health. Borden's followers in Parliament chose Meighen to succeed him as their leader and prime minister.

Prime minister

First term. When Meighen took office as prime minister on July 10, 1920, his government faced serious political problems. Many of its supporters in the West and in rural Ontario had begun to favor the new Progressive Party, organized by dissatisfied farmers, who wanted lower tariffs. In addition, Meighen had little support in Quebec.

Meighen's most notable achievement as prime minister occurred at a conference of British Empire prime ministers in London in 1921. The conference had been called to consider renewal of the Anglo-Japanese Alliance of 1902. Meighen knew the United States disliked the treaty, and he believed Canada and Great Britain would be served best if it expired. Largely because of Meighen's arguments, the conference postponed a decision on renewal. This move helped lead to the Washington Naval Conference of 1921-1922. At this conference, Britain, Japan, France, Italy, and the United States reached an agreement on arms limitation (see **Arms control**).

By 1921, the wartime union of Conservatives and Liberals had fallen apart. Many Liberals had returned to their old party. Meighen led the Conservatives in the general election that year. But they suffered the worst defeat of any Canadian governing party up to that time. They won only 50 of the 235 seats in the House of Commons and placed third behind the Liberals and the Progressives. Meighen himself lost his seat from Portage la Prairie. W. L. Mackenzie King, the Liberal Party leader, replaced Meighen as prime minister on Dec. 29, 1921.

Opposition leader. Meighen set out to rebuild the Conservative Party. In 1922, he won election to the House of Commons from Grenville, Ont., and became leader of the opposition in the House. In the 1925 election, Meighen regained his seat from Portage la Prairie. The Conservatives emerged as the largest group in the House of Commons. But they fell seven seats short of a majority, and King won enough support from the Progressives to remain prime minister.

In 1926, a scandal in the customs department disgraced the King Administration. King asked Lord Byng, Canada's governor general, to dissolve Parliament so a new election could be held. But Byng refused to do so, and King resigned. Byng believed that Meighen, as leader of the largest party in the House of Commons, should have a chance to form a government.

Second term. On June 29, 1926, Meighen again became prime minister. But his government soon met defeat in the House of Commons on a motion charging that its ministers were serving illegally. This time Byng dissolved Parliament at Meighen's request. The Liberals won the election that followed, and King succeeded Meighen as prime minister on September 25.

Meighen, who had also lost his seat, resigned as Conservative leader and retired from public service. By the end of 1926, he was an investment banker in Toronto.

Later years

Meighen began a political comeback in 1932, when Prime Minister Richard B. Bennett appointed him to the Canadian Senate. Bennett had succeeded Meighen as leader of the Conservative Party and had led the party to victory in the 1930 general election. Meighen became government leader in the Senate, and then leader of the opposition in the Senate after King led the Liberals back to power in 1935.

In 1941, the Conservative Party again chose Meighen as its leader. But his political career lasted only a short time longer. Meighen sought election to the House of Commons from York South, in Toronto. However, he was defeated in February 1942 by a socialist who called for social welfare policies. World War II (1939-1945) was underway, and Meighen again came out in favor of the draft. In December, Meighen retired from politics a second time. But before retiring, he arranged for Premier John Bracken of Manitoba to be selected as leader of the newly renamed Progressive Conservative Party. Meighen devoted the rest of his life chiefly to business activities. He died on Aug. 5, 1960, in Toronto.

J. L. Granatstein

Meigs, *megz,* **Cornelia Lynde** (1884-1973), an American author, wrote more than two dozen books for children. Most of them are based on incidents in American history. In 1934, she won the Newbery Medal for *Invincible Louisa,* the life of Louisa May Alcott. Her other works include *Kingdom of the Winding Road* (1915), *Rain on the Roof* (1925), *The Trade Wind* (1927), and *As the Crow Flies* (1927). Meigs wrote many of her books under the pen name Adair Aldon. She was editor in chief and co-author of *A Critical History of Children's Literature* (1953). She also wrote a play, *The Steadfast Princess* (1915).

Cornelia Meigs was born in Rock Island, Ill. She spent her summers in New England. Some of her books relate the New England stories her parents and grandparents told her. She was graduated from Bryn Mawr College, and taught there 18 years. Kathryn Pierson Jennings

Meiji. See Mutsuhito.

Mein Kampf is a book by Adolf Hitler. The title is German for *My Struggle.* In the book, Hitler gave a fanciful account of his life and set down his political ideas. He described the alleged superiority of the German people, and said that the good of Germany ranked above all other values. The book stated Hitler's ideas on "race purity." These beliefs led to World War II and the slaughter of millions of Europeans. *Mein Kampf* was the "bible" for German Nazis and a guide for Nazi sympathizers in other countries. Stefan T. Possony

See also **Hitler, Adolf** (*Mein Kampf*).

Meiosis. See Cell (Cell division; illustration).

Meir, Golda (1898-1978), served as prime minister of Israel from 1969 to 1974. During her political career, she supported large-scale immigration to Israel and major housing and other construction programs. Her main problem as prime minister was the territorial conflict between Israel and several Arab nations. Meir followed a firm but open policy toward the Arabs.

In October 1973, war broke out for the fourth time between Israel and the Arabs. Israel suffered heavy early losses, and Meir's government was severely criticized. As a result, she resigned in June 1974, even though she had led the Labor Party to victory in the December 1973 elections.

Wide World

Golda Meir

Golda Meir was born Golda Mabovitz in Kiev, Ukraine. Her family moved to Milwaukee, Wis., in 1906, and she later taught school there. In 1921, she went to Palestine and joined a collective farm village.

In 1948, part of Palestine became the new nation of Israel. Meir served as Israel's minister of labor from 1949 to 1956 and as minister of foreign affairs from 1956 to 1966. She was secretary-general of the Labor Party from 1966 to 1969.   Ellis Rivkin

Additional resources

Adler, David A. *Our Golda: The Story of Golda Meir.* Penguin, 1986. First published in 1984. For younger readers.
Meir, Golda. *My Life.* Dell, 1976. First published in 1975.
Sachar, Howard M. *A History of Israel: From the Rise of Zionism to Our Time.* Knopf, 1979. *A History of Israel: From the Aftermath of the Yom Kippur War.* Oxford, 1988. First published in 1976 and 1987, respectively. Contain many references to Meir.
Slater, Robert. *Golda: The Uncrowned Queen of Israel: A Pictorial Biography.* Jonathan David, 1981.

Meistersinger. See Mastersinger.

Meitner, *MYT nuhr,* **Lise,** *LEE zuh* (1878-1968), was an Austrian-born physicist who played an essential role in the discovery of *nuclear fission* (the splitting of the nucleus of an atom). From 1934 to 1938, Meitner and German chemists Otto Hahn and Fritz Strassmann worked on the reactions that occur when neutrons bombard uranium nuclei. In December 1938, Hahn and Strassmann discovered that such bombardment produces nuclei of *barium,* a chemical element much lighter than uranium. In January 1939, Meitner and her nephew, Otto Frisch, gave the first explanation of that discovery. Meitner and Frisch described how neutron bombardment causes uranium nuclei to split into nuclei of barium and other elements, and they calculated the enormous energy released. Meitner and Frisch suggested that the process of splitting be called nuclear fission. The work of Meitner, Hahn, Strassmann, and Frisch led to the development of the atomic bomb and other uses of nuclear energy.

Meitner was born in Vienna in 1878. She earned a doctorate in physics from the University of Vienna in 1906. In 1907, she began working with Hahn in Berlin. She and Hahn were among the first to isolate the element protactinium in 1917. A pioneer for women in physics, she became the first head of the physics department at the Kaiser-Wilhelm Institute of Chemistry (now the Max Planck Institute of Chemistry) in 1917.

In 1938, Meitner fled Nazi Germany because she was of Jewish descent. She then worked at the Nobel Insti-

tute for Physics in Stockholm, Sweden. She was a visiting professor at the Catholic University of America in 1946. In 1966, she shared the Enrico Fermi Award with Hahn and Strassmann.   Ruth Lewin Sime

See also **Nuclear energy** (The first artificially created fission reaction).

Mekong River, *MAY kahng,* is the longest river on the Indochinese peninsula. The Mekong is about 2,600 miles (4,180 kilometers) long. It flows southeastward from eastern Tibet, and forms part of the boundary between Thailand and Laos. See **Thailand** (map). The river crosses Laos, Cambodia, and Vietnam before it empties into the South China Sea near Ho Chi Minh City. In the region of the lower delta, the Mekong is known as the Sai Gon River. Ships can sail only about 350 miles (563 kilometers) up the Mekong. Farther inland, the river is interrupted by rapids and sand bars.   H. J. McPherson

Melaka, *muh LAK uh,* also spelled *Malacca* (pop. 88,073), is the capital of Melaka, a state of Malaysia. Melaka lies on the southwest coast of the Malay Peninsula, 125 miles (201 kilometers) northwest of Singapore. For the location of Melaka, see **Malaysia** (map).

Melaka lies in an area that produces pepper, rice, and sage. During the 1400's, the city became the most important commercial port in Southeast Asia. The Portuguese captured the city in 1511. The Dutch seized Melaka in 1641, and the British gained control of the city in 1824. Melaka is no longer a major Asian port.

David P. Chandler

Melanchthon, *muh LANGK thuhn,* **Philipp** (1497-1560), a German humanist and scholar, was Martin Luther's chief associate in starting and leading the Protestant Reformation. Melanchthon wrote the *Loci Communes* (*Commonplaces,* 1521), a widely read handbook that set down Lutheran doctrines in a systematic way for easy reference. He was also the chief author of the Augsburg Confession, which became the basic statement of faith of the Lutheran Church.

Melanchthon had a calmer personality than did Luther. He continually tried to find compromise solutions to issues that divided Protestants and Catholics, and Protestants from each other. Melanchthon declared that many such issues were unimportant for salvation and should not block Christian unity. But he also believed that the Roman Catholic Church had forsaken the true Christian tradition several hundred years after Christ. He especially opposed the power of the popes.

Melanchthon was born near Karlsruhe. Like Luther, he was a professor at the University of Wittenberg. He was a brilliant student of classical literature and of the works of the early church fathers. He has been called the "teacher of Germany" because of his influence on high school and university education in that country.

M. U. Edwards

See also **Luther, Martin; Augsburg Confession; Reformation.**

Melanesia. See Pacific Islands.

Melanin. See Skin (Epidermis; Skin color); Hair (Color and texture); Races, Human (Climatic adaptations).

Melba, Dame Nellie (1861-1931), was a famous Australian soprano. Her real name was Helen Porter Mitchell. She adopted her stage name from Melbourne, Australia. Nellie Melba was born in Richmond, which is a suburb of Melbourne.

Nellie Melba first sang in public at the age of 6 in Melbourne. She made her operatic debut in 1887 in Brussels, Belgium, singing the role of Gilda in *Rigoletto*. She performed in Italy, Russia, Denmark, and England. Nellie Melba made her American debut in New York City in 1893. She was made Dame Commander in the Order of the British Empire in 1918.

Martin Bernheimer

Radio Times Hulton Picture Library
Dame Nellie Melba

D. & J. Heaton, Stock, Boston

Melbourne is Australia's second largest city. It is the capital of the state of Victoria. Beautiful parks line the Yarra River, *above*.

Melbourne (pop. 3,022,157) is the second largest city of Australia. Only Sydney has more people. Melbourne, the capital of the state of Victoria, lies on Port Phillip Bay on the southeastern coast (see **Australia** [political map]). Melbourne is a busy seaport, Australia's chief financial city, and Victoria's commercial and industrial center.

The city and its suburbs cover more than 2,400 square miles (6,219 square kilometers). Downtown Melbourne is on the northern shore of Port Phillip Bay. Important buildings include the State Library of Victoria and Parliament House, where the Victoria legislature meets. The Yarra River runs through Melbourne. Several parks surround the city. The Melbourne Cup, a famous horse race, takes place yearly at Flemington Racecourse.

The Melbourne area is the home of La Trobe, Melbourne, and Monash universities, and a number of colleges. The Victorian Arts Centre, completed in 1984, includes facilities for concerts and plays. The National Gallery of Victoria, an art museum, is part of the Victorian Arts Centre.

The people. Most of Melbourne's residents are of British ancestry. About three-fourths of the people were born in Australia. Many people from Britain, Greece, Italy, and other European countries, and from Southeast Asia, have settled in Melbourne since World War II ended in 1945.

About 78 percent of Melbourne's families own houses. Large suburbs of single-family houses extend east, north, and west of the city. Melbourne has an extensive public transportation system.

Economy. The value of Melbourne's manufactured products totals about 30 percent of Australia's factory output and about 85 percent of Victoria's. The chief products include automobiles, chemicals, food products, machinery, and textiles. The city's more than 10,000 factories employ about 180,000 workers. Wholesale and retail trading and important financial institutions make Melbourne a major commercial center. It is the hub of Victoria's transportation network. Port Melbourne serves oceangoing vessels. The Melbourne area has an

© Barbara Pfeffer from Peter Arnold

A Melbourne shopping mall offers a wide selection of goods for sale. Melbourne is an important center of commerce and industry.

international airport at Tullamarine.

History. Aborigines lived in the Melbourne area before white settlers first arrived. John Batman, an Australian farmer, founded Melbourne in June 1835. Batman represented a group of people from the nearby island of Tasmania who wanted land for sheep farms. He bought 600,000 acres (240,000 hectares) from the Aborigines and paid them with blankets, tomahawks, and other goods. In October 1835, another group of settlers from Tasmania arrived. They were led by John Pascoe Fawkner. A village developed by the Yarra River. The governor of New South Wales later named the village for Viscount Melbourne, the British prime minister.

Melbourne was incorporated as a city in 1847. In 1851, part of New South Wales became a separate colony named Victoria, with Melbourne as its capital. That same year, miners discovered gold in Victoria, and a gold rush began. The city's population jumped from 23,000 in 1851 to 140,000 in 1861. It was Australia's largest city from 1856 until Sydney outgrew it in 1911. Melbourne also served as the capital of Australia from 1901 until 1927, when Canberra replaced it.

World War II (1939-1945) brought new industries and workers to the Melbourne area. Postwar growth was steady, with new industrial development attracting immigrants. The city's population rose from about $1\frac{1}{4}$ million in the early 1950's to about 3 million today.

Peter McLaughlin

Melcher, Frederic Gershom (1879-1963), won the Regina Medal in 1962 for his contributions to children's literature. In 1919, he helped found Children's Book Week. He established the Newbery Medal in 1921 for the outstanding children's book of the year, and the Caldecott Medal in 1937 for the best-illustrated children's book of the year. Born in Malden, Mass., Melcher was coeditor of *Publishers' Weekly* for 40 years. In addition, he served as board chairman of the R. R. Bowker Publishing Company.   Kathryn Pierson Jennings

See also **Caldecott Medal; Literature for children** (Awards).

Mellon, Andrew William (1855-1937), was an American financier. President Warren G. Harding appointed him United States secretary of the treasury in 1921. Mellon served until 1932 under Presidents Harding, Calvin Coolidge, and Herbert Hoover. While Mellon was in office, the U.S. government reduced by $9 billion its debt from World War I (1914-1918), and Congress cut income tax rates substantially.

Mellon was born in Pittsburgh of wealthy parents. In 1886, he joined his father's bank, Thomas Mellon and Sons, and became a shrewd judge of which new businesses and young business people deserved loans. Mellon served as an officer or director of many financial and industrial corporations. He became especially active in the development of the coal, coke, oil, and aluminum industries. By 1921, he had become one of the wealthiest people in the United States. Mellon served as U.S. ambassador to Britain in 1932 and 1933. In 1937, he gave his $25-million art collection to the U.S. government. He also donated $15 million for a museum to house the collection. This museum, the National Gallery of Art in Washington, D.C., opened in 1941 (see **National Gallery of Art**).   James S. Olson

See also **Mellon Foundation, Andrew W.**

Mellon Foundation, Andrew W., is an organization that grants funds to institutions in a number of fields. These fields include higher education; cultural affairs and the performing arts; education and research in health and population; and certain areas of conservation and public affairs. The foundation does not make grants to individuals or to strictly local organizations outside the New York City area. It ranks as one of the 10 wealthiest foundations in the United States. For assets, see **Foundations** (table).

The foundation was established in 1969 in memory of Andrew W. Mellon, an American financier. Mellon's daughter and son, Ailsa Mellon Bruce and Paul Mellon, formed it by combining the Avalon Foundation and the Old Dominion Foundation. Ailsa had set up Avalon in 1940, and Paul established Old Dominion in 1941. The Andrew W. Mellon Foundation has headquarters at 140 East 62nd Street, New York, NY 10021.

Critically reviewed by the Andrew W. Mellon Foundation

Mellophone is a curved brass instrument that resembles a French horn. The player produces tones by blowing into a cup-shaped mouthpiece and vibrating the lips. The player changes notes by adjusting lip tension and fingering the instrument's three valves.

The mellophone was first manufactured in 1860 and was a popular instrument in concert bands from about 1890 to 1930. Today, mellophones are used in marching bands to provide a powerful melodic or harmonic voice in a range between the trumpets and the trombones.

Stewart L. Ross

See also **French horn.**

Melodrama. See **Drama** (Forms of drama; Romanticism).

Melody. See **Music** (Melody).

Melon is the name of the fruit of several plants that belong to the gourd family. Melon plants have trailing or climbing stems that fasten themselves with tendrils to the objects they climb over. *Tendrils* are modified leaves that look like small coils of wire. The fruits, or melons, are round or somewhat egg-shaped. They measure up to 1 foot (30 centimeters) or more across. The fruits vary from tan and yellow to light or dark green. The flesh may be green, white, yellow, orange, pink, or red.

Scientific classification. Melons belong to the gourd family, Cucurbitaceae.   Gary W. Elmstrom

See also **Casaba; Muskmelon; Watermelon.**

Melos. See **Milos.**

Melpomene. See **Muses.**

Meltdown. See **Nuclear energy** (Hazards and safeguards).

Melting point is the temperature at which a substance changes from a solid to a liquid. The melting points of different substances vary considerably. For example, tungsten has an extremely high melting point, 3410 °C, but solid hydrogen melts at the low temperature of −259 °C. The melting point of a material depends partly on whether the material is a *pure substance* or a *mixture.* A pure substance is either a pure element, such as iron, or a simple compound, such as water. A mixture consists of two or more substances that are not chemically combined.

A pure substance melts at a definite temperature or within a narrow temperature range. For example, when iron is heated, its temperature rises until the metal reaches its melting point of 1535 °C. The iron remains at that temperature until all the metal has melted.

Mixtures do not melt at a specific temperature. Simple mixtures, such as brass and steel, melt over a range of temperatures. For example, steel, which is a mixture of iron and other elements, has a melting point of 1400 °C to 1500 °C. Thus, the temperature of steel rises 100 °C during the melting process instead of remaining constant. Such complex mixtures as glass and tar do not melt over a specific temperature range. Instead, these substances gradually become softer and more fluid as their temperature increases.

The melting point of most simple mixtures differs from that of any of the pure substances in the mixtures. Brass, an alloy of copper and zinc, melts over a range of 900 °C to 1000 °C. However, the melting point of copper is 1083.4 °C, and that of zinc is 419.58 °C.

Chemists can determine the purity of a particular substance by finding its melting point. In most cases, a solid is a pure substance if it melts at a specific temperature or over a narrow temperature range. The solid is a mixture if it melts over a much broader temperature range.

The melting point of a substance is affected to some extent by atmospheric pressure. An increase in this pressure raises the melting point of most substances. But an increase in atmospheric pressure lowers the melting point of water and of the few other substances that expand when they freeze. All freezing points specified in this article are based on a pressure of *1 atmosphere* (14.696 pounds per square inch [101.325 kilopascals]), the pressure of the atmosphere at average sea level.

The liquid form of a pure substance freezes at the same temperature at which its solid form melts. Thus, the solid and liquid forms can exist together at the melting point without any temperature change in either. For example, if any amount of ice whose temperature is 0 °C, the melting point of ice, is added to any amount of water whose temperature is also 0 °C, the temperature of the resulting ice water will remain 0 °C. Furthermore, the relative proportions of ice and water will remain the same unless heat is added to the ice water or removed from it. However, if heat is added, the ice will begin to melt. If heat is removed, the water will begin to freeze.

The solid and liquid forms of a mixture can exist together over a range of temperatures. This range is determined by the type and amount of each of the pure substances in the mixture.

Some pure solids do not melt when heated. Instead, they change from a solid to a gas. Such substances as arsenic, dry ice, and iodine go through this process, which is called *sublimation*.   John P. Chesick

See also **Freezing point.**

Melting pot. See United States (Ancestry).

Melville, Herman (1819-1891), ranks among America's major authors. He wrote *Moby-Dick,* one of the great novels in literature, and his reputation rests largely on this book. But many of his other works are literary creations of a high order—blending fact, fiction, adventure, and subtle symbolism. Melville's wealth of personal experience in faraway places was remarkable even in the footloose and exploring world of the 1800's. Melville brought to his extraordinary adventures a vivid imagination and a philosophical skepticism, as well as a

remarkable skill in handling the new American language.

His early life. Melville was born in New York City. The family name was Melvill, and he added the "e" to the name. His father was a merchant from New England. His mother came from an old and socially prominent New York Dutch family. Melville lived his first 11 years in New York City. Following his father's death after suffering a financial and mental breakdown in 1831, the family moved to Albany, N.Y.

Herman Melville by A. W. Twitchell. The Berkshire Athenaeum, Pittsfield, Mass.

Herman Melville

Young, inexperienced, and now poor, Melville tried a variety of jobs between 1832 and 1841. He was a clerk in his brother's hat store in Albany, worked in his uncle's bank, taught in a school near Pittsfield, Mass., and, in 1837, sailed to Liverpool, England, as a cabin boy on a merchant ship. He described this voyage in his novel *Redburn.* Melville returned to America and signed on as a seaman on the newly built whaling ship *Acushnet* for a trip in the Pacific Ocean. From this trip came the basic experiences recorded in several of his books, and above all, the whaling knowledge he later put into *Moby-Dick.*

Melville sailed from New Bedford, Mass., on Jan. 3, 1841. He stayed on the *Acushnet* for 18 months. After the ship put in at Nuka Hiva in the Marquesas Islands, he and a shipmate deserted. The two men headed inland until they accidentally came to the lovely valley of the Typees, a Polynesian tribe with a reputation as fierce cannibals. However, the natives turned out to be gentle and charming hosts. Melville described his experiences with these people in *Typee.*

Melville lived in the valley for about a month. He then joined another whaling ship, but he soon deserted it with other sailors in a semimutiny at Tahiti. After a few days in a local jail, Melville and a new friend began roaming the beautiful and unspoiled islands of Tahiti and Moorea. Melville described his life during these wanderings in the novel *Omoo.*

After short service on a third whaling ship, Melville landed at the Sandwich Islands (now Hawaii), where he lived by doing odd jobs. On Aug. 17, 1843, he enlisted as a seaman on the frigate *United States,* flagship of the Navy's Pacific Squadron. He recounted his long voyage around Cape Horn to the United States in the novel *White-Jacket.*

Melville arrived in Boston Harbor in October 1844. He was released from the Navy and headed home to Albany, his imagination overflowing with his adventures.

His literary career. Melville wrote about his experiences so attractively that he soon became one of the most popular writers of his time. The books that made his reputation were *Typee* (1846); *Omoo* (1847); *Mardi* (1849), a complex allegorical romance set in the South Seas; *Redburn* (1849); and *White-Jacket* (1850).

Melville then began *Moby-Dick,* another "whaling voyage," as he called it, similar to his successful travel books. He had almost completed the book when he met

Nathaniel Hawthorne. Hawthorne inspired him to radically revise the whaling documentary into a novel of both universal significance and literary complexity.

Moby-Dick, or The Whale (1851), on one level, is the story of the hunt for Moby Dick, a fierce white whale supposedly known to sailors of Melville's time. Captain Ahab is the captain of the whaling ship *Pequod.* He has lost a leg in an earlier battle with Moby Dick, and is determined to catch the whale. The novel brilliantly describes the dangerous and often violent life on a whaling ship, and contains information on the whaling industry and a discussion of the nature of whales. On another level *Moby-Dick* is a deeply symbolic story. The whale symbolizes the mysterious and complex force of the universe, and Captain Ahab represents the heroic struggle against the limiting and crippling constrictions that confront an intelligent person.

Melville's popularity began to decline with the publication of his masterpiece. The novel, either ignored or misunderstood by critics and readers, damaged Melville's reputation as a writer. When Melville followed *Moby-Dick* with the pessimistic and tragic novel *Pierre* (1853), his readers began to desert him, calling him either eccentric or mad. The public was ready to accept unusual and exciting adventures, but they did not want ironic, frightening exposures of the terrible double meanings in life.

Melville turned to writing short stories. Two of them, "Benito Cereno" and "Bartleby the Scrivener," rank as classics. Several of the stories were collected in *The Piazza Tales* (1856). But the haunting and disturbing question of the meaning of life that hovered over the stories also displeased the public. In 1855, Melville published *Israel Potter,* a novel set during the Revolutionary War in America. After *The Confidence-Man* (1856), a bitter satire on humanity, Melville gave up writing.

His later life. To make a living, Melville worked as deputy inspector of customs in the Port of New York from 1866 to 1885. For private pleasure he wrote poetry, which he published at his own and his uncle's expense. He toured the Holy Land in 1856 and 1857. The trip resulted in a narrative poem, *Clarel* (1876). The poem presents a powerful picture of a man's struggle to find his faith in a skeptical, materialistic world.

Melville began writing prose again after his retirement. At his death, he left the manuscript of *Billy Budd, Sailor.* This short novel, first published in 1924 and considered Melville's finest book after *Moby-Dick,* is a symbolic story about the clash between innocence and evil, and between social forms and individual liberty.

The 1920's marked the start of a Melville revival among critics and readers. By the 1940's, Americans at last recognized his genius. His reputation has since spread throughout the world.   John Clendenning

Additional resources

Arvin, Newton. *Herman Melville.* Greenwood, 1973. First published in 1950.
A Companion to Melville Studies. Ed. by John Bryant. Greenwood, 1986.
Hillway, Tyrus. *Herman Melville.* Rev. ed. Twayne, 1979.
Melville, Herman. *The Portable Melville.* Viking, 1957.

Melville Island is one of a group of Canadian islands in the Arctic Ocean, north of Canada's mainland. It lies between Prince Patrick and Bathurst islands, and is one of the Parry Islands. See **Canada** [terrain map]). The island covers about 16,300 square miles (42,220 square kilometers). It stretches nearly 200 miles (320 kilometers) from east to west, and about 130 miles (209 kilometers) at its widest north to south point. Frozen seas surround it most of the year. The island is uninhabited, except for visiting scientists and prospectors.

In 1819, Sir William Parry, a British naval officer and explorer, became the first European to reach Melville Island. He was searching for a northwest passage to Asia. The island is governed as part of the Northwest Territories of Canada.   Ian W. D. Dalziel

Membrane is a term used to describe biological structures that cover surfaces and separate spaces in organisms. For example, *cellular membranes* provide the external boundary for cells and divide cells into functional compartments. They serve as barriers to the passage of molecules in and out of cells and between compartments (see **Cell** [Inside a living cell]).

The term *membrane* is also used to describe thin sheets of tissues that cover surfaces or separate spaces in the body. There are three types of these membranes: (1) fibrous, (2) serous, and (3) mucous. These vary greatly in thickness and in the types of cells composing them.

Fibrous membranes are tough and add strength to the parts they cover. They are made up entirely of fibrous connective tissue (see **Tissue** [Animal tissues]). The fibrous membrane that lines the inside of the skull is called *dura mater.* The *periosteum* is a fibrous membrane that covers the bones. The periosteum also serves as an attachment for muscles, and contains the blood vessels and nerves of the bones.

Serous membranes line body cavities that do not open to the outside, such as the thorax and abdomen. They also cover the outside of the digestive organs and support them. Serous membranes secrete a watery fluid that keeps them moist and prevents their sticking to each other or to the organs they touch. A serous membrane lines the *pericardium,* the sac around the heart (see **Heart** [The structure of the heart]). Other serous membranes include the *pleura,* which lines the lung cavities, and the *peritoneum,* which lines the cavity of the abdomen (see **Pleura**). Inflammation of the peritoneum is known as *peritonitis.* A serous membrane called the *synovial membrane* lines the cavities of the joints. It secretes a watery fluid that lubricates the joints and helps them move easily and smoothly. The largest of the synovial cavities is in the knee.

Mucous membranes line organs and passages of the body that open to the outside. A clear, sticky fluid called *mucus* covers mucous membranes (see **Mucus**). Glands just under the membranes produce the mucus. Mucous membranes form the lining of the mouth, throat, alimentary canal, reproductive system, nose, trachea and lungs, the inner surfaces of the eyelids, and the Eustachian tube.   Kermit L. Carraway

Memel. See **Klaipèda.**

Memel River. See **Neman River.**

Memling, Hans (1430?-1494), was a Flemish painter. His name is also spelled *Memlinc.* He is known for his religious paintings, especially of the Madonna and Child enthroned with angels, and for his portraits.

Memling's paintings are characterized by a feeling of sweetness and calm. They show religious stories in narrative detail but without startling dramatic action. Memling combined these personal stylistic characteristics with aspects of earlier Northern European art. He was particularly influenced by Rogier van der Weyden, with whom he may have worked. Memling's most famous paintings are small panels that decorate the Reliquary Shrine of St. Ursula in Bruges, Belgium. Memling was born in Seligenstadt, Germany, but spent most of his life in Bruges.   Linda Stone-Ferrier

See also **Clothing** (picture: The hennin).

Memorial may take the form of a statue, monument, building, or park. For information on specific memorials, see the following articles in *World Book:*

Arc de Triomphe	National Park System
Jefferson Memorial	Sarcophagus
Kennedy Center for the Per-	Statue of Liberty
forming Arts	Unknown soldier
Lincoln Memorial	Washington Monument
Monument	

Memorial Day, also called Decoration Day, is a patriotic holiday in the United States. It is a day to honor Americans who gave their lives for their country. Originally, Memorial Day honored military personnel who died in the Civil War (1861-1865). The holiday now also honors those who died in any war while serving the United States.

Memorial Day is a legal holiday in most states. Most Northern States and some Southern States observe Memorial Day the last Monday in May. This date was made a federal holiday by a law that became effective in 1971. Most of the Southern States also have their own days for honoring the Confederate dead. Mississippi celebrates the last Monday in April as Confederate Memorial Day. Alabama celebrates on the fourth Monday in April. Georgia observes this holiday on April 26. North Carolina and South Carolina celebrate it on May 10. Virginia observes the holiday on the last Monday in May. Louisiana observes it on June 3, and Tennessee has a holiday called Confederate Decoration Day on that date. Texas celebrates Confederate Heroes Day on January 19.

Observance. On Memorial Day, people place flowers and flags on the graves of military personnel. Many organizations, including Boy Scouts, Girl Scouts, and fraternal groups, march in military parades and take part in special programs. These programs often include the reading of Abraham Lincoln's "Gettysburg Address." Memorials are often dedicated on this day. Military exercises and special programs are held at Gettysburg National Military Park and at the National Cemetery in Arlington, Va. To honor those who died at sea, some United States ports also organize ceremonies where tiny ships filled with flowers are set afloat on the water.

Since the end of World War I, Memorial Day has also been Poppy Day. Volunteers sell small, red artificial poppies in order to help disabled veterans (see **Poppy Week**). In recent years, the custom has grown in most families to decorate the graves of loved ones on Memorial Day.

History. Several communities claim to have originated Memorial Day. But in 1966, the United States government proclaimed Waterloo, N.Y., the birthplace of the holiday. The people of Waterloo first observed Memorial Day on May 5, 1866, to honor soldiers killed in the Civil War. Businesses were closed, and people dec-

orated soldiers' graves and flew flags at half-mast.

Major General John A. Logan in 1868 named May 30 as a special day for honoring the graves of Union soldiers. Logan served as commander in chief of the Grand Army of the Republic, an organization of Union veterans of the Civil War. They had charge of Memorial Day celebrations in the Northern States for many years. The American Legion took over this duty after World War I.   Sharron G. Uhler

Memory. See **Computer** (Storing information).

Memory is the ability to remember something that has been learned or experienced. Memory is a vital part of the learning process. If you remembered nothing from the past, you would be unable to learn anything new. All your experiences would be lost as soon as they ended, and each new situation would be totally unfamiliar. Without memory, you would repeatedly have the same experiences for the "first time." You would also lose the richness memory gives to life—the pleasure of happy remembrances as well as the sorrow of unhappy ones.

Scientists know little about what happens in the brain when it stores memories. However, they are almost certain that storing new memories involves both chemical changes in the nerve cells of the brain and changes in their physical structure. Research indicates that these chemical and physical changes occur in a tiny section of the brain called the *hippocampus* when a person stores new memories. The hippocampus is part of a larger structure called the *cerebral cortex,* which controls most higher brain functions. Such functions include problem solving and the use of language. Scientists have found that a memory is acquired by means of a series of solidifying events in the brain. However, more research will be necessary to discover precisely how memories solidify.

The memory system

Psychologists divide a person's memory system into three stages, each of which has a different time span. These stages are called *sensory memory, short-term memory,* and *long-term memory.*

Sensory memory holds information for only an instant. Suppose you look at a picture of a mountain. Information about the mountain passes through your eyes to your sensory memory, which briefly holds a nearly exact image of the picture. However, the image quickly fades, and it disappears in less than a second. For the information to last, you must transfer it rapidly to short-term memory.

Short-term memory can hold a fact as long as you actively think about it. You use short-term memory when you look up a telephone number and repeat it to yourself until you dial it. Unless you continually repeat this information to yourself, it will fade after about 20 seconds. However, some information from short-term memory enters long-term memory, where it may last a long time.

Long-term memory includes a huge amount of information, some of which lasts a lifetime. Information enters long-term memory as a result of either of two factors: (1) repetition or (2) intense emotion. A casual acquaintance, met briefly but on many occasions, will be remembered for a long time. The strong emotions of the first experience of falling in love or of the moments surrounding a car crash help place these events in long-term memory.

Measuring memory

There are three commonly used methods to measure how much a person remembers. These methods are (1) recall, (2) recognition, and (3) relearning. Suppose you give a party and someone asks you a few weeks later who was there. The simplest way to find out how much you remember is to list as many names as you can. This is the method of *recall.*

In *recognition,* the person asking about your guests would give you a list of names. The list would include names of people who were at the party and of others who were not. You could then indicate which people were there. Most people can recognize more facts than they can recall. As a result, most students perform better on multiple-choice tests than on essay tests.

In *relearning,* you would memorize the guest list after apparently forgetting it. Most people relearn information faster than they learned it the first time. Scientists regard the difference in the time required for the original learning and for the relearning as evidence of how much was remembered.

Why people forget

In general, people forget more and more as time passes. An hour after a party ends, you probably could remember most of the people who were there. Two days later, you might recall only a few of the guests. A month later, you probably would remember even fewer. Scientists have devoted much study to why the passage of time makes people unable to remember things they once knew. The chief explanations for forgetting include *interference, retrieval failure, motivated forgetting,* and *constructive processes.*

Interference occurs when the remembering of certain learned material blocks the memory of other learned material. If a friend moves, you may have difficulty recalling his or her new telephone number. The person's old number may keep coming to mind and interfering with your remembering the new one. But after you have thoroughly learned the new number, you may not even be able to recall the old one.

The above example illustrates two types of interference. Previously learned information may hamper a person's ability to remember new material. This hampering process is called *proactive interference* or *proactive inhibition.* Likewise, the learning of new facts may interfere with the memory of something previously learned. Such interference is known as *retroactive interference* or *retroactive inhibition.*

Retrieval failure is the inability to recall information that has been stored in the memory. You probably have had the experience of being unable to think of a name or some other piece of information that was on the tip of your tongue. Later, the information came to you naturally and effortlessly. Such temporary loss of memory, which occurs frequently, is called *retrieval failure.* Scientists compare it to trying to find a misplaced object in a cluttered room. The information is not gone, but neither can it be recalled immediately.

Motivated forgetting is a loss of memory caused by conscious or unconscious desires. Scientists believe we forget many things because we want to do so. Motivated forgetting is related to a psychological process called *repression.* Repression involves forcing unpleasant feelings or painful experiences from the conscious mind into the unconscious. For example, people who like to gamble tend to remember most of the times they won—and forget those when they lost.

Constructive processes involve the unconscious invention of false memories. When you try to remember an event that happened months or years ago, you may recall only a few facts. Using those facts, you fill in the gaps with details that seem to make sense but may be untrue. The process of constructing probable happenings to tell a complete story is called *refabrication* or *confabulation.* Refabricated memories seem real and are almost impossible to distinguish from memories of events that actually occurred.

Improving memory

Memory experts believe that people can, with practice, increase their ability to remember. One of the most important means of improving memory is the use of mental aids called *mnemonic devices* (pronounced *nih MAHN ihk*). Other techniques can also be used to help people improve their memory.

Mnemonic devices include rhymes, clues, mental pictures, and other methods. One of the simplest ways is to put the information into a rhyme. Many people remember the number of days in each month by using a verse that begins, "Thirty days hath September. . . ."

Another method provides clues by means of an *acronym,* a word formed from the first letters or syllables of other words. For example, the acronym *homes* could help a person remember the names of the Great Lakes—Huron, Ontario, Michigan, Erie, Superior.

A mental picture can be provided by the key-word method, which is particularly useful in learning foreign words. Suppose you want to remember that the German word *Gabel* (pronounced *GAH behl*) means *fork.* First, you think of a key word in English that sounds like the foreign word—for example, *gobble.* Next, you connect the two words through a mental image, such as that of a person gobbling food with a fork. From then on, to recall the meaning of *Gabel,* you would remember *gobble* and the stored image linking it to *fork.*

Mental pictures can also be used to remember names. When you meet a person for the first time, pick out a physical feature of the individual and relate it to his or her name. For example, if you meet a very tall man named Mr. Shackley, imagine his bumping his head on the roof of a shack. In the future, this image will help you remember his name when you see or think of him.

To use mnemonic devices, you must first learn them —and often invent them. After mastering a mnemonic device, however, you can use it at any time you wish.

Other ways to improve memory. A good way to ensure remembering a piece of information is to study it long after you think you know it perfectly. This process is called *overlearning.* The more thoroughly you learn something, the more lasting the memory will be.

Another memory aid involves making the surroundings in which you remember material similar to those in which you learned the material. For this reason, football coaches require players to practice under conditions similar to those of an actual game. Students often find it helpful to study in the room where they will be tested.

Still another method centers on organization. Try to organize information by creating a link between something you want to remember and something you already know. Suppose, for instance, that you want to assure recalling that the telephone was patented in 1876. You might do so by remembering that the telephone was patented 100 years after the signing of the Declaration of Independence.

Uncommon memory conditions

Unusually good memory. We sometimes hear of someone who has a "photographic memory," which supposedly works like a camera taking a picture. A person with such a memory would be able to take a quick mental picture of a textbook page or a scene. Later, the person could describe the page or scene perfectly by causing the image to reappear in his or her mind.

No one actually has a photographic memory. However, some people have a similar ability called *eidetic imagery.* An eidetic image is a picture that remains in a person's mind for a few seconds after a scene has disappeared. People who have eidetic imagery can look at a scene briefly and then give a thorough description of the scene based on a mental image. But the image fades quickly and may be inaccurate. Eidetic imagery is rare. Only 5 to 10 percent of all children have this ability, and most of them lose it as they grow up.

Amnesia can result from disease, physical injury, or emotional shock. Many cases of amnesia, even severe ones, are temporary, and the amnesic person regains his or her memory. A person who suffers a brain injury may forget events that occurred just before the injury. This inability to remember past events is called *retrograde amnesia.* The more severe the injury, the greater the memory loss. Football players who receive a blow to the head might forget a few seconds of their lives. Someone who suffers major brain damage in an automobile accident might lose months or even years of memories. Some brain-injured people also have *anterograde amnesia.* This condition involves difficulty remembering events that occur after the injury. Both these types of amnesia also can be produced by emotional shock.   Elizabeth F. Loftus

See also **Alzheimer's disease; Amnesia; Brain** (In thinking and remembering); **Learning; Learning disabilities** (Types); **Senility.**

Additional resources

Gallant, Roy A. *Memory: How It Works and How to Improve It.* Macmillan, 1984. First published in 1980. Also suitable for younger readers.

Gregg, Vernon H. *Introduction to Human Memory.* Routledge, 1986.

Loftus, Elizabeth F. *Memory: Surprising New Insights into How We Remember and Why We Forget.* Ardsley Hse., 1988. First published in 1980.

Rosenfield, Israel. *The Invention of Memory: A New View of the Brain.* Basic Bks., 1988. A discussion of memory research.

Memphis was the first capital of ancient Egypt. According to tradition, Menes, who was the first king of Egypt, founded the city and made it his capital around 3100 B.C. Memphis stood near the site of present-day Cairo. During the Old Kingdom (2686-2181 B.C.), kings built pyramids at Giza and Saqqarah near Memphis. The city was Egypt's capital until the end of the Old Kingdom, and was an important religious and political center until about 330 B.C. Nothing remains of the ancient city itself. However, cemeteries and the pyramids at Giza and Saqqarah stand as reminders of the city's past glory. See also **Egypt, Ancient** (map; History).   Barbara Mertz

Memphis is the largest city in Tennessee. It lies on a bluff on the east bank of the Mississippi River in the southwest corner of the state. Memphis serves as the commercial and industrial center of western Tennessee and parts of neighboring states.

Cotton and river trade accounted for much of the city's early growth. By 1900, Memphis was the world's largest market for cotton and hardwood lumber. The city is still a leader in these activities. But industrial expansion after World War II ended in 1945 made Memphis one of the South's largest urban centers. The city also became a hub of higher education, medical care, and motel development; and a center for the recording and distribution of music.

Memphis was named for the ancient Egyptian capital of Memphis, which lay on the Nile River. Settlers chose the site because the nearby Wolf River flowed into the Mississippi and provided an excellent harbor. The bluff site also furnished protection from floods.

The city covers 288 square miles (746 square kilometers) and is the seat of Shelby County. The Memphis metropolitan area consists of Fayette, Shelby, and Tipton counties in Tennessee; Crittenden County, Arkansas; and De Soto County, Mississippi. The metropolitan area totals 3,092 square miles (8,008 square kilometers).

The Mississippi River flows to the west of Memphis, and the Tennessee-Mississippi state line forms the southern boundary of the city. Memphis suburbs include Arlington, Bartlett, Collierville, Germantown, and Millington, Tenn.; Southaven, Miss.; and West Memphis, Ark., which lies west of the river. Millington is the home of Naval Air Station Memphis. The Naval Air Technical Training Center at this air base trains more naval aircraft maintenance technicians than any other installation in the world.

Downtown Memphis extends $1\frac{1}{2}$ miles (2.4 kilometers) along the Mississippi River. The Memphis Civic Center stands on the north edge of the downtown area. The Civic Center consists of local, state, and federal government buildings. In the southern end of downtown Memphis is Beale Street, where composer W. C. Handy worked as a musician. Handy made the street famous in his song "Beale Street Blues."

Since the late 1970's, Memphis business and political leaders have directed a downtown redevelopment program that has cost more than $750 million. Completed projects include a convention center; Mud Island Park, a theme park that is connected to the downtown area by a monorail; renovation of the Orpheum Theater and the Peabody Hotel; the renewal of Beale Street as an entertainment center; the construction of office and residential buildings; and the Pyramid—a sports and entertainment arena that has a seating capacity of 22,000.

Graceland, the estate of the famous rock singer Elvis Presley, lies in southern Memphis. Presley died in 1977 and was buried on the estate. Each year, hundreds of thousands of people visit the estate.

© Mark E. Gibson, The Stock Market

Memphis is Tennessee's largest city and chief center of commerce, industry, and transportation. Downtown Memphis, *left,* stretches along the east bank of the Mississippi River.

The people. Almost all the people of Memphis were born in the United States. Blacks make up about 55 percent of the city's population. Other ethnic groups, in order of size, include those of German, Irish, and English descent.

Poverty in the black community is a major problem in Memphis. Large numbers of blacks live in crowded, run-down dwellings in areas north and south of the downtown district. Many have little education and few work skills.

Like many other cities, Memphis has had racial problems. In 1968, the civil rights leader Martin Luther King, Jr., was assassinated in Memphis by James Earl Ray, a native of Illinois and an escaped convict. King had gone to Memphis to support a strike by city sanitation workers, most of whom were blacks.

After King's death, the city made efforts to improve living conditions in the black community. Memphis worked with federal agencies to train blacks for jobs and to help blacks establish businesses. An increasing number of blacks began to participate in commerce and in city and state politics. The city has also sponsored major reforms in housing, education, and health care that have focused on the black community.

The economy. Memphis' economy once centered on cotton. The city is still one of the world's largest cotton markets, but a variety of other economic activities have been developed.

Memphis is the trade center of a region consisting of western Tennessee, eastern Arkansas, northern Mississippi, and southeastern Missouri. The city is also a major national distribution center. The Port of Memphis is one of the busiest inland ports on the Mississippi River, handling more than 13 million short tons (12 million metric tons) of freight yearly. The port ships goods to all parts of the world. Major airlines use Memphis International Airport. Memphis is the headquarters of Federal Express, the nation's largest overnight air express delivery company. Truck lines and railroads carry cargo to and from the city. Memphis' location allows overnight truck delivery to almost 40 percent of the nation.

Service industries employ about 83 percent of the workers in Memphis and Shelby County. Health care is the most important service industry. The Memphis Medical Center includes Baptist Memorial Hospital, the largest private, not-for-profit hospital in the United States. The center also includes the world-famous St. Jude Children's Research Hospital; the colleges of dentistry, medicine, nursing, and pharmacy of the University of Tennessee, Memphis; and more than a dozen full-service hospitals. Memphis is also the leading center in the United States for the wholesale trade of hardwood lumber.

Manufacturing and processing employ about 13 percent of the workers of Memphis and Shelby County. The chief manufacturing companies in Memphis produce chemicals, electrical equipment, food and food products, nonelectrical machinery, and paper and related products. Several major food and food-processing companies have plants in Memphis.

Tourism has become a major industry in Memphis, contributing more than $1 billion a year to the local economy. Graceland, the estate of Elvis Presley, draws the most tourists. Memphis has one daily newspaper, *The Commercial Appeal.*

Facts in brief

Population: *City*—610,337. *Metropolitan area*—1,007,306.
Area: *City*—288 sq. mi. (746 km²). *Metropolitan area*—3,092 sq. mi. (8,008 km²).
Altitude: 331 ft. (101 m) above sea level.
Climate: *Average temperature*—January, 40 °F (4 °C); July, 82 °F (28 °C). *Average annual precipitation* (rainfall, melted snow, and other forms of moisture)—52 in. (132 cm).
Government: Mayor-council. *Terms*—4 years for the mayor and for the 13 council members.
Founded: 1819. Incorporated as a city in 1849.

Symbols of Memphis. The red, white, and blue in the flag of Memphis represent the United States and Tennessee, both of which use those colors in their flags. The flag includes the city seal. The steamboat on the seal symbolizes commerce.

Education. The Memphis public school system enrolls more than 100,000 students, about 80 percent of whom are blacks. About 14,000 students in Memphis attend private schools. The city started to desegregate its public schools in 1961. But 10 years later, most black students still attended all-black or mostly black schools. In 1973, under a federal court order, the public school system began busing some black students to mostly white schools, and some white students to all-black or mostly black schools. As a result of the court order, about 30,000 white public school students began attending private schools. Since then, a growing black population in Memphis has created a large black majority in the public schools, and desegregation is no longer a major issue.

Memphis State University, the city's largest institution of higher learning, has an enrollment of about 20,000. Other colleges and universities in Memphis include Christian Brothers University, Harding Graduate School of Religion, LeMoyne-Owen College, Memphis College of Art, Rhodes College, Southern College of Optometry, and the University of Tennessee, Memphis.

Cultural life. The Memphis Symphony Orchestra performs at the Memphis Municipal Auditorium. Local ballet and opera companies are also active in Memphis.

The Memphis Brooks Museum of Art has a collection of Italian Renaissance paintings and sculpture, plus numerous other exhibits. The Dixon Gallery has a noted collection of French impressionism. The Memphis College of Art and several smaller galleries also feature various artwork. The Memphis Pink Palace Museum has exhibits on the natural history of Memphis and the surrounding region.

The Memphis Little Theatre offers a regular season of plays. The Orpheum Theater presents touring Broadway plays and musicals.

The Memphis Public Library consists of a main library and 22 branches. It owns about $1\frac{1}{2}$ million volumes.

Recreation. Memphis has more than 170 parks covering about 5,400 acres (2,200 hectares). Overton Park, east of downtown, has one of the South's largest zoos and an aquarium. Mud Island Park, between the Wolf and Mississippi rivers, features a five-block-long replica of the lower Mississippi Valley. In addition, Shelby Farms covers 5,000 acres (2,000 hectares) at the city's eastern limits. The park includes the 1,000-acre (400-hectare) Agricenter International, a center for agricultural research and exhibits.

The Memphis in May International Festival is one of the largest annual events held in the United States. It honors a different nation each year. A popular feature of the festival is the International Barbeque Contest. The Mid-South Fairgrounds includes the Coliseum and the Liberty Bowl Memorial Stadium. The Mid-South Fair, held in September, presents agricultural and commercial exhibits.

Government. Memphis has a mayor-council form of government. The voters elect a mayor and 13 council members to four-year terms. In 1992, a voting rights lawsuit led to the drawing of new districts, so that Memphis' black majority would be more equally represented on the council. Property and sales taxes provide most of the city's funds.

History. Chickasaw Indians lived in what is now the Memphis area long before white settlers first came there. Hernando de Soto, a Spanish explorer, arrived in the area in 1541 and became the first white person to see the Mississippi River.

City of Memphis

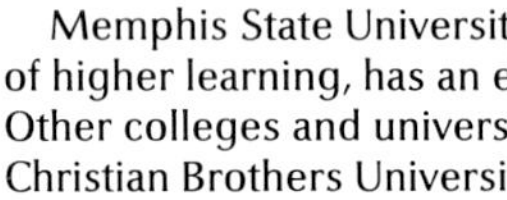

Memphis lies on the Mississippi River in southwestern Tennessee. It is the largest city in the state and an important shipping center. The map shows points of interest in the Memphis area.

☐ City of Memphis
▨ Area outside Memphis
--- State boundary
═══ Main road
— Other road
┼┼┼ Rail line
■ Point of interest

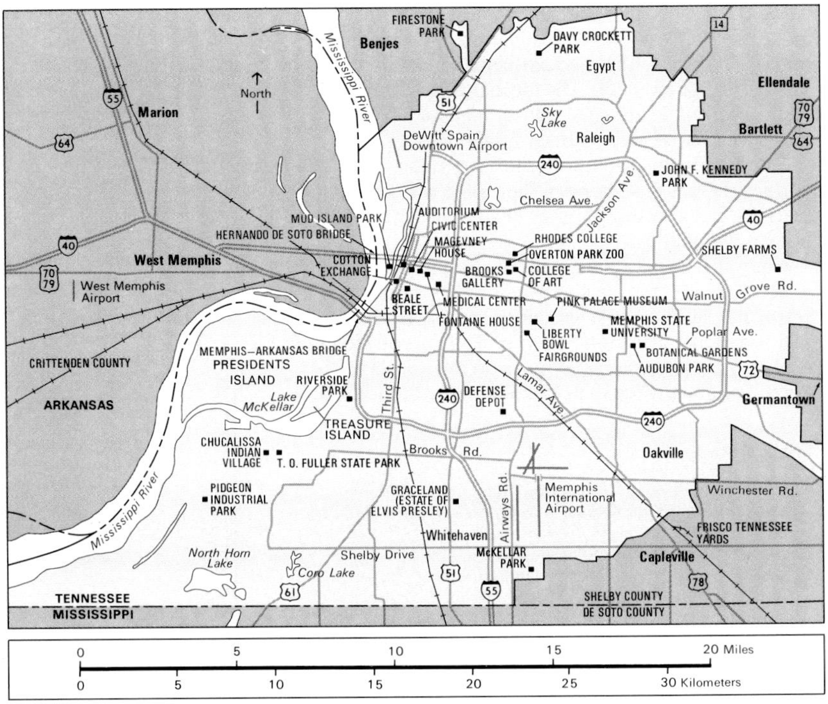

In 1682, the French explorer René-Robert Cavelier, Sieur de La Salle, built Fort Prud'homme near what is now Memphis and claimed the area for France. By the 1700's, France, Britain, and Spain had claimed the Tennessee region. The United States gained control of the area in the late 1700's. In 1818, the U.S. government bought much of western Tennessee from the Chickasaw. General Andrew Jackson, Judge John Overton, and General James Winchester became owners of 5,000 acres (2,000 hectares) of the land. In 1819, the three men organized a settlement there and named it Memphis.

Memphis was incorporated as a city in 1849. In 1860, it had a population of 23,000 and ranked as the South's sixth largest city. After the American Civil War began in 1861, Memphis became a military center for the Confederacy. The city fell to Union forces in 1862. In the 1870's, a series of yellow fever epidemics struck the city. About half the population fled. In 1878, the epidemics killed about 5,200 of the 19,600 people who lived in Memphis. The state legislature took away the city's charter in 1879.

By 1890, river trade had increased, and the population had climbed to 64,500. In 1892, a railroad bridge was completed across the Mississippi at Memphis. The bridge increased trade with the Southwest, and Memphis soon became the world's largest inland center for cotton and hardwood lumber. Memphis regained its charter in 1893. During the late 1800's, many freed slaves moved to Memphis from plantations and small towns. Many worked in the cotton and lumber mills.

In 1909, E. H. Crump was elected mayor of Memphis. Crump became one of the most powerful political bosses in the nation's history. Until his death in 1954, Crump controlled almost all politics in Memphis and some state politics as well.

By 1960, the city's population had grown to 498,000. During the 1960's, a building boom brought many new factories and skyscrapers to Memphis. Memphis International Airport opened in 1963. The area of Memphis increased by about 70 percent through annexation of suburbs. The city's population grew by about 25 percent, largely as a result of this annexation.

In the late 1960's and early 1970's, Memphis suffered from racial conflict and weak political leadership. Recognition of common interests, however, has helped blacks and whites work together in order to resolve racial conflicts in the city. Memphis shifted from a mayor-commission to a mayor-council form of government in 1968.

In 1979, Memphis began a two-year program called the Governor's Job Conference. The conference brought together business and government leaders and citizens from throughout the community to plan economic and social growth. One of the conference's most successful projects was the promotion of Memphis as "America's Distribution Center." By the mid-1980's, the city had become one of the largest distribution centers in the United States.

Since the 1980's, the growing black majority in Memphis has put increased emphasis on the educational and economic needs of the black community. In 1991, the voters of Memphis elected W. W. Herenton mayor. He became the city's first elected black mayor when he took office at the start of 1992.   David C. Vincent

Menagerie. See **Circus** (History); **Zoo** (History).

Menander, *muh NAN duhr* (342?-291? B.C.), was a Greek playwright who wrote more than 100 comedies. We know his work only through fragments of his plays, adaptations of his plots by Roman dramatists Plautus and Terence, and one whole play, *Dyscolos* (The Grouch).

Menander was born and lived in Athens. His comedies dramatize humorous situations, especially in love affairs, in middle-class society. The plays resemble many modern comedies that deal with problems of home life. Menander is noted for his plot construction, characterization, clear style, and sympathetic view of humanity. His plays offer gentle lessons about human relationships, but he intended them primarily to entertain audiences.   Luci Berkowitz

Mencius, *MEHN shee uhs* (390?-305? B.C.), was one of the most influential figures in the development of the Chinese philosophy called Confucianism. Mencius is best known for his belief that human nature is good. He also believed that the people of a nation were justified in deposing or even killing a bad ruler. Mencius defined a bad ruler as one who ignored the people's welfare and governed them unkindly. Many of Mencius' ideas appear in the *Mengzi* (also spelled *Meng-tzu*), a book that is probably a collection of his teachings.

Mencius was born in the state of Zou, in what is now Shantung Province. His real name was Meng Ke. The name *Mencius* is the Latin form of *Mengzi,* a title that means *Master Meng.* Scholars know nothing about Mencius' early life except for information in some unreliable legends.   David R. Knechtges

See also **Confucianism** (Early Confucianism).

Mencken, H. L. (1880-1956), was an American journalist, critic, and editor. His robust, often savagely witty style and his tremendous productivity as a writer brought him distinction in almost every literary form he attempted. From about 1910 to 1940, he was the most important literary figure in the United States.

Henry Louis Mencken was born in Baltimore. He began his journalism career at the age of 18 as a reporter with the *Baltimore Morning Herald.* By the age of 25, he had risen to editor in chief. After the paper closed in 1906, Mencken joined the *Baltimore Sun* as Sunday editor. He worked for the *Sun* for the rest of his career, except for leaves of absence during the two world wars. Mencken became famous for his newspaper columns, in which he enjoyed attacking American taste and culture, ridiculing a wide range of popular beliefs.

In 1905, Mencken published the first book-length study of British playwright George Bernard Shaw. Three years later, he published *The Philosophy of Friedrich Nietzsche,* a study of the German philosopher.

From 1908 to 1923, Mencken wrote about 2,000 book reviews for the magazine *Smart Set,* which he edited with George Jean Nathan from 1914 to 1923. Under Mencken and Nathan, the magazine became a central shaper of literary taste in America. In 1923, Mencken began a 10-year position as founding editor of the *American Mercury.* This magazine of humor and comments about American customs and politics appealed to sophisticated, intellectual readers. During this period, Mencken reached the height of his influence over American culture.

Mencken is best known for his monumental study

The American Language (1919), which he revised and supplemented several times. In it, Mencken examined the development of the English language in America, praising the acceptance of new words and forms of expression as a reflection of the American life style.

A. Aubrey Bodine

H. L. Mencken

Mencken's criticism and essays were collected in the six-volume *Prejudices* (1919-1927). His other works include three autobiographical volumes, *Happy Days, 1880-1892* (1940), *Newspaper Days, 1899-1906* (1941), and *Heathen Days, 1890-1936* (1943). Parts of his diary were published in 1990.   Daniel Mark Fogel

Mendel, *MEHN duhl,* **Gregor Johann,** *GREHG uhr YOH hahn* (1822-1884), an Austrian botanist and monk, formulated the basic laws of heredity. His experiments with the breeding of garden peas led to the development of the science of genetics.

His life. Mendel was born in Heinzendorf, Austria (now Hynčice, near Krnov, in what is now the Czech Republic). His parents were peasants. He was an excellent student and decided to be a teacher. Many teachers at that time were priests. Therefore, in 1843, at the age of 21, Mendel entered the monastery of St. Thomas in Brünn, Austria (now Brno, the Czech Republic). He became a priest in 1847.

At the monastery, Mendel was exposed to many scholars. In 1851, the monastery sent him to study science and mathematics at the University of Vienna. He returned to the monastery in 1853 and taught biology and physics at a local high school for the next 14 years. Mendel's fame came from his research in the monastery garden. In 1868, Mendel was elected abbot of the monastery. From then on, his administrative responsibilities limited his opportunities for research.

His work. In his experiments, Mendel studied the inheritance of seven pairs of traits in garden pea plants and in their seeds. These pairs included (1) rounded or wrinkled seeds and (2) tall or short plants.

Mendel bred and crossbred thousands of plants and observed the characteristics of each successive generation. Like all organisms that reproduce sexually, pea plants produce their offspring through the union of special sex cells called *gametes.* In pea plants, a male gamete, or sperm cell, combines with a female gamete, or egg cell, to form a seed.

Mendel concluded that plant traits are handed down through hereditary elements in the gametes. These elements are now called *genes.* He reasoned that each plant receives a pair of genes for each trait, one gene from each of its parents. Based on his experiments, he concluded that if a plant inherits two different genes for a trait, one gene will be *dominant* and the other will be *recessive.* The trait of the dominant gene will appear in the plant. For example, the gene for round seeds is dominant, and the gene for wrinkled seeds is recessive. A plant that inherits both genes will have round seeds.

Mendel also concluded that the pairs of genes *segregate* (separate) in a random fashion when a plant's gametes are formed. Thus, a parent plant hands down only one gene of each pair to its offspring. In addition, Mendel believed that a plant inherits each of its traits independently of other traits. These two conclusions are known as Mendel's *Law of Segregation* and his *Law of Independent Assortment.* Since Mendel's time, scientists

Brown Bros.

Gregor Mendel

have discovered some exceptions to his conclusions, but his theories in general have been proved.

Mendel's results were published in 1866 but went unnoticed for 34 years. Scientists found the report in 1900 and soon recognized its importance.   Daniel L. Hartl

See also **Genetics** (History); **Heredity** (Mendel's experiments).

Additional resources

Olby, Robert C. *Origins of Mendelism.* 2nd ed. Univ. of Chicago Pr., 1985.
Orel, Vitězslav. *Mendel.* Oxford, 1984.

Mendeleev, *MEHN duh LAY uhf,* **Dmitri Ivanovich,** *DMEE trih ih VAH nuh vihch* (1834-1907), was a Russian chemist who developed a form of the *periodic law,* a basic principle in chemistry. His law states the properties of chemical elements recur in regular patterns when the elements are arranged according to their atomic weight. Mendeleev's work, together with that of the German chemist Julius Lothar Meyer, led to the *periodic table,* a systematic arrangement of the elements (see **Element, Chemical** [Periodic table of the elements]).

In 1869, Mendeleev proposed his arrangement of the elements in order of increasing atomic weight and according to similarity in properties. Mendeleev's table had blank spaces for unknown elements. Later, using the periodic law, he predicted the properties of three unknown elements. His predictions were confirmed by the discovery between 1875 and 1886 of three elements with these properties. Mendeleev also discovered the phenomenon of *critical temperature,* the temperature at which a gas or vapor may be liquefied by pressure. He was born in Tobolsk, Russia.   O. Bertrand Ramsay

Mendelevium, *MEHN duh LAY vee uhm* or *MEHN duh LEE vee uhm,* is an artificially created radioactive element. Its chemical symbol is Md, and its atomic number is 101. It has 13 known isotopes. Its most stable isotope has a mass number of 258 and a half-life of 58 days (see **Radioactivity** [Half-life]). Its heaviest isotope has a mass number of 260 and a half-life of 32 days.

Mendelevium was discovered in 1955 by a team of American chemists consisting of Glenn T. Seaborg, Albert Ghiorso, Bernard G. Harvey, Gregory R. Choppin, and Stanley G. Thompson. They named the element for Russian chemist Dmitri Mendeleev. Mendelevium was first made by bombarding einsteinium—element number 99—with helium ions.   Richard L. Hahn

See also **Element, Chemical; Seaborg, Glenn T.; Transuranium element.**

Mendel's laws. See Heredity (Mendel's experiments); Mendel, Gregor J.

Mendelsohn, *MEHN duhl suhn,* **Eric** (1887-1953), was a German architect noted for his bold geometric style. Mendelsohn attempted to create a new and expressive industrial and commercial architecture. His best-known structure is the Einstein Tower (1924), a laboratory and observatory in Potsdam. The building features sweeping curves typical of Mendelsohn's work.

Eric (also spelled Erich) Mendelsohn was born in Allenstein, East Prussia (now Olsztyn, Poland). He studied architecture in Munich, Germany. His most important German works included the Steinberg, Hermann & Co. factory (1923) in Luckenwalde and the Schocken department stores in Stuttgart (1927) and Chemnitz (1928).

Mendelsohn's Einstein Tower in Potsdam, Germany, is his first major work. He designed the laboratory and observatory to symbolize the scientific investigation of the universe.

AdW/Fröbus

In 1933, Mendelsohn emigrated to England, where he worked with architect Serge Chermayeff. Their best-known collaboration was the De La Warr Pavilion (1935) in Bexhill. Mendelsohn also practiced in Palestine (now Israel) in the late 1930's, designing hospitals in Haifa and Jerusalem. He settled in the United States in 1941. His major U.S. projects included the Maimonides Health Center (1950) in San Francisco and synagogues for several Midwestern cities, including Cleveland and St. Louis.   Leland M. Roth

Mendelssohn, *MEHN duhl suhn,* **Felix** (1809-1847), was a German composer who was widely known and respected in his time. Mendelssohn also gained fame as a conductor and pianist. He also played a significant role in reviving interest in the music of German composer Johann Sebastian Bach. Mendelssohn held high standards of excellence in composition, performance, and musical training that have had an enormous effect on musicians in the 1800's and 1900's.

His life. Mendelssohn was born in Hamburg, Germany. He was the son of a wealthy banker and grandson of the German-Jewish philosopher Moses Mendelssohn. Many of Mendelssohn's ancestors were Jewish, but his father became Protestant after the family moved to Berlin in 1811. At that time, they added Bartholdy to their last name as a sign of their Protestantism. Mendelssohn's full name was Jakob Ludwig Felix Mendelssohn-Bartholdy.

Portrait by Wilhelm Von Schadow. Dr. Felix Wach, Dresden, Germany (Historical Pictures Service, Chicago)

Felix Mendelssohn

Mendelssohn received his first piano lessons from his mother and went on to study with many respected teachers. He made his first public performance as a pianist when he was 9. When he was 10, he joined a choral society in Berlin called the Singakademie. The Singakademie performed Mendelssohn's choral composition "Psalm 19" that same year. In following years, the group presented many of his works. A conductor at the Singakademie, Carl Friedrich Zelter, became Mendelssohn's music teacher. Zelter introduced him to many important musicians and intellectuals, including the German poet Johann Wolfgang von Goethe.

Although Mendelssohn continued performing during his teen-age years, he became increasingly interested in composition. When he was 17, he wrote an overture for *A Midsummer Night's Dream,* a comedy by the English playwright William Shakespeare. Critics consider the overture remarkably mature for a young composer. Mendelssohn later composed additional music for the play, including the well-known "Wedding March."

Mendelssohn's fame as a conductor, composer, and pianist grew rapidly during the 1830's and 1840's. He performed throughout Europe, making 10 trips to Great Britain. Britain's Queen Victoria greatly admired Mendelssohn, and his music was popular with British audiences. Mendelssohn's travels in England and Scotland inspired several compositions, including his overture *The Hebrides* (1832), also called *Fingal's Cave.*

One of Mendelssohn's most significant achievements was his role in reviving the music of Johann Sebastian Bach. In 1829, he conducted a performance of Bach's "Passion According to St. Matthew" (1729) at the Singakademie. It was the first time since Bach's death that this work had been performed. This event and Mendelssohn's enthusiasm for Bach's music generated a great renewal of interest in the music of the composer.

In 1835, Mendelssohn became the conductor of the famous Gewandhaus (Cloth Hall) Orchestra in Leipzig, Germany, a great honor for such a young conductor. The orchestra thrived and became highly respected under his leadership. In 1843, Mendelssohn formed a music academy in Leipzig. He attracted many outstanding musicians to its faculty, including German composer Robert Schumann. In 1837, Mendelssohn married Cécile Jeanrenaud, with whom he had five children. He died from an undiagnosed illness when he was only 38.

His music. Although Mendelssohn composed during the romantic period, his style grew directly from the classical music of the early 1800's. Mendelssohn's music adheres to traditional forms, emphasizes structural clarity, and contains many classical elements, including smooth *progressions* (changes) in harmony and *counterpoint* (combining several melodies at once). But his work has the emotion and dramatic intensity of romantic music. Also, like other romantic composers, Mendelssohn often found inspiration for his music in literature. See **Classical music** (The romantic era).

Mendelssohn wrote 12 early string symphonies, 4 later symphonies for full orchestra, and a choral symphony. The *Scottish Symphony* (1842), the 3rd, and the *Italian Symphony* (1833), the 4th, are the most frequently performed. Most notable among his other works for orchestra are two piano concertos (1831 and 1837) and an outstanding violin concerto (1845). Mendelssohn wrote numerous choral works with religious themes. The oratorios *St. Paul* (1836) and *Elijah* (1846) are the best known. Mendelssohn's other works include eight collections of short piano pieces called *Songs Without Words* (1832-1843), incidental music for the theater, chamber compositions, and several operas.   Daniel T. Politoske

Additional resources

Blunt, Wilfrid. *On Wings of Song: A Biography of Felix Mendelssohn.* Scribner, 1974.
Kupferberg, Herbert. *Felix Mendelssohn: His Life, His Family, His Music.* Scribner, 1972.

Mendelssohn, *MEHN duhl suhn,* **Moses** (1729-1786), was a Jewish philosopher and scholar, and one of the most learned men of his time. Mendelssohn explored a number of philosophical issues. He was a founder of the German *Haskalah,* a religious cultural movement (see **Haskalah**). In his philosophy of religion, Mendelssohn emphasized reason and believed that human beings have an inborn power to know what is good and true.

Mendelssohn wrote several works in German and Hebrew. In *Phädon* (1767), he discussed his belief in the immortality of the soul. In *Jerusalem* (1783), Mendelssohn provided his interpretation of Judaism.

Mendelssohn was born in Dessau, Germany. He moved to Berlin in 1743, where he acquired advanced knowledge of history, Judaism, philosophy, and languages. Mendelssohn took an active part in Jewish cultural life. He worked for civil rights for German Jews and tried to improve Jews' knowledge of German by translating parts of the Bible into that language. In spite of his own traditional observance, Mendelssohn's role in the Berlin Haskalah made him extremely unpopular among Orthodox Jews. His Bible translation was the subject of a major controversy.   Lawrence H. Schiffman

Menelaus, *MEHN uh LAY uhs,* a king of Sparta, was the husband of Helen of Troy. Paris, a Trojan prince, persuaded Helen to elope with him to Troy. Menelaus and his brother, Agamemnon, gathered an army and attacked Troy. After 10 years they took the city, and Menelaus recovered Helen. They wandered for eight years but finally reached Sparta. They lived there for many years. See also **Helen of Troy.**   Cynthia W. Shelmerdine

Menéndez de Avilés, *meh NEHN dehth theh ah vee LEHS,* **Pedro,** *PAY throh* (1519-1574), a Spanish naval captain, founded St. Augustine, the first permanent European settlement in what would become the United States. He established the settlement in Florida. Menéndez also forced French colonists out of Florida and gained control of the territory for Spain.

King Philip II of Spain had selected Menéndez to lead an expedition to Florida in 1565. The main purpose of the mission was to drive out a group of French settlers who had begun colonizing Florida in 1564. The king also wanted Menéndez to colonize Florida for Spain.

In 1565, Menéndez landed in Florida and founded the fortified settlement of St. Augustine. He then led about 500 men in an attack on France's Fort Caroline, near present-day Jacksonville. The Spanish seized the fort, killing about 130 French troops. They also took as prisoners over 200 men, including the French commander, and ruthlessly executed them. Menéndez' victory ended French attempts to colonize eastern Florida. During the next few years, Menéndez established several more fortified settlements in what is now the southeastern United States. He was Spain's governor of Florida from 1568 until his death in 1574.

Menéndez was born in the Asturias region of northern Spain. He became a sailor at the age of 14. He was appointed captain general of Spain's fleet in the West Indies in 1554.   Paul David Nelson

Menes. See **Egypt, Ancient** (Beginnings).

Mengele, *MEHNG geh luh,* **Josef** (1911-1979), a German doctor, personally selected over 400,000 prisoners to die in gas chambers at Auschwitz, a Nazi concentration camp during World War II (1939-1945). He also conducted horrible experiments on inmates, hoping to produce a race of people with blond hair and blue eyes. Camp inmates called him the "Angel of Death."

Mengele was born in Günzburg, Germany. He became a doctor and joined the Nazi Party in 1938. Mengele served at Auschwitz from 1943 until 1945. U.S. troops captured Mengele but freed him before learning of his role at Auschwitz. From 1949 to 1959, he lived in Argentina. In 1959, West Germany issued a warrant for his arrest for committing war crimes and mass murders. Mengele fled first to Paraguay and later to Brazil. He died in 1979. His death was not uncovered until 1985, when his remains were found buried at a cemetery in Embu, Brazil, under a false name. Scientific tests proved the remains to be Mengele's.   Gerald L. Posner

Menhaden, *mehn HAY duhn,* is a fish that lives in the Atlantic Ocean off the Americas from Nova Scotia to Brazil. Its name comes from an Indian word meaning *that which enriches the earth.* Early Indians often used these fish for fertilizing their crops. The menhaden is also called *pogy, mossbunker, bunker, fatback, shad,* and *bugmouth.* It grows from 12 to 18 inches (30 to 46 centimeters) long and weighs from $\frac{3}{4}$ to 1 pound (0.3 to 0.5 kilogram).

Large schools of young menhaden appear along the East Coast of the United States in the summer. They swim near the surface and make easy prey for fishing fleets as well as for sharks, tuna, and other flesh-eating fishes. Menhaden feed chiefly on tiny aquatic organisms called *plankton* (see **Plankton**).

Menhaden can be eaten by humans, but only small quantities are sold for food. Menhaden yield a valuable oil, used in the manufacture of soap, linoleum, oilskin garments, paint, and varnish, and in the tempering of steel. Ground menhaden meal serves as livestock feed, and menhaden scrap is used for fertilizer.

Scientific classification. Menhaden are in the herring family, Clupeidae. They are members of the genus *Brevoortia.*

Robert R. Rofen

Ménière's disease. See Ear (Diseases).

Meninges. See Brain (How the brain is protected); Meningitis.

Meningitis, *MEHN ihn JY tihs,* is a disease that affects the membranes covering the brain and spinal cord. These membranes are called the *meninges.* The disease also affects the *cerebrospinal fluid,* which surrounds the brain and spinal cord. Meningitis results from infection by bacteria, viruses, fungi, or other microbes. This article discusses bacterial and viral meningitis, the two most common forms of the disease.

Meningitis can attack people of all ages, but it most frequently strikes infants and children. Most victims recover completely from the disease. However, bacterial meningitis can cause severe brain damage and even death. Bacterial meningitis also can result in deafness, paralysis, muscle weakness, mental retardation, blindness, and changes in behavior.

People with physical conditions that weaken the body's resistance to infection have the greatest risk of getting meningitis. Such conditions include sickle cell anemia, the lack of a spleen, or the lack of infection-fighting proteins called *immunoglobulins.*

How meningitis develops. In most cases, the bacteria or viruses that cause meningitis inhabit the respiratory organs. The microbes pass into the bloodstream and are carried to the brain, where they infect the meninges and the cerebrospinal fluid. A variety of chemical changes occur in the brain, and the brain may swell.

Many types of bacteria cause meningitis. But most cases of bacterial meningitis result from infection by one of three types of bacteria—*Neisseria meningitidis, Haemophilus influenzae* type b, and *Streptococcus pneumoniae.* Several viruses also cause meningitis.

Symptoms and diagnosis. In general, the symptoms of bacterial meningitis are more severe than those of viral meningitis. The symptoms also vary with the age of the patient. Among infants and young children, the symptoms include fever, nausea, vomiting, loss of appetite, and sleepiness. Some children experience convulsions or uncontrollable jerking of the limbs. Among older children and adults, symptoms often include headache, back pain, muscle aches, and sensitivity to light in the eyes. Many victims also have a stiff neck.

Doctors diagnose meningitis by examining a sample of the patient's cerebrospinal fluid. The sample is obtained by inserting a needle between the vertebrae in the lower part of the back. This procedure is known as a *lumbar puncture* or *spinal tap.* The cerebrospinal fluid of victims of bacterial meningitis contains a high level of protein and a low level of glucose. The fluid of most patients with viral meningitis has a normal or high level of protein and a normal level of glucose. To identify the type of bacterium or virus involved, the patient's cerebrospinal fluid is further tested in various ways.

Treatment and prevention. A patient with meningitis should be under a doctor's care. No specific treatment is effective against viral meningitis. Bacterial meningitis is treated with antibiotics, which greatly reduce the risk of dying from the disease. The antibiotic used depends on the bacteria involved. The most widely used antibiotics for bacterial meningitis are penicillin, ampicillin, chloramphenicol, cefotaxime, and ceftriaxone. Most patients recover from meningitis in several weeks.

Some forms of bacterial and viral meningitis are contagious. Rifampin, an antibiotic, helps protect against the spread of meningitis caused by *Neisseria meningitidis* and *Haemophilus influenzae* type b. Doctors usually administer rifampin to people who come into close contact with a meningitis patient. There are vaccines to protect against certain types of bacterial meningitis. Doctors recommend that all infants be vaccinated for *Haemophilus influenzae* type b meningitis. There are no effective ways to prevent viral meningitis.

Sheldon L. Kaplan

See also Deafness (Diseases); Encephalitis.

Menninger, *MEHN ihng uhr,* **Karl Augustus** (1893-1990), was an American psychiatrist whose writings influenced public attitudes toward mental illness. He helped found the Menninger Clinic, a leading psychiatric center (see **Menninger Clinic**). His most influential book was *The Human Mind* (1930). His other works include *Man Against Himself* (1938), *Love Against Hate* (1942), *The Vital Balance* (1963, with others), *The Crime of Punishment* (1968), and *Whatever Became of Sin?* (1973).

Menninger was born in Topeka, Kans., and he received his M.D. degree from Harvard University. The writings of the Austrian psychiatrist Sigmund Freud interested Menninger, and his writings reflected many of Freud's concepts.   Nancy C. Andreasen

Menninger, *MEHN ihng uhr,* **William Claire** (1899-1966), was a leading American psychiatrist. He and his brother Karl A. Menninger and their father, Charles F. Menninger, founded the Menninger Clinic, a psychiatric center that became internationally famous (see **Menninger Clinic**). During World War II (1939-1945), he served as chief consultant on psychiatry to the surgeon general of the United States Army and won the Distinguished Service Medal. He also became a leader in the Boy Scout movement.

Menninger was born in Topeka, Kans. He received his M.D. degree from Cornell University. His writings include *Psychiatry in a Troubled World* (1948) and *Psychiatry: Its Evolution and Present Status* (1948).

Nancy C. Andreasen

Menninger Clinic, *MEHN ihng uhr,* a nonprofit organization in Topeka, Kans., is one of the world's leading psychiatric centers. The clinic treats mentally ill patients, trains psychiatrists and other mental health professionals, conducts research, and develops programs in the social application of psychiatry.

The clinic includes two psychiatric hospitals—C. F. Menninger Memorial Hospital and Children's Hospital. It also offers a wide range of outpatient services.

The clinic's Karl Menninger School of Psychiatry and Mental Health Sciences is a major training center for mental health professionals. The Menninger Management Institute offers seminars and consultation for leaders in business, government, and medicine. The clinic also does wide research in human behavior.

The Menninger Clinic was established in 1925 by three physicians—Charles F. Menninger and two of his sons, Karl and William. The address of the clinic is P.O. Box 829, Topeka, KS 66601.

Critically reviewed by the Menninger Clinic

See also **Menninger, Karl A.; Menninger, William C.; Kansas** (picture).

Mennonites, *MEHN uh nyts,* belong to a Protestant group that emphasizes a simple style of life and worship. They base their beliefs on the Bible, especially the New Testament. Mennonites try to live according to the Sermon on the Mount (Matt. 5-7). They believe the Bible forbids them from going to war, swearing oaths, or holding offices that require the use of force.

The first Mennonites belonged to a church organized in Zurich, Switzerland, in 1525. The members called themselves *Swiss Brethren.* They believed that church and state should be separate, and that Reformation leaders had not reformed the church enough (see **Reformation**). They also believed that baptism and church membership should be given only to people who are mature enough to make a thorough commitment to the church and demonstrate sincerity in their way of life. These early Mennonites were nicknamed *Anabaptists,* which means *rebaptizers* (see **Anabaptists**). The name *Mennonite* came from Menno Simons, a Roman Catholic priest who led the Anabaptists beginning in the mid-1530's. The Mennonites later split into groups, including the Amish, and became increasingly diverse.

Mennonites often migrated to escape persecution. Many moved to Pennsylvania in the early 1700's and became part of the group called Pennsylvania Dutch (see **Pennsylvania Dutch**). Dutch Mennonites began settling in Polish West Prussia in the 1500's. Some of them moved to Pennsylvania in 1683 after William Penn, the English Quaker who founded Pennsylvania, offered them religious freedom. Many West Prussian Mennonites of Dutch descent moved to Russia in the late 1700's. In the 1870's, many of them moved to Canada and to the Great Plains states. Today, there are about 800,000 Mennonites in 60 countries.   Leland Harder

For pictures of Mennonite life, see **Culture** (A subculture); **Kansas** (Mennonite women). See also **Amish.**

Menominee Indians, *muh NAHM uh nee,* are a tribe that has lived in the Wisconsin and Upper Michigan region for more than 5,000 years. The Menominee once occupied an area of about $9\frac{1}{2}$ million acres (3.8 million hectares). They lived by hunting and gathering food. The name *Menominee* means *wild rice people.* The Indians harvested wild rice from the water by canoe.

Treaties with the United States reduced Menominee lands to a reservation of 235,000 acres (95,000 hectares). Today, the economy of the reservation depends on a lumber operation, including a sawmill.

In 1953, the U.S. government adopted a policy of *termination* as part of a national program to make Indians independent. Termination called for ending federal support and protection of certain reservation Indians. Through this policy, the government abolished the Menominee reservation in 1961. Congress no longer recognized the Menominee as an Indian tribe. It also withdrew the protection and benefits that treaties had guaranteed the Menominee. Termination brought economic hardship and threatened to destroy the tribe's culture.

The Menominee campaigned to have the Menominee termination reversed. In 1973, they regained their treaty rights and tribal status. The government reestablished the Menominee reservation in 1975.   Ada E. Deer

Menopause, *MEHN uh pawz,* is the time in a woman's life when her menstrual periods end. Most women experience menopause, also called *climacteric* (pronounced *kly MAK tuhr ihk*), sometime between the ages of 45 and 50. The length of menopause varies. In some women, the menstrual cycle ends abruptly. In others, the cycle occurs less and less regularly during a period of several months or years before ending. In still others, menopause may be accompanied by irregular bleeding. Such bleeding may indicate a serious problem in the reproductive system and should be discussed with a physician.

Menopause occurs only in human females. It is often called the *change of life* or simply the *change.* Menopause results from changes in the hormones secreted by the pituitary gland and by the ovaries. The ovaries are the organs that produce the eggs necessary for reproduction. The completion of menopause marks the end of a woman's natural childbearing years. Menopause does not alter a woman's ability to enjoy sex.

Various physical and emotional problems are associated with menopause. The most common physical symptoms are sudden heat sensations called *hot flashes.* Others include cold shivers and dry skin. The loss of bone tissue, a condition called *osteoporosis,* is one of the most serious physical symptoms of late menopause (see **Osteoporosis**). Emotional problems include anxiety, depression, and irritability. Some of the symptoms may result from the hormonal changes of menopause. However, other symptoms result from aging or from problems that existed before menopause.

Many of the symptoms can be relieved by treatment with orally administered drugs containing *estrogen* or *progesterone,* both of which are sex hormones. However, such therapy involves some risks and must be supervised by a physician.   Melvin V. Gerbie

See also **Estrogen; Menstruation.**

Menotti, *muh NAHT ee,* **Gian Carlo,** *jahn KAHR loh* (1911-   ), an American composer, wrote some of the most popular operas of the mid-1900's. Unlike most composers, he also writes the *librettos* (words) for his operas and stages most of their premieres. Menotti won the 1950 Pulitzer Prize for music for *The Consul* (1950) and the 1955 prize for *The Saint of Bleecker Street* (1954).

Menotti's first performed opera, *Amelia Goes to the Ball,* was staged in 1938 at the Metropolitan Opera. In 1947, his tragedy *The Medium* (1946) and comedy *The Telephone* (1947) had long runs on Broadway. Menotti's next stage successes were *The Consul,* about political refugees in Europe, and *The Saint of Bleecker Street,* about life in New York City's Italian section. He wrote *Amahl and the Night Visitors,* perhaps his best-known opera, for TV in 1951. Based on the story of the Three Wise Men, it has been rerun often at Christmas.

Menotti was born in Cadegliano, near Milan, Italy, and moved to the United States in 1928. In 1958, he founded the Festival of Two Worlds, an international festival of the arts held each summer in Spoleto, Italy. In 1977, Menotti founded a similar annual festival, Spoleto Festival U.S.A., in Charleston, S.C.   Richard Jackson

Mensheviks, *MEHN shuh vihks,* were members of a group in the Russian Social Democratic Labor Party. In 1903, the party split over a disagreement about membership. V. I. Lenin, a Russian revolutionary, became the leader of the *bolshinstvo* (majority), or Bolsheviks. His opponents became known as the *menshinstvo* (minority), or Mensheviks. The Bolsheviks favored party membership restricted to a small number of professional revolutionaries. The Mensheviks wanted fewer limitations on membership. See also **Bolsheviks; Lenin, V. I.**

Menstruation, *MEHN stru AY shuhn,* is the loss of blood and cells that occurs about once a month in most women of childbearing age. During each month, blood and cells build up in the lining of a woman's *uterus* (womb), a hollow, pear-shaped organ that holds a baby during pregnancy. The thickening of the lining prepares the uterus for pregnancy. If pregnancy does not occur, the lining breaks down. The blood and cells are discharged through the *vagina,* a canal that leads from the uterus to the outside of the body. The process of men-

struation lasts from three to seven days, and this period of time is called the *menstrual period,* or *menses.*

Most girls have their first menstrual period between the ages of 10 and 16. A woman stops having menstrual

Parts of the female reproductive system

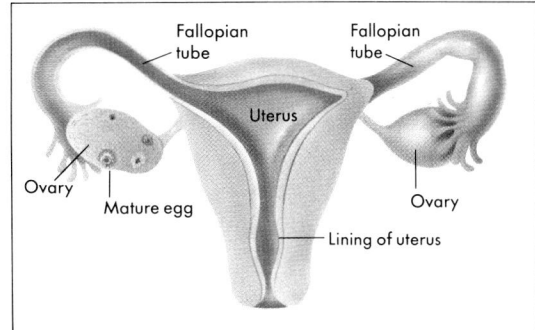

WORLD BOOK illustrations by Charles Wellek

The four phases of the menstrual cycle

Menstrual phase begins about 14 days after an egg leaves the ovary. If the egg is not fertilized, it cannot attach to the uterine wall. It dies and passes out of the body. The ovaries stop supplying hormones to support the uterine lining, which begins to break down and shed. During this shedding, which is called the *menstrual period* or *menses,* most of the lining and about $1\frac{1}{2}$ ounces (44 milliliters) of blood are discharged. The beginning of menses is Day 1 of the menstrual cycle.

Follicular phase. The decrease of estrogen before menses helps the pituitary gland release *follicle-stimulating hormone* (FSH) into the bloodstream. The hormone causes an egg to ripen within a *follicle* (tiny sac) in an ovary. The cells around the growing egg secrete *estradiol,* a form of estrogen. As the estrogen levels rise, uterine bleeding stops and the lining of the uterus thickens to receive a fertilized egg.

Ovulation. The largest egg follicle stimulates the pituitary gland to release a surge of *luteinizing hormone* (LH). This hormone causes *ovulation,* the release of the mature egg from its follicle. The egg travels to the uterus through the *Fallopian tube,* where it may be fertilized by a male sex cell called a *sperm.* Ovulation takes place at about Day 14, or halfway through the menstrual cycle.

Luteal phase. The LH surge causes the empty follicle to form a body of cells called a *corpus luteum* (CL), which secretes estrogen and progesterone. Progesterone further prepares the uterus so a fertilized egg may attach to it. If fertilization occurs, the menstrual cycle stops until after the baby is born. If the egg is not fertilized, the CL decreases secretion of both estrogen and progesterone, and the uterine lining breaks down. As estrogen levels fall, the pituitary releases FSH and more follicles start to develop in the ovary.

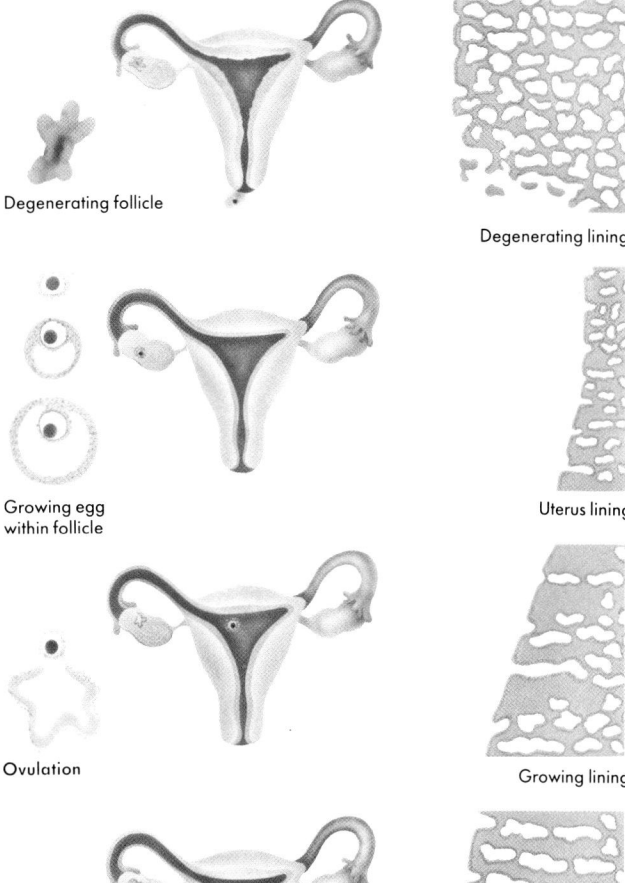

Degenerating follicle

Degenerating lining

Growing egg within follicle

Uterus lining

Ovulation

Growing lining

Corpus luteum

Mature lining

periods during a time of life called *menopause,* which occurs between the ages of 45 and 55 in most women.

The menstrual cycle. Menstruation is part of the *menstrual cycle,* the process that prepares a woman for pregnancy. This cycle repeats itself every 24 to 32 days during the reproductive years of most women. Several hormones regulate the phases of the menstrual cycle.

During menstruation, some *eggs* (female sex cells) begin to mature in the *ovaries,* two organs located near the uterus. As the eggs develop, the surrounding cells release *estradiol* (one of the estrogen hormones) into the bloodstream. As the estrogen level increases, menstrual bleeding stops and the lining of the uterus thickens in preparation for receiving a fertilized egg. The increase in estrogen also causes the pituitary gland to release a hormone that travels to the ovaries and causes the most mature egg to be released. The release of the egg, called *ovulation,* occurs about 14 days before the next menstrual period. The egg travels to the uterus through the *fallopian tube.* After ovulation, the ovary that has just released the egg produces another hormone, *progesterone,* which prepares the uterine wall so that *implantation* (attachment) of the fertilized egg may occur (see **Progesterone**).

Fertilization occurs if the egg unites with a male sex cell called a *sperm* in the fallopian tube. The fertilized egg attaches to the uterine wall and continues its nine-month development into a baby (see **Reproduction, Human**). The *placenta,* an organ that supplies food and oxygen to the baby, secretes hormones that prevent menstruation during pregnancy. If the egg is not fertilized, there is no placenta to secrete hormones. Thus, the uterine lining breaks down and is shed about 14 days after ovulation.

Effects of menstruation. Some women have mild to moderate abdominal cramps a few days before or during menstruation. This discomfort, called *dysmenorrhea,* results from contractions of the uterus and is usually normal. During the days before menstruation begins, some women experience emotional or physical symptoms that may include depression, anxiety, fatigue, headache, body swelling, or pain in the breasts. This condition is called *premenstrual syndrome* (PMS).

Menstruation signifies good health if it occurs regularly and without excessive pain, fatigue, or blood loss. Most women carry on their usual activities. Menstrual discharge can be absorbed either by a *sanitary napkin,* a disposable pad that covers the vaginal opening, or by a *tampon,* a roll of absorbent material worn in the vagina.

The most common reason for a young woman to miss a menstrual period is pregnancy. Other reasons include emotional stress, weight loss, and abnormal hormonal balance. If a woman frequently misses her period or if it occurs less often than every 35 days, she should consult a doctor.   Mona M. Shangold

See also **Estrogen; Estrous cycle; Menopause; Premenstrual syndrome; Toxic shock syndrome.**

Mental health. See Health (Elements of mental health).

Mental illness is any disease of the mind that affects a person's thoughts, feelings, or behavior. Almost everyone has periods of sadness, anger, and fear. However, these periods usually do not last long. Mentally ill people suffer from extreme moods and abnormal thoughts and feelings that may last for years. These disturbances often cause unhappiness and lead to socially unacceptable behavior. They can make it hard for a person to carry out everyday tasks or to get along with people.

Mentally ill people react to their condition in various ways. Some explain their behavior by blaming other people. Others withdraw from reality and seem unaware of their surroundings. In severe cases, mentally ill people may cause physical harm to themselves or to others.

Mental illness affects people in all nations and at all economic levels. However, behavior considered abnormal in one society may be accepted, or even encouraged, in another. Therefore, the definition of mental illness varies from culture to culture. In the United States, about 9 per cent of the people receive treatment for mental illness at some time during their life.

Mentally ill people can get help from various sources. Some patients receive treatment from psychiatrists and psychologists in private practice. Others obtain help at clinics and community mental health centers. In severe cases, patients may require hospitalization because they cannot take care of themselves properly.

Psychiatrists sometimes refer to mental illnesses as *mental disorders, emotional illnesses,* or *psychiatric illnesses.* The legal term *insanity* is used to describe a mental illness so severe that the person is considered not legally responsible for his or her acts. A mental illness that occurs suddenly and requires immediate treatment may be called a *nervous breakdown,* but physicians do not use this term.

Kinds of mental illnesses

The major kinds of mental illnesses may be classified into seven groups: (1) organic disorders, (2) schizophrenia, (3) mood disorders, (4) anxiety disorders, (5) dissociative disorders, (6) personality disorders, and (7) childhood mental disorders. Psychiatrists sometimes also use the terms *neurosis* and *psychosis* to describe the severity of various mental illnesses. A neurosis is a mild disorder that causes distress but does not interfere greatly with a person's everyday activities. Most anxiety disorders and personality disorders are considered neuroses. A psychosis is a severe mental disorder that prevents the individual from functioning in a normal manner. Common psychoses include schizophrenia and manic-depressive disorder.

Organic disorders are mental illnesses known to result from a physical cause, such as a birth defect, a disease, or an injury. The most common organic disorders are delirium and dementia.

Delirium is a disorder in which a person loses awareness of his or her surroundings. People with delirium are easily distracted and confused, and they act and speak in a disorganized manner. They may have *illusions* (distorted visions) or *hallucinations* (sensations with no real basis). Some delirious people become excited and irritable, but others appear listless and withdrawn. This disorder is most common in children and elderly people. Most cases of delirium begin suddenly and last no longer than a week. Causes of delirium include liver or kidney disease, high blood pressure, head injuries, alcoholism, and drug addiction.

Dementia is characterized by a decrease in mental ability, particularly memory and judgment. People with

Play therapy enables mentally ill youngsters to act out their emotional problems with dolls and other toys. For example, a child who is angry with his sister may strike a girl doll. A therapist encourages children to relate such actions to feelings about themselves and other people.

WORLD BOOK photo by Steinkamp/Ballogg

dementia may forget names, conversations, or recent events. They often neglect personal hygiene, disregard social rules, and experience other changes in personality and behavior. Dementia results from the destruction of brain tissue and occurs mainly in elderly people.

Schizophrenia is a severe mental disorder in which a person suffers unpredictable disturbances in thinking, mood, awareness, and behavior. The word *schizophrenia* means a *splitting of the mind.* It refers to the illogical, confused thoughts and actions that characterize schizophrenic behavior.

In most cases, schizophrenia develops gradually. A schizophrenic patient's conversations become unusual and difficult to understand. The patient may often show inappropriate emotions, such as laughing at a sad story or becoming very angry without any obvious cause.

People with schizophrenia commonly have delusions. For example, patients with *paranoid delusions* imagine that other people are following them or trying to harm them. Some schizophrenic patients also have hallucinations. The most common hallucinations are imaginary voices. A schizophrenic patient may believe these voices carry messages from important people or from God.

The delusions, hallucinations, and disorganized speech of schizophrenics are sometimes referred to as *positive symptoms* because they are distortions or exaggerations of normal mental functions. People with schizophrenia also may display *negative symptoms,* which represent a lessening or loss of normal functions. Such symptoms include decreased speech, a blunting of the ability to express emotions, an inability to experience pleasure, and difficulty in sustaining attention.

Mood disorders, also known as *affective disorders,* mainly involve disturbances in the patient's mood. The two chief mood disorders are *depression* (sadness) and *mania* (extreme joy and overactivity). Patients with *bipolar disorder,* also called *manic-depressive disorder,* suffer alternating periods of depression and mania.

Most people with depression feel hopeless and worthless. Many suffer from insomnia and loss of appe-

tite. Other symptoms include headaches, backaches, and chest pains. Some people with depression move and think slowly, but others feel restless. In many cases, the patient has difficulty concentrating and may have terrifying and uncontrollable thoughts. Many people with depression attempt suicide because they believe they have no reason to continue living. Others view suicide as an escape from their problems.

A person with mania feels alert, optimistic, and over-

Mental illness terms

Anxiety is a condition of worry, tension, or uneasiness produced by the anticipation of some danger whose source is largely unknown.

Compulsion is an irresistible impulse to perform a certain action.

Delusion is a false belief that a person maintains in spite of evidence that proves it untrue.

Depression is a mental disorder characterized by feelings of deep sadness, hopelessness, and worthlessness.

Hallucination is the sensation of something that does not really exist.

Illusion is a distorted perception of reality.

Mania means a mental disorder that involves extreme optimism and excessive energy, often accompanied by uncontrollable irritability and anger.

Mood disorder is a mental illness that mainly affects a person's mood.

Neurosis is a mild mental disorder.

Obsession is a recurring thought that a person considers senseless or terrible but cannot ignore.

Organic disorder refers to a mental illness that results from a physical cause, such as a birth defect, a disease, or an injury.

Paranoia is a mental condition in which an individual unjustifiably feels threatened by other people.

Phobia means a strong, unreasonable fear of a particular object or situation.

Psychosis is a severe mental disorder characterized by delusions, hallucinations, and inability to deal with reality.

Schizophrenia is a severe mental disorder characterized by unpredictable thoughts and behavior and a withdrawal from reality.

Unconscious refers to thoughts and feelings that a person is not directly or fully aware of.

confident. However, these feelings may suddenly change to irritability or rage. The mind jumps from one thought to another, and the individual speaks rapidly in a rambling and uncontrollable manner. People with mania move quickly, work energetically, and need little sleep. They move restlessly from project to project but seldom complete any particular task. Most periods of mania begin suddenly, last for a few days or weeks, and then end abruptly.

Anxiety disorders are mental disturbances in which a person experiences unreasonable fears. The four chief types are (1) generalized anxiety, (2) phobias, (3) panic disorder, and (4) obsessive-compulsive disorder.

Generalized anxiety is a persistent fear without obvious cause that lasts a month or longer. Its symptoms include muscle tension, nausea, rapid heartbeat, and hot or cold spells. People with generalized anxiety constantly worry that something terrible will happen to them. This makes them impatient and irritable, and they often find it difficult to get along with other people.

Phobias are persistent, strong fears of certain objects or situations. Common phobias include *agoraphobia,* the fear of large open spaces; and *claustrophobia,* the fear of small enclosed spaces. A person suffering from a phobia has a strong desire to avoid the dreaded object or situation. If forced into contact with the object of the phobia, the individual may panic or become nauseated.

Panic disorder is a sudden, intense feeling of fear. Symptoms include shortness of breath, rapid heartbeat, dizziness, numbness, sweating, and trembling. In most cases, a fear of death accompanies these physical disturbances. Most panic attacks last several minutes, but others continue for several hours. A person may have only one attack, or attacks may recur over a period of months or years. This disorder occurs far more commonly in women than in men.

Obsessive-compulsive disorder is characterized by illogical and uncontrollable impulses that result in *obsessions* or *compulsions.* Obsessions are persistent thoughts that the patient considers senseless or terrible but cannot ignore. The most common obsessions involve thoughts of committing violent acts or of becoming contaminated. Compulsions are actions performed again and again with little purpose, such as repeated handwashing or counting objects.

People with compulsions believe their actions will produce or prevent some future event. They generally realize the senselessness of their behavior and do not enjoy performing it. However, resisting the compulsion causes increased tension, which immediately disappears after the action is performed. In severe cases, a compulsion becomes a person's major activity and thus prevents the individual from leading a normal life.

Dissociative disorders involve a loss or change of identity. In one common dissociative disorder, *psychogenic amnesia,* a person forgets his or her past. In a similar disorder, called *psychogenic fugue,* the individual not only forgets the past but also travels to a new location and assumes a new identity. People who suffer from *depersonalization disorder* feel that they are watching themselves from a distance and have no control over their actions. In *multiple personality disorder,* the individual has two or more distinct personalities, each of which dominates at certain times.

Personality disorders are character traits that create difficulties in personal relationships. For example, *antisocial personality disorder* is characterized by aggressive and harmful behavior that first occurs before the age of 15. Such behavior includes lying, stealing, fighting, and resisting authority. During adulthood, people with this disorder often have difficulty keeping a job or accepting other responsibilities.

Individuals with *paranoid personality disorder* are overly suspicious, cautious, and secretive. They may have delusions that people are watching them or talking about them. They often criticize others but have difficulty accepting criticism.

People who suffer from *compulsive personality disorder* attach great importance to organization. They strive for efficiency and may spend a great deal of time making lists and schedules. But they are also indecisive and seldom accomplish anything they set out to do. They often make unreasonable demands on other people and have difficulty expressing emotions.

Childhood mental disorders. Children may suffer from the same mental disorders that affect adults, but sometimes these disorders produce different symptoms in children. For example, a child with depression may demonstrate the depression by getting into trouble in school. Also, some mental illnesses generally occur only in children. In one such illness, *attention deficit disorder,* the child is disorganized and easily distracted. Most children with this disorder also suffer from *hyperactivity,* a state of almost constant motion. These disturbances often cause learning difficulties in school and behavior problems both in school and at home.

A severe mental disorder called *infantile autism* begins during early childhood. Children with this disorder fail to develop speech and other forms of communication. Autistic children appear detached and unresponsive. They usually stare vacantly, and they have no facial expression. They may become strongly attached to specific objects and repeatedly perform such rhythmic body movements as handclapping and rocking.

Causes of mental illness

Research has shown that mental illnesses have various causes, but the causes are not fully understood. Some mental disorders are due to physical changes in the brain resulting from illness or injury. Chemical imbalances in the brain may cause other mental illnesses. Still other disorders are mainly due to conditions in the environment that affect a person's mental state. These conditions include unpleasant childhood experiences and severe emotional stress. In addition, many cases of mental illness probably result from a combination of two or more of these causes.

Physical changes in the structure of the brain may cause severe mental disorders, including delirium and dementia. Brain damage may result from such causes as head injuries, infections, or inherited defects. Diseases that damage or destroy brain tissue include encephalitis, meningitis, and brain tumors. A disease called *arteriosclerosis* (hardening of the arteries) may damage the brain by reducing its blood supply. This disease mainly attacks middle-aged and older people.

Chemical imbalances in the body may affect a person's thoughts, feelings, and behavior. Research suggests that an imbalance of certain brain chemicals may cause such mental illnesses as schizophrenia and manic-depressive disorder. These chemicals, called *neurotransmitters,* enable the nerve cells in the brain to communicate with one another. People with schizophrenia may have a defect that causes brain cells to release excess amounts of *dopamine,* a neurotransmitter. Mania may result from an excess of dopamine and two other neurotransmitters *norepinephrine* and *serotonin.* A deficiency of these three chemicals may cause depression. See **Brain** (The chemistry of the brain).

Both schizophrenia and manic-depressive disorder sometimes run in families. Studies suggest that this happens because children can inherit a tendency to develop the chemical imbalances involved in these disorders. However, environmental conditions generally determine whether a person with such an inherited tendency will actually become mentally ill.

Childhood experiences that are unpleasant or disturbing may cause unconscious mental conflicts that affect a person throughout life. Most such experiences involve family problems, relationships with other children, or difficulties in school.

Emotional stress may become so severe that it interferes with a person's ability to handle everyday problems. Stress may result from overwork, poor health, financial problems, or family responsibilities. If stress becomes overwhelming, a person may reach the "breaking point" and become mentally ill. The ability to deal with stress depends greatly on a person's physical condition, past experiences, and current problems.

Methods of treatment

Mentally ill people need specialized treatment from mental health professionals, such as psychiatrists and psychologists. Psychiatrists have an M.D. degree and advanced training in the treatment of mental illness. Most psychologists have a Ph.D. degree and practical training in psychology.

Psychiatrists diagnose and treat most cases of serious mental illness. First, a psychiatrist examines the patient to determine if the mental disorder has a physical cause. The psychiatrist also talks with the patient and sometimes with the patient's family. These discussions help the psychiatrist understand the symptoms of the disorder.

A psychologist may help the psychiatrist diagnose mental illnesses. Psychologists give patients special tests that measure a wide variety of personality traits and mental reactions. In a Rorschach test, for example, patients describe what they see in a series of standardized inkblots. These descriptions help the examiner recognize abnormal psychological tendencies. Psychologists also may use various forms of psychotherapy to treat some mental illnesses.

After diagnosing a patient's disorder, the psychiatrist may treat the illness in a number of ways. The major methods of treatment include (1) drug therapy, (2) psychotherapy, (3) electroconvulsive therapy, (4) psychosurgery, and (5) hospitalization.

Drug therapy. Since 1950, scientists have developed a number of medications that have proved extremely successful in the treatment of certain mental disorders. Psychiatrists use *tricyclic antidepressants* to treat pa-

WORLD BOOK photo by Steinkamp/Ballogg

A Rorschach test uses 10 standardized inkblots to help diagnose mental disorders. The patient describes what he or she sees in each blot. A trained examiner interprets the description.

tients with severe depression. In most cases, these drugs restore the depressed patient to normal. *Lithium carbonate* is the most effective drug for patients who suffer from manic-depressive disorder. It reduces the frequency and severity of both the manic and the depressive periods and, in many cases, eliminates them entirely. Medications called *antianxiety drugs* or *tranquilizers* help relieve the tension caused by anxiety disorders. Psychiatrists often use *antipsychotic drugs* to treat schizophrenia. Antipsychotic drugs help relieve hallucinations, delusions, and other symptoms of schizophrenia.

Some drugs used in treating mental illnesses may have serious side effects. Drowsiness and muscle weakness often accompany the use of antianxiety drugs, and antipsychotic drugs may cause restlessness and muscle spasms. Many patients receiving drug therapy become dependent on their medication. If a patient discontinues using prescribed medication, the symptoms of the disorder often return.

Psychotherapy consists of structured discussions and other activities involving a therapist and one or more patients. In general, the goal of psychotherapy is to help patients discover the cause of their mental disorder and improve or correct their condition. A psychotherapist has training in the theories and techniques of psychotherapy. A psychotherapist may be a psychiatrist, a psychologist, or a psychiatric social worker.

Kinds of psychotherapy include (1) analytic, (2) behavioral, and (3) supportive. Some therapists use one of these forms for all patients. Other therapists vary their techniques depending on the individual needs of their patients.

Analytic psychotherapy is based on the theory that mental disorders result from conflicts between conscious and unconscious forces in the mind. The best-known form of analytic therapy is called *psychoanalysis.* Psychoanalysts try to make their patients aware of unconscious mental conflicts and help them find ways to resolve these conflicts. Many analysts use a method called *free association,* in which the patient talks about anything that comes to mind. A psychoanalyst may also question patients about their dreams and childhood memories, which can provide insight into unconscious thoughts and feelings.

Behavioral psychotherapy concentrates on relieving current symptoms of the patient's mental disorder rather than on trying to understand unconscious conflicts. According to behavioral theory, mentally ill people never learned how to deal with everyday problems. Behavioral therapists help patients develop appropriate behavior through such methods as rewarding desirable responses and ignoring or punishing undesirable ones.

Supportive psychotherapy focuses on recent events and personal relationships in the patient's life. The patient and the therapist work as a team to solve the practical problems caused by the mental disorder. Supportive therapists try to help patients appreciate and accept themselves. The therapist encourages patients to discuss their feelings and then provides reassurance and practical advice.

Special techniques may be used in conjunction with any type of psychotherapy. The most widely used techniques include (1) psychodrama, (2) play therapy, and (3) group therapy.

In a psychodrama, a group of patients act out their problems. They may play the roles of themselves and of other people in their lives. Such role-playing encourages the patients to observe their problems from various points of view and thus gain a better understanding of their mental disorder.

Play therapy is used in treating mentally disturbed children. A therapist gives the child dolls and other toys and asks the youngster to tell a story about them. The child generally uses the toys to act out personal con-

David R. Frazier

Psychodrama is a technique used by psychotherapists to help patients view their problems more clearly. In a psychodrama, patients portray themselves and other people in their lives.

flicts. The therapist then helps the young patient relate these play actions to his or her own situation.

Group therapy is any kind of psychotherapy conducted with a group of six or more people. Many patients learn about their own problems by sharing experiences with people who have similar conflicts. The group members also encourage and support one another during times of personal stress.

Electroconvulsive therapy (ECT), also called *electroshock treatment,* involves passing an electric current through the patient's brain for a fraction of a second. The patient becomes unconscious and experiences a convulsion that lasts about one minute. Psychiatrists currently use ECT to treat hospitalized patients who remain depressed and suicidal in spite of drug therapy and psychotherapy. In most cases, ECT shortens the period of depression, but does not prevent future occurrences. ECT also often causes temporary amnesia.

Psychosurgery is used in treating mental disorders that result from an overproduction of chemicals or nerve impulses in a specific area of the brain. Such surgery involves destroying or removing the defective area or cutting the nerve fibers between it and other parts of the brain. The most common type of psychosurgery is a *cingulotomy.* In this operation, the surgeon uses a surgical knife or an electric current to cut through a bundle of nerve fibers called the *cingulum.* The cingulum connects the brain's frontal and temporal lobes and plays a role in controlling emotions.

Psychosurgery has been used to treat patients who suffer from severe depression, compulsions, or anxieties. Psychiatrists generally recommend such surgery only if other methods of treatment have proved ineffective. Most psychiatrists consider psychosurgery unsafe and discourage its use in treating mental illness. Such surgery is rarely performed today, though psychosurgery was often used prior to the development of effective medications during the 1950's.

Hospitalization may be necessary for people with severe mental illnesses who require constant medical attention. In many cases, removing patients from the home environment relieves them of any social or personal stress that may have contributed to the development of mental illness. In addition, a hospital has trained personnel who can prevent patients from harming themselves or others.

In most mental hospitals, patients receive specialized treatment for their particular mental disorder. Trained therapists prescribe medications, supervise psychotherapy sessions, and administer electroconvulsive treatments. In many hospitals, patients and staff members work together to plan hospital routines. This feeling of participation helps patients readjust to everyday activities after they leave the hospital.

History

Early attitudes. Prehistoric peoples believed mental illnesses were caused by evil spirits that possessed the body. Tribal priests performed magical ceremonies, administered potions, and used hypnosis to drive out the evil spirits. Some priests also tried to release the spirits by cutting a hole in the victim's skull.

Many ancient Greeks believed that mental disorders were punishment from their gods, and so they tried to cure these illnesses with prayers and religious ceremonies. About 400 B.C., however, the Greek physician Hippocrates claimed that mental disorders resulted from an imbalance of four body fluids: blood, phlegm, yellow bile, and black bile. For example, depression supposedly resulted from an excess of black bile. The ancient Greek name for this fluid, *melan chole,* is the origin of the word *melancholy,* which means *sadness.*

During the Middle Ages, a belief in witchcraft spread throughout Europe. Many people with mental illnesses were considered witches and were killed by burning, hanging, or drowning. Mentally ill people who managed to escape charges of witchcraft were generally put in prisons or hospitals.

During the 1500's, many European nations built institutions for the mentally ill. One of the most famous was St. Mary of Bethlehem in London, which became widely known as *Bedlam.* The inmates suffered from unsanitary conditions, public beatings, and other harsh treatment. Today, the word *bedlam* means *uproar* and *confusion.*

Humane treatment of mentally ill people began in the late 1700's. During that period, a French physician named Philippe Pinel and William Tuke, a British merchant, worked to improve the conditions of mental institutions in their countries. Through their efforts, many mental hospitals introduced treatments that included fresh air, exercise, and pleasant surroundings.

During the early 1800's, an American physician named Benjamin Rush incorporated the ideas of Pinel and Tuke in his treatment of mentally ill patients at Pennsylvania Hospital in Philadelphia. Dorothea Dix, an American schoolteacher, began visiting mental hospitals throughout the United States in the 1840's. She described the hospitals' miserable conditions to state legislators and persuaded them to pass laws providing state funds for mental institutions.

In 1908, Clifford W. Beers, a former mental patient, wrote a book that described his experiences in three mental hospitals in Connecticut. This book, *A Mind That Found Itself,* stimulated public interest in mental illness. In 1909, Beers helped establish the National Committee for Mental Hygiene (now the National Association for Mental Health). It was made up of psychiatrists, psychologists, and private citizens and worked to promote public understanding of the problems of mental illness. By 1919, the committee had grown into an international organization that provided funds for research in the diagnosis, treatment, and prevention of mental disorders.

Medical approaches to mental illness were first practiced in ancient Greece and Rome and again became standard practice in the late 1800's in Europe. Emil Kraepelin, a German psychiatrist, developed a system of diagnosing and classifying mental disorders in 1883. These classifications were expanded by Eugene Bleuler, a Swiss physician. Bleuler also introduced the practice of examining all areas of a patient's life, not only the symptoms of mental illness. The American psychiatrist Adolf Meyer taught the ideas of Kraepelin and Bleuler in the United States and urged the establishment of psychiatric research centers.

In the early 1900's, the Austrian psychiatrist Sigmund Freud introduced the theory that forces in the unconscious mind strongly influence an individual's personality and behavior. Freud also suggested that conflicts

Illustration from *The History of Psychiatry* by Franz G. Alexander and Sheldon T. Selesnick; © 1966 Harper & Row, Publishers

A rotating chair was used to treat mental disorders during the late 1700's. It supposedly relieved mental illness by increasing the blood supply to the brain.

during early childhood affect the development of the unconscious. These theories became the basis for psychoanalysis and other forms of psychotherapy.

Recent developments. In 1956, for the first time, the number of patients discharged from public mental hospitals in the United States exceeded the number admitted. This trend has continued largely because of the effectiveness of drug therapy, which enables many patients to receive treatment while living at home. However, the release of such large numbers of patients has caused serious problems. Many communities lack adequate counseling services to help mentally ill individuals readjust to everyday life. As a result, former patients often find it difficult to obtain housing and employment.

The success of drug therapy has led to increased interest in finding other effective means of treating mental illness. Much of this work involves searching for links between mental disturbances and genetic defects or other physical disorders.   Nancy C. Andreasen

Related articles in *World Book* include:

Kinds of mental illnesses

Alcoholism	Bulimia	Neurosis
Amnesia	Depression	Phobia
Anorexia nervosa	Hypochondria	Psychosis
Anxiety	Hysteria	Pyromania
Autism	Kleptomania	Schizophrenia
Bipolar disorder		

Treatment

Abnormal psychology	Freud, Sigmund	Psychiatry
Adler, Alfred	Hypnotism	Psychoanalysis
Beers, Clifford W.	Jung, Carl G.	Psychology
Chlorpromazine	Occupational	Psychotherapy
Clinical psychology	therapy (Helping	Shock treatment
Dix, Dorothea L.	the mentally	Tranquilizer
	disabled)	

Other related articles

Catalepsy	Extrovert	Hyperactivity
Delusion	Hallucination	Incompetence

Outline

Questions

How did prehistoric peoples treat mental illnesses?
What is mania? How does it differ from depression?
What drugs do psychiatrists use to relieve anxiety? Schizophre-
  nia? Manic-depressive disorder?
How may emotional stress affect mental functions?
What is supportive therapy?
How is electroconvulsive therapy used in treating mental disor-
  ders?
What is an *obsession*? A *compulsion*?
Who was Clifford W. Beers? What contributions did he make to
  psychiatric research?
How does psychoanalysis help patients understand their mental
  disorders?
What theories did Sigmund Freud introduce that led to the de-
  velopment of psychotherapy?

Reading and Study Guide

See *Mental illness* in the Research Guide/Index, Volume 22, for
  a *Reading and Study Guide.*

Additional resources

Andreasen, Nancy C. *The Broken Brain: The Biological Revolu-
  tion in Psychiatry.* Harper, 1985. First published in 1984.
*Diagnostic and Statistical Manual of Mental Disorders: DSM-
  III-R.* 3rd ed. Am. Psychiatric Assn., 1987.
Gilman, Sander L. *Seeing the Insane: A Cultural History of Mad-
  ness and Art in the Western World.* Wiley, 1982.
Hyde, Margaret O. *Is This Kid "Crazy"? Understanding Unusual
  Behavior.* Westminster, 1983. Also suitable for younger read-
  ers.

Mental retardation is a condition of subnormal intellectual and social development. A mentally retarded
person's intelligence ranks significantly below average,
and the social functioning of such a person is less capable and independent than that of other people of the
same age and cultural group. Almost 3 per cent of the
people of the United States suffer retardation.

Many mildly retarded children are not recognized as
retarded until they start school and fail to learn well.
Most of them are not unusual in appearance. But some
seriously retarded youngsters are identified early in life
because they are slow to sit up, walk, or talk, or because
they have physical disabilities.

Physicians and social workers once advised parents
of the retarded to place their child in a custodial institution. But today, experts believe that all but the most seriously retarded can benefit more by living in a community. In the 1980's, about 4 per cent of the mentally
retarded lived in institutions.

Caring for the retarded at home requires great pa-
tience and understanding. Many parents have difficulty
adjusting to the fact that their child has below average
mental ability. Counseling has helped many parents accept the situation and learn how to help their child.

Degrees of mental retardation. Mental ability can
be measured by IQ—that is, a person's score on an intelligence test (see **Intelligence quotient**). People of average intelligence score from 90 to 109 on such a test. An
IQ of below 70 signifies one of four degrees of mental
retardation: (1) mild, (2) moderate, (3) severe, or (4) profound.

Mildly retarded people have IQ's of 55 to 69. They account for about 90 per cent of the mentally retarded in
the United States. Some are placed in school classes for
the *educable mentally retarded.* Others attend regular
classes. By the time the mildly retarded reach their late
teens, they may be able to do sixth-grade schoolwork.
Many mildly retarded adults can support themselves as
unskilled or semiskilled workers.

Moderately retarded people have IQ's of 40 to 54.
They can make little or no progress in such subjects as
reading, writing, and arithmetic. Most require special
school classes for the *trainable mentally retarded.* They
can learn to care for themselves and to perform useful
tasks at home or in special workshops.

Severely retarded people have IQ's of 25 to 39. They
require training in language, personal hygiene, and getting along with others. Severely retarded individuals
must be cared for throughout life.

Profoundly retarded people have IQ's below 25 and
never advance beyond the mental age of a baby or tod-
dler. Many profoundly retarded people need constant
care to survive, though they may learn to walk and to
recognize familiar faces.

Causes. Mental retardation may result from many different factors. The normal development of a human
being is so complex that almost anything that interferes
with it may contribute to retardation.

Multiple causes. Many mentally retarded individuals
seem to be handicapped by a combination of factors, no
one of which by itself could have produced the retardation. Many mildly retarded children, for example, come
from families with little money, poor health, low educational achievement, poor nutrition, and other disadvantages. Some parents are too discouraged or too overworked to provide a good learning environment for
their children. Furthermore, many different genes contribute to intelligence, and a child may inherit an unlucky combination of many genes.

Single causes. In a small number of cases, a single
cause accounts for most of the retardation. These causes
have such overwhelming effects that normal development is impossible. Single causes may be *genetic* (inherited) or environmental.

Genetic conditions causing mental retardation include the presence of an extra chromosome or an abnormal chromosome in the cells. Chromosomes are cellular structures that contain the heredity-controlling
genes. The presence of an extra chromosome causes
Down syndrome (see **Down syndrome**). The *fragile-X
syndrome* involves an abnormality of the X chromosome, one of the chromosomes that determines a person's sex. This condition affects mostly males. More
rarely, retardation may be caused by the absence of a

necessary chromosome. Retardation may also result from the effects of a dominant gene or a pair of recessive genes that interfere with normal growth or metabolism. *Phenylketonuria* (PKU), a condition in which a person cannot properly transform one kind of amino acid into a related amino acid, results from a pair of recessive genes. PKU causes brain damage if the diet is not controlled. See **Phenylketonuria**.

Environmental causes of mental retardation may occur before, during, or after birth. A child may be retarded if the mother contracts such a disease as *rubella* (German measles) or syphilis during pregnancy. The mental development of a child may also be affected by other factors concerning the mother's health during her youth or while she is pregnant. These factors include her nutrition, her age and general health, and her use of alcohol or drugs. Events at birth can also cause retardation. They include premature birth, injury during delivery, and failure of the newborn to breathe properly. During childhood, retardation can result from such causes as brain infection, head injury, prolonged high fever, swallowing concentrated poisonous substances, or breathing such substances from polluted air.

Prevention. Proper care of the mother before and during pregnancy can prevent many cases of mental retardation. Proper delivery and care of sick or premature infants also help reduce the number of cases. Damage resulting from PKU and a few other disorders can be controlled after birth by a special diet or medication.

Physicians can identify through tests some couples for whom having children would involve a high risk of genetic damage. Many such couples decide not to risk having a defective child. Other tests can reveal certain kinds of genetic conditions in an unborn baby. The parents may then decide to discontinue the pregnancy. See **Genetic counseling**.

Retardation produced by multiple causes is more difficult to prevent. Many experts believe the number of such cases could best be reduced by improving the health, education, and economic level of the poor.

Treatment. The mentally retarded cannot be "cured." But in most cases, a great deal can be done to help their intellectual and social development. Much of this treatment consists of appropriate education or training. In the United States, it is the legal right of every school-age child, no matter how seriously retarded, to have the opportunity to learn to function to the best of his or her ability. In some cases, training can begin in infancy. It may continue until the individual is well established in an adult role.

As retarded children grow up, their education tends to center more and more on the skills they will need as adults. Many mildly retarded adults become good workers and good citizens. Mildly retarded adults who cannot hold a job and moderately to severely retarded adults may work in a *sheltered workshop,* a center that employs disabled people. These men and women live with their families or in homes for the retarded in the community. Only the most severely retarded, who require intensive care, are likely to live permanently in residential facilities without doing any productive work.

Marianne Schuelein

See also **Special education; Special Olympics; Vocational rehabilitation**.

Additional resources

Baroff, George S. *Mental Retardation: Nature, Cause, and Management.* 2nd ed. Hemisphere Pub. Corp., 1986.
Scheerenberger, R. C. *A History of Mental Retardation.* Brookes, 1983.

Mental telepathy. See Telepathy.

Menthol, *MEHN thahl,* is a soft, white substance with a mint odor and a fresh, cool taste. It is widely used as an ingredient in cough and cold medicines, perfumes, and cigarettes. Menthol is found in oil of the leaves of the peppermint plant.

Menthol is a *differential anesthetic*—that is, a substance that causes the loss of some sensations. Therefore, it can be used as a salve that reduces itching. However, menthol also stimulates the *receptor* (receiver) cells in the skin that normally respond to cold. Thus, it gives a sensation of coolness that is unrelated to body temperature. The chemical formula of menthol is $C_{10}H_{20}O$. 　　Dorothy M. Feigl

Mentor was the elderly friend and adviser of Odysseus, the hero of the *Odyssey,* an ancient Greek epic. Before Odysseus (Ulysses in Latin) went to fight in the Trojan War, he made Mentor the guardian of his son, Telemachus. In Mentor's shape, the goddess Athena helped Telemachus search for Odysseus. Today, the word *mentor* means a wise, faithful counselor.

Cynthia W. Shelmerdine

Menuhin, *MEHN yoo ihn,* **Yehudi,** *yuh HOO dee* (1916-　　), is an American violinist who had spectacular success as a child prodigy. He promoted the works of contemporary composers and revived neglected, but valuable, music of the past. He has combined the classical musical style of his early training with jazz and with the music of India and other countries.

Menuhin was born in New York City. At the age of 7 he appeared as a violin soloist with the San Francisco Orchestra. Menuhin has been active in training young musicians, most significantly at a school in Surrey, England, he founded in 1963. His essays and speeches on music and other subjects were collected in *Theme and Variations* (1972). He also wrote *Unfinished Journey* (1977), an autobiography. 　　Stephen Clapp

Mephistopheles, *MEHF uh STAHF uh leez,* is the Devil in a German legend about a magician named Faust. In an anonymously written book called *The History of Johann Faust* (1587), Faust sold his soul to Mephistopheles in return for the Devil's services for 24 years. The name *Mephistopheles* may come from three Greek words meaning *not loving the light* or, possibly, from the Hebrew *mephiz* (destroyer) and *tophel* (liar).

In Johann von Goethe's drama *Faust* (1808, 1832), Mephistopheles is a clever evil spirit who is "part of that force, which would do ever evil, and does ever good." The Devil loses in the end, because the troubles he causes only help humanity to find wisdom and grace. Mephistopheles also appears in the operas *Faust* (1859) by Charles Gounod and *Mefistofele* (1868) by Arrigo Boito, and in Christopher Marlowe's play *The Tragical History of Doctor Faustus* (written about 1588).

Klaus L. Berghahn

Mercantilism, *MUR kuhn tih LIHZ uhm,* was an economic system followed by England, France, and other major trading nations from the 1500's to the late 1700's. Under this system, a nation's government strictly regulated economic affairs to enrich its treasury, especially by ensuring that exports exceeded imports.

Mercantilism was based on two beliefs. First, mercantilists judged a nation's wealth by its stock of gold and silver, rather than by standards of living or other measurements. Second, the mercantilists believed the world had a limited supply of wealth, and so one country could grow rich only at the expense of another.

According to the mercantilists, a nation that did not have gold or silver mines had to rely on foreign trade to become rich. They called for an excess of exports over imports, a situation they termed a *favorable balance of trade*. At that time, gold served as the chief means of settling international debts. A nation that exported more than it imported could collect the difference in gold from the importing countries.

To maintain a favorable balance of trade, mercantilist governments enacted high tariffs and other restrictions on imports. In addition, the governments strongly encouraged the growth of domestic industries. Many nations sought overseas colonies, which served as markets for exports and as sources of raw materials. Mercantilist governments also encouraged population growth, because a large population provided a supply of labor and a market for industrial products. Some nations prohibited the sale of gold and other precious metals to foreigners.

During the late 1700's, the mercantilist systems of many countries were gradually replaced by a policy called *laissez faire*. Under laissez faire, the government played a limited role in economic affairs.

Today, the term *mercantilism* is sometimes used to describe policies that protect domestic industries from foreign competition. In addition, mercantilist efforts to plan economic activity resemble government planning under Communism and socialism. But there are many differences between mercantilism and a socialist or Communist system.   Richard C. Wiles

See also **Colonialism** (Economic policies).

Mercator, *muhr KAY tuhr,* **Gerardus,** *juhr AHR duhs* (1512-1594), was a Flemish geographer who became the leading mapmaker of the 1500's. He won lasting fame because of his world map of 1569. It introduced a new way of showing the roughly ball-shaped earth on a flat sheet of paper. This method, called the Mercator projection, proved ideal for navigation and is still used today.

On a map using the Mercator projection, the *meridians* (lines of longitude) and the *parallels* (lines of latitude) appear as straight lines that cross at right angles. The straight lines, plus the aid of a compass, help navigators plot accurate routes. However, many geographical features on this kind of map are exaggerated in size. See **Map** (Cylindrical projections).

Mercator was born in Rupelmonde, Flanders (now Belgium). His given name was Gerard Kremer, but he adopted the Latin form of this name. Mercator studied at the University of Louvain. Later, he made globes and navigation instruments for Holy Roman Emperor Charles V. In addition, Mercator produced a collection of maps titled *Atlas*. This title marked the first use of the word *atlas* to describe a collection of maps.

John Noble Wilford

Mercator projection. See **Map** (Cylindrical projections).

Mercenary, *MUR suh NEHR ee,* is a person who serves for pay in the armed forces of a foreign country. Most men and women who become mercenaries do so to make money or because they love war and adventure.

In ancient times, Persia, Greece, and Rome used mercenaries. Mercenaries were most common from about 1100 to 1500. At that time, many rulers hired trained professional soldiers to protect their states. Some rulers made money by hiring out their mercenary armies to other states. During the Revolutionary War in America (1775-1783), Great Britain hired German soldiers to fight the American colonists. Such military heroes as Casimir Pulaski of Poland and Baron von Steuben of Prussia—both of whom helped the colonists—are also technically considered mercenaries.

The rise of national armies largely ended the need for mercenaries. Today, a few countries in developing areas use mercenaries instead of or as part of their military forces.   John E. Jessup, Jr.

See also **Army** (Armies in the Middle Ages); **Hessians.**

Gerardus Mercator, *above,* worked out a basic system for mapmaking. His world map of 1538, *left,* shows many of the new lands discovered by explorers, including America.

Merchandise Mart is a major wholesale buying center and one of the largest buildings in the world. The Merchandise Mart stands on the north bank of the Chicago River in downtown Chicago.

Every year, more than $1\frac{1}{2}$ million visitors come to the Merchandise Mart from all parts of the world to purchase new goods. These visitors include architects, interior designers, and gift, floor-covering, and home-furnishing retailers. More than 3,200 manufacturers have permanent displays in the Merchandise Mart. These displays include about $1\frac{1}{4}$ million separate items of merchandise. Special "markets" or shows for buyers are held throughout the year. About 20,000 people work in the Mart.

The Merchandise Mart is 25 stories high. The build-

The Merchandise Mart

The Merchandise Mart, one of the world's largest buildings, covers two city blocks on the north bank of the Chicago River.

ing covers two city blocks, and its total floor space equals almost 95 acres (38 hectares).

Marshall Field and Company built the Merchandise Mart in 1930 at a cost of $32 million. In 1945, the Mart was purchased by Joseph P. Kennedy, former United States Ambassador to Great Britain and father of President John F. Kennedy.

Critically reviewed by Merchandise Mart Properties, Incorporated

Merchandising. See Marketing.

Merchant. See Trade (Early trade).

Merchant marine is a fleet made up of a nation's commercial ships and the men and women who operate them. It includes both cargo and passenger ships.

The importance of a country's merchant marine is measured by its *gross tonnage,* rather than by the number of ships. Gross tonnage is the total space within the hull and enclosed deck space on a ship. Each 100 cubic feet of space in a ship equals 1 gross ton.

Technically, the largest merchant fleet in the world is registered under the flag of Liberia, a tiny African country. However, Liberians own only a few of these ships. Many shipowners from other countries register their vessels in Liberia because taxes are lower there. The United States has the sixth largest merchant marine. Other countries with large merchant marines include Greece, Japan, and Panama. For a list of the world's leading merchant fleets, see **Ship** (table).

The United States merchant marine. The American Colonies had a large merchant fleet before the Revolutionary War started in 1775. By 1800, America's merchant

fleet ranked second in the world only to the British fleet. But much United States shipping was destroyed during the Civil War (1861-1865). Most of the remaining ships became obsolete when steel hulls and steam power were developed.

The United States Shipping Board was created in 1916. It improved the merchant marine by building and purchasing ships and regulating shipping. Since 1950, the Maritime Administration has assisted the merchant marine through programs designed to help U.S. shippers operate modern ships (see **Maritime Administration**).

Careers in the merchant marine. One way to become an officer in the United States merchant marine is to gain admission to the United States Merchant Marine Academy in Kings Point, N.Y. Young people can get information about the academy by writing to the Division of Maritime Academies, Maritime Administration, United States Department of Transportation, Washington, DC 20590. See **United States Merchant Marine Academy**.

A person can also earn an officer's license by studying at a state nautical school. But only a few states have these schools. The courses needed for an officer's license generally require three or four years of study. Seamen can also earn an officer's license by spending three years at sea, working either on the deck or in the engine room to advance in unlicensed ratings. Then they must pass the licensed officer's examination. Young people may obtain unlicensed positions aboard ship if they can get seamen's certificates from the Coast Guard. Wages are set by contracts between shipping companies and maritime unions.

Officers and seamen in the British merchant fleet receive their training by studying on training ships or enrolling in nautical schools for two or three years of study.
Critically reviewed by the Maritime Administration

Additional resources

America's Maritime Legacy: A History of the U.S. Merchant Marine and Shipbuilding Industry Since Colonial Times. Ed. by Robert A. Kilmarx. Westview, 1979.

Bauer, Karl J. *A Maritime History of the United States: The Role of America's Seas and Waterways.* Univ. of South Carolina Pr., 1988.

Petersen, Gwenn B. *Careers in the United States Merchant Marine.* Lodestar, 1983. Also suitable for younger readers.

Sager, Eric W. *Seafaring Labour: The Merchant Marine of Atlantic Canada, 1820-1914.* McGill-Queens Univ. Pr. (Montreal), 1989.

Whitehurst, Clinton H., Jr. *The U.S. Merchant Marine: In Search of an Enduring Maritime Policy.* Naval Institute Pr., 1983.

Merchant Marine Academy. See United States Merchant Marine Academy.

Merchant of Venice. See Shakespeare, William (Shakespeare's plays).

Mercurochrome is the trade name for a weak antiseptic that is used in a water solution. The generic name is *merbromin*. Mercurochrome is one of a group of antiseptics, called *organic mercurials*, that contain mercury. Mercurochrome is a coarse, green powder, but in a water solution it is a deep red. Mercurochrome's chemical formula is $C_{20}H_8Br_2HgNa_2O_6$. Mercurochrome solutions normally do not burn or irritate when applied to wounds.
N. E. Sladek

See also **Antiseptic**.

WORLD BOOK photo

Mercury is a silver-colored liquid at room temperature, *right.*
Most mercury comes from the ore cinnabar, *left.*

Mercury, a silver-colored metal, is one of the chemical elements. Unlike any other metal, mercury is a liquid
at room temperature. It flows so easily and rapidly that it
is sometimes called *quicksilver.* No one knows who discovered mercury, but the ancient Chinese, Egyptians,
Greeks, Hindus, and Romans knew about the metal. It
was named for the swift messenger of the gods in
Roman mythology.

Mercury is used in some types of thermometers and
barometers and in certain other instruments. Mercury
compounds have uses in agriculture and industry. They
once were widely used in such common products as
house paints and paper. As a result, mercury became
widespread in the environment in some places. Mercury, however, is extremely poisonous and can cause illness or death. After many people realized its dangers,
industries and government began trying to reduce the
amount of mercury reaching the environment.

Mercury has the chemical symbol Hg. Its atomic
weight is 200.59 and its atomic number is 80. Mercury
melts at -38.87 °C and boils at 356.58 °C.

Uses. Mercury has many *properties* (qualities) that
make it useful. For example, mercury expands and contracts evenly when heated or cooled. It also remains liquid over a wide range of temperatures. These properties
have prompted its use in thermometers.

Mercury conducts electricity and is used in some
electric switches and relays to make them operate silently and efficiently. Industrial chemical manufacturers
use mercury in *electrolysis cells* to change substances
with electricity. Mercury vapor, used in fluorescent
lamps, gives off light when electricity passes through it.

Various *alloys* (mixtures of metals) containing mercury have many uses. Mercury alloys are called *amalgams.* They include silver amalgam, a mixture of silver
and mercury that dentists use to fill cavities in teeth.
Many dry cell batteries contain amalgams of zinc and
cadmium to prevent impurities from shortening the life
of the battery. See **Amalgam.**

Sources. Mercury is less abundant in the earth's
crust than many other metals. However, because mercury deposits are quite concentrated, it is readily available. Most of the mercury used by people comes from
an ore called *cinnabar.* To obtain pure mercury, refiners
heat cinnabar in a flow of air. Oxygen in the air com-

bines with sulfur in the ore, forming sulfur dioxide gas
and leaving mercury behind.

Before its breakup, the Soviet Union was the leading
producer of mercury. Other mercury-producing countries include Algeria, China, the Dominican Republic,
Finland, Germany, Italy, Mexico, Slovakia, Spain, Turkey,
and the United States.

Compounds. Chemists divide mercury compounds
into two groups: (1) *mercurous* or *mercury (I)* compounds, and (2) *mercuric* or *mercury (II)* compounds.
Mercurous compounds include *mercurous chloride*
(Hg_2Cl_2), also called *calomel,* and *mercurous sulfate*
(Hg_2SO_4). Calomel is an antiseptic used to kill bacteria.
Scientists use mercurous sulfate to speed up certain
tests on organic compounds.

Mercuric compounds include *mercuric chloride*
($HgCl_2$), a powerful poison that surgeons once used to
disinfect wounds. Mercuric chloride is also called *cor-
rosive sublimate* or *bichloride of mercury.* Most ammunition uses *mercuric fulminate* ($Hg[OCN]_2$) to set off its
explosive. Paint manufacturers use *mercuric sulfide*
(HgS) in making a red pigment called *vermilion.* Mercury batteries contain *mercuric oxide* (HgO). Several organic mercuric compounds have important medical
uses. For example, some medicines called *diuretics,*
which physicians use to treat kidney disease, contain
these compounds. The antiseptic *Mercurochrome* is
also a mercuric compound.

Mercury in the environment is hazardous chiefly
because its poisonous compounds have been found in
plants and animals that people use for food. Scientists
have discovered poisonous mercury compounds in
such foods as eggs, fish, grain, and meat. Mercury acts
as a *cumulative* poison—that is, the body has difficulty
eliminating it. Thus, it may collect over a long time,
eventually reaching dangerous levels.

Among the most dangerous mercury compounds are
those containing *methyl mercury.* They can damage
brain cells. In the mid-1950's, more than 100 Japanese
were poisoned by fish that contained large amounts of
methyl mercury. The mercury came from industrial
wastes that had been dumped into the bay where the
fish were caught. In the early 1970's, some tuna and
swordfish sold in U.S. stores were found to contain dangerous amounts of mercury. The U.S. government recalled the fish from the stores and warned the public.

Government and industry are working to keep mercury out of the environment. In the early 1970's, the U.S.
and Canadian governments began to prohibit industrial
dumping of wastes containing mercury. Much mercury
has been put into the environment in other ways. Mercury compounds were once used to prevent fungi from
growing in lumber, paint, paper, and seeds, and to kill
plant fungus diseases. Shipbuilders sold paint containing mercury to prevent marine organisms from growing
on the hulls of ships. In 1972, the U.S. government halted
the use of mercury compounds for most of these purposes.   Raymond E. Davis

Related articles in *World Book* include:

Amalgam	Metallurgy
Barometer	(Amalgamation)
Cinnabar	Thermometer
Environmental pollution	Vermilion
Mercurochrome	

Mercury is the planet nearest the sun. It has a diameter of 3,031 miles (4,878 kilometers), about two-fifths the earth's diameter. Mercury's mean distance from the sun is about 36 million miles (57.9 million kilometers), compared to 67,250,000 miles (108,230,000 kilometers) for Venus, the second closest planet.

Because of Mercury's size and nearness to the brightly shining sun, the planet is often hard to see from the earth without a telescope. At certain times of the year, Mercury can be seen low in the western sky just after sunset. At other times, it can be seen low in the eastern sky just before sunrise.

Orbit. Mercury travels around the sun in an *elliptical* (oval-shaped) orbit. The planet is about 28,600,000 miles (46 million kilometers) from the sun at its closest point, and about 43.4 million miles (69.8 million kilometers) from the sun at its farthest point. Mercury is about 57 million miles (91.7 million kilometers) from the earth at its closest approach.

Mercury moves around the sun faster than any other planet. The ancient Romans named it Mercury in honor of the swift messenger of their gods. Mercury travels about 30 miles (48 kilometers) per second, and goes around the sun once every 88 earth-days. The earth goes around the sun once every 365 days, or one year.

Rotation. As Mercury moves around the sun, it rotates on its *axis,* an imaginary line that runs through its center. The planet rotates once about every 59 earth-days—a rotation slower than that of any other planet except Venus. As a result of the planet's slow rotation on its axis and rapid movement around the sun, a day on Mercury—that is, the interval between one sunrise and the next—lasts 176 earth-days.

Until 1965, astronomers believed that Mercury rotated once every 88 earth-days, the same time the planet takes to go around the sun. If Mercury did this, the sun would seem to stand still in Mercury's sky. One side of the planet would always face the sun, and the other side would always be dark. In 1965, astronomers bounced radar beams off Mercury. The signals returning from one side of the planet differed from those from the other side. Using these beams, the astronomers measured the movement of the opposite sides and found that Mercury rotates once in about 59 days. The 59-day rotation period is two-thirds of the 88-day period that makes up a year on Mercury.

Phases. When viewed through a telescope, Mercury can be seen going through "changes" in shape and size. These apparent changes are called *phases,* and resemble those of the moon. They result from different parts of Mercury's sunlit side being visible from the earth at different times.

As Mercury and the earth travel around the sun, Mercury can be seen near the other side of the sun about every 116 days. At this point, almost all its sunlit area is visible from the earth. It looks like a bright, round spot with almost no visible marks. As Mercury moves around the sun toward the earth, less and less of its sunlit area can be seen. After about 36 days, only half its surface is visible. After another 22 days, it nears the same side of

Hyron Spinrad, the contributor of this article, is Professor of Astronomy at the University of California, Berkeley.

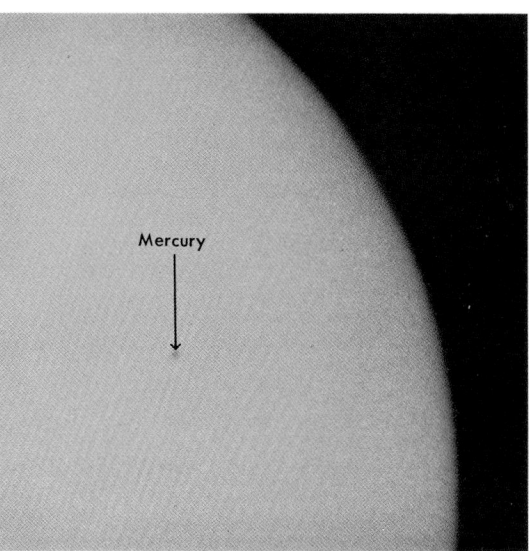

Russ Kinne, Photo Researchers

Mercury appears as a tiny dot against the sun when it is directly between the sun and the earth. Mercury is so small and so near the sun that a telescope is needed to see it at this point.

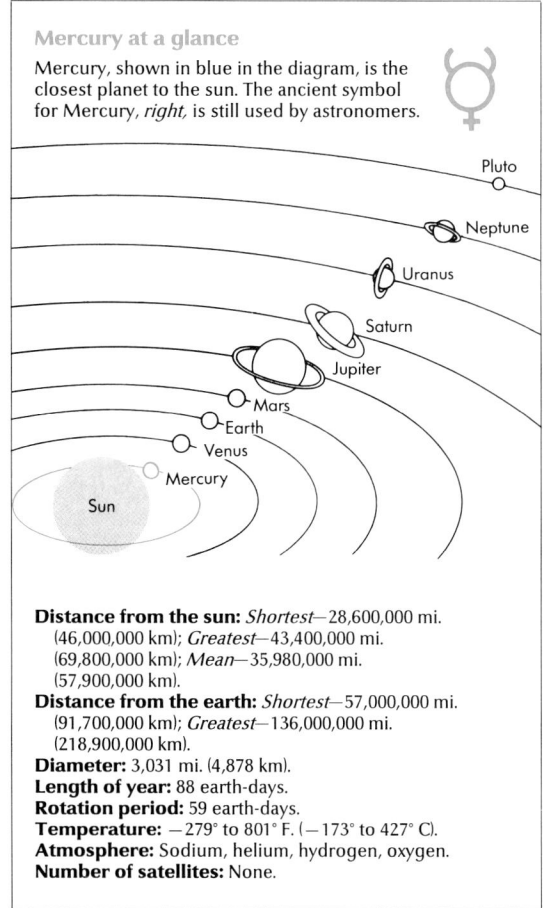

Mercury at a glance

Mercury, shown in blue in the diagram, is the closest planet to the sun. The ancient symbol for Mercury, *right,* is still used by astronomers.

Distance from the sun: *Shortest*—28,600,000 mi. (46,000,000 km); *Greatest*—43,400,000 mi. (69,800,000 km); *Mean*—35,980,000 mi. (57,900,000 km).
Distance from the earth: *Shortest*—57,000,000 mi. (91,700,000 km); *Greatest*—136,000,000 mi. (218,900,000 km).
Diameter: 3,031 mi. (4,878 km).
Length of year: 88 earth-days.
Rotation period: 59 earth-days.
Temperature: −279° to 801° F. (−173° to 427° C).
Atmosphere: Sodium, helium, hydrogen, oxygen.
Number of satellites: None.

NASA

The planet Mercury was first photographed in detail on March 29, 1974, by the U.S. probe *Mariner 10.* The probe was about 130,000 miles (210,000 kilometers) from Mercury.

the sun as the earth, and only a thin sunlit area is visible. The amount of sunlit area that can be seen increases gradually after Mercury passes in front of the sun and begins moving away from the earth.

When Mercury is on the same side of the sun as the earth is, its dark side faces the earth. The planet is usually not visible at this point because Mercury and the earth orbit the sun at different angles. As a result, Mercury does not always pass directly between the earth and the sun. Sometimes Mercury is directly between the earth and the sun. When this occurs, every 3 to 13 years, the planet is in *transit* and can be seen as a black spot against the sun.

Surface and atmosphere. Mercury's surface appears to be much like that of the moon. It reflects about 6 per cent of the sunlight it receives, about the same as the moon's surface reflects. Like the moon, Mercury is covered by a thin layer of minerals called *silicates* in the form of tiny particles. It also has broad, flat plains; steep cliffs; and many deep craters similar to those on the moon. Many astronomers believe the craters were formed by meteors or small comets crashing into the planet. Mercury does not have enough atmosphere to slow down approaching meteors and burn them up by friction.

Although Mercury may have a moonlike surface, its interior appears to resemble that of the earth. Many scientists think the interiors of both planets consist largely of iron and other heavy elements. The discovery of a magnetic field around Mercury led some scientists to believe that the planet has a large core of liquid iron, just as the earth does.

Mercury is dry, extremely hot, and almost airless. The sun's rays are about seven times as strong on Mercury as they are on the earth. The sun also appears about $2\frac{1}{2}$ times as large in Mercury's sky as in the earth's. Mercury does not have enough gases in its atmosphere to reduce the amount of heat and light it receives from the sun. The temperature on the planet may reach 801° F. (427° C) during the day. But at night the temperature may drop as low as −279° F. (−173° C). Because of the lack of atmosphere, Mercury's sky is black, and stars probably can be seen during the day.

Mercury is surrounded by an extremely small amount of helium, hydrogen, oxygen, and sodium. This envelope of gases is so thin that the greatest possible *atmospheric pressure* (force exerted by the weight of gases) on Mercury would be about 0.00000000003 pound per square inch (0.000000000002 kilogram per square centimeter). The atmospheric pressure on the earth is about 14.7 pounds per square inch (1.03 kilograms per square centimeter).

The plant and animal life of the earth could not live on Mercury because of the lack of oxygen and the intense heat. Scientists doubt that the planet has any form of life.

Density and mass. Mercury's *density* is slightly less than the earth's (see **Density**). That is, a portion of Mercury would weigh about the same as an equal portion of the earth. Mercury is smaller than the earth and has much less *mass* (see **Mass**). Mercury's smaller mass makes its force of gravity only about a third as strong as that of the earth. An object that weighs 100 pounds on the earth would weigh only about 38 pounds on Mercury.

Flights to Mercury. The United States *Mariner 10* became the first and only spacecraft to reach Mercury. The unmanned spacecraft flew to within 460 miles (740 kilometers) of Mercury on March 29, 1974. It swept past the planet again on Sept. 24, 1974, and on March 16, 1975. During those flights, the spacecraft photographed portions of the surface of Mercury. It also detected Mercury's magnetic field.

Mariner 10 became the first spacecraft to study two planets. The probe photographed and made scientific measurements of Venus while traveling to Mercury. As the probe flew near Venus, the planet's gravity pulled on the spacecraft, causing it to move faster. Thus, *Mariner 10* reached Mercury in less time and by using less fuel than if it had flown directly from the earth.

In the future, unmanned space probes may go into orbit around Mercury, crash into it, or land on it. The data returned by such probes will give astronomers a better picture of what the planet is like. The probes also may enable scientists to determine how Mercury was formed. Manned exploration of Mercury will be difficult because of its unfavorable surface conditions.

Hyron Spinrad

See also **Evening star; Planet; Solar system; Space exploration.**

Additional resources

Asimov, Isaac. *Venus, Near Neighbor of the Sun.* Lothrop, 1981. Suitable for younger readers. Discusses both Mercury and Venus.

Murray, Bruce G., and others. *Earthlike Planets: Surfaces of Mercury, Venus, Earth, Moon, Mars.* W. H. Freeman, 1981.

Strom, Robert G. *Mercury: The Elusive Planet.* Smithsonian Institution, 1987.

Mercury was the messenger of the gods and the god of roads and travel in Roman mythology. The ancient Romans also worshiped Mercury as the god of commerce, property, and wealth. The words *commerce, merchandise,* and *merchant* are related to his name. The Romans considered Mercury crafty and deceptive. They even saw him as a trickster or thief. Criminals regarded him as their protector. Because Mercury resembled the messenger god Hermes in Greek mythology, he took on many of Hermes' myths.

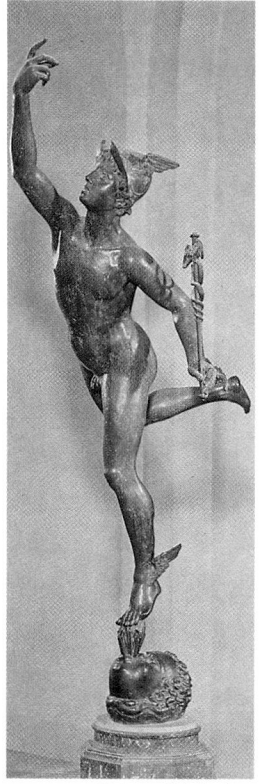

Mercury is a bronze statue by Giambologna of Italy.

The Louvre, Paris, Cossé Brissac collection (Giraudon/Art Resource)

Mercury delivered his messages with miraculous speed because he wore winged sandals called *talaria.* He also wore a broad-brimmed winged hat called a *petasus* and carried a winged staff. The Greeks called the staff a *kerykeion,* from the Greek word for *messenger.* In Latin, the language of the Romans, the word was changed to *caduceus.* Mercury's caduceus had two snakes curled around it. In ancient times, most messengers and travelers wore a hat similar to Mercury's petasus to protect them from the sun. Messengers also carried a staff to identify themselves so they could travel freely. Mercury later became associated with magic and science. His caduceus is frequently confused with the single-snake crutch of Aesculapius, the Roman god of healing.

Mercury was the son of Jupiter, the king of the gods, and Maia, a minor goddess. Artists portrayed him as a handsome young man, with an expression of alertness and intelligence. E. N. Genovese

See also **Hermes.**

Mercury program. See Space exploration (Vostok and Mercury: The first human beings in space).

Mercury vapor lamp. See Electric light.

Meredith, George (1828-1909), was an English novelist and poet. He wrote his novels in a subtle poetic prose, rich in metaphor. His best-known novel, *The Ordeal of Richard Feverel* (1859), is the story of the harm done a young man who is sheltered by his father and educated at home. It is one of several novels written by Meredith in which a duel is fought over a woman. *The Egoist* (1879) and *Diana of the Crossways* (1885) show Meredith's support of the emancipation of women. The heroine exercises freedom of choice in love and marriage.

Meredith thought his poetry had more merit than his novels, and many scholars agree. His *Modern Love* (1862) is one of the finest poetic works of the Victorian Age. It is a long, beautifully written sequence of 16-line sonnets inspired by his unhappy marriage to his first wife, who deserted him. Meredith was born in Portsmouth. He worked for many years as a journalist and literary critic. Sharon Bassett

See also **English literature** (Later Victorian literature).

Meredith, James Howard (1933-   ), was the first black to attend the University of Mississippi. He tried to register at the school in the fall of 1962. He was accompanied by federal marshals, but police and other state officials repeatedly barred his entrance. A large protest group that gathered on the campus rioted against Meredith and the marshals. Two people were killed. However, Meredith succeeded in registering, and federal troops were stationed on the campus to protect him until he graduated in 1963.

United Press Int.

James Meredith

In 1966, Meredith led a march in the South to encourage blacks to vote. A sniper shot him in Mississippi, but he recovered, and later completed the march.

Meredith was born in Kosciusko, Miss. He wrote the book *Three Years in Mississippi* (1966). C. Eric Lincoln

Merganser, *muhr GAN suhr,* is the name of a group of ducks that eat fish. Mergansers have straight narrow bills for grasping their food. Their bills also have notched edges, which is the reason mergansers are sometimes called *sawbills.* Mergansers are found in many parts of the world. The *American, red-breasted,*

WORLD BOOK illustration by Trevor Boyer, Linden Artists Ltd.

The American merganser has a straight narrow bill hooked at the tip and notched at the edges. The bill helps it catch fish.

and *hooded mergansers* live in North America.

Mergansers have crests of feathers on their heads. The males are black and white, and the females are drab brown and gray. The American merganser has a glossy greenish-black head, a dark back, and white neck and sides. The red-breasted merganser is similar, but it has a cinnamon-red breast and a longer crest. The hooded merganser has a large black-and-white crest. All three species have white wing patches.

Scientific classification. Mergansers belong to the family Anatidae. The American merganser is *Mergus merganser*. The red-breasted merganser is *M. serrator*. The hooded merganser is *Lophodytes cucullatus*.   Eric G. Bolen

Mergenthaler, *MUR guhn* THAW *luhr,* **Ottmar,** *AHT mahr* (1854-1899), invented the Linotype typesetting machine. Mergenthaler made a device with a keyboard that composed *matrices* (molds) for letters, and cast an entire line of type at once. He demonstrated and patented the Linotype in 1884. It was first used in 1886. Mergenthaler was born in Württemberg, Germany, and came to the United States in 1872. See also **Linotype.**

Peter M. VanWingen

Merger is the combination of two or more independent companies into a single corporation. In most mergers, a firm acquires the assets and liabilities of a smaller enterprise by purchasing its capital stock. It then takes over the operations of the smaller firm and drops that firm's name. In some mergers, firms of similar size join to form an entirely new corporation.

There are three basic types of mergers—*horizontal, vertical,* and *conglomerate.* Horizontal mergers combine companies in the same field. Vertical mergers join a supplier and a user, such as a tire company and an automobile company. Most conglomerate mergers combine firms in unrelated markets.

Critics of mergers argue that they produce firms that have monopoly power over prices and output. Defenders of mergers maintain that they benefit the public by making companies more efficient and better able to supply their products at reasonable prices.

Robert B. Carson

Meridian. See Greenwich Meridian; Longitude.

Mérimée, *may ree MAY,* **Prosper,** *praws PAIR* (1803-1870), a French author, is best known for his *novelettes* (long short stories). One of them, "Carmen" (1845), was the source for Georges Bizet's opera of the same name (see **Opera** [*Carmen*]). Mérimée's other novelettes include "Mateo Falcone" (1829) and "Colomba" (1840), tales of violence in Corsica. In the fantastic tale "The Venus of Ille" (1837), the hero is apparently killed by a statue.

Mérimée was born in Paris. His first works were *Theatre of Clara Gazul* (1825), a group of plays; and *La Guzla* (1827), a book of ballads. He fooled the public by saying these works were translations. Mérimée wrote during the romantic age, and his work has elements of both romantic and classical literature. It is romantic in the violent passions it portrays, and in the strong personalities of its characters. Mérimée's work is classical in its unemotional presentation, formal style, and its attention to detail.

In the 1850's, Mérimée worked to arouse French interest in Russia and its literature through his essays and translations. As Inspector General of Historic Monuments, he was active in restoring and preserving impor-

tant French monuments. He also wrote much history, in addition to his plays and fiction.   Thomas H. Goetz

Merlin was a magician and prophet who was an adviser to the legendary King Arthur. Various stories about Merlin appear in medieval literature. According to some narratives, Merlin educated Arthur as a youth. Merlin also helped establish the Round Table at which King Arthur's knights sat. He foresaw events of Arthur's reign, including the quest for the Holy Grail and the destruction of King Arthur's castle, Camelot. In addition, Merlin was said to have created the ancient British monument known as Stonehenge. See **Arthur, King.**

The story of Merlin probably originated in legends of a Celtic poet and prophet who lived in the 500's. The earliest detailed account of the Arthurian legends describes Merlin as a wizard and prophet whose father was a devil. In later stories, Merlin falls in love with Vivian, also known as the Lady of the Lake. She uses her magic to imprison him forever.   Edmund Reiss

Mermaid was a mythical creature that lived in the sea. According to popular belief, mermaids were half human and half fish. They attracted mortal men by their beauty and their singing. They would sit and comb their golden hair. A magic cap lay beside them. They would slip the cap on the head of the man they wanted and take him away with them. A human being could live in the sea by wearing the magic cap. There were also mermen, who captured mortal maidens.

Mermen and mermaids are often found in art and poetry. Certain sea animals, such as the seal, the dolphin, and especially the manatee or sea cow, look a little like human beings from a distance. This similarity in appearance may explain the stories. See also **Sirenia.**

C. Scott Littleton

Merovingian dynasty, *MEHR uh VIHN jee uhn,* was a line of Frankish kings who conquered Gaul and surrounding lands beginning in A.D. 486 and ruled until 751. The Franks were Germanic peoples, and Gaul was a region that included present-day France, Belgium, Luxembourg, and southwestern Germany. The name *Merovingian* comes from Merovech, a relative of the first Merovingian ruler, Clovis I.

Clovis I was also the most powerful Merovingian king. He unified the Franks under his rule. By the time he died in 511, he had conquered northern and southwestern Gaul and additional land in what is now western Germany. The kingdom was then divided among four of Clovis' sons, who added southeastern Gaul and other territory to the realm. However, a process of further dividing the kingdom led to numerous civil wars that severely weakened the dynasty. In 751, the last Merovingian king, Childeric III, was replaced by Pepin the Short, the first ruler from the Carolingian dynasty (see **Pepin the Short**).   Bernard S. Bachrach

See also **Clovis I; France** (The Carolingian dynasty); **Franks.**

Merrill, Robert (1919-   ), an American baritone, became one of the world's leading opera stars. He gained recognition for his powerful and resonant voice, which he combined with great warmth and superb technique. Merrill sang all of the major Italian and French baritone operatic roles. He also performed in lighter works, notably in the Broadway musical *Fiddler on the Roof,* and gave many concerts and recitals.

Merrill was born in Brooklyn, N.Y. In 1944, he made his operatic debut in Trenton, N.J., as Amonasro in *Aida*. Merrill made his debut with the Metropolitan Opera in New York City in 1945 in the role of Germont in *La Traviata*. He wrote several books, including an autobiography, *Once More from the Beginning* (1965), and a novel, *The Divas* (1978).   Charles H. Webb

Merrill's Marauders, sometimes called Merrill's Raiders, were about 3,000 United States infantrymen who fought under Brigadier General Frank Merrill during World War II (1939-1945). The Marauders were tough jungle fighters who won fame in the China-Burma-India theater. They went to India in October 1943, after President Franklin D. Roosevelt called for volunteers to take part in a "dangerous and hazardous" mission. In March 1944, after a 100-mile (160-kilometer) march, Merrill's Marauders surprised the enemy by blocking the only Japanese supply line in the Hukawng Valley.   Charles B. MacDonald

Merrimack. See Monitor and Merrimack.

Merrimack River flows through southern New Hampshire and northeastern Massachusetts. The river is formed where the Winnepesaukee and Pemigewasset streams meet at Franklin, N.H. It empties into the Atlantic Ocean at Newburyport, Mass. Textile mills built along the river in the 1800's contributed heavily to the early growth of the cities of Manchester and Nashua, N.H.; and Lawrence and Lowell, Mass. *Merrimack* is an Indian name meaning *swift water*. For the location of the Merrimack River, see **New Hampshire** (physical map).

   Robert L. A. Adams

Merry-go-round is a popular children's ride at amusement parks, carnivals, and theme parks. The ride is also called a *carrousel* (also spelled *carousel*). A merry-go-round basically consists of brightly painted horses and other animals mounted on a circular platform. Benches that resemble chariots may also be mounted on the platform. Riders sit on the animals and benches. A motor causes the platform to revolve. Some animals are attached to poles that move up and down as

Six Flags Great America

A beautiful, two-level merry-go-round entertains children and adults who ride on its benches and brightly colored animals. Most merry-go-rounds play music as they revolve.

the ride moves. On most merry-go-rounds, a mechanical organ plays music while the ride is in motion.

The merry-go-round is the oldest amusement ride still in use. The term *merry-go-round* first appeared as early as 1729 in a poem in an English newspaper. The first known American merry-go-round was operated in Salem, Mass., in 1799.   Don B. Wilmeth

Mersey, *MUR zee,* **River,** is an important trade waterway in northwest England. The river rises in the Pennine Hills, flows southwest past Runcorn, and enters the Irish Sea near Liverpool. The Mersey is about 70 miles (110 kilometers) long.

A system of docks and basins extends along both banks of the *estuary* (mouth) of the Mersey at Liverpool and Birkenhead. A railway tunnel under the river connects the two manufacturing centers. An underwater tunnel for highway traffic was completed in 1934. The Manchester Ship Canal connects Salford and Manchester with the river.   John W. Webb

Merton, Robert King (1910-   ), is an American sociologist. He became known for combining social theory and *quantitative* (statistical) research.

In his book *Science, Technology and Society in Seventeenth Century England* (1938), Merton discussed cultural, economic, and social forces that contributed to the development of modern science. He concluded that many Protestant reformers, including the English Puritans, indirectly helped bring modern science into being by encouraging people to study nature.

In his work *Social Theory and Social Structure* (1949), Merton explored why individuals behave in ways that their society considers abnormal. He explained five types of behavior, ranging from *conformity* to *rebellion*. According to Merton, a person who conforms accepts society's goals and its ways of achieving them. A person who rebels tries to change society with new goals and new ways of reaching them.

Merton is regarded as the founder of a field known as the *sociology of science*. This field focuses on the ways social groups, social organizations, and the values of society influence the development of science.

Merton was born in Philadelphia. He graduated from Temple University in 1931 and earned a Ph.D. degree from Harvard University in 1936. He joined the faculty of Columbia University in 1941.   Neil J. Smelser

Merton, Thomas (1915-1968), a Roman Catholic monk, was the most popular spiritual writer of his time. Merton won fame for his autobiography, *The Seven Storey Mountain* (1948). The book describes Merton's troubled youth and the experiences that led him to become a Catholic in 1938. The book also deals with his entry in 1941 into the Order of Cistercians of the Strict Observance at Our Lady of Gethsemani Monastery, located near Bardstown, Ky. The members of this order, called Trappists, lead strict and studious religious lives. In 1949, Merton was ordained a Catholic priest. In 1965, he retired to a hermitage.

Merton was born in Prades, France, of an American mother and New Zealand father. He grew up in France and England. Merton wrote over 40 books, many of which record his struggle for greater personal integrity. He also wrote widely on Eastern religions. Merton's better-known publications include *The Sign of Jonas* (1953), *New Seeds of Contemplation* (1961), *Conjectures of a*

Guilty Bystander (1966), and *Faith and Violence* (1968). Merton died by accidental electrocution in Bangkok, Thailand.   Richard J. Hauser

Merv is an oasis in central Asia. It covers about 2,000 square miles (5,200 square kilometers) in the vast plateau desert in the southeastern part of Turkmenistan (see **Turkmenistan** [map]).

The Merv has been a center of life and industry for hundreds of years, though it lies in the midst of a great wasteland. The ancient Persians called the Merv "the cradle of the human race." Farming is the chief occupation in the oasis. Some cotton and wool are produced. The ancient town of Merv is in ruins. The modern city, Mary, stands approximately 20 miles (30 kilometers) west of the old site. It was founded by Russians in 1881.

Zvi Gitelman

Merwin, W. S. (1927-   ), is an American poet and translator. He won the 1971 Pulitzer Prize in poetry for his collection *The Carriers of Ladders* (1970).

Merwin's poems are intense and impersonal. They deal with isolation, violence, and death as well as with moral values and the nature of reality. Merwin explores the strangeness of personal experience in "For the Anniversary of My Death." He wrote about nature and animals in two early collections, *The Dancing Bears* (1954) and *Green with Beasts* (1956). His best-known poems are collected in *The Lice* (1967). Later collections include *Writings to an Unfinished Accompaniment* (1973) and *Opening the Hand* (1983).

Merwin has won praise for his translations of Spanish and French literature. His most important translations include *The Poem of the Cid* (1959), *The Song of Roland* (1963), and *Selected Translations, 1968-1978* (1979).

Merwin's prose works are collected in *The Miner's Pale Children* (1970), *Houses and Travellers* (1977), *Unframed Originals* (1982), and *Regions of Memory* (1986). William Stanley Merwin was born in New York City.

Steven Gould Axelrod

Mesa, *MAY suh,* is an isolated hill or mountain that has a flat, tablelike top and steep sides. *Mesa* is a Spanish word meaning *table.* Mesas are found in dry climates. In the United States, they are common in Arizona, Colorado, New Mexico, and Utah.

Dick Skrondahl

A mesa is an isolated flat-topped hill or mountain with steep sides. The rugged bluffs pictured above are part of the colorful high mesa country of northern New Mexico.

Mesas range in size from a few acres or hectares to hundreds of square miles or kilometers. Mesas were once part of larger plateaus or upland areas that were worn away by erosion over a long period of time. The top of a mesa consists of lava, sandstone, or other types of rock that resist erosion. Beneath it lie layers of less resistant rocks, such as siltstone and shale. The lower slopes of a mesa are covered with large blocks of resistant rock, which broke off from the edges of the mesa when the underlying rock eroded.   Lay James Gibson

See also **Butte.**

Mesa, *MAY suh,* Ariz. (pop. 288,091), is one of the largest cities in the state. It lies near the Salt River, about 13 miles east of Phoenix. For location, see **Arizona** (political map).

Mesa is a fast-growing community with a wide variety of businesses. It serves as the retail and service center for eastern Maricopa County. Several medical centers and large shopping malls are located in Mesa. Major businesses in the city produce electronics, helicopters, heavy machinery, and propulsion equipment. Automotive testing and food processing are also important industries. The mainline of the Southern Pacific Railroad serves Mesa.

The city is the home of Mesa Community College and the Arizona Temple of the Church of Jesus Christ of Latter-Day Saints. Mesa's chief tourist attractions include the Arizona Temple Visitors' Center and the Mesa Southwest Museum.

Mesa was founded by Mormons in 1878. The original settlement occupied about 1 square mile (2.6 square kilometers) of elevated ground, overlooking the Salt River Valley. *Mesa* is a Spanish word meaning *table.* Mesa began *annexing* (adding) some of the surrounding area in the 1930's. The city has a mayor-council form of government.   Lay James Gibson

Mesa Verde National Park, *MAY suh vurd* or *MAY suh VUR dee.* Hundreds of years ago, Indians built high cliff dwellings of stone along the canyon walls of a huge plateau in southwestern Colorado. Some of the cliff dwellings are still standing. In 1906, the United States Congress set aside this region as a national park. The park was named Mesa Verde (Spanish for *green table*) because it is covered with forests of juniper and piñon pines. For area, see **National Park System** (table: National parks).

The cliff dwellers built their homes in alcoves along overhanging walls of these canyons partly for protection against other tribes. Cliff Palace, the largest cliff house, contains more than 200 living rooms. About 200 people lived in Cliff Palace at one time. The structure is built much like a modern apartment building. It has sections that are two, three, and four stories high. Cliff Palace also has many underground rooms, known as *kivas,* where the Indians held religious ceremonies. Spruce Tree House, another large ruin in the park, has about 115 living rooms.

Scientists think most of these homes were built in the 1200's. Historians believe the cliff dwellers left this region by 1300 because of a great drought.

Critically reviewed by the National Park Service

See also **Cliff dwellers** (picture); **Colorado** (picture).

Mesabi Range, *muh SAH bih,* is a chain of hills in northeastern Minnesota. The range was once one of the great iron ore mining regions of the world. *Mesabi* is the Indian word for *hidden giant.* Most of the range lies in St. Louis County, which is bordered on the southeast by Lake Superior. The range itself is from 60 to 75 miles (97 to 121 kilometers) northwest of the lake.

The Mesabi Range was first leased for mining in 1890 by Leonidas Merritt, three of his brothers, and three of his nephews. By 1896, 20 mines were producing nearly 3 million short tons (2.7 million metric tons) of ore a year. The ore was so near the surface that *open-pit mining* was used. Iron ore mining at Mesabi declined sharply during the 1900's, but some low grade ore is still mined there.   Thomas J. Baerwald

Mescaline, *MEHS kuh leen,* is a powerful drug that distorts what a person sees and hears and intensifies the emotions. It is obtained from the top, or "button," of the peyote cactus, which grows in parts of Mexico and of the southwestern United States. The Native American Church, which has members from a number of Indian tribes, uses the peyote as a sacrament in religious ceremonies. In the United States, federal law prohibits the possession or use of mescaline except by this church.

The effects of a 350-microgram capsule of mescaline last about 12 hours and resemble those of LSD (see **LSD**). Users may see beautiful color patterns or frightening visions of themselves and others as monsters. A mescaline experience may result in new insights, or it may cause extreme anxiety. A user's personality, the setting, and the dose all affect the experience.

The use of mescaline does not generally produce physical or psychological dependence. But regular users may become unproductive and disinterested in life. In most cases, these reactions end after a person stops taking the drug.   Donald J. Wolk

Meseta. See **Spain** (introduction; The Meseta; picture).

Meshed, *meh SHEHD* (pop. 1,463,508), is one of Iran's largest cities and a leading religious center. It lies on a fertile plain in northeastern Iran. For location, see **Iran** (map). People travel to Meshed each year to visit the gold-domed tomb of Imam Ali Reza, a Muslim leader. Meshed manufactures rugs, shawls, silk goods, porcelain, and jewelry. It also is a trading center for timber, cotton textiles, and animal hides. Meshed was founded around Imam Ali Reza's tomb and became a flourishing town in the 1300's. See **Asia** (picture: Muslims).

Michel Le Gall

Mesmer, *MEHZ muhr,* **Franz Anton** (1734-1815), an Austrian physician, pioneered in the practice of hypnotism. He developed a theory called "animal magnetism," later named *mesmerism.* Mesmer believed that a mysterious fluid penetrates all bodies. This fluid allows one person to have a powerful, "magnetic" influence over another person.

Mesmer was born at Iznang in Austria. His first name has often been given as Friedrich because of a mistake in an early book about him. Mesmer studied medicine in Vienna. He went to Paris to lecture and practice in 1778. His sessions, or *séances,* in which he supposedly "magnetized" patients, created a sensation. But the medical profession considered him a fraud. Mesmer's theories have been discarded, but hypnotism has been accepted as a subject for scientific study and as a means of treating certain disorders. See **Hypnotism** (History).

Hannah S. Decker

Mesolithic Period. See **Stone Age**.

Meson, *MEHS ahn* or *MEHZ ahn,* is a subatomic particle. Mesons form one of the classes of a family of particles called *hadrons.* The other class consists of *baryons,* which include protons, neutrons, and hyperons. All hadrons act upon one another through a force called the *strong interaction,* or the *strong nuclear force.* This force holds an atomic nucleus together.

Mesons are *unstable particles.* Within a fraction of a second after they are created, they *decay* (break down) into lighter particles. Mesons carry a positive or negative electric charge, or they are neutral.

There are many types of mesons. The lightest is called a *pion* or *pi-meson.* It has a mass equal to 15 per cent of the mass of a proton. The heaviest meson, called an *upsilon particle,* is about 10 times as heavy as a proton. Other mesons include *k-mesons* (also called *kaons*) and *psi particles* (also known as *J particles*).

Hideki Yukawa, a Japanese physicist, predicted the existence of mesons in 1935. He thought they would be fundamental particles and would carry the strong interaction, in much the same way as *photons* are carriers of the electromagnetic force (see **Photon**). But physicists have since determined that mesons are not fundamental particles. Instead, each meson consists of two particles that are fundamental, a quark and an antiquark. Physicists now also believe the strong nuclear force is transmitted by particles called *gluons* (see **Gluon**).

In 1937, the American physicist Carl D. Anderson identified a particle as a meson. But researchers found the particle, called a *muon,* was not readily affected by the strong nuclear force, and so could not be classified as a meson. The first known meson was detected in 1947 when Cecil Powell, a British physicist, discovered a pion in a shower of cosmic rays. Today, mesons are made artificially in huge machines called *particle accelerators* (see **Particle accelerator**).   Lee Smolin

See also **Anderson, Carl David; Baryon; Hadron; Psi particle; Yukawa, Hideki.**

Mesopotamia, *MEHS uh puh TAY mee uh,* was an ancient region in which the world's earliest civilization developed. Mesopotamia included the area that is now eastern Syria, southeastern Turkey, and most of Iraq. It extended from the Taurus Mountains in the north to the Persian Gulf in the south, and from the Zagros Mountains in the east to the Syrian Desert in the west. But the heart of the region was the land between the Tigris and Euphrates rivers. The name *Mesopotamia* comes from a Greek word meaning *between rivers.*

Northern Mesopotamia was a plateau that had a mild climate. Parts of it received enough rain for crops to grow. In southern Mesopotamia, a plain of fertile soil left by floodwaters of the Tigris and Euphrates rivers provided rich farmland. But the long, hot summers and little rain in this area made irrigation necessary for agriculture.

The oldest known communities in northern Mesopotamia were villages established in the Zagros foothills by about 7000 B.C. Traces of villages in far southern Mesopotamia date from the 5000's B.C. Sometime before 3500 B.C., new settlers arrived in this region. Scholars do not know where these people originally came from, but the area they settled became known as Sumer. About 3500 B.C., the Sumerians began to build the

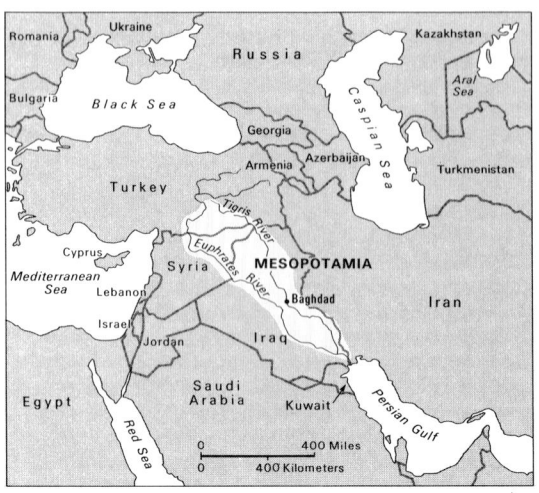

Location of Mesopotamia

world's first cities and to develop its first civilization. About the same time, the Sumerians invented the world's first system of writing. This system, using word-pictures, developed into a system of wedge-shaped characters called *cuneiform* (see **Cuneiform**).

During the 2300's B.C., people originally from the west called Akkadians conquered Sumer. The invaders were Semites—that is, people who spoke a language related to Arabic and Hebrew. The Akkadians and other Semites formed empires that ruled Mesopotamia for much of the period between 2300 and 539 B.C. These Semitic groups included the Babylonians, Assyrians, and Amorites.

In 539 B.C., Mesopotamia became part of the Persian Empire. The Macedonian ruler Alexander the Great conquered the Persians in 331 B.C. Later, the Seleucids, Parthians, Romans, Sassanids, Arabs, and Mongols ruled Mesopotamia. In the A.D. 1500's, the Ottoman Empire began to establish control over the region. Mesopotamia remained part of the Ottoman Empire until the British occupied the area during World War I (1914-1918). In 1921, most of Mesopotamia became part of the newly created nation of Iraq.   John A. Brinkman

Related articles in *World Book* include:

Architecture (Mesopotamian)	Iraq
Assyria	Mitanni
Babylonia	Persia, Ancient
Chaldea	Sumer
Euphrates River	Tigris River

Additional resources

Oppenheim, A. Leo. *Ancient Mesopotamia: Portrait of a Dead Civilization.* 2nd ed. Univ. of Chicago Pr., 1977.
Reade, Julian. *Mesopotamia.* Harvard Univ. Pr., 1991.
Roaf, Michael. *Cultural Atlas of Mesopotamia and the Ancient Near East.* Facts on File, 1990.

Mesosphere, *MEHS uh sfeer,* is a layer of the earth's atmosphere. It lies between the *stratosphere* and the *thermosphere,* the uppermost layer of the atmosphere. The mesosphere begins at an altitude of about 30 miles (48 kilometers) and extends to about 50 miles (80 kilometers).

The temperature of the air in the mesosphere gener-

ally decreases as the altitude increases. At the base of the mesosphere, the temperature averages 28 °F (−2 °C). The lowest temperature in the earth's atmosphere occurs at the top of the mesosphere, called the *mesopause.* In the mesopause over the North and South poles, the air temperature may drop as low as −165 °F (−109 °C). The coldest mesopause temperatures at a pole occur when it is summer there.

Scientists believe the air in the mesosphere may mix, as it does in the *troposphere,* the lowest layer of the atmosphere. The temperature in both layers decreases with increasing altitude. One indication of variable air motion in the mesosphere comes from watching the zigzag trails of meteors passing through it. Thin clouds have also been sighted in the polar regions of the mesosphere during summer.   Veerabhadran Ramanathan

See also **Air** (The mesosphere); **Atmosphere; Stratosphere; Thermosphere; Troposphere.**
Mesozoic Era. See **Earth** (The Mesozoic Era; table); **Dinosaur; Reptile** (The evolution of reptiles).
Mesquite, *mehs KEET,* is the name of a group of thorny, low shrubs that grow in dry climates. The most

Grant Heilman
The mesquite tree thrives in dry climates. It needs little water, and its long roots burrow deeply to obtain moisture.

common species, the *honey mesquite,* is found in the Southwestern United States, Mexico, and the West Indies. It also grows in the Hawaiian Islands, where it was planted by missionaries.

A mesquite needs little water and will grow in deserts too hot and dry for many plants. As parts of the shrub die and decay, they release nitrogen compounds into the soil. As a result, the sandy soil around mesquite often contains enough nitrogen to allow a variety of plants to grow.

In the mid-1900's, mesquite began spreading through rangelands in southwestern North America, displacing large areas of grasses. Ranchers often try to eliminate the shrub because grasses provide better food for cattle and other domestic animals.

When a mesquite has plenty of water, it grows into a large tree. It may become 50 to 60 feet (15 to 18 meters) high with a trunk 3 feet (91 centimeters) across. People use the wood of mesquite for fuel, to make fence posts, and to build dwellings. The seeds or beans serve as food for cattle and horses and were once an important food for the Indians of the Southwest. Two kinds of gum taken from mesquite are used to make candies and Mexican dyes.

Scientific classification. Mesquites belong to the pea family, Leguminosae or Fabaceae. The scientific name for the honey mesquite is *Prosopis glandulosa.* Kimball T. Harper

See also **Tree** (Familiar broadleaf and needleleaf trees [picture]).

Messenger. See **Mercury; Post office** (History).

Messenia, *muh SEE nee uh,* is a *department* (political division) of Greece. It was also an important region in ancient times. Messenia is located in the *Peloponnesus* (Greece's southern peninsula). It has an area of 1,155 square miles (2,991 square kilometers) and a population of about 160,000. Kalamai is the capital of the department. Messenia's farmland is the richest in Greece.

During the Late Bronze Age in Greece (1550-1100 B.C.), eastern Messenia was controlled by King Menelaus of Sparta, and western Messenia by King Nestor of

WORLD BOOK map

Messenia lies in southwestern Greece.

Pylos (now Pilos). According to legend, both Nestor and Menelaus were among the Greek heroes who fought in the Trojan War. In the 1100's B.C., Dorian invaders from the north overran Messenia. Nestor's palace at Pylos was uncovered in 1939 by American archaeologist Carl Blegen. It is considered one of the great monuments of Bronze Age Greece.

In the late 700's B.C., Sparta conquered Messenia and enslaved the people. Messenians revolted unsuccessfully twice, and they stayed under Spartan rule. But in 371 B.C., Thebes defeated Sparta in the Battle of Leuctra and freed the Messenians. The Theban leader Epaminondas helped the Messenians build a new capital and fortress at Messene (now Messini). The walls of that fortress still stand. Messenia remained independent under the protection of Macedonia and the Achaean League until the Romans conquered all of Greece in 146 B.C.

During the Middle Ages (A.D. 400's to the 1500's), Slavs, Franks, Venetians, and Turks occupied Messenia. Frankish and Turkish castles still stand at Kalamai, Koroni, Methoni, and Pilos. Norman A. Doenges

Messerschmitt. See **Airplane** (During World War II).

Messiaen, *mehs YAHN,* **Olivier,** *aw lee VYAY* (1908-1992), was a French composer. His wide-ranging style uses elements of bird calls, church vocal music called *plain song,* and Greek and Hindu rhythms. His 10-movement symphony, *Turangalila* (1949), features some of these techniques. As a German prisoner of war during World War II, Messiaen composed *Quartet for the End of Time* (1941), his most famous work. He also com-

posed *Twenty Glances at the Infant Jesus* (1944) for piano, *Oiseaux Exotiques* (*Exotic Birds,* 1955) for piano and orchestra, and the opera *St. Francis* (1983).

Olivier Eugène Prosper Charles Messiaen was born in Avignon, France. In 1931, he became an organist at the Church of the Holy Trinity in Paris. He became a professor of harmony at the Paris Conservatory in 1942. Messiaen taught and greatly influenced many modern composers, including Pierre Boulez of France and Karlheinz Stockhausen of Germany. The most notable of his extensive writings on music is *The Technique of My Musical Language* (1956). Stephen Jaffe

Messiah, *muh SY uh,* is a person who is thought of as a savior or liberator by his or her followers. The term *messiah* comes from a Hebrew word meaning *anointed one.*

The concept of a Messiah is central to Judaism and Christianity. The term *messiah* originally was applied to ancient Hebrew priests and kings who had been anointed with holy oil. During Biblical times, the Jews looked for a Messiah to deliver them from oppression. They also regarded certain prophets as Messiahs. The term came to refer specifically to a descendant of the great Israelite leader King David. This Messiah would bring an age of justice, peace, and prosperity to Israel. However, Jews vary in their expectations about the nature and mission of the Messiah. Some believe in a personal Messiah who will save those who have been faithful. Others think that an era called the *Messianic Age* will come, when peace and freedom will reign.

The notion of an *eschatological Messiah* developed among some Jewish sects. Such a Messiah would come to announce the end of the world. The Book of Daniel refers to an eschatological Messiah called "Son of Man," who will rule "an everlasting kingdom."

Christians believe Jesus is the promised Messiah. They gave Him the title *Christ,* the Greek word for Messiah. Many Christians also believe the Messiah will come again at the end of the world.

Throughout history, especially during periods of social or political unrest, people have claimed to be Messiahs. Some have temporarily gained large followings. Such people are known as *false Messiahs.* Jill Raitt

See **Judaism** (The Messiah); **Jesus Christ; David.**

Messiah, oratorio. See **Handel, George F.**

Messier, *meh SYAY,* **Charles,** *sharl* (1730-1817), was a French astronomer. He prepared the first catalog of *nonstellar* objects visible from the Northern Hemisphere. Such objects include galaxies, *nebulae* (clouds of dust and gas), and star clusters. Messier began the catalog in the late 1750's and completed it in 1784. His listing, called the *Catalogue of Nebulae and of Star Clusters,* contains 103 nonstellar objects. Messier discovered most of these objects himself. Astronomers still specify the objects in his catalog by their catalog numbers, placing an *M* for *Messier* before the number.

Messier did not originally intend to produce a catalog of nonstellar objects. He specialized in tracking comets and, while searching for them, saw hazy objects that did not change position. Messier concluded that these stellar objects were not comets. He recorded their position in the sky so that other astronomers would not confuse them with comets. Messier also discovered 21 comets.

Messier was born in Badonviller, France, near St.-Dié.

He became chief astronomer of the Marine Observatory in Paris in 1759.   Frank D. Drake

See also **Nebula**.

Messina, *muh SEE nuh* (pop. 255,890), is one of the largest cities in Sicily, an Italian island in the Mediterranean Sea. Messina lies on the northeastern coast of the island, on the Strait of Messina (see **Italy** [political map]). The city serves as a gateway to Sicily. Every day, thousands of people travel by ferry across the less than 2 miles (3.2 kilometers) of water separating Messina and the Italian mainland. Messina, a market center, exports fruit, wine, and other products.

Historians believe that the Greeks founded Messina during the 700's B.C. By 500 B.C., the city had become a well-known Greek colony. Since ancient times, Messina has been fought over by many nations. Earthquakes almost destroyed the city in 1783 and 1908. Messina suffered heavy damage from Allied air raids in 1943, during World War II.   David I. Kertzer

Mestizo, *mehs TEE zoh,* is a Spanish word that comes from the Latin *mixtus,* meaning *mixed.* The word refers to a person with mixed ancestry. A mestizo may be someone of mixed white and black or Malay ancestry. More commonly, the term is applied to a person of mixed white and American Indian parentage, especially in Latin America.   Douglas H. Ubelaker

See also **Latin America** (People; picture).

Meštrović, *MEHSH truh vihch,* **Ivan** (1883-1962), was an internationally known Croatian sculptor. He worked chiefly in marble, wood, and bronze. Much of his sculpture was strongly influenced by Greek classical styles. Religious and patriotic themes dominate Meštrović's art. Meštrović's major works include the marble sculptures *Maiden of Kossovo* (1907) and *Pietà* (1942-1946).

Meštrović was born in Vrpoljc, Dalmatia (now part of Croatia). He learned carving from a master mason in Split. During World War I (1914-1918), he was a leader in the movement to create the nation of Yugoslavia. Meštrović worked and taught mainly in Yugoslavia until the mid-1940's, when he moved to the United States.

Joseph F. Lamb

Metabolism, *muh TAB uh lihz uhm,* is the sum of the chemical processes by which cells produce the materials and energy necessary for life. Metabolism has two phases: (1) *anabolism,* or *constructive metabolism,* during which cells combine molecules to assemble new organic materials, and (2) *catabolism,* or *destructive metabolism,* during which cells break down molecules to obtain energy and release heat. All organisms conduct both phases constantly. This article specifically discusses human metabolism, but the processes are similar in other higher animals.

Control of metabolism. Hormones control both the rate and direction of metabolism. Thyroxine, a hormone secreted by the thyroid gland, determines the rate of metabolism. Hormones secreted by special cells in the pancreas determine whether most of the body's metabolic activity will be anabolic or catabolic. The body conducts more anabolic than catabolic activities after a meal. Eating increases the level of glucose in the blood. The pancreas responds to this high level of glucose by releasing the hormone insulin. Insulin triggers the cells to begin anabolic activities. When the level of glucose is low—for example, when a person is fasting—the pan-

creas releases the hormone glucagon. Glucagon signals the cells to conduct more catabolic processes.

The rate of metabolism when a person is at rest is called the *basal metabolic rate* (BMR). The BMR is a measure of the heat produced by metabolism. This rate varies among people according to sex, age, and body size. Dietitians measure the BMR to determine a person's caloric needs. At one time, physicians used the BMR to detect an overactive or underactive thyroid gland. Since the 1970's, doctors generally have diagnosed such disorders with tests that measure the blood levels of thyroid hormones.

Raw materials of metabolism. Most series of metabolic reactions involve molecules of glucose, fatty acids, or amino acids. The diet is the basic source of these molecules. During digestion, enzymes split dietary proteins into amino acids, dietary fats into fatty acids and glycerol, and dietary *carbohydrates* (starches and sugars) into simple sugars, particularly glucose. These compounds are then absorbed and transported by the blood to the cells.

Anabolism produces complex compounds by combining simpler molecules. During anabolism, cells combine amino acids to form *structural proteins* and *functional proteins.* The body repairs and replaces tissues with structural proteins. Functional proteins perform specific jobs. Functional proteins include enzymes, which speed up chemical reactions; antibodies, which help fight disease; and most hormones, which regulate various body processes.

Cells convert glucose and fatty acids to energy storage compounds during anabolism. Cells in the liver and the muscles combine molecules of glucose to form a storage compound called *glycogen.* Cells in the body's *adipose* (fatty) tissues combine fatty acids with glycerol to form body fat. By a complex series of reactions, excess glucose and amino acids also can be converted into body fat.

Catabolism is the breaking down of glucose, fatty acids, and amino acids to obtain energy and produce heat. The compounds involved in catabolism come either from newly digested food, from the breakdown of storage glycogen or fat, or from the breakdown of body protein.

Glucose catabolism has two steps. The first step, *glycolysis,* works without oxygen. Glycolysis breaks down glucose into pyruvic acid and releases a small amount of energy. If oxygen is present, the pyruvic acid is converted to a compound called *acetyl-coenzyme A* (abbreviated *acetyl-CoA*). The second step of glucose catabolism, the *Krebs cycle,* then takes place. In the Krebs cycle, a series of chemical reactions combines acetyl-CoA with oxygen to produce carbon dioxide and water, and to obtain energy.

The catabolism of fatty acids also has two steps. First, enzymes convert fatty acids to acetyl-CoA. Acetyl-CoA then enters the Krebs cycle. Although amino acids generally serve as building blocks for new proteins, the body may use excess amino acids as an energy source. Before they can be catabolized, amino acids must be chemically altered in the liver or other tissues. They can then enter the Krebs cycle.

About 60 per cent of the energy released during catabolism takes the form of heat. The rest of the energy is stored in the chemical bonds that link atoms in a compound called *adenosine triphosphate,* or *ATP.* When the body needs this energy, enzymes break the bonds and release it. Patricia B. Swan

Related articles in *World Book* include:

Cell (Metabolic diseases)	Spirometer
Food (How the body uses food)	Steroid
Potassium	Thyroid gland

Metacarpal bone. See Hand.
Metacomet. See Philip, King.
Metal forms a large part of the earth on which we live. Nearly 80 per cent of the known elements are metals. Metals are important in all aspects of construction and manufacturing. Industries use metals and combinations of metals called *alloys* to build cars and a wide variety of machinery. Compounds that contain metals are used in drugs, batteries, and many other products.

What metal is. Metals have certain properties that distinguish them from other elements. Metals reflect light and have a shiny appearance. They also are good conductors of electricity and heat. Most metals are *malleable*—that is, they can be hammered into thin sheets. Most metals are also *ductile,* which means that they can be drawn out into wires.

In a chemical reaction with a nonmetal, a metal atom gives up one or more electrons to the nonmetal. For example, the metal sodium (Na) reacts with chlorine (Cl) to form the compound sodium chloride (NaCl). In this chemical reaction, each sodium atom gives up one electron, which has a negative charge, to form a positive sodium ion (Na). The chlorine takes on this electron to become a chloride ion (Cl). The oppositely charged ions bond to form NaCl—common table salt.

The properties of a pure metal are different from the properties of a compound containing the metal. For example, in the metallic state, sodium is shiny and highly malleable, and it is extremely reactive with air. But the compound sodium chloride is colorless and brittle, and is stable in air.

In the earth's crust, most of the metallic elements occur in compounds and not in the metallic state. For example, the earth's crust includes about 8 per cent aluminum, 5 per cent iron, and 4 per cent calcium. All these are present in compounds. A few of the rare and least reactive metals may be found in the metallic state in the earth's crust. These metals include copper, gold, mercury, and platinum. Scientists think the earth's core is mainly made up of nickel and iron in the metallic state.

Combinations of metals retain the properties of metals. These combinations include bronze, bell metal, gun metal, and type metal. Alloys and metals that do not contain iron are referred to as *nonferrous* alloys and metals.

Metals through the ages. Ancient people knew and used many native metals. Gold was used for ornaments, plates, jewelry, and utensils as early as 3500 B.C. Gold objects showing a high degree of culture have been excavated at the ruins of the ancient city of Ur in Mesopotamia. Silver was used as early as 2400 B.C., and many ancient people considered it to be more valuable than gold, because it was rarer in the native state. Native copper also was used at an early date for making tools and utensils, because it was found near the surface of the ground in the native state and could be easily worked and shaped.

Since about 1000 B.C., iron and steel have been the chief metals for construction. Today, supplies of the best iron ore for steelmaking are being exhausted. The same is true for copper, lead, and zinc deposits. Thus, metallurgists substitute aluminum for steel in many cases. The earth's supply of aluminum is almost unlimited.

Magnesium, another light, strong metal, has also become important. It is extracted from sea water and the common rock called *dolomite.* The radioactive metal uranium is used as a fuel in nuclear reactors.
 Duward F. Shriver

Related articles in *World Book* include:

Metals

Actinium	Hafnium	Promethium
Aluminum	Holmium	Protactinium
Americium	Indium	Radium
Antimony	Iridium	Rhenium
Barium	Iron	Rhodium
Berkelium	Lanthanum	Rubidium
Beryllium	Lawrencium	Ruthenium
Bismuth	Lead	Samarium
Cadmium	Lithium	Scandium
Calcium	Lutetium	Silver
Californium	Magnesium	Sodium
Cerium	Manganese	Strontium
Cesium	Mendelevium	Tantalum
Chromium	Mercury	Technetium
Cobalt	Molybdenum	Terbium
Copper	Neodymium	Thallium
Curium	Neptunium	Thorium
Dysprosium	Nickel	Thulium
Einsteinium	Niobium	Tin
Erbium	Nobelium	Titanium
Europium	Osmium	Tungsten
Fermium	Palladium	Uranium
Francium	Platinum	Vanadium
Gadolinium	Plutonium	Ytterbium
Gallium	Polonium	Yttrium
Germanium	Potassium	Zinc
Gold	Praseodymium	Zirconium

Other related articles

Alloy	Metallography
Assaying	Metallurgy
Corrosion	Mineral
Ductility	Mining
Element, Chemical	Rare earth
Malleability	

Metal detector is an instrument used to locate hidden or lost metal objects. It gives off signals in the presence of metal. Detectors are widely used by treasure hunters, who search outdoors for old coins, jewelry, and other valuable relics. Police use metal detectors in criminal investigations. Archaeologists and prospectors also use them.

Metal detectors vary in design and shape, but they all operate in basically the same way. A detector transmits radio waves by means of an antenna. A metal object absorbs some of these waves and reflects them back to the instrument. The detector's receiving circuit amplifies the reflected waves into a strong signal that tells the user of the object's presence.

All detectors can locate metals that lie buried underground or are hidden behind brick or stone walls. Many detectors have a feature called a "discriminating circuit," which distinguishes objects made of valuable metal from those of a nonvaluable material. Metal detectors are manufactured in a number of sizes. Most of these

Garrett Electronics

A metal detector is used to find coins, jewelry, and other valuable objects that are buried underground.

instruments can be easily carried by their users.

Charles L. Garrett

Metal fatigue is the gradual weakening of metal after extensive use. Such weakening is caused by the repeated application of tension, pressure, or other forms of stress. Stress cycles often alter the molecular structure of the materials so that they crack. Metal fatigue usually begins at the surface of a metal piece where small defects, or even minute tool marks, serve as a concentration point for stress. The crack spreads through the piece, eventually making it too weak to carry its normal load. Engineers allow for metal fatigue in planning airplanes, bridges, and machinery. Gordon H. Geiger

Metallography, *MEHT uh LAHG ruh fee,* is the study of the internal structure of metals and alloys. The term also may be applied to the study of ceramics and *composites* (combinations of materials that often include metals). Metallographers determine how materials will react under certain conditions, such as extreme heat or cold. Industry depends on metallography in the creation, testing, and improvement of such products as missiles and spacecraft. Metallographers study material samples with X rays and microscopes. Powerful electron microscopes have helped them develop new kinds of materials. I. Melvin Bernstein

Metallurgical engineering. See Metallurgy; Engineering (Materials engineering).

Metallurgy, *MEHT uh LUR jee,* is the science of separating metals from their *ores* (the minerals or rocks in which they are found), preparing them for use, and improving their performance. Metallurgy falls into two

major divisions: *extractive,* or *process, metallurgy;* and *physical,* or *alloy, metallurgy.*

Extractive metallurgy

Extractive metallurgy deals with taking metals from their ores and *refining* (purifying) them. It includes a wide variety of specialized commercial processes, such as mineral dressing, roasting, sintering, smelting, leaching, electrolysis, and amalgamation.

Mineral dressing occurs between the mining of the ore and the extraction of metals from it. Mineral dressing removes as much of the waste materials as possible from the ore. This process usually begins by grinding the ore so that the metals in it, along with certain nonmetallic materials, separate from the waste. Then the various waste materials may be floated or washed away. In this *flotation process,* crushed ore is *agitated* (set in motion) in water with bubbles of air or gas. Various chemicals or oils that have been added to the water cause the mineral particles to stick to the bubbles. The minerals are then removed in a froth. The waste materials that remain are called *gangue* (pronounced *gang*). The removal of the gangue reduces the amount of ore that must be handled when the metal is extracted. Because this ore has a higher concentration of metal, it can be more economically refined into the final metal.

Roasting removes sulfur and other impurities from the ore. When the ore is heated in air, the sulfur and certain other impurities combine with the oxygen in the air, and pass off as gases. The remaining solid material contains a *metallic oxide* (combination of metal and oxygen) that must be further purified or reduced to yield the pure metal.

Sintering may occur when the temperature at which ores are roasted becomes very high. In this process, fine particles in contact with one another join to form coarse lumps. The joining is caused by surface tension. It is the same force that causes small water drops to combine into larger drops. Sintering is sometimes accompanied by partial melting of the fine particles, but the particles often remain entirely solid during the process. The coarse lumps produced by sintering are easier to handle and use in later processes.

Smelting. After the ores have been subjected to such preliminary processes as dressing, roasting, or sintering, processors begin the actual work of extracting the metal. The usual method of metal extraction is *smelting* (melting the ore in such a way as to remove impurities). In the case of iron, for example, the ore is placed in a huge, brick-lined furnace called a *blast furnace,* and subjected to high heat. Quantities of coke and limestone also are placed in the furnace. As the heat of the furnace is raised, the coke begins to burn and give off carbon monoxide. This gas takes oxygen from the ore, helping to purify the iron.

Many of the other impurities of the ore melt and combine with the limestone to form a liquid collection of *refuse* (waste materials) which is usually lighter than the iron. This refuse rises to the top of the molten metal, and is taken from the furnace as slag. The slag is drawn off from holes in the side of the furnace at a height above the level of the molten iron. The molten iron is still not completely free of impurities. But almost all the iron has been taken from the ore. The metal must now be refined further, usually by causing it to react with oxygen in a furnace.

Leaching. Some metals can be effectively separated from their ores by *hydrometallurgy* (leaching). This is a method of dissolving the metal out of the ore with a chemical solvent. The metal may then be recovered from the chemical solution by a process called *precipitation.* For example, gold is usually separated from its ore by treating the ore with a dilute alkaline solution of sodium cyanide. After the gold is dissolved in the sodium cyanide, it is placed in contact with metallic zinc. This causes all the gold to *precipitate* (separate) from the solution and gather on the metallic zinc.

Electrolysis. After the metal has been taken from its ore by leaching, it is sometimes recovered from the leaching solution by electrolysis. For example, copper is leached from some ores with sulfuric acid. Then it is placed in an electrolytic cell. There, electric current flows from a lead *anode* (positive pole) through the solution to a copper *cathode* (negative pole). The copper particles in the solution have a positive charge. These particles then seek their opposites, or the negatively charged copper cathode. Aluminum and magnesium also are recovered by electrolysis.

Electrolysis is also used to purify the metal. Copper is one of the metals that can be refined by electrolysis. The impure metal is used as the anode. When electric current is passed through the solution, the atoms of pure copper on the anode give up electrons and pass into solution as positively charged particles. These particles pass through the solution toward the cathode. There, they acquire the necessary electrons to become neutral copper atoms. Most impurities are left behind, and a plating of purified copper forms on the cathode.

Amalgamation is a method that is sometimes used to recover gold and silver from their ores. A solution carries finely ground particles of ore over plates covered with mercury. The mercury attracts the metal and combines with it. The mercury forms an alloy, called an *amalgam,* with the gold or silver. Then the amalgam is heated. The heat causes the mercury to come to a boil and pass off as a gas, which is recovered and recycled. This process leaves behind a metallic sponge of pure gold or silver.

Physical metallurgy

Physical metallurgy is the branch of metallurgy that adapts metals for their final use and improves their performance. It includes any operation used to process a refined commercial metal into a finished product.

Different metals may be mixed to create a metal with special properties. Metal mixtures are called *alloys.* For example, mixing steel with nickel and chromium produces a strong, chemically resistant material called *stainless steel.* Heat treatments may improve such properties as strength and *ductility* (ability to be shaped). New metallic alloys include nickel base *super alloys,* which are used in jet engines. *Shape memory alloys* change shape in response to changes in temperature.

Metal is formed into its final shape by casting, rolling, forging, welding, pressing, extrusion, drawing, stamping, and other methods. Surface treatment may include heating and *carburizing* (combining with carbon). A coating may also be applied to the metal's surface. For example, in a process known as *galvanizing,* a thin layer of zinc is applied to iron or steel to prevent rust.

New combinations of metallic and nonmetallic materials, called *composites,* are replacing traditional metallic alloys for many uses. Some composites are made of nonmetallic materials only. These include fiberglass and carbon epoxy, which is used in sports equipment and jet fighters. Another new approach involves the production of powders of metals and nonmetals. For example, in a process called *gas atomization,* droplets of molten metal are sprayed with gas to form very fine solid particles. These particles can be combined at high temperatures and under high pressure to form alloys with special properties.

History

Metallurgy is one of the oldest sciences. The people of prehistoric times knew something of physical metallurgy. For example, the ancient Chinese and Egyptians found gold and silver in their pure state as grains and nuggets, and hammered the metal into many different kinds of ornaments and other objects. The American Indians found large amounts of pure copper in the area near Lake Superior and hammered the metal into weapons, implements, and jewelry.

Sometime before written history began, some of the ancient peoples discovered the simplest principles of smelting metals from their ores. Lead was probably the first metal ever to be separated from its ore by smelting, because this ore is very easy to smelt. But as long as 4,000 years ago, the Egyptians knew how to separate iron from its ore—and iron ore is considered one of the hardest to smelt. By the time of the Assyrian civilization, the smelting of iron ore was a highly developed art. The ancient Assyrians even knew how to change iron into steel. In the Middle Ages, when alchemists were studying ways to make gold from other substances, great advances were made in metallurgy. The alchemists laid the foundations of the modern science of metallurgy. See **Metal** (Metals through the ages).

Careers in metallurgy

A growing demand for new alloys and composites and new treatments for pure metals has increased the importance of metallurgy as a career. *Metallurgists,* also called *metallurgical engineers,* can find jobs in industries that extract, adapt, and use metals. The mining industry also employs large numbers of metallurgists. Other openings are available in other industries, in government, and in research.

Metallurgists and other persons interested in materials production have increased their efforts to explain complex metallurgical behavior in terms of the basic laws of physics and chemistry. They also have extended the use of metallurgical research methods and skills to such nonmetallic materials as ceramics, semiconductors, plastics, organic solids, and glass. The name *materials science* has been given to the field that deals with both metals and nonmetals.

People interested in metallurgy or materials science as a career should have an aptitude in science and should take as many high-school science and mathematics courses as possible. Most jobs require a bachelor of science degree in metallurgical or materials engineering. Most research positions require an advanced degree.   I. Melvin Bernstein

Related articles in *World Book* include:

Alchemy	Flux	Powder metal-
Alloy	Forging	lurgy
Amalgam	Ion microscope	Sintering
Annealing	Iron and steel	Slag
Electrolysis	Machine tool	Solder
Flotation process	Metallography	Zone melting

Metamorphic rock, *meht uh MAWR fihk,* is one of the three main types of rock in the earth's crust. It forms from the other two main types, *igneous* and *sedimentary.* For example, marble is a metamorphic rock that forms from the sedimentary rock limestone. Schist and slate are metamorphic rocks that come from shale.

Metamorphic rock forms when heat or pressure, or both, cause changes in the "parent" rock. One of the changes is the formation of new minerals, called *recrystallization.* The new mineral grains often are larger than the old ones. Also, platy materials, such as mica, may crystallize in parallel planes. When this happens, the rock breaks easily along these planes. This characteristic of metamorphic rocks is called *rock cleavage.*

Several processes can create metamorphic rock. In *contact metamorphism,* heat produced by nearby *magma* (molten igneous rock) causes recrystallization. In *regional metamorphism,* both heat and pressure change rock. Pressure comes from the burial of the rocks deep in the earth's crust. Movements in the earth's crust may also affect the rock by deforming it. These movements are often associated with the formation of mountains. In a less common process, *dynamic metamorphism,* only deformation due to crustal movements alters rock. In *hydrothermal metamorphism,* hot water provides heat that changes the rock. The water often also reacts with the rock, causing chemical changes.   Maria Luisa Crawford

See also **Metamorphism; Rock** (Metamorphic rock).

Metamorphism, *MEHT uh MAWR fihz uhm,* is the set of processes by which rocks are changed in form. During metamorphism, the size, shape, and arrangement of the minerals in rocks are modified. As a result, new minerals may form or existing minerals may increase in size.

Metamorphism is caused by heat or pressure or both, and sometimes fluids. Metamorphism does not involve the melting of rock or the addition or subtraction of chemicals. In *contact metamorphism,* rocks change as a result of contact with a hot *igneous* body, such as a lava flow. The change caused by the heat and pressure im-

posed below the earth's surface is called *regional metamorphism.* Regional metamorphism often occurs over a large area. *Dynamic metamorphism* includes rock changes that result from high pressure and low temperatures, such as those at the surface of a large fault.

John C. Butler

See also **Metamorphic rock; Rock** (Metamorphic rock; table).

Metamorphosis, *MEHT uh MAWR fuh sihs,* is a Greek word that means *transformation.* Biologists use this word to describe the extreme changes in form and appearance that occur in lower animals between the growing phase of life and the mature adult phase.

Such higher animals as cats, dogs, and horses—like human beings—are similar in form and structure to the adult when they are born. They differ chiefly in size from the mature animals. These animals exhibit what is known as *direct development.* When such lower animals as ants, butterflies, and sea urchins emerge from the egg, they appear to be different from their parents. In many of these young animals, major changes in structure and appearance must occur before they become adults.

The changes that occur in the life cycle of a butterfly or a moth are among the most striking examples of metamorphosis. Because butterflies and moths pass through four distinct stages, scientists consider them as examples of *complete metamorphosis.* The first stage is the egg in which the embryo forms. Eggs of butterflies and many moths are deposited on plants that will provide food for the next stage, called the *larva.*

The larva of a butterfly or a moth is also known as a *caterpillar.* Caterpillars may be hairy, spiny, or smooth-skinned. They may be a single color or have striking color patterns. Caterpillars differ from the adult in having suckerlike *prolegs* on the abdomen and chewing mouthparts. The adult lacks prolegs and has sucking mouthparts. In addition, caterpillars have no wings.

Caterpillars grow rapidly, *molting* (shedding) their outer skins several times. After about a month in the larval stage, a butterfly caterpillar deposits a pad of silk on a twig or other support and attaches itself there. Then it molts once more to enter the third stage of metamorphosis, the *pupa.* Many moths form a silken cocoon before molting to the pupal stage. Other moths pupate in underground cells or in plant stems.

The pupa. During the pupal stage, the developing butterfly or moth is inactive. The butterfly pupa, also called a *chrysalis,* is protected only by its abdomen.

Complete metamorphosis of a house fly

During the life cycle of a house fly, the egg hatches into a larva, which eats and grows and then forms a pupa. Inside the pupa, the adult develops and emerges from the pupa shell.

WORLD BOOK illustration by Shirley Wheeler, Oxford Illustrators Limited

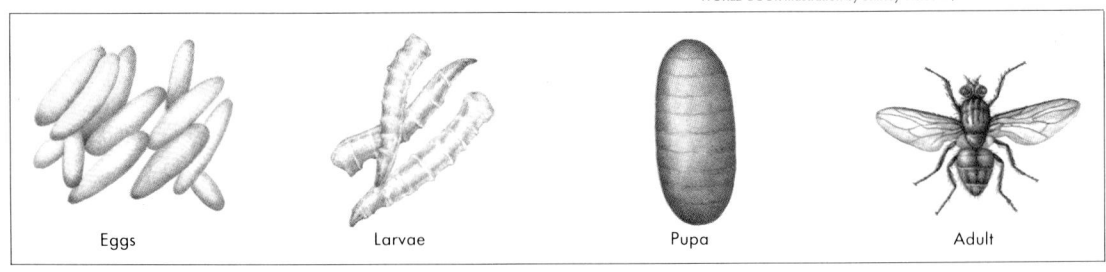

| Eggs | Larvae | Pupa | Adult |

Metamorphosis of a frog

WORLD BOOK illustration by John F. Eggert

Eggs

Tadpoles

Adult

Within the pupal case, larval structures are replaced by those of the adult. Usually there is a another period of inactivity, known as *diapause,* in which even these changes cease. The pupal stage is ideal for passing periods of environmental extremes, such as drought or winter. The pupal stage may last only a few days, or several months, depending on climate and species.

The adult. The adult insect, also called the *imago,* emerges by pushing against its pupal casing, which splits open. The adult crawls onto a twig or other support and pumps blood into its shrunken wings until they are full-size and strong. It then flies away to feed on liquid food, such as flower nectar or tree sap, and carry out its reproductive functions.

Other examples. Beetles, flies, bees, wasps, ants, and many other insects exhibit complete metamorphosis. More primitive insects, including grasshoppers and cockroaches, have only three stages: egg, *nymph* (larva), and adult. This type of metamorphosis, which lacks the pupal stage, is called *incomplete metamorphosis.*

Metamorphosis occurs in most other major animal groups. Among *vertebrates* (animals that have backbones), frogs and toads are the best-known examples. They lay eggs in water, and the eggs hatch into legless tadpoles with tails and gills. A tadpole gradually develops into a four-legged frog, as lungs replace the gills and the tail disappears. Unlike tadpoles, which must live in water, frogs and toads can survive both in and out of water.   Charles V. Covell, Jr.

Related articles in *World Book* include:

Butterfly	Larva
Cocoon	Molting
Fly	Moth
Insect	Pupa

Metaphor, *MEHT uh fuhr* or *MEHT uh fawr,* a figure of speech, is an expression taken from one field of experience and used to say something in another field. For example, when we say, "He's a sly fox," we are using metaphor. That is, we are using the name of an animal to describe a man. A metaphor suggests a comparison without using the word *like* or *as.* The statement "He is *like* a sly fox" or "He is sly *as* a fox" is a simile (see **Simile**).

Everyday speech is rich in metaphors. If we ask someone, "Did you *land* a job today?" the reply may be, "No, not a *bite.*" These words from the special language of *fishing* are used to express thoughts about job-hunting.

Common words actually develop new senses when they are repeatedly used as metaphors. For instance, we hardly realize that in the phrase "table leg," the word *leg* was originally a metaphor. But when told not to "make pigs of yourselves," we are probably aware of the unpleasant comparison the metaphor suggests.

Metaphors are important in the speech of politicians, scientists, and journalists. In 1946, Sir Winston Churchill used the now-famous phrase "iron curtain" to describe an international problem. Scientists speak of the "wave theory of light." And the phrase "priming the pump" is sometimes used to refer to government spending to stimulate a nation's business and industry. In each case, the metaphor has been an important tool of thought.

Great works of literature are enriched by metaphor. Psalm 23 of the Bible is based on a metaphor. It begins with the words, "The Lord is my shepherd," and suggests the relation of God to humanity by considering the relation of a shepherd to sheep. The plays of Shakespeare contain brilliant metaphors, such as the passage in *As You Like It* beginning, "All the world's a stage."

Mixed metaphors, using two or more unrelated metaphors in the same expression, are often unintentionally amusing. An example: "I smell a rat, but we shall nip it in the bud."   Paul B. Diehl

Metaphysical poets, *MEHT uh FIHZ uh kuhl,* is the name given to certain English poets of the 1600's who were influenced by John Donne, the most important member of the group. Donne wrote on both religious and nonreligious subjects. Metaphysical poets who wrote mainly on religious subjects included Richard Crashaw, George Herbert, and Henry Vaughan. Lord Herbert of Cherbury, John Cleveland, Abraham Cowley, and Andrew Marvell wrote mostly on nonreligious topics.

Metaphysical poetry contains irregular, "unpoetic" rhythms and colloquial language. It also sometimes uses far-fetched or outlandish comparisons, either similes or metaphors, called *metaphysical conceits.* The metaphysical conceit often extends a comparison to great length to describe an emotion, idea, or situation.

In the late 1700's, English critic Samuel Johnson first named this group "metaphysical poets" in his *Lives of the Poets* (1779-1781). Johnson criticized their exhibition of learning and especially their use of metaphysical conceits. Despite Johnson's label, however, these poets were actually no more "metaphysical" in the philosophical sense than other thoughtful writers.

After being condemned by critics like Johnson, the metaphysical poets returned to favor in the early 1900's. The essays of T. S. Eliot helped stimulate this revival. Modern poets influenced by the group include Eliot, Wallace Stevens, Hart Crane, Elinor Wylie, and Richard Eberhart.   Gary A. Stringer

See also **Cowley, Abraham; Donne, John; Herbert, George; Marvell, Andrew; Vaughan, Henry.**

Metaphysics, MEHT uh FIHZ ihks, is the branch of philosophy concerned with the basic nature of reality. Its aim is to give a systematic account of the world and the principles that govern it. In contrast to the natural sciences, which study specific features of the world, metaphysics is a more general investigation into the fundamental features of what exists. The metaphysician relies on forms of analysis that depend on pure reason rather than the experimental methods of the natural scientist. Metaphysical speculation has always focused on certain key concepts such as space and time, causality, identity and change, possibility and necessity, universals and particulars, and mind and body.

Space and time. When philosophers want to understand the nature of the universe, they often begin by examining the nature of space and time. Such questions as "Can there be time without change?" and "Is space something distinct from the objects in the universe?" belong to the realm of metaphysics. Some metaphysicians have argued that space and time are *absolute*—that is, independent of any change in the arrangement of the contents of the universe. But according to the *relativistic* account, both space and time can be reduced to the relationships between things in the universe.

Causality. Theories of causality attempt to answer questions about how or why events happen. The concept of causality is closely related to problems of *determinism* and free will. Determinism states that strict causal laws govern all events, even human actions. *Nondeterministic* metaphysical theories claim that events are not controlled by external causes. These theories state that people freely choose their actions, and in any situation could choose otherwise than they actually do.

Identity and change. Studying the relationship between identity and change helps philosophers understand how things can persist through time even though they seem to change. Most people will agree that objects can change without becoming different things. For example, a coat of paint will not transform a house into a different house. However, it is unclear to what extent changes can take place without destroying the original object. Thus, if we gradually replace all the parts of a house, it seems that we will have slowly destroyed the old house and built a new one in its place. Some metaphysical theories distinguish an object's *form,* or organization, from the matter out of which it is made. They argue that the form persists through time and guarantees the identity of the object through changes.

Possibility and necessity. When philosophers want to know how people make judgments of truth, they often examine the concepts of possibility and necessity. These questions are related to issues of *necessary truths* and *contingent truths.* That there are 9 planets in our solar system is a contingent truth, because there could

be 10 planets or even no planets. On the other hand, the fact that $2 + 2 = 4$ is a necessary truth, because it could not be otherwise. Once philosophers have distinguished between possibility and necessity, they can consider whether there are essential properties of objects. If it is a necessary truth that a thing have a certain property, philosophers call that property an *essential* property. Thus, warm-bloodedness is presumably an essential property of dogs, and brownness is only an *accidental* (nonessential) property of some dogs.

Universals and particulars. Thinking about the nature of objects and their properties often leads philosophers to discussions of universals and particulars. A universal is something that many separate things have in common. A particular is an object with many properties. For example, the property of redness is common to many individuals. Some metaphysicians believe there is therefore a universal redness. *Realism* about universals is the doctrine that universals can exist separately from particulars and that there is a universal redness common to all red things. Thus, in a realistic theory, universal redness is something more than the totality of all red things. In contrast, *nominalistic* theories claim that there is no universal redness and that *red* is simply a word that people apply to all red things in the world.

Mind and body. Many metaphysical problems arise from the observation that mind and body seem to interact, even though they appear to have nothing in common. These problems can be phrased in such questions as "Is the mind a physical thing?" and "Are people's minds identical with their brains?" *Dualism* contends that mind and matter are two fundamentally distinct kinds of things. A basic problem for dualism is to explain how a physical process can have a nonphysical effect, or how mental events can result in changes in the physical world. *Monism* denies that mind and matter are two different things. Monism can be either *materialistic,* asserting that only matter exists, or *idealistic,* claiming that mind is basic to everything.

Opinions about metaphysics. The apparent failure to reach widespread agreement on metaphysical issues has prompted some philosophers to insist that these questions are beyond the power of human beings to answer. In the early 1900's, philosophers who called themselves *logical positivists* argued that metaphysical questions were meaningless because no amount of evidence could possibly decide them one way or another.

The positivists' critique of metaphysics was widely accepted in the 1920's and 1930's, but most philosophers today are less inclined to dismiss metaphysical theories. There are no easy answers to metaphysical questions. However, philosophers now believe that they can judge these theories by how well they satisfy people's basic intuitions, and combine with accepted scientific theories to provide a unified view of the world.

Douglas M. Jesseph

See also **Free will; Idealism; Materialism; Philosophy** (Metaphysics; Ancient philosophy); **Positivism.**

Metastasis. See **Cancer** (How cancer develops).

Metaurus, Battle of. See **Army** (table).

Metchnikoff, *mehch nee KAWF,* **Élie,** *ay LEE* (1845-1916), was a Russian biologist. He shared the 1908 Nobel Prize for medicine for his work in *immunology* (the study of immunity). In particular, he discovered the function of *phagocytes.* In the human immune system, phagocytes are white blood cells that attack disease germs. Metchnikoff determined that inflammation at a wound is caused when phagocytes surround germs. Doctors at first opposed his ideas on phagocytes. But his discovery was generally accepted before his death.

Metchnikoff's writings include *Immunity in Infectious Diseases* (1901) and *Lectures on the Comparative Pathology of Inflammation* (1892). He later studied aging. In *The Prolongation of Life* (1905), he suggests that eating cultures of sour milk bacteria, commonly available in yogurt, would slow the aging process.

Metchnikoff was born in Ivanovka, near Kharkov. He studied in Russia and Germany and taught zoology at Odessa University. He joined the staff of the Pasteur Institute in Paris in 1892 and became its subdirector in 1895.   Dale C. Smith

Meteor is a bright streak of light seen briefly in the sky. Meteors are often called *shooting stars* or *falling stars* because they look like stars falling from the sky. Meteors result when chunks of metallic or stony matter called *meteoroids* enter the earth's atmosphere from space. Air friction makes the meteoroid so hot it glows and creates a trail of hot glowing gases. Meteoroids that reach the earth before burning up are called *meteorites.*

Scientists estimate that as many as 200 million visible meteors occur in the earth's atmosphere every day. These and invisible meteorites are estimated to add more than 1,000 short tons (910 metric tons) daily to the earth's weight. We first see most of these meteors when they are about 65 miles (105 kilometers) above the earth. Air friction heats them and the air around them to about 4000 °F (2200 °C), and they burn out at altitudes of 30 to 50 miles (48 to 80 kilometers).

All known meteoroids belong to the solar system of which the earth is a part. They travel in a variety of orbits and velocities about the sun. The faster ones move at about 26 miles (42 kilometers) a second. The earth travels at about 18 miles (29 kilometers) a second. When meteoroids meet the earth's atmosphere head-on, the combined velocity may reach about 44 miles (71 kilometers) a second. Those traveling in the same direction as the earth hit the atmosphere at much slower speeds. Meteors rarely blaze for more than a few seconds. But occasionally one leaves a shining trail that lasts as long as

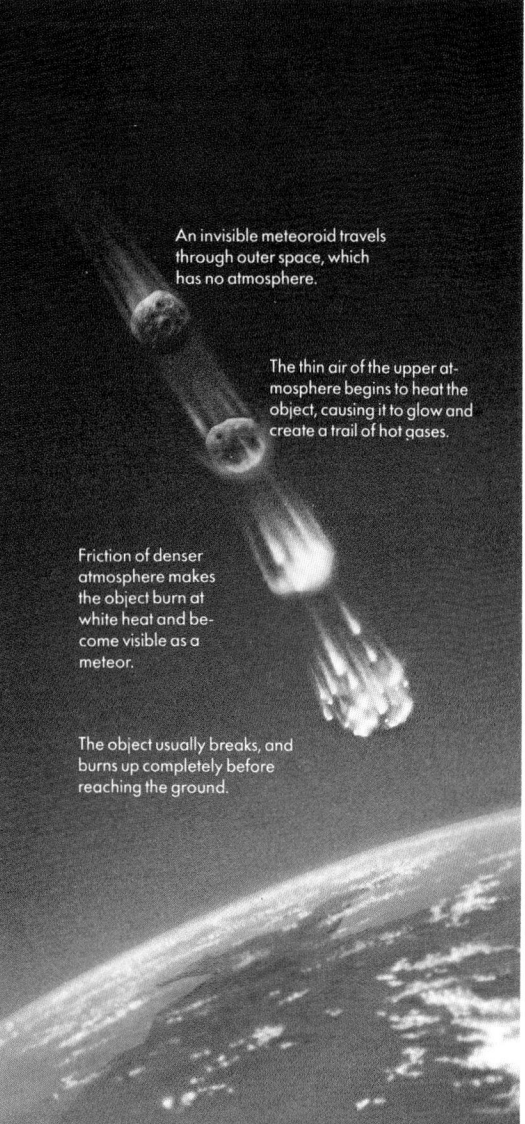

An invisible meteoroid travels through outer space, which has no atmosphere.

The thin air of the upper atmosphere begins to heat the object, causing it to glow and create a trail of hot gases.

Friction of denser atmosphere makes the object burn at white heat and become visible as a meteor.

The object usually breaks, and burns up completely before reaching the ground.

WORLD BOOK illustration by Rob Wood

A meteor appears in the sky whenever an object called a *meteoroid* hurtles into the earth's atmosphere from space.

Meteor Crater Enterprises

The Meteor Crater of Arizona lies between the towns of Flagstaff and Winslow. Scientists believe that a meteorite struck the earth about 50,000 years ago and dug a hole about 4,150 feet (1,265 meters) across and 570 feet (174 meters) deep.

several minutes. Most of the meteors we see were originally no larger than a pinhead or a grain of sand.

Meteor showers. The earth meets a number of swarms of meteoroids every year. At such times, the sky seems filled with a shower of flying sparks. Some swarms of meteoroids have orbits similar to those of comets. These swarms are fragments of comets.

The most brilliant meteoric shower took place on Nov. 13, 1833. The earth encounters this swarm, called the *Leonid* meteor shower, every November. It consists of a great ring of particles that revolves continually around the sun. Another brilliant Leonid meteor shower occurred in 1966. Written records indicate that the Leonid shower was seen as long ago as A.D. 902.

Astronomers name meteor showers after the con-

The Willamette meteorite is the largest meteorite ever found in the United States. It measures about 118 inches (300 centimeters) long and weighs about $15\frac{1}{2}$ short tons (14 metric tons). Rust and atmospheric friction caused pits in one side. It was named after Oregon's Willamette Valley, where it was found in 1902.

P. Hollembeak, American Museum of Natural History

Important meteor showers

Shower	Date
Quadrantid	January 3
Lyrid	April 21
Eta Aquarid	May 4
Delta Aquarid	July 29
Perseid	August 12
Orionid	October 22
Taurid, North	November 1
Taurid, South	November 16
Leonid	November 17
Geminid	December 12

stellations from which they appear to come. The table above lists some of the important annual showers and the dates of their greatest activity.

Meteorites sometimes explode into fragments with a noise that can be heard far away when they strike the earth or its atmosphere. In 1908, the famous Tunguska meteorite exploded several miles or kilometers above the ground in Siberia. People as far as 466 miles (750 kilometers) away saw it in full daylight, and felt its blast at a distance of 50 miles (80 kilometers). The meteorite had a weight estimated at a few hundred tons.

According to one theory, a meteorite caused the dinosaurs to die out about 65 million years ago. The meteorite struck where the village of Chicxulub Puerto is now located, near Progreso, Mexico. The crash spewed dust and other debris into the atmosphere. The debris blocked out so much sunlight that not enough food grew to feed the plant-eating dinosaurs. As these creatures died off, so did the meat-eating dinosaurs that fed on them.

There are two kinds of meteorites, stony and iron. *Stony meteorites* are made up of many stony minerals mixed with particles of iron. Some resemble minerals from volcanoes. *Iron meteorites* consist chiefly of iron combined with nickel.

Scientists collect meteorites for study, because they are thought to be unchanged fragments of the material from which the moon and planets were made. The largest meteorite, located at Hoba West in Namibia, weighs about 66 short tons (60 metric tons). The Hayden Planetarium in New York City owns the Ahnighito, a 34-short-

ton (31-metric-ton) nickel-iron meteorite. Arctic explorer Robert E. Peary brought the Ahnighito to the United States from western Greenland in 1897. Thousands of small meteorites have been found on Antarctica.

In the 1950's, scientists discovered a 400-mile (640-kilometer) wide depression on the eastern shore of Hudson Bay in Canada. This depression may be the earth's largest meteorite crater. Canada also has four other craters found in the 1950's. These are a crater 7 to 8 miles (11 to 13 kilometers) wide at Deep Bay, Saskatchewan; the Chubb crater, 2 miles (3.2 kilometers) wide, on the Ungava Peninsula; and a 2-mile-wide crater at Brent and a crater $1\frac{1}{2}$ miles (2.4 kilometers) wide at Holleford, both in Ontario. The Meteor Crater in Arizona is about 4,150 feet (1,265 meters) wide and 570 feet (174 meters) deep.   Frank D. Drake

See also **Fireball; Leonids; Silliman, Benjamin; Tektite.**

Meteorite. See Meteor.

Meteorological Society, *MEE tee uhr uh LAHJ uh kuhl,* **American,** is an international organization that encourages the study of the atmospheric, oceanic, and related sciences. Most of its members are meteorologists and oceanographers. The society produces educational films, sponsors conferences and workshops, and offers awards and scholarships to college students. It also certifies consulting meteorologists and grants seals of approval to TV meteorologists. The society publishes journals, books, and papers. It was founded in 1919. Headquarters are in Boston, Mass.

Critically reviewed by the American Meteorological Society

Meteorology, *MEE tee uh RAHL uh jee,* is the study of the earth's atmosphere and the variations in atmospheric conditions that produce weather. Meteorologists measure wind, temperature, precipitation, air pressure, and other atmospheric conditions. They also measure chemical substances in the atmosphere, such as carbon dioxide and ozone, that affect the climate. By analyzing data about the atmosphere, meteorologists often can predict weather conditions.

Many meteorologists work as weather observers. They measure weather conditions. Other meteorologists, who are employed as forecasters, analyze weather maps and information from computers and other sources. They use such data to prepare detailed weather reports, make forecasts, and issue warnings of hazardous weather conditions. Forecasters also prepare special weather information, such as data for farmers about water-supply conditions. Some work for government agencies. Others work for private businesses, such as airlines, oil companies, and radio and TV stations.

Many meteorologists conduct research. Some develop computer techniques to improve forecasting or to study thunderstorms and other weather conditions. Others work on the development of improved instruments for observing the weather. Research meteorologists also collect and analyze weather data to study the causes of extreme weather events, such as tornadoes and floods. In addition, researchers study ways to modify the weather. For example, they experiment with cloud seeding to produce rain (see **Rainmaking**).

How meteorologists study the atmosphere. Meteorologists use a wide variety of scientific instruments to gather information about the atmosphere and the weather. These scientists make weather observations from land, in the air, and at sea. Meteorologists use such instruments as thermometers, barometers, and hygrometers to measure basic aspects of the weather. Balloons carrying these instruments measure conditions in the upper atmosphere (see **Balloon** [Scientific uses]). Radar devices determine the location, size, speed, and direction of storms.

Weather satellites, also called meteorological satellites, take pictures of the earth from great altitudes. Meteorologists use these pictures to chart the movement of clouds. In addition, weather satellites measure air temperature and humidity, and help detect storms that develop at sea.

Computers help meteorologists forecast the weather. These machines produce weather maps from observations all over the world. Computers can predict certain elements of weather by solving complex sets of equations that describe the behavior of the atmosphere. Weather forecasting with computers is called *numerical forecasting.*

History. The word *meteorology* comes from *Meteorologica,* the title of a book by the ancient Greek philosopher Aristotle. In this book, Aristotle wrote about his weather observations.

Scientific observation of the weather began in 1593, when the Italian scientist Galileo invented a type of thermometer to measure air temperature. By the late 1700's, instruments had been invented to measure humidity, wind, air pressure, and precipitation. During the 1800's, the use of weather maps enabled people to forecast the weather scientifically.

In the early 1900's, meteorologists began to explain the structure of the atmosphere. For example, the Norwegian meteorologist Vilhelm Bjerknes discovered that the atmosphere contains zones of rapidly changing conditions called *fronts.* Shortly after World War II ended in 1945, the Swedish-American meteorologist Carl-Gustaf Rossby studied *jet streams,* which are atmospheric regions of extremely strong winds. Such findings greatly changed methods of forecasting the weather. In addition, the accuracy of forecasting improved after computers, weather satellites, and other modern instruments came into use.

Cooperation between nations further advanced the study of meteorology. In 1963, the United Nations (UN) approved the *World Weather Watch,* an observation system that maps the weather of many areas of the world.   Margaret A. LeMone

See also **Weather.**

Meter, also spelled *metre,* is the base unit of length in the metric system. Its symbol is *m.* A meter is equal to 39.370 inches. Scientists define the meter as the distance traveled by light in a vacuum during $\frac{1}{299,792,458}$ of a second. From 1960 to 1983, the length of the meter had been defined as 1,650,763.73 wavelengths of the orange-red line of the spectrum of light radiated by the isotope krypton 86, measured in a vacuum. This measurement standard had replaced the platinum-iridium meter bar.

See also **Centimeter; Metric system.**   Thomas T. Liao

Meter, in poetry, refers to the pattern of rhythm in a poem. The pattern may be easy or difficult to hear. Poets who create meters in English usually work within one of three metrical traditions: (1) stress, (2) syllabic, or (3) foot-

verse. For a discussion of meter and examples of the most important meters, see Poetry (**Rhythm and meter**).

Meter is not necessary to poetry. In many poems, the rhythm does not create a pattern (see **Free verse**). The rhythm of such poetry often follows the structures of phrases and clauses, and the arrangement of lines on the page.   Paul B. Diehl

See also **Blank verse; Couplet.**

Meter, Electric. See Electric meter.

Methadone is a drug used in experimental programs that help people overcome addiction to such narcotics as heroin, morphine, or opium. Most of these programs also include counseling to help addicts with psychological, social, and occupational problems.

Methadone itself can cause addiction with symptoms similar to those of heroin addiction. But if people already addicted to heroin, morphine, or opium take methadone, they no longer crave or even enjoy the other drugs. Methadone must be taken orally to produce those effects. If methadone doses are stopped, former drug cravings return. As a result, a former heroin addict may have to take methadone for life.

Lengthy methadone treatment has been criticized as a substitution of one addiction for another. But methadone therapy produces different effects than does addiction to heroin. A heroin user experiences *highs* (extremely happy feelings), dreamlike states, and sleepiness. Most people who are addicted to heroin cannot hold a job or maintain normal social relationships. But a former heroin addict who takes methadone in the prescribed manner has a clear mind and a feeling of well-being. In time, most addicts who are treated with methadone can lead normal lives. Long-term methadone therapy was developed in 1964 by two American physicians, Vincent Dole and Marie Nyswander, a husband-and-wife team.   Donald J. Wolk

See also **Drug abuse** (Treatment of drug abuse).

Methamphetamine, MEHTH am FEHT uh meen, is a powerful drug nicknamed "speed." It quickly produces feelings of joy, strength, and alertness. Methamphetamine gives a user the capacity to work and talk for long periods of time. Misuse of methamphetamine can be dangerous, and the drug can be obtained legally only with a doctor's prescription. Methamphetamine is one of a group of drugs called amphetamines. It has been sold under many brand names, including Methedrine and Desoxyn.

Physicians once prescribed methamphetamine pills for weight control. The pills have also been used to combat fatigue and to help people under tension improve their work. Excess use of methamphetamine causes severe weight loss, pains in muscles and joints, excessive activity, and overconcentration on minor tasks. Some people become suspicious and develop antisocial behavior.

People who stop using methamphetamines may experience withdrawal symptoms. Such an experience suggests that the drug may cause physical dependence. In time, tolerance to the drug develops and the user's body needs larger and larger doses to achieve the same effect. Users may become mentally dependent on the drug if, when they go without it, they find the world cold and demanding. Sudden withdrawal from methamphetamines may cause deep depression, fatigue, or even a temporary *psychosis* (severe mental illness).

Donald J. Wolk

See also **Amphetamine; Drug abuse.**

Methane, *METH ayn,* is an important industrial compound that makes up a large part of natural gas. It is formed when plants decay in places where there is very little air. Methane is often called *marsh gas* because it is found around stagnant water and swamps. It is also the chief substance in *firedamp,* a gas that causes serious explosions in mines.

The chemical industry uses methane as a starting material for many other chemicals. Methane reacts at high temperatures with a limited amount of air to form acetylene and with ammonia to produce hydrogen cyanide. It also undergoes *partial combustion* (incomplete burning), producing hydrogen and carbon monoxide gases. This mixture serves as a source for commercial hydrogen, and for carbon monoxide used in making methyl alcohol (methanol).

Methane is a colorless, odorless gas. It is nontoxic but highly flammable. It is soluble in alcohol but only slightly soluble in water. Methane's chemical formula is CH_4, and it is the first member of the *paraffin* series of hydrocarbons. Mixtures of methane with air, oxygen, or chlorine are explosive. Methane is a significant part of the atmospheres of Jupiter, Saturn, Neptune, and Uranus. Robert C. Gadwood

See also **Acetylene; Damp; Gas** (The composition of natural gas); **Hydrocarbon; Methanol.**

Methanol, *METH uh nohl* or *METH uh nahl,* is a type of alcohol used for many industrial purposes. It is also called *methyl alcohol* or *wood alcohol.* Methanol is a clear, colorless organic compound. It is flammable and highly poisonous. Drinking methanol, or inhaling its fumes for prolonged periods, can cause blindness or death. Methanol also can be absorbed through the skin.

Methanol's chemical formula is CH_3OH. It has a molecular weight of 32.04. It boils at 65 °C and freezes at −94 °C. At 20 °C, its density is 0.7915 grams per cubic centimeter (see **Density**).

Methanol readily dissolves a number of other chemicals. This property makes it an important *solvent* (substance that dissolves other substances) in the manufacture of dyes, medicines, and other products. In addition, methanol mixes readily with water. Solutions of methanol and water function in motor vehicles as antifreezes for windshield washer fluids and fuel lines. Such solutions remain liquid at temperatures that would freeze pure water.

A wide variety of products are manufactured from mixtures of methanol and *ethanol,* which is also called *grain alcohol.* Ethanol is an ingredient of many alcoholic beverages, but mixing it with methanol makes it *denatured* (unfit to drink).

A variety of substances undergo chemical reactions with methanol. For example, oxygen reacts with methanol to produce *formaldehyde,* a chemical used in making plastics. Organic acids react with methanol to form compounds called *esters,* which are used in such products as paints and varnishes. In addition, methanol can be converted to high-octane gasoline, but only by means of an expensive process.

Campers use methanol as fuel in portable stoves. Methanol also can function as a motor fuel in place of gasoline, but its rates of corrosion and combustion differ from those of gasoline. Therefore, such use of pure methanol requires adjustments to the carburetor, other engine parts, and the fuel tank.

Most commercial methanol is produced by heating carbon monoxide and hydrogen under pressure in the presence of a metal oxide catalyst (see **Catalysis**). Mixtures of carbon monoxide and hydrogen can be obtained from such sources as coal, natural gas, petroleum, wood, garbage, or sewage. Robert C. Gadwood

Method acting is the general approach to acting used by most modern American actors. This approach is based upon the idea that actors should achieve a detailed emotional identification with their characters. Actors try to think and feel what their characters would think and feel. Method acting tries to help actors create truthful and deeply felt performances.

The major features of Method acting are taken from the teachings of Russian stage director Konstantin Stanislavski. In 1931, the Group Theatre was organized in New York City by Harold Clurman, Lee Strasberg, and Cheryl Crawford. Using Stanislavski's ideas, the Group developed acting techniques over 20 years marked by lively experimentation and passionate debate. In 1947, several former members of the Group founded the Actors Studio as a place where professional actors could continue to refine their skills. Under Strasberg's direction, the Actors Studio became the most influential American home of Method acting.

Robert Lewis was a founder of the Actors Studio. His book *Method—or Madness* (1958) describes many techniques and exercises of Method acting.

Maarten Reilingh

See also **Theater** (Systems of acting); **Brando, Marlon; Stanislavski, Konstantin.**

Methodists belong to those Protestant denominations that trace their beginnings back to John Wesley, a clergyman of the Church of England. A number of churches throughout the world share the name *Methodist* and a common heritage in Wesley's teaching and organization. The largest is The United Methodist Church, which is predominantly North American. There is no central organization of Methodists, but many denominations are part of the World Methodist Council, a cooperative association. Methodists have followed John Wesley in adopting the teachings and practices of the Church of England. They accept the Bible as the primary rule of faith, with Christian tradition and reason as secondary authorities. They also stress religious experience as an important standard of faith.

Early history. Methodism originated as a movement with groups of students at Oxford University in the late 1720's. They helped each other to be disciplined and methodical in their study, spiritual devotions, and practical good works. These activities earned them the nickname "Methodists." One of the founders was Charles Wesley, and their leader was his brother John. Both brothers, after deep personal experiences of faith in 1738, joined the Evangelical Revival of the 1700's by venturing into open-air preaching.

There were two distinctive features of the Wesleys' preaching and, in turn, of the Methodist movement. The first was a message that invited all to respond to God's gracious reconciliation through Jesus Christ. The second was the incorporation into societies of those who did respond. In the societies, members developed the practical disciplines of a Christian life, primarily through subdivisions of the societies, known as *classes*. The classes met weekly under the spiritual guidance of a class leader, who asked members to give an account of their discipleship according to the General Rules of the Societies (1743).

As the movement spread, John Wesley emerged as its leader and Charles as its poet. Charles composed more than 7,000 hymns, giving Methodists a further distinctive characteristic—the singing of their faith. The *Collection of Hymns* (1780) remains a spiritual classic of the world church. John's major role was to organize the societies into a connected system governed by an annual conference that first met in 1744. Methodism was also noted for John's use of *lay* (unordained) preachers.

John Wesley wanted the societies to remain a reforming movement within the Church of England. However, the resistance of Anglican clergy and the need to provide pastoral supervision for society members led to a separation from the church. Wesley acknowledged this separation in 1784, when he ordained Thomas Coke as the first superintendent of the Methodist church in America. He also gave Coke authority to ordain Francis Asbury to serve in the same capacity.

In 1784, at the Christmas Conference in Baltimore, the Methodist Episcopal Church was formed, with Coke and Asbury becoming its first bishops. The new denomination spread rapidly, chiefly through the work of traveling preachers, known as *circuit riders*, who took Methodism's message to the expanding American frontier.

Social change and division. As Methodism became consolidated, the discipline of the early societies gave way to the less demanding social structure of a church. Tensions developed, some of which were due to unresolved issues of church government following John Wesley's death in 1791. But the deeper reason for the tensions was that Methodism stressed a Christian life style in the world. This emphasis involved its members in the social changes of the 1800's. In England, the major social conflict was the emerging trade union movement. In the United States, it was slavery.

These issues led to many divisions among the Methodists. In Britain, the first was the formation of the Methodist New Connexion in 1797, which was followed by the Primitive Methodists in 1810. In the United States, the divisions resulted in the establishment of the Methodist Protestant Church (1830), the Wesleyan Methodist Connection (1843), and the Free Methodist Church (1860). Several black Methodist churches were also formed, including the African Methodist Episcopal Church (1787), the African Methodist Episcopal Zion Church (1796), and the Colored (later the Christian) Methodist Episcopal Church (1870). The most important dispute over slavery occurred in 1844, dividing the Methodist Episcopal Church into North and South denominations. Doctrinal differences led to the formation of the Church of the Nazarene (1908).

Major reunions took place in Britain in 1932 and in the United States in 1939. The United Methodist Church was formed in 1968. Methodists became part of the United Church of Canada in 1925, and the Uniting Church in Australia in 1977. David Lowes Watson

Related articles in *World Book* include:

African Methodist Episcopal Church	Protestantism (The Methodist movement)
African Methodist Episcopal Zion Church	United Church of Canada
	United Methodist Church
Asbury, Francis	Wesley, Charles
Church of the Nazarene	Wesley, John
Circuit rider	Wesleyan Church
Free Methodist Church	Whitefield, George

Methuselah, *muh THOO zuh luh,* was the son of Enoch, the father of Lamech, and the grandfather of Noah in the Old Testament. According to the Bible, he lived 969 years (Gen. 5: 25-27), making him the oldest Biblical person. The expression "as old as Methuselah" describes a very old person. Babylonians believed some of their heroes lived 36,000 years. Carole R. Fontaine

Methyl alcohol. See Methanol.

Methylbenzene. See Toluene.

Métis, *may TEES* or *may TEE,* refers to people of mixed white and American Indian ancestry who inhabited the Red River Colony (in present-day Manitoba) in the 1800's. The word *métis* means *mixed* in French.

Métis settlements developed in the Red River Colony from contacts between Indians and colonial fur-trading companies. Métis settlers farmed, traded furs, and hunted buffalo. Several culturally distinct métis groups lived in the colony, including French-speaking Roman Catholics and English-speaking Protestants. Most métis also spoke the Cree Indian language.

The métis rebelled in 1869 and 1870, after Canada's government prepared to move white settlers into the Red River area. The area became part of Canada in 1870, but the government promised the métis they would be able to continue to use their land.

Over the next several years, however, the government systematically forced the métis off their land. Many of the English-speaking métis merged into nearby white communities. Many of the French speakers moved into what is now Saskatchewan.

In Saskatchewan, métis again battled the Canadian government, this time in the North West Rebellion of 1885. After the rebellion failed, many métis in Saskatchewan mixed into white communities. Today, many people of partial Indian ancestry in Canada and in certain border areas of the United States refer to themselves as métis. J. M. Bumsted

See also **North West Rebellion; Red River Rebellion; Riel, Louis.**

Metonymy, *muh TAHN uh mee,* is a figure of speech by which a phrase or word is used for a related phrase or word. For example, when we "turn on the light," we actually flip a switch, closing an electric circuit and causing the light. But we give the name of the effect to the cause. When we "listen to records," we really hear music, but we name the cause to mean the effect. When we ask for "another cup," we really mean more coffee. The container symbolizes what it contains. These are common forms of metonymy.

In *synecdoche,* which is related to metonymy, we name the part for the whole. For instance, on board a ship, the order "All hands on deck" calls the crew to assemble on the deck. The word *hands* is used to refer to the members of the ship's crew. Marianne Cooley

See also **Slang** (Figures of speech).

Metre. See Meter; Metric system.

WORLD BOOK photo

Students learn about the metric system by making various measurements with metric units.

Metric system

Metric system is a group of units used to make any kind of measurement, such as length, temperature, time, or weight. No other system of measurement ever used equals the metric system in simpleness. Scientists everywhere make measurements in metric units, and so do all other people in most countries.

The United States customarily uses the *inch-pound* system for most measurements. This system was developed in England from older units, beginning about the 1200's. In 1975, the United States Congress passed the Metric Conversion Act, which called for a voluntary changeover to the metric system. Congress amended the act in 1988, making the metric system the preferred system of weights and measures for U.S. trade and commerce. The 1988 bill required U.S. government agencies to use the metric system for purchases, grants, and other business-related activities by the end of 1992. Federal agencies had begun to make this conversion by the end of 1992. In the early 1970's, the Canadian government began to convert Canada to the metric system. All major countries except Canada and the United States were already using the metric system.

A group of French scientists created the metric system in the 1790's. Since then, the system has been revised several times. The official name of the present version is *Système International d'Unités* (International System of Units), usually known simply as *SI*. The term

Daniel V. De Simone, the contributor of this article, is a consultant for DMS International. He directed the U.S. Metric Study conducted by the government from 1968 to 1971.

metric comes from the base unit of length in the system, the *meter,* for which the international spelling is *metre.*

Using the metric system

The scientists who created the metric system designed it to fit their needs. They made the system logical and exact. Furthermore, it is necessary to know only a few metric units to make everyday measurements.

The metric system is simple to use for two reasons. First, it follows the decimal number system—that is, metric units increase or decrease in size by 10's. For example, a meter has 10 parts called *decimeters.* A decimeter has 10 parts called *centimeters.* Units in the inch-pound system have no single number relationship between them. For example, feet and yards are related by 3's, but feet and inches are related by 12's.

Also, the metric system has only 7 base units that make up all its measurements. The inch-pound system has more than 20 base units for just its common measurements. Inch-pound units used for special purposes add many more base units to that system.

The decimal arrangement. The metric system is a decimal system just as are the U.S. and Canadian money systems. In a decimal system, a unit is 10 times larger than the next smaller unit. For example, a meter equals 10 decimeters just as a dollar equals 10 dimes.

Most metric units have a prefix that tells the relationship of that unit to the base unit. These prefixes are the same no matter which base unit is used. This uniform system also simplifies metric measurement.

Greek prefixes are used to show multiples of a base unit. They make a base unit larger. For example, *hecto* means 100 times and *kilo* means 1,000 times. Latin prefixes are used to show the submultiples of the base unit. They make a base unit smaller. For example, *centi* means

$\frac{1}{100}$ and *milli* means $\frac{1}{1,000}$. The table on page 439 shows all the prefixes, their symbols, and their relationship to the base unit.

An example will illustrate the basic simpleness of a decimal system. Suppose you want to measure the length and width of a room so you can draw a floor plan to scale. Using the inch-pound system, you measure the room with a yardstick and get the length in units of yards, feet, and inches. To find the distance in just feet and inches, you multiply the number of yards by 3. Suppose the room measures 3 yards 1 foot 6 inches long. This measurement equals 10 feet 6 inches.

To prepare the scale drawing, you decide to let one inch of the drawing equal one foot of the room. The 10 feet in the room measurement equal 10 inches on the drawing. But the 6 inches must be divided by 12 to get the fraction of an inch needed to represent them on the drawing. Since $6 \div 12$ equals $\frac{1}{2}$, the correct scale distance for the drawing is $10\frac{1}{2}$ inches.

Using the metric system, you find the room measures 3 meters 2 decimeters long. This measurement can also be written as 3.2 meters. You let one decimeter of the drawing equal one meter of the room. Then, all you do to change the room measurement into the scale measurement is divide by 10. Moving the decimal point one place to the left divides a decimal number by 10. Therefore, the scale distance is 3.2 meters ÷ 10, or 0.32 meter, which equals 3.2 decimeters.

Metric measurement units. Seven *base* (basic) units form the foundation of the metric system. Nearly all everyday measurements involve only four of these units. (1) The *meter* is the base unit for length or distance. (2) The *kilogram* is the base unit for *mass,* the weight of an object when measured on the earth. (3) The *second* is the base unit for time. (4) The *kelvin* is the base unit for temperature. Most people, when measuring in metric units, use *Celsius* temperatures instead of kelvin temperatures. One kelvin is equivalent to one degree Celsius, but the two temperature scales begin at different points. See the section *Temperature measurements* in this article.

The three other base units have specialized uses by scientists and engineers. (5) The *ampere* is the base unit for electrical measurements. (6) The *mole* is the base unit for measuring the amount of any substance involved in a chemical or other reaction. (7) The *candela* is the base unit for measuring the intensity of light.

Every base unit is defined by a *measurement standard* that gives the exact value of the unit. The metric system also includes two supplementary units for measuring angles. These units are the *radian* and the *steradian* (see **Radian**).

All other units in the metric system consist of two or more base units. For example, the unit for speed, *meters per second,* combines the base units for length and time. Such combination units are called *derived units.*

Common measurements

This section describes everyday measurements made by using the metric system. The examples give an approximate number of inch-pound units in each metric unit. For more precise conversions between the two systems, see the *World Book* article on **Weights and measures**. Other articles discuss the specialized metric units used by scientists and engineers. For example, see **Energy** for the metric units related to energy.

Length and distance measurements. The meter is used for such measurements as the length of a rope or of a piano or other large object. It also is used to measure the height of a mountain or the altitude of an airplane. A meter is slightly longer than a yard. Short lengths are measured in centimeters, or they may be measured in *millimeters.* A centimeter equals about $\frac{2}{5}$ of an inch. Books, pencils, and other small objects may be measured in centimeters. A millimeter equals about $\frac{1}{25}$ of an inch. Photographic film, small hardware, and tiny mechanical parts are measured in millimeters.

Long distances, such as those between cities, are measured in *kilometers.* A kilometer equals about $\frac{5}{8}$ of a mile. A short distance, such as that between two buildings on the same block, is measured in meters.

Surface measurements tell how much area something covers. For example, the amount of carpeting needed to cover a floor is measured in square units. Most areas are measured in *square meters.* A square meter equals the surface covered by a square one meter long on each side. It is slightly larger than a square yard. Smaller areas may be measured in *square centimeters* or *square millimeters.*

Land is sometimes measured in units called *hectares.* A hectare equals 10,000 square meters, or about $2\frac{1}{2}$ acres. Large land areas, such as cities and countries, are measured in *square kilometers.* One square kilometer equals about 247 acres, or about $\frac{3}{8}$ of a square mile.

Volume and capacity measurements tell how much space something occupies or encloses. A volume measurement tells the size of a box, and a capacity measurement tells how much the box can hold. Volume and capacity are both measured in cubic units, such as *cubic meters* or *cubic decimeters.* The volume of a box with each side 1 meter long equals 1 cubic meter. A cubic meter contains 1,000 cubic decimeters and equals about $1\frac{1}{3}$ cubic yards.

Most capacity measurements for liquids are made in units called *liters.* A liter equals a cubic decimeter and is slightly larger than a liquid quart. Smaller units include the *deciliter* ($\frac{1}{10}$ of a liter) and the *milliliter* ($\frac{1}{1,000}$ of a liter). A milliliter equals a cubic centimeter.

Weight and mass measurements. The mass of an object is not really the same as its weight because its weight changes with altitude. However, the two measurements are equal at sea level on the earth. The kilogram is a unit of mass. But most people who use the metric system think of the kilogram as a unit of weight.

A kilogram equals about $2\frac{1}{5}$ avoirdupois pounds. The *gram* is used for small weight measurements. A gram equals $\frac{1}{1,000}$ of a kilogram. Manufacturers and shippers weigh bulk goods in *metric tons.* A metric ton equals 1,000 kilograms, or about $1\frac{1}{10}$ short tons in the inch-pound system.

Time measurements. The metric system measures time just as the inch-pound system does for measurements longer than a second. For such measurements, the metric system does not follow the decimal system. For example, 60—not 100—seconds equal a minute, and 60 minutes equal an hour. Time measurements in both systems use a decimal arrangement for units longer than a year. Ten years equal a *decade,* 10 decades are a

The metric system at a glance

Length and distance

Length and distance measurements in the metric system are based on the meter. All units for length and distance are decimal fractions or multiples of the meter. Commonly used units include the millimeter, centimeter, meter, and kilometer.

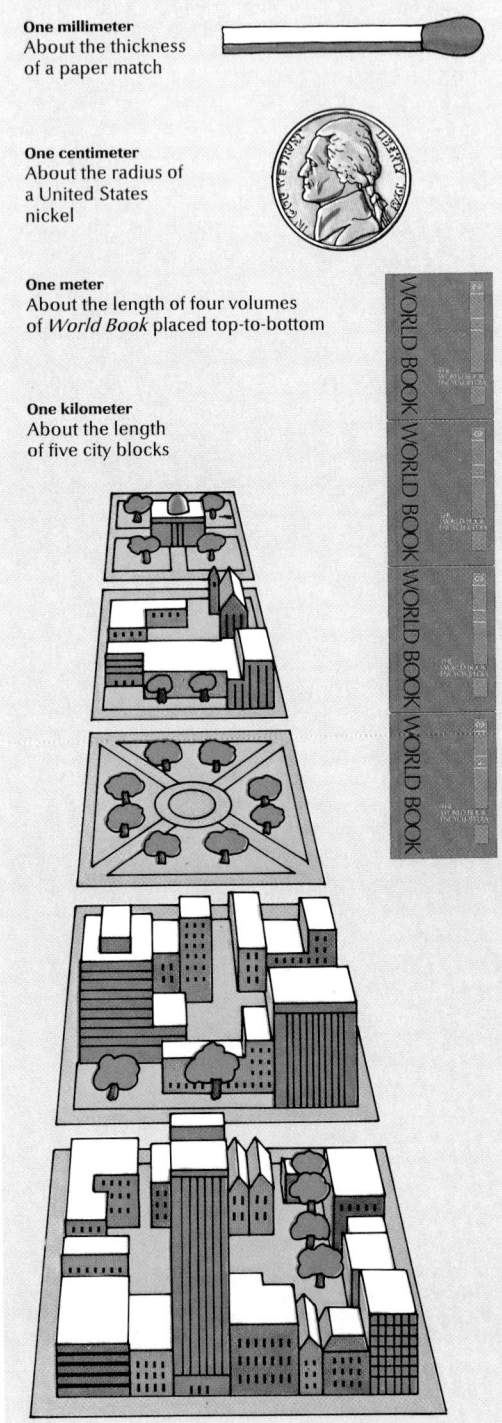

One millimeter
About the thickness of a paper match

One centimeter
About the radius of a United States nickel

One meter
About the length of four volumes of *World Book* placed top-to-bottom

One kilometer
About the length of five city blocks

Surface or area

Surface or area measurements in the metric system are also based on the meter. But area is measured in square units. Common area units include the square centimeter, square meter, hectare (10,000 square meters), and square kilometer.

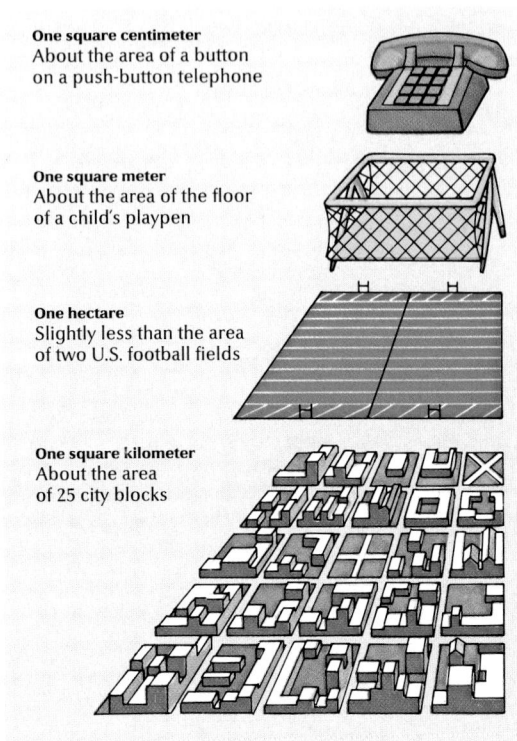

One square centimeter
About the area of a button on a push-button telephone

One square meter
About the area of the floor of a child's playpen

One hectare
Slightly less than the area of two U.S. football fields

One square kilometer
About the area of 25 city blocks

WORLD BOOK illustrations by George Suyeoka

Volume and capacity

Volume and capacity measurements in the metric system are based on the meter, but these measurements are made in cubic units. Common volume and capacity units include the cubic centimeter, liter (1,000 cubic centimeters), and cubic meter.

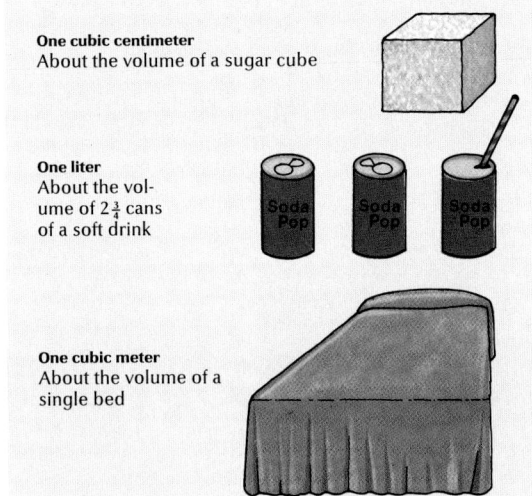

One cubic centimeter
About the volume of a sugar cube

One liter
About the volume of 2¾ cans of a soft drink

One cubic meter
About the volume of a single bed

The illustrations on these pages help show the size of the most common metric units. The metric conversion table will aid in the conversion of measurements into or out of the metric system.

Weight and mass

Weight measurement in the metric system is based on mass, the amount of matter an object contains. The base unit for mass in the metric system is the kilogram. Commonly used weight units include the gram (0.001 kilogram), the kilogram, and the metric ton (1,000 kilograms).

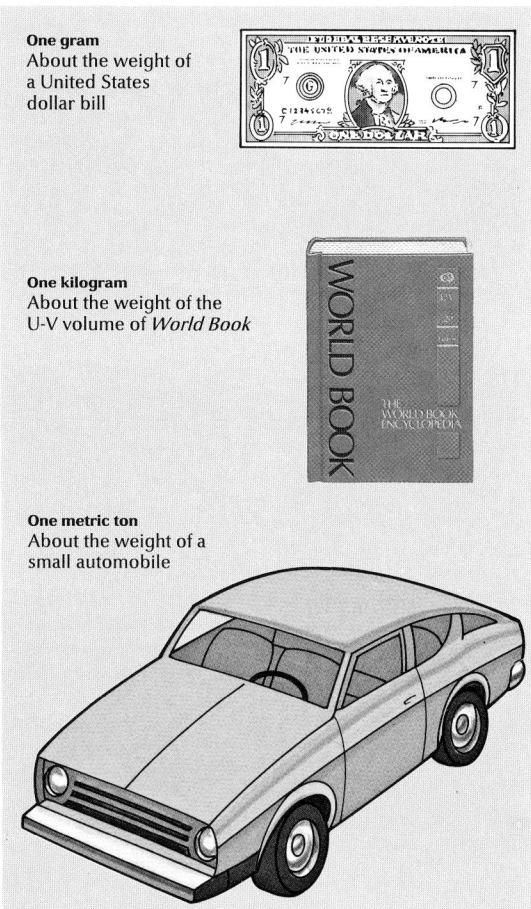

One gram
About the weight of a United States dollar bill

One kilogram
About the weight of the U-V volume of *World Book*

One metric ton
About the weight of a small automobile

Metric conversion table

When you know:	Multiply by:	To find:
Length and distance		
inches (in.)	2.540	centimeters*
feet (ft.)	30.480	centimeters*
yards (yd.)	0.914	meters†
miles (mi.)	1.609	kilometers†
millimeters (mm)	0.039	inches†
centimeters (cm)	0.394	inches†
meters (m)	1.094	yards†
kilometers (km)	0.621	miles†
Surface or area		
square inches (sq. in.)	6.452	square centimeters†
square feet (sq. ft.)	0.093	square meters†
square yards (sq. yd.)	0.836	square meters†
square miles (sq. mi.)	2.590	square kilometers†
acres	0.405	hectares†
square centimeters (cm²)	0.155	square inches†
square meters (m²)	1.196	square yards†
square kilometers (km²)	0.386	square miles†
hectares (ha)	2.471	acres†
Volume and capacity (Liquid)		
fluid ounces (fl. oz.)	29.574	milliliters†
pints (pt.), U.S.	0.473	liters†
pints (pt.), imperial	0.568	liters†
quarts (qt.), U.S.	0.946	liters†
quarts (qt.), imperial	1.137	liters†
gallons (gal.), U.S.	3.785	liters†
gallons (gal.), imperial	4.546	liters†
milliliters (ml)	0.034	fluid ounces†
liters (l)	2.113	pints, U.S.†
liters (l)	1.761	pints, imperial†
liters (l)	1.057	quarts, U.S.†
liters (l)	0.880	quarts, imperial†
liters (l)	0.264	gallons, U.S.†
liters (l)	0.220	gallons, imperial†
Weight and mass		
ounces (oz.)	28.350	grams†
pounds (lb.)	0.454	kilograms†
short tons	0.907	metric tons†
grams (g)	0.035	ounces†
kilograms (kg)	2.205	pounds†
metric tons (t)	1.102	short tons†
Temperature		
degrees Fahrenheit (°F)	$\frac{5}{9}$ (after subtracting 32)	degrees Celsius‡
degrees Celsius (°C)	$\frac{9}{5}$ (then add 32)	degrees Fahrenheit§

*Answer is exact.
†Answer is approximate.
‡Answer is exact only if number of degrees Fahrenheit minus 32 is evenly divisible by 9.
§Answer is exact only if number of degrees Celsius is evenly divisible by 5.

Temperature

Everyday temperature measurements in the metric system are made on the Celsius scale. This scale was once called the centigrade scale. Water freezes at 0 °C and boils at 100 °C.

Metric prefixes

These prefixes can be added to most metric units to increase or decrease their size. For example, a kilometer equals 1,000 meters. Centi, kilo, and milli are the most commonly used prefixes.

Prefix	Symbol	Increase or decrease in unit	
exa (*EHK suh*)	E	1,000,000,000,000,000,000	(One quintillion)
peta (*PEH tuh*)	P	1,000,000,000,000,000	(One quadrillion)
tera (*TEHR uh*)	T	1,000,000,000,000	(One trillion)
giga (*JIHG uh*)	G	1,000,000,000	(One billion)
mega (*MEHG uh*)	M	1,000,000	(One million)
kilo (*KIHL uh*)	k	1,000	(One thousand)
hecto (*HEHK tuh*)	h	100	(One hundred)
deka (*DEHK uh*)	da	10	(Ten)
deci (*DEHS uh*)	d	0.1	(One-tenth)
centi (*SEHN tuh*)	c	0.01	(One-hundredth)
milli (*MIHL uh*)	m	0.001	(One-thousandth)
micro (*MY kroh*)	μ	0.000001	(One-millionth)
nano (*NAY nuh*)	n	0.000000001	(One-billionth)
pico (*PY koh*)	p	0.000000000001	(One-trillionth)
femto (*FEHM toh*)	f	0.000000000000001	(One-quadrillionth)
atto (*AT toh*)	a	0.000000000000000001	(One-quintillionth)

Water at 0°C (ice)   Water at 100°C (steam)

century, and 10 centuries are a *millennium.* For more information about time measurement, see **Time.**

The metric system follows a decimal arrangement for time measurements shorter than a second. Scientists and others who work with electronic equipment, including computers and radar, use such measurements. For example, some electronic computers perform mathematical operations in *microseconds* and *nanoseconds.* A microsecond is $\frac{1}{1,000,000}$ of a second, and a nanosecond is $\frac{1}{1,000,000,000}$ of a second.

Temperature measurements. Most people who use the metric system have thermometers marked in degrees Celsius (°C). Water freezes at 0 °C and boils at 100 °C. The normal body temperature of human beings is 37 °C. Celsius has been the official name of the metric scale for temperature since 1948. But many people still call this scale by its old name of *centigrade scale.* The word *centigrade* means *divided into 100 parts.* The Celsius scale has 100 degrees between the freezing and boiling temperatures of water.

Scientists do not know of any limit on how high a temperature may be. The temperature at the center of the sun is about 15,000,000 °C, for example, but other stars may have an even higher temperature. However, nothing can have a temperature lower than -273.15 °C. This temperature is called *absolute zero.* It forms the basis of the *Kelvin scale* used by some scientists. One degree Celsius equals one Kelvin. Because the Kelvin scale begins at absolute zero, 0 K equals -273.15 °C, and 273.15 K equals 0 °C. See **Absolute zero.**

History

Before the development of the metric system, every nation used measurement units that had grown from local customs. For example, the English once used "three barleycorns, round and dry" as their standard for an inch. Grains of barley varied in size, of course—and so did the inch. As a result, no one could be sure that their measurements of the same thing would be equal.

During the 1600's, some people recognized the need for a single, accurate, worldwide measurement system. In 1670, Gabriel Mouton, a French clergyman, proposed a decimal measurement system. He based his unit of length on the length of one minute ($\frac{1}{21,600}$) of the earth's circumference. In 1671, Jean Picard, a French astronomer, proposed the length of a pendulum that swung once per second as the standard unit of length. Such a standard would have been more accurate than barleycorns because it was based on the physical laws of motion. In addition, a pendulum could have been duplicated easily to provide uniform measurement standards for everyone. Through the years, other people suggested various systems and standards of measurement.

The creation of the metric system. In 1790, the National Assembly of France asked the French Academy of Sciences to create a standard system of weights and measures. A commission appointed by the academy proposed a system that was both simple and scientific. This system became known as the metric system, and France officially adopted it in 1795. But the government did not require the French people to use the new units of measurement until 1840.

In the original metric system, the unit of length equaled a fraction of the earth's circumference. This fraction was $\frac{1}{10,000,000}$ of the distance from the North Pole to the equator along the line of longitude near Dunkerque, France; and Barcelona, Spain. The French scientists named this unit of length the *metre,* from the Greek word *metron,* meaning *a measure.*

The units for capacity and mass came from the meter.

Important dates in the development of the metric system

1670 Gabriel Mouton, a French clergyman, proposed a decimal system of measurement based on a fraction of the earth's circumference.

1671 Jean Picard, a French astronomer, proposed using the length of a pendulum swinging once each second as a standard unit of length.

1790 The National Assembly of France requested the French Academy of Sciences to develop a standard system of weights and measures. The system the academy developed became known as the metric system. Also in 1790, Thomas Jefferson, then U.S. secretary of state, recommended that the United States use a decimal system of measurement. Congress rejected the idea.

1795 France adopted the metric system but allowed people to continue using other measurement units.

1821 John Quincy Adams, then U.S. secretary of state, proposed conversion to the metric system. Congress again rejected the proposal.

1837 France passed a law that required all Frenchmen to begin using the metric system on Jan. 1, 1840.

1866 Congress legalized the use of the metric system in the United States but did not require that it be used.

1870-1875 An international conference on the metric system met to update the system and adopt new measurement standards for the kilogram and meter. Seventeen nations, including the United States, took part in the conference.

1875 The Treaty of the Meter, signed at the close of the 1870-1875 international conference set up a permanent organization, the International Bureau of Weights and Measures, to change the metric system as needed.

1889 New meter and kilogram standards based on those adopted by the 1870-1875 conference were made and sent to countries that signed the Treaty of the Meter.

1893 The United States began defining all its measurement units as fractions of the standard meter and kilogram.

1890's Attempts were made in Congress to change U.S. measurements to metric, but none were successful.

1957 The U.S. Army and Marine Corps adopted the metric system as the basis for their weapons and equipment.

1960 A General Conference of Weights and Measures held by countries using the metric system adopted a revised version of the system.

1965 Great Britain began a changeover to the metric system.

1970 Australia began a scheduled 10-year conversion to the metric system.

1971 A congressional study recommended that the United States make a planned conversion to the metric system.

1975 Canada began a gradual changeover to the metric system.

1975 The United States Congress passed the Metric Conversion Act, which called for a voluntary changeover to the metric system.

1983 A General Conference of Weights and Measures adopted a new measurement standard for the meter.

1988 The U.S. Congress passed the Omnibus Trade and Competitiveness Act. The bill amended the Metric Conversion Act of 1975 and included a provision that called for all federal government agencies to use the metric system for business transactions by the end of 1992.

The commission chose the cubic decimeter as the unit of fluid capacity and named it the liter. The scientists defined the unit for mass, the gram, as the mass of a cubic centimeter of water at the temperature where it weighs the most. That temperature is about 4 °C (39 °F).

The original measurement standards of the metric units have been replaced by more accurate ones, and other units have been added to the system. Whenever necessary, an international group of scientists holds a General Conference of Weights and Measures to revise the system. The General Conference of 1960 named the system Système International d'Unités.

International acceptance. Other nations began to convert to the metric system after 1840, when the French people were first required to use it. By 1850, Greece, the Netherlands, Spain, and parts of Italy had adopted the new units of measurement.

An international metric convention, held from 1870 to 1875, created measurement standards of greater accuracy for length and mass. Seventeen nations, including the United States, took part in this convention. In 1875, they signed the Treaty of the Meter, which set up a permanent organization to change the metric system as necessary. This organization, the International Bureau of Weights and Measures, is based near Paris.

By 1900, 35 nations had adopted the metric system. They included the major countries of continental Europe and South America. By the mid-1970's, almost every country in the world had either converted to the system or planned to do so. The United States is the only major country not to have adopted the metric system.

The United States and the metric system. In 1790, Secretary of State Thomas Jefferson recommended that the United States use a decimal measurement system. Congress rejected the recommendation. In 1821, Secretary of State John Quincy Adams also proposed conversion to the metric system. But Congress again turned down such action. At that time, most U.S. trade was with England and Canada, neither of which was considering changing its measurements. A conversion of U.S. measurements would have interfered with this trade.

The United States showed little interest in the metric system for more than 40 years following Adams' proposal. Meanwhile, the nation's industries developed machines and products based on inch-pound units. Until the mid-1900's, many industries opposed conversion to metric measurements. They believed such a step would require costly changes in their machines and manufacturing methods. In 1866, Congress made the metric system legal in the United States. But it took no action toward requiring the use of metric measurements.

In 1893, the United States based the yard and the pound on fractions of the international metric standards for the meter and the kilogram. But during the next 70 years, only a few metric measurements began to come into daily use. In the 1950's, pharmacists started to use metric units to fill prescriptions. In 1957, the U.S. Army and the Marine Corps began to measure in metric units. During the 1960's, because of the increasing number of foreign automobiles in the United States, many mechanics had to use tools based on the metric system. Also in the 1960's, the National Aeronautics and Space Administration (NASA) began to use metric units.

In 1965, Britain began a changeover to the metric system. Other members of the Commonwealth of Nations, including Canada, later decided to convert. These actions prompted a renewal of U.S. interest in the metric system.

In 1968, Congress authorized a three-year study of metric conversion. This study recommended a step-by-step conversion to the metric system during a period of 10 years. Such a planned conversion would help reduce the cost and problems of changing the nation's measurement system. In 1975, Congress passed a bill that established a policy of voluntary conversion to the metric system. Another bill, passed in 1988, amended the 1975 bill and made the metric system the preferred system of weights and measures for U.S. trade and commerce. In addition, the bill calls for agencies of the federal government to use the metric system for purchases, grants, and other business-related activities. By the end of 1992, this conversion had begun. The Office of Metric Programs in the U.S. Department of Commerce promotes the use of metric units by business and industry.

By the early 1990's, public use of metric units in the United States was still limited. However, U.S. businesses had begun making greater use of metric units, since they were competing in a global market based on the metric system. Today, all U.S. automobiles are designed to metric specifications. Commonly used metric instruments include millimeter wrenches and speedometers that record both miles and kilometers per hour.

Daniel V. De Simone

Related articles in *World Book* include:

Absolute zero	International Bureau	Mole
Ampere	of Weights and	Newton
Candela	Measures	Oersted
Celsius scale	Kilogram	Pascal
Centimeter	Kilometer	Weber
Dyne	Liter	Weights and
Gauss	Meter	measures
Gram	Micrometer	

Outline

I. Using the metric system
   A. The decimal arrange-   B. Metric measurement units
      ment
II. Common measurements
   A. Length and distance measurements
   B. Surface measurements
   C. Volume and capacity measurements
   D. Weight and mass measurements
   E. Time measurements
   F. Temperature measurements
III. History

Questions

Why is a decimal system of measurement easier to work with than a nondecimal system?
What are the seven base metric units?
What do the letters *SI* stand for?
What is a *derived unit*?
What prefix is used to increase a unit by 1,000?
Where was the metric system developed? When?
Why did U.S. industry oppose the metric system?
Where does the term *metric* come from?
What was Gabriel Mouton's proposal for a decimal unit of length?
What did the Treaty of the Meter accomplish?

Additional resources

Level I
Hirsch, S. Carl. *Meter Means Measure: The Story of the Metric System.* Viking, 1973.

Ross, Frank. *The Metric System: Measures for All Mankind.* Phillips, 1974.

Level II

Hahn, James and Lynn. *The Metric System.* Watts, 1975.

Hopkins, Robert A. *The International (SI) Metric System and How It Works.* 3rd ed. AMJ Pub., 1983.

Metroliner. See **Railroad** (Intercity trains).

Metronome, *MEHT ruh nohm,* is an instrument that beats time for musicians. The Dutch inventor Dietrich Winkel invented it. But the German Johann N. Mälzel patented it in 1816. The mechanical type consists of a wooden or plastic box with a pendulum. A movable counterweight is attached to the pendulum. The mechanism ticks as the pendulum moves. The lower the counterweight is set, the faster the machine ticks. Most modern metronomes are small electronic devices. They may tick, display a flashing light, or both.   Thomas W. Tunks

WORLD BOOK photo by Steinkamp/Ballogg

The metronome is a clocklike device with a pendulum that can be adjusted to make a ticking sound at various speeds. Metronomes mark time for people practicing on musical instruments.

Metropolitan is the title of a high-ranking clergyman in the Anglican, Eastern Orthodox, and Roman Catholic churches. He is the head of church province, diocese, or all the Christians in an important city. Like archbishops, metropolitans rank above bishops. They consult with bishops about matters other than regular affairs in the bishop's diocese. A metropolitan also calls and presides over church councils called *synods.* In some Eastern Orthodox Churches, the head of an independent national church is called a metropolitan. See **Archbishop; Patriarch.**   Ralph W. Quere

Metropolitan area consists of a central city and the developed area that surrounds it. The developed area may be made up of such jurisdictions as cities, bor-

oughs, towns, townships, or villages.

In the United States, a metropolitan area is officially called a *Metropolitan Statistical Area.* Two or more adjacent metropolitan statistical areas form a *Consolidated Metropolitan Statistical Area.* U.S. metropolitan areas have at least one city or urban area with a population of 50,000 or more, and include the entire county in which the city is located. Adjacent counties may be considered part of the area, depending on their population density and the number of workers who commute to jobs in the central county. The term *greater* applied to a city refers to a metropolitan area, such as Greater Paris. In England, clusters of small cities around a large city are called *metropolitan counties.*

In developed countries, most people live in metropolitan areas. In the United States, about 80 percent of the people live in the nation's 268 metropolitan statistical areas. In Canada, about 60 percent of the people reside in 25 metropolitan areas.

The development of suburbs

As cities grow, people move beyond official city boundaries, creating suburbs. This process of *suburbanization* has been going on since the late 1800's. Several factors contributed to the development of metropolitan areas. Originally, large numbers of people came from rural areas to central cities in search of employment. This population shift produced overcrowded cities, causing other people to move to outlying areas. The use of automobiles, together with the improvement of roads and highways, increased tremendously following the end of World War II in 1945. As a result, more and more people have settled in communities outside of central cities since the late 1940's.

By 1970, more people in U.S. metropolitan areas lived in suburbs than in central cities. But by the early 1980's, the rate of suburban growth had decreased for a number of reasons. For example, many people moved to the suburbs to avoid such problems of big cities as crime, housing shortages, and racial conflicts. However, as the suburbs grew larger, they developed the same problems. Urban revitalization programs drew some people back to central cities.

People who live in the suburbs of a central city have traditionally considered the city as their workplace because of its commercial and industrial activities. Suburbanites also use the city's cultural, professional, and recreational facilities and services. Since the 1950's, however, many businesses and industries have moved to the suburbs. Today, many suburbanites who once commuted to and from work in the city work, shop, and enjoy various recreational activities in the suburbs.

Problems of metropolitan areas

Government. Most metropolitan areas have no central government to handle problems that affect the entire area. In most cases, government is almost completely decentralized—that is, each city, town, village, or other community in the metropolitan area has its own government. Little or no relationship exists between these governments and that of the central city.

The metropolitan statistical areas in the United States contain such local governmental units as counties, townships, municipalities, school districts, and special districts. Each unit has considerable political independence and establishes its own policies. As a result, government in most metropolitan areas is characterized by overlapping authority, policy conflicts, and lack of cooperation in solving mutual problems.

Many people who live in a metropolitan area may be affected by government policies over which they have little or no control. For example, people who live in suburbs may vote in their suburb and, at the same time, own a business in the central city. Government policy decisions made in the city may affect the business, even though the suburbanite cannot vote on them.

Finances and taxation. The widespread movement from central cities to suburbs affects the financial position of all the communities involved. The central city experiences declining land values and the loss of tax revenues. Also, many people who move into the city are poor, and many who move out are wealthy. As a result, the city provides medical care and other services for large numbers of residents who cannot afford them. The relocation of industries and commercial activities to the suburbs deprives city residents of job opportunities and reduces the city's tax base. However, many suburban communities are almost completely residential. Such suburbs have few taxable businesses, and they therefore often have difficulty raising enough money to provide adequate levels of such essential services as police and fire protection and public education.

Many suburban residents use public facilities in the central city, including museums, parks, and sports arenas, all of which require expensive maintenance. Some cities have tried to tax suburban residents who work in the city or to charge nonresident fees for the use of city facilities. In most cases, suburbanites have successfully resisted such taxes. Some suburbs have attempted to impose a similar tax on city dwellers who work in the suburbs or use suburban facilities. Most of these attempts also have failed.

Property taxes are the major source of revenue for governmental units within a metropolitan area. As a result, the central city and its suburbs compete for such tax-paying developments as manufacturing plants, office buildings, and shopping centers. These types of developments pay high property taxes and use few expensive public services. But in recent years, many metropolitan areas have worked to slow or stop suburban growth in order to reduce the cost of maintaining roads, sewage systems, and other public utilities and to protect the suburban way of life.

Metropolitan area plans

Various types of plans have been devised in attempts to solve the governmental and financial problems of metropolitan areas. These plans try to provide efficient government and a well-balanced economic policy for an entire metropolitan area. In most cases, however, local governments want to retain control over such important activities as education, police and fire protection, and zoning. This desire for local political independence has hampered efforts to develop effective plans. In many countries, the national government and the state or provincial governments handle most issues concerning growth and development of metropolitan areas.

The chief programs used in providing more efficient government and public financing for metropolitan areas include (1) annexation, (2) extramural jurisdiction, (3) county government, (4) special districts, (5) metropolitan federation, and (6) tax sharing.

Annexation. Most cities grew to their present size through annexation, which involves absorbing the outlying areas. Today, however, suburban residents generally oppose this method because they do not want to lose governmental independence.

Extramural jurisdiction. Some states and provinces give central cities governmental control of areas outside their boundaries. For example, Alabama cities have powers for $1\frac{1}{2}$ or 3 miles (2.4 or 4.8 kilometers) outside their city limits, depending on their population. Powers of extramural jurisdiction, also called *extraterritorial powers,* include police protection and sanitary regula-

Metropolitan area of Denver

The Denver Metropolitan Statistical Area (MSA) covers five Colorado counties. The map at the right also shows three other MSA's—Boulder-Longmont, Greeley, and Colorado Springs.

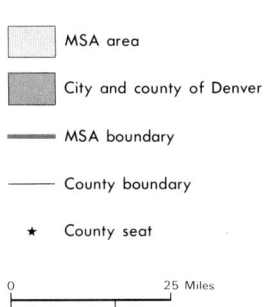

☐ MSA area

▨ City and county of Denver

━━ MSA boundary

── County boundary

★ County seat

0 ———— 25 Miles
0 ———— 25 Kilometers

WORLD BOOK map

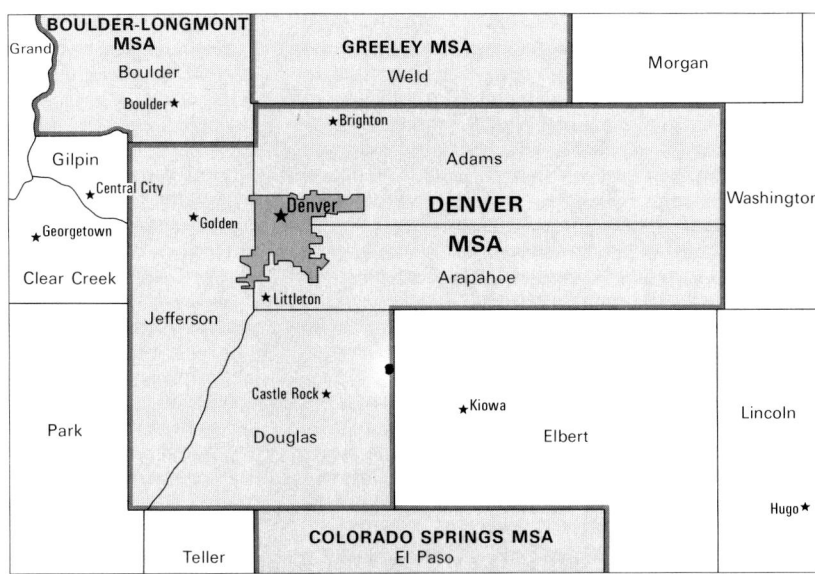

tion. They also may cover taxation of businesses and the control of subdivisions beyond city lines.

County government in some states and provinces provides urban services for areas outside city limits. For example, California has county governments that supply health and welfare assistance, police and fire protection, and other services to such areas.

A metropolitan county government provides urban services for an entire county, including central cities. Dade County, Florida, which includes Greater Miami, operates under a metropolitan county government plan. Voters from Miami and from other cities and districts in the metropolitan area elect members of a governing commission. The commission carries out plans for serving and developing the entire county. Municipalities handle only local affairs.

City-county government operates in a number of cities, including New York City, St. Louis, and San Francisco. It combines city and county functions but does not include suburban development.

Special districts, also called *municipal authorities,* consist of two or more local units in a metropolitan area. They provide one or more specific government services, such as sewage disposal and water distribution. The governing boards of special districts have the power to levy taxes and to spend public money. Many districts also use the revenue from services to pay for construction, maintenance, and operation of facilities.

Districts and authorities have led to increased governmental unity. But they have added to, rather than reduced, the number of governmental units in metropolitan areas. One of the largest and most successful municipal authorities is the Port Authority of New York and New Jersey. It handles port development and transportation within about 25 miles (40 kilometers) of New York City, in New York and New Jersey (see **Port Authority of New York and New Jersey**). The Metropolitan Water District of Southern California serves about 15 million people in 300 communities, including Los Angeles.

Metropolitan federation combines all the local governments of a metropolitan area into a unit called a *federated city.* The local units retain their own identities and carry on certain functions that they are best suited to handle, such as education, zoning, and police protection. The federated city administers the remaining functions for the entire metropolitan area. It has the taxing power to finance such functions, plus the authority to establish and carry out policies.

The Municipality of Metropolitan Toronto merges the city government with five suburban governments. This federation controls land use, road construction, police protection, public transportation, sewage disposal, water supply, and welfare services. The municipalities that belong to the federation are responsible for such functions as fire protection and health services. See **Toronto** (Government; History).

Tax sharing allows communities in a metropolitan area to share the costs and benefits of development. In a tax-sharing plan, part of the revenue a community gains from a new tax-producing development is distributed among other communities that are affected by the development. For example, the construction of a shopping center in one community may cause heavier traffic in neighboring communities. Tax sharing would help the

neighboring communities pay for the increased costs of maintaining their roads.

Since the late 1970's, many metropolitan areas have considered adopting tax-sharing plans. In the United States, such a plan operates in the Minneapolis-St. Paul metropolitan area. Under this plan, the communities contribute tax revenues to the plan according to the amount of increase in the *assessed* (estimated) value of business properties.   Louis H. Masotti

See also **City** (Metropolitan cities; table: 50 largest metropolitan areas); **Megalopolis; Suburb.**

Metropolitan Museum of Art in New York City is the largest art museum in the United States. It includes more than 2 million works of art. The city of New York owns the building, but the collections belong to a corporation that runs the museum under a charter granted in 1870. The museum offers concerts and lectures in a 700-seat auditorium. Its shops sell art books, posters, and reproductions of works of art from the collections.

The collections of ancient art include Egyptian prehistoric pottery, wall paintings, sculpture, and jewelry, and an original Egyptian tomb dated about 2450 B.C. Greek and Roman objects include vases and stone sculptures, bronzes, gems, jewelry, glass, and wall paintings. Etruscan art includes terra cotta work. Art from Mesopotamia, Persia, and Turkey is represented by sculptures, ivories, bronzes, and works in silver and gold.

The collections of Asian art include works from China, Japan, Korea, India, and Southeast Asia dating from 2000 B.C. to the present. They contain paintings, sculpture, ceramics, bronzes, jades, decorative arts, and textiles. The Chinese galleries include monumental Buddhist sculpture and a Chinese scholar's garden court. The collection of Islamic art is the largest in the world. An entire wing is devoted to the arts of Africa, the Pacific Islands, and the Americas.

The collections of European paintings date from the 1400's through the 1800's. The decorative arts collection dates from the Renaissance to the 1900's and includes entire rooms from the palaces and great houses of France, England, and Spain.

The American art collections contain paintings, prints, drawings, decorative arts, and architecture from the colonial period to the 1800's. The museum also has 24 period rooms dating from 1640 to a Frank Lloyd Wright living room built from 1912 to 1915.

Art of the 1900's includes paintings, sculpture, works on paper, and decorative arts. These items are displayed in 22 galleries.

The Uris Center is the center for the museum's educational activities. It offers a library, auditorium, and classrooms. The Costume Institute collection contains clothing from the 1600's to the present from Europe, Asia, Africa, and the Americas.

The Cloisters, located in Fort Tryon Park, is a branch of the museum devoted to medieval art. Its collections include paintings, tapestries, metalwork, sculpture, ivories, and stained glass. The Cloisters also features parts of monasteries and churches from France and Spain, and a lovely outdoor garden.

Critically reviewed by the Metropolitan Museum of Art

Metternich, *MEHT uhr nihk* (1773-1859), served as Austrian minister of foreign affairs from 1809 to 1848. He was the leading European statesman during most of that period, often called the *Age of Metternich.* Metternich was a political conservative who used his power both to protect the Austrian Empire and to support monarchs elsewhere against popular unrest. He was given the additional title of chancellor in 1821.

Metternich tried to maintain a balance of power in Europe. He played a major role at conferences of European leaders, beginning with the Congress of Vienna (1814-1815). This conference determined the rulers and boundaries of Europe after the defeat of Napoleon I. Metternich encouraged European powers to suppress liberal and nationalist activity. He employed a network of spies to inform him of political threats. Uprisings in Europe during 1830 weakened Metternich's power somewhat. He used strict censorship in an attempt to prevent the spread of revolutionary ideas to Austria. In 1848, however, revolution broke out in France and quickly spread to Austria and the rest of Europe. The people of Vienna demanded Metternich's resignation. Metternich resigned in March 1848 and fled to England. Metternich returned to Austria in 1851, but he never held office again.

Metternich was born in Koblenz, in what is now western Germany. His full name was Klemens Wenzel Nepomuk Lothar von Metternich. He began his diplomatic career in 1801 as Austrian minister to Dresden. His marriage to Princess Eleanore Kaunitz, granddaughter of the Austrian chancellor, aided his rise to power. The Austrian emperor gave him the title Prince von Metternich in 1813.   Peter N. Stearns

See also **Austria** (Metternich and revolution); **Vienna, Congress of; Revolution of 1848.**

Meuse River, *myooz,* rises in the Langres Plateau of eastern France, and flows north past Verdun through the Ardennes highlands. The river then flows northeast through Belgium past Namur and Liège. North of Liège, the river enters the Netherlands. Here, it makes a sweeping curve northwest and empties into the North Sea south of Rotterdam. The Meuse River is 575 miles (925 kilometers) long. In Belgium and the Netherlands, it is called the Maas.

Several navigable canals join the Meuse River along its course. Near Toul, France, the Meuse connects with the Marne-Rhine Canal. At Liège, the river is linked with the Albert Canal, which goes to Antwerp. At Maastricht, the Meuse River meets the Juliana Canal.   Hugh D. Clout

Mexicali, *MEHK sih KAL ee* or *MEH hee KAH lee* (pop. 510,664), is the capital and largest city of the Mexican state of Baja California Norte. Mexicali lies across the border from Calexico, Calif. For location, see **Mexico** (political map). The names of both cities are combinations of the words *Mexico* and *California.*

Mexicali was founded in 1903. Today, the city is a center of tourism. Tourists enjoy Mexicali's bullfights, rodeos, dune-buggy races, handicraft exhibits, Mexican and Oriental restaurants, and exclusive shopping district. The city also has a historical museum and numerous examples of modern and old Spanish-style architecture.   Julian C. Bridges

Mexican Americans. See Hispanic Americans.
Mexican bean beetle. See Bean beetle.
Mexican hairless is a dog that has no coat of hair. Its skin is bare, except for a little tuft of hair on its forehead

and a slight fuzz along its tail. The skin is a spotted, pinkish color. A Mexican hairless weighs about 12 pounds (5 kilograms). It has a narrow head and a pointed nose. Its body is lightly built, with a rounded back and a long tail. The Mexican hairless probably originated in China in the 1300's. It was first imported into Mexico by sailors.   Critically reviewed by the American Kennel Club

Mexican turnip. See Jicama.
Mexican War (1846-1848) was fought between the United States and Mexico over disagreements that had been accumulating for two decades. In the course of the war, United States forces invaded Mexico and occupied the capital, Mexico City. By the Treaty of Guadalupe Hidalgo, the United States acquired from Mexico the regions of California, Nevada, and Utah, most of Arizona and New Mexico, and parts of Colorado and Wyoming. But many historians believe the war was an unnecessary attack on a weaker nation.

Causes of the war

Background of the war. In 1835, Texas revolted against the Mexican government, which then controlled the region. Texans established the Republic of Texas in 1836, but Mexico refused to recognize Texas' independence. The Mexican government warned the United States that if Texas were admitted to the Union, Mexico would break off diplomatic relations with the United States. James K. Polk was elected U.S. President in 1844. He favored the expansion of U.S. territory and supported the annexation of Texas. Texas was made a state in 1845, and Mexico broke off relations with the United States. At this point, the dispute could have been settled by peaceful means. But the United States wanted additional Mexican territory, and other quarrels developed.

One of these disputes was the question of the boundary between Texas and Mexico. Texas claimed the Rio Grande as its southwestern border. Mexico said that Texas had never extended farther than the Nueces River. Also, the U.S. government claimed that Mexico owed U.S. citizens about $3 million to make up for lives and

WORLD BOOK map

Campaigns of the Mexican War took place chiefly in Mexico, California, and Texas. The war ended soon after United States troops led by Major General Winfield Scott won a series of major battles and occupied Mexico City.

property that had been lost in Mexico since Mexico's war for independence from Spain ended in 1821. By the 1840's, many Americans demanded that the United States collect these debts by force.

More important was a growing feeling in the United States that the country had a "manifest destiny" to expand westward into new lands (see **Manifest destiny**). The westward movement had brought Americans into Mexican territory, especially California. Mexico was too weak to control or populate its northern territories. Both American and Mexican inhabitants were discontented with Mexican rule. California seemed almost ready to declare itself independent.

Events leading up to the war. In the fall of 1845, President Polk sent John Slidell to Mexico as American minister. Slidell was to offer Mexico $25 million and cancel all claims for damages if Mexico would accept the Rio Grande boundary and sell New Mexico and California to the United States. If Mexico refused to sell the territories, Slidell was to offer to cancel the claims on condition that Mexico agreed to the Rio Grande boundary. While Slidell was in Mexico, a new Mexican president came to power. Both the old and new presidents were afraid their enemies would denounce them as cowards if they made concessions to the United States. They refused to see Slidell, who came home and told Polk that Mexico needed to be "chastised."

Meanwhile, Polk had ordered Major General Zachary Taylor, who was stationed with about 4,000 men on the Nueces River, to advance to the Rio Grande. Taylor reached the river in April 1846. On April 25, a party of Mexican soldiers surprised and defeated a small group of American cavalry just north of the Rio Grande.

Polk had wanted to ask Congress to declare war on Mexico. The news of the battle gave him the chance to say that Mexico had "invaded our territory and shed American blood on American soil." In reality, Mexico had as good a claim as the United States to the soil where the blood was shed. But on May 13, 1846, Congress declared war on Mexico.

The war

The Americans had two aims. They wanted to add to the United States the territory that Mexico had been

asked to sell. They also wished to invade Mexico to force the Mexicans to accept the loss of the territory.

The occupation of New Mexico and California. In June 1846, General Stephen W. Kearny set out with about 1,700 troops from Fort Leavenworth, Kans., to capture New Mexico. In August, the expedition entered the New Mexican town of Santa Fe and took control of New Mexico. The next month, Kearny pushed across the desert to California.

Meanwhile, in June 1846, a group of American settlers led by U.S. Army officer John C. Frémont revolted in California against the Mexican government. This rebellion became known as the Bear Flag Revolt because of the portrayal of a grizzly bear on the settlers' flag. In July, U.S. naval forces under Commodore John D. Sloat captured the California town of Monterey and occupied the San Francisco area. On December 6, Kearny led about 100 troops in the bloody Battle of San Pasqual near San Diego. Reinforcements from San Diego helped save the small American army. In January 1847, U.S. troops under Kearny and Commodore Robert F. Stockton of the Navy won the Battle of San Gabriel near Los Angeles. This victory completed the American conquest of California.

Taylor's campaign. Before war officially began, General Zachary Taylor had driven the Mexicans across the lower Rio Grande to Matamoros in the two battles of Palo Alto and Resaca de la Palma. These battles occurred on May 8 and 9, 1846. On May 18, Taylor crossed the river and occupied Matamoros. After waiting for new troops, he moved his army up the river and marched against the important city of Monterrey. Monterrey fell on September 24, after a hard-fought battle. Before the end of the year, Taylor had occupied Saltillo and Victoria, important towns of northeastern Mexico. However, Mexico still refused to negotiate with the United States.

Polk and his advisers decided to land an army at Veracruz, on the east coast, and strike a blow at Mexico City. Many of Taylor's best troops were ordered to join Major General Winfield Scott, who was placed in charge of the new campaign. President Antonio López de Santa Anna of Mexico commanded the Mexican Army. He learned of the American plans and immediately led a large army against Taylor at Buena Vista, in the mountains beyond Saltillo. Although the Mexican forces nearly overran the U.S. positions, Taylor's troops eventually defeated them. General Taylor became a hero because of his victories and was elected President of the United States in 1848.

Doniphan's victories. In December 1846, Colonel Alexander W. Doniphan led about 850 troops south from Santa Fe to capture the Mexican city of Chihuahua. The American troops defeated a Mexican army at El Brazito on Christmas Day. Doniphan's army won the furious Battle of the Sacramento, fought just outside Chihuahua on Feb. 28, 1847. The Americans occupied the city on March 1.

Scott's campaign. General Scott was at this time the officer of highest rank in the United States Army. With a force of about 10,000 men, he landed near Veracruz on March 9, 1847. Twenty days later he captured the city, and on April 8 he began his advance toward the Mexican capital. The American army stormed a mountain pass at Cerro Gordo on April 17 and 18 and pushed on. Near Mexico City, American troops fought and won the

The Mexican Cession was the land Mexico *ceded* (gave up) to the United States in the Mexican War. The cession covered what are now California, Nevada, Utah, and parts of four other states.

WORLD BOOK map

battles of Contreras and Churubusco on August 19 and 20. The Mexican Army was superior in numbers but poorly equipped and poorly led.

After a two weeks' armistice, the Americans won a battle at Molino del Rey and stormed and captured the hilltop fortress of Chapultepec. On the following day the Americans marched into Mexico City.

The peace treaty. Despite all the American victories, Mexico refused to negotiate a peace treaty. In April 1847, Polk had sent Nicholas P. Trist, Chief Clerk of the Department of State, to join Scott's army in Mexico and attempt to open diplomatic negotiations with Santa Anna. When the armistice of August failed, the President recalled Trist. But Santa Anna resigned shortly after Scott entered the Mexican capital. Mexico established a new government, and it feared that it might lose even more territory if it did not accept the American demands. At the request of the Mexican leaders and General Scott, Trist agreed to remain in Mexico against Polk's orders and negotiate a settlement.

The treaty was signed on Feb. 2, 1848, at the village of Guadalupe Hidalgo, near Mexico City. By this time, many people in the United States wanted to annex all Mexico. But the treaty required Mexico to give up only the territory Polk had originally asked for. The United States paid Mexico $15 million for this territory, known as the Mexican Cession. In 1853, the Gadsden Purchase gave an additional 29,640 square miles (76,767 square kilometers) to the United States (see **Gadsden Purchase**).

Results of the war. The United States gained more than 525,000 square miles (1,360,000 square kilometers) of territory as a result of the Mexican War. But the war also revived the quarrels over slavery. Here was new territory. Was it to be slave or free? The Compromise of 1850 made California a free state and established the principle of "popular sovereignty." That meant letting the people of a territory decide whether it would be slave or free. However, popular sovereignty later led to bitter disagreement and became one of the underlying causes of the American Civil War. See **Compromise of 1850; Popular sovereignty.**

The Mexican War gave training to many officers who later fought in the Civil War. Civil War officers who also fought in the Mexican War included Ulysses S. Grant, William T. Sherman, George B. McClellan, George Gordon Meade, Robert E. Lee, Stonewall Jackson, and Jefferson Davis.

Principal battles

The chief battles of the Mexican War included:

Palo Alto, *PAL oh AL toh,* was one of the earliest battles of the war. General Taylor's troops defeated Mexican forces under General Mariano Arista on May 8, 1846, on a plain northeast of Brownsville, Tex.

Resaca de la Palma, *ray SAH kuh day lah PAHL muh.* A 2,300-man army under Taylor crushed 5,000 Mexican soldiers under Arista in Cameron County, near Brownsville, Tex., on May 9, 1846. General Taylor's two victories allowed him to cross the Rio Grande and to invade Mexico.

Buena Vista, *BWAY nah VEES tah.* Near the ranch of Buena Vista, Mexico, Taylor's force of about 5,000 men defended a narrow mountain pass against Santa Anna's army made up of from 16,000 to 20,000 men. Through this battle, fought on Feb. 22 and 23, 1847, the American forces established their hold on northeastern Mexico.

Cerro Gordo, *SEHR oh GAWR doh,* ranks among the most important battles the Americans fought on the march from Veracruz to Mexico City. A mountain pass near Jalapa, Cerro Gordo lies 60 miles (97 kilometers) northwest of Veracruz. General Scott's 9,000-man force attacked 13,000 Mexicans under Santa Anna, and forced them to flee. The battle, fought on April 17 and 18, 1847, cleared the way to Mexico City.

Churubusco, *CHOO roo VOOS koh.* In the small village of Churubusco, 6 miles (10 kilometers) south of Mexico City, Scott's invading army won another major victory on Aug. 20, 1847. Scott's soldiers stormed the fortified camp of Contreras, then attacked the Mexican force at Churubusco. The Mexicans finally fled, and sought refuge within the walls of the capital city. The Americans had about 9,000 men in the battle; the Mexicans, about 30,000.

Chapultepec, *chuh PUHL tuh PEHK,* was the last battle of the war before the capture of Mexico City. On Sept. 12, 1847, Scott's men attacked Chapultepec, a fortified hill guarding the city gates. The attacks continued the following day until the Mexicans retreated to Mexico City. On September 14, Scott's troops entered the Mexican capital.   Joseph A. Stout, Jr.

Related articles in *World Book* include:

Davis, Jefferson
Frémont, John C.
Grant, Ulysses S. (Early Army career)
Guadalupe Hidalgo, Treaty of
Jackson, Stonewall
Lee, Robert E. (The Mexican War)
McClellan, George B.

Mexico (War with Texas and the U.S.)
Polk, James K.
Santa Anna, Antonio L. de
Scott, Winfield
Taylor, Zachary
Texas (History)
Wilmot Proviso

Additional resources

De Voto, Bernard A. *The Year of Decision: 1846.* Little, Brown, 1943. Classic study of the year the U.S. went to war.
Johannsen, Robert W. *To the Halls of the Montezumas: The Mexican War in the American Imagination.* Oxford, 1985.
Lawson, Don. *The United States in the Mexican War.* Abelard-Schuman, 1976. Suitable for younger readers.
Smith, Justin H. *The War with Mexico.* 2 vols. Peter Smith, 1963. First published in 1919. A classic study.

Bettmann Archive
The Battle of Palo Alto was one of the earliest battles of the war. General Zachary Taylor's troops defeated the Mexicans near Brownsville, Tex., five days before the war officially began.

© E. R. Degginger, Bruce Coleman Inc.

The rugged mountains of Mexico's Sierra Madre Occidental contain deep, steep-walled canyons carved by swiftly flowing streams. Some regions are so wild that they have not been explored on foot. The mountain range borders the western edge of Mexico's wide Central Plateau.

Mexico

Mexico is the northernmost country of Latin America. It lies just south of the United States. The Rio Grande forms about two-thirds of the boundary between Mexico and the United States. Among all the countries of the Western Hemisphere, only the United States and Brazil have more people than Mexico. Mexico City is the capital and largest city of Mexico. It also has the world's largest metropolitan area population.

To understand Mexico, it is necessary to view the nation's long early history. Hundreds of years ago, the Indians of Mexico built large cities, developed a calendar, invented a counting system, and used a form of writing. The last Indian empire in Mexico—that of the Aztec—fell to Spanish invaders in 1521. For the next 300 years, Mexico was a Spanish colony. The Spaniards took Mexico's riches, and the Indians remained poor and uneducated. But the Spaniards also introduced many changes in farming, government, industry, and religion.

During the Spanish colonial period, a third group of people developed in Mexico. These people, who had both Indian and white ancestors, became known as *mestizos*. Today, the great majority of Mexicans are

The contributors of this article are Roderic A. Camp, Professor at the Latin American Studies Center, Tulane University and author of Intellectuals and the State in Twentieth-Century Mexico; *and James D. Riley, Associate Professor of History at the Catholic University of America and author of* Hacendados Jesuitas en Mexico.

mestizos. Some of them think of the Spaniards as intruders and take great pride in their Indian ancestry. A number of government programs stress the Indian role in Mexican culture. In 1949, the government made an Indian the symbol of Mexican nationality. The Indian was Cuauhtémoc, the last Aztec emperor. Cuauhtémoc's bravery under torture by the Spanish made him a Mexican hero.

Few other countries have so wide a variety of landscapes and climates within such short distances of one another. Towering mountains and high, rolling plateaus cover more than two-thirds of Mexico. The climate, land formation, and plant life in these rugged highlands may vary greatly within a short distance. Mexico also has tropical forests, dry deserts, and fertile valleys.

Manufacturing, agriculture, mining, and tourism are all important to Mexico's economy. Leading manufactured products include automobiles, cement, chemicals, clothing, processed foods, and steel. Crops are grown on only about an eighth of Mexico's land. The rest of the land is too dry, mountainous, or otherwise unsuitable for crops. However, Mexico is one of the world's leading producers of cacao beans, coffee, corn, oranges, and sugar cane.

Mexico is rich in minerals. It is the leading producer of silver in the world. The country also has large deposits of copper, gold, lead, salt, and sulfur. Petroleum production has long been important in Mexico. During the 1970's, vast, newly discovered deposits of petroleum greatly increased the importance of the country's petro-

© Harvey Lloyd, The Stock Market

Mexico City is the capital of Mexico and the nation's leading center of culture, industry, and transportation. It ranks as the world's largest metropolitan area in population.

© Steven D. Elmore, The Stock Market

Ruins of an ancient Maya temple stand at Palenque in the state of Chiapas. The temple was built about A.D. 650, during a period when great Indian civilizations thrived in Mexico.

leum industry. More than 6 million tourists visit Mexico each year. The money they spend contributes to the nation's economy.

The Mexicans gained independence from Spain in 1821. A social revolution began in 1910, when the people of Mexico started a long struggle for social justice and economic progress. During this struggle, the government took over huge, privately owned farmlands and divided them among millions of landless farmers. The government established a national school system to promote education, and it has built many hospitals and housing projects.

Since the 1940's, the government has especially encouraged the development of manufacturing and petroleum production. But all these changes have not kept up with Mexico's rapid population growth, and the country faces increasingly difficult economic and social problems. More than a third of the people still live in poverty, and the government keeps expanding its programs to help them.

Government

Mexico is a federal republic with an executive branch, a legislative branch, and a judicial branch or court system. The executive branch, headed by a president, is the decision-making center of the government. It establishes government policies, proposes laws, and controls the distribution of federal tax revenues. Mexico has 31 states and 1 federal district. Each state has an elected governor and legislature. The president appoints the

governor of the Federal District. All Mexicans who are at least 18 years old can vote.

National government. Mexico's president has tremendous influence over the government. All prominent political figures in the executive branch depend indirectly on the president for their jobs. The president introduces many pieces of legislation. Many presidents also have used constitutional amendments to support government policies.

The president appoints a cabinet that directs government operations. Important cabinet members include the secretary of government and the secretary of planning and federal budget. The president is elected by the people to a six-year term and may serve only one term of office. If the president does not finish the term, the legislature chooses a temporary president to serve until a special or regular presidential election is held.

Mexico's legislature is called the General Congress. It consists of a Senate and a Chamber of Deputies. The Senate has 64 members who are elected to six-year terms. The Chamber of Deputies has 500 members. Three hundred of the deputies are elected from the country's electoral districts. The remaining 200 seats are filled by deputies who do not represent a particular electoral district. Members of the Chamber of Deputies serve three-year terms. Members of the General Congress can serve more than one term, but they may not serve consecutive terms.

Local government. State governors are elected by the people to six-year terms and state legislators to

Mexico in brief

General information

Capital: Mexico City.

Official language: Spanish. But about 7 per cent of Mexicans use Náhuatl, Maya, Zapotec, or some other American Indian language.

Official name: *Estados Unidos Mexicanos* (United Mexican States).

National anthem: "Himno Nacional de México" ("National Anthem of Mexico").

Largest cities: (1980 census; 1988 estimate for Mexico City)
Mexico City (10,263,275)
Guadalajara (1,626,152)
Netzahualcóyotl (1,341,230)
Monterrey (1,090,009)
Puebla (835,759)
Ecatepec (784,507)

Flag Research Center

Mexico's flag, adopted in 1821, features a version of the country's coat of arms. The green stands for independence, white for religion, and red for union.

Coat of arms. A legend says the Aztec Indians built their capital Tenochtitlan (now Mexico City) where they saw an eagle perched on a cactus and devouring a snake.

Land and climate

Land: Mexico lies in North America. It is bordered by the United States on the north and by Guatemala and Belize on the southeast. The Gulf of Mexico and the Caribbean Sea lie to the east; the Pacific Ocean to the west and south. A chain of high volcanic mountains extends east-west across southern Mexico, just south of Mexico City. Lower mountain chains extend northwestward from each end of the volcanic chain, forming a great U-shape of mountains. Much of north-central Mexico is a high plateau rimmed by these mountain ranges. The Pacific Coast in the far south is rugged and has densely forested areas. The long peninsula of Baja California in the northwest is mostly desert with some mountains. The Yucatán Peninsula in the southeast is flat and forested. Mexico's chief rivers are the Rio Grande (at the U.S. border) and the Balsas.

Area: 756,066 sq. mi. (1,958,201 km²). *Greatest distances—* north-south, 1,250 mi. (2,012 km); east-west, 1,900 mi. (3,060 km). *Coastline*—6,320 mi. (10,170 km).

Elevation: *Highest*—Pico de Orizaba (also called Citlaltépetl), 18,410 ft. (5,610 m). *Lowest*—near Mexicali, 33 ft. (10 m) below sea level.

Climate: Northwest and north-central Mexico are mostly desert, with hot summers and cool to mild winters. The northeast coast has moderate rainfall with mild winters and warm summers. Central Mexico is dry, with temperatures varying according to altitude. High locations, such as Mexico City, have mild temperatures year-round. Low-altitude locations are warmer. Southern Mexico, including Yucatán, is warm and moist year-round.

Government

Form of government: Presidential democracy.

Chief executive: President (elected to 6-year term).

Legislature: Congress of two houses—64-member Senate and 500-member Chamber of Deputies.

Judiciary: Highest court is the Supreme Court of Justice.

Political subdivisions: 31 states, 1 federal district.

People

Population: *1994 estimate*—95,939,000; *1990 census*—81,140,922. *1999 estimate*—105,147,000.

Population density: 127 persons per sq. mi. (49 per km²).

Distribution: 75 per cent urban, 25 per cent rural.

Major ethnic/national groups: Almost entirely Mexican. Most Mexicans are of mixed American Indian and Spanish ancestry; some are entirely Indian or entirely of European descent; a few have partly black or East Asian ancestry.

Major religions: More than 90 per cent Roman Catholic; some Protestants, Jews, and American Indian religions.

Population trend

Millions

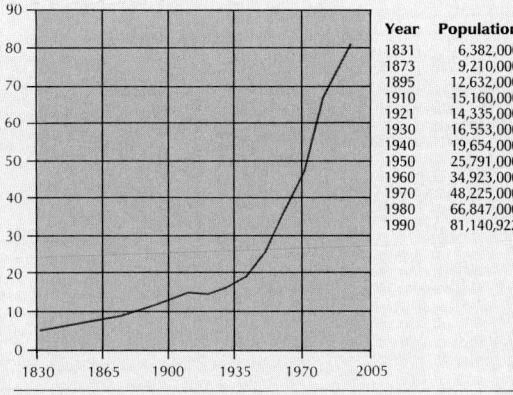

Year	Population
1831	6,382,000
1873	9,210,000
1895	12,632,000
1910	15,160,000
1921	14,335,000
1930	16,553,000
1940	19,654,000
1950	25,791,000
1960	34,923,000
1970	48,225,000
1980	66,847,000
1990	81,140,922

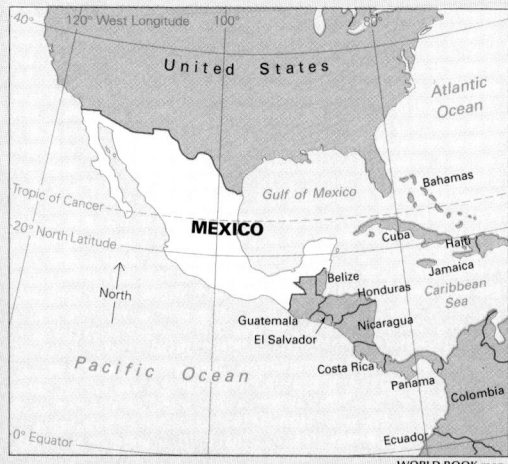

WORLD BOOK map

Economy

Chief products: *Agriculture*—corn, beef cattle, milk, wheat, coffee. *Manufacturing*—processed foods, motor vehicles, iron and steel. *Mining*—petroleum, natural gas, iron ore.

Money: *Basic unit*—new peso. For value in U.S. dollars, see Money (table: Exchange rates).

Gross national product: *1987 total GNP*—$149,395,000,000. *1987 GNP per capita*—$1,820.

Foreign trade: *Major exported goods*—petroleum, motor vehicles and engines, coffee. *Value of exported goods and services*—$32,444,000,000 (1988). *Major imported goods*—industrial machinery, electric and electronic equipment, motor vehicles and parts. *Value of imported goods and services*—$35,349,000,000 (1988). *Main trading partners*—United States, Japan, Spain, Germany.

three-year terms. The president can remove governors from office with the approval of the Senate. Each state is divided into *municipios* (townships). Each municipio has a president and a council elected to three-year terms.

Less than 10 per cent of all tax revenues go directly to state and local agencies. State agencies depend on the national government, and local authorities on state agencies, for funds to carry out public works projects.

Politics. Mexico's dominant political party is the Partido Revolucionario Institucional (Institutional Revolutionary Party), also known as the PRI. The PRI considers itself to be the official promoter of the economic and social goals of the Mexican Revolution. The party was established in 1929 as the *Partido Nacional Revolucionario* (National Revolutionary Party).

Until 1988, the PRI enjoyed nearly absolute domination of Mexican elections. But in 1988 elections, the PRI suffered a setback when opposition candidates won almost half the seats in the Chamber of Deputies, and nearly won the presidency. In 1991 elections, however, the PRI regained a large majority in the Chamber of Deputies. The strongest opposition parties are the *Partido de Acción Nacional* (National Action Party), and the *Partido de la Revolución Democrática* (Democratic Revolutionary Party).

Courts. The highest court in Mexico is the Supreme Court of Justice. It has 21 members and several alternates, all of whom are appointed by the president. The Supreme Court selects members of a circuit and district court system. The highest court in each state is a Superior Court of Justice.

The courts rarely declare a law unconstitutional and generally support the president's policies. But Mexicans may use the courts to protect their individual rights through an *amparo* (protection) procedure. In amparo cases, the courts may decide that a law has resulted in unfair treatment and that an exception should be made, but the law in question is not changed. However, most Mexicans cannot afford to use the legal process.

Armed forces. About 138,000 men and women serve in Mexico's army, navy, and air force. The army is the largest branch of the armed forces. It has about 105,000 members. Mexican men are required to serve part-time for a year in the army after reaching the age of 18.

People

Population. Mexico has about 96 million people. Its population is increasing about $2\frac{1}{4}$ per cent a year, as a result of a traditionally high birth rate and a sharply reduced death rate. About 55 per cent of Mexico's population is under 20 years of age.

Since the early 1950's, improved living conditions and expanded health services have cut the death rate by about two-thirds. The relatively young population and its high rate of growth have placed tremendous pressure on such services as education, health care, and social security.

The strain on basic services is especially serious in urban centers. Many cities lack adequate housing, clean drinking water, and public transportation. Since 1970, the most rapid population growth has occurred in the states of México, Morelos, Campeche, and Quintana Roo.

The high rate of population growth has contributed to a shortage of jobs in Mexico. During the 1980's, far more people entered the labor force than retired, while the economy experienced little growth. This situation has led to a high rate of unemployment. It has also stimulated increasing migration of Mexicans to the United States.

Ancestry. The great majority of the Mexican people are *mestizos* (people of mixed white and Indian ancestry). Their white ancestors were mostly Spaniards who came to what is now Mexico during and after the Spanish conquest of 1519-1521. Their Indian ancestors were living in the region when the Spaniards arrived. Blacks and some Asians are also part of the Mexican population. The nation has some Indians and whites of unmixed ancestry. But most Mexicans think of themselves as mestizos. Being a mestizo is generally a matter of national pride. Most of Mexico's political, business, intellectual, and military leaders are mestizos.

Being an Indian in Mexico does not depend chiefly on ancestry. It is mostly a matter of way of life and point of view. For example, Mexicans are considered Indians if they speak an Indian language, wear Indian clothes, and live in a village where the people call themselves Indians. This is true even if they are actually mestizo or white. In some regions, such as Oaxaca and Yucatán, Indian culture influences the life style of the mestizo population.

Language. Almost all Mexicans speak Spanish, the official language of Mexico and nearly all other Latin-American countries. Many words that are used in the United States came from Mexico. They include *canyon, corral, desperado, lariat, lasso, macho, patio, político, rodeo,* and *stampede.*

Most Mexican Indians speak Spanish in addition to their own ancient language. However, more than 5 million Mexican Indians primarily use an Indian language in daily life. The major Indian languages include Maya, Mixtec, Náhuatl, Otomí, Tarascan, and Zapotec. See **Spanish language.**

Way of life

The way of life in Mexico includes many features from the nation's long Indian past and the Spanish colonial period. But Mexico has changed rapidly during the 1900's. In many ways, life in its larger cities has become similar to that in the neighboring United States. Mexican villagers follow the older way of life more than the city people do. Even in the villages, however, government economic and educational programs are doing much to modernize the people's lives. These programs are bringing the Indian villagers into the general life of Mexico, and making them think of themselves as Mexicans rather than Indians.

Mexican households consist of an average of five or six people. In many homes, several generations of the same family live together. Many women in the cities have jobs, and the women who live in farm areas often help cultivate the fields. Mexican girls do not have as much individual freedom as do girls in the United States and Canada. Farm boys work in the fields, and many young people in the cities have part-time or full-time jobs.

City life. About three-fourths of the people of Mexico live in cities and towns with populations of at least 2,500.

9   **10**   **11**   **12**   **13**   **14**   **15**   **16**

Mexico
political map

- National park (N.P.)
- International boundary
- State boundary
- Expressway
- Other road
- Railroad
- ⊛ National capital
- ★ State capital
- • Other city or town
- □ Ruin

WORLD BOOK map

A
B
C
D
E
F
(C
I

UNITED STATES / Texas

Sherman
Denton
Graham
Fort Worth
Dallas
Corsicana
Tyler
Snyder
Sweetwater
Abilene
Brownwood
Waco
L. Whitney
Palestine
Lufkin
Toledo Bend Res.
San Angelo
Colorado
Killeen
Temple
Huntsville
Bryan
Sam Rayburn Res.
Kerrville
★ Austin
L. Travis
Houston
Beaumont
Port Arthur
San Antonio
Bay City
Galveston
Victoria
Freeport
Port Lavaca
Matagorda I.
San Jose I.
Corpus Christi
Padre I.

Arkansas
Texarkana
Longview
Shreveport
Monroe
Vicksburg
Meridian
Jackson
Mississippi
Louisiana
Alexandria
Natchez
Opelousas
Baton Rouge
Lafayette
New Iberia
New Orleans
Marsh I.
Mississippi Delta
Lake Charles

Texas
STATES
Brownwood
San Angelo
Del Rio
Amistad Res.
Ciudad Acuña
Piedras Negras
Eagle Pass
Nueva Rosita
Sabinas
V. Carranza Res.
Laredo
Kingsville
Nuevo Laredo
McAllen
Harlingen
Brownsville
Reynosa
Matamoros

Gulf of Mexico

Monclova
Villaldama
Sabinas Hidalgo
M.R. Gómez Res.
CUMBRES DE MONTERREY N.P.
Guadalupe
Monterrey
Saltillo
Montemorelos
Nuevo León
Linares
San Fernando
Río Bravo
Madre Lagoon
San Juan
San Fernando
Tamaulipas
Hidalgo
Aramberri
Cedral
Matehuala
Jaumave
Ciudad Victoria
Los Lavaderos
La Pesca
V. Guerrero Res.
Soto la Marina
Charcas
San Luis Potosí
Xicotencatl
Aldama
Ciudad Mante
González
Cerritos
Altamira
Ciudad Madero
★ **San Luis Potosí**
Cárdenas
Valles
Ébano
Tampico
Ríoverde
Tamiahua Lagoon
San Felipe
Tempoal
Cape Rojo
Guanajuato
Jalpan
Tamazunchale
Cerro Azul
★ Guanajuato
Huejutla
Tuxpan
Salamanca
Querétaro
Hidalgo
Poza Rica de Hidalgo
Celaya
Actopan
Papantla
Veracruz
★ **Querétaro**
Acámbaro
San Juan del Río
Tulancingo
Martínez de la Torre
Pachuca
★ **Morelia**
Teziutlán
Misantla
Zitácuaro
Mexico City
Netzahualcóyotl
Tlaxcala
Cuetepec
★ **Jalapa**
Federal District
PICO DE ORIZABA N.P.
Tacámbaro
Toluca
México
Tlaxcala
Veracruz
Ciudad Altamirano
Cuernavaca
Puebla
Córdoba
Alvarado
Taxco
Atlixco
Orizaba
Papaloapan
Morelos
Tierra Blanca
San Andrés Tuxtla
Teloloapan
Iguala de la Independencia
Matamoros
Tehuacán
Cosamaloapan
Frontera
Carmen
Puebla
Miguel Alemán Res.
Coatzacoalcos
Comalcalco
Tabasco
Guerrero
Huajuapan
Acayucan
Cárdenas
Macuspana
Villahermosa
Petatlán
Chilpancingo ★
Tlapa
Tuxtepec
Nochixtlán
Minatitlán
Las Choapas
PALENQUE
Tenosique
Coyuca de Benítez
Tlaxiaco
MONTE ALBÁN
Oaxaca
Ocotlán
Nezahualcóyotl Res.
Matías Romero
Chiapas
Acapulco
Ayutla
Oaxaca
Ixtepec
Cintalapa
Tuxtla
San Cristóbal de las Casas
BONAMPAK
Pinotepa Nacional
Jamiltepec
Tehuantepec
Juchitán
Villa Flores
Arriaga
LAGUNAS DE MONTEBELLO N.P.
Miahuatlán
Salina Cruz
Angostura Res.
Comitán
San Luis
LAGUNAS DE CHACAHUA N.P.
Puerto Escondido
Santa Cruz Huatulco
Gulf of Tehuantepec
Tonalá
Mapastepec
Escuintla
Huehuetenango
GUATEMALA
Puerto Ángel
Huixtla
Quezaltenango
Tapachula
Chiquimula
Mazatenango
⊛ **Guatemala City**
HONDURAS
EL SALVADOR
Tegucigalpa ⊛

Gulf of Mexico

Arrecife Alacrán
Río Lagartos
Cape Catoche
Progreso
Tizimín
Cancún
Cancún I.
Hunucmá
Motul
Mérida
Valladolid
Maxcanú
COBA
Cozumel
Calkiní
Ticul
CHICHÉN ITZÁ
Cozumel I.
Yucatán
Hecelchakán
UXMAL
Peto
TULUM
Campeche
Hopelchén
Quintana Roo
Champotón
EDZNÁ
Felipe Carrillo Puerto
Bay of Campeche
Términos Lagoon
Campeche
BECAN
Chetumal
Chetumal Bay
Escárcega
Pital
Ambergris Cay
CALAKMUL
Candelaria
Orange Walk
Turneffe Is.
Belize City
Belmopan
BELIZE
Roatán I.
Flores
Gulf of Honduras
Puerto Barrios
Puerto Cortés
Cobán
Lake Izabal
San Pedro Sula
Zacapa

Tropic of Cancer
—25°
—30°
—20°
—15°
100°   95°   90°

| 1,000 | | 1,200 | | 1,400 | | 1,600 | | 1,800 Miles |
| 1,600 | 1,800 | 2,000 | 2,200 | 2,400 | 2,600 | 2,800 Kilometers |

The most urban areas of the country include the Federal District and the states on Nuevo León and Baja California Norte. Forty-eight cities have more than 100,000 people. Mexico City, the capital and largest city, has more than 10 million people. Three other cities have more than 1 million people. They are, in order of size, Guadalajara, Netzahualcóyotl, and Monterrey. The metropolitan area of Mexico City, which includes the cities of Netzahualcóyotl, Tlalnepantla, Ecatepec, and Naucalpan, has more than 19 million people and is the largest urban area in the world. See the separate articles on Mexican cities listed in the *Related articles* at the end of this article.

Many Mexican cities and towns began as Indian communities. After the Spaniards arrived, they built the main church and the chief public and government buildings around a *plaza* (public square). The plaza is still the center of city life, even in large cities. In the evenings and on Sunday afternoons, the people gather in the plaza to talk with friends or to listen to music.

The city centers are filled with high-rise buildings, and modern houses and apartment buildings occupy the suburbs. But older parts of towns and cities have rows of homes built in the Spanish colonial style. Most of these houses are made of stone or *adobe* (sun-dried clay) brick. Small balconies extend from some windows. A Spanish-style house also has a *patio* (courtyard), which is the center of family life. This gardenlike area of the

house may have a fountain, flowers, vines, and pots of blooming plants.

All of the large Mexican cities have grown very rapidly because people have moved there from the rural areas to find jobs and a better life. As a result, many cities suffer from serious social and environmental problems. Houses in many of the poor sections are made of scraps of wood, metal, and whatever other materials can be found. Most of them lack electricity and running water. The large number of cars and trucks cause frequent traffic jams. Air pollution is very bad in Mexico City, and it causes many people to suffer from respiratory and eye diseases.

Many people who move to cities have no regular jobs. Others do not earn enough to support themselves. Entire families must work—sometimes at two or three jobs—in order to survive. Many poor people with no skills find jobs as street vendors, construction workers, or street cleaners. Others make a living by washing clothes and cleaning houses. After they have lived in the city for a while, many of the poor find better-paying jobs in factories.

Rural life. About one out of every four Mexicans lives on a farm or in a small village. Most of these farmers live near their fields. The villages are very poor and have little access to such basic social services as health care and education. Most young people leave the villages to find work in the cities and towns.

Mexico map index

States and Federal District

Name	Population	Area In sq. mi.	In km²	Map key
Aguascalientes	684,247	2,112	5,471	G 8
Baja California Norte	1,388,476	26,997	69,921	B 2
Baja California Sur	315,095	28,369	73,475	E 3
Campeche	592,933	19,619	50,812	I 14
Chiapas	2,518,679	28,653	74,211	J 13
Chihuahua	2,238,542	94,571	244,938	D 6
Coahuila	1,906,119	57,908	149,982	D 8
Colima	419,439	2,004	5,191	I 7
Durango	1,384,518	47,560	123,181	F 7
Federal District	19,150,275	571	1,479	I 10
Guanajuato	3,542,103	11,773	30,491	H 9
Guerrero	2,560,262	24,819	64,281	J 9
Hidalgo	1,822,296	8,036	20,813	H 10
Jalisco	5,198,374	31,211	80,836	H 7
México	11,571,111	8,245	21,355	I 9
Michoacán	3,377,732	23,138	59,928	I 8
Morelos	1,258,468	1,911	4,950	I 10
Nayarit	846,278	10,417	26,979	G 7
Nuevo León	3,146,169	25,067	64,924	F 9
Oaxaca	2,650,232	36,275	93,952	J 11
Puebla	4,068,038	13,090	33,902	I 10
Querétaro	952,875	4,420	11,449	H 9
Quintana Roo	393,398	19,387	50,212	H 15
San Luis Potosí	2,020,715	24,351	63,068	G 9
Sinaloa	2,367,567	22,521	58,328	F 6
Sonora	1,799,646	70,291	182,052	C 4
Tabasco	1,299,507	9,756	25,267	I 13
Tamaulipas	2,266,677	30,650	79,384	F 10
Tlaxcala	665,606	1,551	4,016	I 10
Veracruz	6,658,946	27,683	71,699	H 11
Yucatán	1,302,600	14,827	38,402	H 15
Zacatecas	1,251,531	28,283	73,252	F 8

Cities and towns

Acámbaro ......98,126. .H 9	Cancún ....11,348. .G 16	Ciudad Hidalgo* ....72,787. .H 9	Lázaro Cárdenas ......62,355. .I 8	San Juan del Rio ....81,820. .H 9

Acámbaro ......98,126. .H 9
Acapulco .....409,335. .J 9
Acayucan ....52,106. .J 12
Aguascalientes ...359,454. .G 8
Ahome ....254,681. .E 5
Apatzingán ....75,805. .I 8
Atizapán de Zarazoga* ...202,248. .I 10
Atlixco ....91,660. .I 10
Caborca ......50,452. .B 3
Campeche ......151,805. .H 14
Canatlán ......64,953. .F 7

Cancún ....11,348. .G 16
Cardenas ......119,235. .I 13
Carmen ....144,684. .I 13
Celaya ....219,010. .H 9
Cerro Azul ......33,123. .H 10
Chetumal ....38,000. .I 15
Chihuahua ....406,830. .C 6
Chilapa ....73,335. .J 10
Chilpancingo ...98,266. .J 9
Ciudad Delicias ....82,215. .D 7
Ciudad Guzmán ....62,353. .I 7

Ciudad Hidalgo* ....72,787. .H 9
Ciudad Madero ......132,444. .G 10
Ciudad Mante ..106,426. .G 10
Ciudad Obregón ......255,845. .D 4
Ciudad Victoria ......153,206. .F 10
Coatepec ......50,631. .I 11
Coatzacoalcos ....186,129. .I 12
Colima ....100,428. .I 7
Comalcalco ....101,448. .I 13
Comitán ....54,733. .J 13
Compostela ....86,189. .H 7
Córdoba ....126,179. .I 11
Cortazar* ....61,308. .H 9
Cosamaloapan ....103,239. .I 11
Cozumel ....23,270. .H 16
Cuauhtémoc ...85,589. .D 6
Cuautla* ....94,101. .I 10
Cuernavaca ...232,355. .I 10
Culiacán .....560,011. .F 5
Dolores Hidalgo* ....67,358. .H 9
Durango ......321,148. .F 7
Ecatepec* .....784,507. .I 10
El Fuerte ......81,330. .E 5
Ensenada ....175,425. .A 1
Etchojoa* ....66,156. .D 4
Fresnillo ......132,365. .G 8
Garza García* .....81,974. .E 9
Gómez Palacio .....180,011. .E 7
Guadalajara .....1,626,152. .
............†2,244,715. .H 8
Guadalupe ...370,908. .E 9
Guanajuato ....83,576. .H 9
Guasave ......221,139. .E 5
Guaymas ......97,962. .D 4
Hermosillo .....340,779. .C 4
Hidalgo del Parral ....78,994. .D 6
Iguala de la Independencia ....83,328. .I 9
Irapuato .....246,308. .H 8
Jalapa ....212,769. .I 11
Jerez ....55,164. .G 8
Jiutepec* ......69,687. .I 10
Juárez* .....567,365. .B 6
Lagos de Moreno ......84,305. .H 8
La Paz ....130,427. .F 4
La Piedad Cavadas* ....63,608. .H 8

Lázaro Cárdenas ......62,355. .I 8
León ....655,809. .H 8
Lerdo ....73,527. .E 7
Linares ....53,691. .F 9
Los Mochis ...122,531. .E 5
Manzanillo ......73,290. .I 7
Martínez de la Torre ......93,796. .H 11
Matamoros .....57,941. .J 10
Matamoros* ....71,771. .E 8
Matehuala .....61,272. .F 9
Mazatlán ......249,988. .F 6
Mérida ....424,529. .H 15
Mexicali .....510,664. .A 2
Mexico City ....10,263,275. .
............†19,150,000. .I 10
Minatitlán .....145,268. .J 12
Monclova ......119,609. .E 9
Monterrey ....1,090,009. .
............†1,916,472. .I 9
Morelia ......353,055. .I 9
Navojoa ......106,221. .D 5
Netzahualcóyotl ......1,341,230. .I 10
Nogales ....68,076. .B 4
Naucalpan* ....730,170. .I 10
Nuevo Laredo ....203,286. .D 9
Oaxaca ......157,284. .J 11
Ocosingo* ......69,757. .J 13
Ocotlán ....59,196. .H 8
Orizaba ....114,848. .I 11
Pachuca ......135,248. .H 10
Papantla ......146,131. .H 11
Pátzcuaro .....53,287. .I 8
Penjamo* .....105,105. .H 9
Piedras Negras ....80,290. .C 9
Poza Rica de Hidalgo ....166,799. .H 11
Puebla ....835,759. .I 10
Puerto Vallarta ......57,028. .H 7
Querétaro ....293,586. .H 9
Reynosa .....211,412. .E 10
Rio Bravo .....83,522. .E 10
Salamanca ....160,040. .H 9
Salina Cruz ....42,239. .K 12
Saltillo ....321,758. .E 9
Salvatierra* ...94,732. .H 9
San Andrés Tuxtla ......112,104. .I 12
San Cristóbal de las Casas ....60,550. .J 13
San Francisco del Rincón* ....66,575. .H 8

San Juan del Rio ....81,820. .H 9
San Luis ....92,790. .A 2
San Luis Potosí ......406,630. .G 9
San Martín Texmelucan* .....79,504. .I 9
San Miguel de Allende* ......77,624. .H 9
San Nicolás de los Garzas* .....280,696. .E 9
San Pedro .....93,410. .E 8
Santa Catarina* ......89,488. .E 9
Santiago Ixcuintla .....98,935. .G 7
Silao ....77,036. .H 8
Tamazunchale ...76,643. .H 10
Tampico ......267,957. .G 10
Tapachula ....144,057. .K 13
Taxco ....75,912. .I 9
Tecomán ....67,064. .I 7
Tehuacán ....113,107. .I 11
Tehuantepec ...28,443. .J 12
Temapeche* ....91,478. .H 10
Tepatitlán .....78,364. .H 8
Tepic ....177,007. .H 7
Teziutlán ......50,572. .H 11
Tierra Blanca ....70,427. .I 11
Tijuana ....461,257. .A 1
Tlalnepantla ....778,173. .I 10
Tlaquepaque .....177,324. .H 7
Tlaxcala ....35,384. .I 10
Toluca ....357,071. .I 9
Torreón ......363,886. .E 8
Tula* ....57,604. .H 10
Tulancingo ....70,782. .H 10
Tuxpan ....34,079. .G 7
Tuxpan ....96,581. .H 11
Tuxtla ....166,476. .J 13
Uruapan ......146,998. .I 8
Valle de Santiago* ....100,733. .H 9
Valles ....105,625. .G 10
Venustiano Carranza* ....33,059. .I 7
Veracruz ......305,456. .I 11
Villahermosa .....250,903. .I 13
Yuriria* ....65,745. .H 9
Zacapu* ....62,620. .I 8
Zacatecas .....88,807. .G 8
Zamora ......113,474. .H 8
Zapopan ....389,081. .H 7
Zitácuaro ......83,649. .I 9

*Does not appear on map; key shows general location.
†Population of metropolitan area, including suburbs.
Sources: 1988 estimates for states, Federal District, and Mexico City and its metropolitan area; 1980 census for all other places.

Population density

The population of Mexico is concentrated in the south-central region of the country, particularly around Mexico City. The cities shown on the map are among the largest in Mexico.

Major urban centers

● More than 10 million inhabitants

● 1 million to 10 million inhabitants

• Less than 1 million inhabitants

Persons per sq. mi.	Persons per km2
More than 250	More than 100
60 to 250	25 to 100
25 to 60	10 to 25
Less than 25	Less than 10

WORLD BOOK map

The village homes stand along dusty streets that are simple dirt roads or are paved with cobblestones. In most of the villages, a Roman Catholic church stands on one side of the plaza, which forms the center of the community. On the other sides of most village plazas are a few stores and government buildings.

Almost every village, and every city and town, has a marketplace. Going to market is one of the chief activities of the people in farm areas. Men, women, and children take clothes, food, lace, pictures, toys, baskets, or whatever else they wish to sell or trade. They either rent stalls in which to display their goods, or spread the merchandise on the ground. The people spend one day each week at the marketplace chatting with friends and

© Lee Foster, Bruce Coleman Inc.

Modern machinery is used by many Mexican farmers. The government promotes modern farming methods, but some farmers still use hand tools and follow ancient farming practices.

doing business. Farmers often trade their goods instead of selling them, and much bargaining takes place.

The shape and style of village houses vary according to the climate. People on the dry central plateau build homes of adobe, brick, cement blocks, or stone, with flat roofs of red tile, sheet metal, or straw. Some of these houses have only one room, a dirt floor, and few or no windows. The kitchen may be simply a lean-to built of poles and cornstalks placed against an outside wall. If a house does not have a lean-to kitchen, the family may build a cooking fire on the floor. The smoke from the fire curls out through the door and windows.

In areas of heavy rainfall, many houses have walls built of poles coated with lime and clay. This mixture lasts longer in the rain than adobe does. The houses have sloping roofs to allow the water to run off easily. Some Indians in southern Mexico build round houses. In Yucatán, most village houses are rectangular with rounded ends. The roofs are made of palm leaves.

Most Indians live in villages in central and southern Mexico and the Yucatán Peninsula and are poor. Dishonest mestizos have treated many Indians unfairly, sometimes taking their land, exploiting them for cheap labor, or charging them higher prices for goods and services. As a result, conflicts between Indians and wealthier mestizo neighbors have occurred.

Food and drink. Thousands of years ago, the Indians of what is now Mexico discovered how to grow corn. It became their most important food. Today, corn is still the chief food of most Mexicans, especially in rural areas. Mexican cooks generally soften the corn in hot limewater, boil it, and then grind it into meal.

The main corn-meal food is the *tortilla,* a thin flat bread shaped by hand or machine and cooked on an ungreased griddle. It also may be made with wheat flour. The tortilla is the bread of most Mexicans. It can be eaten plain or as part of (1) the *taco,* a folded tortilla filled with chopped meat, chicken, or cheese, and then fried; (2) the *enchilada,* a rolled-up tortilla with a similar

© Chip & Rosa Maria Peterson

© Chip & Rosa Maria Peterson

Extremes of poverty and wealth can be seen in Mexico City. Poor people live in shacks on the outskirts of the city, *top*. Wealthy Mexicans, by contrast, can afford luxury condominiums with tennis courts and swimming pools, *above*.

filling and covered with a hot sauce; or (3) the *tostada*, a tortilla fried in deep fat until it becomes crisp, and served flat with beans, cheese, lettuce, meat, and onions on top.

Many Mexicans eat *frijoles* (beans) that are boiled, mashed, and then fried and refried in lard. Poorer Mexicans may eat frijoles every day, often using a folded tortilla to spoon up the beans. Rice is also boiled and then fried. Other popular foods include *atole* (a thick, soupy corn-meal dish) and *tamales* (corn meal steamed in corn husks or banana leaves, and usually mixed with pork or chicken). Most Mexicans like their foods highly seasoned with hot chili pepper or other strong peppers. Turkey is a popular holiday dish. It is often served with

mole, a sauce made of chocolate, chili, sesame seed, and spices.

The poorer families eat little meat because they cannot afford it. They may vary their basic diet of corn and beans with fruit, honey, onions, tomatoes, squash, or sweet potatoes. Favorite fruits include avocados, bananas, mangoes, oranges, and papayas. The fruit and leaves of the prickly pear, a type of cactus, are boiled, fried, or stewed. Wealthier Mexicans have a more balanced diet.

Popular beverages in Mexico include water flavored with a variety of fruit juices, and cinnamon-flavored hot chocolate cooked with water and beaten into foam. Mexicans also drink coffee, milk, soft drinks, and mineral water. Alcoholic beverages include *mescal, pulque,* and *tequila,* which are made from the juice of the maguey plant, and beer and wine.

Clothing. Mexicans in the cities and larger towns wear clothing similar to that worn in the United States and Canada. The village people wear simple types of clothing that vary according to region and climate. The designs of these clothes date back hundreds of years. In central and southern Mexico, men generally wear plain cotton shirts and trousers, and leather sandals called *huaraches.* Wide-brimmed felt or straw hats called *sombreros* protect Mexican men from the hot sun. During cold or rainy weather, they may wear *ponchos* (blankets that have a slit in the center for the head and are draped over the shoulders). At night, the men may wrap themselves in colorful *serapes,* which are blankets carried over one shoulder during the day. The village women wear blouses and long, full skirts, and usually go barefoot or wear plastic sandals. They cover their heads with fringed shawls called *rebozos.* A mother may wrap her baby to her back with a rebozo.

Some of the villagers' clothing is homemade. Hand weaving was an ancient Indian art, and today the Indians are famous for their beautiful home-woven fabrics. Styles of weaving vary throughout Mexico, and an Indian's region can be identified by the colors and designs of his poncho or serape. For example, blankets with a striped rainbow pattern come from the Saltillo area of the country.

Some Indians wear unusual clothing. Large capes made of straw are worn in Oaxaca state. On holidays, Indian women on the Isthmus of Tehuantepec wear a wide, lacy white headdress called a *huipil grande.* According to legend, this garment was copied from baby clothes that were washed ashore from a Spanish shipwreck. The Indian women thought the clothes were head shawls. In Yucatán, Maya women wear long, loose white dresses that are embroidered around the neck and bottom hem.

Mexicans sometimes wear national costumes on holidays and other special occasions. The men's national costumes include the dark blue *charro* suit, made of doeskin or velvet. It has a *bolero* (short jacket) and tight riding pants with gold or silver buttons down the sides. A flowing red bow tie, spurred boots, and a fancy white sombrero complete the costume.

Probably the best-known women's costume is the *china poblana.* It is usually worn in the *jarabe tapatío,* or Mexican hat dance. A legend says the china poblana was named for a Chinese princess of the 1600's who was kid-

Mexican clothing includes the traditional dress of various Indian groups as well as modern styles. The Huichol Indians embroider their clothes with detailed, colorful patterns, *left*. In cities and large towns, Mexicans wear pants, shirts, and other clothes similar to those worn in the United States and Canada, *right*.

© Richard Steedman, The Stock Market

© Chip & Rosa Maria Peterson

napped by pirates and sold in the slave market. She was brought to Acapulco, where a kindly merchant of Puebla bought her. In Puebla, she dedicated her life to helping the poor. The princess adopted a costume that the local women later imitated. Today, it consists of a full red-and-green skirt decorated with beads and other ornaments, a colorfully embroidered short-sleeved blouse, and a brightly colored sash. See **Clothing** (picture: Traditional costumes).

Holidays. Mexicans celebrate their Independence Days, September 15 and 16, and other holidays with colorful *fiestas* (festivals). Every Mexican city, town, and village also holds a yearly fiesta to honor its local patron saint. Most fiestas begin before daylight with a shower of rockets, loud explosions of fireworks, and ringing of bells. During the fiestas, the people pray and burn candles to their saints in churches decorated with flowers and colored tissue paper. They dance, gamble, hold parades, and buy refreshments in the crowded marketplaces and public square. Fireworks are again set off at night.

In the smaller towns and villages, cockfights and amateur bullfights are also held during fiestas. In the larger towns and the cities, most fiestas include less religious worship than do the village fiestas. The people watch plays and professional bullfights, ride merry-go-rounds and Ferris wheels, and buy goods at merchants' booths.

Guadalupe Day is Mexico's most important religious holiday. It honors the Virgin of Guadalupe, the patron saint of Mexico. Guadalupe Day is celebrated on December 12, when the Virgin is believed to have appeared as an Indian maiden on Tepeyac Hill in Mexico City.

On the nine nights before Christmas, friends and neighbors gather and act out the journey of Mary and Joseph to Bethlehem. These nine ceremonies are called *posadas*. Each night after the posada, the children play the *piñata* game. Piñatas are containers made of earthenware or papier-mâché. Many piñatas are shaped like ani-

mals and are filled with candy, fruit, and toys. A piñata is hung above the heads of the children. Then the youngsters are blindfolded and take turns trying to break the piñata with a stick. After it breaks, the children scramble to collect the scattered presents. On Twelfth-night, 12 days after Christmas, parents fill their children's shoes with presents. See **Christmas** (picture: A Mexican tradition).

Recreation. Soccer is the most popular sport in Mexico, followed by baseball. Boys and men often can be found playing soccer or baseball on vacant lots, and many play on teams in amateur leagues. Mexico also has professional baseball and soccer leagues. Basketball has

© Frederica Georgia, Photo Researchers

Bullfighting is the most popular spectator sport in Mexico. Almost all large cities and many small towns have bullrings.

Worshipers wave palm branches in a church procession through the streets of Puebla on Palm Sunday, *left*. Religion plays an important role in the lives of most Mexicans. More than 90 per cent of Mexico's people are Roman Catholics.

Melinda Berge, Bruce Coleman Inc.

become popular. Jai alai is also a popular sport.

Most Mexicans enjoy watching bullfights. Almost all large cities have bullrings. Mexico City has the largest bullring in the world. It seats about 55,000 people.

On Sundays—the only day most Mexicans do not work—many families go to the park to relax and picnic. Mexicans also enjoy watching movies and television, dancing at nightclubs or discos, and entertaining friends and relatives at home. Many wealthier Mexicans visit the country's historic sites and resorts along the coast.

Religion. More than 90 per cent of Mexico's people belong to the Roman Catholic Church. Mexico also has some Protestants, Jews, and other religious groups.

Roman Catholic missionaries and priests first arrived from Spain in the early 1500's. They baptized millions of Indians. But the rain, sun, and other forces of nature remained an important part of religion to the Indians. Today, millions of Indian villagers still combine ancient religious practices with Catholicism.

During the Spanish colonial period, the Roman Catholic Church was closely linked with the government as the official state church. The church became wealthy and powerful, and prohibited other religions. Beginning in the mid-1800's, the Mexican government greatly reduced the political and economic power of the church by prohibiting churches from owning property and participating in politics. But these laws were not always enforced. In 1991, Mexico's legislature passed constitutional amendments to end these restrictions.

Education. Throughout the Spanish colonial period, the Roman Catholic Church controlled education in what is now Mexico. During the 1800's, the newly independent government and the church struggled for power, and the government won control of the schools. Mexico's present Constitution, adopted in 1917, prohibited religious groups and ministers from establishing schools or teaching in them. But the laws often were not enforced. Changes to the Constitution, passed in 1991, legalized church-owned schools and the teaching of religion in them. Before these changes were passed, about 95 per cent of Mexico's schoolchildren attended public elementary schools. Only about 5 per cent of

schoolchildren attended private elementary schools.

During the early 1900's, less than 25 per cent of Mexico's people could read or write. Since the Revolution of 1910, and especially since the early 1940's, the government has done much to promote free public education. It has built thousands of new schools and established teachers' colleges. The government spends large sums on education each year. Today, almost 90 per cent of all Mexican adults can read and write.

Mexican law requires all children from the age of 6 through 14 to go to school. About 90 per cent of school-age children begin school. However, only about half of these children finish elementary school. More children in urban areas attend and finish school than in rural areas. After kindergarten, a child has six years of elementary school, followed by three years of *basic secondary* school. Graduates of basic secondary school may go on to a three-year *upper secondary* school. Many upper secondary schools are privately run, some by colleges in order to prepare students for college work. Other upper secondary schools offer business and technical courses.

Courses of higher education at Mexico's many universities, specialized colleges, and technical institutes last from three to seven years. The oldest and largest Mexican university is the National Autonomous University of Mexico in Mexico City. It was founded in 1551 and has more than 325,000 students. The Biblioteca Nacional de Mexico (National Library of Mexico) is located on the university's campus. See **Mexico, National Autonomous University of.**

Arts

The arts have been an important part of Mexican life since the days of ancient Indians. The Maya and Toltec Indians built beautiful temples and painted *murals* (wall-paintings) in them. The Aztec Indians composed music and poetry. The Spaniards brought a love for beautiful buildings and for literature. Indian craftworkers built and decorated thousands of churches based on Spanish designs. During the 1900's, Mexico has produced many important architects, painters, composers, and writers.

Architecture of the ancient Indians was related chiefly to religion. The Indians built stone temples on flat-topped pyramids, and decorated them with murals and sculptured symbols. These symbols represented the feathered-serpent god Quetzalcóatl and the Indians' other gods. Many ancient structures still stand near Mexico City and at Chichén Itzá in Yucatán. See **Maya** (Arts and crafts); **Pyramids** (American pyramids).

After the Spanish conquest, the earliest mission churches were designed in a simple style. Later churches, especially those built during the 1700's, took on a more ornamental style. The huge Metropolitan Cathedral in Mexico City, begun in 1573 but not completed for hundreds of years, shows the influence of many different styles of architecture. During the 1900's, many Mexican architects have combined ancient Indian designs with modern construction methods. Their work includes the beautiful buildings of the National Autonomous University of Mexico by Félix Candela and Carlos Lazo, and the striking National Museum of Anthropology in Mexico City by Pedro Ramírez Vázquez. Other examples include the apartment buildings called Jardines de Pedregal by Luís Barragán, and the 44-story Latin-American Tower in Mexico City.

Painting. During the Spanish colonial period, many artists painted murals in churches or portraits of government officials. But Mexican painting is best known for the artists who did their work after the Mexican Revolution of 1910. Beginning in the 1920's, José Orozco, Diego Rivera, and David Siqueiros painted the story of the revolution on the walls of public buildings. Important Mexican painters of later years include Rufino Tamayo and José Luis Cuevas. Since the 1960's, many younger Mexican painters have turned from revolutionary themes and have followed the latest art influences from other countries. See **Painting** (Mexican painting).

© Sergio Dorantes

The National Museum of Anthropology in Mexico City houses priceless displays of ancient Indian art, *above*. The building's interior was designed by architect Pedro Ramírez Vázquez.

Literature. Outstanding colonial writers included the dramatist Juan Ruiz de Alarcón and the poet Sor Juana Inés de la Cruz. In 1816, José Joaquín Fernández de Lizardi published *The Itching Parrot,* probably the first Latin-American novel. After 1910, revolutionary themes became important in novels by such writers as Mariano Azuela and Martín Luis Guzmán. These themes sometimes appear in the works of later writers, such as Carlos Fuentes, Juan Rulfo, and Agustín Yáñez. Leading Mexican poets of the 1900's include Amado Nervo, Octavio Paz, Carlos Pellicer, Alfonso Reyes, and Marco Antonio Montes de Oca. See **Latin-American literature.**

Music. Early Indians used drums, flutes, gourd rattles, and seashells as well as their voices for music and

Fresco (1964); Museum of National History, Mexico City (Giraudon/Art Resource)

The story of the Mexican Revolution is told in murals by David Siqueiros and other well-known Mexican artists. Part of Siqueiros' mural, *left,* shows the revolt led by Emiliano Zapata to gain land for Mexican peasants.

© Bruce Coleman Inc.

The ornate religious architecture of the Spanish colonial period is represented by the Church of San Francisco Acatepec, built in 1730 near Puebla. Its main entrance and towers are decorated with brightly colored tiles that form striking patterns.

dances. This ancient music is still played in some parts of Mexico. Much church music was written in the colonial period. Folk songs called *corridos* have long been popular in Mexico. They may tell of the Mexican Revolution, a bandit or a sheriff, or the struggle between church and state. In the 1900's, Mexican composers including Carlos Chávez and Silvestre Revueltas have used themes from corridos or ancient Indian music.

Today, strolling musical groups called *mariachis* perform along streets and in restaurants. Mariachi groups include singers, and players of guitars, trumpets, and violins. The music of *marimbas*—instruments similar to xylophones—is also popular. Folk dances are important features of Mexican fiestas. In the Mexican hat dance, also called the *jarabe tapatío,* dancers perform a lively sequence with hopping steps and heel-and-toe tapping.

The land

Mexico has six main land regions: (1) the Pacific Northwest, (2) the Plateau of Mexico, (3) the Gulf Coastal Plain, (4) the Southern Uplands, (5) the Chiapas Highlands, and (6) the Yucatán Peninsula. Within these six land regions are many smaller ones that differ greatly in altitude, climate, and land formation. Many kinds of plants and animals also live in Mexico.

The Pacific Northwest region of Mexico is generally dry. The Peninsula of Lower California, the region's westernmost section, consists largely of rolling or mountainous desert. During some years, the desert receives no rain at all. It has a few oases, where farmers in

small settlements grow dates and grapes. The northwestern corner and southern end of the peninsula get enough rain for a little farming. The lowest point in Mexico is in the far northern area, near Mexicali. This area, 33 feet (10 meters) below sea level, is the southern end of the huge Imperial Valley of California.

The most valuable land of Mexico's Pacific Northwest lies along the mainland coastal strip. There, in fertile river valleys, is some of Mexico's richest farmland. The valleys are irrigated with the waters of the Colorado, Fuerte, Yaqui, and other rivers. Steep, narrow mountain ranges extend in a north-south direction in the state of Sonora, east of the coastal plain. The ranges lie parallel to each other and separate the upper river valleys. In these basins are cattle ranches, irrigated farmland, and copper and silver mines.

The Plateau of Mexico is the largest of Mexico's land regions. It has most of the Mexican people and the largest cities. The plateau is the most varied land region, and consists of five sections.

The Cordillera Neo-Volcánica (Neo-Volcanic Chain), a series of volcanoes, extends across Mexico at the plateau's southern edge. Many of the volcanoes are active. The volcanic soils are fertile and receive enough rain for agriculture. Corn, beans, and other crops have been grown on the slopes since the days of the ancient Indian civilizations. The highest point in Mexico is 18,410-foot (5,610-meter) Pico de Orizaba (Citlaltépetl). Southeast of Mexico City are the volcanoes Ixtacihuatl and Popocatépetl, both more than 17,000 feet (5,180 meters) high. To the west is Lake Chapala, Mexico's largest lake. It covers 417 square miles (1,080 square kilometers). See **Ixtacihuatl; Orizaba, Pico de; Popocatépetl.**

The Mesa Central (Central Plateau), which lies north of the Neo-Volcanic Chain on the plateau, is the heart of

Victor Englebert

The Mexican hat dance is a popular Mexican dance. It is often performed by the Ballet Folklórico, a dance company that appears regularly in the Palace of Fine Arts in Mexico City.

Mexico. It averages about 7,000 feet (2,100 meters) above sea level. The rainfall in this section is enough to raise corn or beans, and wheat and barley grow well there. The Aztec capital of Tenochtitlan stood at the southern edge, in the beautiful Valley of Mexico. Mexico City was built on the same site after the Spanish conquest, and became the capital during the colonial period. Today, it is also the country's leading center of culture, industry, and transportation. Several small lakes, including famous Lake Xochimilco, are in the Mexico City area (see **Lake Xochimilco**).

The western part of the Mesa Central is called the *bajio* (flat). This region covers one of the most productive agricultural areas in the country. The bajio also includes the manufacturing centers of Guadalajara, León, Querétaro, and San Luis Potosí.

The Mesa del Norte (Northern Plateau) makes up more than half the Plateau of Mexico. It extends from the Mesa Central north to the United States. The Mesa del Norte is highest in the south and west, with altitudes from 6,000 to 9,000 feet (1,800 to 2,700 meters). In the north and east, it is less than 4,000 feet (1,200 meters) high. Low mountains rise from 2,000 to 3,000 feet (610 to 910 meters) above its plains. This section receives little rainfall except in the higher mountains, where frost is a constant threat to farming. Only in such irrigated places as the Saltillo and Torreón areas is farming really successful.

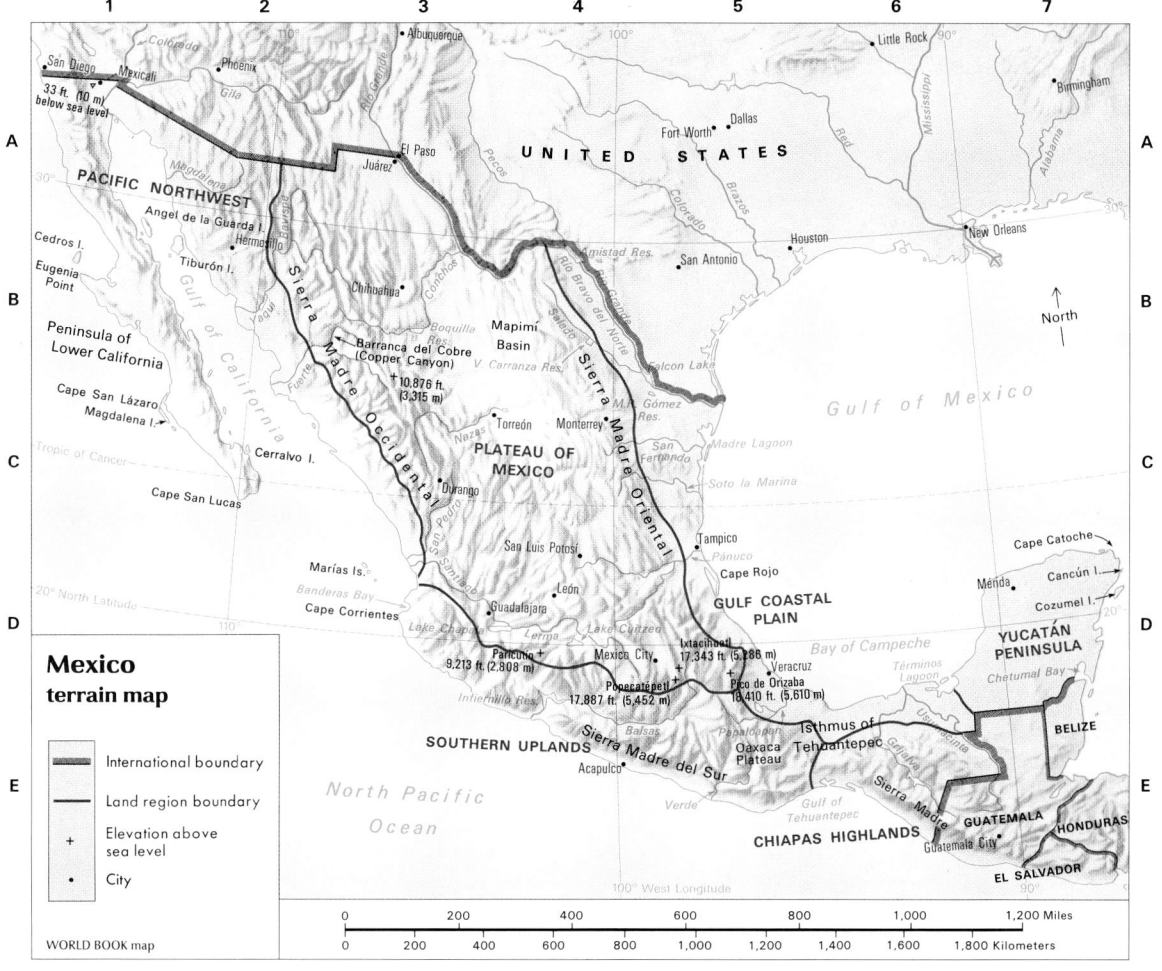

Mexico
terrain map

| International boundary |
| Land region boundary |
| + Elevation above sea level |
| • City |

WORLD BOOK map

Physical features

Amistad Reservoir	B	4	Cape San Lucas	C	2	Isthmus of			Papaloapan River	E	5	Sierra Madre del Sur
Ángel de la			Cedros Island	B	1	Tehuantepec	E	6	Paricutín (volcano)	D	4	(mountains)	E	4
Guarda Island	B	1	Cerralvo Island	C	2	Ixtacíhuatl (volcano)	D	5	Peninsula of Lower			Sierra Madre
Balsas River	E	4	Chetumal Bay	D	7	Lake Chapala	D	3	California	B	1	Occidental
Banderas Bay	D	3	Chiapas Highlands	E	6	Lake Cuitzeo	D	4	Pico de Orizaba	D	5	(mountains)	B	2
Barranca del Cobre			Colorado River	A	1	Lerma River	D	4	Plateau of Mexico	C	4	Sierra Madre
(Copper Canyon)	B	3	Conchos River	B	3	M. R. Gómez			Popocatépetl			Oriental
Bavispe River	B	2	Cozumel Island	D	7	Reservoir	C	4	(volcano)	D	5	(mountains)	C	4
Bay of Campeche	D	6	Eugenia Point	B	1	Madre Lagoon	C	5	Rio Bravo del			Soto la Marina
Boquilla Reservoir	B	3	Falcon Lake	B	4	Magdalena Island	C	1	Norte (river)	B	4	River	C	5
Cancún Island	D	7	Fuerte River	B	2	Magdalena River	A	2	Rio Grande (river)	B	4	Southern Uplands	E	4
Cape Catoche	D	7	Grijalva River	E	6	Mapimí Basin	B	4	Salado River	B	4	Términos Lagoon	D	6
Cape Corrientes	D	3	Gulf Coastal Plain	D	5	Marías Islands	D	3	San Fernando River	C	5	Tiburón Island	B	1
Cape Rojo	D	5	Gulf of California	B	2	Nazas River	C	3	San Pedro River	D	3	Usumacinta River	E	6
Cape San Lázaro	C	1	Gulf of Mexico	C	6	Oaxaca Plateau	E	5	Santiago River	D	3	V. Carranza Reservoir	B	4
			Gulf of Tehuantepec	E	6	Pacific Northwest	A	1	Sierra Madre			Yaqui River	B	2
			Infiernillo Reservoir	D	4	Pánuco River	D	5	(mountains)	E	6	Yucatán Peninsula	D	7

Deserts cover large areas of the Pacific Northwest and Northern Plateau regions of Mexico. The deserts support a wide variety of plant life, including large cactuses called *saguaros.*

The low mountains of the mesa have rich deposits of metal ores. The Spaniards began developing these mines during the 1500's. They also established huge ranches in the nearby dry hills and plains to supply the miners with beef, horses, and mules. In the Durango and Chihuahua areas, *vaqueros* (cowboys) developed skills at riding, roping cattle, and fighting Indians. American cowboys later copied these skills.

The Sierra Madre Occidental is a long mountain range that forms the western rim of the Plateau of Mexico. For hundreds of years, this range was a natural barrier to transportation between the plateau and the west coast. Paved roads and a railroad were not built across it until the 1900's. The range includes some of Mexico's most rugged land. Short, steep streams flowing to the Pacific Ocean have cut canyons more than 1 mile (1.6 kilometers) deep through the mountains. The largest canyon is the spectacular Barranca del Cobre, cut by the Urique River. This deep, wide gorge is so wild that parts of it have not been explored on foot.

The Sierra Madre Oriental, the plateau's eastern rim,

is actually a series of mountain ranges. In many places between the ranges, highways and railroads climb up to the plateau from the east coast. Monterrey, near large deposits of coal and iron ore, is the major center of the Mexican steel industry. See **Sierra Madre.**

The Gulf Coastal Plain. North of Tampico, the plain is largely covered by tangled forests of low, thorny bushes and trees. This section of the plain is generally dry, and farming is possible only along rivers and with the aid of irrigation. South of Tampico, the rainfall increases. The plant life gradually changes southward, and becomes a tropical rain forest in Tabasco. The southern section has some rich farmland.

Many of Mexico's longest rivers flow into the Gulf of Mexico from the coastal plain. They include the Rio Grande, which forms about 1,300 miles (2,090 kilometers) of Mexico's border with the United States. Large petroleum deposits lie beneath the plain and offshore. Huge sulfur deposits occur near the Gulf of Mexico in the Isthmus of Tehuantepec. The isthmus, which is 130 miles (209 kilometers) wide, is the narrowest part of Mexico. See **Gulf of Mexico; Rio Grande.**

The Southern Uplands consist largely of steep ridges and deep gorges cut by mountain streams. The region includes a large, hot, dry valley just south of the Neo-Volcanic Chain. This valley is drained by the Balsas River. The Sierra Madre del Sur, a rugged mountain range, rises southwest of the valley along the Pacific Ocean. The famous beach resort of Acapulco is on this coast. A little farming takes place on the steep mountainsides. The Oaxaca Plateau makes up the eastern part of the Southern Uplands. Monte Albán, an ancient Indian religious center, was built there on a flattened mountaintop. Much of the gold of the Aztec empire probably came from the Oaxaca Plateau.

The Chiapas Highlands have great blocklike mountains that rise more than 9,000 feet (2,700 meters) above sea level. There are also many relatively flat surfaces at high altitudes. These tablelands are farmed by Indians who speak Maya and other ancient languages. Most of

The Central Plateau has some of Mexico's richest farmland. The southern edge of the region includes sugar cane fields that stretch toward the foothills of the volcano Popocatépetl.

Tropical rain forests are found in the southern areas of the Gulf Coastal Plain and on the Yucatán Peninsula. The crowns of the tall trees form a thick canopy that prevents most light from reaching the forest floor.

© Tom McHugh, Photo Researchers

the region's modern farming development is taking place in deep, broad river valleys. With irrigation, farmers grow coffee, fruits, and other crops.

The Yucatán Peninsula is a low limestone plateau with no rivers. Limestone dissolves in water, and rainfall reaches the sea through underground channels dissolved out of the rock. Great pits have formed where the roofs of these channels have fallen in. The pits were the sacred wells of the ancient Maya Indians. The northwestern part of the region is dry bushland. There, leaves of agave plants provide a yellow fiber called *henequen,* which is used in making twine. To the south, the rainfall increases, and tropical rain forests cover the land. See **Yucatán Peninsula.**

Plant and animal life. Forests cover about a fifth of Mexico. The northwestern and central mountains have forests that include ebony, mahogany, rosewood, walnut, and other valuable hardwoods used in making furniture. Large pine forests also grow in the mountains and supply timber for Mexico's pulp and paper industry. Sapodilla trees, which grow in southern Mexico, provide *chicle,* a gumlike substance used in making chewing gum.

Mexico also has a great variety of flowers and cactus plants. The country's thousands of kinds of flowers include azaleas, chrysanthemums, geraniums, orchids, and poinsettias. The northern deserts have hundreds of kinds of cactus plants.

Deer and mountain lions live in Mexico's mountains. The country's northern deserts have coyotes, lizards, prairie dogs, and rattlesnakes. Mexico also has some alligators, jaguars, opossums, and raccoons. Chihuahuas, the world's smallest dogs, originally came from Mexico.

Mexico has hundreds of kinds of birds, including the beautifully colored quetzals of the southern forests. Other birds include flamingoes, hummingbirds, herons, parrots, and pelicans.

Fish and shellfish are plentiful in the coastal waters, lakes, and rivers. The freshwater fish of Mexico include bass, catfish, and trout. Along the Caribbean coast of the Yucatán Peninsula are coral reefs with many kinds of tropical fish. Marlin, swordfish, and tarpon are among the game fish caught in the seas off Mexico's coasts.

Climate

The climate of Mexico varies sharply from region to region. These differences are especially great in tropical Mexico, south of the Tropic of Cancer. In the south, the wide variety in altitude results in three main temperature zones. The *tierra caliente* (hot land) includes regions up to 3,000 feet (910 meters) above sea level. This zone has long, hot summers and mild winters with no frost.

The *tierra templada* (temperate land), from 3,000 to 6,000 feet (910 to 1,800 meters), has temperatures that generally stay between 80° and 50° F. (27° and 10° C). Most crops can be grown there. The *tierra fria* (cold land) lies above 6,000 feet (1,800 meters). Frost is rare in this zone up to 8,000 feet (2,400 meters), but it may occur at almost any time. The highest peaks in the tierra fria are always covered with snow.

In tropical regions of Mexico, most rain falls in summer, usually as short, heavy, afternoon showers. Toward the south, the rainy season begins earlier and lasts longer.

The northern half of Mexico is usually dry and consists largely of deserts and semideserts. The lack of rainfall has limited agricultural development in the north. Only the mountainous sections receive enough rainfall for growing good crops without irrigation. Most of northern Mexico's rainfall also occurs during the summer. But northwestern Lower California receives most of its rainfall during the winter. Above 2,000 feet (610 meters), summer days are hot and nights are cool. During

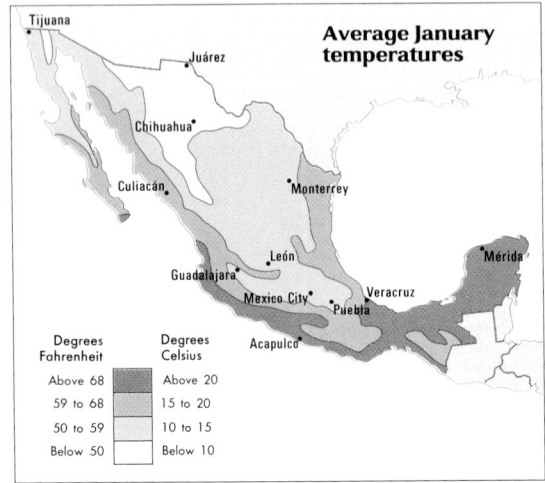

WORLD BOOK map

In winter, Mexico has warm weather in the south and cooler weather in the north and at high elevations. Average January temperatures in Mexico City range from 42° to 66° F. (6° to 19° C).

WORLD BOOK map

In summer, Mexico's climate is warm in the central regions of the country and hot along the coasts. July temperatures in Mexico City range from 53° to 73° F. (12° to 23° C).

Average monthly weather

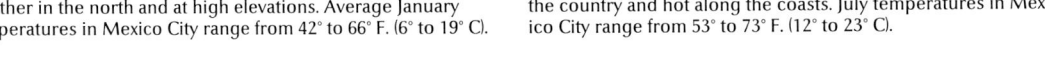

	Mexico City					Monterrey				
	Temperatures F°		C°		Days of rain or snow	Temperatures F°		C°		Days of rain or snow
	High	Low	High	Low		High	Low	High	Low	
Jan.	66	42	19	6	4	68	48	20	9	6
Feb.	69	43	21	6	5	72	52	22	11	5
Mar.	75	47	24	8	9	76	57	24	14	7
Apr.	77	51	25	11	14	84	62	29	17	7
May	78	54	26	12	17	87	68	31	20	9
June	76	55	24	13	21	91	71	33	22	8
July	73	53	23	12	27	90	71	32	22	8
Aug.	73	54	23	12	27	92	72	33	22	7
Sept.	74	53	23	12	23	86	70	30	21	10
Oct.	70	50	21	10	13	80	64	27	18	9
Nov.	68	46	20	8	6	71	55	22	13	8
Dec.	66	43	19	6	4	65	50	18	10	6

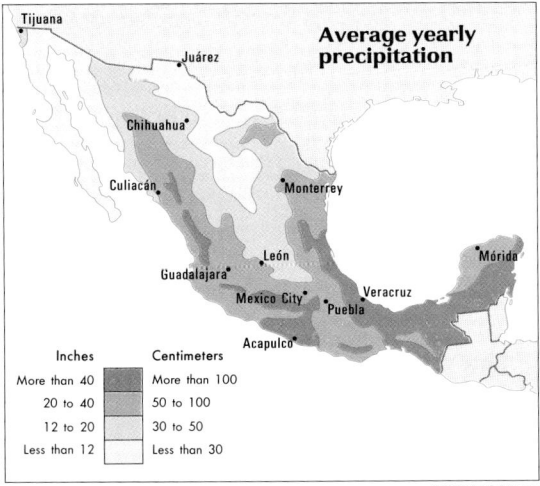

WORLD BOOK map

the winter, days are warm and nights are cold. The coastal lowlands are hot, except on the cool Pacific coast of Lower California.

Most of Mexico's precipitation falls during a rainy season that lasts from June to September. Northern Mexico is generally dry. Heavy rains fall in the south and on the Yucatán Peninsula.

Economy

Until the mid-1900's, the Mexican economy was based on agriculture and mining. Since the 1940's, the government has promoted the development of industry, and Mexico now produces many of the manufactured products its people use.

In the 1970's, Mexico became a major exporter of oil to the United States. Income from oil production, which is controlled by the government, spurred the development of manufacturing and service industries. During the mid- and late 1970's, the price of oil was high. Mexico used its expected income from oil production as collateral to borrow money for many construction projects. But in the early 1980's, the price of oil fell. Mexico found it difficult to repay its loans, and spending had to be severely cut. The economy declined, and many Mexicans lost their jobs. But economic reforms begun in the late

1980's helped the economy revive, and inflation dropped sharply.

Service industries are those economic activities that produce services, not goods. Service industries make up about 55 per cent of the total value of goods and services produced in Mexico. Service industries also provide about 50 per cent of Mexico's jobs. Schools, hospitals, stores, hotels, restaurants, and police and fire protection are included in this group. Banking, trade, transportation, and communication are also service industries.

Manufacturing has expanded rapidly in Mexico since the 1940's. This expansion has led to related developments throughout the entire economy. For example, the production of raw materials for new factories has increased. Banking, marketing, and other services have expanded. Heavy government spending on construction has provided additional housing for the growing industrial centers. Power plants have been built for the new industries, as well as highways and railroads for carrying goods.

Mexico's industrialization has been financed chiefly by the nation's business community. However, the Mexican government and foreign investors have also contributed much.

Mexico City is the leading industrial center. The city and its suburbs manufacture about half of the country's products. Monterrey and Guadalajara are also important manufacturing centers in Mexico. Government programs encourage the spread of industry to other areas. New factories have opened in Chihuahua, Juárez, Mexicali, Puebla, Tijuana, Toluca, Veracruz, and near the oil fields.

Many of the new factories along Mexico's border with the United States manufacture products for export to U.S. companies. These factories, called *maquiladoras,* have become an important part of Mexican industrial growth. They manufacture automobile engines and transmissions and assemble a variety of electrical goods, including stereo systems, computers, televisions, and kitchen appliances.

Mexico's leading products include chemicals, clothing, iron and steel, motor vehicles, processed foods, and processed petroleum. Iron and steel are produced in the Monterrey area and at Lázaro Cárdenas. Other important products made in Mexico include beer, cement, electrical machinery, fertilizers, household appliances, rubber, and wood pulp and paper.

Mexico has long been famous for the skill of its craftworkers. These craftworkers follow beautiful old Indian or Spanish-colonial designs. Their products generally vary by area. The articles made by these craftworkers include silver jewelry from Taxco, glassware and pottery from Guadalajara and Puebla, and handwoven baskets and blankets from Oaxaca and Toluca. Many of the products are sold to tourists.

Agriculture. The various farming regions of Mexico vary greatly in altitude, rainfall, and temperature. As a result, many kinds of crops can be grown. However, most of the country is mountainous or receives little rainfall, and is naturally unsuited for growing crops. Crops are grown on only 12 per cent of the total land area.

The best farmlands are in the southern part of Mexico's plateau. There, rich soils, enough rainfall, and a mild climate permit intensive cultivation. The northern part of the plateau has little rainfall and is used mainly for cattle grazing. Large irrigation projects have developed some rich croplands. Fertile soils are found in the rainy, hot regions of the south and east and in the eastern coastal plains. However, much work must be done to turn them into productive farmlands. This work includes clearing and draining the land, and controlling floods, insects, and plant diseases. The western coast of Mexico has fertile soils. However, much of it is mountainous and dry.

Until the 1900's, most Mexicans made a living by farming land near their villages or working on large estates called *haciendas* for wealthy landowners. The Mexican Constitution of 1917 provided for land reform. By 1964, the government had broken up most of the haciendas and distributed the land to the peasants. Today, agriculture provides about 28 per cent of all jobs but accounts for only about 8 per cent of the total value of goods and services. As a result, most farmers live in deep poverty and are far worse off than people in cities.

The constitution also recognized the old system of *ejidos* (farmlands held in common by communities). On the ejidos, farmers either work on individual sections by themselves, or they work the land as a group and share in the crops. Today, most ejidos are worked in individ-

Economy of Mexico

This map shows the major uses of land in Mexico. It also shows where the leading farm, fishing, mineral, and forest products are produced. It also locates the nation's chief manufacturing centers.

Chiefly cultivated land

Grazing land

Chiefly forest land

Generally unproductive land

Fishing

• Mineral deposit

• Manufacturing center

WORLD BOOK map

Mexico's gross domestic product

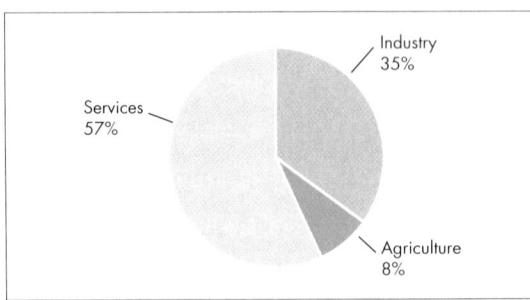

Mexico's gross domestic product (GDP) was $139,991,000,000 in 1987. The GDP is the total value of goods and services produced within a country in a year. *Services* include community, social, and personal services; finance, insurance, and real estate; trade and hotels; transportation and communication; and utilities. *Industry* includes construction, manufacturing, and mining. *Agriculture* includes agriculture, forestry, and fishing.

Production and workers by economic activities

Economic activities	Per cent of GDP produced	Employed workers Number of persons	Employed workers Per cent of total
Trade & hotels	27	3,156,000	14
Manufacturing	26	2,376,000	11
Community, social, & personal services	15	6,440,000	29
Agriculture, forestry, & fishing	8	6,020,000	28
Transportation & communication	7	1,058,000	5
Finance, insurance, & real estate	7	476,000	2
Mining	5	339,000	2
Construction	4	1,904,000	9
Utilities	1	104,000	*
Total	100	21,873,000	100

*Less than half of 1 per cent.
Figures are for 1987. Sources: International Monetary Fund; World Bank.

ual sections. Farmers may pass their land on to their children. By law, they are not allowed to sell or rent the land, though renting is common in practice. Ejidos include about half of Mexico's total cropland. The rest of the nation's cropland consists of small family farms or haciendas that the Mexican government has not broken up.

The Mexican government promotes modern farming methods by means of educational programs, financial aid, and expansion of irrigation and transportation systems. As a result, production has greatly increased in many areas of Mexico. However, ancient farming methods are still used in many other sections, especially on the ejidos.

Mexico's variety of climates enables the country to produce a wide range of crops. More land is used for corn, the people's basic food, than for any other crop. Other major crops include bananas, beans, coffee, cotton, oranges, potatoes, sorghum, sugar cane, and wheat. Mexican farmers also produce avocados, chili peppers, coconuts, grapes, lemons, mangoes, pineapples, safflower seeds, and tomatoes. Many tropical fruits and winter vegetables are exported to the United States. Va-

© Timothy Eagan, Woodfin Camp, Inc.

Beautiful silver objects, including vases, tableware, and jewelry, line the shelves of a shop in San Miguel de Allende, *above.* Mexico is the world's leading producer of silver.

nilla and *cacao,* the plant from which chocolate is made, are raised in tropical wet areas of Mexico.

Livestock is raised throughout Mexico. Beef cattle graze in the dry northern pasturelands. Dairy cattle are raised chiefly in central Mexico. Farmers throughout Mexico also raise chickens, goats, hogs, horses, sheep, and turkeys.

Mining. A wide variety of valuable minerals are mined in Mexico. The country ranks as the world's leading silver producer, mining about a sixth of the world's annual production. Most silver mines operate in the central regions of the country. Mexico is a leading producer of petroleum. It pumps about 900 million barrels of petroleum each year. Oil wells are found chiefly in the states of Campeche, Tabasco, and Veracruz, along the coast and in the Gulf of Mexico. The petroleum industry is operated by a government agency. In addition, Mexico produces much natural gas.

Mexico also mines large quantities of copper, gold, lead, salt, sulfur, and zinc. Other valuable minerals include antimony, bismuth, fluorite, manganese, and mercury. Large iron ore deposits support the nation's growing steel industry.

Fishing industry. Although Mexico has an extensive coastline, fishing accounts for less than 1 per cent of the national income. Important ports include the cities of Ensenada and La Paz on the Baja California Peninsula, Guaymas in the state of Sonora, and Mazatlán in the state of Sinaloa. Fishing crews catch anchovies, oysters, sardines, shrimp, and tuna, much of it for export.

Energy sources. Until the discovery of petroleum and natural gas deposits in Mexico in the 1970's, wood provided most of the energy poor people used for heating and cooking. These deposits have also been a major factor in the development of industry in Mexico, providing cheap fuel oil and natural gas for industrial use. More than 80 per cent of the energy used by industry and business comes from petroleum, and about 16 per cent comes from natural gas. Petroleum and natural gas also generate about 70 per cent of Mexico's electric power. Most of the rest is produced by hydroelectric

Oil refineries in Mexico process large amounts of petroleum. Oil is the country's most valuable natural resource. Petroleum and petroleum products account for more than a third of Mexico's earnings from foreign trade.

© Albano Guatti, The Stock Market

plants. Chicoasen Dam, Mexico's largest hydroelectric plant and one of the world's highest dams, is located on the Grijalva River in the state of Chiapas. The government handles almost all power production and distribution.

Trade. Mexico's chief export is petroleum and petroleum products. The main industrial export is automobile parts. Mexico also exports coffee, fruits and vegetables, and shrimp. Mineral exports include copper, salt, sulfur, silver, and zinc. The leading imports include industrial machinery, electric and electronic equipment, and motor vehicles.

About 70 per cent of Mexico's trade is with the United States, but trade with Western European countries and Japan is increasing. Trade with other Latin-American countries is relatively unimportant. But Mexico is trying to increase it through the Latin American Integration Association, an economic union of Mexico and 10 other Latin-American nations.

Throughout most of the 1980's, Mexico exported more than it imported. However, interest payments on the country's huge foreign debt have greatly strained the Mexican economy.

Tourism. Along with exports of manufactured goods and petroleum, tourism serves as one of Mexico's largest sources of income from abroad. Each year, more than 6 million tourists—mostly Americans—visit Mexico, spending approximately $3 billion. The tourist industry is also a major source of employment for the Mexican population. Tourists visit Mexico City, the old Spanish colonial cities of central Mexico, and the ruins of Mayan Indian cities on the Yucatán Peninsula. Beautiful beach resorts attract many people from the United States and Canada, especially in winter. Popular resort areas include Acapulco, Ensenada, Manzanillo, Mazatlán, Puerto Vallarta, and Zihuatanejo on the Pacific coast, and Cancún and Cozumel Island on the Caribbean coast.

Transportation in Mexico ranges from modern methods to ancient ones. Airlines, highways, and railroads connect all the major cities and towns. But some farmers still carry goods to market on their heads and backs, or by burros and oxcarts.

Mexico has a good highway system. The country has an average of about 1 automobile for every 12 people. Many buses connect Mexico's urban areas.

Mexico City is an important center of international air travel. Guadalajara, Acapulco, Monterrey, and Mérida also have large international airports. Mexico has an extensive government-owned railway network.

Mexico has more than 30 seaports. The major ones include Coatzacoalcos, Tampico, and Veracruz on the Gulf of Mexico, and Guaymas and Salina Cruz on the Pacific Ocean. The nation has a small merchant fleet.

Communication. The first book known to be published in the Western Hemisphere was a catechism printed in Mexico City in 1539. Today, books and magazines published in Mexico City are read widely throughout Mexico and all of Latin America. Mexico has more than 300 daily newspapers, representing many different political opinions. The largest newspapers include *Esto, Excélsior, El Heraldo de México, El Nacional, Novedades, Ovaciones, La Prensa,* and *El Universal,* all published in Mexico City. Other important newspapers include *La Jornada* and *Unomásuno.*

Mexico has an average of about 1 radio for every 4

© Sergio Dorantes

Automobile production is an important manufacturing activity in Mexico. Many of the country's factories produce automobiles or automobile parts for export to the United States.

people and 1 television set for every 9 people. Telephone and telegraph lines connect all parts of the country. The motion-picture industry of Mexico produces more films each year than that of any other Latin-American nation.

History

Ancient times. The first people who lived in what is now Mexico arrived before 8000 B.C. They were Indians of unknown tribes who migrated from the north. These Indians were hunters who lived in small, temporary communities. They followed the herds of buffalo, mammoths, mastodons, and other large animals that roamed the land. About 7500 B.C., the climate became drier. The herds could not find enough grass to eat and died off. The Indians then lived on small wild animals or the berries and seeds of wild plants.

About 7000 B.C., Indians in what is now the Puebla region discovered how to grow plants for food and became farmers. They grew corn, which became their most important food, and avocados, beans, peppers, squashes, and tomatoes. These Indians were among the first people to cultivate these vegetables. They also raised dogs and turkeys for food. As the wandering bands of hunters became groups of farmers, they established permanent settlements.

The growth of villages. By 2000 B.C., large farm villages stood along Lake Texcoco in the fertile south-central Valley of Mexico, and in the southern highlands and forests. The farmers used irrigation to improve their crops. The villages grew and new classes of people developed, including pottery makers, priests, and weavers. Trade in polished stones, pottery, and seashells was carried on with distant communities.

By 1000 B.C., the villagers were building flat-topped pyramids with temples on them. Some villages, including Cuicuilco near what is now Mexico City, became religious centers. Indians came from other communities to worship in the temples. Because these people were farmers, they worshiped gods that represented such natural forces as the rain and the sun. The villages grew into towns, from the Valley of Mexico to the Gulf of Mexico and to the Pacific Ocean, and south to what is now Guatemala.

The Olmec Indians of the southern Gulf Coast made the first great advance toward civilization in the Mexico region. Between about 1200 B.C. and 400 B.C., the Olmec developed a counting system and calendar. They also carved beautiful stone statues. See **Olmec Indians**.

The Classic Period. Great Indian civilizations thrived between A.D. 250 and 900, the Classic Period of Mexico. Huge pyramids dedicated to the sun and the moon were built at Teotihuacán, near what is now Mexico City. In the religious centers of southern Mexico and northern Central America, the Maya Indians built beautiful homes, pyramids, and temples of limestone. They recorded important dates on tall, carved blocks of stone, and wrote in a kind of picture writing. In what is now the state of Oaxaca, the Zapotec Indians flattened a mountaintop and built their religious center of Monte Albán. See **Maya; Zapotec Indians**.

The reasons for the fall of these classic civilizations are not clear. The climate probably became even drier about A.D. 900, and not enough crops could be produced to feed the large population. Perhaps the city people attacked their neighbors to get more land. Or farmers may have revolted against the priests who had ruled them. In the north, wild Chichimec tribes destroyed many cities, including Teotihuacán.

The Toltec and the Aztec. Many wars took place after the Classic Period. The Toltec Indians established an empire during the 900's, with a capital at Tula, north of present-day Mexico City. Toltec influence spread throughout the central and southern regions. This influence included the use of stone pillars to support roofs, the worship of the feathered-serpent god Quetzalcóatl, and human sacrifice in religion. Invading Chichimec tribes destroyed Tula and the Toltec empire about 1200. See **Toltec Indians**.

The Aztec built the last and greatest Indian empire during the mid-1400's. The Aztec empire extended between the Pacific and Gulf coasts, and from the Isthmus

Important dates in Mexico

c. 2000 B.C. Village life developed in the Valley of Mexico.	**1876-1880** and **1884-1911** Porfirio Díaz ruled Mexico as dictator.
c. A.D. 250-900 Great Indian civilizations thrived during the Classic Period.	**1910-1911** Francisco I. Madero led a revolution that overthrew Díaz.
c. 900-1200 The Toltec empire controlled the Valley of Mexico.	**1914** United States forces occupied Veracruz.
1325 (According to legend) The Aztec founded Tenochtitlan (now Mexico City).	**1917** A revolutionary constitution was adopted.
1519-1521 Hernando Cortés conquered the Aztec empire for Spain.	**1920** The government began making revolutionary social and economic reforms.
1810 Miguel Hidalgo y Costilla began the Mexican struggle for independence.	**1929** The National Revolutionary Party was formed.
1821 Mexico won independence.	**1934** The government began a major program of land distribution to farmers.
1824 Mexico became a republic.	**1938** Mexico took over foreign oil company properties.
1836 Texas won independence from Mexico.	**1942-1945** Mexico's industries expanded rapidly during World War II to supply the Allies with war goods.
1846-1848 The United States defeated Mexico in the Mexican War and won much Mexican territory.	**1953** Women received the right to vote in all elections.
1855 A liberal government under Benito Juárez began a period of reform.	**1968** Government troops put down student demonstrations in Mexico City.
1863 French troops occupied Mexico City.	**1970's** Major new petroleum deposits were discovered on the Gulf of Mexico coast.
1864 Maximilian of Austria became emperor of Mexico.	**1985** Two earthquakes struck south-central Mexico, killing about 7,200 people.
1867 Liberal forces led by Benito Juárez regained power.	

A sculpture of the Aztec god Chac-mool, *left,* served as an altar for human sacrifice in religious ceremonies. Human sacrifice played a major role in the Aztec religion.

of Tehuantepec north to the Pánuco River. The Aztec capital, Tenochtitlan, stood on an island in Lake Texcoco at the site of Mexico City. According to legend, Tenochtitlan had been founded in 1325. When the Spaniards arrived in 1519, Tenochtitlan had a population of about 100,000. No Spanish city then had so many people.

The Aztec were fierce warriors who believed it their duty to sacrifice the men they captured in battle to their gods. The people they conquered hated them because every year the Aztec sacrificed thousands of prisoners of war. The Aztec also composed beautiful music and poetry, and were skilled in medicine. They grew rich with gold, silver, and other treasures paid yearly by the cities and tribes they conquered. See **Aztec.**

The Spanish conquest. The Spaniards began to occupy the West Indies during the 1490's, and discovered Mexico in 1517. That year, Diego Velázquez, the governor of Cuba, sent ships under Francisco Fernández de Córdoba to explore to the west and search for treasure. Córdoba found the Yucatán Peninsula and brought back reports of large cities. Velázquez sent Juan de Grijalva in 1518. Grijalva explored the Mexican coast from Yucatán to what is now Veracruz.

Reports of the strangers were carried to the Aztec emperor Montezuma II, or Moctezuma II, in Tenochtitlan. The tales of Spanish guns and horses—which the Indians had never seen before—and of soldiers in armor made him fear that the Spaniards were gods.

A third expedition of about 650 Spaniards sailed from Cuba under Hernando Cortés, or Hernán Cortés, in February 1519. Cortés' 11 ships followed Grijalva's route along the coast. Cortés defeated large Indian armies with his horses and cannons. He founded Veracruz, the first Spanish settlement in what is now Mexico.

Montezuma sent messengers with rich gifts for Cortés, but he also ordered the Spaniards to leave the land. Instead, Cortés marched toward Tenochtitlan. He

was joined by thousands of the Aztec's Indian enemies, who looked on him as the destroyer of the cruel Aztec. Montezuma did not oppose the Spaniards because he feared Cortés was the god Quetzalcóatl. He allowed the invaders to enter Tenochtitlan in November 1519. The Spaniards were far too few to control the great Aztec capital by themselves. Cortés soon seized Montezuma and held him as hostage for the safety of the Spaniards.

In June 1520, the Aztec revolted. After a week of bitter fighting, the Spaniards tried to sneak out of the city. The Aztec discovered them, and hundreds of Spaniards were killed during *la noche triste* (the sad night). The rest, including Cortés, were saved because their Indian friends fought and stopped the Aztec. Six months later,

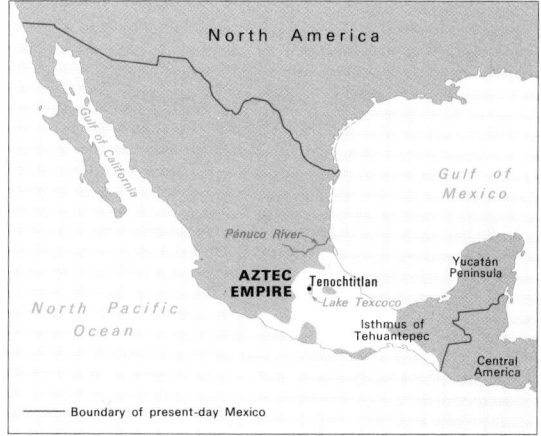

The Aztec empire reached the height of its power during the early 1500's, covering much of what is now south-central Mexico. In 1521, Spaniards led by the explorer Hernando Cortés conquered the Aztec and destroyed their civilization.

From a book by Giovanni Battista Ramusio. Library of Congress

The Aztec capital, Tenochtitlan (now Mexico City), stood on an island in Lake Texcoco. Raised roads connected it with the mainland. This map, published in 1556, is based on one believed to have been drawn by Hernando Cortés, conqueror of the Aztec.

Cortés returned to Tenochtitlan with Spanish forces and a large army of Indians. By May 1521, he had surrounded the Aztec capital with his army and boats, and had cut off the city's food and water. Battles, sickness, and starvation weakened the Aztec army. In August, Cuauhtémoc, the last emperor, surrendered the city. Cortés sent soldiers to take over the rest of the Aztec empire. Some Indians resisted, but most accepted Spanish rule without a fight. See **Cortés, Hernando.**

Spanish rule. After the fighting ended, the Spaniards faced the problem of how to govern the large number of people in the colony. To keep the Indians from revolting, King Charles I of Spain allowed them to speak their own languages and to be governed by their own officials. But he also made a few changes. The Indians had to pay a special tax called a *tribute* and to work for the Spaniards when help was needed. In addition, the Indians were required to convert to Roman Catholicism.

Tenochtitlan and other Indian cities became Spanish cities in which the whites ruled. The whites included *peninsulares* (people born in Spain) and *creoles* (Europeans born in the New World). *Mestizos* (people of mixed white and Indian ancestry) performed labor in the cities. The creoles and mestizos considered themselves superior to the Indians.

During the 1540's, the Spaniards discovered silver mines in the northern part of the colony. The silver brought much wealth to the creoles and peninsulares, and the silver mines drew additional Spanish immigrants. The creoles established estates called *haciendas.* There, they produced food and clothing for the new mining communities. The creoles used the power of the royal government to make the Indians work for them. The Indians lived on the haciendas when they had work. The rest of the time, they lived in their own villages.

The Indians were poor, but they accepted their way of life. They were allowed to live separately according to their customs. As a result, the houses they lived in, the food they ate, and the way they worked changed little over the nearly 300 years of Spanish rule. The king agreed that Spanish laws gave the Indians the right to keep the lands they had owned before the conquest. The Indians found ways to blend the Roman Catholic faith with their own culture, and they respected their Spanish priests.

The Indians considered the king of Spain as their defender. The creoles were at first content to be ruled by Spain because the king was far away and he usually permitted them to govern themselves. The laws were made in Spain, but only a few Spanish officials worked in the colony. The officials could not enforce the laws if the creoles objected. However, in the late 1700's, King Charles III tried to reorganize the government, giving more power to himself and less to the creoles. He also raised taxes. Few creoles sought independence, but many wanted more control of their affairs.

Revolt against the Spaniards. In 1807, French forces occupied Spain and imprisoned King Ferdinand VII. Confusion spread in the colony. Some creoles plotted to seize the colony's government. One of these men was Miguel Hidalgo y Costilla, a priest. Late on the night of Sept. 15, 1810, he called Indians and mestizos to his church in the town of Dolores. He made a speech known as the *Grito de Dolores* (Cry of Dolores), in which he called for a rebellion so that Mexicans could govern

Fresco (1949) by José Clemente Orozco in the State Capitol, Guadalajara (© Robert Frerck)

Miguel Hidalgo y Costilla set off Mexico's War of Independence in 1810. Mexico won freedom from Spain in 1821.

Mexico. Today, late on September 15, Mexico's president rings a bell and repeats the Grito de Dolores. Mexicans celebrate September 16 as Independence Day.

Hidalgo's untrained followers armed themselves and attacked Spanish officials and those who supported the Spaniards. At first, Hidalgo gained support for his cause. But most of his followers were Indians and mestizos, and not creoles. Some Indian communities also refused to support Hidalgo because of the violent ways of the rebels. Hidalgo was forced to retreat. In 1811, Spanish troops captured and executed him.

José María Morelos y Pavón, another priest, continued Hidalgo's struggle. In 1813, Morelos held a Congress that issued the first formal call for independence. The Congress wrote a constitution for a Mexican republic. Morelos hoped to attract the creoles who wanted reform. He succeeded further than Hidalgo. In 1815, however, Morelos too was captured and executed by the Spaniards.

By 1816, Spanish troops had captured or killed almost all of the rebels. Mexico was again at peace, and King Ferdinand VII had returned to the Spanish throne. But the king did not realize that most creoles supported him, and that they still only wanted reform. Instead, the king thought that all Mexicans were traitors to Spain. Ferdinand taxed the creoles and organized a large army to put down any revolutionary movement. His actions convinced many creoles that they no longer could trust Spain.

Independence. In 1820, a revolt by liberals swept Spain. Ferdinand's power weakened, and many creoles saw their chance for revolution. A group of powerful creoles supported Agustín de Iturbide, a military officer. Iturbide had been given command of a Spanish army to crush the last rebel leader, Vicente Guerrero. Instead of fighting Guerrero, Iturbide met with him peacefully. In February 1821, the two leaders agreed to make Mexico independent. They joined their armies and won the support of the liberal and conservative creoles. Only a small part of the Spanish forces in Mexico remained loyal to Spain. By the end of 1821, the last Spanish officials withdrew from Mexico, and Mexico became independent.

Following independence, the creoles could not agree on a form of government. Conservatives wanted a monarchy, but liberals called for a republic. The conservatives, who formed the majority, sought a monarch. They could not persuade a member of the royal family of Spain to be king, and so Iturbide became Emperor Agustín I in 1822. But Iturbide was a poor ruler, and most groups turned against him. In 1823, a military revolt drove him from power.

Mexico's Congress then followed the wishes of the liberals and began to write a constitution for a federal republic. But the creoles still disagreed on how the constitution should be written. Conservatives wanted a strong central government and wanted Roman Catholicism to be the national religion, as it had been under Spanish rule. Liberals wanted the central government to have less power and the states more, and they called for freedom of religion. The groups finally reached a compromise, though many conservative creoles did not support it. In 1824, Mexico became a republic with a president and a two-house Congress heading the national government, and governors and legislatures heading

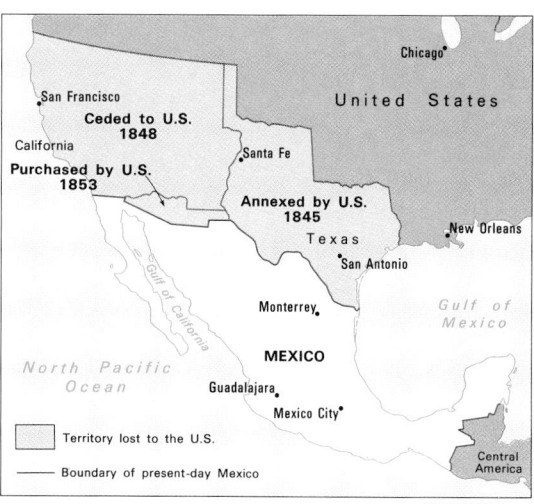

WORLD BOOK map

The Republic of Mexico was established in 1824. It covered much of what is now the Western and Southwestern United States. In the mid-1800's, Mexico lost vast territories to the United States and sold the United States additional lands.

the states. Guadalupe Victoria, a follower of Hidalgo and Morelos, became the first president.

War with Texas and the United States. The mid-1800's was a time of great troubles in Mexico. Many creoles still did not support the Constitution, and Mexicans had little experience in lawmaking and self-government. Military men frequently revolted. One of them, General Antonio López de Santa Anna, became the most important political figure in the country. He was president 11 times between 1833 and 1855. The people elected him president in 1833, and he favored the liberal policies of the government that was temporarily heading the country. But he did not serve right away. In 1834, he joined the conservatives in a revolt against the temporary government, took control, and became a dictator.

Texas was then part of Mexico, but many people from the United States had settled there. When Santa Anna changed the Constitution to give himself more control over the provinces, Americans and Mexicans who supported the liberals in Texas revolted. In 1836, Santa Anna defeated a Texas force in the Battle of the Alamo at San Antonio. But later that year, Texas forces defeated his army at San Jacinto and captured him. Santa Anna signed a treaty recognizing the independence of Texas. In addition to what is now the state of Texas, the new republic of Texas included parts of present-day Colorado, Kansas, New Mexico, Oklahoma, and Wyoming.

The Mexican government did not recognize Santa Anna's treaty. Texas joined the United States in 1845, but Mexico still claimed it. Border disputes developed between Mexico and the United States. In April 1846, U.S. soldiers entered the disputed area and were attacked by Mexican soldiers. In May, the United States declared war on Mexico.

U.S. soldiers occupied what was then Mexican territory in Arizona, California, and New Mexico. In February 1847, U.S. General Zachary Taylor fought Santa Anna—who was again president—in Mexico, at the Battle of Buena Vista near Saltillo. Both sides claimed victory.

Taylor became a national hero in the United States and was elected President the next year. Other U.S. forces landed at Veracruz under General Winfield Scott. In September 1847, Scott captured Mexico City after the bitter Battle of Chapultepec. In this battle, six military students threw themselves from Chapultepec Castle to their deaths, rather than surrender. Today, the Monument to the Boy Heroes stands in Chapultepec Park in their honor.

The Treaty of Guadalupe Hidalgo, signed in February 1848, ended the Mexican War. Under the treaty, Mexico gave the United States the land that is now California, Nevada, and Utah; most of Arizona; and parts of Colorado, New Mexico, and Wyoming. Mexico also recognized Texas, down to the Rio Grande, as part of the United States. Mexico received $15 million from the United States. In the Gadsden Purchase of 1853, the United States paid Mexico $10 million for land in what is now southern Arizona and New Mexico.

For fuller accounts of this period, see the articles on **Alamo; Gadsden Purchase; Guadalupe Hidalgo, Treaty of; Mexican War; San Jacinto, Battle of; Santa Anna, Antonio; Texas** (The Texas revolution).

Reform. The Mexican War exhausted the country's economy, and great political confusion developed. Santa Anna again seized power in 1853 and ruled as a dictator. But the liberals had been gaining strength since the war. In 1855, they drove Santa Anna from power.

Benito Juárez, a Zapotec Indian, and other men gave the liberal movement effective leadership. The liberals promoted the private ownership of land. After they took over in 1855, they passed laws to break up the large estates of the Roman Catholic Church and the lands of Indian villages. In 1857, a new Constitution brought back the federal system of government.

The new reforms resulted in a conservative revolt in 1858. Juárez fled from Mexico City. The liberals declared him president, and he set up a government in Veracruz. During the civil war that followed—the War of the Reform—a conservative government operated in Mexico City. The Catholic bishops supported the conservatives because of the liberals' opposition to the church. In 1859, Juárez issued his Reform Laws in an attempt to end the church's political power in Mexico. The laws ordered the separation of church and state, and the takeover of all church property. The liberal armies defeated the conservatives late in 1860, and Juárez returned to Mexico City in 1861.

The French invasion. The Mexican government had little money after the War of the Reform. Juárez stopped payments on the country's debts to France, Great Britain, and Spain. Troops of the three nations occupied Veracruz in 1862. The British and Spaniards soon left after they saw that the French were more interested in political power than in collecting debts. The French emperor, Napoleon III, took this opportunity to invade and conquer Mexico. French troops occupied Mexico City in 1863. Juárez escaped from the capital.

In 1864, Mexican conservatives, aided by Napoleon III, named Maximilian emperor of Mexico. Maximilian was a brother of the emperor of Austria. Juárez and the liberals fought guerrilla-style battles against Maximilian and the French invaders. In 1866, the United States put pressure on France to remove its troops. This pressure

and the fighting against the liberals were problems for the French. Also, Napoleon III feared war would break out in Europe. In 1867, he withdrew his forces from Mexico. Juárez' forces then captured and shot Maximilian. The conservative movement broke up. Juárez returned to Mexico City, and the country was united behind the liberals. Juárez served as president from 1867 until his death in 1872.

The dictatorship of Porfirio Díaz. Frequent revolts took place again after Juárez' death. In 1876, Porfirio Díaz, a mestizo general, overthrew Juárez' successor. Díaz developed good relations with the conservatives and with some liberal state leaders who cooperated with him. He used his army to control people who opposed him. Díaz served as president from 1876 to 1880, and from 1884 to 1911. The strength of his friends and the fear of his army helped him rule as a dictator. Many people who sided with him became wealthy.

Mexico's economy improved under Díaz. Railroads were built, mines and oil wells developed, and manufacturing industry expanded. But industrial wages were kept low, and attempts to form labor unions were crushed. Indian communities lost their land to big landowners. The great majority of Mexicans remained in poverty and ignorance. The benefits of Mexico's improved economy went chiefly to the big landowners, businessmen, and foreign investors.

The Revolution of 1910. Opposition to Díaz' rule began to grow after 1900. Francisco I. Madero, a liberal landowner, decided to run against him in 1910. During the campaign, Madero became widely popular. Díaz had him jailed until after the election, which Díaz won. Madero then fled to the United States.

In November 1910, Madero issued a call for revolution. He had opposed violence, but he saw no other way to overthrow Díaz. Revolutionary bands developed throughout Mexico. They defeated federal troops, destroyed railroads, and attacked towns and estates. In May 1911, members of Díaz' government agreed to force him from office, in hope of preventing further bloodshed. Díaz resigned and left Mexico, and Madero became president later that year.

Madero meant well, but he could not handle the many groups that opposed him. Some wanted a dictatorship again. Others called for greater reforms than Madero put through. In 1913, General Victoriano Huerta seized power, and Madero was murdered.

Many Mexicans supported Huerta's dictatorship, hoping for peace. But Madero's followers united behind Venustiano Carranza, a state governor, and the bitter fighting continued. President Woodrow Wilson of the United States openly sided with Carranza's revolutionaries. In 1914, U.S. forces seized Veracruz. Wilson hoped to prevent the shipment of arms from the seaport to Huerta's army. Later in 1914, Carranza's forces occupied Mexico City, and Huerta was forced to leave the country. See **Wilson, Woodrow** (Crisis in Mexico).

The Constitution of 1917. The victorious revolutionary leaders soon began to struggle among themselves for power. Carranza's armies fought those of Francisco "Pancho" Villa and Emiliano Zapata. Villa and Zapata demanded more extreme reforms than Carranza planned. In 1915, the United States supported Carranza and halted the export of guns to his enemies. In revenge,

Rebel forces commanded by Emiliano Zapata marched toward Mexico City after the overthrow of Mexican dictator Victoriano Huerta in 1914. Zapata and Francisco "Pancho" Villa struggled for power against revolutionary leader Venustiano Carranza. But by 1916, Carranza controlled most of Mexico.

UPI/Bettmann

Villa crossed the border in 1916 and raided Columbus, N. Mex. His men killed 18 Americans. About five times as many Mexicans also died in the raid. President Wilson sent General John J. Pershing into Mexico, but Pershing's troops failed to capture Villa.

In 1916, Carranza's power was recognized throughout most of Mexico. He called a convention to prepare a new Constitution. The Constitution, adopted in 1917, combined Carranza's liberal policies with more extreme reforms. It gave the government control over education, farm and oil properties, and the Roman Catholic Church. It also limited Mexico's president to one term and recognized labor unions.

Carranza did little to carry out the new constitutional program. In 1920, he was killed during a revolt led by General Álvaro Obregón, who later became president.

Economic and social changes. Obregón distributed some land among the peasants, built many schools throughout the countryside, and supported a strong labor union movement. Plutarco Elías Calles, who had fought Huerta and Villa, became president in 1924. Calles carried on the revolutionary program. He encouraged land reform and enforced constitutional controls over the Roman Catholic Church. The bishops protested by closing the churches from 1926 to 1929. The closing of the churches resulted in a rebellion among the peasants. Emilio Portes Gil became president in 1928, but Calles remained the real power behind the presidency. In 1929, Portes Gil reached an agreement with church officials that allowed the Catholic Church to operate schools and churches without interference. In return, church leaders promised to stay out of political affairs.

Calles formed the National Revolutionary Party in 1929. Until then, Mexican political parties had been temporary groups organized by presidential candidates. The National Revolutionary Party stood for the goals of the Mexican Revolution. It included all important political groups and continues in power today. It was reorganized as the Party of the Mexican Revolution in 1938, and as the Institutional Revolutionary Party in 1946.

By the 1930's, the push for reform had slowed down. Calles and many other old leaders were now wealthy landowners and opposed extreme changes. Younger politicians called for speeding up the revolutionary program. As a result, the National Revolutionary Party adopted a six-year plan of social and economic reform. General Lázaro Cárdenas was named to carry it out.

After Cárdenas became president in 1934, he ended Calles' power. He divided among the peasants more than twice as much land as all previous presidents combined had done. He also promoted government controls over foreign-owned companies and strongly supported labor unions. In 1938, during a strike of oil workers, the government took over the properties of American and British oil companies. The companies and the British government protested angrily. But the U.S. government recognized Mexico's right to the properties as long as the companies received fair payment. In the 1940's, Mexico agreed to make payments to the companies.

The mid-1900's. Mexico's economy grew rapidly in the 1940's. Manuel Ávila Camacho, who was president from 1940 to 1946, did much to encourage industrial progress. World War II also contributed to the nation's industrial growth. Mexico entered the war on the side of the Allies in 1942. It sent an air force unit to the Philippines to fight the Japanese, but its contribution to the war effort was almost entirely economic. The country supplied raw materials and many laborers to the United States. It also made war equipment in factories that the United States helped set up. The value of Mexico's exports had nearly doubled when the war ended in 1945.

The Mexican economy continued to improve after the war. Industry and other economic activities expanded from the late 1940's through the 1960's. New factories made such products as automobiles, cement, chemicals, clothing, electrical appliances, processed foods, and steel. The government expanded highway, irrigation, and railroad systems. Many new buildings went up, especially in Mexico City. Agricultural exports from Mexico to the United States increased. A growing number of

United States tourists in Mexico also helped the economy.

Miguel Alemán Valdés served as president of Mexico from 1946 to 1952. He was followed by Adolfo Ruiz Cortines, who served from 1952 to 1958; Adolfo López Mateos, from 1958 to 1964; and Gustavo Díaz Ordaz, from 1964 to 1970. Under these leaders, Mexico maintained close relations with the United States.

The 1970's. Worldwide problems of recession and inflation led to a decrease in economic production and sharp increases in prices in Mexico during the 1970's. In 1976, Mexico's currency was devalued twice in an effort to stabilize the economy (see **Devaluation**).

Luis Echeverría Álvarez, who was president of Mexico from 1970 to 1976, increased government control over foreign-owned businesses. He also took steps that strained Mexico's friendship with the United States. For example, he improved Mexico's relations with the governments of Cuba and Chile in spite of United States opposition to those governments. Illegal immigration of Mexicans into the United States, plus drug smuggling from Mexico to the United States, caused more problems between the two countries. Echeverría also worked to make Mexico a leader among the developing nations.

José López Portillo became president in 1976. He reduced government controls over both foreign and domestic businesses to encourage more private investment in Mexico. Relations between Mexico and the United States improved somewhat after López Portillo became president.

Vast petroleum deposits were discovered in Mexico during the 1970's. The country's petroleum production and its income from petroleum increased sharply. In the late 1970's, the government greatly increased spending on public works and industry in order to create more jobs.

Recent developments. In spite of Mexico's economic progress since 1940, many people remain poor. Many farmers still lack modern agricultural equipment and irrigation systems, and wages for farm laborers are low. Each year, more Mexicans move from farms to cities in search of jobs. This migration and Mexico's high rate of population growth have helped cause overcrowding and a shortage of jobs in the cities. Every year, many Mexicans move to other countries, especially the United States, to try to make a better living.

The Mexican government expected the income from petroleum to help balance its spending. But by 1981, decreased demand and lower prices for petroleum helped create an economic crisis in Mexico. The government became deeply in debt, and unemployment and prices rose sharply.

In 1982, Miguel de la Madrid Hurtado succeeded López Portillo as president. But Mexico's economic problems continued. These problems worsened during the early 1980's, when thousands of refugees from El Salvador, Guatemala, and Nicaragua entered Mexico and settled in camps near the border in the Chiapas Highlands.

On Sept. 19 and 20, 1985, earthquakes struck south-central Mexico, including Mexico City. They caused about 10,000 deaths and $5 billion in property damage.

During the mid-1980's, opposition to the Institutional

© R. Gaillarde, Gamma/Liaison

Earthquakes devastated south-central Mexico in 1985, killing about 10,000 people. In Mexico City, *above,* the quakes destroyed many buildings and left thousands of people homeless.

Revolutionary Party grew in state and local elections. In 1988, the party's candidate, Carlos Salinas de Gortari, was elected Mexico's president in the closest election in many decades. Many people believed that Salinas won the election by fraud, and he entered office amid much criticism. That same year, an opposition coalition, the National Democratic Front, and an opposition party, the National Action Party, won almost half of the seats in the Chamber of Deputies. As a result, the president no longer could depend on the vote of two-thirds of the Chamber of Deputies required to amend the Constitution.

Salinas promised to remove government restrictions on the economy and to reform Mexican politics. He attempted to stimulate economic growth and overcome Mexico's huge foreign debt by further reducing government ownership of businesses and by encouraging large-scale foreign investment in Mexico. Under these reforms, Mexico's economy improved, and Salinas' party won a huge majority of seats in the Chamber of Deputies in 1991 elections. The government has also taken steps to prevent election fraud, but opponents and observers charged that dishonesty still existed in elections held in the late 1980's and early 1990's.

Roderic A. Camp and James D. Riley

Related articles in *World Book* include:

Biographies

Ávila Camacho, Manuel	Carranza, Venustiano
Cárdenas, Lázaro	Chávez, Carlos

Cortés, Hernando
Cortina, Juan Nepomuceno
Cuauhtémoc
De la Madrid Hurtado,
  Miguel
Díaz, Porfirio
Fuentes, Carlos
Gamio, Manuel
Hidalgo y Costilla, Miguel
Iturbide, Agustín de
Juana Inés de la Cruz
Juárez, Benito P.
López Portillo, José

Maximilian
Montezuma
Obregón, Álvaro
Orozco, José C.
Paz, Octavio
Rivera, Diego
Ruiz Cortines, Adolfo
Salinas de Gortari, Carlos
Santa Anna, Antonio López de
Siqueiros, David
Tamayo, Rufino
Villa, Pancho
Zapata, Emiliano

Cities

Acapulco
Guadalajara
Juárez
Mexicali
Mexico City
Monterrey
Netzahualcóyotl

Nuevo Laredo
Oaxaca
Puebla
Tampico
Taxco
Tijuana
Veracruz

History

Alamo
Aztec
Gadsden Purchase
Guadalupe Hidalgo, Treaty of
Indian, American
Maya
Mexican War

Olmec Indians
San Jacinto, Battle of
Tarascan Indians
Toltec Indians
Yaqui Indians
Zapotec Indians

Physical features

Gulf of California
Gulf of Mexico
Ixtacihuatl
Lake Xochimilco
Orizaba, Pico de
Paricutín

Popocatépetl
Rio Grande
Sierra Madre
Tehuantepec, Isthmus of
Yucatán Peninsula

Other related articles

Adobe
Bullfighting
Cactus
Clothing (pictures)
Feasts and festivals (picture)
Guadalupe Day

Henequen
Hispanic Americans
Latin America
Mexico, National Autono-
  mous University of

Outline

I. Government
  A. National government
  B. Local government
  C. Politics
  D. Courts
  E. Armed forces
II. People
  A. Population
  B. Ancestry
  C. Language
III. Way of life
  A. City life
  B. Rural life
  C. Clothing
  D. Food and drink
  E. Holidays
  F. Recreation
  G. Religion
  H. Education
IV. Arts
  A. Architecture
  B. Painting
  C. Literature
  D. Music
V. The land
  A. The Pacific Northwest
  B. The Plateau of Mexico
  C. The Gulf Coastal Plain
  D. The Southern Uplands
  E. The Chiapas Highlands
  F. The Yucatán Peninsula
  G. Plant and animal life

VI. Climate
VII. Economy
  A. Service industries
  B. Manufacturing
  C. Agriculture
  D. Mining
  E. Fishing industry
  F. Energy sources
  G. Trade
  H. Tourism
  I. Transportation
  J. Communication
VIII. History

Questions

To which ancestral group do most Mexicans belong?
What is the largest main land region of Mexico?
About how much of Mexico can support crops?
How did the discovery of petroleum deposits during the 1970's
  affect the Mexican economy?
What are some words that came from Mexico and are used in
  the United States?
What powers does Mexico's president have?
Who were the *peninsulares*? The *creoles*?
What is the chief food of most Mexicans?
Why did United States forces seize Veracruz in 1914?
What is Mexico's most important religious holiday?

Reading and Study Guide

See *Mexico* in the Research Guide/Index, Volume 22, for a *Reading and Study Guide.*

Additional resources

Level I

Casagrande, Louis B., and Johnson, S. A. *Focus on Mexico: Mod-
ern Life in an Ancient Land.* Lerner, 1986.
Fisher, Leonard E. *Pyramid of the Sun, Pyramid of the Moon.*
Macmillan, 1988. Describes the ancient cultures at the pyra-
mids of Teotihuacan.
Marcus, Rebecca B. and Judith. *Fiesta Time in Mexico.* Garrard,
1974.
Mexico in Pictures. Lerner, 1987.
Rummel, Jack. *Mexico.* Chelsea Hse., 1990.
Stein, R. Conrad. *Mexico.* Childrens Pr., 1984.

Level II

Levy, Daniel C., and Székely, Gabriel. *Mexico: Paradoxes of Sta-
bility and Change.* 2nd ed. Westview, 1987.
Meyer, Michael C., and Sherman, W. L. *The Course of Mexican
History.* 3rd ed. Oxford, 1987.
Oster, Patrick. *The Mexicans: A Personal Portrait of a People.*
Morrow, 1989.
Sabloff, Jeremy A. *The Cities of Ancient Mexico: Reconstructing
a Lost World.* Thames & Hudson, 1989.
Weintraub, Sidney. *A Marriage of Convenience: Relations Be-
tween Mexico and the United States.* Oxford, 1990.

México, a state of Mexico, lies mainly within the beautiful Valley of Mexico. It borders the Federal District,
which has the same boundaries as Mexico City (see
Mexico [political map]). México covers 8,245 square
miles (21,355 square kilometers) and has a population of
11,571,111. Toluca is the capital city. Naucalpan,
Netzahualcóyotl, and Tlalnepantla are major industrial
centers.   James D. Riley

Mexico, National Autonomous University of, is
the largest university in Mexico. It was founded in 1551,
in Mexico City, as the Royal and Pontifical University.
The Roman Catholic Church operated the university
until the government closed it in 1867. It was reopened
in 1910 as the National University of Mexico. The university became *autonomous* (free of government control) in
1929. A new campus was built during the early 1950's.

The university has an enrollment of more than
325,000. Courses are offered in law, philosophy, medicine, science, music, political and social science, commerce, engineering, architecture, and nursing.
          P. A. McGinley

© Byron Augustin from D. Donne Bryant Stock

Mexico City landmarks include the towering Monument to Independence, *above,* honoring heroes of Mexico's independence movement. The monument stands at an intersection of a wide boulevard called the Paseo de la Reforma, the city's major street.

Mexico City

Mexico City is the capital of Mexico and one of the largest cities in the world. About 10 million people live in Mexico City. The metropolitan area of Mexico City, with a population of about 19 million, is the world's largest urban area. About one-fourth of Mexico's people live there. The city is Mexico's center of commerce, higher education, industry, culture, and transportation.

Mexico City lies in central Mexico, about halfway between the Gulf of Mexico and the Pacific Ocean. The city has the same official boundaries as the Federal District of Mexico. The Federal District is a separate political area, similar to the District of Columbia in the United States. The built-up part of Mexico City occupies the northern section of the Federal District, and the rest of the district is rural. The metropolitan area has spread north into the state of México.

Mexico City has long dominated the country economically, politically, and culturally. It was the site of Tenochtitlan (pronounced *tay nohch TEE tlahn*), the capital of the Aztec Indian empire in the 1400's. Spain conquered the Aztec in the 1500's, and the city became the capital of Spain's colony in the Americas. After Mexico became independent in 1821, Mexico City served as the nation's capital through Mexico's years of growth into a modern republic.

As a political and economic center, the city is a magnet for ambitious Mexicans from all walks of life. Its attractions have contributed to its rapid growth and also to its problems. As more and more people moved from

rural Mexico and other cities to the capital, government services could not keep pace with the growing population. In addition, the increase in the number of factories and automobiles in Mexico City created one of the world's worst air pollution problems.

The city

Mexico City is built on ground that once was the lakebed of Lake Texcoco (pronounced *tay SKOH koh*). Surrounded by mountains, the city sits in a natural basin that is 7,349 feet (2,240 meters) above sea level. Mexico City covers 571 square miles (1,479 square kilometers). The metropolitan area extends over about 900 square miles (2,330 square kilometers).

Downtown is the heart of Mexico City. Spanish architecture from the city's colonial period mixes with modern buildings in this section. The center of the downtown section has a layout common to Spanish colonial cities, with a major cathedral and government buildings surrounding a public square. The official name of the central square is Plaza de la Constitución (Constitution

Facts in brief

Population: 10,263,275; met. area, 19,150,000.
Area: 571 sq. mi. (1,479 km²); met. area, about 900 sq. mi. (2,330 km²).
Altitude: 7,349 ft. (2,240 m) above sea level.
Climate: *Average temperature*—December, 54 °F (12 °C); May, 66 °F (19 °C). *Average annual precipitation* (rainfall, melted snow, and other forms of moisture)—29 in. (74 cm). For the monthly weather in Mexico City, see **Mexico** (Climate).
Government: *Chief executive*—head of the Department of the Federal District (appointed by the president).
Founded: 1325 (according to legend).

Roderic A. Camp, the contributor of this article, is Professor of Political Science and Professor of Latin American Studies at Tulane University.

Plaza). But the square, as in many other cities in Mexico, is usually called the Zócalo (Pedestal). The name came from a pedestal erected in the square in the 1840's to hold a monument that was never built. Facing the Zócalo are the City Hall; the Metropolitan Cathedral, Mexico's largest church; and the National Palace, which houses the president's office and cabinet offices. Major government agencies with headquarters near the Zócalo include the Supreme Court of Justice and the Bank of Mexico.

The commercial areas downtown fill with people day and night. Some parts have been closed to automobiles, and pedestrians overflow the sidewalks onto the narrow streets. Historic churches, schools, and museums give the area a colonial flavor. Alameda Park, the downtown section's central park, lies about 1 mile (1.6 kilometers) west of the Zócalo along Avenida (Avenue) Juárez. This street, like several other places in Mexico City, was named for Mexico's President Benito Juárez, who enacted sweeping reforms in the 1850's and 1860's. A few blocks northeast of Alameda Park is Plaza de Garibaldi, where people come to hear the famous *mariachis,* strolling groups of musicians.

Residential and commercial centers have shifted from downtown to the city's southwest section. West of Alameda Park, Avenida Juárez crosses the city's major street, the Paseo de la Reforma (Boulevard of the Reform), named in honor of Juárez' reforms. Reforma is a wide, busy boulevard with beautifully landscaped circles at major intersections. The boulevard crosses the city on a northeast-southwest diagonal for most of its length. At one of its famous intersections stands the Monument to Independence, a golden angel on a tall column.

Reforma passes through Mexico City's largest and

Mexico City

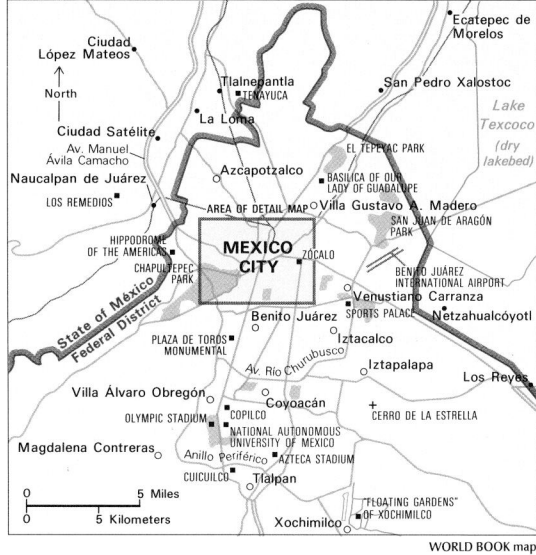

The small map, *top,* shows the location of Mexico City. The map above shows the northern, urban part of the city and many of its points of interest. The southern part of Mexico City consists chiefly of mountains and rural areas.

Central Mexico City

The map at the right shows the downtown area of Mexico City and surrounding residential and commercial neighborhoods.

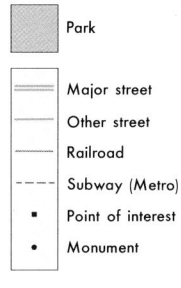

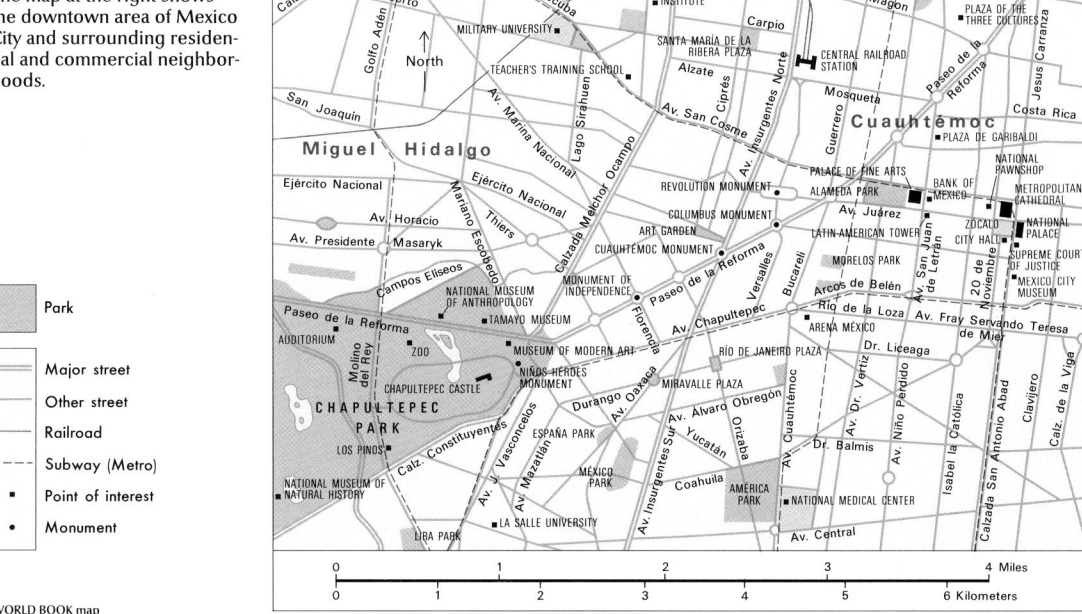

Chapultepec Park is Mexico City's largest park. Every day, thousands of people come to the park to relax, picnic, and visit its many sights. At the entrance to the park zoo, *left,* families gather and vendors sell colorful balloons. The park also includes several of Mexico's leading museums.

© Haroldo de Farla Castro, FPG

most popular park, Chapultepec Park (pronounced *chuh PUHL tuh pehk*). The park includes some of Mexico's leading art and history museums and Chapultepec Castle, the residence of some former Mexican presidents. The presidential residence is now a home called Los Pinos (The Pines) in the southern section of the park.

Mexico City has many neighborhoods, called *colonias.* Some wealthy residential colonias lie west of the park, along the Paseo de la Reforma. Beautiful mansions line Reforma and shady streets in the Lomas de Chapultepec (Hills of Chapultepec) neighborhood. Exclusive shopping districts in the city include the Zona Rosa (Pink Zone), located south of Reforma, and Polanco, a colonia near Chapultepec Park.

Working-class and low-income residential areas sprawl in every direction from downtown Mexico City. Heavy industry is found in the city's northern regions.

The city's south side has become a center of culture. The National Autonomous University of Mexico and the College of Mexico are there. A wealthy colonia called Pedregal (Stony Ground) originated in the 1970's near the university on a field of lava rock left by a now-extinct volcano. Nearby is Perisur, a huge shopping center. Shopping and restaurants are also found along Avenida de los Insurgentes Sur (Avenue of the Insurgents South), a major commercial artery.

Metropolitan area. The Federal District of Mexico is bordered on three sides by the state of México and along its southern boundary by the state of Morelos. Rapid population growth along the México state border has greatly expanded border cities since the 1960's. One of these is Netzahualcóyotl (*NAY tsah wahl KOH yoht uhl*), Mexico's third largest city, which lies east of Mexico City. Netzahualcóyotl has many poor people and serious environmental and health problems, and it lacks basic city services.

West of Mexico City, Reforma joins the highway to Toluca, capital of the state of México. Houses are built on steep hillsides along the highway. Mexico City's growth has spilled over most heavily into the state of México to the northwest, where many factories produce a wide variety of goods. North along the highway to

Querétaro lies a middle-class suburb called Ciudad Satélite (Satellite City).

People

Ethnic groups. Most of Mexico City's people are *mestizos* (people of mixed white and Indian ancestry). They are descended from Spanish settlers and the Indians who were Mexico's original inhabitants. Residents mainly speak Spanish. Two per cent of the city's people speak an Indian language, usually in addition to Spanish.

Immigrants from Europe, the Middle East, and Asia give Mexico City an international flavor. These ethnic groups contribute greatly to the intellectual, commercial, and cultural life of Mexico City.

About 85 to 90 per cent of Mexico City's people are Roman Catholic. The city also has many Jews, Mormons, and Protestants.

Housing. A lack of affordable, good-quality housing is one of Mexico City's most serious problems. People have streamed into the city faster than homes could be built to accommodate them. Federally funded housing for low-income workers, begun in the 1970's, has eased the problem only slightly. Many residences lack safe drinking water, underground sewers, or utilities. Many homes are cardboard shacks, providing little protection. Many others are made from sheets of steel, tin, or other metal, or from asbestos panels. The city also has many middle-class areas with comfortable homes.

Most of Mexico City's buildings—private and public—are made of concrete blocks and cement. Wood is seldom used because it is scarce and expensive.

Education in Mexico City's public school system extends from the elementary grades through the university level. It is supervised by the national government. Most of the schools are seriously underfunded. Many parents who can afford to do so send their children to private schools. There are many private schools in the capital. Most of them are operated by the Roman Catholic Church, though some immigrant groups also have schools.

The capital has more institutions of higher education than anywhere else in the country. Mexico's oldest and largest university is the National Autonomous University of Mexico. Other important schools are the College of Mexico, the National Polytechnic Institute, the Autonomous Technological Institute of Mexico, and the Ibero-American University.

Cultural life and recreation. Mexico City is Mexico's intellectual and cultural center. Many of the country's leading artists and writers live there. The city's most internationally famous group of performers is the Ballet Folklórico. This dance company performs traditional dances in colorful costumes at the Palacio de Bellas Artes (Palace of Fine Arts). The Bellas Artes, a majestic building near Alameda Park, is a performance and exhibition center. The Bellas Artes and many other public buildings in the city are decorated with large murals. The National Palace features a series of murals by Diego Rivera, one of Mexico's most famous painters.

The National Museum of Anthropology, in Chapultepec Park, is one of the world's greatest museums. It displays artworks of the Aztec, Maya, and other ancient Mexican cultures. Also in the park are the Museum of Modern Art and the Tamayo Museum of Contemporary International Art, named for the famous Mexican painter Rufino Tamayo. The Museum of the City of Mexico, near the Zócalo, offers a history of the capital.

Mexico's National Archives are downtown. The city's two most important libraries are at the College of Mexico and the National Autonomous University of Mexico.

Mexico City has baseball, boxing, bullfighting, football, horse racing, jai alai, soccer, swimming, tennis, and many other sports. Soccer is the most popular team sport. In any neighborhood, rich or poor, adults and children can be seen playing the game.

Many people leave the city on weekends. They seek clean air and lush vegetation in such places as Cuernavaca (*KWEHR nuh VAHK uh*), a beautiful city to the south, or Valle de Bravo, a mountain retreat to the west. At the archaeological site of Teotihuacán, people climb towering pyramids for a spectacular view of the ancient Indian city.

Social problems. Mexico City has great difficulty providing adequate schools, transportation, and other

© L. Cherney, Superstock

The National Museum of Anthropology houses such ancient Indian artworks as this sculpture of an Aztec goddess.

public services for its huge and growing population. The city also has a serious crime problem, especially in low-income neighborhoods. In addition, many police and other government officials have been accused of corrupt practices, such as accepting bribes and engaging in criminal activities themselves. Alcoholism, drug addiction, and juvenile delinquency are other serious difficulties in the city.

The city's large number of people creates transportation difficulties. Many workers live far from their jobs and travel an average of about two hours per day to and from work. Because few highways bypass the city, long-distance travelers must drive through it, adding to overcrowded streets. A beltway system to separate local traffic from through traffic has been started.

Environmental problems. Air pollution is Mexico City's most dangerous environmental problem. It is so serious that sometimes children must stay indoors when the government announces air-quality warnings. Many people suffer from breathing problems and eye irritation. The city lies in a bowl-shaped valley. The surrounding mountains keep the wind from blowing away factory smoke, automobile exhaust, and other pollutants. The government has tried to control pollution from cars by closing some downtown streets to traffic. The city also bans about one-fifth of its cars from the road each day of the workweek, with the day a car cannot be driven determined by its license number. In the early 1990's, the government began to impose even stricter pollution controls.

Economy

The Mexico City area ranks first in the country in manufacturing activities and in retail business. It is also the leading center of financial and professional services. The city is the center for Mexico's commercial activity and a major tourist area. In fact, the country's economic development is so concentrated in the Mexico City area that the federal government wants to draw business and industry to other parts of Mexico.

Industry. Mexico City accounts for about half of Mexico's manufacturing activity and almost half of its factory

© Karl Kummels, Superstock

The Palacio de Bellas Artes is a performance and exhibition center famous for the beauty of its architecture.

© Macduff Everton, West Stock

The Mexican stock exchange became one of the world's fastest-growing stock markets in the early 1990's. The exchange, *above,* is located in Mexico City's financial district.

workers. Other major employers are petroleum and mineral refineries and construction companies. About 40 per cent of Mexico's technical and research specialists live in Mexico City.

The federal government ranks as one of the city's chief employers. Many college graduates in architecture, economics, engineering, law, and other fields pursue careers in government. To relieve crowding in Mexico City, the government sought in the 1980's to move federal agencies away from the capital. But few agencies actually relocated.

Finance. Mexico City is the financial center of the nation. More than half of all the country's bank transactions take place there. In 1982, the government took control of all Mexican banks, but it began selling them back to private owners in 1991.

Transportation. Mexico City's location has made it the hub of Mexico's transportation system. Railroads and highways radiate from the city like spokes of a wheel. It is hard to travel north or south in Mexico without passing through the capital. Passenger rail service is extensive in Mexico, but most travel is done by bus. Benito Juárez International Airport, east of downtown, handles direct flights to and from many countries and other Mexican cities.

The Federal District has many local bus routes and one of the best subway systems in the world. Even though new subway and bus routes are added continually, the huge population causes buses and subways to be crowded.

Communication. Mexico City is the country's radio and television broadcast center. Televisa, with offices downtown, is the largest privately owned television network in Latin America. It broadcasts on various channels in Mexico City and throughout the country and even reaches many parts of the United States.

Mexico City publishes more daily newspapers per person than any other city in the world. With 14 dailies, the competition for readership is fierce. A well-read res-

ident of Mexico City may subscribe to half a dozen papers representing various political viewpoints.

City government

Mexico City's government is complicated by its unusual political status as the Federal District. It is similar in some ways to Mexico's 31 states, but it does not have an elected governor and legislature as the others do. The district is run directly by the federal government as the Department of the Federal District (DDF). The head of the DDF is a member of the president's cabinet and is appointed by the president. This official is called the *regente* and functions like a mayor. The DDF is funded mainly by the federal government and absorbs more of the national budget than any other agency.

Many Federal District residents believe that they should elect their own leaders. In response to these feelings, the federal government in the 1980's created a city assembly made up of delegates elected from various wards of Mexico City.

The Federal District elects two senators to Mexico's Senate, as each of the states does. The Federal District also elects 40 members, more than any state, to the Chamber of Deputies, the larger house of Mexico's General Congress.

History

City of the Aztec. By 2000 B.C., farm villages had developed in the Lake Texcoco region. The Aztec Indians founded their capital, Tenochtitlan, on an island in the middle of the lake. According to legend, they established Tenochtitlan in A.D. 1325. From this magnificent city of about 100,000 to 300,000 people, the Aztec ruled a vast empire during the 1400's.

In 1519, the Spanish explorer Hernando Cortés marched on Tenochtitlan. He and his men were welcomed into the city by the Aztec emperor, Montezuma, who thought Cortés was a god. Cortés imprisoned Montezuma and took control of the city. In 1520, the Aztec forced the Spaniards out. Cortés returned with a larger force, conquered the city, and destroyed it in 1521.

Spanish rule. Cortés rebuilt the city, creating a Spanish capital over the ruins. Almost all traces of Aztec architecture were destroyed. Mexico City became the capital of a Spanish colony called New Spain. The colony at its peak extended from present-day Central America to the state of Kansas in the United States. The city regained its former size and grew into the largest city in the Western Hemisphere. After about 30,000 people died in floods in 1629, the Spaniards improved the canal and dike system for draining Lake Texcoco.

Independence. Mexico became independent from Spain in 1821. In 1846, Mexico went to war with the United States over disputed territories. In 1847, Mexico City was captured by U.S. troops after the Battle of Chapultepec. In that battle, six military students jumped from Chapultepec Castle to their deaths rather than surrender. The Monumento a los Niños Héroes (Monument to the Boy Heroes) stands in Chapultepec Park in their honor. United States troops occupied the city until the war ended in 1848. See **Mexican War.**

In 1863, Mexico City fell to invading French troops. From 1864 to 1867, Mexico was governed by an Austrian-born monarch, Maximilian, who gained the throne with the support of France and of Mexican conservatives. Maximilian had the Paseo Imperial (Imperial Boulevard) constructed to connect the National Palace at the Zócalo with his residence, Chapultepec Castle. The street was later renamed the Paseo de la Reforma.

General Porfirio Díaz came to power in 1876 and ruled as a dictator. He modernized Mexico City and added many architectural landmarks. One of the most dramatic of these began as his legislative palace but became the Monument to the Revolution, honoring his overthrow in 1911. Díaz also began the Palacio de Bellas Artes in 1904, though it was not completed until 1934.

Revolution and growth. The Mexican Revolution began in 1910 in opposition to Díaz, forcing him out of office the next year. In February 1913, Mexico City again became the scene of fighting as troops rebelled against the elected president, Francisco I. Madero. This period of fighting became known as the *Decena Trágica,* the Tragic Ten Days. Madero was murdered, and Victoriano Huerta ruled as a dictator until he too was overthrown. For the next several years, revolutionary leaders struggled among themselves for power.

From the 1940's to about 1970, Mexico had an economic boom. Miguel Alemán Valdés, who became president in 1946, began large-scale public works that contributed to this boom and to Mexico City's modernization. From 1940 to 1970, about 3 million Mexicans migrated to the capital. This steady flow of people contributed to the city's rapid growth but also to its social and economic problems. After several years of slower economic growth in the early 1970's, the discovery of vast petroleum deposits in Mexico brought a brief return to prosperity.

Recent developments. In the 1980's, world oil prices and the demand for oil began to drop, triggering a major economic crisis that severely affected Mexico City. The Mexican government had borrowed heavily to finance development programs, expecting oil profits to balance its spending. Instead, the government had trou-

ble paying its debts, and unemployment and prices rose sharply. Many residents of Mexico City lost their jobs because of government cutbacks.

In 1985, a major earthquake with strong aftershocks struck south-central Mexico, including Mexico City, causing about 10,000 deaths. Damage was especially severe because the city had been built on the moist clay soil of a former lakebed. During an earthquake, such soil transmits powerful vibrations and acts like jelly, causing buildings to collapse. About 400 buildings in Mexico City were destroyed, and thousands of others suffered damage. After the quakes, the city enacted tougher building codes and safety standards.

In the early 1990's, Mexico's economy grew stronger. More services came under private rather than government control, and inflation decreased. Mexico City profited most from the country's growing prosperity. Benefits went mainly to the city's middle and upper classes.

In 1991, the government stepped up efforts to improve the city's air quality. It closed dozens of firms for violating environmental laws, including a huge petroleum refinery at Azcapotzalco in northwestern Mexico City. The government also announced a program to replace old taxicabs and buses with new, less polluting vehicles.   Roderic A. Camp

Related articles in *World Book* include:

Aztec	Latin America	México (state)
Cortés, Hernando	(pictures)	Montezuma
Cuernavaca	Mexico (country)	Netzahualcóyotl
Lake Xochimilco		

Outline

I. The city
  A. Downtown
  B. Residential and
    commercial centers
  C. The city's south side
  D. Metropolitan area

II. People
  A. Ethnic groups
  B. Housing
  C. Education
  D. Cultural life and
    recreation
  E. Social problems
  F. Environmental
    problems

III. Economy
  A. Industry
  B. The federal government
  C. Finance
  D. Transportation
  E. Communication

IV. City government

V. History

Questions

What people founded Mexico City?

Who are the "Boy Heroes" honored by a monument in Chapultepec Park?

What is Mexico City's most popular sport?

What are *colonias*?

How does Mexico City rank in size compared to other cities in the world?

Where in Mexico City is the Zócalo?

What is Mexico City's largest park?

What natural disaster damaged the city in 1985?

What is the Zona Rosa?

Why does Mexico City limit the number of cars allowed to drive downtown?

Additional resources

Davis, James E., and Hawke, S. D. *Mexico City.* Raintree, 1990. For younger readers.

Frommer's Mexico City & Acapulco 1991-1992. Prentice-Hall, 1990.

Kandell, Jonathan. *La Capital: The Biography of Mexico City.* Random Hse., 1988.

UPI/Bettmann

During the Mexican Revolution, a series of dictators and revolutionary leaders controlled Mexico City for short periods. Revolutionaries led by Álvaro Obregón entered the city, *above,* after the overthrow of dictator Victoriano Huerta in 1914.

Meyer, Julius Lothar (1830-1895), a German chemist, showed the relation between the atomic weights and properties of the elements. He and the Russian chemist Dmitri Mendeleev independently developed a *periodic table,* which grouped the elements by their atomic weights and properties (see **Element, Chemical** [Periodic table]). Meyer also concluded that elements were composed of several kinds of smaller particles. This idea led other scientists to study the structure of atoms. Meyer was born in Tübingen and was a professor of chemistry at the University of Tübingen from 1876 until his death. See also **Chemistry** (Formation of the periodic table).   Seymour Harold Mauskopf

Meyerbeer, Giacomo (1791-1864), was one of the most popular opera composers of his day. He was born in Berlin, but achieved his greatest success while composing in Paris. The trend in French opera during the 1830's and 1840's was toward grand opera, which emphasized many performers on stage and impressive stage effects. Meyerbeer used this stress on the spectacular in his first Paris opera, *Robert-le-Diable* (1831), which gained him immediate fame. This work was followed by *Les Huguenots* (1836) and *Le Prophète* (1849). *L'Africaine,* perhaps his most interesting opera, was first performed in 1865, after his death. Meyerbeer had an acute sense for building stunning climaxes and for creating spectacular effects. Richard Wagner's early operas owe much to the influence of Meyerbeer's music.
          Thomas Bauman

Miami, *my AM ee,* Fla. (pop. 358,548; met. area pop. 1,937,094), is a world-famous resort city. Its recreational areas and warm weather attract about 13 million visitors yearly. Many retired people move to Miami from other parts of the United States because of the area's climate.

The city is on the southeastern coast of Florida at the mouth of the Miami River. It lies on Biscayne Bay, about $3\frac{1}{2}$ miles (5.6 kilometers) west of the Atlantic Ocean.

The first permanent white settlers of the Miami area built houses on Biscayne Bay. The community, which the settlers named for the Miami River, has grown rapidly as the result of industrial expansion and year-round tourism. Miami is Florida's second largest city. Only Jacksonville has more people.

The city. Miami, the county seat of Dade County, covers about 54 square miles (140 square kilometers) including 20 square miles (52 square kilometers) of inland water. The heart of downtown Miami is the intersection of Miami Avenue and Flagler Street. County government buildings stand nearby.

The Miami-Hialeah metropolitan area covers all of Dade County—2,020 square miles (5,232 square kilometers). This area includes Hialeah, a city that lies about 5 miles (8 kilometers) northwest of Miami, and 25 other cities. The metropolitan areas of Miami-Hialeah and of Fort Lauderdale-Hollywood, Fla., form the Miami-Fort Lauderdale Consolidated Metropolitan Statistical Area.

About 55 per cent of Miami's people were born outside the United States. Cubans make up about two-fifths of the population and they give the city a strong Latin culture. This culture has attracted many banks and companies that handle Latin-American trade. The city also has a large Haitian population. Other population groups include those of English, German, and Italian descent. About 25 per cent of the people in Miami are blacks.

Economy of the Miami metropolitan area depends mostly on tourism, which produces about $4.5 billion annually. Most tourist accommodations operate all year. The city's temperature varies little, averaging 81 °F

Carol Guzy, *The Miami Herald*

Downtown Miami lies on Biscayne Bay, about $3\frac{1}{2}$ miles (5.6 kilometers) west of the Atlantic Ocean. Cruise ships anchor in the bay of this popular resort city.

(27 °C) in summer and 71 °F (22 °C) in winter. For the monthly weather in Miami, see **Florida** (Climate).

The Miami metropolitan area has about 3,000 manufacturing plants. The city is one of the largest centers in the country for the production of clothing. Other products include furniture, metal goods, printed materials, and transportation equipment.

Miami International Airport is one of the nation's busiest terminals. The airport serves as the main air gateway between the United States and Latin America. The Port of Miami handles passenger and cargo ships from many countries. Passenger trains also serve the city. One daily English-language newspaper—the *Herald*—and one Spanish-language daily—*Diario Las Americas*—are published in Miami. The city has about 10 television stations and about 30 radio stations.

Education. The Dade County public school system operates about 280 elementary and secondary schools.

About 325 private and church-supported schools serve the area. Institutions of higher learning in the area include St. Thomas University, Florida International University, Florida Memorial College, Barry University, and the University of Miami. The University of Miami's Rosenstiel Institute of Marine and Atmospheric Sciences is an important center of ocean study. The Miami-Dade County Public Library system consists of a main library and 28 branches.

Cultural life and recreation. Miami has an opera company, two dance companies, and several art galleries and theaters. The Metro Dade Cultural Center in downtown Miami houses the main library, the Center for the Fine Arts, and the Historical Museum of Southern Florida. Other points of interest in the area include Bayside Marketplace, Fairchild Tropical Garden, Lowe Art Museum, Metrozoo, the Seaquarium, and Villa Vizcaya Museum and Gardens. Many visitors attend the an-

WORLD BOOK map

City of Miami

FLORIDA

Miami

Miami, an important tourist center, lies in southeastern Florida. The large map shows the city of Miami. The small map shows the Miami geographical area.

 City boundary
 County boundary
 Expressway
 Other street
 Railroad
 Metrorail (rapid transit)
 ▪ Point of interest
 Park

Miami Geographical Area

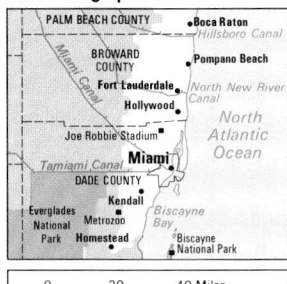

0	20	40 Miles
0	20	40	60 Kilometers

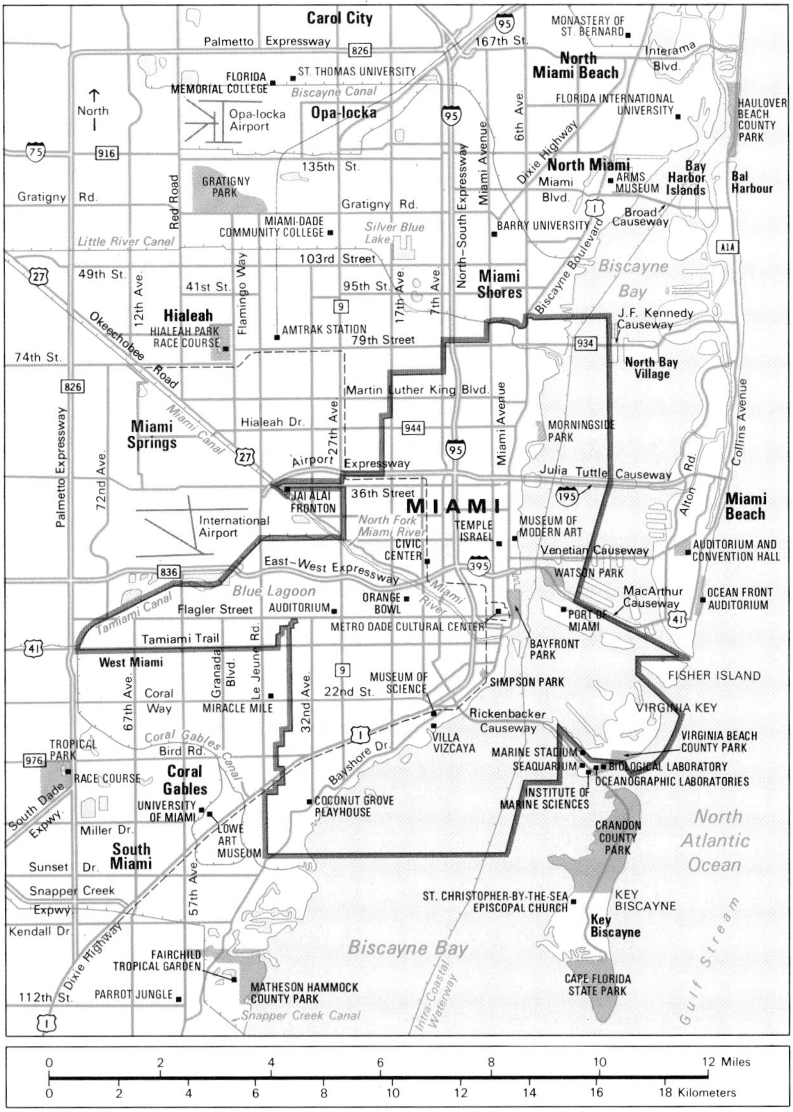

0	2	4	6	8	10	12 Miles
0	2	4	6	8	10	12	14	16	18 Kilometers

nual Orange Bowl football game on New Year's Day. The Miami Dolphins of the National Football League and the Florida Marlins baseball team play their home games in Joe Robbie Stadium. The Miami Heat of the National Basketball Association and the Florida Panthers of the National Hockey League play in the Miami Arena.

Government. Miami has a commission-manager government. The voters elect a mayor and four commissioners to four-year terms. The commission appoints a city manager to direct various government services.

Miami is also governed by a metropolitan county government called *Metro.* The 13-member Dade County Board of Commissioners heads Metro. It administers pollution control, transportation, and other activities that affect the entire county. Metro, the first metropolitan government, was created in 1957.

History. Tequesta Indians lived in what is now the Miami area long before white settlers first arrived. In 1895, Julia D. Tuttle, a Florida pioneer, convinced railroad builder Henry M. Flagler that the area could become rich farmland. She sent him some flowers to show that the land had escaped a killing frost. In 1896, Flagler extended the Florida East Coast Railroad to the area in exchange for land. That same year, Miami was founded and received a city charter. About 1,500 people lived there. The railroad helped Miami's population reach 5,000 by 1910 and 30,000 by 1920.

During the early 1920's, a great real estate boom centered in Miami. People made and lost fortunes with the construction of homes, hotels, and resorts. Just as the boom began to decline in 1926, a destructive hurricane struck the city. Another severe storm hit in 1928. Even so, Miami's population reached 110,000 by 1930.

During World War II (1939-1945), Miami served as an important military training center. The armed services used most of the city's hotels as barracks. Many service personnel settled in Miami after the war. By 1950, the city had a population of 250,000.

Since 1959, when Fidel Castro became dictator of Cuba, hundreds of thousands of Cubans have fled to Miami, about 200 miles (320 kilometers) away. In the late 1970's, many refugees from Haiti also began settling in the Miami area. In 1985, voters elected Xavier L. Suarez mayor. Suarez became the city's first Cuban-born mayor. He was reelected in 1987 and 1989.

Like many other large cities, Miami faces the problems of unemployment and housing shortages, which especially affect the black population. In 1980, racial tension erupted into violence after four white former Dade County policemen were found not guilty of killing a black Miami businessman. The verdict sparked rioting that led to 17 deaths and more than $100 million in damage.

In the mid-1980's, a number of new buildings rose in downtown Miami and on nearby Brickell Avenue, Miami's financial center. These buildings included the 55-story Southeast Financial Center, completed in downtown Miami in 1984, and the 32-story Brickell Bay Office Tower, which opened in 1985. A rapid transit system, Metrorail, began operating in 1984. Metromover, a downtown elevated shuttle line, was added in 1986.

In August 1992, Hurricane Andrew struck Florida. The hurricane came ashore just south of Miami, so the city was spared the brunt of the storm. However, areas in Dade County south of Miami, especially the city of Homestead, were severely damaged. Hurricane Andrew killed at least 40 people in Florida, left about 250,000 homeless, and caused about $20 billion in property damage.   Rick Hirsch

See also **Ferre, Maurice.**

Miami Beach, *my AM ee,* Fla. (pop. 92,639), is one of North America's most famous resort centers. It lies on an island $2\frac{1}{2}$ miles (4 kilometers) across Biscayne Bay from the city of Miami. The island measures 10 miles (16 kilometers) from north to south and is 1 to 3 miles (1.6 to 5 kilometers) wide. Four causeways connect it with the mainland. For location, see **Miami** (map).

The city's major industry is tourism. Its many hotels and other lodging facilities can accommodate over 200,000 visitors. The tropical climate, white sandy beaches, and recreational areas attract over 2 million tourists annually. The city has many parks, fishing piers, playgrounds, beaches, recreation centers, and swimming pools. Tropical trees and shrubs line its streets, and gardens of brilliant flowers border its green lawns. Miami Beach features many buildings designed in the *art deco* style popular in the 1920's and 1930's.

Tequesta Indians lived in the Miami Beach area in the 1400's. A Spanish mission was built in 1567. An attempt by businessmen to start a coconut plantation failed in the 1880's. But John S. Collins, one of the businessmen, pioneered in developing the resort city. Other city founders include Carl G. Fisher, Thomas J. Pancoast, and John N. Lummus. In 1912, rock and sand were pumped from the bottom of Biscayne Bay and spread over mangrove roots and soft sand to create the modern city. Miami Beach was incorporated as a town in 1915. It was incorporated as a city in 1917. The city has a council-manager government.   Rick Hirsch

Miami Indians are a tribe that lived in several areas near the Great Lakes. They were divided into six bands. Two of the bands, the Wea and the Piankashaws, became independent tribes in the early 1800's.

When white explorers first encountered the Miami in the mid-1600's, the tribe lived in the area of present-day Green Bay, Wis. Gradually, the Miami moved south to areas along the Wabash, Great Miami, and Maumee rivers in what are now Illinois, Indiana, and Ohio.

The Miami resembled the Illinois Indians in their language and customs. They lived in dome-shaped wigwams. Their villages were surrounded by large fields of corn, which was the tribe's chief crop.

The Miami had a reputation as skilled warriors. But much of their success in war came from their clever choice of allies. They formed shifting alliances with the French, the British, and neighboring tribes. In 1763, some Miami helped the Ottawa chief Pontiac fight the British in a conflict known as Pontiac's War. During the Revolutionary War (1775-1783), however, the Miami sided with the British because they opposed the expansion of American settlers into their lands.

The Miami and allied tribes, known as the Miami Confederacy, fought against U.S. forces in the Indian wars of the Ohio Valley in the 1790's. Under their most famous war chief, Little Turtle, the Indians won several major battles. However, Major General "Mad Anthony" Wayne defeated the Miami Confederacy in 1794 at the Battle of Fallen Timbers.

In 1846, the U.S. Army tried to force many of the Miami to leave Indiana. Some members of the tribe escaped from the Army and remained in the state. Others were allowed to stay. Those who left eventually settled in Oklahoma. Today, about 3,000 Miami still live in Indiana. About 1,200 members of the tribe make their homes in Oklahoma.   Terry P. Wilson

See also **Indian wars** (Other Midwestern conflicts); **Little Turtle.**

Mica, *MY kuh,* is the name of a group of minerals that contain atoms of aluminum, oxygen, and silicon bonded together into flat sheets. Mica has perfect *cleavage*—that is, it splits cleanly into thin sheets or layers. These sheets of mica are tough, flexible, and elastic. Mica may be colorless, black, brown, green, or violet.

The chief kinds of mica, in order of abundance, are (1) muscovite, (2) biotite, (3) phlogopite, and (4) lepidolite. They differ according to the atoms of various substances that occur in layers between the aluminum-oxygen-silicon sheets and hold the sheets together.

Muscovite contains aluminum and potassium. It is usually colorless but may be pale green. Muscovite got its name because Russians, or "Muscovites," once used it as window glass. Biotite contains iron, magnesium, and potassium and is black. Phlogopite has magnesium and potassium and is pale brown or colorless. Lepidolite contains aluminum and lithium and is pale violet.

Mica is found in *igneous* and *metamorphic* rocks (see **Rock** [Igneous rock; Metamorphic rock]). These rocks glisten if they contain a large amount of mica because the flakes of mica reflect light.

Muscovite and phlogopite serve as insulators in electric appliances. They are also used in *capacitors* and *vacuum tubes* (see **Capacitor; Vacuum tube**). In ground form, muscovite and phlogopite also serve as filler material; lubricants for industrial molds; and coatings in the manufacture of paints, plastics, roofing materials, and wallboard. Lepidolite is a source of lithium, used in long-lasting dry cell batteries and in the manufacture of ceramic and glass products, lubricants, and aluminum. Biotite is transformed by weathering into *vermiculite,* used in construction materials (see **Vermiculite**).

Mica is produced in the form of large sheets or in small pieces called *scrap mica* or *flake mica.* India is the leading producer of sheet mica, followed by Brazil and Madagascar. The use of sheet mica has declined since the 1950's because of high production costs and because synthetic materials have partially replaced it. In addition, the development of transistors and other devices has reduced the use of vacuum tubes, which contain sheet mica. Nevertheless, sheet mica is still used in a variety of electrical and electronic products.

Scrap mica is important in many industries. The United States is the largest producer of scrap mica. Most U.S. mica comes from North Carolina, followed by New Mexico and South Dakota.   Maria Luisa Crawford

Micah, *MY kuh,* **Book of,** is a book of the Hebrew Bible, or Old Testament, named for a Hebrew prophet. Micah lived about 700 B.C., during the reign of King Hezekiah of Judah. *Micah* means "Who is like the Lord?"

The first part of the Book of Micah contains prophecies of punishment against Samaria and Jerusalem for the corruption of their leaders. It also includes prophecies of salvation that say Mt. Zion, the holy mountain in Jerusalem, will be the sacred center where universal peace shall one day spring. The second part of the book contains judgments focusing on the broken relationship between God and Israel, and hopeful prophecies of God reestablishing His love of His people. Famous passages include the summary of true religion (6: 8) and the expectation of the Messiah from Bethlehem (5: 2-5).

The contrast between Micah's prophecies of doom and hope has led scholars to argue that the original book was a collection of speeches from the time of Hezekiah. A group of sayings was probably added later, after the Babylonian Exile, which ended in 538 B.C.   Eric M. Meyers

Mice. See Mouse.

Michael, Saint, is one of the four archangels in both Jewish and Christian scriptures. He is considered the patron angel and guardian of Israel. In art, he is usually portrayed as a warrior. In Revelation 12: 7-9, Michael and his angels fight a dragon. Later tradition identifies him as the angel mentioned in Acts 7: 38 who gave the law to Moses on Mount Sinai. His feast day is the festival of Michaelmas—on September 29 in the West and on November 8 in the Eastern Orthodox Churches (see **Michaelmas**).   Richard A. Edwards

Michaelmas, *MIHK uhl muhs,* is a festival held on September 29 in the Roman Catholic and Anglican churches, and on November 8 in the Greek, Armenian, and Coptic churches. The feast honors Saint Michael the archangel (see **Michael, Saint**). Michaelmas probably originated in the Roman Empire in the A.D. 400's. The festival was particularly important during the Middle Ages when Saint Michael was the patron saint of knights and also one of the patron saints of the Roman Catholic Church.

In Great Britain and several other countries, Michaelmas is one of the four quarter days of the year when rents and bills come due. It is also the beginning of a quarterly court term and an academic term at Oxford and Cambridge. The British celebrate Michaelmas with meals of roast goose, a custom that started hundreds of years ago when people included a goose in their rent payments. An English proverb says, "If you eat goose on Michaelmas Day you will never want money all the year round."   David G. Truemper

Michaelmas daisy. See Aster.

Michel, *MY kuhl,* **Robert Henry** (1923-   ), an Illinois Republican, has been minority leader of the United States House of Representatives since 1981. Michel served as Republican *whip* (assistant leader) of the House from 1975 to 1981. He first won election to Congress as a representative from Illinois in 1956. He served as chairman of the national Republican campaign committee in 1973 and 1974.

As a congressman, Michel maintained a conservative voting record. He supported such policies as increased military spending, reduced funds for social programs, and less government regulation of industry. Michel won respect as a political bargainer who could persuade Democrats to support many Republican programs.

Michel was born in Peoria, Ill. He served in the U.S. Army in Europe from 1943 to 1946. He graduated from Bradley University. From 1949 to 1956, Michel was an administrative assistant to Representative Harold H. Velde, whom he succeeded in Congress.   Lee Thornton

Pietà (1498-1499), St. Peter's Church, Vatican City, Camera Clix

Michelangelo's *Pietà* was the most important work of his youth and established his reputation as a sculptor. The marble statue shows the Virgin Mary cradling Jesus after the Crucifixion.

Michelangelo, *MY kuhl AN juh LOH* or *MIHK uhl AN juh LOH* (1475-1564), was one of the most famous artists in history and a great leader of the Italian Renaissance. He was mainly interested in creating large marble statues, but his endless creative energy also led him to become a great painter and architect, and an active poet. He was also one of the most famous people of his time.

Michelangelo is best known for his treatment of the human body in painting and sculpture. His figures convey a sense of grandeur and power, and arouse strong emotions in many spectators. In size, strength, and emotional intensity, these figures go beyond real people. Michelangelo's figures are both animated and restrained, and seem to possess great spiritual energy. The force, movement, and beauty of his figures broaden our experience of humanity. His work pressed toward the extremes of heroism and tragedy, but is never false or artificial. See the picture of his statue of David with the **David** article.

Early life. Michelangelo was born on March 6, 1475. His full name was Michelangelo Buonarroti. He came from a respectable Florence family, and was born in the village of Caprese, where his father was a government agent. After a brief classical education, he became an apprentice at the age of 12 to the most popular painter in Florence, Domenico Ghirlandajo.

Before his apprenticeship was completed, Michelangelo stopped painting and began working as a sculptor under the guidance of a pupil of the sculptor Donatello. Michelangelo attracted the support of the ruler of Florence, Lorenzo de' Medici, who invited the young artist to stay at his palace. Michelangelo's earliest surviving sculpture is a small unfinished relief of a battle, done when he was about 16. This work shows the obvious influence of ancient Roman marble sculpture belonging to Lorenzo. But the relief also shows the force and movement that became typical of Michelangelo's style. During these years, he began the study of anatomy.

After the Medici family lost power in 1494, Michelangelo began traveling. He lived in Rome from 1496 to 1501. There he had his first marked success when he carved in marble a life-sized statue of the Roman wine god Bacchus. At 23, Michelangelo carved a version of the traditional Pietà subject, the dead Christ in the lap of the mourning Mary. Both figures are larger than life size. This statue, now in St. Peter's Church in Rome, established him as a leading sculptor. The work was plainer and less decorative than most statues of the time, and thus looked stronger and more solemn.

Michelangelo lived in Florence from 1501 to 1505. There he met Leonardo da Vinci. The new democratic government of Florence wanted to display the talents of the city's two outstanding artists. So it asked both Leonardo and Michelangelo to create large battle scenes for the walls of the city hall. Michelangelo's work, now lost, is known to us through his sketches and through copies by other artists. It displayed his expert ability to render human anatomy. On this project, Michelangelo learned from Leonardo how to show flowing and vibrant movement. Leonardo carried this manner of showing life and action further than any previous artist. Amazingly, Michelangelo's ability to project solid forms did not decrease. It was during these years that Michelangelo formed the basis of the style in which he would work for the rest of his life.

From about 1505 on, Michelangelo devoted nearly all his time to large projects. In his enthusiasm for creating grand and powerful works of art, he accepted projects that were far too large for him to complete. The first one was a tomb ordered by Pope Julius II that was to include 40 marble statues. The artist accepted the commission in 1505 and ended the project unsuccessfully 40 years later.

The Sistine Chapel. Julius II was a patron of the arts with a sweeping imagination equal to Michelangelo's. He gave the artist a more practical commission, painting the ceiling of the Sistine Chapel in the Vatican. This project became Michelangelo's most famous work. The frescoes in the chapel show nine scenes from the Old Testament—three scenes each of God creating the world, the story of Adam and Eve, and Noah and the Flood. These are surrounded by 12 larger than life size Old Testament prophets and classical prophetic women called *sibyls*. For examples of these paintings, see the pictures with **Isaiah, Book of; Jeremiah, Book of.**

Michelangelo began the ceiling in 1508 and completed it in 1511. At first, he approached this task in a style resembling his earlier works. But soon he gained confidence and developed new ways of showing tension and power. Michelangelo began the second half with scenes that are much grander and freer in execution, such as *The Creation of Adam,* reproduced in the **Painting** article. Again he progressed to richer and more active compositions. See **David** (picture: *David and Goliath*).

The tomb of Julius II. After he had finished the ceiling, Michelangelo resumed work on the pope's tomb. He carved three famous figures that resemble the painted prophets and decorative figures on the Sistine ceiling. These figures are Moses and two prisoners, sometimes called *The Heroic Captive* and the *Dying Captive.* The figure of Moses, who seems to be filled with terrible anger, was later used as the centerpiece of the tomb. This statue was finally placed in the Church of St. Peter in Chains in Rome. The figures of the two captives may symbolize lands conquered by Julius II or arts and sciences left without support after his death. One of them struggles violently against his bonds, as the other languishes and seems to submit to defeat.

The Medici Chapel. Michelangelo spent the years from 1515 to 1534 working mainly for the Medici family, which had regained control of Florence. He designed and carved tombs for two Medici princes and also designed the Medici Chapel, in which the tombs are placed. Michelangelo left the chapel incomplete when he left Florence in 1534. He never returned to the city, though he was buried there.

Along with the statues of the two young princes, the tombs include the famous figures of Day and Night on one tomb and Dawn and Evening on the other. The figures recline on curving lids, conveying a sense of fate or individual tragedy. They make a great impact on spectators as an intensely significant observation about human destiny. Some read the parts of the monument from floor to ceiling as a symbol of the rising of the soul after its release from the body. Others see the four statues on the curved lids as a sign of the endless movement of time, in which life is only an incident. The tomb containing Dawn and Evening is reproduced in the **Sculpture** article.

Detail from The Vatican Museums

The Crucifixion of Saint Peter was completed by Michelangelo when he was 75. This fresco and a companion work, *The Conversion of Saint Paul,* were commissioned by Pope Paul III.

Florentine *Pietà*, *above,* was intended for Michelangelo's own tomb. The bearded figure at the top of the group is an idealized self-portrait of the sculptor when he was about 75 years old.

The Heroic Captive, *right,* shows the strength and emotional tension found in Michelangelo's sculpture. The 7-foot (2.1-meter) statue was completed in 1516 for the tomb of Pope Julius II.

The Sistine ceiling, *below,* was probably Michelangelo's greatest achievement as a painter. He completed this fresco in 1511. It shows God creating the sun, the moon, and plants.

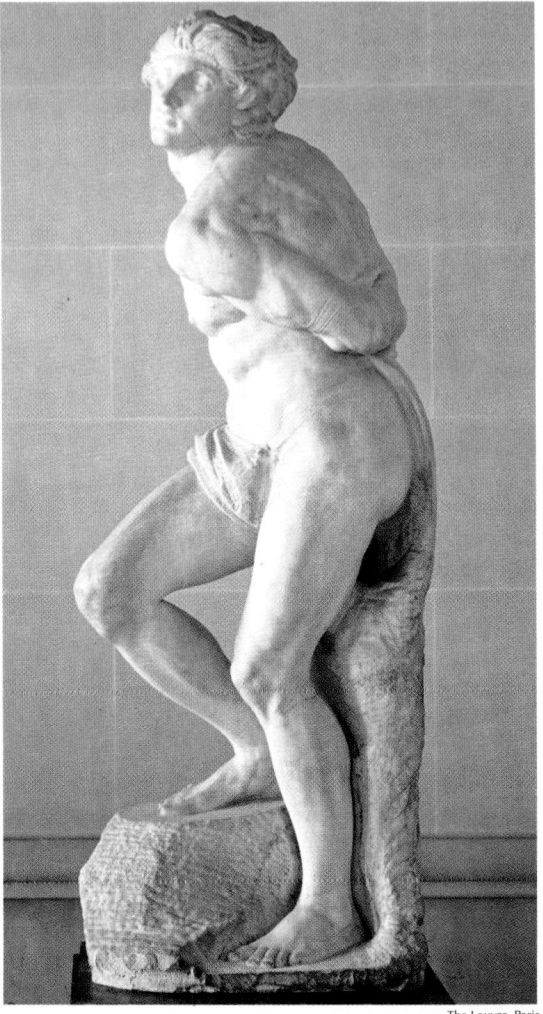

Michelangelo also designed the architecture of the Medici Chapel. He planned the walls like a carved relief, with projections and hollows and long, narrow shapes to give an elongated effect. This approach, resembling carved architecture, is carried further in the entrance hall and staircase to the Laurentian library in Florence, which he designed at the same time.

The Last Judgment. Michelangelo had always favored the republic, so he left Florence after the Medici family had firmly consolidated its rule. He settled in Rome, where he worked for Pope Paul III. During the period from 1534 to 1541, he painted the fresco of *The Last Judgment* for the altar wall of the Sistine Chapel. In a single scene almost as large as the entire ceiling, Michelangelo showed the Resurrection and the judgment of humanity. In response to the commanding gesture of Jesus in the upper center, tombs open and the dead rise to heaven on one side, while on the other side the damned tumble into hell. There they are rowed across a river in a scene based on *The Divine Comedy,* a famous poem by the Italian writer Dante Alighieri. A detail of this fresco appears in **Religion** (A doctrine of salvation).

Later years. The small amount of sculpture in Michelangelo's later years includes works to complete old commissions and two unfinished Pietà groups. He created both Pietàs for his own satisfaction and not for a patron. The Pietà now in the Cathedral of Florence was meant for his own tomb. It is designed as a massive pyramid, with Christ's body slumping down on the ground. In the Rondanini *Pietà,* now in Milan, the marble limbs are reduced to a ghostlike thinness. The bodies seem to lack substance, while the material of the stone is emphasized by the hacking chisel marks left on the unfinished surface. Because of this technique, many modern sculptors, including Henry Moore, admire this work above all others Michelangelo produced.

Michelangelo devoted much time after 1546 to architecture and poetry. In 1546, Pope Paul III appointed him supervising architect of St. Peter's Church, one of Julius II's unfinished projects. Michelangelo worked on the church without salary. By the time he died in 1564, construction had reached the lower part of the dome, which was finished by another architect (see **Rome** [picture: An air view of Rome]). After 1538, he planned a square for the Civic Center of Rome and the buildings facing it. The square is not rectangular. It symbolizes Rome as the center of the world.

Michelangelo's last paintings, finished when he was 75 years old, were frescoes in the Pauline Chapel in the Vatican. They show *The Crucifixion of Saint Peter* and *The Conversion of Saint Paul.* Although they are large, complicated designs like the Sistine Chapel paintings, they are graver, more still and inward. Michelangelo became extremely religious in his last years, during which he made moving devotional drawings comparable to the Rondanini *Pietà.* He also wrote some of his finest poetry during his last years.　　　David Summers

See also *Michelangelo* in the Research Guide/Index, Volume 22, for a *Reading and Study Guide.*

Additional resources

Hibbard, Howard. *Michelangelo.* 2nd ed. Harper, 1985.
Murray, Linda. *Michelangelo.* Thames & Hudson, 1985. First published in 1980.

Michelson, *MY kuhl suhn,* **Albert Abraham** (1852-1931), was the first American citizen to win a Nobel Prize in science. He received the 1907 Nobel Prize in physics for his design of precise optical instruments and for the accurate measurements he obtained with them.

Michelson was born in Strzelno, Poland (then in the domain of Prussia), near Inowrocław. His family emigrated to the United States when he was 2. In 1873, Michelson graduated from the U.S. Naval Academy.

In 1880, while studying in Germany, Michelson designed an instrument to measure the speed of the earth through the *ether.* At that time, scientists believed that all space was filled with a stationary substance, which they called ether. They thought that light must travel in such a substance as ether in order to travel through space. Michelson's instrument, now known as the *Michelson interferometer,* compares the speed of a light beam moving in one direction with that of a beam moving at a right angle to it. By measuring the interference of the two light beams, Michelson believed he could find the velocity of the earth through the ether. He determined from the interference pattern actually produced that the speed of the earth in relation to the ether was zero. In 1887, Michelson refined this experiment with the aid of Edward Morley, an American chemist and physicist. The result was the same as before. Michelson and Morley's experiment helped destroy the ether theory (see **Ether**).

Michelson resigned his naval commission in 1881. He taught physics at the University of Chicago for most of his career.　　　Richard L. Hilt

See also **Interferometer; Relativity.**

Michener, *MIHCH uh nuhr,* **James Albert** (1907-　　), an American author, won the 1948 Pulitzer Prize for fiction for his collection of stories, *Tales of the South Pacific* (1947). The book describes the life of U.S. servicemen among people of the Solomon Islands during World War II. Joshua Logan, Richard Rodgers, and Oscar Hammerstein II based their musical comedy *South Pacific* (1949) on stories in Michener's collection.

Michener's novels include *The Fires of Spring* (1949), *The Bridges at Toko-ri* (1953), *Sayonara* (1954), *Hawaii* (1960), *Caravans* (1963), *The Source* (1965), *Centennial* (1974), *Chesapeake* (1978), *The Covenant* (1980), *Space* (1982), *Poland* (1983), *Texas* (1985), *Alaska* (1988), *Caribbean* (1989), and *The Novel* (1991). He has also written on current events and Oriental art. He was born in New York City.　　　Samuel Chase Coale

Michener, *MIHCH uh nuhr,* **Roland** (1900-1991), was governor general of Canada from 1967 to 1974. In 1967, he became the first governor general to give the Order of Canada, the nation's highest civilian honor. He also awarded the first Order of Military Merit in 1972. He helped promote physical fitness by jogging about 2 miles (3.2 kilometers) a day. He also encouraged all Canadians to learn both English and French.

Daniel Roland Michener was born in Lacombe, Alta. He received a bachelor's degree from the University of Alberta and a law degree from Oxford University in England. Michener served in the Ontario legislature from 1945 to 1948. He was elected to Canada's House of Commons in 1953 and became Speaker in 1957. In 1964, he was appointed High Commissioner to India and Canada's first ambassador to Nepal.　　　Jacques Monet

Tom Algire

Lake of the Clouds is surrounded by the thick forests of the Porcupine Mountains. The lake is in Michigan's Upper Peninsula, one of the two separate land areas that make up the state.

Michigan *The Wolverine State*

Michigan is an important industrial, farming, tourist, and mining state in the Great Lakes region of the United States. It is one of the nation's leading manufacturing states. Michigan leads in the manufacture of automobiles. Detroit, Michigan's largest city, is called the *Automobile Capital of the World* and the *Motor City.* The Detroit area produces more cars and trucks than any other part of the nation. Flint, Pontiac, and Lansing, the state capital, also are important automaking centers. Michigan is a leading state in food processing and steel production.

Michigan touches four of the five Great Lakes—Erie, Huron, Michigan, and Superior. The state's 3,288-mile (5,292-kilometer) shoreline is longer than that of any other state except Alaska. Michigan consists of two separate land areas, called the Upper Peninsula and the Lower Peninsula. The two peninsulas are connected by

---

The contributors of this article are Justin L. Kestenbaum, Professor of History at Michigan State University; and Harold A. Winters, Professor of Geography at Michigan State University.

the Mackinac Bridge, which spans 5 miles (8 kilometers) across the Straits of Mackinac.

Most farming in Michigan takes place in the southern half of the Lower Peninsula. Extensive areas of the Lower Peninsula near the shore of Lake Michigan are excellent for fruit growing. Michigan is among the leading states in the production of apples, cherries, and many other fruits. Michigan leads all other states in the production of dry beans.

Michigan is one of the leading tourist states. About 22 million people visit the state each year. Both the Upper and Lower peninsulas offer resort and recreation facilities, and scenic beauty. In addition to the Great Lakes, Michigan has more than 11,000 smaller lakes. Forests cover more than half the state. Michigan offers excellent hunting and fishing opportunities for outdoor sport enthusiasts.

Michigan is second only to Minnesota in iron ore production. Iron ore is mined in the Upper Peninsula. Michigan's other mining products include petroleum and natural gas. Petroleum and natural gas come from the Lower Peninsula.

Interesting facts about Michigan

The world's oldest agricultural college is Michigan State University. It was founded in 1855 as Michigan Agricultural College. Michigan State is also the oldest U.S. land-grant college.

Mackinac Bridge, designed by David B. Steinman and opened in 1957, connects Michigan's Upper and Lower peninsulas. Michigan is the only state in the continental United States to have such large sections entirely separated by water.

Battle Creek is called the
Cereal Bowl of America. Dr. John H. Kellogg's interest in health foods for patients at the Battle Creek Sanitarium stimulated the ready-to-eat breakfast food industry. Charles W. Post and W. K. Kellogg, John's brother, made the cereal industry a successful commercial venture in the early 1900's. Today, Battle Creek produces more breakfast cereal than any other city in the world.

Cereal Bowl of America

WORLD BOOK illustrations by Kevin Chadwick

The first practical carpet sweeper was invented by M. R. Bissell in Grand Rapids in 1876. The Bissell factory, still located there, is the world's largest manufacturer of carpet sweepers.

The first traffic lines to designate lanes were painted near Trenton in 1911. Edward N. Hines, Wayne County road commissioner, proposed the lines. He called them "center line safety stripes."

First carpet sweepers

The first person to observe digestion was William Beaumont, an Army doctor stationed at Fort Mackinac. He treated Alexis St. Martin, a fur trader who was shot by accident in the abdomen on Mackinac Island in 1822. Beaumont tried patiently to close the wound, but it never healed. Despite his injury, St. Martin lived to the age of 76. He was known as "the man with a window in his stomach." Through this "window," Beaumont gathered information that has proved to be accurate.

Ford Motor Company
Robots weld car bodies at a manufacturing plant in Wixom. Michigan ranks as the leading U.S. automobile manufacturer.

French explorers of the early 1600's were the first Europeans to visit what is now Michigan. France controlled the region for nearly 150 years, but did little to develop it. Great Britain gained control of the Michigan region after defeating France in the French and Indian Wars (1689-1763). In 1787, after the Revolutionary War in America, Michigan became part of the Northwest Territory of the United States. In 1805, Congress established the Territory of Michigan. In 1837, Michigan became the 26th state.

Michigan is named for Lake Michigan. The Chippewa Indians called the lake *Michigama,* which means *great,* or *large, lake.* Michigan is nicknamed the *Wolverine State* because the early fur traders brought valuable wolverine pelts to trading posts in the region. The state is also known as the *Water Wonderland,* because of its many beautiful lakes and streams. Including its share of the Great Lakes, Michigan has more fresh water than any other state. The Upper Peninsula is sometimes called the *Land of Hiawatha* because it is described in Henry Wadsworth Longfellow's poem, *The Song of Hiawatha.*

© Charles E. Zirkle, Image Broker
People relax in an outdoor cafe overlooking downtown Detroit. The modern Renaissance Center, one of the largest renewal projects in United States history, rises in the background.

Michigan in brief

Michigan (brown) ranks 23rd in size among all the states and 7th in size among the Midwestern States (yellow).

General information

Statehood: Jan. 26, 1837, the 26th state.
State abbreviations: Mich. (traditional); MI (postal).
State motto: *Si quaeris peninsulam amoenam, circumspice* (If you seek a pleasant peninsula, look about you).
State song (unofficial): "Michigan, My Michigan." Words by Douglas M. Malloch.

The State Capitol is in Lansing, Michigan's capital since 1847. Detroit served as capital from 1837 to 1847.

Land and climate

Area: 58,513 sq. mi. (151,548 km²), including 1,704 sq. mi. (4,412 km²) of inland water but excluding 38,192 sq. mi. (98,917 km²) of Great Lakes water.
Elevation: *Highest*—Mount Curwood, 1,980 ft. (604 m) above sea level. *Lowest*—572 ft. (174 m) above sea level along Lake Erie.
Record high temperature: 112 °F (44 °C) at Mio on July 13, 1936.
Record low temperature: −51 °F (−46 °C) at Vanderbilt on Feb. 9, 1934.
Average July temperature: 69 °F (21 °C).
Average January temperature: 20 °F (−7 °C).
Average yearly precipitation: 32 in. (81 cm).

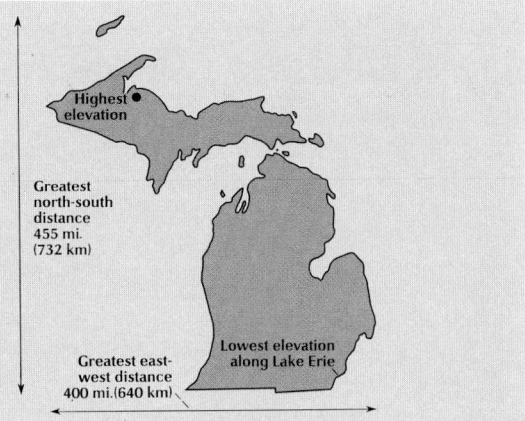

Highest elevation

Greatest north-south distance 455 mi. (732 km)

Greatest east-west distance 400 mi.(640 km)

Lowest elevation along Lake Erie

Important dates

Father Jacques Marquette founded Michigan's first permanent settlement at Sault Ste. Marie.

Michigan became the 26th state on January 26.

| 1620 | 1668 | 1701 | 1837 |

Étienne Brulé of France explored the Upper Peninsula of Michigan.

Antoine Cadillac founded what is now Detroit.

State bird
Robin

State flower
Apple blossom

State tree
White pine

People

Population: 9,328,784 (1990 census)
Rank among the states: 8th
Density: 159 persons per sq. mi. (62 per km²), U.S. average 69 per sq. mi. (27 per km²)
Distribution: 70 percent urban, 30 percent rural
Largest cities in Michigan

Detroit	1,027,974
Grand Rapids	189,126
Warren	144,864
Flint	140,761
Lansing	127,321
Sterling Heights	117,810

Source: U.S. Bureau of the Census.

Population trend

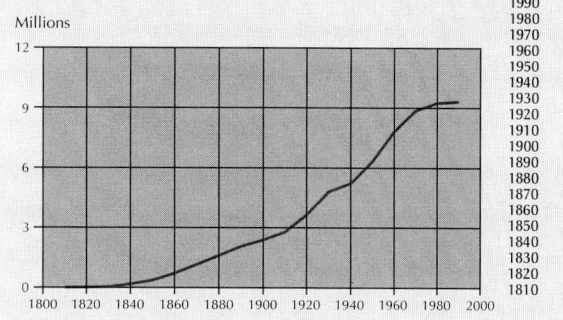

Source: U.S. Bureau of the Census.

Year	Population
1990	9,328,784
1980	9,262,070
1970	8,881,826
1960	7,823,194
1950	6,371,766
1940	5,256,106
1930	4,842,325
1920	3,668,412
1910	2,810,173
1900	2,420,982
1890	2,093,890
1880	1,636,937
1870	1,184,059
1860	749,113
1850	397,654
1840	212,267
1830	31,639
1820	8,896
1810	4,762

Economy

Chief products

Agriculture: milk, corn, hay, beef cattle, hogs.
Manufacturing: transportation equipment, machinery, fabricated metal products, food products, chemicals.
Mining: natural gas, iron ore, petroleum.

Gross state product

Value of goods and services produced in 1991: $190,594,000,000. *Services* include community, social, and personal services; finance; government; trade; and transportation, communication, and utilities. *Industry* includes construction, manufacturing, and mining. *Agriculture* includes agriculture, fishing, and forestry.

Source: U.S. Bureau of Economic Analysis.

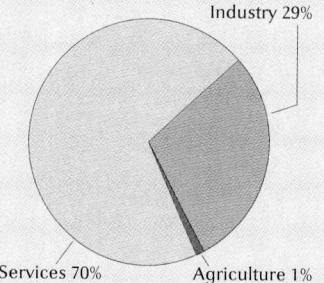

Industry 29%
Services 70%
Agriculture 1%

Government

State government

Governor: 4-year term
State senators: 38; 4-year terms
State representatives: 110; 2-year terms
Counties: 83

Federal government

United States senators: 2
United States representatives: 16
Electoral votes: 18

Sources of information

Tourism: Travel Bureau, Department of Commerce, P.O. Box 30226, Lansing, MI 48909
Economy: Library of Michigan, Information Services, P.O. Box 3007, Lansing, MI 48909
Government: Library of Michigan, Information Services, P.O. Box 3007, Lansing, MI 48909
History: Michigan State Archives, 717 West Allegan Street, Lansing, MI 48918

Michigan workers formed the United Automobile Workers union.

Michigan established a state lottery.

1899 | **1935** | **1964** | **1972**

Ransom E. Olds established Michigan's first automobile factory in Detroit.

A new state constitution went into effect.

Population. The 1990 United States census reported that Michigan had 9,328,784 people. The population had increased $\frac{1}{2}$ per cent over the 1980 figure, 9,262,070. According to the 1990 census, Michigan ranks 8th in population among the 50 states.

About 70 percent of Michigan's people live in urban areas. That is, they live in cities and towns of 2,500 or more people. About 30 percent of the people live in rural areas.

More than 80 percent of the people of Michigan make their homes in one of the state's nine metropolitan areas (see **Metropolitan area**). These are Ann Arbor, Benton Harbor, Detroit, Flint, Grand Rapids-Muskegon-Holland, Jackson, Kalamazoo-Battle Creek, Lansing-East Lansing, and Saginaw-Bay City-Midland. For the populations of these metropolitan areas, see the *Index* to the political map of Michigan. The majority of the people in the state live in the Lower Peninsula. Only about 300,000 people, or approximately 3 percent, live in Michigan's Upper Peninsula.

Detroit is Michigan's largest city, and the seventh largest city in the United States. Other large cities in Michigan, in order of population, are Grand Rapids, Warren, Flint, Lansing, Sterling Heights, Ann Arbor, Livonia, Dearborn, Westland, and Kalamazoo. All of these cities have populations of more than 80,000, and all of them are in the Lower Peninsula. The largest city in the Upper Peninsula is Marquette. It has a population of about 22,000 people.

About 96 out of 100 people in Michigan were born in the United States. Of the more than 350,000 people from other countries who live in the state, the largest group came from Canada.

About 14 percent of Michigan's people are blacks. Other large population groups in the state include people of German, Irish, English, Polish, French, and Dutch descent.

Schools. Roman Catholic missionaries who came to the Michigan region in the 1600's established schools for the Indians. In 1798, Father Gabriel Richard came to Detroit to serve as pastor of Ste. Anne's Roman Catholic Church. He established schools to provide regular classes and vocational training for Indian and white children.

Population density

Most of Michigan's people live in urban areas in the southern half of the Lower Peninsula—especially in and around Detroit. The Upper Peninsula is thinly settled.

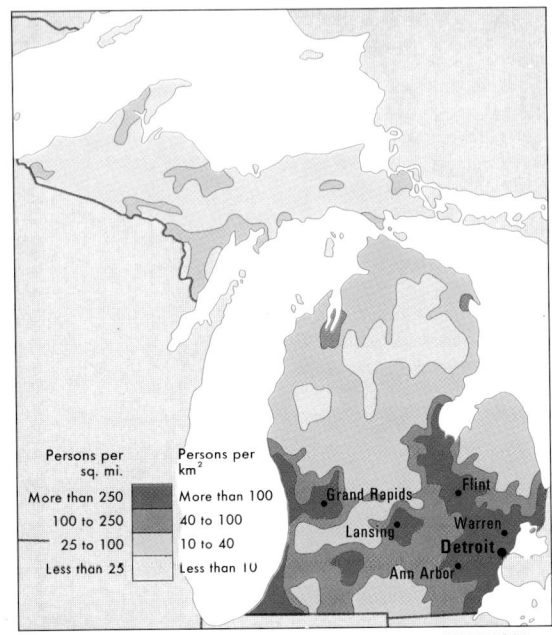

Persons per sq. mi.	Persons per km²
More than 250	More than 100
100 to 250	40 to 100
25 to 100	10 to 40
Less than 25	Less than 10

WORLD BOOK map

In 1809, the territorial legislature passed Michigan's first school law. The law provided for school districts, school taxes, and the building of public schools. In 1827, the legislature provided for community schools maintained by townships. After Michigan entered the Union in 1837, the Legislature approved a statewide system of public education, including a university. The new state Constitution provided for the appointment of a superintendent of public instruction to administer the public school system. The Michigan superintendent of public instruction was the first such administrator in the United States.

Eastern Michigan University, established in 1849, was

University of Michigan

College football is a popular spectator sport in Michigan. The Wolverines of the University of Michigan play their home games at Michigan Stadium in Ann Arbor, *left,* which seats more than 100,000 people.

the first state teachers college west of New York. Michigan State University, founded in 1855, was the first state school to offer agriculture courses for credit. In 1879, the University of Michigan became one of the first state universities to establish a *chair* (special teaching position) in education.

The state board of education directs Michigan's public school system. The state board consists of eight elected members. It appoints the superintendent of public instruction. A Michigan state law requires children from age 6 through 15 to attend school. For the number of students and teachers in Michigan, see **Education** (table).

Libraries. The Library of Michigan—the state library—was founded in Detroit in 1828, when many settlers were moving into the Michigan Territory. This library is now in the Michigan Library and Historical Center in Lansing. It has about 5 million volumes. Michigan has 16 library cooperatives and more than 375 public libraries with about 300 branches. The state provides aid to public libraries and cooperatives.

Libraries of the University of Michigan at Ann Arbor have more than $6\frac{1}{2}$ million volumes. The William L. Clements Library at the university has a famous collection on early America. The Gerald R. Ford Library in Ann Arbor contains the papers of the 38th U.S. President. The Detroit Public Library has the Burton Historical Collection. This collection contains reference works on Michigan and the Great Lakes area. The Walter P. Reuther Library of Wayne State University in Detroit has material relating to the history of labor, Michigan, and the Detroit area.

Museums. The Detroit Institute of Arts was established in 1885. Its collection of paintings and sculptures includes murals by the famous Mexican artist Diego Rivera. The Detroit Historical Museum contains exhibits on the history of Detroit and Michigan. Greenfield Vil-

© Ken Kaminsky

The Detroit Public Library has 25 branches. It features the Burton Historical Collection, a body of reference materials on Michigan and the Great Lakes region.

lage, in Dearborn, is an indoor-outdoor museum complex. The exhibits at Greenfield Village deal with American industrial history and life in the 1700's and 1800's (see **Greenfield Village**).

The Grand Rapids Public Museum features natural history exhibits. The Gerald R. Ford Museum, also in Grand Rapids, features items relating to the life of the former U.S. President. The Michigan Historical Museum in Lansing displays items dating from prehistoric times to the modern industrial era. The Kingman Museum of Natural History in Battle Creek has exhibits of wildlife, prehistoric mammals, and ancient relics. The Alfred P. Sloan, Jr., Museum in Flint features displays on transportation. Mackinac Island has seven museums. One features the instruments of William Beaumont, a surgeon who made major discoveries about digestion.

Universities and colleges

Michigan has 47 universities and colleges that offer bachelor's or advanced degrees and are accredited by the North Central Association of Colleges and Schools. For enrollments and further information, see **Universities and colleges** (table).

Name	Mailing address	Name	Mailing address
Adrian College	Adrian	Kendall College of	
Albion College	Albion	Art and Design	Grand Rapids
Alma College	Alma	Lake Superior State University	Sault Ste. Marie
Andrews University	Berrien Springs	Lawrence Technological	
Aquinas College	Grand Rapids	University	Southfield
Baker College	*	Madonna University	Livonia
Calvin College	Grand Rapids	Marygrove College	Detroit
Center for Creative Studies-		Michigan, University of	*
College of Art and Design	Detroit	Michigan Christian College	Rochester
Center for Humanistic Studies	Detroit		Hills
Central Michigan University	Mount Pleasant	Michigan State University	East Lansing
Cleary College	Ypsilanti	Michigan Technological University	Houghton
Concordia College	Ann Arbor	Northern Michigan University	Marquette
Cranbrook Academy of Art	Bloomfield Hills	Northwood Institute	Midland
Davenport College of Business	Grand Rapids	Oakland University	Rochester
Detroit Mercy, University of	Detroit	Olivet College	Olivet
Detroit College of Business	Dearborn	Sacred Heart Major Seminary/College	
Eastern Michigan University	Ypsilanti	and Theologate	Detroit
Ferris State University	Big Rapids	Saginaw Valley State University	University Cen-
GMI Engineering and			ter
Management Institute	Flint	St. Mary's College	Orchard Lake
Grace Bible College	Grand Rapids	Siena Heights College	Adrian
Grand Rapids Baptist College		Spring Arbor College	Spring Arbor
and Seminary	Grand Rapids	Walsh College of Accountancy	
Grand Valley State		and Business Administration	Troy
University	Allendale	Wayne State University	Detroit
Hillsdale College	Hillsdale	Western Michigan University	Kalamazoo
Hope College	Holland	William Tyndale College	Farmington Hills
Kalamazoo College	Kalamazoo		

*For campuses, see **Universities and colleges** (table).

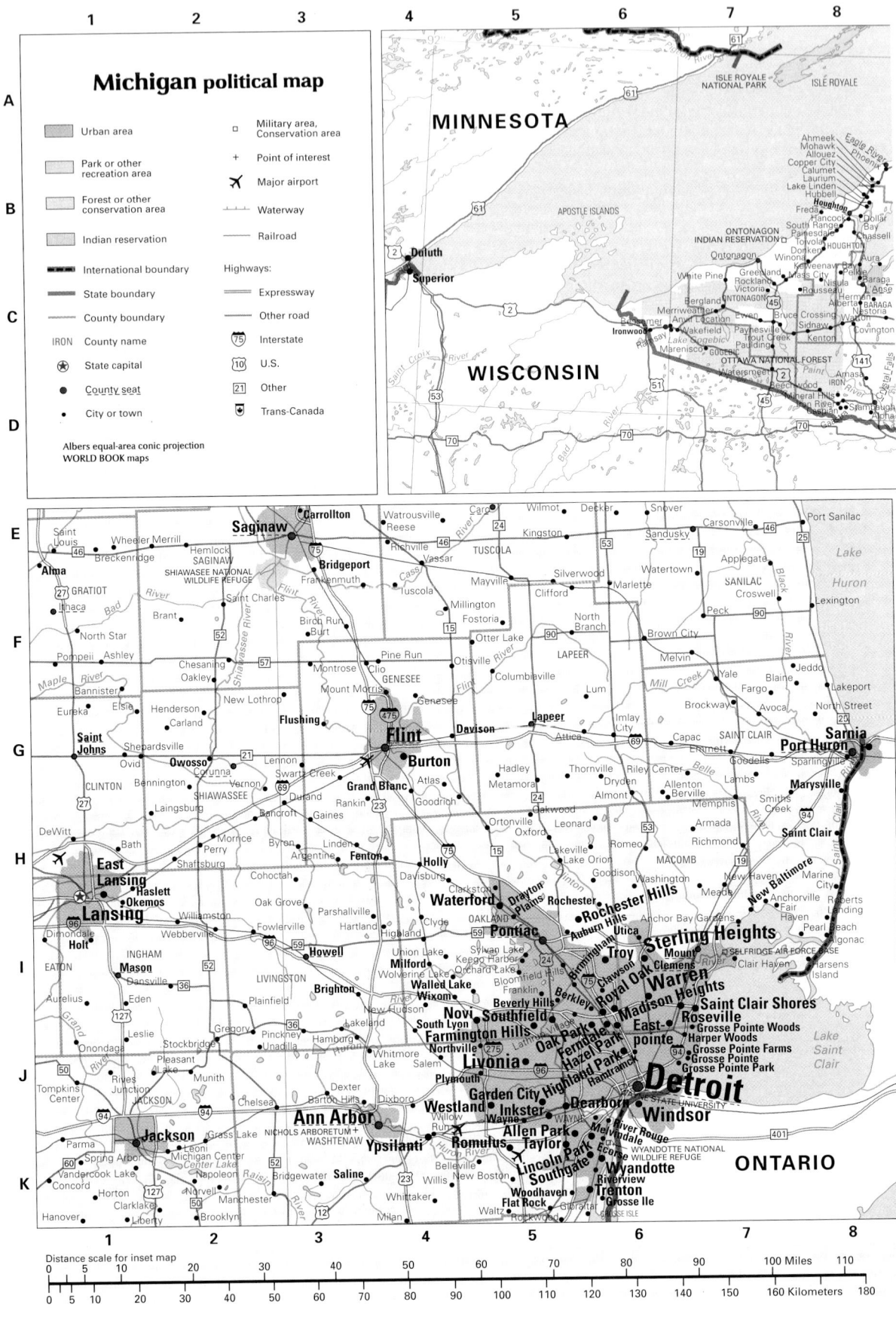

Michigan political map

Legend:

- Urban area
- Park or other recreation area
- Forest or other conservation area
- Indian reservation
- International boundary
- State boundary
- County boundary
- IRON — County name
- ★ State capital
- ● County seat
- • City or town

- □ Military area, Conservation area
- + Point of interest
- ✈ Major airport
- Waterway
- Railroad

Highways:
- Expressway
- Other road
- 75 Interstate
- 10 U.S.
- 21 Other
- Trans-Canada

Albers equal-area conic projection
WORLD BOOK maps

Distance scale for inset map
0 5 10   20   30   40   50   60   70   80   90   100 Miles   110
0 5 10 20 30 40 50 60 70 80 90 100 110 120 130 140 150 160 Kilometers 180

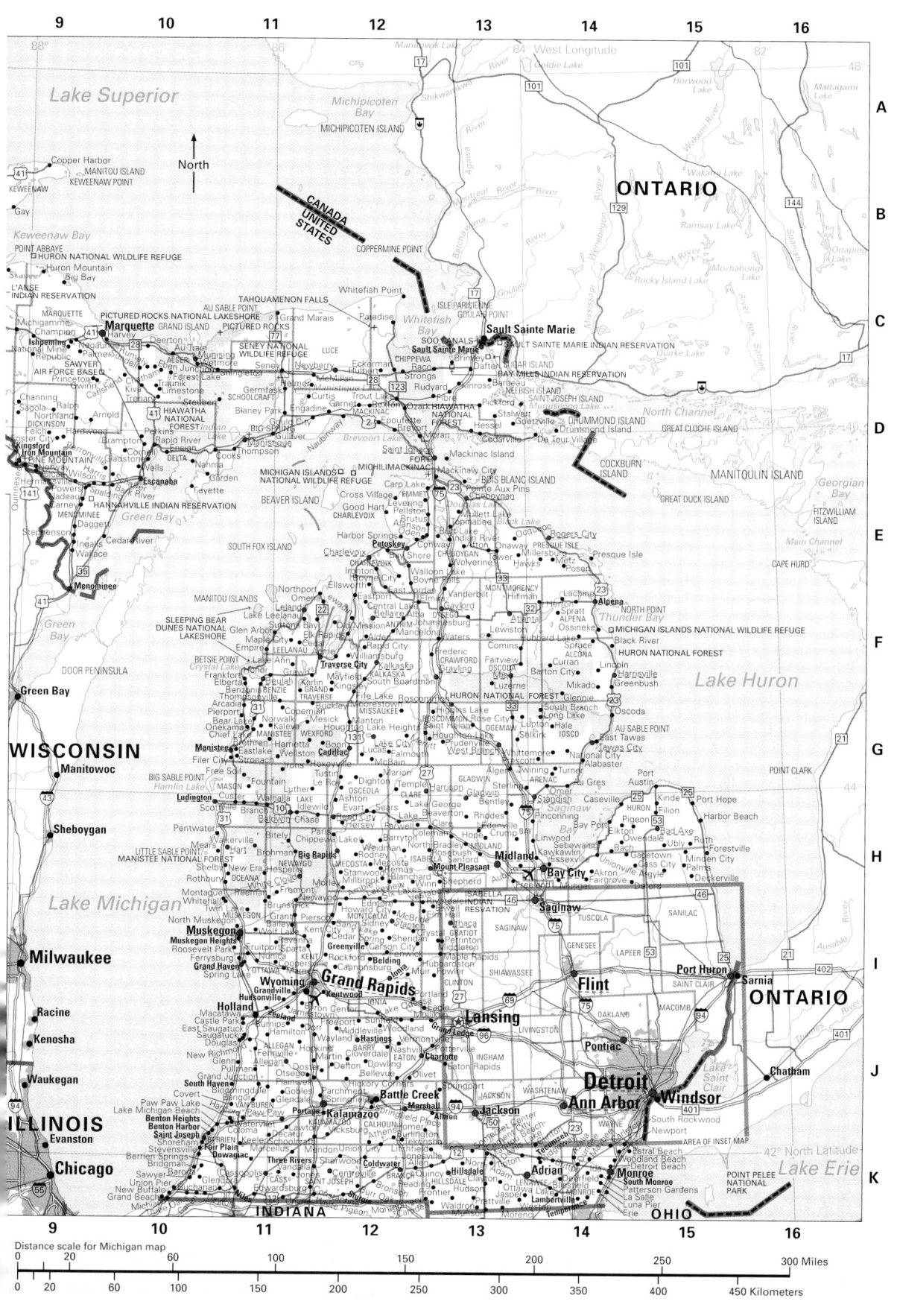

Michigan map index

*Does not appear on map; key shows general location.
†Census designated place—unincorporated, but recognized as a significant settled community by the U.S. Bureau of the Census.
ºCounty seat.
Source: 1990 census. Places without population figures are unincorporated areas.

Michigan has year-round activities for people who love sports and the outdoors. Thousands of lakes, along with many rivers and streams, attract swimmers, water skiers, fishing enthusiasts, and boaters. Thick forests and scenic woodlands appeal to hunters and campers. In winter, many people travel to Michigan for skiing, skating, snowmobiling, tobogganing, iceboat racing, and ice fishing. International ski-flying competitions are held in Ironwood at Copper Peak, one of the world's largest artificially created ski-flying hills. Sightseers are drawn to the many beautiful waterfalls, and dunes, and to the rugged "Copper Country" of the western Upper Peninsula.

One of Michigan's most popular annual events is the weeklong Tulip Festival, held each May in Holland. The people of the city dress in traditional Dutch costumes. The festival includes parades, dancing in wooden shoes, and ceremonial street washing.

Grand Sable Dunes at Pictured Rocks National Lakeshore near Munising

© Rod Planck, Click/Chicago

Places to visit

Following are brief descriptions of some of Michigan's many interesting places to visit:

Arboretums of Michigan have some of the country's finest collections of plants, shrubs, and trees. Leila Arboretum, in Battle Creek, is a landscaped park that has rare plants and a wildlife museum. Nichols Arboretum, in Ann Arbor, is a natural environment that has more than 600 species of trees and shrubs, including about 250 kinds of peonies.

Big Spring, or *Kitchi-ti-ki-pi,* near Manistique, is a pool fed by 16,000 gallons (61,000 liters) of water per minute erupting from its depths. The pool is 45 feet (14 meters) deep and 200 feet (61 meters) across. The water is so clear that visitors can watch coins drift to the bottom of the pool.

Detroit produces more cars and trucks than any other city in the nation. It is the seventh largest city in the United States, and a leading port. The city's Cultural Center includes libraries, museums, and Wayne State University. Greektown is a popular tourist attraction. See **Detroit.**

Fort Michilimackinac, in Mackinaw City, is a reconstruction of the fort built in the 1700's. Buildings include the home of British commander Robert Rogers, and Ste. Anne's Jesuit church. Nearby historic attractions include Mill Creek State Historic Park and *The Welcome,* a ship that dates from the 1700's.

Greenfield Village, in Dearborn, is a collection of historic buildings and landmarks restored by Henry Ford. Greenfield Village includes buildings made famous by such persons as Abraham Lincoln, Thomas Edison, William H. McGuffey, and Stephen Foster. The Henry Ford Museum is next to the village. See **Greenfield Village.**

Kellogg Bird Sanctuary, on Gull Lake near Battle Creek, is a 100-acre (40-hectare) refuge for ducks, geese, pheasants, swans, and other wild birds.

Mackinac Island is a famous resort island in the Straits of Mackinac, between Michigan's Upper and Lower peninsulas. Historic Fort Mackinac stands on the island. No automobiles are permitted on the island. See **Mackinac Island.**

National Ski Hall of Fame, in Ishpeming, pays tribute to famous United States skiers, skiing events, and persons who have made outstanding contributions to the sport.

Pictured Rocks National Lakeshore, near Munising on Lake Superior, has beautifully colored cliffs that have been carved into spectacular shapes by the action of waves. The Grand Sable Dunes are also at Pictured Rocks.

Sleeping Bear Dunes National Lakeshore, near Empire, features a mound of sand shaped like a sleeping bear. The mound rises about 465 feet (142 meters).

Soo Canals, at Sault Ste. Marie, permit ships to travel between Lake Huron and Lake Superior through huge locks. See **Soo Canals.**

Tahquamenon Falls, near Newberry, are among the most beautiful sights of the Upper Peninsula. Henry Wadsworth Longfellow wrote about both the upper and lower falls of the Tahquamenon River in his poem *The Song of Hiawatha.*

Windmill Island Municipal Park in Holland features the only authentic, operating Dutch windmill in the United States. Visitors may purchase flour that has been ground at the windmill.

National forests and parks. Michigan has four national forests. The largest, Ottawa National Forest, lies in the western part of the Upper Peninsula. Hiawatha National Forest is in the central and eastern parts of the Upper Peninsula. Huron National Forest occupies much of the Au Sable River Basin in the eastern Lower Peninsula. Manistee National Forest covers most of the Manistee River Basin in the western Lower Peninsula. Michigan's only national park, Isle Royale, is in northwestern Lake Superior, about 20 miles (32 kilometers) from the mainland of Minnesota. It includes Isle Royale and about 200 nearby small islands. The park has one of the largest remaining herds of great-antlered moose in the United States. Isle Royale National Park is about 48 miles (77 kilometers) from the Upper Peninsula. See **Isle Royale National Park.**

State parks and forests. Michigan has 99 state parks and recreation areas, 6 state forests, and more than 170 roadside parks and rest areas. Michigan's park system has over 14,000 prepared campsites, more than any other state. In addition, the state has about 70 organized winter-sport areas. For information on the state parks and other attractions of Michigan, write to the Michigan Travel Bureau, P.O. Box 30226, Lansing, MI 48909.

Skiing at Crystal Mountain

Michigan Travel Bureau

© Jim Kransberger

Port Huron to Mackinac Island Yacht Race

Annual events

January-March
Tip-Up Town, U.S.A. in Houghton Lake (January); I-500 Snow-mobile Race in Sault Ste. Marie (early February); Invitational Nordic Ski Race in Newberry (mid-March); Snowmobile Festival in Boyne City and Copper Harbor (mid-March).

April-July
Maple Syrup Festival in Shepherd and Vermontville (April); Blossomtime Festival in St. Joseph-Benton Harbor (May); Highland Festival and Games in Alma (May); Grand Prix in Detroit (June); Bavarian Festival in Frankenmuth (June); Muzzle Loaders Festival in Dearborn (June); International Freedom Festival in Detroit (late June-early July); Lumbertown Music Festival in Muskegon (early July); National Cherry Festival in Traverse City (early July); Yacht Races at Mackinac Island from Chicago and Port Huron (July); Ann Arbor Art Fair (July).

August-September
Michigan Festival in East Lansing (early August); Upper Peninsula State Fair in Escanaba (mid-August); State Fair in Detroit (late August); Mackinac Bridge Walk, from St. Ignace to Mackinaw City (Labor Day); Montreux/Detroit Jazz Festival (late August-early September); Michigan Wine and Harvest Festival in Paw Paw and Kalamazoo (mid-September).

October-December
Fall color tours, statewide (October); Red Flannel Days in Cedar Springs (October); Hunting season, parts of Upper and Lower peninsulas (October-November), statewide (November); Christmas at Greenfield Village in Dearborn (December).

© Jim West

Cotswold Cottage in Greenfield Village

© W. Spencer Parshall

Windmill Island Municipal Park in Holland

Land regions. Michigan has two main land regions: (1) the Superior Upland and (2) the Great Lakes Plains.

The Superior Upland extends along Lake Superior and covers the western half of the Upper Peninsula. Much of the region is rugged, rising from about 600 to 1,980 feet (180 to 604 meters) above sea level. Michigan's highest hills are in this region. The Porcupine Mountains in extreme northwestern Michigan rise more than 1,000 feet (305 meters) from the shores of Lake Superior. Mount Curwood is the highest point in the state, 1,980 feet (604 meters) above sea level. Forests cover most of these hills. The Superior Upland has some of the nation's richest iron and copper deposits.

The Great Lakes Plains stretch along the Great Lakes from Wisconsin to Ohio. In Michigan, the region covers the eastern Upper Peninsula and the entire Lower Peninsula. In the Upper Peninsula, parts of the Great Lakes Plains are lowlands covered by swamps. A short growing season and poor soils make many parts of the area unsuitable for farming. The Great Lakes Plains are part of a large Midwestern land region called the *Interior Plains.*

Much of the Lower Peninsula is fairly level, but some parts are rolling and hilly. Parts of the north-central Lower Peninsula rises 1,200 to 1,400 feet (366 to 427 meters) above sea level. Many high bluffs and sand dunes border Lake Michigan. The state's lowest point, 572 feet (174 meters) above sea level, is along the shore of Lake Erie. Parts of the northern Lower Peninsula have sandy wastes, covered with jack pine trees, scrub, and stumps. The southern half of the Lower Peninsula has much good farmland.

Shoreline of Michigan is 3,288 miles (5,292 kilometers) long—more than that of any other state except Alaska. This includes 1,056 miles (1,699 kilometers) of island shoreline. Four Great Lakes border the state—Erie, Huron, Michigan, and Superior. No part of Michigan lies more than 85 miles (137 kilometers) from one of these lakes.

Bays along the Lower Peninsula include Grand Traverse and Little Traverse on Lake Michigan, and Saginaw on Lake Huron. The Upper Peninsula has Whitefish and Keweenaw bays on Lake Superior, and Big Bay de Noc on Lake Michigan. Green Bay touches the southern tip of the Upper Peninsula.

Islands. Michigan's largest island, Isle Royale, covers about 210 square miles (544 square kilometers) in Lake Superior. The Beaver and Manitou islands are in Lake Michigan. Bois Blanc, Mackinac, and Round islands are in Lake Huron, just east of the Straits of Mackinac. Drummond Island, also in Lake Huron, lies off the eastern tip of the Upper Peninsula. The small islands in the Detroit River include Belle Isle and Grosse Ile.

Rivers, waterfalls, and lakes. The chief rivers of the Upper Peninsula include the Escanaba, Manistique, Menominee, Ontonagon, Sturgeon, Tahquamenon, and Whitefish. Principal rivers in the Lower Peninsula are the Au Sable, Clinton, Grand, Huron, Kalamazoo, Manistee, Muskegon, Raisin, Saginaw, and St. Joseph. The Grand River, 260 miles (418 kilometers) long, is the longest in the state. The Detroit, St. Clair, and St. Marys rivers are important for commerce. The Detroit River connects Lakes Erie and St. Clair. Lakes Huron and St. Clair are joined by the St. Clair. The St. Marys River connects Lakes Huron and Superior.

Michigan's Upper Peninsula has about 150 beautiful waterfalls. The best-known falls are the Upper and Lower Tahquamenon Falls on the Tahquamenon River. Other well-known waterfalls include the Agate, Bond, Laughing Whitefish, Miners, and Munising—all in the Upper Peninsula.

Michigan has more than 11,000 inland lakes. The largest is 31-square-mile (80-square-kilometer) Houghton Lake in the north-central Lower Peninsula. Most of the larger lakes are in the Lower Peninsula. They include Black, Burt, Charlevoix, Crystal, Higgins, Mullet, and Torch lakes. Lake Gogebic is the largest lake in the Upper Peninsula.

Plant and animal life. Forests cover more than half of Michigan. Much of the state's forest land is covered

Land regions of Michigan

WORLD BOOK map

Map index

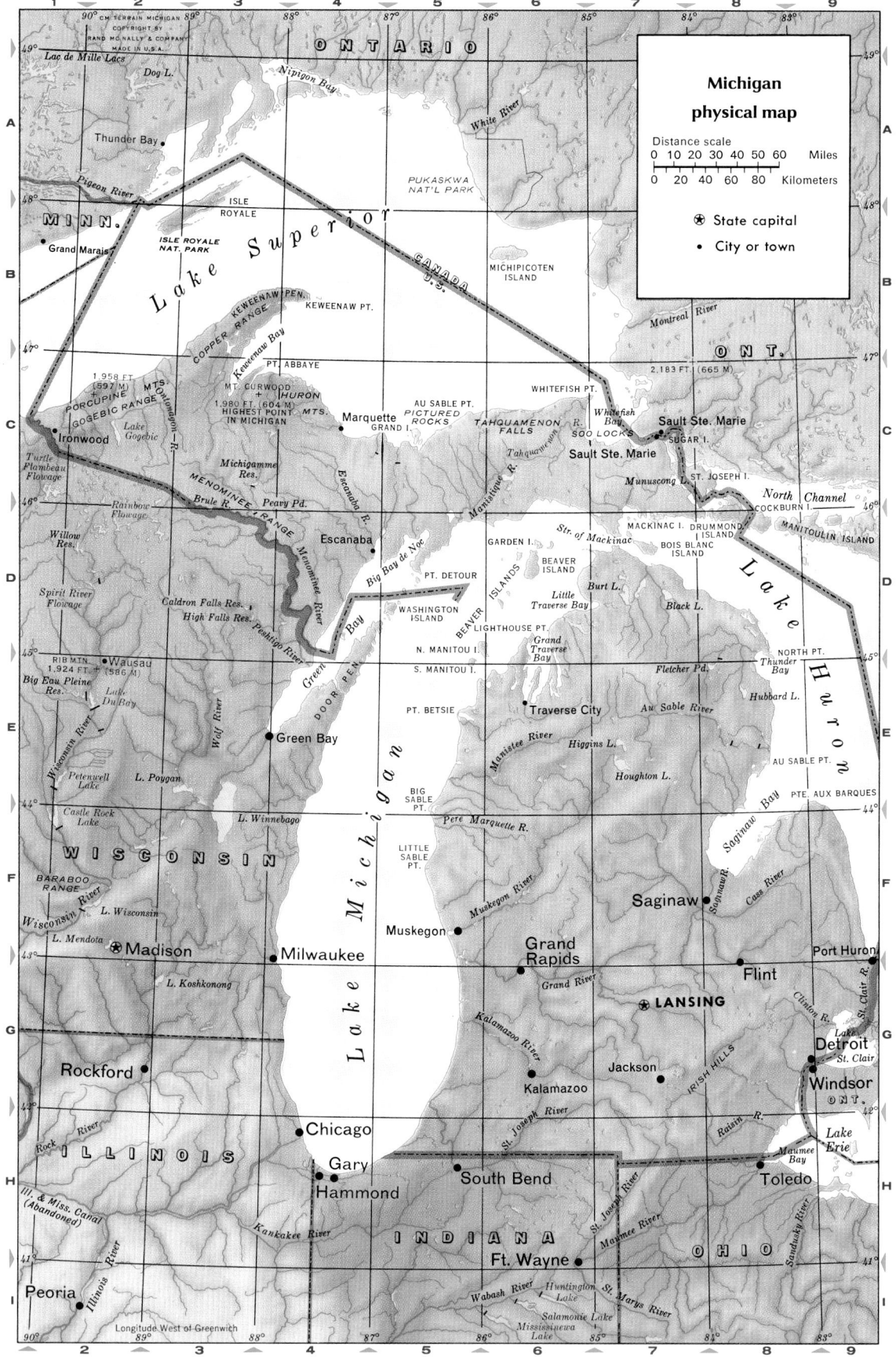

Michigan
physical map

Distance scale
0 10 20 30 40 50 60 Miles
0 20 40 60 80 Kilometers

⊛ State capital
• City or town

ONTARIO

Lac de Mille Lacs
Dog L.
Nipigon Bay
White River
Thunder Bay
PUKASKWA NAT'L PARK
Pigeon River
MINN.
ISLE ROYALE
Grand Marais
ISLE ROYALE NAT. PARK
Lake Superior
MICHIPICOTEN ISLAND
CANADA U.S.
KEWEENAW PEN.
COPPER RANGE
KEWEENAW PT.
Keweenaw Bay
PT. ABBAYE
Montreal River
ONT.
2,183 FT. (665 M)
1,958 FT. (597 M)
PORCUPINE MTS.
GOGEBIC RANGE
MT. CURWOOD
HURON
1,980 FT. (604 M)
HIGHEST POINT IN MICHIGAN
MTS.
Marquette
GRAND I.
AU SABLE PT.
PICTURED ROCKS
TAHQUAMENON FALLS
R.
Whitefish Bay
WHITEFISH PT.
SOO LOCKS
Sault Ste. Marie
Sault Ste. Marie
SUGAR I.
Ironwood
Turtle Flambeau Flowage
Lake Gogebic
Michigamme Res.
Tahquamenon
ST. JOSEPH I.
Munuscong L.
North Channel
COCKBURN I.
MANITOULIN ISLAND
Rainbow Flowage
MENOMINEE RANGE
Brule R.
Peavy Pd.
Escanaba R.
Manistique R.
MACKINAC I.
DRUMMOND ISLAND
BOIS BLANC ISLAND
Lake Huron
Willow Res.
Spirit River Flowage
Caldron Falls Res.
High Falls Res.
Peshtigo River
Escanaba
Big Bay de Noc
PT. DETOUR
WASHINGTON ISLAND
N. MANITOU I.
GARDEN I.
BEAVER ISLANDS
Str. of Mackinac
BEAVER ISLAND
Little Traverse Bay
Burt L.
Black L.
NORTH PT.
Thunder Bay
Hubbard L.
RIB MTN.
1,924 FT. (586 M)
Wausau
Big Eau Pleine Res.
Lake Du Bay
Wolf River
Green Bay
DOOR PEN.
LIGHTHOUSE PT.
S. MANITOU I.
Grand Traverse Bay
Fletcher Pd.
AU SABLE PT.
PTE. AUX BARQUES
Petenwell Lake
L. Poygan
PT. BETSIE
Traverse City
Au Sable River
Higgins L.
Houghton L.
Saginaw Bay
Castle Rock Lake
L. Winnebago
Manistee River
BIG SABLE PT.
Pere Marquette R.
WISCONSIN
BARABOO RANGE
Wisconsin River
L. Wisconsin
LITTLE SABLE PT.
Muskegon River
Saginaw
Saginaw R.
Cass River
L. Mendota
Madison
Milwaukee
L. Koshkonong
Muskegon
Grand Rapids
Grand River
LANSING
Flint
Port Huron
Clinton R.
St. Clair R.
Rockford
Lake Michigan
Kalamazoo River
Detroit
St. Clair
Chicago
St. Joseph River
Jackson
Kalamazoo
IRISH HILLS
Windsor
ONT.
Lake Erie
Gary
Hammond
South Bend
Raisin R.
Maumee Bay
Toledo
ILLINOIS
Ill. & Miss. Canal (Abandoned)
Rock River
Kankakee River
INDIANA
St. Joseph River
Maumee River
OHIO
Sandusky River
Peoria
Illinois River
Ft. Wayne
Wabash River
Huntington Lake
St. Marys River
Salamonie Lake
Mississinewa Lake

Longitude West of Greenwich

Specially created for *The World Book Encyclopedia* by Rand McNally and World Book editors

James P. Rowan

Tahquamenon Falls, near Newberry, are located in the Great Lakes Plains region of Michigan's Upper Peninsula. The broad Upper Tahquamenon Falls is known as the *Little Niagara*.

Michigan probably has more deer than any other state except Texas. Other common fur and game animals in Michigan include badgers, black bears, minks, muskrats, opossums, rabbits, raccoons, red foxes, skunks, squirrels, and weasels. Hundreds of kinds of birds live in the state. Game birds most prized by hunters include ducks, geese, grouse, and pheasants.

Fishes found in Michigan's lakes, rivers, and streams include bass, crappie, perch, pike, salmon, trout, and walleye. Smelt runs occur each spring in streams that empty into parts of Lake Huron and Lake Michigan. Other fishes common in Michigan's waters include alewives, catfish, and chubs. Carp, lake herring, and whitefish are common in the Great Lakes.

by such hardwood trees as aspens, beeches, birches, maples, and oaks. Softwoods cover most of the remaining forest land. These include cedars, firs, hemlocks, pines, and spruces.

Bittersweet, clematis, grapes, moonseed, and several kinds of smilax grow wild in Michigan's thickest forests. Such shrubs as blackberry, currant, elder, gooseberry, raspberry, rose, and viburnum thrive in the more open forest areas. Ferns and mosses grow in the swamps, as do cranberries and lady's-slippers. Such flowers as the arbutus, mandrake, trillium, and violet bloom in late April to early May. Flowers that bloom later in the year include the daisy, iris, orange milkweed, rose, shooting star, and tiger lily. Other common flowers include the aster, chicory, goldenrod, and sunflower.

Average monthly weather

Escanaba						Detroit					
	Temperatures				Days of rain or snow		Temperatures				Days of rain or snow
	F°		C°				F°		C°		
	High	Low	High	Low			High	Low	High	Low	
Jan.	25	10	−4	−12	12	Jan.	32	19	0	−7	13
Feb.	26	9	−3	−13	10	Feb.	34	19	1	−7	11
Mar.	34	18	1	−8	10	Mar.	44	27	7	−3	12
Apr.	46	31	8	−1	10	Apr.	57	36	14	2	13
May	58	42	14	6	11	May	70	47	21	8	11
June	69	52	21	11	11	June	80	58	27	14	10
July	75	58	24	14	11	July	84	63	29	17	9
Aug.	73	57	23	14	10	Aug.	81	61	27	16	9
Sept.	65	50	18	10	12	Sept.	74	55	23	13	8
Oct.	54	40	12	4	10	Oct.	62	43	17	6	7
Nov.	40	28	4	−2	11	Nov.	46	33	8	1	12
Dec.	29	16	−2	−9	11	Dec.	35	23	2	−5	11

Average January temperatures

The Upper Peninsula generally has the coldest winters in the state. Southeastern Michigan has the mildest temperatures.

Average July temperatures

Michigan has warm summers. Temperatures decrease steadily from the south northward to the Upper Peninsula.

Average yearly precipitation

Michigan has a moist climate. Precipitation varies widely in the state. The Upper Peninsula receives heavy snowfalls.

WORLD BOOK   maps

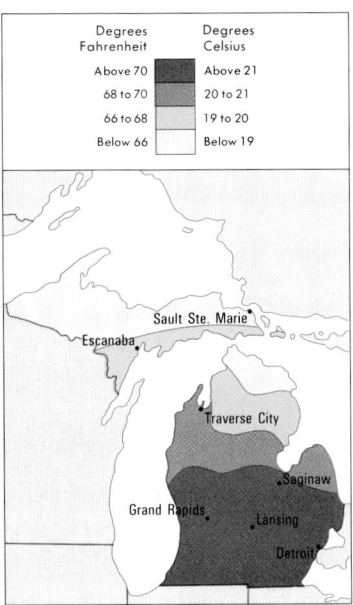

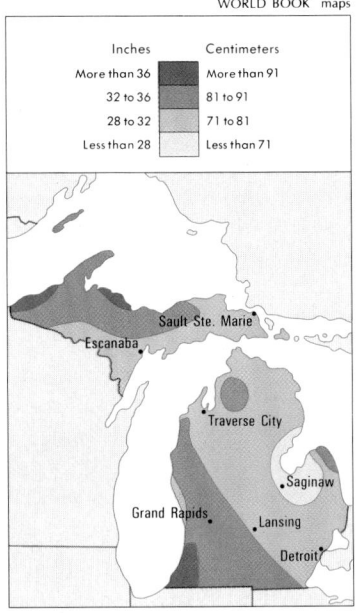

Climate. Michigan has a moist climate with cold winters and warm summers in the south and cool summers in the north. Winds from the Great Lakes bring much cloudiness. About 6 of every 10 days are partly cloudy in summer and about 7 of every 10 days in winter. Fall and winter are especially cloudy in the western Lower Peninsula and the eastern Upper Peninsula.

The Lower Peninsula is generally warmer than the Upper Peninsula. Average January temperatures range from 15 °F. (−9 °C) in the western Upper Peninsula to 26 °F. (−3 °C) in the southern Lower Peninsula. July temperatures average 65 °F. (18 °C) in the eastern Upper Peninsula and 73 °F. (23 °C) in the southern Lower Peninsula. Michigan's record low temperature, −51 °F. (−46 °C),

occurred in Vanderbilt on Feb. 9, 1934. Mio recorded the highest temperature, 112 °F. (44 °C), on July 13, 1936. Air cooled by Lake Michigan in the spring usually prevents the budding of fruit trees until the danger of frosts has passed.

Michigan's yearly *precipitation* (rain, melted snow, and other forms of moisture) ranges from about 26 to 36 inches (66 to 91 centimeters). Annual snowfall in Michigan varies from less than 40 inches (102 centimeters) in the southeastern Lower Peninsula to more than 160 inches (406 centimeters) in the western Upper Peninsula. The state's record snowfall, $276\frac{1}{2}$ inches (702.3 centimeters), occurred at Houghton during the winter of 1949-1950.

Economy

Service industries, taken together, account for about 70 percent of Michigan's *gross state product*—the total value of all goods and services produced in a state in a year. Michigan ranks among the nation's leading manufacturing states. The production of transportation equipment ranks as the state's most important manufacturing industry. Detroit is Michigan's chief manufacturing center. Other important manufacturing cities include Battle Creek, Flint, Grand Rapids, Lansing, Livonia, Pontiac, Saginaw, and Warren.

Important natural gas and petroleum deposits lie under Michigan's Lower Peninsula. Valuable iron ore deposits are in the western Upper Peninsula. The southern Lower Peninsula has the best farmland. Most of the state's livestock and crops are raised in this area. Fruit thrives along the Lake Michigan shoreline of the Lower Peninsula.

Michigan is a leading tourist state. Millions of people visit the state annually and contribute about $6 billion to the economy. Natural attractions, and resort and recreation areas, can be found in many parts of the Upper and Lower peninsulas.

Natural resources of Michigan include fertile soils, rich mineral deposits, widespread forests, and plentiful plant and animal life. For information about the state's forests and plant and animal life, see the *Land and climate* section.

Soil. The Upper Peninsula of Michigan has soils that vary from fertile loams to areas of poor soils and infertile sands. The northern section of the Lower Peninsula has sandy and loamy soils similar to those of the Upper Peninsula of the state. A variety of soils covers former glacial lakebeds next to Saginaw Bay and along the shoreline of eastern Michigan. These glacial soils range from rich, dark-brown or black loams and gray sands, to infertile soils that are shallow and poorly drained. The state's richest soils are in the southern half of the Lower Peninsula.

Minerals. Michigan's Upper Peninsula has vast iron ore and copper deposits. Great stores of iron ore lie in the Marquette Range of the central Upper Peninsula. The Menominee Range in the southern Upper Peninsula, and the Gogebic Range in the western corner, also have enormous iron ore deposits. These iron deposits extend into Wisconsin, and are part of one of the greatest known iron ore regions in the world. The Keweenaw

Production and workers by economic activities

Economic activities	Percent of GSP* produced	Employed workers	
		Number of persons	Percent of total
Manufacturing	25	899,000	23
Community, social, & personal services	19	933,600	24
Finance, insurance, & real estate	17	188,900	5
Wholesale & retail trade	16	926,800	23
Government	11	631,700	16
Transportation, communication, & utilities	7	156,900	4
Construction	3	128,800	3
Agriculture	1	85,300	2
Mining	1	9,100	†
Total	**100**	**3,960,100**	**100**

*GSP = gross state product, the total value of goods and services produced in a year.
†Less than one-half of 1 percent.
Figures are for 1991.
Sources: *World Book* estimates based on data from U.S. Bureau of Economic Analysis, U.S. Bureau of Labor Statistics, and U.S. Department of Agriculture.

Peninsula, which forms the northernmost tip of the Upper Peninsula, is one of the few sources of *native* (pure) copper in the world.

The Lower Peninsula has valuable deposits of petroleum. The largest of these deposits lie in the northwestern and southern parts of the Lower Peninsula. Important deposits of natural gas are also found in the northwestern part of the Lower Peninsula. The Lower Peninsula has deposits of salt. Brines that contain calcium chloride and magnesium are also found in this region of the state. Limestone and shale are widespread in the state. Gypsum deposits lie under part of the Lower Peninsula. Every county in Michigan has deposits of sand and gravel.

Service industries account for 70 percent of Michigan's gross state product. Service industries are concentrated in the state's metropolitan areas, especially the Detroit metropolitan area.

Community, social, and personal services make up the leading service industry in Michigan in terms of the gross state product. This industry also employs more of Michigan's labor force than any other economic activity.

It consists of a variety of service establishments, including doctors' offices and private hospitals, law firms, engineering and research companies, and repair shops. The suburban areas of Detroit have the largest concentration of private health care facilities in Michigan. Engineering and research companies receive much business from the state's automotive industry.

Finance, insurance, and real estate is the second-ranking service industry in Michigan. Detroit is one of the nation's leading banking centers. Major banking companies in the city include Comerica and NDB Bank NA. Banks play a vital role in the economy by providing loans for business expansion. The insurance industry is especially important in Detroit and Lansing. Lansing is the home of Jackson National Life, one of the Midwest's largest insurance companies. Urban renewal projects and the growth of suburban areas have benefited Michigan's real estate companies.

Wholesale and retail trade ranks third among Michigan's service industries. In the wholesale trade sector, distributors of automobiles, automobile parts, groceries, and machinery are most important. The port of Detroit handles much international wholesale trade. Among retail trade establishments, automobile dealerships, discount stores, grocery stores, and restaurants bring in the most income. Troy is the headquarters of K Mart, one of the largest retailing companies in the United States.

Government ranks fourth among Michigan service in-dustries. Government services include public schools and hospitals, and military establishments. The public school system is one of the major employers in the state. State government offices are based in Lansing. The federal and state government have branch offices in Detroit. Detroit's city government employs a large number of people.

Transportation, communication, and utilities rank fifth in importance among Michigan's service industries. Several railroad and trucking companies have large operations in Detroit. The city is the home of Grand Trunk, a major United States railroad company. Television and telephone companies are the major parts of the communications industry. The largest utility company in Michigan is Consumers Power. More information about transportation and communication appears later in this section.

Manufacturing accounts for about 25 percent of the gross state product. Goods manufactured in the state have a *value added by manufacture* of about $63 billion a year. This figure represents the increase in value of raw materials after they become finished products.

Transportation equipment is Michigan's leading type of manufactured product. It provides more than one-third of the state's manufacturing income. Automobiles, buses, trucks, and other vehicles manufactured in Michigan may be seen in all parts of the world. The transportation equipment industries employ about a third of all the industrial workers in the state. Michigan's transpor-

Farm and mineral products

This map shows where the leading farm and mineral products are produced. The major urban areas (shown in red) are the important manufacturing centers.

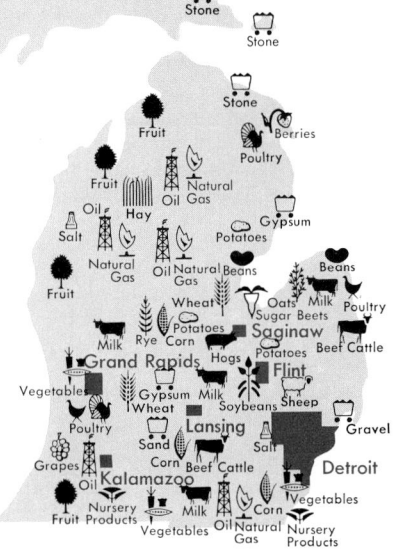

© Linda Kelly-Hassett from Caryle Calvin

Workers test molten steel in a blast furnace in a Detroit steel plant. Michigan ranks among the leading states in producing iron ore and steel. Michigan factories also manufacture metal products.

WORLD BOOK map

tation industries rank high among the nation's users of rubber, plate glass, and upholstery material.

Michigan is the leading manufacturer of automobiles among the states. Detroit is called the *Automobile Capital of the World* and the *Motor City.* Other important automobile-manufacturing cities in Michigan include Dearborn, Flatrock, Flint, Hamtramck, Lansing, Pontiac, Sterling Heights, Wayne, and Wixom. Other vehicles produced in the state include full-sized and light trucks, airplanes, boats, buses, and tanks.

The production of machinery is the second most valuable type of manufacturing activity in Michigan in terms of value added by manufacture. Most of the state's machinery is made in the Detroit area. Machine parts are the leading product of this industry. Machine parts include bearings, chisels, dies, and valves. Other important kinds of machinery are computers, conveyors, engines, machine tools, and pumps.

Fabricated metal products are next in value in Michigan. Products manufactured in the Detroit area account for about half of this total. Grand Rapids and Warren are important producers of fabricated metal products. These goods include cutlery, hand tools, hardware, and other products made from metals.

Food products rank fourth in value. Michigan is among the leading food-processing states. Detroit is the state's largest processor of foods. Grand Rapids is also an important food-processing center. Battle Creek, often called the *Cereal Bowl of America,* produces more breakfast cereal than any other city in the world. Fremont has the largest baby food plant in the United States. The state has important fruit and vegetable canneries and sugar refineries.

Chemicals are Michigan's fifth-ranking manufactured product. Pharmaceuticals are the most important type of chemical product made in the state. Upjohn, one of the nation's largest pharmaceutical manufacturers, is based in Kalamazoo. The Detroit area and several of the southwestern counties also have factories that produce pharmaceuticals. Other important chemical products made in the state include paint, resins, and soaps.

Other manufactured products made in Michigan, in order of value, include printed materials, rubber and plastic products, primary metals, furniture, and paper products. Newspapers and business forms are the major types of printed materials. Factories throughout the state manufacture rubber and plastic products. These products include rubber hoses and gaskets and plastic automotive parts and plumbing supplies. The manufacture of iron and steel is the most important part of the primary metals industry. Aluminum production is also significant. The suburban part of the Detroit metropolitan area is the leading region for the production of primary metals in Michigan. Grand Rapids manufactures much of the furniture made in Michigan. Kalamazoo is a center of the state's paper manufacturing industry.

Michigan is among the leading states in the manufacture of sporting goods and athletic equipment. Such goods are produced, for example, in Muskegon, which has one of the nation's largest plants for making bowling alley equipment.

Agriculture accounts for 1 percent of the gross state product. Farmland covers about a third of the state's land area. Michigan's best farmland is in the southern part of the state. Michigan's approximately 54,000 farms average 200 acres (81 hectares) in size.

Crops provide about 60 percent of the total farm income. The state's leading crops are corn, hay, soybeans, wheat, dry beans, sugar beets, potatoes, cherries, and apples. Crops grown in greenhouses and nurseries are also an important source of income.

The land along Lake Michigan in the Lower Peninsula is one of the most productive fruit-growing belts in North America. Michigan ranks among the leading states in raising apples, blueberries, cantaloupes, cherries, grapes, peaches, pears, plums, and strawberries. Fruit tree blossoms attract many bees in spring, and honey is an important by-product of the fruit industry. Western Michigan has the best climate and soil for growing fruit. Most of the grapes are grown in the

© Joe Viesti

Workers harvest cherries in an orchard in Leelanau County. They use a machine that shakes the trunk of the tree to make the cherries fall. Michigan is the leading cherry-growing area in North America.

southwestern counties. Traverse City is famous for its cherries.

Most of Michigan's vegetable farming takes place in the southern half of the Lower Peninsula. Michigan is the leading producer among the states of dry beans and of cucumbers for pickles. Other important vegetables raised in the state include asparagus, carrots, celery, cucumbers, onions, potatoes, snap beans, sugar beets, sweet corn, and tomatoes. Many farmers in the state raise soybeans, corn, and hay—usually as feed for livestock rather than as cash crops.

Livestock and livestock products provide about 40 percent of the farm income. Milk is Michigan's leading farm product. The state ranks among the leading producers of milk. Beef cattle and hogs are also important farm products. They are raised mainly in the southern half of the Lower Peninsula.

Dairying is important throughout the Lower Peninsula. Zeeland is a center of baby chick hatcheries. Ottawa County has large turkey farms, and chicken, duck, geese, and turkey hatcheries.

Mining accounts for 1 percent of the gross state product. Natural gas, iron ore, and petroleum provide most of the state's mining income.

The northern part of the Lower Peninsula has the largest natural gas fields in Michigan. The leading gas-producing counties are Grand Traverse, Kalkaska, Manistee, and Otsego. Natural gas is piped from these areas to the state's largest cities, where it serves as fuel for heating buildings. Michigan must import natural gas from other states to fully meet its needs. Some of the imported natural gas is stored underground in depleted gas wells.

Michigan ranks second among the states in the production of iron ore. Only Minnesota produces more iron ore. The Marquette area on the Upper Peninsula produces all of Michigan's iron ore. Almost all of the iron ore mined in the state is a low grade of ore called *taconite.* Heavy production of iron ore in Michigan during the early 1900's depleted most of the higher grades of ore. Today, Michigan produces about a fourth of the nation's iron ore. But the importance of iron ore mining has declined greatly in both Michigan and the United States as a whole since 1950.

Michigan has about 6,000 active oil wells. Petroleum production is heaviest in the northwestern and south-central parts of the Lower Peninsula. Michigan petroleum production is not large enough to meet the total demand within the state.

Rogers City has one of the world's largest limestone quarries. Michigan is the leading producer of calcium chloride. It ranks among the leaders in the production of gypsum, iodine, magnesium compounds, peat, and sand and gravel. Large deposits of copper lie in the western part of the Upper Peninsula. These deposits are expensive to mine. As a result, copper is mined in Michigan only when copper prices are high.

Fishing industry. Michigan has an annual fish catch that is valued at approximately 7\frac{1}{2}$ million. The most valuable fishes taken from the Great Lakes include catfish, chubs, lake herring, lake trout, whitefish, and yellow perch. During every spring, workers in the commercial fishing industry take smelts from the state's rivers and streams.

Electric power. Plants that burn coal provide about 70 percent of Michigan's electric power. Nuclear plants provide most of the rest of the state's electricity. Hydroelectric plants and plants that burn gas or petroleum supply only a small amount of power.

Transportation. American Indians and early pioneers in Michigan traveled in canoes along the waterways. The first roads followed Indian trails. The first highway in Michigan was built in the 1820's. It extended from Detroit across the Maumee River into Ohio. The Erie and Kalamazoo Railroad was completed in 1836. Horses pulled the railroad's first cars. In 1837, the Erie and Kalamazoo started to operate what was probably the first steam locomotive west of the Allegheny Mountains. By the mid-1800's, stagecoach routes connected Detroit with Chicago.

The state highway department was established in 1905. In 1908, Michigan became the first state to build a concrete highway—a stretch 1 mile (1.6 kilometers) long in Detroit.

In 1957, the Mackinac Bridge was completed across the Straits of Mackinac. This was the first bridge to connect the Upper and Lower peninsulas. The International Bridge, across the St. Marys River at Sault Ste. Marie, was completed in 1962. It links Michigan with Ontario. This 2-mile (3-kilometer) bridge replaced ferryboats that once carried people across the river. Other links between Michigan and Ontario include a Detroit-to-Windsor bridge, a Detroit-to-Windsor tunnel, and a Port Huron-to-Sarnia bridge.

Today, Michigan has about 117,000 miles (189,000 kilometers) of roads. Six major rail carriers provide freight service in the state. Passenger trains serve the major cities of the Lower Peninsula. Detroit Metropolitan Airport, Michigan's chief air terminal, is one of the world's busiest airports.

Ships from Michigan ports carry huge cargoes of minerals, grain, and manufactured goods across the Great Lakes and through the Great Lakes-St. Lawrence Seaway system to various ports and even other countries. The Soo Canals rank among the busiest ship canals in the Western Hemisphere, even though ice closes the canals from late December to early April.

Detroit is Michigan's largest and busiest port. Other major ports in the state include Alpena, Calcite (near Rogers City), Escanaba, and St. Clair. An automobile ferry service crosses Lake Michigan between Ludington and Manitowoc, Wis. Ferries also serve the Manitou Islands, Beaver Island, Mackinac Island, and Isle Royale.

Communication. Michigan's first regularly published newspaper, the *Detroit Gazette,* was established in 1817. Radio station WWJ in Detroit began broadcasting in 1920. WWJ and Pittsburgh's KDKA were the nation's first regular commercial radio stations. Michigan's first television station, WWJ-TV, began operating in Detroit in 1947.

Michigan has about 50 daily newspapers. Daily newspapers with the largest circulations include the Detroit *Free Press,* the *Detroit News,* the Flint *Journal,* and the *Grand Rapids Press.* Michigan publishers produce about 250 weekly and semiweekly newspapers, several foreign-language papers, and about 185 periodicals. The state has about 40 television stations and about 230 radio stations.

Constitution. Michigan's present Constitution was adopted in 1963 and went into effect in 1964. Earlier constitutions were adopted in 1835, 1850, and 1908.

Constitutional *amendments* (changes) may be proposed in three ways. *Initiative amendments* are introduced by petitions signed by a specified number of voters. *Legislative amendments* are introduced by members of the state Legislature. Legislative amendments must be approved by two-thirds of the members of both houses of the Legislature. Amendments can also be proposed by *constitutional conventions.* Beginning in 1978, and every 16 years thereafter, the voters will decide whether to call a constitutional convention. All proposed amendments must be approved by a majority of the voters who cast ballots on the amendment.

Executive. The Constitution of 1964 increased the governor's term of office from two years to four years. Michigan's governor may serve no more than two terms. The Constitution also increased from two to four years the terms of the lieutenant governor, secretary of state, and attorney general. These officials may serve no more than two terms. Beginning in 1966, each party's candidates for governor and lieutenant governor began running for office as a team. Thus, voters in Michigan cast a single vote for the governor and lieutenant governor together.

The governor, with the consent of the state Senate, appoints various state officials who are not elected. These officials include the treasurer, members of boards and commissions, and department heads. Officials elected to eight-year terms include regents of the University of Michigan, trustees of Michigan State University, governors of Wayne State University, and members of the state board of education.

To run for governor, candidates of major political parties must be nominated by the people in a primary election. Candidates for other statewide elective offices are nominated at party conventions. A *recall* law gives the people the right to vote to remove from office any elected officials other than judges. A specified number of qualified voters must sign a petition in order to hold such a recall vote.

Legislature of Michigan consists of a 38-member Senate and a 110-member House of Representatives. State senators serve four-year terms and may serve no more than two terms. State representatives serve two-year terms and may serve no more than three terms. Legislative sessions begin on the second Wednesday of every January. The sessions adjourn on a date determined by a joint resolution of the two houses—usually December 30.

Courts. Michigan's highest court is the state Supreme Court. This court has seven justices, elected to eight-year terms. The justices elect one of their members to serve as chief justice.

Michigan also has a court of appeals. Eight judges are elected from each of three districts drawn according to population. Michigan has 56 circuits, each with its own circuit court. Circuit courts are the highest trial courts in the state. Each county in Michigan has a probate court and a district court. Six cities in southeastern Michigan have special municipal courts. All appeals, circuit, district, and probate court judges are elected to six-year terms.

The governors of Michigan

	Party	Term
Stevens T. Mason	Democratic	1837-1840
William Woodbridge	Whig	1840-1841
James W. Gordon	Whig	1841-1842
John S. Barry	Democratic	1842-1845
Alpheus Felch	Democratic	1846-1847
William L. Greenly	Democratic	1847
Epaphroditus Ransom	Democratic	1848-1849
John S. Barry	Democratic	1850
Robert McClelland	Democratic	1851-1853
Andrew Parsons	Democratic	1853-1854
Kinsley S. Bingham	Republican	1855-1858
Moses Wisner	Republican	1859-1860
Austin Blair	Republican	1861-1864
Henry H. Crapo	Republican	1865-1868
Henry P. Baldwin	Republican	1869-1872
John J. Bagley	Republican	1873-1876
Charles M. Croswell	Republican	1877-1880
David H. Jerome	Republican	1881-1882
Josiah W. Begole	Democratic and Greenback	1883-1884
Russell A. Alger	Republican	1885-1886
Cyrus G. Luce	Republican	1887-1890
Edwin B. Winans	Democratic	1891-1892
John T. Rich	Republican	1893-1896
Hazen S. Pingree	Republican	1897-1900
Aaron T. Bliss	Republican	1901-1904
Fred M. Warner	Republican	1905-1910
Chase S. Osborn	Republican	1911-1912
Woodbridge N. Ferris	Democratic	1913-1916
Albert E. Sleeper	Republican	1917-1920
Alexander J. Groesbeck	Republican	1921-1926
Fred W. Green	Republican	1927-1930
Wilber M. Brucker	Republican	1931-1932
William A. Comstock	Democratic	1933-1934
Frank D. Fitzgerald	Republican	1935-1936
Frank Murphy	Democratic	1937-1938
Frank D. Fitzgerald	Republican	1939
Luren D. Dickinson	Republican	1939-1940
Murray D. Van Wagoner	Democratic	1941-1942
Harry F. Kelly	Republican	1943-1946
Kim Sigler	Republican	1947-1948
G. Mennen Williams	Democratic	1949-1960
John B. Swainson	Democratic	1961-1962
George W. Romney	Republican	1963-1969
William G. Milliken	Republican	1969-1983
James Blanchard	Democratic	1983-1991
John Engler	Republican	1991-

Local government. The county is Michigan's chief unit of local government. The state's 83 counties are divided into townships. Each county has a county board of commissioners as its legislative body. The board consists of representatives from each part of the county. Other officers include the county clerk, county treasurer, prosecuting attorney, register of deeds, and sheriff.

The Constitution permits counties and cities to have *home rule* (self-government) to the extent that they may frame, adopt, and amend their own charters. However, these powers can be restricted by the Constitution and the Legislature. More than a hundred Michigan cities have the city-manager form of government. Most of the other cities in the state have the mayor-council form. Counties adopting a home rule charter may have a county executive as their chief administrative officer.

Revenue. Sales and income taxes account for about half of the state government's *general revenue* (income).

Other sources of revenue include estate and gift taxes, a lottery, license fees, property taxes, and a value-added tax on businesses. More than 20 percent of the state government's revenue comes from federal grants and programs.

Politics. The Republican Party is strongest in rural areas of Michigan. Democratic strength lies in the Upper Peninsula, and in Detroit and other urban areas.

Since the mid-1800's, Michigan has supported Republican candidates for governor and President far more often than Democratic candidates. For the state's electoral votes and voting record in presidential elections, see **Electoral College** (table). In the mid-1970's and 1980's, Democratic strength increased in elections for state offices. But in 1990, Republicans regained the governor's office.

Michigan's House of Representatives meets in Lansing, the state capital. State representatives serve two-year terms.

© Ken Kaminsky

History

Indian days. About 15,000 Indians lived in the Michigan area when Europeans first arrived. Most of the tribes belonged to the Algonquian language group. They included the Chippewa and Menominee tribes in the Upper Peninsula, and the Miami, Ottawa, and Potawatomi tribes in the Lower Peninsula. The Wyandot, who settled around what is now Detroit, belonged to the Iroquois language group. Only about 3,000 Indians lived in the forests of the Upper Peninsula.

French exploration and settlement. Étienne Brulé of France explored the Upper Peninsula around 1620. He was probably the first white person to visit the Michigan region. Brulé was sent to the Michigan region from Quebec by Governor Samuel de Champlain of New France (Canada).

In 1634, Champlain sent another explorer, Jean Nicolet, to the region to search for a route to the Pacific Ocean. Nicolet sailed through the Straits of Mackinac and explored parts of the Upper Peninsula. In 1660, Father René Ménard, a Jesuit missionary, established a mission at Keweenaw Bay. In 1668, Father Jacques Marquette founded Michigan's first permanent settlement, at Sault Ste. Marie.

During the late 1600's, Father Marquette; Louis Jolliet; René-Robert Cavelier, Sieur de La Salle; and other Frenchmen explored much of the region. They mapped many of the lakes and rivers. By 1700, the French had built forts, missions, and trading posts at several places in both the Upper and Lower peninsulas. In 1701, An-toine de La Mothe Cadillac founded Fort Pontchartrain, which grew into the city of Detroit.

The Michigan region made little progress under the French. Only a few settlers established farms in the region, mostly along the Detroit River. The main French interests were to convert the Indians to Christianity and to develop a profitable fur trade. They also hoped to use the region as a passage to the west.

British control. During the late 1600's and the 1700's, France and Britain struggled to gain control of North America. They fought a series of wars, and the French were defeated in 1763. Britain won most of the French holdings in North America, including the Michigan region. See **French and Indian wars**.

In 1763, during Pontiac's War, Indians massacred the British at Fort Michilimackinac in Mackinaw City. The Indians, led by the Ottawa chief Pontiac, also attacked a number of other forts, killing many of the settlers. Indians attacked Detroit for about five months, but were finally turned away. In 1774, the British made Michigan part of the province of Quebec. The British were more interested in fur trading than in settling the region.

During the Revolutionary War (1775-1783), the British sent raiding parties of Indians and whites from Detroit to attack American settlements. Spain and Britain also fought each other during the Revolutionary War. In 1781, Spanish forces captured Fort St. Joseph in Niles, and held it one day. The Revolutionary War ended in 1783, and the Michigan region came under the control of the United States. The British wanted to hold on to the valuable fur trade as long as possible. They did not surrender Detroit or Fort Mackinac to the United States until 1796.

Territorial period. In 1787, the Michigan region became part of the Northwest Territory—the first territory established by the United States government. In 1800, Congress created the Indiana Territory, which included part of Michigan. The Indiana Territory obtained the entire Michigan region in 1803. In 1805, Congress established the Territory of Michigan. The territory included the Lower Peninsula and the eastern part of the Upper Peninsula.

During the War of 1812, the British captured Detroit and Fort Mackinac. American forces regained Detroit in 1813. The British returned Fort Mackinac to the United States in 1815, after the war ended.

The Erie Canal was completed in 1825. This canal linked the Great Lakes with the Atlantic Ocean and, in doing so, provided a transportation route between the eastern states and the western territories. Many settlers came to Michigan, especially from New York and New England.

In 1835, a convention drew up a state constitution. The people *ratified* (approved) the Constitution on Oct. 5, 1835, and elected 23-year-old Stevens T. Mason as their first state governor. But Congress delayed admitting Michigan to the Union because of a dispute between Michigan and Ohio. The dispute involved a strip of land near Toledo. Congress settled the question in 1836 by giving the 520-square-mile (1,347-square-kilometer) "Toledo Strip" to Ohio, and the entire Upper Peninsula to Michigan.

Progress as a state. Michigan became the 26th state of the Union on Jan. 26, 1837. The western Upper Peninsula soon proved to be a source of many valuable minerals. In 1842, the state obtained Isle Royale and the Keweenaw Peninsula in a treaty with the Indians. Iron-ore mining began near Negaunee in 1845. Large numbers of miners and prospectors soon came to the Upper Peninsula. By the late 1840's, mining was prospering in the state. But the miners needed some way to ship the ore from western Michigan to the iron and steel centers along the Great Lakes. This need was one of the chief reasons for the construction of the Soo Canal, which was completed in 1855 (see **Soo Canals**).

The Republican Party was named in 1854 in Jackson.

Delegates to a Michigan state convention met there on July 6, 1854. They were the first to formally adopt the name *Republican* (see **Republican Party**).

Michigan soldiers fought in the Union Army during the Civil War (1861-1865). General George A. Custer, a famous Union officer, led the Michigan cavalry. On May 10, 1865, the Fourth Michigan Cavalry captured Jefferson Davis, president of the Confederacy, near Irwinville, Ga.

After the Civil War, lumbering became an important industry in Michigan. The construction of sawmills aided the rapid development of manufacturing in the state. Michigan lumber was used in building many cities, towns, and farms of the Midwest. Michigan hardwood lumber helped develop the furniture industry, which started in Grand Rapids in the 1830's. By 1870, Michigan led the nation in lumber production.

Between 1870 and 1900, Michigan's population more than doubled. Agriculture developed as settlers poured into Michigan and cleared the land. Michigan took the lead among the states in the support of public education. Railroads and steamship lines promoted Michigan resorts, and the state's tourist industry began to develop.

The early 1900's brought further industrial expansion. In 1899, Ransom E. Olds founded the Olds Motor Works in Detroit. By 1901, the factory was mass-producing Oldsmobiles. Henry Ford organized the Ford Motor Company in 1903. Detroit soon became the center of the nation's automobile industry. This new industry increased Michigan's population and its prosperity.

In 1914, Henry Ford announced that the Ford Motor Company would share its profits with its workers. Ford also established a minimum wage of $5 a day. At that time, most unskilled workers earned only $1 a day, and skilled workers earned $2.50.

After the United States entered World War I in 1917, Michigan factories built trucks, armored vehicles, airplane engines, and other military products. The improvement of Michigan's highways during the 1920's contributed to the growth of the automobile industry and related businesses. By the late 1920's, Michigan's tourist industry had become a leading source of income in the state.

Depression and recovery. Michigan was hit hard by the Great Depression of the 1930's. Hundreds of thousands of workers lost their jobs. Federal measures to end the depression had important effects in Michigan. The state had more than a hundred Civilian Conserva-

Charles Symon Collection, Bentley Historical Library, University of Michigan

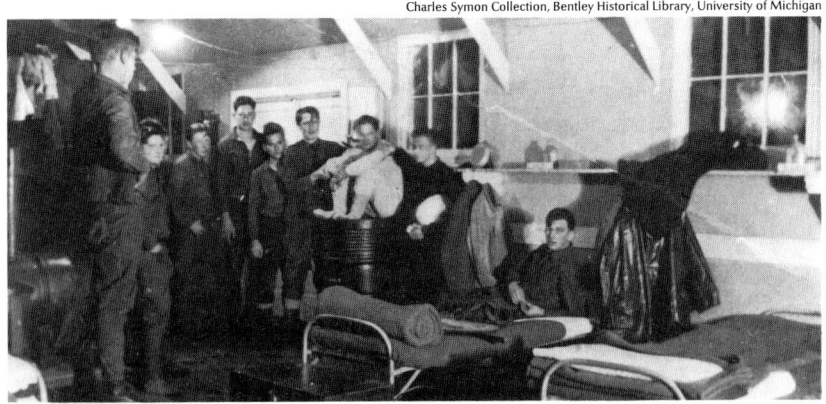

The Civilian Conservation Corps, a government employment program during the Great Depression of the 1930's, had more than 100 camps in Michigan. Young men in the program conserved and developed natural resources by planting trees, building dams, and fighting forest fires.

Historic Michigan

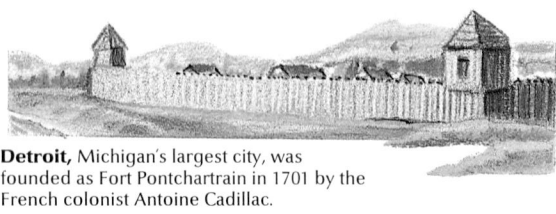

Detroit, Michigan's largest city, was founded as Fort Pontchartrain in 1701 by the French colonist Antoine Cadillac.

The Republican Party formally adopted its name at Jackson in 1854. The party began as a series of antislavery meetings throughout the North earlier that year.

Henry Ford built his first workable automobile in Detroit in 1896. Three years later, Ransom E. Olds established Michigan's first automobile factory in Detroit.

The Soo Canals at Sault Ste. Marie rank among the busiest ship canals in the Western Hemisphere, even though ice closes them from December to April. The first canal on the Michigan side was completed in 1855.

The United Automobile Workers organized in Michigan in 1935. By 1941, the union represented workers at all the major automobile companies.

WORLD BOOK illustrations by Kevin Chadwick

Important dates in Michigan

1620? Étienne Brulé, a French explorer, visited what is now Michigan.

1668 Father Jacques Marquette founded Michigan's first permanent settlement at Sault Ste. Marie.

1701 Antoine Cadillac founded what is now Detroit.

1763 The British took possession of Michigan.

1783 The United States gained Michigan from the British after the Revolutionary War.

1787 Congress made Michigan part of the Northwest Territory.

1800 Michigan became part of the Indiana Territory.

1805 Congress created the Territory of Michigan.

1837 Michigan became the 26th state on January 26. Congress gave Michigan the entire Upper Peninsula.

1845 The Michigan iron mining industry began near Negaunee.

1854 The Republican Party was formally named at Jackson.

1855 The Soo Canal was completed.

1899 Ransom E. Olds established Michigan's first automobile factory in Detroit.

1914 The Ford Motor Company established a minimum daily wage of $5.

1935 Michigan workers formed the United Automobile Workers union.

1942-1945 Michigan's entire automobile industry converted to war production during World War II.

1957 The Mackinac Bridge was opened to traffic between Mackinaw City and St. Ignace.

1964 Michigan's new Constitution went into effect.

1967 Michigan's legislature adopted a state income tax.

1968 Michigan voters approved $435 million in bond issues to expand recreational areas and to fight water pollution.

1972 Michigan established a state lottery.

Mass production of tanks took place at this Chrysler Corporation factory in Detroit during World War II (1939-1945) During the war, Michigan's entire automobile industry switched to manufacturing tanks, planes, and other war materials.

The Archives of Labor and Urban Affairs, Wayne State University

tion Corps (CCC) camps. In these camps, the government employed young men to work on conservation projects. The Works Progress Administration (WPA) employed about 500,000 persons in Michigan to work on public works projects. Before and during the depression, copper mining in other states became less costly than in Michigan. It cost more to mine copper in Michigan because the ore lies so deep in the earth. Michigan's copper mining decreased, and more unemployment resulted in the Upper Peninsula.

In 1935, workers in the automobile industry organized the United Automobile Workers union. In December 1936, the union went on strike at the Fisher Body and Chevrolet plants in Flint. The strikers demanded a *closed shop* (an industry in which only union members can be hired). The union also called for *collective bargaining* (discussion of differences between company and union representatives). The Fisher and Chevrolet plant officials rejected the union's demands. The strikers then locked themselves inside the plants, and fought off police attempts to remove them. The union received collective bargaining rights on Feb. 11, 1937, and the strike ended. After signing a contract with the Ford Motor Company in 1941, the United Automobile Workers represented the workers of all the large automobile companies, and won its chief demands. These demands included higher pay and recognition of the union as representative of the workers.

The mid-1900's. During World War II (1939-1945), Michigan's entire automobile industry switched to manufacturing war materials. The production of airplanes, ships, tanks, and other military equipment brought prosperity back to the state.

G. Mennen Williams, a Democrat, served as governor of Michigan from 1949 to 1960. He helped revive two-party politics in Michigan. Under his leadership, politics became very issue-oriented. Michigan's prosperity continued during his terms in office. Millions of Americans bought new cars and other products that were made in Michigan. The state's mining industry began to recover.

In 1955, a new copper mine opened near Ontonagon. Iron-mining companies in Michigan's Upper Peninsula developed new methods of recovering iron from nonmagnetic ore and new ways of processing ore for shipment to steel plants. In 1957, the Mackinac Bridge was completed, linking the Upper and Lower peninsulas.

The state faced financial problems during the late 1950's and early 1960's. A nationwide recession caused a slump in Michigan automobile sales and production. As a result, other business activities in the state also slowed down. Michigan's financial picture brightened as the nation began to prosper again during the 1960's, and purchases of automobiles and other Michigan products increased.

In 1961, Michigan voters authorized a constitutional convention to revise the outdated state constitution, which had been adopted in 1908. The convention submitted a new constitution to the voters in 1962. They approved the constitution in 1963, and it went into effect in 1964.

George W. Romney, a Michigan businessman, served as the state's governor from 1963 to 1969. Romney, a Republican, had played a leading role in the constitutional convention. As governor, he fought for passage of the new constitution. Romney's administration modernized the state tax structure. New taxes, including a state income tax adopted in 1967, enabled Michigan to increase spending for education, mental health facilities, welfare programs, and other government services. In 1972, Michigan established a state lottery to help raise additional money.

In July 1967, an eight-day riot broke out in a predominantly black section of Detroit. Rioters burned buildings and looted stores. Forty-three people were killed, and about $45 million worth of property was damaged or destroyed.

In 1973, President Richard M. Nixon appointed Congressman Gerald R. Ford of Michigan to succeed Vice President Spiro T. Agnew, who had resigned. Ford became the 38th President in 1974, when Nixon resigned because of his involvement in the Watergate political scandal.

Recent developments. Nationwide recessions during the early 1970's and the early 1980's contributed to slumps in the automobile industry, and unemployment in Michigan rose sharply. By 1980, Michigan had the highest unemployment rate of any state.

A serious financial crisis in the early 1980's forced the state government to cut funding for education, mental health services, welfare programs, and other services. By late 1983, improved automobile sales reduced the state's unemployment, and a temporary increase in the income tax enabled the state to restore program cuts.

In the 1990's, the production of transportation equipment remained the most important manufacturing activity in the state. Michigan continues to lead the nation in automobile production. But Michigan leaders are working to attract new industries to reduce the state's dependence on the automobile industry.

Justin L. Kestenbaum and Harold A. Winters

Study aids

Related articles in *World Book* include:

Biographies

Bieber, Owen F.	Ford, Henry
Cadillac, Antoine de la M.	Ford, Henry, II
Cass, Lewis	Guest, Edgar A.
Chandler, Zachariah	Kellogg, W. K.
Chrysler, Walter P.	Marquette, Jacques
Coughlin, Charles E.	Milles, Carl
Dewey, Thomas E.	Olds, Ransom E.
Dodge brothers	Pontiac
Ford, Gerald R.	Young, Coleman A.

Cities

Ann Arbor	Dearborn	Flint	Holland
Battle Creek	Detroit	Grand Rapids	Lansing

Physical features

Detroit River	Lake Saint Clair	Mackinac Island
Lake Erie	Lake Superior	Manitoulin Island
Lake Huron	Mackinac,	Saint Marys River
Lake Michigan	Straits of	

Other related articles

Greenfield Village	National Music	Petoskey stone
Isle Royale	Camp	Soo Canals
National Park	Northwest Ordinance	War of 1812

Outline

I. People
  A. Population
  B. Schools
  C. Libraries
  D. Museums
II. Visitor's guide
  A. Places to visit
  B. Annual events
III. Land and climate
  A. Land regions
  B. Shoreline
  C. Islands
  D. Rivers, waterfalls, and lakes
  E. Plant and animal life
  F. Climate
IV. Economy
  A. Natural resources
  B. Service industries
  C. Manufacturing
  D. Agriculture
  E. Mining
  F. Fishing industry
  G. Electric power
  H. Transportation
  I. Communication

V. Government
  A. Constitution
  B. Executive
  C. Legislature
  D. Courts
  E. Local government
  F. Revenue
  G. Politics
VI. History

Questions

Why does Michigan have so many cloudy days?

Why did the Michigan region not prosper under French rule?

Why did copper production in Michigan decrease in the early 1900's?

How did Michigan's lumber industry aid the growth of the state?

What Michigan canals rank among the busiest ship canals in the Western Hemisphere?

What territories of the United States did Michigan belong to before becoming a state?

What event brought many settlers to Michigan in the 1820's?

How did Michigan obtain the Upper Peninsula?

What are two of the chief provisions of the Michigan Constitution adopted in 1963?

What city in Michigan is called the *Cereal Bowl of America?*

Additional resources

Level I

Carpenter, Allan. *Michigan.* Rev. ed. Childrens Pr., 1978.
Fradin, Dennis B. *Michigan.* Childrens Pr., 1992.
Stein, R. Conrad. *Michigan.* Childrens Pr., 1987.
Thompson, Kathleen. *Michigan.* Raintree, 1987.

Level II

Clive, Alan. *State of War: Michigan in World War II.* Univ. of Michigan Pr., 1979.
Dorr, John A., Jr., and Eschman, D. F. *Geology of Michigan.* Univ. of Michigan Pr., 1970.
DuFresne, Jim. *Michigan: Off the Beaten Path.* 2nd ed. Globe Pequot, 1990.
Dunbar, Willis F. *Michigan: A History of the Wolverine State.* Rev. ed. by George S. May. Eerdmans, 1980.
Fitting, James E. *The Archaeology of Michigan: A Guide to the Prehistory of the Great Lakes Region.* 2nd ed. Cranbrook Inst., 1975.
Karamanski, Theodore J. *Deep Woods Frontier: A History of Logging in Northern Michigan.* Wayne State Univ. Pr., 1989.
May, George S. *Michigan: An Illustrated History of the Great Lakes State.* Windsor Pubns., 1987.
Michigan Atlas and Gazetteer. 4th ed. DeLorme Pub., 1991.
A Michigan Reader: 11,000 B.C. to A.D. 1865. Ed. by George S. May and H. J. Brinks. Eerdmans, 1974.
A Michigan Reader: 1865 to the Present. Ed. by Robert M. Warner and C. W. Vander Hill. Eerdmans, 1974.
Santer, Richard A. *Michigan: Heart of the Great Lakes.* Kendall-Hunt, 1977.

Michigan, Lake. See Lake Michigan.

Michigan, University of, is a state-controlled coeducational university. The main campus is in Ann Arbor, and there are branch campuses in Dearborn and Flint. The Ann Arbor campus has colleges of architecture and urban planning, art, business administration, dentistry, education, engineering, law, liberal arts, library science, medicine, music, natural resources, nursing, pharmacy, public health, social work, and graduate studies. The Dearborn campus has five schools and colleges and the Flint campus has three.

The University of Michigan is a major research university. Its medical center, an 82-acre complex of patient care, teaching, and research facilities, is one of the largest in the world. Other major research facilities include an institute for social research and a space physics research laboratory. Michigan's library, with $6\frac{1}{2}$ million volumes, ranks as one of the largest academic libraries in the United States.

The University of Michigan was founded in 1817. For the enrollment of the university, see **Universities and colleges** (table).

Critically reviewed by the University of Michigan

Michigan State University is a state-supported co-educational school in East Lansing, Mich. It ranks as one of the largest single-campus institutions of higher education in the United States. Michigan State has colleges of agriculture and natural resources, arts and letters, business, communication arts and sciences, education, engineering, human ecology, human medicine, natural science, nursing, osteopathic medicine, social science, and veterinary medicine. It also has a graduate school. Michigan State also offers programs in lifelong education, international studies, and urban affairs. It grants bachelor's, master's, and doctor's degrees.

The school was founded in 1855 as Michigan Agricultural College. It served as a model for the land-grant colleges and universities founded later in the United States. The university was the first state school to offer courses in agriculture for credit. It took its present name in 1955. For enrollment, see **Universities and colleges** (table).

Critically reviewed by Michigan State University

Mickey Mouse. See **Disney, Walt** (with picture).

Micmac Indians, *MIHK mak,* are a tribe of eastern Canada. They belong to the Algonquian language family. About 12,000 Micmac live on reservations in the provinces of New Brunswick, Nova Scotia, Prince Edward Island, and Quebec.

Large numbers of Micmac, especially young people, work in various cities but maintain close ties with family members on the reservation. Many of these young Indians share their wages with their families.

The Micmac once fished and gathered clams, mussels, and bird eggs from spring to fall. They hunted bears, moose, and small game during the winter. These Indians used birchbark canoes for summer travel, and wooden toboggans and snowshoes in winter. They lived in tepees that they covered with animal skins or birchbark. The Micmac made clothing from pelts and carved utensils from bark. The Micmac had many legends about a superbeing called *Glooscap,* who supposedly shaped much of their landscape.

A few related families usually camped together in bands. Many bands, such as the Bear River band and the Red Bank band, were named after the area where they once lived. A chief called a *sagamore* led each band. He provided his followers with canoes, hunting dogs, and weapons in exchange for fish, game, and pelts.

In the early 1500's, the Micmac traded with French, Portuguese, and Spanish fishermen who visited Canada yearly. When Jacques Cartier, a French explorer, came to Canada in 1534, the Indians traded their furs for beads and knives. The Micmac and the French made an unsuccessful attempt to keep the British out of Canada.

During the early 1700's, the British took control of most of the land occupied by the Micmac. The Indians retreated to remote sections of their land as the British founded settlements along the Atlantic coast. The Micmac came under the authority of the Canadian government in 1867.   Jeanne Guillemin

See also **Prince Edward Island.**

Microbiology, *MY kroh by AHL uh jee,* is the study of microscopic organisms. These organisms are some-

times called *microbes.* They include algae, bacteria, molds, protozoans, viruses, and yeasts. Microbiologists also study such tiny infectious particles as *prions, viroids,* and *plasmids.*

Many biologists specialize in the study of certain kinds of microorganisms. For example, *bacteriologists* work with bacteria, *mycologists* are concerned with fungi, and *virologists* study viruses.

Microorganisms. Nearly all microorganisms measure less than $\frac{4}{1,000}$ inch (0.1 millimeter) across. Many microorganisms must be studied with microscopes that magnify objects at least 1,000 times. Most viruses, plasmids, prions, and viroids are so tiny that they can be seen only with electron microscopes that magnify many thousands of times.

Viruses are called *acellular* microorganisms because they do not have true cell structures. All other microorganisms are *cellular.* They have cell membranes, cytoplasm, and a nuclear body. Bacteria are the smallest single-celled organisms. The smallest bacteria may be as small as $\frac{4}{10}$ of a *micrometer* (a micrometer is $\frac{1}{25,400}$ inch, or .001 millimeter). About 10,000 small viruses could be packed into a cell the size of one of these bacteria. Over a billion of these tiny cells could be packed into one of the largest *microbial* cells—the cells of a certain algae.

Fields of microbiology. Many microbiologists study the relationships between microbes and human beings, animals, and plants. Medical microbiologists investigate the role of microorganisms in human and animal diseases and search for ways to prevent and cure these diseases. Dental microbiologists are concerned with the microorganisms found in the mouth, especially their role in tooth decay. Agricultural microbiologists study plant diseases, the role of microorganisms in soil fertility, and spoilage of agricultural products by microorganisms. Industrial microbiologists use microorganisms to produce such products as alcoholic beverages, amino acids, antibiotics, citric acid, and vitamin C. General microbiologists study the basic features of microorganisms, including ecology, genetics, metabolism, physiology, and structure.

Microorganisms also play an important part in sewage treatment and pollution control. Some microorganisms, such as algae and bacteria, are being grown experimentally for use as food. Yeast is used as an ingredient in a variety of foods. It adds flavor and increases the nutritional value of certain foods, such as potato chips. Advances in genetic engineering also have made microbes more useful to people. Scientists can develop new microbes by transferring genes from one organism to another or by making desirable changes in specific genes.   Robert E. Marquis

Related articles in *World Book* include:

Algae	Protozoan
Bacteria	Viroid
Bacteriology	Virus
Mold	Yeast
Prion	

Additional resources

Gest, Howard. *The World of Microbes.* Science Tech Pubs., 1987.

Teasdale, Jim. *Microbes.* Silver Burdett, 1984.

Microcomputer. See **Computer** (Kinds of computers).

Microcrystalline wax is widely used in making special types of paper for packaging. Paper treated with microcrystalline waxes is strong enough to replace tin and steel in many types of containers. These waxes are extracted from the residual oils driven off during the process of refining petroleum (see **Petroleum** [Refining petroleum]). Microcrystalline waxes were first used during the 1920's.   William B. Harper

Microelectronics. See Electronics (The beginnings of microelectronics; illustration: Devices used in microelectronics).

Microencapsulation is the process of enclosing a substance in a capsule so that the substance can be easily released. Such capsules are made of gelatin, plastic, starch, or other materials. Solids, liquids, and gases can be encapsulated.

Microencapsulation is used in making carbonless copy paper. This paper has a top sheet—coated on the underside with millions of capsules—and a bottom sheet. The capsules release a colorless dye when broken by the pressure of writing or typing. The dye reacts with a thin layer of white clay on the surface of the lower sheet, forming ink. Microencapsulation is also used in making *timed-release* medicines. Such medicines are slowly released in the body so that their effect is extended for as long as 12 hours.   Barry Zimmerman

Microfiche. See Microfilm.

Microfilm is a kind of photographic film on which reduced images of printed and other materials are recorded. Because these images are reduced in size, microfilm can store large amounts of information in a small space. The process of making microfilm copies is called *microphotography.*

People read the material recorded on microfilm by using a *microfilm reader.* This machine enlarges the images on the film and projects them onto a built-in screen. Some microfilm readers, called *reader-printers,* can also produce a paper copy of the enlarged image.

Uses. Microfilm is widely used by libraries, government offices, and banks and other businesses. Libraries save space by storing old newspapers and magazines on microfilm. Inexpensive microfilm copies of rare and fragile books and manuscripts enable many people to read these materials. Some specialized writings have such a small audience it is not practical to publish them in book form. Instead, these specialized writings are stored on microfilm.

Government offices preserve such documents as certificates of birth, marriage, and death on microfilm. This practice saves storage space and allows people to use these records without damaging the paper originals.

Banks keep a record of all checks they handle by storing an image of each check on microfilm. Some businesses use microfilm for recording information directly from computers, thereby eliminating the need for bulky paper computer printouts. On the other hand, computers can be used with microfilm filing systems to locate information and project it onto the reading screen.

Types. Microfilm comes in rolls and rectangular sheets. The term *microform* is sometimes used to refer to both the rolls and the sheets. Banks use rolls 16 millimeters ($\frac{5}{8}$ inch) wide and 100 or 200 feet (30 or 60 meters) long. A 200-foot roll holds copies of as many as 44,000 checks reduced 20 to 50 times in size. Rolls of microfilm 35 millimeters ($1\frac{3}{8}$ inches) wide are used mainly for engineering drawings and other large documents.

Sheets of microfilm are called *microfiche.* Microfiche measures 105 by 148 millimeters ($4\frac{1}{8}$ by $5\frac{13}{16}$ inches). The images on a microfiche are arranged in a grid pattern. A single microfiche may contain images of up to 400 pages reduced 18 to 72 times.

An *ultrafiche* has the same overall dimensions as a standard microfiche, but holds many more images. The images on an ultrafiche are reduced 90 times or more. Businesses use ultrafiche to store such material as parts catalogs and price lists.

Most microfilm is designed so that the images are permanent. Some microfilm is made so that images can be replaced with new material.   John S. O'Callaghan

Micrometer, *my KRAHM uh tuhr,* is a mechanical device that measures small distances or angles. The term *micrometer* comes from Greek words meaning *small measure,* and micrometers are used for precision measurement. A wide variety of scientific and engineering instruments are equipped with micrometers, including telescopes, microscopes, and surveying tools.

A commonly used micrometer called a *micrometer caliper* measures the thickness of objects. It consists of a micrometer *spindle* or screw that turns inside a fixed

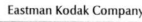

A microfilm system consists of a strip of microfilm, *left,* and a microfilm reader, *below.* On the microfilm are photographically reduced images of many pages of information. The microfilm reader enlarges the images and projects them onto a built-in screen for viewing.

Eastman Kodak Company

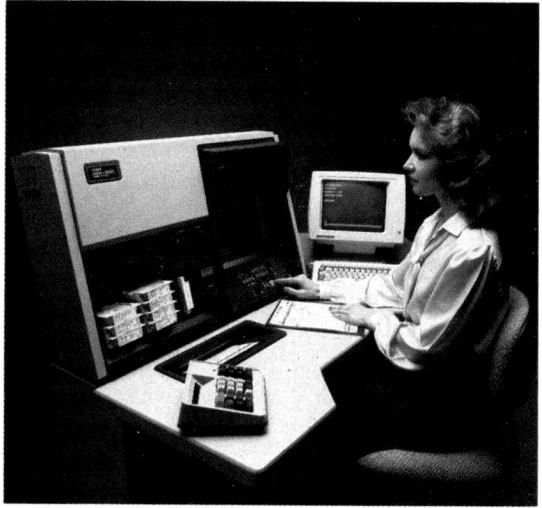

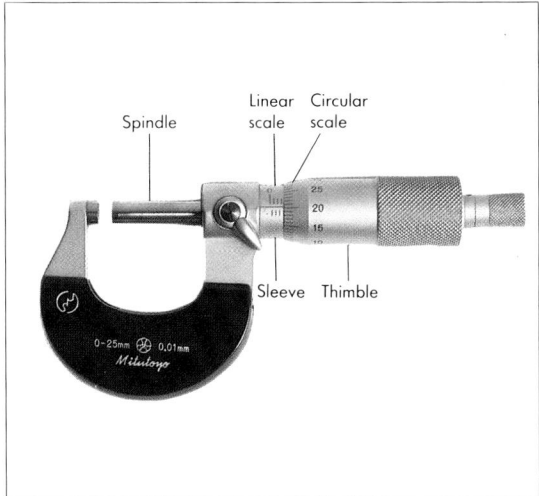

© David R. Frazier Photolibrary

A micrometer caliper measures an object's thickness. This one shows a measurement of just over 3.20 millimeters.

nut. The nut is covered by a *sleeve.* The spindle can be closed on the object to be measured by rotating a part called the *thimble.* The number of turns made by the thimble is measured by two scales, one on the sleeve and the other on the thimble. In many metric micrometers, each rotation of the thimble advances the spindle 0.5 millimeter on the linear scale. The circular scale on the thimble can measure to $\frac{1}{50}$ of 0.5 millimeter, or 0.01 millimeter.   Joseph J. Snoble

See also **Caliper.**

Micrometer, *MY kroh MEE tuhr,* also called *micron,* is a metric unit of length. The symbol for the micrometer is μm. One micrometer is equal to 0.000001 meter, or $\frac{1}{25,400}$ inch.

The micrometer is used to express extremely short distances and the thickness of very thin objects. Scientists express the size of asbestos fibers, colloidal particles, and various other tiny objects viewed under a microscope in micrometers.   Thomas T. Liao

Micronesia. See Pacific Islands.

Microorganism. See Microbiology.

Microphone is a device that changes sound into electric energy. This energy instantly travels over wires or through the air to a loudspeaker or some other instrument that changes it back into sound. Microphones,

which are often called "mikes," are also used in recording sound.

The first microphone was the telephone transmitter, which the American inventor Alexander Graham Bell developed in 1876. Today, microphones are used in announcing over public-address systems and in broadcasting radio and television shows. They are also used in recording the sound for motion pictures and in making compact discs and tape recordings. Citizens band (CB) radios and *ham* (amateur) radios also have mikes.

Microphones of various designs are used for different purposes. CB operators and some entertainers use mikes held in the hand. Other mikes are attached to stands. Still others have an arm called a *boom,* which holds the microphone above a television or movie performer. The boom and microphone can follow the performer in any direction, but they stay out of view of the camera. *Lavalier microphones,* also called *lapel microphones* and *tie-tack microphones,* are fastened to the user's clothing.

Some microphones pick up sound from all directions, but others are sensitive to sound from only certain directions. An *omnidirectional microphone* picks up sound from all around. A *bidirectional microphone* is used for sound coming from the front or from behind, but not from the sides. A *unidirectional microphone* picks up sound from only one direction.

In some microphones, sound produces variations in an electric current. In others, sound generates a current. In all microphones, the current corresponds to the pattern of the sound waves.

Microphones may be classified according to how they change sound into electric energy. The five main

© F. Meylan, Sygma   © David R. Frazier

© B. Barbier, Sygma

Microphones of various designs are used for different purposes. A singer uses a studio microphone, *top left,* in recording music. A person who needs to move around while speaking can wear a headset microphone, *top right.* A boom microphone, *left,* picks up sound on a movie or television set. The boom is an arm that holds the microphone above a performer.

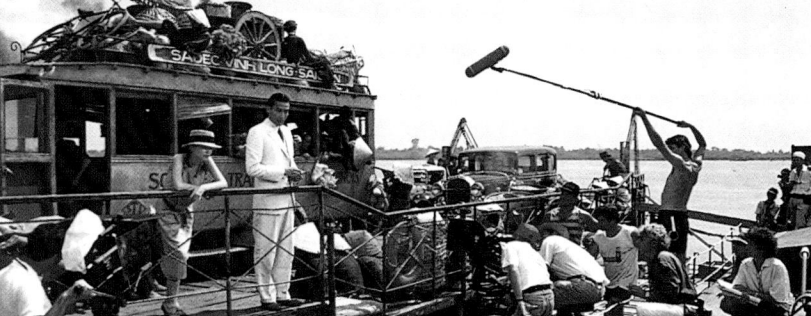

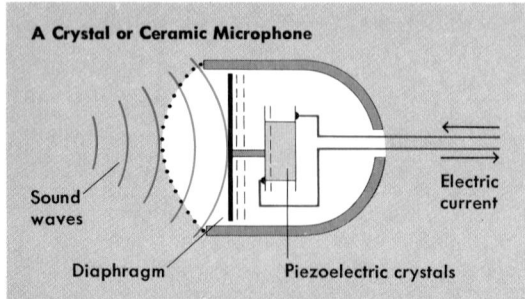

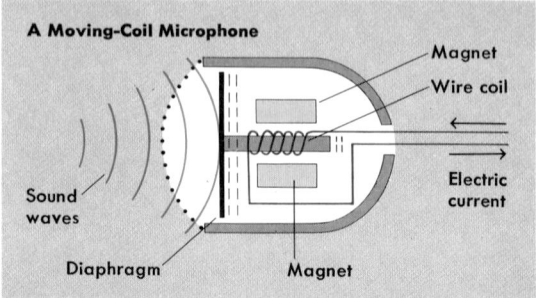

WORLD BOOK diagrams by Arthur Grebetz

Microphones change sound into electric energy. Many microphones have a metal disk called a *diaphragm,* which vibrates when struck by sound waves. In a crystal or ceramic microphone, *left,* the diaphragm vibrates against substances called *piezoelectric crystals,* creating an electric current. In a moving-coil microphone, *right,* the vibrating diaphragm causes a wire coil to move across a magnetic field. This movement produces an electric current in the coil.

types, in order of increasing complexity, are (1) carbon, (2) crystal and ceramic, (3) moving-coil, (4) ribbon, and (5) capacitor. Moving-coil, ribbon, and capacitor mikes can reproduce sound much more accurately than the other types and are used by the movie, radio, recording, and television industries.

Carbon microphones have a small container called a *button,* which is filled with particles of carbon. An electric current from a generator or battery flows through the carbon. A metal disk called a *diaphragm* presses against the button and vibrates when struck by sound waves. The vibrations cause variations in the current running through the carbon. Carbon microphones are used chiefly in telephones.

Crystal and ceramic microphones contain substances called *piezoelectric crystals.* Pressure on these crystals makes them generate an electric current (see **Piezoelectricity**). Crystal and ceramic microphones may or may not have a diaphragm touching the crystals. An electric current is produced by pressure from sound waves that hit the diaphragm or strike the crystals directly. Crystal and ceramic microphones are used in ham radios, home tape recorders, and many public-address systems.

Moving-coil microphones have a wire coil attached to a diaphragm. The coil and diaphragm are suspended in a magnetic field. When sound waves hit the diaphragm, the coil moves across the field. This movement produces an electric current in the coil. Many CB radios have moving-coil microphones.

Ribbon microphones have a metal ribbon suspended in a magnetic field. An electric current is generated when sound waves hit the ribbon and move it across the field. Both ribbon and moving-coil microphones are called *dynamic microphones.* These mikes are classified as *electromagnetic* because they use a magnetic field to change sound into electric energy.

Capacitor microphones, often called *condenser microphones,* have two metal plates set slightly apart. The plates are electrically charged and serve as a *capacitor,* a device that stores a charge. The front plate is flexible and acts as a diaphragm. The back plate cannot move. Sound waves make the front plate vibrate, which causes variations in the electric current from the capacitor. Capacitor microphones are classified as *electrostatic* be-

cause they require an electric charge to change sound into electric energy.

A capacitor microphone produces only a low amount of electrical energy. Therefore, it must have a device called a *preamplifier,* which boosts the mike's signal to a usable level. In most capacitor microphones, called *electrets,* the capacitor is permanently charged and a small battery powers the preamplifier. Electret capacitors are used in hearing aids.   Stanley R. Alten

Related articles in *World Book* include:

Phonograph	Telephone	Wiretapping
Radio	Television	

Microprocessor. See Computer chip.

Microscope is an instrument that magnifies extremely small objects so they can be seen easily. It ranks as one of the most important tools of science. Physicians and biologists, for example, use microscopes to examine bacteria and blood cells. Materials scientists and engineers use microscopes to study the crystal structures within metals and alloys (metal mixtures), and to examine computer chips and other tiny electronic devices. Biology students observe algae, protozoa, and other single-cell organisms under a microscope.

There are four basic kinds of microscopes: (1) *optical,* or *light;* (2) *electron;* (3) *scanning probe;* and (4) *ion.* This article discusses mainly optical microscopes.

How an optical microscope works. An optical microscope has one or more lenses that *refract* (bend) the light rays that shine through, or are reflected by, the specimen being observed (see **Lens**). The refracted light rays make the specimen appear much larger than it is.

The simplest optical microscope is a magnifying glass, which has only one lens (see **Magnifying glass**). The best magnifying glasses can magnify an object by 10 to 20 times.

Magnification power is symbolized by a number and the abbreviation X. For example, a 10X magnifying glass magnifies a specimen by 10 times.

A *compound microscope* uses two or more sets of lenses to provide higher magnifications. Each set of lenses functions as a unit and is referred to as a *lens system.* A compound microscope has an *eyepiece,* or *ocular, lens system,* often called simply the *ocular;* and one or more *objective lens systems,* often called *objectives.*

In microscopes with only one objective, that lens

system and the ocular are mounted at opposite ends of a tube. The objective produces a magnified image of the specimen. The ocular then magnifies this image.

In microscopes with two or more objectives, the objectives are mounted in a rotating *nosepiece* connected to the end of the tube opposite the ocular. The person operating the microscope rotates the nosepiece to align one of the objectives with the opening in the end of the tube. This objective works with the ocular to provide the desired magnification. Many compound microscopes have three objectives that magnify by 4X, 10X, and 40X. When used with a 10X ocular, these microscopes provide magnifications of 40X, 100X, and 400X.

In addition to magnifying a specimen, a microscope must produce a clear image. This capability is called the *resolving power,* or *resolution,* of the microscope. In an optical microscope, the *wavelength* (distance between wave crests) of the light waves that illuminate the specimen limits the resolving power. The wavelength of visible light ranges from about 4,000 to 7,000 *angstroms.* (One angstrom equals 1/10,000,000 millimeter [about 1/250,000,000 inch]). The best optical microscopes cannot resolve parts of a specimen that are closer together than about 2,000 angstroms. To obtain higher resolutions, scientists use other types of microscopes.

Parts of an optical microscope. Most optical microscopes used for teaching have three main parts: (1) the tube, which has already been described; (2) the *foot;* and (3) the *body.* The foot is the base of the instrument. The body is an upright support that holds the tube. At the lower end of the body is a mirror. The specimen lies on the *stage,* a platform above the mirror. The mirror reflects light up through an opening in the stage to illuminate the specimen. The operator can move the tube within the body by turning a *coarse-adjustment knob.* This focuses the microscope. A *fine-adjustment knob*

moves the tube a small distance for final focusing of a high-power objective.

Using an optical microscope. To prepare a microscope for use, turn the nosepiece to bring the objective with the lowest power into viewing position. Next, turn the coarse-adjustment knob to lower the tube until the objective is just above the opening in the stage. Finally, look through the ocular and adjust the mirror so a bright circle of light appears.

Many specimens viewed through a microscope are transparent or have been made transparent. The technique of preparing specimens is called *microtomy* (see **Microtomy**). Specimens are mounted on glass slides that measure 3 inches long and 1 inch wide (76 by 25 millimeters).

To view a slide, place it on the stage with the specimen directly over the opening. Hold the slide in place with clips that are attached to the stage. Look through the ocular and turn the coarse-adjustment knob to raise the objective until the specimen comes into focus. To avoid breaking the slide or the objective, never lower the lens when a slide is on the stage.

Advanced optical microscopes are used in research and have extra-powerful lens systems. Many such microscopes have a 100X objective and a 20X ocular, which together provide a magnification of 2,000X. Some high-powered microscopes have *oil immersion* objectives. The bottom lens of the objective touches a drop of special oil placed on the slide. The oil refracts light in a way that provides a better image at high magnification.

Other microscopes used for research have additional features. For example, a microscope with a *binocular tube* splits the light from the objective into two beams. An ocular for each beam enables the operator to view the specimen with both eyes. *Trinocular tubes* split the light into three beams—one for each eye and one for a

Parts of an optical microscope The diagram at the left shows the external parts of an optical microscope. A person adjusts these parts to view a specimen. The cutaway diagram at the right shows the path that light follows when passing through the specimen and then through the lenses of the microscope.

WORLD BOOK diagram

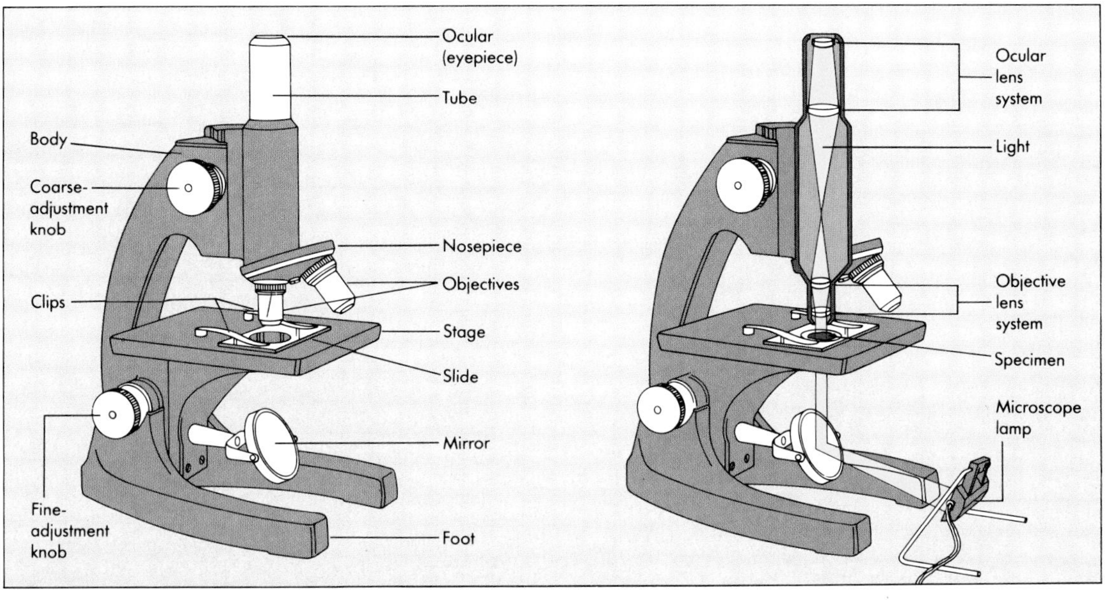

A *World Book* science project

The microscopic world

The purpose of this project is to use a microscope to study the tiny organisms that live in water. The photographs with this project will help you identify the organisms you see. By using a camera that takes time exposures, you can take your own pictures through the microscope.

Materials

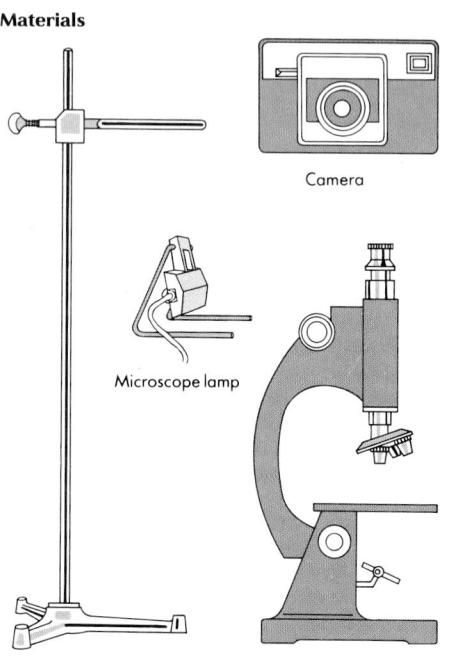

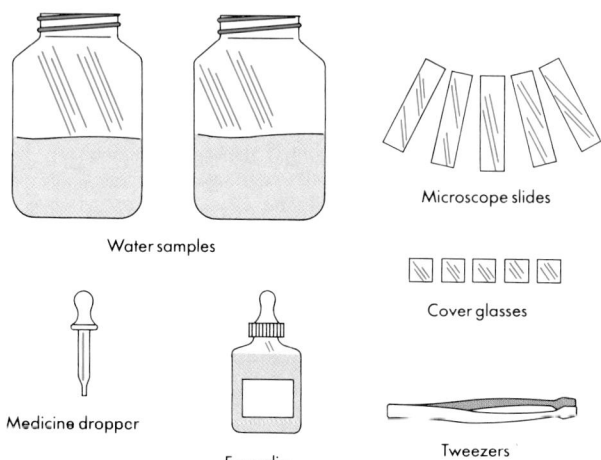

Camera

Water samples

Microscope slides

Cover glasses

Microscope lamp

Medicine dropper

Formalin

Tweezers

Adjustable stand

Microscope

Materials for this project are shown above. The microscope should be able to magnify by at least 400X. With it, you will need microscope slides, cover glasses, and a microscope lamp. Water samples should come from a pond or slow-moving stream. To take pictures, you will need a camera and stand, and formalin to kill the organisms. CAUTION: Formalin is extremely irritating to the eyes and nose. Handle it with care and wash your hands after using it.

WORLD BOOK illustrations by Arthur Grebetz

Preparing and studying the slides

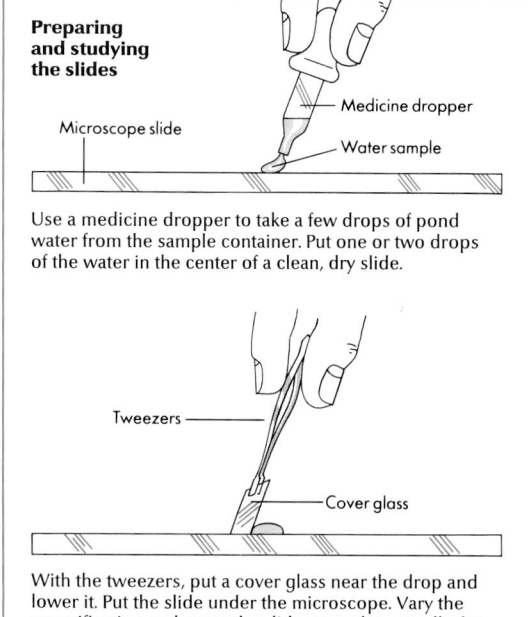

Microscope slide

Medicine dropper

Water sample

Use a medicine dropper to take a few drops of pond water from the sample container. Put one or two drops of the water in the center of a clean, dry slide.

Tweezers

Cover glass

With the tweezers, put a cover glass near the drop and lower it. Put the slide under the microscope. Vary the magnification and move the slide around to see all of it.

Mounting the camera

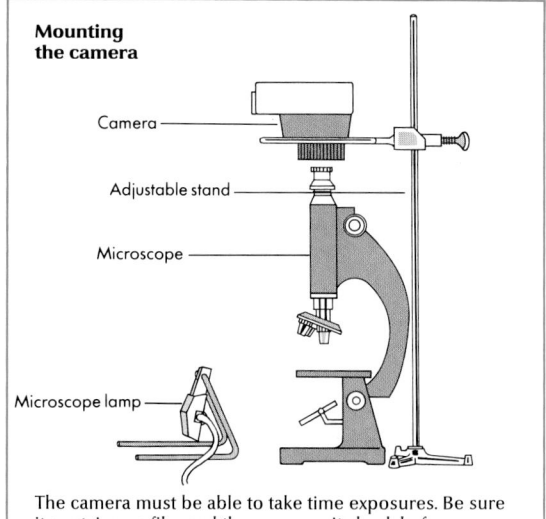

Camera

Adjustable stand

Microscope

Microscope lamp

The camera must be able to take time exposures. Be sure it contains no film and then remove its back before mounting. After focusing the microscope, place the camera on an adjustable stand over it. Put a piece of waxed paper over the camera's back in place of the film. Then open the shutter and move the camera up or down until you get a sharp picture on the waxed paper.

Taking the pictures

The organisms you photograph must be killed with a drop of formalin or they will move and blur the picture. After focusing the camera, close the shutter and load it with film. Be careful when moving the camera that you do not change its height over the microscope. Take the pictures on ordinary black-and-white film. Begin with a time exposure of 5 seconds at 100X magnification. Increase the exposure time if your pictures are too dark, or decrease the exposure time if they are too light. Double the exposure time for each doubling of the magnification.

All photomicrographs by Hugh Spencer except where noted

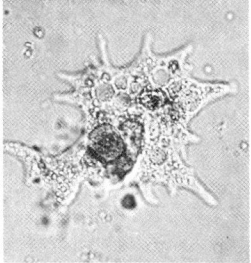

Ameba

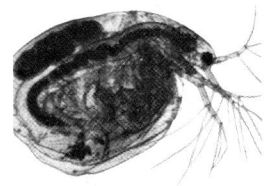

Copepod (Daphnia)

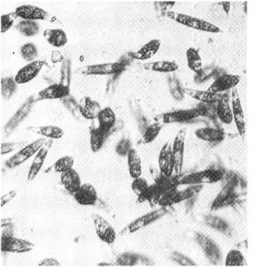

Euglena

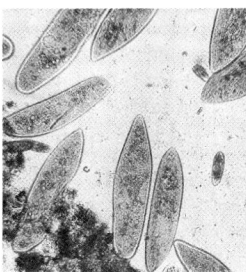

Paramecia

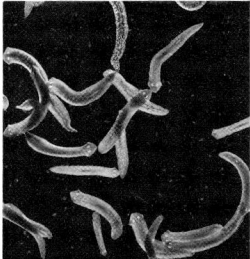

Carolina Biological Supply Company

Planaria

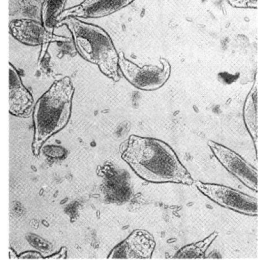

Rotifers

Spirogyra (Green algae)

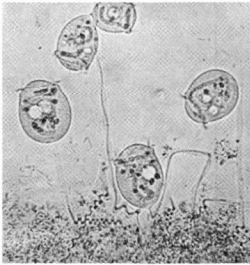

Vorticella

built-in camera. A *stereoscope* microscope provides a three-dimensional view of the specimen. Such a microscope has an objective and an ocular for each eye.

Scientists use special optical microscopes to study details that are not normally visible. For example, a *phase contrast microscope* changes the phase relationship between the light waves passing through the specimen and those not passing through it. This action makes some parts of the specimen appear brighter and other parts darker than normal. Parts of a transparent object that vary in thickness or have certain other optical properties can be made visible in this way.

A *dark-field microscope* prevents light from the lamp from shining directly up the tube. Instead, the microscope uses only light scattered by the specimen. The specimen appears bright against a black background.

A *scanning optical microscope* does not illuminate the entire specimen at once. Instead, the microscope directs a laser beam at a small spot on the specimen. An electronic device called a *photodetector* measures the amount of light reflected from, or shining through, the specimen. The beam then scans the specimen as the photodetector takes measurements at a large number of spots. A computer combines the measurements to produce an image on a TV-like monitor screen.

In a *confocal scanning optical microscope,* a photodetector measures light readings from various depths in the specimen. A computer uses the measurements to create a three-dimensional image. The operator can rotate the image to examine it from any angle.

Other kinds of microscopes. *Electron microscopes* use a beam of electrons rather than a beam of light to produce magnified images. Electron wavelengths are much shorter than those of visible light. As a result, electron microscopes can resolve much finer detail than optical microscopes can. Some electron microscopes can resolve objects that are less than 2 angstroms apart, which is sufficient to reveal the fundamental atomic structure of the specimen.

There are two basic types of electron microscopes. A *transmission electron microscope* passes a broad beam of electrons through a specimen slice a few hundred angstroms thick. A *scanning electron microscope* scans a focused beam across the surface of the specimen. See **Electron microscope.**

Scanning probe microscopes scan a specimen with a sharp point called a *probe.* There are two main types of scanning probe microscopes: (1) the *scanning tunneling microscope* (STM) and (2) the *atomic force microscope* (AFM). In the STM, the probe does not quite touch the specimen. An electric current flows between the probe and the specimen. A computer uses measurements of this current to create an image. An STM can resolve surface atoms that are less than 2 angstroms apart.

In the AFM, the probe gently touches the surface of the specimen. As the probe scans the specimen, it reacts to the roughness of the surface by moving up and down. Electronic devices measure this movement and send their results to a computer, which creates an image. The AFM can produce images of specimens, such as animal tissue, through which electric current does not flow readily. See **Scanning probe microscope.**

An *ion microscope,* also known as a *field-ion microscope,* is used to examine metals. It creates an image of the crystal structure of the tip of an extremely sharp metal needle. An electric field applied to the tip repels charged helium atoms, which spread out and strike a special screen. The screen glows where the atoms strike it, forming an image of the arrangement of atoms in the metal. See **Ion microscope.**

History of the microscope. Engravers probably used water-filled glass globes as magnifying glasses at least 2,000 years ago. The Romans may have made magnifying glasses from rock crystal. Glass lenses of the type now used were introduced in the late 1200's.

Historians generally credit a Dutch spectacle-maker, Zacharias Janssen, with discovering the principle of the compound microscope about 1590. In the 1670's, Anton van Leeuwenhoek, a Dutch amateur scientist, made single-lens microscopes that could magnify up to 270X. Leeuwenhoek was the first person to observe microscopic life and record his observations.

Few improvements occurred until the early 1800's, when better glass-making methods produced lenses that provided undistorted images. German scientists demonstrated the first electron microscope in 1931. The ion microscope was invented in 1951. In 1981, Swiss and West German scientists demonstrated the first scanning tunneling microscope.   Stephen J. Pennycook

See also **Cell** (pictures); **Leeuwenhoek, Anton van; Ultramicroscope; World, History of the** (picture: New scientific devices).

Additional resources

Bleifeld, Maurice. *Experimenting with a Microscope*. Watts, 1988. For younger readers.
Burgess, Jeremy, and others. *Microcosmos*. Cambridge, 1987.

Microtome, *MY kruh tohm,* is a device used to cut materials very thin so that they can be seen in cross sec-

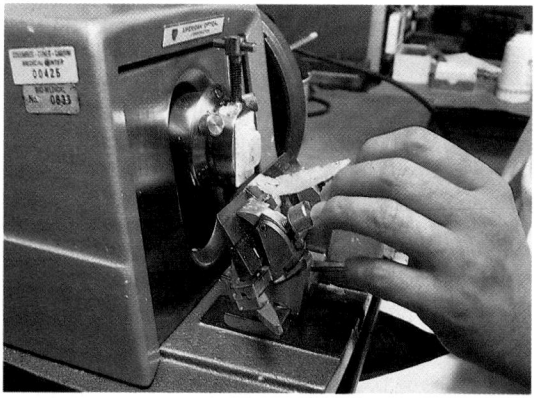

WORLD BOOK photo by Steinkamp/Ballogg
A microtome cuts thin slices of human tissue for examination under a microscope. Wax holds the tissue together so the microtome can slice it thin enough for light to pass through.

tion under a microscope. It has a holder in which the specimen is clamped, a razor-sharp knife, a guide for the knife, and a turnscrew which regulates the thickness of the slice. See also **Microscope; Microtomy.**

Microtomy, *my KRAHT uh mee,* originally meant *microscopic cutting.* But it now means the art of preparing objects for examination with a microscope. Without

preparation, few objects can be properly examined with a microscope (see **Microscope**). A piece of metal, for example, must be highly polished and etched before its structure can be seen with a microscope.

Scientists prepare biological materials either as smears, squashes, wholemounts, or sections. *Smears* are made by applying a thin layer of blood or other organic fluid to a microscopic slide. Technicians dry and stain the layer so the cells can be seen. Geneticists make *squashes* by crushing cells in order to see the number and shape of the chromosomes (see **Chromosome**). *Wholemounts* are prepared from whole microscopic organisms that are killed in a *fixative* to keep their shape. They are then stained. Alcohol removes the water, and clove or cedar oil makes the objects transparent. Technicians next mount the objects in a drop of resin on a glass slide, which they cover with a glass *coverslip* about $\frac{1}{5,000}$ inch (.005 millimeter) thick.

Scientists study plant and animal tissues in *sections* about $\frac{1}{2,500}$ inch (.01 millimeter) thick. The tissues are hardened and dried out, then soaked in wax and shaped into blocks. The wax supports the tissues so they can be sliced into sections on a *microtome* (see **Microtome**). The sections are cemented to slides with egg white and the wax is dissolved. They are then stained and preserved under a coverslip. An *ultramicrotome* is used to prepare specimens for the electron microscope. It cuts sections about $\frac{1}{1,300,000}$ inch (.02 micrometer) thick. The specimens are so thin that the electron beam of the microscope can penetrate them.   Peter Gray

Microwave is a short radio wave. It varies from .03937 inch to 1 foot (1 millimeter to 30 centimeters) in length. Like light waves, microwaves may be reflected and concentrated. But they pass easily through rain, smoke, and fog, which block light waves. They can also pass through the *ionosphere,* which surrounds the earth and blocks or reflects longer radio waves. Thus, microwaves are well suited for long-distance, satellite, and space communications and for control of navigation.

Microwaves first came to public notice through the use of radar in World War II (1939-1945). Today, many satellite communications systems use them. In TV, microwave transmission sends programs from pickup cameras in the field to the TV transmitter. These programs can then be sent via satellites to locations around the world. Microwaves can also cook food in microwave ovens.   Vijai K. Tripathi

See also **Microwave oven; Radar; Radio; Satellite, Artificial; Television; Ultrahigh frequency waves.**

Microwave oven is an appliance that heats food by penetrating it with short radio waves. These waves cause molecules in food to vibrate rapidly. Friction among the moving molecules creates heat, which cooks the food.

Microwave cooking generally takes much less time than cooking with electric or gas ovens. This is because microwave ovens produce heat directly inside the food, but regular ovens cook food gradually, from the outside in. When properly prepared, meats and vegetables cooked in a microwave oven tend to retain more of their natural juices than when cooked by other methods.

Microwaves are produced in a microwave oven by an electronic vacuum tube called a *magnetron.* In most such ovens, these waves travel through a metal chamber

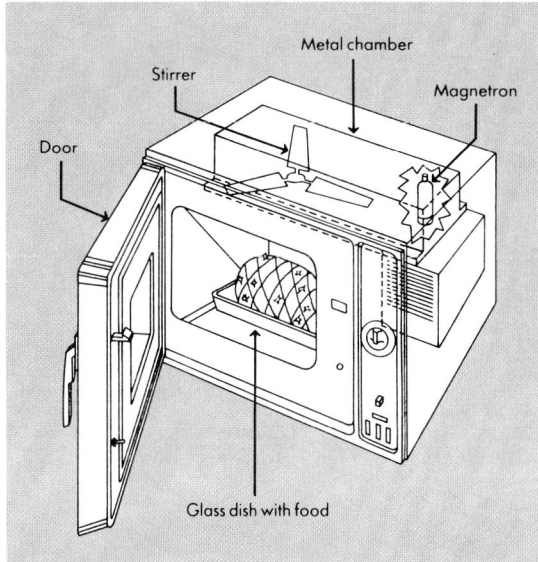

Stirrer

Metal chamber

Magnetron

Door

Glass dish with food

WORLD BOOK diagram

A microwave oven has an electronic vacuum tube called a *magnetron* that produces microwaves. The waves travel through a metal chamber to the *stirrer,* which scatters them into the oven. There, the microwaves penetrate food and cook it quickly.

to the *stirrer,* a device similar to an electric fan. The stirrer scatters the waves around the oven's metal interior. The waves bounce from wall to wall until they enter the food in the oven.

Microwaves penetrate food to various depths, depending on the food's molecular makeup and thickness. For example, microwaves can travel about $1\frac{1}{2}$ inches (3.8 centimeters) into most meats. If the meat is thicker, the waves do not penetrate it completely. Instead, the inner layers of the meat are cooked by heat from the outer layers.

Microwaves pass through glass, paper, and most kinds of china and plastics. Therefore, most containers made of these materials may be used to hold food in microwave ovens. Metal cookware should be avoided because it reflects microwaves, preventing them from entering the food. In addition, metal containers may reflect enough energy back to the magnetron to damage it.

Microwaves that leak from an oven may pose a hazard to people nearby. In addition, such leaks reduce the oven's efficiency. Secure door seals and proper door closure help prevent microwave leakage. Microwave ovens that do not close securely should never be used.

Manufacturers introduced microwave ovens for home use in the 1950's. Sales of these appliances have grown rapidly since the mid-1970's.   Evan Powell

Midas, *MY duhs,* was a character in Greek mythology. He was king of Phrygia, an ancient country in central Asia Minor. The god Dionysus gave Midas the power to turn everything he touched into gold, because he had helped Dionysus' teacher Silenus (see **Dionysus**).

At first, Midas' miraculous power pleased him. But soon it became a curse, because even his food turned to gold the moment he touched it. He prayed to Dionysus to help him, and the god told him to bathe in the river Pactolus. Midas washed himself, and the magic touch

left him. But the sands of the river turned to gold.

Midas acted as judge at a musical contest between Apollo and Pan (see **Apollo; Pan**). He awarded the prize to Pan, and Apollo angrily turned Midas' ears into those of an ass. Midas was ashamed and kept his ears covered. But he could not hide his ears from the slave who was his barber. The slave did not dare tell anyone about the king's ears because he feared punishment. He dug a hole and whispered the truth into it. Reeds grew out of the soil and whispered the secret when the wind blew.

The expression *to have the Midas touch* is used to describe a person who makes money in everything he or she does. A *Midas* is a wealthy person.   Jon D. Mikalson

Middle age refers to an arbitrary period in a person's life between early adulthood and old age. In industrial societies, such as the United States and Canada, this period now usually extends from about the age of 40 to 65. However, there is no noticeable change in physical or behavioral functioning at either of these ages. The range of middle age may vary in different societies. For example, in nonindustrialized countries, people may be considered old by the age of 40.

In Western industrial societies, middle age is often characterized by an inclination to "settle down." Middle-aged people accept obligations and responsibilities, and work harder to develop a consistent pattern of relationships. They tend to place increasing value on their family life and friendships, even if they have successful careers. Many people may feel closer to their own elderly parents, having achieved a deeper understanding of what the older generation went through. Parents often become more open and respectful with their children.

Researchers believe that some middle-aged people may not enjoy this part of life because they fear old age and value youth too much. However, studies of people moving from youth through middle age have found many sources of satisfaction. Some middle-aged people feel that they still have the physical vigor to carry out their plans and responsibilities. Often life satisfaction is enhanced by the skills and experiences acquired over the years. As a result, problems in middle age can often be handled before they become crises.

Each new group of people that enters middle age comes along at a particular point in social history with unique values, pressures, and opportunities. For example, characteristics of middle-aged people today include a greater number of women in the labor force than ever before, a greater emphasis on physical fitness, and a higher divorce rate. Middle-aged people today also face new challenges. These challenges include (1) major changes in the workplace due to the increasing use of computers and (2) increasingly permissive standards of sexual expression. Thus, middle age is far from a quiet, uneventful period of life. But many middle-aged people benefit from their broad life experience and well-developed skills. Many are also enrolling in college and finding other opportunities to make the most of their potential as vital, creative people.   Robert J. Kastenbaum

Additional resources

Brandes, Stanley H. *Forty: The Age and the Symbol.* Univ. of Tennessee Pr., 1985.
Golan, Naomi. *The Perilous Bridge: Helping Clients Through Mid-Life Transitions.* Free Pr., 1986.

"March" from the Duc de Berry's *Les Très Riches Heures* (*The Very Rich Hours*, early 1400's),
an illuminated manuscript by the Limbourg brothers; Musée Condé, Chantilly, France (Giraudon)

Middle Ages

Middle Ages were the period between ancient and modern times in western Europe. Before the Middle Ages, western Europe was part of the Roman Empire. After the Middle Ages, western Europe included the Holy Roman Empire, the kingdoms of England and France, and a number of smaller states. The Middle Ages are also known as the *medieval* period, from the Latin words *medium* (middle) and *aevum* (age). Sometimes the Middle Ages are incorrectly called the *Dark Ages*.

The history of the Middle Ages extends from the end of the Roman Empire to the 1500's. Historians today do not give exact dates for the end of the Roman Empire, because it ended over a period of several hundred

years. This article uses the A.D. 400's as the starting date of the Middle Ages. By that time, the Roman Empire was so weak that Germanic tribes were able to conquer it. The Germanic way of life gradually combined with the Roman way of life to form the civilization which we call *medieval*. Medieval civilization was greatly influenced by the Muslims in Spain and the Middle East, and by the Byzantine Empire in southeastern Europe.

This article tells about life in western Europe between the A.D. 400's and the 1500's. To learn how other civilizations influenced medieval civilization, see the *World Book* articles on **Byzantine Empire; Muslims;** and **Rome, Ancient.** See also **World, History of the.**

The beginnings

The Germanic invasions. The Germanic peoples came from Scandinavia in northern Europe. They began moving into central Europe about 1000 B.C. By the A.D.

Bryce Lyon, the contributor of this article, is Emeritus Professor of History at Brown University and author of The Middle Ages in Western Europe.

Illustration from an illuminated manuscript (1448); National Library of Austria, Vienna

Life in the Middle Ages centered around control of the land. Land was ruled by a powerful lord, defended by his knights, and farmed by his peasants. The lord's home, *left,* a mighty stone castle built for defense, provided protection for the peasants. The Christian church was also an important institution during the Middle Ages. When a town wanted to build a new cathedral, the townspeople sometimes helped construct it, *above.* These community building projects were called *fatigues.*

200's, they occupied regions in the Rhine and Danube river basins along the northern and northeastern boundaries of the Roman Empire. Some Germans adopted the civilization of their Roman neighbors. They traded with Roman merchants, learned to farm the land, and accepted Christianity as their religion.

But most Germans were rough, ignorant people. The Romans called them *barbarians* (uncivilized people). The Germans lived in tribes, each governed by a chief. The few laws that these people had were based on tribal customs and superstition. The tribesmen were fierce in appearance—big, bearded, and clothed in animal skins or coarse linen. They fought with spears and shields, and were brave warriors. The Germans lived mainly by hunting and by a crude type of farming. They worshiped such Scandinavian gods as Odin and Thor. Few Germans could read or write.

During the A.D. 400's, the Germanic tribes began invading Roman territory. By then, the Roman Empire had lost much of its great power, and its armies could not defend the long frontier. The Visigoths invaded Spain about A.D. 416. The Angles, Jutes, and Saxons began to

settle in Britain about 450. The Franks established a kingdom in Gaul (now France) in the 480's. The Ostrogoths invaded Italy in 489. See **Angles; Franks; Goths; Jutes; Saxons.**

Barbarian Europe. The barbarian invasions divided the huge Roman Empire into many kingdoms. The barbarians were loyal only to their tribal chiefs or to their own families. Each tribe kept its own laws and customs. As a result, the strong central and local governments of the Romans disappeared.

In the Roman Empire, a strong system of laws protected the citizens and gave them the safety and security that comes from law and order. Barbarian superstitions replaced many Roman laws. For example, *trial by ordeal* became a common way of determining whether a person was guilty of a crime. The accused person's arm was plunged into a pot of boiling water. Or the person had to pick up a red-hot iron bar with the bare hand. If the burns healed within three days, the person was judged innocent. Otherwise, the accused was hanged. See also **Trial by combat.**

The barbarian invasions also destroyed most of the European trade that the Romans had established. Few people used the great system of stone roads that had encouraged trade and communication among the prosperous cities of the Roman Empire. Without trade, money went out of use almost completely. Most of the people were forced to make their living from farming activities.

By the 800's, most of western Europe was divided into large estates of land called *manors.* A few wealthy landowners, called *landlords* or *lords,* ruled the manors, but most of the people were poor peasants who worked the land. Each village on a manor produced nearly everything needed by its people. This system of obtaining a living from the land was called *manorialism.* See **Manorialism.**

Towns lost their importance under manorial conditions. Most people who had lived in the towns went to the countryside and became peasants on the manors. Some towns were completely abandoned and gradually disappeared. The middle class, which had engaged in trade and industry, also disappeared.

Education and cultural activities were almost forgotten. Almost all state and city schools disappeared. Few people could read or write Latin, which was the language of the well-educated. Even fewer people were educated enough to preserve the little that remained of ancient Greek and Roman knowledge. The great skills of ancient literature, architecture, painting, and sculpture were forgotten.

The Christian church was the main civilizing force of the early Middle Ages. It provided leadership for the people and saved western Europe from complete ignorance.

Little by little, the church made Christians of the barbarians. Although the people of Europe no longer honored one ruler, they gradually began to worship the same God. People called *missionaries* traveled great distances to spread the Christian faith. They also helped civilize the barbarians by introducing Roman ideas of government and justice into their lives.

The popes, bishops, and other leaders of the church took over many functions of government after the Roman emperors lost power. The church collected taxes and maintained law courts to punish criminals. Church buildings also served as hospitals for the sick, and as inns for travelers.

Two church institutions—the *cathedral* and the *monastery*—became centers of learning in the early Middle Ages. Cathedrals were the churches of bishops. Monasteries were communities of men called *monks,* who gave up worldly life to serve God through prayer and work. The monks of some monasteries and the clergy of the cathedrals helped continue the reading and writing of Latin, and preserved many valuable ancient manuscripts. They also set up most of the schools in Europe.

The Carolingian Empire united most of western Europe under one ruler in the late 700's. The *Carolingians* were a family of Frankish kings who ruled from the mid-700's to 987. The most important Frankish rulers were Charles Martel, his son Pepin the Short, and Pepin's son Charlemagne.

Charles Martel united the Frankish kingdom in the early 700's, when he captured lands held by powerful Frankish lords. Pepin the Short strengthened the Carolingians' control over the Frankish kingdom. In 768, Charlemagne became ruler of the kingdom. He then conquered much of western Europe, and united Europe for the first time since the end of the Roman Empire.

In creating their empire, the Frankish rulers depended on the assistance of loyal noblemen called *vassals.* A nobleman became a vassal when he pledged his loyalty to the king and promised to serve him. The king then became a *lord* to his vassal. Most vassals held important positions in the king's army, where they served as *knights.* Many vassals had their own knights, whose services they also pledged to the king.

The Carolingian kings rewarded their vassals by granting them estates called *fiefs.* A fief included the manors on the land, the buildings and villages of each manor, and the peasants who farmed the manors.

The early Middle Ages reached their highest point of achievement during the long rule of Charlemagne. He worked to protect the church from its enemies and to keep the people of Europe united under the church. Although Charlemagne never learned to write, he did improve education. He established a school in his palace at Aachen, and teachers from throughout Europe gathered there. They organized schools and libraries, and copied ancient manuscripts. These activities caused a new interest in learning called the *Carolingian Renaissance.* See **Charlemagne.**

Charlemagne's empire and the revival of learning did not last long after his death. His three grandsons fought each other for the title of emperor. In 843, the Treaty of Verdun divided the empire into three parts, one for each grandson. Soon after, the divided empire was attacked by Magyars, Muslims, and Vikings. By the late 800's, the Carolingian Empire no longer existed.

Feudal Europe

Feudalism. After the end of Charlemagne's empire, Europe was again divided into many kingdoms. Most of the kings had little control over their kingdoms. As a result, hundreds of vassals—with such titles as *prince, baron, duke,* or *count*—became independent rulers of their own fiefs. These noblemen ruled their fiefs through a form of government called feudalism.

Under feudalism, the noblemen who controlled the land also had political, economic, judicial, and military power. Each nobleman collected taxes and fines, acted as judge in legal disputes, and maintained an army of knights within his own territory. He also supervised the farming of the manors on his fief. The fief-holders were the ruling class in Europe for more than 400 years.

A typical member of the ruling class under feudalism was a nobleman, a knight, a vassal, and a lord—all at the same time. He was a nobleman because he had been born into the noble class. He became a knight when he decided to spend his life as a professional warrior. He became a vassal when he promised to serve a king or other important person in return for a fief. Finally, he became a lord when he gave part of his own land to persons who promised to serve him.

Suppose that Sir John, a nobleman, was a vassal of William the Conqueror, king of England and duke of Normandy. When John pledged his loyalty to William, he also promised to supply the king with 10 knights. In return, William gave 20 manors to John as a fief. If the king called his army to battle, John had to go—and take nine other knights with him. If John did not have nine knights living in his household, he hired wandering knights. As payment, John gave each knight one manor as a fief. The knights then pledged their loyalty and service to John. In this way, they became John's vassals, and he became their lord.

A lord and a vassal had rights and duties toward each other. A lord promised his vassal protection and justice, and the vassal gave the lord various services, most of which were military. Feudal warfare was common in Europe. If a lord and his vassal performed their duties, there was peace and good government. But if either disregarded his duties, war broke out between them. The lords fought among themselves as well, because they often tried to seize each other's land. The church, which had its own princes and fiefs, was part of the feudal system, so it also suffered in the warfare. See **Feudalism.**

Feudal government. During the 900's and 1000's, most of western Europe was divided into feudal states. A powerful lord ruled each state as if he were king. The kings themselves ruled only their own royal lands.

In France, the king ruled only the area called the *Île-de-France,* a narrow strip of land centered near Paris. The rest of France was divided into such feudal states as Aquitaine, Anjou, Brittany, Flanders, and Normandy. In some feudal states, no lord was powerful enough to establish a strong government. But in Anjou, Flanders, and Normandy, capable lords provided strong governments. The dukes of Normandy maintained tight control over the noblemen living there. No one could build a castle, collect taxes, regulate trade, or hold important court trials without the duke's permission. Only he could order an army into battle.

Under William the Conqueror, England became the strongest feudal state in Europe. William, who was duke of Normandy, invaded England in 1066. After defeating the Anglo-Saxon army, he became king of England. He then established the feudal system in England by making all landholders his vassals. See **Norman Conquest; Normandy; William I, the Conqueror.**

The strong governments in the feudal states of France

and England provided some peace and security for the people. Strong feudal government allowed rulers in the 1100's and 1200's to establish strong central governments in France and England.

Feudalism did not provide strong government in Germany or Italy. For hundreds of years, powerful dukes fought the kings. Otto I, one of the most powerful German kings, won control over the dukes in the mid-900's. He then tried to create an empire similar to Charlemagne's. After conquering lands east of Germany, Otto invaded Italy. In 962, the pope crowned Otto *Holy Roman Emperor.* The Holy Roman Empire was small and weak, and included only Germany and northern Italy. In time, the German dukes tried to regain control of their

kingdoms, and the empire was continually divided by warfare. Neither Germany nor Italy became united countries until the 1800's.

The power of the church became the single great force that bound Europe together during the feudal period. The church touched almost everyone's life in many important ways. The church baptized a person at birth, performed the wedding ceremony at the person's marriage, and conducted the burial services when the person died.

The church also became the largest landholder in western Europe during the Middle Ages. Many feudal lords gave fiefs to the church in return for services performed by the clergy. At first, feudal lords controlled the

Feudal states of Europe: 1096

Kingdom of France

Holy Roman Empire

This map shows the political divisions of Europe in 1096. France and the Holy Roman Empire were made up of many feudal states, each ruled by a lord. The kings ruled only their own royal lands. In France, the king ruled the Île-de-France, shown in yellow. England was a unified kingdom ruled by William II.

Data for map from *Mediaeval History*, by Bryce Lyon; Harper & Row, 1962.   WORLD BOOK map

church, but it gradually won a large degree of freedom.

Although clergymen did not take a direct part in feudal warfare, they controlled the lords with their own types of weapons. One great power of the church was its threat of *excommunication.* To excommunicate a person meant to cut the person off completely from the church and take away the person's hope of going to heaven. If a lord continued to rebel after being excommunicated, the church disciplined him with an *interdict.* This action closed all the churches on the lord's land. No one on the land could be married or buried with the church's blessing, and the church bells never rang. The people usually became so discontented that they rebelled, and the lord finally yielded to the church.

Life of the people. Europe during the 900's was poor, underdeveloped, and thinly populated. At least half the land could not be farmed because of thick forests or swamps. War, disease, famine, and a low birth rate kept the population small. People lived an average of only 30 years. There was little travel or communication, and fewer than 20 per cent of the people went farther than 10 miles (16 kilometers) from their birthplace.

The people of western Europe consisted of three groups. The *lords* governed the large fiefs and did all the fighting. The *clergy* served the church. The *peasants* worked on the land to support themselves, the clergy, and the lords.

The lords. A lord's life centered around fighting. He believed that the only honorable way to live was as a professional warrior. The lords and their knights, wearing heavy armor and riding huge war horses, fought with lances or heavy swords.

The behavior of all fighting men gradually came to be governed by a system called *chivalry.* Chivalry required that a man earn knighthood through a long and difficult training period. A knight was supposed to be courageous in battle, fight according to certain rules, keep his promises, and defend the church. Chivalry also included rules for gentlemanly conduct toward women. In times of peace, a lord and his knights entertained themselves by practicing for war. They took part in *jousts* (combat between two armed knights) and in *tournaments* (combat between two groups of knights). See **Knights and knighthood.**

The lord lived in a manor house or a castle. Early castles were simple forts surrounded by fences of tree trunks. Later castles were mighty fortresses of stone. In the great hall of the castle, the lord and his knights ate, drank, and gambled at the firesides. They played dice, checkers, and chess.

The lord's wife, called a *lady,* was trained to sew, spin, and weave, and to rule the household servants. She had few rights. If she did not bear at least one son, the lord could end their marriage. Neither the lords nor their ladies thought education was necessary, and few could read or write.

The clergy. Most bishops and other high-ranking clergymen were noblemen who devoted their lives to the church. They ruled large fiefs and lived much like other noblemen. Some of these clergymen were as wealthy and powerful as the greatest military lords.

Monks who lived in a monastery were required to live according to its rules. They had to spend a certain number of hours each day studying, praying, and taking part in religious services. Some monks who were outstanding scholars left the monastery and became advisers to kings or other rulers.

Many peasants who became clergymen served as priests in the peasant villages. Each village priest lived in a small cottage near his church. He gave advice and help to the peasants, settled disputes, and performed church ceremonies. The priests collected fees for baptisms, marriages, and burials. But most priests were as poor as the peasants they served.

The peasants had few rights, and were almost completely at the mercy of their lords. A peasant family worked together to farm both the lord's fields and their own. Peasants also performed whatever other tasks the lord demanded, such as cutting wood, storing grain, or repairing roads and bridges.

Peasants had to pay many kinds of rents and taxes. They had to bring grain to the lord's mill to be ground, bake bread in the lord's oven, and take grapes to the lord's wine press. Each of these services meant another payment to the lord. Money was scarce, so the peasants usually paid in wheat, oats, eggs, or poultry from their own land.

Peasants lived in crude huts and slept on bags filled with straw. They ate black bread, eggs, poultry, and such vegetables as cabbage and turnips. Rarely could they afford meat. They could not hunt or fish because game on the manor belonged to the lord.

The High Middle Ages

Medieval civilization reached its highest point of achievement between the 1000's and the late 1200's. This period is called the *High Middle Ages.*

During the 1000's, many capable lords provided strong governments and periods of peace and security under the feudal system. As a result, the people were able to devote themselves to new ideas and activities.

Economic recovery. As government improved, so did economic conditions. Merchants again traveled the old land routes and waterways of Europe. Towns sprang up along the main trade routes. Most early towns developed near a fortified castle, church, or monastery where merchants could stop for protection. The merchants, and the craftworkers who made the goods sold by the merchants, gradually settled in the towns.

Europe's population began to increase during the 1000's, and many people moved to the towns in search of jobs. At the same time, peasants began to leave the manors to seek a new life. Some became merchants and craftworkers. Others farmed the land outside the towns and supplied the townspeople with food. Medieval towns, which arose mainly because of the growth of trade, encouraged trade. The townspeople bought goods, and also produced goods for merchants to sell.

The peasants learned better ways of farming and produced more and more food for the growing population. Peasants began to use water power to run the grain mills and sawmills. They gained land for farming by clearing forests and draining swamps.

For the first time since the days of the Roman Empire, Europeans took notice of the world beyond their borders. Merchants traveled afar to trade with the peoples of the Byzantine Empire in southeastern Europe. The *Crusades,* a series of holy wars against the Muslims, encouraged European trade with the Middle East (see **Crusades**). Italians in Genoa, Pisa, Venice, and other towns built great fleets of ships to carry the merchants' goods across the Mediterranean Sea to trade centers in Spain and northern Africa. The Italians brought back goods from these seaports. Many of the goods were exports from cities in India and China. Leaders in the towns of northern Germany created the Hanseatic League to organize trade in northern Europe.

Merchants exchanged their goods at great international trade fairs held in towns along the main European trade routes. Each fair was held at a different time of the year, and merchants traveled from one fair to another. The county of Champagne in northeastern France became the site of the first great European fairs. Its towns lay on the trade routes that linked Italy with northern Europe. Flemish merchants brought woolen cloth to the fairs. Italian merchants brought silks, spices, and perfumes from the Middle East, India, and China. Merchants from northern and eastern Europe brought furs, lumber, and stone. The merchants not only traded their goods, but also exchanged ideas about new methods of farming, new industries, and events in Europe and the rest of the world.

Medieval towns. Early towns were only small settlements outside the walls of a castle or a church. As the small towns grew larger, walls were built around them. Soldiers on the walls kept a lookout for attacking armies. The towns were crowded because the walls limited the amount of land available. Houses stood crowded together. The people had to build upward because land was expensive, and many buildings were five or six stories high.

Streets were narrow, crooked, dark, and filthy. Until about 1200, they were not paved. The people threw all their garbage and rubbish into the streets, and disease spread quickly. During the 1200's, the people in some towns began to pave their streets with rough cobblestones. They also took some steps toward increasing sanitation.

A citizen who went out at night took his servants along for protection against robbers. The servants carried lanterns and torches because no town had any street lighting. The wide use of lamps, torches, and candles made fire one of the great dangers for a medieval town. Wealthy citizens had stone and brick houses, but most of the houses were made of wood. A large fire was likely to wipe out a whole town. The city of Rouen, in France, burned to the ground six times between 1200 and 1225.

After the merchants and craftsmen settled in the towns, they set up organizations called *guilds.* A guild protected its members against unfair business practices, established prices and wages, and settled disputes between workers and employers.

Guilds played an important part in town government. When the first guilds were organized, the towns had few laws to protect merchants or craftsmen. Most laws were made and enforced by the lord who owned the land on which a town stood. As the townspeople gained power, they demanded the right to govern themselves. Often, a guild forced a lord to grant the people a charter giving them certain rights of self-government. Guilds led the townspeople's fight for self-government, and so members of guilds often ran the new town governments. See **Guild.**

The decline of feudalism. Economic recovery brought many changes to the social and political organization of Europe. Money came back into use with the growth of trade and industry, the rise of towns, and the crusades. The manorial system began to break down as people grew less dependent on the land. Many peasants ran away from the manors to the towns. Other peasants bought their freedom with money that they made by selling food to the townspeople. The lords of some towns encouraged new settlers to come. Many lords granted freedom to peasants who settled in their towns.

The feudal system, which was based on manorialism, began to break down, too. Ruling lords could pay for military and political service with money instead of fiefs. Their wealth provided better pay for the soldiers and officials they hired. In return, the lords received better service. They and their governments grew increasingly powerful.

Developments in the 1100's and 1200's laid the foundation for the eventual rise of great nation-states in England and France. Such powerful kings as Henry II of England and Louis IX of France forced feudal lords to accept their authority. These kings developed new and better forms of government. They also organized national armies to protect the people, and established royal laws and courts to provide justice throughout the land. See **Henry** (II) of England; **Louis** (IX).

At the same time, small but well-organized governments took form in Flanders, and in Italian city-states including Florence, Genoa, Siena, and Venice.

Learning and the arts during the high Middle Ages were devoted to glorifying God and strengthening the power of the church. From 1100 to 1300, almost all the great ideas and artistic achievements reflected the influence of the church.

Princes and laborers alike contributed money to build the magnificent stone cathedrals that rose above medieval towns. The stained glass windows and sculptured figures that decorated the cathedrals portrayed events in the life of Christ and other stories from the Bible. The cathedrals still standing in the French cities of Chartres, Reims, Amiens, and Paris are reminders of the faith of medieval people. See **Notre Dame, Cathedral of; Reims** (picture).

Increasing contact with Arab and Byzantine civilizations brought back much learning that had been lost to Europe since the end of the Roman Empire. Scholars translated Greek and Arabic writings from these civilizations into Latin, and studied their meanings. More and more scholars became familiar with the writings of the Greek philosopher Aristotle. The scholars argued whether Aristotle's teachings opposed those of the church. A field of thought called *scholasticism* grew out of their discussions and writings (see **Scholasticism**). Among the great teachers and writers of this period were Peter Abelard, Albertus Magnus, and Thomas Aquinas (see **Abelard, Peter; Albertus Magnus, Saint; Aquinas, Saint Thomas**).

Students gathered at the cathedrals where the scholars lectured. Students and scholars formed organizations called *universities,* which were similar to the craftsmen's guilds. From the universities came men to

Illumination (1200's) from a French manuscript;
© Pierpont Morgan Library, New York City

Building a medieval stone wall required great engineering skill. In this illustration, workers cut stone into squares and carry it to a crane. A man powers the crane by walking on the steps of a large moving wheel. Another worker carries mortar up a ladder to the man who cements the pieces of stone together.

serve the church and the new states, to practice law and medicine, to write literature, and to educate others.

The late Middle Ages

Between 1300 and 1500, medieval Europe gradually gave way to modern Europe. During this period, the Middle Ages overlapped the period in European history called the *Renaissance.* For a discussion of the great developments in art and learning during this period, see the *World Book* article on **Renaissance.**

A halt in progress. Although art and learning advanced, other areas of medieval civilization stood still or fell back. Europe had moved forward economically and socially almost without interruption during the high Middle Ages. The population had grown steadily, social conditions had improved, and industry and trade had expanded greatly. These developments in Europe came to an end in the 1300's. The population decreased, the people became discontented, and industry and trade shrank.

Wars and natural disasters played a large part in the halt of European progress. From 1337 to 1453, England and France fought the Hundred Years' War, which interrupted trade and exhausted the economies of both nations (see **Hundred Years' War**). In addition, the breakdown of feudalism and manorialism caused civil war throughout most of Europe. Peasants rose in bloody revolts to win freedom from lords. In the towns, workers

fought the rich merchants who kept them poor and powerless.

To add to the miseries of the people, the *Black Death* killed about a fourth of Europe's population between 1347 and 1352. The Black Death was an outbreak of plague, one of the worst epidemic diseases (see **Plague**). Severe droughts and floods also brought death, disease, and famine.

The growth of royal power. By the 1300's, the breakdown of feudalism had seriously weakened the feudal lords. At the same time, economic recovery had enriched the kings. With the help of hired armies, the kings enforced their authority over the lords. Royal infantry—newly armed with longbows, spears called *pikes,* and guns—defeated armies of feudal knights.

Meanwhile, the kings greatly increased their power by gaining the support of the middle classes in the towns. The townspeople agreed to support the kings by paying taxes in return for peace and good government. These developments gave birth to the nations of modern Europe.

Troubles in the church. The power of the popes grew with that of the kings, and bitter disputes arose between the rulers of church and state. Churchmen took an increasing part in political affairs, and kings interfered in church affairs more and more. The popes sometimes surrendered their independence and gave in to the kings. This happened especially from 1309 to 1377, when the popes ruled the church from Avignon, France. After the popes returned to Rome, disputes over the election of popes divided the church. Two, and sometimes three, men claimed the title of pope. Such disputes hurt the influence of the church. They also caused criticism of church affairs and of church teaching. The religious unity of western Europe was weakened, leading to the Protestant Reformation of the 1500's. See **Christianity** (The division of the church); **Pope** (The troubles of the papacy); **Reformation.**

The growth of humanism. During the late Middle Ages, scholars and artists were less concerned with religious thinking, and concentrated more on understanding people and the world. This new outlook was called *humanism.* The scholars and artists of ancient Greece and Rome had emphasized the study of humanity. Scholars and artists of the late Middle Ages rediscovered the ancient works and gained inspiration from them. Architects began to design nonreligious buildings, rather than cathedrals. Painters and sculptors began to glorify people and nature in their works. Scholars delighted in the study of pre-Christian authors of ancient times. During the late Middle Ages, more and more writers composed prose and poetry not in Latin but in the *vernacular* (native) languages, including French and Italian. This increasing use of the vernacular opened a new literary age, and gradually brought learning and literature to the common people.

The political, economic, and cultural changes of the late Middle Ages gradually changed Europe, and by the early 1500's it was no longer medieval. But the culture and institutions of the Middle Ages continued to influence modern European history.　　　Bryce Lyon

Related articles in *World Book.* For a discussion of political developments in western Europe during the Middle Ages, see the *History* sections of the articles on **Austria; Belgium; Eng-**

land; France; Germany; Italy; the Netherlands; Spain; and Switzerland. Other related articles include:

Outline

I. The beginnings
  A. The Germanic invasions
  B. Barbarian Europe
  C. The Christian Church
  D. The Carolingian Empire
II. Feudal Europe
  A. Feudalism
  B. Feudal government
  C. The power of the church
  D. Life of the people
III. The High Middle Ages
  A. Economic recovery
  B. Medieval towns
  C. The decline of feudalism
  D. Learning and the arts
IV. The late Middle Ages
  A. A halt in progress
  B. The growth of royal power
  C. Troubles in the church
  D. The growth of humanism

Questions

How did the Germanic invasions of the A.D. 400's change European life?
What two church institutions preserved learning during the early Middle Ages?
What were Charlemagne's accomplishments?
What was feudalism? What did it accomplish for Europe?
What were the three classes of medieval society during feudal times?
Why did towns develop during the high Middle Ages?
What was a *fief?* a *manor?* a *vassal?* a *guild?* the *Black Death?*
Why did economic and social progress come to a halt in the late medieval period?
What forces weakened the church in the late Middle Ages?
What was *humanism?* How did it affect medieval society?

Additional resources

Caselli, Giovanni. *The Middle Ages.* Bedrick, 1988. For younger readers.

Corbishley, Mike. *The Middle Ages.* Facts on File, 1990. For younger readers.
Dictionary of the Middle Ages. Ed. by Joseph R. Strayer. 13 vols. Scribner, 1982-1989.
Gies, Frances and Joseph. *Life in a Medieval Village.* HarperCollins, 1990.
The Middle Ages: A Concise Encyclopaedia. Ed. by H. R. Loyn. Thames & Hudson, 1989.
The Oxford Illustrated History of Medieval Europe. Ed. by George Holmes. Oxford, 1990. First published in 1988.

Middle America is a term geographers sometimes use for the area between the United States and South America. Middle America includes Mexico, Central America, and the islands in the Caribbean Sea. These islands are called the West Indies. Spanish is the dominant language in Middle America. For more information, see the *World Book* articles on each country in Middle America. See also **Caribbean Sea; Central America; West Indies.**   Roderic A. Camp

Middle Atlantic States are New Jersey, New York, and Pennsylvania. For information on this region, see **United States** (Regions). See also the articles on the states that make up the region.

Middle class is a group of people between the upper class and the lower class in a society. In the United States, most members of the middle class have a college education and an above-average standard of living. Members of the U.S. middle class are sometimes called *middle Americans.* The term *middle class* first came into general use during the early 1800's in Europe. It referred to the *bourgeoisie* (business class), a group that developed between the aristocrats and the peasants.

Sociologists use the term *social stratification* to describe the process of dividing societies into classes. This process is based on many factors, chiefly a person's occupation. Other factors include income, power, reputation, and wealth. The majority of middle-class people work for a living and do not inherit great wealth. Most middle-class occupations do not involve manual labor. They include those of business owners and managers, clerks, lawyers, physicians, and teachers.

Since the 1950's, the middle class has ranked as the largest class in the United States. From 1974 to 1979, about half the nation's workers had middle-class—that is, nonmanual—occupations. Many values held by middle-class people became the principal values of society. These values included acting according to the moral standards of the community, achieving financial success, advancing in a job, and owning property. During the 1950's and early 1960's, many middle-class people were more concerned with achieving their goals than with changing conditions in society. But from the mid-1960's on, more members of this group, particularly the younger and better educated, became active in society. They objected to certain conditions, rather than simply accepting them. For example, many middle-class Americans supported peace movements and protested racial discrimination.   David J. Maume, Jr.

See also **Social class.**

Additional resources

Baritz, Loren. *The Good Life: The Meaning of Success for the American Middle Class.* Harper, 1990. First published in 1989.
Landry, Bart. *The New Black Middle Class.* Univ. of California Pr., 1987.

© Dallas and John Heaton, Click/Chicago   © Richard Lobell

Ways of life in the Middle East range from modern cities to traditional farms. The city scene above shows a square in Istanbul, Turkey, dominated by a huge *mosque*—an Islamic house of worship. The farming scene shows traditional farming methods being used in southern Lebanon.

Middle East

Middle East is a large region that covers parts of northern Africa, southwestern Asia, and southeastern Europe. Scholars disagree on which countries make up the Middle East. But many say the region consists of Bahrain, Cyprus, Egypt, Iran, Iraq, Israel, Jordan, Kuwait, Lebanon, Oman, Qatar, Saudi Arabia, Sudan, Syria, Turkey, United Arab Emirates, and Yemen. These countries cover about 3,743,000 square miles (9,694,000 square kilometers) and together have a population of about 262 million.

Two of the world's first great civilizations—those of Sumer and Egypt—developed in the area after 3500 B.C. The region also is the birthplace of three major religions—Judaism, Christianity, and Islam.

Since the birth of Islam in the A.D. 600's, Islamic powers have dominated the Middle East. More than 90 per cent of the region's people are Muslims—followers of Islam.

Most of the people of the Middle East are Muslim Arabs. Other religious and ethnic groups include black Africans, Armenians, Copts, Greeks, Iranians, Jews, Kurds, and Turks.

The Middle East is an area of great economic importance as one of the world's major oil-producing regions. It is also a scene of much political unrest and conflict.

People

Ancestry. The people of the Middle East belong to various ethnic groups, which are based largely on cul-

---

The contributors of this article are Dina Le Gall, contributor to Middle East Contemporary Survey *and other publications on the Middle East, and Michel Le Gall, Associate Professor of History at St. Olaf College.*

ture, language, and history. Ethnically, more than three-fourths of the Middle Eastern people are Arabs. Although they live in different countries, the Arabs share a common culture and a common language, Arabic. Iranians and Turks also form major ethnic groups in the region. Smaller groups in the Middle East include Armenians, Copts, Greeks, Jews, Kurds, and various black African groups.

Way of life. Until the 1900's, most Middle Eastern people lived in villages or small towns and made a living by farming. Only a small number lived in cities. Since World War II (1939-1945), many people have moved to urban areas. Today, in most Middle Eastern countries, more than half the people live in cities. Middle Eastern people have strong ties to their families and to their religious and language groups.

In general, city dwellers in the Middle East have a more modern way of life than the rural villagers. In the cities, cars and people move about at a fast pace. People hold jobs in business, education, government, and the media. Television, which is widely viewed, introduces Western ideas and tastes.

In rural areas of the Middle East, the way of life is slowly changing. Better fertilizers, irrigation methods, and machinery have made life easier for some farmers. But many Middle Eastern farmers still use the same kinds of tools and methods their ancestors used hundreds of years ago. Some people of the Middle East are nomads. They live in the desert and herd cattle, goats, and sheep.

Since the mid-1900's, changes have occurred in the status of urban women in the Middle East. Women in rural areas have always done farm work alongside their husbands, but most urban women were confined to their home. Today, many women in the cities have jobs in business, education, and government. For more information on the people of the Middle East, see the *People* section of the various country articles.

Middle East

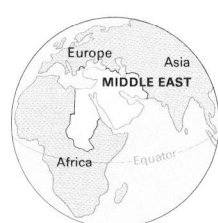

Europe
Asia
MIDDLE EAST
Africa
Equator

★   National capital

•   Other city or town

——   International boundary

—·—·—   Major oil pipeline

▨   Israeli-occupied territory

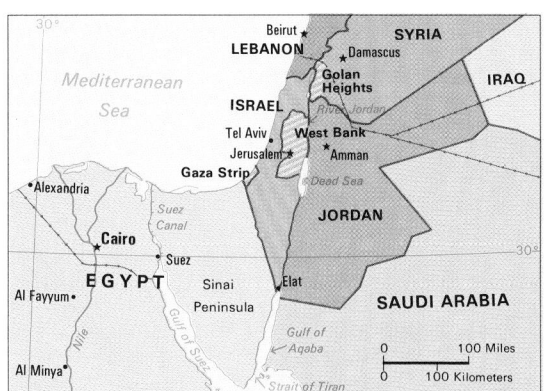

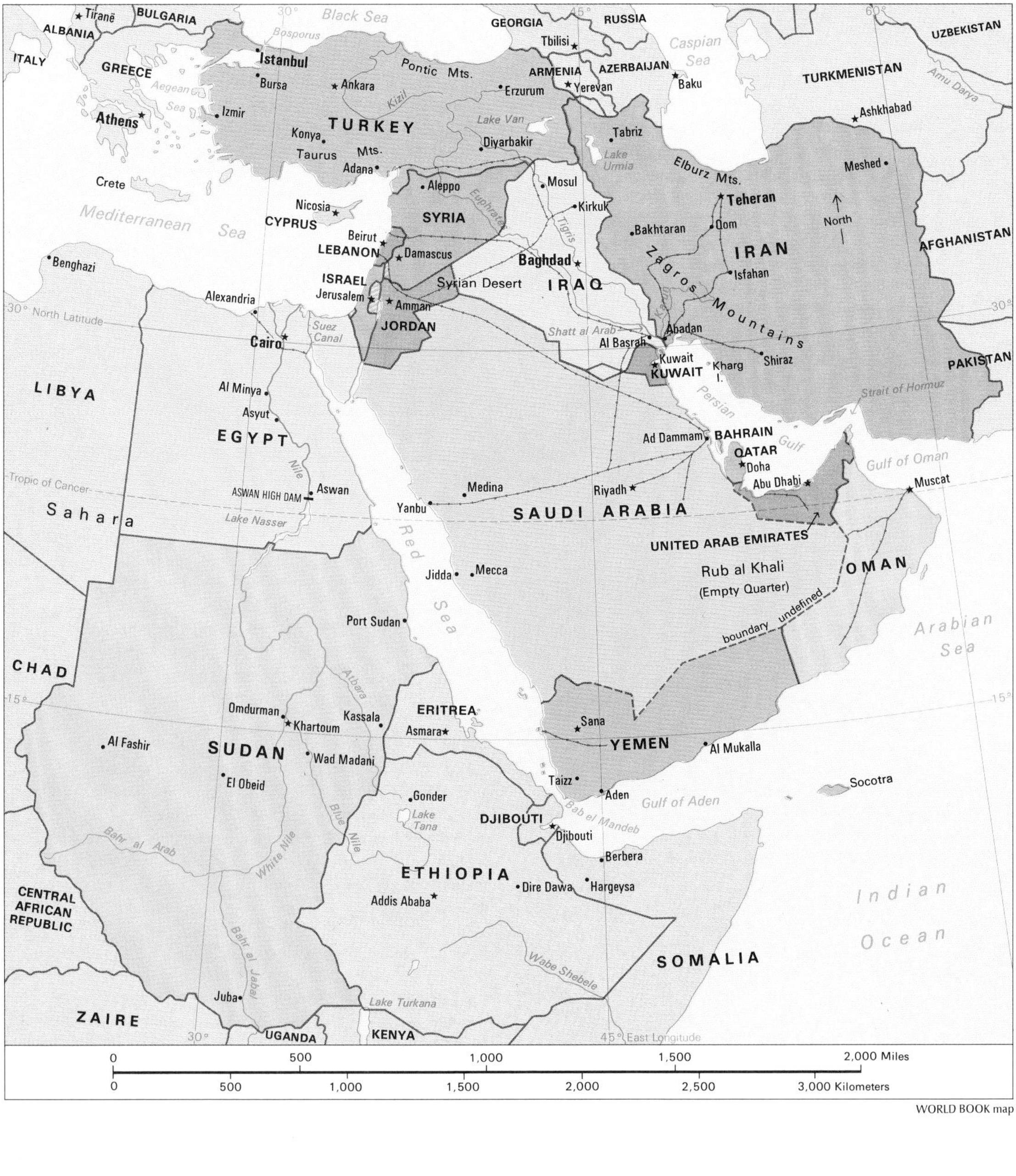

30°
Beirut •★
SYRIA
LEBANON
★ Damascus
Golan Heights
IRAQ
Mediterranean Sea
ISRAEL
River Jordan
Tel Aviv •
West Bank
Jerusalem ★
• Amman
Gaza Strip
Dead Sea
• Alexandria
Suez Canal
JORDAN
Cairo ★
30°
• Suez
EGYPT
Sinai
Peninsula
Elat •
Al Fayyum •
Gulf of Aqaba
SAUDI ARABIA
Al Minya •
0   100 Miles
Strait of Tiran
0   100 Kilometers

★ Tiranë   **BULGARIA**   30°   *Black Sea*   45°   **GEORGIA**   **RUSSIA**   60°
ALBANIA
Bosporus
Tbilisi •
Caspian Sea
UZBEKISTAN
ITALY
GREECE
★ **Istanbul**
Pontic Mts.
★ Erzurum
ARMENIA **AZERBAIJAN**
★ Yerevan
Baku •
TURKMENISTAN
Aegean Sea
Bursa •
★ Ankara
Kizil
Athens ★
• Izmir
TURKEY
Lake Van
Tabriz •
Elburz Mts.
Meshed •
Ashkhabad •
Konya •
Taurus
Mts.
Diyarbakir •
Lake Urmia
Crete
Adana •
Mosul •
North
AFGHANISTAN
Nicosia ★
• Aleppo
• Kirkuk
★ **Teheran**
CYPRUS
SYRIA
• Qom
Mediterranean Sea
Beirut ★
Bakhtaran •
LEBANON
★ Damascus
Baghdad ★
IRAN
• Isfahan
ISRAEL
Syrian Desert
IRAQ
Zagros Mountains
PAKISTAN
Jerusalem ★
★ Amman
Shatt al Arab
Abadan •
30°
JORDAN
Al Basrah •
• Shiraz
Cairo ★
Suez Canal
★ Kuwait
Strait of Hormuz
LIBYA
Alexandria
KUWAIT
Kharg I.
30° North Latitude
Al Minya •
Persian Gulf
Benghazi •
Asyut •
Ad Dammam •
BAHRAIN
EGYPT
QATAR
Gulf of Oman
• Doha
Abu Dhabi ★
Muscat •
Tropic of Cancer
ASWAN HIGH DAM
Aswan •
Medina •
Riyadh ★
UNITED ARAB EMIRATES
Sahara
Lake Nasser
Yanbu •
SAUDI ARABIA
OMAN
Red Sea
Rub al Khali
(Empty Quarter)
Arabian Sea
Jidda •   • Mecca
boundary undefined
CHAD
Port Sudan •
15°
15°
Omdurman •
Kassala •
ERITREA
• Sana
Al Fashir •
★ Khartoum
Asmara ★
YEMEN
• Al Mukalla
SUDAN
• Wad Madani
Socotra •
• El Obeid
Taizz •
• Aden
Gulf of Aden
• Gonder
Lake Tana
DJIBOUTI
Bab el Mandeb
Djibouti •
• Berbera
Blue Nile
ETHIOPIA
• Dire Dawa   • Hargeysa
Indian Ocean
CENTRAL AFRICAN REPUBLIC
Addis Ababa ★
White Nile
Wabe Shebele
SOMALIA
Bahr al Jabal
Juba •
Lake Turkana
ZAIRE
30°
UGANDA
KENYA
45° East Longitude

0   500   1,000   1,500   2,000 Miles
0   500   1,000   1,500   2,000   2,500   3,000 Kilometers

WORLD BOOK map

Hutchison Library

Oil is the Middle East's most important mineral product. Workers at Port Rashid in the United Arab Emirates, *above,* are loading barrels of oil onto oil tankers.

Religion and language. The Middle East is the birthplace of Judaism, Christianity, and Islam. More than 90 per cent of the area's population, including most Arabs, Iranians, and Turks, are Muslims. Christians make up about 7 per cent of the population. The largest Christian groups are the Coptic, Greek Orthodox, and Maronite denominations. Jews, who make up only 1 per cent of the population, live in Israel.

The chief language of the Middle East is Arabic. Written Arabic is the same throughout the region, but the spoken language differs from country to country. Persian is the official language of Iran. People in Turkey speak Turkish. Most Israelis speak Hebrew. Other languages of the Middle East include Baluchi, Greek, and Kurdish.

The land

In the northern part of the Middle East, mountains border interior plateaus. The Pontic Mountains and the Taurus Mountains rise in Turkey, and the Elburz and Zagros mountains extend across Iran.

The southern part of the Middle East is a vast arid plateau. Several large deserts lie in this area. The Western and Eastern deserts of Egypt are part of the Sahara. The Rub al Khali, known in English as the Empty Quarter, stretches across southern Saudi Arabia.

The Middle East has two major river systems—the Tigris-Euphrates and the Nile. The Tigris and Euphrates begin in the mountains of Turkey and flow through Syria and Iraq. In Iraq, the rivers meet and form the Shatt al Arab, which empties into the Persian Gulf. The Nile flows north through Sudan and Egypt to the Mediterranean Sea.

Economy

Agriculture has long been the Middle East's most important economic activity. More than half the people are

farmers. But the discovery of oil in the Middle East in the early 1900's has radically changed the economy of some countries. Oil production has become a major industry. Manufacturing is increasing, particularly the manufacture of products made from oil. In some countries, especially Egypt, tourism is a major industry.

Agriculture. The chief crops of the Middle East include barley, cotton, oranges, sugar cane, tobacco, and wheat. Many Middle Eastern farmers do not own their land. But since World War II, a growing number have become owners of the small farms they work. In such countries as Egypt and Iraq, the amount of farmland has doubled since the late 1800's. The use of fertilizers, improved equipment, and better irrigation methods have helped bring about the increase. But many farmers continue to use traditional machinery and methods. They cannot afford tractors and other heavy equipment.

Mining. Oil is by far the most important mineral product of the Middle East. The region has about three-fifths of the world's known oil reserves. The major oil producers are Iran, Iraq, Kuwait, Oman, Qatar, Saudi Arabia, and the United Arab Emirates. Most of the oil is sold to European countries and Japan. The governments of the oil-producing countries use much of the income from oil sales to build roads, develop new industries, and provide services for their people.

In 1960, some oil-producing countries formed the Organization of Petroleum Exporting Countries (OPEC) to gain more control over oil prices. During the Arab-Israeli War of 1973, some Arab members of OPEC stopped or reduced oil shipments to countries supporting Israel. Prices of oil in those countries rose sharply.

Other minerals mined in the Middle East include coal, iron ore, and phosphates. Coal mines operate in Iran and Turkey. Egypt and Turkey produce iron ore. Jordan supplies a fifth of the world's phosphates.

Manufacturing. The major manufacturing countries of the Middle East are Egypt, Iran, and Turkey. Together, these three countries produce 6 per cent of the world's refined sugar and 5 per cent of its cement and cotton cloth. The Middle East also produces small amounts of fertilizers, paper, and steel. Israel manufactures a variety of specialized technological products, such as computer parts and fighter aircraft. In the late 1960's, the oil-producing countries began to develop industries that make use of oil. These industries include the manufacture of chemicals and plastics.

History

Early civilizations. People lived in parts of the Middle East as early as 25,000 B.C. It was in this region that agriculture began around 8000 B.C. Between 3500 and 3100 B.C., two of the world's earliest great civilizations—those of Sumer and Egypt—developed in the region. The Sumerian civilization developed on the fertile plain between the Tigris and Euphrates rivers (see **Sumer**). It was later absorbed by the Babylonian Empire. The Egyptian civilization arose in the Nile Valley (see **Egypt, Ancient**). About 1900 B.C., a people called the Hittites came to power in what is now Turkey. Other peoples, such as the Hebrews and the Phoenicians, also organized societies in the region.

Beginning in the 800's B.C., a series of invaders conquered these civilizations. The invaders included the Assyrians, the Medes, the Persians, and, finally, Alexander the Great. Alexander conquered the Middle East in 331 B.C. and united it into one empire. He died in 323 B.C. The next 300 years, called the *Hellenistic Age,* brought great achievements in scholarship, science, and the arts.

By 30 B.C., the Romans had conquered much of the Middle East. During Roman rule, Jesus Christ was born in Bethlehem and died in Jerusalem. Christianity spread throughout the Roman Empire, replacing pagan cults. Christianity was the major religion of the Middle East until the rise of Islam in the A.D. 600's.

Islamic empires. Muhammad, the founder of Islam, was born in Mecca in about 570. In 622, he moved to the oasis of Medina, where he became the head of a small religious and political community. After his death in 632, his followers, called Muslims, conquered what are now Egypt, Iraq, and Syria. Many of the conquered people adopted Islam and the Arabic language. By 711, Arab Muslim rule extended from what is now Spain in the west to Iran in the east. Muslims of the Umayyad family ruled these lands from the city of Damascus. In 750, the Abbasid family overthrew the Umayyads and made Baghdad the capital of the Islamic Empire.

During Abbasid rule, groups of Muslim Turks invaded from central Asia. The most important were the Seljuk Turks. They took over Baghdad in 1055, and soon after, they conquered what are now Syria and Palestine. By the end of the 1000's, the Abbasid Empire was declining, and independent dynasties were emerging. In 1258, Mongols from China conquered Baghdad and destroyed the remains of the Abbasid government.

In the 1300's, the *dynasty* (family of rulers) of the Ottoman Turks became established in Anatolia (now Turkey). In the early 1500's the Ottomans added the Arab lands of the Middle East to their empire. By that time, they had also advanced into the Balkan Peninsula and had become a military threat to Europe. In the 1700's and 1800's, the Ottoman Empire declined in power and size in the face of new, strong states that developed in Europe. By World War I (1914-1918), some European countries had gained much economic and political influence in the Middle East.

World War I. During World War I, the Ottoman Empire joined with Germany against Great Britain, France, Italy, and Russia. Arabs who hoped to win independence from the Ottoman Turks supported the European Allies. Britain promised to help create independent Arab governments in the Middle East after the war. But Britain also agreed with France to divide the Middle East into zones of British and French rule and influence. In 1917, Britain issued the Balfour Declaration, which supported the creation of a Jewish homeland in Palestine—but without violating the civil or religious rights of the Arabs there (see **Balfour Declaration**).

In 1923, the defeated Ottoman Empire became the Republic of Turkey. The League of Nations divided most of the Arab lands of the Middle East into mandated territories (see **Mandated territory**). France took control of Lebanon and Syria. Britain received the mandates for Iraq, Jordan (called Trans-Jordan until 1949), and Palestine. Britain also kept control over Egypt, which it had conquered in 1882. The Arabs conducted a struggle for independence in the years after the war. Many territories gained independence in the 1930's and 1940's.

Palestine. In Palestine, Arab mistrust of Great Britain grew during the 1930's. Between 1933 and 1935, more than 100,000 Jewish refugees fled to Palestine from Nazi Germany and Poland. The Jewish immigration alarmed the Palestinian Arabs, who wanted Palestine to become an independent Arab state. In 1936, they called a general strike that almost paralyzed Palestine. They declared the strike would last until the British halted Jewish immigration. But after about five months, the Arabs ended the strike without achieving their goals. However, they continued to oppose British control.

In 1947, Great Britain asked the United Nations (UN) to deal with the Palestine problem. The UN voted to divide Palestine into two states, one Arab and one Jewish. The Jews accepted this solution and established the State of Israel on May 14, 1948. The Arabs, who made up about two-thirds of the population of Palestine, rejected the plan. The next day, five Arab states—Egypt, Jordan, Iraq, Lebanon, and Syria—attacked Israel. The Israelis defeated the Arabs.

When the war ended in 1949, Israel had about half the land that the UN had assigned to the Arab state. Egypt controlled the Gaza Strip, and Jordan occupied and later annexed the West Bank of the Jordan River. The city of Jerusalem was divided between Israel and Jordan. About 700,000 Palestinian Arabs had fled or been driven out of the land that was now Israel. They became refugees in Gaza, the West Bank, Syria, and Lebanon.

Continuing conflict. The 1950's and 1960's were years of radical change in the Middle East. A new generation led by young army officers took over the governments of many Arab states. They overthrew leaders who had cooperated with Great Britain and France. They hoped to bring about a political unification of the Arab world and to remove any European influence. Gamal Abdel Nasser, the leader of Egypt, became the symbol of these hopes. In 1956, Nasser seized the Suez Canal in Egypt from its British and French owners. In response to Nasser's action, Britain, France, and Israel invaded Egypt. Pressure from the United States, the Soviet Union, and other nations forced the invaders to withdraw.

In May 1967, the Arabs believed Israel was planning a major attack on Syria. Nasser sent Egyptian troops into the Sinai Peninsula and closed the Straits of Tiran, the entrance to the Israeli port of Elat. On June 5, the Israeli air force retaliated by destroying most of the air forces of Egypt, Syria, and Jordan. In the following six days, Israel seized the Sinai Peninsula and the Gaza Strip from Egypt, the Golan Heights from Syria, and the West Bank (including East Jerusalem) from Jordan. Almost 1 million Palestinian Arabs came under Israeli rule.

After the Six-Day War, no solution was reached in the Arab-Israeli conflict. The Arabs wanted Israel to withdraw from the land it had conquered. Israel demanded negotiations and Arab recognition of its right to exist.

The Palestine Liberation Organization (PLO), founded in 1964, became an important force in the Middle East after the 1967 war. The PLO is a confederation of Palestinian Arab groups that wants to establish an Arab state in Palestine. It includes associations of lawyers, teachers, laborers, and other groups, as well as guerrilla fighters who staged terrorist attacks and commando raids against Israel. The Arab nations recognized the PLO as the representative of the Palestinian people.

A historic agreement between Israel and the Palestine Liberation Organization (PLO) was signed on Sept. 13, 1993, in Washington, D.C. The two bitter enemies agreed to work to end their conflicts. Following the signing, Israeli Prime Minister Yitzhak Rabin, *far left,* and PLO leader Yasir Arafat, *near left,* shook hands as United States President Bill Clinton looked on.

AP/Wide World

In October 1973, Egypt and Syria launched a surprise attack against Israel. They were driven back by the Israelis. Most of the fighting ended by November.

Attempt at peace. In 1977, Egyptian President Anwar el-Sadat declared his willingness to make peace. In 1978, Sadat, Israeli Prime Minister Menachem Begin, and U.S. President Jimmy Carter held discussions at Camp David in the United States. The discussions resulted in an agreement called the Camp David Accords. Israel agreed to withdraw from Egypt's Sinai Peninsula. Egypt and Israel pledged to negotiate with Jordan and the Palestinians to grant some form of self-rule to the West Bank and the Gaza Strip.

Egypt and Israel signed a peace treaty in 1979, and Israel withdrew from the Sinai. But no progress was made in deciding the future of the Gaza Strip and the West Bank following the treaty.

Recent developments. In the 1970's and 1980's, Islam emerged as a strong force in Middle Eastern politics. The region continued to be troubled by conflicts.

In the 1970's in Lebanon, an uneasy balance between the Muslim and Christian communities collapsed. The conflict was sparked by the presence of armed PLO members in the country. The Muslims supported the PLO fighters, and the Christians opposed them. But at the heart of the conflict was the fact that Lebanon's growing Muslim population demanded more power in the government. The Christians opposed Muslim demands for increased power. In 1975, civil war broke out between various Muslim and Christian forces. In 1991, agreements between the opposing sides led to an end of most of the fighting in Lebanon.

A revolution occurred in Iran in 1979. Muslim religious leader Ayatollah Ruhollah Khomeini and his followers took control of the government. Khomeini declared Iran to be an Islamic republic. In 1980, Iran and Iraq went to war over territorial disputes and other disagreements. The fighting continued for eight years. In August 1988, the two nations agreed to a cease-fire plan.

The Arab-Israeli conflict flared up again at the end of 1987. Arab residents of the Gaza Strip and the West Bank demonstrated against Israel's occupation. Israeli troops killed about 300 protesters. Several Israelis were also killed.

In August 1990, Iraq invaded Kuwait. The United States and other nations sent military forces to Saudi Arabia to defend that country against a possible Iraqi invasion. These nations and Saudi Arabia formed an allied military coalition. In January 1991, war broke out between Iraq and these nations. In February, the allied coalition defeated Iraq and forced its troops to leave Kuwait. For more information, see **Persian Gulf War.**

In October 1991, a peace conference began between Israel on one side, and Middle Eastern Arab nations and Arab residents of the Gaza Strip and the West Bank on the other side. In separate discussions in 1993, Israel and the PLO agreed to recognize each other. On Sept. 13, 1993, they signed an agreement that included steps for ending their conflicts. The agreement provided for the start of a plan for self-government for, and Israel's withdrawal from, the Gaza Strip and the West Bank.

Dina Le Gall and Michel Le Gall

Related articles in *World Book* include:

Countries

Bahrain	Israel	Qatar	Turkey
Cyprus	Jordan	Saudi Arabia	United Arab
Egypt	Kuwait	Sudan	Emirates
Iran	Lebanon	Syria	Yemen
Iraq	Oman		

Other related articles

Arabs	Islam	Petroleum
Desert	Mediterranean Sea	

See also *Middle East* in the Research Guide/Index, Volume 22, for a *Reading and Study Guide.*

Outline

I. People
  A. Ancestry   C. Religion and language
  B. Way of life
II. The land
III. Economy
  A. Agriculture   C. Manufacturing
  B. Mining
IV. History

Questions

What is the major religion of the Middle East?
What is the region's most important mineral product?
Whose discussions resulted in the Camp David Accords?
Why did some oil-producing countries form OPEC?
When did the Middle East become part of the Ottoman Empire?
What were the sources of conflict between Christian and Muslim groups in Lebanon in the 1970's?
When did the PLO become prominent?
What is the chief language of the Middle East?
What did the United Nations do in 1947 regarding Palestine?
Where is the Empty Quarter?

Additional resources

The Cambridge Encyclopedia of the Middle East and North Africa. Ed. by Trevor Mostyn. Cambridge, 1988.
Fisher, Sidney N., and Ochsenwald, William. *The Middle East: A History.* 4th ed. McGraw, 1990.
The Middle East. 7th ed. Congressional Quarterly, 1991.
The Middle East and South Asia. Stryker-Post. Published annually. Also suitable for younger readers.

Middle school is a school designed for students in sixth, seventh, and eighth grade. Some middle schools include fifth grade. In a number of communities, students attend middle school rather than junior high school. Middle schools are sometimes called *intermediate schools.* Middle schools try to meet the special needs of children of the sixth, seventh, and eighth grades. Most children of this age are entering *puberty.* This period of rapid growth marks the end of childhood and the start of physical and sexual maturity. Middle schools try to help students understand the physical and social changes of puberty.

Many middle schools use a method of instruction called *individualized learning,* also called *individualized instruction.* This system enables each student to advance at his or her own speed and receive individual help from the teacher. The schools also use *team teaching,* in which several teachers share the responsibility for teaching a group of students.

Middle schools began in the United States about 1960 and their number has increased steadily. In the 1960's, many schools became overcrowded. To relieve the crowded conditions, some communities built middle schools. In the early 1980's, the United States had about 6,000 middle schools. Donald H. Eichhorn

See also Junior high school.

Middle West. See United States (Regions).

Middleton, Arthur (1742-1787), was a South Carolina signer of the Declaration of Independence. He was a leader in the Revolutionary War in America (1775-1783).

Between 1765 and 1776, Middleton served in the colonial legislature and in the Provincial Congress of South Carolina. While in the congress, he helped write South Carolina's Constitution of 1776. He also served as a member of the first South Carolina Council of Safety, which provided transitional government after the colonial government was overthrown. He was a delegate to the Continental Congress in 1776 and 1777 and to the Congress of the Confederation in 1781. The British captured him in 1780 at the siege of Charleston, S.C. He was born near that city. Robert A. Becker

Midge is any of a large family of small flies. Midges look like tiny mosquitoes, but they do not bite. There are about 2,000 species of midges, about 670 of which live in North America. Midges have slender bodies and long, thin legs. Adult males have feathery antennae. These insects often appear at dusk in large numbers that look like a moving haze.

The *larva* (immature form) of a midge resembles a worm. It may be green, white, or red. Red larvae are often called *bloodworms.* Midge larvae are found in mud, in water, or on decaying plant matter. They are a major source of food for larger insects and fish.

Several families of flies that have the word *midge* as part of their name are not really midges. These include the biting midges, also known as *punkies* or *no-see-ums.* Biting midges have stout bodies and a painful bite. They are seen near lakes and rivers and at the beach. Some people call biting midges *sand flies* (see **Sand fly**).

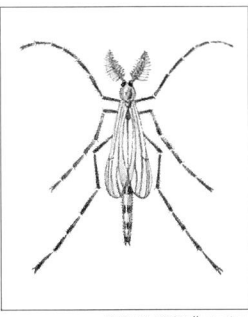

Scientific classification. Midges belong to the midge family, Chironomidae. Biting midges make up the biting midge family, Ceratopogonidae.

WORLD BOOK illustration by James Teason

A common midge

Sandra J. Glover

Midget. See Dwarf.

Midnight sun is a term used for the sun when it can be seen 24 hours a day in the earth's polar regions. At the North Pole, the sun never sets for six months, from about March 20 to September 23. At the South Pole, the sun remains above the horizon from about September 23 to March 20. The length of periods of continuous

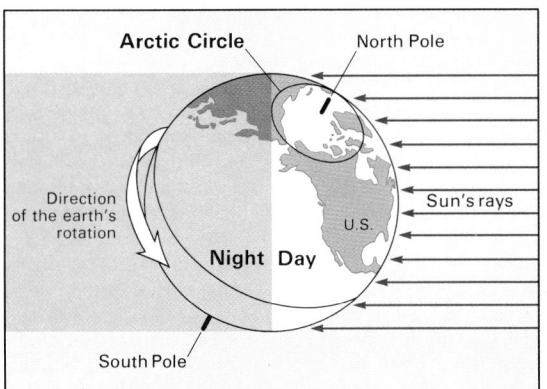

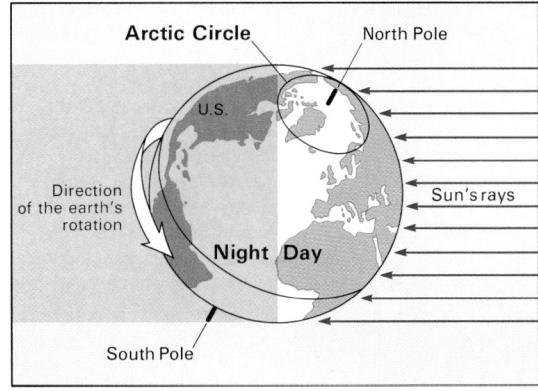

WORLD BOOK graphs

The midnight sun provides continuous sunlight in the Arctic Circle for a few days around June 21, *above.* In the illustration at the left, both the Arctic Circle and the United States are in sunlight. In the illustration at the right, the rotation of the earth has turned the United States away from the sun into darkness, but the Arctic Circle remains in sunlight.

sunlight decreases as the distance from either pole increases. At an imaginary line called the Arctic Circle, such a period occurs for only a few days around June 21. At another imaginary line, the Antarctic Circle, it lasts for a day or two around December 21.

The midnight sun is caused by the tilting of the earth's axis in one direction as the earth travels around the sun. One pole slants toward the sun for six months, while the other pole slants away from the sun and receives no sunlight. As the earth revolves around the sun, it also spins on its axis. This spinning motion makes the sun appear to rise and set at regular intervals, causing day and night on most of the earth.   C. R. O'Dell

See also **Antarctic Circle; Arctic Circle; Day.**

Midway, Battle of. See World War II (The tide turns); Midway Island.

Midway Island lies 1,300 miles (2,090 kilometers) northwest of Honolulu in the Pacific Ocean. It is made up of two islands in an atoll 6 miles (10 kilometers) in diameter. It has an area of 2 square miles (5 square kilometers) and a total coastline of about 20 miles (32 kilometers). Midway has a population of about 470. The United States discovered Midway in 1859, and annexed it in 1867. United States companies built a cable relay station there in 1903, and an airport in 1935. The U.S. Navy Department controls the island.

The Battle of Midway was one of the main naval battles in World War II. From June 4 to June 6, 1942, U.S. land- and carrier-based planes attacked a Japanese fleet approaching the islands. They sank four aircraft carriers and one heavy cruiser. The United States lost the destroyer *Hammann* and the aircraft carrier *Yorktown.*

The Battle of Midway was the first decisive U.S. naval victory over the Japanese in World War II. It crippled Japan's naval air power and ended Japan's attempt to seize Midway as a base from which to strike Hawaii. Many military experts believe it was the turning point in the Pacific campaign.   Robert C. Kiste

See also **World War II** (The tide turns).

Midwestern States are Illinois, Indiana, Iowa, Kansas, Michigan, Minnesota, Missouri, Nebraska, North Dakota, Ohio, South Dakota, and Wisconsin. For information on these states, see **United States** (Regions) and the articles on the states that make up the region.

Midwife is a person who helps women give birth. A midwife also gives care and advice during the patient's pregnancy and after the baby is born. Midwives work in birthing centers, patients' homes, and hospitals.

In the United States, trained midwives are called *nurse-midwives.* They are registered nurses who have been certified by the American College of Nurse-Midwives. Some states require nurse-midwives to have a special license. Other states allow them to practice under their nursing license.

Nurse-midwives emphasize that childbirth is a natural, normal process. They help the family have a safe and satisfying birth experience. Most nurse-midwives accept only patients who will probably have a normal delivery. However, they must be able to recognize signs of difficulty during childbirth. If necessary, a physician is called, or the patient is moved to a hospital.

Lay midwives have no formal training in midwifery. Traditionally, most lay midwives have worked in rural areas that have relatively few doctors. A few states license lay midwives, but lay midwifery is illegal in most states.   Lois Kazmier Halstead

Midwife toad is the name of certain small toads of central and southwestern Europe. Midwife toads are also called *obstetrical toads.* They received their name because the male helps care for the eggs. Adult midwife toads are about 2 inches (5 centimeters) long. The fe-

J. Andrada, Bruce Coleman Ltd.

The male midwife toad carries the fertilized eggs like a bunch of grapes attached to its hind legs until the tadpoles hatch.

male lays from 20 to 60 eggs in two strings. The male fastens them to his legs and carries them until they hatch. He usually hides on land beneath a stone or underground while he carries the eggs. He comes out after dark and bathes the eggs in a pond or stream. After three weeks he takes the eggs into the water, and tadpoles hatch from them.

Scientific classification. Midwife toads belong to the family Discoglossidae. The most common species is *Alytes obstetricans.*   J. Whitfield Gibbons

Mies van der Rohe, *MEEZ van duhr ROH uh,* **Ludwig** (1886-1969), was one of the most influential architects of the 1900's. He won fame for the clean, uncluttered design of his buildings of brick, steel, and glass. His architectural philosophy is sometimes summarized by the phrase "less is more."

Mies, as he was called, was born in Aachen, Germany. He built his first steel-framed building in 1927 at the Werkbund exposition he directed in Stuttgart, Germany. Two years later, he built his famous German Pavilion at an international exhibition in Barcelona, Spain. It featured onyx partition walls, a hovering slab roof, and travertine walls. The building enclosed space in an abstract manner through its asymmetrically placed wall elements that extended beyond the body of the building.

In 1930, Mies became director of the Bauhaus school of design in Dessau, Germany. That same year, he built the Tugendhat house in Brno, Czechoslovakia. This house applied his abstract principles of composition to domestic architecture. In 1932, Mies moved the Bauhaus to Berlin where he remained until it closed in 1933.

Mies moved to the United States in 1938. He became director of the school of architecture, planning, and design at the Armour Institute in Chicago, later the Illinois Institute of Technology (IIT). In 1939, Mies began planning a new campus for IIT. He left the symmetrical steel skeletons of the buildings exposed and combined them with great expanses of glass and carefully arranged panels of brick (see **Architecture** [Ludwig Mies van der

Lake Shore Drive apartments (1950-1952) in Chicago (WORLD BOOK photo by Dan Miller)

Apartment towers by Mies van der Rohe show the geometric simplicity of his steel and glass designs.

Rohe). One of his most praised buildings is the Seagram Building (1958) in New York, which he co-designed with Philip Johnson. It shows his love of fine materials and regular forms that he believed were applicable to any type of building.　　Nicholas Adams

See also **Bauhaus**; **Chicago** (Architecture); **Furniture** (The Bauhaus).

Additional resources

Carter, Peter. *Mies van der Rohe at Work.* Praeger, 1974.
Mies Van der Rohe: Architect as Educator: 6 June through 12 July 1986: Catalogue for the Exhibition. Ed. by Rolf Achilles and others. Univ. of Chicago Press, 1986.
Schulze, Franz. *Mies van der Rohe: A Critical Biography.* University of Chicago, 1985.
Spaeth, David A. *Mies van der Rohe.* Rizzoli, 1985.

Mifflin, Thomas (1744-1800), represented Pennsylvania at the Constitutional Convention of 1787 and signed the Constitution of the United States. Mifflin played only a minor role at the convention, seldom joining in debates. But he was highly popular in Pennsylvania and served the state throughout his life.

Mifflin was born in Philadelphia of Quaker parents. He was elected to the Pennsylvania Assembly in 1772 and became a member of the First Continental Congress in 1774. After the Revolutionary War in America began in 1775, he joined the army and soon became quartermaster general of General George Washington's troops. Mifflin resigned from his post in 1777. About the same time, he became involved in a plot to remove Washington as commander in chief. Mifflin then returned to the Pennsylvania Assembly, where he favored the interests of business. He served in the Congress of the Confederation from 1782 to 1784 and as chief executive of Pennsylvania from 1788 to 1799.　　Richard D. Brown

Mignonette, *MIHN yuh NEHT,* is an attractive garden plant of North America and Europe. Its name comes from a French word that means *little darling.* The mignonette has a low, bushy mass of smooth, soft-green leaves. The tiny flowers grow on tall spikes. The flowers are yellowish-white with reddish pollen stalks inside, and they have a delightful fragrance. Gardeners have produced larger-flowered mignonettes, but they are not as fragrant. Some cultivated varieties make excellent border plants. The mignonette grows best in a cool temperature and a light soil. It is a hardy plant that may be grown from seed plantings in May and July.

WORLD BOOK illustration by Robert Hynes

Mignonette

Scientific classification. The mignonette is in the mignonette family, Resedaceae. Its scientific name is *Reseda odorata.*　　Robert A. Kennedy

Migraine. See Headache.

Migrant labor is a farm labor force that moves into a region temporarily to help harvest and process crops. Migrants usually harvest fruits and vegetables that must be picked as soon as they ripen. Few of these workers settle permanently in any community. In the United States, most migrants are American Indians, blacks, Mexican Americans, Mexicans, or Puerto Ricans. No one knows how many migrants work in the United States. Estimates range from 125,000 to more than a million.

Temporary farmworkers generally receive low wages and often cannot find continuous work. Many migrants do not work in one place long enough to qualify for such government aid as food stamps and disability insurance. They are not protected by federal laws concerning hours, wages, and union membership that cover industrial workers. Many migrant families live in run-down, unsanitary housing. They often lack adequate food or medical care, and many suffer malnutrition or other health problems.

Many migrant workers have difficulty finding other kinds of work because they lack education. Only about a fifth of the migrant children go beyond sixth grade. Migrant youngsters tend to fall behind in their education because they change schools frequently. Some migrant children miss classes because they work to help support their family. Many schools sponsor special programs to promote the education of migrant children who temporarily live in the area. The federal Comprehensive Employment and Training Act of 1973 provided vocational training for adult migrants.

During the late 1960's, the California labor leader Cesar Chavez organized what is now the United Farm Workers of America (UFW). Many farm operators opposed the union, which seeks higher pay for migrants. They believed that increased labor costs would result in smaller profits and higher food prices. By 1970, some growers had signed UFW contracts that provided wage increases. However, most migrants today are not protected by such contracts.   Warren Van Tine

See also **Chavez, Cesar Estrada; United Farm Workers of America.**

Additional resources

Ashabranner, Brent K. *Dark Harvest: Migrant Farmworkers in America.* Dodd, 1985. Suitable for younger readers.
Coles, Robert. *Uprooted Children: The Early Life of Migrant Farm Workers.* Univ. of Pittsburgh Press, 1970.
Shotwell, Louisa R. *The Harvesters: The Story of the Migrant People.* Octagon, 1979. First published in 1961.

Migration, in biology, is the movement of animals to a place that offers better living conditions. Many birds, fishes, insects, and mammals regularly migrate to avoid unfavorable changes in weather or food supply. Human beings also migrate, but they do so for political and social reasons as well as biological ones. For information on human migrations, see **Immigration.**

Biologists use the term *migration* to describe several types of movements. Some biologists, particularly those who study insects, refer to one-way journeys as migrations. Such movements take place when animals leave an area in search of better living conditions, and neither they nor their descendants necessarily return to the original area.

Other biologists refer to the long-term historical changes in the distribution of animals as migrations. But most biologists define migrations as regular, round-trip movements between two areas. Each area offers more favorable living conditions than the other at some point in the animals' lives. This article discusses such regular, round-trip migrations.

Migrations take place on land, in water, or in the air. Some animals migrate only short distances. For example, many frogs and toads make yearly migrations of only a few miles or kilometers between their breeding and nonbreeding homes. Other migrations cover thousands of miles or kilometers. Arctic terns rank among the animals that migrate farthest. These birds travel as much as 22,000 miles (35,400 kilometers) in a year.

Types of migrations. Most migratory animals make (1) daily migrations or (2) seasonal migrations. Other migratory animals make only one or a few round-trip journeys during their lifetime.

Daily migrations take place among many of the small, drifting animals that live in the ocean. These *plankton animals* swim hundreds of feet or meters below the surface during the day. Each night, they migrate to the upper levels of the water.

Seasonal migrations take place twice a year. They occur in connection with periodic changes in temperature or rainfall. There are three main kinds of seasonal migrations: (1) latitudinal migrations, (2) altitudinal migrations, and (3) local migrations.

Bats, seals, and most species of migratory birds perform *latitudinal migrations.* That is, they migrate in basically a north-south direction. Some mountain-dwelling animals make *altitudinal migrations* up and down the mountain slopes. For example, mountain quail and mule deer spend summer in high elevations and move to lower areas in winter. Many tropical birds and mammals make *local migrations.* They move to moister regions of the tropics during the dry season and return to their original homes when the rainy season begins.

Less frequent migrations are made by some animals. For example, salmon are born in freshwater streams but soon migrate to the oceans. After several years, they return to their freshwater birthplaces to breed. Pacific salmon die soon afterward, but some Atlantic salmon swim back to the ocean and return to their birthplaces to breed as many as three times. Female sea turtles also make a number of migrations during their lifetime. Every two or three years, mature female green turtles and loggerhead turtles swim up to 1,400 miles (2,300 kilometers) to the beach where they hatched. There they lay their eggs.

Why animals migrate. Migration enables many species to take advantage of favorable weather and abundant food supplies in areas with changing environments. In some parts of the world, for example, food is plentiful in summer but becomes scarce during the cold winter months. Many animals that live in these regions migrate to warmer climates in the fall. They return in the spring when the weather warms up.

Many migrations are related to reproduction. Numerous animals migrate to breeding areas where their young have the best chance for survival. Migratory birds breed in their summer homes, where the food supply is most abundant. Humpback whales, on the other hand, migrate from their polar feeding grounds to give birth in tropical or subtropical waters. The warm waters provide little food for the adults, but the newborns could not survive in the polar seas.

What triggers migrations. Many animals begin their migrations after unfavorable environmental conditions set in. But among other species, the factors that trigger migrations are more difficult to explain. Many migratory birds, for example, leave their winter homes in the tropics while conditions there are still favorable. Among such species, migration may be triggered by environmental changes that are associated with the onset of warm weather and increased food in their northern breeding grounds. Experiments show that changes in daylength stimulate the migrations of many species of birds. In spring, the increasing hours of daylight trigger the release of certain *hormones* in the bodies of the birds. Hormones are chemical substances that regulate many body functions. In this case, the hormones stimulate preparations for the northward trip.

Besides using environmental clues, many seasonal migrators probably have an inborn "calendar" that tells them when to migrate. Some birds show seasonal migratory behavior even when kept under constant conditions in a laboratory. An inborn timing mechanism may trigger the migration of salmon and other animals that migrate at different stages of their life.

How migrating animals find their way. Research has shown that animals use a number of ways to gather directional information during migrations. Many are guided by the sun, the moon, and the stars. Such travelers must be able to allow for the movements of these heavenly bodies in determining direction. Others follow landscape features, such as rivers or mountain ranges.

Animals rely on more than visual cues when they migrate. Salmon find their way back to their birthplace by recognizing the odors of their home streams. Some animals are guided by changes in temperature, moisture, wind direction, or the earth's magnetic field. Sea dwellers may use information from ocean currents.

Many animals use more than one compass during their migrations. Some species of birds are guided by the sun during the day and the stars at night. Many biologists believe that they use the earth's magnetic field to find their way on cloudy days and nights.

Sometimes, migrating animals are forced from their normal route into an unfamiliar area. In some cases, the "lost" animals seem to be able to determine where they are and how to reach their original destination. This process is called *navigation*. Although there are many examples of what appears to be navigation by animals, scientists know little about how this process works.

Some of the most convincing evidence of animal navigation comes from experiments with shearwaters, sparrows, and homing pigeons. Scientists captured these birds and took them to unfamiliar areas up to thousands of miles or kilometers away. Most of the birds successfully returned to the original capture point.

Other experiments indicate that although young animals are able to migrate, they may not be able to navigate from unfamiliar areas. For example, European starlings normally migrate in a southwest direction from their breeding grounds around the Baltic Sea to wintering areas bordering the English Channel. Scientists captured both adult and young starlings that had reached the Netherlands during a migration. They took the birds to Switzerland and released them. The adult starlings corrected for the move and reached their normal wintering grounds. But the young birds, which were making their first migration, continued to fly southwest. The young birds ended up in Portugal, Spain, and southern France.   Sidney A. Gauthreaux, Jr.

Related articles in *World Book* include:

Animal (Animal migration)	Insect (Hibernation and migration)
Bird (Bird migration)	
Butterfly (Migration)	Seal
Fish (Fish migrations)	Whale (Migrations)

Additional resources

Animal Migration, Orientation, and Navigation. Ed. by Sidney A. Gauthreaux, Jr. Academic Press, 1980.
Baker, R. Robin. *Migration: Paths Through Time and Space.* Hodder & Stoughton, 1982.
The Mystery of Migration. Ed. by R. Robin Baker and others. Viking, 1981. First published in 1980.

Mikado, *muh KAH doh,* was the ancient title of the Emperor of Japan. The term was also used by foreigners. The term *Mikado* comes from the Japanese words that mean *exalted gate.* This shows the reverence the Japanese people held for their ruler.

After Chinese civilization came to Japan in the A.D. 500's, the Japanese came to call their emperor *Tenno,* which means *Heavenly Emperor.* The emperor is never referred to by his personal name. Recent emperors and their reigns are called by a name selected for them. The Emperor Akihito is known as the *Heisei Tenno* or *Heisei Emperor.*

Many historians consider Japan's ruling dynasty the oldest in the world. Japanese legend assigns the date 660 B.C. to the reign of Jimmu, the first Mikado. According to tradition, he descended from the Sun Goddess. Historians consider this date too early, but they trace the same family of emperors back through 125 reigns. The emperors after A.D. 400 are fully historical.

William S. Gilbert and Arthur S. Sullivan wrote a popular operetta, *The Mikado.* See **Gilbert and Sullivan.**
Marius B. Jansen

Mikan, *MY kuhn,* **George** (1924-   ), became the most famous—and perhaps the dominant—basketball player of the 1940's and early 1950's. In 1950, sportswriters selected Mikan as the outstanding college or professional player of the first half of the 1900's. Mikan, who stood 6 feet 10 inches (208 centimeters) tall, used his height, strength, and great hook shot to become the first of basketball's high-scoring centers.

George Lawrence Mikan was born in Joliet, Ill. He played college basketball at DePaul University, where he won all-America honors in 1944, 1945, and 1946. Mikan starred with the Minneapolis Lakers

UPI
George Mikan

professional team from 1947 to 1956. He led the Lakers to National Basketball Association (NBA) championships in the 1948-1949, 1949-1950, 1951-1952, 1952-1953, and 1953-1954 seasons. Mikan scored 11,764 points for the Lakers, an average of 22.6 points per game. Mikan led the league in scoring during the 1948-1949, 1949-1950, and 1950-1951 seasons.   Bob Logan

See also **Basketball** (picture: Outstanding centers).

Miki, *MEE kee,* **Takeo,** *TAH kayoh* (1907-1988), served as prime minister of Japan from December 1974 to December 1976. Miki also headed Japan's Liberal-Democratic Party. He resigned from office after the 1976 elections, in which the Liberal-Democrats retained control of the *Diet* (parliament), but with a smaller margin of victory than in earlier elections. Before and during Miki's term in office, some members of the Liberal-Democratic Party—though not Miki—had been accused of corruption. These charges contributed to the party's setback.

Miki was born in Donari Town on Shikoku Island, Japan. He entered Meiji University in Tokyo in 1929. Miki went to the United States in 1932. While attending universities there, he held such jobs as lecturer and radio broadcaster for Japanese-American audiences. Miki returned to Japan in 1936 and graduated from Meiji University the next year.

In 1937, Miki became the youngest representative ever elected to the Diet up to that time. He won reelection to the Diet a record 16 times. Miki served as deputy prime minister from 1972 to 1974. Through the years, he also held nine Cabinet posts and various offices in his party.   Lewis Austin

Milan, *mih LAN* (pop. 1,634,638), is the second largest city in Italy. Only Rome has more people. Milan ranks as Italy's chief center of finance, manufacturing, and international trade. The city's location in northern Italy, near a pass through the Alps, made it a center of trade as early as the A.D. 100's (see **Italy** [political map]). Many tourists visit Milan to see the city's priceless works of art. Milan is the capital of Lombardy, one of the political regions of Italy. The city's name in Italian is Milano.

The city covers 70 square miles (182 square kilometers). Much of Milan has a modern appearance, but it also includes a number of beautiful ancient buildings.

Milan's large Gothic cathedral stands in the heart of the city, and the nearby area includes many cultural attractions. Music lovers from many parts of the world hear concerts at La Scala, one of the leading opera houses of Europe. The Ambrosian Library is a treasure house of rare books and ancient manuscripts. Masterpieces of Italian painting hang in the Brera Art Gallery, the Gallery of Modern Art, the Poldi Pezzoli Museum, and the Sforza Castle. The fortresslike castle once served as the home of Milan's rulers. Leonardo da Vinci painted *The Last Supper,* one of the most famous masterpieces in history, on a wall of the Monastery of Santa Maria delle Grazie. Visitors to Milan may see this painting, which appears in the **Jesus Christ** article.

Milan has several major universities, including Bocconi University, the Catholic University of the Sacred Heart, and the University of Milan. The city also has several technical institutes.

The 36-story Pirelli Building, one of the tallest business structures in Italy, stands in an area of modern office buildings in the northern part of Milan. Industrial areas and residential suburbs extend from the city in all directions. Like other modern cities, Milan has such problems as air pollution and traffic jams.

People of Milan are called Milanese. They have a reputation for ambition, energy, and skill in business. Many earn their living as management personnel with a business firm or as skilled workers.

Many Milanese like to spend afternoons at a cafe in the city, making business deals or chatting with friends. A favorite gathering place is the Galleria Vittorio Emanuele II, a large, glass-roofed building that includes restaurants and shops. The Galleria, often called the "living room of Milan," stands near the cathedral.

Economy. Milan is the site of Italy's stock market and the headquarters of its major banks. The Italian advertising, publishing, and design and fashion industries are also centered in the city. The Milan area has thousands of small and medium-sized factories and several huge manufacturing plants. Leading products of Milan include chemicals, electric appliances, textiles, tires, and transportation equipment. The city is a hub of major highways and railroad lines, and it has two major airports—Linate and Malpensa.

History. Around 400 B.C., the Celts, a people of western Europe, founded a town on the site of what is now Milan (see **Celts**). In 222 B.C., the Romans conquered the town, which they named Mediolanum. Mediolanum, later called Milan, became a Roman military base and also a center of trade between Rome and central Europe. By the A.D. 200's, it ranked as one of the largest cities of the Roman Empire. Barbaric tribes invaded Milan and other parts of Europe during the late 400's, and the empire fell in 476. The invasions ended trade, and Milan became a small town.

The city regained importance in the 1000's as European trade and commerce expanded. From 1277 to 1535, Milanese nobles governed the city. They hired great art-

The Galleria in Milan is a large glass-roofed building that houses numerous restaurants and shops. The famous landmark is a popular meeting place of the people of Milan.

ists who created beautiful buildings and works of art.

The Spanish Empire took over Milan in 1535, and Austria gained control of the city in 1714. French forces led by Napoleon conquered Milan in 1796, but Austria regained the city in 1815. Milan became part of the Kingdom of Sardinia in 1859 and part of the newly formed Kingdom of Italy in 1861. The city developed some of Italy's first modern industries in the late 1800's.

Benito Mussolini, who ruled Italy as dictator from 1922 to 1943, founded his Fascist movement in Milan in 1919. Allied bombings damaged large areas of Milan during World War II (1939-1945), but the people rebuilt their city. The 1950's and 1960's brought great industrial growth to Milan. Many people came from southern Italy to work in the city's factories. This increase in population led to a severe housing shortage. But in the 1960's and 1970's, the city helped finance the construction of hundreds of new apartment buildings.   David I. Kertzer

For the monthly weather in Milan, see **Italy** (Climate). See also **Milan Cathedral.**

Milan Cathedral is a large church in Milan, Italy. It was begun in 1385, and is primarily Gothic in style. As construction continued for several centuries, the cathedral also has Renaissance and baroque ornament. It was completed in 1813 by the order of Napoleon I.

The cathedral is built of white Carrara marble in the plan of a Latin cross. It is 520 feet (158 meters) long and

Ted Spiegel, Black Star
Milan Cathedral in Italy is one of Europe's largest churches. Its roof is covered with 135 marble spires, each bearing a statue.

205 feet (62 meters) wide. The cathedral is noted for its elaborate decoration, which includes marble spires each bearing a life-sized statue of a saint, Biblical character, or historical figure. There are more than 3,000 statues in the interior and exterior of the cathedral. The cathedral dominates a large public square in the center of the city.   J. William Rudd

Milan Decree was a fundamental step in the *Continental System,* a plan of French Emperor Napoleon I to destroy Britain by ending British trade with continental Europe. Napoleon issued the decree on Dec. 17, 1807.

The Milan Decree supplemented Napoleon's Berlin Decree of 1806, which had begun the Continental System. The Berlin Decree barred British ships from entering ports that were under French control. In early 1807, the British fought the Berlin Decree by issuing the *Orders in Council,* which required neutral ships to stop at British ports before sailing to ports controlled by France. The British loaded the ships with British goods before allowing them to proceed to the French-controlled ports. The Milan Decree said that France could seize any ship that obeyed the Orders in Council.

Although the Milan Decree increased the effectiveness of the Continental System, Napoleon could not adequately enforce it because the British had the most powerful navy afloat. But Napoleon did cause great distress to neutral powers. The decree led the United States to adopt severe acts to protect its commerce. Napoleon eventually convinced the United States that he would withdraw his decree. In this way, Napoleon turned American anger against the British and furnished a cause for the War of 1812 between the United States and Britain.   Eric A. Arnold, Jr.

See also **Continental System; Napoleon I** (Fall from power); **War of 1812** (Causes of the war).

Mildew is the name of several kinds of fungi that attack plants and some products made from plants and animals. The name comes from a Middle English word, *mealdew,* meaning *spoiled meal.* There are two main classes that damage living plants: *powdery mildew* and *downy mildew.* The term *mildew* also can be applied generally to any fungus that grows in a damp place.

Powdery mildews attack green plants. There are about 50 different kinds of powdery mildews, and some of them can attack several different plants. About 1,500 different kinds of flowering plants may be infected by powdery mildew. These include the gooseberry, pea, peach, rose, apple, cherry, and grape.

Powdery mildew usually grows on the surface of the leaves, but it may also grow on the stems and fruits. The mildew forms white blotches that consist of many *hyphae* (threads). These hyphae send out branches that absorb nutrients from the cells of leaves, stems, or fruits. The hyphae also produce cells called *spores* by which the mildew reproduces. Certain *fungicides* (chemical solutions that kill fungi) can be used to protect plants.

Downy mildews produce yellow spots on the upper surfaces of the leaves or young fruits. After a mildew attacks the top of a leaf, small sporelike structures develop from the *stomata* (breathing pores) on the bottom of the leaf. These sporelike structures may produce even tinier spores that swim in the dewdrops on the surface of the leaf. Infections occur as these spores send hyphae into the leaf or fruit tissue.

Downy mildews attack many plants, including grape, cucumber, cabbage, onion, and lettuce. In 1845 and 1846, a fungus that was related to downy mildew almost destroyed the Irish potato crop, and a terrible famine followed. One way to protect plants from downy mildew is to spray them with a copper-based fungicide such as *Bordeaux mixture.* In addition, scientists have developed

Dan Guravich, Photo Researchers

Downy mildew attacks many crop plants. This picture shows a normal soybean leaf and one spotted by downy mildew.

disease-resistant plants that can withstand either downy mildews or powdery mildews, or both classes.

Mildew is a serious problem in damp tropical countries because it attacks clothes unless they are kept dry. Even in temperate regions, clothing should not be allowed to remain wet long.

Mildew may attack bookbindings in damp climates. Books kept in damp or poorly ventilated places also are subject to mildew. To protect books from mildew, keep the volumes in an enclosed, dry bookcase. If books must be stored in an open place, good air circulation will help prevent mildew.

Applying certain chemical solutions to bookbindings may prevent mildew. These solutions, as well as the fungicides used to protect plants from mildews, are highly poisonous and should be used with extreme care.

Scientific classification. Mildews belong to the division Eumycota in the kingdom Fungi. The powdery mildews are in the family Erysiphaceae. The downy mildews are in the family Peronosporaceae.   Joe F. Ammirati

See also **Fungi; Fungicide; Mold.**

Mile is a unit of length. In the inch-pound system of measurement customarily used in the United States, the unit used to measure land distances is the *international*

statute mile, or *international land mile.* It is equal to 5,280 feet or 320 rods.

The mile was first used by the Romans. The Roman mile was about 5,000 feet long and had 1,000 paces, each 5 feet in length. The term *mile* comes from *milia passuum,* the Latin words for *a thousand paces.* In the metric system, the unit used to measure land distances is the *kilometer.* One mile equals 1.609 kilometers.

In 1959, the United States adopted the *international foot,* which was slightly smaller than the foot then in use in the United States. The old foot is now known as the *survey foot* and is used only for surveying. The *survey mile,* which equals 5,280 survey feet, is about $\frac{1}{8}$ inch longer than the international statute mile.

Distances on the sea are measured in *nautical, geographical,* or *sea miles.* The *international nautical mile* used primarily in the United States equals exactly 1.852 kilometers, or approximately 1.151 international statute miles. One international nautical mile equals almost exactly 1 minute of the circumference of the earth's surface. The value of 1.852 kilometers per international nautical mile can be derived by dividing the approximate circumference of the earth—40,000 kilometers—by 360 degrees, dividing the result by 60 (the number of minutes in 1 degree), and rounding to three decimal places.

Richard S. Davis

See also **Knot; League; Weights and measures.**

Miles, Nelson Appleton (1839-1925), a noted American military officer, served in the Civil War, the Indian wars, and the Spanish-American War. He rose to the rank of lieutenant general in the United States Army, the Army's highest rank of his day, without a formal military education. In 1892, he received the Medal of Honor for his service in the Civil War.

Miles was born near Westminster, Mass. He entered the army as a volunteer lieutenant when the Civil War started in 1861. He fought in nearly every battle in the East, suffered several wounds, and won rapid promotion. In 1866, he became a colonel in the regular Army.

From 1869 to 1890, Miles led campaigns against the major Indian tribes in the West. The Army's most successful Indian fighter, he defeated the Apaches and forced Geronimo, one of their fiercest warriors, to surrender in 1886. In 1894, Miles commanded troops sent

Roman mile   about 5,000 feet

Kilometer   3,280.840 feet

International nautical mile   6,076.115 feet

International statute mile   5,280 feet

Different miles measure distances on land, on sea, and in the air. The Roman mile was about 5,000 feet. The metric system uses kilometers to measure distances. A nautical mile equals about $\frac{1}{60}$ of one degree of the distance around the earth. In the 1500's, people in England measured distances in 660-foot furlongs, so Queen Elizabeth I made the statute mile 8 furlongs, or 5,280 feet.

by President Grover Cleveland to Chicago during the Pullman Strike, a violent labor dispute (see **Pullman Strike**). He became Commanding General of the Army in 1895. In the Spanish-American War, Miles led the invasion of Puerto Rico in 1898. In 1901, he was promoted to lieutenant general. He retired in 1903.   James E. Sefton

Milhaud, *mee YOH,* **Darius,** *da RYOOS* (1892-1974), was a French-born composer noted for his works for the stage. Milhaud wrote 15 operas, 13 ballets, and music for other ballets and for motion pictures. The French poet Paul Claudel wrote the *librettos* (words) for several of Milhaud's works, including his famous opera, *Christophe Colomb* (1928). Milhaud's best-known ballet, *La creation du monde* (*The Creation of the World,* 1923), reflects his interest in jazz.

Milhaud was born in Aix-en-Provence in southern France, and this region inspired his *Suite Provençale* for orchestra (1936). Milhaud received his music training at the Paris Conservatory from 1910 to 1915. In 1917 and 1918, he served with the French Embassy in Rio de Janeiro, Brazil, and became acquainted with Brazilian popular music. Milhaud used this music in *Saudades do Brasil* (*Memories of Brazil,* 1920-1921), which he composed for piano and later arranged for orchestra.

During the 1920's, Milhaud belonged to a group of young French composers called *Les Six.* He left France in 1940 during World War II (1939-1945). That year, Milhaud joined the faculty of the music department at Mills College in Oakland, Calif. He retired in 1974.

Richard Jackson

Milhous, *MIHL hows,* **Katherine** (1894-1977), was an American author and illustrator of children's books. She came from a Pennsylvania Dutch background, which influenced her work. Milhous won the 1951 Caldecott Medal for her illustrations for *The Egg Tree* (1950), a picture book she wrote about Pennsylvania Dutch Easter customs. Milhous also wrote and illustrated such picture books as *Lovina: A Story of the Pennsylvania Country* (1940), *Patrick and the Golden Slippers* (1951), *Appolonia's Valentine* (1954), and *Through These Arches: The Story of Independence Hall* (1964). She also illustrated a number of books written by children's authors Alice Dalgliesh and Mabel Leigh Hunt.

Milhous was born in Philadelphia. She studied at the Pennsylvania Academy of Fine Arts.   Jill P. May

Military Academy, United States. See United States Military Academy.

Military aircraft. See Aircraft, Military.

Military discharge ends a person's period of service in the armed forces. Members of the Armed Forces of the United States receive one of five types of discharges: (1) honorable, (2) general, (3) undesirable, (4) bad conduct, and (5) dishonorable.

Honorable discharges are issued to all those whose military behavior has been proper and whose performance of duty has been "proficient and industrious." A person holding such a discharge is entitled to all benefits available to veterans.

General discharges are given to those whose military records do not entitle them to an honorable discharge. A general discharge may be issued if a person has been found guilty by a general court-martial. Veterans with general discharges are eligible for the same benefits as those holding honorable discharges.

Undesirable discharges are given to people considered unfit for military service. They cancel many veteran benefits and prohibit reenlistment in any service.

Bad conduct discharges are given for reasons such as absence without leave, insubordination, and destruction of private property. A bad conduct discharge deprives the holder of all veteran benefits and certain citizenship rights.

Dishonorable discharges may be given for such reasons as theft, desertion, and destruction of government property. They cancel all veteran benefits and some citizenship rights.   Ann Alexander Warren

Military insignia. See Insignia; also the pictures in Air Force, U.S.; Army, U.S.; Marine Corps, U.S.; Navy, U.S.

Military Justice, Uniform Code of. See Uniform Code of Military Justice.

Military police are the trained police maintained by a nation's armed forces. On military installations, these men and women have powers similar to those of civilian police. Military police enforce military laws and regulations, control traffic, prevent and investigate crime, apprehend military absentees, maintain custody of military prisoners, and provide physical security for military personnel and property. In combat situations, military police also maintain custody of prisoners of war. When necessary in combat, military police can be ordered to fight as infantry.

In the United States armed forces, police duties are carried out by Military Police (MP) for the Army and Marine Corps, the Shore Patrol for the Navy and Coast Guard, and the Security Police for the Air Force. The functions of the Shore Patrol are more limited than those of other military police (see **Shore Patrol**).

Ann Alexander Warren

Military school is an institution that educates people and trains them in military arts and sciences. All major countries operate military schools. Many United States military schools are privately operated.

Government military schools. In the United States, each branch of the armed forces has its own military schools. Courses in these schools for enlisted men and women range from the repair of guided missiles to food service. The armed forces maintain service academies, officer-candidate schools, and reserve officers training corps for individuals who are learning to become officers. Service academies of the armed forces are the U.S. Air Force Academy at Colorado Springs, Colo.; the U.S. Coast Guard Academy at New London, Conn.; the U.S. Military Academy at West Point, N.Y.; and the U.S. Naval Academy at Annapolis, Md.

Some military schools prepare officers for duties they may have to perform in peace or war. Schools at the first level cover specialized subjects. Schools at the next level stress command and staff work. They include the Army War College, Naval War College, Air War College, Army Command and General Staff College, College of Naval Command and Staff, Marine Corps Command and Staff College, and Air Command and Staff College. The National Defense University is a joint-service institution and operates at the highest level. It consists of the National War College and the Industrial College of the Armed Forces, both in Washington, D.C., and the Armed Forces Staff College in Norfolk, Va.

Other military schools and colleges train students of junior high school, high school, and college age. Students wear distinctive uniforms, and learn the fundamentals of military training, strategy, and tactics. Leading state-controlled military colleges include the Citadel in Charleston, S.C.; and Virginia Military Institute in Lexington, Va. Some schools that formerly accepted only males now accept females as well.

In other countries. The United Kingdom trains its officers at the Royal Military Academy located in Sandhurst, the Army Staff College in Camberley, the National Defence College in Latimer, and the Royal College of Defence Studies in London. Canada has the Royal Military College of Canada in Kingston, Ont.; Royal Roads Military College near Victoria, B.C.; and Collège militaire royal de Saint-Jean in Saint-Jean, Que. The chief French military school is Saint-Cyr, in Coëtquidan, Brittany. Russia has the Frunze Academy in Moscow.

Ann Alexander Warren

Related articles in *World Book* include:

Armed Forces Staff College
Army War College
Naval War College
Quantico Marine Corps Combat
  Development Command
Royal Military College of Canada

United States Air Force Academy
United States Coast Guard Academy
United States Military Academy
United States Naval Academy

Military science is the study of scientific principles that control the conduct of war. It is also the application of those principles to battle conditions.

Related articles in *World Book* include:

Air force
Air Force, United States
Army
Army, United States
Logistics

Marine Corps, United States
Military training
Navy
Navy, United States
War

Military service, Compulsory. See Draft, Military.

Military training is training in the art and science of war. Modern military training is a great deal more complex than in ancient times. Battles then involved relatively simple formations, weapons, and equipment. Today, fighting troops must understand and be prepared to use mechanized equipment and intricate scientific instruments. They must be backed up by many more service troops than there are actual fighters. During World War II (1939-1945), nations trained both men and women in a variety of jobs. In some countries, women have also engaged in combat.

All soldiers first learn to obey orders. Combat soldiers learn to handle various weapons: machine guns, bayonets, rifles, pistols, and grenades. They learn how to handle explosives. Soldiers assigned to a specialized branch of the army get additional training for a particular job. For example, they may learn to drive a tank, to jump from an airplane, to operate radar, or to build a bridge.

Training schools. In the United States, the Army, Navy, and Air Force maintain a system of schools or training stations for officers and enlisted personnel. Each of these branches also has specialized schools for higher officer training. These schools include the Army War College, the Naval War College, and the Air University. The Armed Forces Staff College and the National Defense University are operated jointly by the services. The National Defense University includes the National War College and the Industrial College of the Armed Forces. The National War College teaches military strategy and related subjects in politics, economics, and social problems. The Industrial College of the Armed Forces prepares military officers for duties connected with *procurement* (purchase) and maintenance of supplies and equipment.

Military training for civilians. Many U.S. colleges and universities have Reserve Officers Training Corps units of the Army, Navy, and Air Force, which offer instruction for prospective officers. Students who successfully complete such training may be eligible for commissions in the regular Army, Navy, or Air Force. The Army also conducts a junior branch of its ROTC in some high schools and preparatory schools. The National Guard and Air National Guard are other volunteer organizations offering training to civilians. The individual states and territories conduct these groups.

Compulsory military training. From the days of the ancient Romans, many European countries have tried some form of enforced military service. France introduced a conscription law in 1792. Germany made the greatest progress in developing a military machine under nationwide conscription. It began its program after the Franco-Prussian War (1870-1871).

In the United States, the federal government first tried compulsory military training during the Civil War (1861-1865). Conscription laws providing for military training for male citizens were also in effect in the United States during World War I (1914-1918) and World War II. The first U.S. peacetime draft law was enacted in 1940.

Ann Alexander Warren

Related articles in *World Book* include:

Air Force, United States
Army, United States
Draft, Military
Marine Corps, United States
Military school

Militia
National Guard
Navy, United States
Reserve Officers Training Corps

Militia, *muh LIHSH uh,* includes all able-bodied persons who are liable to be called into the armed forces in time of national emergency. The militia of the United States includes the Air Force Reserve, Air National Guard, Army National Guard, Army Reserve, Marine Corps Reserve, and Naval Reserve.

Each of the 13 American Colonies required its citizens to enroll and train in the militia. Militiamen formed almost half of the army that fought in the Revolutionary War in America (1775-1783). The U.S. Constitution gave Congress the right to call up the militia to "execute the laws of the Union." The Militia Act of 1792 placed every "free able-bodied white male citizen" from the age of 18 to 45 in the militia. But it left the control and training of these units to each state. The act of 1903 made all male citizens subject to military service. It placed the militia, by then known as the National Guard, under the control of both state governments and the federal government (see **National Guard**).

The governments of ancient Egypt, Greece, and Rome all formed militias. Switzerland's militia system was set up in 1291. Militiamen in feudal England had to keep armor and weapons that were inspected twice a year.

Joel D. Meyerson

See also **Draft, Military** (The history of conscription); **Switzerland** (Defense).

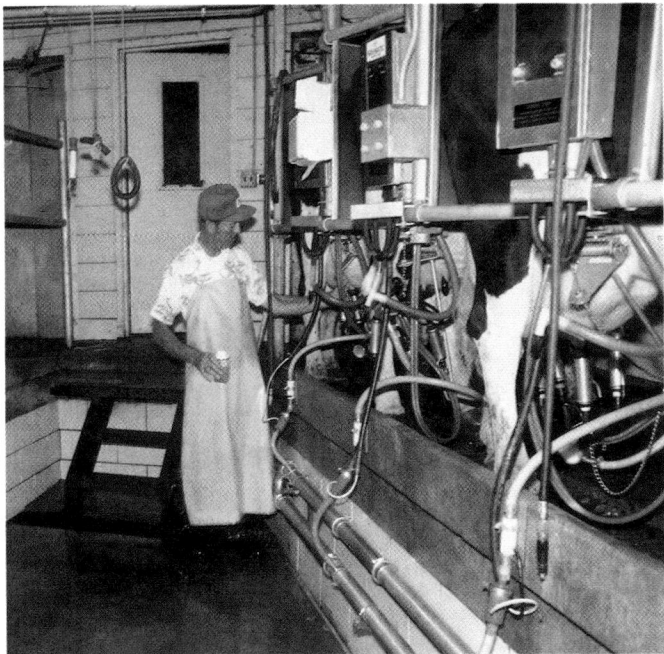

© Melissa Grimes-Guy, Photo Researchers
© Tom Tracy

The production of milk begins at a dairy farm, where machines milk the cows, *left.* The raw milk then goes to a dairy plant for processing. Finally, the milk is packaged, and the containers are stored in a large refrigerated room, *right,* to await delivery to stores and homes.

Milk

Milk is the most nourishing of all foods and a favorite drink of people throughout the world. Milk has almost all the *nutrients* (nourishing substances) that people need for growth and good health. In addition, milk has most of these nutrients in large amounts and in such proportions that they can work as a team to help keep the body strong and healthy.

All female mammals produce milk to nourish their young. But when we think of milk, we generally think of the milk that comes from cows. Cows provide most of the milk used in the United States, Canada, and many other countries. In some parts of the world, however, other animals produce the main supply of milk. Goat milk is popular in parts of Europe, Latin America, Africa, and Asia. Camels provide milk in the desert lands of Arabia, central Asia, and northern Africa. Some South Americans drink llama milk. In Arctic regions, people get milk from reindeer. Sheep provide much of the milk in Greece, Iran, and Turkey. Water buffalo supply milk in Egypt, India, Pakistan, and many countries of Southeast Asia.

Butter, cheese, ice cream, yogurt, and several other foods are made from milk. Milk—or one of its products—is also an ingredient in many foods, such as cakes, casseroles, puddings, and sauces. Milk is also used in mak-

Robert T. Marshall, the contributor of this article, is Professor of Food Science and Nutrition at the University of Missouri-Columbia and the coauthor of The Science of Providing Milk for Man.

ing numerous products besides food. For example, manufacturers use *casein,* the main protein in milk, to make waterproof glues, various plastics, and paints.

This article discusses the food value of cow's milk. It then deals mainly with the U.S. milk industry.

Food value of milk

This section discusses the nutrients in milk. It also examines the importance of milk in the human diet.

Nutrients in milk. The body needs six kinds of nutrients for energy, growth, and the replacement of worn-out tissue. These nutrients are (1) water, (2) carbohydrates, (3) fats, (4) proteins, (5) minerals, and (6) vitamins. Milk has been called "the most nearly perfect food" because it is an outstanding source of these nutrients. But milk is not "the perfect food" because it lacks enough iron and does not provide all vitamins.

Interesting facts about milk

Ancestors of today's dairy cows were wild cattle that roamed the forests of northern Europe many thousands of years ago.

Average yearly milk production per cow in the United States totals about 1,800 gallons (6,800 liters), approximately twice as much as in 1960.

Daily food for a dairy cow ranges from 40 to 60 pounds (18 to 27 kilograms) of feed. In addition, a cow requires 10 to 20 gallons (38 to 76 liters) of water a day.

First dairy cattle in what is now the United States were brought to the Jamestown colony in Virginia in 1611.

Record milk production by a cow in one year is 6,472 gallons (24,499 liters). This is an average of about 18 gallons (68 liters) per day, enough to provide 72 people with 1 quart (0.95 liter) each. A cow in Rochester, Ind., set the record in 1975.

Water is the most vital nutrient. The body needs water to carry out all its life processes. Cow's milk is about 87 per cent water.

Carbohydrates are a major source of energy for the body. The carbohydrate content of milk is mainly *lactose,* or *milk sugar.* In addition to providing energy, lactose helps the body absorb the minerals calcium and phosphorus in milk. Our bones and teeth consist largely of these minerals. Lactose also gives milk its sweet taste. See **Carbohydrate.**

Fats, like carbohydrates, provide energy. They also supply certain fatty acids that the body must have. Fat gives milk its rich flavor. Milk fat also contains vitamins A, D, E, and K and several other substances. One of these substances, *carotene,* gives milk its golden tint. Milk fat appears as tiny *globules.* A drop of milk contains about 100 million such globules. See **Fat.**

Proteins help the body grow and maintain itself. They also supply energy. The proteins in milk are *complete proteins*—that is, they contain all the *amino acids* (protein parts) needed for building blood and tissue. Only egg proteins and the proteins in some meats have a higher food value than milk proteins have. Casein makes up about four-fifths of the protein content of milk. It is found only in milk. See **Protein.**

Minerals, like proteins, help the body grow and remain healthy. Calcium and phosphorus are the most important minerals in milk. In fact, milk is the chief food source of calcium. Other minerals in milk include potassium, sodium, and sulfur and smaller amounts of aluminum, copper, iodine, iron, manganese, and zinc.

Vitamins are essential for growth, maintaining body tissue, and the prevention of such diseases as beriberi and rickets. Milk provides more vitamins—and in larger amounts—than do most other natural foods. Milk is an excellent source of vitamins A and B_2 and a good source of vitamin B_1. Other vitamins in milk include vitamins B_6, B_{12}, C, E, and K and niacin. Milk also has vitamin D, but the quantity is low. Most dairies add extra vitamin D to milk. See **Vitamin.**

All milk—human and animal—contains the same nutrients. The amounts differ, however. Compared with cow's milk, for example, the milk from a water buffalo has 3 times as much fat and $1\frac{1}{2}$ times as much protein but only about three-fourths the sugar. Human milk has fewer proteins and minerals than cow's milk but about $1\frac{1}{2}$ times as much sugar.

In the United States, the federal government requires that *whole* milk sold as food meet certain standards. The government specifies that whole milk must contain at least 3.25 per cent milk fat and 8.25 per cent nonfat milk solids. Some states require a higher percentage of nonfat milk solids in their milk. For example, California requires 8.7 per cent nonfat milk solids in its whole milk. Most cow's milk has about 3.5 per cent milk fat, 5 per cent lactose, 3.5 per cent protein, and 0.7 per cent minerals. The percentages differ somewhat between individual cows and breeds. The quality and composition of milk also depend on what a cow is fed and how the animal is cared for.

Milk in the human diet. Milk is an important part of most people's diet. It is the first food of newborn babies, whether they are breast-fed or bottle-fed. Because of its many nutrients, milk helps the body develop. Children who drink milk grow faster than other children who eat the same kinds of food but do not drink milk. Milk can also help people obtain the nutrients their diet might otherwise lack.

Doctors and nutrition experts disagree on exactly how much milk a person should drink. In general, they recommend that children and teen-agers drink at least three 8-ounce (240-milliliter) glasses a day. Adults should have at least one glass daily. Expectant mothers and mothers who are nursing their babies should drink three or four glasses a day.

Many people cannot drink the recommended amount of milk. For example, some adults can digest only a small amount of milk because their bodies are low in *lactase,* the chemical substance that breaks down milk sugar. In the United States, a small percentage of children are allergic to milk. Finally, many doctors recommend that patients who have a large amount of *cholesterol* in their bloodstream avoid drinking whole milk because of its cholesterol content. Cholesterol is a fatty substance that is found in all animal tissues. However, a high level of cholesterol in the bloodstream may contribute to *arteriosclerosis,* a disease of the arteries that can cause heart attacks. Skim milk contains little cholesterol.

Milk from farm to table

Millions of Americans enjoy pure, fresh milk every day, especially at mealtimes. But few realize the many steps required—first at a dairy farm and then at a processing plant—to get this milk to the dining table.

At a dairy farm, milk is produced under highly sanitary conditions by cows called *dairy cattle.* Most dairy cows in North America are the black and white Holstein-Friesian breed. See **Cattle** (Dairy cattle).

Production. Almost all U.S. dairy farmers use milking machines to milk their cows. Machines are faster and more sanitary than milking by hand. But some dairy farmers still do their milking by hand. See **Milking machine.**

The milk that cows produce is called *raw milk* until it has been pasteurized. Harmful bacteria grow rapidly in raw milk unless the milk is kept clean and cool. Dairy farmers therefore see that their cows and barns are clean, and they sanitize their milking equipment. Most

The composition of cow's milk

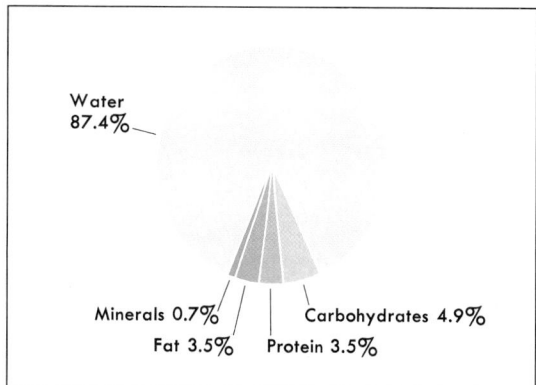

Water
87.4%

Minerals 0.7%   Carbohydrates 4.9%

Fat 3.5%   Protein 3.5%

Source: U.S. Agricultural Research Service.

farmers store raw milk in a refrigerated tank until it can be delivered to a processing plant. As a cow is milked, the milk flows into the tank and is cooled to less than 40 °F (4.4 °C).

Local, state, and federal agencies have set standards of cleanliness for dairy farms and processing plants. To make sure these standards are met, local health inspectors check farms and plants and conduct laboratory tests of milk. Cows are also tested periodically by veterinarians for two diseases, tuberculosis and brucellosis.

Almost all the fluid milk sold for table use in the United States is classified as *grade A.* Most communities have special rules regarding the sanitary conditions under which milk must be produced and processed to be classed as grade A. The rules are largely based on the Grade A Pasteurized Milk Ordinance, a set of recommendations developed by the U.S. Food and Drug Administration (FDA). The states voluntarily adopt this ordinance. Milk moves from state to state with minimal legal restraints. Representatives from various states work together to resolve problems concerning the sanitary quality of grade A milk. Many states also permit the sale of a *manufacturing grade* of milk. It is used chiefly in making such dairy products as butter, cheese, and ice cream.

Marketing. Most dairy farmers are members and joint owners of a dairy *cooperative.* A cooperative picks up the members' raw milk and sells it for them at the highest price to processing plants. Some cooperatives not only pick up the members' milk but also process it. See **Cooperative.**

The U.S. government sets minimum prices that farmers receive for their milk through a *price support program.* Under the program, the government buys dairy products when the farm price of milk falls below a minimum price. In 1986, the government purchased the right to sell milk from about 14,000 producers. These produc-

ers also agreed to sell a large number of their cows and to stay out of the milk production business for at least five years. This action was taken to reduce milk production and bring it more in line with consumer demand.

Transportation. A dairy cooperative operates large tank trucks to transport the milk of its members. At least every other day, a truck picks up milk from various dairy farms in an area and delivers it to a processing plant. The truck's tank is insulated to keep the milk cold, even in hot weather.

At each farm, the milk haulers examine and take samples of the milk before pumping it into the tank. The samples are important because all the milk from the various farms becomes mixed in the tank. The samples from each farm go to the local health department and the milk processor to be tested for composition and quality.

At a processing plant. More than 40 per cent of the milk produced in the United States is processed into various kinds of fluid milk or cream. Most of the rest is made into such dairy products as butter, cheese, and ice cream. A small amount is used to make special types of dairy products, such as *acidophilus milk.* This milk is often used for treating intestinal disorders. The following discussion describes the processing of fresh fluid milk. To learn how some other dairy products are made, see the table *Kinds of milk and milk products* on this page.

As soon as the tank truck arrives at a processing plant, laboratory technicians check the odor, taste, and appearance of the milk. They also measure the fat content, the number of bacteria, the amount of milk solids, and the acidity. Technicians further test the milk during and after processing. All this testing helps ensure the quality and purity of the milk. Milk is the most highly tested of all foods.

After the first tests, the milk is pumped into a large re-

Kinds of milk and milk products

There are many kinds of milk and milk products. They vary widely in flavor, texture, and use. This table briefly describes a few of these foods and the processes by which they are made.

Milk or milk product	Description	Manufacturing process
*Butter	Churned milk fat.	Pasteurized cream mechanically churned, causing its milk fat to form into butter.
*Cheese	Treated curd of milk.	Bacteria or other agent added to milk to form soft curd; liquid part of milk removed from curd; curd then made into different types of cheese.
Cream	Rich milk product containing at least 18 per cent milk fat.	Mechanically separated from nonhomogenized whole milk.
Cultured buttermilk	Low-fat milk with tangy flavor	Acid-producing bacteria added to pasteurized skim of low-fat milk; allowed to ferment until desired taste obtained.
Evaporated milk	Whole milk with about 60 per cent of its water removed; requires no refrigeration until opened.	Pasteurized whole milk heated in a vacuum to remove proper percentage of water; milk then canned, sealed, and sterilized; may also be sterilized first, then canned and sealed.
*Ice cream	Sweet, frozen dairy product.	Cream, concentrated milk, sugar, and flavoring mixed together and frozen; air whipped in to give proper texture.
Low-fat milk	Milk that has about 0.5 to 2 per cent milk fat.	Skim milk mixed with whole milk to obtain proper percentage of milk fat; mixture pasteurized and homogenized.
Skim milk	Milk that has about 0.1 per cent milk fat.	Mechanically separated from nonhomogenized whole milk.
Sour cream	Smooth, firm, tangy cream with at least 18 per cent milk fat.	Acid-producing bacteria added to cream, causing it to sour; cream chilled after proper flavor reached; also made by adding acid and flavoring directly to cream.
*Yogurt	Thick, custardlike form of milk.	Nonfat dry milk mixed with partly skimmed milk; bacteria and flavoring added; mixture ferments, forming tangy curd; curd chilled after desired flavor obtained; fruit and sugar often added.

*Has a separate article in *World Book.*

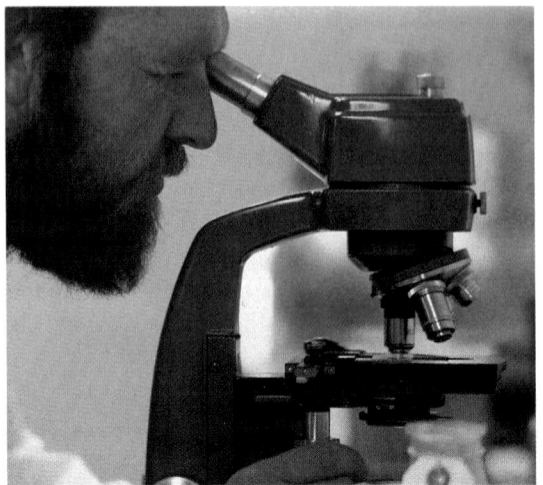

© Terry Wild

Testing milk's quality and purity is a constant activity at a dairy plant. This technician is using a microscope to check bacteria counts in milk samples.

frigerated storage tank. On its way to the tank, the milk passes through a *clarifier.* This machine removes any hair, dust, or similar matter that may be in the milk. After the milk is pumped from the storage tank, it goes through five basic steps. These steps, in order, are (1) separation or standardization, (2) pasteurization, (3) homogenization, (4) fortification, and (5) packaging.

Separation or standardization. Some of the milk that comes from the storage tank is separated. The rest is standardized. In separation, the cream, or fat, is mechan-

ically *skimmed* (separated) from milk. Some of the cream is then either bottled or used to make butter or other dairy products. Some of the remaining *skim milk* is also either bottled or used to make such foods as cottage cheese or cultured buttermilk. The rest of the cream and skim milk is used to standardize the milk that has not been separated.

In standardization, the fat content of milk is regulated. A device called a *Milko-tester* measures the fat content as the milk flows through a pipeline. If the content becomes lower than the desired level, cream is pumped in with the milk. If the fat content becomes higher, skim milk is pumped in. Standardization enables dairies to produce 2 per cent milk and other low-fat milks with a uniform fat content. It also ensures that the fat content of whole milk meets government requirements.

Pasteurization involves heating milk to kill disease-causing bacteria. Nearly all milk sold in the United States is pasteurized. Most is pasteurized by the *high-temperature short-time,* or *HTST, method,* which involves heating milk to 161 °F (72 °C) for 15 seconds and then quickly cooling it. Some milk is pasteurized by the *batch method*—that is, by heating it to 145 °F (63 °C) for 30 minutes. In a method called *ultrapasteurization,* milk is heated to at least 280 °F (138 °C) for 2 or more seconds and then cooled rapidly. Milk treated by any of these methods spoils quickly if not refrigerated. But milk pasteurized by the *ultrahigh-temperature,* or *UHT,* method keeps for months without refrigeration. In this method, milk is heated to about 300 °F (149 °C) for 6 to 9 seconds, then cooled rapidly and stored in sterile containers. UHT-treated milk is also called *sterilized milk.*

Homogenization. Almost all the whole milk and low-fat milk sold in the United States is homogenized. Ho-

How a dairy processes whole milk

After raw milk arrives at a dairy, some of it is separated into skim milk and cream. The rest is processed into whole milk. The first step in the process is *standardization.* A Milko-tester indicates whether cream should be added to increase the fat content or skim milk to lower it. After the proper fat content is reached, the milk is pasteurized, homogenized, and packaged as whole milk.

WORLD BOOK diagram by Lowell Stumpf

Raw Milk

Milko-tester checks fat content

Standardized Milk made by adding skim milk or cream

Skim Milk Storage Tank

Cream Storage Tank

Separator mechanically separates raw milk into skim milk and cream

Pasteurizer heats milk to kill harmful bacteria

Homogenizer breaks up fat globules

Packager fills and seals milk containers

mogenization breaks up the fat globules in milk so the globules do not rise to the top. A machine called a *homogenizer* forces the milk through tiny openings under great pressure. The process increases the number of fat globules and gives every drop of milk the same amount of cream. Milk that has been homogenized tastes richer than nonhomogenized milk. See **Homogenization**.

Fortification improves the food value of milk by adding certain nutrients, especially vitamins and proteins. Most dairies add vitamin D because the quantity is low in milk. They fortify skim milk with protein and vitamin A as well as vitamin D. A few dairies also add other vitamins and some minerals to milk.

Packaging is the final step in the processing of milk. Automatic packaging machines fill and seal milk containers, most of which are paper cartons or plastic bottles. Direct fluorescent light can damage milk that is packaged in certain kinds of plastic containers. It destroys some of the vitamins in milk and can change the milk's flavor. Some plastic containers consist of materials that filter out or reflect fluorescent light.

Refrigerated trucks deliver packaged milk to stores and homes. At one time, home delivery of milk was common in the United States. Today, almost all families buy their milk at a supermarket or other retail store.

The milk industry

Every state in the United States and every Canadian province produces milk. The U.S. dairy industry is concentrated in the *Dairy Belt,* which extends from New York to Minnesota. Wisconsin, California, and New York lead the states in milk production. Quebec and Ontario are the chief milk-producing provinces.

In the United States, milk producers receive about $20 billion a year for their products. The nation has about 1,700 dairy plants. About two-thirds of the plants process fluid milk. These plants employ about 84,000 workers. The rest of the plants make other milk products. Dairy plants process approximately $6\frac{1}{2}$ billion gallons (25 billion liters) of fluid milk yearly—enough to provide each U.S. citizen with 1 cup (0.24 liter) a day. Consumers in the United States buy about $50 billion worth of fluid milk and fluid milk products a year.

Canada has approximately 400 dairy plants. Canadian plants process about 670 million gallons (2.5 billion liters) of fluid milk annually.

History of the milk industry

No one knows when people first used animal milk for food. However, the people of ancient Babylon, Egypt, and India raised dairy cattle as early as 4000 B.C. At that time, the family cow was the chief source of milk. A family used as much milk as it needed and traded or sold the rest to neighbors. This practice is still common in some parts of the world.

In America, the family cow was especially common during colonial times. But by 1850, many U.S. farmers had begun to own several dairy cows and to supply milk to nearby homes. With the growth of cities, local laws prohibited keeping cows within city limits. Farmers outside the cities then began to increase the size of their herds and to establish dairy businesses.

As the dairy industry grew, several cities passed laws to control the sale of milk. Some of these laws made it il-

© Tom Tracy

Packaging machines automatically fill and seal milk containers with tremendous speed. The dairy worker above is adjusting a machine that packages about seventy 1-gallon (3.8-liter) plastic bottles of milk a minute.

legal to add water to milk or to remove cream from it. Boston passed the first such law in 1856. However, none of the early laws set health standards for milk. Many dairies added chemical preservatives to milk. But after some of these chemicals were found to be harmful, laws prohibited their use. Gradually, cities and states began supervising the industry to protect the public health.

Several inventions and new processes helped speed the growth of the milk industry. In 1856, an American inventor named Gail Borden received a patent for the first successful milk-condensing process. About 1885, dairies first used glass jars and bottles, which workers filled by

Leading milk-producing states and provinces

Amount of milk produced in a year

State/Province	Amount
Wisconsin	●●●●●●●●●●●●● 2,803,000,000 gallons (10,611,000,000 liters)
California	●●●●●●●●●●●◐ 2,568,000,000 gallons (9,721,000,000 liters)
New York	●●●●●●◖ 1,347,000,000 gallons (5,099,000,000 liters)
Pennsylvania	●●●●●● 1,205,000,000 gallons (4,561,000,000 liters)
Minnesota	●●●●●◖ 1,146,000,000 gallons (4,338,000,000 liters)
Quebec	●●●◖ 687,000,000 gallons (2,601,000,000 liters)
Texas	●●●◖ 650,000,000 gallons (2,461,000,000 liters)
Michigan	●●●◖ 628,000,000 gallons (2,377,000,000 liters)
Ontario	●●● 615,000,000 gallons (2,328,000,000 liters)
West Virginia	●●◖ 562,000,000 gallons (2,127,000,000 liters)

Figures are for 1992. Sources: U.S. Department of Agriculture; Statistics Canada.

hand. The invention of a bottling machine in 1886 made filling the containers easier and faster.

In 1890, Stephen M. Babcock, an American agricultural chemist, developed a test to measure the fat content of milk. This test still plays a role in the measurement of fat content. In the 1890's, a few dairy plants introduced pasteurization, a process invented by the French scientist Louis Pasteur. Homogenizers gradually came into use after 1900.

In the mid-1980's, researchers and certain dairy farmers in the United States began injecting a *synthetic* (laboratory-produced) substance called *bovine somatotropin* (BST) into test herds to increase the production of milk. This substance, also called *bovine growth hormone,* is almost identical to BST naturally produced by cows. Natural BST stimulates milk production in a cow that has given birth. Synthetic BST supplements the cow's supply of the natural hormone. In 1985, the FDA ruled that milk from the test herds was safe for human consumption. However, the FDA did not make a final decision regarding the commercial use of synthetic BST.

Robert T. Marshall

Related articles in *World Book* include:

Milk and milk products

Butter	Cheese	Kumiss
Buttermilk	Ice cream	Yogurt
Casein		

Milk production

Dairying	Homogenization	Pure food
Dehydrated food	Milking machine	and drug laws
Farm and farming	Pasteurization	

Sources of milk

Camel	Reindeer
Cattle (Dairy cattle)	Sheep
Goat (Products)	Water buffalo
Llama	Yak

Outline

I. **Food value of milk**
   A. Nutrients in milk   B. Milk in the human diet
II. **Milk from farm to table**
   A. At a dairy farm   B. At a processing plant
III. **The milk industry**
IV. **History of the milk industry**

Questions

What are some common food products made from milk?
What is a dairy *cooperative?* What is its purpose?
What are the three leading milk-producing states?
Why are some people able to digest only a small amount of milk?
What happens to milk during pasteurization? During homogenization?
What is *grade A* milk? *Raw milk?*
What do laboratory technicians at processing plants test in milk?
Why is milk such a nourishing food?
What other animals besides cows supply milk for human use?
How do farmers help prevent the rapid growth of bacteria in raw milk?

Milk snake is a type of kingsnake that farmers once believed took milk from cows. Today, scientists know that no snake is physically able to take milk from a cow. However, any snake might drink milk from a pail because of the milk's water content. There are many subspecies of milk snakes. The best-known subspecies is the *eastern milk snake.* Like other kingsnakes, the milk snake eats lizards and rodents. Milk snakes frequently

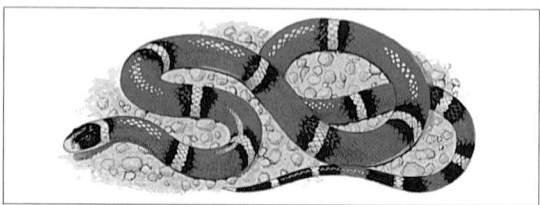

WORLD BOOK illustration by Richard Lewington, The Garden Studios
The milk snake is valuable to farmers because it eats the mice that live in and around farm buildings.

go into barnyards to hunt for rodents that nest there.

The eastern milk snake may be 4 feet (1.2 meters) long. Some other types of kingsnakes grow to be 6 feet (1.8 meters) in length. Eastern milk snakes are gray with dark-bordered chestnut blotches on the back and sides. Milk snakes found in the Western and Southern United States have a pattern of rings or blotches of reddish-orange, black, and either white or yellow.

Scientific classification. The milk snake is a member of the common snake family, Colubridae. Its scientific name is *Lampropeltis triangulum.*   Laurie J. Vitt

See also **Kingsnake.**

Milk sugar. See Sugar (Milk); Milk (Nutrients in milk).
Milking machine is a device that milks cows. Most dairies milk their cows with such machines instead of by hand. The machines cut costs, because they reduce the amount of labor needed to obtain milk. They also help keep the milk clean.

A milking machine consists of a number of tube-shaped cups, a *pulsator,* and hoses. Each cup is composed of a metal shell and a rubber liner. A cow's teats fit into the inner chambers created by the liners. A vacuum in each chamber holds the cup onto the teat. The space between the cup's liner and its shell forms the outer chamber. The pulsator regulates the milking process by changing the pressure in the outer chamber to pull milk from the teat. During the *milking phase,* the pulsator creates a vacuum. During the *rest* or *massage phase,* it produces normal pressure. This alternating pressure, which resembles the sucking of a calf, massages each teat to keep it healthy. After milk is drawn from the teat, the milk flows through the attached hoses and into a pail or pipeline.

Anna Baldwin, a New Jersey farm woman, invented the suction milking machine in 1878. But Carl Gustav de Laval, a Swedish engineer, developed the first commercially successful machine. This device went on the market in 1918.   Sidney L. Spahr

See also **Cattle** (picture: A milking parlor); **Farm and farming** (picture).

Milkweed is the name of more than 100 kinds of plants that have tufts of silky hairs on the seeds and contain a milky juice. The *common milkweed* is one of the best-known milkweeds in North America. It grows along roadsides and in fields and waste places in the eastern United States as far south as Georgia.

The stems of the common milkweed stand from about $3\frac{1}{4}$ to $6\frac{1}{2}$ feet (1 to 2 meters) high and bear large, hairy, pale-green leaves on short stalks. The purplish flowers grow in clusters at the tip of the stem. The flowers bloom from June to August and have a sweet odor that attracts insects. Each flower is shaped so that an in-

E. R. Degginger

The milkweed plant has large seed pods, *left,* that burst open and release the plant's seeds. Some of the seeds grow into new plants, which develop flowers, *right.* Milkweed flowers bloom along roadsides and in fields from June to August.

sect has to walk through masses of pollen before it reaches the nectar. The insect then flies away with two bundles of pollen on its legs and brings about *cross-pollination* when it visits another milkweed of the same kind (see **Pollen** [Cross-pollination]).

By autumn, large, rough seed pods have developed from the flowers of the milkweed. When the pods ripen and burst open, clouds of seeds are scattered by the wind. The milkweed can also reproduce itself from its creeping, underground roots. In 1942, milkweed floss was collected as a wartime substitute for the kapok fiber used in life belts. The milky juice of the milkweed contains small amounts of a rubberlike substance. One of the most attractive milkweeds is the *butterfly weed.*

Scientific classification. The milkweed is a member of the milkweed family, Asclepiadaceae. The scientific name for the common milkweed is *Asclepias syriaca.*   Jerry M. Baskin

Milky Way is the galaxy that includes the sun, the earth, and the rest of our solar system. The Milky Way Galaxy contains hundreds of billions of stars. Huge clouds of dust particles and gases lie throughout the Galaxy. *Milky Way* also refers to the portion of the Milky Way Galaxy that can be seen by the naked eye. On clear, dark nights, it appears as a broad, milky-looking band of starlight stretching across the sky. Dark gaps in the band

are formed by dust and gas clouds that block out light from the stars that lie behind them.

Shape of the Galaxy. The Milky Way is shaped like a thin disk with a bulge in the center. Stars, dust, and gases fan out from the central bulge in long, curving arms that form a *spiral* (coiled) pattern. For this reason, astronomers classify the Milky Way as a *spiral galaxy.* To someone far above the Milky Way, the Galaxy would resemble a huge pinwheel. However, because of our location inside the Galaxy, we see only the hazy light from the strip of stars around the earth.

The flat part of the Milky Way disk contains many young stars and small, irregularly shaped groups of stars called *open clusters,* also known as *galactic clusters.* It also has most of the Galaxy's dust and gases. A vast number of older stars are in the central bulge of the disk. The bulge and disk are surrounded by a sphere of stars known as a *halo.* The halo contains relatively old stars in dense, ball-like groups called *globular clusters.*

Size of the Galaxy. The diameter of the Milky Way is about 100,000 light-years. A light-year is the distance that light travels in one year—about 5.88 trillion miles (9.46 trillion kilometers). The Milky Way is about 10,000 light-years thick at the central bulge and much flatter toward the edges of the disk. Our solar system is located in the outskirts of the Galaxy, about 25,000 light-years away from the center. The distance between the stars in our section of the Milky Way averages about 5 light-years. Stars in the galactic center are about 100 times closer together. Most astronomers estimate that the total mass of the Milky Way is more than 100 billion times that of the sun (see **Mass**). Much of the mass is concentrated toward the center of the Galaxy.

The center of the Galaxy. All stars and star clusters in the Milky Way orbit the center of the Galaxy, much as the planets in our solar system orbit the sun. For example, the sun completes an almost circular orbit of the center once about every 250 million years. Almost all the bright stars in the Milky Way orbit in the same direction. For this reason, the entire galactic system appears to rotate about its center.

The clouds of dust and gases in the Milky Way prevent us from seeing very far into the center of the Galaxy. However, astronomers studying radio waves and infrared rays—which can penetrate the clouds—have

NASA

The Milky Way Galaxy is shaped like a disk with a bulge in the center. Astronomers obtained this image from a camera mounted on a scientific satellite. This camera photographs *infrared* (heat) rays, rather than visible light. The earth is located about 25,000 light-years from the Galaxy's center, roughly half the distance to the Galaxy's edge, so much of the disklike structure of the Milky Way is not shown in this image.

discovered that the central region gives off enormous amounts of energy. Studies with radio and infrared telescopes have also revealed a powerful gravitational force that seems to come from the exact center of the Galaxy. Some astronomers believe that the Milky Way's center is a massive *black hole,* an invisible object whose gravitational pull is so great that not even light can escape from it (see **Black hole**). They think the center's energy is generated when the black hole swallows gas and other matter from the surrounding Galaxy.   Mark Morris

See also **Galaxy; Nebula; Solar system; Star** (Stars in the universe [with picture]).

Additional resources

Bok, Bart J. and P. F. *The Milky Way.* 5th ed. Harvard, 1981.
Gallant, Roy A. *Once Around the Galaxy.* Watts, 1983. Suitable for younger readers.
Kühn, Ludwig. *The Milky Way: The Structure and Development of Our Star System.* Wiley, 1982.

Mill is a *money of account,* or coin term used in keeping accounts in the United States. A mill, which is not a coin, has the value of one-tenth of a cent.

Mill was the family name of three famous British writers—father, son, and the son's wife. They won distinction in philosophy, history, psychology, and economics.

James Mill (1773-1836) established his reputation as a writer with the publication of *A History of British India* (1817). This work was partly responsible for changes in the Indian government. It also won him a job with the East India Company in 1819. He headed the company from 1830 until his death.

In 1808, Mill met Jeremy Bentham, a political economist called the *father of utilitarianism.* The utilitarians believed that the greatest happiness of the greatest number should be the sole purpose of all public action (see **Bentham, Jeremy; Utilitarianism**). Mill adopted the utilitarian philosophy and became Bentham's ardent disciple and the editor of *St. James's Chronicle.*

His writings helped clarify the philosophical and psychological basis of utilitarianism. *Analysis of the Phenomena of the Human Mind* (1829) is a study of psychology. He wrote *Elements of Political Economy* (1821) for his son, and it became the first textbook of English economics. In *Fragment on Mackintosh* (1835), he states his views of utility as the basis of morals.

Mill was born in Scotland and graduated from Edinburgh University, where he studied for the ministry. He became a Presbyterian minister in 1798 but left the ministry in 1802 to become a journalist.

John Stuart Mill (1806-1873) became the leader of the utilitarian movement. Mill was one of the most advanced thinkers of his time. He tried to help the English working people by promoting measures leading to a more equal division of profits. He favored a cooperative system of agriculture and increased rights for women. He served as editor of the *Westminster Review* from 1835 to 1840 and wrote many articles on economics.

His greatest philosophical work, *System of Logic* (1843), ranks with Aristotle's work in that field. Mill applied economic principles to social conditions in *Principles of Political Economy* (1848). His other works include *Utilitarianism* (1863), *On Liberty* (1859), *The Subjection of Women* (1869), and *Autobiography* (1873).

Mill was born in London and was educated by his fa-

ther. By the age of 14, he had mastered Latin, classical literature, logic, political economy, history, and mathematics. He entered the East India Company as a clerk at 17. Like his father, he became director of the company. He retired after 33 years of service and was elected to Parliament in 1865.

Additional resources

Hollander, Samuel. *The Economics of John Stuart Mill.* 2 vols. Univ. of Toronto Press, 1985.
Packe, Michael. *Life of John Stuart Mill.* Macmillan, 1954. A standard source.

Harriet Taylor Mill (1807-1858) was the wife of John Stuart Mill and helped him write many of his works. She called for increased rights for women and workers and greatly influenced Mill's writings in these areas.

Many of John Stuart Mill's writings probably originated from discussions with Harriet. She helped him write *Principles of Political Economy.* Some scholars also consider her the coauthor of *On Liberty, The Subjection of Women,* and *Autobiography,* all of which were published after her death. But only the essay "Enfranchisement of Women" bears her name. It appears in her husband's *Discussions and Dissertations,* a four-volume work published from 1859 to 1875. In the introduction to *On Liberty,* he calls Harriet "the inspirer, and in part the author, of all that is best in my writings."

She was born Harriet Hardy in Walworth, near Durham, England. In 1826, she married John Taylor, a merchant. Harriet met John Stuart Mill about 1830, and they became close friends. Taylor died in 1849, and she married Mill in 1851.   H. W. Spiegel

Millais, *mih LAY,* **Sir John Everett** (1829-1896), an English painter, helped found the Pre-Raphaelite Brotherhood in 1848. The brotherhood was a group of poets and painters who believed that art should present moral messages through uplifting themes. Most of Millais's paintings have literary or religious subjects. He painted detailed and realistic pictures in the Pre-Raphaelite manner until about 1857. He then changed his style, painting sentimental pictures that became extremely popular. He also painted portraits of distinguished Englishmen of his time and illustrated books and periodicals.

Millais was born in Southampton. He was a child prodigy and attended classes at the Royal Academy of Arts when he was only 11 years old.   Douglas K. S. Hyland

See also **Pre-Raphaelite Brotherhood; Carlyle, Thomas** (picture); **Pizarro, Francisco** (picture).

Millar, Kenneth. See **Macdonald, Ross.**

Millay, *mih LAY,* **Edna St. Vincent** (1892-1950), was an American poet. Many of her poems have romantic themes. She wrote about love and death, about the self and the universe, and about the feelings of rebellious youth. In her treatment of these subjects, she combined sentimentality with wit and sophistication.

Millay was born in Rockland, Me., and graduated from Vassar College in 1917. She did some of her best work while very young. "Renascence," a poem about a personal religious experience, was written when she was only 19 years old. *A Few Figs from Thistles* (1920) was one of three works for which she won a Pulitzer Prize in 1923. The other two works were *The Ballad of the Harp-Weaver* and eight sonnets.

Millay's later poetry became increasingly concerned

with modern history. *Conversation at Midnight* (1937) deals with events that were leading to World War II. *The Murder of Lidice* (1942) tells about the destruction of a Czechoslovak town by German troops during the war. Millay was fond of the sonnet form, and her many sonnets were published in 1941. A definitive collection of her poems appeared in 1956. She also wrote several plays, including the one-act poetic fantasy *Aria da Capo* (1919).   William Harmon

Millennium, *muh LEHN ee uhm,* means any period of 1,000 years. But the term is usually used to refer to the period mentioned in the New Testament Book of Revelation (20: 1-6) as the time when holiness will prevail throughout the world (see **Revelation, Book of**).

Some people have interpreted the passage in Revelation as meaning that Christ will reign on earth either before or after the 1,000-year period. These views are known as *premillennialism* and *postmillennialism.*

Because the Book of Revelation frequently uses numbers symbolically, other people have interpreted this passage spiritually. They regard the millennium as the long period of time between Christ's first coming and His second coming. St. Augustine was the first to set forth this view, known as *amillennialism.* It is expressed in *The City of God.*   Joseph M. Hallman

Millepede. See Millipede.

Miller, Arthur (1915-   ), is a leading American playwright. His works record the conflict between the individual and the society which establishes the individual's moral code. Miller showed society's morality as valid in *All My Sons* (1947) and *A View from the Bridge* (1955). But in *Death of a Salesman* (1949), *The Crucible* (1953), *Incident at Vichy* (1964), and *The Price* (1968), he showed its morality as false. *Death of a Salesman,* which received a Pulitzer Prize, is generally considered Miller's masterpiece. It tells of Willy Loman, a traveling salesman who chooses popularity and material success as his goals. Destroyed by his choice, Loman commits suicide in the end. The play typifies Miller's belief that the "common man" is the modern tragic hero.

Miller's work generally follows the Ibsen school of realistic drama. But much of the action in *Death of a Salesman* is seen through Loman's mind, thus establishing Miller's debt to expressionistic drama.

Miller was born in New York City. He was married to actress Marilyn Monroe from 1956 to 1961. His autobiographical play *After the Fall* (1964) partly deals with his relationship with Monroe. Miller's other writings include *Focus* (1945), a novel; *The Misfits* (1961), a motion-picture script; and *The Theater Essays of Arthur Miller* (1978). In his drama *The American Clock* (1980), Miller dealt with memories of his family during the Great Depression of the 1930's. Miller also wrote an autobiography, *Timebends: A Life* (1987).   Mardi Valgemae

Miller, Cincinnatus H. See Miller, Joaquin.

Miller, Dorie (1919-1943), was a famous black American hero of World War II (1939-1945). On Dec. 7, 1941, he was serving as a mess attendant aboard the battleship *West Virginia* at the U.S. naval base on Pearl Harbor in Hawaii. That day, Japan staged a surprise attack on Pearl Harbor, and the *West Virginia* came under heavy fire. Miller had no gunnery training, but he took the place of a dead machine-gun operator and shot down four Japanese aircraft. For this feat, Miller received the Navy Cross, a medal given for great heroism in combat.

Miller was born on a farm near Waco, Tex. He enlisted in the U.S. Navy in 1939. At that time, blacks could serve in the Navy only as cook, steward, mess attendant, or waiter. After the attack on Pearl Harbor, Miller became a steward aboard the aircraft carrier *Liscome Bay.* He was killed when a Japanese submarine torpedo blew up the ship on Nov. 24, 1943.   James L. Stokesbury

Miller, Glenn (1904-1944), was a popular American dance band leader, arranger, and trombonist. Miller's band featured a distinctive sound that he developed by blending a clarinet with four saxophones. The band played smoothly danceable ballads and crisply driving swing numbers. Its hit records included "Moonlight Serenade," the band's theme song; "In the Mood"; "Little Brown Jug"; and "Sunrise Serenade."

Miller was born in Clarinda, Iowa. From 1926 to 1936, he played trombone in several bands, including those of Tommy and Jimmy Dorsey, Red Nichols, Ray Noble, Ben Pollack, and Freddy Rich. Miller formed his first band in 1937. He achieved his greatest success from 1938 until he entered the United States Army Air Forces in 1942. Miller disappeared during an air journey while in the service.   Nat Hentoff

Miller, Henry (1891-1980), became one of the most controversial American authors of his time. His emphasis on sex and his obscene language led to censorship trials and literary quarrels.

Miller's first important book, *Tropic of Cancer* (1934), was banned from publication in the United States until 1961. It was written in Paris where Miller had exiled himself from an America he despised. As in all of Miller's work, the plot is not as important as the message. He believed that modern civilization is diseased. People, to be healthy again, must win freedom from society and glorify the self and the senses.

Tropic of Capricorn (1939) is even more poetic and has a stronger sense of prophecy. It mixes moments of mystic joy with descriptions of what Miller saw as the U.S. cultural wasteland. His nonfiction, such as *The Air-Conditioned Nightmare* (1945), reflects the same concerns in its study of modern American culture. But the work includes studies of some Americans whom Miller felt lived successful lives. Miller's basic position never changed, though his later subjects were more literary. He was born in New York City.   Victor A. Kramer

Miller, Joaquin, *wah KEEN* (1837-1913), was an American poet who wrote about the West. Today, he is better known for his colorful, adventurous life than for the literary quality of his writing. In his poems, Miller intended to praise Americans and their vast new country. A few of his poems were once popular, notably "Alaska," "Crossing the Plains," and "Columbus." But critics no longer take his verse seriously. They consider his style flat and conventional and his technique severely limited.

Miller was born in Liberty, Ind. His real name was Cincinnatus Hiner Miller. He took the first name *Joaquin* after writing a poem defending the Mexican bandit Joaquín Murieta. Miller's family moved to Oregon in 1852. According to his own exaggerated account of his life, his "cradle was a covered wagon, pointed west." In Oregon, Miller began a series of exploits that included gold mining and living with the Digger Indians. He also visited England, where his collection *Songs of the Sier-*

ras (1871) was enthusiastically praised. Miller also wrote novels, plays, and the autobiography *Life Among the Modocs* (1873).   Elmer W. Borklund

Miller, Samuel Freeman (1816-1890), served as an associate justice of the Supreme Court of the United States from 1862 until his death. He is known for writing the court's decision in the Slaughterhouse Cases.

In the Slaughterhouse Cases, the Supreme Court ruled in 1873 that Louisiana could give one meat company the exclusive right to slaughter livestock in New Orleans. Butchers of other companies were allowed to use the slaughterhouses by paying a fee. Many butchers argued that they were denied their rights under the 14th Amendment of the U.S. Constitution. This amendment forbids the states to deny citizens any rights granted by federal law. Miller's interpretation of the law upheld the power of the states to regulate most business without federal interference. The court's decision had the effect of limiting the federal government's power to protect the rights of blacks, most of whom had recently been freed from slavery.

Miller was born in Richmond, Ky. He received an M.D. degree from Transylvania University and practiced medicine for several years. He later instructed himself in the law. In 1850, Miller moved to Iowa, where he became a leading attorney.   C. Peter Magrath

Miller, William Edward (1914-1983), was the Republican nominee for Vice President of the United States in the 1964 election. Senator Barry M. Goldwater and Miller were defeated by a Democratic ticket headed by President Lyndon B. Johnson and Hubert H. Humphrey.

Miller, a New Yorker, served in the U.S. House of Representatives from 1951 to 1965 and was Republican national chairman from 1961 to 1964. He gained a reputation as a tough debater and campaigner, and a good organizer. Miller headed his party's congressional campaign committee in 1960. The Republicans gained 22 seats in the House, even though their presidential candidate, Richard M. Nixon, was defeated. Republican leaders gave Miller much credit for the victories. Miller also became known for his barbed comments about Democrats. Goldwater indicated this was one reason he chose Miller as his running mate.

Miller was born in Lockport, N.Y. He attended the University of Notre Dame and Albany Law School. He served in the Army during World War II, and later helped prosecute German war criminals at the Nuremberg trials. Miller entered politics when Governor Thomas E. Dewey of New York appointed him district attorney of Niagara County in 1948.   Stephen E. Ambrose

Millerites. See Adventists.

Milles, *MIHL luhs,* **Carl** (1875-1955), was a Swedish-American sculptor. He became famous for creating fountains that combine graceful figures with splashing water. Milles studied the art of the past and attempted to create a contemporary classical style. His elongated figures emphasize action and gesture and often have symbolic significance. Milles's works include *Meeting of the Waters* (1940), in St. Louis, Mo., and *Fountain of Faith* (1952), in Falls Church, Va.

Milles was born in Lagga, Sweden, near Uppsala. He came to the United States in 1929 and became a citizen in 1945. He taught for many years at the Cranbrook Academy of Art in Bloomfield Hills, Mich., which has a fine collection of his works. Milles's home in Lidingö, near Stockholm, has been made into a park and museum called the Millesgården.   Joseph F. Lamb

Millet, *MIHL iht,* is any one of a group of grasses that produce small, edible seeds. The seeds are an important source of food in the dry regions of Asia and Africa. People grind the seeds into flour for flat breads and thin, fried cakes, or they use the seeds in making porridges. In the United States, millet seeds, leaves, and stems serve as feed for livestock.

During ancient and medieval times, millet was the chief crop of Europe and parts of Asia and Africa. However, it was unsuited for making yeast-raised breads and eventually lost popularity to wheat and other grains. Today, China, India, and Russia are among the leading countries in producing millet.

There are about 10 species of millet. Most varieties grow 1 to 4 feet (0.3 to 1.2 meters) tall. The seeds develop in a cluster called a *seed head* at the top of the stem. Millet matures rapidly and is sometimes planted as an emergency crop after a previous crop has failed. Many varieties can grow in hotter, drier weather and in less fertile soils than most other grains can. The chief species of millet include (1) *pearl millet,* (2) *foxtail millet,* and (3) *proso millet.*

Pearl millet serves as a major food for many people in India and Africa. Farmers in the southeastern United States grow pearl millet mainly for grazing livestock. More pearl millet is grown in the United States than any other variety. Pearl millet measures up to 15 feet (4.6 meters) tall. Its seed head looks like a long, narrow spike. Pearl millet is also called *cattail millet* or *candle millet.*

Foxtail millet, also called *Italian millet* or *hay millet,* is grown as a food crop in China, Kazakhstan, Russia, and Ukraine. In the United States, farmers in the Great Plains cultivate foxtail millet primarily for hay but also for grain and birdseed. It ranks second to pearl millet in order of production. Foxtail millet normally is $2\frac{1}{2}$ to 5 feet (0.8 to 1.5 meters) tall.

WORLD BOOK illustration by Robert Hynes

Millet

Proso millet, also called *hog millet* or *Hershey millet,* forms a major part of the diets of many Asians. The hulled seeds are eaten as cooked cereal, and the flour from the seeds is often substituted for rice flour. In the United States, proso is used for livestock feed and for birdseed. Its food value for livestock is almost as great as that of corn. However, proso seeds are extremely hard and must be finely ground before being fed to livestock. Proso usually grows from 1 to 2 feet (0.3 to 0.6 meter) tall. It has coarse, hairy stems that make poor hay.

Scientific classification. Millet belongs to the grass family, Poaceae or Gramineae. Pearl millet is classified as *Pennisetum glaucum,* foxtail millet is *Setaria italica,* and proso millet is *Panicum miliaceum.*   Donald J. Reid

See also **Mali** (picture: Farmers in Mali).

Millet, *mee LEH,* **Jean François,** *zhan frahn SWAH* (1814-1875), a French artist, was the most significant painter of peasant life of the 1800's. In 1849, he settled in the village of Barbizon near the forest of Fontainebleau. He spent almost all the rest of his life there painting scenes from rural life. His most popular works include *The Sower* (1850), *The Gleaners* (1857), and *The Angelus* (1859). Such works dignify their subjects, portraying rural life at a time when universal suffrage in France made the peasant an important political force.

Millet was born in Gruchy, near Cherbourg. He was descended from well-to-do farmers in Normandy, and his knowledge of peasant life came from the perspective of a prosperous farmer. Millet's paintings became especially popular with American and French industrialists of the late 1800's. These industrialists appreciated the idea of hard work and social order, which Millet's paintings seemed to endorse. Millet influenced a number of artists, including the famous painters Vincent van Gogh and Georges Seurat.   Richard Shiff

See also **Barbizon School.**

Milligan, Ex parte. See Ex parte Milligan.

Millikan, *MIHL uh kuhn,* **Robert Andrews** (1868-1953) was a distinguished American physicist. He is noted for his measurement of the electrical charge carried by the electron and for his experiments with cosmic rays. Millikan won the Nobel Prize for physics in 1923.

Millikan's Nobel Prize work included a series of experiments, begun in 1909, to study the charge carried by an electron. He sprayed drops of oil into a special chamber and measured how the charges carried by electrons in the drops affected the drops' fall. Millikan's prizewinning work also included another group of experiments that helped prove Albert Einstein's mathematical explanation of the photoelectric effect (see **Einstein, Albert**).

From the 1920's through the 1940's, Millikan compared the intensity of cosmic rays at various latitudes and altitudes. The data Millikan collected helped scientists study how the earth's magnetic field deflects cosmic rays as they arrive from outer space.

Millikan was born in Morrison, Ill. He attended Oberlin College and received a Ph.D. degree from Columbia University in 1895. He taught at the University of Chicago from 1896 to 1921. From 1921 to 1945, he served as the head of the California Institute of Technology.

Daniel J. Kevles

See also **Cosmic rays; Electron; Muon.**

Millipede, *MIHL uh peed,* also spelled *millepede,* is a wormlike, many-legged animal. Millipedes have segmented bodies. Two pairs of legs attach to most of their body segments. The word *millipede* means *thousand-footed,* but no millipede has as many as 1,000 feet. Some *species* (kinds) have up to 115 pairs of legs.

Millipedes range from less than $\frac{1}{8}$ inch (3 millimeters) to up to 9 inches (23 centimeters) long. The animals have round heads that bear a pair of short antennae. Millipedes usually feed on decaying plant life, but some species also attack crops growing in damp soil. They live in dark, damp places, under stones and rotting logs. When they are disturbed, millipedes usually coil up. Many types of millipede give off foul odors. A few species are capable of producing fluids containing cyanide poison. About 7,500 species of millipedes are found throughout the world.

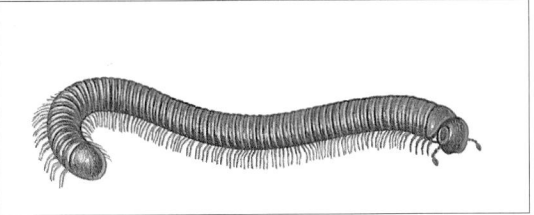

WORLD BOOK illustration by James Teason

The millipede is a wormlike, many-legged animal. Some species have up to 115 pairs of legs.

Scientific classification. Millipedes are classified in the phylum Arthropoda. They make up the class Diplopoda.

Edwin W. Minch

Mills, Robert (1781-1855), was one of the first Americans trained as an architect and engineer. He designed the Washington Monument in Washington, D.C., which for many years was the tallest structure in the world (see **Washington Monument**). Mills designed more than 50 important buildings. They include the United States Post Office, Treasury, and Patent Office buildings in Washington, D.C, and numerous U.S. customs houses and courthouses. His nongovernment buildings include churches and homes. Mills was born in Charleston, S.C.

Leland M. Roth

Milne, *mihln,* **A. A.** (1882-1956), an English author, became famous for his children's stories and poems. Two of Milne's books, *Winnie-the-Pooh* (1926) and *The House at Pooh Corner* (1928), have become masterpieces of children's literature.

Milne based the characters in the Pooh stories on his son, Christopher Robin, and the young boy's stuffed animals. Milne's stories describe the adventures of Christopher Robin and his animal friends in a forest called the Hundred Acre Wood. Some of the characters in the Pooh stories include Winnie-the-Pooh, a bear; Piglet, a small pig; and Eeyore, an old donkey (see **Literature for children** [picture: Winnie-the-Pooh]). In his autobiography, *It's Too Late Now* (1939), Milne told how his son's stuffed animals led to the creation of the characters in the Pooh stories.

In addition to the Pooh stories, Milne wrote two classic collections of children's poems, *When We Were Very Young* (1924) and *Now We Are Six* (1927). He wrote the children's play *Make-Believe* (1918) and adapted Kenneth Grahame's children's book *The Wind in the Willows* into a play, *Toad of Toad Hall* (1929). Milne also created novels, short stories, and plays for adults. He wrote a famous detective novel, *The Red House Mystery* (1922), and a book of short stories called *A Table Near the Band* (1950). His comic plays include *Mr. Pim Passes By* (1919), *The Truth About Blayds* (1921), and *The Dover Road* (1922). He also wrote his *Autobiography* (1939).

Alan Alexander Milne was born in London and graduated from Cambridge University in 1903. From 1906 to 1914, he served as assistant editor of *Punch,* a humor magazine. Milne contributed many comic essays and poems to the magazine.   Carol Tecla Christ

Milne, *mihln,* **David Brown** (1882-1953), was an important Canadian painter. Milne is best known for creating simplified arrangements of flattened forms with short, broken brushstrokes. Milne primarily painted landscapes and still lifes, using either oil paint or water colors. He also made many color prints using a method called *drypoint etching.*

Milne was born near Paisley, Ont. In 1904, he moved to New York City to study art. Several of his works were displayed there in the Armory Show of 1913, a famous exhibit of American and European modern art. Milne lived and painted mostly in rural New York from 1919 to 1928, when he returned permanently to Canada.

Jeremy Adamson

Ollie Matson's House Is Just a Square Red Cloud (1931), an oil painting on canvas; National Gallery of Canada, Ottawa, the Vincent Massey Bequest, 1968

A landscape by David Milne, *shown above,* portrays a rural scene in southern Ontario. The painting is typical of the artist's abstract style and his use of short, broken brushstrokes.

Milnes, *mihlnz,* **Sherrill** (1935-   ), is an American operatic baritone known for his rich voice and great range. Milnes specializes in Italian operas, particularly those by Giuseppe Verdi. He has also appeared in concerts with major American symphony orchestras.

Milnes was born in Hinsdale, Ill., and studied voice at Drake University. He first sang a major role in 1960 with Boris Goldovsky's New England Opera Company, and toured with the company from 1960 to 1965. Milnes has appeared regularly at the Metropolitan Opera in New York City since his debut in 1965 as Valentin in Charles Gounod's *Faust.* He has also sung with other companies throughout the world.   John H. Baron

Milos, *MEE laws,* or Melos, is a Greek island located in the Aegean Sea (see **Greece** [map]). The island of Milos is famous as the place where a remarkable statue of the goddess Venus was found in 1820. This statue is called the Aphrodite of Milos, or the Venus de Milo (see **Venus de Milo**). The island covers about 58 square miles (151 square kilometers) and has about 4,560 people. Its economic activities include tourism and the production of olives and tobacco.

In the Stone Age, Milos was famous for its *obsidian* (volcanic glass), which was used for cutting tools. The Athenians seized the island in 416 B.C., and massacred the men there.   John J. Baxevanis

Milošević, *mee LOH SHEHV ihtch,* **Slobodan,** *SLAW baw duhn* (1941-   ), became president of Serbia, one of the republics that make up Yugoslavia, in 1989. He

was reelected in 1990 and 1992. Milošević is also the most powerful official in Yugoslavia's government.

Milošević became known for his extreme nationalism. In 1990, he abolished the power of self-government held by the Serbian provinces of Kosovo and Vojvodina. Milošević has supplied arms and troops to Serbs living and fighting in Croatia and Bosnia-Herzegovina, two former republics of Yugoslavia that declared independence in the early 1990's. War broke out in the former republics between Serbs, who demanded territory there, and non-Serbs. Milošević has encouraged Serbs to practice the policy of *ethnic cleansing* in an attempt to rid Serbian-held areas of all non-Serbs, particularly in Bosnia-Herzegovina.

Reuters/Bettmann

Slobodan Milošević

Milošević was born in Požarevac, Serbia. After graduating from the University of Belgrade in 1964, he held several positions in the Yugoslav Communist Party. In 1986, Milošević became head of the Central Committee of the League of Communists of Serbia.

Sabrina P. Ramet

Milstein, *MIHL styn,* **Nathan** (1904-1992), was a well-known and beloved violinist. He became known particularly for his interpretations of Bach violin sonatas and the great violin concertos. Milstein was born in Odessa, Ukraine (then part of the Russian empire). Early in his life, he played concerts with the famous pianist Vladimir Horowitz in Russia. Milstein came to the United States in 1929 to make his American debut with the Philadelphia Orchestra. His stature as an artist grew steadily. He continued to perform into his 80's to enthusiastic acclaim.

Stephen Clapp

Miltiades, *mihl TY uh DEEZ* (540?-488? B.C.), was a famous general of ancient Athens. Miltiades defeated the Persians at the Battle of Marathon in 490 B.C., during the wars between Greece and Persia (see **Marathon**).

Miltiades was a member of an aristocratic Athenian family. About 516 B.C., while securing trade routes for Athens, he made himself ruler of what is now the Gallipoli Peninsula in Turkey. He probably fought against Persian forces led by Darius. He lost his throne about 492 B.C. and was forced to flee to Athens. Persians invaded Greece in 490 B.C., and the Athenians made Miltiades a general. Because of his experience in fighting the Persians, he convinced the other generals to attack the enemy at Marathon. After defeating the Persians and driving them from Greece, he commanded a fleet in the Aegean Sea.   Jack Martin Balcer

Milton, John (1608-1674), was an English poet and political writer. He is the author of *Paradise Lost* (1667, revised 1674), considered by many to be the greatest epic poem in the English language. He also wrote *Paradise Regained* (1671) and *Samson Agonistes* (1671). Milton composed the first two of these works, and probably also the last, when he was totally blind.

Milton wrote *Paradise Lost* to "justify the ways of God to man." The 12-book poem retells the Biblical story of the Creation and the fall of Adam and Eve against the backdrop of Satan's rebellion against God and expulsion from heaven (see Doré, Gustave [picture]). *Paradise Regained* is a four-book "brief epic" written, like *Paradise Lost,* in blank verse. Based loosely on the Gospels, it narrates Christ's successful withstanding of Satan's temptations. *Samson Agonistes* tells the Biblical story of Samson in the style of Greek tragic drama. It depicts Samson, betrayed by Dalila (Delilah) and blinded by the Philistines, defeating his captors at the cost of his life.

Milton had a thorough knowledge of classical Greek and Latin authors and was greatly influenced by them. But, as a Protestant, he emphasized the Bible as interpreted by the individual believer. Through his poetry, Milton wanted to do for England "what the greatest and choicest wits of Athens, Rome, or modern Italy, and those Hebrews of old" did for their countries "with this over and above of being a Christian."

His early life and works. Milton was born in London on Dec. 9, 1608. He attended St. Paul's School and then Christ's College at Cambridge University. While at Cambridge, he wrote "On the Morning of Christ's Nativity" (1629) and the companion poems "L'Allegro" and "Il Penseroso" (both 1631?). Although his early training prepared him for a religious career, he came to believe "tyranny had invaded the church." He chose instead to dedicate himself to God's service as a poet. Upon graduating from Cambridge in 1632, he went to Horton, his father's country home, to study and write.

At Horton, Milton wrote two major pieces. *Comus* (1634), a *masque* (dramatic presentation with music), concerns the nature of virtue. Milton wrote the words, and the noted musician Henry Lawes wrote the music. "Lycidas" (1637), considered by many to be the finest short poem in English, is a pastoral elegy commemorating the death of his friend Edward King. In this poem, Milton for the first time subordinated classical sources to a Christian vision as he did in his mature art.

Milton left Horton in 1638 for a 15-month European tour. While in Italy, Milton heard of a growing conflict between the bishops of the Church of England and the Puritans. He returned to England to support the Puritan cause through a series of political writings.

Middle years. Civil discord divided England from 1640 to 1660. King Charles I and the bishops of the Church of England clashed with the Puritans over policies of church and state, and civil war broke out in 1642. The Puritans defeated the King's forces, and Charles was beheaded in 1649. Parliament then established a Commonwealth government led by Oliver Cromwell. See **England** (The Civil War).

During this 20-year period, Milton turned away from poetry to work on behalf of Parliament and the Commonwealth through his prose. In all his writings, he championed radical political and religious views. In *Of Reformation in England* (1641), he criticized the Church of England. In *The Ready and Easy Way to Establish a Free Commonwealth* (1660), he cried out against the prospect of the restoration of King Charles II to the throne. He defended the people's right to choose and depose their rulers in *The Tenure of Kings and Magistrates* (1649).

Milton married 16-year-old Mary Powell in 1643. But their marriage was unhappy. She left Milton after a

Oil portrait on canvas (1629) by an unknown artist; National Portrait Gallery, London (Granger Collection)

John Milton wrote his first well-known poems while a student at Cambridge University. This portrait shows him at age 21.

month or two and did not return for two years. Milton gained notoriety by writing a series of pamphlets in favor of divorce in certain cases. In 1644, he published his most famous prose work, *Areopagitica,* a defense of freedom of the press.

Milton's work and constant study strained his weak eyes, and he was completely blind by 1652. His wife died the same year. He wrote the sonnet "When I Consider How My Light Is Spent" (1655) about his blindness. In 1656, Milton married Katherine Woodcock. She died 16 months later. Milton probably wrote the sonnet "Methought I Saw My Late Espoused Saint" (1658) about her.

Retirement. Charles II was restored to the throne in 1660, and a number of people held responsible for the execution of Charles I were tried and executed. Milton was arrested, but not harmed. He went into retirement and married Elizabeth Minshull in 1663. Milton wrote *Paradise Lost, Paradise Regained,* and probably *Samson Agonistes,* his masterpieces, during his final years. These works are in part a response to his own blindness and the collapse of the Puritans' hopes for the establishment of Christ's kingdom on earth. Milton's major poems fulfill his ambition to "leave something so written to aftertimes, as they should not willingly let it die." They confirm his reputation as England's foremost nondramatic poet.   Peter L. Rudnytsky

Additional resources

The Cambridge Companion to Milton. Ed. by Dennis Danielson. Cambridge, 1989.
Wilson, A. N. *The Life of John Milton.* Oxford, 1983.

Milwaukee Department of City Development

Downtown Milwaukee borders the western shore of Lake Michigan. The city is an important Great Lakes port. The 42-story First Wisconsin Center, *left,* is the tallest building in Wisconsin.

Milwaukee, *mihl WAW kee,* is the largest city in Wisconsin and one of the major industrial centers of the United States. The city ranks as one of the country's leading manufacturers of automobile parts, beer, and electrical and nonelectrical machinery.

Milwaukee lies on the western shore of Lake Michigan, about 90 miles (140 kilometers) north of Chicago. The city's excellent harbor has made Milwaukee an important Great Lakes port.

Milwaukee's name comes from the Milwaukee River. Most historians say that the river's Algonquian Indian name, *Millioke,* means *good land.* Others translate the name as *great council place.* Milwaukee is often called the *Cream City* because of its many old cream-colored brick buildings.

Descendants of German immigrants make up a large part of Milwaukee's population. Business and street names, cultural events, and famous restaurants in Milwaukee are reminders of the city's German heritage.

Solomon Juneau, a French-Canadian fur trader, settled in the Milwaukee area in 1818. He established a town on the east side of the Milwaukee River in 1833. The town later combined with neighboring villages and became Milwaukee.

Trade accounted for much of the city's early growth. During the 1860's, Milwaukee was one of the leading grain markets in the United States. However, by the late 1800's, manufacturing had replaced trade as the city's chief source of income.

The Socialist Party played an important role in local politics during the 1900's. In 1910, Milwaukee became the first major city in the United States to elect a Socialist mayor.

Metropolitan Milwaukee

Milwaukee, the seat of Milwaukee County, covers 106 square miles (275 square kilometers), or about 45 per cent of the county. It extends about 10 miles (16 kilometers) along the shore of Lake Michigan. The city's metropolitan area occupies 1,497 square miles (3,877 square kilometers) and covers four counties—Milwaukee, Ozaukee, Washington, and Waukesha. About 30 per cent of the state's people live in this metropolitan area.

The city. Milwaukee lies on a bluff overlooking a crescent-shaped bay. Three rivers—the Kinnickinnic, the Menomonee, and the Milwaukee—flow through the city to the bay.

The streets of Milwaukee run in a checkerboard pat-

Facts in brief

Population: *City*—628,088. *Metropolitan area*—1,432,149. *Consolidated metropolitan area*—1,607,183.
Area: *City*—106 sq. mi. (275 km²). *Metropolitan area*—1,497 sq. mi. (3,877 km²). *Consolidated metropolitan area*—1,838 sq. mi. (4,760 km²).
Climate: *Average temperature*—January, 22 °F (−6 °C); July, 71 °F (22 °C). *Average annual precipitation* (rainfall, melted snow, and other forms of moisture)—30 inches (76 centimeters). For the monthly weather in Milwaukee, see **Wisconsin** (Climate).
Government: Mayor-council (four-year terms).
Founded: 1830's. Incorporated as a city, 1846.

tern. Many north-south streets have numbers instead of names. The Menomonee Valley, where many manufacturing companies are located, divides the city into the North Side and South Side. The main business district lies north of the valley, and older residential areas and industrial districts are to the south.

Downtown Milwaukee extends west for about 2 miles (3 kilometers) from the lakefront. Banks, department stores, office buildings, restaurants, and specialty shops line Wisconsin Avenue, the city's main street. Government buildings include City Hall on East Wells Street and the County Court House on North 9th Street. At the downtown's west end stand the Bradley Center and the Milwaukee Exposition Convention Center and Arena (MECCA). The Bradley Center hosts sports and other entertainment events. The MECCA consists of the Arena, which hosts chiefly trade shows and conventions; the Auditorium, where exhibitions and stage shows are held; and the Convention Center.

The metropolitan area. A network of freeways connects downtown Milwaukee and its suburbs. West Allis and Wauwatosa, the largest suburbs, lie west of the city. Other suburbs include Cudahy, Oak Creek, Shorewood, and Whitefish Bay. Large shopping centers, such as Bay Shore, Brookfield Square, and Southridge, serve the

Symbols of Milwaukee. The city flag, adopted in 1954, has a large gear to represent manufacturing. It also has symbols for Milwaukee's government, history, and shipping industry. Scenes on the city seal, *right,* stand for education and transportation.

suburbs. The metropolitan areas of Milwaukee-Waukesha and of Racine, Wis., form the Milwaukee-Racine Consolidated Metropolitan Statistical Area.

The people

About 95 per cent of Milwaukee's people were born in the United States. Blacks make up about 30 per cent of the population. Many blacks live in the inner city, close to the downtown area. About 17 per cent of the people have German ancestry. Other groups include people of English, Irish, Italian, Mexican, or Polish de-

City of Milwaukee

Milwaukee lies on the western shore of Lake Michigan. The map at the right shows the city and some of its points of interest. The map below shows Milwaukee and the surrounding area.

City boundary		Expressway
County boundary		Other street
Park		Railroad
	•	Point of interest

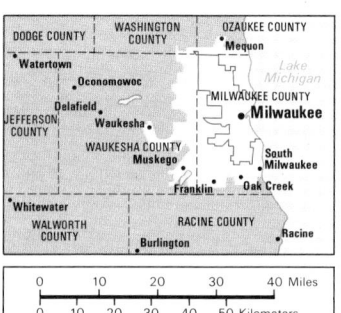

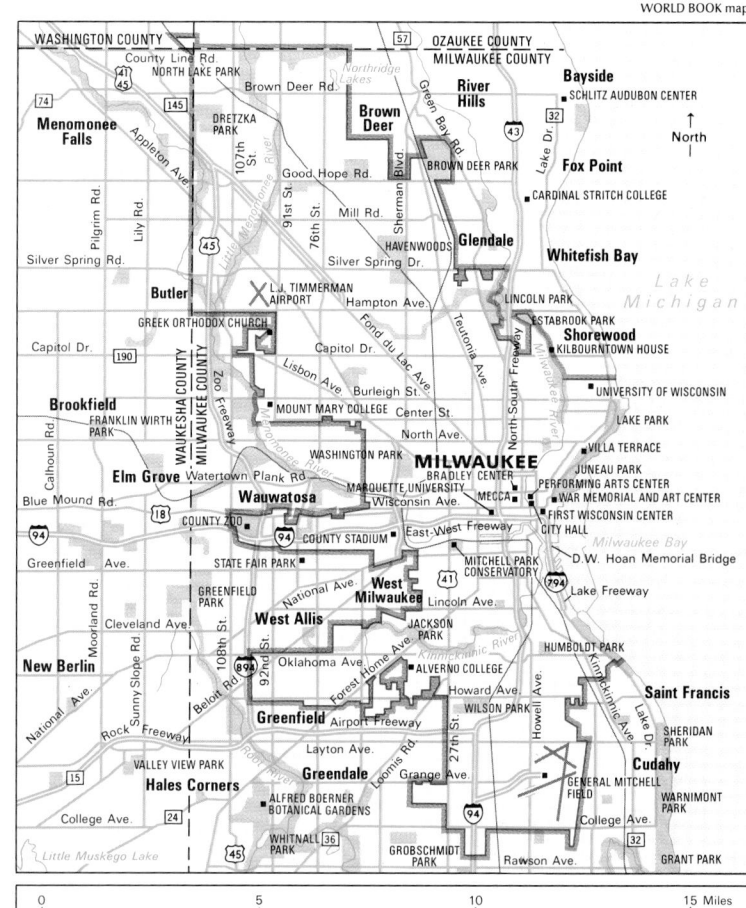

WORLD BOOK maps

The Mitchell Park Conservatory, famous for its huge glass domes, features rare plants and flowers in natural settings.

J. Blank, FPG

scent. Nearly 11 per cent of Milwaukee's residents speak a language other than English at home.

Milwaukee has had some serious racial disturbances. In 1967, riots broke out in the black community. Civil rights groups have organized marches, picketings, and sit-ins to protest discrimination. Various groups work to aid minorities and improve race relations. Poverty is also a major problem in Milwaukee, where 1 out of 5 people lives below the poverty line.

Economy

Industry. The Milwaukee area has about 3,000 manufacturing plants that employ about 23 per cent of the area's work force. The chief products include automobile parts, beer, electrical equipment, and farm and factory machinery. Other industries produce construction and mining equipment, food products, iron and steel forgings, and leather goods.

Finance and trade. The Northwestern Mutual Life Insurance Company, one of the nation's largest insurance firms, is in Milwaukee. Several other major insurance companies and banks are also headquartered there. The wholesale trade of beer, dairy products, and machinery is important to the economy. About 51 per cent of the workers hold jobs in service industries, including about 23 per cent in wholesale and retail trade.

Transportation. Milwaukee's harbor handles about $2\frac{1}{4}$ million short tons (2 million metric tons) of cargo annually. Ships connect the city with about 100 overseas ports by way of the St. Lawrence Seaway.

Passenger trains and five rail freight lines serve Milwaukee. The Milwaukee area has an extensive system of expressways. Milwaukee's main airport is Mitchell Field.

Communication. About 30 radio stations, 6 television stations, including 2 educational stations, and 1 cable TV system serve the Milwaukee area. The Journal Company owns the city's two daily newspapers, the *Milwaukee Sentinel,* published in the morning, and *The Milwaukee Journal,* published in the afternoon.

Education

The Milwaukee public school system includes about 140 elementary and secondary schools, with an enroll-

ment of about 90,000 students. More than 29,000 students attend about 125 parochial and other private schools in the city.

The University of Wisconsin-Milwaukee, the city's largest university, has about 25,500 students. It includes several skyscrapers and dominates the northeast side of the city. About 12,000 students attend Marquette University. Alverno College, Cardinal Stritch College, Concordia University, Mount Mary College, and Wisconsin Lutheran College are also in the area. Training for the Roman Catholic priesthood is provided at the graduate level by St. Francis Seminary in nearby St. Francis.

Other institutions of higher learning in the Milwaukee area include the Medical College of Wisconsin, Milwaukee Institute of Art and Design, and the Milwaukee School of Engineering. The Milwaukee Area Technical College is one of the nation's largest vocational and adult education centers.

The Milwaukee public library system has over 2 million books. It includes 13 branches.

Cultural life

The arts. The city's Performing Arts Center houses the Milwaukee Symphony Orchestra, the Milwaukee Repertory Theater, a choral group, a ballet, and an opera company. The Pabst and Riverside theaters provide elegant settings for stage performances. Blues and rock musicians and other entertainers perform at Milwaukee's many nightclubs.

Museums. The Milwaukee Art Center, in the city's lakefront War Memorial Center, displays American and European paintings and sculpture. The Milwaukee Public Museum contains many natural-history exhibits. It also has a model of a Milwaukee street as it looked in the early 1900's. The Milwaukee County Historical Center features exhibits of local history.

Recreation

Parks. The Milwaukee County Park System includes 140 parks and parkways and covers more than 14,000 acres (5,700 hectares). The largest park, Whitnall Park, occupies about 1,200 acres (486 hectares). The park features the beautiful Alfred Boerner Botanical Gardens, which have more than 1,000 species of flowers. A conservatory in Mitchell Park displays plants of desert, temperate, and tropical climates in their natural settings. The Milwaukee County Zoo has wide moats and glass-enclosed cages, rather than bars. Visitors may tour the zoo in a miniature train or in a rubber-tired zoomobile.

Sports. The Milwaukee Brewers of the American League play baseball in County Stadium. The Green Bay Packers of the National Football League play some of their games there. The Milwaukee Bucks of the National Basketball Association play in the Bradley Center. The nation's top golfers compete in the Greater Milwaukee Open, held every September.

Annual events and places of interest in the Milwaukee area include:

Lakefront Festival of Arts, in late spring. Viewers can see thousands of paintings on the lawns surrounding the Milwaukee War Memorial Center.

Summerfest, an 11-day celebration in late June and early July, features fireworks displays, a Fourth of July parade, and stage entertainment by various ethnic groups. Ethnic festivals are held on the lakefront every weekend from Summerfest until Labor Day.

Greek Orthodox Church of the Annunciation in nearby Wauwatosa. Designed by the famous American architect Frank Lloyd Wright, it features an unusual style of architecture.

Joan of Arc Chapel on the Marquette University campus. This chapel, built in France during the 1400's, was reconstructed on the campus in the 1960's.

Kilbourntown House in Estabrook Park was the home of Benjamin Church, a pioneer architect. Church built it in 1844.

State Fair Park, in suburban West Allis, has facilities for rides, stage entertainment, and automobile races. About 1 million people visit the park during the annual 11-day Wisconsin State Fair in August.

Great Circus Parade, held in July through downtown streets, is the largest parade of its kind in the world. It features classic circus wagons pulled by teams of horses.

Government

Milwaukee has a mayor-council form of government. The voters elect the mayor to a four-year term. The mayor appoints major department heads and members of various boards and commissions. Most of the appointments are subject to approval by the council. The mayor has veto power over some council decisions and may also propose legislation. Milwaukee is divided into 17 districts called *wards*. The voters of each ward elect one representative, called an *alderman,* to the city council, officially called the Common Council. The aldermen serve four-year terms. Property taxes provide nearly half the city's revenue. Other sources of revenue include state and federal aid.

The Milwaukee city government faces many problems, including decreasing revenue and air and water pollution. In an effort to solve these problems, Milwaukee leaders work chiefly with two groups. These groups are the Greater Milwaukee Committee, a voluntary organization of civic leaders, and the Southeastern Wisconsin Regional Planning Commission, which is both state and federally supported.

History

Early development. The Fox, Mascouten, and Potawatomi Indians hunted in the Milwaukee area before the first white settlers came. In 1674, Father Jacques Marquette, a French missionary, stopped at the site. Later, other missionaries and fur traders began to visit the area. One trader, Jacques Vieau, opened a trading post there in 1795. Solomon Juneau, Vieau's clerk and son-in-law, settled in the area in 1818. In 1833, Juneau founded a town on the east side of the Milwaukee River.

During the 1830's, many settlers came from the Eastern United States. They included Byron Kilbourn of Connecticut and George H. Walker of Virginia. Kilbourn set up his own community on the west side of the Milwaukee River. Walker developed the area south of the Menomonee River. In the late 1830's, the settlements combined to form the Village of Milwaukee. Milwaukee received a city charter in 1846, and Juneau became its first mayor. By 1847, the population was about 12,000.

Beginning in the 1840's, many Europeans settled in Milwaukee. They included many Germans, Irish, and Poles. These immigrants played an important role in the city's cultural, economic, and political development.

Economic growth. During the 1850's and 1860's, Milwaukee flourished as a commercial center. Harbor improvements and the construction of roads and railroads helped the city become a leading market for flour and wheat. After 1870, manufacturing became the city's chief economic activity. With the growth of such industries as meat packing and tanning, Milwaukee's population rose to more than 200,000 by 1890.

The 1900's. Industrialization provided a base for the Socialist movement of the late 1800's and 1900's. Milwaukee Socialists did little to promote socialism, which calls for public ownership of industry. Instead, they fought for labor and political reforms and higher social benefits.

In 1910, Milwaukeeans elected Emil Seidel, a Socialist, as mayor. Milwaukee was the first major city in the United States to have a Socialist mayor. Seidel served until 1912. Since then, Milwaukee has had two other Socialist mayors—Daniel W. Hoan, from 1916 to 1940, and Frank P. Zeidler, from 1948 to 1960. The Common Council had a Socialist majority only under Seidel.

After World War II (1939-1945), Milwaukee began a redevelopment program that included construction of freeways and major changes in the downtown and lakefront areas. During the 1950's, the city modernized its harbor to receive ocean ships. These improvements and the opening of the St. Lawrence Seaway in 1959 made Milwaukee an important international port.

Recent developments. Both before and after World War II, Milwaukee's population grew steadily. By 1960, it reached 741,324. But since then, the city's population has decreased. Many people have moved to new residential areas outside the city. By 1990, Milwaukee's population had dropped to 628,088, but some areas outside the city had experienced sharp growth.

In 1968, Milwaukee launched Midtown, an urban renewal project that included industrial, recreational, and residential redevelopment of an area northwest of downtown Milwaukee. The project ended in 1977. In the early 1980's, the Grand Avenue revitalization program focused on the downtown area. This project, completed in 1982, included the reconstruction of older buildings, construction of new ones, and the creation of an enclosed shopping mall.   Michael Juley

Milwaukee Deep. See Deep.

Mimeograph. See Duplicator.

Mimicry, *MIHM ihk ree,* is the condition in which one living organism closely resembles, or mimics, its surroundings or another animal or plant. It is usually the result of similar color or construction. Mimicry may enable the organism to protect itself in its struggle for existence. For example, the monarch butterfly and the viceroy butterfly resemble each other in size, shape, and colors. The monarch is believed to be distasteful to birds, while the viceroy is not. But the viceroy often escapes being eaten by birds because it resembles the monarch.

Another example of mimicry is the *Kallima,* or "dead leaf," butterfly of India, which brings its wings together over its back and places the "tails" of its wings against a twig when it rests. The Kallima escapes notice because the undersides of its wings resemble a dead leaf in color and texture.   George B. Johnson

See also **Animal** (Protective resemblance); **Bird** (Calls and songs; Protection against enemies; pictures); **Protective coloration; Bates, Henry Walter.**

The **mimosa** is a spreading tree with featherlike leaves and blossoms. Mimosas generally grow in warm climates.

© Dick Dietrich, FPG

Mimosa, *mih MOH suh* or *mih MOH zuh,* is the name of a group of trees, shrubs, and herbs that have featherlike leaves. Mimosas grow chiefly in warm or tropical regions. In the United States, they are found from Maryland to Florida and west to Texas. The seeds of mimosas grow in flat pods. The small flowers may be white, pink, lavender, or purple. The *silver wattle,* a shrub with silvery-gray leaves, is widely sold by florists as mimosa. It is closely related to mimosas.

   Scientific classification. Mimosas belong to the pea family, Fabaceae or Leguminosae.   Walter S. Judd

   See also **Sensitive plant.**

Minaret, *MIHN uh REHT* or *MIHN uh reht,* is a tall, usually slender, tower attached to the Muslim house of worship, called a *mosque.* Most mosques have from two to six minarets. From the top of the minaret, a *muez-*

© R. & S. Michaud, Woodfin Camp, Inc.

Minarets are towers attached to Islamic houses of worship called *mosques.* A crier called a *muezzin* summons Muslims to prayer from a balcony near the top of the minaret.

zin (crier) calls the faithful to prayer five times each day. Minarets have one or more balconies where the muezzin can stand. The minaret may be round, square, or many-sided. Most are built of brick or stone, and contain an internal staircase. The minaret is one of the most common features of Islamic architecture.

   Many scholars believe the form of the minaret is derived from the ancient Lighthouse at Alexandria, Egypt, which was completed in the 200's B.C. Among the earliest minarets are those at a mosque in Damascus, Syria, built in A.D. 707. Minarets are common in India, northern Africa, and throughout the Middle East.
   William J. Hennessey

   For pictures of minarets, see **Architecture** (Islamic); **India; Iran; Islamic art; Turkey.**

Minch, The, is a broad strait that separates the island of Lewis with Harris, in the Outer Hebrides, from the west coast of Scotland. For location, see **Scotland** (political map). The average width of the strait is about 30 miles (48 kilometers).   A. S. Mather

Mind. Psychologists, psychiatrists, and philosophers have held many views on the nature of the mind. Even today, they still disagree.

   Early theories of mind held that human beings were made up of two different substances, *mind* and *matter.* Matter was something that could be seen and felt. Matter occupied space and had weight. Mind was a substance present in a person, but it took up no space and could not be weighed, seen, or touched. The mind was divided into several *faculties,* such as will, reason, and memory. Some people thought that the mind, like the muscles, developed through exercise. Thus, the way to strengthen the mind was to give the faculties work to do.

   Some psychologists and philosophers who questioned the mind-substance idea offered the view that mind was the sum total of all a person's conscious states. This meant that the mind was simply a mass of thoughts, memories, feelings, and emotions. At any given moment, there would be only a few things in a person's consciousness, the things to which a person was giving attention; and there would be some other things of which a person was aware without thinking about them, somewhat as we see things "out of the corner of our eye." Below this level of consciousness would be a whole vast mass made up of all the conscious states an individual had experienced since birth. Whenever a new idea or impression made its way into a person's consciousness, all earlier impressions like it or in some way related to it were supposed to rise up into consciousness and welcome the newcomer. In this way, the mind kept growing and rearranging itself.

   The nature of mind. During the 1800's, psychologists began to try out some of these ideas on the nature of mind. For example, one man set himself the task of memorizing nonsense syllables over a period of time, and checking how long it took him each time he tried. He reached the conclusion that a person could memorize and memorize without in any way improving his memory. Other psychologists began to ask why it was, if mind and matter were separate substances, that drugs or illness or a blow on the head could so greatly disturb a person's mind. They wondered also why the mind seemed to fail as people grew very old.

Some of these psychologists went so far as to suggest that perhaps everything a person did could be explained in terms of the body, without using such ideas as mind or consciousness at all. These psychologists held that actual physical movements of the brain and central nervous system could account for all the events we speak of as "mental," if only we knew enough about them. The person who spoke of "mind" or "consciousness," according to this view, was simply an animal impelled through experiences and habits. This animal had built up certain associations in its nervous system, to make specific sounds on specific occasions.

This theory, sometimes called *extreme behaviorism,* made rapid headway among psychologists. However, its limitations soon became apparent. Many modifications of the original viewpoint have been made.

Another view began to develop that perhaps mind, like matter, is just something that happens, and is not a separate, identifiable thing. For example, everyone knows that water is wet. But atoms of hydrogen and oxygen are not wet, and neither are the energy charges that make them up. We can say that wetness is a quality that comes into being when energy charges, organized in the form of hydrogen and oxygen atoms, are brought together to form water. If we break water down into its parts, the wetness is gone, and so is the water itself.

In the same way, mind is a quality that comes into being as people interact with the world around them. According to this theory, mind, like wetness, is something that emerges or comes into being when organisms reach a certain level of complexity in development.

Another theory states that mind is the foundation and the source of feeling, thinking, and willing. This foundation is distinct from the acts which it produces. The mind is the ultimate source of sensations, images, feelings, and thoughts. The thoughts are the mental activities. The *soul* is an even broader concept. It is the source of both mental and other life activities, such as breathing and walking.

Physical and mental relationship. Most people believe that a practical separation between mind and body is impossible. The mind can move the body, as when people decide to flex their muscles. Almost any human reaction has both physical and mental sides, so that people smile with pleasure, frown in anger, or quiver with fear. Physicians tell us that mental states can actually produce heart disease, ulcer of the stomach, kidney trouble, and other diseases.

The body also affects the mind. People can note the difference in their mental state when they are hungry or well-fed, cold or warm, sick or well. It is known also that certain glands have a profound effect upon emotions, attitudes, and behavior. See **Behavior.**

The influence of the mind and the body on each other is difficult to explain. Some people explain it by discarding the mind. Others discard matter in order to explain it. A more common-sense view insists that they both exist and interact. According to the interaction theory, each human being is composed of both body and mind. However, the body and mind are incomplete until they form a unity called a *person,* or *ego.* A human being is a single composite substance made up of two distinct principles. It is the *person* who thinks and remembers, not the mind, and not the body.

The discussion above deals with some of the many questions and problems involved in the nature of mind. The discussion shows that serious work is being done on the subject. No one statement of the nature of mind is acceptable to all authorities. Nancy C. Andreasen

Related articles in *World Book* include:

Emotion	Memory	Suggestion
Intelligence	Psychology	Unconscious

Mind reading is a term loosely applied to various forms of *extrasensory perception (ESP),* especially *telepathy* and *clairvoyance.* Telepathy is an awareness of another person's thoughts, knowledge, or feelings without the aid of the senses of hearing, sight, smell, taste, or touch. Clairvoyance is an awareness of events, objects, or persons without the use of the known senses. The term *mind reading* may be considered a synonym for *telepathy.* But the term has little more than historical interest today because of changing ideas about the concept of the mind. In the past, each person was considered to have a mind more or less independent of his body and behavior. It was also thought that one mind could "read" another mind without using the known senses. Today, scientists do not believe that the mind is independent of the rest of the body. William M. Smith

See also **Extrasensory perception; Telepathy; Clairvoyance; Parapsychology.**

Mindoro. See Philippines (The main islands).

Mindszenty, *mihnd ZEHN tih,* **Joseph Cardinal** (1892-1975), a cardinal of the Roman Catholic Church, was a religious leader in Hungary. For many people, he became a symbol of resistance to Communism.

Pope Pius XII named Mindszenty bishop of Veszprém in 1944, and archbishop of Esztergom and primate of Hungary in 1945. The pope made him a cardinal in 1946. Mindszenty became a main target of the Communist-dominated secret police. In 1949, Mindszenty was convicted of treason by Hungary's Communist government and given a life sentence. He remained under house arrest until 1956, when Hungarian rebels freed him during their revolt. Mindszenty took refuge in the United States Embassy in Budapest and lived there for 15 years.

United Press Int.
Cardinal Mindszenty

In 1971, Mindszenty left Hungary and went into exile in Rome. He did so at the request of Pope Paul VI, under an agreement between the Vatican and the Hungarian government. Mindszenty later settled in Vienna. In 1974, to improve relations between the church and the Hungarian government, the pope removed Mindszenty as primate of Hungary and archbishop of Esztergom.

Mindszenty was born Joseph Pehm in Csehmindszenty. His father was of German ancestry. Mindszenty was ordained a priest in 1915. During the Nazi occupation of Hungary, he changed his name to indicate his complete Hungarian nationality, using the name of his birthplace. John T. Farrell

Mine. See Mining.

Mine warfare is the use of explosive devices called mines to kill enemy troops and destroy their ships, tanks, and other equipment. Some mines explode when a person steps on them. Others explode when run over by a tank or jeep. Mines may be designed to explode when moved or even touched. Naval mines are *detonated* (exploded) by the effects produced by a passing ship. Mines also may be exploded by remote control.

Mines can be positioned to prevent an enemy from entering an area. They can also be used to influence the course traveled by enemy troops or ships. By avoiding mined areas, enemy forces may be forced to take routes where they can be attacked more easily. Mines are inexpensive compared to many other weapons, and persons with little training can put them into place.

There are two chief kinds of mines, *land mines* and *naval mines.*

Land mines

Land mines are planted in the ground. They may be laid out in planned patterns called *mine fields.* Mines may be planted by soldiers or fired into an area by artillery. They also may be dropped by helicopters.

Kinds of land mines. The main types of land mines are: (1) antipersonnel mines, (2) antitank mines, (3) chemical mines, (4) controlled mines, and (5) nuclear mines.

Antipersonnel mines are used to kill or injure enemy soldiers. They have a sensitive *fuse* (triggering device) that is set off by the weight of even a small person. They also may be set off when someone walks into a wire or moves an object to which the mines are wired.

Some antipersonnel mines have small explosive charges and kill only a few persons a short distance away. Others can kill many people more than 200 yards (180 meters) away. Some antipersonnel mines fire an explosive charge that explodes in the air, spraying shrapnel over a large area (see **Shrapnel**).

Mines called *booby traps* explode when they are moved. They are hidden in buildings; under dead soldiers; or in ordinary objects, such as appliances and briefcases, that are likely to be moved by enemy troops.

Antitank mines destroy enemy tanks and other vehicles. These mines are larger than antipersonnel mines. Most types of antitank mines explode only when a weight of more than about 300 pounds (140 kilograms) moves over them. Soldiers can walk safely on antitank mines. But these mines destroy trucks and lightly armored vehicles and at least damage the metal tracks on which tanks move.

Chemical mines release a poison gas when they are triggered. The gas kills or injures unprotected troops.

Controlled mines are placed in position before a battle. They are exploded by remote control when enemy forces approach the mines.

Nuclear mines contain small nuclear devices. These mines are used to blow up concrete bridges or to close off mountain passes. Such jobs would require many tons of conventional explosives. Nuclear mines are small enough to be carried by two persons or in a jeep.

Detecting land mines. Land mines can be detected by several methods. Soldiers may locate mines by crawling along the ground and carefully probing the area ahead with their bayonets. When a mine is found, it is cautiously dug out and the fuse is removed, or its posi-

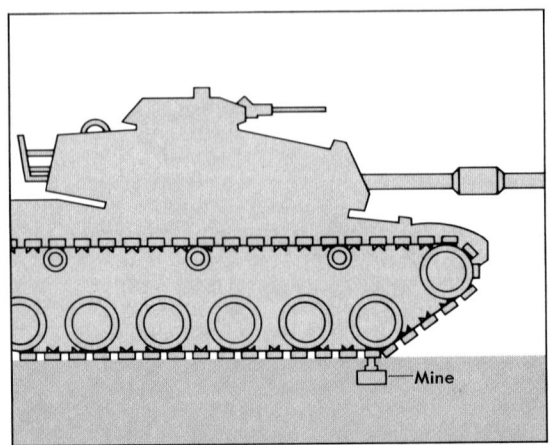

An antitank mine explodes when run over by a tank or other heavy vehicle, *above.* The mine, which is buried close to the surface, is triggered by the pressure of the vehicle.

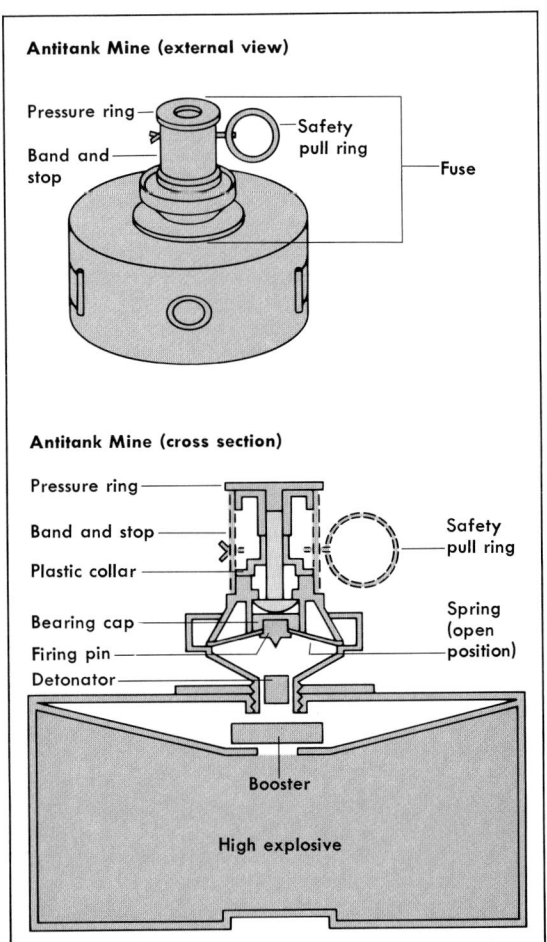

WORLD BOOK diagrams by Steven Liska

The parts of an antitank mine are shown above. The mine is detonated when the pressure ring at the top is forced down into the mine. This action causes the firing pin to hit the detonator, which then sets off the booster. The booster then activates the high explosive, and the mine explodes.

tion is marked so it can be bypassed. Sensitive instruments called *mine detectors* locate mines with metal cases. Mines can be detected more rapidly by a mine-detecting device mounted on a jeep. The jeep stops automatically when the device detects a mine.

After mines have been detected, they may be marked and bypassed, exploded by artillery fire, or blown up by tanks fitted with special rollers or chain devices. The devices trigger the mines when passing over them. Devices called *snakes* are also used to clear minefields. Snakes are long tubes packed with explosives that are detonated in a mined area. The blast sets off nearby mines and clears a path for troops and vehicles.

Naval mines

Naval mines rest on or are anchored to the floor of a body of water. Some naval mines float freely, but such mines are dangerous to friendly ships as well as enemy vessels. Naval mines are laid by surface ships, including vessels called *minelayers,* and by aircraft and submarines. Some naval mines are self-propelled. They are launched from a submarine and travel a few miles before settling on the ocean floor. The CAPTOR mine of the United States Navy is anchored to the ocean bottom. The mine launches a self-guided torpedo after detecting the propeller noise of a passing submarine.

Kinds of naval mines. There are four chief kinds of naval mines. They are (1) acoustic mines, (2) contact mines, (3) magnetic mines, and (4) pressure mines.

Acoustic mines are exploded by the sound of a ship's propellers.

Contact mines are triggered when a ship touches them. They also may be exploded when a ship touches antennas that stick out from the mines.

Magnetic mines are triggered by the magnetic field that surrounds a metal warship. To avoid setting off a magnetic mine, a ship may use a set of electrical cables called a *degaussing belt,* which reduces or neutralizes the magnetic field.

Pressure mines explode when passing ships cause a change in the water pressure around the mines.

Detecting naval mines. Naval mines are difficult to detect and to *sweep* (remove or detonate). They may be fitted with counting devices that allow a certain number of ships to pass before the mines explode. The mines may also be fitted with timers that prevent them from firing for a certain number of hours or days. Ships called *minesweepers* use sonar to locate mines, which are then swept. Minesweeping helicopters tow devices that sweep mines in shallow water. Ships called *minehunters* operate cable-controlled vehicles that examine and destroy mines on the ocean floor.

Acoustic mines are blown up by noisemaking devices towed underwater. The anchor cables of contact mines are cut by instruments towed underwater by mine-sweepers. The mines then float to the surface and are exploded by gunfire. Some magnetic mines are triggered by electrical devices towed by ships. Pressure mines are cleared by having a small, specially equipped ship pass nearby to detonate them.

History

Land mines have been used in warfare for more than 200 years. The term *mine* came from the practice of dig-

© Michael T. J. Kulik

A minesweeping device towed by a helicopter is called a *sled.* The magnetic field produced by the sled detonates magnetic mines that have been planted underwater.

ging tunnels under enemy positions, packing the tunnels with gunpowder, and exploding them. During the Civil War (1861-1865), Union soldiers mined a section of Confederate trenches at Petersburg, Va. The soldiers dug a tunnel more than 500 feet (150 meters) long, placed gunpowder in it, and blew a large crater in the Confederate defenses. During World War I (1914-1918), troops buried artillery shells. These shells exploded when stepped on by a person or run over by a tank or truck. After World War I, mines with wood, metal, or plastic containers were developed. Land mines were widely used during World War II (1939-1945) and later wars.

The first naval mines—floating vessels that contained explosives—were used in the late 1500's. Early types of underwater mines, called *torpedoes,* were sealed wooden containers filled with gunpowder and equipped with a fuse. The fuse was set, and a diver swam under an enemy ship and attached the torpedo to the ship's hull. During the Revolutionary War (1775-1783), David Bushnell, an American inventor, developed the first American submarine equipped with a mine-attaching device. During the Civil War, both the Confederate Navy and the Union Navy used underwater mines. Naval mines were also used extensively in most later wars.   Norman Polmar

Mine Workers of America, United. See United Mine Workers of America.

Miner. See Mining; Coal (How coal is mined; The coal industry [picture: Coal miners]).

Miner, Jack (1865-1944), was a Canadian bird conservationist and researcher of North American bird migrations. He established a bird sanctuary on his farm near Kingsville, Ont., in 1904. Miner studied the migrations of ducks and geese by marking thousands of these birds with numbered metal leg bands, then releasing them. Hunters returned the bands from birds they shot. In this way, Miner learned where the migrating birds went. Friends established the Jack Miner Migratory Bird Foundation in 1931 to help him continue his research. Miner was born John Thomas Miner in Dover Center, Ohio.   G. J. Kenagy

Hornblende

Feldspar

Quartz

Mica

Rocks are made of minerals. A chunk of granite, *left,* contains bits of hornblende, feldspar, quartz, and mica. Alone, these minerals appear as shown, *right.*

Mineral

Mineral is the most common solid material found on the earth. The earth's land and oceans all rest on a layer of rock made of minerals. Rocks on the earth's surface are also made of minerals. Even soil contains tiny pieces of minerals broken from rocks. Minerals are also found on our moon and on Mercury, Venus, and Mars.

Minerals include such common substances as rock salt and pencil "lead," and such rare ones as gold, silver, and gems. There are about 3,000 kinds of minerals, but only about 100 of them are common. Most of the others are harder to find than gold.

People use minerals to make many products. For example, graphite is used for pencil leads. Other products made from minerals include cement for building, fertilizers for farming, and chemicals for manufacturing.

Many people use the term *mineral* for any substance taken from the earth. Such substances include coal, petroleum, natural gas, and sand—none of which is a mineral. However, these substances are commonly known as mineral resources. Certain substances in food and water, such as calcium, iron, and phosphorus, also are called minerals. But mineralogists, the scientists who study minerals, do not consider any of them minerals.

Mineralogists use the term *mineral* to mean a substance that has all of the four following features. (1) A mineral is found in nature. A natural diamond is a mineral, but a synthetic diamond is not. (2) A mineral is made up of substances that were never alive. Coal, petroleum, and natural gas are not minerals because they

were formed from the remains of animals and plants. (3) A mineral has the same chemical makeup wherever it is found. Sand is not a mineral because samples from different places usually have different chemical makeups. (4) The atoms of a mineral are arranged in a regular pattern, and form solid units called *crystals.* The calcium and phosphorus found in milk are not minerals because they are dissolved in a liquid and are not crystals.

This article discusses only substances that mineralogists consider minerals. For information on coal, petroleum, and other products that are taken from the ground, see the articles listed in the *Related articles* section of the **Mining** article. For information on other materials that are often called minerals, see the *World Book* articles on **Food** (How the body uses food) and **Ocean** (Minerals).

Identifying minerals

Minerals vary greatly in appearance and feel. Some minerals have glasslike surfaces that sparkle with color. Others look dull and feel greasy. The hardest minerals can scratch glass. The softest ones can be scratched by a fingernail. Four of the main characteristics of minerals are (1) luster, (2) cleavage, (3) hardness, and (4) color.

Luster of a mineral may be metallic or nonmetallic. Minerals with metallic luster shine like metal. Such min-

David F. Hess, the contributor of this article, is Associate Professor of Geology at Western Illinois University. All photos are courtesy of the Field Museum of Natural History, Chicago, unless otherwise noted.

erals include galena, gold, and ilmenite. Minerals with nonmetallic luster vary in appearance. Quartz looks glassy, talc has a pearly surface, and varieties of cinnabar appear dull and claylike. The luster of a mineral also may differ from sample to sample. Some cinnabar, for example, has a metallic luster rather than a dull luster.

Cleavage is the splitting of a mineral into pieces that have flat surfaces. Minerals differ in the number of directions they split, and in the angles at which the flat surfaces meet. Mica splits in one direction and forms thin sheets. Halite has three cleavage directions, and it breaks into tiny cubes. A diamond may split in four directions, forming a pyramid. Other minerals, such as quartz, do not split cleanly, but break into pieces with irregular surfaces.

Hardness of minerals may be tested by scratching one mineral with another. The harder mineral scratches the softer one, and mineralogists use a scale of hardness based on this principle. Friedrich Mohs, a German mineralogist, invented the scale in 1822. The Mohs hardness scale lists 10 minerals from the softest to the hardest. These minerals are numbered from 1 to 10. The hardness of other minerals is found by determining whether they scratch, or are scratched by, the minerals in the Mohs scale. For example, galena scratches gypsum (number 2), but is scratched by calcite (number 3). Therefore, galena's hardness is $2\frac{1}{2}$—about halfway between that of gypsum and calcite. A person's fingernail has a hardness of about 2.

Color of some minerals depends on the substances that make up the crystals. The black of ilmenite, the red of cinnabar, and the green of serpentine all result from the chemical composition of these minerals. Other minerals get their color from chemical impurities. Pure quartz, for example, has colorless crystals. But tiny amounts of other substances in quartz crystals can give quartz a pink or green tint, or even make it black.

Other identification tests. Some minerals may be recognized by their *habit* (general appearance). Gold is found in the form of nuggets, and diamonds are found

as crystals. Halite may have the form of grains, clumps of crystals, or large chunks. Serpentine asbestos occurs as fibers. Mineralogists can also identify minerals by feeling, tasting, or smelling them. Talc and serpentine feel greasy. Epsomite and halite taste salty, and borax and melanterite taste sweet. Kaolinite has an earthy smell.

A *streak test* uses color to identify a mineral. The mineral is rubbed across a slightly rough, white porcelain plate. The rubbing grinds some of the mineral to powder and leaves a colored streak on the plate. But the streak is not always the same color as the sample. Hematite varies from reddish brown to black, but always leaves a red streak. Chalcopyrite, a brassy yellow mineral, produces a green-black streak.

Many chemical tests can identify minerals. One of the simplest consists of pouring a warm, dilute acid on the sample. If the acid fizzes, the sample belongs to a group of minerals called *carbonates*. Calcite, argonite, and dolomite are examples of carbonates. These minerals contain carbon and oxygen, together with other chemicals. When attacked by acid, the minerals release carbon dioxide gas which forms bubbles in the acid. This test may be made at home, using vinegar for the acid. In the *flame test*, a bit of a mineral is ground into powder near the air holes at the base of a lighted Bunsen burner. Air carries the powder up into the flame. The powder gives the flame a color that identifies the mineral.

Inside minerals

Mineral crystals occur in many sizes. A giant crystal of beryl or feldspar may weigh several tons. Tiny crystals of kaolin may be too small to be studied even with a microscope. Regardless of their size, all crystals are basically the same. They are groups of atoms arranged in a regular pattern.

To imagine what it is like inside a crystal, you can think of "rooms" formed by the crystal's atoms. A room in a copper crystal is formed by 14 copper atoms. The room has an atom at each corner of the floor and ceiling, and an atom at the centers of the floor, the ceiling,-

MOHS HARDNESS SCALE		
MINERAL	HARDNESS	COMMON TESTS
Talc	1	Scratched by a fingernail
Gypsum	2	Scratched by a fingernail
Calcite	3	Scratched by a copper coin
Fluorite	4	Scratched by a knife blade or window glass
Apatite	5	Scratched by a knife blade or window glass
Feldspar	6	
Quartz	7	Scratches a knife blade or window glass
Topaz	8	Scratches a knife blade or window glass
Corundum	9	
Diamond	10	Scratches all common materials

Common identification tests. A mineral's hardness is tested by scratching it against minerals listed in the Mohs scale, *left.* A streak test of hematite, *center,* leaves a red streak. The tester rubs the mineral against rough porcelain and wipes the streak with his finger. *Right,* calcite cleaves into blocks, and mica into sheets.

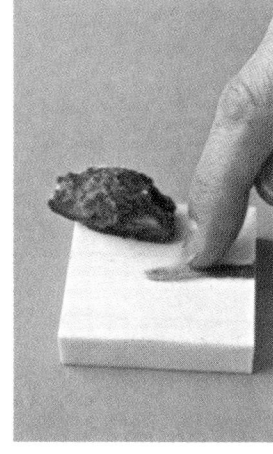

Common minerals with metallic luster

Bornite Cu_5FeS_4. Copper-red with purple-blue tarnish. Hardness 3. Cleaves.

Chalcopyrite $CuFeS_2$. Brassy yellow. Leaves a green-black streak. Hardness $3\frac{1}{2}$-4. Does not cleave.

Copper Cu. Copper-red with brown tarnish. Hardness $2\frac{1}{2}$-3. Does not cleave.

Galena PbS. Bright metallic lead-gray cubes. Hardness $2\frac{1}{2}$. Cleaves to form cubes.

Gold Au. Yellow nuggets, grains, and flakes. Does not tarnish. Hardness $2\frac{1}{2}$-3. Does not cleave.

Graphite C. Steel-gray. Feels greasy. Hardness 1-2. Cleaves into tablets and sheets.

Magnetite Fe_3O_4. Black. Attracted by magnet and may act as magnet. Hardness $5\frac{1}{2}$-$6\frac{1}{2}$. Does not cleave.

Pyrite FeS_2. Pale brassy yellow. Leaves green- to brown-black streak. Hardness 6-$6\frac{1}{2}$. Does not cleave.

Pyrrhotite FeS. Bronze-yellow. Weakly attracted to magnet. Hardness $3\frac{1}{2}$-$4\frac{1}{2}$. Does not cleave.

Rutile TiO_2. Red to black with gem-like luster. Hardness 6-$6\frac{1}{2}$. Cleaves.

Silver Ag. Silver-white (above, as flecks in barite), tarnishing to black. Hardness $2\frac{1}{2}$-3. Does not cleave.

Stibnite Sb_2S_3. Gray columns with black tarnish. Hardness 2. Cleaves in one direction.

Common minerals with nonmetallic luster

Almandine, a garnet, $Fe_3Al_2Si_3O_{12}$. Deep red, brownish-red, or brownish-black. Hardness 7-$7\frac{1}{2}$. Does not cleave.

Azurite $Cu_3(CO_3)_2(OH)_2$. Blue. Hardness $3\frac{1}{2}$-4. Cleaves irregularly.

Calcite $CaCO_3$. Colorless or white when pure. Hardness 3. Rhombohedral cleavage.

Fluorite CaF_2. Green, blue, or purple cubes. Hardness 4. Cleaves in four directions.

Gypsum $CaSO_4 \cdot 2H_2O$. Colorless, white, gray, or yellow to brown. Hardness 2. Cleaves into plates.

Kyanite Al_2SiO_5. Often, pale blue to white. Hardness 4-$7\frac{1}{2}$. Cleaves in one direction.

Malachite $Cu_2(CO_3)(OH)_2$. Bright green. Hardness $3\frac{1}{2}$-4. Cleaves irregularly.

Muscovite $KAl_2(AlSi_3O_{10})(OH)_2$. Colorless. Hardness $2\frac{1}{2}$-3. Cleaves into tablets and sheets.

Potassium feldspar $KAlSi_3O_8$. White to pink. Hardness 6. Cleaves almost at right angles.

Quartz SiO_2. Clear or tinted glassy crystals. Hardness 7. Does not cleave.

Sulfur S. Yellow. Melts and burns with a match. Hardness $1\frac{1}{2}$-$2\frac{1}{2}$. Cleaves irregularly.

Talc $Mg_3Si_4O_{10}(OH)_2$. White, green, or gray. Feels greasy. Hardness 1. Cleaves into tablets and sheets.

and each of the four walls. A copper crystal consists of many of these rooms side by side and one on top of the other. The rooms share copper atoms where they meet. Mineralogists call such rooms *unit cells.*

Most minerals consist of more than one kind of atom. Halite, for example, consists of sodium atoms and chlorine atoms. Other minerals may have as many as five kinds of atoms in complicated arrangements. Some unit cells have six walls instead of four, and others have slanted walls. Such differences in the shape of unit cells produce differences in the shape of mineral crystals.

Chemical bonds are electrical forces that hold atoms together in a crystal. An *ionic bond* results when certain atoms give up some of their electrons to other atoms. Ionic bonds are the most common chemical bond in minerals. A *covalent bond* results when several atoms share electrons. Covalent bonds, which are very strong, occur in such minerals as diamonds, and are common in compounds containing carbon. Chemical bonds can hold two or more atoms together only in definite positions. These positions depend on the size of the atoms, and the number of bonding electrons. The shape and size of the unit cell, in turn, depend on the positions the atoms take when they are bonded together. See **Bond.**

Bonds between atoms are not all equally strong. This variation in bonding strength explains why some crystals can be cleaved. Cleavage can take place in a crystal when the weak bonds lie at a right angle to a flat surface that is called a *cleavage plane.* When the crystal is cut along the cleavage plane, the weak bonds break and the crystal splits, exposing the flat surface.

How minerals grow. Most minerals grow in liquids. For example, some crystals grow in a liquid called *magma* deep inside the earth. This extremely hot substance contains all the kinds of atoms that make up the earth's minerals. When magma cools, some atoms become bonded together and form tiny crystals. The crystals grow by adding layers of atoms to their flat outer surfaces. The new atoms must be the right size, and they must have the right number of bonding electrons to fit into the growing crystals.

Mineral composition and structure are both important in studying and classifying minerals. Some minerals have the same kind of crystal, but differ in one or more of the atoms that make it up. For example, olivine has a basic crystal made of oxygen and silicon atoms. Either iron or magnesium atoms can fit into this crystal. As a result, there are two kinds of olivine—forsterite, which contains magnesium, and fayalite, which contains iron. Mineralogists use the term *isomorphic* for minerals that have the same structure but different compositions.

Some mineral crystals are made of the same kinds of

How atoms are arranged in minerals

 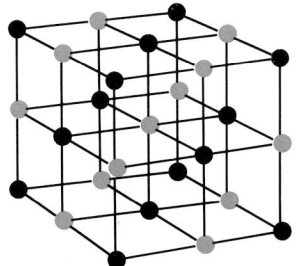 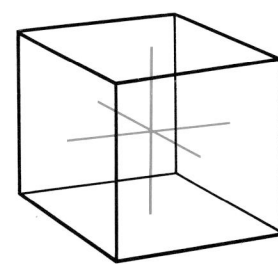

© Breck P. Kent

A halite crystal, *above left,* has four sides and is made up of billions of four-sided unit cells. Each cell, *center,* contains 14 sodium atoms (shown in black) and 13 chlorine atoms (blue). Halite belongs to the isometric crystal system—one of seven systems into which all mineral crystals are grouped. A diagram for the isometric system, *right,* includes three axes (imaginary lines) that show the directions followed by the crystal's edges.

 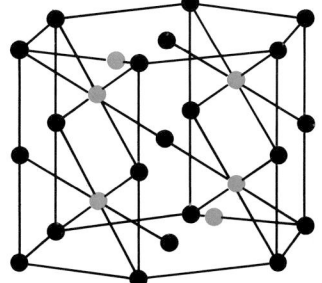 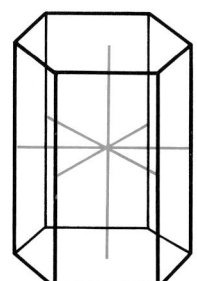

© Breck P. Kent

A corundum crystal, *above left,* has six sides. Its unit cell, *center,* is a six-sided "room" containing 21 oxygen atoms (black) and 6 aluminum atoms (blue). Corundum is in the hexagonal system, *right,* which has four axes.

atoms, but differ in the way the atoms are arranged. For example, diamond and graphite are both made of the element carbon. The carbon in diamond, which is the hardest substance known, is bonded into a blocky framework. The carbon in graphite is bonded into thin, fragile sheets. Mineralogists use the term *polymorphic* to describe minerals that have the same composition but different structures.

The major *classes* of minerals—based on composition and structure—include *elements, sulfides, halides, carbonates, sulfates, oxides, phosphates, and silicates.* The silicate class is especially important, because silicates make up 95 per cent of the minerals, by volume, in the earth's crust. Mineral classes are divided into *families* on the basis of the chemicals in each mineral. Families, in turn, are made up of *groups* of minerals that have a similar structure. Groups are further divided into *species.*

History of mineralogy

Early studies. Minerals were among the first substances that people used and described. Egyptian paintings of 5,000 years ago show that minerals were used in weapons and jewelry, and in religious ceremonies. Theophrastus, a Greek philosopher, wrote a short work on minerals about 300 B.C. Pliny the Elder of Rome wrote about metals, ores, stones, and gems about A.D. 77.

Other early writings about minerals were done by German scientists. These writings include *De Mineralibus* (1262) by Albertus Magnus and *De Re Metallica* (1556) by Georgius Agricola.

The scientific study of mineral crystals began in the 1600's. In 1665, Robert Hooke, an English scientist, showed that metal balls piled in different ways duplicated the shapes of alum crystals. In 1669, Nicolaus Steno, a Danish physician, found that the angles between the faces of quartz crystals were always the same, even though the crystals had different shapes.

By the late 1700's, scientists had studied and described many minerals. But they only guessed at the makeup of crystals and the reasons for their shape. A French scientist, Romé de l'Isle, suggested in 1772 that Steno's discovery could be explained only if the crystals were composed of identical units stacked together in a regular way. During the 1780's, the French scientist René J. Haüy made further studies of these mineral units. He called them *integral molecules.* About 1780, chemists began to develop clearer ideas about the nature of chemical elements. Mineralogists then saw that minerals were made up of chemicals, but they still did not understand their structure.

The 1900's. In the 1900's, X-ray studies provided the key to the internal structure of minerals. In 1912, German scientist Max von Laue sent an X-ray beam through a crystal of sphalerite. The beam was *diffracted* (divided) by the flat surfaces of the crystal. The experiment showed that the atoms in sphalerite are bonded together into sheets which connect to one another at specific angles. From similar experiments, scientists later learned how atoms are arranged into unit cells and, in turn, into crystals. By the 1930's, scientists had used X rays to study and describe many different minerals.

Today, new laboratory instruments are changing the study of minerals. The *electron probe microanalyzer,* linked to a computer, can measure changes in the chemical composition of a single crystal. A *scanning electron microscope* magnifies crystals many thousands of times beyond normal size. Using a special electron microscope, scientists can photograph the shadows or reflections of atoms and molecules. In this way they can observe the internal structure of a mineral crystal.

Mineralogists are still trying to answer many questions. For example, they would like to know how certain minerals are made, and why impurities affect a crystal's mechanical and electrical properties. In addition, mineralogists are constantly finding new uses for minerals and the chemical elements they contain.   David F. Hess

Related articles. For information on the minerals found in specific parts of the world, see the *Economy* section of the articles on each country, state, and province. See also the following articles:

Why some minerals cleave

E. R. Degginger

Graphite, *above,* consists of layers of carbon atoms. Weak bonds hold the layers together and form cleavage planes, *below.* The crystal splits into tablets along these planes.

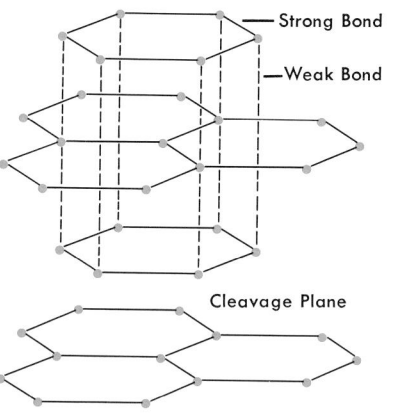

Strong Bond

Weak Bond

Cleavage Plane

Minerals

Alabaster	Cinnabar	Glauconite	Meer-
Amphibole	Columbite	Graphite	schaum
Asbestos	Corundum	Gypsum	Mica
Azurite	Diopside	Hematite	Monazite
Bauxite	Dolomite	Hornblende	Olivine
Beryl	Emery	Ilmenite	Pyrite
Calcite	Feldspar	Kyanite	Pyroxene
Carnotite	Flint	Limonite	Quartz
Chalcocite	Fluorite	Loadstone	Salt
Chalcopyrite	Galena	Malachite	Serpentine

Sillimanite	Talc	Vermiculite
Sphalerite	Trona	Wolframite

Other related articles

See **Gem**; **Metal**; **Mining**; and **Rock** and their lists of *Related articles*. See also the following articles:

Alumina	Clay	Crystal
Bond	Conservation (Min-	Hardness
Ceramics	eral conservation)	

Outline

I. Identifying minerals
   A. Luster   D. Color
   B. Cleavage   E. Other identification tests
   C. Hardness
II. Inside minerals
   A. Mineral crystals   C. How minerals grow
   B. Chemical bonds   D. Mineral composition and
                                    structure
III. History of mineralogy

Questions

Why does quartz have a variety of colors?
What is a unit cell?
What mineral has a salty taste? A sweet taste?
Why can some minerals be split into pieces with flat surfaces?
Why is a synthetic diamond not a mineral?
What did Max von Laue discover about minerals?
What holds together the atoms in a crystal?
How many kinds of minerals are there?
What kind of mineral is a carbonate? Why does acid fizz when
   poured on a carbonate?
How do minerals grow?

Reading and Study Guide

See *Rocks and minerals* in the Research Guide/Index, Volume 22, for a *Reading and Study Guide.*

Additional resources

Cheney, Glenn A. *Mineral Resources.* Watts, 1985. For younger
   readers.
Chesterman, Charles W. *The Audubon Society Field Guide to
   North American Rocks and Minerals.* Knopf, 1979.
Fodor, R. V. *Gold, Copper, Iron: How Metals Are Formed,
   Found, and Used.* Enslow, 1989. Suitable for younger readers.
Klein, Cornelis, and Hurlbut, C. S. *Manual of Mineralogy.* 20th
   ed. Wiley, 1986. First published in 1985.
Medenbach, Olaf, and Wilk, Harry. *The Magic of Minerals.*
   Springer-Verlag, 1989. First published in 1986.
Robbins, Manuel. *The Collector's Book of Fluorescent Minerals.*
   Van Nostrand, 1983.
Simon and Schuster's Guide to Rocks and Minerals. Ed. by Mar-
   tin Prinz and others. Simon & Schuster, 1978.
Symes, R. F., and others. *Rocks & Minerals.* Knopf, 1988. For
   younger readers.

Mineral oil is a clear, colorless, oily liquid with almost no taste or odor. It is also called *liquid paraffin, liquid petrolatum, white mineral oil,* and *white paraffin oil.* Mineral oil is an ingredient in certain medicines and cosmetics. It also serves as a dissolving agent in the manufacture of plastics, and as an industrial lubricant. Mineral oil comes from the distillation of petroleum *fractions* (separated parts) at 600 ° to 750 °F (316 ° to 399 °C). Further refinement purifies the oil. See also **Dis-tillation.**   Geoffrey E. Dolbear

Mineral water, also called *aerated water,* is spring water with a high content of mineral matter or of gas. (The term *aerated* means *charged with gas.*) The mineral matter includes salt, Epsom salt, lime, magnesia, iron, silica, boron, fluorine, and many others, including radioactive substances. The most common gases in mineral water are carbon dioxide and hydrogen sulfide.

In most cases, the water is rain water that has seeped underground through rocks, dissolving mineral matter on the way. Other springs may contain *magmatic* or *juvenile* water, which rises from deep in the earth after forming through a chemical process in rocks. Some of these springs are hot springs. Others have cooled to ordinary temperatures.

People have used mineral water since ancient times to cure such ailments as rheumatism, skin infections, and poor digestion. The temperature of the water, the location, the altitude, and the climate at the springs are all considered in the treatment.

There are thousands of mineral springs in North America. About 800 have at one time had *spas* (resorts) where people used to come for the waters. Most of them are in the East and Midwest. Their popularity has declined since the turn of the century, and many have shut down. The best-known mineral springs today are at Saratoga Springs, N.Y.; Hot Springs, Ark.; and French Lick, Ind. Hot Springs has been made a national park (see **Hot Springs National Park**).

The waters from some foreign springs are imported to the United States. Among these waters are the Apollinaris from Germany, Hunyadi-Janos from Hungary, and Vichy from France. Water taken from mineral springs is sold in sterilized bottles.   Douglas S. Cherkauer

See also **Black Forest.**

Mineralogy. See **Mineral.**

Minerva was one of the most important goddesses in ancient Roman mythology. Minerva resembled the Greek goddess Athena and like her was a virgin goddess. She was the favorite child of Jupiter, the king of the gods. One myth tells of her being born out of Jupiter's head, fully grown and dressed in armor.

Minerva had a variety of functions. Originally, she represented skill in handicrafts, particularly those associated with women, such as spinning and weaving. Later, Minerva came to symbolize general skill. Still later, the Romans worshiped her as the goddess of wisdom. The owl has traditionally been considered wise because it was the bird of Minerva.

The Romans, who believed that warfare involved the higher mental powers, worshiped Minerva as the goddess of the intellectual aspect of war. Most artists showed her wearing armor and a helmet. Minerva carried a magic shield or breastplate called the *aegis.*

E. N. Genovese

See also **Athena; Aegis.**

Mines, Bureau of, is an agency of the United States Department of the Interior. The bureau helps to ensure that the nation has enough copper, lead, silver, zinc, and other nonfuel minerals for its needs. The agency conducts research to develop safe and economical methods for mining, processing, using, and recycling mineral resources. In addition, it investigates ways to use domestic ores as substitutes for imported minerals and ways to decrease the pollution and land damage caused by mining.

The bureau publishes statistics on all phases of nonfuel mineral resource development, including exploration, production, shipments, and prices. The bureau was created in 1910.   Critically reviewed by the Bureau of Mines

Minesweeper. See **Mine warfare** (Detecting naval mines).

Ming dynasty ruled China from A.D. 1368 to 1644, a period of Chinese rule between two foreign conquests. It was preceded by the Mongol Empire and followed by the Manchu dynasty. Ming rulers restored traditional institutions, such as the civil service, which the Mongols had suspended. Chinese authority extended into Mongolia, Korea, Southeast Asia, and the Ryukyu Islands.

Ming means *bright* in Chinese, and the period was important especially in the arts. The imperial palace in Beijing's *Forbidden City* reached its current splendor largely through the efforts of Ming architects. Artists also produced exquisite porcelain, bronze, and lacquerware. During the final century of the Ming dynasty, increasing numbers of Europeans began visiting China and opening it up to foreign influence.   Richard L. Davis

Miniature bull terrier is a small, muscular dog. Except for its smaller size, it is identical to the bull terrier. Breeders in England developed the miniature bull terrier by mating small bull terriers to one another.

The miniature bull terrier stands about 10 to 14 inches (25 to 36 centimeters) high and usually weighs 15 to 30

Augustino J. Napoli
A miniature bull terrier is a small, muscular dog.

pounds (7 to 14 kilograms). It has a long, wide head; small eyes; pointed ears; a short, glossy coat; and a short, straight tail. Miniature bull terriers most commonly are white. They also may be gray, brown, tan, red, or other colors, usually with white markings.

Miniature bull terriers are intelligent, alert, and affectionate. They make good show dogs and pets.
Critically reviewed by the Miniature Bull Terrier Club of America
See also **Bull terrier.**

Miniature pinscher, *PIHN shuhr,* is a toy dog of the terrier family. It comes from the Rhine Valley of Germany. Germans sometimes call it a *reh pinscher* (deer terrier) because it looks like a small deer. It has a wedge-shaped head and black eyes. The dog may be red, black with rust-red markings, or brown with rust-red markings. It resembles the Doberman pinscher but weighs only 6 to 10 pounds (2.7 to 4.5 kilograms). See also **Dog** (picture: Toy dogs).
Critically reviewed by the Miniature Pinscher Club of America

Miniature schnauzer, *SHNOW zuhr,* is a breed of dog that originated in Germany in the 1800's. Breeders developed the dog by mating the standard schnauzer with the affenpinscher. The dog's high spirits and intelli-

gence have helped make it popular in the United States. It is also a good watchdog and ratcatcher.

The dog's coloring may be salt and pepper, black and silver, black and tan, or all black. It has a shaggy beard and long, bushy eyebrows. Most owners have the dog's coat clipped short on top and the beard and eyebrows trimmed. The dog stands 12 to 14 inches (30 to 36 centimeters) tall at the shoulders and weighs about 15 pounds (7 kilograms). See also **Dog** (picture: Terriers).
Critically reviewed by the American Kennel Club

Minibike. See **Motorcycle** (Kinds of motorcycles).
Minim, *MIHN uhm,* is the smallest unit of fluid measure in the apothecaries' system of measurement. Druggists once used this system, but they now measure many prescriptions in metric units. One minim equals 0.062 milliliter, or cubic centimeter. In the apothecaries' system, 60 minims equals one fluid dram, and one fluid dram equals 1/8 of an ounce. One drop of liquid from a medicine dropper contains roughly one minim. The word *minim* comes from the Latin word *minimus,* meaning *smallest.*   Richard S. Davis

Minimum wage is the smallest amount of money per hour that an employer may legally pay a worker. It may be established by law to cover all workers or only those in certain industries. Self-employed persons and employees of small businesses are often not covered by minimum wage laws.

In the United States, about 40 states have minimum wage laws or boards that set minimum wages. The first state law was passed in Massachusetts in 1912. Federal minimum wage legislation became effective when the Fair Labor Standards Act was passed in 1938. The original act set a minimum wage of 25 cents per hour for 1938. The minimum wage has been increased several times by amendments to the Fair Labor Standards Act. Under the latest amendment, passed in 1989, the minimum wage was raised from $3.35 an hour to $3.80 an hour in April 1990 and to $4.25 an hour in April 1991.

The 1989 amendment also established a *training wage* that employers could pay workers under age 20. This wage, which took effect in April 1990, was set at $3.35 an hour or 85 percent of the applicable minimum wage, whichever was greater, for the first 90 days of employment. But few employers used the training wage. Many employers believed that the training wage was difficult to administer or that they would not be able to attract qualified workers at the lower rate. The training wage expired in 1993.

About 80 percent of all private industries are covered by the federal minimum wage. Most states set lower minimum wages than those set by federal legislation, and a few set them higher. In Canada, each province or territory sets its own minimum wage. There is also a minimum wage for employees of the federal government. In the United Kingdom, wage boards set minimum wages for particular industries. In the United Kingdom and other European countries, labor unions and employers set unofficial minimum wages by agreement.

Minimum wage laws were set up to raise wages for low-income workers without substantially reducing their job opportunities. But many economists feel employers do not hire as many low-income workers as they would if no minimum wage existed.   Paul L. Burgess

See also **Fair Labor Standards Act.**

In an open-pit copper mine, miners use power shovels to load the mineral-bearing rock called *ore* onto trucks. The miners remove the ore in horizontal layers called *benches.* The trucks haul ore out of the mine to crushers.

Nicholas Devore III, Bruce Coleman Inc.

Mining

Mining is the process of taking minerals or coal from the earth. Most substances that we get from the earth we obtain by mining. Mining provides iron for making airplanes, automobiles, and refrigerators. Mines also supply salt for food; gold, silver, and diamonds for jewelry; and coal for fuel. We mine stone for buildings, phosphate for fertilizer, and gravel for highways.

Some substances can be mined more cheaply than others because they are found at the earth's surface. Some lie far beneath the surface and can be removed only by digging deep underground. Other mined substances are found in oceans, lakes, and rivers.

People have mined the earth for thousands of years. About 6000 B.C., people dug pits and tunnels to get flint, a hard stone used to make tools and weapons. By 3500 B.C., people were mining tin and copper. They combined these metals to make bronze, a hard *alloy* (mixture of metals) that made better tools and weapons. The ancient Romans probably were the first people to realize that mining could make a nation rich and powerful. Merchants traded valuable stones and metals and brought riches to the Roman Empire. The Romans took over the mines of every country they conquered.

The Roman Empire ended in the A.D. 400's. For about a thousand years, few advancements were made in mining. During the 1400's, coal, iron, and other materials were mined in Europe, especially in Germany, Sweden, and France. Mining also developed in South America. The Inca Indians and other tribes of South America used metals to make tools, jewelry, and weapons.

Mining began in what is now the United States during the early 1700's. French explorers mined lead and zinc in the valley of the Mississippi River. In the mid-

William Hustrulid, the contributor of this article, is Professor of Mining at the Colorado School of Mines.

1800's, miners began to dig up large amounts of coal in Pennsylvania. At about the same time, thousands of people rushed to California hoping to find gold. In the West, the gold rush led to the discovery of copper, lead, silver, and other useful minerals.

Most substances obtained by mining are minerals. A mineral is made of materials that were never alive. Thus, coal, petroleum, and natural gas are not considered true minerals because they were formed from the remains of plants that lived long ago. Coal, however, is obtained by mining. Because this article discusses the recovery of mined substances, it includes both minerals and coal. For information on drilling for oil and natural gas, see the *World Book* articles **Petroleum** and **Gas** (fuel).

Kinds of mining

There are many methods of mining. Each is based on where and how a coal or mineral deposit is found. Some deposits lie at or near the earth's surface, and others are far underground. Some minerals are found as a compact mass, and others are widely scattered. Minerals also vary in hardness and in the ease with which the mineral-bearing material called *ore* can be separated from the surrounding rocks. Some minerals occur in such large bodies of water as oceans and seas, and are obtained by pumping. For a discussion of the methods of mining a particular mineral, see the *World Book* article on that mineral. For details on coal-mining methods, see **Coal** (How coal is mined; illustrations).

Today, most mines are highly mechanized. Hydraulically powered drills bore holes in the ore. Large machines dig and load the ore, and trains, trucks, and conveyors transport it. In underground mines, high-speed elevators called *skips* carry ore to the surface.

Surface mining methods are used when deposits occur at or near the surface of the earth. These methods include placer mining, dredging, open-pit mining, strip mining, and quarrying.

Placer mining is a way of obtaining gold, platinum, tin, and other so-called *heavy minerals* from gravel and sand deposits where nearby water supplies are plentiful. The exact technique used depends on the size and kind of deposit. On a small scale, *panning* may be used to recover gold and other minerals from streams. On a larger scale, miners use a form of placer mining called *sluicing.* In this method, the mineral-bearing gravel and sand are shoveled into the upper end of a slanting wooden trough called a *riffle box.* In the box, they are washed by water. The valuable minerals are heavier than the sand and gravel, and settle in grooves on the bottom of the box. The gravel and sand are washed away. The mineral-bearing gravel and sand may also be moved directly from a deposit into the riffle box by the force of water shooting out through a large nozzle called a *giant.* This process is called *hydraulicking.*

Dredging is used especially where mineral-bearing sand and gravel layers are exceptionally thick. In dredging, a pond or lake must be formed so that a large, bargelike machine called a *dredge* can be floated. An endless chain of buckets is attached to a *boom* (long beam) at the front end of the dredge. The buckets dip into the water when one end of the boom is lowered. They dig up the mineral-bearing sand and gravel and move the material to a bin on the deck of the dredge. The material is taken from the bin and washed in much the same way as in placer mining. After the valuable minerals are collected, the sand and gravel are put on a conveyor belt and dumped back into the pond behind the dredge. By digging forward while disposing of the waste sand and gravel to the rear, the pond and the dredge move ahead as the deposit is mined.

When mining some kinds of loose gravel deposits, machines called *draglines* or *slacklines* are used. These machines have a scoop attached to a high boom. The scoop is pulled back and forth along the deposit to gather material, which is put into a separating bin.

Open-pit mining is used to recover valuable minerals from large, thick *orebodies* (beds or veins of ore) lying close to the surface. First, the miners must remove the *overburden*—that is, the layer of rock and other material that covers the deposit. Then they use explosives to break up great masses of ore-bearing hard rock. The miners mine the deposit in a series of horizontal layers called *benches.* Miners build a road connecting the benches up the sides of the pit. Trucks or trains haul the ore up the road and out of the pit.

Strip mining is a method of obtaining coal and such minerals as phosphate that lie flat near the earth's surface. Strip mining around hills or mountains is called *contour mining* or *collar mining.* Strip mining on flat terrain is called *furrow mining.* In this method, miners cut a furrow and cast the overburden into a ridge parallel to the cut called a *spoil.* They break the ore up with machines or explosives and then use shovels or machines to load the ore into trucks or railroad cars. After removing all the ore from the first cut, the miners cut a new furrow, casting the spoil into the previous cut.

In the past, strip mining had a bad reputation because it caused great destruction in the mined areas. This was especially true in mountainous areas, where strip mining would destroy vegetation on mountainsides and lead to mud slides and severe soil erosion.

Today, mining companies in the United States must plan for *reclamation* of the land before they can begin mining. Reclamation is a process in which the land is restored as closely as possible to its original state. In many cases, the reclaimed land is more valuable than it was before mining. For example, the lakes created in the final cuts of some mined areas have provided excellent fishing and water sports.

Quarrying is a way of mining a deposit that lies at the surface of the earth with little or no overburden. Such rocks and minerals as limestone, gypsum, and mica are produced from quarries. Sand and gravel used for making concrete and large stones used for building are also mined in quarries. Miners have several methods of quarrying. Hard minerals are drilled or are blasted with explosives. Sand and gravel are simply shoveled onto trucks or trains and shipped. Building stones such as marble and granite are sold in natural blocks or pieces. To free these blocks, miners saw, channel, or cut them on four sides, and wedge them free from parent rock.

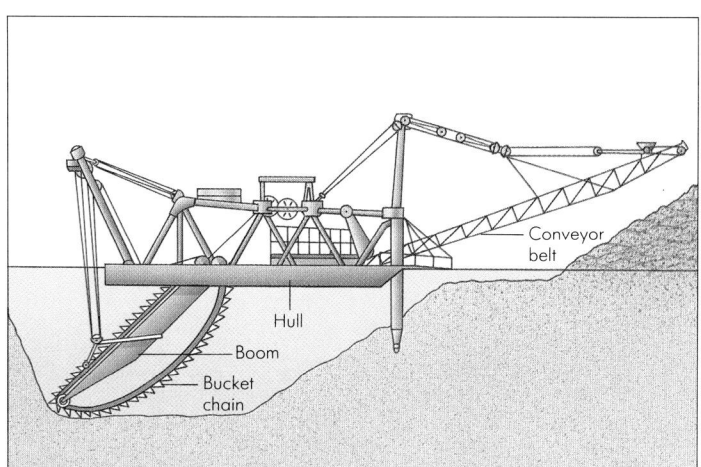

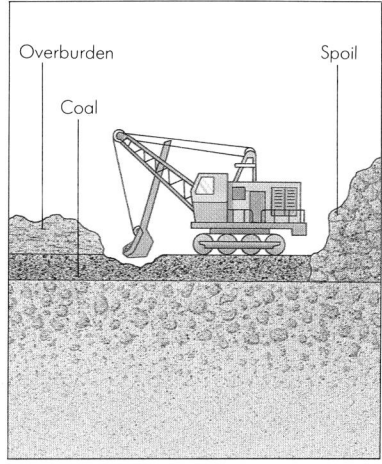

WORLD BOOK illustrations by Oxford Illustrators Limited

Surface mining includes *dredging* and *furrow mining.* In dredging, *left,* buckets on a dredge scoop the ore from the bottom of a pond. In furrow mining, *right,* a power shovel uncovers coal and transfers the overburden to piles called *spoil.* The coal is broken up and loaded onto trucks.

Then the miners hoist the blocks onto trucks or trains.

Underground mining methods are used when the deposit lies deep beneath the earth's surface. First, the miners *drive* (dig) an opening into the mine. A vertical opening is called a *shaft*. A passage that is nearly horizontal, dug into the side of a hill or mountain, is called an *adit*. In coal mining, it is called a *slope*. From these main passages, miners dig systems of horizontal passages called *levels*. A wide variety of mining methods are available for removing the ore. Types of underground mining include (1) room-and-pillar mining, (2) longwall mining, (3) sublevel stoping, (4) cut-and-fill mining, (5) block caving, and (6) sublevel caving.

Room-and-pillar mining is a method of recovering ore from horizontal or nearly horizontal orebodies. Miners excavate the orebody as completely as possible, leaving parts of the ore as pillars to support the *hanging wall* (the rock above the ore vein). Room-and-pillar mining is the most widely used method of underground mining in the United States. Materials commonly mined using this method include coal and the minerals lead, limestone, potash, salt, and uranium.

Longwall mining is also used to dig ore from horizontal seams. Miners use a machine to cut or break ore from a single long face called a *longwall*. Hydraulic roof supports hold up the hanging wall above the miners. As the miners dig farther into the vein, the supports advance with them, and the hanging wall behind them collapses.

Sublevel stoping is used in orebodies with a steep *dip*. A dip is the angle the orebody makes with the horizontal. Miners develop sublevels between the main levels and drill and blast the ore from both the sublevels and main levels. As the ore is removed, empty chambers called *stopes* form. The ore, broken in large vertical slices, falls to the bottom of the empty stopes. There, it is recovered for transport out of the mine.

Cut-and-fill mining is a method of removing ore from vertical veins in horizontal slices, starting at the stope's bottom and advancing upwards. After miners excavate a slice of ore, they fill the stope with waste material called *gangue* or waste sand from ore-processing plants. This material supports the walls and provides a working platform from which to mine the next ore slice.

Block caving is a way of mining such ores as copper and iron when they are scattered throughout the waste material. In this method, the miners dig levels, dividing the orebody into large sections or blocks. Then they undercut each block with a horizontal slot. The pressure of the overlying rock and ore causes the ore above the slot to cave in. Large machines transport the ore to vertical or inclined openings called *ore passes.*

Sublevel caving is used in large, steeply dipping orebodies. Miners divide the orebody into sublevels 25 to 50 feet (7.5 to 15 meters) apart. Each sublevel is developed with a network of *drifts* (horizontal passages) that penetrate the complete ore section.

From the sublevel drifts, the miners drill deep holes into a fan-shaped pattern in the ore section immediately above. The blasting of one fan breaks the ore, causing it to cave into the drift. There, it is loaded and transported to the ore passes.

Pumping methods are used to recover minerals that occur in large bodies of water or that can be changed

A shaft mine

A shaft mine is a system of horizontal and vertical passages through which ore is removed and hauled to the surface. Gold, lead, and other minerals in vertical veins are mined in this way.

WORLD BOOK illustration by Oxford Illustrators Limited

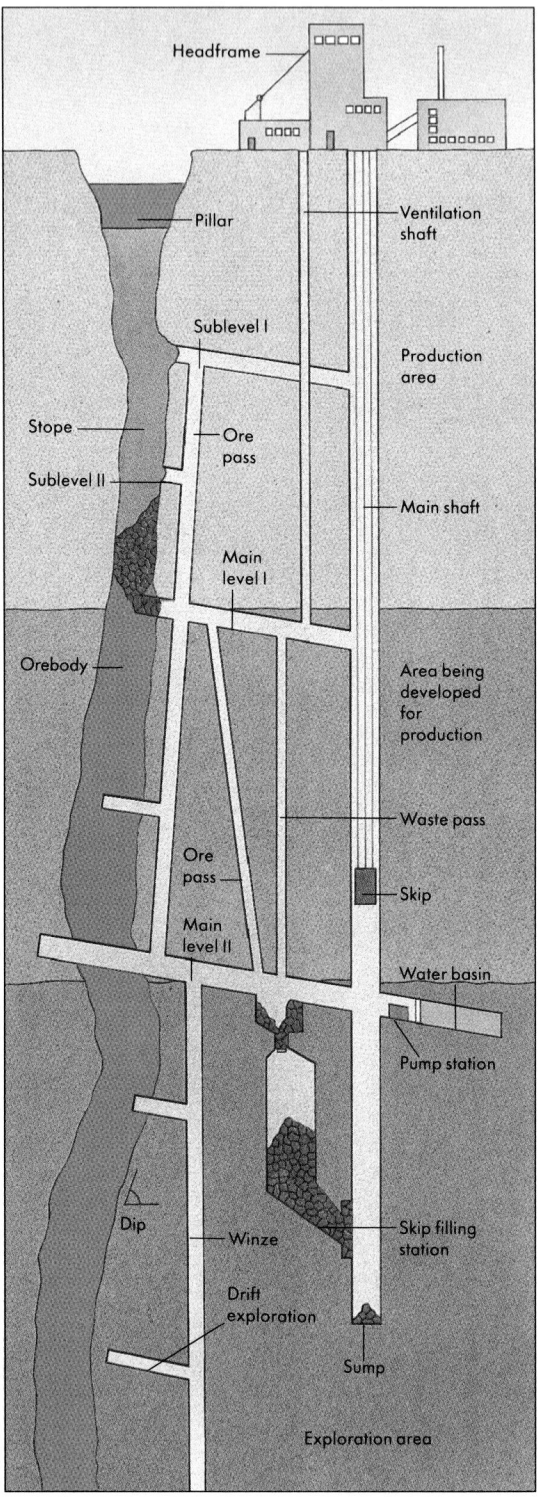

Labels: Headframe, Pillar, Ventilation shaft, Sublevel I, Production area, Stope, Ore pass, Sublevel II, Main shaft, Main level I, Orebody, Area being developed for production, Waste pass, Ore pass, Skip, Main level II, Water basin, Pump station, Dip, Winze, Skip filling station, Drift exploration, Sump, Exploration area

A continuous miner digs coal or ore from horizontal seams deep underground. In a single operation, the machine gouges out the mineral with its rotating cutter and loads it onto a shuttle car.

© Paolo Koch, Photo Researchers

into liquid form. The waters of the ocean and of some lakes, including Great Salt Lake in Utah, contain huge amounts of mineral elements. Miners often obtain them by pumping the water into plants where it is treated. Pumps move large amounts of seawater through *precipitators* (separators) to remove the minerals. Most of the magnesium used today is obtained by this method.

Pumping is sometimes used to get salt from beds beneath the surface of the earth. Mine workers drill holes and circulate water underground to dissolve the salt and form a saltwater solution called *brine*. The brine is then pumped to the surface and taken to a factory. There, the water is evaporated, and the salt forms a solid again. A somewhat similar method called *leaching* is used for some ores that contain copper (see **Copper** [Leaching]).

The Frasch process, another pumping method, is often used in mining sulfur, a mineral that melts easily. The miners bore holes in a buried sulfur bed and inject superheated water. The sulfur then melts and forms a liquid. The miners force the liquid sulfur to the surface by pumping compressed air into the holes. After the sul-

fur cools, it becomes a solid again and can be stored until needed.

The mining industry

In the late 1980's, the annual value of U.S. mining production was about $50 billion. In Canada, the value of mineral production was about $15 billion a year. These figures do not include petroleum and natural gas production because these substances are not obtained by traditional mining methods. But economists often include petroleum and natural gas in mining statistics.

The United States mining industry employs about 400,000 people and offers a wide variety of careers for professional, skilled, and semiskilled workers. Management in the mining industry consists mainly of business people and engineers. These people manage mines, smelters, and refineries, and direct the search for new deposits. They also try to improve mining methods and to develop new operating and engineering practices.

Many universities and colleges offer training for specialized careers in mining industry engineering. A *geological engineer* or *geologist* guides the search for

---

Mining terms

Adit is a nearly horizontal passage from the earth's surface into a mine.

Crosscut is a horizontal or nearly horizontal mine passage that intersects the orebody.

Dip is the angle an ore deposit is inclined from the horizontal.

Drawpoint is a place where ore can be loaded and removed.

Drift is any underground mine passage.

Footwall is the wall or zone of rock under an inclined vein. It is beneath the miners' feet as they excavate the ore.

Gangue is the worthless material mixed with the ore.

Hanging wall is the wall or zone of rock above an inclined vein. It hangs above the miners as they excavate the ore.

Level is the group of drifts and crosscuts made at one depth in an underground mine. Miners usually develop several levels.

Ore pass is a vertical or inclined underground opening through which ore is dropped.

Outcrop is the exposed surface of a deposit.

Overburden is the soil or rock that covers a deposit.

Pillar is a thick post of rock created by removing the surrounding rock.

Quarry is an open or surface excavation from which building stone is usually obtained.

Raise is a passage driven upward from a lower level toward an upper level in an underground mine.

Ramp is an inclined underground opening. It connects levels or production areas and allows the passage of motorized vehicles.

Shaft is a vertical passage from earth's surface into a mine. It is shaped like an elevator shaft.

Skip is a bucket, cage, or wagon in which materials or miners are drawn up or let down a mine shaft.

Stope is an underground excavation formed by the removal of ore between one level and the next in a mine.

Strike is the main horizontal direction of a deposit.

Stripping is the process of removing the overburden.

Sublevel is a system of horizontal underground workings.

Sump is the bottom of a mine shaft where water, sludge, or rocks may collect.

Tunnel is a horizontal underground passage that opens to the surface at both ends.

Vein is a deposit with definite boundaries that separate it from the surrounding rock.

Waste pass is a vertical or inclined opening through which waste material is dumped.

Water basin is a collection area for water that has seeped into a mine or has been piped into the mine and used in drilling. Pumps push this water to the surface.

Winze is a passage that has been driven downward from one level toward a lower level in an underground mine.

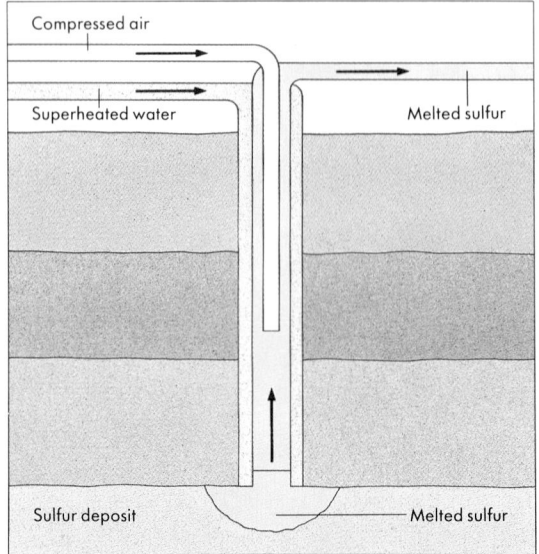

Compressed air

Superheated water   *Melted sulfur*

Sulfur deposit   *Melted sulfur*

WORLD BOOK illustration by Oxford Illustrators Limited

The Frasch method of mining sulfur involves pumping hot water into the deposit through a pipe to melt the sulfur. Compressed air flows into the deposit through a second pipe and forces the sulfur to rise to the surface through a third pipe.

mineral deposits and estimates their value. A *mining engineer* designs the mine and directs the mining process. A *metallurgist* or *metallurgical engineer* directs *beneficiation* (milling, smelting, and refining) of minerals so the company can sell or use them. The mining industry also employs computer specialists, surveyors, and scientists, including chemists and physicists.

Among the workers in mines are people skilled in operating and maintaining various kinds of mining machinery. Other workers include mechanics, electricians, truckdrivers, and laborers. Some people with mining experience are federal or state mine inspectors. They help enforce laws that promote miners' health and safety. Others with mining experience may be involved in the sale of mining equipment, materials, and supplies.

For more on mining careers, write the American Institute of Mining, Metallurgical and Petroleum Engineers, 345 E. 47th Street, New York, NY 10017.   William Hustrulid

Leading mining states and provinces

Value of annual mining production

West Virginia ●●●●●●●●●●●●●●
$4,895,000,000

Kentucky ●●●●●●●●●●●●(
$4,373,000,000

Ontario ●●●●●●●●●●●●(
$4,347,000,000

Arizona ●●●●●●●●(
$2,976,000,000

British Columbia ●●●●●●●(
$2,860,000,000

Figures are in U.S. dollars for 1991 and do not include petroleum or natural gas production. Sources: *World Book* estimates based on data from U.S. Bureau of Mines, U.S. Energy Information Administration, and Statistics Canada.

Related articles in *World Book*. See the article on **Mineral** and the *Economy* section of the various country, state, and province articles. Other related articles include:

Alchemy	Lead	Tin
Assaying	Magnesium	United Mine
Coal	Metal	Workers
Coke	Metallurgy	of America
Copper	Mines, Bureau of	Uranium
Damp	Ore	Well
Diamond	Petroleum	Western frontier
Engineering	Prospecting	life
Gas (fuel)	Quarrying	(The search for
Gem	Safety lamp	gold and silver)
Gold	Salt	Zinc
Iron and steel	Silver	

Outline

I. Kinds of mining
  A. Surface mining methods
  B. Underground mining methods
  C. Pumping methods
II. The mining industry

Questions

What were some of the first substances ever mined?
How do miners recover ore using placer mining?
What are some different methods of surface mining?
What is the overburden?
What is reclamation?
What are some different methods of underground mining?
How do miners obtain sulfur by the Frasch process?
What determines the method used to mine a rock or mineral deposit?
What is the difference between a shaft and an adit?
What are some specialized positions for mining engineers?

Reading and Study Guide

See *Mining* in the Research Guide/Index, Volume 22, for a *Reading and Study Guide*.

Additional resources

Cheney, Glenn A. *Mineral Resources.* Watts, 1985. For younger readers.
Dixon, Colin J. *Atlas of Economic Mineral Deposits.* Cornell Univ. Pr., 1979.
Gregory, Cedric E. *A Concise History of Mining.* Pergamon, 1980.
  Rudiments of Mining Practice. Gulf Pub., 1983.

Mining engineering. See Mining (The mining industry); **Engineering** (Materials engineering).

Minister, in international relations, is a diplomatic agent who represents his or her country in a foreign land. Ministers are appointed by the head of their country and rank below ambassadors. The President of the United States appoints ministers. Like all U.S. diplomatic agents, ministers get their credentials from the secretary of state.

Most countries exchange ambassadors, rather than ministers. The title of minister may be used to designate high-ranking diplomats below the ambassadorial level. In some countries, the name *minister* is also given to high administrative officers who make up the cabinet or executive body (see **Cabinet**).   Robert J. Pranger

See also **Ambassador; Diplomacy; Ministry.**

Minister, in religion, is one who serves. The word minister is a Latin term meaning *servant*. Especially in Protestantism, a minister is an ordained member of the clergy who usually acts as pastor of a congregation. In addition to conducting worship services, an ordained minister usually administers the sacraments, preaches, and assumes responsibility for the pastoral care of the congregation. Lay ministers, who are not ordained, may assist at worship services. For example, they often read parts of the liturgy and lessons and help distribute Communion. In Roman Catholic, Eastern Orthodox, and Anglican churches, priests fill the role of ordained ministers.   Ralph W. Quere

Ministry, in government, is a body of executive officers who advise the head of a country or directly control a nation's affairs. Often, the members are members of parliament and heads of executive departments.

Ministries are part of the governmental setup of countries that have a parliamentary form of government. The ministry of Great Britain has furnished the model for all nations using the parliamentary system.

The British ministry consists of the prime minister and a number of other officers known as the *ministers.* The monarch appoints the prime minister, usually selecting the leader of the party in control of the House of Commons. The monarch's selections of the other ministers are based on the recommendations of the prime minister. British ministers are members of Parliament and are divided into *cabinet ministers* and *ministers not in the cabinet.* Cabinet ministers vary from cabinet to cabinet. Major bills are introduced by ministers.

The British ministry represents the political party or parties that control the House of Commons. When it can no longer get parliamentary support, the ministry resigns.   Robert G. Neumann

See also **Cabinet** (The cabinet system of government); **Prime minister.**

Mink is a small mammal prized for its fur. The luxurious winter pelts of minks have long been in demand by the fur industry, which uses them to make expensive capes, coats, stoles, and other clothing.

Minks have slender bodies and short legs. They weigh from about $1\frac{1}{2}$ to $2\frac{3}{4}$ pounds (0.7 to 1.2 kilograms). They range in length from about 20 to 25 inches (50 to 64 centimeters), not including their bushy tails. Wild minks have brown fur. But minks raised in captivity have been bred to have black, blue, silver-gray, and white coats.

There are two species of minks, the North American mink and the European mink. The North American mink lives throughout most of North America. It is slightly larger than the European mink, which originally lived in northern Europe and northern and central Asia. Only the fur of American minks has commercial value.

How minks live. Minks live in rural and wilderness areas near rivers, streams, marshes, and lakes. They hunt in the water and on land. Their underwater prey include crayfish, frogs, and minnows. Minks, however, have limited underwater vision. Therefore, they often sight their prey from the shore and then dive into the water and try to catch it before it escapes. The double-layered fur of minks helps them hunt in water. The oily outer layer repels water, keeping the mink dry. The soft, thick layer beneath keeps the mink warm.

On land, minks hunt under logs, between rocks, and in rodent burrows for mice, muskrats, rabbits, and snakes. Their chief enemies include bobcats, foxes, and certain types of owls.

Female minks have litters of from 2 to 10 young. They give birth in the spring. The mothers raise and feed the young without help from the males. By the end of their first summer, the young can feed themselves. By the end of their first year, they have established their hunting territories and they can reproduce. Minks rarely live beyond three years.

Minks are legally trapped in winter throughout their range in North America. The pelts of female minks, though smaller than those of males, often are more valuable, because they are less coarse.

Mink ranches. American minks are raised in captivity on *mink ranches,* also called *mink farms,* in many parts of the world. The fur of minks raised on ranches is less likely to be damaged than the fur of wild minks. Many American minks have escaped from ranches in northern Europe. These minks have established wild American mink populations that have nearly caused the extinction of the native European mink.

Scientific classification. Minks belong to the weasel family, Mustelidae. The North American mink is *Mustela vison.* The European mink is *M. lutreola.*   Roger A. Powell

See also **Fur.**

© Tom Brakefield, Bruce Coleman Inc.

Wild minks live in North America, northern Europe, and northern and central Asia. They inhabit rural and wilderness areas near rivers, streams, marshes, and lakes.

© Ray F. Hillstrom

White minks are specially bred on *mink ranches,* also called *mink farms.* Minks raised in captivity have also been bred to have black, blue, and silver-gray fur.

WORLD BOOK photo by Richard Sennott

Minneapolis is the largest city in Minnesota and an important Midwestern economic center. Downtown Minneapolis has many modern buildings. The Minnesota Twins baseball team and the Minnesota Vikings football team play home games at the Hubert H. Humphrey Metrodome, *right.*

Minneapolis, *MIHN ee AP uh lihs,* is the largest city in Minnesota and a major Midwestern center of finance, industry, trade, and transportation. The city also is the home of the University of Minnesota, one of the nation's largest universities. Minneapolis lies in southeastern Minnesota, just west of St. Paul, its "twin city."

The name *Minneapolis* comes from the Indian word *minne,* meaning *water,* and the Greek word *polis,* which means *city.* Minneapolis got its name because of the 22 natural lakes that lie within the city limits. It has the nickname *City of Lakes.*

In the late 1840's, farmers and lumberjacks settled the

Facts in brief

Population: *City*—368,383. *Metropolitan area*—2,464,124.
Area: 59 sq. mi. (153 km²). *Metropolitan area*—4,619 sq. mi. (11,963 km²).
Climate: *Average temperature*—January, 14 °F (−10 °C); July, 74 °F (23 °C). *Average annual precipitation* (rainfall, melted snow, and other forms of moisture)—32 inches (81 centimeters). For the monthly weather in Minneapolis, see **Minnesota** (Climate).
Government: Mayor-council. *Terms*—4 years for the mayor and the 13 council members.
Founded: 1849. Incorporated as a city in 1867.

area that is now Minneapolis. They chose the area because of its broad farmlands and hardwood forests. In addition, the nearby Falls of St. Anthony, on the Mississippi River, supplied water power for their flour mills and sawmills. In 1849, a village called Saint Anthony was established on the east side of the falls. In 1852, settlers on the west side of the falls chose the name Minneapolis for their growing community. Saint Anthony became a city in 1855, and Minneapolis did so in 1867. In 1872, the two cities merged under the name Minneapolis.

From 1882 to 1930, Minneapolis led the world in flour production. After World War II ended in 1945, the city became an important producer of computers, electronic equipment, and farm machinery. Today, service industries, especially education, finance, and retail trade, are the most important economic activities.

Metropolitan Minneapolis

The city covers 59 square miles (153 square kilometers), including 4 square miles (10 square kilometers) of inland water. The Mississippi River divides Minneapolis into two areas, the larger of which is west of the river. Most of the huge University of Minnesota campus lies on the east bank, but part of the campus is on the west bank.

Downtown Minneapolis, on the west bank, faces the Falls of St. Anthony. Nicollet Avenue, the chief shopping street, features an eight-block-long shopping center called Nicollet Mall. The law permits cabs and buses—but not automobiles—to drive on the mall. The Investors Diversified Services (IDS) Center faces Nicollet Mall. It includes the 57-story IDS Tower, the tallest building in Minnesota. The IDS Tower and many buildings near it are connected by the Skyway System. The system consists of enclosed elevated passageways between the buildings. Heated in winter and air-conditioned in summer, the Skyway System provides comfort for people moving about in the area. The city's main financial district is on Marquette Avenue, a block southeast of Nicollet Avenue.

The metropolitan area covers about 4,619 square miles (11,963 square kilometers) and spreads over nine counties in Minnesota and one in Wisconsin. It takes in 176 self-governing communities. Communities in this area include St. Paul, Minnesota's capital and second largest city, and Bloomington, Minnesota's third largest

city. The Minnesota part of the metropolitan area has about $2\frac{1}{2}$ million people—about half the state's population. The Minneapolis and St. Paul business districts are connected by the Interstate 94 expressway.

The people

About 90 per cent of the people in Minneapolis were born in the United States. Blacks make up about 13 per cent of the population. About a tenth of the city's population have German ancestry. Other major groups include people of Norwegian, Swedish, or English descent. Asians, a fast-growing segment of the population, make up about 4.5 per cent of the city's people. About 3.5 per cent of the people are American Indians. Minneapolis has one of the largest American Indian populations of any city in the United States.

Economy

Commerce and industry. Service industries employ about one-third of all Minneapolis workers. Wholesale and retail trade employ about one-fourth, and one-fifth

City of Minneapolis

MINNESOTA

Minneapolis is an industrial city on the Mississippi River. The large map shows the city's major landmarks. The small map shows Minneapolis and its twin city, St. Paul.

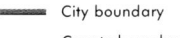

City boundary
County boundary
Expressway
Other street
Railroad
■ Point of interest
Park

Minneapolis-St. Paul area

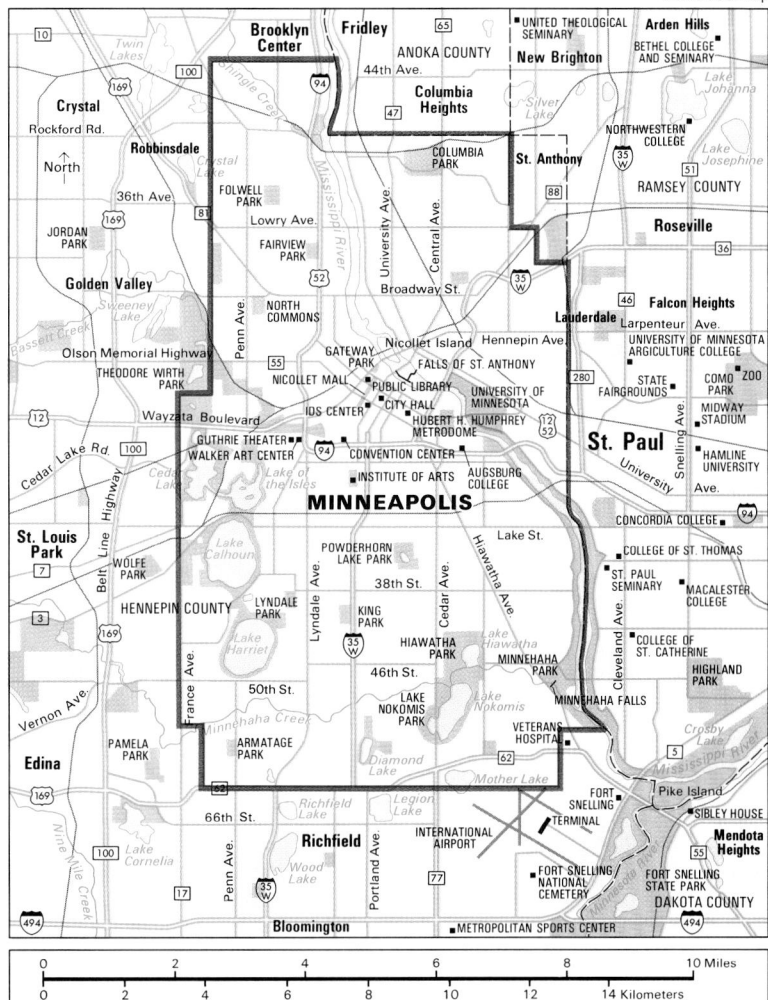

WORLD BOOK map

Alvis Upitis, Shostal

The Nicollet Mall, *above,* a landscaped downtown shopping area, occupies eight blocks along Nicollet Avenue.

of the city's population have jobs in manufacturing. Several major wholesale and retail firms have their headquarters in the city. Minneapolis is a major financial center. It is the headquarters of the Ninth Federal Reserve Bank District, which serves a six-state region.

Minneapolis ranks as a major center for commercial printing and flour milling. Other important economic activities include the production of computer equipment and industrial machinery.

Transportation. Airlines use the Minneapolis-St. Paul International Airport. Six railroad freight lines serve the city, and passenger trains use a terminal in St. Paul. Twenty bridges in Minneapolis cross the Mississippi River. Several major highways, including two interstate routes, pass through the city. The Minneapolis-St. Paul area ranks among the top trucking terminals in the United States. More than 150 trucking companies serve the area.

Communication. Minneapolis has one daily newspaper, the *Star Tribune.* Eight television stations and about 35 radio stations broadcast in the Minneapolis-St. Paul area.

Education

The Minneapolis public school system includes about 50 elementary and high schools with a total of about 40,000 students. Blacks make up about 32 per cent of the enrollment. Asians make up 10 per cent of the enrollment, and Indians account for 8 per cent. The city has a busing program to achieve racial balance in the public schools. About 8,000 students attend 32 parochial and private schools in Minneapolis.

The Twin Cities campus of the University of Minnesota has facilities in Minneapolis and St. Paul. It ranks as one of the nation's largest university campuses. Other institutions of higher learning in Minneapolis include Augsburg College, North Central Bible College, the

Minneapolis College of Art Design, and St. Thomas University.

The Minneapolis Public Library has 16 branches and owns more than a million books. Libraries of the University of Minnesota contain about $3\frac{1}{2}$ million volumes.

Cultural life

The arts. The Minnesota Orchestra has its headquarters at Orchestra Hall near Nicollet Mall. The Guthrie Theater is the home of one of the best-known theater groups in the United States. In addition, Minneapolis is known for its numerous small theater companies and dance groups.

Museums. The Walker Art Center owns one of the country's finest collections of modern art. The Minneapolis Institute of Arts displays masterpieces dating from 2000 B.C. to modern times. The Planetarium of the Minneapolis Public Library features sky shows.

Recreation

Minneapolis has been called the *Vacation Capital* because it serves as the gateway to the lake region of northern Minnesota. The Minneapolis Aquatennial, held every July, features a canoe derby, costume balls, parades, and water ballets. The annual Minnesota State Fair takes place in early fall at the State Fairgrounds in St. Paul. The highlights of the fair include carnival shows and agricultural and industrial exhibits. The Mall of America, a major retail and recreation center in Bloomington, has more than 400 shops and an indoor amusement park.

Parks. Minneapolis has about 150 public parks, which cover about 6,000 acres (2,400 hectares). Most of the parks line the shores of the Mississippi River or surround the many small lakes within the city. Theodore Wirth Park, the largest park in Minneapolis, covers almost 740 acres (300 hectares) and has a wooded area for hiking.

Minnehaha Park includes Minnehaha Falls, which is 53 feet (16 meters) high. The American poet Henry Wadsworth Longfellow made Minnehaha Falls famous in his long poem *The Song of Hiawatha.* See **Minnehaha Falls.**

Summer vacationers enjoy boating and swimming at Lake Minnetonka, which is 12 miles (19 kilometers) long and lies 12 miles southwest of Minneapolis. Many of the city's tourists visit Fort Snelling, the center of the first permanent white settlement in what is now the Minneapolis area.

Sports. The Minnesota Twins of the American League play baseball at the Hubert H. Humphrey Metrodome in Minneapolis. The Minnesota Vikings of the National Football League also play their home games at the Metrodome. The Minnesota Timberwolves of the National Basketball Association play at Target Center.

Government

Minneapolis has a mayor-council form of government. The voters elect the mayor and 13 council members to four-year terms. Property taxes, state aid, and municipal fees provide the city's most important sources of revenue.

In 1967, Minnesota established the Metropolitan Council of the Twin Cities Area. This governmental agency has the power to tax and to sell bonds. It deals with such areawide concerns as health, housing, land use, sewer construction, transportation, waste disposal, and water pollution. The council consists of 14 members and a chairperson, all appointed by the governor of Minnesota.

History

Early days. Sioux Indians once farmed and hunted in what is now the Minneapolis area. In 1680, a Belgian explorer and missionary named Louis Hennepin became the first white person to visit the site. In 1819, the U.S. Army established Fort St. Anthony in a temporary building there. From 1820 to 1822, American soldiers serving under Colonel Josiah Snelling built Fort St. Anthony as a permanent fort. The fort was renamed Fort Snelling in 1825. Fort Snelling served for more than 30 years as a trading center and a gateway to the northern wilderness and the western prairies.

During the 1840's, the great forests of the area attracted lumberjacks from Maine. The lumberjacks built sawmills near the Falls of St. Anthony. In 1849, the village of St. Anthony was established on the east side of the falls. Another community developed on the west side of the falls. In 1852, the settlers chose the name Minneapolis for the village on the west side. St. Anthony became a city in 1855. Minneapolis was incorporated as a city in 1867. In 1872, the two cities merged under the name Minneapolis.

In 1854, grain millers built a large flour mill in Minneapolis to take advantage of the area's rich wheat fields. Flour milling soon became a major industry of Minneapolis. By 1870, Minneapolis ranked as the state's principal lumbering center.

In the 1870's, a flour-sifting device called the *purifier* was perfected in Minneapolis. It enabled millers to produce high-quality flour from inexpensive spring wheat. Large flour mills helped the city grow. By 1880, Minneapolis had 46,887 people.

In 1882, Minneapolis became the world's leading flour-milling center. Both Minneapolis and St. Paul developed into important transportation centers about this time. But Minneapolis grew faster than St. Paul because it had greater industrial development. By 1890, Minneapolis had a population of 164,738.

The 1900's. The increased use of steam-powered machinery during the late 1800's led to rapid growth of the city's lumber industry. From 1899 to 1905, Minneapolis led the world in lumber production. But by 1906, most of the nearby forests had been cut down, and the city's lumber trade declined sharply. The population of Minneapolis grew from 202,718 in 1900 to 301,408 in 1910.

By 1916, General Mills, Incorporated, The Pillsbury Company, and other local firms produced such huge quantities of flour that Minneapolis became known as *Mill City.* But a large increase in freight rates during the 1920's caused the grain companies to establish milling centers in other parts of the country. In 1930, Buffalo, N.Y., replaced Minneapolis as the world's leading center of flour production. That year, Minneapolis had 464,356 people.

Recent developments. Following World War II, Minneapolis became a leader in the manufacture of computers, electronic equipment, and farm machinery.

By 1950, the downtown area had become old and shabby. People and industry began moving from the city to the suburbs during the 1950's. The population fell from 521,718 in 1950 to 482,872 in 1960. Since the 1960's, the population of the Minneapolis metropolitan area has increased, but the number of people living in the city has continued to fall. Since the 1980's, the rate of decline has slowed.

Since the 1950's, private investors have spent large sums of money to redevelop the downtown area. Gateway Center, a renewal project begun in 1958, was largely completed in the mid-1970's. It features apartment and office buildings and covers 18 blocks in the heart of the city. The Nicollet Mall was completed in 1968 and the IDS Center in 1972.

In the late 1980's, the Nicollet Mall underwent a major renovation, and several new department stores opened, giving a needed boost to declining retail trade. In addition, the entertainment district along Hennepin Avenue, was revitalized.   Belvel J. Boyd

See also **Minnesota.**

Minnehaha Falls, *MIHN ee HAH hah,* is a waterfall on Minnehaha Creek in Minneapolis, Minn. *Minnehaha* means *laughing waters* in the Sioux Indian language. The falls are 53 feet (16 meters) high. Over thousands of years, they have cut a deep gorge in the surrounding sandstone and limestone cliffs. Minnehaha Falls is part of a city park and appears on the seal of the city. More than 500,000 people visit the park each year. The American poet Henry Wadsworth Longfellow made the falls famous in *The Song of Hiawatha* (1855), a poem based on Indian legend. A statue of the Indian leader Hiawatha and his wife stands at the top of the waterfall.

Gordon L. Levine

See also **Minnesota** (picture).

Minnesinger, *MIHN uh SIHNG uhr,* was one of a group of German love poets who flourished from the late 1100's to the late 1300's. The minnesingers sang their poetry to music at court festivals.

Minne was an old German word meaning *love.* The minnesingers' expressions of love were regulated by the courtly society that placed much value on form. Courtly love, as many minnesingers portrayed it, was the hopeless love of a knight for a lady of high station. The knight's plea that the lady answer his love was often expressed in feudal terms such as a vassal might use in begging a favor from his lord. The lady usually remained unapproachable.

The doctrines and forms of courtly love developed in southern France and spread to Germany. In addition to ideas of the feudal system, several literary traditions influenced the minnesingers. These included Arabic poetry transmitted from Spain, classical literature such as Ovid's *The Art of Love,* and medieval Latin poetry. The homage paid to the Virgin Mary in the 1100's also contributed to the idealization of women so basic to much of courtly love poetry.

The leading minnesingers included Dietmar von Aist, Kürenberger, Heinrich von Veldeke, Friedrich von Hausen, Heinrich von Morungen, Reinmar von Hagenau, Walther von der Vogelweide, Neidhart von Reuenthal, Tannhäuser, and Ulrich von Lichtenstein.

James F. Poag

See also **Tannhäuser; Walther von der Vogelweide.**

© Steve Solum, West Stock

The Minnesota shoreline stretches along Lake Superior in the northeast part of the state. Rugged cliffs and thick forests provide beautiful wilderness scenery in this region, making it one of Minnesota's most popular vacation areas.

Minnesota   *The Gopher State*

Minnesota is a large state in the Midwestern United States. The state is an important producer of agricultural and manufactured goods. Such service industries as finance and trade are also important to its economy. Minnesota's Twin Cities of Minneapolis and St. Paul form a major metropolitan area of the Midwest. St. Paul is Minnesota's capital, and Minneapolis is the state's largest city.

Southern Minnesota has some of the nation's richest farmland. Thousands of dairy cattle in this area make Minnesota one of the leading milk-producing states. Minnesota is also a major producer of corn, hogs, soybeans, and wheat.

The processing of farm products is a leading manufacturing activity in Minnesota. Large dairy plants, flour mills, and meat-packing plants are found in several parts of the state. Minnesota's other chief manufacturing activity is the production of computers. The Twin Cities and Rochester have large computer companies.

Minneapolis is a leading financial center of the Mid-

west. Retail trade employs many people in the Twin Cities. Duluth has the busiest freshwater port in North America. The Mayo Clinic in Rochester is a world-famous medical center.

Minnesota's scenic beauty, sparkling lakes, and deep pine woods make it a vacation wonderland. Its plentiful game animals and fish attract people who enjoy hunting and fishing. Campers, canoeists, and hikers can explore its vast northern wilderness areas.

The state's history is much the story of the development of its great natural resources. The fur-bearing animals of Minnesota's forests first attracted fur traders. Next, the fertile soil brought farmers, who poured into the region from the Eastern States and from Europe. The thick forests of tall pines attracted lumberjacks from Maine, Michigan, and Wisconsin. Finally, miners came to dig the state's vast deposits of rich iron ore.

The name *Minnesota* comes from two Sioux Indian words meaning *sky-tinted waters*. During the late 1800's, the state's flour mills and dairy products gave Minnesota one of its nicknames—the *Bread and Butter State*. But it is best known as the *Gopher State*. This nickname can be traced to an 1857 cartoon that represented dishonest railroad organizers as striped gophers. Gophers, known for being destructive to farm crops, live mainly in the state's southern and western prairies.

The contributors of this article are William E. Lass, Professor of History at Mankato State University; and Gordon L. Levine, Director of the Alworth Institute for International Studies at the University of Minnesota, Duluth.

Glenn A. Knudsen, Tom Stack & Assoc.

The Crystal Court Mall of the IDS Center in Minneapolis attracts many visitors. Minneapolis is the largest city in Minnesota.

Interesting facts about Minnesota

WORLD BOOK illustrations by Kevin Chadwick

General James Shields was the only person ever elected United States senator by three different states. A Democrat, he served during the middle and late 1800's as senator of Illinois, Minnesota, and Missouri.

The first national farm organization was founded by Oliver H. Kelley of Minnesota. It was called the National Grange, Patrons of Husbandry.

General James Shields

The home thermostat was invented and first manufactured in Minneapolis in 1885, by Alfred M. Butz.

Cellophane transparent tape was invented and patented by Richard Gurley Drew of St. Paul. The Minnesota Manufacturing and Mining Company began producing the tape in 1930.

The busiest freshwater port in North America is the port of Duluth, Minn.-Superior, Wis. The port is also the farthest inland ocean port in the United States.

Port of Duluth

© Rollin Geppert, West Stock

The city of St. Paul lies chiefly along the north bank of the Mississippi River. About half of Minnesota's people live in the Minneapolis-St. Paul metropolitan area.

Minnesota in brief

Symbols of Minnesota

The state flag, adopted in 1957, bears a version of the state seal. The dates *1819, 1858,* and *1893* indicate, respectively, the year of Minnesota's first settlement, the year of statehood, and the year the original flag was adopted. The seal was adopted in 1861. A man plowing symbolizes agriculture and a stump stands for the lumber industry, both important parts of the state's history. An Indian represents Minnesota's Indian heritage.

State flag

State seal

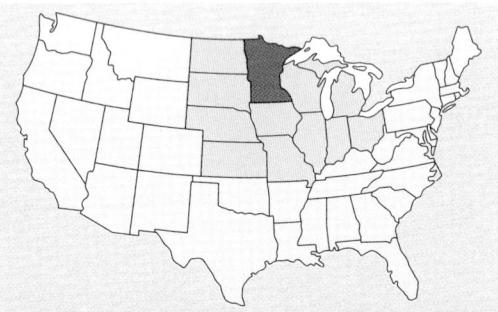

Minnesota (brown) ranks 12th in size among all the states and is the largest of the Midwestern States (yellow).

General information

Statehood: May 11, 1858, the 32nd state.
State abbreviations: Minn. (traditional); MN (postal).
State motto: *L'Etoile du Nord* (The Star of the North).
State song: "Hail! Minnesota." Words by Truman E. Rickard and Arthur E. Upson; music by Truman E. Rickard.

The State Capitol is in St. Paul, the capital of Minnesota since it became a territory in 1849.

Land and climate

Area: 84,397 sq. mi. (218,587 km²), including 4,780 sq. mi. (12,381 km²) of inland water but excluding 2,546 sq. mi. (6,594 km²) of Great Lakes water.
Elevation: *Highest*—Eagle Mountain, 2,301 ft. (701 m) above sea level. *Lowest*—602 ft. (83 m) above sea level along Lake Superior.
Record high temperature: 114 °F (46 °C) at Moorhead on July 6, 1936, and at Beardsley on July 29, 1917.
Record low temperature: −59 °F (−51 °C) at Pokegama Dam on Feb. 16, 1903, and at Leech Lake Dam on Feb. 9, 1899.
Average July temperature: 70 °F (21 °C).
Average January temperature: 8 °F (−13 °C).
Average yearly precipitation: 26 in. (66 cm).

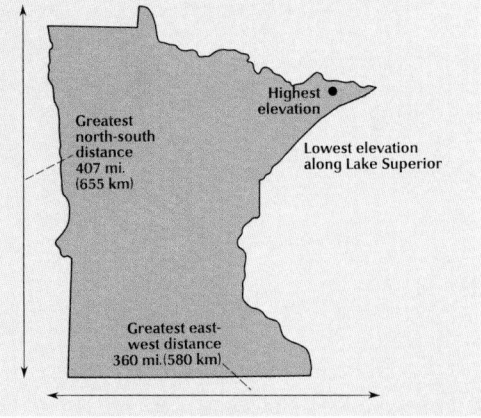

Greatest north-south distance 407 mi. (655 km)

Highest elevation

Lowest elevation along Lake Superior

Greatest east-west distance 360 mi. (580 km)

Important dates

Britain granted the land east of the Mississippi River to the United States.

The U.S. Army built Fort St. Anthony, which was renamed Fort Snelling in 1825.

| 1679 | 1783 | 1803 | 1820-1825 |

Daniel Greysolon, Sieur Duluth, explored Lake Superior's western shore.

The United States obtained the Minnesota area west of the Mississippi through the Louisiana Purchase.

State bird
Common loon

State flower
Pink and white lady's-slipper

State tree
Norway pine

People

Population: 4,387,029 (1990 census)
Rank among the states: 20th
Density: 52 persons per sq. mi. (20 per km²), U.S. average 69 per sq. mi. (27 per km²)
Distribution: 70 per cent urban, 30 per cent rural
Largest cities in Minnesota

Minneapolis	368,383
St. Paul	272,235
Bloomington	86,335
Duluth	85,493
Rochester	70,745
Brooklyn Park	56,381

Source: U.S. Bureau of the Census.

Population trend

Millions

Year	Population
1990	4,387,029
1980	4,075,970
1970	3,806,103
1960	3,413,864
1950	2,982,483
1940	2,792,300
1930	2,563,953
1920	2,387,125
1910	2,075,708
1900	1,751,394
1890	1,310,283
1880	780,773
1870	439,706
1860	172,023
1850	6,077

Source: U.S. Bureau of the Census.

Economy

Chief products

Agriculture: milk, corn, soybeans, beef cattle, hogs.
Manufacturing: machinery, food products, printed materials, fabricated metal products, scientific instruments, electrical equipment, paper products.
Mining: iron ore.

Gross state product

Value of goods and services produced in 1991: $102,319,000,000. *Services* include community, social, and personal services; finance; government; trade; and transportation, communication, and utilities. *Industry* includes construction, manufacturing, and mining. *Agriculture* includes agriculture, fishing, and forestry.

Source: U.S. Bureau of Economic Analysis.

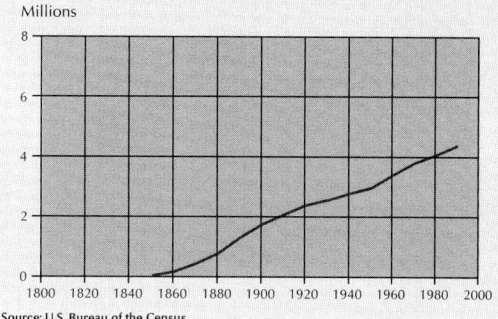

Industry 24%
Services 73%
Agriculture 3%

Government

State government

Governor: 4-year term
State senators: 67; 4-year terms
State representatives: 134; 2-year terms
Counties: 87

Federal government

United States senators: 2
United States representatives: 8
Electoral votes: 10

Sources of information

Tourism: Minnesota Office of Tourism, 100 Metro Square, 121 7th Place East, St. Paul, MN 55101
Economy: Research and Statistics Office, Minnesota Department of Jobs and Training, 390 North Robert Street, St. Paul, MN 55101
Government: House of Representatives Information Office, 175 State Office Building, St. Paul, MN 55155
History: Minnesota Historical Society's History Center, 345 Kellogg Boulevard West, St. Paul, MN 55102

The first shipment of iron ore from the Vermilion Range left Minnesota.

Minnesota adopted a state constitutional amendment establishing a Court of Appeals.

| 1858 | 1884 | 1955 | 1982 |

Minnesota became the 32nd state on May 11.

A large taconite-processing plant began operations at Silver Bay.

People

Population. The 1990 United States census reported that Minnesota had 4,387,029 people. The population of the state had increased $7\frac{1}{2}$ percent over the 1980 census figure, which was 4,075,970. According to the 1990 census, Minnesota ranks 20th in population among the 50 states.

About 70 percent of Minnesota's people live in urban areas. More than half of the people live in the Minneapolis-St. Paul Metropolitan Statistical Area (see **Metropolitan area**). For the names and populations of the state's metropolitan areas, see the *Index* to the political map of Minnesota.

Minneapolis is the largest city in Minnesota. It adjoins St. Paul, Minnesota's capital and second largest city. The Twin Cities, as they are called, serve as the state's leading cultural, financial, and commercial center. Duluth, which lies along the west shore of Lake Superior, is one of the largest cities in Minnesota. Duluth is the westernmost port on the Great Lakes and a major commercial center.

The largest groups of people who settled in Minnesota during the 1800's and early 1900's came from Finland, Germany, Norway, and Sweden. Many also came from Austria, Canada, Denmark, Great Britain, Ireland, Poland, and Russia.

Schools. About 1820, the first school for white children was opened at Fort St. Anthony (later renamed Fort Snelling). Missionaries set up some Indian schools dur-

Population density

Most of Minnesota's residents live in the southeast. About half the people live in the Minneapolis-St. Paul metropolitan area. The north and west are thinly populated.

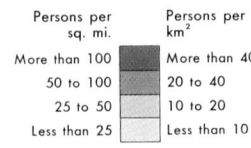

Persons per sq. mi.	Persons per km²
More than 100	More than 40
50 to 100	20 to 40
25 to 50	10 to 20
Less than 25	Less than 10

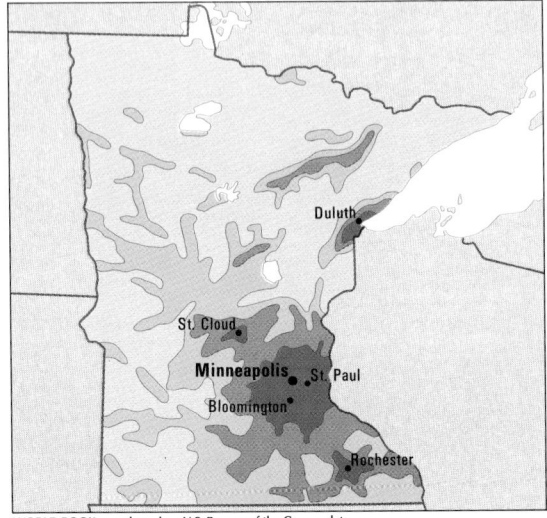

WORLD BOOK map; based on U.S. Bureau of the Census data.

Paul Stafford, © Minnesota Office of Tourism

The Minnesota Twins of the American League play baseball in the Hubert H. Humphrey Metrodome in Minneapolis. The Twin Cities area also has professional basketball and football teams.

Science Museum of Minnesota

The Science Museum of Minnesota in St. Paul features exhibits of science, technology, and natural history. This boy is producing electricity by pedaling a bicycle generator.

The University of Minnesota has facilities in Minneapolis and St. Paul at its Twin Cities Campus. The main quadrangle, *above,* is located in Minneapolis.

ing the 1830's. In 1849, the territorial legislature passed a law providing for the establishment of public schools in Minnesota.

Universities and colleges

Minnesota has 30 universities and colleges that offer bachelor's or advanced degrees and are accredited by the North Central Association of Colleges and Schools. For enrollments and further information, see **Universities and colleges** (table).

Name	Mailing address
Alfred Adler Institute of Minnesota	Hopkins
Augsburg College	Minneapolis
Bethel College	St. Paul
Bethel Theological Seminary	St. Paul
Carleton College	Northfield
Concordia College—Moorhead	Moorhead
Concordia College-St. Paul	St. Paul
Crown College	St. Bonifacius
Dr. Martin Luther College	New Ulm
Gustavus Adolphus College	St. Peter
Hamline University	St. Paul
Luther Northwestern Theological Seminary	St. Paul
Macalester College	St. Paul
Mayo Foundation	*
Minneapolis College of Art Design	Minneapolis
Minnesota, University of	*
Minnesota State University System	*
North Central Bible College	Minneapolis
Northwestern College	Roseville
Northwestern College of Chiropractic	Bloomington
St. Benedict, College of	St. Joseph
St. Catherine, College of	St. Paul
St. John's University	Collegeville
St. Mary's College of Minnesota	Winona
St. Olaf College	Northfield
St. Scholastica, College of	Duluth
St. Thomas, University of	St. Paul
United Theological Seminary of the Twin Cities	New Brighton
Walden University	Minneapolis

*For campuses and founding dates, see **Universities and colleges** (table).

The state board of education directs the state department of education. The board has nine members. They are appointed to four-year terms by the governor with the approval of the state Senate. The governor appoints the department's chief administrative officer, the commissioner of education, to a four-year term, with the approval of the Senate.

In Minnesota, children are required to attend school between their 7th and 16th birthdays. For the number of students and teachers in the state, see **Education** (table).

Libraries. Minnesota has about 330 public libraries. The largest of these libraries serve Minneapolis, St. Paul, and Hennepin County. The libraries of the Twin Cities Campus of the University of Minnesota have about $4\frac{1}{2}$ million volumes, the largest collection in the state. The university has some of the country's largest collections of materials dealing with children's literature, European expansion, and Scandinavia.

Other important library collections in Minnesota include the James J. Hill Reference Library, the Minnesota Historical Society Library, and the State Law Library, all in St. Paul; and the Mayo Medical Library in Rochester. Statewide library networks allow Minnesotans to have access to materials from the state's largest public and university libraries.

Museums. The Minneapolis Institute of Arts is the largest art museum in Minnesota. Its artworks come from many periods and cultures. The Walker Art Center, also in Minneapolis, has an outstanding collection of modern art.

The Science Museum of Minnesota in St. Paul has exhibits dealing with science, technology, and natural history. The Lake Superior Museum of Transportation in Duluth features railroad cars and equipment. The Canal Park Marine Museum in Duluth traces the history of commercial fishing in the upper Great Lakes region.

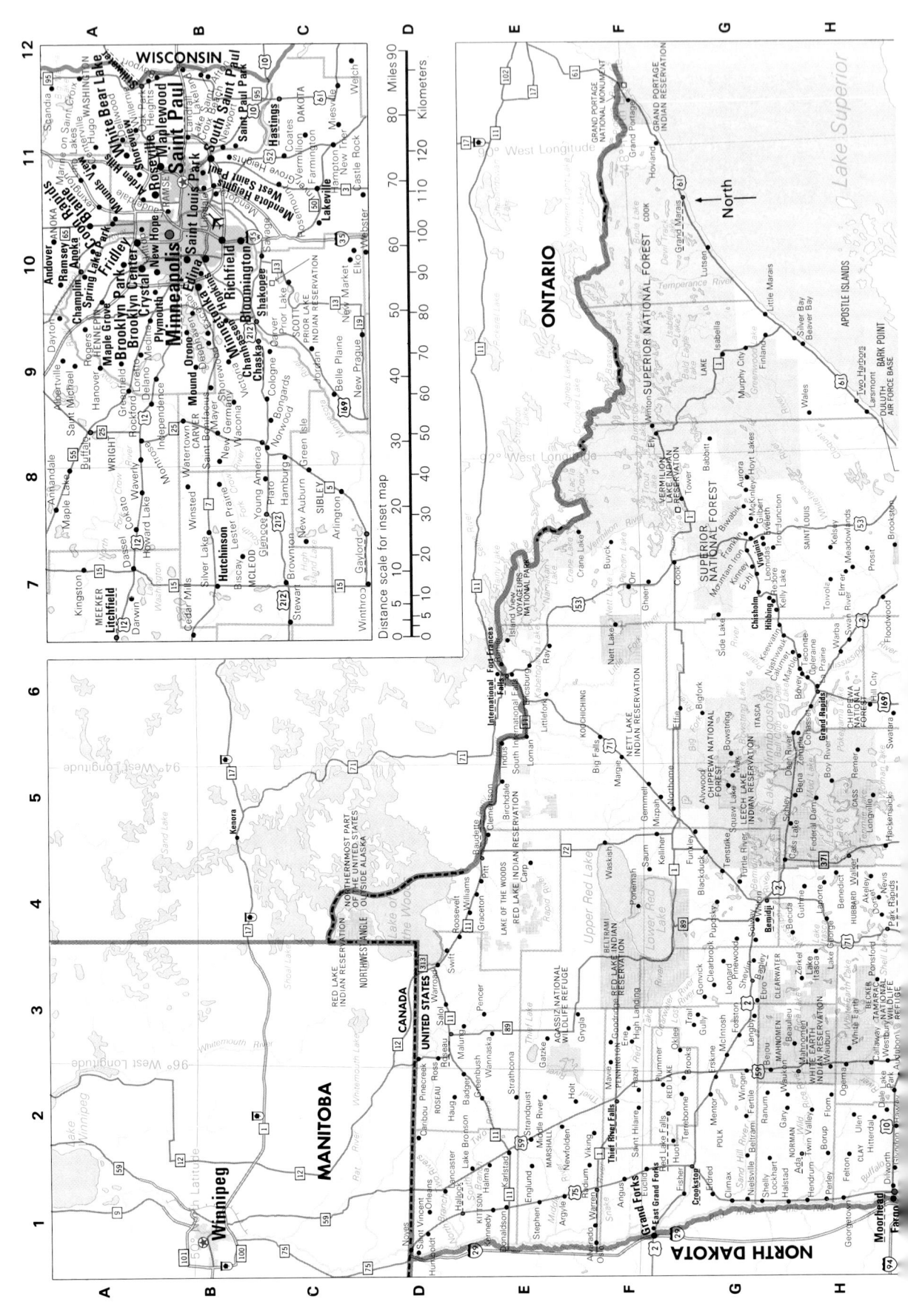

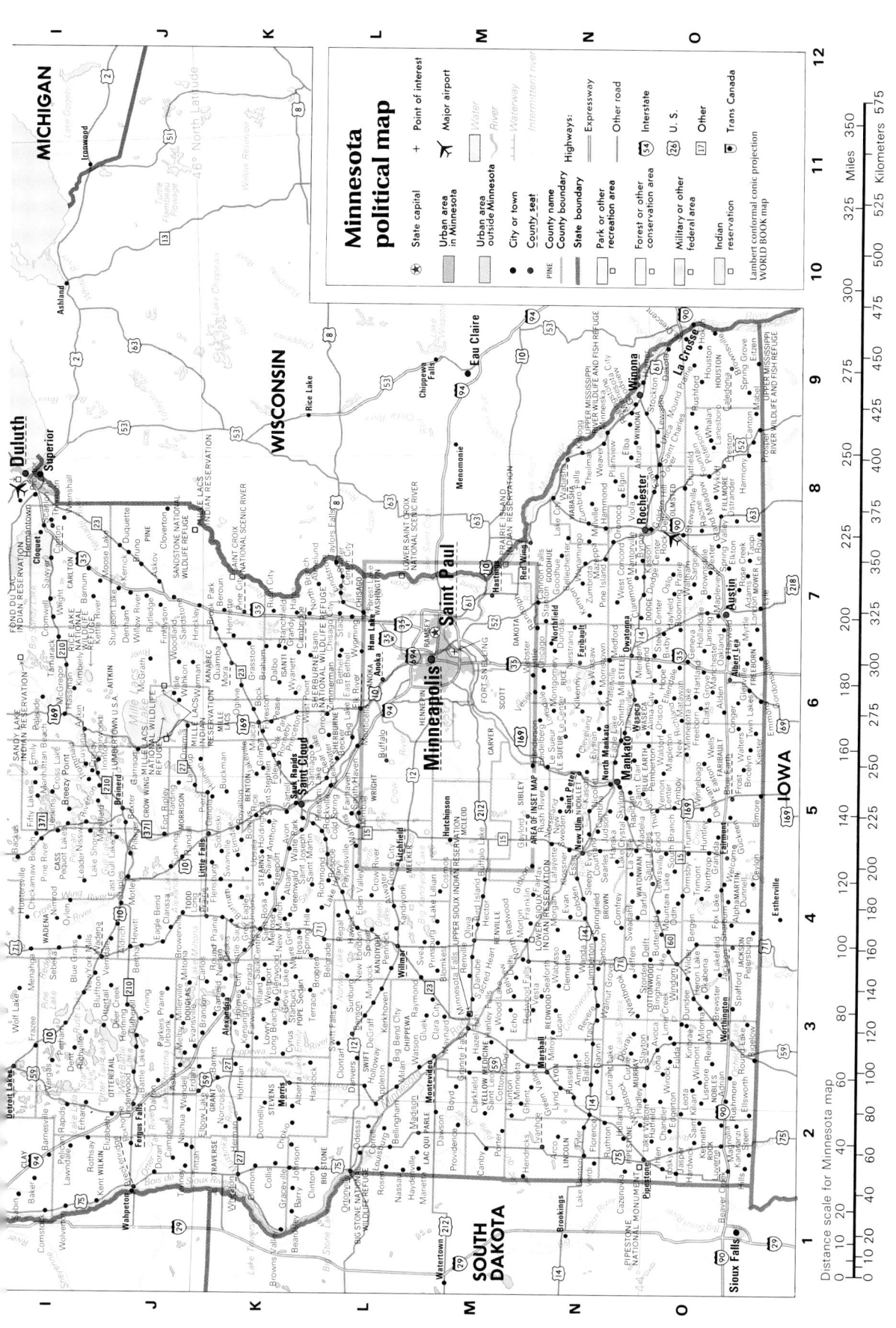

Minnesota political map

Legend:

- ✦ State capital
- ＋ Point of interest
- ✈ Major airport

- Urban area in Minnesota
- Urban area outside Minnesota
- Water
- River
- Waterway
- Intermittent river

- ● City or town
- ● County seat
- County name
- County boundary
- State boundary

Highways:
- Expressway
- Other road
- 54 Interstate
- 26 U.S.
- 12 Other
- Trans Canada

- Park or other recreation area
- Forest or other conservation area
- Military or other federal area
- Indian reservation

Lambert conformal conic projection
WORLD BOOK map

Distance scale for Minnesota map

Miles 0 10 20 40 60 80 100 120 140 160 180 200 225 250 275 300 325 350

Kilometers 0 10 20 40 60 80 100 120 140 160 180 200 225 250 275 300 325 350 375 400 425 450 475 500 525 550 575

MICHIGAN
WISCONSIN
SOUTH DAKOTA
IOWA

Duluth
Superior
Minneapolis
Saint Paul
Rochester
Mankato
Austin
Winona
La Crosse
Eau Claire
Detroit Lakes
Fergus Falls
Alexandria
Saint Cloud
Little Falls
Brainerd
Ashland
Sioux Falls
Watertown
Marshall
Montevideo
Morris
Willmar
Worthington
Pipestone
Albert Lea
Faribault
New Ulm
North Mankato
Saint Peter
Red Wing
Hutchinson
Litchfield
Anoka
Buffalo
Hastings

Minnesota map index

Metropolitan areas

Duluth 239,971
(198,213 in Minn.;
41,758 in Wis.)
Fargo (N. Dak.)-
Moorehead 153,296
(102,874 in N. Dak.;
50,422 in Minn.)
Minneapolis-
St. Paul 2,464,124
(2,413,873 in Minn.;
50,251 in Wis.)
Rochester 106,470
St. Cloud 190,921

Counties

Aitkin ....12,425..J 6
Anoka ....243,641..L 6
Becker ....27,881..H 3
Beltrami ....34,384..F 4
Benton ....30,185..K 5
Big Stone ....6,285..L 2
Blue Earth ....54,044..O 5
Brown ....26,984..N 4
Carlton ....29,259..I 7
Carver ....47,915..M 6
Cass ....21,791..H 5
Chippewa ....13,228..L 3
Chisago ....30,521..K 7
Clay ....50,422..H 2
Clearwater ....8,309..G 3
Cook ....3,868..F 10
Cottonwood ....12,694..O 3
Crow Wing ....44,249..J 5
Dakota ....275,227..M 7
Dodge ....15,731..O 7
Douglas ....28,674..J 3
Faribault ....16,937..O 5
Fillmore ....20,777..O 8
Freeborn ....33,060..O 6
Goodhue ....40,690..N 7
Grant ....6,246..K 2
Hennepin ....1,032,431..M 6
Houston ....18,497..O 9
Hubbard ....14,939..H 4
Isanti ....25,921..K 6
Itasca ....40,861..G 6
Jackson ....11,677..O 4
Kanabec ....12,802..K 6
Kandiyohi ....38,761..L 4
Kittson ....5,767..E 1
Koochiching ....16,299..F 6
Lac qui Parle ....8,924..M 2
Lake ....10,415..G 9
Lake of the Woods ....4,076..E 4
Le Sueur ....23,239..N 6
Lincoln ....6,890..N 2
Lyon ....24,789..N 2
Mahnomen ....5,044..G 3
Marshall ....10,993..E 2
Martin ....22,914..O 4
McLeod ....32,030..M 5
Meeker ....20,846..L 4
Mille Lacs ....18,670..K 6
Morrison ....29,604..J 5
Mower ....37,385..O 7
Murray ....9,660..O 3
Nicollet ....28,076..N 5
Nobles ....20,098..O 2
Norman ....7,975..H 2
Olmsted ....106,470..O 8
Otter Tail ....50,714..J 2
Pennington ....13,306..F 2
Pine ....21,264..J 7
Pipestone ....10,491..N 2
Polk ....32,498..G 2
Pope ....10,745..K 3
Ramsey ....485,765..M 7
Red Lake ....4,525..F 2
Redwood ....17,254..N 3
Renville ....17,673..M 4
Rice ....49,183..N 6
Rock ....9,806..O 2
Roseau ....15,026..D 2
St. Louis ....198,213..H 7
Scott ....57,846..M 6
Sherburne ....41,945..L 6
Sibley ....14,366..M 5
Stearns ....118,791..K 4
Steele ....30,729..N 6
Stevens ....10,634..K 2
Swift ....10,724..L 3
Todd ....23,363..J 4
Traverse ....4,463..K 2
Wabasha ....19,744..N 8
Wadena ....13,154..I 4
Waseca ....18,079..O 6
Washington ....145,896..L 7
Watonwan ....11,682..O 4
Wilkin ....7,516..J 2
Winona ....47,828..N 9
Wright ....68,710..L 5
Yellow Medicine ....11,684..M 2

Cities

Ada ....1,708.°H 2
Adams ....756..O 7
Adrian ....1,141..O 2
Afton ....2,645..B 12
Aitkin ....1,698.°I 6
Akeley ....393..H 4
Albany ....1,548..K 4
Albert Lea ....18,310.°O 6
Alberta ....136..K 2
Albertville ....1,251..A 9
Alden ....623..O 6
Aldrich ....70..J 4
Alexandria ....7,838.°K 3
Alpha ....105..O 4
Altura ....349..N 8
Alvarado ....356..F 1
Amboy ....517..O 5
Andover ....15,216..A 10
Annandale ....2,054..A 8
Anoka ....17,192.°L 6
Apple Valley* ....34,598..M 6
Appleton ....1,552..L 2
Arco ....104..N 2
Arden Hills ....9,199..A 11
Argyle ....636..E 1
Arlington ....1,886..C 8
Ashby ....469..J 3
Askov ....343..J 7
Atwater ....1,053..L 4
Audubon ....411..H 2
Aurora ....1,965..G 8
Austin ....21,907.°O 7
Avoca ....150..O 3
Avon ....970..K 5
Babbitt ....1,562..G 8
Backus ....240..I 5
Badger ....381..D 2
Bagley ....1,388.°G 3
Balaton ....737..N 2
Barnesville ....2,066..I 2
Barnum ....482..I 7
Barrett ....350..K 2
Barry ....40..K 1
Battle Lake ....698..J 3
Baudette ....1,146.°E 4
Baxter ....3,695..J 5
Bayport ....3,200..B 12
Beardsley ....297..K 1
Beaver Bay ....147..H 9
Beaver Creek ....249..O 2
Becker ....902..L 5
Bejou ....110..G 2
Belgrade ....700..L 4
Belle Plaine ....3,149..C 9
Bellechester ....110..N 7
Bellingham ....247..L 2
Beltrami ....137..G 2
Belview ....383..M 3
Bemidji ....11,245.°G 4
Bena ....147..H 5
Benson ....3,235.°L 3
Bertha ....507..J 4
Bethel ....394..L 6
Big Falls ....341..F 6
Big Lake ....3,113..L 6
Bigelow ....232..O 3
Bigfork ....384..G 6
Bingham Lake ....155..O 4
Birchwood Village* ....1,042..L 7
Bird Island ....1,326..M 4
Biscay ....113..B 7
Biwabik ....1,097..G 8
Blackduck ....718..G 4
Blaine ....38,975..A 10
Blomkest ....183..M 4
Blooming Prairie ....2,043..O 7
Bloomington ....86,335..B 10
Blue Earth ....3,745.°O 5
Bluffton ....187..I 3
Bock ....115..K 6
Borup ....119..H 2
Bovey ....662..H 6
Bowlus ....260..K 5
Boy River ....43..H 5
Boyd ....251..M 2
Braham ....1,139..K 6
Brainerd ....12,353.°J 5
Branch* ....2,400..K 7
Brandon ....441..J 3
Breckenridge ....3,708.°J 1
Breezy Point ....432..I 5
Brewster ....532..O 3
Bricelyn ....426..O 6
Brook Park ....125..K 7
Brooklyn Center ....28,887..A 10
Brooklyn Park ....56,381..A 10
Brooks ....158..G 2
Brookston ....107..H 7
Brooten ....589..L 4
Browerville ....782..J 4
Browns Valley ....804..K 1
Brownsdale ....695..O 7
Brownsville ....415..O 9
Brownton ....781..C 7
Bruno ....89..J 7
Buckman ....201..K 5
Buffalo ....6,856.°L 5
Buffalo Lake ....734..M 4
Buhl ....915..G 7
Burnsville* ....51,288..M 6
Burtrum ....172..K 4
Butterfield ....509..O 4
Byron ....2,441..O 7
Caledonia ....2,846.°O 9
Callaway ....212..H 2
Calumet ....382..H 6
Cambridge ....5,094.°K 6
Campbell ....233..J 2
Canby ....1,826..M 2
Cannon Falls ....3,232..N 7
Canton ....362..O 8
Carlos ....361..J 3
Carlton ....923.°I 7
Carver ....744..C 9
Cass Lake ....923..G 4
Castle Rock ....D 11
Cedar Mills ....80..B 7
Center City ....451.°L 7
Centerville ....1,633..A 11
Ceylon ....461..O 4
Champlin ....16,849..A 10
Chandler ....316..O 2
Chanhassen ....11,732..B 9
Chaska ....11,339.°C 9
Chatfield ....2,226..O 8
Chickamaw Beach ....132..I 5
Chisago City ....2,009..L 7
Chisholm ....5,290..G 7
Chokio ....521..K 2
Circle Pines* ....4,704..L 7
Clara City ....1,307..M 3
Claremont ....530..O 7
Clarissa ....637..J 4
Clarkfield ....924..M 3
Clarks Grove ....675..O 6
Clear Lake ....315..L 5
Clearbrook ....560..G 3
Clearwater ....597..L 5
Clements ....191..N 4
Cleveland ....699..N 5
Climax ....264..G 1
Clinton ....574..L 2
Clitherall ....109..J 3
Clontarf ....172..L 3
Cloquet ....10,885..I 8
Coates ....186..C 11
Cobden ....62..N 4
Cohasset ....H 6
Cokato ....2,180..A 8
Cold Spring ....2,459..L 5
Coleraine ....1,041..H 6
Collegeville* ....K 5
Cologne ....563..C 9
Columbia Heights* ....18,910..L 6
Comfrey ....433..N 4
Comstock ....123..I 1
Conger ....143..O 6
Cook ....680..F 7
Coon Rapids ....52,978..A 10
Corcoran* ....5,199..L 6
Correll ....60..L 2
Cosmos ....610..M 4
Cottage Grove* ....22,935..M 7
Cottonwood ....982..M 3
Courtland ....412..N 5
Crane Lake ....F 7
Cromwell ....221..I 7
Crookston ....8,119.°G 1
Crosby ....2,073..I 5
Crosslake ....1,132..I 5
Crystal ....23,788..A 10
Currie ....303..N 3
Cuyuna ....172..I 5
Cyrus ....328..K 3
Dakota ....360..O 9
Dalton ....234..J 2
Danube ....562..M 4
Danvers ....98..L 3
Darfur ....128..O 4
Darwin ....252..A 7
Dassel ....1,082..A 7
Dawson ....1,626..M 2
Dayton ....4,443..A 9
Deephaven ....3,653..B 10
Deer Creek ....303..J 3
Deer River ....838..H 6
Deerwood ....524..L 5
De Graff ....149..L 3
Delano ....2,709..A 9
Delavan ....245..O 5
Delhi ....69..M 3
Dellwood ....887..A 11
Denham ....36..J 7
Dennison* ....152..N 7
Dent ....177..I 3
Detroit Lakes ....6,635.°I 3
Dexter ....303..O 7
Dilworth ....2,562..H 1
Dodge Center ....1,954..O 7
Donaldson ....57..E 1
Donnelly ....221..K 2
Doran ....78..J 2
Dover ....416..O 8
Dovray ....60..N 3
Duluth ....85,493.°I 8
Dumont ....126..K 2
Dundas ....473..N 6
Dundee ....107..O 3
Dunnell ....187..O 4
Eagan* ....47,409..M 6
Eagle Bend ....524..J 4
Eagle Lake ....1,703..N 5
East Bethel ....8,050..L 6
East Grand Forks ....8,658..F 1
East Gull Lake ....687..J 5
Easton ....229..O 5
Echo ....304..M 3
Eden Prairie* ....39,311..M 6
Eden Valley ....732..L 4
Edgerton ....1,106..O 2
Edina ....46,070..B 10
Effie ....130..F 6
Eitzen ....221..O 9
Elba ....220..N 8
Elbow Lake ....1,186.°J 2
Elgin ....733..N 8
Elizabeth ....152..J 2
Elk River ....11,143.°L 6
Elko ....223..C 10
Elkton ....142..O 7
Ellendale ....549..O 6
Ellsworth ....580..O 2
Elmdale ....130..K 5
Elmore ....709..O 5
Elrosa ....205..K 4
Ely ....3,968..F 8
Ely Lake* ....G 7
Elysian ....445..N 6
Emily ....613..I 5
Emmons ....439..O 6
Erhard ....181..I 2
Ericsburg ....E 6
Erskine ....422..G 2
Evan ....83..N 4
Evansville ....566..J 3
Eveleth ....4,064..G 7
Excelsior ....2,367..B 9
Eyota ....1,448..O 8
Fairfax ....1,276..N 4
Fairhaven ....L 5
Fairmont ....11,265.°O 5
Falcon Heights* ....5,380..M 6
Faribault ....17,085.°N 6
Farmington ....5,940..C 11
Farwell ....74..K 3
Federal Dam ....118..H 5
Felton ....211..H 2
Fergus Falls ....12,362.°J 2
Fertile ....853..G 2
Fifty Lakes ....299..I 5
Finland ....G 9
Finlayson ....242..J 7
Fisher ....413..G 1
Flensburg ....213..K 4
Floodwood ....574..H 7
Florence ....53..N 2
Foley ....1,854.°K 5
Forada ....171..K 3
Forest Lake ....5,833..L 7
Foreston ....354..K 6
Fort Ripley ....92..J 5
Fosston ....1,529..G 3
Fountain ....327..O 8
Foxhome ....160..J 2
Franklin ....22..G 7
Franklin ....441..N 4
Frazee ....1,176..I 3
Freeborn ....301..O 6
Freeport ....556..K 4
Fridley ....28,335..A 10
Frost ....236..O 5
Fulda ....1,212..O 3
Funkley ....15..G 5
Garfield ....203..K 3
Garrison ....138..J 5
Garvin ....149..N 3
Gary ....200..G 2
Gaylord ....1,935.°M 5
Gem Lake* ....439..L 7
Geneva ....444..O 6
Genola ....85..K 5
Georgetown ....107..H 1
Ghent ....316..N 2
Gibbon ....712..N 4
Gilbert ....1,934..G 8
Gilman ....192..K 5
Glencoe ....4,648.°C 8
Glenville ....778..O 6
Glenwood ....2,573.°K 3
Glyndon ....862..H 1
Golden Hill ....O 8
Golden Valley* ....20,971..M 6
Gonvick ....302..G 3
Good Thunder ....561..O 5
Goodhue ....533..N 7
Goodridge ....115..F 3
Goodview ....2,878..N 9
Graceville ....671..K 2
Granada ....374..O 5
Grand Marais ....1,171.°G 11
Grand Meadow ....967..O 7
Grand Rapids ....7,976.°H 6
Granite Falls ....3,083.°M 3
Grasston ....119..K 6
Green Isle ....239..C 8
Greenbush ....800..E 2
Greenfield ....1,450..A 9
Greenwald ....209..K 4
Greenwood* ....614..L 5
Grey Eagle ....353..K 4
Grove City ....547..L 4
Grygla ....220..F 3
Gully ....128..G 3
Hackensack ....245..H 5
Hadley ....94..O 2
Hallock ....1,304.°D 1
Halma ....73..E 1
Halstad ....611..G 1
Ham Lake ....8,924..L 6
Hamburg ....492..C 8
Hammond ....205..N 8
Hampton ....363..C 11
Hancock ....723..K 3
Hanley Falls ....246..M 3
Hanover ....787..A 9
Hanska ....443..N 5
Harding ....76..J 5
Hardwick ....234..O 2
Harmony ....1,081..O 8
Harris ....843..K 7
Hartland ....270..O 6
Hastings ....15,445.°M 7
Hatfield ....66..O 2
Hawley ....1,655..H 2
Hayfield ....1,283..O 7
Hayward ....246..O 6
Hazel Run ....81..M 3
Hector ....1,145..M 4
Heidelberg ....73..N 6
Henderson ....746..N 5
Hendricks ....684..M 2
Hendrum ....309..H 1
Henning ....738..J 3
Henriette ....78..K 7
Herman ....485..K 2
Hermantown ....6,761..I 8
Heron Lake ....730..O 3
Hewitt ....269..J 4
Hibbing ....18,046..G 7
Hill City ....469..H 6
Hillman ....45..J 5
Hills ....607..O 2
Hilltop ....749..A 10
Hinckley ....946..J 7
Hitterdal ....242..H 2
Hoffman ....576..K 3
Hokah ....687..O 9
Holdingford ....561..K 5
Holland ....216..N 2
Hollandale ....289..O 6
Holloway ....123..L 2
Holt ....88..E 2
Homer ....O 9
Hopkins ....16,534..B 10
Houston ....1,013..O 9
Hovland ....F 11
Howard Lake ....1,343..A 8
Hoyt Lakes ....2,348..G 8
Hugo ....4,417..A 11
Humboldt ....74..D 1
Hutchinson ....11,523..M 5
Ihlen ....101..O 2
Independence ....2,822..B 9
International Falls ....8,325.°E 6
Inver Grove Heights ....22,477..B 11
Iona ....158..O 3
Iron Junction ....133..G 7
Ironton ....553..I 5
Isanti ....1,228..K 6
Island View ....150..E 6
Isle ....566..J 6
Ivanhoe ....751.°N 2
Jackson ....3,559.°O 4
Janesville ....1,969..N 6
Jasper ....599..O 2
Jeffers ....443..O 3
Jenkins ....262..I 5
Johnson ....46..K 2
Jordan ....2,909..C 9
Kandiyohi ....506..L 4
Karlstad ....881..E 2
Kasota ....655..N 5
Kasson ....3,514..O 7
Keewatin ....1,118..G 7
Kelliher ....348..F 5
Kellogg ....423..N 8
Kelly Lake ....G 7
Kennedy ....337..E 1
Kenneth ....81..O 2
Kensington ....295..K 3
Kent ....131..J 1
Kenyon ....1,552..N 7
Kerkhoven ....732..L 3
Kerrick ....56..J 7
Kettle River ....190..I 7
Kiester ....606..O 6
Kilkenny ....167..N 6
Kimball ....690..L 5
Kinbrae ....18..O 3
Kingston ....131..A 7
Kinney ....257..G 7
La Crescent ....4,311..O 9
Lafayette ....462..N 5
Lake Benton ....693..N 2
Lake Bronson ....272..E 1
Lake City ....4,391..N 8
Lake Crystal ....2,084..N 5
Lake Elmo* ....5,903..M 7
Lake George ....H 4
Lake Henry ....90..L 4
Lake Lillian ....229..M 4
Lake Park ....638..H 2
Lake St. Croix Beach ....1,078..B 12
Lake Shore ....693..I 5
Lake Wilson ....319..O 2
Lakefield ....1,679..O 3
Lakeland ....2,000..B 12
Lakeland Shores* ....291..M 7
Lakeville ....24,854..C 10
Lamberton ....972..N 3
Lancaster ....342..D 1
Landfall Village ....685..B 11
Lanesboro ....858..O 8
Lansing ....O 6
Laporte ....101..H 4
La Prairie ....438..H 6

Artstreet

Minnehaha Falls on Minnehaha Creek in Minneapolis is a beautiful waterfall made famous in Henry Wadsworth Longfellow's poem *The Song of Hiawatha*. The waterfall is 53 feet (16 meters) high.

La Salle ....98..N 4
Lastrup ....112..J 5
Lauderdale ......2,700..B 10
Le Center ......2,006.°N 6
Lengby ....112..G 3
Leonard ....26..G 3
Leonidas ....70..G 7
Leota ....O 2
Le Roy ....904..O 8
Lester Prairie ....1,180..B 8
Le Sueur ....3,714..N 5
Lewisville ....1,298..O 9
Lewisville ....255..O 5
Lexington ......2,279..A 11
Lilydale ....506..B 11
Lindstrom ......2,461..L 7
Lino Lakes ......8,807..A 11
Lismore ....248..O 2
Litchfield ......6,041.°L 4
Little Canada* ..8,971..L 7
Little Falls ....7,232.°J 5
Littlefork ....838..E 6
Long Beach ......204..A 3
Long Lake* .....1,984..M 6
Long Prairie ...2,786.°J 4
Longville ....224..H 5
Lonsdale ....1,252..N 6
Loretto ....404..A 9
Louisburg ....42..L 2
Lowry ....233..K 3
Lucan ....235..N 3
Luverne ....4,382.°O 2
Lyle ....504..O 7
Lynd ....287..N 2
Mabel ....745..O 9
Madelia ....2,237..O 5
Madison ....1,951.°M 2
Madison Lake* ...643..N 5
Magnolia ....155..O 2
Mahnomen .....1,154.°H 2
Mahtomedi* ....5,569..L 7
Manchester ....69..O 6
Manhattan Beach ...61..J 5
Mankato ....31,477.°N 5
Mantorville ......874.°N 7
Maple Grove ...38,736..A 10
Maple Lake ....1,394..A 8
Maple Plain* ...2,005..M 6
Mapleton ....1,526..O 5
Mapleview ....206..O 7
Maplewood ....30,954..B 11
Marble ....618..H 6
Marietta ....211..M 2
Marine on St.
Croix ....602..A 12
Marshall ......12,023.°N 3
Mayer ....471..B 8
Maynard ....419..M 3
Mazeppa ....722..N 7
McGrath ....62..J 6
McGregor ....376..I 6
McIntosh ....665..G 3
McKinley ....116..G 9
Meadowlands ......92..H 7

Medford ....733..N 6
Medicine Lake* ...385..M 6
Medina ....3,096..A 9
Meire Grove .....124..K 4
Melrose ....2,561..K 4
Menahga ....1,076..J 4
Mendota ....164..B 11
Mendota
Heights ......9,431..B 11
Mentor ....94..G 2
Merrifield ....I 4
Middle River .....285..E 2
Miesville ....135..C 12
Milaca ....2,182.°K 6
Milan ....353..L 2
Millerville ....104..J 3
Millville ....163..N 8
Milroy ....297..N 3
Miltona ....181..J 3
Minneapolis ..368,383.°M 6
Minneiska ....127..N 8
Minneota ....1,417..M 2
Minnesota City ...258..N 9
Minnesota Lake ..681..O 6
Minnetonka ...48,370..B 10
Minnetonka
Beach ....573..M 6
Minnetrista* ...3,439..M 6
Mizpah ....100..F 5
Montevideo ....5,499.°M 3
Montgomery ...2,399..N 6
Monticello .....4,941..L 6
Montrose ....1,008..A 8
Moorhead .....32,295.°H 1
Moose Lake ....1,206..J 7
Mora ....2,905.°K 6
Morgan ....965..N 4
Morris ....5,613.°K 2
Morristown ....784..N 6
Morton ....448..M 4
Motley ....441..J 4
Mound ....9,634..B 9
Mounds View ..12,541..A 10
Mountain Iron ..3,362..G 7
Mountain Lake .1,906..O 4
Murdock ....282..L 3
Myrtle ....72..O 7
Nashua ....63..J 2
Nashwauk ......1,026..G 6
Nassau ....83..L 2
Nelson ....177..K 3
Nerstrand ....210..N 7
Nett Lake ....F 7
Nevis ....375..H 4
New Auburn ....463..M 5
New Brighton* .22,207..L 6
New Germany .....353..B 8
New Hope .....21,853..B 10
New London ....971..L 4
New Market ....227..C 10
New Munich ....314..K 4
New Prague ....3,569..D 9
New Richland ...1,237..O 6
New Trier ....96..C 11

New Ulm ....13,132.°N 4
New York Mills ...940..J 3
Newfolden ....345..E 2
Newport ....3,720..B 11
Nicollet ....795..N 5
Nielsville ....100..G 1
Nimrod ....65..I 4
Nisswa ....1,391..J 5
Norcross ....86..K 2
North Branch ...1,867..K 7
North Mankato .10,164..N 5
North Oaks* ....3,386..L 6
North Redwood ...203..M 4
North St. Paul* .12,376..L 7
Northfield .....14,684..N 7
Northome ....283..F 5
Northrop ....276..O 5
Norwood ....1,351..C 8
Oak Park ....K 6
Oak Park Heights .3,486..A 12
Oakdale* ......18,374..M 7
Oakland ....155..L 2
Odessa ....155..L 2
Odin ....102..O 4
Ogema ....164..H 2
Ogilvie ....510..K 6
Okabena ....223..O 3
Oklee ....441..F 3
Olivia ....2,623.°M 4
Onamia ....676..J 6
Ormsby ....159..O 4
Orono ....7,285..B 9
Oronoco ....727..N 7
Orr ....265..F 7
Ortonville ......2,205.°L 2
Osakis ....1,256..K 4
Oslo ....362..F 1
Osseo* ....2,704..L 6
Ostrander ....276..O 8
Ottertail ....313..J 3
Owatonna .....19,386.°N 6
Palisade ....144..I 6
Park Rapids ....2,863.°H 4
Parkers Prairie ...956..J 3
Paynesville ....2,275..L 4
Pease ....178..K 6
Pelican Rapids ..1,886..I 2
Pemberton ....228..O 6
Pennock ....476..L 4
Pequot Lakes ....843..I 5
Perham ....2,075..I 3
Perley ....132..H 1
Peterson ....259..O 9
Pierz ....1,014..J 5
Pike Lake* ....H 7
Pillager ....306..J 5
Pine City .....2,613.°K 7
Pine Island ....2,125..N 7
Pine River ....871..I 5
Pine Springs* ....436..L 7
Pipestone .....4,554.°O 2
Plainview .....2,768..N 8
Plato ....355..C 8
Pleasant Lake .....79..L 5

Plummer ....277..F 2
Plymouth .....50,889..B 10
Porter ....210..M 2
Preston ....1,530.°O 8
Princeton .....3,719..K 6
Prinsburg ....502..M 3
Prior Lake ....11,482..C 10
Proctor ....2,974..I 8
Quamba ....124..K 6
Racine ....288..O 8
Ramsey ....12,408..A 10
Randall ....571..J 5
Randolph ....331..N 7
Ranier ....199..E 6
Raymond ....668..M 3
Red Lake Falls ..1,481.°F 2
Red Wing ....15,134.°N 7
Redwood Falls ..4,859.°N 4
Regal ....51..L 4
Remer ....342..H 5
Renville ....1,315..M 3
Revere ....117..N 3
Rice ....610..K 5
Richfield .....35,710..B 10
Richmond ....965..L 5
Richville ....121..I 3
Riverton ....122..I 5
Robbinsdale* ..14,396..M 6
Rochester ....70,745.°O 8
Rock Creek* ...1,040..K 7
Rockford ......2,665..A 9
Rockville ....579..L 5
Rogers ....698..A 9
Rollingstone .....697..N 9
Ronneby ....58..K 5
Roosevelt ....180..D 4
Roscoe ....141..L 4
Rose Creek ......363..O 7
Roseau ....2,396.°D 3
Rosemount ....8,622..C 11
Roseville ....33,485..B 11
Rothsay ....443..J 2
Round Lake ......463..O 3
Royalton ....802..K 5
Rush City .....1,497..K 7
Rushford ......1,485..O 9
Rushford Village* ..705..O 9
Rushmore ....381..O 2
Russell ....394..N 2
Ruthton ....328..N 2
Rutledge ....152..J 7
Sabin ....495..I 1
Sacred Heart .....603..M 4
St. Anthony ....81..K 4
St. Anthony* ...7,727..L 6
St. Bonifacius ..1,180..B 9
St. Charles ....2,642..O 8
St. Clair ....633..N 5
St. Cloud ....48,812.°K 5
St. Francis* ...2,538..L 6
St. Hilaire ....298..F 2
St. James .....4,364.°O 4
St. Joseph ....3,294..K 5
St. Leo ....111..M 2
St. Louis Park .43,787..B 10
St. Martin ....274..K 4
St. Marys Point* ..339..M 7
St. Michael ....2,506..A 9
St. Paul .....272,235.°M 7
St. Paul Park ...4,965..B 11
St. Peter ......9,421.°N 5
St. Rosa ....75..K 4
St. Stephen ......607..K 5
St. Vincent ......116..D 1
Sanborn ....459..N 4
Sandstone .....2,057..J 7
Sargeant ....78..O 7
Sartell ....5,393..K 5
Sauk Centre ...3,581..K 4
Sauk Rapids ...7,825..K 5
Savage ....9,906..C 10
Scandia ....A 12
Scanlon ....878..I 8
Seaforth ....87..N 3
Sebeka ....662..I 4
Sedan ....63..K 3
Shafer ....368..L 7
Shakopee .....11,739.°C 9
Shelly ....215..G 1
Sherburn ....1,105..O 4
Shevlin ....157..G 3
Shoreview ....24,587..A 11
Shorewood .....5,917..B 9
Silver Bay .....1,894..H 9
Silver Lake ......764..B 7
Skyline ....272..N 5
Slayton ....2,147.°O 3
Sleepy Eye ....3,694..N 4
Sobieski ....199..K 5
Solway ....74..G 4
South Haven .....193..L 5
South International
Falls ....E 6
South St. Paul .20,197..B 11
Spicer ....1,020..L 4
Spring Grove ..1,153..O 9
Spring Hill ....77..K 4
Spring Lake
Park ....6,532..A 10
Spring Park* ...1,571..M 6
Spring Valley ..2,461..O 8
Springfield ....2,173..N 4
Squaw Lake ......139..G 5
Stacy ....1,081..L 7
Staples ....2,754..J 4
Starbuck ....1,143..K 3
Steen ....176..O 2
Stephen ....707..E 1
Stewart ....566..C 7

Stewartville .....4,520..O 8
Stillwater ....13,882.°A 12
Stockton ....529..O 9
Storden ....283..O 3
Strandquist ....98..E 2
Strathcona ....40..E 2
Sturgeon Lake ...230..J 7
Sunburg ....117..L 3
Sunfish Lake* ....413..M 7
Swanville ....324..K 4
Swatara ....J 6
Taconite ....310..H 6
Tamarack ....53..I 7
Taopi ....83..O 7
Taunton ....175..M 2
Taylors Falls ....694..L 7
Tenney ....4..J 2
Tenstrike ....184..G 4
Thief River Falls .8,010.°F 2
Thomson ....132..I 8
Tintah ....74..J 2
Tonka Bay* ....1,472..M 6
Tower ....502..G 8
Tracy ....2,059..N 3
Trail ....67..G 3
Trimont ....745..O 4
Trommald ....80..I 5
Trosky ....120..O 2
Truman ....1,292..O 5
Turtle River ......62..G 4
Twin Lakes ....154..O 6
Twin Valley ......821..H 2
Two Harbors ...3,651.°H 9
Tyler ....1,257..N 2
Ulen ....547..H 2
Underwood ....284..J 2
Upsala ....371..K 4
Urbank ....73..J 3
Utica ....220..O 8
Vadnais Heights* .11,041..L 7
Vergas ....287..I 3
Vermillion ....510..C 11
Verndale ....560..J 4
Vernon Center ...339..O 5
Veseli ....N 6
Vesta ....302..N 3
Victoria ....2,354..B 9
Viking ....103..F 2
Villard ....247..K 3
Vining ....84..J 3
Virginia ....9,410.°G 7
Wabasha ....2,384.°N 8
Wabasso ....684..N 3
Waconia ....3,498..B 9
Wadena ....4,131.°J 4
Wahkon ....197..J 6
Waite Park .....5,020..K 5
Waldorf ....243..O 6
Walker ....950.°H 4
Walnut Grove ....625..N 3
Walters ....86..O 6
Waltham ....170..O 7
Wanamingo ....847..N 7
Wanda ....103..N 4
Warba ....137..H 6
Warren ....1,813.°F 1
Warroad ....1,679..D 3
Warsaw ....N 6
Waseca ....8,385.°N 6
Watertown .....2,408..B 8
Waterville .....1,771..N 6
Watkins ....849..L 5
Watson ....211..M 3
Waubun ....330..H 2
Waverly ....600..A 8
Wayzata* ......3,806..M 6
Webster ....N 6
Welcome ....790..O 4
Wells ....2,465..O 6
Wendell ....159..J 2
West Concord ....871..N 7
West St. Paul .19,248..B 11
West Union ....54..K 4
Westbrook ....853..O 3
Westport ....47..K 4
Whalan ....94..O 8
Wheaton ....1,581..B 8
White Bear Lake .24,704..A 11
White Earth† .....319..H 3
Wilder ....83..O 3
Willernie ....584..A 11
Williams ....212..E 4
Willmar ....17,531.°L 4
Willow River .....284..J 7
Wilmont ....351..O 2
Wilton ....171..G 4
Windom ....4,283.°O 4
Winger ....167..G 2
Winnebago .....1,565..O 5
Winona ....25,399.°N 9
Winsted ....1,581..B 8
Winthrop ......1,279..O 7
Winton ....169..F 8
Wolf Lake ....35..I 3
Wolverton ....158..I 1
Wood Lake ....404..N 3
Woodbury* ....20,075..M 7
Woodland* ....496..M 6
Woodstock ....159..O 2
Worthington ...9,977.°O 3
Wrenshall ....296..I 8
Wright ....144..I 7
Wykoff ....493..O 8
Wyoming ....2,142..L 7
Young America ..1,354..C 8
Zemple ....63..H 6
Zimmerman ....1,350..L 6
Zumbro Falls .....237..N 8
Zumbrota ....2,312..N 7

Visitor's guide

Minnesota is one of the nation's most popular playgrounds. Every year, several million residents and out-of-state visitors spend their vacations in Minnesota. Thousands of sparkling blue lakes attract swimmers, water skiers, and boaters. Fishing enthusiasts find the cool northern waters filled with a great variety of game fish. Wooded parks and deep forests are scattered throughout the state. Skiing, snowmobiling, and ice fishing are favorite winter activities.

Minnesota's long, cold winters are ideal for winter carnivals and sports festivals. The St. Paul Winter Carnival begins the last week in January. The carnival features ice-skating races, and ski-jumping and ice sculpture contests. A snowmobile race is also held across the United States-Canadian border. The Minneapolis Aquatennial, held in July, features boat races, costume balls, and a torchlight parade. Minnesota holds its State Fair in St. Paul from late August through Labor Day.

Minnesota State Fair

The Minnesota State Fair in St. Paul

Glensheen, University of Minnesota

The luxurious living room in Duluth's Glensheen mansion

Places to visit

Forest History Center, in Grand Rapids, includes a reconstructed logging camp of the 1800's. Exhibits trace human life in Minnesota from prehistoric times to the present.

Fort Snelling is a restored military post near Minneapolis. It was established in temporary buildings in 1819 and built as a permanent fort between 1820 and 1825. The fort features demonstrations dealing with life of the 1820's.

Glensheen is a lavish 39-room mansion in Duluth. It was built in 1905 by Chester A. Congdon, a wealthy mining executive.

Ironworld, near Chisholm, features exhibits on the history of mining in Minnesota. It has an outdoor amphitheater, park, and a train that tours two open-pit mines.

Mall of America, in Bloomington, includes 400 specialty shops, 14 movie theaters, 8 nightclubs, 3 department stores, and an indoor amusement park with a roller coaster.

Minnesota Zoo, in Apple Valley, exhibits about 250 species of animals in natural settings.

Murphy's Landing, near Shakopee, is a re-creation of an 1890 pioneer village. It features replicas of pioneer farms, an Indian village, and a fur trader's cabin.

Science Museum of Minnesota, in St. Paul, features science, technology, and natural history exhibits. Its omnitheater shows films on a domed screen that surrounds the audience.

Statues of Paul Bunyan and Babe, in Bemidji, honor the legendary lumberman and his giant blue ox. Brainerd also has huge statues of Paul and his ox.

The Guthrie Theater, in Minneapolis, presents some of the nation's finest dramatic performances.

National parklands in Minnesota include two national monuments—Grand Portage and Pipestone. Grand Portage National Monument, on the northwestern shore of Lake Superior, marks the site of a historic canoe route and trading post. For centuries, Indian peace pipes have been made from the red pipestone found at Pipestone National Monument. Voyageurs National Park, near International Falls, has scenic waterways. For information on other national parklands in the state, see the article on **National Park System.**

National forests. Minnesota has two national forests. Superior National Forest lies in the northeast and includes the Boundary Waters Canoe Area, the nation's only wilderness preserved for canoeists. Chippewa National Forest covers much of Itasca County and parts of Beltrami and Cass counties.

State parks and forests. Minnesota has about 65 state parks and about 45 state forests. For information on the state parks, write to Commissioner, Parks and Recreation Division, Department of Natural Resources, 500 Lafayette Road, St. Paul, MN 55155-4001.

Annual events

January-March
Ice Box Days winter festival in International Falls (January); John Beargrease Sled Dog Race between Duluth and Grand Marais (January); Grand Vinterslass Fest in Grand Rapids (January); International Eelpout Festival in Walker (February); Minnesota Finlandia Ski Marathon in Bemidji (February); St. Paul Winter Carnival (late January-early February).

April-June
Festival of Nations in St. Paul (April or May); Swayed Pines Folk Fest in Collegeville (April); Cinco de Mayo in St. Paul (May); Grandma's Marathon in Duluth (June); Rochesterfest in Rochester (June).

July-September
Art in the Park in Albert Lea (July); Heritagefest in New Ulm (July); Taste of Minnesota food festival in St. Paul (July); Wheels, Wings & Water Festival in St. Cloud (July); Minneapolis Aquatennial (July); Automobile racing at the Brainerd International Raceway in Brainerd (July-August); Fishermen's Picnic in Grand Marais (August); Renaissance Fair in Shakopee (August-September); Minnesota State Fair in St. Paul (August-September); Dozinky: A Czechoslovakian Harvest Festival, in New Prague (September).

October-December
Halloween Festival in Anoka (October); Oktoberfest in New Ulm (October); Folkways of Christmas in Shakopee (December); Christmas in the Village, in Montevideo (December); New Year's Eve Family Events in Minneapolis (December).

Joe Glannetti, the Guthrie Theater
Drama at the Guthrie Theater in Minneapolis

Minnesota Office of Tourism
John Beargrease Sled Dog Race near Duluth

Minnesota Renaissance Festival
The Renaissance Festival in Shakopee

Minnesota Office of Tourism
Tigers at the Minnesota Zoo in Apple Valley

Land and climate

The Boundary Waters area, in northern Minnesota along the United States-Canadian border, is a thickly forested region dotted with magnificent blue lakes.

Gallery North

During the Ice Age, which began about 1¾ million years ago, a series of glaciers moved across Minnesota. Scientists believe the last glacier retreated from the region about 10,000 years ago. As the glaciers advanced south and west across Minnesota, they leveled most of the land. Only a small area in the southeast was untouched. The glaciers created gently rolling plains over most of the state. Thousands of low places formed by the glaciers filled with water. These places became lakes, swamps, or marshes.

Land regions. Minnesota has four major land regions: (1) the Superior Upland, (2) the Young Drift Plains, (3) the Dissected Till Plains, and (4) the Driftless Area.

The Superior Upland is part of the southern tip of the Canadian Shield. The Canadian Shield is a vast area lying over old, hard rock (see **Canadian Shield**). The glaciers had less effect on the hard rock of the Superior Upland than on most other regions of the state. That is why this region includes the most rugged part of Minnesota. The area just north of Lake Superior is the roughest, most isolated part of the state. Eagle Mountain in Cook County is 2,301 feet (701 meters) high. It is Minnesota's highest point. The northeastern tip of the Superior Upland has an arrowhead shape, and is called the *Arrowhead Country.* Most of Minnesota's iron ore deposits are in the Superior Upland.

The Young Drift Plains consist mainly of gently rolling farmlands. Glaciers smoothed the surface of this region, and deposited great amounts of fertile topsoil called *drift* as they melted. The region has some of the nation's richest farmland, and it is the most important farming area in Minnesota. Parts of the Drift Plains are

sandy or stony, and not so well suited for crop farming. *Moraines* can be found in some places, especially in central Minnesota. These are deposits of stones and other earth materials pushed before or along the sides of the glaciers. The moraine areas are hilly and have many lakes. The northernmost tip of the Drift Plains was once part of the bed of Lake Agassiz, a huge lake that drained away at the end of the Ice Age (see **Lake**

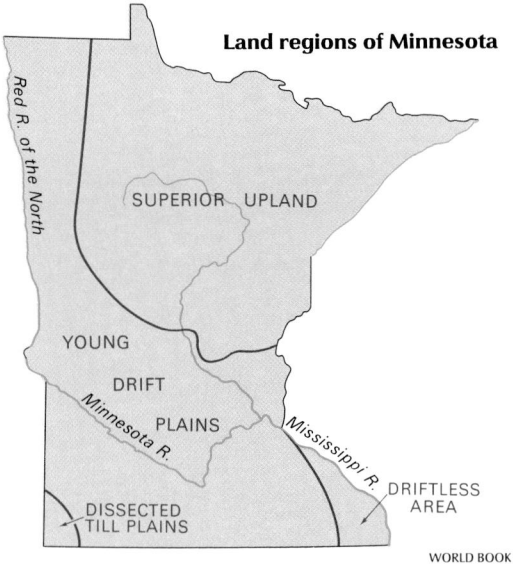

Land regions of Minnesota

SUPERIOR UPLAND

Red R. of the North

YOUNG

DRIFT

PLAINS

Minnesota R.

Mississippi R.

DRIFTLESS AREA

DISSECTED TILL PLAINS

WORLD BOOK map

Map index

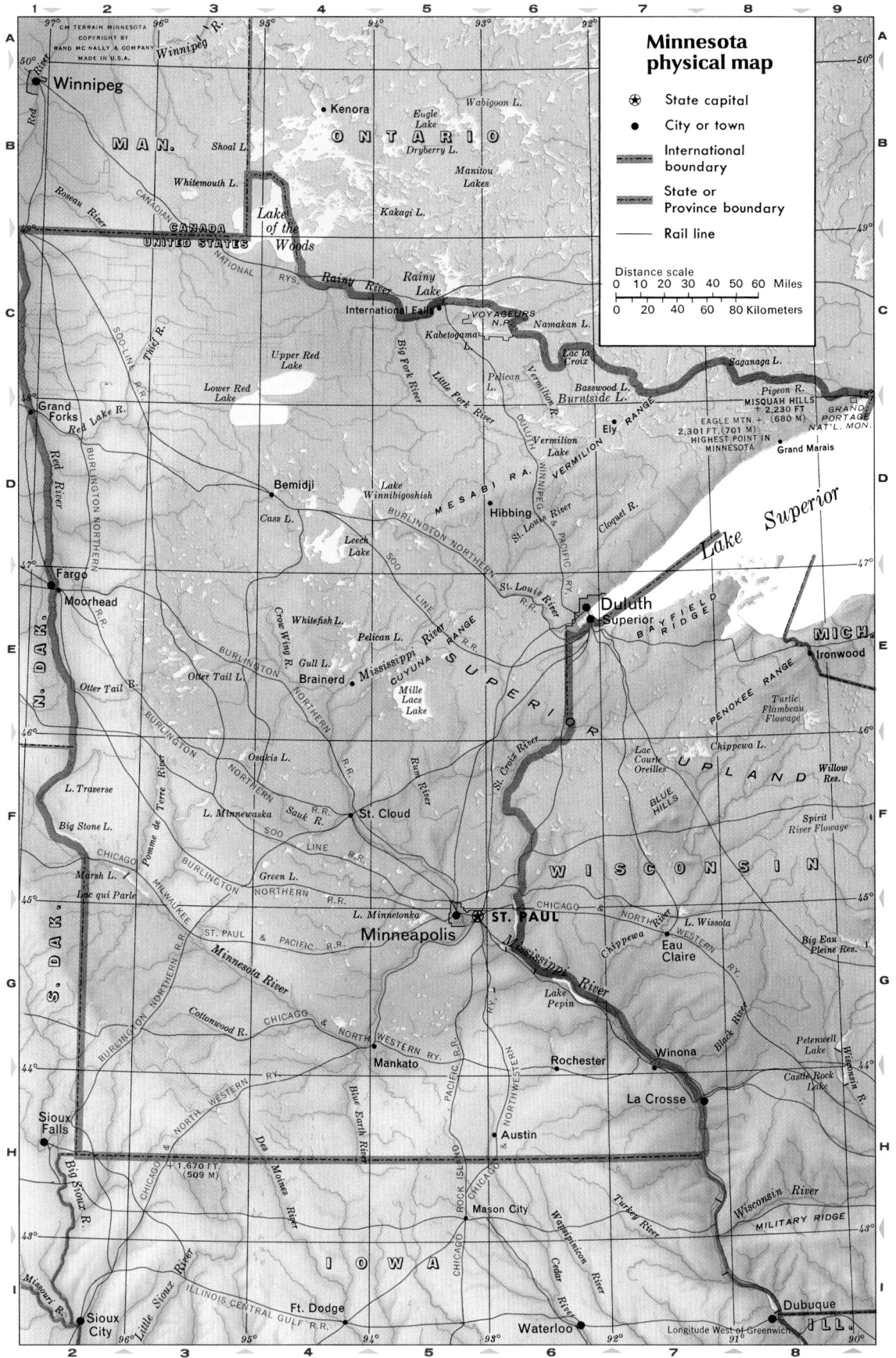

Average January temperatures

Minnesota winters can be bitterly cold. International Falls frequently has the lowest daily temperature in the nation.

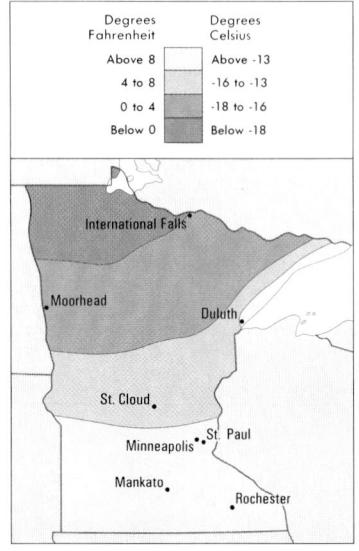

Average July temperatures

Minnesota generally has even temperatures during the summer. The southern half of the state is the warmest.

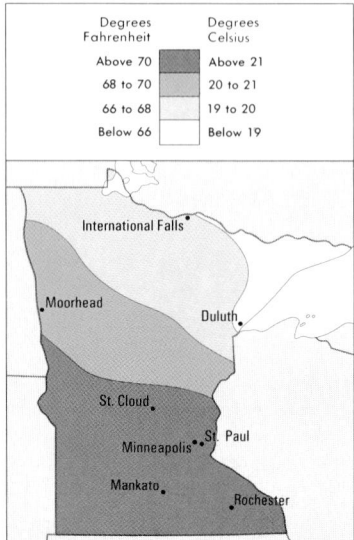

Average yearly precipitation

The east has the greatest amount of precipitation. The amount decreases steadily toward the northwestern part of the state.

WORLD BOOK maps

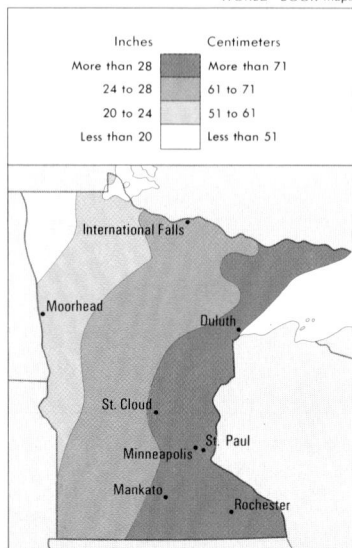

Average monthly weather

	International Falls					Minneapolis-St. Paul			
	Temperatures F.°		C.°		Days of rain or snow	Temperatures F.°		C.°		Days of rain or snow
	High	Low	High	Low		High	Low	High	Low	
Jan.	14	−8	−10	−22	12	23	6	−5	−14	8
Feb.	19	−5	−7	−21	11	27	9	−3	−13	7
Mar.	32	8	0	−13	11	39	23	4	−5	11
Apr.	48	26	9	−3	10	56	36	13	2	9
May	63	38	17	3	12	69	48	21	9	11
June	73	48	23	9	13	79	58	26	14	13
July	79	53	26	12	11	85	63	29	17	11
Aug.	75	51	24	11	12	82	61	28	16	10
Sept.	65	42	18	6	12	73	52	23	11	9
Oct.	52	32	11	0	9	60	41	16	5	7
Nov.	32	16	0	−9	12	41	25	5	−4	8
Dec.	18	0	−8	−18	12	27	12	−3	−11	9

Agassiz). Marshlands and wooded areas lie in parts of this northern section. But most of it is a level and almost treeless plain.

The Dissected Till Plains cover the southwestern corner of Minnesota. There, the glaciers left a thick deposit of *till*—a soil-forming material of sand, gravel, and clay. Streams have *dissected* (cut up) the region. The few level areas in the Dissected Till Plains make excellent farmland.

The Driftless Area lies along the Mississippi River in the southeastern corner of the state. Although glaciers never touched this region, the western part is almost flat. Swift-flowing streams have cut deep valleys into the eastern part of the Driftless Area, giving it a broken surface.

Lakes, rivers, and waterfalls. Minnesota has one of the greatest water areas of any state. Its thousands of in-

land lakes cover more than 4,750 square miles (12,300 square kilometers)—over a twentieth of the state's area. The number of lakes in Minnesota has been estimated as high as 22,000. There are more than 15,000 known lake basins in the state that cover 10 acres (4 hectares) or more. But opinions differ on how large a body of water must be to be properly called a lake.

The largest lake within the state, Red Lake, covers 430 square miles (1,110 square kilometers). Other big lakes in northern Minnesota include Cass Lake, Lake of the Woods, Leech Lake, Vermilion Lake, and Winnibigoshish Lake. Large lakes elsewhere in the state include Big Stone Lake and Lake Traverse, in western Minnesota; and Mille Lacs Lake and Lake Minnetonka, near the center of Minnesota.

Lake Itasca, in north-central Minnesota, is the source of the mighty Mississippi River. It flows out of the lake as a small, clear stream about 10 feet (3 meters) wide and less than 2 feet (61 centimeters) deep.

The Mississippi River and its branches drain about 57 per cent of Minnesota. The Mississippi's chief branches include the Crow Wing, Minnesota, Rum, St. Croix, and Sauk rivers. The Rainy River and the Red River of the North drain the northern and northwestern areas of Minnesota. The St. Louis River and other rivers that empty into Lake Superior drain the land that lies north of the lake.

One of Minnesota's most beautiful waterfalls is Minnehaha Falls, on Minnehaha Creek in Minneapolis. Henry Wadsworth Longfellow made this 53-foot (16-meter) falls famous in his poem *The Song of Hiawatha*. The 49-foot (15-meter) Falls of St. Anthony, on the Mississippi River in Minneapolis, was an important source of power in the early development of Minneapolis. The highest waterfall entirely within the state is 124-foot (38-meter) Cascade Falls, on the Cascade River in Cook

County. Another famous waterfall is High Falls, on the Pigeon River along the Minnesota-Ontario border. High Falls drops 133 feet (41 meters).

Plant and animal life. Forests cover about 35 per cent of Minnesota. Aspen, balsam fir, pine, spruce, and white birch grow in the northern part of the state. Scattered groves of ash, black walnut, elm, maple, and oak grow in the south.

Blackberries, lilies of the valley, raspberries, rue anemones, wild geraniums, and wild roses are found in northern Minnesota. Blueberries, honeysuckles, sweet ferns, trailing arbutus, and wintergreen cover natural openings in the pine forests. Wild flowers that grow in the southern, western, and northwestern parts of Minnesota include asters, bird's-foot violets, blazing stars, goldenrod, and prairie phlox.

White-tailed deer can be found over most of the state. Black bears and moose roam the woods and swamps of the north. Smaller animals found in various parts of Minnesota include beavers, bobcats, foxes, gophers, minks, muskrats, raccoons, and skunks. Quail and ring-necked pheasants feed in the grainfields. Ducks nest in the lakes and swamps during the summer. Fish in Minnesota waters include bass, northern pike, sunfish, trout, and walleye.

Climate. In July, Minnesota averages 68 °F (20 °C) in the north and 74 °F (23 °C) in the south. The record high, 114 °F (46 °C), was set at Beardsley on July 29, 1917, and at Moorhead on July 6, 1936. January temperatures average 2 °F (−17 °C) in the north and 15 °F (−9 °C) in the south. The record low, −59 °F (−51 °C), was set at Leech Lake Dam on Feb. 9, 1899, and at Pokegama Falls (now Pokegama Dam) on Feb. 16, 1903.

Northwestern Minnesota has about 19 inches (48 centimeters) of *precipitation* (rain, melted snow, and other forms of moisture) each year. The southeast receives about 32 inches (81 centimeters) of precipitation a year. Snowfall averages 20 inches (51 centimeters) annually in the southwest and 70 inches (180 centimeters) in the northeast.

Economy

Service industries, taken together, make up nearly three-fourths of Minnesota's *gross state product*—the total value of all goods and services produced in a state in a year. However, manufacturing is the single most important economic activity. It accounts for about a fifth of the gross state product. The Minnesota economy benefits from spending by the thousands of people who vacation in the state during the year.

Natural resources of Minnesota include fertile soil, important minerals, and thick evergreen forests.

Soil is Minnesota's most important natural resource because it is the basis of the state's great farm economy. Minnesota has several types of soil. Most of them were formed from the drift deposited by the glaciers. The color and fertility of the soil indicate the direction from which the ice sheets came. Drift brought from the north was generally gray and more fertile. Drift from the northeast was reddish and less fertile. In some places, different kinds of drift were deposited in layers or mixed. In parts of southern Minnesota, the wind deposited a fine, silty material called *loess* on top of the drift. The loess formed a fertile, rock-free topsoil.

Minerals. The Mesabi Range, in Itasca and St. Louis counties, yields all of Minnesota's iron ore. Most of the ore mined in the Mesabi Range comes from a rock called *taconite* (see **Taconite**). Ore from the Cuyuna Range, located just north of Mille Lacs Lake, contains manganese, an important element in steelmaking. Large deposits of granite are found near St. Cloud and along the upper Minnesota River. Quarries in the southern part of Minnesota produce limestone and sandstone. Sand and gravel are found throughout the state.

Forests cover about 35 per cent of Minnesota. Forests of jack, Norway, and white pine grow in the north. Other northern trees include the aspen, balsam fir, spruce, and white birch. Scattered groves of ash, black walnut, elm, maple, and oak trees grow in the southern part of the state.

Service industries account for 73 per cent of the gross state product of Minnesota. Most of these industries are concentrated in the state's five metropolitan areas.

Finance, insurance, and real estate ranks as Minnesota's leading service industry in terms of the gross state product. Minneapolis is the center of this industry. Real estate is the leading part of this industry because of the large sums of money involved in the buying and selling of homes and other buildings. The Minneapolis area is the headquarters of several major U.S. banks, holding companies, and insurance firms. Another large financial company is based in St. Paul.

Community, social, and personal services form the second-ranking service industry in Minnesota. This industry employs more people in Minnesota than any other industry. It includes a variety of businesses, in-

Production and workers by economic activities

Economic activities	Per cent of GSP* produced	Employed workers	
		Number of persons	Per cent of total
Manufacturing	21	395,800	18
Finance, insurance, & real estate	20	127,500	6
Community, social, & personal services	18	558,500	25
Wholesale & retail trade	16	517,500	23
Government	10	343,200	15
Transportation, communication, & utilities	9	110,200	5
Agriculture	3	112,300	5
Construction	3	75,800	3
Mining	†	7,900	†
Total	**100**	**2,248,700**	**100**

*GSP = gross state product, the total value of goods and services produced in a year.
†Less than one-half of 1 per cent.
Figures are for 1991.
Sources: *World Book* estimates based on data from U.S. Bureau of Economic Analysis, U.S. Bureau of Labor Statistics, and U.S. Department of Agriculture.

cluding private health care, computer programming and data processing, legal services, and automobile repair. Rochester is the home of the Mayo Clinic, one of the world's largest medical centers. The Twin Cities also have large private health care facilities.

Wholesale and retail trade ranks third among Minnesota's service industries. The wholesale trade of automobiles, farm products, and groceries is important in the state. Leading retail businesses include discount stores, food stores, and restaurants. Two of the nation's top retailing companies, Dayton Hudson and Super Valu Stores, are based in the Twin Cities area. Duluth is Minnesota's second major center of wholesale and retail trade.

Government is fourth in importance among service industries in Minnesota. Government services include public schools and hospitals, and military bases.

Transportation, communication, and utilities form the fifth-ranking service industry. Northwest Airlines is based in Eagan. More information about transportation and communication appears later in this section.

Manufacturing, including processing, accounts for 21 per cent of the gross state product of Minnesota. Goods manufactured in the state have a *value added by manufacture* of about $23 billion yearly. This figure represents the increase in value of raw materials after they become finished products.

Machinery is the leading manufactured product in Minnesota in terms of value added by manufacture. Computers are by far the most important kind of machinery produced in the state. Several of the nation's largest computer companies are headquartered in Minneapolis. Computers are also made in the Rochester and St. Paul areas. Computers manufactured in Minnesota range in size from small desktop models to huge super-

Minnesota Department of Energy and Economic Development
Workers prepare corn on the cob in a processing plant in Le Sueur. Minnesota ranks as one of the leading agricultural states. It is sometimes called the *Bread and Butter State.*

Farm, mineral, and forest products

This map shows where the state's leading farm, mineral, and forest products are produced. The major urban areas (shown on the map in red) are the state's important manufacturing centers.

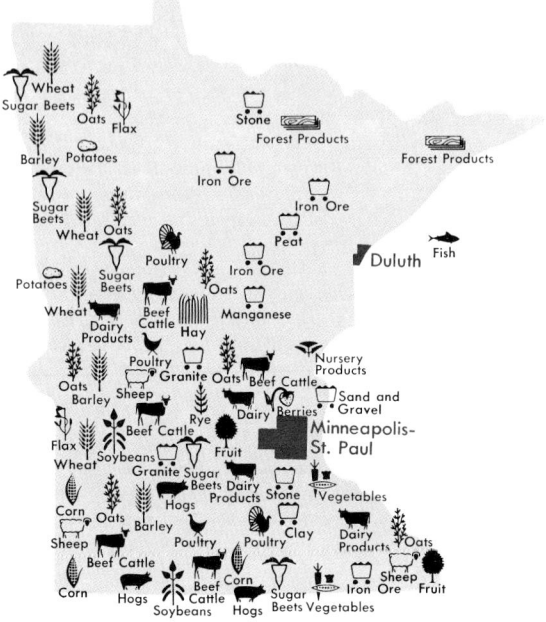

WORLD BOOK map

computers. Minnesota also produces farm and construction machinery.

Food products rank second in value. Meat packing is the most important food-processing activity, and Minnesota is one of the nation's leading meat-packing states. The largest plants are in Albert Lea, Austin, and Duluth. Large poultry-processing plants operate in southern and central Minnesota.

Minnesota ranks among the leading states in the production of flour. Its mills produce large amounts of cake mixes and breakfast cereals. Minnesota ranks high among the states in milk, butter, and cheese production. Soft drink and beer production is also important.

Minnesota is a top producer of canned vegetables. Most of the canning plants are in southern Minnesota. Sugar-beet refineries operate in the Red River Valley and along the Minnesota River.

The production of printed materials is the third most valuable manufacturing activity in Minnesota. Business forms and newspapers are the leading printed materials. Legal books and calendars are also important. St. Paul, Minneapolis, Mankato, and Duluth are the major centers of the state's printing industry.

Other types of products manufactured in Minnesota, in order of value, include fabricated metal products, scientific instruments, electrical equipment, paper products, and transportation equipment. The major types of metal products made in the state are weapons and ammunition, cans, and stampings. Thermostats and other control devices are the leading scientific instruments.

The Twin Cities produce a variety of electrical equipment. Cloquet and Grand Rapids have large paper mills, and Hutchinson has a large plant that manufactures adhesive tape. Trucks, which are made in St. Paul, are the major type of transportation equipment produced in the state.

Agriculture provides 3 per cent of the gross state product. Minnesota ranks among the leading states in annual farm income. Farmland covers about 30 million acres (12 million hectares), or a little more than half the state. Minnesota's approximately 88,000 farms have an average size of 341 acres (138 hectares).

Thousands of Minnesota farmers sell their produce through farm cooperatives. Most of them are dairy cooperatives, but many handle grain and livestock. See **Cooperative.**

Livestock and livestock products provide about 55 per cent of Minnesota's annual income from farm products. Milk is the state's most valuable livestock product. Minnesota has about 1 million dairy cattle. Minnesota is one of the leading milk-producing states. Most of Minnesota's milk is made into butter and cheese.

Hogs and beef cattle are also important sources of livestock income in Minnesota. The state ranks among the leaders in hog production. Southwestern Minnesota has the most hog and cattle farms. Minnesota is also an important producer of eggs and turkeys.

Crops account for about 45 per cent of Minnesota's farm income. Corn is the state's most valuable field crop. Soybeans rank as the second most valuable crop. Minnesota ranks among the leading states in the production of both corn and soybeans. Each of these crops is grown throughout southern Minnesota, as is hay, the third most valuable crop. Much of the state's corn, hay, and soybeans is fed to livestock. The Red River Valley of northwestern Minnesota is famous for its huge wheat crops. Other crops grown in Minnesota include barley, flaxseed, oats, and sugar beets. Peas, potatoes, and sweet corn are the state's leading vegetables. Apples are the leading fruit.

Mining accounts for less than one-half of 1 per cent of Minnesota's gross state product. Iron ore provides about 90 per cent of the state's mining income. Minnesota leads the states in iron ore production. But iron ore mining has declined greatly in importance to the Minnesota economy during the 1900's. Most of the state's remaining iron ore is a low grade called *taconite.* It is mined in the northeastern part of the state.

Quarries in central Minnesota yield unusually fine granite. Limestone is taken from extensive deposits in southern Minnesota. Clay comes from many areas of Minnesota, and is used in making bricks and tile. Sand and gravel are also produced throughout the state.

Fishing industry. Minnesota's annual fish catch is valued at about $6 million. The most valuable fishes taken from the Mississippi River include buffalo fish, carp, catfish, whitefish, and yellow perch. Lake herring, smelt, walleye, and yellow pike are the chief products of the Lake Superior catch.

Electric power. About 65 per cent of Minnesota's electric power is produced by plants that burn coal. Nuclear energy generates about 30 per cent of the state's electric power. Minnesota has two nuclear power plants at Prairie Island near Red Wing and one at Monticello. The state also has hydroelectric plants and plants that burn natural gas. Minnesota must purchase some electric power from other states to fulfill its needs.

Transportation. Minnesota's great network of rivers and lakes provided transportation for the explorers, fur traders, missionaries, and settlers who first entered the region. In the 1820's, the first steamboats sailed on the upper Mississippi. Railroad construction in the state progressed rapidly after 1865. Today, 12 rail lines provide freight service, and passenger trains serve about 10 cities. The Twin Cities form the chief rail center of the Upper Mississippi Valley. They also have the state's busiest airport.

About 129,000 miles (208,000 kilometers) of roads and highways cross the state. Nine-tenths of them are surfaced. The nation's largest bus system, Greyhound Bus Lines, had its start in Hibbing in 1914.

Barges bring coal, oil, and other products to Minnesota ports which lie on the Minnesota, Mississippi, and St. Croix rivers. The barges return with grain and other products from Minnesota. Much of Minnesota's water traffic is on Lake Superior. The harbor at Duluth and Superior, Wis., is the busiest freshwater port in North America and one of the busiest freshwater ports in the world. Grains, iron ore, and coal make up most of the outgoing cargo from this port.

Communication. In 1849, James Madison Goodhue began publishing Minnesota's first newspaper, the *Minnesota Pioneer,* in St. Paul. Today, Minnesota has about 30 daily newspapers and about 290 weekly newspapers. The daily newspapers with the largest circulations include the *Rochester Post-Bulletin,* the *Star Tribune* in Minneapolis, and the *St. Paul Pioneer Press.* Minnesota also publishes about 180 periodicals.

Minnesota's first licensed radio station was WLB (now KUOM), an educational station owned by the University of Minnesota. The station was licensed in Minneapolis in 1922. The first commercial radio station, WDGY, began broadcasting from Minneapolis in 1923. KSTP-TV, Minnesota's first television station, started broadcasting in Minneapolis in 1948. Minnesota now has about 190 radio stations and 18 television stations.

Government

Constitution. Minnesota is still governed under its original constitution, adopted in 1858. The Constitution may be *amended* (changed) in two ways. An amendment may be proposed in the legislature, where it must be approved by a majority of the lawmakers. Next, the amendment must be approved by a majority of the voters in an election.

The Constitution may also be amended by a constitutional convention. A proposal to call such a convention must be approved by two-thirds of the legislature and by a majority of the voters in an election. Proposals made by a convention become law after they have been approved by three-fifths of the voters casting ballots on the proposals.

Executive. The governor of Minnesota is elected to hold office for a four-year term. The governor can be re-elected any number of times.

The lieutenant governor, secretary of state, attorney general, treasurer, and auditor are also elected to four-year terms. The governor appoints the heads of most state departments, boards, and commissions. These officials are appointed to serve terms that range from two to six years.

Legislature consists of a 67-member Senate and a 134-member House of Representatives. Each senator and representative is elected from a separate district. Senators serve four-year terms, and representatives serve two-year terms.

The Minnesota legislature begins its regular session on the Tuesday after the first Monday in January in odd-numbered years. The Constitution of Minnesota limits regular legislative sessions to 120 legislative days over a two-year period. The governor may call special legislative sessions.

Courts. The state Supreme Court, Minnesota's highest court, has a chief justice and six associate justices. The chief justice and the associate justices are elected to six-year terms. In 1982, Minnesota adopted a state constitutional amendment that established a Court of Appeals. The court consists of 16 judges, who are elected to six-year terms.

Minnesota has one district court. It is divided into 10 judicial districts. Each judicial district has three or more judges, who are elected to six-year terms. The district court handles criminal and civil cases. The judicial districts in Hennepin and Ramsey counties also handle cases involving juveniles.

Local government. Minnesota has 87 counties. Each is governed by a board of commissioners, usually consisting of five members. The board's powers include borrowing money, collecting taxes, and determining how funds are to be spent. Board members are elected to four-year terms. Other county officials in Minnesota include the attorney, auditor, coroner, sheriff, and treas-urer. These officials also serve four-year terms.

Minnesota has more than 850 cities. The state constitution allows cities to adopt *home rule* charters. This means that a city may choose the form of government best suited to its needs. About 100 cities operate under home rule charters. Most Minnesota cities use the mayor-council form of government. The rest use the commission or council-manager form.

There are about 1,800 organized townships in Minnesota. Each township is governed by a board of supervisors. The voters elect the supervisors to three-year terms at an annual township meeting.

Revenue. Taxes bring in about two-thirds of the state government's *general revenue* (income). Most of the rest comes from federal grants and programs. Taxes on personal income provide about 40 per cent of the tax revenue. Sales and gross receipts taxes also provide about 40 per cent of the tax revenue. They include a general sales tax and a motor fuels tax.

Politics. During most of its early history, Minnesota strongly favored Republicans for state offices and for President. Between 1858 and 1931, Minnesota had only four Democratic governors. For Minnesota's electoral votes and voting record in presidential elections, see **Electoral College** (table).

In 1918, a third party, the Farmer-Labor Party, was

Minnesota House of Representatives

Minnesota's House of Representatives meets in the House Chambers, *above,* in St. Paul. The Minnesota House consists of 134 members. Representatives serve two-year terms.

The governors of Minnesota

	Party	Term
Henry H. Sibley	Democratic	1858-1860
Alexander Ramsey	Republican	1860-1863
Henry A. Swift	Republican	1863-1864
Stephen Miller	Republican	1864-1866
William R. Marshall	Republican	1866-1870
Horace Austin	Republican	1870-1874
Cushman K. Davis	Republican	1874-1876
John S. Pillsbury	Republican	1876-1882
Lucius F. Hubbard	Republican	1882-1887
Andrew R. McGill	Republican	1887-1889
William R. Merriam	Republican	1889-1893
Knute Nelson	Republican	1893-1895
David M. Clough	Republican	1895-1899
John Lind	Democratic	1899-1901
Samuel R. Van Sant	Republican	1901-1905
John A. Johnson	Democratic	1905-1909
Adolph O. Eberhart	Republican	1909-1915
Winfield S. Hammond	Democratic	1915
Joseph A. A. Burnquist	Republican	1915-1921
Jacob A. O. Preus	Republican	1921-1925
Theodore Christianson	Republican	1925-1931
Floyd B. Olson	Farmer-Labor	1931-1936
Hjalmar Petersen	Farmer-Labor	1936-1937
Elmer A. Benson	Farmer-Labor	1937-1939
Harold E. Stassen	Republican	1939-1943
Edward J. Thye	Republican	1943-1947
Luther W. Youngdahl	Republican	1947-1951
C. Elmer Anderson	Republican	1951-1955
Orville L. Freeman	DFL*	1955-1961
Elmer L. Andersen	Republican	1961-1963
Karl F. Rolvaag	DFL*	1963-1967
Harold E. LeVander	Republican	1967-1971
Wendell R. Anderson	DFL*	1971-1976
Rudy Perpich	DFL*	1976-1979
Albert H. Quie	I-R†	1979-1983
Rudy Perpich	DFL*	1983-1991
Arne H. Carlson	I-R†	1991-

*Democratic-Farmer-Labor.   †Independent-Republicans.

founded in Minnesota. It soon became powerful. In 1944, the Farmer-Labor Party joined with the Minnesota Democratic Party to form the Democratic-Farmer-Labor Party (DFL).

Hubert H. Humphrey, a DFL leader, served in the U.S. Senate from 1949 to 1964 and from 1971 to 1978. Humphrey was Vice President of the United States from 1965 to 1969. He was the Democratic nominee for President in 1968, but lost. Walter F. Mondale of Minnesota also served as Vice President and as a U.S. senator. He was the Democratic nominee for President in 1984, but he lost the election.

In 1975, the Republican Party of Minnesota changed its name to Independent-Republicans of Minnesota. Both the DFL and the Independent-Republicans have much strength in Minnesota today.

History

Indian days. White people first entered the Minnesota region in the last half of the 1600's. They found Sioux Indians in the northern forests. The Sioux lived in dome-shaped wigwams and were skilled hunters. By 1750, large numbers of Chippewa Indians were moving westward into Minnesota. They took over the region's northern forests, and forced the Sioux to move to the southwest. The Sioux became wanderers, and the two tribes remained enemies for many years. See **Indian, American** (Table of tribes).

Exploration. Two famous French fur traders, Pierre Esprit Radisson and Médard Chouart, Sieur des Groseilliers, were the first white men to set foot in Minnesota. They arrived in the area near what is now Two Harbors about 1660.

Another Frenchman, Daniel Greysolon, Sieur Duluth (or Du Lhut), entered Minnesota in 1679. Duluth was an adventurer who hoped to find a water route to the Pacific Ocean. Duluth landed on the western shore of Lake Superior, and then pushed on into the interior of Minnesota. He claimed the entire region for King Louis XIV of France.

In 1680, Father Louis Hennepin, a Belgian missionary, set out from the Illinois region to explore the upper Mississippi. But Sioux Indians captured Hennepin and his two companions. The Indians took them into Minnesota. Although a captive, Hennepin saw much of the region. He became the first white man to visit the site of present-day Minneapolis, where he sighted and named the Falls of St. Anthony. Meanwhile, Duluth heard that Indians had captured three white men. He found the Indians and successfully demanded that they release the captives.

Struggle for control. In 1762, France gave Spain all its land west of the Mississippi River, including much of Minnesota. But the Spaniards did not try to explore or settle the region, and French trappers continued to collect furs there. In 1763, the French and Indian War ended. France lost this war with Great Britain over rival claims in North America. France gave Britain almost all its land east of the Mississippi, including eastern Minnesota. During the next 50 years, the North West Company and other British fur-trading firms established posts in the region.

In 1783, the Revolutionary War ended. Great Britain gave its land south of the Great Lakes and east of the Mississippi River to the United States. This vast area became part of the Northwest Territory, which Congress created in 1787. However, British fur companies continued to trade in the region. The United States did not gain full control of the Northwest Territory until after the War of 1812.

The Louisiana Purchase. In 1800, Napoleon Bonaparte forced Spain to return the region west of the Mississippi River to France. France sold this region, called Louisiana, to the United States in 1803 (see **Louisiana Purchase**). Two years later, Zebulon M. Pike was sent to explore the upper Mississippi and the Minnesota wilderness.

In 1819, the U.S. Army established a fort in temporary buildings. In 1820, American soldiers began building Fort St. Anthony as a permanent fort at the point where

Royal Ontario Museum, Toronto

Fort Snelling in southeastern Minnesota protected settlers and traders in the early 1800's. Canadian artist Paul Kane painted a view of the fort in *Fort Snelling, Sioux Scalp Dance, left.*

Immigrants from Germany, Norway, Sweden, and other European countries came to Minnesota during the 1870's, 1880's, and 1890's. Many became farmers or railroad workers.

Brooks, Minnesota Historical Society

the Minnesota and Mississippi rivers meet. The fort was completed in 1825 and renamed Fort Snelling. It became a center of industry and culture, as well as of military duty. Explorers often used Fort Snelling as a base from which they set out for undiscovered parts of Minnesota. These explorers included Stephen H. Long, William H. Keating, and George W. Featherstonhaugh. In 1832, Henry R. Schoolcraft discovered and named Lake Itasca, the source of the Mississippi River.

Lumbering began in the St. Croix Valley during the late 1830's. In 1837, the Sioux and Chippewa Indians sold their claims to the logging area around the St. Croix River to the U.S. government. Lumberers and settlers soon moved to the area. Settlers founded Minnesota's first towns—St. Paul, St. Anthony (which later merged with Minneapolis), and Stillwater.

Territorial days. Through the years, parts of Minnesota had belonged to the territories of Illinois, Indiana, Iowa, Michigan, Missouri, and Wisconsin, and to the territory and district of Louisiana. On March 3, 1849, Congress created the Minnesota Territory. Its southern, northern, and eastern boundaries were the same as those of the state today. The western boundary extended to the Missouri and White Earth rivers. Alexander Ramsey was appointed as the first territorial governor. About 4,000 white people lived in Minnesota when it became a territory.

In 1851, the Sioux Indians, under pressure from the U.S. government, signed two treaties giving up their rights to a vast area west of the Mississippi River. Most of the land was in southern Minnesota. This new rich territory was opened to white settlement, and newcomers poured in.

Statehood. On May 11, 1858, Congress admitted Minnesota into the Union as the 32nd state. The people elected Henry H. Sibley as the first governor of their state. Sibley had been an agent of the American Fur Company, and had worked for the creation of the Minnesota Territory. Minnesota had a population of about 150,000 when it became a state.

The Civil War began in 1861. Minnesota became the first state to offer troops for the Union armies. In August 1862, when many Minnesota men were away fighting for the Union, the Sioux—then confined to reservations—went to war against the pioneers. The Indians swooped down on frontier towns, killing about 500 settlers and destroying much property. Federal troops helped Minnesota militiamen put down the uprising.

Industrial development occurred rapidly in Minnesota after the Civil War ended in 1865. Railroads expanded across the state, and the old Sioux hunting grounds became wheat lands. Flour mills sprang up throughout the wheat region, but most were in the Minneapolis area. These mills produced such huge quantities of flour that Minneapolis was known as the *Mill City.*

Minnesota waged a vigorous drive to attract newcomers. The state government and the railroads sent pamphlets to Europe, describing the opportunities in Minnesota. During the 1870's, 1880's, and 1890's, thousands of immigrants, especially Germans, Norwegians, and Swedes, settled in the state.

The outstanding event of the late 1800's was the development of rich iron ore resources. In 1884, the first ore was shipped from the Vermilion Range. In 1890, workers employed by Leonidas Merritt and several of his seven brothers discovered ore near Mountain Iron in the Mesabi Range. Two years later, after involving other relatives in their venture, the Merritts shipped the first load of ore from the Mesabi Range.

In 1889, William W. Mayo and his two sons, William and Charles, established the Mayo Clinic in Rochester. The clinic's fame spread rapidly, and the Mayos turned it into a general medical center. The clinic became one of the world's leading medical research centers.

In 1894, a great forest fire swept across about 400 square miles (1,000 square kilometers) of eastern Minnesota. It wiped out the villages of Hinckley and Sandstone. More than 400 people were killed, and property valued at over $1 million was destroyed.

The early 1900's. In 1911, the first shipment of iron ore left the Cuyuna Range. In December 1915, the first operations began at a huge steel mill in Duluth. After the United States entered World War I in 1917, there were heavy demands for Minnesota's products. Great crops of wheat and other grains were raised to feed the armed forces. Iron ore production totaled almost 90 million short tons (82 million metric tons) during 1917 and 1918.

In 1918, Minnesota was struck by another disastrous forest fire. Strong winds fanned a number of small fires into one huge fire that roared across large areas of Carlton and St. Louis counties in the northeast. The fire killed more than 400 people and destroyed property valued at about $25 million.

During the 1890's and early 1900's, many Minnesota farmers joined cooperatives. They joined together to

Historic Minnesota

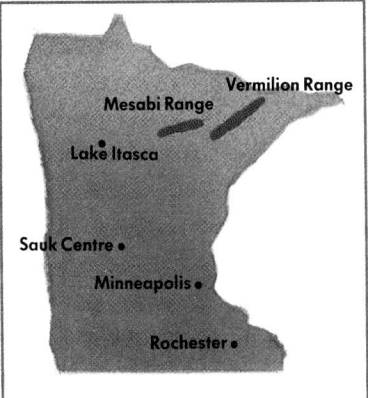

The source of the Mississippi River was discovered in 1832 by Henry Schoolcraft, an American explorer. He traced the river to its origin at Lake Itasca in northwestern Minnesota.

The first flour mill in Minnesota was built at the Falls of St. Anthony in 1823. Minneapolis was one of the world's leading flour centers by the 1870's.

Rich iron deposits were discovered in Minnesota in 1865 by geologist H. H. Eames. The Vermilion Range was first mined in 1884; the Mesabi Range in 1892.

The Mayo Clinic was established at Rochester in 1889 by William W. Mayo and his two sons, William and Charles. It is a leading medical research center.

Sinclair Lewis, an American novelist, was born in Sauk Centre in 1885. He became the first American to win the Nobel Prize for literature.

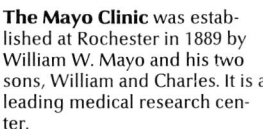

Important dates in Minnesota

WORLD BOOK illustrations by Kevin Chadwick

c. 1660 Pierre Esprit Radisson and Médard Chouart, Sieur des Groseilliers, visited the Minnesota region.

1679 Daniel Greysolon, Sieur Duluth, explored the western shore of Lake Superior.

1680 Louis Hennepin sighted the Falls of St. Anthony.

1783 Great Britain granted the land east of the Mississippi River to the United States.

1803 The United States obtained the Minnesota area west of the Mississippi through the Louisiana Purchase.

1819-1825 The U.S. Army established a fort in temporary buildings in 1819. It built Fort St. Anthony as a permanent fort between 1820 and 1825. The fort was renamed Fort Snelling in 1825.

1832 Henry R. Schoolcraft discovered Lake Itasca, the source of the Mississippi River.

1849 Congress created the Minnesota Territory.

1851 The Sioux Indians gave up their rights to large areas of land west of the Mississippi River.

1858 Minnesota became the 32nd state on May 11.

1862 Minnesota millitiamen and U.S. troops put down a Sioux uprising.

1884 The first shipment of iron ore from the Vermilion Range left Minnesota.

1889 William W. Mayo and his two sons founded the Mayo Clinic in Rochester.

1892 The first ore was shipped from the Mesabi Range.

1944 The Farmer-Labor party joined the Minnesota Democratic party to form the Democratic-Farmer-Labor party.

1964 Minnesota voters approved a constitutional amendment assuring taconite producers that taxes on taconite will not be raised at a higher rate than taxes on other businesses for 25 years.

1982 Minnesota adopted a state constitutional amendment that established the Court of Appeals to relieve the caseload of the state Supreme Court.

provide their own financial and storage services, and transportation for their products. The farmers believed that the railroads, banks, and grain companies charged too much for these services. During the 1920's, the new Farmer-Labor Party supported the farmers. In 1931, Floyd B. Olson became the first Farmer-Labor governor.

The Great Depression of the 1930's hit Minnesota hard. Unemployment was widespread in the cities. About 70 per cent of the iron-range workers in the state lost their jobs. Farm income fell sharply. The state government took many steps to fight the depression, and federal agencies were set up to provide employment and relief.

The mid-1900's. Minnesota's economy recovered during World War II (1939-1945). The state's lumber and mining industries turned out huge amounts of raw materials for the armed forces. But the supply of high-grade iron ore suddenly dropped in the 1950's, as did the demand for the ore. The industry declined and several mines closed.

As a result of the mining slump, the state's iron industry began to develop low-grade taconite ore. Taconite contains about 30 per cent iron in the form of specks of iron oxide.

In 1964, Minnesota voters approved an amendment to the state constitution that boosted investment in the iron industry. The so-called taconite amendment guaranteed that taxes on taconite would not be raised at a higher rate than taxes on other products for 25 years. Previously, iron-mining companies had been taxed at a higher rate, and producers had delayed plans to build taconite plants. After passage of the taconite amendment, producers invested more than $1 billion in taconite plants. But air and water pollution at these plants became a major concern (see **Taconite**).

Many new industries began to operate in Minnesota during the 1950's and 1960's. The products of these industries include aerospace equipment, chemicals, computers, electronic equipment, heavy machinery, and processed foods.

In Minnesota, as in other states, the number of farms and farmworkers decreased. Large numbers of families moved from rural areas to cities. By 1950, the state's total urban population had grown larger than the rural population for the first time. In 1964, a federal court ordered Minnesota to *reapportion* (redivide) its legislative districts to give the city population equal representation in the state legislature.

The Farmer-Labor Party joined the state Democratic Party in 1944 to form the Democratic-Farmer-Labor Party (DFL). In 1975, the Republican Party of Minnesota changed its name to Independent-Republicans of Minnesota.

Recent developments. In 1979, the Minnesota legislature provided state schools with a substantial increase in financial aid. In 1980, the legislature passed major tax relief on income and property taxes.

A major problem facing Minnesota during the 1970's and 1980's was finding ways to develop the state's many natural resources and, at the same time, preserve its natural beauty. Air and water pollution from taconite plants remained a serious concern. In 1978, the Minnesota Supreme Court ordered the Reserve Mining Company of Silver Bay to meet pollution control standards at its taco-

nite-processing plant. In 1980, the company established an on-land waste disposal site and no longer discharged waste into nearby Lake Superior.

Industrialists increased efforts to develop the state's copper-nickel ore deposits and to expand logging operations. However, these efforts met opposition from environmentalists. In 1979, the state legislature removed limits it had imposed in 1974 on copper-nickel ore mining in Minnesota. During the 1980's, a decline in agricultural prices and other farm problems led to economic difficulties in Minnesota's rural areas.

William E. Lass and Gordon L. Levine

Study aids

Related articles in *World Book* include:

Biographies

Blackmun, Harry A.	Mayo, William J.
Burger, Warren E.	Mayo, William W.
Donnelly, Ignatius	McCarthy, Eugene J.
Hennepin, Louis	Mondale, Walter F.
Hill, James J.	Pike, Zebulon M.
Humphrey, Hubert H.	Radisson, Pierre E.
Lewis, Sinclair	Rice, Henry M.
Lindbergh, Charles A.	Stassen, Harold E.
Mayo, Charles H.	

Cities

Duluth	Minneapolis	Saint Paul
Hibbing	Saint Cloud	Stillwater

History

Indian, American (Indians of the Plains)	Louisiana Purchase
	Northwest Territory

Physical features

Lake Agassiz	Minnehaha Falls	Rainy Lake
Lake Superior	Minnesota River	Red River
Mesabi Range	Mississippi River	of the North

Other related articles

Bunyan, Paul
Farmer-Labor Party
Grand Portage National Monument
Voyageurs National Park

Outline

I. People
  A. Population
  B. Schools
  C. Libraries
  D. Museums
II. Visitor's guide
  A. Places to visit
  B. Annual events
III. Land and climate
  A. Land regions
  B. Lakes, rivers, and waterfalls
  C. Plant and animal life
  D. Climate
IV. Economy
  A. Natural resources
  B. Service industries
  C. Manufacturing
  D. Agriculture
  E. Mining
  F. Fishing industry
  G. Electric power
  H. Transportation
  I. Communication
V. Government
  A. Constitution
  B. Executive
  C. Legislature
  D. Courts
  E. Local government
  F. Revenue
  G. Politics
VI. History

Questions

What two cities in Minnesota and Wisconsin make up one of the world's leading ports?

Why was Minnesota nicknamed the *Gopher State*? The *Bread and Butter State*?

Who were some of the early explorers of Minnesota?

What is the state's chief manufacturing industry?

What are some of Minnesota's products?

What is the open-pit method of mining? How much of Minnesota's iron ore is mined by this method?

What political party was founded in Minnesota?

How much of the iron ore mined in the United States comes from Minnesota?

How many state constitutions has Minnesota had?

What major medical center is in Rochester?

Additional resources

Level I

Carpenter, Allan. *Minnesota*. Rev. ed. Childrens Pr., 1978.

Fearing, Jerry. *The Story of Minnesota*. 3rd ed. Minnesota Hist. Soc., 1977.

Fradin, Dennis B. *Minnesota in Words and Pictures*. Childrens Pr., 1980.

The Gopher Reader: Minnesota's Story in Words and Pictures. Ed. by Alice H. Poatgieter and J. T. Dunn. 2 vols. Minnesota Hist. Soc., 1958-1975.

Rosenfelt, Willard E. *Minnesota: Its People and Culture*. Denison, 1973.

Stein, R. Conrad. *Minnesota*. Childrens Pr., 1990.

Level II

Blegen, Theodore C. *Minnesota: A History of the State*. 2nd ed. Univ. of Minnesota Pr., 1975.

Borchert, John R. *America's Northern Heartland*. Univ. of Minnesota Pr., 1987.

Brill, Charles. *Indian and Free: A Contemporary Portrait of Life on a Chippewa Reservation*. Bks. on Demand, 1974.

Gelbach, Deborah L. *From This Land: A History of Minnesota's Empires, Enterprises, and Entrepreneurs*. Windsor Pubns., 1988.

Growing Up in Minnesota: Ten Writers Remember Their Childhoods. Ed. by Chester G. Anderson. Univ. of Minnesota Pr., 1976.

Hanson, Royce, and others. *Tribune of the People: The Minnesota Legislature and Its Leadership*. Univ. of Minnesota Pr., 1989.

Kane, Lucile M., and Ominsky, Alan. *Twin Cities: A Pictorial History of Saint Paul and Minneapolis*. Minnesota Hist. Soc., 1983.

Lass, William E. *Minnesota: A Bicentennial History*. Norton, 1977.

Minnesota in a Century of Change: The State and Its People Since 1900. Ed. by Clifford E. Clark, Jr. Minnesota Hist. Soc., 1989.

Mitau, Gunter T. *Politics in Minnesota*. Rev. ed. Univ. of Minnesota Pr., 1970.

Ojakangas, Richard W., and Matsch, C. L. *Minnesota's Geology*. Univ. of Minnesota Pr., 1982.

Olsenius, Richard. *Minnesota Travel Companion: A Unique Guide to the History Along Minnesota's Highways*. Bluestem, 1982.

They Chose Minnesota: A Survey of the State's Ethnic Groups. Minnesota Historical Society, 1981.

Minnesota, University of, is a state-supported coeducational institution. Its largest and oldest campus, the Twin Cities campus, is in Minneapolis-St. Paul. The university also has campuses in Crookston, Duluth, Morris, and Waseca.

The Twin Cities campus awards bachelor's, master's, and doctor's degrees. A special program allows some juniors and seniors to follow individual courses of study. The Twin Cities campus has colleges of agriculture, architecture, biological sciences, education, home economics, liberal arts, natural sciences, pharmacy, and veterinary medicine; institutes of public affairs and technology; schools of dentistry, journalism, law, management, medicine, nursing, and public health; a continuing education and extension division; and a graduate school.

The Duluth campus offers liberal arts, science, and business courses leading to bachelor's and master's degrees. It also has a two-year School of Medicine. The Morris campus is a four-year liberal arts institution. The Waseca campus has two-year programs in business, the food and fiber industries, horticulture, and human services. The Crookston campus offers two-year programs in arts and sciences, agriculture, business, and hospitality and home economics.

Other university facilities include the Hormel Institute in Austin, the Lake Itasca Forestry and Biological Station in Itasca State Park, the Forestry Research Center in Cloquet, the Cedar Creek Natural History Area near Bethel, the Freshwater Biological Research Center in Navarre, the Natural Resources Research Institute in Duluth, and the Rosemount Research Center. The university also has an agricultural experiment station with six branches.

The University of Minnesota was chartered in 1851 as a preparatory school. The school closed during the Civil War (1861-1865) and reorganized as a four-year college in 1868. For enrollment, see **Universities and colleges** (table). *Critically reviewed by the University of Minnesota*

See also **Minnesota** (picture).

Minnesota River is a large branch of the Mississippi River. The Minnesota flows through a wide valley that was cut by the outlet of Lake Agassiz, an ancient glacial lake (see **Lake Agassiz**). The Minnesota River rises in the Coteau des Prairies (*Little Hills of the Prairie*), a group of hills that are located in northeastern South Dakota. The river flows southeast to Big Stone Lake on the boundary between South Dakota and Minnesota. It follows Big Stone Lake south to Ortonville. There, the Minnesota River flows southeast to Mankato, Minn. The river then turns sharply to the northeast. It flows northeast until it joins the Mississippi River. The Minnesota River enters the Mississippi River south of St. Paul, Minn. For location, see **Minnesota** (physical map).

The Minnesota River is 332 miles (534 kilometers) long. It drains an area of about 16,600 square miles (41,400 square kilometers).

Early explorers and fur traders sailed up the Minnesota River in their westward journeys. Today, the river is an important trade route. *Thomas J. Baerwald*

Minnow is a common name for fish in the carp and minnow family. This is the largest family of freshwater fishes, with about 1,600 species in North America, Europe, Asia, and Africa. Most American minnows are small, less than 6 inches (15 centimeters) long. But a few grow quite large. The *Colorado squawfish,* one of the largest minnows in North America, reaches a length of 2 to 4 feet (61 to 120 centimeters). The *Indian mahseer,* found in rivers and streams throughout India, grows to 9 feet (2. 7 meters) long. Minnows often are difficult to identify because of their uniform size, form, and color.

Minnows are *forage fish*—that is, they furnish the food that allows game fish to reach a large size. Minnows also are used as live bait to catch larger fish. In many places, so many minnows have been caught for bait that there are few left, and some states have outlawed or limited the taking of minnows. Minnows are

WORLD BOOK illustration by Colin Newman, Linden Artists Ltd.

Minnows make up the largest family of freshwater fishes. The common shiner, *above,* is a common North American minnow.

usually caught with nets and are often raised in ponds and fish hatcheries. Some common minnows in North America are the *common shiner,* the *golden shiner,* and the *creek chub.*

Scientific classification. The minnow belongs to the family Cyprinidae. The scientific name for the Colorado squawfish is *Ptychocheilus lucius.* The Indian mahseer is *Barbus tor.* The golden shiner is *Notemigonus crysoleucas;* the common shiner, *Notropis cornutus;* and the creek chub, *Semotilus atromaculatus.*　David W. Greenfield

See also **Chub.**

Minoan civilization. See Aegean civilization; Architecture (Minoan architecture); **Crete; Painting** (Cretan painting).

Minor is a person who is under legal age. In the United States, the legal age was traditionally 21. However, the 26th Amendment to the U.S. Constitution, ratified in 1971, set the minimum voting age at 18. Since then, many states have lowered the legal age—known as the age of majority or adulthood—to 18. In 45 states, the legal age is now 18. In four others—Alabama, Alaska, Nebraska, and Wyoming—it is 19. The general age of majority is still 21 in Mississippi. Many states set 21 as the minimum legal age to possess or drink alcoholic beverages.

Under the law, minors have many privileges that are not given to adults. For example, they are not held responsible for a contract with an adult and can refuse to carry out their part of the bargain. However, minors are usually liable for the reasonable value of certain goods or services that are not provided by a parent, as long as the parent provides essential care. These goods or services, called *necessaries,* include food, clothing, lodging, medical care, and education. The law gives special privileges to minors because they are considered too inexperienced to be fully responsible for their actions. In some states, these privileges can be removed by a court action.

Minors may be held responsible for wrongdoing, such as damages they do to others. However, age and inexperience may be taken into consideration.

Under common law, infants under 7 years old were presumed to be incapable of committing a crime. Between the ages of 7 and 14, this presumption could be rebutted. For children over 14, the presumption was that they had criminal capacity. Punishment today varies with the minor's age and usually differs from that for adults. All U.S. states have special courts for minors (see **Juvenile court**).　Aidan R. Gough

Minor leagues. See Baseball (Minor leagues).

© Luis Castaneon, The Image Bank

Minorca is a Spanish island in the Mediterranean Sea, off the east coast of the mainland of Spain. It is popular with tourists because of its mild climate and pleasant scenery.

Minorca, *mih NAWR kuh,* also spelled *Menorca,* is the second largest island of the Balearic Islands, which lie off the east coast of the mainland of Spain (see **Balearic Islands**). Minorca has an area of 266 square miles (689 square kilometers) and a population of about 57,000. Some iron is mined there. Farm crops include cereals and hemp, and grapes, olives, and other fruits. Metalware, textiles, soap, wine, and sandals are manufactured on the island. Tourism is a major industry. Mahón is the chief city and port. For location, see **Spain** (political map).

Minorca is part of Spain. Both England and France captured the island several times. England ceded Minorca to Spain by the Treaty of Amiens in 1802.
　Edward Malefakis

Minority group is a group of people who differ in some ways from the principal group in a society. Members of minority groups may differ from the principal group, also called the *dominant group,* in speech, appearance, or cultural practices. The dominant group also has greater political and economic power than the minority group. In many cases, the dominant group *discriminates* against minorities—that is, it treats them unfairly. Most members of minority groups have fewer economic, political, and social opportunities than members of the dominant group have.

Social scientists refer to minorities as racial or ethnic minorities. In sociology, a *racial minority* is identified chiefly by one or more distinctive physical characteristics that are shared by members of the group. These may include skin color, type of hair, body structure, and shape of the head or nose. Most anthropologists today reject the idea that the human population can be broken into biologically defined races. However, socially defined racial classifications persist in many societies. Blacks are considered a racial minority in the United States. An *ethnic minority* is identified chiefly by distinctive cultural practices. For example, its language or speaking accent, religion, or manner of living is different from that of the dominant group. The Amish people of the United States and Canada are an ethnic minority. Many Amish dress in plain styles that are different from the clothing worn by most Americans.

Some minority groups combine the characteristics of both racial and ethnic minorities. For example, most Chinese in California in the 1850's were distinguished from other Americans both by their skin and by such cultural characteristics as their language and the style of their clothing.

People in society, especially the members of the dominant group, decide which cultural and physical characteristics are important enough to distinguish people as minorities. For example, the dominant group might decide to use skin color but to ignore hair.

The term *minority* often means *less than half of the whole.* When applied to people, however, the term does not necessarily refer to numerical proportion. Some minority groups actually have more members than the dominant group. For example, blacks form a majority of the population in some cities and counties of the Southern United States. But these blacks have considerably fewer economic and political opportunities than the dominant white group. Thus, blacks in these areas form a *subordinate* (less powerful) group.

How a group becomes a minority

Many minority groups develop when people leave their homeland and settle in another society. Members of the minority may move into the territory of the dominant group either voluntarily or against their will. Or the dominant group may move in and take over the minority's territory. When these groups meet, the dominant group uses its greater economic and military power or other strength to control the minority group.

The enclosing of a minority group within the territory of a dominant group is called *incorporation.* The importing of black Africans to North and South America as slaves from the 1600's to the 1800's was an example of forced incorporation. Immigration is a type of voluntary incorporation. The United States has admitted millions of non-English immigrants from Europe since the late 1700's, and many of these people have become minority groups. Incorporation also occurs when one group annexes territory that adjoins its own. During the 1840's, for example, the United States gained many Spanish-speaking persons when it annexed areas that formerly belonged to Mexico. Annexation has played an especially important role in the history of some European nations. For example, Estonians, Turkish Muslims, and certain other large groups became minorities after czarist Russia annexed their lands.

Some minority groups have resulted from *colonialism.* In colonialism, one nation sends some of its members to gain control over another people's land. This land, which becomes a colony, is used as a source of wealth for the settlers' homeland. The colony's original inhabitants, who have less economic and military power than the settlers, become a minority group. Many European countries, including Belgium, France, Great Britain, Portugal, and Spain, established large colonial empires between the 1400's and the 1900's.

After establishing control over the minority, the dominant group may try to remove them from its territory.

The dominant group may expel the minority, as white Americans did in the 1830's when they forced the Cherokee Indians to move from the Southeastern United States to reservations in what is now Oklahoma. Or the dominant group may attempt complete destruction of the minority. For example, American settlers gained control of North America by killing many of the native Indians. *Genocide* is a form of mass murder in which one organized group—usually a government—systematically kills members of another group. Between 1933 and 1945, the Nazis in Germany persecuted Jews on a regular basis. The Nazis murdered about 6 million Jews.

Relationships between groups

Most dominant and minority groups develop certain patterns in dealing with each other. These patterns include *racial or ethnic stratification, assimilation,* and *internal colonialism.* The dominant group usually controls how these patterns develop.

Racial or ethnic stratification occurs when the dominant group divides the society into classes along racial and cultural lines. Minority groups are given low social and economic positions. For example, many Irish, Italian, and black African immigrants to the United States were assigned such positions by British Americans and other groups that had settled earlier. For periods of varying length, minority groups that live under racial or ethnic stratification suffer segregation, discrimination, and poverty.

Assimilation may develop after the dominant and minority groups have lived together for some time. In this process, the dominant group accepts the minority group into society. Two types of assimilation take place, often at different speeds. In the process of *structural assimilation,* the minority group is partially or wholly admitted into the friendship groups and economic organizations of the dominant group. In the process of *cultural assimilation,* the minority group adopts much of the culture of the dominant group and may lose many of the cultural characteristics that had set it apart. For example, Scandinavian Americans gave up much of their ethnic heritage while undergoing cultural assimilation. Jews, on the other hand, preserved more of their own culture.

Internal colonialism occurs when minority groups achieve political and economic equality slowly or not at all. This pattern typically lasts for many years and in some cases for centuries. In the Western world, many nonwhite minorities have experienced a period of slavery or forced labor followed by many years of discrimination. In the United States, blacks, other non-European minorities, and women have suffered centuries of political, economic, and educational discrimination. Discrimination persists in the United States today, though laws prohibit much of it.

Results of minority status

Minority group members generally recognize that they belong to a less-favored group, and this realization affects their behavior. A sense of isolation and common suffering is a strong social glue that binds them together. Common cultural and physical traits also help unify the minority group. Identification with the minority may continue even after a minority group member is assimilated into the dominant group. For instance, a person of Jewish descent may no longer practice the traditional Jewish religion and may become a member of the dominant group. Yet the person may continue to think of himself or herself primarily as a Jew.

Members of minority groups respond to domination in various ways. For example, some passively adopt the culture of the dominant group. Others try to achieve territorial separation. In the late 1800's, for example, some Jews reacting to discrimination in Europe began a movement called *Zionism* to establish a Jewish nation in Palestine. This movement resulted in the establishment of Israel. Attempts by small groups of black Americans to return to Africa in the 1700's and 1800's are another example of this response to domination. Some members of minority groups use various means to challenge domination. They challenge segregation laws in court, refuse to obey discriminatory laws, and, in some cases, resort to rioting and other forms of violence.

Minorities in the United States

The United States has become the home of many minority groups. These minorities include blacks, Jews, European immigrants, Spanish-speaking Americans, Asian Americans, and American Indians.

Blacks form the largest minority group in the United States. They make up 12 per cent of the population, about 30 million people. Blacks were brought to America as slaves beginning in the early 1600's, and most blacks remained slaves until after the Civil War (1861-1865). But even as they gradually gained legal freedom, most blacks could not assimilate into American life because of widespread discrimination. In the 1960's and 1970's, some blacks reacted to their exclusion from society by starting black nationalist or black power movements. These movements called for separation and the strengthening of black group-identity and political organization.

Jews have often fled to the United States to avoid persecution, only to meet continued discrimination. Today, there are about 6 million Jews in the United States. Many Jews have retained their religious beliefs and many traditional practices.

Other European immigrants who came to the United States often became minority groups. Most of these minorities were eventually assimilated into American society. Before the 1880's, most Europeans who came to the United States were from northern and western Europe. Beginning in the 1880's, most came from southern and eastern Europe. Most European immigrants have come from Austria-Hungary, Germany, Italy, Ireland, Poland, Russia, and the United Kingdom.

Spanish-speaking Americans, also called *Latinos* or *Hispanic Americans,* are primarily of Cuban, Mexican, and Puerto Rican ancestry. The United States has more than 22 million Hispanics, most of whom are of Mexican descent.

Cubans began to migrate to the United States in large numbers during the 1960's, after Cuba came under Communist control. Most have settled in Florida.

Mexicans became incorporated into the United States when the nation acquired what are now large parts of the West and Southwest from Mexico. Since the Mexican War (1846-1848), many Mexicans have migrated to the United States.

Puerto Ricans have migrated to the U.S. mainland in large numbers since World War II (1939-1945). Many have settled in New York City.

Asian Americans include Chinese, Japanese, Filipino, and Vietnamese groups. More than 7 million Asians live in the United States today.

Chinese have often been discriminated against. Some live in city neighborhoods called *Chinatowns.*

Japanese immigrants have often suffered the same injustices as the Chinese. During World War II, many Japanese Americans suffered violations of their constitutional rights. They were forced to leave their homes and businesses and to live in concentration camps in several Western states.

American Indians have suffered centuries of discrimination. Indians were driven from their homes by European settlers and were forced to live on reservations. About 2 million Indians live in the United States today. Many Indians now call themselves *Native Americans.*

Minority groups in other countries

Many nations have minority groups. European countries have often had minority nationality groups living within their boundaries. For example, before World War II, Germans lived in a part of Czechoslovakia called the Sudetenland.

Religious minorities have also lived in Europe. Today, Roman Catholics are a minority in Northern Ireland, and Jews form a minority in parts of Europe.

In South Africa, many whites discriminate against blacks and other nonwhites, though nonwhites make up most of the population. Until 1991, whites followed a government policy of *apartheid* (separateness). Under apartheid, almost all nonwhites were legally segregated from whites and faced official discrimination in education, employment, and many other areas. Nonwhites continue to face official discrimination in voting and politics. In housing, they are still largely segregated from whites.

Many national minority groups live in the Commonwealth of Independent States, which replaced the Soviet Union in 1991. Under Soviet rule during World War II (1939-1945), some of these groups—the Volga Germans, Crimean Tatars, and Kalmuks—were expelled from their homelands, supposedly for disloyalty. Jews suffered discrimination under both czarist and Soviet rule. Today, ethnic tensions remain a threat to social stability in many of the former Soviet republics.   Joe R. Feagin

Related articles in *World Book* include:

Affirmative action	Colonialism	Jews
Asian Americans	Ghetto	Prejudice
Bilingual education	Hispanic	Racism
Black Americans	Americans	Segregation
Civil Rights, Com-	Indian, American	South Africa
mission on		

Additional resources

Daniels, Roger. *Coming to America: A History of Immigration and Ethnicity in American Life.* HarperCollins, 1990.
Harvard Encyclopedia of American Ethnic Groups. Ed. by Stephan Thernstrom. Harvard Univ. Pr., 1980.
Peoples of North America. 40 vols. Chelsea Hse., 1985-1991. Each title in this series focuses on a specific group, including American Indians, black Americans, French Canadians, and others. Also suitable for younger readers.

Minos, *MY nuhs,* was a king of Crete in Greek mythology. He ordered Daedalus, a skilled artisan and inventor, to build the *Labyrinth.* This was a mazelike building in which Minos imprisoned a monster known as the Minotaur. Minos conquered much of Greece, including Athens. He forced the Athenians to send seven young men and seven young women at regular intervals as a sacrifice to the Minotaur. Eventually Theseus, one of the intended victims, killed the Minotaur and eloped with Minos' daughter Ariadne.

Minos imprisoned Daedalus for helping Theseus and Ariadne run away, but Daedalus escaped. Minos pursued Daedalus and finally found him in Sicily. According to one story, Daedalus killed the king by scalding him in a specially constructed bathtub. After his death, Minos and his brother Rhadamanthus became judges in the underworld. Justin M. Glenn

See also **Theseus; Minotaur; Daedalus; Hades.**

Minot, *MY nuht,* **George Richards** (1885-1950), an American physician, was one of the world's greatest authorities on the functions of blood and on blood diseases. In 1926, he announced the liver treatment for pernicious anemia patients. Minot and his co-worker, the American physician William P. Murphy, showed that when the patients were treated with a diet containing a large amount of liver, the anemia disappeared and the red blood count returned to normal. The discovery opened a new era for patients with anemia, which was a disease that had always been fatal. Minot and Murphy received the 1934 Nobel Prize in physiology or medicine for this research. They shared the prize with American physician George H. Whipple, who had made the same discovery.

Minot wrote many articles on blood and its disorders. He also wrote about dietary deficiency. He was coauthor of *Pathological Physiology and Clinical Description of the Anemias* (1936).

Minot was born in Boston, Mass. He received his medical degree from Harvard University in 1912. He was associated with Massachusetts General Hospital from 1918 to 1923. From 1928 to 1948, Minot was professor of medicine at Harvard Medical School and director of the Boston City Hospital's Thorndike Memorial Laboratory. Daniel J. Kevles

Minotaur, *MIHN uh tawr,* in Greek mythology, was a monster with the head of a bull and the body of a man. It was the offspring of a bull and Pasiphae, the wife of King Minos of Crete. Minos kept the Minotaur in the Labyrinth, a mazelike building from which no one could escape. Minos sacrificed seven Athenian youths and seven Athenian maidens to the Minotaur each year. Theseus of Athens finally killed the Minotaur, and escaped from the Labyrinth by following a thread given to him by Minos' daughter, Ariadne. See **Theseus.**

A palace excavated during the 1900's at Knossos in Crete has so many passageways that it resembles the legendary Labyrinth. Paintings found there show bulls and bull-baiting games. William F. Hansen

Minsk (pop. 1,613,000) is the capital of Belarus. In 1991, it became the headquarters of the Commonwealth of Independent States, a loose confederation of nations that were formerly republics of the Soviet Union. Minsk lies on the Svisloch River. For the location of Minsk, see **Belarus** (map).

Factories in Minsk produce ball bearings, machine tools, peat-digging machines, radios, trucks, and tractors. Woodworkers in the city produce prefabricated houses and furniture. Minsk is the home of the Belarusian state university, medical and polytechnic schools, an academy of sciences, a state museum, and an opera and ballet theater.

Minsk suffered heavy damage during the fighting in World War II (1939-1945). After the war, Minsk expanded greatly with the construction of many new factories and new housing for the workers. Theodore Shabad

Minstrel is a term most broadly used to refer to professional entertainers who flourished in Europe during

Detail of a German illuminated manuscript (early 1300s) (Granger Collection)

A German minstrel called a *minnesinger* sang love poetry. Minnesingers were popular during the Middle Ages.

Theseus and the Minotaur (1848), a bronze statue by Antoine Louis Barye; the Walters Art Gallery, Baltimore

The Minotaur in Greek mythology had a bull's head and a man's body. Theseus, a Greek hero, killed it on Crete.

the Middle Ages. Minstrels were chiefly singers and musicians, but many were also storytellers, jugglers, clowns, and tumblers. These wandering performers were known by different names in different countries. They were called *troubadours* and *jongleurs* in France, and *minnesingers* in Germany. They were known as *skalds* in Scandinavia and *bards* in Ireland. The early English minstrel was called a *scop*. The name *minstrel* was used for the later poet-musicians of England.

Some minstrels belonged to the households of kings and nobles. Some traveled about and gave entertainments at the castles along their way. Sometimes they entertained the village folk. The minstrels often made up their own songs and stories as they entertained. But they also repeated ballads and folk tales of the time, thus helping to preserve them. The minstrels began to die out by the late 1400's. The printing press eventually replaced the storytellers.   Don B. Wilmeth

Related articles in *World Book* include:

Bard	Minnesinger	Troubadour
Mastersinger	Skald	Trouvère

Minstrel show was the first uniquely American form of show business. Minstrel shows began in the 1840's and reached their peak of popularity about 1870, though they existed until about 1900. Most minstrel shows were performed by white entertainers who blackened their faces to impersonate blacks. A few black minstrel companies also toured the United States. Minstrel shows reinforced negative images of blacks that lasted long after the shows had disappeared.

In 1846, the American showman E. P. Christy organized the Christy Minstrels, the first important minstrel company. The American composer Stephen Foster wrote many of his best-known songs for the Christy Minstrels (see **Foster, Stephen Collins**). Christy developed the distinctive three-part format for the minstrel show. During the first part, the whole company sat in a semicircle on stage while the master of ceremonies, called the *interlocutor,* and the star performers, named Mr. Bones and Mr. Tambo, exchanged jokes. This part was followed by the *olio,* a variety section that featured such acts as comedy routines, sentimental songs, and dances. The third part of the minstrel show was a one-act skit.

Minstrel companies performed in permanent minstrel theaters in almost every major city in the United States, especially in the Northeast. Companies also toured smaller cities and towns. The unsophisticated and fun-filled shows especially appealed to less educated audiences.   Don B. Wilmeth

Cameramann International, Ltd.

Blank coins—metal disks with no design—flow into a bin at the Denver Mint, *above.* The blanks then are fed into a press that stamps a design on both sides. The press also squeezes ridges on the rims of dimes, quarters, and half dollars.

Mint is a place where coins are made. In the United States and most other countries, only the government may *mint* (manufacture) coins. American mints are supervised by the United States Mint, a division of the Department of the Treasury. Mints now operate in Denver, Philadelphia, San Francisco, and West Point, N.Y. They make only coins. The Bureau of Engraving and Printing in Washington, D.C., makes paper money.

U.S. mints make half dollars, quarters, dimes, nickels, and cents for general circulation. They also make commemorative coins for special occasions and gold and silver bullion coins for investors. For a description of how U.S. coins are minted, see **Money** (Minting coins).

Historians believe the world's first mint was founded during the 600's B.C. in Lydia, now a part of Turkey. Ancient Mediterranean civilizations, including Greece and Rome, used coins in commerce. The use of coins gradually spread throughout Europe and Asia.

The first mint in the United States was established in Boston in 1652. It produced coins under the authority of the General Court of the Massachusetts Bay Colony. The Articles of Confederation of 1781 gave both the U.S.

Culver Pictures

A minstrel show traditionally featured white performers in blackface. The show opened with the entertainers grouped in a semicircle. The men on each end, called Mr. Tambo and Mr. Bones, exchanged jokes with the interlocutor, wearing white gloves in the center.

Congress and the individual states authority to mint money and regulate its value. The first federal mint opened in Philadelphia in 1792 and is still in operation. Other federal mints have operated in Carson City, Nev.; Charlotte, N.C.; Dahlonega, Ga.; Denver; New Orleans; and San Francisco.

Coins were minted in England before the coming of the Romans in A.D. 43. The present British Royal Mint has operated in London since 1810. The Canadian mint was established in Ottawa in 1870 as a branch of the British Royal Mint. It became a part of the Canadian Department of Finance in 1931.   R. G. Doty

See also **Bullion.**

Mint is the name of a large family of plants that grow mostly in temperate regions. There are about 3,500 species of mints. Many are highly fragrant. Their leaves are dotted with small glands that contain aromatic oils. The oils are released when the leaves are crushed.

The leaves of all mint plants grow in pairs on opposite sides of the stem, which in most species is distinctly square. Most mint plants have small, white, bluish, or pinkish flowers. In some species, such as lavender and peppermint, the flowers grow on spikes at the end of the stem. Mint plants usually bear small, roundish fruit that divides into four nutlets when mature.

WORLD BOOK illustration by John D. Dawson

Mint

Mint plants are particularly abundant in the countries that border the Mediterranean Sea. Both the leaves and the oil of mints are used as herbs for flavoring in cooking. The leaves may be used either fresh or dried. Popular cooking mints include marjoram, rosemary, and sage. Such mints as white horehound and peppermint add a cool, sharp flavor to candies. Mints also are used in some medicines and perfumes.

Scientific classification. Mints make up the mint family, Lamiaceae or Labiatae.   Donna M. Eggers Ware

Related articles in *World Book* include:

Balm	Horehound	Patchouli	Sage
Basil	Hyssop	Pennyroyal	Salvia
Bergamot	Lavender	Peppermint	Spearmint
Catnip	Marjoram	Rosemary	Thyme

Minto, Earl of (1845-1914), was a British colonial administrator who served as governor general of Canada from 1898 to 1904. As governor general, he supported sending Canadian volunteer forces to southern Africa to aid British troops in the Boer War (1899-1902). French-speaking Canadians opposed Canadian participation in foreign wars and protested the move. English-speaking Canadians approved it. As a result, the French-speaking group and the English-speaking group became more divided on Canada's role in the British Empire. Minto also promoted land conservation and the creation of the Public Archives of Canada.

The Earl of Minto was born in London. His given and family name was Gilbert John Murray Kynynmond Elliot. In 1891, he inherited the family estate near Hawick, Scot-

land, succeeding his father as Earl of Minto. Minto served as viceroy of India from 1905 to 1910. In that position, he helped bring about reforms that enlarged government councils to include elected Indians for the first time.   Jacques Monet

Minuet is a formal dance that was popular in European courts during the late 1600's and the 1700's. Music for the dance is also called the minuet. Many composers of the late 1600's and the 1700's wrote minuets for orchestra and also for ballets and operas.

The minuet contains a basic step unit that takes 2 measures of $\frac{3}{4}$ time. The tempo has varied over the long history of the dance. A couple moves through a series of figures, at least one of which forms the letter Z. The figures allow the dancers to join hands, separate, and pass or circle one another. Dancers maintain a smooth up-and-down motion but keep their upper bodies erect.

The minuet first became popular about 1670 in the court of King Louis XIV of France. A system of dance notation made the minuet easy to learn from diagrams in books, and the dance soon spread to other courts in Europe.   Dianne L. Woodruff

Minuit, *MIHN yoo iht,* **Peter** (1580-1638), was a Dutch colonial governor who bought Manhattan Island from the Indians in 1626. He paid with trinkets costing 60 Dutch guilders, or about $24 (see **Manhattan Island**). This purchase legalized the occupation of the island by the Dutch West India Company. Minuit made New Amsterdam, a settlement on the southern half of Manhattan Island, the center of the company's activities. Minuit supervised the building of Fort Amsterdam by company employees. The fort was designed primarily to protect the Hudson River mouth, a vital highway for the fur trade. New Amsterdam became an important trade center under the Dutch. The English later renamed the colony New York.

The Dutch West India Company recalled Minuit in 1631 for granting too many privileges to the *patroons* (wealthy landowners). Later, the Swedish government asked him to lead its first expedition to America, and he returned to America in 1638. He built Fort Christina, named after the queen of Sweden, at what is now Wilmington, Del. Shortly after the establishment of the fort, he drowned at sea during a hurricane.

Minuit was born in Wesel, Germany, but moved to the Netherlands as a young man. In 1626, he became the governor and director-general of New Netherland, the Dutch colony in North America.   Oliver A. Rink

Minute is a unit that is used to measure both time and angles. In time, 60 minutes make up one hour. Each minute is divided into 60 seconds. Because an hour is $\frac{1}{24}$ of a day, a minute is $\frac{1}{1,440}$ of a day. In measuring angles, 60 minutes make up one degree. A circle is divided into 360 degrees, and so one minute is $\frac{1}{21,600}$ of a circle. Each minute of an angle is divided into 60 seconds.

The minute in time is an exact measurement, which means exactly so much time. The minute of an angle is an exact portion of a circle, and is independent of the size of the circle. But if the angle is denoted by a linear measurement along the circumference, the distance of a minute depends on the circle's diameter. For example, a minute on a baseball measures only a small fraction of an inch. On the earth's surface a minute is one nautical mile, about 6,076 feet, or 1,852 meters (see **Mile**).

The circle was first divided into 360 degrees by ancient civilizations, either the Babylonians or the Egyptians. The Babylonians figured everything in units, 10's, and 60's instead of 10's and 100's, as we do. The degree was divided into 60 parts and each of these parts was divided into 60 parts. The Romans called the first divisions the *partes minutae primae,* or "first small parts." The second division they called the *partes minutae secundae,* or "second small parts." These terms were finally shortened to *minute* and *second.*   James Jespersen

See also **Degree; Hour; Second.**

Minutemen were volunteer soldiers who fought for the American Colonies against Britain at the beginning of the Revolutionary War in America (1775-1783). Just before the war, they were trained and organized into military companies. They were called *minutemen* because they were ready to fight "at a munute's notice."

When the Massachusetts militia was reorganized in 1774, the Provincial Congress provided that one-third of all the new regiments were to be made up of minutemen. The most famous action of the minutemen occurred on April 19, 1775, at Lexington and Concord, where they fought side by side with the militia. Minutemen groups disappeared when regular armies were formed.   James H. Hutson

See also **Revolutionary War in America** (Lexington and Concord).

Statue by H. H. Kitson; © Michael Philip Manheim, The Stock Solution

A statue of a minuteman stands at Lexington Green in Lexington, Mass., where the first shots of the Revolutionary War were fired. Eight colonists died in the fighting there.

© George E. Jones III, Photo Researchers

At the North Bridge in Concord, Mass., minutemen and the colonial militia drove off British troops. The original bridge no longer exists, but it was rebuilt in memory of the minutemen.

Miocene Epoch. See Earth (table: Outline of the earth's history).

Miquelon. See **Saint-Pierre and Miquelon.**

Mira, *MY ruh,* a giant red star, was one of the first stars of variable brightness to be discovered. In 1596, the German astronomer David Fabricius observed that the star changed over a period of months, dimming and then brightening. Because of this discovery, astronomers named the star *mira* after a Latin word meaning *wonderful.* At its brightest, Mira is about 100 times as bright as it is at its dimmest. Members of an amateur group, the American Association of Variable Observers, make observations of Mira and other variable stars.

Mira has about the same mass as the sun. But if its center were where the center of the sun is, Mira would extend beyond the orbit of Mars. Mira is about 270 light-years away from the earth.   David H. Levy

Mirabeau, *MIHR uh boh* or *mee ra BOH,* **Comte de** (1749-1791), was a French statesman, orator, and leader of the French Revolution (1789-1799). His powerful and eloquent speaking style made him the most forceful enemy of the French royal court. Mirabeau wanted the French government to consist of both a monarch and an elected assembly, like the constitutional monarchy of Britain. His political beliefs were sincere. But Mirabeau was always in debt and had a disgraceful personal life. As a result, neither King Louis XVI of France nor the revolutionaries fully trusted him.

Mirabeau was born in Bignon. His father was a nobleman. Mirabeau's given and family name was Honoré Gabriel Victor de Riqueti. In 1767, he became a cavalry officer in theFrench army. Mirabeau left the army after serving in Corsica in 1769. From 1774 to 1780, he was imprisoned several times for debt and other offenses.

In 1780, Mirabeau moved to the Netherlands. There, he began writing pamphlets attacking the despotism of the French monarchy. These writings made him famous among the middle class throughout Europe. By 1788, Mirabeau had returned to France. In 1789, he was elected to represent Aix-en-Provence in a body called the Estates-General (see **Estates-General**). Despite his noble background, he was chosen as a delegate of the

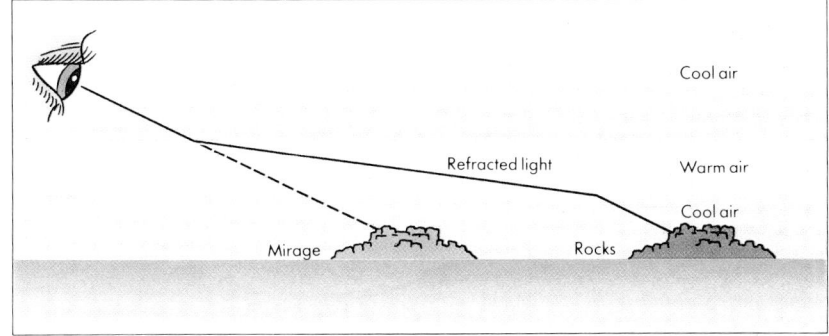

A mirage can be caused by light rays bending when they pass through substances of different densities. In the drawing at the left, light rays from the distant rocks bend as they pass from the cool, heavy air near the surface to the upper warm, light air. This produces a mirage that makes the rocks appear closer than they are.

WORLD BOOK illustration by Sarah Woodward

third estate, which included peasants, working people of the cities, and the middle class. In June 1789, the delegates of the third estate declared themselves the National Assembly of France. They took an oath not to disband until they had written a constitution for France. On June 23, a chief aide of Louis XVI ordered the deputies to leave their meeting place at Versailles. Mirabeau thundered, "Go and tell your master that we are here by the will of the people and that we shall not budge save at the point of a bayonet." The deputies stayed.

Mirabeau was a founder and an active member of the Jacobin Club, a powerful group of revolutionary leaders (see **Jacobins**). In 1791, he was elected president of the National Assembly. Mirabeau urged the king to accept the many reforms adopted by the Assembly and to take his place as a constitutional monarch. The royal family rejected his wise advice. Mirabeau died after a brief illness and was buried as a national hero.   Isser Woloch

Miracle is an event that cannot be explained through the known laws of nature. Miracles are generally associated with religion, but any occurrence can be called a miracle if it has no natural explanation.

The major figures in a religion are often credited with performing miracles. These figures include Jesus Christ in Christianity, Moses and the prophets in Judaism, Muhammad in Islam, and various gods in Hinduism. Many religions also teach that lesser holy figures, such as saints and rabbis, may also perform miracles. People may make pilgrimages to certain sacred places and objects to ask for a miracle. For example, Roman Catholic pilgrims travel to the shrine at Lourdes, France. There they pray to the Virgin Mary to plead with God on their behalf for miraculous cures.

Devout members of a religion believe in miracles and consider them a divine sign. Others have an equally firm belief that there is no such thing as a true miracle. They feel that all so-called miracles can be explained through scientific or psychological knowledge.   Jill Raitt

See also **Jesus Christ** (The miracles); **Shrine; Saint; Lourdes; Ba'al Shem Tov.**

Miracle play is a form of religious drama which was popular in the Middle Ages. It was based on the lives of the saints. At first, the plays were presented as a part of Roman Catholic Church services. But, like the mystery plays out of which they developed, they lost the approval of the church. The plays were driven from the church to the streets or public squares. In England, trade guild members performed these plays on feast days. Miracle plays have been revived from time to time,

but interest in this type of drama has become chiefly literary. See **Drama** (Medieval drama).   Albert Wertheim

Mirage, *muh RAHZH,* is a type of optical illusion. A mirage may occur when a person is driving and sees what seems to be a pool of water lying on a hot paved road ahead. But when the person reaches the spot, the water has disappeared or has seemingly moved farther down the road. Mirages may include distant objects that seem to be closer than they truly are. Other objects, such as a mountain or a ship, may seem to float in the sky. Mirages can be seen in deserts, at sea, or in the Arctic.

The bending of light rays as they pass through air with different temperatures causes a mirage. This bending motion is called *refraction* (see **Refraction**). The most common type of mirage is the *oasis mirage.* Desert travelers sometimes experience it when they see a distant pool of water that appears to be an oasis. But when they reach the spot, they find only dry sand.

An oasis mirage can be produced when light from the sun heats the ground and the air just above it. A ray of light from the sky passes first through the cooler air high above the ground and then into the warmer or hotter air near the ground. The speed of the light increases as it enters the warmer air because fewer air molecules get in the way of the light. The gradual change in the speed of the light forces the ray to change its direction. The ray bends upward just before it reaches the ground.

A person cannot see the path the ray takes. Since the ray is traveling upward when the person sees it, the person thinks that the ray came from a spot on the ground. Hot air above the ground mixes rapidly with other layers of air heated by the sun. As the ray travels through these layers, the hot air causes the ray to ripple or "wiggle." The light of an oasis mirage is blue because it comes from the sky. Therefore, the person concludes that this blue spot must be a pool of water that has small waves. But what the person really sees is part of the sky. The rays that produce mirages are real. Therefore, mirages can be photographed.

Another type of mirage is known as the *Fata Morgana.* Fata Morganas are the most beautiful of all mirages. A Fata Morgana occurs when a layer of hot air traps rays of light coming from the distant objects. Objects such as rocks or chunks of ice appear to be towers of a fairy-tale castle.   Jearl Walker

Miramichi River, *MIHR uh muh SHEE,* is an important waterway in New Brunswick. Its main branches are the Northwest Miramichi River and the Southwest Miramichi River. These two branches meet southwest of Newcastle and form the Miramichi River. The Miramichi, a famous salmon stream, flows northeast and empties into the Gulf of St. Lawrence through Miramichi Bay. Large ships can sail up the Miramichi River to Newcastle, about 30 miles (48 kilometers) from the river's mouth.

T. W. Acheson

Miranda, *mee RAHN dah,* **Francisco de** (1750-1816), a Venezuelan patriot, fought in the American, French, and Spanish-American revolutions. He took the lead in declaring Venezuela's independence from Spain in 1811 (see **Venezuela** [The struggle for independence]). Unsuccessful as a dictator, he surrendered his forces to the Royalists. His former subordinates, including Simón Bolívar, handed him over to the Spanish (see **Bolívar, Simón**). Miranda died in a Spanish dungeon. He was born in Caracas.   Harvey L. Johnson

Miranda v. Arizona, *mih RAN duh,* was a case in which the Supreme Court of the United States limited the power of police to question suspects. The court ruled in 1966 that nothing arrested persons say can be used against them in their trial unless they have been told they have certain rights. For example, suspects must be told they have the right to remain silent, and that anything they say can be held against them. They also must be told they can have a lawyer present during questioning, and, if they cannot afford one, the court will appoint one. If a suspect requests an attorney, the questioning must cease until an attorney is present.

The court's decision reversed the conviction of Ernesto A. Miranda, a Phoenix warehouse worker, on charges of kidnapping and rape. Miranda had confessed to the charges, and his confession was used as evidence against him. But Miranda had not been told of his right to remain silent and had been denied the right to consult a lawyer.

The Supreme Court based its decision on the Fifth and Sixth amendments to the United States Constitution. The Fifth Amendment to the Constitution protects persons from being forced to testify against themselves. The Sixth Amendment to the Constitution guarantees a defendant's right to a lawyer.

Several later Supreme Court decisions limited the scope of the ruling in *Miranda v. Arizona.* In 1971, for example, the court ruled that a confession obtained in violation of the *Miranda* decision can be used at a trial to prove the defendant is lying.   Stanley I. Kutler

See also **Escobedo v. Illinois.**

Miró, *mee ROH,* **Joan,** *hoh AHN* (1893-1983), was a Spanish painter who developed an imaginative and extremely personal style. His highly abstract forms suggest real people and animals as well as fantastic creatures and objects. Many of Miró's paintings contain a story or scene disguised by the apparent abstractness of the shapes and colors. His painting *Landscapes* appears in the **Painting** article.

Miró developed his characteristic style during the 1920's and early 1930's. His mature work portrays a world of fantasy, which he pictured in brightly colored shapes and lively expressive lines. Miró also worked in other art forms, including ceramics, sculpture, and *lithography,* a type of printmaking.

Miró was born in Montroig, Spain, near Barcelona. In 1919 he went to Paris, where he helped establish the surrealism movement in the 1920's.   Pamela A. Ivinski

Mirror is any smooth surface that reflects most of the light striking it. Only a small fraction of the light is absorbed by a mirror. In addition to being nonabsorbent, a surface must be smooth to about $\frac{1}{25,000}$ inch (0.0001 centimeter) to reflect sharp images. Some rough surfaces reflect light, but they scatter it in all directions so that no image is formed.

Most mirrors are made by putting a thin layer of silver or aluminum onto a sheet of high-quality glass. The glass supports the metallic layer and protects its shiny surface. Many mirrors in scientific instruments have the metal coating in front of the glass. A polished sheet of metal—without glass—can also serve as a mirror.

Images reflected by a mirror vary according to the mirror's shape. There are three principal kinds of mirrors: (1) plane mirrors, (2) convex mirrors, and (3) concave mirrors.

Plane mirrors have a flat surface. Most looking glasses are plane mirrors. A line perpendicular to a plane mirror at any point of reflection is called the *normal.* Light strikes the mirror at some angle to the normal, and this angle is known as the *angle of incidence.* Light is reflected back at an equal angle on the other side of the normal. This angle is called the *angle of reflection.* The two angles are always equal.

An image in a plane mirror is a *virtual image,* one that appears to be behind the mirror. It is *erect* (correct end up), but reversed from left to right. The image is the same size as the object it reflects and appears to be equidistant from the mirror.

Convex mirrors are curved like part of the outer surface of a sphere. When a convex mirror is illuminated by

Women and Birds in the Night (1934), an oil painting on canvas; Yale University Art Gallery, Bequest of Kay Sage Tanguy

A painting by Joan Miró shows the simple forms, playful images, and sense of fantasy that are typical of the artist's style.

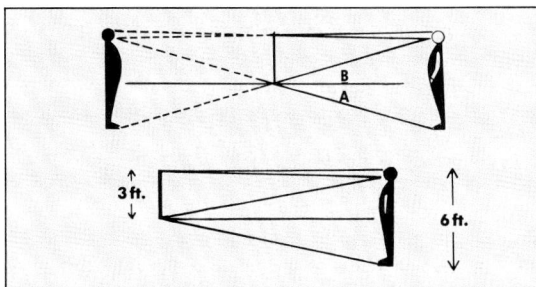

In a plane mirror, the image is at the mirror, but appears to be as far beyond it as the object is in front of it. In a mirror, *top,* the angle of incidence (A) equals the angle of reflection (B). Because of this, a mirror must be at least half the height of a person to reflect a full-length image, *bottom.*

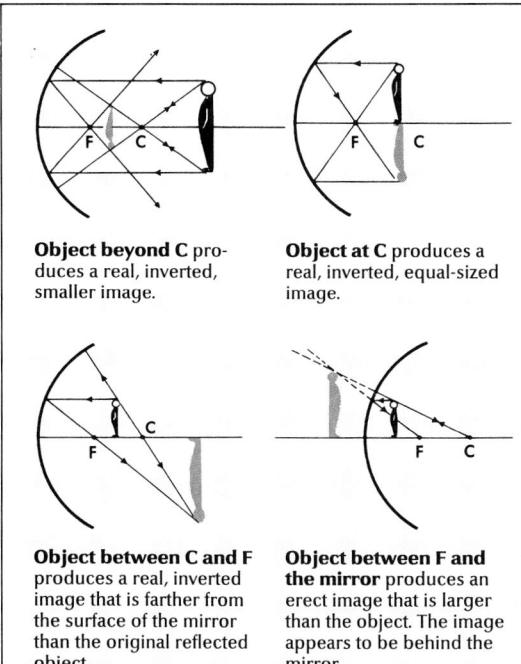

Object beyond C produces a real, inverted, smaller image.

Object at C produces a real, inverted, equal-sized image.

Object between C and F produces a real, inverted image that is farther from the surface of the mirror than the original reflected object.

Object between F and the mirror produces an erect image that is larger than the object. The image appears to be behind the mirror.

In a concave mirror, *above,* such as those used for shaving, the position and size of the *image* (in gray) depend on the position of the *object* (in black) in relation to the mirror's *center of focus* (F) and *center of curvature* (C). The position of the object also determines whether the image is *real* (formed in front of the mirror) or *virtual* (appears formed behind the mirror).

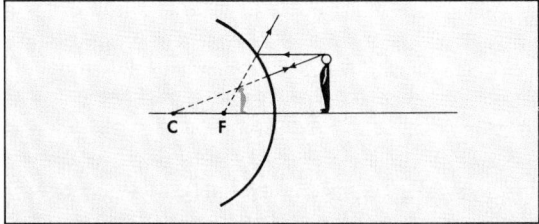

A convex mirror, as pictured in the diagram above, produces an upright image that is much smaller than the object. The image formed appears to be behind the mirror.

parallel rays of light, the reflected light seems to come from a point behind the mirror called the *focus.* The focus is halfway between the mirror and the mirror's *center of curvature,* the center of the sphere of which the mirror is a part.

A convex mirror forms virtual images that are erect and *demagnified*—that is, smaller than the object being reflected. Many automobiles have a convex rearview mirror, which provides a wider field of vision than a plane mirror. But the reflected objects appear farther away than they are because they are demagnified.

Concave mirrors are hollow and curved like part of the inner surface of a sphere. The focus and center of curvature are both in front of the mirror. The focus is a *real focus* because parallel light rays striking the mirror meet at this point when they are reflected. Solar ovens use concave mirrors to focus sunlight.

An image produced by a concave mirror may be either a virtual image or a *real image.* A real image, unlike a virtual one, is formed in front of the mirror and is produced by the actual intersecting of reflected light rays. The properties of an image formed by a concave mirror are determined by the position of the object being reflected. For an object between the mirror and its focus, the image will be virtual, erect, and magnified. Objects beyond the focus, however, produce real images. They may be erect or inverted, and magnified or demagnified, depending on the position of the object.

Concave mirrors include shaving mirrors, make-up mirrors, and mirrors in reflecting telescopes. Concave and convex mirrors both produce somewhat distorted images.   Sandra M. Faber

See also **Aberration; Parabola; Telescope** (Reflecting telescopes).

MIRV. See **Guided missile** (The warhead; diagram).

Miscarriage, also called *spontaneous abortion,* is the accidental or natural ending of a pregnancy before a baby can live outside its mother's body. Studies indicate that 15 to 20 per cent of all diagnosed pregnancies end in miscarriage. But the risk of miscarriage is highest during the first two weeks following *conception* (fertilization), a time at which most women do not even know they are pregnant. Thus, many physicians believe the overall rate of miscarriage, including undiagnosed pregnancies, may actually be as high as 50 per cent.

Up to 60 per cent of all miscarriages occur because of defects in the embryo's *chromosomes.* Chromosomes are tiny, threadlike structures that carry genes. In most miscarriages involving defective chromosomes, the embryo cannot develop normally. A miscarriage may also occur if *progesterone,* a hormone necessary to maintain pregnancy, is not present in sufficient amounts. Some women miscarry because the *uterus,* the organ in which the offspring develops, cannot withstand the pressures of the growing fetus. Some *chronic* (long-term) diseases, such as diabetes and kidney disease, also are linked to miscarriages. Pregnant women with such diseases require close medical attention.   Gretajo Northrop

Misdemeanor is any violation of the law which is less serious than a felony. Assault and battery, the theft of a small sum of money, and other such acts against public safety and welfare, are misdemeanors. So are most traffic offenses. Not all courts draw the same line between misdemeanors and felonies. A felony in one court may

be a misdemeanor in another. People guilty of misdemeanors are usually fined or given a short jail sentence.
See also **Felony.**   George T. Felkenes

Miskolc, *MIHSH kawlts* (pop. 211,660), is a city in Hungary. Miskolc, a busy commercial center, is located on
the Sajó River in the northeast industrial region of Hungary. For the location of Miskolc, see **Hungary** (political
map).

During the 1300's, Miskolc developed as a busy market town and center of the Hungarian wine trade. Handicrafts industries flourished there in the 1700's. Iron
smelting and engineering industries developed during
the 1800's and remain important. Other industries produce cement, furniture, paper, and textiles. The city's
Ottó Herman Museum features noted archaeological exhibits. The Technical University of Heavy Industry provides training in various fields of engineering. Popular
health spas and a resort hotel are located in nearby
Lillafüred, west of Miskolc.   Thomas Sakmyster

Missile, Guided. See Guided missile.

Missile boat is a small, fast warship that can fire
guided missiles. It is used by navies to patrol and defend narrow seas and coastal waters.

Missile boats measure from about 83 to 200 feet (25 to
61 meters) long and can travel up to 40 *knots* (nautical
miles per hour) or faster. They have diesel or gas turbine
engines, or both. Missile boats carry from two to eight
missiles. The missiles can reach enemy ships up to 60
miles (97 kilometers) away. In addition, missile boats
have one or more guns for use against aircraft and small
ships. The barrels of these guns measure up to 3 inches
(76 millimeters) in caliber.

Many missile boats are *hydrofoils* (see **Hydrofoil**). At
high speeds, their hulls are raised above the water by
foils, wing-shaped structures below the surface. These
craft are powered by diesel engines when their hulls are
in the water, and by gas turbines when they are above
the water on their foils.

The first missile boats were built by the Soviet Navy
and went to sea in 1958. The most famous Soviet missile
boat classes, the *Osa* and the *Komar,* have been used by
many navies. In 1967, the Egyptian Navy used Komar
class boats to sink an Israeli destroyer. The Egyptian
boats were in their own harbor when they fired four

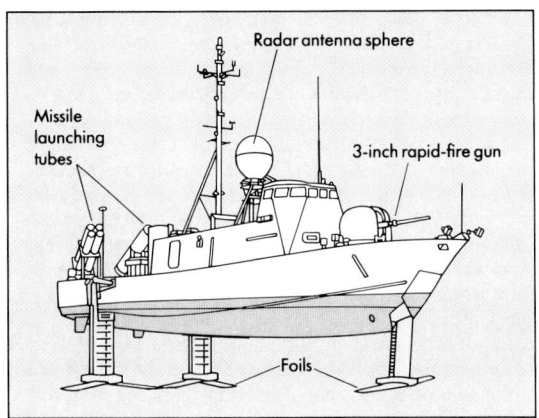

Radar antenna sphere

Missile
launching
tubes

3-inch rapid-fire gun

Foils

WORLD BOOK illustration by George Suyeoka

A missile boat of the U.S. Navy, *above,* can skim over the water
on foils. It can fire up to eight missiles at enemy ships.

missiles at the destroyer, which was $12\frac{1}{2}$ miles (20.1 kilometers) off the coast. The United States and other nations began to develop missile boats following this and
other sinkings by Soviet-built craft. The first U.S. Navy
missile boat, the *Pegasus,* was completed in 1976.

Norman Polmar

Mission life in America thrived for more than 250
years in a belt of North America known as the Spanish
Borderlands. From the 1560's to the 1820's, Spanish missionaries established themselves among the Indians in
this region, which covered a vast area north of Spain's
colonial empire in Latin America. Missions developed in
what are now Georgia, Florida, Texas, New Mexico, Arizona, and California. French missions arose in the Great
Lakes area, and there were some villages of Indian converts to Christianity in New England. Christian missions
also were later established on United States Indian reservations. However, this article focuses on the development, the daily life, and the heritage of the Spanish missions.

In the 50 years after the arrival of Christopher Columbus in 1492, Spain claimed most of the New World. The
pope, as head of the Roman Catholic Church, granted
the Spanish monarchs great authority over the church in
the Americas. As a result, missions became agencies of
the government. The Spanish government paid the missionaries' expenses, hoping they could persuade the Indians to become loyal Spanish citizens, as well as
Roman Catholics. Spain's two chief interests—the protection of its empire and the conversion of the Indians—
usually determined where and when missions would be
established. Spanish soldiers and missionaries came to
Florida from Cuba and the Caribbean. Other missionaries in the Spanish Borderlands came by way of *New
Spain* (Mexico).

Development of the missions

Eastern missions. In the Roman Catholic Church,
missionary work had long been a specialty of certain
groups known as *orders.* Members of one order, the
Society of Jesus (Jesuits), labored and died among the
Indians of the humid south Atlantic coast between 1566
and 1572. Most of the missionaries in the Spanish Borderlands, however, were members of the Order of Friars Minor (Franciscans).

Franciscans operated missions in what are now Florida and Georgia for almost 200 years. By 1655, there
were 38 missions in the area. Because the Indians
moved around a great deal to hunt, fish, and wage war,
the missions often changed locations. At times, European diseases caused many deaths among the Indians.
After the founding of Charleston, S.C., in 1670, English
settlers began to lure surviving Indians away with trade
goods and guns. Some attacked the Indians, often en-
slaving or killing them. By 1708, only a few missions
were left, and in 1763, Spain surrendered Florida to
Great Britain.

Western missions. In 1598, Spain established a colony in the New Mexico area, where Pueblo Indians had
an advanced civilization. The group that settled there included Franciscan missionaries, who sought to control
the colony in the 1600's. Churches were built in about 50
Pueblo towns. In the early 1600's, the friars claimed to
have about 35,000 mission Indians.

Detail of a drawing by William Alexander; Newberry Library, Chicago

Spanish missions in America thrived in parts of the South and West from the 1500's to the 1800's. They introduced Christianity to thousands of American Indians. This drawing, made in 1792, shows Mission San Carlos Borromeo de Carmelo, near what is now Carmel, Calif.

Indians sometimes challenged European colonization because it disrupted their former ways of life. The bloodiest Indian uprising took place in 1680, when the Pueblo Indians drove the outnumbered Spaniards from the New Mexico colony and killed over 400 of them (see **Indian wars** [The Pueblo revolt]). The surviving Spaniards retreated to the El Paso, Tex., area. Twelve years later, they recolonized in New Mexico.

In the 1680's, Spaniards began occupying parts of present-day Texas. Spain relied on missions, *presidios* (forts), and other settlements to prevent the advance of French explorers and traders into the Texas area. Spain also hoped to befriend the powerful Indian tribes of this region, including the Apaches and Comanches. By the mid-1700's, there were a few widely scattered clusters of missions that had survived Indian invasions. Some of the most memorable were the adobe and stone missions in the San Antonio area. These missions were known as the "Alamo chain."

From 1691 to 1711, Eusebio Francisco Kino, a Jesuit missionary, led many expeditions in the area that is now Arizona. These expeditions created a demand for Spanish missionaries and goods throughout the region. The Franciscans replaced the Jesuits in the Arizona region in 1768. They rebuilt San Xavier del Bac, which Kino had founded near Tucson in 1700. The Franciscans remained in the region until the late 1820's. See **Kino, Eusebio Francisco.**

The Spanish settlement of California began in 1769. That year, soldier-settlers and missionaries took possession of the area that became the city of San Diego. The Franciscan Junípero Serra founded the first California mission, known as San Diego de Alcalá, on this site. Serra went on to found 8 more of California's 21 missions before his death in 1784. These missions became home to thousands of Indians. Some of the California missions developed into major agricultural and manufacturing centers.

In 1833 and 1834, the Mexican government seized and redistributed mission properties. This action brought an end to the active role of missions in the

Spanish Borderlands. See **Indian, American** (Indians of the California-Intermountain region); **Serra, Junípero.**

Life at the missions

The Spanish missions fed, clothed, and often housed the Indians who entered them. In return, the Indians agreed to take instruction in Christianity, to observe Spanish customs, and to work for the mission.

Many Spanish missions included dining areas, schools, storerooms, and workshops, as well as living quarters and a church. In most cases, these structures were built of adobe or stone and arranged around a square courtyard. All the missions had farms, and many operated ranches. The California missions became especially productive. In 1834, Indians there herded a total of 396,000 cattle; 62,000 horses; and 321,000 sheep, goats, and pigs. They also harvested 123,000 bushels of grain.

In the mornings, mission Indians attended religious services and received instruction in Catholicism. Some of them learned to read and write in Spanish. During the rest of the day, they worked, usually on the farms. Some Indians learned carpentry, metalworking, and other skills from the missionaries and from outside workers hired to supervise construction of the churches and other mission buildings.

At first, many Indians welcomed the benefits of a more reliable and varied food supply, protection from enemies, and the rich ceremonies of Roman Catholicism. Later, various problems developed. Many Indians objected to the highly structured mission routine and to the fact that they were forbidden to leave without permission. They resented the missionaries' attacks on their former religions and traditions, and they feared the diseases that killed many of their family members. Some of the Indians fled. Others rebelled, often destroying churches and killing missionaries.

Missionaries were able to keep many Indians under mission discipline for several generations. When the missionaries left or the missions closed, however, some Indians returned to their former way of life. Discrimination and a lack of education prevented even skilled Indi-

Mission San José was established in San Antonio, Tex., in 1720. Its many graceful carvings, which attract thousands of visitors yearly, are reminders of Spanish rule in America.

WORLD BOOK photo by Zintgraff Photography

ans from getting good jobs and receiving equal rights among whites.

A visitor's guide

A number of Spanish missions have been maintained through the years, restored, or rebuilt. Following are brief descriptions of some of these Spanish missions.

La Purísima Concepcíon, near Lompoc, Calif., is a state historical monument. It was founded in 1787.

Nombre de Díos, in St. Augustine, Fla., is the oldest U.S. mission. Its first Mass was celebrated in 1565.

Nuestra Señora del Carmen, near El Paso, Tex., was founded by Franciscans in 1682 as a refuge from the Pueblo Revolt of 1680.

San Antonio de Valero, in San Antonio, Tex., is better known as the Alamo. It was the site of a famous battle in 1836, during the Texas Revolution.

Santa Bárbara, in Santa Barbara, Calif., has been called Queen of the California Missions because of its architectural beauty. Today, it is a Franciscan parish.

San Esteban Rey de Acoma, at Acoma, N. Mex., was constructed during the 1630's. It is one of the few churches that survived the Pueblo Revolt of 1680. It stands atop an isolated *mesa* (tableland) 365 feet (111 meters) high.

San José, in San Antonio, Tex., is part of San Antonio Missions National Historical Park. It was founded in 1720 by the Franciscan Antonio Margil de Jesús.

San Juan Capistrano, in San Juan Capistrano, Calif., was established by the Franciscan Junípero Serra in 1776. An earthquake destroyed most of it in 1812.

San Xavier del Bac, near Tucson, Ariz., still serves local Papago Indians. The Jesuit Eusebio Francisco Kino first visited the site in 1692 and founded a mission there in 1700.

John L. Kessel

See also the *History* and *Places to visit* sections of the articles on **Arizona; California; New Mexico;** and **Texas.**

Additional resources

Barton, Bruce W. *The Tree at the Center of the World: A Story of the California Missions.* Ross-Erikson, 1979.

Bowden, Henry W. *American Indians and Christian Missions: Studies in Cultural Conflict.* Univ. of Chicago Press, 1981.

Churchmen and the Western Indians, 1820-1920. Ed. by Clyde A. Milner II and F. A. O'Neil. Univ. of Oklahoma Press, 1985.

Cochran, Alice C. *Miners, Merchants, and Missionaries: The Roles of Missionaries and Pioneer Churches in the Colorado Gold Rush and Its Aftermath, 1858-1870.* Scarecrow, 1980.

Kessell, John L. *The Missions of New Mexico Since 1776.* Univ. of New Mexico Press, 1979.

Lanning, John T. *The Spanish Missions of Georgia.* Scholarly, 1971. First published in 1935.

Missionary is a person sent by a religious group to convert others to his or her faith. Many missionaries also work to provide education, agricultural information, medical care, and other social services to the people they serve.

Religions attract converts in various ways. Buddhist organizations spread the teachings of Buddha throughout the world by sponsoring lectures and meditation sessions. Islamic missionaries conduct worship services and distribute religious literature. Some religions today, including Judaism, have no missionaries because they do not seek converts. Christianity carries on the most extensive missionary activities. This article discusses Christian missionaries.

Men and women may serve as *foreign missionaries* or *home missionaries.* Foreign missionaries leave their own countries and work abroad. Today, the whole world, especially its huge cities, is considered a mission field. Missionaries are sent to other countries from Asia, Africa, and Latin America, as well as from North America and Europe. Home missionaries carry out assignments in their own lands.

There are about 290,000 Christian missionaries. Many missionaries are members of the clergy. Many men and women who are not ordained and do not belong to religious orders serve as *lay missionaries.* There has been a large growth in the number of people serving short terms as missionaries.

Duties. Missionaries explain the teachings of their faith and try to inspire devotion to Jesus Christ. They lead worship services, preach sermons, translate the Bible, write religious materials, organize churches, and guide converts in the practice of their faith.

Many missionaries also use their skills to relieve poverty and disease among the people they serve. Others provide relief from such disasters as earthquakes, famines, floods, and storms. Missionaries usually work through national schools and hospitals. But in some remote areas, they still provide the only education and health care available. Missionaries who have technical skills may train people in business methods, construction trades, or improved farming techniques.

Some missionary organizations direct their efforts to special groups. Such organizations as Inter-Varsity Christian Fellowship, Youth for Christ, Campus Crusade for Christ, and Navigators work with students. Prison Fellowship Ministries works with people in prisons.

Several groups loosely related to Christian denominations place special emphasis on conversion. All Jehovah's Witnesses must work at least 10 hours each month spreading their faith to people on street corners and in private homes. Many Mormons who are young adults or retired people volunteer to spend up to two years as full-time missionaries without pay. Some organizations express their faith chiefly through social work and acts of charity. The Salvation Army is one of the largest such organizations in the world.

Organization. Today, about two-thirds of all Christian missionaries are Roman Catholics, and the rest are Protestants. The fastest-growing groups belong to evangelical Protestant denominations, especially charismatic and Pentecostal churches. More missionaries come from the United States than from any other country.

Several Catholic religious orders devote much of their efforts to missionary activities. These groups include the Catholic Foreign Mission Society of America (Maryknoll) and the Society of Jesus (Jesuits). The Congregation for the Evangelization of Peoples or Propagation of the Faith directs worldwide Catholic mission work. Protestant missionaries are recruited and financed by denominations, church-sponsored organizations, and independent agencies. The Division of World Mission and Evangelism of the World Council of Churches coordinates much Protestant missionary activity. The Evangelical Foreign Missions Association and the Interdenominational Foreign Mission Association perform this service for evangelical Protestants.

History. Christian missionary work began soon after that religion was founded nearly 2,000 years ago. Christianity spread rapidly because of such enthusiastic missionary activity as that of the apostles Peter and Paul. By the 300's, Christianity had spread throughout the Roman Empire, including North Africa. The missionary Saint Patrick brought Christianity to Ireland in the 400's. During the Middle Ages, such Christian missionaries as Saint Boniface converted the people of most European countries. By the 1500's, Roman Catholic missionaries were sailing with European explorers and soldiers to little-known regions of Africa, Asia, and the Americas. During the 1500's and 1600's, Dominicans, Franciscans, and Jesuits and other Catholic orders set up many missions throughout the world.

The Protestant missionary movement began in the 1600's, when Protestant nations of Europe established trading companies and colonies overseas. John Eliot and David Brainerd were famous early missionaries to American Indians. In the 1800's, thousands of missionaries, including William Carey, David Livingstone, and Robert Morrison, worked in the Far East and Africa. The period became known as "the great century" of Protestant missions.

Revivalist preachers, such as Jonathan Edwards and George Whitefield, sought converts among American colonists in the 1700's. Later, revivalists from Baptist, Methodist, and other churches won converts and established congregations on the U.S. frontier. Revivalists of the 1800's and early 1900's gained converts in the growing cities. Now, evangelists such as Billy Graham use large crusades, radio, and television to seek converts.

Many people in mission lands resented foreign missionary activity. This resentment arose partly because missionaries often promoted foreign political and economic interests among the people with whom they worked. Also, missionaries often considered Western ways of life superior to the customs and values of native cultures, which they tried to change. Some missionaries supported governments that ignored the needs of the poor. At the same time, missionaries often won respect for their work in health, education, and other fields.

A strong sense of patriotic unity called *nationalism* swept through many developing countries after World War II ended in 1945. In time, these countries won independence, and the churches there appointed more national leaders to replace the missionaries. Some of the countries opposed missionary activity, seized church-supported schools, and even deported or killed missionaries.

Today, more missionaries than ever before are at work throughout the world. Increasing numbers are being sent by churches in Africa, Asia, Latin America, and many of the Pacific Islands. They use modern methods of communication and scientific studies to help them in their work. They often cooperate with local churches.   James A. De Jong

Related articles in *World Book* include:

Asbury, Francis	Lee, Jason
Boniface, Saint	Marquette, Jacques
Brébeuf, Saint Jean de	Mission life in America
De Smet, Pierre J.	Patrick, Saint
Eliot, John	Salvation Army
Grenfell, Sir Wilfred T.	Schweitzer, Albert
Hennepin, Louis	Serra, Junipero
Jogues, Saint Isaac	Whitman, Marcus
Judson, Adoniram	Whitman, Narcissa
Las Casas, Bartolomé de	Xavier, Saint Francis

Additional resources

Austin, Alvyn J. *Saving China: Canadian Missionaries in the Middle Kingdom, 1888-1959.* Univ. of Toronto Pr., 1986.
Hutchison, William R. *Errand to the World: American Protestant Thought and Foreign Missions.* Univ. of Chicago Pr., 1987.
Neill, Stephen C. *A History of Christian Missions.* 2nd ed. Penguin, 1986.

Missionary Ridge, Battle of. See Civil War (Battle of Chattanooga).

Mississauga, MIHS uh SAW guh (pop. 463,388), is one of the largest cities in Ontario, Canada. It was created in 1976 by combining several villages and towns west of Toronto. For location, see **Ontario** (political map).

Mississauga's downtown area is in the center of the city. It includes the Civic Centre, which is the home of the city government; and Square One, a large shopping and office complex. Canada's busiest airport, Lester B. Pearson International Airport, is located on the northeast side of the city. Mississauga's industries include the production of aerospace equipment, electronic products, scientific instruments, and pharmaceuticals.

Mississauga is located on land purchased from the Mississauga Indians in 1805. Several communities sprung up in the area. The town of Mississauga was incorporated in 1968. In 1976, the Ontario government combined the town and about 110 square miles (290 square kilometers) of towns, townships, and villages to form the city of Mississauga. Many of these communities retain their small-town atmosphere.   Lou Clancy

Mississippi's stately old homes like Rosalie, *above,* a mansion in Natchez, are reminders of life in the Old South. Natchez is the oldest town along the Mississippi River.

Mississippi   *The Magnolia State*

Mississippi is a state that is going through a period of great change. Part of the Deep South of the United States, it was once a land of farmers and quiet towns. It is becoming a state of office workers and busy cities. Since the 1930's, the people of Mississippi have worked to build a modern economy based on industry as well as agriculture.

But tradition still plays an important part in Mississippi life. The people of Mississippi have great pride in their state's history. Mississippi retains many reminders of the Old South. Stately *antebellum* (pre-Civil War) mansions bring back memories of Mississippi plantation life before the Civil War, which began in 1861. Monuments throughout Mississippi recall the heroic deeds of the Confederate soldiers who fought on the state's many battlefields.

Today, most of Mississippi's workers are employed in service industries, which include retail trade and government. Factories also employ many people. The state produces a variety of manufactured goods, including

appliances, clothing, meat products, and ships.

Farmland and forest-covered hills spread over most of the state. Many Mississippi farmlands are used to raise cattle or chickens. Others are used to grow crops. Mississippi ranks among the leading producers of chickens, cotton, and soybeans. The state also has significant deposits of petroleum and natural gas.

Despite the growth in the state's economic base, many of the jobs in Mississippi pay low wages. As a result, the average income in Mississippi is lower than in any other state.

Mississippi takes its name from the mighty river that forms most of its western border. *Mississippi* means the *Great Water,* or the *Father of Waters,* in the language of the Indians who lived in the region in early times. Mississippi's nickname, the *Magnolia State,* comes from the magnolia trees that grow in most parts of the state. Mississippi gardens also have many azaleas and camellias. These flowers bloom for months each year because the climate of Mississippi is generally warm and moist.

The mild climate attracts many tourists to Mississippi. The Mississippi Gulf Coast is a popular vacationland. It has large, sunny beaches that are lined with many fine hotels. Jackson is the capital of Mississippi and the state's largest city.

The contributors of this article are John Ray Skates, Jr., Professor of History, and Robert W. Wales, Professor of Geography, both at the University of Southern Mississippi.

Interesting facts about Mississippi

The world's first heart transplant into a human being was performed by Dr. James D. Hardy at the University of Mississippi Medical Center in Jackson in 1964. Hardy replaced a human heart with the heart of a chimpanzee. The operation introduced important techniques used in later successful human-to-human heart transplants.

First heart transplant

The Pascagoula River is known as the *Singing River.* The sound it makes, best heard in warm months toward evening, resembles the sound of a swarm of bees in flight. According to an Indian legend, a young chieftain of the Pascagoula tribe wooed and won a princess of the rival Biloxi tribe who was already engaged. The furious Biloxi attacked the Pascagoula, demanding the surrender of the offending chieftain. The Pascagoula refused. Realizing they could not escape, they joined hands with the ill-fated couple and walked, singing, into the river.

WORLD BOOK illustrations by Kevin Chadwick

Coca-Cola was first bottled in 1894 by Joseph A. Biedenharn, a candy store owner in Vicksburg.

Grenada was formed in 1836 by the union of two rival towns, Pittsburg and Tullahoma. The union was symbolized by an actual wedding ceremony in which the groom came from Pittsburg and the bride from Tullahoma.

The last world heavyweight bare-knuckle boxing championship was fought in Richburg, near Hattiesburg, in 1889. John L. Sullivan defeated Jake Kilrain in 75 rounds.

Sullivan vs. Kilrain

© D. Donne Bryant

A resort near Biloxi attracts vacationers throughout the year. Biloxi is on the Mississippi Gulf Coast, a popular tourist area with large, sandy beaches and many fine hotels.

© Bruce Roberts, Stills, Inc.

Cattle graze in a Mississippi pasture in a region of black, fertile soil called the *Black Belt* or *Black Prairie.* Mississippi is an important livestock-raising state.

© Richard and Mary Magruder

Jackson is Mississippi's capital and largest city. Known as the *Crossroads of the South,* it serves as a center of commerce, industry, and transportation.

Mississippi in brief

Symbols of Mississippi

The state flag was adopted in 1894. The bars of red, white, and blue are the national colors. A replica of the Confederate battle flag occupies the upper left portion. The state seal, adopted in 1817, bears a modified version of the arms of the United States. The eagle holds an olive branch and arrows, symbolizing the desire for peace but the ability to wage war.

State flag

State seal

Mississippi (brown) ranks 32nd in size among all the states and 7th in size among the Southern States (yellow).

The State Capitol is in Jackson, Mississippi's capital since 1822. Other capitals were Natchez (1798-1802, 1817-1821), Washington (1802-1817), and Columbia (1821-1822).

General information

Statehood: Dec. 10, 1817, the 20th state.
State abbreviations: Miss. (traditional); MS (postal).
State motto: *Virtute et Armis* (By Valor and Arms).
State song: "Go Mis-sis-sip-pi" by Houston Davis.

Land and climate

Area: 47,695 sq. mi. (123,530 km²), including 781 sq. mi. (2,024 km²) of inland water but excluding 591 sq. mi. (1,530 km²) of coastal water.
Elevation: *Highest*—Woodall Mountain, 806 ft. (246 m) above sea level. *Lowest*—sea level along the coast.
Coastline: 44 mi. (71 km).
Record high temperature: 115 °F (46 °C) at Holly Springs on July 29, 1930.
Record low temperature: −19 °F (−28 °C) at Corinth on Jan. 30, 1966.
Average July temperature: 81 °F (27 °C).
Average January temperature: 46 °F (8 °C).
Average yearly precipitation: 56 in. (142 cm).

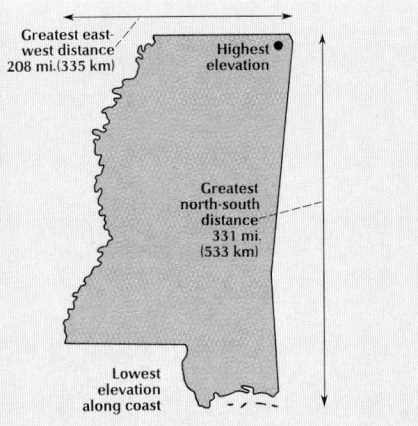

Greatest east-west distance 208 mi.(335 km)

Highest elevation

Greatest north-south distance 331 mi. (533 km)

Lowest elevation along coast

Important dates

Pierre Le Moyne, Sieur d'Iberville, established the first European settlement in Mississippi at Old Biloxi.

| 1540 | 1699 | 1763 |

Hernando de Soto of Spain entered the Mississippi region.

Mississippi became English territory after the French and Indian War.

State bird
Mockingbird

State flower
Magnolia

State tree
Magnolia

People

Population: 2,586,443 (1990 census)
Rank among the states: 31st
Density: 54 persons per sq. mi. (21 per km²), U.S. average 69 per sq. mi. (27 per km²)
Distribution: 53 per cent rural, 47 per cent urban

Largest cities in Mississippi

Jackson	196,637
Biloxi	46,319
Greenville	45,226
Hattiesburg	41,882
Meridian	41,036
Gulfport	40,775

Source: U.S. Bureau of the Census.

Population trend

Millions

Year	Population
1990	2,586,443
1980	2,520,631
1970	2,216,994
1960	2,178,141
1950	2,178,914
1940	2,183,796
1930	2,009,821
1920	1,790,618
1910	1,797,114
1900	1,551,270
1890	1,289,600
1880	1,131,597
1870	827,922
1860	791,305
1850	606,526
1840	375,651
1830	136,621
1820	75,448
1810	31,306
1800	7,600

Source: U.S. Bureau of the Census.

Economy

Chief products

Agriculture: chickens, cotton, soybeans, beef cattle, milk.
Manufacturing: food products, transportation equipment, electrical equipment, wood products, paper products, clothing, furniture.
Mining: petroleum, natural gas.

Gross state product

Value of goods and services produced in 1991: $41,806,000,000. *Services* include community, social, and personal services; finance; government; trade; and transportation, communication, and utilities. *Industry* includes construction, manufacturing, and mining. *Agriculture* includes agriculture, fishing, and forestry.

Source: U.S. Bureau of Economic Analysis.

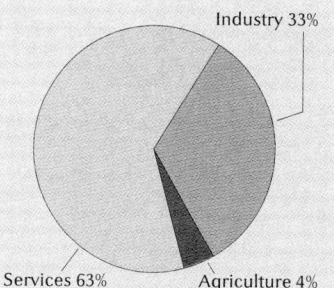

Industry 33%
Services 63%
Agriculture 4%

Government

State government

Governor: 4-year term
State senators: 52; 4-year terms
State representatives: 122; 4-year terms
Counties: 82

Federal government

United States senators: 2
United States representatives: 5
Electoral votes: 7

Sources of information

For information on tourism in Mississippi, write to: Mississippi Division of Tourism, P.O. Box 849, Jackson, MS 39205. The Office of the Governor handles requests for information about the state's economy, government, and history. Write to: Governor, P.O. Box 139, Jackson, MS 39205.

Mississippi became the 20th state on December 10.

A federal court ordered the desegregation of Mississippi schools.

| 1798 | 1817 | 1939 | 1969 |

Congress organized the Mississippi territory.

Petroleum was discovered at Tinsley.

Population. The 1990 United States census reported that Mississippi had 2,586,443 people. The population had increased $2\frac{1}{2}$ per cent over the 1980 figure, 2,520,631. According to the 1990 census, Mississippi ranks 31st in population among the 50 states.

About 53 per cent of Mississippi's people live in rural areas. About 47 per cent of the people live in urban areas. But Mississippi's urban population is growing as people move to the cities where manufacturing industries are being developed. Mississippi's urban population almost tripled between 1930 and 1970. In addition, many Mississippians live on small farms in rural areas, but work in nearby cities.

The largest city is Jackson, the state capital and center of Mississippi's business and financial activities. The state includes all of two metropolitan areas and part of a third (see **Metropolitan area**). Jackson is Mississippi's largest metropolitan area. The metropolitan area of Biloxi-Gulfport-Pascagoula ranks second in population. For the populations of these areas, see the *Index* to the Mississippi political map.

Mississippi's six largest cities, in order of size, are Jackson, Biloxi, Greenville, Hattiesburg, Meridian, and Gulfport. Several of the state's large cities lie on the Mississippi River. These cities include Greenville, Natchez, and Vicksburg.

The 1990 census showed that 36 per cent of the people in Mississippi are blacks. This is a larger proportion of blacks than in any other state. Mississippi's other large population groups include people of Irish, English, German, and American Indian descent.

Schools. The Mississippi public school system was established by the Constitution of 1869. The state set up a board of education and provided that every child

© Joy A. Guravich

A musician performs at the Delta Blues Festival, which is held each September in Greenville.

Population density

Mississippi's population is spread fairly evenly across the state. More than half the people live in rural areas. Almost all the largest cities are in the southern half of the state.

Persons per sq. mi.	Persons per km²
More than 100	More than 40
50 to 100	20 to 40
25 to 50	10 to 20
Less than 25	Less than 10

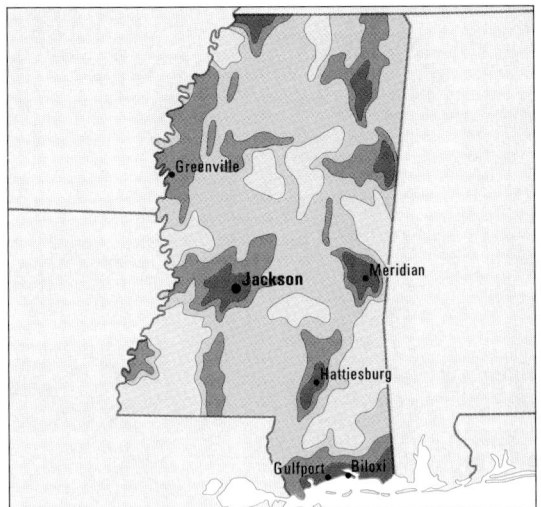

WORLD BOOK map; based on U.S. Bureau of the Census data.

William H. Allen, Jr.

St. Paul's Seafood Festival is held each July in Pass Christian. The festival features arts, crafts, and seafood dinners.

should receive free schooling for four months each year. At first, most Mississippians opposed public schools. The Civil War had caused hard times and the people had little money for school taxes. But by the 1890's, conditions had improved and the public school system had won general approval. In 1904, the state established a textbook commission, now a division within the State Department of Education. The division supplies books to all children in public and private schools. In 1908, Mississippi provided for the establishment of agricultural high schools.

The state school system was reorganized during the 1950's, 1960's, and early 1980's. The aim was to improve the schools by consolidating small districts (see **Consolidated school**). To meet the need for workers in new industry and business, Mississippi has also established a network of vocational-technical training centers at both the high school and junior college levels. The state also has enacted reforms to provide more equal access to learning throughout the state.

Like other Southern states, Mississippi had separate schools for blacks and whites for many years. In 1954, the Supreme Court of the United States ruled that public school segregation on the basis of race is unconstitutional. The first racial integration in Mississippi public schools took place in 1964. Today, all the state's public school districts are integrated. Children from 6 through 16 years of age must attend school.

The state superintendent of public education directs Mississippi's elementary and secondary schools. A nine-member state board of education selects the superintendent. The governor appoints five of the board of education members. The lieutenant governor and the Speaker of the state House of Representatives each appoint two members of the board. For the number of students and teachers in Mississippi, see **Education** (table).

Libraries. The first public library in Mississippi was established in Port Gibson in 1818. Today, there are more than 250 public libraries in the state.

Several college and university libraries in Mississippi have outstanding collections. These collections include the William Faulkner and Stark Young collections at the University of Mississippi, the John C. Stennis Collection at Mississippi State University, and the Lena Y. de Grummond and Cleanth Brooks literature collections at the University of Southern Mississippi. The Mississippi Department of Archives library has the most complete collection of historical information on Mississippi.

Museums. Mississippi has one of the nation's finest historical museums, in the restored Old Capitol in Jackson. Other historical museums include the Old Courthouse Museum in Vicksburg, and the Jefferson Davis Shrine at Beauvoir House near Biloxi. Art museums include the Mississippi Museum of Art in Jackson, the Mary Buie Museum in Oxford, and the Lauren Rogers Library and Museum of Art in Laurel. The Mississippi Museum of Natural Science in Jackson features many exhibits of natural history.

Universities and colleges

Mississippi has 17 universities and colleges that grant bachelor's or advanced degrees and are accredited by the Southern Association of Colleges and Schools. For enrollments and further information, see **Universities and colleges** (table).

Name	Mailing address	Name	Mailing address
Alcorn State University	Lorman	Mississippi University	
Belhaven College	Jackson	for Women	Columbus
Blue Mountain College	Blue Mountain	Mississippi Valley State	
Delta State University	Cleveland	University	Itta Bena
Jackson State University	Jackson	Reformed Theological Seminary	Jackson
Magnolia Bible College	Kosciusko	Rust College	Holly Springs
Millsaps College	Jackson	Southern Mississippi,	
Mississippi, University of	*	University of	Hattiesburg
Mississippi College	Clinton	Tougaloo College	Tougaloo
Mississippi State University	Mississippi State	William Carey College	Hattiesburg

*For campuses and founding dates, see **Universities and colleges** (table).

Mississippi Division of Tourism

The University of Southern Mississippi is located in Hattiesburg. The university's administration building is shown above.

© Tom Kraak, Creative Pictures

The Mississippi State Historical Museum, founded in 1902, is located in the Old Capitol in Jackson.

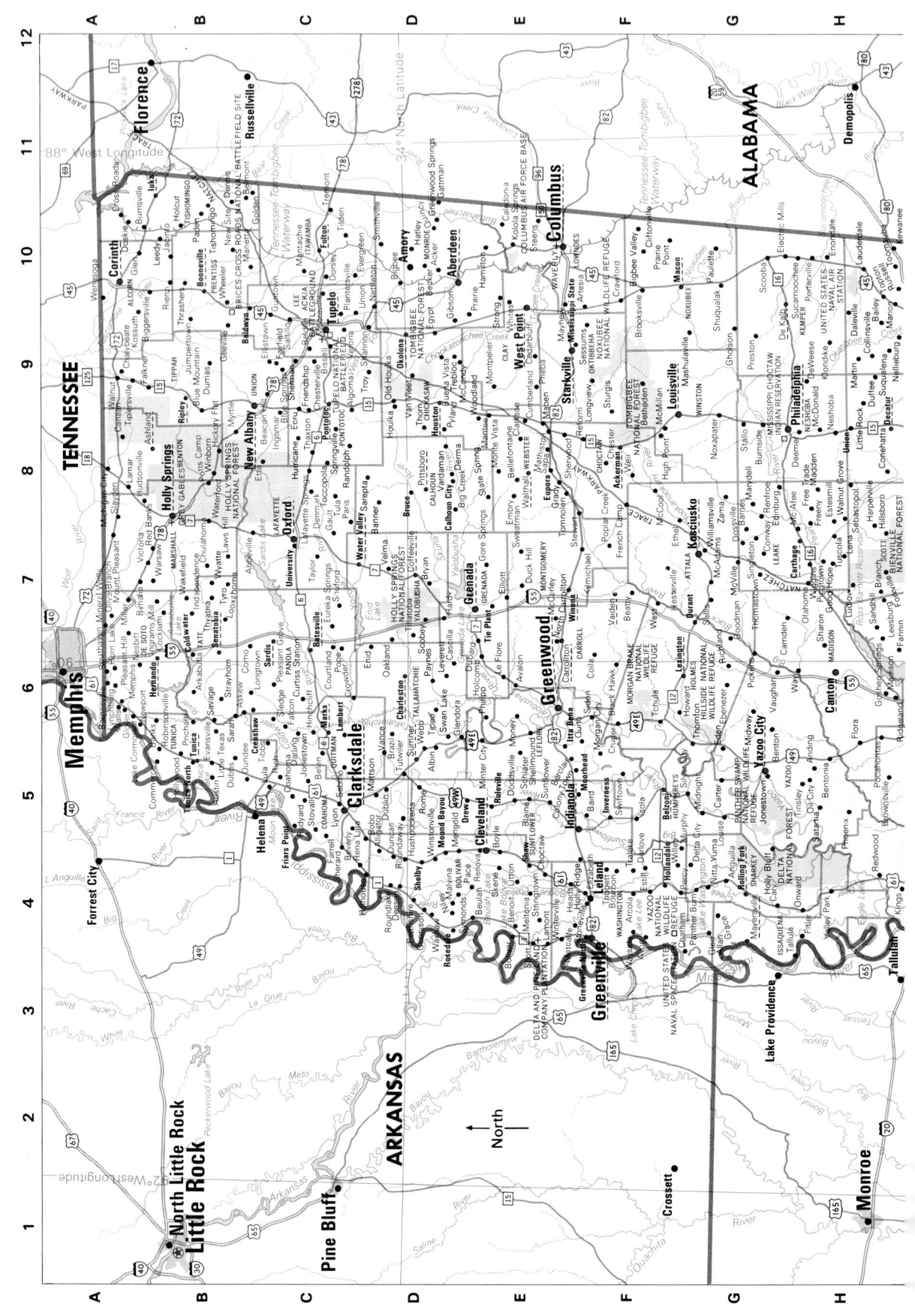

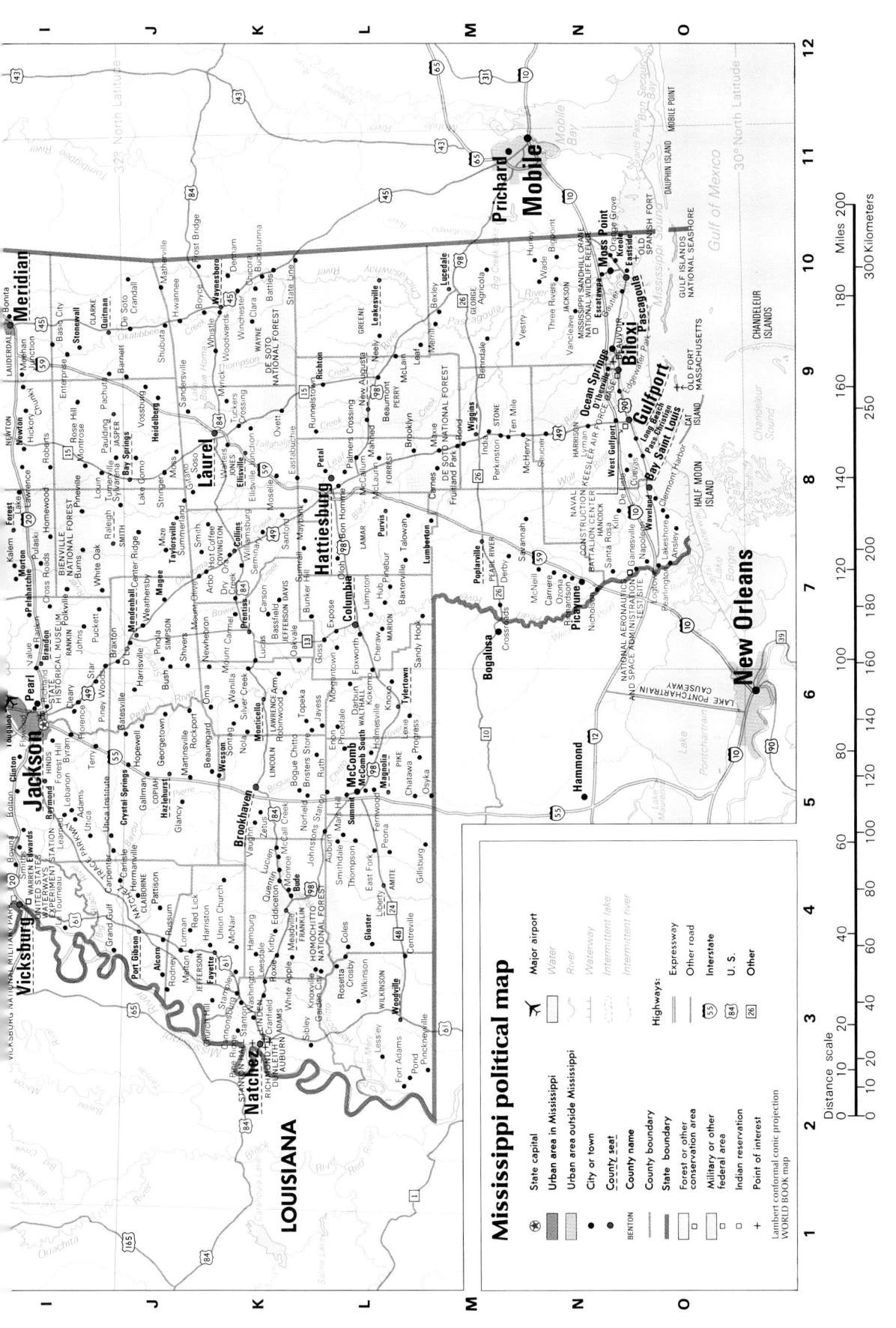

Mississippi political map

⊛	State capital	
	Urban area in Mississippi	
	Urban area outside Mississippi	
●	City or town	
<u>BENTON</u>	County seat	
	County name	
	County boundary	
	State boundary	
	Forest or other conservation area	
	Military or other federal area	
	Indian reservation	
+	Point of interest	
✈	Major airport	

	Water
	River
	Waterway
	Intermittent lake
	Intermittent river

Highways:
	Expressway
	Other road
55	Interstate
84	U. S.
26	Other

Distance scale
0   10   20   30   40 Miles
0   10   20   30   40 50 60 Kilometers

Lambert conformal conic projection
WORLD BOOK map

LOUISIANA

Mississippi map index

Delta Queen Steamboat Co.

The *Delta Queen,* a famous sternwheel riverboat, stops at several Mississippi ports on its tours up and down the Mississippi River. The steam-powered boat was built in 1926.

The Gulf Coast of Mississippi is one of the nation's most popular resort regions. This vacationland has won fame for its large, sunny beaches and fine hotels. In other parts of the state, historic monuments and pleasant wooded areas are the chief attractions. Thousands of visitors also take tours of Mississippi's many old mansions and plantations. There, they can get some idea of what life was like in Mississippi before the Civil War. Pretty hostesses dressed in billowing hoop skirts serve as guides.

Excellent hunting and fishing in about 25 Wildlife Management areas attract many people to Mississippi. Hunters may shoot such animals as wild doves, ducks, geese, quail, turkeys, deer, rabbits, raccoons, and squir-rels. Thousands of Mississippi ponds and lakes have been stocked with fish. People can cast in fresh water for bass, bream, crappies, and other fishes. Or they may sit lazily on the banks of a Mississippi river or pond and wait for catfish to take their bait. Salt-water fishing enthusiasts fight big game fish in the waters off the Gulf Coast of Mississippi.

One of the highlights of Mississippi's many annual events is the Shrimp Festival in Biloxi. This event takes place during the first week of June. The Shrimp Festival marks the opening of the shrimp-fishing season in Mississippi. Highlights of the celebration include a street dance, the crowning of a shrimp queen, and the blessing of the shrimp fleet.

Elvis Presley's birthplace in Tupelo

© Tom Kraak, Creative Pictures

Places to visit

Following are brief descriptions of some of Mississippi's most interesting places to visit:

Capitols, in Jackson, offer many reminders of the state's rich history. The Old Capitol, now the State Historical Museum, was built chiefly by slave labor between 1833 and 1842. Here, Mississippi voted in January 1861 to secede from the Union. The New Capitol, which was built in 1903, houses the state Legislature and the governor's offices.

Churches. The Church of the Holy Trinity in Vicksburg, completed in 1880, has a memorial honoring the Union and Confederate soldiers who fought in the siege of Vicksburg. St. Paul's Episcopal Church in Woodville dates from 1824, and the First Presbyterian Church in Port Gibson from 1829.

Delta Blues Museum, in Clarksdale, includes videotaped presentations, photographs, sound-and-slide shows, and memorabilia of the blues artists and their music.

Elvis Presley's birthplace, at Tupelo in northeastern Mississippi, marks the site where the famous singer was born. The tiny house where Presley spent his early years is now part of Elvis Presley Park.

Florewood River Plantation, in the Delta near Greenwood, is a state park and museum. It has 22 buildings that show what life was like on a cotton plantation before the Civil War.

Fort Massachusetts, on Ship Island, was a Union stronghold during the Civil War. Union forces captured the fort from the Confederates in 1861. Another interesting historic site is the Old Spanish Fort in Pascagoula, one of the oldest buildings on the Gulf Coast. It was part of a settlement and fort built in 1718.

Mount Locust is a restored inn along the Natchez Trace Parkway near Fayette. It was built in 1777 as a stopping place for travelers on the Natchez Trace, an important pioneer route between Natchez and Nashville, Tenn.

Petrified Forest, near Flora, contains giant stone trees dating back 30 million years. Facilities there include a nature trail, a geological museum, a rock and gem shop, and picnic areas.

Smith Robertson Museum and Cultural Center, in Jackson, has exhibits that depict the experience and heritage of black Mississippians from their African roots to the present. The museum is housed in the former Smith Robertson School, the first public school for blacks in Jackson.

Stately old homes in or near Natchez are reminders of the way of life of wealthy Mississippians before the Civil War. These mansions include Auburn (built in 1812), D'Evereux (1840), Dunleith (1856), Edgewood (1860), Gloucester (1804), Linden (1789), Melrose (1845), Monteigne (1853), Richmond (1786), Rosalie (1820), and Stanton Hall (1857). Cedar Grove (1842) and McRaven (1797) are in Vicksburg. Other homes include Waverley (1852) near Columbus, Grey Gables (1830) in Holly Springs, and Hampton Hall (1832) near Woodville.

Jefferson Davis spent his boyhood at Rosemont, near Woodville. At Biloxi stands Beauvoir, Davis' last home. Beauvoir is now a shrine and a museum.

Vicksburg National Military Park honors the siege of Vicksburg, which lasted from May 19 to July 4, 1863. The siege, which ended in a Union victory, was a major turning point of the Civil War. Monuments in the park honor the states represented in the battle. Each state's monument is located at the site where that state's troops drew their battle lines.

National forests. Mississippi has six national forests. The largest of these is De Soto in southeastern Mississippi. The state's other five national forests are Homochitto in the southwest; Bienville, Delta, and Tombigbee in central Mississippi; and Holly Springs in the northern part of the state.

State parks. Mississippi has 27 state parks. For information on these state parks, write to Department of Wildlife, Fisheries and Parks, P.O. Box 451, Jackson, MS 39205.

© Tom Kraak, Creative Pictures

Vicksburg National Military Park

Shostal

Beauvoir, last home of Jefferson Davis

Annual events

January-February
Dixie National Livestock Show and Rodeo in Jackson (February); Mardi Gras festivities in various cities on the Mississippi Gulf Coast (February).

March-June
Garden Club Pilgrimages of Antebellum Homes in Columbus, Holly Springs, Natchez, Port Gibson, Vicksburg, and other communities (March-April); D'Iberville Landing and Historical Ball in Ocean Springs (April); Deposit Guaranty Bank Golf Classic in Hattiesburg (April); Railroad Festival in Amory (April); World Catfish Festival in Belzoni (April); Atwood Blue-grass Festival in Monticello (May); Jubilee Jam Art and Music Festival in Jackson (May); Flea Market in Canton (May); Jimmy Rodgers Memorial Festival in Meridian (May); St. Jude Open Bass Classic in Sardis (May); Blessing of the Fleet and Shrimp Festival in Biloxi (June); National Tobacco Spitting Contest in Raleigh (June).

July-September
Choctaw Indian Fair in Philadelphia (July); Mississippi Deep Sea Fishing Rodeo in Gulfport (July); Watermelon Festival in Mize (July); Crop Day in Greenwood (August); Neshoba County Fair in Philadelphia (August); Delta Blues Festival in Greenville (September); Grand Village of the Natchez Indians Festival in Natchez (September); Seafood Festival in Biloxi (September).

October-December
Mississippi State Fair in Jackson (second week of October); Natchez Fall Pilgrimage in Natchez (October); Scottish Highland Games in Biloxi (November); Sweet Potato Festival in Vardaman (November); Christmas in Natchez (December); Trees of Christmas Festival in Meridian (December).

© Dan Guravich

Blessing of the fleet at the Biloxi Shrimp Festival

Land and climate

Land regions. Mississippi has two main land regions: (1) the Mississippi Alluvial Plain, and (2) the East Gulf Coastal Plain.

The Mississippi Alluvial Plain covers the entire western edge of the state. It consists of fertile lowlands and forms part of the 35,000-square-mile (90,600-square-kilometer) Alluvial Plain of the Mississippi River. The region is quite narrow south of Vicksburg. North of the city, the plain spreads out and covers the area between the Mississippi River and the Yazoo, Tallahatchie, and Coldwater rivers. Floodwaters of the rivers have enriched the soil of the region with deposits of silt. The fertile soil of the Mississippi Alluvial Plain is famous for its large cotton and soybean crops. Most Mississippians call this region the *Delta.*

The East Gulf Coastal Plain extends over all the state east of the Alluvial Plain. Most of the region is made up of low, rolling, forested hills. The coastal plain also has prairies and lowlands. Yellowish-brown *loess* (soil blown by winds) covers the region in the west. Most Mississippians call these deposits the Cane, Bluff, or Loess Hills. The Tennessee River Hills rise in northeastern Mississippi. They include the highest point in the state, 806-foot (246-meter) Woodall Mountain. The Pine Hills, often called the Piney Woods, rise in the southeastern part of the region. They are covered largely with longleaf and slash-pine forests.

The main prairie is called the *Black Belt* or *Black Prairie* because its soil is largely black in color. This long, narrow prairie lies in the northeast section of the state.

The Black Belt stretches through 10 counties. Livestock graze there, and corn and hay grow well on the farmlands of the Black Belt. Small prairies also lie in central Mississippi, east of Jackson. Along the Mississippi Sound, lowlands stretch inland over the southern portion of the region.

Coastline. Mississippi has a coastline of 44 miles (71 kilometers) along the Gulf of Mexico. With bays and coves, it has a total shoreline of 359 miles (578 kilometers). The largest bays include Biloxi, St. Louis, and Pascagoula. The nation's longest sea wall protects about 25 miles (40 kilometers) of coastline between Biloxi and Point Henderson at Pass Christian. Other coastal towns include Bay St. Louis, Gulfport, and Ocean Springs. Deer Island is near the mouth of Biloxi Bay, and a chain of small islands lies off the coast. They include Cat, Horn, Ship, and Petit Bois islands. Mississippi Sound separates them from the mainland.

Rivers and lakes. Mississippi has many rivers and lakes. The nation's most important river, the Mississippi, forms most of the state's western border. Its floodwaters, in earlier times, often deposited silt on the land, and helped make the land fertile. In some years, heavy floods damaged crops and homes. Today, wide *levees* (dikes) help protect many areas against damaging floods (see **Levee; Mississippi River**).

The state has several main river basins. The rivers of the western and north-central basin drain into the Mississippi River. These rivers include the Big Black River and the Yazoo River with its tributaries, the Coldwater,

© Dan Guravich

The Yazoo River flows through the Mississippi Alluvial Plain, a region known to most Mississippians as the *Delta.* The region's fertile soil produces large cotton and soybean crops.

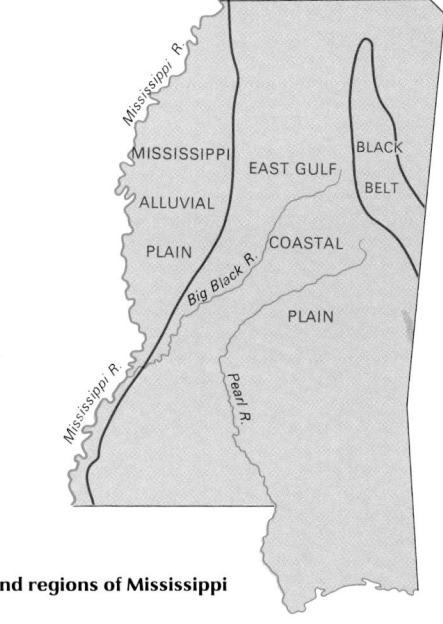

Land regions of Mississippi

Map index

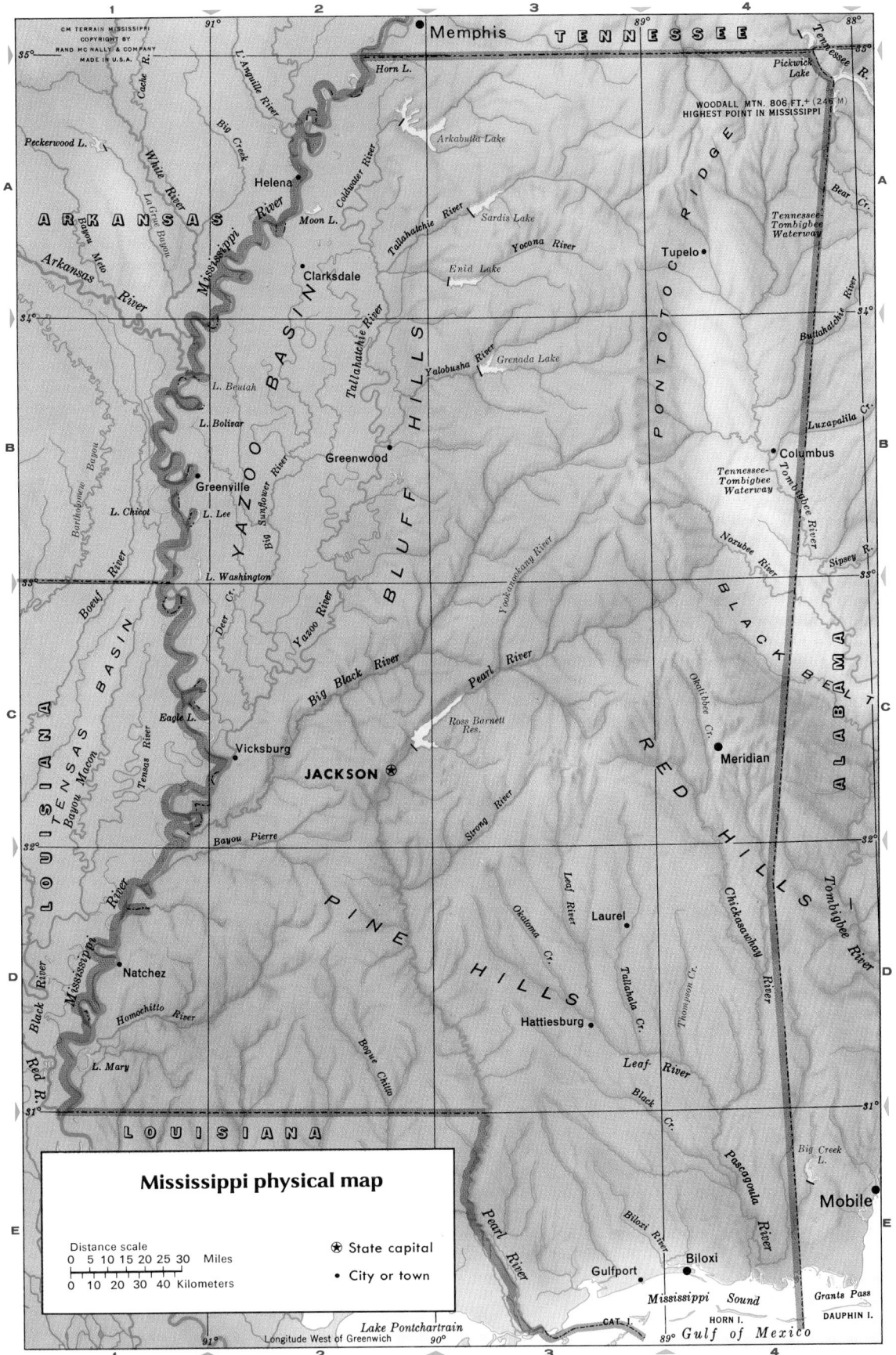

Mississippi physical map

Distance scale

0 5 10 15 20 25 30 Miles

0 10 20 30 40 Kilometers

⊛ State capital

• City or town

WOODALL MTN. 806 FT.⁺ (245 M)
HIGHEST POINT IN MISSISSIPPI

TENNESSEE

ARKANSAS

LOUISIANA

ALABAMA

Memphis

Helena

Clarksdale

Greenwood

Greenville

Vicksburg

JACKSON

Natchez

Tupelo

Columbus

Meridian

Laurel

Hattiesburg

Gulfport

Biloxi

Mobile

YAZOO BASIN

BLUFF HILLS

LOUTENSAS BASIN

ARKANSAS BASIN

PINE HILLS

RED HILLS

BLACK BELT

PONTOTOC RIDGE

Mississippi River

White River

Arkansas River

Cache R.

L'Anguilla River

Big Creek

Coldwater River

Tallahatchie River

Yocona River

Yalobusha River

Tallahatchie River

Sunflower River

Yazoo River

Big Black River

Pearl River

Yockanookany River

Strong River

Bogue Chitto

Leaf River

Okatoma Cr.

Tallahala Cr.

Leaf River

Black Cr.

Pearl River

Biloxi River

Pascagoula River

Chickasawhay River

Thompson Cr.

Noxubee River

Tombigbee River

Buttahatchie River

Luxapalila Cr.

Sipsey R.

Bear Cr.

Tennessee R.

Tennessee-Tombigbee Waterway

Tennessee-Tombigbee Waterway

Okatibbee Cr.

Homochitto River

Black River

Red R.

Mississippi River

Bayou Pierre

Bayou Macon

Tensas River

Deer Cr.

Boeuf River

Bayou Meto

Bayou Bartholomew

LaGrue Bayou

Peckerwood L.

Horn L.

Arkabutla Lake

Moon L.

Sardis Lake

Enid Lake

Grenada Lake

L. Beulah

L. Bolivar

L. Chicot

L. Lee

L. Washington

Eagle L.

Ross Barnett Res.

L. Mary

Big Creek L.

Pickwick Lake

Lake Pontchartrain

Mississippi Sound

Gulf of Mexico

CAT I.

HORN I.

DAUPHIN I.

Grants Pass

Longitude West of Greenwich

35°

34°

33°

32°

31°

91°

89°

88°

90°

Specially created for *The World Book Encyclopedia* by Rand McNally and World Book editors

The Piney Woods cover most of southeastern Mississippi in the state's East Gulf Coastal Plain region. These abundant pine forests provide pine oil, rosin, and turpentine, as well as lumber.

© Dan Guravich

Big Sunflower, and Tallahatchie rivers. Rivers of the eastern basin drain into the Gulf of Mexico. They include the Pearl, Pascagoula, and Tombigbee. Many of Mississippi's lakes are artificially created reservoirs, such as Pickwick Lake in the northeastern corner of the state. Other artificially created lakes include Arkabutla, Enid, Grenada, and Sardis, all of which are in north-central Mississippi. These lakes lie behind flood-control dams. In the early 1960's, the large Ross Barnett Reservoir was built on the Pearl River near Jackson.

The Mississippi River has formed many *oxbow lakes,* mostly north of Vicksburg. These lakes form when a river changes its course to take short cuts (see **Oxbow lake**). Oxbow lakes found in Mississippi include Beulah, Lee, Moon, and Washington. Mississippi also has many slow-moving streams called *bayous.* Some of Mississippi's bayous connect the lakes with the rivers in the Delta. Others link the inland waterways with the Gulf of Mexico.

Plant and animal life. Forests cover more than half of Mississippi. Pine trees are important as a source of lumber. Loblolly, longleaf, and slash pines grow in the Piney Woods area. The shortleaf pine grows in the northern and central sections of the state. Other trees that grow in Mississippi include the ash, bald cypress, cottonwood, elm, hickory, oak, pecan, sweet gum, and tupelo.

The magnolia, an evergreen tree with fragrant white flowers, grows throughout the state. The magnolia is Mississippi's state flower. Many parts of the state also have azaleas, black-eyed Susans, camellias, crepe myrtle, dogwood, redbud, violets, Virginia creepers, and pink and white Cherokee roses.

Animal life in Mississippi includes beavers, deer, foxes, opossums, rabbits, and squirrels. Among the state's game birds are wild doves, ducks, quails, and turkeys. The mockingbird is Mississippi's state bird. Freshwater fish found in the state's waters include bass, bream, catfish, and crappies. In the Gulf waters are crabs, oysters, shrimp, menhaden, mackerel, and speckled trout.

Climate. Mississippi has a warm, moist climate, with long summers and short winters. In July, Mississippi temperatures average about 81° F. (27° C). Winds from the Gulf of Mexico, and frequent thundershowers, cool much of the state during the summers. Even in the interior part of the state, the temperature seldom goes above 100° F. (38° C). However, temperatures of 90° F. (32° C) or higher occur about 55 days a year on the Gulf Coast and more often in the interior. The highest temperature recorded in Mississippi was 115° F. (46° C) at Holly Springs on July 29, 1930.

January temperatures average 46° F. (8° C) in Mississippi. The lowest temperature was −19° F. (−28° C), recorded at Corinth on Jan. 30, 1966. Northern and central Mississippi occasionally have ice and snow. The Gulf Coast ordinarily has a frost-free season of 250 to 300 days.

Mississippi's *precipitation* (rain, melted snow, and other forms of moisture) ranges from about 50 inches (130 centimeters) a year in the northwestern part of the state to about 65 inches (165 centimeters) in the southeastern part. Hurricanes sometimes sweep northward from the Gulf in late summer and fall.

Average monthly weather

	Jackson						Meridian					
	Temperatures				**Days of rain or snow**		**Temperatures**				**Days of rain or snow**
	F°		**C°**				**F°**		**C°**		
	High	**Low**	**High**	**Low**			**High**	**Low**	**High**	**Low**	
Jan.	59	38	15	3	11	Jan.	59	37	15	3	10
Feb.	62	40	17	4	11	Feb.	62	39	17	4	10
Mar.	68	46	20	8	10	Mar.	68	45	20	7	10
Apr.	76	54	24	12	9	Apr.	77	52	25	11	8
May	84	61	29	16	9	May	84	59	29	15	10
June	91	68	33	20	9	June	91	67	33	19	10
July	94	71	34	22	11	July	92	70	33	21	12
Aug.	93	70	34	21	7	Aug.	92	69	33	21	10
Sept.	89	65	32	18	7	Sept.	87	64	31	18	7
Oct.	80	53	27	12	5	Oct.	78	51	26	11	5
Nov.	67	43	19	6	8	Nov.	67	41	19	5	7
Dec.	59	39	15	4	10	Dec.	60	37	16	3	10

Average January temperatures
Mississippi has mild winters. The mildest weather occurs in the far south. Temperatures decrease to the north.

Average July temperatures
Mississippi has hot summers with little temperature variation. The west and south are slightly warmer.

Average yearly precipitation
Mississippi has a rainy climate. The heaviest rains fall in the far south, brought by winds from the Gulf of Mexico.

WORLD BOOK maps

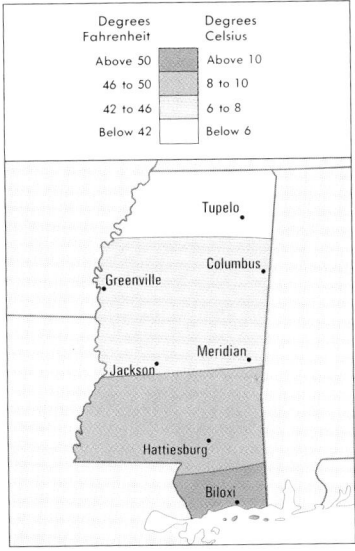

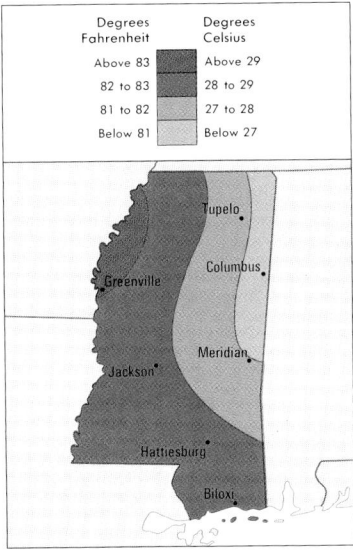

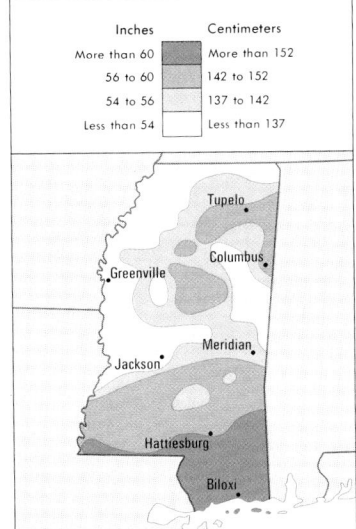

Economy

Service industries, taken together, account for nearly two-thirds of Mississippi's *gross state product*—the total value of all goods and services produced in a state in a year. However, manufacturing is the single most valuable economic activity. It accounts for more than a fourth of the gross state product.

Natural resources of Mississippi include rich soils, abundant water supplies, valuable mineral deposits, and large forests.

Soil and water are the state's most important natural resources. The Mississippi Alluvial Plain has some of the richest soil in the United States. Much of this fertile earth is silt deposited by floodwaters of the Mississippi River. Another fertile area of clay loam soils is in the Black Belt. These soils are gray or black in color. Sandy loam soil covers most of the East Gulf Coastal Plain. Mississippi has great supplies of surface water, and also many wells. Together, they furnish abundant fresh water for home and industrial use.

Minerals. Petroleum is the most valuable mineral resource of Mississippi. The chief oil deposits are in southern Mississippi. The state also has valuable deposits of natural gas. The largest deposits are located in the south-central and southwestern counties.

Mississippi has many kinds of clays that are used by industry. They include bentonite, used to lubricate oil well drills, and fuller's earth, used in refining fats and oils. Other clays are ball clays, kaolin, and certain clays suitable for making brick and tile. Low-grade bauxite is found in an area that extends from Tippah County to Kemper County.

Large deposits of sand and gravel are found in the state. Tishomingo County has large deposits of sandstone. Other mineral resources include iron ore, lignite, limestone, and salt.

Forests cover more than half of Mississippi. They provide the raw materials for a huge output of products that make Mississippi a leading forest industry state. About 120 kinds of trees grow in Mississippi. The most important are the loblolly, longleaf, and slash pines of the Piney Woods area, and the shortleaf pine of northern

Production and workers by economic activities

Economic activities	Percent of GSP* produced	Employed workers Number of persons	Employed workers Percent of total
Manufacturing	28	246,400	25
Wholesale and retail trade	14	197,300	20
Finance, insurance, & real estate	14	38,800	4
Government	13	203,800	20
Community, social, & personal services	13	165,500	17
Transportation, communication, & utilities	9	44,800	5
Agriculture	4	50,800	5
Construction	4	34,600	4
Mining	1	5,600	†
Total	100	987,600	100

*GSP = gross state product, the total value of goods and services produced in a year.
†Less than 1 percent.
Figures are for 1991.
Sources: *World Book* estimates based on data from U.S. Bureau of Economic Analysis, U.S. Bureau of Labor Statistics, and U.S. Department of Agriculture.

and central Mississippi. Other trees include the ash, baldcypress, cottonwood, elm, hickory, oak, pecan, sweet gum, and tupelo. Mississippi conducts a widespread program of planting young trees to replace those that are cut down. Mississippi has about 5,700 tree farms—more than any other state.

Service industries provide 63 per cent of the gross state product of Mississippi. The state's leading service industries are (1) wholesale and retail trade, and (2) finance, insurance, and real estate. The wholesale trade of automobiles, farm and forest products, and petroleum are especially important in Mississippi. Retail trade is one of the leading employers. Major types of retail establishments are automobile dealerships, grocery stores, and restaurants. Jackson is the state's leading center of trade.

Jackson is the state's leading financial city. Most of Mississippi's major insurance and real estate firms are based in the Jackson area, as are the largest banks. Grenada, Gulfport, and Tupelo also have large banks.

Next in importance among Mississippi service industries are (1) government and (2) community, social, and personal services. Both of these industries contribute an equal portion of Mississippi's gross state product. Government services include the operation of public schools and hospitals, and military establishments. State and local education systems are the leading government employers. The distribution of government social services is important because of the many poor people in the state. Major military establishments in the state include Keesler Air Force Base in Biloxi and the John C. Stennis Space Center in Hancock County. The Stennis Space Center is the primary rocket test site of the National Aeronautics and Space Administration (NASA).

Community, social, and personal services include such activities as the operation of private hospitals and doctors' offices, hotels, law firms, and repair shops. More than half of the hotel revenue comes from the Biloxi and Jackson areas. Most people in Mississippi's largest cities have access to quality health care, but many rural areas do not have an adequate number of nearby hospitals or doctors.

The last type of service industry consists of transportation, communication, and utilities. Mississippi's location in the heart of the Southeast and along the Mississippi River makes it an important transportation state. More information about transportation and communication appears later in this section.

Manufacturing accounts for 28 per cent of the gross state product. Goods manufactured in Mississippi have an annual *value added by manufacture* of about $10\frac{1}{2}$ billion. This figure represents the increase in value of raw materials after they become finished products. Mississippi has one of the most diverse manufacturing sectors of any state. Many types of manufactured products contribute a nearly equal amount of income.

Food processing is Mississippi's leading manufacturing activity. Meat packing is especially important. Forest, Laurel, and Morton have large poultry processing plants. Other important food products include beverages, dairy products, grain products, and seasonings.

Transportation equipment ranks second among the state's manufactured products. Large shipyards in Pascagoula build freighters and tankers, making shipbuilding

the most important activity of this industry. The production of motor-vehicle parts is the other major activity.

The production of electrical equipment ranks third among Mississippi's manufacturing activities. Chief products of this industry are appliances, generators, lighting and wiring equipment, motors, stereo systems, and telephones. Important centers of production include Columbus, Jackson, Mendenhall, and Meridian.

Wood products are the fourth-ranking manufactured product. Mississippi ranks among the leading lumber-producing states. Large wood-processing plants operate in Columbus, Laurel, Louisville, and Vicksburg.

Other products manufactured in Mississippi, in order of value, include paper products, clothing, furniture, chemicals, and machinery. Larger paper mills are at Moss Point and Natchez. Factories that produce furniture are located primarily in the northeastern part of the state and near Jackson. The clothing industry employs more people than any other manufacturing activity in Mississippi. Chief products include dresses, shirts, slacks, and work clothes.

Agriculture provides 4 per cent of the gross state product. Mississippi has about 38,000 farms. These farms cover about half the state and have an average size of 337 acres (136 hectares). Livestock farms provide about 55 per cent of the total farm income and crop farms provide about 45 per cent.

Farm, mineral, and forest products

This map shows where the state's leading farm, mineral, and forest products are produced. The major urban area (shown on the map in red) is the state's important manufacturing center.

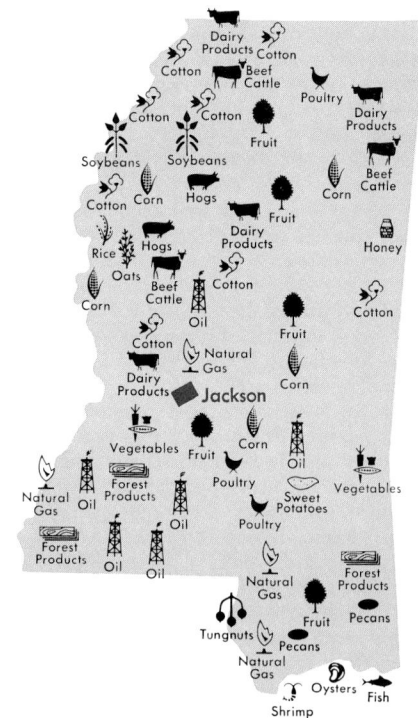

WORLD BOOK map

Harris Barnes, Jr.

Cotton is one of Mississippi's most valuable farm products. These mechanical pickers are harvesting cotton in the Delta.

Broilers (chickens from 5 to 12 weeks old) are the leading livestock product in Mississippi. The largest concentration of poultry farms lies within a triangular region formed by Hattiesburg, Jackson, and Meridian. Some farmers raise hens to produce eggs.

Beef and dairy cattle are also major sources of farm income in Mississippi. The state's cattle farmers benefit from the mild climate, which allows for long growing seasons for feed crops. Cattle farms are common in all regions except the Mississippi Delta. Some farmers raise hogs or sheep.

Cotton and soybeans are the state's most valuable crops. Mississippi ranks among the leading producers of both of these crops. The northwestern part of the state is the major cotton-growing area, and the northeastern part of the state is the major soybean-growing area. Mississippi farmers grow large amounts of corn, grain sorghum, and hay for livestock feed. Other crops include peanuts, rice, and wheat.

Mississippi also produces valuable amounts of cottonseed, greenhouse and nursery products, and pecans. The state's leading vegetables are sweet potatoes, cucumbers, and cowpeas. Important fruits are peaches, watermelons, and muscadine grapes.

Mining accounts for 1 per cent of the gross state product. Petroleum and natural gas account for about 90 per cent of the value of the state's mined products. Petroleum production is heaviest in the region surrounding Laurel in the southeast part of the state. Major production also occurs in the southwest corner of Mississippi. South-central Mississippi has many natural gas wells. Rankin County, just east of Jackson, accounts for a fifth of the state's natural gas production.

Mississippi's other mineral products include clays, crushed stone, and sand and gravel. Clays mined in the state are ball clay, bentonite, common clay, and fuller's earth. Limestone quarries along the state's eastern border are the main source of crushed stone.

Fishing industry. Mississippi is a leading shrimp-fishing state. Biloxi is Mississippi's chief shrimp-packing port. Pascagoula ranks as another center of the state's fishing industry. The saltwater catch includes menhaden, oysters, and red snapper. The freshwater catch in Mississippi includes buffalo fish, carp, and catfish. Mississippi is the leading producer of farm-raised catfish. The Alluvial Plain is the center of the state's thriving catfish farming and processing industry.

Electric power. Coal-burning plants and nuclear plants each generate about 40 per cent of the electricity in Mississippi. Plants that burn natural gas provide most of the rest. Petroleum-burning plants provide a small amount of the state's electricity. A nuclear plant operates in Grand Gulf. Mississippi buys some of its electric power from the Tennessee Valley Authority.

Transportation. Mississippi has one of the finest highway systems in the South. The state has about 73,000 miles (117,000 kilometers) of highways. Jackson has the state's only major commercial airport. About 17 railroads provide freight service, and passenger trains serve about 15 cities in the state.

Mississippi has two major deepwater seaports, Gulfport and Pascagoula. The Mississippi River connects Mississippi with many inland states. The state's leading river ports are Greenville, Natchez, Rosedale, and Vicksburg. The Tennessee-Tombigbee Waterway, which connects the Tennessee and Tombigbee rivers, provides cities in northeastern Mississippi with more direct access to ports on the Gulf of Mexico.

Communication. About 140 newspapers are published in Mississippi, including about 20 dailies. About 35 periodicals also are published in Mississippi. The state has about 150 radio stations and about 20 television stations.

Mississippi's earliest newspapers, all published in Natchez, were the *Mississippi Gazette* (established in 1799), the *Intelligencer* (1801), and the *Mississippi Herald* (1802). The oldest newspaper still published in Mississippi, the *Woodville Republican*, was founded in 1823. Dailies with the largest circulations include *The Sun Herald* of Biloxi and Gulfport, *The Clarion-Ledger* of Jackson, and the *Northeast Mississippi Daily Journal of Tupelo*.

Government

Constitution. Mississippi adopted its present Constitution in 1890. The state had three earlier constitutions, adopted in 1817, 1832, and 1869. The Constitution of 1869 was written so that Mississippi could qualify to re-enter the Union after the Civil War. An *amendment* (change) to the Constitution must be approved by two-thirds of the members of each house of the state Legislature. Then the amendment must be approved by a majority of the people voting on the amendment in an elec-tion. The Constitution may also be amended by a constitutional convention that is called by a majority of each house.

Executive. The governor of Mississippi is elected to a four-year term and may not serve more than two terms. Other executive officers who are elected to four-year terms in Mississippi include the lieutenant governor, secretary of state, treasurer, auditor, attorney general, commissioner of agriculture and commerce, public service and transportation commissioners, and commissioner of insurance.

Legislature of Mississippi consists of a Senate of 52 members and a House of Representatives of 122 members. State legislators are elected to four-year terms. Regular legislative sessions begin on the Tuesday after the first Monday in January each year. Most of the sessions last 90 days. The Legislature may extend the sessions. Every fourth year, the regular session lasts 125 days. The governor may call special sessions.

Courts in Mississippi are headed by the Supreme Court. The people elect the nine Supreme Court justices to eight-year terms. Three are elected from each of three districts that were set up for electing Supreme Court justices. The justice who has served the longest acts as chief justice. All other judges are elected to four-year terms. The chief trial courts are chancery courts, whose judges handle civil and equity cases, and circuit courts, whose judges handle civil and criminal cases. Other courts include county, justice, and juvenile courts.

Local government. The county is the chief unit of local government in Mississippi. The state has 82 counties, each with five districts. The people of each district elect one of the five members of a county board of supervisors, which administers the county. Most cities have the mayor-council form of government. The Legislature controls the county and city governments.

Revenue. Taxation provides almost 60 per cent of the state government's *general revenue* (income). Most of the state's remaining revenue comes from grants received from the federal government and from other United States government programs. The state receives about half of its tax revenue from a sales tax. Other large sources of revenue in Mississippi include individual and corporation income taxes and taxes on motor fuels. Additional state government revenue comes from license fees and taxes levied on alcoholic beverages, insurance, petroleum mining, and tobacco products.

Politics. The Democratic Party has controlled Mississippi politics throughout most of the state's history. Since 1876, almost all Mississippi governors and most state and local officials have been Democrats. Before the 1963 election, Republicans rarely nominated candidates for many state and local offices. As a result, nomination by the Democratic party in primary elections almost always meant election to office. During the 1980's, however, Republican candidates won several U.S. congressional elections. In 1991, Kirk Fordice became the first Republican to be elected governor since 1874.

In presidential elections since 1876, Mississippi has cast its electoral votes for the Democratic candidate in every election except nine—all after 1944. In 1948, Mississippi voted for Governor Strom Thurmond of South Carolina, the nominee of the Dixiecrat Party (see **Dixiecrat Party**). In 1960, the state chose electors who voted for Senator Harry F. Byrd of Virginia rather than for the Democratic nominee, Senator John F. Kennedy of Massachusetts. In 1964, Senator Barry M. Goldwater of Arizona became the first Republican presidential candidate to win in Mississippi since 1872. In 1968, the state's electors voted for George C. Wallace of Alabama. Wallace was the nominee of the American Independent Party (see **American Party**). Republican presidential candidates won in Mississippi in 1972, 1980, 1984, 1988, and 1992. For Mississippi's voting record in presidential elections since 1820, see **Electoral College** (table).

The governors of Mississippi

	Party	Term		Party	Term
David Holmes	* Dem.-Rep.	1817-1820	John M. Stone	Democratic	1876-1882
George Poindexter	Dem.-Rep.	1820-1822	Robert Lowry	Democratic	1882-1890
Walter Leake	Dem.-Rep.	1822-1825	John M. Stone	Democratic	1890-1896
Gerard C. Brandon	Dem.-Rep.	1825-1826	Anselm J. McLaurin	Democratic	1896-1900
David Holmes	Dem.-Rep.	1826	Andrew H. Longino	Democratic	1900-1904
Gerard C. Brandon	Dem.-Rep.	1826-1832	James K. Vardaman	Democratic	1904-1908
Abram M. Scott	Democratic	1832-1833	Edmond F. Noel	Democratic	1908-1912
Charles Lynch	Democratic	1833	Earl L. Brewer	Democratic	1912-1916
Hiram G. Runnels	Democratic	1833-1835	Theodore G. Bilbo	Democratic	1916-1920
John A. Quitman	Whig	1835-1836	Lee M. Russell	Democratic	1920-1924
Charles Lynch	Democratic	1836-1838	Henry L. Whitfield	Democratic	1924-1927
Alexander G. McNutt	Democratic	1838-1842	Dennis Murphree	Democratic	1927-1928
Tilghman M. Tucker	Democratic	1842-1844	Theodore G. Bilbo	Democratic	1928-1932
Albert G. Brown	Democratic	1844-1848	Martin Sennett Conner	Democratic	1932-1936
Joseph W. Matthews	Democratic	1848-1850	Hugh L. White	Democratic	1936-1940
John A. Quitman	Democratic	1850-1851	Paul B. Johnson	Democratic	1940-1943
John I. Guion	Democratic	1851	Dennis Murphree	Democratic	1943-1944
James Whitfield	Democratic	1851-1852	Thomas L. Bailey	Democratic	1944-1946
Henry S. Foote	† Union Dem.	1852-1854	Fielding L. Wright	Democratic	1946-1952
John J. Pettus	Democratic	1854	Hugh L. White	Democratic	1952-1956
John J. McRae	Democratic	1854-1857	James P. Coleman	Democratic	1956-1960
William McWillie	Democratic	1857-1859	Ross R. Barnett	Democratic	1960-1964
John J. Pettus	Democratic	1859-1863	Paul B. Johnson	Democratic	1964-1968
Charles Clark	Democratic	1863-1865	John Bell Williams	Democratic	1968-1972
William L. Sharkey	** Whig-Dem.	1865	William Waller	Democratic	1972-1976
Benjamin G. Humphreys	Whig	1865-1868	Cliff Finch	Democratic	1976-1980
Adelbert Ames	‡ U.S. Mil. Gov.	1868-1870	William F. Winter	Democratic	1980-1984
James L. Alcorn	Republican	1870-1871	William A. Allain	Democratic	1984-1988
Ridgley C. Powers	Republican	1871-1874	Ray Mabus	Democratic	1988-1992
Adelbert Ames	Republican	1874-1876	Kirk Fordice	Republican	1992-

*Democratic-Republican. †Union Democratic. **Whig-Democratic. ‡United States Military Governor.

Indian days. Three powerful Indian tribes once ruled the Mississippi region. The Chickasaw lived in the north and east, the Choctaw in the central area, and the Natchez in the southwest. They held power over the Chakchiuma, Tunica, and Yazoo tribes that lived along the Yazoo River, and the Biloxi and Pascagoula tribes of the Gulf Coast. Between 25,000 and 30,000 Indians lived in the Mississippi region when the first white explorers arrived. See **Indian, American** (table of tribes).

Exploration and early settlement. In 1540, the Spanish explorer Hernando de Soto became the first European to enter the Mississippi region. De Soto reached the Mississippi River in 1541 while searching for gold. The Spanish explorers found no treasure in the region and made no settlements there. In 1682, the French explorer Robert Cavelier, Sieur de la Salle, traveled down the Mississippi River from the Great Lakes to the Gulf of Mexico. Cavelier claimed the entire Mississippi Valley for France, and named it *Louisiana* for King Louis XIV. The region included present-day Mississippi.

In 1699, Pierre le Moyne, Sieur d'Iberville, established the first French settlement of the region at Old Biloxi (now Ocean Springs). In 1716, a second settlement was established by Jean Baptiste le Moyne, Sieur de Bienville, at Fort Rosalie (now Natchez). Three years later, in 1719, the first black slaves were brought to the region from West Africa. They worked in the rice and tobacco fields of the French colonists.

During the early 1700's, a scheme to develop the region was launched by John Law, a Scottish economist. Law's scheme failed and many people lost the money they had invested in his company. However, Law's venture brought much attention to Louisiana. As a result, thousands of settlers were attracted to the region (see **Mississippi Scheme**). Old Biloxi, New Biloxi (now Biloxi), and Fort Louis de la Mobile (now Mobile, Ala.) served as capital of the region at various times during the early 1700's. In 1722, the French made New Orleans, in present-day Louisiana, the capital of the region. At that time, Louisiana made up a vast territory that extended from the Allegheny Mountains to the Rocky Mountains.

Many difficulties delayed development of the region. At first, the Indians fought the settlers. Later, the British battled the French for possession of the newly settled land. In 1730, the French put down an uprising of the Natchez Indians, nearly wiping out the tribe. But in 1736, British troops helped the Chickasaw Indians defeat the French colonists in the northeastern part of present-day Mississippi. That defeat stopped the French from gaining control of the Mississippi Valley. During the French and Indian War (1754-1763), the British and the Chickasaw blocked the French in the lower Mississippi Valley from joining the French forces in the Ohio Valley. The Treaty of Paris, signed after the war, gave the British all the land east of the Mississippi River. Thus, the Mississippi region came under British rule. The southern portion became part of the British province called West Florida. Nearly all of the remaining area became part of the Georgia colony.

Territorial days. During the Revolutionary War (1775-1783), most of the settlers of West Florida remained loyal to Great Britain. But the Indians, trappers, and scouts of the rest of the Mississippi region supported the American Colonies. In 1781, because the British were so busy with their war with the colonies, Spain was able to take over West Florida. Two years later, Great Britain granted West Florida to Spain. After the British lost the war, the Mississippi region north of about the 32nd parallel was made part of the United States. The area between this boundary and the 31st parallel was claimed by both the United States and Spain. This area included the Natchez district. In 1795, the Spanish government accepted the 31st parallel as the border of the United States in the Pinckney Treaty (see **Pinckney Treaty**).

Congress organized the Mississippi Territory in 1798, with Natchez as the capital. Winthrop Sargent became the first governor of the new territory. It was bounded on the south by the 31st parallel, on the west by the Mississippi River, on the north by a line east from the mouth of the Yazoo River, and on the east by the Chattahoochee River. In 1803, the Louisiana Purchase made the Mississippi River part of the United States. Development of the Mississippi Territory was aided because the river allowed Mississippi trading ships to sail to the Gulf of Mexico.

In 1804, Congress extended the Mississippi Territory north to the border of Tennessee. More land was added in 1812. That year, the part of the West Florida Republic lying east of the Pearl River was incorporated into the

"View of Vicksburg," State of Mississippi Department of Archives and History, Jackson (Hiatt-Ford Photography)

The port of Vicksburg was an important stop for Mississippi riverboats in the 1800's. The city is still a major river port.

Currier and Ives lithograph (1884) of a painting by William Aiken Walker; Bettmann Archive

Plantations were a center of rural life in the 1800's. This scene shows field hands picking cotton on a plantation along the Mississippi River. A steamboat sails by in the background.

Mississippi Territory. The republic had been formed in 1810 after American settlers took control of the region from Spain. The republic consisted of the land south of the 31st parallel between the Mississippi River and the Perdido River. With the incorporation of this land, the Mississippi Territory extended over all of present-day Alabama and Mississippi and parts of present-day Florida.

During the War of 1812, the Choctaw Indians under Chief Pushmataha remained friendly to the Americans. The Choctaw joined the Mississippi militia in helping General Andrew Jackson put down uprisings of the Creek Indians and in defeating a British army in the Battle of New Orleans.

Statehood. In 1817, Congress divided the Mississippi Territory into the state of Mississippi and the Alabama Territory. On Dec. 10, 1817, Mississippi was admitted to the Union as the 20th state. The first Mississippi state governor, David Holmes, had been territorial governor since 1809. Columbia, Natchez, and Washington served as the state capital at various times until Jackson became the capital in 1822.

In territorial days, Indian tribes had controlled almost two-thirds of Mississippi. The tribes gradually gave up their lands to the U.S. government. By 1832, most of the Indians had moved to the Indian Territory (now Oklahoma). The lands they left were opened for settlement. Many settlers came from the East to farm the fertile soil of Mississippi. Much of the soil was excellent for growing cotton. Cotton production had increased throughout the South as a result of Eli Whitney's cotton gin, which was invented in 1793.

After 1806, an improved type of cottonseed helped increase Mississippi's cotton production. The improved variety was developed from some seeds brought to Mississippi from Mexico. It was called Petit Gulf, the name of the area in Claiborne County where it was developed. The cotton producers used slave labor to operate large cotton plantations. Mississippi became one of the wealthiest states of the period.

During the 1850's, Mississippi farmers built many levees in the Delta region to control the floodwaters of the Mississippi and Yazoo rivers. In 1858, the legislature set up a board of levee commissioners. A large amount of the swampland in the state was drained and made suitable for farming.

The Civil War and Reconstruction. Most Mississippians did not favor *secession* (withdrawal) from the Union when South Carolina threatened to do so in 1832 (see **Nullification**). But their feelings changed during the next 29 years. The reasons for the change included violations of the Fugitive Slave Law, the struggle over slavery in Kansas, the founding of the Republican Party, and the economic differences between the North and the South. Mississippi became a strong defender of states' rights and of slavery. See **Civil War** (Causes and background of the war).

On Jan. 9, 1861, a convention met in the Old Capitol in Jackson and adopted the Ordinance of Secession. Mississippi became the second state, after South Carolina, to secede from the Union. About five weeks later, Jefferson Davis of Mississippi became president of the Confederacy. He had been a soldier, planter, and a U.S. Senator. Davis also had served as Secretary of War under President Franklin Pierce.

More than 80,000 Mississippi troops served in the Confederate armies. Union and Confederate forces clashed in Mississippi, or on its borders, in many places. Important battles were fought at Corinth, Harrisburg (now Tupelo), Holly Springs, Iuka, Jackson, Meridian, and Port Gibson. In June 1864, at Brice's Cross Roads, Confederate General Nathan Bedford Forrest defeated a larger Union cavalry force. Forrest supposedly explained his military successes by saying that he "got there first with the most men."

The Battle of Vicksburg ranks as the most important military action in Mississippi. The Confederate stronghold in Vicksburg fell to General Ulysses S. Grant's Union forces on July 4, 1863, after a 47-day siege. General Grant's capture of Vicksburg gave the Union control of the Mississippi River. The Union victories at Vicksburg and Gettysburg marked the turning point of the Civil War.

After the war, in 1867, the United States placed

ᵀHistoric ꟽMississippi

The first colonial settlement in the Mississippi Valley was established by Pierre Le Moyne, Sieur d' Iberville, at Old Biloxi (now Ocean Springs) in 1699.

Aaron Burr's preliminary treason trial was held in Washington, Miss., in 1807. Burr had raised a small military force of his own, and was accused of trying to set up a republic in the West.

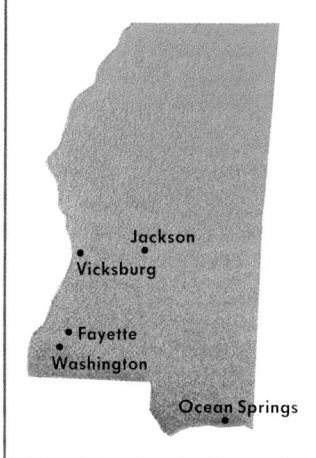

The Ordinance of Secession was adopted by Mississippi on Jan. 9, 1861, making it the second state to withdraw from the Union.

Vicksburg is often called the Gibraltar of the Confederacy. The South controlled the Mississippi River during the Civil War until Vicksburg finally fell in 1863.

Charles Evers was elected mayor of Fayette in 1969, thus becoming the first black mayor in Mississippi since the Reconstruction period (1865-1877).

Important dates in Mississippi

WORLD BOOK illustrations by Kevin Chadwick

1540	Hernando de Soto entered the Mississippi region.
1699	Pierre Le Moyne, Sieur d'Iberville, established the first French colony at Old Biloxi.
1763	Mississippi became English territory after the French and Indian War.
1781	Spain occupied the Gulf Coast.
1798	The Mississippi Territory was organized.
1817	Mississippi became the 20th state on December 10.
1858	Mississippi started a swamp drainage program in the Delta.
1861	Mississippi seceded from the Union.
1863	Union forces captured Vicksburg in the Civil War.
1870	Mississippi was readmitted to the Union.

1939	Petroleum was discovered at Tinsley.
1954	The Mississippi legislature passed a law banning required union membership.
1960	Mississippi passed laws that broadened the tax-free privilege of industrial properties.
1964	Atomic scientists set off the first nuclear test explosion east of the Mississippi River at Baxterville, Miss.
1969	A federal court ordered the desegregation of Mississippi's public schools.
1969	Charles Evers became the first black mayor in Mississippi since Reconstruction. He was elected in Fayette.
1991	Kirk Fordice became the first Republican to be elected governor of Mississippi since 1874.

Mississippi under military rule during the Reconstruction period. Mississippi was readmitted to the Union in 1870, after adopting a new state constitution and ratifying amendments 14 and 15 of the United States Constitution. It took many years for the state to recover from its war losses. After Reconstruction ended in 1876, whites in Mississippi, as in the other Southern states, refused to share political power with blacks. Blacks throughout the South gradually lost most of the rights they had gained after the Civil War. See **Reconstruction.**

The early 1900's were years of progress in industry, agriculture, and education. The construction of railroads provided access to the pine forests of southeast Mississippi, resulting in a boom in the lumber industry. The industry reached a high peak just before World War I began in 1914. New drainage projects in Mississippi opened large swampy areas to agriculture. County agricultural high schools were established in 1908. The state established an illiteracy commission in 1916 to start a special educational program for adults who could not read or write. In 1912, the Mississippi legislature passed laws regulating child labor.

Legislative measures during the 1920's included the establishment of a state commission of education in 1924, of a state library commission in 1926, and of a highway building program in 1929. The first milk condensery in the South opened at Starkville in 1926. Mississippi suffered greatly in the Mississippi River flood of 1927. About 100,000 people fled from their flooded homes in the Delta. The damage to crops and property in Mississippi totaled over $204 million. The next year, Congress made the U.S. Army Corps of Engineers responsible for controlling floods on the Mississippi River.

Economic development. During the Great Depression of the 1930's, Mississippi launched an important program of economic development. The program, called Balancing Agriculture With Industry (BAWI), was helped by special laws passed by the legislature in 1936. These laws freed new industries from paying certain taxes. The laws also allowed cities and counties to issue bonds and use the bond money to build factories for new industries. The BAWI program is administered by the state's Department of Economic Development. In developing the BAWI program, Mississippi became one of the first states to use national advertising to promote new industries. Mississippi's industrial development was strongly aided by the discovery of petroleum at Tinsley in 1939 and at Vaughan in 1940.

The mid-1900's. During World War II (1939-1945), many war plants operated in Mississippi. The port of Pascagoula became an assembly center for ships sailing in convoys. After the war, the state's industrial development continued. In 1954, the legislature passed a right-to-work law. This law provided that no worker has to join a union if he or she does not want to do so. The law became part of the state's constitution in 1960.

During the 1960's, Mississippi worked to attract new industries. The increasing mechanization of agriculture had created a surplus of farm labor, and Mississippi leaders wanted new industries that could employ former farm workers. The legislature passed laws in 1960 broadening the tax-free position of industry. In 1963, a huge oil refinery was built in Pascagoula. In 1964, the state set up the Mississippi Research and Development Center. The center encourages new industries to move into the state and helps established companies expand. By 1966, more Mississippians worked in manufacturing than in agriculture. But Mississippi still had relatively little industry compared to many other states, and most of its workers earned low incomes. In 1968, the Ingalls shipyards began an expansion program in Pascagoula. In other coastal areas, the tourist industry boomed.

Like many other states, Mississippi has had racial problems. The state's constitution had provided for segregated schools. But in 1954, the Supreme Court of the United States ruled that compulsory segregation of public schools was unconstitutional. Efforts by civil rights groups to bring about integration were sometimes met with violence. In 1962, two persons were killed in riots that broke out when James Meredith enrolled as the first black student at the University of Mississippi. In 1963, Medgar Evers, Mississippi field secretary of the National Association for the Advancement of Colored

UPI/Bettmann Newsphotos

Medgar Evers, *center,* became the field secretary of the National Association for the Advancement of Colored People (NAACP) in Mississippi in 1954. He worked to help blacks win civil rights until a sniper shot and killed him on June 12, 1963.

People (NAACP), was shot and killed. In 1964, three civil rights workers were murdered near Philadelphia, Miss. Both white and black leaders in Mississippi spoke out against the violence.

In the fall of 1964, the first public schools in Mississippi began to desegregate. In 1969, the U.S. Supreme Court ordered an immediate end to all segregated public schools. As a result, a federal court in New Orleans ordered 33 Mississippi school districts to desegregate by December 1969. Many white people opened segregated private schools and enrolled their children. Also in 1969, Charles Evers, brother of Medgar, was elected mayor of Fayette. He became the first black mayor in Mississippi since Reconstruction.

Recent developments. The incomes of Mississippi families rose steadily in the 1970's, although they remained low by national standards. A number of new industries moved to the state, and by the mid-1980's, about a fourth of Mississippi workers were employed in manufacturing. But thousands of farm workers in the Delta region are jobless because of the increased use of machinery on farms. Large numbers of high school and college graduates leave Mississippi to find jobs.

Mississippi faces the challenge of fully developing its economic program. In addition, local and state government is still organized to meet the needs of an agricultural, rural society and needs to be modernized to deal with economic problems effectively. Mississippi hopes to keep young people from leaving the state by attracting industries that require higher skills and pay higher wages. To attract such industries, many cities are working to improve transportation and other services and to increase cultural and educational opportunities.

John Ray Skates, Jr., and Robert W. Wales

Study aids

Related articles in *World Book* include:

Biographies

Bruce, Blanche K.
Davis, Jefferson
De Soto, Hernando
Evers (family)
Faulkner, William
George, James Z.

Lamar, Lucius Q. C.
Revels, Hiram R.
Welty, Eudora
Williams, Tennessee
Wright, Richard

Cities

Biloxi
Jackson

Natchez
Vicksburg

History

Black Americans
Civil War
Confederate States of America
Louisiana Purchase

Mississippi Scheme
Natchez Trace
Reconstruction

Physical features

Gulf of Mexico
Mississippi River

Tombigbee River

Outline

I. People
  A. Population
  B. Schools
  C. Libraries
  D. Museums
II. Visitor's guide
  A. Places to visit
  B. Annual events
III. Land and climate
  A. Land regions
  B. Coastline
  C. Rivers and lakes
  D. Plant and animal life
  E. Climate
IV. Economy
  A. Natural resources
  B. Service industries
  C. Manufacturing
  D. Agriculture
  E. Mining
  F. Fishing industry
  G. Electric power
  H. Transportation
  I. Communication
V. Government
  A. Constitution
  B. Executive
  C. Legislature
  D. Courts
  E. Local government
  F. Revenue
  G. Politics
VI. History

Questions

Which region of Mississippi is famous for its large soybean and cotton crops? Why is its soil so fertile?

What special event marks the opening of Mississippi's shrimp-fishing season?

How does Mississippi protect its valuable trees?

Why did the early Spanish explorers make no settlements in the Mississippi region?

Why does the Battle of Vicksburg rank as one of the most important battles of the Civil War?

How does Mississippi try to attract new industries?

What does Mississippi's name mean?

Why did public opinion in Mississippi about secession change during the 29 years before the Civil War?

Why did Mississippi adopt a new constitution in 1869?

What kind of program did Mississippi institute during the depression to help improve its economy?

Additional resources

Level I
Carpenter, Allan. *Mississippi.* Rev. ed. Childrens Press, 1978.
Fradin, Dennis B. *Mississippi in Words and Pictures.* Childrens Press, 1980.
Thompson, Kathleen. *Mississippi.* Raintree, 1987.

Level II
An Anthology of Mississippi Writers. Ed. by Noel E. Polk and James R. Scafidel. Univ. Press of Mississippi, 1979.
Atlas of Mississippi. Ed. by Ralph D. Cross and Robert W. Wales. Univ. Press of Mississippi, 1974.
Harris, William Charles. *The Day of the Carpetbagger: Republican Reconstruction in Mississippi.* Louisiana State Univ. Press, 1979.
A History of Mississippi. Ed. by Richard A. McLemore. 2 vols. Univ. Press of Mississippi, 1973.
Kirwan, Albert D. *Revolt of the Rednecks: Mississippi Politics, 1876-1925.* Harper, 1965. First published in 1951.
Mississippi: Conflict and Change. Ed. by James W. Loewen and Charles Sallis. Rev. ed. Pantheon, 1982.
A Mississippi Reader: Selected Articles from "The Journal of Mississippi History." Ed. by John E. Gonzales. Mississippi Historical Society, 1980.
Newton, Carolyn. *Outdoor Mississippi.* Univ. Press of Mississippi, 1974.
Skates, John Ray, Jr. *Mississippi: A Bicentennial History.* Norton, 1979.
Welty, Eudora. *One Time, One Place: Mississippi in the Depression; A Snapshot Album.* Random House, 1971.
Wharton, Vernon L. *The Negro in Mississippi, 1865-1890.* Greenwood, 1984. First published in 1947.

University of Mississippi

Farley Hall at the University of Mississippi houses much of the university library's Blues Archive.

Mississippi, University of, is a state-supported co-educational school with campuses in Oxford and Jackson, Miss. The main campus, in Oxford, has a college of liberal arts, a graduate school, and schools of business administration, education, engineering, law, pharmacy, and accountancy. The University of Mississippi Medical Center in Jackson includes schools of dentistry, medicine, nursing, and health-related professions. The university grants bachelor's, master's, and doctor's degrees.

The university's library features materials by and about such Mississippians as the noted authors William Faulkner and Stark Young. Faulkner's Nobel Prize and important manuscripts are kept in the library. The library also includes the Blues Archive. The university owns and maintains Faulkner's home, Rowan Oak, near the main campus. The collections at the University Museums include antique scientific instruments and Greek and Roman coins, pottery, and sculpture.

The university's Center for the Study of Southern Culture promotes education and scholarship on the American South through a wide variety of programs, including annual conferences on Faulkner and on regional history. The federally funded National Center for Physical Acoustics, which conducts research on sound, is located on the Oxford campus and managed by the university.

The university was founded in 1844 and opened in 1848. For enrollment, see **Universities and colleges** (table).   Critically reviewed by the University of Mississippi

Mississippi Bubble. See Mississippi Scheme.

Mississippi River is one of the chief rivers of North America and the second longest river in the United States. Only the Missouri is longer. The Mississippi flows 2,340 miles (3,766 kilometers) from its source in northwestern Minnesota to its mouth in the Gulf of Mexico. The Mississippi and its tributaries drain almost all the plains that lie between the Appalachian Mountains and the Rocky Mountains. This drainage basin covers 1,247,300 square miles (3,230,490 square kilometers) and includes the nation's most productive agricultural and industrial areas.

The Mississippi is the nation's chief inland waterway. It carries agricultural goods, industrial products, and raw materials. Ships can travel the river for more than 1,800 miles (2,897 kilometers) from Minneapolis, Minn., to the Gulf of Mexico. The river ranges in depth from 9 feet (2.7 meters) to 100 feet (30 meters) during most of its course. The river reaches its widest point— about $3\frac{1}{2}$ miles (5.6 kilometers)—just north of Clinton, Iowa, in a backwater formed by Lock and Dam No. 13.

The Mississippi, which is sometimes called "Old Man River," has played a vital role in the history of the United States. During the 1500's and 1600's, it provided a route for Spanish and French explorers. With the coming of steamboats in the 1800's, the Mississippi became a great transportation and trade route. The famous American author Mark Twain described the river vividly in his book *Life on the Mississippi* (1883).

The course of the Mississippi. The Mississippi begins as a small, clear stream that rushes out of Lake Itasca in northwestern Minnesota. The river flows northward and then eastward, linking a series of lakes.

The Mississippi begins to curve southward near Grand Rapids, Minn. As it flows between Minneapolis and St. Paul, Minn., it is joined by the Minnesota River. Beginning with its junction with the St. Croix River, the Mississippi forms part of the boundary between Minnesota and Wisconsin. It is also part of the boundaries of eight other states. Illinois, Kentucky, Tennessee, and Mississippi are to the east, and Iowa, Missouri, Arkansas, and part of Louisiana are on the western shore.

Two major tributaries, the Illinois River and the Missouri River, join the Mississippi above St. Louis. The muddy waters of the Missouri mix with the clear waters of the Mississippi, and the Mississippi takes on the muddy color for which it is known in the South.

The Ohio River flows into the Mississippi at Cairo, Ill., doubling the Mississippi's volume of water. This junction divides the upper Mississippi from the lower Mississippi. South of Cairo, the flood plain of the Mississippi forms a fertile valley. The valley is over 50 miles (80 kilometers) wide in some places. The river winds back and forth through this valley and forms broad loops. It sometimes changes its course and cuts off the loops, creating horseshoe-shaped lakes called *oxbow lakes.* Along its lower course, the Mississippi deposits soil particles called *silt* along its banks. The silt builds up and forms embankments known as *natural levees.*

The Arkansas River joins the Mississippi about 50 miles (80 kilometers) north of Greenville, Miss. North of Marksville, La., the Red River enters the Mississippi flood plain, but most of its flow continues into the Atchafalaya River. About a fourth of the Mississippi's water also goes into the Atchafalaya.

Mississippi River

▭ Mississippi River drainage basin	✳ State capital
— International boundary	• City or town
— State or provincial boundary	■ Point of interest
	– Mississippi River lock and dam

As the Mississippi approaches the Gulf of Mexico, it deposits large amounts of silt to form a delta. The Mississippi Delta covers about 13,000 square miles (33,700 square kilometers). South of New Orleans, the river breaks up into several channels called *distributaries,* which enter the Gulf of Mexico. They include Main Pass, North Pass, South Pass, and Southwest Pass. The Mississippi River system empties over 640, 000 cubic feet (18,100 cubic meters) of water per second into the gulf. This discharge totals about 133 cubic miles (554 cubic kilometers) of water per year.

Commerce. The Mississippi River carries about 60 percent of the freight that is transported on the nation's inland waterways. About 460 million short tons (420 million metric tons) of freight are transported on the Mississippi annually.

Most commercial freight on the Mississippi travels on large barges pushed by tugboats. Between Minneapolis and Cairo, the southbound freight consists mainly of agricultural products, such as corn, soybeans, and wheat. Coal and steel products from the Ohio River system are transported north. South of Cairo, goods from the Ohio double the Mississippi's traffic. Most of the cargo consists of southbound agricultural goods, coal, and steel products. At Baton Rouge, La., petrochemical products, aluminum, and petroleum are added to the barge traffic. Beginning at Baton Rouge, the Mississippi deepens and allows passage of oceangoing vessels. The greatest volume of traffic on the Mississippi moves between New Orleans and Southwest Pass.

Floods and flood control. From time to time, the Mississippi has caused serious floods. The floods occur when rain and melting snow bring unusually large amounts of water into the Mississippi. The river then

Milt and Joan Mann

The source of the Mississippi River is Lake Itasca in north-western Minnesota. The Mississippi begins as a small, clear stream but it later reaches a width of about $3\frac{1}{2}$ miles (5.6 kilometers) in a backwater north of Clinton, Iowa.

overflows into the surrounding flood plain. Especially destructive floods occurred in 1927, 1937, 1965, 1973, 1982, 1983, and 1993. See **Flood.**

Dams and levees have provided some protection against flooding by the Mississippi River. A series of dams along the Missouri and Ohio rivers control the amount of water that enters the Mississippi. The Mississippi itself was dammed north of St. Louis. Along the lower course of the Mississippi, the natural levees have been heightened and new levees built to prevent flooding. Dredging of the river channel not only increases the amount of water the river can carry, but also aids navigation on the river. In addition, areas of land that are called *floodways* provide outlets for draining off water

when the river reaches flood level.

Animal and plant life. The Mississippi River and its valley support many kinds of animals and plants. Such freshwater fishes as bass, sunfish, and trout live in the clear waters of the upper Mississippi. Carp, catfish, and buffalo fish are found in the muddy waters of the lower Mississippi.

The most common animals in the Mississippi Valley are mink, muskrats, opossums, otters, and skunks. Large rodents called *nutrias* live in the swamps and marshlands of the delta area (see **Nutria**). This area also provides winter nesting grounds for ducks, geese, and other migratory birds. Pelicans, herons, and egrets live in the area throughout the year.

Forests of hardwood trees, such as basswood, hickory, maple, and oak, grow in the upper Mississippi Valley. South of Cairo, the forests consist mainly of baldcypress, sweet gum, southern oak, and tupelo trees.

Pollution seriously threatens the wildlife of the Mississippi. Fertilizers and insecticides used on farms are washed into the river, and industries empty wastes into its waters.

Since the 1970's, steps have been taken to prevent further pollution of the river. For example, federal regulations prohibit farmers from using certain insecticides and other harmful chemicals.

History. The Mississippi was formed about 2 million years ago at the beginning of the Pleistocene Ice Age. During this period, glaciers covered much of the Northern Hemisphere. Melting ice from the glaciers was carried to the Mississippi by both the Missouri and Ohio rivers.

Various Indian tribes, including the Illinois, the Kickapoo, the Ojibway, and the Santee Dakota, lived in the upper Mississippi Valley. The name *Mississippi,* which means *big river,* came from these tribes. The lower valley was the home of such tribes as the Chickasaw, the Choctaw, the Natchez, and the Tunica.

The first European to travel on the Mississippi was

Robert H. Glaze, Artstreet

Along the upper course of the Mississippi, forests of hardwood trees and steep bluffs line the river's banks in many areas. The river often cuts off areas of land, creating islands.

Robert H. Glaze, Artstreet

The port of New Orleans, on the Mississippi River, is the busiest port in the United States. Ships from all parts of the world dock at the wharves along the Mississippi.

U.S. Army Corps of Engineers

Southwest Pass, a channel of the Mississippi, flows into the Gulf of Mexico. The greatest volume of traffic on the Mississippi moves between New Orleans and Southwest Pass.

the Spanish explorer Hernando de Soto. He crossed the river in 1541 near what is now Memphis. In the early 1680's, the French explorer Sieur de La Salle traveled on the river and claimed the Mississippi Valley for France.

France lost all of its territories on the mainland of North America as a result of the French and Indian War (1754-1763). Great Britain gained the land east of the Mississippi, and Spain took over the land west of the river. After the Revolutionary War in America (1775-1783), the United States took control of the British territories. In 1800, France regained the land west of the Mississippi. The United States bought this land from France in the Louisiana Purchase of 1803.

After the entire Mississippi Valley became part of the United States, settlers and traders set out on the river in flatboats, keelboats, and rafts. The importance of the river as a transportation and trade route increased with the development of steamboats in the early 1800's. Mississippi River cities, including St. Louis, Memphis, and New Orleans, served as supply centers for the westward movement.

During the Civil War (1861-1865), the Mississippi served as an invasion route for the Union forces. The capture of such river cities as New Orleans, Memphis, and Vicksburg, Miss., divided the Confederacy in half and assured victory for the North. After the war, railroads soon took over most of the river's former steamboat traffic. The completion of the Eads Bridge in 1874, connecting St. Louis and East St. Louis, Ill., provided a major rail crossing over the river. Many more bridges were built during the years that followed.

The importance of the Mississippi as a transportation route has increased greatly since the 1920's. No other means of transportation can move masses of heavy, bulky cargo as cheaply as the barges and tugboats on the mighty river.   John Edwin Coffman

Related articles in *World Book* include:

Delta	Inland waterway	Levee
De Soto, Hernando	Jetty	Louisiana
Hennepin, Louis	La Salle, Sieur de	

Mississippi Scheme was a wild financial project formulated in France in 1717. John Law, a Scottish economist, originated the scheme, which resulted in the organization of a business firm called the Mississippi

Company. The French *regent* (temporary ruler), Philippe, Duke of Orléans, gave the company a *monopoly* (exclusive rights) to carry on far-reaching business operations in French-held Louisiana and Canada. At first, the scheme won widespread approval. Thousands of Frenchmen bought shares in Law's company without really knowing how their money was to be used. But when the stockholders discovered that the company actually did little to develop business enterprises in America, they became frightened and began to sell their shares at greatly reduced prices. The result was a financial panic in 1720, known as the bursting of "The Mississippi Bubble." A few investors who sold their shares early at high prices made huge profits. But others suffered heavy losses. The scheme failed, but it helped advertise Louisiana and brought thousands of settlers and slaves to the colony.   Maarten Ultee

Mississippi State University is a coeducational school in Mississippi State, Miss. It receives state and federal support. It has colleges of agriculture, arts and sciences, business and industry, education, engineering, and veterinary medicine; schools of accountancy, architecture, and forest resources; and a graduate school. Courses lead to bachelor's, master's, and doctor's degrees. The university includes an agricultural and forestry experiment station, an agricultural extension service, a boll weevil research laboratory, and a chemical regulatory laboratory. It is noted for its aerospace research facilities and a seed technology laboratory. The school was founded in 1878, and took its present name in 1958. For enrollment, see **Universities and colleges** (table).   Critically reviewed by Mississippi State University

Mississippi University for Women is a state-controlled coeducational school in Columbus, Miss. Founded in 1884, it was the first public college for women in the United States. The school became coeducational in 1982. Its undergraduate curriculum emphasizes liberal arts and professional preparation programs. Master's degrees are available in education and nursing. The university houses the Mississippi School for Mathematics and Science, a residential high school for gifted students.   Critically reviewed by Mississippi University for Women

Mississippian Indians. See Mound builders.
Mississippian Period was the early part of the Carboniferous Period in the Paleozoic Era of geologic history. See Earth (table: Outline of the earth's history).
Missoula, *muh ZOO luh* (pop. 42,918), is one of the largest cities in Montana. It lies in the west-central part of the state, on the Pacific slope of the Rocky Mountains (see **Montana** [political map]).

Missoula's main industries are the production of wood and paper products. The city is the site of the University of Montana. It also serves as the headquarters of Region One of the United States Forest Service. Nearby is a training center for Forest Service fire fighters. North of Missoula is the Rattlesnake National Recreation Area and Wilderness, which covers about 61,000 acres (25,000 hectares).

The name *Missoula* comes from a Flathead Indian word meaning *by or near the cold, chilling waters.* The word might refer to Hell Gate Canyon, just east of Missoula, where Blackfeet Indians ambushed Flathead Indians. Missoula was founded in 1860. It has a mayor-council government.   Bradley Hurd

© Dan Engle, Ozark Photo Services

The Ozark Plateau of southern Missouri is a beautiful region of forests, caves, large lakes, and clear streams. A stream rushes by an old mill, *above,* in this popular vacation area.

Missouri   *The Show Me State*

Missouri, *muh ZOOR ee* or *muh ZOOR uh,* is an important industrial and farming state of the Midwest region of the United States. Its location and its two great rivers have made Missouri a center of water, land, and air transportation.

The mighty Mississippi River forms Missouri's eastern border. The wide Missouri River winds across the state from west to east. A wealth of food, manufactured products, and raw materials is shipped on these waterways—the nation's longest rivers. Kansas City and St. Louis rank among the chief U.S. air and rail terminals. They also are among the nation's top trucking centers. About 15 major commercial airlines serve the state. Railroad passenger trains and freight lines, and many major highways also crisscross Missouri.

Vast fields of golden grain and green grasses cover the state's rolling plains in the north and west. Swift streams tumble through the rugged, wooded plateau of southern Missouri. This scenic region, called the

The contributors of this article are Stephen Kneeshaw, Professor of History at the College of the Ozarks; and Dale Robert Martin, Associate Professor of Geography at Northeast Missouri State University.

Ozarks, is one of the major recreation areas of the Midwest.

Most of Missouri's workers are employed in service industries, which include government, health care, and retail trade. The state's factories turn out large numbers of airplanes and automobiles. Some manufacturing activities, such as meat packing and fertilizer production, are related to Missouri's huge farm output. Missouri ranks among the leading producers of beef cattle, corn, hogs, and soybeans.

Missouri is sometimes called the *Mother of the West* because it once lay at the frontier of the United States. The state supplied many of the pioneers who settled the vast region between Missouri and the Pacific Ocean. St. Louis, St. Charles, Independence, St. Joseph, and Westport Landing (now Kansas City) served as jumping-off places for the westbound pioneers. The historic Santa Fe Trail led from Independence to the rich, faraway Southwest. Thousands of settlers also followed the Oregon Trail from Independence to the Pacific Northwest. Furs brought from the Northwest made St. Louis the fur capital of the world.

During the Civil War, Missourians were torn between their loyalties to the South and to the Union. After the war, manufacturing developed rapidly, and St. Louis

WORLD BOOK illustrations by Kevin Chadwick

Interesting facts about Missouri

The world's first school of journalism opened at the University of Missouri at Columbia in 1908.

The first parachute jump from an airplane was made March 1, 1912, by Captain Albert Berry at Jefferson Barracks, St. Louis. He jumped from an altitude of 1,500 feet (460 meters). His parachute was a modified hot-air balloon.

First parachute jump

The first public school kindergarten was opened in 1873 by the St. Louis Board of Education. Susan Elizabeth Blow taught the class of 68 students.

The world's largest producer of corncob pipes is Washington, Mo. Factories there make about 6 million corncob pipes each year.

Ice cream cones were first served at the 1904 Louisiana Purchase Exposition world's fair in St. Louis.

© Robert Lee II

Downtown St. Louis has many modern buildings. Some of these buildings surround the Old Courthouse, *center.*

Ice cream cones

and Kansas City grew into industrial giants. Agriculture also expanded, and Missouri became a great farming state.

Many outstanding Americans have lived in Missouri. They include Harry S. Truman, the 33rd President of the United States; Mark Twain, the creator of Tom Sawyer and Huckleberry Finn; Walt Disney, the famous motion-picture producer; Eugene Field, the beloved children's poet; General John J. Pershing, commander of U.S. forces in Europe during World War I; George Washington Carver, the great scientist; Joseph Pulitzer, the famous journalist; General Omar N. Bradley, a brilliant commander in World War II; and Thomas Hart Benton and George Caleb Bingham, noted painters.

The state's name comes from the Missouri River. The word *Missouri* probably came from an Indian word meaning the *town of the large canoes.* Missouri's nickname is the Show Me State. This nickname is usually traced to a speech by Congressman Willard Duncan Vandiver of Missouri in 1899. Speaking in Philadelphia, Vandiver said: ". . . frothy eloquence neither convinces nor satisfies me. I am from Missouri. You have got to show me."

Jefferson City is Missouri's capital, and Kansas City is the largest city.

© R. Hamilton Smith

Farmers harvest corn from the rich, fertile soil of Missouri's plains region. Fields of grain or green grasses cover most of northern Missouri. It is a leading corn-producing state.

Missouri in brief

Symbols of Missouri

The state flag, adopted in 1913, has stripes of red, white, and blue that symbolize loyalty to the Union. The coat of arms in the center is surrounded by a ring of 24 stars, which show that Missouri was the 24th state. On the state seal, adopted in 1822, two grizzly bears support a shield featuring symbols of Missouri on the left and the arms of the United States on the right. The bears represent the state's strength and the bravery of its citizens.

State flag

State seal

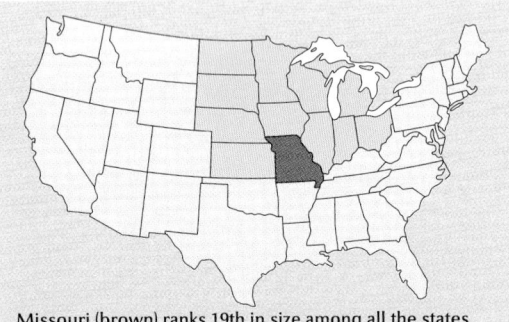

Missouri (brown) ranks 19th in size among all the states and 6th in size among the Midwestern States (yellow).

General information

Statehood: Aug. 10, 1821, the 24th state.
State abbreviations: Mo. (traditional); MO (postal).
State motto: *Salus populi suprema lex esto* (The welfare of the people shall be the supreme law).
State song: "Missouri Waltz." Words by J. R. Shannon; music from a melody obtained from John V. Eppel.

The State Capitol is in Jefferson City, Missouri's capital since 1826. Earlier capitals were St. Louis (1820) and St. Charles (1821-1826).

Land and climate

Area: 69,709 sq. mi. (180,546 km²), including 811 sq. mi. (2,100 km²) of inland water.
Elevation: *Highest*—Taum Sauk Mountain, 1,772 ft. (540 m) above sea level. *Lowest*—230 ft. (70 m) above sea level, along the St. Francis River near Cardwell.
Record high temperature: 118 °F (48 °C) at Clinton on July 15, 1936, at Lamar on July 18, 1936, and at Union and Warsaw on July 14, 1954.
Record low temperature: −40 °F (−40 °C) at Warsaw on Feb. 13, 1905.
Average July temperature: 78 °F (26 °C).
Average January temperature: 30 °F (−1 °C).
Average yearly precipitation: 40 in. (102 cm).

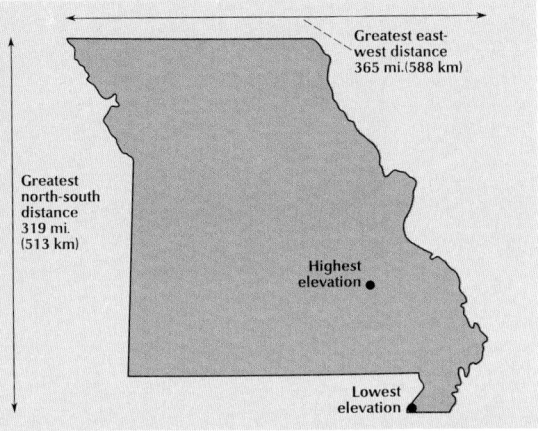

Greatest east-west distance 365 mi.(588 km)

Greatest north-south distance 319 mi. (513 km)

Highest elevation ●

Lowest elevation ●

Important dates

Pierre Laclède Liguest and René Auguste Chouteau established St. Louis.

Missouri became the 24th state on August 10.

| 1682 | 1764 | 1812 | 1821 | 1854 |

La Salle claimed the Mississippi Valley, including Missouri, for France.

Congress made Missouri a territory.

Border warfare began between antislavery Kansans and proslavery Missourians.

State bird
Bluebird

State flower
Hawthorn

State tree
Flowering dogwood

People

Population: 5,137,804 (1990 census)
Rank among the states: 15th
Density: 74 persons per sq. mi. (28 per km²), U.S. average 69 per sq. mi. (27 per km²)
Distribution: 69 percent urban, 31 percent rural

Largest cities in Missouri

Kansas City	435,146
St. Louis	396,685
Springfield	140,494
Independence	112,301
St. Joseph	71,852
Columbia	69,101

Source: U.S. Bureau of the Census.

Population trend

Millions

Year	Population
1990	5,137,804
1980	4,916,759
1970	4,677,623
1960	4,319,813
1950	3,954,653
1940	3,784,664
1930	3,629,367
1920	3,404,055
1910	3,293,335
1900	3,106,665
1890	2,679,185
1880	2,168,380
1870	1,721,295
1860	1,182,012
1850	682,044
1840	383,702
1830	140,455
1820	66,586
1810	19,783

Source: U.S. Bureau of the Census.

Economy

Chief products

Agriculture: soybeans, beef cattle, hogs, corn, hay.
Manufacturing: transportation equipment, chemicals, food products, fabricated metal products, printed materials, electrical equipment, machinery.
Mining: limestone, lead, coal.

Gross state product

Value of goods and services produced in 1991: $106,883,000,000. *Services* include community, social, and personal services; finance; government; trade; and transportation, communication, and utilities. *Industry* includes construction, manufacturing, and mining. *Agriculture* includes agriculture, fishing, and forestry.

Source: U.S. Bureau of Economic Analysis.

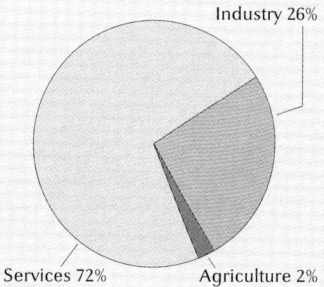

Industry 26%

Services 72%

Agriculture 2%

Government

State government

Governor: 4-year term
State senators: 34; 4-year terms
State representatives: 163; 2-year terms
Counties: 114

Federal government

United States senators: 2
United States representatives: 9
Electoral votes: 11

Sources of information

Tourism: Division of Tourism, P.O. Box 1055, Jefferson City, MO 65102
Economy: Department of Economic Development, P.O. Box 1157, Jefferson City, MO 65102
Government: Governor's Office, P.O. Box 720, Capitol Building, Room 217B, Jefferson City, MO 65102
History: Department of Natural Resources, Division of Parks, Recreation, and Historic Preservation, P.O. Box 176, Jefferson City, MO 65102

Missouri became a battleground during the Civil War.

The 630-foot (192-meter) Gateway Arch in St. Louis, the tallest U.S. monument, was completed.

1861-1865   **1904**   **1965**   **1986**

The Louisiana Purchase Centennial Exposition was held in St. Louis.

Missouri's government began operating a statewide lottery.

Population. The 1990 United States census reported that Missouri had 5,137,804 people. The state's population had increased $4\frac{1}{2}$ percent over the 1980 census figure, 4,916,759. According to the 1990 census, Missouri ranks 15th in population among the 50 states.

About two-thirds of the people in Missouri live in urban areas. Most of them live in metropolitan areas. Missouri has six metropolitan areas (see **Metropolitan area**). The largest one is the St. Louis area, which extends into Illinois and has a population of about $2\frac{1}{2}$ million. Other metropolitan areas in Missouri are Columbia, Joplin, Kansas City, St. Joseph, and Springfield. For the populations of these metropolitan areas, see the *Index* to the political map of Missouri.

Kansas City is the state's largest city, and St. Louis ranks second. They rank among the nation's chief transportation, grain, and livestock centers.

Approximately 11 percent of the people living in Missouri are blacks. Other large population groups in the state include people who are of German, Irish, English, American Indian, French, Italian, Dutch, and Scotch-Irish descent.

Schools. Missouri's first school was a private elementary school established in St. Louis in 1774. In 1820, Missouri's first constitution included a provision for establishing a system of public education. The system did not start operating until 1839, however.

Population density

More than two-thirds of Missouri's people live in urban areas. Kansas City and St. Louis are the state's largest urban areas.

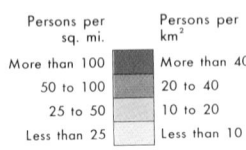

Persons per sq. mi.	Persons per km²
More than 100	More than 40
50 to 100	20 to 40
25 to 50	10 to 20
Less than 25	Less than 10

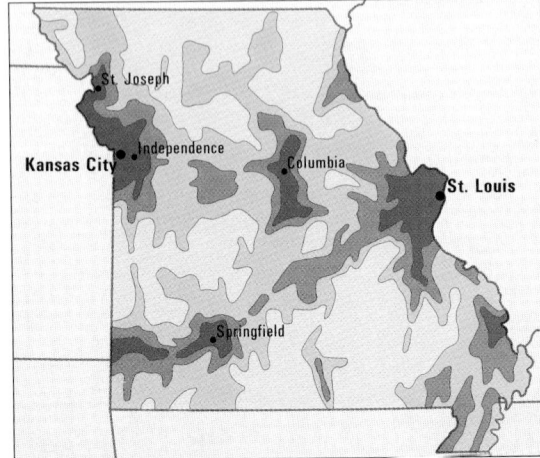

WORLD BOOK map; based on U.S. Bureau of the Census data.

© Nathan Benn, Woodfin Camp, Inc.

Children in Hannibal compete in the National Tom Sawyer Fence Painting Contest. This event honors Mark Twain, who created the Tom Sawyer character. Twain grew up in Hannibal.

© Gary Allen, Impact Press Group

Washington University is one of several universities and colleges in St. Louis. Brookings Hall, *above,* houses the university's main administration offices.

The state board of education supervises Missouri's public school system. The board of education has eight members appointed by the governor to eight-year terms. One term expires each year. The board appoints a commissioner of education. The commissioner serves as the chief administrative officer of the Department of Elementary and Secondary Education. All children between the ages of 7 and 16 must attend school. For the number of students and teachers in Missouri, see **Education** (table).

Libraries. Many of Missouri's public libraries grew out of public school libraries. Some started as *subscription libraries,* in which members contributed money and used the books free of charge.

In 1865, the St. Louis public library was established. It was supported by money from the school board and by fees and donations. In 1893, the library became tax-supported.

Today, Missouri has approximately 170 public libraries and about 70 college and university libraries. The library of the University of Missouri at Columbia is the largest library in Missouri.

Museums. Missouri's largest art museums are the St. Louis Art Museum in St. Louis and the Nelson-Atkins Museum of Art in Kansas City. The St. Louis Art Museum has a collection from many countries and periods. The Nelson-Atkins Museum owns noted collections of Oriental and American art. The Capitol in Jefferson City houses a museum that has collections of Missouri materials. These materials have historical, geological, scientific, and cultural interest.

The Missouri Historical Society building in Forest Park in St. Louis displays trophies and gifts received by Charles A. Lindbergh, the aviator. The Harry S. Truman Library in Independence exhibits the souvenirs of the 33rd President.

Nelson-Atkins Museum of Art

Missouri Division of Tourism

Harry S. Truman Library in Independence

The Nelson-Atkins Museum of Art in Kansas City

Universities and colleges

Missouri has 49 universities and colleges that offer bachelor's or advanced degrees and are accredited by the North Central Association of Colleges and Schools. For enrollments and further information, see **Universities and colleges** (table).

Name	Mailing address	Name	Mailing address	Name	Mailing address
Aquinas Institute of Theology	St. Louis	**Harris-Stowe State College**	St. Louis	**Research College of Nursing**	Kansas City
Assemblies of God		**Kansas City Art Institute**	Kansas City	**Rockhurst College**	Kansas City
Theological Seminary	Springfield	**Kenrick-Glennon Seminary**	St. Louis	**St. Louis College of**	
Avila College	Kansas City	**Lincoln University**	Jefferson City	**Pharmacy**	St. Louis
Central Methodist College	Fayette	**Lindenwood College**	St. Charles	**St. Louis University**	*
Central Missouri State University	Warrensburg	**Logan College of Chiropractic**	Chesterfield	**St. Paul School of Theology**	Kansas City
Cleveland Chiropractic College		**Maryville University**	St. Louis	**Southeast Missouri State**	
of Kansas City	Kansas City	**Midwestern Baptist Theological**		**University**	Cape Girardeau
Columbia College	Columbia	**Seminary**	Kansas City	**Southwest Baptist**	
Conception Seminary College	Conception	**Missouri, University of**	*	**University**	Bolivar
Concordia Seminary	St. Louis	**Missouri Baptist College**	St. Louis	**Southwest Missouri State**	
Covenant Theological Seminary	St. Louis	**Missouri Southern State College**	Joplin	**University**	Springfield
Culver-Stockton College	Canton	**Missouri Valley College**	Marshall	**Stephens College**	Columbia
Deaconess College of Nursing	St. Louis	**Missouri Western State College**	St. Joseph	**Washington University**	St. Louis
DeVry Institute of Technology	Kansas City	**Northeast Missouri State**		**Webster University**	St. Louis
Drury College	Springfield	**University**	Kirksville	**Westminster College**	Fulton
Eden Theological Seminary	Webster Groves	**Northwest Missouri State**		**William Jewell College**	Liberty
Evangel College	Springfield	**University**	Maryville	**William Woods College**	Fulton
Fontbonne College	St. Louis	**Ozarks, College of the**	Point Lookout		
Hannibal-LaGrange College	Hannibal	**Park College**	Parkville		

*For campuses and founding dates, see **Universities and colleges** (table).

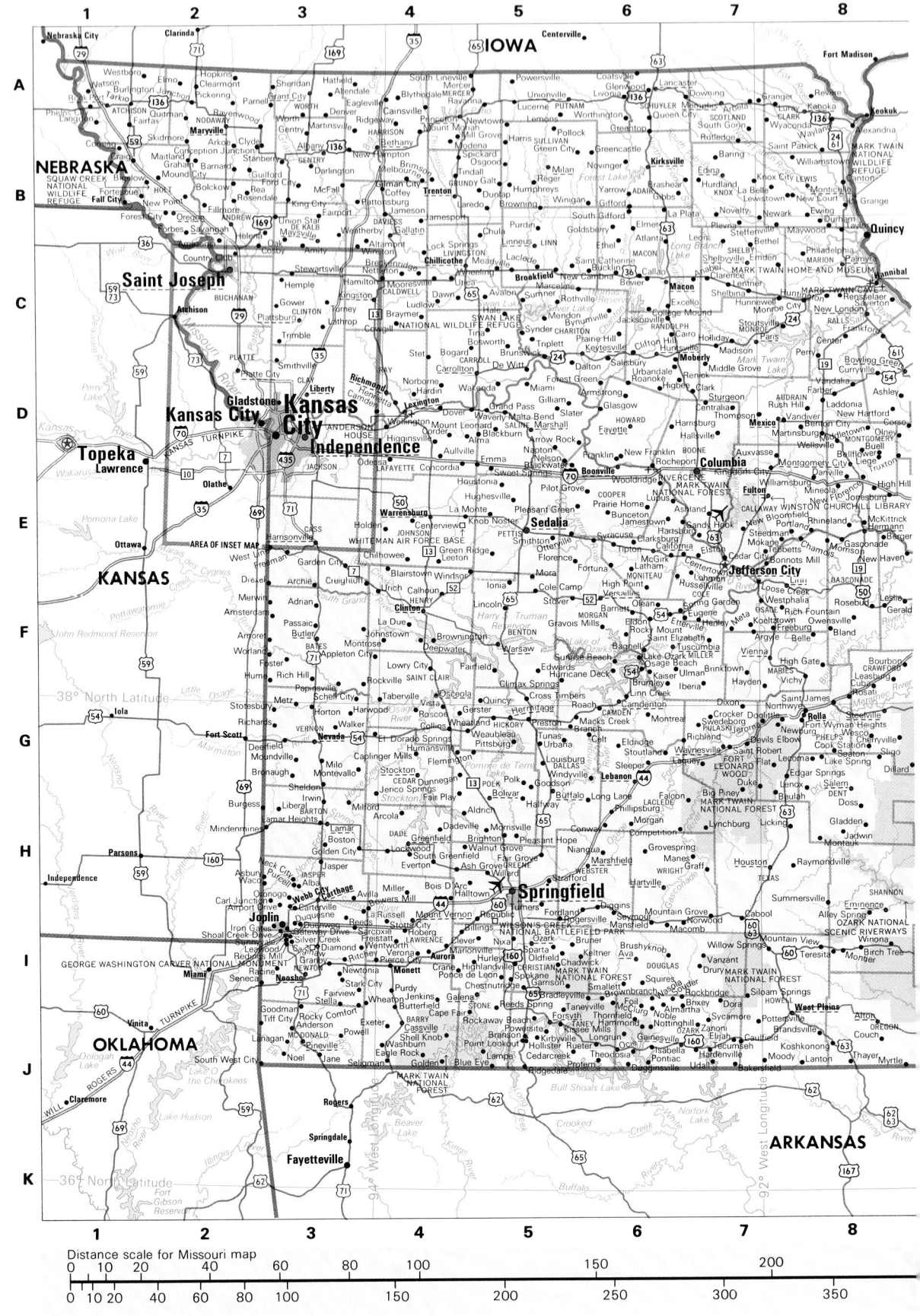

Distance scale for Missouri map

0 10 20   40   60   80   100   150   200

0 10 20   40   60   80   100   150   200   250   300   350

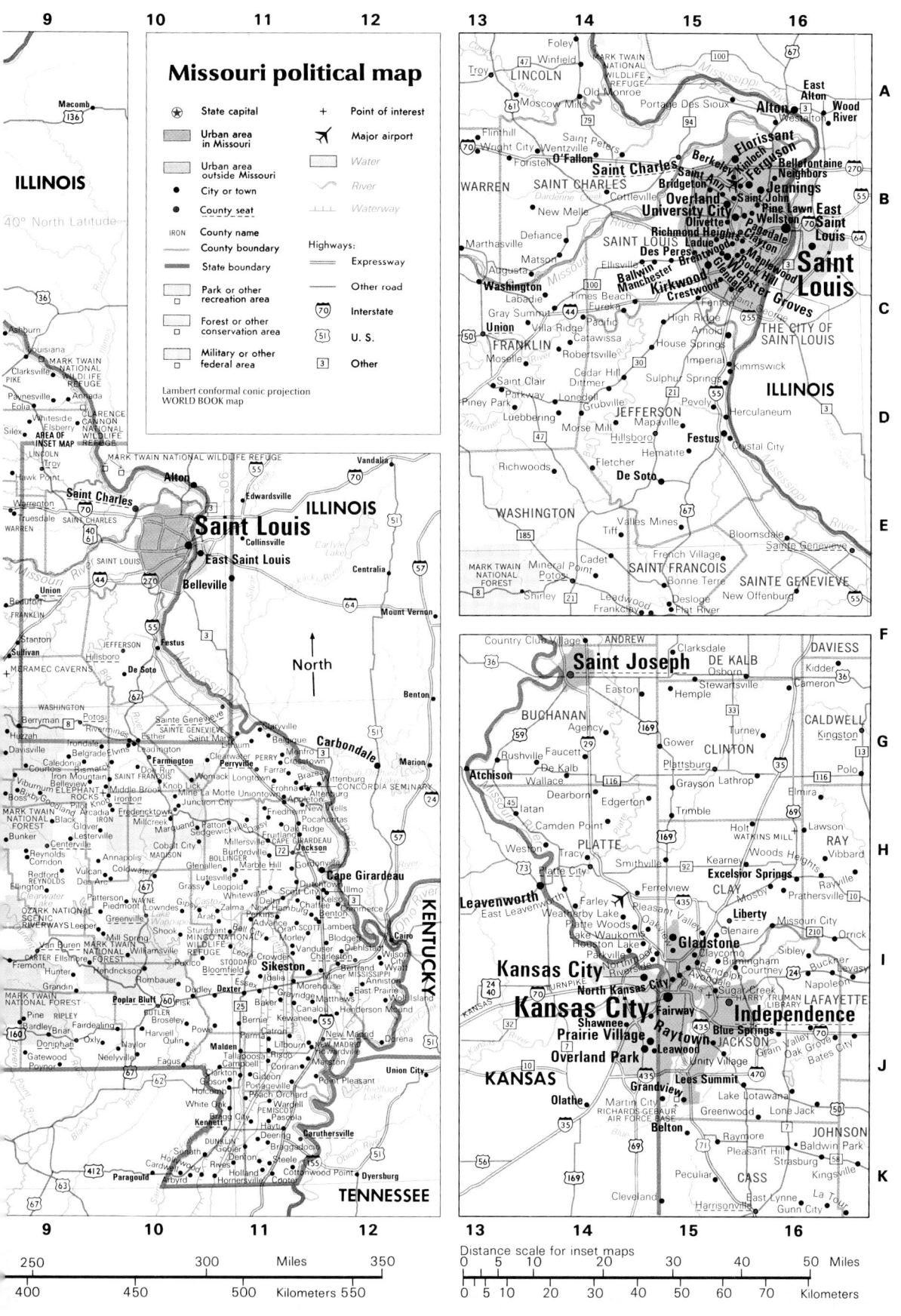

Missouri political map

Legend

- ⊛ State capital
- Urban area in Missouri
- Urban area outside Missouri
- ● City or town
- ● County seat
- IRON County name
- County boundary
- State boundary
- Park or other recreation area
- Forest or other conservation area
- Military or other federal area
- ✛ Point of interest
- ✈ Major airport
- Water
- River
- Waterway

Highways:
- Expressway
- Other road
- 70 Interstate
- 51 U.S.
- 3 Other

Lambert conformal conic projection
WORLD BOOK map

North

ILLINOIS

TENNESSEE

KENTUCKY

KANSAS

Distance scale for inset maps
0 5 10   20   30   40   50 Miles
0 5 10   20   30   40   50   60   70 Kilometers

250   300   Miles   350
400   450   500   Kilometers   550

Missouri map index

Place	Population	Key	
Jefferson City	35,481°	E	7
Jennings	15,905	B	16
Jerico Springs	247	G	4
Jonesburg	630	E	8
Joplin	40,961	I	3
Josephville*	445	E	9
Junction City	326	H	10
Kahoka	2,195°	A	8
Kansas City	435,146	D	3
Kearney	1,790	H	16
Kelso	526	H	12
Kennett	10,941°	K	11
Keytesville	564°	C	6
Kidder	241	F	16
Kimberling City*	1,590	J	5
Kimmswick	135	D	15
King City	986	B	3
Kingdom City	112	E	7
Kingston	279°	C	4
Kingsville	279	K	16
Kinloch	2,702	B	15
Kirksville	17,152°	B	6
Kirkwood	27,291	C	15
Knob Noster	2,261	E	4
Knox City	262	B	7
Koshkonong	198	J	8
La Belle	655	B	7
Laclede	410	C	5
Laddonia	581	D	8
Ladue	8,847	B	15
La Grange	1,102	B	8
Lake Lotawana	2,141	J	16
Lake Mykee Town*	257	E	7
Lake Ozark	681	F	6
Lake St. Louis*	7,400	E	9
Lake Tapawingo*	761	E	3
Lake Waukomis	1,027	I	15
Lake Winnebago*	741	E	3
Lakeland*	351	F	6
Lakeshire*	1,467	E	10
Lakeside*	38	F	6
Lakeview*	110	F	6
Lamar	4,168°	H	3
Lamar Heights	176	H	3
Lambert	36	I	12
La Monte	995	E	5
Lanagan	501	J	3
Lancaster	785°	A	6
La Plata	1,401	B	6
Laredo	205	B	5
Larussell	114	I	4
Lathrop	1,794	C	3
La Tour	87	K	16
Lawson	1,876	H	16
Leadington	201	G	10
Leadwood	1,247	F	15
Leasburg	289	F	8
Leawood	736	I	3
Lebanon	9,983°	G	6
Leeds*		I	15
Lees Summit	46,418	J	16
Leeton	632	E	4
Lemay*†	18,005	F	10
Leonard	90	B	7
Leslie	134	F	8
Levasy	279	I	16
Lewis and Clark Village*	142	C	2
Lewistown	453	B	7
Lexington	4,860°	D	4
Liberal	684	H	3
Liberty	20,459°	D	3
Licking	1,328	H	7
Lilbourn	1,378	J	11
Lincoln	874	F	5
Linn	1,148°	F	7
Linn Creek	232	G	6
Linneus	364°	B	5
Lithium	7	G	11
Livonia	126	A	6
Lock Springs	57	C	4
Lockwood	1,041	H	4
Lohman	154	F	7
Lone Jack	392	J	16
Longtown	107	G	11
Louisburg	115	G	5
Louisiana	3,967	C	9
Lowry City	723	F	4
Lucerne	51	A	5
Ludlow	147	C	4
Lupus	39	E	6
Luray	70	A	7
Lutesville		H	11
Mackenzie*	148	E	10
Macks Creek	272	G	5
Macon	5,571°	C	6
Madison	518	C	7
Maitland	338	B	2
Malden	5,123	J	11
Malta Bend	289	D	5
Manchester	6,542	C	15
Mansfield	1,429	I	6
Maplewood	9,962	B	15
Marble Hill	1,447°	H	11
Marceline	2,645	C	5
Marionville	1,920	I	4
Marlborough*	1,949	E	10
Marquand	278	H	10
Marshall	12,711°	D	5
Marshfield	4,374°	H	6
Marston	691	J	11
Marthasville	674	B	13
Martinsburg	337	D	8
Martinsville		A	3
Maryland Heights*	25,407	E	10
Maryville	10,663°	A	2
Matthews	614	I	12
Maysville	1,176°	B	3
Mayview*	279	D	4
McFall	142	B	3
McKittrick	66	E	8
Meadville	360	C	5
Memphis	2,094°	A	7
Mendon	207	C	5
Mercer	297	A	5
Merwin	75	F	3
Meta	249	F	7
Metz	91	G	3
Mexico	11,290°	D	7
Miami	142	D	5
Middletown	217	D	8
Midway*		I	3
Milan	1,767°	B	5
Milford	22	H	3
Mill Spring	252	I	10
Millard*	71	B	6
Miller	753	H	4
Milo	76	G	3
Mindenmines	346	H	3
Miner	1,218	I	12
Mineral Point	384	E	14
Missouri City	348	I	16
Moberly	12,839	C	6
Mokane	186	E	7
Moline Acres*	2,710	E	10
Monett	6,529	I	4
Monroe City	2,701	C	8
Montgomery City	2,281°	E	8
Monticello	106°	B	8
Montrose	440	F	4
Mooresville	100	C	4
Morehouse	1,068	I	11
Morley	683	I	11
Morrison	160	E	8
Morrisville	293	H	5
Mosby	194	H	16
Moscow Mills	924	A	13
Mound City	1,273	B	2
Moundville	140	G	3
Mount Leonard	96	D	5
Mount Moriah	104	A	4
Mount Vernon	3,726°	I	4
Mountain Grove	4,182	I	7
Mountain View	2,036	I	8
Murphy*†	9,342	F	10
Napoleon	233	I	16
Naylor	642	J	10
Nick City	132	H	3
Neelyville	381	J	10
Nelson	181	D	5
Neosho	9,254°	I	3
Nevada	8,597°	G	3
New Bloomfield	480	E	7
New Cambria	223	C	6
New Florence	801	E	8
New Franklin	1,107	D	6
New Hampton	320	B	3
New Haven	1,757	E	9
New London	988°	C	8
New Madrid	3,350°	J	12
New Melle	486	B	14
Newark	82	B	7
Newburg	589	G	7
Newtonia	204	I	3
Newtown	115	A	5
Niangua	459	H	6
Nixa	4,707	I	5
Noel	1,169	J	3
Norborne	856	D	4
Normandy*	4,480	E	10
North Kansas City	4,130	I	15
North Lilbourn*	157	J	11
North Wardell*	135	J	11
Northmoor	441	I	15
Northwoods*	5,106	E	10
Northwye		G	8
Norwood	449	I	6
Norwood Court*	888	E	10
Novelty	143	B	7
Novinger	542	B	6
Oak Grove*	402	F	9
Oak Grove	4,565	J	16
Oak Ridge	202	H	11
Oakland*	1,593	E	10
Oakland Park*	89	I	3
Oaks	130	I	15
Oakview	351	I	15
Oakwood*	212	D	3
Oakwood Manor*		D	3
Oakwood Park*	213	D	3
Odessa	3,695	D	4
O'Fallon	18,695	B	14
Old Monroe	242	A	14
Olean	106	F	6
Olivette	7,573	B	15
Olympian Village*	752	F	10
Oran	1,164	I	11
Oregon	935°	B	2
Oronogo	595	H	3
Orrick	935	I	16
Osage Beach	2,599	F	6
Osborn	400	F	16
Osceola	755°	G	4
Osgood	53	B	5
Otterville	507	E	5
Overland	17,987	B	15
Owensville	2,325	F	8
Ozark	4,243°	I	5
Pacific	4,350	C	14
Pagedale	3,771	B	16
Palmyra	3,371°	C	8
Paris	1,486°	C	7
Parkdale*	212	F	10
Parkville	2,402	I	14
Parkway	277	D	13
Parma	995	J	11
Parnell	157	A	3
Pasadena Hills*	1,165	E	10
Pasadena Park*	532	E	10
Pascola	120	K	11
Passaic	40	F	3
Pattonsburg	414	B	4
Paynesville	54	D	9
Peculiar	1,777	K	15
Penermon*	94	I	11
Perry	711	D	8
Perryville	6,933°	G	11
Pevely	2,831	D	15
Phelps City	32	A	1
Phillipsburg	170	H	6
Pickering	171	A	2
Piedmont	2,166	I	10
Pierce City	1,382	I	4
Pilot Grove	714	E	6
Pilot Knob	783	H	10
Pine Lawn	5,092	B	16
Pineville	580°	J	3
Platte City	2,947°	D	2
Platte Woods	427	I	15
Plattsburg	2,248°	C	3
Pleasant Hill	3,827	K	16
Pleasant Hope	360	H	5
Pleasant Valley	2,731	I	15
Pocahontas	90	H	11
Pollock	66	A	5
Polo	539	G	16
Poplar Bluff	16,996°	I	10
Portage Des Sioux	503	A	15
Portageville	3,401	J	11
Potosi	2,683°	G	9
Powersville	38	A	5
Prairie Home	215	E	6
Prathersville	130	H	16
Preston	136	G	5
Princeton	1,021°	A	4
Purcell	359	H	3
Purdin	217	B	5
Purdy	977	I	4
Puxico	819	I	10
Queen City	704	A	6
Quitman	47	A	2
Qulin	384	J	10
Randolph	60	I	15
Ravenwood	409	A	3
Raymondville	425	H	8
Raymore	5,592	K	15
Raytown	30,601	J	15
Rayville	170	H	16
Rea	62	B	3
Redings Mill	204	I	3
Reeds	88	I	3
Reeds Spring	411	I	5
Renick	195	D	6
Republic	6,292	I	5
Revere	133	A	8
Rhineland	157	E	8
Rich Hill	1,317	F	3
Richards	106	G	3
Richland	2,029	G	6
Richmond	5,738°	D	4
Richmond Heights	10,448	B	15
Ridgely*	57	C	2
Ridgeway	379	A	4
Risco	434	J	11
Ritchey	62	I	3
Rivermines	459	G	10
Riverside	3,010	I	15
Riverview*	3,242	E	10
Rocheport	255	D	6
Rock Hill	5,217	C	15
Rockaway Beach	275	J	5
Rock Port	1,438°	A	1
Rockville	193	F	4
Rogersville	995	I	5
Rolla	14,090°	G	8
Roscoe	100	G	4
Rosebud	380	F	8
Rosendale	186	B	2
Rothville	100	C	5
Rush Hill	121	D	8
Rushville	306	G	13
Russellville	869	F	6
Rutledge	74	B	7
Saginaw	384	I	3
St. Ann	14,489	B	15
St. Charles	54,555°	E	10
St. Clair	3,917	D	13
St. Elizabeth	257	F	7
St. George	1,270	C	15
St. James	3,256	G	8
St. John	7,466	B	15
St. Joseph	71,852°	C	2
St. Louis	396,685‡	E	10
St. Martins*	717	F	7
St. Marys	461	G	11
St. Paul*	1,192	E	9
St. Peters	45,779	B	14
St. Robert	1,730	G	7
St. Thomas*	263	F	7
Ste. Genevieve	4,411°	G	11
Salem	4,486°	G	8
Salisbury	1,881	D	6
Sappington*†	10,917	E	10
Sarcoxie	1,330	I	3
Savannah	4,352°	B	2
Schell City	292	G	3
Schuermann Heights*		E	10
Scott City	4,292	H	12
Sedalia	19,800°	E	5
Sedgewickville	138	H	11
Seligman	593	J	4
Senath	1,622	K	10
Seneca	1,885	I	3
Seymour	1,636	I	6
Shelbina	2,172	C	7
Shelbyville	582°	C	7
Sheldon	464	G	3
Sheridan	174	A	3
Shoal Creek Drive	296	I	3
Shoal Creek Estates	21	I	3
Shrewsbury*	6,416	E	10
Sibley	367	I	16
Sikeston	17,641	I	11
Silex	197	D	9
Silver Creek	513	I	3
Skidmore	404	A	2
Slater	2,186	D	5
Smithton	532	E	5
Smithville	2,525	D	3
South Gifford	64	B	6
South Gorin	130	A	7
South Greenfield	112	H	4
South Lineville	40	A	5
South West City	600	J	3
Spanish Lake*†	20,322	E	10
Sparta	751	I	5
Spickard	326	B	4
Springfield	140,494°	H	5
Stanberry	1,310	B	3
Stark City	127	I	3
Steele	2,395	K	11
Steelville	1,465°	G	8
Stella	132	I	3
Stewartsville	732	C	3
Stockton	1,579°	G	4
Stotesbury	42	G	3
Stotts City	235	I	4
Stoutland	207	G	6
Stoutsville	26	C	7
Stover	964	F	5
Strafford	1,166	H	5
Strasburg	124	K	16
Sturgeon	838	D	7
Sugar Creek	3,982	I	15
Sullivan	5,661	F	9
Summersville	571	H	8
Sumner	140	C	5
Sundown	35	I	6
Sunnyvale		I	3
Sunrise Beach	181	F	6
Sunset Hills*	4,915	E	10
Sweet Springs	1,595	E	5
Sycamore Hills*	667	E	10
Syracuse	185	E	6
Table Rock Townsite	100	J	5
Tallapoosa	174	J	11
Taneyville	279	I	5
Taos*	802	F	7
Tarkio	2,243	A	1
Tarrants	43	D	9
Tarsney Lakes*		D	3
Thayer	1,996	J	8
Theodosia	235	J	6
Times Beach		C	15
Tina	199	C	5
Tindall	46	B	4
Tipton	2,026	E	6
Town and Country*	9,519	E	10
Tracy	287	H	14
Trenton	6,129°	B	4
Trimble	405	C	3
Triplett	58	C	5
Troy	3,811°	D	9
Truesdale	285	E	9
Turney	155	C	3
Tuscumbia	148°	F	6
Twin Oaks*	506	E	10
Umber View Heights	34	G	4
Union	5,909°	F	9
Union Star	432	B	3
Unionville	1,989°	A	5
Unity Village	138	J	15
University City	40,087	B	15
Uplands Park*	499	E	10
Urbana	350	G	5
Urich	498	F	4
Valley Park*	4,165	E	10
Van Buren	893°	I	9
Vandalia	2,683	D	8
Vandiver	75	D	7
Vanduser	187	I	11
Velda*	1,597	E	10
Velda Village Hills*	1,315	E	10
Verona	546	I	4
Versailles	2,365°	F	6
Viburnum	743	G	9
Vienna	611°	F	7
Vinita Park*	2,001	E	10
Vinita Terrace*	338	E	10
Vista	50	G	4
Waco	86	H	3
Wakenda	89	D	5
Walker	283	G	3
Walnut Grove	549	H	4
Wardell	325	J	11
Wardsville*	513	F	7
Warrensburg	15,244°	E	4
Warrenton	3,564°	E	9
Warsaw	1,696°	F	5
Warson Woods*	2,049	E	10
Washburn	362	J	4
Washington	10,704	C	13
Watson	137	A	1
Waverly	837	D	5
Wayland	391	A	8
Waynesville	3,207°	G	7
Weatherby	91	B	3
Weatherby Lake	1,613	I	14
Weaubleau	436	G	4
Webb City	7,449	H	3
Webster Groves	22,987	C	15
Weldon Spring Heights	82	E	10
Wellington	779	D	4
Wellston	3,612	B	16
Wellsville	1,430	D	8
Wentworth	138	I	4
Wentzville	5,088	B	14
West Line	98	E	3
West Plains	8,913°	J	7
Westboro	182	A	2
Weston	1,528	H	14
Westphalia	287	F	7
Westwood*	309	E	10
Wheatland	363	G	5
Wheaton	637	I	4
Wheeling	284	C	5
Whiteman AFB†	4,174	E	4
Whiteside	79	D	9
Whitewater	103	H	11
Wilbur Park*	522	E	10
Willard	2,177	H	5
Williamsville	391	I	10
Willow Springs	2,038	I	7
Wilson City	210	I	12
Winchester*	1,678	E	10
Windsor	3,044	E	4
Winfield	672	A	14
Winona	1,081	I	8
Winston	251	C	4
Wittenberg		G	12
Woods Heights	708	H	16
Woodson Terrace*	4,362	E	10
Wooldridge	54	E	6
Worth	103	A	3
Worthington	86	A	6
Wright City	1,250	B	13
Wyaconda	347	A	7
Wyatt	376	I	12
Zalma	83	I	11

*Does not appear on map; key shows general location.
†Census designated place—unincorporated, but recognized as a significant settled community by the U.S. Bureau of the Census.
‡Independent city, not part of any county.

°County seat.
Source: 1990 census. Places without population figures are unincorporated areas.

Missouri's mild climate and many attractions make the state a popular vacationland. Missouri has abundant wildlife, rugged hills, rushing streams, and peaceful woodlands to delight hunters, hikers, and photographers.

People who like to fish can try their luck for bass, trout, and other fish in the state's clear, spring-fed streams. Hunting for foxes and raccoons in the hills of

Missouri has long been a favorite sport. Visitors can take guided boat trips down rapid streams. The state's most unusual sights include such natural wonders as great bubbling springs and deep caverns.

Missouri's best-known annual event is perhaps the VP Fair. This celebration is held in early July in St. Louis. The fair attracts millions of people for Independence Day festivities.

Broom making in Silver Dollar City

Missouri Division of Tourism

Places to visit

Following are brief descriptions of some of Missouri's many interesting places to visit:

Branson, a town in the southwest Missouri Ozarks, offers country music performances by major artists. Its nearly 30 music theaters attract up to 5 million visitors each year.

Gateway Arch, in St. Louis, commemorates the city's role in the settlement of the West. The arch rises 630 feet (192 meters) and ranks as the tallest monument constructed in the United States. Small trains carry visitors to the top.

Harry S. Truman Library, in Independence, opened in 1957. The building houses about $3\frac{1}{2}$ million documents and mementos of Truman's presidency.

Lake of the Ozarks, in central Missouri, is one of the largest artificially created lakes in the world. Its shoreline is more than 1,300 miles (2,090 kilometers) long. The lake and the areas around it form a popular resort and recreation center.

Mark Twain Cave, near Hannibal, is a cave that Mark Twain learned about as a boy. In *The Adventures of Tom Sawyer,* Tom and his friend Becky Thatcher get lost in this cave.

Mark Twain Home and Museum, in Hannibal, is the restored boyhood home of the writer. The museum has many objects connected with Mark Twain's life.

Meramec Caverns, near Sullivan, is a legendary hideout of the outlaw Jesse James. The first room of this huge cave is large enough to hold 300 automobiles.

Pony Express Stables, in St. Joseph, are preserved to help trace the heritage of the famed Pony Express. Express riders

carried United States mail between St. Joseph and Sacramento, Calif., from April 1860 to October 1861.

Silver Dollar City, near Branson, is a reconstruction of an 1890's American mining town. Craftworkers show how Conestoga wagons were built and demonstrate such crafts as candle dipping and glass blowing.

Winston Churchill Memorial and Library, in Fulton, was formerly the Church of St. Mary Aldermanbury. It was dismantled and moved from London after World War II, and rebuilt on the campus of Westminster College in Fulton. Winston Churchill delivered his famous "iron curtain" speech on the campus in 1946.

National forest and parklands. Mark Twain National Forest, Missouri's only national forest, lies in the southern part of the state. Ulysses S. Grant National Historic Site, near St. Louis, is the estate occupied by Grant in the years immediately preceding the Civil War. George Washington Carver National Monument, near Diamond, honors the famous Missouri-born scientist. For more information on these and other national parklands in Missouri, see the map and tables in the *World Book* article on **National Park System.**

State forests and parks. Missouri has 100 state forests. Indian Trail, the largest, covers 13,253 acres (5,363 hectares) in Dent County. Missouri has 47 state parks and 25 state historic sites that provide outdoor recreation and preserve the state's heritage. For information about Missouri's state parks, write to Director, Division of Parks, Recreation and Historic Preservation, Box 176, Jefferson City, MO 65102.

© Jim Curley, Impact Press Group

Jour de Fete (Festival Day) in Ste. Genevieve

Annual events

January-March
St. Patrick's Day Parade in Kansas City (March 17); National Intercollegiate (NAIA) Basketball Tournament in Kansas City (March).

April-June
Dogwood Festival in Camdenton (April); Storytelling Festival in St. Louis (May); Maifest Celebration in Hermann (May); Valley of Flowers Festival in Florissant (May); Scott Joplin Ragtime Festival in Sedalia (June).

July-September
VP Fair in St. Louis (July); National Tom Sawyer Fence Painting Contest in Hannibal (July); Blessing of the Fleet in Hazelwood (July); State Fair in Sedalia (August); Jour de Fete (Festival Day) in Ste. Genevieve (August); Ozark Empire Fair in Springfield (August); Cotton Carnival in Sikeston (September); Country Club Plaza Art Fair in Kansas City (September); The Great Forest Park Balloon Race in Kirkwood (September); National Crafts Festival in Silver Dollar City, near Branson (September-October).

October-December
Robidoux Festival in St. Joseph (October); American Royal Rodeo, Livestock and Horse Show in Kansas City (November); Ozark Mountain Christmas near Branson (November-December).

Missouri Division of Tourism

Mark Twain Museum and Home in Hannibal

Missouri Division of Tourism

Meramec Caverns near Sullivan

© Robert Lee II

Climatron at Missouri Botanical Garden in St. Louis

Land and climate

Land regions. Missouri has four main land regions. These are, from north to south: (1) the Dissected Till Plains, (2) the Osage Plains, (3) the Ozark Plateau (or Ozarks), and (4) the Mississippi Alluvial Plain.

*The **Dissected Till Plains** lie north of the Missouri River. Glaciers once covered this region. The great ice sheets left a rich, deep deposit of soil-forming materials especially suited to the growing of corn. Many slow-moving streams drain the rolling surface of this land region.

*The **Osage Plains** lie in western Missouri. This is a region of flat prairie land, broken in places by low hills. Glacial ice never covered the region, and the soil is not as rich as that of the Dissected Till Plains. The chief crops are corn and other grains.

*The **Ozark Plateau** is the state's largest land region. Forested hills and low mountains give it scenic beauty. The plateau rises from 500 to 1,700 feet (150 to 518 meters) or more above sea level. In the extreme southwestern corner of the state, a high, wooded tableland has soil especially good for gardening and raising strawberries. The river valleys are about the only level land in the Ozark region. The plateau is one of the nation's major tourist areas because of its many caves, large springs and lakes, and clear, fast-flowing streams.

The St. Francois Mountains rise in the southeast. This series of granite peaks, knobs, and domes covers about 70 square miles (180 square kilometers). The St. Francois Mountains do not form a continuous range. They rise more or less in groups, usually of two or three peaks. The St. Francois Mountains make up the highest and most rugged part of the state. One of the peaks, Taum Sauk (1,772 feet, or 540 meters), is the highest point in Missouri.

*The **Mississippi Alluvial Plain** covers the southeastern corner of Missouri. This region was once a swampy wilderness. Much of the area has been cleared and drained, and the soil is unusually rich for farming. Cotton, soybeans, and rice are important crops. The southern part of the plain is known as the *Boot Heel* because of its shape.

Rivers and lakes. Missouri owes much of its commercial and industrial importance to the two largest rivers in the United States—the Mississippi and the Missouri. These rivers and their branches provide water highways for transportation, water supplies for cities and industries, and hydroelectric power for homes and factories.

The Current River is one of Missouri's most beautiful rivers. It starts from Montauk Spring in the Ozarks, which has a daily flow of about 40 million gallons (150 million liters). The river's name comes from the swift flow of its cold, sparkling waters. Like the Black, James, St. Francis, and other rivers of the Ozark Plateau, the Current is noted for its game fish. Other rivers favored by fishermen include the Gasconade, Little Piney, Meramec, and White.

The Harry S. Truman Reservoir, an artificially created lake, is the largest lake in the state. The reservoir covers about 55,600 acres (22,500 hectares). The second largest lake is Lake of the Ozarks. It covers about 55,300 acres

© Robert M. Lindholm

A colorful, tree-covered cliff is reflected in a pool of an Ozark stream. The Ozark Plateau region of southern Missouri has some of the most beautiful wilderness in the United States.

Land regions of Missouri

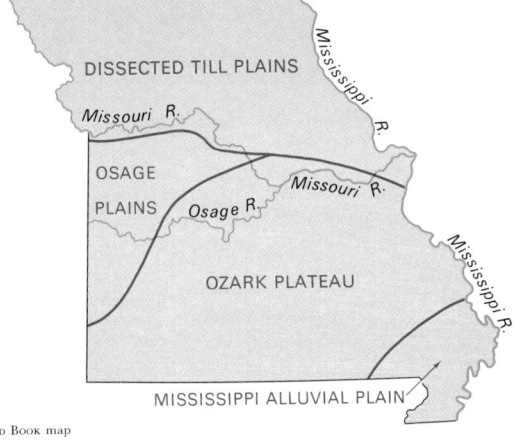

WORLD BOOK map

Map index

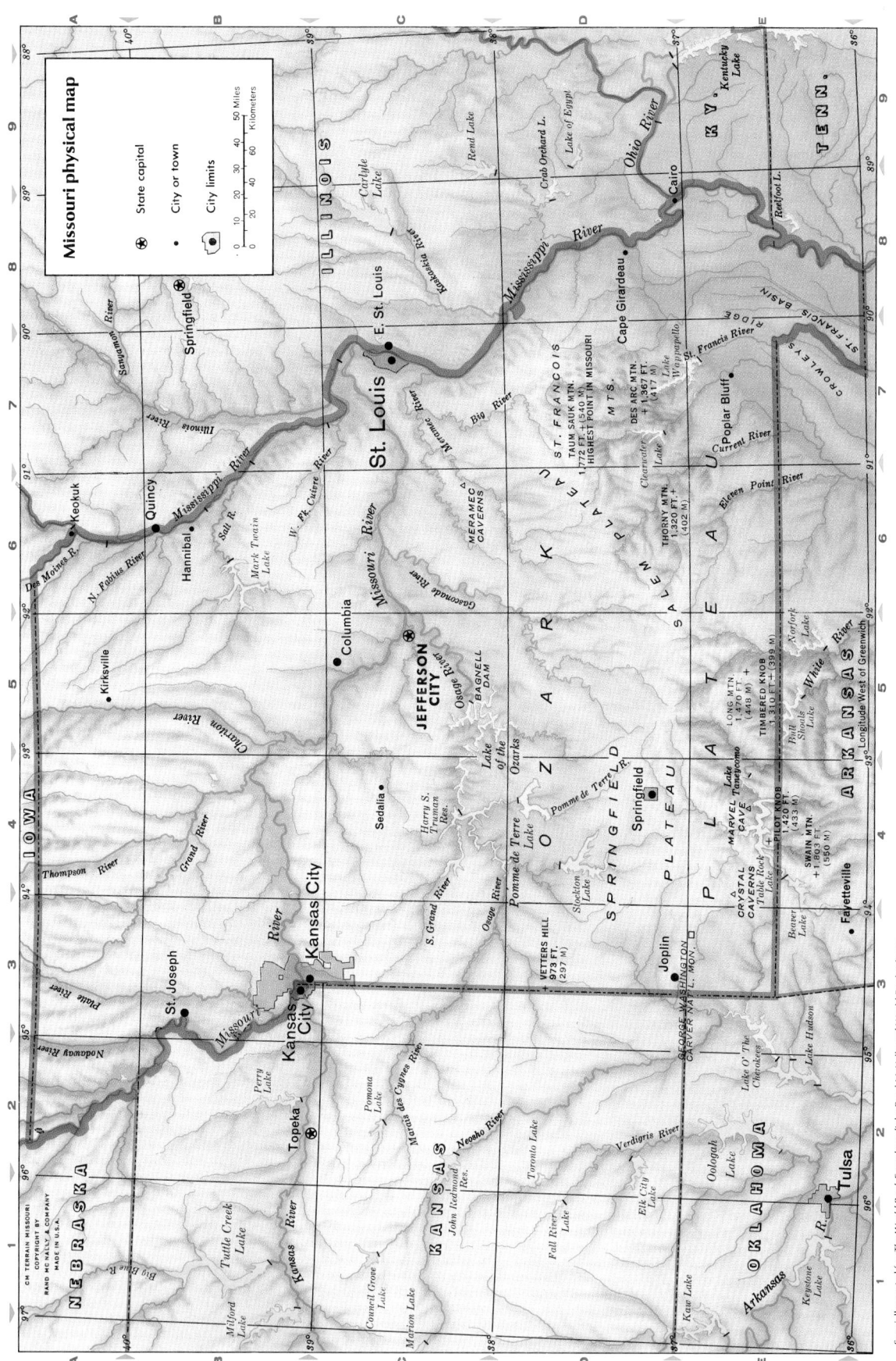

Missouri physical map

State capital
City or town
City limits

50 Miles
0 10 20 30 40 60
Kilometers

NEBRASKA

IOWA

ILLINOIS

KENTUCKY

TENN.

KANSAS

OKLAHOMA

ARKANSAS

Big Blue R.
Milford Lake
Tuttle Creek Lake
Kansas River
Thompson River
Nodaway River
Des Moines R.
N. Fabius River
Sangamon River
Illinois River
Keokuk
Quincy
Hannibal
Salt R.
Mark Twain Lake
Kickapoo Creek

St. Joseph
Platte River
Missouri River
Kansas City
Kansas City
Topeka
Perry Lake
Pomona Lake
Marais des Cygnes River
John Redmond Res.
Council Grove Lake
Marion Lake
Toronto Lake
Neosho River
Verdigris River
Fall River Lake
Elk City Lake
Oologah Lake
Keystone Lake
Arkansas R.
Tulsa

Springfield
Springfield
Sedalia
Columbia
Kirksville
Chariton River
Grand River
S. Grand River
Osage River
Pomme de Terre Lake
Stockton Lake
Harry S. Truman Res.
Lake of the Ozarks
Bagnell Dam
Osage River
JEFFERSON CITY

St. Louis
E. St. Louis
Mississippi River
Missouri River
Meramec River
Gasconade River
W. Ft. Cuivre River
Big River
MERAMEC CAVERNS

Lake Hudson
Lake O' The Cherokees
Beaver Lake
Fayetteville
Bull Shoals Lake
Norfork Lake
White River
Joplin
GEORGE WASHINGTON CARVER NAT'L MON.
VETTERS HILL 973 FT. (297 M)
CRYSTAL CAVERNS
MARVEL CAVE
PILOT KNOB 1,420 FT. (433 M)
SWAIN MTN. 1,803 FT. (550 M)
TIMBERED KNOB 1,310 FT. (399 M)
LONG MTN. 1,470 FT. (448 M)
Pomme de Terre
Table Rock Lake
Taneycomo Lake

OZARK PLATEAU
SPRINGFIELD PLATEAU

SALEM PLATEAU
ST. FRANCOIS MTS.
TAUM SAUK MTN. 1,772 FT. (540 M) HIGHEST POINT IN MISSOURI
DES ARC MTN. 1,367 FT. (417 M)
THORNY MTN. 1,320 FT. (402 M)
Clearwater Lake
Eleven Point River
Current River
Poplar Bluff
Lake Wappapello
St. Francis River
Cape Girardeau
ST. FRANCIS RIDGE
CROWLEYS RIDGE
ST. FRANCIS BASIN

Ohio River
Cairo
Kentucky Lake
Reelfoot L.
Crab Orchard L.
Lake of Egypt
Rend Lake
Carlyle Lake
Kaskaskia River

91° Longitude West of Greenwich

Specially created for *The World Book Encyclopedia* by Rand McNally and World Book editors

(22,400 hectares). Lake of the Ozarks was also artificially created. Other artificially created lakes include Pomme de Terre, Table Rock, and Taneycomo.

Springs and caves. About 10,000 springs bubble from the ground in the Ozark Plateau. More than a hundred springs have a daily water flow of over 1 million gallons (3.8 million liters) each. The largest is Big Spring, near Van Buren. It has an average flow of about 278 million gallons (1,052 million liters) of water a day. Missouri also has about 30 mineral springs.

More than 1,450 caves have been found in Missouri. Underground streams formed these caves beneath the Ozarks. One of the largest caves, Marvel Cave, is near Branson. The cave has 10 miles (16 kilometers) of passageways. Every year, about 20 marriages are performed in Bridal Cave, near Camdenton.

Plant and animal life. Forests cover about a third of Missouri, chiefly the southern part of the state. The state's forests are made up largely of hardwoods. Most of the forests consist of various types of oak or hickory. The state also has large growths of such trees as ash, bald cypress, cottonwood, elm, maple, shortleaf pine, and sweet gum.

Asters, dogwood, goldenrod, milkweed, roses, sweet Williams, verbenas, violets, and many kinds of mint and hawthorn grow throughout Missouri. Prairie blossoms include anemones, meadow roses, turtleheads, and white snakeroots. Mistletoe grows on many trees on the Mississippi Alluvial Plain region of Missouri. The Ozark Plateau probably has more flowers than any other region in the state.

White-tailed deer are the most numerous of Missouri's big-game animals. Other animals include beavers, cottontail rabbits, foxes, muskrats, opossums, raccoons, skunks, and squirrels. The most common birds are the blue jay, cardinal, mockingbird, purple finch, and woodpecker. Baltimore orioles, goldfinch, and whippoorwills are also seen.

The bobwhite quail is Missouri's most plentiful game bird. Fish found in Missouri's lakes, rivers, and streams include bass, bluegills, catfish, crappies, jack salmon, and trout.

Climate. Winters and summers are milder in the mountain areas of Missouri than in the lower-lying plains. In July, the average temperature is about 78° F. (26° C). The state's record high temperature is 118° F. (48° C). It was set at Clinton on July 15, 1936; at Lamar on July 18, 1936; and at Union and Warsaw on July 14, 1954.

The average January temperature is about 30° F. (−1° C). Missouri's record low temperature of −40° F. (−40° C) was set at Warsaw on Feb. 13, 1905. The average yearly *precipitation* (rain, melted snow, and other forms of moisture) ranges from about 50 inches (130 centimeters) in the southeast to 30 inches (76 centimeters) in the northwest. The growing season in Missouri ranges from 225 days in the southeastern part of the state to 170 days in the northern part.

Average monthly weather

	Kansas City					St. Louis				
	Temperatures				Days of		Temperatures			Days of
	F°		C°		rain or		F°		C°	rain or
	High	Low	High	Low	snow		High	Low	High Low	snow
Jan.	39	21	4	−6	7	Jan	41	26	5 −3	9
Feb.	44	25	7	−4	7	Feb.	45	29	7 −2	9
Mar.	54	34	12	1	9	Mar.	54	37	12 3	11
Apr.	66	46	19	8	11	Apr.	66	47	19 8	12
May	75	56	24	13	12	May	75	57	24 14	12
June	85	66	29	19	11	June	85	67	29 19	11
July	91	71	33	22	8	July	90	72	32 22	8
Aug.	89	69	32	21	9	Aug.	88	70	31 21	8
Sept.	81	60	27	16	7	Sept.	80	62	27 17	7
Oct.	70	49	21	9	7	Oct.	70	52	21 11	7
Nov.	54	35	12	2	6	Nov.	54	38	12 3	8
Dec.	42	25	6	−4	7	Dec.	44	29	7 −2	9

Average January temperatures

Missouri has a broad range of winter temperatures. The north is the coldest while the south averages above freezing.

Average July temperatures

Summers in Missouri are milder in the mountainous south than in the lower-lying plains. The far north is also milder.

Average yearly precipitation

Precipitation varies widely in the state, with the southeast getting the most. The northern part of Missouri is the driest.

WORLD BOOK maps

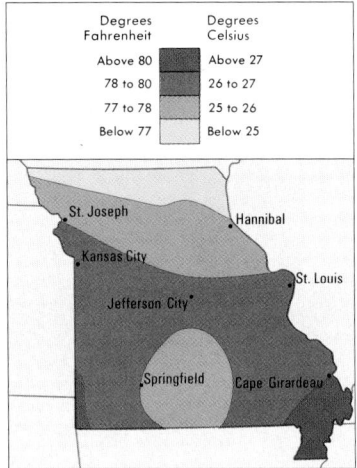

Degrees Fahrenheit	Degrees Celsius
Above 32	Above 0
28 to 32	-2 to 0
24 to 28	-4 to -2
Below 24	Below -4

Degrees Fahrenheit	Degrees Celsius
Above 80	Above 27
78 to 80	26 to 27
77 to 78	25 to 26
Below 77	Below 25

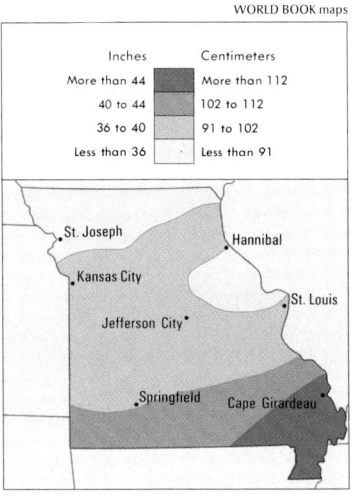

Inches	Centimeters
More than 44	More than 112
40 to 44	102 to 112
36 to 40	91 to 102
Less than 36	Less than 91

Service industries, taken together, make up nearly three-fourths of Missouri's *gross state product*—the total value of all goods and services produced in a state in a year. However, manufacturing is the single most important economic activity.

Natural resources of Missouri include fertile soils and large mineral deposits.

Soil. The soils of the Dissected Till Plains are mainly glacial soils (clay mixed with sand and gravel) and *loess* (a brownish wind-blown dust). A band of rich loess, often more than 50 feet (15 meters) deep, lies along the Missouri River. The Osage Plains have soils of medium fertility, ranging from dark-brown loam to lighter-colored sandy or silt loams.

Brown limestone soils cover most of the southwestern part of the Ozarks. Elsewhere in the Ozarks, the soils are shallow and stony. The Mississippi River has deposited rich soils on the Mississippi Alluvial Plain. Rich alluvial soil also lies along the Missouri River.

Minerals. The state's most important metal is lead. Lead is found in Iron, Reynolds, and Washington counties. Copper, silver, and zinc are also recovered by processing the lead ore. Large fire clay deposits occur in east-central Missouri. An important barite reserve lies south of St. Louis. Limestone, Missouri's leading quarry product, is found in most of the state. Dolomite, granite, marble, and sandstone are also quarried.

Coal is found in about half of the state, in an area extending from the southwest to the northeast. Missouri's coal reserves total about 6 billion short tons (5.4 billion metric tons). The state has deposits of iron ore in the eastern Ozarks. Missouri also has small amounts of oil and natural gas along its western border. Other minerals found in the state include cobalt, manganese, nickel, sand and gravel, and tungsten.

Service industries account for 72 percent of the gross state product. Most of the service industries are concentrated in Missouri's six metropolitan areas.

Community, social, and personal services form the leading service industry in Missouri in terms of the gross state product. The industry includes such activities as the operation of doctors' offices and private hospitals, hotels, data processing services, and professional sports franchises. St. Louis and its suburbs are the leading area for most of these activities. Columbia, Kansas City, and Springfield are also major centers of health care in Mis-

Production and workers by economic activities

Economic activities	Percent of GSP* produced	Employed workers	
		Number of persons	Percent of total
Manufacturing	22	415,300	17
Community, social, & personal services	19	579,300	24
Wholesale and retail trade	16	548,500	23
Finance, insurance, & real estate	15	136,400	6
Government	11	370,800	15
Transportation, communication, & utilities	11	152,000	6
Construction	4	88,100	4
Agriculture	2	118,000	5
Mining	†	4,700	†
Total	100	2,413,100	100

*GSP = gross state product, the total value of goods and services produced in a year.
†Less than one-half of 1 per cent.
Figures are for 1991.
Sources: *World Book* estimates based on data from U.S. Bureau of Economic Analysis, U.S. Bureau of Labor Statistics, and U.S. Department of Agriculture.

souri. Professional sports teams in Kansas City and St. Louis make an important contribution to the state's economy.

Wholesale and retail trade is the second-ranking service industry in terms of the gross state product. The wholesale trade of farm products is important in Kansas City, St. Joseph, St. Louis, and Springfield. St. Louis is a major national center for the wholesale trade of automobiles. The wholesale trade of groceries is significant in all of Missouri's urban areas. Leading retail establishments include automobile dealerships, department stores, and restaurants. The St. Louis and Kansas City areas are the leaders in retail trade in Missouri.

Finance, insurance, and real estate form the third most important service industry in Missouri. St. Louis and Kansas City are both among the Midwest's leading financial cities. Each city is the home of a district branch of the Federal Reserve Bank. The largest commercial banks and insurance companies in Missouri are located in St. Louis.

Missouri's next most important service industries are

McDonnell Douglas Corp.

Airplane manufacturing is a major industry in the St. Louis area. The factory at left is producing F-15 Eagle fighter planes.

(1) government and (2) transportation, communication, and utilities. Each of these two industries contributes an equal portion of the state's gross state product. Government services include the operation of public schools, public hospitals, and military bases.

Transportation services are important to Missouri's economy. A major moving company is headquartered in Fenton. Many railroads have large operations in Kansas City and St. Louis. Some firms use barges on the Mississippi and Missouri rivers to transport freight. Telephone companies form the largest part of the communications sector. More information about transportation and communication can be found later in this section.

Manufacturing accounts for 22 percent of the gross state product. Goods manufactured in the state have a *value added by manufacture* of approximately $26 billion a year. This figure represents the increase in value of raw materials after they become finished products. The state has more than 8,400 factories. Most of these factories are located in the Kansas City and St. Louis metropolitan areas.

The production of transportation equipment is Missouri's leading manufacturing activity by far. Factories produce airplanes, barges, railroad cars, truck and bus bodies, and truck trailers. Missouri ranks high in automobile and truck production. Fenton, Kansas City, and Wentzville have automobile plants. Claycomo and Fenton manufacture trucks. St. Louis is one of the leading areas in the United States for the production of military aircraft. Factories in northern St. Louis County manufacture F-15 Eagle and F-18 Hornet supersonic fighter planes.

Chemicals rank second in value among Missouri's manufactured products. This industry includes the production of fertilizer, insecticide, paint, pharmaceuticals, and soap. The St. Louis area accounts for about half of the state's total chemical manufacturing.

Food products rank third in value added by manufacture. One of the nation's largest dairy-processing plants is in Springfield. St. Louis ranks as a leading beer-brewing center of the United States. Kansas City, which is located in the heart of the nation's winter-wheat belt, has large flour mills.

Other products manufactured in Missouri, in order of value, include fabricated metal products, printed materials, electrical equipment, and machinery. Fabricated metal products manufactured in the state include cans, doors, and ammunition.

Agriculture provides 2 percent of Missouri's gross state product. Missouri has about 107,000 farms. The average farm covers 284 acres (115 hectares). Farmland covers more than 30 million acres (12 million hectares) of Missouri, or about two-thirds of the state.

Livestock and livestock products account for about 55 percent of Missouri's farm income. Missouri ranks among the leading producers of beef cattle, hogs, and turkeys. Beef cattle and hogs provide most of the income for the state's livestock farmers. Southwest Missouri is the most important area for raising beef cattle. Large numbers of dairy cattle are also raised there. Hog farms are important throughout the state. Farmers in central Missouri raise the most turkeys. Chickens and sheep can also be found on some of the farms in the state.

Crops account for about 45 percent of Missouri's farm income. Soybeans are the state's most valuable farm product. Missouri is among the leading growers of soybeans, corn, and grain sorghum. These crops are used mainly for livestock feed. Soybeans are also used to make oil. Northern Missouri has the largest soybean production. The heaviest concentration of corn farms is in the central part of the state. Eastern Missouri grows the most grain sorghum. Farmers also raise large amounts of cotton, hay, and wheat in Missouri.

Apples, peaches, and grapes are Missouri's most valuable fruits. Truck farms near St. Louis grow a variety of vegetables. Greenhouse and nursery products are important in the Kansas City and St. Louis areas.

Farm, mineral, and forest products

This map shows where the leading farm, mineral, and forest products are produced. The major urban areas (shown in red) are the important manufacturing centers.

WORLD BOOK map

© R. Hamilton Smith

A combine harvests Missouri soybeans.

Mining accounts for less than one-half of 1 per cent of Missouri's gross state product. Lead, limestone, and coal provide most of the mining income.

Missouri leads the states in lead production. Lead is mined in Iron and Reynolds counties in the southeastern part of the state. Copper, silver, and zinc are also produced from the lead mines. Most of the state's limestone comes from quarries near the Mississippi River. Limestone is made into cement and crushed stone for roadbeds. Coal comes mainly from surface mines in Randolph County in the northeast. Other mineral products include clays, iron ore, and sand and gravel.

Electric power. Coal-fired steam plants generate about 80 per cent of Missouri's electric power. A large hydroelectric power plant at Bagnell Dam in the Ozark Plateau generates electricity mainly for the St. Louis area. A nuclear power plant in Callaway County supplies electricity mainly for eastern and central Missouri.

The Taum Sauk Project near Lesterville is one of the largest pumped-storage hydroelectric plants in the United States. The plant stores and uses the same supply of water over and over again. The water is pumped from a lower reservoir to a higher one. When the water is released from the upper reservoir and flows to the lower one, its flow is used to generate electricity.

Transportation. Missouri's central location, its nearness to raw materials, and the great Mississippi and Missouri waterways have made the state a leading transportation center in the nation.

Lambert Airport in St. Louis and Mid-Continent International Airport in Kansas City are among the busiest airports in the Midwestern United States. Small airports and private airstrips are scattered throughout the state.

St. Louis and Kansas City are among the largest United States railroad centers. About 20 rail lines provide freight service, and passenger trains serve about 10 cities in the state.

Missouri has about 120,000 miles (190,000 kilometers) of roads and highways. About 95 per cent of the state's roads and highways are surfaced. The first land traffic in Missouri followed old Indian trails. In 1860 and 1861, St. Joseph was the eastern terminal of the pony express mail system. The famous Oregon and Santa Fe trails ran from Independence. Today, Kansas City and St. Louis rank among the nation's leading trucking centers.

Boats and barges can use the Mississippi River for 490 miles (789 kilometers) along the state's eastern border. The Missouri River has about 550 miles (890 kilometers) of commercially navigable waters in the state. St. Louis is one of the busiest inland U.S. ports.

Communication. Two famous Missouri journalists made newspaper history. They founded the state's leading papers and influenced journalism across the country. William Rockhill Nelson, founder of *The Kansas City Star,* fought for government reform. Joseph Pulitzer, who founded the *St. Louis Post-Dispatch,* established the Pulitzer Prizes (see **Pulitzer Prizes**).

The first Missouri newspaper, the *Missouri Gazette,* began publication in St. Louis in 1808. Today, Missouri has about 50 daily newspapers and about 260 weeklies. Newspapers with the largest daily circulations include *The Kansas City Star* and the *St. Louis Post-Dispatch.* Missouri publishers also issue about 205 periodicals.

The first radio station in Missouri, WEW of St. Louis University, began broadcasting in 1921. The state's first television station, KSD-TV, started in 1947 in St. Louis. There are now about 220 radio stations and about 25 television stations.

Government

Constitution of Missouri was adopted in 1945. The state had three earlier constitutions, adopted in 1820, 1865, and 1875. An amendment to the Constitution may be proposed by a majority of the members of the state legislature. Or it may be proposed by a petition signed by 8 per cent of the voters in two-thirds of the state's congressional districts. To become part of the Constitution, an amendment must be approved by a majority of the voters voting on the amendment. The Constitution requires that the people vote every 20 years, starting in 1962, on whether to call a convention to amend the Constitution.

Executive. The governor of Missouri is elected to a four-year term and is limited to two terms. The governor appoints many of the key officials of state government agencies. The other top state officials are the lieutenant governor, secretary of state, state treasurer, attorney general, and state auditor. These officials are elected to four-year terms.

Legislature of Missouri is known as the General Assembly. It consists of a Senate of 34 members and a House of Representatives of 163 members. Missouri has 34 senatorial districts and 163 representative districts. Voters in each senatorial district elect one senator. Voters in each representative district elect one representative. Senators serve four-year terms and may serve no

more than two terms. Representatives serve two-year terms and may serve no more than four terms.

In 1966, a commission *reapportioned* (redivided) the House of Representatives to provide equal representation on the basis of population. Beginning in 1971, both the House and Senate districts have been redrawn every 10 years, based on U.S. census results.

The General Assembly meets every year on the Wednesday after the first Monday in January. The General Assembly's session lasts until the Friday following the second Monday in May. The governor may call special sessions of the Assembly. Special sessions may also be called by petition by three-fourths of the members of the Senate or three-fourths of the members of the House of Representatives.

Courts in Missouri are headed by the state Supreme Court, composed of seven judges. The state court of appeals has three districts—the Western district in Kansas City, the Eastern district in St. Louis, and the Southern district in Springfield. The governor appoints the judges of the Supreme Court and the appeals courts for 12-year terms. They are selected from candidates proposed by nonpartisan commissions. Appointed judges must be approved by the voters in the next general election. When their term expires, they must again be approved by the voters to remain in office. Every two years, the

Supreme Court selects one member to serve as chief justice.

The state constitution also provides for circuit courts, associate circuit courts, and municipal courts. Circuit-court judges serve six-year terms, and the rest serve four-year terms. Judges of circuit and associate circuit courts in Jackson, Platte, Clay, and St. Louis counties—and in the city of St. Louis—are selected like the judges of the Supreme Court. The people elect all other Missouri judges.

Local government. Voters in Missouri's 114 counties elect local officials. These officials generally include three commissioners of the county commission, a sheriff, recorder of deeds, prosecuting attorney, collector of revenue, assessor, treasurer, coroner, public administrator, and surveyor. The county commissioners serve as the chief administrators of the county. They are responsible for health, welfare, and public works in the county, and set the county tax rate. The constitution provides that any county with more than 85,000 residents, or any city with over 10,000 people, may organize its government in the way that best suits its people. Like most Missouri cities, St. Louis has a mayor-council form of government. But St. Louis is an independent city and is not

Missouri's House of Representatives meets in the state capitol in Jefferson City. Representatives serve two-year terms.

© Chris Wilkins, Impact Press Group

The governors of Missouri

	Party	Term		Party	Term
Alexander McNair	*Dem.-Rep.	1820-1824	David R. Francis	Democratic	1889-1893
Frederick Bates	*Dem.-Rep.	1824-1825	William Joel Stone	Democratic	1893-1897
Abraham J. Williams	*Dem.-Rep.	1825-1826	Lon V. Stephens	Democratic	1897-1901
John Miller	*Dem.-Rep.	1826-1832	Alexander M. Dockery	Democratic	1901-1905
Daniel Dunklin	Democratic	1832-1836	Joseph W. Folk	Democratic	1905-1909
Lilburn W. Boggs	Democratic	1836-1840	Herbert S. Hadley	Republican	1909-1913
Thomas Reynolds	Democratic	1840-1844	Elliott W. Major	Democratic	1913-1917
Meredith M. Marmaduke	Democratic	1844	Frederick D. Gardner	Democratic	1917-1921
John C. Edwards	Democratic	1844-1848	Arthur M. Hyde	Republican	1921-1925
Austin A. King	Democratic	1848-1853	Sam A. Baker	Republican	1925-1929
Sterling Price	Democratic	1853-1857	Henry S. Caulfield	Republican	1929-1933
Trusten Polk	Democratic	1857	Guy B. Park	Democratic	1933-1937
Hancock Lee Jackson	Democratic	1857	Lloyd C. Stark	Democratic	1937-1941
Robert M. Stewart	Democratic	1857-1861	Forrest C. Donnell	Republican	1941-1945
Claiborne F. Jackson	Democratic	1861	Phil M. Donnelly	Democratic	1945-1949
Hamilton R. Gamble	Union	1861-1864	Forrest Smith	Democratic	1949-1953
Willard P. Hall	Union	1864-1865	Phil M. Donnelly	Democratic	1953-1957
Thomas C. Fletcher	‡Rad. Rep.	1865-1869	James T. Blair, Jr.	Democratic	1957-1961
Joseph W. McClurg	‡Rad. Rep.	1869-1871	John M. Dalton	Democratic	1961-1965
B. Gratz Brown	†Lib. Rep.	1871-1873	Warren E. Hearnes	Democratic	1965-1973
Silas Woodson	Democratic	1873-1875	Christopher S. Bond	Republican	1973-1977
Charles H. Hardin	Democratic	1875-1877	Joseph P. Teasdale	Democratic	1977-1981
John S. Phelps	Democratic	1877-1881	Christopher S. Bond	Republican	1981-1985
Thomas T. Crittenden	Democratic	1881-1885	John Ashcroft	Republican	1985-1993
John S. Marmaduke	Democratic	1885-1887	Mel Carnahan	Democratic	1993-
Albert P. Morehouse	Democratic	1887-1889			

*Democratic-Republican.   †Liberal Republican.   ‡Radical Republican.

part of any county. It is governed by a mayor, a 28-member Board of Aldermen, and the board president.

Revenue. Taxes bring in about two-thirds of Missouri's *general revenue* (income). The federal government provides about a fourth of the revenue. Missouri receives about half its revenue from a sales tax, individual and corporation income taxes, a gasoline tax, and vehicle licenses. Taxes are also collected on cigarettes, liquor, property, and other items. A statewide lottery also contributes to the state's revenue.

Politics. Missouri voters tend to favor Democratic candidates over Republicans, but the balloting is usually close. During the 1900's, Missouri has voted for the winner in all except two presidential elections—in 1900 and 1956. For its voting record in presidential elections since 1820, see **Electoral College** (table).

St. Louis and Kansas City vote strongly Democratic, but the region around St. Louis is Republican. Northeastern Missouri, most of the counties along the Missouri River, and southeastern Missouri are Democratic. North-central and southwestern Missouri are Republican. About 30 counties switch back and forth between the two major parties. The party that wins these counties generally controls the state legislature.

History

Indian days. Indians known as mound builders lived in the Missouri region long before white men came there. The Indians built large earthwork mounds that still may be seen in various sections of the state (see **Mound builders**). Many tribes of Indians lived in Missouri when the white man first arrived. The Missouri Indians dwelt in what is now east-central Missouri. The Osage, a tribe of unusually tall Indians, lived and hunted in the areas to the south and the west. Other tribes included the Fox and the Sauk Indians, who lived in the north. See **Indian, American** (table of tribes).

Exploration and settlement. The daring French explorers Father Jacques Marquette and Louis Jolliet were probably the first white people to see the mouth of the Missouri River. In 1673, they marked the spot where the Missouri joins the Mississippi. In 1682, another French explorer, René-Robert Cavelier, Sieur de La Salle, traveled down the Mississippi River and claimed the Mississippi Valley for France. La Salle named the region *Louisiana* in honor of King Louis XIV.

During the years that followed, French trappers and fur traders established trading posts along the river. French missionaries, eager to convert the Indians, founded a number of missions. Indian tales of gold and silver attracted other Frenchmen. These adventurers found lead and salt in what is now St. Francois County and remained to mine these minerals. About 1700, Jesuit missionaries established the first white settlement in Missouri, the Mission of St. Francis Xavier. They built it near the present site of St. Louis. The mission was abandoned in 1703 because of unhealthful swamps nearby. About 1735, settlers from what is now Illinois established Missouri's first permanent white settlement, at Ste. Genevieve. In 1764, Pierre Laclède Liguest and René Auguste Chouteau founded St. Louis.

By a secret treaty, signed in 1762, France gave up all its territory west of the Mississippi River to Spain. France and Spain had been allies in the Seven Years' War (see **Seven Years' War**). The Spaniards encouraged pioneers from the East to come to the region, and settlers poured into the Spanish land. One of the pioneers was Daniel Boone, the famous frontiersman. He moved to what is now St. Charles County in 1799, after the Spanish had granted him about 850 acres (340 hectares) of land. In 1800, the Spanish appointed Boone a *syndic,* or judge (see **Boone, Daniel**).

Napoleon Bonaparte, the ruler of France, forced Spain to return the territory west of the Mississippi to France in 1800. By that time, much of present-day Missouri had been explored and many communities had been established. Napoleon, badly in need of money to finance his wars in Europe, sold the Louisiana Territory to the United States in 1803 (see **Louisiana Purchase**). The northern part of the territory was called Upper Louisiana, and included the present state of Missouri. Upper Louisiana extended northward from the 33rd parallel to Canada, and westward to the Rocky Mountains. In 1812, Congress organized the Missouri Territory.

In late 1811 and early 1812, three of the strongest earthquakes ever to hit the United States struck Missouri's New Madrid area. Scientists believe they measured 8 or higher on the Richter scale and were probably more severe than the great San Francisco earthquake of 1906. Fortunately, not many people lived in the region. Property damage and the death toll thus were small compared with the earthquakes' violence.

Territorial days. The Missouri Territory began with a population of more than 20,000. The farming and mining industries were well established, and schools and churches had been built. So many settlers poured into the territory that the Indians became aroused by the loss of their ancient hunting grounds. For several years, the Indians led bloody raids on the frontier settlements.

In 1812, war broke out between the United States and Great Britain (see **War of 1812**). The British gave weapons to the Indians and encouraged them to attack the Missouri pioneers. The settlers built forts and block-houses for protection. Even after the war between the United States and Britain ended, the Indians continued to raid many settlements. The attacks ended in 1815, when the Indians and U.S. government officials signed a peace treaty at Portage des Sioux.

Statehood and expansion. In 1818, Missouri asked Congress to be admitted into the Union. The territory had been settled mainly by Southerners who had brought black slaves with them. Missouri's application for admission as a slave state caused a nationwide dispute between slavery and antislavery sympathizers. This dispute was not settled until 1820, when Congress passed the Missouri Compromise. Under this legislation, Missouri entered the Union as a slave state on Aug. 10, 1821. A census in 1820 showed that the territory had 66,586 people, including 10,222 slaves. Missourians elected Alexander McNair as the first governor.

When Missouri entered the Union, it was the western frontier of the nation. The fur trade was the state's most

Historic Missouri

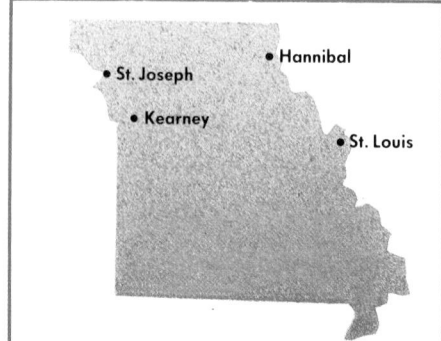

Lewis and Clark started their famous journey to the Pacific Northwest from near St. Louis in 1804. They gave the United States a strong claim to the great Oregon region.

The Missouri Compromise, passed by Congress in 1820, brought Missouri into the Union the next year as a slave state.

Mark Twain, a great American author, was born in 1835 in Florida, Mo. He grew up in Hannibal.

Jesse James, one of the nation's most celebrated bandits, terrorized Missouri for about 16 years following the Civil War. He was born near Centerville (now Kearney).

The Dred Scott Decision was made by the U.S. Supreme Court in 1857. It prevented Missouri slave Dred Scott from gaining freedom, and added to the North-South conflict.

The pony express linked St. Joseph with Sacramento, Calif., in 1860 and 1861. Riders carrying mail on this route covered almost 2,000 miles (3,200 kilometers) in about 10 days.

WORLD BOOK illustrations by Kevin Chadwick

Important dates in Missouri

1673 Father Jacques Marquette and Louis Jolliet probably became the first white people to see the mouth of the Missouri River.

1682 René-Robert Cavelier, Sieur de la Salle, claimed the Mississippi Valley, including Missouri, for France. He named the region *Louisiana.*

c. 1735 Settlers established Missouri's first permanent white settlement, at Ste. Genevieve.

1762 France gave the Louisiana region to Spain.

1764 Pierre Laclède Liguest and René Auguste Chouteau established St. Louis.

1800 Spain returned the Louisiana region to France.

1803 France sold the Louisiana region to the U.S.

1812 Congress made Missouri a territory.

1815 Indian attacks on Missouri settlements ended when the Indians and United States government officials signed a peace treaty at Portage des Sioux.

1821 Missouri became the 24th state on August 10.

1837 Missouri gained its six northwestern counties as a result of the Platte Purchase.

1854 Border warfare began between antislavery Kansans and proslavery Missourians.

1861-1865 Missouri became a battleground during the Civil War.

1904 The Louisiana Purchase Exposition was held in St. Louis.

1931 Bagnell Dam on the Osage River was completed, forming the Lake of the Ozarks.

1945 Harry S. Truman of Independence became the 33rd President of the United States.

1965 The last section of the stainless steel Gateway Arch was put in place in St. Louis. The nation's tallest monument, it is 630 feet (192 meters) high.

1986 Missouri began operating a statewide lottery.

important industry. In 1822, John Jacob Astor organized a St. Louis branch of the American Fur Company. Within the next 12 years, Astor ruined or bought out most other fur companies. He had a near monopoly on the fur trade west of the Mississippi River.

In 1836, Congress approved the purchase from the Indians of an area known as the Platte Country. By presidential proclamation, it became part of Missouri in 1837. This region extended the northern part of Missouri's western border to the Missouri River.

Since the 1820's, Missourians had been carrying on a regular trade with Mexicans over the Santa Fe Trail. This famous trail linked Independence, Mo., with Santa Fe in the Southwest. Tremendous wealth from the Southwest poured into Missouri, and Independence became a busy, thriving village. The great Oregon Trail, which thousands of settlers followed to the Pacific Northwest, also began in Independence. See **Santa Fe Trail; Oregon Trail.**

The Civil War. In 1857, the Supreme Court of the United States issued the historic Dred Scott Decision. The court ruled that Scott, a Missouri slave, was merely property and did not have citizenship rights. The ruling greatly increased ill feeling between the North and the South (see **Dred Scott Decision**). Meanwhile, many Missourians who lived near the western border of the state feared that the newly organized Kansas Territory would become a free state. As more and more antislavery families settled in Kansas, scattered warfare broke out between Missourians and Kansans (see **Brown, John; Kansas** ["Bleeding Kansas"]). Kansas became a free state in 1861. Fighting between Kansas and Missourians continued into the Civil War.

Missouri became the center of national interest in 1861. The nation wondered whether Missouri would *secede* (withdraw) from the Union and join the Confederacy. Early in 1861, Governor Claiborne F. Jackson recommended that a state convention be called to determine the will of the people. The convention was held in February and March. Jackson and some members of the convention were strongly pro-South, but the convention voted to remain in the Union. Most Missourians wanted to stay neutral if war should come.

After the Civil War began in April 1861, President Abraham Lincoln called for troops from Missouri. Governor Jackson refused Lincoln's call. Union soldiers and the Missouri state militia, which Jackson commanded as governor, clashed at Boonville on June 17, 1861. This battle was the first real fighting of the Civil War in Missouri. The Union troops, under General Nathaniel Lyon, routed the militiamen and gained control of northern Missouri. Jackson and his militiamen retreated to southwestern Missouri, where they reorganized. They then advanced to Wilson's Creek, near Springfield. There, in August, the militiamen and Confederate troops defeated the Union forces in a bloody battle.

On July 22, the state convention had met again. It voted to remove pro-Confederate state leaders from office. The convention replaced them with pro-Union men. Hamilton R. Gamble became governor. In September 1861, Jackson called for the legislature to meet in Neosho in October. Not enough members attended to hold a legal session. But those present voted to secede from the Union and join the Confederacy.

The Confederate forces controlled a foothold in southwestern Missouri until March 1862, when Union forces defeated them at Pea Ridge, Ark. In 1864, General Sterling Price tried to recapture Missouri for the South in a daring raid. He was defeated at Westport, which is a part of present-day Kansas City. Price's defeat marked the end of full-scale fighting in the state. Throughout the war, however, bands of both Union and Confederate guerrillas terrorized the Missouri countryside. These guerrillas burned and looted towns and murdered innocent people.

After the war ended in 1865, Missouri adopted a new constitution. It included a clause that denied the right to vote to anyone who refused to swear that he had not sympathized with the South. This unpopular clause was repealed in 1870.

Progress as a state. Between 1850 and 1870, big changes took place in Missouri. St. Louis and Kansas City became important transportation centers. The frontier disappeared. Trade with Mexico over the Santa Fe Trail ended. The fur trade grew less important, although St. Louis remained one of the world's great fur markets. Tenant farmers replaced the relatively few slaves who worked the fields.

In 1875, Missouri adopted a new constitution. It reestablished the governor's term from two to four years. It also established a state railroad commission to regulate rates and shipping conditions.

For almost 20 years after the Civil War, many former Confederate guerrillas turned to crime. They held up banks, stagecoaches, and trains. In 1881, Governor Thomas T. Crittenden began a campaign to stop the outlaws. He offered a $5,000 reward for the arrest of Jesse James, one of the most notorious bandits. James was killed by one of his own gang in 1882.

The Louisiana Purchase Exposition was held in St. Louis in 1904. This world's fair attracted almost 20 million visitors from the United States and other countries. A popular exhibit featured automobiles. One of the automobiles had been driven all the way from New York City to St. Louis under its own power.

In 1905, Governor Joseph W. Folk began one of the state's most progressive administrations. Missouri adopted statewide primary elections and began political, social, and industrial reforms. Laws were passed calling for the inspection of working conditions in Missouri's factories. Other laws regulated child labor and public utilities in the state.

After the United States entered World War I in 1917, Missouri's mining, manufacturing, and agriculture expanded to supply the nation's armed forces. General John J. Pershing, who was born in Linn County, became commander in chief of the United States forces in France. General Enoch H. Crowder, born in Grundy County, became the first director of the Selective Service System.

Bagnell Dam, an important source of electric power for the St. Louis area, was completed in 1931. The waters held back by the dam formed Missouri's Lake of the Ozarks. Many Missourians lost their jobs during the Great Depression of the 1930's, and farmers suffered because of low prices. Under Governor Guy B. Park, the number of state government employees was cut and operating costs of government were reduced. The federal

The Louisiana Purchase Exposition, also known as the St. Louis World's Fair, was held in the city in 1904. Visitors there saw early types of automobiles and tasted the first ice cream cones.

government set up several agencies in Missouri to provide employment and relief.

The mid-1900's. During World War II (1939-1945), many new industries were developed in Missouri to provide supplies for the armed forces. In 1944, U.S. Senator Harry S. Truman of Independence was elected Vice President. He became President after President Franklin D. Roosevelt died in 1945. Truman was elected to a full term as President in 1948.

New industrial plants boosted Missouri's economy during the 1950's. An electronics plant opened in Joplin, and factories in St. Louis and Neosho began producing parts for spacecraft. A uranium-processing plant went into operation in Weldon Spring.

During the 1960's, Missouri conducted a strong drive to attract more industries. It also encouraged tourism, which became a $500-million business annually. The mining industry in Missouri expanded during the 1960's with the discovery of iron ore deposits in Crawford, Dent, Franklin, Iron, and Washington counties.

By the early 1960's, most public schools in Missouri were desegregated. The state constitution had provided for segregated schools. But in 1954, the Supreme Court of the United States ruled that compulsory segregation of public schools was unconstitutional.

Recent developments. Urban problems increased in Missouri during the 1970's. In St. Louis and Kansas City, for example, many middle-class families moved to the suburbs. The population shift drained the cities of much financial support. Inadequate transportation and increasing crime added to problems of Missouri's cities. The big cities are attempting to redevelop their downtown areas to attract new businesses and tourists.

Missouri's farming community suffered during a national farm crisis in the mid-1980's. Many farmers could not afford to keep their farms. A number of Missouri's industries also suffered during this period as foreign trade restrictions were loosened. Shoe manufacturing and automobile manufacturing were the hardest hit.

Missouri also faced environmental problems. Runoff from new land developments muddied lakes and robbed the land of topsoil. Toxic substances, such as pesticides, were found in fish. Contamination from landfills and septic tanks threatened ground water supplies. In the early 1980's, high levels of dioxin, a poisonous substance, were discovered in Times Beach near St. Louis, and in other Missouri areas. The U.S. government bought all the homes and businesses in Times Beach. A cleanup program was begun in 1991. The cleanup was expected to last about 10 years.

Missouri was also challenged by financial problems in the 1980's. The state needed more money for education, health and welfare programs, environmental programs, and new bridges and highways. In 1986, Missouri began a state lottery to increase its revenue.

Missouri sometimes suffers from flooding along the Mississippi-Missouri river systems. Major floods struck in 1993 as a result of heavy rains. They damaged billions of dollars worth of property and crops in Missouri.

In spite of Missouri's problems, the state's economy remains strong. Missouri's farms continue to produce large quantities of livestock, soybeans, corn, wheat, and cotton. St. Louis, Kansas City, and some smaller cities annually report many new and expanded factories. The state's aerospace industry continues to thrive. In addition, tourism has become a billion-dollar industry for Missouri. St. Louis, Kansas City, and Springfield attract major conventions of business, religious, and political organizations. The Ozarks draw vacationers from a wide area.   Stephen Kneeshaw and Dale Robert Martin

Related articles in *World Book* include:

Biographies

Atchison, David R.	Eagleton, Thomas F.
Benton, Thomas Hart (senator)	Field, Eugene
Benton, Thomas Hart (painter)	Gephardt, Richard Andrew
Blair (Francis P., Jr.)	James, Jesse
Bradley, Omar N.	Nelson, William R.
Brown, Benjamin Gratz	Pulitzer, Joseph
Carver, George Washington	Truman, Harry S.
Chouteau (family)	Twain, Mark

Cities

Columbia	Jefferson City	Saint Louis
Hannibal	Kansas City	Springfield
Independence	Saint Joseph	

History

Civil War	Louisiana Purchase
Dred Scott Decision	Missouri Compromise
Latter Day Saints, Reorganized	Pony express
Church of Jesus Christ of	Santa Fe Trail
Lewis and Clark Expedition	Western frontier life

Physical features

Mississippi River	Missouri River	Ozark Mountains

Other related articles

Fort Leonard Wood
George Washington Carver National Monument
Osage Indians

Outline

I. People
  A. Population
  B. Schools
  C. Libraries
  D. Museums
II. Visitor's guide
  A. Places to visit
  B. Annual events
III. Land and climate
  A. Land regions
  B. Rivers and lakes
  C. Springs and caves
  D. Plant and animal life
  E. Climate
IV. Economy
  A. Natural resources
  B. Service industries
  C. Manufacturing
  D. Agriculture
  E. Mining
  F. Electric power
  G. Transportation
  H. Communication
V. Government
  A. Constitution
  B. Executive
  C. Legislature
  D. Courts
  E. Local government
  F. Revenue
  G. Politics
VI. History

Questions

From which Missouri city did the famous Santa Fe and Oregon trails run?
What is Missouri's leading crop?
Which political party has been stronger in Missouri's history?
To what two rivers does Missouri owe much of its commercial and industrial importance?
Why is Missouri sometimes called the *Mother of the West?* Why was it nicknamed the *Show Me State?*
What are Missouri's chief manufactured products?
Which economic activity employs the most Missourians?
What two Missouri journalists influenced journalism across the country?
What was the Missouri Compromise? The Dred Scott Decision?
Why did national interest focus on Missouri in 1861?

Additional resources

Level I

Carpenter, Allan. *Missouri.* Rev. ed. Childrens Press, 1978.
Fradin, Dennis B. *Missouri in Words and Pictures.* Childrens Press, 1980.
Thompson, Kathleen. *Missouri.* Raintree, 1985.

Level II

Chapman, Carl H. and E. F. *Indians and Archaeology of Missouri.* Rev. ed. Univ. of Missouri Press, 1983.
Eckberg, Carl J. *Colonial Ste. Genevieve: An Adventure on the Mississippi Frontier.* Patrice, 1985.
Greene, Lorenzo J., and others. *Missouri's Black Heritage.* Forum Press, 1980.
History of Missouri. Univ. of Missouri Press. Vol. 1, *1673 to 1820,* by W. E. Foley (1971); Vol. II, *1820 to 1860,* by P. McCandless (1972); Vol. III, *1860 to 1875,* by W. E. Parrish (1973); Vol. V, *1919 to 1953,* by R. S. Kirkendall (1986). Multivolume work, publication in progress.
Meyer, Duane G. *The Heritage of Missouri.* 3rd ed. River City Pubs., 1982.
Nagel, Paul C. *Missouri: A Bicentennial History.* Norton, 1977.
Rafferty, Milton D. *Historical Atlas of Missouri.* Univ. of Oklahoma Press, 1982. *Missouri: A Geography.* Westview, 1983.

Missouri, a ship. See **World War II** (Victory in the Pacific).

Missouri, University of, is a coeducational state university system. It has four campuses.

The University of Missouri-Columbia campus grants degrees in agriculture, arts and science, business and public administration, education, engineering, fine arts, forestry-fisheries-wildlife, human environmental sciences, journalism, law, library and information science, medicine, nursing, social work, and veterinary medicine. Its school of journalism, founded in 1908, is the oldest in the world.

The University of Missouri-Kansas City campus grants degrees in arts and sciences, basic life sciences, business and public administration, computer science and telecommunications, dentistry, education, law, medicine, music, nursing, and pharmacy. It was founded as the privately controlled University of Kansas City in 1929. It became part of the University of Missouri in 1963.

The University of Missouri-Rolla campus offers degrees in arts and sciences, engineering, and mines and metallurgy. It was founded in 1870.

The University of Missouri-St. Louis campus grants degrees in arts and sciences, business administration, education, nursing, and optometry. It was founded as an urban campus of the University of Missouri in 1963.

Each campus also provides a graduate program. The University of Missouri was founded in 1839 in Columbia. It is the oldest state university west of the Mississippi River. For enrollment, see **Universities and colleges** (table).   Critically reviewed by the University of Missouri

Missouri Compromise was a plan agreed upon by the United States Congress in 1820 to settle the debate over slavery in the Louisiana Purchase area. It temporarily maintained the balance between free and slave states.

In 1818, the Territory of Missouri, which was part of the Louisiana Purchase, applied for admission to the Union. Slavery was legal in the territory, and about 10,000 slaves lived there. Most people expected Missouri to become a slave state. When the bill to admit Missouri to the Union was introduced, there were an equal number of free and slave states. Six of the original 13 states and five new states permitted slavery, while seven of the original states and four new states did not. This meant that the free states and the slave states each had 22 senators in the U.S. Senate. The admission of Missouri threatened to destroy this balance.

This balance had been temporarily upset a number of times, but it had always been easy to decide whether states east of the Mississippi River should be slave or free. Mason and Dixon's Line and the Ohio River formed a natural and well-understood boundary between the two sections. No such line had been drawn west of the Mississippi River. In addition, some parts of Missouri Territory lay to the north of the mouth of the Ohio River, while other parts of it lay to the south.

A heated debate broke out in Congress when Representative James Tallmadge of New York introduced an amendment to the bill enabling Missouri to become a state. Tallmadge proposed to prohibit the bringing of any more slaves into Missouri, and to grant freedom to the children of slaves born within the state after its admission. This proposal disturbed Southerners, who found cotton growing by means of slave labor increasingly profitable, and feared national legislation against slavery. Because the free states dominated the House of Representatives, the slave states felt they must keep the even balance in the Senate.

The Tallmadge Amendment passed the House, but the Senate defeated it. During the next session of Congress, Maine applied for admission to the Union. Missouri and Maine could then be accepted without upsetting the Senate's balance between free and slave states, and the Missouri Compromise became possible.

The compromise admitted Maine as a free state and authorized Missouri to form a state constitution. A territory had to have an established constitution before it could become a state. The compromise also banned slavery from the Louisiana Purchase north of the southern boundary of Missouri, the line of 36° 30' north latitude, except in the state of Missouri.

The people of Missouri believed they had the right to decide about slavery in their state. They wrote a constitution that allowed slavery and that restricted free blacks from entering the state.

Before Congress would admit Missouri, a second Missouri Compromise was necessary. Henry Clay, the Speaker of the House, helped work out this agreement. It required the Missouri legislature not to deny black citizens their constitutional rights. With this understanding, Missouri was admitted to the Union in 1821.

In 1848, Congress passed the Oregon Territory bill, which prohibited slavery in the area. President James K. Polk signed the bill because the Oregon Territory lay north of the Missouri Compromise line. Later proposals tried to extend the line by law across the continent to the Pacific Ocean. These efforts failed. The Missouri Compromise was repealed by the Kansas-Nebraska Act of 1854 (see **Kansas-Nebraska Act**).   William E. Foley

Additional resources

Dangerfield, George. *The Awakening of American Nationalism, 1815-1828*. Harper, 1965. Includes a lengthy discussion of the Missouri Compromise.
Fehrenbacher, Don E. *Slavery, Law, and Politics: The Dred Scot Case in Historical Perspective*. Oxford, 1981. Includes a discussion of the Missouri Compromise.
Moore, Glover. *The Missouri Controversy, 1819-1821*. Univ. of Kentucky Pr., 1953. The standard presentation.

Missouri River is the longest river in the United States. It flows 2,540 miles (4,090 kilometers) from its source, the Jefferson River at Red Rock Creek in southwestern Montana, to its mouth on the Mississippi River. The Missouri drains an area of about 529,000 square miles (1,371,100 square kilometers). This drainage basin includes all or parts of 10 U.S. states and 2 Canadian provinces.

The Missouri has large amounts of mud in its water. Early explorers and Indians called it the *Big Muddy,* and farmers have described it as "too thick to drink and too thin to plow." The source of the river's name is unclear. The river may have been named after an Indian village called *OueMessourit* or *Ou-Missouri* located near its mouth. The village name means *town of the large canoes.*

The course of the Missouri. The headwaters of the Missouri are at Red Rock Creek in southwestern Montana, where the Jefferson River, a small rushing stream high in the Rocky Mountains, begins. At Three Forks, Mont., the Jefferson joins the Madison and Gallatin rivers to form the Missouri.

The Missouri flows north from Three Forks and cuts through a spectacular gorge called the Gates of the Mountains. Then it bends toward the northeast and plunges down a series of waterfalls known as the Great Falls of the Missouri. The city of Great Falls, Mont., at the foot of the waterfalls, is named for these waterfalls. From Great Falls, the Missouri winds eastward across Montana. In North Dakota, the river makes a great bend southward. Then it flows southeast across South Dakota.

The Missouri forms part of the boundary between South Dakota and Nebraska. It turns south at Sioux City, Iowa, and flows between Iowa and Nebraska. The river also forms the Nebraska-Missouri boundary and part of the Missouri-Kansas boundary. At Kansas City, Mo., the river turns east again. It flows across Missouri and joins the Mississippi River about 20 miles (32 kilometers) north of downtown St. Louis. Every second, the Missouri empties an average of 76,300 cubic feet (2,161 cubic meters) of water into the Mississippi.

The Missouri, like most rivers, has an upper, middle, and lower part. The upper Missouri is a clear, rapid-flowing stream in the mountains of western Montana. The middle Missouri begins just below Great Falls, where the river leaves the mountains and moves onto the Great Plains. The middle Missouri is slower and muddier than the upper part. The lower Missouri is the slowest and muddiest part. It begins just downstream from Yankton, S. Dak., and extends to the Mississippi.

The Platte River is the longest branch of the Missouri. Other major tributaries include the James, Kansas, Milk, Osage, and Yellowstone rivers.

Navigation. The Missouri River was once used for commercial navigation along most of its course. Today, almost all traffic upstream from Sioux City is recreational, but commercial activity thrives on the lower Missouri. The commercial river traffic is extremely important to farmers of the western part of the Midwest. It carries their goods to market and brings them fertilizer and other farm supplies. The chief ports on the river are Kansas City, Mo.; Omaha, Nebr.; and Sioux City.

Commercial traffic on the Missouri totals more than $3\frac{1}{4}$ million short tons (3.2 million metric tons) of freight yearly. Freight headed downstream consists mainly of such farm products as corn, sorghum, soybeans, and wheat. Upstream cargoes include benzine, cement, fertilizer, lime, paint, and phosphate. Most of the freight travels on barges pushed by powerful tugboats. A navigation channel at least 300 feet (91 meters) wide and 9 feet (2.7 meters) deep is maintained on the river between Sioux City and the Mississippi.

Dams and reservoirs. A series of six huge dams form a nearly continual chain of long, winding reservoirs along the middle Missouri River. These dams, in order from north to south along the river, are Fort Peck, Garrison, Oahe, Big Bend, Fort Randall, and Gavins Point. About 60 smaller dams and reservoirs are on tributaries of the Missouri. See **Fort Peck Dam; Fort Randall Dam; Garrison Dam.**

Flooding was once a serious problem on the Missouri. In spring, excess water from melting snow often caused the river to overflow, causing widespread damage. The six large dams on the middle Missouri have nearly eliminated this problem. The reservoirs of the dams store excess water in spring and gradually release it during the rest of the year, thus greatly reducing floods downstream.

The dams and their reservoirs also provide other services. Hydroelectric powerhouses at the dams generate electricity used by farms, homes, and industries throughout the middle Missouri Basin. Millions of visitors use the reservoirs annually for boating, fishing, swimming, and water skiing. Water from the reservoirs is also used to irrigate farmland and serve cities along the river.

Wildlife and conservation. The Missouri and its valley provide a rich habitat for a wide variety of wildlife. Bears, deer, elk, moose, and other large animals live in the mountainous upper Missouri Valley. Smaller animals, such as beavers, foxes, muskrats, rabbits, skunks, and weasels, are common along the middle and lower parts of the river. Fishes of the cool, clear upper Missouri include graylings and rainbow trout. Bass, bullheads, catfish, carp, and perch inhabit the warmer, muddier waters below Great Falls.

The upper Missouri River flows through forests of fir, hemlock, and spruce trees. The middle and lower sections of the river wind through grasslands. Forests of cottonwoods, hickories, oaks, poplars, and willows also lie along the middle and lower sections of the Missouri.

At one time, pollution threatened much of the wildlife along the Missouri. Pesticides and other chemicals used by farmers were washed into the river, and industries dumped wastes into it. These substances poisoned fish and other wildlife. Today, federal laws ban certain pesticides, and industrial discharges into the river are carefully controlled. As a result, the quality of the water is gradually improving.

History. The Missouri River was formed about 20 million years ago, during the late Tertiary Period. During the Pleistocene Ice Age, about 2 million years ago, the river marked the southern and western edge of many of the huge ice sheets that covered the land.

The Missouri River Basin was the home of several Indian tribes. The Wind River Shoshone and Atsina lived near the headwaters of the river, in western Montana. Several buffalo-hunting tribes occupied the Missouri Basin between eastern Montana and the Mississippi.

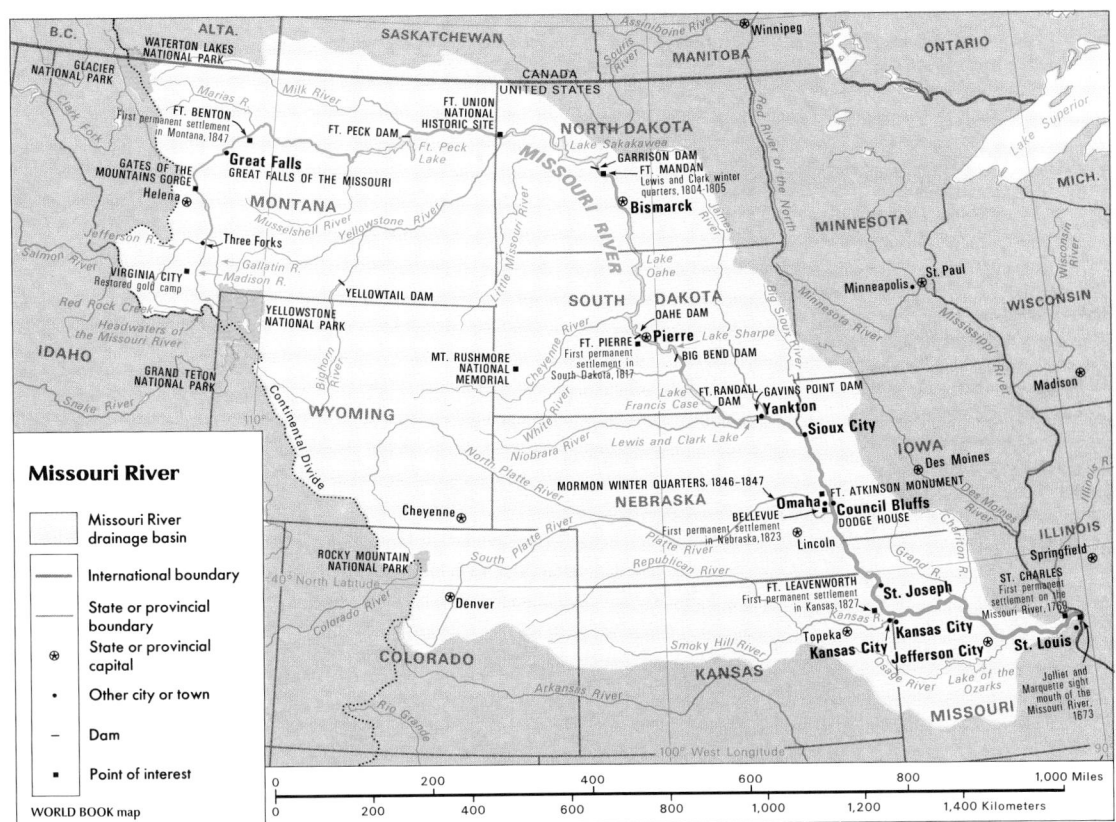

Missouri River

- Missouri River drainage basin
- International boundary
- State or provincial boundary
- ⊛ State or provincial capital
- • Other city or town
- − Dam
- ▪ Point of interest

WORLD BOOK map

They included the Arikara, the Assiniboine, the Dakotah (Sioux), the Hidatsa, the Kansa, the Missouri, and the Omaha. Many of these tribes spent much of their time on the grasslands away from the river. But the Missouri was a valuable water source, a favorite hunting ground, and an important route for their canoes.

The first whites to see the Missouri River were the explorers Jacques Marquette of France and Louis Jolliet, a French Canadian. They reached the mouth of the Missouri in 1673 while exploring the Mississippi. The United States bought the Missouri River Basin from France in 1803 as part of the Louisiana Purchase. From 1804 to 1806, two Americans, Meriwether Lewis and William Clark, explored the territory drained by the Missouri. See **Lewis and Clark expedition**.

During the early 1800's, the Missouri became one of the main transportation routes of the fur trade in the West. At first, keelboats hauled furs and supplies on the river. Steamboat traffic began on the Missouri in 1819, and steamers soon became the chief means of transportation. Many pioneers who traveled west in the mid-1800's went at least part of the way on a Missouri steamer. Traffic on the Missouri declined after railroads were built in the West during the late 1800's. But today, the lower Missouri River is an important commercial waterway.

Major floods struck along the river in 1943, 1947, 1951, 1952, and 1993. But the six huge dams on the middle Missouri and the smaller dams on the tributaries have greatly reduced the threat of disastrous flooding. These dams make up the heart of the Missouri River Basin Project. This program, authorized by Congress in 1944, is a flood control, electric power, and irrigation project. The program calls for construction of 137 dams and reservoirs on the Missouri and its tributaries. The entire project probably will not be completed until after the year 2000.   John Edwin Coffman

Mist. See Fog.

Mistletoe is a plant that grows as a parasite on the trunks and branches of various trees. The *American mistletoe* and the *European mistletoe* grow most often on apple trees. They also may grow on other trees, such as the lime, hawthorn, sycamore, poplar, locust, fir, and occasionally on oak. The *dwarf mistletoe* is a small variety that grows on pines in the Eastern United States.

Mistletoe is an evergreen with leathery, oblong leaves. It has tiny yellow flowers that bloom in February and March. Birds eat the white, shiny fruits called berries. The berry seeds cling to the bills of birds and are scattered when birds sharpen their bills against the bark of trees. The berries may be poisonous to people.

Mistletoe is associated with many traditions and holidays, especially Christmas. Historians say the Druids—ancient priests of the Celts—cut the mistletoe that grew on the sacred oak and gave it to the people for charms. In Teutonic

WORLD BOOK illustration by Robert Hynes

American mistletoe

mythology, an arrow of mistletoe killed Balder, son of the goddess Frigg. Early European peoples used mistletoe as a ceremonial plant. The custom of using mistletoe at Christmastime probably comes from this practice. In many countries, tradition says that a person caught standing beneath mistletoe must forfeit a kiss.

Scientific classification. Mistletoe belongs to the mistletoe family, Loranthaceae. The scientific name for the American mistletoe is *Phoradendron serotinum*. The dwarf mistletoe is *Arceuthobium pusillum*.   James S. Miller

See also **Christmas** (Christmas decorations); **Oklahoma** (picture: State flower); **Parasite**.

Mistral, *mee STRAL,* **Frédéric,** *fray day REEK* (1830-1914), was a famous French poet who won the 1904 Nobel Prize for literature. He wrote in modern Provençal, the language of southern France. Mistral led a movement of the 1800's called the *Felibrige,* which tried to revive the literary tradition and enrich the language of the medieval troubadours (see **Troubadour**).

In 1859, Mistral published his masterpiece, *Mirèio* (also called *Mireille*), an epic describing the tragic love of a farmer's daughter in the valley of the Rhône River. The poem's success did much to gain sympathy for the Provençal revival in literature. In addition to *Song of the Rhône* (1897) and other poems, Mistral compiled *Lou Tresor dóu Felibrige* (1876-1886), a dictionary of *langue d'oc,* the general term used for the dialects of southern France. He was born near Arles.   Jean-Pierre Cauvin

Mistral, *mees TRAHL,* **Gabriela,** *gah bree EH lah* (1889-1957), was the pen name of Lucila Godoy Alcayaga, a Chilean poet and educator. In 1945, she became the first Latin-American writer to win the Nobel Prize for literature. Her spare, plain style with its often Biblical flavor gave Spanish-American poetry a fresh direction. She was a student of folk verse, particularly children's rhymes and lullabies, and drew on these forms in developing her poetry. Her best-known books of poetry include *Desolation* (1922), *Tenderness* (1924), *Felling of Trees* (1934), and *Wine Press* (1954).

Mistral was born in Vicuña, Chile. She was a rural schoolteacher and later became a prominent educator in Chile. She served in the foreign service of Chile and at the League of Nations. Mistral taught in the United States in the 1930's.   Naomi Lindstrom

Mitanni, *mih TAN ee,* was an ancient kingdom in northern Mesopotamia. The kingdom was located in what is now southeastern Turkey. The Mitannians used horses and were skilled in the use of chariots in war. The neighboring Hittites learned how to use chariots in warfare from the Mitannians. In the 1400's B.C., the Mitannians fought the Egyptians for control of Syria. But both kingdoms feared the rise of Hittite power. A Mitannian princess married into the Egyptian royal family as a sign of unity. About 1370 B.C., however, the Hittites defeated the Mitannians. Civil war further weakened them, and the kingdom was finally absorbed into the Assyrian Empire by about 1350 B.C.   Thomas W. Africa

Mitchel, John Purroy (1879-1918), was elected reform mayor of New York City in 1913. His election ended, for a time, control by Tammany Hall, a notorious political group. Mitchel reduced the city debt, fought dishonesty in the city's police department, and set up a relief fund and workshops for the unemployed. However, a number of Mitchel's actions angered powerful interests, and he lost his bid for reelection in 1917.

Mitchel was born in Fordham, N.Y., and graduated from New York Law School. In 1906, as a commissioner of accounts for the city, he exposed dishonest practices of two borough presidents, the fire department, and the licenses bureau.　　　Charles B. Forcey and Linda R. Forcey

Mitchell, Arthur (1934-　　), was the first black American to dance with a major classical ballet company. He performed with the New York City Ballet from 1955 to 1970.

Mitchell was born in New York City and attended the School of American Ballet. In 1955, he joined the New York City Ballet. His major roles included the part of Puck in *A Midsummer Night's Dream* and the *pas de deux* (dance for two persons) in *Agon.*

General Billy Mitchell stands, *left,* during his court-martial. Later events proved that his airpower theories were correct.

first controlled the development of aviation in the U.S. Army. Mitchell learned to fly in 1916, and became air adviser to General John Pershing in World War I (1914-1918). He was in Europe when the United States entered the war, and quickly got in touch with Allied air leaders. Major General Hugh M. Trenchard, head of the British Royal Flying Corps, greatly influenced Mitchell. Mitchell commanded several large air units in combat, including the largest concentration of Allied airpower of the war, during the Battle of St.-Mihiel. Mitchell had become a brigadier general by the time the war ended.

After the war, Mitchell became assistant chief of the Air Service, and the leading advocate of an air force independent of the Army and the Navy. He found a natural resistance among leaders of the older services, and appealed to the public through books, magazine articles, newspaper interviews, and speeches. Because airplanes were then limited in size and range, many people thought his claims for airpower were exaggerated. But he persuaded many others, especially after a 1921 experiment when he sank three former German ships—a destroyer, a cruiser, and a battleship—with aerial bombs. He repeated this success in tests against three obsolete U.S. battleships. However, Mitchell failed to achieve his goal, perhaps partly because he was often violent in argument and bitter in his condemnation of military superiors who disagreed with his ideas.

William Mitchell was born in Nice, France, of American parents. He wrote *Our Air Force* (1921), *Winged Defense* (1925), and *Skyways* (1930).　　　Alfred Goldberg

Additional resources

Davis, Burke. *The Billy Mitchell Affair.* Random Hse., 1967. Concentrates on his military career and court-martial.
Hurley, Alfred F. *Billy Mitchell: Crusader for Air Power.* Rev. ed. Indiana Univ. Pr., 1975.

© Martha Swope

Arthur Mitchell danced with Allegra Kent in George Balanchine's modern ballet *Agon* at the New York City Ballet, *above.*

In 1969, Mitchell formed the Dance Theatre of Harlem, a professional ballet company in New York City's chief black community. The company is best known for its varied repertoire, including a version of the 1841 romantic ballet *Giselle* the company set in the Louisiana bayou. Mitchell directs the company, teaches in the school, and composes dances. As a *choreographer* (creator of dances), Mitchell created such works as *Holberg Suite* (1970), *Rhythmetron* (1972), and *Manifestations* (1976).　　　Dianne L. Woodruff

Mitchell, Billy (1879-1936), a United States Army general, was one of the most controversial figures in American military history. An early and vigorous advocate of airpower, he was court-martialed for defiance of his superiors in 1925. He resigned from the Army rather than accept a five-year suspension. He was branded at first as an extremist and insurgent. But early in World War II (1939-1945), events confirmed many of Mitchell's predictions. In 1946, the United States Congress authorized the Medal of Honor for Mitchell.

Mitchell enlisted in the Army as a private at the start of the Spanish-American War in 1898. He remained in the Army and rose rapidly in the Signal Corps, which

Mitchell, George John (1933-　　), a Democrat from Maine, became majority leader of the United States Senate in 1989. Mitchell had been appointed to the Senate in 1980 to complete the unexpired term of Edmund S. Muskie. Muskie resigned his Senate seat to become secretary of state under President Jimmy Carter. Mitchell won election to a full six-year term in 1982 and was reelected in 1988.

Mitchell was born in Waterville, Me. He graduated from Bowdoin College in 1954. In 1960, he earned a law degree from Georgetown University. From 1960 to 1962, Mitchell worked as a trial lawyer at the U.S. Department of Justice. He served as an assistant to Senator Muskie from 1962 to 1965. From 1966 to 1968, Mitchell was chairman of the Democratic Party in Maine. He was elected to the Democratic National Committee in 1969 and served on the committee until 1977. From 1977 to 1979, he was U.S. attorney for the state of Maine. From 1979 to 1980, he served as U.S. district judge for that state.   Lee Thornton

Mitchell, Margaret (1900-1949), an American author, wrote *Gone with the Wind* (1936), one of the most popular novels of all time. It won the 1937 Pulitzer Prize for fiction.

Gone with the Wind is a story of the South during the Civil War, written from the Southern point of view. The story begins just before the outbreak of the war in 1861. It describes the impact of the conflict on the South and ends during the postwar Reconstruction period. The two main characters— the Southern belle Scarlett O'Hara and the dashing Rhett Butler—rank among the best-known figures in American fiction. The motion picture *Gone with the Wind* (1939) became one of the most popular films ever made.

United Press Int.
Margaret Mitchell

Mitchell was born in Atlanta, Ga., where much of the action of *Gone with the Wind* takes place. She wrote the novel over a period of 10 years. *Margaret Mitchell's "Gone with the Wind" Letters: 1936-1949* was published in 1976. Alexandra Ripley wrote a continuation of the Mitchell novel that was published in 1991 as *Scarlett: The Sequel to Margaret Mitchell's Gone with the Wind.*
          Noel Polk

Mitchell, Maria (1818-1889), an American astronomer, became known for her studies of sunspots and of satellites of planets. She discovered a new comet in 1847. Although she was largely self-educated, she served as professor of astronomy at Vassar College from 1865 to 1888. Mitchell was elected into several learned societies. In 1848, she became the first woman member of the American Academy of Arts and Sciences. She later became a fellow of the society. She was elected to the Hall of Fame for Great Americans in 1905. Mitchell was born in Nantucket, Mass.   C. R. O'Dell

Mitchell, Wesley Clair (1874-1948), was an American economist known for his studies of the rise and fall in business activity. Mitchell collected data about prices, production, and other factors in periods of prosperity and during economic slumps. He then determined the probable causes of the recurring increase and decrease in economic activity called the *business cycle.*

Mitchell pioneered the use of detailed statistics in economic studies. During his time, most economists developed theories based on only a few observations. Mitchell believed economic theories should be sup-

ported by a large amount of statistical evidence. Most economists today use the combined theoretical and statistical approach begun by Mitchell.

In 1920, Mitchell helped found the National Bureau of Economic Research. This private nonprofit organization conducts research on a variety of economic problems. Mitchell served as the organization's director from 1920 to 1945. See **National Bureau of Economic Research.**

Mitchell was born in Rushville, Ill. He taught economics at Columbia University from 1913 to 1919 and from 1922 until 1944. His books include *Business Cycles* (1913) and *Business Cycles: The Problem and Its Setting* (1927).
          Barry W. Poulson

Mite is the common name for a type of small animal related to ticks. Mites and ticks are not insects. They are related to spiders and scorpions.

Some mites live on land, while others live in water. Some are too small to be seen easily with the naked eye and must be studied under a microscope. The adult usually has a saclike body with a slight dividing line between its abdomen and thorax, and has four pairs of legs. The mouth has piercing and grasping organs. The digestive system begins in the sucking beak. The young larvae of most species hatch from eggs and have six legs. They shed their skins and change into nymphs with eight legs. After one or more other moltings, the nymphs change into adults.

Many kinds of mites live at least part of their lives as parasites. They suck the blood of animals or the juice from plants, and eat cell tissues as well. Other mites eat feathers, cheese, flour, cereal, drugs, and other stored products. Several kinds of mites burrow into the skin of people and other mammals, especially horses, cattle, and sheep. They cause the skin to break out and itch, forming scabs and mange. The troublesome *chiggers,* or *red bugs,* which torment people in the woods, are larvae of mites. Another kind which attacks people is a long wormlike mite which burrows into the hair follicles and the oil glands. All these mites except the last can be repelled by sulfur preparations.

Several kinds of mites attack poultry. The best-known of these species is the common *chicken mite,* which sucks the blood of its victims at night and hides in cracks during the day.

Sometimes a mite called the *red spider* destroys greenhouse plants. The *pearleaf blister mite* damages fruit trees. *Gall mites* form small lumps on leaves and twigs. Unlike other mites, they have only two pairs of legs. *Clover mites* attack plants and fruit trees. In late au-

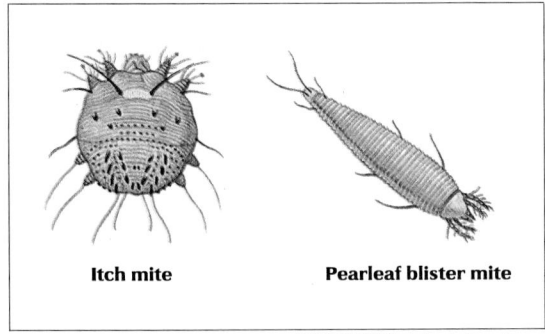
Itch mite   Pearleaf blister mite

WORLD BOOK illustrations by James Teason

tumn, large numbers of these mites often move indoors to avoid the cold weather. Other mites attack bulbs and roots of plants. A few species prey on plant lice, or aphids, and others on insects and grasshopper eggs. Many species live in the soil and help break down dead plant and animal tissues.

Scientific classification. Mites belong to the order Acarina. The scientific name for the itch mite of human beings is *Sarcoptes scabiei*. The skin mite of horses and cattle is *Psoroptes ovis*. The chicken mite is *Dermanyssus gallinae*. The red spider is *Tetranychus bimaculatus*, or some closely related species.

Edwin W. Minch

See also **Chigger; Mange; Parasite; Tick.**

Mithra, *MIHTH ruh,* was a god of the tribes of the Aryans who settled in ancient Persia. Mithra, also known as Mithras, is the same god as Mitra, the sun god who appears in the ancient literature of Hinduism called the Vedas. According to Zoroastrian religious tradition, Mithra was the god of light, closely associated with the sun. Mithra was said to be an ally of the supreme god Ahura Mazda. Under Ahura Mazda's leadership, Mithra and other gods fought against Angra Mainyu, the Zoroastrian god of evil (see **Zoroastrianism**).

The Persians spread the worship of Mithra, called Mithraism, throughout Asia Minor. The cult became popular, especially among Roman soldiers and slaves. By about A.D. 100, they had spread it into Europe. Mithraism ranked as a principal competing religion of Christianity until the 300's. Robert William Smith

Mithridates VI, *MITH rih DAY teez* (120?-63 B.C.), was king of Pontus, an area in what is now Turkey. One of Rome's most dangerous enemies, Mithridates opposed Roman expansion into Asia Minor.

Mithridates fought three wars against Rome. The first of these wars occurred in 90 B.C., when Rome's Italian allies in central and southern Italy revolted. Mithridates drove the Romans from Asia. He ordered every Roman citizen in Asia Minor killed—an estimated 80,000 people were put to death.

When Rome attacked Mithridates' allies in Greece, he sent two armies there. But Sulla, a Roman general, defeated them, and Mithridates had to make peace in 84 B.C. The greatest war broke out in 75 B.C. when Rome took over Bithynia, a region adjoining Pontus. The Roman general Pompey drove Mithridates out of Asia Minor. Mithridates planned to continue the war from the Crimea in what is now southern Ukraine. But his son, Pharnaces, rebelled against him. Mithridates had himself killed by a bodyguard. Clive Foss

Mitosis. See **Cell** (Cell division; illustration).

Mitral valve prolapse, sometimes called MVP, is a common heart valve disorder. The mitral valve is between the left atrium and the left ventricle of the heart. It has two *leaflets* (flaps) that control the blood flow. MVP occurs when one or both of the leaflets are enlarged or have extra tissue. MVP is usually harmless. However, major complications can occur, including a blood clot in the brain and an infection called *infective endocarditis* involving the mitral valve as well as other valves. MVP appears twice as often in women as in men. It is most commonly a hereditary disorder.

Some people with MVP have no symptoms. However, most patients experience a rapid or irregular heartbeat, shortness of breath, light-headedness, and chronic fa-

tigue. Many patients also suffer from migraines, eating and sleeping disorders, an overactive or inflamed thyroid gland, diarrhea, and cold hands and feet. Emotional stress often magnifies the symptoms.

Doctors generally prescribe regular exams and aerobic exercise for people who have MVP. Patients also are advised to restrict their intake or use of high-carbohydrate foods, caffeine, and decongestants. Some patients may need beta-blockers and specific antiarrhythmic medication. More severe cases may require surgery to repair or replace the valve or to insert an electronic regulator, such as a pacemaker or defibrillator. Carl E. Eybel

See also **Heart** (Valves; illustration: Parts of the heart; Valve disease).

Mitropoulos, *mih TRAHP uh luhs,* **Dimitri** (1896-1960), was a symphony orchestra and opera conductor. He conducted a wide repertory and was particularly successful with works of the 1900's. He won praise for the passion and sweep of his interpretations.

Mitropoulos was born in Athens, Greece. He received the most important part of his music education in Berlin as a student of Ferruccio Busoni, an Italian composer and pianist. After building a European reputation, Mitropoulos made his United States debut in 1936 with the Boston Symphony Orchestra. From 1937 to 1949, he was chief conductor of the Minneapolis Symphony Orchestra. He was the principal conductor of the New York Philharmonic Orchestra from 1949 to 1958. From 1954 until his death, Mitropoulos was also a conductor at the Metropolitan Opera, where he specialized in operas of Giuseppe Verdi and Richard Strauss. Martin Bernheimer

Mitterrand, *MEE tehr ahn,* **François Maurice** (1916-   ), was elected president of France in 1981 and reelected in 1988. Mitterrand, leader of the Socialist Party, became the country's first leftist president since 1958. His party also gained control of Parliament in 1981. During his campaign, Mitterrand proposed a socialist program of expanding government control of businesses. After his election, the government bought controlling interests in some important businesses in France. In 1986, Conservatives won control of Parliament. Mitterrand lost some of his powers as a result of the Conservative victory. The Socialists regained much of their power as a result of the 1988 elections, but the party lost power in the 1993 elections. Under Mitterrand, France joined the allied forces in the 1991 Persian Gulf War against Iraq (see **Persian Gulf War**).

Mitterrand was born in Jarnac, near Cognac. He graduated from the University of Paris in 1938. He served in the army during World War II and was wounded and imprisoned by the Germans in 1940. He escaped in 1941 and joined the resistance movement.

Mitterrand served in the National Assembly, the most powerful house of the French Parliament, from 1946 to 1958 and from 1962 until he became president. He was a member of

Wide World Photos
François Mitterrand

the less powerful Senate between his terms in the National Assembly. Mitterrand began his political career as a moderate. His political views shifted toward left wing socialism, and he became a leading opponent of conservative government policies during the 1960's and 1970's.   Michael M. Harrison

Miwok Indians, *MEE wahk,* is the name of three groups in northern California who speak related languages. The three are (1) the Lake Miwok, who traditionally lived south of Clear Lake; (2) the Coast Miwok, who made their homes near the Pacific coast just north of present-day San Francisco; and (3) the Eastern Miwok, who lived in central California, south of what is now Sacramento (see **California** [physical map]).

Traditionally, each of the three Miwok groups consisted of smaller units called *tribelets.* A typical tribelet was made up of several villages. Each Lake or Eastern Miwok tribelet had its own hereditary chief. Each Coast Miwok tribelet chose two chiefs—one male and one female—and a female ceremonial leader, or *maien.*

The Miwok lived in houses made of bark, grass, and other materials. Some homes stood partly underground and were covered with branches and earth. For food, the Miwok fished and hunted and gathered acorns and other wild plant foods.

In the early 1800's, Spaniards captured many Miwok to work as laborers on missions and ranches. In the 1820's and 1830's, some Miwok banded together to fight for their territory and posed a threat to white settlers. The United States Army killed numerous Miwok in a series of massacres in the 1850's. Many Miwok still live in California. Some dwell on *rancherias,* small tracts of land reserved for Indian use.   Victoria D. Patterson

Mix, Tom (1880-1940), became one of America's most famous motion-picture cowboys. He entered the movies in 1910. His expert horsemanship and easygoing manner made him a star. He appeared in such Western movies as *Riders of the Purple Sage* (1925). Mix and his horse, Tony, were given a reception by the Lord Mayor of London in 1925.

Mix was born in Mix Run, Pa., near Du Bois. He joined the army to fight in the Spanish-American War (1898). But he was not involved in combat duty.
        Louis Giannetti

Culver
Tom Mix

Mixed economy. See **Capitalism** (In a mixed economy); **Economics** (Mixed economies).

Mixed numbers. See **Fraction** (Fraction terms).

Moa, *MOH uh,* is any one of about 13 *species* (kinds) of extinct birds that once lived on the North Island and the South Island of New Zealand. Moas ranged in size from those as big as a large turkey to some that were 10 to 13 feet (3 to 4 meters) tall. Moas could not fly. They had small heads, long necks, stout legs, and no wings. They ate fruits and leaves.

Moas lived in New Zealand when the *Maoris,* the Polynesians who settled the country, arrived there about

WORLD BOOK illustration by Trevor Boyer, Linden Artists Ltd.
The moa is an extinct bird that looked somewhat like an ostrich. Some small moas lived in New Zealand until the 1700's.

1,000 years ago. Hunting and the destruction of the moa's lowland forest habitat probably led to the bird's extinction several hundred years later. Some small species of moas were native to mountains on the South Island and may have survived there until the 1700's.

Scientific classification. Moas belong to the moa order, Dinornithiformes, and the family Dinornithidae.   Alan Feduccia

Moabite stone. This ancient stone bears some of the earliest writing in Hebrew-Phoenician characters. The stone is of black basalt. It is about 3 feet 8 inches (112 centimeters) high and 2 feet 3 inches (68 centimeters) wide. F. A. Klein, a missionary, found it in 1868 at Diban, in ancient Moab. The writing on it was probably carved by a Moabite scribe about 865 B.C. It is a good example of the Hebrew-Phoenician characters used at the time.

When the French in Constantinople wanted to buy the stone, the Arabs of Diban broke the priceless, irreplaceable monument into many parts, hoping to get more money by selling the pieces separately. The French collected the larger pieces. A French Embassy official in Constantinople had also made a papier-mâché impression of the stone before it was broken.

The 34-line inscription tells of the deeds of Mesha, king of the Moabites, in his wars against the kings of Israel and against the Edomites. For a description of part of this conflict from the point of view of the people of Israel, see II Kings 3: 4-27. The restored stone is in the Louvre, in Paris.   William A. Ward

Moat. See **Castle.**

Mobile, *moh BEEL* (pop. 196,278; met. area pop. 476,923), is Alabama's second largest city and its only seaport. Only Birmingham has more people. Mobile lies on the Mobile River where the river flows into Mobile Bay, 31 miles (50 kilometers) north of the Gulf of Mexico (see **Alabama** [political map]).

Mobile is one of the nation's oldest cities. A French-Canadian explorer founded it in 1702 as Fort Louis de la Mobile. He named the fort after the nearby Mobile, or Mabila, Indians, who belonged to the Choctaw tribe. Mobile is called the *City of Six Flags* because six governments have controlled it. France, Great Britain, and Spain ruled Mobile during the 1700's. Then the United States, the Republic of Alabama, the Confederate States of America, and again the United States flew their flags there.

The city extends west of the Mobile River and covers 160 square miles (414 square kilometers). It is the seat of Mobile County. The Mobile metropolitan area spreads over all of Baldwin and Mobile counties, 2,957 square miles (7,659 square kilometers).

The 34-story First National Bank Building is the tallest structure in downtown Mobile. The Municipal Auditorium and Theater occupies 12 acres (5 hectares) in the center of the city. The Brookley Industrial Complex in southeast Mobile is a former Air Force base.

About 98 per cent of Mobile's people were born in the United States. Approximately two-fifths are blacks. Mobile's public schools belong to the Mobile County school system, the largest school system in Alabama. The system has about 50 elementary schools, 20 junior high schools, and 15 senior high schools, with a total enrollment of more than 68,000 students. There are also many private and parochial schools in the city. Mobile is

Louvre, Paris

The Moabite stone bears a historical inscription describing the deeds of a Moabite king. It was carved about 865 B.C.

the home of Mobile College, Spring Hill College, and the University of South Alabama.

Mobile has 6 TV stations, 15 radio stations, and 2 daily newspapers—the *Press* and the *Register.* The Mobile Public Library has 5 branches and a bookmobile.

Mobile sponsors a symphony orchestra and a small opera company. The Municipal Auditorium and Theater presents such events as America's Junior Miss program, ballet, basketball games, circuses, and horse shows. The city celebrates Mardi Gras each year (see **Mardi Gras**). The Historic Mobile Preservation Society and other groups maintain several homes as they were in the 1800's. A variety of historic aircraft are displayed in Battleship Park, which is located along Mobile Bay. The park also includes the battleship U.S.S. *Alabama,* which fought in World War II (1939-1945), and the U.S.S. *Drum,* a World War II submarine. Mobile's Earnest F. Ladd Memorial Stadium is the home of the annual Senior Bowl football game between teams of top college players. Bellingrath Gardens, south of the city, displays flowers, shrubs, and trees from throughout the South. Several streets in Mobile and its suburbs form the 35-mile (56-kilometer) Azalea Trail, where thousands of azalea plants bloom every spring.

Economy of Mobile is based on manufacturing, state and federal government operations, and shipping. The city has over 200 factories. Its largest industry produces paper and wood pulp used for paper. Other products include bakery goods, cement, chemicals, clothing, furniture, naval supplies, paint, rayon, refined oil, and seafood. The major government employers are the U.S. Corps of Engineers and the U.S. Coast Guard.

The Port of Mobile is one of the busiest ports in the Southern United States. It handles large amounts of coal, iron ore, petroleum products, and forest products. Shipyards at the port repair and maintain ships that service the port. In 1985, the Tennessee-Tombigbee Waterway opened Mobile's harbor to about 16,000 miles (26,000 kilometers) of navigable inland waterways (see **Tombigbee River**). The waterway connects the Tennessee River with the Tombigbee River.

Five railroads and more than 60 trucking companies provide freight service to Mobile. No railroad passenger trains stop there, but several bus lines and about 130 steamship firms serve the city. Airlines use Mobile Municipal Airport just outside Mobile. Three tunnels carry automobile traffic under the Mobile River.

Government. Mobile has a mayor-council form of government. The voters elect a mayor and seven council members to four-year terms. Mobile gets most of its revenue from taxes on licenses, property, and sales.

History. Jean Baptiste Le Moyne, Sieur de Bienville, a French-Canadian explorer, founded Fort Louis de la Mobile in 1702. Sieur de Bienville established the fort as a trading post and a French outpost to control nearby Indians. In 1711, river floods forced the colony to move 27 miles (43 kilometers) south to the present site of Mobile.

France gave Mobile to Great Britain in 1763 after the French and Indian War (1754-1763). Spain captured Mobile in 1780, and the United States seized it in 1813. Mobile was incorporated as a city in 1819.

Mobile became an important seaport during the early 1800's as cotton production flourished in the South. The Civil War Battle of Mobile Bay, won by Union forces

Mobile, a major U.S. port, lies on the Mobile River. The 34-story First National Bank Building, *center,* towers over downtown Mobile.

Mobile Chamber of Commerce

under Rear Admiral David G. Farragut, closed Mobile's port in August 1864. The city fell nine months later and was the last Southern stronghold to surrender.

The Civil War crippled cotton production in the South, and Mobile suffered economically. However, exports of lumber and naval supplies and imports of general cargo gradually strengthened the city's economy. By the beginning of World War I (1914-1918), Mobile was again a thriving seaport. Between World War I and World War II (1939-1945), Mobile became a shipbuilding and railroad center. In 1940, workers finished building the Bankhead Tunnel. The tunnel carries automobile traffic under the Mobile River. It was the first underwater tunnel built in the South. Construction of an Army Air Forces supply base in Mobile during World War II and an expanding paper industry after the war boosted the city to its greatest period of growth. Mobile's population increased from 78,720 in 1940 to 202,779 in 1960.

Mobile's economy suffered again during the 1960's, when the federal government gradually closed Brookley Air Force Base in the city. In 1964, Mobile began Task Force 200, a plan to encourage industrial development in the city. As part of the project, Mobile purchased the abandoned military base in 1969 and created the Brookley Aerospace and Industrial Complex, now called the Brookley Industrial Complex. The city leases buildings and land in the complex to industry. From 1964 to 1969, Task Force 200 expanded Mobile's industrial employment by more than 16,000 jobs.

As in other cities both North and South, public school integration was a major problem in Mobile during the 1960's. Federal court orders forced Mobile to integrate some schools beginning in 1963. As the result of a 1968 ruling by a U.S. Court of Appeals, the city established widespread school integration in 1970. Many white people then set up private schools for their children.

Mobile rebuilt much of its downtown area during the 1960's. Housing projects and office buildings replaced hundreds of old structures. Wrecking crews cleared other areas to make way for an interstate highway system. Two more automobile tunnels under the Mobile River opened in 1975.   John Irvin Sellers

See also **Alabama** (pictures; Climate; History); **Bienville, Sieur de; Iberville, Sieur d'.**

Mobile, *MOH beel,* is a type of sculpture that originated during the early 1900's. A mobile is distinctive from other types of sculpture in that it achieves its expression or meaning through movement. Traditional sculpture achieves its expression through the arrangement of solid stationary forms.

Most mobiles are frail constructions of rodlike projections that are loosely joined together. Objects of various sizes and shapes are delicately balanced so they can swing freely in an infinite variety of moving arcs. Sculptors use many materials, textures, and colors for mobiles. A typical mobile could include colored disks, spheres, and wires, or cut and bent sheets of metal.

Most mobiles are suspended from above, so they can move freely. Some are pivoted on a base. Sculptors plan mobiles to present artistic interest not only in their ac-

Metal construction (1978) by Alexander Calder; National Gallery of Art, Washington, D.C. (© Ken Firestone)

A mobile is a type of sculpture that moves through the action of air currents. Most mobiles consist of abstract metal shapes carefully balanced and suspended from wires attached to rods.

tual shape, but also in the moving shadows they cast on walls and the floor. Mobiles usually move as the result of natural currents of air. A few are designed to move through mechanical power.

A mobile's shape and design are important, but its aesthetic value depends on its movement. The constantly swinging projections form arcs that cut invisible shapes out of space. A mobile's real design emerges from this variety of space shapes and from their relationships to one another and to the hanging objects.

Artists of many cultures in different times have created objects that depend on movement for some part of their expression. The first mobile is often attributed to the Russian painter and designer Alexander Rodchenko, who experimented in 1920 with suspended unpowered moving structures made of wood. But an American sculptor, Alexander Calder, was the first artist to create a true mobile, in which movement is the basic aesthetic purpose. Calder is regarded as the foremost creator of mobiles. Calder also created sculptures called *stabiles,* which are huge, stationary constructions of abstract design made from steel plates.

The word *mobile* was first used by the French painter Marcel Duchamp to describe the hand-powered and motor-driven sculptures that Calder exhibited in Paris in 1932. It is most generally associated with the type of unpowered mobile that Calder began making in 1934, using wire and painted tin shapes. Deborah Emont Scott

See also **Calder, Alexander; Sculpture** (Form and treatment; picture: *Red Petals*).

Mobile Bay, Battle of. See **Civil War** (Battle of Mobile Bay).

Mobile home, *MOH buhl,* is a movable, factory-built house. Mobile homes have built-in wheels. However, they usually move only when a truck hauls them to a homesite. Today, mobile homes are designed as permanent, year-round residences. As a result, the term *manufactured home* has begun to replace *mobile home.*

Mobile homes range from 48 to 70 feet (15 to 21 meters) in length and 12 to 28 feet (3.7 to 8.5 meters) in width. They may consist of several units that are joined at the homesite. The houses typically have a living room, kitchen, two or more bedrooms and bathrooms, and closets and cabinets. The homes are sold fully equipped with carpeting, draperies, kitchen appliances, and a furnace. Many of them are sold with furniture. The owner may add such features as an air conditioner, an automatic dishwasher, and a garbage disposal unit. A mobile home may rest on blocks, on a concrete slab, or on a basement. Once installed, the house is connected to electricity, gas, and water supply lines.

In the United States, more than 12 million people live in about 6 million mobile homes. Many of the houses stand in mobile-home communities on lots that the residents rent or own. In some neighborhoods, mobile homes occupy lots alongside traditional houses.

Mobile homes cost less to own and maintain than do most other houses. In 1976, the U.S. government established standards for the construction of mobile homes.
Bruce Butterfield

Mobile River, *moh BEEL,* is a short river that helps drain the delta at the head of Mobile Bay in southwestern Alabama (see **Alabama** [physical map]). The river begins where the Alabama and Tombigbee rivers meet.

The Mobile flows southward for about 45 miles (72 kilometers) before it empties into the Gulf of Mexico through Mobile Bay. The river is connected by the Tombigbee River to the Tennessee-Tombigbee Waterway, which opened in 1985. This waterway helps link the port at Mobile with inland ports on the Tennessee and Ohio rivers. The Mobile River provides transportation for coal, wood products, and other cargo. The river was named for the Mobile, or Mabila, Indians who once lived near its mouth. Neal G. Lineback

Möbius strip is a continuous loop with a half-twist in it. You can make a Möbius strip by taking a rectangular strip of paper, turning over one end (twisting it 180 degrees), and joining the ends. Although the original strip had two sides, the Möbius strip has only one. To check this, draw a line down the strip's middle until you reach the place where you started. You will find that the line runs around "both sides" of the strip. Similarly, a Möbius strip has only one edge. If you run your finger along its edge, you will return to your starting place after going around all the edge there is. If you cut the strip "in two"

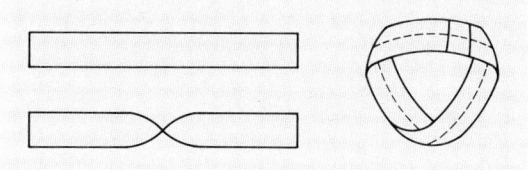

along the line you have drawn, it will remain one loop but will have two sides. The Möbius strip is named after August F. Möbius, the German mathematician who discovered it in the mid-1800's. Mary Kay Corbitt

Mobutu Sese Seko, *moh BOO too SAY say SAY koh* (1930-   ), has been president of Zaire since 1965. Zaire, formerly the Belgian colony of Belgian Congo, became an independent nation in 1960. The nation was called Congo until 1971.

For more than 25 years, Mobutu had complete power. Until 1990, Zaire had only one political party, which supported Mobutu's policies. That year, Mobutu announced governmental reforms under which opposition parties were allowed to form. In 1991, a national conference was held to rewrite the constitution and prepare for multiparty elections. But Mobutu suspended the conference several times.

In 1991, Mobutu agreed to share power with a prime minister and a cabinet. In 1992, a national conference elected a prime minister, cabinet, and a legislature. However, in 1993, Mobutu dismissed the prime minister and cabinet, and a new prime minister was appointed. But the previous prime minister refused to accept the dismissal.

Mobutu was born in the village of Lisala. He served in the Belgian colonial army from 1949 to 1956. He

© Lochon, Gamma-Liaison
Mobutu Sese Seko

became chief of staff of his country's army in July 1960. He took control of the government in September, after disputes between civilian leaders began. Mobutu returned control of the government to civilians in February 1961. Left wing rebellions began in Zaire in 1964. In November 1965, Mobutu took control of the government again and became president.

Mobutu's original name was Joseph Désiré Mobutu. He adopted the name Mobutu Sese Seko in 1972, shortly before he ordered all Zairians with European names to adopt African names.   Robert I. Rotberg

Moby-Dick. See Melville, Herman.

Moccasin, *MAHK uh suhn,* is a soft, slipperlike shoe originally worn by North American Indians. The Indians made moccasins from the skin of deer and other animals and decorated them with beads or porcupine quills. These shoes had no heels and were closely fitted. Most were of ankle length. Others extended to the knee.

The term *moccasin* also refers to a shoe construction. Genuine moccasins were made of a single piece of leather forming the bottom and sides of the shoe. A second piece, called the *plug,* formed the top of the shoe. In modern forms of moccasins, the sole may have more than one piece of material for greater protection and longer wear.   Ruth Schachter

See also **Indian, American** (picture: The Woodland Indians); **Shoe** (Kinds of shoes; picture).

Moccasin flower. See Lady's-slipper.

Moccasin snake. See Water moccasin.

Mock orange is the name of a group of shrubs native to North America, eastern Asia, and Europe. Garden species are sometimes called *syringas.* Mock orange plants are covered with small, white or cream-colored flowers that may grow singly or in clusters. The flowers of some species have purple spots at the base of the petals. In most species, the flowers are fragrant, but some species have odorless flowers. The plants generally reach a height of no more than 10 feet (3 meters), but a few species may grow 15 feet (4.5 meters) high.

Mock oranges generally bloom in late spring, often for only a few weeks. Breeders have produced many hybrids of mock oranges.

Scientific classification. Mock oranges belong to the saxifrage family, Saxifragaceae. They make up the genus *Philadelphus.*   Fred T. Davies, Jr.

Mockingbird is the name of more than 30 species of birds native to the Western Hemisphere. The *northern mockingbird,* also called *common mockingbird* or simply *mockingbird,* is famous for its ability to imitate the sounds of other birds. One naturalist reported a northern mockingbird that imitated the songs of 32 different birds in 10 minutes. The bird's own song is one of the most versatile birdsongs. The bird lives throughout the United States and Mexico and in parts of Canada.

The northern mockingbird has an ashy-white breast and an ash-gray coat. Its wings and tail are darker gray with white markings. Males and females have almost the same coloring, but the female has a little less white. The mockingbird grows from 9 to 11 inches (23 to 28 centimeters) long. It has a long slender body and tail.

Mockingbirds build their nests in thickets, low trees, and bushes. They lay from four to six greenish-blue or bluish-white eggs spotted with brown. Mockingbirds help people by eating insects and weed seeds. They

Hal H. Harrison from Grant Heilman

A mockingbird feeds its young insects and seeds. Mockingbirds can imitate the songs of many kinds of birds.

often pick insects off the radiators of parked cars. They also eat wild fruits and can damage fruit crops. The birds can be aggressive, especially when nesting.

Scientific classification. Mockingbirds belong to the mockingbird family, Mimidae. The scientific name for the northern mockingbird is *Mimus polyglottos.*   Donald F. Bruning

Mode, in statistics, is that value in any group that occurs most frequently. Suppose a boy counts the eggs in 77 birds' nests. He finds that 4 nests have 1 egg each, 65 have 2 eggs each, 5 have 3 eggs, and 3 have 4 eggs. The nests that contain 2 eggs are by far the most common. Thus, 2 is the *mode,* or *modal value,* in this group. The mode is a type of *average* that is often useful in the study of statistics.   Doris F. Hertsgaard

See also **Average; Mean; Median; Statistics** (Probability).

Model . . . See articles on models listed under their key word, as in **Airplane, Model.**

Model Parliament was the name given in the 1800's to the parliament that met at Westminster, in England, in 1295. When Edward I of England ordered the parliament to meet, he summoned not only churchmen and nobles, but also two knights elected from each county and two townsmen from each of many towns. For this reason, the parliament was considered representative of early assemblies from which today's British Parliament gradually emerged. But research indicates that knights and townsmen had been summoned before 1295, and some later parliaments included only nobles and churchmen. See also **Parliament.**   John Gillingham

Model T. See Ford, Henry (with picture).

Modeling. See Sculpture (The sculptor at work).

Modeling is a profession in which people display clothing and other products or illustrate various situations. Models of all ages pose for photographers and painters and work in fashion shows and exhibits.

Kinds of models. Different kinds of models specialize in a variety of assignments, but any model may work in more than one field. *Fashion models,* wearing the latest styles of clothing, jewelry, and accessories, pose for photographs that appear in magazines, newspapers, and catalogs. These models also display clothes in stores and fashion shows. *Commercial models* help sell many kinds of products in stores and wholesale showrooms and at exhibits and trade shows. They also appear in advertisements and television commercials.

Many publications hire *illustration models* to appear in pictures with articles and stories. *Artist's models* pose for art classes and individual artists. Clothing designers and patternmakers employ *fitter's models* for fitting clothes in all sizes in which the garments will be made.

Physical requirements for modeling. A model's basic requirement is physical attractiveness. A woman need not be beautiful, nor a man handsome, to be a model. But a model must appear desirable according to the ideal of the time. He or she also should be well groomed and graceful. A youthful appearance is necessary for most modeling, especially fashion modeling.

Size is vital in fashion work. Most fashion models are young women who wear a size 8 or 10 dress. A female model should be at least 5 feet 8 inches (175 centimeters) tall to display clothes to their best advantage. Most male models wear a size 40-regular suit and are at least 6 feet (183 centimeters) tall. A fitter's model must have the exact dimensions required for a standard size. Height is not as important for illustration models or for models who specialize in modeling such items as jewelry or shoes. They must have well-proportioned hands, legs, and feet. *Photographic models,* who pose for the camera, must be thin to appear attractive on film.

A model's work. Modeling may seem glamorous and exciting, but it is difficult, demanding work. Models sometimes work for long periods under hot, bright lights. Advertisers plan ads far in advance, and so models may be required to pose in bathing suits in winter and in heavy coats during the summer. A model must be able to follow directions, and must have some acting ability in order to portray any mood desired by a client.

A model who is photographed earns an hourly fee for his or her time. But for a fashion show, a model may work for a specific fee. Artist's models charge lower fees because artists operate on smaller budgets and their work requires more time. The fees of models who perform in TV commercials are determined by contracts with the television and motion-picture actors' unions.

Models are photographed at a photographer's studio. Photographs also may be taken *on location* in other buildings, outdoors, or in another city or country.

Model agencies represent models in dealing with clients. An agency accepts assignments for a model, sends bills to clients, and collects money owed the model. The agency receives a percentage of the model's earnings as a commission. Successful models are registered with a licensed model agency.

A client arranges with an agency to hire a model for a certain length of time on a particular day. This arrangement is called a *booking.* The booking may be for appearing in a fashion show, making a TV commercial, or posing for a photographer or artist.

Careers. Modeling is a highly competitive field, and most models have only a short career because a youthful appearance is so important. With the growing interest in the concerns of older people in the United States, some models are now able to work for many years. Nevertheless, the average modeling career still lasts only one to three years.

Employers generally prefer models who have had training or actual experience in the field. A man or woman who wants to become a model can attend modeling and self-improvement classes. These classes teach such skills as poise, grooming, the use of makeup, and the selection of attractive clothing and accessories.

© Larry Day

Models pose for a photographer, who positions them for a fashion advertisement. Although modeling may seem to be glamorous, it requires hard, tiring work and long hours.

Courses in dance, drama, and speech are also useful.

Most models are selected for a particular assignment on the basis of their *portfolio.* A model's portfolio consists of a series of photographs that show him or her in a variety of poses with different facial expressions. Female models also pose wearing a variety of hairstyles. Models also give potential clients a short series of photos called a *composite.* A composite includes a model's height and other physical characteristics and the name of the agency to contact.

In the United States, most modeling activity takes place in Atlanta, Chicago, Dallas, Los Angeles, and New York City. New York City is the center of most national advertising, and professional models find their best opportunities there. Modeling jobs are available in certain small cities, but most of the assignments outside large metropolitan areas involve only part-time work.

Some successful models become identified with a single company or product. A few gain fame as celebrities and personally endorse certain products. Many people have used a modeling career as a stepping stone to some other interesting professions. These former models are employed in such fields as advertising, fashion merchandising, public relations, publishing, and retail buying. Models who make TV commercials gain experience that can be helpful for an acting career in television or the movies. This experience can also lead to executive positions in various areas of the entertainment field.   Critically reviewed by the World Modeling Association

Additional resources

Anderson, Marie P. *Model: A Complete Guide to Becoming a Professional Model.* Doubleday, 1989. First published in 1988.
Beirne, Barbara. *Under the Lights: A Child Model at Work.* Carolrhoda, 1988. For younger readers.
Goldman, Larry. *Becoming a Professional Model.* Morrow, 1986. Deals with both male and female models.

Moderate Republican. See Reconstruction (The radicals and the moderates).

Modigliani, *moh* DEE *lee AH nee,* **Amedeo,** *AH meh DEH oh* (1884-1920), was an important Italian artist of the early 1900's. His favorite subject was the single figure. He painted many portraits. Modigliani's other favored theme was the reclining female nude.

Modigliani was a brilliant draftsman and his creative use of line is a notable aspect of his style. He preferred oval and cylindrical forms. Most of his subjects have elongated bodies, long necks, and oval heads. The simplification and distortion of the figures in his paintings, drawings, and sculptures show his interest in black African sculpture. The elegance of his creations also suggests the influence of his friend, the sculptor Constantin Brancusi. Even though Modigliani's portrait subjects

An oil portrait on canvas of Juan Gris (about 1917); Metropolitan Museum of Art, New York City, Bequest of Miss Adelaide Milton de Groot

A typical Modigliani portrait shows a single figure with a long neck and little expression against a simple background.

were molded by his recognizable style, they retain their individuality. His painting *Gypsy Woman with Baby* is reproduced in the **Painting** article.

Modigliani was born in Livorno. He settled in Paris in 1906. He was a colorful and restless character whose early death was linked to alcohol and drug abuse.

Pamela A. Ivinski

Modoc Indians, *MOH dahk,* are a small tribe closely related to the Klamath Indians. Until the 1860's, the Modoc lived at the California and Oregon border, mainly in the Lost River Valley and around Tule Lake. In winter, they lived in shelters that were partly underground. In warm months, they lived in wood houses

covered with mats made from tall marsh plants called *tules.* They also used tules to make rafts, baskets, and shoes. The Modoc fished, hunted, and gathered wild vegetables for food. Modoc leaders came from wealthy families, but the tribe made political decisions at assemblies where everyone was permitted to speak.

In 1864, the United States government relocated the Modoc tribe to the Klamath Reservation in Oregon. Kintpuash, a Modoc leader also known as Captain Jack, could not tolerate the reservation and returned home with part of the tribe. In 1872, the United States Army tried to force them to return to the reservation. The tribe fled to an area near Tule Lake. From there, about 60 Modoc warriors fought off more than 1,000 soldiers for five months. The Army eventually defeated the Modoc, executed their leaders, and exiled most of the tribe to Oklahoma.

Today, about 200 Modoc live in Oklahoma. The site of the Modoc war with the Army is now Lava Beds National Monument in California.   Victoria D. Patterson

See also **Captain Jack.**

Moebius strip. See Möbius strip.

Moffat Tunnel, *MAHF uht,* is one of the longest railroad tunnels in the world. It cuts through James Peak in Colorado for 6.23 miles (10.03 kilometers).

Moffat Tunnel has two separate *bores* (tubes). The largest, 24 by 16 feet (7 by 5 meters), is used for trains. The other bore, 8 by 8 feet (2.4 by 2.4 meters), carries water from the Fraser River to Denver. Engineers bored through rock from each side of the Continental Divide, at an elevation of 9,200 feet (2,800 meters). The tunnel shortened the distance between Salt Lake City and Denver by 176 miles (283 kilometers). By using the tunnel, trains avoid snowstorms, snowslides, and steep grades. The tunnel was named for David H. Moffat, American banker and railroad builder. It was leased to the Denver & Salt Lake Railroad.   Boyd C. Paulson, Jr.

Mogadishu, *MAW gah DEE shoo* (pop. 750,000), is the capital and largest city of Somalia. Mogadishu, sometimes spelled *Mogadiscio,* is also the country's chief port. It is located about 140 miles (225 kilometers) north of the equator on the southeast coast of Somalia, which borders the Indian Ocean (see **Somalia** [map]).

Mogadishu has Arab- and Western-style buildings. Its modern harbor handles many of Somalia's exports, including bananas, cattle, and hides. The city's chief industries process foods.

Historians believe that Arabs founded Mogadishu in the 900's. Arab sultans ruled the city for centuries. Italy gained control of the city in 1889 and later made it the capital of the colony of Italian Somaliland. The Italians built the city's central section. In 1960, Italian Somaliland and neighboring British Somaliland became the independent state of Somalia, with Mogadishu as its capital. In 1991, much fighting took place in Mogadishu between government forces and rebels. The city suffered heavy damage.   Stephen K. Commins

Mogollon, *moh guh YOHN,* is the name of prehistoric Indians who lived in southeastern Arizona and southwestern New Mexico from about 500 B.C. to A.D. 1200. Scientists believe they disappeared about A.D. 1250. The early Mogollon lived in villages of pit-houses. Later, they built crude one-story pueblo villages. The Indians gathered wild berries and seeds and later hunted and farmed corn. They used crude stone tools. The Mogollon made tobacco pipes of stone or baked clay. They decorated pottery with figures and geometric designs in red and brown or black and white. The pottery of the Mimbres people, a branch of the Mogollon, was among the finest made anywhere in North America north of Mexico.   Alfonso Ortiz

Mogul Empire, *MOH gul,* or Mughal Empire, ruled most of India in the 1500's and 1600's. Life in Mogul India set a standard of magnificence for its region of Asia, and the empire had peace, order, and stability. The centralized government of the empire provided a model for later rulers of India. A distinctive culture developed that blended Middle Eastern and Indian elements, and the Persian language became widely used.

Babar, a prince from what is now Afghanistan, founded the Mogul Empire in 1526. His grandson Akbar established its governmental structure. Akbar, who ruled from 1556 to 1605, controlled north and central India and Afghanistan. Jahangir, Akbar's son, ruled from 1605 to 1627 and was a patron of painting. His son Shah Jahan reigned from 1627 to 1658, during the height of the Mogul period. He encouraged architecture and built the famous Taj Mahal as a tomb for his wife. Shah Jahan's son Aurangzeb took the throne from his father in 1658 and imprisoned Shah Jahan.

The Mogul emperors were Muslims who ruled a largely Hindu nation. Under Akbar, Hindu warriors served as Mogul generals and governors. Other Hindus were administrators and clerks. Later, Aurangzeb imposed a tax on the Hindus and destroyed many of their temples. The Mahrattas, Hindu warriors of Central India, revolted and seriously weakened the empire.

The Mogul Empire began to break up soon after Aurangzeb's death in 1707. Moguls continued to rule a small kingdom at Delhi until Great Britain took control of India in the 1800's.   J. F. Richards

See also **Akbar; Aurangzeb; Babar; India** (The Mogul Empire); **Shah Jahan.**

Mohair is the name given to the hair of the Angora goat. This animal is native to Asia Minor and also is raised in South Africa and the United States. The name *mohair* is also applied to the lustrous, long-wearing fabrics produced from the hair of the Angora goat.

Mohair is smooth and resilient. It is often blended with other fibers. In many blends, mohair gives the surface of the fabric a glossy appearance. Mohair is often used to make decorative fabrics, draperies, and clothing, especially summer suits. It is also used in fabrics that must withstand rough wear, such as furniture upholstery.   Robert A. Barnhardt

See also **Goat** (picture: Angora goats).

Mohammad. See Muhammad.

Mohammad Reza Pahlavi, *moh ham AD reh ZAH pah lah VEE* (1919-1980), was the *shah* (king) of Iran from 1941 to 1979. He was overthrown in 1979 by a mass movement of Iranians led by Ayatollah Ruhollah Khomeini, a Muslim religious leader. As shah, Mohammad Reza carried out many economic and social reforms. But they did little for most Iranians, and he was a dictatorial ruler. Alternate spellings for parts of his name include *Mohammed, Muhammad, Riza,* and *Pahlevi.*

Mohammad Reza was born in Teheran. He succeeded his father, Reza Shah Pahlavi, as shah. Reza had refused

to cooperate with the Allies during World War II (1939-1945), and they forced him to abdicate. After Mohammad Reza became shah, he let the Allies keep troops in Iran and send supplies through Iran to the Soviet Union.

Beginning in the mid-1940's, the shah's authority was challenged by Iranian Communists and by nationalists led by Mohammad Mossadegh. In 1951, the nationalists forced the shah to appoint Mossadegh prime minister. Continuing opposition forced the shah to leave Iran in 1953. But with American help, Mossadegh was ousted, and the shah became Iran's most powerful leader.

In the 1960's, the shah began a program to distribute land to some peasant farmers. In the 1960's and 1970's, he used part of Iran's oil revenue to promote social and economic development. He expanded programs dealing with literacy and health care, and built many schools, airports, highways, railroads, dams, and irrigation facilities. He also bought much military equipment. Economic change led to rapid migration from rural areas to cities and increased the income gap between rich and poor.

Although Iran had a parliament and a cabinet, the shah controlled the government. His vast power aroused much opposition, especially from students, intellectuals, religious leaders, and industrial workers. His critics accused him of denying freedom of speech and other rights and of using secret police and military force to silence opponents. They also claimed his spending policies and government corruption were ruining Iran's economy. Many conservative Muslims said some of his policies violated teachings of the Muslim religion.

In January 1979, during the mass movement against him, the shah left Iran. His government was overthrown in February. While living in Mexico, the shah became ill. In October 1979, he was admitted to a hospital in the United States. In November, Iranian revolutionaries took over the United States Embassy in Teheran. They held as hostages a group of U.S. citizens, most of whom worked for the embassy. They said they would not release the hostages unless the U.S. government returned the shah to Iran for trial. The government refused to do so. The shah moved to Panama in December 1979 and to Egypt in March 1980. He died in Egypt in July 1980. The hostages were released in January 1981.   Nikki R. Keddie

See also **Iran** (Reforms and growing unrest).

Mohammed. See Muhammad.

Mohammedanism. See Islam; Muslims.

Mohave Indians, *moh HAH vee,* are a tribe who live in Colorado, Arizona, and Nevada along the Colorado River. Traditionally, the Mohave lived in isolated groups of related families. They built houses made of a frame of logs and poles thatched with plant material and covered with sand. Some houses were large enough for many families to live together.

The Mohave farmed the rich soil created by the spring flooding of the Colorado River. They planted corn, beans, pumpkins, melons, and wheat. They also fished in the river with nets or basketry scoops, hunted, and gathered wild plants.

The Mohave thought of themselves as a single nation within a defined territory. Unlike many other California tribes, whose small villages had little involvement with other villages of the same tribe, the Mohave moved freely from one settlement to another throughout the territory. They had hereditary chiefs, but such positions as war leader and *shaman* (spiritual leader or doctor) went to individuals believed to have received special powers in dreams. In the Mohave religion, knowledge and power came from dreams.

In the late 1700's, there were about 3,000 Mohave Indians. Today, more than 900 Mohave reside on the Fort Mojave Reservation near Needles, Calif. Over a thousand Mohave live south of Parker, Ariz., on the Colorado River Reservation.   Victoria D. Patterson

Mohawk Indians are a tribe of Iroquois Indians who once occupied an area near the Mohawk River in central New York. Today, most of the tribe's approximately 10,000 members live in Canada. More than a fourth live on the Six Nations Indian Reserve near Brantford, Ont. Other Mohawk live in New York.

Mohawk warriors were known for their fierceness and skill in battle. The term *Mohawk* comes from an Indian word that means *they eat living things.* Mohawk men hunted bear, deer, and other animals. Mohawk women raised corn, beans, and squash and gathered nuts, berries, and edible plants. The Mohawk lived in large bark-covered dwellings called *long houses.*

The Mohawk were one of the five tribes that, by the early 1600's, had joined together to form an organization known as the *Iroquois League* or the *Five Nations.* The other tribes were the Cayuga, Oneida, Onondaga, and Seneca. No one knows exactly when the league was formed. About 1722, the Tuscarora joined the league, which then became known as the *League of the Six Nations.* The Mohawk's land made up the easternmost part of the Iroquois territory.

The league became divided over which side to support during the Revolutionary War in America (1775-1783). The Mohawk and three other Iroquois tribes supported the British, largely because of the influence of a Mohawk leader named Joseph Brant (see **Brant, Joseph**). After Britain lost the war, many Mohawk and other Iroquois moved to Canada. Some Mohawk took up new occupations, including craftwork and lumberjacking. Since the late 1800's, many Mohawk have specialized in construction work on skyscrapers and bridges.

In recent years, the Mohawk have been involved in several disputes over land claims and other matters. In 1990, a land dispute broke out between some Mohawk and residents of the town of Oka, Que., near Montreal. An armed Mohawk group blocked access to the disputed land in March. This action led to a stand-off with police and Canadian armed forces that lasted until late September, when the last of the Mohawk group surrendered. Other Mohawk, acting in sympathy, blockaded a major bridge over the St. Lawrence River from July to early September. The Canadian government purchased the disputed land during the stand-off and, in negotiations with the Mohawk, has offered to turn it over to them. Negotiations have also taken place over treaty rights and other issues.   Robert E. Powless

See also **Iroquois Indians.**

Mohawk River is the largest tributary of the Hudson River. The Mohawk rises in central New York, about 20 miles (32 kilometers) north of Rome. It flows southeast for 148 miles (238 kilometers) and enters the Hudson River about 10 miles (16 kilometers) north of Albany.

The Mohawk River was named for the Mohawk Indians who lived in the west part of the Mohawk Valley.

The valley has served as a transportation route from the Hudson Valley to the Great Lakes region since colonial days. Two railroads, a highway, and the main branch of the New York State Barge Canal System run along the Mohawk for much of its length.   Michael K. Heiman

Mohawk Trail was a route westward along the Mohawk River from the Hudson River to the Great Lakes. The Iroquois Indian confederacy, a league of Indian tribes that included the Mohawk Indians, occupied the land it crossed. In pioneer days, thousands of settlers traveled westward along this route. Its importance declined after the building of the Erie Canal in 1825. A railroad and a modern highway now follow the course of the trail.   Robert E. Powless

Mohegan Indians became a powerful tribe in New England during colonial times. They lived along the Thames River in Connecticut, and the name *Mohegan* refers to the tides of the Thames near the Connecticut coast. The Mohegan are often confused with the Mohican, a tribe invented by the American writer James Fenimore Cooper in his novel *The Last of the Mohicans.*

The Mohegan Indians formed part of the Pequot tribe until the Pequot War broke out in New England in 1637. The Mohegan then helped the New England colonists destroy the Pequot. The Mohegan chief, Uncas, remained friendly with the colonists and helped them in other Indian wars. In turn, the colonists supported the Mohegan in their disagreements with other tribes.

During the 1700's, white settlers in Connecticut gradually forced the Mohegan Indians off much of their land. Large numbers of Mohegan also died from diseases introduced by whites. In 1775, many of the remaining Mohegan joined a mixed group of Christian Indians in a community in New York called Brotherton. In the 1820's, the federal government moved these Indians to Wisconsin. Today, their descendants live on the Stockbridge Reservation in northeastern Wisconsin. Some descendants of the Mohegan still live in Ledyard and North Stonington, Conn.   T. Brasser

See also **Uncas.**

Mohican Indians. See Mohegan Indians; Mahican Indians.

Mohs scale. See Mineral (Hardness).

Moi, Daniel Toroitich arap (1924-   ), became president of Kenya in 1978. He had been vice president from 1967 until 1978. He became president when Jomo Kenyatta, Kenya's first president, died. As president, Moi promoted good relations with the United States and other Western nations during the Cold War.

Early in Moi's presidency, his Kenya African National Union (KANU) was the only political party in Kenya, though other parties were not banned by law. But after an unsuccessful coup against him in 1982, Moi backed a change in the Constitution that made KANU the only legal political party. The one-party state led to protests by Kenyans, and threats by Western nations to stop fi-

© Tannenbaum, Sygma

Daniel T. arap Moi

nancial aid to Kenya. In 1991, the Constitution was amended to allow for a multiparty system. Elections were held in December 1992, and Moi was elected president by the voters.

Moi was born near Nakuru, Kenya. He worked as a schoolteacher from 1945 to 1957. Moi was active in the negotiations that led to Kenya's independence from Britain in 1963.   Stephen K. Commins

Moiré pattern, *mwah RAY* or *maw RAY,* is a pattern of lines formed when two regularly spaced patterns overlap but are not aligned. For example, the illustration with this article shows the moiré pattern produced by two misaligned, overlapping patterns of circles. In this case, lines seem to stream from the center of the figure.

The word *moiré* comes from the name of a ribbed fabric made since the 1400's. Overlapping pieces of silk

A moiré pattern of wide curving lines results where two groups of narrow-lined circles overlap.

or window screens often produce moiré patterns. Many *optical art,* or *op art,* paintings also have moiré patterns. The patterns create an illusion of shimmer, as though some hidden feature of the paintings were vibrating.

Scientists use moiré patterns to detect abnormalities in surfaces and motions, because any change in a moiré pattern is highly magnified. For example, a slight movement of one circle in the illustration would noticeably change the moiré pattern.   Jearl Walker

Mojave Desert, *moh HAH vee,* in southeastern California, is a vast desert wasteland covering about 25,000 square miles (64,700 square kilometers). It lies between the Sierra Nevada and the Colorado River (see **California** [physical map]). The Pacific Ocean once covered this region. Over a long period, high mountains rose and blocked the entry of water from the sea. Volcanic mountains erupted and covered the region with lava, mud, and ashes. Today, many small isolated mountain ranges and extinct volcanoes break up the great stretches of sandy soil. Dry lake beds form the world's chief source of boron, a mineral used for jet-engine and rocket fuels and for nuclear reactor controls.   John Edwin Coffman

Molasses is a thick, sweet, sticky syrup. It is yellowish or dark brown. Molasses is used for brewing, cooking, candymaking, and distilling alcohol, and as a livestock feed.

Most molasses is obtained as a by-product in the manufacture of sugar from sugar cane. Therefore, countries that grow sugar cane produce most of the world's molasses (see **Sugar cane**). In the United States, Florida and Hawaii are centers of molasses production.

Molasses is the liquid that remains after sugar crystals are removed from concentrated cane juice. Molasses may be made by the *open kettle method* or by the *vacuum pan method.* In the open kettle method, the cane juice is boiled in a large open pan. After it has been boiled several times, most of the water evaporates. The syrup that remains receives additional boiling until it becomes a stiff mass of syrup and crystals called *massecuite.* The massecuite is placed in barrels with tiny holes in the bottom. The molasses seeps through these holes, leaving sugar crystals inside the barrels.

Large sugar factories generally use the vacuum pan method, in which the massecuite is boiled in large, covered vacuum pans. After being boiled several times, it is thoroughly stirred in a mixer. The mixture is then spun in rotating containers called *centrifuges.* The centrifuges have walls of fine copper mesh that permit the molasses to pass through but hold the sugar crystals.

Further boiling of the molasses produces varying grades. The molasses left after several boilings is called *blackstrap.* It is used in fertilizer and is commonly mixed with hay to serve as feed for farm animals. The distillation of molasses produces ethyl alcohol, which is used in the chemical industry and as a combustion fuel. Molasses is also distilled to make rum.   Paul H. Moore

Molasses Act was a British law passed in 1733 to change a pattern of trade in the American Colonies. It placed a duty of sixpence on each gallon of molasses imported into British colonies from areas not ruled by Britain, and also put duties on imported sugar and rum. Molasses was used to make rum, and New England had a rich rum industry. Because of lower prices, the New Englanders bought more rum in the French West Indies than in the British West Indies. Planters in the British West Indies thus requested duties on molasses in hopes of curbing the trade with the French. But New England smugglers avoided paying the duties.   Pauline Maier

Mold is a hollow form. See **Cast and casting**.

Mold is a type of fungus that often grows on food. Like mushrooms, mildews, and all other fungi, molds have no *chlorophyll*—the green coloring matter that plants use to manufacture food. Molds live on food made by plants or animals, or on decaying matter. Some molds live as parasites on animals, plants, or other fungi.

Many common molds can grow on bread, fruit, and other food. The *black bread mold* often forms a cottony, soft, white growth on damp bread. The mold gets its name from the dark-colored *spores* (tiny reproductive bodies) that it soon produces. A group of molds known as the *blue molds* also may grow on bread. A green mold often grows on various kinds of cheeses. Other molds, called *water molds,* are found in water and soil.

Molds develop from spores. When a spore of the black bread mold settles on damp food, it swells and begins to grow by producing tiny *hyphae* (threads). The hyphae form a tangled mass called a *mycelium,* which in turn produces aerial hyphae called *stolons.* Rootlike structures known as *rhizoids* anchor the stolons in the food. As the black bread mold matures, many upright *fruiting bodies* form above the rhizoids. Each fruiting body has a spore case, called a *sporangium,* at its end. A sporangium looks like a miniature pinhead and contains thousands of spores. When the spore case matures and breaks open, the spores are carried away by air currents. These spores may settle on damp foods and grow, starting the reproductive cycle over again. Some molds, such as *Penicillium,* produce chains of spores at the tips of certain hyphae, called *conidiophores.*

Moldy foods generally should be thrown away. But certain cheeses, such as Roquefort, owe their flavor to a mold that grows in them and ripens them. Molds are also useful because they fertilize soil by breaking up dead organisms and waste material. *Penicillium* molds produce the drug penicillin (see **Penicillin**).

Scientific classification. Molds belong to the division Eumycota in the kingdom Fungi. They are in the classes Hyphomycetes, Oomycetes, and Zygomycetes.   Joe F. Ammirati

See also **Fungi; Mildew; Mycotoxin; Slime mold.**

Moldavia. See **Moldova; Romania** (Land regions).

Moldova, *mawl DOH vuh,* is a country in south-central Europe bordered by Romania on the west and by Ukraine on the other three sides. From 1940 to 1991, Moldova was a republic of the Soviet Union. It was called the Moldavian Soviet Socialist Republic, or simply Moldavia. With the collapse of the Soviet Union in 1991, the republic declared its independence.

Moldova belonged to Romania before it became part of the Soviet Union, and it shares Romania's language, history, and culture. Moldova has especially close ties with a region in eastern Romania that is still called Moldavia. For much of their history, Moldova and the Romanian region of Moldavia were united.

Moldova covers 13,012 square miles (33,700 square kilometers) and has a population of 4,521,000. Chisinau, called Kishinev under the Soviets, is the capital.

Government and politics

Political power in Moldova is divided between the president, Parliament, and the Council of Ministers. Voters elect the president to a five-year term. The Parliament has 365 members, who are also elected to five-year terms. The president appoints the Council of Ministers.

The country's largest political party is the Moldovan Popular Front, which supports reunification of Moldova with Romania. The National Alliance for Independence supports independent statehood. It is made up of about 10 political, cultural, and professional organizations. The Joint Council of Work Cooperatives is the major political force in an industrial region on the east bank of the Dnestr (also spelled Nistru) River in eastern Moldova. Many of the people in this region, called Trans-Dnestr, are of Russian or Ukrainian descent and oppose union with Romania. The activities of the Communist Party—which had been the only party under Soviet rule—were outlawed in 1991.

People

Ethnic groups and language. Moldova is the most densely populated of all the former Soviet republics. About two-thirds of the people are ethnic Moldovans. Most of the rest of the population is made up of Russians; Ukrainians; Gagauz, a Turkic people; and Bulgarians. More than half of the people of Moldova live in rural areas, clustered in villages. Most of these people work as farmers.

Moldova

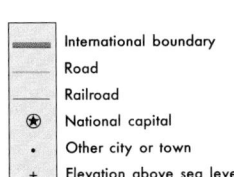

▬▬▬	International boundary
▭	Road
—	Railroad
⊛	National capital
•	Other city or town
+	Elevation above sea level

WORLD BOOK maps

Facts in brief

Capital: Chisinau.
Official language: Romanian.
Official name: Republica Moldova (Republic of Moldova).
Area: 13,012 sq. mi. (33,700 km²). *Greatest distances*—north-south, 210 mi. (340 km); east-west, 165 mi. (265 km).
Elevation: *Highest*—Mount Balaneshty, 1,407 ft. (429 m). *Lowest:* Dnestr River at southeastern border, 80 ft. (25 m).
Population: *Estimated 1994 population*—4,521,000; density, 347 persons per sq. mi. (134 per km²); distribution, 53 percent rural, 47 percent urban. *1989 census*—4,337,592. *Estimated 1999 population*—4,682,000.
Chief products: *Agriculture*—eggs, grain, grapes, milk, sugar beets. *Manufacturing*—construction materials, refrigerators, tractors, washing machines.
National anthem: *"Deşteapta-te, Române"* ("Romanian, Arise").
Money: *Basic unit*—ruble.

A. Boulat, Sipa Press

Rich farmland covers three-fourths of Moldova, and the country's economy is based largely on agriculture. Farmers load bales of hay, which will be used as feed for cattle.

The country's official language is Romanian. The Moldovans used the Roman alphabet in writing their language. Under Soviet rule, they were forced to adopt the Cyrillic alphabet, which is used to write the Russian language. But in 1989, the republic's parliament ordered a return to the Roman alphabet.

Religion. Most Moldovans are Eastern Orthodox Christians. From 1940 until the late 1980's, the Soviet Union forbade religious instruction in Moldova and discouraged church attendance. In 1990, the Soviet Union restored religious freedom.

Education. Moldovan children are required to attend school from the ages of 6 to 18. Almost every Moldovan 15 years of age or older can read and write. The Moldovan State University is in Chisinau. The Academy of Sciences in that city oversees the workings of about 30 academic institutes.

Land and climate

Most of Moldova consists of hills broken by river valleys. The highest elevations are in the scenic forests of the central region. The country's tallest peak is Mount Balaneshty, which rises 1,407 feet (429 meters) in the Kodry Hills in west-central Moldova. Lush uplands and *steppes* (grassy plains) cover much of northern and eastern Moldova. A large plain stretches across the south.

Moldova has more than 3,000 rivers, but only 8 are longer than 60 miles (95 kilometers). The country's main waterway is the Dnestr River, which flows through eastern Moldova. The Prut River flows along the western border, between Moldova and Romania.

Rich, black soil that is good for farming covers three-fourths of the country. In the north and along the Dnestr, where the most fertile soils are, farmers grow fruits, sugar beets, and some grain. Less rich soils in the south are used for corn, wheat, and sunflowers.

The animals found in Moldova include wolves, badgers, wild boars, and Siberian stags. The rivers hold carp, pike, and perch. Such animals as hares, muskrats, and foxes are hunted for their fur.

Temperatures average about 25 °F (−4 °C) in January and about 70 °F (21 °C) in July. The average annual precipitation provides about 20 inches (50 centimeters) of rain, snow, and other forms of moisture.

Economy

Moldova has a developing economy supported mainly by agriculture. The central and southern regions produce grapes for wine. Farms in the south also grow corn and winter wheat. The northern and central regions have fruit orchards and fields of grain. Moldova's other crops include sugar beets, sunflowers, and tobacco. Dairy farming, hog farming, and cattle raising are also important.

Moldova's chief industries process food and other agricultural products and manufacture construction materials, refrigerators, television sets, tractors and other agricultural machinery, and washing machines. The country has plants for canning fruits and vegetables, refining sugar from sugar beets, and making wine. Other plants process furs and make footwear and silk and woolen garments.

Moldova's chief trading partners are former Soviet republics, especially Russia and Ukraine; and other countries of Eastern Europe. Its major exports include wine, leather and fur, and clothing. Its main imports include fuel, automobiles, and electronic items.

History

Early days. From about 700 B.C. until about A.D. 200, the region that is now Moldova was under the control of Iranian peoples from central Asia—first the Scythians and later the Sarmatians. From about A.D. 200 until the A.D. 1200's, various other peoples from the west and east invaded and ruled the area. These invaders included the Goths, Huns, Avars, and finally the Mongols (also called the Tatars). The people of Moldova gradually united and by the mid-1300's, they formed an independent state under a single ruler, a prince. The state was called the principality of Moldavia. It included present-day Moldova, then called Bessarabia, and an area between the Moldavian Carpathian Mountains and the Prut River in modern Romania. For a map showing the principality of Moldavia in 1350, see **Romania** (History).

Ottoman and Russian rule. The Ottoman Empire, based in present-day Turkey, gained control of the principality of Moldavia by the early 1500's. The Ottomans ruled the region until 1812, when Russia took control of Bessarabia. The Treaty of Paris that ended the Crimean War in 1856 gave southern Bessarabia to the principality of Moldavia, following Russia's defeat in that war. In 1861, the principality of Moldavia united with the principality of Walachia, now a region in present-day Romania, to form the new nation of Romania. Russia regained southern Bessarabia in 1878.

Romanian and Soviet rule. After World War I (1914-1918), all of Bessarabia became part of Romania. The Soviet Union, which had been formed as a Communist state under Russia's leadership in 1922, refused to recognize Bessarabia's unification with Romania. In 1924, the Soviets established the Moldavian Autonomous Soviet Socialist Republic (A.S.S.R.) in the Trans-Dnestr region. In 1940, during World War II, the Soviet Union seized Bessarabia. The Soviets merged most of Bessarabia with part of the Moldavian A.S.S.R. to form the Moldavian Soviet Socialist Republic. Bessarabia became part of Romania again in 1941, but the Soviet Union regained it in 1944.

Breakup of the Soviet Union. The Moldavian Supreme Soviet, as the republic's legislature was then called, declared in 1990 that its laws took precedence over those of the Soviet Union. Moldavia also changed its name to Moldova.

In August 1991, conservative Communist officials failed in an attempt to overthrow Soviet President Mikhail S. Gorbachev. During the upheaval that followed, Moldova and several other republics declared their independence. In December, the Soviet Union was dissolved.

Moldova's leaders restored many of the country's ties to Romania. They reintroduced Romanian history as a basic subject in the school curriculum and sent thousands of Moldovans to study in Romanian schools. They adopted the Romanian national anthem.

Threats to Moldovan unity. In 1990—before Moldova became independent—both the Gagauz people in southern Moldova and Russians and Ukrainians in the Trans-Dnestr region had announced that they were forming independent states. Many of these people objected to the 1989 law that made Romanian the official language. In March 1992, fighting between ethnic Moldovans and separatists in the Trans-Dnestr broke out. In July, a peacekeeping force, consisting of Moldovans, Russians, and non-separatists from Trans-Dnestr, entered the region, and fighting ceased.

Vladimir Tismaneanu

See also **Bessarabia; Chisinau; Commonwealth of Independent States; Romania.**

Mole is a small, thick-bodied mammal that lives underground. The mole is a fast, tireless digger. It has a narrow, pointed nose, a wedge-shaped head, and large forelegs. Its front paws, which turn outward, have long, broad nails. The forelegs work like shovels, scooping out the earth. The mole's hind legs are short and powerful. The animal is almost blind, with tiny eyes that are shaded by overhanging fur or skin. A mole does not have external ears, but it hears well.

A mole's home can be recognized by a cone-shaped mound of earth above it. This mound is considerably larger than the slightly raised roofs of the tunnels the animal makes when digging for food. Moles eat primarily worms and insects. Their diggings often spoil gardens and fields, and farmers set traps in the animals' tunnels.

Mole fur has been used in making coats and jackets. Furriers prefer bluish-gray mole fur, but they also use black, brownish-black, and paler shades. Moleskin is lightweight, warm, soft, and thick. But it does not wear well and has lost popularity through the years.

The eastern mole is found from Massachusetts and Florida to central Texas. It is 5 to 8 inches (13 to 20 centimeters) long, including a tail that measures about 1 inch (2.5 centimeters) in length. It weighs from $1\frac{1}{2}$ to 5 ounces (43 to 140 grams) and eats nearly its own weight

Charles E. Mohr, Photo Researchers

A mole searches for earthworms and other food by digging tunnels with its sharp claws and powerful legs. It is nearly blind, but it does not need keen vision in its underground tunnels.

in food every day. The eastern mole lives almost its entire life underground. It tunnels near the surface when searching for food. Most eastern moles live in nests about 1 foot (30 centimeters) underground.

The star-nosed mole has a fringe of fleshy *tentacles* (feelers) around its nose. It has dark, blackish-brown fur on its upper parts, shading to a paler color underneath. The animal's long, hairy tail thickens at the base. The star-nosed mole lives in southeastern Canada and in the Eastern United States as far south as Georgia. It likes to live near water and usually builds its home in the damp, muddy soil of a swamp or along the shore of a brook or pond. The star-nosed mole is an expert swimmer. In the winter, the star-nosed mole burrows deep into the soil to avoid frost. See **Mammal** (illustration: The star-nosed mole).

The European mole builds a home that has many underground chambers. There is one central chamber that is connected to other smaller, round rooms. Passageways extend from these rooms in all directions. One passage, called the *bolt run,* serves as an exit in case of danger. The other passages lead to feeding grounds. In the central chamber is a nest. Three or four baby moles are born in early spring. The European mole is about the same size as the eastern mole.

Moles also live in parts of Asia. The largest species of all moles is the *Russian desman,* which is about 14 inches (36 centimeters) long, including the tail. It lives in southeastern Europe and central western Asia. The smallest species are the shrew moles and long-tailed moles of Asia and the Pacific Coast of North America. They are about 5 inches (13 centimeters) long, including their tails.

Scientific classification. Moles belong to the mole family, Talpidae. The scientific name for the eastern mole is *Scalopus aquaticus.* The star-nosed mole is *Condylura cristata.* The European mole is *Talpa europaea.* The Russian desman is *Desmana moschata.*   Hugh H. Genoways

Mole is a unit used in chemistry to measure the amount of a substance. One mole of any substance contains about 602,213,670,000,000,000,000,000 (602.214 billion trillion) of the *elementary entities* that make up the substance. These entities can be molecules, atoms, ions, electrons or other subatomic particles, or groups of particles. The large number is called the *Avogadro constant,* in honor of Italian physicist Amedeo Avogadro.

The mole is a base unit in the metric system of measurement. The symbol for the mole is *mol.* The mass in grams of 1 mole of a substance is the same as the number of *atomic mass units* (amu's) in one elementary entity of that substance. One amu is $\frac{1}{12}$ the mass of one atom of carbon-12. Carbon-12 is the *isotope* (form) of carbon whose atomic nucleus contains 6 protons and 6 neutrons (see **Isotope**). Thus, one atom—the elementary entity—of carbon-12 has a mass of 12 amu's, and 1 mole of carbon-12 has a mass of 12 grams.   Peter A. Rock

Mole is a colored growth on the skin. It consists of cells that contain *melanin,* a dark pigment. Moles may be present at birth and are often called *birthmarks.* But most first appear during childhood or adolescence.

Moles may occur on any part of the body. They vary in size and may be flat or raised. They range from light brown to bluish-black. Most moles are small and do not change in appearance. Some have long, dark hairs.

Moles are extremely common—on the average, adults have about 40. The tendency to have many moles runs in families. Most moles are hardly noticed, but conspicuous moles may be considered unattractive by some people. Such moles can be removed by surgery.

The great majority of moles are harmless. In rare cases, however, a mole can develop into a cancerous tumor called a *melanoma.* A melanoma may start as a mole that changes color, itches, becomes sore, enlarges, grows crusty, or bleeds. Melanomas may destroy surrounding healthy tissue and may spread cancer to other parts of the body. Most of these tumors are curable if they are diagnosed and treated early. Therefore, any change in a mole should be reported to a physician immediately.   Yelva Liptzin Lynfield

See also **Skin** (Tumors); **Birthmark**.

Mole cricket is a type of large insect that burrows in the ground like a mole. Its short front legs, like the mole's legs, are specially suited for burrowing. Most mole crickets also have wings and can fly. Mole crickets live in tropical and temperate regions. They live underground in burrows and also may be found in damp basements. Mole crickets eat insect larvae, earthworms, and root and tuber crops, including potatoes.

The most common species of mole cricket in North America is the *northern mole cricket.* It measures about $1\frac{1}{2}$ inches (4 centimeters) long and is velvety brown in

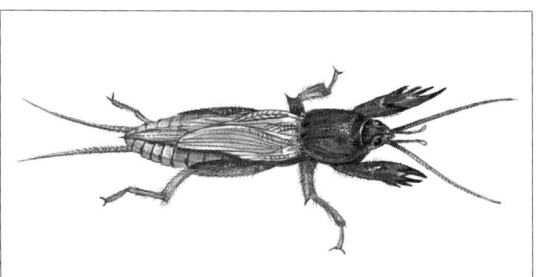

WORLD BOOK illustration by John F. Eggert
A mole cricket burrows in the ground like a mole. This illustration shows a northern mole cricket.

color. The *changa,* a mole cricket of Puerto Rico, is the worst insect pest of the sugar crop.

Scientific classification. Mole crickets make up the mole cricket family, Gryllotalpidae. The scientific name for the northern mole cricket is *Neocurtilla hexadactyla.* The changa is *Scapteriscus vicinus.*   Betty Lane Faber

Mole-rat is a type of small rodent. Mole-rats live in Africa and around the Mediterranean. They spend their entire lives underground. One of the most interesting species is the *naked mole-rat,* which lives in the hot, dry areas of Kenya, Ethiopia, and Somalia. Naked mole-rats live in organized communities. They are the only known mammals whose social behavior resembles that of such insects as bees, ants, and termites.

Naked mole-rats are about $3\frac{1}{3}$ inches (8.5 centimeters) long and weigh 1 to 2 ounces (28 to 57 grams). These animals appear hairless but actually have thinly scattered hair on their bodies. They are nearly blind, but they can feel objects with their whiskers and their body hair. They use their long front teeth to dig tunnels. Their body temperature varies with the temperature of their surroundings. Naked mole-rats communicate by means

WORLD BOOK illustration by John F. Eggert
A naked mole-rat has wrinkled skin and scattered hair.

of complex vocalizations. They eat the underground parts of plants, such as roots and bulbs.

Each colony of naked mole-rats consists of 75 to 80 individuals. Within a colony, only one female has *pups* (young). Other females that attempt to reproduce are attacked. The breeding female has one to three mates and can produce more than 100 offspring each year. The other colony members help the breeders by carrying out specific activities. Smaller members find and transport food, clear tunnels, and build nests. Larger members excavate tunnels and protect the colony from enemies, such as poisonous snakes.

Scientific classification. Mole-rats belong to the families Bathyergidae and Spalacidae. The scientific name for the naked mole-rat is *Heterocephalus glaber.*   Paul W. Sherman

Molecular biology is the study of those molecules that direct molecular processes in cells. For example, genetic information is stored in large molecules in the cells of organisms. The way in which these molecules convert their information into chemical reactions gives an organism its particular characteristics and is essential for its life. Molecular biology is a relatively new area of biology and has provided a greater understanding of "what life is" and "how life works."

The beginning of molecular biology. The term *molecular biology* was first defined in 1938 by the American mathematician Warren Weaver as "those borderline areas in which physics and chemistry merge with biology." At that time, many physicists and chemists were investigating the biochemical processes that occur in living cells. Some studied the basic chemical "building blocks" of living cells, which include amino acids, lipids, and simple carbohydrates. Other scientists studied molecules thousands and even billions of times larger than the basic building blocks. These molecules are known as *macromolecules*. There are two chief kinds of macromolecules—nucleic acids and proteins.

The nucleic acid *DNA* (deoxyribonucleic acid) is the chief macromolecule in *chromosomes,* the cell structures that control heredity. In 1953, biologists James D. Watson of the United States and Francis H. C. Crick of Great Britain proposed a model for the structure of DNA. They correctly suggested that a molecule of DNA looks like a twisted ladder, or *double helix.* The rungs of the ladder consist of pairs of compounds called *bases.* Just before a cell divides, the DNA ladder breaks lengthwise, separating the pairs of bases. The bases in each half ladder then attach to free bases, forming base pairs that are identical to the original ones (see **Cell** [DNA—the wondrous ladder]). This discovery indicated how information stored in DNA molecules could be transmitted, both to the new cells formed by cell division and to other parts of the cell, for the manufacture of proteins.

In the 1950's, molecular biologists formulated two important biological concepts—(1) the central dogma and (2) the genetic code. The central dogma states that DNA's instructions for making proteins are transmitted from DNA through *RNA* (ribonucleic acid). The genetic code refers to the sequences of bases in DNA and RNA molecules that determine the biological function of these macromolecules. For example, in a DNA molecule, a sequence of bases that provides instructions for making a specific protein is called a *gene.* A single molecule of DNA may contain thousands of genes. See **Cell** (RNA—the master copy; The genetic code).

Molecular biology today focuses primarily on determining why only some genes are expressed in certain cells. French scientists performed early research of this type in the 1960's. Using *E. coli* bacteria, they showed that certain proteins can activate or "shut off" genes.

During the 1980's, advances in genetic engineering enabled scientists to study gene regulation in the cells of higher plants and animals. Such research has added greatly to the understanding of many biological processes. For example, molecular biologists have identified several genes that can cause cancer in human beings. These genes, called *oncogenes,* are normally inactive in adults but may be activated by viruses, chemicals, or other agents. If scientists determine which agents activate oncogenes, new methods of treating cancer may be developed.   Perry B. Hackett, Jr.

Additional resources

Biological Science: A Molecular Approach. Ed. by Toby Klang. 6th ed. Heath, 1990.
Darnell, James E., and others. *Molecular Cell Biology.* Scientific Am. Bks., 1986.
Rees, Anthony R., and Sternberg, M. J. E. *From Cells to Atoms: An Illustrated Introduction to Molecular Biology.* Blackwell Scientific, 1984.

Molecular mass. See Molecule (Individual molecules).

Molecule is one of the basic units of matter. It is the smallest particle into which a substance can be divided and still have the chemical identity of the original substance. If the substance were divided further, only molecular fragments or atoms of chemical elements would remain. For example, a drop of water contains billions of water molecules. If one of those water molecules were separated from the rest, it would still behave as water. But if that water molecule were divided, only atoms of the elements hydrogen and oxygen would remain.

Individual molecules. Molecules are made up of atoms held together in certain arrangements. Scientists use chemical formulas to show the composition of molecules. For example, a water molecule consists of two hydrogen atoms and one oxygen atom, and it has the formula H_2O. A molecule's size and shape depends on the size and number of its atoms. A molecule that consists of two atoms, such as nitric oxide (NO), is called a *diatomic* molecule. A molecule made up of three atoms, such as water, is called a *triatomic* molecule. A large molecule, such as DNA, can contain millions of atoms.

Atoms link together in molecules through strong attractive forces called *bonds* (see **Bond** [chemical]). The shape of a molecule depends upon two factors: (1) The atoms tend to take up positions relative to one another such that the bonds formed are the strongest of all the bonds that this particular group of atoms could form. (2) Atoms that are not bonded to each other tend to move far apart. For example, an ammonia molecule has the shape of a *tetrahedron* (a pyramidlike figure with four faces). It consists of three hydrogen atoms attached to a nitrogen atom. Normal butane molecules have 4 carbon atoms arranged in a zigzag chain with 10 hydrogen atoms attached. Large protein molecules can form long spiral chains.

The mass of a molecule is indicated by its *molecular mass.* Molecular mass can be found by adding the *atomic masses* of all the atoms in a molecule. The molecular mass of carbon dioxide (CO_2) can be found by adding the atomic mass of carbon, which is 12, and the masses of the 2 oxygen atoms, which are about 16 each. Carbon dioxide has a molecular mass of about 44. A molecule's mass can also be measured with an instrument called a *mass spectrometer.*

Polar molecules and ionic substances. Each atom in a molecule consists of a positively-charged nucleus surrounded by a cloud of negatively-charged electrons. In a *neutral* molecule, the positive and negative charges are evenly balanced throughout the molecule. In *polar* molecules, the charges are not evenly balanced. In a polar molecule, more positive charge collects at one location in the molecule and more negative charge collects at a different location. Some molecules are magnetic because of the way the electrons are unevenly distributed within the molecule.

Almost all gases, most common liquids, and many solids are made up of neutral or polar molecules. But some substances are made up of units called *ions* (atoms or groups of atoms with a positive or a negative charge). These substances are called *ionic substances.*

Salts are examples of ionic substances. For example, sodium chloride, common table salt, consists of positive sodium ions and negative chloride ions. Electric forces among the ions hold them together in a regular framework. Metals are also different from molecular substances. In addition to positive ions, metals consist of a large number of electrons that move about freely throughout the metal.

Molecules and matter. Molecules are held together in a group by electrical forces called *Van der Waals forces*. These forces are usually weaker than those that hold a molecule itself together. The force between molecules depends on how far apart they are. When two molecules are widely separated, they attract each other. When they come very close together, they repel each other.

In a solid, the molecules are so arranged that the forces which attract and repel are balanced. The molecules vibrate about these positions of balance, but they do not have enough energy to move to different parts of the solid. As the temperature of a solid is raised, the molecules vibrate more strongly. When the Van der Waals forces can no longer hold the molecules in place, the solid melts.

In a liquid, the molecules move about easily, but they still have some attractive force on one another. These forces are strong enough to keep the liquid together. Certain organic compounds called *liquid crystals* have properties of both liquids and solids. Within a particular temperature range, such a compound flows like a liquid, but has a more ordered molecular arrangement. Its molecules line up side by side and form tiny groups or clusters that slide past one another in certain directions. See **Liquid crystal**.

In a gas, the molecules move about so fast that the attractive forces have little effect on them. When two molecules in a gas collide, the repelling force sends them apart again. Therefore, gas molecules fill a container completely, because they move freely through all the space available.

Most substances can be changed into solids, liquids, or gases by either raising or lowering their temperatures. The temperature at which these changes occur—and also other characteristics of a substance—depends on the size, shape, and mass of the molecules and also on the strength of the Van der Waals forces between them.

Under certain conditions, two molecules may collide with enough energy to react and form one or more new molecules. The process by which many small molecules combine chemically to produce a large molecule is called *polymerization* (see **Polymerization**). Molecules can also break down into smaller molecules. Causes of molecular disintegration include ultraviolet light, fast-moving electrons, and nuclear radiation.

Studying molecules. Scientists can study some molecules directly with an *electron microscope*. This method provides a picture of a molecule, but the picture is often too blurred to see fine details. A *scanning tunneling microscope* produces an image of some individual atoms in a solid substance. Scientists also study molecules indirectly. For example, they study solids by *X-ray diffraction*. The way a solid deflects X rays tells them about the size, shape, and arrangement of its molecules. Scientists also use *neutron diffraction* and *electron diffraction* to study solids. They pass a beam of *neutrons* (uncharged particles) or electrons through a solid, and observe how the beam is affected. Electron diffraction can also be used to study gases.

Scientists also learn about molecules by studying the way they absorb or give off light. Each kind of molecule absorbs or gives off certain colors of light. This group of

Diagrams of some common molecules Scientists study chemical compounds to learn how many atoms of each element are in the molecules and how these atoms are joined to each other. With this information, diagrams of molecules can be drawn with balls representing the individual atoms.

WORLD BOOK diagram

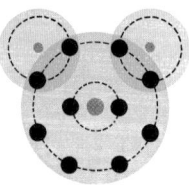

A molecule of water forms when two atoms of hydrogen and one of oxygen, *above,* join together in sharing their electrons, *below.* The electrons fill the vacancies in all the atoms.

Water Molecule

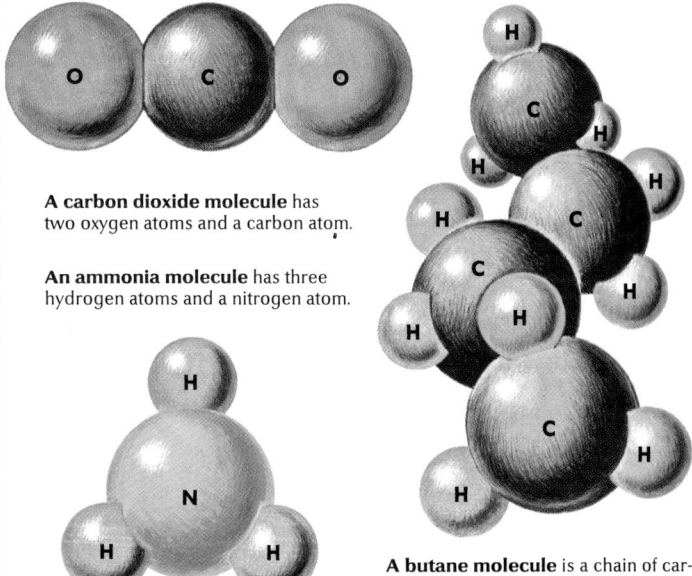

A carbon dioxide molecule has two oxygen atoms and a carbon atom.

An ammonia molecule has three hydrogen atoms and a nitrogen atom.

A butane molecule is a chain of carbon atoms with hydrogen atoms.

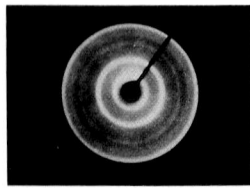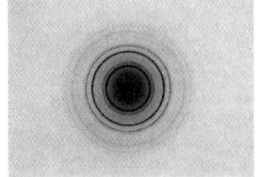

E. R. Degginger

Diffraction patterns are produced on photographic film when X rays or electrons pass through molecules of various substances. X rays produced the pattern at the left, and electrons made the one at the right.

colors makes up the molecule's *spectrum.* By studying the spectrum of a substance, scientists can find the sizes and shapes of its molecules, the strength of the forces that hold the atoms together in the molecules, and the way the electrons move about in the molecules.

Melvyn C. Usselman

Related articles in *World Book* include:

Atom	Ion	Liquid
Chemistry	Light (Other sources	Matter
Gas (matter)	of light)	Solid

Molière, *mohl YAIR* (1622-1673), was the stage name of Jean Baptiste Poquelin, the greatest French writer of comedy. Molière's plays emphasize one broad principle: the comic contrast between how people see themselves and how others see them.

Molière experimented with many drama forms. During his short career, he wrote farce, high comedy, satire, and comedy-ballets. He wrote equally well in verse and prose. Molière was also a fine actor and director.

Molière was born in Paris, the son of a prosperous upholsterer. He earned a law degree, but he never practiced law. In 1643, he and some friends founded the Illustre-Théâtre. From 1645 to 1647, the troupe toured France. In 1658, a performance attracted the attention of Louis XIV. The king gave Molière a permanent theater and asked him to write court entertainments.

Molière had no strong philosophy, but he had a knack for choosing controversial subjects that would attract public interest. His plays generally favor youth, love, and nature against age, selfishness, and efforts to imitate nobility. In 1662, *The School for Wives,* his first masterpiece in verse, satirized the narrow education given to girls of the middle class as well as an old man's claims to the love of his young female ward. As a result, he was attacked by extremist religious groups in France. *Tartuffe,* or *The Imposter* (1664), was a satire on religious hypocrisy. It aroused such great church opposition that the play could not be performed for several years. Opposition from the church also forced *Don Juan,* or *The Stone Feast* (1665), to close after a short run. Molière then satirized universal human failings in *The Misanthrope* (1666), *The Miser* (1668), *The Learned Ladies* (1672), and other plays.

Molière in the Role of Caesar. Portrait by Nicolas Mignard, Comédie Française, Paris (National Photographic Service, Versailles)

Molière

Late in his career, Molière wrote a series of comedy-ballets in which the dramatic script was accompanied by interludes of song and dance, somewhat like today's musical comedies. These works include *George Dandin* (1668), *The Would-Be Gentleman* (1670), and *The Imaginary Invalid* (1673). Carol L. Sherman

See also **French literature** (Classical drama); **Drama** (French neoclassical drama).

Additional resources

Fernandez, Ramon. *Molière: The Man Seen Through the Plays.* Octagon, 1980. Reprint of the 1958 English edition. First published in France in 1929.

Palmer, John L. *Molière.* Harcourt, 1930. A standard biography.

Molina, Tirso de. See Tirso de Molina.

Mollusk, *MAHL uhsk,* is a soft-bodied animal that has no bones. Snails, slugs, clams, mussels, oysters, squids, and octopuses are mollusks. Most mollusks have a hard shell that protects their soft bodies. Some, such as cuttlefish and squids, have no outside shell. A special shell grows inside their bodies. This shell is called a *cuttle-bone* in cuttlefish and a *pen* in squids. A few kinds of mollusks, including octopuses and certain slugs, have no shell at all. For additional information on mollusk shells and how they are formed, see **Shell.**

All mollusks have a skinlike organ called the *mantle.* In mollusks with outside shells, the mantle makes the shell. The edges of the mantle release liquid shell materials and add them to the shell as the mollusk grows. In mollusks with no outside shell, the mantle forms a tough cover around the body organs.

Mollusks live in most parts of the world. Some kinds of mollusks live in the deepest parts of oceans. Others are found on the wooded slopes of high mountains. Still others live in hot, dry deserts. Wherever mollusks live, they must keep their bodies moist to stay alive. Most land mollusks live in damp places such as under leaves or in soil.

The importance of mollusks

Mollusks are used mainly for food. People in many parts of the world eat mollusks every day. Most Americans do not eat them nearly so often. The most popular kinds used as food in the United States are clams, oysters, and scallops. Mollusk shells are made into many useful products, including pearl buttons, jewelry, and various souvenir items. Perhaps the best-known mollusk products are the pearls made by pearl oysters.

Some mollusks are harmful to people. For example, certain small, freshwater snails of the tropics carry worms that cause an often fatal disease called *schistosomiasis.* Shipworm clams drill into rope, wooden boats, and wharves and cause millions of dollars worth of damage a year.

Kinds of mollusks

Mollusks make up the largest group of water animals. There are about 50,000 known kinds of living mollusks, and scientists find about 1,000 new species every year. The fossils of about 100,000 other species of mollusks have also been found.

The mollusks make up a *phylum* (major division) of the animal kingdom. The scientific name of the phylum is *Mollusca,* a Latin word meaning *soft-bodied.* To learn

Giant snail

Mark Boulton, Bruce Coleman Ltd.

Flame scallop

Alex Kerstitch

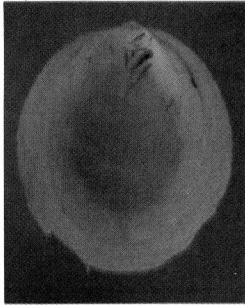

Robert Robertson

Monoplacophoran

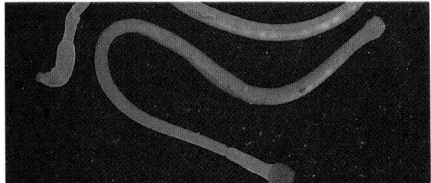

Robert Robertson

Aplacophoran

Tooth shell

Frieder Sauer, Bruce Coleman Ltd.

Lined chiton

Jeff Foott, Bruce Coleman Ltd.

Octopus

Jane Burton, Bruce Coleman Ltd.

where the phylum fits into the animal kingdom, see **Animal** (table: *A classification of the animal kingdom*).

There are seven *classes* (large groups) of mollusks. They are (1) univalves or Gastropoda, (2) bivalves or Bivalvia or Pelecypoda, (3) octopuses and squids or Cephalopoda, (4) tooth shells or Scaphopoda, (5) chitons or Polyplacophora, (6) Monoplacophora, and (7) Aplacophora.

Univalves or gastropods (Gastropoda) are the largest class of mollusks. They include limpets, slugs, snails, and whelks. Most kinds of univalves have a single, coiled shell. The name *univalve* comes from Latin words meaning *one shell.* But some kinds of univalves, including garden slugs and the sea slugs called *nudibranchs,* have no shells after the larval stage.

The name *Gastropoda* comes from Greek words meaning *belly* and *foot.* Gastropods seem to crawl on their bellies, but actually they use a large, muscular foot. The foot spreads beneath the body, and its muscles move in a rippling motion that makes the animal move forward. Most sea snails and some land snails have a lidlike part called an *operculum* on the back of the foot. When danger threatens, the snail draws back into its shell and the operculum closes the shell opening.

Certain kinds of univalves have two pairs of *tentacles* (feelers) on their heads. One pair helps the animals feel their way about. Some species have an eye on each of

the other two tentacles. Others have no eyes at all. A univalve also has a ribbon of teeth. This ribbon, called a *radula,* works like a rough file and tears apart the animal's food. Most univalves that eat plants have thousands of weak teeth. A few kinds eat other mollusks, and have several dozen strong teeth.

Bivalves (Bivalvia or Pelecypoda) form the second largest class of mollusks. They include clams, oysters, mussels, scallops, and shipworms. All bivalves have two shells held together by hinges that look like small teeth. The shells of bivalves are usually open. When the animals are frightened, strong muscles pull the shells shut and hold them closed until danger has passed.

Bivalves have a strong, muscular foot. Many kinds of these animals move about by pushing the foot out and hooking it in the mud or sand. Then they pull themselves up with the foot. Some bivalves, such as the geoduck and razor clam, use the foot to dig holes. They push the foot downward into mud or sand. First the foot swells to enlarge the hole, and then it contracts and pulls the shell into the burrow. The Pholas clam can dig holes even in hard clay or soft rock.

Bivalves have no head or teeth. They get oxygen and food through a muscular *siphon* (tube). The siphon can be stretched to reach food and water if the animal is buried in mud or sand. Bivalves feed on plant cells material, which is filtered from the water by the gills.

Octopuses and squids (Cephalopoda) are the most active mollusks. The argonaut, cuttlefish, and nautilus also belong to this group. All the species in the group live in the ocean.

The word *Cephalopoda* comes from Greek words meaning *head* and *foot*. A cephalopod seems to be made up of a large head and long arms that look like feet. Octopuses and squids have dome-shaped "heads" surrounded by arms. Octopuses have eight arms, and squids have eight arms and two tentacles. The arms grow around hard, strong, beaklike jaws on the underside of the head. These jaws tear the animal's prey, and are far more dangerous than the arms. Octopuses use their arms and squids use their tentacles and arms to capture prey and pull it through their jaws. Octopuses and squids eat fish, other mollusks, and shellfish.

Tooth shells (Scaphopoda) have slender, curving shells that resemble tusks. These mollusks are often called *tusk shells.* The word *Scaphopoda* comes from Greek words that mean *boat* and *foot.* A tooth shell has a pointed foot that looks somewhat like a small boat. All tooth shells live in the ocean, where they burrow in the mud or sand. The top of the shell sticks up into the water. Tooth shells have no head or eyes. They feed on one-celled organisms that are swept into the mouth by tentacles.

Chitons (Polyplacophora) have flat, oval bodies covered by eight shell plates. The plates are held together by a tough girdle. The name *Polyplacophora* comes from Greek words that mean *many, shell,* and *bearer.* This name refers to the eight overlapping pieces of a chiton's shell. Chitons have a large, flat foot. They can use the foot to move about, but they usually cling firmly to rocks. When they are forced to let go of the rocks, they roll up into a ball. Chitons have a small head and mouth, but they have no eyes or tentacles. Their long radula has many teeth, which some chitons use to scrape seaweed from rocks for food.

Monoplacophora live in the deep parts of the ocean, and most are found only as fossils. The name *Monoplacophora* comes from Greek words meaning *single, shell,* and *bearer.* Monoplacophorans have one shell that is almost flat, like a limpet shell. They are unusual because they have several pairs of gills, six or more pairs of kidneys, and many ladderlike nerve centers. Like other mollusks, they have a mantle. They also have a radula. Little is known about their habits.

Aplacophora are rarely seen, wormlike mollusks covered with small spines. The name *Aplacophora* comes from Greek words that mean *no shell.*

Robert Robertson

Related articles in *World Book* include:

Abalone	Cowrie	Mussel	Shell
Argonaut	Cuttlefish	Nautilus	Shipworm
Chiton	Geoduck	Octopus	Slug
Clam	Limpet	Oyster	Snail
Cockle	Mother-of-	Periwinkle	Squid
Conch	pearl	Scallop	Whelk

Molly is the name of a group of small, colorful fish popular in home aquariums. Mollies are *live-bearers—* that is, they give birth to live, fully formed young. Most other fishes reproduce by laying eggs. Mollies are closely related to the guppy, another type of live-bearer (see **Guppy**).

The sailfin molly has a large fin along its back and a large tail fin. It is a popular aquarium fish.

Mollies are native to freshwater streams of South America, Central America, and the Southern United States. They sometimes enter pools and lagoons that have seawater mixed with fresh water. Adult mollies range in size from 3 to 6 inches (8 to 16 centimeters). Most species are naturally bluish or silvery-olive with various spots and bars. Male mollies are usually more colorful than females and have larger fins.

Favorite aquarium species include the *Amazon molly,* the *sailfin molly,* and the *shortfin molly.* Selective breeding has resulted in numerous colorful varieties of mollies that would not normally occur in nature.

Scientific classification. Mollies belong to the family of live-bearing fishes, Poeciliidae. They are in the genus *Poecilia.*

John E. McCosker

Molly Maguires was the popular name for members of a secret society of immigrant Irish coal miners in the United States. Their name was based on a legendary Irish heroine who supposedly led a revolt of peasant farmers against rent collectors in the 1600's. The members of the secret society occasionally dressed in women's clothing to surprise their enemies. The society took part in violent labor conflicts between mine owners and workers in Pennsylvania during the 1870's. The group was accused of using murder and terror against its enemies. Ten members convicted of murder were executed on June 21, 1877.   David Brody

Molnár, *MOHL nahr,* **Ferenc,** *FEH rehnts* (1878-1952), became the most widely known Hungarian dramatist of his time. He specialized in writing light romantic comedies with witty dialogue. In *The Guardsman* (1910), a jealous husband pretends to be his own rival. *The Glass Slipper* (1924) presents a comic version of the Cinderella story. *Liliom* (1909), a more serious play about an amusement park barker, later served as the basis for the Rodgers and Hammerstein musical *Carousel.* Molnár's other popular comedies include *The Devil* (1907), *The Swan* (1920), and *The Play's the Thing* (1926).

Molnár was born in Budapest. He studied law and worked as a journalist before turning to drama. In addition to his plays, he wrote several novels and many humorous character sketches and essays. In 1940, Molnár moved to the United States and later became an American citizen.   Gerald M. Berkowitz

Molokai. See Hawaii (The islands).

Molotov, *MAHL uh tawf,* **Vyacheslav Mikhailovich,** *vyah cheh SLAHF mih KHY lah vihch* (1890-1986), became widely known during two terms as foreign minister of the Soviet Union. He was demoted in 1957 for his opposition to Nikita S. Khrushchev, first secretary of the Soviet Communist Party. He was expelled from the Communist Party's Presidium and sent into virtual exile as ambassador to Outer Mongolia. In 1960, he became the Soviet delegate to the International Atomic Energy Agency. The Soviet Communist Party attacked him in 1961 and he returned to Moscow. In 1962, Molotov was expelled from the party, and the Supreme Soviet (legislature) ordered his name removed from all Soviet towns, buildings, and objects that had been named after him. He was reinstated as a party member in 1984.

From 1939 to 1949 and from 1953 to 1956, Molotov served as commissar (later called minister) of foreign affairs. He helped create the Soviet Union's policy of hostility to the West, particularly to the United States. He attacked the North Atlantic Treaty Organization (NATO) as an agency that would lead to another war. He proposed a collective security treaty for European countries that would exclude the United States.

Molotov joined the Bolshevik Party at the age of 16 (see **Bolsheviks**). Beginning in 1906, he engaged in various revolutionary activities. He was arrested and exiled twice, but returned to help plan the Bolshevik revolution. After the Bolshevik (now Communist) Party seized power in Russia in 1917, he received several important political promotions. He served as premier of the Soviet Union from 1930 to 1941.

Molotov was born in the Kirov region of European Russia. His family name was Skriabin, but he changed it to Molotov, which derives from *molot,* the Russian word for *hammer.*   Melvin Croan

Molting is the process by which an animal sheds worn hair, skin, scales, feathers, or fur and grows a new body covering. Molting often occurs at a definite time each year known as the animal's *molting season.*

The process of molting varies with different animals. Some animals have a hard outer covering, called an *exoskeleton,* that is too firm to expand as the animal grows. These animals, including crabs, lobsters, and insects,

E. R. Degginger

A molting snake rubs its nose against a rough surface, such as a rock or tree trunk, until its skin breaks away. Then it slides out of the old skin, leaving it turned inside out. The process takes only a few minutes. This snake is an albino corn snake.

must periodically shed their outer shell and grow a new one. The old exoskeleton becomes detached by fluid that appears beneath it. A new, soft exoskeleton grows in folds beneath the old, detached covering. The animal presses against the old exoskeleton, causing it to split, and wriggles out. The new exoskeleton then unfolds and hardens. Caterpillars of several kinds of butterflies shed their skin as many as five times as they grow. Adult insects do not molt. Lobsters, crabs, and similar animals molt irregularly throughout life.

Many reptiles also molt throughout life. Snakes and lizards shed and replace their entire skin. Alligators and crocodiles shed and replace each of their scales individually. This pattern of molting is similar to that of birds.

Birds shed their feathers at least once a year and grow a new set. Some songbirds molt three times a year, but not all feathers are shed each time. A complete molt typically takes four to six weeks and occurs in late summer. Worn feathers are pushed out by new ones in a regular pattern. In most birds, a feather used for flying is shed only after the one next to it is partly regrown. Thus, the bird maintains its ability to fly. Ducks, geese, and swans shed all their flight feathers at once and are flightless during their molting season. Large birds may require more than a year to molt completely, or they may molt almost continuously. In many birds, molting also plays an important part in courtship. Old, dull feathers are replaced by brightly colored ones that help attract a mate.

Many mammals shed their hair each spring. Some animals replace body parts during their molting season. For example, deer replace their antlers. The lemming, an animal similar to a guinea pig, and the ptarmigan, a grouselike bird, replace their claws.   Edward H. Burtt, Jr.

Moltke, *MAWLT kuh,* **Helmuth Karl von** (1800-1891), was a Prussian military genius. He ranked next to Prince Otto von Bismarck as a builder of the German Empire.

Moltke was appointed to the Prussian general staff in 1832. He became chief of staff in 1858. As chief of staff, Moltke prepared the military plans for the wars with Denmark in 1864, with Austria in 1866, and with France in 1870. His campaigns always succeeded. Moltke's greatest triumph was the Prussian victory over France. His armies won decisively at Sedan on Sept. 2, 1870. Metz fell in October, and the Prussian armies entered Paris in triumph (see **Franco-Prussian War**).

Moltke was born in the duchy of Mecklenburg-Schwerin and grew up in the city of Lübeck. He graduated from the Royal Military Academy in Copenhagen. His nephew Helmuth von Moltke served as commander of the German Army in France at the beginning of World War I.   Charles W. Ingrao

Moluccas. See **Indonesia** (The Moluccas); **Netherlands** (Recent developments).

Molybdenum, *muh LIHB duh nuhm,* is a hard, silvery-white metallic element. Its high melting point, which is 2617° C, makes it one of the strongest and most widely used *refractory* (heat-resistant) metals. When *alloyed* (mixed) with steel, molybdenum improves that metal's toughness and strength, especially at high temperatures. It also increases the heat and chemical resistance of certain nickel-based metals when alloyed with them.

Molybdenum is used in making aircraft and missile

parts. It is also an important trace element in plant nutrition. Molybdenum compounds have many industrial uses, particularly as catalysts in the refining of petroleum. In addition, molybdenum sulfide is used as a high temperature lubricant under conditions where most oils decompose. Molybdenum oxide is used in the manufacture of stainless steel and high-speed tools.

Molybdenum is found in molybdenite and a number of other minerals. In the United States, concentrated deposits of molybdenite occur in Colorado. Canada and Chile also produce molybdenite. Carl Wilhelm Scheele, a Swedish chemist, discovered molybdenum in 1778. The element has the chemical symbol Mo. Its atomic number is 42, and its atomic weight is 95.94. Molybdenum boils at 4612 °C.   R. Craig Taylor

Mombasa, *mahm BAH suh* (pop. 442,369), is the second largest city of Kenya, after Nairobi. Mombasa is a busy seaport on the east coast of Africa (see **Kenya** [map]). It handles most of the international shipping of Kenya; and of Uganda, Rwanda, Burundi, and eastern Zaire, which lie inland. The city has an oil refinery, an international airport, and a modern section with large government buildings and many resort hotels.

Persian and Arab traders settled at what is now Mombasa as early as the 700's. The city became an important port in the 1200's, when ivory, gold, timber, and slaves were shipped from Africa to other lands. Mombasa was controlled by Portugal for most of the period from 1528 until 1698, and by Oman from 1698 until 1887. Great Britain controlled the city from 1887 until 1963, when Kenya became an independent nation.   Stephen K. Commins

Moment, in physics, is the product of a quantity multiplied by a particular distance from a *fulcrum,* or axis. *Moment of force,* also called *torque,* is an example. A 100-pound person sitting 10 feet from the center of a seesaw produces a torque of 1,000 pound-feet.

Moment of inertia is the product of an object's mass multiplied by the square of its distance from an axis. It indicates how easy or hard it is to start or stop a spinning motion. The larger the moment of inertia is, the more torque is needed to change the rate of spin.

Lucille B. Garmon

See also **Lever** (Law of equilibrium).

Momentum, *moh MEHN tuhm,* in physics, was called the quantity of motion of a moving body by the English scientist Sir Issac Newton. When a baseball bat is swung, it has a momentum that depends on its mass and how fast it moves. The force exerted on the ball when the bat hits it depends on the rate of change in the bat's momentum.

To calculate the momentum of any moving object, multiply its *mass* (quantity of matter) by its *velocity* (speed and direction). An automobile that weighs 2,200 pounds has a mass of 1,000 kilograms. When driving north at 5 meters per second (about 11 miles per hour), it has a momentum of 5,000 (1,000 × 5) kilogram meters per second toward the north. An 11,000-pound truck has a mass of 5,000 kilograms. To have the same momentum as the car, the truck must drive north at only 1 meter per second (about 2 miles per hour).

An important law of physics states that momentum is conserved when two bodies act on each other without outside forces. If two objects collide, the total momentum of both objects after the collision equals their total

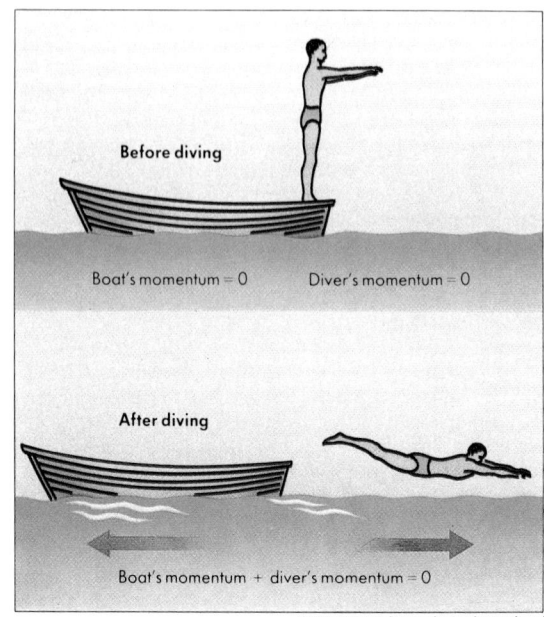

WORLD BOOK diagram by Sarah Woodward

Total momentum stays the same during a dive from a boat. The boat and diver move in opposite directions. The boat's momentum is opposite and equal to the diver's momentum.

momentum before collision. If the two objects have zero total initial momentum, their total final momentum also is zero. Thus, the momentum gained by one is equal and opposite to the momentum gained by the other. When a person dives off a still rowboat, the boat moves in a direction opposite to that of the dive. The boat's final momentum is equal and opposite to the person's final momentum, so that the total final momentum is zero, as it was before the dive.   Leon N. Cooper

See also **Force; Mass; Motion; Velocity.**

Mona Lisa. See **Da Vinci, Leonardo** (Return to Florence; picture).

Monaco, *MAHN uh koh,* is one of the smallest countries in the world. It has an area of only about $\frac{1}{2}$ square mile (1.5 square kilometers). Monaco lies on the French Riviera, which borders the Mediterranean Sea. France borders it on the other three sides.

Monaco is a popular tourist resort, with many luxury hotels, clubs, flower gardens, and places of entertainment. One of its chief attractions is the famous Monte Carlo gambling casino. Monaco is also known for such automobile sports events as the Monte Carlo Rally and the Monaco Grand Prix.

The towns of Monaco and Monte Carlo sit on cliffs overlooking the Mediterranean. Monaco is the capital. Prince Rainier III rules from a castle, part of which was built in the 1200's. Monaco's official language is French. The citizens of Monaco are called *Monégasques.*

Government. Monaco is a *principality* (ruled by a prince). The prince represents Monaco in international affairs, including the signing of treaties. Under the terms of a treaty that was signed with France in 1918, if the royal family of Monaco produces no male heirs, the principality will come under French rule.

A minister of state, under the authority of the prince,

Monaco

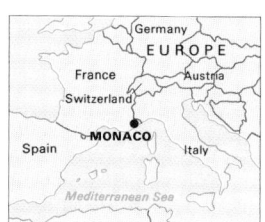

☐	Urban area
▨	Park
▬	International boundary
—	Road
—	Railroad
+	Elevation above sea level

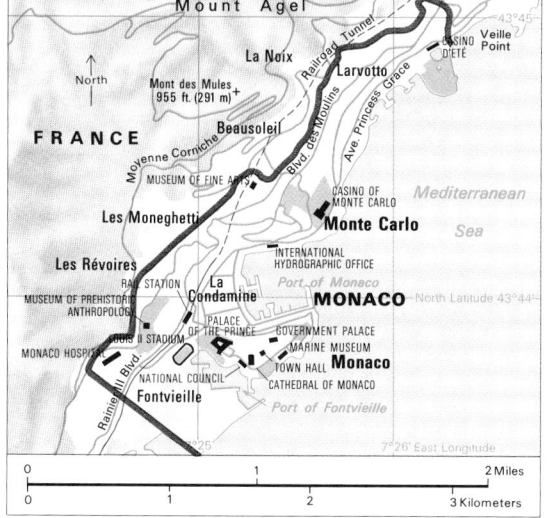

WORLD BOOK maps

heads the government. The minister is a French civil servant chosen by the prince. Three councilors who are responsible for finance, police and internal affairs, and public works assist the minister of state. The 18-member National Council shares the legislative powers with the prince. Citizens of Monaco elect National Council members to five-year terms. The Council must approve changes in Monaco's Constitution.

People. Only about a seventh of Monaco's people are Monégasque. More than half its residents are French, and most of the others are Americans, Belgians, British, and Italians. Most people in Monaco speak French. Most Monégasque citizens converse in a dialect called Monégasque, which is based on French and Italian.

Many wealthy people from other countries make Monaco their home because the principality has no income tax. But since 1963, most French people living in Monaco have had to pay income tax at French rates.

The state religion is Roman Catholicism. There is

Facts in brief

Capital: Monaco.
Official language: French.
Area: 0.58 sq. mi. (1.49 km²).
Population: *Estimated 1994 population*—29,000; density, 50,000 persons per sq. mi. (19,463 persons per km²); distribution, 100 per cent urban. *1982 census*—27,063. *Estimated 1999 population*—30,000.
Chief products: Beer, candy, chemicals, dairy products.
Flag: The flag has two horizontal stripes, red and white. See **Flag** (picture: Flags of Europe).
Money: *Basic unit*—French franc. See **Money** (table).

complete freedom of worship. Monaco's primary schools are run by the church. The principality also has a high school and a music academy.

The Monaco government awards the Rainier III prize for literature each year to a writer in the French language. Monaco's libraries include the Princess Caroline Library, which specializes in children's literature. Monaco also has a marine museum, a prehistoric times museum, a zoo, and botanical gardens. The marine museum has several rare exhibits, one of the world's leading aquariums, and a laboratory for research.

The Grand Theater of Monte Carlo presents performances by some of the world's greatest singers and ballet dancers. Leading musical conductors and soloists perform with Monaco's national orchestra.

Land. Monaco lies at the foot of Mt. Agel (3,600 feet, or 1,100 meters). In places, Monaco stretches only 200 yards (180 meters) inland from the Mediterranean.

Monaco has four distinct parts—three towns and a small industrial area. Monaco, the old town and former fortress, stands on a rocky point 200 feet (61 meters) high. It is dominated by the royal palace. Monte Carlo has the famous gambling casino, the opera house, hotels, shops, beaches, and swimming pools. La Condamine, a port area, lies between the towns of Monaco and Monte Carlo. The industrial zone, called Fontvieille, lies west of the town of Monaco.

The country has a mild winter climate, with an average January temperature of 50 °F (10 °C). Summer temperatures rarely exceed 90 °F (32 °C). On the average, rain falls only 62 days a year.

Economy. Commerce and manufacturing account for about two-thirds of Monaco's income. The country's chief products include cosmetics, glass, pharmaceuticals, precision instruments, and processed foods. Tourism contributes much to the economy. Each year, more than 600,000 tourists from all parts of the world visit the principality. A company called the Société des Bains de Mer, which is partly owned by the government, operates the casino and most of the hotels, clubs, beaches, and other places of entertainment. Monaco's colorful postage stamps are popular with collectors. Postage

E. Nagele, FPG

Monte Carlo is a tourist resort in Monaco. The town lies on the French Riviera coast of the Mediterranean Sea.

stamps are an important source of income in Monaco.

Monaco is an important center for business. Many foreign companies have headquarters in Monaco because of the low taxation there.

The principality of Monaco has a local bus service. The main highway on the coast passes through Monaco, carrying motorists who are traveling between France and Italy. A railroad connecting France and Italy also runs through Monaco. The principality transmits its own radio and television programs. Its television transmitter is located on top of Mt. Agel, in French territory.

History. Monaco's museum contains much evidence, including remains and tools, of early peoples in the area. Phoenicians from the eastern Mediterranean probably settled in Monaco in about 700 B.C. In Greek and Roman times, Monaco was an important trading center, and its harbor sheltered ships from many lands.

The Genoese, from northern Italy, gained control of Monaco in the A.D. 1100's. They built the first fort there in 1215. In 1308, the Genoese granted governing rights over Monaco to the Grimaldi family of Genoa. The Grimaldi family first allied itself with France. During the early 1500's to mid-1600's, the family sought protection from Spain. Palace revolts and violence marked this period in Monaco's history. Prince Jean II was murdered by his brother Lucien in 1505. Lucien was later murdered by a relative. Prince Honoré I was drowned by some of his subjects during a revolt in 1604.

France seized control of Monaco in 1793, during the French Revolution. But the Congress of Vienna restored control to the Grimaldi family under the protection of Sardinia in 1814. France seized some of Monaco's territory in 1848, but the territory was returned in 1861.

The princes of Monaco ruled as absolute monarchs until 1911, when Prince Albert I approved a new constitution. Later rulers included Prince Albert, known as the *Scientist Prince.* He did important marine research and founded the famous Oceanographic Museum. Prince Louis II ruled from 1922 until 1949, except for the German occupation during World War II. His grandson Prince Rainier III succeeded him. In 1956, Rainier married American motion-picture star Grace Kelly, who took the title of Princess Grace. They had two daughters and a son. The son, Prince Albert, is heir apparent.

In 1959, Prince Rainier dissolved the National Council and appointed a National Assembly. In 1962, under pressure from France, he restored the National Council and granted Monaco a new constitution. The constitution provided votes for women and abolished the death penalty. In 1963, under pressure from France, Monaco taxed business profits for the first time.

Since the early 1980's, Monaco has reclaimed land from the sea for developing new beaches. In addition, a new sports complex, two marinas, and several condominium buildings have been built. In 1982, Princess Grace died following an automobile accident near Monaco.   Janet L. Polasky

See also **Rainier III; Kelly, Grace; Monte Carlo**.

Monarch butterfly. See Butterfly (picture).

Monarchy is a form of government in which one person who inherits, or is elected to, a throne is head of state for life. These persons, or monarchs, have different titles, including *king, emperor,* or *sultan,* in various governments. The old idea of monarchy maintained that the power of the monarch was absolute. It sometimes held that the monarch was responsible only to God. This doctrine became known as "the divine right of kings" (see **Divine right of kings**).

Revolutions destroyed much of the power of monarchs. In the 1640's, the English Parliament raised an army, defeated King Charles I, and condemned him to death. In 1688, the English people feared James II would restore the Roman Catholic faith, and forced him to give up his throne. The French Revolution of 1789 limited the power of Louis XVI, and in 1793 the revolutionists put him to death. As a result, *limited,* or *constitutional,* monarchy developed, in which the monarch's duties are largely ceremonial and symbolic. In modern constitutional monarchies, the executive power is usually exercised by a prime minister and Cabinet. Great Britain, Norway, Denmark, Sweden, and Japan are modern constitutional monarchies.   Alexander J. Groth

Related articles in *World Book* include:

Coronation	Emperor	King	Sultan
Czar	Kaiser	Queen	

Monastery. See Monasticism; Monk; Cloister.

Monasticism, *muh NAS tuh sihz uhm,* is a special form of religious community life. People who practice monasticism separate themselves from ordinary ways of living so they can follow the teachings of their religion as completely as possible. Men who adopt a monastic life are called monks and live in a monastery. Monastic women are called nuns and live in a convent.

Monasticism has an important part in several major religions. The word comes from the Greek word *monos,* meaning *alone.* The first Christian monastics were called *ones who live alone* because they lived by themselves in the desert. Later, groups of them gathered together and formed communities that followed a life of prayer and self-discipline. Today, the members of monastic communities also follow this kind of life.

Christian monasticism began in Egypt about A.D. 271, when Saint Anthony of Thebes went alone into the desert to lead a holy life. Others soon followed. In the

John Topham, The Image Works

Benedictine monks in a French abbey walk under a covered passage called a cloister. Such monks live away from the outside world, devoting themselves to prayer, study, and work.

early 300's, Saint Pachomius, another desert holy man, gathered some of these hermits into monasteries.

Monasticism became especially influential in Europe during the early Middle Ages. At that time, Europe had thousands of monasteries that were great centers of learning. After about 1200, however, Christian monasticism began to be replaced by orders of wandering friars. It has never regained its former influence. See **Middle Ages** (The Christian church).

Life in a Christian monastic community involves work, prayer, and meditation. A monastery or convent may be in a rural area or in a city. It may consist of a small, walled-in group of huts or a huge complex that houses hundreds of people. But it is designed to isolate its people from the world outside. Christian monasticism also includes an extremely important element called the *rule,* a set of guidelines by which members of a monastic group live. Its essential purpose is to set specific times each day for study, work, prayer, and other activities. Eastern Orthodox monastic groups base their rule on the teachings of Saint Basil of Caesarea, who lived in the 300's. The Rule of Saint Benedict of Nursia, written in the 500's, is the model for most Roman Catholic groups.

In addition to following a rule, Christian monks and nuns take three vows—*poverty, chastity,* and *obedience.* The vow of poverty requires a person not to own any private possessions. The vow of chastity obligates a monk or nun to have no sexual relations. The vow of obedience requires a person to always follow the decisions of the leader of the monastic community.

There are several Christian monastic orders. Each of these groups of monasteries or convents follows the same rule and shares a common leadership. There are also many nonmonastic orders. The members of these groups dedicate their lives to preaching and service, rather than to prayer and meditation.

Non-Christian monasticism. A number of non-Christian religions also have monastic communities. For example, monasticism in Buddhism began in the 500's B.C., about 800 years before Christian monasticism. Buddha, the founder of the religion, taught his followers to give up their family, work, and material things. Early Buddhist monks and nuns spent most of their time as wandering *mendicants* (holy beggars). Today, few Buddhist nuns are left, and most Buddhist monks live in monasteries. Buddhist monks are the only preachers of their religion. A highly detailed rule called the *Vinaya* guides everything they do. See **Buddhism.**

The monks and nuns of Jainism, an ancient religion of India, still live much as the first Buddhist monastics did. They are wandering mendicants who lead extremely strict lives and strive never to harm any living creature, not even an insect. See **Jainism.**

Hinduism has had religious hermits since ancient times. But they were never well organized until about A.D. 800, when a great teacher named Sankara founded an order with four monasteries. Since then, about 10 large orders and many small ones have developed.

The influence of monasticism today has declined almost everywhere. Perhaps the chief reason for this decline has been widespread *secularism* (doubt of the value of religion). Christian monastic groups have lost members who question the value of the traditional vows, especially the vow of chastity. In addition, Communist governments have persecuted Buddhist monastics in China, Tibet, and parts of Southeast Asia. Most Hindu monastic orders also have fewer members.

On the other hand, there has been renewed interest in monasticism among some religious groups. The Ramakrishna Mission, a modern Hindu order involved in social work, has attracted a large following in India and in other parts of the world. Tibetan Buddhist exiles have founded successful monasteries in the United States. The Lutheran and Dutch Reformed churches and several other Protestant groups have also started monastic communities. Nancy E. Auer Falk

Related articles in *World Book.* See **Religious life** and its list of *Related articles.* See also the following articles:

Cloister	Hermit	Roman Catholic
Convent	Library (Libraries of	Church (The rec-
Essenes	the Middle Ages)	ognition of
Fakir	Monk	Christianity)

Additional resources

Brooke, Christopher N. *Monasteries of the World: The Rise and Development of the Monastic Tradition.* Crescent Bks., 1982. First published in 1974 as *The Monastic World, 1000-1300.*
Levi, Peter. *The Frontiers of Paradise: A Study of Monks and Monasteries.* Weidenfeld & Nicolson, 1988.

Monazite, *MAHN uh zyt,* is a heavy, yellow-brown mineral. It is a compound of phosphates (phosphorus and oxygen) of the rare-earth metals and thorium. Its chemical formula is $(Th, Ce, La, Y)PO_4$. Monazite is one of the chief sources of thorium, a nuclear fuel used in some nuclear reactors. Monazite is also an important source for the rare-earth elements and compounds, used widely in glass and metal manufacturing.

Monazite occurs naturally in granite rocks and pegmatite veins. As these rocks weather and break up, the monazite settles in deposits in riverbeds and beach sand. Commercial supplies of monazite are taken from sand. The monazite is usually separated from other collected minerals by an electromagnetic process. The most important monazite deposits occur in India and Brazil. Other monazite deposits are found in the United States, Australia, Sri Lanka, Malaysia, Indonesia, Canada, and South Africa. Rodney C. Ewing

Monck, George. See Monk, George.

Monck, *muhngk,* **Viscount** (1819-1894), was the first governor general of the Dominion of Canada. The Dominion was formed by a union of British North American colonies in 1867. Monck served as governor general for about a year. He had been governor general of British North America from 1861 to 1867. During that period, Monck strongly supported the Canadian confederation movement, which led to formation of the Dominion. He asked Sir John A. Macdonald, a confederation leader, to be the Dominion's first prime minister.

Charles Stanley Monck was born in Tipperary, Ireland. He became the fourth Viscount Monck in 1849. Monck, a Liberal, was elected to the British House of Commons in 1852. He was a lord of the treasury from 1855 to 1858 in the government led by Viscount Palmerston. Monck was knighted in 1869. Jacques Monet

Moncton, *MUHNGK tuhn,* New Brunswick (pop. 57,010), is a major transportation and distributing center for the Maritime Provinces of Canada. The Maritime Provinces are New Brunswick, Nova Scotia, and Prince Edward Island. Moncton lies on the Petitcodiac River near the Bay of Fundy (see **New Brunswick** [political map]). Railroads and highways connect Moncton to Nova Scotia. A railway and ferry provide service to Prince Edward Island. Daily air flights link Moncton with other parts of Canada. The city has several industries. It is the home of the University of Moncton. For the monthly weather, see **New Brunswick** (Climate).

The famous *bore* (tidal wave) of the Petitcodiac River rushes past Moncton twice a day. It comes up from the Bay of Fundy. The wall of water measures about 24 inches (61 centimeters) high. See **Bay of Fundy**.

Germans from Pennsylvania first settled Moncton in 1763. The town, then known as *The Bend*, became a shipbuilding center. The name was changed to Moncton in 1885, and a city charter was granted in 1890. During World War II (1939-1945), the city's airport was used to train British and Canadian air forces. Moncton has a mayor-council form of government.   T. W. Acheson

Mondale, Walter Frederick (1928-   ), was Vice President of the United States from 1977 to 1981 under President Jimmy Carter. Before becoming Vice President, Mondale had been a U.S. senator from Minnesota. He was known as a liberal who supported government action in many fields. Mondale was the Democratic nominee for President in 1984. He lost to his Republican opponent, President Ronald Reagan.

Early life. Mondale was born in Ceylon, Minn. His father was a Methodist minister. Walter, the sixth of seven children, was nicknamed Fritz as a boy. He graduated from the University of Minnesota in 1951 and from the university's law school in 1956. He practiced law in Minneapolis until 1960. In 1955, Mondale married Joan Adams (1930-   ) of St. Paul, Minn. The Mondales had three children—Theodore (1957-   ), Eleanor Jane (1960-   ), and William (1962-   ).

Political career. Mondale began his political career in May 1960, when Governor Orville L. Freeman of Minnesota appointed him attorney general of the state. Mondale had managed Freeman's third successful campaign for the governorship. Mondale was elected to a full term as state attorney general in November 1960 and won reelection in 1962.

In 1964, Governor Karl F. Rolvaag appointed Mondale to the U.S. Senate to replace Hubert H. Humphrey, who had been elected Vice President of the U.S. Mondale won election to a full term in 1966 and was reelected in 1972. As a senator, Mondale became known for his liberal views. He voted for bills that favored civil rights, consumer protection, education reform, and campaign financing reform.

The 1976 Democratic National Convention nominated Mondale for Vice President. In the election, Carter and Mondale defeated their Republican opponents, President Gerald R. Ford and Senator Robert J. Dole of Kansas.

As Vice President, Mondale took on many assignments. His duties included visiting foreign nations and advising Carter.

Wide World

Walter F. Mondale

In the 1980 presidential election, Carter and Mondale again became the Democratic nominees. But they were defeated in their bid for a second term by their Republican opponents, Ronald Reagan and George Bush.

In 1984, the Democratic National Convention nominated Mondale for President and, at his request, Representative Geraldine A. Ferraro of New York for Vice President. Ferraro was the first woman ever chosen for the vice presidency by a major U.S. political party. In the election, Mondale and Ferraro were defeated by Reagan and Bush. In 1993, President Bill Clinton appointed Mondale U.S. ambassador to Japan.   Finlay Lewis

See also **Carter, Jimmy; Ferraro, Geraldine A.; Vice President of the United States** (Growth of the vice presidency).

Monday is the second day of the week. The word comes from the Anglo-Saxon *mōnandaeg,* which means the *moon's day.* In ancient times, each of the seven days of the week was dedicated to a god or goddess. Monday was sacred to the goddess of the moon.

Black Monday is the name given to Easter Monday, April 14, 1360. On this day, many of the troops of King Edward III of England, who were fighting the French, died on horseback outside Paris due to cold weather.

Blue Monday is a term used in the United States to indicate that it is a dismal day. It is the day the workweek begins.   Jack Santino

See also **Labor Day; Week.**

Mondrian, *MAWN dree AHN,* **Piet,** *peet* (1872-1944), was a Dutch painter known for his rigidly geometric style. He influenced modern architecture and commercial design as well as painting.

Mondrian used straight black lines in horizontal and vertical patterns on a white background. In many paintings, he used pure primary colors to fill in rectangles created by these lines. Mondrian's final paintings have brightly colored lines, rather than black ones. All his important works feature smooth surfaces with no sign of brushstrokes. His *Lozenge Composition in a Square* is reproduced in the **Painting** article.

Mondrian called his style *neoplasticism.* It is also called *De Stijl* (*The Style*), after a magazine published from 1917 to 1928 by Mondrian and the Dutch painter Theo Van Doesburg. Mondrian published many of his theories of art in this magazine. He regarded neoplasticism as an attempt to unify the arts and give people an orderly environment of beauty.

Mondrian was born in Amersfoort. During the early 1900's, he developed his geometric style through several series of increasingly abstract paintings of buildings and trees. Mondrian lived in Paris from 1919 to 1938. He settled in New York City in 1940.   Willard E. Misfeldt

Monel metal, *moh NEHL,* is an important alloy of nickel and copper. It contains about 67 per cent nickel and 30 per cent copper. The rest is made up of such elements as aluminum, iron, manganese, or titanium. Monel metal looks like nickel. It is about as hard as steel and can be forged and drawn into wire or other shapes. It is easier to prepare than nickel, for some ores already contain nickel and copper in suitable proportions. Thus, the alloy is sometimes cheaper than pure nickel.

Monel metal generally resists corrosion, showing hardly any damage from steam, seawater, hot gas, air, or acids. This property makes it useful in sheet-metal work,

Monet's *Water Lilies* was one of a series the artist painted near the end of his life, when he was almost blind. The emphasis on light and color gives the picture an almost abstract quality.

E. G. Buehrle Collection, Zurich, Switzerland

in chemical plants, and on ships. It is used for pump fittings, propellers, and condenser tubes; as a covering for sinks and soda fountains; and for containing and transporting acids. I. Melvin Bernstein

Moneran, *muh NIHR uhn,* also called *prokaryote* (pronounced *proh KAR ee oht*), is the name of a group of primitive one-celled organisms. Monerans make up the kingdom Monera. This kingdom consists of blue-green algae, also called *cyanobacteria,* and bacteria. Monerans live alone or in clusters called *colonies.* The individual organisms can be seen only with a microscope, but some colonies are visible with the unaided eye. Monera is one of the five kingdoms of living things recognized by most scientists. The other kingdoms are Animalia (animals), Fungi (fungi), Plantae (plants), and Protista (protists). Some scientists classify monerans as part of either the protist or plant kingdom.

Most biologists believe monerans are among the oldest types of organisms. Unlike all other living cells, monerans do not have a nucleus surrounded by a membrane. But they do have a nuclear area that contains DNA, the substance that controls heredity. Monerans also lack typical *organelles,* structures that perform functions in other cells (see **Cell** [Inside a living cell]).

Monerans live throughout the world, even where no other life can survive. For example, blue-green algae live in the water of hot springs as well as in frozen wastelands. Free-living bacteria dwell throughout the soil and water, and parasitic species live within nearly all multi-celled plants and animals. Irwin Richard Isquith

See also **Algae; Bacteria; Protist.**

Monet, *moh NAY* or *maw NEH,* **Claude** (1840-1926), a French painter, was a leader of the impressionist move-ment. He influenced art by trying to paint his personal, spontaneous response to outdoor scenes or events. Earlier artists had also painted outdoor studies rapidly—almost in shorthand. But they used such studies as "notes" for more elaborate pictures painted in the studio. Monet was the most important of the artists who first allowed their initial impressions of outdoor scenes to stand as complete works. He was especially concerned with the effect of outdoor light and atmosphere. This concern can be seen in his *Old St. Lazare Station, Paris* (1877), which is reproduced in the **Painting** article, and in his *La Grenouillère* (1869).

Monet was born in Paris. In 1874, he exhibited a landscape called *Impression: Sunrise* (1872) in a show. This patchily textured work caused one critic to skeptically call the entire show *impressionist,* which gave the movement its name.

Monet's fascination with light led him to paint several series of pictures showing the effect of sunlight on a subject. For example, he painted views of a cathedral or of a haystack under changing atmospheric conditions and at different hours of the day. In 1883, Monet settled in Giverny, near Vernon. There, at his country home, he painted garden scenes and a series of large pictures of water lilies. The swirling colors of the lilies influenced later abstract painters. Albert Boime

Additional resources

Gordon, Robert, and Forge, Andrew. *Monet.* Abrams, 1983.
House, John. *Monet: Nature into Art.* Yale, 1986.
Seitz, William. *Claude Monet.* Abrams, 1982.

Monetarism. See **Economics** (New solutions for old problems).

Naira (Nigeria)

5 pounds (Great Britain)

500 lire (Italy)

1000 yen (Japan)

5 shekels (Israel)

Franc (Switzerland)

5 francs (Belgium)

10 riyals (Saudi Arabia)

10 new pesos (Mexico)

Mark (Germany)

Dollar (Canada)

Franc (France)

Quarter (United States)

Bills and coins from around the world look different and have different names because each nation has its own system of money. The money from nearly all countries consists of paper or of copper, nickel, and other metals that have little value by themselves.

Money

Money is anything that is generally accepted by people in exchange for the things they sell or the work they do. Gold and silver were once the most common forms of money. But today, money consists mainly of paper bills, coins made of various metals, and checking account deposits.

Each country has its own basic unit of money. In the United States, for example, the basic unit is the U.S. dollar. Canada uses the Canadian dollar, France the franc, Great Britain the pound, Japan the yen, Mexico the new peso, and Russia the ruble. The money in use in a country is called its *currency*.

Money has three main uses. First, and most important, it is a *medium of exchange*—that is, something people will accept for their goods or services. Without a medium of exchange, people would have to trade their goods or services directly for other goods or services. If you wanted a bicycle, you would have to find a bicycle owner willing to trade. Suppose the bicycle owner wanted skis in exchange for the bike and you did not own skis. You would then have to find something a ski owner or ski maker wanted and trade it for skis to give the bicycle owner. Such trading, called *barter*, can take much time. A modern, industrialized country could not function without a medium of exchange.

A second use of money is that it serves as a *unit of account*. People state the price of goods and services in terms of money. In the United States, people use dollars to specify price, just as they use hours to express time and miles or kilometers to measure distance.

A third use of money is as a *store of wealth*. People can save money and then use it to make purchases in the future. Other stores of wealth include gold, jewels, paintings, real estate, and stocks and bonds.

The contributors of this article are R. G. Doty, Curator of the National Numismatic Collection of the Smithsonian Institution; and Stanley Fischer, Vice President of Development Economics and Chief Economist at the World Bank. The photographs for this article were taken for World Book *by James Simek, unless otherwise credited. Some rare examples of money were provided through the courtesy of Deak-Perera Chicago, Inc.; the Rare Coin Company of America, Inc.; and the Jeffery S. Zarit Company. Current U.S. paper money pictured in this article is shown in black and white because color reproduction is prohibited by law.*

Christiana Dittmann, Rainbow
Barter at a Peruvian marketplace

Cowrie shells (Africa, Asia, and Australia)

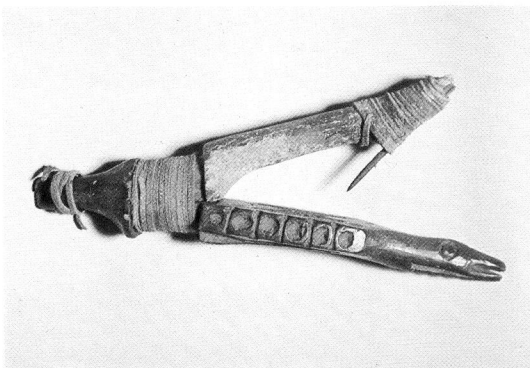

Fishhook (Northwest Coast of North America)

Trade beads (Africa)

The development of money began as people came to accept certain goods as mediums of exchange. Before then, all people, like those at the upper left, used *barter* (the exchange of goods for other goods) to get what they wanted. The other pictures show former mediums of exchange.

Any object or substance that serves as a medium of exchange, a unit of account, and a store of wealth is money. To be convenient, however, money should have several qualities. It should come in pieces of standard value so that it does not have to be weighed or measured every time it is used. It should be easy to carry so that people can carry enough money to buy what they need. Finally, it should divide into units so that people can make small purchases and receive change.

In the past, people used beads, cocoa beans, salt, shells, stones, tobacco, and other things as money. But above all, they used such metals as copper, gold, and silver. These metals made convenient, durable money.

Today, most money consists of paper. The paper itself is of little value, but it is accepted in exchange. People accept pieces of metal or paper in exchange for work or goods for only one reason: They know that others will take the same metal or paper in exchange for the things they want. The value of money therefore results from the fact that everyone will accept it as payment.

How money developed

Early people had no system of money as we know it. To get the things they wanted, people used the barter system of trading. Gradually, people learned that almost everyone would accept certain goods in exchange for any product or service. These goods included animal hides, cattle, cloth, salt, and articles of gold or silver. People began to use such merchandise as mediums of exchange, much as we use money.

Many people still use barter, especially in the developing countries of Africa, Asia, and Latin America. Millions of families in these countries live by farming and produce barely enough food to meet their own needs. As a result, they seldom acquire any money and must use barter to obtain the things they want. People in industrial countries also turn to barter if money becomes scarce or worthless. For example, barter became widespread in Germany after the country's defeat in World War II (1939-1945). German money became almost worthless, and people refused to take it. Instead, they bartered for most goods and services. They also used cigarettes, coffee, and sugar, which were in short supply, as mediums of exchange.

The first coins may have been made during the 600's B.C. in Lydia, a country in what is now western Turkey. The coins were bean-shaped lumps of *electrum,* a natural mixture of gold and silver. The coins had a stamped design to show that the king of Lydia guaranteed them to be of uniform value. The designs saved people the trouble of weighing each coin to determine its value. Traders accepted these coins instead of cattle, cloth, gold dust, or other goods as a medium of exchange. Other countries saw the advantages of the Lydian coins and began to make their own coins.

Many historians believe that coins were also invented independently in ancient China and in India. At first, the Chinese used knives, spades, and other metal tools as mediums of exchange. As early as 1100 B.C., they began to use miniature bronze tools instead of real ones. In time, the little tools developed into coins.

Coins today have many of the same features that they had in ancient times. For example, they have a government-approved design stamped on them, like the coins of ancient Lydia.

The development of paper money began in China, probably during the A.D. 600's. The Italian trader Marco

Polo traveled to China in the 1200's and was amazed to see the Chinese using paper money instead of coins. In a book about his travels, Polo wrote: "All his [the Chinese emperor's] subjects receive it [paper money] without hesitation because, wherever their business may call them, they can dispose of it again in the purchase of merchandise they may require."

In spite of Polo's description, Europeans could not understand how a piece of paper could be valuable. They did not adopt the use of paper money until the 1600's, when banks began to issue paper bills, called *bank notes,* to depositors and borrowers. The notes could be exchanged for gold or silver coins on deposit in the bank. Until the 1800's, most of the paper bills in circulation were notes issued by banks or private companies rather than by governments.

Some of the first paper currency in North America consisted of playing cards. This playing-card money was introduced in Canada in 1685. Canada was then a French

The first coins and bills

One of the first coins was this bean-shaped gold *stater, above.* It was made in Lydia during the 500's B.C.

Miniature tools, such as the spade and hoe at the right, were mediums of exchange in China as early as 1100 B.C.

An ancient Greek coin called a *tetra-drachm* was issued during the 400's B.C. The front of the coin, *above left,* had a portrait of the goddess Athena. An owl was stamped on the back, *above right.*

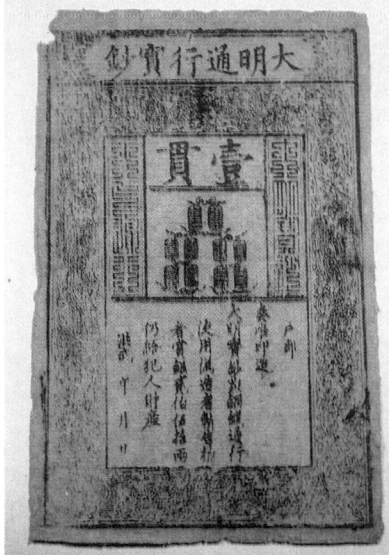

Paper money was first used in China. This bill was printed on bark paper in the 1300's.

Playing-card money was used in Canada when it was a French colony during the 1600's and 1700's. The colonial governor signed the back of each card.

Money in the American Colonies

Money was scarce in the American Colonies. Paper currency was seldom used, and the British did not allow the colonies to mint coins. As a result, the colonists used any foreign coins they could get. Indian wampum and other goods also circulated as money.

The oak-tree shilling was one of the first coins made in Massachusetts. The colony began to issue coins like the one above in 1660.

The escudo was used throughout the Americas. The 8-escudo coin above was minted in the reign of King Ferdinand VI of Spain.

Wampum, which consisted of beads made from shells, was used by the Indians to decorate garments and keep records. The colonists, who had few coins, used it as money. Most wampum was made into necklaces or belts.

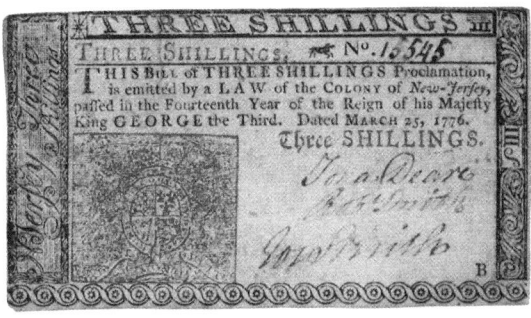

A 3-shilling note, left, was issued by the colony of New Jersey in 1776. A number of colonies issued their own paper currency.

colony. Money to pay the French soldiers stationed there had to be shipped from France. Shipments were often delayed, however, and cash grew so scarce that the colonial government began to issue playing cards as currency. Each card was marked a certain value and signed by the governor. Such playing-card money circulated for more than 70 years.

History of United States currency

In the American Colonies, money was scarce. England did not furnish coins and forbade the colonies to make them. The English hoped to force the colonies to trade almost entirely with England. One way of doing so was by limiting the money supply. Without money, the colonists could not do business with traders in other countries who demanded payment in cash. But the colonists could buy products from English traders with *bills of exchange.* They got these documents from other English traders in exchange for their own goods.

The American colonists used a variety of goods in place of money. These goods included beaver pelts, grain, musket balls, and nails. Some colonists, especially in the tobacco-growing colonies of Maryland and Virginia, circulated receipts for tobacco stored in warehouses. Indian wampum, which consisted of beads made from shells, was mainly used for keeping records. But Indians and colonists also accepted it as money.

The colonists also used any foreign coins they could get. English shillings, Spanish dollars, and French and Dutch coins all circulated in the colonies. Probably the most common coins were large silver Spanish dollars called *pieces of eight.* To make change, a person could chop the coin into eight pie-shaped pieces called *bits.* Two bits were worth a quarter of a dollar, four bits a half dollar, and so on. We still use the expression *two bits* to mean a quarter of a dollar.

In 1652, the Massachusetts Bay Colony became the first colony to make coins. It produced several kinds of silver coins, including a *pine-tree shilling* and an *oak-tree shilling,* which were stamped with a tree design. Massachusetts continued to issue coins for 30 years in defiance of an English law that said only the monarch could issue them. The colony dated all coins 1652, no matter when they were made, probably to get around the law. In 1652, there was no monarch in England. Thus, the colonists could claim the coins were minted at a time when royal authority did not exist.

Massachusetts also became the first colony to produce paper money. In 1690, the colonial government issued notes called *bills of credit.* The bills were receipts for loans made by citizens to the colonial government. Massachusetts used the bills to help finance the first French and Indian war, a war between English and French colonists for control of eastern North America.

The first United States currency. During the mid-1700's, Great Britain tried to tighten its control over the American Colonies with new taxes, stricter trade regulations, and other laws. Friction between the Americans and the British mounted. In 1775, the Revolutionary War broke out between the two sides. The next year, colonial leaders meeting as the Second Continental Congress declared independence and founded the United States of America. To help finance the war for independence, each state and the Continental Congress began to issue paper money.

As war expenses mounted, the states and Congress printed more and more money. Congress itself issued about $240 million in notes called *continentals*. So many continentals were printed that by 1780 they were almost worthless. Americans began to describe any useless thing as "not worth a continental." The experience with

continentals was so bad that the U.S. government did not again issue paper currency for widespread use until the 1860's.

The United States won the Revolutionary War in 1783, but the struggle left the American monetary system in disorder. Most of the currencies circulated by the states had little value. The U.S. Constitution, adopted in 1788, corrected this problem by giving Congress the sole power to coin money and regulate its value. In 1792, an act of Congress set up the first national money system in the United States. The act made the dollar the basic unit of money. It also put the nation on a system called the *bimetallic standard,* which meant that both gold and silver were legal money. The value of each metal in relation to the other was fixed by law. For years, 16 ounces (448 grams) of silver equaled 1 ounce (28 grams) of gold.

The act also established a national mint in Philadel-

Money in the new nation

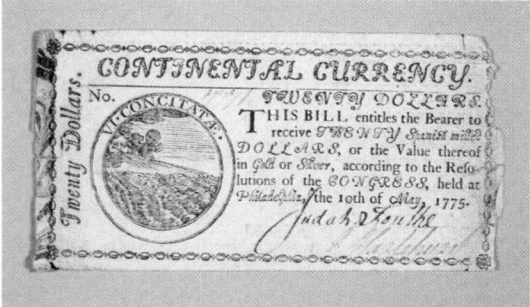

Continental currency was issued by the Continental Congress to help finance the Revolutionary War (1775-1783). So many of these notes were printed that they became almost worthless.

The écu, a French coin, was one of many foreign coins that circulated in the United States after the nation won independence. A 1793 law made these coins part of the U.S. monetary system.

The Spanish dollar, or piece of eight, was another foreign coin that circulated in the new nation. The coin shown at the far left and center was minted in Mexico in 1790. These dollars could be chopped into eight pieces, called *bits,* or into quarters, *near left,* called *two bits.*

A $10 gold piece called an *eagle* was issued by the U.S. Mint from 1795 to 1933. The eagle shown above dates from 1795. It has a liberty cap on the front and an eagle on the back.

Bank notes were the most common paper money in the United States until the 1860's. Banks vowed to exchange their notes for gold or silver. The State Bank of Illinois issued this note in 1840.

Later United States money
U.S. currency of the 1800's and early 1900's included silver coins, gold pieces, and various types of paper money. Many bills, including gold and silver certificates, could be exchanged for gold or silver coins on demand. The use of these two metals as money is called the *bimetallic standard*.

Silver dollar (1800)

U.S. Assay Office $50 gold piece (1851)

$20 gold double eagle (1865)

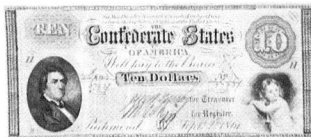

Confederate $10 bill (1861)

$5 legal tender note (about 1862)

$50 gold certificate (about 1882)

$20 national bank note (about 1882)

$50 silver certificate (about 1891)

Federal Reserve $10 bill (about 1914)

phia. The mint produced $10 gold coins called *eagles,* silver dollars, and other coins.

Americans continued to use many foreign coins in addition to their new currency. A law passed in 1793 made these coins part of the U.S. monetary system. The value of a foreign coin depended on how much gold or silver it had. In 1857, Congress passed a law removing foreign coins from circulation.

The rebirth of paper money. During the early 1800's, the only paper money in the United States consisted of hundreds of kinds of bank notes. Each bank promised to exchange its notes on demand for gold or silver coins. But numerous banks did not keep enough coins to redeem their notes. Many notes therefore were not worth their *face value*—that is, the value stated on them. As a result, people hesitated to accept bank notes.

The soundest bank notes of the early 1800's were issued by the two national banks chartered by the U.S. government. The First Bank of the United States was chartered by Congress from 1791 to 1811, and the Second Bank of the United States from 1816 to 1836. Both banks supported their notes with reserves of gold coins, and people considered the notes as good as gold.

Paper money as we know it today dates from the 1860's. To help pay the costs of the Civil War (1861-1865), the U.S. government issued about $430 million in paper money. The money could not be exchanged for gold or silver. The bills were called *legal tender notes* or *United States notes.* But most people called them *greenbacks* because the backs were printed in green. The government declared that greenbacks were *legal tender*—that is, money people must accept in payment of public and private debts. Nevertheless, the value of greenbacks depended on people's confidence in the government. That confidence rose and fell with the victories and defeats of the North in the Civil War. At one time, each greenback dollar was worth only 35 cents in gold coin. In the South, the Confederate States also issued paper money. It quickly became almost worthless.

In 1863 and 1864, Congress passed the National Bank Acts, which set up a system of privately owned banks chartered by the federal government. These national banks issued notes backed by U.S. government bonds. Congress also taxed state bank notes to discourage banks from issuing them, and people from using them. As a result, national bank notes became the country's chief currency.

Some greenbacks also continued to circulate. The government announced that, beginning in 1879, it would pay gold coins for greenbacks. The U.S. Depart-

Portrait on bill:

William McKinley

Grover Cleveland

James Madison

Salmon P. Chase

Illustrations by U.S. Bureau of Engraving and Printing by special permission of the Chief, U.S. Secret Service, Dept. of the Treasury. Further reproduction in whole or in part is strictly prohibited.

Large U.S. bills include Federal Reserve notes in denominations of $500, $1,000, $5,000, and $10,000, *above*. The government began withdrawing such bills from circulation in 1969.

ment of the Treasury gathered enough gold to redeem all the greenbacks likely to be brought in. But as soon as people knew they could exchange their greenbacks for gold, they were not anxious to do so. The fact that the Treasury paid out only gold coins meant the country was operating on an unofficial *gold standard*, rather than the bimetallic standard of the early 1800's. The gold standard is a system in which a nation defines its basic monetary unit as worth a certain quantity of gold and agrees to redeem its money in gold on demand.

The new national banks system eliminated the confusion that had existed when hundreds of different bank notes were in circulation. But the system did not provide for the federal government to increase the supply of money when needed. Shortages of money contributed to a series of economic slumps during the late 1800's. Many people called for the government to provide more money by coining unlimited amounts of silver. Such a policy was called *free silver*, and the argument over free silver became an important political issue.

The dispute reached a climax during the presidential election of 1896. The Republican candidate, William McKinley, favored the gold standard. McKinley defeated William Jennings Bryan, the Democratic candidate, who supported free silver (see **Free silver**). In 1900, Congress passed the Gold Standard Act, which officially put the nation on a gold standard. The United States went on and off the gold standard several times and finally abandoned it in 1971 (see **Gold standard**).

The United States suffered from repeated monetary difficulties until 1913, when Congress passed the Federal Reserve Act. This act created the Federal Reserve System, a central banking system that controls the nation's money supply.

United States currency today consists of coins and paper money. Under federal law, only the Department of the Treasury and the Federal Reserve System may issue U.S. currency. The Treasury issues all coins and a type of paper money known as *United States notes*. The Federal Reserve issues paper currency called *Federal*

United States coins

Cent
Abraham Lincoln/Lincoln Memorial

Nickel
Thomas Jefferson/Monticello

Dime
Franklin D. Roosevelt/
Torch and sprigs of laurel and oak

Quarter
George Washington/Eagle

Half dollar
John F. Kennedy/Presidential seal

Dollar
Susan B. Anthony/Eagle

Federal Reserve notes

Federal Reserve notes make up nearly all the paper money in the United States. The notes are issued by the 12 Federal Reserve Banks in the Federal Reserve System. The photographs on this page show the front and back of the seven bills now being issued: $1, $2, $5, $10, $20, $50, and $100.

George Washington

The Great Seal

Thomas Jefferson/Signing of the Declaration of Independence

Abraham Lincoln/Lincoln Memorial

Alexander Hamilton/U.S. Treasury

Andrew Jackson/The White House

Ulysses S. Grant/U.S. Capitol

Benjamin Franklin/Independence Hall

Illustrations by U.S. Bureau of Engraving and Printing by special permission of the Chief, U.S. Secret Service, Dept. of the Treasury. Further reproduction in whole or in part is strictly prohibited.

Reserve notes. All U.S. currency carries the nation's official motto, *In God We Trust.*

Coins come in six *denominations* (values): (1) penny, or 1 cent; (2) nickel, or 5 cents; (3) dime, or 10 cents; (4) quarter, or 25 cents; (5) half dollar, or 50 cents; and (6) $1. All coins are made of *alloys* (mixtures of metals). Pennies are copper-coated zinc. Nickels are a mixture of copper and nickel. Dimes, quarters, half dollars, and dollars are made of three layers of metal. The core is pure copper, and the outer layers are an alloy of copper and nickel.

Dimes, quarters, half dollars, and dollars have ridges called *reeding* or *milling* around the edge. Reeding helps blind people recognize certain denominations. For example, the reeding on a dime distinguishes it from a penny, which has a smooth edge.

Federal law requires that coins be dated with the year they were made. Coins also must bear the word *Liberty* and the Latin motto *E Pluribus Unum,* meaning *out of many, one.* This motto refers to the creation of the United States from the original Thirteen Colonies.

Mints in Denver and Philadelphia make most coins for general circulation. Mints in San Francisco and West

Chief features of a Federal Reserve note

Seal and letter of the Federal Reserve Bank that issued the note

Seal of the Department of the Treasury

Serial number

Serial number

Year when the note was designed

Number of the Federal Reserve Bank that issued the note

Printing plate identification numbers

Point, N.Y., make mostly commemorative coins to mark special occasions, and gold and silver bullion coins for investors. People buy bullion coins for the value of the metal. Coins made in Denver are marked with a small *D*. A *P* appears on most coins made in Philadelphia. Some coins made in San Francisco are marked with an *S* and some in West Point with a *W*.

Paper money. Federal Reserve notes make up nearly all the paper money issued in the United States today. About $195 billion of these notes were in circulation during the mid-1980's. They come in seven denominations: $1, $2, $5, $10, $20, $50, and $100. The notes are issued by the 12 Federal Reserve Banks in the Federal Reserve System. Each note has a letter, number, and seal that identify the bank which issued it. In addition, each note bears the words *Federal Reserve note* and a green Treasury seal. Until 1969, Federal Reserve Banks also issued notes in four large denominations: $500, $1,000, $5,000, and $10,000.

The only other paper money issued in the United States today consists of United States notes. The Treas-ury issues them in the $100 denomination only. These notes, which are the descendants of Civil War green-backs, carry the words *United States note* and a red Treasury seal. The Treasury keeps about $323 million in United States notes in circulation. All Federal Reserve and United States notes bear the printed signatures of the secretary of the treasury and the treasurer of the United States.

How money is manufactured

Two agencies of the U.S. Department of the Treasury manufacture currency. The United States Mint makes coins, and the Bureau of Engraving and Printing produces paper money.

Minting coins. The production of a new coin begins with artists' proposed designs for the coin. After government officials select a design, an artist constructs a large clay model of the coin. Most models are about eight times the size of the finished coin. The artist does not add details because the clay is too soft. Instead, the artist makes a mold of the clay model and then makes a

How coins are made   The United States Mint makes all U.S. coins. Bars of metal are rolled into strips about the thickness of the finished coins. A machine punches coin-sized disks, called *blanks,* out of the metal strips. The blanks are fed into a *coining press,* which stamps a design on both sides of each blank.

Designing a new coin starts with a number of sketches. After a design has been selected, an artist makes a large model of the coin.

Reducing the design to coin size is done by a *reducing lathe.* This machine traces the model coin and carves it in miniature on a steel *hub.*

Cutting the hub is done by a sharp tool on the other end of the reducing lathe. The hub is heat-treated to harden it and used to make a set of coin-stamping *dies.*

Screening the blanks removes imperfect ones. The perfect blanks are fed into the coining press, which uses the coin-stamping dies to produce the design.

Inspecting the newly minted coins helps find defective ones. Imperfect coins are melted down, and the metal is then used over again.

United States Mint, Philadelphia (WORLD BOOK photos)

Counting and bagging the finished coins is done by machines. The mint ships the coins to Federal Reserve Banks for distribution to the public.

plaster cast from the mold. The plaster is hard enough to enable the artist to carve fine details. A machine called a *reducing lathe* traces the finished plaster model and carves the design, reduced to coin size, onto a soft piece of steel called a *master hub.* The master hub is heat-treated to harden it. A special machine takes an impression of the hub to make a set of steel tools called *master dies.* These dies are used to stamp copies of the master hub called *working hubs.* The working hubs are employed, in turn, to make *working dies,* which stamp the coins. The master hub and master dies are stored and used to make more hubs and dies after the first ones wear out.

Bars of metal are heated and squeezed between heavy rollers into strips the thickness of a coin. A machine punches out smooth disks of metal, called *blanks,* from the strips. The blanks are the size of coins but have no design. The blanks are fed into an *upsetting machine,* which puts a raised rim around the edge of each one. Then, they are fed into a *coining press.* The press uses two working dies to impress the coin's design on both sides of each blank in one operation. The press also reeds the edge of all coins except pennies and nickels.

The mint ships the finished coins to Federal Reserve Banks for distribution to commercial banks. The Reserve Banks also remove worn and damaged coins from circulation. The mint melts these coins and uses the metal to make new coins.

Printing paper money. The production of a new bill begins when artists sketch their designs for it. The secretary of the treasury must approve the final design. Engravers cut the design into a steel plate. A machine called a *transfer press* squeezes the engraving against a soft steel roller, making a raised design on its surface. After the roller is heat-treated to harden it, another transfer press reproduces the design from the roller 32 times on a printing plate. Each plate prints a sheet of 32 bills. Separate plates print the two sides of the bills.

Many people believe the paper used for money is made by a secret process. But the government publishes a detailed description of the paper so private companies can compete for the contract to manufacture

How paper money is made   The Bureau of Engraving and Printing makes all U.S. paper currency. The bureau uses special paper and ink that have been manufactured to its specifications to produce long-lasting money. High-speed presses print sheets of 32 bills each. The sheets are then cut into separate bills.

Designing a new bill begins with a number of artist's drawings. The United States secretary of the treasury must approve the final design for a new bill.

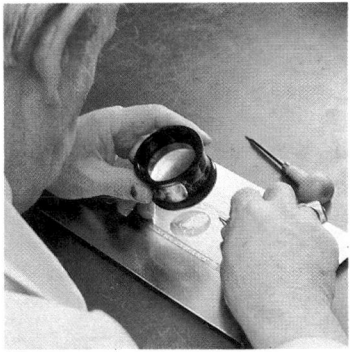
Making an engraving. An engraver cuts the design into a steel plate. A machine called a *transfer press* copies the engraving 32 times on a printing plate.

Inspecting the printing plate ensures that it has no flaws. During printing, paper will be forced into the engraved lines of the plate to pick up ink.

Printing is done by fast presses that print thousands of sheets an hour. Separate plates print the front and back of the bills. Serial numbers are added later.

Inspecting the new bills. The printed sheets are cut in half and examined. The inspectors mark any imperfect bills. Later, such bills are replaced.

Bureau of Engraving and Printing (WORLD BOOK photos)

Counting and stacking are done by a machine that puts the bills in order of their serial numbers and bands them in stacks of 100 for delivery to banks.

it. A U.S. law forbids unauthorized people to make any type of paper similar to that used for money.

The Bureau of Engraving and Printing uses high-speed presses to print sheets of paper currency. The design is printed first. Then the seals and serial numbers are added in a separate operation. The sheets are cut into stacks of bills. Imperfect bills are replaced with new ones called *star notes.* Each star note has the same serial number as the bill it replaces, but a star after the number shows that it is a replacement bill. The bills are shipped to Reserve Banks, which distribute them to commercial banks.

Most $1 bills wear out after about 18 months in circulation. Larger denominations last for years because they are handled less often. Banks collect worn-out bills and ship them to Federal Reserve Banks for replacement. The Reserve Banks destroy worn-out money in shredding machines.

Money and the economy

The quantity of money in a country affects the level of prices, the rate of economic growth, and therefore the amount of employment. If the money supply increases, people have extra money to buy things, and their demand for products grows. In response to the growing demand, manufacturers hire more workers to increase output. Earnings rise and spending increases, leading to further economic growth. However, if output cannot keep pace with demand, prices will increase. A continuing rise in prices is called *inflation.* Inflation may cause problems for people whose income does not keep pace with rising prices.

If the money supply shrinks, people have less to spend. Goods and services remain unsold. Prices fall. Manufacturers cut back on production, and many businesses lay off workers.

The main economic goals of nearly all nations are to promote economic growth and high employment with a minimum increase in prices. A government's chief methods of promoting these goals are by its *monetary policy* and its *fiscal policy.* Monetary policy refers to how a government manages the nation's money supply. Fiscal policy refers to a government's taxing and spending programs. To stimulate the economy, a government may increase the money supply, reduce taxes, or boost its own spending. The following discussion deals mainly with monetary policy. For information on fiscal policy, see **Economics** (Economic stability).

The value of money is defined by economists as the quantity of goods and services that the money will buy. If prices go up or down, the value of money also changes. A major aim of any government's monetary policy is to keep prices stable and thus preserve the value of money, also called its *purchasing power.* Today, people worry most about inflation, which lowers the value of money. If prices double, for example, a dollar buys only half as much as before, and so the value of money has dropped one-half. You sometimes read or hear such a statement as "A dollar today is worth 42 cents." That statement means a dollar today buys only as much as 42 cents bought at an earlier time. The earlier time chosen for comparison is called the *base period.* Another way of describing the same price rise is to say that prices have risen 138 per cent since the base pe-

riod. The *rate of inflation* is the rate at which prices in general are rising and the rate at which the value of money is falling.

Rapid, uncontrolled inflation can severely damage a country's economy. For example, prices in Germany increased 10 billion times from August 1922 to November 1923. Such severe inflation is called *hyperinflation.* The value of the German mark dropped so sharply and so rapidly that employers paid workers twice a day. Marks became so worthless that no one would take them, and people began to use barter instead of money. Employers paid workers by giving them some of the goods they produced. People spent so much time trading for the things they needed that production nearly came to a halt. The hyperinflation ended after the government introduced a new currency.

Inflation has many causes. But in most cases, prices cannot continue to rise without increases in the quantity of money. There never has been severe inflation without a large expansion in a nation's money supply.

Definitions of the money supply. The money supply includes more than just coins and paper money. In fact, checking account deposits are the most common form of money in the United States and many other countries. In the United States, about three-fourths of all payments are made by check. Checks are a safe and convenient medium of exchange. In addition, a canceled check provides written proof that payment was made.

Economists define the money supply in various ways, depending on which assets they include in their measurements. The definitions change as the banking system changes. Two major definitions of the U.S. money supply are called M-1 and M-2.

M-1 consists of checking account deposits, also called *demand deposits;* traveler's checks; and currency. In the late 1980's, M-1 totaled about $800 billion.

M-2 consists of M-1 plus money invested in savings accounts at commercial banks, at mutual savings banks, and at savings and loan associations. Such savings, called *time deposits,* are not immediately available to make purchases. The saver first has to withdraw the money, and the bank can require advance notice of withdrawal. However, most people can easily convert their savings to cash or checking deposits. M-2 amounted to approximately $3,200 billion in the late 1980's.

How the money supply is determined. The size of a nation's money supply is determined differently if the nation uses *commodity money* or *fiat money.* Commodity money typically consists of valuable metals, especially gold or silver. Fiat money is of little value itself. But it has value because people are willing to accept it. To increase the likelihood of people accepting its money, a government may make the currency legal tender. Then, the law requires people to accept the money at face value.

If a nation uses commodity money, the money supply is determined by the cost of producing the metal and the rate of production. During the late 1800's and early 1900's, the United States and many other countries were on the gold standard, which is a commodity money system. Each nation promised to redeem its currency for a specified amount of gold. For example, a U.S. dollar was officially valued at about 26 grains (1.7 grams) of gold.

The amount of money countries could issue depended on how much gold was being mined in the world. A decline in gold output during the 1870's and 1880's slowed the growth of the money supply and caused prices to fall. The economic problems ended only after the discovery of new gold fields in South Africa and after the invention of a more efficient method of extracting gold from the rocks in which it is found.

The United States and most other countries today are on the fiat money system. Under this system, the money supply does not depend on the production of any commodity. Instead, the national government controls the money supply. The government does so through its *central bank,* which is a government agency in most countries. A nation's central bank issues currency, regulates the activities of the country's commercial banks, and performs other financial services for the government. The Federal Reserve System is the central bank of the United States. The central bank of Canada is the Bank of Canada. Other central banks include the Bank of England in Great Britain, the Banque de France in France, and the Deutsche Bundesbank in Germany.

How the Federal Reserve System adjusts the money supply

The Federal Reserve System, the central bank of the United States, regulates the nation's money supply. This chart shows how the Federal Reserve puts more money into circulation. To shrink the money supply, the Federal Reserve takes opposite actions.

WORLD BOOK diagram by David Cunningham

The Board of Governors of the Federal Reserve System reviews data on employment, industrial output, inflation, and other economic trends. It decides to increase the money supply.

The discount rate is the interest rate banks pay to borrow from the Federal Reserve. Lowering the rate encourages banks to grant loans.

Open-market operations involve buying and selling government securities. To boost the money supply, the Federal Reserve buys securities.

The reserve requirement is the amount of money banks must keep on reserve. Lowering the requirement lets banks make more loans.

An open-market trader of the Federal Reserve buys securities from dealers and pays by check. The dealers deposit the checks in their banks, which must put part of the money on reserve but can lend the rest.

The money supply expands when banks make more loans because of a lower discount rate, open-market purchase, or lower reserve requirement.

The role of the Federal Reserve System. The Federal Reserve System, often called simply the *Fed,* has 12 regional Federal Reserve Banks. Each bank is responsible for a Federal Reserve District. Most large commercial banks belong to the system. They use the Reserve Bank in their district much as people use a bank in their community. Each member bank must keep a certain sum of money either as currency in its vaults or as deposits at its Reserve Bank. This sum is a percentage of the member bank's own deposits and is called a *reserve requirement.* The reserve requirement is set by the Federal Reserve. A bank may withdraw any excess deposits at the Reserve Bank to get currency when needed. It may also borrow from the Reserve Bank. The Federal Reserve has the authority to set reserve requirements for all deposit-taking institutions.

The Federal Reserve can control the money supply in several ways. It may raise or lower the *discount rate,* which is the interest rate that commercial banks pay to borrow from Reserve Banks. Or the Federal Reserve may raise or lower reserve requirements. Raising the discount rate or the reserve requirement reduces the ability of banks to make loans and thus shrinks the money supply. Lowering the discount rate or the reserve requirement has the opposite effect on the money supply.

However, the Federal Reserve's chief means of adjusting the money supply is by buying and selling government securities. These activities are called *open-market operations.* If the Federal Reserve wants to increase the quantity of money, it makes an *open-market purchase.* It buys government securities from banks and other businesses and from individuals. The Federal Reserve pays for the securities with a check. The sellers now have more money than before, and so there is more money in the economy. When the sellers deposit the checks at their bank, the supply of money may increase further. Under Federal Reserve rules, a member that receives new funds must put a portion on reserve in its district Reserve Bank. The bank then can lend or invest the rest. As a result, the quantity of money in the economy will rise by even more than the amount of the open-market purchase. To reduce the money supply, the Federal Reserve sells securities in an *open-market sale.*

The Federal Reserve's ability to control the money supply might make it seem easy to adjust the supply to promote the government's economic goals. For example, the Federal Reserve could expand the money supply whenever unemployment increased, thus creating more jobs. It could reduce the money supply whenever inflation occurred, thus holding prices down. But use of monetary policy to control the economy is far more difficult than it seems.

Monetary policy is often ineffective because changes in the money supply do not affect the economy immediately. If the effect of a change is long delayed, it may strike the economy at the wrong time. For example, the Federal Reserve might decide to increase the money supply in the hope of reducing joblessness within six months. But the drop in unemployment might not come for a year or more, and it might happen at a time when unemployment had already begun to fall for other reasons. Instead of reducing joblessness, the Federal Reserve's action might then only fuel inflation.

The Federal Reserve's task is also difficult because it is likely to increase unemployment when it tries to reduce inflation, and vice versa. If the Federal Reserve fights inflation by reducing the money supply, employers may cut back on production and more workers will lose their jobs. If the Federal Reserve boosts the money supply to create more jobs, price increases may follow. In such cases, the Federal Reserve may have difficulty deciding what to do. Some economists believe that the best way to fight inflation and unemployment is by a gradual, continuous increase in the money supply instead of frequent adjustments.

International finance

Much trade takes place between nations. For example, Americans buy French cheese and Japanese automobiles, and the French and Japanese buy American airplanes and blue jeans. Most imported goods must be paid for in the currency of the selling country. An automobile dealer in the United States who buys Japanese cars gets yen by buying them from a bank at the current *exchange rate.* An exchange rate is the price of one nation's currency expressed in terms of another country's currency. If the exchange rate were 100 yen to the U. S. dollar, for example, the American would have to buy $12,000 in yen to pay for a Japanese automobile that cost 1.2 million yen.

Exchange rates are determined in foreign exchange markets. The rates vary from day to day in relation to international demand for various currencies. If Americans buy more Japanese products, for example, the U.S. demand for yen increases and the yen rises in price against the dollar. This system is known as *floating exchange rates* or *flexible exchange rates.*

Most countries do not allow the exchange rate for their currency to float freely, however. Each country has holdings of foreign currency. If the exchange rate falls too far, the government will use some of its foreign holdings to buy enough of its own currency to stabilize the exchange rate.

The balance of payments is the difference between a nation's receipts of foreign currency and its expenditures of foreign currency. A nation's balance of payments affects its exchange rate. The world price of a country's currency tends to rise if the country's receipts exceed its expenditures. This condition is called a *balance-of-payments surplus.* A nation's currency will tend to decline on world markets if more money flows out of the country than comes in. This condition is called a *balance-of-payments deficit.*

The primary influences on the balance of payments are income levels and rates of inflation. Suppose income levels rise more quickly abroad than in the United States. People in other countries then will increase their imports of American goods. The United States will export more than it imports, creating a balance-of-payments surplus and causing the world price of U.S. dollars to increase. If inflation causes prices to rise more quickly in the United States than abroad, foreign goods become cheaper for Americans to buy and they import more. This situation creates a balance-of-payments deficit and causes the U.S. dollar to drop in price.

International reserves. Each country has official holdings of foreign currency that it uses to stabilize ex-

Exchange rates

An exchange rate is the price of one country's currency in terms of another country's currency. Exchange rates vary from day to day, depending on the international demand for different currencies. This table shows the exchange rate in United States dollars for many world currencies on July 2, 1993.

Country	Monetary unit	Price in U.S. dollars
Algeria	Dinar	$ .05
Argentina	Peso	1.00
Australia	Dollar	.67
Austria	Schilling	.08
Bahamas	Dollar	1.00
Bahrain	Dinar	2.65
Bangladesh	Taka	.03
Barbados	Dollar	.50
Belgium	Franc	.03
Belize	Dollar	.50
Bolivia	Boliviano	.23
Brazil	Cruzeiro	.00002
Burma	Kyat	.16
Burundi	Franc	.004
Cameroon	Franc	.003
Canada	Dollar	.78
Central African Republic	Franc	.003
Chile	Peso	.002
China	Yuan	.17
Colombia	Peso	.001
Costa Rica	Colon	.007
Cuba	Peso	.76
Cyprus	Pound	1.99
Czech Republic	Koruna	.03
Denmark	Krone	.15
Dominica	Dollar	.37
Dominican Republic	Peso	.08
Ecuador	Sucre	.0005
Egypt	Pound	.30
El Salvador	Colon	.11
Ethiopia	Birr	.20
Fiji	Dollar	.65
Finland	Markka	.18
France	Franc	.17
Germany	Mark	.59
Ghana	Cedi	.002
Greece	Drachma	.004
Guatemala	Quetzal	.18
Guyana	Dollar	.008
Haiti	Gourde	.08
Honduras	Lempira	.16
Hong Kong	Dollar	.13
Hungary	Forint	.01
Iceland	Krona	.01
India	Rupee	.03
Indonesia	Rupiah	.0005
Iran	Rial	.0006
Iraq	Dinar	3.22
Ireland	Pound	1.44
Israel	Shekel	.36
Italy	Lira	.0006
Jamaica	Dollar	.04
Japan	Yen	.009
Jordan	Dinar	1.43
Kenya	Shilling	.02
Korea, South	Won	.001
Kuwait	Dinar	3.32
Lebanon	Pound	.0006
Liberia	Dollar	$ 1.00
Libya	Dinar	3.35
Luxembourg	Franc	.03
Madagascar	Franc	.0005
Malaysia	Ringgit	.38
Malta	Lira	2.60
Mexico	Peso	.32
Mongolia	Tughrik	.003
Morocco	Dirham	.11
Nepal	Rupee	.02
Netherlands	Guilder	.53
New Zealand	Dollar	.54
Nicaragua	Gold córdoba	.16
Niger	Franc	.003
Nigeria	Naira	.04
Norway	Krone	.14
Oman	Rial	2.60
Pakistan	Rupee	.04
Panama	Balboa	1.00
Papua New Guinea	Kina	1.02
Paraguay	Guarani	.0006
Peru	Sol	.49
Philippines	Peso	.04
Poland	Zloty	.00006
Portugal	Escudo	.006
Qatar	Riyal	.27
Romania	Leu	.001
Russia	Ruble	.0009
Rwanda	Franc	.007
Saudi Arabia	Riyal	.27
Senegal	Franc	.003
Sierra Leone	Leone	.002
Singapore	Dollar	.62
Somalia	Shilling	.0004
South Africa	Rand	.22
Spain	Peseta	.008
Sri Lanka	Rupee	.02
Sudan	Pound	.008
Swaziland	Lilangeni	.30
Sweden	Krona	.13
Switzerland	Franc	.66
Syria	Pound	.05
Taiwan	Dollar	.04
Tanzania	Shilling	.003
Thailand	Baht	.04
Trinidad and Tobago	Dollar	.18
Tunisia	Dinar	1.01
Turkey	Lira	.00009
Uganda	Shilling	.0008
United Arab Emirates	Dirham	.27
United Kingdom	Pound	1.51
United States	Dollar	1.00
Uruguay	Peso	.25
Venezuela	Bolivar	.01
Yugoslavia	Dinar	.0000005
Zaire	Zaire	.0000002
Zambia	Kwacha	.002
Zimbabwe	Dollar	.15

Source: BankAmerica Corporation.

change rates and to pay international debts. These holdings are called *international reserves*. The U.S. dollar plays a special role in international reserves, partly because the United States is one of the world's leading trading nations. Many countries keep nearly all their international reserves in U.S. dollars, and most countries are willing to accept payment in dollars. To some extent, the U.S. dollar thus functions as an international medium of exchange.

The International Monetary Fund (IMF) is an organization that works to improve financial dealings between countries. The International Monetary Fund has introduced a type of international reserves called *Special Drawing Rights (SDR's)*. Member countries of the IMF can use these reserves to settle accounts among themselves. Unlike other reserves, SDR's exist only as entries on the account books of the IMF. Some economists think SDR's eventually will become widely used as an international medium of exchange.

R. G. Doty and Stanley Fischer

Related articles in *World Book.* See **Bank** and **Economics.** See also the following articles:

Modern currencies

Cent	Lira	Quetzal
Dime	Mark	Rial
Dollar	Nickel	Ruble
Drachma	Penny	Rupee
Franc	Peseta	Shekel
Guilder	Peso	Yen
Half dollar	Pound	Yuan
Kopeck	Quarter	

Historical currencies

Denarius	Florin	Pine-tree shilling
Doubloon	Greenback	Shilling
Ducat	Guinea	Sou
Eagle	Piece of eight	Talent
Farthing		

Negotiable instruments

Bill of exchange	Negotiable instrument
Bond	Note
Check	Savings bond
Draft	Traveler's check
Money order	

Government agencies

Farm Credit System
Federal Deposit Insurance Corporation
Federal National Mortgage Association
Federal Reserve System
Treasury, Department of the

International finance

Balance of payments	European Monetary System	International Monetary Fund
Bretton Woods	Exchange rate	Special drawing rights
Convertibility	International Finance Corporation	
Devaluation		
Eurodollar		

Other related articles

Barter	Free silver
Bullion	Gold (Money)
Coin collecting	Gold standard
Colonial life in America (Money)	Gresham's law
	Income
Counterfeiting	Indian, American (Money)
Depreciation	Inflation
Depression	Investment

Legal tender	Silver (Uses of silver)
Mill	Trade (The use of money)
Mint	Wampum

Outline

I. How money developed
  A. The first coins
  B. The development of paper money
II. History of United States currency
  A. The first United States currency
  B. The rebirth of paper money
  C. United States currency today
III. How money is manufactured
  A. Minting coins
  B. Printing paper money
IV. Money and the economy
  A. The value of money
  B. Definitions of the money supply
  C. How the money supply is determined
  D. The role of the Federal Reserve System
V. International finance
  A. The balance of payments
  B. International reserves

Questions

How did people obtain the things that they needed before money?
What organization controls the supply of money in the United States?
What motto appears on all U.S. money?
Where was the first paper money used?
What were some of the things that people in the past used as money?
How does inflation affect the value of money?
Where are U.S. coins manufactured?
How did the expression *two bits,* which means 25 cents, originate?

Additional resources

Level I
Bungum, Jane E. *Money and Financial Institutions.* Lerner, 1991.
Cribb, Joe. *Money.* Knopf, 1990.
Drobot, Eve. *Amazing Investigations: Money.* Prentice-Hall, 1987.
Wallace, G. David. *Money Basics.* Prentice-Hall, 1984.
Wilkinson, Elizabeth. *Making Cents: Every Kid's Guide to Money—How to Make It, What to Do with It.* Little, Brown, 1989.

Level II
Moore, Carl H., and Russell, A. E. *Money: Its Origin, Development, and Modern Use.* McFarland, 1987.
Pick, Albert. *Standard Catalog of World Paper Money.* Ed. by Neil Shafer and C. R. Bruce II. 2 vols. 6th ed. Krause, 1990.
Ritter, Lawrence S., and Silber, W. L. *Money.* 5th ed. Basic Bks., 1984.
Schwartz, Anna J. *Money in Historical Perspective.* Univ. of Chicago Pr., 1987.

Money market fund is a mutual fund that invests only in short-term securities. The term *money market* refers to the buying and selling of such securities. Money market funds are also known as *liquid asset funds, cash funds,* or *money funds.*

Many institutions need to borrow money for short periods of time—a year or less. Such institutions include the federal government, banks and other financial firms, and corporations. The securities that these institutions sell in the money market yield returns closely tied to current interest rates. Common types of money market securities include Treasury bills and certificates of deposit.

Like all other mutual funds, money market funds pool the money of many investors and pay them interest. The interest rate paid varies, depending on market condi-

UNITED STATES OF AMERICA POSTAL MONEY ORDER 15-800/000

36454738691

SAMPLE

SERIAL NUMBER   YEAR MONTH DAY   POST OFFICE   U. S. DOLLARS AND CENTS

PAY TO   FROM
STREET   STREET
CITY   STATE   ZIP   CITY   STATE   ZIP

MONEY ORDER   COD NO. OR USED FOR

⑆00000800 2⑈   36454738691⑈

A **U.S. domestic postal money order** can be purchased at any United States post office. The post office fills in the amount of the money order. The purchaser adds his or her name and address and the name and address of the person who should receive payment.

WORLD BOOK photo

tions. But it generally exceeds the rate small investors can get in savings accounts that have limits on interest rates.

The United States government does not insure the money in money market funds. However, money market funds invest mainly in low-risk securities and are considered safe.

Money market funds developed during the early 1970's. Their low initial investment, high yields, and safety led to spectacular growth. However, that trend ended in 1982, when the federal government allowed savings institutions to offer federally insured accounts that provided yields similar to those of money market funds.

There are more than 450 money market funds in the United States. Their net assets total more than $260 billion.   Carol S. Greenwald

See also **Investment** (Mutual funds); **Mutual fund**.

Money order is a document directing that a sum of money be paid to a certain person. Many banks and stores and all United States and Canadian post offices sell money orders.

Money orders resemble checks and thus provide a safe way to send money through the mail. A purchaser fills out a money order and mails it to the person named. The person receiving the order may cash it at a bank or post office.

U.S. postal money orders may be either domestic or international. A domestic money order may be sent anywhere within the United States. Domestic orders also may be sent to Antigua and Barbuda, the Bahamas, Barbados, Belize, the British Virgin Islands, Canada, Dominica, Grenada, Jamaica, Montserrat, St. Christopher and Nevis, St. Lucia, St. Vincent and the Grenadines, and Trinidad and Tobago. An international money order may be sent to any of the approximately 75 countries that honor them.

The highest face value of any single domestic or international money order is $700. No individual may purchase postal money orders exceeding $10,000 in face value on any day. The fee for a domestic postal money order is 75 cents. The fee for an international money order is $3.00.

A postal money order may be cashed at any time after the date of issue. Postal money orders may be endorsed only once. The United States Postal Service refunds the value of its money orders if they are lost or stolen in the mail.

Canadian postal money orders cannot have a face value of more than $999. However, an unlimited number may be purchased. The fee is $1.75 for money orders issued in Canada for payment in Canada. The fee for payment in the United States and its territories and possessions is $2.45. For most other countries, the fee is $4.50.

Critically reviewed by the Canada Post Corporation and the U.S. Postal Service

Mongol Empire was the biggest land empire in history. Its territory extended from the Yellow Sea in east-

Canada Post Corporation

CANADIAN POSTAL MONEY ORDER 🍁 *MANDAT DE POSTE CANADIEN*

PAY TO
PAYEZ À

SPECIMEN   NOT VALID FOR MORE THAN
                  VALIDE
                  JUSQU'À CONCURRENCE DE
                  $200 00

Serial No.   Day   Month   Year   Office No.   Fee Code   Currency   Amount

1748898126   210576   313394   7   CAN$ ◆1234

Nº d'ordre   Jour   Mois   Année   Nº bureau   Code de droit   Monnaie   Montant

SENDER
ENVOYEUR   Account No.   Numéro du compte
ADDRESS
ADRESSE

⑆00000⑈ 127⑈

A **Canadian postal money order** is printed in both English and French. It has spaces for the sender's name and address and for the name of the person receiving the money.

The Mongol Empire covered most of Asia. It began under Genghis Khan during the early 1200's and pushed into eastern Europe for a period in the mid-1200's. The empire reached its greatest extent under Kublai Khan in the late 1200's. The Mongols controlled most of India from the 1500's to the 1700's. The original Mongol homeland makes up what is now Mongolia.

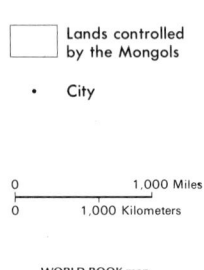

Lands controlled by the Mongols

• City

0   1,000 Miles
0   1,000 Kilometers

WORLD BOOK map

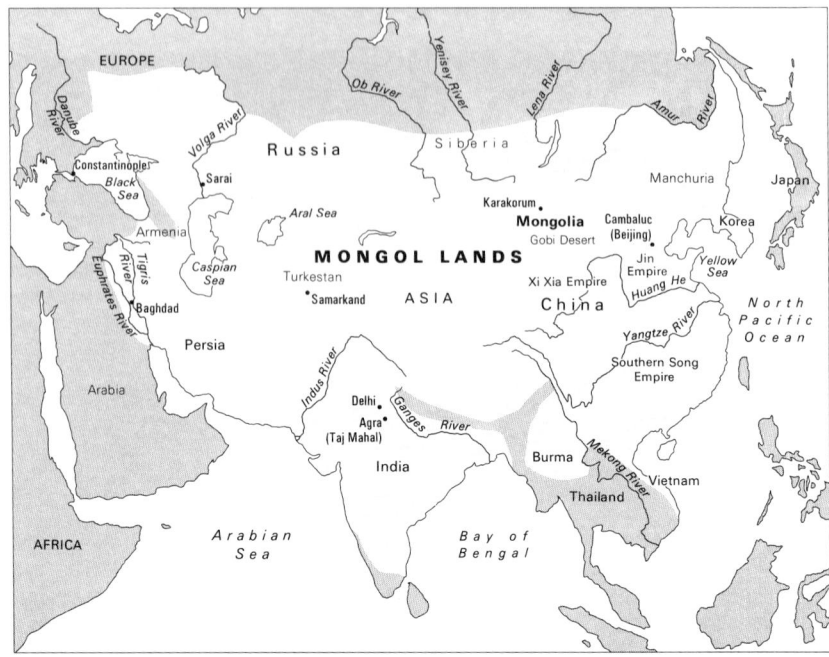

ern Asia to the borders of eastern Europe. At various times it included China, Korea, Mongolia, Persia (now Iran), Turkestan, and Armenia. It also included parts of Burma, Vietnam, Thailand, and Russia.

The Mongols, who eventually became known as the Tatars, were the most savage conquerors of history. But this vast empire helped increase contacts between peoples of different cultures. Migrations fostered these contacts and promoted trade. Roads were built to connect Russia and Persia with eastern Asia. Many Europeans came to China, and Chinese went to Russia and other parts of Europe. Printing and other Chinese inventions such as paper, gunpowder, and the compass may have been introduced to the West during Mongol times.

The Mongols originally consisted of loosely organized nomadic tribes in Mongolia, Manchuria, and Siberia. They lived in felt tents called *yurts*, and raised ponies, sheep, camels, oxen, and goats. They ate mainly meat and milk. Every Mongol man was a soldier and learned to ride and use a bow and arrow skillfully.

Early empire

Genghis Khan. In the late 1100's, Temüjin, a Mongol chieftain who later became known as Genghis Khan, rose to power as *khan* (see **Khan**). He began to unify and organize the scattered Mongol and other nomadic tribes into a superior fighting force. Genghis Khan was shrewd, ruthless, ambitious, and a strict disciplinarian. After he became the undisputed master of Mongolia, and "lord of all the peoples dwelling in felt tents," he set out on a spectacular career of conquest.

Genghis Khan aimed to train the best-disciplined and most effective army of his time. As part of his military strategy, he formed an officer corps from Mongols who were trained in military tactics. These men were then stationed with various tribes as a training force. The

Mongol tribes specialized in the art of siege. They used storming ladders and sandbags to fill in moats. Besiegers approached fortress walls under the protection of gigantic shields. Each tribe prepared a siege train, which consisted of special arms and equipment.

Invasions. Genghis Khan wanted to conquer China. He attacked first Xi Xia, a state along the northwestern border of China. Xi Xia represented the Chinese military pattern, with Chinese-trained armies and Chinese-built fortresses. In this campaign, Genghis Khan could evaluate his armies and train them for war against China.

The Mongols subdued Xi Xia, and then turned to North China. There the Ruzhen tribe of the Manchu people had established the Jin dynasty. Genghis Khan chose spring for his assault on China, so that his horses would have food when crossing the Gobi Desert. Warriors carried everything they needed on the march, and each rider had a spare horse. The hordes drove herds of cattle for food in the desert. The Mongol conquest of North China took several decades. It was not completed until 1234, after Genghis Khan's death.

In 1218, Genghis Khan broke off his attack on China and turned west toward central Asia and eastern Europe. His armies charged into the steppes of Russia and the Muslim lands, including Persia. They came within reach of Constantinople (now Istanbul) and destroyed much of Islamic-Arabic civilization.

All along their routes, the Mongol armies ruthlessly eliminated any resistance. They spread terror and destruction everywhere. When conquered territories resisted, the Mongols slaughtered the population of entire cities.

Genghis Khan died in 1227. The Mongols pushed into Europe under Ogotai, a son of Genghis Khan. In 1241, about 150,000 Mongol riders laid waste a large part of Hungary and Poland, threatening the civilization of western Europe. Ogotai died in the midst of this campaign. His death forced the Mongol generals to break off the campaign and return to Mongolia to elect a new khan.

Later empire

Kublai Khan, a grandson of Genghis Khan, completed the conquest of China in 1279, after attacking the Song dynasty in South China. Kublai Khan's Yuan dynasty lasted until 1368. He established the Mongol winter capital at Cambaluc (also spelled *Khanbalikh*), the site of present-day Beijing. Further attempts to extend the Mongol Empire to Japan were unsuccessful. Mongol warriors fought unsuccessfully at sea and in the tropical climate of Southeast Asia.

The Mongols under Kublai Khan had a reputation for greater tolerance than that shown under earlier Mongol rulers. Kublai permitted the existence of various religions. He enlisted the services of Muslims, Christians, Buddhists, and Taoists. He supported Confucianism and Chinese political ideas, though he avoided having too many Chinese in high offices. In Persia and other Islamic lands, many Mongols adopted Muslim customs and the Muslim faith.

European contacts. Marco Polo was one of the most famous Europeans to travel to the Orient at this time. His travel records contain much interesting information about the Mongols. His reports of beautiful Chinese cities and the riches of the country he called *Cathay* did much to arouse the interest of Europeans in exploring the possibilities of trade with the Orient. Many Europeans, including Christopher Columbus, then sought to go to the Orient by the sea route.

The Khan expressed a desire to have more missionaries sent to China. Dominican and Franciscan missionaries were welcomed by the Khan in Cambaluc. A Franciscan, John of Montecorvino, built a church in the capital and converted many people to Christianity.

Decline. The Mongol Empire did not last long, because it was too big and had no unity of culture. Actually, it began to disintegrate shortly after it reached its peak of expansion in the late 1200's. The Mongols were dauntless fighters, but had little experience in administration. They relied upon other peoples to look after their affairs. They brought foreigners into China to avoid total reliance on the Chinese. The Mongols temporarily suspended the Chinese civil service system to allow these other peoples to assume positions.

Corrupt government and incompetent administration resulted in revolts in different parts of the empire. Even before the fall of the Yuan dynasty in China, the Mongols had lost control of many of their conquered lands. In some areas, they had never succeeded in firmly establishing their rule after their military conquests. Even at the peak of his power, Kublai Khan's authority did not extend to such distant places as Persia and Russia. The Mongols also lacked a firm hold in Southeast Asia.

Breakup. When Kublai Khan died, his empire broke up into several parts. These smaller empires were the Golden Horde on the steppes of southern Russia and the Balkans, the Mongolian-Chinese Yuan Empire, and the realm of the Ilkhans in western Asia. A revolution in China in the 1300's ended the Yuan dynasty and restored Chinese rule in the form of the Ming dynasty.

The great Timur, or Tamerlane, a descendant of Genghis Khan, joined some of the Mongol empires together again and extended his rule over much of Asia in the late 1300's. A descendant of Tamerlane named Babar established a powerful Mongol state in India in 1526. Babar's realm was called *the Kingdom of the Great Moguls.* The term *Mogul* comes from the Persian word *mughul,* meaning *a Mongol.* A Mogul emperor, Shah Jahan, built the beautiful Taj Mahal in the early 1600's. The British destroyed the Mogul kingdom after it had begun to break up in the 1700's.   Richard L. Davis

Related articles. See the *History* sections of the various countries where Mongols ruled, such as **China** (History). See also the following:

Genghis Khan	Mongolia	Shah Jahan
Kublai Khan	Polo, Marco	Tamerlane

Additional resources

The Mongol Conquests: Time Frame AD 1200-1300. Time-Life Books, 1989.

Medieval Tartar Huts and Waggons, drawing by Quinto Cenni. From *The Book of Sir Marco Polo* by Colonel Sir Henry Yule, London, published by John Murrey, 1903 (Newberry Library)

Mongols of the Middle Ages, *above,* often carried their tents on large wooden wagons when moving. A team of many oxen drew the wagon. The driver stood in the entrance of the tent.

A modern nomadic Mongolian family, *left,* lives in tents similar to those of medieval times. The collapsible felt tents provide protection from the extreme heat and cold.

Mongolia

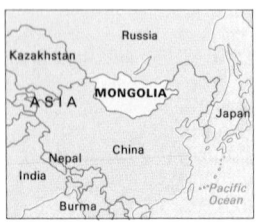

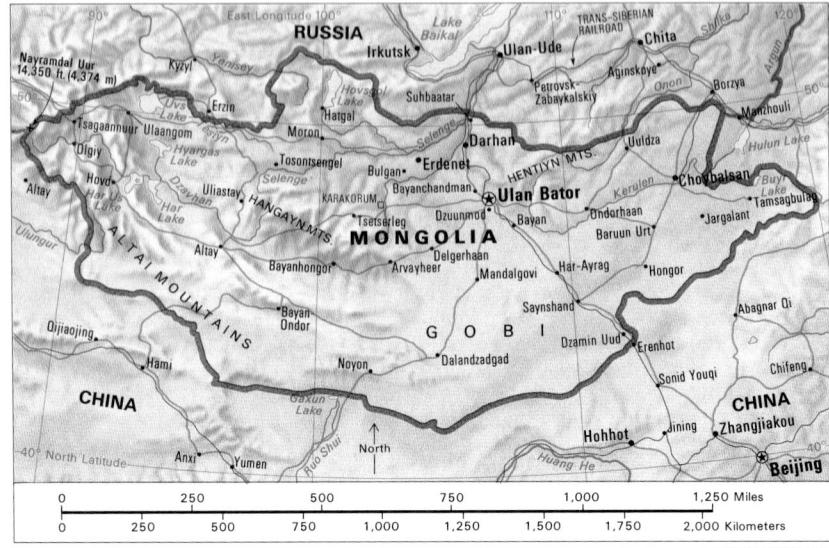

International boundary

Road

Railroad

⊛ National capital

• Other city or town

+ Elevation above sea level

WORLD BOOK maps

Morgan, David. *The Mongols.* Basil Blackwell, 1986.
Saunders, John J. *The History of the Mongol Conquests.*
  Routledge, 1971.

Mongolia, *mahng GOH lee uh,* is a country that lies between China and Russia in east-central Asia. It is a rugged land. Plateaus and towering mountain ranges cover much of the country. The bleak Gobi Desert blankets much of southeastern Mongolia. Temperatures are usually very cold or very hot. Mongolia's little rainfall occurs in a few summer storms.

Many Mongolians raise livestock for a living. Mongolian herders once wandered over the grassy plateaus where their animals grazed. Today, many of these herders work on cooperative livestock farms that are set up by the government. Industry employs an increasing number of people.

Mongolia is the original home of an Asian people called *Mongols.* The Mongols built the largest land empire in history during the 1200's. They conquered an area from eastern Asia to eastern Europe. China ruled Mongolia from the 1680's to 1911. Mongolia was then called *Outer Mongolia.* A Mongol region to the south, called *Inner Mongolia,* is still part of China.

Government. Mongolia's president, the most powerful official in the country, is elected by voters to a four-year term. The president is the head of the armed forces and nominates the prime minister, who carries out the day-to-day operations of government. The prime minister and president nominate the ministers who make up the Cabinet.

Mongolia's people elect members of a national legislature called the State Great Khural to four-year terms. The 76-member State Great Khural makes decisions regarding domestic and foreign affairs. It also *appoints* (approves) the prime minister and Cabinet.

Communists gained control of Mongolia's government in 1921. The Communist Party became Mongolia's only political party. In 1990, Mongolia adopted a democratic, multiparty system of government. The Communist Party broke up, and many new parties were formed. The strongest of these new parties, the Mongolian Peo-

ple's Revolutionary Party, is made up mostly of former Communist Party members.

For administrative and judicial purposes, the country is divided into 18 provinces called *Aimags* and three independent cities. These cities are Ulan Bator, Mongolia's capital, and Darhan and Erdenet.

The people. Nearly all the people of Mongolia are Mongols. Some Chinese, Kazakhs, and Russians also live in Mongolia. The official language of Mongolia is Mongolian. Mongolian has several dialects. Most of the people speak Khalkha Mongolian, which is the official dialect. Mongolian is written in a special form of the Cyrillic alphabet, the alphabet of the Russian language. There is, however, a growing movement to replace the Russian alphabet with an old Mongolian alphabet. *Lamaism* (a form of Buddhism) and Shamanism are the chief religions in Mongolia. Religious practice was discouraged under Communist rule, but Mongolia's democratic government permits greater religious expression.

About half of Mongolia's people live on livestock farms. The farms are like huge ranches with small towns in the center. The central buildings include houses, offices, shops, and medical posts for the people and ani-

Facts in brief

Capital: Ulan Bator.

Official language: Mongolian.

Area: 604,829 sq. mi. (1,566,500 km²). *Greatest distances*—east-west, 1,500 mi. (2,414 km); north-south, 790 mi. (1,271 km).

Population: *Estimated 1994 population*—2,433,000; density, 4 persons per sq. mi. (2 per km²); distribution, 53 per cent urban, 47 per cent rural. *1989 census*—2,043,400. *Estimated 1999 population*—2,765,000.

Chief products: *Agriculture*—camels, cattle, goats, grain, horses, meat, milk, potatoes, sheep, vegetables. *Manufacturing and processing*—building materials, felt, processed foods, soap, textiles. *Mining*—coal, petroleum.

Flag: Vertical stripes of red, blue, and red, with gold symbols on the left stripe. The flag was adopted in 1992. See **Flag** (picture: Flags of Asia and the Pacific).

Money: *Basic unit*—tughrik. See **Money** (table).

mals. The state runs some farms for raising crops.

Few Mongolians still follow the traditional way of life of nomadic herders. Those who do, journey from place to place with their animals. They live in felt tents called *ger* or *yurts,* which help protect them from the intense heat and cold. The government is gradually settling the nomads on farms.

The Mongolian State University was founded in Ulan Bator in 1942. The country has teacher training colleges and technical schools where students study such subjects as agriculture, economics, and medicine.

Land. No part of Mongolia lies less than 1,700 feet (518 meters) above sea level. The Altai Mountains in western Mongolia rise to more than 14,000 feet (4,270 meters). A high plateau lies between the Altai Mountains and the Hangayn Mountains in central Mongolia. This plateau has many lakes. Uvs Lake, the largest, covers about 1,300 square miles (3,370 square kilometers). Dense forests cover the Hentiyn Mountains, northeast of Ulan Bator. Eastern Mongolia is a lower plateau of grassland. It becomes less fertile as it nears the Gobi, a bleak desert area from southeastern Mongolia into Inner Mongolia.

Mongolia gets very hot and very cold. Temperatures ranging from −57 to 96 °F (−49 to 36 °C) have been recorded in Ulan Bator. Snowfall and rainfall are usually light. Heavy rains may occur in July and August. Violent earthquakes sometimes shake Mongolia.

Economy. Under Communist rule, the state owned and operated most factories and farms in Mongolia. But since Communist rule ended, Mongolia has worked to reduce government control of industry. Livestock-raising is the backbone of the economy. Herders keep over 20 million animals, more than half of them sheep. Other animals include camels, cattle, goats, and horses. Cattle make up about 35 per cent of the country's exports, and wool about 40 per cent. Mongolia also exports dairy products, furs, hides, and meat.

The number of animals raised in the country has decreased since the mid-1900's. During the same period, farmers have greatly increased their production of grains and other crops.

Manufacturing and construction are of major importance to the Mongolian economy. Building materials, processed foods, tent frames and felts, wool and woolen fabrics, furniture, glass and china, soap, and matches rank among the chief manufactured products. Mongolia has rich deposits of coal, copper, gold, iron, and petroleum.

Mongolia's main railroad connects Ulan Bator with Russia's Trans-Siberian railroad in the north and with Chinese railroads in the south. The country has about 47,000 miles (75,600 kilometers) of roads. Most of these are dirt roads. Mongolia and Russia trade goods over Hovsgol Lake and the Selenge River. Air service links Ulan Bator with other countries and with provincial capitals in Mongolia.

Mongolia's leading daily newspaper is *Unen* (*Truth*). The country also has 9 other newspapers and 13 periodicals. There are also 18 provincial newspapers in Mongolia.

History. Various groups of Mongols were united under Genghis Khan in the early 1200's. Genghis Khan and his grandson Kublai Khan extended the Mongol Empire from Korea and China westward into Europe. The empire broke up in the late 1300's. See **Mongol Empire**.

Mongol princes reunited Mongolia in the late 1500's and converted the people to Lamaism. In the early 1600's, the Manchu rulers of Manchuria gained control of Inner Mongolia. The Manchus conquered China in 1644 and seized Outer Mongolia in the 1680's. Mongolia, like China, had little contact with other nations during the 1700's and the 1800's. See **Manchus**.

The Mongolians drove Chinese forces out of Outer Mongolia in 1911. They appointed a priest, called the *Living Buddha,* as king, and appealed to Russia for support. In 1913, China and Russia agreed to give Outer Mongolia control over its own affairs. Legally, Outer Mongolia remained Chinese territory. But, in fact, it came largely under the control of Russia. In 1920, during Russia's civil war, anti-Communist Russian troops occupied Outer Mongolia and ruled it through the Living Buddha. Mongolian and Russian Communists gained control of Outer Mongolia in 1921. They established the

On the Mongolian plains, wandering nomads live in collapsible tents called *ger* or *yurt, right.* The dwelling is made of layers of felt covered with canvas or hide. The enclosed pen, *foreground,* is for livestock. The government is gradually settling the nomads on farms.

Mongolian People's Republic in 1924, after the Living Buddha died. The Soviet Union was formed in 1922 under Russia's leadership, and it existed until 1991. Mongolia supported the Soviet Union in the Soviet-Chinese dispute for leadership of the Communist world.

In the late 1980's, reforms resulted in more freedom for people in the Soviet Union and Communist countries of Eastern Europe. Influenced by these changes, people in Mongolia held demonstrations in early 1990 for more freedom. As a result, the country's Communist Party gave up its monopoly on power and a multiparty system was adopted. Free elections were held in July 1990. Communists won a majority of seats in the legislature.

New elections were held in June 1992. By then, the Communist Party had broken up. In the election, the Mongolian People's Revolutionary Party, mostly made up of former Communist Party members, won a large majority of the legislative seats.   Andrew C. Hess

Related articles in *World Book* include:

Altai Mountains	Gobi
China (History)	Horse (graph)
Clothing (picture: Traditional	Kublai Khan
costumes)	Lamaism
Genghis Khan	Ulan Bator

Mongolism. See Down syndrome.

Mongoose, *MAHNG goos,* is the name of several closely related small animals that live in Africa and southern Asia. They are related to the civet and the genet (see **Civet**). The common mongoose is about 16 inches (41 centimeters) long and has stiff, yellowish-gray hair that is grizzled with brownish-black. It has a fierce disposition but can be tamed.

The mongoose is best known for its ability to kill snakes. It is not immune to poison, but its swiftness allows it to seize and kill poisonous snakes such as the cobra. The mongoose also kills mice, rats, poultry, wild birds, and other small animals. It also eats birds' eggs.

The mongoose has been introduced into Jamaica, Cuba, Puerto Rico, Hawaii, and other parts of the world to destroy hordes of rats. However, in most cases, the mongooses have done more damage to native birds than to the rats. Mongooses cannot be brought into the United States without a permit from the Bureau of Sport Fisheries and Wildlife. A permit is granted only if the animal will be used in a zoological exhibit or for educational, medical, or scientific purposes.

Scientific classification. The mongoose belongs to the family Herpestidae. There are about 17 genera. One genus, *Herpestes,* includes many Asiatic mongooses.   Gary A. Heidt

Mongrel. See Dog (Kinds of dogs).

Monitor is the name of a group of about 30 kinds of lizards that live in the Solomon Islands, New Guinea, Australia, the East Indies, southern Asia, and Africa. In Australia, monitors are called *goannas.* A monitor has a long head and neck, and a narrow, deeply forked tongue. The body is usually black or brown with yellow bands, spots, or mottling. The legs are short and powerful, and the tail has a whiplike end. Monitors are usually at least 4 feet (1.2 meters) long. One, the *Komodo dragon,* is often 10 feet (3 meters) long. This species lives on the Lesser Sunda Islands of Indonesia.

When a monitor is cornered, it stands high on its legs and puffs up its body. This display makes the animal look larger than it is. A monitor may also defend itself by using its tail like a whip or by biting with its sharp teeth.

A monitor will eat almost any animal it can kill, including other reptiles, birds, mammals, insects, and crustaceans. Many monitors live near water, and they are all good swimmers and divers. When they swim, they hold their legs against their sides, driving forward by weaving their bodies and tails. Monitors lay eggs, and climb well. The best-known species are the Komodo dragon, the *Nile monitor* of Africa, and the *water monitor,* which lives from India to northern Australia.

Scientific classification. Monitors are in the monitor family, Varanidae. The scientific name for the Komodo dragon is *Varanus komodoensis;* the Nile monitor, *V. niloticus;* and the water monitor, *V. salvator.*   Laurie J. Vitt

See also **Komodo dragon; Lizard** (picture).

Monitor. See Television (The control room).

Monitor and Merrimack fought a famous naval battle in the American Civil War (1861-1865). The two ships were called *ironclads* because they had been covered with iron. The battle, which ended with little damage to either the Union's *Monitor* or the Confederacy's *Merrimack,* focused worldwide attention on the importance of armor-plated ships. It was also one of the first sea battles in which the opposing ships were maneuvered entirely under steam power.

The *Merrimack,* or *Merrimac,* originally was a wooden frigate. Union troops sank it when they evacuated the Navy yard at Portsmouth, Va., after the war began in 1861. Confederate forces raised the ship and covered it with iron plates. They renamed it *Virginia,* though it is often referred to by its original name.

Peter Jackson, Bruce Coleman Ltd.

A mongoose prepares to eat a snake it has killed. The mongoose can fight snakes successfully because of its ability to dodge and pounce with lightning speed.

On March 8, 1862, the *Virginia* sank two Union ships at Hampton Roads, Va., and ran three others aground. The *Virginia* returned the next day, but it found a Union ironclad, the *Monitor,* waiting. The *Monitor* was built of iron as well as being ironclad. John Ericsson, a Swedish-American inventor, had designed this "cheese box on a raft" for the Union (see **Ericsson, John**).

The two ships battled for more than three hours. But their shells had little effect on either vessel, and the battle ended in a draw. Within the year, however, both ships were lost. The *Virginia* was destroyed to keep it from being captured by the Union. The *Monitor* filled with water and sank while being towed at sea in a storm.

In 1974, Duke University scientists announced that they had located the *Monitor* at the bottom of the Atlantic Ocean. They reported that the ship lay about 16 miles (26 kilometers) south of Cape Hatteras, off the coast of North Carolina.   Gabor S. Boritt

See also **Civil War** (First battle between ironclads).

Monitoring station receives and measures signals from radio transmitters. These signals come from such sources as AM and FM radio stations, television stations, radios in airplanes and ships, and amateur radios. Some countries use monitoring stations as "listening posts" to obtain information from other countries.

In the United States, the Federal Communications Commission (FCC) operates 13 monitoring stations. In Canada, the Department of Transport operates four stations. Both government agencies issue transmitter licenses and enforce operating regulations determined by national laws and international laws and treaties. Monitoring stations measure radio transmissions often to make certain the stations are operating under these regulations and the terms of their licenses.

The United States and Canada maintain many mobile monitoring vehicles. Long-range direction finders help locate sources of radio interference, unauthorized transmitters, and aircraft and ships in distress.

During World War II (1939-1945), the FCC operated as many as 102 monitoring stations, supported by automobiles with direction finders. This equipment was used to uncover radio transmitters operated by enemy agents.

Critically reviewed by the Federal Communications Commission

Monk is a man who has separated himself from ordinary ways of life to devote himself to his religion. Monks have played a prominent role in Christianity, especially in the Roman Catholic and Eastern Orthodox churches. Monks are also important in certain types of Buddhism, Jainism, Islam, and Hinduism.

Monks devote themselves to work, study, and prayer. To become a monk, a man must join a religious order. After a period of training, he is initiated into the order in a formal ceremony. As part of the initiation, a Christian monk takes vows of *poverty, chastity,* and *obedience,* promising to own no property, to refrain from sexual activity, and to obey superiors. In many orders, monks live in communities called *monasteries.* Each order follows its own set of guidelines, called a *rule.*   Jill Raitt

See also **Monasticism; Religious life; Buddhism** (The sangha).

Monk, George (1608-1670), was an English general and naval commander. His name is also spelled Monck. He helped restore King Charles II to the English throne in 1660.

Monk joined the army at the age of 17. He commanded Irish troops for the king in the English Civil War in the 1640's, which ended with the triumph of Parliament and the English political and military leader Oliver Cromwell (see **Cromwell, Oliver**). The parliamentary troops defeated Monk in 1644 and imprisoned him in the Tower of London for two years. Cromwell then offered to free him if he would serve in the army of the Commonwealth of England. Monk did so and was made a lieutenant general.

He served the Commonwealth as commander in chief of Scotland from 1651 to 1652 and from 1654 to 1659. He helped command the English Navy in 1652 and 1653, and he defeated the Dutch in several naval battles.

After the death of Cromwell in 1658, Monk made possible the peaceful return of King Charles II. The Presbyterian members who had been driven out of Parliament in 1648 were brought back. Their presence in Parliament made certain a majority in favor of restoring Charles. Monk quietly shifted the armed forces throughout England to prevent any chance of an uprising.

Monk led Parliament in bringing back Charles II in 1660. Charles rewarded Monk by giving him a large pension and by making him Duke of Albemarle, *privy councilor* (adviser to the king), and lord lieutenant of Devon and Middlesex (now part of London). Monk was born in the English county of Devon.   Charles Carlton

See also **Restoration.**

Monk, Thelonious, *thuh LOH nee uhs* (1917-1982), was an American composer, pianist, and bandleader. He gained recognition as one of the most adventurous and influential musicians in jazz. Monk's music is intensely rhythmic and often humorous. But his daring use of dissonance and his unique piano style made him a controversial figure. Many of his compositions, including "Round Midnight," "52nd Street Theme," "Epistrophy," and "Straight No Chaser," have become jazz standards.

Thelonious Sphere Monk was born in Rocky Mount, N.C., and grew up in New York City. He was closely associated with the bebop (or bop) movement in the early 1940's. In the early 1950's, Monk formed the first in a series of small jazz groups. He usually led quartets but occasionally formed an orchestra for concerts and recordings. The groups included several important tenor saxophonists, including Sonny Rollins, John Coltrane, and Charles Rouse.   Gary Giddins

Monkey is one of many kinds of small, lively mammals that rank among the most intelligent animals. Scientists classify monkeys—together with human beings, apes, lemurs, and lorises—in the order Primates, the highest order of mammals. The intelligence of monkeys enables them to adapt to a broad range of environments. Their liveliness makes them favorites in zoos. Because of the similarities between monkeys and humans, scientists have used monkeys in research on human behavior and disease. For example, a blood substance called the *Rh factor* was discovered during experiments with the rhesus monkey (see **Rh factor**).

There are about 200 species of monkeys. Most of them live in tropical regions in Central and South America, Africa, and Asia. Most species live in forests and some spend their entire life in the trees. Some African and Asian species live in *savannas* (grasslands with scattered trees) and spend most of their life on the ground.

Francisco Erize, Bruce Coleman Ltd.; E. R. Degginger

Monkeys live in many kinds of environments. Spider monkeys, *left,* dwell in forests of Central and South America. They swing and run swiftly among the tree branches. Baboons, *above,* roam African *savannas* (grasslands with scattered trees). They feed on the ground and sleep in caves or trees.

But even these monkeys sleep in trees—or on steep cliffs—for protection at night. All monkeys live together in various kinds of groups.

Monkeys vary greatly in size. The smallest species, the pygmy marmoset, measures only about 6 inches (15 centimeters) long, not including the tail. The mandrill, one of the largest species, may grow as long as 32 inches (81 centimeters), not including the tail.

Scientists classify monkeys into two major groups, New World monkeys and Old World monkeys. New World monkeys live in Central and South America, and Old World monkeys are found in Africa and Asia. The two groups differ in several ways. For example, New World monkeys have nostrils spaced widely apart. The nostrils of Old World monkeys are close together. Most kinds of New World monkeys have 36 teeth. Old World monkeys have 32 teeth, as do humans. Some species of New World monkeys can grasp objects with their tail, but no Old World monkey can.

New World monkeys have a remarkable variety of sizes, shapes, and colors. Scientists divide them into two main groups: (1) marmosets and tamarins; and (2) all other New World species, including capuchins, dourou-coulis, howlers, spider monkeys, squirrel monkeys, woolly monkeys, and woolly spider monkeys. All New World monkeys are *arboreal*—that is, they live in trees.

Old World monkeys include baboons, colobus monkeys, guenons, langurs, and macaques. Some Old World monkeys, including colobus monkeys and langurs, are *leaf-eating monkeys* and live mainly in trees. Many other Old World monkeys live on the ground. Among the monkeys that live on the ground, the males may be twice as large as the females. See the *Related articles* at the end of this article for a list of the monkeys about which *World Book* has separate articles.

Many people believe that apes—chimpanzees, gib-bons, gorillas, and orangutans—are monkeys. But monkeys and apes differ in several ways. For example, apes are more intelligent than monkeys. Most monkeys have a tail, but none of the apes do. Monkeys are smaller than most apes. Apes are expert climbers. Monkeys generally run, jump, and leap among tree branches.

Human activities have greatly reduced the number of monkeys throughout the world. Some people hunt monkeys for food. Others catch them for pets. The clearing of land for agricultural, housing, and industrial developments has reduced the amount of living space available to monkeys. A number of species of New World and Old World monkeys are threatened with extinction.

The body of a monkey

All monkeys, including those that live on the ground, are the descendants of monkeys that live in trees. As a result, all monkeys have a body primarily suited for living in and moving through trees. For example, monkeys have long arms and legs that help them climb, leap, and run. They also can use their hands and feet to grasp

Where monkeys live

The yellow areas of this map show the parts of the world in which monkeys live. Most species of monkeys live in the tropics.

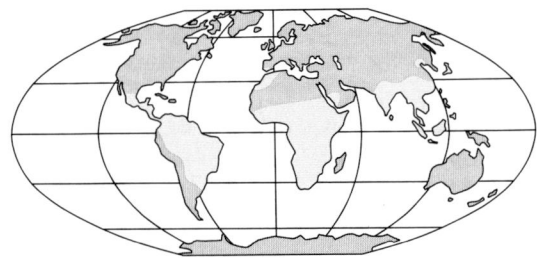

The skeleton of a guenon monkey

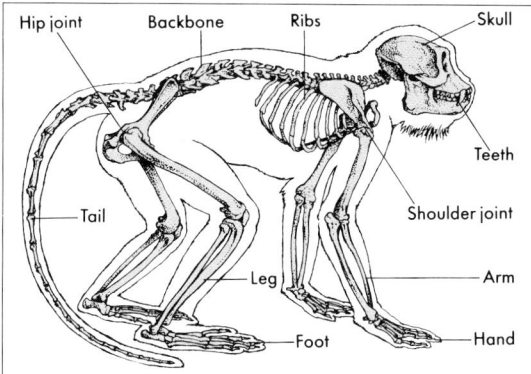

WORLD BOOK illustration by John D. Dawson

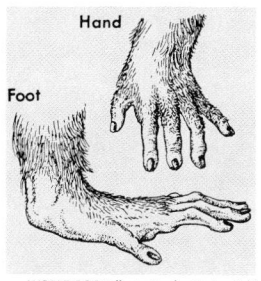

WORLD BOOK illustration by Marion Pahl

A monkey's hands and feet both can grasp objects. The big toe of a monkey looks and moves like a thumb.

Shelly Grossman, Woodfin Camp, Inc.

A monkey's tail provides balance for running and jumping. A spider monkey, *above,* can swing by its tail.

objects—including tree branches. Most species have a long tail that helps them keep their balance. Some New World monkeys can use their tail like a hand to grasp branches and food while moving through the trees.

Head. Monkeys, unlike many other mammals, depend more on their eyes than their nose to gather information about their surroundings. They have large eyes that face forward. They can see in depth and distinguish colors. Their eyes help them judge distances and tell the size, shape, and ripeness of food.

Some monkeys, including baboons, mandrills, and sakis, have large, heavy jaws and eat grass and leaves. Smaller monkeys, such as marmosets and squirrel monkeys, have smaller, lighter jaws. They eat mostly fruit and insects. Many kinds of Old World monkeys have cheek pouches much like those of hamsters and squirrels. The pouches enable the monkeys to store food temporarily. No New World monkey has these pouches.

Arms and legs. Monkeys usually walk and run on all fours, either on tree branches or on the ground. Most species have legs that are slightly longer than their arms. Many kinds of monkeys can stand and even run on their legs, but only for a short period of time. Monkeys usually stand or run on their legs when carrying food, peering over high grass, or threatening enemies or members of the group.

Hands and feet. Old World monkeys have *opposable* thumbs—that is, the thumb can be placed opposite any of the other fingers. This enables a monkey to grasp

small food items. Most kinds of New World monkeys have thumbs that are only partly opposable. Their thumbs also do not move so freely as those of Old World monkeys. Two kinds of New World monkeys— spider monkeys and woolly spider monkeys—have only tiny thumbs or no thumbs at all. Among Old World monkeys, colobus monkeys have no thumbs.

The feet of most monkeys are larger and more powerful than their hands. All monkeys have five toes on each foot. The big toes look and function much like thumbs, giving the monkey an extra pair of grasping "hands." Marmosets and tamarins have claws on their fingers and toes, except for their big toes, which have a nail. All other kinds of monkeys have flat or flattish nails on all their fingers and toes.

Tail. Most monkeys that live on the ground have a shorter tail than do most that live in trees. Arboreal monkeys may have a tail longer than their body. They use their tail for balancing on tree branches. They also use it as an *air brake*—that is, to slow themselves down when they leap from branch to branch. Some New World monkeys, including howlers, spider monkeys, and woolly monkeys, can grasp objects with their tail. The tail of such monkeys has bare skin at the end. The tail of other monkeys is completely covered with hair.

The life of a monkey

Monkeys in captivity live longer than other animals of similar size. They also live longer than most other kinds of mammals, except apes and human beings. Capuchins may live 40 years. Baboons and some macaques may live 30 years. Life spans are shorter in the wild because of disease and other factors.

Food. Most kinds of monkeys eat almost anything they can find. Their food includes birds and birds' eggs, flowers, frogs, fruit, grass, insects, leaves, lizards, nuts, and roots. Baboons may catch and eat such animals as newborn antelope.

Leaves make up about 40 per cent of the food eaten by banded langurs and over 80 per cent of the food of black and white colobus monkeys. All leaf-eating monkeys have sharp crests on their back teeth for shredding leaves. They also have large salivary glands and a large stomach that is divided into compartments. Such specialized structures help leaf-eating monkeys digest their coarse food. Unlike other Old World monkeys, leaf-eating monkeys do not have cheek pouches.

R. C. Hermes, NAS   Lanceau, Agence de Presse Jacana

New World and Old World monkeys can be identified by their noses. The nostrils of New World monkeys, such as the woolly monkey, *left,* are widely spaced. Those of Old World monkeys, such as the mangabey, *right,* are close together.

Douc langur
Pygathrix nemaeus nemaeus
Found in Laos and Vietnam
and on the island of Hainan
Body length: 22 to 32 inches
(56 to 81 centimeters)*

De Brazza's guenon
Cercopithecus neglectus
Found in central and eastern
African forests
Body length: 16 to 24 inches
(41 to 61 centimeters)*

Red uakari
Cacajao rubicundus
Found in eastern Peru and
northwestern Brazil
Body length: 14 to 19 inches
(36 to 48 centimeters)*

Woolly monkey
Lagothrix lagothricha
Found in the upper Amazon River
basin of South America
Body length: 15 to 23 inches
(38 to 58 centimeters)*

Douroucouli
Aotus trivirgatus
Found in forests of most of
South America and Panama
Body length: 10 to 19 inches
(25 to 48 centimeters)*

Patas monkey
Erythrocebus patas
Found in African grasslands
from Tanzania northward
Body length: 23 to 29 inches
(58 to 74 centimeters)*

Red colobus
Colobus badius
Found in tropical rain forests
of Africa
Body length: 18 to 24 inches
(46 to 61 centimeters)*

Proboscis monkey
Nasalis larvatus
Found in Borneo
Body length: 21 to 30 inches
(53 to 76 centimeters)*

*not including the tail

WORLD BOOK illustrations by Helmut Diller

E. R. Degginger

Vervets are among the commonest monkeys in Africa. Some may be found in city parks. They live in bands of from 6 to 20 members. Vervets feed and travel in trees and on the ground.

Young. Most kinds of monkeys give birth to one baby at a time. But marmosets and tamarins sometimes produce twins or even triplets. Scientists do not know the length of pregnancy of many species of monkeys, but the females of some species carry their young inside their bodies for about $4\frac{1}{2}$ months to about 8 months.

Most baby monkeys depend completely on their mother for food and security. They nurse on her milk for a few weeks to two years, depending on the species. A baby monkey hangs onto its mother almost from the moment of birth by grasping her fur. The mother carries the infant until it can travel safely on its own. At first, the infant clings to its mother's underside. Later, the young monkey rides on its mother's back. Among three kinds of New World monkeys—douroucoulis, marmosets, and titis—the father may carry the young on his back, giving them to the female for feeding.

Group life. All species of monkeys live together in social groups. New World monkey groups seldom consist of more than 20 members. Old World monkey groups usually have from 30 to 100 members. There are three kinds of monkey groups: (1) family groups, (2) multimale groups, and (3) one-male groups.

Family groups consist of an adult male, an adult female, and their young. At least three kinds of New World monkeys—sakis, titis, and owl monkeys—live in family groups. Three Old World species may also live in family groups. They are De Brazza's guenons, Mentawi Island langurs, and Hamlyn's owl-faced monkeys.

Multimale groups may consist of a number of adult males, about twice as many adult females, and their young. Most New World monkeys live in such groups, including capuchins, howlers, spider monkeys, squirrel monkeys, and marmosets. Many Old World monkeys, including langurs, macaques, and most baboons, also live in multimale groups.

One-male groups consist of one adult male, several adult females, and their young. Young adult males and females may also belong to the group. Certain species of Old World monkeys live in such groups. They include guenons, geladas, and hamadryas baboons.

In general, monkeys that live in trees have a looser social organization than do monkeys that live on the ground. For example, most guenons and mangabeys live in trees and form one-male groups of which the male is the leader. But he does not have strong leadership, and he has little control over the actions of other members of his group. The females in the group may mate with other males. Members of his group may leave, and new members may join. But monkeys that live on the ground, including most baboons, live in groups that are more tightly organized. A multimale baboon group is *closed*—that is, few members leave and few strangers join the group. Several dominant males control the group's movements, stop fights within the group, punish group members, and protect the group against enemies. The dominant males sometimes prevent other males in the group from mating with the females.

Scientists believe monkeys that live in trees have looser groups because these species are safer than those that live on the ground. The worst enemies of monkeys that live in trees are large eagles. Eagles kill adult and young monkeys with their powerful claws. Monkeys that live on the ground have many other enemies, including cheetahs, hyenas, jackals, leopards, and lions. These monkeys spend time in areas that have no nearby trees into which they can escape. As a result, they must be tightly organized under strong leaders so they can avoid danger or defend themselves.

Monkeys that live on the ground defend themselves chiefly by threatening their enemies. If a cheetah approaches a group of baboons, for example, the leaders of the group gather together to face the danger. Each male baboon shows his long canine teeth and barks. If

Oxford Scientific Films from Bruce Coleman Inc.

Rhesus monkeys, which are found in India, live in tightly organized groups. Like other ground-dwelling monkeys, they depend on group organization for defense.

these actions do not frighten the cheetah away, the baboons may attack.

Communication. Monkeys communicate with one another in various ways. For example, a male rhesus monkey threatens members of its group by staring, opening its mouth and showing its teeth, bobbing its head, and slapping the ground with its hands. *Social grooming* helps maintain friendly relations between baboons. In grooming, one baboon carefully cleans the fur of another. Both animals seem to find satisfaction in this activity. Baboons spend several hours a day grooming.

Scientific classification. Marmosets and tamarins make up the marmoset family, Callitrichidae. All the other New World monkeys belong to the New World monkey family, Cebidae. Old World monkeys make up the Old World monkey family, Cercopithecidae.   Randall L. Susman

Related articles in *World Book* include:

Animal (Animals of the tropical forests; Intelligence of animals; pictures)	Colobus	Marmoset
	Comparative psychology (picture)	Primate
		Proboscis monkey
		Rhesus monkey
	Guenon	Spider monkey
Ape	Howler	Squirrel monkey
Baboon	Langur	Tamarin
Barbary ape	Macaque	Titi
Capuchin	Mandrill	Woolly monkey

Additional resources

Level I
Hoffman, Mary. *Monkey.* Raintree, 1984.
Selsam, Millicent E., and Hunt, Joyce. *A First Look at Monkeys and Apes.* Walker, 1979.

Level II
Berger, Gotthart. *Monkeys and Apes.* Arco, 1985.
Napier, John R. and P. H. *The Natural History of the Primates.* MIT Pr., 1985.

Monkey bread. See Baobab.

Monkey flower is the name given to a large group of herbs and small shrubs. These plants have flowers with *two lips,* an upper lip made up of two joined petals and a lower lip of three joined petals. The petals often have spots that make the flower look more like a monkey's face.

There are many different species, growing from 6 to 36 inches (15 to 91 centimeters) high. They grow in South and North America, mostly on the Pacific Coast. Monkey flowers can be grown in gardens, garden borders, and greenhouses. They grow well in shady places and should be given plenty of water. Some of the shrubby kinds do not require much care.

Scientific classification. Monkey flowers belong to the figwort family, Scrophulariaceae. They make up the genus *Mimulus.* One kind is *M. luteus.*   W. Dennis Clark

Monmouth, *MAHN muhth,* **Duke of** (1649-1685), was an Englishman who led an unsuccessful rebellion against King James II. Monmouth was the illegitimate son of Charles II and a Welsh woman named Lucy Walter, and was a pretender to the throne of England.

Monmouth was born James Scott in Rotterdam, the Netherlands. His father became King Charles II in 1660 after Richard Cromwell lost power. Charles called Scott back to England and made him Duke of Monmouth.

In 1685, Charles II died and his brother James II became king. Monmouth claimed to be the legitimate heir to the throne, on the false grounds that his parents had married. After consulting with supporters in the Netherlands, he landed at Lyme Regis, near Weymouth, and is-

sued a proclamation declaring James a usurper, tyrant, and murderer. He rallied about 4,000 men in southwestern England to overthrow James. But he was defeated at the Battle of Sedgemoor, near Taunton, and taken to the king. Before a court headed by Lord Jeffreys, he begged for his life. But he was imprisoned in the Tower of London and executed.   Charles Carlton

Monnet, *moh NAY,* **Jean,** *zhahn* (1888-1979), a French businessman and statesman, led the movement to unify Western Europe in the 1950's and 1960's. He has been called the Father of the European Community. Monnet proposed the European Coal and Steel Community in 1950 and was its president from 1952 to 1955. He set up the Action Committee for a United States of Europe and was its president from 1956 to 1975. He helped create the European Atomic Energy Community (Euratom) and the European Economic Community (Common Market), both formed in 1957. See **European Community**.

Monnet was born in Cognac. His career as an international financial adviser began when he helped organize Allied supply operations in World War I (1914-1918). From 1919 to 1923, he was deputy secretary general of the League of Nations. In World War II (1939-1945), he was an economic adviser to the American, French, and British governments and later became a member of the French provisional government. He created the Monnet Plan, a five-year recovery plan for France that was adopted in 1947. Monnet soon realized that France's recovery depended on a revived European economy. He also became convinced that the nations of Europe, acting separately, could no longer deal with Europe's economic and political problems. As a result, he began working to develop a United States of Europe.

Monnet received many honors. In 1963, he became one of the first Europeans to receive the Presidential Medal of Freedom, the highest civilian medal awarded by the United States.   Alexander Sedgwick

Monoclonal antibody is a specialized type of protein molecule produced in the laboratory. Similar antibodies are produced naturally by the immune systems of animals and human beings when foreign substances, such as bacteria and viruses, invade the body. Antibodies can neutralize these substances by attaching to their *antigens.* Natural antibodies in blood are a mixture of many antibodies that react with many antigens, thus serving as the body's front-line defense against disease. But solutions of monoclonal antibodies act against a specific antigen and can be made in large quantities. They have shown promise in medical research, including the detection and treatment of cancer.

A monoclonal antibody is produced in a test tube or culture dish by combining a tumor cell with a type of white blood cell called a *B cell.* The resulting hybrid cell, called a *hybridoma,* has properties of both the tumor cell and the B cell. Like the B cell, the hybridoma produces a specific antibody. Like the tumor cell, the hybridoma can grow and reproduce indefinitely in the laboratory. The hybridoma produces identical cells called *clones,* which in turn can survive in the laboratory and produce large quantities of monoclonal antibodies. Most monoclonal antibodies are produced from the cells of laboratory animals, usually mice. Human monoclonal antibodies also have been developed. In one technique of producing human monoclonal antibodies,

B cell IR (immune response) genes are inserted into a bacterial cell, which can reproduce indefinitely.

Researchers use monoclonal antibodies to attach to and identify various cell types and in certain diagnostic tests for bacteria and viruses. For example, in some allergy detection tests, monoclonal antibodies are used to identify the substance that causes the allergy. Scientists eventually hope to use monoclonal antibodies for early cancer detection. Monoclonal antibodies could be "tagged" with radioactive material, enabling doctors to locate tumors when only a few malignant cells are present. In cancer therapy, anticancer drugs could be combined with monoclonal antibodies, which would deliver these drugs to cancer cells without harming surrounding healthy tissue.   Arlene R. Collins

See also **Immunity**.

Monocotyledon, *MAHN uh KAHT uh LEE duhn,* is a type of flowering plant that has one *cotyledon* (leafy structure within the plant's seed). The leaves of most monocotyledons have parallel veins. The flower parts usually grow in multiples of three. About 40,000 species of plants are monocotyledons, including bananas, pineapples, and corn. See also **Cotyledon**.

Monomer, *MAHN uh muhr,* is any molecule that can combine with identical molecules or certain other molecules to form a long, chainlike molecule called a *polymer*. All plastics and rubbers are made of polymers. Polymers also are used in such products as paints, waxes, glues, and lubricants. Heat, pressure, or chemical treatment may be used to cause monomers to combine. See also **Polymer; Polymerization**.   Peter A. Rock

Monongahela River, *muh NAHN guh HEE luh,* provides river transportation between the rich coal fields of southwestern Pennsylvania and the steel factories at Pittsburgh. The river is formed where the Tygart and West Fork rivers meet in Marion County, West Virginia. It winds northeast across the boundary of Pennsylvania to the mouth of the Cheat River. Here it flows north until it unites with the Allegheny at Pittsburgh to form the Ohio River. The Monongahela is 128 miles (206 kilometers) long. Boats can sail on the river in Pennsylvania. The name *Monongahela* comes from an Indian word that means *river with sliding banks*.   William C. Rense

Mononucleosis, *MAHN uh NOO klee OH sihs,* also called *infectious mononucleosis,* is a mild infectious disease marked by a large increase in the number of abnormal *lymphocytes,* a type of white blood cell. The disease gets its name from these *mononuclear* (single nucleus) cells. Mononucleosis occurs most often in young adults but also strikes children and older people.

Mononucleosis is caused by the Epstein-Barr (EB) virus, one of the herpesviruses. Direct contact between people—kissing, for example—can spread the disease. The chief symptoms include chills, fever, sore throat, and fatigue. Mononucleosis is sometimes called *glandular fever* because swelling occurs in the lymph glands, especially those in the neck. Symptoms may also include enlargement of the spleen, inflammation of the mouth and gums, skin rash, jaundice, and an enlarged liver.

Depending on the seriousness of the case, most doctors recommend mild to complete bed rest for a mononucleosis patient. The disease is not fatal, and most patients recover within three to six weeks.

A blood test called the Paul-Bunnell test can determine whether a person has mononucleosis. A sample of the *serum* (clear liquid) of the patient's blood is mixed with sheep's blood. If the patient has the disease, the sheep's blood cells will stick together.   Stanley Yachnin

See also **Herpesvirus; Epstein-Barr virus**.

Monopoly and competition are two kinds of business conditions. In a monopoly, one company or a cooperating group of companies controls the supply of a product or service for which there is no close substitute. In competition, a number of rival firms compete to sell similar goods or services to buyers.

The extent of rivalry between sellers, rather than the number of sellers in a market, determines whether there will be monopoly or competition. In some industries that have only a few sellers, those companies compete vigorously. Each firm tries to offer a better or cheaper product. Other industries have many sellers, but the companies act together as a monopoly would.

Kinds of monopoly and competition. Economists divide market conditions into four major categories: (1) monopoly, (2) pure competition, (3) monopolistic competition, and (4) oligopoly.

In a monopoly, a single firm is the only supplier of a product or service for which buyers cannot easily find a substitute. Monopolies are extremely rare. In the United States, the U.S. Postal Service and some public utilities, such as electric, gas, water, and local telephone companies, are monopolies. A firm may be a monopoly because the market is too small to support others. A grocery store in a small isolated town may be a monopoly.

In pure competition, an industry consists of a large number of producers that sell nearly identical products. Pure competition is also rare. In the United States, the sale of wheat and certain other agricultural products comes closest to this form of competition.

In monopolistic competition, many rival companies sell different varieties of the same product or service. Each of these firms has a monopoly on its own variety of the product, but there are many close substitutes. An example of monopolistic competition in the United States is the clothing industry, in which hundreds of manufacturers sell different styles of clothing.

In an oligopoly, a small number of companies dominate an industry. The policies of each company greatly influence those of the other firms because so few sellers are involved. In the United States, the automobile and computer industries are oligopolies.

Causes and effects of monopolies. A monopoly may develop for a number of reasons. For example, a company may achieve the same volume of production more cheaply than its competitors because of greater efficiency. The more efficient firm may drive other producers out of business and achieve a monopoly.

In some industries, monopolies result from *entry barriers,* which are obstacles that prevent new companies from entering the market. Entry barriers include licenses and patents, which give a business the exclusive right to produce a particular product. A monopoly may also exist because a company controls the supply of a raw material required to make a product.

The reactions of rival firms to one another's policies play a key role in determining the degree of monopoly or competition. For example, a firm would hesitate to lower its prices if it thought its competitors would quickly match the cuts. All the rivals would have lower profits, and none would increase its share of sales.

Monopolies generally set prices higher than they would if there were competitive firms that could produce at similar cost. Thus, monopolies generally make larger profits than competitive firms do. Unfortunately, a monopoly may sell a product of poor quality without suffering a loss in sales.

However, some economists believe monopolies may be useful. For example, a monopoly may be more efficient than a group of competing firms. Some experts also believe monopolies promote research and invention because large companies can sponsor more research programs with their additional profits. However, studies have shown that many companies do not increase their research budgets after taking over an industry.

History. Some of the earliest monopolies were European shipping companies that operated during the Renaissance under royal charters. Kings, queens, and other rulers gave these companies exclusive rights to trade with people in Asia and other regions.

During the late 1800's and early 1900's, many business leaders in the United States tried to reduce competition. In some industries, many small firms merged to form large corporations. In other industries, corporations formed monopolistic combinations called *trusts,* in which a group of managers controlled prices and production without a formal merger. Some trusts cut prices to force smaller firms out of business. The trusts then limited production and raised prices. Huge trusts monopolized many fields, including the railroad, steel, and petroleum industries.

The abuse of monopolies and trusts led to a number of federal laws. The Sherman Antitrust Act of 1890 banned any trust or other combination that interfered with interstate or foreign trade. In 1911, the government used this act to break up the Standard Oil Company into more than 30 separate, competing firms. The Clayton Antitrust Act of 1914 made it illegal for corporations to group together under interlocking boards of directors. This law also prohibited several unfair business practices that large firms had used to eliminate smaller rivals. The Celler-Kefauver Act of 1950 tightened control over mergers that might reduce competition.

Today, antitrust laws are enforced by the Federal Trade Commission (FTC) and the Antitrust Division of the Department of Justice. The FTC can order a company to stop unfair methods of competition. The Antitrust Division investigates and prosecutes businesses that violate antitrust regulations.

The federal government and most state governments have special laws to control public utilities. Government regulation replaces competition in setting prices and establishing standards of service for these utility companies.   Henry J. Aaron

Related articles in *World Book* include:

Antitrust laws	Conglomerate	Public utility
Business	Industry	United States,
(Competition)	(Industrial organi-	History of the
Capitalism	zation)	(Monopolies)
Cartel	Merger	

Additional resources

Frazer, Tim. *Monopoly, Competition, and the Law: The Regula-tion of Business Activity in Britain, Europe, and America.* St. Martin's, 1988.
Kefauver, Estes. *In a Few Hands: Monopoly Power in America.* Pantheon, 1965.
Mueller, Willard F. *A Primer on Monopoly and Competition.* Random Hse., 1970.

Monorail is a railroad that has only one rail. Monorail cars run along a rail above or below them. Cars that run above the track have either a gyroscopic device to balance them, or guide wheels that grip the side of the rail to keep the cars from falling over (see **Gyroscope**).

There are two types of suspended monorail systems. In the older type, the cars hang freely from wheels on a rail. The newer "split-rail" type suspends the cars from two rails spaced closely together and housed in one enclosure. The enclosure ensures quieter operation, and also keeps the track dry.

Monorail cars can be powered by electric motors, gas turbines, or gasoline engines. Rubber wheels cut noise considerably. Monorails are faster and cheaper to operate and maintain than two-rail elevated or subway lines. The smaller amount of friction in monorails allows greater speeds with less operating cost.

The first monorail system, built in Wuppertal, Germany, in 1901, still carries passengers. Many U.S. cities have studied the possibility of building monorail systems that can be built quickly and can operate above a busy street. Ground supports for such systems require little space because monorails have only one rail.

The first monorail train in the United States began operating at Disneyland in Anaheim, Calif., in 1957. Other monorails are located at Seattle, Wash.; Dallas, Tex.; Lake Arrowhead, Calif.; Pomona, Calif.; New York City; and Lake Buena Vista, Fla. Tokyo, Japan, built an 8.2-mile (13.2-kilometer) monorail system for use during the 1964 Olympic Games there.   Gus Welty

Sally Wayland

A monorail train glides above a pool at Walt Disney's EPCOT Center in Lake Buena Vista, Fla. Supports for monorail tracks take up little space, leaving the ground free for other uses.

Monosodium glutamate (MSG) is a white, crystalline substance used in the preparation and processing of many foods. Although MSG has a slight flavor of its own, its chief effect is to bring out the tastes of such foods as meats, vegetables, seafood, soups, sauces, and casseroles.

Monosodium glutamate forms when sodium is added to an amino acid called *glutamic acid* (see **Amino acid**). Chemically, MSG is a sodium salt. However, it does not taste like table salt, which is sodium chloride, and it contains only one-third the sodium of table salt. Its taste is different from the four common categories of taste—salt, sour, sweet, and bitter. In 1908, Japanese chemist Kikunae Ikeda discovered MSG's ability to improve the flavor of food.

Since the late 1960's, some people have reported suffering various discomforts due to eating MSG. However, studies of people who say they have experienced these discomforts have failed to prove that MSG caused them. Experiments with animals have shown that force-feeding or injecting MSG can damage sections of the immature brain. But studies in which MSG is added to the normal diet of animals have revealed no damage.

Two agencies of the United Nations, the Food and Agriculture Organization and the World Health Organization, jointly reviewed the safety of MSG. In 1988, they concluded that MSG is not a health hazard. In 1990, the European Community's Scientific Committee for Food reached the same conclusion. In the United States, the Food and Drug Administration lists MSG as "generally recognized as safe."   Andrew G. Ebert

Monotheism. See **Religion** (Belief in a deity).

Monotreme. See **Mammal** (Reproduction; picture: Monotremes).

Monotype is a machine used to produce metal type for printing. The Monotype is noted for producing high-quality work. It has been used for printing fine books as well as catalogs, magazines, and other printed material. The Monotype has been replaced by *photocomposition* in most printing. Photocomposition is a form of typesetting that produces images of type characters on photosensitive film or paper (see **Printing** [Typesetting]).

How the Monotype works. The Monotype machine consists of a *keyboard* and a *casting machine.* The keyboard is a typewriterlike composing machine. There are 225 keys on the board, and each key represents a separate letter or character. As a key is depressed, a corresponding code of small holes is punched in a paper ribbon or tape. A counter shows the space taken for each character. The operator knows from the counter exactly how much space has been used in each line and can *justify* the line—that is, make it the right length.

The casting machine is a miniature foundry that produces the type. It may be in a different location than the keyboard. The perforated tape from the keyboard is fed through the casting machine. The machine "reads" the code and selects the *matrix* (mold) corresponding to each coded character. Each character is then cast in metal as an individual unit. The cast types are delivered in the required order and justification for printing.

History. Printing with movable metal type was invented in the 1400's. Since then, printers have desired a method of type composition that would increase the speed, reduce the labor, and maintain the quality of hand composition. Tolbert Lanston, an American inventor, spent 13 years developing the Monotype machine to meet this demand. In 1887, he applied for a patent for his idea, though he did not have a model of the machine. John Sellers Bancroft, a machinist, developed the Monotype to virtually its final stage by 1899. The Monotype was widely used until the 1960's, when it was gradually replaced by photocomposition for most printing purposes.   J. C. McCracken

See also **Printing** (Typesetting).

Monroe, Harriet (1860-1936), was an American poet and editor. She founded *Poetry: A Magazine of Verse* in Chicago in 1912 and served as its editor until her death. Her magazine helped initiate and develop modern American poetry. Although Monroe became famous chiefly as an editor, she also wrote poetry, including *You and I* (1914) and *The Difference* (1924). Her autobiography, *A Poet's Life: Seventy Years in a Changing World,* was published in 1938, after her death. Monroe was born in Washington, D.C.   Bonnie Costello

How a Monotype works

Lewis Mitchell, McKenzie-Harris

Lewis Mitchell, McKenzie-Harris

A Monotype sets type in two operations. First, the operator strikes keys on a keyboard, *left,* to punch holes, representing characters, in a paper tape. The tape is fed into the casting machine, *right,* which selects a mold for each character. Molten metal is then poured into the molds.

5th President of
the United States 1817-1825

| Madison | Monroe | Adams |
| Daniel D. Tompkins |
4th President	5th President	6th President	Vice President
1809-1817	1817-1825	1825-1829	1817-1825
Democratic-Republican	Democratic-Republican	Democratic-Republican	

Detail of an oil painting on wood panel (1817) by Gilbert Stuart; Pennsylvania Academy of the Fine Arts, Philadelphia

Monroe, James (1758-1831), is best remembered for the Monroe Doctrine, which he proclaimed in 1823. This historic policy warned European countries not to interfere with the free nations of the Western Hemisphere.

Monroe became President after more than 40 years of public service. He had fought in the Revolutionary War in America. During the first years after independence, he had served in the Virginia Assembly and in the Congress of the Confederation. He later became a United States senator; minister to France, Spain, and Great Britain; and governor of Virginia. During the War of 1812, he served as secretary of state and secretary of war at the same time.

In appearance and manner, Monroe resembled his fellow Virginian, George Washington. He was tall and rawboned, and had a military bearing. His gray-blue eyes invited confidence. Even John Quincy Adams, who criticized almost everyone, spoke well of Monroe.

At his inauguration, Monroe still wore his hair in the old-fashioned way, powdered and tied in a queue at the back. He favored suits of black broadcloth with knee breeches and buckles on the shoes. To the people, he represented the almost legendary heroism of the generation that led the country to freedom.

As President, Monroe presided quietly during a period known as "the era of good feeling." He looked forward to America's glorious future, the outlines of which emerged rapidly during his presidency. The frontier was moving rapidly westward, and small cities sprang up west of the Mississippi River. Monroe sent General Andrew Jackson on a military expedition into Florida which resulted in the acquisition of Florida from Spain. Rapidly extending frontiers soon caused Americans to consider whether slavery should be permitted in the new territories. The Missouri Compromise "settled" this problem for nearly 30 years by setting definite limits to the extension of slavery in land lying within the Louisiana Purchase area.

Early life

Boyhood. James Monroe was born in Westmoreland County, Virginia, on April 28, 1758. His father, Colonel Spence Monroe, came from a Scottish family that had settled in Virginia in the mid-1600's. The family of his mother, Elizabeth Jones Monroe, came from Wales, and also had lived in Virginia for many years. James was the eldest of four boys and a girl.

James studied at home with a tutor until he was 12 years old. Then his father sent him to the school of Parson Archibald Campbell. The boy had to leave home early in the morning and tramp through the forest to reach Campbell's school. He often carried a rifle and shot game on the way. At the age of 16, James entered the College of William and Mary. However, the stirring events of the Revolutionary War soon lured him into the army.

Soldier. Although only 18, Monroe was commissioned a lieutenant. He soon saw action, fighting at Harlem Heights and White Plains in the fall of 1776. His superior officers praised Monroe for gallantry in the Battle of Trenton, where he was wounded in the shoulder. During the next two years, he fought at Brandywine, Germantown, and Monmouth.

In 1778, Monroe was promoted to lieutenant colonel and sent to raise troops in Virginia. He failed in his mission, but it greatly influenced his future career. It brought him into contact with Thomas Jefferson, then governor of the state. Monroe began to study law under

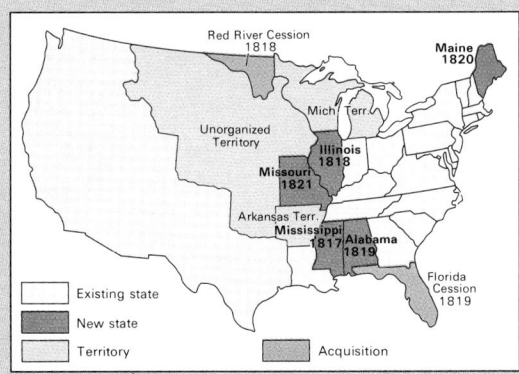

Five states joined the Union during Monroe's term. The Red River and Florida cessions increased the size of the United States.

The U.S. flag had 15 stars when Monroe took office in 1817. Nine stars were added during his term—five in 1818, one in 1819, two in 1820, and one in 1822.

The world of President Monroe

The Supreme Court of the United States established the doctrine of implied powers in 1819. The court ruled that the federal government has powers in addition to those specified in the Constitution. Implied powers are those necessary to carry out specified powers.

The first steamship crossing of the Atlantic Ocean was made by the American ship the *Savannah* in 1819.

Literature published during Monroe's Administration included "Thanatopsis" (1817) by the American poet William Cullen Bryant; "A Visit from St. Nicholas" (1823) attributed to the American scholar Clement Moore; and *Persuasion* (1818) by the British novelist Jane Austen.

The first landing in Antarctica took place in 1821. The crew of an American seal-hunting ship went ashore at Hughes Bay, near the tip of the Antarctic Peninsula.

The first public high school in the United States opened in Boston in 1821.

The Santa Fe Trail, blazed by William Becknell in 1821, opened the Southwestern United States to trade.

Greece proclaimed its independence from Turkey and declared itself a republic in 1821. Also in that year, Brazil gained its independence from Portugal.

The Latin-American wars of independence ended in 1824 when the armies of the Venezuelan general Simón Bolívar defeated the Spaniards. This victory ended Spanish power in South America. In the same year, Mexico became a republic.

Jefferson's guidance, and became a political disciple and lifelong friend of his teacher.

Political and public career

Monroe began his public career in 1782, when he won a seat in the Virginia Assembly. In 1783, he was elected to the Congress of the Confederation, where he served three years (see **Congress of the Confederation**). Monroe did not favor a highly centralized government. But he supported moderate measures intended to let Congress establish tariffs. Monroe worked to give pioneers the right to travel on the Mississippi River. He also aided Jefferson in drafting laws for the development of the West. Two hurried trips to the western region had left Monroe unimpressed with its beauty or fertility. But he still believed that the West would be important in the future growth of the country.

State politics. In 1786, Monroe settled down to practice law in Fredericksburg, Va. But politics drew him like a magnet. He ran for the Virginia Assembly and won easily. He remained in the assembly four years.

Important dates in Monroe's life

1758 (April 28) Born in Westmoreland County, Virginia.
1783 Elected to the Congress of the Confederation.
1786 (Feb. 16) Married Elizabeth Kortright.
1790 Elected to the United States Senate.
1794 Named minister to France.
1799 Elected governor of Virginia.
1811 Appointed secretary of state.
1814 Named secretary of war.
1816 Elected President of the United States.
1820 Reelected President.
1823 Proclaimed the Monroe Doctrine.
1831 (July 4) Died in New York City.

In 1788, Monroe served in the convention called by Virginia to ratify the United States Constitution. His distrust of a strong federal government aligned him with Patrick Henry and George Mason, who opposed the Constitution. But Monroe offered only moderate opposition, and he gracefully accepted ratification.

Monroe's family. In 1786, Monroe married 17-year-old Elizabeth Kortright (June 30, 1768-Sept. 23, 1830), the daughter of a New York City merchant. The couple had two daughters, Eliza and Maria, and a son, but the boy died at the age of 2. Monroe's admiration for Jefferson

Library of Congress

Monroe's birthplace in Westmoreland County, Virginia, no longer exists. This drawing shows one artist's idea of how the house looked. Today, a historical marker stands near the site.

Detail of an oil portrait on canvas (1796) by Benjamin West; © Mrs. Gouverneur Hoes, White House Historical Association (photography by the National Geographic Society)

Elizabeth Kortright Monroe followed the President's wishes in observing strict social etiquette at the White House.

became so strong that in 1789 he moved to Charlottesville, Va. There he built Ash Lawn, not far from Jefferson's estate, Monticello.

U.S. senator. Monroe ran against James Madison for the first United States House of Representatives, but lost. In 1790, the Virginia legislature elected him to fill a vacancy in the U.S. Senate. As a senator, Monroe aligned himself with Madison and with Jefferson, then secretary of state, in vigorous opposition to the Federalist program of Alexander Hamilton. Assisted by such leaders as Albert Gallatin and Aaron Burr, the three Virginians founded the Democratic-Republican Party. This party developed, some historians believe, into the modern Democratic Party (see **Democratic-Republican Party**).

Opposition to Washington. In 1794, President George Washington appointed Monroe minister to France. The President knew that Monroe opposed many administration policies, but he needed a diplomat who could improve relations with the French. He also knew that Monroe strongly admired France.

During talks in France, Monroe criticized the Jay Treaty between the United States and Britain as "the most shameful transaction I have ever known." Furious, Washington recalled Monroe in 1796. See **Jay Treaty.**

Upon his return, Monroe became involved in a bitter personal dispute with Hamilton that nearly led to a duel. The quarrel resulted from the publication of materials that slandered Hamilton. Monroe was blamed, but denied responsibility. Hamilton eventually dropped his charges. The quarrel, and the humiliation of being recalled from France, made these years among the unhappiest in Monroe's life.

Diplomat under Jefferson. In 1799, Monroe was elected governor of Virginia. In this post, he played an important part in preserving democratic processes dur-

ing the tense years following passage of the Alien and Sedition Acts (see **Alien and Sedition Acts**). Early in 1803, President Thomas Jefferson sent Monroe to Paris to help Robert R. Livingston negotiate the purchase of New Orleans. By the time Monroe reached France, Napoleon had offered the astonished Livingston the entire Louisiana Territory. Monroe urged Livingston to accept the offer without waiting to consult Jefferson, and they arranged for the treaty. See **Louisiana Purchase.**

Jefferson was pleased with Monroe's initiative, and sent him to Madrid to help Charles Pinckney purchase the Floridas from Spain. They failed, but Jefferson still had confidence in Monroe. The President named him minister to Great Britain. In 1806, Monroe helped conclude a trade treaty that was so unsatisfactory that Jefferson refused to submit it to the Senate.

Monroe felt his usefulness in London had ended, and returned home in 1807. He became a reluctant candidate for the nomination to succeed Jefferson as President. But Madison won the nomination and the presidency. Monroe served in the Virginia Assembly until he again was elected governor in 1811.

Secretary of state. Monroe resigned as governor after about three months to accept President Madison's appointment as secretary of state. As his first task, he attempted to reach some understanding with the British over the impressment of American sailors. But he soon concluded that war could not be avoided.

At the beginning of the War of 1812, Monroe was eager to take command of the army. But Madison convinced him to stay in the Cabinet. Secretary of War John Armstrong was forced to resign in 1814 because of neglect of duty during the burning of Washington, D.C. Madison asked Monroe to become secretary of war while continuing as secretary of state. Monroe held both offices for the rest of the war. After he took over the War Department, American armies won several brilliant victories. These triumphs greatly increased Monroe's popularity. See **War of 1812.**

In 1816, while still secretary of state, Monroe was elected President of the United States. He received 183 electoral votes to 34 for Senator Rufus King of New York, the Federalist candidate. For votes by states, see **Electoral College** (table). Monroe's running mate was Governor Daniel D. Tompkins of New York.

Monroe's Administration (1817-1825)

The years of Monroe's presidency are generally known as "the era of good feeling." The Federalist Party had disappeared after the election of 1816, and nearly everyone belonged to the Democratic-Republican Party. The country prospered because of fast-growing industries and settlement of the West. A depression in 1818-1819 caused only a temporary setback.

"The American System" provided the chief issue of Monroe's first term. House Speaker Henry Clay of Kentucky advanced this plan. The American System proposed to strengthen nationalism in two ways: (1) construction of new roads and canals to open the West, and (2) enactment of a protective tariff to encourage Northern manufacturers and develop home markets.

Monroe distrusted the American System because he doubted that the federal government had the power for these activities. Monroe studied the program during a

$3\frac{1}{2}$-month tour of the North and West. But this trip did not change his "settled conviction" that Congress did not have the power to build roads and canals.

Clay continued his fight, and finally won Congress over to his side. In 1822, Monroe vetoed a bill providing for federal administration of toll gates on the Cumberland Road. He urged a constitutional amendment to give Congress the power to promote internal improvements. In 1824, Monroe signed the Survey Act, which planned improvements in the future.

Clay had more success in pushing through the protective tariff, the second part of his American System. Congress had already raised tariff rates in 1816, and it further increased the duty on iron in 1818. In 1824, Congress raised tariff rates in general.

Life in the White House. The British had burned the White House during the War of 1812, and the mansion had not been rebuilt when Monroe took office. The new President maintained his residence on I Street, near 20th Street, for nine months. On New Year's Day, 1818, President and Mrs. Monroe held a public reception marking the reopening of the White House.

Monroe had observed court etiquette during his trips to Europe, and decided to adopt a strict social attitude for the White House. Partly because of ill health, Mrs. Monroe received only visitors to whom she had sent invitations. She refused to pay calls, sending her elder daughter, Mrs. Eliza Hay, in her place. Soon all Washington buzzed about the "snobbish" Mrs. Monroe.

As time passed, the public realized that Mrs. Monroe had followed the President's wishes in establishing protocol. During Monroe's second term, her Wednesday receptions became popular. The visit of the Marquis de Lafayette on New Year's Day, 1825, added a touch of splendor to the last months of Monroe's term.

Beginnings of sectionalism. In 1818, Missouri applied for admission to the Union as a slave state. The House of Representatives aroused anger in the South by passing a bill to admit Missouri with the provision that no more slaves could be brought into the state. The Sen-

Jack E. Boucher, Historic American Buildings Survey, National Park Service

Monroe's I Street residence served as the president's home for the first nine months of his term while the White House was being rebuilt. It had been destroyed during the War of 1812.

Vice President and Cabinet

Vice President	*Daniel D. Tompkins
Secretary of state	*John Quincy Adams
Secretary of the treasury	*William H. Crawford
Secretary of war	*John C. Calhoun
Attorney general	Richard Rush
	William Wirt (1817)
Secretary of the navy	Benjamin W. Crownin-shield
	Smith Thompson (1819)
	Samuel L. Southard (1823)

*Has a separate biography in WORLD BOOK.

ate defeated this provision, and Congress eventually agreed on a bill known as the Missouri Compromise. This law permitted slavery in Missouri, but banned it from the rest of the Louisiana Purchase region north of the southern boundary of Missouri. Monroe avoided interfering with these debates. But he said he would not sign a bill placing any special restraints on Missouri's admission to the Union. See **Missouri Compromise.**

War with the Seminole. Since the War of 1812, Americans in Georgia had been harassed by bands of Indians in Spanish Florida. In 1817, fighting broke out between the Seminole Indians and settlers in southern Georgia. Monroe ordered Major General Andrew Jackson to raise a militia and put down the uprising. Jackson chased the Indians into the Everglades of Florida. Then he captured Pensacola, the Spanish capital of Florida.

Jackson's easy conquest convinced the Spanish that they could not defend Florida. In 1819, they agreed to give Florida to the United States in return for the cancellation of $5 million in American claims against Spain.

Diplomatic achievements. Monroe's Administration marked one of the most brilliant periods in American diplomacy. The Rush-Bagot Agreement, signed with Great Britain in 1817, prohibited fortifications on the Great

---

Quotations from Monroe

The following quotations come from some of Monroe's speeches and writings.

National Honor is National property of the highest value.
First Inaugural Address, March 4, 1817

The American continents . . . are henceforth not to be considered as subjects for future colonization by any European powers.
Annual Message to Congress, Dec. 2, 1823

We owe it, therefore, to candor, and to the amicable relations existing between the United States and those powers to declare that we should consider any attempt on their part to extend their system to any portion of this hemisphere as dangerous to our peace and safety. With the existing colonies or dependencies of any European power we . . . shall not interfere. But with the Government . . . we could not view any interposition for the purpose of oppressing them, or controlling in any other manner their destiny, by any European power, in any other light than as the manifestation of an unfriendly disposition toward the United States.
Annual Message to Congress, Dec. 2, 1823

In a government founded on the sovereignty of the people the education of youth is an object of the first importance. In such a government knowledge should be diffused throughout the whole society, and for that purpose the means of acquiring it made not only practicable but easy to every citizen. . . .
Speech to the Virginia Legislature, Dec. 7, 1801

The Monroe Doctrine warned European nations against interfering in the affairs of countries in the Western Hemisphere. This picture shows Monroe, *standing,* explaining the doctrine to his Cabinet. Monroe proclaimed the doctrine to guarantee the freedom of newly independent nations in Latin America.

Culver

Lakes. In 1818, Britain agreed to the 49th parallel as the boundary between the United States and Canada from Lake of the Woods on the Minnesota-Ontario border as far west as the Rocky Mountains. The British also consented to joint occupation of the Oregon region. American diplomats convinced Spain to give up its claims to Oregon in 1819, and the Russians agreed to a similar pact in 1824.

Reelection. In the election of 1820, Monroe was unopposed for the presidency. Monroe received every vote cast in the electoral college but one. William Plumer, an elector from New Hampshire, cast his vote for John Quincy Adams.

The Monroe Doctrine. During the Napoleonic Wars, the Spaniards had become deeply involved in European affairs, and took little interest in their American colonies. Most of the colonies took advantage of this situation and declared independence from Spain. The Latin-American revolutions aroused great sympathy in the United States. As early as 1817, Henry Clay had begun a campaign for recognition of these new countries. In March 1822, Monroe finally recommended that their independence be recognized. In December 1823, the President proclaimed the historic Monroe Doctrine in a message to Congress. This doctrine has remained a basic American policy ever since.

The era of good feeling ended before Monroe finished his second term. Unlike the situation which followed the retirement of Jefferson and Madison, there was no outstanding figure who was the overwhelming choice to become the next President. Four men fought for the office. None won a majority of the votes, and the House of Representatives chose John Quincy Adams. See **Adams, John Quincy** (Election of 1824).

Later years

Monroe retired to Oak Hill, his estate near Leesburg, Va. He served for five years as a regent of the University of Virginia. In 1829, he became presiding officer of the Virginia Constitutional Convention. His wife died on Sept. 23, 1830, and was buried at Oak Hill. Long public service had left Monroe a poor man, and he was too old to resume his law practice. Late in 1830, his financial distress forced him to move to New York City to live with his daughter. Monroe died there on July 4, 1831. In 1858, his remains were moved to Hollywood Cemetery in

Richmond, Va. His law office in Fredericksburg has been preserved as a memorial.   Ralph Ketcham

Related articles in *World Book* include:

Adams, John Quincy	Jefferson, Thomas	President
Clay, Henry	Louisiana Purchase	of the U.S.
Hamilton, Alexander	Madison, James	Tariff
Jackson, Andrew	Missouri	Tompkins,
Jay Treaty	Compromise	Daniel D.
	Monroe Doctrine	War of 1812

Outline

I. Early life
    A. Boyhood   B. Soldier
II. Political and public career
    A. State politics
    B. Monroe's family
    C. U.S. senator
    D. Opposition to Washington
    E. Diplomat under Jefferson
    F. Secretary of state
III. Monroe's Administration (1817-1825)
    A. "The American System"   D. War with the Seminole
    B. Life in the White House   E. Diplomatic achievements
    C. Beginnings of   F. Reelection
        sectionalism   G. The Monroe Doctrine
IV. Later years

Questions

What two Cabinet posts did Monroe hold at once?
Why did Monroe oppose "The American System"?
What term is often used to describe the period of Monroe's Administration? Why?
How did Monroe display initiative during negotiations for the purchase of Louisiana?
How did slavery become an issue in Monroe's presidency?
How did Monroe meet Thomas Jefferson?
Why were Monroe and his wife unpopular during their early years in the White House?
How did Monroe arouse the hostility of George Washington while serving as minister to France?
What was the Monroe Doctrine?
How did Monroe contribute to the founding of his country?

Additional resources

Ammon, Harry. *James Monroe: The Quest for National Identity.* McGraw, 1971.
Cresson, William P. *James Monroe.* Shoe String, 1971. First published in 1946.
Fitz-gerald, Christine M. *James Monroe: Fifth President of the United States.* Childrens Pr., 1987. For younger readers.
Stefoff, Rebecca. *James Monroe: 5th President of the United States.* Garrett Educational, 1988. For younger readers.
Wetzel, Charles. *James Monroe.* Chelsea Hse., 1989. Suitable for younger readers.

Monroe, Marilyn (1926-1962), was an American motion-picture actress. Her great beauty made her a world-famous sex symbol. But in spite of her success in films, Monroe had a tragic life. She died at the age of 36 from an overdose of sleeping pills. Since her death, she has become one of the most written-about film stars in history.

Monroe's real name was either Norma Jean Baker or Norma Jean Mortenson. She was born in Los Angeles and made her film debut in 1948 in *Dangerous Years.*

Monroe soon won attention with small roles in *The Asphalt Jungle* (1950) and *All About Eve* (1950). Her most successful dramatic roles were in *Bus Stop* (1956) and *The Misfits* (1961). She appeared as a comedienne in *Gentlemen Prefer Blondes* (1953), *The Seven-Year Itch* (1955), and *Some Like It Hot* (1959). Monroe appeared in 28 films. She was married to former baseball star Joe Di-Maggio in 1954, and they were divorced that same year. Monroe was married to playwright Arthur Miller from 1956 to 1961.

United Press Int.

Marilyn Monroe

Louis Giannetti

Additional resources

Conway, Michael, and Ricci, Mark. *The Complete Films of Marilyn Monroe.* Citadel, 1986.
Monroe, Marilyn. *My Story.* Stein & Day, 1974.
Summers, Anthony. *Goddess: The Secret Lives of Marilyn Monroe.* Macmillan, 1985.

Monroe Doctrine was set forth by President James Monroe in a message he delivered to the Congress of the United States on Dec. 2, 1823. It supported the independent nations of the Western Hemisphere against European interference "for the purpose of oppressing them, or controlling in any other manner their destiny." The doctrine said also that the American continents were "henceforth not to be considered as subjects for future colonization by any European powers." This statement meant that the United States would not allow new colonies to be created in the Americas, nor would it permit existing colonies to extend their boundaries.

Origins. The Monroe Doctrine grew out of conditions in Europe as well as in America. The three leading absolute monarchies of Europe were Russia, Austria, and Prussia. They had pledged themselves to "put an end to the system of representative government, in whatever country it may exist in Europe." The United States feared that these three powers (sometimes called the *Holy Alliance*) might also try to suppress representative government in the Americas.

During and after the Napoleonic Wars, most of the Spanish colonies in America had taken advantage of unsettled conditions in Europe to break away from the mother country. As they won independence, these colonies formed themselves into republics with constitutions much like that of the United States. Only Brazil chose to keep its monarchy when it declared its independence from Portugal.

After Napoleon's downfall in 1815, the monarchy was restored in Spain, and it seemed possible that the Holy Alliance might try to restore Spain's colonies as well. The French monarchy, which had followed the policy of the Holy Alliance to the point of actually suppressing a democratic revolution in Spain, was also suspected of intending to help Spain regain its former American possessions. A rumor that France was on the point of doing so spread over Europe during 1823.

This threat disturbed not only the United States, but Great Britain as well. As free republics, the Spanish-American nations traded with Britain. If they became colonies again, whether of Spain or of France, their trade with Great Britain would certainly be cut down. Britain had steadily opposed the doctrine of the Holy Alliance and had few allies in Europe. George Canning, the British foreign minister, proposed to Richard Rush, the American minister in London, that Britain and the United States issue a joint warning against aggression by European countries in the Americas.

President Monroe was at first inclined to accept the British offer. Former Presidents Jefferson and Madison strongly favored the idea. With Great Britain "on our side," Jefferson argued, "we need not fear the whole world." But Monroe's Secretary of State, John Quincy Adams, said that the United States should not "come in as a cock-boat in the wake of the British man-of-war." He urged that the United States alone make the kind of statement Canning had in mind. He said that the British would use their sea power to prevent European intervention in America whether they had an agreement with the United States or not. Thus the United States would have all the advantages of joint action without entering into what amounted to an alliance with Britain. Moreover, a strictly American declaration would clearly apply to Britain as well as to other European countries.

Monroe finally decided to follow Adams' advice and proclaimed the Monroe Doctrine. He used practically the same words in the doctrine that Adams had used when he first proposed it to him. See also **Adams, John Quincy** (Secretary of state).

Results. Until the late 1800's, Europe's respect for the rights of the smaller American nations rested less upon the Monroe Doctrine than upon fear of the British Navy. A possible exception to this rule occurred in the 1860's, shortly after the Civil War, while the wartime Army and Navy of the United States were still strong. During those years, the attitude of the American government encouraged Emperor Napoleon III to give up an attempt to set up a European kingdom in Mexico. It was not until the 1880's, when the United States began to enlarge its new Navy of modern steel ships, that the United States again had enough power to enforce the Monroe Doctrine. Great Britain and other countries generally ignored the doctrine until the 1890's.

The Monroe Doctrine also served to express U.S. interest in increasing its trade with the other countries of the Western Hemisphere. However, Europe continued to get the larger share of Latin-American trade, most of which went to Great Britain.

In some ways, the Monroe Doctrine strained relations between the United States and the Latin-American countries. The nations that the doctrine supposedly protected resented the way the United States assumed superiority over them. They also feared "The Colossus of the North" more than they feared any European nation.

The Monroe Doctrine in action. In the 1800's, the doctrine was seldom invoked. President James Polk referred to it in 1845 during a dispute with Great Britain over Oregon. Secretary of State William Seward acted partly on the basis of the doctrine when he denounced French intervention in Mexico in the 1860's. President Grover Cleveland used it when he threatened to take strong action against Great Britain in 1895 if the British would not arbitrate their dispute with Venezuela.

The Roosevelt Corollary. In the early 1900's, President Theodore Roosevelt gave new meaning to the Monroe Doctrine. He claimed that wrongdoing on the part of the smaller American nations might tempt European countries to intervene in those nations, either to collect debts or to defend the lives and property of Europeans. According to Roosevelt, the Monroe Doctrine required the United States to prevent European intervention by intervening itself. Under this "big stick" policy, the United States sent troops into the Dominican Republic in 1905, into Nicaragua in 1912, and into Haiti in 1915. See **Roosevelt, Theodore** (Foreign policy).

In general, President Woodrow Wilson continued Roosevelt's policy. Wilson promised that the United States would "never again seek one additional foot of territory by conquest." But as President, he interfered in a revolution in Mexico and tried unsuccessfully to obtain support for intervention from other Latin-American countries. See **Wilson, Woodrow** (Crisis in Mexico).

The "Good Neighbor Policy." After World War I ended in 1918, the United States worked to improve relations with Latin America. Herbert Hoover made a good-will tour of South America before he took office as U.S. President in 1929. During his Administration, Hoover moved away from the policy of U.S. intervention in Latin America.

Hoover's successor as President was Franklin D. Roosevelt. Roosevelt's policy toward the Latin-American countries became known as the "Good Neighbor Policy." Under it, Roosevelt abandoned the practice of intervention and tried to expand trade with Latin America. He also sought Latin-American cooperation in defending North and South America from countries located outside the Western Hemisphere.

During the Hoover and Roosevelt administrations, the United States gradually withdrew its forces from the smaller American countries it had occupied and gave up the special privileges it had claimed. By a series of trade agreements, it cut down high tariff barriers that had done much to keep the Americas apart. Conferences on inter-American affairs were held at Montevideo, Uruguay, in 1933; at Buenos Aires, Argentina, in 1936; at Lima, Peru, in 1938; and at Havana, Cuba, in 1940.

During World War II (1939-1945), fear of Nazi aggression brought the American republics somewhat closer. The republics met at Rio de Janeiro, Brazil, in 1942; at Mexico City, Mexico, in 1945; and at Petropolis, Brazil, near Rio de Janeiro, in 1947. They set up the Organization of American States at a meeting in Bogotá, Colombia, in 1948. See also **Roosevelt, Franklin D.** (Good Neighbor Policy); **Pan-American conferences.**

The Monroe Doctrine and isolationism. Some people have confused the Monroe Doctrine with the policy of *isolationism,* or staying out of international political and economic affairs. The original statement of the Monroe Doctrine did affirm an earlier U.S. policy of isolation from Europe. That policy had been set forth by President George Washington in his Farewell Address of 1796. However, the Monroe Doctrine did not express a U.S. policy of isolation from the rest of the Western Hemisphere. On the contrary, it implied that in that hemisphere the United States would play a more active role.

Mark T. Gilderhus

See also **Monroe, James** (The Monroe Doctrine).

Additional resources

May, Ernest R. *The Making of the Monroe Doctrine.* Harvard, 1975.
The Monroe Doctrine: Its Modern Significance. Ed. by Donald M. Dozer. Rev. ed. Arizona State Univ. Ctr. for Latin American Studies, 1976.
Perkins, Dexter. *A History of the Monroe Doctrine.* Little, Brown, 1963. Reprint of 1955 revised edition.

Monrovia, *muhn ROH vee uh* (pop. 421,058), is the capital and chief city of Liberia. It stands on the Atlantic Coast at the mouth of the St. Paul River and has a modern, well-developed harbor. For location, see **Liberia** (map). It is the educational and cultural center of the country. The University of Liberia is in the city.

Monrovia was named for James Monroe, President of the United States from 1817 to 1825. The city was founded in 1822 by the American Colonization Society as a place to resettle freed slaves from the United States.

Mark W. DeLancey

Monsoon, *mahn SOON,* is a seasonal wind that blows over the northern part of the Indian Ocean, especially the Arabian Sea, and over most of the surrounding land areas. The monsoon blows continually from the southwest from April to October. It blows from the northeast from November to March.

Monsoons are generated by the difference in the heating and cooling of air over land and sea. During the summer, radiant energy from the sun heats land surfaces far more than it does sea surfaces. The strongly heated air over the land rises and is replaced by a southwesterly wind carrying warm, moist air from the Indian Ocean. Water vapor in the rising air condenses and forms clouds and rain. This process releases large amounts of heat, which helps drive monsoons.

In winter, the land is cooled much more than the sea. The cool air over the land sinks and spreads out to the sea as a dry northeasterly wind.

The southwesterly monsoon brings heavy rains to southern and southeastern Asia, including Bangladesh, Burma, India, and Thailand. The strength of the southwesterly monsoon—and the time in April that it begins—affects agriculture in southern Asia. Abnormal monsoons can destroy a region's crops and livestock and disrupt its economy. Monsoons also blow over the coasts of northern Australia, eastern Asia, parts of Africa and the Southwestern United States.

Richard A. Dirks

See also **Asia** (Climate).

Monster. See Dracula; Dragon; Frankenstein; Loch Ness monster. See also the *Monsters and creatures* section of the *Related articles* with the **Mythology** article.

Mont Blanc, *mawn BLAHN* or *mahnt BLAHNGK,* is the highest mountain in the Alps and one of the most famous peaks in Europe. Mont Blanc is often called the *monarch of mountains.* Its name is French for *white mountain.*

Mont Blanc rises 15,771 feet (4,807 meters) on the border between France, Italy, and Switzerland. The base of the mountain is a huge mass of granite which extends into all three countries. Its highest peak is in southern France. Mont Blanc is about 30 miles (48 kilometers) long and 10 miles (16 kilometers) wide. Thick woods and swift streams cover its lower slopes. But above 8,000 feet (2,400 meters), there is always a thick blanket of snow. Mont Blanc has several large glaciers. Its most famous glacier is Mer de Glace (Sea of Ice). A scientific laboratory was built on Mont Blanc in 1893.

Jacques Balmat and Michel Paccard first climbed Mont Blanc in 1786. Today, it is easily climbed, and it is a resort center. People can ride up 6,287 feet (1,916 meters) to Mer de Glace on a cog railway. For those who prefer to climb, there are shelters to aid them in their 50- to 60-hour journey. The world's highest aerial tramway goes up Aiguille du Midi, a lower peak of Mont Blanc. In 1965, the Mont Blanc tunnel, linking France and Italy, was opened for auto traffic. Howell C. Lloyd

See also **Alps** (map); **Mountain** (picture chart).

Mont Cenis Tunnel. See Fréjus Tunnels.

Mont Pelée, MAWN *puh LAY,* is an active volcano on the north end of Martinique in the French West Indies. It rises 4,583 feet (1,397 meters) above sea level.

The volcano erupted violently in 1902, after lying dormant since 1851. Floods of mud loosened by the eruption devastated the slopes of the mountain. A heap of lava 1,000 feet (300 meters) high formed in the crater. A slender spire of rock was thrust up another 1,000 feet from the crater. An avalanche of red-hot lava and clouds of hot gas swept down the mountain, destroying the city of St.-Pierre and killing about 38,000 people. Only one person, a man in prison in the city's dungeon, escaped alive. Milder eruptions occurred between 1929 and 1932. The French government maintains a volcano observatory on Mont Pelée. Gustavo A. Antonini

Mont-Saint-Michel, *mawn san mee SHEHL,* is a large rock that juts from the waters of Mont-St.-Michel Bay off the northwestern coast of France. An abbey founded in the 900's sits at the top of the rock, and a small town lies on the slopes. For location, see **France** (terrain map). See also **France** (picture: Mont-St.-Michel).

Hugh D. Clout

Montagnais Indians, MAHN *tuh NYAY,* are a tribe that once hunted and fished throughout the southern Labrador Peninsula in Canada. The name *Montagnais* comes from a French word meaning *mountain people.* The tribe received this name from French explorers, probably because of the rugged terrain of their land.

The Montagnais were nomads who traveled in small bands consisting of about 50 to 100 related people. They lived almost completely by hunting and fishing because the growing season was too short for farming. Each band needed a large territory in which to hunt and fish.

Montagnais bands moved as the seasons changed in search of game. They spent the winter in the forests hunting moose and caribou, using toboggans and snowshoes for travel. They lived in lodges constructed partly underground and covered with snow or earth. In the summer, they camped along the St. Lawrence River and other waterways, and traveled by canoe to fish for salmon and eel. Their summer homes were cone-shaped tents covered with skins or bark.

The Montagnais owned few material goods. Nearly all their possessions consisted of tools, weapons, and utensils used to catch and prepare food.

In 1603, the French explorer Samuel de Champlain became the first European to encounter the Montagnais. The tribe soon became partners of the French in the fur trade. The Montagnais maintained a trading center on the St. Lawrence from which they controlled the trade between neighboring tribes and the French. During the 1600's, many Montagnais died in battle with the Iroquois. Guns obtained from European traders enabled the Montagnais to kill more game. By the early 1700's, however, large animals had become scarce, and many Montagnais died of starvation or disease.

Today, many Montagnais continue to rely on hunting and fishing to make a living. About 7,000 Montagnais live on nine reserves in Quebec. James A. Tuck

Montaigne, *mahn TAYN,* **Michel Eyquem de,** *mee SHEHL eh KEHM duh* (1533-1592), a French writer, is considered by many the creator of the personal essay. Writers up to the present time have imitated his informal, conversational style. Montaigne's essays reveal his independent mind and sound judgment, his charm and wit, and his wealth of experience in life and literature. The most original aspect of the essays was Montaigne's goal to make himself the subject matter of his writings. He first began publishing his essays in 1580, adding to them as life and experience provided him with new insights and understanding. He wrote a total of 107 essays, including the long "Apology for Raymond Sebond" with its famous skeptical motto, "What do I know?"

Montaigne was born in his family's castle near Bordeaux, into a family that had recently bought its way into the nobility. Montaigne studied law, and became a minor legal official in 1554. He retired in 1570 to devote himself to writing. From 1581 to 1585, he was mayor of Bordeaux. Montaigne immortalized his friendship with French writer Étienne de La Boétie in the essay "Of Friendship." Mary B. McKinley

See also **Essay** (Personal essays).

Montale, *mohn TAH lay,* **Eugenio,** *ay oo JAYN yoh* (1896-1981), was an Italian lyric poet and literary critic. He received the 1975 Nobel Prize for literature.

Montale was born in Genoa and spent much of his youth in Monterosso, a small town on the shore of the Ligurian Sea. This rugged coastline setting inspired many of the images of his early verse. Montale's first book of poetry was *Cuttlefish Bones* (1925). The poems stress the themes of the modern individual's loss of faith, the impossibility of human happiness, and the powerlessness of poetry to transform reality. The collection *The Occasions* (1939) further developed these themes. Later volumes of poems include *The Storm and Other Poems* (1956), and *Notebook of Four Years* (1977, published in English as *It Depends: A Poet's Notebook*).

Montale wrote a number of autobiographical short stories published in *The Butterfly of Dinard* (1956). Many of his essays were collected in *Act of Faith* (1966) and *Away from Home* (1968). Montale also became known for his masterful Italian translations of such English-language poets as Emily Dickinson, T. S. Eliot, and William Shakespeare. Richard H. Lansing

E. R. Degginger

Glacier National Park, located in northwestern Montana, has many steep, rugged peaks such as Grinnell Point, *above*. The park also has more than 50 glaciers and about 250 lakes. The Rocky Mountains cover the western two-fifths of the state. To the east lie the Great Plains.

Montana *The Treasure State*

Montana is the fourth largest state of the United States. Only Alaska, Texas, and California have larger areas than Montana. Western Montana is a land of tall, rugged mountains. There, miners dig deep into the earth to tap the state's vast deposits of copper, gold, and silver. Eastern Montana is a land of broad plains. The view from these vast, open plains has earned Montana a nickname, *The Big Sky Country*. On the plains, herds of cattle graze on the prairie grasses, wheat grows in the fertile soil, and wells bring up petroleum from deep under the ground. Eastern Montana also has the largest coal reserves in the United States. Billings is the largest city in Montana.

The name *Montana* comes from a Spanish word meaning *mountainous*. Early travelers, who saw the sun glistening on the lofty, snow-capped peaks, called the area the *Land of Shining Mountains*. These mountains

---

The contributors of this article are Harry W. Fritz, Professor of History at the University of Montana; and Katherine Hansen, Associate Professor of Geography at Montana State University.

contained a wealth of gold and silver, which gave the state another nickname, the *Treasure State*. Glacier National Park has mountain peaks so steep and remote that they have never been climbed.

Early Montana was Indian country. But gold was discovered in Montana in 1862, and great numbers of eager prospectors rushed to the area. Mining camps sprang up overnight, and wealth came to the territory. But the gold also brought problems. Outlaws spread terror in the mining camps until groups of citizens called *vigilantes* took the law into their own hands. The vigilantes hanged many outlaws and drove others away. Montana was the scene of another struggle—the Indians' last efforts to keep their land. The last stand of Lieutenant Colonel George A. Custer was fought in Montana. In addition, the final battles of the Nez Perce War were fought in the state.

The mountains, the battlefields, the old gold camps, and the vast, lonely distances of Montana still make a visitor feel close to the American frontier. In the state's capital, Helena, the main street is called Last Chance Gulch. The name comes from a gold camp that once stood on that site. Even today, when a basement is dug for a building in Helena, the digging sometimes produces gold dust.

Interesting facts about Montana

Grasshopper Glacier, near Cooke City, is named for the swarms of grasshoppers that became trapped in its ice long ago and can still be seen.

Benton Lake National Wildlife Refuge, in north-central Montana, is one of the most productive waterfowl nesting sites in the United States. About 25,000 waterfowl and 10,000 shore birds are raised there annually.

Bibles were first placed in hotel rooms in October 1908 in Iron Mountain (now Superior). The Gideons placed them in the Superior Hotel.

One of the richest deposits of gold ever found in the United States was discovered at Alder Gulch (now Virginia City) in 1863. Within a year, about 10,000 people had settled within 10 miles (16 kilometers) of the site.

Gideon Bibles

Giant Springs

Giant Springs, in Great Falls, is among the largest springs in the world. Each day, about 390 million gallons (1.5 billion liters) of water gush out of the ground there.

More gem sapphires are found in Montana than in any other state.

Great Falls is Montana's second largest city, and one of only two metropolitan areas in the state. It was named for nearby falls of the Missouri River.

A petroleum refinery in Billings processes Montana oil. Montana has valuable reserves of petroleum and coal.

Montana in brief

Symbols of Montana

The state flag, adopted in 1905, displays an adaptation of the state seal within a field of blue. The word *MONTANA* was added to the flag in 1981. On the state seal, adopted in 1893, the mountains and the Great Falls of the Missouri River symbolize Montana's vast natural resources. The plow stands for agriculture, and the pick and shovel represent mining. The state motto is on a ribbon.

State flag

State seal

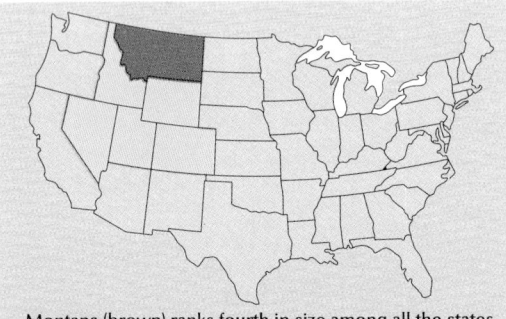

Montana (brown) ranks fourth in size among all the states and first in size among the Rocky Mountain States (yellow).

General information

Statehood: Nov. 8, 1889, the 41st state.
State abbreviations: Mont. (traditional); MT (postal).
State motto: *Oro y Plata* (Gold and Silver).
State song: "Montana." Words by Charles C. Cohen; music by Joseph E. Howard.

The State Capitol is in Helena, Montana's capital since 1875. Earlier capitals were Bannack (1864-1865) and Virginia City (1865-1875).

Land and climate

Area: 147,047 sq. mi. (380,849 km²), including 1,490 sq. mi. (3,859 km²) of inland water.
Elevation: *Highest*—Granite Peak, 12,799 ft. (3,901 m) above sea level. *Lowest*—1,800 ft. (549 m) above sea level along the Kootenai River in Lincoln County.
Record high temperature: 117 °F (47 °C) at Glendive on July 20, 1893, and at Medicine Lake on July 5, 1937.
Record low temperature: −70 °F (−57 °C) at Rogers Pass on Jan. 20, 1954.
Average July temperature: 68 °F (20 °C).
Average January temperature: 18 °F (−8 °C).
Average yearly precipitation: 15 in. (38 cm).

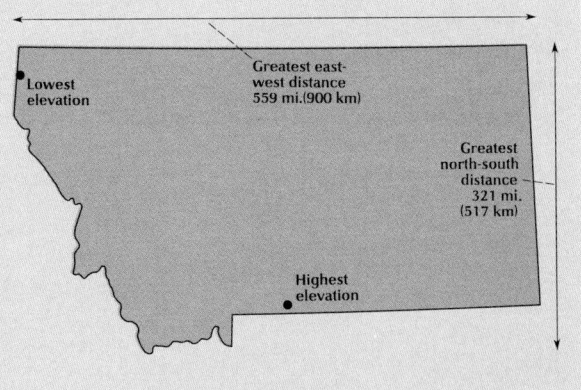

Lowest elevation

Greatest east-west distance 559 mi.(900 km)

Greatest north-south distance 321 mi. (517 km)

Highest elevation

Important dates

Lewis and Clark explored parts of Montana on their journey to and from the Pacific.

Gold was discovered on Grasshopper Creek.

| 1803 | 1805-1806 | 1846 | 1862 | 1889 |

Eastern Montana became U.S. territory through the Louisiana Purchase.

Northwestern Montana became U.S. territory through the Oregon treaty with England.

Montana became the 41st state on Nov. 8.

State bird
Western meadowlark

State flower
Bitterroot

State tree
Ponderosa pine

People

Population: 803,655 (1990 census)
Rank among the states: 44th
Density: 5 persons per sq. mi. (2 per km²), U.S. average 69 per sq. mi. (27 per km²)
Distribution: 52 per cent urban, 48 per cent rural
Largest cities in Montana

Billings	81,151
Great Falls	55,097
Missoula	42,918
Butte	33,941
Helena	24,569
Bozeman	22,600

Source: U.S. Bureau of the Census.

Population trend

Thousands

Year	Population
1990	803,655
1980	786,690
1970	694,409
1960	674,767
1950	591,024
1940	559,456
1930	537,606
1920	548,889
1910	376,053
1900	243,329
1890	142,924
1880	39,159
1870	20,595

Source: U.S. Bureau of the Census.

Economy

Chief products

Agriculture: beef cattle, wheat, hay, barley.
Manufacturing: wood products, food products.
Mining: coal, copper, gold, petroleum.

Gross state product

Value of goods and services produced in 1991: $14,639,000,000. *Services* include community, social, and personal services; finance; government; trade; and transportation, communication, and utilities. *Industry* includes construction, manufacturing, and mining. *Agriculture* includes agriculture, fishing, and forestry.

Source: U.S. Bureau of Economic Analysis.

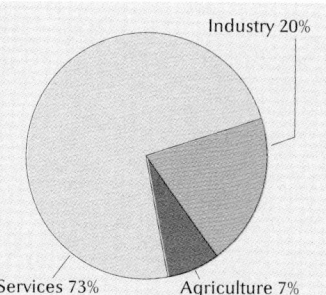

Industry 20%
Services 73%
Agriculture 7%

Government

State government

Governor: 4-year term
State senators: 50; 4-year terms
State representatives: 100; 2-year terms
Counties: 56

Federal government

United States senators: 2
United States representatives: 1
Electoral votes: 3

Sources of information

Tourism: Department of Commerce, Montana Promotion Division, 1424 9th Avenue, Helena, MT 59620
Economy: Department of Commerce, Census and Economic Information Center, 1424 9th Avenue, Helena, MT 59620
Government: Montana Legislative Council, Room 138, State Capitol, Helena, MT 59620
History: Montana Historical Society, 225 N. Roberts Street, Helena, MT 59620

The U.S. Congress established Glacier National Park.

The first oil wells in the Montana section of the Williston Basin started production.

1910 **1940** **1951** **1973**

Fort Peck dam was completed.

A new state constitution went into effect.

Population. The 1990 United States census reported that Montana had 803,655 people. The state's population had increased 2 per cent over the 1980 census figure, 786,690. According to the 1990 census, Montana ranks 44th in population among the 50 states. Montana has about 48,000 American Indians, most of whom live on reservations. They make up about 6 per cent of the state's population.

About 52 per cent of the people live in urban areas, and about 48 per cent live in rural areas. Billings and Great Falls are the only cities of more than 55,000 people, and they are the only metropolitan areas in the state (see **Metropolitan area**). For the populations of Billings and Great Falls, see the *Index* to the political map of Montana.

Universities and colleges

Montana has nine universities and colleges that offer bachelor's or advanced degrees and are accredited by the Northwest Association of Schools and Colleges. For enrollments and further information, see **Universities and colleges** (table).

Name	Mailing address
Carroll College	Helena
Eastern Montana College	Billings
Great Falls, College of	Great Falls
Montana, University of	Missoula
Montana College of Mineral Science and Technology	Butte
Montana State University	Bozeman
Northern Montana College	Havre
Rocky Mountain College	Billings
Western Montana College of the University of Montana	Dillon

Stu White

Cowboys on a wild horse hunt near Cascade try to capture wild horses for use on a ranch. Some of Montana's farmland is used for livestock grazing. Many of the state's farms cover as many as 7,000 acres (2,800 hectares).

Population density

Slightly more than half the people of Montana live in urban areas. The most densely populated areas are in the west and the south. Billings is the largest city.

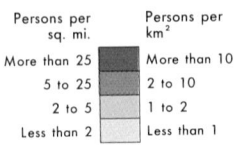

Persons per sq. mi.	Persons per km²
More than 25	More than 10
5 to 25	2 to 10
2 to 5	1 to 2
Less than 2	Less than 1

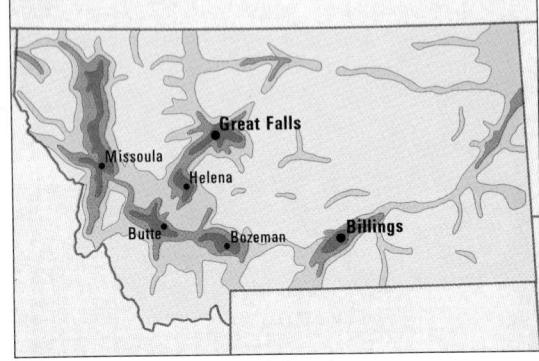

WORLD BOOK map; based on U.S. Bureau of the Census data.

Most of Montana's cities began as mining towns, or as centers of trade for farm and ranch areas. For example, Butte grew from a mining camp. So did Helena, the state capital. Missoula developed as an agricultural trade center.

Schools. Montana's first schools were started in mining camps in the early 1860's. These schools had private teachers who charged tuition. The Roman Catholic Church organized a boarding school for Indians in the Flathead Valley in 1864. The Legislature provided for free public schools in 1893 and for county high schools in 1897.

Today, Montana's public schools are supervised by an elected superintendent of public instruction and a Board of Public Education that is appointed by the governor. The superintendent serves a four-year term. Each county and most school districts have a superintendent of schools. Montana's two largest universities are Montana State University in Bozeman and the University of Montana in Missoula.

Libraries. The library of the state historical society in Helena features the world's largest collection of materials on the history of the Montana region. The libraries of the University of Montana and Montana State University also have good collections of regional materials. The library at Eastern Montana College in Billings has a large collection of material on Custer and the Battle of the Little Bighorn. Montana has about 110 public libraries.

Museums. The Montana Historical Society in Helena features exhibits on the development of the state and a fine collection of paintings and sculpture by famous cowboy artist Charles M. Russell. Great Falls also has a Russell museum. The Museum of the Rockies in Bozeman has exhibits of the geology, fossils, archaeology, and history of the Rocky Mountains. The Museum of the Plains Indians and Craft Center in Browning has collections of historic and contemporary arts of the Plains Indians. The World Museum of Mining is in Butte. Other museums are at Big Hole National Battlefield, Wisdom; and Little Big Horn Battlefield National Monument.

Montana map index

*Does not appear on map; key shows general location.
†Census designated place—unincorporated, but recognized as a significant settled community by the U.S. Bureau of the Census.
°County seat.

‡City of Anaconda and Deer Lodge County are consolidated as Anaconda-Deer Lodge County.
**City of Butte and Silver Bow County are consolidated as Butte-Silver Bow.
Source: 1990 census. Places without population figures are unincorporated areas.

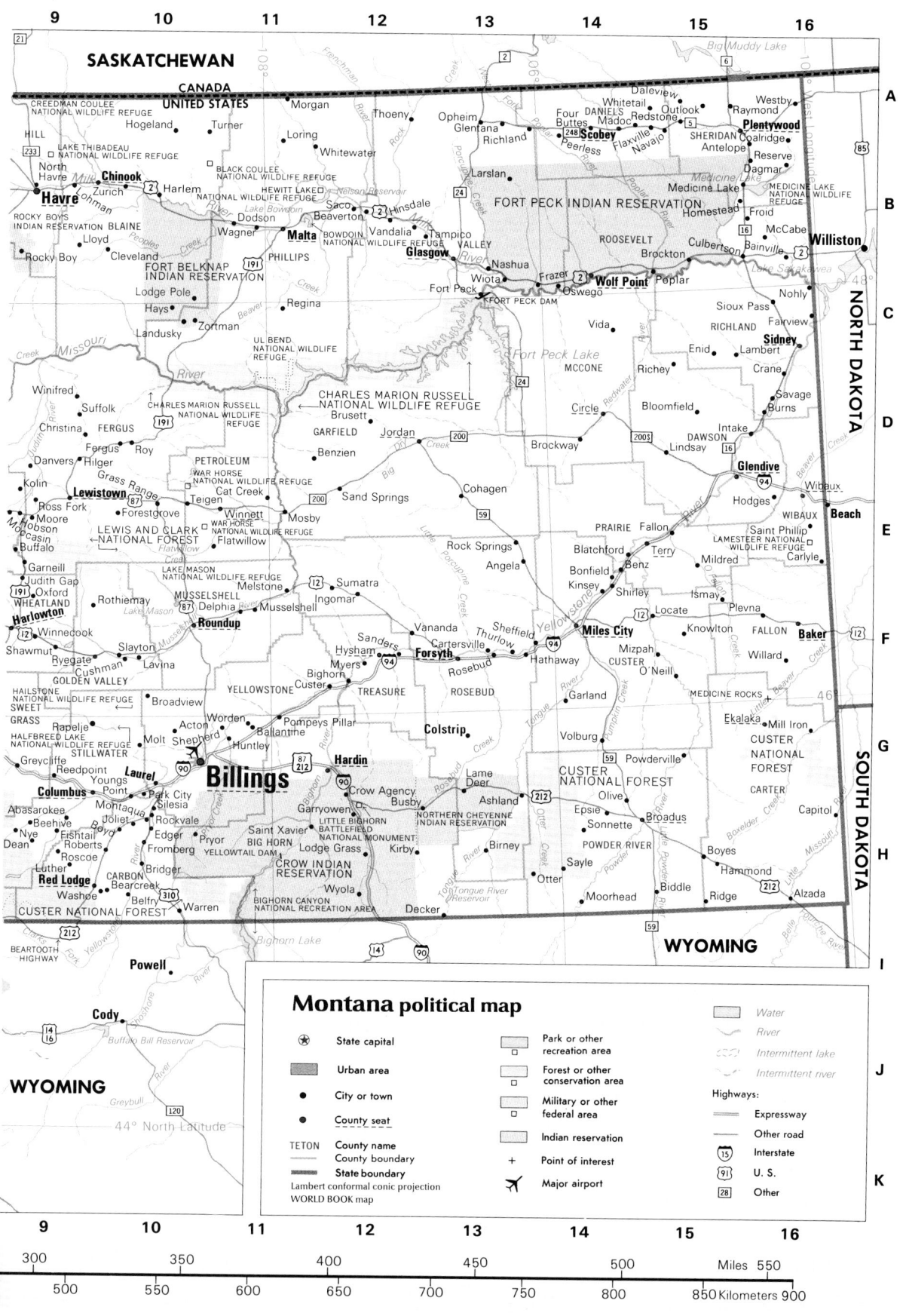

Montana political map

⍟	State capital
	Urban area
●	City or town
●	County seat
TETON	County name
	County boundary
	State boundary

Lambert conformal conic projection
WORLD BOOK map

	Park or other recreation area
	Forest or other conservation area
	Military or other federal area
	Indian reservation
+	Point of interest
✈	Major airport

	Water
	River
	Intermittent lake
	Intermittent river

Highways:

═══	Expressway
───	Other road
15	Interstate
91	U.S.
28	Other

Miles
300 350 400 450 500 550

500 550 600 650 700 750 800 850 900 Kilometers

Few states equal Montana in attractions for outdoor recreation. People from all over the world travel to Montana to fish, camp, and hike. Montana's mountains and lakes are perfect for winter activities, such as ice fishing, snowshoeing, snowmobiling, and skiing. Lovers of the outdoors also enjoy the state's national parks, national forests, dude ranches, ski lodges, summer resorts, and other attractions. Montana's wide-open spaces are home to a wide variety of birds and animals that are no longer found in many other states. Trips to old ghost towns and to Indian battle sites in Montana interest history enthusiasts.

Montana's Western heritage is reflected in the rodeos and Indian ceremonies that are held throughout the state. Almost every Montana town has a rodeo. Nationally ranked riders compete for large cash prizes in some rodeos. In others, hometown cowboys and cowgirls show their skill. Rodeo owners buy wild horses in a May Bucking Horse Sale in Miles City. Indians on Montana's reservations perform colorful dances and ceremonies.

Places to visit

Following are brief descriptions of some of Montana's most interesting places to visit.

Beartooth Highway leads from Red Lodge to Yellowstone Park. It is open from June to September. Motorists on this route see spectacular mountain views as they wind over the Beartooth Plateau, which is 11,000 feet (3,350 meters) high.

Flathead Lake recreation area, in northwestern Montana, offers boating, fishing, and swimming. The lake is the largest naturally occurring freshwater lake in the United States west of the Mississippi River.

Fort Peck Dam, near Glasgow, is one of the world's largest dams. It forms Fort Peck Lake, which is popular for boating, fishing, camping, and sightseeing.

Giant Springs, near Great Falls, discharges 270,000 gallons (1,020,000 liters) of water a minute. This spring was sighted by Lewis and Clark in 1805.

Glacier National Park, in northwestern Montana, includes a large area of majestic mountain scenery. It has more than 50 glaciers that lie on the mountain slopes. Several of its rugged peaks have never been climbed. See **Glacier National Park**.

Helena has many historical points of interest. Attractions include the State Capitol, St. Helena's Cathedral, and the original governor's mansion.

Medicine Rocks, near Ekalaka, lie in the badlands of eastern Montana. Wind and water carved these sandstone rocks into unusual shapes.

National Bison Range, near Missoula, includes about 19,000 acres (7,690 hectares) and a herd of from 300 to 500 bison. The range was established in 1908.

Virginia City, near Dillon, has been restored to look as it did in 1865, when it was one of the nation's richest gold camps.

Yellowstone National Park lies mainly in northwestern Wyoming, but three of the five park entrances are in Montana. These entrances are located near Cooke City, Gardiner, and West Yellowstone. See **Yellowstone National Park**.

Other national parklands in Montana include the sites of two famous Indian battles. These sites, preserved by the federal government, are at the Little Bighorn Battlefield National Monument, south of Hardin; and Big Hole National Battlefield, at Wisdom. See **National Park System**.

National forests. Eleven national forests lie either entirely or partly in Montana. The largest of these are Beaverhead, Flathead, Gallatin, Kootenai, Lewis and Clark, and Lolo. The others are Bitterroot, Custer, Deerlodge, Helena, and Kaniksu.

State parks and forests. Montana has 89 state parks, monuments, and recreational areas. For further information, write to the Montana Promotion Division, Department of Commerce, Helena, MT 59620.

Ray Atkeson

Virginia City near Dillon

Annual events

January-March

National Outdoor Speedskating Championship in Butte (January); Governor's Cup 500 Sled Dog Race, from Helena to Seeley Lake (February); Winter Carnival in Whitefish (February); C. M. Russell western art auction and exhibition in Great Falls (March); Winter Carnival in Red Lodge (March).

April-June

Cherry Blossom Festival in Polson (May); Miles City Jaycee Bucking Horse Sale (May); College National Finals Rodeo in Bozeman (June); Governor's Cup Marathon in Helena (June); Music Festival in Red Lodge (June); Montana Traditional Jazz Festival in Helena (June).

July-September

Home of Champions Rodeo in Red Lodge (July); Libby Logger Days (July); State Fiddler's Contest in Polson (July); North American Indian Days in Browning (July); Wild Horse Stampede rodeo in Wolf Point (July); Yellowstone River Float, Livingston to Billings (July); Festival of Nations in Red Lodge (August); Northwest Montana Fair and Rodeo in Kalispell (August); State Fair and Rodeo in Great Falls (August); Sweet Pea art festival in Bozeman (August); Western Montana Fair and Rodeo in Missoula (August); Threshing Bee and Antique Show in Culbertson (September).

October-December

Bison Roundup near Moiese (October); Northern International Stock Show and Rodeo in Billings (October); Bald Eagle Gathering near Helena (November); Fall Camp for Cross-Country Skiers in West Yellowstone (November); Christmas Stroll in Bozeman (December).

Great Falls Advertising Federation

C. M. Russell art auction in Great Falls

Robert C. Gildart

Miles City bucking horse contest

Robert C. Gildart

Gary Wunderwald, Montana Travel Promotion

Festival of Nations in Red Lodge

North American Indian Days in Browning

Land and climate

Land regions. Montana has two major land regions. They are (1) the Great Plains and (2) the Rocky Mountains.

The Great Plains of Montana are part of the vast Interior Plain of North America that stretches from Canada to Mexico. In Montana, this high, gently rolling land makes up the eastern three-fifths of the state. The land is broken by hills and wide river valleys. Here and there, groups of mountains rise sharply from the plains. These ranges include the Bears Paw, Big Snowy, Judith, and Little Rocky mountains. In the southeast, wind and water have created badland areas of gullies and colorful columns of red, yellow, brown, and white stone.

The Rocky Mountains cover the western two-fifths of Montana. This is a region of unusual beauty. The valleys have flat, grassy floors, and the mountains are forested with fir, pine, spruce, and other evergreens. In southwestern Montana, valleys may extend 30 to 40 miles (48 to 64 kilometers) between mountain ranges. In the northwest, most valleys are narrow—from 1 to 5 miles (1.6 to 8 kilometers) wide. Snow covers the higher mountains 8 to 10 months each year. There are many permanent snowfields and a few active glaciers in the higher mountain ranges. The glaciers that once covered this land carved the highest mountains into jagged peaks. The glaciers retreated, leaving many clear, cold lakes.

There are more than 50 mountain ranges or groups in this area. The most important ranges include the Absaroka, Beartooth, Beaverhead, Big Belt, Bitterroot, Bridger, Cabinet, Crazy, Flathead, Gallatin, Little Belt, Madison, Mission, Swan, and Tobacco Root. The highest peaks rise in south-central Montana north of Yellowstone Park. Granite Peak in Park County is the highest mountain. It rises 12,799 feet (3,901 meters).

Faults (fractures in the earth's outer rocky shell, along which movement has taken place) create the danger of earthquakes in this region. The worst quake period recorded was in 1935, when more than 1,200 shocks were felt in 80 days in the Helena area.

Rivers and lakes. Montana is the only state drained by river systems that empty into the Gulf of Mexico, Hudson Bay, and the Pacific Ocean. The Missouri River system drains into the Gulf of Mexico by way of the Mississippi River. The Columbia system includes the Clark Fork and drains into the Pacific Ocean. The Belly, St. Mary's, and Waterton rivers reach Hudson Bay through the Nelson-Saskatchewan river system.

Montana's most important rivers are the Missouri and its branch, the Yellowstone. These rivers drain about six-sevenths of the state. The Missouri starts in southwestern Montana, as a smaller stream called the Jefferson River. At Three Forks, Mont., the Jefferson, Madison, and Gallatin rivers meet, and from this point the river is called the Missouri. The Missouri flows north past Helena, then through a deep scenic gorge called the Gates of the Mountains. It then curves eastward. Fort Peck Dam, on the Missouri in northeastern Montana, is one of the largest earth-fill dams in the United States. The Missouri leaves Montana at the North Dakota border. The main tributaries of the Missouri in Montana are the Marias, Milk, Sun, and Teton.

The Yellowstone flows north out of Yellowstone Park and then runs east and somewhat north. It joins the Missouri in North Dakota. The chief branches of the Yellowstone—the Bighorn, Clarks Fork, Powder, and Tongue rivers—flow into it from the south.

The *Continental Divide* winds through Montana. This height of land separates the waters running west into the Pacific Ocean from those that run east to the Atlantic Ocean.

The major rivers west of the divide are the Kootenai and the Clark Fork of the Columbia. The chief branches of the Clark Fork are the Bitterroot, Blackfoot, Flathead, and Thompson rivers. These western streams drain only about one-seventh of the land, but they carry as much water as the eastern Montana rivers.

One of Montana's largest lakes is Flathead Lake, which covers about 189 square miles (490 square kilometers) in the northwest. The largest artificially

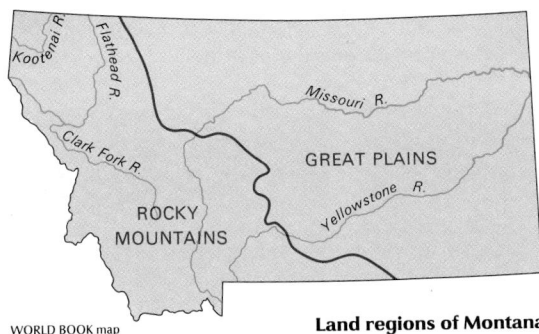

WORLD BOOK map

Land regions of Montana

Map index

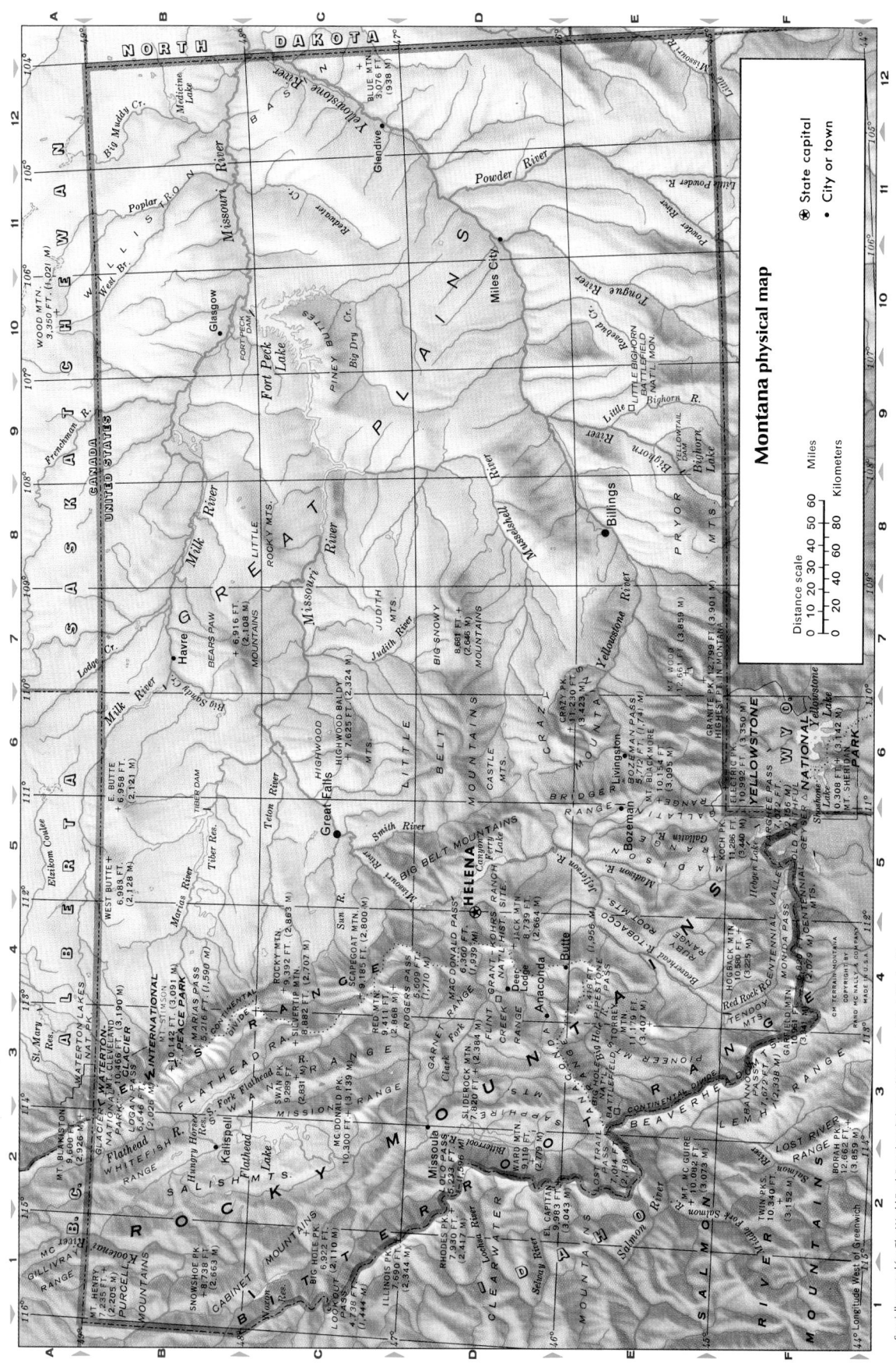

Montana physical map

Distance scale

| Miles | 0 10 20 30 40 50 60 |
| Kilometers | 0 20 40 60 80 |

⊛ State capital
• City or town

Specially created for *The World Book Encyclopedia* by Rand McNally and World Book editors

created lake is Fort Peck Lake, on the Missouri River, which covers 383 square miles (992 square kilometers). Other important lakes include Canyon Ferry Lake and Hungry Horse and Tiber reservoirs. Yellowtail Dam, which was completed in 1966, creates a lake 71 miles (114 kilometers) long in Montana and Wyoming.

In 1967, army engineers began building the Libby Dam on the Kootenai River in northwestern Montana. The dam, which went into full operation in 1975, produces 525,000 kilowatts of power and provides flood control. It created Lake Koocanusa, which is 90 miles (145 kilometers) long and extends 42 miles (68 kilometers) into Canada. The dam is part of the Libby Dam hydroelectric project, which was completed in 1984. The $373-million project was made possible by the Columbia River Treaty between Canada and the United States.

Plant and animal life. Forests cover about one-fourth of Montana. Common trees include ashes, alders, aspens, birches, cedars, firs, larches, pines, and spruces. Flowers include the aster, bitter root, columbine, daisy, dryad, lily, lupine, poppy, and primrose. Grasslands cover much of the state.

Montana has large numbers of big-game animals. Deer are found both on the plains and in the mountains. Pronghorns thrive on the plains. Bear, moose, mountain goats, mountain sheep, bison, and elk live in the mountains. Such small fur-bearing animals as beaver, mink, and muskrat are found there. Common game birds include wild ducks and geese, grouse, pheasants, and partridges. Montana's many high, cold streams and lakes are famous for trout and grayling, two kinds of game fish.

Climate. Montana's climate varies considerably from one area to the other because the state is so large and has such great differences in elevation. The region west of the Continental Divide has cooler summers and warmer winters than the area east of the divide. In the western part of the state, the average January tempera-

Average monthly weather

	Butte						Great Falls					
	Temperatures				Days of rain or snow		Temperatures				Days of rain or snow
	F° High	F° Low	C° High	C° Low			F° High	F° Low	C° High	C° Low	
Jan.	28	0	−2	−18	9	Jan.	32	14	0	−10	8
Feb.	33	5	1	−15	9	Feb.	35	15	2	−9	8
Mar.	40	14	4	−10	10	Mar.	43	22	6	−6	9
Apr.	51	26	11	−3	9	Apr.	56	33	13	1	8
May	61	33	16	1	11	May	66	42	19	6	11
June	69	40	21	4	13	June	73	49	23	9	13
July	80	45	27	7	10	July	84	55	29	13	8
Aug.	78	42	26	6	7	Aug.	81	53	27	12	7
Sept.	66	34	19	1	7	Sept.	69	44	21	7	7
Oct.	55	27	13	−3	7	Oct.	59	37	15	3	6
Nov.	41	16	5	−9	7	Nov.	45	26	7	−3	7
Dec.	31	6	−1	−14	8	Dec.	35	18	2	−8	6

Ray Atkeson

The Yellowstone River winds through Paradise Valley in the Rocky Mountain region of south-central Montana. Flat, fertile valleys stretch as far as 40 miles (64 kilometers) in this region.

Average January temperatures

Montana has cold winters. The region west of the Continental Divide has milder winters than the area east of the divide.

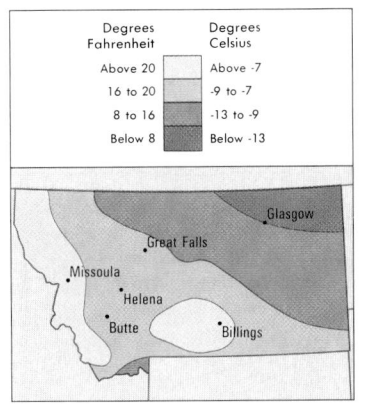

Degrees Fahrenheit	Degrees Celsius
Above 20	Above -7
16 to 20	-9 to -7
8 to 16	-13 to -9
Below 8	Below -13

Average July temperatures

The state has mild summers with wide variations between the warmer east and cooler west and central areas.

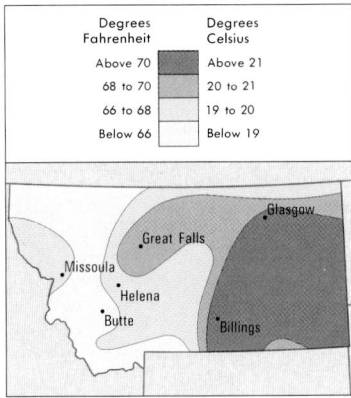

Degrees Fahrenheit	Degrees Celsius
Above 70	Above 21
68 to 70	20 to 21
66 to 68	19 to 20
Below 66	Below 19

Average yearly precipitation

Much of Montana has a dry climate. The mountainous western area receives more precipitation than the plains region.

WORLD BOOK maps

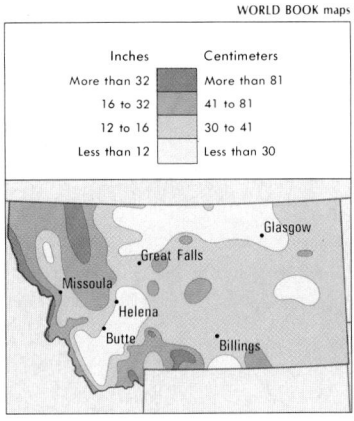

Inches	Centimeters
More than 32	More than 81
16 to 32	41 to 81
12 to 16	30 to 41
Less than 12	Less than 30

ture is about 20 °F (−7 °C). Eastern Montana's January average is around 14 °F (−10 °C). July temperatures average 64 °F (18 °C) in the west, and 71 °F (22 °C) in the east. The state's record high temperature of 117 °F (47 °C) was recorded at Glendive on July 20, 1893, and at Medicine Lake on July 5, 1937. Before Alaska became a state in 1959, Rogers Pass had the lowest U.S. temperature ever recorded, −70 °F (−57 °C) on Jan. 20, 1954.

Most of Montana, except the western edge, has an-nual *precipitation* (rain, melted snow, and other forms of moisture) of 13 to 14 inches (33 to 36 centimeters). The western mountain areas receive more moisture than the plains. Snowfall in Montana ranges from 15 inches (38 centimeters) to 300 inches (760 centimeters) annually.

In winter, a *chinook* wind sometimes blows down the eastern mountain slopes. This warm, dry wind often melts the snow and exposes grazing land, allowing ranchers to graze cattle for part of the winter.

Economy

The service industries play a major role in Montana's economy. Taken together, they account for about three-fourths of the *gross state product*—the total value of goods and services produced in the state in a year. They also employ about four-fifths of the state's workers. Major activities included in service industries are education, health care, real estate, trade, and tourism. Service industries are especially important in urban areas.

In the rural areas of Montana's plains, major economic activities include cattle ranching, wheat farming, and the mining of coal and petroleum. In the mountains, metal mining and logging are important. Most of the manufacturing done in Montana involves the processing of farm and forest products.

The federal government owns about a fourth of the land in Montana. Federal agencies control livestock grazing, logging, and mining in those areas.

Natural resources of Montana include vast reserves of minerals and large areas of cropland, grassland, and forestland.

Soil. The soils of northern Montana are a mixture of clay, sand, and gravel left by melting glaciers. Much of the soil in the south was formed from the sediments of shallow seas that covered the area millions of years ago. Soils deposited by floods are found along the rivers and in the western valleys. The mountain soils were formed as mountain rocks eroded. In a few areas, fertile *loess* (wind-blown dust) lies in a thick layer.

Minerals. Montana has huge deposits of two important minerals—coal and petroleum. Montana's coal reserves lie under much of the plains region. Petroleum deposits also lie under the plains. Some of the petroleum deposits contain natural gas.

The western mountains of Montana have large ore reserves. This ore contains copper, gold, lead, platinum, silver, and zinc. Other mineral reserves include barite, clay, gemstones, gypsum, limestone, molybdenum, palladium, phosphate rock, sand and gravel, talc, and vermiculite.

Grasslands. About two-thirds of Montana is used for grazing. The most important grasses are buffalo grass, blue grama, and Western wheat grass.

Forests cover about 23 million acres (9.3 million hectares), or about one-fourth of Montana. About $8\frac{1}{2}$ million acres (3.4 million hectares) are not available for logging. Some forests are in national parks and other reserves. Others are too poor in quality or too far from transportation to be useful. About half of the $14\frac{1}{2}$ million acres (5.9 million hectares) of commercial timber is still virgin forest. Douglas-fir is the most important tree for logging. Cedar, pine, and spruce also are important.

Paul Conklin

Coal is one of Montana's most valuable minerals. This worker is preparing to blast surface coal from a seam near Colstrip.

Service industries account for 73 per cent of the gross state product in Montana. The state's leading service industries are (1) finance, insurance, and real estate and (2) community, social, and personal services. Real estate is a major part of the state's economy because of the large sums of money involved in the buying and selling of homes and other property. Many small investment companies are based in Montana.

Community, social, and personal services consist of a

Production and workers by economic activities

Economic activities	Per cent of GSP* produced	Employed workers Number of persons	Employed workers Per cent of total
Finance, insurance, & real estate	17	13,800	4
Community, social, & personal services	17	77,000	23
Wholesale & retail trade	14	81,100	25
Government	14	71,000	22
Transportation, communication, & utilities	11	20,300	6
Manufacturing	7	21,700	7
Construction	7	11,200	3
Agriculture	7	27,500	8
Mining	6	6,000	2
Total	100	329,600	100

*GSP = gross state product, the total value of goods and services produced in a year.
Figures are for 1991.
Sources: *World Book* estimates based on data from U.S. Bureau of Economic Analysis, U.S. Bureau of Labor Statistics, and U.S. Department of Agriculture.

variety of businesses, including doctors' offices and private hospitals, motels, law firms, and repair shops. Billings and Great Falls are the leading centers of health care in Montana.

Next in importance among Montana's service industries are (1) wholesale and retail trade and (2) government. Wholesale and retail trade is the state's leading employer. The wholesale trade of food products, mineral products, and motor vehicles is important in Montana. Major types of retail businesses include discount and grocery stores, gas stations, and restaurants.

Government services include the operation of public schools and hospitals, military bases, and Indian reservations. The public school system employs many people. State government offices are based in Helena. A missile base lies near Great Falls.

Transportation, communication, and utilities rank last in importance among the state's service industries. The transportation industry is vital to Montana's economy because goods must often be shipped great distances to reach markets. Trucking firms and railroads are the major means of transporting freight. Oil pipelines are also an important part of the transportation system. Telephone companies are the most important part of the communications sector. Utilities supply electricity, gas, and water service. More information about transportation and communication appears later in this section.

Agriculture contributes 7 per cent of the gross state product. Farms and ranches cover about two-thirds of the state's land area.

Livestock and livestock products provide about half of Montana's farm income. Beef cattle are the state's leading farm product. Some of the nation's largest cattle ranches are in Montana. Farmers raise beef cattle throughout the state. They also raise dairy cattle, mainly in the river valleys of western Montana. Sheep graze in many parts of the state. The region just east of the Rocky Mountains has many hog farms.

Crops provide about half of Montana's farm income. Wheat is the state's major crop. Wheat production is heaviest in the north-central and northeastern parts of the state. This region produces mainly spring wheat. Winter wheat is grown in the southern part of the state. Barley and hay are also important crops in Montana. Farms in the area north of Great Falls grow much of the

barley. Hay grows throughout Montana. The state is also an important producer of potatoes and sugar beets. Sweet black cherries are Montana's major fruit crop.

Mining provides 7 per cent of Montana's gross state product. Coal and petroleum are the state's leading mineral products. Almost all of Montana's coal is *subbituminous* (soft) coal obtained from surface mines in Big Horn and Rosebud counties. The Powder River and Williston basins, in eastern Montana, lead in petroleum production. Other oil-producing areas include Carbon, Musselshell, Pondera, Rosebud, and Toole counties.

Montana's metals output varies widely, depending on prices and labor conditions. The state is an important source of gold, silver, copper, and lead. Many mines in the Rocky Mountain region yield metal ores. Some of the ores contain more than one type of metal. Gold provides more income than any other metal mined in Montana. The state's largest gold mine is near Whitehall. Several metal mines lie in central Montana. Stillwater County has the nation's only mine that yields platinum-group metals.

Montana leads the nation in the production of talc and vermiculite, which are used primarily for insulation. Other mineral products in Montana include gypsum, used in wallboard; limestone, used in cement; natural gas; and sand and gravel.

Manufacturing in Montana accounts for 7 per cent of the gross state product. Goods made there have a *value added by manufacture* of about $1\frac{1}{4}$ billion a year. Value added by manufacture represents the increase in value of raw materials after they become finished products.

The manufacture of lumber and wood products is Montana's leading manufacturing activity. The state has about 70 sawmills, most of them in the mountainous regions of far western Montana. Flathead, Gallatin, Lincoln, and Missoula counties produce much lumber. Columbia Falls, Libby, and Missoula have plywood plants. Other wood products include pencils, prefabricated houses, and telephone poles.

Food processing is the second most important manufacturing activity in Montana. The Billings and Great Falls areas are the state's chief food-processing centers. Meat packing, milk processing, grain milling, and soft drink bottling are major parts of the industry.

**Farm,
mineral, and
forest products**

This map shows where the state's leading farm, mineral, and forest products are produced. The major urban areas (shown on the map in red) are the state's important manufacturing centers.

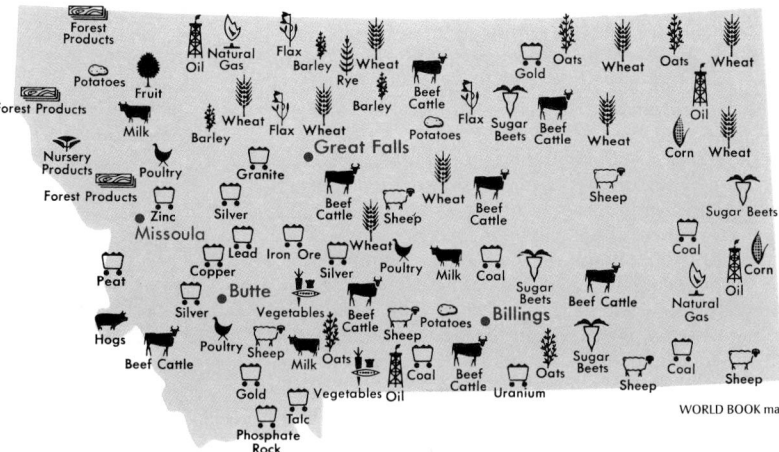

WORLD BOOK map

Other products manufactured in Montana include aluminum, printed materials, refined petroleum, concrete, paper products, and primary metals.

Electric power. Plants that burn coal provide about 55 per cent of Montana's electric power. Hydroelectric plants produce almost all of the remaining power.

Transportation. Montana has about 71,000 miles (114,000 kilometers) of roads, and about 25 per cent of them have a paved surface. Billings has the state's busiest airport. Three railroads provide freight service in Montana, and passenger trains serve about 10 cities.

The Utah & Northern, the first railroad in Montana, entered the area in 1880.

Communication. Montana has about 65 newspapers, including about 10 dailies. The largest papers are *The Billings Gazette* and the *Great Falls Tribune.* The first important newspaper, the *Montana Post,* appeared in Virginia City in August 1864. The first radio station, KFBB, began broadcasting at Great Falls in 1922. The first television stations, KXLF-TV and KOPR-TV, began operating in Butte in 1953. Today, the state has about 95 radio stations and about 15 television stations.

Government

Constitution of Montana went into effect in 1973. It replaced a Constitution that had been adopted in 1889 and amended about 30 times. Amendments may be proposed by (1) a two-thirds vote of the State Legislature, (2) a petition signed by a certain number of voters, or (3) a constitutional convention. To be adopted, a proposed amendment must be approved by a majority of the citizens voting in an election.

A constitutional convention may be proposed by either a two-thirds vote of the Legislature or a petition signed by a certain number of voters. Approval of proposals by a majority of the voters in an election is required in order to call a constitutional convention. The constitution requires that the people vote at least once every 20 years on whether to call a constitutional convention.

Executive. The governor and lieutenant governor of Montana serve a four-year term and may be reelected any number of times. But they may not serve more than two terms in succession. These officials must remain out of office for eight years before serving in the same office again. The governor has powers of appointment involving key officials in 17 executive departments and many state institutions. The governor also has strong veto powers over legislation. For example, the governor

may veto individual items in an *appropriation* (money) bill and sign the rest of the bill into law.

The attorney general, auditor, secretary of state, and superintendent of public instruction are elected to four-year terms. These officials follow the same term limits as the governor and lieutenant governor.

Legislature consists of a 50-member Senate and a 100-member House of Representatives. Each of the 50 senatorial districts in Montana elects one senator, who serves a four-year term and may serve no more than two terms. Each of the 100 representative districts in the state elects one representative, who serves a two-year term and may serve no more than four terms.

Regular legislative sessions are held in odd-numbered years. Sessions begin on the first Monday in January and are limited to 90 legislative days. Special sessions may be called by the governor or the Legislature.

In 1965, Montana's legislative districts were *reapportioned* (redivided) to provide equal representation based on population. The districts were reapportioned again in 1971, 1974, and 1983.

Courts. The highest court of appeals in Montana is the state Supreme Court. It consists of six associate justices and one chief justice. Justices of the Supreme Court are elected by the voters to eight-year terms. The trial courts for major civil and criminal cases are the district courts. District court judges are elected to six-year terms from each of 20 judicial districts. Municipal courts, police courts, and justice of the peace courts handle less serious cases.

Local government. Fifty-three of the state's 56 counties elect three county commissioners to govern the county. The commissioners serve six-year terms. Elected chief executives administer two of the other counties, and a manager appointed by commissioners runs the remaining county. About 120 of Montana's cities and towns have a mayor-council government. Several other cities in Montana, including Bozeman, Great Falls, and Helena, use the council-manager system.

Revenue. State taxes and fees provide about 50 per cent of the state government's *general revenue* (income) in Montana. Most of the rest comes from federal grants and programs. Much of the tax revenue in the state comes from income taxes and a tax on coal production. The state government also taxes motor fuels, property, and other items. Montana has no general sales tax.

Politics. In the early days, the Democratic Party dominated Montana politics. Many people voted Democratic

The governors of Montana

	Party	Term
Joseph K. Toole	Democratic	1889-1893
John E. Rickards	Republican	1893-1897
Robert B. Smith	*Dem.-Pop.	1897-1901
Joseph K. Toole	Democratic	1901-1908
Edwin L. Norris	Democratic	1908-1913
S. V. Stewart	Democratic	1913-1921
Joseph M. Dixon	Republican	1921-1925
John E. Erickson	Democratic	1925-1933
Frank H. Cooney	Democratic	1933-1935
W. Elmer Holt	Democratic	1935-1937
Roy E. Ayers	Democratic	1937-1941
Sam C. Ford	Republican	1941-1949
John W. Bonner	Democratic	1949-1953
J. Hugo Aronson	Republican	1953-1961
Donald G. Nutter	Republican	1961-1962
Tim M. Babcock	Republican	1962-1969
Forrest H. Anderson	Democratic	1969-1973
Thomas L. Judge	Democratic	1973-1981
Ted Schwinden	Democratic	1981-1989
Stan Stephens	Republican	1989-1993
Marc Racicot	Republican	1993-

*Democrat-Populist

because they came to Montana from the traditionally Democratic South. Montanans joked that part of the Confederate Army never surrendered, it just retreated to Montana.

During the 1900's, the Republican and Democratic parties have shared power in Montana. About two-thirds of the state's governors have been Democrats.

The state usually elects Democrats to the United States Senate.

Montana has given its electoral votes to the Republican candidate in about 60 per cent of the presidential elections. For more information on the state's voting record in presidential elections, see **Electoral College** (table).

History

Indian days. Before the white settlers arrived, two groups of Indian tribes lived in the region that is now Montana. The Arapaho, Assiniboine, Atsina, Blackfeet, Cheyenne, and Crow tribes lived on the plains. The mountains in the west were the home of the Bannock, Flathead, Kalispel, Kutenai, and Shoshone tribes. Other nearby tribes such as the Sioux, Mandan, and Nez Perce hunted in the Montana region.

Exploration. French trappers may have visited the Montana area as early as the 1740's. The American explorers Meriwether Lewis and William Clark led their expedition across Montana to the Pacific Coast in 1805. They returned in 1806 and explored parts of Montana both going and coming. After 1807, fur traders became active there. In 1841, Jesuit missionaries established St. Mary's Mission, the first attempt at a permanent settlement, near what is now Stevensville. In 1847, the American Fur Company built Fort Benton on the Missouri River. The town that formed there is Montana's oldest continuously populated town.

The United States got most of what is now Montana as part of the Louisiana Purchase (see **Louisiana Purchase**). The northwestern part was gained by treaty with Great Britain in 1846. At various times, parts of Montana were in the territories of Louisiana, Missouri, Nebraska, Dakota, Oregon, Washington, and Idaho.

The gold rush. In 1862, prospectors found gold in Grasshopper Creek in southwestern Montana. Other gold strikes followed, and wild mining camps grew around the gold fields. These included Bannack, Diamond City, Virginia City, and others.

The mining camps had almost no effective law enforcement. Finally, the citizens took the law into their own hands. One famous incident involved the two biggest gold camps—Bannack and Virginia City. The settlers learned that their sheriff, Henry Plummer, was actually an outlaw leader. The men of Bannack and Virginia City formed a *vigilance committee* to rid themselves of the outlaws. These vigilantes hanged 21 men, including Plummer, in January 1864. The vigilantes adopted as their symbol the numbers 3-7-77. These numbers may have referred to dimensions of a grave—3 feet wide, 7 feet deep, and 77 inches long. Or the symbol may have been associated with masonic ritual because many of the vigilantes were members of the Masons, a fraternal organization. Many outlaws were hanged or driven from Montana.

Many of the early prospectors came from the South, some from Confederate Army units that broke up early in the Civil War (1861-1865). One of the major gold fields was called Confederate Gulch, because three Southerners found the first gold there.

During the boom years, gold dust was the principal money. For example, missionaries did not pass collection plates at services. They passed a tin cup for gold dust. Chinese laundries even found gold in their wash water when they had finished washing the miners' clothing.

Sidney Edgerton, an Idaho official, saw the need for better government of the wild mining camps. At the time, Montana was part of the Idaho territory. Edgerton traveled to Washington, D.C., to lobby for territorial status. Montana became a territory on May 26, 1864, and Edgerton served as its first governor.

The cattle industry began in Montana in the mid-1850's, when Richard Grant, a trader, brought the first herd to the area from Oregon. In 1866, Nelson Story, a cattleman, drove a thousand longhorn cattle from Texas to Montana. Story's herd started the Montana cattle industry in earnest. The coming of the Northern Pacific Railroad in 1883 opened the way to the eastern markets and caused even more growth. However, disaster struck the cattle industry in the bitterly cold winter of 1886-1887. Cattle died by the thousands during the severe winter. Ranching continued after this, but on a smaller scale.

Indian fighting. Two of the most famous Indian campaigns in American history were fought in the Montana Territory. On June 25, 1876, Sioux and Cheyenne Indians wiped out part of the 7th Cavalry Regiment under Lieutenant Colonel George A. Custer. This famous battle, known as "Custer's Last Stand," was fought near the Little Bighorn River in southeastern Montana. The last serious Indian fighting in Montana started when the U.S. gov-

Montana Historical Society

The gold rush brought prospectors to Montana. Helena, shown above in 1866, sprang up after gold was discovered at Last Chance Gulch in 1864.

ʼHistoric ꝶMontana

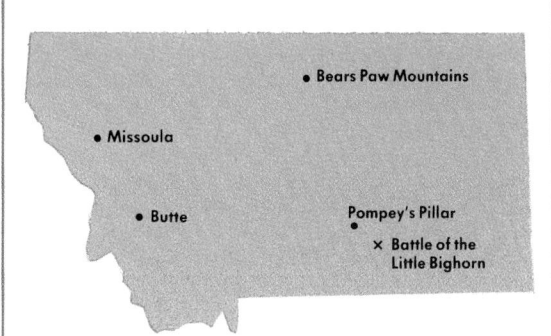

- Bears Paw Mountains
- Missoula
- Butte
- Pompey's Pillar
- × Battle of the Little Bighorn

Pompey's Pillar, a famous landmark for pioneers migrating westward, rises 200 feet (61 meters) above the Yellowstone River. Explorer William Clark first saw it in 1806.

Copper mining increased in 1882 after copper was discovered in the Anaconda silver mine in Butte.

Custer's Last Stand took place in 1876 when Custer and about 210 of his troops were killed in the Battle of the Little Bighorn.

Chief Joseph and the Nez Perce Indians surrendered to federal troops at Bears Paw Mountains in 1877. This ended Indian fighting in Montana.

Jeannette Rankin of Missoula was the first woman to serve in the United States Congress. She was elected to the U.S. House of Representatives in 1916.

WORLD BOOK illustrations by Kevin Chadwick

Important dates in Montana

1803 Eastern Montana became U.S. territory through the Louisiana Purchase.

1805-1806 Lewis and Clark explored part of Montana on their journey to and from the Pacific Coast.

1846 The Oregon treaty with England made northwestern Montana part of the United States.

1862 Gold was discovered on Grasshopper Creek.

1864 Congress established the Montana Territory.

1876 The Sioux and Cheyenne Indians defeated U.S. Cavalry troops at the Battle of the Little Bighorn.

1877 Chief Joseph and the Nez Perce Indians surrendered to federal troops after several battles.

1880 The Utah & Northern Railroad entered Montana.

1883 The Northern Pacific Railroad crossed Montana.

1889 Montana became the 41st state on Nov. 8.

1910 Congress established Glacier National Park.

1940 Fort Peck Dam was completed.

1951 The first oil wells in the Montana section of the Williston Basin started production.

1955 The Anaconda Aluminum Company dedicated a $65-million plant at Columbia Falls.

1966 Construction of Yellowtail Dam was completed.

1973 A new state constitution went into effect.

1984 The Libby Dam hydroelectric project, begun in 1967, was completed.

ernment tried to move the Nez Perce Indians from their lands in Oregon. Chief Joseph of the Nez Perce led his tribe toward Canada through Montana. The Indians and U.S. troops fought several small battles in Idaho, and then a two-day battle at Big Hole in southwestern Montana. Troops under Colonel Nelson A. Miles captured Chief Joseph's Indians about 40 miles (64 kilometers) from the Canadian border. See **Indian wars** (The Sioux wars; The Nez Perce War).

Statehood. Between 1880 and 1890, the population of Montana grew from about 39,000 to nearly 143,000. The people of Montana first asked for statehood in 1884, but they had to wait five years. Finally, Montana was admitted to the United States as the 41st state on Nov. 8, 1889. Joseph K. Toole of Helena became the first governor of the state.

Much of Montana's growth during the 1880's and 1890's came because of the mines at Butte. The earliest mines produced gold. Then silver was discovered in the rock ledges of Butte Hill. Later, the miners found rich veins of copper. Miners came to Butte from Ireland, England, and other areas of Europe. Smelters were built in Anaconda and Great Falls, and more men were hired to operate them. Butte Hill became known as the *Richest Hill on Earth.*

Marcus Daly and William A. Clark led the development of Butte copper and controlled many of the richest mines. The two men became rivals in both business and politics. The great wealth produced by the mines gave both men great power. Daly built the town of Anaconda and spent large sums of money in a campaign to make it the state capital. Clark opposed Daly's plan, and the voters picked Helena as the capital.

Clark wanted to be a U.S. senator, but Daly opposed him. In the campaign of 1899, Clark was accused of bribery. He won the election but resigned rather than face an investigation by a Senate committee. Two years later, Clark won his Senate seat in a second election. He was helped by F. Augustus Heinze, another mineowner. Heinze had arrived in Butte long after Daly and Clark became millionaires. But Heinze became wealthy through clever use of mining law and court suits.

First Daly, then the others sold their properties to a single corporation, which became the Anaconda Company. The company organized an electric power company, built a railroad, and constructed dams. It also controlled forests, banks, and newspapers. Anaconda became so important in the life of the state that Montanans referred to it simply as "The Company."

Progress as a state. During the early 1900's, Montana made increasing use of its natural resources. New dams harnessed the state's rivers, providing water for irrigation and electric power for industry. The extension of the railroads assisted the processing industries. New plants refined sugar, milled flour, and processed meat. In 1910, Congress created Glacier National Park, which became an attraction for the tourists.

Jeannette Rankin of Missoula, a leader in the campaign for women's rights, was elected to the U.S. House of Representatives in 1916. She was the first woman to serve in Congress. She won fame in 1941 as the only member of Congress to vote against U.S. entry into World War II. Rankin said she did not believe in war and would not vote for it.

Depression years. Montana suffered during the Great Depression of the 1930's. Demand for the state's metals dropped because of the nationwide lag in production. Drought contributed to the drop in farm income brought on by the depression.

However, state and federal programs continued to develop Montana's resources during the 1930's. The building of the giant Fort Peck Dam helped provide jobs. Completion of the dam in 1940 provided badly needed water for irrigation. Other projects included insect control, irrigation, rural electrification, and soil conservation. Construction of parks, recreation areas, and roads also continued under government direction.

The mid-1900's. Montana's economy boomed during World War II (1939-1945). The state's meat and grain were in great demand, and its copper and other metals were used in the war effort. After the war, lower prices for grain reduced agricultural income. Many people moved from farming areas to towns and cities to find jobs. Some small farming towns were abandoned.

Montana's petroleum industry expanded rapidly in the early 1950's, when major oil fields were discovered in the Williston Basin along the Montana-North Dakota border. Wells in the new Montana fields began pumping oil in 1951. In 1955, the Anaconda Aluminum Company opened a $65-million plant in northwestern Montana, and aluminum products became important to the state's economy. During the 1960's, Anaconda spent more than $50 million to improve operations at the Butte mines and to make better use of the remaining ore there.

Tourism grew as an important source of income in Montana during the mid-1900's. The state developed more parks and historic sites, and private developers opened dude ranches, summer resorts, and skiing centers. Such ski areas as Big Mountain, near Whitefish, helped extend the tourist season through winter.

The state's irrigation and water conservation programs were also expanded. In 1966, Yellowtail Dam on the Bighorn River in southern Montana was completed. This dam provides water for electric power, irrigation, and recreation. Work began in 1967 on the $373-million Libby Dam hydroelectric project on the Kootenai River in northwestern Montana. The power plant there began operation in 1975. The project was completed in 1984.

Recent developments. In 1972, Montana voters narrowly approved a new state Constitution. The Constitution went into effect in 1973.

Montana's gas, oil, and coal industries expanded rapidly during the 1970's, when an energy shortage developed in the United States. Coal production increased sharply, from less than 3 million to almost 40 million tons per year. Huge, open-pit strip mines operated at Colstrip and other southeastern Montana sites. The Montana Power Company built four coal-fired electric power plants at Colstrip. A 30 per cent coal severance tax contributed needed funds to the state. But in the early 1980's, fuel prices fell, and Montana's production leveled off.

Montana's traditionally important industries experienced major difficulties during the 1980's. Farmers suffered hardships brought on by drought, low farm product prices, and reduced sales to foreign markets. The lumber industry cut fewer logs than in the past.

In addition, the mining industry lost thousands of jobs. The Anaconda Company, once the leading mining company in the state, gave up copper mining and smelting altogether.

Montana today remains a state rich in natural resources. But technological changes have cost jobs. State leaders seek to broaden the economy and ensure a successful future for the state by expanding the manufacturing and travel, recreation, and retirement industries. The Science and Technology Alliance, a state agency created in 1985, helps finance research to look for new uses for raw materials.   Harry W. Fritz and Katherine Hansen

Study aids

Related articles in *World Book* include:

Biographies

Custer, George A.
Joseph, Chief
Mansfield, Mike
Rankin, Jeannette

Russell, Charles M.
Sitting Bull
Wheeler, Burton K.

Cities

Billings
Butte

Great Falls
Helena

History

Bozeman Trail
Lewis and Clark expedition
Louisiana Purchase

Western frontier life
Westward movement

National parks and monuments

Glacier National Park
Little Bighorn Battlefield National Monument
Yellowstone National Park

Physical features

Missouri River
Rocky Mountains

Yellowstone River

Other related articles

Assiniboine Indians
Cheyenne Indians
Crow Indians
Fort Peck Dam

Indian, American
Kutenai Indians
United States (picture: Fields of wheat)

Outline

I. People
  A. Population
  B. Schools
  C. Libraries
  D. Museums

II. Visitor's guide
  A. Places to visit
  B. Annual events

III. Land and climate
  A. Land regions
  B. Rivers and lakes
  C. Plant and animal life
  D. Climate

IV. Economy
  A. Natural resources
  B. Service industries
  C. Manufacturing
  D. Mining
  E. Agriculture
  F. Electric power
  G. Transportation
  H. Communication

V. Government
  A. Constitution
  B. Executive
  C. Legislature
  D. Courts
  E. Local government
  F. Revenue
  G. Politics

VI. History

Questions

What three great river systems drain Montana?
What minerals are most important to Montana?
What is Montana's most valuable farm product?
What Montana artist won fame for his paintings and sculptures of the West?
What two famous Indian battles were fought in Montana during territorial days?
Why is Montana called the *Treasure State?*
What expedition explored Montana in 1805-1806?
Why did early Montanans usually vote for Democrats?
Which two famous parks lie at least partly in Montana?
Why does Montana's climate vary so greatly?

Additional resources

Level I
Fradin, Judith B. and D. B. *Montana.* Childrens Pr., 1992.
Heinrichs, Ann. *Montana.* Childrens Pr., 1991.
LaDoux, Rita. *Montana.* Lerner, 1992.
Lang, William L., and Myers, R. C. *Montana: Our Land and People.* 2nd ed. Pruett, 1989.

Level II
Cunningham, Bill. *Montana Wildlands.* American Geographic Publishing, 1990.
Farr, William E., and Toole, K. R. *Montana: Images of the Past.* Pruett, 1978.
Hamilton, James McLellan. *History of Montana: From Wilderness to Statehood, 1805-1970.* 2nd ed. Binford, 1970.
Malone, Michael P. *The Battle for Butte: Mining and Politics on the Northern Frontier, 1864-1906.* Univ. of Washington Pr., 1985. First published in 1981.
Malone, Michael P., and others. *Montana: A History of Two Centuries.* 2nd ed. Univ. of Washington Pr., 1991.
McRae, W. C., and Jewell, Judy. *Montana Handbook.* Moon Pubns., 1992.
Petrik, Paula E. *No Step Backward: Women and Family on the Rocky Mountain Mining Frontier, Helena, Montana, 1865-1900.* Montana Hist. Soc. Pr., 1987.
Spence, Clark C. *Territorial Politics and Government in Montana, 1864-89.* Univ. of Illinois Pr., 1975. *Montana: A Bicentennial History.* Norton, 1978.

Montana, Joe (1956-   ), ranks among the greatest quarterbacks in professional football history. Montana is known for his leadership, his accurate passing, and his durability. He led the San Francisco 49ers of the National Football League (NFL) to Super Bowl victories at the end of the 1981-1982, 1984-1985, 1988-1989, and 1989-1990 seasons. Montana holds several Super Bowl passing records as well as an NFL record for passing for more than 3,000 yards in each of six seasons.

Joseph C. Montana was born in Monongahela, Pa. He attended the University of Notre Dame from 1975 to 1979. He led Notre Dame to the unofficial national college football championship in 1977. Montana was selected by San Francisco in 1979 in the third round of the college players' draft and became the team's starting quarterback in 1981. Montana was traded to the Kansas City Chiefs in 1993.   Carlton Stowers

Montana, University of, is a coeducational state-supported school in Missoula, Mont. It includes a college of arts and sciences and schools of fine arts, forestry, law, business administration, education, journalism, and pharmacy. The university awards associate, bachelor's, master's, doctor of education, and doctor of philosophy degrees. It also has a biological station, and a 30,000-acre (12,000-hectare) forest experiment station. In addition, it operates a bureau of business and economic research, a wildlife research unit, a wood chemistry laboratory, an immunological research institute, a center for Asian studies and ethics in public affairs, and the Montana Entrepreneurship Center. The university was chartered in 1893. It is part of the Montana University System. For enrollment, see **Universities and colleges** (table).

Montana State University is a state-assisted coeducational school in Bozeman, Mont. The university has colleges of agriculture, arts and architecture, business, education, engineering, letters and sciences, and nursing. Courses lead to bachelor's, master's, and doctor's degrees. The Engineering Experiment Station, the Montana Agricultural Experiment Station, and the Montana Cooperative Extension Service are connected with the university.

Montana State University was founded in 1893. It is part of the Montana University System. For enrollment, see **Universities and colleges** (table).

Montcalm, *mahnt KAHM* or *mawn KAHLM,* **Marquis de,** *mahr KEE duh* (1712-1759), a French general, was killed in one of the last great battles between the French and British in America. Montcalm was wounded on the Plains of Abraham in the battle for the city of Quebec. He died in the city a few hours later. The British commander, General James Wolfe, also died in the action.

Montcalm defeated the British in the first part of the French and Indian War (1754-1763). He captured Oswego and Fort William Henry on Lake George, and successfully defended Ticonderoga. But lack of support from the French government handicapped him.

Detail of a portrait by an unknown artist. Marquis de Montcalm, Paris (Public Archives of Canada)

Marquis de Montcalm

As the war progressed, Montcalm realized that a decisive battle would be fought between the French and British at Quebec. He gathered his main forces to defend the city, and threw back the first British attacks. But Wolfe appeared with his whole force on the Plains of Abraham on Sept. 13, 1759. Montcalm led the French attack, but his troops broke under the heavy fire of the British. The American historian Francis Parkman described Montcalm's death in this battle in the dramatic climax of his book *Montcalm and Wolfe* (1884).

Louis Joseph de Montcalm-Gozon was born in France, near Nîmes. He joined the French army at the age of 12, and became a captain at 17. By 1756, he had become commander of the French troops in America.

Fred W. Anderson

See also **French and Indian wars** (The French and Indian War); **Quebec, Battle of; Wolfe, James.**

Monte Carlo, *MAHN tee KAHR loh* (pop. 11,599), is the tourist region of the principality of Monaco. It lies on the Riviera, 9 miles (14 kilometers) from Nice, France, and overlooks the Mediterranean Sea. Monte Carlo is a popular resort area. Exports from the Monte Carlo region include olive oil, oranges, and perfumes.

Monte Carlo has been famous as a gambling center since the middle of the 1800's. It has a government-owned casino and two privately owned gambling establishments. Citizens of Monaco are forbidden to gamble

Eric Carle, Shostal

Monte Carlo is a luxurious resort on the Mediterranean coast. It is famous for its elaborate gambling casino, *above,* which was built in the 1870's. The building is set in tropical gardens.

at any of these facilities. But each year thousands of visitors come to play roulette, baccarat, and other games of chance.   Janet L. Polasky

See also **Monaco.**

Monte Cassino, *MAHN tee kuh SEE noh,* is an abbey in Italy, located between Rome and Naples. Here St. Benedict founded the Roman Catholic Benedictine order (see **Benedictines**). About A.D. 529, St. Benedict sought refuge from persecution inside the ruined city of Cassino. Later, St. Benedict and his followers built the monastery on a height above the town.

The Benedictine order at Monte Cassino reached the height of its influence from 1058 to 1087. Abbot Desiderius, who later became Pope Victor III, ruled it during that time. The monks of Monte Cassino produced manuscripts and paintings which became famous throughout the world. In 1071, a new abbey church was consecrated. It was named a cathedral in 1321.

In 1866, when Italy dissolved many of its monasteries, Monte Cassino became a national monument. Its buildings held a monastery, a school for laymen, and two seminaries. The abbey's library contained an excellent collection of manuscripts. During World War II, the Allied advance was held up at Cassino and the abbey was bombarded. But most of its treasures were saved. By 1952, the Italian government had rebuilt the buildings along their original lines. They put the masterpieces of the monastery on public display.   Stanley K. Stowers

Monte Cristo, *MAHN tee KRIHS toh* or *MOHN tay KREES toh,* is a small, barren Italian island in the Mediterranean Sea. For location, see **Italy** (terrain map). The island covers 4 square miles (10 square kilometers). In ancient times it was known as *Oglasa.* It became famous through Alexandre Dumas' novel, *The Count of Monte Cristo.* The novel tells how the hero discovered a treasure there. Most of the island is a mountain of granite, rising 2,000 feet (610 meters) above sea level. Benedictine monks once had a monastery on Monte Cristo. But they abandoned it after pirates attacked them in 1553. More than 300 years later, the Italian government tried to establish a *penal colony* (prison settlement) on Monte Cristo. It soon gave up the attempt.   David I. Kertzer

Montenegro, MAHN *tuh NEH groh,* is one of the two republics of Yugoslavia. Serbia is the other. In 1918, Montenegro became part of the Kingdom of the Serbs, Croats, and Slovenes, later renamed Yugoslavia. In 1946, Yugoslavia was organized as a federal state consisting of six republics, one of which was Montenegro. Between June 1991 and March 1992, four of the republics—Bosnia-Herzegovina, Croatia, Macedonia, and Slovenia—declared their independence. In April 1992, Montenegro joined Serbia in forming a new, smaller Yugoslavia.

Montenegro covers 5,333 square miles (13,812 square kilometers) and has about 606,000 people. Montenegro's name in Serbo-Croatian, the republic's language, is *Crna Gora,* which means *black mountain.* The capital and largest city is Podgorica (formerly Titograd). About 132,000 people live in Podgorica.

Government. A president heads Montenegro's government. A 125-member assembly makes the republic's laws. The voters elect the president and the assembly members to 4-year terms. The Montenegrin Democratic Party of Socialists (formerly the Montenegrin League of Communists) is the republic's chief political party.

People. About 68 percent of the people of Montenegro are Montenegrins, a people closely related to the Serbs. Like the Serbs, the Montenegrins speak Serbo-Croatian, use the Cyrillic alphabet, and, traditionally, have belonged to the Serbian Orthodox Church. Minority groups in Montenegro include Albanians, Muslim Slavs, and Serbs. Children in Montenegro are required to attend school between the ages of 7 and 15. Montenegro has a university in Podgorica. Montenegro's urban population began to grow in the 1950's, as people moved to the cities to seek jobs. Between 1953 and 1981, the percentage of city dwellers rose from 14 to about 50 percent.

Land and climate. Mountains cover most of Montenegro, and thick forests grow over much of the republic. A narrow strip of land lies along the Adriatic Sea. Most of Montenegro has cold, snowy winters. Summers are warm in the valleys but cool in the mountains. The coast has a mild climate.

Economy. When Montenegro was part of the larger Yugoslavia, it had one of the weakest economies of the six republics. For many years, a poor network of roads and railroads held back economic development. But the opening in 1976 of a railroad line between Bar, Montenegro's major seaport, and Belgrade, Yugoslavia's capital, improved the transportation system and helped the economy somewhat.

Montenegro has large deposits of bauxite, coal, and lead. Factories manufacture aluminum, cement, iron and steel, and paper. The most important crops are corn, olives, potatoes, tobacco, and wheat. Farmers also grow cherries, figs, grapes, peaches, pears, and plums, and raise cattle, hogs, and sheep.

Tourism is a major source of income for Montenegro. Many vacationers come to Montenegro's coast to enjoy the warm climate and scenic beaches. People who fish, hike, hunt, and ski also visit the mountains.

Montenegro has airports in Ivangrad, Podgorica, and Tivat. The leading daily newspaper is *Pobjeda.*

History. Present-day Montenegro became part of the Roman Empire in about 11 B.C. Slavs settled in the region in the 600's. Montenegro became part of Serbia in

Montenegro

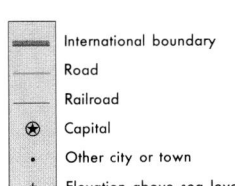

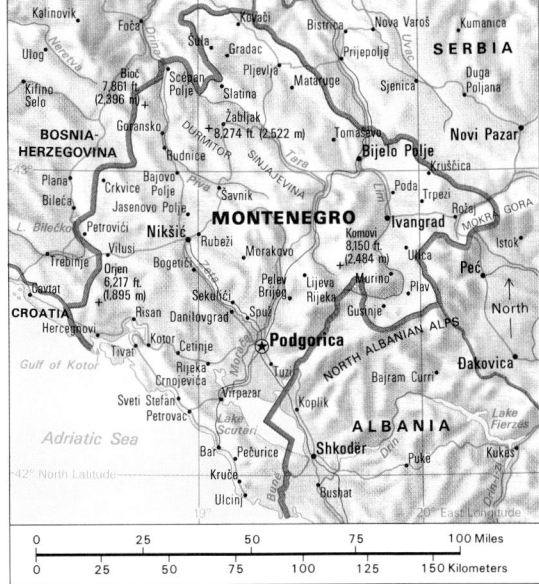

WORLD BOOK maps

Montenegro is one of the two republics of Yugoslavia. Serbia is the other. Montenegro lies on the Balkan Peninsula of Europe.

the late 1100's. The Ottoman Empire, based in modern-day Turkey, defeated the Serbs in the Battle of Kosovo Polje in 1389. Local nobles ruled the country on behalf of the Ottomans until 1516. That year, Serbian Orthodox bishops of the monastery at Cetinje began to rule part of Montenegro. By the late 1700's, their rule extended to the entire country. In 1852, Montenegro's ruler took the title of prince, and the position of bishop became a separate office.

In 1878, the Congress of Berlin, a meeting of European leaders, formally recognized Montenegro as independent. The congress granted new lands to Montenegro, about doubling its size. Prince Nicholas took the throne in 1860 and declared himself king in 1910.

In the early 1900's, a movement to unite Serbs and other Slavic peoples gathered strength in the region. In 1918, townspeople deposed the king, and Montenegro became part of the new Kingdom of the Serbs, Croats, and Slovenes. But rural villagers organized militias to resist incorporation into the kingdom. Their resistance continued until the mid-1920's.

During World War II (1939-1945), Italian and then German troops occupied parts of Montenegro. A resistance movement led by a group of Communists called Partisans fought the Italian and German troops. By 1945, the Communists had gained control of all of Yugoslavia. In

Montenegro's coastline rises sharply to the mountains at Petrovac, a town on the Adriatic Sea. Olive trees grow on the mountain slopes surrounding the town. Montenegro's name in Serbo-Croatian means *black mountain,* and mountains cover most of the republic.

Schmied, ZEFA

1946, Montenegro became one of the six republics of Yugoslavia.

In 1990, Montenegro held its first multiparty elections. Momir Bulatović, a Communist, was elected president. Between June 1991 and March 1992, four Yugoslav republics—Croatia, Slovenia, Macedonia, and Bosnia-Herzegovina—declared their independence. In April 1992, Serbia and Montenegro formed a new Yugoslavia. See **Serbia; Yugoslavia.**   Sabrina P. Ramet

Monterey, MAHN *tuh RAY,* Calif. (pop. 31,954), is a port city that lies along the southern end of Monterey Bay (see **California** [political map]). It is on the Monterey Peninsula, home to many artists and writers.

Sebastián Vizcaíno, a Spanish explorer, landed in what is now Monterey in 1602. The area was settled in 1770, when the Spaniards founded a *presidio* (military fort) there. The city was California's capital under Spanish and Mexican rule, and its capital as a United States territory until 1850.

Today, the Salinas-Seaside-Monterey metropolitan area has a population of 355,660. Tourists, conventions, and military bases provide much of the area's income. Monterey has restored many of its historic buildings. The Monterey Bay Aquarium is one of the world's largest aquariums. The Defense Language Institute, a language school for U.S. military personnel, and the Naval Postgraduate School are in the city. Monterey has a mayor-council-manager government.   Lewis A. Leader

Monterrey, *mohn tehr RAY* (pop. 1,090,009; met. area pop. 1,916,472), is Mexico's fourth largest city. Only Mexico City, Netzahualcóyotl, and Guadalajara have more people. Monterrey lies in a fertile valley near the Texas border (see **Mexico** [political map]). The Pan American Highway links Monterrey with Laredo, Tex., 140 miles (225 kilometers) northeast. Many Mexican Americans live in Monterrey. It is known for its iron and steel foundries, and for its breweries. More than 500 factories produce textiles, cement, and other products. A natural gas pipeline between Texas and Monterrey aided the city's industrial growth. Monterrey has old Spanish-style buildings and many modern structures. The nearby Technological Institute attracts many U.S. students. Spanish settlers founded Monterrey about 1560. It was incorporated as a city in 1596.   James D. Riley

Montesquieu, MAHN teh SKYOO (1689-1755), was a French philosopher. His major work, *The Spirit of the Laws* (1748), influenced the writing of many constitutions, including the Constitution of the United States.

Montesquieu believed that laws underlie all things—human, natural, and divine. One of philosophy's major tasks was to discover these laws. It was difficult to study humanity because the laws governing human nature were complex. Yet Montesquieu believed these laws could be found by *empirical* (experimental) methods of investigation (see **Empiricism**). Knowledge of the laws would ease the ills of society and improve life.

Montesquieu said there were three basic types of government—monarchal, republican, and despotic. A monarchal government had limited power placed in a king or queen. A republican government was either an aristocracy or a democracy. In an aristocracy, only a few had power. In a democracy, all had it. A despotic government was controlled by a tyrant, who had absolute authority. Montesquieu believed legal systems should vary according to the basic type of government.

Montesquieu supported human freedom and op-

Bettmann Archive

Montesquieu

posed tyranny. He believed that political liberty involved separating the legislative, executive, and judicial powers of government. He believed that liberty and respect for properly constituted law could exist together.

Montesquieu, whose real name was Charles de Secondat, was born near Bordeaux. He inherited the title Baron de la Brède et de Montesquieu. He gained fame with his *Persian Letters* (1721), which ridiculed Parisian life and many French institutions. He also criticized the church and national governments of France. Montesquieu was admitted to the French Academy in 1727. He lived in England from 1729 to 1731 and came to admire the English political system.   James Creech

Montessori, *MAHN tuh SAWR ee,* **Maria** (1870-1952), was an Italian educator and physician. She won international fame for designing an educational system to aid children in the development of intelligence and independence. Her educational approach became known as the *Montessori method* (see **Montessori method**). Montessori schools exist worldwide.

Montessori was born in Chiaravalle, near Ancona, Italy. She became the first Italian woman to receive a medical degree when she graduated from the University of Rome in 1896. Early in her medical career,

Granger Collection
Maria Montessori

Montessori worked with children in mental asylums. In 1899, she became codirector of the State Orthophrenic School for underdeveloped children. The educational methods she devised were so successful that her learning-disabled students passed reading and writing examinations for normal children. In 1907, she opened her first school, where she taught normal preschool children from poor families. Montessori lectured extensively on her methods throughout the world and wrote several books, including *The Montessori Method* (1912) and *The Absorbent Mind* (1949).   Paula P. Lillard

Montessori method, *MAHN tuh SAWR ee,* is an educational system designed to aid children in the development of intelligence and independence. The system was developed by Maria Montessori, an Italian educator and physician, in the early 1900's (see **Montessori, Maria**). Thousands of schools throughout the world use the Montessori method.

Montessori educators establish special environments to meet the needs of students in three distinct age groups: infancy to $2\frac{1}{2}$ years, $2\frac{1}{2}$ to $6\frac{1}{2}$ years, and $6\frac{1}{2}$ through 12 years. The students learn through activities that involve exploration, manipulation, order, repetition, abstraction, and communication.

Children from infancy through the age of 6 develop mentally through their senses. Thus, Montessori educators encourage students in the first two age groups to use their senses of touch, sight, hearing, smell, and taste to explore and manipulate materials in their immediate environment. Children from 6 through 12 years of age can deal with abstract concepts based on their newly developed powers of reasoning, imagination, and cre-

ativity. Montessori educators assist these children by presenting special lessons and materials. After a presentation, instructors help the students explore the topic independently. In most cases, the students carry out their exploration in groups made up of classmates who are of different ages and who have chosen to work with one another. The groups then report their findings to the entire class, both orally and in writing.

The Association Montessori Internationale (AMI) sets international standards for the education of Montessori teachers and teacher trainers and for Montessori schools. In the United States, the American Montessori Society (AMS) also trains teachers and certifies schools. However, many U.S. schools that use the name *Montessori* do not have AMS or AMI certification.

The AMS has headquarters at 150 Fifth Avenue, New York, NY 10011. AMI headquarters are in Amsterdam in the Netherlands.   Paula P. Lillard

Additional resources

Hainstock, Elizabeth G. *The Essential Montessori.* Rev. ed. New American Lib., 1986.
Kramer, Rita. *Maria Montessori: A Biography.* Addison-Wesley, 1988. First published in 1976.
Lillard, Paula P. *Montessori: A Modern Approach.* Schocken, 1988. First published in 1972.

Monteux, *mawn TUH,* **Pierre** (1875-1964), was a leading French conductor of the 1900's. He conducted a broad repertory with great authority and finesse, using a technique notable for its restraint.

Monteux was born in Paris. He first gained attention as a conductor in 1911 with the Diaghilev Ballets Russes. He conducted several important premieres for this ballet company, particularly the first performance of Igor Stravinsky's *The Rite of Spring* (1913).

In 1917, Monteux went to the United States to conduct at the Metropolitan Opera. From 1919 to 1924, he conducted the Boston Symphony Orchestra. Monteux conducted in Europe from 1924 to 1936. He conducted the San Francisco Symphony Orchestra from 1936 to 1952. From 1960 until his death, Monteux served as principal conductor of the London Symphony Orchestra.

Martin Bernheimer

Monteverdi, *MAHN tuh VAIR dee,* **Claudio,** *KLOW dyoh* (1567-1643), was an Italian composer. His works greatly influenced the change from the strict style of Renaissance music to the emotional style of the baroque movement (see **Baroque**).

He is often considered the first important composer of opera, and his *Orfeo* (1607) the first modern opera. Only two of his other operas have survived in complete form—*The Return of Ulysses* (1641) and *The Coronation of Poppea* (1642), a great masterpiece.

Monteverdi was a genius at composing for orchestra. In writing for strings, he pioneered in using an agitated effect called *tremolo* and a plucking technique called *pizzi-*

Bettmann Archive
Claudio Monteverdi

cato. He was also one of the great composers of religious music and madrigals (see **Madrigal**). Monteverdi's *Vespers* (1610) combined church chants with devices that were previously associated with *secular* (nonreligious) music using chords. These devices included *arias* (vocal solos) and *recitative* (speech recited to music).

Monteverdi was born in Cremona. From 1590 to 1612, he was employed as a musician and composer by the Duke of Mantua. From 1613 until his death, Monteverdi was choirmaster of the Cathedral of St. Mark in Venice. Beginning in 1637, he also served as composer for the first public opera house in Venice.   Charles H. Webb

Montevideo, *MAHN tuh vih DAY oh* (pop. 1,247,920), is the capital, largest city, and chief port of Uruguay. It lies at the midpoint of Uruguay's coast, where an *estuary* (bay) called the Río de la Plata meets the Atlantic Ocean. For location, see **Uruguay** (map).

The center of the city is Independence Plaza, a park surrounded by highly decorative buildings. These buildings include the Government House, the Museum of Natural History, the Salvo Palace, the Solís Theatre, and the Victoria Plaza Hotel. The Avenida 18 de Julio runs east from the plaza and passes through the main business district. This avenue gets its name from July 18, 1830, the date Uruguay adopted its first constitution. West of the plaza, an arch leads to a historic district called Old Town. Old Town has many buildings that date from the 1700's or 1800's.

Most of Montevideo's people are of Spanish, Italian, or other European descent. About two-fifths of all Uruguayans live in Montevideo. Most people in Montevideo dwell in single-family houses or modern apartment buildings. There are few slums. The city has an excellent system of public education and is the home of the University of the Republic and the Technical University of Uruguay. However, many young Uruguayans leave the city following college to take advantage of more job opportunities in nearby Argentina or Brazil.

The Uruguayan government employs more than half of the workers of Montevideo. The city's important industries include textile manufacturing, banking, and tourism. Most of Uruguay's exports and imports pass through Montevideo's port.

Montevideo was founded in 1726 by Bruno Mauricio de Zabala, the Spanish colonial governor of Buenos Aires, Argentina. Beginning in the late 1800's, the city expanded rapidly as the result of heavy immigration from European countries, including Spain, France, Great Britain, Italy, and Hungary. This heritage makes Montevideo seem much like a European city.   Nathan A. Haverstock

See also **Uruguay** (pictures).

Montezuma, *MAHN tee ZOO muh,* was the name of two Aztec rulers of Mexico (see **Aztec**). The name is also spelled *Moctezuma* or *Motecuhzoma.*

Montezuma I (1390?-1469?) became emperor in 1440. He won fame as a military leader who expanded the boundaries of the Aztec Empire to the Gulf of Mexico. He started a vast public works program. He built a huge dike that kept the waters of Lake Texcoco from flooding his capital, Tenochtitlan (now Mexico City), and built an aqueduct to bring fresh water from the springs of Chapultepec to his capital.

Montezuma II (1480?-1520), the great-grandson of Montezuma I, was Emperor of Mexico when the Spaniards came. He ruled from 1502 to 1520. During his reign, he extended the Aztec domain as far south as Honduras. Like Montezuma I, he built many temples, water conduits, and hospitals. But his people disliked him for his appointments of favorites and his heavy taxation. The last New Fire Ceremony occurred in 1507 under his reign. It was a rite designed to ensure the continuance of the world for another cycle.

He and his people believed that Hernando Cortés, the leader of the Spaniards, was Quetzalcóatl, the White God of the Aztec, who had sailed away many years before but promised to return. At first, Montezuma welcomed the Spaniards with gifts of golden ornaments. Later, he tried to keep them from entering Tenochtitlan, but it was too late. Cortés captured the city and the Emperor. The Indian people attacked the palace and Mon-

Robert Harding Picture Library Ltd.

Independence Plaza, *foreground left,* is an attractive park in the heart of Montevideo. Both historic and modern buildings surround the plaza. The Salvo Palace—the tall, ornate building in this scene—is a landmark of the city.

Montezuma II, *far left,* was an Aztec emperor who ruled in Mexico from 1502 to 1520. This illustration shows his coronation as emperor. The Aztec empire was at the height of its power when Montezuma's rule began. But the empire fell to the Spaniards shortly after his death.

Illustrated manuscript (1579) by Friar Diego Duran; National Library, Madrid (Granger Collection)

tezuma tried vainly to calm them. But he was stoned to death. Several American writers have used the dramatic meeting between Montezuma and Cortés as the theme of their books.   William H. Gilbert

See also **Cortés, Hernando**.

Montezuma Castle National Monument, *MAHN tee ZOO muh,* is in central Arizona. It contains a five-story cliff-dwelling ruin in a niche in the face of a cliff. The monument was established in 1906. It includes Montezuma Well. For area, see **National Park System** (table: National monuments). For location, see **Arizona** (physical map).

Montfort, *MAHNT fuhrt* or *mawn FAWR,* **Simon de,** *see MAWN duh* (1208?-1265), an English statesman and soldier, contributed to the growth of parliamentary government in England. He has been called "the father of the House of Commons."

For many years, Montfort was a favorite of King Henry III. But he lost favor because of his desire for political reform. Henry III wanted to rule as he pleased, and Montfort led a rebellion aimed at limiting the king's power by law. King Henry and his son (later Edward I) took up arms, but Montfort captured them both at the battle of Lewes in 1264. Shortly after, Montfort assembled a parliament that won him fame.

Parliament had been only another name for the king's Great Council of barons and prelates, though some commoners had served in the past. Montfort wished to give more people a voice in affairs. He called to this Parliament of January 1265 two representatives from each shire and two from each town and borough.

Montfort was killed a few months later in the battle of Evesham. His tomb became an English shrine.

Montfort was born in France. When he was 21, he came to England to claim the lands and title formerly held by his great-grandfather. Ten years later, he received the title Earl of Leicester.   John Gillingham

Arizona Office of Tourism

Montezuma Castle National Monument, in central Arizona, includes a five-story cliff-dwelling ruin, *above.* The dwelling was built by American Indians between A.D. 1000 and 1300.

Montgolfier brothers, *mahnt GAHL fee uhr* or *mawn gawl FYAY,* were French papermakers who invented the hot-air balloon. Jacques Étienne Montgolfier (1745-1799) and Joseph Michel Montgolfier (1740-1810) experimented with large bags filled with hot gases produced by burning wool and moist straw.

The Montgolfier brothers were born in Annonay. They first launched small balloons in 1782 and demonstrated a larger balloon in June 1783. In September, they launched a balloon carrying a sheep, a duck, and a rooster as King Louis XVI looked on. The next month, a French scientist, Jean F. Pilâtre de Rozier, ascended in a Montgolfier balloon anchored to the ground. On Nov. 21, 1783, he and a French nobleman, the Marquis d'Arlandes, made the first human free flight in history. They drifted over Paris for about 25 minutes in a Montgolfier balloon.   Richard P. Hallion

See also **Airplane** (First manned flights [picture]); **Balloon** (History; picture).

Montgomery, *mahnt GUHM uh ree* or *muhn GUHM rih,* Ala. (pop. 187,106; met. area 292,517), is the state capital and an agricultural center of the South. The city is known as the *Cradle of the Confederacy.* Southerners established the Confederate States of America there in 1861, and the city was the first Confederate capital. It lies on three hills along the Alabama River in south-central Alabama. For location, see **Alabama** (political map).

Two towns—East Alabama and New Philadelphia—united in 1819 and formed a single city. The people named it Montgomery in honor of Brigadier General Richard Montgomery, a Revolutionary War hero.

Description. Montgomery, the seat of Montgomery County, covers about 133 square miles (344 square kilometers). Alabama State University, Faulkner University, Huntingdon College, and campuses of Auburn University and Troy State University are in Montgomery.

Tourist attractions include the State Capitol, the Montgomery Museum of Fine Arts, and the Old North Hull Street Historic District. The district, which lies near the Capitol includes over 20 buildings from the 1800's. The First White House of the Confederacy is in Montgomery. It was the home of Jefferson Davis, who was president of the Confederacy. See **Alabama** (picture: State Capitol).

Government operations—on the federal, state, and local levels—and retail and wholesale trade have an important part in the city's economy. Government activities and trade each employ about 20 per cent of Montgomery's work force. Federal employers include nearby Gunter and Maxwell Air Force bases. Montgomery's chief industries include the manufacture of furniture, glass products, machinery, paper, and textiles.

Government and history. Montgomery has a mayor-council government. The mayor and the nine city council members are elected to four-year terms.

Alibamu and Creek Indians lived in what is now the Montgomery area before white settlers arrived. In 1817, a group led by Andrew Dexter of Massachusetts founded the town of New Philadelphia at the site of present-day Montgomery. That same year, a group headed by General John Scott of Georgia established Alabama Town nearby. In 1818, Scott's group moved its town nearer to New Philadelphia and renamed its settlement East Alabama. After the two towns united and

© Arvis D. Williams

The First White House of the Confederacy was in Montgomery, the capital of Alabama. Jefferson Davis lived here in 1861.

formed Montgomery in 1819, commerce and population increased. The city became the state capital in 1846. Its population grew slowly but steadily during the late 1800's and early 1900's. It leveled off in the 1960's.

The civil rights leader Martin Luther King, Jr., lived in Montgomery and began his crusade there in 1955. In 1956, Montgomery became one of the first Southern cities to stop racial segregation on buses. See **King, Martin Luther, Jr.**

In 1973, the United States Army Corps of Engineers completed a project that included construction of three dams on the Alabama River. The dams enabled barges to travel on the river for the first time. This development helped to increase trade in Montgomery. In 1985, workers completed a theater complex to house the Alabama Shakespeare Festival. The complex, situated in 200 acres (90 hectares) of meadowland, includes two theaters; costume, scenery, and properties workshops; administrative offices; a cafe; and a gift shop. In 1989, a memorial to people who were killed in the civil rights movement in the United States was dedicated in Montgomery.

William Thomas Johnson, Jr.

Montgomery, *mahnt GUHM uh ree* or *mahnt GUHM ree,* **Bernard Law** (1887-1976), was a British Army commander in World War II. His victories in North Africa and Europe made him the idol of Great Britain.

Montgomery was born in London. He became an infantry lieutenant in 1908. At the outbreak of World War II in 1939, Montgomery was a major general. He took command of the Third Division and led it for nine months in France. He was rescued with his men from Dunkerque in May 1940 (see **Dunkerque**). Montgomery then commanded the defense zone of southeastern England, where he prepared defenses against an expected German invasion.

In 1942, Montgomery took command of the Eighth Army in North Africa and restored its weakened morale. That Octo-

United Press Int.

Lord Montgomery

ber, he attacked German Field Marshal Erwin Rommel's Afrika Korps at El Alamein, Egypt, and eventually drove the Germans into Tunisia.

After the African campaign, Montgomery took part in the invasion of Sicily and in early fighting on the Italian mainland. He then helped plan the invasion of France. Montgomery led the 21st Army Group that landed in Normandy in June 1944 and was promoted to field marshal in August.

After the war, Montgomery became head of the British zone of occupation in Germany. In 1946, he received the title Viscount Montgomery of Alamein in recognition of his war service. He served as chief of the British Imperial General Staff from 1946 to 1948, and then as chairman of the commanders in chief of the Western European Union from 1948 to 1951. Montgomery served as Deputy Supreme Allied Commander of the North Atlantic Treaty Organization (NATO) from 1951 to 1958.

Ian F. W. Beckett

Montgomery, *mahnt GUHM uh ree* or *mahnt GUHM ree,* **Lucy Maud** (1874-1942), was a Canadian author best known for her novel *Anne of Green Gables* (1908). The novel describes an adolescent girl's search for independence from the adult world. Montgomery based it on her childhood experiences living with her grandmother at Cavendish in the Canadian province of Prince Edward Island. The novel's lovable heroine and pleasing setting on Prince Edward Island gained Montgomery an international reputation. Montgomery described Anne's career and marriage in seven later novels.

Montgomery was born in Clifton (now New London), P.E.I. After attending Dalhousie University, she worked as a journalist and teacher in Halifax, N.S. Montgomery moved to Cavendish in 1898 to take care of her grandmother, who was ill. There, she began writing short stories and poems for children's magazines. Montgomery was awarded the Order of the British Empire in 1935. The Green Gables Farmhouse at Cavendish, believed to be the scene of Montgomery's famous novel, is now a national museum. See **Prince Edward Island** (picture).

Rosemary Sullivan

Month. The calendar year is divided into 12 parts, each of which is called a *month.* But the word *month* has other meanings. Several kinds of months are measured by the moon's motion. At one point in the moon's path, it is closest to the earth. This point is called the *perigee.* The time the moon takes to revolve from one perigee to the next is an *anomalistic month.* This period averages 27 days, 13 hours, 18 minutes, and 33.1 seconds.

If the moon were looked at from a distant star it would seem to make a complete revolution around the earth in 27 days, 7 hours, 43 minutes, and 11.5 seconds. This period is a *sidereal month.* The *proper lunar month,* which is called the *synodical month,* is the period between one new moon and the next, an average of 29 days, 12 hours, 44 minutes, and 2.8 seconds.

The synodical month is one of three natural divisions of time. The other two are the rotation of the earth on its axis, or a day, and the revolution of the earth around the sun, or a year. Another astronomical month is the *solar month,* which is one twelfth of a solar year. The solar month is the time taken by the sun to pass through each of the 12 signs of the zodiac (see **Zodiac**).

Our calendar months vary in length from 28 days to 31 days. The lengths of calendar months have no relation to astronomy. At first the 12 months were 29 and 30 days alternately. Later, days were added to the months to make the year come out closer to a *solar year*—the time the earth takes to go once around the sun.

In the Gregorian calendar which we use today, each day of the month is called by its number. June 1 is the "first of June," and so on. The ancient Greeks divided the month into 3 periods of 10 days, and the French Revolutionary calendar used months of equal length divided into 3 parts of 10 days each. The fifteenth day of the month was called the fifth day of the second decade.

The Roman system was even more complicated. The Roman calendar had three fixed days in each month, the *calends,* the *nones,* and the *ides.* The Romans counted backward from these fixed days. They would say something would happen, for example, three days before the nones. The calends were the first day of the month. The ides were at the middle, either the 13th or 15th of the month. The nones were the ninth day before the ides, counting both days. When the soothsayer told Julius Caesar to "beware the Ides of March," he meant a very definite day. James Jespersen

See also the articles in *World Book* on each month of the year. See also **Calendar; Day; Ides; Moon** (How the moon moves).

Monticello, *MAHN tih SEHL oh* or *MAHN tih CHEHL oh,* is the home Thomas Jefferson designed and built for himself on a hilltop just outside Charlottesville, Va. He started planning Monticello in 1768, and construction began in 1770. The first part was completed in 1775, but alterations and expansions continued until 1809.

In designing Monticello, Jefferson drew on his knowledge of local traditions, ancient Roman buildings, and especially the work of Andrea Palladio, an Italian architect of the 1500's. Palladio's Villa Rotonda near Vicenza, Italy, is the major source for Monticello's symmetrical plan and central dome. Jefferson also added several original and practical elements, such as a revolving desk and an enclosed bed that opened onto both his bedroom and study. William J. Hennessey

See also **Jefferson, Thomas** (picture).

Montmorency River, *MAHNT muh REHN see,* is a short, swift river in Quebec. It is named for the Duc de Montmorency, an admiral of France. The river rises in Snow Lake and flows southward for about 62 miles (100 kilometers). It empties into the Saint Lawrence River about 6 miles (10 kilometers) northeast of Quebec City. Montmorency Falls, which are about 150 feet (46 meters) wide and 251 feet (77 meters) high, lie at the mouth of the river. They are Quebec's highest waterfall.

Carman Miller

Montpelier, *mahnt PEEL yuhr,* Vt. (pop. 8,247), the state capital, stands along the Winooski River in the central part of the state (see **Vermont** [political map]). The life insurance industry and the state government employ many of the city's people. Other industries include printing and the manufacture of plastics, machinery, and stone-finishing and sawmill equipment. Montpelier lies on an old Indian trade route. It is the home of Vermont College, a campus of Norwich University. Chartered in 1780, Montpelier became a city in 1895. It has a council-manager government. See also **Vermont** (picture: The State House). Kevin Goddard

George Hunter

Montreal is Canada's chief transportation center. Downtown Montreal lies between Montreal Harbour, on the St. Lawrence River, and tree-covered Mount Royal, *background.*

Montreal

Montreal, *MAHN tree AWL,* is the largest city in Quebec and the largest French-speaking city in the world after Paris. About two-thirds of Montreal's people have French ancestors and speak French. More people live within the city limits of Montreal than live within the city limits of any other Canadian city. However, Toronto has the country's largest metropolitan area population. As a result, some people consider Montreal Canada's largest city, while others give that distinction to Toronto.

Montreal ranks as one of the world's largest inland seaports and as Canada's chief transportation center. It is also a major center of Canadian business, industry, culture, and education.

Montreal is one of North America's most interesting cities. It lies on an island and is the only city on the continent built around a mountain. Montreal covers about two-fifths of the Island of Montreal at the place where the St. Lawrence and Ottawa rivers meet in southern Quebec. A tree-covered mountain, Mount Royal, rises 763 feet (233 meters) in the city's center.

Montreal has some of Canada's tallest office buildings, largest department stores, and most luxurious hotels. Its downtown area includes the world's largest network of underground stores and restaurants.

The city has a fascinating waterfront area called *Old Montreal.* In this area, old stone buildings line narrow, cobblestone streets and impressive monuments stand in historic squares. Montreal also has outstanding museums, theaters, and universities.

Robin B. Burns, the contributor of this article, is Professor of History at Bishop's University.

In 1535, Jacques Cartier of France became the first European explorer to reach the site that is now Montreal. Cartier climbed to the top of the mountain and named it *Mont Réal* (Mount Royal). The first permanent European settlement on the site was established in 1642. That year, Paul de Chomedey, Sieur de Maisonneuve—a former officer in the French Army—brought a small group of Roman Catholic missionaries and settlers to the island from France. The settlement was first called *Ville-Marie* (Mary's City) in honor of the Virgin Mary. But by the early 1700's, it had become identified with the mountain, and was called *Montreal.*

Today, Montreal faces problems common to other large cities. These problems include unemployment, poverty, declining quality of public services and facilities, and a changing population. Many French-speaking people are moving to the suburbs, while immigrants from other countries are moving to the city. As a result, there is social and political tension between people who support the growing ethnic diversity of Montreal and people who wish to maintain the city's French character.

Facts in brief

Population: 1,017,666. *Metropolitan area population*—3,127,242.

Area: 74 sq. mi. (192 km²). *Metropolitan area*—1,355 sq. mi. (3,509 km²).

Altitude: 187 ft. (57 m) above sea level.

Climate: *Average temperature*—January, 15 °F (−9 °C); July, 70 °F (21 °C). *Average annual precipitation* (rainfall, melted snow, and other forms of moisture)—40 in. (102 cm). For information on the monthly weather in Montreal, see **Quebec** (Climate).

Government: Mayor-council. *Terms*—4 years for the mayor and the 50 council members.

Founded: 1642. Incorporated as a city in 1832.

Montreal lies on the triangular Island of Montreal. The island is about 32 miles (51 kilometers) long, and 10 miles (16 kilometers) wide at its widest point. The city of Montreal occupies 74 of the 182 square miles (192 of the 471 square kilometers) that the island covers. The city lies on two separate parts of the island—one near the center and one in the north. The Montreal metropolitan area, called *Greater Montreal,* covers 1,355 square miles (3,509 square kilometers). It includes all of the Island of Montreal, nearby Jésus Island, several smaller islands, and parts of the Quebec mainland around the islands.

Montreal was built on a series of terraces that rise from the bank of the St. Lawrence River west to Mount Royal. At shore level are port facilities and warehouses and wholesale trade establishments. Old Montreal lies on the lowest terraces, near the riverfront. Farther up are the towering office buildings and busy stores of downtown Montreal. Mount Royal, which most Montrealers call "the mountain," rises west of this area. Montreal's chief residential districts lie north, south, and west of Mount Royal. Many industrial plants line the St. Lawrence River and Boulevard St.-Laurent (St. Lawrence Boulevard).

Boulevard St.-Laurent, one of Montreal's chief streets, runs through the center of the city. It divides Montreal into two sections. Montrealers call the sections the *East End* and the *West End.* Geographically, however, the sections are more nearly the northern and southern parts of the city.

Old Montreal borders the St. Lawrence River between Berri and McGill streets. Many of its old buildings stand side by side with tall, modern structures. Charming restaurants, historic houses, and *boutiques* (small retail stores) line the area's narrow streets. Several of these streets are paved with cobblestones.

Old Montreal has many reminders of Montreal's rich history. The city's oldest church, Notre-Dame-de-Bon-Secours, stands on Rue St.-Paul (St. Paul Street) in the northern part of Old Montreal. This Roman Catholic stone church was built in 1771 on the foundations of an earlier building. The St. Sulpice Seminary, the oldest building in Montreal, is on Rue Notre-Dame (Notre-Dame Street) at the south end of Old Montreal. Ville-Marie's first priests opened it in 1685, and their followers have lived in the building ever since.

Two of Montreal's most historic *places* (squares) are near the seminary. Across Rue Notre-Dame is Place d'Armes (Parade Ground). The first clash between Ville-Marie's founders and the Iroquois Indians took place there in 1644. The Maisonneuve Monument in the square honors the city's founder. A few blocks east of the seminary, on Rue St.-Paul, is Place Royale (Royal Square). This square was the site of Fort Montreal, built by Ville-Marie's pioneers in 1642.

Important banks and insurance companies border Place d'Armes. Government buildings, including several courthouses and Hôtel de Ville (City Hall), line Rue Notre-Dame a few blocks north of Place d'Armes.

Downtown Montreal lies west of Old Montreal. It has some of Canada's tallest buildings, busiest department stores, and finest hotels.

Several downtown streets have special characteris-

tics. Boulevard René-Lévesque (René Lévesque Boulevard), a wide street that crosses the heart of downtown Montreal, is known for its skyscrapers. The city's best-known one, the Royal Bank of Canada Building, rises 615 feet (187 meters) at René-Lévesque and University Street. It towers over Place Ville-Marie, one of the city's chief office centers. The bank building is shaped like a cross. The height and shape of the building have made it a city landmark.

Rue Ste.-Catherine (St. Catherine Street), a block away from René-Lévesque, is noted for its department stores, restaurants, and theaters. Sherbrooke Street, two blocks away from Rue Ste.-Catherine, attracts many visitors because of its luxurious antique shops, art galleries, and hotels.

One of Montreal's liveliest sections lies beneath the downtown streets. This section is called the *Underground City.* There, over 200 restaurants and stores and several motion-picture theaters border a network of passageways and squares. The network is the largest development of its kind in the world.

Metropolitan area. Greater Montreal is Canada's second largest urban area. Only the Toronto Census Metropolitan Area is larger. About 3,100,000 people, or about 11 percent of Canada's people, live in Greater Montreal. About 75 cities and towns make up the Montreal metropolitan area. Montreal is by far the largest of these communities. But more than two-thirds of the people in the metropolitan area live outside the city.

Laval, on Jésus Island, ranks as Montreal's largest suburb. It has a population of about 314,000. Longueuil, with about 130,000 people, is the largest suburb on the east shore of the St. Lawrence River. Westmount, an independent residential city on Mount Royal, lies entirely within Montreal's city limits.

Barbara K. Deans

Rue de la Montagne (Mountain Street), in downtown Montreal, has some of the city's most charming restaurants. Several of them feature French cooking.

About 77 percent of Montreal's people were born in Canada. French Canadians are by far the largest group in the city.

Signs throughout the city appear mainly in French. Since the end of World War II in 1945, hundreds of thousands of immigrants from Europe have settled in Montreal. Today, people of many nationalities and ethnic backgrounds live in the city.

Roman Catholics make up about four-fifths of Montreal's population. Most of the Catholics are of French descent. The majority of English-speaking Montrealers are Protestants. Anglicans, Presbyterians, and members of the United Church of Canada form the city's largest Protestant denominations. Jews make up another large religious group in Montreal. About 3 percent of the city's population is Jewish.

Ethnic groups. About two-thirds of the people in Montreal have French ancestry. Other ethnic groups, in order of size, include Italians, British, Jews, Greeks, and blacks.

In the Montreal metropolitan area, people of French ancestry account for almost 60 percent of the population. People of British and of Italian descent each make up about 7 percent of the population. Other large groups in the city are, in order of size, Jews, Greeks, blacks, Chinese, and Portuguese. More than 25 percent of the people in Montreal are descended from more than one ethnic group.

Nearly 70 percent of Montrealers rent their dwellings. Large numbers of French Canadians rent apartments in the East End. However, more and more French Canadians are buying homes in the western suburbs, where the majority of the people are English-speaking.

Almost half of Montreal's people speak both French and English. About 400,000 people in the city only speak French, and about 100,000 people in Montreal only speak English.

Montreal's economy was once controlled by private companies that used English as the language of business. As a result, Montrealers needed a good knowledge of English to obtain a well-paying job. Since 1977, however, the Quebec government has required all

Rus Arnold

Montreal's *Métro* riders enter and leave the city's subway system through some of the world's most attractive stations. The Champ-de-Mars station, *above,* features colored windows. Other stations have decorated walls.

Paul Baich, Pictorial Parade

Shoppers and office workers relax or enjoy an outdoor lunch in the plaza of the Place Ville-Marie, a downtown office complex with a shopping center.

Gerry Souter, Van Cleve Photography

The Underground City, a shopping area beneath Montreal's downtown streets, features over 200 stores and restaurants. Escalators in major hotels serve the system, the largest development of its kind in the world.

Montreal

QUEBEC

• Montreal

Montreal lies on the St. Lawrence River in southern Quebec. The top map shows the Montreal metropolitan area, which consists of about 75 cities and towns. Many people who live in these communities commute daily to and from their jobs in Montreal. The city covers about two-fifths of the Island of Montreal. The map at the bottom shows the major parks, points of interest, and streets in the downtown area of Montreal.

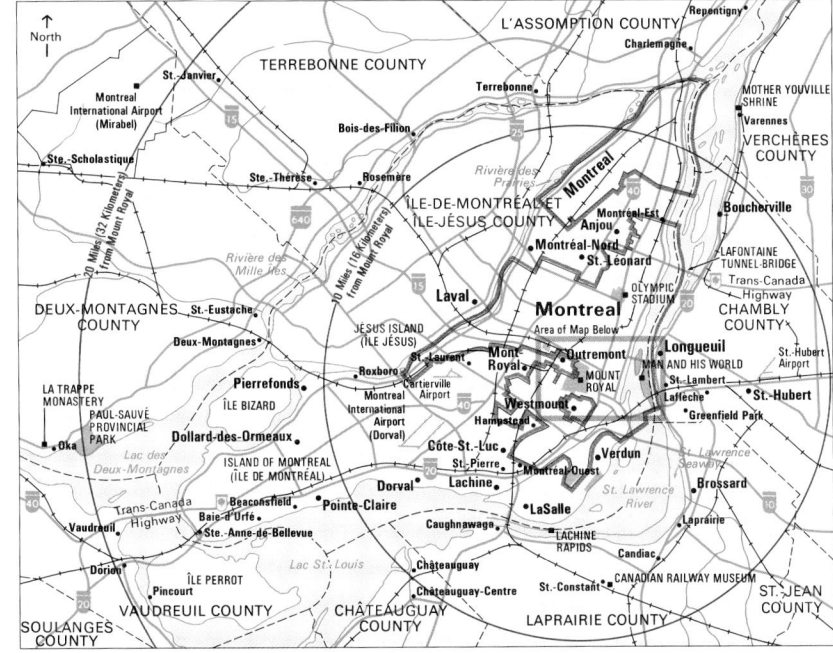

WORLD BOOK maps

Park

City boundary

County boundary

Highway or street

Rail line

Subway (Métro)

Point of interest

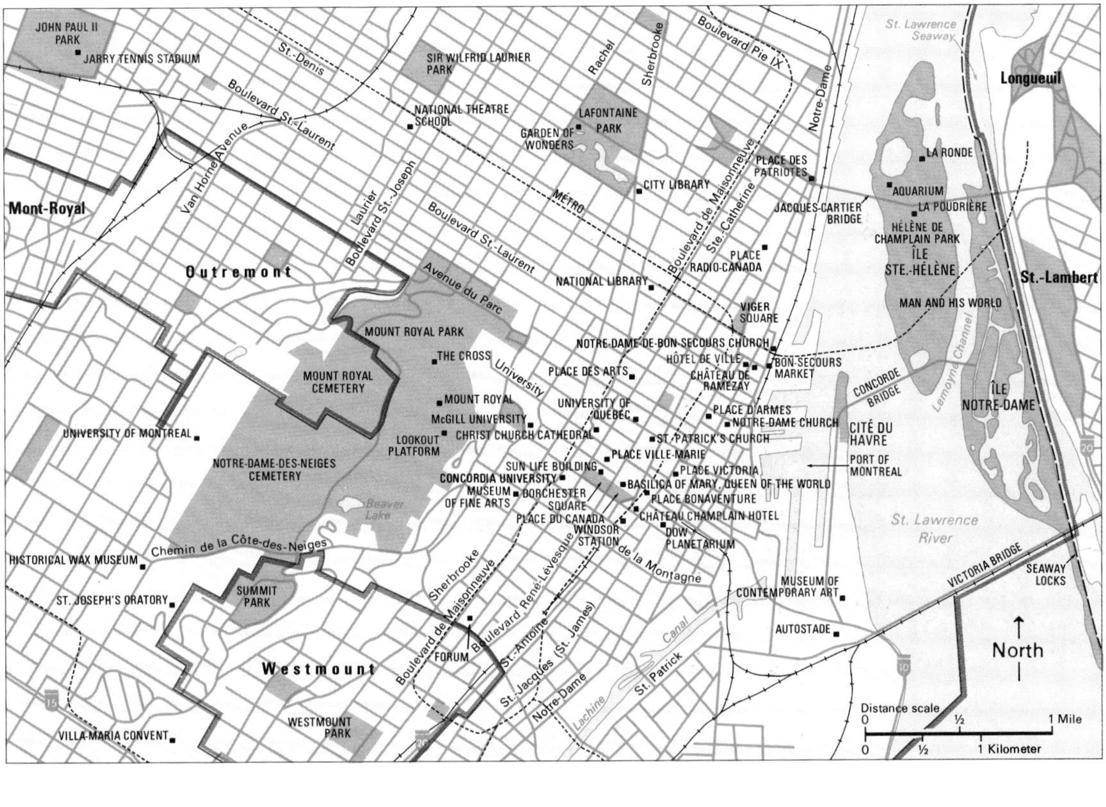

companies that employ 50 or more people to use French as the language of business.

Housing. Montreal has a lower proportion of single-family houses and a higher proportion of apartment buildings than any other Canadian metropolitan area. Most of the houses are located in the West End. A number of luxurious mansions lie on the slopes of Mount Royal.

Most of the apartments in Montreal are in the East End. Rows of two- or three-story apartment buildings with outside staircases are a common sight there. Apartment buildings in this style, constructed chiefly during the 1920's and 1930's, were designed to make maximum use of inside space.

Montreal is the site of one of the world's most unusual apartment developments. This development, called Habitat, stands on Cité du Havre, a strip of land that extends into the St. Lawrence River. Designed by Canadian architect Moshe Safdie, Habitat consists of 158 apartments that look like a stack of concrete boxes. One apartment's roof serves as the terrace of another. See **Safdie, Moshe** (picture).

Montreal has many new houses and tall, modern

Barbara K. Deans

Balconies and outdoor staircases are a distinctive feature of many apartment buildings in Montreal's East End. Most French-speaking Montrealers live in this section of the city.

apartment buildings. But the city also has old and run-down dwellings. The worst housing in Montreal is in the East End. During the 1960's, the city redeveloped 107 acres (43 hectares) in an area called Little Burgundy. The project included the construction of 1,200 apartments at a cost of about $30 million. However, nearly 10 times more dwellings were torn down than were rebuilt. Since the 1960's, efforts have been made to repair old dwellings.

Education. Montreal has an unusual public school system. The system is organized on the basis of language and religion. Four kinds of schools exist within the public school system. They are (1) Roman Catholic schools that teach entirely in English, (2) Roman Catholic, French-language schools, (3) Protestant, English-language schools, and (4) Protestant, French-language schools.

Most Jewish students attend either the Protestant schools or private Jewish schools. The public school system has about 300 schools. A Roman Catholic school board administers about 225 of them. A Protestant school board runs the rest. Montreal also has a number of nonreligious private schools.

Montreal is the home of two of Canada's most famous universities, the University of Montreal and McGill University. The University of Montreal is the largest university outside of France in which all the courses are taught in French. McGill University, which is one of the country's oldest universities, was founded in 1821. Other institutions of higher learning in Montreal include Concordia University, an English-language university; and the University of Quebec, which teaches classes in French.

The University of Montreal, McGill University, and Concordia University are privately owned but largely publicly financed. The province controls the University of Quebec.

Social problems. In the early 1990's, Montreal had a high rate of unemployment. Poverty was also a problem in the city. Nearly one out of every four Montrealers lived below the poverty line. A growing number of people who could afford private homes were moving from the city to the suburbs.

In 1974, the Quebec government made French the official language of the province. Since then, many English-speaking people, and some important companies that conduct business in English, have left Montreal and Quebec because they were unwilling or unable to adapt to the necessity of using French. However, the number of people whose first language is French has declined since this time, while the number of immigrants who seek to learn English has increased. Many French-speaking Montrealers are alarmed at this situation. They support the government of Quebec's policies, which require immigrants to attend French-language schools and restrict the display of English-language signs in public.

Many people who have immigrated to Montreal since the 1980's have complained that the city's government has been slow to provide for equal opportunities. Tensions have also grown between Montreal's police department and the city's black community.

Montreal is Canada's chief transportation center. It ranks second only to Toronto among the top Canadian centers of finance, industry, and trade.

Montreal's location contributes much to the city's economic importance. Montreal lies on the St. Lawrence River at the entrance to the St. Lawrence Seaway. This location has helped make it one of the world's leading inland seaports. Waterways in the Montreal area also provide a large supply of low-cost hydroelectric power. This supply, about a twelfth of the hydroelectric power produced in Quebec, has helped attract many industries to the city. In addition, Montreal lies in the most fertile and productive agricultural region of Quebec. As a result, the city has become an important food-processing center.

Transportation. The St. Lawrence River links Montreal with the Atlantic Ocean, about 1,000 miles (1,600 kilometers) to the northeast. The St. Lawrence Seaway extends shipping services 1,300 miles (2,090 kilometers) inland. It makes Montreal a major stopover point for ships sailing between the Great Lakes and the Atlantic (see **Saint Lawrence Seaway**).

Montreal Harbour stretches 15 miles (24 kilometers) along the west bank of the St. Lawrence River. It serves about 3,000 oceangoing or coastal and inland vessels and handles over 23 million short tons (21 million metric tons) of cargo yearly. Montreal is one of the largest grain ports in the world. Each year, between 3 million and 4 million short tons (2.7 million and 3.6 million metric tons) of grain are shipped from Montreal Harbour.

Montreal ranks as Canada's largest railroad center. CP Rail and the Canadian National Railways, the nation's two transcontinental rail lines, have their headquarters in the city. These railroads carry freight east to the Atlantic seaboard and west to the Pacific Coast. Several railways connect Montreal and a number of cities in the United States. In 1968, the Canadian National Railways began operating North America's first turbine-powered passenger train between Montreal and Toronto.

Major airlines use Montreal International Airport (Dorval), which lies just southwest of the city, and Montreal International Airport (Mirabel), northwest of Montreal. Air Canada, the nation's largest commercial airline, has its headquarters in the city. The International Civil Aviation Organization also has its headquarters in Montreal.

More than 10 major highways serve Montreal. The Trans-Canada Highway, which runs from coast to coast, crosses downtown Montreal 100 feet (30 meters) underground. Nearly 20 railroad and highway bridges connect the Island of Montreal with Laval and the opposite shore of the St. Lawrence River.

Montreal's subway, called the *Métro,* carries passengers between the downtown area and the outskirts of the city in less than 20 minutes. It can serve up to 60,000 riders an hour. The Métro, which opened in 1966, is one of the world's quietest subways. It was the first subway in the Western Hemisphere to use rubber tires. Buses also provide public transportation in Montreal.

Industry. Manufacturing is the leading source of employment in Greater Montreal. The more than 7,000 factories in the area employ about a fourth of its workers.

These plants produce about $25 billion worth of goods yearly. They account for about two-thirds of Quebec's industrial production.

Greater Montreal's leading industries are the manufacture of transportation equipment and food processing. The area's chief food products are beer, canned goods, and sugar. Petroleum refineries in Montreal produce about a tenth of Canada's gasoline.

Greater Montreal is also one of Canada's major centers for the manufacture of chemicals, clothing, and tobacco products. The area also leads Quebec in the production of electrical machinery, electronic equipment, and fur products.

Trade and finance. Companies in Greater Montreal play an important role in Canada's foreign trade. These companies handle about 15 percent of the import business in the nation and about 7 percent of its export business.

Montreal area companies also account for about 10 percent of the wholesale and retail trade in Canada and about 55 percent of such trade in Quebec. Wholesale companies, which sell goods to retail stores, employ more than 75,000 workers in Greater Montreal. Area retail stores employ about 160,000 workers. These stores include some of Canada's largest department stores. Place Bonaventure, in downtown Montreal, is one of the largest commercial buildings in the world. It has more than 3 million square feet (300,000 square meters) of space to display goods.

More than 40 percent of Canada's financial companies are in Greater Montreal. Banks, credit organizations, savings firms, and other financial companies in the area employ over 90,000 people. Loans by these companies contribute to the growth of business and industry throughout Canada.

The Bank of Montreal, founded in 1817, was the first bank in Canada. The Royal Bank of Canada, the country's largest bank, has its headquarters in Montreal. The Montreal Stock Exchange is the oldest stock market in the country. The stock exchange opened in the city in 1874.

Communication. Four daily newspapers are published in Montreal. Three of the papers—*La Presse, Le Devoir,* and *Le Journal de Montréal*—are written in French. *The Gazette* is the only Montreal daily that is written in English. *Le Journal de Montréal* has the largest circulation of any of Quebec's daily newspapers. *The Gazette* was the first newspaper published in Montreal. It was founded in 1778.

Fifteen radio stations broadcast from the city, seven of them in French and eight in English. Station CFCF of Montreal was Canada's first radio station. It began broadcasting in 1919.

Montreal has five television stations. Three of them broadcast in the French language and two in English. The French-language network of the Canadian Broadcasting Corporation (CBC) is based in Montreal. More French-language television programs are produced in Montreal than in any other city in the world except Paris. Television station CBFT, one of the first two Canadian stations, began broadcasting from Montreal in 1952. The other pioneer station was CBLT of Toronto.

Prazak, Miller Services

Beaver Lake in Mount Royal Park

Barbara K. Deans

Ski area on Mount Royal

Quebec Department of Tourism

The Place des Arts

Montreal is one of North America's leading cultural centers. It has outstanding dance, drama, and musical groups, and its art galleries, libraries, and museums rank among the finest in Canada. The city is also known for its many beautiful churches and well-planned parks. Montreal's sports attractions include professional baseball and hockey.

Each year, about 6 million tourists visit Montreal. Many restaurants in Montreal specialize in French cooking. Visitors can also find restaurants featuring Chinese, Greek, Italian, or other kinds of cooking.

The arts. The world-famous Montreal Symphony Orchestra and the Montreal Metropolitan Orchestra make their home in the city. Montreal also has Les Grands Ballets Canadiens, a major dance company; two jazz dance companies; and about 40 French-language theater groups, including Le Théâtre du Nouveau Monde, Le Théâtre du Rideau Vert, and Le Théâtre Jean Duceppe. The Centaur Theater features English-language productions. Many annual art festivals take place in Montreal, such as the International Jazz and World Film festivals. The Théâtre des Amèriques festival is held every two years in the city.

Place des Arts at Rue Ste.-Catherine and St. Urbain Street is one of North America's finest centers for the performing arts. The Montreal Opera and many of Montreal's other leading cultural groups entertain at the center. The center includes the Salle Wilfrid-Pelletier concert hall, which can seat 3,000 people. A second structure houses the smaller Maisonneuve and Port-Royal theaters, both of which offer stage productions.

Libraries. Montreal's public library system is called the Montreal City Library. It consists of a main library and 23 branches. The system owns about 2,200,000 books written in French, 450,000 in English, and 50,000

Notre-Dame Basilica

Rus Arnold

in other languages. Other libraries in Montreal include the Fraser-Hickson Library, the Jewish Public Library, the Quebec National Library, and the libraries of the city's four universities.

Museums. The Montreal Museum of Fine Arts at Sherbrooke and Drummond streets displays paintings by leading Canadian artists. It also has collections of furniture, glass, lace, and silver from Canada and many works of art from Asia and South America. It is one of the oldest museums in Canada. It was founded in 1860.

The Musée d'Art Contemporain (Museum of Contemporary Art) is located at Place des Arts. It exhibits modern works of art from Europe and North America. The Château de Ramezay, in Old Montreal, is a history museum. The building dates from 1705. It was once the home of Claude de Ramezay, second French governor of Montreal. The McCord Museum of Canadian History is on Sherbrooke Street across from McGill University.

The David M. Stewart Museum, on Île Ste.-Hélène, has exhibits on the history of Quebec's European settlement. Dow Planetarium at Rue St.-Jacques (St. James Street) and Peel Street features programs on the space age. The Archaeological and History Museum at Place Royale features displays on the early history of Montreal. The Canadian Center for Architecture is housed in an old mansion on Boulevard René Lévesque.

Churches. Montreal is famous for its more than 300 churches. Several of them are noted for their Gothic-style architecture. St. Patrick's Church, in downtown Montreal, serves English-speaking Roman Catholics. Notre-Dame Basilica in Old Montreal, is attended by French-speaking Catholics. This church has two towers, one of which houses a huge bell. This bell, which is called *Le Gros Bourdon* (The Great Bell), weighs 12 short tons (11 metric tons). Notre-Dame Basilica is also noted

Notre-Dame-de-Bon-Secours Church

Hellmut Walter Schade

Ellefson, Miller Services

St. Joseph's Oratory

for its magnificently carved wooden interior.

Notre-Dame-de-Bon-Secours is another well-known church in Old Montreal. Some Montrealers call it *the Sailors' Church*. A statue of the Virgin Mary on the roof is believed to perform miracles to help sailors.

The Cathedral-Basilica of Mary, Queen of the World, stands in the heart of the downtown area. The designers of this church patterned it after St. Peter's Basilica in Vatican City. The church serves as the seat of the Catholic archdiocese of Montreal. The seat of the Anglican diocese, Christ Church Cathedral, is also in downtown Montreal. St. Joseph's Oratory stands on the west slope of Mount Royal. Every year, more than 2 million people visit this Roman Catholic shrine.

Parks. The Montreal park system includes about 400 parks and playgrounds. These recreation areas cover a total of more than 5,000 acres (2,000 hectares). Visitors can ride through Mount Royal Park, on Mount Royal, in horse-drawn carriages in summer or in sleighs during winter. The park was designed by Frederick Law Olmsted, who designed New York City's Central Park. The park includes Beaver Lake, a popular spot for ice-skating during the winter.

Montrealers also enjoy activities at Lafontaine and Maisonneuve parks. Lafontaine Park, at Sherbrooke and Amherst streets, has a lake for boating. Maisonneuve Park, at Sherbrooke and Pie IX Boulevard, includes the city's Botanical Gardens. The Montreal Insectarium and the Chinese Garden, the largest of its kind outside China, are on the grounds of the Botanical Gardens.

Sports. The Montreal Canadiens of the National Hockey League play in the Forum. Olympic Stadium is the home of the Montreal Expos baseball team of the National League. The stadium features the world's first retractable dome, which was completed in 1987.

Winter sports are a major attraction in the Montreal area. As many as 5,000 skiers and tobogganers may rush to Mount Royal after a snowfall. Skiing is also popular in the nearby Laurentian Mountains.

Other places to visit. Many of Montreal's most interesting places to visit are described in earlier sections of this article. For example, Old Montreal, discussed in *The City* section, has many attractions. Other popular places to visit in Montreal include lookout platforms on Mount Royal, a 135-acre (55-hectare) amusement park called La Ronde, and the Métro.

Two lookout platforms on the mountain offer visitors magnificent views of the Montreal area. From an observation area on the west slope, visitors can gaze over Montreal's tree-lined streets, spired churches, towering office buildings, and old stone houses. An iron cross rises 100 feet (30 meters) near this platform. The cross, illuminated at night, is a memorial to Ville-Marie's survival of a flood in 1642. The other platform is on the south slope. It overlooks residential communities in the city.

La Ronde lies on Île Ste.-Hélène, near the former site of Expo 67, a world's fair held in Montreal in 1967. La Ronde is open during the summer months.

The Métro is one of the world's most attractive subways. Brightly colored mosaics and basket-weave designs decorate many of its ceramic walls. Because of these decorations, the Métro has been called "the largest underground art gallery in the world."

Montreal Olympic Park

Olympic Stadium, *above left,* in northeastern Montreal, is home to the Montreal Expos of the National League. The stadium was built for the 1976 Summer Olympic Games. The low building to the right is the Biodôme, a natural-science museum.

Organization. Montreal has a mayor-council form of government. The voters elect the mayor and the 50 members of the City Council to four-year terms.

The mayor acts as the administrative head of the city government. He or she supervises the various departments of the city's government. A seven-member executive committee prepares the city budget and proposes new laws. The committee consists of the mayor and six City Council members.

The City Council appoints the council members to the executive committee and elects one of them chairman. The City Council passes the city's laws. It also appoints and dismisses directors of city departments and adopts the annual city budget.

Montreal gets some of its government services from an agency called the Montreal Urban Community Council. The council, created by the Quebec legislature in 1969, serves all the cities and towns on the Island of Montreal and nearby Île Bizard (Bizard Island). It administers such services as fire protection, law enforcement, long-range planning, public health, public transportation, sanitation, traffic control, and water supply. The council consists of the mayor and all the council members and the mayor of each of the other communities.

The city of Montreal has an annual budget of about $1.9 billion. Only three other Canadian government budgets are larger—the federal government's and those

Symbols of Montreal. The city flag and the coat of arms of Montreal include the national flowers of France (fleur-de-lis), England (rose), Scotland (thistle), and Ireland (shamrock). Immigrants from these lands played key roles in the city's growth.

of Ontario and Quebec provinces. More than 40 percent of Montreal's revenue comes from taxes on property. The rest of the city's funds come from taxes on sales, businesses, water, and amusements, and from aid given by the province.

Problems. Like most other big cities, Montreal has difficulty finding ways to pay for the rapidly rising costs of government services. The major problems faced by Montreal's government include building more low-cost housing, providing higher pay for city employees, and maintaining the city's *infrastructure* (public services and facilities).

History

Algonquin and Iroquois Indians lived in the Montreal region before European settlers arrived. The area's rivers and lakes provided the Indians with a plentiful supply of fish. The waterways also served as excellent transportation routes.

Exploration. In 1535, the French explorer Jacques Cartier sailed up the St. Lawrence River. The Lachine Rapids, south of what is now Montreal, prevented Cartier from going farther by ship. He then explored the Island of Montreal and found the Iroquois village of Hochelaga at the foot of Mount Royal. Several thousand Indians lived in the village. Another famous French explorer, Samuel de Champlain, visited the site of Montreal in 1603 and 1611. By that time, the Iroquois had abandoned the site.

French settlement. In 1639, Jérôme Le Royer, Sieur de la Dauversière, a French tax collector, formed a company in Paris to establish a colony on the Island of Montreal. In 1641, the company sent a Roman Catholic missionary group to the island to convert the Indians to Christianity. The group, led by Paul de Chomedey, Sieur de Maisonneuve, arrived in 1642. The colonists built a fort at what is now Place Royale in Old Montreal and established the settlement of Ville-Marie.

Iroquois Indians attacked the colony, hoping to stop the profitable fur trade that the French had established with the Algonquin and Huron. The Huron were the chief rivals of the Iroquois. Despite the attacks, the colony prospered as a religious center and fur-trading post. The French and the Iroquois made peace in 1701.

By the early 1700's, Ville-Marie had become known as

Montreal. It had a population of about 3,500 in 1710 and was the commercial heart of France's North American empire, called *New France*. Montreal's location on the St. Lawrence River made it an important center of trade. European goods passed through Montreal on the way to the North American west. The St. Lawrence also linked Montreal to the rich supplies of furs in Canada's interior. Montreal's location near the Ottawa River made it the gateway to the valuable forests of the Canadian northwest.

British settlement. British troops under General Jeffery Amherst captured Montreal in 1760, during the French and Indian War (1754-1763). The surrender of Montreal marked the end of the fighting in this war and led to the collapse of New France. The Treaty of Paris, signed in 1763, officially ended the French and Indian War and made Canada a British colony. A few English-speaking settlers then came to Montreal.

General Richard Montgomery's American forces occupied Montreal in November 1775, during the Revolutionary War in America (1775-1783). Benjamin Franklin and other American diplomats tried to gain French-Canadian support against the British. But their efforts failed, partly because most French Canadians regarded the war as just a quarrel between Britain and its colonies. In June 1776, the arrival of British troops forced the American soldiers to withdraw, and Montreal became a British possession again.

Fur traders in Montreal founded the North West Company as a rival to the Hudson's Bay Company fur trade. The new firm was organized in the 1770's.

Lithograph (1843) by James Duncan; Public Archives of Canada

Montreal's waterfront district was the city's chief center of activity in the early 1800's, *above.* Today, the district is known as *Old Montreal* and has many historic sites.

Montreal began to expand toward the north and the south on the Island of Montreal in the late 1700's. English-speaking merchants began to establish businesses in Montreal during this period. They gradually gained control of the town's economy. A major cause of this development was that many French merchants had returned to France after British troops captured the city in 1760.

The early 1800's. By 1800, Montreal's population had reached 9,000. Canada's first steamboat, the *Accommodation,* sailed the St. Lawrence River from Montreal to Quebec in 1809. In 1821, the Hudson's Bay Company bought the North West Company. The Hudson Bay area then became the chief market for furs, and Montreal declined as a fur-trading center.

The Lachine Canal, which crosses the southern edge of Montreal, opened in 1825. It provided a detour for small vessels around the Lachine Rapids and led to a sharp increase in trade and travel between Montreal and the Great Lakes. Shipping replaced fur trading as Montreal's chief industry, and Montreal grew in importance as a port.

In 1832, Montreal was incorporated as a city. From 1844 until 1849, it served as the capital of the Province of Canada. By 1850, the city's population had soared to about 50,000. For a short period, the majority of Montreal's population was English-speaking.

The growing city. Montreal continued to develop as a transportation center during the mid-1800's, when railways linked it to Portland, Maine; and areas west of Toronto. Investment by wealthy English-speaking merchants helped Montreal become a major industrial center during this period. Many industries were built along the Lachine Canal. Thousands of British immigrants and French Canadians from other parts of Quebec came to Montreal to find jobs in the new factories.

By 1871, about 107,000 people lived in Montreal. About half of these people were of French ancestry.

The Canadian Pacific Railway Company (now CP Rail), based in Montreal, completed Canada's first transcontinental railroad in 1885. The railroad attracted more industry and brought new prosperity to the city. By 1901, Montreal's population had risen to 267,730. The *annexation* (addition) of several neighboring communities helped it reach 467,986 by 1911.

The war issue. During World War I (1914-1918), Canada fought on the side of the Allies, which included France, Britain, and the United States. Many of the French Canadians in Montreal supported the government's policy and volunteered for the war, along with the city's English-speaking citizens. In 1917, Canada's government introduced a military draft. Many French Canadians opposed this policy.

During World War II (1939-1945), a military draft again caused unrest among French Canadians. In 1940, Montreal Mayor Camillien Houde urged Montrealers to defy a Canadian government plan to register all the men and women in the country. Houde charged that the registration would lead to a military draft for overseas service. Most French Canadians opposed a draft, and Canadian government leaders had pledged not to establish one. Federal authorities arrested Houde and kept him in a prison camp until 1944. Tensions increased when the Canadian government introduced a draft for overseas service in 1944.

The changing city. By the early 1950's, Montreal's population had topped 1 million. During the late 1950's, the city entered a period of great economic growth. In 1958, a city development program enlarged Montreal Harbour. The opening of the St. Lawrence Seaway in 1959 attracted hundreds of industries.

During the 1960's, a construction boom in the downtown area of Montreal gave the city a new skyline. Private developers tore down old structures throughout the area and replaced them with huge banks, hotels, and office buildings. The two tallest skyscrapers in Montreal, the 49-story Royal Bank of Canada Building and the 47-story Place Victoria, were completed during this period.

Other important downtown developments of the 1960's included Place Bonaventure, a trade mart, and the Place des Arts, a cultural center. An underground shopping network also was constructed.

The city built new highways and a new subway, the Métro, to help serve visitors attending Expo 67, an international exhibition held in Montreal in 1967. More than 50 million people attended the exhibition.

In 1975, the Montreal International Airport (Mirabel) opened. Montreal hosted the 1976 Summer Olympic Games. Construction for the event included housing facilities for the athletes and a new sports stadium. Montreal officials began to rent the housing to the public in 1978. The city's professional baseball team, the Montreal Expos, began playing in the stadium in 1977. Jean Drapeau served as mayor of Montreal from 1954 to 1957 and again from 1960 until 1986.

The separatist movement. In 1960, the Rassemblement pour l'Indépendence Nationale (Assembly for National Independence) was founded in Montreal. Its chief aim was to bring about the separation of Quebec from the rest of Canada and make the province an independent nation.

The Front de Libération du Québec (Quebec Liberation Front), a terrorist organization known as the *FLQ,* began to use violence to promote separatism in 1963. At first, the FLQ attacked armories and other symbols of the federal government. The organization soon became involved in labor disputes. During the period from 1963 to 1968, the FLQ claimed responsibility for bombings and armed robberies in the Montreal area.

In October 1970, members of the FLQ kidnapped British Trade Commissioner James R. Cross and Quebec Labor Minister Pierre Laporte. Canadian Prime Minister Pierre Trudeau, a French Canadian born in Montreal, sent federal troops to Montreal and other Quebec cities to guard government officials. The murder of Laporte later in the month increased tension in Montreal. The federal troops were withdrawn in January 1971, after police arrested four members of the FLQ and charged them with the kidnapping and murder of Laporte. Cross's kidnappers had released him after government officials guaranteed the kidnappers safe passage to Cuba.

Recent developments. In 1982, Montreal annexed the northern suburb of Pointe-aux-Trembles. The annexation of that suburb increased the area of Montreal by about 10 percent. Development of downtown Montreal continued in the 1980's. But many of the development projects stressed the preservation of the city's architectural heritage. The city also adopted a long-range urban development plan.

In 1992, Montreal marked its 350th anniversary with several construction projects and year-long celebrations. The Museum of Contemporary Art moved to a new home at Place des Arts. Two new museums, the Archaeological and Historical Museum and a science center called the Biodôme, also opened.   Robin B. Burns

Study aids

Related articles in *World Book* include:

Biographies

Amherst, Lord Jeffery	La Vérendrye, Sieur de
Bourassa, Henri	Papineau, Louis Joseph
Cartier, Jacques	Trudeau, Pierre Elliott
D'Youville, Saint Marguerite	Vanier, Georges Philias

History

French and Indian wars
Hudson's Bay Company
North West Company
Revolutionary War in America

Other related articles

Canada (pictures)	Quebec (pictures)
Laval	Saint Lawrence River
Ottawa River	Saint Lawrence Seaway

Outline

I. The city
  A. Old Montreal
  B. Downtown Montreal
  C. Metropolitan area
II. People
  A. Ethnic groups
  B. Housing
  C. Education
  D. Social problems
III. Economy
  A. Transportation
  B. Industry
  C. Trade and finance
  D. Communication
IV. Cultural life and places to visit
  A. The arts
  B. Libraries
  C. Museums
  D. Churches
  E. Parks
  F. Sports
  G. Other places to visit
V. Government
  A. Organization
  B. Problems
VI. History

Questions

How do major problems in Montreal differ from those in other cities?
Why did the Iroquois Indians attack Ville-Marie in the 1600's?
Why is Montreal's public school system unusual?
Who founded Montreal? When?
What are Montreal's two most important industries?
How does Montreal's location contribute to its economic importance?
What governments in Canada have larger annual budgets than Montreal?
Why has the Métro been called the "world's largest underground art gallery"?
What is Habitat? Who designed it?
What is Montreal's *Underground City?*

Montreal, University of, or Université de Montréal, is a private, coeducational university in Montreal, Que. All courses are conducted in French. They lead to bachelor's, master's, and doctor's degrees. The university has faculties of architecture, arts and science, business administration, dentistry, education, engineering, graduate

University of Montreal

The University of Montreal, the largest French-language university outside France, stands on the slopes of Mount Royal.

studies, law, medicine, music, nursing, optometry, pharmacy, physical health and education, theology, and veterinary medicine. It also offers interdisciplinary studies. The faculty of continuing education conducts evening and summer courses. A large computer center serves all university departments. Research is conducted in all fields of study, especially in the medical, natural, physical, and social sciences. The university includes the Polytechnic School, or École Polytechnique; and a business school, the École des Hautes Études Commerciales.

The University of Montreal was founded in 1876. It was controlled by the Roman Catholic Church until 1967, when it became nondenominational. For enrollment, see **Canada** (table: Universities and colleges).

Critically reviewed by the University of Montreal

Montréal-Nord, *mawn ray AL nawr,* Quebec (pop. 85,516), lies on Montreal Isle, and adjoins the northeast section of the city of Montreal (see **Quebec** [political map]). In English, the city's name is *Montreal North.* It produces furniture, food products, and electric appliances. Founded in 1915, Montréal-Nord became a city in 1959. It has a mayor-council form of government.

Hubert Charbonneau

Monts, *mawn,* **Sieur de** (1560?-1630?), a French explorer and colonizer, settled the region of Acadia in Canada. King Henry IV of France made de Monts a lieutenant general and governor of Acadia. The king also granted him a monopoly over the fur trade in Acadia on the condition that he bring settlers into the region.

De Monts sailed for America in March 1604 with Jean de Biencourt de Poutrincourt and Samuel de Champlain. They explored the Bay of Fundy and settled at the mouth of the Saint Croix River. In 1605, they founded Port Royal, Nova Scotia. De Monts then returned to France, leaving Poutrincourt as governor.

De Monts never returned to Canada. His monopoly over the fur trade ended in 1608. But he remained active in the trade until 1617. In 1608, de Monts sent Champlain to Canada to found Quebec, establish a warehouse, and explore the country. De Monts was born in Saintonge, France. His given and family name was Pierre du Gua.

John A. Dickinson

See also **Acadia; Annapolis Royal; Champlain, Samuel de; Poutrincourt, Jean de Biencourt de.**

Montserrat, *MAHNT suh RAT,* is one of the Leeward Islands in the West Indies. It is a British dependency. It lies about 250 miles (402 kilometers) southeast of Puerto Rico (see **West Indies** [map]). Montserrat has an area of

38 square miles (98 square kilometers) and a population of 11,900. It has three groups of mountains. The highest group is the Soufrière Hills, which rise to about 3,000 feet (910 meters) in the southern part of the island. Sea-island cotton, limes, and vegetables are the chief crops. The capital is Plymouth.

Christopher Columbus reached Montserrat in 1493 during his second voyage to the Western Hemisphere. Columbus named the island after a mountain in Spain. Irish settlers came to Montserrat in 1632, and today many of the people speak with a *brogue* (Irish accent). The English and French fought for possession of Montserrat for about 150 years. Britain has controlled the island since 1783. In 1989, Hurricane Hugo struck Montserrat, killing 10 people and severely damaging most of the buildings on the island.   Gustavo A. Antonini

Montserrat, *MAHNT suh RAT,* is a mountain and a famous monastery near Barcelona in eastern Spain. The mountain's highest peak is 4,054 feet (1,236 meters) above sea level. Its name probably means *saw-toothed mountain,* referring to its jagged peaks.

The monastery of Montserrat, built in the 700's or 800's, is about 20 miles (32 kilometers) northwest of Barcelona. Many pilgrims visit the restored church to see the *Black Virgin,* patron saint of Catalonia. Christopher Columbus brought Indians to pay homage at this church.   George Kish

Monument is a structure, usually a building or statue, built in memory of a person or an event. *National monuments* are places of historic, scientific, or scenic interest set aside by a government as public property. They include such structures as historic forts and such natural features as canyons. For a list of national monuments that have separate articles in *World Book,* see **National Park System** (table).   William J. Hennessey

Mood is a person's state of mind or outlook on life. Everyone's mood may change from day to day, or, sometimes, from hour to hour. But in certain mental illnesses, usually called *bipolar disorder* or *manic-depressive disorder,* the patient's mood is obviously disturbed. Patients may be sad, or happy and excited, for no visible reason. Their mood changes often. Some psychiatrists believe that the basic trouble with such patients is a disturbance of their mood. They have suggested calling such illnesses *primary mood disturbances.* Psychoanalysts believe that an apparently unexplainable mood can be caused by unconscious thoughts, wishes, or guilt feelings. But there is as yet no data to prove this belief.

Paula J. Clayton

Mood, or *mode,* is a term applied to verb forms that distinguish among certain kinds of meaning. For example, the verb *is* in "He is my brother" is an *indicative* mood form—that is, it states a fact. But the verb *were* in "if he were my brother" is a *subjunctive* mood form—that is, it expresses a condition contrary to fact.

Some languages have elaborate mood forms, but in English not many contrasts remain between the indicative and the subjunctive mood. For the verb *be,* the indicative forms of the present tense are *I am, you are, he is, we are,* and *they are.* The subjunctive forms are *I be, you be, he be, we be,* and *they be.* In the past tense, the indicative forms are *I was, you were, he was, we were,* and *they were,* and the subjunctive forms are *I were, you were, he were, we were,* and *they were.* Other verbs have a distinction at only one point: the third person singular of the present tense. For instance, *she calls* is indicative, but *she call* is subjunctive.

Subjunctive uses. Although the subjunctive has limited forms and uses in English, it is useful as a way of expressing a wish, a request, urgency, or a condition contrary to fact:

> I wish it *were* true. (wish)
> She asked that we *be* admitted. (request)
> It is necessary that he *stay*. (urgency)
> If words *were* deeds, we would be finished. (condition contrary to fact)

Older English usage employed the present subjunctive frequently in clauses introduced by *if* and *though,* such as "If it *be* he, let him be admitted," and "Though she *call* repeatedly, I shall not answer."

Other older uses of the subjunctive survive in many expressions, most of which are blessings or prayerful wishes: *God bless you, Long live the king, Heaven forbid, Suffice it to say,* and *God be with you.*

Imperative mood. The term *imperative mood* is commonly given to verbs that express commands or requests. "*Stop* the music," "*Leave* the room," and "*Give* this to your mother" are examples. In English, the imperative form is the *base* (simple) form of the verb. Imperative sentences usually have no subjects, and the omission of the subject is one of the chief signals that the sentence is a command or a request. But sometimes, imperative sentences do have subjects, as in "You do it, George."

Verb phrases. The terms *mood* and *mode* are also applied sometimes to verb phrases like *might go, should stay,* and *may try.* Words like *may, might, should,* and *would* are often called *modal auxiliaries.* They express the same meanings conveyed by mood endings on the verb in such languages as Greek or Latin. In English, however, modern grammarians usually limit the term *mood* to the indicative, subjunctive, and imperative forms, omitting the modals.   William F. Irmscher

Moodie, Susanna (1803-1885), was a Canadian author. Her best-known book is her autobiography, *Roughing It in the Bush* (1852). The book gives an accurate account of the hardships of pioneer life in Canada in the 1830's. But it also includes humorous stories and lively sketches of people living on the Canadian frontier. Moodie based the book on her experiences as a pioneer farmer in what is now Ontario.

Moodie was born into a wealthy family in Bungay, England, near Norwich. Her maiden name was Susanna Strickland. In 1832, she married Lieutenant J. W. D. Moodie, an officer in the British army. In that year, Moodie immigrated with her husband to the area north of Lake Ontario in what was then called Upper Canada. From 1839 to 1851, Moodie wrote fiction and poetry for the *Literary Garland,* a Canadian magazine.
   Rosemary Sullivan

Moody, Dwight Lyman (1837-1899), was an American evangelist. He founded the interdenominational Moody Memorial Church, the Moody Bible Institute, and the Moody Press in Chicago (see **Moody Bible Institute**). He also established a private high school for girls and another for boys near Northfield, Mass.

Moody was born in East Northfield, Mass. He left a job as a clerk in a Boston shoe store to become a shoe salesman in Chicago in 1856. He devoted all his time to

Sunday school and YMCA activities after 1860. He conducted great evangelistic campaigns in the United States and Britain, appearing with Ira D. Sankey, a gospel singer and hymn writer.   Henry Warner Bowden

Moody, Helen Wills. See Wills, Helen N.
Moody, Maryon Elspeth. See Pearson, Lester Bowles (Education and war service).

Moody, William Vaughn (1869-1910), was an American dramatist, poet, teacher, and literary historian. Critics hailed his play *The Great Divide* (1906) as a landmark in American drama because of its frank, naturalistic treatment of the collision between eastern puritanism and western frontier individualism. Moody planned a verse *trilogy* (three related plays) on the theme of "the unity of God and man." He completed *The Masque of Judgment* (1900) and *The Fire Bringer* (1904), but died before finishing the third play, *The Death of Eve.* He also wrote *The Faith Healer* (1909).

Moody's *Poems* (1901) contain the well-known lyrics "Gloucester Moors" and "The Quarry." While teaching at the University of Chicago, Moody wrote *History of English Literature* (1902) with Robert Morss Lovett. Moody was born in Spencer, Ind.   Frederick C. Wilkins

Moody Bible Institute, in Chicago, is an independent school that trains pastors, missionaries, and church-related workers. It offers bachelor's degrees, graduate and adult-education classes, and conducts a worldwide correspondence school. The institute operates 11 radio stations, the Moody Broadcasting Network, and Moody Press Publishers, and publishes *Moody Monthly* magazine. The Moody Institute of Science, in Whittier, Calif., produces religious and science films.

Dwight Lyman Moody, an evangelist, founded the institute in 1886. He established it to educate men and women in spreading the message of the Bible to the poor and working classes.
   Critically reviewed by the Moody Bible Institute
   See also **Moody, Dwight Lyman.**

WORLD BOOK photo by Steinkamp/Ballogg

The Moody Bible Institute offers college-level Christian service training. Its headquarters, *above,* are in Chicago.

Moon

The moon was photographed by the Apollo 11 astronauts during their return trip to the earth. They had made the first landing on the moon. The astronauts landed on the Sea of Tranquility, a large, dark-colored lava plain. The highland areas of the moon are lighter in color.

Moon is the earth's nearest neighbor in space. In 1969, this huge natural satellite of the earth became the first object in space to be visited by human beings.

The moon is the brightest object in the night sky, but it gives off no light of its own. When the moon "shines," it is *reflecting* (casting back) light from the sun. On some nights, the moon looks like a gleaming silver globe. On others, it appears as a thin slice of light. But the moon does not change its size or shape. Its appearance seems to change as different parts of it are lighted by the sun.

The moon travels around the earth once about every $27\frac{1}{3}$ days. The average distance between the centers of the earth and the moon is 238,857 miles (384,403 kilometers). A rocket journey from the earth to the moon and back takes about six days.

Because the moon is relatively close to the earth, it seems much larger than the stars and about the same size as the sun. The moon measures about 2,160 miles (3,476 kilometers) across. This distance is about a fourth the diameter of the earth and 400 times smaller than that

of the sun. If the moon were seen next to the earth, it would look like a tennis ball next to a basketball.

The earth is not the only planet with a moon. For example, Jupiter has 16 known satellites. The earth's moon is the sixth largest of the more than 40 natural satellites of the planets. For more information on natural satellites, see the separate planet articles.

The moon has no life of any kind. Compared with the earth, it has changed little over billions of years. The moon has no air, wind, or water. On the moon, the sky is black—even during the day—and the stars are always visible. At night, the rocky surface becomes colder than any place on the earth. In the day, the temperature of the rocks is slightly higher than that of boiling water.

Through the centuries, people have gazed at the moon, worshiped it, and studied it. The long-time dream of traveling to the moon became history on July 20, 1969, when astronaut Neil A. Armstrong of the United States set foot on it.

Space flights and moon landings have provided many facts about the moon. Moon exploration has also helped solve many mysteries about the earth, the sun, and the planets. For more information on moon exploration, see the *World Book* article on **Space exploration**.

The contributor of this article is Paul Gorenstein, Supervisory Astrophysicist at the Smithsonian Astrophysical Observatory.

NASA

NASA

The far side of the moon has a rugged surface. The large crater in the center of the photograph is International Astronomical Union Crater No. 308. It is about 50 miles (80 kilometers) wide. The lunar footprint at the right was made by Edwin E. Aldrin, Jr., an Apollo 11 astronaut.

The moon at a glance

Age: About 4,600,000,000 (4.6 billion) years.

Distance from the earth: *Shortest*—221,456 miles (356,399 kilometers); *Greatest*—252,711 miles (406,699 kilometers); *Mean*—238,857 miles (384,403 kilometers).

Diameter: About 2,160 miles (3,476 kilometers).

Circumference: About 6,790 miles (10,927 kilometers).

Surface area: About 14,670,000 square miles (38,000,000 square kilometers).

Rotation period: 27 days, 7 hours, 43 minutes.

Revolution period around the earth: 27 days, 7 hours, 43 minutes.

Average speed around the earth: 2,300 miles (3,700 kilometers) per hour.

Length of day and night: About 15 earth-days each.

Temperature at equator: *Sun at zenith over maria,* 260° F. (127° C); *Lunar night on maria,* −280° F. (−173° C).

Surface gravity: About $\frac{1}{6}$ that of the earth.

Escape velocity: $1\frac{1}{2}$ miles (2.4 kilometers) per second.

Mass: $\frac{1}{81}$ that of the earth.

Volume: $\frac{1}{50}$ that of the earth.

Atmosphere: Little or none.

WORLD BOOK diagram

The diameter of the moon is about 2,160 miles (3,476 kilometers), or about a fourth of the earth's diameter. If the moon were placed on top of the United States, it would extend almost from San Francisco to Cleveland.

The moon's surface. When seen with the unaided eye from the earth, the moon looks like a smooth globe with dark and light patches of gray. Field glasses or a small telescope will bring into view the features first seen by Galileo, the Italian scientist of the 1600's.

The dark patches on the moon are broad, flat plains that Galileo may have thought were covered with water. He called them *maria* (singular, *mare*), a Latin word meaning *seas.* Today, we know the maria are lowlands of rock covered by a thin layer of rocky soil. Most of the light gray parts of the moon's surface are rough and mountainous. These areas are called *highlands.* The maria occur mainly on the near side of the moon, which faces the earth. The far side is nearly all highlands.

Most of the maria were formed from 3.3 to 3.8 billion years ago by great flows of *lava* (molten rock) that poured out and cooled on the moon's surface. The lava that formed the maria has filled in the low places on the moon. Some of the low places, such as the Imbrium Basin in the Sea of Rains, are giant craters. The lava filling these craters forms round maria.

Craters are the most numerous features of the moon's surface. The moon has craters within craters and even connected craters. Scientists estimate that the moon has half a million craters that are more than 1 mile (1.6 kilometers) wide. A total of about 30 thousand billion craters are at least 1 foot (30 centimeters) wide.

Most of the small craters are simple bowl-shaped pits with low rims. Most craters from 5 to 10 miles (8 to 16 kilometers) wide have high walls and level floors. Many craters wider than 15 miles (24 kilometers) have hilly floors or central peaks. Large craters are rimmed by mountains and have steep, terraced walls. The largest crater, the Imbrium Basin, is about 700 miles (1,100 kilometers) wide. Its floor is covered by dark lava, which forms one eye of the familiar "man in the moon."

Certain craters on the moon are called *ray craters.* These craters are surrounded by light gray streaks known as *rays.* The rays look like splashes of bright material and extend out in many directions. Around Tycho, a crater 54 miles (87 kilometers) wide, a few rays are 10 to 15 miles (16 to 24 kilometers) wide and can be traced for nearly 1,000 miles (1,600 kilometers). Swarms of small *secondary craters* in the rays probably were formed by rocks thrown out of the ray craters. The rays probably are mixtures of broken rocks thrown from the ray craters and rock fragments splashed out of the secondary craters. Scientists know that the ray craters were formed late in the moon's history because their rays cross over maria, mountains, and other craters.

Billions of small craters on the moon have been formed by the impact of *meteoroids,* solid objects that travel through space. Many meteoroids also hit the earth's atmosphere. Most melt or break up high in the air, producing streaks of light called *meteors.* Only the largest reach the earth's surface fast enough to dig a crater. The moon's lack of atmosphere means that even tiny meteoroids form craters. Erosion on the moon works so slowly that craters only 1 foot (30 centimeters) in diameter remain for millions of years.

Many large craters on the moon probably were formed when *comets* or *asteroids* hit the moon. These bodies also travel around the sun, but they are much larger than meteoroids. The moon's largest and oldest

Schmidt Crater, on the western edge of the Sea of Tranquility, is 7 miles (11 kilometers) wide. The moon has billions of craters. The largest is about 700 miles (1,100 kilometers) wide.

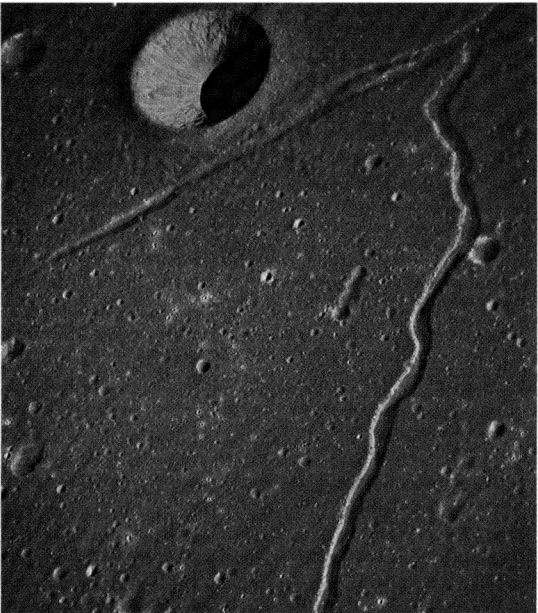

A winding rille, *right,* is one of several long, narrow valleys on the moon that probably were caused by flowing lava. Maskelyne G Crater, *top,* is about 4 miles (6 kilometers) wide.

craters may have been created by the impact of *planetesimals,* solid objects that perhaps crashed together and formed the moon itself.

A few craters on the moon look like volcanic craters on the earth. Some of these craters are found on the tops of small mountains or in the centers of low, rounded hills. In other places, craters are lined up in a row just as volcanoes on the earth commonly are lined up. Many of the lunar craters that resemble volcanoes are found on the lava plains.

The mountainous areas of the moon are scattered with huge craters. All the major mountain ranges of the moon appear to be the broken rims of these huge cra-

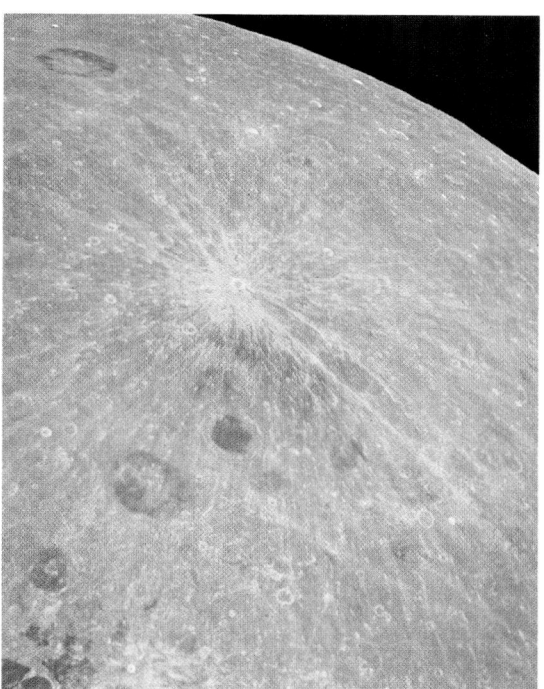

NASA

Rays of bright material spread from some craters across the moon's surface. This ray crater on the far side of the moon was photographed by the Apollo 13 astronauts.

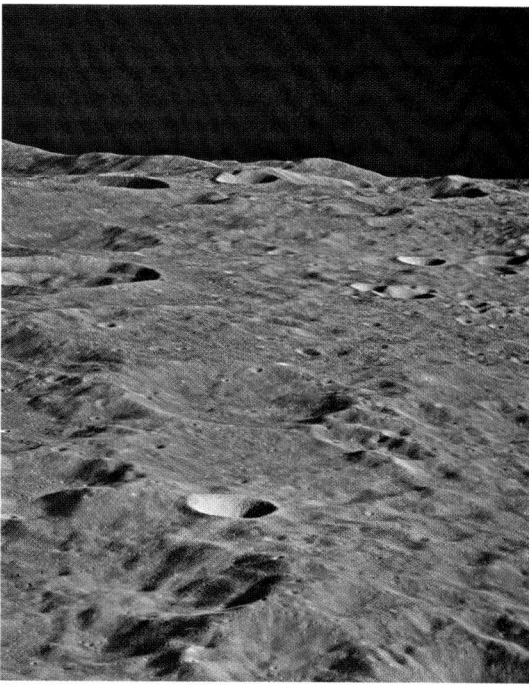

NASA

The surface of the moon's far side has more craters and mountains than that of the side that faces the earth. The far side has fewer "seas," and its craters appear smooth and worn.

NASA

A basalt rock returned by the Apollo 11 astronauts resembles lava rock from volcanoes on the earth. Gases escaping from the molten rock caused the holes.

NASA

A breccia rock collected from a crater during the Apollo 12 mission consists of soil and rock pieces squeezed together and coated with glass.

NASA

The oldest rock found on the moon is this Apollo 12 sample. It has high radioactivity and is more than 4 billion years old.

ters. The rugged Apennine Mountains, near the Sea of Rains, rise about 20,000 feet (6,100 meters). The Leibnitz Mountains, near the moon's south pole, are at least 26,000 feet (7,920 meters) high. They are about as tall as the highest mountains on the earth.

The moon also has long, narrow valleys called *rilles*. Most rilles are straight and probably were formed when the moon's outer crust was cracked, and sections of the surface dropped down. *Sinuous rilles* are winding channels that look much like dry riverbeds. They probably were formed by the flow of lava on the maria.

What the moon is made of. Scientists have learned much about the composition of the moon by studying

rocks and soil brought back by U.S. astronauts. But many questions will remain unanswered until samples can be taken from a number of places on the moon.

Moon soil collected by the first Apollo astronauts was dark gray to brownish gray. It consisted of bits of rock and glass, and scattered chunks of rock. The soil was formed by repeated grinding and churning of the moon's surface as meteoroids hit it and craters were formed. Soil on the maria generally is from 5 to 20 feet (1.5 to 6 meters) deep. About half of it consists of bits of glass. Some soil grains are microscopic glass balls.

Nothing lives in moon soil. The soil contains no plant or animal fossils. But some earth plants grow better

The labels on the map include:

Pythagoras, W. Bond, Strabo, Sea of Cold (Mare Frigoris), Bay of Dew, Jura Mountains, Plato, Endymion, Aristoteles, Hercules, Atlas, Alps, Alpine Valley, Bay of Rainbows, Straight Range, Mount Pico, Eudoxus, Franklin, Messala, Geminus, Mairan, Sea of Rains (Mare Imbrium), Aristillus, Archimedes, Caucasus, Autolycus, Posidonius, Lake of Dreams, Taurus Mountains, Cleomedes, Timocharis, Marsh of Decay, Apollo 15 landing, Sea of Serenity (Mare Serenitatis), Macrobius, Struve, Aristarchus, Apennines, Haemus Mountains, Apollo 17 landing, Marsh of Sleep, Sea of Crises (Mare Crisium), Cardanus, Kepler, Carpathians, Eratosthenes, Sea of Vapors (Mare Vaporum), Plinius, Copernicus, Seething Bay, Manilius, Marginal Sea, Reinhold, Sea of Tranquility (Mare Tranquillitatis), Lansberg, Central Bay, Julius Caesar, Agrippa, Maskelyne, Foaming Sea, Riccioli, Apollo 12 landing, Hipparchus, Schmidt, Apollo 11 landing, Sea of Fertility (Mare Fecunditatis), Grimaldi, Riphaeus Mountains, Apollo 14 landing, Ptolemaeus, Apollo 16 landing, Delambre, Gutenberg, Smyth's Sea, Letronne, Fra Mauro, Albategnius, Cyrillus, Theophilus, Pyrenees, Langrenus, Goclenius, Gassendi, Alphonsus, Abulfeda, Sea of Nectar (Mare Nectaris), Colombo, Vendelinus, Mersenius, Arzachel, Abulfeda, Catharina, Santbech, Sea of Moisture (Mare Humorum), Sea of Clouds (Mare Nubium), Straight Wall, Altai Scarp, Fracastorius, Petavius, Mercator, Pitatus, Purbach, Piccolomini, Humboldt, Campanus, Regiomontanus, Furnerius, Walter, Deslandres, Orontius, Stöfler, Maurolycus, Janssen, Schickard, Wilhelm, Tycho, Maginus, Pitiscus, Longomontanus, Cuvier, Schiller, Scheiner, Clavius, Manzinus, Vlacq, Blancanus, Curtius

WORLD BOOK map based on U.S. Air Force photographic mosaic

Moon—near side

Map index

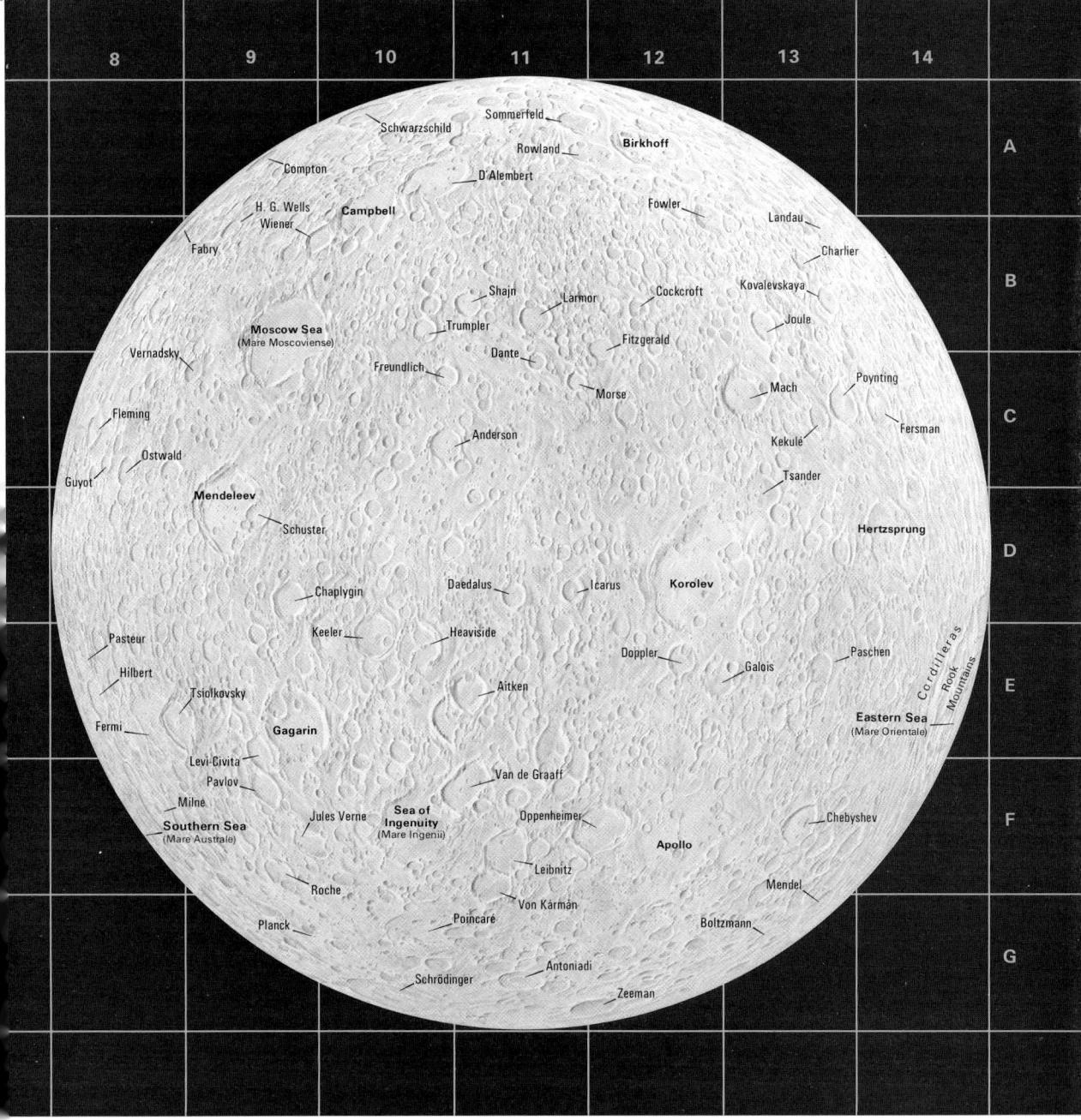

WORLD BOOK map by Bernardo Guiliano; adapted from the U.S. Air Force Lunar Chart

Moon—far side

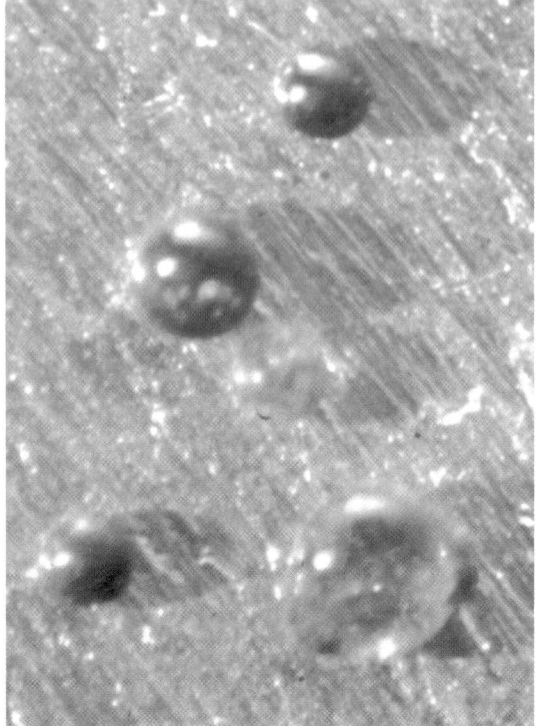

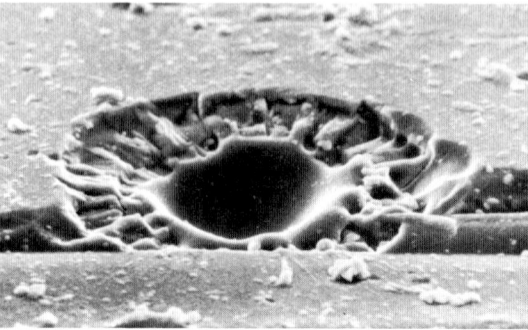

Microcraters on some moon samples can be seen only with a microscope. This crater, magnified 1,700 times, was formed by the high-speed impact of cosmic dust on broken glass particles.

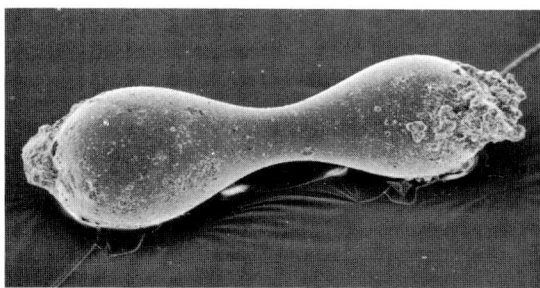

Tiny colored glass balls are found in much lunar soil. The spherules shown above are about the size of a period. These samples were brought back by the Apollo 11 astronauts.

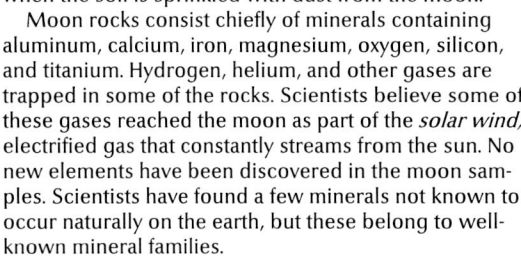

A dumbbell-shaped blob is one of the glassy objects that are found in the moon's soil. Such objects probably were formed when meteoroids struck the moon, splattering molten droplets.

when the soil is sprinkled with dust from the moon.

Moon rocks consist chiefly of minerals containing aluminum, calcium, iron, magnesium, oxygen, silicon, and titanium. Hydrogen, helium, and other gases are trapped in some of the rocks. Scientists believe some of these gases reached the moon as part of the *solar wind,* electrified gas that constantly streams from the sun. No new elements have been discovered in the moon samples. Scientists have found a few minerals not known to occur naturally on the earth, but these belong to well-known mineral families.

Two main types of rock have been collected by the astronauts. One type is *basalt,* a hardened lava and the most common volcanic rock on the earth. The lava rocks are mainly crystals of feldspar, pyroxene, and ilmenite. These minerals were formed at about 2200° F. (1200° C). They prove that part of the moon was extremely hot when the maria were formed. The second type of rock, called *breccia,* is made of soil and pieces of rock squeezed together when hit by falling objects.

The moon's outer crust seems stiff and strong, but much remains to be learned about its interior. On the Apollo 13 flight, mission controllers sent part of the giant Saturn rocket crashing into the moon. The resulting *seismic* (earthquakelike) vibrations lasted about four hours. These long-lasting vibrations had not been expected by scientists.

Gravity. Astronauts walk easily on the moon, even though they wear heavy equipment. They feel light be-

cause the force of gravity on the moon's surface is six times weaker than that on the surface of the earth. A boy or girl who weighs 60 pounds on the earth would weigh only 10 pounds on the moon. Gravity is weaker on the moon because the moon's *mass* (the amount of matter a body contains) is about 81 times smaller than the earth's mass. In 1968, scientists found that the force of gravity differs slightly from place to place on the moon. They believe the slight difference is caused by large concentrations of mass in many of the round maria. Scientists have used the term *mascons* to describe these areas, but the cause of mascons is not yet known.

Atmosphere and weather. The moon has little or no atmosphere. If the moon ever did have a surrounding layer of gases, it would have leaked away into space because of the moon's weak gravity. As a result of its lack of atmosphere, the moon has no weather, no clouds, no rain, and no wind. There is no water on its surface. Astronauts on the moon must carry air with them to breathe. They must talk to each other by radio because there is no air to carry sound.

Temperature. The surface of the moon gets much hotter and colder than any place on the earth. At the moon's equator, noon temperatures on the maria are as high as 260° F. (127° C). Temperatures drop below −280° F. (−173° C) during the two-week lunar night. In some deep craters near the moon's poles, the temperature is always near −400° F. (−240° C). Space suits protect astronauts from the heat and cold.

The orbit of the moon. The moon travels around the earth in an *elliptical* (oval shaped) path called an *orbit.* One such trip around the earth is called a *revolution.* The moon moves at an average speed of about 2,300 miles (3,700 kilometers) per hour along its 1.4-million-mile (2.3-million-kilometer) orbit.

The moon also travels with the earth as the earth circles the sun every $365\frac{1}{4}$ days, an earth year. The moon actually moves from west to east in the sky. But it seems to move from east to west as it rises and sets because the earth spins much faster than the moon revolves around the earth.

Because the moon's orbit is oval, the moon is not always the same distance from the earth. The point where the moon comes closest to the earth is 221,456 miles (356,399 kilometers) away. This point is called the moon's *perigee.* The moon's farthest point from the earth is 252,711 miles (406,699 kilometers) away. This point is the moon's *apogee.*

The gravitational pull of the earth keeps the moon in its orbit. If the earth or its gravitational force were to suddenly disappear, the moon would no longer orbit the earth. But the moon would still move in orbit around the sun.

Scientists measure the moon's revolution around the earth in *synodic months* and *sidereal months.* A synodic month—which equals about $29\frac{1}{2}$ days—is the period from one new moon to the next new moon. It is the time that the moon takes to revolve around the earth in relation to the sun. If the moon started on its orbit from a spot exactly between the earth and the sun, it would return to almost the same place in about $29\frac{1}{2}$ days. A synodic month equals a full day on the moon. This *lunar day* is divided into about two weeks of light and about two weeks of darkness.

A sidereal month—about $27\frac{1}{3}$ days—is the time the moon takes to make one trip around the earth in relation to the stars. If the moon's revolution were to begin on a line with a certain star, it would return to the same position about $27\frac{1}{3}$ days later.

A synodic month is longer than a sidereal month because the earth travels around the sun while the moon travels around the earth. By the time the moon has made one revolution around the earth, the earth has revolved $\frac{1}{13}$ of the way around the sun. Therefore, the moon has to travel slightly farther to be in the same position in relation to the sun.

Rotation. The moon rotates completely on its *axis* (an imaginary line through its north and south poles) only once during each trip around the earth. The moon rotates from west to east, the same direction that it travels around the earth. At its equator, the moon rotates at a speed of about 10 miles (16 kilometers) per hour. When you look up at the moon, you always see the same side.

How the moon gets its light

The moon gives off no light of its own. It shines by reflecting sunlight. Like the earth, half of the moon is always lighted by the sun's direct rays, and the other half is always in shadow. At times during the month, only a small slice of the moon's side that faces the earth is in full sunshine. The moon appears as a thin, bright *crescent. Earthshine* (sunlight reflected by the earth), dimly lights the moon's "dark" side when it faces the earth. Because the moon is made up chiefly of dark gray rocks and dust, it reflects only 10 per cent of the light it receives.

WORLD BOOK diagram

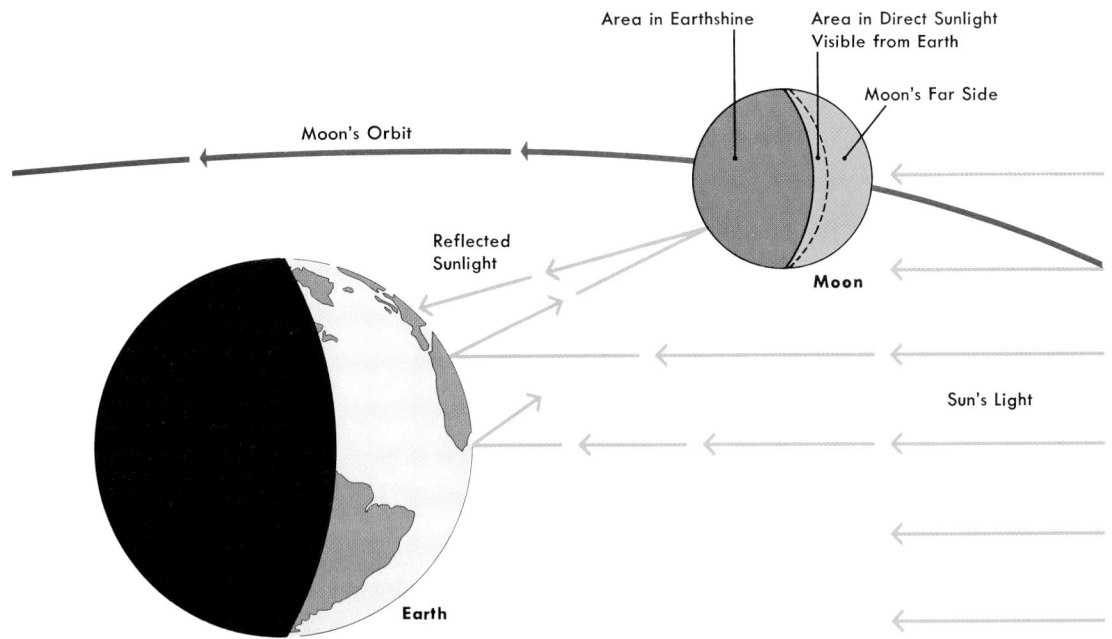

Area in Earthshine

Area in Direct Sunlight Visible from Earth

Moon's Far Side

Moon's Orbit

Reflected Sunlight

Moon

Sun's Light

Earth

The moon is held in this position by gravitational forces. We know that the moon is rotating because we can see only one side of it. If the moon did not rotate, we would be able to see its entire surface.

Sometimes we can see a short distance around the *limb* (edge) of the moon. The moon seems to swing from side to side and nod up and down during each revolution. These apparent motions are called *librations.* They are caused by slight changes in the moon's speed of revolution and by a five-degree tilt of the moon's orbit to the orbit of the earth. At different times, the librations enable us to see a total of 59 per cent of the moon's surface from the earth. The other 41 per cent of the moon's surface can never be seen from the earth. The moon's far side was a complete mystery until Oct. 7, 1959, when a Soviet rocket orbited the moon and sent back a few pictures of one far side area to the earth. On Dec. 24, 1968, the Apollo 8 astronauts became the first people to see the far side.

The phases of the moon. During a synodic month, we can see the moon "change" from a slim crescent to a full circle and back again. These apparent changes in the moon's shape and size are actually different conditions of lighting called *phases.* They are caused by changes in the amount of sunlight reflected by the moon toward the earth. The moon seems to change shape because we

see different parts of its sunlit surface as it orbits the earth. Like the earth, half the moon is always lighted by the sun's rays except during eclipses. Sometimes the far side of the moon is in full sunlight even though it is out of view.

When the moon is between the sun and the earth, its sunlit side—the far side—is turned away from the earth. Astronomers call this darkened phase of the moon a *new moon.* In the new moon phase, the side of the moon that faces the earth is dimly lighted by *earthshine,* which is sunlight that is reflected from the earth to the moon.

A day after a new moon, a thin slice of light appears along the moon's eastern edge. The line between the sunlit part of the moon's face and its dark part is called the *terminator.* Each day, more and more of the moon's sunlit side is seen as the terminator moves from east to west. After about seven days, we can see half of a full moon. This half-circle shape is half of the moon's side that is exposed to sunlight and is the part that can be seen from the earth. This phase is called the *first quarter.* About seven days after the first quarter, the moon has moved to a point where the earth is between the moon and the sun. We can now see the entire sunlit side of the moon. This phase is called *full moon.* A full moon seems bright on a clear night. But a whole sky of

Why the moon has phases

The moon seems to change shape from day to day as it goes through *phases.* The moon changes from *new moon* to *full moon* and back again every $29\frac{1}{2}$ days. The phases are caused by the moon's orbit around the earth as the earth and moon travel around the sun. Half of the moon is always in sunlight, but varying amounts of the lighted side are visible from the earth. As the moon and earth move along their orbits, more of the sunlit part is seen until it shines as a full moon. Then less and less of the sunlit part is seen until the dark new moon returns.

WORLD BOOK diagram

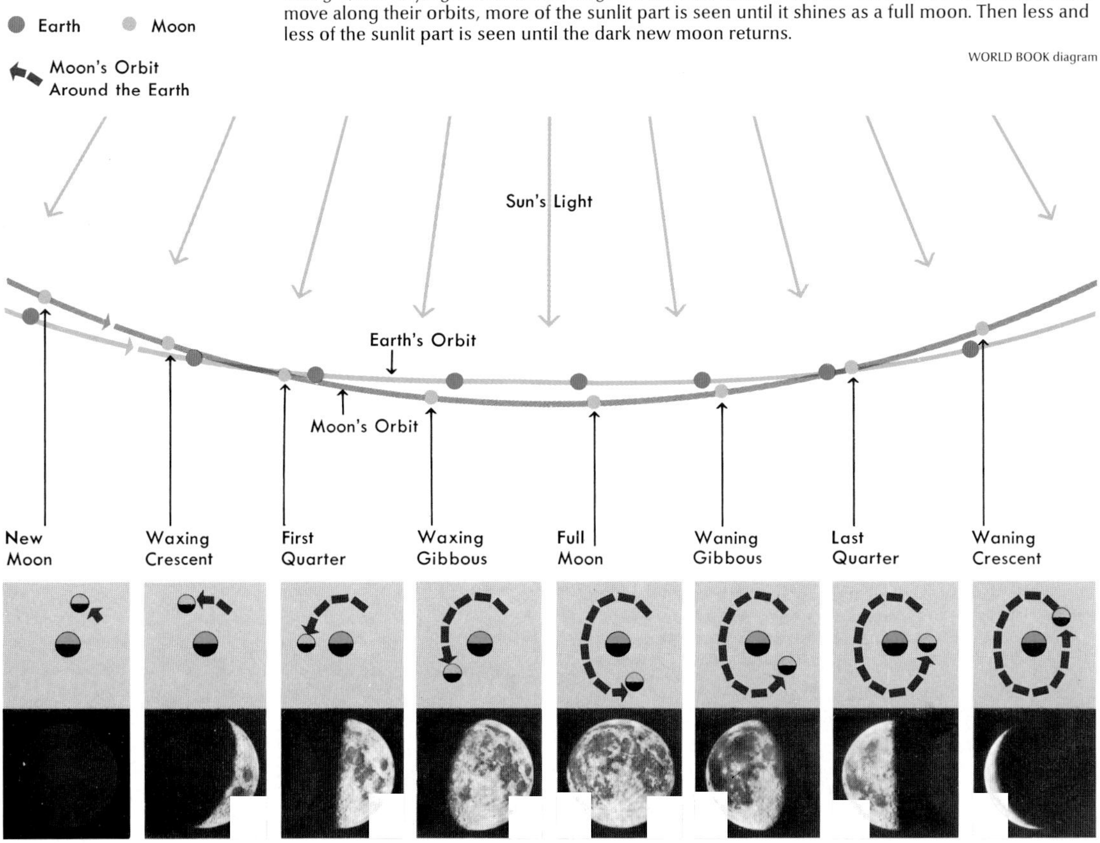

● Earth   ● Moon

← Moon's Orbit Around the Earth

Sun's Light

Earth's Orbit

Moon's Orbit

| New Moon | Waxing Crescent | First Quarter | Waxing Gibbous | Full Moon | Waning Gibbous | Last Quarter | Waning Crescent |

full moons would be only about a fifth as bright as the sun.

About seven days after full moon, we again see half of a full moon. This phase is called the *last quarter,* or the third quarter. After another week, the moon returns to a point between the earth and the sun for the new moon phase.

As the moon changes from new moon to full moon, it is said to be *waxing.* During the period from full moon back to new moon, the moon is said to be *waning.* When the moon appears smaller than half of a full moon, it is called *crescent.* When the moon looks larger than half of a full moon, yet is not a full moon, it is called *gibbous.*

The moon rises and sets at different times. In the new moon phase, it rises above the horizon with the sun in the east and travels close to the sun across the sky. With each passing day, the moon rises an average of about 50 minutes later and drops about 12 degrees farther behind in relation to the sun.

By the end of a week—at the first quarter phase—the moon rises at about noon and sets at about midnight. In another week—at full moon—it rises as the sun sets and sets as the sun rises. At last quarter, it rises at about midnight and sets at about noon. A week later—back at new moon—the moon and the sun rise together in the east.

Eclipses. The light of the sun causes both the earth and the moon to throw shadows into space. When a full moon passes through the earth's shadow, we see an *eclipse* of the moon. During a lunar eclipse, the moon is a dark reddish color. It is faintly lighted by red rays from the sun that have been *refracted* (bent) by the earth's atmosphere.

During another kind of eclipse, the new moon passes directly between the earth and the sun. When part or all of the sun is hidden by the moon, we see a *solar eclipse* (an eclipse of the sun). Solar eclipses occur where the shadow of the moon passes across the earth. The apparent size of the sun and the moon just happens by accident to be nearly equal. See **Eclipse.**

The moon and tides. Since ancient times, man has watched the rising and falling of the water level along the seashore. Just as the earth's gravity pulls on the moon, the moon's gravity pulls on the earth and its large bodies of water. The moon's gravity pulls up the water directly below the moon. On the other side of the earth, the moon pulls the solid body of the earth away from the water. As a result, two bulges called *high tides* are formed on the oceans and seas. As the earth turns, these tidal bulges travel from east to west. Every place along the seashore has two high tides and two low tides daily. See **Tide.**

Why we see only one side of the moon

When we look at the moon, we always see the same side. This is because the moon turns once on its axis in the same time that it circles the earth. Astronomers call the moon's motion *synchronous* rotation. The force of gravity always keeps the same side of the moon toward the earth. This diagram shows why one side of the moon can never be seen from the earth. As the moon turns, a moon landmark such as a crater, shown as a red dot, stays in about the same position during the month. Sometimes the landmark is hidden in the dark part of the moon facing the earth. But because it does not move to the side of the moon opposite the earth, we know that we are seeing only one side of the moon. If the moon did not turn in its journey around the earth, the landmark would gradually seem to move across the visible surface of the moon. It would disappear around the moon's western edge and return to view on the moon's eastern edge about 14 days later.

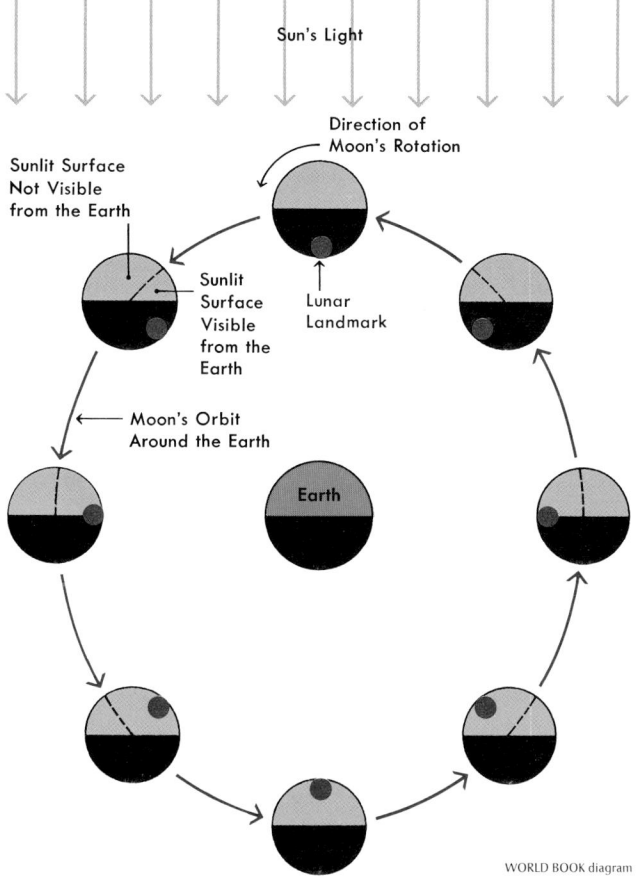

Sun's Light

Direction of Moon's Rotation

Sunlit Surface Not Visible from the Earth

Sunlit Surface Visible from the Earth

Lunar Landmark

Moon's Orbit Around the Earth

Earth

WORLD BOOK diagram

Age and history. The earth and meteorites that have fallen on the earth are more than $4\frac{1}{2}$ billion years old. Largely as a result of this evidence, most scientists assume that the entire solar system—including the moon—was formed at about the same time. However, none of the lunar rocks brought back to the earth by the Apollo astronauts has been proved to be more than 4.2 billion years old. Scientists have determined that some of the rocks are at least that old by using the potassium-argon method of dating. This method was used because the rocks contain radioactive potassium 40, which changes into argon gas 40 at a constant rate. Scientists measure the relative amounts of potassium and argon present in a rock and then use the ratio to calculate the rock's age.

The oldest lunar rocks, however, actually may be more than 4.2 billion years old. High temperatures may have driven away the argon gas that had formed in the rocks by 4.2 billion years ago. The temperature of the rocks could have been raised to such levels by a bombardment of meteorites or by some other event.

Most of the large craters in the highlands of the moon were formed when many large solid bodies from space struck the moon. Scientists believe this bombardment took place between 3.9 and 4.2 billion years ago. Also during this period, other solid bodies probably struck the earth and other planets. As time went on, fewer bodies were left in space and the number that struck the moon gradually decreased.

The maria formed when lava flowed out on the lunar surface between 3.3 and 3.8 billion years ago. The maria are smoother than the highlands because the lava covered the old craters on the lowlands.

Scientific theories have been developed to explain how the moon was formed. But more scientific exploration is needed before the mystery can be solved.

The moon was once much closer to the earth than it is now. Early in its history, it may have been only about 10,000 miles (16,000 kilometers) from the earth. The earth also may have been spinning 10 times faster than it does today. The moon's orbit is still becoming larger as the earth spins more slowly. These changes are caused by friction from the tides, which slows the earth's rotation and forces the moon into a larger orbit.

In 1879, George H. Darwin, an English mathematician,

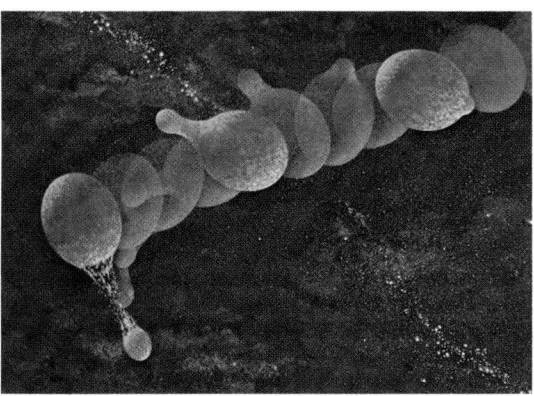

WORLD BOOK diagram by Herbert Herrick

The "escape" theory of the moon's origin says that the earth and the moon were once a single body. The sun's gravity caused a bulge on one side of the fast-spinning earth. A lopsided dumbbell formed, and the bulge broke away and became the moon.

WORLD BOOK diagram by Herbert Herrick

A third moon formation theory says that the moon was formed at about the same time as the earth and in the same region of space. The two bodies were made from huge whirlpools of gas and dust that were left over when the sun was formed.

WORLD BOOK diagram by Herbert Herrick

The "capture" theory of the moon's formation says that the moon was once a planet that traveled around the sun. At some point along its orbit, the moon was captured by the earth's gravity and became a satellite of the earth.

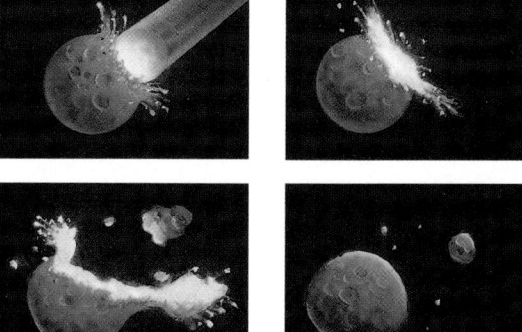

WORLD BOOK illustration by Rob Wood, Stansbury, Ronsaville, Wood Inc.

The "collision" theory proposes that a large body from space smashed into the earth and knocked a mass of solid material from the earth's mantle. This material orbited the earth and eventually united into a single mass to form the moon.

suggested that the earth and the moon were once a single body. Shortly after the earth was formed, according to his theory, called the "escape" theory, a huge bulge was produced on the earth by the attraction of the sun. The earth was spinning much more rapidly than it is today, and the bulge eventually broke away from the earth. Other scientists have pointed out that the material of the bulge probably would have become extremely hot and may have broken up into many pieces. Later, the pieces may have fallen together again to form the moon. A second theory, called the "capture" theory, states that the moon was formed as a separate planet that followed its own orbit around the sun. Every few years, the moon came close to the earth because their orbits were similar. During one of these close passes, the moon was captured in the earth's gravitational field.

A third theory is that the earth and moon were formed close to each other from a disk of gas and dust around the sun. They were formed as a double-planet system, much like the systems of double stars that are common in our galaxy. The large craters created early in the moon's history may have been formed by the impact of smaller moons that were circling the earth, or by planetesimals that were orbiting the sun.

A fourth theory is that a large body from space collided with the earth after its iron core was formed. The resulting impact caused an explosion that blew material from the earth's *mantle* (shell of rock between the core and surface) into outer space. This material began to orbit the earth and eventually united into a single body to form the moon. Supporters of this theory say that rocks and other materials discovered on the moon are similar to those found on the earth and could have originated from the earth's mantle.

The moon in history

Measuring time. Since ancient times, people have measured time by the phases of the moon. The American Indians recorded that a harvest or a hunt took place a certain number of "moons" ago. People in Muslim countries still use a calendar with 354 days, or 12 synodic lunar months. Jews use the lunar calendar to establish the dates of religious holidays. Christians observe Easter on a date that varies each year because it is related to the full moon. The words *month* and *Monday* come from Old English words related to *moon.*

Mythology. Early peoples thought the moon was a powerful god or goddess. The ancient Romans called their moon goddesses Luna and Diana. Diana was also the goddess of the hunt and used a moon crescent for a bow and moonbeams for arrows. The moon goddesses of the ancient Greeks were Selene and Artemis. The Greeks and Romans also believed in a goddess called Hecate who was said to have three faces—as Hecate, she was the moon in its dark form; as Artemis (Diana), she was the waxing moon; and as Selene (Luna), she was the full moon. The early Egyptians honored the moon god Khonsu. The Babylonians knew the moon as Sin, sometimes called Nannar, the most powerful of the sky gods. Some American Indian tribes believed the moon and the sun were brother and sister gods. Today, some peoples still worship the moon.

Legend and folklore. Many peoples who did not think of the moon as sacred believed that it influenced life. Early philosophers and priests taught that the moon was related to birth, growth, and death because it waxed and waned. Some people feared eclipses as signs of famine, war, or other disasters. According to one superstition, sleeping in moonlight could cause insanity. The word *lunatic,* which means *moonstruck,* comes from *luna,* a Latin word meaning *moon.* Even today, many people believe the moon affects the weather. Others think seeds grow especially well when planted during a waxing moon. The moon is important in *astrology,* a popular *pseudo* (false) science.

Legends of various lands told how the "man in the moon" had been imprisoned there for stealing or for breaking the Sabbath. Some people saw other figures in the moon's markings. These figures include Jack and Jill, a beautiful woman, a cat, a frog, and a rabbit.

Many people once believed that some form of life existed on the moon. The ancient Greek writer Plutarch told of moon demons that lived in caves. Johannes Kepler, a German astronomer of the 1600's, wrote that lunar craters were built by moon creatures. In 1822, F. P. Gruithuisen, another German astronomer, told of discovering a "lunar city." In the 1920's, the American astronomer W. H. Pickering declared that insects might live on the moon. Many scientists hoped that certain chemicals might be found on the moon to give clues as to how life began on the earth.

Literature and music. Many authors and poets have written about the moon and have described its beauty. In *A Midsummer Night's Dream,* the famous English playwright William Shakespeare compared the moon to "a silver bow new-bent in heaven." In "The Cloud," the English poet Percy Bysshe Shelley described the moon

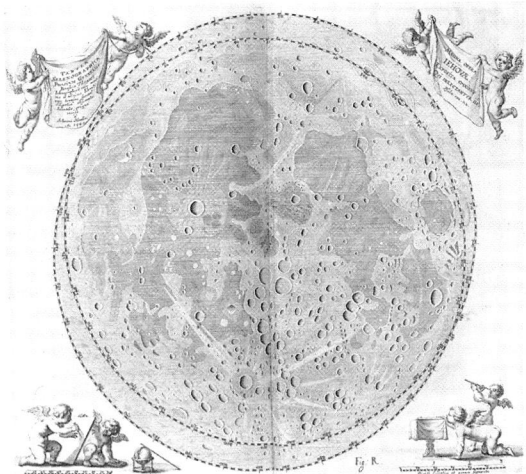

Illustration by Johann Hevelius from *Selenographia,*
Gdańsk, 1647. University of Chicago Library

An early moon map was drawn in 1645 by Johann Hevelius, a city official of Gdańsk, Poland. Hevelius, an amateur astronomer, charted about 250 lunar formations with a telescope.

Milestones in moon study

c. 2200 B.C. The Mesopotamians recorded lunar eclipses.

500's B.C. The Babylonians predicted the dates of eclipses.

c. 459 B.C. Anaxagoras, a Greek philosopher, noted that the moon's light came from the sun and explained eclipses.

c. 335 B.C. Aristotle, a Greek philosopher, used lunar eclipses to prove that the earth was ball-shaped.

c. 280 B.C. Aristarchus, a Greek astronomer, found a way to measure the moon's distance from the earth.

c. 150 B.C. Hipparchus, a Greek astronomer, measured the period of the moon's revolution around the earth.

c. 74 B.C. Posidonius, a philosopher born in Syria, explained the effect of the moon and the sun on the earth's tides.

A.D. c. 150 Ptolemy, an astronomer in Egypt, discovered the irregularity of the moon's motion in its orbit. His largely incorrect writings became the chief astronomical authority for 14 centuries.

1543 Nicolaus Copernicus, a Polish astronomer, published a book reviving the idea that the earth was a moving planet. Present-day astronomy is based on Copernicus' work.

c. 1588-1598 Tycho Brahe, a Danish astronomer, made observations leading to theories about the moon's motion.

c. 1600-1609 Johannes Kepler, a German astronomer, discovered the oval shaped orbits of the planets.

1609-1610 Galileo, an Italian scientist, made the first practical use of the telescope to study the moon.

c. 1645 Johann Hevelius, a Polish pioneer of moon mapping, charted more than 250 moon formations.

1687 Sir Isaac Newton explained the basis for the moon's motion and its tidal effect on the earth.

c. 1828 F. P. Gruithuisen, a German astronomer, suggested meteoroids as a cause of some lunar craters.

1850's William C. Bond and J. A. Whipple, of Harvard Observatory, took photographs of lunar features.

1920's Bernard Lyot, a French astronomer, concluded that a layer of dust covered the moon's surface.

1930 The American astronomers Edison Pettit and S. B. Nicholson obtained the first reliable lunar temperatures.

1946 The U.S. Army Signal Corps bounced radio waves from the moon's surface.

1959 The Soviet Union launched *Luna 2,* the first spaceship to hit the moon. The Soviet Union's *Luna 3* sent the first pictures of the moon's far side back to the earth.

1964-1965 U.S. spacecraft *Rangers VII, VIII,* and *IX* took the first close-up television pictures of the moon.

1966 The Soviet Union's *Luna 9* became the first spacecraft to make a soft landing on the moon.

1968 The Apollo 8 astronauts flew 10 orbits around the moon.

1969 The Apollo 11 and Apollo 12 astronauts landed on the moon. They collected samples, took photographs, set up experiments, and explored the nearby area.

1970 The Soviet Union's *Luna 16* became the first unmanned spacecraft to return soil samples from the moon.

as "that orbèd maiden, with white fire laden, whom mortals call the moon. . . ."

Other writers have told of imaginary space flights to the moon. During the A.D. 100's, the Greek writer Lucian described a hero who was lifted to the moon after his ship got caught in a waterspout. In the 1600's, the French author Cyrano de Bergerac wrote of a moon ship that used a form of rocket propulsion. The French novelist Jules Verne blasted his characters to the moon from a cannon 900 feet (270 meters) long in *From the Earth to the Moon* (1865). In *The First Men in the Moon* (1901), the English writer H. G. Wells described an antigravity substance that sent travelers to the moon.

The moon has also been a favorite topic of musicians. A piano sonata written by Ludwig van Beethoven, the famous German composer, is known as the *Moonlight Sonata. Clair de lune,* meaning *moonlight,* is the title of musical works by at least three French composers, including Claude Debussy. Popular songs have included "By the Light of the Silvery Moon" and "Moon River."

Moon study. Some ancient peoples believed that the moon was a rotating bowl of fire. Others thought it was a mirror that reflected the earth's land and seas. In spite of such beliefs, early astronomers worked out many correct ideas about the moon's size, shape, motion, and distance from the earth. In 1609, Galileo used a crude telescope for the first scientific study of the moon's surface.

Knowledge about the moon increased as *selenographers* (scientists who study moon geography) drew improved maps of the lunar surface. With the development of cameras and photography in the mid-1800's, the moon could be photographed in detail.

The space age, which began in 1957, opened a new chapter in the study of the moon. On Sept. 12, 1959, the Soviet Union launched *Luna 2,* which was the first artificial object to reach the moon. By 1990, the Soviet Union

and the United States had launched about 30 unmanned spacecraft that either landed on the moon or passed close enough to send back useful information. From 1966 to 1968, the United States landed five Surveyor spacecraft on the moon. These lunar probes took almost 90,000 detailed photographs and also sent back information on the moon's composition. During the same period, the United States launched five Lunar Orbiters that photographed 98 per cent of the moon's surface. These spacecraft paved the way to a manned landing by showing that the moon's surface would hold the weight of a spacecraft and by locating suitable landing sites. On July 20, 1969, Apollo 11 landed on the moon. Firsthand exploration and study of the moon had begun. In July 1971,

NASA

A lunar rover, *right,* was first used on the moon by Apollo 15 astronauts in July 1971. It carried James B. Irwin, *above,* and David R. Scott over 17 miles (27 kilometers) on the moon.

NASA

An Apollo 16 astronaut, John W. Young, explored the moon's surface in 1972. In the background is some of the equipment used to take measurements and collect mineral samples.

the Apollo 15 astronauts were the first to travel on the moon in a powered vehicle called a *lunar rover.*

In December 1972, Apollo 17 astronauts made the sixth and last manned landing in the Apollo program. In this program, a total of 12 astronauts set foot on the moon. These astronauts explored lunar highlands, maria, craters, and rilles. They took thousands of photographs of the lunar landscape. Apollo astronauts gathered many samples of moon rocks and soil and provided scientists with enough material for years of study. The astronauts also set up various scientific experiments. For example, Apollo 17 astronauts placed instruments into holes they drilled into the moon's surface. These instruments measured the amount of heat escaping from the moon. Such measurements help scientists learn about the moon's early history.

Future exploration on the moon. For years to come, scientific exploration will be the main reason for traveling to the moon. Someday, a scientific base may be built there. For short periods, astronaut-scientists could explore the surrounding area and conduct experiments at a temporary base. Later, these stations might be enlarged into permanent moon colonies where 50 to 100 people could live and work for months or even longer. Some scientists believe moon bases should be built underground for protection against the sun's radiation, extremes of heat and cold, and meteoroids.

Perhaps scientists will one day set up telescopes on the moon. The earth's atmosphere limits the study of faraway stars and galaxies. Astronomers on the moon would have a clearer view of the universe. Looking even farther into the future, some scientists think the moon could be used as a place to launch or refuel flights into deep space. Rockets could travel from the moon to the other planets on less power than is needed to travel to the planets from the earth. However, most scientists predict that earth-orbiting space stations will be better places than the moon to place telescopes and to launch deep space missions. Lunar exploration also may be car-

ried out by unmanned surface vehicles sent to the moon but controlled from the earth. The Soviet Union's *Lunokhod 1* was the first such vehicle to explore the lunar surface. It landed on the moon on Nov. 17, 1970.

Today, the moon is a symbol of the peaceful exploration of space. No nation owns the moon. In 1967, more than 90 nations signed a space exploration treaty. It declares that neither the moon nor any other natural body in outer space may be claimed by any country or be used for military purposes.   Paul Gorenstein

Study aids

Related articles in *World Book* include:

Artemis	Diana	Meteor	Solar system
Astrology	Eclipse	Monday	Space
Astronaut	Galileo	Month	exploration
Astronomy	Gravitation	Observatory	Tektite
Baily's beads	Harvest	Orbit	Telescope
Calendar	moon	Planetarium	Tide
Crescent	Luna	Satellite	

Outline

I. What the moon is like
  A. The moon's surface
  B. What the moon is made of
  C. Gravity
  D. Atmosphere and weather
  E. Temperature

II. How the moon moves
  A. The orbit of the moon
  B. Rotation
  C. The phases of the moon
  D. Eclipses
  E. The moon and tides

III. How the moon was formed
  A. Age and history
  B. Scientific theories

IV. The moon in history
  A. Measuring time
  B. Mythology
  C. Legend and folklore
  D. Literature and music
  E. Moon study
  F. Future exploration on the moon

Questions

What causes the phases of the moon?
Why do astronauts on the moon's surface weigh only $\frac{1}{6}$ of the amount they weigh on earth?
What are four theories of how the moon was formed?
What are *maria?* How were they probably formed?
Why does the same side of the moon always face the earth?
How much of the moon's surface can be seen from the earth?
How does the moon affect tides on earth?
When did the first artificial object reach the moon?
What makes the moon "shine"?
What is the moon's mean distance from the earth?

Reading and Study Guide

See *Moon* in the Research Guide/Index, Volume 22, for a *Reading and Study Guide.*

Additional resources

Level I
Asimov, Isaac. *The Earth's Moon.* Gareth Stevens, 1988.
Couper, Heather, and Henbest, Nigel. *The Moon.* Watts, 1986.
Hughes, David W. *The Moon.* Facts on File, 1989.

Level II
Cadogan, Peter H. *The Moon—Our Sister Planet.* Cambridge, 1981.
Cherrington, Ernest H., Jr. *Exploring the Moon Through Binoculars and Small Telescopes.* Rev. ed. Dover, 1984.
Hockey, Thomas A. *The Book of the Moon: A Lunar Introduction to Astronomy, Geology, Space Physics, and Space Travel.* Prentice-Hall, 1986.
Long, Kim. *The Moon Book.* Johnson Bks., 1988.

Moonflower is an attractive flower in the morning-glory family. It is a climbing vine that may grow 10 feet (3 meters) high. Its broad, heart-shaped leaves block sunlight and make an excellent screen for porches. The moonflower's pure white trumpet-shaped flowers may

WORLD BOOK illustration by Christabel King

The moonflower is an attractive climbing vine. The plant has broad, heart-shaped leaves and white trumpet-shaped flowers. Its large leaves make it a good sunscreen for porches.

be 3 to 6 inches (8 to 15 centimeters) across. These strongly scented flowers open at night and close in sunlight. The moonflower grows quickly. The parts of the plant aboveground die every year, but the roots remain alive. New parts grow from the roots each year.

Scientific classification. The moonflower is a member of the morning-glory family, Convolvulaceae. Its scientific name is *Ipomoea alba.*   Daniel F. Austin

Moonies. See **Cult.**

Moonstone is a whitish variety of the mineral called *feldspar* (see **Feldspar**). Moonstone can be cut and used as a gem. It is a birthstone for June. Light will shine through it, but not so clearly as through glass. The stone also reflects light with a bluish to pearly-colored sheen that comes from inside the stone. Sri Lanka produces many moonstones.   John C. Butler

See also **Birthstone; Gem** (picture).

Moor is a large area of open wasteland. A layer of peat that is usually wet covers some moors. The word is most often applied to the moors of Scotland and other parts of the British Isles, where heather grows in abundance. But there are also moors in northwest Europe and North America. Sphagnum moss grows on most moors, especially in North America. Many moors have special names. See also **Peat.**   John W. Webb

Moore, Clement Clarke (1779-1863), an American scholar, is generally considered the author of the popular Christmas ballad "An Account of a Visit from St. Nicholas." The ballad is also known as "A Visit from St. Nicholas" and by its first line, " 'Twas the Night Before Christmas." According to tradition, Moore wrote the poem in 1822 as a Christmas present for his children. The poem was first published anonymously in the *Troy* (N.Y.) *Sentinel* on Dec. 23, 1823. Some people have

claimed that Henry Livingston, Jr., actually wrote the poem. Livingston was a New York land surveyor who also composed poetry.

Moore was born in New York City. He was a Biblical scholar and taught Greek and Oriental literature in the Episcopal seminaries of New York City from 1821 to 1850.   Robert J. Myers

See also **Santa Claus** (Santa's appearance).

Moore, Douglas Stuart (1893-1969), was an American composer, best known for his operas on American subjects. He won the 1951 Pulitzer Prize for music for *Giants in the Earth,* based on Ole Rölvaag's novel about the hardships of Norwegian farmers in the Dakota Territory in the 1800's. Moore's most successful work, *The Ballad of Baby Doe* (1956), concerns a Colorado mining tycoon. *The Devil and Daniel Webster* (1939) is based on Stephen Vincent Benét's short story set in New England. Moore's other compositions include the symphonic suite *Pageant of P. T. Barnum* (1924) and the symphonic poem *Moby Dick* (1928).

Moore was born in Cutchogue, N.Y. He became a professor of music at Columbia University in 1926 and was head of its music department from 1940 to 1962. He wrote two books on music appreciation, *Listening to Music* (1932, enlarged 1937) and *From Madrigal to Modern Music* (1942).   Richard Jackson

Moore, G. E. (1873-1958), a British philosopher, thought of philosophy as a rational approach to practical questions about the real world. In *ethics,* the branch of philosophy that deals with the nature of right and wrong, he was interested in how we know what is good. In his most widely read book, *Principia Ethica* (1903), Moore argued that we know good actions from bad ones by intuition, not by analyzing behavior according to logical concepts. Intuition must be used because it is not possible to define the idea of good.

Moore favored common sense as the best approach to argue against *idealism.* Idealism is the belief that the existence of things depends on the mind and ideas (see **Idealism**). He thought that common sense leads us to assume that material objects do exist independently of the mind.

Moore's impact on British philosophy was as much a result of his style as of his ideas. His habit of asking sharp and disturbing questions was compared to Socrates' method of posing questions. Moore's clear writing was compared to that of Plato. His other books include *Ethics* (1912), *Philosophical Studies* (1922), and *Some Main Problems in Philosophy* (1953).

George Edward Moore was born in London. He graduated from Trinity College in Cambridge where he taught from 1911 until 1939. Moore was editor of the philosophical journal *Mind* from 1921 until 1947.

David H. Richter

Moore, George Augustus (1852-1933), was an Irish author. His novels show the influence of Honoré de Balzac's realism and Émile Zola's naturalism. *Confessions of a Young Man* (1888) is a clever portrayal of experimental painters in Paris. *Esther Waters* (1894) is a grim story of a servant girl's misfortunes. *Héloïse and Abelard* (1921), an account of a famous medieval love story, is his fictional masterpiece. It is considered one of the few great imaginative reconstructions of life in the Middle Ages.

Moore was born in County Mayo. He worked to establish a native Irish drama and helped bring about the Irish Literary Revival. He described his efforts in *Hail and Farewell* (1911-1914), a memoir. *Avowals* (1919) and *Conversations in Ebury Street* (1924) are autobiographical works in the form of dialogues.   Sharon Bassett

Moore, Henry (1898-1986), is considered the greatest English sculptor of the 1900's. Moore used holes in his work to emphasize its three-dimensional quality. The holes create a sense of mass. Moore associated the openings with ". . . the mysterious fascination of caves in hillsides and cliffs." A good example is Moore's elmwood *Reclining Figure* (1936), which is reproduced in **Sculpture** (Modern international sculpture).

Much of Moore's later work is based on the human form. Moore's bronze *Family Group* (1949) shows how he simplified his human figures, treating the proportion freely. His figures are composed of flowing *convex* (curving outward) and *concave* (curving inward) forms that create rich contrasts of light and dark. A good example is his stone *Family Group* (1955).

Several of Moore's later works, such as his *Reclining Figure* (1965) at Lincoln Center in New York City, are outdoor pieces. These large bronze works combine the human form with cliff or rock formations. His abstract works, which resemble wood or stone objects shaped by natural forces, convey a mysterious quality.

Moore was born in Castleford, near Leeds. He attended the Leeds School of Art and the Royal College of Art in London. As a young sculptor, Moore was inspired by Mexican and African carvings, and his early work shows the simple and monumental quality of such art.

Joseph F. Lamb

See also **Hirshhorn Museum and Sculpture Garden** (picture).

Moore, Marianne (1887-1972), ranks with Emily Dickinson among America's finest woman poets. Although some of her verse is difficult to understand, Moore crafted her poems superbly. She generally used poetic forms in which the controlling element is the number and arrangement of syllables rather than conventional patterns of meter.

Moore's subjects—often birds, exotic animals, and other things in nature— may seem to limit her range, but she used them

Wide World

Marianne Moore

as symbols of honesty and steadfastness. These virtues mark her work, from *Poems* (1921) through *Complete Poems* (1967) and her critical prose collected in *Predilections* (1955). Her *Collected Poems* won the 1952 Pulitzer Prize for poetry. *The Complete Prose of Marianne Moore* was published in 1986, after her death.

Marianne Moore was born in St. Louis, and became a teacher and a librarian. As the editor of *The Dial* magazine from 1925 to 1929, Moore played an important part in encouraging young writers and publishing their work.   William Harmon

See also **Poetry** (Rhythm and meter).

Moore, Thomas (1779-1852), an Irish poet, wrote the words for some of the best-loved songs in the English language. They include "Believe Me If All Those Endearing Young Charms," "The Last Rose of Summer," and "Oft in the Stilly Night." Moore wrote much light, serious, and satirical verse, and much prose. His works were as widely read in his day as the works of Lord Byron and Sir Walter Scott. But he is remembered today mostly for his verse set to music.

Moore was born in Dublin and graduated from Trinity College. He studied law for a time in London. His works include a translation of Anacreon's poems (1800); *Lalla Rookh* (1817), a romance; and a biography of Byron (1830).   William Harmon

Moores Creek National Battlefield. See **National Park System** (table: National battlefields).

Moorhen. See **Gallinule.**

Moorish art. See **Islamic art.**

Moors is a term that commonly refers to Muslims who speak Arabic and live in northwestern Africa. The term also refers to Muslims of Spanish, Jewish, or Turkish descent who live in northern Africa. Muslims of Arab descent who live in Sri Lanka are also called *Moors. Moro,* another form of the word, refers to Muslims who live in the southern Philippines.

In ancient history, the Romans called the people of northwestern Africa *Mauri* and the region they lived in *Mauritania.* These people belonged to a larger group of African people called *Berbers.* Many of the Berbers became Muslims, and they adopted Arabic in addition to their own Berber language. They became known as Moors.

The Moors joined the Arabs in conquering Spain during the 700's. Much of what is regarded as Moorish civilization of the Middle Ages was largely Arabic. The Moors lost much of their land in Spain by the late 1200's. In 1492, Ferdinand and Isabella of Spain conquered Granada, the last Moorish kingdom in Spain. In 1500, they ordered the people of Granada to either become Christians or leave the region. Those who stayed were called *Moriscos.*   James W. Brodman

See also **Alhambra; Arabs; Boabdil; Granada.**

The Surrender of Seville (1634) by Francisco Zurbarán, The Trustees of the Grosvenor Estates, London. By kind permission of His Grace The Duke of Westminster DL (Photographic Records Ltd.)

Moors surrendered Seville to Ferdinand III in 1248. The Moors lost much of their land in Spain by the late 1200's.

Moose live in northern regions that have dense forests and many lakes and swamps. A cow moose and her calf, *left,* stroll along a shore. About 10 days after birth, a moose calf can travel with its mother. A bull moose, *right,* has heavy antlers that it sheds each year.

Moose is the largest member of the deer family. The largest kind of moose lives in Alaska. These moose stand up to $7\frac{1}{2}$ feet (2.3 meters) high at the shoulder and weigh as much as 1,800 pounds (816 kilograms).

Moose inhabit northern forests throughout the world. In Europe, they are known as elk and live in northern Scandinavia and eastward through Siberia. In North America, moose live in Canada and Alaska and southward into the Rocky Mountains to Utah and Colorado. They also live in parts of Maine, Michigan, Minnesota, New Hampshire, and North Dakota.

The body of a moose. A moose has big shoulders that form a hump. Its long legs and broad hoofs make the moose a strong swimmer and help it to walk in marshy areas and through deep snow. Moose fur is brownish-black on the upper parts, and grayish-brown on the belly and lower legs. A flap of skin and fur, called a *bell,* hangs from the moose's throat. Most moose stand about $6\frac{1}{2}$ feet (2 meters) high at the shoulder and weigh 800 to 1,400 pounds (360 to 640 kilograms).

The male moose, called a *bull,* has antlers. Moose antlers are shaped like the palm of a hand with many short, pointed fingers. Bulls shed their antlers every winter and then begin to grow new ones in the spring. A pair of moose antlers may measure 5 to 6 feet (1.5 to 1.8 meters) wide and weigh as much as 85 pounds (39 kilograms).

The life of a moose. The moose's mating season lasts a few weeks in the fall. A bull will roam about in search of a female moose, called a *cow.* Both bulls and cows make calling sounds in the mating season, and a bull will move toward a calling cow. If a bull finds another bull with a cow, the bulls fight with their antlers to see which one will mate with her. A mature bull may mate with several cows in one mating season. Moose calves are born in the spring. A cow has one, two, or, rarely, three calves. A calf's fur is reddish-brown. A calf stays with its mother until she chases it away the next spring before having her next calf.

Moose eat woody plants, especially twigs of willows and such shrubs as hazel, dogwood, and mountain maple. In addition, moose eat plants that grow under the surface of shallow water. They wade into streams and ponds and put their heads underwater to get a mouthful of plants. They usually raise their heads to watch for enemies while they chew.

Moose usually live alone and do not form herds as do North American elk and caribou. However, sometimes a group of three or four moose will stay in one spot if the food there is plentiful.

The chief enemies of moose are bears and wolves. A wolf pack or a bear will kill and eat a calf if the calf can be separated from its mother. Once a moose is full-grown, even a wolf pack cannot kill it unless it is old or weak. A moose does not begin to suffer from old age until it is about 12 years of age or more.

Although moose and white-tailed deer both live in forests and eat similar food, the two animals are usually not found together in great numbers. Deer carry a disease that rarely is fatal to them but often kills moose. This disease is caused by a tiny worm. The worm lives harmlessly on the surface of a deer's brain or spinal cord. In a moose, however, the worm burrows into the central nervous system and causes paralysis and, eventually, death.

Moose and people. Before Europeans came to North America, the moose was an important source of food for Indians. Settlers hunted moose until the animals became scarce in some areas. They also cut down most of the forests where moose lived. Eventually, restrictions were placed on moose hunting in many areas, and some forests were allowed to regrow. Today, moose have become numerous enough to allow some hunting in some areas.

Scientific classification. Moose belong to the deer family, Cervidae. They are *Alces alces.*   L. David Mech

See also **Animal** (picture: Animals of the temperate forests); **Deer; Elk.**

Moose, Loyal Order of, is a fraternal order that has branches in the United States, Canada, and Great Britain. Each of the more than 1 million members is required to have unquestionable devotion to his country's flag and loyalty to democratic government. Members take part in many civic and philanthropic endeavors.

The Loyal Order of Moose was founded in Louisville, Ky., in 1888. Headquarters are in Mooseheart, Ill., about 40 miles (64 kilometers) west of Chicago. Here the order maintains "Child City," a home and school for orphans and other children who have no parental care—especially for the children of Moose members who have died. The home was founded in 1913 and includes more than 110 buildings. It provides academic, vocational, and spiritual training.

Loyal Order of Moose emblem

Moosehaven, "City of Contentment," lies on the St. Johns River, 14 miles (23 kilometers) from Jacksonville, Fla. This model home for the dependent aged of the Moose has 22 modern buildings, including a health care center. Critically reviewed by the Loyal Order of Moose

Moose Jaw (pop. 33,593) is a center for service industries and manufacturing in southern Saskatchewan. It lies at the meeting point of Thunder Creek and the Moose Jaw River. For location, see **Saskatchewan** (political map). Farmers and ranchers of the surrounding area send their products to Moose Jaw's grain elevators and stockyards. They also rely on the city for many service needs, such as health care. Industries in Moose Jaw include the manufacture of asphalt, chemicals, clothing, and food products. Moose Jaw was chartered in 1884 and became a city in 1903. It has a mayor-council government. Adrian A. Seaborne

Moose River drains many streams and rivers of northern Ontario. It is only 75 miles (121 kilometers) long. But the streams and rivers that empty into it drain 42,100 square miles (109,000 square kilometers) of northern Ontario. The river is formed where the Mattagami and Missinaibi streams join. It empties into James Bay. For location, see **Ontario** (physical map). George B. Priddle

Mora, *MOH ruh,* **Juan Rafael** (1814-1860), served as president of Costa Rica from 1849 to 1859. He was called "National Hero" for defending Central America against an American adventurer, William Walker, in 1856 and 1857 (see **Walker, William**). Mora established public schools in Costa Rica and made elementary education compulsory. He encouraged the coffee industry, built public buildings, and gave Costa Rica its first national bank and its first street-lighting system.

Rebels drove Mora from Costa Rica in 1859. He returned in 1860, but was defeated in a revolt and was executed at Puntarenas. Mora was born in San José.

John A. Booth

Moraine, *muh RAYN,* is the earth and stones that a glacier carries along and deposits when the ice melts. Moraine also means a band of such material in a glacier or on its surface, or an uneven ridge of material deposited at the edge of the melting ice. On each side of a glacier in a mountain valley are rock fragments that have rolled onto the ice from nearby slopes. These rock fragments form a *lateral moraine.*

When two mountain glaciers unite, they form a compound glacier. The lateral moraines between them merge into a *medial moraine* along the middle of the compound glacier. When the ice front of a mountain glacier or continental ice sheet remains stationary, the melting ice deposits rocks carried by the glacier. These rocks form an *end moraine* or *terminal moraine*—that is, an irregular ridge with hills and hollows. Some end moraines formed by the great ice sheets and mountain glaciers of the Ice Age are long ranges of hills. A *ground moraine* is a thin, uneven layer of material deposited beneath the ice or at its edge as the ice margin retreats. A *recessional moraine* forms when a retreating glacier pauses for a long time. Donald F. Eschman

See also **Glacier.**

Moral education is instruction focused on questions of right and wrong. Moral education also includes the development of *values,* the standards by which people judge what is important, worthwhile, and good.

People receive moral education from many sources, including their family, church, friends, and teachers—and even television. Schools have always been involved in such education, either intentionally or unintentionally. For example, many stories for young readers include a moral lesson. During the 1970's, educators in the United States began to develop special teaching methods to help students deal with moral questions.

Methods of moral education

Schools use four chief methods in moral education. These methods are (1) inculcation, (2) values clarification, (3) moral development, and (4) value analysis. Some schools use a combination of these methods in an approach called *comprehensive moral education.*

Inculcation is an effort to teach children the values that educators believe lead to moral behavior. These values include honesty, compassion, justice, and respect for others. One way of teaching such standards is to provide appropriate praise and punishment. Another means is to have teachers reflect the desired values in their own behavior.

Values clarification helps students develop their own values and moral standards by teaching them a decision-making process. The learning procedures stress setting goals, choosing thoughtfully from alternatives, and acting on one's own convictions.

Moral development helps students improve their ability to judge moral questions. This method is based on the theory that people progress from lower to higher stages of moral reasoning. According to the theory, people progress from making moral decisions based on self-interest, to seeking the approval of others, to following rules, to respecting the rights of others, and so on. At the highest moral level, an individual might oppose the laws of society if they conflict with moral principles that are even higher.

Educators stimulate moral development primarily by having students discuss difficult questions called *moral dilemmas.* One dilemma might be, "Should Heintz steal food to feed his starving family?" Educators also stimulate moral development by establishing *just schools,* in which students govern themselves according to the principles of fairness and justice.

Value analysis helps students apply techniques of logic and scientific investigation to matters involving values. Teachers stress the importance of exploring all alternatives, of gathering and evaluating the facts, and of making a logical decision.

Arguments about moral education

Some people oppose the teaching of moral education in schools. Many of these individuals feel that only the family and church should provide such instruction. Others argue that moral education takes class time that should be used for such basic subjects as reading, writing, and mathematics.

Surveys indicate that most parents favor some form of moral education in schools. Supporters of such education argue that the family and church need help in teaching moral behavior. Many believe that schools in a democratic society must teach such values as hard work, honesty, fairness, cooperation, tolerance, and respect. Howard Kirschenbaum

Morale is the general attitude or outlook of an individual or a group toward a specific situation. It influences, and is influenced by, such factors as optimism, confidence, and determination. Morale may seriously affect both well-being and performance, and is closely related to what is called *esprit de corps.* When morale is "high," the sense of confidence of an individual or a group are generally good, resulting in a high level of performance. When morale is "low," performance is usually correspondingly poor.

Business executives, military officers, college deans, athletics coaches, and other leaders have learned to analyze the morale in their groups. They recognize that the level of morale is a decisive factor in determining group or individual achievement. Kenneth J. Gergen

See also **Alienation; Group dynamics.**

Morality play is a form of drama that flourished in the 1400's. The morality play developed from the mystery play, which dramatized Biblical events, and the miracle play, which dramatized the lives of saints. Morality plays were essentially dramatized sermons. Their general theme was the struggle between good and evil for the allegiance of the human soul.

The style of the morality play was usually allegorical, with the actors portraying such figures as Virtue, Vice, Riches, Poverty, Knowledge, Ignorance, Grace, or the Seven Deadly Sins. The play was centered on an allegorical figure sometimes called Mankind or Humanity. The figure represented common people and their souls. The antagonist of the Mankind figure was usually the Vice figure, who sometimes appeared as the Devil or under several other names. Often Vice was a comic figure full of tricks and disguises. But despite his comedy, Vice represented eternal damnation for the Mankind figure foolish enough to be deceived by him. Unlike the mystery plays, which were performed by amateurs, morality plays were performed by professional and sometimes traveling actors. Albert Wertheim

See also **Miracle play; Mystery play; Drama** (Medieval drama); **English literature** (Early English drama).

Moratorium, *MAWR uh TAWR ee uhm,* is a postponement of the time for payment of debts or financial obligations. It is accomplished by executive or legislative decree. The moratorium delays legal action on debts. But the moratorium does not release the debtor from the obligation to pay. It merely postpones the day the debt is due.

A moratorium has frequently been declared following a money panic, political or industrial upheaval, or national calamity, such as flood or earthquake. However, today moratorium refers mostly to the postponement of payment on commercial debts. The instruments of the credit system, such as bills of exchange, drafts, and bank deposits, are the kinds of things that are affected by a moratorium.

Moratoriums were used only on occasions of public disaster before World War I (1914-1918). Great Britain declared the first war moratorium in 1914 on bills of exchange that were due in London. President Franklin D. Roosevelt declared a moratorium in 1933 to save the financial system of the United States from complete collapse. During the 1980's, groups of commercial banks in industrial countries declared moratoriums on the repayment of loan principal by developing countries. Joanna H. Frodin

Moravia, *moh RAY vee uh,* is a geographic region of the Czech Republic. The region covers 10,076 square miles (26,097 square kilometers) and has a population of about 4 million. Brno is the largest city of Moravia and the second largest of the Czech Republic. Only Prague has more people. Moravia's name in the Czech language is *Morava.*

Moravia lies in the eastern part of the Czech Republic. The region slopes southwest from the Carpathian and Sudeten Mountains to the Morava River. The Morava empties into the Danube River, one of the chief waterways of Europe.

Flat, fertile farmland makes up most of Moravia. The principal crops of the region include barley, corn, flax,

Czech Travel Bureau

Pernštejn Castle in Moravia has served as a fortress and as an aristocratic residence. The castle, completed in the early 1500's, is one of Moravia's major architectural monuments.

oats, rye, sugar beets, and wheat. Many farmers also raise beef and dairy cattle.

The Czech Republic's largest coal mines and an important industrial district are located around the city of Ostrava, in northern Moravia. The Ostrava area has large steelworks and other heavy industries. Moravian factories also produce chemicals, leather goods, machinery, shoes, textiles, and tractors.

Almost all the people of Moravia are Czechs, a Slavic people who speak the Czech language. Many Moravians belong to the Roman Catholic Church. Moravia has two universities and several technical schools.

After the A.D. 400's, Slavic tribes settled in Moravia. During the 800's, these tribes united with other Slavic tribes and formed the Great Moravian Empire, which included a large part of central Europe. Beginning in the late 800's, the Magyars (Hungarians) invaded the Great Moravian Empire, and in time they destroyed it.

In the early 900's, Moravia became part of the territory ruled by the Duke of Bohemia. In 1526, Bohemia and Moravia came under the rule of the Habsburg family of Austria (see **Habsburg, House of**). The Habsburgs ruled the Czechs for almost 400 years.

In October 1918, shortly before World War I ended, the independent republic of Czechoslovakia was established, with Moravia as one of its provinces. During World War II (1939-1945), German troops occupied Czechoslovakia. The Germans set up Moravia and Bohemia as a single protectorate within Germany. This protectorate was dissolved after Soviet and United States forces drove the German troops from Czechoslovakia in 1945. In 1949, Czechoslovakia replaced its provinces, including Moravia, with smaller administrative units. In 1992, Czechoslovakia ceased to exist and the two independent countries of the Czech Republic and Slovakia were created in its place. Moravia became part of the Czech Republic.

WORLD BOOK map

Moravia, which is a region in the eastern part of the Czech Republic, has industrial cities, rich mineral deposits, and fertile farmland. Brno is the largest city.

Vojtech Mastny

See also **Brno**.

Moravian Church, *maw RAY vee uhn,* is a Protestant denomination that was formed after the death of religious reformer John Hus in Bohemia. In 1457, some supporters of the martyred Hus organized themselves as the *Unitas Fratrum* (Unity of Brethren). They stressed the sole authority of the Bible; simplicity in worship; receiving the Lord's Supper in faith without authoritative human explanation; and disciplined Christian living. In 1467, the group established its own ministry. Despite suppression, the Brethren flourished and were an important religious force by the time of Martin Luther. See **Brethren; Hus, John**.

The Brethren suffered great persecution during the Thirty Years' War (1618-1648). The group revived during

the Pietist movement in Germany in the early 1700's. Pietists were Christians—mainly Lutherans—who wanted to return to the simple life of the early Christians. Beginning in 1722, refugees from Moravia under the leadership of Count von Zinzendorf reorganized the church. It then became known as the Moravian Church. The group built Herrnhut, a town on the count's estate in Saxony. Herrnhut became the base for the missionary activity of the Moravian Church throughout the world, especially among developing countries. The church has always been noted for its missionary work. As a result, most Moravians live in Africa or the Caribbean area. Today, the denomination has about 515,000 members.

Moravians first immigrated to America in 1735. The church has two headquarters—in Bethlehem, Pa., and Winston-Salem, N.C. The church has three orders of the ministry—bishops, presbyters, and deacons. Provincial and district *synods* (conferences) of ministers and the laity administer the church.

Critically reviewed by the Moravian Church

Moray. See **Eel**.

Mordant, *MAWR duhnt,* is a chemical that combines with dyes to prevent them from dissolving easily. The dye alone might wash out, but the compound formed by the dye and the mordant will not, so the color is long lasting. Common mordants include salts of chromium, iron, aluminum, tin, or other metals. These are basic or metallic mordants. They are used with two kinds of dyes, acid dyes and direct dyes. Tannic acid, lactic acid, and oleic acid are other common mordants. These are acid mordants, and they combine with another group of dyes called basic dyes. The compounds of basic mordants with dyes are called *lakes*. When alizarin, an acid dye, is mordanted with a basic aluminum salt, it colors cotton cloth a bright red, called *Turkey red*. See also **Lake** (dye). Howard L. Needles

More, Saint Thomas (1477?-1535), was a great English author, statesman, and scholar. He served as lord chancellor, the highest judicial official in England, from 1529 to 1532. But More resigned because he opposed King Henry VIII's plan to divorce his queen. He was beheaded in 1535 for refusing to accept the king as head of the English church. More has since become an example of the individual who places conscience above the claims of *secular* (nonreligious) authority. The Roman Catholic Church declared him a saint in 1935.

His life. More was born in London, probably in 1477 but perhaps in 1478. He studied at Oxford University. More began his legal career in 1494, and became an undersheriff of London in 1510. By 1518 he had entered the service of King Henry VIII as royal councilor and ambassador. He was knighted and made undertreasurer in 1521, and was chancellor of the Duchy of Lancaster from 1525 to 1529.

More became lord chancellor after Cardinal Wolsey

Detail of an oil portrait by Hans Holbein the Younger, the Frick Collection, New York

Saint Thomas More

was dismissed late in 1529. At that time, Henry VIII was engaged in a bitter battle with the Roman Catholic Church. He wanted to divorce Catherine of Aragon so he could marry Anne Boleyn. More resigned his office because he could not support the king's policy against the pope. In April 1534, More was imprisoned for refusing to swear to the Oath of Supremacy, the preamble to a law called the Act of Succession. The oath stated that Henry VIII ranked above all foreign rulers, including the pope. More was convicted of high treason on *perjured* (falsely sworn) evidence and was beheaded on July 6, 1535.

Character and writings. More's personality combined intense concern for the problems of his day and spiritual detachment from worldly affairs. He was a devoted family man, and lived a plain, simple private life. He was famed for his merry wit. Yet to the people of his day, More was a contradictory figure—he was merriest when he seemed saddest and was saddest when he appeared most happy. He was a patron of the arts. His friends included the humanist Erasmus and the artist Hans Holbein.

More's sympathetic philosophy is best reflected in *Utopia* (written in Latin in 1516). *Utopia* is an account of an ideal society, with justice and equality for all citizens. This masterpiece gave the word *utopia* to European languages. More also produced much English and Latin prose and poetry. He wrote his finest English work, *A Dialogue of Comfort Against Tribulation,* while in prison. His other works include *The History of King Richard III* (written in English in 1513?) and a series of writings in Latin in which he defended the church against Protestant attacks. Gary A. Stringer

See also **Utopia; Renaissance** (Desiderius Erasmus and Saint Thomas More).

Additional resources

Chambers, Raymond W. *Thomas More.* Univ. of Michigan Pr., 1958. First published in 1935.
Guy, John. A.*The Public Career of Sir Thomas More.* Yale, 1980.
Kenny, Anthony J. P. *Thomas More.* Oxford, 1983.
Marius, Richard C. *Thomas More: A Biography.* Knopf, 1984.

Morelos y Pavón, José María. See Mexico (Revolt against the Spaniards).

Mores, *MAWR ayz,* are customs that reflect a society's ideas about right and wrong. Examples of mores include the prohibitions in many societies against murder, cannibalism, and *incest* (sexual relations between closely related persons). People who violate the mores of their society face disapproval and punishment. The term *mores* comes from a Latin word that means *customs.*

Most people believe the well-being of their society depends on the enforcement of its mores. Many societies have enacted laws that reflect their own mores (see **Law** [The development of law]). Mores are a type of *folkway,* but not all folkways are considered as important as mores to the society's welfare. Examples of less strongly held folkways include wedding and funeral traditions and table manners. The violation of such folkways produces only a mild reaction, such as surprise or scorn.

The term *mores* was introduced in English by William Graham Sumner, an American sociologist, in his book *Folkways* (1906). Sumner pointed out that mores vary from one society to another. In most cases, each society believes that its own mores are the most natural and de-

sirable ones. Sumner called this belief *ethnocentrism.*

Most mores remain unchanged from generation to generation, but some change over a period of time. For example, many people in the United States once believed in the segregation of whites and blacks. Today, however, many people think all individuals should have equal access to housing, education, jobs, and public facilities. Michael Moffatt

See also **Custom; Sumner, William Graham.**

Morgagni, *mawr GAH nyee,* **Giovanni Battista,** *jaw VAHN nee baht TEES tah* (1682-1771), an Italian anatomist and pathologist, became known as "the father of pathological anatomy." He discovered and described many diseases of the heart and blood vessels. Morgagni's book, *On the Seats and Causes of Diseases* (1761), became a landmark in the history of pathology (see **Pathology**). Morgagni believed that disease results from a breakdown in tissues and organs, producing abnormal changes that can be seen during an autopsy.

Morgagni graduated from the University of Bologna. He became a professor of theoretical medicine at the University of Padua in 1712. He was appointed as the first professor of anatomy in 1715. Morgagni was born in Forlì, Italy. Matthew Ramsey

Morgan is the family name of three great American bankers.

Junius Spencer Morgan (1813-1890) founded the Morgan financial empire. As a young man, he made a fortune in the dry-goods business, and in 1854 he became a member of the London banking firm of George Peabody and Company. The company's name later was changed to J. S. Morgan and Company, and the firm became a famous international banking house with headquarters in London. Morgan was born in what is now Holyoke, Mass.

John Pierpont Morgan (1837-1913), a son of Junius Spencer Morgan, became one of the greatest financiers in the United States. He joined his father's banking firm in 1856. Morgan was a member of the firm of Dabney, Morgan & Company from 1864 to 1871. In 1871, Morgan and the Drexel family of Philadelphia established the firm of Drexel, Morgan & Company. Morgan reorganized the firm under the name of J. P. Morgan & Company in 1895.

Morgan's firm became a leader in financing American business and in marketing bond issues of the U.S. government. It also sold bonds of the British government. Morgan helped organize the United States Steel Corporation in 1901. He was active in financing the International Harvester, American Telephone and Telegraph, and General Electric companies. Morgan and his associates served as directors of corporations, banks, railroads, public utility companies, and insurance firms. In 1912, he was investigated by a congressional committee because of his financial power, but nothing discreditable was revealed.

Brown Bros.

John Pierpont Morgan

After the panic of 1893, Morgan helped reorganize many railroads, including the Northern Pacific, Erie, Southern, and the Philadelphia and Reading. In 1904, the Supreme Court of the United States dissolved the Northern Securities Company because it violated the Sherman Antitrust Act. Morgan and other financiers had created the company in order to control key railroads in the West.

In 1895, Morgan's firm sold all of a $62 million government bond issue. The sale ended a gold shortage in the U.S. Treasury. During the panic of 1907, Morgan loaned money to banks to keep them from closing.

Morgan made many gifts to education and charity. He founded the Lying-in Hospital in New York City and gave a large sum to the Harvard Medical School. Morgan was an ardent Episcopalian and gave a substantial share of the funds to build the Cathedral of Saint John the Divine in New York City.

He was a great art collector and gave many valuable pictures, statues, and books to American libraries and museums. Some of his most famous collections were loaned to the Metropolitan Museum of Art in New York, which he helped found. Morgan was a famous yachtsman. He was active in defending the America's Cup in international yachting several times.

Morgan was born in Hartford, Conn. He was educated at the University of Göttingen in Germany.

Additional resources

Allen, Frederick L. *The Great Pierpont Morgan.* Harper, 1949. A standard biography.
Carosso, Vincent P. *The Morgans: Private International Bankers, 1845-1913.* Harvard Univ. Pr., 1987. Includes information on J. P. Morgan.
Sinclair, Andrew. *Corsair: The Life of J. Pierpont Morgan.* Little, Brown, 1981.

John Pierpont Morgan, Jr. (1867-1943), was the son of John Pierpont Morgan. When his father died in 1913, Morgan took over many of the financial posts J. P. Morgan had held. Morgan succeeded his father as chairman of the board of United States Steel.

Morgan's firm became an official wartime purchasing agent for Great Britain in the United States in 1914. In this position, he placed contracts for the manufacture of food and munitions. The J. P. Morgan Company handled most of the postwar international loans, including many dealing with reparations. Morgan was appointed a member of the commission to revise the Dawes Plan in 1929 (see **Dawes Plan**).

Like his father, Morgan made large gifts to education and the arts. In 1923, he dedicated his father's library as an institution of research. Under the terms of the gift, the library will be kept intact as a complete unit until March 31, 2013, a hundred years from the date of his father's death. In 1920, Morgan gave his house in London to the United States for use as the residence of the U.S. ambassador. Morgan was born at Irvington, N.Y., and graduated from Harvard University.   W. H. Baughn

Morgan, Daniel (1736-1802), served as an American officer in the Revolutionary War. He joined the Revolutionary forces in 1775 as a captain. He volunteered to go with Benedict Arnold on his expedition to Quebec and was taken prisoner there. On his release in 1776, he became a colonel in charge of a Virginia regiment. He organized a corps of sharpshooters in 1777 that helped

General Horatio Gates in his battles against General John Burgoyne. Morgan resigned from the army in 1779. But he was recalled in 1780 and became a brigadier general. He commanded the American troops at the victory at Cowpens, S.C., in 1781.

After the war, he helped put down the Whiskey Rebellion in 1794 in western Pennsylvania (see **Whiskey Rebellion**). He served as a Federalist from Virginia in the U.S. House of Representatives from 1797 to 1799. Morgan was probably born in Hunterdon County, New Jersey.   Paul David Nelson

Morgan, Garrett Augustus (1877-1963), was an American inventor. He developed a number of devices, including versions of the gas mask and traffic light.

Morgan developed a gas mask in 1912. His device included an airtight canvas hood that was worn over the head. The hood was connected to a special breathing tube that hung to the ground. Many police departments and fire departments throughout the United States became equipped with Morgan's gas mask. In 1916, Morgan used his device to rescue more than 20 workers who were trapped in a smoke-filled water tunnel in Cleveland.

Ebony Magazine

Garrett Augustus Morgan

Morgan patented his traffic light in 1923. His device looked much different from the traffic signals used today. However, like modern traffic signals, the device Morgan patented had red, yellow, and green lights. Soon after Morgan received the patent for his traffic light, he sold the rights to the General Electric Company for $40,000.

Morgan was born in Paris, Ky. He moved to Cleveland in 1895.   Raymond W. Smock

Morgan, Sir Henry (1635?-1688), was the most famous English *buccaneer* (pirate). In his day, England and Spain were rivals for trade and colonies. Morgan raided Spanish ships and towns in Spain's colonies in the West Indies, Central America, and South America. In 1671, he caused the destruction of Panama City, Panama, the largest Spanish city in Central America.

Early career. Morgan was born in Wales. Little is known of his early life. In 1655, he arrived in the West Indies as a soldier with an English expedition. This expedition captured the Spanish colony of Jamaica. By 1666, Morgan had become a buccaneer. Thomas Modyford, the new English governor of Jamaica, thought the buccaneers were Jamaica's best defense, and he directed them to attack the Spaniards.

In 1668, Morgan led about 500 English buccaneers in a raid on Portobelo, Panama. Morgan proved his skills as a commander by capturing the city. At one point he used captives, including priests and nuns, as a human shield while attacking a fortress.

In 1669, Morgan gathered about 500 buccaneers and eight ships for a raid on Maracaibo, Venezuela. On his way home to Jamaica, he easily defeated three Spanish warships that had been sent to capture him.

Morgan returned to Jamaica to discover that England and Spain were negotiating a peace treaty. With the treaty nearly approved, Modyford hesitated to permit the buccaneers to attack the Spanish again. But after a Spanish attack, and before news of the signing of the treaty had reached Jamaica, Modyford let Morgan sail again.

Attack on Panama. In December 1670, Morgan sailed for Panama in his final and most famous raid. He led a force of 38 ships and about 2,000 men. He captured several towns and finally faced the Spanish army just outside Panama City in 1671. The Spaniards stampeded a herd of cattle at the buccaneers, but Morgan's men scattered the cattle and slaughtered the Spanish army. Some Spaniards then set fires in Panama City in hopes of slowing the buccaneers' progress. The fires got out of control and destroyed the city. The Spaniards had earlier moved their wealth out of the city, and the buccaneers found little loot to share.

Shortly after Morgan reached Jamaica in 1671, Sir Thomas Lynch succeeded Modyford as governor of Jamaica. The English government had decided to replace Modyford because of his support of the buccaneers. The new governor arrested Morgan for his attack on Panama and sent him to England for trial. But King Charles II forgave Morgan and knighted him in 1674. Morgan was appointed deputy governor of Jamaica in 1674 and served until 1683.   Robert C. Ritchie

Additional resources

Earle, Peter. *The Sack of Panama: Sir Henry Morgan's Adventures on the Spanish Main.* Viking, 1982.
Pope, Dudley. *The Buccaneer King: The Biography of Sir Henry Morgan, 1635-1688.* Dodd, 1977.
Roberts, Walter A. *Sir Henry Morgan, Buccaneer and Governor.* Covici, 1933.
Syme, Ronald. *Sir Henry Morgan, Buccaneer.* Morrow, 1965. For younger readers.

Morgan, John Hunt (1825-1864), a Confederate general, led a group of daring men, called Morgan's Raiders, during the Civil War (1861-1865). His troops, a group of volunteer cavalrymen, raided public property, burned bridges, took horses, and captured railroad supplies. They also caused severe losses among Union troops. Morgan never commanded more than 4,000 men, but it is said he captured as many as 15,000 soldiers.

In 1863, Morgan was ordered to invade Kentucky and draw General William S. Rosecrans' army from Tennessee. Morgan went farther than he was ordered. He broke through the federal lines in Kentucky and crossed the Ohio River into Indiana. A flood caused the river to rise, and Morgan could not return to Confederate territory. He was captured in July 1863, and was imprisoned in Columbus, Ohio.

Morgan escaped the next November and continued his raids. He was defeated in Kentucky, in June 1864. He went to Greeneville, Tenn., where he was surrounded and shot by Union troops in September 1864. Morgan was born in Huntsville, Ala. He spent his boyhood in Kentucky.   Frank E. Vandiver

Morgan, Justin (1748-1798), owned and gave his name to a horse that was the original stallion of the breed of Morgan horses. The breed became famous for its strength, endurance, and speed (see **Horse** [Saddle horses; picture]). When the horse was a colt, Morgan re-

ceived it from a farmer in payment of a debt. This unusual stallion died in 1821 at the age of 29.

Morgan was born in West Springfield, Mass. He moved to Randolph, Vt., in 1788, and became a schoolteacher, singing master, and town clerk.   Steven D. Price

Morgan, Lewis Henry (1818-1881), was an American anthropologist who founded the comparative scientific study of kinship systems. He studied the family relationships of American Indians and other peoples to determine their similarities and differences. Unlike most other anthropologists of his time, Morgan learned many of his facts firsthand by traveling and by observing living Indians.

Morgan also became famous for his theory of social evolution. According to this theory, the history of human culture was a process of *evolution* (gradual development) from lower to higher forms. Morgan believed that people pass through three stages of development: (1) savagery, (2) barbarism, and (3) civilization. So-called primitive peoples, whose technology was less advanced than that of Western nations, supposedly represented the earlier phases of evolution.

Morgan was born near Aurora, N.Y., and became a lawyer. He began anthropological research after joining a club dedicated to studying Indian ways of life. Morgan never held an academic post but achieved widespread recognition for his studies. His books include *Systems of Consanguinity and Affinity of the Human Family* (1871) and *Ancient Society* (1877).   Igor Kopytoff

Morgan, Thomas Hunt (1866-1945), an American geneticist, won the 1933 Nobel Prize in physiology or medicine for his work on heredity described in *The Theory of the Gene* (1926). He showed through his experiments that certain characteristics are transmitted from generation to generation through genes (see **Heredity** [The birth of genetics]).

Morgan studied the laws of heredity by using the fruit fly (*Drosophila melanogaster*) for experiments in breeding. His research clarified the physical basis for the linkage and recombination of hereditary traits. He was the first to explain sex-linked inheritance, that some traits pass to only one or the other sex. Morgan and his associates proved that genes are arranged on the chromosomes in a fixed linear order (see **Chromosome**).

He began his experiments at Columbia University, where he was professor of biology from 1904 to 1928. He was director of the William G. Kerckhoff Biology Laboratory at the California Institute of Technology from 1928 to 1941. He wrote *Evolution and Genetics* (1925), *Experimental Embryology* (1927), and was coauthor of *The Mechanism of Mendelian Heredity* (1915).

Morgan was born in Lexington, Ky. He studied at the University of Kentucky, McGill University, the University of Edinburgh, and received his Ph.D. from Johns Hopkins University. His many honors included membership in the Royal Society (1919).   Alan R. Rushton

Morgan's Raiders. See Morgan, John Hunt.
Morgantown, W. Va. (pop. 25,879), is the home of West Virginia University. Manufacturing plants there make brass plumbing fixtures, hand-blown glass, and textiles. Limestone quarries and two of the world's largest coal mines are located near the city. Morgantown lies on the banks of the Monongahela River, 72 miles (116 kilometers) south of Pittsburgh (see **West Virginia**

[political map]). Colonel Zackquill Morgan founded Morgantown about 1766. The city was known as Morgan's Town when it was chartered in 1785. It has a council-manager government. John Samsell

Morgenthau, MAWR guhn THAW, **Henry, Jr.** (1891-1967), served as United States secretary of the treasury from 1934 to 1945 under Presidents Franklin D. Roosevelt and Harry S. Truman. During World War II (1939-1945), Morgenthau organized the Victory Bond campaign that raised more than $200 billion. He proved efficient in the treasury post, although he probably would have preferred to be secretary of agriculture.

Morgenthau lived near Roosevelt's Hyde Park (N.Y.) estate, and they were close friends. When Roosevelt became governor of New York in 1929, he named Morgenthau head of his Agricultural Advisory Commission. Morgenthau served briefly in 1933 as chairman of the Federal Farm Board and then as governor of the Farm Credit Administration. He also served as undersecretary of the treasury before he was named secretary in 1934.

During World War II, he proposed the Morgenthau Plan for Germany. It would have eliminated most of Germany's heavy industries, and ended German military power. It was never adopted. Morgenthau took a leading part in the 1944 Bretton Woods (N.H.) international monetary conference. He was born in New York City.

Harvey Wish

Mörike, MUHR ih kuh, **Eduard,** AY doo AHRT (1804-1875), was a German lyric poet. He overcame the vagueness that characterizes much romantic poetry. Some of his work suggests a pleasant, untroubled atmosphere. But Mörike's most admired poems are about single objects or moments in time, such as an old lamp in a summer house, or two lovers as they disappear around a corner.

Mörike also wrote prose. *Mozart on His Journey to Prague* (1855) is considered a masterpiece of short German prose. It is a charming story about Mozart, delicately clouded by an awareness of the young composer's approaching death. Mörike also wrote *Painter Nolten* (1832), a subtle psychological novel.

Mörike was born in Ludwigsburg. He became a Protestant minister in 1834. But he retired in 1843 to devote himself to writing. Jeffrey L. Sammons

Morison, Samuel Eliot (1887-1976), was an American historian, teacher of history, and winner of two Pulitzer Prizes. His *Admiral of the Ocean Sea,* a life of Columbus, won the prize in 1943, and his *John Paul Jones* received it in 1960. His other books include *History of United States Naval Operations in World War II* in 15 volumes (1947-1962), *The Intellectual Life of Colonial New England* (1960), *One Boy's Boston* (1962), *The Oxford History of the American People* (1965), *The European Discovery of America: The Northern Voyages* (1971), and *The European Discovery of America: The Southern Voyages* (1974).

Morison was born in Boston and was educated at Harvard University and in Paris. In 1915, he became a teacher of history at Harvard. He served in World War I (1914-1918) and World War II (1939-1945). Morison was elected to the American Academy of Arts and Letters in 1963. Merle Curti

Morisot, maw ree ZOH, **Berthe,** bairt (1841-1895), was a French painter and an important member of the

impressionist movement. Many of her pictures portray women, often with their children, in scenes of everyday domestic life. She painted such subjects in a light, delicate style. Morisot also painted landscapes, many with women and children. In addition to her oil paintings, she was noted for her water colors and pastel works.

Morisot was born in Bourges and moved to Paris in 1851. She studied with the noted landscape artist Camille Corot in the 1860's. Morisot first exhibited in the Salon of 1865. She met the artist Edouard Manet in 1868, and they became close friends. He painted many portraits of her, and she married his brother in 1874. She and Manet influenced each other's work in the 1870's.

Morisot participated in the first impressionist show in 1874. After 1880, her work was influenced by the style and colors of the impressionist artist Pierre Auguste Renoir. Ann Friedman

Oil painting (1870); National Gallery of Art, Washington, D.C., Chester Dale Collection

A typical Morisot painting, *The Mother and Sister of the Artist,* portrays two women in a scene from everyday life.

Morley, Thomas (1557 or 1558-1602), was an English composer of the Renaissance period. He is best known for his lighthearted unaccompanied vocal pieces known as *madrigals* (see **Madrigal**).

Morley's most popular madrigal is *Now is the month of Maying,* with its nonsense refrain "Fa la la." Another popular Morley song is *It was a lover and his lass,* with words from William Shakespeare's comedy *As You Like It.* Morley's songs for two voices, called *canzonets,* are still used as models by music theory students.

Morley was born in Norwich. He was educated at Oxford University and became a noted music teacher. In 1597, he published a composition textbook, written as a dialogue, which tells us much about how music was taught and written in his time. Morley also made arrangements for a *consort,* a group of instruments used in the theater of his day. Joscelyn Godwin

Mormon cricket is not really a cricket but belongs to the family of katydids and long-horned grasshoppers. It can be very harmful to crops. The Mormon cricket lives in the Western United States and as far east as Kansas.

Mormon crickets are brown, black, or green and grow about 2 inches (5 centimeters) long. They have small wings but cannot fly. In summer, the female Mormon cricket lays its eggs one at a time in the ground. The young hatch the next spring and are full-grown by summer. Farmers use poisonous powder and baits to kill Mormon crickets. In 1848, a swarm threatened to ruin the crops of the Mormons in Utah. But flocks of gulls suddenly appeared and ate the insects.

Scientific classification. The Mormon cricket belongs to the family Tettigoniidae. It is *Anabrus simplex.*

Betty Lane Faber

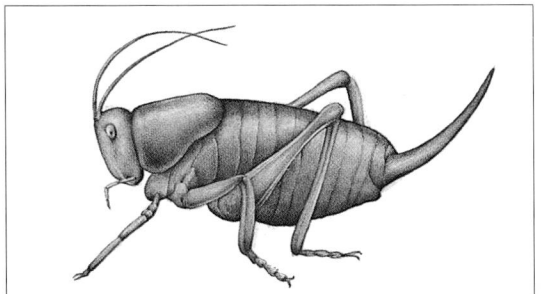

WORLD BOOK illustration by Shirley Hooper, Oxford Illustrators Limited

The Mormon cricket is very destructive to crops in the Western United States. It has small wings but cannot fly.

Mormons is the name commonly given to members of The Church of Jesus Christ of Latter-day Saints. They are so called because of their belief in the *Book of Mormon.* They claim that the Church as established by Christ did not survive in its original form, and was restored in modern times by divine means through a modern prophet, Joseph Smith. Thus, they believe their church is the true and complete church of Jesus Christ restored on earth. Mormons are more correctly called *Latter-day Saints,* using the word "saint" in its Biblical sense to mean any member of Christ's church.

The church has almost 7 million members. Many Mormons live in the western United States, and church headquarters are in Salt Lake City, Utah. The church is also established in most other countries of the world.

Several other churches accept the *Book of Mormon,* but are not associated with the church described in this article. The largest of these is the Reorganized Church of Jesus Christ of Latter Day Saints, which has headquarters in Independence, Mo.

Church doctrines

Mormon beliefs are based on ancient and modern revelations from God. Many of these revelations are recorded in scriptures. These scriptures include the Bible, the *Book of Mormon, Doctrine and Covenants,* and the *Pearl of Great Price.*

Mormons regard the Bible as the word of God, but they believe that it is not a complete record of all that

God said and did. The *Book of Mormon* is a history of early peoples of the Western Hemisphere. Mormons teach that the *Book of Mormon* was divinely inspired, and regard it as holy scripture. The *Book of Mormon* was translated by Joseph Smith from golden plates which he said he received from the angel Moroni. *Doctrine and Covenants* contains revelations made by God to Smith. The *Pearl of Great Price* contains writings of Smith and his translation of some ancient records.

Mormons believe in a unique concept of God. They teach that this concept was revealed by God through Joseph Smith and other prophets. Mormons believe that the Supreme Being is God the Father, who is a living, eternal being having a glorified body of flesh and bone. The human body is made in the image of God.

Mormons teach that God the Father created all people as spirit-children before the earth was made. They regard Jesus Christ as the first spirit-child the Supreme Being created. They believe that Christ created the world under the direction of God the Father. This is why Mormons also refer to Christ as the Creator. Jesus Christ came down to earth and was born of the Virgin Mary. He was the only one of God's spirit-children begotten by the Father in the flesh. He is divine.

Jesus Christ died on the cross for the sins of all humanity and brought about the resurrection of all. He lives today as a resurrected, immortal being of flesh and bone.

God the Father and Jesus Christ are two separate be-

Detail of an oil painting on canvas (1966) by Ken Riley; Church Office Building, Salt Lake City, Utah (The Church of Jesus Christ of Latter-day Saints)

Joseph Smith, *left,* the founder of the Mormon Church, said he received engraved plates from the angel Moroni. Smith translated them into the scriptures called the *Book of Mormon.*

ings. Together with the Holy Ghost, they form a Trinity, Godhead, or governing council in the heavens. The Holy Ghost is a third personage, but is a spirit without a body of flesh and bone.

Mormons claim that their doctrine is the one which Jesus and His apostles taught. They believe that the first principles and ordinances of the gospel are faith in Jesus Christ; repentance; baptism by immersion for the remission of sins; and the laying on of hands for the gift of the Holy Ghost. They believe that a person must be called of God by those who have the authority in order to preach the gospel and to administer its ordinances.

Mormons believe in life after death and in the physical resurrection of the body. The spirit, awaiting the resurrection of the body, continues in an intelligent existence. During this time, persons who did not know the gospel in life may accept it after death. Mormons believe, for this reason, that living persons can be baptized on behalf of the deceased. In this ceremony, a living Mormon acts as a representative of the dead person and is baptized for that person. Other rites are performed for the dead.

Since Mormons believe in life after death, they believe that family life continues after death. Marriages performed in a Mormon temple are for eternity, and not just for this life. Mormons believe in a final judgment in which all people will be judged according to their faith and works. Each person will be rewarded or punished according to merit.

Some Mormons practiced *polygamy* (the practice of a man having more than one wife at the same time) as a religious principle during the mid-1800's. But the church outlawed the practice in 1890 after the Supreme Court of the United States ruled it illegal.

They believe in upholding the civil law of the country in which they are established. For example, they believe the Constitution of the United States is an inspired document. Mormons in the United States are urged by their religion to uphold its principles.

Church organization

Mormons regard the organization plan of their church as divinely inspired. They have no professional clergy. But all members in good standing, young and old, can participate in church government through several church organizations. A body called the General Authorities heads the church. It consists of the President and two counselors; the Council of the Twelve Apostles; the Patriarch of the church; the First Quorum of the Seventy; and the three-member Presiding Bishopric.

Under the General Authorities are area leaders and then regional and local organizations called stakes and wards. Each *stake* (diocese) is governed by a president and two counselors, who are assisted by an advisory council of 12 men. A stake has between 2,000 and 10,000 members. A *ward* (congregation) is governed by a bishop and two counselors. Wards have an average of 500 to 600 members.

Worthy male members of the church may enter the priesthood, which is divided into two orders. The *Aaronic* (lesser) order is for young men 12 to 18 years old. The *Melchizedek* (higher) order is for men over 18. Each order is subdivided into *quorums* (groups). Mormons believe that the priesthood provides authority to act in God's name in governing the church and in performing religious ceremonies.

Several auxiliary organizations assist the priesthood. The Sunday School, the largest auxiliary organization, provides religious education for adults and children. The Women's Relief Society helps the sick and the poor, and directs women's activities. The Young Men and Young Women organizations provide programs for

Ayer Collection, Newberry Library

Mormon pioneers left Nauvoo, Ill., in 1846, on the way west to the valley of the Great Salt Lake in Utah. The Mormons had established the city of Nauvoo only seven years earlier. But it became a hotbed of anti-Mormon feeling. Many of the saints were killed and their homes and fields burned. After Joseph Smith's death, Brigham Young led the pioneers.

Paul Markow & Associates from FPG

The Mormon Temple in Salt Lake City, Utah, is a magnificent six-spired granite structure of The Church of Jesus Christ of Latter-day Saints.

teen-agers. The Primary Association sponsors classwork and recreation for children 3 to 11 years old.

The church operates an extensive educational system. It provides weekday religious education for high school students in about 1,900 *seminaries* located near public high schools in 42 states and six foreign countries. The church conducts 66 weekday religious *institutes* for Mormon students near college campuses. It also maintains fully accredited colleges and universities in Utah, Idaho, and the Pacific Islands. Best known of these is Brigham Young University in Provo, Utah.

Mormons assist aged, handicapped, and unemployed members through a voluntary *welfare program.* Projects directed by the wards and stakes help the poor.

Voluntary contributions from members and income from church-operated businesses support the church. Most members give a *tithe* (one-tenth of their annual income) to the church. Thousands of young men and women and retired people work from 18 to 24 months in a worldwide missionary program without pay.

History

Revelations. During the early 1800's, Joseph Smith, the son of a New England farmer, received a series of divine revelations. According to Smith's account, God the Father and Jesus Christ appeared to him near Palmyra, N.Y., in 1820. They advised him not to join any existing church and to prepare for an important task. Smith said he was visited by an angel named Moroni three years later. Moroni told him about golden plates on which the history of early peoples of the Western Hemisphere was engraved in an ancient language. In 1827, Smith received the plates on Cumorah, a hill near Palmyra. His translation of the plates, called the *Book of Mormon,* was published in 1830. Smith and his associates founded the church on April 6, 1830. It grew rapidly, and had 1,000 members by the end of the first year.

Mormons in the Middle West. Mormon communities were established at Kirtland, Ohio, and Independence, Mo., during the early 1830's. Smith moved the church headquarters to Kirtland in 1831, and the town was the center of the church for almost eight years. He instituted the basic organization and many of the present doctrines there. The first Mormon temple was completed there in 1836.

The 1830's were years of growth, but serious problems arose at the same time. Disputes among some church members themselves, the collapse of a Mormon bank in 1837, and conflict with non-Mormon neighbors broke up the Kirtland community. In 1838, Smith and his loyal followers moved to Missouri, and joined other Mormons there. But trouble again arose. The Missouri Mormons had been driven from Independence in 1833, many settling in a town called Far West, in northern Missouri. In the fall of 1838, mobs attacked the Mormons in several of their settlements. In the "massacre at Haun's Mill," 17 Mormons, including some children, were killed. Joseph Smith and other leaders were

FPG

The Mormon Tabernacle stands next to the Mormon Temple in Salt Lake City. The Tabernacle has a 325-member choir that has won worldwide fame through concerts. The huge organ, begun in 1866, still contains some of the original pipes.

arrested on what Mormons believe were false charges. Ordered out of Missouri, more than 5,000 Mormons fled to Illinois in late 1838 and early 1839. Smith escaped from prison in the spring of 1839 and rejoined his people in Illinois.

They founded the city of Nauvoo, which became one of the state's largest cities. The rapid growth of Nauvoo, and the important part Mormons played in state politics made non-Mormons suspicious and hostile again. One faction set up a newspaper to fight Smith, who had become a candidate for President of the United States. The paper was destroyed, and Smith was blamed for it. He, his brother Hyrum, and other leaders were arrested and jailed. On June 27, 1844, a mob attacked the jail. Smith and his brother were shot and killed.

The Mormons in Utah. Brigham Young became the next church leader. Mobs forced the Mormons out of Illinois in 1846. Joseph Smith had planned to move his people to the Great Basin in the Rocky Mountains. This plan was now put into effect by Young. In 1847, Young led the advance party of settlers into the Great Salt Lake valley. The population of the region grew rapidly, and by 1849, the Mormons had set up a civil government. The Mormons applied for admission to the Union as the *State of Deseret,* but Congress created the Territory of Utah in 1850 instead, and appointed Young governor.

Trouble with non-Mormons began again. It was falsely reported in Washington, D.C., that the Mormons were rebelling. Anti-Mormon public opinion caused President James Buchanan to replace Young with a non-Mormon governor and to send troops to Utah in 1857. The trouble that followed has been called the Utah War or the Mormon War. The conflict ended in 1858 when Young accepted the new governor and President Buchanan gave full pardon to all concerned.

The number of Utah settlements increased until the territory's population reached 140,000 in 1877. Congress continued to oppose the practice of polygamy, and the church outlawed the practice in 1890. A Mormon ambition was realized in 1896 when Utah was admitted to the Union as the 45th state.

Mormons today have won a reputation as a temperate, industrious people who have made their churches monuments to thrift and faith. Their meeting houses are in many ways model community centers. They include facilities for worship, learning, and recreation. There are 47 temples built or planned worldwide. The temples are devoted entirely to religious ceremonies, and are open only to faithful Mormons. All other Mormon meeting places, chapels, and recreation halls are open to the general public.

The promotion of music and the arts has long been important to the Latter-day Saints. The 325-voice Mormon Tabernacle Choir in Salt Lake City is famous for its broadcasts, telecasts, and concert tours. The choir, now more than a hundred years old, has been heard on United States radio networks since 1929.

Critically reviewed by The Church of Jesus Christ of Latter-day Saints

Related articles in *World Book* include:

Deseret	Salt Lake City
Latter Day Saints, Reorganized	Smith, Joseph
Church of Jesus Christ of	Utah (History; pictures)
Nevada (Early settlement)	Young, Brigham
Polygamy	

Additional resources

Arrington, Leonard J., and Bitton, Davis. *The Mormon Experience: A History of the Latter-Day Saints.* Knopf, 1979. Suitable for younger readers.
Hansen, Klaus J. *Mormonism and the American Experience.* Univ. of Chicago Pr., 1981.
O'Dea, Thomas F. *The Mormons.* Univ. of Chicago Pr., 1964. First published in 1957.
Shipps, Jan. *Mormonism: The Story of a New Religious Tradition.* Univ. of Illinois Pr., 1987. First published in 1985.

Morning-glory is the name of a family made up mainly of climbing plants. Garden morning-glories are among the best-known plants in this group. Others are

WORLD BOOK illustration by Christabel King

A garden morning-glory has dark heart-shaped leaves and colorful flowers shaped like a funnel.

the *bindweed, jalap, moonflower, scammony,* and *sweet potato.* The morning-glory grows rapidly and twines about nearby objects. Its vines grow from 10 to 20 feet (3 to 6 meters) high. It is widely used as a covering for posts, fences, and porches.

Garden morning-glories have dark green leaves shaped like a heart. The flowers are shaped like a funnel and are of various shades and mixtures of purple, blue, red, pink, and white. The fragrant flowers open in the morning but close in the sunlight later in the day. The seeds may be soaked in water overnight to soften the seed covering and make sprouting easier. Japanese varieties of morning-glories have flowers 7 inches (18 centimeters) in diameter. Their flowers are mixtures of purple, rose, and violet. The morning-glory is the flower for September.

Scientific classification. Morning-glories belong to the morning-glory family, Convolvulaceae. Common garden morning-glories include *Ipomoea purpurea, I. nil,* and *I. tricolor.*

Daniel F. Austin

Related articles in *World Book* include:

Bindweed	Flower (picture: Garden annuals)	Moonflower
Dodder		Sweet potato

Morning sickness. See Pregnancy.
Morning star. See Evening star.

Rabat, Morocco's capital, lies on the Atlantic Ocean. The wall was originally built along the coast to protect Rabat from enemy attack by sea. About half of all Moroccans live in cities.

Morocco

Morocco, *muh RAHK oh,* is a country in the northwestern corner of Africa. It is bordered by the Mediterranean Sea on the north and the Atlantic Ocean on the west. The Strait of Gibraltar, which connects the Mediterranean and the Atlantic, separates Morocco from Spain by only about 8 miles (13 kilometers). Fertile plains lie along Morocco's coasts, and forested mountains stretch across the middle of the country from southwest to northeast. Beyond the mountains lies a sun-baked desert, the Sahara. Rabat is Morocco's capital, and Casablanca is the largest city.

Nearly all Moroccans are of mixed Arab and Berber descent. But the people make up two distinct ethnic groups—Arab and Berber—depending mainly on whether they speak Arabic or Berber. Almost all Moroccans are Muslims. Farming is the chief occupation, and more than half the people live in rural areas. France and Spain controlled Morocco from the early 1900's until it won independence in 1956.

Government

National government. Morocco is a constitutional monarchy headed by a king. Its Constitution gives the king broad powers. For example, he commands the armed forces, may issue orders that have the force of law, and controls the major government agencies.

The day-to-day work of Morocco's government is carried out by a prime minister and a Cabinet of other min-

Kenneth J. Perkins, the contributor of this article, is Associate Professor of History at the University of South Carolina.

isters, all appointed by the king. The Chamber of Representatives makes Morocco's laws. Its 306 members serve six-year terms. The people elect two-thirds of the members. The rest are chosen by representatives of local governments, professional organizations, and other groups. All citizens who are 20 years of age or older may vote.

Local government. Morocco is divided into 35 *provinces* and 6 *prefectures.* Rabat makes up one prefecture, and Casablanca the other five. A governor appointed by

A busy market place occupies the heart of Moroccan cities. Many city dwellers wear Western-style clothing, though women who follow Islamic tradition still cover their face with a veil.

the king heads each province and prefecture. The provinces are further divided into smaller units. The national government controls all local governments.

Politics. Morocco's Istiqlal (Independence) Party promotes the spread of Arab culture and reforms based on Islamic teachings. The Union Socialiste des Forces Populaires (Socialist Union of Popular Forces) backs broad socialist reforms. The conservative Mouvement Populaire (Popular Movement) generally supports the king's policies. Other parties include the Rassemblement National des Indépendents (National Assembly of Independents) and a small Communist group.

Courts. Morocco's highest court is the Supreme Court. Lower courts include appeals courts, regional courts, and *sadad* (conciliation or peace) courts.

Armed forces. Morocco's army, navy, and air force have about 149,000 members. Men may be drafted for $1\frac{1}{2}$ years of service after they reach the age of 18.

People

Population and ancestry. Morocco has about 28 million people. About half of the people live in cities, and about half live in rural areas. Morocco has an annual population growth rate of about $2\frac{1}{2}$ per cent—higher than that of most countries.

Almost all Moroccans are of mixed Arab and Berber ancestry. Berbers lived in what is now Morocco as long as 3,000 years ago. Arabs began to move into the area during the 600's. Over the years, the two groups intermarried so extensively that today there are few Moroccans of unmixed Arab or Berber ancestry. People are identified as Arabs or Berbers chiefly by their main language, Arabic or Berber. According to Morocco's government, Arabs form nearly 65 per cent of the population, and Berbers make up the rest. Most Arabs live in cities or along the Atlantic coast. Most Berbers live in mountain areas.

Languages. Arabic is the official language of Morocco. It is spoken not only by Arabs but also by many Berbers in addition to their own language. A large number of Arabs and Berbers also speak French or Spanish.

Religion. Islam is Morocco's official religion. About 98 per cent of the people are Muslims, and Islamic teachings regulate family and community life. Morocco also has some Christians and Jews.

Facts in brief

Capital: Rabat.
Official language: Arabic.
Official name: Kingdom of Morocco.
Area: 172,414 sq. mi. (446,550 km²). *Greatest distances*—north-south, 565 mi. (910 km); east-west, 730 mi. (1,170 km). *Coastline*—1,140 mi. (1,835 km).
Elevation: *Highest*—Jebel Toubkal, 13,665 ft. (4,165 m) above sea level. *Lowest*—sea level.
Population: *Estimated 1994 population*—27,587,000; density, 160 persons per sq. mi. (62 per km²); distribution, 52 per cent urban, 48 per cent rural. *1982 census*—20,449,555. *Estimated 1999 population*—30,803,000.
Chief products: *Agriculture*—wheat, barley, corn, sugar beets, citrus fruits, potatoes, tomatoes. *Fishing*—sardines, mackerel, tuna, anchovies. *Manufacturing*—fertilizers, petroleum products, processed foods, textiles, leather goods, cement, chemicals. *Mining*—phosphate rock.
Money: *Basic unit*—dirham. See **Money** (table).

Way of life. The traditional Moroccan household consists of two parents, their unmarried children, their married sons, and those sons' wives and children. When the father dies, each married son begins his own household. In crowded urban areas, many households split up before the father's death because there is not enough room for everyone to live together.

Housing in rural Morocco varies according to climate and available building materials. Many people in the southern part of the country live in houses of dried mud bricks. In other rural areas of Morocco, houses are made of wood and stone. Many houses have only one large room. This room serves as kitchen, living room, sleeping quarters, and barn. People gather at a weekly outdoor market called a *souk* to buy and sell goods and chat with neighbors. In desert regions, some Moroccans lead a nomadic life and live in tents.

Many urban Moroccans live in small attached houses. Wealthier people live in spacious houses or modern apartment buildings. Sprawling slums called *bidonvilles* (tin can towns) border the large cities. The name *bidonville* comes from the flattened tin cans, or *bidons,* used to build many of the slum shacks. Severe overcrowding exists in the *medinas* of Morocco's large cities. The me-

Symbols of Morocco. Morocco's national flag was officially adopted in 1915. It features a five-pointed green star against a red background. The green star appears again on the country's coat of arms. The coat of arms also shows the Atlas Mountains, a sun, two lions, and a crown. An inscription in Arabic at the bottom reads, *If You Assist God, He Will Also Assist You.*

WORLD BOOK map
Morocco lies in northwestern Africa. It borders Algeria, Western Sahara, the Atlantic Ocean, and the Mediterranean Sea.

dinas are the original city settlements, from which large metropolitan areas have grown.

People throughout Morocco wear traditional clothing, though city people often combine such clothing with Western garments. Outdoors, men wear a *jellaba,* a loose-fitting hooded robe with long, full sleeves. A *burnoose* is a similar but heavier garment worn chiefly by rural men. Most men wear a turban or a brimless cap. One type of cap, called a *fez,* is named for the Moroccan city of Fez. This red, flat-topped cap is now usually worn only for formal occasions.

Like men, women wear a jellaba as an outer garment. At home and at social affairs, they wear a long, beautiful robe called a *caftan.* Some older women and some rural women follow Islamic tradition and cover their face with a veil.

Food and drink. Foods made of barley and wheat form the basis of most Moroccans' diet. The national dish is *couscous.* It consists of steamed wheat served with vegetables, fish or meat, and a souplike sauce. Moroccans like pastries made with honey and almonds. The national drink is mint tea.

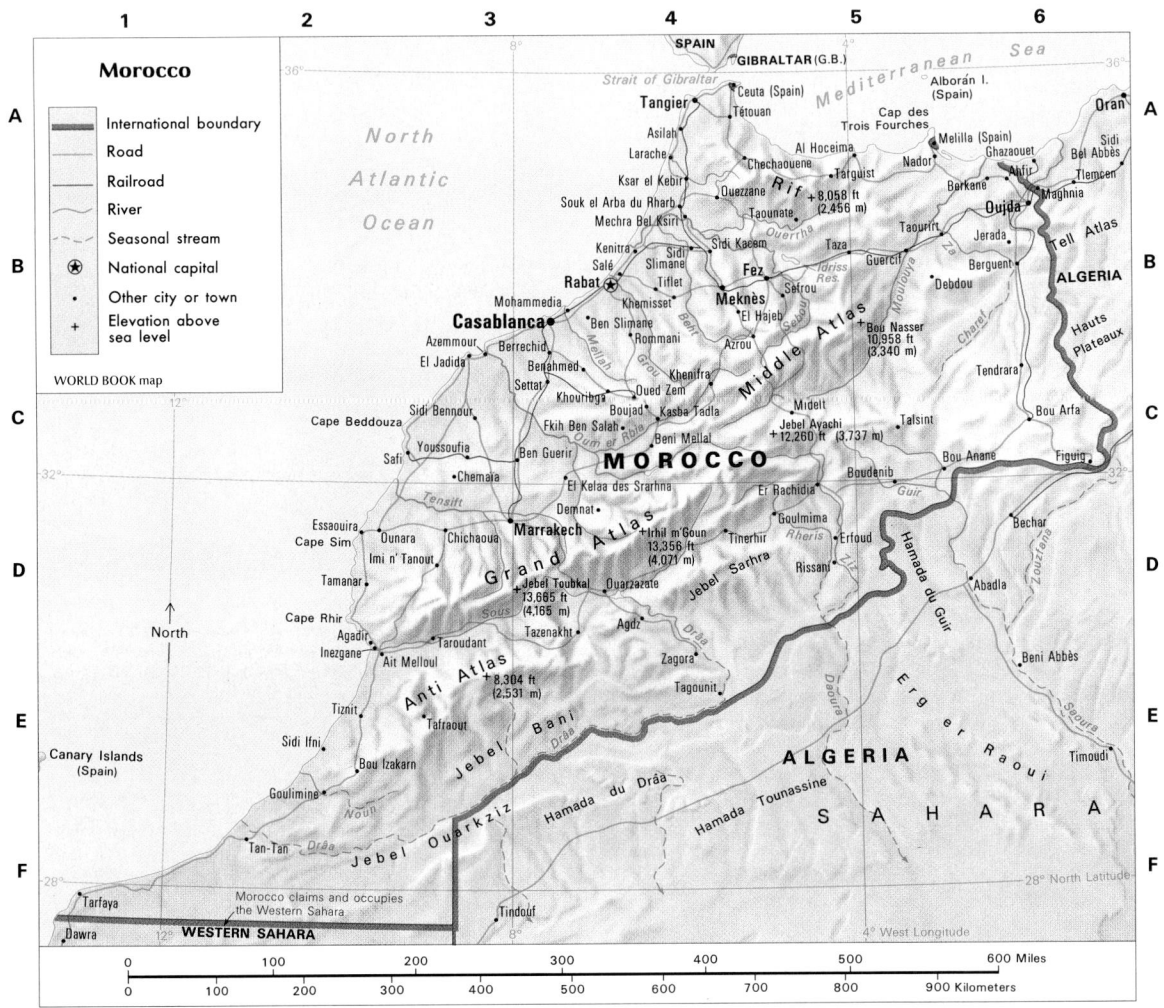

Morocco map index

Source: 1982 census.

Recreation. Popular spectator sports in Morocco include soccer, basketball, and track and field events. Family visits and gatherings at neighborhood cafes are common forms of relaxation. The people also enjoy many local and religious festivals throughout the year.

Education. Morocco provides free elementary and high school education. Classes are taught in Arabic and French. Children from 7 through 13 years old are required to attend school, but less than 70 per cent of them do so. Attendance is especially low in rural areas, which have a lack of teachers and schools. In addition, many rural boys stay at home to help their families farm the land. Moreover, many parents place less value on education for girls than for boys. Only about 20 per cent of all Moroccans aged 15 or older can read and write. Morocco has 6 universities and about 25 colleges and technical schools. The largest university, Muhammad V University in Rabat, has about 27,000 students.

The arts. Moroccans have long been known for their fine leather goods, rugs, pottery, and metalware. Many Moroccan arts reflect Spanish and French influences as well as Arabic and Berber traditions. For example, traditional Moroccan folk music and folk dances are often combined with the styles of the Andalusian region of southern Spain. French influences can be seen in painting, sculpture, and drama. Modern Moroccan authors, whether writing in Arabic or French, have often dealt with problems of cultural identity and have protested continuing French influences in Morocco.

The land and climate

Land regions. Morocco has three major land regions. They are (1) the Coastal Lowlands, (2) the Atlas Mountain Chain, and (3) the Sahara.

The Coastal Lowlands border the Mediterranean Sea and the Atlantic Ocean. The land gradually rises from the Atlantic coast and forms a plateau that extends to the mountains. Rich farmland in the Coastal Lowlands is irrigated by water from the region's many shallow rivers. Most of Morocco's crops are grown there.

The Atlas Mountain Chain crosses the middle of Morocco from southwest to northeast. The heavily forested chain has three distinct ranges: (1) the Anti Atlas in the southwest; (2) the Grand Atlas, also called Haut Atlas, in the central area; and (3) the Middle Atlas, or Moyen Atlas, in the northeast. The Rif, a group of mountains in the far north, are sometimes included in the Atlas chain.

The Sahara lies east and south of the Atlas Mountains. It is a barren region of sand dunes, rocks, stones, and scattered oases.

Climate. Most of Morocco has two seasons, rainy and dry. The rainy season generally lasts from October or November to April or May. Nearly all the rainfall occurs in this period. Annual rainfall varies in each region. It averages 9 inches (229 millimeters) in Marakkech and 21 inches (533 millimeters) in Rabat. Droughts sometimes occur in the dry season, from May or June to September or October. January temperatures average 66° F. (19° C) in Marrakech and 63° F. (19° C) in Rabat. June temperatures average 91° F. (33° C) in Marrakech and 77° F. (25° C) in Rabat.

Economy

Morocco has a developing economy based mainly on agriculture and mining. The government controls the mining industry, most transportation and communication services, and some manufacturing industries. However, most farms and businesses are privately owned.

Agriculture and fishing employ about 40 per cent of all workers in Morocco. The chief crops include wheat, barley, corn, sugar beets, citrus fruits, potatoes, tomatoes, olives, and beans. More than a third of Morocco's farmland is owned by only 3 per cent of the nation's farmers. Their large farms produce about 85 per cent of all the crops. Most farmers own fewer than 10 acres (4 hectares). The chief livestock are sheep, goats, and dairy cattle. Morocco is one of Africa's leading fishing countries. Sardines, mackerel, tuna, and anchovies are caught off the coasts. Much of the catch is canned for export or processed for fertilizers or animal feed.

Service industries employ more than 40 per cent of Morocco's workers. Tourism is a major service industry. Nearly 2 million tourists, most of them from western Europe, visit Morocco each year. Many service industries

Fertile farmland occupies a valley in the Atlas Mountains near the city of Fez. The Atlas Mountains cross Morocco from southwest to northeast. They separate the coastal plains from the Sahara.

An industrial plant in Safi processes phosphate rock into chemicals called *phosphates.* Morocco leads the world in the export of phosphate rock and is a top producer of phosphates.

workers are employed by hotels, restaurants, and resorts. The government and institutions that provide community services hire many other service workers. Service industries employees also include people in trade, transportation, and communication.

Manufacturing provides jobs for about 15 per cent of all Moroccan workers. Most manufactures are produced for local use. They include processed foods; textiles; leather goods; cement; chemicals; paper; and metal, rubber, and plastic products. Fertilizers and petroleum products are produced chiefly for export. Casablanca is the main industrial center.

Mining employs less than 2 per cent of Morocco's labor force but is highly important to the economy. Morocco is the world's largest exporter of *phosphate rock,* which is used to produce fertilizers and other chemicals. Morocco has about two-thirds of the world's known reserves of phosphate rock. Other minerals include iron ore, lead, zinc, coal, copper, and natural gas.

Energy sources. About three-quarters of Morocco's energy needs are supplied by imports, mostly of oil. The rest of the nation's energy requirements comes from its own coal, natural gas, and hydroelectric resources.

Trade. Phosphate rock and phosphate products account for about half of Morocco's export income. Other exports include fruits, fish, vegetables, clothing, and such handicrafts as leather goods and rugs. The chief imports are oil, industrial equipment, and food and other consumer goods. The nation's key trading partners include France, Spain, Germany, and Italy.

Transportation and communication. Highways and government-owned railroads link all major Moroccan cities with one another and with key agricultural and mining areas. Only about 5 per cent of the people own a car, but private and government-operated bus service reaches nearly all parts of the country. Most of Morocco's trade is handled at Casablanca. Tangier is the main passenger port. The government-controlled Royal Air Maroc provides international airline service.

About 10 privately owned daily newspapers, printed in both Arabic and French, are published in Rabat and Casablanca. The government controls radio and TV broadcasts. TV programs are broadcast in Arabic and

French, and radio programs in Arabic, French, Berber, Spanish, and English. About 10 per cent of Morocco's people own a radio, and about 4 per cent own a TV set.

History

Farming communities existed in what is now Morocco at least 8,000 years ago. By 1000 B.C., Berbers had migrated to the region. They may have come from Europe, southwestern Asia, or northeastern Africa. From about A.D. 40 to the 600's, the region was ruled, in turn, by the Romans, Vandals, and Byzantines.

Arab conquest. During the 680's, Arabs from the Arabian Peninsula invaded Morocco. Many Berbers adopted the religion of the Arabs, Islam. But they resented the Arabs' political control.

In the late 700's, an Arab leader named Idris ibn Abdallah united the region's Berbers and Arabs under his rule, thereby creating the first Moroccan state. He also founded the Idrisid *dynasty* (series of rulers from the same family), which governed Morocco for almost 200 years. The country's rulers came to be called *sultans.* Fez, the Idrisid capital, developed into a major religious and cultural center of the Islamic world.

From about 1050 through the mid-1400's, Morocco was ruled by three Islamic Berber dynasties. At various times, the Berber empires covered much of northern Africa and extended into the Christian lands of Spain and Portugal. But by the 1200's, the Christians had begun to drive the Muslims from Portugal and Spain.

Corsairs and sharifs. The last Muslims were driven from Spain in the 1500's. Meanwhile, Spain and Portugal had begun to seize territory on Morocco's coasts. The rivalry between Muslims and Christians contributed to widespread naval warfare in the western Mediterranean. Private warships commanded by Muslim *corsairs* attacked ships and coastal towns of Christian nations. In addition, Muslim and Christian corsairs attacked one another's ships and ports. The port of Salé was a major base for Moroccan corsairs.

Arab tribes and families of *sharifs* helped lead Moroccans' opposition to the Christian seizures of their territory. Sharifs were descendants of Muhammad, the prophet of Islam. In the mid-1500's, a sharifian family named the Saadians gained control of Morocco and founded a dynasty that ruled until the mid-1600's. Since then, the Alawis, another sharifian family, have been Morocco's reigning dynasty.

French and Spanish control. Through treaties and military victories, France and Spain established control over the economic and political affairs of Morocco by the early 1900's. Sultan Hassan I, who ruled from 1873 to 1894, had tried to modernize Morocco's government and its army. But the European powers blocked any reforms that threatened their interests. Hassan was succeeded by his son Abd al-Aziz.

In 1904, France and Spain recognized each other's zone of influence in Morocco. Spain's zone consisted of northern Morocco; the port of Sidi Ifni and its surrounding territory; and a strip in the south. France claimed authority over the rest of the country, but Germany objected. The major powers met in 1906 in Algeciras, Spain, to discuss France's growing power in Morocco. The conference upheld Morocco's independence, though France and Spain kept their special privileges.

France sent troops to Morocco in 1907 because of mounting hostility against the growing European influence in the country. The presence of French forces further enraged the Moroccans. Abd al-Aziz was overthrown by his brother Abd al-Hafidh in 1908. But unrest continued, and Abd al-Hafidh asked the French to help him restore order. In 1912, Abd al-Hafidh signed the Treaty of Fez with France. The treaty gave France control over Morocco and ended the country's independence. Spain was granted control of its zone of Morocco by France. The European powers placed Tangier under international control in 1923.

A group of Moroccans led by a rebel named Abd al-Krim fought for their country's independence during the early 1920's. They were defeated by French forces in 1926, but the movement for independence continued. In 1934, a group of Moroccans drew up the Plan of Reforms. It called for a reinterpretation of the Treaty of Fez that would guarantee Moroccans' political rights. France rejected the plan. Following widespread demonstrations in 1937, France arrested or exiled leaders of the independence movement.

Independence. Morocco was the scene of fighting between Allied and Axis forces during World War II (1939-1945). In 1943, U.S. President Franklin D. Roosevelt and British Prime Minister Winston Churchill met in Casablanca to discuss war plans. That same year, the Istiqlal (Independence) Party was formed to work for Morocco's freedom.

Sultan Muhammad V supported the Istiqlal Party. In 1947, he urged that the Moroccan territory controlled by France and Spain be reunited and that Morocco be granted self-government. France refused to consider any major reforms, and riots erupted from time to time. In 1953, the French sent Muhammad into exile and imprisoned some Istiqlal leaders. The sultan's exile angered many Moroccans, and acts of violence became common. New Istiqlal leaders formed the National Liberation Army, which openly fought French troops. To restore order, the French brought Muhammad back in late 1955 and promised to grant Morocco its freedom.

On March 2, 1956, Morocco became independent of France. In April, Spain gave up nearly all its claims in northern Morocco. The international city of Tangier again became part of Morocco in October.

Constitutional monarchy. Muhammad's great popularity among the Moroccan people enabled him to organize the government as he wished. In 1957, he changed his title from sultan to king as part of his plan to make Morocco a constitutional monarchy. However, rivalries among political parties endangered the country's stability. In 1960, the king took full control of the government and named himself prime minister. He died suddenly in 1961. Muhammad's son, Hassan II, then became king and prime minister. In 1962, Morocco adopted its first Constitution. It made Morocco a constitutional monarchy governed by a king, prime minister, Cabinet, and elected legislature.

Unemployment and high inflation were among the problems facing Morocco in the early 1960's. Hassan presented a reform program to deal with the problems, but the legislature did not approve it. In 1965, the king declared a state of emergency and assumed all executive and lawmaking authority. The state of emergency lasted until 1970, when the people approved a new Constitution and elected a new legislature.

Hassan again took control of Morocco's government in 1972, after military officers had tried for the second time to assassinate him. Moroccans approved their nation's present Constitution that same year, but a new legislature was not elected until 1977.

Recent developments. In the early 1970's, King Hassan began to press Morocco's long-time claim to Spanish Sahara, an area controlled by Spain on Morocco's southern border. Mauritania also wanted parts of the area. But the Polisario Front, an organization in Spanish Sahara, demanded independence. In 1976, Spain gave up the area to Morocco and Mauritania. Morocco claimed the northern part, and Mauritania the southern. The area came to be called Western Sahara.

The Polisario Front continued to demand independence for Western Sahara. Fighting broke out between the Front and troops from Morocco and Mauritania. Algeria and Libya provided military aid to the Front. In 1979, Mauritania gave up its claim to Western Sahara. Morocco then claimed the entire area. Fighting between Morocco and the Polisario Front continued.

The cost of the fighting in Western Sahara drained the economy of Morocco. The economy also suffered when the world market price of phosphate rock, Morocco's chief export, dropped sharply in the 1980's.

A cease-fire between Moroccan forces and those of the Polisario Front was declared in September 1991. The cease-fire plan also called for a *referendum* (direct vote) to determine whether Western Sahara would become independent or a part of Morocco.   Kenneth J. Perkins

Related articles in *World Book* include:

Outline

Questions

What is the ancestry of almost all Moroccans?
Why is school attendance especially low in rural Morocco?
What serious economic problems does Morocco have today?
What is a *souk*? A *burnoose*? Couscous?
Who created the first Moroccan state? When?
Morocco is the world's largest exporter of what product?
What is the chief occupation in Morocco?
Who introduced Islam into Morocco? When?
Where are most of Morocco's crops grown?

Moroni (pop. 26,000) is the capital and largest city of Comoros. Moroni lies on the west coast of Grande Comoro island. For location, see **Comoros** (map).

Moroni is the nation's center of government, trade, and tourism. It is home of the nation's main *mosque* (Muslim house of worship), chief *lycée* (secondary school), and sole international airport. The architecture in Moroni shows an Arab influence. Arabs ruled the Comoros Islands from the 1400's until the 1800's, when France gained control. Moroni became the capital of Comoros in 1962, after the nation declared its independence from France in 1961 (see **Comoros** [History]).

Leroy Vail

Morpheus, *MAWR fee uhs* or *MAWR fyoos,* was a god of dreams in Greek mythology. He was one of the sons of Hypnos, the god of sleep. He took human form and appeared to people in their sleep. To be "in the arms of Morpheus" means to be asleep, and the drug morphine is named after him.   Justin M. Glenn

Morphine is a drug used to relieve severe pain and to treat several other medical problems. Some people use morphine because it makes them feel happier. In the United States, federal laws prohibit the use of this drug except when prescribed by a physician.

People who use morphine regularly may in time become addicted to it. If they stop their usual dose, they will feel ill for several days unless they take medicine for this *withdrawal sickness.* Withdrawal sickness may include abdominal cramps, back pains, chills, diarrhea, nausea, vomiting, and weakness.

Morphine makes severe pain bearable and moderate pain disappear. The drug also stops coughing and diarrhea, checks bleeding, and may help bring sleep. Doctors give patients morphine only if other medicines fail. Besides being addictive, morphine interferes with breathing and heart action and may cause vomiting.

Small doses of morphine leave the mind fairly clear. Larger doses cloud the mind and make the user feel extremely lazy. Most morphine users feel little hunger, anger, sadness, or worry, and their sex drive is greatly reduced. Most people with mental or social problems feel happy after using morphine, even though their problems have not really been solved.

Some morphine addicts can give up the drug fairly easily with medical help. But an addict with many problems—mental, physical, or social—may find morphine hard to give up. Personal counseling, controlled living situations, and such medicines as methadone may help addicts solve their problems and stop taking morphine (see **Drug abuse; Methadone**).

Morphine is made from opium, and heroin is manufactured from morphine. These three drugs have similar effects. However, heroin is the strongest and opium is the least powerful. See **Heroin; Opium.**   Donald J. Wolk

Morphology, *mawr FAHL uh jee,* is the branch of science that deals with the structure of animals, plants, and nonliving matter. Morphology most often involves the study of living things. It includes such areas as *cytology,* the study of cell structure; *histology,* the study of tissue structure; and *anatomy,* the study of the structure of whole organisms. In geology, morphology is the study of the external form of rocks.   Lawrence C. Wit

Morrill, Justin Smith (1810-1898), was a United States political leader. He represented Vermont in the

U.S. House of Representatives from 1855 to 1867, and in the U.S. Senate from 1867 to 1898. He proposed the Morrill Act of 1862, which established land-grant colleges and universities (see **Land-grant university**). He introduced the Morrill Tariff Act of 1861. He also helped found the Republican Party and helped pass legislation that established the present Library of Congress. Morrill was born in Strafford, Vt.   Dan L. Flores

Morrill acts. See Land-grant university.

Morris, Desmond (1928-   ), is a British zoologist. He has written or coauthored more than a dozen books that have increased popular interest in the behavior of animals and human beings. Morris has also helped make films and television programs that explore the social behavior of animals.

Morris' best-known books are *The Naked Ape* (1967) and *The Human Zoo* (1969). These books, written from the viewpoint of a zoologist, discuss the basic elements of animal behavior in human beings. Morris examines the ways that humans behave socially in modern-day urban society. *The Naked Ape* became widely popular, but some scientists criticized it because they thought its entertainment value outweighed its scientific value. Morris also wrote *The Biology of Art* (1962) and *The Mammals: A Guide to the Living Species* (1965). With his wife, Ramona Morris, he wrote *Men and Snakes* (1965), *Men and Apes* (1966), and *Men and Pandas* (1966). Desmond John Morris was born in Purton, England, near Swindon.   G. J. Kenagy

Morris, Esther Hobart (1814-1902), led the fight for women's suffrage in Wyoming. Through her efforts, the territory of Wyoming passed a women's suffrage law in 1869 that became a model for later suffrage laws. When Wyoming became a state in 1890, it was the first state to permit women to vote.

Born Esther McQuigg in Tioga County, New York, she settled in the Wyoming territory in 1868. She became the first woman justice of the peace in the United States in 1870. A statue of Morris represents Wyoming in Statuary Hall in the United States Capitol in Washington, D.C.   Louis Filler

Morris, Gouverneur, *GUHV uhr NEER* (1752-1816), was an American statesman and diplomat. He headed the committee that wrote the final draft of the Constitution of the United States. Much of the credit for the wording in the Constitution belongs to him.

Morris was suspected of sympathies for Great Britain at the outbreak of the Revolutionary War in America in 1775. But he soon proved himself to be one of the most active American patriots. He served as a leading member of the New York constitutional convention in 1776. He was a member of the Second Continental Congress from 1778 to 1779. The brilliant and energetic Morris headed several committees of Congress and acted as draftsman of important documents. He was one of General George Washington's most able supporters in Congress during the Revolutionary War. Morris attracted the attention of Robert Morris, financial agent of Congress, and served as assistant superintendent of finance from 1781 to 1785.

Morris was elected a Pennsylvania delegate to the Constitutional Convention of 1787. He spoke 173 times—more often than any other delegate—and favored a strong, centralized government controlled by the wealthy. In 1789, Morris went to Paris as a financial agent. From 1792 to 1794, he was minister to France. From 1800 to 1803, he was a U.S. senator from New York. Morris was also a key figure in promoting the construction of the Erie Canal. He was born in Morrisania (now part of New York City).   Richard D. Brown

Morris, Lewis (1726-1798), was a signer of the Declaration of Independence from New York. He served in the Continental Congress from 1775 to 1777, where he worked on committees supervising supplies of ammunition and military stores. Morris served in the New York state legislature from 1777 to 1790. He was a brigadier general of the New York militia during the Revolutionary War. He was born in Morrisania (now part of New York City) and was a half brother of Gouverneur Morris (see **Morris, Gouverneur**).   Gary D. Hermalyn

Morris, Robert (1734-1806), a Pennsylvania merchant and banker, was one of six people who signed both the Declaration of Independence and the Constitution of the United States. Morris became one of the wealthiest people in the American Colonies. He raised great amounts of money to support the Continental Army during the Revolutionary War in America (1775-1783). Because of this, he was known as "the financier of the American Revolution."

Morris was born in or near Liverpool, England. He came to the American Colonies at the age of 13. Morris' energy and intelligence helped him become an important member of a Philadelphia shipping and banking firm at the age of 20.

From 1775 to 1778, Morris served in the Second Continental Congress. This congress adopted the Declaration of Independence in 1776. He was superintendent of finance of the United States from 1781 to 1784. The treasury of the new country had all but collapsed because of the Revolutionary War in America. Morris improved the unsettled financial condition by establishing the Bank of North America, which opened in 1782. Through Morris' efforts, the Continental Army had supplies and money that helped it win a decisive victory in the Battle of Yorktown. This victory ensured the success of the revolution.

After the war, Morris expanded his fortune through commercial and real estate undertakings. He attended almost every session of the Constitutional Convention of 1787 but played a minor role. Morris represented Pennsylvania as a United States senator from 1789 to 1795. By the time he left the Senate, Morris had invested heavily in unsettled land throughout the nation. By the late 1790's, however, his credit had collapsed. Morris was sent to debtor's prison in 1798. He was released in 1801, and spent the last years of his life living in near poverty.
          Richard D. Brown

See also **Philadelphia** (The Revolutionary War period); **Washington, George** (Recall to duty).

Morris, William (1834-1896), was an English poet, artist, and socialist reformer. He fell in love with medieval culture and acquired a deep knowledge of English Gothic architecture. Morris wanted to replace the mass-produced objects of his time with the beauty and individuality he saw in medieval art.

Morris retold many myths and epics. His own favorite was *The Story of Sigurd the Volsung, and the Fall of the Nibelungs* (1876), a translation of the Volsunga Saga of

Teutonic mythology. Morris' romantic narrative *The Life and Death of Jason* (1867) recounts the adventures of the Greek mythological hero. His other major poetry includes *The Defence of Guenevere and Other Poems* (1858); and *The Earthly Paradise* (1868-1870), a poem modeled on Geoffrey Chaucer's *The Canterbury Tales.*

Morris became interested in interior design as an art form. In 1861, he founded a company that produced furniture, wallpaper, stained glass, tapestries, and other decorative articles for the home. His experiments in furniture led to the design of the popular Morris chair.

Morris created his own publishing company, the Kelmscott Press, in 1890. The press printed artistic editions of distinguished literary works. It stimulated artistic book design and printing in other countries. See **Book** (picture: A beautiful book; The 1800's).

In his later years, Morris became a lecturer and propagandist for socialist solutions to problems created by the Industrial Revolution. He wrote the romances *A Dream of John Ball* (1888) and *News from Nowhere* (1891), both landmarks of the English socialist movement. Morris was born in Walthamstow, near London.
          Harold Orel

See also **Architecture** (Early modern architecture in Europe).

Morrison, Toni (1931-   ), a black American novelist, won the 1988 Pulitzer Prize for fiction for *Beloved* (1987). The novel tells the story of a former slave tragically haunted by memories of her life in slavery and the baby she killed to save the child from that fate. *Beloved* demonstrates Morrison's lyrical style, vivid characterizations, and ability to persuade readers to accept the unusual as real. Her masterful use of language makes her one of the best American writers of the 1900's.

Morrison's first two novels, *The Bluest Eye* (1970) and *Sula* (1973), focus on the lives of black women and girls. In *Song of Solomon* (1977), a man learns that he must reject his father's self-centered materialism and discover strength in love for friends. In *Tar Baby* (1981), a black American man and woman fail to sustain their relationship because of class differences. *Jazz* (1992) is set in Harlem during the 1920's. It takes its themes from the power of jazz music.

Morrison has also published a collection of essays, *Playing in the Dark* (1992). She edited *Race-ing Justice, En-gendering Power: Essays on Anita Hill, Clarence Thomas, and the Construction of Social Reality* (1992). She was born in Lorain, Ohio.   Nellie Y. McKay

Morse, Samuel Finley Breese (1791-1872), was a famous American inventor and painter. He received the patent for the first successful electric telegraph in the United States. He also invented the Morse code, used for many years to send telegraphic messages (see **Morse code**). In addition, Morse helped found the National Academy of Design and served as its first president.

Early years. Morse was born on April 27, 1791, in Charlestown, Mass. His family was devoutly Calvinist, and its conservative religious beliefs influenced Morse throughout his life.

Morse attended Yale University. While there, he studied chemistry with Benjamin Silliman and natural philosophy with Benjamin Day. Both men also lectured on the new science of electricity. From Silliman, Morse learned about batteries and constructed several of his own. However, Morse was an indifferent student. His real passion was art.

Brown Bros.

Samuel F. B. Morse

Morse graduated from Yale in 1810. The following year, he obtained reluctant permission from his parents to study art abroad. He studied in London with two American-born masters—Washington Allston and Benjamin West. He also studied at the Royal Academy of Arts, where he learned the "Grand Style" of art, which featured themes from history and mythology. In 1813, his first and only sculpture, a figure of the dying Hercules, won critical acclaim and a gold medal in the Adelphi Society of Arts competition. In 1815, having spent all the funds his parents could spare, Morse regretfully returned home.

Morse as artist. Back in the United States, Morse was unable to secure an income from the historical painting he regarded as his true calling. In order to earn money, he began painting portraits of members of fashionable society. Although he considered this type of painting to be inferior to true art, he became successful at it. Among his famous subjects were President James Monroe, the poet William Cullen Bryant, and the inventor Eli Whitney. Morse's portrait of the French soldier and statesman Marquis de Lafayette became the best known of all his paintings.

Despite his success as a portrait painter, Morse continued to struggle financially. In 1822, he finished work on a painting that depicted the House of Representatives in session with recognizable portraits of more than 80 members. He planned to charge admission for viewing it, but the public was largely indifferent. Several years later, Morse made another attempt with an elaborate painting of the interior of the Louvre museum in Paris. But this scheme met with the same disappointing result.

In 1826, Morse and 30 other American artists founded the National Academy of Design. Morse was chosen president, an office he held continuously until 1845.

From 1829 to 1832, Morse traveled in Europe, perfecting his artistic technique. In 1832, he was appointed professor of painting and sculpture at the University of the City of New York (now New York University). He later became professor of the literature of the arts of design there. About this time, Morse began his involvement in the *nativist movement.* This movement regarded immigration and Roman Catholicism as threats against an authentic American republic. Morse wrote a number of passionate articles supporting these positions. In 1836, he ran for mayor of New York City on the Native American ticket but lost the election.

In the mid-1830's, Morse was denied an important commission he had hoped to obtain to paint historical murals for the Rotunda of the Capitol in Washington, D.C. Frustrated once again in his dream of devoting himself to art, Morse shifted his attention to the telegraph. After 1837, he did not paint again.

Morse as inventor. Morse diligently pursued a number of schemes in an effort to acquire an independent livelihood that would enable him to support himself as a serious artist. Among these projects were the invention of a pump for fire engines and a marble-cutting machine to reproduce statues mechanically. The most successful of these efforts, however, was the telegraph.

Morse had been interested in electricity since his student days at Yale. In 1827, for example, he attended a series of lectures on electricity given at Columbia University by the American chemist James Freeman Dana. Then, during his return voyage from Europe aboard the ship *Sully* in 1832, Morse discussed with several other passengers the possibility of transmitting "intelligence" at a distance by electricity. He theorized in his diary that transmission could be based on a single circuit using underground wires. He also improvised possible codes.

Work on the telegraph went slowly. Too poor to buy insulated wires on reels, he bought wire in pieces and soldered the pieces together. He wrapped the wire—bit by bit—with cotton thread. He built his instruments from old clockworks and art equipment.

Morse was scientifically inexperienced and baffled by a variety of technical problems. In early 1836, he began to work jointly on the telegraph with Leonard Gale, who taught chemistry at the University of the City of New York. Gale alerted Morse to the work of Joseph Henry, a

Oil painting on canvas (1825); Art Commission of the City of New York (WORLD BOOK photo by E. E. Smith)

Samuel F. B. Morse first won recognition as a painter. His portrait *Marquis de Lafayette, above,* shows his artistic skill.

The first public telegraph message, sent from Washington to Baltimore in 1844, was recorded on tape, *left*.

Smithsonian Institution

Morse built a port rule, *left,* to operate the key of his telegraph. The key established a circuit that allowed current to pass to the receiver.

Smithsonian Institution

physicist at the College of New Jersey (now Princeton University), who had built a crude electromagnetic acoustic device several years earlier. By the end of 1837, Morse and Gale had built an electromagnetic telegraph based on Henry's work. This device could send messages 10 miles (16 kilometers) on wire strung around Morse's workroom.

Another key collaborator on the project was Alfred Vail, a skilled mechanic with access to a machine shop. He had approached Morse and offered him funds and assistance. Morse promptly made him a partner.

In 1837, Congress sought proposals for a telegraph system to connect the financial market of New York City with the cotton market of New Orleans. Only Morse proposed an electric system, but Congress would not advance funds for a small experimental line. In 1840, Morse was granted a U.S. patent for his telegraph. In its 1841-42 session, Congress once more failed to act on Morse's telegraph bill.

Finally, in 1842, his work received a favorable report from the Committee on Commerce. In 1843, Congress granted him $30,000 to build a test line between Baltimore and Washington, D.C. On May 24, 1844, Morse demonstrated the line by tapping out the famous message, "What hath God wrought!" Morse earned national praise for his device, but the government did not buy his patents or sponsor a national telegraph.

The next decade saw hard-fought legal and economic battles between Morse and some of his original associates. One fight involved his refusal to acknowledge Joseph Henry's key theoretical contributions to the telegraph. In 1859, discouraged from years of fighting, Morse and his partners sold their patent rights.

Later life. After gaining recognition at home and abroad for his part in developing the telegraph, Morse focused his attention on politics. He continued his support of the nativist movement. He was also an ardent antiabolitionist, believing that slavery had been ordained by the Bible. He was active in the Democratic Party. He ran for Congress in 1854 but lost the election.

By the 1860's, Morse had finally achieved a degree of financial security. He became a vice president of the new Metropolitan Museum of Art and a trustee of Vassar College. He also made donations to Yale and to various religious and moral societies. In 1871, the telegraph industry honored him with a statue in Central Park in New York City.   Carolyn Marvin

See also **Clinton, De Witt** (picture); **Telegraph**.

Additional resources

Kloss, William. *Samuel F. B. Morse*. Abrams, 1988.
Mabee, Carleton. *American Leonardo: A Life of Samuel F. B. Morse*. Octagon, 1969. First published in 1943.
Staiti, Paul J. *Samuel F. B. Morse*. Cambridge, 1989.

Morse, Wayne Lyman (1900-1974), served as United States senator from Oregon, first as a Republican, then as a Democrat. He was elected in 1944 and in 1950 as a Republican. Calling himself an "independent Republican," Morse withdrew from the Republican Party in 1952 and supported the Democratic Party's presidential candidate Adlai E. Stevenson. Morse became a Democrat in 1955, and was reelected to the Senate as a Democrat in 1956 and 1962. He lost bids for reelection in 1968 and 1972. His major interests in the Senate included labor-management relations, Latin-American affairs, and international law. In the 1960's, Morse became one of the most outspoken critics of United States involvement in the Vietnam War.

Morse was born in Madison, Wis. He graduated from the University of Wisconsin in 1923, and earned law degrees at the University of Minnesota and at Columbia University. Morse began teaching law at the University of Oregon in 1929. He served as dean of the university's law school from 1931 through 1944.   James I. Lengle

Morse code is a system of sending messages that uses short and long sounds combined in various ways to represent letters, numerals, and other characters. A short sound is called a *dit;* a long sound, a *dah.* Written code uses dots and dashes to represent dits and dahs.

The code is named for the American inventor and painter Samuel F. B. Morse, who patented the telegraph in 1840. In the past, telegraph companies used *American*

Alphabet

A ●■	O ● ●
B ■●●●	P ●●●●●
C ●● ●	Q ●●■●
D ■●●	R ● ●●
E ●	S ●●●
F ●■●	T ■
G ■■●	U ●●■
H ●●●●	V ●●●■
I ●●	W ●■■
J ■●■●	X ●■●●
K ■●■	Y ●● ●●
L ■	Z ●●● ●
M ■■	& ● ●●●
N ■●	$ ●●●■●●●

Numerals

1 ●■■●	6 ●●●●●●
2 ●●■●	7 ■■●●
3 ●●●■	8 ■●●●●
4 ●●●■●	9 ■●●■
5 ●●●●●	0 ■■■■■

Punctuation

●■●■	●●■■●●	●●● ●●	■●●■●●
Comma	Period	Semicolon	Interrogation

Alphabet

A ●■	J ●■■■	S ●●●
B ■●●●	K ■●■	T ■
C ■●■●	L ●■●●	U ●●■
D ■●●	M ■■	V ●●●■
E ●	N ■●	W ●■■
F ●●■●	O ■■■	X ■●●■
G ■■●	P ●■■●	Y ■●■■
H ●●●●	Q ■■●■	Z ■■●●
I ●●	R ●■●	

Numerals

1 ●■■■■	6 ■●●●●
2 ●●■■■	7 ■■●●●
3 ●●●■■	8 ■■■●●
4 ●●●●■	9 ■■■■●
5 ●●●●●	0 ■■■■■

Punctuation and other signs

●■●■●■	■■●●■■	●●■■●●
Period	Comma	Interrogation
■■■●●●	■●■●■●	●■●■●●
Colon	Semicolon	Quotation marks
●●●■■■●●●	■●■	●■●●●
SOS	Start	Wait
●■●●●■●	●■●	●●●●●●●●
End of message	Understand	Error

WORLD BOOK chart

Morse code uses short and long sounds, written as dots and dashes. Telegrams were once sent in American Morse code, *left.* Amateur radio operators still use international Morse code, *right.*

Morse Code to transmit telegrams by wire. An operator tapped out a message on a *telegraph key,* a switch that opened and closed an electric circuit. A receiving device at the other end of the circuit made clicking sounds and wrote dots and dashes on a paper tape. Today, the telegraph and American Morse Code are rarely used.

The *International Morse Code* was derived from the American Morse Code for use by radio telegraphers. Today, only amateur and maritime radio operators still use this code regularly. Military and commercial operators may also use it when radio signals are too weak for other systems to work. In this code, a dah is three times as long as a dit. Between the sounds that represent a character, there is an interval of silence as long as one dit. Between letters are three such intervals; between words, seven intervals.

Critically reviewed by the American Radio Relay League

See also **Morse, Samuel F. B.; Telegraph.**

Mortality rate. See Birth and death rates.

Mortar is a short-range weapon that is used to reach nearby targets that are protected by hills or other obstacles. A mortar fires a shell on a high arc that enables it to clear obstacles. It has a higher angle of fire, shorter barrel, and lower muzzle *velocity* (speed) than a gun or a howitzer. Mortars are light, can be moved easily, and have great firepower. For example, the 81-millimeter mortar can fire an 11-pound (5-kilogram) shell nearly 3 miles (4.8 kilometers).

A mortar consists of a tube closed at the *breech* (bottom) end, that rests on a base plate. Two adjustable legs support the muzzle end. Soldiers fire the mortar by dropping the ammunition down the muzzle. When the ammunition reaches the bottom, it strikes the firing pin, which explodes the *primer.* Most mortar shells have fins to prevent them from tumbling in the air. Artillery mortars have *bore* diameters of 105 millimeters or larger. Infantry mortars have diameters that are less than 105 millimeters.

Before World War II (1939-1945), armies used heavy, stubby mortars. Large mortars were also used to defend coastlines. But howitzers have largely replaced these heavy mortars in present-day warfare. The lightweight and easily moved infantry mortar became an important weapon during World War II.   Frances M. Lussier

See also **Civil War** (picture).

Morte Darthur. See Malory, Sir Thomas.

Mortgage is a loan agreement that enables a person to borrow money to buy a house or other property. The property is used as security for the loan. The lender may take possession of the property if the loan is not repaid on time. Almost all mortgages involve real estate.

A mortgage actually consists of two legal documents. One document, called a *note,* specifies the amount of the loan, the repayment terms, and other conditions of

U.S. Army

81-mm mortars, *above,* are lightweight and easy to move. They have a maximum firing range of about 3 miles (4.8 kilometers).

the agreement. The other document is the mortgage it-self, which gives the lender legal claim to the property if the loan is not repaid. The term *mortgage* commonly re-fers to the entire loan agreement. The lender is called the *mortgagee,* and the borrower is the *mortgager.*

A person can obtain a mortgage from a bank, insur-ance company, mortgage company, savings and loan as-sociation, or other financial institutions. The interest rate and other terms vary from lender to lender. Most mort-gage agreements require the mortgager to repay the loan in monthly installments over a period of 20 years or more. Part of each payment goes toward the unpaid bal-ance of the loan, called the *principal,* and part toward the interest. As the borrower pays off the loan, more of each monthly payment goes toward the principal, and less toward the interest. The mortgager gradually in-creases the *equity,* which is the value of the property beyond the amount owed on it.

If the borrower misses a number of payments or vio-lates any other condition of the agreement, the lender may *foreclose* the mortgage. Foreclosure is a legal pro-cedure by which the lender takes over the mortgaged property. The lender then may sell the property, keep the amount owed, and give the borrower the rest. More than one mortgage may be placed on a property. If fore-closure occurs, the holder of the *second mortgage* gets nothing until the claims of the first have been met.

Two United States government agencies, the Federal Housing Administration (FHA) and the Department of Veterans Affairs, guarantee some home mortgage loans against loss to the lender. Loans unprotected by a gov-ernment agency are called *conventional loans.*

Mortgage loans have traditionally been a popular in-vestment for financial institutions because of the great safety of such loans. During periods of rapidly rising prices, however, lenders may hesitate to tie up their money in mortgages. Interest rates soar during these periods of *inflation,* but most mortgages pay interest at a fixed rate throughout their term. Thus, a lending insti-tution that issues a 25-year mortgage at 8 per cent inter-est may lose an opportunity to lend the money later at 12 per cent. Inflation also drives down the purchasing power of money. As a result, the dollars that lenders get back have less buying power than the dollars they lent. Therefore, in periods of inflation, many lending institu-tions charge an additional fee called *points* for granting a mortgage loan. Each point equals 1 per cent of the amount of the loan. The fee is regarded as prepaid inter-est and must be paid when the mortgage is signed.

To counteract the effects of inflation, lending institu-tions have developed other types of mortgages. In a *graduated-payment mortgage,* the borrower makes lower monthly payments for the first few years and higher payments later. In a *variable-rate* or *adjustable-rate* mortgage, the interest rate rises and falls in relation to current interest rates. In a *growing-equity mortgage,* monthly payments increase between 3 and 7 per cent yearly until the balance is paid. In a *balloon-payment mortgage,* payments are lower for the first few years and then a large single payment repays the remaining balance.   Mark J. Riedy

See also **Federal Home Loan Mortgage Corporation; Federal National Mortgage Association; Government National Mortgage Association.**

Mortician. See Embalming (Modern embalming).

Morton, John (1724-1777), was a Pennsylvania signer of the Declaration of Independence. He served in the Continental Congress from 1774 to 1777. Morton began his political career in 1756 as a member of the Pennsyl-vania Assembly. He served in the Assembly for nearly 20 years and was also an associate judge of the Pennsylva-nia state Supreme Court. He was one of the state's four delegates to the Stamp Act Congress in 1765. Morton was born in Ridley, Pa.   Robert J. Taylor

Morton, Julius Sterling (1832-1902), an American political leader and nature lover, established the first United States observance of Arbor Day (see **Arbor Day**). Morton was secretary of agriculture from 1893 to 1897 in President Grover Cleveland's Cabinet. He was secre-tary of the Nebraska territory from 1858 to 1861, and also served as acting governor for several months. He was born in Adams, N.Y., and received degrees from the Uni-versity of Michigan and Union College. Nebraska placed a statue of Morton in the United States Capitol in 1937.

Arthur A. Ekirch, Jr.

See also **Nebraska** (Places to visit [Arbor Lodge]).

Morton, Levi Parsons (1824-1920), served as Vice President of the United States from 1889 to 1893, under President Benjamin Harrison. He also was minister to France from 1881 to 1885, and governor of New York in 1895 and 1896. Morton was a Republican. His political success started in 1879 when he was elected to a term in the House of Representatives from New York.

He entered the banking business during the Civil War, and became a prominent New York City banker. His company, through its London branch, was fiscal agent of the United States from 1873 to 1884. He taught school and owned a dry goods firm in New Hampshire before he became a banker. He was born in Shoreham, Vt.   Irving G. Williams

Morton, Oliver Perry (1823-1877), served as gover-nor of Indiana during the Civil War and as a Republican United States senator from 1867 until his death. He was elected lieutenant governor in 1860, and became gover-nor in 1861 when Governor Henry Lane resigned to enter the Senate. As governor, Morton helped raise vol-unteer troops. He raised money through his own efforts to support troops when the Indiana legislature refused to grant him funds. Morton was born in Wayne County, Indiana. Indiana placed a statue of Morton in the U.S. Capitol in 1900.   James E. Sefton

Morton, William Thomas Green (1819-1868), an American dentist, made the first public demonstration of ether in 1846. Crawford W. Long used ether during surgery in 1842, but he did not publish his discovery until 1849 (see **Long, Crawford W.**).

Morton first used ether in a tooth extraction at the suggestion of Charles T. Jackson, a professor of chemis-try at Harvard University. He used it again in 1846 in an operation performed by John C. Warren at the Massa-chusetts General Hospital. This public demonstration marked a turning point in the acceptance of anesthesia by the medical community. The method spread rapidly to Great Britain, France, and other countries.

In 1850, the French Academy of Science awarded the Montyon prize of 5,000 francs jointly to Jackson and Morton. Both men claimed sole credit for the discovery, and Morton refused to share the prize. A bitter quarrel and lawsuits followed, and Morton was ruined financially. The U.S. Congress set up a committee to examine the rival claims, but it could not reach a decision. Morton was born in Charlton, Mass.   Edwin S. Munson

See also **Anesthesia; Ether; Medicine** (History [picture: Ether anesthesia]).

Mosaic, moh ZAY ihk, is an art form in which small pieces of colored glass, stone, or other material are set into mortar. The pieces, called *tesserae* or *tessellae,* fit together to form a picture. Most mosaics decorate ceilings, floors, and interior walls, but some are used for such exterior surfaces as pavements and outside walls. Since the mid-1500's, mosaics have also been used to decorate furniture and objects of personal adornment as well as for architectural ornament.

People in ancient Mesopotamia may have made mosaics as early as the 3000's B.C. However, the widespread use of mosaics began during the 300's B.C. in areas ruled by Greece. The Greeks later taught mosaic design to the Romans, who developed their own style of the art form during the A.D. 100's and 200's. The Romans spread mosaic art throughout the Roman Empire.

In the 500's, mosaics became the major decorative art form of the Byzantine Empire, which included parts of the eastern Mediterranean area. Mosaics of religious scenes decorated the walls and ceilings of many Byzantine churches. The finest Byzantine mosaics were made from the 900's to the 1300's. With the end of the Byzantine era in the 1400's, mosaic art declined. But it was revived during the mid- and late 1500's in the Italian cities of Florence and Rome.

Through the centuries, peoples of various other cultures have created mosaic art. For example, Muslims in India and Persia made mosaics, as did the Aztec and Mayan Indians of Latin America. Architects in Mexico have used mosaics to decorate modern buildings.

John W. Keefe

See also **Byzantine art; Indiana** (People [picture]); **Shell** (picture: Shell mosaic).

Mosaic disease, moh ZAY ihk, is the name of a group of plant diseases caused by certain viruses. The leaves of affected plants become mottled with light- and dark-green blotches. The disease usually stunts the growth of plants and may cause flowers to become streaked and twisted. Plants attacked by the disease include beans, carnations, corn, orchids, potatoes, sweet peas, tobacco, and wheat, and such weeds as burweed and milkweed. Insects called *aphids* often transmit the virus from diseased plants to healthy ones. People may spread certain mosaic viruses by handling plants after smoking tobacco products made from infected tobacco. There is no cure for diseased plants, and they should be removed. Such plants should never be used for cuttings because every part is infected.   Jerry T. Walker

Mosby, MOHZ bee, **John Singleton** (1833-1916), was a famous Confederate ranger during the Civil War. He joined the Confederate cavalry in 1861, and began his independent ranger activities in 1863. His raids on Union bases and camps were so effective that part of north-central Virginia became known as "Mosby's Confederacy." After the war, Mosby practiced law and held several public offices. He was born in Powhatan County, Virginia.   Frank E. Vandiver

The Good Shepherd (about A.D. 430) from the Mausoleum of Galla Placidia, Ravenna, Italy (Madeline Grimoldi)

An early Christian mosaic, *left,* portrays Jesus Christ as a shepherd. The sheep tended by Christ symbolize human souls. The detail shown above left illustrates how the unknown artist arranged many colored pieces to create the scene.

© Chip Hires, Gamma/Liaison

The center of Moscow contains many historic buildings. The Savior Tower, *with clock,* is a main entrance to the Kremlin. St. Basil's Cathedral, with its colorful spires, lies outside the Kremlin. Red Square, *right,* has been the site of many parades and other gatherings.

Moscow

Moscow, *MAHS kow* or *MAHS koh*, is the capital of Russia and one of the largest cities in the world. More than $8\frac{3}{4}$ million people live in Moscow. Moscow is the cultural, communications, government, industrial, scientific, and transportation center of Russia. It lies in western Russia, in the European part of the country. The Moscow River, for which the city was named, flows through the city.

Moscow emerged as the most powerful Russian city in the late 1400's. The princes of Moscow played a leading role in uniting various Russian lands and in conquering non-Russian peoples and territories. Moscow became the capital of the Russian Empire and was the home of Russia's *czars* (emperors) until 1712, when the capital was moved to St. Petersburg. Moscow again became the Russian capital in 1918, after the Bolsheviks (later called Communists) took control of the country. In 1922, Russia and three other republics united to form the Union of Soviet Socialist Republics. Moscow was chosen as the Soviet capital.

The Communists lost power in the Soviet Union in August 1991. In December, the Soviet Union was dissolved. Russia and other former Soviet republics became independent countries. Most of the republics, including Russia, formed a non-Communist Common-

Jaroslaw Bilocerkowycz, the contributor of this article, is Associate Professor of Political Science at the University of Dayton and author of Soviet Ukrainian Dissent: A Study of Political Alienation.

wealth of Independent States. Moscow remained the capital of Russia. The city of Minsk, in Belarus, was named headquarters of the commonwealth.

The city

Layout of Moscow. Moscow is built in the shape of a wheel. This shape can be traced to the city's early history, when rings of fortifications were built to protect it from attack. Today, wide boulevards extend from the city's center, forming the spokes of the wheel. They cross circular boulevards, which make up the inner and outer rims of the wheel. A major highway circles Moscow. Past the highway lies the Green Belt, a ring of forests and parks covering about 695 square miles (1,800 square kilometers).

The oldest and busiest sections of Moscow lie near the Kremlin, a huge walled fortress at the city's historic center. Just north and east of the Kremlin is the main business, commercial, and administrative district. Encircling this area and the Kremlin are Moscow's main shopping streets and many cultural buildings. Most of the

Facts in brief

Population: 8,801,000; metropolitan area, 8,967,000.
Area: 339 sq. mi. (879 km²).
Climate: *Average temperature*—January, 15 °F (−10 °C); July, 65 °F (18 °C). *Average annual precipitation* (rainfall, melted snow, and other moisture)—25 in. (64 cm).
Government: City Soviet of about 500 deputies, elected to five-year terms. Mayor directly elected by the people.

city's new residential and industrial districts lie in the outermost rings.

Famous landmarks. At the heart of the city stands the Kremlin. This old fortress was the center of the Soviet Union's government until that nation was dissolved in 1991. Since then, it has been the center of the Russian government. Inside its walls, which extend almost $1\frac{1}{2}$ miles (2.4 kilometers), are beautiful cathedrals and palaces, as well as government buildings. Some of the cathedrals date from the 1400's. Many czars are buried in the Cathedral of the Archangel Michael. The Grand Kremlin Palace was built in the early 1800's as an imperial residence. The building later was the meeting place of the Supreme Soviet, the parliament of the Soviet Union. In 1992, Russia's Congress of People's Deputies met in the Grand Kremlin Palace. The Palace of Congresses, built in 1961, is used for cultural performances and government meetings and receptions. From 1961 to 1990, it also housed Soviet Communist Party meetings. See **Kremlin.**

Red Square lies just outside the Kremlin walls. This large plaza, about $\frac{1}{4}$ mile (0.4 kilometer) long, took its name in Russian from an old word meaning both *beautiful* and *red.* Huge military and civilian parades were held in Red Square in order to celebrate various special occasions.

Opposite the Kremlin on Red Square is GUM, the country's largest department store. It was completed in the early 1890's and remodeled in 1953. The initials GUM come from three Russian words that mean State Department Store. St. Basil's Cathedral—a Russian church famous for its many colorful, onion-shaped domes—is also on Red Square. Originally built over 400 years ago to honor several military conquests, this building is now part of the State Historical Museum. The Russia Hotel, one of the world's largest hotels, is near Red Square.

The Russian Parliament building, where Russia's Supreme Soviet meets, lies west of the Kremlin.

People

People of Moscow are called *Muscovites.* Moscow's population is a mixture of many nationalities. Russians are by far the largest group in Moscow. Other nationalities include Jews, Ukrainians, Tatars, Belarusians, and Armenians. Moscow does not have separate ethnic neighborhoods. The government has attempted to limit the number of people who live in Moscow.

Housing. Most Muscovites live in small, one- or two-room apartments. The majority of these apartments are in high-rise buildings erected since the 1950's. Despite the growth of housing units, Muscovites suffer housing shortages and complain of poor building quality. Families often wait years to get their own apartment. Some employers provide housing for their workers.

Education. Moscow has about 75 institutes of higher education. Two are universities—Moscow State University and the Russian University of People's Friendship. The others are specialized institutes that train students in specific fields, such as engineering or medicine.

Moscow State University ranks as the largest university in Russia. Established in 1755, it has over 28,000 students. The Russian University of People's Friendship, established in 1960, draws students mainly from Africa, Asia, and Latin America.

Like all Russian children, Moscow youngsters must attend school from age 6 to 17. Moscow has about 1,300 elementary schools and general high schools, and about 150 technical or vocational high schools.

Religion. From 1917 through the 1980's, the Communist government of the Soviet Union discouraged the practice of all religions. As a result, many Muscovites do not follow any religious faith. Many others, however,

Moscow

Location of Moscow

Green belt or park

International boundary

City boundary

Road or street

Railroad

Canal

• Point of interest

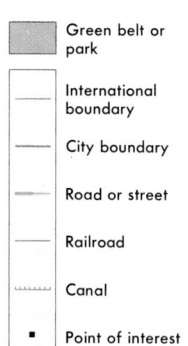

Greater Moscow

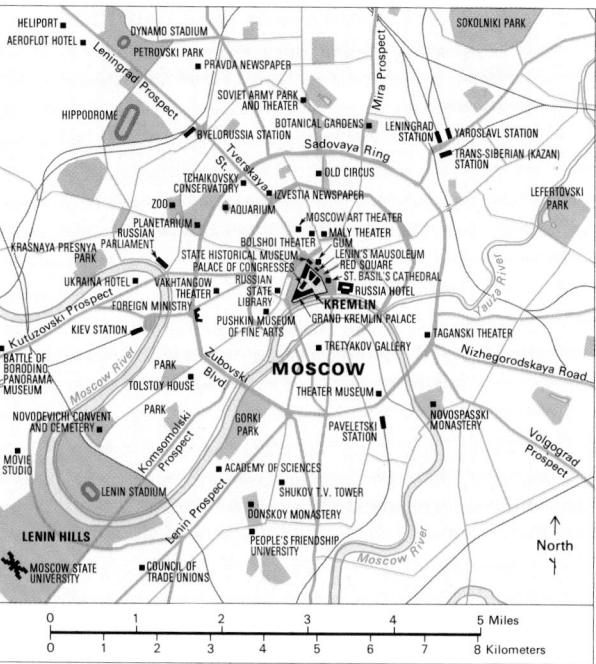

The Bolshoi Theater Ballet of Moscow is an internationally known ballet company. Bolshoi performers are known for their great skill and vigorous, dramatic dancing. This photo shows a Bolshoi performance of the famous French romantic ballet *Giselle.*

ZEFA

have continued to practice a religion. Most religious Muscovites of Russian nationality belong to the Russian Orthodox Church. Some old and beautiful Orthodox churches were made into museums after 1917. In 1990, the Soviet government ended all religious restrictions. Places of worship that had been closed for decades were reopened.

Non-Russian Muscovites belong to many religious groups, including Baptists, Jews, Muslims, and Roman Catholics. Moscow has a few Catholic and Protestant churches, two Jewish synagogues, and an Islamic mosque.

Social problems. During the late 1980's, crime became a growing problem in Moscow. In part, the increase in crime was due to the loosening of formerly strict police controls. It also stemmed from economic hardships—including serious shortages of food, clothing, and other goods—which have grown more serious since the 1980's. Crime has also been fueled by a high rate of alcoholism.

Homelessness has also become a problem in Moscow. The homeless people include refugees who have fled ethnic violence in other parts of the country.

Moscow has long suffered from pollution problems. For many years, industrial growth was emphasized with little concern for the environment. Exhaust from factories and automobiles fouled the air. Poor water and sewage treatment also caused problems. Muscovites have begun using high-technology equipment and energy-saving devices to control pollution. They have also begun closing or moving some factories that pollute.

Cultural life

Arts. Moscow has long been a center of Russian and world culture. The Bolshoi Theater presents operas and ballets. The ballet company, called the Bolshoi Theater Ballet, has become internationally known and admired. Dancers from all over the country are trained at the Bolshoi Theater's school. A symphony orchestra performs at the Tchaikovsky Concert Hall in Moscow. The city also features a number of famous drama theaters, including the Maly and Moscow Art theaters.

Museums and libraries. Moscow has about 75 museums and many art galleries. The State Historical Museum attracts many students of Russian history. The

Central Lenin Museum and the Central Museum of the Revolution have exhibits on the Russian Revolution. Dazzling treasures that belonged to the czars are displayed in the Armory Museum in the Kremlin. The Tretyakov Gallery contains a collection of traditional art. The Russian National Exhibition Center highlights science and technology.

Over 1,200 main libraries operate in Moscow. The Russian State Library is the largest library in Russia and one of the largest in the world. See also **Library** (Eastern Europe and Russia; picture: Russian State Library).

Entertainment and recreation. Moscow has many recreational facilities. The huge Lenin Stadium sports complex was completed in 1956 and later expanded for the 1980 Olympics. The complex includes Lenin Stadium, which seats about 103,000 people. The stadium is used mainly for soccer, the country's most popular sport, and for track events. The athletic complex also includes swimming pools and smaller sports arenas.

Gorki Park is Moscow's most popular amusement center. It features an outdoor theater and facilities for boating, ice skating, and tennis. The park covers about 300 acres (120 hectares) and opened in 1925.

The Arbat is a popular district of downtown Moscow.

© Jean S. Buldain, Berg & Associates

Gorki Park in Moscow offers many activities, such as boating, amusement rides, ice skating, tennis, and theater.

ZEFA

The Arbat is a popular district of downtown Moscow. It has many shops, restaurants, and bookstores. Street artists, such as the one above, make the Arbat a colorful place to visit.

© Jean S. Buldain, Berg & Associates

The Metro is Moscow's subway system. It is famous for its many elegant subway stations, each of which is decorated in a different style. The one above is the Kievskaya station.

It has many small shops, restaurants, and bookstores. Folk music, roving artists, and political debates make the Arbat a lively section of town.

Chess is a popular pastime for Muscovites, and many chess champions play at the city's Central Chess Club. The Moscow Zoo is a popular attraction. The Moscow Circus is one of the finest circuses in the world.

Economy

Most Muscovites work in state-controlled enterprises. Many are employed by agencies of the national or city governments. Others work in factories, stores, or other businesses owned by the state. Since 1991, some businesses in Moscow have come under private ownership.

Manufacturing. Moscow is the most important industrial city in Russia. Its factories produce a wide variety of goods. These include automobiles, buses, chemicals, dairy products, electrical machinery, measuring instruments, processed foods, steel, textiles, and trucks.

Transportation. Moscow serves as Russia's transportation center. Highways and railways extend in all directions from the city to most parts of the country. Moscow has four major airports, the largest of which is in Domodedovo, south of the city. Sheremetyevo International Airport handles most international flights. The Moscow Canal links the city to the Volga, Europe's longest river.

The people of Moscow are proud of their subway system, the Metro. It has about 140 subway stations, which are the fanciest in the world. Many look like palace halls and are decorated with chandeliers, marble panels, paintings, stained glass, and statues. The Metro opened in 1935. It has about 140 miles (225 kilometers) of track. Over 7 million passengers ride it daily.

Communications. Many magazines, journals, and newspapers are published in Moscow. These include the important national newspapers *Pravda* (*Truth*) and *Izvestia* (*News*). Other popular publications published in Moscow include the newspapers *Trud* (*Labor*), *Komso-*

molskaia Pravda (*Youth Communist League Truth*), and the political magazine *Argumenty i fakty* (*Arguments and Facts*). *Evening Moscow* and the *Moscow News* are the city's local papers.

Radio Moscow, operated by the government, broadcasts programs on four channels. The Central Television Studios are also government operated. They transmit programs on two national network channels. Moscow also has several local channels and receives local programs from St. Petersburg.

Government

Moscow is governed by a *City Soviet* (City Council) of about 500 deputies elected to five-year terms. Each deputy represents an election district called a *ward*.

Before 1990, only one candidate ran for election in each ward. The candidate was elected unless most voters crossed his or her name off the ballot. In the March 1990 city election, two or three candidates could run for each position on the City Soviet. Candidates from opposing political organizations were nominated by individuals or groups. Voters crossed the name of the candidates they opposed off the ballots. A candidate had to receive at least 50 per cent of the vote in his or her ward to win. In cases where no candidate received 50 per cent of the vote, a runoff election was held.

Before 1991, members of the City Soviet elected one deputy to be chairman, or mayor. In June 1991, the people of Moscow elected their mayor directly. Later in 1991, the executive branch of the city government was reorganized. Moscow was divided into 10 administrative districts. Each administrative district is headed by a prefect who is appointed by the mayor. The prefects and their staffs administer city services and policies in their areas. Moscow is also divided into local districts. Each district government is responsible for local affairs.

History

The rise of Moscow. It is not known when Moscow was first settled. The first recorded reference to the

Moscow in the 1100's was a wooden fortress on a hill. The Kremlin now stands at this location. The nearby Moscow River was an important trade route.

Sovfoto

© Shone, Gamma/Liaison

Jubilant Muscovites celebrated a failed coup in August 1991. Several Communist officials had attempted to overthrow the president of the Soviet Union, Mikhail S. Gorbachev. But in December, Gorbachev resigned, and the Soviet Union was dissolved.

town is in an early Russian historical chronicle under the year 1147. At that time, Moscow was a possession of Yuri Dolgoruki, a Russian prince who ruled the surrounding region. The town lay on important land and water trade routes, and it grew and prospered. During the 1200's, Tatar invaders from Asia conquered Moscow and other Russian lands. The Russian princes were forced to recognize the Tatars as their rulers and pay them taxes. During the 1300's, the Moscow princes collected taxes in their region for the Tatars. The Moscow princes expanded their territory greatly by buying lands or seizing them from rival princes.

By the late 1400's, Moscow had become the most powerful Russian city. Moscow threw off Tatar control during the late 1400's under Ivan III (the Great). His grandson, Ivan IV (the Terrible), was crowned czar of all Russia in 1547. Moscow was his capital.

Moscow grew rapidly during the 1600's. The czars built palaces in the Kremlin, and nobles built mansions. New churches and monasteries arose, and industries developed. In 1712 Peter I (the Great), moved the capital to St. Petersburg. However, Moscow remained an important center of culture and trade.

Destruction and rebirth. In the fall of 1812, invading French troops under Napoleon I sought to capture Moscow. The French and Russian armies fought a major battle at Borodino, just outside Moscow. The French army won the battle and entered Moscow without a struggle. Most of the people had left the city. Soon afterward, fires destroyed most of Moscow. Historians believe that most of the fires were set by retreating Russians, but that others were started by looting troops from Napoleon's army. After about a month, the French troops left and began a disastrous retreat through the cold Russian winter. See **Napoleon I** (Disaster in Russia).

The rebuilding of Moscow began almost immediately. New residences were built and factories began to appear. By the mid-1800's, Moscow had emerged as the railway and industrial center of Russia. The city's population grew rapidly, passing 1 million by 1900.

Early 1900's. In 1905 and in 1917, fierce revolutions against the czar took place in several Russian cities, including Moscow. In the 1917 revolution, the government fell to the Bolsheviks, who moved the capital back to Moscow in 1918.

Moscow grew rapidly during the 1930's. During World War II (1939-1945), German troops advanced almost to the city but never captured it. Governmental bodies and industrial factories were moved to the eastern part of the country. German air raids damaged Moscow, but in 1941 the German forces were stopped. The Battle of Moscow was an important victory for the Soviet Union because it proved that the Germans could be defeated. See **World War II** (The invasion of the Soviet Union; On the Soviet front).

Recent developments. Since the 1950's, thousands of apartment buildings have been built in Moscow. Some are 25 stories high. In 1960, the city's boundaries were expanded, more than doubling the city's area. The 1980 Summer Olympic Games were held in Moscow, the first Soviet city ever to host the Olympics.

In 1990, Moscow held its first democratic election for the City Soviet. Democratic reformers won a majority of the seats. In August 1991, Moscow became the center of protests that helped end a coup aimed at overthrowing the president of the Soviet Union, Mikhail S. Gorbachev. But on Dec. 25, 1991, Gorbachev resigned, and the Soviet Union was dissolved. Russia and other former Soviet republics formed a Commonwealth of Independent States. Moscow remained Russia's capital, but Minsk was chosen as headquarters of the commonwealth.

Jaroslaw Bilocerkowycz

Related articles in *World Book* include:

Outline

V. Government
VI. History

Questions

How did Moscow become the most powerful Russian city?
What is the Green Belt?
Which art form is the Bolshoi Theater most famous for?
What efforts has the city made to control pollution?
What is the Metro?
How are candidates elected to the City Soviet?
Why was the Battle of Moscow important in World War II?
What makes Moscow the transportation center of Russia?
What is the Arbat?
Why did crime become a growing problem in Moscow?

Moscow Art Theater became one of the most influential theaters of the 1900's. It presents plays by major Russian authors and has made several tours of Western countries. One of its founders, Konstantin Stanislavski, developed his *Method* style of acting at the theater. The style stresses psychological realism in the interpretation and presentation of plays. In the Method style, actors and actresses define a role by saying, "If I were this character, I would. . . ." Actors and actresses also define a role by drawing on relevant experiences from their own lives. The style has had great impact on Western theater.

The Moscow Art Theater was founded in 1898 by Stanislavski and Vladimir Nemirovich-Danchenko. Its production in 1898 of Anton Chekhov's *The Sea Gull* started his career as a successful playwright.

Albert Wertheim

See also **Stanislavski, Konstantin.**

Moseley-Braun, *brawn,* **Carol** (1947-　　), became the first black woman to be elected to the United States Senate when she won a U.S. Senate seat in 1992. Moseley-Braun, a Democrat from Illinois, decided to run for the Senate after Clarence Thomas gained Senate confirmation as a justice of the Supreme Court of the United States—despite charges that he had sexually harassed a female co-worker. Moseley-Braun, who was considered a liberal, received strong support from women voters. In the Senate, Moseley-Braun and California Senator Dianne Feinstein became the first women to serve on the powerful Senate Judiciary Committee.

© Robert Trippett, Sipa Press
Carol Moseley-Braun

Moseley-Braun was born in Chicago. She earned a law degree from the University of Chicago in 1972 and was an assistant U.S. attorney from 1973 to 1977. She served in the Illinois House of Representatives from 1979 to 1989, when she became the recorder of deeds in Cook County, Illinois. Guy Halverson

Moselle River, *moh ZEHL,* a branch of the Rhine River, rises in the Vosges Mountains in eastern France. It flows northeastward for 319 miles (513 kilometers) and empties into the Rhine in Koblenz, Germany. It is called the *Mosel* in Germany. Much of the Moselle is very shallow. A 170-mile (274-kilometer) canal enables barges to go about 200 miles (320 kilometers) up the river. The fa-

mous Moselle wines are made along the river's banks. Major ironworks and steelworks lie along the Moselle in eastern France. The beautiful river valley in Germany attracts many tourists. The Moselle was the scene of bitter fighting during World War I (1914-1918) and World War II (1939-1945). Frank Ahnert

Moses was the principal leader and teacher of the Israelites and one of the most important characters in the Bible. He led his people out of slavery in Egypt to their homeland in Canaan, later called Palestine. At Mount Sinai, Moses declared the Ten Commandments as the law for his people. There, the Israelites were established as a nation under Moses' leadership.

Moses was a political organizer, a military chief, a diplomat, a lawmaker, and a judge as well as a religious leader. He kept the Israelite nation united during its years of wandering in the desert between Egypt and Canaan. The Bible pays tribute to Moses in the following passage: "And there arose not a prophet in Israel like unto Moses, whom the Lord knew face to face, in all the signs and the wonders, which the Lord sent him to do in the land of Egypt to Pharaoh. . ." (Deut. 34: 10).

The first five books of the Bible—Genesis, Exodus, Leviticus, Numbers, and Deuteronomy—are called the "Five Books of Moses," or the *Pentateuch.* The story of Moses' life is in the books of Exodus, Leviticus, Numbers, and Deuteronomy. However, the books do not mention Moses as the author. Biblical scholars believe that the stories in the Five Books of Moses were passed orally from generation to generation until they were written down between about 1000 and 400 B.C.

Early life. Moses was born in Egypt near the end of the 1300's B.C. He was the descendant of Hebrew slaves who had migrated from Canaan to Egypt hundreds of years earlier. The Egyptians had enslaved the Hebrews and forced them to build large cities and palaces.

According to the Bible, the population of the Hebrews eventually grew so large that the Egyptian pharaoh feared they could not be controlled. Therefore, at about the time of Moses' birth, the pharaoh ordered all male Hebrew children killed. Moses' mother hid the baby in a basket in the rushes on the bank of the Nile River. The pharaoh's daughter found the infant and raised him, with the help of Moses' own mother. This account of Moses' escape from death shows that he would become a great man.

Moses was given an Egyptian name and received an Egyptian education, but he retained his Hebrew identity. As an adult, Moses saw an Egyptian beating a Hebrew. He killed the Egyptian and fled into the desert. While living there, he married Zipporah, the daughter of Jethro, a priest of the Midianite tribe. They had two sons, Gershom and Eliezer.

Moses settled in the land of Midian. There, he lived as a shepherd. One day, according to the Bible, God spoke to him from a burning bush. He commanded Moses to return to Egypt and lead the Hebrews to the land that had been promised to Abraham, the ancestor of the Hebrews (see **Abraham**). Moses argued that he could not perform such a difficult project. However, Moses accepted God's commandment to lead the Hebrews from Egypt.

The Exodus. Moses joined his older brother, Aaron, while returning to Egypt, and they met with the pharaoh.

Moses reportedly told the pharaoh, "Let my people go" (Exod. 5: 1), but the Egyptian ruler refused to do so. He punished the Hebrews by increasing their workload.

According to the Bible, the Egyptians were then afflicted with nine terrible plagues. But after each one, the pharaoh continued to refuse to let the Hebrews leave. The 10th and final plague killed the pharaoh's oldest son and all first-born Egyptian sons. But the Hebrews remained unharmed.

The 10th plague caused the pharaoh and the Egyptian people great grief. The pharaoh finally agreed to let the Hebrews leave Egypt. Their flight from Egypt is called the *Exodus.* The pharaoh soon regretted losing so many slaves and sent his army to recapture them. According to the Book of Exodus, God led the Hebrews through the wilderness to a body of water traditionally identified as the Red Sea. However, because the Hebrew text actually says "sea of reeds," most modern scholars believe the body of water was actually the marshy lands east of the Nile Delta, well north of the Red Sea. As the pursuing Egyptians drew closer, God commanded Moses to lift a rod and stretch his hand over the sea to divide the waters. The parting of the waters enabled his people to cross safely. The Egyptian soldiers followed the Hebrews but drowned when the waters flowed back into place.

The covenant with God. Moses led the Hebrews across the Red Sea into the desert. They journeyed to Mount Sinai, where they entered into a *covenant* (agreement) with God. Under the terms of the covenant, the Hebrews became the new nation of Israel. The covenant provided that all the Israelites would live under God's eternal love and protection. In exchange, they would be ruled by God and obey His laws.

The basis of the covenant consisted of the Ten Commandments and laws found in the "Book of the Covenant," a set of God-given rules and guidelines. According to the Bible, Moses received the Ten Commandments and other laws from God on Mount Sinai. The Ten Commandments and the laws of the "Book of the Covenant" became part of what is known as the "Torah of Moses." These laws defined the Israelites' relationship with one another and with God. Moses also established an administrative and legal system for the Israelites to help carry out the laws of the covenant.

While Moses was receiving the Ten Commandments, the Israelites became impatient. They wanted a god that they could see. As a result, the Israelites built a golden calf and began to worship it. The Israelites thought the golden calf represented the God who had led them out of Egypt.

After Moses came down from the mountain, he found his people dancing before the idol. He became so angry that he smashed the stone tablets on which the Ten Commandments had been inscribed. Many Israelites died soon afterward, and the people believed that the deaths were a punishment for their sin. Moses later carved a new copy of the Ten Commandments into other stone tablets.

The Biblical story also describes how Moses organized the nation's official forms of worship. The Israelites' religious activities centered on a movable structure called the *Tabernacle.* The Tabernacle served as an official meeting place for God and the people, and it sym-

bolized His relationship with the Israelites (see **Tabernacle**). The people reestablished the old Hebrew holidays as national celebrations. The Exodus became a theme of the renewed festivals. The springtime holiday *Passover* celebrates the Israelites' escape from Egypt (see **Passover**).

Journey to Canaan. The Israelites are reported to have spent 40 years wandering in the desert between Egypt and Canaan. They lived under harsh conditions and often complained to Moses. The people also became impatient and frustrated, and they challenged Moses' authority as a religious and political leader. In addition, they questioned their faith in a God they could not see.

Moses often asked for God's help to care for his people. He frequently obtained food and water for the Israelites under God's direction. Throughout their long wanderings in the desert, Moses served as an intermediary between God and the Israelite people.

Hostile tribes apparently attacked the Israelites several times in the desert, but Moses always led his people to victory. He also foresaw the many difficulties that the Israelites would encounter in Canaan.

When the Israelites reached Canaan, God allowed Moses to see the new land but not to enter it. According to the Bible, Moses did not cross the Jordan River into Canaan because he had not followed one of God's instructions (Num. 20: 1-13). God had told Moses to obtain water for the Israelites by speaking to a rock. Water would then flow from the rock. But instead of speaking

Miniature (about 1320) from the *Golden Haggadah* of Barcelona, Spain; British Library, London

Moses was an Israelite leader. This painting shows events from his life. At the upper right, an angel in a burning bush appears to Moses. At the upper left, Moses and his wife return to Egypt from Midian and meet his brother Aaron. At the lower right, the brothers perform a miracle for the elders of Israel. At the lower left, Moses and Aaron appear before the pharaoh.

Grandma Moses Properties, New York City
(Polaroid Land Photograph)

Grandma Moses, *above,* was a popular American folk artist. The gaily colored *Out for Christmas Trees, left,* shows the innocence and charm of her paintings. She took her subjects from memories of her life on farms in northern New York and Virginia.

Oil painting on canvas; © 1987, Grandma Moses Properties, New York City

to the rock, Moses struck it. Joshua, an assistant of Moses, led the people into Canaan.

Moses died in God's favor at an advanced age. According to the Book of Deuteronomy, God buried Moses on Mount Nebo in the desert. Carol L. Meyers

See also **Aaron; Deuteronomy; Exodus; Jews** (The Exodus); **Joshua; Pentateuch.**

Additional resources

Auerbach, Elias. *Moses.* Wayne State Univ. Pr., 1975. First published in West Germany in 1953.
Buber, Martin. *Moses: The Revelation and the Covenant.* Humanities Pr., 1988. First published in England in 1946.
Encyclopaedia Judaica. 17 vols. Ed. by Cecil Roth and Geoffrey Wigoder. Keter Pub., 1982. See the article "Moses" in Vol. XII, pp. 371-411.
Jagersma, H. *A History of Israel in the Old Testament Period.* Fortress, 1982.
Roshwald, Mordecai and Miriam. *Moses: Leader, Prophet, Man.* Yoseloff, 1969. A standard work.

Moses, Grandma (1860-1961), was an American folk artist. She started painting when she was in her 70's and remained active until near her death. She never had an art lesson. Grandma Moses painted simple but realistic

scenes of rural life. These colorful and lively pictures were based on memories of her own youth in the late 1800's. Critics have praised her work for its freshness, innocence, and humanity.

Grandma Moses was born Anna Mary Robertson in Washington County, New York. She was married to Thomas Salmon Moses in 1887. For many years, she embroidered pictures on canvas. She began to paint when arthritis made it difficult for her to hold embroidery needles. An art collector first discovered her paintings in the 1930's. She was represented in a show at the Museum of Modern Art in New York City in 1939. Her first one-artist show was in 1940. Her autobiography, *My Life's History,* was published in 1952. Sarah Burns

Moses, Phoebe Ann. See Oakley, Annie.
Moshav. See Israel (Rural life).
Moshoeshoe. See Lesotho (History).
Moslems. See Muslims.
Mosque, *mahsk,* is a building used for Muslim worship. Some mosques are simple assembly halls for prayer. *Cathedral,* or *Friday, mosques* are large, elaborate buildings designed to house all the adult believers

Milt and Joan Mann

The interior of a mosque, *left,* has an arch called a *mihrab.* The mihrab is set in the wall nearest to the Muslim holy city of Mecca, the direction worshipers must face when they pray. To the right of the mihrab stands a pulpit called a *mimbar.* The interior is decorated with quotations in Arabic from the Koran, the Muslim holy book.

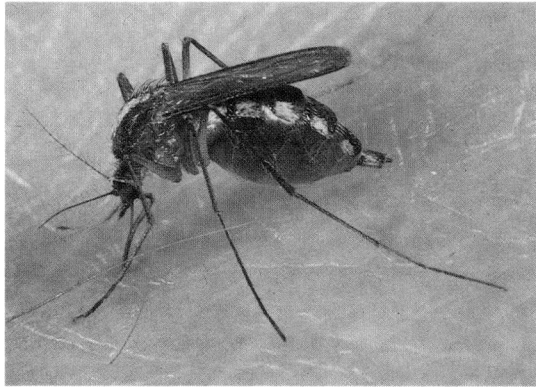

© Robert K. Washino

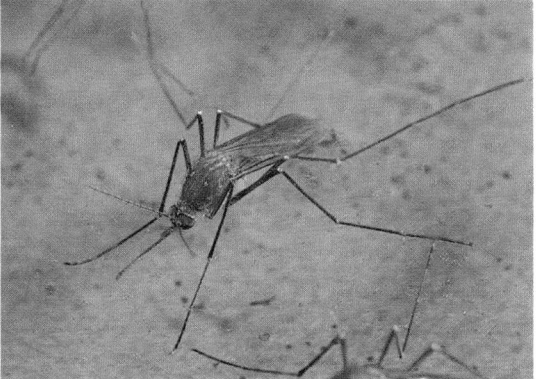

© E. R. Degginger

Mosquitoes live throughout the world. Certain kinds transmit diseases when they "bite." These photographs show an *Anopheles* mosquito, *top,* and a *Culex, bottom.* Some *Anopheles* mosquitoes carry malaria. *Culex* mosquitoes transmit encephalitis.

in a community. Mosques also have served as places of religious instruction, as tombs, and as temporary homes for traveling scholars.

A typical mosque has a courtyard surrounded by four halls called *iwans.* In most cases, there is a fountain or well for ceremonial washing in the courtyard. The inner wall closest to the holy city of Mecca has a decorative niche or arch called a *mihrab,* which indicates the direction Muslims must face when praying. In numerous mosques, flat surfaces are decorated with painted or tile patterns or with scriptural quotations in elegant handwriting called *calligraphy.* Most mosques have from one to six towers called *minarets,* from which *muezzins* (criers) call the faithful to prayer. Many mosques contain a pulpit, called a *mimbar.*   William J. Hennessey

For other pictures of mosques, see **Afghanistan; Africa** (The arts); **Architecture** (Islamic architecture); **Asia** (Way of life in Southwest Asia); **Iran; Islam; Islamic art; Minaret.**

Mosquitia. See Mosquito Coast.

Mosquito is an insect that spreads some of the worst diseases of people and animals. Certain kinds of mosquitoes carry the germs that cause such serious diseases as encephalitis, malaria, filariasis, and yellow fever. When a mosquito "bites," it may leave germs behind. Many kinds of mosquitoes do not spread diseases,

but they have painful "bites." Many of the mosquitoes that are associated with disease live in the hot, moist lands near the equator. But mosquitoes are found in all parts of the world, even in the Arctic.

There are more than 3,000 species of mosquitoes. About 150 species live in the United States. Biologists classify species of mosquitoes into about 35 groups, each called a *genus.* For example, the common house mosquito, which may transmit certain kinds of parasitic worms, belongs to the genus *Culex.* This species and other members of its genus may also carry encephalitis viruses. Some mosquitoes in the genus *Anopheles* carry malaria, and some in the genus *Aedes* transmit yellow fever virus.

People control insects in many ways. Small amounts of chemical insecticides kill mosquitoes when sprayed in homes, garages, and other buildings. Thick mists of insecticides may be sprayed into fields, forests, and gardens. People also control mosquitoes by destroying the places where they breed. Mosquitoes lay their eggs in marshes, swamps, and pools of still water, and tree holes, tires, and tin cans that contain standing water. Such places may be drained, or the surface of the water may be covered with thin layers of oil or insecticides.

Since the 1960's, scientists have turned increasing attention to the biological control of insects, including mosquitoes. Programs are designed to control certain insects without damaging other elements of the environment. One such program uses fish that eat mosquito *larvae* (young). Another uses the spores of a bacterium, *Bacillus thuringiensis,* to kill the larvae.

Most kinds of mosquitoes are from $\frac{1}{8}$ to $\frac{1}{4}$ inch (3 to 6 millimeters) long. One of the largest is the American gallinipper. It grows about $\frac{5}{8}$ inch (16 millimeters) long.

The hum of a mosquito is the sound of its wings beating. A mosquito's wings move about 1,000 times a second. A female's wings make a higher tone than a male's wings, and the sound helps males find mates.

Mosquitoes are *flies* (insects with two wings). The word *mosquito* is Spanish and means *little fly.*

The body of a mosquito

The mosquito's slender body has three parts: (1) the head, (2) the thorax, and (3) the abdomen. The insect's body wall is thin and elastic. Fine hair and thin scales grow on the body and on the wings. Most kinds of mosquitoes are black, brown, gray, or tan. Many species have white or light-colored markings on their backs, legs, or wings. A few kinds are bright blue or green, and seem to shine with coppery or golden lights.

Head. The mosquito has a large, round head that is joined to the thorax by a short, thin neck. Two huge *compound* eyes cover most of the head. These eyes, like those of most other kinds of insects, are made up of thousands of six-sided lenses. Each lens points in a

Facts in brief

Number of eggs: 100 to 300 at a time, depending on species. As many as 1,000 a year for each female.

Length of life: Up to 30 days or more for females; about 7 to 10 days for males.

Where found: All parts of the world.

Scientific classification: Mosquitoes belong to the fly order Diptera. They make up the family Culicidae.

The body of a mosquito

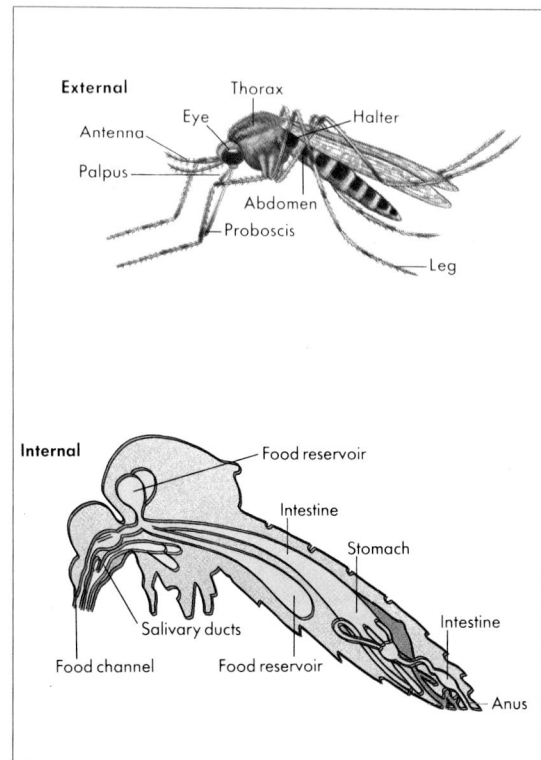

The heads of mosquitoes

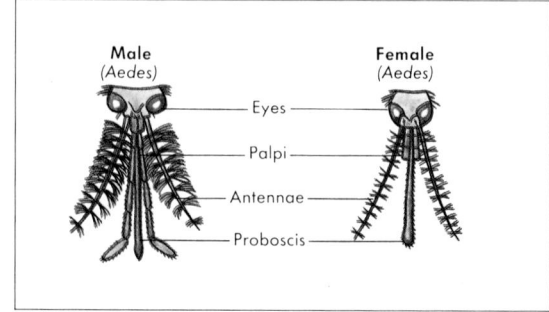

How a mosquito "bites"

A mosquito stabs a victim's skin with sharp stylets hidden in the proboscis. As the insect pushes the stylets down, they curve and enter a blood vessel. The *labium* (lower lip) slides out of the way.

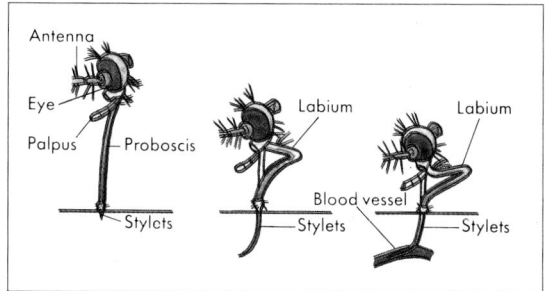

WORLD BOOK illustrations by Oxford Illustrators Limited

slightly different direction and works independently. A mosquito cannot focus its eyes for sharp vision, but it quickly sees any movement. The eyes are always open, even when the insect rests.

A mosquito hears and smells with its two antennae, which grow near the center of its head between the eyes. The antennae of a female mosquito are long and covered with soft hair. The male's antennae are also long, and have bushy hairs that give a feathery appearance.

The mouth of a mosquito looks somewhat like a funnel. The broadest part is nearest the head, and a tubelike part called the *proboscis* extends downward. A mosquito uses its proboscis to "bite," and as a straw to sip liquids, its only food. The males and females of many species sip plant juices.

How a mosquito "bites." Only female mosquitoes "bite," and only the females of a few species attack human beings and animals. They sip the victim's blood, which they need for the development of the eggs inside their bodies.

Mosquitoes do not really bite because they cannot open their jaws. When a mosquito "bites," it stabs through the victim's skin with six needlelike parts called *stylets,* which form the center of the proboscis. The stylets are covered and protected by the insect's lower lip, called the *labium.* As the stylets enter the skin, the labium bends and slides upward out of the way. Then saliva flows into the wound through channels formed by the stylets. The mosquito can easily sip the blood be-

cause the saliva keeps it from clotting. Most people are allergic to the saliva, and an itchy welt called a "mosquito bite" forms on the skin. After the mosquito has sipped enough blood, it slowly pulls the stylets out of the wound, and the labium slips into place over them. Then the insect flies away.

The amount of blood taken varies greatly among individual mosquitoes. Some may sip as much as $1\frac{1}{2}$ times their own weight at a time.

Thorax. The mosquito's thorax is shaped somewhat like a triangle, with the broadest part above and the narrowest part underneath. Thin, flat scales of various colors form patterns on the upper part of the thorax of certain kinds of mosquitoes. These patterns help identify different species. One kind of mosquito that spreads yellow fever has a U-shaped pattern formed by white scales on a background of dark scales.

Strong muscles are attached to the inside wall of the thorax. These muscles move the mosquito's legs and wings. A mosquito has six long, slender legs, and each leg has five major joints. A pair of claws on each leg helps the insect cling to such flat surfaces as walls and ceilings. The mosquito uses all its legs when it walks, but usually stands on only four of them. Many kinds of mosquitoes rest on their four front legs. Some kinds hold their two hind legs almost straight out behind them, but others curve their legs over their backs. White scales form bands on the legs of some species.

Mosquitoes have two wings, unlike most other kinds of insects, which have four wings. The wings are so thin

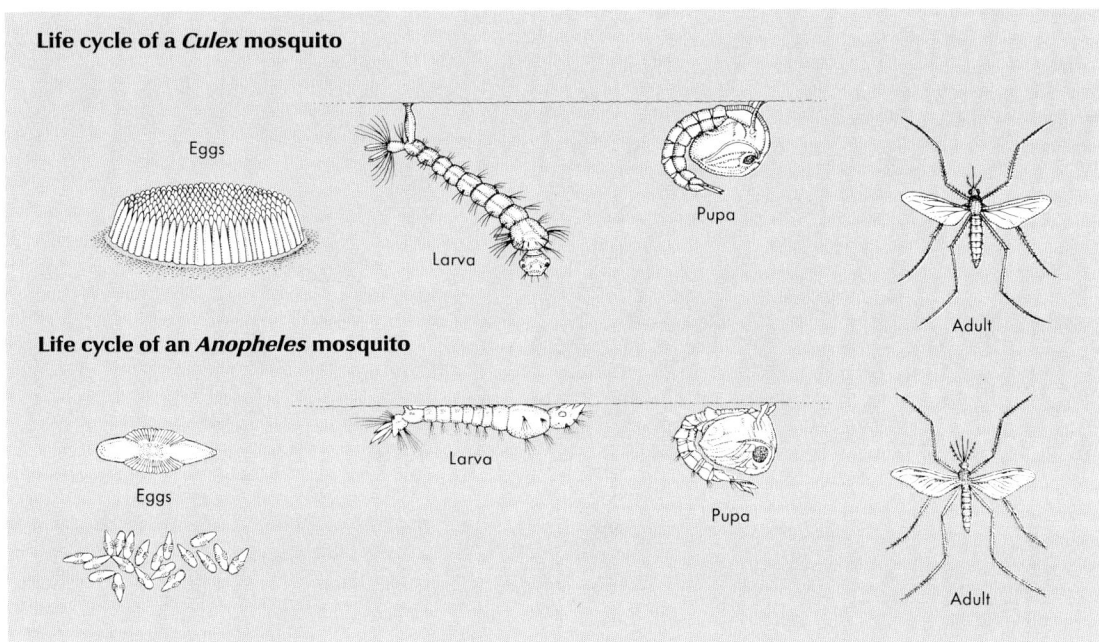

Life cycle of a *Culex* mosquito

Eggs

Larva

Pupa

Adult

Life cycle of an *Anopheles* mosquito

Eggs

Larva

Pupa

Adult

WORLD BOOK illustration by Patricia Wynne

that the veins show through. The veins not only carry blood to the wings, but also help stiffen and support them. Thin scales cover the veins and the edges of the wings. The scales rub off like dust when anything touches them. Some species of mosquitoes may have scales of beautiful colors.

Instead of hind wings, which most other insects have, a mosquito has two thick, rodlike parts with knobs at the tips. These parts, called *halteres,* give the mosquito its sense of balance. The halteres vibrate at the same rate as the wings when the insect flies.

A mosquito lifts itself into the air as soon as it beats its wings. It does not have to run or jump to take off. In the air, the mosquito can dart quickly and easily in any direction. The halteres keep the insect in balance. A mosquito must beat its wings constantly while it is in the air. It does not glide during flight or when coming in for a landing as do butterflies, moths, and most other flying insects. A mosquito beats its wings until its feet touch a landing place.

Abdomen of a mosquito is long and slender, and looks somewhat like a tube. Some kinds of mosquitoes have an abdomen with a pointed end. Other kinds have an abdomen with a rounded end. The shape of the abdomen helps scientists identify the species.

A mosquito breathes through air holes called *spiracles* along the sides of its body. The abdomen has eight pairs of spiracles, and the thorax has two pairs. Air flows into the holes, and tubes carry the air from the spiracles to all parts of the mosquito's body.

The life of a mosquito

A mosquito's life is divided into four stages: (1) egg, (2) larva, (3) pupa, and (4) adult. At each stage the mosquito's appearance changes completely, and the insect lives a different kind of life. In warm climates, some species develop from newly hatched eggs into adults in only a

week. In the cold climate of the far north, mosquito eggs may remain dormant from autumn until late spring. They hatch in May or June, and take a month or more to grow into adults.

Egg. A female mosquito lays from 100 to 300 eggs at a time, depending on the species. One female may lay as many as 3,000 eggs during her lifetime. The eggs are laid through an opening at the tip of the female's abdomen. The females of most species of mosquitoes lay their eggs in water or near it, but each species has a favorite spot. Some like quiet swamps, and others prefer salt marshes. Still others lay their eggs in hidden pools that form in tin cans, rain barrels, gutters, fallen logs, or hollow tree stumps.

Among some species, the females drop their eggs one at a time. Frilly, transparent parts on the shell keep each egg afloat until it hatches. The females of other species arrange their eggs in groups that look somewhat like rafts. The female rests on the surface of the water while she lays her eggs, which are narrow at the top. With her hind legs, she carefully pushes the eggs, wide ends downward, into raftlike groups. The eggs of most kinds of mosquitoes hatch in two or three days in warm weather.

All mosquito eggs must have moisture to hatch, but not all species lay their eggs in water. Certain mosquitoes, called floodwater mosquitoes, drop their eggs in moist soil on flood plains and on irrigation sites. The eggs hatch after a flood takes place—perhaps a year later. Other species, sometimes called pond mosquitoes, lay their eggs in hollow places left by ponds that have dried up. The eggs hatch after rains fill the ponds with water. Not all of the eggs of these mosquitoes hatch after the first rain. They must be soaked by a second or even a third rain before they hatch into larvae.

Larva of a mosquito is often called a *wriggler* because it is so active. The wrigglers of most species move about by jerking their bodies through the water.

A wriggler looks somewhat like a worm or a caterpillar. A thin, skinlike shell covers its body. The wriggler has a broad head, with two short, bushy antennae on each side. It has two eyes behind the antennae, near the back of the head. Its mouth is on the underside of the head, near the front. Long hairs called *mouth brushes* grow around the jaws and sweep food into the wriggler's mouth. Unlike an adult mosquito, a wriggler can open its jaws and chew its food. It eats tiny aquatic life, including one-celled organisms called *protozoans,* and other wrigglers.

A wriggler breathes through a tubelike *siphon* (air tube) at the rear of its body. To get air, it pushes its siphon above the surface of the water.

The larvae of certain swamp mosquitoes do not have to come to the surface for air. They get air from the leaves, stems, and roots of various underwater plants. The larva of one kind of swamp mosquito has a breathing tube with two sharp tips. It uses one tip to hold itself to the plant, and moves the other tip back and forth in the plant tissue to get the oxygen stored there.

The larvae of many species of mosquitoes grow quickly. They *molt* (shed their skins and grow new ones) four times in 4 to 10 days. After the last molt, the larvae change into pupae. The larvae of some species spend the winter in hibernation. They change into pupae early in spring.

Pupa. A mosquito pupa is shaped somewhat like a comma. The head and thorax are rolled into a ball, and the abdomen hangs down like a curved tail. A thin "skin," like that of the larva, covers the pupa's body. The pupa breathes through trumpet-shaped tubes attached to the top of its thorax. The pupa sticks these tubes out of the water to get air. The pupa of certain swamp mosquitoes, whose larva gets air from underwater plants, pushes its tubes into the plant. After this pupa has changed into an adult, it pulls out the tubes or breaks them off and leaves them in the plant. The pupa then swims to the surface.

The pupae of most species of insects do not move, but almost all kinds of mosquito pupae can swim. These pupae are sometimes called *tumblers* because they roll and tumble in the water.

A mosquito pupa does not eat. It changes into an adult in two to four days. The pupal "skin" splits down the back, and the adult mosquito pushes its head and front legs out. The insect then pulls out the rest of its body.

Adult. After the adult mosquito leaves the pupal "skin," its wings dry quickly and it flies a short distance away. Most species of mosquitoes spend their whole lives within 1 mile (1.6 kilometers) of the place where they hatched. A few kinds may travel as far as 20 miles (32 kilometers) away to find food or mates.

A female mosquito attracts a mate by the high-pitched sound made by her wings. The males are deaf for the first 24 to 48 hours of their lives, until the hairs on their antennae are dry.

The females of some species must sip blood before they can lay eggs that will hatch. Each species of female prefers the blood of certain kinds of animals. Some feed only on frogs, snakes, or other cold-blooded animals. Other mosquitoes prefer birds. Still other mosquitoes

suck the blood of cows, horses, and people.

Male mosquitoes may live only about 7 to 10 days, but females may live up to 30 days or more. The females of some species live through the winter in barns, garages, houses, caves, or in the bark of logs. Some species spend the winter as eggs or as larvae. They develop into adults in spring.   E. W. Cupp

Related articles in *World Book* include:

DDT	Gorgas, William C.
Dengue	Guppy
Dragonfly	Insecticide
Elephantiasis	Malaria
Finlay, Carlos Juan	Reed, Walter
Fly	Yellow fever

Mosquito Coast, also called Mosquitia, is a strip of land that lies along the east coast of Nicaragua and the northeast coast of Honduras. It has an area of over 32,500 square miles (84,175 square kilometers) and extends for about 200 miles (320 kilometers) from the San Juan River in Nicaragua to the Aguan River in Honduras. The southern part makes up the department of Zelaya in Nicaragua. The northern part lies in the departments of Gracias a Dios and Colón in Honduras. The Mosquito Coast received its name from the Miskito (also spelled *Mosquito*) Indians.   Gary S. Elbow

See also **Honduras** (The Northeastern Plain, map); **Nicaragua** (map).

Mosquito hawk. See Nighthawk.

Moss is any of a variety of small, green, nonflowering plants found throughout the world. Mosses tend to grow close together in large numbers. They often form soft, dense mats on rocks, at the base of trees, or on soil. Most mosses live on land in moist, shady places. But some are found in dry environments, and others grow in lakes, ponds, or rivers. Most mosses measure less than 6 inches (15 centimeters) in height.

There are more than 9,000 species of mosses, over 1,200 of which grow in the United States and Canada. Common species include *granite mosses* and *peat mosses*. Granite mosses are found on rocks in mountainous regions and the Arctic. Peat mosses, also called *Sphagnum,* grow in bogs and other marshy areas. Other common mosses include the *hairy cap moss* and the *stair-step moss*. Hairy cap mosses grow chiefly on soil, often in thick tufts. Stair-step mosses sometimes form dense carpets covering large areas of ground.

All mosses belong to a scientific class called Musci. Other kinds of plants have the word *moss* as part of their common name but are not really mosses. These plants include Spanish moss, reindeer moss, and club mosses. See **Club moss; Reindeer moss; Spanish moss.**

The structure of mosses. Unlike flowering plants, mosses do not have true roots. But they have threadlike structures called *rhizoids* that resemble roots. The rhizoids anchor the plant to the surface from which it grows. A short stem grows from the rhizoids. It is covered by tiny leaves in a spiral pattern. The leaves contain chlorophyll, a green substance the plant uses to make food. In many cases, a vein runs the length of the leaf from the stem to the tip. This vein, called the *costa* or *midrib,* strengthens the leaf and transports food and water.

How mosses live. Many mosses grow in moist or aquatic environments. However, certain mosses can sur-

Runk/Schoenberg from Grant Heilman   Robert McKenzie, Tom Stack & Assoc.   Tom and Pat Leeson, Photo Researchers

Mosses tend to grow in bunches, and they often form dense mats that cover large areas. There are more than 9,000 species of mosses worldwide. Three types of mosses common in North America are peat moss, *left,* granite moss, *center,* and hairy cap moss, *right.*

vive extremely dry conditions. Their need for water changes with the amount of water available in the environment. During dry periods, these mosses may turn dull brown and appear dead. But they become green and fresh-looking again as soon as it rains. Other, short-living mosses are found in prairies and other habitats that have exceptionally dry summer months. These mosses grow during the rainy months of spring and die when summer begins.

Mosses grow and reproduce in two phases—as *sporophytes* and *gametophytes.* This kind of life cycle is called *alternation of generations.*

During one phase, the moss plant is called a gametophyte. The gametophyte is the plant familiarly recognized as the moss. A mature gametophyte produces *gametes* (male sperm cells or female egg cells). The gametes form in special organs that grow from the top of the stem. The organs that produce sperm cells are called the *antheridia.* Those that produce egg cells are known as the *archegonia.* About half of all mosses bear

John Shaw, Tom Stack & Assoc.

Sporophytes of hairy cap mosses rise high above the ground, *above.* Each sporophyte consists of a long stalk ending in podlike capsules that contain tiny, seedlike spores.

both antheridia and archegonia on the same plant. When the antheridia become ripe and damp enough, they burst and release hundreds of sperm cells. Some of these cells may reach an archegonium, where one may unite with an egg cell to form a *zygote.*

The formation of the zygote begins the second phase of the moss life cycle. During this phase, the zygote develops into a sporophyte. This plant grows attached to the gametophyte. It consists of a long, erect stalk called a *seta,* with a podlike *capsule* at the end. Microscopic structures called *spores* form in the capsule. A capsule may contain from four to more than a million spores, depending on the species.

In most mosses, the mouth of the capsule is covered by a lidlike *operculum.* In peat mosses, when the spores ripen, the operculum comes off explosively and the spores shoot into the air. In most other mosses, tiny toothlike structures around the mouth of the capsule control the release of spores. These structures, called the *peristome,* remain closed under wet conditions. In dry conditions, they open to discharge spores. If a spore falls on a damp area, it may sprout into a branching, threadlike *protonema.* Buds from the protonema then grow into gametophytes, completing the life cycle.

The importance of mosses. Mosses play an important part in the lives of many small animals. A number of small animals, including certain mites and spiders, live in mosses. Some birds use moss fibers to build or line their nests. Weevils in New Guinea have been found with mosses growing on their backs. The mosses serve as camouflage for these insects.

Mosses also help the environment. Peat mosses can hold large quantities of water. This characteristic helps prevent soil erosion and flooding. Mosses also store minerals and other nutrients. After mosses die, they *decompose* (break down) and release the nutrients. Other plants then use these nutrients to grow.

In some regions of the world, decaying mosses and other plant matter accumulate in marshy fields over numerous years and form *peat.* Many such peat bogs are located in Canada, Russia, and northern Eu-

Motels serve millions of guests each year. Most motels are located near highways, on the outskirts of towns, or near airports. All motels provide free parking facilities, and many have restaurants. Some, such as the motel shown here, have swimming pools.

Artstreet

rope. The peat may be dried and used as fuel. See **Peat**.

Peat mosses have a spongy texture and are very absorbent. Many gardeners use them to keep young plants from drying out. In addition, peat mosses are used in the cultivation of mushrooms and as packing material. Peat mosses also contain chemicals that kill germs. Some American Indians used peat mosses for diapers. In World War I (1914-1918), peat mosses were used as dressings for wounds. See **Peat moss**.

Scientific classification. Mosses form the class Musci in the division Bryophyta. Peat mosses make up the genus *Sphagnum*.   Dale H. Vitt

See also **Hornwort; Liverwort; Plant** (pictures: Bryophytes); **Spore** (picture: Some kinds of spores).

Mossadegh, Mohammad. See **Iran** (The nationalist movement).

Mössbauer, *MAWS bow uhr,* **Rudolf Ludwig** (1929-   ), a German physicist, shared the 1961 Nobel Prize in physics for research into gamma rays. He discovered the "Mössbauer Effect," a method of producing gamma rays with a precise, predictable wavelength. This enables physicists to use gamma radiation to make precise measurements. The "Mössbauer Effect" was later used to confirm some predictions made by Albert Einstein in his relativity theory. Mössbauer was born in Munich and received his Ph.D. from the technical institute there. He became professor of experimental physics at the institute (now called the Technical University of Munich) in 1964.   Richard L. Hilt

Motel is an establishment that provides overnight lodging, chiefly for automobile travelers. Most motels are located near busy interchanges of major highways, on the outskirts of towns, or near airports. All motels provide free parking facilities from which guests can reach their rooms directly. Some motels have restaurants and swimming pools.

The word *motel* comes from a combination of the words *motor* and *hotel*. Motels are also called *motor hotels, motor inns,* or *motor lodges.* The United States has more than 15,000 motels. Canada has about 4,000.

The number of rooms in a motel can range from fewer than 10 to more than 200. Many large motels are in the downtown areas of cities. Most of them provide the same services and charge approximately the same rates as commercial hotels (see **Hotel** [Commercial

hotels]). On the other hand, most roadside motels offer fewer dining and other services, and they charge lower rates than the majority of hotels. The casual atmosphere of these motels, plus their convenient location on or near highways, appeals to large numbers of motorists.

Most motels do not require reservations because many automobile travelers cannot be sure where they will spend the night. Almost all roadside motels have large signs that tell whether vacant rooms are available. Motorists can see these signs and do not have to leave their cars to find out if a motel has any vacancies.

Roadside motels use highway billboards to advertise their location and the services they provide. These billboards are often located at various points for several miles along the major highways leading to a motel.

The first motels, called *tourist cabins,* were established during the early 1900's, when people began to travel by automobile. Tourist cabins originated in the Western United States, where people could not travel the long distances between towns in one day. These establishments also served fishermen, hunters, and other vacationers in remote areas.

The motel industry grew rapidly during the mid-1900's. People began to travel longer distances by car and needed places to stay along the way. The establishment of *motel chains,* which consist of two or more motels owned by one person or company, also stimulated motel development.

Through the years, several major motel chains have expanded by means of *franchises.* Under this system, an individual or a company buys a franchise—that is, the right to own and operate a motel in the chain. The purchaser runs the motel in the same manner and under the same name as the other motels in the chain. The franchise owner pays the chain a percentage of the motel's income. The owner has the advantage of operating a motel with a well-known name and reputation.

In the 1970's, several companies established chains of *budget motels.* The rates at these motels may be as low as half of those of other motels. Budget motels have small rooms and provide fewer services than more expensive motels. They do not have restaurants, and many have no swimming pools. Some budget motels in areas with cool climates do not provide air conditioning.

Glenn Withiam

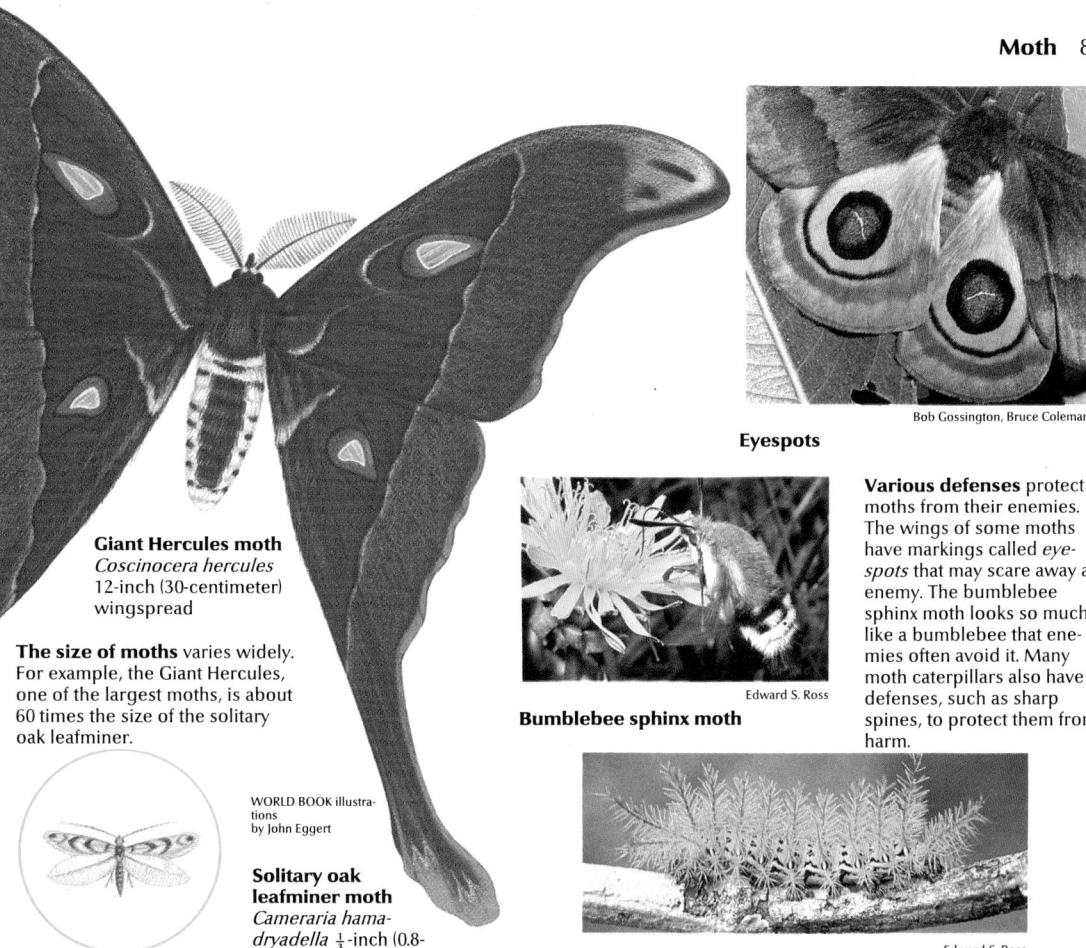

Giant Hercules moth
Coscinocera hercules
12-inch (30-centimeter)
wingspread

The size of moths varies widely.
For example, the Giant Hercules,
one of the largest moths, is about
60 times the size of the solitary
oak leafminer.

WORLD BOOK illustrations
by John Eggert

**Solitary oak
leafminer moth**
*Cameraria hama-
dryadella* $\frac{1}{3}$-inch (0.8-
centimeter) wingspread

Bob Gossington, Bruce Coleman Inc.

Eyespots

Edward S. Ross

Bumblebee sphinx moth

Various defenses protect
moths from their enemies.
The wings of some moths
have markings called *eyespots* that may scare away an
enemy. The bumblebee
sphinx moth looks so much
like a bumblebee that enemies often avoid it. Many
moth caterpillars also have
defenses, such as sharp
spines, to protect them from
harm.

Edward S. Ross

Caterpillar with spines

Moth is any of a wide variety of insects closely related
to butterflies. All butterflies and almost all moths have
two pairs of wings—a pair of large front wings and a
pair of smaller hind wings. Moths and butterflies together form the insect group *Lepidoptera*. The name
Lepidoptera comes from two Greek words: *lepis*, meaning *scale*; and *pteron*, meaning *wing*. The name refers to
the fine, powdery scales that cover the wings of butterflies and moths.

Moths live throughout the world, except in the
oceans. They inhabit steamy jungles near the equator,
and they have even been found on icecaps in the Arctic.
Moths vary greatly in size. The largest moths are the
Giant Hercules of Australia and the Giant Owl Moth of
South America. They have a wingspread of about 12
inches (30 centimeters). The smallest moths have wing-
spreads of about $\frac{1}{8}$ inch (0.3 centimeter). These moths
belong to a group called *leafminers.*

Like butterflies, moths change in form as they develop into adults. Only the adult form of a moth has
wings. Female adult moths lay many tiny eggs that hatch
into wormlike caterpillars. A caterpillar eats almost constantly, and it grows rapidly. After it is fully grown, the
caterpillar forms a shell-like covering around itself.
Within this shell, the insect goes through its final
changes. Eventually, the insect breaks out of the shell as
a fully developed adult moth.

Moths differ from butterflies in a number of important ways. For example, most moths fly at dusk or at
night. The majority of butterflies fly during the day.
Among most moths, the hind wing is attached to the
front wing by a hook or set of hooks, called a *frenulum.*
Butterflies lack a frenulum. In addition, most butterflies
have antennae that widen at the ends and resemble
clubs. The antennae of most moths are not club-shaped.

Some moths are regarded as pests because their caterpillars feed on and damage trees, food plants, or
clothing. However, many others are valuable to people
and nature. People use caterpillars of certain moths to
produce silk. Many adult moths help pollinate flowers.

The bodies of moths

A moth's body, like that of any insect, has three main
parts. They are: (1) the head, (2) the thorax, and (3) the abdomen.

The head bears the moth's eyes, antennae, and
mouthparts. These structures are the insect's most important sense organs.

Eyes. Moths have two large *compound eyes* on each
side of the head. These eyes consist of many separate
lenses, each of which supplies a complete image of part
of the moth's surroundings. Compound eyes are specially designed to help an insect spot movements, such
as the approach of an enemy.

The anatomy of a moth   A moth's body has three main parts: (1) head, (2) thorax, and (3) abdomen. The head bears the major sense organs, the thorax supports the wings and legs, and the abdomen contains various internal organs. The drawings below show external and internal features of a typical female moth.

WORLD BOOK illustrations by Zorica Dabich

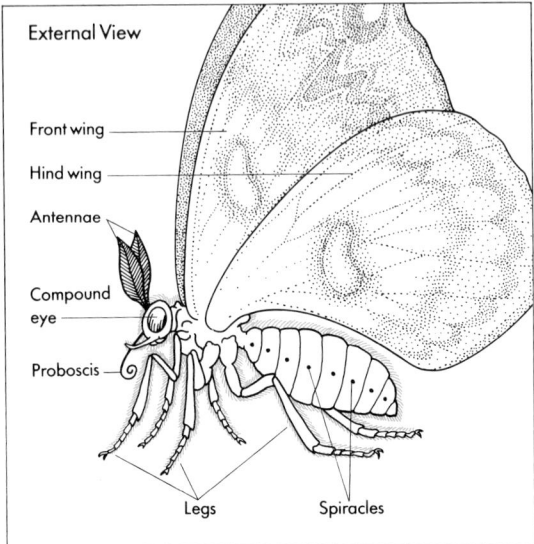

External View

Front wing

Hind wing

Antennae

Compound eye

Proboscis

Legs

Spiracles

Internal View

Circulatory system
Digestive system
Nervous system
Reproductive system
Respiratory system

Head   Thorax   Abdomen

Brain   Heart   Spiracles

The life cycle of a moth

A moth goes through four stages of development: (1) egg, (2) larva, (3) pupa, and (4) adult. A female moth lays many tiny eggs, which hatch into larvae, or caterpillars. A caterpillar spends its life eating and growing. When fully grown, it forms a shell and becomes a pupa. The insect goes through its final changes within the shell. It emerges from the shell as an adult. These photos show stages in the development of a *Cecropia* moth.

Lyna M. Stone, Bruce Coleman Inc.
Female laying eggs

E. R. Degginger, Bruce Coleman Inc.
Larva

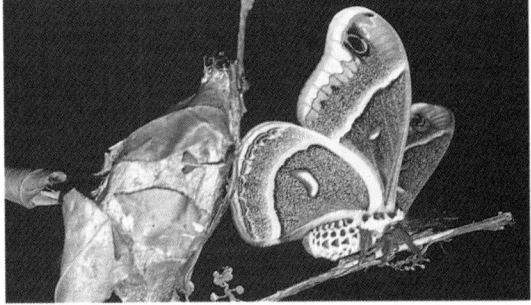

© Michael Lustbader, Photo Researchers
Pupal shell and adult

Antennae. Two antennae stick out from between a moth's eyes. Moths use their antennae chiefly to smell. The antennae are extremely sensitive to chemicals in the air. Female moths release chemicals called *pheromones* into the air to attract males for mating. The antennae of a male moth can "smell" a female as far as 5 miles (8 kilometers) away.

Mouthparts. Adult moths feed mostly on liquids, such as flower nectar and the juice of fruits. They suck up their food through a long, hollow tongue called a *proboscis.* The proboscis coils under the head when not in use.

The thorax forms the middle section of a moth's body. Attached to the thorax are the legs and wings of the insect.

Legs. Adult moths have three pairs of legs. Each leg consists of five segments. Joints connect the segments. Taste organs grow at the tips of the legs.

Wings. Two membranes form each of a moth's wings. A network of hollow tubes called *veins* supports the wings. Tiny scales cover the membranes and give the wings their colors and patterns. The females of some species lack wings and cannot fly.

The abdomen contains the organs of reproduction and the major organs of digestion. Tiny holes called *spiracles* on the sides of the abdomen lead into the insect's respiratory system. Oxygen enters the moth's body through the spiracles.

The life cycle of moths

Every moth goes through four stages of development: (1) egg, (2) larva, (3) pupa, and (4) adult. The process of development through several different stages is called *metamorphosis.*

The egg. Female moths lay their eggs one at a time or in masses, usually in summer or fall. A female moth may lay from a few to more than 18,000 eggs. Most moth eggs measure less than $\frac{1}{25}$ inch (1 millimeter) across and are round or oval. Often, the female deposits the eggs on the kinds of plants that her offspring like to eat. The eggs of most species hatch within a week. The eggs of some species do not hatch until spring.

The larva, or caterpillar, that crawls out of the egg is made up of 14 segments, including a head. Caterpillars have three pairs of legs near the front of the body. Most caterpillars also have five pairs of leglike *prolegs*, farther back on the body. Many moth caterpillars are extremely colorful, and some have fierce-looking spines or bristles.

Caterpillars have chewing mouth parts. Moth caterpillars chiefly eat leaves and other plant parts. They may also feed on wood, the larvae of other insects, and hair. Many moth caterpillars feed on clothing and other materials made of wool, which is sheep's hair.

A short structure called the *spinneret* sticks out below the mouth. The caterpillar sends out an almost continuous stream of liquid silk through the spinneret. The silk quickly hardens to a slender thread that gives the caterpillar a foothold as it crawls about.

Caterpillars grow to their full size within a month or several months, depending on the species and other factors. Like other insects, they shed their skin several times as they grow. This process is called *molting*.

The pupa. The final molt transforms the caterpillar into a *pupa*, an inactive stage during which dramatic physical changes occur. The caterpillar may spin a protective, silken cocoon around itself for the pupal stage. The insect fastens the cocoon to a tree limb or some other solid object. Inside the cocoon, the insect forms a protective shell of a substance called *chitin*. Some moth caterpillars do not spin cocoons. Instead, they burrow into the ground or hide under loose bark before forming a chitin shell.

During the pupal stage, the insect does not move about. But within the chitin shell, the wormlike caterpillar changes into an adult moth. This change, called *pupation*, takes a few days or several months, depending on the species.

The adult. At the end of pupation, the adult moth breaks out of its chitin covering. If the moth has wings, it pumps blood into the wings to expand them and soon flutters off in search of food or a mate. Most adult moths live only a few days to a few weeks, but some may survive six months or more. A few adult moths do not feed and live only a few days.

Migration

Many moths need warm air temperatures for their flight muscles to work. As a result, moths are most common in the summer and fall. Only a few species live actively through the winter as adults. These moths must "heat up" their flight muscles before flying by rapidly vibrating their wings.

Some moths avoid cold weather by migrating to warmer regions. For example, the hummingbird hawk moth migrates from the British Isles to southern Europe in the fall. Moths may also migrate to avoid other unfavorable conditions. Bogong moths of Australia migrate from lowland pastures to the mountains during the summer to avoid extreme heat. In the mountains, where food is scarce, these moths enter a resting state called

Cary Wolinsky, Stock, Boston

Colorful cocoons of the *Bombyx mori* moth fill a silk grower's frame, *above*. Silk is obtained by unraveling the cocoons. Caterpillars of the moth are shown crawling across the frame.

Norman Owen Tomalin, Bruce Coleman Inc.

The gypsy moth caterpillar is a serious forest pest. Each year, gypsy moth caterpillars destroy vast areas of forestland in eastern North America by stripping trees of their leaves.

diapause to save their energy. In the fall, they again become active and return to the lowlands to mate.

Defenses against enemies

Moths have many enemies. For example, certain wasps lay their eggs on or inside moth caterpillars. The wasp larvae feed on the body fluids of the caterpillar and eventually kill it. Other animals prey on adult moths. These predators include spiders, birds, and bats.

Moths have developed various ways of protecting themselves against predators. By flying primarily at night, moths avoid many daytime predators. Many moths have coloring that blends with their surroundings. For example, certain moths look like the bark or leaves of a tree. Some moths have wing markings that resemble the eyes of a larger animal. These eyespots may frighten away predators.

The caterpillars of some moths are bad-tasting or even poisonous to predators. Such caterpillars may have vivid markings. An animal that eats one of these caterpillars will most likely avoid eating another caterpillar with similar markings.

The importance of moths

The best-known benefit of moths to human beings is probably the production of silk. In China, people have used a species of moths called *Bombyx mori* to produce silk for more than 4,000 years. To obtain the silk, workers unravel the moth's cocoon into a single, long thread. The thread is then combined with thread from other cocoons and woven into silk fabrics.

Moths are important in the pollination of certain flow-

Some North American moths

There are more than 100,000 species of moths worldwide. These drawings show members of six of the largest moth families. All the moths shown live in North America. The caterpillar of each species is also illustrated. The scientific name of the species appears in italics.

Giant silkworm moths and royal moths

Tussock moths

WORLD BOOK illustrations by John Eggert

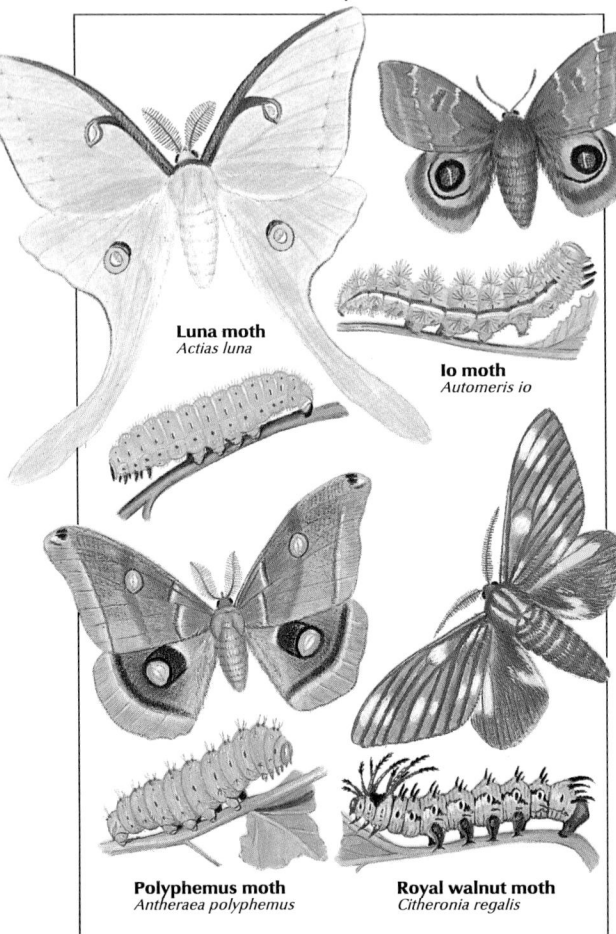

Luna moth
Actias luna

Io moth
Automeris io

Polyphemus moth
Antheraea polyphemus

Royal walnut moth
Citheronia regalis

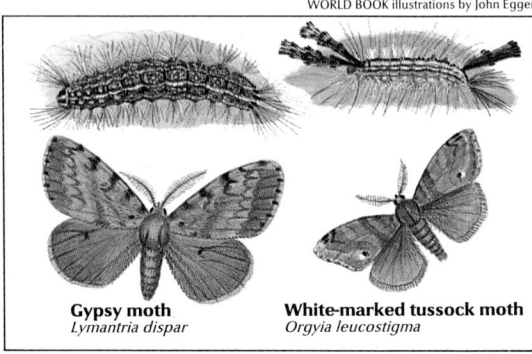

Gypsy moth
Lymantria dispar

White-marked tussock moth
Orgyia leucostigma

Tiger moths

Isabella tiger moth
Pyrrharctia isabella

Great tiger moth
Arctia caja

ers. Pollination occurs when a moth visits flowers to feed on nectar. Grains of pollen stick to the moth's body as it feeds and then rub off on other flowers the insect visits. Some flowers that bloom only at night depend on night-flying moths for pollination.

Moth caterpillars eat leaves and other plant parts. They cause extensive damage to crops and forests each year. Some species feed on woolen fabrics and other animal products. The caterpillars of a group of moths known as *clothes moths* may damage woolen garments.

Kinds of moths

There are more than 100,000 species of moths. They are grouped into various families, according to common physical features. This section describes six of the most common families of moths. The scientific name of the family is given in parentheses after the common name.

Owlet moths and underwing moths (Noctuidae) total more than 20,000 species and form the largest family of moths. Most of these moths are small to medium in size. The majority of species are dull-colored, but

many underwing moths have bands of bright colors on the hind wings.

Both owlets and underwings have a special hearing organ called a *tympanum* on the thorax. This organ can pick up high-frequency sounds made by bats. Upon hearing a bat, these moths may fly in an irregular pattern to avoid being eaten. Many caterpillars in this family, including cutworms and army worms, cause serious damage to crops.

Tiger moths (Arctiidae) consist of about 10,000 species. They are small to medium in size. Many have brightly colored patterns on their wings. Many caterpillars in this family also have bright coloring and may be covered with a dense mat of long hairs. A common caterpillar of this type is the *woollybear caterpillar*. It grows into the Isabella tiger moth. Tiger moth caterpillars feed on plants, including poisonous ones. The poison stays in the moths into adulthood and helps protect them from animals that might otherwise eat them.

Measuringworm moths (Geometridae) make up about 12,000 species. Most are small with relatively

Hawk moths (sphinx moths)

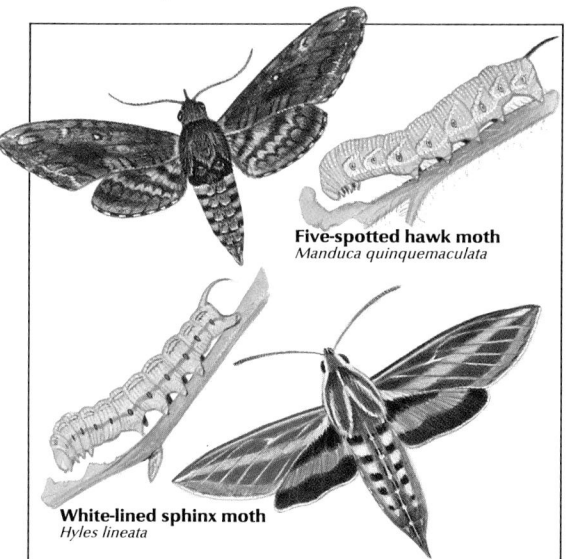

Five-spotted hawk moth
Manduca quinquemaculata

White-lined sphinx moth
Hyles lineata

Measuringworm moths

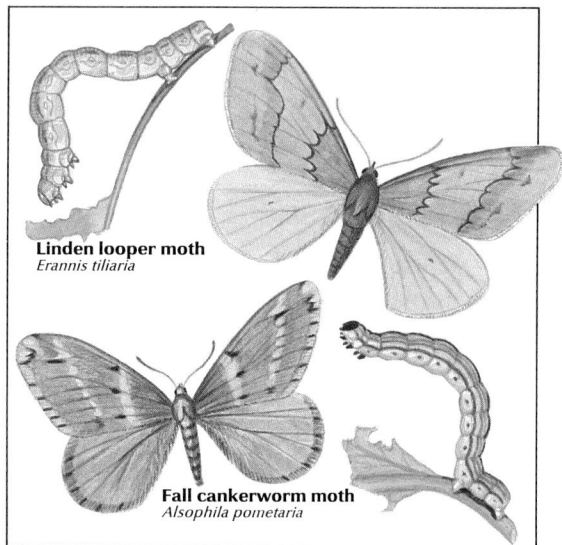

Linden looper moth
Erannis tiliaria

Fall cankerworm moth
Alsophila pometaria

Owlet moths and underwing moths

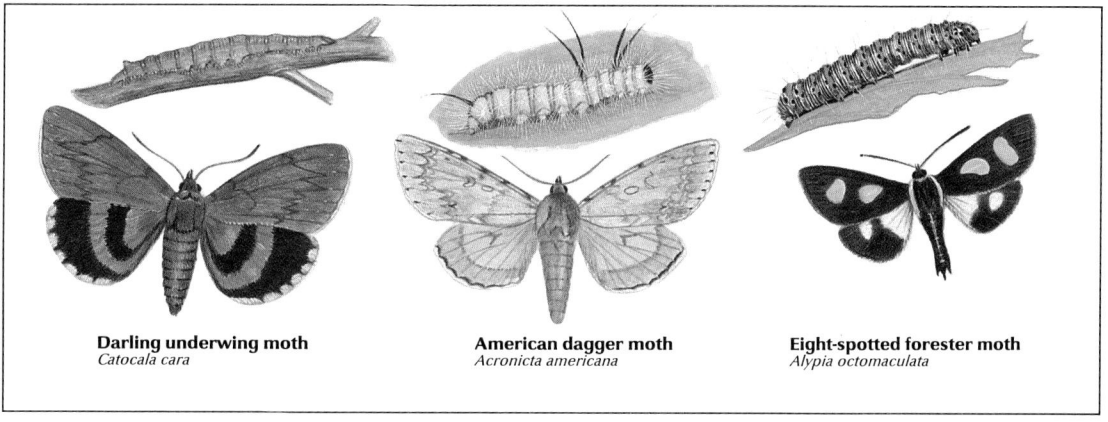

Darling underwing moth
Catocala cara

American dagger moth
Acronicta americana

Eight-spotted forester moth
Alypia octomaculata

large wings. The females of several species lack wings.

The caterpillars in this family are commonly called *measuring worms* or *inchworms* because of their unusual crawl. They crawl by alternately looping their bodies into the air and then extending their front legs to straighten themselves. Some inchworms, such as cankerworms, seriously damage trees. Several species of inchworms found in Hawaii can catch and eat flies.

Tussock moths (Lymantriidae) number about 2,000 species. Adult tussocks do not have working mouthparts and so they cannot feed. They live only a few days or weeks. These medium-sized moths typically have dull coloring. The females of some species rarely fly. In other species, the females have no wings at all.

The caterpillars of tussock moths are very hairy. Many have bunches of longer hairs, called *tussocks*, on their backs. In some species, these hairs cause skin irritation if touched. Many tussock caterpillars are serious pests of North American forests. One well-known species, the caterpillar of the gypsy moth, destroys vast areas of eastern forestland each year by eating leaves.

Hawk moths (Sphingidae), also called *sphinx moths*, total about 1,000 species. Many of them have bright coloring. Hawk moths are swift flyers and beat their wings so rapidly that they are often mistaken for hummingbirds. Some species of hawk moths resemble bumblebees or wasps.

Hawk moth caterpillars have a curved, hornlike structure near the end of the abdomen. For this reason, they are often called *hornworms*. The tobacco hornworm and the tomato hornworm seriously damage crops.

Giant silkworm moths and royal moths (Saturniidae) consist of about 1,300 species. In general, the members of this family are brightly colored and have dark or transparent eyespots on the hind wings. Some species, including the luna moth and the Giant Hercules moth, have a long, taillike extension on each hind wing. Giant silkworm moths and royal moths do not feed, and thus they live only a few days.

The caterpillars of many species have stiff bristles on their bodies. In some species, the tips of the bristles contain irritating chemicals. Many caterpillars in this family feed on trees and shrubs and can cause considerable damage. The cocoons of several Asian species produce a coarse silk known as *tussah silk*. But the species most commonly used in the production of commercial silk belongs to another family.　　　Bernd Heinrich

Related articles in *World Book*. The article on **Butterfly** has much information that also applies to moths. See also the following articles:

Army worm	Hawk moth
Browntail moth	Insect (pictures)
Caterpillar	Leafminer
Codling moth	Measuring worm
Corn borer	Peach moth
Corn earworm	Pink bollworm
Cutworm	Spruce budworm
Death's-head moth	Tent caterpillar
Gypsy moth	Tussock moth

Additional resources

Brewer, Jo, and Winter, Dave. *Butterflies and Moths: A Companion to Your Field Guide.* Prentice-Hall, 1986.
Covell, Charles V., Jr. *A Field Guide to the Moths of Eastern North America.* Houghton, 1984.
Ivy, Bill. *Moths.* Grolier, 1986. For younger readers.
Watts, Barrie. *Moth.* Silver Burdett, 1990. For younger readers.

Mother Carey's chicken. See Petrel.

Mother Goose is a name that has been associated with children's literature for hundreds of years. Mother Goose appears as the author of countless collections of tales and rhymes in many languages. However, no one knows if an actual Mother Goose ever existed. Some scholars believe that Mother Goose is based on a real person, but others say that Mother Goose is a fictional character.

Who was Mother Goose? Scholars who believe Mother Goose actually existed have several theories about her identity. According to one theory, she was the Queen of Sheba, who lived in Biblical times. Others suggest she was Queen Bertha, the mother of the great medieval military leader Charlemagne. Queen Bertha, who died in 783, was nicknamed "Queen Goose-Foot" or "Goose-Footed Bertha."

Another theory proposes that the original Mother Goose was a woman named Elizabeth Goose (or Vergoose or Vertigoose), who lived in colonial Boston. The woman enjoyed entertaining her grandchildren with the songs and rhymes she remembered from her own childhood. Her son-in-law, Thomas Fleet, supposedly collected those songs and rhymes and published them in 1719 as *Songs for the Nursery, or Mother Goose's Melodies.* However, no copy of this book has ever been found, and most scholars doubt that the book ever existed.

Some Mother Goose books pictured her as an old woman with a crooked nose and large chin, usually telling stories to a group of children. Other editions have pictured Mother Goose as an old woman with a tall hat and a magic wand, riding through the air on the back of a goose.

The history of Mother Goose literature. Most of the rhymes and verses that appear in Mother Goose books existed long before they were published. Many of them originated in England and were based on folk songs, ballads, street cries, and tavern songs. A number included humorous or satirical verses that were based on real people, events, or customs. These early rhymes were written to entertain adults. Before 1800, the only

rhymes that were written for small children were alphabet rhymes, lullabies, and verses that accompanied games.

Mother Goose was popular in France as early as the mid-1600's, when the name was attached to collections of tales. In 1697, Charles Perrault, a French writer, published a book called *Histories or Tales of Past Times, with Morals.* The front of the book had an engraving of an old woman sitting by a fireplace, apparently telling stories to three listeners. A sign on the wall read, "Contes de Ma Mère L'Oye" ("Tales of Mother Goose"). Perrault's collection popularized eight tales that may have been known at the time, including "Sleeping Beauty," "Red Riding Hood," and "Cinderella."

Perrault's book was translated into English by Robert Samber and published in England in 1729. An engraving of an old woman was included in this edition, with a sign on the wall reading "Mother Goose's Tales." The name was adopted for the title when the tales were reissued in 1768 by the John Newbery publishing house. The same publishers issued a collection of rhymes in 1781, which they called *Mother Goose's Melody.* "Ding Dong, Bell" and "Little Tom Tucker" were among its 51 rhymes. The book also contained 16 songs from plays written by William Shakespeare. *Mother Goose's Melody* was reprinted several times in England.

The first Mother Goose book published in America was a reprint of Newbery's *Mother Goose's Melody,* issued by Isaiah Thomas in 1786. The Boston publishing firm of Munroe and Francis published *Mother Goose's Quarto, or Melodies Complete* about 1825. It was reprinted in 1833 as *The Only True Mother Goose Melodies* and consisted of 169 rhymes, including an 11-verse version of "London Bridge." Since the early 1800's, the name of Mother Goose has been firmly associated with collections of rhymes.　　　Marilyn Fain Apseloff

See also **Literature for children** and its *Books to read* section; **Nursery rhyme; Newbery, John; Perrault, Charles.**

Additional resources

The Annotated Mother Goose: Nursery Rhymes Old and New. Ed. by William S. and Ceil Baring-Gould. Crown, 1982. Contains background information about the rhymes.
Delamar, Gloria T. *Mother Goose: From Nursery to Literature.* McFarland, 1987.
One Misty Moisty Morning: Rhymes from Mother Goose. Illus. by Mitchell Miller. Farrar, 1971. Includes lesser-known rhymes.
The Random House Book of Mother Goose. Ed. and illus. by Arnold Lobel. Random House, 1986.

Mother Jones. See Jones, Mary Harris.

Mother-of-pearl. Certain shellfish, such as pearl oysters, abalones, and freshwater mussels produce shells lined with a lustrous, rainbow-colored material. This material is called *mother-of-pearl,* or *nacre* (pronounced *NAY kuhr*). It varies in color from pale grayish-blue and pink to purple and green. Shells containing mother-of-pearl are found off the coasts of tropical countries, particularly around the South Sea Islands, the Philippine Islands, Australia, Panama, and Lower California.

Mother-of-pearl has long been commercially valuable. It has been used for ornamentation, in the manufacture of buttons, and in the inlay for various works of art, particularly those made of wood and silver. People

© Breck P. Kent, Animals Animals

Bluish-purple mother-of-pearl lines the shell of a pearl oyster, *above*. Mother-of-pearl is found off tropical coasts in the shells of various sea animals.

of many island cultures have bartered mother-of-pearl for other goods. Today, mother-of-pearl is commonly used in making jewelry, such as pearl necklaces, and for decorative pocketknife handles.   M. Patricia Morse

See also **Pearl** (Cultured pearls).

Mother of Presidents. See Ohio; Virginia.

Mother of States. See Virginia.

Mother of the West. See Missouri.

Mother Teresa. See Teresa, Mother.

Mother's Day is set apart every year in honor of motherhood. On the second Sunday in May, many families and churches make a special point of honoring mothers. Many people follow the custom of wearing a carnation on Mother's Day. A colored carnation means that a person's mother is living. A white carnation indicates that a person's mother is dead.

A day for honoring mothers was observed many years ago in England. It was called *Mothering Sunday,* and came in mid-Lent. Yugoslavs and people in other nations have observed similar days.

Julia Ward Howe made the first known suggestion for a Mother's Day in the United States in 1872. She suggested that people observe a Mother's Day on June 2 as a day dedicated to peace. For several years, she held an annual Mother's Day meeting in Boston.

United Press Int.

Anna Jarvis

Mary Towles Sasseen, a Kentucky schoolteacher, started conducting Mother's Day celebrations in 1887. Frank E. Hering of South Bend, Ind., launched a campaign for the observance of Mother's Day in 1904.

Three years later, Anna Jarvis of Grafton, W. Va., and Philadelphia, began a campaign for a nationwide observance of Mother's Day. She chose the second Sunday in May, and began the custom of wearing a carnation. On May 10, 1908, churches in Grafton and Philadelphia held Mother's Day celebrations. The service at Andrews Methodist Episcopal Church in Grafton honored the memory of Anna Jarvis' own mother, Mrs. Anna Reeves Jarvis.

At the General Conference of the Methodist Episcopal Church in Minneapolis, Minn., in 1912, a delegate from Andrews Church introduced a resolution recognizing Anna Jarvis as the founder of Mother's Day. It suggested that the second Sunday in May be observed as Mother's Day.

Mother's Day received national recognition on May 9, 1914. On that day, President Woodrow Wilson signed a joint resolution of Congress recommending that Congress and the executive departments of the federal government observe Mother's Day. The next year, President Wilson was authorized to proclaim Mother's Day an annual national observance.   Sharron G. Uhler

Motherwell, Robert (1915-1991), an American painter, was a leading member of the abstract expressionist school. Motherwell became famous for several series of paintings. But his large body of work includes many widely varied themes ranging from violent and large menacing shapes to tender, intimate forms.

Motherwell began his best-known series, *Elegies to the Spanish Republic,* in 1948 and continued it through the 1970's. This group of more than 100 paintings deals

Elegy to the Spanish Republic LV (1960), an oil painting on canvas; Contemporary Collection of the Cleveland Museum of Art

A Motherwell painting is part of the artist's series called *Elegies to the Spanish Republic.* Most of these paintings consist of black oval between vertical panels on a light background.

with his emotional reaction to the Spanish Civil War (1936-1939). Motherwell used colors and designs that suggest characteristics of Spain's landscape. In the mid-1950's, he created the *Je t'aime* series, which features broad, freely applied brush strokes. During the 1940's and 1950's, Motherwell also produced collages. In the early 1960's, he painted a series called *Beside the Sea.* These works have simple shapes and sharp color combinations that represent the sea and splashing waves.

Motherwell was born in Aberdeen, Wash. He worked in many techniques, including etchings, lithographs, and illustrated books. Motherwell also wrote essays on art and edited a series of books by modern artists.

Dore Ashton

See also **Abstract expressionism.**

Motion. See Parliamentary procedure (Motions).

Motion occurs when an object changes its location in space. *Motion* is a relative rather than an absolute term. An object may be in motion with regard to another object, but may be stationary with respect to a third object. For example, suppose you are riding on a train and you pass a person standing alongside the tracks. The person standing along the tracks will see you and everyone else on the train as being in motion. But the person sitting next to you on the train will be stationary with respect to you.

Everything in the universe is in motion. Even as you sit reading this page, you are moving very rapidly because the earth is rotating on its axis. You are also moving with the earth as it revolves around the sun. In addition, the sun, the earth, and the rest of the planets in our solar system are involved in the general rotation of our galaxy within the universe.

The difference in motion between yourself and the object that you are looking at is called *apparent motion*. For example, suppose you are riding in a car on the highway and another car is moving slightly faster than yours. You will see the other car as being in a small apparent motion relative to your car. Your car becomes your *frame of reference.*

There are two important forms of motion. One is called *rectilinear motion,* in which objects move in straight lines. This motion normally occurs when objects are moving freely. Motion along a curved path is called *curvilinear motion*. In curvilinear motion, objects are pushed sideways by a force.

Qualities of motion

Velocity. The rate of motion is usually referred to as *speed*. The term *velocity* describes both the speed of an object and its direction. When a car moves along a curve and the speedometer does not change, the car is said to be moving at a constant speed. But the car's velocity is changing because its direction of motion is changing. Both speed and velocity can be expressed in various units of measurement that describe how far an object travels in a period of time. These units include miles per hour, feet per second, and centimeters per second. When both the speed and direction of an object are constant, the motion of the object is said to be *uniform.*

Acceleration occurs whenever the velocity of an object changes. Acceleration is how much the velocity has changed in a period of time. It is expressed in such terms as miles per hour per second, feet per second per second, or centimeters per second per second. For example, if a car traveling 3 miles per hour in its first second, travels 6 miles per hour in its second second, and 9 miles per hour in the third second, it is said to have a uniform acceleration of 3 miles per hour per second. The velocity of the car has increased 3 miles per hour for each second of motion.

A decrease of the velocity of an object over time is called *negative acceleration* or *deceleration.* For example, when a car brakes while approaching a stop sign, it decelerates. Both acceleration and deceleration can be *variable* (changeable) as well as uniform.

One situation where uniform acceleration occurs is when a ball is rolled down an inclined plane. The uniform acceleration of the ball will be twice the distance the ball rolls during its first second of movement. For example, a ball that rolls 1 foot in the first second has an acceleration of 2 feet per second per second. The distance the ball will have traveled and the velocity it will have reached after an interval of time can also be determined. The distance can be found using the formula $S = \frac{1}{2}at^2$, where S is the distance, a is the acceleration, and t is the time elapsed. The velocity (v) can be found with the formula $v = at$. Therefore, if a ball has a uniform acceleration of 2 feet per second per second, after 2 seconds it will have traveled 4 feet and its velocity will be 4 feet per second.

Similarly, if a car accelerates at a constant rate of 10 feet per second per second, after 5 seconds its velocity will be 50 feet per second, and it will have traveled 125 feet. After 10 seconds, the car's velocity will be 100 feet per second, and it will have traveled 500 feet.

Uniform acceleration also occurs when an object falls freely through the air. In this case, gravity provides a constant acceleration of 32 feet per second per second (9.8 meters per second per second). For example, a ball falling under gravity will have traveled 16 feet (4.9 meters) in 1 second and 64 feet (19.6 meters) in 2 seconds. But objects do not actually fall quite this fast because of the resistance of the air. In formulas where gravitational acceleration applies, the symbol g—for gravity—replaces a.

Momentum and kinetic energy. The momentum (p) of a moving object equals its mass (m) multiplied by its velocity (v); $p = mv$. An object with momentum also has *kinetic energy*. This energy, which is often called the *energy of motion,* is the energy a body possesses because of its motion. The kinetic energy (E) of an object is one-half of its mass multiplied by the square of its velocity. The formula is written $E = \frac{1}{2}mv^2$. When the formula is written in terms of the momentum of the object, it is $E = \frac{1}{2}pv$.

The kinetic energy of an object increases with the square of its velocity. For example, an automobile moving at 60 miles an hour has four times the energy it would have at 30 miles an hour. This increase in kinetic energy is why high-speed collisions are so much more

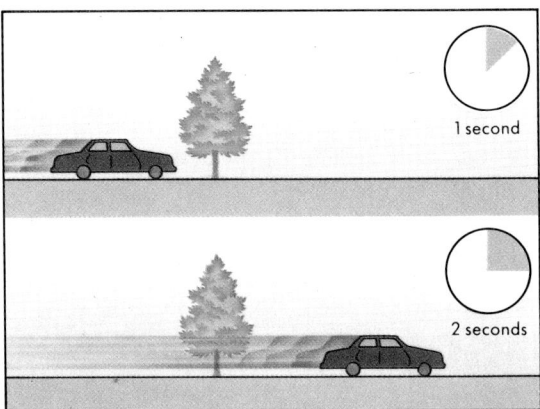

WORLD BOOK illustration by Sarah Woodward

Motion can be described in terms of speed, which measures how far an object travels in a certain length of time. If the car above moves at a speed of 50 feet (15 meters) per second, in 2 seconds it will have traveled 100 feet (30 meters).

dangerous and damaging than low-speed collisions. When a moving object collides with another object, energy and momentum are transferred. The energy given up by the moving object is called the *impact.* Objects moving at high velocity have high impact if they strike another object.

Objects obtain momentum and kinetic energy from forces acting on them for a period of time. The longer the time of action, the larger the momentum and kinetic energy. In such sports as tennis and golf, players follow through with their rackets and clubs so that force is applied to the ball for the longest time possible. As a result, the ball travels faster and has greater momentum and kinetic energy.

How friction affects motion

If we roll a ball along the ground, we notice that it slows down and stops even though no apparent force is being applied to it. The ball slows down and stops because of *friction.* Friction is resistance to motion. Air is one of the most common causes of friction. Automobiles and airplanes are streamlined to make them move more easily through the air.

But friction is also a help. Without it people could not walk on the earth. Instead, they would slide. We would not be able to nail two boards or screw metal objects together because friction holds them in place. When we apply the brakes on a car or a bicycle, it is friction that slows down the wheels.

In many instances, we try to reduce friction by making the surfaces of objects move more easily over one another. Smoothing out surfaces or placing another substance, such as a lubricating oil, between two solid surfaces reduces friction. Rotating objects such as roller bearings, ball bearings, and wheels may also greatly reduce friction. They make it easier to push such large, heavy objects as beds or automobiles.

Newton's laws of motion

In the 1600's, the English scientist and mathematician Sir Isaac Newton proposed three laws of motion. Newton's laws concern the ideal motion of objects and do not take into account air resistance or other friction. However, these laws have enabled scientists to describe a wide variety of motions.

The first law states that an object moving in a straight line will continue to move in a straight line unless acted upon by an outside force. This law also states that an object at rest will stay at rest unless a force moves it. Newton's first law is known as the *principle of inertia.* Inertia is the property of matter that makes an object stay in motion if it is moving or remain motionless if it is not moving. Forces that change an object's motion must first overcome the inertia of the object. The greater an object's mass, the harder it is to put the object into motion or change its velocity. Inertia serves as a measurement of how hard it is to get an object moving. See **Inertia.**

The second law describes how an object changes its motion when a force is applied to it. The change of motion depends on the magnitude of the force and the mass of the object. A heavier object will change its motion less under a given applied force than will an object of lighter weight. Therefore, if the same force is applied

to two objects, the change of motion of the lighter-weight object will be greater. Newton's second law also states that the effect of a given force is always in the direction of the force. For example, if an object is pushed toward the west, it moves that way and not toward the east. Newton's second law may be written as $F = ma$, where F is the applied force. Scientists use this formula to describe motion of all kinds of objects.

According to Newton's second law, forces cause changes in the motion of objects. Suppose a person fires a bullet horizontally from the muzzle of a gun. Newton's first law says that the bullet will continue to travel on a straight line forever if no forces act upon it. However, the earth's gravity does act on the bullet. As a result, the bullet will fall toward the ground. This fall occurs because the force of gravity pulls the bullet downward at right angles to the direction of travel.

If the rifle is fired horizontally from a height above the earth of 16 feet (4.9 meters), the bullet will be accelerated by gravity and hit the ground in one second—the same time it would take a freely falling body to drop. Because of gravity, rifles or any other type of gun have a limited range of distance they can shoot. In addition, bullets must be shot slightly upward to increase the range and make up for the drop.

The third law of motion states that for each action there is an equal and opposite reaction. For example, when hot gases escape from a rocket engine during take-off, the rocket is propelled upward. The downward motion of the gases from the rocket generates a reaction of the rocket upward. This reaction helps the rocket overcome air resistance and fly into space. There are many other examples of Newton's third law. When a rifle fires a bullet, the firing of the bullet is the action and the recoil of the rifle is the reaction. Both are caused by the expanding gas of the exploding gunpowder. Rotating lawn sprinklers propel a spray of water in one direction while rotating in the other direction.

Sometimes the reaction is such that it cannot be easily seen. When you throw a ball against a wall and the ball bounces back, you do not see the wall moving in the opposite direction. But there is a small motion of the area of the wall that was hit. If the ball bounces from the ground, the earth also draws back, but the mass of the earth is so great that we cannot see its motion.

Modifications of Newton's laws, particularly his second law, were proposed in the early 1900's by the German-born physicist Albert Einstein. For example, Einstein concluded that, based on his own *special theory of relativity,* the mass of an object can change with its velocity. But this effect is only important at velocities that are near that of the speed of light, which is 186,282 miles (299,792 kilometers) per second. See **Relativity.**

Gregory Benford

Related articles in *World Book* include:

Motion, Perpetual. See Perpetual motion machine.

Motion pictures provide entertainment for millions of people throughout the world every day. The musical fantasy *The Wizard of Oz, above,* has been an audience favorite since it was released in 1939. Judy Garland, its young heroine, became one of the most popular stars in movie history.

Motion picture

Motion picture is a series of images recorded on film or tape that appear to move when played through a film projector or a videotape player. Also known as movies, film, or cinema, the motion picture is one of the most popular forms of art and entertainment throughout the world. It is also a major source of information.

Every week, millions of people go to the movies. Many millions more watch movies that are broadcast on television or are played back on a videotape player.

But movies are much more than just entertainment. The motion picture is a major art form, as are, for example, painting and drama. Artists express themselves by using paint and dramatists by using words. Filmmakers express their ideas through a motion-picture camera. By using the camera in different ways, the filmmaker can express different points of view. A filmmaker may film scenes for a picture in a desert, on a mountain, and in a large city. Filmmakers can also film scenes from different angles. Later, through a process called *editing,* they can select the angle that most effectively expresses a dramatic point. Through editing, the filmmakers can also show events happening at the same time in different places.

Movies have become a gigantic industry. A typical feature-length film costs several million dollars to make and requires the skills of hundreds of workers. Highly technical devices, including cameras, sound-recording equipment, and projectors, are needed to film and show movies. In fact, motion pictures could not exist without many of the scientific and technical discoveries made since the late 1800's. For this reason, movies have been called the art form of the 20th century.

We can enjoy many forms of art and entertainment by ourselves. We can enjoy reading a story or looking at a painting alone. But we usually enjoy a motion picture most when we watch it as part of an audience. An exciting scene increases in suspense when we feel the tension sweeping through a large group of viewers. A film usually makes less of an impact if we see it in a nearly empty theater or alone at home.

The movies have a brief history, compared to such art forms as music and painting. Movies date back only to the late 1800's. By the early 1900's, filmmakers had already developed distinctive artistic theories and techniques. However, motion pictures received little scholarly attention until the 1960's. Since then, thousands of books have been published about every aspect of filmmaking and film history. Many universities and colleges offer degrees in motion pictures, and many more offer film courses.

In addition to their artistic and entertainment values, movies are also widely used in education, especially as teaching aids. Teachers use such films in classes on ge-

The contributors of this article are Michael Rabiger, Director of the Documentary Center at Columbia College in Chicago; Robert Sklar, Professor of Cinema Studies at New York University; and Nicholas Tanis, Associate Professor of Film and Television at New York University.

Culver

Kobal Collection/SuperStock

Silent movies established the power of film. Silent stars, such as Charlie Chaplin, *left,* gained worldwide fame. The 1925 Soviet classic *The Battleship Potemkin, right,* showed how film could be used as propaganda. It featured this scene of civilians being massacred by their government.

ography, history, mathematics, and the physical and social sciences. Movies use slow motion, animation, and other special techniques to demonstrate processes that otherwise could not be seen or studied thoroughly. For example, a film can speed up the formation of crystals so a class can study this process.

Television stations use motion pictures to inform as well as to entertain their viewers. TV stations frequently present *documentaries.* A documentary is a nonfiction movie that tries to present factual information in a dramatic and entertaining way. Documentaries deal with a variety of subjects, such as environmental pollution and the history of presidential elections. Made-for-TV movies may deal with sensitive social issues within the framework of a regular entertainment movie.

Millions of people enjoy taking their own motion pictures with small motion-picture cameras. Some of these cameras can also record sound as they are filming. Home movies began to develop as a hobby during the 1920's, following the invention of low-cost film that could be used in small cameras. The popularity of home movies has increased over the years with the improvement in cameras and projectors, the introduction of color and sound film, and the development of home video recorders that play back on TV sets.

This article deals mainly with feature-length motion pictures made for exhibition in theaters and on videocassettes and television. For information on home movies, see **Video camera; Videotape recorder** (In the home).

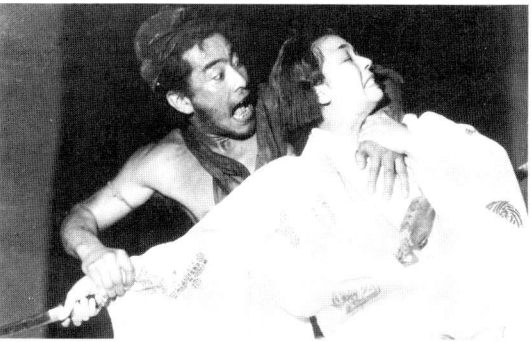

Kobal Collection/SuperStock

Filmmaking is an international art form. *Rashomon, above,* was the first Japanese film to gain a large Western audience.

© Universal City Studios, Inc., from AP/Wide World

Moviemaking is a major industry. *E.T.: The Extra-Terrestrial, above,* earned more than $200 million at the box office.

How motion pictures are made

© Mikki Ansin, Gamma/Liaison

Shooting the movie is actually one of the later stages in making a motion picture. First comes a great deal of planning and development. The movie above is being shot on a *sound stage*—a large soundproof building especially designed for filmmaking.

Making a feature film calls for a special blend of art and business skills. A Hollywood motion picture may take less than six months to more than two years to create. It can cost less than $250,000 or more than $50 million. On a large budget film, several hundred people will be employed.

Although the film cast and crew may include hundreds of members, the people who perform two key functions remain at the center of the filmmaking process: the *producers* and the *director.* The producers are the chief business and legal managers of the film. Usually, one or more *executive producers* from the film company supervise the work of the producer of the specific motion picture. By choosing the director and other key members of the creative team, and by supervising the budget, the producers exert great influence over the creative part of the film production.

The director is responsible for guiding the creative efforts of the screenwriters, cast, and crew. By influencing the film's shooting schedule and the equipment and personnel needs of the film, the director plays a major role in shaping the budget.

Each film presents a different set of problems for the producers and director. Some movies call for extensive traveling to distant locations. Others call for complicated special effects. Some need elaborate sets or an intimate and delicate acting style. Regardless of the particular challenges, each film will pass through five stages to reach its audience. These stages occasionally overlap, but they occur in the following order: (1) development, (2) preproduction, (3) production, (4) post-production,

and (5) distribution. This section describes the first four stages. The fifth stage—distribution—is discussed in the section *The motion-picture industry.*

Before the late 1940's, almost all American movies were produced by major studios in or near Hollywood, Calif. Today, most movies are made by independent film producers. The following section describes chiefly how a motion picture is made by an independent producer. However, the key personnel and many of the steps also apply to films made by the major studios. For information on the "studio era," see the *History* section.

Development

Developing the story. All feature films begin with an idea for a story. The idea can come from a newspaper article, from someone's imagination, or from an existing book or play. The idea may be as complicated as a 30-page outline or as simple as a single sentence. No one person is responsible for finding an interesting source for a film story. Movie ideas come from screenwriters, producers, directors, actors and actresses, agents, and friends of the filmmaker.

After a good idea has been identified, the producer or director must find a screenwriter with the ability and sensitivity to turn that idea into a story that will work as a movie. Once commissioned, the screenwriter works closely with the project's originator to develop the characters and to construct the story based on the original idea. The screenwriter's job is to create the document that will serve as the blueprint for producing the film. This document is the *screenplay.*

The script contains the dialogue, a description of the action, and the camera angles for each scene. The script supervisor records the director's instructions on the script, *above*.

When looking for a *property* (story) to film, producers also review scripts prepared by screenwriters working on "spec." "Spec" means that the screenwriter has not been contracted—or even informally asked—to write a script based on someone else's idea. Instead, the writer is speculating that his or her own idea will be sold to a producer or studio.

A writer working on spec sends an original script to an agent who will market it. The agent shows the script to producers and studio executives who may be interested in purchasing and producing it. If they are interested, they can purchase the script outright or—for a reduced fee—they can *option* it. By taking an option on a script, producers acquire the exclusive rights to the script for a limited time. During that time, they explore the possibility of producing the script. If they decide to produce it, they then buy the script. If they want more time to decide, they can renew the option. If the option is not renewed, the screenwriter keeps the option fee and has the right to sell the script to another producer.

Acquiring financing. After obtaining a property, most independent producers must secure financial backing for the project. As a first step, they usually try to interest a successful director or a recognized actor or actress in the film. Associating a proven director or star with the project helps assure investors that the movie will have box-office appeal. Choosing the director and leading performer is one of the most important steps in the production of a film—not only because it helps in obtaining financing, but also because each star-director-producer team will interpret a script differently.

In another major step before approaching potential investors, the producers prepare an estimated budget and a shooting schedule. They consider the expected size of the film's audience, the amount of money realistically required to create the film, and the amount of money they can expect to raise from investors.

After the producers are satisfied with the estimated budget and shooting schedule, they put together the film's "package." The package consists of the budget, script, shooting schedule, and key creative people who will make the film. Based on the package, the producers seek funds from banks, studios, or private investors. The money will be raised if the creative team's experience and "name recognition" value are strong and the budget

The director works to achieve a desired result in a scene. The director above explains his ideas about an upcoming shot to an actress. Below, he listens to a suggestion from a technician.

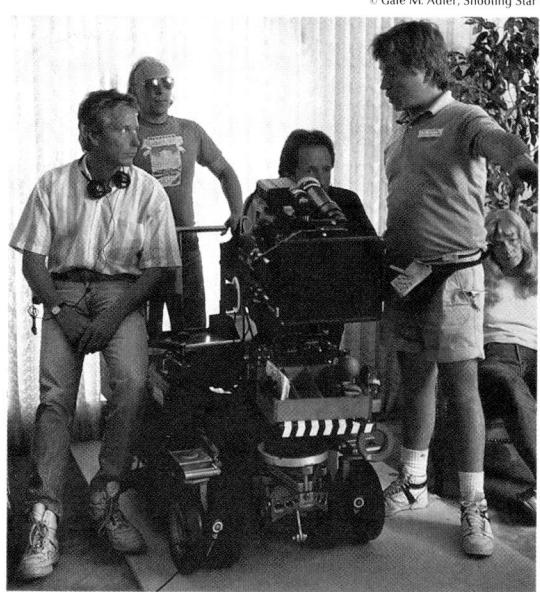

seems low enough for the film to make a profit. In some cases, the package will be so strong that the producers will also be able to sell the project to a distributor at this stage. Once the funds are secured, the actual planning of the production can begin.

Preproduction

During the preproduction stage, the producers, the director, and other key crew members create a detailed plan of action for turning the script into a motion picture. This involves planning for all the creative decisions, personnel choices, equipment, and material necessary to make the film. The goal is to anticipate and solve all problems likely to be encountered in producing the motion picture.

The preproduction period can take as little as two

weeks to six months or more. By the end of this period, the crew is a well-organized group with a common goal. They understand the deadlines they face to complete the film, and they have all the major materials ready so they can execute their plan smoothly.

The preproduction period is the beginning of intense collaboration among the members of the production team. At the center of these collaborations are the producers and the director. They develop and carry to the members of the crew their overall vision of the film. Through a series of meetings and discussions with the cast and crew, they decide upon the specific interpretations of the look and sound of the script.

Reviewing the script. All phases of preproduction start with a careful reading and analysis of the script. The director examines the script to understand the story and to develop a vision of the most effective way to translate the script into film and sound images. Suggestions from members of the creative team often lead to further revisions of the script. The director also develops ideas on casting, costuming, set design, photography, and editing.

Assembling the production team. Working closely with the producers, the director hires a crew. The director will try to choose craftworkers who, because of their experience and understanding of filmmaking, will develop and enhance the director's idea of the film.

The production manager is one of the key positions in the team. The production manager develops the actual budget and shooting schedule. Working under the producers, the production manager will supervise the production and authorize all expenditures.

The director of photography, or *cinematographer,* is responsible to the director for achieving the best possible visual look for the film. The director of photography supervises the camera crew, and designs and executes the lighting pattern of the movie.

The art director is responsible for designing and creating the sets. He or she makes blueprints and sometimes models of the sets. Once the designs are approved, the art director oversees their construction.

The costume designers and their crew are responsible for designing and making the costumes. They may also purchase costumes for the production. In preparing their work, the designers must consider the work of the director of photography and the art director. The colors and patterns used on walls and in the lighting will affect the work of the costume designers. They can create a feeling of harmony by designing costumes that blend with the background. If the costumes clash with the sets, the audience can be subtly informed that the characters are out of place with their surroundings.

Through a series of meetings, the director and the heads of the various production departments discuss their understanding of the script and how to translate it into props, costumes, hairstyles, color, lighting, compositions, and camera movements. This close collaboration and exchange of ideas will lead to the planning of the film's design.

During the preproduction period, a crucial decision faces the producers, director, director of photography, and the art director. They must decide whether to film each scene on a *sound stage*—an artificial set constructed in a building—or on *location*—a real place that

© Gale M. Adler, Shooting Star

The director of photography, *right,* tries to create the best look for the movie. The director of photography supervises the camera crew and designs and executes the film's lighting.

resembles the one depicted in the story. This decision affects both the look and the budget of the film. Most films combine both location and sound stage filming. The advantages and disadvantages of each technique are discussed under *Production.*

Developing the shooting schedule is the job of the production manager. Knowing how the director wants the film to look gives the production manager a feeling for how long and how difficult the filming will be. A number of variables help determine how many days the crew will need to shoot the film. These variables include traveling to distant locations, construction of elaborate sets or lighting setups, and planning long and complex camera movements. By knowing how many days will be needed, the production manager can plan a schedule for shooting the motion picture.

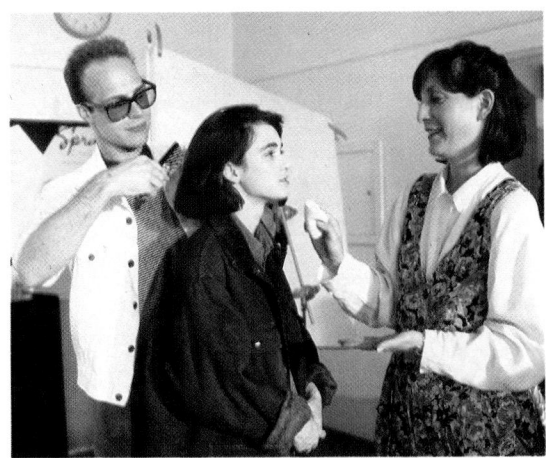

© Gale M. Adler, Shooting Star

Makeup artists apply cosmetics to help an actress's coloring look natural under the bright lights needed for filming.

© Gale M. Adler, Shooting Star

The costume designer creates the motion picture's costume designs, oversees their production, and makes sure they suit the actors and actresses.

To save time and money, the production manager plans a schedule in which most of the scenes will be shot out of the order in which they appear in the script. For example, if scenes one, five, and nine all take place in the same living room, it will save time and expense to shoot them all at once. This way, the crew only has to set up the lights once and the production manager only has to organize the materials needed on that set once. If the scenes were shot in the order in which they appear in the script, the crew would have to set up its equipment three separate times.

Preparing the final budget. With the shooting schedule prepared, the production manager can begin laying out the actual cost of the film. The manager must stay within the guidelines of the estimated budget and the amount of money raised from the investors. The manager can specify what equipment to use and how much it will cost, and can decide how much time will be needed to edit the film. A shorter time will be required if the director plans the film carefully in the preproduction stage. More time will be needed if the director *improvises* on the set. Improvising means that, as the film is being shot, the director works to discover the best way to play a dramatic moment or find the most appropriate camera position.

The production manager makes a final budget after reviewing the script for its costume, location, and acting needs, and after identifying the necessary equipment and size of the crew. The final budget includes *above the line* costs and *below the line* costs. The above the line costs are the salaries for key actors and actresses, the fees for the producers and director, and the purchase of the script and other creative fees. Below the line costs include crew salaries, equipment rentals, insurance costs, film and sound stock purchases, and rent for editing rooms. The producers and the director then review the budget and shooting schedule. They may request adjustments to figures they feel are unrealistic.

During the preproduction period, the producers and production manager refine the budget. They plan how the budget will be spent day by day until the film is completed and ready for distribution. The production manager and the assistant director work with the heads of the various departments so they can plan their work to meet the needs of the schedule and the budget.

Assembling the cast. As the budget and shooting schedule are being completed, the director works with the producers and casting director to complete the cast. The casting director's job is to screen the applicants. He or she sometimes considers hundreds of actors and actresses for each major role in a film. Through a series of auditions and interviews, the selection is narrowed down to a few candidates for each role. At an audition, a

© Gale M. Adler, Shooting Star

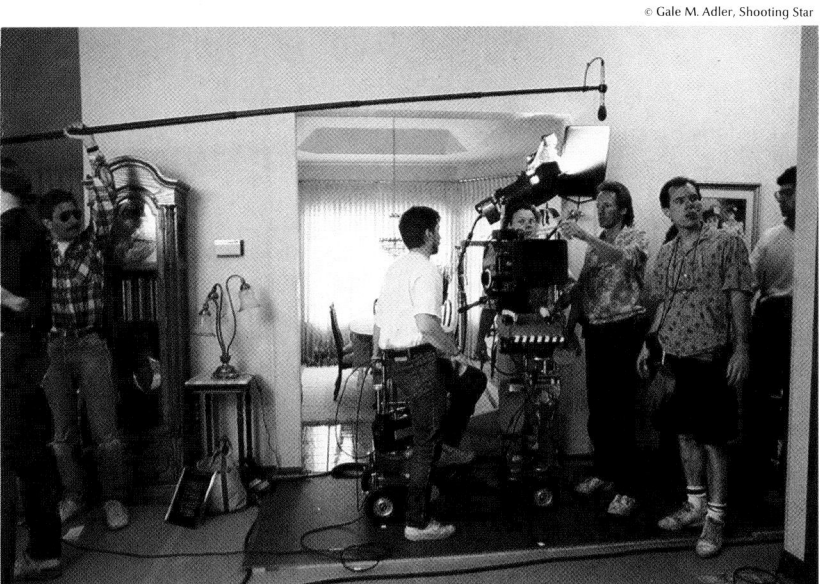

Preparing to shoot a scene, the various technicians set up their lights while another crew places the sound gear in position to record the action on audiotape. Adjustments in equipment placement may be made to film different versions of a single shot.

performer may be asked to read from the script or to act in a scene previously prepared. The director and producers select the final cast from the pool of performers identified by the casting director. Actors and actresses are chosen for their talent and their ability to blend with other performers to create a team performance. The actors and actresses are also selected for how appropriate they are for the role, based on their appearance, temperament, and the director's interpretation of the role.

Holding rehearsals. If time permits and the performers are available, rehearsals take place before shooting. During rehearsals, the director and the cast explore the characters and script together. They read through the script and discuss the story and the role each character plays in it. They then act out the scenes and rework them to fit their talents and interpretations. They may use improvisation to explore each character and the possible ways to play a scene.

Not all directors hold preproduction rehearsals. Some only discuss the story and characters with performers at this time. They prefer to wait until the actors and actresses are actually on the set to rehearse each scene. Performers with small parts usually meet the director for the first time the day their scene is shot.

Production

During the preproduction period, the filmmakers imagine the movie they want to make. They gather the people and materials needed to realize their idea. During the production period, the movie-as-imagined is brought to life and recorded on film and audiotape. The creative work of the preproduction period is continued and extended. However, instead of working with words or drawings or budgets on paper, the filmmakers work with actors and actresses and the materials of real life.

Filming on a sound stage. A sound stage is a hangarlike building in which sets can be built. Shooting on a sound stage enables the production team to design and build the sets to exact specifications. It allows them to place the camera exactly where they desire, and to create precise scale and details in their sets. Achieving the desired lighting is easier because each stage has a grid of pipes suspended from the ceiling. This grid allows the director of photography to hang each lighting unit with precision. The stage is enclosed, which eliminates noise and distractions from the outside world. Working on a stage saves time when setting up, and it eliminates moving the film's company from place to place because everything is shot right on the sets.

The disadvantage of filming on the sound stage is the extra cost. Constructing sets is much like building a house. A designer must make architectural plans of the set. Carpenters must build it and the set must be painted and furnished.

Filming on location. The advantage of shooting on a location is that the set already exists, for example, a skyscraper, a mountain, or a harbor. Additions can be made to the location to create the appropriate look. If, for instance, the scene needs a driveway but there is none at the site, a false driveway can be added.

The main disadvantage of shooting on location comes from the fact that locations were not designed for filmmaking. The filmmakers may not have the room to spread out their equipment and freely move the camera.

© Shooting Star

Building a set usually takes place on a sound stage. The art director is responsible for designing the sets. After the designs are approved, the art director oversees their actual construction.

They must bring in generators to supply enough electricity for their lights. The location is more difficult to protect from outside intrusions, such as pedestrians, noise from traffic and airplanes, and changes in light throughout the day. The cast and crew must be transported to the locations, which may be in distant parts of the world. The personnel must be fed and housed. However, the success of many films comes from the authentic look and feel of the location, which outweigh the disadvantages.

Some filmmakers shoot outdoor scenes on a *back lot,* an open air area on studio property. A back lot set is a re-creation of an exterior, such as a city street. Filming on a back lot saves time and money that would be consumed shooting on location. However, the results may be less authentic-looking than location shooting.

Preparing to shoot. The location or the set on the sound stage must be carefully prepared before the camera can interpret the action. The shooting day usually starts very early. Trucks begin arriving with lights, props, and camera and sound equipment at 6 or 7 a.m. The *set decorator* arranges the props. Hairdressers and makeup artists arrive just before the performers. The actors and actresses spend from one to several hours having their hair and makeup prepared for each day's shoot. The craft services crew puts out coffee and donuts for the crew as they set up. The director and assistants review the schedule for that day's work. The director of photography directs electricians called *gaffers* in setting up the lights.

The set must be lit brightly enough for an image to be made on film. Lighting a scene is one of the most time-consuming and important aspects of film production. Lighting creates a mood or a tone for each scene. The lighting director or director of photography uses contrast as a major tool. Contrast is the relative brightness of a character or object against surrounding shadows

Filming on location provides a movie with realistic settings that might be difficult, as well as more costly, to create at a studio. But on-location shooting also has disadvantages. For example, personnel and equipment must be transported to the location, which can present problems in isolated areas.

© Mikki Ansin, Gamma/Liaison

and darkened areas. A happier, more upbeat mood can be created by lowering the contrast and making the scene brighter. A scene filled with shadows and set off by a few small areas of bright light is usually more somber. In a mystery movie, a threatening tone can be developed in a darker scene emphasizing heavily contrasting light. An audience sits in expectation, waiting for something or someone to jump out of the shadows.

As the lighting is being adjusted, the performers and director come to the set. They review their work from the rehearsal period, focusing on their characters' actions and reactions in the upcoming scene. For unlike live theater, where the performer acts in a continuous time sequence, film requires a performer to work in fragments of scenes. Each shot in a film seldom covers more than a minute or two of the film's story, and, as explained earlier, the scenes themselves are shot out of order. Consequently, film performers must develop their characters without the help of continuity, and the actors and actresses must have a strong sense of the film's time sequence. Acting in fragments does have some advantages, however, over stage acting. In the movies, the performer can concentrate on the very short sequences of dialogue or movement that go into a given shot.

Shooting the movie. After the lighting preparation is completed, the director and performers go onto the set and rehearse in front of the camera operator and a technician called the *sound mixer*. The director works with actors and actresses to polish their performances. In addition, the camera operator checks to be sure that the photography will be satisfactory, and the sound mixer makes certain that a good clear audio recording can be made. Then the shot is recorded on film and audiotape. Usually, there are several *takes* (versions) of each shot.

The director may call for a retake to improve upon a performance or to ask for a different interpretation of the scene. The performer may want to try a new approach, or the camera operator may want to improve the framing of the shot or the camera movement.

© Eva Sereny, Sygma

Lighting is responsible for much of a scene's dramatic effect. In this shot from a horror film, the shadowy background contrasts with the brightly lit faces to heighten the tension.

Much of the shot's impact depends on the choice of camera lens and position, and on the *blocking* of actors and actresses. A long, or *telephoto,* lens makes a scene look flat. A *wide-angle* lens deepens space. Camera position influences how an audience understands a scene. For example, if a camera is placed so that it looks at a character through a fence or a set of bars, the audience will probably feel that the character is closed in, almost imprisoned.

Blocking refers to how the performers move during a scene. If a character moves toward the camera and grows large in the frame, he or she will take attention away from the other performers in the frame. If characters walk away from the camera, the audience will feel that the figures are isolated or vulnerable or less important, depending upon the preceding action and scenes.

A device called a *clapstick* is used to keep track of the takes and shots—information that will be needed during the post-production stage. A clapstick consists of a slate attached to two hinged boards. The slate is marked with the number of each scene and take. The clapstick is photographed before each take, thus visually identifying the scene number and the take number. A member of the camera crew also says aloud the scene and take numbers, and then immediately claps the two boards together to make a sharp sound. The spoken information and clapping noise are recorded on the sound track, creating an audio record just as the slate preserves a visual record of the filming.

After each take, the director consults with the performers, the director of photography, and the camera operator. They decide on any adjustments that could improve the shot. Traditionally, they had to rely on their instincts of how the take will look on the film. Since the 1970's, however, many directors have used a *video assist* to help judge the takes as they are being shot. The video assist is a video recording system attached to the motion-picture camera. It records an image on videotape at the same time the camera is filming. The videotape can be examined immediately after shooting, an advantage over the camera film, which must first be processed in a laboratory. The video assist thus provides the filmmakers with a faster way to judge the work in each shot, allowing them to determine what improve-

ments need to be made in the next take.

On a low-budget film, only three or four takes may be made from each camera setup. On a big-budget film, as many as 50 takes might be made. After the director is satisfied with a take, it is *printed*—that is, sent to the laboratory for processing. A copy called a *work print* is then made for the editing phase.

After all the takes of a shot have been made, the crew, supervised by the director of photography, sets up the lights and camera angle for the next shot. The performers go to their dressing rooms, or to their trailers if they are on location, to wait for the crew to complete its work. Meanwhile, the director talks to the designers about the next day's set. The director may also meet with the producers and production manager to discuss the schedule, budget, or other production-related matters. At the end of the day, if the work is on location and completed, the crew packs up the equipment and moves the company to the next location.

Post-production

The production stage provides the raw materials from which the motion picture will be constructed. This raw material consists of fragments of film and audiotape. The fragments record the characters, places, and events that make up the film's story and interpretation. Post-production is the stage during which the raw material is edited into a motion picture. Editing refers to the total process of putting a movie together in a final form. In many ways, editing resembles the writing stage of film-making. But instead of constructing the story out of words, the editor and director select the best shots and dialogue. They use them to lay out the movie's structure and to determine its moment-to-moment shape.

Throughout the process, the editors pay close attention to the rhythm and tempo of the film. They carefully choose where each shot begins and how it flows into the next shot. If necessary, the film can be reinterpreted during editing to take advantage of its strengths and to diminish its weaknesses.

Preliminary steps. The editing process begins after a sequence of important steps to prepare the *camera original* and the sound track for editing. The camera original is the film exposed during the production stage. First, the work print must be made by the film laboratories after the camera original has been processed. The work print is used during the editing to preserve the camera original from damage. The sound track must be copied onto a tape the same width as the film. Matching the size of the film and tape allows the editor to put the sound track and picture on the same machine while editing.

Next, the sound must be brought into *synchronous* relationship with the picture. This means the sound must be placed so it exactly matches the action in the picture. For example, when an actor speaks on the film, the audience should hear his voice at the same time. On the film, an assistant editor marks the clapstick frame where the boards close. The assistant then marks the corresponding clapstick sound on the sound track. Lining up this sound and the appropriate picture frame creates the synchronous relationship. The assistant editor has to find and establish this synchronous relationship for every shot in the film. After the film and sound

© Gale M. Adler, Shooting Star

A clapstick is a hinged board used to keep track of the takes, scenes, and other important information during actual filming.

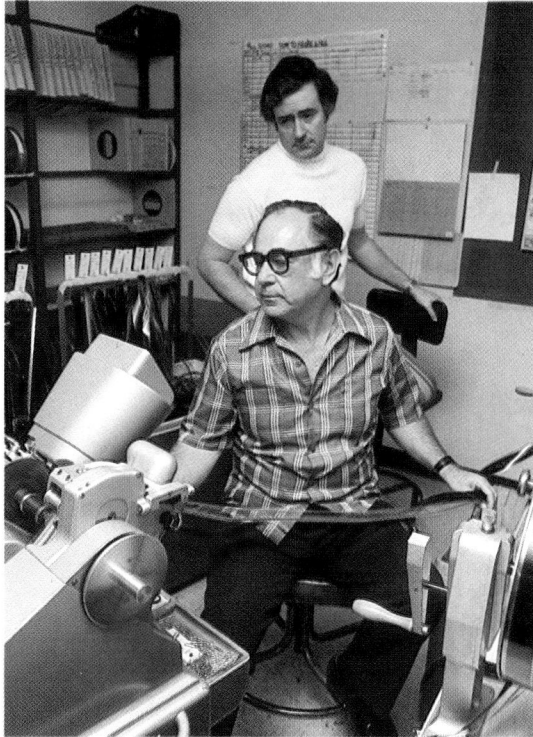

The editor operates a machine called the Moviola. The editor examines the film on the Moviola screen and selects the desired shots. The editor then organizes them to tell the film's story.

have been "synced up," the assistant editor makes a detailed written record of each shot. This written log enables the editors to keep track of the thousands of feet of exposed film.

The rushes. Next, the director and editor screen this raw, unedited footage, called *rushes,* or *dailies.* They discuss which shots to use and sketch out how the shots should be arranged. These screenings usually take place at the end of each day's shooting during production—an example of how the different stages of making a movie overlap. The editor, director, producers, and other crew members see the footage from scenes filmed the previous day. In this way, they can check on the quality of their work. If necessary, they can adjust their approach. They can reshoot a single shot or an entire scene before leaving a location. They can also create new scenes to fill in gaps in the story they did not realize existed. Most important, they can begin the actual editing process.

The rough and fine cuts. Based on the discussions with the director and producers, the editor begins to assemble the selected footage and put it in order. This preliminary version of the film is called the *rough cut.* It follows the order of the screenplay, using the shots selected by the director.

After the rough cut is completed, the editor screens it with the director. Based upon their response, different takes of shots may be used, and the order of scenes may be changed. Scenes that fail to add to the storytelling might be dropped. The editor makes these adjustments, which clarify and strengthen the story and refine it

Special effects create illusions. The top picture shows a painting on glass called a *matte* painting. The black area blocks out light. The middle picture shows a shot from a real set, also with a black area. At the bottom, the matte painting and the shot of the set—this time photographed with live actors—have been combined to create the finished scene.

closer to its final shape. This version is called the *fine cut.*

This cut is then screened and analyzed with the producers. To get a fresh opinion, friends and fellow filmmakers not involved with the production are also invited. Adjustments again are made to improve the story and the filmmaking. The director continues to supervise cuts until he or she is satisfied, given the limitations of the budget and the post-production schedule. The producers or the studio can then take over and polish, revise, or completely restructure the film as they see fit.

Adding music and sound effects. During the editing, the composer and sound editor join the other filmmakers. Some composers want to be involved from the initial planning of the film to absorb its mood and to understand its development. Most composers, however, are brought in during or after the rough cut has been completed.

The composer and sound editor will screen the film with the director, identifying appropriate moments for sound effects and music. They discuss the kind of music the film calls for and the instruments that will be used in recording the music. Sometimes the discussions result in a scene being reedited. The director may decide that a passage of dialogue can be effectively replaced by music.

As the composer prepares and records the music, the sound editor adds sound effects, background noises, and additional dialogue. These sounds contribute to the character and impact of the film and strengthen the desired illusion. After the picture has been *locked* and the sound editing completed, the filmmakers take the *final* or *frozen* cut to its final production phases.

Mixing the sound. The various sounds and music are blended together onto one track during a *mixing session* in a mix studio. Several technicians—usually a dialogue mixer, a sound effects mixer, and a music mixer—sit behind a large console with many volume and sound effects controls. In front of them is a screen on which the film is projected. The director watches the film with them as the mixers follow carefully prepared charts known as *cue sheets.* These sheets indicate when each sound occurs in the film's sound tracks. The mixers work together under the leadership of the dialogue mixer. They adjust the relative volume and sound quality of each sound to emphasize the most important sounds.

The answer print. Once the sound has been mixed, the camera original is then edited, shot for shot, to exactly match the final cut of the work print. Next, the laboratories print a new copy on a single, continuous piece of film. They then copy the mixed sound track along the edge of this new print, creating an *answer print.* This version includes the movie's titles and credits, as well as optical effects—such as dissolving from one shot to another—that were decided upon during the editing. The film also contains the final mixed sounds in the sound track. Small adjustments can be made at this point. By reprinting, individual shots can be made darker or lighter or their color can be adjusted.

When the filmmakers believe their work is complete, they preview the picture for an outside audience. Based on the audience's response, whole scenes may be reedited and reprinted. After the filmmakers are satisfied with the film's appearance, the post-production stage is complete. The product is now ready for distribution to its audience.

In a mixing session, technicians called *mixers* blend the individual sound tracks for the dialogue, music, and sound effects onto a master tape. The mixers watch the screen action as they operate controls on their *sound console* to switch on and balance the various sounds.

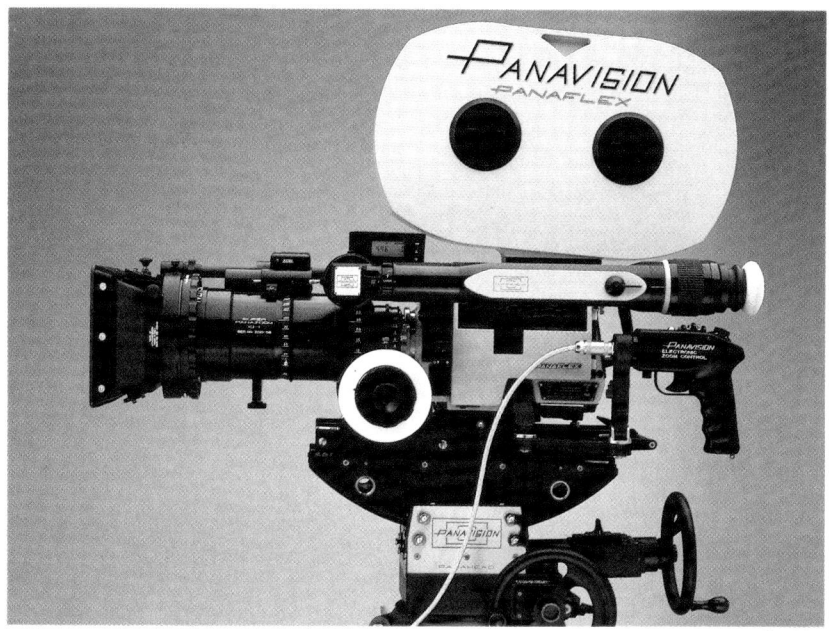

Panavision

A 35-millimeter motion picture camera is a complex piece of equipment. The film is housed in a lightproof, soundproof *magazine* that is mounted atop the camera. Unexposed film unwinds from a reel in the magazine's *supply chamber.* As the film moves through the camera, it is exposed by light entering through the lens and winds onto a reel in the *take-up chamber.* Knobs on the side of the camera focus the lens and wheels at the base of the camera adjust its position.

As we watch a motion picture, we are actually watching many thousands of individual still pictures called *frames.* Each new frame shows an image slightly different from the image in the preceding frame. When a single image is flashed upon a screen, the human eye continues to see it for one-tenth of a second after the screen has gone black. Because of this phenomenon, called *persistence of vision,* we see a continuous flow of action when viewing a series of images flashed in rapid succession.

The camera. In principle, a movie camera is like a still camera except that it takes many pictures each second. In addition, the camera mechanism is precision-engineered to run almost noiselessly to avoid interfering with sound recording.

The camera lens focuses an image, consisting of light rays, upon a single frame of unexposed film. The image boundaries are precisely defined by a rectangular opening called the *aperture.* After the frame has been exposed, a revolving shutter closes, temporarily shielding the aperture from further light. A metal tooth called a *claw* automatically engages the *sprocket holes* on the side of the film. The claw quickly moves the exposed frame down, pulling a fresh frame into position. While a *register pin* holds the unexposed frame in exact position, the shutter revolves and a burst of light exposes the new frame.

The film's stop-start movement is called *intermittent motion.* This cycle takes place 24 times a second for sound film. For slow-motion filming, the camera mechanism is run faster. For faster motion, the mechanism is run slower than 24 frames a second. The images are then projected at the normal 24 frames a second.

Unexposed film is loaded into the *supply chamber* of a lightproof *magazine,* which can be rapidly mounted and removed from the camera body. After the film has been exposed, it passes into the magazine's *take-up*

chamber. It is then unloaded in the dark and sent to a film laboratory for processing.

The film is made of light-sensitive chemicals called *emulsion* coated on a flexible plastic strip called a *base.* Any camera can use either black-and-white or color film. Film length is expressed in feet, but the standard widths are given in millimeters.

The oldest film in current use is 35 millimeters (about $1\frac{3}{8}$ inches) wide. This size was originally introduced in the United States in 1899 and soon became the standard width for making motion pictures. Almost all film shot for theater exhibition is 35 millimeters wide. Film shot for television and for classroom use is 16 millimeters (about $\frac{5}{8}$ of an inch) wide. Home movie film is 8 millimeters (about $\frac{1}{4}$ inch) wide. The wider the film, the larger the area of the frame and the greater the image's res-

The shutter controls the length of time that light strikes the film. When the shutter is open, light travels through the lens and an opening called the *aperture* onto the unexposed film. The register pin holds the film motionless until one frame has been exposed. The shutter closes, and the pin then withdraws. A claw is next inserted into the sprocket holes. It pulls the film to the next frame. This cycle is repeated 24 times a second.

WORLD BOOK diagrams by Mas Nakagawa

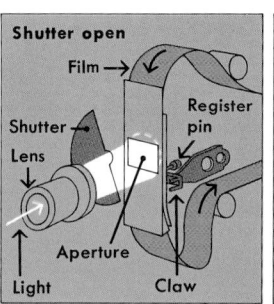

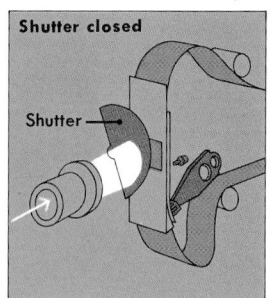

olution (detail). Movies projected in theaters show the largest image and thus use the largest film size. Occasionally, a filmmaker will shoot a movie using 70-millimeter ($2\frac{3}{4}$-inch) film, which is extremely costly but produces exceptionally sharp images on the screen.

The sound track is a narrow band recorded on the side of the film image. For information on how the sound is mixed and recorded on magnetic tape before being transferred to the film, see the section *How motion pictures are made.* The sound track appears on the film as a photographic recording that can be optically played back through a projector.

The sound is transferred from the magnetic tape to the photographic film by means of a *galvanometer,* an instrument that reacts to varying electric currents. At the heart of the galvanometer is a coil of wire that turns when an electric current passes through it. The direction and distance that the coil turns varies according to the direction and strength of the electric current. In this case, the current is produced by the magnetic sound recording. A wedge-shaped beam of light is projected onto a mirror attached to the coil on the galvanometer. As the coil quivers in response to the sound recording, the mirror vibrates accordingly, which in turn makes the reflection of the wedge-shaped beam tremble. This

The sound track is photographed on film by a beam of light, shown by the dashed line. The beam shines from a recording lamp through a lens that shapes it into a wedge and focuses it on a mirror. This mirror vibrates in response to the electrical impulses made by the magnetic tape recording of the sound track. The vibrating mirror reflects the wedge-shaped beam up and down across a slit in another lens. This exposes a pattern of light on the film. The pattern is converted into sound when the film is run through a projector.

WORLD BOOK illustration by Arthur Grebetz

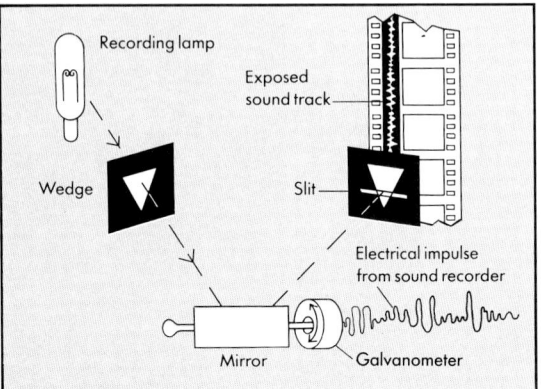

The projector mechanism projects the film image on a screen and also reproduces the sound. The projector has sprockets that pull the film through its mechanism. A rotating shutter prevents light from reaching the film until each frame is stationary. To reproduce the sound, an exciter lamp sends a narrow beam of light through the photographic sound track. The variations of light emerging on the other side shine into a photoelectric cell and are converted into electrical impulses. The tiny impulses are then greatly amplified and fed into the theater loudspeaker system.

WORLD BOOK illustration by Arthur Grebetz

Rotating shutter

Drive sprocket

Projection lens

Projection light source

Screen

Speaker

Photoelectric cell

Exciter lamp

Amplifier

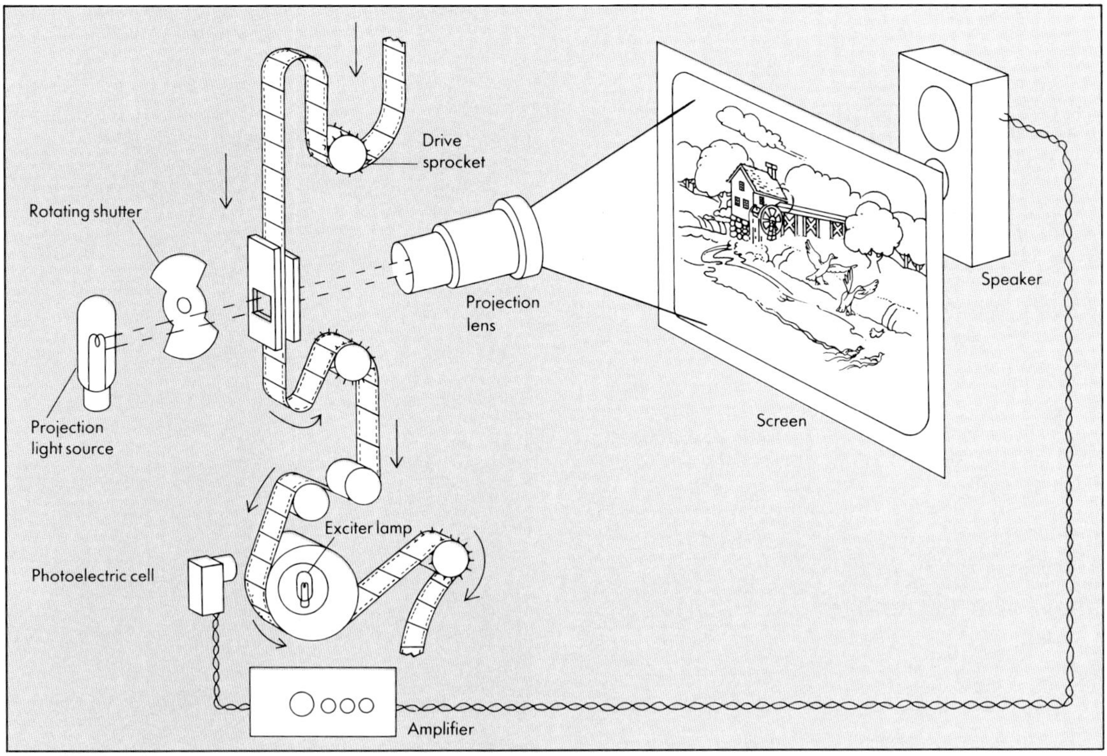

8 mm   16 mm   35 mm

Eastman Kodak

Film for home movies is 8 millimeters wide. TV and classroom movies are shot on 16-millimeter film. Most theater movies use 35-millimeter film. Two white bands of sound track run down the left side of the 16- and 35-millimeter films.

trembling beam is reflected through a slit-shaped aperture and onto the film. This action produces a continuously changing area of exposed film called a *variable-area sound recording.*

The projector reproduces the film sound track and throws the visual images onto a screen. Like a camera, the projector has sprockets that pull the film through its mechanism. It also uses the intermittent-motion principle to hold each frame stationary during the projection. Some of the earliest cameras could even be adapted to serve as projectors.

In the modern projector, a rotating shutter prevents light from reaching the film until each frame is stationary. Then the shutter allows the bright light source to shine through the film and project the image through the focusing lens onto the screen. To minimize a flickering image, the shutter produces two short flashes of light for each projected frame instead of one long one. In a single second of film projected at 24 frames a second, there are 48 flashed images. Some projectors use a pulsing light source, which eliminates the need for a shutter.

The projector mechanism must allow for different principles of sound and film reproduction. At the point where the image is being projected onto the screen, the film is moving in the intermittent, start-and-stop fashion just described. However, sound can only be *read* (reproduced) from film in continuous motion. To resolve this problem, the *sound head*—the device that reads the sound track—scans the film after it is past the lens and is again moving in a continuous motion. To permit the image and its matching sound to be reproduced at the same time, the sound must be recorded ahead of its

corresponding image on the film. In 35-millimeter film, for example, the sound track is advanced 21 frames ahead of its corresponding image.

To reproduce the sound, an *exciter lamp* sends a narrow beam of light through the photographic sound track. The variations of light emerging on the other side shine into a photoelectric cell, where light is converted into electrical impulses. These tiny electrical impulses are then greatly amplified and fed into the theater loudspeaker system. If a motion picture has a stereo or quadraphonic sound track, multiple sound tracks are recorded on magnetic strips coated on the release print. The strips are read by a projector equipped with magnetic replay heads.

The screen. The typical theater screen is made of white plastic stretched on a metal or wooden frame. The screen is coated with millions of tiny glass beads. The beads make a highly reflective surface that looks equally bright no matter where the viewer sits in the theater. Screens vary in size, depending upon the size of the theater in which they are used. The trend has been toward smaller screens to fit the smaller multiple-screen theaters that have emerged in shopping centers during the late 1900's.

The sound system's loudspeakers are placed behind the screen, which has thousands of small holes that allow the sound to pass through. There are 20 to 30 holes per square inch (3 to 6 per square centimeter). The holes are too tiny to be seen by the audience, so the sound seems to come from the picture itself.

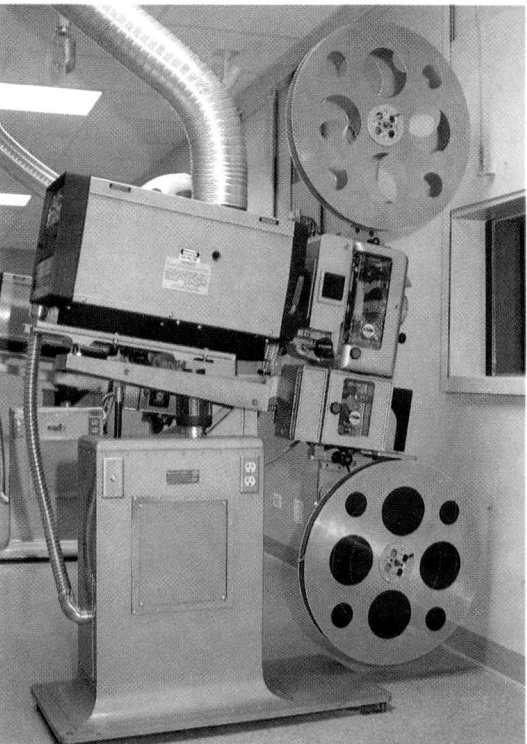

Cineplex Odeon Theatres (WORLD BOOK photo by Ralph Brunke)
A 35-millimeter projector is used to show motion pictures in theaters. The projector shown above is equipped with a soundhead that can convert the sound track into four-channel stereo.

Movies are a billion-dollar industry. Americans pay more than $4¼ billion yearly to see movies. The payroll for workers in the U.S. film industry totals about $6 billion. There are more than 23,000 screens showing movies throughout the United States.

The motion-picture industry is divided into three branches—production, distribution, and exhibition. From about 1915 to the late 1940's, large movie studios controlled all three branches of the U.S. movie industry. The studios not only made the films, they distributed them to the theaters, the biggest and most important of which they owned.

In 1948, the Supreme Court of the United States ruled that studio control over production, distribution, and exhibition was an illegal monopoly. The court ordered the motion-picture studios to give up their role as exhibitors. By 1953, most of the Hollywood studios had sold their movie theaters.

Also during the late 1940's, the studios began to curtail their role in the production of movies, partly because of economic competition from television. The studios discovered that, in most cases, they could earn more money by financing and distributing movies made by independent producers.

This section deals with the distribution and exhibition branches of the movie industry. For information about production see the section *How motion pictures are made.* This section also describes attempts by government and private organizations to censor movies and the industry's own attempts at self-regulation. The section ends with a discussion of film festivals and awards.

Distribution. Distributors are responsible for advertising the film and delivering it to its audience in theaters and in homes through television and videocassettes. Major studios serve as the distributor for most American films. The remainder are handled by independent distribution companies.

Some producers are able to secure distribution before the film is even made. At this early stage, distributors might be interested in the movie because of its star or because the film will be a sequel to a popular film. If the producers have not obtained distribution before filming, they usually wait until the final print of the film is made before presenting it to distributors.

The distributor charges the film's producer a fee of 30 to 50 per cent of all the money the film takes in. A new producer may have to pay a larger fee to attract a distributor than does an established producer with a record of profitable films. Distributors also charge for making the copies of the film sent to the theaters. In addition, they charge for advertising and publicizing the film. The costs of copying the film, advertising, and publicity come out of the first money the film takes in. The producer receives money only after these costs and the distribution fees have been deducted. The distributor can thus make a profit on a picture, while the film's producer may earn nothing.

After the producers and distributor arrange a distribution deal, the distributor carefully identifies the film's audience. The distributor generally arranges for *sneak previews* to judge the film's effectiveness and to identify its main audience. At a sneak preview, the distributor assembles an audience that may be chosen for such characteristics as age, income level, or occupation. During

the screening, the distributor's staff usually watches the audience, observing their reactions and level of enjoyment. Afterward, the audience may be asked to fill out information cards on their reaction to the film. They may also meet with the distributor's staff to discuss their reactions. After reviewing the preview responses, the distributor designs the advertising campaign and decides how to release the film most effectively. Sometimes the audience responses prompt the distributor to ask the producer to reedit or reshoot parts of the film.

Films with a broad appeal will receive widespread distribution, perhaps opening in more than 2,000 theaters across the country on the same day. Films with more specialized audience appeal generally open in a few carefully selected theaters in various cities. Widespread distribution is intended to quickly reach the broadest possible audience. The narrower or *platform* approach tries to build and sustain interest in the film over a period of time with good critical reviews and positive word-of-mouth from pleased viewers.

Most advertising campaigns are designed to make their heaviest impact for the first two or three weeks of a film's release. If the campaign attracts the right audience and these viewers enjoy the film, they will tell their friends and thus sell the movie to a new audience.

A second campaign is sometimes designed to appeal to a different portion of the public. For example, the film may be an action movie with a star not usually associated with action films. The first campaign might reach out to that part of the public interested in action movies. The second campaign would be designed to attract that part of the public interested in seeing the star. The advertising campaign and the film's theatrical release also prepare the way for the film's release on videocassette, which has become a major market for distributors. Some films are released directly on videocassette, bypassing theatrical release entirely.

If the motion picture can earn three times its budget in ticket sales during its first year of domestic release, the producers and their investors will begin to make a profit. The film will then be considered a commercial success. Other sources of revenue include foreign distribution and sales to broadcast and cable television.

Exhibition. Financial arrangements for exhibiting a movie can be extremely complicated and may vary from film to film. In the simplest arrangement, the distributor charges an exhibitor a flat fee. More commonly, however, the exhibitor pays the distributor a percentage of the weekly box-office profits (box office receipts minus theater operating expenses), often with a certain minimum payment guaranteed. For example, a distributor may require 90 cents of every dollar of profit from an exhibitor during the first week's ticket sales if the film is expected to be a hit. The percentage would then decline in succeeding weeks of the film's run at the theater. Typically, however, the exhibitor keeps about 50 cents out of every dollar collected from ticket sales. The other 50 cents goes for costs of distribution and production. The flat fee or percentage the exhibitor pays the distributor is called the film's *rental.*

Theater owners place bids with distributors for the films they want to exhibit. The limited number of films produced has forced exhibitors to bid higher and higher against one another for the right to rent especially desirable films. Exhibitors, in turn, have raised ticket prices. The higher prices have helped make the public more selective in its moviegoing. However, the industry still sells more than 1 billion movie tickets each year in the United States.

Censorship and self-regulation. During the first half of the 1900's, several state and local governments had censorship boards that reviewed all movies before they could be shown in their areas. Some civic and religious groups also had boards that advised members whether they believed a movie to be offensive.

Censorship remained an important factor in the American movie industry until the 1950's. Beginning in 1952, the Supreme Court made a series of decisions that undercut the legality of the local and state boards. In 1965, the last strong state censorship board—that of New York state—went out of existence.

The motion-picture industry's efforts to regulate itself date back to 1922, when the movie studios established the Motion Picture Producers and Distributors of America. This organization reviewed movie scripts before filming began, to delete material that the organization felt might be considered offensive.

In 1945, the organization became the Motion Picture Association of America. In 1968, the association adopted a classification system. Instead of reviewing scripts before production, the association rates the completed film as to its suitability for various ages. The association classifies films into five categories: *G*—general, all ages admitted; *PG*—all ages admitted, but parental guidance suggested; *PG-13*—all ages admitted, but parents are strongly cautioned to give special guidance for attendance by children under 13; *R*—restricted, persons under 17 must be accompanied by a parent or guardian; *NC-17* —persons under 17 not admitted.

Festivals and awards. The first major film festival was held in Venice, Italy, in 1932. Today, hundreds of festivals are held annually. The largest and probably best-known festival is held in Cannes, France. Other important festivals take place in Venice, Berlin, London, Moscow, New York City, and San Sebastián, Spain.

The best-known movie awards are made each spring by the Academy of Motion Picture Arts and Sciences.

© Academy of Motion Picture Arts and Sciences ®

The Oscar is a gold-plated bronze statue presented to winners of the Academy Awards. The statue received its name in 1931, when an Academy librarian said it resembled her Uncle Oscar.

These awards, called the *Academy Awards,* or *Oscars,* are presented for outstanding achievements in filmmaking during the preceding year.

A number of organizations of critics issue annual film awards, including the National Society of Film Critics and the New York Film Critics Circle. The Hollywood Foreign Press Association gives the annual Golden Globe Awards. The best-known awards given annually in other nations come from the British Academy of Film and Television Arts. Its awards resemble the Oscars.

Academy Award winners*

Best picture

1927-28	Wings	1950	All About Eve	1972	The Godfather
1928-29	The Broadway Melody	1951	An American in Paris	1973	The Sting
1929-30	All Quiet on the Western Front	1952	The Greatest Show on Earth	1974	The Godfather, Part II
1930-31	Cimarron	1953	From Here to Eternity	1975	One Flew Over the Cuckoo's Nest
1931-32	Grand Hotel	1954	On the Waterfront	1976	Rocky
1932-33	Cavalcade	1955	Marty	1977	Annie Hall
1934	It Happened One Night	1956	Around the World in 80 Days	1978	The Deer Hunter
1935	Mutiny on the Bounty	1957	The Bridge on the River Kwai	1979	Kramer vs. Kramer
1936	The Great Ziegfeld	1958	Gigi	1980	Ordinary People
1937	The Life of Émile Zola	1959	Ben-Hur	1981	Chariots of Fire
1938	You Can't Take It with You	1960	The Apartment	1982	Gandhi
1939	Gone with the Wind	1961	West Side Story	1983	Terms of Endearment
1940	Rebecca	1962	Lawrence of Arabia	1984	Amadeus
1941	How Green Was My Valley	1963	Tom Jones	1985	Out of Africa
1942	Mrs. Miniver	1964	My Fair Lady	1986	Platoon
1943	Casablanca	1965	The Sound of Music	1987	The Last Emperor
1944	Going My Way	1966	A Man for All Seasons	1988	Rain Man
1945	The Lost Weekend	1967	In the Heat of the Night	1989	Driving Miss Daisy
1946	The Best Years of Our Lives	1968	Oliver!	1990	Dances with Wolves
1947	Gentleman's Agreement	1969	Midnight Cowboy	1991	The Silence of the Lambs
1948	Hamlet	1970	Patton	1992	Unforgiven
1949	All the King's Men	1971	The French Connection		

*Academy Awards are presented each spring for outstanding achievements in filmmaking during the preceding year.

(Continued on next page)

Best achievement in directing

1927-28	Frank Borzage (*Seventh Heaven*),	1960	Billy Wilder (*The Apartment*)
	Lewis Milestone (*Two Arabian Knights*)	1961	Robert Wise and Jerome Robbins (*West Side Story*)
1928-29	Frank Lloyd (*The Divine Lady*)	1962	David Lean (*Lawrence of Arabia*)
1929-30	Lewis Milestone (*All Quiet on the Western Front*)	1963	Tony Richardson (*Tom Jones*)
1930-31	Norman Taurog (*Skippy*)	1964	George Cukor (*My Fair Lady*)
1931-32	Frank Borzage (*Bad Girl*)	1965	Robert Wise (*The Sound of Music*)
1932-33	Frank Lloyd (*Cavalcade*)	1966	Fred Zinnemann (*A Man for All Seasons*)
1934	Frank Capra (*It Happened One Night*)	1967	Mike Nichols (*The Graduate*)
1935	John Ford (*The Informer*)	1968	Sir Carol Reed (*Oliver!*)
1936	Frank Capra (*Mr. Deeds Goes to Town*)	1969	John Schlesinger (*Midnight Cowboy*)
1937	Leo McCarey (*The Awful Truth*)	1970	Franklin J. Schaffner (*Patton*)
1938	Frank Capra (*You Can't Take It with You*)	1971	William Friedkin (*The French Connection*)
1939	Victor Fleming (*Gone with the Wind*)	1972	Bob Fosse (*Cabaret*)
1940	John Ford (*The Grapes of Wrath*)	1973	George Roy Hill (*The Sting*)
1941	John Ford (*How Green Was My Valley*)	1974	Francis Ford Coppola (*The Godfather, Part II*)
1942	William Wyler (*Mrs. Miniver*)	1975	Milos Forman (*One Flew Over the Cuckoo's Nest*)
1943	Michael Curtiz (*Casablanca*)	1976	John Avildsen (*Rocky*)
1944	Leo McCarey (*Going My Way*)	1977	Woody Allen (*Annie Hall*)
1945	Billy Wilder (*The Lost Weekend*)	1978	Michael Cimino (*The Deer Hunter*)
1946	William Wyler (*The Best Years of Our Lives*)	1979	Robert Benton (*Kramer vs. Kramer*)
1947	Elia Kazan (*Gentleman's Agreement*)	1980	Robert Redford (*Ordinary People*)
1948	John Huston (*The Treasure of the Sierra Madre*)	1981	Warren Beatty (*Reds*)
1949	Joseph L. Mankiewicz (*A Letter to Three Wives*)	1982	Sir Richard Attenborough (*Gandhi*)
1950	Joseph L. Mankiewicz (*All About Eve*)	1983	James L. Brooks (*Terms of Endearment*)
1951	George Stevens (*A Place in the Sun*)	1984	Milos Forman (*Amadeus*)
1952	John Ford (*The Quiet Man*)	1985	Sydney Pollack (*Out of Africa*)
1953	Fred Zinnemann (*From Here to Eternity*)	1986	Oliver Stone (*Platoon*)
1954	Elia Kazan (*On the Waterfront*)	1987	Bernardo Bertolucci (*The Last Emperor*)
1955	Delbert Mann (*Marty*)	1988	Barry Levinson (*Rain Man*)
1956	George Stevens (*Giant*)	1989	Oliver Stone (*Born on the Fourth of July*)
1957	David Lean (*The Bridge on the River Kwai*)	1990	Kevin Costner (*Dances with Wolves*)
1958	Vincente Minnelli (*Gigi*)	1991	Jonathan Demme (*The Silence of the Lambs*)
1959	William Wyler (*Ben-Hur*)	1992	Clint Eastwood *(Unforgiven)*

Best performance by an actress

1927-28	Janet Gaynor (*Seventh Heaven, Street Angel, Sunrise*)	1961	Sophia Loren (*Two Women*)
		1962	Anne Bancroft (*The Miracle Worker*)
1928-29	Mary Pickford (*Coquette*)	1963	Patricia Neal (*Hud*)
1929-30	Norma Shearer (*The Divorcee*)	1964	Julie Andrews (*Mary Poppins*)
1930-31	Marie Dressler (*Min and Bill*)	1965	Julie Christie (*Darling*)
1931-32	Helen Hayes (*The Sin of Madelon Claudet*)	1966	Elizabeth Taylor (*Who's Afraid of Virginia Woolf?*)
1932-33	Katharine Hepburn (*Morning Glory*)	1967	Katharine Hepburn (*Guess Who's Coming to Dinner*)
1934	Claudette Colbert (*It Happened One Night*)		
1935	Bette Davis (*Dangerous*)	1968	Katharine Hepburn (*The Lion in Winter*),
1936	Luise Rainer (*The Great Ziegfeld*)		Barbra Streisand (*Funny Girl*)
1937	Luise Rainer (*The Good Earth*)	1969	Maggie Smith (*The Prime of Miss Jean Brodie*)
1938	Bette Davis (*Jezebel*)	1970	Glenda Jackson (*Women in Love*)
1939	Vivien Leigh (*Gone with the Wind*)	1971	Jane Fonda (*Klute*)
1940	Ginger Rogers (*Kitty Foyle*)	1972	Liza Minnelli (*Cabaret*)
1941	Joan Fontaine (*Suspicion*)	1973	Glenda Jackson (*A Touch of Class*)
1942	Greer Garson (*Mrs. Miniver*)	1974	Ellen Burstyn (*Alice Doesn't Live Here Anymore*)
1943	Jennifer Jones (*The Song of Bernadette*)	1975	Louise Fletcher (*One Flew Over the Cuckoo's Nest*)
1944	Ingrid Bergman (*Gaslight*)	1976	Faye Dunaway (*Network*)
1945	Joan Crawford (*Mildred Pierce*)	1977	Diane Keaton (*Annie Hall*)
1946	Olivia de Havilland (*To Each His Own*)	1978	Jane Fonda (*Coming Home*)
1947	Loretta Young (*The Farmer's Daughter*)	1979	Sally Field (*Norma Rae*)
1948	Jane Wyman (*Johnny Belinda*)	1980	Sissy Spacek (*Coal Miner's Daughter*)
1949	Olivia de Havilland (*The Heiress*)	1981	Katharine Hepburn (*On Golden Pond*)
1950	Judy Holliday (*Born Yesterday*)	1982	Meryl Streep (*Sophie's Choice*)
1951	Vivien Leigh (*A Streetcar Named Desire*)	1983	Shirley MacLaine (*Terms of Endearment*)
1952	Shirley Booth (*Come Back, Little Sheba*)	1984	Sally Field (*Places in the Heart*)
1953	Audrey Hepburn (*Roman Holiday*)	1985	Geraldine Page (*The Trip to Bountiful*)
1954	Grace Kelly (*The Country Girl*)	1986	Marlee Matlin (*Children of a Lesser God*)
1955	Anna Magnani (*The Rose Tattoo*)	1987	Cher (*Moonstruck*)
1956	Ingrid Bergman (*Anastasia*)	1988	Jodie Foster (*The Accused*)
1957	Joanne Woodward (*The Three Faces of Eve*)	1989	Jessica Tandy (*Driving Miss Daisy*)
1958	Susan Hayward (*I Want to Live!*)	1990	Kathy Bates (*Misery*)
1959	Simone Signoret (*Room at the Top*)	1991	Jodie Foster (*The Silence of the Lambs*)
1960	Elizabeth Taylor (*Butterfield 8*)	1992	Emma Thompson *(Howards End)*

Best performance by an actor

1927-28	Emil Jannings (*The Way of All Flesh, The Last Command*)	1944	Bing Crosby (*Going My Way*)
1928-29	Warner Baxter (*In Old Arizona*)	1945	Ray Milland (*The Lost Weekend*)
1929-30	George Arliss (*Disraeli*)	1946	Fredric March (*The Best Years of Our Lives*)
1930-31	Lionel Barrymore (*A Free Soul*)	1947	Ronald Colman (*A Double Life*)
1931-32	Fredric March (*Dr. Jekyll and Mr. Hyde*), Wallace Beery (*The Champ*)	1948	Laurence Olivier (*Hamlet*)
1932-33	Charles Laughton (*The Private Life of Henry VIII*)	1949	Broderick Crawford (*All the King's Men*)
1934	Clark Gable (*It Happened One Night*)	1950	José Ferrer (*Cyrano de Bergerac*)
1935	Victor McLaglen (*The Informer*)	1951	Humphrey Bogart (*The African Queen*)
1936	Paul Muni (*The Story of Louis Pasteur*)	1952	Gary Cooper (*High Noon*)
1937	Spencer Tracy (*Captains Courageous*)	1953	William Holden (*Stalag 17*)
1938	Spencer Tracy (*Boys Town*)	1954	Marlon Brando (*On the Waterfront*)
1939	Robert Donat (*Goodbye, Mr. Chips*)	1955	Ernest Borgnine (*Marty*)
1940	James Stewart (*The Philadelphia Story*)	1956	Yul Brynner (*The King and I*)
1941	Gary Cooper (*Sergeant York*)	1957	Alec Guinness (*The Bridge on the River Kwai*)
1942	James Cagney (*Yankee Doodle Dandy*)	1958	David Niven (*Separate Tables*)
1943	Paul Lukas (*Watch on the Rhine*)	1959	Charlton Heston (*Ben-Hur*)

Best performance by an actor *(continued)*

1960	Burt Lancaster (*Elmer Gantry*)		1978	Jon Voight (*Coming Home*)
1961	Maximilian Schell (*Judgment at Nuremberg*)		1979	Dustin Hoffman (*Kramer vs. Kramer*)
1962	Gregory Peck (*To Kill a Mockingbird*)		1980	Robert De Niro (*Raging Bull*)
1963	Sidney Poitier (*Lilies of the Field*)		1981	Henry Fonda (*On Golden Pond*)
1964	Rex Harrison (*My Fair Lady*)		1982	Ben Kingsley (*Gandhi*)
1965	Lee Marvin (*Cat Ballou*)		1983	Robert Duvall (*Tender Mercies*)
1966	Paul Scofield (*A Man for All Seasons*)		1984	F. Murray Abraham (*Amadeus*)
1967	Rod Steiger (*In the Heat of the Night*)		1985	William Hurt (*Kiss of the Spider Woman*)
1968	Cliff Robertson (*Charly*)		1986	Paul Newman (*The Color of Money*)
1969	John Wayne (*True Grit*)		1987	Michael Douglas (*Wall Street*)
1970	George C. Scott (*Patton*)		1988	Dustin Hoffman (*Rain Man*)
1971	Gene Hackman (*The French Connection*)		1989	Daniel Day-Lewis (*My Left Foot*)
1972	Marlon Brando (*The Godfather*)		1990	Jeremy Irons (*Reversal of Fortune*)
1973	Jack Lemmon (*Save the Tiger*)		1991	Anthony Hopkins (*The Silence of the Lambs*)
1974	Art Carney (*Harry and Tonto*)		1992	Al Pacino (*Scent of a Woman*)
1975	Jack Nicholson (*One Flew Over the Cuckoo's Nest*)			
1976	Peter Finch (*Network*)			
1977	Richard Dreyfuss (*The Goodbye Girl*)			

Best performance by an actor in a supporting role

1927-35	No Award
1936	Walter Brennan (*Come and Get It*)
1937	Joseph Schildkraut (*The Life of Émile Zola*)
1938	Walter Brennan (*Kentucky*)
1939	Thomas Mitchell (*Stagecoach*)
1940	Walter Brennan (*The Westerner*)
1941	Donald Crisp (*How Green Was My Valley*)
1942	Van Heflin (*Johnny Eager*)
1943	Charles Coburn (*The More the Merrier*)
1944	Barry Fitzgerald (*Going My Way*)
1945	James Dunn (*A Tree Grows in Brooklyn*)
1946	Harold Russell (*The Best Years of Our Lives*)
1947	Edmund Gwenn (*Miracle on 34th Street*)
1948	Walter Huston (*The Treasure of the Sierra Madre*)
1949	Dean Jagger (*Twelve O'Clock High*)
1950	George Sanders (*All About Eve*)
1951	Karl Malden (*A Streetcar Named Desire*)
1952	Anthony Quinn (*Viva Zapata!*)
1953	Frank Sinatra (*From Here to Eternity*)
1954	Edmond O'Brien (*The Barefoot Contessa*)
1955	Jack Lemmon (*Mister Roberts*)
1956	Anthony Quinn (*Lust for Life*)
1957	Red Buttons (*Sayonara*)
1958	Burl Ives (*The Big Country*)
1959	Hugh Griffith (*Ben-Hur*)
1960	Peter Ustinov (*Spartacus*)
1961	George Chakiris (*West Side Story*)
1962	Ed Begley (*Sweet Bird of Youth*)
1963	Melvyn Douglas (*Hud*)
1964	Peter Ustinov (*Topkapi*)
1965	Martin Balsam (*A Thousand Clowns*)
1966	Walter Matthau (*The Fortune Cookie*)
1967	George Kennedy (*Cool Hand Luke*)
1968	Jack Albertson (*The Subject Was Roses*)
1969	Gig Young (*They Shoot Horses, Don't They?*)
1970	John Mills (*Ryan's Daughter*)
1971	Ben Johnson (*The Last Picture Show*)
1972	Joel Grey (*Cabaret*)
1973	John Houseman (*The Paper Chase*)
1974	Robert De Niro (*The Godfather, Part II*)
1975	George Burns (*The Sunshine Boys*)
1976	Jason Robards (*All the President's Men*)
1977	Jason Robards (*Julia*)
1978	Christopher Walken (*The Deer Hunter*)
1979	Melvyn Douglas (*Being There*)
1980	Timothy Hutton (*Ordinary People*)
1981	Sir John Gielgud (*Arthur*)
1982	Louis Gossett, Jr. (*An Officer and a Gentleman*)
1983	Jack Nicholson (*Terms of Endearment*)
1984	Haing S. Ngor (*The Killing Fields*)
1985	Don Ameche (*Cocoon*)
1986	Michael Caine (*Hannah and Her Sisters*)
1987	Sean Connery (*The Untouchables*)
1988	Kevin Kline (*A Fish Called Wanda*)
1989	Denzel Washington (*Glory*)
1990	Joe Pesci (*GoodFellas*)
1991	Jack Palance (*City Slickers*)
1992	Gene Hackman (*Unforgiven*)

Best performance by an actress in a supporting role

1927-35	No Award
1936	Gale Sondergaard (*Anthony Adverse*)
1937	Alice Brady (*In Old Chicago*)
1938	Fay Bainter (*Jezebel*)
1939	Hattie McDaniel (*Gone with the Wind*)
1940	Jane Darwell (*The Grapes of Wrath*)
1941	Mary Astor (*The Great Lie*)
1942	Teresa Wright (*Mrs. Miniver*)
1943	Katina Paxinou (*For Whom the Bell Tolls*)
1944	Ethel Barrymore (*None But the Lonely Heart*)
1945	Anne Revere (*National Velvet*)
1946	Anne Baxter (*The Razor's Edge*)
1947	Celeste Holm (*Gentleman's Agreement*)
1948	Claire Trevor (*Key Largo*)
1949	Mercedes McCambridge (*All the King's Men*)
1950	Josephine Hull (*Harvey*)
1951	Kim Hunter (*A Streetcar Named Desire*)
1952	Gloria Grahame (*The Bad and the Beautiful*)
1953	Donna Reed (*From Here to Eternity*)
1954	Eva Marie Saint (*On the Waterfront*)
1955	Jo Van Fleet (*East of Eden*)
1956	Dorothy Malone (*Written on the Wind*)
1957	Miyoshi Umeki (*Sayonara*)
1958	Wendy Hiller (*Separate Tables*)
1959	Shelley Winters (*The Diary of Anne Frank*)
1960	Shirley Jones (*Elmer Gantry*)
1961	Rita Moreno (*West Side Story*)
1962	Patty Duke (*The Miracle Worker*)
1963	Margaret Rutherford (*The V.I.P.s*)
1964	Lila Kedrova (*Zorba the Greek*)
1965	Shelley Winters (*A Patch of Blue*)
1966	Sandy Dennis (*Who's Afraid of Virginia Woolf?*)
1967	Estelle Parsons (*Bonnie and Clyde*)
1968	Ruth Gordon (*Rosemary's Baby*)
1969	Goldie Hawn (*Cactus Flower*)
1970	Helen Hayes (*Airport*)
1971	Cloris Leachman (*The Last Picture Show*)
1972	Eileen Heckart (*Butterflies Are Free*)
1973	Tatum O'Neal (*Paper Moon*)
1974	Ingrid Bergman (*Murder on the Orient Express*)
1975	Lee Grant (*Shampoo*)
1976	Beatrice Straight (*Network*)
1977	Vanessa Redgrave (*Julia*)
1978	Maggie Smith (*California Suite*)
1979	Meryl Streep (*Kramer vs. Kramer*)
1980	Mary Steenburgen (*Melvin and Howard*)
1981	Maureen Stapleton (*Reds*)
1982	Jessica Lange (*Tootsie*)
1983	Linda Hunt (*The Year of Living Dangerously*)
1984	Dame Peggy Ashcroft (*A Passage to India*)
1985	Anjelica Huston (*Prizzi's Honor*)
1986	Dianne Wiest (*Hannah and Her Sisters*)
1987	Olympia Dukakis (*Moonstruck*)
1988	Geena Davis (*The Accidental Tourist*)
1989	Brenda Fricker (*My Left Foot*)
1990	Whoopi Goldberg (*Ghost*)
1991	Mercedes Ruehl (*The Fisher King*)
1992	Marisa Tomei (*My Cousin Vinnie*)

The first successful photographs of motion were pictures of a horse. Eadweard Muybridge, a British photographer in the United States, took them in the 1870's using a row of still cameras.

Since earliest times, people have been interested in portraying things in motion. During the late 1800's, developments in science helped stimulate a series of inventions that led to projected motion pictures on celluloid film. These inventions laid the foundation for a new industry and a new art form.

The first successful photographs of motion were made in 1877 and 1878 by Eadweard Muybridge, a British photographer working in California. Muybridge took a series of photographs of a running horse. For his project, Muybridge set up a row of cameras (first 12, then 24) with strings attached to their shutters. When the horse ran by, it broke each string in succession, tripping the shutters.

The invention of motion pictures. Muybridge's feat influenced inventors in several countries to work toward developing devices to record and re-present movie images. These inventors included Thomas Armat, Thomas Alva Edison, C. Francis Jenkins, and Woodville Latham in the United States; William Friese-Greene and Robert W. Paul in Great Britain; and the brothers Louis Jean and Auguste Lumière and Etienne-Jules Marey in France. Through their efforts, several different types of motion-picture cameras and projectors appeared in the mid-1890's.

Edison's company displayed the first commercial motion-picture machine at the World's Columbian Exposition in 1893. Edison called his machine the *kinetoscope*. It was a cabinet showing unenlarged 35-millimeter black-and-white films running about 90 seconds. An individual watched through a peephole as the film moved on spools. Kinetoscope parlors opened in a number of cities. However, they were soon replaced by projection machines that threw greatly enlarged pictures on a screen. These new machines allowed many people to view a single film at the same time.

The Lumière brothers held a public screening of projected motion pictures on Dec. 28, 1895, in a Paris cafe. Edison, adapting a projector developed by Armat, presented the first public exhibition of projected motion pictures in the United States on April 23, 1896, in a New York City music hall.

Early motion pictures. Film screenings soon became a popular entertainment. In large cities, motion pictures played on vaudeville programs, in music halls, and in amusement arcades. Traveling projectionists brought the films to smaller cities and country towns. The most popular subjects included re-creations of current news events, such as battles in the Spanish-American War of 1898, and dramatized folk tales.

Films were made without recorded synchronized sound. However, exhibitors sometimes accompanied the images with music or lectures, or even used off-screen live actors to provide dialogue. Later, printed *titles* were inserted within the films. The titles gave dialogue, descriptions of action, or commentary. Titles permitted the international circulation of films, because translated titles could easily replace the originals.

Edison's company dominated the early years of American moviemaking through its control of patents on filmmaking equipment. Edwin S. Porter, who worked for Edison as a director and cameraman, became a leader in shifting film production from current events toward storytelling. Porter's 1903 film, *The Great Train Robbery*, portrayed a train robbery and the pursuit and capture of the robbers. The 11-minute Western became a sensational hit.

The nickelodeon. Porter's film and the storytelling movies that followed opened the way for a major breakthrough in motion-picture exhibition—the *nickelodeon* theater. Beginning about 1905, thousands of these theaters opened in American cities, mostly in commercial

The first important movie was *The Great Train Robbery,* *above,* directed by Edwin S. Porter in 1903. It described a train robbery and the pursuit and capture of the bandits. Porter was the first director to use modern film techniques to tell a story.

The first movie theaters were called *nickelodeons.* Most nickelodeons were stores converted into theaters by adding chairs. They charged 5 cents. They showed silent movies, while a pianist played music that suited the action on the screen.

areas or in immigrant neighborhoods. Many small stores were converted to nickelodeons by adding a screen and folding chairs. Admission was only 5 cents, much less than competing entertainment. Nickelodeons attracted a large new audience for movies, and laid the foundation for the growing profitability and expansion of the movie industry.

The birth of Hollywood. In the early years of American filmmaking, most movies were produced in New York City and New Jersey, though some were made in Chicago, Florida, and elsewhere. As the industry developed, filmmakers began working more and more in southern California. They were drawn by a climate suitable for year-round outdoor shooting and by the availability of varied scenery.

By the time World War I broke out in Europe in 1914, a number of companies had established studios in and around the Hollywood district of Los Angeles. After the war ended in 1918, American movies became dominant worldwide and the name "Hollywood" came to stand for the values and style of American movies.

D. W. Griffith was the most influential film director during the early years of Hollywood. Griffith pioneered many of the stylistic features and filmmaking techniques that became established as the Hollywood standard. His work brought wider appreciation to the movies as art and helped films attract a more educated and wealthier audience.

Griffith directed hundreds of short films between 1908 and 1913, and a number of feature-length films in later years. Throughout his career, which ended about 1930, he advanced a variety of stylistic improvements. Many filmmakers before and after Griffith regarded movies as filmed theater. They placed the camera a set distance from the performers, photographing the scene from a single viewpoint as a spectator would see it in the theater. Griffith liberated camera movement. He continually shifted the camera to different distances from the action. He established the close-up shot of a face, a part of a body, or an object as a basic part of film style. Using the close-up, Griffith also led his players toward an acting style of greater realism and psychological

The Birth of a Nation, directed by D. W. Griffith in 1915, was the first American motion-picture epic. The film dealt with the American Civil War and the period that followed. The movie featured spectacular battle scenes.

depth than was common at that time.

Griffith also revolutionized film editing. Instead of filming an entire scene in one shot, or a few shots, he broke up scenes into many shots, filming from different angles and distances. He extended this idea of film editing to include action at different locations so that the story moved swiftly from place to place in a style called *cross-cutting*. Griffith emphasized a quicker tempo of shots, of movement from place to place, and movement within a scene. As a result, his films established a breadth, freedom, and swift pace that characterized the treatment of time and space in later American motion pictures.

Griffith's most famous, and controversial, work was the epic *The Birth of a Nation* (1915). The film portrayed the American Civil War (1861-1865) and the following Reconstruction period through the eyes of two families, one Northern and one Southern. The film was praised as the first great American work of cinema art, but also criticized as racist for its portrayal of blacks and its sympathetic treatment of the Ku Klux Klan.

Movies become big business. About the time *The Birth of a Nation* was released, movie companies were developing a "star system" similar to those of other performing arts, such as theater and opera. Publicizing performers became the most effective means of promoting movies and attracting large audiences. The first highly paid and most popular motion-picture stars included dramatic performers Douglas Fairbanks, Sr., and Mary Pickford, cowboy actor William S. Hart, and comedian Charlie Chaplin.

Before World War I, foreign-made films were strong competition for American movies in the United States, especially mystery serials from France and historical epics from Italy. But during the war, European governments diverted raw material from their film industries for military needs. American movie companies seized the opportunity to become the world's strongest film industry. Their successes enabled producers to spend money on lavish costumes and expensive sets. The studios created a sense of glamour around American motion-picture stars that appealed to audiences throughout the world.

Within the United States, competition among movie companies led the most powerful studios toward *vertical integration*. This term describes the system in which a studio owned production facilities, distribution channels, and movie theaters. Vertical integration gave the studios control of all three major elements of filmmaking: production, distribution, and exhibition.

A few movie companies came to dominate the industry—Columbia, Fox, Metro-Goldwyn-Mayer, Paramount, RKO, United Artists, Universal, and Warner Brothers. They adopted a system in which producers supervised a movie's development from script to postproduction. Producers, who were usually businessmen rather than film artists, kept a close watch on budgets and schedules. As far as possible, all the people working on the film—the director, writers, designers, crew, and cast—were drawn from the studio payroll.

Vertical integration enabled the companies to use their studio stages efficiently and maintain a high volume of production. But the system placed an even greater emphasis on movie stars and familiar, repeatable *genre* movies. A genre film is a specific type, such as a Western or a crime melodrama.

Filmmaking in Europe. While American movies remained popular and profitable, more demanding viewers in the 1920's began to look to Europe for new developments in film art. Moviemakers in European countries often competed against American domination of their own theaters by developing distinctive film styles. This goal was perhaps achieved most successfully in Germany. There, many film directors, writers, and designers were also active in other arts, including painting and live theater.

In subject matter, German filmmakers stressed fantasy and legend, and also an intense psychological realism not often attempted in American films. The Germans often treated themes in a style drawn from a movement in the arts called *expressionism* (see **Expressionism**). Expressionist films used nonrealistic sets and unusual camera angles to represent a character's inner feelings. The best-known and most influential expressionist film was *The Cabinet of Dr. Caligari* (1919), directed by Robert Wiene.

One artistic approach in German cinema stressed lighting and camera movement. German filmmakers created a threatening visual mood to accompany their tales of the supernatural by making scenes darker than normal and by emphasizing contrasting light and shadow. A famous example is the horror movie *Nosferatu* (1922), directed by Friedrich Murnau. The same director also made *The Last Laugh* (1924), which told its story entirely through the visual images of the camera, eliminating descriptive and dialogue titles.

Filmmaking made advances in Russia, too, particularly after the Bolshevik (Communist) revolution of 1917. In 1922, the Soviet Union was formed under Russia's leadership, and it existed until 1991. In the Soviet Union, movies gained attention as an important medium for education and propaganda. Soviet filmmakers emphasized

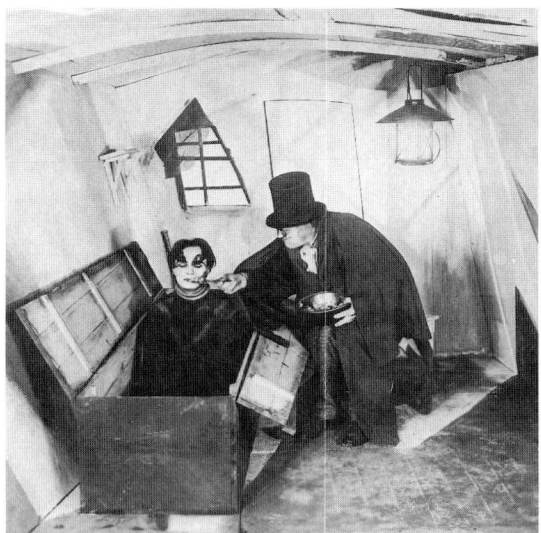

Kobal Collection/SuperStock

The Cabinet of Dr. Caligari (1919) was a famous silent German horror film. The distorted sets reflect the twisted mind of the madman who narrates the story.

film editing, refining the *montage.* Montage is a technique in which many separate shots are used to create a single point.

Soviet director Sergei Eisenstein developed theories of how the arrangement of shots could create associations in the mind of the audience and stimulate emotions and ideas (see **Eisenstein, Sergei Mikhailovich**). Eisenstein put his ideas into practice in such important films as *The Battleship Potemkin* (1925), which raised the Soviet silent cinema to equality with German films in artistic prestige and influence.

The silent film classics from Germany and the Soviet Union, as well as France, Scandinavia, and elsewhere, were not experienced as silent by audiences. In most large theaters, the films were accompanied by music, often prepared specifically for the film and played by a large orchestra.

American film companies showed their respect for European artistic advances by inviting many foreign filmmakers from Germany, Sweden, Great Britain, and elsewhere to work in Hollywood. Friedrich Murnau moved to Hollywood about 1926. Even more widely known were performers like Sweden's Greta Garbo, who became one of the greatest stars of American motion pictures.

The movies talk. During the 1920's, engineers in the United States and Germany were working to develop a technology that could add synchronous recorded sound to movies. By the mid-1920's, a few systems were ready for demonstration.

The first sound film to create a sensation was *The Jazz Singer* (1927). Although silent for much of its length, in a few scenes the popular American entertainer Al Jolson sang and spoke in synchronous sound. The film used a system in which the sound from a mechanically re-corded disc was mechanically synchronized with the film strip. This system was soon replaced by one that used electronic signals to record the sound directly on the film strip. The sound-on-film system was widely used by 1929.

The coming of sound marked a turning point in motion-picture history. Some historians claim sound was actually a setback for the artistic development of movies. The emphasis on sound, and the expense of developing it, limited other technological advances that filmmakers had been experimenting with in the 1920's. For instance, a wide-screen process demonstrated by French director Abel Gance in *Napoléon* (1927) was not generally introduced until the 1950's. What was affected the most, perhaps, was a kind of poetic cinema represented by such silent films as *The Passion of Joan of Arc* (1928), directed by Carl Dreyer of Denmark. Such films survived more as an experimental art form than as part of mainstream commercial motion pictures.

With the introduction of sound, motion pictures went through an awkward period of adjustment. Cameras had to be enclosed in soundproof boxes because the microphones picked up motor noise. More importantly, directors had to learn how best to take advantage of sound. But this adjustment period was brief. By 1931, one of Germany's major silent film directors, Fritz Lang, had made *M,* a sound film that remains a masterpiece of cinema. In 1928, Walt Disney issued *Steamboat Willie,* the first animated short film to use synchronized sound. For more information about animation in motion pictures, see **Animation; Disney, Walt**.

In Hollywood, sound introduced greater changes in personnel than in film style. Sound brought with it a flood of directors, dialogue writers, and, especially, performers from the Broadway theater. A number of silent

Hollywood musicals of the 1930's became noted for their elaborate staging. Dance director Busby Berkeley staged this spectacular World War I musical number in *Gold Diggers of 1933.*

Scene from *Gold Diggers of 1933* (1933), directed by Mervyn Le Roy; the John Springer Collection, Bettmann Archive

screen stars, notably Greta Garbo and the comedy team of Stan Laurel and Oliver Hardy, successfully made the transition to sound. However, others did not, either because of unsuitable voices or problems with what the studios considered excessive salaries.

Movies in the 1930's. Two important new genres in American movies came from Broadway in the 1930's, the musical and the gangster picture. Both came to symbolize Hollywood's contribution to national culture during the Great Depression that followed the stock market crash of 1929. Gangster films like *The Public Enemy* (1931), directed by William Wellman, and *Scarface* (1932), directed by Howard Hawks, dramatized the violence and disorder that accompanied the illegal manufacture and sale of alcoholic beverages during the prohibition era (1919-1933). Such musicals as *Gold Diggers of 1933* (1933) portrayed a spirit of cooperation and optimism intended to combat the economic depression. The film was one of many Hollywood musicals in the 1930's that featured spectacular dance sequences created by Busby Berkeley.

The Great Depression had a strong impact on the American film industry. Interest in sound pictures had nearly doubled annual movie theater attendance in the late 1920's. But the economic crisis greatly reduced attendance, causing many theaters to close. Nearly all the movie companies lost money, and several declared bankruptcy. No major studios shut down, however.

By the mid-1930's, American movie companies again began to prosper. They launched what many consider one of the greatest periods of popular entertainment filmmaking. During the middle and late 1930's, Hollywood produced major hits in nearly all the familiar genres. In particular, the horror film gained new prominence and the sound comedy emerged as a leading film style. The horror cycle actually began in 1931 with *Dracula,* directed by Tod Browning, and *Frankenstein,* directed by James Whale.

Among the comedy films of the 1930's, one of the most popular types was the *screwball comedy.* These movies often portrayed the zany antics of wealthy characters. One classic screwball comedy was *It Happened One Night* (1934), directed by Frank Capra and starring Clark Gable and Claudette Colbert. Another example

Kobal Collection/SuperStock

Screwball comedies were popular during the 1930's. Many portrayed the zany antics of wealthy characters. Katharine Hepburn and Cary Grant starred in *Bringing Up Baby* (1938).

was *Bringing Up Baby* (1938), directed by Howard Hawks and starring Cary Grant and Katharine Hepburn.

The arrival of sound gave new emphasis to the role of language in cinema. Many countries strengthened their film industries out of national pride in their language and culture. Some countries restricted the importation of American movies, in order to encourage their domestic film industry. In most countries, the dialogue of foreign films was translated into the home language. In the United States, however, such films were almost always played in their original version, with printed English subtitles projected on the bottom of the film.

The leading film-producing nations of Europe during the silent era, Germany and the Soviet Union, were displaced during the first decade of sound movies by Great Britain and France. Alfred Hitchcock led the emergence of British cinema. Hitchcock directed a number of internationally successful thrillers, including *The Thirty-Nine Steps* (1935) and *The Lady Vanishes* (1938). In France, Jean Renoir made a series of films during the 1930's that shrewdly observed social attitudes of the time, notably

Robert Donat and Madeleine Carroll in a scene from *The Thirty-Nine Steps* (1935); Bettmann Archive

The Thirty-Nine Steps was one of director Alfred Hitchcock's earliest successes. He made the thriller in England in 1935. Hitchcock later settled in the United States. His best English and American suspense films are noted for their humorous touches and their brilliant camerawork.

Culver

Grand Illusion was a classic antiwar film directed by Jean Renoir of France in 1937. The motion picture is set in a German prisoner of war camp for officers in 1917, during World War I.

Grand Illusion (1937) and *Rules of the Game* (1939).

The rise of dictatorships in Germany and the Soviet Union hampered filmmaking in those countries during the 1930's. After Adolf Hitler seized power in Germany in 1933, a number of German filmmakers went into exile. Many settled in the United States. Fritz Lang began an important career as an American film director with *Fury* (1936). Renoir went to Hollywood after the German conquest of France early in World War II (1939-1945). Hitchcock had already left Great Britain for Hollywood in 1939, though not for political reasons.

The United States did not enter the war until late 1941, and America's prewar period closed triumphantly with two celebrated films. One was *Gone with the Wind* (1939), a Civil War drama directed by Victor Fleming and starring Clark Gable and Vivien Leigh. The other was *Citizen Kane* (1941). A young American director and actor named Orson Welles produced, directed, and starred in this story of a powerful American newspaper publisher. In this film, Welles and his cinematographer, Gregg Toland, experimented with startling camera angles and dramatic lighting techniques. The film's brilliant photography helped make it one of the most honored films in cinema history.

Movies and World War II. The role of movies in education and propaganda was far more appreciated during World War II than in World War I. After the United States entered the conflict, Hollywood contributed to the war effort through traditional entertainment movies and through government service. Fiction films like *Casablanca* (1943) dramatized the war struggle using the traditional screen narrative devices of a love story and individual heroism. The film, directed by Michael Curtiz and

starring Humphrey Bogart and Ingrid Bergman, became one of the most popular motion pictures in American film history.

American directors such as John Ford, William Wyler, John Huston, and George Stevens entered military service and produced important documentary films about the war. Working for the U.S. Army Signal Corps, Frank Capra supervised the "Why We Fight" documentary series, which explained the causes of the war and American war aims.

Postwar realism. The impact of the war led many European directors to make movies that focused on society and its problems. This impulse resulted in the emergence of the first important postwar European film movement, *neorealism.*

Neorealist directors were concerned primarily with portraying the daily life of ordinary people. They mainly filmed on location rather than on a studio set, and they used mostly nonprofessional actors and actresses. These qualities gave neorealist films a gritty, almost documentary look.

Italian director Roberto Rossellini made the first internationally significant neorealist films. Rossellini's *Open City* (1945) and *Paisan* (1946) told of the struggle to liberate wartime Italy from its own Fascist government and the later German occupation of the country. Probably the most famous of the neorealist films was *The Bicycle Thieves* (1948), directed by Vittorio de Sica. It follows a workingman and his young son as they search for a stolen bicycle. The Italian government regarded the treatment of social problems in these films as harmful to the country's image internationally and passed a law in 1949 hampering their export. The law effectively ended the neorealism movement in Italy.

Bettmann Archive

Orson Welles produced, directed, and starred in *Citizen Kane* (1941). This biography of a powerful newspaper publisher is famous for its experimental photographic effects.

Scene from *The Bicycle Thieves* (1949),
directed by Vittorio De Sica; Culver Pictures

Italian films gained international attention after World War II with such realistic movies as *The Bicycle Thieves*. The film concerned a man and his son searching for a stolen bicycle.

Thanks to the international impact of neorealism, films and filmmakers previously little known outside their home countries began to gain international recognition. Some of this acclaim resulted from screenings at film festivals. Japanese director Akira Kurosawa brought attention to his country's distinguished film tradition with *Rashomon* (1950). The Latin-American film industry gained recognition with *Los Olvidados* (1950), made in Mexico by Spanish director Luis Buñuel.

Postwar American movies. Like European filmmakers, many American directors entered the postwar era with a desire to make films that were socially relevant. But political, legal, and economic influences led Hollywood to fall back on familiar genres. The conservative political atmosphere of the postwar years discouraged filmmakers from taking risks in subject matter. In 1948, the U.S. Supreme Court effectively banned vertical integration by requiring studios to rid themselves of their theaters, thus eliminating studio control of movie exhibitions. The studio system suffered from that court ruling

and declining film attendance in the early 1950's due to the increasing popularity of television. Studios never regained the power they once had.

Year after year during the 1950's, movie attendance steadily decreased. There was a brief upswing in 1953 and 1954 when the industry introduced wide-screen processes such as CinemaScope and Cinerama. These processes temporarily lured the curious away from their television sets. Still, Hollywood's production volume fell from about 550 films per year before World War II to about 250 a year during the 1950's. Independent production began to take over from the studio system, though studios still functioned as distributors. International co-productions became common, mingling stars from many countries.

The art film revival. The reduction in Hollywood film production created renewed interest in art films, much as in the 1920's. During the 1950's, a number of theaters in the United States specialized in showing films by foreign directors. Serious filmgoers sought out works by such directors as Federico Fellini of Italy and Ingmar Bergman of Sweden. Fellini became known for such highly personal comedy-dramas as *La Strada* (1954) and *Nights of Caberia* (1957). Bergman won fame for such brooding and symbolic dramas as *The Seventh Seal* and *Wild Strawberries* (both 1957). Such motion pictures reminded American moviegoers of the possibilities of film art—at a time when many people saw Hollywood as a place dominated by gimmicks and old, overworked formulas.

The New Wave in France. One place where the Hollywood movie remained appreciated was France. There, young film critics praised John Ford, Howard Hawks, and certain other studio directors for bringing a unique visual style and personal viewpoint to standard genre films. Under the influence of critical writings from France, the artistic qualities of Hollywood films began to be appreciated more than ever before.

The chief goal of the young French critics, however, was to revive what they saw as a stuffy French film industry. Leaving writing for directing, they were to become leaders of the French *New Wave.* Their impact on filmmaking of the 1960's was as profound as that of Italian neorealism several years earlier. Such films as *The 400 Blows* (1959), directed by François Truffaut, and

Max Von Sydow, *right,* in a scene from *The Seventh Seal* (1957); Culver

The Seventh Seal helped make Swedish director Ingmar Bergman one of the most widely discussed directors in motion-picture history. Bergman gained fame for a series of films that combined dramatic photography, sensitive acting, and often obscure philosophical and religious themes.

Jean-Paul Belmondo and Jean Seberg in a scene from *Breathless* (1960); Bettmann Archive

Breathless was one of the first New Wave hits. It was directed by Jean-Luc Godard and based on a story by François Truffaut, who later became a major New Wave director.

Breathless (1960), directed by Jean-Luc Godard, marked the emergence of a new generation of influential movie directors.

Claude Chabrol is credited with starting the New Wave with *Le Beau Serge* (1958). Louis Malle gained recognition as an important New Wave director with *The Lovers* (1958). Other major directors who emerged from the New Wave included Jacques Rivette and Eric Rohmer.

The years 1959 and 1960 proved to be a key moment in cinema development. Besides the works of Truffaut and Godard, a number of other films showed that a widespread artistic revival was underway. These films included *Hiroshima, Mon Amour* (1959), a French film

Peter Bull, *left*, and Peter Sellers, *right*, in a scene from *Dr. Strangelove* (1964); Granger Collection

Dr. Strangelove was a 1964 film that created controversy because it took a comic and satirical view of the possibility of a nuclear war between the United States and the Soviet Union.

directed by Alain Resnais; Fellini's *La Dolce Vita* (1960); and Alfred Hitchcock's *Psycho* (1960).

Movies in the 1960's. The decade of the 1960's saw the appearance of *Cinema Novo* in Brazil, a movement that resembled neorealism. It attempted to combine political subject matter with bold cinema techniques. Such directors as Nagisa Oshima in Japan and Bernardo Bertolucci in Italy became part of the international film scene. Stanley Kubrick, an American director working in England, made a number of popular and influential films. The best known was *Dr. Strangelove or: How I Learned to Stop Worrying and Love the Bomb* (1964). The film is a dark comedy that satirizes the serious subjects of conflict between the United States and the Soviet Union and the threat of nuclear destruction. Kubrick also directed *2001: A Space Odyssey* (1968), a science-fiction work about future space travel and humanity's self-renewal.

During the 1960's, Eastern European films made their mark on the world scene for the first time. Polish director Roman Polanski's *Knife in the Water* (1962) was the first major international success from Eastern Europe. Czechoslovak cinema soon captured worldwide attention with a series of comic films that criticized social and political conditions. The best known included *Loves of a Blonde* (1965) and *The Firemen's Ball* (1967), directed by Milos Forman; and *Closely Watched Trains* (1966), directed by Jiri Menzel. These movies were popular with audiences but not with government officials, and the movement ended when Soviet troops invaded Czechoslovakia in 1968.

Several Eastern European filmmakers, including Polanski and Forman, emigrated to Hollywood, where they could pursue their craft with greater artistic freedom. Forman won the 1975 Academy Award as best director for *One Flew Over the Cuckoo's Nest.*

For several reasons, the American film industry did not fully participate in the world cinema renaissance of the 1960's. Theater attendance continued to suffer in the United States from the availability on television of both old and more recent films, as well as made-for-TV movies. Traditional methods and higher production costs slowed the Hollywood studios' response to new trends and younger talents. Only in the late 1960's did opportunities open up for a new generation of filmmakers. Their impact began to be felt in the 1970's, stimulated by new ways in which motion pictures were marketed to the public.

Changes in Hollywood. For many years, movies were released slowly, first in a few big cities, then fanning out across the country to smaller cities and towns. In the early 1970's, the movie companies discovered that they might gain greater financial returns by releasing a film in hundreds of cities at the same time, supported by national television advertising.

The new distribution method was used experimentally on director Francis Ford Coppola's *The Godfather* (1972), a much-anticipated film based on a best-selling novel about organized crime. The results were impressive. *The Godfather* became the most commercially successful film produced to that time—dethroning *Gone with the Wind,* which had reigned as box-office champion for more than 30 years. In addition, Coppola was the first of Hollywood's younger directors to make a

Marlon Brando in a scene from *The Godfather* (1972); © Steve Schapiro, Gamma/Liaison

The Godfather was a dramatic account of two generations of a family in the United States who live by organized crime. The motion picture set box-office records in the early 1970's.

major impact. His success helped open the door for other young filmmakers.

Steven Spielberg and George Lucas became the most successful of the new generation of filmmakers who surfaced in the 1970's. They established a remarkable record for producing and directing popular films, be-

ginning with *Jaws* (1975), directed by Spielberg. Lucas' science-fiction movie *Star Wars* (1977) was the first of many highly popular new movies to come from Hollywood's own adventure, military, and science-fiction genres instead of a best-selling book.

Spielberg and Lucas succeeded with old-fashioned genre movies modernized with spectacular visual effects. Lucas produced two more films in the *Star Wars* series, *The Empire Strikes Back* (1980) and *Return of the Jedi* (1983). Spielberg and Lucas teamed up to make three films that re-created the daredevil adventures of action movies of the 1930's and 1940's. Lucas produced and Spielberg directed the adventure movies *Raiders of the Lost Ark* (1981), *Indiana Jones and the Temple of Doom* (1984), and *Indiana Jones and the Last Crusade* (1989).

As co-producer and director, Spielberg made the most commercially successful film in history, *E.T.: The Extra-Terrestrial* (1982). The motion picture was a sentimental fantasy about an intelligent creature from outer space lost on earth.

Recent developments. Adventure movies and fantasies were not the only motion pictures that revived the enthusiasm of American movie audiences. A group of young comic actors gained wide appeal, most prominently Bill Murray and Dan Aykroyd, featured in *Ghostbusters* (1984), and Eddie Murphy, star of *Beverly Hills Cop* (1984).

The hits of the 1980's revived and transformed the American movie industry. Budgets soared as filmmakers sought to achieve a mix of star attraction and special effects. The gap grew wider between Hollywood's emphasis on blockbuster hits and the more modest resources and goals of moviemakers from other countries. Critics argued that too many American films aimed at the youth market and ignored the tastes and concerns of adults. In the 1980's, as in the 1920's and 1950's, artistic developments seemed to come from outside the United States.

South Australian Film Corporation

Australian films gained an international audience in the late 1970's and 1980's with movies like *Breaker Morant,* which dealt with an episode in the Australian Army during the Boer War.

Harrison Ford in a scene from *Raiders of the Lost Ark* (1981); © Sygma

Raiders of the Lost Ark was a traditional Hollywood adventure movie that featured spectacular modern special effects. It was one of several popular films directed by Steven Spielberg.

© Gamma/Liaison

Rain Man was a big hit of the late 1980's. This 1988 film about two brothers starred two of Hollywood's most popular actors, Dustin Hoffman, *left,* and Tom Cruise, *right.*

In the 1980's, however, the artistic advances centered less on style and more on subject matter. From Asia, Africa, the Middle East, Australia, and elsewhere, came films whose visions of history, culture, and social relations were little known to audiences in other countries. Examples include *My Brilliant Career* (1980) from Australia and *The Official Story* (1985) from Argentina. Movies throughout the world became more accessible than ever before. This availability resulted from the widespread popularity of videocassette technology, film courses in schools and colleges, film festivals, and screenings in museums.

The ability of films from distant places to find audiences in North America also encouraged some American moviemakers to work outside the big-budget, commercially oriented Hollywood film industry. Perhaps the most important figure among the non-Hollywood type of director has been Woody Allen. He aimed his comedies at adult, urban moviegoers, and achieved considerable success with such films as *Annie Hall* (1977) and *Hannah and Her Sisters* (1986). Susan Seidelman directed the hit *Desperately Seeking Susan* (1985), casting rock music star Madonna in one of the leading roles. Spike Lee became a leading black voice in American cinema with *School Daze* (1988), *Do the Right Thing* (1989), and *Jungle Fever* (1991).

During the 1980's, motion pictures continued to be pulled between the two poles that have influenced their development throughout the century: the small-budget art film and the big-budget, mass-audience movie. New means of distribution—particularly cable TV and videocassettes—have helped foster filmmaking throughout the world, resulting in an increased variety of na-

tional and cultural viewpoints in film. At the same time, Hollywood has continued to exert its powerful attraction on both foreign and American independent moviemakers for its financial resources and access to a vast audience. The majority of popular films internationally continue to be big-budget Hollywood movies like *Batman* (1989) and the Lucas-Spielberg adventure dramas.

Michael Rabiger, Robert Sklar, and Nicholas Tanis

Study aids

Related articles in *World Book* include:

Actors and actresses

Allen, Woody	Fields, W. C.	Marx brothers
Anderson, Dame Judith	Fonda, Henry	Mix, Tom
	Fonda, Jane	Monroe, Marilyn
Astaire, Fred	Gable, Clark	Newman, Paul
Autry, Gene	Garbo, Greta	Nicholson, Jack
Barrault, Jean-Louis	Garland, Judy	Olivier, Laurence
Barrymore (family)	Gish, Dorothy	Pickford, Mary
Beatty, Warren	Gish, Lillian	Poitier, Sidney
Bergman, Ingrid	Grant, Cary	Reagan, Ronald W.
Bogart, Humphrey	Guinness, Sir Alec	Redford, Robert
Brando, Marlon	Hepburn,	Redgrave, Sir Michael
Cagney, James	Katharine	
Chaplin, Charlie	Hoffman, Dustin	Rogers, Roy
Chevalier, Maurice	Hope, Bob	Rogers, Will
Cooper, Gary	Ives, Burl	Sinatra, Frank
Crosby, Bing	Jolson, Al	Stewart, James
Davis, Bette	Karloff, Boris	Streep, Meryl
Dean, James	Kaye, Danny	Streisand, Barbra
De Niro, Robert	Keaton, Buster	Temple, Shirley
Dietrich, Marlene	Kelly, Gene	Tracy, Spencer
Eastwood, Clint	Kelly, Grace	Valentino, Rudolph
Fairbanks,	Laughton, Charles	
Douglas, Sr.	Laurel and Hardy	Wayne, John
Fairbanks,	Lloyd, Harold	Welles, Orson
Douglas, Jr.	Clayton	West, Mae

Directors and producers

Allen, Woody	Flaherty, Robert J.	Lucas, George
Antonioni, Michelangelo	Ford, John	Nichols, Mike
	Godard, Jean-Luc	Redford, Robert
Beatty, Warren	Goldwyn, Samuel	Renoir, Jean
Bergman, Ingmar	Griffith, D. W.	Scorsese, Martin
Buñuel, Luis	Hawks, Howard	Sennett, Mack
Capra, Frank	Henson, Jim	Spielberg, Steven
Clair, René	Hitchcock, Alfred	Sturges, Preston
Coppola, Francis F.	Huston, John	Truffaut, François
Cukor, George	Kazan, Elia	Von Sternberg,
De Mille, Cecil B.	Kubrick, Stanley	Josef
De Sica, Vittorio	Kurosawa, Akira	Welles, Orson
Disney, Walt	Lang, Fritz	Wilder, Billy
Eisenstein,	Lee, Spike	Wyler, William
Sergei	Lean, Sir David	Zinnemann,
Fellini, Federico	Lubitsch, Ernst	Fred

Other related articles

Academy of Motion Picture Arts and Sciences	Copyright	Television
	Drama	Theater
	Edison, Thomas A.	Walt Disney Company
Animation	Hollywood	
Audio-visual materials	Lumière brothers	Western frontier life (Entertainment)
	Method acting	
Camera	Sound	
Cartoon	Technicolor	

Outline

I. How motion pictures are made
    A. Development   C. Production
    B. Preproduction

Questions

What was a *screwball comedy*?
Where and when was the first film festival held?
What is a *take*?
Who participates in a *mixing session*?
What were the characteristics of *neorealism*?
Who is responsible for the visual look of a film?
What is a *variable-area sound recording*?
How does filming on a sound stage differ from filming on location?
What is an *option* on a screenplay?
How does a *video assist* aid a director?

Additional resources

General

Balcziak, Bill. *Movies*. Rourke, 1989. For younger readers.
Dick, Bernard F. *Anatomy of Film*. 2nd ed. St. Martin's, 1990.
Eisenstein, Sergei M. *The Film Sense*. Harcourt, 1969. Reprint of 1947 revised edition. *Film Essays and a Lecture*. Princeton, 1982.
Halliwell, Leslie. *Halliwell's Filmgoer's and Video Viewer's Companion*. 9th ed. Harper, 1990. *Halliwell's Film Guide*. 8th ed. 1991.
Kawin, Bruce F. *How Movies Work*. Macmillan, 1987.
Konigsberg, Ira. *The Complete Film Dictionary*. New American Lib., 1989. First published in 1987.
Manchel, Frank. *Film Study: A Resource Guide*. Rev. ed. Fairleigh Dickinson, 1987.

Making motion pictures

Bernstein, Steven. *The Technique of Film Production*. Focal Pr., 1988.
Clemens, Virginia P. *Behind the Filmmaking Scene*. Westminster, 1982. A guide to careers in the motion-picture industry. Also suitable for younger readers.
Dmytryk, Edward. *On Filmmaking*. Focal Pr., 1986.
Giannetti, Louis D. *Understanding Movies*. 5th ed. Prentice-Hall, 1990.
Russo, John. *Making Movies: The Inside Guide to Independent Movie Production*. Delacorte, 1989.
Schwartz, Perry. *Making Movies*. Lerner, 1989. For younger readers.
Sherman, Eric. *Frame by Frame: A Handbook for Creative Filmmaking*. Acrobat, 1987.

History and criticism

Bohn, Thomas W., and Stromgren, R. L. *Light and Shadows: A History of Motion Pictures*. 3rd ed. Mayfield Pub. Co., 1987.
History of the American Cinema. Scribner, 1990-. Multivolume work, publication in progress. Titles include *The Emergence of Cinema: The American Screen to 1907*, by Charles Musser (1990); and *The Transformation of Cinema, 1907-1915*, by Eileen Bowser (1990).
Kael, Pauline. *State of the Art*. Dutton, 1985. *Hooked*. 1988. *5001 Nights at the Movies*. Rev. ed. Holt, 1991. *Movie Love: Complete Reviews, 1988-1991*. Dutton, 1991.
Mast, Gerald. *A Short History of the Movies*. 4th ed. Macmillan, 1986.
The Motion Picture Guide. Ed. by Jay R. Nash and S. R. Ross. 10 vols. CineBooks, 1985-1987. Updated with annual supplements.
Slide, Anthony. *The International Film Industry: A Historical Dictionary*. Greenwood, 1989.
World Cinema Since 1945. Ed. by William Luhr. Ungar, 1987.

In addition to the works listed, many books that begin with the title *The Films of . . .* cover stars, directors, and decades in film history. Examples are *The Films of Mae West* by Jon Tuska (Citadel), *The Films of Fritz Lang* by Frederick W. Ott (Citadel), and *The Films of the Twenties* by Jerry Vermilye (Citadel).

Motion sickness is a condition in which motion causes extreme nausea. The sufferer becomes pale and perspires. If the motion persists, he or she vomits. Many people affected by motion sickness also experience belching, headaches, apathy, and sleepiness.

Motion sickness occurs in response to the movements of ships, automobiles, buses, trains, aircraft, and spacecraft. It may be called seasickness, carsickness, trainsickness, or airsickness, depending on the source of the motion. More than half the astronauts and cosmonauts who have flown in large spacecraft have experienced a type of motion sickness called *space adaptation syndrome*. Aboard spacecraft, as aboard ships, motion sickness usually appears during the first day of travel. It generally disappears after a few days, as the traveler gets used to the motion.

Motion sickness typically results from the effects of unusual motion on a person's *vestibular system*, the organs of balance in the inner ear (see **Ear** [The sense of balance]). Motions that cause sickness exceed the limits that the vestibular system can accurately report to the brain. In such cases, the vestibular system reports false information about bodily motions that conflicts with information reported by vision and the other senses. For example, the vestibular system might report that the body is moving upward, while the person's eyes report that the body is moving downward. People or animals that lack the vestibular system are immune to motion sickness.

Research has shown that the vestibular system, in addition to its role in balance, functions as part of the body's mechanism for detecting poisons. When certain poisons are present in a person's blood, the vestibular system malfunctions and reports false information. After receiving this false information, the brain causes vomiting, which empties the person's stomach of the poison before more of it can be absorbed into the bloodstream. Research suggests that motion sickness occurs when the brain interprets the false information from the vestibular system as being the result of poisoning. The brain then triggers vomiting as the appropriate action.

To help avoid or reduce motion sickness, a person should keep head movements to a minimum—by holding the head against a headrest, for example—and look at the distant horizon straight ahead. These actions prevent conflict between the motion information reported by the eyes and the vestibular organs. In addition, certain drugs help prevent motion sickness if taken before traveling. Some professional pilots with recurrent motion sickness have used biofeedback training to learn to control such body functions as heart rate and skin temperature (see **Biofeedback**). For reasons not yet understood, voluntary control of such functions during exposure to motion situations can help control the symptoms of motion sickness.   K. E. Money

See also **Dramamine**.

Motivation commonly refers to anything that causes people to behave as they do. Most people have a clear sense of what it feels like to be motivated to do something. But scientists have found it difficult to define motivation. When studying motivation, most psychologists and behavioral scientists focus on two specific aspects of motivated behavior—the arousal of behavior and the direction of behavior.

Arousal of behavior involves whatever brings an organism to action. Arousal means being "stirred up" or "ready for action." It may result from stimuli inside or outside the body. Inside, or internal, stimuli include the sensation of dryness that produces thirst and the stomach contractions that cause hunger pangs. Outside, or external, stimuli include the heat that causes pain when a person touches a hot burner.

An aroused organism's response to stimuli depends on habits and other ways of acting that it has learned. Based on such learning, the organism may act either aimlessly or highly purposefully in a particular situation.

Direction of behavior is determined by several influences. These influences include an organism's habits, skills, and basic capacities.

Motives themselves may also direct behavior. For example, differing motives may direct the behavior of two football coaches when their teams face much stronger opponents. One coach's behavior may be motivated by—that is, directed toward—competition or winning. That coach may concentrate on seeking an upset victory. However, the behavior of the other coach may be motivated by the players' feelings and may focus on keeping the players from being discouraged by the probable loss.

Physiological conditions can direct behavior by making organisms sensitive to stimuli from the environment. For example, many types of birds may become sensitive to available mates and also direct their behavior toward nest building when the birds' hormones reach a certain level.

Kinds of motives. Most behavioral scientists place all motives into one or more of three groups. These groups are (1) homeostatic motives, (2) nonhomeostatic motives, and (3) learned, or social, motives.

Homeostatic motives include hunger, thirst, respiration, and excretion. They work to keep the body in a balanced internal state. The term *homeostasis* refers to the body's tendency to maintain such a balanced internal state. Many homeostatic motives are set in motion either by bodily deficits or bodily excesses. When the body needs water, for example, changes occur that cause thirst and motivate the person to seek something to drink.

Nonhomeostatic motives include sex, such maternal activity as nest building, and curiosity about the environment. These motives are aroused by occasional forces. In the absence of such forces, nonhomeostatic motives may be inactive. In contrast, the needs for food, water, and air—homeostatic motives—have almost continuous influence.

Learned motives, or *social motives,* include curiosity, a desire for novelty, and needs for such things as achievement, power, social affiliation, and approval. These motives seem to develop through experience, especially through social experience, such as early experi-

ence in the family or with friends during adolescence. Learned motives continue to evolve and influence behavior throughout life. However, their exact origins are not clear. Some babies have strong needs for social affiliation that may result from conditions during pregnancy and birth as well as, perhaps, other factors.

The three kinds of motives often overlap. For example, desire for new experiences may be homeostatic as well as learned. This is because people differ as to the level of novel stimulation their homeostatic mechanisms seek to maintain. As a result, some people always seem to be looking for something new while others seem overly content with the familiar.

Theories of motivation. Some general theories of motivation identify a limited number of central motives, such as sex and death instincts, from which other motives develop. Other theories support a single, main motive in human development, such as a person's need for power or to fully realize his or her potential.

In contrast, some psychologists argue that many different motives guide behavior. These motives include needs for order, understanding, and independence. Other theories of motivation try to identify the physiological mechanisms underlying a wide range of motives. For example, researchers exploring the relations between behavior and brain function have identified chemical and electrical processes in the brain that influence behavior in people and animals.

Applications. Motivation plays an important role in informal relationships, but also in highly structured relationships, such as those found in industry and education. In industry, managers use motivation techniques to promote cooperation between employers and employees. Such cooperation enables employees to satisfy certain needs through their jobs, including security, career interests, and respect. If employees expect their jobs to help satisfy these needs, they will probably be more motivated to achieve the company's business objectives.

In education, teachers often use rewards to motivate students to learn. They may also motivate students to find satisfaction in the learning activity itself by emphasizing the value of being able to work through problems. Such an approach encourages students' mastery of problem-solving techniques and an increased expectancy of success in future tasks.   Edwin B. Fisher, Jr.

See also **Adler, Alfred; Developmental psychology** (Psychoanalytic theory; Cognitive theory); **Learning** (How we learn; Efficient learning); **Maslow, Abraham; Perception** (Factors affecting perception); **Psychology.**

Motivation research tries to learn why people choose things they buy. It also seeks to find out what people learn from advertising. Motivation researchers explore the feelings and points of view of consumers. They use knowledge from psychology, sociology, and other social sciences to interpret these emotions and attitudes. Motivation researchers interview people in a conversational way, and sometimes give them tests that must be analyzed by psychologists and sociologists. This type of research has shown that people do not shop with only price and quality in mind. They may buy something to impress others, or to keep up with their group. People may also buy something to imitate someone they admire.   Bonnie B. Reece

See also **Advertising** (Research).

Motmot, *MAHT maht,* is the name of a family of birds related to kingfishers. Motmots live in Central and South America. In most, the tail feathers wear off easily and the end of the tail looks like two tennis rackets. The bird swings its tail from side to side when it is perched, perhaps because predators are likely to spring at the moving tail, rather than at the motionless bird.

Motmots have handsome feathers colored blue, black, green, and cinnamon. The birds range from 6 $\frac{1}{2}$ to 20 inches (17 to 51 centimeters) long. Motmots like to live alone, usually in gloomy forests.

WORLD BOOK illustration
by Trevor Boyer, Linden Artists Ltd.
Motmot

Some nest in rock crevices, but most nest in tunnels they bore in river banks or in the ground. The female lays three or four eggs. Motmots eat insects, reptiles, and fruit. The motmot has a *serrated* (saw-edged) bill.

Scientific classification. Motmots belong to the motmot family, Momotidae.   David M. Niles

Moton, *MOHT uhn,* **Robert Russa,** *RUHS uh* (1867-1940), was a black American educator. He succeeded his friend Booker T. Washington as president of Tuskegee Institute (now Tuskegee University) in 1915 (see **Tuskegee University**). Moton worked for racial good will. In 1930, he was chairman of the Commission on Interracial Cooperation. He received the Spingarn Medal in 1932.

At the request of President Woodrow Wilson, Moton went to France in 1918 to study conditions affecting black soldiers in World War I. He served in 1930 as chairman of the U.S. Commission on Education in Haiti. Moton wrote several books, including *Racial Good Will* (1916), *What the Negro Thinks* (1929), and his autobiography, *Finding a Way Out* (1920). He was born in Amelia County, Virginia, a descendant of an African tribal chief. Moton was taught by his mother. He graduated from Hampton Institute.   Claude A. Eggertsen

Motor. See **Engine; Electric motor; Rocket; Starter** (with picture).

Motor car. See **Automobile.**

Motor fuel tax. See **Gasoline tax.**

Motor home. See **Recreational vehicle.**

Motor scooter. See **Motorcycle.**

Motorbike. See **Motorcycle.**

Motorboat racing is an exciting, competitive sport that tests the performance of motorboats and the skill of drivers. Every year, thousands of people compete in a variety of motorboat races. Racing categories are based on such factors as the size of the boat, the shape of its hull, and the location and power of its engine.

Motorboat races are held throughout the year on lakes, rivers, and oceans in many parts of the world. In the United States, most events are sponsored and approved by the American Power Boat Association (APBA). Founded in 1903, the APBA sponsors races, establishes rules of competition, and conducts speed trials. It also jointly sponsors races with the Canadian Boating Federation. The APBA is the national authority for the Union of International Motorboating (UIM). The UIM governs international competition and is the official authority for world speed records.

Racing boat designs

Racing boats differ from recreational boats in design and equipment. Most recreational boats use standard marine engines designed for safe, dependable performance. The hull may vary in length from 9 to 100 feet (2.7 to 30 meters). Racing engines and hulls are specially designed for speed, endurance, and handling. Racing boat lengths range from 9 to 50 feet (2.7 to 15 meters).

Hull designs. Racing boats have two basic hull designs—*displacement* and *planing.* Motorboats with displacement hulls ride in the water. Those with planing hulls skim over the water's surface on a cushion of air.

Most motorboats with displacement hulls are known as *flatbottoms.* These boats have flat bottoms with gently sloped sides and range from 9 to 17 feet (2.7 to 5.2 meters) long. Flatbottoms may have inboard or outboard engines. Inboard engines are inside the hull. Outboard engines are outside, usually at the rear of the boat. Flatbottoms with outboard engines are called *runabouts.* The driver of a flatbottom is in front of the engine. The driver sits in inboards or kneels in most outboards.

Hydroplanes are the most common planing boats. They have flat or only slightly curved bottoms and hulls. This design allows the pressure of the water to lift the boat and keep it on the surface of the water as long as the boat moves rapidly. A short float called a *sponson* on each side of the hull helps lift the boat's front end as it increases speed. Some hydroplanes can reach speeds up to 200 miles (320 kilometers) per hour. However, they require much room to make turns. The driver usually sits in front of the engine. However, in some inboards the driver sits behind the engine. Hydroplanes range from 11 to 28 feet (3.4 to 8.5 meters) long.

Other racing boats may have a V-bottom hull or a tunnel hull. A V-bottom hull has steeply slanted sides and a pointed bottom. Motorboats with this hull perform well in rough water. They range from 17 to 50 feet (5.2 to 15 meters) long. Tunnel-hulled boats are similar to hydroplanes in that they ride on a cushion of air. But a tunnel hull has sponsons that extend the length of the boat, creating a "tunnel" down the middle of the boat.

Engine designs. Racing motorboats are powered by gasoline, diesel, jet, or turbine engines. Most boats operate with a single engine. However, some oceangoing boats may have as many as four engines. Some racing categories require *stock engines,* which are made in a factory and are not allowed to be *modified* (changed). Other racing classes allow modification of the motor.

In most races, inboard racing boats must use standard automobile engines. But large inboard hydroplanes may also use aircraft engines. Outboard motorboats use only marine engines. Many manufacturers produce marine models designed for high performance.

The propeller is one of the most important pieces of equipment on a racing boat. Propellers are designed to increase the boat's speed and to provide efficient handling. They may have two, three, or four blades.

Safety equipment is required for all motorboat racing. All drivers must wear approved helmets and life jackets. Some life jackets are fitted with special collars to prevent neck injuries. In addition, most boats have a "kill switch" that is designed to protect drivers who get thrown from their boats. The switch attaches to the driver's life jacket. The engine automatically shuts off if the switch becomes detached from the jacket while the motor is running. This precaution protects drivers from being injured by their boats if they fall into the water. Oceangoing boats must have fire extinguishers and first-aid kits. Some hydroplanes carry an oxygen supply for the driver as an added safety precaution.

Types of racing

The APBA formulates rules and conducts races in nine motorboat categories: (1) stock, (2) modified, (3) professional, (4) outboard performance craft, (5) inboard, (6) inboard endurance, (7) unlimited, (8) offshore, and (9) drag. Each racing category is divided into classes based on engine and hull specifications.

There are four basic kinds of motorboat races: (1) circle, or closed course, (2) endurance, (3) drag, and (4) offshore. Circle racing is open to most classes of motorboats and takes place on circular or oval courses of varying lengths. Endurance races also cover oval courses. In many endurance races, drivers complete as many laps of the course as possible within a specific amount of time. Time limits range from 10 minutes to more than 7 hours. Boats that are designed for drag racing compete on short, straight courses. This type of race

emphasizes the boat's ability to accelerate quickly. Most offshore races are held in ocean waters. Some of the larger offshore boats may race distances of more than 200 miles (320 kilometers). Hydroplanes are generally raced in circle competition, while flatbottoms compete both in circle and drag racing. Boats with V-bottom hulls are used primarily in offshore and endurance races.

About 3,000 drivers compete in nearly 400 APBA events each year. Many members also serve as referees, inspectors, and scorers. The Gold Cup, the APBA's most important hydroplane race, was first held on the Hudson River in 1904. It is raced by unlimited hydroplanes over a 2- or $2\frac{1}{2}$-mile (3.2- or 4-kilometer) circular course. The Gold Cup record speed for one lap is 131.387 miles (211.447 kilometers) per hour, set by Chip Hanauer in 1983.　　Critically reviewed by the American Power Boat Association

See also **Hydrofoil; Hydroplane; Outboard motor.**

Motorcycle is a two- or three-wheeled vehicle powered by a gasoline engine mounted midway between the front and rear wheels. A motorcycle has a much heavier and stronger frame than a bicycle, the vehicle from which it was developed. People in many parts of the world use motorcycles for transportation or ride them for recreation and sport. Many police departments use motorcycles for pursuit and traffic control because these vehicles can be maneuvered easily through traffic. Some fire departments use motorcycles to transport medical personnel to accident scenes. Many motorcyclists call their machines "bikes."

In the United States and Canada, motor vehicle laws affect the operation of motorcycles as well as of auto-

Rusty Rae, American Power Boat Association

A hydroplane skims across the water, riding on a cushion of air. The bottom of its hull is flat or only slightly curved.

Rick Cline, American Power Boat Association

A flatbottom has gently sloped sides and a flat bottom. The boat may have engines either inside or outside the hull.

Forest Johnson, American Power Boat Association

A V-bottom hull has steeply slanted sides and a pointed bottom. The boat performs especially well in rough water.

Rusty Rae, American Power Boat Association

A tunnel hull has long floats called *sponsons* that extend the length of each side, creating a "tunnel" down the middle.

Bill Wood, American Motorcyclist Association

© Lee Balterman from Marilyn Gartman

WORLD BOOK photo

Motorcycles can be used for both recreation and transportation. For some riders, a motorcycle offers the thrill of competing in races. For others, it helps in performing a job. Messengers and police officers value the "bike" for its ability to maneuver easily through traffic.

mobiles and other kinds of vehicles. In a few states and provinces, a motorcyclist needs only a regular driver's license. However, nearly all the states and provinces require cyclists to have a motorcycle operator's license, for which a person must pass a test. One test used by many licensing agencies is the Motorcycle Operator Skills Test (MOST). In order to pass this test, cyclists must be able to demonstrate skill in handling a motorcycle. Many states and provinces also require cyclists to wear safety helmets and protection for their eyes.

Motorcycling is popular throughout the world. In regions where gasoline is usually more expensive, such as East Asia, Europe, and South America, motorcycles are regarded as convenient and inexpensive transportation. In the United States and Canada, motorcycles are widely used for recreation, as well as for transportation to jobs. In urban areas, motorcycles help to reduce traffic congestion and air pollution.

Kinds of motorcycles. Manufacturers produce motorcycles in a variety of sizes, types, and weights. The two main kinds are (1) those designed primarily for use on streets and other paved surfaces, and (2) those intended chiefly for off-road riding. The first group consists of street and touring bikes and motor scooters. The second group includes trail bikes and a variety of other related off-road vehicles.

Street bikes are used on roads and highways for short or long trips and for in-town riding. They weigh from 235 to 500 pounds (110 to 230 kilograms) and can travel at all legal highway speeds.

Touring bikes are street bikes that carry special equipment for long-distance travel. For example, many touring bikes are equipped with windshields to provide extra protection against the wind, and compartments to carry luggage. Touring bikes weigh from 500 to 900 pounds (230 to 410 kilograms) and can usually travel at

greater speeds than street bikes can.

Trail bikes can travel on rough country trails, climb hills, and cross streams. They have deeply grooved tires that provide traction on gravel and other rough surfaces. They weigh from 150 to 250 pounds (68 to 110 kilograms).

Motor scooters are not technically motorcycles, because their engine is mounted over or directly in front of the rear wheel. They are also more compact than motorcycles and designed for use at lower speeds. In addition, the driver of a motor scooter sits with both feet on a floorboard.

Minibikes and minicycles have motorcycle-type engines but weigh less and are more compact than most motorcycles. They are not built for use on paved roads.

Motorbikes include *mopeds* (pronounced *MOH pehdz*), which are started by pedaling. Mopeds have an automatic transmission, and can reach a speed of 30 miles (48 kilometers) per hour.

The parts of a motorcycle. A motorcycle has five major parts: (1) the engine, (2) the transmission system, (3) the wheels, (4) the brakes, and (5) the controls. A frame of steel or chrome tubing holds them together.

The engine of a motorcycle has one to six cylinders. It operates on either a two-stroke or four-stroke cycle (see **Gasoline engine** [Cycle]).

The transmission system of most motorcycles consists of four, five, or six gears. Racing models may have as many as eight speeds, and some small models have as few as two.

The wheels. Most street motorcycles have steel- or aluminum-rimmed wheels with tubeless tires similar to those on automobiles. However, many off-road bikes have rubber tubes inside the tire to hold compressed air. Motorcycle tires have a rounded tread pattern that provides the traction needed for leaning through turns.

The *front forks,* an extension of the frame, help hold the front wheel in place. They serve as a suspension system that cushions the rider against bumps. A *rear swing arm* allows the rear wheel to move up and down, providing additional stability when riding over bumps.

The brakes. A motorcycle has front- and rear-wheel brakes, which work separately. The front brake supplies most of the stopping force.

The controls. The rider uses various hand and foot controls to operate the motorcycle. Most older bikes have a kick starter, but a large number of recent models are equipped with an electric starter instead. A hand twist grip controls the throttle, which regulates the speed of the engine. A hand lever on the left handlebar operates the clutch. A hand lever on the right handlebar controls the front brake, and a foot pedal controls the rear brake. Most motorcycles have a second foot control for shifting gears.

Motorcycle safety. The Motorcycle Safety Foundation in the United States and the Canada Safety Council in Canada have developed courses to promote motorcycle safety. These classes, which are offered by many community colleges, high schools, and police departments, are designed to develop good riding habits. They also stress the importance of proper cycling clothes, such as a helmet, goggles, gloves, and boots.

Motorcycling as a sport enables cyclists to compete in such events as dirt-track races, *enduros* (endurance races), and cross-country races. Dirt-track racing is the most popular type of motorcycle competition. It includes races run on flat, oval tracks and *motocrosses,*

Mercedes-Benz

The first gasoline-powered motorcycle was invented in 1885 by Gottlieb Daimler, a German engineer.

which are run on rugged courses that have jumps, hills, and other obstacles.

Most motorcycle competition is governed by the American Motorcyclist Association (AMA), which has headquarters in Westerville, Ohio. The AMA sponsors a number of annual races. A point system established by the AMA determines a racing champion each year. Cyclists receive points for winning official races or for placing high in the events. The racer who earns the most points becomes Grand National Champion.

History. The first gasoline-powered motorcycle was invented in 1885 by Gottlieb Daimler, a German engi-

Parts of a motorcycle

Harley-Davidson Motor Co., Inc.

Rear-view mirror
Throttle
Front brake lever
Turn signal lights
Seat for passenger
Turn signal light
Speedometer
Rider's seat
Headlight
Battery
Fuel tank
Taillight and stoplight
Engine
Front fork
Fender
Gearshift pedal
Tire
License plate bracket
Rear brake pedal
Tire valve
Muffler
Timer
Kickstand
Front brake disk
Rear brake
Transmission
Exhaust pipe
Air cleaner
Footrest

neer. He attached a four-stroke piston engine to a wooden bicycle frame. For the next few years, motorcycles remained largely experimental. During the early 1900's, they developed into useful vehicles. Today's motorcycles have the same general appearance as earlier models. But modern bikes are easier to handle, and they have stronger frames, more powerful engines, and more efficient brakes.   Gregory B. Harrison

Mott, Lucretia Coffin, *loo KREE shuh* (1793-1880), was a leader of the abolitionist and women's rights movements in the United States. Mott helped establish two antislavery groups, and she and Elizabeth Cady Stanton, another reformer, organized the nation's first women's rights meeting.

Mott was born in Nantucket, Mass. Her family were Quakers, and she taught at a Quaker school near Poughkeepsie, N.Y., in 1808 and 1809. She moved to Philadelphia in 1809. Mott became a Quaker minister in 1821 and, like many other Quakers, was active in the abolitionist movement. She became known for her eloquent speeches against slavery. In 1833, Mott helped found the American Anti-Slavery Society and the Philadelphia Female Anti-Slavery Society. She helped organize the Anti-Slavery Convention of American Women in 1837.

In 1840, Mott went to London as a delegate to the World Anti-Slavery Convention. However, the men who controlled the meeting refused to seat her and the other women delegates. Mott met Stanton, who was attending the meeting with her husband. The two women were angered by the convention's

Detail of a portrait by Joseph Kyle, from the collection of Mrs. Alan Valentine (R. E. Condit)
Lucretia Mott

action and pledged to work for women's rights.

In 1848, Mott and Stanton called a women's rights convention in Seneca Falls, N.Y., where the Stantons lived. The men and women at this meeting passed a Declaration of Sentiments. This series of resolutions demanded more rights for women, including better educational and job opportunities and the right to vote.

After 1848, Mott began to speak widely for both abolition and women's rights. She also wrote a book, *Discourse on Woman* (1850). It discussed the economic, educational, and political restrictions on women in the United States and other Western nations. After slavery was abolished in the United States in 1865, Mott supported the movement to give blacks the right to vote. In 1864, she and other Quakers had founded Swarthmore College.   June Sochen

See also **Stanton, Elizabeth Cady.**

Mott Foundation, Charles Stewart, is a private foundation that donates money to nonprofit organizations involved in improving the quality of community life through education, social welfare, economic development, and environmental management. It ranks as one of the wealthiest foundations in the United States. For assets, see **Foundations** (table).

Charles S. Mott, a director of the General Motors Cor-

poration, established the foundation in 1926. Each year, the foundation awards about 450 grants in all 50 states. It also makes international grants. The Mott Foundation has headquarters at 1200 Mott Foundation Building, Flint, MI 48502.

Critically reviewed by the Charles Stewart Mott Foundation

Mouflon. See **Sheep** (Wild sheep).

Mould. See **Mold** (plant).

Moulting. See **Molting.**

Moultrie, *MOHL tree* or *MOOL tree,* **William** (1730-1805), was an American military leader during the Revolutionary War in America (1775-1783). Fort Moultrie in the Charleston (S.C.) harbor was named for Moultrie (see **Fort Moultrie**).

Moultrie entered the Continental Army at the start of the war, and became a brigadier general after his brave defense of Charleston harbor against the British fleet in 1776. He defeated the British again at Beaufort in 1779. Moultrie was captured when Charleston surrendered in 1780. He was set free in a prisoner exchange in 1782 and became a major general. Moultrie was governor of South Carolina from 1785 to 1787 and 1792 to 1794. His *Memoirs of the American Revolution* was published in two volumes in 1802. He was born in Charleston.

Paul David Nelson

Mound bird is a name applied to several species of birds that build mounds for nests. Mound birds are also called *megapodes.* They are found from the Nicobar Islands in the Indian Ocean to the Philippines and Australia. Mound birds are dull-colored, and most are about the size of a chicken.

Mound birds lay 8 to 10 pinkish eggs in mounds of soil mixed with leaves and other plant material. They scrape the mounds together with their large feet. The plant material gives off heat as it decays. This heat and the heat of the sun hatch the eggs. The birds use the same mounds for many years, adding to them each season. Some mounds become more than 14 feet (4 meters) high and 70 feet (21 meters) around. The female places each egg in a hole that she digs in the top of the mound. The young birds hatch in six weeks.

Scientific classification. Mound birds make up the megapode family, Megapodiidae.   Bertin W. Anderson

M. D. England, ARDEA

A mound bird lays its eggs in mounds of decaying plants. The decaying material releases heat, which hatches the eggs.

© Tony Linck

Great Serpent Mound, near Hillsboro, Ohio, was built by the Adena peoples. The mound resembles a huge snake from the air and measures about $\frac{1}{4}$ mile (0.4 kilometer) long. The Adena, who began building mounds about 700 B.C., used the monuments as burial places.

Mound builders were early North American Indians who built large monuments of earth. They built the mounds as burial places and as platforms to hold temples and the houses of chiefs. Thousands of mounds still stand in Canada and the United States. They were built entirely by workers who carried loads of earth on their backs. The mound builders had no horses or oxen and no wheeled vehicles. Many of the mounds consist of several hundred tons of dirt, stone, and other materials.

People once believed the Indians could not have built such huge structures. They thought the mound builders were a lost race who disappeared from North America before the Indians came. But scientists have found Indian-made objects in the mounds, proving that the builders were Indians. According to another theory, Indians learned mound building from the Vikings, who explored part of the east coast of North America about A.D. 1000. But the Indians began to build mounds at least 7,000 years ago, long before the Vikings arrived.

The mound builders were not a single group of people. Many groups of Indians practiced mound building, especially those who lived in the valleys of the Mississippi and Ohio rivers and in the Great Lakes region. The three main mound-building peoples were the *Adena*, the *Hopewell*, and the *Mississippian*.

The Adena culture began to build large mounds about 700 B.C. in what is now southern Ohio. The people lived in small villages and supported themselves by hunting, fishing, gathering wild plants, and perhaps a little farming. They were skilled at a variety of crafts, such as pottery and jewelry making.

The Adena built mounds as burial places. Many Adena mounds are single heaps of earth, and some have ditches around them. The Adena made these monuments by piling dirt, stones, or other materials over the dead. The size of a mound increased as bodies were added to it. Most of the dead were buried in simple graves in the mounds. However, the bodies of village leaders and other high-ranking people were placed in log tombs before being covered with earth. Such tombs also held a few gifts for the dead person. A common gift was a tobacco pipe made of clay or carved from soft stone. One of the largest Adena burial mounds, Grave Creek Mound in Moundsville, W. Va., is about 70 feet (20 meters) high.

The Adena also built ridges of earth to surround their sacred sites, and some mounds shaped like animals. One famous Adena mound is Great Serpent Mound, near Hillsboro, Ohio. It looks like a huge snake from the air and measures about $\frac{1}{4}$ mile (0.4 kilometer) long.

The Adena traded with other Indians, and mound building spread to those groups. Mounds similar to those of the Adena were built by prehistoric Indians in several areas, including what are now New York, New Jersey, and Vermont.

The Hopewell culture flourished from about 100 B.C. to about A.D. 500. It extended throughout present-day Ohio, Indiana, Michigan, Illinois, Wisconsin, Iowa, and Missouri. The people cultivated a variety of crops, including corn and squash. Farming enabled Hopewell communities to support more people than the Adena villages did. The Hopewell also developed a vast

An eagle made of rocks spreads across the top of a circular mound near Eatonton, Ga. Many mounds in the Southeastern United States were built by Indians who belonged to the Mississippian culture.

trade network. Hopewell traders obtained shells and shark teeth from what is now Florida and *pipestone*, a soft stone used to make pipes, from present-day Minnesota. They also got volcanic glass from the Wyoming area and silver from what is now Ontario. Many of these materials were made into gifts to bury with the dead.

The Hopewell cremated some of their dead and put the ashes in burial mounds. They placed the ashes or the unburned dead in log tombs similar to the ones made by the Adena. The tombs contained many gifts, such as beads, bracelets, pipes, pots, tools, and weapons. The Hopewell believed a person's spirit used these articles in the next world.

The Hopewell built many more mounds than did the Adena. Many Hopewell sites consist of many mounds surrounded by a ridge. The largest site, called the Newark Earthworks, is in Newark, Ohio. It has several large earthen structures, including an octagonal ridge that

surrounds about 50 acres (20 hectares) of land.

The Hopewell trade network collapsed by about A.D. 500, and the people no longer built as many earthen mounds. Scholars do not know exactly why the Hopewell culture declined. However, many archaeologists believe that other Indian groups were growing and outbreaks of war were increasing at that time.

The Mississippian culture lasted from about 700 until the 1700's, after the arrival of European settlers. It developed primarily in what became the southern United States and in the Mississippi Valley area. The Mississippian people raised livestock and grew crops. They built some of the earliest cities of North America.

The largest Mississippian city was Cahokia, in present-day Illinois. It had a population of nearly 40,000 and probably had a complex form of government. Monk's Mound, the largest mound in Cahokia, is bigger at the base than the Great Pyramid of Egypt. Monk's

Monk's Mound, built by the Mississippian peoples, is the largest of over 100 mounds near Cahokia, Ill. It covers about 16 acres (6 hectares) and is bigger at the base than the Great Pyramid of Egypt.

Mound rises about 100 feet (30 meters) and covers about 16 acres (6 hectares). Cahokia had more than 100 other mounds. Many were burial mounds, and others served as foundations for temples or for the houses of city officials.

The Mississippian people adopted many customs from the Indians of what is now Mexico, with whom they may have traded. Like the Mexican Indians, the Mississippians built large, flat-topped temple mounds in the center of their cities. At the top of each stood one or more temples, where religious ceremonies were held. Temple mounds still stand in many cities, including Moundville, Ala.; Macon, Ga.; and Winterville, Miss.

Many southern Mississippian people practiced a religion that anthropologists call the *Southern Cult*. This cult borrowed many customs and symbols from Mexican Indian religions. For example, much Southern Cult artwork includes a flying human figure that has winglike tattoos around the eyes. Artists also decorated many articles with spiders and woodpeckers, which they believed had special powers. The Indians probably practiced human sacrifice as part of their religion.

The Mississippian civilization continued to grow until the 1500's, when diseases brought by European explorers killed many of the people. Only one Mississippian group, the Natchez Indians, survived long enough to be fully described by the Europeans.

Other mound builders. One of the largest mound sites in the United States is Poverty Point, near Epps, La. The main part of the site consists of a group of six octagonal terraces, one within the other. The largest octagon has a diameter of about 4,000 feet (1,200 meters). Poverty Point is probably more than 3,000 years old. Many scientists think the people who designed Poverty Point were influenced by the religious monuments of Mexico's Olmec Indians.

In what is now Ohio, descendants of the Hopewell known as the *Fort Ancient culture* built earthen forts. The name of the culture comes from one of their largest forts, Fort Ancient. The remains of the fort surround more than 100 acres (40 hectares) of land. They are located on a hill above the Little Miami River, near Lebanon, Ohio.

Prehistoric Indians in what are now Iowa, Minnesota, and Wisconsin built hundreds of large burial mounds in the shape of birds, bears, panthers, and other animals. A bird mound near Madison, Wis., has a wingspread of more than 600 feet (180 meters). Near Baraboo, Wis., a mound shaped like a standing man measures more than 210 feet (63 meters) from head to toe. Other major mound sites include Lizard Mounds, near Milwaukee, and Effigy Mounds National Monument, near McGregor, Iowa.   Dean Snow

Related articles in *World Book* include:

Effigy Mounds National Monument
Indian, American (The first Americans; picture)
Mound City Group National Monument
Ohio (Places to visit; picture)

Additional resources

Korp, Maureen E. *The Sacred Geography of the American Mound Builders*. Edwin Mellen Pr., 1990.
Le Sueur, Meridel. *The Mound Builders*. Watts, 1974. Also suitable for younger readers.
Myron, Robert. *Shadow of the Hawk: Saga of the Mound Builders*. Putnam, 1964. Also suitable for younger readers.
Silverberg, Robert. *Mound Builders of Ancient America: The Archaeology of a Myth*. Ohio Univ. Pr., 1986. First published in 1968.

Mound City Group National Monument, near Chillicothe, Ohio, contains a large group of prehistoric mounds enclosed within earthen walls. These burial grounds were built by the Hopewell Indians between 200 B.C. and A.D. 500. The monument was established in 1923. For area, see **National Park System** (table: National monuments). See also **Mound builders**.
Critically reviewed by the National Park Service

Mount Ararat. See Ararat.

Mount Assiniboine, *uh SIHN uh BOYN*, rises on the boundary between the Canadian provinces of British Columbia and Alberta. It forms part of the Continental Divide. The peak lies 20 miles (32 kilometers) south of Banff and stands 11,870 feet (3,618 meters) high. The mountain was first climbed in 1901. For the location of Mount Assiniboine, see **British Columbia** (physical map).   Graeme Wynn

Mount Carmel, *KAHR muhl,* is a mountain in northwestern Israel. It extends 13 miles (21 kilometers), from the Esdraelon Valley to the south coast of the Bay of Haifa. Its peak rises 1,791 feet (546 meters) above sea level. For the location of Mount Carmel, see **Israel** (terrain map).

Mount Cook is the highest peak (12,349 feet, or 3,764 meters) in New Zealand. It is in the Southern Alps in Mount Cook National Park, in the west-central part of New Zealand's South Island. The Maoris called it *Aorangi*. It was named Mount Cook for Captain James Cook, the English navigator who was one of the first Europeans known to have seen it. See also **Mountain** (diagram: Major mountains).   W. B. Johnston

Mount Desert Island is an island off the coast of Maine. For location, see **Maine** (physical map). Mount Desert has about 9,600 people. It covers 144 square miles (373 square kilometers). Cadillac Mountain, the highest peak, rises 1,530 feet (466 meters) above sea level. Acadia National Park, established on the island in 1919, was the first national park east of the Mississippi River. In 1604, French explorer Samuel de Champlain became the first European to reach Mount Desert. See also **Acadia National Park; Champlain, Samuel de.**
Paul B. Frederic

Mount Elbrus, *ehl BROOS,* is the highest mountain in Europe. It rises 18,510 feet (5,642 meters) in the Caucasus Mountains. Mount Elbrus is located in southwestern Russia (see **Russia** [terrain map]). Over 20 glaciers, covering about 55 square miles (142 square kilometers), descend from the mountain. See also **Mountain** (diagram: Major mountains).   Leslie Dienes

Mount Etna, *EHT nuh,* is one of the most famous volcanoes in the world. It rises 11,122 feet (3,390 meters) on the eastern coast of the island of Sicily. Part of the mountain's base, which is about 100 miles (160 kilometers) around, extends to the Mediterranean Sea.

Mount Etna (sometimes spelled *Aetna*) makes a colorful picture with its snow-covered peaks, the forests growing on its slopes, and the orchards, vineyards, and orange groves about its base. The region around Etna is the most densely populated area of Sicily. Nearby are the cities of Catania and Acireale, and 63 villages.

Mount Etna is one of the world's most famous active volcanoes. It has erupted at least 260 times since its first recorded eruption in about 700 B.C. This eruption took place in 1983.

The first recorded eruption of Mount Etna occurred about 700 B.C. There have been at least 260 eruptions since then, some extremely violent. About 20,000 people were killed in an earthquake that accompanied a 1669 eruption. Several towns were destroyed in 1950 and 1951. Violent eruptions in 1960 ripped a hole in the mountain's east side. Eruptions also occurred several times since then.   Howell C. Lloyd

See also **Mountain** (diagram: Major mountains); **Volcano** (The study of volcanoes).

Mount Everest is the highest mountain in the world. It rises about $5\frac{1}{2}$ miles (8.9 kilometers) above sea level. It is one of the mountains that make up the Himalaya, on the frontiers of Tibet and Nepal, north of India (see **Nepal** [map]).

Surveyors disagree on the exact height of Mount Everest. A British government survey in the middle 1800's set the height at 29,002 feet (8,840 meters). The 1954 Indian government survey set the present official height at 29,028 feet (8,848 meters). But a widely used unofficial figure is 29,141 feet (8,882 meters).

Mount Everest was named for Sir George Everest (1790-1866), a British surveyor-general of India. Tibetans call Mount Everest *Chomolungma.* Nepalese call the mountain *Sagarmatha.*

Many climbers have tried to scale Mount Everest since the British first saw it in the 1850's. Avalanches, crevasses, and strong winds have combined with extreme steepness and thin air to make the climb difficult. On May 29, 1953, Sir Edmund Hillary of New Zealand and Tenzing Norgay, a Nepalese Sherpa tribesman, became the first men to reach the top. They were members of a British expedition led by Sir John Hunt. It left Kathmandu, Nepal, on March 10, 1953, and approached the mountain from its south side—which had been called unclimbable. As the climbers advanced up the slopes, they set up a series of camps, each with fewer members. The last camp, one small tent at 27,900 feet (8,504 meters), was established by Hillary and Norgay, who

Mount Everest, in the Himalaya range on the frontier of Tibet and Nepal, is the highest mountain in the world. The lofty, snow-covered peak rises about $5\frac{1}{2}$ miles (8.9 kilometers) above sea level.

reached the summit alone. See **Hillary, Sir Edmund P.**

In 1956, a Swiss expedition climbed Mount Everest twice. The expedition also became the first group to scale Lhotse, the fourth highest peak in the world and one of the several summits that make up the Mount Everest massif.

In 1963, Norman G. Dyhrenfurth led a United States expedition that climbed Mount Everest. On May 1, James W. Whittaker, accompanied by Nepalese guide Nawang Gombu, became the first American to reach the top of the mountain. He climbed to the summit from the south. Thomas F. Hornbein and William F. Unsoeld, members of the same expedition, became the first people to scale the difficult west ridge. They reached the top on May 22.

On September 24, 1975, Dougal Haston and Doug Scott became the first climbers to reach the top of Mount Everest by climbing the mountain's southwest face. Haston and Scott were part of a British expedition. On May 10, 1980, two members of a Japanese expedition, Takashi Ozaki and Tsuneo Shigehiro, became the first people to reach the top from the north.

On May 5, 1988, two expeditions reached the top of Mount Everest from opposite sides for the first time. The climbing teams consisted of members from China, Japan, and Nepal. A team of three began in Nepal and climbed the mountain's south face. A team of eight began its climb of the north face in Tibet.

Some Sherpa tribesmen claim a creature they call the *Yeti,* or *Abominable Snowman,* lives around Mount Everest. But climbers have not seen it.   Sir Edmund P. Hillary

See also **Abominable Snowman; Mountain** (picture chart); **Asia** (picture).

Additional resources

Bonington, Christian. *Everest, the Hard Way.* Random Hse., 1976. *The Everest Years: A Climber's Life.* Viking Penguin, 1987.
Burgess, Al, and Palmer, Jim. *Everest Canada: The Ultimate Challenge.* Stoddart (Don Mills, Ont.); Beaufort Bks., 1983. The story of the first Canadians to climb Mount Everest.

Unsworth, Walt. *Everest: A Mountaineering History.* Houghton, 1981.

Mount Fuji, *FOO jee,* is the highest mountain in Japan (12,388 feet, or 3,776 meters). Mount Fuji lies on the island of Honshu, about 60 miles (97 kilometers) west of Tokyo. The Japanese call the mountain *Fuji-yama* or *Fuji-san.* Fuji has long, symmetrical slopes. Its top often is hidden by clouds. Its crown of snow melts in summer. The Japanese have long considered it a sacred mountain, and more than 50,000 pilgrims climb to its summit every year. The top contains an inactive volcano crater. See also **Japan** (picture); **Mountain** (picture chart).
          Kenneth B. Pyle

Mount Godwin Austen. See **K2.**

Mount Hood is an inactive volcano in the Cascade Mountain Range of northern Oregon. It rises about 30 miles (48 kilometers) south of the Columbia River. The mountain is 11,239 feet (3,426 meters) high. It has many glaciers. See also **Mountain** (picture chart); **Oregon** (pictures).

Mount Kanchenjunga, *KAHN chuhn JUNG guh,* also called Kinchinjunga, *KIHN chihn JUN gah,* is one of the highest mountains in the world. It rises 28,208 feet (8,598 meters). The mountain is part of the Himalaya, and stands about 100 miles (160 kilometers) east of Mount Everest, between Nepal and the Indian state of Sikkim. A British expedition climbed Mount Kanchenjunga for the first time in 1955. See also **Mountain** (picture chart).
          James A. Hafner

Mount Kenya, *KEHN yuh* or *KEEN yuh,* is an extinct volcanic cone in central Kenya, East Africa, 70 miles (110 kilometers) from Nairobi. It is 17,058 feet (5,199 meters) high, the second tallest mountain in Africa. Mount Kenya has glaciers on its slopes. Sir Halford Mackinder, an Englishman, first climbed it in 1899.

See also **Mountain** (picture chart).

Mount Kilimanjaro. See **Kilimanjaro.**

Mount Kosciusko, *KAHZ ee UHS koh,* is the highest peak in Australia. It rises 7,310 feet (2,228 meters). It is in

E. Streichan, Shostal

Mount Fuji, overlooking Lake Kawaguchi, rises 12,388 feet (3,776 meters) on the Japanese island of Honshu. It has been considered sacred since ancient times. Each summer, thousands of Japanese make a pilgrimage to the top.

the Snowy Mountains range of the Australian Alps, in southeastern New South Wales. Mount Kosciusko is 240 miles (390 kilometers) southwest of Sydney. See also **Mountain** (picture chart).

Mount Logan is the highest peak in Canada and the second highest peak in North America. Only Mount McKinley in Alaska is higher (see **Mount McKinley**). Mount Logan rises 19,524 feet (5,951 meters) and is part of the Saint Elias Range in the southwest corner of the Yukon Territory. It lies in Canada's Kluane National Park among the world's largest concentration of ice fields and glaciers. The peak was named for Sir William E. Logan, director of the Geological Survey of Canada from 1842 to 1869. It was first climbed by a joint United States-Canadian team in 1925.   G. Peter Kershaw

See also **Mountain** (picture chart); **Yukon Territory** (map).

Mount Lucania, *loo KAY nee uh,* is the ninth highest mountain in North America. It rises 17,150 feet (5,227 meters) in Canada's Kluane National Park, in the southwestern corner of the Yukon Territory. Mount Lucania is one of the peaks of the Saint Elias Mountains.

See also **Saint Elias Mountains.**

Mount Makalu, *MUH kuh loo,* is one of the highest mountains in the world. Makalu stands in the Himalaya about 10 miles (16 kilometers) southeast of Mount Everest, on the border between Nepal and Tibet. The mountain's highest peak, Makalu I, rises 27,824 feet (8,481 meters). Makalu II is 25,130 feet (7,660 meters) high. In 1955, a group of French mountaineers led by Jean Franco became the first people to climb to the top of Makalu.

James A. Hafner

See also **Mountain** (picture chart).

Mount Mansfield. See Green Mountains.

Mount Marcy. See Adirondack Mountains.

Mount Mazama. See Crater Lake.

Mount McKinley, in south-central Alaska, is sometimes called the *top of the continent* because it has the highest peak in North America. The mountain actually has two peaks—the South Peak, which is 20,320 feet (6,194 meters) high; and the North Peak, which rises 19,470 feet (5,934 meters). For many years, the height of the South Peak was believed to be 20,269 feet (6,178 meters). But in 1956, after 10 years of surveys, the U.S. Geological Survey established the height as 20,320 feet (6,194 meters).

Mount McKinley is part of the Alaska Range. It was named for William McKinley, who served as President of the United States from 1897 to 1901. The Athabaskan Indians of Alaska called the mountain *Denali,* which means *The Great One* or *The High One.* Mount McKinley is the chief scenic attraction of Denali National Park. The north side of the mountain represents one of the world's greatest unbroken *precipices* (steep cliffs).

Between 1903 and 1913, at least 11 expeditions tried unsuccessfully to climb to the summit of Mount McKinley. In 1906, Frederick A. Cook claimed to have been the first person to reach the summit. But his claim was disputed, and it was found to be false in 1910 (see **Cook, Frederick A.**).

Also in 1910, a group of miners and prospectors, known as the Sourdough party, climbed Mount McKinley. They said they had reached the top and claimed to have erected a flagpole at the summit. In 1913, Hudson

Stuck, Harry P. Karstens, and two companions became the first people to successfully climb to the top of the South Peak. From there, they sighted the flagpole planted by the Sourdough party on the slightly lower North Peak. In 1932, Alfred D. Lindley, Harry J. Liek, Erling Strom, and Grant Pearson reached the top of the South Peak. Two days later, they climbed the North Peak, thus becoming the first people to ascend both peaks.   Claus-M. Naske

See also **Alaska** (picture); **Denali National Park; Mountain** (picture chart).

Mount McKinley National Park. See Denali National Park.

Mount Meron. See Israel (The land).

Mount Mitchell, in western North Carolina, is the highest point east of the Mississippi River. It is 6,684 feet (2,037 meters) high and is in Mount Mitchell State Park, 20 miles (32 kilometers) northeast of Asheville. The peak is part of the Black Mountains.

Mount Nebo, *NEE boh,* was the peak in the Mount Pisgah range from which Moses saw the Promised Land. According to the Bible (Deut. 34: 5), he died there. Mount Nebo is probably Jabal an Naba, in present-day Jordan. A shrine to the Babylonian god Nebo may have stood on the mountain.   Peter Gubser

See also **Mount Pisgah.**

Mount of Olives is a low range of hills about $\frac{1}{2}$ mile (0.8 kilometer) east of Jerusalem. It is also called Mount Olivet. According to the Bible, Jesus went down from Olivet to make His triumphal entry into Jerusalem. Each night of His last week, He returned to Olivet (Luke 21: 37) until the night of His betrayal. Acts 1 names Olivet as the place from which He rose into Heaven. The Church of the Ascension is located on Mount Olivet where the Ascension is supposed to have occurred.

Bruce M. Metzger

See also **Gethsemane; Jerusalem** (illustration: Jerusalem at the time of Jesus Christ); **Jesus Christ** (The Passion [The trial]).

Mount Olympus. See Olympus.

Mount Palomar Observatory. See Palomar Observatory.

Mount Parnassus. See Parnassus.

Mount Pisgah, *PIHZ guh,* is a small mountain range located in central Jordan. According to the Bible (Deut. 34:1), Moses saw the Promised Land from its highest peak, Mount Nebo. The peak towers 2,631 feet (802 meters) high.

The Pisgah range rises east of the River Jordan. The northern half of the Dead Sea lies southwest of the range. This mountain range was part of the ancient kingdom of Moab in Palestine. According to the Bible, Balak, a king of Moab, built his seven altars for the prophet Balaam on Mount Pisgah, offered sacrifices, and asked Balaam to curse the people of Israel (Num. 22-24).

Peter Gubser

See also **Mount Nebo.**

Mount Rainier, *ruh NIHR* or *RAY neer,* in Mount Rainier National Park, near Seattle, is the highest mountain in the state of Washington. The peak is 14,410 feet (4,392 meters) above sea level. Gassy fumes still rise from Mount Rainier's great volcanic cone, but its deeply cut slopes show that the volcano was largely formed long ago. Automobile roads lead through fine forests of cedar and fir to Rainier. Mountain torrents, patches of red heather, and white avalanche lilies line these scenic routes.

Explorer George Vancouver saw the mountain peak from his ship in 1792. Vancouver named it for his friend and fellow British naval officer Peter Rainier. Hazard Stevens and P. B. Van Trump were the first people to climb to the mountain's top. They climbed it by way of the Gibraltar Route in 1870. The climb to the top is a test of endurance. Even shorter climbs are challenging because of the mountain's deep crevasses, ice caves, and steep cliffs.

Paradise Valley perches at 5,400 feet (1,650 meters) on the slope near the timber line on Mount Rainier. Paradise Valley lies between the Nisqually and Paradise glaciers. Twenty-five glaciers feed the swift streams and tumbling waterfalls that roar through the glacial valleys. Wild flowers of many colors border the glaciers. The Nisqually and the Cowlitz glaciers are the most often explored of the ice regions in the park. The 90-mile (140-kilometer) Wonderland Trail encircles the mountain.

Jois C. Child

See also **Mountain** (picture chart).

Mount Rainier National Park, *ruh NIHR* or *RAY neer,* is in west-central Washington, near Seattle. The park was established in 1899 to preserve the natural beauty of majestic, ice-clad Mount Rainier. For the area of Mount Rainier National Park, see **National Park System** (table: National parks).

An old 14,410-foot (4,392-meter) volcanic cone, Mount Rainier bears a glacier system over 35 square miles (90 square kilometers) in extent. Twenty-five "rivers of ice" originate at or near its summit.

Covering the lower slopes of the mountain are magnificent forests of Douglas-fir, western hemlock, and western redcedar. Blacktail deer and mountain goats are among the animals that visitors may see in the national park.

To enjoy fully the park's spectacular scenery and interesting natural phenomena, visitors must hike or ride horseback. One park trail—the 90-mile (140-kilometer) Wonderland Trail—circles the peak and enters remote areas. In winter, Paradise Valley, on the south side of Mount Rainier, is popular for cross-country skiing. It rises 1 mile (1.6 kilometers) high.

Critically reviewed by the National Park Service

See also **Mount Rainier.**

Mount Royal. See Montreal.

Mount Royal Park. See **Quebec** (Places to visit); Montreal (Parks; picture: Beaver Lake in Mount Royal Park).

Mount Rushmore National Memorial is a huge carving on a granite cliff called Mount Rushmore in the Black Hills of South Dakota. Mount Rushmore National Memorial shows the faces of four American Presidents: George Washington, Thomas Jefferson, Theodore Roosevelt, and Abraham Lincoln. The head of Washington is as high as a five-story building (about 60 feet, or 18 meters). The height of the head is to the scale of a human being 465 feet (142 meters) tall.

The American sculptor Gutzon Borglum designed the Mount Rushmore memorial and supervised most of its work. Workers used models that were one-twelfth actual size to obtain measurements for the figures. The workers cut the figures from Mount Rushmore's granite cliff by means of drills and dynamite. Work on the me-

Shostal

Mount Rushmore is a memorial to four great Americans. It has the largest figures of any statue in the world. The head of George Washington, *above left,* is as high as a five-story building. The other heads, *left to right,* are Thomas Jefferson, Theodore Roosevelt, and Abraham Lincoln.

morial began in 1927 and continued, with lapses, for over 14 years. Borglum died in 1941, before the memorial was completed, and his son Lincoln finished the work.

Mount Rushmore stands in the mountains 25 miles (40 kilometers) from Rapid City. The memorial rises 5,725 feet (1,745 meters) above sea level, and more than 500 feet (150 meters) above the valley. Thus, Mount Rushmore stands taller than the Great Pyramid of Egypt (see **Pyramids**). The memorial is part of the National Park System.

Critically reviewed by the National Park Service

See also **Borglum, Gutzon; South Dakota** (picture).

Mount Saint Helens is a volcano in the Cascade Mountains, 95 miles (153 kilometers) south of Seattle, Wash. The volcano has erupted several times since 1980. Fifty-seven people died in the 1980 eruptions. The eruptions also caused hundreds of millions of dollars of damage to the surrounding area. The volcanic explosions blasted away more than 1,000 feet (300 meters) from the peak and created a huge crater. The volcano's elevation after the 1980 eruptions was 8,364 feet (2,549 meters) above sea level. The eruptions of Mount St. Helens were the first to occur in the continental United States outside Alaska since 1917, when Lassen Peak in northern California last erupted. Since mid-1980, the volcano has had more than 20 eruptions where lava has been released and hundreds of eruptions where ash was spewed into the air.

Mount St. Helens has erupted many times in the past 4,500 years, but it was inactive from 1857 until 1980. Hot ash and rocks from the 1980 eruptions started forest fires and melted snow on the upper slopes of the mountain. The resulting floods and mud slides washed away buildings, roads, and bridges. Explosions flattened millions of trees. The eruptions also spread a thick layer of volcanic ash over a wide area, destroying crops and wildlife and blanketing cities. Geologists expect Mount St. Helens to continue to erupt from time to time.

Jois C. Child

See also **Mountain** (picture chart); **Washington** (picture: The eruptions of Mount St. Helens).

Additional resources

Lauber, Patricia. *Volcano: The Eruption and Healing of Mount St. Helens.* Bradbury, 1986. For younger readers.
Shane, Scott. *Discovering Mount St. Helens: A Guide to the National Volcanic Monument.* Univ. of Washington Pr., 1985.

Mount Shasta towers 14,162 feet (4,317 meters) above sea level in northern California. It rises almost 10,000 feet (3,000 meters) above the low mountains on which it rests. Mount Shasta is the southernmost of the great volcanoes in the Cascade Range between northern California and the Canadian border. For location, see **California** (physical map). Successive lava flows over thousands of years made Mount Shasta. The mountain is not considered an active volcano, but it has a hot spring near its summit.

A newer and smaller volcanic cone, called *Shastina,* lies on the western slopes of Shasta, about 2,500 feet (762 meters) below the summit. It has an almost perfectly preserved summit crater. Five small valley glaciers are found high on the sides of the peak, above 10,000 feet (3,000 meters). Roger Barnett

See also **Mountain** (picture chart).

Mount Sinai. See **Sinai**.

Mount Vernon was the home of George Washington. It lies in Fairfax County, Virginia, about 15 miles (24 kilometers) south of Washington, D.C. The tomb of George and Martha Washington is also located at Mount Vernon. More than a million tourists visit this national shrine each year. The present estate covers about 500 acres (202 hectares).

Washington lived at Mount Vernon as a farmer before he was called upon in 1775 to take command of the Continental Army in the Revolutionary War. When the war ended, he came back to Mount Vernon to retire. But his service to his country was not finished. In 1789, he was elected as the first President of the United States. At the end of his second term as President, Washington returned to the estate to live quietly until his death two years later.

The buildings. The mansion is a large, comfortable building with white pillars. It stands on a high bluff overlooking the Potomac River. There are 20 rooms in the $2\frac{1}{2}$-story building. The attic has dormer windows. The mansion is built of wood, but the board siding on the outside is arranged to make it look like stone. The house has great dignity and beauty.

George Washington's father, Augustine, built the main section of the house during the 1730's. The elder Washington called the country estate the Little Hunting Creek Plantation. George Washington's elder half brother, Lawrence, inherited the property in 1743. He renamed it Mount Vernon in honor of Admiral Edward Vernon, his former commander in the British Navy.

Roger Werths, Woodfin Camp, Inc.

Mount St. Helens caused many deaths and enormous damage in southwestern Washington after erupting in 1980, *above.* The eruptions were the first in the continental United States outside Alaska since 1917.

Mount Vernon Ladies' Association

Mount Vernon, the estate of George Washington, covers about 500 acres (202 hectares) in Fairfax County, Virginia. It includes a mansion, *center rear,* and about 15 smaller buildings.

B. Glander, Shostal

The mansion is a $2\frac{1}{2}$-story building with 20 rooms. It is made of wood.

Mount Vernon Ladies' Association

Washington's bedroom is on the second floor of the south addition to the mansion. Washington died in this bed in 1799.

Robert Srenco, Shostal

The Mount Vernon kitchen, a two-room building, stood near the mansion. The kitchen's west room is shown above.

Mount Vernon Ladies' Association

The small dining room at Mount Vernon was the scene of many dinners during the late 1700's.

George Washington inherited Mount Vernon in 1761. He added the *piazza,* a two-story porch along the river side of the house, after returning from the Revolutionary War. See **Virginia** (picture).

The inside of the house has been restored as nearly as possible to its original state. Many of the original furnishings have been returned.

About 15 smaller buildings stand at the sides and behind the mansion. Some were living quarters for servants and craftworkers. Others housed farm tools and animals. Nearly everything Washington's family needed was grown or made on the plantation, which at that time totaled about 7,600 acres (3,075 hectares).

The grounds and the tomb. The grounds around the mansion add to the beauty of the estate. A wide, green lawn sweeps away from the east porch and ends in a park at the foot of the hill. Flower gardens and fruit and shade trees surround the buildings on the estate. Washington himself planted many of the trees that still flourish. The simple ivy-covered tomb where George and Martha Washington are buried stands at the foot of a hill, south of the house.

A national shrine. By 1853, the estate was in a run-down condition because it could not be maintained as a self-supporting farm. Then a group of women formed the Mount Vernon Ladies' Association to save the grounds and buildings of Mount Vernon. These women aroused public interest in the project. Gifts of money from people in all parts of the country enabled them to buy the estate. They restored buildings that had fallen into ruin and repaired the mansion. They recovered many of the original articles of furniture and decoration. John Augustine Washington, Jr., the last private owner of Mount Vernon, presented the estate with the key of the Bastille, which is exhibited in the central hall. The French statesman Marquis de Lafayette had given the key of the French fortress to Washington in 1790, during the French Revolution. Other valuable personal articles of the Washington family were also placed in the house. Thus, this historic place was saved to become a memorial. The Mount Vernon Ladies' Association now cares for the estate.

In 1931, the United States government completed the scenic Memorial Highway from Washington, D.C., to Mount Vernon. The road follows the banks of the Potomac River.

Critically reviewed by the Mount Vernon Ladies' Association

See also **Washington, George**.

Additional resources

De Forest, Elizabeth K. *The Gardens and Grounds at Mount Vernon: How George Washington Planned and Planted Them.* Univ. Pr. of Virginia, 1982.
Miller, Natalie. *The Story of Mount Vernon.* Childrens Pr., 1965. For younger readers.
Mount Vernon: A Handbook. Mount Vernon Ladies' Assoc., 1985. First published in 1974.
Lewis, Taylor, Jr., and Young, Joanne. *Washington's Mount Vernon.* Holt, 1973. A book of photographs.

Mount Vernon, N.Y. (pop. 67,153), is a historic suburb of New York City (see **New York** [political map]). The first permanent settlement in the Mount Vernon area, called Eastchester, was established in 1664. In 1735, a New York newspaper publisher named John Peter Zenger was put on trial for criticizing the governor of the New York colony for interfering in an election held in Eastchester. Zenger's trial, in which he was found innocent of libel charges, helped establish the principle of freedom of the press in the United States.

In 1851, the Industrial Home Association of New York bought land for a community of homes there for workers who wanted to avoid the high rents and overcrowding of New York City. It named the community Mount Vernon, after the home of George Washington, the first U.S. President. Mount Vernon was incorporated as a village in 1853 and chartered as a city in 1892. Old St. Paul's Episcopal Church, used by the British as a hospital during the Revolutionary War in America (1775-1783), still stands in Mount Vernon. It was named a national historic landmark in 1943. Mount Vernon has a mayor-council form of government.   John Kenneth White

Mount Vesuvius. See **Vesuvius**.

Mount Washington is the highest peak in New Hampshire and in the Northeastern United States. It rises 6,288 feet (1,917 meters) in the Presidential Range of the White Mountains. It lies in a resort area. In the summer, the summit can be reached by hiking trails, automobile road, or cog railway. See also **New Hampshire** (picture); **White Mountains**.   Robert L. A. Adams

Mount Whitney, one of the highest mountains in the United States, rises 14,495 feet (4,418 meters). Snow-capped Mount Whitney lies in the southern part of the Sierra Nevada Range of California. Its granite pinnacles and domes rise sharply to more than 10,000 feet (3,000 meters) above the Owens Valley to the east. Mount Whitney was named for Josiah Dwight Whitney (1819-1896), state geologist of California.   Roger Barnett

See also **Mountain** (diagram: Major mountains).

Mount Wilson Observatory is an astronomical observatory in southwestern California. It stands on Mount Wilson, 5,710 feet (1,740 meters) above sea level, about 10 miles (16 kilometers) northeast of Pasadena.

George Ellery Hale, an American astronomer, founded the observatory in 1904. It originally specialized in the study of the sun and is still a leading center for research on the magnetic fields and the velocities of the solar surface. The observatory has two solar telescopes, which are mounted in towers 150 and 60 feet (46 and 18 meters) high.

The observatory also has one reflecting telescope with a diameter of 60 inches (1.5 meters). This instrument is used to study stars. Astronomers made many important discoveries with a 100-inch (2.5-meter) reflecting telescope that the observatory operated until 1985. The American astronomer Edwin P. Hubble discovered the expansion of the universe with the aid of this instrument (see **Universe** [Size of the universe]).

Until 1980, the Mount Wilson Observatory was operated jointly by the Carnegie Institution of Washington, D.C., and the California Institute of Technology at Pasadena. In 1980, the Carnegie Institution assumed sole administrative control of the Mount Wilson Observatory. The Carnegie Institution continued to operate the observatory until 1989. That year, administrative control of the observatory was transferred to the Mount Wilson Institute, a private organization.

Critically reviewed by the Mount Wilson Institute

See also **Palomar Observatory; Telescope**.

Mount Zion. See **Jerusalem** (West Jerusalem).

Majestic mountain peaks tower above their surroundings. These mountains, part of the rugged Rocky Mountain system, rise along the Athabaska River in Alberta, Canada.

Mountain

Mountain is a landform that stands much higher than its surroundings. Mountains generally are larger than hills, but what people call *hills* in one place may be higher than what people call *mountains* elsewhere. For example, the Black Hills of South Dakota and Wyoming stand higher above their surroundings than do the Ouachita Mountains of Arkansas and Oklahoma.

Mountains generally have steep slopes and sharp or slightly rounded peaks or ridges. Many geologists consider an elevated area a mountain only if it includes two or more zones of climate and plant life at different altitudes. In general, the climate becomes cooler and wetter with increasing elevation. In most parts of the world, a mountain must rise about 2,000 feet (600 meters) above its surroundings to include two climate zones.

A mountain may be a single peak, such as a lone volcano, or it may be part of a mountain range. A group of mountain ranges forms a mountain system. The Pacific Mountain System, for example, is made up of the Cascade Range and several other mountain ranges along the west coast of North America.

Mountains occur in the ocean as well as on land. Many islands are mountains on the ocean floor whose peaks rise above the surface of the water. The world's longest mountain system—the Mid-Atlantic Ridge—is almost totally underwater. It stretches more than 10,000 miles (16,000 kilometers) from the North Atlantic Ocean nearly to Antarctica. Some of the ridge's highest peaks form such islands as Iceland and the Azores.

The height of a mountain is usually expressed as the

Donald F. Eschman, the contributor of this article, is Professor Emeritus of Geology at the University of Michigan.

distance that its peak rises above sea level. Mount Everest, long considered the world's highest mountain, rises 29,028 feet (8,848 meters) above sea level, according to a 1954 survey. Later surveys have suggested new heights for Mount Everest, as well as for K2, which is also called Mount Godwin Austen or Dapsang. Some surveys suggest that K2 may be a few feet higher than Mount Everest. Someday, scientists may measure the mountains again and reach a final conclusion about their heights.

Mauna Kea, a volcano on the island of Hawaii, has the world's largest rise from base to peak. From the volcano's base on the floor of the Pacific Ocean to its peak 13,796 feet (4,204 meters) above the ocean surface, Mauna Kea rises a total of 33,476 feet (10,203 meters)— more than 6 miles.

The importance of mountains

Mountain ranges are important because they determine the climate and water flow of surrounding regions. Mountains are also important for the plants and animals they support, and as a source of minerals. Mountain ranges influence human activities, shaping patterns of transportation, communication, and settlement.

Climate. Mountain ranges strongly affect air movements and precipitation patterns. The temperature of the air drops as altitude increases. Cold air cannot hold as much moisture as warm air can. As a result, when warm, moist air moves up the windward slope of a mountain, it cools and the water vapor it holds condenses into water droplets. The water then falls on the windward slope as rain or snow.

By the time air passes the crest of a mountain, it has lost most of its moisture. For this reason, the side of the mountain away from the wind, called the *leeward side,* is drier than the windward side. The dry area on the leeward side of a mountain range is called a *rain shadow.* Many of the world's deserts lie in rain shadows.

Water flow. Mountains affect the availability of water for vast areas. Because so much precipitation falls on mountain slopes, many rivers have their headwaters in mountain regions. The Rio Grande and the Colorado River, for example, receive nearly all their water from mountains. Much of the snow in high mountains melts only during the summer. Thus, mountains act as reservoirs, feeding streams and rivers even during periods of summer drought.

Because of their steep slopes and abundant water flow, mountainous areas make good locations for hydroelectric plants, which convert the energy of falling water into electric power. Mountainous Norway produces nearly all its electricity from water power.

Plants and animals. Because mountains include diverse conditions at different elevations, they provide environments suitable to many kinds of plant and animal life. Few living things survive in the bitter cold of snow-capped mountain peaks. Just below the snowfields, however, a variety of small animals such as chinchillas and pikas make their home. A few sure-footed large animals such as mountain goats and sheep also live there. These animals feed on shrubs, mosses, and other plants that grow above the *timber line,* the line beyond which trees will not grow because of the cold.

Below the timber line, many mountains have large forests filled with a wide range of plant and animal life. Many areas of the western United States are too dry to support trees except in the cooler, wetter climate of the mountains. The lumber industry in such regions depends on timber grown in mountainous areas. Many animals that are important to the fur industry or for big game hunting also live in the mountains.

Minerals. Much of the world's mineral resources come from mountainous regions. Mountains are formed by such geologic processes as volcanic eruptions and earthquakes. These processes may bring valuable minerals near the surface, where they can be mined.

Human activities. In many parts of the world, mountains have long served as barriers, hindering transportation, settlement, and communication. The isolation of mountain communities has created much diversity of cultures. In Switzerland's Alps, for example, the people speak hundreds of dialects of four different languages.

Mountains are also important recreation areas. Each year, millions of people vacation in mountainous areas to camp, hike, ski, climb, or just to enjoy the fresh air and spectacular views.

How mountains are formed

Mountains are created over long periods of time by tremendous forces in the earth. Since the early 1960's, earth scientists have developed a theory called *plate tectonics* that explains the formation of mountains and other geologic features. According to this theory, the earth's outer shell is made up of about 30 rigid plates of various sizes. The continents and the ocean basins make up the outermost part of these plates. The plates are in slow, continuous motion. Most mountain building occurs along boundaries between plates.

There are five basic kinds of mountains, depending on the process by which they were formed: (1) *volcanic mountains,* (2) *fold mountains,* (3) *fault-block mountains,* (4) *dome mountains,* and (5) *erosion mountains.*

Major mountain ranges may include more than one of these kinds. The Front Range of the Rocky Mountains in Colorado, for example, began as fold mountains. Later, geologic forces pushed up large blocks of earth's crust in the range, creating fault-block mountains.

Volcanic mountains, such as Washington's Mount Rainier and Japan's Mount Fuji, form when molten rock from deep within the earth erupts and piles up on the surface. As a result, volcanic mountains consist chiefly of *igneous rocks,* such as basalt and rhyolite, which are formed when molten material cools and solidifies. Igneous rocks are one of the three major types of rocks. The other types, *sedimentary rocks* and *metamorphic rocks,* can be found in mountains formed by other processes.

Much volcanic mountain building takes place in areas called *subduction zones.* In these zones, two of the huge plates making up the earth's crust collide, and the edge of one plate is thrust under the edge of the other in a process called *subduction.* Friction and the earth's heat cause the material in the sinking plate to melt and rise to the surface, creating volcanic eruptions. Such volcanic activity resulting from subduction formed the Cascade Range in North America, the Andes Mountains of South America, and the Himalaya in Asia.

If the subduction zone lies under an ocean, the volcanic activity there may form a chain of islands called an *island arc.* The Aleutian Islands of Alaska and the Mariana Islands in the Pacific Ocean are such island arcs.

Volcanic mountain building in the ocean is also associated with the separation of plates. Molten rock from the earth's interior wells up between two plates, creating a submerged mountain range called a *mid-ocean ridge.* The Mid-Atlantic Ridge formed in this way. As the molten rock cools and the plates continue to move apart, the solidified material becomes new ocean floor.

The formation of still other volcanic mountains is independent of the action of the plates. Earth scientists believe that these mountains originate from *mantle plumes* —columns of molten rock that rise from deep inside the earth. These plumes are stationary in relation to the plates moving above them. When the molten rock nears the surface, it forms a pocket of intense heat, or *hot spot,* that erupts as a volcano. Over a long period of time, as the plate above the plume moves, the plume creates a line of volcanoes. The Hawaiian Islands formed in this manner as the Pacific Plate moved in a northwesterly direction over a stationary plume.

Fold mountains, such as the Appalachian Mountains in the eastern United States and the Alps in Europe, form when two plates meet head-on and their edges crumple. Fold mountains consist mainly of sedimentary rocks, such as limestone and shale, which form when *sediments* (particles of older rock and plant and animal remains) settle to the bottom of bodies of water and harden. Heat and pressure change some of the rocks into metamorphic rocks, such as marble and slate.

The thickest deposits of sedimentary rock generally accumulate along the edges of continents. When plates and the continents riding on them collide, the accumulated layers of rock crumple and fold like a tablecloth that is pushed across a table. This creates fold mountains in which the wrinkling of the rock layers may range from gentle, wavelike patterns to sharp, complex folds with extensive *faulting* (fracturing) of the layers. Much of the Appalachian Mountains consists of gently folded rock. Europe's Alps, however, are so sharply folded that a person climbing in some areas may cross the same layer of rock several times during a single ascent. The first time the layer is right side up, the next time upside down, then right side up again, and so on. In such intensely folded and faulted mountains, molten rock may push up from the earth's interior into the sedimentary layers, creating veins of granite and other igneous rocks. Heat and pressure caused by the weight of the upper rock layers may change sedimentary rock in the deeper layers into metamorphic rock, such as schist.

Fault-block mountains consist of huge blocks of the earth's crust that have been tilted or pushed up along a fracture line called a *fault*. The Teton Range in Wyoming, the Wasatch Range in Utah, the Sierra Nevada in California, and the Harz Mountains in Germany are fault-block mountains. Some blocks are pushed up between two separate faults. More commonly, a block is tilted up along one side of a single fault.

In fault-block mountains, the steep slope of the uplifted blocks results in rapid erosion of the exposed rock. The debris created by this erosion accumulates at the base of the mountain. Many of the isolated mountains of western Arizona, western Utah, and Nevada are fault-block mountains separated by broad plains filled with such debris.

Dome mountains, such as the Black Hills of South Dakota and the Adirondack Mountains of New York, form where geologic forces lift the earth's crust into a broad bulge or dome. Because the dome is raised above its surroundings, it is vulnerable to increased erosion. Layers of sedimentary rock covering the dome erode, exposing underlying igneous and metamorphic rock. This harder underlying rock then erodes irregu-

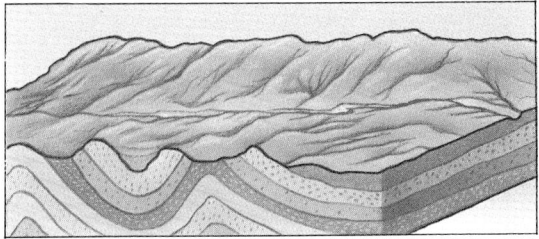

WORLD BOOK illustration by Paul D. Turnbaugh

Fold mountains form when sections of the earth's crust collide. Such collisions cause layers of rock in the crust to crumple and fold, often creating the wavelike patterns shown above.

WORLD BOOK illustration by Paul D. Turnbaugh

Fault-block mountains form when huge blocks of the earth's crust are pushed up along a fracture line called a *fault*. Such blocks may also be pushed up between several faults, *above*.

larly. As a result, peaks and valleys are formed.

Erosion mountains. A few mountains, such as the Catskill Mountains in New York, result from the erosion of a thick pile of sedimentary rock. This type of mountain is all that remains of a plateau after rivers or glaciers erode the plateau to form peaks and valleys.

Major mountain systems

The Appalachian Mountains extend from Alabama to the Gaspe Peninsula in Canada—a distance of about 1,500 miles (2,400 kilometers). They are composed mainly of folded and faulted sedimentary and metamorphic rock layers. Many scientists think that the Appalachian Mountains and the entire Appalachian region, which extends to the island of Newfoundland, were formed by three collisions of the North American Plate with other plates, beginning about 435 million years ago. The last collision was between the North American and African plates about 250 million years ago.

The Rocky Mountains stretch for about 3,300 miles (5,300 kilometers) from New Mexico into Alaska. The Rockies include fold, fault-block, and volcanic mountains. They began to form about 100 million years ago and were lifted again during the past 25 million years.

The Pacific Mountain System consists of two parallel chains of mountains that run for about 2,500 miles (4,000 kilometers) from southern California to Alaska. One chain, the Coast Ranges, includes the Olympic Mountains of Washington, many islands off the coast of British Columbia, and part of Alaska's coast and coastal islands. The Coast Ranges consist mostly of marine sediments but contain much volcanic rock in some areas. The other chain in the Pacific System consists of the Sierra Nevada of California, the Cascade Range of Oregon and Washington, the Coast Mountains of British Columbia, and the Alaska and Aleutian ranges. Both chains began forming about 240 million years ago, and have been further uplifted within the past 63 million years.

The Andes Mountains stretch along the west coast of South America for about 4,500 miles (7,200 kilometers). They are composed largely of igneous rocks, most of which were formed by volcanic eruptions within the past 65 million years. The volcanic activity has resulted from the subduction of the Nazca Plate, which underlies the Pacific Ocean west of South America and is pushing beneath the South American Plate. The Andes and the Pacific Mountain System are part of the *Ring of Fire,* a belt of subduction zones that encircles the Pacific and includes most of the world's volcanoes. The southernmost section of the Ring of Fire consists of the mountains of Antarctica, including an extension of the Andes called the Antarctic Peninsula.

The Tethyan Mountain System (pronounced *TEE thee uhn*) extends across Africa, Europe, and Asia for well over 7,000 miles (11,000 kilometers). It includes the Atlas Mountains of northwestern Africa, the Alps and the Carpathian Mountains in Europe, and the Caucasus Mountains between Europe and Asia. In Asia, it continues through the Zagros Mountains, the Pamirs, the Karakoram Range, and the Himalaya.

The mountains of the Tethyan System consist largely of highly deformed sedimentary and igneous rocks that have been folded and faulted within the past 80 million years. Earth scientists consider the system to be a result

Mountains of the world

Some famous mountains

Name	In feet	In meters	Location	Interesting facts
Aconcagua	22,831	6,959	Andes in Argentina	Highest peak in the Western Hemisphere
Annapurna	26,504	8,078	Himalaya in Nepal	Highest mountain climbed until 1953
Ararat	17,011	5,185	Eastern Plateau in Turkey	Noah's Ark supposed to have rested on Ararat
Chimborazo	20,561	6,267	Andes in Ecuador	For many years thought to be the highest mountain in the Western Hemisphere
Cotopaxi	19,347	5,897	Andes in Ecuador	One of the world's highest active volcanoes
Ixtacihuatl	17,343	5,286	Plateau of Mexico	Aztec name for *white woman*
Jungfrau	13,642	4,158	Alps in Switzerland	Electric railroad partway up the mountain
K2, or Mount Godwin Austen, or Dapsang	28,250	8,611	Karakoram, or Mustagh, in Kashmir	Second highest mountain in the world
Kilimanjaro	19,340	5,895	Isolated peak in Tanzania	Highest mountain in Africa
Lassen Peak	10,457	3,187	Cascade in California	One of the few active U.S. volcanoes
Matterhorn	14,692	4,478	Alps on Switzerland-Italy border	Favorite for daring mountain climbers
Mauna Kea	13,796	4,205	Island of Hawaii	World's greatest rise from base to peak
Mauna Loa	13,677	4,169	Island of Hawaii	World's largest volcano
Mont Blanc	15,771	4,807	Alps on France-Italy-Switzerland border	Highest mountain in the Alps
Mount Cook	12,349	3,764	Southern Alps in New Zealand	Highest peak in New Zealand
Mount Elbrus	18,510	5,642	Caucasus in Russia	Highest mountain in Europe
Mount Etna	11,122	3,390	Island of Sicily	Volcano known to have erupted over 260 times
Mount Everest	29,028	8,848	Himalaya on Nepal-Tibet border	Highest mountain in the world; first scaled in 1953
Mount Fuji	12,388	3,776	Island of Honshu in Japan	Considered sacred by many Japanese
Mount Hood	11,239	3,426	Cascade in Oregon	Inactive volcano with many glaciers
Mount Kanchenjunga, or Kinchinjunga	28,208	8,598	Himalaya on Nepal-India border	Third highest mountain in the world
Mount Kenya	17,058	5,199	Central Kenya	Base straddles the equator
Mount Kosciusko	7,310	2,228	Australian Alps	Highest peak in Australia
Mount Logan	19,524	5,951	St. Elias in Canada	Highest peak in Canada
Mount Makalu	27,824	8,481	Himalaya on Nepal-Tibet border	Fourth highest mountain in the world
Mount McKinley	20,320	6,194	Alaska Range in Alaska	Highest peak in North America
Mount Rainier	14,410	4,392	Cascade in Washington	Highest peak in Washington
Mount St. Helens	8,364	2,549	Cascade in Washington	One of the few active U.S. volcanoes
Mount Shasta	14,162	4,317	Cascade in California	Famous for its twin peaks
Mount Whitney	14,495	4,418	Sierra Nevada in California	Highest mountain in California
Olympus	9,570	2,917	Greece	Considered home of the gods by early Greeks
Pico de Orizaba	18,410	5,610	Plateau of Mexico	Highest peak in Mexico
Pikes Peak	14,110	4,301	Front Range in Colorado	Most famous of the Rocky Mountains
Popocatépetl	17,887	5,452	Plateau of Mexico	Aztec name for *smoking mountain*
Vesuvius	4,190	1,277	Italy	Only active volcano on the mainland of Europe

Each mountain listed has a separate article in *World Book*.

Sources: Rand McNally & Company; U.S. Geological Survey.

Major mountains of the Western Hemisphere

WORLD BOOK illustration by Robert Addison

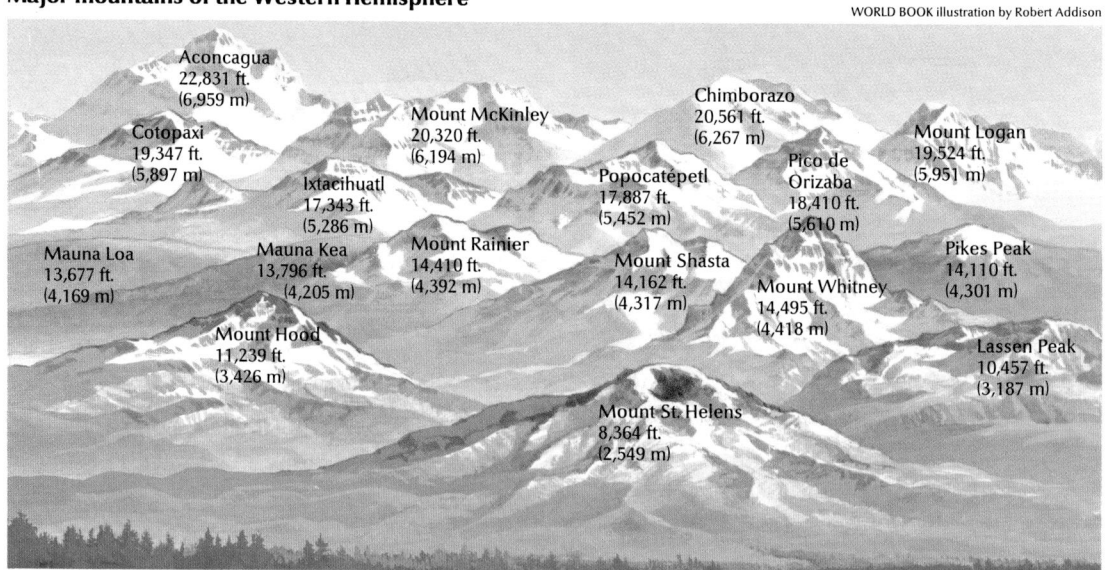

Location of the mountains

This map locates the mountains listed in the table *Some famous mountains* and illustrated in the diagrams *Major mountains of the Eastern Hemisphere* and *Major mountains of the Western Hemisphere.* The diagrams also show how the mountains compare in height.

WORLD BOOK map

Mount McKinley
Mount Logan
NORTH AMERICA
Mount St. Helens
Mount Rainier
Mount Shasta
Mount Hood
Lassen Peak
Pikes Peak
Mount Whitney
Mauna Kea
Mauna Loa
Ixtacihuatl
Popocatépetl
Pico de Orizaba
Cotopaxi
Chimborazo
SOUTH AMERICA
Aconcagua
Pacific Ocean
Atlantic Ocean
Equator
EUROPE
Mont Blanc
Jungfrau
Matterhorn
Vesuvius
Olympus
Mount Etna
Mount Elbrus
Ararat
ASIA
K2
Annapurna
Mount Makalu
Mount Everest
Mount Kanchenjunga
Mount Fuji
Pacific Ocean
AFRICA
Mount Kenya
Kilimanjaro
Indian Ocean
AUSTRALIA
Mount Kosciusko
Mount Cook
ANTARCTICA

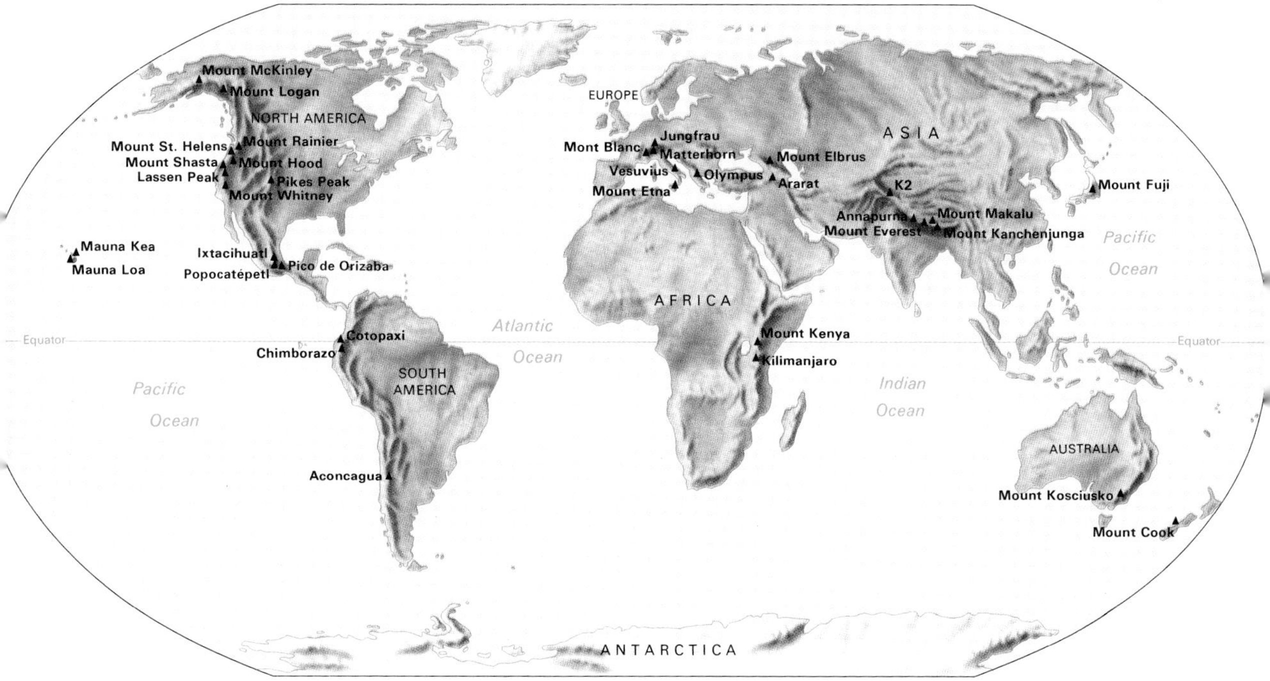

Major mountains of the Eastern Hemisphere

WORLD BOOK illustration by Robert Addison

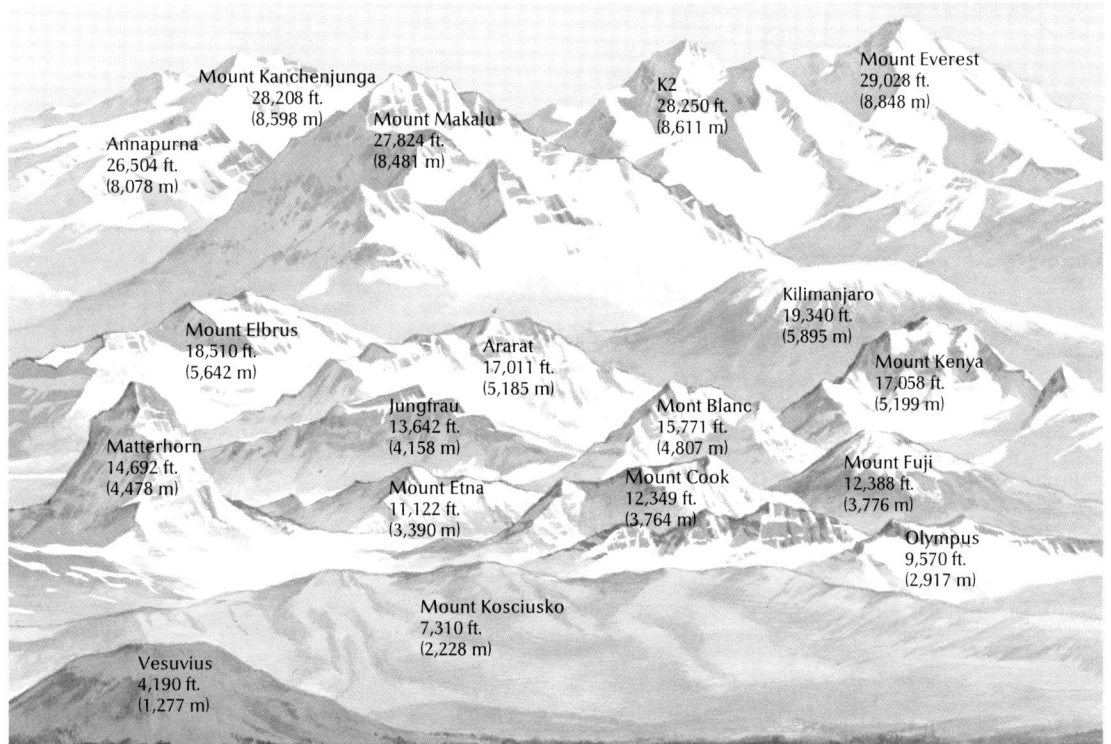

Mount Kanchenjunga 28,208 ft. (8,598 m)
Annapurna 26,504 ft. (8,078 m)
Mount Makalu 27,824 ft. (8,481 m)
K2 28,250 ft. (8,611 m)
Mount Everest 29,028 ft. (8,848 m)
Kilimanjaro 19,340 ft. (5,895 m)
Mount Elbrus 18,510 ft. (5,642 m)
Ararat 17,011 ft. (5,185 m)
Mount Kenya 17,058 ft. (5,199 m)
Jungfrau 13,642 ft. (4,158 m)
Mont Blanc 15,771 ft. (4,807 m)
Matterhorn 14,692 ft. (4,478 m)
Mount Cook 12,349 ft. (3,764 m)
Mount Fuji 12,388 ft. (3,776 m)
Mount Etna 11,122 ft. (3,390 m)
Olympus 9,570 ft. (2,917 m)
Mount Kosciusko 7,310 ft. (2,228 m)
Vesuvius 4,190 ft. (1,277 m)

of the African, Arabian, and Indian plates colliding into the Eurasian Plate. Earthquakes occur frequently along the Tethyan System, indicating that mountain building is still taking place.

Studying mountains

Why geologists study mountains. Geologists study mountains because such study provides important and useful knowledge. Analysis of the structure, composition, and distribution of mountains yields information about the geologic forces that shape the earth and about the makeup of the earth's interior. Geologists also study mountains to learn about the history of the earth, including the formation of earth's major features.

The study of mountains has led to the discovery of rich mineral deposits and is necessary in the ongoing search for useful mineral resources. Knowledge of mountain geology helps engineers design and build mountain roads, railroad beds and tunnels, and dams.

Measuring mountains. Accurately determining the location and height of mountains is particularly important for geographers and mapmakers. They often use aerial photography, in which an airborne camera takes a series of overlapping photographs of an area. Mapmakers then use a process called *photogrammetry* to create maps from the photographs.

Artificial satellites and high-flying aircraft provide accurate data about location and altitude by means of instruments called *radar altimeters.* A radar altimeter sends radio signals down to the earth and receives the signals after they have been reflected from the ground. It computes the distance to the ground based on the speed of the radio waves and the time they took to travel to the ground and back. Mountain surveyors also use a similar technique called *laser ranging,* in which a laser beam is bounced off an object to determine its distance.   Donald F. Eschman

Related articles in *World Book.* See the articles on the mountains listed in the table *Some famous mountains* in this article. See **Volcano** and its list of *Related articles.* See also the following articles:

Africa, Asia, and the Pacific

Altai Mountains	Krakatau	Tian Shan
Atlas Mountains	Mount Carmel	Ural Mountains
Himalaya	Mount of Olives	Yablonovyy Moun-
Hindu Kush	Mount Pisgah	tains
Khyber Pass	Pamirs	

Europe

Alps	Caucasus	Parnassus
Apennines	Mountains	Pennine Chain
Ben Nevis	Hekla	Pyrenees
Carpathian	Montserrat	Stromboli
Mountains		

North America

Adirondack Mountains	Great Divide
Allegheny Mountains	Great Smoky Mountains
Appalachian Mountains	Green Mountains
Black Hills	Kilauea
Blue Ridge Mountains	Mount Rushmore
Canadian Shield	National Memorial
Cascade Range	Mount Washington
Catskill Mountains	Olympic Mountains
Clingmans Dome	Ozark Mountains
Coast Ranges	Paricutin
Cumberland Mountains	

Rocky Mountains	Sierra Madre	Teton Range
Saint Elias Moun-	Sierra Nevada	Wasatch Range
tains	Stone Mountain	White Mountains
Selkirk Mountains		

South America

Andes Mountains	Ojos del Salado
El Misti	Pichincha

Other related articles

Altitude	Hill
Animal (Animals	Mountain climbing
of the mountains)	Mountain pass
Avalanche	Ocean (The land at the bottom
Butte	of the sea)
Cordillera	Plant (picture: Plants of
Divide	the high mountain tundra)
Earth (How the earth	Plate tectonics
changes)	Weather (Geographical
Erosion	features)
Gap	World (graph: Highest
Geology	mountain on each
Glacier	continent)

Outline

I. The importance of mountains
A. Climate	D. Minerals
B. Water flow	E. Human activities
C. Plants and animals	

II. How mountains are formed
A. Volcanic mountains	D. Dome mountains
B. Fold mountains	E. Erosion mountains
C. Fault-block mountains	

III. Major mountain systems
A. The Appalachian Mountains
B. The Rocky Mountains
C. The Pacific Mountain System
D. The Andes Mountains
E. The Tethyan Mountain System

IV. Studying mountains
A. Why geologists study mountains
B. Measuring mountains

Questions

How were the Hawaiian Islands formed?
What is the *Ring of Fire?*
The Tethyan Mountain System stretches across which three continents?
What are the five basic kinds of mountains?
What is the world's longest mountain system?
How does a radar altimeter measure the height of mountains?
What is the world's highest mountain?
What is a *rain shadow?*
How are fold mountains formed?
What is the theory of *plate tectonics?*

Additional resources

Level I
Bain, Iain, and McDonald, Albert. *Mountains and People.* Silver Burdett, 1982.
Bramwell, Martyn. *Mountains.* Watts, 1986.
George, Jean C. *One Day in the Alpine Tundra.* T. Y. Crowell, 1984.

Level II
The Anatomy of Mountain Ranges. Ed. by Jean-Paul Schaer and John Rodgers. Princeton, 1987.
Beckey, Fred W. *Mountains of North America.* Bonanza, 1986. First published in 1982.
Jerome, John. *On Mountains: Thinking About Terrain.* Harcourt, 1978.
National Geographic Soc. *America's Magnificent Mountains.* The Society, 1980.
Price, Larry W. *Mountains & Man: A Study of Process and Environment.* Univ. of California Pr., 1981.
Ricciuti, Edward R. *Wildlife of the Mountains.* Abrams, 1979.

Mountain ash is the name for a group of trees and shrubs that grow in the Northern Hemisphere. They grow chiefly in high places. The *American mountain ash* grows from Newfoundland south to northern Georgia. A mountain ash has compound leaves made up of several separate leaflets. The white flowers grow in large, flattened clusters. The orange-to-red fruits are clusters of berrylike *pomes.*

Mountain ash is valuable as wildlife food and as an ornamental tree for lawns and gardens. The wood from the *European mountain ash,* or *rowan tree,* may be used for making tool handles. Superstitious people once believed the rowan tree would drive away evil spirits.

Scientific classification. The mountain ash belongs to the rose family, Rosaceae. The scientific name for the American mountain ash is *Sorbus americana.* The rowan tree is *S. aucuparia.*   Norman L. Christensen, Jr.

See also **Tree** (Familiar broadleaf and needleleaf trees [picture]).

Mountain avens is a small, hardy plant that grows wild in the northern and arctic regions. It is the floral emblem of Canada's Northwest Territories. The plant has small, saucer-shaped, yellow or white flowers. It grows on high ledges and rocky slopes in North America, Europe, and Asia.

Scientific classification. The mountain avens belongs to the rose family, Rosaceae. It is genus *Dryas.* The scientific name for the yellow mountain avens of the Canadian Rockies is *D. drummondii.* The common mountain avens is *D. octopetala.*

Mountain beaver, also called *sewellel,* is a rodent that lives along the Pacific coast and in nearby mountains. Mountain beavers, which are not related to true beavers, have lived on earth longer than any other rodent. They lived in North America at least 60 million years ago. They are also called *boomers* and *whistlers,* though they do not make booming or whistling noises. *Sewellel* is a Chinook Indian word meaning *robe.*

Mountain beavers are about 1 foot (30 centimeters) long and look like large voles rather than like beavers (see **Vole**). They have a short, thick body, short legs, a short tail, and small eyes and ears. Their fur is thick and short. Mountain beavers live in groups called *colonies.* They live in tunnels they dig in the banks of streams.

Scientific classification. The mountain beaver is the only surviving member of the mountain beaver family, Aplodontidae. Its scientific name is *Aplodontia rufa.*   Clark E. Adams

Mountain climbing is the sport of climbing mountain slopes to reach their peaks. It is also called *mountaineering* or *Alpinism.*

Mountain climbing as a sport started in Europe when people began to ascend peaks simply for the challenge and adventure. Most of the major mountains, except those in the most remote parts of the world, have been climbed. The tallest peak in North America, located on Mount McKinley, was first climbed in 1913. In 1953, Sir Edmund Hillary of New Zealand and Tenzing Norgay of Nepal became the first to reach the summit of Mount Everest in Asia, the world's highest mountain. See **Mount McKinley; Mount Everest.**

Mountaineers still try to be the first to conquer a tall peak. But the main focus of the sport has become the exploration of new routes up the most challenging mountains. Mountaineers are also attracted to established routes that are very difficult or particularly enjoyable.

Styles of mountain climbing. Mountaineers today place great importance on the style of ascent. Experienced mountaineers typically climb in teams of two or more, but they sometimes climb alone for the increased challenge and solitude.

The traditional method of climbing a peak is called the *expedition style.* In this style, large teams of mountaineers set ropes on difficult terrain and establish a network of well-stocked camps.

Mountaineers consider *Alpine style climbing* the purest and most challenging way to climb a peak. Mountaineers begin at the base of a peak and climb to its summit without returning for additional supplies or equipment. The Alpine style requires a rapid ascent because the climbers are limited to the provisions they can carry in their packs. Retreat from a route without the camps and ropes of expedition style is often more difficult and dangerous.

Challenge of the Himalaya. Many mountain ranges offer outstanding climbing challenges. But the immense peaks of the Himalaya, the world's highest mountains, are regarded as the greatest test in mountaineering. Himalayan climbing is particularly difficult and hazardous because of the high altitudes, extreme cold, and severe weather. The sport's new frontier has become the attempt to reach the summit of these peaks without bottled oxygen, large numbers of support climbers, and expedition style tactics.

Basic mountaineering equipment and methods. Mountaineers use climbing ropes, tied around the waist or into a waist harness, to protect them if they fall. On snow and ice slopes, mountain climbers ascend with the aid of ice axes and a set of metal spikes called *crampons* attached to the bottom of climbing boots.

In difficult terrain, climbers use a technique called *belaying* to stop a fall. In belaying, a lead climber ascends while a second climber releases the rope from a secure position. While advancing, the lead climber inserts pieces of gear into the snow, ice, or cracks in the rock, securing the rope to them with a *snap link* or *karabiner.* The lead climber then belays the second climber, who removes the pieces of gear so that they may be used again.

Climbers descend from the summit by the easiest or quickest route. Often they *rappel* steep sections. Rappelling is a way of sliding down the climbing rope.

Mountain climbing safety. Mountaineering is a hazardous sport. Mountain storms can bring high winds and very cold temperatures that make climbing extremely difficult. Mountaineers also face such dangers as avalanches, ice and rock falls, and hidden cracks in the rock. At high elevations, such altitude sicknesses as pulmonary and cerebral edema can be life threatening.

Mountaineers can overcome these dangers by taking adequate precautions. They should observe the weather and note any changes in barometric pressure. On high peaks, mountaineers must allow themselves time to adjust to the reduced amount of oxygen. Climbing with helmets helps protect against falling ice and rock.

Different routes on a mountain require different levels of climbing skill. Mountaineers should select a climb that is within their ability. They must also know when to retreat if the weather changes or the climb becomes too difficult or dangerous.

Mountain climbing schools and clubs. There are many mountain climbing guide services in the United States. Two schools that provide instruction in mountain climbing are the National Outdoor Leadership School, P.O. Box AA, Lander, WY 82520; and Outward Bound, Inc., 384 Field Point Road, Greenwich, CT 06835. Information about mountain climbing clubs can be obtained by writing to the American Alpine Club, 113 East 90th Street, New York, NY 10028.   Mark B. Hesse

See also **Alps** (Climbing the Alps); **Hillary, Sir Edmund; Himalaya; Mount Rainier.**

Additional resources

The Climber's Handbook. Ed. by Audrey Salkeld. Sierra Club, 1987.

Kelsey, Michael R. *Climbers and Hikers Guide to the World's Mountains.* 2nd ed. Kelsey Pub., 1984.

Mitchell, Richard G., Jr. *Mountain Experience: The Psychology and Sociology of Adventure.* Univ. of Chicago Pr., 1983.

Mountaineering: The Freedom of the Hills. Ed. by Ed Peters. 4th ed. Mountaineers, 1982.

Mountain goat is a white, woolly animal that lives on steep cliffs high in the mountains of western North America. The animal roams across mountains in Alaska, western Canada, and Montana, Idaho, and Washington. The mountain goat is a type of *goat antelope*. It looks more like a goat than an antelope but is only distantly related to true goats and sheep.

Most mountain goats stand from 3 to 4 feet (90 to 120 centimeters) tall at the shoulder. The males are larger than the females. Thick underfur and a long, hairy, white overcoat protect the mountain goat against severe winds and bitter cold in winter. The animals have short, powerful legs with large black hoofs and are sure-footed climbers. The *billy* (male) has slender horns that may measure as much as 1 foot (30 centimeters) long. The horns of the *nanny* (female) may be slightly longer. The female uses its horns to defend a *territory* (area) against other mountain goats. Adult females dominate males and can force even large males to leave an area.

The billy usually lives alone except during the mating season in November. The nanny's *gestation* (pregnancy)

David C. Fritts, Animals Animals

The mountain goat has short, sharp horns and a beard. Strong legs enable it to move about easily on rocky cliffs. A woolly coat provides protection against cold mountain winds.

period lasts about six months, and she gives birth to a single kid or twins during the spring. Nannies and their kids live in groups during the summer and by themselves in their territory during winter. Mountain goats eat grasses, sedges, lichens, and the leaves and twigs of shrubs.

Scientific classification. The mountain goat belongs to the bovid family, Bovidae. Its scientific name is *Oreamnos americanus.*   Valerius Geist

Mountain laurel is an evergreen plant that grows naturally in eastern North America. As a shrub, it stands 5 to 10 feet (1.5 to 3 meters) tall. As a tree, it reaches 30 feet (9 meters) high or more. The mountain laurel has pink or white flowers, which may have purple markings. Its glossy, dark leaves are oblong and pointed at the ends. The leaves and nectar of the mountain laurel are poisonous. The plant is also called *kalmia.* Mountain laurels are often used in landscaping, and the plant has been introduced into western North America and Great Britain.

Scientific classification. Mountain laurel is in the heath family, Ericaceae. Its scientific name is *Kalmia latifolia.*

James L. Luteyn

Mountain lion is a large wild animal of the cat family. Mountain lions once lived throughout the forests of the United States and southern Canada. When settlers moved in, they drove this animal out. The number of mountain lions has been greatly reduced in both these countries, except in large national and state or provincial parks. Today, mountain lions live chiefly in western provinces and states from British Columbia and Alberta to California and New Mexico. Small numbers dwell in southeastern Canada and New England and southward through the Appalachian Mountains. They are also found in uninhabited areas of Florida and certain other parts of the South. Mountain lions are more common outside the United States and Canada. They live throughout much of Mexico, Central America, and southward to the tip of South America.

Early settlers called the animal *cougar,* or mountain lion. They thought it was a female lion. Other names for this animal are *catamount* and *puma.* Especially in the eastern states, it is known as *panther,* a name also given to several other kinds of cat (see **Panther**).

An adult mountain lion may be either a gray color or a reddish or yellowish color called *tawny.* Its hairs are fawn-gray tipped with reddish-brown or grayish. This animal has no spots, and in this way it is different from the jaguar. The throat, the insides of the legs, and the belly are white, and the tip of the tail is black. Some mountain lions are solid black. A full-grown animal may be 5 feet (1.5 meters) long or more, not counting the tail, which is 2 to 3 feet (61 to 91 centimeters) long. The heaviest mountain lion on record weighed 227 pounds (103 kilograms). The body is slender, and the legs are long. The head is round and rather small.

Mountain lions have from one to five cubs at a time, generally two years apart. The average number is three. The cubs weigh about 1 pound (0.5 kilogram) at birth. They are covered with fur and are blind. They are lighter brown than their parents. The cubs have large brownish-black spots on the body and dark rings on the short tail. Adults care for their young until they are able to survive alone. Young lions need about two years to develop

Maurice Hornocker

A mountain lion may reach a length of 5 feet (1.5 meters) or more, not counting its tail. Among the cats of North and South America, only the jaguar is larger. Mountain lions hunt and kill deer, elk, and smaller prey, such as rabbits.

Warren Garst, Van Cleve Photography

Mountain lion cubs are covered with dark spots that disappear as the animals grow older. Cubs stay with their mother for up to two years.

enough skill in hunting to find their own food. They may live to be 10 to 20 years old.

The cry of the mountain lion can be terrifying. It sounds like a person screaming in pain. The animal also has a soft whistle call.

A mountain lion usually hunts at night, sometimes traveling long distances in pursuit of game. Its chief prey are deer and elk. Occasionally, a mountain lion will kill a bighorn sheep. In need it will feed on small mammals—even skunks and porcupines. A mountain lion keeps under cover while stalking its prey. It then leaps out upon the animal, breaking the animal's neck or dragging it down to the ground.

Ranchers regard mountain lions as pests. But the big cats seldom kill calves or other domestic animals. Biologists believe that mountain lions should be controlled but not killed off, because these big cats play an important part in the animal world. Like most other large predators, mountain lions feed mainly on weak, sick, or old prey. Such animals can be burdens to their herds. By killing them, mountain lions help strengthen the herds. Mountain lions are very unlikely to attack people.

Scientific classification. The mountain lion is a mammal that belongs to the cat family, Felidae. Its scientific name is *Felis concolor.*   Thomas L. Poulson

Mountain men. See Fur trade (The 1800's); Westward movement (Exploration).

Mountain nestor. See Kea.

Mountain pass is a passageway over a mountain barrier. Passes generally occur at low points on mountain watersheds, or in valleys between mountain ridges. The importance of a mountain pass depends on the need for communication between the people who are living on each side.

Well-known passes include Donner (7,088 feet, or 2,160 meters) in California; Brenner (4,508 feet, or 1,374 meters) between Italy and Austria; and Khyber (3,370 feet, or 1,027 meters) between Pakistan and Afghanistan.

H. J. McPherson

Mountain sheep. See Bighorn (with pictures).

Mountain sickness. See Altitude sickness.

Mountaineering. See Mountain climbing.

Mountbatten, Louis (1900-1979), a member of the royal family of Great Britain, distinguished himself as a military leader and as the last *viceroy* (ruler) of the British colony of India. He served as chief of combined British operations during World War II (1939-1945). Mountbatten later became first sea lord, Great Britain's highest naval officer. As viceroy of India, he helped arrange for that country's independence.

Mountbatten was born in Windsor, England. His given and family name was Louis Francis Albert Victor Nicholas Battenberg. He was the son of Prince Louis of Battenberg. Mountbatten joined the Royal Navy in 1913. He studied at the Royal Naval College. When World War II began, he was commander of the destroyer *Kelly.* German bombers sank the ship in the Battle of Crete in 1941. Half the *Kelly*'s crew of 240 was killed. The rest, including Mountbatten, clung to the wreckage for four hours under enemy fire before being rescued. In 1942, he became chief of combined operations. He led a task force that planned raids on German-occupied areas in Europe. He took command of the Allied forces in Southeast Asia in 1943 and led the reconquest of Burma and Peninsular Malaysia from Japan.

Mountbatten was named viceroy of India in March 1947. He skillfully supervised the end of British rule in India in spite of deep rivalries among many of India's Hindu and Muslim inhabitants. The arrangement included the division of the country into the Hindu-dominated nation of India and the smaller Muslim-dominated nation of Pakistan. In August 1947, Mountbatten was chosen the first governor general of independent India. He returned to naval service in June 1948. Mountbatten was first sea lord from 1955 to 1959 and chief of the British defense staff from 1959 to 1965.

Mountbatten retired in 1965. He was killed when a bomb exploded his fishing boat off the coast of Ireland. The Irish Republican Army, a terrorist group seeking Northern Ireland's independence from Britain, claimed responsibility for the bombing.   James L. Stokesbury

Mountbatten-Windsor. See Windsor (family).

Mounted Police. See Royal Canadian Mounted Police.

Mourning. See Funeral customs.

Mourning dove is an American bird with a sad, cooing call. It breeds in southeastern Alaska and from southern Canada to Mexico, and winters as far south as Panama. The bird is about 12 inches (30 centimeters) long. It flies swiftly, and its wings make a whistling sound as they move through the air.

WORLD BOOK illustration by Trevor Boyer, Linden Artists, Ltd.

The mourning dove has grayish-brown feathers. Its long tail tapers to a point and has a white border.

The mourning dove places its nest, built loosely of twigs, in a tree or bush or on the ground. The female lays two white eggs. The young hatch in about two weeks and leave the nest in about two more weeks. Young birds put their beaks in the parents' throats and feed on partly digested food mixed with a fluid called *crop milk.* Mourning doves eat weed seeds and insects.

Scientific classification. The mourning dove belongs to the pigeon and dove family, Columbidae. It is *Zenaida macroura.*

Edward H. Burtt, Jr.

See also **Dove** (picture); **Pigeon; Turtledove.**

Mouse is a small animal with soft fur, a pointed snout, round black eyes, rounded ears, and a thin tail. The word *mouse* is not the name of any one kind of animal or family of animals. Many kinds of *rodents* (gnawing animals) are called mice. They include small rats, hamsters, gerbils, jerboas, lemmings, voles, harvest mice, deer

Cy La Tour

A house mouse eats stolen grain.

mice, and grasshopper mice. All these animals have chisellike front teeth that are useful for gnawing. A rodent's front teeth grow throughout the animal's life.

There are hundreds of kinds of mice, and they live in most parts of the world. They can be found in the mountains, in fields and woodlands, in swamps, near streams, and in deserts. Probably the best known kind of mouse is the house mouse. It lives wherever people live, and often builds its nest in homes, garages, or barns. Some kinds of white house mice are raised as pets. Other kinds are used by scientists to learn about sickness, to test new drugs, and to study behavior.

House mice

House mice probably could be found in the homes of people who lived during ancient times. Those mice probably stole the people's food, just as mice do today. The word *mouse* comes from an old Sanskrit word meaning *thief.* Sanskrit is an ancient language of Asia, where scientists believe house mice originated. House mice spread from Asia throughout Europe. The ancestors of the house mice that now live in North and South America were brought there by English, French, and Spanish ships during the 1500's.

House mice always seem to be busy. Those that live in buildings may scamper about day or night. House mice that live in fields and forests usually come out only at night. All house mice climb well and can often be heard running between the walls of houses.

Body of a house mouse is $2\frac{1}{2}$ to $3\frac{1}{2}$ inches (6.4 to 8.9 centimeters) long without the tail. The tail is the same length or a little shorter. Most house mice weigh $\frac{1}{2}$ to 1 ounce (14 to 28 grams). Their size and weight, and the length of their tails, differ greatly among the many varieties and even among individuals of the same variety.

The fur of most house mice is soft, but it may be stiff and wiry. It is grayish-brown on the animal's back and sides, and yellowish-white underneath. House mice raised as pets or for use in laboratories may have pure white fur, black or brown spots, or other combinations of colors. The tail is covered by scaly skin.

A house mouse has a small head and a long, narrow snout. Several long, thin whiskers grow from the sides of the snout. These whiskers, like those of a cat, help the mouse feel its way in the dark. The animal has rounded

Facts in brief

Common name	Scientific name	Gestation period	Number of young	Where found
*House mouse	*Mus musculus*	18-21 days	4-7	Worldwide
American harvest mouse	*Reithrodontomys fulvescens*	21-24 days	1-7	North and South America
Grasshopper mouse	*Onychomys leucogaster*	29-38 days	3-4	North America
Deer mouse	*Peromyscus maniculatus*	21-27 days	1-9	North and South America

*The house mouse belongs to the family of Old World rats and mice, Muridae. The American harvest, grasshopper, and deer mice belong to the family of New World rats and mice, Cricetidae.

ears, and its eyes look somewhat like round black beads. A mouse can hear well, but it has poor sight. Probably because house mice cannot see well, they may enter a lighted room even if people are there.

Like all other rodents, mice have strong, sharp front teeth that grow throughout the animal's life. With these chisellike teeth, mice can gnaw holes in wood, tear apart packages to get at food inside, and damage books, clothing, and furniture.

Food. A house mouse eats almost anything that human beings eat. It feeds on any meat or plant materials that it can find. Mice also eat such household items as glue, leather, paste, and soap. House mice that live out of doors eat insects, and the leaves, roots, seeds, and stems of plants. Mice always seem to be looking for something to eat, but they need little food. They damage much more food than they eat.

Homes. House mice live wherever they can find food and shelter. Any dark place that is warm and quiet makes an excellent home for mice. A mouse may build its nest in a warm corner of a barn, on a beam under the roof of a garage, or in a box stored in an attic or basement. The animal may tear strips of clothing or upholstery to get materials for its nest. It may line the nest with feathers or cotton stolen from pillows. House mice that live in fields or woodlands dig holes in the ground and build nests of grass inside. They may line the nests with feathers or pieces of fur.

Young. A female house mouse may give birth every 20 to 30 days. She carries her young in her body for 18 to 21 days before they are born. She has four to seven young at a time. Newborn mice have pink skin and no fur, and their eyes are closed. They are completely helpless. Soft fur covers their bodies by the time they are 10 days old. When they are 14 days old, their eyes open. Young mice stay near the nest for about three weeks after birth. Then they leave to build their own nests and start raising families. Most female house mice begin to have young when they are about 45 days old.

Enemies. People are probably the worst enemies of the house mouse. They set traps and place poisons where mice can easily find them. Almost every meat-eating animal is an enemy of house mice. Cats and dogs hunt mice in houses and barns. Coyotes, foxes, snakes, and other animals capture them in forests and woodlands. Owls, hawks, and other birds of prey swoop down on them in fields and prairies. Rats and even other mice are also enemies. House mice may live as long as a year in a hidden corner of an attic or basement. But they have so many enemies that few wild mice survive more than two or three months. Some mice kept as pets or in laboratories may live six years.

House mice avoid their enemies by hiding. A mouse seldom wanders far from its nest. It spends most of its time within an area of about 200 feet (61 meters) in diameter. Wherever possible, the mouse moves along paths protected by furniture, boxes, or other objects. The mouse scampers as fast as it can across the open spaces between the objects. House mice do not like water and try to avoid it, but they can swim.

Some other kinds of mice

American harvest mice look like house mice, but are smaller and have more hair on their tails. Most

J. M. Conrader

White-footed mouse and her young

Jane Burton, Photo Researchers

Harvest mouse

Grasshopper mouse

Cordell Andersen, NAS

American harvest mice also have much larger ears. Harvest mice live from southwestern Canada and the western half of the United States to Ecuador. They also live in the Eastern United States south of the Potomac and Ohio rivers. Some kinds of harvest mice live in salt marshes and in tropical forests, but most species prefer open grassy regions.

Harvest mice build their nests in places where tall grass grows. They weave leaves of grass into ball-shaped nests that are 6 to 7 inches (15 to 18 centimeters) in diameter. The mice build their nests 6 to 12 inches (15 to 30 centimeters) above the ground in branches of bushes or on stems of grass. Harvest mice are excellent climbers and use the plant stems as ladders to reach their nests. They grasp the plant stems with their tails as they climb. Harvest mice also make nests in the ground.

These mice eat green plant sprouts, but they prefer seeds. They pick seeds off the ground, or they "harvest" seeds from plants by bending the plant stems to the ground where they bite off the seeds.

A female harvest mouse has one to seven young at a time. She carries the young mice in her body for 21 to 24 days before they are born. When the young are about 2 months old, they may start their own families.

Grasshopper mice are about the same size as house mice, but they look fatter and have stubby tails. Their fur is brown or gray above and white underneath. They probably got their name because they eat grasshoppers. These mice are found in the dry regions and deserts of the Western United States, and in northern Mexico. Grasshopper mice live wherever they can find shelter in the ground. They often use burrows that were abandoned by such rodents as gophers, ground squirrels, and deer mice.

The female grasshopper mouse carries her young inside her body for 29 to 38 days. Usually three or four young are born at a time. The young mice become adults when they are about three months old.

Grasshopper mice are most active at night, when they come out of their burrows to hunt. Unlike most other mice, grasshopper mice prefer to eat meat rather than plants. They eat any animal they can overpower, including insects, worms, and other mice. Their favorite foods are grasshoppers and scorpions. Grasshopper mice hunt their prey much as cats do. They creep up to their victims and attack quickly. Grasshopper mice are the only mice that make howling noises at night.

The skeleton of a mouse

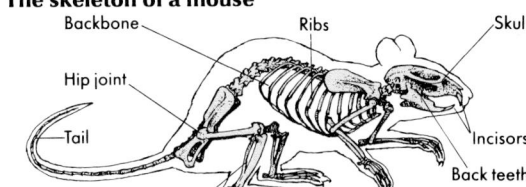

WORLD BOOK illustration by John D. Dawson

Mouse tracks

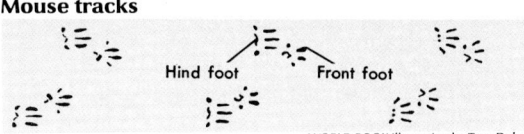

Hind foot   Front foot

WORLD BOOK illustration by Tom Dolan

© Breck P. Kent, Animals Animals

A laboratory mouse is tested to determine its ability to learn in a simple *T maze, above.* Researchers place the mouse in the maze and time how long it takes to find the food. After a few repetitions, the mouse learns to find the food more quickly.

Deer mice, sometimes called *white-footed mice,* measure 6 to 8 inches (15 to 20 centimeters) long. Their tails are $2\frac{1}{2}$ to 4 inches (6 to 10 centimeters) long. The fur on their upper parts is gray or brown, and the belly fur is white. The ears of these mice are large in relation to the size of their bodies. There are more than 50 species of deer mice. They are found from northern Colombia throughout North America as far north as Alaska and Labrador. They live in every kind of region—mountains, plains, deserts, forests, and swamps.

Deer mice build their nests in tunnels they dig, or in hollow logs, tree stumps, or cracks in rocks. The mice may go into houses to find soft materials such as cloth or cotton for their nests. They usually build several nests a year because they move out when a nest gets soiled.

A female deer mouse gives birth to one to nine young at a time. She carries them in her body for 21 to 27 days before birth. The young live in the nest for three to six weeks, and then leave to build nests of their own.

Deer mice usually rest during the day and look for food at night. They eat berries, fruits, leaves, nuts, seeds, and insects. When excited, these mice thump their front feet rapidly on the ground.   Clyde Jones

See also Rat; Rodent; Jumping mouse; Vole.

Mouse Tower is a tower on a small island in the Rhine River near Bingen, Germany. A famous legend tells that Archbishop Hatto of Mainz built the tower. According to the legend, during a famine in 974, the cruel archbishop lured the poor and needy of the town into a barn and then set it on fire. As the people shrieked among the flames, the archbishop called out, "Hear, hear how the mice squeak!" Soon afterward, a swarm of mice came to avenge the deaths. The bishop fled to the tower, but the mice swam across the Rhine and devoured him.

The city of Mainz had two archbishops named Hatto during the Middle Ages, but neither burned starving people in barns and neither was eaten by mice. *Mäuseturm,* the German name for the Mouse Tower, appears to be a form of *mautturm,* which means *toll tower.* The tower was probably built in the 1200's as a place for collecting tolls from boats on the Rhine.   C. Stephen Jaeger

Mousorgski, Modest. See Mussorgsky, Modest.

Mouth is the part of the body that is adapted for taking in food. The lips at the mouth opening help us drink and pick up our food. Inside, we have two rows of teeth, one above the other, to grind and crush food into pulp that can be swallowed and digested. Salivary glands in the walls and floor of the mouth give off saliva, which mixes with our food as we chew it. Saliva helps us swallow dry foods and aids digestion of sugars. See **Saliva.**

The mouth cavity is lined with mucous membrane. The roof of the mouth consists of a bony front part, called the *hard palate,* and a soft part in the rear, called the *soft palate.* The hard palate forms a partition between the mouth and nasal passages. The soft palate arches at the back of the mouth to form a curtain between the mouth and *pharynx* (back part of the throat). During swallowing, the soft palate closes the nasal passages from the throat to prevent food from entering the nose. The pharynx connects the mouth and nose with both the *esophagus* (tube that carries food to the stomach) and the *trachea* (windpipe that carries air to the lungs). A flexible bundle of muscles extends from the floor of the mouth to form the *tongue.* The tongue not only helps us to eat, swallow, and talk, but it contains almost all the sense organs of taste (see **Taste**).

Harmful germs may enter the body through the mouth. The mouth should be kept clean to help ward off disease. The mouth cavity is an excellent breeding place for germs because it is warm and moist.

The teeth should be cleaned thoroughly at least twice a day, and the mouth should be rinsed out after every meal. The teeth should be brushed lengthwise as well as crosswise, to remove particles of food. Jagged teeth may damage the mucous membrane and lead to infection. Periodontitis (diseased gums) causes bone loss around the teeth, which may eventually make teeth become loose and fall out. Disease of the teeth may cause the body to become infected by bacteria. Trench mouth, also called *Vincent's infection,* is an infection of the

mouth. Painful cankers may also attack the mucous membrane that lines the mouth.   Raymond L. Burich

Related articles in *World Book* include:

Canker	Periodontitis
Cold sore	Teeth
Dentistry	Tongue
Palate	Trench mouth

Movie. See Motion picture.

Mowat, *MOW uht,* **Farley** (1921-   ), is a Canadian author who has written widely about the wildlife and peoples of northern Canada. In many of his books, Mowat tells captivating stories that also explore serious ecological and conservation issues.

Mowat was born in Belleville, Ont. His first book, *People of the Deer* (1952), describes the life of the deer-hunting Ihalmiut Eskimos, a people whose population had declined from 7,000 in 1890 to 40 in 1949. The book criticizes the Canadian government for policies that led to the destruction of the Ihalmiut and their way of life. Mowat's *Never Cry Wolf* (1963) portrays a young biologist who studies wolves in the northern wilderness. This book argues that wolves are not vicious animals but play a necessary and useful role in nature. Other books by Mowat that deal with wildlife issues include *A Whale for the Killing* (1972) and *Sea of Slaughter* (1984).

Mowat also wrote the biography *Woman in the Mists: The Story of Dian Fossey and the Mountain Gorillas of Africa* (1987). This book became the basis for the movie *Gorillas in the Mist* (1988).   Rosemary Sullivan

Mowat, Sir Oliver (1820-1903), a Canadian statesman, served as prime minister and attorney general of Ontario from 1872 to 1896. During his administration, Mowat introduced the ballot in municipal and provincial elections and extended the voting franchise. He fought to obtain more political rights for the provinces.

Mowat was also one of Canada's Fathers of Confederation. These individuals were planners of the union of British colonies that formed the Dominion of Canada in 1867. Mowat was knighted in 1892. He was lieutenant governor of Ontario from 1897 until his death. He was born in what is now Kingston, Ont.   David Jay Bercuson

Moynihan, Daniel Patrick (1927-   ), a Democrat from New York, has been a member of the United States Senate since 1977. He became chairman of the Senate Finance Committee in 1993. Moynihan served as U.S. ambassador to the United Nations in 1975 and 1976.

An authority on the problems of cities and of minority groups, Moynihan first became known for his books and articles on immigration, the antipoverty program, and black family life. From 1966 to 1969, he headed the Joint Center of Urban Studies at Harvard University and Massachusetts Institute of Technology. He served as counselor to the President under Richard M. Nixon in 1969 and 1970. Moynihan returned to Harvard in 1971 as professor of education and urban politics. He remained on the Harvard faculty until 1976. Moynihan served as the nation's ambassador to India from 1973 to 1975.

Moynihan was born in Tulsa, Okla., but grew up in New York City. He graduated from Tufts University and received a doctorate from Tufts's Fletcher School of International Law and Diplomacy. He was an assistant to Governor Averell Harriman of New York in the 1950's and served in the U.S. Department of Labor from 1961 to 1965.   David S. Broder

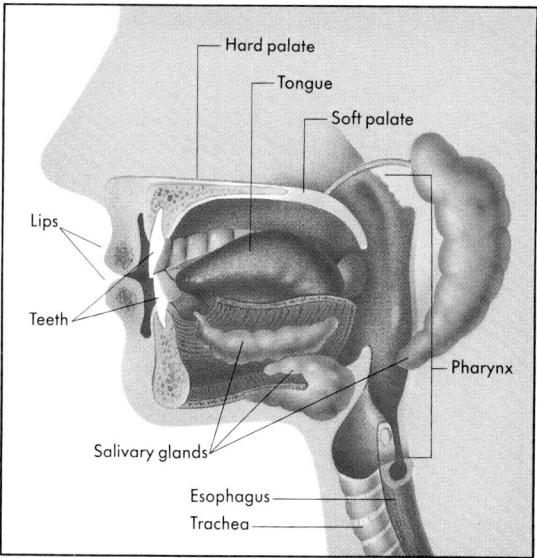

WORLD BOOK illustration by Charles Wellek

The mouth is adapted for taking in food. Food is ground by the teeth, and moistened and partly digested by saliva. The tongue tastes and mixes the food and aids in swallowing. The tongue, teeth, and lips also help form the sounds of human speech.

Mozambique, *моʜ zuhm BEEK,* is a country on the southeast coast of Africa. It covers 309,496 square miles (801,590 square kilometers) and has a population of about 17 million.

About two-thirds of the Mozambicans live in rural areas. Most of the urban centers lie near the coast. Maputo is the capital, largest city, and chief port. Mozambique is noted for its many fine harbors. Its excellent port facilities are used by some neighboring countries. Mozambique was governed by Portugal from the early 1500's until 1975, when it became independent after a 10-year struggle against Portuguese rule.

Government. Until 1990, the Front for the Liberation of Mozambique, or Frelimo, was Mozambique's only legal political party. That year, a new constitution was adopted that legalized all political parties. Multiparty presidential and legislative elections were planned. Until the elections are held, the leader of Frelimo was scheduled to remain as president. Members of the national legislature, who were appointed by Frelimo, were

Facts in brief

Capital: Maputo.
Official language: Portuguese.
Official name: *República de Moçambique* (Republic of Mozambique).
Area: 309,496 sq. mi. (801,590 km²). *Coastline*—1,556 mi. (2,504 km). *Greatest distances*—north-south, 1,100 mi. (1,770 km); east-west, 680 mi. (1,094 km).
Elevation: *Highest*—Mt. Binga, 7,992 ft. (2,436 m). *Lowest*—sea level.
Population: *Estimated 1994 population*—17,417,000; density, 56 persons per sq. mi. (22 per km²); distribution, 66 per cent rural, 34 per cent urban. *1980 census*—12,117,000. *Estimated 1999 population*—19,883,000.
Chief products: Cashews, cassava, coconuts, cotton, shrimp, sugar cane.
Flag: The flag has three broad, horizontal stripes of green, black, and yellow separated by narrow white bands. To the left is a red triangle with a yellow star. The star holds a book with a hoe and a rifle crossed over it. See **Flag** (picture: Flags of Africa).
Money: *Basic unit*—metical.

also scheduled to remain in office.

People. Almost all Mozambicans are black Africans. Other groups, including Arabs, Europeans, and Pakistanis, make up less than 1 per cent of the population. Most of the blacks belong to groups that speak one of the Bantu languages. The largest of these groups, the Makua-Lomwe, account for about 40 per cent of the population of Mozambique. Few blacks can speak Portuguese, the country's official language. Some Mozambicans speak English when conducting business activities.

Most Mozambicans are farmers, but their techniques are extremely simple. Some farmers use the *slash-and-burn* method, which involves cutting and burning forest

Mozambique

- National park (N.P.)
- ⎯⎯ International boundary
- ⎯⎯ Road
- ⎯⎯ Railroad
- ⊛ National capital
- • Other city or town
- + Elevation above sea level

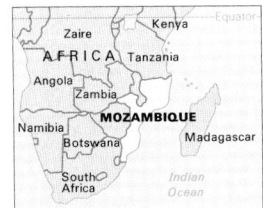

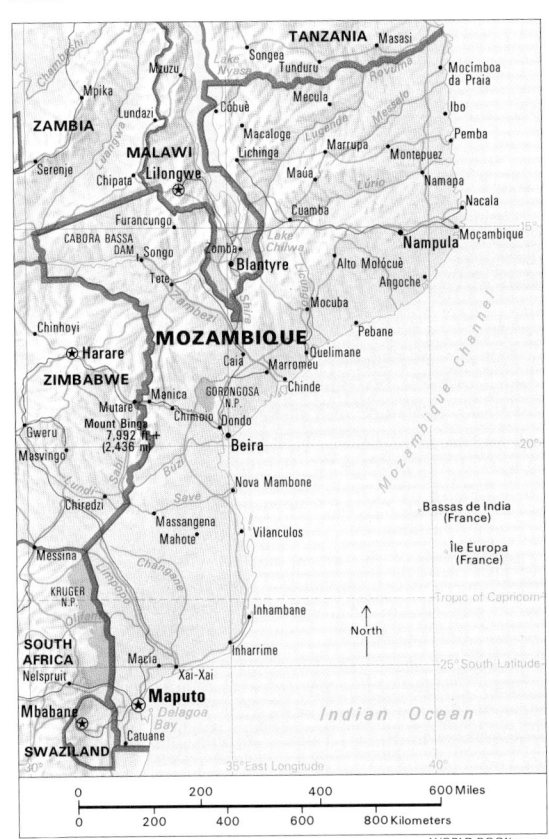

0 | 200 | 400 | 600 Miles
0 | 200 | 400 | 600 | 800 Kilometers

WORLD BOOK maps

© Jean Gaumy, Magnum

Maputo, the capital of Mozambique, is a leading African port. Ships from many countries carry cargo to and from the city. Maputo lies on Delagoa Bay, an inlet of the Indian Ocean.

© Jean Gaumy, Magnum

An outdoor market, where people buy food and other goods, serves as a shopping center in many parts of Mozambique. The market shown above is located in the capital, Maputo.

trees to clear an area for planting. Farmers in some areas of the country use more modern techniques.

About 55 per cent of the people of Mozambique practice traditional African religions. Many of this group are *animists,* who believe that everything in nature has a soul. Others worship the spirits of their ancestors. About 30 per cent of the people are Christians, mostly Roman Catholics. Many of the remaining people are Muslims.

Only about 15 per cent of Mozambique's people 15 years of age or older can read and write, but the government has begun programs to improve education. A university was established in Maputo in 1962.

Land and climate. Almost half of Mozambique is covered by a flat plain that extends inland from the coast. The land rises steadily beyond the plain, and high plateaus and mountains run along much of the western border. Sand dunes and swamps line the coast. Grasslands and tropical forests cover much of the country.

Many sizable rivers flow east through Mozambique into the Indian Ocean, and their basins have extremely fertile soil. Cashew trees and coconut palms grow throughout the country. Animal life in Mozambique includes crocodiles, elephants, lions, and zebras.

Mozambique has a basically tropical climate, but temperatures and rainfall vary considerably in different areas. Temperatures average 68 °F (20 °C) in July and 80 °F (27 °C) in January. About 80 per cent of the annual rainfall occurs from November to March. The rainfall ranges from 16 to 48 inches (41 to 122 centimeters).

Economy of Mozambique is not well developed. Agriculture is Mozambique's major economic activity. The nation is a leading producer of cashews. Other important crops include coconuts, cotton, sugar cane, and cassava, a starchy root. Some people catch fish and shrimp in the Indian Ocean. Mozambique's economy depends partly on payments by South Africa, Zimbabwe, Swaziland, and Malawi for the use of railroads and port facilities. Maputo and Beira are the chief seaports. Also, many Mozambicans work in South Africa.

Industrial development has been slow and has occurred mainly in the food-processing and oil-refining industries. Coal is mined in central Mozambique. The Cahora Bassa Dam in the northwest produces electric power, much of which is transmitted to South Africa.

Most of Mozambique's roads are unpaved. Several railroads link Mozambican ports with other African countries. The chief airport is at Maputo. Three daily newspapers are published in the country.

History. People have lived in what is now Mozambique since the 4000's B.C. Bantu-speaking people settled there before A.D. 100. Arabs lived in the area by the 800's. Portuguese explorers first visited Mozambique in 1497. They established a trading post there in 1505, and the country became a slave-trading center. But most of Mozambique was undeveloped until the 1900's.

Through the years, Portuguese control of Mozambique was threatened by Arabs, Africans, and some European nations. In 1885, Africa was divided among various European powers, and Mozambique was recognized as a Portuguese colony. It was often called Portuguese East Africa. Borders similar to those of present-day Mozambique were established in 1891.

Towns and railroads were built in Mozambique during the late 1800's and early 1900's, and the Portuguese population rose. In the 1950's, many blacks became increasingly discontented with white Portuguese rule.

© Susan Meiselas, Magnum

At an open-air school in Mozambique, children learn the basics of mathematics. The government of Mozambique has begun programs to improve education. But about three-fourths of the people 15 years of age or older still cannot read and write.

Frelimo was established in 1961 as a guerrilla movement. It began military attacks against the Portuguese in 1964 and gained control of part of northern Mozambique. Fighting continued for 10 years.

Portugal agreed in 1974 to grant independence to its colonies. Mozambique became independent on June 25, 1975. Frelimo—which based its policies on the philosophy of Karl Marx and V. I. Lenin, two founders of Communism—took over the government. Its government gained control of all education, health and legal services, housing, farmland, and major industries. Most of the Portuguese left Mozambique at that time.

In 1976, Mozambique closed its border with Rhodesia (now Zimbabwe) to protest that country's white minority government. This action cost Mozambique much income from Rhodesian use of its railroads and ports. Also, Mozambique limited the number of its workers in South Africa, which has a white minority government.

Border fighting broke out between Mozambican and Rhodesian troops. Many black Rhodesians fled to Mozambique to use bases there in their fight against the Rhodesian government. In 1980, blacks gained control of Rhodesia's government, and the country's name was changed to Zimbabwe. Friction between Mozambique and that country ended (see **Zimbabwe** [History]). Mozambique aided guerrilla forces that opposed the South African government. South Africa gave aid to guerrillas who were fighting against Mozambique's government. In 1984, Mozambique and South Africa signed a treaty in which both countries agreed to stop giving assistance to the guerrillas. But the guerrillas in Mozambique, called the National Resistance Movement, or Renamo, continued fighting in Mozambique. The fighting disrupted farming and other economic activities.

In the early 1980's, Mozambique's government decided to permit the increase of private enterprise. It began helping some people to start their own businesses and began a shift from the Communist-style state farms to private and family-run farms. In 1989, the government officially ended its Marxist economic policies.

In the 1980's and early 1990's, droughts and the disruption resulting from the civil war caused food shortages that led to malnutrition and starvation for millions of people. Direct peace talks between Frelimo and Renamo began in 1990, and the groups signed a peace agreement in 1992. Until 1990, Frelimo was Mozambique's only legal political party. New parties began to register legally in 1992. Multiparty elections were to be held, possibly in mid-1994.   L. H. Gann

See also **Maputo.**

Mozart, *MOHT sahrt,* **Wolfgang Amadeus,** *AM uh DAY uhs* (1756-1791), an Austrian composer, is considered one of the greatest and most creative musical geniuses of all time. With Joseph Haydn, he was the leading composer of the classical style of the late 1700's. Mozart died before his 36th birthday, but he still left more than 600 works.

His life

Mozart was born in Salzburg. His father, Leopold, was the leader of the local orchestra, and also wrote an important book about violin playing. At the age of 3, Wolfgang showed signs of remarkable musical talent. He learned to play the harpsichord, a keyboard instrument that preceded the piano, at the age of 4. He was composing music at 5, and when he was 6, he played for the Austrian empress at her court in Vienna.

Before he was 14, Mozart had composed many works for the harpsichord, piano, or the violin, as well as orchestral and other works. His father recognized Wolfgang's amazing talent and devoted most of his time to his son's general and musical education. While serving as his teacher, Leopold took Wolfgang on concert tours through much of Europe. Wolfgang composed, gave public performances, met many musicians, and played the organ in many churches. In 1769, like his father before him, he began working for the archbishop of Salzburg, who also ruled the province. The Mozarts often quarreled with the archbishop, partly because Wolfgang was often absent from Salzburg. The archbishop dismissed young Mozart in 1781.

Mozart was actually glad to leave Salzburg, a small town, and seek his fortune in Vienna, one of the music capitals of Europe. By this time people took less notice of him, because he was no longer a child prodigy. But he was a brilliant performer and active as a composer.

Mozart married in 1782. He earned his living in Vienna by selling his compositions, giving public performances, and giving music lessons. None of these activities produced enough income to support his family. Mozart even traveled to Germany for the coronation of a new emperor, but his concerts there did not attract as much attention as he hoped. Mozart died in poverty on Dec. 5, 1791.

His works

Operas. Mozart excelled in almost every kind of musical composition. Several of his 22 operas gained wide recognition before and after his death, and they still please audiences all over the world. *The Marriage of Figaro* (1786) and *Don Giovanni* (1787) are operas Mozart composed with words in Italian. *The Magic Flute* (1791) has German texts. Each of these operas contains *arias* (songs for single voices), *recitative* (rapidly sung dialogue), *ensembles* in which several people sing at the same time, and choruses. The orchestra provides an ever-changing expressive accompaniment. The drama ranges from comedy to tragedy.

Symphonies. Mozart wrote over 40 symphonies, many of which are performed today. Some originally were *overtures* (orchestral introductions) for operas, and last only a few minutes. His later symphonies, which are the most popular, are full-length orchestral compositions that last 20 to 30 minutes. Most consist of four *movements* (sections). His last and most famous symphony, Number 41 (1788), is nicknamed the *Jupiter.*

Church music. Mozart composed a great amount of church music, most of it for performance at the Salzburg Cathedral. He wrote Masses and shorter pieces called *motets;* and he set psalms to music, especially for the vespers (afternoon or evening) service. The music is beautiful and varied. It includes choral and solo parts, usually with accompaniment by organ and orchestra. Mozart's best-known sacred work is the *Requiem* (Mass for the Dead). He began it in 1791 and while writing it seems to have become concerned about his own death. Parts of the *Requiem* were composed during his final illness. He died before the work was finished.

Other works. Mozart wrote other, generally lighter, orchestral works, called *serenades.* Some were intended for outdoor performance. One has become well known as *Eine kleine Nachtmusik* (*A Little Night Music,* 1787). Mozart also wrote many compositions called *concertos* for a solo instrument such as violin or piano, with orchestral accompaniment. He often played the solo part.

Throughout his life Mozart composed *chamber music*—works for a small number of instruments in

A Mozart family portrait from about 1780 shows the young Wolfgang seated next to his sister, Nannerl, who was a noted pianist. Their father, Leopold, *right,* gained recognition as a violinist and composer. A portrait of Wolfgang's mother, Anna Maria, hangs on the wall.

which only one musician plays each part. Mozart concentrated on string quartets (two violins, viola, and cello). He was influenced in this by Haydn, whose quartets he admired, and to whom he dedicated six quartets.

Mozart's sonatas for keyboard (harpsichord or piano) and for violin and keyboard are outstanding. The piano was then still fairly new and was widely played by amateurs. More than any other composer, Mozart helped to make the instrument popular.

His style. In spite of his hardships and disappointments, much of Mozart's music is cheerful and vigorous. He had a sense of humor and liked puns and practical jokes. He composed many lighter works. These works include the opera *Così Fan Tutte* (*All Women Are Like That,* 1790), much of his early instrumental music, and *canons* (rounds) with nonsense words.

Mozart also produced deeply serious music. His most profound works include his late piano concertos, several string quartets, the string quintet in G minor, and his last three symphonies—E flat major, G minor, and the *Jupiter.* Larger works contain both serious and light elements, as does *Don Giovanni.*

Mozart belonged to the Order of Freemasons and wrote several compositions for their meetings. Some scenes from his fairy-tale opera *The Magic Flute* were inspired by Masonic traditions and beliefs.

A catalog of Mozart's works was first prepared by Ludwig Köchel (1800-1877), a German music lover. Mozart's works are still identified by the numbers Köchel assigned to them. A famous music and theater festival held each summer in Salzburg features his works.

Daniel T. Politoske

See also **Classical music** (The classical period); **Opera** (Mozart; the opera repertoire). For a *Reading and Study Guide,* see *Mozart, Wolfgang Amadeus,* in the Research Guide/Index, Volume 22.

Additional resources

The Mozart Compendium: A Guide to Mozart's Life and Music. Ed. by H. C. Robbins Landon. Schirmer Bks., 1990.
Sadie, Stanley. *The New Grove Mozart.* Norton, 1982.

MS. See **Multiple sclerosis.**

Mubarak, *muh BAHR ak,* **Hosni,** *HAHS nee* (1928-), became president of Egypt in October 1981. He succeeded Anwar el-Sadat, who was assassinated by Islamic fundamentalist extremists. As president, Mubarak continued Sadat's policies, including the fulfillment of the 1979 peace agreement between Egypt and Israel (see **Egypt** [Egypt today]). He has allowed more political and journalistic freedom than Sadat had. Mubarak faces strong opposition from Islamic extremists in Egypt, who also challenged Sadat's policies and Egypt's negotiations with Israel.

In August 1990, Iraq invaded and occupied Kuwait. Mubarak played a leading role in organizing Arab opposition to Iraq. Egypt and other Arab nations and the United States and other Western nations

State Information Service of Egypt
Hosni Mubarak

formed a military coalition against Iraq. In February 1991, the coalition drove the Iraqis out of Kuwait. See **Persian Gulf War.**

Violence by Islamic extremists increased greatly in the early 1990's in Egypt. These people attacked Egyptian Christians, foreign tourists, and other foreigners. In 1992, Mubarak's government began raiding extremist strongholds and making arrests.

Mubarak was born in Kafr-El-Meselha, a village about 80 miles (130 kilometers) north of Cairo. He graduated from Egypt's Military Academy in 1949, and its Air Force Academy in 1950. He then served as a fighter pilot and a bomber squadron commander in the Egyptian Air Force. He commanded the air force from 1972 to 1975, when Sadat appointed him vice president.

Malcolm C. Peck

Mucilage, *MYOO suh lihj,* is a thick, sticky substance usually made by dissolving gum in water, or in some other liquid. The purpose of mucilage is to cause two substances to *adhere* (stick together). Therefore, mucilage is classified as an *adhesive.* The exact ingredients of mucilage vary with the adhesive's planned uses. Gum arabic dissolved in hot water makes gum-arabic mucilage. When aluminum sulfate is added to the solution, the adhesive may be used to make paper stick to glass. Dissolving *dextrin* (a substance made from starch) in cold water makes a mucilage that is used on postage stamps. Glue and gelatin also are used to make mucilage.

James Nelson Rieck

See also **Glue; Gum arabic.**

Muckrakers were a group of writers in the early 1900's who exposed social and political evils in the United States. They wrote about such problems as child labor, prostitution, racial discrimination, and corruption in business and government. In 1906, President Theodore Roosevelt labeled them *muckrakers* because he felt they were concerned only with turning up filth. But these writers increased public awareness of social problems and forced government and business to reform.

Nearly all the muckrakers were journalists who wrote for inexpensive monthly magazines, including *American Magazine, Collier's, Cosmopolitan, Everybody's Magazine,* and *McClure's Magazine.* Some historians and novelists were also called muckrakers.

Muckraking gained much support from the public after *McClure's* published three exposés in 1903. The articles included investigations of corrupt city government by Lincoln Steffens and of the Standard Oil Company by Ida M. Tarbell. Many articles by muckrakers later appeared as books, including *The Shame of the Cities* (1904) by Steffens and *History of the Standard Oil Company* (1904) by Tarbell. Other prominent muckrakers were Samuel Hopkins Adams, Ray Stannard Baker, Charles E. Russell, and Upton Sinclair.

The muckrakers helped prepare the way for many reforms in the United States. Sinclair's novel *The Jungle* (1906) exposed unsanitary conditions in the meat-packing industry and led to the nation's first pure food laws. Other reforms included the direct election of U.S. senators and greater government regulation of business. Muckraking disappeared by about 1912, partly because the public lost interest. David Chalmers

See also **Sinclair, Upton; Steffens, Lincoln; Tarbell, Ida M.**

Mucoviscidosis. See Cystic fibrosis.

Mucus, *MYOO kuhs,* is a thick, clear, slimy fluid found in the nose, mouth, and other organs and passages that open to the outside of the body. It is made up mostly of a compound of protein and sugar. This fluid is produced by cells in the mucous membranes and covers the surfaces of the membranes.

Mucus performs two principal duties. It provides lubrication for material which must pass over the membranes, such as food passing down the *esophagus* (food tube). It also catches foreign matter and keeps it from entering the body. The mucous membranes of the nose, sinuses, and *trachea* (windpipe) are covered with fine hairlike structures known as *cilia.* The cilia contain microscopic muscles that enable them to rhythmically move back and forth. The motions of the cilia cause the mucus to carry bacteria and dust up the trachea to the nose and throat where it can be swallowed or blown out.   Jerome C. Goldstein

See also **Cold, Common; Cystic fibrosis; Membrane; Mouth; Nose.**

Mud hen. See Coot.

Mudd, Samuel Alexander (1833-1883), was the doctor who set John Wilkes Booth's leg after Booth assassinated United States President Abraham Lincoln in 1865. Mudd claimed he did not recognize Booth. A military court found Mudd guilty as an accessory after the fact in the assassination. Sentenced to life imprisonment, Mudd saved many prisoners and guards in a yellow fever epidemic. In 1869, he was pardoned by President Andrew Johnson and freed from prison. Mudd was born in Charles County, Maryland.   Mark E. Neely, Jr.

Mudpuppy is a large salamander that lives in American ponds, streams, lakes, and rivers. They may grow as much as 17 inches (43 centimeters) long, but an 8-inch (20-centimeter) animal may be full-grown.

The mudpuppy has a slimy body. It may be dark brown, gray-brown, or black, usually with darker spots. It has a powerful flat tail and four weak legs. It has deep purplish-red external gills behind its short, flat head. The mudpuppy is also called the *water dog.*

Mudpuppies live in the Great Lakes, the Mississippi River, and ponds and streams as far south as Georgia and as far west as Texas. Mudpuppies usually stay in 2 to 8 feet (0.6 to 2.4 meters) of fresh water, especially among water plants. They attach their yellow eggs to

E. R. Degginger

The mudpuppy is a type of salamander. It has a powerful flat tail and four weak legs. It lives in American ponds and streams and eats crayfish, fish eggs, and other water animals.

some object lying under about 4 feet (1.2 meters) of sunny water. The young are about $\frac{3}{4}$ inch (19 millimeters) long when they hatch. Mudpuppies eat crayfish, fish eggs, and other water animals. They usually hunt during the hours of dawn or dusk. Mudpuppies may remain active throughout the year.

Scientific classification. The mudpuppy belongs to the family Proteidae. The scientific name for the most common mudpuppy is *Necturus maculosus.*   Don C. Forester

Muffler is a device that greatly reduces the exhaust noise of an engine. Mufflers are used on nearly all automobiles. The exhaust of a gasoline engine originates in the cylinders. When the exhaust leaves the cylinders, it is at a much higher temperature and pressure than the outside air (see **Gasoline engine**). If released directly into the air from the cylinders, the exhaust would expand suddenly, producing a loud, sharp noise. In the muffler and in other parts of the exhaust system, the gases are allowed to expand gradually and to cool. The pressure is thereby reduced, and little noise results when the exhaust is released.   William H. Haverdink

Mugabe, *moo GAH bay,* **Robert Gabriel** (1924-), became head of the government of Zimbabwe in 1980. Mugabe heads the country's largest political party, the Zimbabwe African National Union-Patriotic Front (ZANU-PF). During the 1970's, Mugabe helped lead the country's black nationalists in a military and political struggle to end white-minority rule. Nearly all the people of Zimbabwe are black, but whites controlled the

How a muffler works

A muffler reduces the noise made by exhaust gases from a gasoline engine. The device passes the gases through perforated pipes called *louver tubes.* These tubes enable the gases to expand and cool so that the gases do not produce a loud noise when they reach the outside air. *Resonating chambers* also help deaden exhaust noise by absorbing some of the sound produced by the gases as they flow through the muffler.

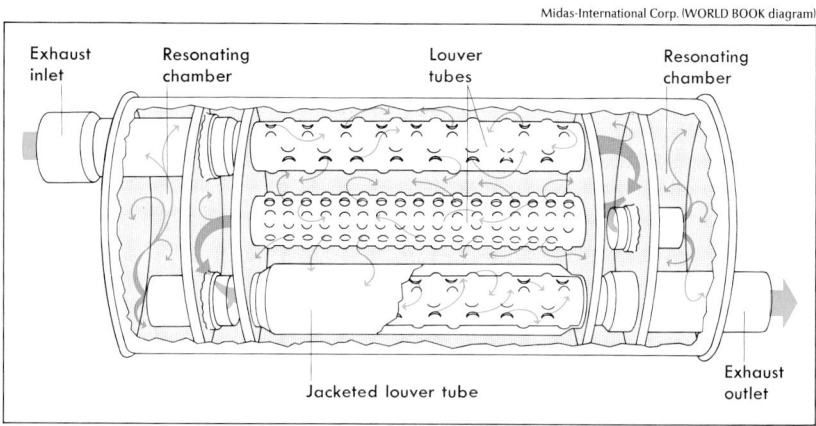

Midas-International Corp. (WORLD BOOK diagram)

Exhaust inlet

Resonating chamber

Louver tubes

Resonating chamber

Jacketed louver tube

Exhaust outlet

government from about 1890 to 1979. See **Zimbabwe** (History).

A supporter of Marxist ideals, Mugabe has worked to establish a one-party socialist state. But conflicts between the Shona and the Ndebele, Zimbabwe's largest ethnic groups, at first blocked his efforts. The Shona tended to support Mugabe's ZANU-PF, while most of the Ndebele supported Joshua Nkomo's Zimbabwe African People's Union. In 1989, Mugabe and Nkomo merged their parties. The new party, headed by Mugabe, retained the name ZANU-PF. In 1990, ZANU-PF rejected Mugabe's proposal for instituting a one-party state, but other parties have little power.

© Allan Tannenbaum, Sygma
Robert Mugabe

Mugabe was born in Kutama, near what is now Harare, Zimbabwe. In 1963, he helped found ZANU-PF. The white government jailed him from 1964 to 1974. He became prime minister after his party won a parliamentary majority in 1980. In 1987, Parliament elected Mugabe to the new post of executive president. The voters reelected him in 1990.

Sanford J. Ungar

Mughal Empire. See Mogul Empire.

Mugwumps were influential Republicans who refused to support their party's presidential candidate, James G. Blaine, in 1884. The Mugwumps, who supported government reform, did not trust Blaine and believed he opposed reform. They worked for the Democratic candidate, Grover Cleveland. In the election, Cleveland narrowly defeated Blaine. See also **Cleveland, Grover** (Election of 1884). Robert W. Cherny

Muhammad, *moo HAM uhd* (A.D. 570?-632), was a prophet whose life and teachings form the basis of the Islamic religion. The name *Muhammad* means *Praised One.* There are several common spellings of the name, including *Mohammad, Mohammed,* and *Mahomet.* Muslims believe Muhammad was the last messenger of God. They believe he completed the sacred teachings of such earlier prophets as Abraham, Moses, and Jesus. Muslims respect Muhammad but do not worship him.

Muhammad was one of the most influential men of all time. He felt himself called to be God's prophet. This belief gave him the strength to bring about many changes in Arabia. When Muhammad began to preach in the 600's, Arabia was a wild, lawless land. The fierce tribes of the deserts fought continual bloody wars.

In Mecca, a city in southwestern Arabia, there was much suffering among the poor. Most of the people worshiped many gods, and prayed to idols and spirits.

Muhammad brought a new message to his people from God. He taught that there is only one God, and that this God requires people to make *Islam* (submission) to Him. Muhammad replaced the old loyalty to tribes with a new tie of equality and allegiance among all Muslims. He also preached against the injustice of the wealthy classes in Mecca, and tried to help the poor.

During his lifetime, Muhammad led his people to unite in a great religious movement. Within a hundred years after his death, Muslims carried the teachings of Muhammad into other parts of the Middle East, into northern Africa, Europe, and Asia. Today, there are Muslim communities throughout the world.

Early life. Muhammad was born in Mecca. His father died before his birth, and his mother died when he was a child. His grandfather, and later Abu Talib, his uncle, became his guardians. For a time, Muhammad lived with a desert tribe. He learned to tend sheep and camels. According to tradition, he joined his uncle on caravan journeys through Arabia to Syria. He probably attended assemblies and fairs in Mecca, where he may have heard people of different faiths express their ideas.

At the age of 25, Muhammad entered the service of Khadija, a wealthy widow of about 40. He later married her. They had two sons and four daughters. The sons died young. One daughter, Fatima, married Ali, son of Abu Talib. Many Muslims trace their descent from Muhammad through this couple (see **Fatimid dynasty**).

His religious life. The most sacred shrine in Mecca was the Kaaba. It had a black stone, believed to be especially sacred, in one corner. When Muhammad was 35, a flood damaged the Kaaba. Because of his moral excellence, Muhammad was chosen to set the sacred stone back into place (see **Kaaba**). Later, when Muhammad was meditating alone in a cave on Mount Hira, a vision appeared to him. Muslims believe the vision was of the angel Gabriel, who called Muhammad to serve as a prophet and proclaim God's message to his people.

At first, Muhammad doubted that his vision had come from God. But his wife Khadija reassured him. She became his first disciple. For a time, no more revelations came, and Muhammad grew discouraged. Then Gabriel

S. M. Amin, *Aramco World* Magazine
The burial place of Muhammad is the Prophet's Mosque in Medina, Saudi Arabia, *above.* Muhammad died in Medina in A.D. 632. He had fled there from Mecca in 622. Most Muslims who make a yearly pilgrimage to Mecca visit this mosque.

came again, and told him, "Arise and warn, magnify thy Lord . . . wait patiently for Him." At first, Muhammad may have told only relatives and friends of the revelations. But soon he began to preach publicly. Most people who heard him ridiculed him, but some believed. Abu Bakr, a rich merchant, became a disciple. Omar (Umar Ibn al-Khattab in Arabic), a Meccan leader, persecuted Muhammad at first, but later accepted him as a prophet.

The Hegira. Muhammad continued to preach in Mecca until several calamities took place. First, both Khadija and Abu Talib died. Also the people of Mecca began to hate Muhammad for his claims and his attacks on their way of life. Finally, in A.D. 622, Muhammad fled north to the nearby city of Medina, then called Yathrib. His emigration to Medina is called the *Hegira*. It is considered so important that the Muslim calendar begins with the year of the Hegira. The people of Medina welcomed Muhammad. His preaching and statesmanship soon won most of them as followers.

His teachings. Muhammad was now the head of both a religion and a community, and he made his message law. He abolished idol worship and the killing of unwanted baby girls. He limited *polygyny* (marriage to more than one wife at a time) and restricted divorce. He reformed inheritance laws, regulated slavery, and helped the poor. He also banned war and violence except for self-defense and for the cause of Islam.

Muhammad seems to have expected Jews and Christians to accept him as a prophet. At first he was friendly toward them. He chose Jerusalem as the direction to be faced in prayer, similar to the Jewish practice. He also set aside Friday as a Muslim day of congregational prayer, perhaps because the Jews began their Sabbath preparations then. But the Jews of Medina conspired against him with his enemies in Mecca. Muhammad angrily drove them from the city and organized a purely Muslim society. To symbolize the independence of the new religion, he ordered Muslims to face Mecca, instead of Jerusalem, when praying.

The Meccans went to war against Muhammad and his followers. They attacked Medina several times but were always driven back. In 630, Muhammad entered Mecca in triumph. He offered pardon to the people there, most of whom accepted him as the Prophet of God. He destroyed the pagan idols in the Kaaba, prayed there, and made it a *mosque* (house of worship). Muhammad died two years later in Medina. His tomb is in the Prophet's Mosque in Medina (see **Medina**).   Charles J. Adams

Critically reviewed by Ali Hassan Abdel-Kader

Related articles in *World Book* include:

Additional resources

Cook, Michael A. *Muhammad.* Oxford, 1983.
Schimmel, Annemarie. *And Muhammad Is His Messenger: The Veneration of the Prophet in Islamic Piety.* Univ. of North Carolina Pr., 1985.

Muhammad II, *moo HAM uhd* (1432-1481), also known as Mehmed II or Mehmet II, was the seventh *sultan* (ruler) of the Ottoman Empire. He is sometimes called *The Conqueror* because he conquered Constantinople (now Istanbul), capital of the Byzantine Empire, in 1453. His victory ended that empire, which once ruled much of Africa, Europe, and the Middle East.

Muhammad became sultan in 1444 but was deposed in 1446. He regained power in 1451 and ruled until 1481 as one of the greatest Ottoman sultans. Muhammad extended Ottoman rule in the Balkans, Asia Minor, and the Crimea. He also reorganized the empire's administrative system and rebuilt Istanbul, which had badly deteriorated in the last days of the Byzantine Empire.

Muhammad was well-educated. He knew several languages and used ideas from other cultures to his empire's advantage.   Justin McCarthy

See also **Ottoman Empire** (Expansion and decline).

Muhammad, *moo HAM uhd,* **Elijah,** *ih LY juh* (1897-1975), was the major leader of the Nation of Islam, commonly known as the Black Muslims. This organization combines religious beliefs with black nationalism. Muhammad favored racial separation and wanted to establish a black nation within the United States.

Muhammad was born in Sandersville, Ga. His given and family name was Elijah Poole. In 1923, he moved to Detroit, where he worked on an automobile assembly line. In 1930, he met the founder of the Black Muslims, W. D. Fard (or Wali Farad). Fard eventually chose this devoted disciple as his chief aide and gave him the Muslim name Muhammad.

After Fard disappeared in 1934, Muhammad led a number of Black Muslims to Chicago, where he established the organization's main headquarters. He also set up the worship of Fard as Allah and himself as the Messenger of Allah and head of the Black Muslims. Muhammad built on the teaching of Fard and combined aspects of Islam with the black nationalism of black leader Marcus Garvey. Aided by his chief disciple, Malcolm X, Muhammad built the movement and encouraged its rapid spread in the 1950's and 1960's.   Lawrence H. Mamiya

Wide World

Elijah Muhammad

See also **Black Muslims.**

Muhammad Ali, the boxer. See **Ali, Muhammad.**

Muhammad Ali, *moo HAM uhd AH lee* (1769-1849), ruled Egypt from 1805 to 1848. He used French and other European advisers to help modernize Egypt and to increase its wealth and power. Under him, the Egyptian government and army came to be patterned after those of European countries. But he did not encourage democracy. He kept power firmly in his own hands.

Muhammad Ali was born in Kavalla, then part of the Turkish-based Ottoman Empire and now in Greece. In 1801, he helped evict French invaders from Egypt as an officer in the Ottoman army. The Ottoman *sultan* (prince) named him governor of Egypt in 1805. In 1831, Muhammad Ali turned against the sultan and attacked Ottoman forces, gaining temporary control of an area that now includes Syria. In 1841, the Ottoman Empire granted him and his family the hereditary right to rule Egypt. His descendants held this right until 1953, though they usually ruled under British control.   Justin McCarthy

See also **Egypt** (Muhammad Ali and modernization).

Muhammad Reza Pahlavi. See Mohammad Reza Pahlavi.

Muhammadanism. See Islam; Muslims.

Muhlenberg, *MYOO luhn burg,* **Henry Melchior** (1711-1787), was a key figure in organizing Lutheran churches in America. Muhlenberg was born in Einbeck, Germany. In 1741, he responded to a request from Lutherans in the Philadelphia area for a pastor. When he arrived from Germany in 1742, he found the Lutheran movement disorganized and weak. Muhlenberg worked to teach Lutheran beliefs and build a strong, stable, religious identity among Lutheran colonists. He was the leader of the Pennsylvania Ministerium, which oversaw Lutheran expansion throughout the colonies and provided missionary pastors for new churches until the late 1700's.

Muhlenberg's oldest son, John, a Lutheran minister, served in the United States Congress (see **Muhlenberg, John Peter Gabriel**). His second son, Frederick Augustus Conrad, also a Lutheran minister, served as the first Speaker of the U.S. House of Representatives from 1789 to 1791 and also from 1793 to 1795. Frederick's grandson William, an Episcopal clergyman, founded Flushing Institute, one of the first church-sponsored U.S. schools, which opened in 1828.   Charles H. Lippy

Muhlenberg, *MYOO luhn burg,* **John Peter Gabriel** (1746-1807), a Lutheran minister, became a colonial military leader during the Revolutionary War in America (1775-1783). He later was elected to the United States Congress.

Muhlenberg served at churches in New Jersey from 1760 to 1771 and then became a minister in Woodstock, Va. There, after a Sunday service in 1776, Muhlenberg removed his robe to reveal a military uniform. He enrolled men in his parish into a regiment and became its colonel. He commanded troops at the battles of Brandywine and Germantown in Pennsylvania; Monmouth, N.J.; and Yorktown, Va., and rose to the rank of major general. Pennsylvania elected him to three terms in the U.S. House of Representatives—1789 to 1791, 1793 to 1795, and 1799 to 1801.

Muhlenberg was born in Trappe, Pa. A statue of him represents Pennsylvania in the U.S. Capitol. His father, Henry M. Muhlenberg, helped found the Lutheran Church in America.   Henry Warner Bowden

Muir, *myoor,* **John** (1838-1914), an explorer, naturalist, and writer, campaigned for the conservation of land, water, and forests in the United States. His efforts influenced Congress to pass the Yosemite National Park Bill in 1890, establishing both Yosemite and Sequoia national parks. Muir helped persuade President Theodore Roosevelt to set aside 148 million acres (59,900,000 hectares) of forest reserves. A redwood forest near San Francisco was named Muir Woods in 1908 in his honor.

Muir tramped through many regions of the United States, Europe, Asia, Africa, and the Arctic. He spent six years in the area of Yosemite Valley and was the first person to explain the valley's glacial origin. In 1879, Muir discovered a glacier in Alaska that now bears his name. He called California "the grand side of the mountain" and owned a large fruit ranch there. In 1892, he founded the Sierra Club, which became a leading conservation organization (see **Sierra Club**). Muir wrote a number of books, including *The Mountains of California* (1894), *Our*

National Parks (1901), and *The Yosemite* (1912).

Muir was born in Dunbar, Scotland. His family moved to Wisconsin when he was 11. He grew up on a farm and developed a great love of nature. As a boy, he attracted attention with his inventions. He entered the University of Wisconsin at the age of 22. Muir supported himself by teaching and by doing farm work during the summer. His interests included botany and geology.   Stephen Fox

See also **Conservation** (picture: Vast areas were set aside as national parks).

Muir Woods National Monument, *myoor,* near San Francisco, has one of California's most famous redwood groves. William Kent, a California statesman, donated Muir Woods to the United States. It was established in 1908. For the area of the monument, see

Richard Frear, National Park Service

Muir Woods National Monument features a grove of towering redwood trees. The monument is located in a coastal valley just north of San Francisco.

National Park System (table: National monuments).
Critically reviewed by the National Park Service

Mujibur Rahman, *MOO jee bur RAH mahn* (1920-1975), became the first prime minister of Bangladesh in January 1972. Mujibur Rahman (known as Mujib) resigned as prime minister in January 1975 and took office as president of Bangladesh. Military leaders of the country overthrew Mujib's government and killed him in August 1975.

Mujib's rise to national leadership followed 25 years of political activity in East Pakistan (now Bangladesh). During that period, he was held as a political prisoner for a total of more than 10 years.

In 1970, Mujib became the unrivaled leader of the East Pakistanis. That year, the Awami League, the party headed by Mujib, won a majority of the seats in an assembly that was to write a new constitution for Pakistan. Mujib met with the West Pakistani leaders to discuss the proposed constitution. But the talks broke down, and civil war erupted between East and West Pakistan. The government imprisoned Mujib in West Pakistan. He was released after Bangladesh gained independence in December 1971. He returned home to a hero's welcome and to the tasks of building and leading a new nation.

Mujib was born in the village of Tungipara, 60 miles (97 kilometers) southwest of Dhaka. He graduated from Islamia College in Calcutta and studied law for a short time at Dhaka University. Stanley J. Heginbotham

See also **Bangladesh** (History).

Mukden. See Shenyang.

Mulatto, *muh LAT oh,* is a person of mixed white and black descent. The term *mulatto* also applies to those who have one white and one black parent. The child of a white person and a mulatto is a *quadroon.* Mulattoes vary in appearance. Some have dark skins and kinky hair and some do not. The word *creole* is often confused with *mulatto.* In the United States, a creole is a white Southerner of French or Spanish ancestry. See also **Creole; Latin America** (People; picture); **Mestizo.**

Douglas H. Ubelaker

Mulberry is any of a group of ornamental trees and shrubs that have small, round, sweet fruits. The fruits, also called mulberries, are white, purple, or red. Each consists of a cluster of tiny one-seeded fruits. Mulberry flowers are greenish white and grow in cylindrical clusters that hang from stalks on the branches. The plants have oval or heart-shaped ridged leaves.

White mulberries play an important role in the silk industry. Their leaves provide food for silkworms, from whose cocoons silk fabrics are woven. The chief kind of white mulberry used as silkworm food is the silkworm mulberry. Most silkworm mulberries come from China. Russian mulberries, another important type of white mulberries, are the most widely planted mulberries in the United States. They are sturdy shrubs that grow well as hedges, and so growers use them as windbreaks.

Red mulberries, also called American mulberries, grow wild throughout most of the eastern and central sections of the United States. Farmers feed their fruit to hogs and poultry. Black mulberries are grown throughout Europe for their juicy, crimson-black fruit. The fruit is eaten fresh and used in making preserves and wines.

Scientific classification. Mulberries belong to the mulberry family, Moraceae. White mulberries are *Morus alba.* Silk mulberries are *M. alba,* var. *multicaulis.* Russian mulberries are *M. alba,* var. *tatarica.* Red mulberries are *M. rubra,* and black mulberries are *M. nigra.* Max E. Austin

See also **Silk; Tree** (Familiar broadleaf and needleleaf trees [picture]).

Mulch is any material that is spread over soil so that air can get through, but less water can evaporate from the soil. Mulch may be made of manure, straw, hay, clover, chaff, alfalfa, corncobs, leaves, sawdust, wood chips, and many other substances. It is often applied about 2 to 3 inches (5 to 8 centimeters) thick. It helps keep water in the soil by reducing evaporation, and it also decays and enriches the soil. It also reduces the number of weeds that would otherwise grow up to compete with plant crops. Mulch is valuable to home gardeners, but it often costs more than commercial fertilizers.

Taylor J. Johnston

Muldoon, Robert David (1921-1992), served as prime minister of New Zealand from 1975 to 1984. He became the leader of the National Party in 1974. Muldoon took office as prime minister after leading his party to victory over the Labour Party in the 1975 election. His party won again in 1978 and 1981, and Muldoon remained as prime minister. However, the Labour Party defeated Muldoon's party in the 1984 election, ending Muldoon's term.

Muldoon was born in Auckland, New Zealand. He served in the army during World War II and studied cost accounting in England after the war ended in 1945. He became an expert accountant and is a partner in an Auckland accounting firm. Muldoon first won election to Parliament in 1960. He served as minister of finance from 1967 to 1972 and as deputy prime minister in 1972. Muldoon was knighted in 1984. Andrew Stone

Mule is a domesticated, hybrid animal that results from crossing a *mare* (female horse) and a *jack* (male donkey). The offspring of a male horse (stallion) and a female ass (jenny) is called a *hinny.* Other mulelike hybrids were bred during ancient times from horses and onagers. Mules were once popular work animals throughout the world. Some breeders even raised certain types of large donkeys in order to produce sizable mules.

A mule looks somewhat like both its parents. Like the jack, a mule has long ears, short mane, small feet, and a tail with a tuft of long hairs at the end. From the mother it gets a large, well-shaped body and strong muscles. She also gives it a horse's ease in getting used to harness. The father gives the mule a braying voice, surefootedness, and endurance. Like the jack, a mule saves its strength when it is forced to work hard and for a long time. A mule is less likely to suffer from overwork than a horse.

Mules are hardy and resist disease well. Unfortunately, mules do not have offspring of their own, except in extremely rare cases. Animals which cannot have offspring are said to be *sterile.* All male mules and most female mules are sterile. A few female mules have produced young after they were bred to male asses or to stallions.

Mules can remain strong under much harsh treatment and work, but they work better if they are treated

© Eric & David Hosking

The black mulberry tree bears crimson-black fruit. This tree is grown throughout Europe, where its juicy fruit is eaten fresh and is used to make preserves and wines.

Garry D. McMichael, Photo Researchers

A mule can be used to pull a plow and do other hard work on farms and plantations. Mules are sure-footed and have strong muscles. They have been used as work animals throughout the world.

with kindness. When owners take proper care of their mules, the mules will do as much work as horses, and they will do the work under more harsh conditions. The hardiness of mules makes them suitable for work in construction camps, mines, and military zones.

In the United States, over nine-tenths of all the mules have worked on farms and plantations. Most of them have been used in the South.　　Geo. H. Waring

See also **Coal** (picture: A Pennsylvania mine of the late 1800's); **Donkey; Glanders.**

Mule deer is a beautiful deer that has large, furry ears similar to those of a mule. This grayish- to brownish-colored deer stands about 3 to $3\frac{1}{2}$ feet (91 to 107 centimeters) high, and has large, branching antlers. It has a peculiar stiff-legged gait that enables it to swiftly bound over the roughest trails. Mule deer live from northern Mexico north to the southern parts of Alaska and Canada's Yukon Territory, and from northern Texas and eastern North Dakota west to the Pacific Coast. In the Pacific Northwest, mule deer are called *black-tailed deer.*

Grant Heilman

The mule has long ears, a short mane, and a tail tipped with long hairs. It is the offspring of a male donkey and a female horse. Mules usually cannot have offspring of their own.

Ray Richardson, Animals Animals

Mule deer have large, furry ears that look somewhat like those of a mule. In this photograph, a buck, *right,* guards a doe during mating season. Mule deer live in western North America.

Mule deer eat a wide range of vegetation, including grasses and the buds, leaves, and twigs of shrubs and small trees. They also may eat agricultural crops. Mule deer are normally active only around dawn and dusk. They may live in herds of 5 to 20 animals, spending the summer in hills and mountains and the winter in valleys.

Scientific classification. Mule deer are in the deer family, Cervidae. Their scientific name is *Odocoileus hemionus*.

Gregory K. Snyder

See also **Deer**.

Mullein, *MUHL uhn,* also called *mullen,* is the name of a group of plants native to Europe and Asia. There are more than 250 kinds of mulleins. Three kinds grow in the United States and southern Canada. The *common mullein* is found in rocky pastures, along roadsides, and in waste places. It grows to 6 feet (1.8 meters) high and has a thick, woolly stem and thick, velvety leaves. Yellow flowers grow in clusters in the form of a spike at the top of the stalk. The smaller *moth mullein* has smooth, deeply veined leaves. Both the stem and leaves of these plants irritate the skin when touched. The *white mullein* grows in the Eastern United States. A thin, powdery down covers this plant.

WORLD BOOK illustration by Robert Hynes
Common mullein

The leaves of the common mullein were formerly used to make a tea for treating coughs, nervous disorders, and inflammations. Certain mulleins often grow as weeds. They may be controlled by cutting the flower stalks before the seed forms or by spraying with a *herbicide* (chemical weedkiller).

Scientific classification. Mulleins belong to the figwort family, Scrophulariaceae. The scientific name for the common mullein is *Verbascum thapsus*. The moth mullein is *V. blattaria*. The white mullein is *V. lychnitis*.   Kenneth A. Nicely

Mullens, Priscilla. See Alden, John and Priscilla.
Muller, *MUHL uhr,* **Hermann Joseph** (1890-1967), was an American geneticist. By exposing fruit flies to X rays, Muller proved that X rays can produce *mutations* (sudden changes in genes). The results of this work, published in 1927, brought him the 1946 Nobel Prize for physiology or medicine.

Muller was born in New York City. He began his research on heredity with Thomas Hunt Morgan while a student at Columbia University. They studied the linkage of genes and the crossing over of chromosome strands that occur during genetic recombination, a process that takes place just before cells divide. Muller became a professor of zoology at Indiana University in 1945.

Alan R. Rushton

See also **Heredity** (The birth of genetics).
Müller, *MYOO luhr,* **Paul Hermann** (1899-1965), a Swiss chemist, won the 1948 Nobel Prize for physiology or medicine for discovering the insect-killing properties of DDT (dichloro-diphenyl-trichloroethane). His last

name is also spelled *Mueller.* DDT first was produced in Austria in 1873, but Müller discovered DDT's value as an insect killer in 1939. DDT was used during World War II (1939-1945) to kill body lice that carried typhus. Müller was born in Olten, Switzerland. See also **DDT**.

Eric Howard Christianson

Mullet, *MUHL iht,* is the name of two different families of silvery-blue fish with stout bodies. Mullets are from 1 to 2 feet (30 to 61 centimeters) long and have blunt heads and small mouths. The teeth, if any, are very weak. Great numbers of these fish live close to the shore in nearly all temperate and tropical waters. Their flesh is wholesome and has a good flavor. The *striped mullet* is the largest of all the species, weighing from 10 to 12 pounds (4.5 to 5.4 kilograms). Striped mullets are plentiful around the Florida Keys and on the Gulf Coast. The *liza* and the *white mullet* live in the same areas as the striped mullet and are about as large.

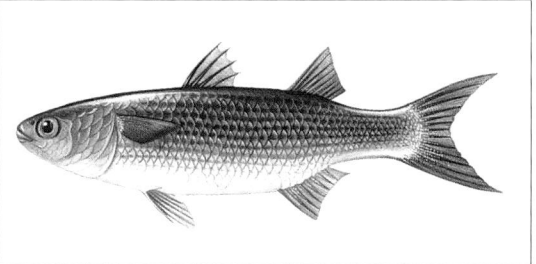

WORLD BOOK illustration by Colin Newman, Linden Artists Ltd.
A mullet has a stout, silvery-blue body. Mullets are plentiful in coastal waters in most warm regions of the world. The flesh of these fish has a good flavor.

Surmullets, or *red mullets,* are small, brightly colored fish that live chiefly in warm seas. They have small mouths and weak teeth. Two long feelers called *barbels* hang like strings from the chin of the red mullet.

Scientific classification. Mullets make up the mullet family, Mugilidae. The striped mullet is *M. liza*, and the white mullet is *M. curema*. Red mullets belong to the goatfish family, Mullidae.   William J. Richards

Mulliken, Robert Sanderson (1896-1986), an American chemist, won the 1966 Nobel Prize for chemistry. He received the award for his *molecular-orbital theory,* which he adopted in 1925. This theory describes the arrangement of electrons in molecules.

The electrons of an atom orbit its nucleus. Scientists once believed that the electrons continued to orbit the individual atomic nuclei after atoms had combined to form a molecule. But Mulliken showed that each atom's outermost electrons can orbit the entire molecule. Most scientists accept this theory.

The molecular-orbital theory has been applied in such fields as biological and industrial research. For example, scientists have used the theory to study the structure of proteins, plastics, and a number of other complex compounds.

Mulliken was born in Newburyport, Mass. He graduated from the Massachusetts Institute of Technology in 1917 and received a Ph.D. degree from the University of Chicago in 1921. Mulliken taught at the university from 1928 to 1961.   Daniel J. Kevles

Brian Mulroney

Peter Bregg

Prime Minister of Canada
1984-1993

Turner
1984

Mulroney
1984-1993

Campbell
1993

Mulroney, *muhl ROO nee,* **Brian** (1939-   ), served as prime minister of Canada from 1984 to 1993. Mulroney had been chosen leader of the Progressive Conservative Party in 1983. Before 1983, Mulroney had been a lawyer and business executive and had never been elected to a public office. But he led the Conservatives to a landslide victory in the election of 1984 and succeeded John N. Turner as prime minister. Mulroney remained in office after the general election of 1988. In 1993, he resigned as prime minister and leader of the Progressive Conservative Party. He was succeeded by Kim Campbell, the minister of national defence.

During college and law school in the late 1950's and early 1960's, Mulroney had held many leadership positions in Progressive Conservative student groups. After graduating, he practiced law and served on party committees. In 1977, Mulroney became president of the Iron Ore Company of Canada. He held that position until he became Progressive Conservative Party leader.

Mulroney's friends knew him to be charming and persuasive. Associates rated him as an able negotiator who at times was tough and cautious.

As prime minister, Mulroney faced the challenges of keeping the province of Quebec a part of Canada and of leading the country through an economic recession. His efforts to amend the Canadian Constitution to satisfy Quebec separatists failed. His economic proposals, including the introduction of a new federal sales tax, lost him popularity. However, Mulroney achieved a major goal in 1988 when he signed a free-trade agreement with the United States. In 1992, he signed a pact that extended the agreement to include Mexico.

Early life

Boyhood. Mulroney was born on March 20, 1939, in Baie-Comeau, Que. His full name is Martin Brian Mulroney, but he prefers to be called Brian Mulroney. He was the third oldest of the six children of Benedict M. Mulroney and Irene O'Shea Mulroney. Brian's father was

an electrician for a paper company in Baie-Comeau.

Brian became an excellent tennis player as a teenager and won the Baie-Comeau Junior Tennis Championship. He attended local schools until he was 13 years old. Then his parents sent him to St. Thomas College, a boys' school in Chatham, N.B.

College education. In 1955, at the age of 16, Mulroney entered St. Francis Xavier University in Antigonish, N.S. He earned honors in political science and developed an interest in politics. Mulroney's parents had supported the Liberal Party. But Brian came to admire Robert L. Stanfield, leader of the Nova Scotia Progressive Conservative Party, and joined the Conservative club at the university. He was elected president of the club in 1958. In 1959, he received a B.A. degree.

Mulroney then enrolled at Dalhousie University in Halifax, N.S., to study law. Later in 1959, he was elected executive vice president of the Progressive Conservative Student Federation of Canada. In 1960, he transferred to Laval University Law School in Ste.-Foy, Que. In 1961, he became leader of the Progressive Conservative club at Laval. Mulroney received his law degree in 1963.

Early business career

Young lawyer. After graduating from law school, Mulroney joined the Montreal law firm of Ogilvy, Re-

Important dates in Mulroney's life

1939   (March 20) Born in Baie-Comeau, Que.
1959   Graduated from St. Francis Xavier University.
1959   Elected executive vice president of Progressive Conservative Student Federation.
1973   (May 26) Married Mila Pivnicki.
1974   Became member of Cliche Royal Commission.
1977   Became president of Iron Ore Company of Canada.
1983   Elected leader of Progressive Conservative Party.
1984   (Sept. 17) Became prime minister of Canada.
1988   Led Conservatives to victory again.
1993   (June 25) Resigned as prime minister and leader of the Progressive Conservative Party.

nault. He specialized in labor law. His involvement with the Progressive Conservative Party continued to grow. He served on its policy committee from 1966 to 1971 and on the finance committee of the Quebec Progressive Conservative Party from 1966 to 1974.

On May 26, 1973, Mulroney married Mila Pivnicki (1953-   ) of Montreal. The Mulroneys had four children, Caroline (1974-   ), Benedict (1976-   ), Robert Mark (1979-   ), and Daniel (1985-   ).

In May 1974, Mulroney was appointed to the Cliche Royal Commission, which was established to investigate violence in Quebec's construction industry. He frequently appeared on the evening television news and began to gain national prominence.

First bid for leadership. In 1975, Progressive Conservative leader Robert L. Stanfield announced his intention to retire. Mulroney's work on the Cliche commission had impressed influential members of the Progressive Conservative Party, and they urged him to become a candidate for the leadership. Mulroney accepted the challenge and ran a strong campaign. The party met to choose its new leader in February 1976. Mulroney finished third in the voting.

Business executive. In June 1976, Mulroney joined the Iron Ore Company of Canada as executive vice president of corporate affairs. He had done some legal work for the Quebec-based company and was chosen for his new job by the company's president, William Bennett. In 1977, Bennett retired, and Mulroney succeeded him as president. The firm had long been troubled by labor strikes and was deeply in debt. Mulroney settled the labor disputes and led the company to record profits.

During the early 1980's, decreased demands for steel led to a sharp drop in iron ore prices. Iron ore is used to make steel, and the Iron Ore Company suffered large losses. As a result, the company closed its mine in Schefferville, Que., in 1982. Mulroney arranged a compensation and relocation program for the 285 employees who lost their jobs.

Career in government

Election as party leader. Joe Clark of Alberta had led the Progressive Conservative Party to power in the general election of 1979. But the Liberals regained control in a general election the next year. Opposition to Clark's leadership then began to grow.

Early in 1983, Clark resigned and called a party convention for June to select a new leader. Mulroney became a major candidate for the leadership even though he had never won election to a public office. His supporters felt that his Quebec connections would help strengthen the party's prospects in that province, a traditional stronghold of the Liberal Party. Quebec had about a fourth of Canada's population.

Clark tried to regain his position at the convention, but Mulroney's fresh appeal and Quebec background helped carry him to victory. Mulroney was the first Progressive Conservative leader ever to win that position without any experience in an elected office. Two months later, he easily won election to the Canadian House of Commons from a district in Nova Scotia.

The 1984 election. Prime Minister Pierre Trudeau retired in 1984. He was succeeded in late June 1984 by John N. Turner, a Toronto lawyer who had held several Cabinet positions in the governments headed by Lester B. Pearson and Trudeau. Turner called a general election for Sept. 4, 1984.

At the time of the campaign, Canada's economy was slowly recovering from a recession. The unemployment rate was still high, standing at 11 percent of the labor force. Mulroney promised that a new Conservative government would create jobs and increase industrial productivity and foreign investment. In the election, he led the Progressive Conservative Party to a huge victory. The party won 211 of the 282 seats in the House of Commons. It captured 58 of Quebec's 75 seats, the most the Conservatives had ever won there. Mulroney took office as prime minister on September 17.

Prime minister. Mulroney faced many problems during the early part of his term. The economy grew only slightly, unemployment remained high, and the federal budget deficit rose sharply. Mistakes and blunders by the Cabinet also hurt Mulroney's image. By May 1986, five ministers had resigned under severe public criticism. The next month, Mulroney moved half his ministers into new jobs. He also retired two, fired four, and added eight other ministers.

The Meech Lake accord. In 1987, Mulroney helped bring about an agreement that was partly designed to win Quebec's acceptance of the Canadian Constitution. Quebec had earlier refused to accept the Constitution because the document did not recognize the province as a distinct society in Canada. On June 3, 1987, Mulroney and Canada's 10 provincial heads of government signed a constitutional agreement that proposed such recognition. The agreement, called the Meech Lake accord, also included other constitutional changes and was sent to the provincial legislatures for ratification. However, the accord was never ratified.

Many opponents of the Meech Lake accord believed that it would have granted Quebec's provincial government too much power over the rights of individuals in Quebec—especially over the rights of Quebec's English-speaking minority. Most people in Quebec speak French. Eight of the 10 provinces ratified the accord, but Manitoba and Newfoundland withheld their support. As a result, many Quebecers began to demand increased independence for Quebec from the rest of Canada.

Free trade and the 1988 election. On Jan. 2, 1988, Mulroney and United States President Ronald Reagan signed a major trade pact between Canada and the United States. The agreement called for the elimination of all tariffs and many other trade barriers by 1999. However, the Liberal Party opposed the agreement and blocked its ratification in the Canadian Senate.

John N. Turner, the Liberal Party leader, demanded that Mulroney call a general election to let Canadians express their approval or disapproval of the agreement. The Liberal senators promised to ratify the pact if the Progressive Conservatives won the election.

Mulroney called a general election for Nov. 21, 1988. The Progressive Conservatives won a majority of the seats in the House of Commons, and Mulroney continued as prime minister. After the general election, the Canadian Senate approved the free-trade agreement, and the pact went into effect on Jan. 1, 1989.

Other economic developments. In April 1989, the Mulroney government proposed a federal budget de-

Andrew Clark, Office of the Prime Minister

The Mulroney family. Standing are son Benedict, *left,* and daughter Caroline, *right.* Seated are son Robert Mark, Mulroney, son Daniel Nicholas Dimitri, and Mulroney's wife, Mila.

signed to reduce Canada's large budget deficit. The new budget called for tax increases and spending cuts.

To help raise revenue, Mulroney's government proposed a controversial new federal sales tax. The tax, called the *goods and services tax* (GST), applied to almost all goods and services sold in Canada. It replaced a tax that had covered fewer purchases. Most Canadians opposed the new tax, but it went into effect in 1991.

In April 1990, Canada was struck by a recession that ended seven years of economic growth. By March 1991, 10.5 percent of Canadian workers were unemployed. Mulroney's government was criticized for not doing enough to end the recession. By mid-1991, support for Mulroney dropped sharply.

In 1992, Mulroney signed the North American Free Trade Agreement (NAFTA) between Canada, the United States, and Mexico. This pact built on the Canada-U.S. free-trade agreement by calling for the gradual elimination of tariffs and certain other trade barriers between those two countries and Mexico. NAFTA required ratification by the national legislatures of the three countries.

The Persian Gulf War. In 1991, the Mulroney government authorized the participation of the Canadian Armed Forces in the Persian Gulf War. Canadian pilots flew bombing missions over Iraq and Kuwait from their station in Qatar, a country near Saudi Arabia.

The constitutional crisis. After the failure of the Meech Lake accord, Quebec's ruling Liberal Party adopted a platform demanding sole authority in the province over such matters as agriculture, energy, and trade. It also demanded a role in forming Canada's for-

eign policy. It announced that it would ask Quebecers to vote on the separation of Quebec from the rest of Canada if the Canadian government did not agree to its demands by the fall of 1992. Mulroney supported more independence for Quebec but strongly opposed separation. In 1991, he appointed former prime minister Joe Clark minister for constitutional affairs. In this post, Clark worked to preserve Canada's national unity.

In September 1991, Mulroney introduced a new plan to revise the Constitution. The plan provided for recognition of Quebec as a distinct society, the replacement of Canada's appointed Senate with an elected one, and self-government for Canada's native peoples. It also proposed the transfer of some federal powers to the provinces. A parliamentary committee soon met to discuss and gather public opinion on the plan.

In August 1992, Clark and 10 provincial heads of government agreed to a set of constitutional amendments based on Mulroney's plan. To go into effect, the amendments required ratification by the provinces. In addition, Mulroney called for a nationwide vote on the amendments. The vote was held in October, and most Canadians, including majorities in Quebec and each of five other provinces, voted against the accord.

In February 1993, Mulroney announced his resignation as prime minister and leader of the Progressive Conservative Party. He said he had lost enthusiasm for governing. He called a party convention to be held in June to choose his replacement. Defence Minister Kim Campbell won the party leadership, and she was sworn in as prime minister on June 25. Mulroney returned to private life and the practice of law.   Kendal Windeyer

See also **Campbell, Kim.**

Multilateral aid. See Foreign aid.

Multimedia, *MUHL tih MEE dee uh,* is a computer-controlled combination of text, graphics, sound, photographs, motion pictures, and other types of media. Multimedia programs have a variety of applications in education, entertainment, job training, and other areas.

The hardware needed to run multimedia programs usually includes a personal computer with a large-capacity memory, high-quality video and audio systems, and a *CD-ROM* drive. CD-ROM's resemble audio compact discs, and they can store the enormous amount of data required for a multimedia program. Some systems enable users to record video and audio on a computers' hard disk drive to create their own multimedia programs. Personal computers enable users to *interact* with multimedia programs—that is, users become active participants rather than passive observers.

For example, a multimedia program could employ an interactive story to improve a user's Italian language skills. The story might involve a search for an apartment in Rome. The program could begin with a motion-picture clip showing a couple walking past several apartment buildings. The user would select a building and listen to the conversation between the landlord and the couple. At the end of the conversation, the user could decide to continue searching or to choose an apartment in that building. At any point during the story, the user could access the program's dictionary or request a translation of the dialogue. Thus, the program incorporates motion pictures, sound, and text into an interactive story that enables users to practice Italian.

Many computer programs combine several types of media, such as text, graphics, animation, and sound. But most computer programs do not offer television and movie clips or digital stereo sound. Such high-quality video and audio distinguish multimedia from other programs. In the early 1990's, multimedia made up only a small percentage of all computer programs.

Glorianna Davenport

Multinational corporation is a business organization that is based in one country and has branches, subsidiaries, and plants in many countries. Such organizations carry out substantial amounts of financing, production, sales, and research and development in their foreign operations.

Multinational corporations, also called *MNC's* and *transnational corporations,* have developed since World War II ended in 1945. MNC's can have great economic power. The largest MNC's include Exxon, Ford, General Motors, and Royal Dutch/Shell, each of which has reported annual sales of greater than $75 billion. This figure is larger than the gross national products of more than 80 percent of the world's countries.

The main reasons firms develop into MNC's are (1) to obtain control over the supply of resources, (2) to take advantage of the lower costs of foreign labor and materials, (3) to avoid paying tariffs on imported goods, and (4) to avoid high production costs and taxes associated with certain operations in the home country.

Operation. Most multinational corporations are based on manufacturing or minerals industries. They operate in fields that involve frequent technological change, including the production of computers, drugs, and electronic equipment. A typical firm in such fields has a large research organization in the country in which it has its headquarters. There, the firm develops new products and manufacturing processes. It then trains workers in its foreign plants to use these new skills. Some multinational corporations grant foreign companies a license to use their methods and processes instead of setting up plants of their own.

A multinational firm may have a few plants in one country that produce complete products to be sold in several countries. In other cases, plants in many countries may each make parts of the finished products. This process gives the MNC a larger area from which to choose the most economical locations for specialized plants. The corporation can then sell its products at lower prices than would otherwise be possible.

Debate over MNC's. The economic role of multinational corporations has aroused widespread international debate. In the United States, for example, some labor groups believe that U.S. MNC's have increased unemployment at home by establishing operations in other countries. However, some studies have indicated that MNC's have preserved or created more jobs for U.S. citizens than they have eliminated. Another concern is that, by shifting production operations overseas, U.S. MNC's decrease the flow of funds earned by U.S. exports. However, MNC defenders argue that such actions by U.S. MNC's are offset by foreign-based MNC's locating production operations within the United States.

Abroad, many people oppose U.S. multinational corporations because of their control over local economies and the profits they earn. But supporters of MNC's emphasize the contributions of an MNC's technology and capital to economic development.   Robert B. Carson

Multiple birth is the birth of more than one infant from the same pregnancy. Twins, triplets, quadruplets, and quintuplets are all examples of multiple birth. Most animals give birth to more than one offspring at a time. Human beings usually have only one baby at a time. This article discusses multiple births in human beings.

Kinds of multiple births. Most multiple births in humans involve twins. Twins occur about once in every 89 births. By contrast, triplets occur about once in every 7,900 births, and quadruplets occur about once in 705,000 births.

The two most commonly recognized types of twins are *fraternal* and *identical.* Fraternal twins may be of the same sex or consist of a brother and a sister, with each individual having a different genetic makeup. Identical twins are always of the same sex and have an identical genetic makeup. They generally are more difficult to tell apart physically than are fraternal twins.

Researchers have found that the rate at which identical twins occur—about 4 times in every 1,000 births—is fairly constant. The birth rate of fraternal twins, however, is highly variable. For example, fraternal twins occur more frequently among black people, particularly black Africans, than among people of European ancestry, including white Americans. Fraternal twins are least common among Asians. Scientists do not know why such variations exist.

How multiple births occur. In pregnancies that produce a single infant, one of the mother's ovaries releases an egg that joins with a sperm from the father. The fertilized egg, called a *zygote,* develops into a baby.

In multiple births, the process of development is somewhat different. For example, in pregnancies involving fraternal twins, also called *dizygotic twins,* the moth-

Gerard Smith, Monkmeyer

Nancy Hays, Monkmeyer

Twins, the most common human multiple birth, occur about once in 89 births. Identical twins often look much alike, *top.* Fraternal twins may resemble each other only slightly, *above.*

er's ovaries release two eggs at about the same time. Each egg is fertilized by a separate sperm, producing two zygotes, each with different genetic characteristics. As a result, fraternal twins may look no more alike than brothers or sisters who are not twins. Identical twins, also called *monozygotic twins,* originate from a single zygote. Early during the mother's pregnancy, the zygote's cell mass divides into two parts. The two parts develop into separate individuals who have the same genetic makeup. Scientists believe that *Siamese twins,* also known as *conjoined twins,* develop from a zygote that fails to separate completely (see **Siamese twins**).

Multiple births involving three or more infants occur through processes similar to the development of twins. For example, if the mother's ovaries release three, four, or five eggs and each of the eggs becomes fertilized, fraternal triplets, quadruplets, or quintuplets will be born. A zygote that divides into more than two parts will result in the birth of identical triplets, quadruplets, or quintuplets. If two eggs are fertilized and one of them splits in two, the mother will give birth to triplets consisting of identical twins and one nonidentical baby.

Fertility drugs. The use of *fertility drugs* is associated with a higher than normal rate of multiple births. Fertility drugs help some women who have previously been infertile become pregnant. The drugs cause a woman's ovaries to release an egg about once a month. In some cases, fertility drugs cause the release of several eggs at the same time and thus increase the possibility of multiple birth. Use of *clomiphene citrate,* one of the most widely taken fertility drugs, results in twins about once in 12 births.   Melvin V. Gerbie

Additional resources

Alexander, Terry P. *Make Room for Twins: A Complete Guide to Pregnancy, Delivery, and the Childhood Years.* Bantam, 1987.
Novotny, Pamela P. *The Joy of Twins: Having, Raising, and Loving Babies Who Arrive in Groups.* Crown, 1988.

Multiple sclerosis, *sklih ROH sihs,* often called MS, is a disease of the nervous system. It is characterized by repeated attacks of nervous system damage, followed by recovery. The time and severity of attacks are unpredictable. The illness can cause serious disabilities, including paralysis of the legs and partial loss of vision. MS afflicts more women than men. Most patients begin to have symptoms of MS when they are from 20 to 25 years old. MS is the most common cause of disability for people under the age of 45 in the United States.

MS is characterized by scattered areas of inflammation and by destruction of *myelin* in the white matter of the brain and spinal cord. Myelin is a fatty substance that surrounds and protects certain nerve fibers. Many small, hard, platelike areas of scar called *plaques* appear throughout the myelin and interfere with the normal function of nerve pathways. The word *sclerosis* comes from a Greek term that means *hard* and refers to the plaques.

The symptoms of MS depend on which areas of the brain and spinal cord are affected. Therefore, the symptoms differ with each attack. In time, more and more plaques develop in the victim's myelin, causing new symptoms. Physicians diagnose MS chiefly from the symptoms. A medical technique called *magnetic resonance imaging* (MRI) can aid in diagnosis by producing images of the brain, thereby ruling out other diseases or revealing the telltale plaques.

The first symptoms may appear suddenly, but they may also start slowly and gradually worsen. Difficulty walking is commonly the first problem. Loss of vision, double vision, loss of balance, and weakness in an arm or leg may also occur. Numbness or tingling may occur in the fingers or elsewhere, and problems of coordination are also common. After several days to several weeks, these symptoms decrease and may disappear entirely. New attacks appear unpredictably after periods of recovery lasting months to years. In a small number of patients, symptoms are progressive with no apparent recovery between attacks. About a third of MS patients become seriously disabled, but few die from MS.

Physicians do not know the cause of MS. Population studies indicate that MS may be caused by a virus that infects people before they are 15 years old. The virus may produce an abnormal reaction in the body's immune system. Normally, the body protects itself from disease by producing substances called *antibodies,* which fight infection. In MS, a defect in the immune system may allow antibodies or white blood cells to destroy myelin.

Certain genes that control the body's immune system are associated with MS. Scientists think the immune system, under the control of genes, reacts with an unidentified environmental factor—probably a virus—to produce a condition that can lead to MS. Adrenocorticotropic hormone (ACTH) is the most widely used therapy. Certain drugs that affect the immune system are also helpful. These include imuran, cytoxan, copolymer I, cyclosporine, and interferons.   William J. Weiner

Additional resources

Matthews, Walter B. *Multiple Sclerosis: The Facts.* 2nd ed. Oxford, 1985.
Rosner, Louis J., and Ross, Shelley. *Multiple Sclerosis.* Prentice-Hall, 1987.

Multiplication is a short way of adding or counting equal numbers. Multiplication is one of the four basic operations in arithmetic along with addition, subtraction, and division.

Suppose you want to know how much six gumballs will cost. The gumballs are 5¢ each. You can find the answer by addition: $5+5+5+5+5+5=30$. Six gumballs

Multiplication terms

Annexing zeros is a quick way of multiplying by 10, 100, 1,000, and so on. It means placing zeros at the end of the number being multiplied.

Carry, in multiplication, means to change a number from one place in the product to the next. A 10 in the 1's place is carried to the 10's place.

Multiplicand is the number that is multiplied. In $4 \times 8 = 32$, 8 is the multiplicand.

Multiplication fact is a basic statement in multiplication, such as $6 \times 3 = 18$.

Multiplier is the number that does the multiplying. In $4 \times 8 = 32$, 4 is the multiplier.

Partial product is the result of multiplying a number by one digit of the multiplier. It is used when the multiplier has two or more digits.

Product is the answer or result of multiplication. In $4 \times 8 = 32$, 32 is the product.

The 100 multiplication facts

0	1	2	3	4	5	6	7	8	9
×0	×0	×0	×0	×0	×0	×0	×0	×0	×0
0	0	0	0	0	0	0	0	0	0

0	1	2	3	4	5	6	7	8	9
×1	×1	×1	×1	×1	×1	×1	×1	×1	×1
0	1	2	3	4	5	6	7	8	9

0	1	2	3	4	5	6	7	8	9
×2	×2	×2	×2	×2	×2	×2	×2	×2	×2
0	2	4	6	8	10	12	14	16	18

0	1	2	3	4	5	6	7	8	9
×3	×3	×3	×3	×3	×3	×3	×3	×3	×3
0	3	6	9	12	15	18	21	24	27

0	1	2	3	4	5	6	7	8	9
×4	×4	×4	×4	×4	×4	×4	×4	×4	×4
0	4	8	12	16	20	24	28	32	36

0	1	2	3	4	5	6	7	8	9
×5	×5	×5	×5	×5	×5	×5	×5	×5	×5
0	5	10	15	20	25	30	35	40	45

0	1	2	3	4	5	6	7	8	9
×6	×6	×6	×6	×6	×6	×6	×6	×6	×6
0	6	12	18	24	30	36	42	48	54

0	1	2	3	4	5	6	7	8	9
×7	×7	×7	×7	×7	×7	×7	×7	×7	×7
0	7	14	21	28	35	42	49	56	63

0	1	2	3	4	5	6	7	8	9
×8	×8	×8	×8	×8	×8	×8	×8	×8	×8
0	8	16	24	32	40	48	56	64	72

0	1	2	3	4	5	6	7	8	9
×9	×9	×9	×9	×9	×9	×9	×9	×9	×9
0	9	18	27	36	45	54	63	72	81

You do not need to write the names every time, but it is important to keep the columns straight when multiplying larger numbers. An understanding of place value is important in learning multiplication. See **Decimal system** (Multiplication).

Multiplication facts. A statement such as $6 \times 5 = 30$ is a *multiplication fact*. It consists of a multiplier, a multiplicand, and a product. You should use addition to discover the multiplication facts. For example, $5+5+5+5+5+5=30$. After discovering a multiplication fact, you should memorize it. By knowing the 100 multiplication facts, you can learn to multiply any numbers.

Most of the multiplication facts are easy to learn. If you play a game and score 0 four times, your score is 0, because $4 \times 0 = 0$. Zero multiplied by any number is zero. Any number multiplied by zero is also zero. You have now learned 19 of the multiplication facts!

If you make a score of 1 four times, your score is 4, because $4 \times 1 = 4$. Similarly, $5 \times 1 = 5$, $6 \times 1 = 6$, and $8 \times 1 = 8$. One multiplied by any number is that number. Any number multiplied by one is also that same number. You now know 17 more multiplication facts.

The two boxes of eggs shown below illustrate an important rule in multiplication.

Each box contains 12 eggs. You can look at the box of eggs at the left in two ways. You might say that there are six rows of eggs with two eggs in each row. Or, you could say that there are two rows of eggs with six eggs in each row.

You can also look at the box of eggs at the right in two ways. You might say that there are four rows of eggs with three eggs in each row. Or, you could say that there are three rows of eggs with four eggs in each row. The multiplication facts that show this are:

$$6 \times 2 = 12 \qquad 4 \times 3 = 12$$
$$2 \times 6 = 12 \qquad 3 \times 4 = 12$$

The examples of the boxes of eggs illustrate that *numbers can be multiplied in any order,* which is known as the *commutative property of multiplication.* The products will always be the same. Knowing this rule cuts down the number of multiplication facts to be learned from 100 to 55.

Knowing the *squares* is helpful in learning the multiplication facts. A square is a number multiplied by itself. Here are the squares that help to learn the facts:

$$2 \times 2 = 4 \qquad 5 \times 5 = 25 \qquad 8 \times 8 = 64$$
$$3 \times 3 = 9 \qquad 6 \times 6 = 36 \qquad 9 \times 9 = 81$$
$$4 \times 4 = 16 \qquad 7 \times 7 = 49$$

will cost 30¢. However, it is easier to learn that six 5's are 30. Learning facts like this is the basis of multiplication.

Learning to multiply

Many people learn multiplication only by memorizing its facts and rules. Often people do not understand the methods that they are using. The best way for a person to learn how to multiply is to find out how multiplication works.

Writing multiplication. Operations in arithmetic are shown by symbols. The symbol of multiplication is ×. The statement $6 \times 5 = 30$ means "six 5's are 30." People also say, "5 multiplied by 6 is 30," or they can say "6 times 5 is 30."

The number that is being multiplied, or added together a number of times, is called the *multiplicand.* The number that does the multiplying, or the number of multiplicands to be added, is called the *multiplier.* The result, or answer, is called the *product.* A multiplication problem is usually written like this:

$$\begin{array}{r} 5 \\ \times 6 \\ \hline 30 \end{array}$$

    Multiplicand
    Multiplier
    Product

You can make pictures of the squares with dots. Here are the dot pictures of the squares of six and seven:

If you add a row of six dots to the first picture, you will have seven 6's. This shows that $36+6=42$ or $7\times6=42$. If you take away a row of dots from the second picture, you will have six 7's. This shows that $49-7=42$ or $6\times7=42$. Making dot pictures can help you learn the multiplication facts. For example, you can make a square containing four dots to show 2×2. Another square containing nine dots shows 3×3. A third square could show 4×4, and so on.

Learning the multiplication facts takes time and study. But knowing the multiplication facts is necessary to become skilled at multiplying. You can become even better at arithmetic if you learn the division facts as you learn the multiplication facts. The division facts are the opposite of the multiplication facts. See **Division** (Division facts).

Multiplying by one digit

Any number from 0 to 9 is called a *digit*. The number 26 is a two-digit number. The number 514 is a three-digit number. A digit gets its value from the place it occupies in a number. The first place on the right is for 1's, the next to the left is for 10's, the next for 100's, and so on. For example, in the number 347, the 3 means three 100's, the 4 means four 10's, and the 7 means seven 1's. Depending on its place, the digit 2 may mean two 1's, (2), two 10's (20), two 100's (200), or two 1,000's (2,000). You combine the idea of place value with the multiplication facts to multiply large numbers.

Here is an example of the steps needed to work a multiplication problem using more than one multiplication fact. There are 32 students in a class. Each student uses one sheet of paper a day. How many sheets of paper will be needed for three days? We could solve the problem by using addition: $32+32+32=96$. The class will need 96 sheets of paper for three days. Multiplication is quicker and easier. The number 32 is three 10's and two 1's. The basic idea is to multiply first the 1's by 3 and then the 10's.

$$\begin{array}{r} 32 \\ \times 3 \\ \hline 96 \end{array}$$

First, you multiply the two 1's by 3. This is $3\times2=6$. You write the 6 in the 1's place in the product. Next, you multiply the three 10's by 3. This is $3\times30=90$. The 90 is nine 10's, and you write the 9 in the 10's place in the product. The answer is 96.

You multiply a larger number by one digit in much the same way:

$$\begin{array}{r} 302 \\ \times 4 \\ \hline 1208 \end{array}$$

First, you multiply the two 1's by 4. This is $4\times2=8$. You write the 8 in the 1's place in the product. Next, you multiply the 0 or "no" 10's by 4. This is $4\times0=0$. You write the 0 in the 10's place in the product. Then you multiply the three 100's. This is $4\times300=1,200$. You write the 12 in the 100's and 1,000's place in the product. The answer is 1,208.

When you multiply a large number by one digit, you must multiply each digit of the larger number—the 1's, 10's, 100's, 1,000's, and so on—one at a time. As you do the multiplication, you must write down the products of each of these multiplications—the 1's, 10's, 100's, 1,000's, and so on.

How to carry in multiplication

Students learn how to "carry" when they learn addition. When you add several numbers, there may be a 10 in the sum of the 1's column. You carry or add this 10 to the 10's column, usually by writing a small 1 above the 10's column. Carrying in multiplication is similar to carrying in addition:

Addition	Multiplication
$^1 12$	
12	
12	$^1 12$
12	$\times 8$
12	$\overline{96}$
12	
12	
12	
$\overline{96}$	

When you add the eight 12's, the eight 2's total 16, or one 10 and six 1's. You write the six 1's in the 1's place in the sum. You add the 10 to the column of eight 10's by writing a 1 at the top of that column. Adding the 1's in the 10's column gives you nine 10's. You write nine 10's in the 10's place in the sum. To multiply 8×12, you multiply the 1's first. This is $8\times2=16$. You write the six 1's in the 1's place in the product. You write a 1 to be added to the product of 8×1 in the 10's place. This is $8\times1=8$ and $8+1=9$. You write the nine 10's in the 10's place in the product. *Be sure to multiply first. Then add the "carry number" to the product.*

Multiplying by large numbers

A multiplier that has more than one digit introduces a new idea in multiplication. This idea is the use of the *partial product*. You can learn this idea best from an example.

Jim wants to know how many cartons of milk his school used last month. It used 312 cartons each day for 23 days.

$$\begin{array}{r} 312 \\ \times 23 \\ \hline 936 \\ 624 \\ \hline 7176 \end{array}$$

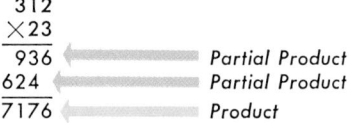

Partial Product
Partial Product
Product

The multiplier, 23, has two digits. It has two 10's and three 1's. You must use these as separate parts. First, you multiply 312 by the three 1's. This is $3\times2=6$. You write the 6 in the 1's place in the product. Then, $3\times1=3$ and $3\times3=9$. You write the 3 and the 9 in the 10's and 100's places in the product. This product of 3×312 is a partial product. Next, you multiply 312 by the two 10's. You write the product of this multiplication below the first product. You start this new partial product one place to the left, in the 10's place, because 312 is now being multiplied by 10's, not by 1's. First, $2 \times 2 = 4$. This is four 10's. You write the 4 below the 10's place in the first product. Next, $2 \times 1 = 2$ and $2 \times 3 = 6$. You write the 2 and the 6 in the 100's and 1,000's places of the second partial product. Now, the two partial products must be added together. The first partial product is 3×312 or 936. The second partial product is 20×312 or 6,240. Thus, $936 + 6,240 = 7,176$. The answer is that the school uses 7,176 cartons of milk in 23 days.

Multiplying by a three-digit multiplier is the same as by a two-digit multiplier. But there are three partial products instead of two. When you use the 100's part of the multiplier in a problem with a three-digit multiplier, remember to write this product beginning in the 100's place.

```
    123
  ×234
    492  ←——— First Partial Product
    369  ←——— Second Partial Product
    246  ←——— Third Partial Product
  28782  ←——— Product
```

Notice that the partial product of 2×123 is started in the 100's column directly under the 2.

You do not write "carry numbers" when you are multiplying by larger numbers. You must carry in your mind. If you wrote in carry numbers, you could easily confuse them with the carry numbers from another part of the multiplier.

Multiplying by zero

Zeros in combination with other digits represent 10's, 100's, 1,000's, and so on. When there are zeros in a multiplier, you can shorten the work of multiplication.

```
    14            14
  ×20          ×20
    00          280
   28
  280
```

In the example at the right, you can see that there will be no 1's in the 1's place. So you can write a 0 to show the 1's place, and write the product of the two 10's on the same line. This shortens the work.

You must be careful when you use this method with a three-digit multiplier that ends in zero. The difficulty comes in placing the second partial product:

```
    214
  ×320
   4280
    642
  68480
```

You begin the second partial product in the 100's place, because 3, the part of the multiplier being used, represents 100's. You should always check the place of the

multiplier when you write its partial product.

An easy way to multiply by 10, 100, 1,000, and other multiples of 10 is to *annex zeros*. This means to place zeros at the end of a number.

$$10 \times 2 = 20 \qquad 100 \times 2 = 200 \qquad 1,000 \times 2 = 2,000$$

Stated as a rule, this means that *to multiply by* 10, *annex a zero to the multiplicand. To multiply by* 100, *annex two zeros to the multiplicand. To multiply by* 1,000, *annex three zeros to the multiplicand.*

You can extend this method:

$$400 \times 12 = 4,800$$

You multiply 12 by 4, and annex two 0's.

When you multiply larger numbers, there may be a zero in the 10's place of the multiplier.

```
      423
    ×302
      846
   12690
  127746
```

In this case, you write a zero in the 10's place of the second partial product. This is to make sure you start the next partial product in the 100's place.

How to check multiplication

You should always check the answer in multiplication to be sure you have solved the problem correctly. You have seen that numbers can be multiplied in any order and the product remains the same. For example, $2 \times 4 = 8$ and $4 \times 2 = 8$. The best way to check a product is to change the places of the multiplier and multiplicand and do the multiplication again.

```
    15        12          342          153
  ×12      ×15        ×153        ×342
    30        60         1026          306
    15        12         1710          612
  180      180          342          459
                          52326        52326
```

The products are the same, but the partial products are different. If you make a mistake one way, you probably will not make it the other way. If your answers are different, you can locate your mistake.

When you multiply a large number by one digit, you can check it easily by dividing the product by the single digit. See **Division** (Short division).

```
    3425            3425
     ×5         5√17125
   17125
```

Multiplication rules

These five rules will help you solve problems in multiplication.

1. Remember that multiplication is a short way of adding equal numbers. The multiplier tells you how many times a number is to be multiplied.

2. Learn the meaning of the multiplication facts and learn to recall the facts quickly. Remember that a number multiplied by zero is zero and that a number multiplied by one is the same number. Also remember that zero multiplied by any number is zero.

3. Remember the methods for multiplying by one or more digits. You multiply the 1's, 10's, 100's, and 1,000's of the multiplicand one after the other and write the result in the product. When the multiplier has two or more digits, you must use partial products.

4. Place value has great importance in multiplication. Always keep the columns straight, and start the product under the digit you are using in the multiplier.

5. Learn to check the answer after working a problem in multiplication. You can do this by changing the places of the multiplier and multiplicand, and doing the multiplication again.

Fun with multiplication

Many of the games that can be played using the addition, subtraction, and division facts can be changed a little for the use of multiplication facts.

Product! is played by a group of children sitting in a circle. The leader picks a number, such as 5. The player next to the leader begins with 1, and the group counts around to the left. When the counting comes to a product of 5, the player calls "Product!" instead of the number. The counting goes like this: "1, 2, 3, 4, Product!, 6, 7, 8, 9, Product!", and so on. A player who forgets to say "Product!" is out, and the winner is the last player left.

Finger multiplying can be fun. By using fingers, you can multiply 5, 6, 7, 8, or 9 by 5, 6, 7, 8, or 9.

Suppose you want to multiply 8×6. Close the fingers of both hands. Open 3 fingers on the left hand. The 5 closed on the right hand and the 3 open stand for 8. Now open 1 finger on the right hand. The 5 that were closed and the 1 now open on the right hand stand for 6. Now 3 fingers should be open on the left hand and 1 finger open on the right. This is the 10's digit of the answer. Add the fingers open: $3 + 1 = 4$. There are four 10's in the answer. The closed fingers give the 1's digit. There are 2 fingers closed on the left hand and 4 fingers closed on the right hand. Multiply these to get the 1's

digit. This is $2 \times 4 = 8$. Add the 10's and the 1's. Four 10's and eight 1's are 48. This shows that $8 \times 6 = 48$.

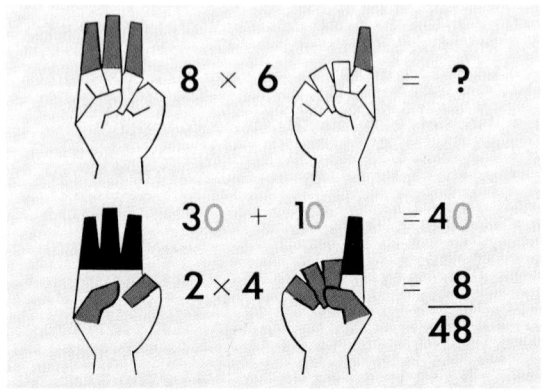

Another example is 9×7. Start with the fingers closed. Open 4 fingers on the left hand for 9 $(4 + 5 = 9)$. Open 2 fingers on the right hand for 7 $(5 + 2 = 7)$. Add the fingers open: $4 + 2 = 6$. This is the 10's digit. There is 1 finger closed on the left hand and 3 fingers closed on the right hand. Multiply these for the 1's digit. This is $1 \times 3 = 3$. Add the six 10's and the three 1's: $60 + 3 = 63$. This shows that $9 \times 7 = 63$.   John M. Smith

Related articles in *World Book* include:

Addition	Decimal system	Mathematics
Algebra	Division	Numeration sys-
(Multiplication)	Factor	tems
Arithmetic	Fraction	Subtraction

Outline

I. Learning to multiply
  A. Writing multiplication   B. Multiplication facts
II. Multiplying by one digit
III. How to carry in multiplication
IV. Multiplying by large numbers
V. Multiplying by zero
VI. How to check multiplication
VII. Multiplication rules
VIII. Fun with multiplication

Practice multiplication examples

1.	275 ×608	4.	840 ×364	7.	804 ×708	10.	307 ×400	13.	479 ×900	16.	358 ×679
2.	790 ×200	5.	300 ×705	8.	700 ×700	11.	906 ×368	14.	680 ×509	17.	478 ×297
3.	600 ×320	6.	500 ×457	9.	305 ×930	12.	947 ×350	15.	960 ×470	18.	689 ×698

19. How many stamps does Jim have in his stamp book? The book has 5 pages with 48 stamps on each page.

20. How much will 5 books cost at $2.25 each?

21. Pat rides her bicycle at a speed of 8 kilometers per hour for 3 hours. How far will she ride?

22. How far will Mr. Scott's automobile go on 10 gallons of gasoline? It goes 26 miles on 1 gallon.

23. Eggs cost 89¢ a dozen. How much will 6 dozen cost?

24. Four mothers plan to bring a dozen cookies each for a picnic. How many cookies will there be?

Answers to the practice examples

1. **167,200**	5. **211,500**	9. **283,650**	13. **431,100**	17. **141,966**	21. **24 kilometers**
2. **158,000**	6. **228,500**	10. **122,800**	14. **346,120**	18. **480,922**	22. **260 miles**
3. **192,000**	7. **569,232**	11. **333,408**	15. **451,200**	19. **240 stamps**	23. **$5.34**
4. **305,760**	8. **490,000**	12. **331,450**	16. **243,082**	20. **$11.25**	24. **48 cookies**

Mumford, Lewis (1895-1990), was an American social critic, philosopher, and historian. Many of his books explore the relation between modern people and their environment. Several of them deal with city planning. *The City in History* (1961) won the 1962 National Book Award for nonfiction. It describes how human civilization is expressed in the development of cities.

Mumford wrote a four-volume philosophy of civilization called *The Renewal of Life.* The series included *Technics and Civilization* (1934), *The Culture of Cities* (1938), *The Condition of Man* (1944), and *The Conduct of Life* (1951). He also wrote several histories of architecture and studies of American culture. He was born in Flushing, N.Y. In 1975, Queen Elizabeth II of Great Britain knighted Mumford for his contributions to city planning in Great Britain.

Mummy is an embalmed body that has been preserved for thousands of years. The ancient Egyptians believed that the dead lived on in the next world, and that their bodies had to be preserved forever as they were in life. They believed that the body would serve a person in the next world and therefore spent much effort in developing methods of embalming. Thousands of years later, archaeologists found the preserved bodies in tombs. Many museums have one or more Egyptian mummies. The most famous are probably those of Ramses II and Tutankhamen, who were *pharaohs* (rulers) of Egypt.

Scientists now know what materials and processes the Egyptians used to mummify bodies. The process was simple when mummifying began, and gradually became more elaborate. Wealthy persons could afford a more expensive treatment than the poor. Ancient texts state that a complete treatment required 70 days. Embalmers removed the brain through a nostril by using a hook. They removed the internal organs, except the heart and kidneys, through an incision such as a surgeon makes. They usually filled the empty abdomen with linen pads, and sometimes with sawdust. Then they placed the body in natron (sodium carbonate) until the tissues were dried out. Finally, they wrapped the body carefully in many layers of linen bandages and placed it in a coffin. Sometimes there were two or more coffins, one inside the other. The coffins were made of wood or stone, and were either rectangular or shaped like the wrapped mummy. The mummy in its coffin was then placed in a tomb, along with many objects of daily use. The ancient Egyptians believed that the dead would need this equipment in the next world.

The dry climate in some parts of the world, such as Peru, Mexico, and Egypt, preserves dead bodies almost as well as Egyptian embalming methods did. Such naturally preserved bodies are sometimes called mummies also. The word *mummy* comes from *mumiya,* an Arabic word for embalmed body.   Leonard H. Lesko

See also **Embalming; Pyramids; Ramses II; Tutankhamen.**

Mumps is a contagious disease that causes painful swelling below and in front of the ears. Mumps is also called *parotitis* because it affects chiefly the *parotid* (salivary) glands in the cheeks. The swelling occurs in these glands. Mumps is caused by a virus in the saliva of an infected person.

Symptoms appear about 18 days after contact with

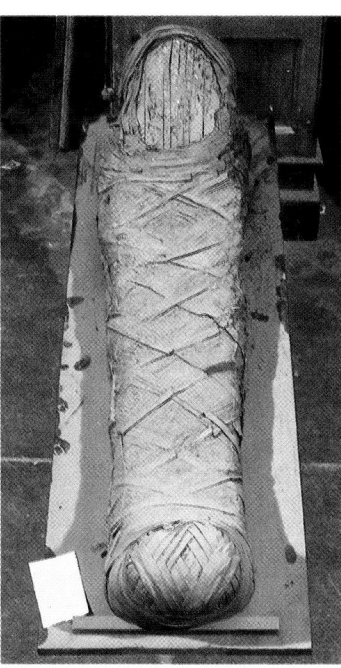

University Museum, University of Pennsylvania   Field Museum of Natural History, Chicago   Field Museum of Natural History, Chicago

Peruvian and Egyptian mummies show how these ancient peoples cared for their dead. The body of a Peruvian girl was wrapped in a seated position in a patchwork cloth bundle called a *mummy bale, left.* A false head stuffed with cotton fabric peers out from the bale. Egyptian mummies, *center and right,* were wound tightly with linen and then laid out in painted coffins.

the mumps virus. They include fever, headache, muscle ache, and sometimes vomiting. Then swelling begins in one or both parotid glands. The pain of the swollen glands may make it difficult for the patient to chew or swallow. Mumps may also attack the salivary glands under the jaw. The swelling lasts about a week.

Most cases of mumps are not serious. But the disease may also affect other parts of the body. The mumps virus may attack the central nervous system, causing extremely high fever, severe headache, and nausea. It causes particularly painful swelling when it occurs in one or both testicles of an adult male. The virus also can infect the ovaries of a female. It only rarely makes a man or a woman *sterile* (unable to produce children).

About a third of the people who become infected with the mumps virus do not develop any symptoms. But they can still infect others. A person with mumps can transmit the disease as early as seven days before the swelling appears and up to nine days after.

No drug affects the mumps virus in a person who has the disease. But a mumps vaccine, which became available in the late 1960's, provides *immunity* (protection) from the disease.   Neil R. Blacklow

Munch, *moongk,* **Edvard** (1863-1944), was a Norwegian artist. His most important works show individuals as helpless, isolated, and tormented by emotions.

Munch was born in Løten, near Oslo. His early paintings often deal with morbid themes linked to his frequent experiences with illness and death as a child. In 1889 he moved to Paris. There he learned how to express his ideas through line, color, and figure distortion from the style of such French artists as Paul Gauguin. Munch explored difficult relationships between men and women in works from 1892 to 1908 while he lived in Germany. Many of these works vividly express an emotion, such as fear, jealousy, a terrifying sense of isolation, or sexual desire. They rank among the earliest examples of expressionism, an art movement that attempts to convey the individual's inner feelings (see **Expressionism**). Munch returned to Norway in 1909. His late work became more realistic and less concerned with disturbing themes.

Munch was a talented printmaker. His woodcuts and lithographs were essential to the revival of graphic art that took place in the late 1800's. Munch was especially skillful with color prints.   Pamela A. Ivinski

Munchausen, *MUHN* CHOW *zuhn,* **Baron,** was the name given to the narrator and central figure in an anonymous booklet of tall tales, *Baron Munchausen's Narrative of His Marvellous Travels and Campaigns in Russia.* It was first published in England in 1785. The booklet sold so widely that enlarged editions began to pour from the printing presses. These used extravagant boasts. The German translation appeared in 1786. The author was an exiled German professor living in London named Rudolph Erich Raspe (1737-1794).

A real Baron Karl Friedrich Hieronymus Münchhausen (1720-1797) was a German aristocrat and officer who served in the Russian army in two wars against the Turks. Raspe may have known him. Münchhausen may have told some good stories, but he disapproved of the great lies the book attributed to him. Münchhausen tried in vain to escape the visitors that the publication brought to him. He died in grief at being named the world's biggest boaster. His name is still used to describe an exaggerator or boaster.   Klaus L. Berghahn

Mung bean. See Bean (Kinds of beans).

Munich, *MYOO nihk* (pop. 1,266,549), is the third largest city in Germany. It ranks next in population to Berlin and Hamburg. Munich lies in the southeastern part of Germany on the Bavarian plain. For location, see **Germany** (political map).

The German name for Munich is *München,* which means *Place of the Monks.* Tradition says that this name goes back to the 700's, when an outpost of the rich abbey of Tegernsee was stationed there.

Munich is well remembered today for its connection with the Nazi Party, which developed out of a small political group founded there in 1919. Munich was the site of Adolf Hitler's "Beer Hall Putsch" of 1923. Hitler attempted a revolution to seize power at a mass meeting in a Munich beer hall (see **Hitler, Adolf** [The Beer Hall Putsch]). In 1938, Great Britain, Italy, France, and Germany signed an agreement at Munich to give Czechoslovakia's Sudetenland to Germany (see **Munich Agreement**).

The Isar River flows through Munich toward the Danube River. The Maximilianeum, the seat of the Bavarian Parliament, lies along the banks of the Isar in Munich. It was built in the mid-1800's.

Munich lies less than 100 miles (160 kilometers) from Brenner Pass in the Alps on the border between Austria and Italy. The location of Munich has made the city a major transportation center linking northern and southern Europe.

Industries. Munich is one of the country's most important centers of economic activity. Its major in-

Casein on paper (1893); National Gallery, Oslo, Norway

Edvard Munch's painting *The Scream* illustrates the feeling of anguish and inner torment that appears in many of his works.

David Falconer, Frazier Photolibrary

Munich's New City Hall stands in the busy Marienplatz, a large square in the old section of the city.

dustries include electronics, food processing, printing and publishing, and the production of chemicals, machine tools, optical instruments, and textiles. Munich is well known for its breweries. Munich was formerly famous for its handicrafts and for its production of stained glass for church windows.

Important buildings. Three of the most famous buildings in Munich are the Cathedral, the Palace, and the German Museum. But beautiful palaces, churches, and public buildings can be found throughout the city. The German Museum is one of the most famous museums in the world for exhibits in technology and science. The imposing State Library contains over a million books and more than 50,000 manuscripts. The National Theater, one of the largest theaters in Germany, was bombed and destroyed during World War II (1939-1945). It was completely restored after five years of labor. The building was reopened officially in 1963.

Three famous museums were almost destroyed by the bombings during World War II. They were the old Pinakothek, the new Pinakothek, and the Glyptothek. Some of the valuable paintings and sculptures in these museums were saved, reassembled, and exhibited after the war.

Ludwig-Maximilian University in Munich has about 25,000 students, and a library of over 700,000 volumes. Founded in 1471, the university was moved to Munich from Landshut in 1826.

History. Munich was founded in 1158 by Duke Henry the Lion. In 1255, the city became the seat of a family of nobles called the House of Wittelsbach. The Wittelsbachs ruled Munich and the rest of Bavaria until World War I ended in 1918. From 1919 to the end of World War II, Munich was a stronghold of Nazism (see **Nazism**). Allied bombings destroyed much of the city during World War II. After the war, Munich was rebuilt

in a way that restored much of its traditional appearance.   Melvin Croan

Munich Agreement, *MYOO nihk,* approved in September 1938 in Munich, Germany, was the acceptance by Great Britain and France of Germany's demand for certain territory in Czechoslovakia. The agreement involved the Sudetenland region of Czechoslovakia, which had about 800,000 Czechs and 2,800,000 people of German ancestry. This region covered about 11,000 square miles (28,500 square kilometers). It included most of Czechoslovakia's industry, communications network, military outposts, and vital natural defenses. The agreement included a promise by Germany to end its aggressive expansion, and Britain and France viewed it as an attempt to avoid war. But Germany violated the agreement, drawing Europe closer to the beginning of World War II (1939-1945).

Background. German dictator Adolf Hitler had claimed that the government of Czechoslovakia was unfair to the German residents of the Sudetenland and that their land should be part of Germany. He had prepared his troops for a military take-over of the region.

Neville Chamberlain, prime minister of Great Britain, attempted to reach a peaceful settlement. He twice met with Hitler in September, but the negotiations failed. Finally, Chamberlain suggested a conference including leaders Édouard Daladier of France and Benito Mussolini of Italy. It took place in Munich on September 29 and 30 and resulted in the Munich Agreement.

The pact allowed Germany to occupy the Sudetenland. In return, Hitler promised that the Sudetenland would be the "last territorial claim I have to make in Europe." The agreement further provided for establishment of an international commission to supervise the occupation, elections in other areas of dispute, a joint guarantee for the independence of the diminished Czechoslovakia, and adjustment of claims made by Poland and Hungary. Only the first and last provisions occurred. The Munich Agreement at first seemed to avoid war. Chamberlain reported to cheering crowds in England "peace with honor" and "peace in our time."

Consequences. A few months after the conference, Hitler broke his promise and had German troops take control of Czechoslovakia. The Soviet Union lost faith in the ability of Britain and France to preserve peace and made a pact with Germany to avoid war. Hitler came to believe Britain and France would not honor their pledge to defend Poland and launched an attack on that country on Sept. 1, 1939. Britain and France promptly declared war on Germany, and World War II began.

The Munich Agreement became a classic example of an ill-advised policy of *appeasement* (concession). After Munich, agreements with an aggressive nation were thought to invite war rather than prevent it. Such agreements are still sometimes referred to as "another Munich."   Diane Shaver Clemens

Municipal government. See City government.

Muñoz Marín, *moo NYOHS mah REEN,* **Luis,** *loo EES* (1898-1980), was the first elected governor of Puerto Rico and its chief political leader for over 25 years. Previous governors had been appointed by the President of the United States. Muñoz Marín served as governor from 1949 to 1965. Under his leadership, Puerto Rico became a self-governing commonwealth of the United

States in 1952. He also began Operation Bootstrap, a comprehensive development program that brought land reform, roads, and schools to neglected areas of Puerto Rico (see **Puerto Rico** [Building a democracy]).

Muñoz Marín was born in San Juan. He studied law in the United States. In 1938, he organized the Popular Democratic Party in Puerto Rico.   Nathan A. Haverstock

Munro, Alice (1931-   ), is a Canadian short-story writer. Munro's fiction excels in revealing the larger and darker meanings in seemingly ordinary events. She describes a fractured and changing world, in which characters search for ways to unify their experiences.

Munro was born in Wingham, Ont. Her given and family name was Alice Ann Laidlaw. She was married to James Munro from 1951 to 1976. Her first collection of stories, *Dance of the Happy Shades* (1968), explores life in a fictional small Ontario town similar to the one in which she was born and raised. *Lives of Girls and Women* (1971) is a series of linked stories. The book follows Del Jordan from her childhood through a series of crises she experiences in religion, sex, and art.

Many of Munro's later stories depict the complications of marriage and the difficulties her characters encounter in knowing their own motivations. They have been collected in *Something I've Been Meaning to Tell You* (1974), *Who Do You Think You Are?* (1978, published in the United States as *The Beggar Maid*), *The Moons of Jupiter* (1982), *The Progress of Love* (1986), and *Friend of My Youth* (1990).   Ronald B. Hatch

Munro, Hector Hugh (1870-1916), was a British writer who wrote under the pen name Saki. Munro is best known for his unsettling and cleverly constructed short stories, often with trick endings. Many of the stories satirize British society of the early 1900's. Munro also wrote two novels, *The Unbearable Bassington* (1912) and *When William Came* (1913). *The Complete Works of Saki* was published in 1976.

Munro was born in Akyab (now Sittwe), Burma. He was taken to England when he was 2 years old. Munro became a well-known London journalist. He died in battle in France during World War I.   Garrett Stewart

Munsee Indians, *MUN see,* formed the Wolf clan of the Delaware Indian tribe. The Munsees lived around the headwaters of the Delaware River and along the Hudson River, and they were called the people of the stony country. White settlers drove them from the Delaware River region about 1740, and the Munsees settled along the Susquehanna River. They later migrated to other areas, largely the Midwest and Southwest in the United States and the Canadian province of Ontario. See **Delaware Indians.**   Roberta Miskokomon

Munsey, *MUN see,* **Frank Andrew** (1854-1925), was a pioneer publisher of low-priced magazines and newspapers. He had little education or financial backing but made nearly $20 million. He started *Munsey's Magazine* in 1889. The magazine's circulation reached 650,000 by 1900. Munsey built a successful grocery chain and used his profits to buy 17 newspapers. He often bought competing papers and combined them into one. Munsey was born in Mercer, Me.   John Eldridge Drewry

Muon, *MYOO ahn,* is a type of elementary particle that closely resembles an electron but has a greater mass. An elementary particle does not consist of smaller units. Both muons and electrons belong to a family of such

particles called *leptons.* The muon carries a negative charge like an electron, but it is about 207 times heavier. Muons are *unstable,* and so they *decay* (break down) to form electrons and other lighter particles.

The muon was discovered independently by two groups of scientists in 1937. These groups were Carl D. Anderson and Seth H. Neddermeyer of California Institute of Technology and Jabez C. Street and Edward C. Stevenson of Harvard University. Scientists have learned about magnetic fields in certain substances by observing muon decay in those materials.   Stanley G. Wojcicki

See also **Electron; Lepton; Meson.**

Mural is a picture or design on a wall or ceiling. Most murals decorate interiors of buildings, but some are used as exterior ornament. Murals usually relate to the architecture they decorate. Murals can alter a viewer's perception of space by creating illusionary openings in walls and ceilings. They can also make space appear more confining. Most murals are public art, meant to be seen and understood by a broad audience.

Artists have used several techniques to create murals,

© 1976 Cityarts Workshop, Inc.

Exterior murals were a popular American art form during the 1960's and 1970's. The mural shown above, called *Women Hold Up Half the Sky,* is on a building wall in New York City. It portrays some of the roles played by women in modern society.

Biblical scenes painted by the Italian artist Giotto cover the walls of the Scrovegni, or Arena, Chapel in Padua, Italy. These beautiful frescoes, which date from the early 1300's, rank among the masterpieces of Italian mural painting.

Fratelli Fabbri Editori, Milan, Italy

including fresco, the most common technique; encaustic; tempera; oil painting; and enamel or ceramic on metal. Sometimes, artists paint on a canvas that is later attached to a wall in a technique called *marouflage.* Some murals, called *mosaics,* are designs composed of pieces of glass, stone, or other material.

The mural is one of the oldest art forms. Prehistoric people decorated caves with murals of animals. Ancient Egyptians painted murals with flat, linear images. Greeks and Romans decorated walls with pictures of gardens, buildings, gods, and heroes. The greatest European murals were created during the Renaissance. The Italian artist Giotto revolutionized mural painting in the early 1300's with his dramatic and realistic Biblical scenes. In the 1400's and 1500's, Italian artists, such as Andrea Mantegna, Masaccio, Piero della Francesca, and Raphael, further developed Giotto's style. The greatest mural painter of the Renaissance was Michelangelo. Baroque and rococo artists of the 1600's and 1700's drew on Renaissance techniques to paint murals that made walls and ceilings seem to dissolve into space.

Mural art declined in prominence in the 1800's. However, at the end of the century, French painter Puvis de Chavannes and American John La Farge had revived the art form. Murals gained popularity in Mexico during the 1920's when José Clemente Orozco, Diego Rivera, and David Siqueiros created murals depicting Mexican legends and history. In the 1930's and early 1940's, the U.S. government sponsored over 2,000 murals in public buildings by such artists as Thomas Hart Benton, Reginald Marsh, and Ben Shahn. Since the 1960's, many artists have painted murals to draw attention to poverty, racism, and other social and political issues, thus permitting murals to serve as propaganda art.

John W. Keefe

See also **Fresco** and its list of related articles; **Mexico** (Arts); **Mosaic; Benton, Thomas Hart; Painting** (Materials and Techniques).

Murasaki Shikibu, *MOO rah SAH kee SHEE kee BOO* (A.D. 975?-1031?), also called Lady Murasaki, is the most famous writer of early Japanese literature. Her long novel *The Tale of Genji* is generally considered the greatest work of Japanese fiction. The novel begins with the romantic adventures of Prince Genji, the "Shining Prince." He exemplifies courtliness and the unique Japanese sensitivity to nature. The tone grows somber as the book follows the next two generations of Genji's family. The themes of death, frustration in love, and a Buddhist sense of human impermanence dominate the story. Lady Murasaki flawlessly handled a large cast of characters, portraying them with a psychological realism that did not appear in Western literature until centuries later.

Lady Murasaki was one of several gifted writers who served as ladies in waiting to Japanese empresses during the 1000's. In addition to *The Tale of Genji,* she wrote poetry and a diary famous for its witty portrayal of her contemporaries.   Mark Morris

Murat, *myoo RA,* **Joachim,** *zhoh ah KEEM* (1771?-1815), was the most famous French cavalry commander under Emperor Napoleon I. From 1808 to 1814, Murat ruled the Kingdom of Naples in southern Italy as King Joachim I. Napoleon made him a general in 1799 for defeating the Turks in Egypt. Murat's cavalry attacks helped Napoleon win battles at Austerlitz, Jena, and Friedland between 1805 and 1807.

Murat deserted Napoleon when the emperor was defeated at Leipzig in 1813. But when Napoleon escaped from his prison on the island of Elba in 1815, Murat tried to win all Italy for him. The Austrians, however, defeated Murat. After the Battle of Waterloo in 1815, he was quickly captured, condemned, and executed.

Murat was born in Bastide, France, near Cahors.

In 1800, he married Napoleon's sister Caroline, a step that helped his career. Eric A. Arnold, Jr.

Murder. When one person intentionally kills another without legal justification or excuse, the crime is called *murder*. The clearest example of this is a case where one person deliberately kills another because of hatred, envy, or greed. But there are also situations where a killing is considered murder even when no specific intent to kill exists. For example, a person who accidentally kills someone while committing a robbery is guilty of murder. The fact that the person is committing a serious crime indicates that he or she has a reckless disregard for human life and safety. This takes the place of intent to kill. The penalty for murder is a long prison sentence or death. But many national, state, and provincial governments have done away with the death penalty.

A killing that has legal justification is called *justifiable homicide*. For example, a killing in self-defense would be a justifiable homicide. The law regards a purely accidental killing as an *excusable homicide*. For example, if a pedestrian steps in front of a carefully driven automobile and is killed, the accident would be considered an excusable homicide. When a person in a fit of anger intentionally kills another person after the victim has provoked the attack, the killing is called *voluntary manslaughter*. When a person's death results from reckless driving or other extreme negligence on the part of the killer, the offense is called *involuntary manslaughter*. The penalties in most cases of manslaughter are less severe than those for murder. Charles F. Wellford

See also **Capital punishment; Crime; Homicide; Manslaughter**.

Murdoch, *MUR dahk,* **Dame Iris** (1919-   ), is a British novelist known for her philosophical novels. Her characters face difficult moral choices in their search for love and freedom and are often involved in complex networks of love affairs. Some critics have complained that Murdoch's characters are mere puppets used to act out philosophical ideas. But others have praised her fiction for its wit and psychological insight.

Some of Murdoch's novels expose the dangers of abstract systems of behavior that can cut people off from spontaneous, loving relationships. *Under the Net* (1954) and *A Fairly Honourable Defeat* (1970) are examples. *The Bell* (1958) examines the relationships among the members of a religious commune. In *A Severed Head* (1961), Murdoch portrays three couples whose unfaithful sexual conduct illustrates their shallow, self-centered philosophies. Her other novels include *The Black Prince* (1973), *The Sea, The Sea* (1978), *The Good Apprentice* (1986), and *The Book and the Brotherhood* (1988).

Jean Iris Murdoch was born in Dublin. She lectured in philosophy from 1948 to 1963 at Oxford University in England. Murdoch was made Dame Commander of the Order of the British Empire in 1987. Jane Marcus

Murdoch, *MUR dahk,* **Rupert** (1931-   ), is an Australian-born publisher who owns many newspapers and magazines in Australia, the United Kingdom, the United States, and other countries. His publications range from *The Times* of London, an influential British daily, to the *Star,* a sensational U.S. weekly. He is also owner or part-owner of a motion-picture studio, TV stations, and book-publishing firms. Murdoch is known for making financially struggling operations profitable.

Murdoch's most extensive holdings are in Australia, where he controls over half of the nation's newspaper circulation. His newspapers there include *The Australian,* a national daily, and the *Daily Mirror* and *Daily Telegraph* of Sydney. He also is part-owner of one of the nation's airlines. Murdoch controls his properties through News Corporation Limited and its subsidiaries.

In the United States, Murdoch's publications include the *Boston Herald,* the *San Antonio Express-News,* and *New York, New Woman,* and *TV Guide* magazines. He also owns 20th Century-Fox Film Corporation. In the United Kingdom, he publishes the *News of the World, The Sun, The Times,* and several other newspapers.

Keith Rupert Murdoch was born in Melbourne. In 1985, he became a U.S. citizen. Michael Emery

Muriatic acid. See Hydrochloric acid.

Murieta, *moo ree AY tah,* **Joaquín,** *hwah KEEN,* was the name given to a famous bandit during the California gold rush of the mid-1800's. He became a hero of Spanish-speaking people who had been discouraged from entering the gold fields because of a $20 monthly tax placed on foreign miners in 1850. No one knows if a real Joaquín Murieta existed. There were as many as five bandits in the gold fields known only as *Joaquín.* In July 1853, California rangers killed two Mexicans and later identified one of them as Joaquín Murieta. But this person's true background is unknown.

The legend of Murieta grew after publication of the book *The Life and Adventures of Joaquín Murieta, The Celebrated California Bandit* (1854) by the American writer John Rollin Ridge. Ridge described Murieta as a peaceful miner who became an outlaw after white Americans stole his claim and attacked his family. The story became believable because of later references to Murieta in works by respected writers, including American historians Hubert H. Bancroft and Theodore Hittell and the Chilean poet Pablo Neruda. Feliciano M. Ribera

Murillo, *moo REE lyoh,* **Bartolomé Esteban,** *BAHR toh loh MAY ays TAY bahn* (1618-1682), was a Spanish painter of the 1600's. He is considered the best interpreter of the gentle, optimistic side of Christianity. He is known for the warmth and humanity of his paintings.

Murillo's painting *The Immaculate Conception* shows the delicate beauty and fine shadings of light and atmosphere that characterize his work. Like many of Murillo's paintings, this work has a gentleness critics of the early 1900's found too sentimental. Today, his complex spiraling compositions, fluid brushwork, fine drawing, and subtle colors are much admired. Murillo also painted dignified and flattering portraits and scenes of daily life. He is one of the few artists who created realistic and sympathetic paintings of children.

Murillo was born in Seville. His paintings before 1645 were influenced by the realism and dark coloring found in the work of artists from southern Spain. In 1645, the Franciscan Order in Seville gave Murillo his first important commission. In that same year, Murillo visited painter Diego Velázquez in Madrid. There he was also inspired by Flemish and Venetian masters. In his later work, Murillo became more concerned with problems of light, color, and atmosphere. By 1660, he was Spain's most popular painter. Marilyn Stokstad

Murmansk, *moor MAHNSK* (pop. 472,000), is Russia's chief port on the Arctic Ocean. It is the world's largest city north of the Arctic Circle. The warm Gulf Stream keeps the harbor free of ice the year around. Murmansk stands on a level, treeless plain on the northern part of the Kola Peninsula. It borders the Kola Inlet, an arm of the Arctic Ocean. For the location of Murmansk, see **Russia** (political map).

Murmansk is a fishing and shipbuilding center. It has fish canneries; metal, woodworking, and net and barrel factories; and refrigerating plants. Exporters ship fish, lumber, and minerals. The city has a polar research station. A railroad links Murmansk with St. Petersburg. Murmansk was founded in 1915. During World War II (1939-1945), the Allies used the port to ship supplies to parts of the Soviet Union that were controlled by Germany.   Zvi Gitelman

Murphy, Audie, *AW dee* (1924-1971), won fame as the most decorated United States soldier of World War II (1939-1945). He received 24 medals from the U.S. government, 3 from France, and 1 from Belgium. He later became a motion-picture actor.

Audie Leon Murphy was born in Kingston, Tex., near Greenville. He enlisted in the Army in 1942 and was appointed a second lieutenant in 1944. Murphy served in North Africa and Europe. On Jan. 26, 1945, German forces attacked his unit near Colmar, France. Murphy jumped on a burning tank destroyer and used its machine gun to kill about 50 enemy troops. He received the Medal of Honor, the nation's highest military award.

Oil painting on canvas (1678); Prado Museum, Madrid (MAS)

Murillo's *The Immaculate Conception* honors the Virgin Mary's freedom from original sin. The painting shows the spiritual quality typical of the artist's later work.

Murphy began his motion-picture career in 1948. His films included *The Red Badge of Courage* (1951) and *To Hell and Back* (1955). Murphy died in an airplane crash.

Samuel J. Ziskind

U.S. Army
Audie Murphy

Murphy, Emily Gowan (1868-1933), was a Canadian social reformer and author. She helped win legal and political rights for Canadian women.

In the early 1900's, Murphy helped establish a court in Edmonton, Alta., that handled cases involving women. From 1916 to 1931, she served as the court's first judge and as the first woman magistrate in the British Empire. A book she wrote about drug abuse, *The Black Candle* (1922), helped lead to the passage of drug laws in Canada.

In 1927, Murphy led a group of five women in a court battle to determine whether women were "persons" under the British North America Act, which then served as Canada's constitution. The Privy Council in England, the highest judicial authority in the British Empire, ruled in the women's favor in 1929. The council's ruling enabled women to serve in the Canadian Senate.

Murphy wrote several books under the pen name of "Janey Canuck," including *The Impressions of Janey Canuck Abroad* (1901) and *Janey Canuck in the West* (1910). Murphy was born in Cookstown, Ont.   Patricia Monk

Murray, James (1721?-1794), was a British soldier who became the first British governor of Quebec. He was born near Edinburgh, Scotland, and went to America in 1757. He fought the French at Louisbourg in 1758.

Murray served as one of the three brigadiers under General James Wolfe in the successful battle against the French on the Plains of Abraham outside Quebec City. After the victory, Murray was left in command of the city. He later defended it against a French army led by General François de Lévis.

Murray was made governor of the Quebec region in 1760. Three years later, when French rule ended, he became governor of the main area gained from the French in Canada. He faced many problems in the relations between the English and the Indians and between the French Canadians and English officers and merchants. Some men working under him accused him of favoring the French. Murray was recalled to England in 1766. But he was cleared of all charges.   Phillip Buckner

Murray, Philip (1886-1952), succeeded John L. Lewis as president of the Congress of Industrial Organizations (CIO) in 1940, and held that post until his death. He helped establish World War II government labor policies. He saw to it that the CIO unions kept their "no-strike" pledge during the war. He also served on the National Defense Mediation Board.

Murray rose to his CIO position after 36 years as a labor union organizer and leader. He advanced in the United Mine Workers to the post of vice president, which he held from 1920 to 1942. Murray ended a long friendship with John L. Lewis soon after he succeeded him as president of the CIO.

When the CIO began organizing the steel industry in 1935, Murray became chairman of the organizing committee. He served as the first president of the United Steelworkers of America from 1942 to 1952. In the late 1940's, Murray led a successful fight to oust Communist-dominated unions from the CIO. He led the steelworkers in three national strikes after World War II. Pensions and union security were two of the major issues of these strikes.

Murray was born in Blantyre, Scotland, the son of a coal miner. In 1902, he moved to the United States with his family, and began working in the mines at the age of 16. He argued with a mine foreman soon after he started, and lost his job. The other miners went on strike in sympathy with him. Murray served on Woodrow Wilson's War Labor Board and on the National Bituminous Coal Production Committee during World War I. He was the coauthor, with Morris L. Cooke, of *Organized Labor and Production* (1940).   Jack Barbash

Murray River is the longest permanently flowing river in Australia. It is also an important source of irrigation. The Murray River system includes the Darling, Lachlan, and Murrumbidgee rivers, and drains an area larger than that of France and Spain combined. For location, see **Australia** (terrain map).

The Murray rises in the Australian Alps near the eastern boundary of Victoria. It flows northwestward and forms the boundary between Victoria and New South Wales. It then crosses eastern South Australia and empties into Encounter Bay, south of Adelaide. The Murray River is 1,609 miles (2,589 kilometers) long. With the Darling River, it forms a system 2,310 miles (3,718 kilometers) long. Small recreational boats operate on the Murray. But the river is not navigable into the interior by ships.

A system of dams helps irrigate about $1\frac{1}{2}$ million acres (610,000 hectares) of land. The dams were built under the Murray River Agreement made in 1915 by New South Wales, South Australia, and Victoria. The Snowy Mountains Scheme—begun in the mid-1900's—includes 16 large dams and several small ones. It directs water into the Murray and Murrumbidgee rivers. It provides hydroelectric power for Victoria and New South Wales, and enough water to irrigate about 1,000 square miles (2,600 square kilometers).

One result of the irrigation has been a high salt content in the soil over a large area. The Murray-Darling Basin Commission was established in 1988 to try to solve this ecological problem.   D. N. Jeans

See also **Darling River**.

Murre, *mur,* is a type of sea bird that lives on rocky coasts of the North Atlantic and North Pacific. Great colonies consisting of thousands of murres crowd the rock ledges during the breeding season. A murre is from 16 to 17 inches (41 to 43 centimeters) long. It has short wings. The bird is brownish-black above and white on the breast and throat.

The female murre hatches a single large, pointed egg, which it lays on the bare stone. The egg varies from white to blue and green and usually has black, brown, or lavender spots.

Scientific classification. Murres make up the genus *Uria* in the auk family, Alcidae. The scientific name for the common murre is *Uria aalge.*   Fritz L. Knopf

Murrow, Edward R. (1908-1965), was an American radio and television broadcaster. He won fame during World War II (1939-1945) for his on-the-scene radio broadcasts describing German bombing attacks on London. His listeners in America could hear the bombs exploding in the background.

Egbert Roscoe Murrow was born near Greensboro, N.C. He changed his name to Edward while in college. Murrow became European director of the Columbia Broadcasting System (CBS) in 1937. He turned to radio newscasting shortly before World War II.

Edward R. Murrow Foundation
Edward R. Murrow

Murrow narrated the TV program, "See It Now," from 1951 to 1958. He started a new style of TV newscasting with on-the-scene reporting that told about issues in everyday terms. In the most famous show of the series, Murrow attacked Joseph R. McCarthy. McCarthy was a U.S. senator whose investigations of Communist influence in the government had caused a national controversy (see **McCarthy, Joseph R.**). From 1953 to 1959, Murrow narrated "Person to Person," a TV program that featured interviews with famous people in their homes. He served as director of the U.S. Information Agency from 1961 to 1964.   Keith P. Sanders

Muscat, *MUHS kat* (pop. 30,000; met. area pop. 250,000), is the capital of Oman. It lies on the country's northeast coast, along the Gulf of Oman (see **Oman** [map]). Muscat, also spelled *Masqat,* became Oman's chief seaport and trading center in the 1500's. In the early 1970's, the main port and trade activities were

WORLD BOOK illustration by Trevor Boyer, Linden Artists Ltd.
The common murre is a sea bird that nests in colonies on the rocky coasts of the North Atlantic and North Pacific.

shifted to the nearby suburb of Matrah. Muscat is important because of its location on the Gulf of Oman, the route for oil tankers leaving the Persian Gulf. Two Portuguese forts that date from the late 1500's and the palace of the sultan of Oman, built in the 1970's, dominate the city. Muscat has many old, one- and two-story whitewashed buildings. Most of the people work in commerce or for the government.

Muscat and its more modern suburbs are called the Capital Area. The Capital Area is a booming district that includes an international airport, an oil tanker loading zone, military bases, and a deepwater port. Muscat dates from ancient times. Portugal controlled Muscat from about 1507 to 1650.   Robert Geran Landen

Muscat and Oman. See Oman.

Muscle is the tough, elastic tissue that makes body parts move. All animals except the simplest kinds have some type of muscle.

People use muscles to make various movements, such as walking, jumping, or throwing. Muscles also help in performing activities necessary for growth and for maintaining a strong, healthy body. For example, people use muscles in the jaw to chew food. Other muscles help move food through the stomach and intestines, and aid in digestion. Muscles in the heart and blood vessels force the blood to circulate. Muscles in the chest make breathing possible.

Muscles are found throughout the body. As a person grows, the muscles also get bigger. Muscle makes up nearly half the body weight of an adult.

This article primarily discusses the muscles of human beings. The last section describes muscles in other animals.

Kinds of muscles

The human body has more than 600 major muscles. About 240 of them have specific names. There are two main types of muscles: (1) skeletal muscles and (2) smooth muscles. A third kind of muscle, called *cardiac muscle,* has characteristics of both skeletal and smooth muscles. It is found only in the heart.

Skeletal muscles help hold the bones of the skeleton together and give the body shape. They also make the body move. Skeletal muscles make up a large part of the legs, arms, abdomen, chest, neck, and face. These muscles vary greatly in size, depending on the type of job they do. For example, eye muscles are small and fairly weak, but the muscles of the thigh are large and strong.

All muscles are made up of cells called *muscle fibers.* Each skeletal muscle is composed of thousands of long, cylindrical muscle fibers. When viewed under a microscope, these fibers show alternating light and dark bands called *striations.* For this reason, skeletal muscles are also called *striated muscles.* The striations occur because thick and thin *filaments* (strands) repeatedly overlap each other. The thick filaments consist of a protein called *myosin.* The thin filaments are made up chiefly of the protein *actin.*

Muscle fibers have a variety of other specialized parts. Each skeletal muscle fiber has many elements called *nuclei.* These nuclei contain growth-producing substances that repair or remake various parts of the muscle fiber as they wear out. Each muscle fiber also

Kinds of muscles

The human body has three kinds of muscles: skeletal, smooth, and cardiac. Skeletal muscle fibers have bands called *striations.* Each fiber also has many core elements called *nuclei.* Smooth muscles have no striations and only one nucleus in each fiber. Cardiac muscle has striations and a single nucleus in each fiber.

WORLD BOOK illustrations by Charles Wellek

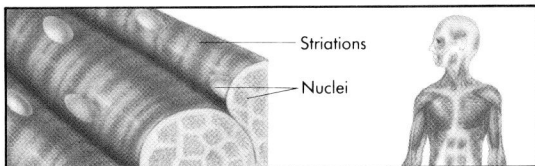

Skeletal muscles

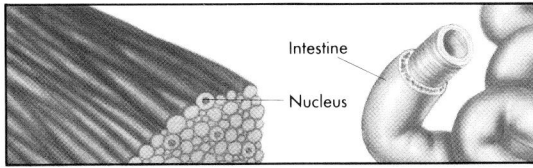

Smooth muscles

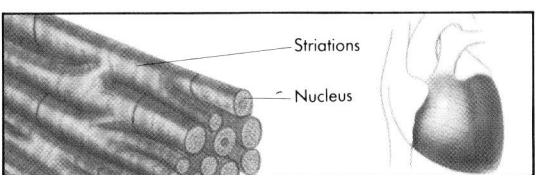

Cardiac muscle

has thousands of tiny sausage-shaped *mitochondria.* These structures produce the energy that the fiber needs in order to live and do its work.

Muscle fibers are held together by *connective tissue.* The ends of most skeletal muscles are joined to bones by a tough, flexible connective tissue called *tendon.* One end of the muscle is attached to a bone that does not move when the muscle *contracts* (draws together). This end of the muscle is called the *origin.* The other end, called the *insertion,* is attached to a bone that moves when the muscle contracts.

When a person stands erect, many skeletal muscles contract to make the body rigid. The skeletal muscles also can make one part of the body move while another part stays stiff. Skeletal muscles act both ways because they work in pairs. One muscle of each pair is called the *flexor.* It bends a joint and brings a limb closer to the body. The other muscle, the *extensor,* does the opposite. For example, the *biceps* muscle in the front of the upper arm is a flexor. When this muscle contracts, the elbow bends and the forearm and hand move toward the shoulder. The *triceps* muscle in the back of the upper arm is an extensor. When it contracts, the elbow straightens and the forearm and hand move away from the shoulder. At the same time, the biceps relaxes so the triceps can pull it back to its original length.

Skeletal muscles contract and pull on the bones they attach to when a nerve stimulates them. They usually move *voluntarily* (under conscious control) and are sometimes called *voluntary muscles.* But skeletal muscles also may move *involuntarily* (without conscious control). For example, involuntary movement occurs when a person jerks his or her hand away from a hot object before thinking about doing it.

Skeletal muscles adapt to exercise in special ways, depending on how they are required to work. For example, muscles grow larger and stronger if a person lifts heavy weights for a short period of time each day. Such exercise causes muscle nuclei to increase production of thick and thin filaments in each exercised muscle fiber. In addition, bone and tendon grow stronger. Muscles adapt differently if a person regularly performs lighter exercise for long periods—such as 30 minutes of bicy-

cling, running, or swimming. In this case, muscle fibers increase their ability to produce energy needed to keep up such muscular work.

Smooth muscles are found in various organs of the body. For example, smooth muscles are found in the walls of the stomach, intestines, blood vessels, and bladder. The fibers of smooth muscles are not striated like those of skeletal muscles. They also are smaller than skeletal muscle fibers and have only one nucleus.

Smooth muscles operate slowly and automatically in a natural, rhythmic pattern of contraction followed by relaxation. In this way, they control various body processes. For example, the steady action of smooth muscles in the stomach and intestines moves food along for digestion. Because they are not under conscious control

Skeletal muscles   The human body has more than 600 major muscles. About 240 of these muscles have specific names. The illustrations below show some of the most important external skeletal muscles. These muscles are identified by their Latin names, which are the names used by medical personnel.

WORLD BOOK illustrations by Charles Wellek

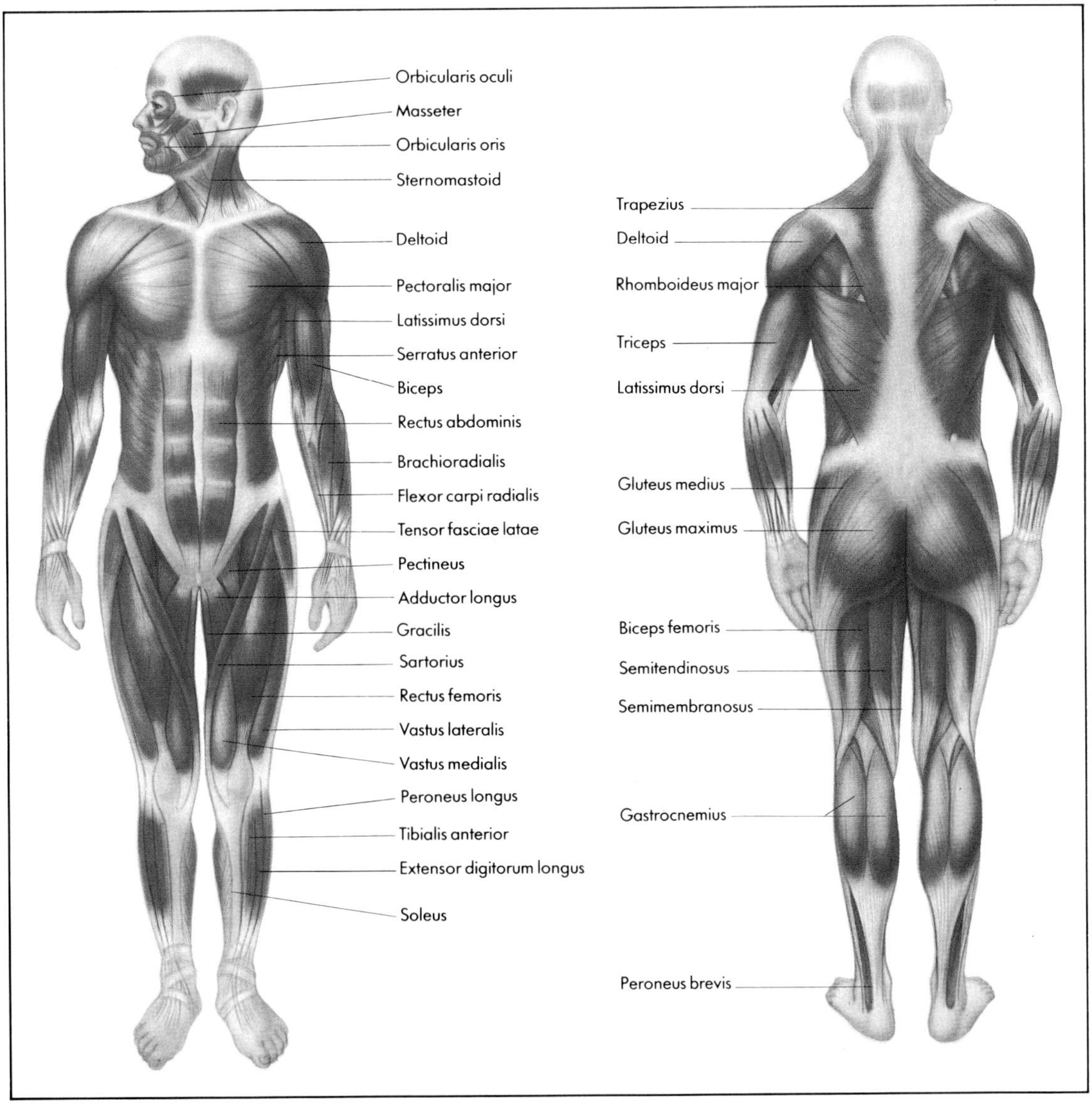

Front view labels:
- Orbicularis oculi
- Masseter
- Orbicularis oris
- Sternomastoid
- Deltoid
- Pectoralis major
- Latissimus dorsi
- Serratus anterior
- Biceps
- Rectus abdominis
- Brachioradialis
- Flexor carpi radialis
- Tensor fasciae latae
- Pectineus
- Adductor longus
- Gracilis
- Sartorius
- Rectus femoris
- Vastus lateralis
- Vastus medialis
- Peroneus longus
- Tibialis anterior
- Extensor digitorum longus
- Soleus

Back view labels:
- Trapezius
- Deltoid
- Rhomboideus major
- Triceps
- Latissimus dorsi
- Gluteus medius
- Gluteus maximus
- Biceps femoris
- Semitendinosus
- Semimembranosus
- Gastrocnemius
- Peroneus brevis

How skeletal muscles move a limb

Skeletal muscles work in pairs, as shown in the example below. The elbow straightens when the triceps muscle *contracts* (draws together). The elbow bends as the biceps muscle contracts.

WORLD BOOK illustrations by Charles Wellek

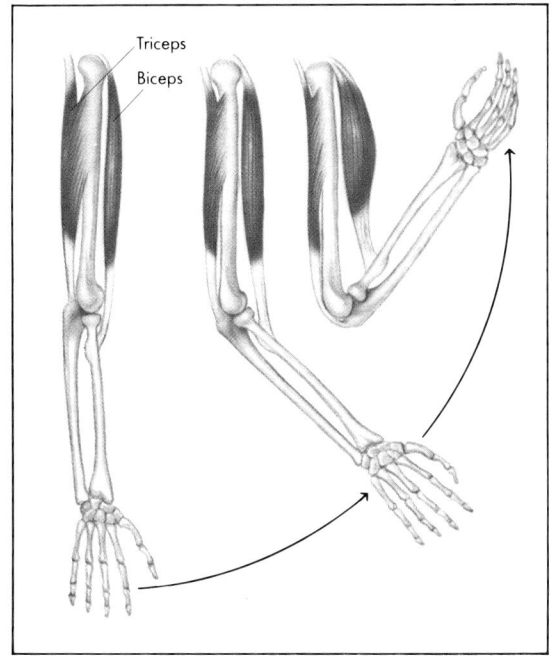

by the brain, smooth muscles are also known as *involuntary muscles.*

Smooth muscles are stimulated by a special set of nerves that belong to the *autonomic nervous system,* and by body chemicals (see **Nervous system** [The autonomic nervous system]). In certain circumstances, the autonomic nerves and hormones act to change the speed and strength of smooth muscle contractions. For example, they slow the pace of contractions in the intestines if a person feels fear or anxiety. They can even stop contractions in the intestines if these feelings become severe. For this reason, people under emotional stress often find it difficult to digest food.

Cardiac muscle makes up the walls of the heart. When cardiac muscle cells contract, they push blood out of the heart and into the arteries. The blood then circulates throughout the body, bringing nourishment to all body cells. Cardiac muscle has characteristics of both skeletal and smooth muscles. Like skeletal muscle fibers, cardiac muscle cells have striations. Like smooth muscle fibers, each cardiac muscle cell has only one nucleus and contracts automatically.

The heart also contains a group of specialized cells called the *sinoatrial node,* or *S-A node.* The S-A node starts up each contraction of the cardiac muscle by giving off rhythmic signals to neighboring muscle cells. As these cells contract, they cause others to contract as well. By this process, all the cardiac muscle cells contract together. The autonomic nerves that stimulate the S-A node control how often the cardiac muscle contracts. The S-A node thus acts as the heart's "pacemaker," because it determines how often the heart beats to

pump blood through the body. For further information about the heart, its parts, and how they work, see **Heart.**

How muscles work

All muscles contract when they are stimulated. Scientists have done much research to determine how muscles contract and how they are stimulated.

How muscles contract. During the mid-1900's, the English scientist H. E. Huxley developed what has become the most widely accepted theory to explain how muscles contract. This theory, called the *sliding filament theory,* proposes that the muscle fiber's thick myosin filaments have numerous small projections. These projections, called *myosin cross-bridges,* spring away from the myosin filaments when the muscle fibers are stimulated. These cross-bridges attach themselves to the thin actin filaments that run parallel to the myosin filaments. The cross-bridges pull on the actin filaments, causing them to slide between the myosin filaments. As the actin filaments slide, they pull the ends of the muscle toward its middle, making the muscle fibers shorten.

In order for the myosin cross-bridges to work, the substance *adenosine triphosphate* (*ATP*) must be produced by muscle cells. ATP provides the energy to slide actin filaments. It is produced when oxygen in muscle fibers combines with chemicals from food. Each muscle fiber contains only a small amount of ATP. When muscles work hard, the body's ability to turn food and oxygen into energy increases to make the needed ATP.

How muscles are stimulated. Muscle cells are excitable because the membrane of each cell is electrically charged. Thus, a muscle cell is said to have *electric potential.* This electric potential results from the presence of sodium and potassium *ions* (electrically charged particles) on each side of the membrane. Potassium ions easily move through the membrane and accumulate in the cell. Sodium ions do not enter the cell as easily. In addition, the membrane has a special mechanism that pumps potassium into the cell and pumps sodium out. Consequently, the cell normally contains much potassium but little sodium.

Muscle cells are stimulated by nerves or by hormones, depending on the muscle involved. When the muscle cell is stimulated, its electric potential changes rapidly. The excited membrane allows sodium to rush into the cell and potassium to flow out. The sodium-potassium pumping mechanism quickly reverses this change, returning the cell to its normal condition.

The change in electric potential in the muscle cell triggers the release of calcium from storage areas inside the cell. The calcium then builds up in the cell and eventually causes the actin filaments to attract myosin cross-bridges and produce contraction. The cell relaxes when the level of calcium drops back to normal.

Disorders of the muscles

Muscles function through an amazing coordination of many elements. Occasionally, however, the normal operation of muscles is disturbed. For example, a person may experience painful cramps of certain skeletal muscles if he or she exercises too hard or for a long time. Skeletal muscle cramps involve *spastic* (sudden and violent) muscle contractions. No one knows exactly why such cramps occur. They probably result from having too much or too little salt in the fluids surrounding muscle fibers. With proper rest and nutrition, the body can correct the problem, and cramping stops. Cramps also may develop in smooth muscle organs, such as the stomach and intestine. Doctors use heat, massage, and medicines in treating cramps. See **Cramp.**

Hard muscular work also may cause skeletal muscles to become sore. In severe cases, the soreness may last up to four days. The cause of muscle soreness is not completely understood, but it probably involves damage to muscle and connective tissue. With proper exercise, the muscles and body can adapt to strenuous muscle work and greatly reduce the risk of tissue damage.

Numerous diseases affect skeletal muscles. Two major classes of muscle diseases are (1) *muscular atrophy diseases* and (2) *myopathies.* Atrophy diseases attack and damage the nervous system, including nerves that stimulate muscles. As a result, muscles progressively shrink and become weak. Amyotrophic lateral sclerosis—also called ALS or Lou Gehrig's disease—is an example of an atrophy disease (see **Amyotrophic lateral sclerosis**). Muscular weakness also occurs in myopathies. In these diseases, however, weakness results because the muscle itself does not function properly. Certain myopathies, such as various *muscular dystrophies,* are characterized by gradual wasting away of skeletal muscles (see **Muscular dystrophy**).

Muscles in other animals

All of the more advanced animals have some kind of muscle tissue. The muscles of human beings and those of other animals have many similarities. For example, humans and other *vertebrates* (animals with backbones) have three kinds of muscles—skeletal, smooth, and cardiac. Some *invertebrates* (animals without backbones), such as insects, have striated muscles. Other invertebrates, such as scallops and squids, have both striated and smooth muscles. In most cases, the muscles of other animals operate in much the same way as human muscles. However, the speed at which striated muscles contract varies widely among species. In general, contractions occur faster in a small animal, such as the rat, than in a large animal like the cow.   Paul A. Molé

Related articles in *World Book* include:

Diaphragm	Muscular dystrophy	Tetany
Human body (The	Myasthenia gravis	Tongue
muscular system;	Tendon	
Trans-vision)		

See also *Muscular system* in the Research Guide/Index, Volume 22, for a *Reading and Study Guide.*

Additional resources

Hoyle, Graham. *Muscles and Their Neural Control.* Wiley, 1983.
Showers, Paul. *You Can't Make a Move Without Your Muscles.* T. Y. Crowell, 1982. For younger readers.
Silverstein, Alvin and V. B. *The Muscular System: How Living Creatures Move.* Prentice-Hall, 1972.
Vevers, Gwynne. *Muscles and Movement.* Lothrop, 1984. For younger readers.

Muscle sense, also called *conscious proprioception,* is one of two senses that tells a person what position parts of the body are in. The other sense is sight. A person walking down the street knows the position of the legs without looking at them. *Proprioceptors* (nerves) in the joints, muscles, and tendons of the legs are sensitive to pressure and tension. The proprioceptors send information about the state of the joints, muscles, and tendons to the brain. The brain combines the information, enabling the person to sense the position of the body and to influence movement. There are proprioceptors for most parts of the body.   Daniel S. Barth

Muscle Shoals is an area of the Tennessee River Valley in northwestern Alabama. It is commonly referred to as *the Shoals.* The area was named for a section of shallow water and rocky rapids that presented a major obstacle to river navigation during the 1800's. The Shoals lie east of the cities of Florence, Tuscumbia, and Sheffield. The town of Muscle Shoals was developed at the west end of the rapids and became a city in 1923.

The Tennessee Valley Authority, created by Congress in 1933, controls two dams at Muscle Shoals (see **Tennessee Valley Authority**). Wilson lies at the west end of the area, and Wheeler, about 15 miles (24 kilometers) east. The dams raise the water level above the rapids and form lakes that hold the season's rainfall. The dams have improved river navigation because the water in the lakes ensures a more nearly uniform depth of water during wet and dry weather. Both dams provide hydroelectric power. Wheeler also controls floods.

Two nitrate plants were completed at Muscle Shoals in 1918, under the National Defense Act of 1916. They were built because it was feared World War I might cut off nitrate from Chile.   David C. Weaver

Muscular dystrophy, *DIHS truh fee,* is a name for certain types of serious muscle diseases. The disorders weaken *skeletal muscles*—that is, the muscles that hold the bones of the skeleton together and move them. Therefore, muscular dystrophies seriously affect movement and posture. Skeletal deformities are often associated with this group of diseases.

All types of muscular dystrophy are inherited. They are caused by a defect in one or more of the genes important to muscle function. Some types are inherited as a *dominant gene abnormality,* while others are inherited as a *recessive gene abnormality* or a *sex-linked recessive gene abnormality.* In dominant gene abnormality, a person who inherits the defective gene from either parent will develop the disease. In recessive gene abnormality, a person must inherit the defective gene from both parents to develop the disease. In sex-linked recessive gene abnormality, women are not affected but may pass on the defective gene to their children. A boy will develop the disease if he inherits the defective gene. Doctors have not found a cure for muscular dystrophy.

The four most common muscular dystrophies are *Duchenne, facioscapulohumeral, limb-girdle,* and *myotonic.* There are also other types of muscular dystrophy.

Duchenne muscular dystrophy is the most common and most rapidly progressive of the childhood muscle diseases. In most cases, the first sign of the disease is difficulty in walking at an early age, from 2 to 6 years old. Later, the patients fall frequently and cannot run. Walking and standing become more difficult, and a wheelchair is needed by adolescence. The disease eventually affects most muscles of the body. Doctors use antibiotics for lung complications and balanced nutrition for overall health in an effort to extend the life expectancy of the patients. Stretching exercises and braces reduce muscle shortening and joint deformities. These treatments may improve the patient's mobility. Duchenne dystrophy is inherited as a sex-linked recessive gene abnormality. It affects only boys.

In 1986, scientists identified the genes that cause Duchenne dystrophy. The following year, they reported the discovery of a protein called *dystrophin* whose absence in muscle tissues causes the disease. Today, researchers are attempting to improve muscle function in Duchenne patients by injecting normal genes or muscle cells into the defective muscle tissues.

Facioscapulohumeral and limb-girdle muscular dystrophies are slowly progressive and usually become evident in adolescence or early adult life. They affect both men and women. Most patients have a normal life expectancy, though with increasing disability. Facioscapulohumeral dystrophy primarily affects the muscles of the face, shoulder, and upper arm. It is inherited as a dominant gene abnormality. Limb-girdle dystrophy primarily affects the muscles of the arms, shoulders, legs, and hips. It is inherited as a recessive gene abnormality.

Myotonic muscular dystrophy is the most common adult dystrophy. It usually causes slowly progressive weakness of the muscles of the fingers, hands, forearms, feet, and lower legs. Along with the onset of weakness, the muscles become periodically *myotonic* (stiff). In addition, patients may develop nonmuscular disorders, including eye cataracts and diabetes. This disease can affect both men and women. It is inherited as a dominant gene abnormality.

Other muscular dystrophies include *Becker, congenital,* and *distal.* Becker is similar to but less severe than Duchenne dystrophy. Congenital dystrophy involves early weakness at birth. Distal dystrophy initially involves the small muscles of the hands and feet.

Michael S. Hudecki

Muscular system. See Muscle; Human body (The muscular system).

Muses, *MYOOZ ehz,* were nine goddesses of the arts and sciences in Greek and Roman mythology. In Greek mythology, they were the daughters of Zeus, the king of the gods; and Mnemosyne, the goddess of memory. Each Muse ruled over a certain art or science. Calliope was the Muse of epic poetry; Erato, love poetry; Euterpe, lyric poetry; Melpomene, tragedy; Thalia, comedy; Clio, history; Urania, astronomy; Polyhymnia, sacred song; and Terpsichore, dance.

The Greeks believed the Muses lived on Mount Olympus with their leader, the god Apollo. Like him, the Muses remained young and beautiful forever. They could see into the future, which few other gods could do. They also had the ability to banish all grief and sorrow. The Muses had pleasing, melodic voices and often sang as a chorus. Early Greek writers and artists called on the Muses for inspiration before beginning to work. Any one or all of the Muses could be asked for help, even though each governed a special art or science.

The Muses played an important part in Roman mythology, though the Roman worship of Muses was borrowed from the Greeks. The Romans believed that Jupiter, the king of their gods, was the father of the Muses.

Several words come from the Greek word *Mousa,* meaning *Muse.* They include *museum,* which originally meant *temple of the Muses;* and *music,* which meant *art of the Muses.*   C. Scott Littleton

See also **Mythology** (picture: The Muses).

Museum is a place where a collection of objects illustrating science, art, history, or other subjects is kept and displayed. At various museums, visitors can learn how people lived and worked in early times, what makes a work of art a masterpiece, or how electricity works. Some people also consider the term *museum* to apply to such educational institutions as planetariums, botanical gardens, zoos, nature centers, and even libraries.

Museum of Science and Industry, Chicago (WORLD BOOK photo)

The Metropolitan Museum of Art, New York, Rogers Fund, 1932

Museums preserve many interesting and beautiful objects from the past. The exhibit on the left traces the development of aircraft and railroad equipment. The dining room on the right, designed by architect Robert Adam for a London house of the 1760's, is displayed in its original form.

Historic villages are reconstructions of towns from various periods in history. Old Sturbridge Village, *above,* in Massachusetts shows life in a New England community of the early 1800's.

A museum collects, cares for, and researches the objects it displays. It also keeps a *study collection* of undisplayed objects. These objects—sometimes called *artifacts*—are often studied by students and researchers.

Kinds of museums

There are three main kinds of museums: (1) art museums, (2) history museums, and (3) science museums.

Art museums preserve and exhibit paintings, sculpture, and other works of art. The collections of some art museums include work from many periods. Famous museums of this type include the Louvre in Paris and the Metropolitan Museum of Art in New York City.

Some museums specialize in artworks of one period. For example, the Museum of Modern Art in New York City displays works created since the late 1800's. Other museums exhibit only one type of art. The Museum of International Folk Art in Santa Fe, N. Mex., for example, specializes in folk art from around the world.

Many art museums also have special exhibits. They borrow works of art from individuals or other museums for such exhibits, which usually last several weeks.

History museums illustrate the life and events of the past. Their collections include documents, furniture, tools, and other materials. Many cities and states have historical societies that operate history museums. Most of these museums have exhibits on local history.

Other types of history museums include *living history museums.* Museums of this type include *living history farms, historic houses,* and *historic villages.* These museums show how people lived or worked during a certain period. On living history farms, workers demonstrate how crops were planted and harvested in earlier times. Historic houses, such as Mount Vernon, George Washington's home near Alexandria, Va., have been restored to their original condition and are open to the public. Williamsburg, a historic village in Virginia, has restored and reconstructed buildings that date from the 1700's. In this village, costumed interpreters demonstrate how early colonists performed such tasks as cooking, making shoes, and printing newspapers.

Science museums have exhibits on the natural sciences and technology. *Museums of natural history* exhibit displays of animals, fossils, plants, rocks, and other objects and organisms found in nature. Most of them, including the National Museum of Natural History in Washington, D.C., have exhibits on ecology and the evolution of human beings. Many museums of natural history have special exhibits on dinosaurs and other topics.

The exhibits in *science-technology museums* explain the operations of various types of machines and industrial methods or trace the development of a particular field of technology. Visitors to the Museum of Science and Industry in Chicago can take a guided tour through a realistic reproduction of a coal mine. The National Air and Space Museum in the Smithsonian Institution in Washington, D.C., has exhibits on the history of aviation and space travel.

Other types of museums feature exhibits on only one subject. The Circus World Museum in Baraboo, Wis., has the world's largest collection of circus wagons. The National Baseball Hall of Fame and Museum in Cooperstown, N.Y., shows highlights of baseball history and displays the uniforms of famous players. Other museums specialize in such subjects as automobiles, clocks, and dolls.

Museums that display materials from several fields of study are called *general museums. Children's* or *youth museums* have exhibits designed to explain the arts and sciences to young people.

A few museums display reproductions or copies of objects. For example, some historical museums have life-sized figures sculptured from wax or plastics. Most of these figures are realistic likenesses of important people in history. The figures are dressed in appropriate costumes and placed in lifelike settings.

Functions of museums

Museums perform three main functions. These institutions (1) acquire new materials, (2) exhibit and care for materials, and (3) provide various special services.

Acquisition of materials. Every new object that a museum adds to its collection is called an *acquisition.* Many acquisitions are gifts from people who collect such items as paintings, precious stones, or sculpture.

An electronic exhibit, such as the one shown above, may require the participation of museum visitors.

Odyssey Productions

Exhibits must be carefully prepared before being displayed. The anthropologist's assistant shown above is cleaning fossils at the National Museum of Kenya in Nairobi.

Other gifts include items that have been kept in a family for many generations, such as a quilt or a journal of an ancestor.

Sometimes a museum buys an item needed to fill a gap in one of its collections. Museum employees may find new materials on archaeological expeditions or field trips. Museums also borrow materials or entire exhibits from other museums. Acquisitions are received by the museum *registrar,* a staff member who records the description of each object. Every acquisition is photographed and given a number. Museum officials determine the value of each object and insure it for that amount.

Exhibition and care of materials. Various members of the museum staff prepare the materials for exhibition. The museum *curator* may conduct research to learn more about objects. Museum *conservators* clean, preserve, or restore objects before they are exhibited.

The curator decides how materials are displayed. For example, a new object may be added to an existing exhibit or become part of a special exhibit. It may be hung on a wall or placed in a case. *Designers* plan and create displays. They build cases and furniture for the displays and set up lights and electric wiring. *Preparators* create display backgrounds and prepare materials for exhibit. Every exhibit receives a label that gives visitors some information about it. Descriptions of all objects appear in the museum's catalog as well.

Museums also protect their exhibits from loss or damage. The doors and windows of many museums have alarms in addition to locks. Exhibit cases are locked, and some may be connected to alarms. Guards patrol museums. Museums may use special light bulbs and devices that control humidity and temperature to protect objects from environmental damage.

Special services. Many museums have an *education department* that gives lectures and classes on the muse-

um's collection. Most museums offer gallery talks, guided tours, and other programs for children and adults. Other activities provided by museums include art festivals, concerts, and hobby workshops. Many museums publish bulletins and pamphlets that describe current and future exhibits. Museums also furnish scholars with research materials and the use of special laboratories and libraries. *Evaluation specialists* determine how well the museum meets the educational needs of the public. Some museums serve as places where local artists can exhibit their work.

History

The word *museum* comes from the Greek word *mouseion.* In ancient Greece, the mouseion was the temple of the *Muses,* the goddesses of arts and sciences. In the 200's B.C., the word was used for a library and research area in Alexandria, Egypt.

Early museums. Throughout history, churches have performed some of the functions of museums. Many worshipers enjoy viewing church furnishings and decorations, including paintings, sculpture, and other art.

During the A.D. 1400's and 1500's, European explorers brought back samples of animal and plant life from North and South America and eastern Asia. They also brought objects made by craftworkers of those regions. Many Europeans collected such materials. Some placed their collections in cabinets that lined the walls of long, narrow rooms called *galleries.* The collections themselves were called *cabinets.*

In the 1500's and 1600's, royal families hired famous artists and craftworkers to create luxurious art objects and furnishings. Today, the Uffizi Palace in Florence, Italy, and other museums own these collections.

The first public museum, the *Ashmolean,* opened in 1683 at Oxford University in England. The museum featured a collection of *curiosities* (rare or strange objects) donated by Elias Ashmole, an English scholar.

Museums of the 1700's. In the mid-1700's, a Swedish botanist named Carolus Linnaeus developed a system of classifying plants and animals. For many years, as a result of his work, scientists concentrated more on putting organisms into various groups than on acquiring new knowledge. Collections of scientific specimens were used mainly for classification purposes.

During the late 1700's, scholars began to study and organize large and complex collections of all kinds. Valuable works of art were separated from objects of little artistic worth. At about this time, people began to use the word *museum* to describe a place where collections could be seen and studied.

The demand for public museums grew in the 1700's, a period when people began to believe that education should be available to everyone. In 1759, the British Museum in London opened with exhibits of manuscripts, plant specimens, and curiosities. These materials had once belonged to the collections of kings and noblemen. In 1750, the Palais de Luxembourg was opened on certain days for the public to view the French royal art collection. During the French Revolution (1789-1799), the government moved the royal collection to the Louvre, which became a public museum in 1793.

Early United States museums. In 1773, the Charleston Library Society opened the first museum in the

American Colonies. It featured objects related to the natural history of South Carolina. In the 1780's, Charles Willson Peale, a painter who studied natural history, opened a museum in his Philadelphia home. Peale's museum displayed animal and mineral specimens and portraits of Thomas Jefferson, George Washington, and other heroes of the Revolutionary War.

In 1866, George Peabody, a Massachusetts banker, gave large sums of money to Harvard and Yale universities for the establishment of science museums. Many colleges and universities then began to use donations from wealthy people to establish museums.

By 1876, the United States had over 200 museums. In that year, the Centennial Exposition was held in Philadelphia. This world's fair included exhibits from various parts of the world. Its exhibits influenced the construction of an increasing number of museums.

Early Canadian museums. In 1842, Abraham Gesner, a geologist and inventor, established the first museum in Canada, the New Brunswick Museum, in Saint John, N.B. The museum featured plants and animals, rocks and minerals, and Indian relics. Later in 1842, Sir William Logan, the director of the Geological Survey of Canada, established a natural science museum in Montreal. This museum eventually became the Canadian Museum of Nature and is now located in Ottawa.

The Montreal Museum of Fine Arts, Canada's first art museum, was founded in 1860. It featured works by Canadian and other artists.

Museums today. Public interest in museums has grown during the late 1900's. Such events as the American Bicentennial Celebration in 1976 have helped raise interest in cultural activities. Museums have also begun to offer exhibits that better respond to the interests of larger numbers of people rather than to mainly those of the scholar.

Museum operations are funded by several sources. These sources include foundations and corporations; national, local, and state governments; and individuals. Some museums charge admission and sell reproductions or gifts relating to their exhibits. Some offer food services, movies, or concerts for a fee. Museums also may earn money by selling duplicate or less desirable items from their collections.

Careers

Most of the museum jobs described in this article require a college degree. Museums hire men and women with training in such fields as art history, history, and library science. The staffs of many museums also include archaeologists, botanists, geologists, zoologists, and other scientists. Many colleges and universities offer training in museum management and techniques. Several offer degrees in museum studies. Many museums offer internships and work-study programs for students at the graduate and undergraduate levels.

Critically reviewed by the American Association of Museums

Related articles in *World Book* include:

Museum of Modern Art, in New York City, is known throughout the world for its matchless overview of art from 1880 to the present. Its collections include more than 100,000 paintings, sculptures, drawings, prints, photographs, architectural models and plans, and design objects, ranging from audio equipment to textiles. In addition, the museum houses 10,000 motion pictures and 3 million movie *stills* (photographs).

The museum arranges special exhibitions that feature the work of specific artists, styles, or movements. Many of these exhibitions tour worldwide. In addition, the museum presents daily film showings.

The museum also publishes books and scholarly catalogs. Its library contains more than 80,000 books, periodicals, and catalogs, as well as an archive of materials for research and reference.

The museum's original building, built in 1939, is one of the city's best examples of the International Style. It was designed by American architects Edward Durell Stone and Philip Goodwin. Architect Philip Johnson designed a remodeling and expansion in the 1950's and 1960's, and Cesar Pelli added a new wing in 1984.

The Museum of Modern Art was founded in 1929. It is located at 11 W. 53rd Street. It is a nonprofit educational institution supported by admission fees, memberships, contributions, and publication sales and services.

Critically reviewed by the Museum of Modern Art

Museum of Science and Industry, in Chicago, is the oldest, largest, and most popular contemporary science and technology museum in the United States. It is designed to further public understanding of science and the use of science in industry by presenting enlightening and entertaining exhibits, educational programs, and other activities.

The museum opened in 1933 and now has over 600,000 square feet (56,000 square meters) of floor space. Its annual attendance of about $4\frac{1}{2}$ million makes it one of Chicago's leading tourist attractions.

The museum focuses chiefly on the physical and life sciences, engineering, and mathematics. Many of its exhibits demonstrate scientific and industrial advances and their applications for the present and the future. The museum emphasizes informal science education, and most of the exhibits are three-dimensional and encourage participation by visitors. For example, visitors may push a button to activate a demonstration, or walk into a life-sized display. Visitors to the museum may also take a trip through a coal mine, go aboard a submarine, stroll down a reconstructed street of 1910, and watch chicks hatch.

Many exhibits are presented as a public service by industrial firms, trade associations, professional societies, government agencies, and foundations. The museum staff develops other exhibits and activities.

The museum is housed in a restored classical style building from the World's Columbian Exposition of 1893. The major areas opened after restoration of the building was completed in 1940. The museum was founded largely through the efforts of Julius Rosenwald, a Chicago businessman and philanthropist. He contributed $3 million to help establish the museum.

Critically reviewed by the Museum of Science and Industry

See also **Chicago** (picture).

Mushet, *MUHSH eht,* **Robert Forester** (1811-1891), was an English metallurgist. In 1870, he patented a special tungsten steel that had remarkable self-hardening qualities. It was especially suitable for machine tools, because it retained its cutting edge, even when red-hot from friction. Mushet also helped improve the Bessemer process of steelmaking. He discovered that adding an iron-manganese alloy called *spiegeleisen* to molten steel helped recarburize the steel. This discovery led to improvements in the strength of the steel (see **Iron and steel** [History]). Mushet was born in Coleford, England.

Bruce E. Seely

Mushroom is any of a variety of fleshy, umbrella-shaped *fungi.* Mushrooms most commonly grow in woods and grassy areas. There are about 3,300 species of mushrooms throughout the world. About 3,000 of these species grow in the United States and Canada.

Keith Gunnar, West Stock

Mushrooms are umbrella-shaped fungi found in many areas where green plants grow. Like other types of fungi, mushrooms live on food substances produced by green plants.

In the past, scientists considered mushrooms and other fungi as nongreen plants. Today, the fungi are most commonly regarded as a separate kingdom of living things. Like other fungi, mushrooms differ from green plants in that they lack *chlorophyll,* the green substance such plants use to make food. Instead, mushrooms survive mainly by absorbing food material from living or decaying plants in their surroundings.

A mushroom consists of two main parts: (1) the mycelium and (2) the fruiting body. The mycelium grows just beneath the surface of the soil and absorbs food materials. This part may live and grow many years. The umbrella-shaped fruiting body grows from the mycelium and lives only a few days. During that time, it produces tiny reproductive cells called *spores* from which new mushrooms grow. The fruiting body of the fungus is the part most people consider the mushroom.

Mushrooms vary greatly in size and color. They measure from about $\frac{3}{4}$ inch (1.9 centimeters) to about 15 inches (38 centimeters) in height. The diameter of the top of a mushroom ranges from less than $\frac{1}{4}$ inch (0.6 centimeters) to about 18 inches (46 centimeters). Most mushrooms have a white, yellow, orange, red, or brown color. Some are blue, violet, green, or black.

Many species of mushrooms are tasty and safe to eat. But others have a bad taste, and some are poisonous. A few of the poisonous species can be fatal if eaten. Mushrooms that are either poisonous or have a bad taste are often referred to as *toadstools.*

Parts of a mushroom

The mycelium of a mushroom consists of many white or yellow, threadlike filaments called *hyphae.* The hyphae absorb food and water for the developing mushroom and help hold it upright. In most mushrooms, the filaments form a loose weblike mycelium. But in some mushrooms they are bundled into long strands that look like shoelaces. The strands are called *rhizomorphs.*

The fruiting body of the mushroom is made up of tightly woven filaments. It consists of a *stalk* topped by a rounded *cap.* Most species of mushrooms have thin, vertical, knifelike growths called *gills* on the underside of the cap. The gills spread outward from the center of the cap like the spokes of a wheel. Species that do not have gills have densely packed, parallel *tubes* under the cap. Tiny, club-shaped cells called *basidia* cover the outer surface of the gills or the inner surface of the tubes. The basidia of most mushrooms produce four microscopic *spores.* The spores are reproductive cells from which new mycelia grow.

In some mushrooms, a clothlike membrane called a *veil* protects the gills or tubes as the mushroom develops. As the cap grows wider, the veil tears. But it remains draped around the stalk, forming a ring called an *annulus.* Sometimes, a veil covers the entire mushroom. When the veil breaks, it leaves a cup called a *volva* or other remains at the base of the stalk. It also may leave warts or patches on the top of the cap.

The life of a mushroom

How a mushroom obtains food. Mushrooms need carbohydrates, proteins, certain vitamins, and other nutrients. To obtain this food, the mycelium releases proteins called *enzymes* from its hyphae. The enzymes con-

Parts of a mushroom The drawing at the left, *below,* shows the chief parts of a mushroom. The other drawings show the details of the underside of the cap, which consists of either gills, *center,* or tubes, *right.* Tiny basidia on the gills or tubes produce the spores from which new mushrooms grow.

WORLD BOOK illustrations by Patricia J. Wynne

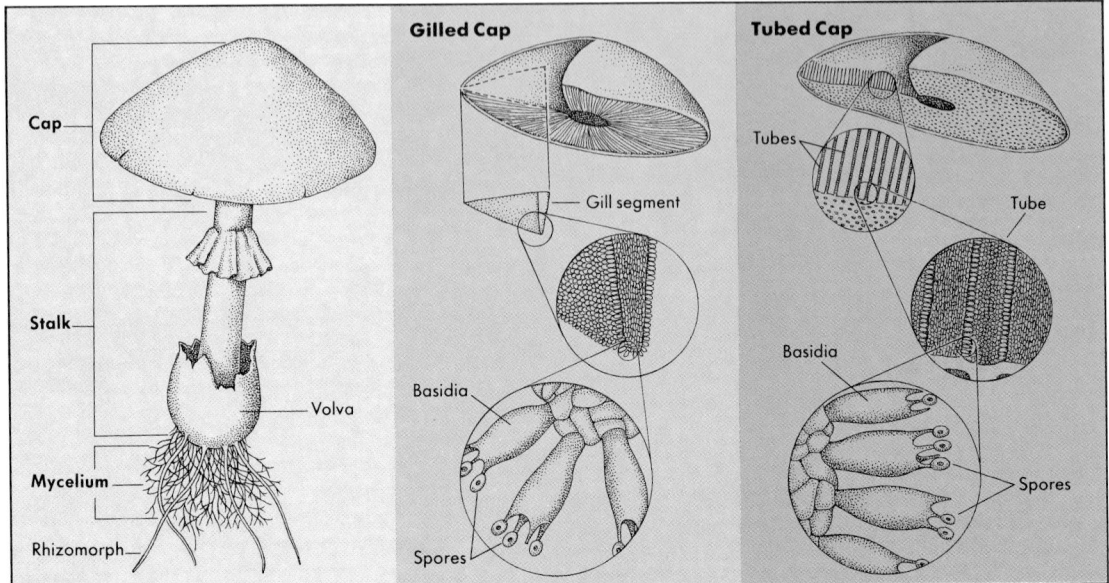

vert the materials on which the hyphae grow into simpler compounds that are absorbed by the mycelium.

Many species of mushrooms are *saprophytes*—that is, they live on dead or decaying materials. Some of these species obtain their food from dead grass or decaying plant matter, or from *humus* (soil formed from decaying plant and animal matter). Other species attack decaying wood, such as fallen trees, old stumps, and even the timber of houses. A few species live on the *dung* (solid body wastes) of animals that graze on grass.

Some mushrooms grow on living plants, especially trees. Such mushrooms are called *parasites.* A few of these mushrooms cause disease and may eventually kill the plants on which they feed.

Other mushrooms grow in or on roots of living green plants without causing harm. This type of association, called a *mycorrhiza,* benefits both the mushroom and the green plant. The mushroom's mycelium absorbs water and certain materials from the soil and passes these on to the plant. In turn, the plant feeds the mushroom. Mushrooms form mycorrhizas with a number of trees—including Douglas-fir, hemlocks, larches, oaks, pines, and poplars—and certain other plants.

How a mushroom grows. Typically, a mature mushroom releases hundreds of millions of spores. The slightest air current can carry the spores great distances. However, only a few spores land in places with enough food and moisture for survival.

If a spore reaches such a place, it begins to grow by sending out a hypha. The hypha lengthens from its tip, branches out, and eventually produces a mycelium. Knots about the size of a pinhead develop on the mycelium. These knots, called *buttons,* will become mature mushrooms. As a button grows, the cap and stalk become recognizable. Soon, either gills or tubes develop under the cap. Then very quickly, the stalk shoots up

and the cap unfolds like the opening of an umbrella. Much of this growth results from the lengthening of cells as they absorb water. This is why mushrooms seem to pop up overnight after a heavy rain. Most mushrooms reach their maximum height in about 8 to 48 hours.

The fruiting bodies of mushrooms die and decay after releasing their spores. But the mycelia often continue to live. In many cases, mycelia produce mushrooms year after year for many years.

Fairy rings. In some grassy areas, rings of greener grass or of bare soil may be seen. Each year, mushrooms grow along the edge of these rings. Such rings are called *fairy rings.* In ancient times, people believed that the rings were footprints left by fairies dancing at night. The mushrooms that appeared were thought to be seats on which the tired fairies sat.

Actually, fairy rings develop in response to the growth of mycelia in soil. Mycelia tend to grow in all directions from a central point, forming an expanding circle. At the edge of the circle, nutrients released by the activity of the mycelia stimulate the growth of grass. As a result, the circle of grass directly above these mycelia may appear greener than its surroundings. Just inside this circle, the grass may die because the growing mycelia absorb nutrients from the surrounding soil. Fairy rings of bare soil may then appear near the inner edge of the circle. If the soil remains undisturbed and no obstacles stop the growth of the mycelia, fairy rings can become extremely large and last for many years. For example, some grasslands in Colorado have fairy rings that measure about 200 feet (60 meters) in diameter. Scientists believe these rings are over 300 years old.

Kinds of mushrooms

Mushrooms belong to a scientific group called Eumycota. This group is divided into classes, orders, and fam-

S. Rannels, Grant Heilman

Joy Spurr

Mushrooms get food from the substances they grow on. Those in the top photo grow on dead wood, and those in the bottom photo on plant roots.

Kit Scates

A fairy ring of mushrooms grows in a field, *above*. It develops because the mushrooms' rootlike mycelia grow outward from a central point. The mushrooms that grow from these mycelia form an expanding circle.

How mushrooms reproduce

Mushrooms reproduce by releasing spores. A spore grows into branched, threadlike filaments that make up the *mycelium*. A knoblike *button* forms on the mycelium. It eventually develops a cap and stalk and becomes a mature mushroom.

WORLD BOOK illustration by Patricia J. Wynne

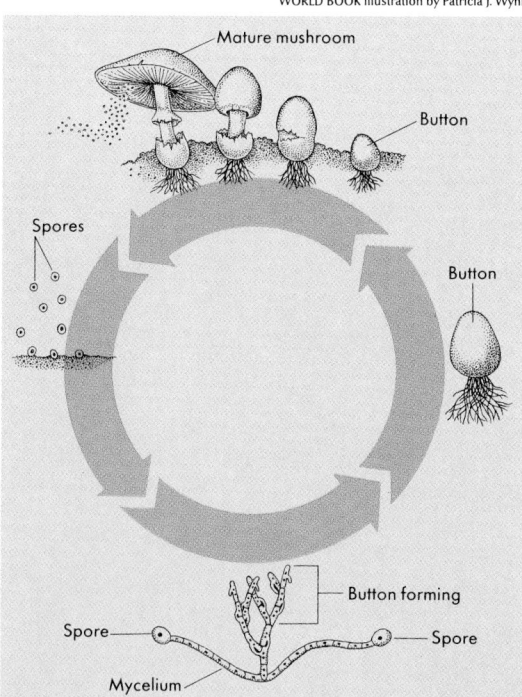

Mature mushroom

Button

Spores

Button

Button forming

Spore

Spore

Mycelium

ilies of mushrooms and other fungi according to common physical characteristics. *Mycologists* (scientists who study fungi) do not agree on the number of families of mushrooms. But most mycologists list mushrooms as *agarics* or *boletes*. Agarics have gills under their caps, and boletes have tubes. Many agarics and boletes are nonpoisonous, but some are poisonous.

In the following discussion, mushrooms are divided into two general groups: (1) poisonous and (2) nonpoisonous. There is no simple test to distinguish a nonpoisonous mushroom from a poisonous one. Therefore, people should not eat a wild mushroom unless they are absolutely certain that it is harmless. All the mushrooms mentioned grow in North America.

Nonpoisonous mushrooms. There are more than 2,000 species of harmless mushrooms. The best-known agaric of these species is the *table mushroom.* This good-tasting mushroom is commercially cultivated. It is available in supermarkets across the United States and Canada. When young, a table mushroom has a white or tan cap with pink gills. As the mushroom matures, the gills turn brown. The table mushroom's closest relative is the *field mushroom.* This species grows on lawns and in meadows throughout North America. It looks much like the table mushroom.

Three other common, wild agarics are the *fairy-ring mushroom,* the *oyster mushroom,* and the *parasol mushroom.* The fairy-ring mushroom grows in grassy areas, such as golf courses. It has a dull-yellow or tan cap with white gills. The oyster mushroom is one of the best-tasting wild mushrooms. It has a large, white cap that resembles an oyster shell. Oyster mushrooms commonly grow in clusters on wood, especially logs and stumps. The parasol mushroom grows on the ground in woods. This species has a pointed cap with brown

Some mushrooms of North America

About 3,000 species of mushrooms grow in North America. Twenty-one of them are illustrated below. They are divided into two groups: (1) agarics and (2) boletes. Agarics have gills under their caps, and boletes have tubes. The scientific name of each mushroom appears in italics.

● Poisonous
◐ Nonpoisonous

WORLD BOOK illustrations by John Eggert

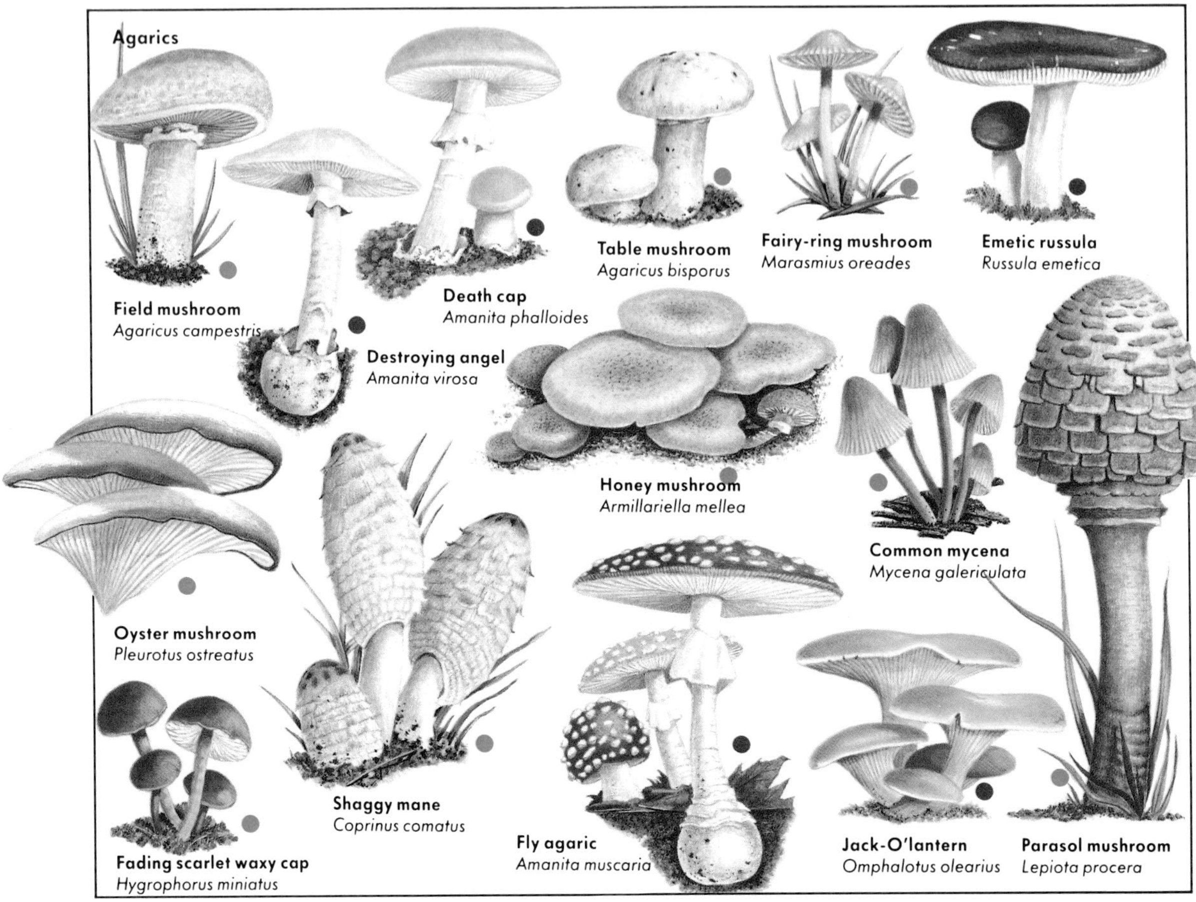

Agarics

Field mushroom
Agaricus campestris

Death cap
Amanita phalloides

Table mushroom
Agaricus bisporus

Fairy-ring mushroom
Marasmius oreades

Emetic russula
Russula emetica

Destroying angel
Amanita virosa

Honey mushroom
Armillariella mellea

Common mycena
Mycena galericulata

Oyster mushroom
Pleurotus ostreatus

Fading scarlet waxy cap
Hygrophorus miniatus

Shaggy mane
Coprinus comatus

Fly agaric
Amanita muscaria

Jack-O'lantern
Omphalotus olearius

Parasol mushroom
Lepiota procera

Boletes

Larch suillus
Suillus grevillei

Slippery Jack
Suillus luteus

Frost's bolete
Boletus frostii

Aspen scaber stalk
Leccinum insigne

Mock oyster
Suillus cavipes

Edible bolete
Boletus edulis

Old man of the woods
Strobilomyces floccopus

scales on top, and a tall, slender stalk with an annulus. It is most common in New England.

The *inky caps* are an unusual group of agarics. At maturity, their gills blacken and melt away drop by drop. The liquid can be used as a substitute for ink. Inky caps grow in the spring or fall.

The *milky lactarias* are a group of colorful, summer agarics. There are many species. They all show drops of milky liquid when their gills are cut. The *indigo lactaria* has a beautiful blue stalk, cap, and gills.

A number of boletes grow widely in North America. The *old man of the woods* has a shaggy, scaly, grayish-black cap with grayish-white tubes. The *slippery Jack* has a slimy, reddish-brown cap. The *edible bolete* has a fat, reddish-brown cap and a thick, white stalk.

Many large, nonpoisonous fungi commonly thought of as mushrooms actually are not mushrooms. The *bracket fungi* form shelflike growths on tree trunks. These fungi commonly have tubes on the underside of their caps. Many bracket fungi do not have stalks. The *chanterelles* are mushroomlike fungi with funnel-shaped caps. The delicious and fragrant *golden chanterelle* is a delicacy prized by gourmets. The *puffballs* are ball-shaped fungi, white to tan in color. They range in size from smaller than a golfball to larger than a basketball. When a puffball matures, its spores become dry and powdery. If touched, the puffball breaks open and the spores escape in a smokelike puff.

Other nonpoisonous fungi closely related to mushrooms include *stinkhorns* and *morels*. The stinkhorns have a tall stalk capped with greenish slime that contains spores. These fungi smell like decaying flesh. Insects attracted to the odor eat the slime and then fly away to deposit the spores in other locations. The morels are among the most flavorful fungi. They have a tan stalk and a darker, cone-shaped cap. The cap, covered with ridges and pits, looks like a sponge.

Poisonous mushrooms produce poisonous chemical compounds called *toxins.* Most toxic mushrooms are not fatal to people if eaten. However, toxic mushrooms may cause nausea, diarrhea, headaches, or other disorders.

A few species of mushrooms have toxins that can cause death. When a person eats these mushrooms, the symptoms of illness may not appear for several hours. The first symptoms include abdominal pain, violent vomiting, and weakness. The toxins of some deadly mushrooms damage the liver. Others attack the kidneys. In most cases, unless immediate medical treatment is given, the victim dies.

Some of the deadliest mushrooms belong to a group called the *amanitas.* These mushrooms have both a volva and an annulus. The *destroying angel* is an especially beautiful, all-white amanita that grows in the summer and fall. The toxins of the destroying angel have killed many people. Another amanita, the *fly agaric,* usually has a bright yellow, orange, or red cap with white warts on top. This species received its name from its use in killing flies. People sprinkled sugar on the mushroom to attract flies. The flies died after feeding on the mushroom.

The *Jack-O'lantern mushroom* causes nausea and diarrhea if eaten. It tends to grow in clusters at the base of oak tree stumps. It has a bright orange cap and gills. The Jack-O'lantern got its name because the cap and gills glow in the dark.

The importance of mushrooms

Mushrooms help keep soil fertile for the growth of plants. As mushrooms grow, they cause the decay of the materials from which they obtain food. This process releases important minerals into the soil. Plants use these minerals to grow and stay healthy.

Mushrooms are an important source of food for insects and many small animals. Red squirrels collect mushrooms in the summer and let them dry on tree branches. Then they store them for use as a winter food.

People eat mushrooms fresh in salads. They also use mushrooms to flavor gravies, eggs, meats, spaghetti sauce, soups, and other food. It is difficult to describe the flavor of a mushroom. Some people say mushrooms have a mild taste. Others say the flavor is nutlike, bitter, or peppery. Many people describe the odor of mushrooms as earthy. Mushrooms are rich in B vitamins and such minerals as potassium, phosphorus, and iron.

Mushroom cultivation is an important industry in the United States and other countries. Most mushrooms are cultivated in specially designed mushroom houses, where growers carefully control such conditions as temperature and moisture. Caves also are ideal for mushroom cultivation because of their consistently cool temperature and dampness. Pennsylvania, which has many caves, has long ranked as one of the major U.S. mushroom-growing regions.

Scientific classification. Mushrooms are classified in the division Eumycota in the kingdom Fungi. They belong to the class Hymenomycetes.   Sally E. Gochenaur

See also **Fungi.**

Additional resources

Lincoff, Gary H. *The Audubon Society Field Guide to North American Mushrooms.* Knopf, 1981.
Phillips, Roger. *Mushrooms of North America.* Little, Brown, 1991.
Selsam, Millicent E. *Mushrooms.* Morrow, 1986. For younger readers.

Musial, Stan (1920-   ), ranks as one of the greatest baseball players of all time. Nicknamed *Stan the Man,* Musial was a star outfielder and first baseman for the St. Louis Cardinals between 1941 and 1963. He won seven National League batting titles, and had a .331 lifetime batting average. Musial played in 3,026 National League games. Only Pete Rose and Henry Aaron played in more games in the league. Musial held the National League record for most base hits (3,630) until 1981, when the record was broken by Pete Rose.

Stanley Frank Musial was born in Donora, Pa. He has been a vice president of the Cardinals since 1963. He was director of the President's Council on Physical Fitness from 1964 to 1966. He was elected to the National Baseball Hall of Fame in 1969.

Dave Nightingale

Wide World

Stan Musial

WORLD BOOK photo by Donald Stebbing

A symphony orchestra and chorus

Photo Reserve from Click

A combo playing jazz

Steve Smith, Wheeler Pictures

An English rock group

Michael Saffle

A string quartet playing chamber music

A variety of musical performances, as shown above and on the next page, suggests some of the many forms of music. But whatever the form, all music is sound arranged for artistic effect.

Music

Music is sound arranged into pleasing or interesting patterns. It forms an important part of many cultural and social activities. People use music to express feelings and ideas. Music also serves to entertain and relax.

Music is a performing art. It differs from such arts as painting and poetry, in which artists create works and then display or publish them. Musical composers need musicians to interpret and perform their works, just as playwrights need actors to perform their plays. Thus, most musical performances are really partnerships between composers and performers.

Music also plays a major role in other arts. Opera combines singing and orchestra music with drama. Ballet and other forms of dancing need music to help the dancers with their steps. Motion pictures and TV dra-

mas use music to help set the mood and emphasize the action. Also, composers have set many poems to music.

Music is one of the oldest arts. People probably started to sing as soon as language developed. Hunting tools struck together may have been the first musical instruments. By about 10,000 B.C., people had discovered how to make flutes out of hollow bones. Many ancient peoples, including the Egyptians, Chinese, and Babylonians, used music in court and religious ceremonies. The first written music dates from about 2500 B.C.

Today, music takes many forms around the world. The music of people in Europe and the Americas is known as *Western music.* There are two chief kinds of Western music, *classical* and *popular.* Classical music includes symphonies, operas, and ballets. Popular music includes country music, folk music, jazz, and rock music. The cultures of Africa and Asia have developed their own types of classical and popular music.

This article deals with the importance of music, musical instruments, the elements of music, and the system used for writing down music. It also includes information on the various types of Western and non-Western

R. M. Longyear, the contributor of this article, is Professor of Music at the University of Kentucky.

Milt and Joan Mann

A sitar player performing Indian music

Milt and Joan Mann

A marching band in a parade in Calgary, Canada

Owen Franken, Stock, Boston

Mariachi players at an outdoor cafe in Mexico City

Photo Reserve from Click

A folk singer performing in concert

music and on careers in music. For information about the history of Western music, see the *World Book* articles **Classical music** and **Popular music**.

The importance of music

Music plays an important part in all cultures. People use music (1) in ceremonies, (2) in work, and (3) in personal and social activities.

In ceremonies. Nearly all peoples use music in their religious services. One kind of religious music seeks to create a state of mystery and awe. For example, some cultures have special musical instruments played only by priests on important occasions, such as harvest ceremonies and the burials of chiefs. Similarly, much Western church music attempts to create a feeling of distance from the daily world. Other religious music helps produce a sense of participation among worshipers. The singing of hymns by a congregation is a good example of this function of religious music.

Many nonreligious ceremonies and spectacles also use music. They include sports events, graduations, circuses, parades, and the crownings of kings and queens.

In work. Before machines became important, people had to do much difficult or boring work by hand. Laborers sang songs to help make their work seem easier. For example, crews aboard sailing ships sang *chanteys,* songs with a strong, regular beat. The sailors pulled or lifted heavy loads in time to the beat. Today, the wide use of machines has made the singing of work songs rare in industrialized societies. However, many offices and factories provide background music for workers.

In personal and social activities. Many people perform music for their own satisfaction. Singing in a chorus or playing a musical instrument in a band can be very enjoyable. Music provides people with a way to express their feelings. A group of happy campers may sing cheerful songs as they sit around a campfire. A sad person may play a mournful tune on a guitar.

Many famous rulers have used music to help them relax. According to the Bible, David played the harp to help King Saul take his mind off the problems of ruling Israel. Kings Richard I and Henry VIII of England composed music. Other leaders have performed music. For example, Presidents Harry S. Truman and Richard M.

Nixon of the United States played the piano.

People use music at a variety of social occasions. At parties and dinners, music often is played for dancing or simply for listening. In some countries, a young man shows that a young woman is special to him by serenading her or by sending musicians to play and sing for her.

Musical instruments

A musical sound, called a *tone,* is produced when air vibrates a certain number of times each second. These vibrations are called *sound waves.* Sound waves must be contained in some way so that the performer can control the pitch, loudness, duration, and quality of the tone. Whatever contains the sound waves must also provide *resonance*—that is, it must amplify and prolong the sound so the tone can be heard.

The vocal cords produce musical sounds in the human voice. These two small folds of tissue vibrate and create sound waves when air passes them from the lungs. The throat and the cavities in the head provide the resonance needed for singing.

Most musical instruments have a string, a *reed* (thin piece of wood or metal), or some other device that creates sound waves when set in motion. Musical instruments can be grouped in five major classes. These classes are (1) stringed instruments, (2) wind instruments, (3) percussion instruments, (4) keyboard instruments, and (5) electronic instruments.

Musical instruments have evolved throughout history. For example, 200 years ago, brass instruments did not have valves, and woodwind instruments had very few keys. Such features were added to modernize the instruments and to make them easier to play. As a result, the tone quality of the instruments also changed. In the late 1900's, many instruments have been restored or built on original models so that the music of early composers can sound as originally intended.

Stringed instruments produce tones when the player makes one or more strings vibrate. There are two basic types of stringed instruments: (1) bowed stringed instruments and (2) plucked stringed instruments.

Bowed stringed instruments are played by drawing a bow back and forth across the strings. The pressure of the bow on the strings produces vibrations that are amplified by the body of the instrument. Most bowed instruments have four strings. Each of the strings is tuned

Musical instruments

The instruments shown below are grouped in four major classes: (1) stringed instruments, (2) wind instruments, (3) percussion instruments, and (4) keyboard instruments. The fifth major class of mu-

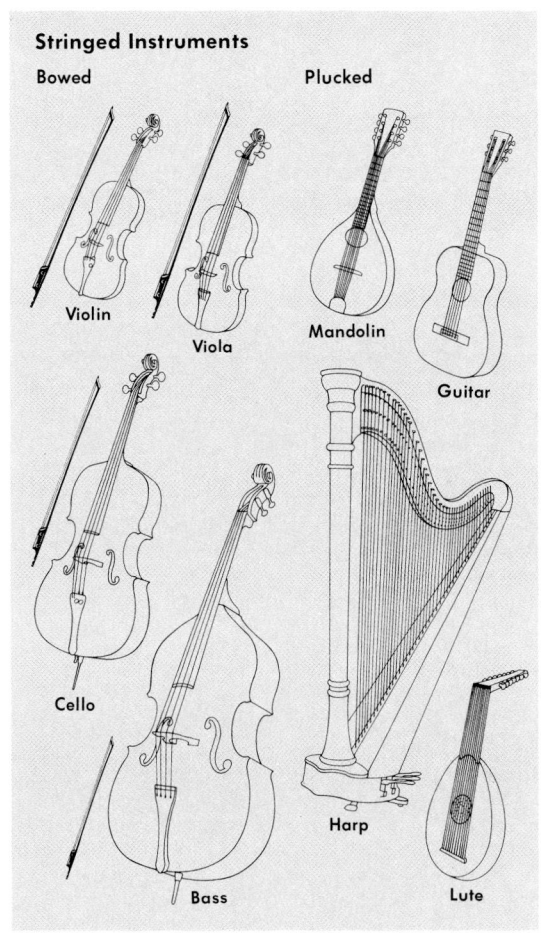

Stringed Instruments

Bowed

Plucked

Violin

Viola

Mandolin

Guitar

Cello

Harp

Bass

Lute

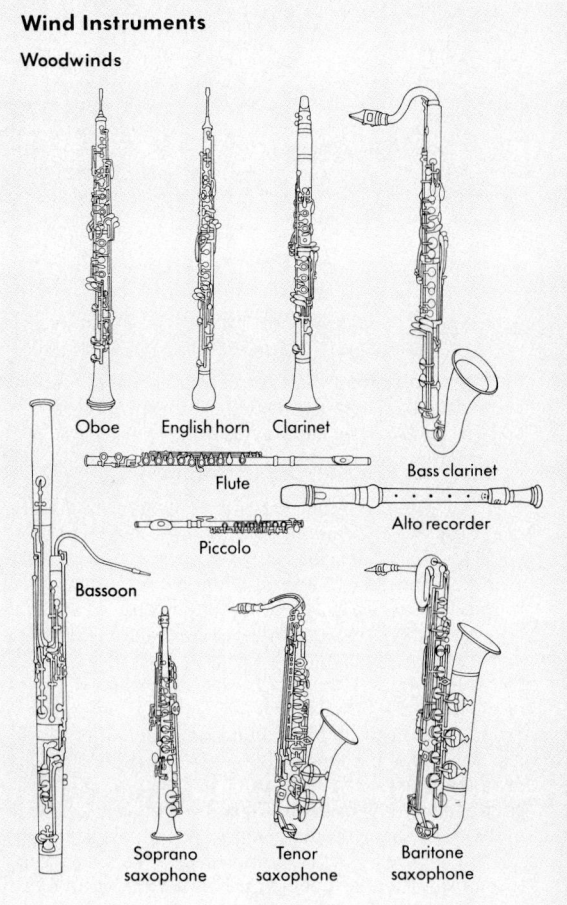

Wind Instruments

Woodwinds

Oboe

English horn

Clarinet

Bass clarinet

Flute

Alto recorder

Piccolo

Bassoon

Soprano saxophone

Tenor saxophone

Baritone saxophone

to a different pitch. To produce other pitches, the musician shortens the strings by pressing down on them with the fingers.

The main bowed instruments, in descending order of pitch and ascending order of size, are the violin, viola, violoncello or cello, and string bass. These instruments form the heart of a symphony orchestra. Violins in an orchestra are divided into *first violins* and *second violins*. The first violins play higher-pitched parts of musical compositions than the second violins.

Plucked stringed instruments are played by plucking the strings with the fingers or a pick. The guitar is the most common plucked stringed instrument. It has 6 to 12 strings. The harp, another important plucked instrument, has up to 47 strings. It produces the most tones of any stringed instrument. Other plucked stringed instruments include the banjo, lute, lyre, mandolin, sitar, ukulele, and zither. The strings of the violin and other bowed instruments also may be plucked to produce special effects. This style of playing on a bowed instrument is called *pizzicato.*

Wind instruments are played by blowing into or through a tube. There are two chief types. They are (1) woodwind instruments and (2) brass instruments.

All woodwind instruments except the saxophone at one time were made of wood. Today, many are made of metal or other materials. In such woodwinds as recorders, the player blows through a mouthpiece into the instrument. In some other woodwinds, such as flutes and piccolos, the player blows across a hole in the instrument. Still other woodwinds, called *reed instruments,* have one or two reeds attached to the mouthpiece. The reeds vibrate when the musician blows on them. The clarinet and saxophone are the chief single-reed instruments. Double-reed instruments include the bassoon, English horn, and oboe.

The player controls the pitch by placing the fingers on holes in the instrument or on keys that cover holes. In this way, the player lengthens or shortens the column of air that vibrates inside the instrument. The piccolo and flute have the highest pitches of woodwinds, and the bassoon and contra bassoon, the lowest.

Brass instruments are played in a different way from that of woodwinds. The player presses the lips against the instrument's mouthpiece so that they vibrate like reeds when the player blows. By either tensing or relax-

sical instruments—electronic instruments—is not represented in these illustrations. Electronic instruments include electric guitars, electric pianos, electronic organs, and synthesizers.

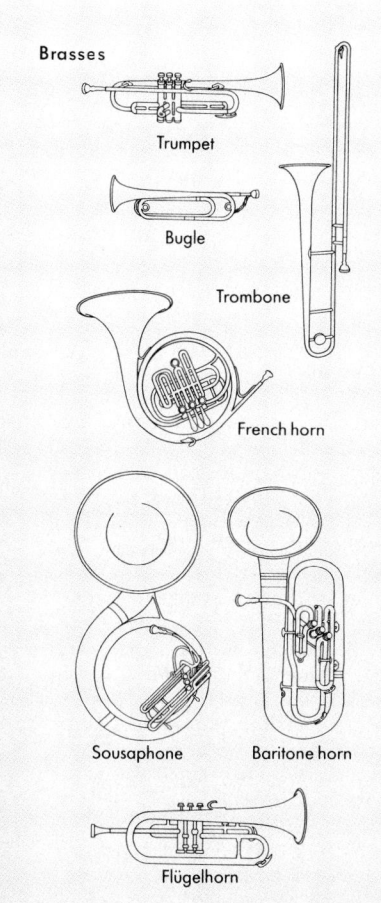

Brasses
Trumpet
Bugle
Trombone
French horn
Sousaphone
Baritone horn
Flügelhorn

Percussion Instruments

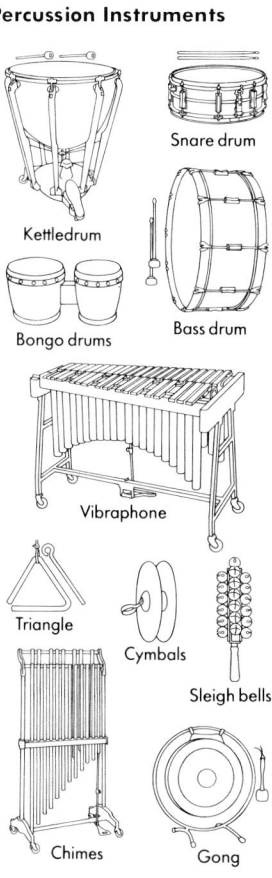

Kettledrum
Snare drum
Bongo drums
Bass drum
Vibraphone
Triangle
Cymbals
Sleigh bells
Chimes
Gong

Keyboard Instruments

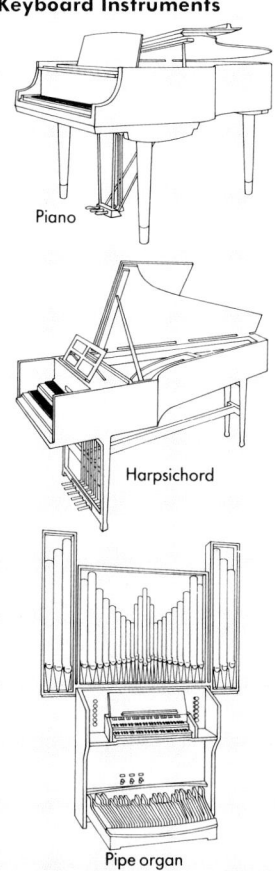

Piano
Harpsichord
Pipe organ

ing the lips, the player produces different pitches. With most brass instruments, the player can further control the pitch with valves that lengthen or shorten the tube through which the air is blown.

The chief brass instruments in an orchestra are the French horn, trumpet, trombone, and tuba. The French horn and trumpet have high pitches, and the trombone and tuba have lower pitches. The trombone has a slide instead of valves. The performer pulls the slide back and forth to control the pitch of the instrument. Other brass instruments, including the baritone horn and sousaphone, are used in bands.

Percussion instruments are sounded by shaking them or by hitting them with a stick or a mallet. Drums are the most common percussion instruments. Most Western drums do not produce a range of pitches. But kettledrums, also called *timpani,* can be tuned to various pitches by adjusting the tension of the drumheads. Glockenspiels and xylophones have a series of bars that produce a range of pitches. Other percussion instruments include castanets, cymbals, gongs, marimbas, and tambourines.

Keyboard instruments have a series of keys connected with a device that produces tones. The musician presses the keys to make sounds. The most popular keyboard instruments are the piano, harpsichord, and pipe organ. The keys on a piano activate small hammers that strike strings. On a harpsichord, the keys control a mechanism that plucks strings. Pressing a key on a pipe organ opens a pipe through which a column of air vibrates. The player operates some pipes by pressing pedals with the feet.

Electronic instruments include those that generate sounds by electricity and those that electronically amplify sounds produced by an instrument. The most common electronic instrument is the electric guitar. It makes louder and more varied tones than an ordinary guitar. Electric guitars, electric pianos, and electronic organs are widely used in rock music. An electronic instrument called a *synthesizer* is used to create original sounds or to imitate the sounds of other musical instruments. Some synthesizers are operated by computer.

The elements of music

A composer uses five basic elements to create a piece of music. These elements are (1) tone, (2) rhythm, (3) melody, (4) harmony, and (5) tone color.

Tone is any musical sound of definite pitch. Most music is based on a *scale,* a particular set of tones arranged according to rising or falling pitch. Western musicians name the tones, or *notes,* of a scale with the first seven letters of the alphabet—A, B, C, D, E, F, and G. The letters are repeated every eight notes. The distance between a note and the next highest note with the same name, such as C to C, is called an *octave.* The higher note has twice as many vibrations per second as the lower note, and the two notes sound very similar. A note may be raised or lowered slightly in pitch to produce a tone halfway between it and the note next to it. The half tone above a note is called its *sharp,* and the half tone below a note is called its *flat.*

The notes in a scale are separated by *half steps* or *whole steps.* In Western music, a half step is the shortest distance between two notes. The distance between a

Some types of scales

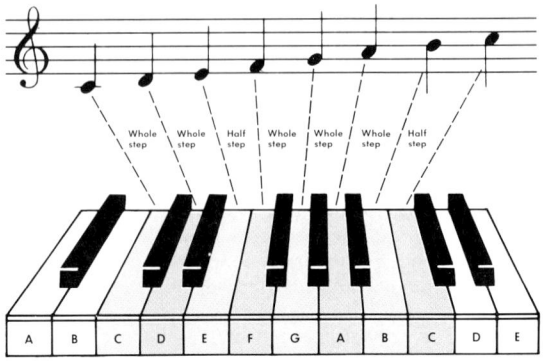

The C major scale has a half step between its third and fourth notes and between its seventh and eighth notes. You hear it when you play the white keys from C to C on the piano.

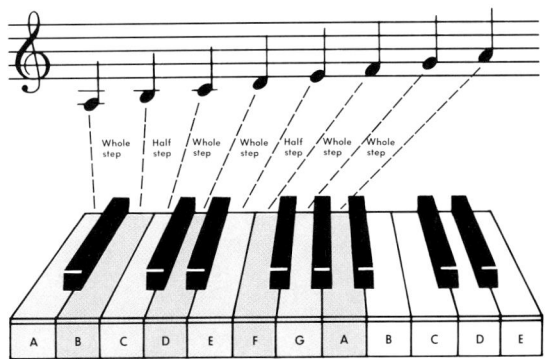

The natural minor scale follows a pattern of one whole step, one half step, two whole steps, one half step, and two whole steps. This scale is often used in folk music.

note and its sharp or flat is a half step. A whole step equals two half steps—the distance from C to D or from D to E, for example. The steps in a scale are commonly called *degrees.*

Most Western composers have based their music on *diatonic scales.* A diatonic scale has eight notes to an octave arranged in a pattern of half steps and whole steps. There are two main types of diatonic scales, *major scales* and *minor scales.* The scales differ in the location of the half steps. A major scale has a half step between its third and fourth degrees and between its seventh and eighth degrees. Thus, the notes of a major scale are arranged in this order: two whole steps, one half step, three whole steps, and one half step. The *natural minor scale* follows a pattern of one whole step, one half step, two whole steps, one half step, and two whole steps. Two other minor scales, the *harmonic minor scale* and the *melodic minor scale,* follow other patterns of steps. However, all minor scales have a half step between the second and third degrees of the scale.

The notes of a diatonic scale vary in importance. The main note, called the *tonic,* is the first degree of the scale. The tonic serves as the tonal center of the scale, and all other notes are related in some way to the tonic.

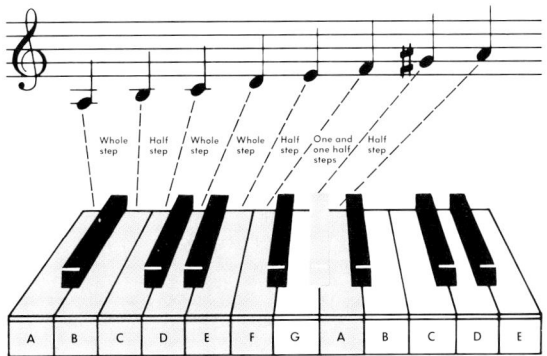

The harmonic minor scale has one and one half steps between its sixth and seventh notes. This wide leap provides a bridge to the *tonic,* or main note, at the octave.

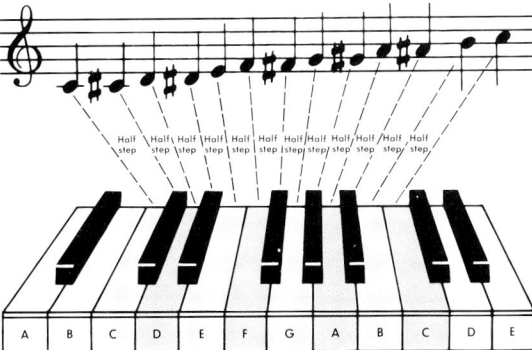

The chromatic scale consists entirely of half steps and has 12 notes to an octave. You hear this scale when you play all the white and black keys from C to C on the piano.

The tonic also gives the scale its name. For example, C is the tonic in the C major and C minor scales.

Next to the tonic, the most important notes of a scale are the fifth degree, called the *dominant,* and the fourth degree, called the *subdominant.* The seventh degree is called the *leading tone* because it leads to the tonic at the octave.

A *chromatic scale* consists entirely of half steps. It has 12 notes to an octave, rather than 8. You can hear the chromatic scale if you play all the white and black keys from one C to the next C on a piano. After 1850, composers increasingly used notes from the chromatic scale to make their music more colorful. During the 1920's, the Austrian composer Arnold Schoenberg developed a type of music based on this scale. This music, called *12-tone music,* has no tonal center.

Rhythm is the way the composer arranges notes in time. Every note has a certain duration as well as a definite pitch. Some notes may last a short time, and others a relatively long time. Rhythm helps give music its character. For example, a familiar piece of music sounds much different if the music is performed with all its notes the same length. The piece of music sounds strange because it lacks the variety of the short and long notes that make up its normal rhythm.

Another important element of rhythm is *accent.* Most composers build their music on a pattern of regularly occurring accents. Certain types of music have a fixed pattern of accent. For example, a waltz follows a strong-weak-weak pattern, *ONE two three ONE two three.* A march has a strong-weak pattern, *ONE two ONE two.*

Some composers create different rhythms by accenting beats that are normally unaccented. This technique, known as *syncopation,* has been widely used in jazz and ragtime music.

Melody. The composer combines pitches and rhythms to create a melody, or tune. The American composer Aaron Copland said, "Melody is what the piece is about." When we hear a piece of music, we most often remember its melody.

Some short pieces of music have only one melody. Longer pieces may consist of different melodies to give the music contrast and variety. A melody repeated throughout a composition is called a *theme.* Composers often use a part of a melody or theme to develop musical ideas. Such a part is called a *motive.* The first four notes of German composer Ludwig van Beethoven's fifth symphony form a motive. By repeating and varying these four notes, Beethoven developed a theme for the first part of this work that recurs through the entire symphony.

Harmony. Most Western music is based on the idea of sounding notes together. The sounding together of three or more notes is called *harmony.*

Harmony involves the use of various *intervals* (distances between notes) in a scale. Intervals are named according to the number of degrees they cover in a major scale. For example, an interval from A to C covers three degrees—A, B, and C—and is called a *third.* An interval spanning five degrees, such as A to E or C to G, is a *fifth.* Fourths, fifths, and eighths are called *perfect intervals.* Seconds, thirds, sixths, and sevenths can be either *major intervals* or *minor intervals.* Perfect intervals and major intervals can be *augmented* (raised a half step). Perfect intervals and minor intervals can be *diminished* (lowered a half step).

Composers use intervals to create *chords*—combinations of three or more notes sounded at the same time. Chords may be built on any note. The most common type of chord is the *triad,* which consists of three tones, each a third apart. For example, a chord that consists of the notes C, E, and G is a major triad. A chord with the notes C, E flat, and G is a minor triad.

The *tonic triad,* or *tonic chord,* is the most important

Triadic chords

Combinations of three or more notes are called *chords.* A *triad* is a chord made up of three notes, each a third apart, such as C, E, and G in a major scale. The most important triads in a musical composition are the *tonic, dominant,* and *subdominant.*

| Tonic Triad | Subdominant Triad | Dominant Triad | Tonic Triad |

chord in a piece of music. It is built on the tonic note of the scale. The second most important chord is the *dominant chord,* and the third is the *subdominant chord.* The dominant chord is built on the fifth note of the scale, and the subdominant chord on the fourth. In the C major scale, the tonic chord is formed by C, E, and G; the dominant chord by G, B, and D; and the subdominant chord by F, A, and C. Any note in the diatonic scale can be harmonized with one of the chords—the tonic, dominant, or subdominant. Many simple songs are harmonized by using only these chords.

Most Western composers use a harmonic system based on the tonic and dominant tones of the scale. The composer fixes the tonic tone and thus a specific *key* (tonal center) firmly in the listener's mind. The composer may then *modulate* (shift) from one key to another by adding sharps or flats to the music. Generally, these sharps or flats prepare the dominant or tonic of the new key. Modulation adds variety and may emphasize a contrasting section of a work. In most cases, the composer eventually returns to the original key.

Another important element of harmony is *cadence.* Cadence is a succession of chords that end a musical work or one of its sections. Most pieces of classical music end with an *authentic cadence,* which consists of a dominant chord followed by a tonic chord. A *plagal*

Cadences

A series of chords that ends a piece of music is called the *cadence.* Most classical music ends with an *authentic cadence.* Many hymns use a *plagal cadence.* Examples appear below.

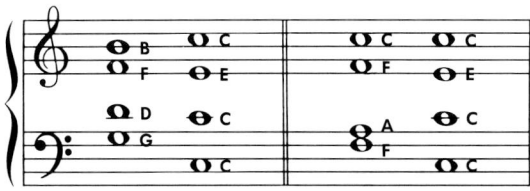

Authentic Cadence   Plagal Cadence

cadence consists of a subdominant chord followed by a tonic chord. The "Amen" ending of a hymn is an example of a plagal cadence.

Harmony has been a part of Western music for more than 1,000 years. However, Western composers' ideas about harmony have changed considerably over the centuries, particularly their ideas about *consonance* and *dissonance.* Harmony that sounds smooth and pleasant is consonant. Harmony that sounds rough and tense is dissonant. Generally, the notes that belong to the major and minor triads are considered consonant intervals, and all other intervals are dissonant.

Composers use harmony chiefly for music that has a melody and accompaniment. Some musical compositions consist of two or more melodies played at the same time. This form of music is called *counterpoint.*

Tone color, also called *timbre,* is the quality of a musical sound. Tone colors produced by different musical instruments vary widely. For example, a melody that seems dark and mournful when played on the English horn may sound bright and merry when played on the flute. Composers take advantage of tone color in *orches-*

tration (writing or arranging music for a musical group). They combine tone colors much as an artist puts together colors in creating a painting.

Musical notation

Through the years, composers developed a system for writing down music so it could be performed by musicians. This system is called *notation.* Notation indicates (1) the pitch of tones; (2) the time values, or duration of

Pitch

Composers use a *staff* to indicate the pitch of notes. A *clef sign* determines the name of each line and space of the staff. The main kinds of clefs are shown below.

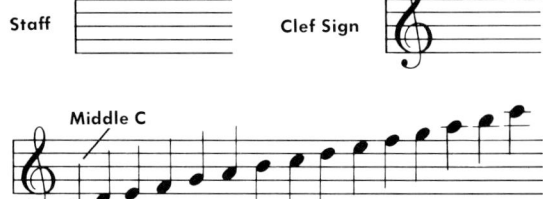

The treble clef, or *G clef,* fixes the G above *middle C* (the C nearest the middle of the piano keyboard) on the second line from the bottom of the staff. It is used for high notes.

The bass clef, also called the *F clef,* locates the F below middle C on the second line from the top of the staff. This clef is used in music that has low notes.

The C clef (alto) fixes middle C on the third line of the staff. It is chiefly used in music for the viola.

The C clef (tenor) locates middle C on the second line from the top of the staff. It is used for cello and bassoon music.

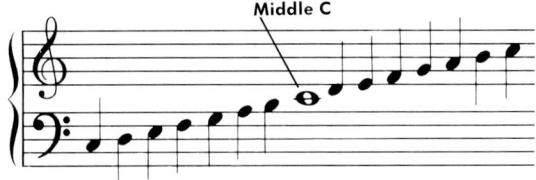

The grand staff combines the treble and bass clefs.

the tones; and (3) expression—that is, the composer's ideas about how the music should be performed.

Indicating pitch. Composers use *staff notation* to express pitch. In this system, sighs called *notes* represent tones. The notes appear on a *staff*, which consists of five horizontal lines and the four intervening spaces. Each line and space represents a certain pitch. Short *ledger lines* indicate pitches above or below the staff.

A *clef sign* at the left end of the staff determines the names of each line and space. Most music is written in either *treble clef* or *bass clef.* High notes, such as those for the violin and flute, appear in treble clef. This clef is often called the *G clef.* It fixes the G above *middle C* (the C nearest the middle of the piano keyboard) on the second line from the bottom of the staff. Lower notes appear in *bass clef,* also called *F clef.* The bass clef fixes the F below middle C on the second line from the top of the staff.

Composers use both treble clef and bass clef for piano and harp music. The *C clef* is used in music for the viola, and sometimes in music for the bassoon, cello, and trombone. This clef fixes middle C in a position that minimizes the number of ledger lines.

A *staff signature,* or *key signature,* appears at the right of the clef sign. It consists of sharp signs (♯) or flat signs (♭) that indicate which notes should always be played sharp or flat. Each staff signature can indicate either of two keys—one major key and one minor key. For example, two sharps can mean the key of either D major or B minor.

The composer may show a change from the staff signature by placing an *accidental* in front of a note. An accidental is the sign for a sharp, a flat, or a *natural* (♮). Any note not marked by a sharp or a flat is a natural. The natural sign cancels a sharp or a flat.

Indicating time values. Staff notation enables composers to indicate how long each note should be held. The *whole note* has the longest time value of any note. The second longest note is the *half note,* then the *quarter note,* the *eighth note,* the *sixteenth note,* the *thirty-*

Staff signatures

The *staff signature,* or *key signature,* tells what key the music is written in. If the music has no flats or sharps, it may be in the key of C major or its *relative minor,* A minor. Each major key has a relative minor, and each minor key has a relative major.

C Major or A Minor

G Major or E Minor

D Major or B Minor

A Major or F Sharp Minor

E Major or C Sharp Minor

B Major or G Sharp Minor

F Sharp Major or D Sharp Minor

C Sharp Major or A Sharp Minor

F Major or D Minor

B Flat Major or G Minor

E Flat Major or C Minor

A Flat Major or F Minor

D Flat Major or B Flat Minor

G Flat Major or E Flat Minor

C Flat Major or A Flat Minor

Time values

The shape of a note or rest indicates how long it lasts. The notes and rests shown below, from left to right, are whole, half, quarter, eighth, sixteenth, thirty-second, and sixty-fourth.

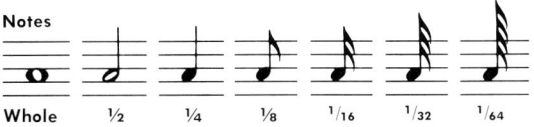

Notes: Whole, ½, ¼, ⅛, 1/16, 1/32, 1/64

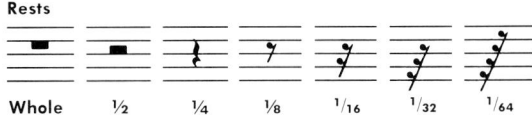

Rests: Whole, ½, ¼, ⅛, 1/16, 1/32, 1/64

A whole note has the same time value as two half notes or four quarter notes or six eighth notes plus two eighth rests. A dot at the right of a note increases its time value by half. For example, a dotted half note equals a half note plus a quarter note.

second note, and so on. Each time value is divided by two to find the next smallest note value.

The shape of a note shows its time value. Whole notes and half notes have an open oval shape. Notes with shorter values have solid oval shapes. All notes except whole notes have *stems.* To indicate notes with shorter values than the quarter note, composers attach *flags* to the stems. An eighth note has one flag; a sixteenth note, two flags; and a thirty-second note, three flags. In a series of short notes, the composer connects the note stems with *beams* instead of attaching a flag to each stem.

A dot at the right of a note increases its duration by

half. For example, a dotted half note equals a half note plus a quarter note. Duration may also be increased by a *tie,* a curved line that connects consecutive notes of the same pitch. The total duration of tied notes equals that of the notes combined.

Periods of silence are an important part of a piece of music. The composer uses markings called *rests* to indicate silence in music. The various shapes of rests indicate their time values. A composer groups the notes and rests in a piece of music into units of time called *measures* or *bars.* The composer uses *bar lines* to separate measures on the staff. The way beats are grouped in measures is called the *meter.*

Meter is indicated by the *time signature,* a fraction that appears at the beginning of a piece of music. The numerator of the fraction tells the number of beats in a measure. The denominator tells what kind of note—half, quarter, or eighth—receives one beat. Music with a $\frac{2}{4}$ meter, for example, has two beats to a measure and a quarter note as the beat unit. One measure of $\frac{2}{4}$ may have a half note, two quarter notes, four eighth notes, or

Time signatures

The *time signature* is a fraction that tells the number of beats in each measure and what kind of note receives one beat. For example, a signature of $\frac{4}{4}$ has four beats, and a time signature of $\frac{3}{4}$ has three. Both have a quarter note as the beat unit.

some other combination totaling two beats. A $\frac{4}{4}$ meter, sometimes written as *C,* has four quarter notes to a measure. Other commonly used meters are $\frac{3}{4}$ and $\frac{6}{8}$.

Many modern composers create irregular rhythms by changing the time signature several times during a piece of music. These composers also may use unusual time signatures, such as $\frac{5}{4}$ or $\frac{11}{16}$.

Musical terms

Accelerando, *ak sehl uh RAHN doh* or *aht chay lay RAHN doh,* means gradually speeding up the tempo.
Accidentals are sharps, flats, and naturals not included in a key signature.
Adagio, *uh DAH joh* or *uh DAH zhee oh,* means slow.
Ad libitum, *ad LIHB uh tuhm,* indicates that the musician may play a composition with great freedom.
Agitato, *AH jee TAH toh,* means played in a restless or excited manner.
Allegro, *uh LAY groh* or *uh LEHG roh,* means fast and lively.
Andante, *ahn DAHN tay* or *an DAN tee,* means smooth and flowing, at a moderate speed.
Animato, *AH nee MAH toh,* means lively or animated.
Appassionato, *ahp PAHS syoh NAH toh,* means with great feeling.
Cadence, *KAY duhns,* is a series of chords that brings a composition or one of its sections to a conclusion.
Cantabile, *kahn TAH bee lay,* means songlike.
Chord is a combination of three or more tones played at the same time.
Clef is a sign that fixes the positions of notes on the lines and spaces of the staff.
Counterpoint is music that consists of two or more melodies played at the same time.
Crescendo, *kruh SHEHN doh,* means growing louder.
Decrescendo, *DEE kruh SHEHN doh* or *DAY kruh SHEHN doh,* means growing softer.
Diminuendo, *duh MIHN yu EHN doh,* means gradually growing softer.
Espressivo, *EHS preh SEE voh,* means with expression.
Flat is the half step below a given tone, with the same letter name as that tone. A flat is also the sign used to show that a tone should be lowered a half step.
Forte, *FAWR tay,* means loud.
Fortissimo, *fawr TIHS uh moh,* means very loud.
Interval is the distance between two notes. The interval consisting of the notes C and E is called a *third* because E is the third note of a diatonic scale from C to C. Likewise, C and F is a *fourth,* C and G a *fifth,* C to A a *sixth,* and so on.
Key is the particular scale used for a piece of music. It is based on a certain note, called the *tonic.*
Largo means extremely slow.
Ledger line is a short line drawn above or below the staff. It is used for notes too high or too low to appear on the staff.
Legato, *lih GAH toh,* means smoothly connected.
Maestoso, *MAH ehs TOH soh,* means majestic.

Measure is a unit of musical time containing an indicated number of beats.
Meter is the arrangement of beats in a piece of music. It is indicated by the *time signature,* a fraction that appears at the beginning of the piece.
Mezzo, *MEHT soh* or *MEHZ oh,* means medium. It modifies other terms, as in *mezzo forte* (moderately loud).
Moderato, *MAHD uh RAH toh,* means playing in moderate tempo.
Modulation, *MAH ju LAY shuhn,* is moving from one key to another key in a musical composition.
Molto, *MOHL toh,* means very or much. It modifies other terms, as in *molto allegro* (very fast).
Motive is a series of notes repeated throughout a piece of music.
Natural is a note that is neither sharp nor flat. A natural is also the sign used to cancel a preceding sharp or flat.
Octave is an interval of eight notes.
Pianissimo, *PEE uh NIHS uh moh,* means very soft.
Piano, *pee AH noh,* means soft.
Più, *pyoo,* means more. It modifies other terms, as in *più presto* (faster).
Prestissimo, *prehs TIHS uh moh,* means as fast as possible.
Presto means extremely fast.
Rallentando, *RAHL lehn TAHN doh,* or **Ritardando,** *REE tahr DAHN doh,* means gradually slowing the tempo.
Scale is a series of tones from one tone to its octave, arranged according to pitch.
Sforzando, *sfawr TSAHN doh,* means played with a sudden, strong accent.
Sharp is the half step above a given tone, with the same letter name as that tone. A sharp is also the sign used to show that a tone should be raised a half step.
Staccato, *stuh KAH toh,* means with distinct tones, sharply separated from one another. The tones are performed as rapidly as possible.
Staff consists of five horizontal lines and the spaces between them. Notes are written on the lines and spaces.
Tempo is the characteristic speed of a piece of music.
Theme is the main melody of a musical composition.
Tremolo, *TREHM uh loh,* means playing in a quivering or trembling style.
Vibrato, *vee BRAH toh,* means a slight wavering in pitch, occurring so quickly that it sounds like a single pitch.
Vivace, *vee VAH chay,* means played in a lively manner or with great speed.

Another important element of time in music is *tempo*. The tempo tells how slowly or quickly the beat unit should be played. Composers sometimes show tempo by a *metronome mark,* which indicates the number of beats per minute. The musician can then follow the tempo by using a *metronome,* a timekeeping machine that can be adjusted to tick off each beat. Composers also may use a number of Italian words to indicate tempo. For example, the word *adagio* means *slowly,* and the word *allegro* means *fast.* These Italian words are used because Italian musicians had the greatest influence in Europe during the 1600's and 1700's, when composers first used words to indicate tempo.

Indicating expression. To affect a listener's feelings, music must be expressive. Composers use various words and symbols to indicate the kind of expression they want in a piece of music.

Some directions indicate *articulation*—that is, how a series of notes should be connected. A curved line over or under notes means that the notes should be con-

Expression

Composers use words and symbols to show the kind of expression they want in music. For example, a curved line over notes indicates that the notes should be played *legato* (smoothly). A dot over notes means they should be played *staccato* (sharply separated).

Legato   Staccato

nected smoothly. This style of playing is called *legato.* A dot over or under notes indicates that they should be played as short notes with silence between them. Musicians call this type of articulation *staccato.*

Composers use certain Italian words or their abbreviations to indicate *dynamics* (loudness or softness). For example, the word *pianissimo* (or *pp*) means *very soft,* and the word *fortissimo* (or *ff*) means *very loud.* Other directions, also in Italian, concern the emotional quality of the music. For example, *dolce* means *sweetly,* and *cantabile* means *songlike.*

Music around the world

Western music is the music of people of European ancestry. It is the major form of music in Europe, North America, South America, and Australia. People in some Asian countries—for example, China, Korea, and Japan—also enjoy Western music. Western music can be divided into three main types: (1) classical music, (2) popular music, and (3) folk music.

Classical music, also called *art music,* is composed according to certain rules and performed by musicians from written music. It includes symphonies and music for opera and ballet.

Classical composers have written different styles of music during different periods of history. For example, most classical music composed in the late 1700's stresses simplicity and elegance. But much classical music of the late 1800's is highly imaginative and emotional. Music written by great classical composers of the

past provides as much enjoyment today as when it was written. See **Classical music.**

Popular music includes many kinds of music, such as country music, jazz, rock music, and music from musical comedies and motion pictures. Popular music, or *entertainment music,* is generally much simpler than classical music. However, some pieces written as popular music hundreds of years ago are performed as classical music today. In addition, many great classical composers wrote some tunes in the style of the popular music of their time. Thus, the line between popular and classical music is flexible, not hard and fast.

Country music is derived from the folk music of rural whites of the Southern United States and other American traditional music. Country music is played from memory or *improvised* (spontaneously varied) from an existing song. See **Country music.**

Jazz first became popular about 1900 among blacks of the Southern United States. It combines the complex rhythms of African music and the harmony of Western music. Jazz musicians have experimented with many kinds of instruments and styles. Most jazz features much improvisation. See **Jazz.**

Rock music is a mixture of blues, country music, jazz, and American and British entertainment music. It is easier to understand than classical music or jazz. Styles of rock music frequently change, but such music always has a strong beat and a simple melody and rhythm. See **Rock music.**

Folk music consists of the traditional songs of a people. Most folk songs begin in rural communities. One person makes up a song, and other people hear it and learn to sing it. Some folk songs have been passed on in this way for hundreds of years. Many composers, including Edvard Grieg of Norway and Antonín Dvořák of Czechoslovakia, have used folk music in their works. See **Folk music.**

Asian music sounds different from Western music because the scales, instruments, and composing techniques used are different. For example, a scale in Western music has 12 steps to an octave. But the Arab scale

De Wys, Inc.

Bulgarian folk musicians and dancers perform a *dance song.* Dance songs are a type of folk music composed to accompany folk dances.

has 17 steps to an octave, and the Indian scale has 22 steps. Such scales are called *microtonal* because they are made up of *microtones*—that is, intervals smaller than a half step. The chief types of Asian music are those of (1) China, (2) Japan, (3) India, (4) the Arab countries, and (5) Indonesia.

Chinese music began more than 2,000 years ago. Orchestras with hundreds of musicians performed at early Chinese religious ceremonies and court festivities. Today, all Chinese plays are set to music. *Peking opera,* also called *Beijing opera,* is the most popular form of Chinese drama. It combines dialogue, music, dancing, and acrobatics.

The principal Chinese musical instruments are the *quin* (ch'in) and the *pipa,* two plucked stringed instruments. Chinese musicians also play bowed stringed instruments, flutes, and percussion instruments, especially bells, drums, and gongs. The basic scale of Chinese music has five notes, most commonly F, G, A, C, and D. Traditional Chinese music has no harmony.

Japanese music was influenced by the court music of China. Japanese court music, called *gagaku,* dates from the A.D. 700's. Japanese orchestras consist of *shakuhachi* (bamboo flutes), gongs, drums, and such plucked stringed instruments as the *samisen* and the *koto.*

Music is an essential part of Japanese theater. The *no play,* a form of Japanese drama developed in the 1300's, features solo and choral singing with accompaniment by a small orchestra. A large orchestra provides background music for the *kabuki,* a dance-drama.

Japanese music has no harmony but makes use of microtones and free rhythm. The basic scales are the natural minor scale and a major scale with the fourth note raised a half step—for example, the C major scale with an F sharp instead of an F.

Indian music is one of the few kinds of non-Western music that have become internationally popular. It first flourished in Hindu temples and the courts of the *maharajahs* (great kings) of India. A soloist sings or plucks a stringed instrument, such as the *vina* or the *sitar.* The soloist may be accompanied by a drummer and a musician playing a *tambura,* a lutelike instrument.

The notes of the Indian scale are arranged in various patterns called *ragas.* Each raga has a special meaning and may be associated with a particular mood, emotion, season, or time of day. The performer chooses an appropriate raga, plays it, and then improvises on it.

Arab music is the music of the Arab nations of the Middle East and northern Africa. The main Arab instruments include flutes; drums; and two plucked stringed instruments, the *oud* and the *qanun.* Most Arab songs have instrumental accompaniment. However, musical instruments may not be used in Muslim worship. The chief Muslim religious music consists of calls to prayer sung by criers called *muezzins* and the chanting of passages from the Koran, the sacred book of the Muslims.

Indonesian music is noted for orchestras called *gamelans.* These orchestras consist of drums, gongs, and xylophones and are used to accompany puppet plays. Gamelan music has a kind of harmony because the instruments play different melodies at the same time.

African music is the music of black peoples who live south of the Sahara. These peoples use music in almost every aspect of their lives, especially religious ceremo-

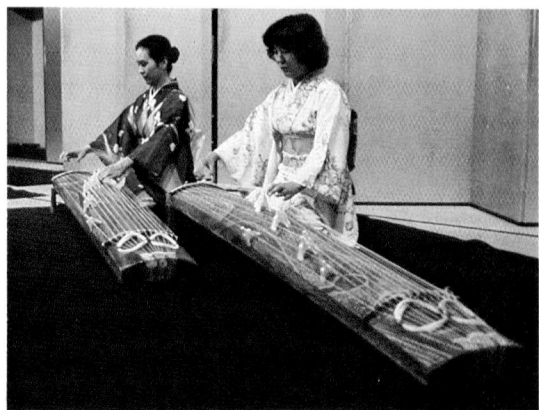

Don Smetzer, Click/Chicago

Japanese music is often played on plucked stringed instruments called *kotos, above.* Other Japanese instruments include gongs, banjolike *samisens,* and *shakuhachi* (bamboo flutes).

nies, festivals, and social rituals. Many Africans believe that music serves as a link with the spirit world.

Drums are the most important instruments in African music. Some drums are made of animal skins and may be played with the fingers. Others consist of hollow logs that the performer beats with sticks. African musicians also play flutes, xylophones, and stringed instruments. One kind of instrument, called the *sansa* or *mbira,* consists of a number of metal strips attached to a piece of wood. The musician plays the instrument by plucking the strips with the fingers or thumbs.

Most African music features complex rhythms. The musicians create these rhythms by combining different patterns of beats played on drums and iron bells or produced by handclapping. Some African songs have harmony. In many songs, a leader sings a phrase and then the chorus repeats the phrase or sings a refrain. Elements of African music appear in jazz, spirituals, and the popular music of Brazil and the Caribbean.

American Indian music is the traditional music of the Indians of North and South America. Much of it de-

Robert Frerck

An Indonesian gamelan orchestra consists of drums, gongs, and xylophones. Gamelan music has a kind of harmony because the instruments play different melodies.

veloped before Europeans arrived in the Americas.

American Indians almost always perform music as part of an activity. For example, music and dancing play an important part in Indian religious ceremonies and such tribal rituals as rain dances and hunting dances. Indian religious leaders called *medicine men* and *medicine women* sing songs as they treat the sick. The Indians also use songs in various social situations, such as courtship and trading. Many Indians compose their own songs. In the past, they said that they learned these songs from spirits that appeared to them in dreams.

Most American Indian music consists of singing accompanied by drums or rattles. Much of this vocal music uses a five-note scale—A, C, D, F, G. Some Indian groups also perform flute music. In parts of Latin America, the music of the Indians mixed with the folk music of their Spanish conquerors. This mixture produced distinctive types of popular music and dance.

Careers in music

Careers in music provide many personal rewards. But such careers require talent and dedication. Only a person willing to devote a great deal of time to study and practice should consider a career in music.

A young person interested in a musical career should start lessons in school and with a private teacher. After finishing high school, the student should enroll in a *conservatory* (specialized music school) or study music at a college or university. In addition to formal lessons, the student should practice and study independently.

Most people who study music want to become professional performers or composers. But competition is keen among musicians, and relatively few earn a living solely by performing or composing. Careers in popular music are difficult to achieve and offer little security. A rock group that suddenly becomes popular may fall out of favor just as quickly. Musicians perform in orchestras or in small groups that play in theaters, nightclubs, and television studios. A few with exceptional talent give solo recitals or perform as soloists with orchestras or opera companies. Composers may work as songwriters or arrange music for TV shows and commercials.

Teaching offers the largest number of career opportunities in music. Many composers and performers earn a living by teaching. Music teachers must have at least a bachelor's degree in music. Most college and university music teachers have a doctor's degree.

Other jobs in the field of music include positions as church organists or choir directors. Music critics review performances for newspapers or magazines. Specialists called *music therapists* work with patients in hospitals and nursing homes. These musicians use music to arouse feelings that help patients get better. Many people make, repair, or sell musical instruments. Large musical organizations, such as symphony orchestras and opera companies, employ concert managers, librarians, secretaries, and other workers.   R. M. Longyear

Related articles in *World Book.* See the *Arts* section of the articles on various countries, such as **China** (The arts). See also the following articles:

Biographies

For biographies of people in the field of music, see the lists of *Related articles* at the end of **Classical music; Hymn; Jazz; Musical comedy; Opera; Piano; Popular music;** and **Violin.**

John Running, Stock, Boston

American Indian music often features singing and dancing accompanied by rattles. American Indians almost always perform music as part of an activity, such as a religious ceremony.

Kinds of music

Aleatory music	Folk music	Oratorio
Ballet	Hymn	Popular music
Blues	Jazz	Ragtime
Chamber music	Musical comedy	Reggae
Country music	Opera	Rock music
Electronic music	Operetta	

Elements of music

Counterpoint	Pitch	Tone
Harmonics	Rhythm	Treble
Harmony	Sound	
Key		

Musical forms

See the list of *Related articles* with **Classical music.** See also:

Barbershop quartet singing	Calypso
	Skald

Musical instruments

Accordion	Conga drum	Harp	Spinet
Bagpipe	Cornet	Harpsichord	Synthesizer
Balalaika	Cymbal	Horn	Tambourine
Banjo	Drum	Jew's-harp	Theremin
Bass	Dulcimer	Lute	Tom-tom
Bassoon	English horn	Lyre	Triangle
Bell	Fife	Mandolin	Trombone
Bongo drums	Flageolet	Marimba	Trumpet
Bugle	Flügelhorn	Oboe	Tuba
Calliope	Flute	Ocarina	Ukulele
Castanets	French horn	Organ	Vibraphone
Celesta	Glockenspiel	Piano	Viol
Cello	Gong	Piccolo	Viola
Chimes	Guitar	Pipe	Violin
Clarinet	Hand organ	Recorder	Virginal
Clavichord	Harmonica	Saxophone	Xylophone
Concertina	Harmonium	Sitar	Zither

Other related articles

American Society of Compos-
  ers, Authors and Publishers
Band
Carillon
Cecilia, Saint
Compact disc
Composer
Greece, Ancient (The arts)
High-fidelity system
Indian, American (Music and
  dancing)
Japan (picture: Court musicians)
Metronome

Motion picture (Adding music
  and sound effects)
Muses
Music Clubs, National Federa-
  tion of
National anthem
National Music Camp
Orchestra
Pulitzer Prizes (Music)
Recording industry
Suzuki method
Tuning fork
Western frontier life (Music)

Outline

I. The importance of music
  A. In ceremonies
  B. In work
  C. In personal and social
    activities

II. Musical instruments
  A. Stringed instruments
  B. Wind instruments
  C. Percussion instruments
  D. Keyboard instruments
  E. Electronic instruments

III. The elements of music
  A. Tone
  B. Rhythm
  C. Melody
  D. Harmony
  E. Tone color

IV. Musical notation
  A. Indicating pitch
  B. Indicating time values
  C. Indicating expression

V. Music around the world
  A. Western music
  B. Asian music
  C. African music
  D. American Indian music

VI. Careers in music

Questions

How do composers indicate silence in music?
What is Western music? Why does Asian music sound different
  from Western music?
What career opportunities are available to music students?
What is a *staff signature*? A *time signature*?
How do minor scales and major scales differ?
What is *counterpoint*?
What is the difference between *tone* and *tone color*?
How does a musician play a brass instrument?
What is a *theme*? A *motive*?
What is the major difference between music and such arts as
  painting and poetry?

Reading and Study Guide

See *Music* in the Research Guide/Index, Volume 22, for a *Reading and Study Guide.*

Additional resources

Level I

Ardley, Neil. *Music: An Illustrated Encyclopedia.* Facts on File,
  1986. *Music.* Knopf, 1989.
Berger, Melvin. *The Science of Music.* Crowell-Collier, 1989.
Gerardi, Bob. *Opportunities in Music Careers.* VGM Career,
  1991.
McLeish, Kenneth and Valerie. *The Oxford First Companion to
  Music.* Oxford, 1982.

Level II

Baskerville, David. *Music Business Handbook & Career Guide.*
  5th ed. Sherwood Co., 1990.
Encyclopedia of Music in Canada. Ed. by Helmut Kallmann and
  others. Univ. of Toronto Pr., 1981.
The New Grove Dictionary of American Music. Ed. by H. Wiley
  Hitchcock and Stanley Sadie. 4 vols. Grove's Dictionaries, 1986.
The New Grove Dictionary of Music and Musicians. Ed. by Stan-
  ley Sadie. 20 vols. Grove's Dictionaries, 1980.

Music box is an instrument that plays tunes automatically. Steel pins protrude from a rotating cylinder driven
by clockwork or a spring. The pins pluck metal teeth of

various lengths, producing soft, high-pitched sounds of
great delicacy. Several teeth may be tuned to the same
note, so the box can repeat notes rapidly. Music boxes
may be connected with clocks, and play certain tunes on
the hour. Music-box movements are built into watches,
toys, and other everyday objects.

Early music boxes had tiny flute pipes instead of
teeth, and gave an organlike sound. Joseph Haydn wrote
many charming pieces for the instrument. In the 1800's,
some inventors developed music boxes that had as
many as 400 teeth.   André P. Larson

Music Clubs, National Federation of, is the largest charitable music organization in the world. The federation is devoted to developing and maintaining high
music standards in the United States and its possessions. It has about 600,000 members. Persons may join
the federation as individuals or through music clubs,
school clubs, choirs, choruses, conservatories, dance
groups, or symphony orchestras.

The federation offers many awards and scholarships.
Winners of the "Young Artist Auditions" receive $5,000
each. These awards are given every two years. The federation also sponsors "Cavalcade for Creative Youth,"
and the Victor Herbert-ASCAP Annual Awards in Composition for Juniors and Students.

The federation commissions works by American composers, and sponsors American Music Month and Parade of American Music in February and National Music
Week in May. In addition, the federation publishes
Music Clubs Magazine and *Junior Keynotes.* The National Federation of Music Clubs was founded in 1898.
Its headquarters are at 1336 N. Delaware St., Indianapolis, IN 46202.

Critically reviewed by the National Federation of Music Clubs

Musical comedy is a type of play that tells a story
through a combination of spoken dialogue, songs, and
dances. Musical comedies are also called *musicals.*

Paul Robert Perry

A music box creates music mechanically. To produce notes,
steel pins on a rotating cylinder pluck metal teeth of various
lengths. A spring or clockwork mechanism drives the cylinder.

Most of them are light in tone and contain much humor. Musical comedies developed in the United States during the late 1800's and have become a unique American contribution to world theater. Many of the best-known songs in popular music originated in musical comedies.

Musical comedy differs in several ways from other types of stage works that have music. For example, the *revue* has songs, dances, and skits but tells no story. The *opera* and *operetta* resemble musical comedy, but most of them have much less spoken dialogue. In addition, most operas use classical music, while nearly all musicals use popular music. Some plays may include songs or instrumental music, but the play remains dramatically complete without the music.

Most major American musical comedies are first presented in New York City, normally on Broadway. The more successful musicals later tour throughout the country and may even be performed in other countries.

Elements of musical comedy

A typical musical comedy consists of four basic elements. These elements are (1) the book, (2) the music, (3) the lyrics, and (4) dancing.

The book is the musical's story. It is sometimes called the *libretto.* The book provides shape and structure to a musical. A successful book integrates the dialogue, music, lyrics, and dancing. Some books are written specifically for a musical. Others are adaptations of other literary forms, especially novels, short stories, or plays. In some cases, the composer writes the book for a show, but most books are written by playwrights or other professional writers.

The music in a musical comedy may be vocal, instrumental, or both. In most shows, the music has a melodic form that the audience can easily remember. In the early history of musical comedy, the music served primarily to entertain audiences and show off the talents of the performers. But by the 1940's, the music began to serve a more dramatic function. Today, it is expected to help create characterization, advance the plot, and develop important situations or action. The composer works with the author of the book to determine where the music can most effectively be used in the story.

The lyrics may be written by the composer or by another person, called a *lyricist.* If the musical involves both a composer and a lyricist, the two must work closely together to ensure that the lyrics fit the music. In many songs, the lyrics contribute to telling the story or describing a character's feelings. The best lyrics are actually skillful poems set to music.

Dancing is one of the most distinctive elements of musical comedy. Some dances are meant only to entertain the audience. But many dances help tell the story or set a mood. Many shows employ a person called a *choreographer,* who creates dances especially for the show. In some cases, a show's director serves as the choreographer. Most dances in musical comedy are light and rhythmic, but some musicals include long dance pieces that resemble classical ballet.

The history of musical comedy

The first musicals. American musical comedy developed from a blend of American popular entertainment and the more classical elements of the European musi-

Billy Rose Theater Collection, The New York Public Library.

The Black Crook is generally considered the first American musical comedy. It opened in 1866. The poster above reflects the show's emphasis on beautiful women and elaborate sets.

cal stage. The basic American influences were vaudeville, minstrel shows, and burlesques. All three types of entertainment had singing, dancing, and comedy, but none had a unifying story. European influences included the ballet, various forms of opera, and a form of elaborate spectacle called an *extravaganza.*

Most scholars believe that *The Black Crook* (1866) marked the beginning of American musical comedy. The show was noted for its spectacular scenery and emphasis on beautiful women. *The Black Crook* was based on European models. A truly American form of musical theater began to appear with *The Brook* (1879). This show included American themes and attempted to integrate the story with the songs and dances.

During the late 1800's and early 1900's, the European-style operetta was perhaps the most popular form of musical theater in America. Three European-born composers—Rudolf Friml, Victor Herbert, and Sigmund Romberg—were the most important composers of operetta in the United States.

A number of American composers and performers attempted to create a more American form of musical theater. In 1879, vaudeville stars Edward Harrigan and Tony Hart presented *The Mulligan Guards' Ball.* This show was the first in a series of *Mulligan Guards'* comic plays with music. The series dealt with recognizable American types and realistic scenes of everyday life. During the early 1900's, composer-actor George M. Cohan wrote the book, music, and lyrics for a number of high-spirited musicals. Such Cohan shows as *Little Johnny Jones*

(1904) and *Forty-Five Minutes from Broadway* (1906) helped turn American musical comedy from European traditions toward a more native American style.

Musical comedy matures. During World War I (1914-1918) and the years immediately afterward, American musical comedy took shape as a unique form of musical theater. Composer Jerome Kern ranks as probably the most influential figure in bringing musical comedy to maturity. From 1915 to 1918, Kern composed the music for a series of sophisticated musicals. Most of the shows had a book and lyrics by the English playwrights P. G. Wodehouse and Guy Bolton. These musicals were known as the "Princess shows" because they were presented in the Princess Theatre in New York City. The Princess shows had small casts and modern, everyday settings. The shows brought a more natural, informal style to musicals.

In 1927, Kern and lyricist Oscar Hammerstein II completed *Show Boat,* a milestone in the development of musical comedy. *Show Boat* presented believable characters in a realistic manner and had a genuinely dramatic book. In addition, the show dealt with racial discrimination and other serious issues that were rarely mentioned in musicals of the time. *Show Boat* also featured some of the most popular songs in the history of musical comedy, notably "Ol' Man River."

In 1931, a political satire called *Of Thee I Sing* opened in New York City. George Gershwin composed the music and his brother, Ira, wrote the lyrics. The noted playwright George S. Kaufman was co-author of the book. The show became the first musical to win the Pulitzer Prize for drama. The award helped raise the status of musical comedy to the level of serious theater. The sharp attacks on American political life also broadened the range of subjects considered suitable for musicals.

A number of major composers and lyricists flourished during the 1920's and 1930's. In addition to George Gershwin and Jerome Kern, the leading composers included Irving Berlin, Cole Porter, Arthur Schwartz, and Vincent Youmans. The top lyricists included Howard Dietz, Ira Gershwin, Otto Harbach, and E. Y. Harburg. Composer Richard Rodgers and lyricist Lorenz Hart formed perhaps the most outstanding partnership of the period. One of their best-known musicals, *Pal Joey*

(1940), introduced a realistic, adult view of such themes as love and sex into musical comedy.

The modern musical. The modern era of musical comedy began in 1943 with the premiere of *Oklahoma!* by Richard Rodgers and Oscar Hammerstein II. The show revolutionized musical comedy through the skill with which the authors integrated the story, music, and dancing. Rodgers and Hammerstein rapidly became the most popular team in the history of musical comedy. Their hits included *Carousel* (1945), *South Pacific* (1949), *The King and I* (1951), and *The Sound of Music* (1959).

A number of teams contributed popular musicals during the 1950's and 1960's. Composer Frederick Loewe and lyricist Alan Jay Lerner created *My Fair Lady* (1956), one of the most popular shows of the century. Composer Leonard Bernstein and lyricist Stephen Sondheim wrote *West Side Story* (1957), a musical based on William Shakespeare's *Romeo and Juliet.* The show featured brilliant choreography by Jerome Robbins. Composer Jerry Bock and lyricist Sheldon Harnick collaborated on *Fiddler on the Roof* (1964). In 1983, *A Chorus Line,* created by choreographer Michael Bennett with music by Marvin Hamlisch, became the longest-running musical in Broadway history. When it closed in 1990, it had achieved a record of 6,137 performances.

Musical comedy today. Since the late 1960's, musicals have been noted for their enormous range of subjects and styles. *Hair* (1967) dealt with American young people of the 1960's who rebelled against society during the Vietnam War. *Grease* (1972) was a rock 'n' roll musical about high school life during the 1950's.

Many critics consider Stephen Sondheim the most creative figure in musical comedy today. Sondheim began his career as a lyricist but soon began to write both the words and music for his shows. Sondheim gained praise for the wit and sophistication of his lyrics and for the originality of his subject matter. His best-known shows include *Company* (1970), *A Little Night Music* (1973), *Sweeney Todd* (1979), *Sunday in the Park with George* (1984), and *Into the Woods* (1986).

The British composer Andrew Lloyd Webber is probably the most commercially successful composer of his time. Lloyd Webber was the key figure in the international success of British musicals since the early 1970's.

Scene from the original production; Brown Brothers

Show Boat helped start a new era of musical comedy in 1927. The show had realistic characters and situations and introduced some of the most popular songs in musical comedy history.

Scene from the original production; Bettmann Archive

Oklahoma! began the age of the modern musical comedy in 1943. It revolutionized musicals through the way its dancing, songs, and dialogue combined to develop plot and characters.

Sunday in the Park with George is based on the life of the French painter Georges Seurat. The show opened in 1984. Stephen Sondheim, the composer and lyricist, gained praise as the most creative figure in musical comedy in the 1970's and 1980's.

© Martha Swope

His hits include *Jesus Christ Superstar* (1971), *Evita* (1978), *Cats* (1981), and *Phantom of the Opera* (1986). Such spectacular musicals represent three trends in musical theater of the late 1900's. They are (1) a lack of notable American musicals, (2) more emphasis on lavish staging and settings, and (3) a movement away from the conventional book musical and the adoption of structures similar to the conventions of opera.

Because of the huge cost of staging musicals, only audience-pleasing spectacles seem to succeed. Some producers have tried to present shows with small casts and few changes of scenery to keep costs low, but such shows have rarely succeeded.   Don B. Wilmeth

Related articles in *World Book* include:

Berlin, Irving	Hammerstein,	Operetta
Bernstein, Leonard	Oscar, II	Porter, Cole
Brice, Fanny	Hart, Lorenz	Robbins, Jerome
Burlesque	Herbert, Victor	Rodgers, Richard
Cohan, George M.	Kern, Jerome	Romberg, Sig-
Dancing (picture:	Lerner, Alan Jay	mund
American musical	Lloyd Webber,	Sondheim, Ste-
comedy)	Andrew	phen
Friml, Rudolf	Loesser, Frank	Vaudeville
Gershwin, George	Minstrel show	Weill, Kurt

Additional resources

Bordman, Gerald M. *American Musical Comedy: From "Adonis" to "Dreamgirls."* Oxford, 1982. *The American Musical Theatre: A Chronicle.* 2nd ed. 1992.
Smith, Cecil, and Litton, Glenn. *Musical Comedy in America.* 2nd ed. Theatre Arts, 1981.

Musical instrument. See Music (Musical instruments).

Musicians, American Federation of, is a labor union affiliated with the American Federation of Labor and Congress of Industrial Organizations (AFL-CIO) and the Canadian Labour Council. Its official name is the American Federation of Musicians of the United States and Canada. It has local unions in the United States, Canada, and Puerto Rico. The union claims jurisdiction over almost all workers in the field of music. Such workers include performers, arrangers, orchestra librarians, conductors, and composers.

The American Federation of Musicians has reached many collective-bargaining agreements with such employers as recording companies, symphony orchestras, theatrical producers, and the motion-picture and television industries. These agreements set such employment conditions as minimum wages, pension contributions, and health benefits.

The union was founded in 1896 in Indianapolis. It has headquarters at 1500 Broadway, Suite 600, New York, NY 10036. For membership, see **Labor movement** (table).

Critically reviewed by the American Federation of Musicians

Musil, *MOO sihl,* **Robert** (1880-1942), was an Austrian author best known for his long novel *The Man Without Qualities.* The first two volumes were published in 1930 and 1933. Musil died before completing the work. A fragment of the third volume was published in 1943.

The novel deals with both philosophical and political themes. The story takes place in Vienna in 1913 and concerns a man named Ulrich, who decides to become a "man without qualities." The character refuses to use his skills as an engineer and mathematician and instead concentrates on seeking ethical and spiritual values. The novel describes the moral and political decline of Austria-Hungary. It also analyzes the cultural crisis in Europe that led to World War I (1914-1918), especially the difficulty of finding stable meaning in the world of modern science.

Musil was born in Klagenfurt. His first major work was *The Confusions of Young Törless* (1906), a novel about adolescence. He also wrote essays and short stories, and two plays.   Russell A. Berman

Musk is a raw material that is used in perfumes. It is formed in a gland in the abdomen of the male musk deer, an animal that lives high in central, eastern, and northeastern Asia. When the gland is dried, the musk forms into grains. The perfume ingredient is an oil that is removed from the grains with alcohol. People have hunted musk deer for their scent glands since ancient times. In 1934, scientists developed a synthetic form of musk that has largely replaced natural musk.

Patricia Ann Mullen

Musk deer is a type of small deer that roams the mountainous forests and brushlands of central, eastern, and northeastern Asia. It gets its name from a musk gland in the male's abdomen. Males use the musk to mark their territories. The musk is highly prized for scenting perfumes and soaps. In some regions, musk deer have been hunted so extensively for their musk that they are nearly extinct.

Musk deer have no antlers, but the upper canine teeth form small tusks. These deer stand from 20 to 24

Gerald Cubitt

The musk deer, *above,* has two upper teeth that form small tusks. Musk deer roam mountainous areas in many parts of Asia.

inches (51 to 61 centimeters) tall at the shoulders and about 2 inches (5 centimeters) higher at the rump. The hind legs are longer and heavier than the front legs. Musk deer have a thick layer of coarse, brittle hair that is yellowish-brown to dark brown at the surface and white at the base. The hair's color pattern helps camouflage the deer, and the thick coat protects the animal from the harsh weather found at high elevations.

Unlike most deer, musk deer generally live alone. They are most active at morning and evening, feeding on grass, lichens, roots, and twigs of shrubs. Musk deer mate in January, and the female bears a single spotted fawn about 160 days later.

Scientific classification. Musk deer form the subfamily Moschinae in the deer family, Cervidae.   Gregory K. Snyder

Musk hog. See Peccary.

Musk ox is a large, shaggy mammal that lives in the Far North. Adult *bulls* (males) measure about 4 to 5 feet (1.2 to 1.5 meters) tall at the shoulder and weigh as much as 900 pounds (410 kilograms). The *cows* (females) are smaller. Both sexes have horns that meet on the forehead to form broad, flattened bulges and curve downward, outward, and upward to sharp tips. The horns of the bulls are massive and are used in fighting other bulls for the cows during the breeding season. The bulls have a gland under their eyes that leaves a musky odor when rubbed on branches of bushes or trees.

Musk oxen are covered over most of their bodies with long, shaggy, dark brown hair. A dense undercoat of fine, soft hair keeps out cold and moisture. Musk oxen have humped shoulders; short, sturdy legs; and broad *cloven* (divided) hoofs. The animals use their hoofs to scrape through snow for such food as willow and pine shoots, grass, lichens, and mosses.

Musk oxen once roamed throughout the North American Arctic. However, they were hunted almost to extinction during the 1800's and early 1900's. Since 1917, laws have protected musk oxen from hunters and the number of these animals has increased. Today, musk oxen live mainly in Arctic coastal areas of Canada and Greenland. They have also been reestablished in Alaska and in far

northern parts of Europe and Asia.

Scientific classification. The musk ox belongs to the bovid family, Bovidae. It is *Ovibos moschatus.*   Thomas L. Poulson

See also **Animal** (picture: Animals of the polar regions).

Muskellunge, *MUHS kuh luhnj,* is the largest fish of the pike family. It may reach a length of 6 feet (1.8 meters) and weigh about 100 pounds (45 kilograms). But most muskellunges are from $2\frac{1}{3}$ to 4 feet (0.7 to 1.2 meters) long and weigh 5 to 36 pounds (2 to 16 kilograms). The maximum life span of a muskellunge is about 25 years. The muskellunge looks much like the common pike. But, unlike the common pike, the muskellunge has no scales on the lower half of its head. Muskellunges may be brown, gray, green, or silver. Most have dark bars or spots on their side, but some are plain.

WORLD BOOK illustration by John F. Eggert

The muskellunge is a large North American pike.

The muskellunge lives in the lakes and quiet rivers of southern Canada. It also is found in the upper Mississippi Valley, the Great Lakes, and the St. Lawrence and Ohio rivers. Many people consider the muskellunge among the best of food fishes.

The "musky" is a prize among fishing enthusiasts. Its tremendous size and strength make a stout line and a heavy hook necessary. It rarely is found far from cover in the waters where it lives. Large adults feed on other large fish, ducks, muskrats, and other vertebrates.

Scientific classification. The muskellunge belongs to the pike family, Esocidae. Its scientific name is *Esox masquinongy.*

David W. Greenfield

Musket was the firearm that infantry soldiers used before the perfection of the rifle. The name was first used in Italy in the 1500's to describe heavy handguns. It may have come from the Italian word *moschetto,* meaning *young sparrowhawk,* or from the name of an Italian inventor, Moschetta of Feltro.

A musket had a smooth *bore* (inside of the barrel). By contrast, a rifle bore has curved grooves.

Early muskets were 6 or 7 feet (1.8 to 2.1 meters) long and weighed as much as 40 pounds (18 kilograms). They fired either single round balls or round balls with smaller lead balls called *buckshot.* They were loaded from the muzzle. The first muskets were *matchlocks,* guns in which a cord match set off the powder charge. They were followed by *wheel locks,* in which a revolving wheel set off sparks; *flintlocks,* in which a flint struck a piece of steel to make sparks; and *caplocks,* in which an explosive cap set off the powder charge. Muskets were so inaccurate that it was difficult to hit a target more than 100 yards (91 meters) away. But the military used muskets long after the development of the first accurate rifle in about 1655. Muskets were considered more convenient because a musket ball slid easily down the barrel. Rifle bullets had to be pounded down to fit into the grooves.   Douglas M. Wicklund

See also **Blunderbuss; Flintlock; Harquebus; Powder horn.**

Muskie. See Muskellunge.

Muskie, Edmund Sixtus (1914-   ), a Maine Democrat, served in the U.S. Senate from 1959 to 1980. In 1980 and 1981, he was secretary of state under President Jimmy Carter. Muskie was the Democratic nominee for Vice President of the United States in 1968. Vice President Hubert H. Humphrey and Muskie were defeated by their Republican opponents, Richard M. Nixon and Governor Spiro T. Agnew of Maryland.

Early life. Muskie was born on March 28, 1914, in Rumford, Me. His father, a tailor, had come to the United States from Poland in 1903. He changed the family name from Marciszewski. Edmund's mother, who came from Buffalo, N.Y., recalled that he was a quiet boy who "wouldn't even play with other children, he was so bashful."

Edmund worked his way through Bates College in Lewiston, Me. He was elected to Phi Beta Kappa and graduated in 1936. He graduated from Cornell University Law School in 1939 and started to practice law in Waterville, Me. Muskie served as a naval officer during World War II.

Political career. Muskie began his political career in 1946, when he was elected to the Maine House of Representatives. He was reelected in 1948 and 1950 and became minority leader of the Democrats in the House. In 1954, he was elected Maine's first Democratic governor since the 1930's. He was reelected governor of the heavily Republican state in 1956. As governor, Muskie promoted economic and educational improvements and stepped up control of water pollution.

Muskie was the first Democrat ever elected to the U.S. Senate by Maine voters. He campaigned for, but did not win, the 1972 Democratic presidential nomination. In the Senate, Muskie served on the Foreign Relations Committee and as chairman of the Budget Committee. He was also assistant majority *whip* (leader) from 1966 until 1980.   James I. Lengle

See also **Humphrey, Hubert H.**

Muskmelon is the fruit of a type of plant that belongs to the gourd family. Muskmelons include cantaloupes, honeydew melons, and casabas. The melons vary in the color and texture of the rind and the color of the flesh. The flesh of the melon is eaten as a dessert or as a breakfast fruit.

The variety of muskmelon commonly referred to as cantaloupe in the United States has yellow-orange flesh and a yellow-brown rind covered with a tangle of ridges or netting. The flesh of a ripe cantaloupe is sweet and has a musky odor. It is a good source of vitamins A and C. However, scientists do not consider this melon to be a true cantaloupe. True cantaloupes grow in Europe. Their flesh is similar to that of cantaloupes grown in the United States, but the rind is harder and warty and lacks the netting.

Honeydew melons have a smooth, green rind and green or white flesh. Casabas have a wrinkled rind. Like

WORLD BOOK illustration by Lorraine Epstein

The cantaloupe is a popular variety of muskmelon.

honeydew melons, casabas have green or white flesh. These melons do not have the musky odor of cantaloupe. All muskmelons have seeds that are attached to a netlike fiber in the center of the melon.

Muskmelons require a long growing season. They have the best flavor and sweetness when grown in a hot, dry climate. In the United States, high-quality melons can be grown in almost every state. In cool areas, growers plant seeds in greenhouses and later transplant them to the field after the last frost. Seeds are planted in warm soil in rows about 6 feet (180 centimeters) apart. The plants are later thinned to one plant about every 2 feet (60 centimeters).

Most muskmelons grow on vines that creep along the ground. The leaves have three to seven lobes. Blossoms open for only one day, and the flowers must be pollinated that day for the plant to bear fruit. Honey bees, which are attracted to the yellow blossoms, pollinate the plants. As a cantaloupe begins to ripen, the rind lightens in color and the fruit begins to *slip* (separate) from the stem. However, most honeydew and casaba melons do not slip from the stem. Fruit growers cut these melons from the vine and then store them until they are fully ripe.

Scientists do not know for sure where muskmelons originally grew. However, many closely related plants originated in Africa and Asia, and many experts believe that muskmelons also originated there thousands of years ago. Muskmelons were introduced into Central America as early as 1516 and into the American Colonies by the early 1600's.

Scientific classification. Muskmelons belong to the gourd family, Cucurbitaceae. The scientific name for muskmelons is *Cucumis melo*. The cantaloupe of the United States is *C. melo,* variety *reticulatus.* Honeydew melons and casabas are *C. melo,* variety *inodorus.*   Gary W. Elmstrom

See also **Casaba; Melon; Gourd.**

Muskoka Lakes, *muh SKOH kuh,* are a group of scenic lakes in the rocky uplands of southern Ontario. The swift-flowing Muskoka River drains the Muskoka Lakes into Georgian Bay. The lakes lie from 100 to 125 miles (160 to 200 kilometers) north of Toronto. Lake Muskoka, the largest of the group, covers 54 square miles (140 square kilometers). Lake Joseph, Lake of Bays, Rosseau Lake, and hundreds of smaller lakes lie nearby. Many streams and waterfalls are in the area.

The lake district is one of the most famous summer-resort regions in North America. Well-known resort centers include Bala, Baysville, Bracebridge, Dorset, Gravenhurst, and Port Sydney. The area has forests of balsam fir, pine, and spruce. Birch and maple trees add color to the region each autumn.   George B. Priddle

Muskrat is an animal that lives near streams, ponds, and rivers. Muskrats get their name from the musklike odor they emit during the breeding season. They live in many parts of North America and have been introduced in some parts of Europe.

Muskrats are suited to life in the water. They use their scaly tails, which are flattened vertically, to help them swim and steer. Their hind feet are fringed with stiff, weblike hairs. Muskrats grow from 16 to 26 inches (41 to 66 centimeters) long, including a 10-inch (25-centimeter) tail. Their light-brown fur is sold as "Hudson seal" after the coarse *guard hairs* have been removed. Muskrat meat, properly prepared, is tasty and sometimes is sold as "marsh rabbit."

Muskrats live in burrows that they dig in the banks of streams. They often damage dikes and levees as they dig. They also make winter houses by plastering such plants as cattails and reeds together with mud. These houses stand out on the icy, snow-covered marshes. Muskrat houses usually have more than one underwater entrance.

Muskrats eat vegetation, especially cattails, bul-rushes, and the roots of water plants. They sometimes eat clams, crayfish, and snails. Minks, raccoons, coyotes, owls, hawks, and alligators prey on muskrats.

Female muskrats give birth to as many as three litters of 1 to 11 young each year. As a result, the muskrat population of an area often increases rapidly. Muskrats are born blind and nearly without fur. The furred young are often called *kits.* Muskrats fight a great deal among themselves. Many of them travel about—even as far as 20 miles (32 kilometers)—to find new homes.

Muskrats are rodents. They are related to lemmings and voles but are larger than these animals. A small, round-tailed muskrat inhabits Florida.

Scientific classification. Muskrats belong to the subfamily Microtinae of the mouse and rat family, Cricetidae. The muskrat

Leonard Lee Rue III, Bruce Coleman Ltd.
A muskrat lives near water and has a long tail.

is classified as *Ondatra zibethicus.*   Charles A. Long

See also **Fur; Trapping.**

Musky. See Muskellunge.

Muslims, *MUHZ luhmz,* also spelled *Moslems,* are people who practice the religion of Islam, preached by Muhammad in the A.D. 600's. *Muslim* is an Arabic word that means *one who submits* (to God). There are Muslim communities throughout the world today. They form the majority of the population in the Middle East, North Africa, and such south and southeast Asian nations as Bangladesh, Indonesia, Malaysia, and Pakistan. There are about 200,000 Muslims in the United States.

The first Muslims, the Arabs, began in the 600's to set up an empire that eventually stretched from the Atlantic Ocean to the borders of China. This empire absorbed many peoples and their cultures. The Muslims have been called the standardbearers of learning during the Middle Ages. They transmitted much of the knowledge of the ancient world, and helped lay the foundations for Western culture. Arab Muslims made such an impact on the Middle East that today much of the area is known as the *Arab world.* Arabic is its major language, and Islam its chief religion.

Early period

Before Muhammad. Islam first began in Arabia. In ancient times, the pagan Arabs were organized into tribes which formed two distinct groups. By 100 B.C., the southern tribes had established several Arab kingdoms. One of the northern tribes, the Quraysh, later gained control of Mecca. This city lay on the main trade route from what is now Yemen to Syria and Egypt. They built the city into a powerful commercial center.

At that time, the Arabs worshiped nature and idols. Their chief gods were al-Lat, al-Uzza, and Manat. The Kaaba, the most famous shrine in Arabia, stood in Mecca. The city attracted religious pilgrims, traders, and settlers from all Arabia and neighboring countries. Jews and Christians mixed freely with the Arabs. Many Arabs were converted to Judaism and Christianity.

The prophet. Muhammad was born about A.D. 570, and grew up in Mecca. He belonged to the Quraysh tribe. Muhammad was disturbed by the injustices of life in Mecca and by the people's worship of idols. When he was about 40, he had a vision in which he was called to be a prophet of God. He began to preach the punishment of evildoers. He urged the Arabs to worship God and to accept him as God's prophet.

The people of Mecca were frightened and angered by Muhammad's preachings, and began to oppose him. Muhammad went secretly to Medina (then called Yathrib), a town about 200 miles (320 kilometers) from Mecca. The people there had agreed to accept him as God's messenger and ruler. Muhammad's *Hegira,* or *Emigration,* took place in A.D. 622. Muslims count that year as the beginning of the Islamic Era. Muhammad began to attack caravans from Mecca. In 630, through diplomacy, he occupied the city. See **Muhammad.**

The spread of Islam

The first caliphs. After Muhammad's death in 632, leaders called *caliphs* led the Muslims. The first four caliphs, called the *rightly guided,* and several famous Arab military leaders accomplished the first major expansion of the Muslim world. This expansion gave the Arabs an important place in world history.

Muhammad gained control of most of Arabia when he took Mecca. But some tribes revolted after his death. Abu Bakr, the first caliph, subdued them and restored them to Islam. He also sent successful Arab forces into the Byzantine provinces of Syria and Palestine, and the Persian province of Iraq. These *holy wars* continued under the caliphs Omar (Umar Ibn al-Khattab in Arabic), who ruled from 634 to 644, and Uthman, who ruled from 644 to 656. The Muslims occupied the Persian capital of Ctesiphon. They also annexed the Byzantine provinces of Syria, Palestine, and Egypt, and part of North Africa. The Persians failed in their last attempt to regain their empire during the caliphate of Ali, who ruled from 656 to 661.

The Umayyad caliphs, who ruled from 661 to 750, led the Arab Muslims to new victories. The caliphate was founded by the caliph Muawiya. He was a member of the aristocratic Meccan family of Umayyah, from which the caliphate takes its name. The Umayyads established their capital at Damascus in 661. They fought the Turkish tribes in Central Asia, sent an expedition into Sindh in India, and reached the borders of China. Under these caliphs, the Muslims also fought the Byzantines in Asia Minor and around the Mediterranean Sea. They twice laid siege to Constantinople (now Istanbul), but without success. The Muslims captured Cyprus, Rhodes, and Sicily, and completed the conquest of North Africa. Many Berbers were converted to Islam.

The Umayyads then turned to Europe, and invaded Spain in 711. A Muslim army crossed the Pyrenees Mountains and marched through southern France until Charles Martel turned it back in 732 in fighting that began near Tours and ended near Poitiers. Many historians regard this battle as one of the most important ever fought, because it determined that Christianity, rather than Islam, would dominate Europe.

Gaining converts. The caliphs did not conquer new lands to gain converts, but many conquered peoples embraced Islam. Unlike the Byzantine Christians, the Muslim conquerors granted a large measure of religious tolerance. All non-Muslims had to pay a special tax in return for not serving in the Muslim army. But many worked as officers and tax collectors in the civil administration and as doctors and tutors at the court. At first, only a few were converted to Islam. Gradually, the Muslims produced their own administrative and professional classes. Beginning about 750, conversion to Islam increased until Islam became the predominant religion in most of the conquered lands.

Division of Islam. From the time of Muhammad's death in 632, several separate groups competed for leadership among the Muslims. In 750, two branches of Muhammad's family, the *Abbasids* and the *Alids,* overthrew the Umayyad caliphate. Dissatisfied Persians helped them. But a youthful Umayyad prince, Abd al-Rahman, escaped and made his way across North Africa to Spain. He subdued and pacified the rival Arab and Berber factions and established the Umayyad dynasty of Spain. The dynasty lasted from 756 to 1031. It had its capital at Córdoba.

In the East, the victors quarreled among themselves. The Abbasids outwitted the Alids and established the

Shostal
The Mosque of Omar, or Dome of the Rock, in Jerusalem covers the rock, *foreground,* from which Muhammad is believed to have ascended to heaven.

Abbasid caliphate, also called the Caliphate of Baghdad. They ruled from 750 to 1258, and built the new capital city of Baghdad. Gradually, the Abbasid empire decayed, and independent dynasties sprang up. The Abbasid empire received its death blow when Baghdad fell to the Mongols in 1258. The Alids, driven underground, agitated as a political and religious minority. One of their religious leaders, Ubaydullah, claimed descent from Fatima, the daughter of Muhammad. He founded the Fatimid dynasty, which lasted from 909 to 1171. This dynasty ruled North Africa, Egypt, Syria, Palestine, the Hejaz, and Yemen. Cairo, Egypt, was its capital. See **Fatimid dynasty.**

Muslim influence in Europe

The Crusades. The Muslims threatened Christian Europe, and several wars resulted. The Christians of eastern and western Europe forgot their differences, and united in a series of wars called the *Crusades.* The Christians conquered Palestine and parts of Syria, and captured Jerusalem in 1099. But a great Muslim general, Saladin, recaptured it in 1187. The crusaders lost ground, and retreated from Acre (now ʿAkko), their last stronghold in Syria, in 1291. See **Crusades.**

Muslim learning. As a result of their conquests, Muslims came into contact with Greek science and philosophy, and Persian history and literature. The Arabs became learned in these fields, and developed a new science and literature of their own in Arabic. Muslim geographers explored many new areas. They also spread knowledge of other discoveries, including the Chinese inventions of paper and gunpowder, and the Hindu system of numerals (see **Arabic numerals**).

The Muslims not only honored learning, but also developed distinctive arts (see **Islamic art**). They also founded many academies and universities. Muslim scholars of many nations traveled freely throughout the

Muslim world. European scholars traveled to Muslim countries, especially Spain, to study Islamic philosophy, mathematics, and medicine. They translated major Arabic works into Latin, the language of learning of the West. In this way, much of the knowledge of the classical world was preserved during the Middle Ages.

The Muslim Turks

Arabs dominated the early spread of Islam, and created the Muslim empire. An alien group, the Turks, invaded Muslim lands, and built their empire on the remains of the Abbasid empire.

The Seljuk Turks. Muslim Turks of Central Asia challenged the Abbasid Caliphate of Baghdad in the 1000's. They were first led by Seljuk, and were named for him. The weak caliph had to receive them and honor their leader Tughril as *sultan.* The Seljuk Turks gained control of the Abbasid caliphs, but the Fatimites fought the Turkish invaders. The Seljuks, who were *Sunnite* Muslims, were among Islam's strongest supporters. After their last strong leader, Malikshah, died in 1092, they split into rival groups. See **Seljuks.**

The Ottoman Turks. Various newly converted Turkish tribes served with the Seljuks. One group, the Ottoman Turks, took their name from their leader Osman, also called Othman. They seized Anatolia in the 1300's and established the Ottoman dynasty. This dynasty held power until 1922 and ruled the greatest Muslim state of modern times. The Ottoman Turks fought the Mongols and put an end to the Byzantine Empire when they seized Constantinople in 1453. Their empire expanded rapidly in Asia and Europe. They conquered the Mameluke dynasty in Egypt in the early 1500's. The Turkish sultans then assumed the title of *caliph.* They fought Christian Europe successfully until halted at Vienna in 1683.

Muslims today

Colonialism. In 1700, three great Muslim empires existed: the Mogul Empire in India, the Safavid Empire in Persia (now Iran), and the Ottoman Empire in Asia Minor (now Turkey). The Mogul and Safavid empires came under the influence of European powers such as Great Britain and Russia and gradually disappeared. European expansion and economic control seriously weakened the Ottoman Empire. By 1900, European colonial powers dominated most of the Muslim world. The French established themselves in North Africa, and the Dutch took Indonesia. Britain occupied Egypt and the Sudan, set up an empire in India, and ruled Malaya. In the 1900's, Italy seized territories in North Africa and the Levant.

European ideas also penetrated into Muslim countries and brought about many changes. Modern education and economic reform spread. The Muslim peoples wanted to be up to date, strong, and independent.

Independence. Most Muslim peoples gained their independence in the 1900's. They form a highly important group of nations that stretches from the Atlantic Ocean to the Philippines. Some of the world's busiest trade and communications routes cross their territories. The chief problems of the newly independent Muslim countries have been to achieve stable governments and to feed their people. Some Muslim nations, such as Bangladesh, Egypt, and Sudan, have too many people living on too little land. Other countries lack the moisture and fertile soil needed to produce food. None is truly industrialized yet. Old quarrels and conflicting interests keep the Muslim peoples from being united. But they are bound by religious and cultural ties and a determination to resist colonialism. Charles J. Adams

See the articles on countries where Muslims live, such as **Egypt**. See also **Islam** with its *Related articles.*

Additional resources

Al Faruqi, Ismail R. and L. L. *The Cultural Atlas of Islam.* Macmillan, 1986.
Muslim Peoples: A World Ethnographic Survey. 2 vols. 2nd ed. Ed. by Richard V. Weekes. Greenwood, 1984.

Muslims, Black. See Black Muslims.

Muslin, *MUHZ luhn,* is a closely woven white or unbleached cloth made from corded cotton yarn. It is named for the city of Mosul, in Iraq, where it was first made. The British call sheer cotton fabrics *muslin.* In the United States, *muslin* means a firm cloth for everyday use. Wide muslin is called *sheeting.* Christine W. Jarvis

Mussel, *MUHS uhl,* is a water animal with a soft body inside a hard shell. Mussels live in the ocean and in fresh water. Their shell consists of two pieces called *valves.* The valves are joined by a hinge and can be opened and closed.

Sea mussels are found attached to rocks and other hard objects on the ocean floor. They often form large mats covering vast areas. They anchor themselves to rocks by means of long, silky threads secreted by a special gland. Sea mussels feed on tiny organisms that are part of the *plankton* (see **Plankton**). These organisms are filtered by the mussels' gills from the surrounding seawater. Several kinds of sea mussels can be eaten. One of these, the *blue mussel,* is also the most common sea mussel. It lives along most coasts. Its shell is bluish-black on the outside and pearly blue inside. It grows to about 3 inches (8 centimeters) in diameter.

Freshwater mussels are found buried in sand bars in rivers, streams, and freshwater lakes. They once were a valuable source of *mother-of-pearl,* which lines the inside of their shells. The mother-of-pearl was used chiefly to make buttons. See **Mother-of-pearl.**

Scientific classification. Mussels are members of the class Bivalvia in the phylum Mollusca. Sea mussels belong to the family Mytilidae. The common blue mussel is *Mytilus edulis.* Freshwater mussels are in the family Unionidae. M. Patricia Morse

See also **Aquaculture; Shell** (pictures); **Zebra mussel.**

Mussels have soft bodies protected by hard shells.

Musset, *myoo SAY,* **Alfred de** (1810-1857), was a French dramatist and poet. Most of his plays were meant to be read rather than performed on stage. Musset is best known for a series of comedies of manners. These works, known collectively as *Comédies et Proverbes,* reflect a witty, poetic style and deep insights into human behavior. His plays deal with the pain of love and with the conflict between innocence and cynical sophistication. Musset's *Lorenzaccio* (1834) was a historical drama set in Florence, Italy. It was first staged in 1896.

Musset was born in Paris. He believed that poetry should express the innermost feelings of the writer and that suffering is essential for the creation of good literature. Among his most famous poems are *Nuits (Nights),* published between 1835 and 1837. They describe his sorrow after the end of his love affair with the famous woman writer George Sand.   Dora E. Polachek

Mussolini, *MOO suh LEE nee* or *moos SOH LEE nee,* **Benito,** *beh NEE toh* (1883-1945), founded fascism and ruled Italy for almost 21 years, most of that time as dictator. He dreamed of building Italy into a great empire, but he led his nation to defeat in World War II (1939-1945) and was executed by his own people.

Early life. Mussolini was born in Dovia, near Forlì, in northeastern Italy. He earned a teaching certificate and briefly taught in an elementary school. From 1902 to 1904, he lived in Switzerland, where he increased his knowledge of socialism. Mussolini served in the Italian military in 1905 and 1906, and then taught school again and became a local socialist leader. In 1909, he went to Trent, Austria (now Trento, Italy), and worked for a socialist newspaper. But Austrian authorities expelled him from Austria for revolutionary activities.

In 1912, Mussolini became editor of the Italian Socialist Party's official newspaper. In this paper, he supported Italian involvement in World War I (1914-1918). Many socialists criticized this position. He then resigned as editor and, in November 1914, founded his own newspaper, *Il Popolo d'Italia,* in which he urged Italy to enter the war against Germany and Austria-Hungary. Later that month, the Socialist Party expelled Mussolini. Italy entered the war in 1915, and Mussolini served in the army until he was wounded in 1917.

United Press Int.

Benito Mussolini used dramatic poses. Clenched fist, jutting jaw, and theatrical actions were all part of his fiery speeches. He gained the support of millions of Italians.

Fascist dictator. In 1919, Mussolini founded the *Fasci di Combattimento* (Combat Groups). This movement appealed to war veterans with a program that supported government ownership of national resources and that put the interests of Italy above all others. In 1921, he transformed the Fasci into the National Fascist Party, adopting a more conservative program to gain the support of property-owning Italians. The Black Shirts, armed squads who supported Mussolini, used violence to combat anti-Fascist groups. In 1922, the Black Shirts staged a March on Rome and forced King Victor Emmanuel III to appoint Mussolini prime minister.

In 1925, Mussolini declared a dictatorship. He abolished other political parties and imposed government control on industry, schools, and the press and police. In 1929, he signed agreements that settled long-standing disputes between the government and the Roman Catholic Church. He also sought to make Italy a *corporate state,* in which the government would help resolve disputes between employers and workers. The powerful Mussolini was called *Il Duce* (The Leader).

Foreign policy. Mussolini sought to make Italy a major power and to create an Italian colonial empire. He invaded and conquered Ethiopia in 1935 and 1936. But this action was condemned by Britain, France, and other countries and drove Mussolini toward an alliance with the German dictator, Adolf Hitler. In 1936, he joined Hitler in sending troops to fight in the Spanish Civil War in support of the rebel leader General Francisco Franco. In 1939, Italy conquered and annexed Albania.

World War II began in 1939, and France and Britain declared war on Germany. After Germany had almost conquered France in 1940, Mussolini entered the war and invaded France. A few days later, France surrendered. But Mussolini's troops soon suffered serious setbacks in North Africa and Greece. They met even stronger opposition after the Soviet Union, and later the United States, joined the war against Italy and Germany.

In July 1943, members of the Italian government deposed Mussolini and restored authority to the king, who then had Mussolini arrested. Mussolini was rescued by German commandos and became the head of a puppet government in northern Italy. In the spring of 1945, the German forces in northern Italy collapsed. On April 27, 1945, Italians opposed to fascism captured Mussolini as he attempted to escape to Switzerland. The next day, he was shot to death.   Philip V. Cannistraro

See also **Fascism; Italy** (History).

Additional resources

Lyttle, Richard B. *Il Duce: The Rise and Fall of Benito Mussolini.* Atheneum, 1987. Suitable for younger readers.
Mack Smith, Denis. *Mussolini.* Knopf, 1982.

Mussorgsky, *moo SAWRG skee* or *MOO sawrg skee,* **Modest,** *moh DEHST* (1839-1881), a Russian composer, was one of the most original composers in the history of Russian music. Mussorgsky was an undisciplined genius with powerful ideas rather than a polished style. He introduced bold and unusual features into his work.

Mussorgsky's place in music rests primarily on his operas and songs. His *Boris Godunov* (1874) is often considered the greatest Russian opera. This opera reflects the composer's interest in native themes and the Russian people. Mussorgsky was a fine singer and pianist and wrote many works for solo voice and for piano. As a song composer, his style ranges from lyrical romances to realistic songs. A number of his realistic songs are set to texts he wrote after observing incidents from everyday Russian life. In these songs Mussorgsky showed a special gift for creating an appropriate vocal line for the rhythms and inflections of Russian speech. His major contribution to piano literature is *Pictures at an Exhibition* (1874). This work is also performed in a version orchestrated in 1922 by the French composer Maurice Ravel.

At the time of his death, Mussorgsky left several unfinished works, including the operas *The Marriage* (Act 1 only, written 1868), *Khovanshchina* (written from 1872 to 1880), and *The Fair at Sorochinsk* (written from 1874 to 1880). Other Russian composers, particularly Mussorgsky's friend Nikolai Rimsky-Korsakov, completed his scores for performance. They corrected features they considered crude by revising much of the music, especially the harmonies and orchestration. The orchestral work *Night on Bald Mountain* (1886) came from Rimsky-Korsakov's reworking of music that had been incorporated into *The Fair at Sorochinsk*. Rimsky-Korsakov's versions of *Khovanshchina* and *Boris Godunov* have most often been performed. Mussorgsky was born in Karevo, near Pskov.   Edward V. Williams

See also **Opera** (Nationalism; *Boris Godunov*).

Mustache. See Beard.

Mustafa Kemal. See Atatürk, Kemal.

Mustang is the name of certain horses that once roamed wild over parts of the American West. Mustangs are descendants of horses brought to America by the Spanish. A large population of wild mustangs developed from the mid-1600's to the mid-1800's. *Mustang* perhaps came from the Spanish word *mesteños* or *mestengo,* meaning *strayed,* or *ownerless, horses.* See also **Cowboy** (His horse).   Geo. H. Waring

Mustard is the name of a family of leafy, annual plants that grow in temperate regions of the Northern Hemisphere. People use a powder or paste made from the seeds of certain mustard plants in salad dressing, to flavor meat, and in preparing pickles and some fish.

Mustard has deep-green leaves that are large, thick,

WORLD BOOK illustration by John D. Dawson

The dark green leaves of the mustard plant make an excellent summer vegetable that is high in vitamin content.

and jagged in shape. The leaves may be harvested while still tender and eaten as greens. The leaves become inedible after the plant sends up its seed stalk.

Mustard is an easy crop to grow. Farmers sow the seeds for the spring crop about two weeks before the last frosts of spring. The seeds for fall crops should be sown about 50 days before the first autumn frosts. Popular varieties include black and white mustard.

Black mustard grows to a height of 6 feet (1.8 meters) or more. Black mustard plants have bright yellow flowers, with smooth pods that lie close to the stem. The seeds are dark brown. Black mustard is the chief source of commercial mustard products.

White mustard grows only about 2 or 3 feet (61 to 91 centimeters) in height. The plant has stiff branching stems, hairy leaves, bristly pods, and small brilliant yellow flowers. Its seeds are yellowish.

Mustard greens are an excellent source of vitamins A, B, and C. In addition, their bulk and fiber tend to have a mildly laxative effect. The oil in mustard seeds gives mustard its strong flavor. It also makes mustard a valuable household remedy. Mixed with warm water, mustard can be used to cause vomiting. It also has been used in a plaster applied to the body to relieve pain.

Scientific classification. Mustards belong to the mustard family, Brassicaceae or Cruciferae. The scientific name for black mustard is *Brassica nigra.* White mustard is *B. hirta.* Most mustards used for greens are *B. juncea.*   Hugh C. Price

Mutation is a change in the hereditary material of an organism's cells. By altering this material, a mutation changes certain traits. Some mutations produce obvious changes. For example, the variety of grape called *Concord* is the result of a mutation. This mutation caused a wild grapevine to produce grapes that were bigger and sweeter than before. Mutations may be transmitted to future generations.

Hereditary material consists of *genes* and *chromosomes.* Genes, which are composed of a substance called *deoxyribonucleic acid* (DNA), determine the hereditary traits of an organism. The genes are lined up along the chromosomes, which are microscopic threadlike bodies. A mutation can affect an individual gene or an entire chromosome. A gene mutation occurs if there are slight chemical changes in DNA. Sickle cell anemia is a blood disease caused by a gene mutation. In a person with this disease, a minor change occurs in the DNA of a gene that controls the production of red blood cells. A chromosome mutation occurs if the number or arrangement of chromosomes changes. Down's syndrome is a mental and physical disorder caused by a chromosome mutation. The disorder occurs if a person is born with an extra copy of a certain chromosome.

Scientists do not know what causes most mutations, even though these changes occur at known rates. Some mutations are caused by such agents as ultraviolet light, X rays, and certain chemicals. Others are caused by *transposable elements*—certain segments of DNA that can change position within the chromosones. Agents that cause mutations are called *mutagens.* The type of mutation that will be caused by a mutagen cannot be predicted.

An organism can pass a mutation on to its offspring only if the mutation affects cells that produce eggs or sperm. This type of mutation is called a *germinal muta-*

tion. The other type of mutation, called a *somatic muta-tion,* occurs in other cells of the body.

A mutation may or may not have a visible effect on the organism that carries it. Most mutations that cause a visible change are harmful. However, some of these mutations enable an organism to survive and reproduce better than other members of its species. Such beneficial mutations—if they are germinal—are the basis of evolution. If the mutant organism passes a beneficial trait on to its offspring, they also will have an advantage in survival and reproduction. After many generations, most members of the species will have the trait.

Breeders use mutations to produce new or improved species of crops and livestock. They do this by breeding certain plants and animals that have one or more favorable mutations. These plants and animals are called *sports.* Daniel L. Hartl

Related articles in *World Book* include:

Antibiotic (Resistance to antibiotics)	Evolution (Mutation)
	Heredity
Breeding	Races, Human (Mutations)
Cell (Metabolic diseases)	Sport
De Vries, Hugo	

Mutiny is any unlawful attempt by military personnel to seize or set aside military authority. The term often refers to an unlawful attempt by a crew to take command of a naval ship. United States military law defines two types of mutiny. One type involves the use of violence or creation of a disturbance by one or more persons acting individually. The second type of mutiny involves two or more people who jointly refuse to obey orders or perform military duties. This type of mutiny need not involve a disturbance. In the United States, the maximum punishment for mutiny is death. See also **Bligh, William; Sepoy Rebellion.** Robert C. Mueller

Mutsuhito, *MOOT soo HEE taw* (1852-1912), reigned as emperor of Japan from 1867 to 1912. Japan developed into an industrial and military power during his reign. He introduced Western ideas into Japan.

He began his reign in a period of confusion. Japan had been ruled by shoguns, or ruling lords, for hundreds of years (see **Shogun**). Japanese noblemen persuaded the shogun to resign in 1867, and restored the ruling power to Emperor Mutsuhito. He adopted as his title *Meiji* (enlightened rule). He is known as the *Meiji emperor.* See **Japan** (History).

Mutsuhito set out to equal the military and economic power of the West. His government sponsored industries, gave the farmers title to their land, instituted education for all his people, and developed up-to-date military forces. He introduced a strong, Prussian-style constitution.

Japan defeated China in 1895, and Russia in 1905. Mutsuhito made an alliance with England in 1902, and added Korea to Japan's territory in 1910. These developments established Japan as a great power.

Mutsuhito was born in Kyoto, a year before Commodore Matthew Perry arrived in Japan. He was enshrined as a god after his death. Marius B. Jansen

See also **Tokyo** (Shrines and temples; picture).

Mutton is meat obtained from sheep that are more than a year old and, in most cases, that weigh more than 100 pounds (45 kilograms). Mutton differs from lamb, which is the meat obtained from sheep less than a year old. Mutton is less tender and has a stronger flavor than lamb. In addition, mutton has a darker color than lamb. This color ranges from dark pink to deep red.

Mutton is a good source of protein, B vitamins, phosphorus, and iron. It is a popular food in Australia, Great Britain, and New Zealand. However, people in Canada and the United States eat very little mutton, and it is usually not available in supermarkets. Donald H. Beermann

See also **Lamb.**

Mutual company is a business owned by the users of the service it provides. Mutual companies include many insurance companies, banks, savings and loan associations, cooperatives, and credit unions. The government gives mutual companies special tax treatment because they do not seek *profit* in the usual sense. Instead, they pass on any *profits* to their members in the form of lower costs or insurance premiums, or higher interest paid on savings deposits. Robert B. Carson

Mutual fund is a company that pools money from many investors and uses it to buy stocks and other securities. The investors receive shares of the mutual fund. The price of a share rises or falls, according to the market prices of securities owned by the fund.

A mutual fund has no fixed number of shares of stock. An investor may buy additional shares from the company at any time. For this reason, mutual funds are also called *open-end investment companies.* They differ from *publicly traded investment funds,* formerly called *closed-end investment companies,* which have a fixed number of shares that are sold on a stock exchange.

Mutual funds are either *load funds* or *no-load funds.* Load funds authorize dealers to sell shares in the fund to investors. The price of a share equals the *net asset value* per share plus a *load.* The net asset value is a price determined by the stock market value of the securities in the fund. The load is a sales charge that includes a commission for the dealer. An investor in a no-load fund buys shares for their net asset value directly from the fund. There is no sales charge. If investors in any mutual fund want to sell their stock, they must sell it back to the fund. The fund must buy its shares back for their approximate net asset value.

Some mutual funds, called *growth funds,* invest mostly in common stocks of companies that have grown rapidly. *Balanced funds* seek more *diversification* (distribution of investments) to reduce risk. They build a *portfolio* (list of securities) that includes bonds as well as stocks. *Income funds* seek higher current income by acquiring bonds and preferred stocks that offer higher than average dividend or interest yields. *Money market funds* invest in Treasury bills and other securities that yield returns closely tied to interest rates. Money market funds usually provide protection against inflation because interest rates rise when inflation is expected to increase. But the rise in interest rates may not provide complete protection.

People buy shares of mutual funds largely because the funds employ professional investment managers. These experts select stocks or bonds that they believe are likely to yield the most profit for the investor. A mutual fund also enables people to own a number of securities. As a result, a mutual fund shareholder has less chance of losing money than a person who invests in only one security. Mutual funds appeal particularly to the small investor because they offer diversification and professional management.   Carol S. Greenwald

See also **Money market fund.**

Mutualism. See Symbiosis.

Mwanamutapa Empire. See Zimbabwe (History).

Myanmar, Union of. See Burma.

Myasthenia gravis, *MY uhs THEE nee uh GRAV ihs,* is a noncontagious disease characterized by progressive weakness of the skeletal muscles. This weakness increases with physical activity but can be partially relieved by rest. The disease afflicts all age groups and both sexes but occurs most frequently among women from 15 to 30 years old and men 40 to 70 years old.

Myasthenia gravis affects primarily the skeletal muscles of the face, neck, arms, and legs (see **Muscle**). Symptoms may include a drooping eyelid; difficulty in chewing, swallowing, and talking; fatigue; and general muscle weakness. Diagnosis can be difficult because the early symptoms are slight and may come and go.

Most researchers believe myasthenia gravis results from a defect at a *neuromuscular junction,* the point where a nerve impulse is transmitted to a muscle. Normally, a substance called *acetylcholine* is released from the nerve ending. Acetylcholine becomes attached to acetylcholine receptor molecules on the muscle surface, causing the muscle to contract. In myasthenia gravis, something causes the acetylcholine receptor molecules to become blocked or to decrease in number.

Researchers suspect that myasthenia gravis is an *autoimmune disease.* In such diseases, the body's immune system, which normally attacks harmful bacteria and viruses, attacks the body's own tissues. The immune system of myasthenia gravis patients appears to attack acetylcholine receptor molecules.

With medication, most patients with myasthenia gravis can live almost completely normal lives. Doctors usually treat symptoms of the disease with drugs, either *anticholinesterases* or *immunosuppressives.* Removal of the thymus gland, a part of the immune system, may be helpful, particularly during the early stages of the illness. In certain advanced cases, a procedure called *plasmapheresis* may be used. In this procedure, the physician withdraws the patient's blood and filters out the immune substances that may be attacking the muscle receptors. The purified blood is then returned to the patient.   Michael S. Hudecki

See also **Thymus.**

Mycenae, *my SEE nee,* was a city in ancient Greece, located 6 miles (10 kilometers) north of Argos in the southern peninsula. German archaeologist Heinrich Schliemann uncovered five royal graves at the site of Mycenae in 1876. This discovery started the study of the Bronze Age on the Greek mainland. These graves, known as the *Shaft Graves,* contained jewels, bronze weapons, and other bronze, gold, and silver objects.

Mycenae was the leading political and cultural center on mainland Greece from about 1400 to 1200 B.C. The Late Bronze Age on the Greek mainland from 1550 to 1100 B.C. is often called the *Mycenaean* period. The city became famous for its royal palace, walled fortress, and beehive-shaped tombs for kings. The tombs can still be seen. The city collapsed during the late 1100's B.C., probably as a result of natural disasters and barbarian invasions. It never regained its power.   Norman A. Doenges

See also **Aegean civilization** (The Mycenaean culture); **Architecture** (Mycenaean architecture); **Ship** (Minoan and Mycenaean ships).

Mycotoxin, *MY kuh TAHK suhn,* is any one of a number of poisonous chemicals produced by fungi. Mycotoxins form on moldy food crops and other plants, though not all molds produce mycotoxins. Crops most often infected by mycotoxins include peanuts, corn, rice, and wheat. Foods or livestock feed made from contaminated crops can poison people and animals. Meat and milk products from animals that have eaten infected grain also may harm humans. Government agencies in the United States and other countries check mycotoxin levels in food and animal feed.

Dampness promotes the formation of molds that produce mycotoxins. Such molds tend to develop in hot, humid regions, but they can also form in cold climates. During the 1940's, for example, thousands of people in the Soviet Union died from eating grain that was left in snow-covered fields and became contaminated. Proper harvesting, drying, and storage of crops help prevent molds that produce mycotoxins from forming.

Research on a group of mycotoxins called *aflatoxins* has suggested that mycotoxins cause other illnesses besides food poisoning. For example, scientists have discovered that feeding low doses of aflatoxin B_1 to laboratory animals can cause liver cancer. As a result, the United Nations' International Agency for Research on Cancer classifies this mycotoxin as a substance that can produce human cancer.   George S. Bailey

Myelitis, *MY uh LY tihs,* is inflammation of the spinal cord. It is often caused by a virus or other infection. Poliomyelitis, multiple sclerosis, and rabies are forms of myelitis. Symptoms of myelitis diseases often include backache and paralysis.   Marianne Schuelein

Myna, *MY nuh,* is the name of several kinds of birds in the starling family. Myna birds are native to India, Burma, and other parts of Asia.

The *common myna* is about the size of an American robin. Its colors range from rich wine-brown on the

WORLD BOOK illustration by John Rignall, Linden Artists Ltd.

The talking myna can imitate human speech even better than a parrot can. This glossy, purplish-black bird measures about 12 to 15 inches (30 to 38 centimeters) long.

lower breast to deep black on the head, neck, and upper breast. It has a splash of white on the lower edge of its wings, and its bill and legs are a bright yellow. This myna feeds on plants, insects, and worms. It often builds its nest in crevices of buildings. It is a noisy bird that is common about yards and buildings. It is often seen among chickens or perched on the backs of cattle. People have released the common myna into the wild in many tropical Pacific islands, including Hawaii, where the bird is now abundant.

Talking mynas are sometimes kept as pets. Many imitate the human voice and can talk, sing, and whistle.

Scientific classification. Mynas are in the starling family, Sturnidae. The common myna is *Acridotheres tristis.* The talking myna is *Gracula religiosa.*   David M. Niles

Myocardial infarction. See Coronary thrombosis.
Myocarditis, *MY oh kahr DY tihs,* is inflammation of the muscle tissue that forms the heart's wall. This muscle, called the *myocardium,* performs the pumping work of the heart. Mild cases of myocarditis may remain undetected. Severe cases can lead to *heart failure,* in which the heart cannot pump enough blood for the body's needs.

Causes of myocarditis include rejection of transplanted tissue and reactions to viruses and toxic chemicals. But in most cases, the cause is never identified.

Many symptoms of heart disease may accompany myocarditis. These symptoms include weakness, shortness of breath, and accumulation of fluids. Irregular heartbeats and enlargement of the heart may also accompany myocarditis. Doctors can detect these two signs with X rays and *electrocardiograms* (measurements of heart activity). However, to reach a final diagnosis of myocarditis, doctors must examine the heart tissue through a microscope. The tissue is obtained with a *catheter,* a long tube that is inserted into the heart by way of a blood vessel.

There is no established treatment for myocarditis. Many patients recover completely. Others live for years with the condition. Some myocarditis patients die from heart failure, which may occur during periods of acute inflammation of the myocardium or years after inflammation.   Toby R. Engel

Myopia. See Nearsightedness.
Myrdal, *MIHR dahl,* **Alva Reimer** (1902-1986), a Swedish diplomat and sociologist, gained fame for promoting nuclear disarmament and world peace. From 1962 to 1973, she headed Sweden's delegation to the United Nations Disarmament Conference in Geneva, Switzerland. Myrdal shared the 1982 Nobel Peace Prize with Alfonso García Robles of Mexico. She was the author of *The Game of Disarmament* (1976) and *War, Weapons, and Everyday Violence* (1977), plus several other books and numerous articles on disarmament.

Myrdal was born in Uppsala, Sweden. She graduated from the University of Stockholm and received a master's degree from the University of Uppsala. Myrdal became Sweden's first woman ambassador. From 1955 to 1961, she served as the country's ambassador to four nations at the same time—Burma, Ceylon (now Sri Lanka), India, and Nepal. Myrdal was a member of Sweden's parliament from 1962 to 1970. She served as minister of disarmament and church affairs in the Swedish Cabinet from 1967 to 1973. Her husband, Gunnar Myrdal, won

the 1974 Nobel Prize in economics. The Myrdals were the only married couple to win the Nobel Prize in different categories.   James W. Vander Zanden
Myrdal, *MIHR dahl,* **Gunnar** (1898-1987), was a Swedish sociologist and economist. He gained fame for his thorough studies of major world problems. His book *An American Dilemma: The Negro Problem and Modern Democracy* (1944) is considered an outstanding study of race relations in the United States. Myrdal's studies of the economic and social development of underdeveloped nations led him to write *Asian Drama: An Inquiry into the Poverty of Nations* (1968). This book tries to tell why so many people of southern Asia are poor, and what, if anything, can be done about it.

Myrdal shared the 1974 Nobel Prize in economics with Friedrich von Hayek of Austria. His wife, Alva R. Myrdal, was a winner of the 1982 Nobel Peace Prize (see **Myrdal, Alva R.**).

Karl Gunnar Myrdal was born in Gustafs, near Sandviken, Sweden. He received a law degree and a doctor of laws in economics degree from the University of Stockholm. He was minister of commerce in the Swedish Cabinet from 1945 to 1947. He served as executive secretary of the United Nations Economic Commission for Europe from 1947 to 1957. In 1960, he became director of the Institute of International Economic Studies in Stockholm.   James W. Vander Zanden
Myrrh, *mur,* is a fragrant gum resin that has been used as a raw material for perfumes since ancient times. It also has been burned as an incense, and used in medicines and in *embalming* (preserving bodies). The Bible says that one of the wise men brought Jesus a gift of myrrh (Matt. 2). Myrrh comes from trees of the genus *Commiphora* found mainly in Saudi Arabia and Ethiopia. The tree discharges the resin from between the outer layers of the bark, and the resin falls to the ground. The perfume ingredient is an oil obtained by heating the resin to produce a vapor, then cooling the vapor.

Patricia Ann Mullen

Myrtle, *MUR tuhl,* is an attractive evergreen shrub or small tree. It grows wild in regions along the Mediterranean Sea and temperate regions of Asia. Some people in the United States cultivate it as an ornamental plant. The myrtle has shiny leaves and fragrant white flowers. The leaves, bark, and blue-black berries are also fra-

© Giuseppe Mazza

The myrtle has shiny leaves and fragrant flowers.

grant. Manufacturers use them in making perfume. The bark is used in tanning industries of southern Europe. Ancient Greeks thought myrtle was sacred to the goddess of love, Aphrodite. They used it in festivals.

The *common periwinkle* is often called *running myrtle.* It has creeping stems and attractive blue flowers.

Scientific classification. Common myrtles belong to the myrtle family, Myrtaceae. Their scientific name is *Myrtus communis.* The common periwinkle is in the dogbane family, Apocynaceae. It is *Vinca minor.*   Walter S. Judd

See also **Bayberry; Guava; Pimento.**

Mysteries, in religion, are secret ceremonies. They may be witnessed or participated in only by people who belong to, or are about to join, the group that practices them. A person joins a group that practices mysteries by undergoing a process of initiation. This process ordinarily includes indoctrination, moral testing, and a rite of purification. Those who are initiated promise never to reveal the group's secret ceremonies and doctrines. Mysteries have been part of many religions. The secrets of early mysteries were so well kept that our knowledge of them is incomplete.

Mysteries were important in ancient Greece and in ancient Rome, beginning in the 600's B.C. One of the most famous Greek mysteries was practiced by a cult in the city of Eleusis near Athens. In late summer, members of the cult performed what were known as the Eleusinian Mysteries. These mysteries were based on the worship of Demeter—the goddess of agriculture, fertility, and grain. Initiation into the cult included a symbolic cleansing in seawater. Those who joined the cult were promised happiness in an afterlife.

In ancient Rome, mysteries were practiced by members of a cult called *Mithraism.* Mithraism, which was practiced only by men, became popular among Roman soldiers. Cult members worshiped Mithra, the god of light who was originally worshiped by inhabitants of Persia. Initiation into Mithraism included a symbolic washing in the blood of a sacrificial animal.

Other mysteries practiced in ancient times were connected with the worship of the god Dionysus in Greece or the goddesses Cybele and Isis in Rome. Mysteries also became part of religious worship in early Christianity. Christians received the Eucharist in secret rituals. However, after Christianity became the official religion of the Roman Empire in the early 300's, the sacraments became more public.   Jill Raitt

See also **Demeter; Mithra.**

Mystery play, a form of Biblical drama, was popular in England from the 1370's until about 1600. Mystery plays were produced and acted by local trade and craft organizations called *guilds.* The term *mystery play* came into use because guilds were sometimes known as *masteries* or *mysteries.* The plays were also called *Corpus Christi plays* because most were presented during the feast of Corpus Christi in late May or June.

Mystery plays dramatized stories from both the Old and New Testaments. Popular subjects included the life of Christ, Adam and Eve, Abraham and Isaac, and Noah and the Flood. Many mystery plays combined biblical scenes with references to local places and events. The plays were staged outdoors, probably on large carts called *pageant wagons.* These wagons were drawn through a town to various places where spectators stood in the street or watched from nearby houses. Each guild in a town was responsible for one episode or play. Mystery plays were presented in cycles of several related dramas. A cycle may have taken one or two days.

The authors of mystery plays, though unknown, were probably members of the guild. Texts of cycles of mystery plays from the towns of Chester, Wakefield, and York have been preserved.   Albert Wertheim

See also **Drama** (Medieval drama); **Miracle play; Morality play.**

Mystery story. See Detective story.

Mystic Seaport, a reconstructed waterfront village, is a reminder of maritime life in the days of the great sailing ships. It lies on the Mystic River in Mystic, Conn. For location, see **Connecticut** (political map).

Waterfront buildings and shops typical of the early and mid-1800's stand along Mystic Seaport's cobblestone streets. The *Australia,* the oldest American schooner afloat, and the *Charles W. Morgan,* New England's last wooden whaleship, are moored at the Seaport's docks. Sea Scouts and other youths learn sailing skills aboard these famous old sailing ships. Mystic Seaport also has one of the finest collections of clipper ship models in America. The Marine Historical Association established Mystic Seaport in 1929. Each year, thousands of tourists visit the village.   John L. Allen

See also **Connecticut** (picture).

Mysticism, *MIHS tuh sihz uhm,* is the belief that God or spiritual truths can be known through individual insight, rather than by reasoning or study. All the major religions include some form of mysticism.

A person who has mystical experiences is called a *mystic.* Most mystics find such experiences difficult to describe. Many say they have visions or hear inner voices that reveal a spiritual truth. Some mystics feel that their spirits fly out of their bodies or become possessed by a higher power. During these experiences, mystics may feel ecstasy or great peace.

Mystics differ in their practice and experiences, even within the same religion. However, most mystics share three basic goals: (1) knowledge of a spiritual reality that exists beyond the everyday world, (2) spiritual union with some higher power, and (3) freedom from selfish needs and worldly desires. To attain these goals, most mystics undergo some form of self-discipline. For example, they may isolate themselves from material comforts and other people. In addition, their discipline may involve extremes of mental and physical activity. Buddhist mystics may meditate for hours or even days without moving. Jews who belong to the Hasidic group often shout and twist their bodies while praying. Some members of the Islamic Sufi sect go into a trance as they perform a whirling dance.

Mysticism has played a prominent role in many religions. Devout Buddhists and Hindus may dedicate their lives to the mystical search for direct spiritual experience. Christian mystics have included several Roman Catholic saints and the Quakers. In Islam, Judaism, and other religions that emphasize the role of a supreme God, mystics may believe that their experiences result from divine actions. In religions in which many gods are worshiped, such as Hinduism and Taoism, mystics may attribute their insights to their own individual efforts.

Nancy E. Auer Falk

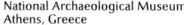

National Archaeological Museum,
Athens, Greece

© Lee Boltin

Ny Carlsberg Glyptotek,
Copenhagen, Denmark

The gods and goddesses of mythology served many functions. The Greeks worshiped Athena, *left,* as the goddess of wisdom and warfare. Xipe Tótec, *center,* was the Aztec god of vegetation. The ancient Egyptian god Anubis, *right,* helped judge the souls of dead people in the underworld.

Mythology

Mythology. People have always tried to understand why certain things happen. For example, they have wanted to know why the sun rises and sets and what causes lightning. They have also wanted to know how the earth was created and how and where humanity first appeared.

Today, people have scientific answers and theories for many such questions about the world around them. But in earlier times—and in some parts of the world today—people lacked the knowledge to provide scientific answers. They therefore explained natural events in terms of stories about gods, goddesses, and heroes. For example, the Greeks had a story to explain the existence of evil and trouble. The Greeks believed that at one time the world's evils and troubles were trapped in a box. They escaped when the container was opened by Pandora, the first woman. Such stories are known as *myths,* and the study of myths is called *mythology.*

In early times, every society developed its own myths, which played an important part in the society's religious life. This religious significance has always separated myths from similar stories, such as folk tales and legends. The people of a society may tell folk tales and leg-

ends for amusement, without believing them. But they usually consider their myths sacred and completely true.

Most myths concern *divinities* (divine beings). These divinities have *supernatural* powers—powers far greater than any human being has. But in spite of their supernatural powers, many gods, goddesses, and heroes of mythology have human characteristics. They are guided by such emotions as love and jealousy, and they experience birth and death. A number of mythological figures even look like human beings. In many cases, the human qualities of the divinities reflect a society's ideals. Good gods and goddesses have the qualities a society admires, and evil ones have the qualities it dislikes.

By studying myths, we can learn how different societies have answered basic questions about the world and the individual's place in it. We study myths to learn how a people developed a particular social system with its many customs and ways of life. By examining myths, we can better understand the feelings and values that bind members of society into one group. We can compare the myths of various cultures to discover how these cultures differ and how they resemble one another. We can also study myths to try to understand why people behave as they do.

For thousands of years, mythology has provided material for much of the world's great art. Myths and mythological characters have inspired masterpieces of architecture, literature, music, painting, and sculpture.

C. Scott Littleton, the contributor of this article, is Professor of Anthropology at Occidental College and the author of The New Comparative Mythology.

Most myths can be divided into two groups—*creation myths* and *explanatory myths.* Creation myths try to explain the origin of the world, the creation of human beings, and the birth of gods and goddesses. All early societies developed creation myths. Explanatory myths try to explain natural processes or events. The Norse, who lived in medieval Scandinavia, believed that the god Thor made thunder and lightning by throwing a hammer at his enemies. The ancient Greeks believed that the lightning bolt was a weapon used by the god Zeus. Many societies developed myths to explain the formation and characteristics of geographic features, such as rivers, lakes, and oceans.

Some explanatory myths deal with illness and death. Many ancient societies—as well as some primitive present-day societies—believed that a person dies because of some act by a mythical being. The people of the Trobriand Islands in the Pacific Ocean believed that men and women were immortal when the world was new. When people began to age, they swam in a certain lagoon and shed their skin. They quickly grew new skin, renewing their youth. One day, a mother returned from the lagoon with her new skin. But her unexpected youthful appearance frightened her little daughter. To calm the child, the mother returned to the lagoon, found her old skin, and put it back on. From then on, according to this myth, death could not be avoided.

Some myths, through the actions of particular gods and heroes, stress proper behavior. The ancient Greeks strongly believed in moderation—that nothing be done in excess. They found this ideal in the behavior of Apollo, the god of purity, music, and poetry. Myths about national heroes also point up basic moral values. The story about young George Washington's confession that he had cut down his father's cherry tree has no basis in fact. Yet many people like to believe the story because it emphasizes the quality of honesty.

Mythical beings fall into several groups. Many gods and goddesses resemble human beings, even though they have supernatural powers. These gods and goddesses were born, fell in love, fought with one another, and generally behaved like their human worshipers. These divinities are called *anthropomorphic,* from two Greek words meaning *in the shape of man.* Greek mythology has many anthropomorphic divinities, including Zeus, who was the most important Greek god.

Another group of mythical beings includes gods and goddesses who resemble animals. These characters are called *theriomorphic,* from two Greek words meaning *in the shape of an animal.* Many theriomorphic beings appear in Egyptian mythology. For example, the Egyptians sometimes represented their god Anubis as a jackal or a dog.

A third group of mythical beings has no specific name. These beings were neither completely human nor completely animal. An example is the famous sphinx of Egypt, which has a human head and a lion's body.

Human beings play an important part in mythology. Many myths deal with the relationships between mortals and divinities. Some mythical mortals have a divine father and a mortal mother. These human characters are called *heroes,* though they do not always act heroically in the modern sense. Most stories about heroes are called *epics* rather than myths, but the difference between the two is not always clear.

Mythical places. Many myths describe places where demons, gods and goddesses, or the souls of the dead live. Most of these places are in the sky or on top of a high mountain. The people believed that the divinities could see everything, and so they located them in a place higher than mortals could reach.

Mythical places exist in the mythologies of most peoples. Perhaps the most sacred place in Japanese mythology is Mount Fuji, the tallest mountain in Japan. During part of their history, the Greeks believed their divinities lived on a mythical Mount Olympus that was separate from the visible Mount Olympus in northern Greece.

The Greeks also believed in mythical places beneath the ground, such as Hades, where the souls of the dead lived. The Norse believed in Hel, an underground home for the souls of all dead persons, except those killed in battle. The souls of slain warriors went to Valhalla, which was a great hall in the sky. The Eskimos believe that their sea goddess, Sedna, lives in a world under the ocean.

Mythical symbols. In their mythologies, people used many symbols to help explain the world. The Greeks symbolized the sun as the god Helios driving a flaming chariot across the sky. The Egyptians represented the sun as a boat.

The separation of the earth from the sky is described in many mythologies. According to Egyptian mythology, the god Shu, *standing center,* raised the sky goddess, Nut, away from her husband, the earth god, Geb, *lying down.* Nut's body thus formed the heavens.

Animals, human beings, and plants have all stood for ideas and events. Some peoples adopted the serpent as a symbol of health because they believed that by shedding its skin, the serpent became young and well again. The Greeks portrayed Asclepius, the god of healing, holding a staff with a serpent coiled around it. Today, that staff symbolizes the medical profession. It is often confused with the *caduceus* of the god Mercury, which has two snakes coiled around it. In Babylonian mythology, the hero Gilgamesh searched for a special herb that made anyone who ate it immortal. Plants can also have opposite meanings. In the Bible, Adam and Eve ate the forbidden fruit and lost their immortality.

Comparing myths. We study the similar myths of various societies by comparing them to one another. We can compare these myths on the basis of their generic, genetic, or historical relationships.

Generic relationships among myths are based on the way people react to common features in their environment. For example, the Maoris of New Zealand and the ancient Greeks both had myths that described how the earth became separated from the sky.

Genetic relationships. A large society may develop a particular myth. Then, for some reason, the society breaks up into several separate societies, each of which develops its own version of the myth. These myths have a genetic relationship.

Myths about the Greek god Zeus and the ancient Indian god Indra have a genetic relationship. The two gods resemble each other in many ways. For example, each is a sky god, and each uses a lightning bolt as his chief weapon. These similarities can be explained by the fact that the ancient Greeks and the people of ancient India descended from a common culture, the Indo-European community. The Indo-Europeans lived several thousand years ago in the area north of the Black Sea, in southeastern Europe. This culture worshiped a warrior god who ruled the sky. One group of Indo-Europeans migrated westward to what is now Greece. There, they developed a sky god who became known as Zeus. Another group of Indo-Europeans, the Aryans, migrated southward into northern India. They developed the warlike sky god Indra.

Historical relationships appear when similar myths develop among cultures that do not share a common origin. For instance, many ancient Near and Middle Eastern societies had a myth in which several generations of sons overthrew their fathers, who ruled as gods or kings. Variations of this myth appeared in Greece and Iran, among the Hittites in what is now Turkey, and among the Phoenicians in what is now Lebanon. Many scholars believe all versions of the myth came from a Babylonian myth dating from about 2000 B.C.

In the 700's B.C., the Greek poet Hesiod wrote a long poem called the *Theogony.* In this poem, Hesiod described the origin of the world and the history of the gods. The *Theogony* contains Greek myths that have generic, genetic, and historical relationships with myths of other cultures. For example, Hesiod describes how the earth became separated from the sky. This myth is generically related to a similar Maori myth. Zeus, a major figure in the *Theogony,* genetically resembles the Indian god Indra. Hesiod also wrote about successive generations of Greek gods being overthrown by their sons. This myth is historically related to similar myths in other cultures of the ancient Near and Middle East.

Oil painting on canvas by N. A. Abilgaard; Royal Museum of Fine Arts, Copenhagen, Denmark

The creation of life is the subject of many myths. According to a Teutonic myth, the giant Ymir and the cow Audhumla became the first living things. They were born out of melting ice. Audhumla's milk fed Ymir. As the cow licked the ice for its salt, she freed the body of Buri, a second giant. Buri was the ancestor of the first race of gods.

The Nile River plays an important part in Egyptian mythology. As the Nile flows northward through Egypt, it creates a narrow ribbon of fertile land in the midst of a great desert. The sharp contrast between the fertility along the Nile and the wasteland of the desert became a basic theme of Egyptian mythology. The creatures that live in the Nile or along its banks became linked with many gods and goddesses.

The Great Ennead. The earliest information we have about Egyptian mythology comes from *hieroglyphics* (picture writings) on the walls of tombs, such as the burial chambers in pyramids. These "pyramid texts" and other documents tell us that from about 3200 to 2250 B.C. the Egyptians believed in a family of nine gods. This family became known as the *Great Ennead,* from the Greek word *ennea,* meaning *nine.* The nine gods of the Great Ennead were Atum, Shu and Tefnut, Geb and Nut, Osiris, Isis, Nephthys, and Horus.

The term *Ennead* later came to include other deities as well. One of these deities was Nun, who symbolized a great ocean that existed before the creation of the earth and the heavens. Another of these deities was the sun god, called Re or Ra. The Egyptians considered Re both the ruler of the world and the first divine pharaoh.

The first god of the Great Ennead was Atum. He was sometimes identified with the setting sun. Atum also represented the source of all gods and all living things. Re created a pair of twins, Shu and his sister, Tefnut. Shu was god of the air, which existed between the sky and the earth. Tefnut was goddess of the dew. Shu and Tefnut married and also produced twins, Geb and his sister, Nut. Geb was the earth god and the pharaoh of Egypt. Nut represented the heavens. Geb and Nut married, but the sun god Re opposed the match and ordered their father, Shu, to raise Nut away from Geb into the sky. Shu's action separated the heavens from the earth. Nut had speckles on her body, and the speckles became the stars.

The Osiris myth. In spite of their separation, Geb and Nut had several children. These included three of the most important divinities in Egyptian mythology—Osiris, Isis, and Seth.

Important divinities in Egyptian mythology

The ancient Egyptians portrayed many of their gods and goddesses with human bodies and the heads of birds or other animals. The divinities held or wore objects symbolizing their power. For example, the god Osiris held a scepter and a whip, which represented the authority of gods and divine pharaohs.

WORLD BOOK illustrations by George Suyeoka

Horus   Hathor   Anubis   Isis   Nephthys   Osiris

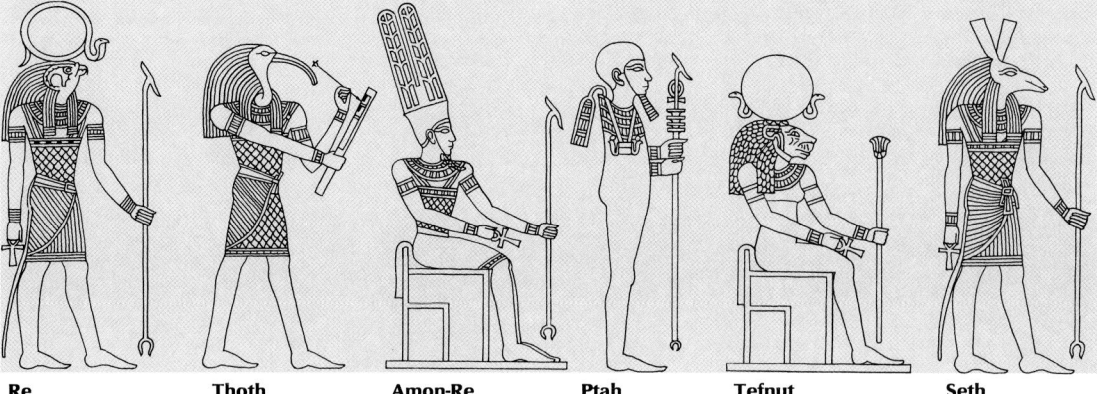

Re   Thoth   Amon-Re   Ptah   Tefnut   Seth

Originally, Osiris may have been god of vegetation, especially of the plants that grew on the rich land along the Nile. The goddess Isis may have represented female fertility. Seth was god of the desert, where vegetation withers and dies from lack of water.

Geb retired to heaven. Osiris then became pharaoh and took Isis as his queen. Seth grew jealous of Osiris' position and killed him. In some versions of this myth, Seth cut Osiris' body into pieces, stuffed the pieces into a box, and set the box afloat on the Nile. Isis refused to accept her husband's death as final. She searched for Osiris' remains with the aid of her sister Nephthys and several other gods and goddesses. Isis finally found the remains of Osiris. With the help of other divinities, she put the body together, restoring Osiris to life. Osiris then became god of the afterlife.

Seth had become pharaoh of Egypt after killing Osiris. But Horus, son of Osiris and Isis, then overthrew Seth and became pharaoh. Thus, the forces of vegetation and creation—symbolized by Osiris, Isis, and Horus—triumphed over the evil forces of the desert, symbolized by Seth. But more important, Osiris had cheated death. The Egyptians believed that if Osiris could triumph over death, so could human beings.

Other Egyptian divinities included Hathor, Horus' wife; Anubis; Ptah; and Thoth. Hathor became the protector of everything feminine. Anubis escorted the dead to the entrance of the afterworld and helped restore Osiris to life. The Egyptians also believed that Anubis invented their elaborate funeral rituals and burial procedures. Ptah invented the arts. Thoth invented writing and magical rituals. He also helped bring Osiris back to life.

Many animals appear in Egyptian mythology. The falcon was sacred to Horus. The scarab, or dung beetle, symbolized Re (see **Scarab**). The Egyptians considered both the cat and the crocodile as divine.

Between 1554 and 1070 B.C., various local divinities became well known throughout ancient Egypt. Some of them became as important as the gods and goddesses of the Ennead. The greatest of these gods was Amon. His *cult* (group of worshipers) originally centered in Thebes. In time, Amon became identified with Re, and was frequently known as Amon-Re. Amon-Re became perhaps the most important Egyptian divinity.

The influence of Egyptian mythology. The divinities of ancient Egypt and the myths about them had great influence on the mythologies of many later civilizations. Egyptian religious ideas may also have strongly affected the development of Judaism and Christianity.

During the 1300's B.C., the pharaoh Amenhotep IV chose Aton as the only god of Egypt. Aton had been a little-known god worshiped in Thebes. Amenhotep was so devoted to the worship of Aton that he changed his own name to Akhen*aton.* The Egyptians stopped worshiping Aton after Akhenaton died. However, some scholars believe the worship of this one divinity lingered among the people of Israel, who had settled in Egypt, and became an important part of the religion that was developed by the Israelite leader Moses. These scholars have suggested that the Jewish and Christian belief in one God may come from the cult of Aton. See **Akhenaton.**

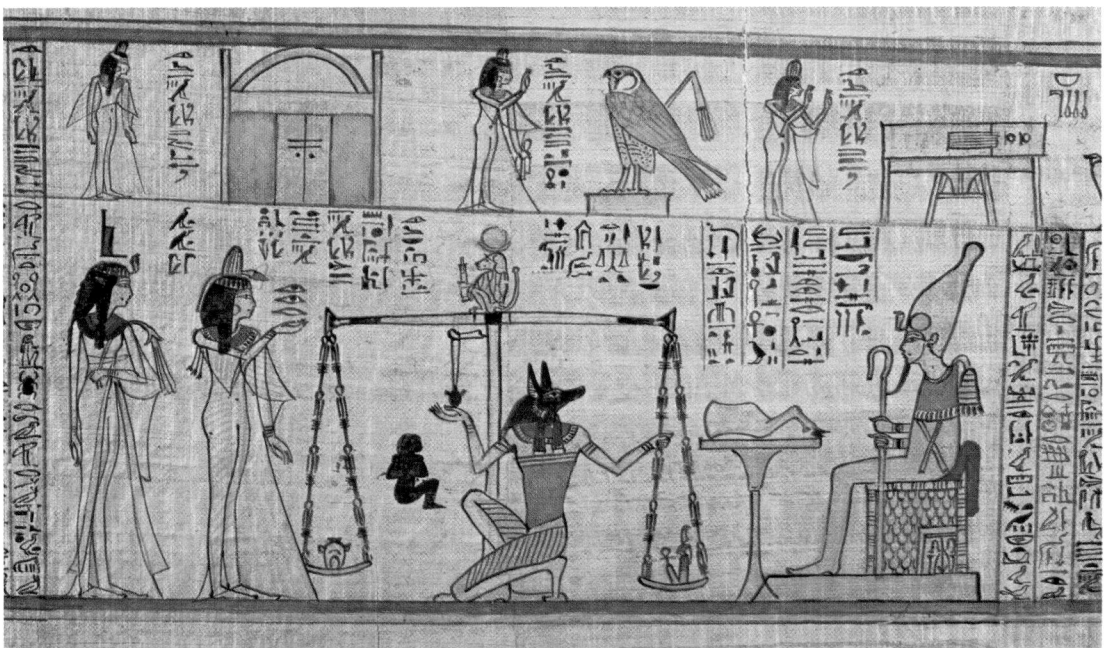

Detail of a papyrus scroll (about 1025 B.C.); Metropolitan Museum of Art, New York City, Museum Excavations and Rogers Fund, 1930

Osiris, Egyptian god of the afterlife, judged the souls of the dead. In this scene, the jackal-headed god Anubis uses a balance scale to weigh a human heart, in the left pan, against objects representing truth and justice, in the right pan. Osiris, sitting at the right, makes the judgment.

The earliest record of Greek mythology comes from clay tablets dating back to the Mycenaean civilization, which reached its peak between 1400 and 1200 B.C. This civilization consisted of several cities in Greece, including Mycenae. The clay tablets describe the chief Mycenaean god as Poseidon. He reappeared in later Greek mythology as a major figure. The god Zeus, who later became the chief god in Greek mythology, played a lesser part in Mycenaean myths.

About 1200 B.C., the Mycenaean civilization fell. During the 1100's B.C., Dorians from northwestern Greece moved into lands that had been held by the Mycenaeans. In the next 400 years, known as the Dark Age of ancient Greece, the Dorian and Mycenaean mythologies combined, helping form classical Greek mythology. See **Dorians.**

The basic sources for classical Greek mythology are three works that date from about the 700's B.C.: the *Theogony* by Hesiod and the *Iliad* and the *Odyssey,* attributed to Homer. Hesiod and Homer rank among the greatest poets of ancient Greece. The *Theogony* and the *Iliad* and *Odyssey* contain most of the basic characters and themes of Greek mythology.

The creation myth. The *Theogony* includes the most important Greek myth—the myth that describes the origin and history of the gods. According to the *Theogony,* the universe began in a state of emptiness called *Chaos.*

The divinity Gaea, or Earth, arose out of Chaos. She immediately gave birth to Uranus, who became king of the sky. Gaea mated with Uranus, producing children who were called the *Titans.*

Uranus feared his children and confined them within the huge body of Gaea. Gaea resented the imprisonment of her children. With Cronus, the youngest Titan, she plotted revenge. Using a sickle provided by Gaea, Cronus attacked Uranus and made him *impotent* (unable to breed children). Cronus then freed the Titans from inside Gaea. Because Uranus was impotent, Cronus became king of the sky. During his reign, the work of creating the world continued. Thousands of divinities were born, including the gods or goddesses of death, night, the rainbow, the rivers, and sleep.

Cronus married his sister Rhea, who bore him three daughters and three sons. But Cronus feared that he, like Uranus, would be deposed by his children. He therefore swallowed his first five children as soon as they were born. To save her sixth child, Zeus, Rhea tricked Cronus into swallowing a stone wrapped in baby clothes. Rhea then hid the infant on the island of Crete. After Zeus grew up, he returned to challenge his father. He tricked Cronus into drinking a substance that made him vomit his children. The children had grown into adults while inside their father. Zeus then led his brothers and sisters in a war against Cronus and the other Ti-

Detail of a painting (300's B.C.) on a Greek vase; the Louvre, Paris

The Greek gods fought the giants after the gods had defeated the Titans. The giants were born from the blood of Uranus, father of the Titans. In this scene, Zeus, *center,* strikes at the giants with a thunderbolt. Hercules, *kneeling,* aims an arrow at a giant. Athena, *lower left,* attacks another giant with her spear.

The Building of the Trojan Horse (about 1760), an oil painting by Giovanni Domenico Tiepolo;
Wadsworth Atheneum, Hartford, Conn., Ella Gallup Sumner and Mary Catlin Sumner Collection

The Greeks built the Trojan horse, hid several soldiers inside, and left it outside the walls of
Troy. The Trojans believed the horse was a gift from the Greeks and pulled it into the city. After
dark, the soldiers sneaked out and opened the city gates for the Greek army.

tans. Zeus and his followers won the war. They exiled
the Titans in chains to Tartarus, a dark region deep
within the earth. The victorious gods and goddesses
chose Zeus as their ruler and agreed to live with him on
Mount Olympus. The divinities who lived on Olympus
became known as *Olympians.*

Greek divinities can be divided into several groups.
The earliest group was the Titans, led by Cronus. The
most powerful group was the Olympians. Several ranks
of divinities existed among the Olympians. The top rank
consisted of six gods and six goddesses. The gods were
Zeus, ruler of all divinities; Apollo, god of music, poetry,
and purity; Ares, god of war; Hephaestus, blacksmith for
the gods; Hermes, messenger for the gods; and Poseidon, god of earthquakes and the ocean. The goddesses
were Athena, goddess of wisdom and war; Aphrodite,
goddess of love; Artemis, twin sister of Apollo and goddess of hunting; Demeter, goddess of agriculture; Hera,
sister and wife of Zeus; and Hestia, goddess of the
hearth.

Three important gods became associated with the 12
Olympians. They were Hades, ruler of the underworld
and brother of Zeus; Dionysus, god of wine and wild
behavior; and Pan, god of the forest and pastures.

There were several groups of minor divinities in
Greek mythology. Beautiful maidens called *nymphs*
guarded various parts of nature. Nymphs called *dryads*
lived in the forest, and nymphs called *Nereids* lived in
the sea. Three goddesses called *Fates* controlled the
destiny of every man. The *Muses* were nine goddesses
of various arts and sciences. All these divinities became
the subjects of specific myths and folk tales.

Greek mythology also has a number of partly mortal,
partly divine beings called *demigods.* Heracles (called
Hercules by the Romans) probably ranked as the most
important demigod. Heracles symbolized strength and
physical endurance. Another demigod, Orpheus, became known for his beautiful singing.

Nearly all the Greek gods, goddesses, demigods, and
other divinities became the subjects of cults. Many cults
became associated with cities. People of Delphi, famous
for its *oracle* (prophet), especially worshiped Apollo (see
Delphi). People of Athens looked to Athena as their protector. Ephesus became the center of the cult of Artemis.
The Temple of Artemis in Ephesus was one of the Seven
Wonders of the Ancient World (see **Seven Wonders of
the Ancient World**).

Greek heroes became almost as important as the divinities in Greek mythology. Heroes were largely or entirely mortal. They were born, grew old, and died. But
they still associated with the divinities. Many heroes
claimed gods as their ancestors.

Most Greek heroes and heroines can be divided into
two main groups. The first group came before the Trojan War, and the second group fought in the war.

The most famous heroes before the Trojan War include Jason, Theseus, and Oedipus. Jason led a band of
heroes called the Argonauts on a search for the fabu-
lous Golden Fleece, the pure gold wool of a sacred ram.
Theseus killed the Minotaur, a monster with the body of
a man and the head of a bull. Oedipus, the king of
Thebes, unknowingly killed his father and married his
mother. Oedipus' story has been popular with artists
and writers for more than 2,000 years.

Detail of a marble relief from a
Greek coffin; the Louvre, Paris

The Muses were Greek goddesses of the arts and sciences. They included Terpsichore (dance), holding a lyre; Urania (astronomy), with a globe; and Melpomene (tragedy), with a mask.

Painting (420 to 410 B.C.) on a Greek cup; courtesy of
the Museum of Fine Arts, Boston, Pierce Fund

The centaurs, in Greek mythology, were part human and part horse. In one myth, pictured here, a centaur attempted to attack Deianira, the wife of Hercules. But Hercules rescued her.

The Trojan War was fought between Greece and the city of Troy. The war began after Helen, wife of the king of Sparta, fled to Troy with Paris, son of the Trojan king. The Greeks organized an army to attack Troy and bring Helen back to Greece. Our knowledge of the war comes chiefly from the *Iliad* and *Odyssey.*

The Greek heroes who participated in the Trojan War included Agamemnon, the commander in chief; Mene-laus, Helen's husband; and Odysseus (Ulysses in Latin), the clever general who formed a plan that finally led to Troy's defeat. Achilles was the most famous Greek warrior, and the major Trojan heroes were Hector and Paris. The gods and goddesses participated in the war almost as much as the heroes. Nearly all the divinities sided with the Greeks. The major exception was the goddess of love, Aphrodite.

Greek and Roman divinities

Many gods and goddesses of Greek mythology held similar positions in Roman mythology. For example, each mythology had a goddess of love. The Greeks called her Aphrodite. The Romans called her Venus. The table below lists the most important Greek and Roman divinities.

Greek	Roman	Position
Aphrodite	Venus	Goddess of love
Apollo	Apollo	God of light, medicine and poetry
Ares	Mars	God of war
Artemis	Diana	Goddess of hunting and childbirth
Asclepius	Aesculapius	God of healing
Athena	Minerva	Goddess of crafts, war, and wisdom
Cronus	Saturn	In Greek mythology, ruler of the Titans and father of Zeus; in Roman mythology, also the god of agriculture
Demeter	Ceres	Goddess of growing things
Dionysus	Bacchus	God of wine, fertility, and wild behavior
Eros	Cupid	God of love
Gaea	Terra	Symbol of the earth and mother and wife of Uranus
Hephaestus	Vulcan	Blacksmith for the gods and god of fire and metalworking
Hera	Juno	Protector of marriage and women. In Greek mythology, sister and wife of Zeus; in Roman mythology, wife of Jupiter
Hermes	Mercury	Messenger for the gods; god of commerce and science; and protector of travelers, thieves, and vagabonds
Hestia	Vesta	Goddess of the hearth
Hypnos	Somnus	God of sleep
Pluto, or Hades	Pluto	God of the underworld
Poseidon	Neptune	God of the sea. In Greek mythology, also god of earthquakes and horses
Rhea	Ops	Wife and sister of Cronus
Uranus	Uranus	Son and husband of Gaea and father of the Titans
Zeus	Jupiter	Ruler of the gods

To many people, Roman mythology largely seems a copy of Greek mythology. The Romans had come into contact with Greek culture during the 700's B.C., and afterward some of their divinities began to reflect the qualities of Greek gods and goddesses. But before that time, the Romans had developed their own mythology. In fact, many of the basic similarities between Roman and Greek mythology can be traced to the common Indo-European heritage shared by Rome and Greece.

Roman divinities. Before the Romans came into contact with Greek culture, they worshiped three major gods—Jupiter, Mars, and Quirinus. These gods are known as the *archaic triad,* meaning *old group of three.* Jupiter ruled as god of the heavens and came to be identified with Zeus. Mars was god of war. He occupied a much more important place in Roman mythology than did Ares, the war god in Greek mythology. Quirinus apparently represented the common people. The Greeks had no similar god.

By the late 500's B.C., the Romans began to replace the archaic triad with the *Capitoline triad*—Jupiter, Juno, and Minerva. The triad's name came from the Capitoline Hill in Rome, on which stood the main temple of Jupiter. In the new triad, Jupiter remained the Romans' chief god. They identified Juno with the Greek goddess Hera and Minerva with Athena.

Between the 500's and 100's B.C., additional Roman mythological figures appeared, nearly all based on Greek divinities. These Roman divinities, with their Greek names in parentheses, included Bacchus (Dionysus), Ceres (Demeter), Diana (Artemis), Mercury (Hermes), Neptune (Poseidon), Pluto (Hades), Venus (Aphrodite), and Vulcan (Hephaestus).

In addition to Greek-inspired divinities, the Romans worshiped many native gods and goddesses. These included Faunus, a nature spirit; Februus, a god of the underworld; Pomona, goddess of fruits and trees; Terminus, god of boundaries; and Tiberinus, god of the Tiber River.

Romulus and Remus. In their mythology, the Romans—unlike the Greeks—tried to explain the founding and history of their nation. Thus, the Romans came to consider their divinities as historical persons. The best example of this historical emphasis is the story of Romulus and Remus, the mythical founders of Rome.

The ancient Romans believed that Romulus and Remus were twins born of a mortal mother and the war god, Mars. Soon after their birth, they were set afloat in a basket on the Tiber River. A she-wolf found the babies and cared for them. Finally, a shepherd discovered the twins and raised them to adulthood.

Romulus and Remus decided to build a city at the spot on the Tiber where the wolf had found them. In a quarrel, Romulus or one of Romulus' followers killed Remus. Romulus then founded Rome, supposedly in 753 B.C. The Romans believed that Romulus became the city's first king and established most of the Roman political institutions.

The seven kings. According to Roman mythology, Romulus was the first of seven kings who ruled Rome from its founding until the early 500's B.C. The kings after Romulus were Numa Pompilius, Tullus Hostilius,

Ancus Marcius, Lucius Tarquinius Priscus, Servius Tullius, and Lucius Tarquinius Superbus. The seven kings became known for various achievements. For example, Numa started many of Rome's basic religious institutions. Tullus Hostilius was a warlike king who conquered the Albans, an Italian tribe that lived southeast of Rome.

There is little evidence that the seven early kings of Rome ever existed or that any of the events connected with their reigns ever took place. Some scholars believe these kings probably originated as divinities, whom the Romans converted into historical figures. The kings and the gods have many similarities. For example, Romulus resembles Jupiter because both were primarily rulers, not military leaders. Tullus Hostilius resembles Mars.

The *Aeneid.* During the 200's B.C., the Romans tried to relate the origins of their divinities to Greek myths. About the time of the birth of Christ, the Roman poet Virgil wrote an epic poem called the *Aeneid.* Virgil modeled the *Aeneid* on the *Iliad* and the *Odyssey* by Homer. Virgil tried to connect the origins of Rome to the events that followed the fiery destruction of Troy by the Greeks.

The *Aeneid* traces the wanderings of the Trojan hero Aeneas, who escaped unharmed from the burning city. He stopped for a time in the city of Carthage in northern Africa. There, he rejected the love of Dido, queen of Carthage. He then sailed for Italy and, in time, landed near the mouth of the Tiber River. After many adventures, Aeneas founded a town. Aeneas' son, Ascanius, later moved the town to Alba Longa, where Romulus and Remus were born. Virgil thus connected the founding of Rome with the Trojan War, a significant event in Greek mythology. See **Aeneid.**

Relief on a Roman altar (A.D. 124); Museo Nazionale Romano, Rome (photo by Raymond V. Schoder)

Romulus and Remus were the mythical founders of Rome. A wolf nursed the twins, *lower left,* after they were abandoned as babies. One of the shepherds, *above,* later found the boys.

Many thousands of islands lie scattered throughout the Pacific Ocean. A rich tradition of myths and mythological figures flourished among the numerous cultures of the islands until the late 1800's, when many of the people became Christians. Some non-Christian cultures have retained their traditional mythologies. In addition, some Christians have kept parts of their native mythologies. See **Pacific Islands.**

Creation myths. Some cultures of the Pacific Islands believed that heaven and the earth always existed. These cultures therefore developed no myths about the creation of the world. Many cultures also assumed that the ocean, which plays such a vital part in Pacific Islands life, always existed.

Some island cultures believed that gods created the world. Other cultures thought the world developed slowly from a great emptiness. According to this myth, the earth and the sky first existed close together and then separated. Several versions of the myth explain how this separation occurred. One example comes from the Maoris of New Zealand. The Maoris have a myth in which the sky, Rangi, loved the earth, Papa. Rangi and Papa gave birth to many gods, who became crushed in the embrace of their parents. In order to survive, the gods separated the earth and the sky, so that life could exist between them.

Pacific Islands divinities. Many similarities existed among the major divinities of the Pacific Islands cultures. Many islanders worshiped a god called Tangaroa. In the New Hebrides (now Vanuatu), he and another divinity ruled the world jointly. In Tahiti, he was a human being who became a divinity.

The most famous demigod among the islands of Polynesia was Maui. According to some myths, Maui created the Hawaiian Islands by fishing them up from the ocean. One of the Hawaiian Islands is named after him. The Polynesians also credited this demigod with teaching human beings how to make fire and do other useful things.

The people of the Pacific Islands believed in the existence of little people similar to the dwarfs and elves of European folklore. The Hawaiians called these people the *menehune.* Pacific Islanders believed the menehune were responsible for events that could not otherwise be explained. For example, if a worker finished a job faster than expected, the menehune was given the credit for the worker's unexplainable speed. If a wall was so old that nobody could remember who built it, the people decided the menehune must have put it up.

Wood sculpture with beaten bark cloth, 22 ½ inches (57 centimeters) high; Museum of Man, Paris

The fire goddess Pele was worshiped in many parts of Polynesia. The Hawaiians believed she lived in the volcano Kilauea. When the goddess became angry, the volcano erupted.

Mana and taboo. The idea of *mana* was important in Pacific Islands mythology. The islanders considered mana an impersonal, supernatural force that flowed through objects, persons, and places. A person who succeeded at a difficult task had a large amount of mana. However, a warrior's defeat in battle showed that the warrior had lost mana. The islanders believed certain animals, persons, and religious objects had so much mana that contact with them was dangerous for ordinary people. These mana-filled beings and objects were thus declared *taboo* (forbidden to touch). The islanders believed a person who touched a taboo object would suffer injury or even death. See **Taboo.**

African mythology

A wide variety of mythologies has developed among the many peoples that live in Africa south of the Sahara. Some of these mythologies are simple and primitive. Others are elaborate and complicated.

The majority of African peoples worship prominent features in nature, such as mountains, rivers, and the sun. Most of these peoples believe that almost everything in nature contains a spirit. Some spirits are friendly, but others are not. Spirits may live in animals, plants, or lifeless objects. Worshipers pray or offer gifts to the spirits to gain their favor and obtain particular benefits from them.

Ancestor worship forms part of many African mythologies. Many Africans believe that, after death, the souls of their ancestors are reborn in living things or in objects. For example, the Zulus refuse to kill certain kinds of snakes because they believe the souls of their ancestors live in those snakes.

Magic plays a major role in the traditional religions of Africa. Priests have great influence among many African peoples because the priests are believed to have magical powers. Many Africans wear charms to protect themselves from harm.

According to several African mythologies, many divinities live in temporary homes on the earth called *fetishes* (see **Fetish**). Fetishes vary from simple stones to beautifully carved images. Some African groups believe that fetishes protect them from evil spells and bring them good luck.

The Ashantis make up the largest native group in Ghana, a small country in western Africa. In many ways, the mythology of the Ashantis illustrates African mythology in general.

Many Ashantis believe that a supreme god called Nyame created the universe. Nyame heads a large group of divinities, most of whom descended from him. Some of these divinities serve as protectors of specific villages or regions. Others represent geographic features. The Ashantis regard rivers as the most sacred geographic feature. They also associate many divinities with specific occupations and crafts, such as farming and metalworking.

Among the Ashanti divinities, only the earth goddess lacks a specific fetish. The Ashantis believe the earth itself is the fetish of the earth goddess. A group of priests supervises the worship of fetishes. The Ashantis believe that their priests possess certain special powers. For example, according to the Ashantis, the priests can persuade a fetish to speak through the lips of a human agent called a *medium*. A priest usually serves as the medium for the fetish. For more information on African mythology, see the *Religions* section of the article **Africa**.

Wooden statue, 31 ½ inches (80 centimeters) high; Musée Royale de l'Afrique Centrale, Tervuren, Belgium (Art Reference Bureau)

Fetish figures like this one of the Songe, a people of Zaire, are used to protect village property. Animal skin, beads, and other materials are added to increase a figure's powers.

Celtic mythology

The Celts were an ancient people of Indo-European origin. Most Celts lived in what is now southwestern Germany until about 500 B.C. They then began settling throughout western Europe, especially in the British Isles. See **Celts**.

Most of our information on Celtic mythology is about mythical characters and events in the British Isles, particularly in Ireland. During the Middle Ages, Irish monks preserved many ancient Celtic myths in several collections of manuscripts. The most important collection of manuscripts is the *Lebor Gabala (Book of Conquests)*, which traces the mythical history of Ireland. Another important collection of manuscripts, *The Mabinogion,* comes from Wales. The first four stories in this collection are called the "Four Branches of the Mabinogi." These stories describe the mythical history of Britain. The Welsh myths show a much stronger Christian influence than do the Irish myths. The Welsh myths also tend to emphasize human characters. The Irish myths deal more with divinities.

The Irish cycles. A great deal of Irish Celtic mythology concerns three important *cycles* (series of related stories). These cycles are (1) the mythological cycle, (2)

the Ulster cycle, and (3) the Fenian cycle.

The mythological cycle, the oldest cycle, is preserved in the *Lebor Gabala.* The cycle describes the early settlement of Ireland through a succession of invasions by five supernatural races. The most important race was the Tuatha De Danann, or People of the Goddess Danu. The Tuatha De Danann was the fourth of the five invading races. They defeated two other races, the Firbolgs and the Fomoirans, and were in turn defeated by the Sons of Mil, also called the Milesians. The Tuatha De Danann were the source of most of the divinities that the Irish people worshiped before they became Christians in the A.D. 400's.

The Ulster cycle centers on the court of King Conchobar at Ulster, probably about the time of Christ. The stories deal with the adventures of Cuchulainn, a great Irish hero who can also be considered a demigod. In some ways, he resembled the Greek hero Achilles. But unlike Achilles and other Greek heroes, Cuchulainn had many supernatural powers. For example, he could spit fire in battle. He was also a magician and poet.

Many stories about Cuchulainn appear in the Ulster cycle. Probably the best known is *The Cattle Raid of*

Cooley. In this story, Queen Mave of Connaught ordered a raid on Ulster to capture a famous brown bull. Cuchulainn single-handedly fought off the invaders until the queen's forces finally captured the bull. However, the Ulster warriors led by King Conchobar came to Cuchulainn's aid and drove the invaders out of the country. Queen Mave plotted revenge against Cuchulainn and several years later used supernatural means to cause his death. See **Cuchulainn.**

The Fenian cycle describes the deeds of the hero Finn MacCool and his band of warriors known as the *Fianna*. Finn and the Fianna were famous for their great size and strength. In addition, Finn was known for his generosity and wisdom. Although divine beings and supernatural events play a part in these stories, the central characters are human. Some scholars believe the events in the Fenian cycle may reflect the political and social conditions in Ireland during the A.D. 200's.

The most famous story in the Fenian cycle is called "The Pursuit of Diarmuid and Grainne." In this story, Finn was to marry Grainne, the daughter of an Irish king. However, she fell in love with Diarmuid, Finn's friend and nephew, and persuaded Diarmuid to elope with her. Finn and his warriors pursued the lovers. Much of the story concerns the adventures of Diarmuid and Grainne as they fled Finn.

Finally, Finn caught Diarmuid and Grainne and indirectly caused the death of Diarmuid. At first, Grainne hated Finn, but he courted her until she became his wife. See **Finn MacCool.**

Welsh myths. Two races of divinities appear in Welsh mythology—the Children of Don and the Children of Llyr. Both races partly resemble the Tuatha De Danann in Irish mythology, possibly because many Irish Celts migrated to Britain and brought their mythology with them.

The most famous Welsh myths concern King Arthur and his knights. The mythical King Arthur was probably based on a powerful Celtic chief who lived in Wales

Scene from the Gundestrup caldron (80 B.C.); National Museum of Denmark, Copenhagen

The Celtic god Cernunnos protected horned animals. He is shown wearing horns. He holds a collar, representing cosmic truth, and a snake, symbolizing prosperity and good fortune.

during the A.D. 500's. Some stories about Arthur and his knights can be traced to such early Welsh literature as the "Four Branches of the Mabinogi." One of these stories tells of the knights' search for the Holy Grail, the cup Christ used at the Last Supper. Some scholars say the Christian myth of the Holy Grail originated in this story.

Teutonic mythology

Teutonic mythology consists of the myths of Scandinavia and Germany. It is sometimes called *Norse* mythology, after the Norsemen who lived in Scandinavia during the Middle Ages. The basic sources for Teutonic mythology consist of two works, called *Eddas*. They were oral poems that were written down in the 1200's (see **Edda**). Other information on Teutonic mythology comes from legends about specific families and heroes and from German literary and historical works of the Middle Ages.

The creation of life. According to the Eddas, two places existed before the creation of life—Muspellsheim, a land of fire, and Niflheim, a land of ice and mist. Between them lay Ginnungagap, a great emptiness where heat and ice met. Out of this emptiness came Ymir, a young giant and the first living thing. A second creature soon appeared, a cow named Audumla. Ymir lived on Audumla's milk. As Ymir matured, he gave birth to three beings. He bore them from his armpits and

from one leg. The first divine family was thus born.

Meanwhile, a second giant, Buri, was frozen in the ice of Niflheim. Audumla licked the ice off his body, freeing him. Buri created a son named Bor, who married the giantess Bestla. They had three sons—Odin, Ve, and Vili. The sons founded the first race of gods.

The construction of the world. After Odin became an adult, he led his brothers in an attack on the giant Ymir and killed him. Odin then became supreme ruler of the world. The gods defeated the giants in battle, but the giants planned revenge on their conquerors.

Odin and his brothers constructed the world from Ymir's body. His blood became the oceans, his ribs the mountains, and his flesh the earth. The gods created the first man from an ash tree and the first woman from an elm tree. They also constructed Asgard, which became their heavenly home. Valhalla, a great hall in Asgard, was the home of warriors killed in battle.

Many divinities lived in Asgard. These divinities were

called the *Aesir,* just as the leading Greek gods and goddesses were called the Olympians. The ruler of Asgard was Odin. Thor, Odin's oldest son, was god of thunder and lightning. Balder, another of Odin's sons, was god of goodness and harmony. Other divinities included Bragi, the god of poetry, and Loki, the evil son of a giant. The most important goddesses included Frigg, Odin's wife; Freyja, goddess of love and beauty; and Hel, goddess of the underworld.

A giant ash tree known as Yggdrasil supported all creation. In most accounts of Yggdrasil, the tree had three roots. One root reached into Niflheim. Another grew to Asgard. The third extended to Jotunheim, the land of the giants. Three sisters called Norns lived around the base of the tree. They controlled the past, present, and future. A giant serpent called Nidoggr lived near the root in Niflheim. The serpent was loyal to the race of giants defeated by Odin. It continually gnawed at the root to bring the tree down, and the gods with it.

Teutonic heroes. Sigurd the Dragon Slayer probably ranks as the most important hero in Teutonic mythology. He appears in a Scandinavian version of German myths about a royal family called the Volsungs. Sigurd became the model for the mythical German hero Siegfried, who appears in the *Nibelungenlied,* a famous German epic of the Middle Ages. Other heroes in Teutonic mythology include Starkad, who was a mortal friend of Odin's, and the Danish warrior Hadding. See **Nibelungenlied.**

The end of the world. Unlike many other major Western mythologies, Teutonic mythology includes an *eschatology* (an account of the end of the world). According to Teutonic mythology, there will be a great battle called *Ragnarok.* This battle will be fought between the giants, led by Loki, and the gods and goddesses living in Asgard. All the gods, goddesses, and giants in the battle will be killed, and the earth will be destroyed by fire. After the battle, Balder will be reborn. With several sons of dead gods, he will form a new race of divinities. The human race will also be re-created. During Ragnarok, a man and woman will take refuge in a forest and sleep through the battle. After the earth again becomes fertile, the couple will awake and begin the new race of human beings. The new world, cleansed of evil and treachery, will endure forever.

American Indian mythology

At the time that Christopher Columbus landed in the New World, Indians lived throughout North and South America. The Indians had many different ways of life and many distinct mythologies. But all the mythologies shared several features. Most Indians believed in the supernatural, including a great variety of gods. The Indians created elaborate religious ceremonies through which they hoped to gain supernatural powers to aid them in searching for food or in fighting enemies. Indian mythologies have many heroes who gave man his first laws and established basic social institutions. Many mythologies describe the end of the world through some great disaster, such as a fire or flood. For more information on the religion of the Indians, see **Indian, American** (Religion).

The Aztec Indians of central Mexico developed one of the most interesting Indian mythologies. The Aztec established a highly advanced civilization that lasted from the A.D. 1300's to 1521. In 1521, Spanish troops led by Hernando Cortés conquered the Aztec. Advanced cultures, such as those of the Toltec and Maya, had existed in Mexico before the Aztec came to power. The Aztec borrowed many of their divinities from these earlier Indian cultures. In addition, the Aztec conquered many of the neighboring Indian peoples. As these peoples became part of the Aztec empire, many of their divinities became part of the Aztec mythology. The Aztec thus developed an extremely complicated mythology, composed of gods of earlier Indian civilizations, their own gods, and gods of the peoples they had conquered.

The Aztec believed the universe had passed through four ages called *suns* and that they were living in the fifth sun. The gods had ended each previous sun with a worldwide disaster and then created a new world. At the end of the first sun, the world was destroyed by jaguars. At the end of the second sun, a hurricane de-

Illustration from the *Codex Borbonicus,* Library of the National Assembly, Palais Bourbon, Paris

The Aztec god Quetzalcóatl was a god of the wind and the protector of the arts. His portrait shows how the Aztec clothed their divinities in colorful and complicated religious symbols.

stroyed the earth. At the end of the third sun, fire rained from the sky and destroyed the world. At the end of the fourth sun, the world ended with a flood. The Aztec believed they were living in the fifth sun and that the world would end with an earthquake.

The chief Aztec divinity was probably the war god, Huitzilopochtli. The Aztec worshiped Tezcatlipoca, a sun god, under four forms, each identified with a specific color and direction. Almost every Indian civilization in Mexico worshiped the god Quetzalcóatl. The Aztec associated him with the arts. Tláloc, the rain god, was probably the oldest god in Aztec mythology. His wife or sister, Chalchiuhtlicue, was goddess of running water. She protected newborn children, marriage, and innocent love. Tlazoltéotl was goddess of pleasure and guilty love. Farming formed the basis of the Aztec economy, and so the people worshiped many agricultural divinities. The most important of these divinities included Centéotl, the maize god; Chicomecóatl, the goddess of agricultural abundance; and Xipe Totec, the god of vegetation.

In Aztec mythology, souls of the dead lived in separate places, depending on how death occurred. For example, a place called Tonatiuhichan was reserved for warriors and victims of religious sacrifices. Other places were reserved for persons who had drowned or for women who had died in childbirth. Most souls passed to Mictlan, an underworld ruled by Mictlantecuhtli and his wife, Mictlancíhuatl. A statue of Xólotl, an Aztec god of death, is reproduced in the introduction to the **Sculpture** article.

Human sacrifice played an important role in Aztec religion. The Aztec held great ceremonies and festivals during which they offered human hearts to Huitzilopochtli and the other major divinities. The Aztec slashed open the chests of their sacrificial victims and tore out their hearts. Most of the victims were prisoners of war. The Aztec considered the victims as representatives of the gods themselves. During the period up to their deaths, some victims were dressed in rich clothing, given many servants, and treated with great honor. The Aztec believed that the souls of the sacrificial victims flew immediately to Tonatiuhichan and lived there forever in happiness.

How myths began

For at least 2,000 years, scholars have speculated about how myths began. Some believe myths began as historical events that became distorted with the passage of time. Others think myths resulted from an attempt to explain natural occurrences that people could not understand. Scholars have also developed other theories of how myths began. None of these theories answers all the questions about myths, but each contributes to an understanding of the subject.

Euhemerus' theory. Euhemerus, a Greek scholar who lived during the late 300's and early 200's B.C., developed one of the oldest known theories about the origin of myths. He was one of the first scholars to suggest that all myths are based on historical facts. Euhemerus believed that scholars had to strip away the supernatural elements in a myth to reach these facts. For example, he felt that Zeus was probably modeled on an early king of Crete who had such great power that he inspired many supernatural tales. Euhemerus' theory has one basic weakness. In most cases, modern scholars lack enough historical evidence to determine whether a mythical figure ever existed.

Müller's theory. Friedrich Max Müller was a German-born British language scholar of the late 1800's. He suggested that all gods and mythical heroes were representations of nature, especially the sun. To Müller, nearly all major divinities and heroes were originally a symbol for the sun in one of its phases. Thus, the birth of a hero stood for the dawn. The hero's triumph over obstacles stood for the sun at noon, its highest point. The hero's decline and death expressed the sunset.

Müller decided that by the time such basic texts as the *Theogony* and the *Rig-Veda* appeared, the symbolic purpose of the gods and heroes had long been forgotten. Instead, people had come to believe in the divinities and heroes themselves. For example, the ancient Greeks believed that the sun god Helios drove his flaming chariot, the sun, across the sky every day. This belief began in an earlier attempt to express symbolically how each day the sun rose in the east and set in the west.

Today, few scholars take Müller's main theories seriously. However, he and his followers did influence most later theories about the origin of myths.

Tylor's theory. Sir Edward Burnett Tylor was an English anthropologist of the 1800's. He believed that myths began through people's efforts to account for unexplainable occurrences in dreams. According to Tylor, the first idea about the supernatural was the belief that a soul lived within the human body. While the body slept, the soul could wander freely and have many adventures. These adventures appeared to people in dreams. People then came to believe that animals had souls. Finally, they decided that everything in nature had a soul. They could then explain, according to Tylor, such natural events as the eruption of a volcano. Gradually, people came to believe that the souls controlling natural occurrences could answer prayers for protection or special favors. The idea that all things in nature have souls is called *animism* (see **Animism**). Tylor considered animism the first step in the development of human thought—and the basis of myths.

Frazer's theory. Sir James George Frazer was a Scottish anthropologist of the late 1800's and early 1900's. He believed that myths began in the great cycle of nature—birth, growth, decay, death, and rebirth.

Frazer's theory developed from his attempt to explain an ancient Italian *ritual* (ceremony) conducted at Nemi, near Rome. At Nemi, there was a sacred grove of trees. In the middle of the grove grew a huge oak tree associated with the god Jupiter. A priest presided over the grove and the oak tree. Frazer's curiosity and interest were aroused by the way priests were replaced. To be-

The Trojan warrior Aeneas receives weapons from his mother, Venus, to use in the Trojan War. Aeneas survived Troy's defeat by the Greeks and founded a colony in Italy. The ancient Romans traced their origin as a nation to Aeneas. According to the ancient Greek scholar Euhemerus, all myths are based on historical events, such as the Trojan War.

Venus, Mother of Aeneas, Presenting Him with Arms Forged by Vulcan (1635), an oil painting on canvas by Nicolas Poussin; Art Gallery of Ontario, Toronto, gift of the Reuben Wells Leonard estate, 1948

come the priest, a man had to kill the current priest with a branch of mistletoe taken from the top of the oak. If the man succeeded, he proved that he had more vigor than the presiding priest and thus had earned the position.

Frazer's study of the Nemi ritual developed into one of the most ambitious anthropological works ever attempted, *The Golden Bough* (12 volumes, 1890-1915). In writing this work, Frazer made a broad study of ancient and primitive mythologies and religions. He concluded that the priests at Nemi were killed as a sacrifice. The ancient Italians believed that when a priest began to lose his vigor, so did Jupiter. As Jupiter became less vigorous, so did the world. For example, winters became longer and the land became less fertile. To keep the world healthy, the priest, representing Jupiter, had to be killed and then reborn in the form of the more vigorous slayer.

Frazer wrote that societies throughout the world sacrificed symbols of their gods to keep these gods—and thus the world—from decaying and dying. According to Frazer, this theme of the dying and reborn god appears in almost every ancient mythology, either directly or symbolically. Frazer therefore concluded that myths originated from the natural cycle of birth, growth, decay, death, and—most important—rebirth.

The ritualist theory. Closely related to Frazer's ideas were those of the so-called *ritualists.* The ritualists believed that myths derive from rituals or ceremonies. The first scholar to develop this theory was Jane Ellen Harrison, a British classicist of the late 1800's and early 1900's and a colleague of Frazer's. Harrison argued that people create myths in order to justify already established magical or religious rituals. Harrison believed that many

myths become the scripts for such rituals.

Fitzroy Richard Somerset, known as Lord Raglan, an English nobleman of the early 1900's, was perhaps the most influential of the ritualists. His best-known theory concerns the life of the typical hero figure. Raglan pointed out that all heroes or hero-gods share a number of common characteristics. He suggested a "ritualistic formula" that included an unusual or difficult conception, a youthful exile, a triumphant return to claim a rightful inheritance, a successful reign followed by a final downfall, and a mysterious death in which the hero's mortal remains disappear. Thus, Raglan regarded such figures as Moses, King Arthur, Robin Hood, and Leif Ericson as fictitious.

Today, few mythologists seriously consider this theory. It is now generally believed that myths and rituals are equally ancient and that it is impossible to prove that one is older than the other. Other modern scholars have disproved Raglan's assumption that all heroes are fictitious. However, by emphasizing the sacred contexts in which many myths are told, the ritualists broadened the scope of mythology and influenced other scholars.

Malinowski's theory. Bronislaw Malinowski was a Polish-born British anthropologist of the early 1900's. He disagreed with Tylor that myths began as prescientific attempts to explain dreams and natural occurrences. Instead, Malinowski emphasized the psychological conditions that lead people to create myths.

According to Malinowski, all people recognize that a frontier exists between what people can and cannot explain logically. Malinowski said people create myths when they reach this frontier. For example, early human beings lacked the scientific knowledge to explain thunder logically, and so they decided it was caused by a god using a hammer. Malinowski believed that people had to create such myths in order to relieve the tension brought on by their not knowing why something happens.

Jensen's theory. Adolf E. Jensen, a German anthropologist of the early and middle 1900's, was influenced by the ideas of Frazer and the ritualists. While conducting field research among an Indonesian tribe called the Wemale, Jensen discovered a myth-ritual associated with the beautiful and virtuous goddess called Hainuwele. Falsely accused of all kinds of crimes, Hainuwele was torn to pieces by an angry mob. Later, her body parts were buried around the edge of the village. From each part sprouted one of the major Wemale food plants. In the Wemale dialect, a figure such as Hainuwele is called a *dema*.

Jensen suggested that similar *dema deities* exist in the mythologies of a variety of primitive cultures in the Pacific Islands, Africa, and North and South America. Other modern scholars have discovered dema deities in several Near Eastern and Indo-European mythologies. Examples include the Babylonian goddess Tiamat, from whose corpse the sky god Marduk formed the world, and the Norse giant Ymir, whose dismembered remains served a similar purpose in Teutonic mythology. Although dema deities are probably not universal, they are extremely widespread and may play an important role in most of the world's mythologies.

Lévi-Strauss's theory. Many modern scholars have applied the methods developed by linguists to the study of mythology. These scholars believe that a set of interpreted myths serves as a form of language. People use myths to express—for the most part unconsciously—their deeply held ideas about themselves and their relationship to the world around them. This approach to mythology is often referred to as *structuralism.*

Claude Lévi-Strauss, a modern French anthropologist,

is the best-known supporter of structuralism. According to Lévi-Strauss, a myth's basic purpose is to resolve an otherwise unresolvable contradiction. Illustrating this theory is his interpretation of the Oedipus myth. In this ancient Greek story, Oedipus, the king of the city of Thebes, unknowingly kills his father and marries his mother. When the truth is revealed to him, Oedipus leaves Thebes with his children and dies in exile.

In explaining the meaning of the Oedipus myth, Lévi-Strauss groups together episodes that share common characteristics. He also considers the whole story, not simply the part that Oedipus plays in it. In the story, Oedipus' great-grandfather, Cadmus, kills a dragon, and Oedipus himself kills a monster called the Sphinx. Lévi-Strauss suggests that both actions reflect people's triumph over the forces of nature, represented by the dragon and the Sphinx.

However, a contrasting theme also appears in the myth. The Greek word *Oedipus* means *swollen foot,* and Oedipus' father, Laius, and his grandfather, Labdacus, also had names that refer to difficulties in walking. The choice of names reflects the extent to which humanity can never escape nature. According to Lévi-Strauss, such themes must be fully explored before one can understand the "deep structure" of the Oedipus myth. Lévi-Strauss believes such corresponding deep structures exist in all myths.

Some scholars argue that Lévi-Strauss's theories are too subjective. Other critics claim that his structural models are too far removed from the actual mythological texts to say anything meaningful about them. Nevertheless, the structuralist approach has had a profound impact on modern mythological studies. The idea that myths and other traditional narratives reflect a deep-seated model of some sort is accepted by most anthropologists and by most scholars who study myths, legends, and folklore.

What mythology tells us about people

Many social scientists have developed theories telling how we can learn about people from the myths they tell. Some of these theories stress the role of myths in understanding society as a whole. Other theories emphasize the place of mythology in understanding why an individual acts in a certain way.

Mythology and society. During the late 1800's and early 1900's, the French sociologist Émile Durkheim developed several important theories on what he felt was the real meaning of myths. Durkheim believed that every society establishes certain social institutions and values, which are reflected in the society's religion. Therefore, according to Durkheim, most of a society's gods, heroes, and myths are really *collective representations* of the institutions and values of that society or of important parts within it. These representations determine how the individuals in the society think and act. By examining a society's myths, Durkheim believed, a sociologist can discover its social institutions and values.

Georges Dumézil, a modern French scholar, was influenced by Durkheim's ideas in the study of Indo-

European mythology. According to Dumézil, the principal Indo-European divinities were collective representations of the *caste* (class) system common to several ancient Indo-European peoples. In ancient India the gods Mitra and Varuna represented the Brahman castes—the highest castes in Hindu society, made up of priests and scholars. The god Indra represented the warrior castes, which ranked below the Brahmans. The Ashvin twins represented still lower castes—farmers and herders. The relation between these divinities reveals what the Hindus considered proper conduct among the castes.

One ancient Indian myth tells that Indra killed a monster that threatened the peace and security of the gods. But the monster happened to be the chaplain of the gods and therefore a divine Brahman. As a result, Indra felt he had committed a great sin because he had killed a Brahman. This myth illustrates the ancient Indian belief that under no circumstances should a member of one caste harm a member of a higher caste.

Mythology and the individual. In the early 1900's, the Swiss psychoanalyst Carl Jung developed a controversial theory about how myths reflect the attitudes and behavior of individuals. Jung suggested that everyone has a *personal* and a *collective* unconscious. An individual's personal unconscious is formed by the person's experiences in the world as filtered through the senses. An individual's collective unconscious is inherited and shared by all members of the person's race.

Jung believed that the collective unconscious is organized into basic patterns and symbols, which he called *archetypes*. Myths represent one kind of archetype. Other kinds include fairy tales, folk sagas, and works of art. Jung believed that all mythologies have certain features in common. These features include characters, such as gods and heroes, and themes, such as love or revenge. Other features include places, such as the home of the gods or the underworld, and plots, such as a battle between generations for control of a throne. Jung suggested that archetypes date back to the earliest days of humankind. By studying myths and other archetypes, Jung believed, scholars could trace the psychological development of particular races as well as of all humankind.   C. Scott Littleton

Study aids

Related articles in *World Book* include:

Egyptian mythology

Amon	Re
Anubis	Serapis
Hathor	Seth
Horus	Sphinx
Isis	Thoth
Osiris	

Greek mythology
Gods and goddesses

Aeolus	Hades	Pan
Aphrodite	Hebe	Persephone
Apollo	Hecate	Poseidon
Ares	Helios	Prometheus
Artemis	Hephaestus	Rhea
Asclepius	Hera	Satyr
Athena	Hermes	Selene
Atlas	Hestia	Titans
Cronus	Hypnos	Triton
Demeter	Morpheus	Uranus
Dionysus	Muses	Zeus
Graces	Nereus	

Heroes and characters from Homer

See the separate articles **Homer**; **Iliad**; and **Odyssey**. See also the following articles:

Achilles	Hector	Orestes
Agamemnon	Hecuba	Paris
Ajax the Greater	Helen of Troy	Penelope
Ajax the Lesser	Iphigenia	Priam
Cassandra	Laocoön	Scylla
Circe	Lotus-eaters	Sirens
Clytemnestra	Menelaus	Ulysses
Electra	Mentor	

Other heroes and characters

Adonis	Deucalion	Narcissus
Amazons	Endymion	Niobe
Andromeda	Europa	Nymph
Antigone	Eurydice	Oedipus
Arachne	Ganymede	Orion
Arethusa	Hercules	Orpheus
Argonauts	Hero and Leander	Pandora
Cadmus	Hesperides	Perseus
Castor and Pollux	Io	Phaëthon
Charon	Jason	Pygmalion
Daedalus	Medea	Sisyphus
Damon and Pythias	Midas	Tantalus
Daphne	Minos	Theseus

Monsters and creatures

Argus	Cerberus
Centaur	Chimera

Cyclops	Hydra	
Giant	Medusa	
Gorgons	Minotaur	
Griffin	Pegasus	
Harpy	Phoenix	

Events, objects, and places

Aegis	Gordian knot	Oracle
Ambrosia	Hellespont	Parnassus
Atlantis	Labyrinth	Styx
Cornucopia	Lethe	Tartarus
Delphi	Mysteries	Thebes
Elysium	Olympia	Trojan War
Epidaurus	Olympus	Troy
Golden Fleece		

Roman mythology

Aeneas	Lares and Penates
Aeneid	Luna
Androcles	Lupercalia
Aurora	Mars
Bacchus	Mercury
Ceres	Minerva
Cupid	Neptune
Diana	Pluto
Dido	Psyche
Fates	Quirinus
Faun	Romulus and Remus
Fortuna	Saturn
Furies	Saturnalia
Genius	Sibyl
Janus	Venus
Juno	Vesta
Jupiter	Vulcan

Celtic mythology

Arthur, King	Irish literature (The Golden
Cuchulainn	Age)
Finn MacCool	Tristan

Teutonic mythology

Balder	Nibelungenlied	Skald
Brunhild	Norns	Snorri Sturluson
Edda	Odin	Tannhäuser
Elf	Saga	Thor
Frey	Siegfried	Tuesday
Freyja	Sigurd	Valhalla
Loki		

Other related articles

Astarte	Gilgamesh, Epic of
Bulfinch, Thomas	Indian, American
Campbell, Joseph	(Religion)
Folklore	Lévi-Strauss, Claude
Frazer, Sir James G.	Malinowski, Bronislaw

Marduk
Moon (Mythology)
Pyramus and Thisbe

Sun (Mythology and sun worship)
Tylor, Sir Edward B.

Outline

I. What myths are about
  A. Mythical beings
  B. Mythical places
  C. Mythical symbols
  D. Comparing myths
II. Egyptian mythology
  A. The Great Ennead
  B. The Osiris myth
  C. Other Egyptian divinities
  D. The influence of Egyptian mythology
III. Greek mythology
  A. The creation myth
  B. Greek divinities
  C. Greek heroes
IV. Roman mythology
  A. Roman divinities
  B. Romulus and Remus
  C. The seven kings
  D. The *Aeneid*
V. Celtic mythology
  A. The Irish cycles
  B. Welsh myths
VI. Teutonic mythology
  A. The creation of life
  B. The construction of the world
  C. Teutonic heroes
  D. The end of the world
VII. Mythology of the Pacific Islands
  A. Creation myths
  B. Pacific Islands divinities
  C. Mana and taboo
VIII. African mythology
IX. American Indian mythology
X. How myths began
  A. Euhemerus' theory
  B. Müller's theory
  C. Tylor's theory
  D. Frazer's theory
  E. The ritualist theory
  F. Malinowski's theory
  G. Jensen's theory
  H. Lévi-Strauss's theory
XI. What mythology tells us about people
  A. Mythology and society
  B. Mythology and the individual

Questions

What is the difference between a *generic* and a *genetic* relation-
ship among myths?
What is the function of a *fetish* in African mythology?
In Egyptian mythology, what was the *Great Ennead*?
What is the importance of the *Theogony* in Greek mythology?
How does a myth differ from a folk tale?
What is the function of a *creation* myth? An *explanatory* myth?
What is the theory of *collective representation*?
In Pacific Islands mythology, what is *mana*? What is *taboo*?

What is the *mythological cycle* in Celtic mythology? The *Ulster cycle*?

Reading and Study Guide

See *Mythology* in the Research Guide/Index, Volume 22, for a *Reading and Study Guide.*

Additional resources

Level I

Aulaire, Ingri d' and E. P. d'. *d'Aulaire's Book of Greek Myths.* Doubleday, 1962. *Norse Gods and Giants.* 1967.
Barber, Richard W. *A Companion to World Mythology.* Dela-corte, 1979.
Bierhorst, John. *The Mythology of North America.* Morrow, 1985.
Branston, Brian. *Gods & Heroes from Viking Mythology.* Schocken, 1982.
Colum, Padraic. *The Children of Odin: The Book of Northern Myths.* Macmillan, 1984. *The Golden Fleece and the Heroes Who Lived Before Achilles.* 1983. First published in 1920 and 1921, respectively.
Coolidge, Olivia E. *Greek Myths.* Houghton, 1949. *Legends of the North.* 1951.
Fisher, Leonard E. *Theseus and the Minotaur.* Holiday Hse., 1988.
Gates, Doris. *A Fair Wind for Troy.* Viking, 1976.
Gerstein, Mordicai. *Tales of Pan.* Harper, 1986.
Hamilton, Virginia. *In the Beginning: Creation Stories from Around the World.* Harcourt, 1988.

Level II

Bell, Robert E. *Dictionary of Classical Mythology: Symbols, At-tributes, & Associations.* ABC-Clio, 1982.
Bulfinch, Thomas. *Bulfinch's Mythology: The Age of Fable; The Age of Chivalry; Legends of Charlemagne.* Available in various editions since first published in 1855, 1858, and 1863, respec-tively.
Campbell, Joseph. *The Masks of God: Primitive Mythology.* Vi-king, 1959. *The Masks of God: Oriental Mythology.* 1962. *The Masks of God: Occidental Mythology.* 1964. *The Masks of God: Creative Mythology.* 1968. *Historical Atlas of World My-thology.* Harper, 1983-. Multi-volume work, publication in progress. *The Power of Myth.* Doubleday, 1988.
Cotterell, Arthur. *A Dictionary of World Mythology.* Putnam, 1979. *The Macmillan Illustrated Encyclopedia of Myths and Legends.* Macmillan, 1989.
Crossley-Holland, Kevin. *The Norse Myths.* Pantheon, 1980.
Frazer, James G. *The Illustrated Golden Bough.* Doubleday, 1978.
Hamilton, Edith. *Mythology.* Little, Brown, 1942.
Ions, Veronica. *Egyptian Mythology.* Rev. ed. Bedrick, 1983. *In-dian Mythology.* Rev. ed. 1984. Myths of India.
Larousse World Mythology. Ed. by Pierre Grimal. Smith Pubs., 1989. First published in 1965.
Mythologies of the Ancient World. Ed. by Samuel Noah Kramer. Doubleday, 1961.
Mythology of All Races. Ed. by John A. MacCulloch, and others. Littlefield, Adams, no date. First published in 1932.
Piggott, Juliet. *Japanese Mythology.* Rev ed. Bedrick, 1983.
Pinsent, John. *Greek Mythology.* Rev. ed. Bedrick, 1983.
Puhvel, Jaan. *Comparative Mythology.* Johns Hopkins, 1987.

Myxedema. See **Thyroid gland** (Underactive thyroid).
Myxomatosis. See **Rabbit** (Diseases).

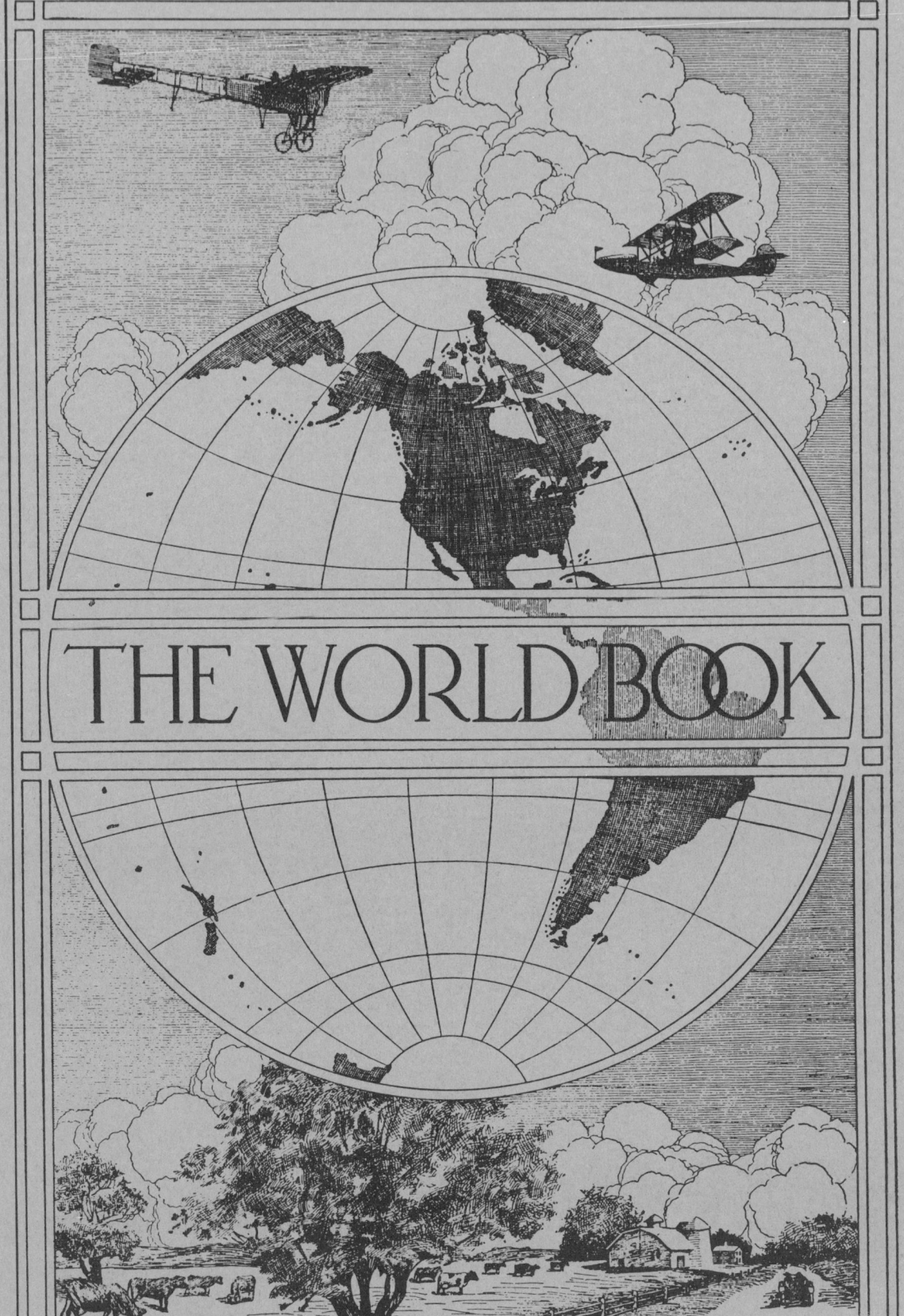